1 MONTH OF
FREE
READING

at
www.ForgottenBooks.com

By purchasing this book you are eligible for one month membership to ForgottenBooks.com, giving you unlimited acccss to our entire collection of over 1,000,000 titles via our web site and mobile apps.

To claim your free month visit:
www.forgottenbooks.com/free909682

ISBN 978-0-265-91896-8

PIBN 10909682

DEPARTMENT OF THE INTERIOR,

CENSUS OFFICE.

FRANCIS A. WALKER, Superintendent,
Appointed April 1, 1879; resigned November 3, 1881.

CHAS. W. SEATON, Superintendent,
Appointed November 4, 1881.

REPORT

ON

COTTON PRODUCTION IN THE UNITED STATES;

ALSO EMBRACING

AGRICULTURAL AND PHYSICO-GEOGRAPHICAL DESCRIPTIONS

OF THE

SEVERAL COTTON STATES AND OF CALIFORNIA.

EUGENE W. HILGARD, Ph. D.,

PROFESSOR OF AGRICULTURE, UNIVERSITY OF CALIFORNIA, FORMER PROFESSOR AT THE UNIVERSITY OF MISSISSIPPI, AND STATE GEOLOGIST,

SPECIAL AGENT IN CHARGE.

PART I.
MISSISSIPPI VALLEY AND SOUTHWESTERN STATES.

WASHINGTON:
GOVERNMENT PRINTING OFFICE
1884.

SUBJECTS OF THIS REPORT.

PART I.

PART II.

APPENDIX.

ii
2

Ch--- 3.17 ... HA.

LETTER OF TRANSMITTAL.

DEPARTMENT OF THE INTERIOR,
CENSUS OFFICE,
Washington, D. C., October 1, 1883.

Hon. H. M. TELLER,
    Secretary of the Interior.

   SIR: I have the honor to transmit herewith the report upon Cotton Culture, forming the fifth and sixth volumes of the final report upon the Tenth Census.
   I have the honor to be, very respectfully, your obedient servant,

C. W. SEATON,
Superintendent of Census.

INTRODUCTORY LETTER.

BOSTON, MASS., *June* 9, 1883.

Under the provisions of the eighteenth section of the act of March 3, 1879, authorizing the Superintendent of Census to "employ experts and special agents to investigate in their economic relations the manufacturing, railroad, fishing, mining, and other industries of the country", it was thought that the cotton culture of the South had a very strong claim to be considered among the most important subjects of such special investigation: first, because of the vast contribution made therefrom to the aggregate production of wealth; second, because this crop is so largely exported, which fact would give the widest possible interest to all information relating to the conditions of its production; third, because of the great and almost revolutionary changes in the system of cultivation which during the past fifteen or twenty years have been in progress throughout the cotton region, making the present a peculiarly appropriate time for a thorough survey of this industry; fourth, because, while other sections of the country afforded many subjects for extended special investigation in the census, cotton culture was the main interest of a group of eleven or twelve states.

In setting on foot the proposed investigation into the cultivation of cotton the Census Office was peculiarly fortunate in securing the services, as chief special agent, of Professor Eugene W. Hilgard, now of the University of California, but for many years a professor in the University of Mississippi, and the head of the geological and agricultural survey of that state. Besides rare powers of mind and high scientific attainments, coupled with the advantages derived from long and careful study of the subject-matter of the investigation, Professor Hilgard possessed the commanding qualification of being the author of that method of soil investigation which, after protracted debate, has been fully established to the approval of the agricultural chemists of the United States.

It is scarcely a matter of wonder that so great a work as was undertaken three years ago in this direction should be found, in the result, somewhat altered from its projected dimensions. In a word, the work, as it is now sent to press, contains vastly more of local and particular descriptions of the cotton lands of the South and somewhat less of general discussion and of historical and comparative matter than was first contemplated. This has been due to an increasing sense of the importance of the former element of the report, and also to the failure of the chief special agent to obtain all the assistance which was anticipated, and to the consequent necessity imposed upon him of doing with his own hands much of the local work. This, combined with the effects of grave and persistent ill-health, has caused Professor Hilgard to abridge that general discussion of the cotton-growing industry in the past as well as in the present, in other countries as well as in the United States, which formed so prominent a feature of the original plan.

No words could exaggerate the sense I have of the zeal, intelligence, and spirit of devotion with which this work has been pursued by Professor Hilgard under the gravest disadvantages. His regretted failure to obtain the services of *collaborateurs* in certain important cotton states has been in no small degree compensated by his exceptional good fortune in securing the assistance of Dr. R. H. Loughridge, first as a reporter upon the great states of Georgia and Texas, and subsequently as a general assistant upon the entire work.

FRANCIS A. WALKER.

v

GENERAL DISCUSSION

OF THE

COTTON PRODUCTION OF THE UNITED STATES;

EMBRACING

THE COTTONSEED-OIL INDUSTRY, METHODS AND UTILITY OF SOIL INVESTIGATION,

AND

TABLES OF COTTON FIBER MEASUREMENTS.

————————

E. W. HILGARD, PH. D.,
SPECIAL AGENT IN CHARGE.

TABLE OF CONTENTS.

TABLE OF CONTENTS.

LETTER OF TRANSMITTAL.

UNIVERSITY OF CALIFORNIA, *May* 31, 1883.

In submitting to the public the series of reports on cotton production the editor deems it not unnecessary to explain briefly the causes leading to their present form, and particularly to the great predominance of the special descriptive over the general part.

As originally outlined by ex-Superintendent Walker, the report was to embrace, besides the merely statistical matter, a measurably complete discussion of cotton production, not only in the United States, but elsewhere, and in the past as well as in the present, "the results themselves being used to indicate the probable movement in the immediate future. In a word, the figures of the returns should be set into a philosophical discussion of the subject-matter to which they relate. In regard to the cotton of the South, the field of actual culture should be defined, and within that field the soils treated of, as far as possible, mapped, the methods of culture discussed, the labor system described, and the American cotton botanically considered and compared as to its adaptations to the uses of the manufacturer with the cotton of other countries. So far as might be, it would be agreeable to the general plan that the discussion should outrun the field of actual present cultivation and take up the question as to the regions of the United States to which the culture might profitably be extended. Historical matter might be introduced to the extent that should appear desirable. Previous official reports and the literature of the subject could be brought under contribution, though the work should in the main consist of fresh, original matter."

Although feeling considerable hesitation in regard to his physical ability to carry out this programme successfully from his distant point of location, the writer, upon finding several gentlemen prominently identified with the agricultural interests of their respective states willing to lend their aid in the premises, finally accepted the general charge of the work, including the elaboration of such portions as might not find other hands.

In pursuance of this general arrangement, the several states were placed in charge of the following gentlemen: North Carolina, Professor W. C. Kerr, state geologist and member of the board of agriculture; Tennessee, Professor James M. Safford, professor of geology at Vanderbilt University, Nashville, and state geologist; South Carolina, Major Harry Hammond, of Beech Island, formerly of the State University of Georgia, and prominently identified with agricultural progress in his state; Alabama, Professor Eugene A. Smith, professor of chemistry and geology in the University of Alabama, and state geologist. The latter also took charge of the state of Florida, while Professors Safford and Kerr added to their respective states such portions of the contiguous states of Kentucky and Virginia, respectively, as could be considered cotton-producing. Georgia was placed in charge of Dr. R. H. Loughridge, formerly assistant in the Georgia geological survey, and thoroughly familiar with that state; and he was also charged with a rapid exploration of the state of Texas, of which he had long been a resident, as well as of the Indian territory, in which his boyhood was spent. Subsequently, the elaboration of a description of the state of Arkansas, from the reports of Dr. David Dale Owen and other sources, and likewise of the cotton-growing part of Missouri, also fell to him. In all cases the materials furnished by the geological surveys of the states were first utilized, and the existing gaps filled, so far as means would allow, by exploration, and essentially by the further analysis of representative soils, mostly carried out in the laboratory of the University of Alabama. Numerous samples of cotton were also obtained, and the measurements of their respective dimensions, strength, etc., were undertaken by Professor J. M. Ordway, of the Massachusetts Institute of Technology. The results of this part of the investigation will be found tabulated in the following pages.

The writer originally hoped to restrict his own state work to Mississippi, of which state he was geologist for a number of years; but in the course of time Louisiana and California were added to his share, from the difficulty of finding other persons qualified by previous acquaintance with these states. This cumulation of special work upon his hands, added to that of general supervision and regular professional duties, must be held accountable for the deviation from the original plan in cutting short to an unfortunate extent the general and, in some respects, most important portion of this report. Moreover, as the answered schedules came in, it was found that they contained a large amount of information regarding the agricultural features and capacities of the cotton states such as is needed by immigrants and investors, yet cannot be found in a connected and authentic form in any publications now extant. It was then concluded to add to the more general description of each state brief descriptions of each of its counties, with such abstracts from the schedule reports as might add to the practical interest. Had it been foreseen how great an increase of labor was involved in this expansion of the original plan the decision might have been against it. But it is believed that if the consequent abridgment of the general part has somewhat diminished the interest of this volume for those directly concerned in the world's cotton trade and production, as well as for the general student, its direct value to the states concerned, and to those who are to seek their homes and fortunes in their inviting climates, has been materially increased. The general discussion can reach those interested through the columns of the periodical press, while the facts wanted by the intending settler can ordinarily be ascertained by him only through personal observation or through the reports of interested parties, mostly very vague as regards the natural features, while profuse in examples of individual cases of well-doing, and in business advertisements. The latter feature is of course rigorously excluded from the contents of this volume; and however desirable it might have been to go somewhat beyond the mere statement of the means of communication and give some data regarding the chief towns, the rapid mutability of such matters in the United States, and the difficulty of avoiding *ex parte* statements and invidious comparisons, with their train of wounded sensibilities, rendered such additions clearly inexpedient. It should therefore be distinctly understood that this omission is intentional and general, and that the descriptions are intended to include only such matter as in the nature of the case is immutable or subject to slow change only, such as the natural features and the predominance of industries or industrial practice that have been found adapted to them.

It is not claimed, nor under the circumstances can it be reasonably expected, that mistakes have been entirely avoided and no important omissions made. The time and means at command were wholly inadequate for a work making such claims. But it is believed that in using the utmost diligence to secure the assistance and co-operation of the men whose life study has been given to the objects in view, and whose past or present official position has enabled them to gain the most comprehensive view of the natural and industrial features of their respective states, it has been possible to bring within this volume a larger foundation of solid and well-digested facts than could have been obtained by any of the ordinary methods of transient commissions or traveling observers, with their almost inevitable sequence of superficial observations and hasty generalizations and conclusions. If the merits as well as the faults of the work shall result in a fuller appreciation by the state and federal governments, as well as by the public, of the benefits to be derived from a closer attention to the study and intelligent as well as intelligible description of the agricultural features and peculiarities of the several portions of the United States, the object of our somewhat arduous labors will have been attained. It is but bare justice to say that these have been materially lightened by the uniform and appreciative courtesy and helpfulness of ex-Superintendent Walker, under whose administration the bulk of the work was done.

EUGENE W. HILGARD,

Chief Special Agent.

PART I.

STATISTICS AND GENERAL DISCUSSION

OF

COTTON PRODUCTION IN THE UNITED STATES.

AGRICULTURAL MAP

OF THE

COTTON STATE

Compiled from the MS. Maps of the State

under the direction of

EUG. W. HILGARD, PH.

Special Agent

1882.

*ERRATUM.—The lands on the Rio Grande in S. W. Texas should have been given the tint indicated by No. 19.

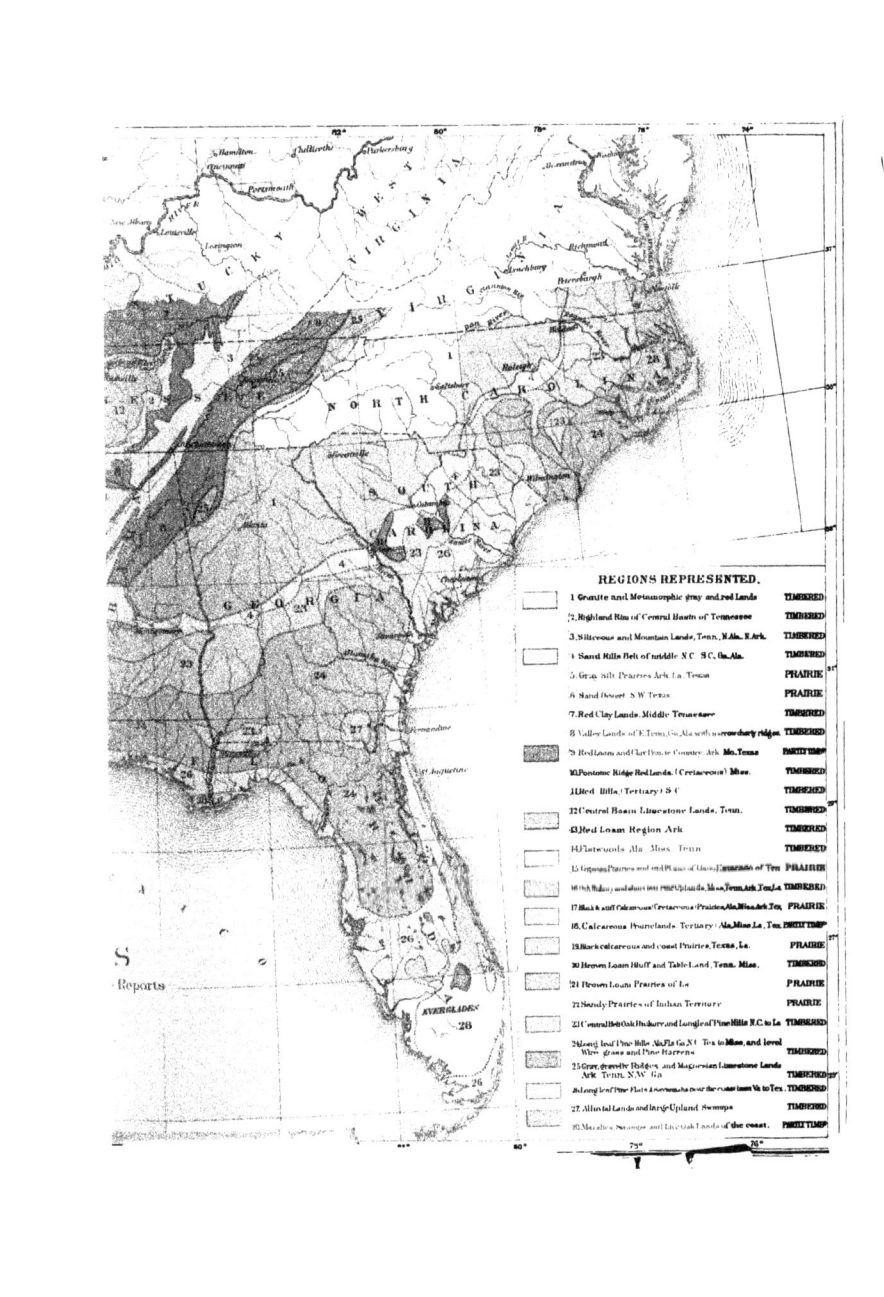

REGIONS REPRESENTED.

1 Granite and Metamorphic gray and red Lands		TIMBERED
2. Highland Rim of Central Basin of Tennessee		TIMBERED
3. Siliceous and Mountain Lands, Tenn., N.Ala., N.Ark.		TIMBERED
4 Sand Hills Belt of middle N.C. S.C, Ga. Ala.		TIMBERED
5. Gray Silt Prairies Ark. La. Texas		PRAIRIE
6 Sand Desert S.W Texas		PRAIRIE
7. Red Clay Lands. Middle Tennessee		TIMBERED
8 Valley Lands of E. Tenn. Ga. Ala. with a narrow cherty ridge.		TIMBERED
9 Red Loam and Clay Pine-tree Country Ark. Mo. Texas		PARTLY TIMB.
10. Pontotoc Ridge Red Lands. (Cretaceous) Miss.		TIMBERED
11.Red Hills.(Tertiary) S.C		TIMBERED
12 Central Basin Limestone Lands. Tenn.		TIMBERED
13 Red Loam Region Ark		TIMBERED
14 Flatwoods Ala. Miss. Tenn		TIMBERED
15 Grassy Prairies and small Plains of Limestone lands of Tex		PRAIRIE
16 Oak Ridges and short-leaf Pine Uplands, Miss. Tenn. Ark. Tex. La.		TIMBERED
17 Black stiff Calcareous Cretaceous Prairies Ala. Miss. Ark. Tex.		PRAIRIE
18. Calcareous Prairielands . Tertiary : Ala. Miss. La. Tex.		PARTLY TIMB.
19 Black calcareous and coast Prairies Texas, La.		PRAIRIE
20 Brown Loam Bluff and Table-Land. Tenn. Miss.		TIMBERED
21 Brown Loam Prairies of La		PRAIRIE
22 Sandy Prairies of Indian Territory		PRAIRIE
23 Central Belt Oak Hickory and Longleaf Pine Hills N.C. to La.		TIMBERED
24 Long leaf Pine Hills Ala. Fla. Ga. N.C Tex. to Miss. and level Wire-grass and Pine Barrens		TIMBERED
25 Gray Gravelly Ridges and Magnesian Limestone Lands Ark. Tenn. N.W. Ga		TIMBERED
26 Long leaf Pine Flats Anomalous over the coast bum Va. to Tex.		TIMBERED
27 Alluvial Lands and large Upland Swamps		TIMBERED
28 Marshes Swamps and Live Oak Lands of the coast.		PARTLY TIMB.

STATISTICS AND GENERAL DISCUSSION.

REVIEW OF THE GENERAL SOIL MAP OF THE COTTON STATES.

[It was intended to present under this head a general review and summary of the agricultural features and statistics of cotton production in the southern states, but the necessary closing of the census work at a fixed date precludes any extended comments.]

This map represents, so far as the smallness of the scale will permit, the chief soil regions of the cotton-growing states in thirteen colors, most of which are made to represent several distinct features, belonging, however, to districts so widely separated that no confusion can arise from this joint use, the meanings of which are indicated in the legend. (a) Since differences of soil necessarily find their expression in the vegetation covering the ground, the designations of the regions are largely based upon the characteristics in regard to tree growth.

It is apparent at a glance that in the coastward portion of the cotton states the agricultural divisions (Nos. 28, 26, 24, 23, 4) form, roughly speaking, belts more or less conforming or parallel to the present coast-line, while inland they are measurably governed on the east by the location and trend of the Alleghany range (Nos. 1, 3, 8), and farther west by the great northward prolongation of the Gulf of Mexico that existed at the end of the Cretaceous period, and was gradually filled up nearly to the present shore-line during the succeeding Tertiary period (Nos. 17, 14, 16, 18, 27). In the axis of this great embayment, which had its head near Cairo, Illinois, lies the alluvial plain of the Mississippi river, bordered and underlaid mostly by early Quaternary deposits lying in a Tertiary trough several hundred feet in depth. The greater part of Texas belongs to the western portion of the ancient embayment, and we find there, only in inverted order (as regards east and west), the same or corresponding formations and soils as those met with east of the Mississippi river in traveling toward the southern end of the Appalachian region; that is, we pass first from the recent to the older *alluvium*, consisting largely of heavy calcareous or "prairie" soils; thence again across calcareous black prairies derived from the *Tertiary* formations (18) to a broader belt of *Cretaceous* black prairies (17), which in their turn are followed, in part at least, by black calcareous prairie soils, derived from the *Carboniferous* limestones. Between these several prairie belts there intervene east of the Mississippi more or less of sandy or loam uplands, not of prominently calcareous character (16, 23), while in Texas the prairies corresponding to the four ages of limestones mostly adjoin each other directly.

It thus appears that, from the Chattahoochee west to the Nueces river of Texas, calcareous soils are widely prevalent; and the parallel map of intensity of cotton production shows a marked increase of the cotton culture whenever one of these calcareous belts is reached.

East of the Chattahoochee, and northeastward to the James, few prominently calcareous soil areas are met with, and all such are rather local and of small extent. The soils here, being derived from the eastern slope of the Alleghanies, are prevalently of a light siliceous character, and below the break of the highlands into the coast plains (or what is popularly known as "the falls of the rivers") they are but rarely influenced by the underlying Tertiary marls. They are mostly what, in a wide application of the term, might be termed "alluvial" soils, chiefly of early Quaternary origin; and, aside from the narrow "live-oak belt" of the immediate coast, the long-leaf pine is their characteristic tree. This pine, as analysis shows, is everywhere an indication of soils poor in lime; and experience shows that until the use of fertilizers becomes part of the agricultural system only the bottom lands of a long-leaf pine area are usually utilized for cotton production. Hence the great pine belts of the Gulf coast produce but very little cotton, while on the Atlantic border, with the use of fertilizers, the culture is more extended.

---

a Owing to the failure of the printer to furnish proof-sheets of the map before striking off the edition, the following erratum requires notice:

The region along the Rio Grande river in Texas should have the same color as the coast and southern prairie region No. 19, on the east of the "Desert".

Discrepancies are apparent in some instances between this general map and the several state maps, which are in part due to differences in depth of color, and in part to the fact that changes were made in some of the state maps by their authors after the entire edition of this general map was printed. The most apparent among these occurs in North Carolina, where the *sand-hills region* (of the general map) have in the state map been merged into the oak uplands or metamorphic region; and the region of *long-leaf pine hills*, which is very prominent here, is there narrowed down and shows its limits more in detail and with a different shade of color.

Inland the proportion of lime in the soils usually increases, and correspondingly the long-leaf pine gradually gives way to the short-leaf species and an increasing proportion of oaks and hickories, until finally the latter alone occupy the ground. With local modifications, this order of things holds good pretty generally from Virginia to eastern Louisiana, but by far most strikingly so in the Gulf states east of the Mississippi. In the bottom plain of the latter, near the line between Arkansas and Louisiana, we find the maximum of cotton production on natural soils (see page 14) on the highly calcareous and otherwise also profusely fertile "buckshot" soils of the great valley, with which only some of those of Red River bottom can dispute precedence. Under their influence cotton culture is carried far into Missouri, while in the hill country to the eastward and westward, in Kentucky and in northwestern Arkansas, it forms but a subordinate feature. In Texas again the Tertiary and Cretaceous prairie regions (Nos. 16 and 17) produce the bulk of upland cotton, while in the coast prairie region the river bottoms are almost alone employed in its production thus far; and westward of the Cretaceous prairie region, where the rainfall becomes more scanty, it has not yet had time to establish itself on a permanent footing, save locally.

While natural advantages thus clearly point to the Mississippi valley and regions immediately adjacent as the natural and future center of cotton production in the United States, it is interesting to notice to how great an extent these advantages are at present balanced by a more rational, thorough, and systematic culture of the less fertile soils of the Atlantic cotton states. The following table shows the total production of the several soil regions given on the map, as well as the partial production of each in the Atlantic cotton states on the one hand, and of the states west of the Chattahoochee on the other. The figures are, of course, only approximate, being based upon the returns by counties, which very often embrace within their areas small sections of other regions outside of the chief region to which each county is referred:

TABLE I.—APPROXIMATE AREA AND COTTON PRODUCTION OF EACH OF THE AGRICULTURAL REGIONS OF THE COTTON-PRODUCING STATES.

Agricultural regions.	Approximate land area.	COTTON PRODUCTION.				
		Total.	Atlantic states.	Mississippi valley and Gulf states.	Seed-cotton product per acre.	
					Claimed for fresh land.	Average yield for 1879.
	Square miles.	*Bales.*	*Bales.*	*Bales.*	*Pounds.*	*Pounds.*
Total...............	710,265	5,755,359	1,801,179	3,954,180	....	507
Metamorphic region..........................	66,605	967,720	896,435	71,285	500–800	496
Siliceous and mountain lands................	22,770	25,500	....	25,500	600–800	496
Sand- and red-hills region..................	6,660	53,355	53,355	....	300–500	561
Gray-silt prairies of Arkansas.............	1,585	27,189	....	27,189	1,000	865
Central basin of Tennessee.................	5,450	48,778	....	48,778	1,000	570
Valley lands of east Tennessee, northwestern Georgia, and Alabama	16,340	99,855	46,619	53,236	800–1,000	600
Red-loam region of Arkansas...............	18,520	144,964	....	144,964	1,000	828
Pontotoc ridge of Mississippi.............	590	22,768	....	22,768	1,000–1,600	555
Red-loam region of northwestern Texas.....	27,000	10,931	....	10,931	500–800	380
Valley of the Tennessee...................	5,080	94,087	....	94,087	1,000–1,500	471
Oak and short-leaf pine uplands............	37,190	944,517	....	944,517	500–1,000	612
Black prairie region.......................	39,225	753,552	....	753,552	800–1,000	456
Coast prairies of Texas and Louisiana......	51,135	136,269	....	136,269	600–1,000	365
Brown-loam table-lands, bluff region, and cane hills	13,950	558,292	....	558,292	1,000–1,200	684
Magnesian limestone lands of Arkansas and Missouri	12,480	49,756	....	49,756	1,000–1,200	798
Oak, hickory, and long-leaf pine uplands...	52,980	906,353	656,501	249,852	400–700	486
Long-leaf pine hills.......................	74,478	100,717	77,213	23,504	400–600	272
Pine flats, savannas, and coast lands......	48,499	79,650	79,056	794	500–1,000	543
Mississippi river alluvial lands...........	29,467	616,063	....	616,063	1,500–2,000	1,068
Other alluvial lands.......................	5,557	104,931	....	104,931	1,500–2,000	783
Indian territory...........................	3,400	17,000	....	17,000	1,800–1,900	969
Marsh lands................................	7,837	....	....	....	....	....
Flatwoods of Mississippi, Alabama, and Tennessee (a)	2,030	....	....	....	....	....
Gypsum region of Texas.....................	17,490	....	....	....	....	....
Llano Estacado of Texas....................	92,927	....	....	....	....	....

a A narrow belt, and its cotton production not separately ascertained.

TABLE II.—TOTAL POPULATION, TILLED LAND, COTTON PRODUCTION, AND AVERAGE PRODUCT PER ACRE FOR THE UNITED STATES.

States in the order of cotton production.	Total land area.	Approximate area over which cotton is planted.	POPULATION.			TILLED LAND.				COTTON PRODUCTION.			Average product per acre.			Total in tons.		Percentage of total production of the bales.
			Total.	White.	Colored.	Acres.	Per cent. of tilled.	Acres per square mile.	Per cent. tilled land.	Acres.	Bales.	Rank in prod. not per acre.	Fraction of a bale.	Seed-cotton.	Lint.	Seed.	Lint.	Cotton-seed.
	2	3	4	5	6	7	8	9	10	11	12	13	14	15	16	17	18	19
	Sq. mls.												Lbs.	Lbs.	Lbs.	Lbs.		
Total	965,305	547,065	16,807,316	11,022,857	5,784,459	79,496,877	13.72	68	16.21	14,480,019	5,755,359		0.39	567	189	376	1,363,849	2,770,417	100.00
Mississippi	46,340	46,340	1,131,597	479,398	652,199	4,924,530	16.60	106	42.77	2,106,215	963,111	7	0.46	657	219	438	223,739	457,478	16.73
Georgia	58,980	a57,580	1,542,180	816,906	725,274	7,693,292	20.37	130	31.63	2,617,138	814,441	13	0.31	444	148	296	193,429	388,856	14.15
Texas	262,290	b108,000	1,591,749	1,197,237	394,512	7,628,530	4.54	29	28.30	2,178,435	c805,284	11	0.37	555	185	370	201,321	402,642	13.99
Alabama	51,540	51,540	1,262,505	662,185	600,320	6,134,198	18.60	119	37.90	2,330,086	693,654	14	0.30	429	143	286	166,168	332,336	12.16
Arkansas	53,045	53,045	802,525	591,531	210,994	3,431,900	10.11	63	30.31	1,042,976	e608,256	4	0.58	831	277	554	152,064	304,128	10.57
South Carolina	30,170	30,170	995,577	391,105	604,472	3,786,090	19.85	134	36.52	1,384,349	522,548	12	0.38	546	182	364	124,105	248,210	9.08
Louisiana	45,420	d37,820	939,946	454,954	484,992	2,907,935	8.63	65	34.48	864,787	508,569	3	0.59	840	280	560	120,785	241,570	8.84
North Carolina	48,580	e42,580	1,399,750	867,242	532,508	5,926,087	19.06	122	15.07	898,153	389,598	9	0.44	621	207	414	92,529	185,058	6.77
Tennessee	41,750	f37,750	1,542,359	1,138,631	403,528	7,700,941	28.52	184	9.33	723,562	330,621	7	0.46	651	217	434	78,522	157,044	5.74
Florida	54,240	g47,640	269,493	142,905	126,588	587,472	2.56	16	27.67	245,595	54,997	15	0.22	318	106	212	13,062	26,902	0.96
Missouri	68,735	15,000	2,168,380	2,022,826	145,554	13,203,756	20.02	192	h0.24	82,116	c20,318	2	0.63	900	300	600	5,079	10,158	0.35
Virginia	40,125	4,000	1,512,565	880,858	631,707	7,358,030	28.63	183	h0.61	45,040	19,595	9	0.44	621	207	414	4,654	9,308	0.34
Indian territory	64,690	2,000								35,000	17,000	6	0.49	699	233	466	4,037	8,075	0.30
Kentucky	40,000	13,000	1,648,690	1,377,179	271,511	8,387,910	32.60	209	h0.03	2,667	1,367	5	0.51	729	243	486	325	650	0.02
California (i)	155,980		864,694	767,181		6,606,102	6.62	42		j375	j295	1	0.79	1,125	375	750	70	140	

a Omitting counties north of the Blue Ridge.
b Omitting western Texas.
c 500-pound bales.
d Omitting marsh lands.
e Omitting the mountain division.
f Omitting Unaka and Cumberland region.
g Omitting Everglades.
h Of tilled land in the cotton region.
i This state is not included in the general summary.
j These do not represent the acreage or number of bales actually produced in the state, but from one locality only. The enumeration schedules sent to this state did not include cotton.

TABLE III.—COUNTIES IN EACH STATE HAVING THE HIGHEST COTTON PRODUCTION.

States in the order of average product per acre.	Average product per acre (fraction of a bale).	COUNTIES HAVING HIGHEST TOTAL PRODUCTION.				COUNTIES HAVING HIGHEST PRODUCT PER ACRE. (a)			
		Name.	Rank in product per acre in the state.	Cotton acreage.	Bales. 475 lbs.	Product per acre, fraction of a bale.	Name.	Rank in total production in state.	Cotton acreage.	Bales.	Product per acre, fraction of a bale.
	1	2	3	4	5	6	7	8	9	10	11
California (b)	0.79	Merced		375	795	0.79	Merced	1	375	795	0.79
Missouri	0.68	Dunklin	2	11,100	7,364	0.66	Pemiscot	5	2,777	2,045	0.75
Louisiana	0.59	Tensas	9	68,668	41,160	0.60	East Carroll	2	40,107	36,180	0.90
Arkansas	0.58	Pulaski	4	45,426	34,568	0.76	Chicot	3	28,941	25,338	0.94
Tennessee	0.46	Graves	6	960	417	0.46	Hickman	3	451	254	0.56
Mississippi	0.46	Shelby		92,630	48,388	0.50	Lake	22	3,249	2,412	0.74
Mississippi	0.46	Washington	3	68,409	54,873	0.67	Issaquena	27	18,782	16,150	0.88
North Carolina	0.44	Wake	7	56,916	30,115	0.50	Brunswick	61	385	344	0.62
Virginia	0.44	Southampton	1	11,500	5,200	0.45	Greenville	2	8,500	4,100	0.48
Texas	0.37	Fayette	33	58,353	24,766	0.42	Bowie	11	11,509	7,958	0.69
South Carolina	0.38	Edgefield	18	92,797	35,894	0.39	Marlborough	10	41,251	23,785	0.58
Georgia	0.31	Burke	54	87,359	29,172	0.33	Polk	41	16,774	8,126	0.48
Alabama	0.30	Dallas	45	115,631	33,584	0.29	Baldwin	62	1,384	638	0.46
Florida	0.22	Jefferson	4	37,500	10,36d	0.28	Levy	10	3,693	1,251	0.34

a Omitting those counties whose production is less than 100 bales, except in the case of California.
b Merced was the only county in California producing cotton during the census year.

It should be kept in mind that in the case of the cotton crop the data collected by the enumerators during June, 1880, necessarily refer to the cotton crop of 1879, at least so far as the product is concerned. It may be questioned whether the same is in all cases true (as should have been the case) of the acreage reported; for, unless specially admonished by the enumerators, the producers would be very likely to give them the acreage of 1880, which would be most readily present to their minds. Since the acreage of 1880 was doubtless greater than that of the preceding year, this error would tend to depress the calculated average production per acre to some extent.

In Table II the cotton-producing states are arranged, in the order of their rank, according to total production in 1879. The first column gives the state areas; the second the approximate areas of each state over which cotton is planted; the three following the population of these states, divided according to color, as bearing upon the question so much and contradictorily discussed as to "who produces the cotton". The next group of three columns gives the number of acres of tilled land, the percentage of these as referred to the total areas, and the number of acres tilled per square mile. Columns 9 to 19 give details of production; No. 9, the percentage of tilled land devoted to cotton culture; 10, the corresponding number of acres in cotton; 11, the number of bales produced; 12, the number indicating the rank of each state among the fifteen as to the average product per acre; 13, the fraction of a bale (of 475 pounds) produced per acre; 14, the corresponding product in pounds of seed-cotton; 15 and 16, the corresponding amounts in pounds of lint and cottonseed, (a) respectively. Columns 17 and 18 give the totals in tons of 2,000 pounds of lint and cottonseed produced, and 19 gives the respective percentages contributed by each state to the grand total.

From the reports received in answer to schedules sent, as well as from statements received from the prominent cotton-shipping ports, it appears that, outside of Texas, Arkansas, and Missouri, the average weight of the "bale" may be assumed to have been 475 pounds in 1879. Upon this basis, and upon the commonly-accepted average proportion of one part of lint to two of seed in the "seed-cotton" as it comes from the field, are based the data given in columns 14 to 19. In the case of other states, the number of bales given is that reported by the enumerators; but as their average weight was about 500 pounds, this figure has served as the basis of all others concerning these states.

In Table III the states are arranged in the order of rank according to average product per acre, as given in column 12, Table II. In the ten columns following are given the names, acreage in cotton, total production in bales, and average product per acre of the "banner counties" of each state, considered, first, in relation to total production, and then in respect to highest product per acre. The rank of counties according to the first point of view is, of course, largely accidental, on account of their unequal areas; yet it is the one most commonly looked to by the producers. The figures under the second head, however, are of the greatest intrinsic significance, the last column showing irrefragably the effect of the fertility of the soil, of intelligent culture, or of both combined.

SUMMARY DISCUSSION OF COTTON PRODUCTION IN THE UNITED STATES.

The accompanying map, compiled from the several state maps (which may be found in the respective state reports), gives a general view of the regions of varying intensities of cotton acreage as compared with the total land area throughout the cotton states.

The regions of high percentage devoted to cotton (10 to 20 per cent. of the total area) are confined almost exclusively to the central portions of Mississippi, Alabama, and Georgia, the cotton acreage averaging above 65 acres per square mile within the respective areas. Small patches (representing counties) of the same occur in North Carolina, Tennessee, and Texas.

Regions of maximum intensity of cotton culture above 20 per cent. of the total area form two prominent belts (shown by the deepest shade of color), one lying along the Mississippi river within the alluvial region, while the other embraces the black prairie region from northeastern Mississippi, southeastward nearly through the central portion of Alabama. The cotton acreage within these belts averages 130 acres per square mile, and upon them was produced in 1879 about 753,550 bales of cotton. A penumbral region of very sparse culture is seen almost to surround, both inland and along the coast, the cotton-producing portion of the states, while outlying areas (representing isolated counties) occur in Kentucky.

A comparison of the total population of the states of the cotton belt proper, from North and South Carolina to Texas, shows in all but two cases an approximation to the proportion of one bale for every two inhabitants. These exceptional states are Mississippi and Arkansas, in which the ratio is from two-thirds to over three-fourths of a bale per head. No obvious relation between the total production and the number, or the ratio to the total number of the colored population, is discernible in the footings by states. Such a relation, however, can be shown in the detailed discussion of the agricultural subdivisions of each state.

I now proceed to discuss the determining causes of the position occupied by each of the states in the column of total production (No. 11 of Table II), as well as in that showing average product per acre (No. 1 of Table III).

---

a I venture upon the innovation of spelling "cottonseed" as one word, as is done in the case of flaxseed or linseed, moonseed, etc., in order to obviate the occurrence of such grammatical monstrosities as "cotton seed oil cake meal", and similarly constituted expressions that can hardly be avoided unless such a change is made. In the above case, "cottonseed-oilcake meal" will be understood at a glance.

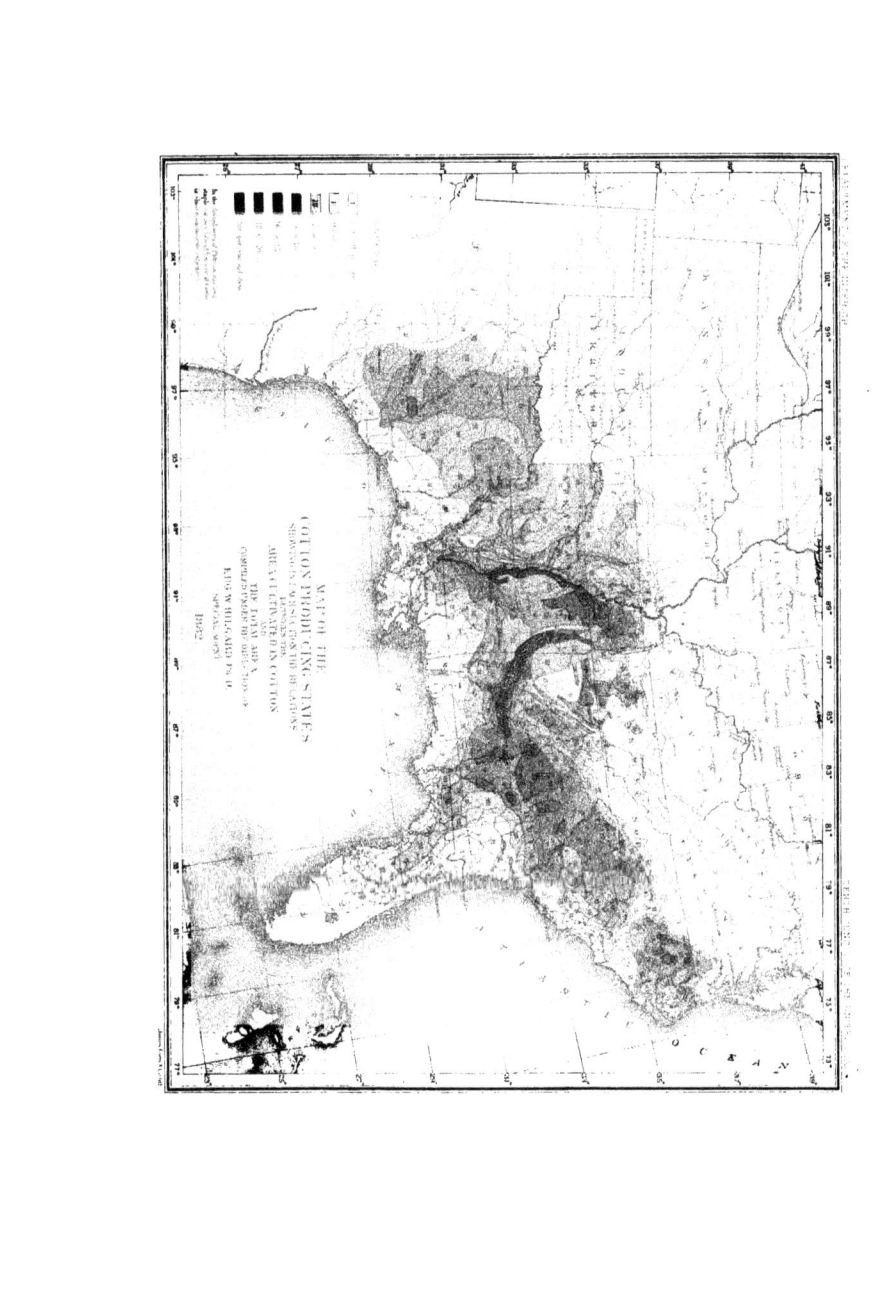

MAP OF THE
COTTON PRODUCING STATES

1882

Mississippi stands first in total production, while sixth in population, among the cotton states, thus bringing up its product to 0.85, or over eight-tenths of a bale *per capita*. At first blush, in view of the great fertility and large area of the Mississippi ("Yazoo") bottom within the limits of the state, the inference would be that the high position of the state's production is due to these fertile lowlands; but a detailed discussion of the areas of production shows that a little over one-fourth (25.5 per cent.) only of the cotton product of the state comes from the Yazoo bottom, while over one-half of the whole is produced in what might be termed the first-class uplands, viz, the table-land belt bordering the Mississippi bluff and the two prairie belts. The remaining one-fourth is grown scatteringly over the sandy uplands, bearing more or less of the long- and short-leaf pine, that form about one-half the area of the state.

It thus appears that the high production of Mississippi is due to the fact that quite one-half of its territory is occupied by soils of exceptional fertility, coupled with the circumstance that cotton culture is the one pursuit to which the population devotes itself.

Table III, columns 5 and 11, shows that Washington county, fronting on the Mississippi river and extending east to the Yazoo river, is the county of the state, as well as of the United States, having the largest total production, but the adjoining county of Issaquena exceeds Washington by 1 per cent. in product per acre, having 0.87 of a bale, or 413 pounds of lint, equal to 1,239 pounds of seed-cotton per acre. Issaquena stands third in this respect in the United States, East Carroll, Louisiana, and Chicot county, Arkansas, ranking above it. Even with the imperfect tillage and incomplete picking of the crop now prevailing in the Yazoo bottom the present average product per acre is over three-quarters of a bale; and, estimating the lands reclaimable by simple exclusion of the Mississippi overflows at only three millions of acres, the annual production could thus readily be raised to 2,250,000 bales in the Yazoo bottom alone without any change in the methods of culture. With improved cultivation the production could easily be brought up to 5,000,000 bales; and thus, with a similar improvement in the culture of the uplands, it is evident that the state of Mississippi alone could produce the entire crop now grown in the United States. (*a*)

Georgia stands second in total production, but examination shows that the causes which place the state so near to the highest in position are widely different from those obtaining in Mississippi. With half a million more inhabitants than Mississippi, the cotton product of Georgia is a little over half a bale (0.53) *per capita*, and the average product per acre is but two-thirds of that of Mississippi (0.31 to 0.46). A detailed examination of the soils of Georgia shows that her area of what in Mississippi are considered first- and second-class soils is very limited— far more so than is the case in the neighboring state of Alabama; yet Georgia stands slightly ahead of Alabama in the average cotton product per acre, and is only a trifle behind in production per capita (0.53 to 0.55). In other words, the high position of Georgia is due, not to natural advantages, but to better cultivation of the soil, the use of fertilizers, and the thrift of an industrious population. Reports also show a considerable extension of the area of cotton culture to and even beyond the Blue Ridge.

The geographical position of *Alabama* between the states standing at the head of the list gives double interest to the question regarding the causes of her position in the same, which would be the third place but for the enormous area of Texas, where the sparse population has thus far picked the best lands. Alabama is a newer state than Georgia, and there reach into it from Mississippi the two belts of rich prairie lands which terminate short of the Chattahoochee. Northern Alabama is almost identical in its agricultural features with northern Georgia, and we should therefore expect to find a much more marked difference in favor of Alabama than is shown in the figures quoted. The inference seems irresistible that, while Mississippi is still partly within the period of the first flush of fertility and Georgia has reached the stage when the use of fertilizers is renovating her fields, the soils of Alabama have passed the first stage, and her population has not yet realized the necessity of sustaining the soil's powers by fertilization.

Cotton culture in *Florida* is chiefly confined to that part of the state lying adjacent to Georgia. This is mostly pine land, and is cultivated without manure; hence the low product of less than a quarter of a bale per acre. Notwithstanding this, there has been a respectable increase in production since 1870, though not so large as that of the population; a circumstance doubtless due to the prominent position which the culture of tropical fruits has assumed during the past decade, and to which most of the new-comers have given their attention. No cotton is returned from that portion of the state lying south of Tampa bay, and but little from the coasts, as well as from the extreme western part. The cotton-growing counties show an average product of 0.26, or a little over a quarter of a bale per acre. A considerable proportion (15,532 bales, or 28.2 per cent.) of this product is long-staple or sea-island cotton, of which the state produces nearly the entire supply at present. It should be kept in mind that the bales of long-staple cotton have an average weight of 350 pounds only, and that the proportion of lint to seed is reckoned as one to three, instead of one to two, as in the uplands cotton.

Tennessee presents the striking fact of a total production of less than half of that of Alabama, but with an average product per acre one-half greater, equal even to that of Mississippi. The cause of this state of things

---

a So far from being an overestimate, the above statement does not adequately state the possibilities within reach of careful culture. Fully 1,000 pounds of lint has repeatedly been picked off an acre of the "buckshot" soil of the Yazoo bottom.

becomes apparent when we circumscribe the regions of production in accordance with the natural divisions of the state. It then appears that the portion of Tennessee lying east of the "central basin", (a) from the eastern highland rim to the line of North Carolina, and comprising about one-third of the area of the cotton-growing state, produces only about 1 per cent. of the total amount of cotton, while 84 per cent. of this total is produced in the country lying between the Tennessee and Mississippi rivers, on the extreme west. More than this, within this region the average production *per inhabitant* is 0.57 of a bale and a little less (0.47 of a bale) *per acre*, while the average for the entire state per inhabitant is only 0.21 of a bale. Again, of the above 84 per cent., 70 belongs to the two tiers of counties lying nearest to the Mississippi river. Of these only a small portion is bottom land of the Mississippi river, the greater part by far being gently rolling uplands ("table-lands"), such as form also a large body in northwestern Mississippi, and extend, gradually narrowing, as far south as Baton Rouge, Louisiana.

It thus appears that the cotton production of Tennessee is concentrated upon a comparatively small area of highly productive lands, the rest being devoted preferably to grain, grasses, tobacco, and other industries, to which the soils and climates are more specially adapted; while in the other cotton-growing states cotton is very generally grown as a matter of course, regardless of other cultures, of which the partial pursuit, at least, would in the end be more profitable than exclusive cotton-planting.

Arkansas produces its 608,000 bales (in round numbers) on somewhat over a million of acres, making the average product per acre 0.58 (slightly lower than that of Louisiana) and the average per inhabitant 0.76 of a bale. A cursory examination shows that by far the greater portion of the cotton produced comes from the eastern and southern portions of the state, which contain a large proportion of bottom lands, while in the extreme northern and northwestern counties but little cotton is grown. The form of the returns makes it difficult to segregate the production of the uplands and lowlands in this case; but the product per acre of the bottom county of Chicot stands second to the highest on the list, and it is safe to assume that, on detailed discussion, the average production of uplands and lowlands will be found, respectively, to be about the same as in Louisiana. In both states alike the use of fertilizers in the large-scale production of cotton may be regarded as wholly insignificant in its influence on the general result.

In the case of *Louisiana*, as in that of Tennessee, a considerable portion (about one-fourth) of the state is devoted mainly to other cultures than that of cotton, the sugar-cane gaining precedence in the lowland country lying south of the mouth of Red river, in which only about 6 per cent. of the total amount of cotton is produced, but at the average rate of 0.80 bale per acre. Nearly the same or a slightly higher average per acre is obtained in the alluvial lands north and west of the mouth of Red river, and in the Red river valley itself. The small parish of East Carroll, in the northeastern corner of the state, has the highest average product per acre of any county in the cotton states (0.95 of a bale), and stands second in total production within the state. It will be noted that East Carroll lies opposite Issaquena county, Mississippi, and adjoins Chicot county, Arkansas, both representing maxima of product per acre in their respective states; and there can be no doubt that were the riverward portion of Washington county, Mississippi, segregated from the less productive interior portion its product per acre (0.87) would equal that of Issaquena (0.88). *We have here apparently the center of maximum cotton production on natural soils in the United States, and probably in the world.*

The average product per acre in the uplands of Louisiana (0.41) is approximately half that of the lowlands; and as the average for the state is 0.59, it follows that somewhat more than half the acreage in cotton belongs to the uplands, while the lowlands yield nearly two-thirds of the entire amount. This predominance of lowland cotton explains the higher average product per acre in Louisiana as compared with Mississippi, where less than one-third of the cotton production comes from the Yazoo bottom lands. Within the cotton-growing region proper the average production is approximately 0.95 of a bale *per inhabitant*, but as this figure excludes the entire population of the city of New Orleans, so largely interested in cotton, it is not fairly comparable with the proportion existing in other states. If one-half the population of the city be taken as mainly interested in cotton, the *per capita* proportion would stand 0.80 bale.

The great state of *Texas*, while first in population, stands third in the list of total cotton production among the cotton states. The fact shown by the figures of acreage and total production, viz, that in the average product per acre (0.37) it stands eleventh in rank, will be a surprise to most persons, and is doubtless in part to be accounted for as an accident of the season, the year 1879 having been an unusually dry one, and therefore especially unfavorable to a country having a scanty rainfall, and in which so large a proportion of the staple is grown on upland soils. Among these the heavy black-prairie soils, so highly productive in favorable seasons, are notoriously the first to suffer from drought. It is probable that in ordinary seasons the average product per acre in Texas would approach more nearly that of Mississippi or South Carolina.

A discussion of the returns shows that 52 per cent. of the cotton product of Texas is grown in the northeastern portion of the state, north of the thirty-second parallel and east of the ninety-eighth meridian, and that within this region the production is highest in the counties adjoining Red river, the product averaging 0.54 bale per acre. South of the thirty-second parallel the average yield is 0.34 bale per acre. The coast counties produce but little cotton; inland, between Red river and San Antonio, about 35 per cent. of the total product is grown on black-

---

a The "central basin" includes the valleys of the Cumberland, Duck, and Elk rivers, with tributaries.

prairie land, the average product per acre on such land being (in 1879) 0.34 bale per acre. A comparison of the returns of the present census with those of the preceding one shows that within the last decade the region of cotton production has extended westward 75 miles. On the south but very little cotton is grown south and west of the Nueces river.

Compared to the area of fertile lands susceptible of cotton culture, the present cotton acreage of Texas is almost insignificant.

The cases of the two *Carolinas* with respect to cotton production are nearly alike, and may as well be considered together. In both states the average cotton product per acre is high as compared with that of Georgia and Alabama, and in the case of North Carolina approaches that of Mississippi itself. Without entering into details on the subject of the distribution of cotton production in these states, it may be broadly stated that the culture of cotton is reported to have greatly extended of late, even up the slopes of the Blue Ridge itself. Among the causes leading to this gratifying result reports received show that the use of fertilizers, and, with it, better methods of culture, are foremost. In other words, these two members of the original union of thirteen have been the first to place cotton culture upon a permanent foundation by adopting a system of regular returns to the soil; and the high product per acre, as compared with Georgia and Alabama on the one hand and with Mississippi on the other, exhibits tellingly the tide-wave advancing westward, the ebb of the first native fertility in Alabama and Florida, the rising tide of restored productiveness in the Carolinas, with Georgia on the westward slope of the wave, on which it is rising and showing distinctly a higher product per acre in its eastern than in its western portion, where the use of fertilizers is much less extended.

2.—THE BORDER COTTON STATES.

The concentration of cotton culture upon the most fertile lands, already so apparent in Tennessee, becomes even more so in *Missouri*, the most northerly region of large-scale cotton production. It appears from Table III that Missouri stands at the head of the list for cotton product per acre cultivated in that crop, and it seems singular that this should be the case at the extreme northern limit of cotton culture; but the anomaly disappears when we locate the area of production, and it becomes apparent that it embraces almost exclusively the highly fertile lowlands lying at the head of the great "Saint Francis bottom", in the southeastern corner of the state. Their product per acre must therefore be compared with that of others of a similar character, e. g., that of the Yazoo bottom; here, as is partly shown in Table III, the average product ranges between 0.80 and 0.88 of a bale per acre, to offset the 0.66 to 0.75 shown by the Missouri cotton area. Assuming the soils to be similar in average fertility in either region, the difference is manifestly due to the comparatively short season for the development of the cotton-plant in the latitude of the Missouri cotton region; and for the same reason cotton is there grown only on those lands whose high fertility insures the most rapid development. Taking these points into consideration, the product per acre seems high, owing, perhaps, to careful cultivation by white labor.

The cotton production of *Kentucky* pertains, in the main, to what has been appropriately styled the "penumbral" region of that industry. The bulk is produced in the counties lying adjacent to western Tennessee and to the Mississippi river, the latter embracing portions of the rich bottom, with an average product per acre of from 0.48 to 0.56 of a bale. Eastward the cotton is grown in small patches, mostly for home consumption. Such small tracts being well cultivated, the product per acre is comparatively high, even so as to reach the average of the counties bordering on the Mississippi river, doubtless through the use of manure.

In *Virginia* the cotton-producing region is confined to ten counties lying in the southeastern portion of the state, adjacent to North Carolina, and corresponding in their surface features and soils to the chief cotton-producing portion of the latter state. Accordingly the average product per acre of both states is the same, viz, 0.44 bale or 621 pounds of seed-cotton. A comparison with the returns of the census of 1870 shows a material increase of area as well as of total production of cotton in Virginia within the last ten years, as cotton was then produced in fifteen counties, with a reported product of 183 bales, as against 19,595 bales now shown from ten counties The change indicates a tendency to the concentration of cotton culture in the southeastern portion of the state.

In the *Indian territory* the area of cotton production extends as far north as Tahlequah, in the Cherokee nation, and a few miles north of Muscogee, Creek nation; but the great bulk of the crop is produced south of the Canadian river, and in the Red River region from the Arkansas line as far west as Caddo, on the Missouri, Kansas and Texas railroad.

In the case of *California* no cotton was reported by the enumerators, but a special examination showed that cotton was grown during the census year in one locality, viz, on the bottom lands of the Merced river, to the extent shown in the table, the yield having been about a 400-pound bale per acre. The staple has at various times, however, been successfully grown in localities scattered throughout the Sacramento and San Joaquin valleys; but the limitation of the local market, and the great distance from the centers of manufacture, has thus far restricted production. The culture is, however, on the increase, since not only the excellence of the staple, but other natural causes, more specially referred to in the report on the state, seem to point to it as a promising industry in the future.

In *Arizona* successful experiments in cotton culture have been made, but not as yet to the extent of marketing the product. The perennial character which the plant assumes there, as well as in southern California, may ultimately turn the balance in favor of its cultivation.

MEASUREMENTS OF COTTON FIBER,

MADE UNDER DIRECTION OF

JOHN M. ORDWAY,

PROFESSOR OF METALLURGY AND INDUSTRIAL CHEMISTRY AT THE MASSACHUSETTS INSTITUTE OF
TECHNOLOGY, BOSTON.

11

23

MEASUREMENTS OF COTTON FIBER.

[NOTE.—The cotton samples of which measurements have been made were received in response to a circular sent out by the Census Office, through the special agents in charge of the subject of cotton production in the several states, to the same persons who had responded to the schedule questions regarding cotton culture. It was requested that one or several good average bolls should be sent with their seed-cotton still adherent; that the variety of the cotton should be stated, as well as the kind of soil on which it had been grown; whether manure has been used, and if so, what kind, and how much; whether the land was fresh or had been cultivated for some length of time, etc.

The extent of the response made is shown in the tables. Four hundred and fifty samples were received in time for the measurements, the proper means and appliances for which were devised by Professor Ordway and used under his personal supervision. Details regarding these, as well as the difficulties encountered, are given by him in the subjoined communication. A brief discussion of the results is added by the editor.

It is to be regretted that, in consequence of a misunderstanding, the state of Tennessee is but very scantily represented among the samples examined.—E. W. H.]

Professor EUGENE W. HILGARD:

DEAR SIR: For making trials of the *length* of cotton fibers we used at first a microscope with a "mechanical stage", whose right and left sliding-piece had been graduated and furnished with a vernier, so as to read to hundredths of a millimeter. The single fiber was spread out straight on a glass slide with the help of a camel's-hair pencil wet with water, and it was then covered with another strip of thin glass having an up and down line ruled in the middle of its length. This cross-line was needed to divide the fiber, so that half of the length could be taken at a time, as the stage allowed a motion of only about 20 millimeters at once.

It requires patience and practice to straighten the fibers properly, and absolute exactness is hardly attainable. After acquiring some experience in handling the fibers, the young ladies, who performed most of the work, found it possible to make pretty nice determinations by direct measurement with a pair of dividers and a scale graduated to twentieths of a millimeter. So a part of the lengths were obtained with the microscope and a part by the direct method.

Most of the samples had not been picked or ginned, and so, in most cases, the fibers were detached directly from the seed at the time of trial.

In determining the *widths* (a) several fibers at a time were compressed dry and measured in different parts with a Jackson eye-piece micrometer, the value of the divisions, for the one-fifth inch objective used, being determined by reference to a standard stage micrometer made by Rogers, of the Harvard College observatory. The figures of width given in the table are averages of four fibers, each measured in five places.

Width alone does not indicate the fineness of the flattened cells, and tensile strength ought, in strictness, to be referred to the area of the cross-section. I therefore desired very much to measure also the thickness of the fibers, but hitherto I have been unable to get an apparatus for untwisting the fibers under the microscope, and without such an apparatus it seems hardly possible to see and determine the natural thickness. It is exceedingly difficult to make exactly transverse sections of such fibers as cotton, and if sections are made with the help of paraffine or gelatine the original size is not likely to remain unaltered. The stage twister would probably enable one to find the comparative amount of twist in fibers, and no doubt the practical value of cotton depends, in no small measure, on the number of turns per millimeter.

---

a It should be understood that the fiber of cotton is, when young, a thin, hollow cylinder filled with liquid. In ripening the liquid disappears and the cylinder contracts into a flat band, with thickened edges (looking in cross-section somewhat like two commas placed points together), and assumes more or less of a twist. It is this peculiar form that allows even very short cotton fiber to be easily spun, a good deal depending upon the extent of the twist, the width, and the form of the upturned edges.—E. W. H.

12
24

I could devise no means of making trustworthy, comparable determinations of *tensile strength* except with single fibers. As the breaking strain of a single fiber is at best but a very small force, rarely exceeding 12 grams, after a due consideration of possible methods it seemed best to resort to the simplest, that of direct weighting. But to get clamps light enough for such fine work is not so very easy. I made very small forceps of hickory wood, with a hinge of thin brass, secured by brass hoops, the points being covered with thin wash-leather, glued on. The grip was tightened by a brass link with a wooden wedge. For the upper stationary holder a wooden clothes-pin with a strong spring was whittled to a narrow point and the tips were covered with wash-leather. The fiber being securely clamped, it was hung vertically, and to the spring hinge of the lower clamp was hooked a scale-pan of thin cardboard with hangers of fine wire. Weights were very carefully added, a tenth of a gram at a time, till the fiber broke. No account was made of such ruptures with a light strain as showed that the fiber was cracked or otherwise defective.

In finding the *relative amounts of fiber and seeds* five average seeds were weighed, with their coats, in a balance sensitive to tenths of a milligram; the fibers were then pulled off, and the remaining furzy or smooth seeds were weighed. Of course the seeds were taken as they came, air-dried. They were mostly about a year old, and the kernels were not as yet very much shrunken.

Respectfully yours.

JOHN M. ORDWAY.

EXPLANATION OF TABLES.

In the following tables the first column of figures shows the reference numbers of the specimens, running consecutively through the states and counties, arranged in alphabetical order.

The arrangement of specimens in each state is, as far as possible, according to soil classification; in some instances, however, the nature of the land on which certain samples of cotton were grown was either not given at all by the sender or was stated in an indefinite manner by reference to a soil number described by him in the county reports. Fertilizers were probably used on many of the soils in the states east of Mississippi, though not generally reported.

Samples collected at different times of the season may exhibit differences independent of the nature of the soil, especially when taken late, under the possible influence of frosts and early rains.

The measurements are recorded in both the English and metric measures and weights. The first and sixth columns give the average length of five fibers; the minimum and maximum are shown by the columns on the right. The second and ninth columns contain the average width of four fibers, measured each in five places, making the average of twenty measurements. These measurements are given in thousandths of an inch and in millimeters. The minimum and maximum of the twenty observations are also given in millimeters.

The third and twelfth columns represent the weight in grains and grams required to break single fibers. The number in each case is the average of either ten or five good results, doubtful trials not being recorded. Minima and maxima are given at the right.

The fourth and fifteenth columns express the weight in grains and grams of five seeds with the lint on.

The fifth column makes known the percentage of lint which was picked from the five gross seeds.

ALABAMA.

Number of sample.	Character of soil.	County.	Cotton variety.	Sender.
	SANDY LANDS.			
8	Sandy upland, unmanured....................................	Bullock..........		W. M. Stakely..............
12	Sandy upland	Clarke.....		S. Forwood................
14	Sandy upland, unmanured..................................	Coffee		M. G. Stoudenmer.............
10	Sandy, gravelly upland	Clarke		S. Forwood......... .....
27	Pine sandy land...	Marion		M. Nesmith................
46 a	Gray sandy soil, yellow-pine land, fertilized	Wilcox		Felix Tait ....
46 b	Gray sandy soil, yellow-pine or scrub post-oak land, fertilized	...do		.......do ....
48 a	Coarsest sandy pine upland, new, no fertilisers.................	Washington		R. M. Campbell ....
48 b	Old gray soil, Vivion place, no fertilizers	...do		.......do ....
48 d	Piny woods, poor sandy land, no fertilisers.................	...do		.......do ....
48 c	Piny woods, poor sandy land, with yard manure	...do		.......do ....
48 e	Piny woods, gray sandy land, with composts	...do		.......do ....
1	Gray sandy lands (flats of creeks), poor	Barbour		H. D. Clayton ....
15	Light sandy soil	Crenshaw		G. W. Thagard.............
9	Black-jack land	Bullock...........	Hunt and Dixon	M. L. Stinson .:.......... ..
17	Gray "barrens" land......................................	Jackson		W. F. Hunt ....
34	Fine sandy "barrens" land, with 200 pounds of guano per acre.........	Madison		T. B. Kelly...............
30	Gray gravelly upland, manured...........................	Saint Clair.......		J. W. Inzer ....
31	......do	...de		.......do ....
28	Black sandy land	Marion		M. Nesmith...............
11	Sandy land, clay subsoil	Clarke		S. Forwood ....
13	Gray gravelly land	Cleburne		J. H. Bell ....
21	Gray gravelly land, lightly manured.....................	Lee.............		J. T. Harris ....
34	Gray gravelly land, manured............................	Tallapoosa.......		D. A. G. Ross ....
	HEAVY AND CALCAREOUS LANDS.			
7	Black land, unmanured	Bullock..........		W. M. Stakely ....
26	Black and loose soil......................................	Marengo.........	Early bolls	W. A. Stickney ....
49 a	Stiff prairie soil	Washington		R. W. Campbell ....
49 b	Black prairie or lime land, loose and mellow	...do		.......do ......
49 c	Red prairie soil	...do		.......do ......
47 c	Slough prairie soil	Wilcox		Felix Tait ....
47 b	Ridge prairie soil	...do		.......do ....
3	Light gray lime lands, Cowikee uplands	Barbour		H. D. Clayton ....
	BOTTOM LANDS.			
44	Brown loam of creek bottoms	Winston		F. C. Burdick ....
33	Bottom lands...	Talladega.........		H. M. Bart ....
5	Lowland	Barbour	...	H. Hawkins ....
4	Best Cowikee bottom land	...do		H. D. Clayton ....
36	Bottom land, fertilized...................................	Tallapoosa........		D. A. G. Ross ....
37	Stiff river bottom land	Tuscaloosa	Long staple	J. B. Maxwell ....
38	......do	...do ..:.......	Ramesses.................	.......do ......
40	......do......	...do ....a.....	Golden Prolific	.......do ......
50	Big Black river bottom land	Washington		R. M. Campbell ....
45 b	First quality Alabama river bottom land	Wilcox		Felix Tait ....
29	Swamp or marsh land.....................................	Marion		M. Nesmith...............
	RED AND CLAY LANDS.			
6	Clay uplands, unmanured................................	Bullock..........	Hunt and Dixon	M. L. Stinson ....
22	Red land	Lee..............		J. T. Harris ....
25 a	Post-oak or mulatto soil, "cedar soil"...................	Marengo.........		W. A. Stickney ....
25 b	...... do................	...... do.......		.......do ......
35	Red land, fertilized......................................	Tallapoosa........		D. A. G. Ross ....
38	Red clay upland	Tuscaloosa	Ramesses.................	J. B. Maxwell ....
41	......do......	...do........	Golden Prolific	.......do ......
45 a	Red land, oak, hickory, and short-leaf pine	Wilcox		Felix Tait ....
2	Coarse, red sandy land, clay subsoil.....................	Barbour		H. D. Clayton ....
16	Red-clay lands...	Jackson		W. F. Hunt ....
19	Table-lands, newly cultivated	Lauderdale		J. H. Simpson ....
18	Table-lands, old lands cultivated 75 years	...de		.......do ......
20	Table-lands, fine red, sandy, gravelly soil	...de	First picking	J. W. Morgan ....
23	Red limestone land, partly manured.....................	Madison		T. B. Kelly...............

26

ALABAMA.

LENGTH, IN INCHES.	WIDTH, IN 1/1000 OF AN INCH.	BREAKING WEIGHT, IN GRAINS.	Weight of 5 seed with the lint, in grains.	Percentage of lint.	LENGTH, IN MILLIMETERS.			WIDTH, IN 1/1000 OF A MILLIMETER.			BREAKING WEIGHT, IN GRAMS.			Weight of 5 seed with the lint, in grams.	Number of sample.
Average of 4 fibers.	Average of 4 fibers.	Average of 10 or 15 results.			Average of 5 fibers.	Minimum.	Maximum.	Average of 4 fibers.	Minimum.	Maximum.	Average of 5 or 10 results.	Minimum.	Maximum.		
1	2	3	4	5	6	7	8	9	10	11	12	13	14	15	
1.043	0.791	148.8	....	....	26.51	21.9	28.3	20.1	10.0	30.0	9.64	7.9	11.5	....	6
0.847	1.004	182.3	11.11	31.25	21.58	21.0	22.1	25.5	15.6	33.3	8.87	7.4	10.6	0.72	12
1.004	0.906	108.4	13.60	35.59	25.50	28.7	27.2	23.0	16.6	30.0	6.70	5.0	7.6	0.725	14
1.214	1.095	182.4	11.43	30.40	30.84	25.1	32.7	24.2	16.6	33.3	8.58	7.2	12.6	0.740	10
1.015	0.744	196.1	14.89	32.12	25.80	21.2	28.3	18.9	13.3	23.3	10.07	8.4	10.6	0.985	27
1.266	0.906	142.3	10.67	26.47	32.16	24.7	37.5	23.0	16.6	30.6	9.22	7.3	12.6	0.685	46 a
1.037	0.878	172.5	12.42	31.68	26.34	25.2	28.2	22.3	16.6	26.6	11.18	8.9	14.7	0.805	46 b
0.925	1.031	192.9	13.74	33.14	23.50	20.6	27.5	26.2	20.0	33.3	12.44	8.5	7.4	0.890	46 c
0.931	1.066	123.3	9.41	36.06	23.54	22.4	26.1	27.8	23.3	30.0	8.03	6.3	11.2	0.810	42 b
0.789	0.827	143.4	9.49	35.77	20.04	19.0	20.9	21.0	13.3	26.6	9.29	8.6	10.1	0.615	46 d
0.922	0.819	114.2	13.04	26.02	23.42	20.9	26.1	20.8	16.6	23.3	7.40	5.7	9.2	0.845	46 e
1.023	0.868	147.5	12.85	31.87	26.00	25.0	26.7	22.0	16.6	26.6	9.56	7.7	13.8	0.800	46 d
0.990	0.890	142.6	11.72	38.16	25.14	22.9	29.2	22.6	20.0	26.6	9.21	8.0	11.3	0.760	1
1.048	0.760	149.4	13.97	34.80	26.62	26.0	28.6	19.3	13.3	23.3	7.66	7.1	9.0	0.905	15
0.963	0.839	115.8	10.65	34.78	24.46	24.1	25.9	21.3	13.3	26.6	9.45	7.7	11.7	0.890	9
0.906	0.768	145.5	12.50	31.43	25.30	22.7	27.5	19.5	16.6	26.6	9.43	7.7	13.0	0.975	17
1.063	0.878	142.3	11.73	34.87	27.52	25.2	34.6	22.3	16.6	26.6	9.32	7.4	13.7	0.780	34
1.076	1.153	162.6	....	....	27.34	26.6	28.2	29.3	20.0	43.3	8.88	8.0	10.9	....	30
1.156	1.027	184.5	13.73	35.76	29.36	26.1	34.2	26.1	20.0	46.6	8.72	8.1	11.4	0.825	31
0.964	0.592	130.1	14.43	36.87	25.00	21.5	27.1	22.4	16.6	33.3	7.78	6.1	12.0	0.936	38
0.848	0.772	140.1	13.50	30.25	21.54	19.5	23.7	19.6	14.6	26.6	9.08	7.2	11.2	0.810	11
0.966	0.794	113.0	8.26	27.10	24.54	22.4	25.8	19.4	13.3	23.3	7.33	6.3	8.9	0.335	13
0.981	0.940	140.0	10.11	36.79	24.42	22.4	29.3	23.3	10.0	26.6	9.10	6.7	12.8	0.555	21
0.864	0.913	108.1	13.13	31.46	21.94	20.8	22.9	23.2	13.3	33.3	10.89	9.6	12.5	0.390	34
1.129	0.988	127.6	....	....	28.54	25.6	31.8	25.1	16.6	30.0	8.28	6.5	12.0	....	7
1.104	0.940	115.8	14.04	28.02	28.04	27.2	29.5	34.1	16.6	36.6	7.87	6.9	8.9	0.910	38
1.178	0.892	122.2	15.90	33.49	29.94	26.4	34.1	21.9	16.6	33.3	7.98	7.1	9.5	1.080	49 a
1.114	0.896	122.2	14.74	30.96	28.30	26.5	33.1	22.7	10.0	30.0	7.92	7.1	9.5	0.965	49 b
1.023	0.941	152.1	10.96	30.90	26.00	25.1	26.7	24.4	13.3	30.0	9.92	8.1	14.3	0.710	49 c
1.089	0.717	144.5	12.43	36.64	28.74	25.9	30.1	18.1	10.0	26.6	7.65	7.3	11.0	0.805	47 a
0.917	0.768	138.3	13.35	32.27	23.30	22.0	25.1	19.5	10.0	26.6	8.96	7.1	10.4	0.955	47 b
0.990	0.690	121.3	13.04	34.67	25.16	22.0	26.6	17.0	10.0	23.3	7.86	6.9	9.0	0.790	7
0.942	0.811	129.5	11.50	36.80	23.95	22.3	25.8	20.6	16.6	30.0	8.39	7.1	10.0	0.745	44
0.974	1.047	180.6	11.43	31.08	24.74	22.7	25.8	26.6	20.0	33.3	8.46	7.2	13.2	0.740	33
1.075	0.995	87.8	12.27	30.82	27.31	24.6	29.0	23.5	16.6	30.0	5.66	4.4	8.2	0.795	5
1.089	0.728	133.7	14.20	36.41	26.40	25.0	28.7	18.5	13.3	23.3	8.99	7.1	10.5	0.930	4
0.968	0.626	136.4	14.04	37.36	24.34	21.0	27.1	15.9	10.0	26.6	8.84	6.6	12.1	0.910	36
1.109	0.986	124.2	11.06	32.90	28.16	26.2	29.1	22.0	16.6	26.6	8.05	6.3	13.3	0.775	37
1.089	0.897	140.4	13.58	34.06	25.40	25.0	27.9	22.3	20.0	33.3	9.10	7.6	13.3	0.890	30
1.016	1.074	266.7	10.11	41.96	25.80	22.3	28.7	27.3	16.6	36.6	12.92	10.6	17.0	0.655	46
1.301	0.740	141.1	13.19	36.65	33.06	30.4	36.6	18.6	13.3	23.3	8.14	7.7	10.9	0.984	39
1.177	0.860	163.3	11.51	33.98	33.90	34.5	33.9	17.5	13.3	23.3	10.18	8.5	14.4	0.768	45 b
0.990	1.061	151.4	11.03	32.36	25.14	23.0	26.7	26.7	10.0	30.0	9.81	9.2	12.3	0.715	29
1.006	0.963	122.0	14.97	30.92	25.56	23.4	27.3	20.4	13.3	26.6	7.97	6.2	9.9	0.970	8
1.007	0.774	136.6	13.95	36.64	25.56	21.5	33.3	18.4	6.6	26.6	8.51	6.3	12.6	0.863	22
0.860	1.181	118.7	11.43	35.78	21.84	20.4	23.0	30.0	23.3	40.0	7.69	6.3	10.3	0.740	25 a
0.920	0.906	132.7	13.58	30.00	23.36	23.3	24.6	23.0	16.6	36.6	8.50	6.7	11.8	0.880	25 b
1.101	0.902	162.5	14.38	31.31	27.96	26.0	32.5	22.9	16.6	36.6	10.55	8.5	14.4	0.990	35
0.961	0.748	86.3	9.49	30.06	24.40	24.9	25.7	19.0	16.6	23.3	5.58	5.0	6.6	0.615	36
1.408	0.870	134.2	15.58	38.75	35.92	31.6	39.9	22.1	16.6	26.6	8.05	6.7	9.6	0.800	41
0.945	1.306	146.1	13.19	34.50	24.02	21.8	27.3	34.0	23.3	36.6	9.47	8.2	13.1	0.850	45 a
0.968	0.986	100.4	10.73	30.20	24.60	23.1	27.6	25.1	20.0	33.3	6.74	5.5	7.9	0.710	3
1.175	0.791	117.3	14.76	29.68	29.78	26.3	34.9	20.1	16.6	26.6	7.60	6.3	8.7	1.065	16
0.875	1.004	197.3	10.96	34.06	22.22	19.1	25.9	25.5	16.6	30.0	12.78	10.3	15.3	0.710	18
0.873	1.016	197.5	10.96	28.60	23.14	20.0	35.1	25.8	20.0	33.3	12.83	10.9	15.3	0.710	18
1.056	0.913	189.0	13.73	33.72	26.89	25.2	29.4	23.2	13.3	26.6	9.01	7.0	13.8	0.825	30
1.045	0.799	187.8	10.96	32.40	26.54	25.6	27.6	20.3	10.0	30.0	8.98	7.3	10.4	0.710	28

27

ALABAMA—Continued.

Number of sample.	Character of soil.	County.	Cotton variety.	Sender.
	RED AND CLAY LANDS—continued.			
32	Red loam valley land	Talladega		H. M. Burt
42	Uplands	Winston		G. W. Hogg
43	....do	....do		....do
	Average of all			

Longest, No. 43; shortest, No. 48 d. Widest, No. 45 a; narrowest, No. 36. Strongest, No. 40;

ARIZONA.

51	Valley lands, Hayden's Ferry	Maricopa		C. T. Hayden
52	Valley lands	Pima	Chinese	W. A. Cunningham
53	....do	Yuma	Second-year plant	Lieut. J. M. E. Hyde, U. S. A.
54	Valley lands, Salt River valley			R. A. Loughridge
	Average of all			

Longest, No. 51; shortest, No. 53. Widest, No. 52;

ARKANSAS.

56	Timbered upland, sandy	Arkansas		J. H. Moore
57	Black gravelly loam	Boone		
58	Sandy loam, ridge land	....do		
61	Black sandy land, flat	Crittenden		A. A. Brewer
62	Dark loam	....do		....do
66	Sandy upland, clay subsoil	Grant		W. W. Cleveland
59	Brown clay loam bottom land	Boone		
56	Arkansas river alluvial land	Arkansas		J. H. Moore
60	....do	Conway		W. C. Stout
64	Dark sandy alluvial land	Garland	Third picking	J. J. Sumpter
65	Light sandy bottom land	....do	....do	....do
67	Lowland	Grant		W. W. Cleveland
63	Buckshot land	Crittenden		A. A. Brewer
	Average of all			

Longest, No. 66; shortest, No. 56. Widest, No. 56; narrowest, No. 55. Strongest, No. 60;

CALIFORNIA.

93	Red gravelly bench land, National ranch	San Diego	2-year old plant	F. H. Kimball
91	Red plateau soil, 2,000 feet altitude	Napa		H. Kimball
68	Alluvial loam, alkaline	Kern	Texan smooth seeds	
69	....do	....do	Golden Prolific	
70	....do	....do	Dickson smooth seeds	
71	....do	....do		
72	Alluvial loam	Merced	Peeler	
73	Alluvial loam, Buckley's ranch	....do	....do	
74	....do	....do	....do	
75	Alluvial loam	....do	Mexican	
76	Alluvial loam, Peck's ranch	....do	Dickson	
77	Alluvial loam, Wilcox place, Mariposa creek	....do	....do	
78	....do	....do	Alabama	
79	Alluvial loam, Hopeton	....do	Dickson	W. A. Grado
80	Alluvial loam, Mariposa creek	....do		J. L. Strong
83	Alluvial loam	Tulare	Seed from Saint Louis prize bale	....do
84	....do	....do	Excelsior	....do
85	....do	....do	Matagorda	....do
86	Alluvial loam, Mussel Slough	....do		
	Average of all			

Longest, No. 86; shortest, No. 70. Widest, No. 70; narrowest, No. 86. Strongest, No. 70;

ALABAMA—Continued.

LENGTH, IN INCHES. Average of 4 fibers.	WIDTH, IN 1/1000 OF AN INCH. Average of 4 fibers.	BREAKING WEIGHT, IN GRAINS. Average of 10 or 15 results.	Weight of 5 seed with the lint, in grains.	Percentage of lint.	LENGTH, IN MILLIMETERS.			WIDTH, IN 1/1000 OF A MILLIMETER.			BREAKING WEIGHT, IN GRAMS.			Weight of 5 seed with the lint, in grams.	Number of sample.
					Average of 5 fibers.	Minimum.	Maximum.	Average of 4 fibers.	Minimum.	Maximum.	Average of 5 or 10 results.	Minimum.	Maximum.		
1	2	3	4	5	6	7	8	9	10	11	12	13	14	15	
0.683	0.858	136.5	11.86	33.11	22.42	20.4	25.2	21.8	16.6	26.6	8.85	7.9	10.4	0.770	32
1.049	9.896	111.2	12.73	33.94	26.64	25.0	35.3	23.8	16.6	26.6	7.21	6.3	8.5	0.835	42
1.427	1.279	144.8	11.11	37.50	36.25	30.3	47.5	32.5	20.0	44.6	8.88	7.2	12.8	0.790	43
1.027	0.896	137.8	12.38	32.96	26.09	19.0	47.5	23.75	6.6	44.6	8.98	4.4	17.4	0.868	

weakest, No. 38. Heaviest, No. 16; lightest, No. 13. Most lint, No. 40; least lint, No. 48 c.

ARIZONA.

1.192	0.965	140.7			30.28	28.3	32.9	24.5	17.4	33.9	9.12	7.9	9.7		51
0.904	1.193	143.7			22.96	17.7	27.5	26.2	17.4	35.6	9.80	8.4	11.8		52
0.745	0.972	138.6	11.50	24.16	18.98	16.3	22.9	24.7	17.4	31.3	8.96	7.5	10.7	0.745	53
1.034	0.770	115.1	12.42	31.67	26.28	25.0	28.7	19.8	13.3	26.6	7.46	6.3	8.3	0.806	54
0.969	0.957	133.7	11.96	27.91	24.61	16.3	32.9	24.3	13.3	35.6	8.71	5.8	11.8	0.775	

narrowest, No. 54. Weakest, No 54; strongest, No. 52.

ARKANSAS.

0.965	1.154	132.3	11.88	31.17	34.52	23.0	36.0	29.3	23.3	46.6	8.50	7.2	9.8	0.770	56
0.953	1.008	103.5	14.27	29.19	24.92	19.6	29.8	23.6	16.6	30.0	6.71	6.2	9.2	0.925	57
1.026	0.984	184.3	13.12	38.23	26.06	23.6	28.3	25.0	16.6	30.0	8.79	7.1	11.8	0.850	58
1.088	0.795	121.0	9.42	32.78	27.65	25.8	28.7	26.2	10.0	30.0	7.84	6.2	10.0	0.610	61
0.972	0.803	132.9	13.19	33.92	34.69	26.9	31.0	30.4	10.0	30.0	8.61	6.8	11.0	0.855	62
1.143	0.807	128.4	11.57	37.33	29.04	26.2	30.6	20.5	16.6	23.3	8.32	7.4	9.4	0.750	66
1.039	0.854	117.6	14.61	28.64	26.40	20.8	31.4	21.7	13.3	30.0	7.62	6.7	9.9	0.980	59
1.050	0.723	131.6	14.35	36.10	27.30	24.0	31.8	18.6	13.6	26.6	8.54	7.5	10.5	0.930	55
1.031	1.095	185.2	22.14	35.69	36.21	23.0	38.5	26.3	13.3	34.6	12.00	10.1	15.6	1.435	60
1.124	0.980	172.2	11.19	35.88	28.54	24.3	36.0	25.1	20.0	30.0	7.92	7.2	9.8	0.735	64
1.032	1.004	162.1	13.27	29.65	26.23	23.6	28.8	25.3	20.0	30.0	10.50	9.6	12.3	0.800	65
0.986	0.787	142.6	11.73	33.55	25.35	22.8	27.8	20.0	16.6	30.0	9.24	8.5	11.8	0.700	67
0.992	0.906	125.0	12.81	30.72	25.13	23.7	26.7	25.3	20.0	33.0	8.10	7.5	8.6	0.890	63
1.036	0.917	134.7	13.36	32.85	26.31	19.6	31.8	23.3	10.0	46.6	8.67	6.2	15.6	0.866	

weakest, No. 57. Heaviest, No. 60; lightest, No. 61. Most lint, No. 58; least lint, No. 59.

CALIFORNIA.

0.992	0.906	174.9	14.36	39.78	22.91	20.4	25.9	23.0	17.4	33.0	11.33	9.5	14.1	0.930	82
1.397	0.984	168.6	9.67	38.87	33.20	26.8	37.7	25.0	17.4	29.6	10.66	8.6	12.4	0.629	81
0.996	0.967	161.7	15.19	35.20	23.36	21.4	28.9	24.8	17.4	34.6	10.48	9.8	11.8	0.790	68
0.961	1.016	132.8	13.19	38.08	25.43	22.3		28.8	18.1	33.1	1.90	7.8	8.7	0.888	69
0.977	1.128	133.2	10.03	38.48	21.07	18.2	33.0	27.5	18.4	43.5	8.13	7.0	9.7	0.950	70
1.122	0.923	145.1	12.96	35.71	26.50	22.4	32.6	23.5	20.0	30.0	9.40	7.7	11.3	0.840	71
0.870	0.854	112.9			22.22	16.8	26.0	21.7	11.8	26.1	7.32	6.7	8.4		72
0.978	0.913	133.7			24.83	21.2	29.4	23.2	17.4	29.6	8.80	7.6	9.8		73
1.431	0.953	172.5	15.82	33.90	36.25	32.6	39.3	34.2	14.5	35.6	11.16	9.0	13.5	1.025	74
0.943	0.996	166.2			23.96	17.5	29.6	25.3	19.2	29.6	12.90	8.2	13.9		75
0.965	1.050	171.0	9.96	32.56	24.22	23.4	27.7	26.9	17.4	34.3	11.14	10.1	13.7	0.645	76
0.850	0.957	165.0	10.72	33.81	21.66	18.4	26.3	24.3	13.0	33.0	10.56	9.0	12.2	0.595	77
1.114	0.906	110.8	31.19	23.45	28.30	24.3	31.3	23.0	13.0	33.0	7.18	5.6	9.4	0.795	78
1.053	1.004	175.6			26.75	22.7	32.5	25.5	17.4	33.0	11.33	8.8	13.9		79
0.960	0.900	151.8			24.62	22.6	26.5	20.1	16.6	23.3	9.84	7.7	11.3		80
1.154	0.779	121.0	13.97	34.81	29.31	27.1	31.0	19.8	13.3	26.6	7.84	7.0	10.0	0.905	83
1.182	0.858	142.3	16.28	33.64	30.02	26.5	32.5	21.8	16.6	36.6	9.23	8.3	10.2	1.055	84
1.143	0.846	112.6	12.58	30.06	29.04	27.0	32.5	21.5	13.3	26.6	7.30	6.5	8.2	0.83^	85
1.689	0.756	115.5	10.36	27.81	42.38	46.0	44.0	19.2	16.6	23.3	7.68	6.2	10.0	0.65?	86
1.079	0.921	144.6	12.56	32.01	27.40	16.8	44.0	23.4	11.8	43.5	9.37	5.6	14.1	0.815	

weakest, No. 78. Heaviest, No. 84; lightest, No. 81. Most cotton, No. 82; least cotton, No. 78.

FLORIDA.

Number of sample.	Character of soil.	County.	Cotton variety.	Sender.
87 a	Old pine lands, sandy, manured with 300 pounds of phosphate per acre	Alachua	Sea Island	P. B. Turpin
87 b	Old pine lands, sandy, not manured	...do	...do	...do
88 a	...do	...do	...do	...do
88 b	Old pine lands, sandy, manured with 12 bushels of cottonseed per acre	...do	...do	...do
90 a	Sandy pine lands, manured	Clay	...do	L. D. Wall
90 b	Sandy pine lands, unmanured	...do	...do	...do
89 a	Sandy pine lands, clay subsoil, commercial fertilizers	...do	...do	...do
89 c	Sandy pine lands, clay subsoil, barn-yard manure	...do	...do	...do
89 b	Sandy pine lands, clay subsoil, no manure	...do	...do	...do
92 a	Sandy, "pepper and salt" land, no manure	...do	...do	...do
93	Sandy, gray soil, new land	Columbia	...do	G. B. Smithson
94	Sandy, gray soil, cultivated 30 years, no manure	...do	Smooth seeds	...do
95	Sandy, gray soil, cultivated 30 years, manured	...do	...do	...do
96 a	Light gray soil, with clay subsoil, old land	...do	Worth 35 cents per pound	...do
96 b	...do	...do	Worth 25 cents per pound	...do
96 c	...do	...do	Worth 7 cents per pound	...do
96 d	...do	...do	Worth 5½ cents per pound	...do
97	Light gray soil, old land	...do	"Rattoon" or "Stand over" cotton of two years' growth. Sprouts from root and produces second crop.	...do
101	Rolling pine land, fine sandy loam, clay subsoil	...do		T. R. Collins
102	Yellow sandy soil, clay subsoil	...do		...do
98	...do	...do		J. D. Zackey
99	...do	...do		...do
107	Common pine land, rather poor, lightly fertilized	Hillsborough	Sea Island	W. F. White
109 b	Gravelly pine land	Marion	...do	I. S. Binnecker
110 a	New pine land	...do	...do	...do
111	"Salt and pepper" sandy land	...do	...do	...do
113 a	Coarse gravelly soil, not manured	Suwannee		G. B. Deale
113 b	Light gray, sandy, not manured	...do	King	...do
114 a	Level piny woods, sandy	Volusia	Coarse or old cotton	D. J. McBride
114 b	Level piny woods	...do	Bolter, or finest	...do
115	Light brown soil	...do	Sea Island	W. A. McBride
116	Dark brown soil	...do	...do	D. J. McBride
117	Light sandy soil	...do	...do	William Arnett
92 a	Pine land, clay subsoil	Clay		O. Budington
92 b	...do	...do		...do
91	Hummock land	...do		L. D. Wall
103	...do	Columbia		T. R. Collins
109 a	Light sandy hummock land	Marion		I. S. Binnecker
110 b	Red hummock land	...do		...do
100	...do	Columbia		J. D. Zackey
104	Sandy upland	Gadsden	Short staple	Jesse Wood
105	Clay upland	...do	...do	...do
112	Mahogany land, manured lightly	Santa Rosa		J. M. McGehee
106	Red clay hummock	Gadsden		Jesse Wood
108	Low hummock land	Hillsborough	"Florida Cecil hemp"	W. F. White
	Average of all			

Longest, No. 96 d; shortest, No. 104. Widest, No. 100; narrowest, No. 106. Strongest, No. 96;

GEORGIA.

118	Sandy, long-leaf pine and wire-grass land	Appling	First boll to open	Benjamin Milliken
122	Poor sandy upland soil, no manure	Burke	Herlong	W. B. Jones & Sons
123	Sandy upland soil	...do	Jones upland, long staple	...do
124	...do	...do	Jones upland, long staple, prolific.	...do
125	Sandy coast lands	Camden		P. T. Grass
144	Sandy, pine, and wire-grass land	Lowndes		J. C. Cook
146	Sandy pine land, not manured	Muscogee		
156	Old gray sandy land, cultivated 40 years, manured	Stewart	Bahamian bolls at joints; 48 bolls a pound of lint, 5 locks per boll.	J. B. Latimer

30

FLORIDA.

LENGTH, IN INCHES.	WIDTH, IN 1/1000 OF AN INCH.	BREAKING WEIGHT, IN GRAINS.	Weight of 5 seed with the lint, in grains.	Percentage of lint.	LENGTH, IN MILLIMETERS.			WIDTH, IN 1/1000 OF A MILLIMETER.			BREAKING WEIGHT, IN GRAMS.			Weight of 5 seed with the lint, in grams.	Number of sample.
Average of 4 fibers.	Average of 4 fibers.	Average of 10 or 15 results.			Average of 5 fibers.	Minimum.	Maximum.	Average of 4 fibers.	Minimum.	Maximum.	Average of 5 or 10 results.	Minimum.	Maximum.		
1	2	3	4	5	6	7	8	9	10	11	12	13	14	15	
1.554	0.732	89.0	12.81	31.82	39.48	36.8	43.2	18.6	15.3	23.3	5.84	5.4	6.0	0.830	87 a
1.514	0.590	99.4	15.30	29.96	38.48	33.4	42.0	15.0	10.0	16.6	6.44	4.6	7.3	0.985	87 b
1.441	0.791	168.2	12.27	32.07	36.60	33.4	37.9	20.1	12.3	22.3	10.90	9.7	11.7	0.796	88 a
1.268	0.800	84.3	12.19	25.32	32.23	29.3	34.6	22.6	16.6	36.6	5.46	4.7	6.6	0.790	88 b
1.014	0.909	115.1	12.47	29.01	25.76	22.9	29.6	23.1	16.6	30.0	7.46	7.2	8.3	0.810	90 a
1.046	0.724	123.4	13.03	26.62	26.58	22.7	32.6	18.4	13.3	26.6	8.00	6.7	9.0	0.845	90 b
1.664	0.831	108.1	12.66	31.73	42.26	44.8	48.3	21.1	16.6	30.0	6.65	5.3	7.0	0.885	89 a
1.246	0.806	151.6	15.20	32.48	31.66	28.9	35.0	22.0	13.3	30.0	9.82	8.7	11.4	0.965	89 c
1.189	0.827	147.9	14.03	28.02	30.20	27.7	32.2	21.0	16.6	28.3	9.58	8.3	10.4	0.910	89 b
1.110	0.752	167.4	21.14	23.35	28.20	26.1	30.1	19.1	16.6	26.6	10.20	8.7	11.0	1.370	92 c
1.552	0.929	192.3	14.43	32.08	39.36	36.5	43.0	23.6	16.6	30.0	8.87	6.5	10.6	1.935	93
1.504	0.799	118.2	14.28	16.75	40.50	36.0	47.0	20.3	13.3	30.0	7.86	5.9	9.9	0.925	94
1.586	0.722	129.0	13.12	30.58	40.28	39.3	47.8	18.6	16.6	30.0	8.96	7.7	9.8	0.850	95
1.600	0.933	118.2			40.86	36.4	59.5	23.7	16.6	26.6	7.95	5.5	8.4	....	96 a
1.576	0.819	140.1	....	....	40.04	37.8	42.7	30.8	13.3	22.3	9.08	7.8	10.4	....	96 b
1.194	0.728	106.1			30.32	30.0	33.6	18.5	13.3	23.5	6.88	5.4	7.1	....	96 c
1.916	0.547	105.2			48.52	47.6	49.5	13.9	10.6	16.6	6.66	5.3	8.1	....	96 d
1.367	0.917	196.5	14.12	34.04	34.74	32.0	36.2	23.3	20.0	30.0	8.20	5.9	8.9	0.915	97
1.366	0.747	185.6	12.81	27.71	34.74	33.7	36.3	19.0	13.3	30.0	8.80	8.5	10.4	0.880	101
1.403	0.811	185.5	10.80	35.71	37.02	34.1	40.4	20.6	16.6	26.6	8.78	3.0	14.4	0.700	102
0.930	0.977	175.0	15.12	35.71	34.90	23.0	35.5	34.8	20.0	38.3	11.94	10.1	13.9	0.980	98
1.080	0.866	117.3	12.43	32.18	27.43	26.5	29.5	22.0	16.6	36.6	7.60	7.1	7.9	0.870	99
1.340	0.846	98.5	9.86	50.76	34.06	31.3	39.3	21.5	16.6	22.3	6.38	6.3	6.5	0.585	107
1.673	0.701	162.7	10.43	30.97	42.50	38.5	47.2	17.8	13.3	22.3	10.34	9.3	13.0	0.675	100 b
1.681	0.797	101.8	10.11	11.45	42.70	37.5	51.3	20.0	16.0	26.6	6.90	5.6	8.9	0.955	110 a
1.433	0.699	138.9	14.93	28.03	36.30	34.5	28.5	17.5	13.3	30.0	8.16	7.3	9.2	0.990	111
1.868	0.677	86.1	13.80	27.78	47.44	38.7	54.5	17.2	10.0	23.2	5.34	4.2	6.4	0.900	112 a
1.806	0.896	117.6	12.81	25.30	40.64	35.8	46.8	22.5	13.3	23.3	7.62	7.2	8.5	0.880	112 b
1.720	0.701	86.7	10.49	30.88	43.70	38.9	40.0	17.8	13.3	23.3	5.82	5.3	6.9	0.690	114 a
1.739	0.799	102.5	11.88	28.97	44.18	38.2	50.2	20.3	16.6	23.3	5.84	6.0	7.4	0.770	114 b
1.480	0.831	127.7	13.11	25.88	37.54	32.6	41.8	21.1	13.3	26.7	7.93	6.4	15.7	0.850	115
1.381	0.811	113.1	11.42	19.50	35.08	30.2	39.9	20.6	13.3	26.7	7.93	6.0	12.0	0.740	116
1.327	0.819	138.0	12.38	33.12	33.80	37.5	40.5	20.8	13.3	26.6	8.94	7.8	10.6	0.815	117
1.609	0.728	134.4	13.50	25.73	40.68	37.4	43.6	18.5	13.3	23.3	8.06	7.5	8.4	0.873	92 a
1.187	0.620	115.7	11.96	29.04	30.16	28.3	32.0	16.0	13.3	20.0	7.50	5.9	8.9	0.778	92 b
1.872	0.909				34.84	25.8	38.7	23.1	16.6	36.6					91
1.344	0.661	130.0	18.04	28.96	34.14	30.0	37.1	16.8	13.3	30.0	7.78	7.1	8.7	0.845	103
1.118	0.732	138.9	11.50	20.80	28.40	23.9	30.5	18.6	13.3	23.3	8.00	8.6	9.5	0.745	100 a
1.508	0.740	120.1	10.80	36.43	40.60	34.2	43.6	18.7	13.3	23.3	7.73	7.3	8.6	0.700	110 b
1.141	1.213	112.7	14.12	35.51	28.98	34.9	32.1	30.8	23.3	33.3	7.80	6.4	8.3	0.915	100
0.854	0.899	166.4	10.49	36.76	21.70	20.9	23.3	21.3	13.3	36.3	10.78	9.1	12.7	0.680	104
0.907	0.960	155.4	10.43	36.56	23.04	10.0	27.0	34.3	16.6	33.3	10.07	8.9	12.9	0.870	103
0.904	0.780	196.6	10.72	31.88	22.96	20.9	26.4	19.3	16.6	30.0	8.90	8.0	9.4	0.900	115
1.061	0.480	121.9	10.88	34.75	27.46	24.3	29.0	12.2	8.3	96.6	7.90	7.4	8.9	0.900	106
1.205	0.760	118.2	9.18	31.00	33.14	29.6	33.3	19.3	16.6	28.3	7.86	9.8	10.1	0.595	108
1.384	0.702	134.1	12.04	29.14	35.15	30.0	36.5	20.2	9.3	26.3	8.04	4.2	15.7	0.819	

Weakest, No. 115 a. Heaviest, No. 92 c; lightest, No. 107. Most lint, No. 104; least lint, No. 119 a.

GEORGIA.

1.018	0.945	180.2	13.77	41.57	25.90	34.5	27.4	34.8	20.0	26.6	11.66	10.6	13.9	0.800	118
1.050	1.294	181.3	13.04	28.84	26.66	34.8	29.7	31.1	20.0	46.6	8.50	7.4	11.0	0.780	122
1.390	1.161	116.5	15.20	26.95	35.06	27.6	37.7	30.4	23.3	33.3	7.55	6.7	9.0	0.965	126
1.572	0.896	115.9	11.58	29.10	39.94	31.4	45.3	22.5	16.6	26.6	7.93	6.7	9.0	0.945	134
1.263	0.681	81.6	10.42	25.92	31.83	28.4	35.0	17.3	13.3	20.0	5.28	4.4	6.5	0.675	125
1.049	0.829	127.5	11.78	28.28	26.66	23.5	28.1	21.3	16.0	36.6	8.26	7.6	9.1	0.760	144
1.060	1.043	165.9	13.58	33.52	27.15	23.3	30.7	26.5	20.0	33.3	10.62	8.9	11.9	0.880	146
1.108	0.896	....	18.60	36.10	28.14	26.2	30.1	22.8	16.6	33.3	....			1.205	156

GEORGIA—Continued.

Number of sample.	Character of soil.	County.	Cotton variety.	Sender.
157	Gray sandy lands...	Sumter	....	S. S. Bird...............................
162	Gray sandy pine lands...	Tattnall	....	John Hughey.........................
163	Sandy pine lands	...do	Bahamian bolls at joints; 48 bolls a pound of lint, 8 locks per boll.	......do ....
	LANDS WITH CLAY SUBSOILS (METAMORPHIC).			
119	Gray sandy land	Bibb	....	W. D. W. Johnson ....
126	Sandy granitic soil...	Campbell	Matagorda..................	Georgia Department of Agriculture.
127	Gray sandy soil...	Carroll..........	....	R. H. Springer....................
131	.....do	Coweta	Improved cluster and sea island.	R. N. Carmichael ....
132	.....do	...do	Barnes' Improved	Georgia Department of Agriculture.
133	.....do	De Kalb	Cheatham and Dixon Improved.	W. B. Frances ....
134	.....do	Gwinnett	....	R. D. Winn ....
139	.....do	Henry	Petit Gulf	Georgia Department of Agriculture.
140	....	Jackson	Herlong	W. J. Colquitt ....
141	Gray sandy soil, first quality...	Lincoln	....	N. A. Crawford ....
143	Coarse and gravelly, third quality	...do	....	......do ....
147	Oak and hickory upland, not manured	Muscogee	....	J. C. Cook ....
148	Coarse sandy upland, manured with 250 pounds guano and 600 pounds of stable manure per acre.	Newton	....	J. P. Walker ....
149	Coarse sandy upland, cultivated 22 years, manured with 400 pounds of guano and 1,000 pounds of compost per acre.	....do	....	......do ....
152	Gray sandy upland, first grade, manured with 55 pounds of old dry stable manure per acre.	Paulding	....	J. R. Prewett ....
150	Gray sandy upland, second grade, manured with 300 pounds of barn-yard manure per acre.	....do	Green seed..................	......do ....
150	Gray sandy land, with 500 pounds of dissolved bones and 1 ton of compost of cottonseed and manure per acre.	Talbot	....	W. R. Gorman ....
165	Gray sandy land	Troup	....	W. P. Beasley......................
166	......do	...do	....	......do ....
167	......do	...do	Jones' Improved	J. F. Jones........................
	CLAY LANDS (METAMORPHIC).			
120	Red or mulatto land...	Bibb	....	W. D. W. Johnson ....
121	Red or mulatto land (new land)	... do	Frost-bitten	......do ....
135	Chocolate or yellow soils...	Gwinnett	....	R. D. Winn ....
136	Red clay land	...do	....	......do ....
137	Mulatto land, good, fertilized.	Hancock..........	Hunt's Prolific, 185 bolls per stalk of 4 feet.	Georgia Department of Agriculture.
138	Mulatto land, poor, fertilized.	...do	Stalk 3 feet high	......do ....
142	Clay land, second quality.	Lincoln	....	N. A. Crawford ....
151	Red upland, fertilized with 300 pounds of night-soil manure per acre.......	Paulding	....	J. R. Prewett ....
160	Red clay land	Talbot	....	W. R. Gorman ....
164	......do	Troup	....	W. P. Beasley......................
158	Red land (buhr-stone, Tertiary)..	Sumter	....	S. S. Bird..........................
	LANDS OF NORTHWEST GEORGIA.			
128	Gravelly ridge lands (Quebec)	Chattooga	....	A. B. McCutchen..................
129	Upland soil	...do	....	A. P. Algood ....
130	Gray gravelly land..	...do	Third picking	C. D. Hill.........................
168	Gray sandy soil, red-clay subsoil, no manure................................	Walker	Late picking	F. M. Young........................
158 b	Gray gravelly land..	Polk	Jones' Improved	S. M. R. Byrd......................
158 a	Red land	.. do	...do	......do ....
	Bottom lands.			
146	River bottom lands, fertilized with 200 pounds of phosphate per acre.....	Muscogee	....	J. C. Cook ....
154	Brier creek bottom land, sandy...	Scriven	Dixon Prolific	G. R. Black........................
155	Brier creek bottom land, alluvial..	...do	Rio Grande	......do ....
161	Creek bottom land...	Talbot	....	W. R. Gorman ....
	Average of all..			

GEORGIA—Continued.

LENGTH, IN INCHES.		WIDTH, IN 1/1000 OF AN INCH.	BREAKING WEIGHT, IN GRAINS.	Weight of 5 seed with the lint, in grains.	Percentage of lint.	LENGTH, IN MILLIMETERS.			WIDTH, IN 1/1000 OF A MILLIMETER.			BREAKING WEIGHT, IN GRAMS.			Weight of 5 seed with the lint, in grams.	Number of sample.
Average of 4 fibers.	Average of 4 fibers.	Average of 10 or 15 results.				Average of 5 fibers.	Minimum.	Maximum.	Average of 4 fibers.	Minimum.	Maximum.	Average of 5 or 10 results.	Minimum.	Maximum.		
1	2	3	4	5	6	7	8	9	10	11	12	13	14	15	
0.942	0.820	128.8	10.57	35.76	23.92	19.5	25.9	21.3	16.6	26.6	8.02	7.0	9.4	0.685	187
0.897	0.866	152.1	11.50	35.57	22.52	19.0	31.4	22.0	15.8	30.0	9.86	8.1	11.6	0.745	162
1.342	0.976	139.6	10.80	30.00	34.10	30.6	36.6	24.8	13.3	36.6	8.40	7.5	9.8	0.700	163
1.086	0.858	151.7	9.49	39.02	27.90	26.8	29.6	21.8	16.6	26.6	9.82	8.1	14.0	0.815	119
0.954	1.126	136.8	10.63	35.50	33.72	30.7	36.9	28.6	20.0	33.3	8.22	7.4	10.1	0.690	120
1.062	0.732	140.7	11.19	36.55	26.72	25.3	28.2	18.6	10.0	26.6	9.13	7.6	10.7	0.735	127
1.272	0.797	128.8	15.50	25.24	34.96	32.0	35.9	19.5	16.6	28.2	8.02	6.2	11.7	1.010	131
0.870	1.051	115.3	11.11	37.50	22.10	18.6	34.4	26.7	29.2	33.3	7.47	8.4	9.8	0.720	132
1.140	1.063	119.0	12.65	34.14	28.96	26.9	30.1	27.0	20.0	43.3	7.71	6.2	9.8	0.820	123
1.246	1.290	145.4	15.06	29.55	31.54	28.5	35.4	32.0	22.3	46.0	9.42	8.0	11.2	1.015	134
1.156	0.795	131.8	12.25	32.20	29.38	26.4	32.9	30.2	13.2	30.0	8.52	6.7	10.3	0.885	139
0.901	0.768	140.6	10.65	35.50	22.88	19.5	23.8	18.5	13.3	28.3	9.11	7.8	11.1	0.690	140
0.934	0.862	156.1	12.81	34.10	23.44	20.0	25.4	21.0	10.0	30.0	10.25	9.1	12.0	0.830	141
1.040	0.909	167.1	12.04	28.41	26.42	22.2	28.2	23.1	10.0	33.3	10.82	9.6	12.1	0.780	142
1.334	1.069	127.7	12.81	31.92	33.90	31.9	36.2	26.9	20.0	36.6	8.92	7.4	11.1	0.820	147
0.806	0.831	167.5	11.50	34.89	20.48	19.0	22.5	21.1	12.3	22.2	9.56	8.0	13.1	0.745	148
0.989	0.748	130.1	10.34	31.34	24.97	21.3	31.0	19.0	19.0	26.6	7.78	7.1	9.5	0.870	149
1.028	0.760	126.7	11.65	33.77	26.06	23.0	28.8	18.3	16.6	23.3	8.17	6.5	9.7	0.755	152
1.182	1.004	119.7	13.19	31.56	30.06	28.4	31.1	25.5	20.0	33.3	7.76	6.7	9.8	0.855	154
1.115	0.870	144.8	15.90	33.96	28.33	34.0	32.2	22.1	16.6	30.0	9.38	7.8	10.0	1.030	159
1.071	0.900	149.4	12.45	34.14	27.20	25.4	29.5	23.1	30.0	26.6	9.68	8.8	10.5	0.820	165
0.881	0.779	140.8	11.42	35.11	22.38	21.4	23.2	19.8	13.2	26.6	8.96	7.9	10.4	0.740	166
0.934	1.004	157.4	16.21	33.90	23.72	21.1	25.7	25.5	20.0	30.0	10.30	8.5	13.0	1.180	167
1.114	1.141	125.0	13.58	30.11	28.31	25.4	31.8	20.0	22.3	12.3	8.10	6.9	9.3	0.880	120
1.025	0.760	110.2	......	......	26.04	23.6	29.9	19.3	13.3	23.3	7.14	5.9	8.1	......	121
0.906	0.614	164.5	13.89	35.00	23.00	20.0	25.4	15.6	19.3	33.3	10.66	9.3	13.7	0.900	133
1.112	1.290	150.1	15.06	33.00	28.34	26.4	30.7	31.0	20.6	43.3	9.73	8.4	13.2	1.015	136
0.819	1.183	134.5	11.65	31.12	20.80	18.6	22.3	29.8	22.3	32.2	8.07	6.8	10.6	0.755	137
0.952	0.921	125.3	9.88	34.37	24.18	23.3	27.4	23.4	13.3	33.3	8.12	7.1	13.3	0.640	138
0.919	0.945	179.3	13.50	36.36	23.34	20.6	25.6	24.0	16.6	33.3	11.61	9.0	13.7	0.855	142
1.007	0.917	149.7	13.61	39.77	25.58	23.8	27.7	22.3	16.6	33.3	9.79	8.8	10.4	0.880	151
1.078	0.878	193.8	11.11	36.80	27.34	23.8	29.5	22.3	13.2	30.0	12.56	9.1	13.1	0.720	160
1.207	0.988	102.1	13.56	34.54	30.64	28.7	34.2	24.6	20.0	26.6	6.62	6.1	7.9	0.815	161
0.909	0.850	119.8	10.34	32.82	25.38	24.5	27.1	21.6	18.3	30.0	7.70	7.9	8.4	0.870	172
1.105	0.889	148.8	10.13	37.78	......	24.5	30.0	21.3	16.6	22.3	8.42	7.1	10.0	1.175	128
1.116	1.181	143.1	14.88	32.79	28.42	26.9	30.6	26.7	20.0	22.3	10.18	8.4	13.6	0.930	129
0.870	0.820	125.0	11.73	35.52	24.62	20.5	29.5	20.0	16.6	26.6	8.10	7.1	8.8	0.780	130
1.172	0.712	116.7	13.56	30.61	29.78	27.5	32.0	18.1	13.3	20.0	7.56	6.8	9.3	0.815	103
0.818	0.668	131.6	17.44	36.28	20.72	19.6	21.4	17.6	16.6	23.3	8.52	7.6	9.7	1.130	153 b
1.012	0.858	148.1	10.10	34.85	25.70	23.5	26.4	21.8	16.6	26.6	9.60	7.8	11.3	6.080	153 a
1.206	0.949	129.3	11.96	27.74	30.66	26.0	35.6	24.1	20.0	30.0	8.36	6.8	9.5	0.775	145
1.142	0.917	121.0	7.95	37.86	29.02	27.1	35.5	22.3	16.6	30.0	7.84	6.1	10.1	0.515	134
0.965	0.732	134.1	11.11	31.94	25.02	23.6	27.2	18.5	13.3	28.3	8.69	7.6	9.9	0.720	155
1.063	1.025	147.5	16.90	35.16	27.00	25.3	29.0	26.6	13.3	30.0	9.56	7.8	14.3	1.005	101
1.066	0.913	196.0	12.80	33.18	27.09	18.6	37.7	23.2	10.0	46.6	8.85	4.4	14.3	0.830	

weakest, No. 175; heaviest, No. 156; lightest, No. 154. Most lint, No. 118; least lint, No. 104.

3 C P

INDIAN TERRITORY.

Number of samples.	Character of soil.	County.	Cotton variety.	Sender.
170	Alluvial land, first class	Pottawatomie	....	E. A. Carnbrew ....
169	Alluvial land, old-land class	...do	....	....de ....

LOUISIANA.

Number of samples.	Character of soil.	PARISH.	Cotton variety.	Sender.
171	Light sandy soil	Bienville	....	T. J. Butler ....
175	Hill land	Catahoula	McClendon's Prolific	M. Dempsey ....
176	Hill land, side of hill	...do	....do	....do ....
178	Upland sandy soil	De Soto..........	Dixon's Cluster, late	A. V. Roberts..............
179	.....do	... do	Peeler, late	....de..............
183	Light sandy loam	Saint Tammany .	....	W. C. Warren..............
185 b	Land sloping toward bottom, cultivated 30 years, manured.	Tangipahoa.....	....	W. H. Garland ....
186	Table-land, not manured	...do	....	B. L. Gullett............
187 a	{ Table-land, long-leaf pine, red and white oaks, subsoil red or yellow { loam, manured.	...do	....	....do ....
187 b		...do	....	
190	Light sandy upland loam	Vernon	....	R. T. Wright..............
173	Red soil....................................	Bienville........	....	T. J. Butler ....
188	Black prairie upland	Vernon	....	R. T. Wright ....
172	Bottom land	Bienville........	....	T. J. Butler ....
174	Creek bottom land....................................	Catahoula	McClendon's Prolific	M. Dempsey ....
177	Dark sandy bottom land ....?	De Soto..........	Peeler	A. V. Roberts ....
180	Hummock land....................................	Morehouse	Boyd's Prolific........	A. S. Keller ....
181	Gum lands....................................	...do	African	....de ....
182	Red river alluvial land	Red River	Peeler............	B. W. Marston ....
184	River bottom	Saint Tammany .	....	W. C. Warren ....
191	Bottom land	Winn	Petit Gulf............	W. T. Jones ....
192	Sandy hummock....................................	...do	Herlong............	....do ....
189	Dark clay loam, lowland....................................	Vernon	....	R. T. Wright ....
185 a	Creek bottom land....................................	Tangipahoa......	....	W. H. Garland ....
	Average of all			

Longest, No. 179; shortest, No. 187 b. Widest, No. 186; narrowest, No. 183. Strongest, No. 185 a.

MISSISSIPPI.

Number of samples.	Character of soil.	COUNTY.	Cotton variety.	Sender.
193	Gravelly hill land, sandy subsoil....................................	Amite	Heavily manured............	J. R. Galtney ....
201	Light sandy loam	La Fayette	Fresh............	P. Fernandes ....
202	.....do	...do	Old land, not manured......	....de ....
200	.....do	... de	Old land, highly manured......	....do ....
203	Dark sandy loam	... do	....	Ira B. Orr ....
209	Dark loam or hill land	Warren......	Cultivated 3 years............	L. Wailes ....
208	.....do	...do	Cultivated 25 years............	....de ....
204	Sandy bottom lands	Lee	First picking............	H. L. Holland ....
205	.....do	... do	Second picking............	....do ....
206	.....do	...do	Third picking............	....do ....
207	.....do	Panola............	....	D. R. Stewart ....
196	Clay loam soil....................................	Hinds	............#............	H. O. Dixon ....
197	.....do	...do	Manured; cultivated 20 years.	......do ....
198	.....do	...do.	Cultivated 22 years............	......do ....
194	Black prairie soil	Clarke............	Cultivated 10 years............	J. W. Wilbourn..............
195	.....do	...de	Cultivated 40 years............	......do ....
199 a	.....do	Jasper............	New ground	S. G. Loughridge..............
199 b	.....do	...de	Cultivated 20 years............	......do ....
	Average of all			

Longest, No. 200; shortest, No. 202. Widest, No. 200; narrowest, No. 196. Strongest, No. 200; weakest, No. 193.

INDIAN TERRITORY.

					LENGTH, IN MILLIMETERS.			WIDTH, IN 1/1000 OF A MILLIMETRE.			BREAKING WEIGHT, IN GRAMS.				
LENGTH, IN INCHES.	WIDTH, IN 1/1000 OF AN INCH.	BREAKING WEIGHT, IN GRAINS.	Weight of 5 seed with the lint. In grains.	Percentage of lint.										Weight of 5 seed with the lint, in grams.	Number of sample.
Average of 4 fibers.	Average of 4 fibers.	Average of 10 or 15 results.			Average of 5 fibers.	Minimum.	Maximum.	Average of 4 fibers.	Minimum.	Maximum.	Average of 5 or 10 results.	Minimum.	Maximum.		
1	2	3	4	5	6	7	8	9	10	11	12	13	14	15	
1.022	1.043	126.2	12.50	31.46	25.98	24.2	28.1	26.5	23.3	30.0	8.12	6.8	12.0	0.810	170
1.140	0.768	112.4	14.35	32.26	28.96	23.3	31.1	19.5	10.0	26.6	7.28	6.6	8.5	0.930	169

LOUISIANA.

1	2	3	4	5	6	7	8	9	10	11	12	13	14	15	
1.116	0.846	123.2	15.28	34.85	28.34	24.0	32.0	21.5	13.2	26.6	7.98	7.2	9.5	0.900	171
1.077	0.952	112.0	11.65	31.12	27.35	23.4	30.7	24.2	16.6	33.3	7.96	4.9	14.7	0.755	173
1.106	0.917	84.6	12.19	36.66	28.08	20.9	40.6	23.3	20.0	26.6	5.48	6.5	8.6	0.790	176
1.062	0.819	109.9	12.42	33.54	25.48	22.5	30.0	29.8	16.6	35.6	7.13	6.2	8.1	0.905	178
1.267	0.795	82.1	13.50	29.14	32.18	30.4	34.4	20.1	13.3	26.6	5.32	6.1	7.0	0.875	179
1.151	0.634	142.4			29.25	22.7	36.9	16.1	6.6	26.0	9.23	7.3	11.9		182
1.075	0.716	141.1	12.04	30.19	27.30	24.5	30.5	16.2	13.3	26.7	9.14	7.9	11.4	0.780	185 b
0.902	1.263	120.1	13.12	38.29	22.92	21.5	24.4	32.1	26.6	36.6	7.78	6.0	10.5	0.850	186
1.152	1.146	149.4	13.50	32.00	29.26	26.2	31.9	29.1	20.0	40.0	9.08	8.7	12.2	0.875	187 a
0.962	0.651	115.6	13.74	29.21	21.90	19.5	28.2	21.1	16.6	33.3	7.49	6.1	14.8	0.890	187 b
1.028	0.906	120.3	13.27	33.96	26.12	24.0	28.5	25.3	13.3	33.3	7.80	7.1	9.1	0.795	190
1.214	0.846	131.8	11.19	33.10	30.84	28.4	32.7	21.5	16.6	26.6	8.34	7.9	10.7	0.725	173
1.001	1.004	178.5	12.89	32.33	25.44	22.8	29.0	25.5	20.0	30.0	11.24	9.4	13.3	0.835	188
1.104	0.790	122.4	10.88	33.46	28.04	24.5	31.6	20.3	16.6	23.3	8.58	6.6	9.6	0.705	172
1.084	0.692	135.5	16.36	32.07	27.53	24.7	31.6	17.6	13.3	23.3	8.78	7.8	10.2	1.060	174
1.220	0.873	151.9	15.66	32.57	30.96	25.8	34.7	22.3	16.6	26.6	9.34	8.6	11.4	1.015	177
1.011	0.907	117.4	11.11	34.02	25.68	23.2	27.2	20.5	6.6	33.3	7.61	5.3	11.7	0.730	180
1.039	0.783	69.0	12.35	34.37	26.40	21.9	31.3	19.9	13.3	30.0	4.47	3.0	6.1	0.900	181
1.014	0.880	94.4	13.19	30.48	25.76	23.0	37.3	21.4	16.6	26.6	6.13	5.7	6.8	0.855	182
1.039	0.657	123.0			26.91	21.2	30.3	16.7	6.6	26.6	7.97	6.8	10.2		184
1.004	1.008	123.7	8.03	35.04	27.80	24.9	31.9	25.8	16.6	33.3	8.02	6.7	10.4	0.585	191
0.987	0.917	138.0	11.80	43.79	25.08	22.7	27.5	23.3	16.6	36.6	8.94	7.4	11.9	0.705	192
1.029	1.058	157.0	16.28	31.38	26.15	24.2	29.3	25.8	13.3	33.3	10.04	8.3	12.8	1.055	189
1.032	1.004	214.5	15.74	39.21	26.22	22.0	31.6	25.8	16.7	40.0	13.90	11.0	16.2	1.020	185 a
1.069	0.882	127.5	13.01	33.08	27.15	19.5	40.6	22.4	6.6	40.0	8.20	3.0	13.2	0.843	

weakest, No. 181. Heaviest, No. 174; lightest, No. 191. Most lint, No. 192; least lint, No. 181.

MISSISSIPPI.

1	2	3	4	5	6	7	8	9	10	11	12	13	14	15	
1.041	1.020	109.9			26.45	22.2	32.7	25.9	17.4	33.9	7.12	6.2	7.8		199
1.055	0.909	123.3			26.80	20.7	32.6	23.1	17.4	31.3	8.12	7.7	9.7		201
0.810	0.929	117.6			20.58	17.7	26.5	23.6	13.0	30.1	7.82	6.0	8.3		202
1.282	1.061	161.4			32.56	30.1	38.0	27.4	20.8	34.5	10.46	8.4	12.4		200
1.069	0.932	184.6			27.16	23.0	30.6	23.7	17.4	30.4	8.72	8.7	11.0		208
1.012	1.010	144.8			26.43	23.3	27.6	24.3	17.4	28.5	8.98	8.3	10.0		209
0.998	0.990	167.0			25.23	21.1	33.8	24.6	18.7	34.2	9.86	9.1	10.8		206
1.007	1.027	188.2	11.11	31.94	25.00	20.4	29.1	20.1	16.1	30.0	8.44	6.9	9.8	0.720	204
1.022	0.941	146.3	9.11	35.59	25.95	24.9	27.3	22.9	17.4	30.4	9.48	8.0	12.7	0.580	205
1.009	0.968	123.0	11.27	33.23	25.62	20.5	30.0	24.6	13.7	34.6	8.10	6.4	10.5	0.780	208
1.170	0.945	130.5			28.72	22.8	36.6	24.0	17.4	33.9	9.04	7.0	11.6		207
1.008	0.984	186.2	13.84	33.25	27.90	24.1	30.6	25.0	17.4	36.5	10.13	8.9	12.4	0.845	196
1.080	0.896	142.0	11.27	32.87	27.44	25.0	28.5	22.6	13.2	34.6	9.26	7.5	11.0	0.730	197
1.216	0.768	145.4	12.73	34.54	30.74	30.1	31.6	19.5	16.6	23.3	9.42	7.8	11.8	0.825	198
0.923	0.903	113.3	13.58	29.26	23.42	17.1	31.6	22.9	11.3	30.1	7.34	6.6	8.3	0.815	194
1.015	0.965	116.7	12.35	31.87	25.80	22.6	29.6	34.5	17.4	31.2	7.56	6.1	10.5	0.800	195
0.906	0.933	116.4	14.83	33.33	25.10	22.0	27.5	23.7	20.0	26.7	7.34	7.0	8.6	0.960	199 a
1.099	1.039	145.1	12.65	34.13	27.90	26.0	32.0	28.4	23.3	30.0	9.40	8.0	11.3	0.829	200 b
1.047	0.957	134.3	12.11	34.01	26.61	17.1	38.0	24.3	13.0	39.1	8.70	6.0	13.7	0.785	

Heaviest, No. 199 a; lightest, No. 205. Most lint, No, 194; least lint, No. 195.

MISSOURI.

Number of sample.	Character of soil.	County.	Cotton variety.	Sender.
	MISSISSIPPI ALLUVIAL LANDS.			
212	Dark sandy loam, cultivated 20 years, no manure	Dunklin	Java Prolific	E. J. Langdon
215	Dark sandy upland	Stoddard		J. P. Walker
210	Dark prairie loam, cultivated 10 years, no manure	Dunklin	Matagorda Silk	E. J. Langdon
211	Dark prairie loam, cultivated 20 years, no manure	...do	Red River	E. J. Langdon
213	Lowland	Stoddard		J. P. Walker
214	...... do	... do		...do
	Average of all			

Longest, No. 210; shortest, Nos. 215 and 213. Widest, No. 214; narrowest, No. 210. Strongest, No. 210;

NORTH CAROLINA.

	SANDY UPLANDS.			
220	Sandy loam of coast region, fertilized with compost	Beaufort	Dickson's Early Cluster	R. W. Wharton
221	Sandy, somewhat clayey loam, with compost of muck, cottonseed, ashes, and phosphate.	....do		...do
230 a	Upland soil, with barn-yard manure	Craven		C. Duffy, jr
230 b	Upland soil, with compost of cottonseed and phosphate	...do		...do
231 a	Light sandy soil, barn-yard manure	...do		...do
231 b	Light sandy soil, with cottonseed and phosphate compost	... do		...do
234	Sandy soil	Cumberland		W. G. Hall
235	Sandy loam	Duplin		J. A. Bryan
238	...... do	Greene		R. C. D. Braman
241	Sandy, piny woods	Halifax	Braswell	J. M. Smith
242	Gray sandy loam	... do		J. H. Parker
243	Light sandy loam	... do		...do
245	Gray sandy loam, piny woods, manured with cottonseed	... do		...do
246	Gray upland soil (near creeks), manured with 100 pounds of sea-fowl guano and 25 bushels of cottonseed per acre.	Harnett	Not well grown	H. C. McNeill
247	Dark gray loam, little sand, yellow-clay subsoil	...do		... do
249	Gray sandy, pine, oak, and hickory land, sandy-clay subsoil	Johnson		R. J. Holt
250	Light sandy land, clay subsoil, oak and hickory	Jones		H. C. Foscue
255	Dark gray soil, clay subsoil	Martin		J. R. Lanier
271	Gray sandy loam	Pasquotank		...do
272	Piny woods, sandy land	Bitt		P. Joyner
273	Light sandy soil	...do		...do
274	Sandy, gravelly soil	Richmond		R. L. Steele
275	Sandy soil	... do		...do
255	Upland soil	Wilson		G. W. Stanton
225	Light sandy loam, pine, oak, etc	Carteret		A. Oaksmith
260 a	Sandy, gravelly pine upland, manured	Moore		M. McQueen
250 b	......do	...do		J. H. McDonald
260 c	......do	...do		J. W. Johnson
260 d	Sandy, gravelly pine upland, manured with 200 pounds of guano per acre	...do		J. C. Ferguson
260 e	Sandy, gravelly pine upland	...do		William Blue
261	Sandy uplands	...do		J. C. Campbell
262	Lands of Pocket creek	...do		...do
263	Sandy uplands	...do		N. R. Bryan
264	Lands of Governor's creek	...do		N. M. Ferguson
265	Sandy uplands	.. do		S. M. Carter
266	......do	...do		E. J. Harrington
267	Sandy pine, oak, and hickory flats, with clay subsoil	New Hanover		A. R. Black
	BOTTOM LANDS.			
219	Dark alluvial soil, slightly manured with guano	Beaufort		R. W Wharton
223 a	Lowland soil, manured with cottonseed and phosphate compost	Craven		C. Duff, jr
223 b	Lowland soil, manured with cottonseed and barnyard manure	...do	Stalk matured 94 bolls	... do
239	Sandy land, Roanoke river	Halifax	Peeler	J. M. Smith
240	..... do	...do	Johnson	... do
256	Light sandy creek lands	Martin		J. R. Lanier
257	Low bottom lands	... do	Opens late	...do
284	Bottom land, no manure	Wayne	Picked late	J. Robinson
277	Light sandy loam, yellow-clay subsoil	Tyrrell		Eph. Leigh
233	Stiff clay hummock land	Craven		J. Humphrey
250 e	Dark gray soil, second bottom Crawley creek, no manure	Moore		John C. Campbell

38

MISSOURI.

LENGTH, IN INCHES.		WIDTH, IN THS OF AN INCH.	BREAKING WEIGHT, IN GRAINS.	Weight of 5 seed with the lint, in grains.	Percentage of lint.	LENGTH, IN MILLIMETERS.			WIDTH, IN THS OF A MILLIMETER.			BREAKING WEIGHT, IN GRAMS.			Weight of 5 seed with the lint, in grams.	Number of sample.
Average of 4 fibers.	Average of 4 fibers.	Average of 10 or 15 results.				Average of 5 fibers.	Minimum.	Maximum.	Average of 4 fibers.	Minimum.	Maximum.	Average of 5 or 10 results.	Minimum.	Maximum.		
1	2	3	4	5	6	7	8	9	10	11	12	13	14	15	
1.075	0.811	197.0	12.72	26.93	27.30	22.5	33.4	20.6	16.6	26.6	8.68	8.0	9.4	0.825	212
0.907	1.047	181.3	11.86	29.51	23.04	22.6	34.3	26.6	22.3	30.0	8.50	6.6	10.2	0.745	213
1.390	0.779	188.3	15.82	28.90	32.02	34.5	37.1	19.8	13.3	32.3	11.88	10.0	13.5	1.025	210
1.240	0.896	100.9	14.12	31.14	31.50	36.4	37.1	22.5	16.6	30.0	8.84	5.1	8.2	0.915	211
0.980	0.905	192.1	11.73	34.21	24.88	23.1	34.1	22.0	16.6	30.0	8.56	7.4	10.9	0.780	213
1.130	0.909	184.0	10.65	32.61	28.89	35.4	41.6	22.1	20.0	26.6	8.62	7.3	9.6	0.690	214
1.096	0.890	196.4	12.76	31.62	27.90	22.5	41.6	22.6	13.3	30.0	8.84	5.1	13.5	0.827	

weakest, No. 211. Heaviest, No. 210; lightest, No. 214. Most lint, No. 213; least lint, No. 210.

NORTH CAROLINA.

1	2	3	4	5	6	7	8	9	10	11	12	13	14	15	
1.043	0.795	141.4	12.11	33.73	26.82	24.1	28.4	20.2	16.6	26.6	9.16	7.2	10.9	0.795	290
1.045	0.661	136.4	10.73	36.97	26.54	25.1	29.6	16.8	10.0	26.6	8.84	7.2	11.4	0.606	221
1.041	0.878	145.4	11.81	26.79	26.44	31.1	30.4	22.3	16.6	30.0	9.42	7.9	13.4	0.765	290a
1.049	1.027	150.6	13.04	26.08	26.84	25.3	29.1	26.1	20.0	22.3	10.34	8.6	11.7	0.845	290b
0.996	0.909	121.0	8.87	34.78	25.29	24.1	26.6	23.1	20.0	26.6	7.84	5.4	8.4	0.575	291a
0.841	1.067	134.7	11.73	40.13	21.36	17.2	24.6	27.1	16.6	26.6	8.08	6.1	9.6	0.780	291b
0.896	0.968	145.0	14.82	27.50	22.51	20.9	24.8	25.1	20.0	30.0	9.40	8.0	11.2	0.960	234
1.040	0.929	161.1			26.42	25.2	29.8	23.6	13.3	30.0	10.44	9.5	11.4		235
0.921	0.839	172.5	14.04	34.06	23.40	26.7	27.6	21.3	20.0	29.3	11.18	8.9	13.0	0.910	236
0.956	1.057	116.3	13.12	35.29	24.28	22.1	25.4	25.3	20.0	26.6	7.54	5.9	8.8	0.850	241
1.032	0.780	131.7			26.24	21.1	30.2	19.3	13.3	23.3	6.83	5.7	10.1		242
0.963	0.827	139.6	13.12	29.41	27.00	25.1	29.7	21.9	16.6	26.6	6.40	7.0	9.8	0.850	243
1.077	0.760	175.6	14.48	32.62	27.36	24.6	29.6	19.3	16.6	22.3	11.44	6.9	13.4	0.933	245
1.018	1.229	153.2	13.19	35.79	25.86	25.2	26.6	21.0	23.3	40.0	9.96	8.1	11.1	0.855	246
1.805	0.874	164.3			25.52	23.8	26.6	22.2	13.3	30.6	10.65	8.6	14.7		247
1.308	0.752	166.6	13.12	26.29	30.68	28.3	33.2	14.1	16.6	22.3	8.91	5.3	10.0	0.850	249
1.018	0.626	171.2			25.78	22.6	26.5	15.9	6.6	22.3	11.10	10.6	11.7		250
1.023	0.964	167.5	11.50	26.34	25.96	21.5	23.4	25.0	13.3	30.0	8.62	8.2	11.1	0.745	255
	1.094							26.6	20.0	30.0					271
1.019	0.896	160.3	13.50	37.03	25.53	34.0	29.5	22.8	16.6	30.0	10.38	9.1	11.6	0.810	272
1.045	0.787	120.1	14.43	38.15	26.54	21.7	22.8	20.0	10.0	26.6	7.78	8.8	9.3	0.935	272
0.988	0.738	130.5			25.36	21.3	29.1	18.6	13.3	23.3	8.04	8.2	10.0		274
1.042	0.748	140.1			26.46	23.1	29.0	19.0	13.3	26.6	8.96	7.0	12.7		275
1.017	1.071	119.8			25.82	23.8	27.9	27.2	16.6	33.3	7.76	7.1	9.0		285
0.696	0.787	107.4	10.08	33.84	17.66	15.4	18.8	20.0	10.0	26.6	6.96	5.1	7.7	0.650	225
1.190	1.067	130.5	13.19	38.62	30.24	29.3	33.1	27.1	20.0	33.3	8.46	7.8	10.8	0.790	260a
1.182	0.945	118.3	13.19	26.07	29.53	25.6	31.5	24.0	20.0	30.0	7.96	6.9	8.1	0.790	260b
1.322	1.181	119.1	13.41	28.30	33.58	30.6	37.8	30.0	26.6	33.3	7.72	6.4	11.1	0.830	260c
1.698	1.195	164.7	13.43	33.54	24.86	35.1	37.5	29.8	23.3	36.6	6.72	5.9	8.8	0.905	260d
1.138	0.990	188.8	14.81	33.13										0.911	260e
1.370	0.804	154.8			27.42	31.3	32.1	25.0	16.6	33.3	10.92	8.6	11.5		261
1.608	1.003	133.3			27.76	27.0	28.9	25.5	20.0	33.3	8.04	7.1	9.5		262
1.225	1.004	132.1			31.13	27.7	35.7	26.5	20.0	33.3	8.56	7.6	9.8		263
1.162	1.043	135.2			28.05	34.7	33.9	26.5	20.0	33.3	8.04	6.8	11.0		264
1.034	0.791	142.9			26.26	34.0	26.3	20.1	10.0	26.6	9.26	8.3	10.1		265
1.139	0.908	126.3	10.49	23.35	28.68	27.4	31.0	22.0	20.0	26.6	8.18	7.0	10.7	0.680	266
0.915	0.906	128.3	13.50	29.71	23.24	22.0	25.1	23.0	20.0	26.6	8.04	7.4	12.1	0.875	267
1.226	0.909	107.1	12.88	29.94	31.14	29.5	32.6	23.1	20.0	26.6	6.94	5.1	8.9	0.825	219
1.076	1.027	113.6	10.11	35.87	27.34	25.7	30.1	26.1	12.3	33.5	7.36	5.9	8.8	0.855	232a
1.131	1.067	116.7	12.81	31.82	28.72	25.7	31.9	27.1	20.0	33.3	7.56	6.0	9.4	0.830	232b
1.045	0.968	176.2	12.19	22.27	26.62	19.9	24.9	25.1	20.0	26.6	11.43	10.1	12.9	0.790	239
0.912	0.896	114.6	9.65	38.40	23.16	21.6	25.6	22.5	16.6	30.0	7.43	6.2	9.5	0.625	240
0.985	1.015	108.9	9.36	32.41	25.03	23.2	27.3	25.6	20.0	30.0	7.06	6.1	10.3	0.640	256
0.992	0.934	128.4	9.96	27.21	24.62	23.1	25.3	16.1	13.3	30.0	8.22	7.4	9.3	0.615	257
0.931	0.929	118.2	10.26	37.39	23.10	30.1	27.5	23.6	16.6	33.3	7.66	6.5	10.1	0.665	264
1.073	0.858	176.9	14.97	35.18	27.40	25.5	29.3	21.8	16.6	26.6	11.46	7.9	13.8	1.080	277
0.965	1.051	126.8	15.43	19.50	24.52	22.6	25.8	26.7	20.0	30.0	8.23	6.6	12.1	1.000	283
1.273	0.910	123.1	14.66	34.30	32.32	29.1	37.0	22.6	20.0	26.6	7.98	6.1	11.3	0.950	239a

NORTH CAROLINA—Continued.

Number of sample.	Character of soil.	County.	Cotton variety.	Sender.
	RED OR CLAYEY LANDS.			
244	Heavy clay soil, manured with cottonseed and guano....................	Halifax......	....	J. H. Parker..................
269	Stiff land (coast)..	Pamlico......	....	J. S. Lane....................
270	Clay soil..	Pasquotank......	....	C. W. Hollowell..........
282	Clay uplands, manured with guano...............................	Wayne........	....	J. Robinson................
283	Clay uplands, no manure..	...do....	....	.........do..............
248	Dark loam upland, little sand, yellow-clay subsoil, manured with 30 bushels of cottonseed per acre.	Harnett..........	Not fully grown.............	H. C. McNeill.............
258 a	Red and dark gravelly upland, manured with 250 pounds of guano per acre..	Moore........	....	A. H. Cameron...........
258 b	Red and dark gravelly upland soil..............................	...do....	....	D. M. Sinclair...........
258 c	......do......	...do....	....	R. M. McRae.............
258 d	......do......	...do....	....	M. Ferguson.............
258 e	......do......	...do....	....	J. C. Campbell...........
250 a	Red and dark gravelly upland soil, no manure..................	...do....	....	R. McDonald.............
250 b	Red and dark gravelly upland soil, manured with 200 pounds guano per acre.	...do....	....	B. F. Clegg..............
250 d	Red and dark gravelly upland soil, no manure..................	...do....	....	F. Campbell.............
250 e	Red and dark gravelly upland soil, manured with 200 pounds guano per acre	...do....	....	A. B. Harrington.........
	OAK UPLANDS HAVING CLAY SUBSOILS.			
216	Sandy upland...	Alamance......	....	J. A. Graham..........
217	Sandy and gravelly upland.....................................	Anson........	....	W. E. Smith...........
218	......do......	...do....	....	......do.............
222	Sandy upland...	Caldwell......	Edwards....	......do.............
223	......do......	...do....	......do....	......do.............
224	......do......	...do....	......do....	......do.............
226	Sandy loam, pine, hickory, poplar..............................	Chatham.......	....	J. W. Scott.............
227 a	Gray and sandy land..	Cleaveland......	....	J. R. Logan.............
227 b	......do......	...do....	....	......do.............
227 d	......do......	...do....	....	......do.............
227 e	Red and gray sandy land......................................	...do....	....	......do.............
227 c	......do......	...do....	....	......do.............
228 a	Gray sandy land..	...do....	....	......do.............
228 b	......do......	...do....	....	......do.............
228 c	......do......	...do....	....	......do.............
228 e	......do......	...do....	....	......do.............
228 f	Red and gray sandy land......................................	...do....	....	......do.............
229	Gray and sandy land..	...do....	....	......do.............
237	Gray and gravelly land.......................................	Franklin......	....	W. F. Greene...........
256	Sandy loam..	Granville......	....	J. B. Hunter...........
252	Gray sandy land..	Lincoln......	....	W. A. Graham...........
251	Upland soil..	...do....	....	Elisha Ballard..........
253	......do......	...do....	....	John J. Phifer..........
268	Gray sandy land..	Orange......	....	C. W. Johnson..........
276	Gray gravelly land...	Stanley......	....	M. T. Waddill..........
280	Gray sandy loam...	Union......	....	H. M. Houston..........
279	Gravelly land..	...do....	....	......do.............
281	Upland..	...do....	....	......do.............
228 d	Red land..	Cleaveland......	....	J. R. Logan.............
254	Red-clay land...	Lincoln......	....	W. A. Graham...........
278	Coarse, gravelly mulatto upland, oak, black-jack, and pine growth........	Union......	....	H. M. Houston..........
	Average of all........			

Longest, No. 258 b; medium, No. 228 a; shortest, No. 225. Widest, No. 248–227 b; medium, No. 258 b–284; narrowest, No. 250. Strongest, No. 251; medium, No. 228 d;

SOUTH CAROLINA.

290	Sandy highlands, Edisto island.................................	Charleston......	....	I. J. Mikell..................
293 a	Light sandy land, James island................................	...do....	....	W. G. Hinson..............
293 b	......do......	...do....	....	......do..............
294	......do......	...do....	....	E. L. Rivers.............
295	Light sandy land, John's island...............................	...do....	Sea island....	W. E. Trip..............
296 a	Light sandy land...	...do....	Santee long-staple.............	J. S. Porcher.............
296 b	......do......	...do....	....	......do..............
296 c	......do......	...do....	....	......do..............
299	High sandy pine land, clay subsoil.............................	Colleton......	....	G. Varn.................
301	Sandy pine lands, clay subsoil.................................	Hampton......	....	H. H. Peeples...........
298	Light sandy loam, clay subsoil.................................	Aiken......	....	P. F. Hammond...........

33

NORTH CAROLINA—Continued.

LENGTH, IN INCHES.	WIDTH, IN 1/1000 OF AN INCH.	BREAKING WEIGHT, IN GRAINS.	Weight of 5 seed with the lint, in grains.	Percentage of lint.	LENGTH, IN MILLIMETERS.			WIDTH, IN 1/10 OF A MILLIMETER.			BREAKING WEIGHT, IN GRAMS.			Weight of 5 seed with the lint, in grams.	Number of sample.
Average of 4 fibers.	Average of 4 fibers.	Average of 10 or 15 results.			Average of 5 fibers.	Minimum.	Maximum.	Average of 4 fibers.	Minimum.	Maximum.	Average of 5 or 10 results.	Minimum.	Maximum.		
1	2	3	4	5	6	7	8	9	10	11	12	13	14	15	
1.241	0.850	121.6	11.96	32.90	31.54	26.2	36.6	21.6	16.6	26.6	7.88	7.1	8.7	0.775	244
1.126	0.894	96.2	12.19	26.58	28.66	23.1	30.2	22.7	16.6	30.0	6.36	5.4	7.2	0.790	269
0.852	0.900	125.2	12.96	29.97	21.64	26.1	22.6	23.1	30.0	25.6	8.12	6.4	16.2	0.840	270
0.965	0.860	168.5	11.57	37.32	24.50	20.1	28.0	22.0	16.6	30.0	10.72	8.1	15.8	0.750	262
1.022	0.984	148.5	11.50	34.24	25.98	21.5	25.4	25.0	13.3	30.0	9.63	8.2	11.1	0.745	263
1.084	1.022	139.5	10.96	35.91	27.54	22.7	31.8	26.0	22.3	33.3	9.04	7.8	16.2	0.710	248
1.037	0.984	117.6	11.57	30.67	26.34	25.1	29.8	25.0	16.6	30.0	7.62	6.1	9.6	0.750	256 a
1.337	0.929	112.4	11.37	31.39	34.46	30.0	34.0	23.6	16.6	26.6	7.28	6.2	8.5	0.860	256 b
1.196	1.035	127.7	15.97	31.46	30.36	27.0	33.1	26.3	16.6	36.6	10.22	7.3	12.5	1.035	256 c
1.251	0.925	118.8	14.20	33.58	31.78	27.0	34.5	23.5	16.6	26.6	7.76	6.4	9.2	0.920	256 d
1.174	0.701	168.3	13.97	32.04	29.14	26.0	32.6	17.8	12.3	23.3	10.58	8.8	11.6	0.905	256 e
1.347	0.835	138.0	12.27	33.96	34.22	31.8	36.2	21.2	13.3	26.6	8.94	6.4	11.2	0.795	350 a
1.328	0.949	130.5	11.65	33.77	33.75	31.0	36.5	24.1	20.0	30.0	8.46	6.7	10.1	0.753	350 b
1.010	0.878	139.8	13.81	32.40	25.66	24.0	28.3	22.3	13.3	26.6	9.04	7.1	11.4	0.806	350 d
1.220	0.689	127.8	14.74	30.89	30.98	25.6	35.3	17.0	13.3	23.3	8.26	7.1	9.8	0.965	350 e
1.178	1.022	150.6	....	....	29.93	26.6	31.9	26.0	20.0	36.6	9.78	8.1	11.1	....	316
0.976	0.925	110.6	....	....	24.94	21.8	29.3	23.5	20.0	26.6	7.18	6.1	8.9	....	317
0.960	0.850	113.4	10.03	33.84	24.12	22.3	26.4	21.6	16.6	26.6	7.48	5.7	9.6	0.650	318
0.875	0.941	147.7	11.42	29.73	22.22	20.4	24.6	22.9	16.6	33.3	9.57	7.7	16.2	0.740	322
1.126	0.870	132.9	11.73	30.36	25.82	24.8	33.8	22.1	16.3	30.0	8.68	7.6	11.3	0.760	323
0.946	0.896	130.5	10.03	34.15	24.04	23.2	25.4	22.8	13.3	33.3	6.51	4.9	8.1	0.650	324
1.005	0.787	134.4	10.96	34.63	25.54	21.4	27.7	20.0	10.0	26.6	8.06	6.6	10.4	0.710	326
0.806	0.906	126.7	....	....	22.74	19.8	23.9	23.0	13.3	33.3	8.21	7.0	9.9	....	327 a
1.086	1.220	98.8	....	....	27.60	24.3	29.1	31.0	26.6	34.6	5.06	3.9	5.9	....	327 b
1.064	0.929	135.7	....	....	27.04	25.0	29.0	23.6	16.6	36.3	8.99	7.0	10.1	....	327 d
0.896	1.059	133.1	....	....	22.74	20.0	27.4	26.9	20.0	33.3	8.63	7.1	14.4	....	327 e
0.911	1.066	113.1	....	....	23.14	21.7	25.4	27.6	20.0	33.3	7.33	4.7	8.2	....	327 c
1.069	1.136	140.7	....	....	26.92	24.6	30.3	28.8	20.0	44.0	8.13	6.7	12.7	....	328 a
1.011	1.020	114.5	....	....	25.70	23.3	27.6	25.9	16.6	40.0	7.42	6.6	9.2	....	328 b
1.050	1.138	100.1	....	....	26.06	25.5	28.6	28.9	13.3	36.6	6.49	4.3	13.6	....	328 c
1.131	0.980	158.1	....	....	28.72	26.0	31.5	24.9	20.0	30.0	10.25	8.6	13.2	....	328 e
0.919	0.890	140.7	....	....	23.34	21.1	25.4	22.6	13.3	33.3	9.13	7.3	13.2	....	328 f
1.016	0.831	121.6	....	....	25.81	24.9	27.3	21.1	16.6	26.6	7.88	6.6	10.6	....	329
0.995	0.896	107.7	....	....	25.26	22.7	26.8	22.0	13.3	36.0	6.96	5.0	8.2	....	334
1.185	1.035	145.3	....	....	29.60	27.2	34.2	26.3	22.3	30.0	9.42	8.1	10.9	....	337
1.048	0.945	104.3	10.56	36.16	26.62	23.5	27.0	24.0	13.3	26.6	6.76	5.9	8.9	0.685	253
1.078	1.035	170.9	14.66	37.89	27.33	23.7	29.3	26.3	16.6	23.3	11.06	9.1	13.9	0.950	251
1.111	1.122	117.0	11.93	33.16	28.24	27.5	28.4	28.5	13.3	36.3	7.64	5.2	16.1	0.715	252
0.972	0.867	132.2	....	....	24.70	20.9	28.4	20.5	16.6	23.3	8.57	7.3	11.7	....	368
1.335	0.866	117.6	11.19	28.27	33.90	32.1	37.2	22.0	13.3	30.0	7.62	6.3	8.6	0.725	276
1.017	0.896	163.9	....	....	25.83	24.0	26.6	22.8	16.6	33.3	10.32	8.6	12.6	....	399
0.971	0.949	138.2	....	....	24.67	21.4	28.5	24.1	20.0	36.6	9.02	7.3	13.2	....	279
1.198	0.744	161.3	....	....	30.62	28.4	32.5	18.9	16.0	30.0	8.6	6.6	13.4	....	381
1.118	0.880	108.7	....	....	18.12	33.4	31.6	16.0	20.0	26.6	8.00	7.1	10.6	....	268 d
1.082	1.047	105.2	12.27	33.96	27.50	25.4	30.3	26.6	20.0	30.0	6.82	5.2	7.4	0.795	354
1.003	0.968	105.3	....	....	25.47	22.9	27.7	24.6	13.3	33.3	6.82	5.4	8.7	....	278
1.058	0.929	192.7	12.55	33.21	26.87	15.4	37.2	23.6	6.6	40.0	8.60	3.9	16.2	0.813	

weakest, No. 269. Heaviest, No. 277; medium, No. 272; lightest, No. 240. Most lint, No. 231 b; medium lint, No 278; least lint, No. 233.

SOUTH CAROLINA.

1.996	0.878	116.5	13.80	27.77	49.94	45.1	53.0	22.3	16.6	30.0	7.16	5.6	9.3	0.900	290
1.780	0.720	71.2	11.42	29.05	45.20	43.0	52.0	18.3	16.6	23.3	4.68	3.0	7.5	0.740	293 a
1.429	0.850	96.2	10.65	37.68	36.30	31.5	33.8	21.6	16.6	26.6	6.43	4.5	10.0	0.690	293 b
1.431	0.882	103.1	9.42	31.94	36.36	26.5	44.3	22.4	16.6	30.0	6.52	5.2	7.7	0.610	294
1.520	0.945	96.8	11.19	32.19	46.22	42.0	48.4	24.0	20.0	23.3	5.40	5.2	10.6	0.735	296
1.606	0.909	104.9	11.96	39.03	42.22	40.8	44.2	23.1	13.3	30.0	6.76	5.3	6.0	0.775	296 a
1.732	0.799	112.9	11.42	33.38	44.00	41.6	47.0	26.3	12.3	26.7	7.26	5.6	9.3	0.760	296 b
1.927	0.966	96.3	10.73	30.94	48.06	46.0	53.2	22.0	16.7	30.0	5.30	4.1	6.6	0.606	296 c
1.218	0.984	132.1	14.20	28.80	30.94	29.6	32.0	25.0	16.6	33.3	7.96	7.2	8.7	0.920	299
1.023	1.086	157.1	13.03	31.41	25.99	23.1	34.9	27.6	22.3	36.6	10.18	8.3	12.6	0.780	301
1.045	0.898	111.4	7.95	31.95	26.54	24.6	27.8	22.8	20.0	26.6	7.22	6.1	9.6	0.513	286

39

SOUTH CAROLINA—Continued.

Number of sample.	Character of soil.	County.	Cotton variety.	Sender.
305	Light sandy soil...	Marlborough		C. S. McCall.
300	Light sandy soil, clay subsoil..................................	Orangeburgh	Long staple..................	O. N. Bowman.
284	Gray sandy pine lands...	Barnwell..........		W. R. Rice ....
289	Light and poor sandy pine lands................................	....do		....do ....
303	Gray uplands, clay subsoils, with 180 pounds of manure per acre.......	Lexington		F. J. Harman ....
304	Red or mulatto lands manured with 195 pounds of fertilizer per acre......	....do		....do ....
287	Mulatto land..	Barnwell..........		W. B. Rice..........
307	Stiff reddish soil	Marlborough		C. S. McCall.
300	Red-clay lands	Fairfield..........		G. H. McMaster......
297	Dark red bottom lands	Colleton		G. Varn.
306	Blackish soil...	Marlborough		C. S. McCall.
302	Dark loam soil of rivers, lightly manured......................	Lexington		F. J. Harman ....
298	Light and sandy hummock land	Colleton		G. Varn.
301	Lowlands of Edisto island	Charleston		I. J. Mikell..........
302	Marsh or salt land of Edisto island............................	....do		....do ....
	Average of all			

Longest, No. 300; shortest, No. 302.   Widest, No. 304; narrowest, No. 295 a.   Strongest, No. 289;

TENNESSEE.

309 a	Table-land, no manure...	Madison		R. C. Harbert ....
310 b	Table-land, old, with barn-yard manure.........................	...do		....do ....
310 a	Table-land, cultivated five years, no manure...................	...do		....do ....
311 a	Hill land, no manure..	...do		....do ....
311 b	Hill land, manured	...do		....do ....
311 a	Hill land...	...do	Rusty cotton	....do ....
300 b	Second bottom land	...do		....do ....
	Average of all			

Longest, No. 310 b; shortest, No. 311 a.   Widest, No. 311 b; narrowest, No. 309 a.   Strongest, No. 309 a;

TEXAS.

	TIMBERED SANDY UPLANDS.			
312	Sandy lands...	Angelina	Worm-proof cotton	E. L. Robb ....
313	Sandy upland soil...	Bastrop..........		
321	Sandy loam soil...	Dallas		J. P. Cole ....
324	Light sandy soil..	Denton		J. W. Evans ....
322	Dark sandy soil...	....do		....do ....
329	Very light sandy soil...	De Witt		A. G. Stevens ....
337	Light sandy soil	....do		....do ....
340	Sandy upland soil...	Gonzales..........		
341	......do..	Gregg		J. D. Woodward ....
345	......do..	Grimes		R. D. Blackshear. ....
353	Sandy pine land of rivers......................................	Kendall..........		C. H. Clans.
351	Sandy pine land	Jasper	Hybrid cotton	L. C. White.
357 a	Sandy post oak, manured	Lee	Schubach, or storm proof	R. H. Flaniken.
357 b	Sandy post oak, manured..	....do	....do	....do ....
356 a	Sandy post oak, not manured	....do	....do	....do ....
356 b	Sandy post oak, manured from cowpen...........................	....do	....do	....do ....
354	Sandy post oak and prairie.....................................	....do		C. B. Longley ....
362	Sandy timbered land....	McLennan..........		
372	Sandy land..	Walker........		J. F. Fisher ....
348	Stiff sandy land	Harrison........		W. J. Caven ....
350 a	Stiff post oak sandy land	Lee		R. H. Flaniken ....
	PRAIRIES.			
350 b	Brown prairie land..	Lee		R. H. Flaniken.
364	Brown loam prairie land...	Navarro	Schubach, or storm proof....	
373	Upland prairie..	Walker........	Smooth seeds	J. F. Fisher ....
330	Black sandy prairie soil..	Ellis		
330	...... do...	Erath..........		J. G. O'Brien ....
331	Lighter sandy prairie soil......................................	... do		....do ....

40

SOUTH CAROLINA—Continued.

LENGTH, IN INCHES.		WIDTH, IN TENS OF AN INCH.	BREAKING WEIGHT, IN GRAINS.	Weight of 5 seed with the lint, in grains.	Percentage of lint.	LENGTH, IN MILLIMETERS.			WIDTH, IN TENS OF A MILLIMETER.			BREAKING WEIGHT, IN GRAMS.			Weight of 5 seed with the lint, in grams.	Number of sample.
Average of 4 fibers.	Average of 4 fibers.	Average of 10 or 15 results.				Average of 5 fibers.	Minimum.	Maximum.	Average of 4 fibers.	Minimum.	Maximum.	Average of 5 or 10 results.	Minimum.	Maximum.		
1	2	3	4	5	6	7	8	9	10	11	12	13	14	15	
0.909	0.976	126.8	9.34	22.22	23.06	20.0	23.7	24.8	20.0	33.3	8.22	6.6	9.1	0.605	305
0.901	1.102	127.8	11.73	28.94	22.88	20.2	24.8	28.0	16.6	38.3	8.28	7.4	12.0	0.760	306
1.068	1.142	146.3	12.66	34.14	27.14	26.5	30.3	29.0	23.3	33.3	9.48	8.3	10.9	0.820	268
0.992	0.776	160.3	14.12	31.14	25.19	22.2	26.1	19.7	10.0	30.0	10.39	8.5	14.3	0.915	289
1.020	1.126	155.5	11.81	33.33	25.92	23.0	31.1	28.6	23.3	45.6	10.06	7.5	13.2	0.765	302
0.779	1.182	143.5	11.27	32.19	19.78	16.7	24.9	30.0	26.6	36.6	9.29	7.7	10.3	0.730	304
0.931	0.846	125.3	12.42	31.02	23.65	22.1	25.6	21.5	16.6	28.3	8.12	6.9	9.3	0.805	287
1.062	1.141	113.0	14.35	29.57	27.00	24.2	29.2	28.0	20.0	36.6	7.32	6.5	9.4	0.890	307
0.956	1.146	98.7	10.03	33.86	24.36	20.3	28.6	29.1	23.3	33.3	6.46	4.3	9.5	0.850	300
1.000	0.973	115.7	12.89	31.72	24.65	21.5	34.3	24.7	13.3	40.0	7.50	6.3	9.4	0.835	297
1.094	1.047	131.8	13.03	39.48	27.60	26.5	29.3	26.6	13.3	40.0	8.54	8.0	9.1	0.780	306
0.766	1.102	142.7	13.12	35.88	19.46	17.6	21.3	26.0	23.3	33.3	9.25	8.7	10.9	0.850	308
1.000	0.907	143.1	12.04	35.88	25.40	20.1	26.0	20.5	16.6	23.3	9.27	6.9	12.1	0.845	296
1.162	0.949	108.8	11.04	32.16	29.54	21.8	42.5	24.1	16.6	30.0	7.05	5.5	8.9	0.715	291
1.460	0.760	92.0	12.42	32.91	37.08	31.7	42.9	18.8	13.3	26.6	5.96	4.6	7.9	0.805	292
1.234	0.957	120.3	11.80	31.62	31.34	16.7	53.2	24.3	13.3	45.6	7.79	3.0	14.3	0.765	

weakest, No. 292 a. Heaviest, No. 307; lightest, No. 296. Most lint, No. 293 b; least lint, No. 290.

TENNESSEE.

0.868	0.764	180.7	11.96	35.48	22.06	20.7	22.6	19.4	6.6	30.0	11.71	7.7	15.5	0.775	309 a
1.131	0.862	115.3	12.73	29.60	28.74	27.3	30.4	22.4	16.6	30.0	7.47	6.9	8.7	0.825	310 b
0.986	0.894	132.5	13.16	31.64	25.04	21.3	29.4	22.7	13.3	30.0	8.57	7.1	11.6	0.790	310 e
0.841	0.890	151.1	10.87	36.62	21.36	19.0	22.0	22.6	16.6	36.6	9.79	7.1	13.7	0.685	311 e
0.896	1.180	139.5	12.19	30.37	23.80	21.3	13.9	30.2	16.6	46.6	9.04	7.1	11.3	0.790	311 b
0.831	0.776	79.6	11.96	37.41	20.86	17.4	22.9	19.7	13.3	33.3	5.16	3.6	8.1	0.775	311 e
1.036	0.862	135.0	14.96	30.52	26.33	23.6	29.4	22.4	16.6	30.0	8.62	7.0	13.1	0.950	309 b
0.922	0.896	133.3	12.33	33.10	25.21	17.4	30.4	22.6	6.6	46.6	8.64	3.6	15.5	0.799	

weakest, No. 311 c. Heaviest, No. 309 b; lightest, No. 311 e. Most lint, No. 311 a; least lint, No. 311 b.

TEXAS.

1.146	0.764	156.5	16.25	32.91	29.16	27.3	22.5	16.9	16.6	22.3	10.14	8.5	12.3	1.185	212
0.994	0.709	113.6	6.26	33.43	25.24	22.9	24.6	18.0	13.3	23.3	7.36	6.7	8.0	0.635	213
1.187	1.062	160.6	14.12	33.74	29.38	26.2	33.0	27.0	23.3	36.6	10.43	7.7	14.7	0.915	221
1.088	0.854	176.4	14.66	34.21	27.63	25.0	32.4	21.7	16.6	36.6	11.43	9.3	14.3	0.950	224
1.094	0.733	196.7	14.43	32.51	27.78	25.5	30.7	18.6	13.3	23.3	8.96	7.7	10.5	0.935	223
0.996	0.799	127.1	14.12	36.21	25.31	22.3	27.6	30.3	10.0	26.6	8.24	6.9	8.9	0.915	226
0.906	0.897	188.9	14.82	31.77	25.30	23.4	25.6	22.6	16.6	30.0	12.24	10.1	14.7	0.960	227
1.114	0.917	61.1	9.03	29.91	28.30	25.1	31.9	23.3	16.6	36.6	3.96	3.7	4.4	0.585	264
1.005	0.791	129.1	13.35	32.30	25.52	22.9	28.5	20.1	16.6	23.3	8.30	7.8	9.2	0.909	241
1.076	0.911	121.8	10.11	36.56	27.33	26.0	36.6	30.0	16.6	36.6	7.80	6.7	10.3	0.655	244
1.162	0.787	121.7			29.56	27.1	30.6	22.5	16.6	26.6	10.23	7.5	11.3		251
1.153	0.858	138.0	17.21	23.73	29.30	27.5	23.0	21.8	16.7	30.0	8.94	7.7	10.4	1.115	357 a
1.374	0.736	143.8	17.13	36.83	34.90	32.9	38.3	18.7	16.7	23.3	9.23	8.0	11.3	1.110	357 b
1.075	0.791	136.4	16.13	31.91	27.30	25.3	31.4	30.1	13.3	36.6	8.84	7.7	11.0	1.175	358 a
1.147	1.260	134.6	17.59	27.19	29.14	26.1	30.3	33.0	20.0	43.3	8.72	8.0	9.7	1.140	358 b
1.085	1.062	153.4	15.05	29.74	27.56	24.6	29.9	27.0	23.3	33.3	9.94	8.1	12.9	0.975	354
1.032	0.909	125.9	9.65	28.80	26.22	23.4	27.8	23.1	20.0	30.0	8.16	7.3	10.2	0.625	342
0.819	0.900	146.6	5.71	32.43	20.80	16.0	24.3	23.1	20.0	30.0	9.50	8.1	14.8	0.370	372
1.390	0.827	127.9	14.94	31.87	35.06	32.7	36.5	21.0	13.3	33.3	8.29	7.3	9.1	0.910	348
1.036	0.976	135.8	15.74	28.92	26.33	23.3	30.0	24.6	20.0	30.0	8.80	8.3	9.5	1.020	350 a
1.075	0.819	154.0	15.66	27.93	27.32	27.0	30.6	16.6	16.7	26.7	9.98	8.7	10.8	1.015	359 a
1.138	0.968	106.0	13.27	37.20	28.92	27.6	30.2	25.1	16.6	30.0	7.00	5.5	8.5	0.880	364
1.097	0.811	123.5	14.20	32.60	27.88	26.5	29.1	20.6	16.6	26.6	8.00	6.4	9.6	0.920	373
1.065	0.768	141.7	10.34	36.56	27.06	24.9	29.1	19.5	13.3	23.3	9.18	8.3	10.0	0.670	329
1.115	0.674	109.7	12.35	33.12	28.34	26.5	29.9	22.2	16.6	33.3	7.11	4.8	10.4	0.800	330
0.879	0.941	145.9	12.89	32.99	23.84	19.6	28.6	23.9	16.6	33.3	9.41	5.4	13.2	0.855	391

41

TEXAS—Continued.

Number of sample.	Character of soil.	County.	Cotton variety.	Sender.
	STIFF LANDS, MOSTLY PRAIRIES.			
300	Red land (timbered)	Lee		Mrs. E. R. Wilson
315	Stiff black prairie soil	Bell	Hafley's Golden Leaf	M. Maedgen
316	.....do	...do	Planted late	...do
317	.....do	Bosque		T. W. Archibald
320	Stiff black prairie land	Dallas		J. F. Cole
322	.....do	...do	Storm-proof cotton	F. Henaley
325	.....do	Denton		J. W. Evans
326	.....do	De Witt		A. G. Stevens
332	.....do	Erath		J. G. O'Brien
323	Stiff black prairie, valley	...do		...do
334	Stiff black prairie land	Falls		E. P. Lea
339	.....do	Fayette	Late picking	
346	Stiff black prairie, hog-wallow soil	Grimes		C. H. Rhinger
347	Stiff black prairie land	Harris		S. P. Christian
349	.....do	Hood	Cheatham Prolific	
352	.....do	Kendall		C. H. Clauss
365	Stiff black prairie land, valley	San Saba		
367	Stiff black prairie land	Travis	Matagorda Silk	J. J. Wheeler
369	.....do	...do	5-lock Silk	...do
370	.....do	Victoria		
371	Stiff black prairie land	Walker	Nankin	J. F. Fisher
	BOTTOM LANDS.			
336 a	Red river bottom sediment land	Fannin		Gideon Smith
336 b	.....do	...do		...do
337 c	Red river bottom sandy land	...do		...do
337 d	.....do	...do		...do
338 e	Red river valley, cultivated 30 years	...do		...do
338 f	.....do	...do		...do
344	Brazos river bottom lands	Grimes		R. D. Blackshear
350	Brazos river second bottom soil	Hood		
351	Brazos river second bottom sandy soil	McLennan		
335	Brazos river black alluvial hummock	Falls		E. P. Lea
314	Colorado river valley soil	Bastrop		
319	Colorado river dark alluvial soil	Colorado		
368	Colorado river valley soil	Travis	5-lock cotton	
318	Oyster creek red soil	Brazoria		J. M. Kirkland
374	Rio Grande valley soil		From stalk, first year growth	Rev. J. G. Hall
375	.....do		From stalk, second year growth	...do
376	.....do		From stalk, fourth year growth	...do
342	Second bottom land	Gregg		J. D. Woodward
343	.....do	...do		...do
355	Yegua creek bottom soil	Lee		C. B. Longley
356	.....do	...do		...do
362	Chambers creek valley soil	Navarro	Schubach, or storm proof	
366	Bottom land	Shelby		
377	Coast lands		Sea-island cotton	
	Average of all			

Longest, No. 377; shortest, No. 372. Widest, No. 358 b; narrowest, No. 313. Strongest, No. 327;

VIRGINIA.

360	Sandy soil and subsoil, manured as in No. 378	Southampton	Williams	W. H. Doughty
362	Light gray sandy soil	Sussex		J. D. Thornton
364	Medium upland	...do		...do
378	Gray sandy loam, red sandy clay subsoil, manured with 30 bushels of cottonseed meal, 100 pounds of guano, 100 pounds of kainit, and 50 pounds of plaster per acre.	Southampton	Williams	W. H. Doughty
379	Gray sandy loam, bluishclay subsoil, with 200 pounds of superphosphate per acre.	...do	Mixed, third picking	...do
381	Light sandy soil, red sandy clay subsoil	...do		J. D. Pretlow
382	.....do	...do		...do
385	Stiff bottom land	Sussex		J. D. Thornton
	Average of all			

Longest, No. 380; shortest, No. 382. Widest, No. 379; narrowest, No. 385. Strongest, No. 380;

TEXAS—Continued.

LENGTH, IN INCHES		WIDTH, IN 1/1000 OF AN INCH	BREAKING WEIGHT, IN GRAINS	Weight of 5 seed with the lint, in grains	Percentage of lint.	LENGTH, IN MILLIMETERS			WIDTH, IN 1/1000 OF A MILLIMETER			BREAKING WEIGHT, IN GRAMS			Weight of 5 seed with the lint, in grams	Number of sample.
Average of 4 fibers.	Average of 4 fibers.	Average of 10 or 15 results.				Average of 5 fibers.	Minimum.	Maximum.	Average of 4 fibers.	Minimum.	Maximum.	Average of 5 or 10 results.	Minimum.	Maximum.		
1	2	3	4	5	6	7	8	9	10	11	12	13	14	15	
1.074	0.962	91.4	5.86	42.10	27.29	22.9	26.9	25.1	20.0	30.0	5.92	5.0	7.3	0.380	300
1.170	0.787	171.4	12.89	32.98	27.92	22.3	30.4	20.0	10.6	26.6	11.11	8.4	14.6	0.835	315
0.865	0.977	136.2	17.44	33.62	21.97	20.4	29.2	24.8	20.0	30.0	8.13	7.5	9.9	1.130	316
0.945	0.831	101.0	12.11	29.96	24.02	22.7	25.5	21.1	16.6	26.6	6.54	4.3	9.5	0.785	317
1.036	0.976	130.7	20.32	22.57	26.06	25.0	26.5	24.8	20.0	26.5	7.82	6.6	10.6	1.320	320
0.927	0.811	115.4	11.96	33.40	23.54	23.0	24.5	20.6	16.6	26.6	7.48	5.5	9.6	0.775	322
0.961	1.075	131.8	16.74	40.00	24.42	22.6	26.8	27.3	23.3	33.3	8.54	5.0	10.6	1.065	325
1.365	6.839	114.8	8.72	31.64	34.68	22.5	36.5	21.2	16.6	30.0	7.44	5.6	10.2	0.565	326
0.857	1.071	118.8	11.42	33.13	21.78	19.6	22.9	27.2	23.3	34.6	7.70	6.6	10.5	0.740	332
1.048	0.986	113.7	7.16	33.32	26.56	24.3	29.1	22.8	16.6	26.6	7.34	6.0	7.9	0.485	333
1.006	1.635	154.0	10.88	36.29	25.57	22.8	27.6	26.3	20.0	33.3	10.06	7.5	11.5	0.705	334
1.165	0.760	90.4	13.81	31.04	29.56	26.3	31.6	19.3	13.3	23.3	5.86	4.2	6.7	0.895	339
0.991	0.827	109.3	12.07	30.93	25.18	24.3	27.2	21.0	16.6	26.6	7.06	6.2	7.9	0.905	346
1.031	0.843	128.2	15.62	28.29	26.12	24.2	28.4	21.4	10.0	30.0	8.31	7.7	10.0	1.025	347
1.116	0.917	144.2	10.95	30.09	28.36	26.3	30.5	23.3	20.0	30.0	9.34	7.0	12.0	0.710	349
1.059	0.850	125.4	....	....	26.90	25.3	30.7	21.6	16.6	26.6	8.13	6.4	13.1	....	352
1.094	0.894	167.7	12.60	34.97	27.78	25.9	29.9	22.7	16.6	30.0	10.86	8.2	14.4	0.875	365
1.200	1.165	144.2	11.88	31.16	30.48	28.2	32.9	29.6	20.0	30.0	9.34	8.4	10.8	0.770	367
1.052	1.015	146.3	....	....	26.67	24.3	29.5	25.8	16.6	33.3	9.48	7.0	10.6	....	369
1.150	0.827	139.6	13.60	26.40	29.22	25.8	29.6	21.0	16.6	23.3	8.96	7.9	8.6	0.880	370
0.979	0.890	137.0	11.96	25.16	24.88	22.3	26.6	22.6	20.0	26.6	8.88	7.8	10.5	0.775	371
0.941	1.212	72.2	16.26	31.75	23.90	22.7	25.7	30.8	23.3	43.3	4.74	4.1	5.2	1.055	336 a
0.904	1.047	152.5	13.35	32.35	25.00	21.0	27.8	26.6	16.3	40.0	9.88	9.0	10.6	0.965	336 b
1.102	0.949	154.3	12.35	37.50	27.98	27.3	28.5	24.1	16.6	33.3	10.00	8.7	11.3	0.800	337 c
0.880	0.929	140.7	12.60	30.86	22.36	19.0	26.0	23.6	16.6	30.0	9.13	8.4	11.0	0.810	337 d
0.994	0.850	91.4	11.57	34.33	25.26	22.7	26.6	21.6	13.3	30.0	5.92	5.6	6.4	0.750	338 e
1.020	0.962	102.8	11.37	32.06	25.90	21.9	27.2	24.6	13.3	33.3	6.66	6.0	8.3	0.750	338 f
1.001	0.894	141.7	10.49	30.14	25.42	21.1	26.6	22.7	16.6	30.0	9.18	7.4	11.7	0.650	344
1.056	0.839	154.6	9.18	37.81	26.82	21.6	35.1	21.3	16.6	26.6	10.02	8.9	12.2	0.585	350
1.009	0.366	134.2	12.60	32.57	25.64	24.5	27.0	22.0	16.6	26.6	7.46	7.1	7.7	0.875	351
1.016	0.866	140.1	11.96	32.25	25.80	20.3	30.0	22.0	16.6	30.0	9.02	8.2	10.1	0.773	353
1.187	0.791	111.4	12.19	27.21	30.14	26.5	32.5	20.1	10.0	26.6	7.22	6.8	7.6	0.790	354
1.104	1.006	127.4	14.51	32.97	28.05	25.4	29.4	26.6	20.0	33.3	8.36	6.7	9.7	0.940	719
1.130	0.909	152.4	10.57	33.57	28.73	25.7	32.1	23.1	16.6	30.0	11.82	8.8	15.0	0.685	368
1.163	1.004	141.7	14.51	35.88	29.54	25.7	32.3	27.8	6.6	36.6	9.18	7.7	11.4	0.940	318
1.174	0.909	167.7	12.04	30.76	29.83	27.6	32.0	23.1	20.0	30.0	10.22	8.5	11.6	0.780	374
1.117	0.732	143.2	12.26	31.44	28.38	20.3	31.2	18.6	10.0	26.6	9.28	8.1	11.3	0.795	375
1.115	0.957	118.2	12.35	34.10	28.34	25.6	30.4	24.3	20.0	30.0	7.66	7.1	8.7	0.965	376
1.000	0.851	144.6	....	....	25.40	20.6	28.9	21.1	16.6	26.6	9.27	8.5	10.5	....	342
1.132	0.878	140.9	....	....	28.73	22.3	31.9	22.3	10.0	33.3	9.13	7.5	9.4	....	343
1.052	0.821	122.2	15.13	27.04	26.76	24.5	29.3	21.1	16.6	26.6	7.92	7.0	10.1	0.980	355
1.043	0.827	156.3	15.36	26.64	26.50	22.3	31.4	21.0	16.6	26.6	10.36	9.0	13.0	0.995	366
0.556	0.835	141.7	13.27	25.74	22.24	20.1	26.1	21.2	16.6	30.0	9.18	7.2	12.6	0.890	362
1.109	0.800	143.7	13.06	26.31	......	......	......	22.6	20.0	26.6	9.44	8.2	9.6	1.000	777
1.717	0.010	112.3	....	....	43.22	36.7	46.1	13.2	16.6	30.0	7.27	6.2	9.0	....	377
1.075	0.897	132.8	12.07	32.94	27.13	16.0	46.1	22.0	6.6	43.3	8.60	3.7	15.0	0.855	

weakest, No. 340. Heaviest, No. 320; lightest, No. 372. Most lint, No. 360; least lint, No. 371.

VIRGINIA.

1.366	1.004	142.3	12.43	30.45	34.70	31.0	43.3	25.5	20.0	30.0	9.22	7.0	12.0	0.870	380
0.883	0.886	124.7	13.27	38.95	22.42	18.6	27.1	22.5	16.6	26.6	8.07	6.6	9.4	0.860	383
1.069	0.791	127.6	11.88	33.47	27.16	26.1	28.3	20.1	13.3	26.6	8.27	7.1	10.1	0.770	384
1.063	1.008	117.6	15.74	29.90	26.48	26.5	27.2	25.6	13.3	33.3	7.62	5.4	11.5	1.020	376
1.067	1.114	127.2	15.59	36.62	27.11	25.1	29.9	23.8	23.3	40.0	8.24	7.0	9.5	1.010	379
0.946	1.094	199.8	14.12	34.97	24.04	23.0	26.0	27.8	30.0	33.3	9.06	7.0	14.1	0.915	381
1.116	1.904	122.0	16.06	31.25	26.36	27.4	32.0	25.5	20.0	33.3	8.56	7.5	11.0	1.040	382
0.964	0.669	97.2	11.96	41.93	24.48	32.7	26.0	17.0	10.0	36.6	6.30	5.6	8.3	0.775	385
1.060	0.945	126.1	14.00	34.44	26.94	18.6	43.3	24.0	10.0	40.0	8.17	5.4	14.1	0.907	

weakest, No. 385. Heaviest, No. 382; lightest, No. 384. Most lint, No. 385; least lint, No. 378.

TABLE SHOWING MAXIMA AND MINIMA OF THE POINTS INCLUDED IN THE MEASUREMENTS FOR THE SEVERAL STATES.

LENGTH OF FIBER.

State.	No. of sample.	County.	Character of soil.	Inches.	No. of sample.	County.	Character of soil.	Inches.
			LONGEST.				SHORTEST.	
Alabama	43	Winston	Upland soil	1.427	48 d	Washington	Old land, pine woods, poor, not manured.	0.789
Arkansas	86	Grant	......do	1.142	56	Arkansas	Timbered upland	0.965
Arizona	51	Maricopa	Valley land	1.192	52	Yuma	(Bell from plant two years old, not cultivated.)	0.745
California	86	Tulare	Dark alluvial loam, light, somewhat alkaline.	1.669	70	Kern	Alluvial loam, somewhat alkaline.	0.837
Florida	96 d	Columbia	Light gray soil, old land (sea-island cotton).	*1.010	104	Gadsden	Sandy table-land	0.854
Georgia	124	Burke	Sandy uplands (Jones' long staple)	1.372	148	Newton	Coarse sandy upland, fertilized	0.806
Indian territory	160		Alluvial lands	1.140	170		Alluvial lands	1.023
Louisiana	179	De Soto	Upland sandy land (late)	1.367	187	Tangipahoa	Table-land, long-leaf pine and oak, manured.	0.862
Mississippi	200	La Fayette	Light sandy upland, old land, highly manured.	1.282	202	La Fayette	Light sandy upland, old land, unmanured.	0.810
Missouri	210	Dunklin	Dark prairie loam, cultivated ten years, not manured.	1.260	215	Stoddard	Lowland	0.907
North Carolina	254 b	Moore	Red and dark gravelly upland soil.	1.357	225	Carteret	Light sandy loam	0.686
South Carolina	290	Charleston	Sandy highland, Edisto island (sea island).	*1.996	302	Lexington	Dark loam river soil, manured	0.766
Tennessee	310 b	Madison	Table land (old land manured)	1.131	311 a	Madison	Hill land	0.821
Texas	348	Harrison	Stiff sandy land	1.390	372	Walker	Sandy land	0.819
Virginia	380	Southampton	Sandy soil and subsoil, manured	1.366	383	Sussex	Light gray sandy soil	0.883
All the states	86	Tulare, Cal.	Dark alluvial loam, Mussel Slough.	1.669	225	Carteret, N. C.	Light sandy loam	0.686

* Sea-island cotton omitted from the averages of the United States.

WIDTH OF FIBER.

State.	No. of sample.	County.	Character of soil.	Inches.	No. of sample.	County.	Character of soil.	Inches.
			WIDEST.				NARROWEST.	
Alabama	43 d	Wilcox	Red land, oak, hickory, and pine..	1.208	36	Tallapoosa	Stiff river bottom land	0.626
Arkansas	56	Arkansas	Timbered upland	1.154	55	Arkansas	Alluvial of Arkansas river	0.722
Arizona	52	Pima	Valley land	1.108	54		Salt river valley	0.779
California	70	Kern	Alluvial loam, alkaline	1.062	86	Tulare	Dark alluvial loam, alkaline	0.756
Florida	100	Columbia		*1.212	106	Gadsden	Red clay hummock	*0.436
Georgia	134	Gwinnett	Gray sandy land, clay subsoil..	1.206	135	Gwinnett	Chocolate or yellow soil (clayey)..	0.614
Indian territory	170		Alluvial lands	1.043	169		Alluvial lands	0.768
Louisiana	186	Tangipahoa	Table-land, not manured	1.263	183	Saint Tammany	Light sandy loam	0.694
Mississippi	200	La Fayette	Light sandy upland, old land, highly manured.	1.061	196	Hinds	Clay loam, cultivated 22 years...	0.768
Missouri	215	Stoddard	Lowland	1.047	212	Dunklin	Dark sandy loam, cultivated 30 years, not manured.	0.811
North Carolina {	246	Harnett	Gray upland soil, fertilized ..... }	1.230	280	Union	Gray sandy loam	0.596
	227 b	Cleaveland	Gray sandy soil					
South Carolina	304	Marlborough	Light sandy soil	1.181	298 a	Charleston	Sandy land, James island	0.729
Tennessee	311 b	Madison	Hill land, manured	1.180	309 a	Madison	Table-land, not manured	0.764
Texas	358 b	Lee	Sandy post-oak soil, unmanured ..	1.980	312	Bastrop	Sandy upland soil	0.700
Virginia	379	Southampton	Gray sandy loam, clay subsoil, manured.	1.114	385	Sussex	Black stiff bottom land	0.609
All the states	46 a	Wilcox, Ala	Red land	1.208	135	Gwinnett, Ga.	Chocolate or yellow soil (clayey)..	0.614

* Sea-island cotton omitted from the averages for the United States.

MAXIMA AND MINIMA OF THE POINTS INCLUDED IN THE MEASUREMENTS FOR THE SEVERAL STATES—Continued.

STRENGTH OF FIBER.

State.	STRONGEST.				WEAKEST.			
	No. of sample.	County.	Character of land.	Breaking weight.	No. of sample.	County.	Character of land.	Breaking weight.
				Grains.				*Grains.*
Alabama	40	Tuscaloosa	Stiff river bottom land	204.7	38	Tuscaloosa	Red clay upland	65.3
Arkansas	60	Conway	Arkansas river bottom land	185.3	57	Boone	Black gravelly loam	103.5
Arizona	52	Pima		143.7	54		Salt river valley	115.1
California	79	Merced	Alluvial loam	175.6	78	Merced	Alluvial loams	110.8
Florida	96	Columbia		*175.0	113 a	Suwannee	Coarse gravelly soil, not manured	*80.1
Georgia	100	Talbot	Red clay lands	193.8	125	Camden	Coast lands (sea-island cotton)	81.5
Indian territory	170		Bottom lands	126.2	169		Bottom lands	113.4
Louisiana	185 d	Tangipahoa	Creek bottoms	214.5	181	Morehouse	Gum lands	69.0
Mississippi	200	La Fayette	Light sandy loam, old, and heavily manured	161.4	193	Amite	Gravelly hill land, heavily manured	109.9
Missouri	210	Dunklin	Dark prairie loam, cultivated 10 years, not manured	183.2	211	Dunklin	Dark prairie loam, cultivated 20 years, not manured	100.9
North Carolina	251	Lincoln	Sandy upland soil	179.9	260	Pamlico	Stiff land	96.2
South Carolina	289	Barnwell	Poor, light, sandy pine lands	180.2	298 a	Charleston	Sandy land, James Island	72.2
Tennessee	300 a	Madison	Table-land, no manure	180.7	311 a	Madison	Hill land	79.6
Texas	327	De Witt	Light sandy land	188.0	340	Gonzales	Sandy upland	61.1
Virginia	380	Southampton	Sandy soil and subsoil, manured	142.3	385	Sussex	Stiff black bottom land	97.2
All the states	185 a	Tangipahoa, La.	Creek bottoms	214.5	340	Gonzales, Tex	Sandy upland	61.1

* Sea-island cotton omitted from the average for the United States.

WEIGHT OF FIVE SEEDS WITH LINT.

State.	GREATEST.				LEAST.			
	No. of sample.	County.	Character of land.	Weight of 5 seed with lint.	No. of sample.	County.	Character of land.	Weight of 5 seed with lint.
				Grains.				*Grains.*
Alabama	18	Jackson	Red clay land	16.76	13	Cleburne	Gravelly land	8.28
Arkansas	60	Conway	Arkansas river bottom land	22.14	61	Crittenden	Black sandy land	9.42
Arizona	54		Salt river valley	12.42	53	Yuma	(No cultivation; from plant of second year.)	11.50
California	84	Tulare	Alluvial loam	16.28	81	Napa	Red plateau land (altitude of 2,000 feet)	9.57
Florida	92 c	Clay	Sandy, "pepper and salt" land, no manure	*21.14	107	Hillsborough	Rather poor pine land	*9.02
Georgia	156	Stewart	Gray sandy land, 40 years' culture, manured	18.60	184	Scriven	Sandy bottom land	7.95
Indian territory	169		Bottom lands	14.95	170		Bottom lands	12.50
Louisiana	174	Catahoula	Creek bottom land	16.96	191	Winn	de	9.03
Mississippi	199 a	Jasper	Black prairie, new land	14.82	205	Lee	Sandy bottom land	9.11
Missouri	210	Dunklin	Dark prairie loam, cultivated 10 years, not manured	15.82	214	Stoddard	Lowland	16.05
North Carolina	277	Tyrrell	Light sandy loam, clay subsoil	16.67	240	Halifax	Sandy river land	8.05
South Carolina	307	Marlborough	Red stiff soil, clay subsoil	14.35	286	Aiken	Light sandy loam, clay subsoil (long staple upland)	7.95
Tennessee	209 b	Madison	Hill land, manured	14.66	311 c	Madison	Hill land, not manured	10.57
Texas	320	Dallas	Black prairie land	20.33	373	Walker	Sandy land	5.71
Virginia	387	Southampton	Light sandy soil, red subsoil	16.95	364	Sussex	Medium upland soil	14.68
All the states	60	Conway, Ark	River bottom land	22.14	373	Walker, Tex	Sandy land	5.71

* Sea-island cotton omitted from the average for the United States.

MAXIMA AND MINIMA OF THE POINTS INCLUDED IN THE MEASUREMENTS FOR THE SEVERAL STATES—Continued.

PERCENTAGE OF LINT ON THE SEED.

State.	GREATEST.				LEAST.			
	No. of sample.	County.	Character of land.	Per cent.	No. of sample.	County.	Character of land.	Per cent.
Alabama	40	Tuscaloosa	Stiff river bottom land	41.98	48 e	Washington	Piny woods land, fertilized	34.62
Arkansas	58	Boone	Sandy loam ridge land	38.23	59	Boone	Brown clay loam	28.64
Arizona	54		Salt river valley	31.67	53	Yuma	(From boll of plant of second year)	24.16
California	89	San Diego	Red gravelly bench land, cotton of 2-year old plant	39.78	78	Merced	Alluvial loam	23.45
Florida	104	Gadsden	Sandy table-land	36.76	110 a	Marion	New pine land, sandy	*11.45
Georgia	118	Appling	Sandy pine woods and wire-grass land	41.57	164	Troup	Red clay land	34.54
Indian territory	169		River bottom land	32.26	170		River bottom land	31.46
Louisiana	102	Winn	Sandy hummock	43.79	182	Red River	Red river alluvial land	29.46
Mississippi	194	Clarke	Black prairie soil, cultivated 10 years.	39.26	196	Clarke	Black prairie soil, cultivated 40 years.	31.87
Missouri	213	Stoddard	Lowlands	34.21	219	Dunklin	Dark sandy loam, cultivated 30 years, unmanured.	28.36
North Carolina	221 b	Craven	Light sandy soil, manured	46.13	223	Craven	Stiff clay hummock land	18.50
South Carolina	293 b	Charleston	Light sandy soil (James island)	37.68	290	Charleston	Highland, sandy (Edisto island)	27.77
Tennessee	311 a	Madison	Hill land	37.41	311 b	Madison	Hill land, manured	30.97
Texas	360	Lee	Red land upland	42.10	371	Walker	Black prairie soil	22.16
Virginia	385	Sussex	Stiff black bottom land	41.98	378	Southampton	Gray sandy loam, clay subsoil, manured.	29.90
All the states	192	Winn, La	Sandy hummock land	43.79	223	Craven, N.C	Stiff clay hummock land	18.50

* Sea-island cotton omitted from the averages of the United States.

AVERAGES FOR EACH STATE.

State.	No. of samples.	Length.	Width, per inch.	Breaking weight.	Weight of 5 seed.	Percentage of lint.
		Inches.		Grains.	Grains.	
Alabama	60	1.027	0.896	137.8	12.98	32.96
Arkansas	13	1.036	0.917	134.7	13.36	32.85
Arizona	4	0.969	0.957	133.7	11.96	27.91
California	19	1.079	0.921	144.6	12.58	32.01
Florida*	45	1.364	0.783	124.1	12.64	29.14
Georgia	83	1.086	0.913	135.9	12.80	33.18
Indian territory	2	1.061	0.905	119.3	13.42	31.87
Louisiana	24	1.069	0.882	127.5	13.01	33.06
Mississippi	18	1.047	0.957	134.3	12.11	34.01
Missouri	6	1.096	0.890	196.4	12.76	31.62
North Carolina	54	1.058	0.929	132.7	12.55	33.21
South Carolina	26	1.234	0.957	130.3	11.86	31.66
Tennessee	7	0.992	0.808	133.3	12.29	33.10
Texas	72	1.075	0.897	122.6	13.07	32.34
Virginia	8	1.060	0.945	126.1	14.00	34.44
Total	450					

* Mostly sea-island cotton.

SUMMARY.

The following table shows the number of samples which have the given respective fiber lengths in the several states.

"Short" staple signifies under 0.98 inches, or 25 millimeters; "medium" means from 0.98 to 1.17 inches, or 25 up to 30 millimeters; "long" staple denotes 1.18 to 1.57 inches, or 30 to 40 millimeters; "extra" includes those that are 1.58 inches, or 40 millimeters or more.

State.	Short.	Medium.	Long.	Extra.	All.
Alabama	22	23	5	....	60
Arizona	2	1	1	....	4
Arkansas	3	10	......	....	13
California	9	6	3	1	19
Florida	4	7	20	14	45
Georgia	16	26	10	......	52
Indian territory	......	2	......	....	2
Louisiana	2	19	3	....	24
Mississippi	2	14	2	....	18
Missouri	2	2	2	....	6
North Carolina	22	58	14	....	94
South Carolina	7	9	4	6	26
Tennessee	4	3	......	....	7
Texas	11	55	5	1	72
Virginia	3	4	1	....	8
Total	109	249	70	22	450

GENERAL AVERAGES FOR THE UNITED STATES.

		Least.	Medium.	Most.	Extra.	All.
Length	inches	0.91	1.07	1.22	*1.72	1.19
	millimeters	23.03	27.09	38.44	43.63	27.89
Width	₁/₁₀₀₀ inch	0.93	0.91	0.86	0.80	0.91
	₁/₁₀₀₀ millimeter	23.60	23.20	22.40	20.40	23.00
Strength	grains	134.30	122.80	126.50	109.90	125.60
	grams	8.70	7.96	8.20	7.12	8.14

* Sea-island cotton.

PERCENTAGES OF DIFFERENT LENGTHS.

Short, or under 0.98 inches long 24
Medium, or from 0.98 to 1.17 inches long 55
Long, or from 1.18 to 1.56 inches long 16
Extra, or 1.57 inches and more 5

The "extra" and the "long" appear, from the character of the seeds, to have come mostly from what Todaro describes as *Gossypium maritimum* (sea-island cotton). The "short" and "medium" correspond to *Gossypium hirsutum* and *Gossypium herbaceum*. Florida makes the best show as to quality, sea-island cotton being predominantly grown.

REMARKS ON THE FIBER MEASUREMENTS.

BY E. W. HILGARD.

Several unforeseen difficulties present themselves in the attempt to deduce general truths from the results of the measurements. First among these is the uncertain nomenclature of the varieties grown. It soon became evident also, as the samples came in, that the same variety of cotton occasionally received different names, and different varieties the same name, so that an element of uncertainty was introduced into the comparison designed to elicit the influence of different soils and climates upon the quality of the staple to the extent to which different varieties might differ in these respects. It was attempted to obtain, through correspondence, accurate and authentic descriptions of the prominent varieties; but from a variety of causes the success was not encouraging, it being evident that the subject requires a thorough sifting by a competent person in the cotton-fields themselves. Again, it was not always possible to obtain samples grown on the soil-varieties that had been accurately studied, and perhaps in the majority of cases the exact nature of the soil had to be inferred from the description of its natural plant or timber growth and of the region of country in which it occurred. It would, of course, have been feasible to supplement these data afterward, and it may perhaps still be done; but want of farther means compels for the present the publication of the data as they are with but little comment.

It is well known that of all experimental studies those referring to agriculture must guard most carefully against hasty conclusions based upon scanty premises and short experience. In the present case, so many factors present themselves as possibly influencing the several points ascertained in the processes of measurement that sweeping inferences regarding any one of them cannot be safely made. But what can be done is to deduce probable indications of the proper direction to be given to future researches, which should be conducted on a uniform and well-elaborated plan, at the several agricultural colleges or experiment stations in the cotton states.

It is greatly to be regretted that, as it now appears, the material received and examined was little adapted to the definite determinations of the questions mooted, being composed of such samples only as chanced to be sent by persons responding to the circular. Had it been feasible to collect samples systematically from the several soil regions, such as the great bottom, the prairie belts, sandy pine lands, etc., of the several states, much more definite conclusions could have been reached, and perhaps could be eliminated even now did time permit. As it is, the best form in which the results foreshadowed can be presented is that of tables showing the maxima and minima of length, width, strength, etc., for the several states. These certainly afford much food for reflection, and show how well a closer investigation of this interesting and important subject would be rewarded. It is true that (as was pointedly remarked by Mr. Edward Atkinson in a letter to the editor on this subject) the commercial grading of the staple, as at present practiced, takes but little account of anything save the length and color, and, to a limited extent, of the luster and fineness of the fiber, the determining points being, first, freedom from trash, and, next, the greater or less injury done to the staple in ginning. The latter point especially is coming to be more and more appreciated, and it is getting to be understood that the high velocities of the saw cylinder, adopted for the sake of an increased output of lint, are seriously detrimental to the quality and especially the strength of the fiber—that a considerable proportion of the fibers is actually cut in two, while a still larger one is sharply bent and thereby weakened at or near the middle, greatly diminishing the aggregate strength of thread made of such material. This is among the considerations that have so strongly recommended the use of the "Clement attachment", with its gently-acting wire brush, instead of the saws; there being no occasion to hasten the ginning beyond the immediate requirements of the carding-machines, the cutting or tearing as well as the sharp bending ("knicken") of the fiber is altogether avoided, and the same cotton will make a stronger thread. It is sometimes thought that the substitution of the Macarthy (cylinder) gin for the saw gin would obviate the greater part of the damage done in ginning; but the experiments made in India and England show that, with an equal output of lint, the knife of the Macarthy gin does nearly or quite as much damage to the staple as the teeth of the saw gin.

So long, then, as the grading and commercial value of cotton depends less upon its natural quality than upon the greater or less care with which it is prepared for market the points of which the measurements are here recorded are only contributory, and not governing, as regards the commercial value of a given product. Yet it is obvious that even thus a knowledge of the peculiarities of the cotton from the several soil regions and varieties is of great importance; for it is manifest that a low and weak fiber must be ginned more slowly than a short and strong one, in order to give the product the highest market value compatible with what may be considered a reasonable output of the gin. The cotton-grower will then know how to balance his operations as between speed and output of the gin, in order to secure the best pecuniary returns in each particular case. At present few pay any attention to these points, and cottonseed cotton having a staple of extra length is ginned at the same speed as, and perhaps even mixed with, short staple from poor pine lands.

The following points are suggested by even a cursory inspection of the preceding tables:

1. *Length of fiber.*—The maximum of all cottons necessarily falls to South Carolina (1.966) and Florida (1.910) as the representatives of the long-staple or sea-island variety. Limiting comparisons to the upland or short-staple cottons, California stands first (1.669), Georgia second (1.552), Alabama third (1.427), and Texas fourth (1.380);

while Virginia and North Carolina come in almost equal for the fifth place. A rapid review discovers no obvious relation of these maxima to upland or lowland soils, and so far as the imperfect testimony goes the upland cottons seem to be longer than those from the lowlands, except in the case of California. The minimum of length (0.695) comes from North Carolina, from a light sandy loam soil. The next shortest comes from a plant bearing in its second year, at Yuma, Arizona, that was growing among weeds in an abandoned garden. Another two-year-old plant, growing near National City, San Diego, also yields a somewhat short, yet respectable fiber. It should be noted that, with the exception of the sample from California (No. 70), all the shortest samples were grown on uplands.

2. *Width of fiber.*—The widest fiber comes from Alabama "red land"; it is at the same time quite short (0.945 inch). With the exception of California and Missouri, all the widest fibers come from uplands, and the width of those from the two excepted states is quite low. Among the minima Florida, with its fine and long sea-island staple, stands foremost. Outside of this the lowest minima are from bottom lands, and it would therefore seem pretty well shown that the river-bottom staple is narrower, and therefore probably finer,(*a*) than that of the uplands.

3. *Strength of fiber.*—The strongest fiber comes from Tangipahoa parish, Louisiana, and was grown on creek-bottom land, of which nothing is known in detail except that it is very sandy, and, for such soil, rich in vegetable matter. The next strongest comes from "stiff river-bottom land" in Tuscaloosa county, Alabama, and a very weak one, oddly enough, from red-clay upland of the same state and county. As all the Alabama samples were strictly new cotton, this is a remarkable result not to be explained by a possible deterioration of the fiber. Fortunately, the two soils referred to have been analyzed and show a remarkable difference in their percentages of phosphoric acid, the latter being very high in the bottom land and extremely low in the upland soil. Time has not permitted the verification of a similar relation in other cases, but the general "run" of soils appears to point that way. It would be curious to find that the strength of cotton fiber depends materially upon the same substance whose presence or absence determines the strength of the bony fabric of animals.

4. *Weight of five seeds with lint attached.*—The maximum weight (22.14) comes from the rich bottom land of the Arkansas river; the next in weight (21.14), curiously enough, from the poor sandy pine upland of Florida; the third heaviest (20.32), from the black prairie land of Texas. It seems difficult to reconcile this diversity of origin with the idea of any common cause; still, inspection of the table shows that the light weights or minima are nearly all from sandy land, both upland and lowland, while the heavier weights come prevalently from heavy and mostly very productive soils. The contrast between the third heaviest weight from Dallas and the lightest (5.71) from Walker county, Texas, is telling, the one being from prairie land, and the other from light sandy upland. It is well known to cotton-growers that the bolls are usually largest on the fertile bottom lands, and it is currently supposed that the seeds are there the heaviest; but nothing is known regarding the number of seeds carried by each, or whether these are usually more numerous in the lowlands or the uplands. These points acquire the greatest practical interest in connection with the next item.

5. *Percentage of lint and seed.*—The proportion commonly assumed to exist between these is that the lint forms about one-third (33.3 per cent.) of the weight of the seed-cotton. The average shown in the table is considerably higher than this, for the natural reason that the gin is not as effective in making a complete separation as the hand, and that a good deal of cotton remains with the seed. Another cause is the dry condition of the seeds when weighed, they having in part been over a year from the picking; while the weight to which the planter refers his product of lint is that obtained in weighing the pickers' daily gatherings, when the seed-cotton is fresh, and in many cases moist or partly wet from dews or showers. The lint alone being always weighed dry, all the losses in drying as well as in ginning tend to lower the lint percentage obtained in practice. Comparing the data in the table, we find the maximum lint percentage (43.79) to come from a sandy creek hummock land in Winn parish, Louisiana, and the minimum (11.45) from new sandy pine land in Marion county, Florida. This is so far below the rest that it must be supposed to have been long-staple cotton, to which in practice the proportion of one of lint to three of seed is assigned; but it is exceedingly low even for that. This sample was not very long, and broke with 101 grains—a very weak fiber. Of the rest, the lowest percentage occurs in stiff clay hummock land from Craven county, North Carolina; and next to this stands a sample from Red river alluvial land from Red River parish, Louisiana. This is one of the best cotton-growing regions of the South, where as much as a thousand pounds of lint per acre has been grown on fresh land; and it confirms the current impression that in the seed-cotton from the great bottoms the seed is heavier than elsewhere. In the case before us it implies the gathering of fully 5,000 pounds of seed-cotton per acre—a somewhat startling figure. There can be no doubt that a close and more extended investigation of this point would lead to important practical results.

Influence on soil and location on cotton fiber.—In regard to the influence of soils and location on the dimensions, strength, and relative abundance of the cotton fiber in seed-cotton Texas seems to offer the best opportunity for a comparison from which at least the element of diversity of climate is sensibly eliminated. It offers, moreover, the advantage of a considerable diversity of soils, strongly characterized and rather numerously represented among those analyzed, as well as a uniform absence of any method of soil improvement calculated to modify the nature of

a "Fineness," properly speaking, involves not only the width but the cross section, i.e., width multiplied into thickness. As the latter has not been measured, it cannot be taken into account; and practically what is here designated as "width" is the measure of commercial "fineness" and "coarseness".

the soil, such as manuring, underdraining, etc. The subjoined table presents the results of a classification of Texas cotton samples and corresponding measurements, upon the basis of the soils upon which they were grown, into four divisions. Of these, the first, that of "black prairie soils", represents soils in general of a rather heavy clay nature, black with humus, in part at least highly calcareous, and in all cases moderately so, and possessing from fair to high percentages of mineral plant-food. In the second class, "sandy-uplands," the texture of the soil is generally light, the amount of humus only moderate, the supply of lime low to deficient, but the supply of phosphoric acid and potash fair to high. The soils of the "river bottoms" differ from the prairie soils mainly in that they are lighter and usually less calcareous, but few being very decidedly so; the supply of humus is rather less, as is also that of potash, but phosphoric acid is mostly high. As to the fourth class, "creek bottoms," the four samples falling into this class seem to represent the alluvial soils of the sandy uplands—sandier than the bottom soils of the large rivers, usually lighter in texture, and with smaller percentages of phosphoric acid, potash, and lime, and mostly also of humus:

Character of lands.	No. of samples.	Length.	Width.	Breaking weight	Weight of 5 seeds, with lint.
		Inches.	Inch.	Grains.	Grains.
Stiff black prairie lands	20	1.049	0.921	135.7	12.64
Sandy upland soils	16	1.059	0.855	136.4	12.65
River bottoms (alluvial)	12	1.048	0.975	138.2	12.61
Creek bottoms (dark loams)	5	1.017	0.840	141.8	14.59

The result of these comparisons may be thus stated: The fiber from the creek bottoms is the shortest, finest, and strongest, and the one yielding the largest weight of seed. That from sandy uplands is the longest, and next in fineness, strength, and weight of seed to the creek-bottom staple. The fibers from the prairie lands and the great alluvial bottoms are of the same length, and are considerably greater than that of the creek-bottom product, but decidedly less than that of the uplands. The river-bottom fiber is the widest of all and in strength is slightly behind that of the uplands. The prairie cotton is somewhat finer, but its strength is considerably behind that of all the rest.

Should these results be substantiated by further comparisons, they would be of very considerable practical importance in the grading of cotton for manufacture. Two factors, however, are lacking, viz, the thickness of the cotton bands, as well as the relative twist, a matter discussed by Professor Ordway on page 18. The determination of these, however, would require appliances to be constructed for the specific purpose.

The comparison of averages of measurements by states must of course be taken with a great deal of allowance for the accidental predominance of the products of certain districts from which the larger number of samples was obtained, as, e. g., in the case of South Carolina and Florida, where long-staple cotton predominates. In the older states it is, moreover, vitiated by long cultivation and the occasional use of heavy manuring, the influence of which is very apparent in some cases where manured and unmanured ground of the same character can be compared. Cases in point are given in the table below:

No. of sample.	Character of lands.	Length.	Width.	Breaking weight.	Weight of 5 seeds, with lint.	Percentage of lint.
	ALABAMA.	Inches.	Inches.	Grains.	Grains.	
48 c	Pine-woods soil, fertilized with yard and fowl-house scrapings	0.922	0.819	114.2	15.04	26.62
48 e	Pine-woods soil, fertilized with compost of cottonseed; lime, and lot scrapings	1.023	0.866	147.6	12.35	31.87
48 d	Pine-woods, old land, not fertilized	0.789	0.827	143.4	9.43	35.77
	MISSISSIPPI.					
201	Light sandy loam, fresh	1.055	0.909	125.3		
202	Light sandy loam, old land, unmanured	0.810	0.929	117.6		
203	Light sandy loam, old land, highly manured	1.282	1.051	161.4		
209	Dark loam or hill land, cultivated three years	1.012	1.016	144.8		
208	Dark loam or hill land, cultivated twenty-five years	0.994	0.990	147.5		
190 a	Black prairie land, fresh	0.996	0.923	116.4	14.62	32.83
190 b	Black prairie land, cultivated twenty years	1.006	1.089	145.1	12.65	34.12
194	Black prairie land, cultivated ten years	0.923	0.902	213.3	12.56	39.96
195	Black prairie land, cultivated forty years	1.015	0.965	116.7	12.35	31.87
	TEXAS.					
356 a	Sandy post-oak land, unmanured	1.075	0.791	136.4	18.12	31.91
356 b	Sandy post-oak land, manured from cow-pen	1.147	1.280	134.6	17.69	27.19
357 a	Sandy post-oak land, manured	1.153	0.858	135.0	17.21	32.73
357 b	Sandy post-oak land, manured	1.274	0.794	143.3	17.13	36.89

In the case of the Alabama pine-woods soil, No. 48, the shortness of the fiber, the small weight of the five seeds, and the large percentage of lint are eloquent of the difference between this product and that from fresh or manured land, both in quantity and quality. The same inference as to length of fiber is apparent in the first group of Mississippi samples, Nos. 201, 202, and 203, in which the fiber from unmanured land is one-fifth shorter than that from the fresh land and one-third shorter than that from the highly manured land; and the comparison in the case of Nos. 208 and 209 points in the same direction. In the case of the black prairie land the reverse occurs; the comparison of the fresh land, No. 199 a, with the same cultivated twenty years, and that of Nos. 194 with 195, each show an increased length of fiber with longer cultivation, with a nearly corresponding increase of width. This is quite intelligible in so far as rich, heavy prairie land really improves by cultivation for some time, becoming more friable and affording better opportunity for full development; while the sandy uplands soon become " tired", and yield a short and indifferent fiber.

THE PRODUCTION AND USES OF COTTONSEED

AND THE

COTTONSEED-OIL INDUSTRY,

BY

E. W. HILGARD.

THE COTTONSEED-OIL INDUSTRY.

The following circular was sent by the Census Office to all cottonseed-oil mills then known to exist, as well as to a number of prominent cotton-planters, for the purpose of obtaining data regarding the cottonseed-oil industry and the uses of cottonseed:

DEPARTMENT OF THE INTERIOR,
CENSUS OFFICE,
Washington, D. C., April 5, 1880.

SIR: The subjoined schedule of questions, relating to the cottonseed-oil industry, is transmitted to you, with the request that you fill the blanks as far as possible, and return them, at as early a period as convenient, in the inclosed envelope.

In order that the object of these questions may be fully understood, it is desirable to call attention to the high importance of the development of the cottonseed-oil industry with reference to its influence upon the production of cotton itself.

Since cottonseed constitutes on an average somewhat more than two-thirds by weight of the crop taken from the cotton-field, it is obvious that the progress of soil exhaustion, or the maintenance of fertility, must depend mainly upon the use made of cottonseed itself. As a matter of fact, however, it is proved by chemical analysis, corroborated by the experience of the older cotton-growing states, that the importance of cottonseed to the soil is far greater than is indicated by its proportion to the lint crop; for out of 45 pounds of mineral plant-food withdrawn from the soil by the seed-cotton required to make a 400-pound bale but a little over four pounds are contained in the lint, the rest remaining in the seed. In other words, the withdrawal of one crop of cottonseed from the soil is equivalent to the drain created by *ten* crops of lint. Practically, cotton lint could be grown indefinitely upon most of the better class of soils without other return than the cottonseed itself.

The oil extracted from the seed, however, contains little that is of any consequence to the soil. The seed-cake and hulls would be nearly as good as the whole seed. The seed-cake *without* the hulls would be equivalent to more than three-quarters of the seed when returned to the field as a manure.

The cottonseed-oil manufacture, therefore, does not only not detract necessarily from the returns to the soil, but puts the most important portion of the crop into a far more convenient shape for use, both for feed and manure, than the raw cottonseed.

It is desired, by the aid of the data furnished by you, to place this important subject clearly and authentically before the cotton-growers, showing them by the irresistible logic of figures that the cottonseed-oil mill is to them the means of utilizing a waste product, increasing materially their home supply of available stock feed, and at the same time of maintaining the fertility of their soil, instead of paying heavy tolls to manufacturers of chemical fertilizers, transportation companies, and provision merchants.

Late experiments having appeared to indicate that among the most available and profitable modes of returning cottonseed or its oil-cake to the fields is the feeding of sheep, thus producing cotton and wool on the same field, as it were, any data you may be able to furnish on this and related points will be especially welcome.

Many persons to whom this circular may be sent, who are not manufacturers of cottonseed-oil, will be able to reply to all the questions in respect to the use of the seed, hulls, and meal for feed and for manure, and they are urgently requested to give such replies, especially as to the feeding of sheep and the effect of cottonseed thus used upon the production of wool.

Respectfully,

FRANCIS A. WALKER,
Superintendent of Census.

In response to the above circular replies were received from twenty cottonseed-oil mills, about double that number being in existence at the time. The substance of the replies is given partly in tabular form and partly under the head of the schedule questions. In some of these is apparent a scantiness of definite data regarding the manufacture; but, fortunately, such data can mostly be supplemented from the statements of others on the same points. The industry has now so far passed beyond the experimental stage that few important technical secrets can lie within the scope of the information asked for.

A number of letters from planters addressed on the subject were also received, and of these abstracts are hereinafter given.

The accompanying table exhibits, in a convenient form, the answers received to a portion of the inquiries; while another portion is of necessity placed under the heads of the respective questions.

COTTONSEED-OIL MILLS—REPLIES TO QUESTIONS.

	Names.	Location.	Tons of seed used. Daily.	Tons of seed used. Yearly.	Estimated gallons of oil. Daily.	Estimated gallons of oil. Yearly.	Hullers.	Presses.	Boxes.
							No.	No.	No.
1	Crescent City Oil Company	New Mechanicham, La	150		5,550		4	12	340
2	Maginnis Oil Works	New Orleans, La		3,500		115,500	6	12	200
3	Planters' Oil Company	...do		20,000		640,000	6	14	84
4	Iberia Oil Mill	New Iberia, La	10		330		1	2	12
5	Hamilton Oil Mills	Shreveport, La	60		1,020		3	3	68
6	Yazoo Oil Works	Yazoo City, Miss			1,100		1	6	22
7	Refuge Oil Works	Refuge, Miss	40		1,240		3	4	60
8	Friar's Point Oil Mill	Friar's Point, Miss			1,360		3	3	45
9	Augusta Oil Company	Augusta, Ga	20		600		1	6	
10	Savannah Oil Company	Savannah, Ga	30		900		1	3	22
11	Galveston Oil Company	Galveston, Tex					5	10	150
12	Calvert Oil Company	Calvert, Tex			800		3	2	30
13	Bryan Manufacturing Company	Bryan, Tex		5,000		162,500	1	4	104
14	Brenham Oil Mill (burned)	Brenham, Tex							
15	Callahan Oil Works	Hempstead, Tex	40		1,280				
16	Schumacher Oil Mill	Navasota, Tex	20		800		1	4	
17	Cottonseed-Oil Mills	Raleigh, N.C	(a)		50				
18	Southern Oil Works	Memphis, Tenn	60		1,820				
19	Panola Oil and Fertilizing Company	...do	75		2,400		3	6	90
20	Hope Oil Company	...do					1	8	

a Three hundred bushels of seed per day.

COTTONSEED-OIL MILLS—REPLIES TO QUESTIONS.

PRODUCT PER TON.				Cottonseed used in a season.	Source of supply.	Average price.	COTTONSEED-CAKE.				
Kernels.	Hulls.	Oil-cake.	Crude oil.				Amount sold at home to farmers.	As cake or meal.	Uses.		
									Feed.	Manure.	
Lbs. 1,000	Lbs. 1,000	Lbs. 775	Galls. 57½	Tons. 12,725¼	Mississippi River valley, Texas, and a little from Alabama.	$10	25 per cent	Meal	Some (b)	Chiefly	1
		700	30-35	17,000	Mississippi, Louisiana, Texas, Alabama, and Florida.	$12-$15	10 per cent	Meal	Yes	Yes	2
Various	Various	Various	Various	20,000	Mississippi River and tributaries, Alabama, and Texas.	Various	Small	Meal	Small	Chiefly	3
e 615	1,385	730	22	1,290	Bayou Teche and Opelousas	$6	All	Meal	Not much	Mostly	4
1,000	1,000	About 700	22	12,000	Bayou Wincey and Red river to Kiamitia; eastern and northern Texas.	$9	Very little	Meal	Little (d)		5
1,000	1,000	720	30-35	2,500 Half season lost.	Yazoo and Tallahatchee rivers.	$7.50 to $8.50, delivered.	None	Meal	Yes	No	6
1,000	1,000	770-785	30-32	7,000	Mississippi river from Vicksburg to Helena.	$9.50, or $7 net to farmers.	None	Some meal	Yes	Yes	7
		700-720	34-36	3,509	Vicksburg to Memphis	$9 to $9.50	None	5 per cent. meal.	Yes	None	8
1,000	1,000	730-740	25-35	867	Georgia and South Carolina	$9 to $11.50	Half	Meal			9
				First season.	Georgia, South Carolina, and Florida.						10
Not yet in operation.					Texas	$6 at railroad stations.					11
500	1,500	763½	20	2,273	Robertson county	$5	Small amount.	Meal	Yes		12
1,240	760	850	22½	2,344 Short supply.	Brazos, Burleson, and Robertson counties.	$7	Small	Meal	Mostly	Some	13
						$4.50, delivered.	Most of it is shipped to Liverpool.				14
900	1,100	750	28-35	3,000	Immediate vicinity and stations on the Houston and Texarkana railroad.	$6	Small am't, 50 tons per year.	Meal	Yes	Yes	15
1,000	1,000	750	30	2,000	Neighborhood.	$6 to $9	Very small	Meal	Mostly	Some	16
1,000	1,000	1,100	22	400	East and Middle North Carolina	$10	All	Meal	Yes	Yes	17
				10,000	Southern states		None		Yes	Yes	18
1,000	1,000	Varies	Varies	10,000	Neighboring states	$7 to $12	Two-thirds	Meal	Yes	Yes	19
					Tennessee, Mississippi, and Arkansas.	$6	2 per cent.	Meal	Yes	None	20

b Increasing demand for this purpose.
c The huller does nothing but grind or cut the seed; the shake divides or separates the kernels from the hulls; 1 to 3¼.
d Increasing; dairymen use it liberally and profitably.

The above partial statement of the seed worked and products marketed by the cottonseed-oil mills is supplemented by a summary given by Hon. Henry V. Ogden, of New Orleans, in a lecture delivered at Atlanta, Georgia, May 26, 1882. He says:

Taking my estimate of the consumption of seed by the forty-one oil-mills this season, the proportion and value of the total product may be summed up as follows:

410,000 tons seed, yielding 35 gallons crude oil to the ton, is 14,350,000 gallons, worth 30 cents per gallon.	$4,305,000
Same amount of seed, yielding 22 pounds cotton lint to the ton, is 9,020,000 pounds cotton, worth 8 cents per pound	721,600
And yielding also 750 pounds oil-cake to the ton, is 137,277 tons (a) of cake, at $20 per ton...............	2,745,540
Makes the total value of the manufactured products ...., ...	7,772,140
Deduct the sum paid for the seed, say...	4,100,000
And there remains for value gained in manipulation of seed..	3,672,140

Other oil-mills (from which no reports have been received) are located as follows:

Louisiana: 2 in New Orleans and 1 in Baton Rouge.

Mississippi: 1 each in Columbus, Greenville, Natchez, Meridian, Jackson, and Vicksburg.

Texas: 1 each in Dallas and Sherman.

Arkansas: 2 in Helena, and 1 each in Pine Bluff and Little Rock.

Alabama: 1 each in Selma and Montgomery.

Tennessee: 4 in Memphis, 2 in Nashville, and 1 in Jackson.

Missouri: 2 in Saint Louis.

OTHER ANSWERS TO SCHEDULE QUESTIONS.

1. Do you refine your oil yourself, or is there a growing tendency to the establishment of separate refineries?

The oil is refined in *Crescent City, Maginnis, Planters, Panola, Hope, Southern* and *Refuge* mills. In the others the crude oil is shipped to refineries. *Maginnis:* We purchase crude oil from other mills. *Iberia:* The mills of New Orleans do the refining. *Refuge:* We know of no tendency to establish separate refineries. *Friar's Point:* We sell the oil in the crude state. *Calvert and Bryan:* There is a tendency to the establishment of refineries. *Callahan and Panola:* The tendency is for oil-mills to refine their own oil.

2. What knowledge have you of the use of cottonseed or meal as a manure for sugar-cane, and of its effect on the production of sugar?

Bryan: It causes the cane to grow rapidly and mature quickly, giving a longer time to sweeten; 400 pounds of meal per acre has been known by a number of planters to increase the yield from 50 to 100 per cent. per acre. *Friar's Point:* We consider it one of the best fertilizers for sugar-cane, and sell large quantities for that purpose. *Refuge:* We are told by buyers that it is the finest that can be found; it also applies to cotton and corn. *Yazoo:* Sugar-planters in the Lower Mississippi region prefer it over any other fertilizer. *Hamilton:* Sugar-planters claim an increased yield of 33⅓ per cent. from its use. *Iberia:* Very beneficial, and is extensively used on cane, particularly stubble cane. *Maginnis* and *Planters:* Meal for sugar-cane is good. *Panola:* Have been told by sugar-planters that in some years (cold seasons) it increases the yield 100 per cent.

3. Do you use any process or machine prior or subsequent to the hulling process for removing lint left by the gin or the short fur of the seed?

The "linter" or gin, usually the Carver patent, is used in all of the mills except the Shreveport mill, which uses only a screen for removing trash, etc.; the Raleigh mill uses nothing at all.

4. Do you find it a paying process, whether as to the value of the shoddy produced or the increased yield of oil?

Crescent Mills: It pays about $1 25 per ton and facilitates hulling, which otherwise would be almost impossible. *Maginnis Mills:* Depends on the price of the seed. *Planters:* It forms part of the product procured from seed. *Iberia:* Not only necessary, but pays. *Hamilton:* Protects machinery from breaks. *Yazoo:* Adds to receipts and facilitates hulling. *Refuge:* The value of the lint we get. *Augusta:* Not very profitable after deducting labor and extra machinery. *Calvert:* In both respects. *Bryan:* The value of the lint, the most profitable part of the business. *Callahan:* It is profitable because of the lint. *Schumacher:* It is essential to free the cake from lint. *Panola and Hope:* It only enables us to hull easier.

5. Do you find any sale for cottonseed hulls for packing, stock feed, or any other purpose?

Crescent City: For stock feed entirely. *Planters:* For packing and stock feed. *Iberia:* For fuel. *Hamilton:* For stock feed. Think it would make paper; and would make a fine absorber for making manures. *Yazoo:* No; cannot give them away; planters would not move them for their value. *Refuge:* For stock feed and fertilizers. *Friar's Point and Augusta:* No use. *Calvert:* For packing and for stock feed. *Bryan:* To some extent for packing; a good demand for stock feed and for fuel. *Brenham:* Were used as fuel in the oil-mill. *Callahan:* For packing, stock feed, fuel, and manure; stock prefer them to the seed. *Schumacher:* To a small extent; some for packing, but mostly for stock feed. *Raleigh:* Some as manure for corn and potatoes. *Hope:* Some for food. *Southern and Panola:* For food and for fuel.

a 2,940 pounds each.

6. Please state what, according to your best information, are the merits or demerits of cottonseed-meal for either food or manure.

Maginnis: Good for both. *Planters:* Its value as cattle food is well established, and English statistics show it as being the best flesh and fat former known. For fertilizers its use is increasing every year. *Iberia:* All that we make is used by the sugar-planters on the Teche for fertilizing, and is considered a necessity. On stubble cane the effect is good, warming the ground and giving the plant an early start. *Hamilton:* Our practical experience proves it a nutritious, cheap, and valuable food for cattle and sheep, and creates the richest and largest flow of milk from cows than any other food ever used. It cannot be surpassed as a fertilizer. *Yazoo:* Excellent for either; is a good flesh former and also a cooling food; is superior to any other for milch cows, sheep, and working cattle. *Refuge:* It fattens cows, and is also a fine milk-producing food. *Calvert:* Good for food; as a manure I don't think it will do in a dry climate. *Bryan:* Has no superior as food for cattle and sheep in producing flesh. A Texas cow will quite often yield one-half more milk if fed on this meal, and at all times will increase her milking capacity fully one-third. The finest looking crops of cotton and corn on the uplands in this county are where about 400 pounds of meal were used per acre. *Callahan:* Good for both, especially as food for milch cows. *Raleigh:* Nothing can be better as a food to produce milk or for work oxen; it has been used with great success for seven years on cotton land, mixed half and half with good acid phosphate. *Panola* (Memphis): It is the equal of any food known; as a fertilizer for some crops it is unsurpassed. *Hope* (Memphis): Best product known for food; recommended as a fertilizer by all who have tried it.

7. What patent or style of huller is preferred ?

Crescent City, Hamilton, Refuge, Friar's Point, Savannah, Calvert, Callahan, Hope and *Panola* prefer Wells' patent of Memphis, Tennessee. *Planters'* and *Galveston* prefer the Keihmuller patent. *Maginnis* and *Yazoo* prefer either Wells' or Keihmuller's patent. *Iberia* and *Augusta* prefer Callahan's patent, Dayton, Ohio. *Bryan:* Callahan's for a small and Wells' for a large mill. *Raleigh:* Old style Stone and Demond mill, of Cincinnati, Ohio.

8. Please give such other information or suggestions regarding possible and desirable improvements in this industry as may be pertinent to the object of these inquiries.

Iberia: We are anxious to have all cultivators of the soil and cotton producers give us the seed and take the meal therefrom for fertilizers. We would like to convince them that the cottonseed, divested of its lint and oil, is a better fertilizer than the raw seed; and it will pay us to work the seed for the oil and lint (extra), giving to the farmer the meal; resulting from his seed; 100 tons of seed gives 40 tons of meal; this is a fair average. *Yazoo:* Refined cottonseed-oil is superior to lard for cooking; not only for salad oil, but for all purposes for which lard is used. In taste it is superior and sweeter, and, being vegetable, is easier digested, less heat producing, and therefore, principally in this climate, a healthier food. *Bryan:* We are using a double mat of our own make for pressing the oil out of the seed, which has increased our working capacity fully 50 per cent. Instead of making six cakes, weighing 8 pounds each, we make twelve cakes, weighing 6 pounds each, at each pressing, without any additional labor save that of packing the cakes in sacks for shipment. *Panola:* We think our home farmers and dairymen stand in their own light in not using the meal or cake more extensively. Nearly the whole of the product is exported to Europe for cattle feed. *Hope:* Much more care should be exercised by planters to preserve their seed in good condition, *so that it may not become heated;* the value is nearly destroyed by heating.

9. Do you use the hulls for fuel ? If so, are they sufficient to make all the steam you need ?

They are not used in *Raleigh.* In all other mills they are used, and make all the steam needed. *Crescent City:* Also sell a great many. *Hamilton:* On grate-bars, longer than for wood. *Yazoo:* 33⅓ per cent. left. *Refuge:* Use only one-half of what is made. *Brenham:* Four hullers will make hulls sufficient for fuel. *Southern:* Depends on the amount of machinery to be run.

10. Are the ashes of the hulls valued as a manure ? If so, for what cultures chiefly, and what price is paid for them ?

No use is made of the ashes as a manure in *Calvert, Callahan,* or *Brenham* mills. In others they are usually valued, but in *Iberia, Hamilton* (Shreveport), *Yazoo, Friar's Point,* and *Bryan* no price is put on them. *Crescent City:* Price $12; mixed with cottonseed meal for sugar-cane. *Maginnis:* From $6 to $14 per ton. *Planters:* Sugar-cane. *Iberia:* We don't sell any. Usual price, $12. *Hamilton:* Don't use them. Give them to friends as manure for vegetable and flower gardens. *Refuge:* Price, $9 per ton. Used for sugar-cane. *Augusta:* From $18 to $20; for most field crops. *Bryan:* But little demand; good for corn; washerwomen use them in preference to wood ashes for making soap. *Hope* and *Panola:* Price, $10 per ton.

ABSTRACT OF LETTERS REGARDING USES OF COTTONSEED.

W. C. STOUT, HAWKSTON, CONWAY COUNTY, ARKANSAS.—The introduction of small cottonseed-oil mills (if profitable) in the interior owned by joint-stock companies would most likely lead to a greater appreciation of the value and uses of cottonseed and its products. At no time and in no place have the farmers ever realized one-half the value of their seed. Fed in the raw state, as from the gin, cottonseed is worth to the farmer half as much as corn. As manure it is worth much more than the price obtained. From $8 to $10 per ton have been paid for seed at the mills. Taking from this the cost of shipping, etc., it is safe to say that the farmer realizes not more than $4 per ton for what is worth to him at home 18 bushels of corn. The sale of the seed at present prices is a ruinous exhaustion of the soil without an adequate return.

JOSEPH B. JONES, HERNDON, GEORGIA.—A very large percentage of cottonseed is still returned to the soil for manure, either in its pure or natural raw state or in the form of a compost. Perhaps 85 to 90 per cent. of all the seed (except what is reserved for planting) is thus used, the remainder being used for food for stock. I have been familiar with its use as food for cattle and sheep for the past fifty years, and know it to be excellent for fattening both; but they must be fed with care and in moderation. The seed has never been regarded as reliable and safe for hogs unless fed in combination with other food, nor have I ever been able to get horses to eat it kindly in any form, either alone or in combination. The cottonseed-meal (free from oil) is, however, the best for all purposes; and, if the hulls remain with it, it is especially good for fertilizers. I prefer, however, the natural seed, in compost, as a fertilizer.

DR. M. W. PHILLIPS, OXFORD, MISSISSIPPI.—Experience has shown that cattle fed on cottonseed, and a very little, in days in excellent condition during the winter; thirty or forty years ago I fed my cows on boiled cottonseed, cooked until easily crushed between forefinger and thumb. There was a demand for all the butter I could spare, and no one complained of *white butter*.

Since 1831 all of my cottonseed was used for manure, except that for planting. I had been taught to let the seed rot in the rains and sun; but after about forty years I determined to let the seed rot in the earth. As an experiment I hauled out sound seed in January to the field and drilled it in the row intended for cotton and turned two furrows on it. I bedded on this in April and planted cotton. This covered 20 acres. Another 20 acres I manured with the rotted seed, most of it as compost. Visitors pronounced the cotton crop from the first to be the best.

I am of the opinion that cottonseed used in stables as litter for stock, to be crushed under foot in part and to be mixed with the dung and saturated with urine, would enhance its value from two to four fold.

On land lying well, cultivated well, all seed and stalks returned to it, the crops will not decline (or very slowly); but to let land become exhausted and then try to bring it back will take more than the seed.

D. L. PHARES, WOODVILLE, MISSISSIPPI.—There is nothing better for food than cottonseed-meal in small quantities, say one or two pounds per day, mixed with hay, etc., and fed to a cow or horse. For manure it is the most valuable known to me. Its use is profitable for crops, except, perhaps, winter oats. Cottonseed sown broadcast and plowed in with winter oats increases the crop from 200 to 400 per cent.

I. H. MOORE, OAKLEY, ARKANSAS.—I know nothing practically of feeding oil-cake to sheep, as the raw seed is cheaper, and has so far been satisfactory. There is no doubt that if the seed from 100 bales of cotton (47 tons) was fed to 500 sheep, running on 100 acres of land, the land would be better and more evenly manured than if the seed in the raw state was plowed in. Cow-peas also raised and sheep pastured on them would be very highly beneficial and restore the old cotton lands of the south. My own experience this winter with feeding sheep on cottonseed has been successful. My flock now consists of 31 old ewes, 16 ewe lambs one year old, and 43 lambs. Three-fourths of the ewes had twins. Last year there were only 31 lambs. Some of the ewes this winter had so much milk that I had to milk them to keep the bag from spoiling. I have fed more seed this year than last. I now feed about two pounds per day to each sheep, or about one ton of seed for each 10 sheep for the winter. The seed is worth at the gin about $3 per ton, or 30 cents for each sheep, and their manure is fully worth the seed.

I am satisfied that the south can, with cottonseed and winter pasture of rye, oats, barley, or wheat, winter 75,000,000 sheep and still have seed sufficient to plant. The more I see of Bermuda grass the more I am satisfied that it will yet prove a great blessing to the south.

PROSPECTIVE MAGNITUDE OF THE COTTONSEED-OIL INDUSTRY AND INFLUENCE UPON SOIL FERTILITY.

The following table shows, for 1879, the amount of cottonseed not needed for seed, and which might have been used in the manufacture of the oil. The second group of columns gives the possible products of such manufacture for the year, assuming that each ton of cottonseed is divided half-and-half into hulls and kernels after the removal of 22 pounds of adherent cotton, and that each ton yields 35 gallons of crude oil. The third group of columns gives the market value of these products, as well as the total for all, the hulls being valued, weight for weight, like pine cord-wood, at $5 per cord, and the ashes at $10 per ton for manurial purposes. The fourth group gives the selling value of the raw cottonseed which would be received by the producer at an average of $7 per ton. In the last column is placed the valuation of the cottonseed, or its equivalent in cottonseed-cake, according to the customary valuation of the ingredients of commercial fertilizers, as deduced from the best analyses. For the percentage composition of cottonseed ash and the ammonia equivalent of the seed the data given in the report of the North Carolina experiment station for 1882 have been adopted; for the ash percentage of the seed the figure 4.0 has been adopted, instead of 3.67, as given on page 95 of that report for the dry substance, but, making an allowance of 7.7 per cent. of moisture, makes the actual figure used 3.70. This increase is justified by the results of ash determinations made by myself with Mississippi uplands cottonseed and by Anderson with seed from South Carolina. The average of the Mississippi seed was 4.2 for the dry substance. Anderson's determinations run even higher than this.

COTTONSEED PRODUCTION OF 1879, THE POSSIBLE OIL-MILL PRODUCTS, WITH THEIR MARKET VALUATIONS, AND THE MANURE VALUE OF SEED IN EXCESS OF THAT REQUIRED FOR PLANTING.

States.	I. COTTONSEED OF 1879.			II. POSSIBLE OIL-MILL PRODUCTS FROM EXTRA SEED OF 1879.				III. MARKET VALUE OF PRODUCTS.						IV.	
	Total.	Reserved for seed. (a)	Convertible into oil and cake.	Crude oil.	Oil-cake.	Cotton from linter.	Hulls.	Crude oil.	Oil-cake.	Cotton from linter.	Hulls. Fuel.	Hulls. Ash.	Hulls. Total.	Selling price of seed.	Manure value of the seed or respective oil-cake.
	Tons.	Tons.	Tons.	Gallons.	Tons.	Tons.	Tons.	Dollars.	Dollars.	Dollars.	Dollars.	Dollars.	Dollars.	Dollars.	Dollars.
The United States	2,270,417	236,718	2,581,696	68,609,465	948,387	27,848	1,288,001	18,562,820	18,987,740	4,455,680	4,419,064	247,600	54,693,523	17,721,893	48,076,922
Alabama	323,336	35,446	293,890	10,296,150	110,209	3,233	143,712	3,065,845	3,204,180	517,280	513,052	28,740	6,949,097	2,057,230	5,348,786
Arkansas	304,126	17,300	296,919	10,043,163	107,594	3,156	140,303	3,012,649	2,151,880	504,960	500,883	28,050	6,196,431	2,008,423	5,221,926
Florida	26,902	4,052	22,850	790,750	8,669	251	11,174	296,925	171,380	40,150	39,891	2,340	493,596	159,950	415,870
Georgia	386,858	43,181	343,677	12,028,695	128,879	3,780	168,058	3,608,609	2,577,580	604,800	599,967	33,610	7,424,566	2,405,739	6,254,921
Indian territory	8,075	412	7,663	268,205	2,873	84	3,748	80,461	57,460	13,440	13,336	750	165,491	53,841	130,487
Kentucky	650	44	606	21,210	227	7	296	6,363	4,540	1,120	1,056	50	13,129	4,343	11,022
Louisiana	241,570	14,269	227,301	7,955,535	85,288	2,500	111,150	2,386,661	1,704,780	400,000	396,806	23,230	4,910,457	1,591,107	4,136,873
Mississippi	457,478	34,720	422,758	14,796,530	158,534	4,650	206,729	4,438,959	3,170,680	744,000	738,022	41,350	9,133,011	2,959,306	7,694,196
Missouri	10,158	530	9,628	336,980	3,610	106	4,708	101,094	72,380	18,960	16,808	950	208,012	67,396	173,230
North Carolina	185,058	14,736	170,322	5,961,270	63,871	1,874	83,387	1,788,381	1,277,420	299,340	297,335	16,050	3,678,696	1,192,254	3,099,860
South Carolina	248,210	23,510	225,700	7,899,500	84,632	2,468	110,367	2,369,830	1,692,780	397,260	394,010	22,070	4,875,970	1,578,900	4,107,740
Tennessee	157,044	11,922	145,122	5,079,270	54,421	1,596	70,965	1,523,781	1,088,430	255,360	253,345	14,190	3,135,096	1,015,854	2,641,220
Texas	402,543	35,944	366,698	12,834,430	137,512	4,034	179,315	3,850,329	2,750,240	645,440	640,155	35,880	7,922,094	2,566,596	6,673,904
Virginia	9,308	743	8,565	299,775	3,212	94	4,180	89,922	64,240	15,040	14,955	840	185,007	59,965	155,883

a The estimates of tons of cottonseed in this and all of the state reports are based upon the generally accepted ratio of two of seed to one of lint; whereas the majority of correspondents place the proportion of seed much higher. This would therefore give a greater weight of seed actually produced than above tabulated, and this excess, with the amount given in the second column of figures, would make a reserve of more than two bushels per acre for planting.

The figures of the table are sufficiently eloquent. Assuming as the nearest approximation to the actual amount of seed worked in 1879-'80 by the forty-one mills the figures given by Mr. Ogden, we find that somewhat over one-seventh of the available seed has been actually worked. Had all been similarly treated, the cotton-planters would have received something over $17,000,000 for the raw seed, which would have been converted into products worth about $54,000,000. But not the least significant item is found in the last column, viz: That *in order to replace the drain upon their fields resulting from the sale of the seed the planters would have had to purchase commercial fertilizers of the estimated value of over forty-six millions; they could have purchased back the oil-cake itself (nearly equal to the fertilizers required) by paying for it about a million more (or $18,987,740) than what they originally could have obtained for their seed ($17,721,893), a saving of $27,080,182 over the value of the commercial fertilizers,* thus showing the oil-cake to be by far the cheapest fertilizer in the market.

Considering that, on account of its better keeping qualities and better adaptation for feed, the oil-cake is more valuable than the seed it represents, the cotton-grower can afford this advance of about 40 cents per ton; and the near balancing of the aggregate values in the home market is a curious instance of the self-adjustment of values under the laws of trade. Still, as regards his soil, the cotton-grower loses the ingredients contained in the hulls; whereas, had he retained the seed and returned it directly to the soil, the replacement would have been so nearly complete as to relieve him entirely from the need of purchasing fertilizers, at least for cotton production. (a)

From the pecuniary standpoint of the maintenance of fertility by a direct return of the cottonseed alone to the soil, as against the need of purchasing, instead, commercial fertilizers (with all the cost of manufacture, transportation, commissions, etc., heaped upon them), the sale of cottonseed at ruling prices is a transaction too absurd to be tolerated for a moment. For although the valuations attached by the chemists to the ingredients of fertilizers are (in the case of the better class at least) usually somewhat above the price paid by the farmer, yet such difference is insignificant compared to that between the seventeen and three-quarter millions received for the seed and the forty-six millions to be paid for fertilizers in order to replace the drain upon the soil. If the cottonseed-oil industry involved such an alternative, it could not stand for a moment so soon as the state of facts became generally known.

But such is far from being the case; and the near equality of the market values of the totals of cottonseed and seed-cake suggests at once the utmost simplicity of transactions between the oil manufacturer and the producer, such as was suggested by me in the southern press years ago. It is that, since the producer is interested in having his surplus cottonseed transformed into the convenient seed-cake, he can afford to let the manufacturer take the remaining lint, oil, and hulls as toll, provided the cake be integrally returned to him, and by him either directly,

a See the circular on page 43 and the table of "soil ingredients withdrawn by various crops," page 50.

or through his cattle, to the soil. The return thus made will still leave cotton one of the least exhaustive crops known, and give the farmer the benefit of a manufacturing industry at home that reacts in many ways to increase the prosperity of the whole. It is true that, in order to render this simple condition of barter possible, cottonseed-oil mills should be established in all large cotton-growing districts; perhaps best as joint-stock concerns, so as to reduce the expense of transportation, as well as the intervention of middlemen, to a minimum. Few more important steps toward the maintenance of fertility in the cotton states could be taken; for as matters stand at present the sale of cottonseed to the oil-mills is on the increase, and yet, as will be seen from the schedule answers from the several states, the use of cottonseed cake or meal within the cotton states is altogether insignificant. Almost the whole of it flows out in a steady stream from the oil-mills to Old and New England, while a costly return stream of commercial fertilizers sets in the reverse direction. When once the full bearing of this matter is understood by cotton-growers, few can have doubts as to the course to be pursued for the preservation of their fields. Either the seed as a whole or the corresponding seed-cake must in common sense go back to the soil.

The following table, based upon data obtained from the investigation of the question in the state of Mississippi, has often been used by the writer to make plain to audiences of farmers the peculiar advantages enjoyed by the cotton-grower as regards the maintenance of the productiveness of his soil. Potash and phosphoric acid, being the most valuable of the mineral ingredients contained, are segregated from the rest of the ash ingredients. The figures refer to the product of an acre of good upland soil as commonly obtained in Mississippi:

Soil ingredients withdrawn by various crops.

	Potash.	Phosphoric acid.
	Pounds.	*Pounds.*
One bale of cotton:		
1,350 pounds of seed-cotton .. { 400 pounds of lint make 4 pounds of ash, containing	1.6	0.5
950 pounds of seed make 41 pounds of ash, containing	14.7	15.2
Total seed-cotton	16.3	15.7
Of the 41 pounds of ash in the seed—		
The hulls, weighing 475 pounds, contain 9.5 pounds of ash.		
The oil-cake, weighing 368 pounds, contain 31.0 pounds of ash.		
The oil, weighing 107 pounds, contains 0.5 pounds of ash.		
950 41.0		
Fifteen bushels of wheat:		
The grain makes 15 pounds of ash, containing	5.5	9.0
Two tons of straw make 200 pounds of ash (silica, 128 pounds), containing.	8.0	3.0
Total	13.5	12.0
Thirty-five bushels of corn:		
The grain makes 25 pounds of ash, containing...........................	6.0	13.0
Two tons of stalks, etc., make 200 pounds of ash (50 pounds silica), containing.................	15.0	16.0
Total	21.0	29.0

One lesson conveyed by this table, viz, that the removal of one crop of cottonseed depletes the soil to the same extent as that of ten crops of cotton lint, has already been referred to in the introductory circular. The comparison with other crops shows that none approaches cotton in respect to the slight exhaustion caused by the sale of the chief merchantable product, the lint, the relation being somewhat as if, in the case of corn, the shucks were only removed while returning the stalks and ears integrally; a proceeding under which most soils would improve instead of deteriorating indefinitely. That this is not only theoretically but practically true, and that the conscientious return to the soil of each field of the cottonseed produced on it *from the beginning of cultivation* will, in the case of all soils of fair natural strength, maintain their cotton production undiminished almost indefinitely, has been repeatedly shown by actual experience in the older states. Of course the same is not true of soils that, through long-continued cropping without returns, have been carried to the verge of exhaustion, *i. e.*, of unprofitableness in cultivation. When this has been done, much more than the simple return of the cottonseed is needed for the time being; yet when the land has once again been placed in good condition, so that it would produce full crops without manure for several years, the rule that holds good for fresh soils would again apply to them. (*a*)

---

a See the writer's discussion of this subject in the *Rural Carolinian* for November and December, 1869.

RETURN OF COTTONSEED TO THE SOIL WITHOUT THE INTERVENTION OF OIL-MILLS.

A.—DIRECT.—It is well known that cottonseed is readily killed by "heating" when kept in large, and especially wet, piles; that the kernels shrink and become brown, and that finally a strong odor of ammonia announces that a large proportion of this most valuable fertilizing substance is escaping. Intelligent farmers have therefore long since been in the habit of letting the seed heat and "kill" in the ground, so as to let the earth absorb the ammonia, or else to compost the pile with muck, plaster, or other proper absorbents. In the former practice it has been found that the use of fresh cottonseed, and still more that of seed-cake meal, is liable to kill seedlings in the immediate neighborhood. This has been attributed to the excessive evolution of ammonia; but some observations having led me to doubt this explanation, I made, in 1871 and 1872, a series of observations and experiments at the University of Mississippi as to the best methods of using these fertilizers and the causes of the occasional bad effects. The latter became abundantly apparent upon submitting a quantity of fresh oil-cake meal to fermentation with a moderate amount of water. Within twenty-four hours a pungent odor, but not of ammonia, became very perceptible in the heated mass; and upon distillation I obtained a not inconsiderable quantity of a very ill-flavored alcohol. The deadly effects of this substance upon the delicate rootlets of seedlings is easily understood, and also the simple method that may be adopted to avoid all trouble from this source, by a "heating" of the seed or seed-cake meal previous to putting in the ground; provided, of course, that the fermentation is stopped short by drying or other means before the evolution of ammonia begins. This confirms the soundness of the long-established practice of "killing the seed" before using it in close connection with other seeds. Meal not previously heated may be used with impunity, provided it is thoroughly mixed with a large proportion of earth. In connection with the same experiments it was found that when the wetted meal is first composted with plaster to absorb the ammonia, and then allowed to sour, it acts most energetically upon bone-meal, and even bone-ash, in rendering them efficacious as fertilizers; thus replacing in a very good measure the effect of sulphuric acid in performing the same service under the hands of the manufacturers of fertilizers, but at nominal expense and at home.

Decomposition of whole seed in the soil.—Another series of experiments was made to test the progress of the decomposition of whole cottonseed buried in the soil. Seed that had been used abundantly under a "seed-bed" of sweet potatoes was examined six months afterward. By far the greater proportion of the seeds were still whole, a number having been perforated either by the rootlets or by insects. The whole seeds were very light, and contained a brown, shrunken kernel, which, upon analysis, was found to contain fully 75 per cent. of the mineral ingredients of the original seed, of which a similar number from the same lot was examined. It was plain that the sweet potatoes and the weeds following them had during all that time been unable to extract from the oily seeds more than a small proportion of their plant-food, but had been benefited chiefly by the ammonia that was given off in the shape of gas at first, and that subsequent crops would get the chief benefit of the mineral plant-food in succeeding years. This result is in accordance with the oft-repeated assertion of cotton-growers that cottonseed put in the ground whole benefits corn more than cotton during the first year. Corn will bear a heavy application of ammoniacal manures, whereas cotton is liable to run to weed and boll poorly under their influence. After the corn has taken up the ammonia during the first season, cotton gets the full benefit of the phosphates and potash the next year.

The experiment shows, in addition, the benefit of the removal of the oil from the seed when desired for manure. The "whole" kernel is completely "preserved in oil" during the first season, and resists the decay which would render its ingredients accessible to plants; whereas, when freed from the oil, as in oil-cake meal, the process of decomposition is unchecked, and the entire stock of plant-food goes to the use of the crop the first season. This is an additional reason for converting the spare seed into oil-cake meal, even for manurial purposes.

B.—INDIRECT RETURN THROUGH THE MANURE OF ANIMALS FED WITH SEED OR SEED-CAKE.—It should be kept in mind that the manure of cattle fed with cottonseed or oil-cake is of especial value as a fertilizer for cotton and should be carefully preserved from waste. By far the safest method of obtaining complete returns to the soil is, in this as in other cases, the use as feed for sheep, which distribute the fertilizer in the most perfect manner, at the same time producing another fiber—wool—from the refuse of the same field that grew the cotton. The plan of "growing cotton and wool on the same field", so strongly advocated by Mr. Edward Atkinson, has been successfully tried by several persons, among them Mr. I. H. Moore, of Oakley, Arkansas, whose experience is given in a preceding page. There seems to be no valid reason why the advantages obtained by him through the feeding of sheep with cottonseed should not be realized by others; but it is true that to do so would involve a material change of policy in southern farming: first, as regards the growing of pasture grasses for the season when the seed is not available (although cake-meal would always be), and second, as regards the raising of the numberless dogs that infest the southern states, each laborer being allowed to keep as many curs as he pleases; and dogs are shown, statistically, to be more numerous, and, according to the shows and valuations made of them, to be more highly valued in some of the states than the useful but unattractive sheep. Southern farmers will soon, however, have to make a serious choice between the two races of domestic animals.

SOIL INVESTIGATION.

INTRODUCTION
TO THE
DESCRIPTION OF STATES,
BY
E. W. HILGARD.

SOIL INVESTIGATION.

A full and accurate knowledge of the agricultural features and other industrial resources of a state is of the most direct and obvious importance to every one concerned in industrial pursuits. It is wanted by the immigrant or settler seeking a new home suitable to his tastes and resources, as well as by the large farmer and capitalist desiring to locate and invest to the best possible advantage. Most of the older states have long ago satisfied this demand in some form; mostly in connection with the public surveys, usually named, from their fundamental feature, geological surveys, but commonly charged as well with the full investigation of the other industrial features of the state. The demand for this kind of information is shown by the publication of numerous pamphlets and newspaper articles, describing more or less fully and correctly certain regions recommended for settlement; but the fact that these publications emanate largely from interested parties, and are compiled by persons unused to accurate observation of natural phenomena and not possessed of the means for thorough investigation, greatly reduces the usefulness of the large amount of correct information thus conveyed. Even the more ambitious class of publications in book form, purporting to give full descriptions of regions, states, or territories, are largely compilations from this class of literature, and, apart from the climatic, commercial, and general topographical data, rarely convey much of that specific, technical, and local information that is so necessary to the seeker for a permanent home, and which he must usually, after all, obtain at the expense and trouble of a personal visit.

Of the state surveys that have given close and specific attention to the agricultural features the first survey of Kentucky and that of Arkansas, by Dr. David Dale Owen, stand first in order of time. Dr. Owen was profoundly impressed with the advantages that a closer and more rational knowledge of the peculiarities of their soils would give those desiring to cultivate them rationally; and his assistants were instructed to gather from the mouths of the inhabitants all information extant in regard to the production, peculiarities, merits, and demerits of the several soils, and also to collect carefully samples of the same, noting all details as to depth, subsoil, drainage, "lay," natural vegetation, etc. These soil samples were afterward subjected to chemical analysis according to a definite and uniform method, and from a comparison and discussion of these Dr. Owen hoped to gain important data, not only with regard to these particular soils, but also with respect to the general functions of soils in vegetable nutrition, the cheapest and most needful modes of improving each one, and of maintaining its productiveness. These views are set forth in the text, especially of the first volume of the Kentucky report, and the effort to carry them into effect is apparent throughout these volumes. Dr. Owen's early death prevented him from entering upon a more general discussion of the subject and of the results deducible from the entire work.

When placed in charge of the geological and agricultural survey of the state of Mississippi the writer earnestly endeavored to carry out more fully the views suggested to him on the occasion of a personal visit by Dr. Owen; and finding before him a field containing an unusually great variety of strongly characterized soils, offering a wide and most interesting scope for comparison, he soon found himself engaged on a field of research almost unexplored and with but few landmarks left by previous investigators; most of the latter, too, pointing away from it, as being hopelessly intricate and beyond the power of our present means of research. But as the work progressed there came glimpses of light and results quite in accord with the general presumptions upon which the hope of ultimate success rested; and with these before him, in the face of much indifference and adverse criticism, much of his life-work has been given to this speciality of physical and chemical soil investigation.

In the "report on the geology and agriculture of the state of Mississippi", printed in 1860, but not published until after the war, the writer adopted the express segregation of the subject into a "geological" portion, into which scientific facts and discussions are freely introduced, and an "agricultural" one, containing a description of the agricultural features of the state, subdivided into "regions", which of course conform more or less to the geological divisions, but at the same time correspond to well-defined and popularly recognized areas of similar agricultural conditions. In this second part of the report, intended for popular comprehension and use, all more recondite scientific or technical language is avoided as much as possible. The soil analyses made up to the time of its going to press are communicated in connection with the descriptions of the several regions concerned, and their meaning is interpreted in accordance with the still somewhat dim understanding then acquired upon such a slender basis of well-observed facts. Subsequently this basis was much enlarged by a number of additional analyses made as the survey work progressed; but these, in consequence of the stoppage of the work and the removal of the writer from the state, were never published. They are now given in full in the report on the state of Mississippi.

The plan adopted of giving, in connection with the census reports on cotton production, a more or less detailed description of the agricultural features of the cotton states, regarding which but little definite information had thus far been accessible to the general public, afforded an excellent opportunity for enlarging the scope of the comparisons of soil composition beyond that afforded by the state of Mississippi. A limited number of analyses of the more important soils of each of the states concerned was, at the writer's request, authorized by the Superintendent; and with the co-operation of state surveys and the utilization of such material as was already extant the field of comparison has thus been extended over the cotton states from North Carolina to Texas, as well as to California, as will be noted in the several reports.

REMARKS ON THE METHODS OF SOIL INVESTIGATION AND ON THE INTERPRETATION AND PRACTICAL UTILITY OF CHEMICAL SOIL ANALYSES.

In view of the emphatic condemnation of chemical soil analysis, as a practically useless expenditure of energy and money, that has in the past been pronounced by a number of prominent scientists, both in this country and in Europe, it is not superfluous to advert in this place to the causes of these opinions, and to point out the extent of their truth and fallacy in connection with a presentation of the methods pursued in the present work, by which these objections are measurably done away with. In the absence of such a discussion, much that follows would be unintelligible, and might seem baseless or arbitrary assumption. (a)

The claim of soil analysis to practical utility has always rested on the general supposition that, "other things being equal, productiveness is, or should be, sensibly proportional to the amount of available plant-food within reach of the roots during the period of the plant's development;" provided, of course, that such supply does not exceed the maximum of that which the plant can utilize when the surplus simply remains inert.

The above statement has been, either tacitly or expressly, admitted as a maxim by those who have attempted to interpret soil analyses at all; it being thoroughly in accordance with the accumulated experience of agriculturists, and with their cry for "enough manure", that has been so potent a factor in the development of agricultural science and of rational agriculture itself. Its acceptance is implied in the search for the solvent that shall represent correctly the action of the plant itself on the soil ingredients; and I shall take it for granted in this discussion, while strongly emphasizing the importance of concomitant physical conditions, that, it is universally admitted that the *ultimate* analysis of soils affords little or no clew to their agricultural value. Such agents as fluohydric acid and alkaline carbonates go by far deeper than the solvents naturally acting in soils bearing vegetation will go within the limits of time in which we are interested.

Many attempts have been made to find solvents whose action on soils would so nearly represent the agents subservient to the needs of vegetation that conclusions as to the present agricultural value of a given soil could be deduced therefrom. It is needless to recite the long list of such solvents suggested since soil analysis attracted attention. From fluohydric acid to water charged with carbonic acid (the latter extensively employed by Dr. D. D. Owen) the acid solvents have all signally failed to secure even an approximation to the result desired, viz, a consistent agreement between the quantitative determinations, or the percentages of plant-food found in the several soils, and the actual experience of those who cultivate them.

It has been attempted by the German experiment-stations, under Wolff's initiative, to gain an approximation to the relative availability of parts of the soil's store of plant-food by consecutive extractions with acid solvents of different strength, beginning with distilled water, and ending with boiling oil of vitriol or fluohydric acid. It can hardly be wondered that this laborious process, with solvents arbitrarily chosen, and without any known relation to the solvent action exerted by roots, should have found so little acceptance, and has, on the contrary, perhaps rather served to confirm the common impression of the uselessness of soil analysis, especially when contrasted with the huge amount of work, ending after all in mere guesses. We vainly seek in the recorded results of such investigations for any such ray of light on the functions of the several soil ingredients as would even remotely justify the labor involved. They rather tend to justify the remark of a distinguished American agricultural author, that he "would rather trust an old farmer to tell him about the value of a soil than the best chemist alive".

The old farmer, however, is not always at hand, especially in the newer portions of the United States, where such *prima facie* judgment is most especially needed, since upon it depends so largely the future of the settler for weal or woe. And even when the old farmer is at hand, he is very frequently sadly at fault when asked such simple but pregnant questions as these: Is the soil likely to be durable? What crops adapted to the climate will bring the highest returns and insure the longest duration of fertility under rational treatment? In which direction

a In the following discussion the language adopted is largely that of an article on the subject, published in the *American Journal of Science* for September, 1881.

will the natural defects or the impending exhaustion of the soil first make themselves felt, and how can they best be countervailed? However, if the old farmer can train his judgment in this matter so as to make shrewd guesses, the agricultural chemist ought to be able to do a great deal better, for he should know all that the farmer does, and a great deal more beside. In addition, he should bring to bear on the whole subject a well-trained mind, accustomed to accurate observation and logical reasoning; but this cannot possibly be accomplished without bringing to bear upon the study of soils the best resources of chemical and physical examination combined—a subject that has too long been put aside upon the mere assertion, based upon imperfect methods of investigation, that its pursuit led to no practical results.

Assuredly, the chemist who does no more than to give the farmer a column of figures summing up to one hundred or nearly so, opposite another column of unintelligible names, acts simply as an analytical machine; and even to the best of such machines the remark above quoted will most truly apply. Soil analyses do not, like the assay of an ore, interpret themselves to the layman; and it is a matter of history that the attempt to so interpret them in the analyses made under the auspices of the German experiment-stations was chiefly instrumental in the rejection of this method of investigation, the results being altogether discordant with the indications of practice upon the basis of a mere comparison of percentages of plant-food.

One great difficulty in the way of definite conclusions from the analyses of European soils is that virgin soils are there practically non-existent, the arable soils having nearly all been at some time subjected to cultivation, and, concurrently, to the use of fertilizers, thus veiling their original characteristics and rendering extremely difficult, to say the least, the taking of any sample of soil that shall represent correctly, in all respects, the whole of any large field or district. In the United States it is our special privilege to be still able to secure specimens of the soils of by far the greater portion of the country that even the plow has never yet touched, and where manure, outside of the flower and vegetable garden, is an unknown quantity. We can find on these soils their original vegetation, which is so largely used by the settler as a means of diagnosing the actual productiveness of the land he proposes to clear and of prognosing its durability, and there can be no doubt that in so doing he is thoroughly right. The virgin soil and its vegetation are the outcome of long ages of coadaptation by the processes of natural selection, and they present to us an array of ready-made culture experiments whose cogency can rarely be approached by those of our experiment stations within less than a life-time. The observant farmer or settler attaches to each tree or herb a more or less definite significance, based upon experience as regards the character and productiveness of the parent soil. A soil naturally timbered with a large proportion of walnut, wild cherry, or, as at the south, with the "poplar" or tulip tree, is at once selected as sure to be both productive and durable, especially if the trees be large. He knows well that the black and Spanish oaks frequent only "strong" soils, and that an admixture of hickory is a welcome addition; while the occurrence of the scarlet oak at once lowers the land in his estimation, and that of pine still more so. However much opposed to the cocklebur in his fields, he welcomes it as a sure sign of a good cotton soil, as much as though he had seen the latter itself growing for a series of years.

It is this sound empiricism that at present gives the old farmers the advantage over "the best chemist alive" in judging of the value and adaptations of soils. But it is certainly the chemist's fault if he fails to avail himself of these long observed facts, and to expand them into something more definite and thorough than intuitive empiricism.

Taking for granted the soundness of the principle involved in judging the productiveness and other peculiarities of soils from their natural vegetation, and having gained a large array of additional data from personal observation in the field, I have then sought to ascertain, by close chemical and physical examination of the soils in their natural condition, the causes that determine this natural selection on the part of certain species of trees and herbaceous plants, while at the same time observing closely the behavior of such soils under cultivation, their special adaptations, etc. It goes without saying that this can be done most successfully where, as in the western and southern states, virgin soils are still obtainable, where the use of manure is unknown, and where the simple history of each field can easily be gathered from the lips of the settler who first broke the sod.

It is evident that when used in this connection, and made uniformly and systematically, with a definite problem in view, each soil analysis becomes an equation of condition; and that by the proper treatment of a large number of such analyses, by a logical process of elimination, the problem of the function and value of each soil-ingredient or soil-condition can be approached with a better prospect of a solution in accordance with *natural* conditions than can be expected from cultures upon artificial soils or in solutions.

My first trials of the efficacy of this method of investigation were made upon the soils of the state of Mississippi, which, fortunately, present extreme variations in character in almost every direction and upon every key, so to speak, of the soil scale. Some of the conclusions reached in that work have been given in published papers; but the wider scope afforded in the work embodied in the present volumes has served to extend and rectify the first conclusions, and gives them a definiteness which renders it desirable to sum up the present condition of the investigation with the record of facts now published.

The *taking of representative soil specimens* is, of course, a matter of first importance, and sometimes of no little difficulty. All those analyzed under my direction have been taken in accordance with printed directions hereinafter given, with care in the selection of proper localities, the discrimination between soil and subsoil, a record of depth, natural vegetation, behavior in cultivation, etc. As heretofore stated, I find that with such care it is perfectly practicable to obtain samples representing typically soil areas of many thousands of square miles, especially so when the subsoils are taken as the more reliable indices. On the other hand, a collection of soil samples taken without such discrimination, care in selection, and accompanying statements regarding "lay", depth, subsoil, etc., is as hopeless a riddle as can be placed before an investigator, so far as practical utility is concerned.

DIRECTIONS FOR TAKING SOIL SPECIMENS.

First. Do not take samples indiscriminately from any locality you may chance to be interested in, but consider what are the two or three chief varieties of soil which, *with their intermixtures*, make up the cultivable area of your region, and carefully sample these first of all.

Second. As a rule, and whenever possible, take specimens only from spots that have not been cultivated, and are otherwise likely to have been changed from their original condition of "virgin soils"—*e. g.*, not from ground frequently trodden over, such as roadsides, cattle-paths, or small pastures, squirrel holes, stumps, or even the foot of trees, or spots that have been washed by rains or streams, so as to have experienced a noticeable change, and not be a fair representative of their kind.

Third. Observe and record carefully the normal vegetation, trees, herbs, grass, etc., of the average land; avoid spots showing unusual growth, whether in kind or quality, as such are likely to have received some animal manure or other outside addition.

Fourth. Always take specimens from more than one spot judged to be a fair representative of the soil intended to be examined as an additional guarantee of a fair average.

Fifth. After selecting a proper spot, pull up the plants growing on it and scrape off the surface lightly with a sharp tool, to remove half-decayed vegetable matter not forming part of the soil as yet. Dig a vertical hole, like a post-hole, at least 20 inches deep. Scrape the sides clean, so as to see at what depth the change of tint occurs which marks the downward limit of the surface soil, and record it. Take at least half a bushel of the earth above this limit, and on a cloth or paper break it up and mix thoroughly, and put up at least a quart of it in a sack or package for examination. This specimen will ordinarily constitute the "soil". Should the change of color occur at a less depth than 6 inches, the fact should be noted, but the specimen taken to that depth nevertheless, since it is the least to which rational culture can be supposed to reach.

In case the difference in the character of a shallow surface soil and its subsoil should be unusually great, as may be the case in tule or other alluvial lands or in rocky districts, a separate sample of that surface soil should be taken besides the one to the depth of 6 inches.

Specimens of salty or "alkali" soils should, as a rule, be taken only toward the end of the dry season, when they will contain the maximum amount of the injurious ingredients which it may be necessary to neutralize.

Sixth. Whatever lies beneath the line of change, or below the minimum depth of 6 inches, will constitute the "subsoil". But should the change of color occur at a greater depth than 12 inches, the "soil" specimen should nevertheless be taken to the depth of 12 inches only, which is the limit of ordinary tillage; then another specimen from that depth down to the line of change, and then the subsoil specimens beneath that line. The depth down to which the last should be taken will depend on circumstances. It is always desirable to know what constitutes the foundation of a soil down to the depth of 3 feet at least, since the question of drainage, resistance to drought, etc., will depend essentially upon the nature of the substratum. But in ordinary cases 10 or 12 inches of subsoil will be sufficient for the purposes of examination in the laboratory. The specimen should be taken in other respects precisely like that of the surface soil, while that of the material underlying this "subsoil" may be taken with less exactness, perhaps at some ditch or other easily accessible point, and should not be broken up like the other specimens.

Seventh. All peculiarities of the soil and subsoil, their behavior in wet and dry seasons, their location, position—every circumstance, in fact, that can throw any light on their agricultural qualities or peculiarities—should be carefully noted and the notes sent with the specimens. Unless accompanied by such notes, specimens cannot ordinarily be considered as justifying the amount of labor involved in their examination.

DETAILS OF SOIL INVESTIGATION.

PHYSICAL SOIL EXAMINATION.—The first step, after recording the aspect of the soil or subsoil under examination, is the separation of the coarser portions—gravel, coarse sand, and bog-ore grains—which cannot be accounted as exerting any important direct influence upon vegetation or the tilling qualities of the soil. I have drawn the limit of the "fine earth" at the diameter of half a millimeter, which is at the same time the upper limit of convenient use of the hydraulic method of mechanical soil analysis. Crushing with a rubber pestle and sifting are the ordinary preparations, but in the case of hard-baked clay soils boiling and passing the creamy magma through the sieve is sometimes necessary. The nature of the coarser portions is noted, and their proportion to the fine earth is determined by weighing.

The fine earth thus obtained is reduced to a condition of tilth, and then its "moisture-coefficient" determined by exposure to an atmosphere *fully* saturated with aqueous vapor at such uniform temperature as may be at command, in a layer not exceeding 1 millimeter in thickness, for a convenient time, not less than seven hours. As stated in a previous paper, I have in these determinations come to results differing materially from those obtained by Knop, Schübler, and others, probably because of the more complete fulfillment of the conditions of full saturation of air as well as of soil. I have found that for some soils the absorption-coefficient varies but little between 7° and 25° C under these conditions, but always *increases* with the elevation of the temperature; while in others this increase is considerable, approximating to 0.1 per cent. for each degree Centigrade from 14° up to 35°, the highest limit thus far observed. With a *half-saturated* atmosphere the direction of change is reversed, the amount absorbed *decreasing* as the temperature rises, but to an extent varying with the degree of saturation. This general fact is in accord with Knop's observations, but it is evident that the law deduced by him can hold good only for a definite degree of undersaturation, which must be introduced as an essential condition, and which he has failed to establish definitely. (a)

Again, I find that, contrary to the conclusions reached by Adolph Mayer, this coefficient exerts an exceedingly important influence upon the agricultural qualities of soils. All those having at 15° C. an absorption-coefficient less than 2 per cent. are in practice droughty soils. The ordinary upland loams not easily damaged by drought have coefficients ranging from 4 to 8 per cent. Those ranging higher are mostly heavy clay soils, whose resistance to drought is very high when they are well tilled, but, from a variety of causes, very low when tillage is shallow and imperfect. Mayer's experiments on the wilting of plants in drying soils, from which he deduces as probable the maxim that the hygroscopic coefficient of soils is a matter of indifference to plants, are entirely nugatory. His plants *in pots* were not under the conditions in which field crops are when called upon to resist drought, whether from drying winds or hot sun. Here the continuous rise of moisture from the subsoil tends to keep up the supply to the water roots, while at the same time the nutrition of some plants, as is well-known, continues almost unabated in air-dry soils so long as there is no injurious rise of temperature in consequence of that dryness. But that is precisely the point where a high moisture-coefficient comes into play, by preventing, in consequence of evaporation, a rise of temperature that, under similar circumstances, would prove fatal to the surface roots of the crop in soils of low absorptive power. In fact, Mayer's conclusion is at variance with the ordinary experience of centuries, repeated every day in the droughty regions of the south and of the Pacific coast. It takes more than flower-pot experiments to invalidate the universal designation of soils of low hygroscopic power as "droughty".

A discussion of the numerous moisture determinations hereinafter given, in connection with the chemical analyses of the corresponding soils, shows that the moisture-coefficient depends essentially, in ordinary soils, upon one or more of four substances, viz (in the order of their efficacy), *humus, ferric hydrate, clay,* and *lime*. It varies in cultivable soils from about 1.5 to 23 per cent. at 15° C. in a saturated atmosphere. A pure clay rarely exceeds 12 per cent.; ferruginous clays show from 15 to 21 per cent.; some calcareous clay soils rise nearly as high, while peaty soils rise to 23 per cent. and even more. The efficacy of the ferric hydrate depends essentially upon a state of fine division. When merely incrusting the sand-grains or aggregated into bog-ore grains, it of course exerts little or no influence, although the analysis may show a high percentage. Sometimes soils highly colored show but a small iron percentage, while yet, on account of very fine diffusion, the advantages referred to are realized.

MECHANICAL ANALYSIS.—It would have been very desirable to extend farther the investigation of the physical constitution of a number of representative soils by the aid of the processes and instrument devised by me ten years ago, (b) but the limits of time and expense assigned to the soil-work under my charge forbade such expansion. The subject has, however, received some additional light from work done in the agricultural laboratory of the University of California on soils of that state, as well as (under the auspices of the Northern Transcontinental Survey) on those of Washington territory. These analyses, partly reported in their proper connection, only serve to confirm the conclusion, previously reached by me, that an intelligent understanding of the physical qualities of soils, their relation to tillage, moisture, and heat, cannot be reached without a more definite and intimate knowledge of the physical constitution of soils, and that to the attainment of such definite knowledge the precautions noted as necessary in the papers above alluded to are the very minimum. This is true, especially as regards the accurate determination of true plastic clay, as contradistinguished from the non-plastic but extremely fine sediments, with which it has always heretofore been weighed conjointly. In irrigation countries especially the facility with which the soil "takes" the water is of first importance, and this factor depends upon the presence or absence of a certain proportion of (true) clay and on certain ratios between the coarser and finer sediments, the ascertainment of which lies completely beyond the possibilities of the methods and instruments employed by the German experiment-stations, and in some cases as yet try severely the capabilities of those devised by me. The entire subject needs a close revision, involving no small amount of labor, but eminently worthy of the attention of the experiment-stations.

a See *Report of the California College of Agriculture* for 1882, p. 54; also *Trans. of the Am. Ass'n of Agr. Chemists*, vol. I, 1883.
b See articles on "The silt analysis of soils and clays" and "Silt analyses of Mississippi soils and subsoils", in *Proc. Am. Ass'n Adv. Sci.*, 1873; *Am. Jour. Sci.*, Oct. and Nov., 1873, and Jan., 1874. Also, article "On the flocculation of particles", *Am. Jour. Sci.*, Feb., 1879

CHEMICAL ANALYSIS—METHODS.—In the selection of the *solvent for making the soil extract* to be analyzed I have been guided by the consideration that minerals not sensibly attacked by several days' hot digestion with strong hydrochloric acid are not likely to furnish anything of importance to *agriculture* within at least a generation or two. If this assumption seems arbitrary, it at least commends itself to common sense. The heavy draught made upon the soil by the removal of crops cannot be sensibly affected by the minute additions made to the available plant-food by the atmospheric or root action on such refractory minerals.

Regarding the *strength of acid* to be used in the extraction of the soils, and the *time* necessary to secure the solution of the important substances, I have caused investigations to be made by Dr. R. H. Loughridge (*Am. Journal*, Jan., 1874, p. 20) on a subsoil selected for its representative position and derivation—a drift soil covering, probably, some 15,000 square miles in the uplands of western Tennessee and Mississippi, and one perhaps as fully "generalized" in its origin as can be obtained. The result of this investigation was that hydrochloric acid of about the specific gravity of 1.115 seems to exert the maximum effect, and that the extraction is practically complete after a water-bath digestion of five days. An excess of time of digestion results simply in higher percentages of alumina and soluble silica, or, what is equivalent, in a farther decomposition of kaolinite particles.

These conditions of digestion have been substantially maintained in all the soil analyses made under my direction. It may be said that what is true as regards the drift soil used in Dr. Loughridge's investigation may not be necessarily so in regard to other soils. I hope before long to test this point with regard to soils lying nearer, both in time and space, to their parent rocks, but it is obvious that which will depend upon the nature of the latter. In the case of soils derived from the close-grained and resistent basalts of Oregon and Washington, for example, the action is soon at an end and left, a plainly recognizable mineral powder is left, the acid acting apparently only on what has been prepared by atmospheric action; but in the case of argillites and other rocks, in which there has been more or less formation of zeolitic material of variable resistance, the extraction appears to be less prompt and its cessation less definitely marked. This, however, refers more especially to the dissolution of potash and alumina, while that of available lime and phosphoric acid seems to be very promptly accomplished far within the limits of the five days' digestion. As will be noted hereafter, these two ingredients really, as a rule, govern most largely the character and agricultural value of soils, variations in the potash percentages being of much less immediate concern. I therefore incline to consider the five days' term of digestion with acid of 1.115 specific gravity as adequate for all ordinary purposes to be gained by the determination of the mineral ingredients of soils, apart from the data derived from extraction of the humus according to the method of Grandeau.

The *methods of analysis* used by me are substantially those given in the *Kentucky Report*, volume I, by Dr. Robert Peter, with such changes as the progress of analytical chemistry suggested. It is substantially the usual course of a silicate analysis after "aufschliessung", using Bunsen's method of boiling with sal ammoniac for the separation of manganese from iron and alumina, and (at present) the permanganate process for the separation of the latter two. After the precipitation of lime, the ammoniacal salts are destroyed by aqua regia, finally using nitric acid in excess; after evaporation to dryness and filtering from silica floccules, sulphuric acid is precipitated by a few drops of baric nitrate, the precipitate being afterward purified; after filtration, the nitrates are decomposed by sublimed oxalic acid in a platinum dish and gently ignited, the alkalies leached out and determined as usual, excess of baryta removed, manganese and magnesia being separated in the residue from the alkali separation. In the insoluble portion of the soil the amount of silica soluble in sodic carbonate is also determined by difference after ignition.

Phosphoric acid is determined by means of ammonic molybdate on a separate portion of three to four grams of fine earth, which has first served for the determination of "volatile matter", or loss by ignition, consisting of organic matter and combined water. While this latter determination is necessary to the "summing up" of the analytical statement, it is not in itself very instructive, as it leaves the relative amounts of the two substances altogether indefinite. A determination of the organic matter by combustion, or by extraction with potash lye, is also unsatisfactory, because of the impossibility of excluding from these determinations a large amount of comminuted but altogether crude and unhumified vegetable matter, which becomes very obvious under the microscope or in the process of silt analysis. I have therefore adopted for the determination of active humus the admirable method of Grandeau, by the aid of which at least a uniform *minimum* determination becomes possible.

I have not devised any method for the direct determination of the *water of hydration*, although there are cases in which it would be very desirable to have this item for the determination of the condition of the alumina and ferric oxide.

I have in a few cases determined the amount of *silica soluble* in boiling solution of sodic carbonate in the *crude* soil. But this determination is often beset with almost insuperable mechanical difficulties, from the diffusion of the clay in the alkaline liquid. It does not appear to promise results of sufficient importance to justify such labor; the more as, by the method of Grandeau, the actual available amount of silica can probably be better determined.

As regards the determinations of *nitrogen* and its compounds in the virgin soils thus far analyzed, I have omitted them in part from want of time and proper appliances for these delicate determinations, and partly from a doubt of their present usefulness. The constant variation and interconvertibility of nitrates and ammonia compounds renders their determination at any given time of interest for that time only; and as the nitrogen percentage of the mold of natural soils adapted to agriculture (a) is not likely to vary much, the humus percentage may probably be taken as roughly proportional to the total nitrogen of the soil. The tendency of natural soils rich in humus is notoriously toward the production of excess of foliage; the special effect of the excessive use of nitrogenous manures, and the use of the latter, very rarely produces any notable beneficial effect on naturally unproductive soils. While, therefore, a full investigation of this subject is of course called for, I have thought that among the many problems to be solved this could best afford to wait. The analyses have, however, made it abundantly obvious that a fulfillment of the *conditions of nitrification* is in all natural soils a primary condition of their thriftiness, as will be more specially noted hereafter.

It may not be unnecessary to state that scarcely in any case have reagents commercially obtainable been found sufficiently pure for the purposes of soil analysis. In the work done under my charge all the reagents have been especially prepared or purified in the laboratory itself. Porcelain beakers only have been used in the digestions, and generally every possible precaution has been taken to insure correctness in the determination of the minute percentages of the important ingredients. Numerous repetitions have in most cases confirmed the correctness of the work, which can, moreover, be measurably controlled by an experienced eye when once the general character of the region concerned is known. Errors are usually traced to omissions to protect the vessels and reagent bottles from dust and to the use of "old" chlorhydric acid or ammonia, these reagents being scarcely fit for use after standing for as much as a month in a glass vessel. They have therefore, as a rule, been currently prepared in small quantities. For the determination of humus, according to Grandeau, about 10 grams of fine earth are commonly used, the treatment with acidulated water being continued until the lime reaction ceases, then washing until the chlorine reaction stops, when the dilute ammonia water dissolves the true humus, leaving the unhumified organic matter untouched. After evaporation and weighing the residue is ignited and the ash weighed, and in it the "available phosphoric acid" determined by means of molybdate.

INTERPRETATION OF THE ANALYTICAL RESULTS.

Having obtained, as above outlined, the percentage composition of a soil, how are we to interpret these percentages to the farmer? What are "high" and "low" percentages of each ingredient important to the plant, whether as food or through its physical properties?

The first question arising in this connection is, naturally, whether all soils, having what experience proves to be high percentages of plant-food when analyzed by the processes above given, show a high degree of productiveness.

So far as my experience goes, this question can for virgin soils be unqualifiedly answered in the affirmative; provided only that improper physical conditions do not interfere with the welfare of the plant.

But it does not therefore follow, as was at first supposed, that the converse is true, and that low percentages necessarily indicate low production. This will be apparent from a simple consideration.

Suppose that we have a heavy alluvial soil of high percentages and producing a maximum crop in favorable seasons. We may dilute this soil with its own weight, or even more, of coarse sand, thereby reducing the percentages to one-half or less; and yet it will not only not produce a smaller crop, but it is more likely to produce the maximum crop every year, on account of improved physical conditions. If we compare the root system of the plants grown in the original and in the diluted soil, we will find the roots in the latter more fully diffused, longer, and better developed, not confined to the crevices of a hard clay, but permeating the entire mass, and evidently having fully as extensive a surface-contact with the fertile soil particles as was the case in the undiluted soil.

How far may this dilution be carried without detriment?—The answer to this question must largely be experimental, and must vary with different plants and soils, which is precisely what the farmers' experience has long since shown. A plant capable of developing a very large root-surface can obviously make up by greater spread for a far greater dilution than one whose root-surface is in any case but small. The former flourishes even on "poor, sandy" soils, while the latter succeeds, and is naturally found on "rich, heavy" ones only, although the absolute amount of plant-food taken from the soil may be the same in either case.

Now, the conditions here supposed are frequently fulfilled in nature, and more especially so in alluvial soils. Among many striking examples that might be given are the analyses of two soils about equally esteemed for the production of cotton, both equally durable, so far as experience has gone, and yet differing in their percentages of mineral plant-food to the extent of from three to five times. (See Nos. 390 and 68 in the subjoined table.) No. 88 is also a highly esteemed soil, while No. 214 is practically worthless; yet the percentage differences are only such as for many purposes would be considered neglectable. Again, No. 206, with higher percentages of most ingredients than the two preceding, is considered as being "of no account".

a Excluding therefrom "sour" soils.

Comparative table of some Mississippi soils.

	HIGHLY PRODUCTIVE.		MEDIUM.	ALMOST WORTHLESS.	
	Buckshot soil.	Middle Homochitto.	Shell hummock soil.	Pine meadow soil.	Pine hills soil.
	Issaquena county.	Franklin county.	Hancock county.	Jackson county.	Smith county.
	No. 390.	No. 88.	No. 68.	No. 214.	No. 206.
Insoluble matter	71.767	92.184	96.082	96.592	93.257
Potash	1.104	0.148	0.045	0.061	0.256
Soda	0.235	0.044	0.057	0.050	0.045
Lime	1.349	0.122	0.096	0.022	4.129
Magnesia	1.005	0.212	0.114	0.060	0.180
Brown oxide of manganese	0.119	0.284	0.053	0.045	0.145
Peroxide of iron	5.818	1.188	0.516	0.450	1.251
Alumina	10.530	3.219	0.484	0.848	2.556
Phosphoric acid	0.304	0.079	0.097	0.021	0.080
Sulphuric acid	0.024	0.045	Trace.	Trace.	0.024
Water and organic matter	7.369	2.697	3.018	2.377	2.330
Total	100.383	100.197	100.544	99.445	100.027

In cases like these, which are not at all infrequent, the mere percentage of plant-food in the soil showing the low figures would lead to a most erroneous estimate of its agricultural value, and the showing made by such comparisons as the above seems at first blush to be a desperate one for the practical value of soil analysis; yet it seems also as though the agricultural chemist could hardly shirk the responsibility of at least trying to account for such glaring anomalies before he declares himself incompetent.

Now, when, in addition to the above figures, we know the fact that in soils such as Nos. 68 and 88 the food-roots can exercise their functions to the depth of 3 or 4 feet, while in the richer soil (No. 390), with ordinary cultivation, they will rarely reach to a greater depth than 12 or 15 inches, the equal productiveness becomes much more intelligible, for it implies that in making the comparison we must multiply the percentages of the two former soils by three or four, which makes them quite respectable. As between soils Nos. 88 and 214, the chemist should know that below the 12 inches represented in the analysis of No. 214 there is nothing but a pure sand underlaid by an impervious clay. As to No. 206, nearly the same occurs, except that at about 20 inches depth there underlies a loam subsoil of fair resources. But such soils occupy thousands of square miles in Mississippi alone. It is a matter of no small consequence whether they can be made profitably cultivable; and, if so, how. If the agricultural chemist can do nothing to help the farmer in solving such problems, his practical utility will be limited, indeed.

From among the multitude of examples of close correspondence of plant-food percentages with the practical estimate of farmers, in cases where there is no material difference in the penetrability or other physical qualities of the soils compared, I select two analyses of Florida soils, known respectively as "first" and "second class", as deduced from the experience in cultivation.

Analyses of Florida pine lands.

	MARION COUNTY.	COLUMBIA COUNTY.
	First class.	Second class.
	No. 6.	No. 7.
Insoluble matter	94.460 } 96.125	95.830 } 96.509
Soluble silica	1.665	0.679
Potash	0.180	0.117
Soda	0.088	0.064
Lime	0.072	0.058
Magnesia	0.089	0.042
Brown oxide of manganese	0.056	0.040
Peroxide of iron	0.221	0.234
Alumina	0.915	0.473
Phosphoric acid	0.110	0.092
Sulphuric acid	0.001	0.058
Water and organic matter	1.884	1.807
Total	99.939	99.493
Hygroscopic moisture	2.138	1.643
absorbed at	26.1 C.°	24.5 C.°

Here the amount of inert matter in both soils is almost identical, though slightly greater in the second-class soil, in which, moreover, the loss shown in summation is probably chiefly attributable to mechanical loss (dusting) during ignition; but the difference in the important ingredients—potash, lime, and phosphoric acid—is striking and uniformly in the same direction, as is also the significant item of "soluble silica", which is farther discussed on page 73. The inferior soil is also more droughty, as is indicated by its low moisture coefficient. It is said to produce, when fresh, from 400 to 500 pounds of seed-cotton per acre, as against from 500 to 700 pounds in the case of the first. Both, however, soon fall below even this production unless sustained by fertilizers.

It is obvious, then, that without a knowledge of the respective depths and penetrability of two soils a comparison of their plant-food percentages will be futile. Nor is it feasible to agree upon a certain depth to which all soils analyzed should be taken. The surface soil, with its processes of humification, nitrification, oxidation, carbonic acid solution, etc., in full progress, must always be distinguished from the subsoil in which these processes are but feebly developed, and where the store of plant-food, in which it is generally richer than the surface soil, is comparatively inert. Hence the obvious importance of specimens correctly taken, and the necessity of intelligent and accurate observations on the spot.

I have attempted to make allowance for the cases of dilution, as above noticed, by combining the results of the mechanical with those of chemical analysis. In the investigation made by Dr. Loughridge of the several sediments obtained in the mechanical analysis of the typical soil above referred to it appeared that plant-food practically ceased to be extracted from sediments exceeding 5 millimeters hydraulic value; and in recalculating the percentages of soils *of the same general derivation*, after throwing out the coarser sediments, we often find very striking approximations to identity of percentage composition, as well as of proportionality *inter se*. It is obvious, however, that this cannot be generally true, since inert clay or impalpable silt must often come in as dilutents. Nevertheless, I consider the mechanical analysis of soils (carried out by the method heretofore described by me, and *not* in accordance with that of the German experiment-stations) as an almost indispensable aid in judging fully of the agricultural peculiarities of soils, especially when these cannot be personally examined in the field.

The concentration of the available portion of the plant-food of soils in their finest portions is almost a maxim already, scarcely needing the corroboration afforded by the investigation of Dr. Loughridge, above quoted. A "strong soil" is invariably one containing within reach of the plant a large amount of impalpable matter; although the reverse is by no means generally true. Striking corroborations of this maxim are afforded by the steady increase of certain plant-food percentages (notably that of potash) in the deposits of streams as we descend, and the proverbial richness of "delta soils" is exactly in point. Compare in this respect the composition of an alluvial "front-land" soil from Sunflower county, Mississippi, with that of corresponding "front-land" of Bayou Terrebonne, in the Houma country of Louisiana, and with that of a "back-land" soil from the latter locality, representing the slack-water deposits back from the bayou ridge.

Comparative analyses of highly fertile lands of Mississippi and Louisiana.

	SUNFLOWER COUNTY, MISSISSIPPI.	TERREBONNE PARISH, LOUISIANA.	
	Front-land.	Front-land.	Back-land.
	No. 276.	No. 229.	No. 240.
Insoluble matter	87.806 } 91.904	75.120 } 81.505	35.480 } 55.242
Soluble silica	4.098	6.980	20.762
Potash	0.236	0.797	1.081
Soda	0.119	4.488	8.181
Lime	0.182	0.681	0.720
Magnesia	0.336	0.562	0.884
Brown oxide of manganese	0.048	0.018	0.014
Peroxide of iron	1.848	2.822	7.101
Alumina	2.566	7.274	12.446
Phosphoric acid	0.182	0.105	0.146
Sulphuric acid	0.042	0.366	0.246
Water and organic matter	2.012	4.400	12.830
Total	100.362	90.528	100.431
Hygroscopic moisture	4.070	8.610	12.830
absorbed at	14 C.°	12 C.°	12 C.°

The increase in the percentages of potash, lime, and alumina is sufficiently striking, the latter indicating the increase of fine clayey and easily decomposible material in the soils. As between the two Louisiana soils, the increase of phosphoric acid is also striking, but the easy solubility of the phosphates in marshy regions renders their distribution somewhat capricious when compared with upland or other soils not subject to long submersion.

But the chemist's task does not stop at these considerations of physical constitution. A comparison of the composition of soils of known productiveness, and characterized in their natural state by certain invariable features of plant-growth, soon reveals the existence of definite relations, not only to the *absolute amounts* of certain ingredients present in the soil, but also to their *relative proportions*. No ingredient exerts in these respects a more decided influence than *lime*, its advent in relatively large proportion, other things remaining equal, changing at once the whole character of vegetation, so as to be a matter of popular remark everywhere. Only it is not popularly known, nor has it been definitely recognized by agricultural chemists thus far, that it is the *lime* that brings the change.

FUNCTIONS OF LIME.—The evidence afforded of this fact by the analyses hereinafter recorded is overwhelming. It is very often obvious to the eye in the rich black "prairie spots" formed where a calcareous material approaches the surface so as to take part, exceptionally, in soil formation; and whatever may be the cause of the disabilities ascribed in Europe to the "poor chalk soils", in the United States the "rich limestone soils" are at least equally proverbial. Thus far he that runs may read, and the agricultural chemist who travels with his eyes open cannot fail to recognize the facts familiar to all farmers. But it is interesting to find that, even where the eye fails to see the effect on the aspect of the soil, analysis invariably corroborates the presumptive evidence afforded by the natural choice of certain trees and smaller plants. Almost all the trees which the "old farmer" habitually selects as a guide to a good "location" (a) are such as frequent calcareous soils, using the term, however, in a somewhat different meaning from that usually given it; that is, I find that, in order to manifest itself unequivocally in the tree-growth, the lime percentage should not fall much below 0.1 per cent. in the lightest sandy soils; in clay loams not below a fourth of 1 per cent., 0.25, and in heavy clay soils not below 0.5, and may advantageously rise to 1 and even 2 per cent. Beyond the latter figure it seems in no case to act more favorably than a less amount, unless it be mechanically.

These are mere statements of facts, amply exemplified in the analyses of soils accompanied by a statement of their natural vegetation. The subjoined analyses may serve as examples:

Table of Mississippi soils, showing relations between lime and clay.

	KEMPER COUNTY.		JASPER COUNTY.		PONTOTOC COUNTY.
	Stiff red soil.	Black prairie soil.	Hogwallow prairie soil.	Black prairie soil.	Flatwoods soil.
	No. 141.	No. 139.	No. 242.	No. 195.	No. 230.
Insoluble matter	84.565 } 87.784	67.078	76.738	77.488	77.854
Soluble silica	13.219 }				
Potash	0.431	0.600	0.525	0.384	0.733
Soda	0.277	0.136	0.190	0.066	0.106
Lime	0.540	1.871	0.424	1.728	0.178
Magnesia	0.836	1.002	0.674	0.881	0.831
Brown oxide of manganese	0.079	0.245	0.550	0.128	0.167
Peroxide of iron	7.089	0.748	4.121	3.890	5.890
Alumina	16.071	13.068	16.069	7.680	10.302
Phosphoric acid	0.187	0.033	0.063	0.104	0.052
Sulphuric acid	0.009	0.077	0.059	· 0.005	0.032
Water and organic matter	6.922	9.453	5.738	7.773	3.689
Total	100.226	99.911	99.165	100.128	99.863
Humus	0.781	1.277	0.729	....	0.806
Available inorganic	3.286	1.086	2.168	....	1.806
Hygroscopic moisture	13.100	11.500	6.830	13.780	9.330
absorbed at	11 C.°	8 C.°	Air-dried.	16 C.°	22 C.°

All these are very stiff soils, the first two from the Cretaceous prairie region, and lying in close proximity on hillsides; the third and fourth from the Tertiary prairie region, also not very far apart. The two black soils (Nos. 139 and 195) bear a most characteristic "lime" growth of trees, and are very productive, although No. 139 does not last well. The other soils bear only oaks. No. 141 is fairly productive in good seasons and with good tillage, but No. 242 is considered practically worthless, and bears a growth of scrubby black-jack oak only. No. 230 is very stiff gray clay soil, whose inferior lime percentage is indicated in the tree-growth by the addition of pine to the black-jack and post oaks. Comparing these with each other and with the sandy soils Nos. 68 and 88 of a previous table, which also bear the lime growth, the maxim above stated appears well established, being moreover corroborated throughout the series of analyses made. It is, besides, altogether in accord with the experience of agriculturists

a Of these, those most generally recognized in the Mississippi valley are the black walnut, wild cherry, sycamore, wild plum, crab-apple, the linden, *most* hickories, ash, chestnut, black, white, and *certain forms* of the other oaks; in the south, in addition, the tulip-tree or "poplar". hackberry, pecan, large, stout sassafras, large grape-vines, and others.

as to the effects of the use of lime as a fertilizer ,on clay-soils, on which it can be advantageously used in large quantities, while small dressings will suffice on lighter ones. There can be no doubt that lime acts in these cases, partially at least, by its peculiar effect on the tillableness of clays, investigated almost simultaneously by Schloesing and myself in 1872, and to which I have applied the term "flocculation". A certain proportion of it is necessary to render the plant-food of heavy clay soils physically accessible to vegetation, and where there is little clay little lime is needed to secure this result; but, after making full allowance for this action, some very obvious chemical relations to other soil ingredients require consideration.

A chemical effect produced by the presence of large percentages of lime in the soils seems to be a kind of "aufschliessung", an energizing or rendering active of that which otherwise would remain inactive. This becomes evident at once in the smaller insoluble residues from the acid treatment yielded by such soils, there being then oftentimes a complete dissolution of the alumina, a large part of which ordinarily remains behind in the shape of clay (kaolinite particles). It would seem that, as regards the silicates, the carbonate of lime in soils performs gradually, in a measure, the same functions as the caustic lime in Lawrence Smith's method of silicate "aufschliessung", doubtless in consequence of the formation of zeolitic compounds readily attacked by solvents.

From the evidence afforded by the analyses, (a) I should summarize as follows : The advantages resulting from the presence of an adequate supply of lime in soils :

a. A more rapid transformation of vegetable matter into *active* humus (*matière noire*), which manifests itself by a dark or deep black tint of the soil.

b. The retention of such humus, against the oxidizing influences of hot climates; witness the high humus percentages of such soils, as against all others, in the southern states. (b)

c. Whether through the medium of this humus, or in a more direct manner, it renders adequate for profitable culture percentages of phosphoric acid and potash so small that, in the case of deficiency or absence of lime, the soil is practically sterile.

d. It tends to secure the proper maintenance of the conditions of nitrification, whereby the inert nitrogen of the soil is rendered available.

e. It exerts a most important physical action on the flocculation, and therefore on the tillability, of the soil.

f. In the same connection it tends to increase the absorption coefficients of soils for moisture and other gases.

g. The efficacy of lime in preventing "running to weed" in fresh soils, and in favoring the production of fruit, is conspicuously shown in a number of cases.

I may add that in the great majority of soils (excepting those that are extremely sandy) the lime percentage is greater in the subsoil than in the surface soil. This is doubtless the result of the easy solubility of calcic carbonate in the soil water, which carries it downward, and thus tends to deplete the surface soil. This fact is strikingly shown in the results of Loughridge's investigation on the composition of the several sediments into which the subsoil under investigation had been resolved. (c) In the summation of the percentages found in the sediments most of the substances determined appear nearly as in the original soil; but of 0.27 per cent. of lime in the latter, only 0.09 reappear in the summation, and a similar loss is shown in the case of phosphoric acid. These two important ingredients had to a large extent been dissolved out by the distilled water used in the process of sedimentation. Practically, the same observation has been made in the formation of crusts of lime carbonate in the drains laid in calcareous or marled soils.

This controlling influence of lime renders its determination alone a matter of no small interest, since its deficiency can very generally be cheaply remedied, avoiding the use of more costly fertilizers. To this extent at least the agricultural chemist can render the old farmer an undoubted service.

As to "a" and "b", the points mentioned therein are apparent upon a mere inspection of the humus determinations given in the last table and throughout the entire series of reports. Ordinary upland soils show from 0.4 to 0.75 per cent. of *matière noire*; the prominently calcareous soils, from 1 to 1.5, and even more. Their familiar black tint tells of the same fact, which is moreover altogether in accord with what we know of the effects of alkalies upon vegetable matter, and with the experience of manure-makers everywhere, only the carbonate of lime in the soil acts more slowly than the hydrate. As to point "c", we have an indication of the same action in the case of marls, whose small percentages of potash and phosphates act so energetically, and in which we so often find the potash in the highly available form of glauconite grains; also in the displacement of potash from zeolitic compounds by lime or lime salts. It is manifestly of the utmost importance for the interpretation

a It will be noted that these axioms regarding the effects of lime in the soil are largely those already recognized in agricultural science: but as they have here been arrived at by the process of direct soil investigation, they are summarily presented in that connection

b The contrary results obtained heretofore in experiments made with soils mixed with lime, which showed a more rapid oxidation of the organic matter than the unlimed soils, are not valid as against the case of soils in their natural condition. It was well known before that nitrification proceeded more rapidly under the artificial circumstances there created; but the *crenacausis* so induced tells largely upon the unhumified organic matter, while the black tint of calcareous soils is due to the efficacious and difficultly oxidable *matière noire*, to the formation of which lime, like potash, contributes so powerfully.

c See *Am. Jour. Sci.*, Jan., 1874, p. 18; also, *Proc. Am. Ass'n Adr. Sci.*, 1873, p. 80.

and utility of soil analyses; and while the reader of these reports will find the truth of the maxim abundantly exemplified in its pages, it may be desirable to adduce some prominent examples in its support. These of course have to be sought chiefly among the less productive soils, but can also be noted in the preceding table; as in the case of the black prairie soil of Kemper, whose very small phosphoric acid percentage suffices, in the presence of much lime, to render it at first more productive than No. 141, with over five times the amount of phosphates, the potash supply being ample in both cases. But before proceeding to discuss this issue a general summary of the usual percentages, as shown in the analyses, together with the general conclusions deduced therefrom, must be given.

PLANT-FOOD PERCENTAGES.—The *phosphoric acid* percentage is that which, in connection with that of lime, seems to govern most commonly the productiveness of our virgin soils. In any of these less than five-hundredths (0.05) must be regarded as a serious deficiency, unless accompanied by a large amount of lime. In sandy-loam soils one-tenth (0.1), when accompanied by a fair supply of lime, secures fair productiveness for from eight to fifteen years; with a deficiency of lime, twice that percentage will only serve for a similar time. The maximum percentage thus far found in an upland soil by my method of analysis is about a quarter of 1 per cent (0.25) in the splendid table-land soils of West Tennessee and Mississippi; in the best bottom (" buckshot ") soil of the Mississippi, three-tenths (0.3); in that of a black prairie of Texas, 0.46 per cent., and in a red-clay soil from Tennessee, 0.563 per cent., this being the highest figure that has come under my observation. It implies the presence in each acre of soil taken to the depth of 6 inches of 11,000 pounds of phosphoric acid.

The *potash percentages* of soils seem in a large number of cases to vary with that of "clay"; that is, in clay soils they are usually high, in sandy soils low; and since subsoils are in all ordinary cases more clayey than surface soils, their potash percentage is also almost invariably higher. One and three-tenths (1.3) per cent. of potash is the highest percentage obtained by my method of extraction, and that from the same soil that afforded the second highest phosphate percentage also, the "buckshot" of the Mississippi bottom, noted for its high and uniform production of cotton. As the same soil contains 1.4 per cent. of lime, and is jet black with humus, it may well serve as the type of a fertile soil.

The potash percentage of heavy clay upland soil and clay loams ranges from about 0.8 to 0.5 per cent., lighter loams from 0.45 to 0.30, sandy loams below 0.3, and sandy soils of great depth may fall below 0.1 consistently with good productiveness and durability, the former depending upon the amounts of lime and phosphoric acid with which it is associated. Virgin soils falling below 0.06 in their potash percentage seem, in most cases that have come under my observation, to be deficient in available potash, its application to such soils being followed by an immediate great increase of production. Sometimes, however, a soil very rich in lime and phosphoric acid shows good productiveness despite a very low potash percentage; (a) and, conversely, a high potash percentage seems capable of offsetting a low one of lime.

Since but few soils fall below this minimum, my general inference has been that potash manures are not among the first to be sought for after the soils have become "tired" by exhaustive culture. The universal preference given to phosphatic and nitrogenous fertilizers in the west and south is in accord with this inference. In the older portions of the United States "kainit" is becoming more important, while in the alkali lands of California soluble potash salts often impregnate the soil water, and will probably never need to be supplied by manure.

In all soils not specially impregnated with sea or other salts the amount of *soda* extracted by the acid is considerably *below* that of potash in the same soil, varying mostly from one-eighth to one-third of the percentage of the latter. When much more is found in such soils a repetition of the determination will usually show that the separation from magnesia was imperfectly made. I can trace no connection between the soda percentage and any important property of the soil, any more than in the case of *magnesia* and *manganese;* albeit none of these is ever absent from ordinary soils. In the majority of cases the percentage of magnesia is greater than that of lime, frequently about double; but it does not seem capable of performing to any appreciable extent the general functions of lime in soil-making.

Sulphuric acid is found in very small quantities only, even in highly fertile soils. From two- to four-hundredths of one per cent. (0.02 to 0.04) seems to be an adequate supply, but it frequently rises to one-tenth (0.1) per cent., rarely higher.

Chlorine I have as a rule left undetermined, on account of its constant variability and universal presence in waters and acknowledged slight importance to useful vegetation.

Iron, in the shape of ferric hydrate finely diffused, appears to be an important soil ingredient on account of its physical, and partly also its chemical, properties. The universal preference given to "red lands" by farmers is sufficiently indicative of the results of experience in this respect, and I have taken pains to investigate its causes. The high absorptive power of ferric hydrate for gases is probably first among the benefits it confers. Red soils resist drought better than similar soils lacking the ferric hydrate.

---

a See, for example, soils Nos. 1 and 2, Florida, which are among the best upland soils in the state, producing, when fresh, as much as 1,500 pounds of seed-cotton.

From 1.5 to 4 are ordinary percentages of ferric oxide, occurring even in soils but little tinted. Ordinary ferruginous loams vary from 3.5 to 7 per cent.; highly colored "red lands" have from 7 to 12 per cent., and occasionally upward to 20 per cent. and more.

Of course, a large amount of ferric hydrate facilitates the tillage of heavy clay soils, and its color tends to the absorption of heat; but I incline strongly to the belief that the benefits of its presence are not confined to physical action. From the fact that highly ferruginous soils rarely have a high percentage of humus, it appears that the former acts as a carrier of oxygen to the latter, and thus probably favors, especially, nitrification.

On the other hand, such soils are the first liable to damage from imperfect drainage, overflows, etc. The reduction of the ferric hydrate to ferrous salts, most commonly in the subsoil, manifests itself promptly by the "blighting" of the crop. But under natural conditions this can rarely occur, because a frequent recurrence of conditions favoring reduction will inevitably result in a gradual bleaching of the soil and an accumulation of its iron in the subsoil in the form of bog-ore or "black pebble".

The percentages of *alumina* are but an imperfect indication of the amount of *clay* in the soil. As before remarked, they are always found larger in calcareous soils, other things being equal, and the amount dissolved continues to increase long after the rest of the important substances have been extracted if the digestion with acid be prolonged, doubtless in consequence of the slow action on the larger kaolinite particles. But the first portions are dissolved with great promptness; and if all were in combination as hydrous silicate, it is obvious that the amount of silica soluble in boiling solution of sodic carbonate should bear a certain ratio to that of the alumina. In all later analyses this determination of "*soluble silica*" in the residue remaining after digestion with acid and evaporation has been made. Curiously enough, it is but rarely that the amount of silica dissolved satisfies the requirement for combining with the alumina into kaolinite, and in a *very* few cases there is an excess of silica over that requirement. In numerous cases the silica falls so far below the amount corresponding to the alumina as to raise a serious question as to the combination in which the latter occurs in the soil, the *hydrate* (gibbsite) being almost the only possible one, apart from zeolitic minerals. Perhaps this fact may serve to explain some of the otherwise incomprehensible variations in the physical properties of soils whose chemical and mechanical analysis would seem to make them almost identical. In some of the Tertiary prairie soils of the southern states, moreover, there seems to occur still another amorphous mineral, related to or identical with *saponite*, which sometimes occurs in segregated masses, and imparts to these soils very peculiar and unwelcome properties in tillage. We are evidently as yet very far from a full understanding of the mechanical constitution of soils.

I have in a few cases determined the amount of *silica soluble* in boiling solution of sodic carbonate in the *crude* soil. But this determination is often beset with almost insuperable mechanical difficulties, from the diffusion of the clay in the alkaline liquid, and does not appear to promise results of sufficient importance to justify such labor; the more, as by the method of Grandeau the actual available amount of silica can probably be better determined.

As regards the *determination of humus*, I have not yet been able to extend the method of Grandeau for humus extractions over a sufficient number of widely-different soils of well known characteristics to consider the claim of its furnishing a definite measure of the available plant-food in the soil as definitely established. There can be no reasonable doubt that what *is* extracted by Grandeau's ammonia-water is at the command of the solvents employed by plants; the only question is, to what extent plants can readily go beyond. This, of course, requires extended culture experiments on a great variety of soils. The determination of the *phosphoric acid* and *silica in the residues* from the ignition of Grandeau's extracts have already furnished most important data concerning the cause of the productiveness of some soils having comparatively a low percentage of phosphates; and here again there is evidence of a direct connection with the more or less calcareous nature of the soils. The facts thus far elicited are not sufficiently numerous to prove or disprove definitely Grandeau's claim as to the direct connection of the results with the soil's present productiveness, and I hope to carry the study of the subject to a more definite conclusion hereafter. The figures given opposite the heading "available inorganic" in the analyses are often suggestive, but can justify no conclusions until they shall have been fully analysed; a task involving no small amount of labor. Silica and ferric oxide seem ordinarily to form the bulk of this ash. There is a class of soils, poor in lime, in which the ammonia solution is of a pale yellow, instead of the usual dark tint, but darkens during evaporation, probably by oxidation of crenic into apocrenic acid.

As exemplifications (which might be indefinitely multiplied) of the *effects of increased lime percentages* in rendering soils thrifty, *i. e.*, productive for the time being, as the result of the increased availability of plant-food when present even in small quantities, I give the following instances:

Analyses of Louisiana soils.

	PINE WOODS SUBSOIL.	OAK AND HICK-ORY RED SUBSOIL.	ANACOCO PRAIRIE SOIL.
	Vernon parish.	Sabine parish.	Vernon parish.
	No. 134.	No. 165.	No. 171.
Insoluble matter	77.870 } 82.265	49.130 } 72.870	53.190 } 74.290
Soluble silica	4.395	23.450	21.100
Potash	0.247	0.202	0.332
Soda	0.083	0.065	0.064
Lime	0.097	0.268	1.398
Magnesia	0.339	0.290	0.735
Brown oxide of manganese	0.041	0.146	0.149
Peroxide of iron	3.214	5.324	4.520
Alumina	9.918	15.222	11.963
Phosphoric acid	0.972	0.088	0.047
Sulphuric acid	0.086	0.050	0.123
Water and organic matter	3.546	5.509	7.285
Total	99.908	99.604	100.287
Hygroscopic moisture absorbed at	8.790 26.6 C.°	12.140 25.6 C.°	13.110 25.5 C.°

In these soils the potash percentage is only fair in Nos. 134 and 171; in No. 165, rather low, according to the usual run of soils of the state. The phosphoric acid is low in all, highest in the pine-hill soil, and deficient, according to the usual standard, in the other two. The pine-hill soil will produce about 500 pounds of seed-cotton per acre for a few years; the Sabine upland soil from 800 to 1,000 pounds, when fresh, but soon declining. The Anacoco prairie soil has yielded from 1,200 to 1,500 pounds per acre for fifteen years, and is still doing fairly well. Had the soil corresponding to No. 134 been analyzed in place of the subsoil, the percentages would have been somewhat diminished all around and the comparison would have been more striking. As it is, the lime percentages are respectively 0.097, 0.268, and 1.398.

Some examples from Mississippi are given in the first table of this paper; but the following are more particularly illustrative of the influence of lime, especially in counteracting a deficiency in the amount of phosphoric acid:

Analyses of Mississippi soils.

	BLACK PRAIRIE SOILS.		LONG-LEAF PINE SOILS.	
	Noxubee county.	Kemper county.	Smith county.	Pike county.
	No. 170.	No. 180.	No. 206.	No. 218.
Insoluble matter	64.644 } 75.704	67.078	98.297	80.801
Soluble silica	11.060			
Potash	0.366	0.699	0.259	0.218
Soda	0.074	0.196	0.065	0.076
Lime	1.254	1.371	0.129	0.034
Magnesia	0.716	1.003	0.180	0.306
Brown oxide of manganese	0.119	0.245	0.146	0.072
Peroxide of iron	4.557	5.748	1.281	2.402
Alumina	8.918	13.068	2.356	3.782
Phosphoric acid	0.068	0.098	0.030	0.088
Sulphuric acid	Trace	0.077	0.024	0.086
Water and organic matter	8.466	6.458	2.330	3.448
Total	100.241	99.911	100.027	100.212
Hygroscopic moisture absorbed at	14.290 20 C.°	11.450 8 C.°	2.480 19 C.°	4.110 21 C.°

All these soils are low in phosphates, the two prairie soils, both highly productive at first, and for 15 to 20 years, then falling off rather suddenly. The two pine soils, Nos. 206 and 218, would scarcely produce 500 pounds of seed-cotton per acre when fresh, and that only for three or four years. Many similar examples may be culled from the analyses of Texas and Alabama soils.

It is quite apparent that where the phosphoric acid percentage is very high the effect on vegetation and productiveness in cultivation is similar to that resulting from the presence of large lime percentages with less phosphates. Usually, however, high phosphates are associated with at least a fair proportion of lime. The following examples of soils from northwestern Georgia are illustrative :

Analyses of Georgia soils.

	WALKER COUNTY.		POLK COUNTY.
	Cherty lands.	Valley lands.	Red valley land.
	No. 506.	No 505.	No. 517.
Insoluble matter................................	81.470 } 88.926	88.680 } 91.398	67.819 } 73.896
Soluble silica................................	7.456	1.718	5.307
Potash	0.422	0.178	0.334
Soda	0.277	0.065	0.068
Lime	0.197	0.047	0.296
Magnesia	0.878	0.031	0.392
Brown oxide of manganese	0.178	0.041	0.084
Peroxide of iron................................	1.969	1.730	6.234
Alumina................................	3.650	2.677	3.721
Phosphoric acid	0.411	0.186	0.042
Sulphuric acid	0.193	0.041	0.238
Water and organic matter	4.405	2.980	10.015
Total	100.926	99.391	99.975
Hygroscopic moisture	6.310	4.840	9.770
absorbed at	13 C.°	14 C.°	16 C.°

Of these soils, No. 506, having a very high percentage of phosphoric acid and only a moderate supply of lime, is very productive. Nos. 505 and 517, one with high lime and low phosphoric acid, the other with the proportions reversed, are both about equally productive.

The effect of a large lime percentage in *increasing the amount of silica and alumina dissolved* in the extraction by acid is abundantly illustrated in the analyses of prairie soils from Mississippi, Alabama, and Texas. A glance at the columns giving the percentages of these substances in the tables will show this relation ; but it will also be noted that while in calcareous clay soils it exists almost invariably there are cases in which a considerable percentage of soluble silica is not accompanied by any notably large proportion of lime. As this occurs usually in sandy or pervious soils, it is possible that these are cases in which the lime has been gradually removed by the well-known leaching process. At all events, no exact numerical proportionality between the present lime percentage and the soluble silica can be established.

In many cases of lime percentages rising to between 1 and 2 and even more carbonic acid is not reported at all, although a qualitative test for that substance was in all cases made. A most striking case is that of the soil and subsoil Nos. 9 and 10, Tennessee, in which, respectively, 6.5 and 8.4 per cent. of lime is present, and yet scarcely a trace of gas is evolved on treatment with acid. The lime consequently exists in the shape of a (zeolitic) silicate, in which doubtless the potash and alumina so abundantly present have a share ; for the soluble silica shown in the table is not remote enough to combine with the alumina into kaolinite.

RELATIONS OF LIME TO HUMUS AND THE AVAILABLE PHOSPHORIC ACID IN THE "MATIÈRE NOIRE".—As remarked above, the determinations of the phosphoric acid contained in the soil extract, according to Grandeau, are not as yet sufficiently numerous to warrant definite conclusions as to the relations of the several soil ingredients to this factor. In some cases in which considerable lime is present the humus extract does not show a very large proportion of available phosphoric acid, but in some cases all, and in others a large proportion of the total phosphoric acid of the soil, is found in the humus extract, and in all such cases the lime percentage is relatively large. Thus in the two soils from the Houma region of Louisiana one-half of the total phosphoric acid of the soil is found in the humus extract ; and in the "sugar-bowl" delta lands of the Brazos river, of Texas, as well as in the bottom of the Colorado river of the west, in southern California, the whole of the contained phosphoric acid is extracted with the humus. All these are soils of extraordinary productiveness. In nearly all the cases of soils poor in lime in which the determination has thus far been made the amount of phosphoric acid appearing in the humus extract is small, varying usually from one-fourth to one-tenth of the total amount in the soil, and even less.

It cannot be doubtful that a thorough investigation of this subject would lead to results not only interesting, but of great practical importance ; but the amount and character of the work involved is such as to place it almost beyond the power of any single investigator, and commensurate only with the scale of a public work.

PART II.

STATISTICS AND AGRICULTURAL DESCRIPTIONS

OF THE

COTTON STATES,

WITH A PRELIMINARY DISCUSSION OF THE GENERAL FEATURES OF THE ALLUVIAL PLAIN OF THE MISSISSIPPI RIVER BELOW THE MOUTH OF THE OHIO.

BY

E. W. HILGARD.

GENERAL FEATURES OF THE ALLUVIAL PLAIN OF THE MISSISSIPPI RIVER BELOW THE MOUTH OF THE OHIO.

The agricultural features of the Mississippi bottom and delta plain are so intimately connected with the geology and topography of this region that a succinct preliminary statement of these must of necessity precede the discussion of its soils. This statement will apply, with some local modifications, to the great alluvial plain from the confluence of the Ohio down to the shores of the Gulf of Mexico.

To the eye of the casual observer the alluvial region appears substantially as a plain, forest-covered throughout—what are called "prairies" being in most cases simply old Indian clearings. Closer observation, and still more the leveling instruments of the surveyor, soon reveal the fact that, as a general rule, the banks of the water-courses are the highest points; that, in other words, each stream has its bed in the axis of a ridge that accompanies it throughout. This ridge is formed of the deposits of the stream itself, and from it the land slopes off gently, until, midway between two water-courses, we usually find a low cypress swamp lying from 2 to 6 feet below the banks, and sometimes even below the ordinary water-level of the streams. This state of things will be best understood by reference to the subjoined diagram (a) representing a section across two "bayous" (b) and the intervening lands and swamp, and of the underground strata as shown in wells and bluff banks.

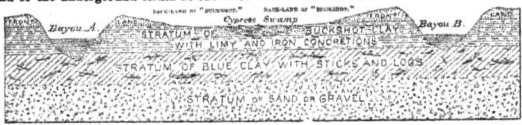

Ideal section across two bayous in the Mississippi bottom, showing surface-structure.

What is true of the smaller streams or bayous holds no less, of course, as regards the larger streams and the great Mississippi itself. The subjoined sections across the Mississippi bottom (one from the main river to the Yazoo bluff, the other from the same to the west bank of the Washita river, about Monroe, Louisiana,) exhibit the same features on the large scale. It will be seen that the bank of the Mississippi river at Melrose Landing, Bolivar county, Mississippi, is 20 feet above that of the Yazoo, due east from that point; while the banks of the Washita river near Monroe, Ouachita parish, Louisiana, are about 10 feet below the level of the banks of the Mississippi near the mouth of the Yazoo.

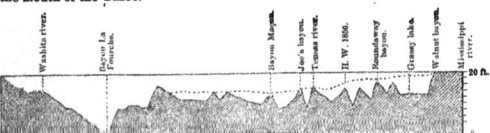

Section showing surface of Mississippi bottom, and high-water mark of 1850, from banks of Mississippi river above Vicksburg, west to the Washita river, below Monroe, Ouachita parish, La. (From Report on the Mississippi river, by Humphreys and Abbot, Plate No. IV.) Distance, about 70 miles.

a See "Remarks on the Geology of the Mississippi Bottom", by Eugene A. Smith, in *Proc. of the Am. Ass'n for the Adv. of Sci.,* 1871, p. 53.

b The French Creole term *bayou* applies properly to water channels branching *out* from the main stream and carrying *off* a portion of its water. Since this office is performed in time of flood by almost every stream in the alluvial plain (whereby the natural current is not uncommonly reversed for some time), the name has come to be applied indiscriminately to all the water-courses of that plain, and thence has been largely transferred in Louisiana to the upland streams also.

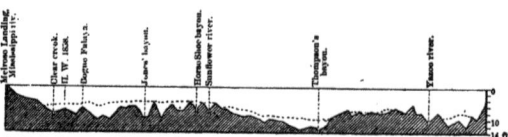

Section showing surface of Mississippi bottom, and high-water mark of 1858, from Melrose Landing, Bolivar county, Miss., east to the Yazoo bluff. Distance, about 75 miles.

A glance at the surface profiles across the great bottom explains the primary importance of preventing the waters of the Mississippi from passing the natural or artificial barriers on its own banks; for, these once passed, the flood descends with a considerable velocity upon the lower ground inland, and not unfrequently reaches the foot of the bluff on either side. There are numerous natural channels through which a partial discharge of floods in this direction takes place wherever not artificially prevented, as has perhaps too frequently been done. Among the more important of such "passes" is the Yazoo pass; the bayous connecting the heads of the Sunflower river with the Mississippi; Jack's bayou and bayou Vidal, forming connections with the Tensas river; and lower down, bayous Plaquemine and Manchac. The opening or closing of these important connections in time of flood, involving the exposure or protection of certain regions, has been from time to time the subject of passionate discussion, in connection with the question of the maintenance of levees or embankments intended to confine the Mississippi river within its banks.

The floods of the Mississippi occur in the six months from December to June, but are usually distinguished as "the spring rise" and "the June rise". The spring rise, broadly speaking, is caused by the spring rains and melting of the snows in the nearer and level portion of the Mississippi valley, from the Alleghanies westward to the great plains; it most commonly occurs in March and April, and when it subsides in time does not materially interfere with the planting of crops in the bottom-lands, where the growing season is several weeks longer than in the adjacent uplands. The second or June rise is caused by the melting of snows in the Rocky mountain region, and is frequently aggravated by persistent rains in the nearer portions of the basin, resulting in a concurrence of the mountain floods, carried by the Missouri and Arkansas rivers, with those of the Ohio and direct tributaries north and south of the same. The June rise, occurring after all the expense of pitching crops has been incurred, is, on that account, usually chargeable with the largest amount of direct damage. When, as is sometimes the case, the putting in of crops is altogether prevented by a continuation of the high water through spring to the end of June, the planter has at least saved a heavy cash outlay, and may more readily make up for the loss of a year's crop during a succeeding favorable season. The average height of the June rises appears to be at least not below that of the spring rises.

In whatever direction the solution of the question of protection of the Mississippi alluvial plain from overflows may ultimately be found, it is certainly the vital question for the development of the immense agricultural resources of this region, as much as is that of irrigation in other portions of the United States. In either case, a few years' respite from inundation or from drought is apt to bring about a relaxation of the efforts for a final settlement of the question, and to induce the investment of large sums in improvements, which are then ruthlessly swept away by one or two seasons' excess, or deficiency, of the vital fluid. In the case of the Mississippi bottom this insecurity has largely restricted cultivation to the soils of the higher ground immediately adjacent to the water-courses.

The high land near the bayous — the "front-land" — is not, however, distinguished by its position alone. As a rule, it is a "light" soil, a loam, sometimes quite sandy, and, on the whole, the more so as the stream depositing it is larger; hence, on the banks of the Mississippi itself, we frequently find it almost too sandy for cultivation. Old abandoned water-courses are also thus frequently marked by ridges of sandy or loam soil, whose timber growth always differs more or less from that of the "back-land", by the presence of the cottonwood and the comparative scarcity or absence of the trees denoting a heavy soil, such as sweet-gum and swamp-chestnut oak.

The immediate banks of the Mississippi river are, as a rule, occupied by a growth of cottonwood trees, sloping up from the seedling near the water's edge to the full-grown forest tree a hundred yards inland, and producing the impression of an elevated, sloping bank. This tree thus serves to fix and consolidate the sandy deposits, checking the current and causing slack-water sediments to form during high water, which ultimately constitute the cultivable soil. Opposite caving shores of bends, and in the eddies below islands, the forming alluvial soil is similarly occupied, the low, gently sloping banks constituting the "battures" and (in the case of islands) "tow-heads". Below Red river, these are chiefly occupied by willows, which are better adapted to the warm climate than the cottonwood.

The "back-land", occupying the landward slope between the front-land and the cypress swamp, is of a totally different nature from the present deposits of the streams, while closely resembling the clayey soil now in process of formation in the swamps. Its special name of "buckshot" is due, partly to the occurrence in it of rounded ferruginous concretions, which cause the same name to be applied to the (of course entirely different) white silt soils elsewhere, and partly to its peculiarity of crumbling into small, roundish-angular fragments in drying; a property to which much of its agricultural value is due, since it thus combines the great intrinsic fertility of a heavy soil with the easy tillability of a light one. The dark-tinted "buckshot" soils are the most highly esteemed for productiveness and durability, being in these respects probably exceeded by few, if any, soils in the world.

Examination of the strata in the banks of the streams, and of those found in digging wells, shows that the dark-colored clay stratum from which the "buckshot" soil is derived underlies the whole of the Mississippi bottom from Memphis to the delta, its thickness commonly varying from 8 to 30 feet, 12 to 15 being the usual one. Into this clay stratum, evidently formed at the time when the entire bottom plain was a continuous swamp, the present streams have excavated their beds, and upon it they now deposit their alluvium. The comparatively firm nature of the banks formed by this "buckshot" clay prevents to a great extent the continual shifting of the smaller channels, so apt to occur in the alluvial plains of other rivers. In the larger channels, however, and especially in that of the main Mississippi, the depth of water and its velocity in times of flood becomes so great as to reach and wash away the sandy or gravelly strata which underlie the clay; and thus undermined the latter breaks off and tumbles into the water in large fragments. It is thus that the "neck" separating from each other the two limbs of a bend is frequently washed away, forming a "cut-off" and, for the time being, making an island of the land in the bend. Generally, however, the entrances to the old river bed are filled up by the deposits formed in the slack water, connection with the newly-formed bed at ordinary stages of water ceases, and a crescent-shaped lake remains in the place of the old channel. These lakes are abundant along the larger streams of the bottom plain, and their banks, being high and dry, are often the preferred sites for residences.

Except as to the kinds of trees forming the timber, these general features of the great bottom suffer but little change as we descend the river until we reach the region of comparatively slack water, below Baton Rouge. From the junction of the Ohio river down to the Mississippi state line, below Memphis, the Mississippi river generally keeps within a short distance of the eastern uplands, so that only comparatively small tracts of bottom land lie within the states of Kentucky and Tennessee (about 320 and 600 square miles respectively), while the foot of the bluff is washed by the river at Columbus and Hickman, Kentucky, and at the four "Chickasaw bluffs" in Tennessee, on the most southerly of which stands the city of Memphis. From the latter point the river turns diagonally (southwestward) across the bottom, striking the high lands of Arkansas near Helena. The bottom plain lying to the northward of this cross-cut in Missouri and Arkansas is popularly known as the *St. Francis bottom* (6,300 square miles), that stream flowing near its western edge and joining the main river a few miles above Helena. Similarly, the extensive area of bottom lying to the southward, in the state of Mississippi, and along whose eastern edge flows the Yazoo river, is known as the *Yazoo bottom* (7,100 square miles); it terminates at Vicksburg, where the great river once more strikes the eastern bluff after having made a great bow to the westward, at the vertex of which it receives the Arkansas river. From Vicksburg to Baton Rouge, Louisiana, where it enters the delta plain proper, the Mississippi river remains within a short distance of the eastern highlands, which it frequently strikes, forming high and steep bluffs at several points, as at Grand Gulf, Rodney, Natchez, Ellis' Cliffs, and Port Hudson, small patches only of alluvial land remaining on the eastern side.

The bottom plain west of the river, from the northeast corner of Louisiana (where the bayou Tensas diverges from the main river) down to the mouth of Red river, is known as the *Tensas bottom* (about 3,115 square miles), and lies wholly within the state of Louisiana.

Of these three chief divisions of the great bottom the Tensas bottom proper is altogether uninterrupted by any ridges above the highest overflows. In the Yazoo bottom there is a long, narrow ridge, entirely above present overflows, extending from the region opposite Helena, Arkansas, to the northern end of Honey island, Holmes county, Mississippi. It is thus about eighty miles in length, and varies from two to six miles in width. Its soil and timber-growth are different from those of the rest of the bottom, dogwood being a largely prevalent tree; it is, in its northern portion, known as the "Dogwood ridge". Its soil is very productive, and approaches in character that of the "front-lands" of the larger bayous.

The St. Francis bottom is much more intersected and diversified by ridges of varying elevation and character. Some of these are true upland ridges, extending in from, and connected more or less with, the mainland. Others are isolated islands of such land, and others again are of a character approaching that of the "Dogwood ridge" of the Yazoo bottom, just referred to. These will be found described in detail in the portion of the report relating to the state of Arkansas.

The same feature is continued into Louisiana, in the upland ridges dividing the flood-plains of bayous Maçon, Bœuf, and Bartholomew from each other, and that of the latter from the bottom of the Washita. Minor ridges of less elevation, and more nearly related to the present alluvium, occur at various points, as is indicated on the map of Louisiana.

The country bordering on the main Mississippi, from Red river down to New Orleans, is popularly known as the "upper coast", in contradistinction to the "lower coast", which embraces the river country from New Orleans to the mouths. The belts of cultivated land lying along the other larger streams (Atchafalaya, Têche, Lafourche, &c.), are habitually referred to by the names of the streams, not as "bottoms", but "country".

In approaching the tide-water region, the crescent-shaped lakes, so characteristic of the alluvial plain above, become rarer, and lakes formed merely by the widening of the stream beds, as well as marsh basins, take their place. The lands lying nearest the channels are still the highest, and those chiefly cultivated; but the difference in the character of the "front-land" and "back-land" becomes less striking, the bayou lands not being as sandy, nor the modern cypress or marsh land as clayey, as is the case in corresponding positions in the Yazoo and Tensas bottoms, where the stiff "buckshot" clay of the ancient swamp contrasts strongly with the sandy sediments deposited from the more swiftly-flowing streams. The tide-water bayous deposit usually a fine silt.

In the tide-marsh region proper these bayou-land ridges, mostly distinguishable at a distance by their groves of live-oak timber, skirt the bayous up to within 8 to 20 miles of the Gulf shore, gradually narrowing, and finally disappearing insensibly in the reedy marsh or grassy prairie of the coast; of which but little, so far, has been brought under cultivation.

The mouths or "passes" of the main Mississippi, unlike the bayous, and in fact unlike any other river in the world, extend rapidly to seaward, independently of the mainland, and far beyond it, by building up narrow banks of a stiff, clayey material on either side. These banks are not formed of the material at present carried by the river, but of clayey masses upheaved from the bottom of the river channel, inside the bar, and generally known as "mud lumps". They form most formidable obstructions to navigation, and frequently compel a change of the river channel, at least for a time; those in the axis of the current may ultimately be washed away, but those arising near the edge remain and serve as a basis for the accumulation of more deposit. Thus the banks are finally elevated above ordinary water-level, and effectually divide, with their tough material, the river current from the sea. The soil thus formed is very fertile, but too much impregnated with salt for immediate cultivation. In the upper portion of the lower delta, above the head of the passes, older soil of this character has produced fine crops of rice.

88

INDEX TO GENERAL DISCUSSION.

REPORT

ON THE

COTTON PRODUCTION OF THE STATE OF LOUISIANA,

WITH A DISCUSSION OF

THE GENERAL AGRICULTURAL FEATURES OF THE STATE.

BY

EUGENE W. HILGARD, Ph. D.,

PROFESSOR OF AGRICULTURE AT THE UNIVERSITY OF CALIFORNIA, FORMERLY AT THE UNIVERSITY OF MISSISSIPPI,
AND STATE GEOLOGIST OF MISSISSIPPI;

SPECIAL CENSUS AGENT.

TABLE OF CONTENTS.

TABLE OF CONTENTS.

LETTER OF TRANSMITTAL.

UNIVERSITY OF CALIFORNIA,
Berkeley, Alameda Co., Cal., April 18, 1881.

HON. FRANCIS A. WALKER,
Superintendent of Tenth Census, Washington, D. C.

DEAR SIR: I transmit herewith a tabular presentation of results of the census enumeration in the state of Louisiana, so far as these concern the production of cotton; also, a report on the physico-geographical and agricultural features of the state of Louisiana, prepared in accordance with your instructions, and with the plans subsequently outlined by me and approved by you, for a more instructive and readable presentation of the enumeration-results relating to the culture and production of cotton, than can be given by the tabular and graphic methods alone. Unlike the publications made on the latter basis, it is intended, not alone for the statistician and student of political economy, but for the information of the general public, and more especially for that of intending settlers and immigrants.

It has always been a matter of surprise to me that out of so many state surveys, so few have given this important subject the benefit of systematic investigation and presentation for popular use. In my own work in several states, I have throughout considered this as the most immediately important object to be compassed, as bearing most directly upon the life-pursuit of the vast majority of the population; and it has seemed to me that the greater part of the want of appreciation and the reverses with which state surveys have proverbially had to contend, are directly traceable to an omission to conform, in this respect, to the natural and, I think, just expectations of the agricultural population. It is difficult to see on what ground the study and publication of the most recondite details of geology, lithology, and paleontology, should have precedence of the fundamentally important work that concerns directly the productive industries; yet this has been the course very commonly pursued, usually at the cost of premature, and at least temporary, stoppage of the entire work, with enormous losses of valuable material and of personal knowledge acquired by the members of the corps.

It thus happens that, in the case of some states whose geological structure is very accurately known, no concise physico-geographical and agricultural description as yet exists; although by a close abstraction and collation of data scattered through the published reports, such a one may be laboriously obtained. As this process will generally be undertaken only by few and specially interested persons, the result is that the general public remains uninformed as to the facts most broadly obvious to the inhabitants themselves and most essential to those contemplating immigration, yet inaccessible except through personal travel, private correspondence, or the *ex parte* representations of interested parties. Even where state bureaus of immigration exist, the information to be obtained is usually of a fragmentary and unsatisfactory character, and incapable of conveying to the seeker for a new home the kind of knowledge he desires in order to make his choice intelligently.

It has been my endeavor, in the compilation of the present report, to supply this deficiency, so far as the state of Louisiana is concerned, and more especially with reference to the industry under my immediate charge, viz, the production of cotton.

v
99

The sources of information available for the present paper, apart from data existing in encyclopedias, have, in the main, been the following :

For the topography of the Mississippi bottom and delta, the *Report on the Mississippi River, by Humphreys and Abbot.*

For the classification and analyses of the soils of the Mississippi bottom, the *Manuscript Notes and Reports of Dr. Eugene A. Smith,* now of the University of Alabama, state geologist and special agent in charge of the subject of cotton culture in the states of Alabama and Florida. The manuscripts referred to form part of the unpublished records of the geological survey of Mississippi, courteously placed at our disposal by the board of trustees of the University of Mississippi, at Oxford. The field-work was done by Dr. Smith, under my direction as state geologist of Mississippi, in the year 1871.

The chief sources of information regarding the rest of the state are, in the order of time :

Manuscript notes and published papers, the results of an expedition undertaken by the writer in November and December, 1877, under the auspices and at the expense of the Smithsonian Institution, for the investigation of the geology of southern Louisiana, and especially of the rock-salt deposit of Petite Anse island. The route was from Vicksburg down the Mississippi river to its mouths, landing at various points on the way; then via New Orleans and New Iberia to Petite Anse island, Weeks' island or Grande Côte, and Côte Blanche, on the Gulf coast.

Manuscript notes and published reports and papers relating to a geological and agricultural reconnaissance of Louisiana, undertaken by the writer, under the auspices of the New Orleans Academy of Sciences and of the Louisiana state bureau of immigration, in May and June, 1869. The route lay from New Orleans, via New Iberia, to Opelousas and Chicotville; thence, west to the Calcasieu river and down that stream, through the Calcasieu prairie, to lake Charles; thence, north to the Anacoco region and to Sabinetown, Texas; thence, via Manny, to Mansfield, De Soto parish; thence, crossing Red river, to Coushatta chute, and north to the salines of Bienville parish, and, via Winfield and Funne Louis, to Harrisonburg, and to Waterproof, in Tensas parish. This expedition determined the general geological structure of Louisiana and its main agricultural and topographical features. (a) Eleven out of the twenty-five soil analyses, hereinafter given, were made at the time, of specimens then collected; and most of the remainder are of samples of the same collection.

Almost simultaneously with the expedition just referred to, a *Geological and Topographical Survey* of the state was begun, under the auspices of the University of Louisiana, at Baton Rouge, and was continued for three years by Professors Samuel H. Lockett and H. V. Hopkins of that institution. The excellent work done by these gentlemen, during that time, has remained almost unnoticed, in consequence of the limited number of copies (200 each) printed of their annual reports. The latter so far amplify and complement the data obtained by me personally, as to leave no considerable portion of the state entirely undescribed; and I have thus been enabled to draw a measurably complete picture of the whole. As it is scarcely possible to give credit separately to the observations of each, and of myself, I can only state broadly, that by far the greater part of all the data not referring to portions of the state visited by me (as above noted), is derived from these reports; and that particularly the admirable and summary descriptions given of a number of parishes by Professor Lockett have, in some cases, been almost literally transcribed by me from his reports. This is especially true of the alluvial parishes from Pointe Coupée to Terrebonne, and from Vermillion to Cameron; also as regards those lying along, and north of, the North Louisiana and Texas railroad. A few valuable data have also been obtained from the *Botanical reports* of Mr. A. Featherman, accompanying the reports above referred to.

Some data and soil specimens were also obtained by Special Agent Dr. R. H. Loughridge, on the route from Shreveport to Bastrop, on his return from the Indian territory in 1880.

Finally, some general information has been derived from the returned schedules of questions on cotton culture, sent out by the Census Office. From some cause, these responses have not been as numerous as could be desired, and, as a consequence, the cultural and commercial details from some portions of the state are very imperfect. It

·) See the following publications: On the Geology of Louisiana, and the Salt-dome Deposit of Petite Anse island, American Journal of Science, January, 1869 ; Final Memoir on same, Smithsonian Contr. to Science, No. 248, June, 1872. Preliminary Report of a Geological Reconnaissance of Louisiana, De Bow's Review, September, 1869; American Journal of Science, November, 1869. Report on the Geological Age of the Mississippi Delta (examination of the shells brought up from the artesian well bored at New Orleans in 1854). Report of U.S. Engineer Department, 1870. On the Geology of the Delta, and the Mud Lumps of the Passes of the Mississippi, American Journal of Science, vol. 1, 1871. On the Geological History of the Gulf of Mexico, ibid., December, 1871. On some points in the Geology of the Southwest, ibid., November, 1872. Supplementary and Final Report of a Geological Reconnaissance of Louisiana, New Orleans, 1873.

is perhaps to be regretted that sugar-cane and rice were not provided for in our inquiries, inasmuch as nearly the whole of southern Louisiana was thus thrown outside of the scope of our questions, and has furnished only meager reports or none at all in some parishes.

The following is the general arrangement of the subject-matter, adopted in this report:

1. The tabulated results of the enumeration, so far as they concern the production of cotton, form the opening portion of this report. For convenience of discussion, I have thought it best to place on one table only the data relating to areas, population, and the production of cotton, making a separate one serve for the comparison of the several crops. Among the latter, I have selected those which, being of prime necessity, influence in either a direct or inverse ratio the production of cotton. Corn (maize) and sweet potatoes are, almost throughout the cotton-growing states, considered next in importance to cotton, as being the staple food-crops, upon whose success and production, as compared to cotton, the question of profit and loss chiefly turns.

2. A brief general outline of the physical geography of the state.

3. Description of the several agricultural regions, with analyses of soils and discussion thereof.

4. Separate descriptions of the several parishes, grouped under the heads of the agricultural regions to which they predominantly belong. In determining the group to which parishes embracing several distinct agricultural features should be assigned, I have endeavored to follow popular usage, and the character of the chief areas of production, rather than mere predominance of area; but in some cases the grouping might perhaps as well have been made otherwise. Each parish-description is preceded by statistical data relating to area, population, distribution of woodland and other agricultural divisions, production of cotton and other chief crops. The figures regarding areas are the results of map measurements made with care in the case of regional fractions; and in view of the discrepancies existing between the various maps of the state, and the more or less uncertain location of the limits of the several agricultural areas, these figures have, as a rule, been placed at the number divisible by five, nearest to the one actually resulting from the measurement; thus avoiding an apparent pretense of accuracy greater than the state of our knowledge at present warrants. County areas, population, and production are, of course, given in accordance with the results of the Tenth Census. In the case of parishes (counties) from which schedules have been received, abstracts of the latter, embracing answers to schedule-questions 1 to 39 inclusive (i. e., those relating to the natural features and cotton production of the several soils), and those relating to the direction, mode, and cost of shipment, are appended.

5. A summary of the rest of the subject-matter of the schedules, relating to agricultural practice, is placed under headings embracing either one or several correlated questions; special answers are sometimes given, with the name of the parish from which the answer comes.

One point of great importance may, however, even now be noted and in a measure commented on. This is: the wide discrepancy between the capabilities of the soils of the several regions as reported by the inhabitants, and their *actual* production as resulting from a comparison of the acreage with the number of bales reported. The average weight of the latter, as given by the New Orleans Cotton Exchange, was, in 1879, about 475 pounds; and on this basis the fraction of bales and weight of lint produced per acre, as given in the tables, has been deduced; also, by multiplication by the number 3, the average product expressed in "seed-cotton". It will be seen from a comparison of the figures so obtained with those given in reports from the several parishes, that the actual product per acre varies usually between 60 and 50 per cent. of the product claimed, and only in few cases rises to 70 per cent., the latter in the case of the fresh soils of the river parishes.

This state of things may well give rise to serious reflections as to the causes of such wide discrepancies. Something may be credited to a natural and unconscious bias on the part of the reporters, to give the best possible account of their region, and, therefore, exceptional and maximum results, instead of averages, as showing what can be done under favorable circumstances. It is hardly to be regretted that this should be so, since the actual averages are easily obtained from the returns, and we are thus enabled to compare possibilities with actual performance.

Three chief causes present themselves as contributing to the result expressed in the latter, viz: unfavorable seasons; accidents from insects, diseases, overflows, &c.; and imperfect tillage and culture.

101

The first-mentioned cause is, of course, not controllable. The growing season of 1879 was somewhat dry, and a falling off of the cotton crop to the extent of one-third was a common estimate, though it may be questioned that it was justified by the general result. The second category already embraces much that is preventable by energetic and concerted action on the part of the producers. But even supposing that the crop of 1879 (which is the one to which the enumeration refers) was actually cut short by an unfavorable season, and accidents, to the extent claimed, there still remains a wide margin to be accounted for by the third cause, viz, imperfect culture.

Upon this point the answers given to the schedule-questions, and tabulated in Part III, throw important light. The shallow tillage and the rarity of fall-plowing, both tending to aggravate the washing away of the best portion of the soil by the winter-rains, are conspicuous among the probable factors; so far as tillage is concerned. As regards the general system of culture, the failure to rotate crops sufficiently, the imperfect return even of the cotton-seed to the soil, and the rarity of any effort to maintain its original productiveness by the other means known to advanced agriculture, are patent. It is a curious comment upon human nature, that the nearest approach to actual maintenance of the original product is found in some of the least productive regions, viz, in the pine flats of eastern Louisiana. Here the use of manure has already become a recognized part of the system, and the fact, that high production thus maintained pays better than to cultivate a large area of poor land, is being appreciated.

Many other interesting and important practical conclusions, that might be deduced from the data here given, are best left for a fuller consideration based upon more extended comparisons.

Very respectfully, your obedient servant,

EUGENE W. HILGARD.

102

TABULATED RESULTS OF THE ENUMERATION.

TABLE I.—AREA, POPULATION, TILLED LAND, AND COTTON PRODUCTION.
TABLE II.—PRODUCTION OF LEADING CROPS.

TABLE I.—AREA, POPULATION, TILLED LAND, AND COTTON PRODUCTION.

Parishes.	Areas.	POPULATION.						TILLED LAND.				COTTON PRODUCTION.			Product per acre.		
		Total population.	Male.	Female.	White.	Color'd.	Average per square mile.	Acres.	Average per square mile.	Per cent. of area.	Per cent. of tilled land in cotton.	Area in cotton.	Total bales (475 lbs.).	Bale.	Seed cotton.	Lint.	Cotton, acres per square mile.
	Sq. mls.											Acres.			Lbs.	Lbs.	
The State	45,420	939,946	468,754	471,192	454,954	484,992	20.7	2,507,895	55.2	8.6	34.9	864,787	508,569	0.59	540	280	19.0
ALLUVIAL REGION.																	
North of Red river.																	
East Carroll	400	12,134	6,325	5,809	1,023	11,111	30.3	56,793	142.0	22.2	70.7	40,167	38,180	0.95	1,353	451	100.4
West Carroll	380	2,776	1,402	1,374	1,339	1,437	7.3	10,071	26.5	4.1	54.7	5,517	4,012	0.73	1,041	347	14.5
Morehouse	842	14,206	7,086	7,120	3,547	10,659	16.9	57,279	68.1	10.6	49.8	28,590	23,481	0.82	1,170	390	34.0
Ouachita	640	14,685	7,384	7,301	4,502	10,183	22.9	48,947	76.3	11.9	50.5	20,040	18,729	0.64	912	304	48.4
Caldwell	535	5,767	2,886	2,881	2,870	2,897	10.8	18,267	34.1	5.3	54.8	9,919	6,504	0.96	936	313	18.5
Richland	578	8,440	4,430	4,010	5,161	5,279	14.6	31,409	54.3	8.5	50.2	15,809	11,831	0.74	1,053	351	27.3
Franklin	596	6,495	3,280	3,215	2,701	3,794	10.9	22,064	37.0	5.8	57.0	13,563	5,472	0.67	954	318	21.1
Madison	672	13,906	7,087	6,819	1,261	12,645	20.7	48,395	72.0	11.3	58.1	28,103	23,361	0.83	1,182	394	41.8
Tensas	612	17,815	9,039	8,776	1,071	16,344	29.1	78,679	126.6	20.1	64.3	50,555	41,959	0.83	1,182	394	82.6
Concordia	680	14,914	7,026	7,388	1,320	13,594	21.9	45,816	67.4	10.4	91.8	42,044	33,110	0.79	1,125	375	61.8
Catahoula	1,278	10,277	5,345	5,032	5,724	4,553	7.5	29,823	21.6	3.4	53.3	15,885	11,766	0.74	1,056	352	11.5
Total	7,313	121,415	61,696	59,725	29,019	92,396	16.6	447,883	61.2	9.6	62.2	278,192	221,115	0.79	1,125	375	38.0
South of Red river.																	
Avoyelles	862	16,747	8,065	8,682	8,483	8,264	19.7	84,787	99.5	15.6	26.0	22,722	18,255	0.77	1,098	366	27.8
Rapides	1,498	23,563	11,964	11,599	9,512	14,051	15.7	76,149	50.8	7.9	33.6	25,622	17,990	0.70	996	332	17.1
Pointe Coupée	575	17,785	9,102	8,683	4,785	13,000	30.9	56,394	98.4	15.4	42.6	24,136	18,935	0.78	1,110	370	42.0
West Baton Rouge	210	7,667	3,965	3,702	2,252	5,415	36.5	26,753	127.4	19.9	14.1	3,784	2,426	0.64	912	304	18.0
Iberville	646	17,544	8,892	8,652	4,784	12,760	27.2	42,122	65.2	10.2	1.8	771	579	0.75	1,068	356	1.2
Saint Martin	818	12,663	6,327	6,336	5,783	6,880	20.5	39,876	64.5	10.1	17.4	6,943	2,322	0.33	456	152	11.3
Assumption	227	17,010	8,631	8,379	8,938	8,072	52.0	36,511	111.7	17.4	0.8	295	119	0.42	600	200	0.8
Ascension	273	16,895	8,506	8,389	5,968	10,927	45.3	27,908	101.6	15.9	5.4	1,265	592	0.46	657	219	3.4
Saint James	208	14,714	7,630	7,064	4,850	9,864	47.8	54,975	177.5	27.7	.....	......	....	.....	......	......	....
Saint John Baptist	190	9,686	5,023	4,663	3,855	5,831	51.0	20,213	152.8	24.0	.....	......	....	.....	......	......	....
Saint Charles	264	7,161	3,719	3,442	1,401	5,760	25.2	21,171	74.5	11.6	.....	51	47	0.92	1,311	437	0.2
Total	5,681	161,435	82,434	79,011	60,611	100,824	27.5	508,750	86.0	13.4	17.1	86,586	61,275	0.71	1,011	337	14.7
Tide-water parishes.																	
Jefferson	395	13,166	6,184	5,962	4,864	7,302	30.8	19,767	50.0	7.8	.....	......	......	.....	......	......	....
Orleans	187	216,090	100,892	115,198	156,367	57,723	1,155.6	4,436	23.7	3.7	.....	7	12	1.71	2,436	812	.....
Saint Bernard	880	4,405	2,437	1,968	2,104	2,301	6.5	11,860	17.4	2.7	5.2	348	146	0.50	840	280	0.4
Plaquemines	930	11,575	6,242	5,338	4,254	7,321	13.4	36,906	39.7	6.2	.....	......	......	.....	......	......	....
Lafourche	1,024	19,113	9,761	9,352	11,282	7,831	18.7	44,802	43.7	6.8	.....	......	......	.....	......	......	....
Terrebonne	1,306	17,957	9,300	8,657	8,613	9,344	9.9	46,403	22.4	3.5	.....	......	......	.....	......	......	....
Saint Mary	648	19,891	10,564	9,327	6,717	13,174	30.7	86,326	103.4	16.0	.....	......	......	.....	......	......	....
Cameron	1,845	2,416	1,216	1,200	2,087	329	1.6	5,743	3.7	0.6	28.0	1,662	696	0.38	543	181	1.1
Total	7,215	303,613	146,596	157,017	196,288	105,325	42.1	230,235	31.9	5.0	0.8	1,917	794	0.41	585	195	0.3
BLUFF REGION.																	
West Feliciana	370	13,309	6,822	6,487	2,267	10,522	34.6	28,895	75.0	12.2	72.7	21,072	11,810	0.56	796	360	57.0
East Feliciana	453	13,192	7,341	7,791	4,497	10,695	31.9	53,218	108.1	16.9	54.2	28,389	11,098	0.39	555	185	58.7
East Baton Rouge	443	18,963	10,688	9,098	7,108	12,852	45.2	49,826	96.6	14.1	39.5	11,808	5,756	0.49	600	232	26.7
Total	1,355	37,999	24,731	24,175	13,885	33,984	37.5	131,228	97.1	15.2	49.4	61,548	28,664	0.47	666	223	47.5
ATTAKAPAS REGION.																	
Iberia	582	16,676	8,532	8,144	8,100	8,576	28.7	49,504	85.2	13.3	15.0	7,443	2,482	0.33	474	157	12.8
Lafayette	262	13,235	6,708	6,527	7,694	5,541	50.5	62,704	239.3	37.4	20.0	12,517	5,489	0.38	990	133	47.8
Saint Landry	2,276	40,004	20,538	19,466	20,473	19,531	17.6	197,370	60.4	9.4	30.7	42,135	23,148	0.55	783	261	18.3
Vermillion	1,226	8,728	4,364	4,364	5,771	1,957	7.1	25,330	20.7	3.2	9.4	2,379	597	0.33	327	109	1.9
Total	4,346	78,643	40,142	38,501	43,038	35,605	18.1	275,008	63.3	9.9	23.4	64,474	29,656	0.46	687	219	14.8
LONG-LEAF PINE REGION.																	
Calcasieu	3,400	12,484	6,473	6,011	9,919	2,565	3.7	14,003	4.1	0.6	10.7	1,468	514	0.34	498	166	0.4
Vernon	1,540	5,160	2,520	2,640	4,783	277	3.4	16,303	10.6	1.7	29.4	4,791	1,662	0.35	498	166	3.1
Grant	642	6,188	3,096	3,092	3,288	2,868	9.6	24,094	37.5	5.9	44.4	11,155	5,158	0.46	657	219	17.4
Winn	979	5,846	2,914	2,932	4,797	1,049	6.0	22,548	23.3	3.6	32.7	7,379	3,002	0.41	585	195	7.6
Livingston	600	5,258	2,694	2,564	4,353	905	8.8	10,467	17.4	2.7	37.0	3,876	1,344	0.35	498	166	6.5
Saint Helena	423	7,504	3,803	3,701	3,328	4,176	17.7	28,385	66.9	10.4	48.3	13,626	5,328	0.39	555	185	32.2
Tangipahoe	790	9,638	4,882	4,756	5,508	4,030	12.2	21,021	26.6	4.2	35.5	7,462	2,584	0.34	543	181	9.7
Saint Tammany	923	6,887	3,521	3,366	4,258	2,629	7.5	5,395	4.2	0.7	5.8	225	102	0.45	642	214	0.3
Washington	669	5,190	2,635	2,555	3,475	1,715	7.8	18,224	27.3	4.3	35.0	6,371	2,338	0.37	528	176	9.5
Total	9,966	64,155	32,538	31,617	43,753	20,402	6.4	156,840	16.0	2.5	35.6	56,309	22,382	0.40	570	190	5.7

TABLE I.—AREA, POPULATION, TILLED LAND, AND COTTON PRODUCTION—Continued.

Parishes.	Area.	POPULATION.						TILLED LAND.			COTTON PRODUCTION.						
		Total population.	Male.	Female.	White.	Color'd.	Average per square mile.	Acres.	Average per square mile.	Per cent. of area.	Per cent. of tilled land in cotton.	Area in cotton.	Total bales (475 lbs.).	Product per acre.			Cotton, acres per square mile.
														Bale.	Seed cotton.	Lint.	
OAK UPLANDS.	Sq. mls.											Acres.			Lbs.	Lbs.	
Sabine	1,008	7,344	3,691	3,653	5,486	1,858	7.3	18,524	18.4	2.9	32.1	5,932	2,313	0.39	535	185	5.9
Natchitoches	1,290	19,707	9,760	9,947	7,638	12,069	15.3	58,969	45.7	7.1	45.4	26,784	15,320	0.57	813	271	20.8
De Soto	856	15,003	7,722	7,881	5,116	10,487	18.2	82,239	96.1	15.0	46.0	37,807	11,298	0.30	426	142	44.2
Caddo	832	26,296	13,157	13,139	6,921	19,375	30.9	93,409	112.0	17.5	48.5	46,238	20,963	0.45	642	214	54.4
Bossier	773	16,042	8,189	7,853	3,256	12,786	20.8	69,430	89.8	14.0	53.5	37,122	25,074	0.68	969	323	48.3
Webster	612	10,005	5,143	4,862	4,822	5,683	16.3	42,402	69.3	10.7	38.7	16,461	6,255	0.38	543	181	26.8
Red River	386	8,573	4,347	4,226	2,507	6,066	22.2	33,930	87.9	13.7	56.6	19,200	11,512	0.60	856	283	49.7
Bienville	856	10,442	5,234	5,208	5,455	4,987	12.2	45,089	52.7	8.2	40.6	18,242	7,208	0.40	570	190	21.3
Jackson	590	5,328	2,636	2,692	2,925	2,403	9.0	26,604	45.1	7.0	38.1	10,138	3,753	0.37	528	176	17.2
Lincoln	465	11,075	5,555	5,520	6,177	4,896	22.8	108,084	222.9	34.8	21.2	22,990	9,723	0.42	600	209	47.4
Claiborne	796	18,837	9,460	9,377	8,541	10,296	23.7	126,000	158.3	24.7	36.0	46,567	19,568	0.42	600	200	58.5
Union	910	13,526	6,739	6,787	8,014	5,512	14.9	62,061	68.9	10.8	45.2	28,366	11,692	0.41	585	195	31.1
Total	9,414	162,778	81,633	81,145	66,358	96,430	17.3	769,331	81.7	12.8	41.0	315,760	144,683	0.46	657	219	33.5

TABLE II.—PRODUCTION OF LEADING CROPS.

Parishes.	COTTON.		SUGAR-CANE.			CORN.		SWEET POTATOES.		RICE.		OATS.	
	Acres.	Bales (475 lbs.).	Acres.	Sugar (hhds.).	Molasses (gallons).	Acres.	Bushels.	Acres.	Bushels.	Acres.	Pounds.	Acres.	Bushels.
ALLUVIAL REGION.													
North of Red river.													
East Carroll	40,157	28,180				7,115	125,691	15	925			15	250
West Carroll	5,517	4,012				3,868	58,062	27	3,545			9	215
Morehouse	28,590	28,481	78		10,601	17,846	288,294	496	19,156			301	3,566
Ouachita	29,040	18,729	36		4,100	13,142	130,993	379	22,810			143	1,158
Caldwell	9,919	6,304	39		2,192	5,717	53,312	182	17,609	3	2,625	188	1,016
Richland	15,809	11,631	3		455	9,878	140,855	66	6,643			19	195
Franklin	12,963	8,472				7,295	100,708	149	20,670			94	1,290
Madison	26,103	23,391				7,797	127,459	140	5,830			15	250
Tensas	50,855	41,850				11,427	205,797	271	23,892				
Concordia	42,044	35,110				6,114	109,333	162	16,098			7	75
Catahoula	15,835	11,766	24		2,100	11,094	134,083	264	23,161			35	509
Total	278,192	221,115	180		20,448	100,734	1,473,557	2,151	173,337	3	2,625	826	9,216
South of Red river.													
Avoyelles	23,722	18,355	800	1,374	90,635	21,402	456,039	510	36,917	178	201,300	13	340
Rapides	25,622	17,990	1,875	1,892	134,531	29,366	488,270	322	26,814	2	923	108	2,481
Pointe Coupée	24,136	18,235	6,027	4,933	334,985	14,817	305,470	188	11,962			5	75
West Baton Rouge	3,784	2,426	6,400	5,225	471,385	7,262	170,591	68	4,554			17	340
Iberville	771	279	16,687	15,279	1,220,515	11,991	331,596	52	3,431	5,129	3,196,500	16	230
Saint Martin	3,942	2,322	3,525	3,253	151,617	11,283	211,995	412	36,427	7	3,187		
Assumption	285	119	12,945	11,931	789,898	14,055	356,995	138	9,022	1,420	226,880	6	40
Ascension	1,285	592	15,545	13,497	844,381	6,112	110,137	341	14,103	616	323,001	38	380
Saint James			15,227	14,251	1,017,352	11,303	189,700	129	12,595	5,870	2,718,586		
Saint John Baptist			9,453	9,614	586,562	2,888	89,906	3	148	696	501,900		
Saint Charles	51	47	7,787	8,802	560,755	1,287	11,915	28	1,829	1,320	609,943		
Total	86,598	61,276	94,561	91,105	6,295,800	131,762	2,622,714	2,011	151,194	13,236	6,794,450	266	3,976
TIDE-WATER PARISHES.													
Jefferson			6,196	6,041	529,620	2,065	30,210	88	4,252	1,841	825,774		
Orleans	7	13	1,162	864	72,300	35	310	48	2,189	1,332	1,229,240		
Saint Bernard	248	146	2,879	3,373	149,580	395	6,945	215	11,572	1,807	1,027,200		
Plaquemines			12,684	14,017	970,324	1,767	30,469	46	855	10,181	6,909,904		
Lafourche			12,349	11,185	822,943	16,018	292,968	321	27,362	9,782	4,592,334		
Terrebonne			15,390	13,751	897,855	14,338	291,833	480	30,406	705	307,554		
Saint Mary			17,306	16,536	913,842	11,302	216,074	136	5,568				
Cameron	1,662	636	51	10	3,087	2,726	43,355	184	13,991	12	7,050		
Total	1,917	794	67,947	65,777	4,360,652	48,646	905,764	1,507	96,213	25,610	14,799,106		
BLUFF REGION.													
West Feliciana	21,972	11,810	29	4	7,220	9,000	140,595	271	20,712	5	5,000	64	1,425
East Feliciana	28,368	11,098	169	9	18,520	16,522	206,907	1,067	57,394	19	7,226	501	7,752
East Baton Rouge	11,308	5,756	3,584	3,366	292,650	11,735	211,449	443	27,727	6	750	218	3,453
Total	61,348	28,664	3,775	3,379	318,390	37,287	558,951	1,781	105,833	30	12,976	783	12,630
ATTAKAPAS REGION.													
Iberia	7,443	2,462	6,501	6,399	297,654	23,760	506,430	917	54,413	83	21,380	165	1,270
Lafayette	12,517	8,489	788	631	30,589	21,713	350,904	469	27,905	110	40,063		
Saint Landry	43,135	23,148	3,711	2,677	190,927	57,411	831,181	1,376	62,643	356	246,543	21	1,725
Vermilion	2,379	557	1,574	1,295	66,672	13,554	166,709	360	14,440	606	368,022	7	66
Total	64,474	29,656	11,569	11,202	586,152	116,418	1,856,924	3,122	160,301	1,605	676,609	283	3,061
LONG-LEAF PINE REGION.													
Calcasieu	1,492	514	87	28	3,676	7,995	98,317	517	40,234	600	367,234	327	3,057
Vernon	4,791	1,662	22		2,870	8,230	74,224	284	32,838	31	10,985	582	5,083
Grant	11,156	5,156				6,177	95,179	22	1,890				
Winn	7,279	3,002	41		3,730	5,588	81,951	350	27,024	4	4,000	986	7,931
Livingston	3,876	1,344	137	48	8,989	2,936	33,911	290	35,122	166	81,050	91	975
Saint Helena	13,926	5,228	114	1	10,147	10,340	152,775	661	52,775	68	23,722	1,115	11,053
Tangipahoa	7,932	2,934	396	136	42,346	6,617	82,268	677	61,962	248	194,080	3,256	24,944
Saint Tammany	225	102	90	14	7,513	1,224	16,086	441	30,202	127	49,719	108	1,370
Washington	6,971	2,333	68		7,210	7,974	85,306	480	43,561	264	166,915	1,793	15,936
Total	86,596	22,382	925	234	87,181	53,371	699,807	3,721	324,988	1,508	898,475	7,908	70,349

COTTON PRODUCTION IN LOUISIANA.

TABLE II.—PRODUCTION OF LEADING CROPS—Continued.

Parishes.	COTTON.		SUGAR-CANE.			CORN.		SWEET POTATOES.		RICE.		OATS.	
	Acres.	Bales (475 lbs.).	Acres.	Sugar (hhds.).	Molasses (gallons).	Acres.	Bushels.	Acres.	Bushels.	Acres.	Pounds.	Acres.	Bushels.
OAK UPLANDS.													
Sabine	5,962	2,212	85	....	9,589	7,971	60,897	191	19,821	2	1,000	427	4,856
Natchitoches	26,784	15,820	28	....	1,875	17,871	151,945	197	19,541	3	1,500	362	8,211
De Soto	27,807	11,296	34	9	2,897	31,080	156,965	732	54,526	....	....	618	5,200
Caddo	44,228	20,962	1	....	52	28,169	156,118	815	25,209	1	600	446	4,100
Bossier	37,133	25,075	7	....	444	20,152	176,620	175	12,458	....	....	1,041	13,725
Webster	16,401	6,355	120	16	10,409	14,894	126,270	336	36,545	....	....	2,556	29,617
Red River	19,200	11,512	9	....	1,042	10,596	52,250	88	9,009	....	....	88	1,065
Bienville	18,242	7,205	108	....	11,067	19,255	117,293	305	24,019	....	....	2,004	13,912
Jackson	10,138	2,753	52	....	5,155	9,372	63,049	206	20,465	....	....	1,543	10,615
Lincoln	23,900	9,723	223	....	36,903	21,602	150,165	265	20,543	....	....	2,654	17,071
Claiborne	46,567	19,566	99	....	10,115	42,930	323,188	471	44,736	....	....	4,394	28,175
Union	28,208	11,592	60	....	5,261	26,551	197,302	229	18,034	....	....	1,097	7,861
Total	315,760	144,522	895	19	88,625	244,584	1,772,572	5,020	307,044	6	4,000	17,428	130,708
Total for the State	964,787	508,569	121,592	171,706	11,606,242	742,728	9,889,689	17,923	1,212,110	42,000	23,163,211	26,361	229,849

PART I.

PHYSICO-GEOGRAPHICAL AND AGRICULTURAL FEATURES

OF THE

STATE OF LOUISIANA.

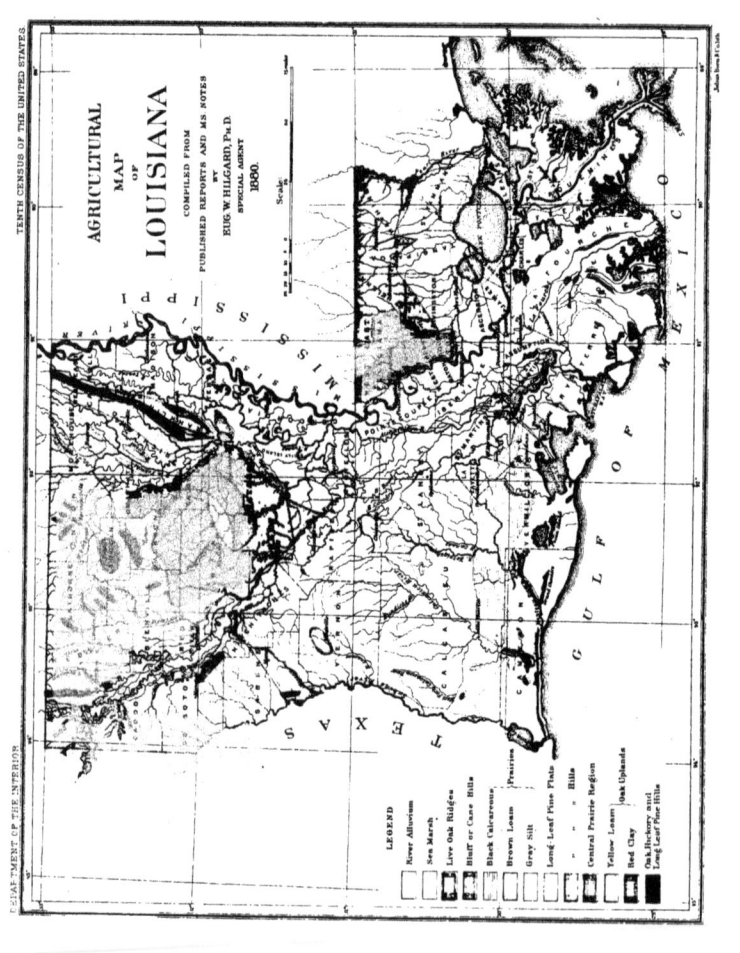

AGRICULTURAL
MAP
OF
LOUISIANA

COMPILED FROM
PUBLISHED REPORTS AND MS NOTES
BY
EUG. W. HILGARD, Ph.D.
SPECIAL AGENT
1880.

Scale:

LEGEND

River Alluvium
Sea Marsh
Live Oak Ridges
Bluff or Cane Hills
Black Calcareous
Brown Loam
Gray Silt
Long-Leaf Pine Flats
Hills
Central Prairie Region
Yellow Loam
Oak Uplands
Red Clay
Oak, Hickory and
Long-Leaf Pine Hills

MISSISSIPPI

TEXAS

GULF OF MEXICO

OUTLINE OF THE PHYSICAL GEOGRAPHY

OF THE

STATE OF LOUISIANA.

Louisiana is situated between the meridians of 89° and 94° W. longitude, and between the parallels of 28° 56′ and 33° N. latitude. By far its greater portion (about 37,030 square miles) lies west of the Mississippi river. There is a not inconsiderable uncertainty in respect to its total area, which is commonly given at 41,346 square miles; but according to map measurements lately made, is greater by several thousand square miles, viz, about 45,420 square miles, exclusive of fresh-water lakes, land-locked bays, and of lake Pontchartrain; of this area about 20,100 square miles is lowland belonging to the alluvium of the Mississippi and Red rivers, and to the marsh region of the coast; the rest, or over one-half of the state, being uplands of varying character.

CLIMATE.—Owing to its nearness to the Gulf of Mexico and the prevalence of winds from that direction, the climate of Louisiana is much less extreme than that of the states lying farther north; the summer heat being less oppressive, though more prolonged, and the winter's average temperature (52.8° at New Orleans, 45.4° at Shreveport) very mild, though liable at times to sudden and severe "cold snaps" brought on by northwesterly storms, which restrict the culture of tropical fruits on a large scale to the immediate neighborhood of the Gulf coast. On such occasions the temperature may fall to 17° even at New Orleans, and to 15° in northern Louisiana. November, December, and January are the coldest months—June, July, and August the hottest; the temperature ranging from 74° to 98°, with a mean of 81.6° at New Orleans, while at Shreveport the range of temperature within the same months is from 64° to 95°, with a mean of about 81°.

The rain-fall at New Orleans amounts to nearly 73 inches annually; at Shreveport about 47 only, but increases slightly toward the Mississippi valley. At New Orleans the rain-fall is most copious during the three hottest months, and somewhat less during the three coldest; during both, about 40 inches of rain-fall is received, the rest of the annual precipitation being more or less evenly distributed over the spring and autumn. The summer rains frequently come accompanied by violent thunder-storms from the northwest; but the southwest is the regular rain wind. The same holds true, more or less, all over the state, the regular summer showers being considered as highly conducive to the welfare of the cotton crop, providing they are not too much prolonged at any one time.

GEOLOGICAL FEATURES.—The figures given above show sufficiently the incorrectness of the impression, very generally prevailing, that Louisiana is "wholly alluvial". Even as regards population, a comparison of that of the alluvial region with that of the upland portion of the state, exhibits the fact that nearly forty-seven per cent. of the entire population, outside of the city of New Orleans, belongs to the uplands, and that among this portion is found not less than six-tenths of the rural white population of the state.

Strictly speaking, even a large portion of the flood plains of the Mississippi and Red rivers is not properly alluvial, the soils being directly derived from deposits formed at a time considerably anterior to the existence of the present river channels. Such is the case with the greater part of the heavy "buckshot" soils which occupy the portions of the bottom where certain strata of dark-colored clay come to the surface. These clays underlie the entire plain, from the Gulf coast as high as Memphis and Shreveport, at depths varying from one to forty feet; and appear to be absent only where the river or its branches have cut them away. They appear to have been deposited at a time when the whole of the valleys was one continuous swamp, without any very definite channels.(a)

These "buckshot" clays are but the older portion of the "Champlain" formation (most definitely exhibited at the Port Hudson bluff), whose higher strata form the "bluff-lands" and "cane-hills" on the eastern border of the Mississippi trough, and the Attakapas prairies, as well as the "Five Islands" in southwestern Louisiana.

---

a See on this subject the writer's "Memoir on the Geology of Lower Louisiana and the Rock-Salt Deposit of Petite Anse", in Smithsonian Contr. Sci., No. 248; also papers in the Amer. Jour. Sci.

North of these prairies, and participating in the general southward dip of the formations of the state, there appear at or near the surface the beds of sand and gravel belonging to the "Stratified Drift"; and these are found capping especially the higher ridges which occur more or less abundantly all over the upland portion of the state. They are seen in the bed of the Mississippi river just above the Port Hudson bluff, but rise northward and form part, or sometimes almost the whole, of the high "bluffs" on either side of the valley. The brown and black sandstone fragments, so common on the crests of sandy ridges in northwestern Louisiana, belong to this drift formation, whose most southern exposure of gravel is found overlying the salt deposit of Petite Anse.

North of the sand and gravel belt bordering the prairies and pine flats, we reach the territory of the Tertiary formations. The most southerly (and therefore newest) of these is the "Grand Gulf" group of blue, green, and white clays and claystones, and clay-sandstones. These rise into high ridges as we advance northward in the parishes of Vernon, Sabine, Natchitoches, Grant, and Catahoula, forming a prominent hilly belt across the state, and terminating in the remarkable hills of Sicily island (see below).

Northward again of this transverse ridge we find, in Sabine, Grant, and Catahoula parishes, a narrow belt, within which the calcareous marls and limestones of the marine Tertiary ("Vicksburg and Jackson") groups approach the surface, and form a country more or less spotted with small prairies ("Central prairie region"). This belt abuts in high ridges on the valley of the Washita in Caldwell parish (see below), and here chiefly the huge fossil bones of the zeuglodon are found.

So far, the geological strata show a definite dip southward to the Gulf; but northward of the prairie belt the dip seems to relate more or less to a (mostly subterranean) ridge or "backbone" of older rocks—Cretaceous limestone—which appears to extend from the prairie region of southwestern Arkansas, in a southeast direction, diagonally across western Louisiana, marking approximately the "divide" between the Washita and Red rivers, and reaching the Gulf shore at the rock-salt deposit of Petite Anse, which undoubtedly is a part of the same formation as that from which, in northern Louisiana, numerous salt springs flow. These springs or "licks" occur in flats in Webster, Bienville, and Winn parishes; some of them have been utilized for the manufacture of salt, and in all of them the Cretaceous limestone is found within a short distance from the surface, and of great thickness. Near Winfield this limestone rises into a ridge 75 feet above the surrounding country. A similar ridge, but much lower, exists near Chicotville, in St. Landry parish. It is again found overlying the great sulphur bed in the artesian wells of Calcasieu, but at a depth of 300 feet; and it will doubtless be struck below the rock-salt bed of Petite Anse.

Around these outcropping summits of the Cretaceous ridge are found (in northwestern Louisiana) fossiliferous rocks, mostly ferruginous and red, or sometimes calcareous, of Tertiary age (Upper Claiborne or Lower Jackson group). Between the more or less isolated knolls or ridges of this character (forming what is known as the "Red Lands"), the country is generally more level, and underlaid by strata of dark-colored clays and sands, frequently associated with beds of lignite, and more rarely with limited seams of fresh-water limestone. Such is, more or less, the geological character of all the uplands of eastern Louisiana, northward of the central belt of calcareous prairies above alluded to; the upper portions of the ridges being here, as elsewhere, composed of, or capped by, the irregularly-bedded sands of the Stratified Drift. On the ridge lands lying between the Mississippi and the Washita, in northeastern Louisiana, the sandy materials of the Port Hudson bluff seem to cover the Tertiary strata.

The well-waters obtained within the latter are apt to be somewhat hard from lime and magnesian salts, and sometimes fetid, where dark-colored clays or lignites underlie.

RIVERS AND DRAINAGE.—The prominent feature of the state is that it embraces the widest part of the alluvial plain, as well as the delta, of the great Mississippi river. The area of the alluvial and marsh lands properly derivable from that river is about 13,635 square miles; that of the bottoms of the other larger streams, before their entrance into the valley, about 1,725 square miles; that of marsh lands west of the delta, 4,225 square miles; other minor swamp and alluvial and marsh areas, about 625 square miles; forming an aggregate of 19,200 square miles, or not quite one-half of the area of the state.

Almost all the larger streams of this alluvial region diverge from the main Mississippi, or from Red river, and hence receive the name of "bayous". They constitute so many additional outlets for the water of the main rivers in time of flood, and form an intricate network, whose cross-connections, and even the direction of current under different circumstances, are not easily realized or remembered. Some one of the larger bayous is found flowing, as a rule, along the edge of the bottom plain, at the foot of the uplands (Washita river north, and bayous Bœuf, Cocodrie, and Tèche south, of Red river).

The delta proper forms an approximately semi-circular projection about 70 miles beyond the general coast line (drawn from about the mouth of Pearl river to Côte Blanche bay); and beyond this still, the present mouths or "passes" of the main river stretch about 35 miles to seaward, forming the curious "Goose Foot", a form of mouth, of which, with its attendant "mudlumps", the Mississippi river furnishes the only example thus far known. A belt of marsh 20 to 30 miles wide forms the outer and much-broken edge of the delta, and a few low, outlying islands are off-shore. A similar marsh-belt borders the mainland from Vermilion bay to the Sabine, with an unbroken shore line, and altogether without islands.

Next to the Mississippi river and its alluvial plain, Red river and its valley, extending from the northwest corner to the middle (north and south) of the state, forms the most prominent feature of the topography of Louisiana. Its entrance into the main valley is popularly considered the point of division between "north" and "south" Louisiana, since, on the river at least, it marks the beginning of sugar-cane culture, and a gradual decrease of cotton production to the southward.

The valley of the Washita river, though in reality extensive, is so soon merged into those of the bayous branching out from the Mississippi river in southeastern Arkansas, that its individuality is, in a measure, lost. That of the Sabine is too little known and settled to attract attention.

The upland portion of the state is naturally divided into three main bodies, to wit: 1. The portion lying between the Mississippi valley and Red river, north of the latter stream. 2. The area south of Red river, between it, the Sabine, and the coast marshes. 3. The uplands of eastern Louisiana, lying between the Mississippi and Pearl rivers.

The rivers of the northern section flow either southeastward into the Washita (D'Arbonne, Castor, Dugdemona, and their branches); or southward into Red river (Bodeau, Dorchite, Black lake, Saline). Those of the southern section (apart from small tributaries of the Sabine river), into the Gulf of Mexico; the Mentau and Calcasieu being the chief ones.

The streams of eastern Louisiana have a southeast trend, and empty either into lakes Maurepas and Pontchartrain (Amite, Tickfaw, Tangipahoa, Tchefunctee), or into Pearl river (Bogue Chitto).

ELEVATION ABOVE THE SEA.—From the coast marshes, lying at high-water level, the surface of the Mississippi delta rises to about 15 feet above mean Gulf level in the latitude of New Orleans. Near Baton Rouge, at the head of the delta proper, the maximum elevation is about 34 feet; at the mouth of Red river, nearly 50 feet; near Natchez, 66 feet; on the Arkansas line, about 130 feet; the average fall of the river between the two last-named points being not quite four inches per mile. The above figures are those given for high-water level at the respective points, when usually a few high points on the immediate river banks remain above water. From these banks there is a more or less rapid downward slope to the landward edge of the bottom plain, as stated more in detail farther on.

South of the parallel of 30° 45' (about the latitude of Port Hudson) the surface of the uplands is, almost throughout, apparently level, but in reality ascends gradually to an elevation of 100 to 150 feet above tide-level at its northern limit. This level country is partly treeless (Attakapas prairies), partly timbered more or less densely, chiefly with the long-leaf pine (pine flats of Calcasieu, and of eastern Louisiana).

North of the line above given, the uplands become more rolling, in places hilly and broken (southern Rapides, Vernon, southern Natchitoches), and are timbered almost throughout. The timber tree prevailing almost altogether in the middle and southern portion of western Louisiana, as well as in eastern Louisiana, is the long-leaf pine; while the northwestern parishes (north of a line laid through Manny, Sabine parish, and Bastrop, Morehouse parish), form a region of rolling oak-uplands, whose varying fertility is indicated by a greater or less admixture of the short-leaf pine on the one hand, and of hickory on the other.

As regards the general elevation of the uplands of northern Louisiana, the highest ridges in Claiborne and Union parishes probably rise as much as 500 feet above the sea. The highest point traversed by the line of the North Louisiana and Texas railroad (Arcadia) lies about 390 feet above the Gulf of Mexico.

AGRICULTURAL SUBDIVISIONS OR REGIONS.—In accordance with the prominent and easily recognized characteristics given above, the agricultural features of the state may conveniently be considered under the following general subdivisions:

1. *The Alluvial Region*, subdivided into—
    a. The alluvial region north of Red river.
    b. The alluvial region of Red river.
    c. The alluvial region south of Red river.
    d. The marsh region of the coast and lakes.
2. *The Bluff Region of western Louisiana.*
3. *The Attakapas Prairie Region*, embracing the three features of—
    a. The black calcareous prairie.
    b. The brown loam prairie.
    c. The gray silt, or pine prairie.
4. *The Long-leaf Pine Region*, subdivided into—
    a. The pine flats.
    b. The pine hills.
5. *The Central Prairie Region.*
6. *The Oak Uplands Region*, with four chief soil-varieties, viz—
    a. The red lands.
    b. The brown loam or table lands.
    c. The pale yellow loam lands.
    d. The gray pine flats.

8 C P

Of these four soil varieties, only the red land areas are sufficiently well defined to admit of being mapped even approximately; the rest being intricately interspersed, with all degrees of transition from each to the others.

THE ALLUVIAL REGION.

The alluvial portion of Louisiana, including therein both the marine and the river alluvium, embraces about 19,200 square miles, or nearly one-half of the area of the state, and by far its most fertile agricultural lands; equaled by few, and surpassed by none in the world in productive capacity, whenever the waters of the rivers that traverse them shall have been put under such control that their annual rise, instead of being, as now, a dreaded scourge, shall be the means of assuring the success of crops beyond peradventure, and of maintaining permanently the fertility of the soils, as those of the Nile have done in Egypt from time immemorial.

For the purpose of description, the alluvial territory of Louisiana may be conveniently classified into these four divisions:

1. Region north of the mouth of Red river.
2. Alluvial region of Red river.
3. Alluvial region south of Red river.
4. Tide-water region of the coast and lakes.

I.—THE ALLUVIAL REGION NORTH OF RED RIVER.

Of the parishes comprehended within these limits, only East Carroll, Madison, Tensas, and Concordia are wholly alluvial; the rest—Morehouse, West Carroll, Richland, Franklin—consist in part of upland ridges, isolated from the main body of the uplands of northern Louisiana by the broad and fertile alluvial tracts bordering the Washita river and bayous Bartholomew and Boeuf. The latter lands are claimed by their inhabitants to be at least equal in fertility to any in the state; while the ridges alluded to are on the whole, even as uplands, of inferior quality, being largely timbered with scrubby black-jack and post oaks, mingled with black gum and more or less of the short-leaf pine: the latter sometimes predominating altogether on the poorer portions.

Thus, in traveling westward from the Mississippi on the Arkansas line, the level alluvium continues for about 8 miles; when, after crossing the bayou Maçon and Tiger bayou, there is a sudden rise into pine uplands with a sandy loam soil. This is the upper end of the *Bayou Maçon hills*, here 8 miles wide, which hence extend 80 miles to the southward, widening to 20 miles near Winnsboro, Franklin parish. Crossing this ridge we descend into the alluvial plain of the bayou Boeuf, also about 8 miles in width, and profusely fertile. Traversing this bottom we reach uplands once more, viz, the northern portion of the ridgy tract occupying a large part of Morehouse parish and known as the *Bastrop hills*, whose width on the state line is but a little over 4 miles, but increases to nearly double during a southwest course of 34 miles. Westward of this upland ridge lies the alluvial plain of the bayou Bartholomew, about 4 miles wide, which again is separated from the bottom of Washita river by a tongue of ridgy land reaching in from Ashley county, Arkansas, to near the junction of the two streams.

The Washita river borders, on the east, the main body of the uplands of northern Louisiana, and its alluvium forms part of the (largely upland) parishes of Union, Ouachita, Caldwell, and Catahoula.

The soil of these ridges, as may be inferred from the timber growth they bear, is prevalently of the character of the "pale sandy loam" soil described as prevailing extensively in northern Louisiana. The sandy or silty pine-flat soil is also represented quite extensively.

Of these three upland peninsulas, the most westerly one, between the Washita and bayou Bartholomew (90 square miles), is the smallest and, on the whole, the least fertile; much of the soil being quite sandy, with an indifferent growth of scrub oaks and short-leaf pine. There are some "prairies" on it, partly with a sandy soil, partly a whitish clayey silt, with ferruginous dots or concretions. The former are very poor, while the latter will probably here, as on the same tract in Ashley county, Arkansas, be found capable of profitable cultivation when properly drained. Seymour's and Dubute prairies are the principal ones, the latter being liable to the Washita overflow.

The middle one of the three upland tracts, the Bastrop hills, rising as much as 50 and 60 feet above the bottom plain, and embracing an area of about 200 square miles, is, on the whole, perhaps, the most fertile; being mostly gently rolling uplands, with a yellow loam soil, timbered with black-jack and post oaks, black gum, hickory, and some short-leaf pine on the uplands, and wide bottoms densely wooded with sweet gum and cypress. The cotton product of these uplands, when fresh, is from 450 to 500 pounds of seed-cotton per acre. The western slope, toward bayou Bartholomew, is gentle, but there is a bluff descent toward the bayou Boeuf; along the foot of this eastern slope lie prairies Mer Rouge and Jefferson. These are fine, fertile tracts, of a few sections each, largely with a black loam soil underlaid by red or yellow loam subsoil, and entirely above overflow; hence, they are nearly all under cultivation. They have little tree growth, save a few clumps of hawthorn, and there was a great deal of sumac (*Rhus copallina*), from the autumnal tints of which the name of "Mer Rouge" was derived.

114

The most easterly and most extensive of the three ridges, embracing nearly 24 townships, or 842 square miles, is likewise highest and most abrupt on its eastern border, in the "Bayou Maçon hills", which rise 15 to 25 feet above the alluvial plain. In the northern half of its course, the eastern flank of this belt bears a strip of pine (short-leaf in the northern, long-leaf in the southern portion), which then trends farther west and surrounds the town of Winnsboro, where it is 5 miles wide. The rolling country lying to the westward of this pine belt, in Richland and Franklin parishes, resembles the Bastrop hills in its soil, timber growth, and agricultural qualities. But the southern portion of the Bayou Maçon hills proper, lying to eastward of the pine belt, has a rich brown loam subsoil, and resembles in its timber growth and agricultural value the "bluff" part of Sicily island, presently to be noticed.

The uplands belt extends close to the fork of Boeuf river and Deer creek, whose alluvium here is quite narrow. Across the Boeuf, in the fork between it and the Washita, there is a narrow loam upland ridge, about 18 miles in length, extending into the fork of the two rivers.

Sicily island, surrounded by the waters of Washita, Deer creek, and bayous Maçon and Tensas, is about 25 miles long and about 12 in average width. About two-thirds of this is low, overflowed bottom lands, while the rest, adjoining the Washita river, is partly abrupt and rocky long-leaf pine hills (the only tract of this kind east of the Washita), partly (on the eastern foot of the hill lands) a level bluff plateau, 20 to 25 feet above overflow, and quite similar in its soil, timber, and agricultural features to the "bluff" lands of West Feliciana and East Baton Rouge. Its southern portion especially is esteemed to be one of the most fertile upland tracts of Louisiana, and is covered with large cotton plantations, whose usual product is nearly one bale of lint per acre. The natural timber growth is exceptionally vigorous and dense, consisting of a great variety of oaks, beech, tulip tree ("poplar"), magnolias, sweet gum, ash, &c., with a great abundance of grapevines. In the northern portion the bluff lands are not so fertile, resembling altogether the Bayou Maçon hills.

On the mainland opposite, at the foot of the pine hills of Catahoula and Rapides, we find in Catahoula prairie (at the north end of Catahoula lake) and Hollowell's prairie (between Saline bayou and Red river) isolated tracts of lands somewhat similar to prairie Mer Rouge, on the edge of the Bastrop hills (see above), but not quite so productive, the soil being partly a whitish silt, with ferruginous "black gravel". Hollowell's prairie passes to the westward into a level oak plateau, from which a gradual admixture of pine forms a transition to the pine hills.

In this connection should be mentioned the Avoyelles prairie, the only outlier of upland in the alluvial region south of Red river, and forming on the banks of that river the last bluff bank seen in descending it. It lies directly opposite the Hollowell's prairie region, and the two are not unlike in their soil and general character. The Avoyelles prairie, while on the one hand resembling the bluff lands at Port Hudson, is on the other also closely related to the "brown loam prairie" of the Opelousas region.

The character of the parishes fronting on the Mississippi river, north of the parish of Avoyelles, has been sufficiently described above (see "Features of the alluvial plain of the Mississippi below the mouth of the Ohio", et seq.), and differs from that of the parishes south of the mouth of Red river in having, on the whole, a smaller proportion of swamp areas, and hence a larger one of land reclaimable by simple exclusion of the annual overflows.

The lands of the Tensas river are especially noted as yielding large crops of high-grade cotton; and being largely of the heavy black "buckshot" clay character, they may well be deemed almost inexhaustible. Most of this land is originally heavily timbered; but at some points, where it becomes very calcareous, it forms limited prairies, with clumps of locust, crab, and plum, which are also highly productive, and, notwithstanding the clayeyness of their soil, quite easily tilled. Details regarding these parishes will be found in Part II, under the proper heads.

Soils of the alluvial region above the mouth of Red river.

No detailed examinations or analyses of the soils forming the main body of the alluvial plain of the Mississippi in Louisiana have as yet been made. There can be little doubt, however, that they are substantially similar to those of the Yazoo bottom, lying opposite; and a table of analyses made of the latter is therefore here subjoined.

Analyses of soils from the Yazoo bottom, Mississippi.

No. 395. *Soil of the "Dogwood ridge"*, a belt of land above overflow, running from Moon lake near Delta, Coahoma county, to Honey island, Holmes county. The specimen was taken on the plantation of Gov. J. L. Alcorn, between Swan lake and Cypress brake, Coahoma county. The vegetation is dogwood, sweet gum, holly, ash, sassafras, and what is called "prickly pear" by the inhabitants. The soil is a light sandy loam, pale yellow in color, and shows no change to the depth of two feet; represented by the sample analyzed. It is easily tilled, and quite as productive as the darker bottom soils. When turned up and exposed to the sun, it turns dark like the other soils.

No. 396. *A light "buckshot" clay*, taken from the edge of a depression or pond, near where the preceding specimen was obtained. It is light yellow in color, and similar to the clay in the bank of Sunflower river.

Nos. 376 and 377. *Soil and subsoil of front-land of Indian bayou*, taken near C. Gillespie's, range 5 west, township 19, section 33, Sunflower county. The soil is grayish and rather sandy, and was taken to the depth of 5 inches. The subsoil is close, whitish clay with reddish flecks, and less "jointy" than the same clay from Sunflower river and Silver creek. The specimen was taken to the depth of 5 to 18 inches. The timber-growth is hickory, holly, sweet gum, water, willow, red, and swamp-chestnut oaks, dogwood, ash, maple, and an undergrowth of cane. This "white" land is not much esteemed by farmers.

No. 354. *Bottom soil of the Tallahatchie river*, range 1 east, township 24, Tallahatchie county, taken to the depth of 12 inches. A dark-colored and rather light loam, a good representative of the front-lands of the upper Yazoo, Tallahatchie, and Cold-Water bottoms.

No. 394. *Soil of Sunflower river front-land ridge*, taken on the bank at Buck's ferry, Issaquena county. It is a stiff, pale gray loam, with yellowish or orange flecks, so that when worked up the soil is somewhat yellow. Specimen taken to the depth of 10 inches; it is underlaid at 4 to 6 feet by "buckshot" clay. The prominent trees are sweet gum, maple, willow oak, elm, ash, and hackberry.

No. 390. *"Buckshot" soil of Deer creek back-land*, from the plantation of J. D. Hill, near Steel's bayou, Issaquena county. It is a stiff, dark-colored clay soil, traversed by numerous cracks, and mottled with spots of ferruginous matter. Upon drying it breaks up into little angular fragments. It is exceedingly fertile and there is no change in its character for 10 feet. The timber growth is sweet gum, pecan, water and willow oak, hackberry, and honey locust; an undergrowth of cane covers most of the land. The specimen was taken to the depth of 12 inches.

Yazoo bottom soils.

	COAHOMA COUNTY.		TALLAHATCHIE COUNTY.	SUNFLOWER COUNTY.		ISSAQUENA COUNTY.	
	Dogwood ridge soil.	Light colored "buckshot" clay.	Tallahatchie bottom soil.	Indian bayou front-land soil.	Indian bayou front-land subsoil.	Sunflower river front-land soil.	Deer creek "buckshot" soil.
	No. 395.	No. 396.	No. 354.	No. 276.	No. 277.	No. 394.	No. 390.
Insoluble matter........................	83.886 } 90.908	75.512 } 86.406	87.146 } 91.944	87.896 } 91.934	87.896 } 91.714	71.164 } 84.670	51.063 } 71.767
Soluble silica...........................	7.022	10.895	4.798	4.038	3.818	13.506	20.704
Potash................................	0.292	0.606	0.301	0.226	0.305	0.401	1.204
Soda...................................	0.086	0.145	0.084	0.116	0.079	0.191	0.235
Lime..................................	0.259	0.386	0.901	0.153	0.147	0.406	1.340
Magnesia..............................	0.596	0.972	0.385	0.256	0.392	0.696	1.065
Brown oxide of manganese..............	0.086	0.138	0.188	0.048	0.050	0.011	0.119
Peroxide of iron.......................	2.691	2.804	2.130	1.848	2.812	3.345	5.818
Alumina...............................	3.692	4.437	2.151	2.565	3.996	6.889	10.529
Phosphoric acid........................	0.143	0.278	0.112	0.162	0.283	0.185	0.304
Sulphuric acid.........................	0.010	0.007	0.005	0.042	....	0.016	0.034
Water and organic matter..............	2.007	4.401	2.644	3.013	1.499	2.748	7.309
Total............................	100.770	100.596	100.205	100.363	99.779	100.038	100.383
Hygroscopic moisture...................	3.945	5.043	4.786	4.067	5.684	7.365	14.305
absorbed at...........................	10 C.°	12 C.°	22 C.°	14 C.°	15.5 C.°	15 C.°	15 C.°

Of these soils, the first (No. 395) is probably unrepresented in Louisiana, though probably frequent in the "St. Francis bottom" in Arkansas. The rest are types of the prominent soil-varieties occurring equally on both sides of the Mississippi north of the mouth of Red river. The Tallahatchie bottom soil (No. 354) is from near the edge of the bottom on the Tallahatchie river in Tallahatchie county. It is noteworthy that its phosphates are lowest of all the soils here shown; while the phosphoric-acid percentages in the older deposits, represented by Nos. 390, 396, and 377, are extraordinarily high.

Without entering into a detailed discussion of these soils in this place, it is important to call attention to the fact that in its store of plant-food of all kinds, the "buckshot" soil stands pre-eminent above all the rest, and well justifies its reputation of being the most productive and durable soil of the great bottom. Unlike most other clay soils it may be tilled at almost any time when the plow can be propelled through it, because, on drying, it crumbles spontaneously into a loose mass of better tilth than many an elaborately tilled upland soil. It is of such depth that the deepest tillage, even by the steam plow, would not reach beyond the true soil material; and its high absorptive power secures crops against injury from drought. At the same time (owing doubtless to its being traversed by innumerable fine cracks, and underlaid by gravel or sand) it drains quite readily. In good seasons, a large part of the cotton crop grown ·on this soil has often been left unpicked for want of labor after taking off 1,500 to 1,800 pounds of seed-cotton to the acre. Two bales of lint per acre can undoubtedly be produced on such soils, with fair culture and good seasons.

The following analyses show the character of some of the soils of the alluvial plain of the bayou Boeuf, which separates the Bastrop hills from the Bayou Maçon peninsula:

No. 237. *Front-land soil*, from bottom of bayou Boeuf, ¼ mile north of Girard, Richland parish, taken to a depth of 10 inches; light and sandy; color: gray; vegetation: willow and chestnut white oaks, maple, ash, sweet gum.

No. 238. *Subsoil* of the above; a sandy clay; color: red; taken to a depth of 10 to 20 inches.

No. 236. *Stiff back-land soil* from 4 miles north of Girard; taken to a depth of 12 inches; a stiff, ash-colored clay; vegetation: chestnut white oak and sweet gum, with dwarf palmetto.

Bayou Boeuf bottom soils.

	Front land soil.	Front-land sub-soil.	Back-land soil.
	No. 237.	No. 238.	No. 236.
Insoluble matter.......................	90.120 } 22.746	78.370 } 85.056	81.800 } 86.503
Soluble silica........................	2.626	6.686	4.703
Potash...............................	0.146	0.234	0.220
Soda.................................	0.078	0.092	0.135
Lime.................................	0.154	0.186	0.365
Magnesia.............................	0.017	0.295	0.610
Brown oxide of manganese	0.065	0.155	0.170
Peroxide of iron.....................	1.980	4.104	4.022
Alumina..............................	3.205	6.369	3.946
Phosphoric acid	0.215	0.147	0.144
Sulphuric acid.......................	0.034	0.234	0.180
Water and organic matter	1.597	2.978	4.150
Total	100.257	99.849	100.415
Hygroscopic moisture	3.010	5.731	5.796
absorbed at.......................	26.6 C.°	26.6 C.°	26 C.°

Except as to its lower potash-percentage, this front-land soil is very similar in composition to the front-land soil from Indian bayou, Sunflower county, Mississippi, the analysis of which is given above. The latter is considered a second-class soil in its locality of occurrence, but it must be remembered that it is there compared with such soils as the black "buckshot", probably one of the most fertile soils in the world. The great depth and good drainage of these front-land soils compensate in a large measure for their comparatively lower percentage of plant-food.

The "back-land" of the bayou Boeuf does not agree in composition and general character with any of the "buck-shot" proper of the Yazoo bottom, but resembles more nearly the "middle-land" of the higher portions of the plain between the Sunflower and Yazoo. Its large lime percentage should render it thrifty, although its phosphates are rather deficient. Its present cotton product is about 1,800 pounds of seed-cotton per acre.

Soils of the bottom ridges.

The following analyses exemplify the character and composition of the soil of the Bastrop hills and of the southern portion of prairie Mer Rouge, the latter probably representing the better class of the "black gravel" (sometimes called also "buckshot") prairies of this entire region:

No. 232. *Sandy loam soil*, from undulating upland 2 miles east of Bastrop, taken to the depth of 12 inches; color: pale yellow; vegetation: oak, hickory, and short-leaf pine.

No. 233. *Subsoil* of the above, taken to a depth of 12 to 18 inches; color: yellow; heavier than the surface soil.

No. 234. *Light prairie soil*, from the southern portion of prairie Mer Rouge; a gray, powdery silt, easily tilled; produces 675 pounds of seed-cotton per acre.

No. 235. *Subsoil* of the above, taken 8 to 18 inches deep; color, grayish yellow; scarcely heavier than the soil.

Upland soils of the Bastrop region, Morehouse parish.

	Bastrop hills soil.	Bastrop hills subsoil.	Prairie Mer Rouge soil.	Prairie Mer Rouge subsoil.
	No. 232.	No. 233.	No. 234.	No. 235.
Insoluble matter	81.700 } 87.450	68.600 } 81.340	89.840 } 93.196	90.650 } 94.086
Soluble silica	5.750	12.650	3.350	3.436
Potash	0.442	0.344	0.131	0.155
Soda	0.296	0.070	0.066	0.085
Lime	0.101	0.120	0.155	0.127
Magnesia	0.230	0.440	0.070	0.288
Brown oxide of manganese	0.396	0.229	0.096	0.135
Peroxide of iron	3.546	4.733	1.870	1.731
Alumina	4.868	9.231	1.080	1.798
Phosphoric acid	0.099	0.111	0.178	0.093
Sulphuric acid	0.079	0.093	0.061	0.210
Water and organic matter	2.544	3.376	3.297	1.906
Total	100.040	100.261	99.670	100.204
Hygroscopic moisture	5.471	8.441	3.278	2.648
absorbed at	29 C.°	29 C.°	28 C.°	26.5 C.°

The loam soil of the Bastrop hills is almost identical in composition with that of the second-class oak uplands of Mississippi, in which the short-leaf pine forms an ingredient of the timber. While having a fair potash-percentage, it is but scantily provided with phosphates, which will soon require to be added; moreover, its lime-percentage is too low for thriftiness, and should be increased by liming. Its physical properties, so far as these can be judged by the absorption of moisture, are satisfactory, but would be improved by deep culture.

The gray silt soil of the southern portion of prairie Mer Rouge, which seems to be similar to that of Hollo-well's, Dubute, and North Avoyelles prairies, is evidently not of much durability, but is kept productive for the time being by its comparatively large lime-percentage and the accumulation of vegetable mold on the surface soil. Its low moisture-coefficient and the formation of bog ore (black pebble) in the subsoil seem to indicate that it is inclined to be leachy, and is not well drained. It is said to have originally produced 1,400 pounds of seed-cotton per acre; at present the product is about 1,100 pounds.

The soil of the northern part of prairie Mer Rouge and that of prairie Jefferson is quite different, being black (or sometimes red) and much heavier, and several feet in depth; below the black subsoil a stratum of yellowish sand is found. The cotton product of this soil is 1,500 to 1,800 pounds of seed-cotton per acre.

II.—THE RED RIVER BOTTOM REGION.

The usual width of the alluvial plain of Red river, in Louisiana, is from 8 to 10 miles (narrowing to 3 at Colfax, Grant parish), while that of the Mississippi bottom between Vicksburg and the mouth of Red river is from 30 to 35. Below the junction of the two valleys, the aggregate width is about the sum of the above figures.

The area of the bottom lands of Red river, within the state of Louisiana, is about 1,425 square miles.

The general topographical features of Red river bottom nearly resemble those of the Mississippi bottom already described, modified materially at only two points, viz, the rapids below Alexandria, caused by the traversal of the river by a Tertiary sandstone formation; and in the extreme northwest portion of the state, by the existence of the great raft. In the rest of its course, Red river is a fine, swiftly-flowing stream, which has cut a well-defined channel, 700 to 800 feet wide, with steep and mostly very solid banks, into strata of red, and, lower down, blue or green clay, which evidently antedate the present river; precisely as is the case with the "buckshot" clays of the Mississippi itself. And just as the soils formed from the latter are scarcely distinguishable from those now forming in the cypress swamps, so the "back-lands" of Red river bottom are formed in part directly from the older red clays, partly from the more modern deposits of the slack-water and low swamp lying back from, or between, the bayous. The soils deposited directly by the river, or by the larger bayous diverging from it, are light and loamy, but rarely sandy; and, where cultivation is established, it usually extends to the very brink of the river bank, unless levees should intervene. The latter, however, are scarcely used on that part of the river lying above the rapids, while those on the portion lying below form a necessary link in the chain of those erected against the floods of the Mississippi. When the latter occur, Red river is transformed into a still back-water as high up as Alexandria.

Its own freshets occur at irregular times, being due to rains occurring below the raft, which are rapidly poured into it by numerous short streams, and cause it to rise at Alexandria as much as 47 feet above low-water mark. They are, of course, of correspondingly short duration, and a moderate rise does little damage, from the fact that the banks are mostly from 25 to 40 feet above low-water.   The effects of the rains occurring above the raft region is so moderated by the numerous lake reservoirs existing there, that in general they merely serve to maintain the river in fair boating condition through the season.

The great raft is the result of what would be called a "jam" by the loggers of the North, formed of a matted mass of fallen trees, partly still afloat, partly water-logged and sunken, which extends across the river channel for between 20 and 30 miles, in the region above Shreveport.   It is advancing up the river, by the addition of drift-wood at its upper end, at the rate of about a mile per annum, while at the lower it is gradually receding as the logs decay; and the solid masses, here frequently overgrown with willow and cottonwood trees, are separated by spaces of clear water.   The damming-up of the river caused by this obstruction compels its water to seek lateral outlets in numerous and frequently shifting bayous and lakes that, to a great extent, exist only on the maps, except in time of high-water.   All the bottom lands in the raft region are thus subject to frequent overflows, and not capable of cultivation or permanent reclamation so long as the raft exists.   Dead forests still standing in the lake beds, prove that this state of things is of comparatively recent date.

The soils of the Red river bottom, below the raft, are substantially of four kinds, viz :

1. *Front-land soil.*—Near the river and . the main bayous there is a yellowish-red or reddish loam soil, light and easily tilled; deep and very productive.   In the "back bottom," further from the channels, this soil becomes gradually heavier and more difficult to till, and forms—

2. *Back-bottom soil.*—Also very productive, and, doubtless, more lasting than No. 1.   Both obviously alluvial.

3. *Bottom-prairie soil.*—A black, calcareous soil, fully 12 inches in depth; timber—large ash, water oak, cottonwood, hackberry, and honey locust—occurs in patches; very productive; "a capital soil."

4. *Wazy soil.*—Also in patches; an exceedingly heavy, close, intractable clay, mostly in low ground.   It bears a curiously stunted, or rather stationary, growth of hackberry, ash, and elm; trees thirty years old being no larger than we usually see them after three or four; besides these it bears large overcup oaks.   It seems to be practically worthless, at least for the present.

The last two soils are doubtless derived from the older clay strata seen in the river banks—No. 4 from the stiff red and brown non-calcareous clays, while No. 3 is similar to the "buckshot" prairie soil of the Tensas bottom, and derives from the lighter calcareous clays of the ancient swamp formation.

The following analyses throw some light on the peculiarities of these soils, and of the materials concerned in their formation.

No. 39. *Front-land subsoil*, from the banks of Red river, 6 miles above Coushatta Chute, Red River parish.   Specimen taken from the face of the bluff bank of the river, about 12 inches below the surface, from a stratum of alluvial loam 5 feet thick, and seemingly the same throughout.

No. 40. *Stiff red clay, with calcareous concretions*, from the same locality as No. 39, but lying beneath it 7 to 8 feet deep, and doubtless the material from which the older "back-land" soils are formed; or, where it is calcareous, the black-bottom prairie, No. 55.

No. 55. *Black-bottom prairie soil*, taken not far from same locality as the above, to the depth of 12 inches.

Red River bottom soils.

[Red River parish, south side, above Coushatta Chute.]

	Reddish alluvial loam.	Red calcareous clay.	Dark bottom-prairie.
	No. 39.	No. 40.	No. 55.
Insoluble matter	90.480 } 94.480	55.750 } 63.220	78.180 } 84.710
Soluble silica	4.000	7.470	6.530
Potash	0.215	0.462	0.614
Soda	0.003	0.358	0.064
Lime	0.217	8.071	0.485
Magnesia	0.585	.3.055	1.041
Brown oxide of manganese	0.384	0.075	0.349
Peroxide of iron	1.866	5.975	3.303
Alumina	1.415	6.682	4.229
Phosphoric acid	0.221	0.280	0.151
Sulphuric acid	0.036	0.001	0.016
Carbonic acid	....	3.913	....
Water and organic matter	1.292	5.819	4.920
Total	100.523	100.491	99.776
Hygroscopic moisture	3.080	....	3.320
absorbed at	21 C.°	....	20.5 C.°

On the whole, the most prevalent, and, in an agricultural point of view, the most important of these soils, is the one formed by the reddish alluvial loam, so characteristic of the present deposits of Red river: Its thickness near the river is seen to vary from 5 to 7 feet (the usual depth) to as much as 17 feet, without any material change. It is very productive, readily yielding in ordinary seasons 2,000 to 2,500 pounds of seed-cotton per acre, and rarely failing, even in extreme seasons, except by actual overflow. The staple rates as good and fair middling.

In comparing this soil with the front-land soils of the Yazoo bottom, and especially with that of Indian bayou (Nos. 376, 377), and the "Dogwood ridge soil" from Coahoma (No. 393), we find, on the whole, a great similarity in composition, however different their aspect. The Red river soil contains less clay and humus, and correspondingly more fine silex, and its hygroscopic power is quite low. But it is richer in phosphates, and, for a soil containing 94.5 per cent. of inert matter, very rich in lime. Its red tint, as the analysis shows, is not due to any large amount of iron oxide, but simply to its fine diffusion; while in the corresponding soils of the Mississippi bottom, it is largely in the form of granules and bog-ore concretions, and can therefore exert but little beneficial influence upon the physical character of the soils. The most unexpected feature exhibited by this analysis, is the fact that in none of these soils the sulphates are present to any unusual extent. It has been usual to ascribe the extraordinary thriftiness of the Red river soils to the gypsum supposed to be brought down from the great gypsum formation of the Llano Estacado, traversed by the river; but it is evident that whatever effect the presence of that substance may originally have exerted upon the decomposition of the soil minerals, it has been so altered *in transitu* that only the lime has remained in shape of carbonate, while the sulphuric acid has been carried into the Gulf. The lime carbonate is so abundant in the older deposits forming the river banks, as to be frequently accumulated in the form of nodules. Moreover, it manifests itself in the black-bottom prairie soil (No. 55) with 0.5 per cent. of lime, and in the red clay (No. 40) from which the dark prairie soil is originally derived.

It will be seen that there is a considerable difference between the composition of the latter and the "buckshot" soil of the Yazoo bottom, the latter being by far the richer in plant-food, and less extreme in its physical qualities. It probably approaches much more nearly, in most respects, the bottom prairies of the Tensas region.

The region bordering upon the Atchafalaya, and especially the bayous Boeuf, Cocodrie, and Courtableau, in Rapides, St. Landry, and even as far as the Tèche, are partly of the same character as those of Red river bottom proper, partly of a mixed type. The peculiar red tints of the Red river deposits appear in the banks of the Atchafalaya, at low stages of water, alternating with the darker or grayish sediments derived from floods of the Mississippi, and impart their character to a large portion of the bordering lands.

Outside of the Red river and Atchafalaya alluvial plains, the peculiar red tints appear in the older alluvium of some of the western tributaries, and also on the bayou Vermillion, which doubtless owes its name to this circumstance.

Along the Tèche, nearly to its junction with the Atchafalaya, the red clay soil appears for a few hundred yards on each side of the stream, where it abuts against the black prairie. It is very fertile, though in places somewhat heavy. The red clay soil of the bayou Vermillion bottom lands contrasts strikingly with that of the brown loam prairie, into which its valley is cut.

The following analysis of this soil shows its character, and its relations with the Red river soils:

No. 210. *Bottom subsoil*, from the flood plain of bayou Vermillion, near Vermillionville, Lafayette parish. Surface soil only a few inches in thickness, a little lighter than the subsoil, mahogany tint. Subsoil: orange-red, quite heavy, taken from 8 to 15 inches depth. Timber: water oak, tulip tree (poplar), magnolia, ash, hackberry, elm, of rather inferior size as compared with trees on the hummock above.

Bayou Vermillion bottom subsoil.

	No. 210.
Insoluble matter	64.290 } 79.640
Soluble silica	15.410
Potash	0.742
Soda	0.126
Lime	0.226
Magnesia	1.192
Brown oxide of manganese	0.160
Peroxide of iron	4.936
Alumina	10.904
Phosphoric acid	0.006
Sulphuric acid	0.226
Water and organic matter	5.627
Total	100.360
Hygroscopic moisture	5.703
absorbed at	26.6 C.°

This soil is here subject to annual overflow, and somewhat difficult to till when wet. Farther below, where the bottom widens, it is lighter, from admixture of upland washings, bears much live oak, and is very fertile. It will be noted that its potash-percentage is very high, while that of phosphoric acid is quite low, and would soon need replenishing by the use of phosphate manures. Its lime-percentage is sufficiently large for thriftiness, but could doubtless be advantageously increased by liming, both for improving tilth and rendering other plant-food available. Green-manuring is indicated as one of the most beneficial improvements needed.

III.—THE ALLUVIAL REGION SOUTH OF RED RIVER.

Almost throughout the parishes embraced in this division (southern Avoyelles, western St. Landry, Pointe Coupée, West Baton Rouge, Iberville, St. Martin, Ascension), as well as in the "marsh parishes" farther to seaward, sugar-cane is the preferred crop, being considered more profitable than cotton. The latter, however, succeeds admirably, the question of its production being mainly a commercial one, though also somewhat influenced by the frequent occurrence of heavy rain storms during the picking season, which interfere with the gathering of the crop.

The surface features of the region may be briefly expressed thus: "Excellent alluvial lands, intersected by an intricate network of bayous, along which the cultivated lands chiefly lie; between, tangled swamps mainly occupied by the cypress, and often extensive canebrakes; cane forming the undergrowth in a large portion of the 'back lands', but becoming less prominent, on the whole, as we approach the marsh regions." (a)

The width of the cultivated, or at least cleared, "coast" belt along the main river, varies usually from one and a half to two and a half sections or miles; and is commonly occupied by extensive and well-improved sugar plantations, whose large sugar-houses, fine residences, and regularly arranged laborers' quarters give them the appearance of villages. The immense fields are bounded in the distance by the dark line of the swamp or forest. The latter, in its higher portions, consists largely of lowland oaks (water, white, chestnut, willow, and overcup), sweet and black gums, sycamore, cottonwood, honey locust, sassafras, pecan, &c., with cypress, sweet and tupelo gums, and willow in the swamps proper.

Along the bayous inland, the higher and therefore cultivated lands also form belts, of greater or less width, sensibly in proportion to the size of the stream, from a quarter to two miles wide. These belts are not always continuous, but interrupted by stretches of low swamp, through which the bayou has not formed a definite bank, as is the case on bayou Courtableau, in St. Landry. Or, the high land may be all on one side, while the other is low, as is frequently the case on the Atchafalaya river. Again, detached bodies of high land, not obviously related to any larger water-course at present in existence, are sometimes found at distances of from 4 to 10 miles from the bayous, and when cleared are known as "brulées", from the burning of the timber required to make them available for cultivation. The shifting of the bayou channels and washing-away of barriers in time of high-water, as well as the even now frequent formation of new bends and cut-offs, explains this state of things.

The high and more or less sandy banks of the numerous crescent-shaped lakes left as the remnants of the formation of cut-offs, whether by the main river or the larger bayous, form the best residence-sites; their stable grassy slopes and still, clear water contrasting favorably with the shifting shores and the ever-threatening and surging muddy current of the river. Especially in the more southerly portion of the region the magnolia, live oak, and pecan form most attractive groves wherein to locate a home, whose only natural drawback is the endless struggle against the implacable mosquito. Many handsome residences, surrounded by these beautiful trees, well-kept lawns and shrubbery such as belongs only to plant-houses farther north, are seen especially on the "coast" of Pointe Coupée, West Baton Rouge, and Iberville.

The soils of this region have not as yet been examined in detail, or analyzed. They appear, on the whole, to be less varied or extreme in their character than those higher up the stream, the front-lands being less sandy, but more of the character of a light loam, made up of fine materials; while the transition to the back-lands is more gradual, and these themselves do not appear to be quite as clayey as the "buckshot" soils of the Yazoo bottom. It is probable that in most cases the latter is deeper underground than is the case above, and instead, the modern cypress swamp soils form the back-land. The high fertility and durability of the alluvial lands, however, remain the same, or if different in any general point, it may be that the front lands are even more productive than is the case northward. This is claimed by the inhabitants, and the statement is in a measure sustained by the analyses made of the lands of bayou Black, in the Houma region, as given below. The high percentages of lime, potash, and humus there shown indicate a gradual increase of these ingredients toward the south, which would of course be partially attained already at intermediate points. More definite information on these points is, however, very much to be desired.

From the descriptions of the parishes belonging to this division, as given in Part II, a fuller understanding of their peculiarities may be gained.

IV.—THE TIDE-WATER REGION.

Within this division may be embraced the parishes of St. James, St. John Baptist, St. Charles, Jefferson, Orleans, St. Bernard, Plaquemines, Lafourche, Terrebonne, St. Mary, southern Iberia, southern Vermillion, and Cameron.

Throughout this region the influence of the tides makes itself felt in the bayous, except at times of high water. The country is a dead level, except in so far as alluvial ridges, elevated as much as 7 feet above the marsh prairies,

a Lockett, 2d. Rep. of the Topogr. Survey of Louisiana, p. 3, &c.

and of varying width, accompany the river, as well as the larger bayous, to within a distance of 8 to 20 miles from the sea shore; where they gradually become lost in the grassy prairie or rush-grown marsh, which skirt either the sea-shore or that of some of the numerous lakes with which the region is dotted, and whose intricate channels and cross-connections, frequently changing from year to year, it is not easy to trace.

On the main river this region is entered soon after passing Donaldsonville, when, on approaching St. James village, the marshes forming the head of the lake and bayou Des Allemands may be seen within a few miles south of the river bank. Opposite St. Charles village, the bordering belt has widened to about 9 miles, but now the marshes bordering lake Pontchartrain appear in sight on the north. The rear of the city of New Orleans touches the marsh, which thenceforward accompanies the river on its course to the Gulf, at a distance varying from 2 to 6 miles; until, a little above the forts (Jackson and St. Philip), it closes in upon the banks, and so continues to the mouths of the passes.

On the whole of this "lower coast" the culture of sugar-cane, rice, and tropical fruits prevails, and cotton is scarcely seen. The soils are light, but very deep and fertile. Immediately along the river banks is the sandy soil of the "willow batture"; a few hundred yards inland the live oak occupies the ground and marks the best soil. In the upper and wider portions of the "coast" the dark cypress-swamp forest forms the back-ground of the plantations, and this in its turn is bordered to seaward by the marsh. But in the narrower portions the cypress swamp is wanting, and the live-oak ridge slopes off gently into the grassy prairie or "round-rush" marsh.

On the bayous the state of things is very much the same. The live-oak ridges are sometimes interrupted for some distance, and then reappear in the marsh as long, conspicuous islands, marking the course sometimes of the present bayou channel, sometimes one that has long been deserted by the current. Such, also, has probably been the origin of the fertile islands or "ridges" in the sea-marsh of southwestern Louisiana, such as Pecan island, and similar strips of live-oak land fringing the lakes and shore in Cameron and Vermillion parishes.

The largest body of cultivatable land in this region is that which is traversed by bayous Lafourche and Terrebonne, and, forming the most fertile portions of the parishes of the same names, is known as the Houma and Thibodeauxville country. Here, also, the sugar-cane, rice, and tropical fruits are the staple production, and no cotton is cultivated. The front-land soil is light, many feet in depth, and supposed to be inexhaustible. That of the back-lands is more stiff, and very dark colored from vegetable matter, as is usually the case in the cypress-swamp soils.

The only soils from this region thus far analyzed are the two following, taken at the request of Hon. William H. Harris, commissioner of agriculture and immigration for Louisiana, by Mr. Jos. A. Gagne, of Houma, in the vicinity of that place.

No. 239. *Bayou Terrebonne front-land soil.*—Timber, originally: live oak, sweet gum, and magnolia. A fine, silty soil, with no visible sand grains; pulverulent, of a pale dun tint when wet, and barely plastic; unchanged to the depth of several feet, varying according to locality; specimen taken to the depth of 12 inches.

No. 240. *Back-land soil*, from same locality. Lies about 5 feet lower than No. 239; growth: cypress; taken to the depth of 12 inches; black, much more stiff than the front-land soil; not in cultivation, being undrained.

Soils from Houma, Terrebonne parish.

	Bayou Terrebonne front-land soil.	Bayou Terrebonne back-land soil.
	No. 239.	No. 240.
Insoluble matter	75.136 } 81.505	35.480 } 56.242
Soluble silica	6.369	20.762
Potash	0.787	1.931
Soda	0.089	0.131
Lime	0.631	0.730
Magnesia	0.552	0.884
Brown oxide of manganese	0.018	0.014
Peroxide of iron	3.822	7.101
Alumina	7.274	15.446
Phosphoric acid	0.105	0.146
Sulphuric acid	0.365	0.246
Water and organic matter	4.400	18.820
Total	99.528	100.481
Humus	0.863	5.067
Available inorganic matter	0.372	0.906
Available phosphoric acid:		
Referred to whole soil	.0.014	0.022
Hygroscopic moisture	3.907	15.822
absorbed at	12 C.°	12 C.°

A comparison of the composition of these soils with that of the Yazoo bottom, given above, shows some interesting facts. The Terrebonne front-land soil, as compared with Nos. 376 and 394, respectively, from Sunflower and Issaquena counties, and there occupying a similar position with regard to the bayous, shows nearly double the percentages of potash and lime, while on the other hand the percentage of phosphoric acid is not only not increased, but even materially less; not higher than is usually found in second-class upland soils. There is a remarkably high percentage of sulphuric acid; in other respects, though slightly more clayey than the Yazoo soils (as shown by the alumina-percentage and the higher moisture-coefficient), there is not much difference.

Comparing the "back-land" from Houma with the "buckshot" soil from Issaquena county, we find a general agreement in the extraordinarily high percentage of potash (over 1 per cent.), also a large amount of lime and very large ones of soluble alumina and silica, implying that the clayey portion is in the finest state of division. Concurrently the moisture-absorption is very unusually high in both cases, and in both, probably, the amount of humus is very large. The two have evidently been formed under analogous circumstances and from similar materials, as is a priori probable from their similar geological position. The only material difference is in the percentage of phosphoric acid which, in the Houma soil, is only half of that in the Issaquena "buckshot". Whether this difference is a constant one or not, is an open question, to be determined by farther analysis; but, constituted as is the Houma soil in other respects, a scarcity of that ingredient is likely to be felt in its cultivation for many years to come.

The marsh lands.

On the passes of the Mississippi, and on that portion above, called the "Neck", the formation of solid land has occurred by the aid of quite a different process, peculiar to the Mississippi river mouths so far as known. This process is the upheaving of the bottom near the mouths, and the formation of mudsprings on the islands so produced, which are known by the name of "mudlumps", and form serious impediments to navigation. They are sometimes built up to the height of 12 or 15 feet, and their material being mostly quite clayey, they are not much subject to washing, but are gradually degraded by rains and storms to the tide-level. Being thus enlarged, the successive "lumps" are gradually connected by the deposition of sediment in the channels separating them, and thus are formed the narrow, continuous shores along each of the passes, which form so exceptional a feature of the Mississippi mouths. The soil of these lumps is mostly quite firm, not easily washed away, and becomes quite productive in the course of time, producing fair vegetables as well as rice. Thus far, however, the last-named crop is the only one whose cultivation has been attempted on any large scale in the marshes of the Louisiana coast, and there can be little doubt that a very large portion of the marsh area will be found susceptible of this use.

As regards the reclamation of the sea-marsh proper for purposes of cultivation, it should be noted that it is progressing slowly along the main river and the larger bayous by a gradual filling-in with sediment, close upon which follows the occupancy of the more solid ground by the willow, the bayberry (*Myrica Carolinensis*), bay galls (*Persea Carolinensis*), the *Baccharis halimifolia*, and in the smaller and more land-locked marshes stunted maple, cypress, and black gum aid in the process. The marsh occupied by the round-rush (*Scirpus lacustris*, (a) tule of California) is comparatively firm, and when protected from the tides can often be made to produce after some years; while that occupied by sedges (cutting-rush, jonc coupant, *Cyperus*) is a practically bottomless, semi-fluid mass of decaying vegetation. The immediate sea-beach is in most cases sandy.

THE BLUFF REGION.

This division embraces only a narrow belt of country, lying adjacent to the Mississippi river, between Baton Rouge and the Mississippi state line. Its average width, east and west, is about 13 miles, and its length about 50; total area, about 650 square miles. It comprehends nearly the whole of East Baton Rouge, the western part of East Feliciana, and nearly all of West Feliciana.

In the northern part of the latter parish the surface of this belt is still rather hilly and broken, as is the case in the adjoining portion of Mississippi, and the summits of the ridges rise several hundred feet in sight of the river. To the southward, however, they soon flatten out, the elevation becomes rapidly less, and is reduced to about 70 to 80 feet above high-water at Port Hudson, and to from 40 to 45 at Baton Rouge. South of the latter point the highlands line swerves to the eastward, and the country along the river is at the level of the general flood-plain.

The soil of this gently rolling "bluff plateau" is usually a rich, brown loam, greatly resembling that of the southern part of Sicily island (see above), which it also resembles in its timber growth—water, willow, swamp-chestnut, and post oaks, hickory, beech, magnolia, locust, tulip tree, and some linden, with, originally, a heavy undergrowth of cane, now destroyed. The brown loam is from 4 to 7 feet in depth, being then underlaid by more or less calcareous silts belonging to the Loess formation, which is so strongly developed in Mississippi, and will be found fully described in that connection. At the foot of the river bluff we sometimes (as at Port Hudson) find the dark-colored clays with calcareous and ferruginous concretions, fossil wood, stumps, &c., which also underlie the Yazoo bottom, and from which the "buckshot" soil is there derived. This clay is at times exhibited in the deep ravines with steep sides that have been scored into the bluff plateau wherever the land has been denuded of timber or thrown out of cultivation. A great deal of damage has already resulted from the neglect of this source of injury.

a Lockett, Rep. Topogr. Surv. La., 1870, p. 35.

The brown loam soil of this region may be considered as first-class upland, and when fresh has readily yielded a 400-pound bale, or 1,300 to 1,400 pounds, of seed-cotton per acre. Most of it, however, has been in cultivation for a long time (this having been one of the earliest-settled regions on the Mississippi), and has been greatly exhausted by improvident cultivation. The soil is, however, so strong naturally and so readily susceptible of improvement of any kind, that its restoration to full productiveness is a mere question of time, at least where the encroachment of ravines has not rendered the process too difficult and costly.

There are some local exceptions to the productiveness of the region, in limited tracts of a white and almost barren soil, with an irregular growth of crab-apple and hawthorn. One of these tracts ("Bullard's plains") is 7 miles from Baton Rouge, on the Bayou Sara road; the other, 5 miles east of Port Hudson. They probably represent outcrops of a white, sandy silt which appears at certain levels in the Port Hudson bluff.

Almost the entire bluff country is occupied by the Bermuda grass, which affords pasture throughout the summer. Besides cotton, corn and sweet-potatoes are the common crops. But the soil and climate are well adapted to the growth of a great variety of fruits, among which the grape would seem likely to be very successful.

THE ATTAKAPAS PRAIRIE REGION.

This division, indicated on the map by the various shades of yellow and brown, embraces the following parishes and parts of parishes: the middle portion of Iberia, all of Lafayette, northern Vermillion, all the upland portion of St. Landry lying south of the heads of bayou Nezpiqué, all of Calcasieu parish lying east of the Calcasieu river, save the extreme northeast corner, and most of the region south of the west fork of Calcasieu and west of the main river.

Except in its most easterly portion, the prairie region is as yet but very thinly settled, and is occupied chiefly by roaming herds of cattle and horses. Yet, its balmy climate, tempered by the sea-breeze, and the fertility of its soils, cannot fail to make it in the future what is now true of a small portion: the "garden of Louisiana".

This region, which is level or only slightly rolling, and mostly treeless, save in narrow strips along the main water-courses, presents three distinct types of soil, between which there are, of course, all degrees of transition, viz: the *black* (calcareous) *prairie*, the *brown loam prairie*, and the *gray silt* or *pine prairie*.

I.—THE BLACK PRAIRIE.

The black calcareous prairie forms an irregular belt, from 7 to 20 and more miles in width, and embraces an area of about 1,280 square miles, along the northern border of the sea-marsh. The land is so nearly level that its drainage is very slow, and collects into numerous shallow basins and ponds (*marais*), which serve as watering-places for stock. From these, shallow, reedy channels (*coulées*), showing scarcely any movement of the water, lead toward the larger water-courses, or to the sea-marsh. There is no natural timber save an occasional honey-locust or plum thicket, but sycamores and China trees (*Melia*) are planted around the scattered homesteads. The open prairie is little settled as yet, though very fertile; the lands bordering the marsh and the streams being preferred for the culture of the sugar-cane, which forms the chief crop. Corn and cotton, however, succeed finely wherever planted in the black prairie, from Iberia to lake Charles.

The black-prairie soil is moderately heavy in tillage, strongly calcareous, 12 to 18 inches in depth, and underlaid by a pale yellow subsoil clay filled with white calcareous concretions (known as "white pebble").

No. 230. *Black-prairie soil*, taken about midway between Petite Anse island and New Iberia; depth, 10 inches without change of color; below this depth it becomes more grayish, with an increasing amount of rounded, partly calcareous, partly ferruginous, concretions (or black pebble); gray loam at 2 to 3 feet; vegetation: grasses, mainly *Panicum* sp., and *Andropogon* (broom-sedge), with *Vernonia* (iron-weed). Color: deep black; soil quite heavy, not as much so as the prairie soils of Mississippi and Alabama, but does not crumble on drying like the latter.

Iberia black-prairie soil.

	No. 230.
Insoluble matter	67.210 } 77.170
Soluble silica	9.960
Potash	0.207
Soda	0.172
Lime	1.737
Magnesia	1.484
Brown oxide of manganese	0.205
Peroxide of iron	2.779
Alumina	4.829
Phosphoric acid	0.208
Sulphuric acid	0.114
Carbonic acid	2.000
Water and organic matter	8.596
Total	99.621
Hygroscopic moisture	10.690
absorbed at	12.7 C.°

This soil differs materially in several respects from most of the prairie soils of Mississippi and Alabama. It contains but little clay, and a large amount of fine siliceous silt. Its percentage of phosphoric acid is quite high, but that of potash comparatively quite low. Hence the extensive withdrawal of the latter ingredient, consequent upon the practice of burning the bagasse, is likely to lead to rapid exhaustion in this respect. The large amount of lime and humus accounts for its present thriftiness.

II.—THE BROWN LOAM PRAIRIE.

This soil occupies the higher and more northerly portions of the prairies east of bayou Cannes, and northward of the black-prairie belt, with which, however, it interlaces so intimately and extensively that it is difficult to draw a definite line of demarkation between them. I estimate the total area occupied by this class of soils at about 1,100 square miles.

The brown loam subsoil of this kind of prairie comes to the surface, more or less, on the whole of the ridge which, rising near Peigneur lake, skirts on the west the great valley, attaining near Washington an elevation of 40 to 50 feet above the latter. Immediately along the bayou Tèche there is a wooded strip of land with live and other lowland oaks, with hackberry, sycamore, honey-locust, &c., also seen along some of the "coulées". The ridge proper, however, about 4 miles wide, is treeless, and takes successively the names of Côte Gelée, Grand Côteau, and Opelousas hills. To the westward it slopes off gradually and insensibly into the level prairie, where the brown loam is covered by a dark surface soil, which, on the whole, decreases in depth to the northward and westward, becoming at the same time lighter colored and less thrifty, until it passes into the gray silty soils of the pine prairies. To the southward, this ridge was doubtless originally continuous to the western headland of Berwick's bay, where the "island" of Belle Isle formed its southern extremity. Of the intermediate portion, there now remain the four elevations (or islands in the sea-marsh) of Côte Blanche, Grande Côte, Petite 'Anse (noted for its rock-salt mine), and Orange island on the shore of lake Peigneur. The general character of the soils of these islands and of the Côte Gelée ridge is almost identical, as will be seen from the analyses given below. The islands were originally, however, clothed with forest and a heavy undergrowth of cane, and their soil is highly productive.

The vegetation of the brown loam prairies is remarkably little varied. Grasses, embracing two or three species of *Paspalum*, with a sprinkling of *Andropogon* or broom-sedge, dispute the ground with white clover. The iron-weed and wild indigo (*Baptisia*) are the chief representatives of herbaceous growth, added to which is, in most regions, the *Helenium tenuifolium* or bitter-weed, whose bright green grass-like leaves often grievously disappoint the hungry beast of burden, and impart an intensely bitter taste to the milk of cows feeding on it for want of something better. But few bright-tinted flowers relieve the monotony of the green surface. In summer there is excellent pasturage, but it is only in the southern portion that it is sufficiently abundant for the winter sustenance of stock.

The prairie extending southwestward from Grand Côteau toward Mentau river, and watered by bayous Plaquemine Brulée, Queue de Tortue, and their branches, receives the general name of Mentau prairie. Here, as farther east, the surface is variegated with ponds, "marais", and "coulées", and by occasional timbered islands or oases called "coves". The soil is light, and on that account is said to be improved by the trampling of cattle. Even with the poor culture now given it by the few who engage in farming, from 35 to 40 bushels of corn per acre is produced, while cotton has scarcely been tried in the western portion of the region. The lowlands along the streams produce cotton, corn, cane, and rice.

Prairie Faquetique, lying between bayous Mallet and Cannes, and prairie Marmou, between the latter and the Nezpiqué, are also occupied chiefly for grazing purposes. The soil of prairie Marmou is said to resemble greatly that of the corresponding portion of the Calcasieu prairie, though somewhat more fertile.

The Côte Gelée, Vermillian, Grand Côteau, and Opelousas prairies, when reasonably well cultivated, produce from 1,000 to 1,200 pounds of seed-cotton per acre, the staple rating as fair middling. Cotton is by far the most prominent culture. Corn is produced for home consumption only, yielding 30 to 40 bushels per acre. Cultivation is generally very shallow, and doubtless for that reason the actual cotton product per acre has greatly decreased in the older districts.

The following analyses of subsoils from different portions of this region convey a fair idea of their composition:

No. 197. *The surface soil of the Opelousas prairie*, taken about half-way between Opelousas and Ville Plate, on the prairie plateau dividing the waters of bayou Cocodrie from those of the Mentau, was about 10 inches deep, of a grayish black tint, not very clayey. The vegetation, same as above stated in general.

No. 226. *Subsoil of Opelousas prairie*, taken at the point mentioned, was taken at 10 to 18 inches depth; color, a tawny brown.

No. 227. *Subsoil of the Côte Gelée*, taken near its southern extremity, on a hillside, of the same tint, at 6 to 12 inches depth.

No. 229. *Subsoil of Grande Côte or Weeks' island*, taken at from 10 to 20 inches depth.

195

Brown-loam prairie soils.

	ST. LANDRY PARISH.		LAFAYETTE PARISH.	IBERIA PARISH.
	Opelousas prairie soil.	Opelousas prairie subsoil.	Côte Gelée subsoil.	Grande Côte subsoil.
	No. 197.	No. 226.	No. 227.	No. 229.
Insoluble matter	86.810 } 90.150	74.740 } 81.700	75.390 } 83.700	72.200 } 82.330
Soluble silica	3.340	6.960	8.310	9.130
Potash	0.189	0.315	0.335	0.408
Soda	0.138	0.013	0.019	0.056
Lime	0.148	0.251	0.133	0.202
Magnesia	0.234	0.264	0.691	0.628
Brown oxide of manganese	0.086	0.081	0.145	0.126
Peroxide of iron	1.941	4.783	4.296	4.758
Alumina	2.068	7.723	6.479	7.704
Phosphoric acid	0.226	0.183	0.157	0.108
Sulphuric acid	0.007	0.011	0.052	0.083
Water and organic matter	4.816	4.860	4.536	4.024
Total	100.053	99.996	100.531	100.559
Hygroscopic moisture	5.420	8.740	7.780	8.900
absorbed at	24 C.°	21 C.°	19 C.°	20.5 C.°

The most obvious difference between these materials and the black-prairie soil from Iberia is the smaller amount of lime, being over six times less than in the latter. Hence the comparative unthriftiness. The analysis of the surface soil also shows a slightly smaller amount of potash, and very much less of vegetable mold. Doubtless the application of lime or plaster would result in a very great improvement. The phosphates, likewise, are in smaller quantity, yet not deficient. As in the case of the Iberia soil, there is here a very great predominance of fine siliceous material over the clay. In this, as in other respects, deep culture, enabling the roots to draw upon the store of plant-food in the subsoil, is sure to be of excellent effect.

III.—THE GRAY SILT, OR PINE PRAIRIES.

This kind of prairie, whose soil is a grayish silt with too little clay to render it retentive, is most extensively developed in Calcasieu, east of the river of that name; but tracts of it are found east of the Nezpiqué and Mentau, such as Pine prairie, near Chicotville; Marmou prairie, also, is stated to be partly of this character. It occupies an area of about 1,075 square miles.

In the northern and poorer portion, the soil is grayish, often ashy, full of bog ore spots; subsoil at 6 to 8 inches is sometimes a mass of black gravel, and underlaid at the depth of a few feet by a putty-like, very siliceous clay, almost impervious to water. The soil is very poor, the growth of grasses coarse, such as *Luzula, Carex, Juncus, Andropogon*, some *Paspalum*; while the *Aletris aurea, Allium mutabile, Linum Virginicum, Baptisia leucophœa* and *leucantha, Psoralea melilotoides*, and a variety of *Polygala*, impart to this barren prairie a much more cheerful aspect than is that of the green and fertile, but flowerless, prairies of Opelousas. Clumps and groves of the long-leaf pine, mostly occupying the singular mounds or hillocks characterizing this part of Louisiana, dot the prairie and lend variety to the landscape, the view being limited by the timbered belts bordering the water-courses on either side; but there is no sign of settlements, save herds of cattle and an occasional "corral".

To the southward the quality of the soil gradually improves, the long-leaf pine being partially replaced by black-jack and post oaks, and the sweeter grasses prevailing more generally. Among the fertile timbered "coves", that of Hickory Flat is the largest, and well settled. Around the heads of water-courses (such as Serpent bayou) there are extensive marshy flats tenanted by water-fowl and (farther south) by alligators. In some of these, excellent crops of rice are grown by the "Acadian" inhabitants; that grain, with eggs and milk, forming almost their sole sustenance. Sandy pine ridges occasionally diversify the southern portion of these prairies, and small crops of corn have been grown there; yet there is little change in the general features until, near the latitude of lake Charles, we reach the edge of the calcareous coast prairie.

For examination, a specimen of soil was taken in the open prairie, about 3 miles south of Serpent bayou (about section 11, township 8 south, range 6 west).

No. 195. *Soil of Pine prairie*, from range 6 east, township 8, 3 miles south of the crossing of Serpent bayou, Calcasieu parish. Vegetation: clumps of black-jack and post oaks, and long-leaved pine, scattered over the prairie. On the grassy surface, the prevalent plants are the two or three oft-mentioned species of *Paspalum*, some *Luzula, Juncus, Andropogon; Leptopoda fimbria, Obeliscaria laciniata, Rudbeckia hirta, Echinacea purpurea, Silphium squarrosum; Baptisia leucophœa, Psoralea melilotoides, Mimosa strigillosa. Polygala*, two species; *Styrax pulverulenta.* Depth taken, 10 inches. Soil gray, somewhat ashy, with brown, ferruginous spots, and small particles of bog ore, which, sifted out, amounts to 0.15 per cent.

126

Pine prairie soil.

	No. 195.
Insoluble matter..	92. 630 } 94. 660
Soluble silica	2. 030
Potash	0. 148
Soda	0. 041
Lime..	0. 262
Magnesia	0. 140
Brown oxide of manganese....	0. 035
Péroxide of iron	1 110
Alumina...	1. 700
Phosphoric acid	0. 038
Sulphuric acid...	0. 061
Water and organic matter	. 2. 614
Total	100 818
Hygroscopic moisture	3. 160
absorbed at................................, ...	13 C.°

According to this analysis, this soil is not as poor, on the whole, as might have been expected; save as regards phosphates and magnesia, in which it is very deficient. It is sadly in need of something to render it more retentive, *i. e.*, clay or vegetable mold; but if properly drained, might be susceptible of profitable improvement and cultivation by some green-manuring and use of bone-meal. Like similar soils in southern Mississippi, it now bears only small-seeded plants; there being a want of the seed-forming ingredients.

The larger streams traversing the prairie region are bordered by timber belts of varying width and character. On the waters of Vermillion river, these "hummock" lands are very fine, better than the prairie adjoining, and timbered with water, basket, scarlet, and live oaks, magnolia, tulip tree, sweet gum, and hackberry. On the heads of bayous Cannes and Plaquemine the timber indicates a somewhat less generous soil, not so well drained, and often full of bog-ore gravel; such tracts being usually marked by thickets of red haw and crab. The level lands timbered with oak, hickory, and elm, on the eastern heads of the Nezpiqué, are in spring often covered with standing water. The same is true of the country on the western heads of the same stream, which is timbered exclusively with the long-leaf pine, and is almost a dead level, full of boggy patches with crawfish holes and aquatic plants, among the latter the *Asclepias paupercula,* the vermilion-colored milkweed of the seacoast marshes. The soil is whitish and very poor, fit only for pasture, and, perhaps, rice culture. Frequently there is a dense growth of candleberry (*Myrica cerifera* and *Carolinensis*), bay galls (*Laurus Carolinensis*), and a variety of whortleberries (*Vaccinium*); and where these prevail exclusively, we have impenetrable thickets, popularly designated as "bay galls", the undisputed resort of the bear, panther, and wild cat. Along the main stream, however, there extends a belt of rolling land several miles wide, with a fine growth of the long-leaved pine, and some good agricultural tracts.

The Calcasieu river itself is bordered by a timber belt of pine, on the level of the prairie; and in the bottom (subject to overflow, but very fertile, and from one to two miles wide) there is a fine growth of beech, magnolia, bay, sweet gum, lowland oaks, &c.

As in the brown loam prairies east of the Nezpiqué, there are in the gray silt prairie occasional "coves" or islands of fertile, timbered upland. One such is the "Hickory Flat" tract in northeastern Calcasieu, which bears a good growth of oaks and hickories; and the "Big Woods" cove in southwestern Calcasieu, which bears the character of the live-oak ridges of the coast.

THE LONG-LEAF PINE REGION.

This division embraces, in western Louisiana, the following parishes and parts of parishes: all that part of Calcasieu lying north of the West fork and west of the main Calcasieu river; all of Vernon, except the Anacoco prairie region; all of Rapides outside of Red river-bottom; the southern portion of Natchitoches, and adjoining southeast corner of Sabine; nearly the whole of the parishes of Grant and Winn; a portion of southern Bienville, and nearly all of southern Jackson; and a considerable part of the upland portion of Ouachita, Caldwell, and · Catahoula, as indicated in the map by the green tints, covering altogether about 7,260 square miles.

East of the Mississippi river, the long-leaf pine covers most of the country lying northward of lakes Pontchartrain and Maurepas, excepting only the belt of "bluff" lands bordering the Mississippi river, and the belts of marsh bordering the lakes named. It therefore embraces nearly all of the parishes of St. Tammany, Washington, Tangipahoa, Livingston, and St. Helena, and the greater part of East Feliciana, about 3,280 square miles.

Over all this area the long-leaf pine (*Pinus australis*) either forms the exclusive timber tree outside of the bottoms of the streams, or is only occasionally intermingled to any material extent with oaks (black-jack and post).

and at times entirely replaced by the short-leaf species (*P. mitis*). The extent to which this replacement occurs is usually a fair measure of the quality of the soil; that on which the long-leaf pine prevails exclusively being in most cases a very sandy loam of little native fertility or durability. Hence cultivation is, in the long-leaf pine region, commonly restricted to the bottoms and lower hillsides, and to such ridges, as by the admixture of the other trees mentioned, show a better class of soil. Such are, for example, the Anacoco prairie, the Sugartown country on Bundick's creek, in Calcasieu, and many other similar cases. The main adaptation of the region, however, is for grazing and lumbering purposes; and large quantities of ship timber, as well as sawn lumber, are shipped from the Calcasieu, as well as from other parts of the region rendered accessible by navigable streams or railroads.

Since the long-leaf pine, within the latitudes of its occurrence, follows measurably a certain quality of soil, it may naturally be expected that it will often be found beyond the limits of its main bodies, where sandy ridges run out into other soil regions. We thus frequently find it occupying the crests of dividing ridges in the oak uplands of northern Louisiana, and, not uncommonly, isolated tracts, or outliers, considerably beyond the limits indicated in the map.

Within the long-leaf pine region of Louisiana we find two different surface characters, accompanied also by more or less difference in the soils and minor vegetation. These are popularly designated as the *pine flats*, and the *pine hills* proper.

THE PINE FLATS.

The pine flats prevail in the southern part of the region (as indicated on the map by the ruled shade of green), both in eastern and western Louisiana. In Calcasieu, west of the river of that name, they are sharply defined on the south by the West fork, southward of which (aside from a narrow belt of pine woods immediately along the stream) lie marshy pine prairies. To the northward, the pine flats are limited by Bundick's creek, and by the pine hills which form the divide between the West fork waters and those of bayou Anacoco. East of the Calcasieu river, a tract of wet pine flats lies between that river and the Nezpiqué, as mentioned above. From this there is a gradual transition to the pine prairie lands by a thinning-out of the timber growth.

The soil of the pine flats proper in this region is not materially different from that of the pine prairies, with which its herbaceous growth has much in common. It is a whitish or gray, unretentive silt, with brown ferruginous or rusty spots, increasing downward, and indicating a lack of drainage. The cause is found, at the depth of 18 to 30 inches, in a compact, whitish or bluish subsoil, full of bog-ore gravel, and consisting generally of siliceous silt compacted by clay, or sometimes of true clay, almost impervious to water, and of the consistence of putty, where it is brought up by the crawfish that commonly inhabit the lower tracts. The roots of the pines themselves remain above this water-sodden substratum, and hence hurricanes uproot them with great ease.

In the better-drained portions, a very pale yellow, silty loam is found in the place of the white "crawfishy" subsoil. This is especially the case to the northward, as in Calcasieu. Beyond Dry bayou, about 20 miles on a direct line from the West fork, where the wet glades and their peculiar vegetation disappear, the country becomes gently rolling, and thus forms an insensible transition from the coast flats to the pine hills.

The pine-flat region of eastern Louisiana, embracing the greater part of Livingston and St. Tammany, and the southern half of Tangipahoa parish, differs in some respects from the flats of Calcasieu. A heavy, gray clay underlies most of the region, sometimes coming to the surface and forming an intractable, ill-drained soil, at others covered with a sandy or silty, and often very poor soil. The shores of lake Pontchartrain are partly fringed with wet glades, partly with a belt, sometimes several miles wide, of sweet gum and lowland oaks, having a fair though ill-drained soil. Inland of these the level pine-woods set in, consisting partly (in St. Tammany) of short-leaf pine, but generally of the long-leaved species. Along some of these streams (especially the Amite) there are fine belts of forest land, with oaks, beech, dogwood, gums, magnolia, and some short-leaf pine, with a good grayish-brown or chocolate-colored, easily tilled soil, with a foundation of sandy, red clay. The settlements therefore are located chiefly along these streams; the fertility of the soil decreasing as we recede from them. The pasturing of stock, lumbering, and, to some extent, the manufacture of turpentine and charcoal, are thus far the chief industries.

THE PINE HILLS.

A sandy, pale yellow subsoil, covered a few inches deep by a tawny or gray, sometimes ashy, but more generally light, sandy, surface soil, characterizes the long-leaf pine hills from Texas to Georgia. In accordance with this great uniformity of soil, their other features—surface conformation, undergrowth, and even herbaceous growth—are remarkably little varied in this long distance. The pervious soil and subsoil, often underlaid by loose, pervious sand at the depth of 1½ to 3 feet, prevents the formation of deep gullies or abrupt banks. Hence the dividing ridges are mostly broad and gently rolling plateaus, whose valleys are often without any definite water-channels in their upper portions; wells in such regions sometimes finding only sand for a hundred and fifty feet. Then strong springs of clear freestone-water will be found gushing out in the deeper valleys, where the water is shed by the clay or rock strata into which the channels of the streams are cut.

The long-leaf pine forest is mostly open, so that a wagon can frequently traverse it with little more difficulty than the open prairie. The shade of the pine being very light, grasses and other plants requiring sunshine flourish underneath them, thus affording an excellent pasture, which fact has made stock-breeding the earliest industry of this region.

The uplands are usually exhausted by a few years' culture in corn or cotton; the crops being often fairly remunerative for the time, especially on tracts where a notable amount of oak and hickory mingles with the pine. In general, however, the bottoms of the larger streams are alone looked to for cotton production in the long-leaf pine hills. As in the prairies and flats, we find in them occasionally oases of fertile land; usually ridges timbered with oak, and some short-leaf pine.

Soils of the pine hills.

The following analysis of a subsoil sample from this region shows well the character of the pale yellow loam that underlies the shallow surface soil, and upon which the durability and quality of these long-leaf pine lands essentially depends.

No. 134. *Pine woods subsoil*, from section 9, township 2, range 9 west, on the heads of Bundick's creek, Vernon parish. Open, undulating pine woods, with some small hickory, black-jack, and black gum among the long-leaf pine. Surface soil gray, ashy, to the depth of 8 inches; subsoil a pale yellow moderately light loam, taken from 8 to 18 inches depth.

Pine hills subsoil.

	No. 134.
Insoluble matter	77.870 } 82.265
	4.395 }
Soluble silica	
Potash	0.347
Soda	0.083
Lime	0.097
Magnesia	0.339
Brown oxide of manganese	0.041
Peroxide of iron	3.314
Alumina	9.918
Phosphoric acid	0.072
Sulphuric acid	0.086
Water and organic matter	3.546
Total	99.908
Hygroscopic moisture	6.790
absorbed at	26.6 C.°

The composition of this subsoil is very similar to that of the long-leaf pine soils analyzed from Mississippi, given elsewhere, and not inferior to that of many soils profitably cultivated in cotton in Georgia and the Carolinas. Their prominent defect is, here as elsewhere, a scarcity of phosphates and of lime; hence unthriftiness. But the physical qualities of these soils are far from undesirable, and, while manure and deep tillage must be employed to render them productive, they are quite susceptible of permanent improvement.

THE ANACOCO PRAIRIE.

A very unusual occurrence of a fertile island in this region is the "Anacoco prairie", in Vernon parish. This is caused by the approach to the surface of a stratum of calcareous clay, which appears generally only on the hillsides in the form of bands of black-prairie and red clay soils, whose washings have imparted fertility to the valley soils. At some points (as on the Anacoco prairie proper) this limy clay has itself formed the surface, and more or less large and continuous tracts of very fertile black-prairie soil, producing excellent cotton. The district over which these prairie spots and general improvement of soil extend, lies between the extreme heads of the main Calcasieu river and the eastern branches of bayou Anacoco, a tributary of the Sabine river, and embraces about one and a half townships. The surface is quite rolling, and presents within a small compass an extraordinary variety of soils, from the poorest sandy pine hills to the richest upland prairie and prairie bottoms, all of which can sometimes be observed on a single hillside slope. Hence farms are mostly small, but in many cases exceedingly productive, though thus far suffering from want of communication with the outside world.

An analysis of the typical black soil of the main Anacoco prairie (forming on Prairie creek a strip about 3 miles long by three-fourths wide) gave the following result:

No. 171. *Anacoco prairie soil*, from John Smart's place, on Prairie creek, section 33, township 3 north, range 9 west. Here the black-prairie soil reaches to a depth of about 20 inches, is rather sandy above, quite heavy below, and underlaid by a heavy gray clay, passing into clay marl. Farther down the soil crumbles on drying, like the Mississippi "buckshot" and black-prairie soils, and is easily tilled when in good condition; washes badly on the hillsides. Produces 40 bushels of corn and a bale of cotton per acre, and has lasted remarkably well, though plowed but a few inches deep. Depth of sample taken, 12 inches.

9 C P

Anacoco prairie soil.

	No. 171.
Insoluble matter...	53. 190 } 74. 290
Soluble silica	21. 100 }
Potash...	0. 532
Soda...	0. 064
Lime	1. 598
Magnesia...	0. 735
Brown oxide of manganese	0. 149
Peroxide of iron	4. 520
Alumina..	11. 363
Phosphoric acid	0. 647
Sulphuric acid..	0. 123
Water and organic matter	7. 266
Total	100. 287
Hygroscopic moisture	13. 110
absorbed at...	25. 5 C.°

It will be noted that, in its chemical composition, this soil differs but little from the (Cretaceous) prairie soils of the northeastern prairie region of Mississippi, especially that from Monroe county (No. 172, Miss.). The Anacoco soil is poorer in phosphates, but it must be remembered that it has been in cultivation, without return, for about twenty years, while the Mississippi soil was a virgin one. As it is, however, it illustrates strikingly how, in presence. of a large amount of lime in the soil, a very small phosphate-percentage will suffice for the needs of crops.

The red and yellow clay soils, mentioned above, seem to differ from the black-prairie soil, mainly in the absence. of, or poverty in, lime. They are designated as "hog wallow", and deemed of "little account"; mainly, it seems, on account of the difficulty of tillage in wet seasons, and liability to injury from drought.

THE CENTRAL PRAIRIE REGION.

The central prairie region constitutes a narrow belt, rarely exceeding 10 miles in width, traversing the state. in a northeasterly and southwesterly direction from the region between Harrisonburg and Columbia, on the. Washita river, to the Sabine river below Sabinetown, on the western border of Texas. Its distinctive character. is the occurrence of prairies, mostly small, partly of the black calcareous soil, partly of that stiff and intractable. kind popularly known as "hog-wallow" from its rough, lumpy surface—the result of the mud-cracks which form in it during the dry season, and, being partially filled up with dry earth, compel a bulging of the ground whenever. wetted by rains.

Both kinds of soil are almost directly derived from underlying strata of the marine Tertiary (Jackson and Vicksburg groups), which frequently form outcrops in the washes and ravines. Where these strata are calcareous, they form black-prairie soil, which is more or less clayey or light, according to the nature of the strata from which it is derived. The "hog-wallow" soil is the result of the disintegration of clay beds poor in lime, and in consequence. producing an unthrifty and heavy, intractable soil. The better quality of the latter soil bears a fair growth of post. oak: the poorer, only a little grass and a few hawthorn bushes. The black prairie is naturally covered with a. luxuriant growth of grass, interspersed with clumps of wild plum and crab, as well as hawthorn (of larger size. than on the "hog-wallow"), and honey locust.

Both kinds of level "prairie" tracts are rarely more than a few miles in extent, being interrupted by ridges. stretching in from the adjacent territory of the long-leaf pine, or oak-uplands region. These ridges may thus have. black prairie or "hog-wallow" prairie at their bases, red or yellow loam with oak and hickory on their flanks, and on their crests the sandy soil bearing the long- or short-leaf pine. To designate or map out these prairies and intersecting ridges would require a very detailed survey. Hence the outline given on the map must be understood. as simply circumscribing the limits within which the several kinds of prairie soils occur at all. The whole region is exceedingly similar to the central prairie region of the state of Mississippi, (a) and its soils are doubtless of similar. composition, as they are alike in respect to their agricultural qualities and defects; the black prairies being mostly exceedingly fertile, and yielding large returns of a fine staple of cotton; while the "hog-wallow" tracts can only in very favorable seasons sustain a respectable position as cotton-producing soils. In the level portions of the "hog-wallow", especially, as well as in some portions of the black prairie where the stiff subsoil underlies near the surface, the cotton is liable to "rust" or, probably rather, *blight*, consequent upon an unhealthy condition of the tap-root, induced by the undrained and close subsoil.

a See the description and discussion of the region of the same name in that state.

One obstacle to the settlement of this region, is the difficulty of obtaining a water supply in wells, no water being found usually within 80 or 100 feet of the surface, and, when obtained, of poor quality, being impregnated with soluble salts of lime and magnesia. This difficulty could probably here, as in the corresponding part of Mississippi, be overcome by the boring of artesian wells; but nothing of the kind has thus far been attempted.

In the part of this region lying along the Washita river, in Catahoula and Caldwell parishes, the surface is hilly, and sometimes broken, but the soil is fertile, black-prairie spots appear on the hillsides, and the forest growth includes, besides oaks, a good deal of hickory, walnut, wild plum, hawthorn, and crab-apple.

In the portions lying adjacent to Red river, the general features above described are, on the whole, much less pronounced. In the region drained by the waters of lake Jatt, in Grant and Winn parishes, long-leaf pine hills are the predominant feature, varied only here and there by small prairie spots. Similarly, the hilly country drained by Casatche bayou, in Natchitoches parish, is mainly of a pine hills character; the Tertiary strata cropping out frequently near the base of the hills, and giving rise to small tracts or patches of black, or "hog-wallow", soil, as the case may be. Farther southwest, on the waters of the Toreau, the prairie feature is still more feebly developed, and the rolling oak-uplands of southern Sabine have a fine oak growth of black, Spanish, and white oaks, hickories, ash, elm, and some short-leaf pine. The surface soil is rather light, with a very red, and somewhat heavy subsoil at 8 to 9 inches. Within a few miles of the edge of the Sabine bottom, there is a strip of genuine "red land" soil, as indicated on the map. Here, as farther north, this soil is found to be especially lasting, and very productive of grain.

No. 165. A sample of the *red loam subsoil* of the rolling oak-uplands, just referred to, lying between the Toreau and Sabine rivers, in southern Sabine parish, was taken in a level tract, timbered as above noted. The surface soil and immediate subsoil down to 10 to 12 inches, resemble those of the pine hills, and the herbaceous growth is not much better than in the latter. The subsoil was taken at from 12 to 18 inches depth; it is a moderately heavy loam, glaringly orange-red, without any coarse sand. The analysis gave the following result:

Red-loam upland subsoil, Sabine parish.

	No. 165.
Insoluble matter	49.120 } 72.570
Soluble silica	23.450
Potash	0.202
Soda	0.065
Lime	0.268
Magnesia	0.290
Brown oxide of manganese	0.146
Peroxide of iron	5.224
Alumina	15.282
Phosphoric acid	0.033
Sulphuric acid	0.050
Water and organic matter	5.509
Total	99.694
Hygroscopic moisture	12.140
absorbed at	25.6 C.°

The high lime-percentage, and the extraordinarily large amount of soluble silica and alumina, together with the high moisture-coefficient, at once recall the fact that these soils are underlaid at no great depth by the calcareous clays of the Tertiary formation, and explain the prevalence of such trees as ash, black and white oaks, on what appears very much like any other pine-upland soil, near the surface. There is, however, a marked deficiency in phosphoric acid, in consequence of which these lands would soon require the restoration of that ingredient. But deep-rooted crops, like cotton, with deep tillage, would doubtless be profitable on this soil for a number of years.

The limited prairie region on the waters of the bayou Anacoco, in Vernon parish, which in many respects greatly resembles the central prairie region, is treated of in connection with the long-leaf pine region, in which it forms a small but fertile oasis (see above).

THE OAK UPLANDS REGION.

The rolling, or sometimes hilly, oak uplands, to be considered under this head, form the prominent and characteristic feature of northwestern Louisiana, outside of the bottom of Red river and the long-leaf pine hills.

There are substantially four different kinds of soil, that, with their intermixtures, represent the agricultural resources of the uplands of this region, viz: the *red lands*, the *brown loam lands*, the *pale sandy loam lands*, and the *gray pine-flats soil*. These soils, however, are so irregularly spotted about among the ridges and valleys, that only a detailed sectional map could fully represent the respective areas of occurrence. For the purposes of the present work, it must suffice to indicate on the map some of the main features of their distribution, supplementing the same in the descriptions of the several parishes.

Red lands.

A striking feature of most of the better class of upland soils in northwestern Louisiana, is the deep orange or "red" tint of the subsoil, due to a large percentage of ferric hydrate (iron rust), very evenly and finely distributed through the mass, and imparting to it, in a high degree, the qualities of ferruginous soils. Not unfrequently the iron is also found in concretionary pebbles, up to masses of considerable size, constituting available deposits of good limonite ore; or, again, it may be so abundantly present in the finely pulverulent form only, as to tint with its red dust all exposed objects, during dry seasons. The "red lands" having a good "lay", and not rendered uncultivatable by an excess of ferruginous gravel or limonite nodules, are among the most highly esteemed soils of this portion of the state, although often most unpromising in their aspect; they being not only productive, but especially very durable. The usual timber growth is oak and hickory, almost always associated with more or less of the short-leaf pine; the greater or less prevalence of the black oak and hickories over the pine and inferior oaks (post and black-jack) being a fair index of the relative fertility of different tracts. The "red lands" proper, which prevail most extensively north of the Red river, in Lincoln, Jackson, Claiborne, and Bossier parishes, are usually hilly, and sometimes rather broken for cultivation; but some of these unpromising-looking lands have been cultivated in corn and cotton for thirty and forty years, without a sensible diminution of their productiveness. This best class of "red-land" soil is a loam rather than a clay, in consequence of the cementation of the soil particles by the iron. Occasionally this feature, carried to excess, interferes with the penetration of the roots, rendering the soil too gravelly or stony; but in that case good tillage improves it very much. Three samples of these character-istic red soils have thus far been analyzed, with the results given below.

No. 184. Red-lands subsoil, taken 7 miles southeast of Mansfield, De Soto parish, on the Pleasant Hill road. The surface soil is gray, rather sandy, about 5 inches in depth. The subsoil, taken from 5 to 12 inches depth, is glaringly orange red; full of ferruginous gravel. At 12 inches there underlies a bed of limonite-ore nodules. The timber is not large, consisting of short-leaf pine, Spanish and post oaks, and hickory, the roots scarcely able to pene-trate the ore bed below.

No. 48. Dolet hills subsoil.—In the hilly country bordering the Red river bottom on the south, in De Soto and Natchitoches parishes (the Dolet hills country), the glaringly red subsoil also prevails largely, but is quite a heavy clay, and the forest growth it bears (black-jack, post, and scarlet, with a little black, oaks) is under-size on the uplands, while walnut, ash, and tulip trees appear in the narrow bottoms. A specimen of the heavy red subsoil was taken on a hillside about two miles from Granning's ferry over the bayou Pierre. The surface soil is only a few inches deep, a little more sandy and grayish; depth to which the subsoil was taken, 5 to 15 inches.

No. 231. Red-lands soil, from near Vienna, Lincoln parish. This is a typical red-land district. There is mostly a shallow, sandy surface soil, 2 or 3 inches deep, but often the red subsoil itself comes to the surface, as in the case of the land from which the sample was taken to the depth of 10 inches. Timber, oak and hickory, with short-leaf pine; said to be a very lasting and fairly productive soil.

Red lands soil and subsoils.

	DE SOTO PARISH. (S. 6, T. 11, R. 12 W.)		LINCOLN PARISH.
	South of Mans-field subsoil.	Dolet hills sub-soil.	Vienna soil.
	No. 184.	No. 48.	No. 231.
Insoluble matter	74.720 } 81.290	71.800 } 79.250	48.055 } 64.130
Soluble silica	6.560	7.450	16.075
Potash	0.218	0.287	0.270
Soda	0.187	0.006	0.008
Lime	0.148	0.055	0.130
Magnesia	0.438	0.449	0.430
Brown oxide of manganese	0.213	0.066	0.210
Peroxide of iron	8.617	8.966	15.927
Alumina	4.908	7.118	11.720
Phosphoric acid	0.152	0.179	0.805
Sulphuric acid	0.054	0.007	0.090
Water and organic matter	3.379	4.230	7.074
Total	99.565	100.785	100.922
Hygroscopic moisture	5.675	8.090	14.118
absorbed at	24.6 C.°	21.8 C.°	28 C.°

The composition of the soil No. 231 shows good cause for its productiveness and durability in the high percentage of phosphoric acid, and the high degree of decomposition shown by the large amount of soluble silica and alumina, indicating the availability of its store of plant-food. Moreover, the high percentage of iron, as shown by the moisture-coefficient, renders it almost drought-proof. Its lime-percentage is not high and could advantageously be increased by liming.

No. 184 is behind the one just referred to, both as to phosphoric acid and potash and moisture-coefficient, though somewhat ahead in respect to lime. Where it is sufficiently deep, it will doubtless prove very productive.

No. 48 is a very close and heavy soil, and its composition shows a deficiency in lime, which is so especially needed in land of this character. With this addition, thorough tillage, and the practice of green-manuring for the purpose of introducing the deficient vegetable matter, it would doubtless prove a very productive and durable soil, as apparently similar land in the same region is known to be.

Doubtless much of the heavy red subsoil mentioned repeatedly, is richer in nutritive ingredients than the last one mentioned; none probably is poorer. But I think the necessity for applying lime exists in all, judging by the usual vegetation.

Brown loam.

In the rolling uplands or broad ridges of Sabine, De Soto, and Caddo, as well as at some other points, we find a light orange or brown loam subsoil, covered by from 6 to 10 inches of a somewhat lighter soil, timbered mainly with good-sized black and Spanish oaks (*Quercus tinctoria* and *falcata*), with some post and black-jack oaks interspersed. The country covered by this soil is very similar to the table-lands region of northern Mississippi, and maintains a fair degree of fertility after long exhaustive cultivation, to which it has largely been subjected. Its quality improves as we descend from the dividing ridges, and especially on the gentler slope toward the Sabine; where the "Grand Cane" region in western De Soto forms one of the most fertile tracts in northwestern Louisiana. Here the oaks mingle with, and are gradually almost replaced by, beech, tulip tree ("poplar"), maple, elm, ash, hickory, and walnut, all large trees, indicating a generous, durable, and easily-tilled soil.

The brown loam soils are doubtless similar in composition to the "table-land soils" of Mississippi.

Pale loam.

A pale yellow, sandy loam subsoil prevails largely in the more level portions of northern Louisiana; the surface soil being grayish and sometimes rather ashy, and bearing a growth of post, black-jack, and some scarlet oaks, black gum, and more or less short-leaf pine. It is a third-rate soil, somewhat better than the pine-hills soil, but not thrifty, and wearing out beyond the limits of profitable culture, in the course of seven or eight years. When fresh it yields about 500 pounds of seed-cotton per acre, and 20 bushels of corn. It covers large areas in the northern parishes, and passes gradually on the one hand into the "red lands" (whose red subsoil is always a mark of improvement in quality, and is accompanied by an increase of the hickories among the timber), and on the other into the brown loam or table-land soil described above. The only Louisiana soil of this character thus far analyzed, is from the upland portion of Morehouse parish, known as the Bastrop hills, and more specially considered in another place.

No. 232. *Sandy loam soil*, from the undulating uplands 2 miles east of Bastrop; taken to the depth of 12 inches. Pale yellow, with little coarse sand. Vegetation: oak, hickory, short-leaf pine.

No. 233. *Subsoil of the above*, taken at the depth of 12 to 18 inches. Yellow, somewhat heavier and deeper tinted than the surface soil.

Bastrop hills soil, Morehouse parish.

	MOREHOUSE PARISH.	
	Bastrop hills soil.	Bastrop hills subsoil.
	No. 232.	No. 233.
Insoluble matter	81.700 } 87.450 5.750 }	68.890 } 81.540 12.650 }
Soluble silica		
Potash	0.442	0.344
Soda	0.296	0.070
Lime	0.101	0.120
Magnesia	0.239	0.440
Brown oxide of manganese	0.396	0.228
Peroxide of iron	3.546	4.788
Alumina	4.868	9.281
Phosphoric acid	0.099	0.111
Sulphuric acid	0.079	0.088
Water and organic matter	2.544	3.876
Total	100.040	100.281
Hygroscopic moisture	5.471	9.441
absorbed at	20 C.°	20 C.°

This soil is almost identical in composition with that of the short-leaf pine uplands of Mississippi, and like these will soon require the supplementing of its somewhat scanty supply of phosphates, while its thriftiness should be increased by liming. Its potash-supply is fair, as is also its retention of moisture; but both can be advantageously increased by deep culture.

Pine flats.

In ill-drained tracts (as in the Black lake country in Natchitoches and Red River parishes, as well as in many of the lake regions on both sides of Red river) the subsoil becomes whitish by the formation of concretions of bog ore or black pebble; and thus the soil becomes poorer than in the uplands, unless enriched by sediment. This kind of "pine-flat soil" is about the least esteemed in this region; even its timber growth being rather indifferent, and often quite stunted.

In Bossier parish, between bayous Bodcau and Dorchite, there is a long level tract, extending from the Arkansas line to lake Bistineau. Much of it is sandy or ashy pine land, some heavier and "crawfishy", with a white clay subsoil. Where well drained (as near Cotton valley) some of this land is quite productive; farther south, some of it forms small prairies of a white soil covered with grass and thorn bushes, and very unproductive. These gray flats form a striking contrast to the "red-land ridges" to which they are frequently adjacent.

Most of the country northward of the main D'Arbonne, in Claiborne and Union parishes, forms level or slightly undulating plateaus between the larger streams, near which alone the country is sometimes somewhat broken. This plateau land has partly a soil intermediate in character between the brown and the pale yellow loam lands mentioned above; the subsoil often taking an orange or red tint at 18 or 20 inches, and thus occasionally, when near the surface, forming a kind of "red land". In part, again, it has a gray, somewhat ashy or sandy soil, underlaid by gravel at 18 to 24 inches; or sometimes by gray clay, and when this comes near the surface, it forms a heavy gary soil intermixed with gravel or broken rock, popularly called "cowhide" land. These soils have not been sufficiently examined, and none have been analyzed; but the fact that the country is well settled with small, thrifty farms, proves that they respond kindly to fair treatment. Some details regarding them will be found in the descriptions of the respective parishes.

GENERAL REMARKS ON COTTON PRODUCTION IN LOUISIANA.

TABLE III.—SHOWING POPULATION AND COTTON PRODUCTION IN EACH AGRICULTURAL REGION OF LOUISIANA.

Agricultural region.	Area.	POPULATION.			COTTON PRODUCTION.									
		Total.	White.	Colored.	Acres.	Bales (475 pounds).	Average per acre.				Total in tons.		Percentage of the state's total production.	Cotton acreage per square mile.
							Bales (475 pounds).	Seed-cotton.	Lint.	Seed.	Lint.	Seed.		
Alluvial region:	Sq. mls.							Lbs.	Lbs.	Lbs.				
North of Red river	7,813	121,415	29,019	92,396	278,192	221,115	0.79	1,125	375	750	52,515	105,080	43.5	35.0
South of Red river	5,681	181,435	80,611	100,824	86,598	61,275	0.71	1,011	337	674	14,553	29,106	12.0	14.7
Tide-water parishes	7,215	303,613	198,288	105,325	1,917	794	0.41	585	195	390	188	376	0.2	0.2
Bluff region	1,295	47,907	13,887	34,020	61,542	28,664	0.47	660	228	446	6,808	13,616	5.6	47.2
Atakapas region	4,946	78,643	43,038	35,605	64,474	28,656	0.46	657	219	438	7,043	14,086	5.8	14.8
Long-leaf pine region	9,956	64,155	43,752	20,402	56,598	22,862	0.40	570	190	380	5,316	10,632	4.4	5.7
Oak uplands	9,414	163,778	66,356	96,430	315,780	144,863	0.46	607	219	438	34,362	68,734	26.5	33.5
Total for the state	45,430	959,946	454,954	484,992	864,787	506,569	0.50	840	280	560	120,785	241,570	100.0	19.0

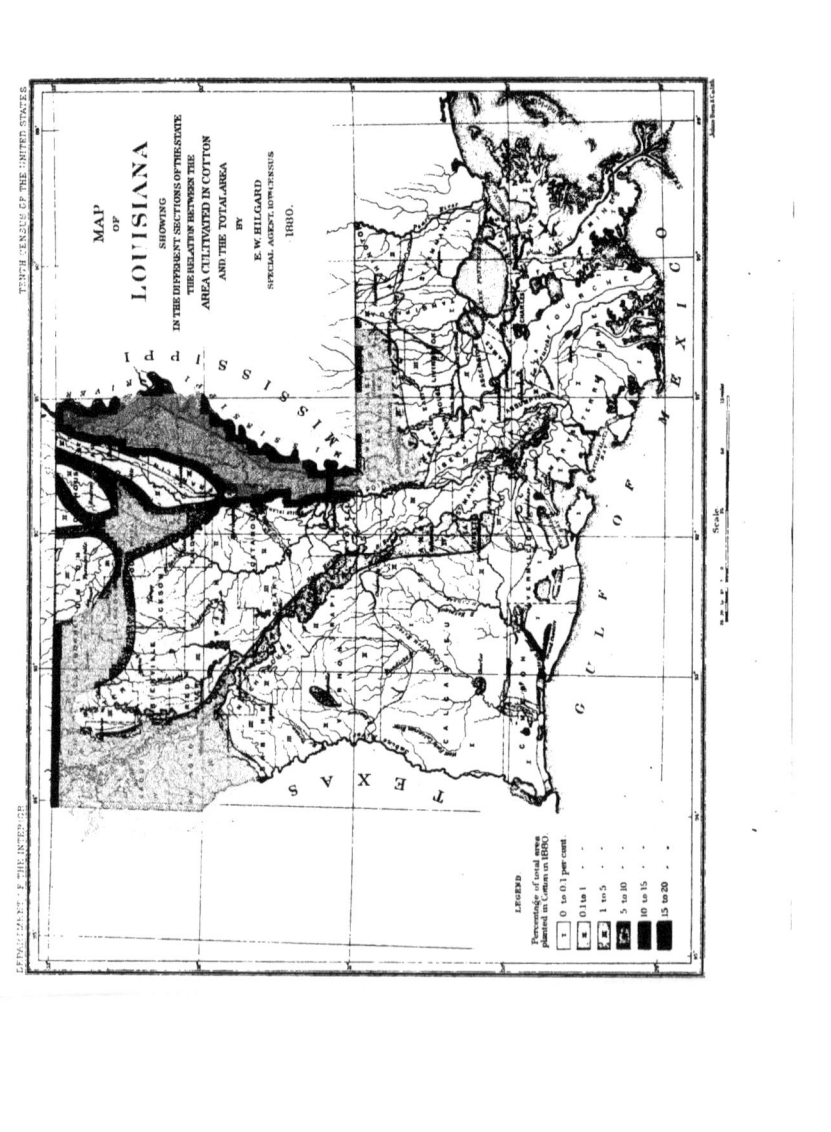

MAP
OF
LOUISIANA
SHOWING
IN THE DIFFERENT SECTIONS OF THE STATE
THE RELATION BETWEEN THE
AREA CULTIVATED IN COTTON
AND THE TOTAL AREA
BY
E. W. HILGARD
SPECIAL AGENT, 10TH CENSUS.
1880.

LEGEND
Percentage of total areas
planted in Cotton in 1880.

0 to 0.1 per cent.
0.1 to 1
1 to 5
5 to 10
10 to 15
15 to 20

Scale

TABLE IV.—SHOWING "BANNER COUNTIES" AS REGARDS PRODUCTION AND PRODUCT PER ACRE IN EACH AGRICULTURAL REGION OF LOUISIANA.

Regions according to product per acre.	Average product per acre.	COUNTIES IN EACH REGION HAVING HIGHEST TOTAL PRODUCTION.					COUNTIES IN EACH REGION HAVING HIGHEST PRODUCT PER ACRE.					
		Name.	Rank in product per acre in the state.	Cotton acreage.	Total production.	Product per acre.	Name.	Rank in total production in the state.	Cotton acreage.	Total production.	Product per acre.	Rank in product per acre in the state.
	Bales.				Bales.	Bales.				Bales.	Bale.	
Alluvial region, north of Red River	0.79	Tensas	4	50,556	41,859	0.83	East Carroll	2	40,167	38,160	0.95	2
Alluvial region, south of Red River	0.72	Pointe Coupée	8	24,196	18,935	0.78	Saint Charles	50	51	47	0.92	3
Bluff region	0.47	West Feliciana	28	21,072	11,810	0.56	West Feliciana	15	21,072	11,810	0.56	28
Attakapas region	0.46	Saint Landry	24	42,135	23,148	0.55	Saint Landry	7	42,135	23,148	0.55	24
Oak uplands region	0.46	Bossier	15	37,133	25,073	0.68	Bossier	4	37,133	25,073	0.68	15
Tide-water parishes	0.41	Cameron	39	1,002	636	0.33	Orleans	51	7	12	1.71	1
Long-leaf pine region	0.40	Saint Helena	27	13,636	5,825	0.39	Grant	29	11,155	5,156	0.46	36

"Banner county" of the state as regards total production, Tensas, 41,859 bales.

"Banner county" of the state as regards product per acre (omitting those whose production is less than 100 bales), East Carroll, 1,353 pounds of seed-cotton.

DISTRIBUTION OF PRODUCTION IN THE STATE AT LARGE.—The most broadly obvious fact, rendered apparent by a glance at the map showing the relative areas given to cotton culture in the state, or by an inspection of Tables II and III, is the decrease of cotton production as we advance southward. Seventy-eight and a half per cent. of the entire cotton crop of the state is produced north of the latitude of the mouth of Red river; 12 only in the alluvial region south of Red river, and in the tide-water parishes two-tenths of 1 per cent. only; no cotton at all being reported by seven of these in 1880.

Since cotton is successfully grown in all tropical countries, this decrease is evidently not caused by the lower latitude as such; and the fact that the decrease is equally apparent in the rich alluvial parishes and in those occupied by the long-leaf pine proves that it is not attributable to a difference in the soils.

· An inspection of Table II (see first of the report) shows that, so far as the alluvial parishes are concerned, it is the replacement of cotton culture by that of the sugar-cane that causes the decrease. To this, as we approach the tide-water region, is added the culture of rice in increasing proportion.

The inference is that these crops are found to be more profitable than cotton, where the soil and climate are suitable. As regards the latter, the late and early frosts liable to occur in the region north of Red river shorten the season too much for the safety of the sugar-cane, but not for that of the cotton crop; hence it is only southward of that popularly recognized dividing line between north and south Louisiana that cane gradually gains precedence in the lowlands, while in the uplands bordering the great valley, and fairly settled, cotton culture continues far to southward, even reaching the gulf shore at the "Five islands", among which Petite Anse and Côte Blanche have possessed extensive cotton plantations. Apart from these, cotton is little seen in the tide-water region, even the culture of the long-staple having become almost extinct.

It is to be regretted that in consequence of the specific nature of the questions embraced in the schedules, but few of those sent to the cane-growing parishes have elicited any replies conveying positive information. In answer to direct questions as to the reasons for the overwhelming preference given to cane, two have been given. One, and the chief, is that "cane is more profitable than cotton where it can be grown", the implication being that while cotton has to compete with all the rest of the cotton growing states, sugar-cane is almost a monopoly of Louisiana, and is more or less protected by the import duties on sugar. Some have added that the frequency of showers during the picking season interferes somewhat with the gathering of the crop, besides tending to depress its grade in the market. An inspection of the rain tables thus far available does not seem to show any general difference in the distribution of the rainfall as between the region north and that south of the mouth of Red river; yet it may be that an examination of the number of rainy days in each month would corroborate the assertion made. Nevertheless, it is not at all likely that the difference is so great as to interfere with the adoption of cotton as the chief crop of the now cane-growing region, in case commercial changes or the competition of sorghum sugar should render sugar production less profitable.

As regards the uplands in the same latitude, the fact that cane requires a deep, moist soil, and deeper culture than cotton, explains the fact that even in the more fertile portions of the Attakapas prairies, in La Fayette and Saint Landry, cotton is, with corn, the preferred crop. The decrease of the culture to westward occurs not only in the case of cotton, but holds as regards all branches of agriculture except stock raising on the natural pasture, which is altogether the predominant industry, the population being very sparse. The soils of these westerly portions of the Attakapas region are also, on the whole, less productive than in the portions lying adjacent to the

Mississippi valley; yet soils inferior to theirs are profitably employed in cotton growing in the southeastern states. The same is more or less true of the portion of east Louisiana lying north of lakes Maurepas and Pontchartrain.— Saint Tammany, and the southern part of Tangipahoa, where stock raising and lumbering predominate at present. It is by comparison with the profusely fertile soils of the more immediate valley and delta plain of the Mississippi river that the soils of these regions are now frequently designated as "too poor to pay for cultivation". But cotton is profitably grown in Georgia, South Carolina, and Florida on land at least no better than that of the pine flats and gray silt prairies of southern Louisiana; and the time will come when these will be equally esteemed as available agricultural lands. In one case only does the cotton product per acre descend as low as is commonly the case in northern Florida and adjacent parts of Georgia on unmanured lands, viz, 0.23 bale in Vermillion parish; and this is probably due to imperfect culture by the Creole population, rather than to poverty of the soil.

DISTRIBUTION OF COTTON PRODUCTION AMONG THE AGRICULTURAL REGIONS.—Table III shows that the *alluvial region* north of Red river mouth, constituting 16.1 per cent. of the state's area, produces 43.5 per cent. of the whole cotton crop; 12 per cent. more is the product of the alluvial region lying south of the mouth of Red river. To this should be added the product of the alluvial bottom or Red river itself; but the form of the returns does not admit of its direct segregation from the totals of the parishes within which (above Rapides) it is mainly embraced. A near approach to such separate estimate can, however, be derived from the average product per acre given for the parishes concerned, viz: Natchitoches, Red River, Bossier, and Caddo. Allowing for the uplands portion of these parishes the general average of 0.40 of a bale, deducible from the average of the rest of the oak uplands region, and for the Red River bottom a slightly higher average product than that of the northern portion of the Mississippi alluvial region, viz, 0.84 bale per acre, the cotton acreages of these Red river parishes that should be assigned to the lowlands can be deduced from the excess of their averages above that of the upland parishes (viz, 0.40 bale). Making the calculation on this basis, we find that of the total product of 72,873 bales reported from these parishes, 39,335 are to be credited to the Red River bottom lands, making 7.7 per cent. of the state's total production. Including with these amounts the 0.2 per cent. grown in the tide-water parishes, we find that at least 63.4 per cent. of the state's total cotton crop is grown in the lowlands of the two great rivers, within not quite one-third of the area of the state. Since in the upland regions also a large part of the cotton crop is grown on bottom lands, it is obvious that an unusually large proportion of Louisiana cotton is of lowland growth, and this circumstance has doubtless much influence in imparting to "Orleans" cotton its character and commercial reputation.

Next to the alluvial region, the *oak uplands* of northwestern Louisiana contribute the largest share of the balance. / Deducting from their tabulated quota the 7.7 per cent. estimated to belong to Red River bottom lands, we still have 20.7 per cent. coming from this upland region, as against 15.9 from all the rest of the upland parishes; the respective areas being to each other as 3 to 5.

The three *bluff parishes*, though constituting less than 2.9 of the state's area, contribute nevertheless 5.6 per cent. of the total cotton product, having the largest cotton acreage per square mile among the regions as a whole; nearly one-half of their area being given to this culture. The fact that they are among the earliest settled and most readily accessible portions of the state has doubtless largely influenced the choice and extent of the culture; but in addition, their generally light and calcareous soils are especially adapted to cotton culture, the crop, though only moderate in the yield per acre, rarely failing.

The *Attakapas region* is not readily comparable in regard to cotton acreage and production as a whole with other portions of the state, on account of its sparsely-settled condition, due largely to remoteness, as well as to historical and social causes. With an area three and one-third times greater than the bluff parishes, its cotton product is practically the same, and nearly ten-elevenths of this amount is produced in La Fayette and Saint Landry, or rather, as regards the latter parish, in the eastern half of the same, the western being merely a great cattle pasture up to this time. The small parish of La Fayette, with its 239.3 acres of tilled lands per square mile, of which one-fifth is occupied by cotton, gives a fairer idea of the capabilities of the region than can be derived from the average of the whole.

As to the *long-leaf pine region*, the smallness of its contribution of 4.4 per cent. of the state's production, from over one-fifth (21.9 per cent.) of its area, is also primarily due to sparseness of settlement; the population forming only 6.8 per cent. of that of the state. That it is not due alone to poverty of soil is apparent from the high product per acre (0.40 bale), being not very far behind that of the Attakapas region. In estimating the possible future production, however, it must not be forgotten that the lands now occupied by cotton are chiefly the bottoms of the streams, which may be estimated to constitute from 7 to 10 per cent. of the total area, the uplands being much less productive, and as yet but little under tillage.

In the *tide-water parishes*, as remarked before, commercial considerations restrict the growing of cotton to occasional spasmodic efforts, so that no general conclusions unfavorable to cotton-growing can justly be drawn from their statistics. All the cotton reported in 1880 seems to have been "uplands", or short staple. As regards the culture of sea-island or long-staple cotton, which before the war flourished at some points in the marsh parishes, the fact that the deep but fairly fertile soils on which it succeeds best elsewhere are of comparatively rare occurrence near the Louisiana coast may militate against a wide extension of this industry, so profitable where the natural

136

conditions are favorable. That the latter exist in the "live-oak ridges" of Cameron and Vermillion, experience has already established; but it seems likely that the same is true of the seaward portions of Saint Mary's, Terrebonne, and Lafourche, where similar lands lie along the bayous, and on the landward edge of the marshes toward the Attakapas prairies. It may well happen that there, and even in a part of the Houma country, the sugar-cane will before long be at least partially replaced by the long-staple cotton.

ACREAGE IN COTTON.—The graphic representation of the ratios between acreage in cotton and total areas given in the map conveys the general facts in this respect better than can be done in words or figures; the more as its shades are outlined, not by counties, but from data derived partly from detailed returns, partly from correspondence or personal observation. The causes and details of this distribution, however, require closer consideration.

As between uplands and lowlands, the summation by parishes, as per tables, places the cotton acreage in the lowlands at 42.4 per cent. of the state's total. But by making the proper allowance for the bottom portion of the Red River parishes, on the assumption explained above, the lowland acreage is raised to 46.8 per cent., or within 3.2 per cent. of half the cotton acreage of the state.

COTTON ACREAGE IN THE SEVERAL REGIONS.—The acreage table resulting from the summation by parishes gives to the *oak uplands region* the greatest total acreage. But when the correction, above made, for the Red River lowlands is applied, the acreage of the region is reduced by the 48,017 acres thus transferred to the lowlands, viz, to 267,743, or 31.0 per cent. of the total cotton acreage of the state, or somewhat over three-fifths of the total of the lowlands. Deducting from the total area of the oak uplands region the 950 square miles belonging to the Red River bottom above Rapides, we find for the uplands proper a cotton acreage of 31.6 per square mile, while that of the Red River bottom region embraced within these counties is 50.5. It thus appears that the Red River bottom, as a whole is exceeded in its cotton acreage per square mile only by three of the alluvial parishes, viz: East Carroll, Tensas, and Concordia; and by three of the upland parishes, viz: East and West Feliciana, and Claiborne, the latter itself belonging to the oak uplands division.

As regards the *lowland division* north of Red river, the summations by parishes here also give results not fully representing the facts of the case on account of the large upland areas of comparatively low production embraced within the group. Thus West Carroll, Caldwell, and Catahoula give in nearly all the columns of Tables I and II figures strikingly below those of the exclusively alluvial parishes; and the same is true, to a less extent, of Richland and Franklin. It would be difficult to apply to the returns, as furnished, corrections similar to those made in the case of the Red River parishes, save upon the assumption that practically all the cotton grown in this group is produced in the lowlands. That this assumption is not very wide of the truth is proved by the figures of the columns showing product per acre, which, apart from the extraordinary product of East Carroll, oscillate not very far from 1,000 pounds of seed-cotton per acre. It is for this reason that the parishes above named, though having a largely preponderating upland area, have nevertheless been placed in the lowland group. Making the calculation on the above basis for the (partly upland) parishes of West Carroll, Morehouse, Ouachita, Caldwell, Richland, Franklin, and Catahoula, we find an average acreage of 52.2 per square mile for the whole group, but ranging from 25.0 in the case of West Carroll to 85.4 in that of Ouachita. The varying productiveness and availability of the alluvial lands, with the greater or less facility of communication with market, explain sufficiently such differences, while it is often difficult to follow them in detail. The cause of the marked preference given to cotton in East Carroll, for example, with its 100.4 acres in cotton per square mile, may lie mainly in the high production per acre, this parish having the maxima in the state in both respects. But the causes of this high production are doubtless themselves complex, and operate similarly in the adjoining counties of Chicot, Arkansas, and Washington, Mississippi, where similar maxima are observed.

Of the parishes of the group lying south of Red river mouth, Rapides shows an apparent anomaly in an acreage (17.1) lower than Avoyelles (27.3), and less than half of that of Pointe Coupée (42.0), the latter lying far to southward. As a matter of fact, by far the greater portion of the cotton product of Rapides comes from the Red River bottom lands, which constitute nearly one-third of its surface, and are as productive and as well settled as any portion of the Red River country. Assigning all the acreage to the lowlands, we find 53.9 per square mile of the 475, doubtless an excess; but making all probable allowance for the uplands, especially north of Red river, the density of cotton culture in the bottom will still remain higher than that of Avoyelles, and is probably not far from that of Pointe Coupée. Southward of the latter the proximity to the cotton-growing uplands affects West Baton Rouge on the one hand and Saint Martin on the other; but southward the sugar-cane overshadows all the *tide-water* parishes, scarcely requiring mention in this connection.

In the *bluff region* as a whole the cotton acreage reaches its maximum (47.3), its average being exceeded by only nine parishes in the state, and the highest acreage within it (viz: 58.7 in East Feliciana) only by East Carroll, Tensas, and Concordia, half of all the tilled land being in cotton, as against an average of 70 in the four river parishes (East Carroll, Madison, Concordia, and Tensas) with which a comparison can properly be made, and of 62.1 for the whole of the group north of Red river mouth. Indian corn is here, as elsewhere in the cotton-growing region, the chief competitor of cotton for the occupancy of the ground.

The unequal distribution of cotton production in the *Attakapas region* has already been alluded to, as also the fact that ten-elevenths of the total cotton product belong to Saint Landry and La Fayette, as does five-sixths of the total acreage. A large proportion of both factors, as regards Saint Landry, is derived from the portion of the parish belonging to the great alluvial plain. The parish of La Fayette, on the contrary, is almost wholly uplands, and one-fifth (20.0) of its tilled lands is devoted to cotton, the rest being mainly corn. While the cotton acreage per square mile in Iberia (12.8) is only a little over one-fourth as much as in La Fayette (47.8), yet the proportion of its tilled lands given to cotton culture (15.0) is three-fourths as great as in La Fayette. Moreover, it is reported to be on the increase, and certainly the soil of the Iberia prairies is eminently well adapted to cotton.

The causes of the relatively and absolutely small production and acreage of cotton in the *long-leaf pine region* have already been alluded to. It is as a whole the most sparsely settled portion of the state, as is apparent from its having the smallest percentage of tilled lands of all the regions, viz, 2.5 per cent., and a population of only 6.4 per square mile. Of the tilled lands, however, over one-third (35.6 per cent.) is devoted to cotton, showing the adaptability of its soils to that industry, which is also sustained by the relatively large cotton product per acre (0.40 bale). The causes leading to this result are more fully considered below, under the proper head.

PRODUCT PER ACRE.—As might be expected, the returns show the maxima of production per acre to occur in the *lowlands* of the Mississippi, northward of Red river; and the alluvial bottom of the latter must be credited with at least equal productiveness, according to the details of local observation. Eliminating as much as possible the influence of the upland production upon this factor, we find that the average of actual product per acre in the great bottoms may be assumed to be in the neighborhood of 0.84 bale, or 409 pounds of cotton lint per acre; the maximum occurring in East Carroll (0.95), the minimum among the purely alluvial parishes in Concordia (0.79 bale). Thence southward, there appears a pretty regularly progressive decrease, broken only by the extraordinary case of the 51 acres in Saint Charles, which, of course, cannot be counted in drawing averages, and the low product of Saint Martin, where the influence of an upland area is apparent.

The cause of the decrease southward is not obvious. It may be partly due to the fact that in the southern alluvial parishes the enormously productive "buckshot" soil is more frequently covered by the lighter and less thrifty modern alluvial deposits, and to some extent to the preference given to sugar-cane as the chief crop, upon which the best part of the land and care is bestowed.

But the above average, though nearly twice as great as that of the uplands at large, is but a partial index of the capabilities of the soil. Almost throughout the bottoms the land is owned in large tracts, and the entire business of production is managed in a "wholesale" style, which is little conducive to obtaining the best possible results from each acre. Moreover, as the population table shows, the work of cultivation is almost exclusively done by negroes, to a large extent not even under the direct supervision of whites. To those acquainted with the character of the southern negro, this clearly means that, on the whole, the work is done very roughly and superficially, even when the laborer's personal interest is directly involved in the amount produced. The negro, even more than the white planter, believes in cultivating as much land as possible when desiring to increase production; the idea of "intense culture", requiring close attention and thorough work throughout, is antagonistic to his instincts. It thus happens not unfrequently that in favorable seasons labor enough to pick all the cotton cannot be obtained, and the last picking, or a part thereof, is left in the fields. When special care and deep tillage has been given, and all the cotton picked, 1,000 and even 1,200 pounds of lint has been produced per acre in numerous cases, both in the Red River valley and on the buckshot lands of the Yazoo and Tensas bottoms. There is, evidently, no reason save a slovenly habit why a product twice as great as that now shown by the returns should not be the rule instead of the exception. The reply given in answer to question No. 1, p. 77, from Concordia, stating that the depth of tillage is "4 to 5 inches in sandy lands, 2 to 3 in black (*i. e.*, buckshot) lands", characterizes the state of things in this respect most fully and tersely. The sandy lands are plowed deeper, because it is easier; the heavy clay "buckshot" lands are merely scratched, even when a two-mule team is used (see question 2, same page), in order to get over more ground, and the roots of the crop are left to penetrate the subsoil as best they may. The labor thus left to be performed by the roots is certainly the most dearly paid for; it may be accomplished by them with comparative ease in favorable seasons, but in less favorable ones is certain to weigh heavily in the year's balance on the loss side of the ledger.

While, then, the sandy or "front-lands" may be presumed to be worked now up to within a reasonable approach to their maximum production, the best and most durable soils—those of the "buckshot" character—are certainly yielding a product far below their natural capacity, and may doubtless readily be made to yield double that amount. It is at present impossible to estimate the relative proportion of the two kinds of soil under cultivation, or naturally existing; the more as a permanent protection against overflows would render available a large "back-land" area, mostly of the buckshot character, that at present is practically irreclaimable swamp.

Taking into consideration all these circumstances, which at present tend to depress both the product per acre and the total production of the lowland region, its future possibilities under a more rational system of culture, and security against floods, cannot but be estimated very high.

Passing to the uplands, we find the next highest product per acre reported from the *bluff region* of east Louisiana. Analyzing the returns, however, it will be seen that those from West Feliciana and East Baton Rouge include the product of not inconsiderable lowland areas, that cannot be segregated from that of the uplands. That from East Feliciana, again, includes the product of a considerable long-leaf pine area, so that the average is doubtless somewhat lower than corresponds to the average production of the "bluff" lands alone, which would probably be from 0.41 to 0.42 bale per acre. These lands have been under cultivation a long time, and have been severely injured by the washing away of the rich black surface loam from the hill lands, which are said to have originally yielded a (400-pound) bale of lint per acre with ease. The excellent deep subsoil still existing will doubtless enable these lands to recover from their present depressed production whenever a system of small farming shall have replaced that of the plantation. This change is now in gradual progress, and the prevailing opinion seems to be that the product per acre has increased during the last decade.

The average product given for the *Attakapas region* likewise requires a correction on account of the large lowland portion of Saint Landry, whose product cannot be segregated in the returns as made. La Fayette and Iberia (0.28 and 0.33 bale, respectively) may be regarded as giving a fair index of the production of the Attakapas uplands under the present system of culture, in which, judging from the small proportion of negroes in the population, a large amount of white labor is engaged. The practice involves, however, neither rotation nor the use of fertilizers, and but very indifferent tillage of a soil of very good native fertility, that could easily be made to yield at least 0.50, i. e., half a bale of lint on an average, since 400 pounds has frequently been obtained under favorable natural conditions. This applies to the upland portion of Saint Landry (the Opelousas prairies) as well. The low product of Vermillion is probably to be accounted for on the ground of very imperfect culture by the Acadian population, and cannot be taken as proof of the decrease of native fertility in the Vermillion bayou lands.

The *long-leaf pine region* as a whole shows an unexpectedly high average product (0.40 bale) as compared with the long-leaf pine lands of the states east of the Mississippi. Two factors contribute to the latter end, viz, the thus far almost exclusive use of lowlands (creek bottom land) for cultivation; and secondly, the use of fertilizers, especially in east Louisiana, where uplands are to some extent occupied. It is thus (as appears from the special report from that parish) that the high product per acre credited to Saint Tammany (0.45 bale) was obtained, while in the case of Grant and Winn, not only the lowlands, but also the uplands, partake somewhat of the character of the adjacent oak uplands region. Eliminating these from the calculation of averages, we find 0.37 bale as the average for the six remaining parishes, 0.38 being that for the four lying east of the Mississippi (Saint Helena, Tangipahoa, Livingston, and Washington) and 0.346, or, say, 0.35, for Vernon and Calcasien. In neither of the latter two has manure or other fertilizers been used, but the Calcasieu cotton is altogether grown on creek bottom land, while in Vernon both the bottoms and a limited area of black prairie contribute to the product. In the east Louisiana parishes not only bottom land, but also second bottom and upland, *fertilized*, enter into the producing area; and it is predicable that hereafter cotton will be largely grown on this basis in a large portion of the long-leaf pine region, which has been comparatively neglected so long as there was an abundance of richer land, and within easier reach of market, at low prices. The analyses of its soils show the uplands, as well as the lowlands, to be far from poor when compared with the soils of the southern Atlantic states, and in almost every case they are capable of profitable production under a rational system of culture. The part of the region lying north of Red river, in which the oak and hickory always intermingle more or less with the pine ("Oak, hickory, and long-leaf pine region") proves the higher native fertility of the soil thus indicated by the high product per acre of the parishes of Grant and Winn, competing in this respect with Bossier and Union. Here again, however, the production is almost confined to creek bottom land, while in the last-mentioned parishes the figure given is the general average from uplands as well as lowlands.

The correction necessary in the average per acre resulting from the summation by parishes in the case of the *oak uplands region* has already been referred to above. Excluding from the calculation of averages the parishes of Caddo, Bossier, Red River, and Natchitoches, which include nearly all of the Red River bottom lands, we obtain for the rest an average of nearly 0.39 bale; but excluding also the exceptionally low average of De Soto (0.30) with its broken ridge lands and comparatively narrow valleys, long under cultivation, we find for the rest an average of almost precisely 0.40 bale per acre, the figure upon which the calculation of the acreage in cotton of the 'Red River valley has been based. The difference in favor of the product of Sabine (0.39), so similar to De Soto in its agricultural and surface features, is readily accounted for by the small proportion of "tilled lands" in the former parish (2.9 against 15.0 in De Soto), indicating that chiefly bottom lands are in cultivation thus far; while in De Soto a large proportion of ridge or plateau land is under tillage. The average figure is, however, only slightly changed whether Sabine be counted in or omitted.

The oak uplands being a region of small farms, largely worked by whites (as is shown by the almost even balance of the two races), is of especial interest as being probably nearer to a permanent condition than any other part of the state. The large proportion of tilled lands in the parishes of Lincoln and Claiborne (34.8 and 24.7 per cent.) speaks of the extensive cultivation of the uplands, and a glance at the soil map shows as one cause thereof the large area of fertile and durable "red lands", whose influence on the product per acre is manifest in the high figure (0.42 bale) for both parishes. In both, likewise, the acreage of cotton and corn is nearly equal, and both together form only 41.3 and 71.0 per cent., respectively, of the total tilled area, thus showing an unusual diversification of crops. In contrast with this, it is curious to note that in the adjacent and naturally very similar parish of Union these two crops occupy over 85 per cent. of the tilled area, cotton having 45 per cent.—a circumstance probably due to better facilities for shipment to market, via the Washita river; for the same relation appears in the case of Bienville, where lake Bistineau forms an available highway.

COTTON PRODUCT AND ACREAGE PER CAPITA OF POPULATION AND PERCENTAGE OF TILLED LAND GIVEN TO COTTON CULTURE.—These relations are of especial importance as regards the question of cotton production by white labor, and must therefore be discussed with reference to the ratio between the races.

Considering, first, the points of maxima and minima of these factors, we find at a glance that the maximum of 3.1 bales *per capita* coincides with three other maxima, viz, that of a predominance of the negro over the white race of 10.8 to 1; a cotton acreage of 100.4 to the square mile; and a product per acre of 0.95 bale—all in the parish of East Carroll. It seems difficult to escape from the inference suggested by this concurrent testimony, of an intimate correlation between the negro race and the precious staple. We vainly seek, however, for a corresponding concurrence of minima, since these occur from independent causes, notably the growing of cane. The smallest proportion of negro population occurs in Vernon, where there are 12.6 whites to one negro, being more than an inversion of the ratio existing in East Carroll. But Vernon, as well as the adjoining parish of Calcasieu, is so thinly settled (tilled lands being 1.7 and 0.6 per cent. of the respective areas) that no conclusions can be drawn from the present condition of agriculture. The proper comparison must be with the other parishes north of Red river, within the cotton zone proper.

We thus find that in the four strictly alluvial cotton parishes of East Carroll, Madison, Tensas, and Concordia, the negro population exceeds the whites in the proportion of over ten to one (average 10.4 to 1), the disproportion diminishing slightly as we advance southward; and in the same region, the acreage in corn stands to that in cotton in the ratio of nearly 5 to 1. Passing Red river there is a sudden change; the numbers of the two races are nearly equal in Avoyelles, and the corn acreage is little below that of cotton; while sugar-cane has not as yet materially influenced either. Southward, in the cane-growing region proper, the negro population again becomes predominant in numbers, but rarely exceeding the ratio of two to one white, and frequently approaching equality; in Lafourche even falling below this, to the proportion of three whites to two negroes. This clearly indicates that cane culture in the lowlands is very much less dependent upon negro labor than is that of cotton; and doubtless correlative with this is the fact that the cane acreage rarely differs widely from the figure showing the total population in the cane-growing parishes; while the cotton acreage in the lowlands north of Red river usually exceeds the numbers of the population in a ratio varying from two to three and one-third. The obvious inference is that cotton requires a larger proportion of purely manual labor, e. g., in the picking of cotton, as against the wholesale methods employed in harvesting cane. The culture of the latter, also, seems to favor a diversity of crops more than does that of cotton, since it rarely occupies more than one-third of the tilled area; while in the cotton-growing parishes, over one-half is very commonly given to cotton culture, and in one case (Concordia) nearly 92 per cent. of the whole tilled area is thus occupied, showing that but an insignificant proportion of the necessaries of life is grown at home.

It is claimed by the inhabitants of southern Louisiana that their lowlands, so long as they are not invaded by the yellow fever, are more healthy than those lying north of Red river, where the malarial influences can be resisted by few whites for any great length of time. Though opposed to the general impression on the subject, there is much weighty testimony in favor of this claim; and its correctness would account in a measure for the larger proportion of whites in the sugar-cane region.

Passing to the uplands of north Louisiana, and again excluding from direct comparison those parishes which include large areas of the Red River bottom lands, the influence of which cannot be segregated, we find the correlation between the negro population and cotton production, acreage, etc.; only partially sustained. Considering, again, the group of exclusively upland parishes north of Red river—Webster, Bienville, Jackson, Lincoln, Claiborne, and Union—and comparing them among themselves, we do not find that the percentage of the tilled lands in cotton is directly related to the ratio between the two races. The maximum of 45.2 per cent. occurs in Union, where the whites predominate in the proportion of 8 to 5.5; the minimum in Lincoln, where the ratio is nearly as 6 to 5; Claiborne, where the negro population is considerably in excess, shows nearly the same figure (36.0) as the average of the group (34.7) for the percentage of the tilled land in cotton, against 70.0 per cent. in the four representative lowland parishes. Union ranges with Natchitoches in this respect (45.2 and 45.4), although the latter embraces a very large proportion of Red River bottom lands; the total cotton acreages of the two, likewise, do not differ widely. Yet in Union the whites exceed the negroes in the proportion of 8 to 5.5, while in Natchitoches the proportion is nearly as 8 to 16 or 1 to 2. In Natchitoches the cotton is mainly grown on the lowlands of Red river, which form one large body; in Union, as the small percentage of tilled lands (10.8) shows, most of the cotton is also grown on bottom lands, (a) but the land is in small tracts (creek bottoms) and not as productive as the Red River bottom (0.41 bale against 0.84). The comparison of these two parishes shows well some of the determining points in the concentration of the negro population, which evidently gravitates to large continuous tracts of fertile land, which it occupies regardless of malaria, to the almost exclusion of the whites, wherever cotton culture (which appears to be the preferred industry) predominates. The small and thrifty farms in the uplands are less to his taste; their isolation interferes with the

---

a According to detailed measurements in north Louisiana and Mississippi the percentage of bottom land in the whole area ranges from 7 to about 10 per cent.

eminently social instincts of the race, and the more painstaking and varied modes of culture required on the less productive upland soils, with the greater need of the exercise of judgment and economy, are uncongenial to the habits of the vast majority. But it is quite evident that in these uplands the whites have successfully taken hold of cotton production, and the fact that the corn acreage is almost even with that of cotton, leaving a respectable balance to be occupied by divers other crops, proves that the self-sustaining plan of husbandry is being adopted.

In the *bluff region*, the two Felicianas, with their large predominance of negro population and cotton acreage (72.7 and 54.3 per cent. of the tilled areas), show the prevalence of the plantation policy which has been handed down from the time of settlement. East Feliciana, with its large proportion of inland country, shows less of this disproportion than West Feliciana, which has a considerable lowland area on the river.

In the *Attakapas region*, outside of thinly-settled Vermillion, the white population predominates somewhat over the negroes (nearly 12 : 11), as in the oak upland parishes; but the acreage given to cotton is only 23.4 per cent. of the tilled lands, corn and other food crops and cane receiving a large share.

In the *long-leaf pine region*, as a whole, the whites outnumber the negroes in the proportion of over two to one (2.14 to 1). Nevertheless, the average proportion of tilled lands occupied by cotton culture is 35.6 per cent., being over half that in the representative alluvial parishes (70.0), and about the same as that of the oak uplands proper (34.7). This near agreement is interesting, inasmuch as these parishes are largely remote from market and therefore of necessity self-sustaining in the matter of food crops. The above figures, therefore, afford some insight into *the proportion of provisions that require to be imported from the outside, wherever the proportion of tilled land occupied by cotton much exceeds one third of that area.*

Table I shows this disproportion between cotton acreage and tilled land to be greatest in the river parishes north of Red river (62.2), next in the Bluff region (50.5), and in the Red River parishes in the lowlands of which the ratio is doubtless about the same as in the Mississippi bottom. It is a concomitant of the wholesale planting, or plantation system, in which, even under good business management, it has but too often led to financial ruin. In its transmission, by force of habit and example, to the small farms, it proves doubly disastrous, since it results in keeping the farmer and laborer under a perennial load of indebtedness to the commission merchant, through the pernicious system of advances upon crops yet to be planted or growing. The answers to schedule questions 30 and 48 (pp. 83, 84) are eloquent on this point, and although the tenor of the answers to question 45 shows that the need of a change in this respect is being appreciated, yet the progress in the right direction seems to be slow. It cannot be doubted that this state of things has a large share in preventing the introduction of a better system of culture than the answers returned now show to exist. The shallow tillage of from 2 to 4 inches, subsoiling being scarcely known as yet; the "turning-out" of "tired land" without a thought of the benefits of fallow tillage resulting in injury rather than benefit to uplands so "rested"; the imperfect practice or total omission of rotation; the insignificant extent to which fertilizers, or any modes of fertilization, are thus far employed, including the inadequate appreciation of the high value of cotton-seed or cotton-seed cake as a return to the soil, especially for cotton production; and, not least, the waste of energy in the ever-repeated fight against an overwhelming host of weeds which a few years' consistent effort would to a great extent subdue once for all—all this speaks of a condition of agricultural methods still far removed from what can be claimed to be permanently possible, or rational even under existing circumstances, viz, as producing the best pecuniary results even for the time being.

Cultivating too much land indifferently, instead of carrying a small area to high productiveness, is in Louisiana as elsewhere in the southwest, the besetting sin of most farmers. How gratefully and profitably cotton responds to high culture has now been too often and pregnantly demonstrated to admit of question. In the present condition of most of the soils covered by cotton, improved tillage alone would allow of the maintenance and even increase of production, while diminishing the area to a considerable extent and thus making room for provision crops on lands already improved, and cutting loose from the mischievous practice of advances on provisions at least, which compel the producer to pay numerous heavy commissions and freight charges upon what he is perfectly able to produce at home. To plant cotton as a money crop, after subsistence is provided for, and to cultivate smaller areas well, while husbanding the powers of the soil, are two maxims that cannot be too strongly commended to the observance of Louisiana cotton growers.

Table of analyses of Louisiana soils and subsoils.

* Humus, 9.90; available phosphoric acid, 0.084.　† Humus, 3.007; available phosphoric acid, 0.262.　‡ Bog ore 0.15.

PART II.

AGRICULTURAL DESCRIPTIONS

OF THE

PARISHES OF LOUISIANA.

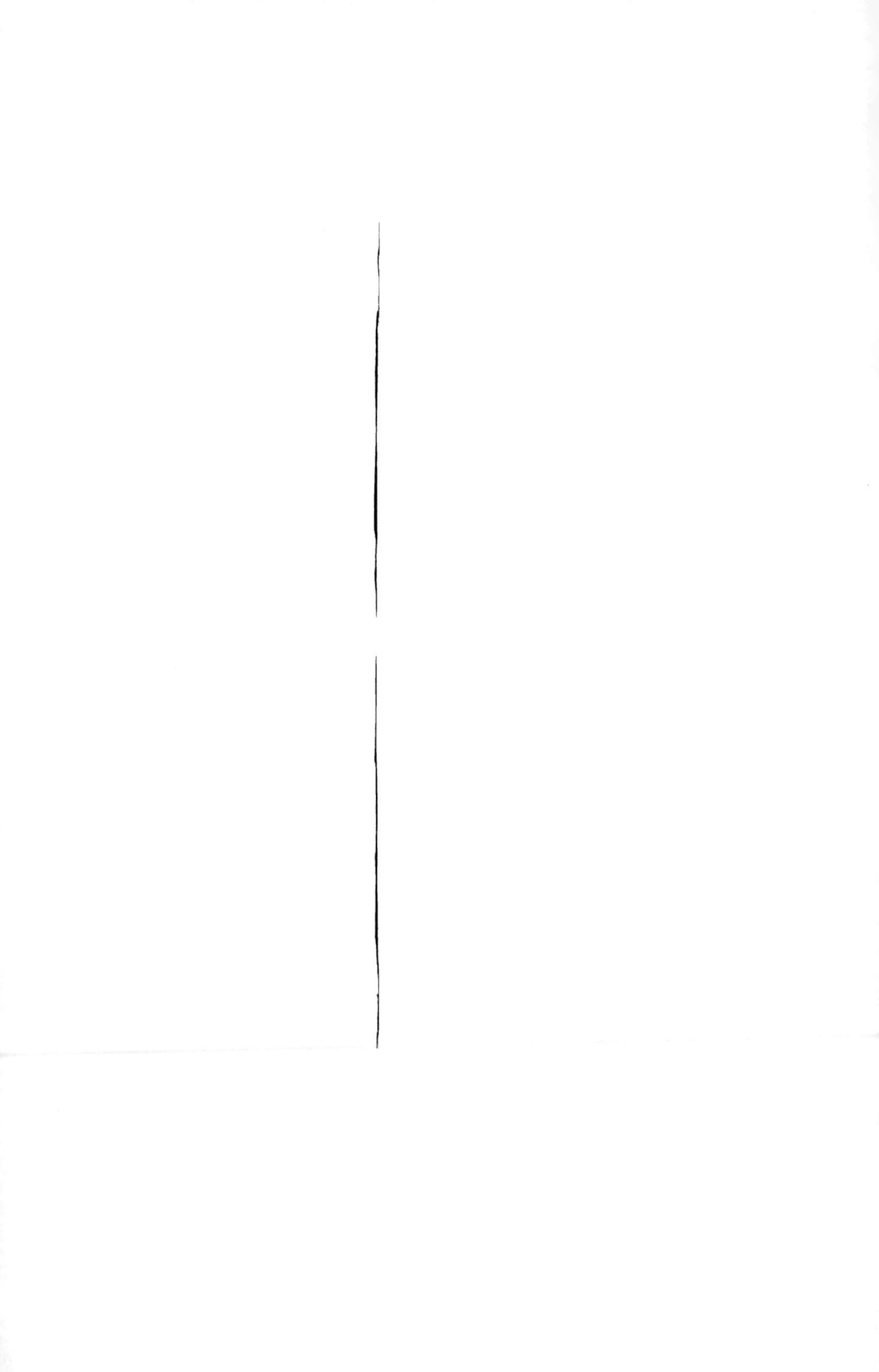

AGRICULTURAL DESCRIPTIONS

OF THE

PARISHES OF LOUISIANA.

The parishes are here grouped under the heads of the several agricultural regions, previously described, to which each predominantly belongs, or, in some cases, under that to which it is popularly assigned. Each parish is described as a whole. When its territory is covered in part by several adjacent soil-regions, its name will be found under each of the several regional heads in which it·is concerned, with a reference to the one under which it is actually described. In the lists of parishes placed at the head of each group, the names of those described *elsewhere* are marked with an asterisk (*); and the reference to the head under which these are described, will be found in its place, in the order of the list, in the text itself.

The descriptions of the parishes embracing portions of the bottom of Red river, above Rapides, are placed under the heads of the corresponding upland regions.

The regional groups of parishes are placed in the same order as that in which the regional descriptions themselves are given.

The statements of areas, of woodland, prairie, &c., refer to the original state of things, irrespective of tilled or otherwise improved lands.

Appended to the description of each parish from which a report or reports have been received, is an abstract of the main points of such reports, so far as they refer to natural features, production, and communication. Those portions of the reports referring to agricultural and commercial practice, are placed in a separate division (Part III), following that of the parish descriptions. In making the abstracts of reports, it has been necessary, in most cases, to change somewhat the language of the reporter, while preserving the sense. In some cases statements palpably incorrect or overdrawn have been altogether omitted, while sometimes explanatory words have been added, placed in parentheses.

ALLUVIAL REGION.

The following parishes lie wholly or partly within the alluvial region of the Mississippi river or its bayous: East Carroll, West Carroll, Morehouse, Ouachita, Caldwell, Richland, parts of Franklin, Madison, Tensas, Concordia, Catahoula, Avoyelles, Rapides, St. Landry*, Pointe Coupée, West Baton Rouge, Iberville, St. Martin, Assumption, Ascension, St. James, St. John Baptist, St. Charles.

The following embrace, besides alluvium, large areas of sea marsh or marsh prairie: Jefferson, Orleans, St. Bernard, Plaquemines, Lafourche, Terrebonne.

Marsh parishes west of the mouth of the Atchafalaya: St. Mary, southern Iberia*, southern Vermillion*, Cameron.

EAST CARROLL.

Population: 12,134.—White, 1,023; colored, 11,111.
Area: 400 square miles.—Woodland, all. All alluvial lands.
Tilled land: 56,793 acres.—Area planted in cotton, 40,167 acres; in corn, 7,115 acres; in sweet potatoes, 15 acres.

Cotton production : 38,160 bales; average cotton product per acre, (the highest in the cotton states), 0.95 bale, 1,353 pounds seed-cotton, or 451 pounds cotton lint.

10 c p

43

. East Carroll parish is wholly alluvial, fronting on the Mississippi river, and bounded west by the bayous Maçon and Tensas. The latter diverges from the Mississippi river in the northeastern portion of this parish, at Bunch's bend, and, passing through lake Providence, takes a southwest direction.

No details regarding the agricultural features of this parish have reached me. It is doubtless similar in general to Madison and Tensas parishes.

WEST CARROLL.

Population: 2,776.—White, 1,339; colored, 1,437.

Area: 380 square miles.—Woodland, all. Alluvial land, 220 square miles; oak uplands, 100 square miles; pine lands, 60 square miles.

Tilled land: 10,071 acres.—Area planted in cotton, 5,517 acres; in corn, 3,868 acres; in sweet potatoes, 27 acres.

Cotton production: 4,012 bales; average cotton product per acre, 0.73 bale, 1,041 pounds seed-cotton, or 347 pounds cotton lint.

West Carroll, a parish lately formed, lies between bayous Maçon and Bœuf, but includes only a narrow belt of alluvium lying along these streams, the main body being an upland ridge similar to the Bastrop hills, constituting the most northerly portion of the upland peninsula, which, farther south, forms part of the parishes of Richland and Franklin (see above), under the general designation of "Bayou Maçon hills". This ridge rises rather abruptly from the bottom plain of the bayou Maçon to the height of 20 feet. It is composed of a sandy, yellow loam, and its eastern portion is timbered with short-leaf pine. In the western, the post and black-jack oaks predominate over the pine, but the soil is rather thin. The westward slope, toward bayou Bœuf, is gentle, and the land improves as we descend: the yellow loam subsoil being apparent for some distance into the Bœuf alluvial plain. The soil of the latter is highly productive. Nearly all the cotton grown in this parish is produced in the alluvial belts.

MOREHOUSE.

Population: 14,206.—White, 3,547; colored, 10,659.

Area: 842 square miles.—Woodland, all but about 20 square miles of prairie. Oak uplands, 294 square miles; alluvial land, 548 square miles.

Tilled land: 57,379 acres.—Area planted in cotton, 28,590 acres; in corn, 17,846 acres; in sweet potatoes, 496 acres; in sugar-cane, 78 acres.

Cotton production: 23,481 bales; average cotton product per acre, 0.82 bale, 1,170 pounds seed-cotton, or 390 pounds cotton lint.

Morehouse parish embraces two chief features, viz, the alluvial plains skirting bayous Bartholomew and Bœuf, and the Washita river, and the two upland peninsulas reaching down from Arkansas, on the eastern and larger one of which the town of Bastrop is situated. These ridges and the prairies at their foot have been fully described in Part I. Regarding the bottom plains of the bayous mentioned, it is noteworthy that their subsoil is often a red clay, not unlike that of Red river bottom, although it is hardly supposable that it can have come from that river. It may be derived from the adjacent upland ridges; in any case it is curious that, in overflowed ground, that color should have been retained. This can only be due to excellent drainage; and this doubtless has something to do with the high fertility of these detached alluvial areas, whose product is, by the inhabitants, reported at 450 pounds of cotton lint per acre. This is especially stated of the back-lands of bayou Bœuf, where the cotton scarcely ever rusts, while, singularly enough, the "rust" is said to appear in some years on the sandy front-lands.

The Washita bottom seems to lie lower, and therefore to be more liable to overflows, than the bottom lands of the Bœuf and Bartholomew. It is not as much in cultivation as the former, but its cotton product is said to be scarcely behind either in quality or quantity.

ABSTRACT OF THE REPORT OF A. S. KELLER, BASTROP.

The lands of the parish are a good deal diversified, and may be thus described: First, "gum lands," whose soil is very black in color, with a good deal of sand, rendering tillage easy. The timber is sweet gum, cottonwood, and pawpaw, with occasionally some red oak interspersed. Second, prairie lands of Mer Rouge and Jefferson, which are light and sandy, but not so rich as the "gum lands". Third, the stiff cane lands, which have a very black soil, hard to cultivate, especially when wet. These lands are very productive in good seasons, but are not much sought after on account of the difficulty of tillage. Their timber-growth is cottonwood, sweet gum, white and red oaks, and ash, with an immense amount of cane undergrowth. Fourth, are the hummock lands, with light and somewhat sandy soil, not so productive as those of the second class. Timber: red and white oaks, dogwood, hickory, black gum, &c.

All of the lands above described are alluvial, contiguous to the bayous Bœuf, Bartholomew, Bonne Idée, and De Gallion, and are almost level. On the "gum lands" the surface soil is from 2 to 4 feet deep, on prairie lands from 14 to 24 inches, and about the same on the hummock lands; on the cane lands from 24 to 36 inches. In all these the subsoil is yellow sand. The hummock lands have a stiff, grayish clay subsoil.

Besides these there are the pine uplands, which are not cultivated to any great extent, and are mainly valuable for their timber. Their soil is a reddish or yellow clay, rather stiff. Washing and gullying does serious damage on these uplands.

The lower lands are drained by ditching. Cotton constitutes about two-thirds of all crops. Corn, sweet and Irish potatoes, sugar-cane for molasses, oats, German millet, &c., are produced, but cotton seems to be the product to which the soil is best adapted. The average height of the stalk is 4½ feet, but varies according to the age of the land. It runs to weed when the weather is too wet. Cultivating altogether with sweeps is thought to be a remedy for this. The seed-cotton product on fresh land is from 1,500 to 2,500 pounds per acre, of which from 1,350 to 1,460 pounds is needed to make a 450-pound bale in a dry year; in wet years it takes more. After ten years' cultivation the cotton product runs from 900 to 1,500 pounds per acre, according to the season. It then takes from 1,575 to 1,675 pounds of seed-cotton to make a 450-pound bale—the staple is not so long as that from fresh land. The most troublesome weed o' the lowland is the cocklebur. About 10 per cent. of land once cultivated now lies out for want of laborers.

146

The chief shipping-time is from October to March. Cotton is shipped mainly to New Orleans; from Monroe by rail at $2 50 per bale, or from Point Pleasant, on bayou Bartholomew, by water at $1 25 per bale. Boats also run to Monroe during a part of the year, in which case freight is less. When the waters are too low for navigation the railroad to Vicksburg charges what it pleases.

OUACHITA.

Population : 14,685.—White, 4,502; colored, 10,183.
Area : 640 square miles.—Woodland, all. Alluvial land, 340 square miles; long-leaf pine hills, 190 square miles; oak uplands, 110 square miles.
Tilled land : 48,847 acres.—Area planted in cotton, 29,040 acres; in corn, 13,143 acres; in sweet potatoes, 379 acres; in sugar-cane, 36 acres.
Cotton production : 18,729 bales; average cotton product per acre, 0.64 bale, 912 pounds seed-cotton, or 304 pounds cotton lint.

Ouachita parish, nearly equally divided between upland on the west and lowland on the east, has long-leaf pine hills of the usual character in its southwestern portion; the lower slopes of the ridges bearing an oak growth, while the crests are sandy and covered with long-leaf pine, the latter gradually disappearing as the bayou Castor is approached.

The northwestern portion has hilly oak-uplands with admixture of short-leaf pine, as in the adjoining part of Union parish. Among the oak and hickory timber of these uplands, the large-leaved magnolia (*Magnolia macrophylla*) is noteworthy, being rare elsewhere in the state. It usually denotes a soil rich in lime, and therefore thrifty. In the lowland swamps the genuine tupelo (*Nyssa uniflora*) forms a prominent (and, in Louisiana, somewhat unusual) feature.

Between the long-leaf pine hills and the oak uplands west of Monroe, there lies an extensive cypress brake, known as Chênière au Tondre, embracing about seven square miles. Numerous bayous emptying into this brake overflow much land, and render it difficult to reclaim.

The area lying east of the Washita river is wholly alluvial, except only a narrow upland ridge, with oaks and short-leaf pine, which lies between the river and bayou Lafourche. Much of the alluvial land is above any overflow experienced so far. This is especially the case with "the Island", lying between the Washita river and bayou De Siard, which is considered the garden spot of the region, producing both corn and cotton in great perfection.

On the Washita river, near Monroe, the prevalent timber growth is water oak, sycamore, honey locust, and black locust, indicating a soil containing much lime.

The river and navigable bayous render the alluvial country very easy of access, and afford great facilities for transportation of produce.

CALDWELL.

Population : 5,767.—White, 2,870; colored, 2,897.
Area : 535 square miles.—Woodland, all. Long-leaf pine hills, 170 square miles; alluvial land (Washita and Bœuf), 170 square miles; central prairie region, 145 square miles; oak uplands, 50 square miles.
Tilled land : 18,267 acres.—Area planted in cotton, 9,919 acres; in corn, 5,717 acres; in sweet potatoes, 182 acres; in sugar-cane, 39 acres.
Cotton production : 6,504 bales; average cotton product per acre, 0.66 bale, 939 pounds seed-cotton, or 313 pounds cotton lint.

Most of western Caldwell is a rough, broken, pine country, cut up by the several branches of bayou Castor. On the dividing ridge between bayou Castor and Washita river, however, a different feature prevails, as far north as several miles beyond Mount Pleasant. The country is also broken and ridgy, the ridges, especially near the Washita, running in the main parallel to that river, on which they occasionally form precipitous bluffs. These ridges have a dark-colored, loamy soil, giving evidence of the presence of lime by the absence of the long-leaf pine, and the prevalence of the better class of upland oaks, hickory, wild plum, and red haw or thorn. The best of this kind of country is in the neighborhood of Grandview, so called from the fine prospect over the Mississippi alluvial plain that is there presented. Between Grandview and Columbia there is a prairie (prairie Du Côte) about a mile in diameter, almost round, and with a yellow loam soil. The soil is very fertile, and is treeless except a few hawthorn bushes. East of the Washita river is mainly the alluvial bottom, subject to overflow, except a long narrow ridge of upland that runs down between Washita and Bœuf rivers, reaching nearly to their junction.

ABSTRACT OF THE REPORT OF W. B. GRAYSON, COLUMBIA.

The uplands are rolling, sometimes level table-lands, and vary greatly in soil. The soil principally cultivated in cotton is the black, sandy soil, with clay foundation, of the Washita bottom. Its timber growth is sweet gum, lowland oaks, elm, poplar (tulip tree), beech, cypress, &c. It varies from a fine sandy to a gravelly loam of gray, mahogany, or blackish tint; depth, 2 feet or more; underlaid by sand. It tills easily in dry, and with some difficulty in wet seasons, and is then late in getting into condition for planting. Cotton, corn, potatoes, peas, and oats are the chief crops of the region; cotton, mainly in the lowlands, and forms one-half of the crops. It grows from 6 to 8 feet in height. In warm, wet weather it may run to weed; this can be checked by plowing close to the stalks. The bottom soil yields about 1,500 pounds of seed-cotton per acre, of which 1,460 pounds are required for a 450-pound bale; rates from low to good middling in market. On older lands the staple is not so long as on fresh land. Tie-vine and cocklebur are the most troublesome weeds. Cannot tell what amount of land lies turned out. After resting awhile the river bottom land produces well. Shipments are made by (Washita) boat to New Orleans, at $1 per bale.

RICHLAND.

Population : 8,440.—White, 3,161; colored, 5,279.
Area : 578 square miles.—Woodland, all. Oak uplands, 288 square miles; alluvial land, 250 square miles; pine lands, 40 square miles.

Tilled land : 31,409 acres.—Area planted in cotton, 15,809 acres; in corn, 9,378 acres; in sweet potatoes, 66 acres; in sugar-cane, 3 acres.

Cotton production : 11,631 bales; average cotton product per acre, 0.74 bale, 1,053 pounds seed-cotton, or 351 pounds cotton lint.

Richland parish embraces two chief features : the alluvial plain of Bœuf river (here intersected by numerous bayous), and the western portion of the upland peninsula lying between the alluvial belts of the Bœuf and bayou Maçon up to Big creek, which traverses that peninsula in a northeast and southwest direction, and forms most of the line between Richland and Franklin parishes. In the northeast corner of the parish the line extends eastward to the bayou Maçon, and thus includes a portion of the alluvial bottom of the latter, as well as a portion of the pine belt which runs along the eastern edge of the uplands.

The alluvium of the Bœuf seems to be somewhat varied with higher tracts or ridges, above overflow, and of an upland character, and rather sandy. A sandy tract of this kind lies between bayou Lafourche and Bœuf river, on the Monroe and Winnsboro road, and smaller ones occur elsewhere. The alluvium proper is of a reddish tinge, apparently from the admixture of red upland soil; it is highly productive.

The uplands east of the Bœuf are gently rolling, the ridges generally running parallel to Big creek. The timber is mainly oaks with some hickory; the land being on the whole quite similar to that of the Bastrop hills, in Morehouse parish.

The transportation of cotton to market is either by steamer, on the Bœuf river direct to New Orleans, or by rail to Vicksburg and thence by river.

FRANKLIN.

Population : 6,495.—White, 2,701; colored, 3,794.

Area : 596 square miles.—Woodland, all. Oak upland, 241 square miles; alluvial land, 170 square miles; pine lands, 160 square miles; bluff (Bayou Maçon hills), 25 square miles.

Tilled land : 22,054 acres.—Area planted in cotton, 12,563 acres; in corn, 7,235 acres; in sweet potatoes, 149 acres.

Cotton production : 8,472 bales; average cotton product per acre, 0.67 bale, 954 pounds seed-cotton, or 318 pounds cotton lint.

Franklin parish is chiefly rolling upland, embracing the southeasterly portion of the Maçon peninsula, and a narrow belt of the alluvium lying between bayou Maçon and the eastern edge of these uplands. It contains also, in its southwestern portion, a similar band of the alluvial plain of bayou Bœuf.

Almost all the streams of the Maçon peninsula run parallel to its longer axis, in a southwesterly direction, which is also of course the prevailing trend of its ridges. Thus we find the pine belt, which, at the northern end of the peninsula, is met with on the eastern edge of the upland (see description of West Carroll parish). This pine belt is nearly level, with a thin, sandy soil, and occupies nearly the middle of the upland tract lying between the Maçon alluvium and Big creek, widens as it progresses southwestward, attaining its maximum width of 5 miles about Winnsboro, and runs out along Turkey lake. The pine in its southern portion is chiefly of the long-leaved species. The oak lands lying on either side of the pine belt are fairly productive; the bottoms of the streams are excellent. The land of the Bayou Maçon hills proper, rising from the edge of the plain, improves in its southern portion and becomes similar, in its soil and productiveness, to that of Sicily island opposite, across Deer creek.

ABSTRACT OF REPORT OF A. F. OSBORN, WINNSBORO.

About one-fifth of the parish is what is designated "swamp", that is, alluvial land of bayous Maçon and Bœuf. The soil of these lands is mostly heavy "buckshot", gray intermingled with brown, and about 18 inches deep; the subsoil is lighter than the surface-soil, variegated from whitish-gray to yellowish-brown, mixed with sand; hence it is easier to till than the ordinary surface-soil, and is nearly or quite as fertile. The surface-soil is crumbly in dry weather and easy to till; in wet seasons very clammy and difficult to work. The natural timber-growth is lowland oaks, sweet gum, swamp hickory, hackberry, box-elder, black and honey locusts, maple, sycamore, cottonwood, and, in low grounds, cypress. The soil is best adapted to cotton, and six-tenths of the improved land is occupied by this crop. It is most productive when 6 feet high; is inclined to run to weed when the soil is fresh; topping is resorted to by some, to restrain this tendency. In fresh land the seed-cotton product ranges from 1,500 to 2,500 pounds per acre, of which 1,520 make a 450-pound bale of lint, middling staple. After fifteen years' cultivation the product, in good years and with good culture, will still range from 1,200 to 2,000 pounds, about 1,432 being then needed for a 450-pound bale. The staple from old land is considered to be of finer texture than from fresh land.

About 25 per cent. of land once in cultivation now lies turned out.

The most troublesome weeds are crab-grass, cocklebur, careless-weed, tea-weed, buffalo-weed.

West of bayou Maçon and east of bayou Bœuf and Big creek, there are undulating table-lands, interspersed with cypress brakes and flats, some 15 miles wide east and west, and 35 miles north and south. Timber on higher lands : oaks with hickory and, in part, pine; on lower lands : oaks, black walnut, hickory, sweet and black gums, maple, sassafras, beech, poplar (tulip tree), magnolia, dogwood, wild cherry, honey and black locusts, &c.

The soil is a fine, sandy one, from brown through buff and gray to whitish in lowlands, about 8 inches deep; subsoil heavier than surface-soil, putty-like, yellowish tint, sometimes impervious, occasionally containing black gravel underlaid by sand, blue mud and sand alternately, 12 feet from surface. Where this subsoil comes to the surface no crops do well, although it tills easily.

The soil is best adapted to cotton and sweet potatoes; cotton occupies about six-tenths of the land cultivated, and attains the height of 6 to 8 feet. It seems to boll equally well at either height. On newly cleared land it sometimes inclines to run to weed; topping is resorted to, but with doubtful advantage. Seed-cotton product, from 1,300 to 1,400 pounds per acre, of which 1,520 pounds make a 450-pound bale usually; sometimes only 1,350 are required; clean staple rates middling. After fifteen years' cultivation the product is 1,100 pounds; in very favorable seasons as high as 1,350 pounds per acre; about the same amount of seed-cotton needed for a bale; staple of somewhat finer texture than that from fresh land.

Crab-grass is the chief pest on this soil, also careless-weed, &c.

About 25 per cent. of this land now lies turned out; it improves by this if kept from washing, and will sometimes produce as much as fresh land; but it washes and gullies very rapidly on slopes if neglected, and is thus soon ruined. In most cases the valleys are injured by these washings of the uplands, the yellow clayey subsoil covering up the valley soil so deeply that roots fail to reach it. Little is done to prevent this trouble; horizontalizing is very successful when properly managed.

Cotton shipments are made, from September to February, by rail and steamboat to New Orleans. Rates of freight per bale are: by rail, $2; by steamboat, in low water, $2 to $2 25, or, in high water, $1 25 to $1 50.

MADISON.

Population: 13,908.—White, 1,261; colored, 12,645.
Area: 672 square miles.—Woodland, all. All alluvial lands.
Tilled land: 48,395 acres.—Area planted in cotton, 28,103 acres; in corn, 7,797 acres; in sweet potatoes, 140 acres.

Cotton production: 23,391 bales; average cotton product per acre, 0.83 bale, 1,182 pounds seed-cotton, or 394 pounds cotton lint.

Madison parish is included between the Mississippi river and bayou Maçon, with Tensas river traversing its western half. In this respect, as well as in its soils and forest growth, it greatly resembles Tensas parish, as described below. The same is true as regards the occupancy of the cultivated lands by cotton as the chief crop. No details of its agricultural features have been accessible to me. The following general statement is made by Mr. A. C. Gibson, of Waverley station, on the Vicksburg and Texas railroad:

The entire parish is alluvial, level, intersected by bayous, but no hills; all subject to overflow; only protected from inundation by levees. It is in the center of the genuine cotton-producing belt.

Timber is sweet gum, oaks, hackberry, pecan, persimmon, cottonwood; cypress in the swamps. The soil varies from sandy loam to a prairie-like clay ("buckshot"); color, blackish or black; most of it warm and well drained (by underlying sand), easy to till, warm and early. It is best adapted to cotton, and three-fourths of the cleared land is occupied by that crop; the rest is in corn. Five feet is the average height of the cotton plant. It inclines to run to weed in wet seasons, but can be restrained by shallow cultivation. The land, when fresh, will produce 500 pounds of lint per acre; on old land about 400, and on the latter 1,520, pounds of seed-cotton is needed for a 450-pound bale. The staple from old land rates about the same as from fresh. It is a shade finer, but not so strong.

Cocklebur and crab-grass are the most troublesome weeds.

About one-half of lands once in cultivation now lie turned out; when again cultivated these lands yield as well as ever, after the first year.

Cotton is shipped chiefly in November, and to New Orleans; the rate of freight is $2 25 per bale.

TENSAS.

Population: 17,815.—White, 1,571; colored, 16,244.
Area: 612 square miles.—Woodland, all. All alluvial lands.
Tilled land: 78,679 acres.—Area planted in cotton, 50,555 acres; in corn, 11,427 acres; in sweet potatoes, 271 acres.

Cotton production: 41,859 bales; average cotton product per acre, 0.83 bale, 1,182 pounds seed-cotton, or 394 pounds cotton lint.

Tensas parish is very similar to Madison and Concordia in its location, surface, and soils. It is wholly alluvial. The bayou Maçon forms most of its western boundary, the Mississippi river the eastern one. The Tensas river meanders through its western portion, from north to south, joining the bayou Maçon in the southern part, and thenceforth forming the boundary of Catahoula parish. The Tensas river is perhaps the stream in whose alluvial plain the fertile "buckshot" soil is most predominant in Louisiana; and Tensas parish has often laid claim to the highest cotton product per acre of the alluvial parishes. It has a comparatively small area of cypress swamp, and while the majority of the large cotton plantations lie along the bayous, on account of facility of tillage and communication, there is a vast area of cultivatable back-land still covered with a dense and beautiful forest growth, awaiting the hand of the husbandman to prove its splendid productiveness. The most densely settled portion of the parish is on the Tensas river, and especially on Choctaw and Tiger bayous, in the southern portion, and it would be difficult to find a more profusely fertile country. In some of the cleared regions the levelness of the fields and their shining black furrows, with honey locust and crab-apple forming clumps here and there, reminds one forcibly of the prairie regions of the West and South. Overflows are the only drawback, and sometimes prevent planting at the proper time; but frosts come late, and in the best seasons so much is grown that a portion of the abundant cotton product is often left in the fields, for want of time and force to gather it all. The staple grown on the Tensas "buckshot" soils is claimed to be the type of high quality lowland, or "Orleans" cotton.

CONCORDIA.

Population: 14,914.—White, 1,320; colored, 13,594.
Area: 680 square miles.—Woodland, all. All alluvial land.
Tilled land: 45,816 acres.—Area planted in cotton, 42,044 acres; in corn, 6,114 acres; in sweet potatoes, 162 acres.

Cotton production: 33,110 bales; average cotton product per acre, 0.79 bale, 1,125 pounds seed-cotton, or 375 pounds cotton lint.

Concordia parish is almost surrounded by large streams of the bottom plain, the east fronting on the Mississippi, and the west on Tensas and Black rivers (the latter formed by the junction of the Tensas and Washita), and bounded on the south by Red river. It is wholly alluvial, and one of the largest of the cotton-growing parishes; the uncultivated lands are densely timbered with the usual bottom growth. There is an unusual proportion of the black "buckshot" land in Concordia, the river front alone being sandy; and the producing capacity of the lands is reported as very high.

ABSTRACT OF REPORT OF W. D. SHAW, BLACK HAWK.

The river front is sandy land; farther back, a coarse or fine sandy loam, dark-colored. The "buckshot" soil varies from gray to black, and is from 1 to 6 feet in depth. The subsoil is generally heavier than the surface soil, and lighter in color, sometimes greenish-yellow (this probably where there is much lime in the mass), or brown, varying greatly according to location. The "buckshot" is somewhat difficult to till in wet seasons, and is late when ill-drained.

Cotton, corn, and sweet potatoes are the chief products; of these, cotton occupies nine-tenths of the cultivated lands. It is most productive when about 5 feet in height; inclines to run to weed when crowded and weedy; to prevent this, it must be well thinned and kept clean. The yield per acre is from 1,400 to 1,800 pounds of seed-cotton, of which about 1,575 pounds go to make a 450-pound bale. After fifty years' cultivation, the "buckshot" land still yields about one-half of the above product; but it takes only about 1,590 pounds of seed-cotton for a bale of lint, which rates somewhat lower than that from fresh land.

The most troublesome weeds here are indigo, cocklebur, and tie-vine (Convolvulus).

Two shipments of cotton per week, while ginning, are made to New Orleans; rate of freight per bale is $1.

ABSTRACT OF REPORT OF GEO. S. WALTON, BOUGÈRES.

Soils, light sandy loam on the river front, for one-half to three-quarters of a mile; then begins the black land, which is partly black loam, partly black "buckshot". The latter two form about two-thirds of the land. The "buckshot" is heavy, and in wet weather very sticky and difficult to till. The same kinds of soil are found all the way to the (Catahoula) hills, and from the Arkansas line to the Gulf. The thickness of the soil differs greatly from place to place, varying from one to several feet; the subsoil is sometimes fine sand, and again stiff clay; sometimes a hard-pan, impervious to water.

The soil is best adapted to cotton, and three-quarters of the lands planted are in cotton. The height of the stalk varies from 4½ to 8 feet; from 5½ to 7 feet is the best height for yield. In rainy seasons, and with deep plowing, the cotton inclines to run to weed; by light cultivation, or the use of sweeps, the tendency can be checked. The land, when fresh, will yield from 1,500 to 2,000 pounds of seed-cotton per acre, of which from 1,520 to 1,575 pounds make a 450-pound bale of lint. This staple rates first-class in market when clean. After twenty years' cultivation, the product runs from 1,000 to 1,500 pounds per acre; 1,350 to 1,500 pounds of seed-cotton then make a standard bale, the staple rating somewhat lower than that from fresh land, but still much better than uplands.

The weeds most troublesome are cocklebur and black-vine.

About one-fourth of the land once cultivated now lies out. When taken into cultivation again it will produce almost as well as at first, after the first year.

Shipping of cotton begins early in September; it is sent by steamboat to New Orleans. Rate of freight is 75 cents per bale.

CATAHOULA.

Population: 10,277.—White, 5,724; colored, 4,553.

Area: 1,378 square miles.—Woodland, 985 square miles. Alluvial land, 550 square miles; long-leaf pine hills, 460 square miles; central prairie region, 240 square miles; bluff land (Sicily island), 30 square miles; oak upland, 38 square miles; Catahoula lake, 60 square miles.

Tilled land: 29,823 acres.—Area planted in cotton, 15,885 acres; in corn, 11,094 acres; in sweet potatoes, 264 acres; in sugar-cane, 24 acres.

Cotton production: 11,766 bales; average cotton product per acre, 0.74 bale, 1,056 pounds seed-cotton, or 352 pounds cotton lint.

Catahoula parish embraces a great variety of soils, as will be apparent from a glance on the map. Its western or upland portion is largely of the true pine-hills character, but to northward the sandy hill-land is interrupted by the lowland belt of the central prairie region, which occupies the northwestern portion of the parish. East of the Washita river, the alluvial plain of the Mississippi, here known as the Tensas bottom, forms the main feature, the only exception being the detached mass of upland on "Sicily island", which is separated from the mainland by the Washita river and bottom, and from the great bottom plain by several connected bayous. This island, which has attracted a good deal of attention, from its unusual position and character, has been sufficiently described already (see map), as has also the Catahoula prairie, on the mainland. The pine hills of southwestern Catahoula, though not differing materially in aspect from the usual character, are not generally abrupt. Near the edge of the Washita bottom their soil is frequently very pebbly, but seems on the whole to be better than that farther west, as appears from the subjoined report, and from the fact of being better settled. The "prairie region", lying north of the pine hills is also quite hilly, especially in its eastern portion, where the black-prairie soil often lies high up on the ridges, which are heavily timbered on their slopes with lime-loving trees, walnut, tulip tree, &c. In the western portion of the tract the "hog-wallow" soil and post-oak flats are more prevalent, varied with spots of true black prairie. The largest of the black-prairie tracts lies in the fork of bayous Castor and Dugdemona, in Winn parish (Pendarvis' prairie).

ABSTRACT OF THE REPORT OF MICHAEL DEMPSEY, JENA.

(Refers to townships 7, 8, 9, and 10, ranges 2 and 3—the southwestern portion of the parish, between Little river and Catahoula lake.)

The country is hilly and rolling, some parts level; the bottom lands are small and confined to the numerous creeks of the uplands; their soil is alluvial, with a mixture of gray and yellow sand. The soils are very variable in color, depth, and quality; some as shallow as 2 inches, or as deep as 2 feet (in bottoms); the latter is the best; a mahogany-colored soil, called "mulatto" land (on hillsides?), is next best, and most largely cultivated. The timber (in the uplands) is yellow or pitch (long-leaf) pine, with more or less oaks and hickory, increasing toward the bottoms; in the bottoms, beech, ash, sweet and black gums, poplar, maple, sassafras, wild cherry, dogwood, &c. Except in the pine lands, the subsoil is mostly heavier than the surface soil. The crops grown are cotton (about half of each farm), corn, peas, sweet and common potatoes, sugar-cane, tobacco, oats, turnips, melons, pumpkins, and all kinds of vegetables. Cotton varies in height from 2 to 8 feet on the several soils. It will run to weed in wet seasons; can be restrained by topping in July or early in August. One thousand pounds of seed-cotton per acre can be produced (on "mulatto" land†), when the land is fresh; 600 to 700 pounds after five years' cultivation. 1,575 pounds on an average are needed for a 450-pound bale. Crab-grass, tea-weed, and tie-vine are the most injurious weeds. Very little land lies turned out; a great deal has been newly taken in during the last ten years. Lying-out improves it for a few years. When cultivated, the land washes readily on slopes, and heavy damage is thus done, but can be prevented by circling. The valleys are rather improved by the washings of the light upland soils. The latter are damaged to the extent of 5 per cent. annually, in wet years more. Little has been done to check the damage; where circling and hillside ditching has been done, the lands are well preserved.

Cotton is shipped to New Orleans, by steamer, at $1 50 per bale.

AVOYELLES.

Population: 16,747.—White, 8,483; colored, 8,264.

Area: 852 square miles.—Woodland, all. Bluff prairie, 40 square miles; oak uplands, 65 square miles; alluvial, 747 square miles.

Tilled land: 84,787 acres.—Area planted in cotton, 23,722 acres; in corn, 21,403 acres; in sweet potatoes, 510 acres; in sugar-cane, 890 acres; in rice, 178 acres.

Cotton production: 18,355 bales; average cotton product per acre, 0.77 bale, 1,098 pounds seed-cotton, or 366 pounds cotton lint.

Of Avoyelles parish, all but about a hundred square miles is alluvial, the Red river and Atchafalaya forming its northern and eastern boundaries, respectively.

The upland is substantially prairie land, in part sparsely timbered, including, on the mainland, part of the promontory between the flood-plains of the Mississippi and Red river (known as Hollowell's prairie), and two "islands", evidently outliers from that promontory, of which the larger is known as Avoyelles prairie.

The parish town of Marksville lies nearly in the center of Avoyelles prairie. The surface of the latter is elevated about 30 feet above high-water of Red river, sometimes forming steep bluff banks. The soil of the southern portion of the Avoyelles prairie resembles, altogether, that of the bluff plateau of West Feliciana, and is similarly productive of cotton, corn, &c. The portion of the prairie lying north of Marksville is less productive, has grayish or whitish silt soil, with ferruginous concretions, and resembles in this respect the greater portion of Hollowell's and Catahoula prairies, and prairie Dubute, farther north. The smaller island is reported to be of a sandy character, with soil and timber resembling the pine hills of the mainland.

The alluvial lands of western Avoyelles parish are mainly of the same character as those of Rapides, being chiefly derived from the sediments of Red river. In the Atchafalaya country, however, the sediments of the Mississippi and Red river frequently alternate in the banks, and there is a greater prevalence of the lighter alluvial soils of the Mississippi river.

RAPIDES.

Population: 23,563.—White, 9,512; colored, 14,051.

Area: 1,498 square miles.—Woodland, all. Long-leaf pine hills, 900 square miles; Red river bottom, 475 square miles; oak uplands, 123 square miles.

Tilled land: 76,149 acres.—Area planted in cotton, 25,622 acres; in corn, 29,366 acres; in sweet potatoes, 232 acres; in sugar-cane, 1,875 acres; in rice, 2 acres.

Cotton production: 17,990 bales; average cotton product per acre, 0.70 bale, 996 pounds seed-cotton, or 332 pounds cotton lint.

The parish of Rapides, as outlined since the formation of the parishes of Vernon and Grant, embraces substantially but two main features, viz, the pine-hill uplands, constituting about two-thirds of the area; and the Red river bottom lands, which form the productive portion.

The pine-hill lands west of Red river are rolling and hilly, with the usual sandy, infertile soils, and the narrow but fairly fertile bottoms of the streams. The great swamp formed by the bayou Cocodrie, on part of the southern line of the parish, is a noteworthy feature.

The uplands east of Red river, within this parish, are nearly of the same character as the pine lands on the west side, although the bottoms of the streams are on the whole wider, and produce a fine quality of upland cotton. Toward the point where the alluvial plain of Red river proper terminates (near the "Egg bend", opposite the Avoyelles prairie), the long-leaf pine is gradually replaced by the short-leaved species, oak-growth increases and finally becomes prevalent, and the open woods pass insensibly into an open plain, forming part of "Hollowell's prairie", the main body of which lies within the limits of Avoyelles parish.

The portion of Red river bottom lying within Rapides parish is claimed by its inhabitants to be the most fertile portion of the Red river alluvial lands. Messrs. C. J. Barstow and George L. Haygood give the following description of the soils occurring near Cheneyville, Rapides parish, in the bayou Boeuf country.

Three kinds of soils may be distinguished :

1. Light, sandy, alluvial soil near the bayous, forming about one-half of the cultivatable land of the region; it is of an orange tint, which shades off into—

2. (About three-tenths of the land.) Dark brown or "mahogany" back-land, the clayeyness increasing at the same time. Both back- and front-land yield from 2,000 to 2,500 pounds seed-cotton per acre, of which 1,542 pounds are required for a 450-pound bale; the best height of the stalk being 5 to 5½ feet. After forty or fifty years' cultivation, the yield is still 1,400 pounds, and the staple better; 45 per cent. of these soils is in cotton.

3. Besides these, there is a heavy red clay, or "buckshot" soil, in the lower back-lands, somewhat difficult to till in wet seasons. On this, cotton is most productive at 4 feet, yielding 1,000 pounds seed-cotton when fresh; staple rating low middling. About 20 per cent. of this land is in cotton.

The timber on all these soils is about the same, viz, lowland oaks, sweet gum, hackberry, cottonwood, sycamore, and cypress. The ordinary weeds (which are least troublesome on No. 3) are bind-weed, cocklebur, and crab-grass. All the lands are drained by ditches only.

This description applies for 30 miles up and down bayou Boeuf.

Cotton is shipped, usually as fast as it can be got ready, by water to New Orleans; the rate of freight is $1 50 per bale.

The lands cultivated in cotton are the first and second bottoms of Red river and its bayous, also sandy bottom lands on the waters of Spring and Flaggon creeks.

The Red river bottom lands are about half-and-half sandy front-land and stiff clay back-land, both along the main river and the bayous. The timber is ash, oak (basket or chestnut-white), gum, hackberry, honey locust, mulberry, pecan, walnut, haw, elm, cypress; elm and sweet gum more especially on the stiff lands.

The soil of the front-lands is brown or brownish-yellow; a clay loam, more or less heavy, averaging about 3 feet in thickness. Just under the soil there is generally found a coarse, light sand for about 8 to 10 inches, then clay for 6 or 8 feet. The soil, when well broken, drains well, and tills easily in both wet and dry seasons, and hence is always early, thus enabling planters to plant as soon as frost will permit, the seed being frequently in the ground by March 10. This sometimes renders replanting necessary, but the danger from the caterpillar is greatly lessened. Besides cotton, which occupies about one-third of this soil, corn, sugar-cane, oats, rice, sweet potatoes, and other vegetables grow well, but cotton and corn yield most heavily on the stiff land. When in 5-foot rows, cotton grows about 5 feet high, but is most productive when planted in checks 2 by 3 feet. Continuous rains and continued working favor running to weed; to avoid it, shallow cultivation only should be given. The land, when fresh, readily yields one and a half bales, or from 2,000 to 2,600 pounds of seed-cotton per acre; that from the first picking requires about 100 pounds more for a bale of lint than that from the second. The staple from fresh land is somewhat longer and coarser than that from land long under cultivation, but after fifty years' cultivation without manure, such land still yields one bale per acre. Perhaps one-fourth of such land now lies out; rest improves it. The most trouble-some weeds on this soil are: coco-, Bermuda-, wire-, blue-, and crab-grass; of others, tie-vine.

The stiff back-lands have a heavy clay soil, of yellow to blackish tint, to the depth of about 3 feet, where they are underlaid by coarse sand. The timber is like that on the front-land, but more gum, elm, sycamore, and pawpaw. The soil tills easily in all seasons when once broken; is well adapted to cotton and corn, and one-half of it being in the former crop. The stalk grows to the height of 7 feet, but is most productive at 5 feet. The product is from one and a half to two bales per acre on fresh land. It takes about 1,760 pounds for a 450-pound bale. After seven years' cultivation, the seed-cotton product is about 1,800 pounds per acre; the staple a little better than at first. The weeds are cocklebur, rag-weed, tie-vine.

The sandy loam of the pine-woods creek bottoms may constitute about one-tenth of the lands of the parish. These bottoms are timbered with lowland oaks, a little ash, holly, magnolia, sweet gum, beech, cherry, dogwood, box-elder. It is a fine sandy loam, blackish from vegetable mold to the depth of from 4 to 12 inches. The subsoil is red or blue clay, underlaid by sand or gravel at 3 to 4 feet. The soil tills readily in all seasons. Corn, cotton, and sugar-cane are planted; about one-third of the cultivated region being in corn. On new land the cotton sometimes runs to weed; 4 to 5 feet is the usual height. The seed-cotton product on fresh land is about 1,700 pounds, and about that amount is needed for a bale. After three years' cultivation the product is about 900 pounds, and the staple then rates somewhat higher; perhaps one-sixth of such land once cultivated now lies out; it is improved by rest, but should have manure when again taken in. Crab-grass, tie-vine, and rag-weed are the most troublesome weeds.

ST. LANDRY.

(See under "Attakapas prairie region".)

POINTE COUPÉE.

Population : 17,785.—White, 4,785 ; colored, 13,000.
Area : 575 square miles.—Woodland, all. Alluvial throughout.
Tilled land : 56,594 acres.—Area planted in cotton, 24,136 acres ; in corn, 14,817 acres ; in sweet potatoes, 188 acres ; in sugar-cane, 6,027 acres.
Cotton production : 18,935 bales ; average cotton product per acre, 0.78 bale, 1,110 pounds seed-cotton, or 370 pounds cotton lint.

The parish of Pointe Coupée is altogether of the alluvial character, lying as it does between the Atchafalaya and Mississippi rivers. Large plantations line all the water-courses, along which there are tracts of higher land, from 1 to 2½ miles in depth, on the landward edge of which the grizzly, moss-curtained cypress forest limits the view. Between these high border belts, lie low, and thus far unreclaimed, cypress swamps, forming a large part of the surface. The floods in this parish reach a greater height than in any other portion of the Mississippi valley, and the "Great Morganza" and the "Grand Levee", 15 to 18 feet in height, have been built to restrain them. These levees protect from overflow no fewer than thirteen of the most productive parishes of the state.

Sugar-cane is one of the principal and most important crops of the parish. The plantations are generally well improved, and the residences, sugar-houses, and laborers' quarters, usually located close to the banks of the numerous bayous and "old river" lakes, oftentimes form exceedingly attractive pictures. The sloping banks are turfed to the clear water's edge with Bermuda-grass, and are shaded by groves of gigantic oaks, sycamores, and sweet gums.

Considerable belts of cultivated lands lie along the following bayous: Atchafalaya, Moreau, Couteau, Letsworth, Latanache, Cow-head, Fisher's, and especially bayou Fordoche.

WEST BATON ROUGE.

Population : 7,667.—White, 2,252 ; colored, 5,415.
Area : 210 square miles.—Woodland, all. Alluvial throughout.
Tilled land : 26,753 acres.—Area planted in cotton, 3,784 acres ; in corn, 7,263 acres ; in sweet potatoes, 68 acres ; in sugar-cane, 6,400 acres.
Cotton production : 2,420 bales ; average cotton product per acre, 0.64 bale, 912 pounds seed-cotton, or 304 pounds cotton lint.

West Baton Rouge is wholly alluvial, being included between the Mississippi river on the east, and bayous Poydras and Grosse Tête on the west. The main body of its available lands lies along the Mississippi river, the landward depth of this "coast" belt being from 1½ to 2½ miles. Then begin the swamp lands, which make up much the larger part of the parish, and extend almost uninterruptedly to the western boundary. Of the many bayous within these back-lands, bayous Poydras, Clause, and lake Clause have fine lands and some handsome plantations on their borders. The other bayous are generally unsettled.

The forest growth of the higher lands is composed of water, chestnut white, willow, and pin oaks, sweet and black gums, sycamore, ash, pecan, sassafras, honey locust, cottonwood, &c., with cypress, sweet and tupelo gums, and willow in the swamps. There are also in the interior extensive canebrakes, where the wild cat, bear, and panther are still found.

The lands along the bayous are highly productive, sugar-cane being the chief crop, with cotton and corn as subsidiaries. The parish has no town or village within its limits, as yet.

IBERVILLE.

Population: 17,544.—White, 4,784; colored, 12,760.
Area: 646 square miles.—Woodland, all. Alluvial throughout.
Tilled land: 42,122 acres.—Area planted in cotton, 771 acres; in corn, 11,991 acres; in sweet potatoes, 52 acres; in sugar-cane, 16,687 acres; in rice, 3,129 acres.
Cotton production: 579 bales; average cotton product per acre, 0.75 bale, 1,068 pounds seed-cotton, or 356 pounds cotton lint.

Iberville parish lies between the bayou Grosse Tête and the Mississippi river on the east, and the upper Grand river and its chain of lakes and bayous bordering the parish of St. Martin, on the west. It is wholly alluvial; belts of cultivatable and highly productive lands lie along most of the bayous to the depth of one-half to two miles, especially in the northern portion, those along bayous Grosse Tête, Maringuin, and Deglaize. Between the Grosse Tête and Maringuin there is an extensive swamp, occupying nearly the whole space between them, just north of Grand river. A similar swamp extends between the Maringuin and Deglaize, from the northern boundary of the parish to lake Oksibe. The lands lying on the forks of Alabama bayou, and between them and Grand river, are also occupied by plantations.

In the southern part of the parish, along lower Grand river and its tributaries, bayous Pigeon and Sorrel, the lands have been partially cleared, and are of fine quality, but the overflows prevent their occupation to a great extent. Bayou Plaquemine, connecting Grand river with the Mississippi, is a large navigable stream, and is thickly settled along both of its banks. The court-house town of Plaquemine has a flourishing business in the shipment of agricultural produce and (cypress) lumber.

The "coast" of Iberville is remarkable for the highly improved condition and great extent of its plantations, there being many handsome residences, surrounded by parks of live oak and pecan trees. Cleared lands lie also along bayou Goula and Manufactory bayou, extending back almost to lake Natchez, by which they are thoroughly drained. The rice crop for 1879 was 2,198,550 pounds.

ST. MARTIN.

Population: 12,663.—White, 5,783; colored, 6,880.
Area: 618 square miles.—Alluvial lands, 518 square miles. Woodland, 460 square miles. Lowland prairie, 58 square miles; upland prairie, 100 square miles.
Tilled land: 39,876 acres.—Area planted in cotton, 6,942 acres; in corn, 11,283 acres; in sweet potatoes, 412 acres; in sugar-cane, 3,525 acres; in rice, 7 acres.
Cotton production: 2,232 bales; average cotton product per acre, 0.32 bale, 456 pounds seed-cotton, or 152 pounds cotton lint.

This parish, greatly reduced in area since the creation of Iberia parish, is predominantly alluvial land, lying between the bayou Tèche and the Atchafalaya river, while the portion lying west of the Tèche, between it and bayou Tortue, is mainly rolling prairie of the "brown loam" character.

The Tèche is here, as in Iberia, bordered by a narrow belt of live-oak groves, whose branches shade the narrowing, but still deep and navigable, stream. The narrow band of Red river alluvium also continues on both sides, on the eastern shading off gradually into the alluvial prairie, which here borders the stream instead of the woodlands, the belt varying from 3 to 5 miles in width. Eastward of these there lie arable lands, densely wooded with a growth of lowland oaks, ash, sweet gum, pecan, sycamore, magnolia, &c. Here, as elsewhere, the culture of sugar-cane occupies nearly all the cultivated alluvial lands, which are profusely fertile. Still farther east, toward the Atchafalaya, the land becomes more low and wet, and is occupied mainly by cypress and tupelo gum. Butte à la Rose is on a tract of higher land on the Atchafalaya.

West of the Tèche (which is navigable to St. Martinsville during most of the year), the prairies average about 3 miles in width. They are bounded on the west by the wooded lands along bayous Vermillion and Tortue. In the southern part of the prairies in this parish, woodlands also occur along bayous Capucin and Cypress, and on Cypress island. Lake Martin, near Breaux bridge, is one of the largest of the prairie "ponds" characteristic of the region, and is a pretty sheet of water.

ASSUMPTION.

Population: 17,010.—White, 8,938; colored, 8,072.
Area: 327 square miles.—Woodland, all. All alluvial land.
Tilled land: 36,511 acres.—Area planted in cotton, 285 acres; in corn, 14,055 acres; in sweet potatoes, 138 acres; in sugar-cane, 12,945 acres; in rice, 1,420 acres.

Cotton production: 119 bales; average cotton product per acre, 0.42 bale, 600 pounds seed-cotton, or 200 pounds cotton lint.

Assumption, though not bordering on the Mississippi river, is a rich alluvial parish throughout. Its prominent hydrographic feature is the bayou Lafourche, which, after leaving the main Mississippi, a little above Donaldsonville, traverses the eastern part of the parish, and along which the improved and cultivated lands chiefly lie. This belt of highly fertile land is about 20 miles in length within the parish, and has a width, on either side of the Lafourche, of from 1 to 1½ mile. It is closely settled, and presents the appearance of one continuous town, with many handsome residences and plantation buildings.

In addition to this continuous tract of open land there are, east and west of the Lafourche, detached bodies of cleared and settled land, called "brulées". Of these, the principal ones are the Sacramento, Grand Bayou, Pierpart, St. Vincent, Big and Little Texas, and L'Abadie "brulées". These lie at distances varying from 4 to 10 miles from the main body of the bayou, and are not inferior in fertility.

The banks of the Attakapas canal, which connects the Lafourche, at Napoleonville (the parish town), with lake Verret, are also settled and under cultivation, as is the western shore of lake Verret, where there are some extensive and well-improved plantations. The eastern shore of this lake has a few scattered settlements, whose inhabitants are engaged in hunting, fishing, and lumbering. The remaining portions of the parish, not specially mentioned, are wooded and mostly swampy.

Sugar-cane and corn, with a little cotton, form the products of the parish.

According to the statement of Mr. Lewis Guion, of Napoleonville, what little cotton is produced in the parish is almost exclusively grown in small patches in the "brulées", back from the main streams. It grows vigorously and bolls well, but the caterpillar and army-worm are very prevalent; and this, coupled with the fact that at the picking season rains are liable to prevail, and with the high price of labor in the sugar-belt, renders cotton culture unprofitable in this region.

ASCENSION.

Population: 16,895.—White, 5,968; colored, 10,927.
Area: 373 square miles.—Woodland, all. All alluvial land.
Tilled land: 37,908 acres.—Area planted in cotton, 1,285 acres; in corn, 6,112 acres; in sweet potatoes, 241 acres; in sugar-cane, 15,545 acres; in rice, 616 acres.
Cotton production: 592 bales; average cotton product per acre, 0.46 bale, 657 pounds seed-cotton, or 219 pounds cotton lint.

Ascension parish is throughout alluvial; the portion fronting on the Mississippi river is identical in character with that of the "coast" of Iberville; the parish is almost entirely a sugar-growing one, and the lands highly productive. The parish town, Donaldsonville, is a thriving village of about 2,000 inhabitants, and at one time was inclined to dispute precedence with New Orleans and Baton Rouge. No detailed data regarding the portion of the parish lying east of the Mississippi river have come into my possession. It appears that lake Maurepas, which on the north and east is bordered by such extensive swamps, is edged by only a narrow fringe of the same south of the Amite river, where it adjoins this parish, which would thus seem to possess an unusual proportion of cultivatable land.

ST. JAMES.

Population: 14,714.—White, 4,850; colored, 9,864.
Area: 308 square miles.—Woodland, 253 square miles. Alluvial land, 253 square miles; marsh and marsh prairie, 55 square miles.
Tilled land: 54,675 acres.—Area planted in cotton, none; in corn, 11,303 acres; in sweet potatoes, 139 acres; in sugar-cane, 15,227 acres; in rice, 5,870 acres.

The parish of St. James, north of the river, resembles more the river parishes farther north, than those of the delta plain proper. The highlands near the river are highly productive and densely settled, and mostly occupied by sugar plantations. Northward of this belt, the drainage is toward lake Maurepas, through bayou Des Acadiens and Mississippi bayou, which head a few miles from the main river. The belt of marsh land, fringing the shores of lake Maurepas, is only from three-quarters to one mile wide, and the land along the bayous south of the river, the cultivated border belt, of the usual width of from 2½ to 3 miles, is somewhat abruptly terminated by the marsh prairies that border the lake Des Allemands, which thence extend westward as a belt about 6 miles in width, a little beyond the principal meridian of the survey, about half-way between the river and bayou Lafourche. The rice crop for 1879 was 2,718,586 pounds.

ST. JOHN BAPTIST.

Population: 9,686.—White, 3,855; colored, 5,831.
Area: 190 square miles.—Woodland, all. Nearly all alluvial land.
Tilled land: 29,213 acres.—Area planted in cotton, none; in corn, 2,888 acres; in sweet potatoes, 3 acres; in sugar-cane, 9,453 acres; in rice, 696 acres.

This small parish, reaching southward to the lake Des Allemands and its bordering marshes, while to the northward it embraces the neck of land that separates lakes Pontchartrain and Maurepas, is in most respects similar to St. Charles (see below). Between the main river and lake Maurepas, it comprehends a fine expanse of agricultural land of great productiveness and in a high state of cultivation. Fields of sugar-cane and market gardens occupy most of the cultivatable lands in the parish. The region between the two lakes is partly marsh prairie, partly cypress swamp, rendered almost impenetrable by a thick undergrowth of saw palmetto. The prairie on the border of lake Pontchartrain is partly of the "trembling" character, which is perceptible even to the passer-by on the great highway—the New Orleans and Chicago railroad—that traverses it. A few cultivated spots and settlements exist in this region also.

154

ST. CHARLES.

Population: 7,161.—White, 1,401; colored, 5,760.

Area: 284 square miles.—Woodland, 234 square miles; marsh and marsh prairie, 50 square miles. Alluvial land, 234 square miles.

Tilled land: 21,171 acres.—Area planted in cotton, 51 acres; in corn, 1,287 acres; in sweet potatoes, 28 acres; in sugar-cane, 7,787 acres; in rice, 1,320 acres.

Cotton production: 47 bales; average cotton product per acre, 0.92 bale, 1,311 pounds seed-cotton, or 437 pounds cotton lint.

The parish of St. Charles embraces a comparatively large area of fine, cultivatable lands, forming belts of about 3 miles wide on either side of the river. Beyond this "coast belt", which is in a high state of cultivation and thickly settled, the ground becomes lower, and more or less swampy, until, along lake Des Allemands and the upper portion of the bayou of the same name, we find a border belt of marsh, 2 or 3 miles in width. This feature becomes less pronounced to the southward, on the lower part of the bayou, where the cypress-swamp land closely approaches the bayou. Across the latter, in Lafourche parish, lies the great grassy prairie Des Allemands. North of the river we find, beyond the cultivated coast belt, a swamp and marsh region from 5 to 6 miles wide, bordering lake Pontchartrain.

JEFFERSON.

Population: 12,166.—White, 4,864; colored, 7,302.

Area: 395 square miles.—Woodland, 170 square miles; marsh and marsh prairie, 225 square miles. Alluvial, 170 square miles.

Tilled land: 19,767 acres.—Area planted in cotton, none; in corn, 2,065 acres; in sweet potatoes, 88 acres; in sugar-cane, 6,136 acres; in rice, 1,841 acres.

Jefferson parish stretches from lake Pontchartrain on the north, to the head of Barataria bay on the Gulf coast. Most of the tillable lands lie in the northern portion, along the Mississippi river, just west of, as well as opposite to, the city of New Orleans. The relatively high banks of the Mississippi, on which the towns of Algiers and Gretna are located, form a dividing ridge, from the south side of which the water drains southward through bayou Barataria and its connections into Barataria bay. On the higher land accompanying this bayou, as well as bayou Dauphine or Des Familles, there are some fine sugar-plantations, although the tillable lands are of little depth, and from about the junction of the two bayous, near the eastern end of lake Washa, the marsh prairie closes in upon their banks.

In this southern portion, the surface of the parish is almost entirely covered by swamp, marsh prairie, and sea marsh, traversed by an intricate network of bayous and dotted with lakes, resorts of fishermen and duck-hunters only. Numerous shell-heaps form the only elevations in the level plain; they are almost exclusively composed of the "clam" or gnathodon, and will doubtless in the future be made profitable for the making of roads, as are those on lake Pontchartrain.

Through Verret canal, light-draught steamers and other craft can pass from the Mississippi, near Algiers, into bayou Barataria, and Harvey's canal establishes a similar communication farther west. Barataria bayou is navigable, and through its connections the waters of the Gulf are reached without difficulty. Prior to the construction of the South pass jetties, this route was strongly urged as the most desirable outlet for the shipping from New Orleans, and it may even yet become of considerable importance for the coasting trade, since there is but little current to be encountered in making the passage up from Barataria bay.

The shore of lake Pontchartrain, at the northern end of the parish, is bordered by 4 to 5 miles of marsh prairie, whose landward limit is marked by a belt of live-oak, forming the background of the landscape as seen from the river. The lands intervening between the live-oak belt and the river are thickly settled and highly productive of sugar.

ORLEANS.

Population: 216,090.—White, 158,367; colored, 57,723.

Area: 187 square miles.—Alluvial land, 80 square miles; marsh, 107 square miles.

Tilled land: 4,436 acres.—Area planted in cotton, 7 acres; in corn, 35 acres; in sweet potatoes, 48 acres; in sugar-cane, 1,162 acres; in rice, 1,332 acres.

Cotton production: 12 bales; average cotton product per acre, 1.71 bales, 2,436 pounds seed-cotton, or 812 pounds cotton lint.

The city of New Orleans and its suburbs, with a population of 216,090, covers nearly all of the higher land lying within Orleans parish. The rear of the city itself almost touches the swamp land, originally timbered with cypress, passing into the marsh prairie that borders lake Pontchartrain with a depth of from 3 to 4 miles. The Great Levee protects the city-front from the flood-waters of the Mississippi; but the enemy not uncommonly finds its way to the rear, through breaks in levees above or below, not so well cared for, when the northern part of the city suffers more or less from water. Bayous St. John and Gentilly, heading near that part of the city, then serve to convey the overflow into lake Pontchartrain.

The New Orleans and Mobile railroad traverses the portion of the parish lying between lakes Borgne and Pontchartrain, a region of little else than swamp and marsh prairie, of which small tracts are gradually being reclaimed for market gardens. The body of those supplying the New Orleans vegetable market lie, however, above the city, in the adjoining parishes of Jefferson, St. Charles, and St. John Baptist. Rice crop, 1,239,240 pounds.

ST. BERNARD.

Population: 4,405.—White, 2,104; colored, 2,301.
Area: 680 square miles.—Woodland, 5 square miles; marsh and marsh prairie, 675 square miles. Alluvial ridges, 25 square miles.
Tilled land; 11,850 acres.—Area planted in cotton, 248 acres; in corn, 395 acres; in sweet potatoes, 215 acres; in sugar-cane, 2,870 acres; in rice, 1,807 acres—yield, 1,027,200 pounds.
Cotton production: 146 bales; average cotton product per acre, 0.59 bale, 840 pounds seed-cotton, or 280 pounds cotton lint.

The parish of St. Bernard embraces but small and incontinuous tracts of land susceptible of cultivation at the present time. The strip of high land lying on the left bank of the Mississippi, about the "English turn" of the river within this parish, is only about three-quarters of a mile wide. Beyond, the cypress swamp takes possession, and beyond that, on the shore of lake Borgne, we find the marsh prairie, about 3 or 4 miles wide at this point.

A narrow strip of live-oak land also lies on the bayou Terre-aux-Boeufs, and on a few others of the bayous. The rest of the parish, so far as I have been able to learn, is occupied by marsh prairie and sea marsh, cut up by bayous and innumerable inlets, frequented only by hunters and fishermen in pursuit of their game. To all but these, notwithstanding its nearness to the commercial metropolis of the Southwest, this region is in a great measure a *terra incognita*.

The Chandeleur islands are said to resemble those of the Mississippi sound, being low and sandy, with an occasional sandhill blown up by the wind. Their growth is mostly scrub with a few pitch pines. They are visited only occasionally by oystermen's and fishermen's crafts.

PLAQUEMINES.

Population: 11,575.—White, 4,254; colored, 7,321.
Area: 930 square miles.—Woodland, 285 square miles; marsh and marsh prairie, 645 square miles. Alluvial land, 285 square miles (along main river).
Tilled land: 36,908 acres.—Area planted in cotton, none; in corn, 1,767 acres; in sweet potatoes, 46 acres; in sugar-cane, 12,084 acres; in rice, 10,181 acres—yield, 6,609,954 pounds.

The cultivatable lands of Plaquemines parish lie wholly along both banks of the Mississippi river. Just below the city of New Orleans, these belts of comparatively high land, are from 1 to as much as 3 miles wide, but gradually decrease in width as we descend the river, until, at forts St. Philip and Jackson, the marsh closes in upon the banks of the great river itself.

Down to the forts, the aspect of this "lower coast" is pretty much the same. Nearest the river, and highest above water-level, are the sandy " willow battures", where the willow, mingled with, and occasionally replaced by, the cottonwood, forms the predominant growth. Beyond lies a belt of woodland, timbered chiefly with live oak, magnolia, and cottonwood, often deeply veiled with "long moss". This woodland belt denotes the richest and most durable soils of the region, and is mostly occupied by sugar plantations and orange orchards. Still beyond these, loom in the distance the somber-hued, moss-curtained denizens of the cypress swamp, their tops forming a level platform sharply defined against the horizon. Between the swamp and the water's edge, to seaward, there usually intervenes a zone of rushes, with here and there a stunted cypress, bay, or candleberry bush, where the salt-water has but slight access.

Of these four belts, either or both of the middle ones may locally be absent. The "cypress" is the rule below the forts; thence to the mouths of the "passes" the willow batture and rush-grown marsh alone form the barrier between the river and the sea, which, in the portion known as " the Neck" is often so exceedingly narrow, as to make it a matter of surprise to the novice that the river does not break through almost anywhere, and thus shorten its course to the sea. There are, indeed, a few connecting bayous naturally formed, and many more excavated by the duck-hunters who frequent this region and supply the New Orleans market. In reality, the narrow barrier is not as frail as it seems, being composed not so much of river sediment as of tough clay, ejected in a semi-fluid condition by the singular mud volcanoes or "mud lumps", that form a unique feature of the Mississippi mouths, and so greatly impede their navigation. They are originally formed by the bulging up of the bottom on and inside of the bar, followed by the breaking out of a mud-spring, which in the end forms an island consisting of tough clay. These islands remain undisturbed along the margin of the channel, and the intervals between them are gradually filled up, partly from their own mass, partly from river sediment. Thus a canal with solid clay walls is being built by the river out into the Gulf, and hence the singular shape of its mouths, which are often compared to the web-feet of water-fowl. The bank that stands directly in the way of the current of the main river, at the "head of the passes", consists of mud-lump clay, and thus, resisting washing away as readily as solid rock, it has divided the current of the great river into the several "passes".

At numerous points (as at Stake island, in the Southwest pass), the mud-lump islands rise as much as 15 feet above the sea-level, though more commonly their height is from bare emergence to 8 or 10 feet. The waves alone make but little impression upon the tough material of the mud lumps; but when the mud springs cease to eject their fluid mud, sun-cracks are formed on the surface, and huge fragments cleave off into the water, where they are soon leveled by the waves, forming mud banks, while the remnant stands up as a steep cliff, whose height is usually greatly overestimated by the passer-by, and their shrubby growth exaggerated into trees. Only one of these islands, Stake island in the Southwest pass, is inhabited. The rest are the resort of sea-fowl, and sometimes of their enemies, the mink and otter.

Few efforts at cultivation of the soil have been made in the marsh region below the forts, and the light-houses and pilot-stations almost alone constitute the resident population. A few settlers' houses are seen on the main river below the forts, and on Southwest pass, where some vegetables have been successfully grown. The dwellings are all on piles, for the sake of safety in time of flood or storm-tides.

Doubtless the culture of rice could be successfully pursued in a large portion of these marshes, thus far left, as their undisputed domain, to the alligator and the mosquito. The portion of the "coast" above the forts is almost entirely devoted to the culture of sugar-cane and tropical fruits.

LAFOURCHE.

Population : 19,113.—White, 11,282; colored, 7,831.
Area : 1,024 square miles.—Woodland, 295 square miles; marsh and marsh prairie, 729 square miles. Alluvial land, 295 square miles.
Tilled land : 44,802 acres.—Area planted in cotton, none; in corn, 16,018 acres; in sweet potatoes, 331 acres; in sugar-cane, 12,249 acres; in rice, 9,732 acres—yield, 4,602,334 pounds.

Lafourche is a long, narrow parish, lying on both sides of the navigable bayou from which it takes its name, its length being from 80 to 85 miles, its width never exceeding 20. The northern portion is similar to Assumption, the rich belt of sugar-cane land continuing to follow the course of the bayou Lafourche; it is in a high state of cultivation to within 25 miles of the Gulf coast. After passing Thibodeauxville, the depth of the high lands gradually diminishes, and toward the lower part of the parish the sea marsh encroaches to within a few hundred yards of the banks of the bayou. For some distance below the site of any plantations, the ridge along the bayou is covered with a dense growth of live oaks. These are gradually crowded out by the rank grass of the marsh, which borders the Lafourche for the last fifteen miles of its seaward course.

Narrow belts of arable lands are also found along bayous Cheeby and Chattamahan, in the northern part of the parish, and along the borders of the lake Des Allemands, lake Boeuf and its outlet, bayou Boeuf. Bayous De la Vacherie, Coquille, and Middle bayou, near the center of the parish, also have some extensive and very fine tracts of improved lands upon their borders. Along the bayou Des Allemands and lake Salvador only a few scattered localities lie high enough to be inhabited. In the western part of the parish, on bayou Blen and some of the smaller bayous, some live-oak ridges exist, and small isolated tracts of a similar nature are occasionally seen in the open, low, grassy prairies, which form the prevalent feature of the Gulf coast of the state inside of the sea marsh proper. Immense tracts on the borders of the lakes are of the "trembling prairie" character, the surface consisting of matted roots and decayed marsh vegetation, sometimes half afloat upon underground sheets of water. Cattle graze upon these prairies, although they vibrate at every tread, and the small-hoofed breeds cannot sustain themselves on account of the continuous paddling motion required for safety.

Outside of these prairies, the tidal sea-marsh presents to the Gulf a ragged edge of islands, peninsulas, and inlets, and is traversed by an intricate maze of tide-water bayous, into which only the duck-hunter cares to penetrate.

The predominant crop of Lafourche is sugar-cane, and next to it, rice and corn. Tropical fruits—oranges, bananas, and figs—are also largely produced.

TERREBONNE.

Population : 17,957.—White, 8,613; colored, 9,344.
Area : 1,806 square miles.—Woodland, 306 square miles; marsh prairie and marsh, 1,500 square miles. Alluvial land, 306 square miles.
Tilled land : 40,403 acres.—Area planted in cotton, none; in corn, 14,338 acres; in sweet potatoes, 459 acres; in sugar-cane, 15,390 acres; in rice, 705 acres.

In total area, Terrebonne is one of the largest parishes of the state, but it contains within its limits a vast extent of salt-marsh, of "trembling", and open, wet prairies.

In the northeastern quarter of the parish there rise a number of bayous, which traverse it from north to south; the most important of these are bayous Terrebonne, Bleu, Petit Caillou, Du Chien, Grand Caillou with its branches, bayou Au Large, and Cade. Running in a westerly direction, there are bayous Black, Chuckahoula, Tigre, L'Ours, Chêne, and Penchant. These bayous are at first narrow, shallow streams, frequently becoming perfectly dry in the summer and autumn; but they gradually increase in breadth and depth, until they become navigable for the smaller class of steamboats. In wet seasons they become large streams, and are of great importance in affording outlets for the flood-waters of the Mississippi. Along all these bayous is a (relatively) high ridge of excellent land, which, however, is not as deep here as farther above, rarely exceeding forty acres (a quarter of a mile) in depth; as on bayous Terrebonne, the Caillous, Black, and Chuckahoula. On others, as on bayou L'Ours, the bordering ridge is often barely wide enough for the public road which follows its windings. In the vicinity of Houma, however, and at several other points, the ridges of contiguous bayous meet and crowd out the intervening swamp, so as to form large tracts under one continuous ownership. Elsewhere, Terrebonne is a region of small farms rather than of extensive plantations. The cultivable ridges accompany the bayous to within from 10 to 20 miles of the sea, when the ridge becomes a live-oak grove for some miles farther, and finally, the salt-marsh closes in upon the bayou. The products of Terrebonne are the same as those of Lafourche—chiefly sugar-cane, with rice, some corn, and tropical fruits. Within the parish are many large lakes, such as lake Long, on its eastern boundary, lakes Quitman, Washa, De Cade, and numerous other smaller sheets of water. On the coast are several important indentations, namely, Timbalier, Terrebonne, Caillou, and Atchafalaya bays; and beyond, there lies a chain of islands, of which the largest are Timbalier and Last islands. These are occasionally swept by storm-tides, but the latter, despite a catastrophe thus caused some time ago, is still occupied as a place of resort. The lakes and bays are frequented chiefly by duck-hunters and fishermen.

ST. MARY.

Population : 19,891.—White, 6,717; colored, 13,174.
Area : 648 square miles.—Woodland, 305 square miles; marsh and marsh prairie, 333 square miles; black prairie (Cyprès Mort), 10 square miles. Two islands, 4 square miles. Alluvial land, 381 square miles.
Tilled land : 66,326 acres.—Area planted in cotton, none; in corn, 11,302 acres; in sweet potatoes, 136 acres; in sugar-cane, 17,396 acres.

The parish of St. Mary consists almost entirely of alluvial lands (the cultivatable portions bordering the various bayous) and of sea marsh; the Cyprès-Mort prairie, in the northwestern portion south of the Tèche, and the islands of Côte Blanche and Belle Isle, being the only exceptions.

On the bayou Tèche, the tillable lands vary in depth from 1 to 3, and in places even 5, miles. All those lying on the eastern side are subject to overflow at the highest stages of the Mississippi river, though at no time has it been known to reach above Centreville. The height of the banks of the Tèche at Franklin is 13 feet above the Gulf level, and at the northern line of the parish, 15 feet. On the other bayous within the parish, the depth of the tillable lands is only from a half to one mile, as on Berwick's bay, bayous Boeuf, Shaffer, and Atchafalaya. Fine bodies of cultivated lands are also found on bayous Salé and Cyprès-Mort, those on bayou Salé being considered the best sugar lands in the parish, while the "Cyprès-Mort woods" are remarkable for their beautiful groves of live oak, ash, magnolia, sweet gum, and cypress. The soil here is a dark alluvial loam, several feet in depth, and very easily tilled. The soil of the Tèche lands is of a lighter tint, and above the town of Franklin the red tint of the Red river alluvium is occasionally observable. Sugar-cane is by far the predominant crop; the cotton shown by the returns being chiefly produced on the island of Côte Blanche. The latter, resembling altogether in its features the islands of Petite Anse and Grande Côte, mentioned in the description of Iberia parish, lies on the shore of Côte Blanche bay, is almost circular, and rises 180 feet above tide-water; area, about 2,000 acres. It was originally heavily timbered with oak, magnolia, &c., with an undergrowth of cane, but is now almost entirely cleared.

Belle Isle, the smallest of the chain of five islands, lies on the western headland of Atchafalaya bay. Its area is only 350 acres; its character substantially the same as that of Côte Blanche.

IBERIA.

(See under "Attakapas prairie region".)

VERMILLION.

(See under "Attakapas prairie region".)

CAMERON.

Population : 2,416.—White, 2,087; colored, 329.

Area : 1,545 square miles.—Woodland, 50 square miles; marsh and marsh prairie, 1,495 square miles. Live-oak ridges, 50 square miles; black prairie, 50 square miles.

Tilled land : 5,743 acres.—Area planted in cotton, 1,662 acres; in corn, 2,726 acres; in sweet potatoes, 184 acres; in sugar-cane, 51 acres; in rice, 12 acres.

Cotton production : 636 bales; average cotton product per acre, 0.38 bale, 543 pounds seed-cotton, or 181 pounds cotton lint.

Cameron parish, originally part of Calcasieu, is mainly sea marsh, embracing at the north from 50 to 100 square miles of the Calcasieu prairie, and in its southern portion the following habitable spots: the island of Grande Chénière; a narrow ridge along the Mermentau pass to its mouth; thence to the mouth of Calcasieu pass; thence, still along the Gulf coast, and but a short distance from it, to the mouth of Sabine pass; also Hackberry island, in the western part of Calcasieu lake; a part of St. John's island, in the southern part of the same lake, and along Calcasieu pass to its mouth; also, at a few points along Sabine pass, and along Johnson's bayou, Black bayou, and a few others emptying into Sabine lake. All of these lands, though above the ordinary tidal overflow, are subject to the unusual high floods produced by long-continued gales from the south, and nearly all have at times suffered from these extraordinary floods. Still, the lands are so good, and the climate generally so fine, that the inhabitants cling to their homes in spite of occasional disasters.

The marketable productions of Cameron are cotton, rice, corn, cattle, fish, oysters, game, oranges, figs, and bananas. (a)

BLUFF REGION.

(Comprising West Feliciana, East Feliciana, and East Baton Rouge parishes.)

WEST FELICIANA.

Population : 12,809.—White, 2,287; colored, 10,522.

Area : 370 square miles.—Woodland, all. Bluff land, 220 square miles; alluvial land (Mississippi bottom), 110 square miles; oak uplands, 40 square miles.

Tilled land : 28,985 acres.—Area planted in cotton, 21,072 acres; in corn, 9,000 acres; in sweet potatoes, 271 acres; in sugar-cane, 22 acres; in rice, 5 acres.

Cotton production : 11,810 bales; average cotton product per acre, 0.56 bale, 798 pounds seed-cotton, or 266 pounds cotton lint.

The parish of West Feliciana comprehends substantially two kinds of lands, outside of small portions of the Mississippi bottom lying east of the river, viz: the bluff lands, forming a belt varying from 10 to 15 miles wide

---

a Lockett, Report of the Topographical Survey of Louisiana, 1870, p. 35.

east and west, which skirt the Mississippi river from Vicksburg to Baton Rouge and constitute the main body of the parish, and rolling oak and pine uplands, with a more or less sandy loam soil, timbered with oaks and some short-leaf pine.

The bluff lands are quite hilly and broken in the northern part of the parish, forming sharp-backed ridges elevated several hundred feet above the river, with narrow valleys intervening. In some places (especially inland) there are larger or smaller areas of level or gently rolling plateau-land, with a yellow or brown loam soil on the tops of the ridges, and, in such cases, the slopes of the latter are less abrupt and have an excellent soil, resulting from the intermixture of the brown loam of the hill-tops with the marly silt that forms the body of the ridges. Where the silt itself forms the cultivated soil, the latter, though productive, is somewhat droughty, being very light and porous, so that the water of the streams sinks below the surface very rapidly, and springs exist only where the older sandstones and clays shed the water (see report on Mississippi, "Cane-hills region").

In the southern portion of the parish the ridges gradually become less high and abrupt, and the rolling plateau character which prevails in East Feliciana, and East Baton Rouge, becomes more prevalent, and the farms increase in area. Near the river, however, deep, narrow valleys with steep sides are still common.

The oak uplands in the northeastern portion of the parish are altogether similar to those described as forming the middle portion of East Feliciana.

ABSTRACT OF THE REPORT OF R. H. RYLAND, BAYOU SARA.

The lowlands of the Mississippi river are very rich, producing splendid crops of cotton.

The upland is table-land, from hilly to rolling and almost level. The original timber is magnolia, sweet gum, oaks, beech, black walnut, and wild cherry.

The land was originally very rich; much of it is now worn and gullied; level tracts still good; soil, a loam or clay loam; the former brown to nearly black and rather light; the latter from grayish-brown to red. These soils frequently alternate or are mixed. The subsoil is mostly clay, heavier than surface soil.

Cotton, corn, and potatoes are the chief crops to which the soil is well adapted. Cotton forms about two-thirds of the crop; 4 to 6 feet is the usual height of cotton on the uplands; it runs to weed in wet weather; no remedy applied. Fresh land yields 1,500 pounds of seed-cotton per acre, of which from 1,350 to 1,575 pounds make a 450-pound bale, the staple rating middling. After eight to ten years' cultivation, the land yields 600 to 1,000 pounds; in bottoms, 800 to 1,200. About the same amount of seed-cotton is needed for a bale, but it is not quite so long in staple nor so heavy in body. The most troublesome weeds are rag-weed, careless-weed, and cocklebur.

Perhaps as much as one-fourth of upland once cultivated lies out; when taken into cultivation it produces well for a few years. It gullies readily on slopes, serious damage being done. The lowlands are rather benefited by the washings. Little is being done to check the damage now, but before the war, horizontalizing and hillside ditching were successfully practiced.

Cotton is shipped, as soon as it is ready, by river to New Orleans; rate of freight is 50 to 75 cents per bale.

EAST FELICIANA.

Population : 15,132.—White, 4,497; colored, 10,635.

Area : 483 square miles.—Woodland, all. Long-leaf pine hills, 403 square miles; bluff land, 80 square miles.

Tilled land : 52,218 acres.—Area planted in cotton, 28,368 acres; in corn, 16,522 acres; in sweet potatoes, 1,067 acres; in sugar-cane, 169 acres; in rice, 19 acres.

Cotton production : 11,098 bales; average cotton product per acre, 0.39 bale, 555 pounds seed-cotton, or 185 pounds cotton lint.

The eastern portion of East Feliciana is a rolling plateau-land, rising in the northern part upward of 100 feet above the Mississippi river, but in the southern, at Port Hudson, declining to between 60 and 70 feet. Deep and rather abrupt ravines are cut into the plateau by the small streams that flow directly toward the Mississippi, while on the eastward slope, toward the Comite, they descend more gently. The belt of "bluff" lands, with their light and fertile soil, is here about 13 miles wide, their general character and timber growth being as described in East Baton Rouge (see below).

Beyond the point mentioned, the short-leaf pine begins to intermingle with the timber growth of the "bluff"; for a short distance there are alternations and intermixtures of the pine and bluff soils, and then the pine predominates, and with post, black-jack, and some Spanish oaks, continues on to the edge of the Comite bottom, in the direction of Clinton, the parish town. The Comite and its branches have quite extensive bottoms of very fertile land, partly swamp. East of the Comite, the country becomes more broken and the soil poorer, the pine predominating over the oaks, and mingling with the long-leaved species. Finally, east of the Amite river, the open long-leaf pine country sets in.

It is claimed that the uplands, timbered with oak and short-leaf pine, between the Comite and Amite, produce as much as half a bale of cotton per acre. This, however, is certainly considerably above the average product, and probably refers more especially to the lands of the Comite proper.

The shipment of products is made almost entirely from various landings on the Mississippi river to New Orleans.

EAST BATON ROUGE.

Population : 19,966.—White, 7,103; colored, 12,863.

Area : 442 square miles.—Woodland, all. Bluff land, 282 square miles; alluvial land, 85 square miles; long-leaf pine hills, 75 square miles.

Tilled land : 40,026 acres.—Area planted in cotton, 11,808 acres; in corn, 11,735 acres; in sweet potatoes, 443 acres; in sugar-cane, 3,584 acres; in rice, 6 acres.

Cotton production : 5,756 bales; average cotton product per acre, 0.49 bale, 699 pounds seed-cotton, or 233 pounds cotton lint.

The parish of East Baton Rouge is essentially a "bluff" parish, there being only a small area of the "oak and pine uplands" character in the northeastern corner. Two small areas of Mississippi bottom are also within the parish limits; and an alluvial tract stretches in along Ward's creek, from bayou Manchac.

At the northwestern corner of the parish, the plateau still rises to about 70 feet above the Mississippi river, but at Baton Rouge descends to about 40 feet only. A short distance below the town the bluff terminates, taking a sweep southeastward, parallel to bayou Manchac, and forms the northern limit of the delta plain proper.

At Baton Rouge, and eastward as well as northward, the bluff plateau is almost level or gently undulating, but much cut into by deep and abrupt ravines, which have been greatly enlarged in consequence of the denudation resulting from deforesting, and turning-out of the older lands.

The soil of the "bluff plateau" is a light buff-colored loam at the surface, but the dark orange-yellow subsoil lies quite near the surface. At most points, these uplands (which were among the earliest settled in the state) were originally covered with an open forest of magnolias, oaks (especially the swamp-chestnut oak), beech, sweet gum, sassafras, &c., with a prevailing undergrowth of tall cane. The soil was a black, deep, easily tilled loam, whose fertility was so satisfactory, that few felt tempted to invade the bottoms. In the course of time, what with the removal of the timber and cane, and shallow tillage, the original soil is scarcely to be seen anywhere, and cane has become a myth. Fortunately for the country, the Bermuda-grass early took possession of the ground abandoned by the cane and the planter, and prevented a great deal of damage by washing; at the same time it forms an excellent pasture during the greater part of the year, and yet does not seem to trouble the cultivated fields in the guise of the "wire-grass", that is such a dreaded pest in the hill country. The rich and deep subsoil loam is thus retained on the uplands, and needs only deep and thorough tillage and rational treatment to restore it to its original fertility. The upland plantations were gradually abandoned by the large planters from the time at which the reclamation of the bottom lands began, and the bluff country has become more and more a land of small farms; thus, under more thrifty management, it is resuming its natural position in the scale of productiveness.

Cotton is by far the predominant crop, but the soil is adapted to a great variety of crops, and more especially to fruits; among these it is probable that the grape would be one of the most successful. Very little has, as yet, been done in this direction.

There are a few local exceptions to the fertility of the bluff plateau, where certain white materials, visible at the Port Hudson bluff, come to the surface. Such is the case with "Bullard's plains", about 7 miles north of Baton Rouge, and another locality about 5 miles east of Port Hudson (in East Feliciana). These are level tracts, with a white soil, putty-like when wet, and almost barren; an irregular growth of crab and hawthorn is all that is found on them.

Communication with market is via Baton Rouge to New Orleans by river.

ATTAKAPAS PRAIRIE REGION.

(Comprising parts of the parishes of Iberia, St. Martin,[*] St. Landry, Vermillion, and Calcasieu,[*] and the whole of Lafayette.)

IBERIA.

Population: 16,676.—White, 8,100; colored, 8,576.

Area: 582 square miles.—Woodland, 185 square miles; dry prairie, 130 square miles; sea marsh, 267 square miles. Bottom, 175 square miles; three islands, 10½ square miles.

Tilled land: 49,604 acres.—Area planted in cotton, 7,443 acres; in corn, 23,740 acres; in sweet potatoes, 917 acres; in sugar-cane, 6,501 acres; in rice, 33 acres.

Cotton production: 2,482 bales; average cotton product per acre, 0.33 bale, 471 pounds seed-cotton, or 157 pounds cotton lint.

This parish presents a considerable variety of features. About two-fifths of its area belong to the great bottom plain which borders the left bank of the bayou Tèche. Within this alluvial area lie Grande and Fausse Pointe lakes, which are in their turn bordered by extensive cypress swamps. The higher portion of the bottom lands, lying along bayou Tèche, with a width of from 1 to 3 miles, has (except within 50 yards of the bayou) a black loam soil, 2 to 2½ feet in depth, timbered with lowland oaks, ash, magnolia, sweet gum, hackberry, &c. It is chiefly devoted to the culture of sugar-cane.

Immediately along the bayou Tèche there lies a strip of red clay land, from 30 to 50 yards wide, on each side above ordinary overflows, and about 6 feet below the level of the upland prairie. It is timbered with beautiful live oaks, and is very fertile—evidently a portion of the alluvial deposits of Red river, made long ago.

From this red-land terrace there is a more or less sudden ascent of from 2 to 6 feet, into the black prairie intervening between the river lands and the sea marsh. It is here a good deal intersected by "coulées", and notably by the "Grand Marais", a fresh-water marsh, about 1 mile wide, extending for some 10 miles in a northwestern and southeastern direction, at a distance of 3 or 4 miles from the Tèche, and forming the extreme head of bayou Cyprès-Mort. The cultivated lands lie mainly along the Tèche, the open prairie being as yet but little cultivated, although well adapted to the culture of cotton. This is partly due to the fact that they are so nearly level, that the water "seems unable to determine which way to flow", and drainage ditches are needed to relieve the soil early in the season for planting purposes.

In the sea marsh of this parish lie the two "islands" of Petite Anse (2,240 acres) and Grande Côte or Weeks' island (2,300 acres). These are tracts of upland, of the character of the brown loam prairie, but originally densely wooded, and having an undergrowth of tall cane among the oaks and magnolias. Their highest points rise, respectively, to 160 and 180 feet above the sea-level. Their products are chiefly upland cotton, and in the lower lands some sugar-cane; Petite Anse is noted for its great rock-salt mine.[a] Another similar "island" lies in the

----

a For a detailed description of this region see Smithsonian Contribution to Science, No. 248.

prairie, on the shore of lake Peigneur; its area is about 2,250 acres, and its chief product has given it the name of "Orange island".

Communication and shipment of products is by steamers on the Tèche, or by the Louisiana and Texas railroad, to New Orleans.

ST. MARTIN.

(See under "Alluvial region".)

LAFAYETTE.

Population : 13,235.—White, 7,694; colored, 5,541.

Area : 262 square miles.—Woodland, 32 square miles; brown loam prairie, 148 square miles; black calcareous prairie, 82 square miles.

Tilled land : 62,704 acres.—Area planted in cotton, 12,517 acres; in corn, 21,713 acres; in sweet potatoes, 469 acres; in sugar-cane, 783 acres; in rice, 110 acres.

Cotton production : 3,489 bales; average cotton product per acre, 0.28 bale, 399 pounds seed-cotton, or 133 pounds cotton lint.

The small parish of Lafayette embraces chiefly level or slightly rolling uplands, of the brown loam prairie character; in its southern portion about 50 square miles of prairie is of the black calcareous type. About one-eighth of its area is wooded and bottom land; the timber occurs chiefly along the edge of the plateau toward the bayou Tortue, along the bayou Vermillion and bayou Carancro, where it forms the "Carancro hills". The timber belts are from one-half to one mile in width; the timber is water, live, basket, and scarlet oaks, magnolia, sweet gum, tulip tree, and hackberry, indicating a warm, generous soil.

The prairie is high and rolling near the eastern line of the parish, and, in its southern portion especially, bears the name of Côte Gelée. The brown loam prairie is mainly occupied by the culture of corn and cotton, while on the black prairie some sugar-cane is grown. The black prairie yields, when fresh, from 1,100 to 1,300 pounds of seed-cotton per acre; the brown loam prairie averages about 200 pounds less. The staple of both is stated to be excellent. Cotton culture prevails mainly in the eastern portion of the parish, while in the western the breeding of neat-cattle and horses is prominent, abundant pasturage being afforded by the prairie grasses.

Communication and shipment of products are by steamers down the Tèche, or by the Louisiana and Texas railroad, to New Orleans.

ST. LANDRY.

Population : 40,004.—White, 20,473; colored, 19,531.

Area : 2,276 square miles.—Woodland, 1,020 square miles; upland prairie, 1,256 square miles. Oak uplands, 150 square miles; pine lands, 250 square miles; Mississippi bottom, 600 square miles.

Tilled land : 137,370 acres.—Area planted in cotton, 42,135 acres; in corn, 57,411 acres; in sweet potatoes, 1,376 acres; in sugar-cane, 2,711 acres; in rice, 856 acres.

Cotton production : 23,148 bales; average cotton product per acre, 0.55 bale, 783 pounds seed-cotton, or 261 pounds cotton lint.

The western or upland portion of the parish of St. Landry consists predominantly of prairie, partly of the brown loam, partly of the gray silt character, with some black prairie occupying the extreme southwestern portion. The areas covered by these are, respectively, about 825, 268, and 163 square miles.

Narrow timber belts extend along most of the streams, and are more especially developed at the heads of these, in the northwestern part of the parish. Thus a considerable belt of long-leaf pine timber extends along the Nezpiqué, and an oak-upland tract of some 90 square miles along bayou Chicot (see map).

Corn and cotton are the chief products of this upland portion, but the greater part is thus far devoted to the pasturage of stock, chiefly neat-cattle and horses. A great deal of cotton is produced in the prairie region lying between the bottom and bayou Plaquemine Brulée, notably in the region of St. Charles or Grand Coteau, and in the neighborhood of Opelousas. Shipments are made by water down bayous Cocodrie and Tèche. The product is from 800 to 1,200 pounds of seed-cotton per acre, and the staple, when clean, rates as first and second class uplands. The corn product, occupying about half the area cultivated, is from 30 to 45 bushels per acre.

The eastern portion of the parish forms part of the great bottom plain, lying between the Atchafalaya river and the uplands, along the foot of which are bayous Cocodrie, Boeuf, Courtablean, and Tèche. All these derive their waters mainly from Red river, and their alluvium is predominantly of the character described under that head.

ABSTRACT OF THE REPORT OF ELBERT GANTT, WASHINGTON.

Cotton, sugar-cane, and corn are the principal crops grown, with rice and sweet potatoes as secondary ones. The cane is grown almost wholly in the alluvial lands, yielding 2 to 3 hogsheads of sugar per acre. The only lands that do not produce well are the cypress swamps (undrained), which lie back from the bayous. The land along the bayous is a blackish loam, very easily tilled, 10 to 20 inches in depth. Beneath lies either a red or bluish clayey subsoil, or a coarse sandy one.

Cotton forms over 50 per cent. of the crops grown. On the lowlands the product on fresh land is about 2,000 pounds of seed-cotton per acre, of which about 1,470 pounds make a 450-pound bale. After six years' cultivation, without manure, the yield is from 1,200 to 1,400 pounds of seed-cotton. The staple rates the same in the market in either case—fair to good middling when clean.

The cotton plant tends to run to weed in very wet seasons. No remedy is applied. The most troublesome weeds are smart-weed and crab-grass, the latter very troublesome in wet seasons. There are no bottom lands turned out of cultivation.

Cotton is shipped to New Orleans. Shipping begins early in October, and continues until all is shipped. Rate of freight per bale is $1 25 to 1 50.

60 COTTON PRODUCTION IN LOUISIANA.

VERMILLION.

Population: 8,728.—White, 6,771; colored, 1,957.

Area: 1,226 square miles.—Woodland, 100 square miles; prairie, 280 square miles; sea marsh, 826 square miles; live-oak ridges, 20 square miles.

Tilled land: 25,330 acres.—Area planted in cotton, 2,379 acres; in corn, 13,554 acres; in sweet potatoes, 360 acres; in sugar cane, 1,574 acres; in rice, 606 acres.

Cotton production: 537 bales; average cotton product per acre, 0.23 bale, 327 pounds seed-cotton, or 109 pounds cotton lint.

The northern portion of Vermillion parish is chiefly level prairie, similar in character to that of Iberia. A timbered belt extends along Vermillion river and its tributaries, and here the cultivated lands mainly lie. A narrow belt of timber also follows the bayou Queue de Tortue, and the Mentau river and lake. But little of the open prairie is in cultivation, it being chiefly devoted to pasturage; but it is susceptible of profitable tillage, and improves for several years after breaking up. The breed of small ponies commonly reared, is but ill-adapted to the work of ploughing and cultivating. The cattle also are not the best of beef stock, and worthless as milkers.

The sea marsh, forming the southern part of the parish, is mostly impassable, and no attempts to reclaim it have thus far been made. Cultivated tracts are on Pecan island, a sinuous ridge in the marsh, about 7 miles from the beach. This is densely timbered with pecan trees, and, besides the nuts of this tree, has produced sea-island cotton, also cane, and tropical fruits in abundance, the soil being a rich black loam of great depth. It comprehends about 10,000 acres. No long-staple cotton has of late been grown there. Petite Chénière island, on the coast east of Pecan island, is similar in its character and productions.

Besides the products above mentioned, game and poultry are sent to market from this parish in considerable quantities. The inhabitants are largely of French-Canadian origin—"Acadians".

CALCASIEU.

(See under "Long-leaf pine region".)

THE LONG-LEAF PINE REGION.

(Comprising, west of the Mississippi: all of Vernon, and parts of Calcasieu, Sabine*, Natchitoches*, Rapides*, Grant, Winn, Bienville*, Jackson*, Ouachita*, Caldwell*, and Catahoula*. East of the Mississippi: East Feliciana*, Livingston, St. Helena, Tangipahoa, St. Tammany, Washington.)

CALCASIEU.

Population: 12,484.—White, 9,919; colored, 2,565.

Area: 3,400 square miles.—Woodland, 1,870 square miles: long-leaf pine flats, 1,385 square miles; long-leaf pine hills, 285 square miles; oak uplands, 35 square miles; Sabine swamp, 165 square miles. Marsh and marsh prairie, 235 square miles; gray silt prairie, 855 square miles; black calcareous prairie, 440 square miles.

Tilled land: 14,003 acres.—Area planted in cotton, 1,493 acres; in corn, 7,995 acres; in sweet potatoes, 517 acres; in sugar-cane, 67 acres; in rice, 600 acres.

Cotton production: 514 bales; average cotton product per acre, 0.34 bale, 486 pounds seed-cotton, or 162 pounds cotton lint.

Calcasieu, the largest parish of the state, and but very thinly settled, is thus far chiefly devoted to the pasturage of large herds of cattle and horses, and in the wooded portions is accessible by navigable streams for lumbering purposes.

East of the main Calcasieu river, and south of the west fork, almost all is prairie to the edge of the sea marsh. In the northeast corner of the parish, about 75 square miles of wet pine flats lie east of the Calcasieu. To the southward of these extends the Calcasieu (gray silt) prairie, interrupted only by the fertile "cove" of Hickory flat. This prairie pastures large herds of cattle and horses, and the few inhabitants grow rice in the marshy flats on the streams. In its southern portion, on English bayou and bayou Lacacine, fine crops of corn are grown, and the black-prairie soil prevails more or less until the sea marsh is reached. Of this latter, since the formation of Cameron parish, Calcasieu embraces only about 170 square miles.

West of the Calcasieu river, and between the west fork and the marsh, the gray-silt pine prairie again prevails, with many marshy flats interspersed. The Big woods form a remarkable fertile "cove" in this region.

North of the west fork of Calcasieu river (sometimes called Houston bayou on maps, a name not known to the inhabitants), and west of the main river, the long-leaf pine forest covers all but a strip of cypress swamp along the west fork and the Sabine river, varying from 1 to 5 miles in width (on the Louisiana side), and embracing some 200 square miles. The rest, except about 300 square miles of pine-hill lands lying between the east fork of Calcasieu river and Bundick's creek, is of the "pine-flats" character, covering about 1,720 square miles. The chief settlements of the region lie on Bundick's and Sugar creeks, where a good loam subsoil renders the soil both durable and fertile.

Cotton has thus far been produced in Calcasieu to a very limited extent only.

Shipments are made to New Orleans by rail, or by coasting vessels via Calcasieu pass.

162

VERNON.

Population: 5,160.—White, 4,783; colored, 377.
Area : 1,540 square miles.—Woodland, all but about 10 square miles of black prairie. Anacoco prairie region, 60 square miles; long-leaf pine hills, 1,430 square miles; long-leaf pine flats, 50 square miles.
Tilled land : 10,303 acres.—Area planted in cotton, 4,791 acres; in corn, 8,320 acres; in sweet potatoes, 284 acres; in sugar-cane, 22 acres; in rice, 31 acres.
Cotton production : 1,662 bales; average cotton product per acre, 0.35 bale, 498 pounds seed-cotton, or 166 pounds cotton lint.
This parish is almost throughout of the "pine-hills" character, with the exception of the "Anacoco prairie region" described above, where the bulk of the cotton grown in the parish is produced. The great distance from market, and the difficult communication through the hilly country lying between the Anacoco prairie and Red river, have stood greatly in the way of its settlement.
The bottoms of the heads of Calcasieu river on the east, and of the tributaries of the bayou Anacoco on the west (especially that of bayou Castor), are productive, and will, in time, be brought under cultivation. On the eastern head-tributaries of Bundick's creek, and especially on Sugar creek, there are prosperous settlements, the bottoms being wide, and even the uplands of fair productiveness, as shown by a considerable admixture of oaks with the pine growth.

ABSTRACT OF THE REPORT OF R. T. WRIGHT, ANACOCO.

(Refers to township 3, range 16; resides on section 15.)

The land is hilly and rolling, partly upland prairie, on the waters of East and West Anacoco creeks. The upland soils vary greatly from one ridge to another, in tracts of from 10 to 40 acres. They are chiefly of three kinds: black upland-prairie, dark clay-loam soil of the two branches of Anacoco and Prairie creeks, and light, sandy upland soil.

The chief one is the black prairie, it forming about one-fifth of the lands in the region, from 5 to 10 miles either way. Its natural timber is hickory, oak, haw, ash, dogwood, persimmon. Its color is black to the depth of over 2 feet. The subsoil is a tough, yellow clay, which becomes very hard when first exposed, but by cultivation pulverizes. It is quite impervious while undisturbed. It is underlaid by hard, white soapstone rock at 4 feet. The land tills with difficulty in wet seasons, but is well drained, and early and warm. Corn, cotton, sweet potatoes, sugar-cane, and rice are produced. The soils seem best adapted to cotton, which is one-half of all crops planted. It is most productive at 6 feet, but reaches 8 feet in height. Too much rain makes it run to weed, and topping will help to make it boll. Fresh land produces from 1,500 to 2,000 pounds of seed-cotton per acre; 1,350 pounds make a 450-pound bale. When clean, it rates in market as low middling. After eight years' cultivation the yield is 1,400 to 1,500 pounds, and a little more is needed to make a bale, but it rates the same in market as that from fresh land. Cocklebur and tie-vine are the most troublesome weeds. Perhaps one-tenth of such land originally cultivated is turned out; when again taken in, it produces 800 to 1,000 pounds per acre. It is a little subject to gullying, but hillside ditches prevent damage.

The dark, sandy-loam soil is timbered with gum, hickory, beech, and pine. It is a brown, fine sandy loam; forms about one-third of the lands; half of it is planted in cotton; will yield about 1,600 pounds of seed-cotton per acre when fresh; the staple rates low middling. After eight years' cultivation it will yield 800 pounds. About one-sixth of it lies turned out; will produce 1,000 to 1,200 pounds when again cultivated. No serious damage is done by washing on hillsides. Weeds : crab-grass and tie-vine.

The light, sandy soil is a grade lower than the preceding, in the amount and quality of the staple produced.

Cotton in the lowlands is liable to be late, and to take the rust; hence the uplands are preferred.

Cotton is shipped to Alexandria; freight, $2 per bale.

SABINE.

(See "Oak-uplands region".)

NATCHITOCHES.

(See "Oak-uplands region".)

RAPIDES.

(See "Alluvial region".)

GRANT.

Population : 6,188.—White, 3,320; colored, 2,868.
Area : 642 square miles.—Woodland, all but small strips of prairie in central prairie region, covering 110 square miles; long-leaf pine hills, 482 square miles; Red river bottom, 50 square miles.
Tilled land : 24,004 acres.—Area planted in cotton, 11,155 acres; in corn, 8,177 acres; in sweet potatoes, 22 acres.
Cotton production : 5,158 bales; average cotton product per acre, 0.46 bale, 657 pounds seed-cotton, or 219 pounds cotton lint.
Grant is one of the new parishes formed since the war, from portions of the territory of Rapides and Winn. Its soils are more varied than is the case in the latter parish, inasmuch as it embraces a small portion of the Red river bottom and also of the "central prairie region", the rest being long-leaf pine lands, similar in character to those of the southern part of Winn, with some level lowlands resembling those on Black lake in Red River parish, and timbered with short-leaf pine, and lowland oaks.

In the northeastern portion of the parish the face of the country is largely level, the soil consisting partly of heavy gray clay, timbered with post oak and short-leaf pine ("hog-wallow"), partly of small, incontinuous tracts or belts of black prairie, either timberless, or only with clumps of hawthorn and crab-apple, and groups of honey locust. These soils are ill-drained, and partly on that account, partly because of the difficulty of obtaining a supply of water, not as much settled as their intrinsic fertility would warrant.

Little river is skirted, mostly on its western side, by a hummock or second bottom, timbered mainly with lowland oaks, and above overflow; the bottom itself is often overflowed to the depth of 6 to 8 feet, but is densely wooded, and full of cypress sloughs. Little river is a navigable stream for small steamers, at all times of the year, to the junction of bayou Castor.

Shipments are made by Red river steamers (or occasionally on Little river) to New Orleans.

WINN.

Population : 5,846.—White, 4,797; colored, 1,049.

Area : 970 square miles.—Woodland, all but small strips of prairie in the central prairie region, covering 30 square miles; long-leaf pine hills, 850 square miles; oak uplands, 90 square miles.

Tilled land : 22,548 acres.—Area planted in cotton, 7,379 acres; in corn, 8,588 acres; in sweet potatoes, 250 acres; in sugar-cane, 41 acres; in rice, 4 acres.

Cotton production : 3,002 bales; average cotton product per acre, 0.41 bale, 585 pounds seed-cotton, or 195 pounds cotton lint.

The surface of Winn parish is rolling, rarely hilly, and its greater part is covered with long-leaf pine forest, affording a great deal of fine timber. Such is especially the case in the western portion; in the eastern, and particularly to southward, the long-leaf pine is mainly restricted to the upper portions of the ridges, while their flanks have a good growth of upland oaks, and short-leaf pine. Where this is the case, we mostly find the dark orange-colored subsoil of the "red lands" underlying the light gray surface soil; while higher up on the ridges the pale-yellow loam is predominant. Hence there is, in the country bordering on the Dugdemona river and its larger tributaries, a considerable amount of good farming upland, on which very fair crops of cotton and corn are produced. The bottoms, however, are not very wide, and being subject to overflow, are as yet but little cultivated. Want of easy communication with the outside world, has stood greatly in the way of the settlement of this region, whose reputation as a farming country is not nearly as good as it deserves to be. A tract of true black prairie (Pendarvis' prairie) lies within this parish, in the fork of Dugdemona river and bayou Castor.

A curious feature of this parish are the salt licks, low flats with salt springs, and usually underlaid by limestone (of the Cretaceous formation), occurring at several points, as Price's lick, Drake's salt-works on Saline bayou, Cedar lick, near Winfield, and others. Of the same geological origin is the limestone hill, a few miles west of Winfield, an isolated mass of Cretaceous limestone, from which excellent lime (much needed in the improvement of the pine lands) is made. At Louisville, in the northeastern part of the parish, a small tract of black prairie is formed by one of these limestone masses approaching the surface.

Cotton is hauled to landings on Red or Washita rivers, and thence goes by steamer to New Orleans.

ABSTRACT OF THE REPORT OF W. T. JONES, WINFIELD.

(Description refers to township 12, range 2 west, in northeastern Winn.)

This is a rolling pine country, with some "hog-wallow" prairie. Cotton does best in the lowlands, although in good seasons the uplands do well also. The creek bottoms (such as that of Kyiche creek) are timbered with lowland oaks, hickory, ash, and some walnut. The soil is dark-colored, light, easily tilled; at 6 inches depth a lighter subsoil underlies. Corn, cotton, sugar-cane, oats, and sweet potatoes are grown. Cotton occupies about one-half of the cultivated land; grows from 4 to 6 feet high, the higher the better. Draining will prevent it from running to weed in wet seasons. The yield per acre is 1,000 pounds of seed-cotton on fresh land; 1,350 pounds required for a 450-pound bale of lint, which rates well in market. After fifteen years' cultivation this land yields about 800 pounds, and perhaps 50 pounds more of seed-cotton is then needed for a bale, the staple being about the same. About one-fourth of such land, once cultivated, now lies out.

The pine uplands gully readily on slopes, and serious damage is done to them, but none to the lowlands.

Cotton is hauled from here to landings on the Washita river, and shipped to New Orleans by boat; freight, $1 50.

BIENVILLE.

(See "Oak-uplands region".)

JACKSON.

(See "Oak-uplands region".)

OUACHITA.

(See "Alluvial region".)

CALDWELL.

(See "Alluvial region".)

CATAHOULA.

(See "Alluvial region".)

EAST FELICIANA.

(See "Bluff region".)

LIVINGSTON.

Population : 5,258.—White, 4,265; colored, 993.
Area : 600 square miles.—Woodland, all. Long-leaf pine flats, 390 square miles; long-leaf pine hills, 122 square miles; alluvial land, 88 square miles.
Tilled land : 10,467 acres.—Area planted in cotton, 3,876 acres; in corn, 3,936 acres; in sweet potatoes, 399 acres; in sugar-cane, 127 acres; in rice, 166 acres.
Cotton production : 1,344 bales; average cotton product per acre, 0.35 bale, 498 pounds seed-cotton, or 166 pounds cotton lint.

Most of the good land of Livingston parish lies along the Amite river, elevated from 25 to 30 feet above the low bottom; with an undulating surface, and a timber growth consisting of oaks, beech, gums, dogwood, short-leaf pine, and some scattering magnolias. The soil is grayish-brown or chocolate-colored, overlying a red, sandy clay subsoil, a fine growth of grass, on even the abandoned lands, forming excellent pasturage for stock. This belt is only a few miles in width, and as we recede from the Amite river the soil becomes poorer; the rest of the parish consisting mainly of broad, level tracts of open long-leaf pine forest, with a whitish unproductive soil. Intersecting these level pine regions are various streams, tributaries of the Amite and Tickfaw, running north and south, with broad, marshy, dense swamp bottoms, often covered with such thick canebrakes as to be absolutely impassable. These canebrakes serve as pasture for cattle in winter, enabling them to keep in fine condition throughout the year. Pine timber, turpentine, and cattle form the chief products of this portion of the parish. In its northeastern portion the land is more rolling, and has a reddish loam subsoil, gradually passing into the lands bordering upon the Amite river.

Communication is partly via Baton Rouge and the Mississippi river, partly by rail on the New Orleans and Chicago railroad.

ST. HELENA.

Population : 7,504.—White, 3,328; colored, 4,176.
Area : 423 square miles.—Woodland, all. Long-leaf pine hills, 413 square miles; pine flats, 10 square miles.
Tilled land : 28,285 acres.—Area planted in cotton, 13,626 acres; in corn, 10,540 acres; in sweet potatoes, 661 acres; in sugar-cane, 114 acres; in rice, 68 acres.
Cotton production : 5,328 bales; average cotton product per acre, 0.39 bale, 555 pounds seed-cotton, or 185 pounds cotton lint.

St. Helena parish, outside of the bottoms and immediate hummocks of the Amite and Tickfaw rivers, is a rolling, sometimes only gently undulating, pine-woods country, covered with open long-leaf pine forest. The soil is mostly a pale, sandy loam, underlaid at a few inches depth by a pale-yellow, sandy subsoil, changing to grayish in the more level portions, with bog-ore spots. These pine-woods soils are, as usual, of little native fertility, "giving out" in a few years; but they are nevertheless quite susceptible of improvement, and the region being esteemed very healthy, is, by many, preferred as a place of residence, to more fertile districts. Thrifty farmers can, by the aid of fertilizers, cultivate profitably such portions of the parish as lie within easy reach of transportation. The streams afford water-power for manufactures, and fuel is abundant.

ABSTRACT OF THE REPORT OF MR. H. C. NEWSOM, GREENSBURG.

In range 25 east, township 2 south, the lands cultivated are, first bottom lands of Darling's and other creeks, tributaries of Amite river, and rolling table-land, whose soils vary considerably from ridge to ridge, in tracts of from 5 to 40 acres.

The most important soil is the black, clayey loam, constituting about half of the land. It is timbered with pine, oak, hickory, gum, beech, &c. The dark surface-soil is about 6 inches thick; then comes a subsoil of heavy red or yellow clay. The soil tills with some difficulty in wet seasons, being rather ill-drained. The crops produced here are corn, cotton, sweet potatoes, and oats; the soil is apparently best adapted to cotton, which occupies half of the land cultivated. The plant attains a height of from 0 to 6 feet, and is most productive at from 4 to 6 feet. It may run to weed in wet seasons, and topping is resorted to to restrain it. The product is from 800 to 1,000 pounds of seed-cotton, rating low middling; it takes 1,350 pounds for a 450-pound bale. After six years' cultivation, the production comes down to 400 pounds per acre. Less seed-cotton is then needed for a bale, and the staple compares favorably with that from fresh land. Very little land lies turned out; it produces well when again taken into cultivation. The uplands wash and gully readily on slopes, and the damage thus done is serious to both uplands and lowlands. Hillside ditching has been successfully used to check the damage.

The soil next in importance is that of the heavy bottom lands, being about one-fourth of the cultivated lands. It is timbered with beech, gum, magnolia, oaks, &c. It is generally a black clay loam, about 6 inches thick, and with a subsoil of stiff, heavy, yellow clay. It tills easily in dry seasons, with difficulty in wet ones, and is liable to be late, being ill-drained. About one-half the crop planted on it is of cotton; the plant inclines to run to weed, and deep culture and topping is used to restrain it. Fresh land will yield 1,000 pounds of seed-cotton; after eight years' cultivation, 800 pounds; rates as low middling. Cocklebur is the worst weed on both these soils.

The pine lands, with a coarse sandy soil, constitute perhaps one-fourth of the land of the region. The soil is four inches deep, blackish; the subsoil is somewhat heavier, usually a pale-yellow color, and leachy. It is underlaid by sand and gravel at 10 to 15 feet. When fresh, this land will produce 500 pounds of seed-cotton; after five years, about 300 pounds; it must be fertilized to produce well.

Cotton in the bottoms is subject to rust in very hot weather, especially where the hillsides are allowed to wash down on the fields. Such weather also favors the cotton-worm.

Shipments are made by rail to New Orleans; freight, $2 per bale.

TANGIPAHOA.

Population : 9,638.—White, 5,608; colored, 4,030.

Area : 790 square miles.—Woodland, all. Long-leaf pine flats, 390 square miles; long-leaf pine hills, 320 square, miles; alluvial land, 80 square miles.

Tilled land : 21,021 acres.—Area planted in cotton, 7,682 acres; in corn, 6,617 acres; in sweet potatoes, 677 acres; in sugar-cane, 396 acres; in rice, 248 acres.

Cotton production : 2,934 bales; average cotton product per acre, 0.38 bale, 543 pounds seed-cotton, or 181 pounds cotton lint.

Tangipahoa parish resembles, in its northern portion, the parish of St. Helena, being a rolling or level pine-woods country, with a soil that, if not naturally productive, is quite susceptible of improvement; and on account of its healthfulness and the easy communication afforded by the Great Northern railroad, the region is becoming of importance, both for its lumber and manufacturing advantages, and the inducement it affords for summer residence to the citizens of New Orleans.

Amite City, the parish town, is situated in level pine woods, altogether resembling those of eastern Livingston, both as to soil and timber, the latter being almost exclusively the long-leaf pine, which is largely utilized by sawmills. The same face of country continues as far south as Pontchatoula; beyond that point there begin the willow and cypress swamps and grassy prairies that lie between lakes Pontchartrain and Maurepas, and thus continue up to the city of New Orleans.

ABSTRACT OF THE REPORT OF ROBERT LYNNE, INDEPENDENCE.

The soil chiefly under cultivation is in the first bottoms of the streams, forming perhaps 7 per cent. of the lands of the parish. The soil is a sandy loam, dark brown, friable, and easily tilled until the humus is consumed, when it becomes more tenacious. Its timber is magnolia, beech, iron-wood, sweet and black gums, cypress in low spots; receding from the streams, this timber becomes mixed with hickory, dogwood, and some smaller growth. The subsoil is generally yellow clay, sometimes gray and red in spots. These last are not easily penetrated by the plow when wet, and are rather impervious to water. The subsoil contains some flinty and angular pebbles, and is underlaid by sand and gravel at 14 feet. The soil is easily tilled at all times.

Corn, cotton, and sweet potatoes are produced; peas, sweet potatoes, and strawberries seem to do particularly well on the natural soil, but when manured it will produce anything. About one-third of the tilled land is planted in cotton. It grows to 4½ feet the first five years, then lower; never grows too tall. Stable-manure and frequent rains make it run to weed; the application of lime, ashes, plaster, or bone-meal, alone or mixed with well-rotted manure, will restrain it.

The land when fresh produces about 700 pounds of seed-cotton per acre, of which it takes 1,406 pounds to make a 450-pound bale, the staple rating low middling and middling. After four years' cultivation, without manure, the yield is 400 pounds of seed-cotton per acre, and the staple does not rate as well.

The soil next in importance is that of the hummocks or second bottoms, which form about 5 per cent. of the land, and lie between the pine lands and the bottoms. Its timber is white oak, hickory, poplar, and dogwood, with occasionally (short-leaf) pine, and beech. The soil is a brown loam, about 4 inches thick; subsoil red or gray, sometimes almost impervious, intermixed with a few pebbles. Sand with some gravel underlies at 20 feet. This soil is well drained and easy to till; it is well adapted to sweet potatoes and peas. About half of it is planted in cotton, which grows about 4 feet high, never too tall, and never runs to weed. The product on fresh land is about 600 pounds per acre, about 1,400 being needed for a 450-pound bale. Staple rates low middling to middling. After four years' cultivation, without manure, the product is about 300 pounds seed-cotton, staple not rating quite so high in market as before.

Crab-grass is the only weed requiring to be kept down; if this is done, no others will trouble.

Very little land lies out; when taken into cultivation again it produces well for two years, and then is "dead".

The washings of the uplands benefit both these soils.

Pine land forms from 88 to 90 per cent. of our land. Timber—pine, with oak (post)—here and there. Surface soil only an inch or two deep; hence the subsoil usually gives the color. This is red, yellow, gray, often with some pebbles, and almost impervious to water. It is underlaid by sand with some gravel at 16 to 40 feet, according to altitude.

Without manure, this soil produces almost nothing; with it, almost anything, including sugar-cane. Very little of this land is cultivated, and only with manure. Its slopes are not steep enough to wash to any extent.

Cotton is shipped by rail to New Orleans as soon as it is packed; the distance is 60 miles; rate of freight per bale is $1 50.

The report of W. H. Garland, Amite City, agrees substantially with the preceding; but places the estimate of creek-bottom and hummock lands at 20 per cent., these bottoms being from 200 to 600 yards wide. Half the agricultural labor is devoted to cotton production; the plant is rather inclined to run to weed; by selection of seed and manuring, this tendency can be restrained. A compost made of cottonseed, stable-manure, lime, saltpeter, and earth (as prescribed by Mr. B. D. Gullett), yields excellent results.

ST. TAMMANY.

Population : 6,887.—White, 4,258; colored, 2,629.

Area : 923 square miles.—Woodland, 765 square miles. Long-leaf pine flats, 540 square miles; long-leaf pine hills, 95 square miles; alluvial and marsh lands, 288 square miles.

Tilled land : 3,895 acres.—Area planted in cotton, 225 acres; in corn, 1,224 acres; in sweet potatoes, 441 acres; in sugar-cane, 90 acres; in rice, 127 acres.

Cotton production : 102 bales; average cotton product per acre, 0.45 bale, 642 pounds seed-cotton, or 214 pounds cotton lint.

St. Tammany is almost altogether a "pine-flat" parish, the undulating or level surface being covered by open (mostly long-leaf) pine forests, with the exception of the marshes along the lower course of Pearl river, and a portion of lake Pontchartrain, which forms the southern boundary. At Mandeville, the lake shore is fringed with a lowland belt, having a timber growth of large sweet gum, swamp chestnut, water, and post oaks. The ground here and elsewhere has a good deal of bitter-weed (*Helenium tenuifolium*), as in the prairies of Opelousas. Outside of this belt, short-leaf pine is the exclusive growth, and prevails very generally, with a little oak, northward to Covington, the parish town. The banks of bayou Phalia are 20 to 30 feet high, and show the same clays as seen on the lake shore.

ABSTRACT OF THE REPORT OF MILTON BURNS, COVINGTON.

(This report refers to the western portion of the parish, drained by bayou Phalia.)

The upland has many small creeks running through it, with fine water and water-power. Cotton culture has been but recently introduced into the parish, and not over 150 bales have been grown, annually. Sugar-cane, also but recently introduced, is the favorite crop. Formerly stock-breeding, lumbering, and the burning of brick and charcoal were the only industries.

The soil of the upland is a light sandy loam, about 6 inches deep, with a red clay foundation, not easily pervious to water. Natural growth is pine; about three-fourths of the land is of this character. Gravel is usually found at the depth of 15 feet.

The soil of the bottoms is a sandy loam, with vegetable mold, and a yellow clay foundation. The bottoms are from 1 to 3 miles wide, and timbered with oaks (water and willow, chiefly), hickory, gums, magnolia, dogwood, holly, beech, poplar, and cypress.

The chief crops produced are sugar-cane, oats, peas, sweet potatoes, and corn, to all of which the soil is well adapted. Cotton will grow to the height of 5 feet, and inclines to run to weed only in excessively wet weather. Without fertilizers, the yield is about one-half bale per acre; 1,350 pounds of seed-cotton are needed for a 450-pound bale. The staple rates as low middling, when clean. After four years' cultivation without fertilizers, the yield is reduced to about one-fourth of a bale, and 1,460 pounds of seed-cotton are needed for a 450-pound bale. The staple then rates as good ordinary. Crab-grass is the only weed of note. No land is turned out, but the area cultivated is increasing. The uplands do not suffer from washing or gullying.

Cotton is shipped chiefly by lake steamer to New Orleans at the rate of 25 cents per bale; shipping begins in September, and continues till January.

WASHINGTON.

Population: 5,190.—White, 3,475; colored, 1,715.
Area: 668 square miles.—Woodland, all. Long-leaf pine hills, all.
Tilled land: 18,224 acres.—Area planted in cotton, 6,371 acres; in corn, 7,974 acres; in sweet potatoes, 480 acres; in sugar-cane, 68 acres; in rice, 264 acres.
Cotton production: 2,338 bales; average cotton product per acre, 0.37 bale, 528 pounds seed-cotton, or 176 pounds cotton lint.

The parish of Washington consists almost altogether of undulating, sometimes rolling, pine woods, like those of northern Tangipahoa and St. Helena. The open long-leaf pine forest covers all but the bottoms and narrow first terraces or "hummocks" of the streams. Of these, the Bogue Chitto, traversing the middle of the parish, is the principal one. Cultivation is restricted to the lands along the water-courses, the pine lands being naturally unproductive, although, as in Tangipahoa, quite susceptible of culture by the aid of fertilizers. Stock-raising and lumbering are prominent among the industries of the inhabitants, and sheep would be especially profitable but for the depredations of dogs. The turpentine industry, also, is to some extent pursued, but is greatly interfered with, by the burning of the grass practiced by the stock-raisers.

The bottom of Pearl river is mostly subject to overflow, but is of high fertility wherever reclaimed.

Lumber is rafted down the streams to Pearl river and tide-water. The western part of the parish is accessible by the New Orleans and Chicago railroad.

THE OAK-UPLANDS REGION.

{Comprising—whole or part of—Sabine, Natchitoches, De Soto, Caddo, Bossier, Webster, Red River, Bienville, Jackson, Lincoln, Claiborne, Union, Ouachita*, Morehouse*, Richland*, Franklin* parishes.)

SABINE.

Population: 7,044.—White, 5,486; colored, 1,558.
Area: 1,005 square miles.—Woodland, all. Oak uplands, 656 square miles; central prairie region, 200 square miles; long-leaf pine hills, 150 square miles.
Tilled land: 18,524 acres.—Area planted in cotton, 5,952 acres; in corn, 7,971 acres; in sweet potatoes, 191 acres; in sugar-cane, 85 acres.
Cotton production: 2,313 bales; average cotton product per acre, 0.39 bale, 555 pounds seed-cotton, or 185 pounds cotton lint.

Sabine parish, as a whole, is occupied by rolling oak-uplands, excepting only a few townships in the southeastern corner, where the long-leaf pine prevails, as it does in the adjoining portions of Vernon and Natchitoches parishes. From these hilly, long-leaf pine lands, whose soil is sandy and unthrifty, there is rather a sudden transition to the better soils of the "central prairie region", beginning west of the bayou Torean. Here oaks, mingled with more or less of short-leaf pine, prevail; the pale-yellow subsoil gives place to a deep-tinted orange or red clayey loam on the hills, while in the valleys there are occasional black-prairie spots, and trees indicative of the limy ingredients of the Marine Tertiary formation prevail. See an analysis of a subsoil from this region. Belts of deep red soils, derived from a shelly ironstone that underlies them, are occasionally found. Lands of the character described form a band 6 or 7 miles wide, running in a northeast direction from the Sabine river to the line of Natchitoches parish, where the long-leaf pine again sets in. Ridges, crested by the latter, run out into the uplands northward of Manny; but on the flanks of these, as well as in the valleys, a good oak-growth mingled with short-leaf pine prevails, and so continues toward De Soto parish, on the dividing ridge between the Sabine and Red rivers. The lands on bayous Negrete and San Patricio are reputed to be the best of the region, and greatly superior to those on the Red river side of the divide. A fine staple of cotton is grown on these lands, which are both productive and lasting.

Communication with the New Orleans market is via landings on Red river.

This is a rolling-upland parish, with numerous creek and bayou bottoms; the latter have a stiff, heavy, gum soil, subject to overflow in the back-lands, while the front-lands are sandy and characterized by beech timber. The creek bottoms are the most important for cotton culture, forming quite one-half of the land on which cotton is grown. The timber is lowland oaks, sweet gum, hickory, holly, and magnolia. The soil is a clay loam, sometimes putty-like; color, from yellow to blackish, and black when containing lime; it is 15 to 24 inches deep; the subsoil is heavier and more sticky, but becomes similar to the surface soil under tillage. Heavy or pipe clay underlies at 5 feet. Corn, cotton, sweet potatoes, peas, oats, and rice are grown, the last to a small extent only, but yields well on the stiff soil. The bayou bottoms are best adapted to cotton, and 40 to 50 per cent. of their land is in that crop. The stalk grows from 4 to 6 feet high; is most productive at 4 feet, being inclined to run to wood on this soil in regular seasons, and doing best in dry ones. Close, deep plowing will restrain it; when well advanced, topping. From 1,200 to 1,500 pounds of seed-cotton per acre are produced, of which from 1,350 to 1,400 pounds make a 450-pound bale. The staple rates good middling when clean; fifteen years' cultivation make little difference in quality or quantity of product. Very little of this land lies out; some has been in cultivation for forty years; when resting four or five years, it produces almost as well as when fresh.

The sandy front-land, or beech soil, forming about one-fourth of the cultivated lands, is more generally planted in corn and potatoes. Its timber is beech, magnolia, white oak, holly, wild peach, &c. It admits of earlier planting than the back-lands, being well drained. Cotton grows 6 to 8 feet high when the land is fresh; six feet is best. About 1,200 pounds of seed-cotton is the product on fresh land, staple, &c., the same as on the back-land. Crab-grass is the most troublesome weed on both of these soils. Cotton in these lowlands is subject to injury in cold, wet seasons, but fruits so much better, and is so much less liable to shedding, that we prefer the lowlands to the uplands for cotton culture.

Hummock, or uplands soil, forms about one-fourth of the tillable lands. The timber is post, red, and black oaks. The soil is fine and sandy, of an orange-red tint, from 12 to 15 inches depth. The subsoil is heavier, and clay is found at a depth of two feet. It tills easily at all times; it is mainly given to the culture of corn and potatoes. Cotton grows from 3 to 5 feet, best at the latter height; it yields 800 to 1,000 pounds of seed-cotton per acre. About 1,050 pounds of seed-cotton are required for a bale; it rates low middling, and about the same after six years' cultivation, when the yield falls to 600 or 700 pounds. A good deal of such land lies turned out, and without manure it is worthless for further cultivation. It washes on slopes, but the valleys are benefited by the washings, and "we let it go". Cotton is hauled to Natchitoches, and generally sold there.

NATCHITOCHES.

Population: 19,707.—White, 7,638; colored, 12,069.

Area: 1,290 square miles.—Woodland, all. Long-leaf pine hills, 600 square miles; oak uplands, 300 square miles; Red river bottom, 390 square miles.

Tilled land: 58,969 acres.—Area planted in cotton, 26,784 acres; in corn, 17,871 acres; in sweet potatoes, 197 acres; in sugar-cane, 28 acres.

Cotton production: 15,320 bales; average cotton product per acre, 0.57 bale, 813 pounds seed-cotton, or 271 pounds cotton lint.

Natchitoches is one of the oldest parishes in the state, and, although nearly one-half of its area is hilly pine land, it ranks third in population, and fifth in cotton production, among the upland parishes. The chief area of production is, of course, the portion of Red river bottom embraced within its limits, and the oak uplands adjoining the same on either side.

South of the old town of Natchitoches, and outside of Red river bottom, the uplands are mainly of the pine hills character, varied only in the hilly, broken country on bayou Casatche by the occasional appearance of limestone, and of lime-loving trees in the deep, narrow valleys, while the bluff banks of the river at Natchitoches and Grand Ecore are crowned with pines. To the north-westward, however, beyond Spanish lake, the pine is absent, and rolling oak-uplands, with an admixture of short-leaf pine among the timber, and with a reddish loam soil of fair fertility, take the place of the pine hills. These oak uplands are substantially identical in character with those of the adjoining parishes of Sabine and De Soto.

North of Red river, the long-leaf pine appears on the bluff at Campti, forming a tract isolated from the main body of the long-leaf pine hills farther north and east, by the lowlands bordering on Black lake, with their growth of oaks and short-leaf pine.

Seven-eighths of all the land cultivated is the red alluvial soil of the Red river bottom. The timber is pecan, oak, ash, elm, hackberry, locust, cypress. The (front-land) soil is porous, as much as 20 feet in depth; pretty well drained. The crops grown are cotton, corn, sweet potatoes, and some tobacco for home use. Cotton and sweet potatoes are the chief crops, the former occupying two-thirds of the cultivated land. The plant frequently attains a height of 8 feet, but is most productive at 5 feet. The land produces 2,000 pounds of seed-cotton when fresh; after fifteen years' cultivation, about 1,800. About 1,460 pounds are needed for a 450-pound bale of lint; the staple rates good middling. Perhaps one-eighth of land once cultivated lies out now; when again cultivated it produces nearly as well as fresh land. The most troublesome weeds are cocklebur and rag-weed.

The prevalence of south winds is thought to be especially favorable to the growth and productiveness of cotton.

Communication with market is by Red river steamers to New Orleans; freight on cotton $1 per bale.

DE SOTO.

Population: 15,603.—White, 5,116; colored, 10,487.

Area: 856 square miles.—Woodland, all. Oak uplands, 836 square miles, of which 60 square miles are "red lands"; bottom (Red river), 20 square miles.

Tilled land: 82,239 acres.—Area planted in cotton, 37,807 acres; in corn, 31,080 acres; in sweet potatoes, 733 acres; in sugar-cane, 34 acres.

Cotton production: 11,298 bales; average cotton product per acre, 0.30 bale, 426 pounds seed-cotton, or 142 pounds cotton lint.

De Soto parish may be classed as a good oak-upland parish, with generally a durable soil, having a subsoil of yellow or orange-colored loam. The divide between Red and Sabine rivers crosses the parish diagonally, a little east of its middle; the parish town of Mansfield being located on it. On the Red river side, the country is rather hilly and broken, the subsoil rather clayey, prevalently of a deep red tint, and not very thrifty on the hills, though very productive in the valleys (Dolet hills). Numerous lakes, and an intricate network of shifting bayous, lie at the foot of these hills, on the western edge of the Red river bottom; of which but little is, however, included within the limits of this parish. On Rambin's bayou there is a post-oak flat tract, some 2 or 3 miles in width, which bears a luxuriant growth of forest trees, but is almost devoid of undergrowth, except a few hawthorn bushes. The surface is covered with countless little knolls, similar to those prevailing in the prairies of the Attakapas parishes. This is probably a heavy soil, requiring drainage to render it productive.

The streams on the Sabine side are larger, the country is more gently rolling, the valleys wider, and the soil more of the character of the "yellow loam table-lands" of Mississippi, the short-leaf pine appearing only in isolated patches to northward of Mansfield, and not at all to westward. The Grand Cane country, on the Sabine slope, on the bayou of that name, is reputed to be the richest part of the parish; the forest growth is luxuriant, and consists of beech, tulip-tree ("poplar"), red, white, pin, chestnut, water, and other oaks, maple, elm, hickory, walnut, magnolia, &c. These lands produce as much as 1,400 pounds of seed-cotton per acre.

Parts of De Soto parish are among the oldest settled in northern Louisiana, and in the uplands not inconsiderable damage has been done by the washing away of the soil and gullying of the fields, in consequence of their having been "turned out" after years of exhaustive cultivation. This is especially the case where the subsoil is underlaid by sand, as frequently happens. Numerous moderately large and well-kept farms, with neat houses and out-buildings, impart to this parish an air of comfort and prosperity scarcely marred by the war.

ABSTRACT OF REPORT OF A. V. ROBERTS, MANSFIELD.

The soil of the uplands, from Red river to the Sabine, is a sandy loam, varying in quality and timber according to location. The top soil is dark colored, sometimes to the depth of 12 inches, with more or less sand and gravel of various colors, and more or less productive. The subsoil is more clayey, usually reddish, and by intermixture with the top soil makes brown and mahogany colors. Sometimes rock is found at 5 to 15 feet. Cotton, corn, sweet potatoes, some oats, peas, and sorghum, are cultivated on the uplands; the soil seems best adapted to cotton, and one-half of the land now cultivated is in cotton. The cotton grows from 4 to 6 feet in height. When fresh the land produces from 800 to 1,200 pounds of seed-cotton per acre; from 1,460 to 1,520 pounds are needed for a 450-pound bale; the lint, when clean, rates middling to good middling. After ten years' cultivation, if maintained by horizontalizing, the product is 600 to 800 pounds; not much difference in quality of lint; a shade below. Perhaps 25 to 50 per cent. of such land once in cultivation now lies turned out; it improves thereby, unless washed away or trodden by stock. The most troublesome weeds are cocklebur and crab-grass.

The bottom lands of bayou Bonnechose have a dark and rather stiff soil, a little more sandy near the bayou; depth from 2 to 3 feet. Tills easily in dry seasons; somewhat troublesome in wet ones. Crops the same as in the uplands, with a little sugar-cane. Two-thirds of the bottom land in cultivation is in cotton; the yield is from 1,200 to 1,800 pounds per acre when fresh, 1,000 pounds after ten years' cultivation. It is but little different in quality from the uplands product, or in the amount needed for a bale. It rates good middling when clean. The most troublesome weeds are cocklebur, crab-grass, careless-weed, tie-vine, and morning-glory. Perhaps 10 per cent. of bottom land once cultivated lies turned out; produces well when again cultivated, though not as well as fresh land.

The timber of the uplands is oaks and hickory chiefly, with more or less short-leaf pine, according to quality. The bottoms have ash, sassafras, gum, beech, magnolia, walnut, ironwood, hackberry, chinquapin, persimmon, maple, witch-hazel, cottonwood, maple, &c.

Most farmers sell their cotton at the nearest market, or at Shreveport. Buyers, and those who ship, send their cotton to New Orleans by water, or from Shreveport by rail; rate of freight per bale is $1 50.

Remarks on cotton production.

Cotton production has certainly increased during the past ten years. The one reason is that the number of persons engaged in its cultivation has increased. Whether farming is carried on under the share or wages system, only cotton and corn are raised, excepting the small sweet-potato patch which every tenant has. Cotton is the chief crop, the only product upon which the farmer can depend for money. Every one, white or black, who tills the soil, produces cotton as the chief crop. It is true that there has been an increase in the relative amount of corn, potatoes, sugar-cane, sorghum, oats, peas, &c., produced, and in the attention paid to rearing horses, cattle, and sheep. Relatively more cotton is now produced by white labor than formerly. Less cotton is now produced by negroes than twelve or fifteen years ago, not even as much as they produced in the days of slavery. It is believed that half the cotton of the uplands is produced by white labor, even in our state.

CADDO.

Population: 26,296.—White, 6,921; colored, 19,375.

Area: 852 square miles.—Woodland, all. Oak uplands, 695 square miles; Red river bottom, 157 square miles.

Tilled land: 95,409 acres.—Area planted in cotton, 46,238 acres; in corn, 23,169 acres; in sweet potatoes, 315 acres; in sugar-cane, 1 acre.

Cotton production: 20,963 bales; average cotton product per acre, 0.45 bale, 642 pounds seed-cotton, or 214 pounds cotton lint.

The upland portion of Caddo parish resembles, on the whole, the corresponding portion of De Soto; but it is greatly "cut up" by numerous lakes and bayous, and in the northern portion by the overflowed lands and lakes caused by the Red river raft. The uplands and second bottoms are, almost throughout, good farming lands.

In the southwest portion we find the continuation of the dividing ridge between Red and Sabine rivers, already described under the head of De Soto parish. The bottoms of the streams here, as well as farther north, are overflowed, and quickly become impassable in wet weather.

Northward of this region the dividing ridge between the waters of Boggy bayou and Cross lake runs east and west, and on its eastern termination stands Shreveport, the second city in the state (population, 11,017), and connected by rail with Vicksburg on the one hand, and with the Texas system of railways on the other.

Northward of Shreveport, the raft gives the character to the country; the lower lands being overflowed, and converted into lakes, swamps, and bayous, of very variable extent, at every freshet (caused by a rise above). Some of these lakes contain tracts of dead forest still standing, but on the subsidence of a flood, appear as mere mud flats. The country between Cross and Soda lakes is otherwise hilly, as is, on the whole, the country bordering Red river bottom. Numerous hilly islands appear both in the lakes and in the country intervening between Red river and bayou Pierre; the bottoms are mainly settled immediately along the streams. In the northeast corner of the parish there is a dense cypress brake, covering about half a township.

The cotton produced is mainly sold to merchants at Shreveport by the producers; shipments to New Orleans are made by the Red river steamers, which reach Shreveport during the greater part of the year; and during the season of low water, cotton is also sent by rail through Texas to New Orleans as well as to St. Louis.

BOSSIER.

Population: 16,042.—White, 3,256; colored, 12,786.

Area: 773 square miles.—Woodland, all. Oak uplands, 553 square miles, of which about 80 square miles are "red land"; alluvial land, 220 square miles.

Tilled land: 69,420 acres.—Area planted in cotton, 37,133 acres; in corn, 20,153 acres; in sweet potatoes, 175 acres; in sugar-cane, 7 acres.

Cotton production: 25,078 bales; average cotton product per acre, 0.68 bale, 969 pounds seed-cotton, or 323 pounds cotton lint.

Bossier parish is a good deal varied in its surface and soil, and is one of the best cotton parishes in the state. Its southwestern portion is formed by Red river bottom, which, between Benton and Shreveport, is protected from overflow by levees, and grows splendid cotton. A detailed account of this region is given below, in the report of Mr. Fort.

The oak-upland country lying between Red river bottom and lake Bistineau, in Bossier and Webster parishes, is known as "the Point", and is somewhat peculiar in its soils; its surface varies from hilly to level. This region is more specially described below by Mr. Fort; its prevailing soil is said to produce, when fresh, 1,000 pounds of seed-cotton per acre.

Northward of the Point, lands timbered with short-leaf pine, black oak, hickory, and dogwood, form the prevailing feature, but varied by belts of different lands running north and south. Thus between Red river and Cypress bayou there is a belt 6 miles wide of a fair rolling, upland farming country. East of Cypress bayou there is a belt of red ridge-lands from the Arkansas line to the mouth of the bayou; these are broken sometimes with high hills covered with red, ochreous rocks, ferruginous earth, &c. East of this ridge there is a belt of level post-oak land, which is nearly continuous from the "Point" to the Arkansas line. These flats are scarcely if at all cultivated, and in wet weather become almost impassable; in the southern portion (as east of Bellevue) there are treeless tracts—"prairies"—with a white soil and very unproductive; surface covered with grass and thorn bushes. Farther south there are again ridgy lands, partly of red rocky soil.

About half the cotton is sold to local buyers; these and others send it to New Orleans by water, or from Shreveport by rail. Rates of freight per bale are $1 to $1 50.

ABSTRACT OF THE REPORT OF B. F. FORT, BELLEVUE. (a)

The Red river bottom averages in width 7 miles, with a length of 65 miles in Bossier and Caddo.

The local climate is as follows: Heavy rains in March and April; dry May; droughty June; seasonable July and August; dry and pleasant September, October, November, and first half of December, and fine for picking. Summer weather in May; 85° to 100° heat in June, not sultry; 85° to 100° heat in shade in July and August, and very sultry. Drought and heat of June delay the coming of the caterpillar. Heavy rains of April melt down the stiff plowed land of back-lands, and make it friable for the balance of the season.

The soils may be classified as follows: 1. Sandy loam, fronts a quarter of a mile wide on each bank of river; half the tilled soil, but only one-fourteenth of the whole bottom. 2. Stiff, red back-lands; nearly half the tilled soil and about five-sevenths of whole bottom. 3. Stiff, red, lateral bayou lands—a fraction only of those tilled; about one-fourteenth of whole; one-fourteenth like bottom and bayou beds.

The *chief one* is designated as "front-lands"; proportion, one-half the cultivated, one-fourteenth of whole bottom; occurs on the whole front on the river, and a short distance down large outgoing bayous; growth: cottonwood, ash, hickory, sweet gum, red oak, and mulberry. It is a light silt and fine sandy loam, reddish gray, several feet in depth. It tills easily in wet and in dry seasons, and is early, warm, and well drained.

Crops: cotton, chiefly, and some corn. The soil is best adapted to cotton. Two-thirds of the crops planted, perhaps more, are of cotton. Usual height of cotton on old-cleared land, 3 feet; for best production higher. Cotton runs to weed in wet seasons; no remedy is used. Seed-cotton product on fresh land, 2,000 pounds per acre; for a 450-pound bale, 1,350 pounds dry, after housing a few weeks; 1,460 pounds dry from field. Staple from fresh land rates good middling in market, when clean. After six years' cultivation (unmanured), 1,700 pounds,

---

a Mr. Fort's intelligent report on the cotton lands of Red river bottom is given almost in full, as a matter of especial interest.

and the same amount of seed-cotton needed per bale; staple a little shorter, but seed somewhat lighter. Troublesome weeds: crab-grass, cocklebur, tie-vine, morning-glory, and cow-pea. No land of this character now lies turned out; old land taken into cultivation produces as well as new.

Soil No. 2.—Designated stiff lands or back-lands, form five-sevenths of the whole bottom, and nearly half the tilled soil; much of it is not reclaimed from overflow; it extends from Washington, St. Landry parish, to Little River, Arkansas. Timber growth: red oak, cotton-wood, ash, hackberry, cypress, pecan, and sweet gum. It is a heavy clay loam; color: brown, mahogany, blackish, and dark-brownish red. Much has no different subsoil within reasonable depth; but a considerable portion has the river deposit a foot below the surface. This subsoil is lighter than the surface soil, being a fine, black, sandy loam. The soil tills easily in wet weather and after breaking up in the spring, and can be plowed after heavy rains. Soil best adapted to cotton; proportion of cotton planted, two-thirds of crops. This is our best soil, and I believe it is the best cotton land in the world. I have it from four different witnesses, viz, R. W. Dougherty, R. T. Glinson, F. J. Smith, and James B. Pickett, that each have known 1,000 pounds of cotton lint to be raised on it to the acre, without manure. It is now being gradually reclaimed from overflow, and can all be reclaimed, within a small fraction, at no great expense per acre. It requires two mules for breaking up in the spring, but for after-cultivation one mule suffices. Tie-vines cause it to be "swept"(a) every two weeks till the latter part of August. This is the land for steam cultivation in the future. The most productive and usual height of cotton is 5 feet. The plant does not incline to run to weed, except on new land; no remedy to restrain it and favor bolling is used. Seed-cotton product and quality of staple, the same as from the front-lands.

The seed-cotton product, after six years' cultivation, is 2,000 pounds per acre (the land is never known to tire); same amount as above needed for a bale; staple, same as that from fresh land. The troublesome weeds are cocklebur, tie-vine, morning-glory, and cow-pea. No land lies turned out.

Soil No. 3.—Designated as bayou lands. These differ but little from No. 2, being a little stiffer and closer to the subsoil, which is often poor. Proportion of this land is small, say one-twentieth of bottom; tilled soil, perhaps one-fourteenth of the entire cultivated lands. I only know it to occur bordering Red Chute bayou, townships 16 to 18 inclusive. Growth: red and overcup oaks, bastard pecan, ash, sweet gum, locust. The soil is a heavy clay loam, brownish, mahogany, blackish, and dark reddish brown. Thickness of surface soil, 6 to 8 inches; subsoil heavier or occasionally lighter than surface soil; underlaid sometimes by white sandstone and sometimes by blue clay, and generally by poor subsoil; rather impervious to water; tills easily in dry and wet seasons after breaking in spring, but is hard to break; it takes two mules. The soil is best adapted to cotton, of which two-thirds of all crops is planted. The height usually attained by cotton is 3 feet; at 4 feet it is most productive; does not incline to run to weed. Seed-cotton, per acre, on fresh land, 1,700 pounds. Seed-cotton for a 450-pound bale, 1,350 pounds, dry from cotton-house; 1,450 pounds, when dry from field; staple rates as middling in market, when clean. Seed-cotton product, per acre, after six years' cultivation, the same as before in quantity and quality. Troublesome weeds are cocklebur and tie-vine. One-fourth or one-fifth of this land lies turned out, but is being recultivated; produces as at first, when again taken into cultivation.

Soils of the "Point country".—No. 1, gray oak and hickory land; No. 2, reddish oak land; No. 3, black-jack ridges. No. 1, designated Point lands, are peculiar to the Point; proportion, three-fourths of cultivated land, and occurs throughout the Point country. Timber: post, black, and red oaks, hickory, short-leaf pine (scattering), and black jack. It is a fine silt or fine, sandy loam; blackish, 4 inches deep; subsoil, a yellowish, sandy loam, not fertile, underlaid by sandy clay at 1¼ foot; tills easily in wet and dry seasons, when broken up in the spring.

Crops.—Cotton, mainly; corn, sweet potatoes, and cow-peas; best adapted to cotton, which constitutes two-thirds of all the crops planted. Height.—Three feet, and, generally speaking, the higher the plant, the more productive it is.

Seed-cotton on fresh land: 1,000 pounds; amount for a 450-pound bale the same as for the bottom; rates as middling in market. Seed-cotton produced after six years' cultivation (unmanured): 700 pounds; staple shorter than on fresh land, but the seed is lighter.

Troublesome weeds.—Crab-grass, hog-weed, and occasionally cocklebur.

Land turned out, one-third; does not improve when again taken into cultivation, as cows pasture on it and tramp it too close; it is slow to grow up in trees.

Soil No. 2 has no common designation; proportion, perhaps one-fourth, and occurs scattered over the Point. Growth: black and post oaks, black jack, and an occasional short-leaf pine. It is a heavy clay loam, light brown to 2 inches depth; subsoil same as surface, but infertile; underlaid by sandy clay; tills easily, when broken up in the spring; proportion of cotton planted, two-thirds; height, 2½ feet; more productive when higher.

Seed-cotton product per acre on fresh land, 700 pounds; after six years' cultivation (unmanured), 400 pounds; staple shorter than on fresh land. No troublesome weeds.

Land turned out, one-half; serious damage done by washing. No damage done to valleys from washing of uplands.

Soil No. 3, designated as "black-jack ridges"; proportion, one-fifth or one-sixth; none cultivated, because sterile; occurs only in the Point. Growth, black jack. It is a light, fine, sandy loam; whitish gray; 1 inch deep. Subsoil sandy, leachy; underlaid by sand to some depth.

Middle and northern Bossier, on the borders of Bodcau and Cypress bayous.—Here there are three chief varieties of soil, viz. (1) gray, sandy loam of the level or undulating short-leaf pine country; (2) rocky red hills and branch bottoms adjacent; (3) flats. The chief one is gray lands or pine land; it occupies two-thirds of the region, extending from township 17 to Arkansas line, and east and west through the parish. Timber, short-leaf pine, black and red oaks, hickory, dogwood, and black gum. The soil is a fine, sandy loam, gray, blackish, and sometimes brownish, showing iron in soil; thickness, 6 inches when fresh. The subsoil is a yellowish, sandy loam, lighter than surface, and rather close, not fertile; underlaid by sandy clay at 1¼ foot. It tills easily in wet and dry seasons.

Crops.—Cotton, chiefly; corn, oats, sweet potatoes, sorghum, and cow-peas. The soil is best adapted to cotton because of the climate; proportion of cotton planted, two-thirds; height attained by cotton, 3 feet, and the higher the better, unless in very wet seasons.

Seed-cotton product on fresh land, 800 pounds; staple, middling when clean; after six years' cultivation the product is 600 pounds; staple somewhat shorter and seeds lighter; the weeds are crab-grass and hog-weed. About one-third of such land once cultivated lies out; this is not thought to benefit the land until after several years' growth of small pines. The land washes readily on slopes, but being so nearly level, no damage is done to them.

Soil No. 2.—Designated "red lands"; proportion, one-sixth, and occurs from Arkansas line south to township 17, in strips. Timber: black and red oaks, black jack, scattering short-leaf pine, and hickory. It is a heavy clay loam, or clay with ironstone and broken gravel; color, brownish, mahogany, blackish, and chocolate. Thickness of surface soil, 3 inches. Subsoil same, but somewhat stiffer; some is hard-pan and nearly impervious to water; contains soft, broken ironstone gravel, underlaid by clay at one-half foot. It tills easily in wet and dry seasons, after breaking up in the spring and when well drained. The soil is best adapted to cotton, and, next, to oats. Proportion of cotton to other crops planted, two-thirds; the highest is most productive; does not incline to run to weed under any circumstances.

a With a "sweep" plow.

171

Seed-cotton product per acre, when land is fresh, 800 pounds. Some small area of this red land is the finest upland in the parish, and has quite a fame. To see such splendid crops on pure red clay is astonishing. What is in the soil to produce that effect, is not known. I think these lands would succeed well in wine-grapes. A great deal of this red ironstone land, however, produces the same as gray lands. Drought hurts it worse, perhaps, than it does the gray, but wet seasons hurt less. Much iron ore overlies parts of it, but an expert stated, some time ago, that this ore would be hard to smelt. Seed-cotton needed for a bale, same as that from the other soils. Staple rates as middling in market, when clean, and from fresh land. Product, after six years' cultivation, 600 pounds per acre, and same amount needed for a bale as on fresh land, but staple is shorter. Weeds are not troublesome; crab-grass grows a little. Land turned out, about one-third. When this land is again taken into cultivation, it is worse than when turned out. It will not grow up in trees quickly. Soil does not wash on slopes.

Soil No. 3.—Flats; proportion, one-third; none cultivated, but reclaimable. This soil occurs from township 17 north, to Arkansas. Growth: post and water oaks, and short-leaf pine; sometimes small haw and sweet gum. It is a heavy, fine silt, or fine, sandy loam, crawfishy, and whitish gray. Thickness of surface soil, 1 inch; character of subsoil about same as surface. Some is hard-pan, impervious to water, and underlaid by sandy clay at 2 or 3 feet. Tillage very difficult in wet and dry seasons, or when ill-drained. A ditch will not draw, and only surface drainage can be adopted. Soil best adapted to cotton, which can, by great labor, be produced.

The report of Mr. J. W. Hayes, of Red Land, on the northern portion of Bossier parish, agrees substantially with the statements of Mr. Fort; as does that, also, of C. L. Tidwell.

WEBSTER.

Population: 10,005.—White, 4,322; colored, 5,683.
Area: 612 square miles.—Woodland, all. Oak uplands, 430 square miles; alluvial land, bayou Dorchite, 137 square miles; bayou Bodcau, 45 square miles.
Tilled land: 42,402 acres.—Area planted in cotton, 16,401 acres; in corn, 14,824 acres; in sweet potatoes, 385 acres; in sugar-cane, 120 acres.
Cotton production: 6,255 bales; average cotton product per acre, 0.38 bale, 543 pounds seed-cotton, or 181 pounds cotton lint.

Webster parish, formed, since the war, from portions of Bienville and Bossier, has for its central feature the broad alluvial bottom of bayou Dorchite, which, in its southern portion, is covered by the waters of lake Bistineau, while in its northwestern portion lies the flood plain of bayou Bodeau, whose channel here divides the parish from Bossier. Black lake bayou forms the parish line on the southeast.

Between bayous Bodcau and Dorchite a long level country extends from the Arkansas line to lake Bistineau. This country is variable in quality; some is poor and sandy, covered with a growth of short-leaf pine; some white and "crawfishy", putty-like, with a growth of dogwood and post oak, and is little better than the pine lands, while other portions, where well drained (as, e. g., near Cotton valley), are fine cotton and corn lands. East of the alluvial plain of bayou Dorchite the country is rolling or hilly, and partly of the "red lands" character, partly also level and occupied by the gray soil characterizing the pine flats, on which water oak and black gum are prominent. This is the case in the country adjoining lake Bistineau, and on Black lake bayou. Generally speaking, it is a country of small but well-kept farms.

(No mention is made anywhere of the alluvial plains of the two bayous, which are doubtless subject to frequent overflows.)

The communication of Webster parish with the markets is partly by land to Shreveport, partly direct, via steamers on Red river and lake Bistineau, to New Orleans.

RED RIVER.

Population: 8,573.—White, 2,507; colored, 6,066.
Area: 386 square miles.—Woodland, all. Red river bottom, 165 square miles; oak uplands, 221 square miles.
Tilled land: 33,930 acres.—Area planted in cotton, 19,200 acres; in corn, 10,566 acres; in sweet potatoes, 88 acres; in sugar-cane, 9 acres.
Cotton production: 11,512, bales; average cotton product per acre, 0.60 bale, 855 pounds seed-cotton, or 285 pounds cotton lint.

The small parish of Red River, lately formed, includes two chief varieties of lands, viz, the Red river bottom and the level or rolling uplands, forming a kind of dividing plateau between the Grand bayou of Black lake and Red river. These uplands are, in general, of the pale-yellow loam or the gray pine-flat character, the timber being short-leaf pine, with post and some Spanish oaks, and much scrubby black jack. A poor soil in the lower, ill-drained portions of the region, but fair where larger Spanish oaks appear among the timber, when the subsoil also assumes a darker yellow or reddish tint. The water of the somewhat sluggish streams is frequently dark-tinted, from the vegetable matter of the swampy areas of the district, which are characterized by the common occurrence of the wax myrtle (*Myrica cerifera*).

Red river, at ordinary stages of water, flows in a deep, narrow channel, cut 35 to 40 feet deep into solid blue and red clays; hence its overflows are always first felt in the "back-lands" traversed by the numerous bayous; and the "front-lands" on the banks of the main river are comparatively exempt from inundation. The soil of the latter is light, of a reddish tint, and is claimed to produce strictly first-class cotton. Large and flourishing plantations occupy the banks of the river for many miles above and below Coushatta chute

ABSTRACT OF THE REPORT OF B. W. MARSTON, EAST POINT.

(Refers to Red river alluvial lands, township 14, range 11 west.)

The two chief soils are sandy front-lands and stiff, black back-lands. The former constitutes three-fourths of the lands, reaching one mile back from the river banks. Cottonwood ash elm pecan hackberry haw elder cover part ... the timber. The soil is sandy loam, from orange-red through mahogany to black; depth, 1 to 10 feet; underlaid by quicksand, with chalybeate water. It is easily tilled at all times, and well drained. Cotton and corn are grown, the former being two-thirds of all crops.
172

It will grow as much as 10 feet in height, but is most productive at 5; runs to weed in wet weather, and sunshine only can restrain it. Fresh land will produce from 1,500 to 4,500 (†) pounds of seed-cotton per acre, of which 1,460 make a 450-pound bale. The production scarcely decreases sensibly The fresher the land the better the staple; rates as fair to good middling. Cocklebur, coffee-weed, and hog-weed are chiefly troublesome. The river banks sometimes cave badly.

Shipments are made by boat to New Orleans, from August to May; freight, per bale, $1 50, or less when there is competition.

BIENVILLE.

Population: 10,442.—White, 5,455; colored, 4,987.

Area: 856 square miles.—Woodland, all. Oak uplands, 756 square miles, of which about 10 square miles are "red lands"; long-leaf pine hills, 100 square miles.

Tilled land: 45,089 acres.—Area planted in cotton, 18,242 acres; in corn, 19,255 acres; in sweet potatoes, 305 acres; in sugar-cane, 108 acres.

Cotton production: 7,208 bales; average cotton product per acre, 0.40 bale, 570 pounds seed-cotton, or 190 pounds cotton lint.

Bienville parish is mainly gently rolling and rather sandy oak-uplands, not unfrequently almost level, especially in the western portion. Post oak and short-leaf pine are there the prevailing timber trees, intermingled more or less with other oaks and hickory, according to the quality of the land. The pale-yellow loam soil is predominant. In the level portions the gray pine-flat soil is largely developed, and then the water oak and black gum form a characteristic ingredient of the timber. Most of the flats bordering the streams are of this character, as is also the country bordering on lake Bistineau.

The red subsoil appears in spots, generally where the country becomes more rolling, and is often accompanied by rolled gravel, as well as by iron-ore (limonite) concretions. This is more especially the case in the southeastern portion, where tracts of hilly red lands occur, the ridges in the southerly portion having more or less long-leaved pine on their crests, while oak-growth, sometimes intermingled with short-leaf pine, covers the hillsides. At Brushy valley and northward, the red-land feature is quite prevalent, and excellent crops of cotton are made, both in the uplands and in the bottoms of the streams, which are here not so liable to overflow, and possess less of the pine-flats character. There is also a good deal of very sandy hill land, which washes very badly when turned out after cultivation.

Not far from Brushy valley is a salt-lick flat, known as Rayburn's lick, where much salt was made during the war. It is underlaid by gypsum and (Cretaceous) limestone, from which good lime can be burned. The use of this on the soil of the region would be very beneficial. A similar lick is "King's", near the northeast corner of Red River parish, where the limestone occurs in even greater abundance and of the best quality. A similar limy spot occurs in the northeastern portion of the parish, near Quay post-office, on the heads of Dugdemona bayou.

A good deal of fine pine timber might be obtained in this parish.

Communication with the New Orleans market is via landings on Red river and steamers on lake Bistineau.

ABSTRACT OF THE REPORT OF T. J. BUTLER, RINGGOLD.

This country has a great variety of soil and lands, some poor pine-barrens, some post-oak "hog-wallows", and then fine oak and hickory uplands, with fertile creek and branch bottoms. The latter part of the season is usually so dry as to cut off the late cotton crop. Sometimes frost in October will do the same.

The chief kinds of soil are the following: 1. Light sandy upland loam. 2. Stiff branch- and creek-bottom soils, very black. 3. Stiff red land, generally hilly.

About one-half of the lands are of the first kind for 2 or 3 miles west, 15 or 20 miles south, and a long distance east and north. The timber is short-leaf pine, oak, hickory, gum, &c. The surface soil is 6 to 12 inches deep, and is a fine sandy loam of a whitish-gray or brown tint. The subsoil is lighter. Usually at 4 inches (below the soil line?) it changes from light-yellow on the hills to a redder hue, until it reaches red clay. It contains some rounded, white gravel, tills with facility in dry seasons, is easily and well drained. Cotton, corn, peas, sweet potatoes, and sugar-cane are produced. Cotton and corn succeed best, and the former occupies about one-half of the cultivated land. The cotton grows from 4 to 7 feet in height, produces best at about 5 feet, inclines to run to weed in wet seasons like 1880. This may be remedied by topping during August. Fresh land produces from 1,000 to 1,200 pounds of seed-cotton per acre, about 1,350 being needed for a 450-pound bale. The staple rates high in market; after four years' cultivation, not quite so well, the product being then from 700 to 1,000 pounds. The only troublesome weed is crab-grass.

Perhaps three-quarters of the land cultivated in cotton before the war lies out. When taken into cultivation it will produce from 700 to 800 pounds per acre, but it often suffers serious damage from washing on slopes, and little has been done toward checking this damage. Hillside ditching is successful in doing so.

2. The branch-bottom soils constitute about one-fifteenth of the lands. The timber is hickory, gum, ash, and walnut. About one-half of the crops grown on these soils is cotton, which grows to 7 feet in height. The seed-cotton product is from 1,200 to 1,500 pounds per acre, 1,500 being required for a bale of lint. The product is but little reduced in quality or quantity by four years' cultivation. Crab-grass is the most troublesome weed.

3. The red lands constitute but a small portion of the soils. It occurs in spots. The timber is oak, pine, and hickory. It is clay. loam, brown or orange-red, 5 to 6 inches deep, and then underlaid by a stiff red clay. It contains rounded and angular iron-gravel, is well drained, and easily tilled, even in wet seasons. The seed-cotton product is 1,200 pounds from fresh land, decreasing but little from year to year. Crab-grass is most troublesome.

JACKSON.

Population: 5,328.—White, 2,925; colored, 2,403.

Area: 590 square miles.—Woodland, all. Oak uplands, 340 square miles, of which about 50 square miles are "red lands"; long-leaf pine hills, 250 square miles.

Tilled land: 26,604 acres.—Area planted in cotton, 10,138 acres; in corn, 9,572 acres; in sweet potatoes, 266 acres; in sugar-cane, 52 acres.

Cotton production: 3,753 bales; average cotton product per acre, 0.37 bale, 528 pounds seed-cotton, or 176 pounds cotton lint.

The northern and greater portion of Jackson parish is rolling oak-uplands, in which the pine-flat feature is much less common than in Bienville, the soil being chiefly of the pale-yellow loam type, with more or less of the red-lands subsoil. The latter feature becomes very prominent north of Vernon, where the true red-land ridges, with their unpromising-looking but very productive and durable soil, occupy a considerable portion of the surface. Southeast of Vernon also, on the bayou Castor, there is a good farming region, rolling uplands, timbered with oaks, hickory, dogwood, and chinquapin, mixed with some short-leaf pine on the hills, and with ash, beech, elm, sweet and black gums in the bottoms.

In the southern part of Jackson parish the long-leaf pine prevails altogether on the higher ridges and on the crests of the lower ones; but, as in Bienville, the slopes are largely timbered with oaks, mixed with short-leaf pine, and are fairly productive.

A small tract of calcareous black prairie, underlaid by limestone, is said to occur near Rochester, in this parish. It is doubtless similar in its origin to the salt-lick spots in Winn and Bienville.

Communication is chiefly via landings on Red river, but also partly with the Washita country.

LINCOLN.

Population: 11,075.—White, 6,177; colored, 4,898.

Area: 485 square miles.—Woodland, all. Oak-uplands red-lands, about 240 square miles; yellow loam, &c., 245 square miles.

Tilled land: 108,084 acres.—Area planted in cotton, 22,990 acres; in corn, 21,602 acres; in sweet potatoes, 265 acres; in sugar-cane, 232 acres.

Cotton production: 9,723 bales; average cotton product per acre, 0.42 bale, 600 pounds seed-cotton, or 200 pounds cotton lint.

Lincoln parish, formed lately from portions of adjoining parishes, is, *par excellence*, the red-land parish of the state. It may be estimated that quite half of its surface is occupied by the red soils, and is often quite hilly and almost too broken for cultivation. This is especially the case in the northwestern portion, where rough red rocks are strewn all over the country; but wherever cultivatable, these rocky lands have proved very productive and durable. The rest of the parish is more gently rolling, and has a yellow loam soil with more or less of the red subsoil. The timber is oak and hickory, mingled more or less with short-leaf pine. The degree of this admixture, and the size of the trees, form very good indications of the relative productiveness of the several varieties of soil. Cotton, corn, and sweet potatoes are largely produced; the farms are small, but well kept, and many small villages are scattered through the country.

Communication with markets is mainly with the Washita country. The projected line of the Northern, Louisiana and Texas railroad traverses this parish.

CLAIBORNE.

Population: 18,837.—White, 8,541; colored, 10,296.

Area: 796 square miles.—Woodland, all. Oak uplands, of which 60 square miles are "red lands".

Tilled land: 126,000 acres.—Area planted in cotton, 46,567 acres; in corn, 42,920 acres; in sweet potatoes, 471 acres; in sugar-cane, 99 acres.

Cotton production: 19,568 bales; average cotton product per acre, 0.42 bale, 600 pounds seed-cotton, or 200 pounds cotton lint.

The entire parish of Claiborne consists of oak uplands, which, south of the bayou D'Arbonne, are sometimes quite hilly and broken (just south of Homer, the dividing ridge between the D'Arbonne and Black lake waters, is almost mountainous), and largely interspersed with "red-land" ridges; the more gently rolling lands having a gray sandy soil, underlaid by the red subsoil. North of the main (or south) fork of the D'Arbonne, there are slightly rolling or almost level plateaus between the streams, near which alone the country becomes at times somewhat broken. The gray surface soil, underlaid by a yellow or reddish subsoil, prevails here altogether; the timber growth being upland oaks, intermingled more or less with the short-leaf pine and hickory, and ash, beech, elm, &c., in the bottoms. It is a good upland farming region, resembling in many respects northern Sabine; the farms are usually small and well cultivated, with many small villages, in these respects the exact reverse of the state, of things in the southern part of the state.

ABSTRACT OF THE REPORT OF J. Y. DAVIDSON, HOMER.

The surface is generally rolling enough to carry off water readily; some land is level, some hilly.

The soil most prevalent here (township 21, range 6) is a deep sandy one, of a gray color. Its timber growth in uplands is oak, pine, gum, beech, hickory, and ash. Its depth is from 18 to 24 inches; its subsoil is sometimes clay, sometimes gravel and sand; at 10 feet often "black dirt". It is free from all stones, tills easily at all times, and is generally well drained. Cotton forms about one-half of all crops; corn, oats, potatoes, and peas are also grown. The usual height of the cotton-stalk is 3½ to 4 feet; it sometimes runs to weed with too much rain; plowing helps this—topping is questionable. Fresh land will produce 1,900 pounds of seed-cotton, of which about 1,350 pounds make a 450-pound bale. The staple rates middling in market. After twenty years' cultivation the yield is 800 pounds; on a well-manured plot 2,000 pounds were grown last year. About the same amount of seed-cotton is required from old, as well as from fresh land, to make a bale of lint, but the staple of that from old land is not quite so good. The most notable weeds are hog-weed, rag-weed, and crab-grass. Perhaps one-tenth of such land, once cultivated, lies out for want of labor. When taken into cultivation again, it will produce 1,000 pounds of seed-cotton per acre. Little if any damage is done by washing on slopes of this soil.

The red lands form about 10 per cent. of the lands of the region. Their timber is the same as that of the gray soil. The soil is an orange-red clay loam or clay to the depth of about one foot, where a stiff clay, rather impervious to water, underlies. This contains some hard, black gravel, both rounded and angular. Tillage somewhat difficult in dry seasons; drainage good. Seems best adapted to grain. One-half of it is planted in cotton: the stalk is about 5 feet high; too much rain makes it run to weed, but deep plowing will remedy this. ＿＿＿＿＿＿＿＿＿＿＿＿ ＿＿＿＿＿ per acre or about 1,000 are required for a 450-pound bale. After ten years' cultivation, the yield is 700 pounds. Staple rates middling from fresh; not quite so good from old land. Crab-grass, hog-weed, and rag-weed are the most troublesome weeds. About 10 per cent. of such land, once cultivated, lies out for want of laborers. When taken into cultivation it produces nearly as well as fresh land. It washes readily on slopes, but by horizontalizing and hillside ditching, much land has been saved.

There is another soil, called gravelly, thin, or "cowhide" land, forming about 10 per cent. of the lands in the region. It is timbered with oak, pine, gum, and beech. The soil is a coarse, sandy or gravely clay, whitish gray, about 6 inches deep; subsoil mostly heavier than surface soil, but sometimes sandy, often impervious, with flinty, white gravel; is well adapted to cotton, producing 800 pounds of seed-cotton per acre, rating middling. After ten years' cultivation the product is 500 pounds.

Crab-grass is most troublesome on this soil; about 20 per cent. of such land, once cultivated, now lies out; it does not produce well when again cultivated; is badly damaged by washing, and nothing has been done to check the injury.

Cotton shipments are made from November to March to New Orleans, by steamboat, at $1 50 per bale.

UNION.

Population : 13,526.—White, 8,014; colored, 5,512.

Area : 910 square miles.—Woodland, all. Oak uplands, 840 square miles (one-fifth red and "mulatto" land); alluvial land (Washita), 70 square miles.

Tilled land : 62,661 acres.—Area planted in cotton, 28,308 acres; in corn, 25,551 acres; in sweet potatoes, 229 acres; in sugar-cane, 60 acres.

Cotton production : 11,692 bales; average cotton product per acre, 0.41 bale, 585 pounds seed-cotton, or 195 pounds cotton lint.

Union parish resembles, generally, that of Claiborne, though on the whole there is perhaps more poor or uncultivatable land.

The country between the forks of the D'Arbonne consists of high, level, dividing ridges, broken only near the streams, as in Claiborne, the soils also being similar. The best farming districts lie on the smaller tributaries.

The northwestern part, between the D'Arbonne waters and bayou L'Outre, is more hilly; much of the hills, however, being of the red-lands character. Farmersville is on a red-land ridge, and the road thence to Sperrysville leads over a continual succession of hills and valleys, with much ironstone, underlaid by pebbly beds. The region is pretty well settled, with small, but thriving, farms.

The northeastern portion is rather hilly, and the soil largely red, but rather sandy and thin; the region more thinly settled. A small area of the Washita bottom is here included within the parish.

Southeast of Farmersville, toward Trenton, in Ouachita parish, there is, for five miles, a broken, hilly country too broken for cultivation; thence southward the country is more level and a better farming region.

The forest growth, in uplands as well as in bottoms, is the same as in Jackson and Claiborne parishes.

ABSTRACT OF THE REPORT OF J. E. TRIMBLE, FARMERSVILLE.

The uplands are hilly or rolling, and there is a little prairie. There are two chief varieties of upland soil, viz, sandy loam and red, stiff land. The former comprehends fully three-fourths of the lands in the parish. Its timber growth is short-leaf pine, oak, hickory, dogwood, in the uplands; sweet gum, bay, mulberry, ash, &c., in the lowlands. The soil, to the depth of 10 to 12 inches, is fine, sandy clay loam, of a yellow, brown, or mahogany tint. The subsoil is heavier, and frequently contains small, dull red, angular sandstone gravel and rocks. The soil tills easily at all times, and is warm and early. The crops grown are corn, cotton, sweet potatoes, peas, small grain, sugar-cane, tobacco; the two last, with cotton, seem to be best adapted to the soil. Cotton forms about one-half of the crops planted; usual height of stalk, 4 feet. In rainy seasons and on fresh land it sometimes runs to weed; this is remedied by topping. The seed-cotton product on fresh land is 1,000 to 1,500 pounds per acre, of which about 1,350 are needed for a 450-pound bale. The lint, when clean, rates in market as middling to fair middling. After five years' cultivation the product is 500 to 800 pounds, about 1,460 being then needed for a 450-pound bale; the staple is shorter, and not so strong; will class as good ordinary or low middling. The most troublesome weeds are rag-weed, cocklebur, hog-weed, and butter-weed.

About 10 per cent. of this upland is turned out for want of laborers; when again taken up it will yield from 750 to 1,000 pounds of seed-cotton per acre. The soil washes or gullies readily on slopes, but the injury done is not generally serious; the valleys are benefited by the washings. Horizontalizing has been practiced with good effect.

The red or "mulatto" lands occur most frequently in the southwestern part of the parish, but more or less in all, forming about one-fifth of the land. Timber: short-leaf pine, oaks, gum, mulberry, hickory, sumach. It is mostly a gravelly clay loam, very sticky, of a brown or mahogany tint. The subsoil is red clay, containing flinty, white, rounded gravel, underlaid by gravel or rock at 3 to 10 feet. It tills easily in dry seasons, and with difficulty when wet; is rather cold, and late in spring. It is apparently best adapted to corn and grain; about half is planted in cotton; the stalk is about 4 feet high; the seed-cotton product, 800 to 1,200 pounds; rates as middling in market; no material difference after five years' cultivation. The same weeds prevail as on the other soil. None of this land lies turned out; it washes readily on slopes, with serious damage; the lowlands are not injured thereby.

In the lowlands, on the streams and bayous, the natural growth is oak, hickory, and swamp pine. The soil is black clay loam, several feet in depth; subsoil lighter than surface. About two-thirds of the crops on these lands is cotton. The seed-cotton product on fresh land is from 2,000 to 3,000 pounds, the stalk attaining a height of 6 to 8 feet; the staple rates as good middling. No change in quantity or quality of product has as yet been noticed after years of cultivation.

Cotton is shipped during the fall by rail and steamboat to New Orleans; rates of freight per bale vary from 75 cents to $3.

OUACHITA.
(See "Alluvial region".)

MOREHOUSE.
(See "Alluvial region".)

RICHLAND.
(See "Alluvial region".)

FRANKLIN.
(See "Alluvial region".)

PART III.

CULTURAL AND ECONOMIC DETAILS

OF

COTTON PRODUCTION.

REFERENCE TABLE

OF

REPORTS RECEIVED FROM LOUISIANA PARISHES.

ALLUVIAL REGION.

Morehouse.—A. S. KELLER, Bastrop, November 14, 1880. Location, township 20 north, range 6 east. Describes the lands of the parish, upland and lowland.

Caldwell.—W. B. GRAYSON, Columbia. Refers to Washita bottom, ranges 3 and 4, township 12.

Catahoula.—MICHAEL DEMPSEY, Jena, November 9, 1880. Refers to townships 7, 8, 9, and 10 north, in ranges 2 and 3 east; pine uplands of southeastern part of parish.

Madison.—A. C. GIBSON, Waverly station, October 19, 1880. Refers to the entire parish; Mississippi alluvium.

1. *Concordia.*—W. D. SHAW, Black Hawk, January, 1880. Refers to townships 2 and 3 north, range 8 east; Mississippi alluvium.

2. *Concordia.*—GEO. S. WALTON, Boughrea, October 21, 1880. Refers to the entire parish; Mississippi alluvium.

1. *Rapides.*—C. J. BARSTOW and GEORGE S. HAYGOOD, Cheneyville, January 8, 1880. Refer to townships 1 and 2 south, ranges 2 and 3 east; alluvium of Red river.

2. *Rapides.*—P. H. HYNSON, Alexandria, December 1, 1880. Refers to uplands north of Red river.

BLUFF REGION.

West Feliciana.—R. H. RYLAND, Bayou Sara, August 9, 1880. Refers to the entire parish; "bluff upland" or cane hills.

ATTAKAPAS PRAIRIE REGION.

St. Landry.—ELBERT GANTT, Washington, December 20, 1879. Refers to the alluvial lands of the Red and Mississippi river bottoms.

LONG-LEAF PINE REGION.

Vernon.—R. T. WRIGHT, Anacoco, November 15, 1880. Refers to township 3 north, range 10 west; Anacoco prairie region.

Natchitoches.—JOSEPH HENRY, Willow P. O., February 19, 1881.

Winn.—W. T. JONES, Winfield, November 25, 1880.

St. Helena.—H. C. NEWSOM, Greensburg, March 2, 1881.

1. *Tangipahoa.*—WILLIAM H. GARLAND and B. D. GULLETT, Amite City, December 1, 1880. Refer to the entire parish.

2. *Tangipahoa.*—ROBERT LYNNE, Independence, April 15, 1880. Refers to the entire parish.

St. Tammany.—MILTON BURNS, Covington, November 13, 1880. Refers to the entire parish.

OAK-UPLANDS REGION.

De Soto.—A. V. ROBERTS, M. D., Mansfield, November 5, 1880. Refers mainly to township 13 north, range 13 west.

1. *Bossier.*—B. F. FORT, Bellevue, January 12, 1880. Refers to townships 15 to 23 (inclusive) north, ranges 11 to 14 (inclusive) west, or all of Red river bottom in Bossier and Caddo parishes.

2. *Bossier (and part of Webster).*—B. F. FORT, Bellevue, January 12, 1880. Refers to townships 16 and 17 north, ranges 10, 11, and 12 west; being Bossier Point, or country between lake Bistineau and Red river bottom.

3. *Bossier.*—B. F. FORT and C. L. TIDWELL, Bellevue, January 10, 1880. Refer to uplands in townships 18, 19, and 20 north, ranges 11, 12, and 13 west, or central Bossier.

4. *Bossier.*—B. F. FORT, Bellevue, January 12, 1880. Refers to townships 21, 22, and 23 north, ranges 11 and 12.

5. *Bossier.*—J. W. HAYES, Red Land. Embraces about the same territory as the preceding, and is substantially identical in tenor.

Red River.—B. W. MARSTON, East Point. Refers to Red river bottom, township 14, range 11 west.

Sabine.—D. W. SELF, Mill Creek, February 8, 1881.

Bienville.—T. J. BUTLER, Ringgold, February 4, 1881. Refers to the whole parish.

Claiborne.—J. T. DAVIDSON, Homer, May 10, 1880. Refers mainly to township 21 north, range 6 west.

Union.—J. E. TRIMBLE, Farmersville, November 28, 1879. Location, township 21 north, range 1 east. Refers to the entire parish.

Franklin.—A. F. OSBORN, Winnsboro, January 16, 1880. Refers to the entire parish.

SUMMARY OF ANSWERS TO SCHEDULE QUESTIONS ON DETAILS OF COTTON CULTURE.

TILLAGE, IMPROVEMENTS, ETC.

1. Usual depth of tillage (measured on land-side of furrow)?

Saint Landry and *Vernon:* 6 to 12 inches; spring plowing is deep. *Concordia:* 4 to 6 inches on sandy lands and 2 to 3 on black lands. *Morehouse, Catahoula, Winn, Saint Helena, Tangipahoa,*

De Soto, Sabine, Claiborne, and *Union:* 4 inches. *Rapides:* usually 3; successful farmers plow 8 inches deep. *Other parishes:* 2¼ and 3 inches; sometimes more.

2. What draft is employed in breaking up?

Caldwell: 2 mules on river-bottom land, 1 on creek bottoms. *Winn, Saint Helena, Saint Tammany, Bossier, Bienville, Claiborne,* and

Union: 1 mule or horse. *Other counties:* Usually 2.

3. Is subsoiling practiced? If so, with what implements, and with what results?

Union: But little; with one plow following another. In corn the experiment has been successful, but not so in cotton. *Tangipahoa:* To a small extent; with Murphy's subsoil plow good

results. *Rapides:* Very little; with common subsoil plow, good results. *Other parishes:* It is not practiced.

4. Is fall plowing practiced? With what results?

In 18 parishes very little or not at all. *Saint Landry* and *Vernon:* Yes, with good results. 2. *Rapides:* It does not pay in this

soil with hired labor. *Claiborne:* It has not resulted beneficially where tried.

5. Is fallowing practiced? Is the land tilled while lying fallow, or only "turned out"? With what results in either case?

Morehouse: Occasionally; the land is allowed to rest until rebedded for planting again. Among the results the production is increased one-fourth and after-cultivation is made easier. *Other parishes:* It is not practiced at all. Lands are by some "turned out". *Rapides, De Soto,* and *Franklin:* Land is improved by being "turned out" for rest, if stock be kept off; if grazed and trodden continually it is less benefited. 2. *Bossier:* No; land is only "turned out", but is not improved thereby.

3. *Bossier:* No; but some land is "turned out"; it is not tilled while lying fallow, because the labor is engaged in the care of the growing crops.

4. *Bossier:* No; the land is only "turned out", and does not improve short of twenty years, or until covered by a growth of pines. If pastured and tramped by cattle and horses the land is not improved, but is often injured.

6. Is rotation of crops practiced? If so, of how many years' course, in what order of crops, and with what results?

Morehouse: Yes; with corn, sweet potatoes, and oats; but chiefly with cotton and corn; as a result both crops are increased one-fifth at least.

Caldwell: Yes; with corn, cotton, sweet potatoes, and oats. Cotton is planted about two seasons successively before changing to other crops; rotation improves all crops in the course.

Catahoula: Yes; with cotton, corn, sweet potatoes, sugar-cane, oats, and tobacco (for home consumption); the land is relieved of cotton only one year at a time, other crops vary as the farmer chooses; as a result, the soil lasts much longer.

Madison and *Bossier:*

Concordia: Yes; with corn, sweet potatoes, oats and cow-pease. Pease are generally planted on corn land when the after-cultivation of the corn is completed, or they follow oats in the same season; in either case cotton is planted on such land the year following. As a result, the cotton crop is increased fully one-fourth.

.1. *Rapides:* To some extent; cotton is relieved every third year by corn and cow-pease with very good results.

2. *Rapides:* Yes; with cotton, corn, sweet potatoes, and oats. Farmers aim to vary their crops every year; results are good.

Saint Landry: Yes; with, and in the order of, sugar-cane, pease, corn and peas, sugar-cane, etc.; with good results.

Vernon: Yes; with cotton, corn, oats, and sweet potatoes; usually corn two years. cotton two years, and oats one year. As a result, the soil is improved and cultivation becomes easier.

Natchitoches: Yes; with corn, cotton, and sweet potatoes.

Winn: A crop is not planted more than three times on the same land.

Saint Helena, West Felicians: Yes; with corn and cotton alternately; with good results.

1. *Tangipahoa:* Yes; usually cotton two seasons, followed by oats in January; when these are harvested, cow-pease are immediately sown, a part of which crop is cut for hay and the balance is plowed under. The next season corn is planted, and this is again followed by cotton.

Saint Tammany: Yes; with corn, oats, and sweet potatoes, one year in each, with good results.

De Soto: Yes; chiefly to the extent of alternating cotton and corn; on the bottom lands, oats and potatoes are raised only in "patches".

Red River: Yes; cotton is alternated with corn, sweet potatoes, oats, or with anything; or, by some cotton is planted successively on the same land indefinitely; results are good in all cases.

Sabine: Yes; a course of rotation consists of about three crops of cotton, two of corn, and one of oats. As a result cotton increases in yield on worn lands.

Bienville: Very little; with cotton, corn, and oats; results are good where it is practiced.

Claiborne: Yes; generally with cotton, corn, oats, and pease, and a rest; in four-years' courses. With such rotation, the return of cotton-seed to the soil and some manure, good results are obtained.

Union: Yes; with corn, cotton, grain (oats, barley, or rye), and pease, in the order given; always with beneficial results.

Franklin: To some extent; chiefly with corn, considerably with oats, and a little with sweet potatoes. Cotton is planted two or three years successively, then corn, pease, oats, and potatoes for the same length of time, then cotton again. Cotton yields more when it follows corn, oats, or potatoes, and *vice versa.*

7. What fertilizers, or other direct means of improving the soil, are used by you, or in your region? With what results? Is green-manuring practiced? With what results?

Natchitoches, Morehouse, Winn, and *Bienville:* Cotton-seed and some stable manure is used. Results good, increasing the yield in Morehouse one-fourth. Green-manuring is not practiced in these parishes, or in Saint Helena, Bossier, and Franklin.

Caldwell: Cotton-seed and stable-manure are used; always with good results. Green-manuring is not practiced; but cow-pease are raised and plowed under after they are dead.

Catahoula: Recently cotton-seed, stable, and barn-yard manures have been applied; where this has been properly done the crops have been nearly doubled. Manures are rarely applied for growing cotton, but cotton is greatly benefited by manures previously applied for other crops. Cow-pease are planted to shelter the soil from the sun, and prevent its washing by rains, and to serve as forage for stock, for which purposes they are very good.

Madison: Planters try to use cotton-seed as manure, but as a rule the renter is a negro, who sells his seed. Lands here are wonderfully improved by manuring. Green-manuring with cow-pease is practiced to a small extent with the most favorable results.

Saint Landry Concordia: Very little of any kind is used at all. A *few* planters return all their cotton-seed to the soil; the practice produces good results. Green-manuring is practiced with cow-pease; with good results.

Rapides: Barn-yard manure and cotton-seed to some extent; always with good results. Green-manuring is practiced with cow-pease; as a result, the product of the following season is increased by one-third. Some think it best to let the pea mature and rot with the vine.

West Feliciana: None are used on land near the Mississippi river or shipping points. On other lands cotton-seed is used; it greatly improves any crop for which it may be applied. Green-manuring with cow-pease is practiced very little, but with good results.

Vernon: The chief means are stable-manure, cotton-seed, and muck from the swamps; they increase the yield by one-third. Green-manuring is practiced by drilling cow-pease closely in rows, and turning under the crop while it is ripening; the production is thus increased and the cultivation of the soil is made much easier.

Saint Helena: Stern's superphosphate and bone-meal are used by some with very satisfactory results.

1. *Tangipahoa:* Stern's fertilizer is used to a considerable extent, but the best farmers regard it as a stimulant rather than a fertilizer; it increases production, but its benefits are doubtful. A sloping plain of pine land bordering a creek bottom, which produced three-fourths of a bale-per acre this year (1880), has received, during the past seven or eight years, nothing but 500 pounds per acre each year of Mr. B. D. Gullet's compost, which is a mixture of a moderate quantity of cotton-seed, 36 bushels of earth, 18 of stable manure, 12 of saltpeter, 4 of lime, and 2 of salt. Green-manuring is also practiced; cow-pease are used with good results.

2. *Tangipahoa:* Cow-pen manure, bone-dust, superphosphates, cottonseed-meal, and cotton-seed; with beneficial and profitable results. Green-manuring is not practiced, but a few efforts have been made with cow-pease and with success.

Saint Tammany: Stable and cow-pen manures, cotton-seed, raw bones, and superphosphate of lime. They double the yield of cotton. Green-manuring is practiced a little; cow-pease are used; the results are nearly equal to those of the fertilizers mentioned.

De Soto: None are used on bottom lands.

1. *Bossier:* Occasionally corn is manured with cotton-seed, and the crop increased three-fold.

2. *Bossier:* What cotton-seed not fed and what manure not wasted are put on the land; with very good results.

3, 4. *Bossier:* Cotton-seed and barn-yard manure are used with good results; but they are insufficient in quantity.

Red River: Cotton-seed and stable-manure are used with good results. Green-manuring with cow-pease is also practiced with good results.

Sabine: The land usually receives nothing more than the return of its cotton stalks.

Claiborne: Cotton-seed and barn-yard manure are used; by practicing, in addition, rotation of crops and resting, the fertility of the soil can be maintained. Green-manuring is not practiced, but cow-pease are raised and fed off by stock.

Union: Stable-manure, cotton-seed, and occasionally some commercial fertilizers are used with benefit to crops planted. Green-manuring is practiced with cow-pease sometimes; the results are excellent for corn.

Franklin: Cotton-seed is sown broadcast, or sometimes a small quantity is thrown upon each hill of corn at planting time; crops are increased one-fourth as a result.

8. How is cotton-seed disposed of? If sold, on what terms, or at what price?

Morehouse: Along the navigable streams it is sold; elsewhere it is fed to stock, and to some extent returned to the soil; its price is $9 (cash) per ton.

Caldwell: A great deal is fed to cattle, and sold at $10 to $12 per ton.

Catahoula: It is fed to cattle and sheep, and used as manure; the price is 10 cents per bushel. There are usually 37 bushels of cotton-seed for each 450-pound bale of lint. By applying 50 bushels of seed to an acre of poor land that will not produce 8 bushels of corn, it will cause such land to yield 25 bushels of corn. The same amount improves rich land, but not in the same ratio. Cotton exhausts land less than any other crop, while the seed, applied in the quantities mentioned, restores fertility better than any other fertilizer. When used for this purpose, the seed should be sown in furrows and covered in

January, so that all that comes up may be killed by frosts. Its effect is not so great on a cotton crop the first year, but its good results are apparent for many years. Some share-laborers sell their seed, to the disadvantage of the farm. A ton of seed is sometimes sold for $6; while, if put on 2 acres of poor land, for producing corn, sugar-cane, tobacco, or Irish potatoes, it is worth more than $25.

Madison: It is sold to the country merchant, who ships it to New Orleans; price $2 to $7 per ton.

Concordia: It is sold for cash at $7 to $10 per ton.

Rapides: It is sold, and to some extent used as manure; the price is from $4 50 to $6 per ton.

West Feliciana: It is generally sold to corn-growers at $8 to $10 per ton.

180

Saint Landry: It is sometimes sold to oil-factories in New Orleans for $10 per ton; at other times it is returned to the soil.

Vernon: It is returned to the soil; when sold, the price is $7 per ton.

Natchitoches: It is used as manure, and some is sold to oil-mills at $5 per ton.

Winn: It is used as manure and feed; price 10 cents per bushel.

Saint Helena: It is generally used as manure for growing corn; price $3 to $6 per ton.

Tangipahoa: It is fed to cows in winter; what is left is returned to the soil in spring, for growing corn; when sold, the price is $10 per ton.

Saint Tammany: It is returned to the soil.

De Soto: Along the river it is sold to oil-factories; where it is not conveniently near shipping points it is fed to stock, returned to the soil, or *wasted.*

1. *Bossier:* It is generally sold to oil-factories for $8 per ton; some is fed.

2, 3, 4. *Bossier:* It is fed and returned to the soil; none is sold except for planting, and at about 10 cents per bushel of 25 pounds.

Red River: It is used as manure and sold, generally at a low price, which is attributable to a combination of steamboat men and oil-companies.

Union, Sabine, Bienville, and *Claiborne:* It is usually fed to stock, or applied to corn land as manure; it is never shipped, but occasionally changes hands at 10 cents per bushel.

Franklin: The surplus is sometimes fed to stock in winter, but it is generally sold for $6 to $7 per ton (cash).

9. Is cottonseed-cake used with you for feed? Is it used for manure, alone or composted, and for what crops?

Concordia: Very little is used for manure: those who have tried it find it a very effective fertilizer. 2 *Rapides:* As manure, either drilled in rows or scattered broadcast. *Saint Landry:* Sometimes fed to cows and used as manure.

Tangipahoa: No; but cottonseed-meal in connection with other food is used for dairy cows by one farmer. Cottonseed-cake is used for manure, alone and mixed with bone-dust for growing corn, cotton, cane, and strawberries; best for sugar-cane. *Other parishes:* Not used for any purpose.

PLANTING AND CULTIVATION OF COTTON.

10. What preparation is usually given to cotton-land before bedding up?

None in *Morehouse, Natchitoches, Winn, Saint Helena, Bossier, Red River, Sabine, Bienville, Claiborne, Union,* and *Franklin.* Spring-plowing in other parishes. *Rapides* and *Saint Landry:*

Sometimes fall-plowing. *Vernon:* Fall-plowing and solid, flat, breaking, and spring-plowing.

11. Do you plant in ridges, and how far apart?

This is the custom in all of the parishes. *Madison* and *Concordia:* 5 to 7 feet. *Other counties:* Usually 4 to 6 feet; sometimes 3 feet.

12. What is your usual planting time?

Rapides, Saint Landry, and *Concordia:* March 15 or 20 to April 30. *Caldwell:* March 25 to April 30. In eight parishes as early as April 1. In *Morehouse, West Feliciana, Bossier, Claiborne, Union,*

Franklin, Catahoula: From 5th to 10th of April. In *Tangipahoa, Saint Tammany,* and *Bienville,* 20th and 15th of April.

13. What variety of seed do you prefer? How much seed is used per acre?

Many varieties are named, usually two or more in a parish. The following are the varieties with number of times mentioned: Dixon, 9 times, Hurlong 8, Peeler 4, Boyd Prolific 4, Petit Gulf 3, African 1, McClenden 1, China 1, Pine 1, "Javy" 1, Early Simpson 1, Golden Prolific 1, South American 1, and Chambers' Improved Prolific 1.

Catahoula: The McClenden Prolific, received from the Department of Agriculture at Washington. The Peeler seed produces our best staple, but does not yield enough per acre. The

Hurlong, or green seed ranks next. The Dixon yields well, but is deficient in quality. The old Petit Gulf, or Mexican, holds its own, while the improved varieties (of which we have many) degenerate after two or three years. One to three bushels of seed, sometimes 4 or 5, are used per acre. *Catahoula:* 4 are not too many on poor land. *Vernon:* 1, if drilled, or one-half if planted in hills. *Tangipahoa:* 1 with careful planting. *De Soto:* 2½ to 4 with the "planter".

14. What implements do you use in planting?

A scooter or bull-tongue plow for opening and a harrow for covering, in all of the parishes. Planting is done by hand usually.

15. Are "cottonseed-planters" used in your region? What opinion is held of their efficacy or convenience?

They are used only in *Morehouse, Concordia, Rapides, Tangipahoa, De Soto, Red River,* and to some extent in *Saint Landry, Claiborne,* and *Natchitoches.*

Where used opinions are favorable. *Catahoula:* On old stumpless lands they save half the labor of man and beast. *Concordia:* Good only on smooth, level land. *Tangipahoa:* They plant more economically and uniformly than by hand. *De Soto:* Liked on sandy and light soils. *Red River:* Good when the

soil is in good condition, and that depends on seasons. On the same land, they are not liked in some parishes. *Caldwell:* Profitable only on very large plantations. *West Feliciana:* Not considered economical. *Bossier:* Negroes stick to old methods. *Claiborne:* Not considered as being worth "the trouble to operate them. *Franklin:* They will not pay on our rough lands.

16. How long, usually, before your seed comes up?

Catahoula and *Natchitoches:* 3 or 4 days if soil is warm and moist. *Madison* and *Franklin:* Early planting, 10 days; late planting, 5 days. *Bossier:* Early planting, 15 days; late planting,

8 days. *Concordia* and *Bienville:* 10 to 14 days. *Claiborne, Winn, West Feliciana:* 7 or 8 days. *Other parishes:* Time is indefinite and dependent on the weather.

17. At what stage of growth do you thin out your "stand", and how far apart?

In most of the parishes thinning out is begun when the plant attains a height of 2 or 3 inches, or when the third or fourth leaf appears. It is then from 10 to 18 days old and is "chopped out" with hoes, leaving at first several plants in

a bunch, a hoe's width apart. When after-cultivation begins, it is further thinned to single plants, at distances of 10 to 15 or 24 inches, according to character of land.

181

18. Is your cotton liable to suffer from " sore shin" ?

Very little in *Saint Landry, Winn, Saint Tammany, De Soto, Claiborne* and *Union.* It is in other parishes. *Madison, West Fe-* *liciana,* and *Catahoula:* If bruised with the hoe. *Other par-* *ishes :* In cool springs, if planted too early.

19. What after-cultivation do you give, and with what implements ?

Morehouse: The sweep and hoe are used as long as grass and weeds continue to grow, and as long as the laborers will work.

Caldwell: Deep plowing, with the turning plow until buds (" forms") are well formed, then shallow cultivation with small sweeps.

Catahoula: Four workings, with plows, hoes, harrows, sweeps, cultivators, and every conceivable implement that will kill grass and keep the soil in good order until August 1.

Concordia: Plowing and hoeing; at first the beds are kept as high as possible, and are gradually worked down as the sea- son advances.

Rapides: Scrape, bar off, thin to bunches, plow the dirt *to* the row and plow out the middles. Repeat this as often as necessary. Some use cultivators and harrows.

Winn: Bar off, partially thin out, throw dirt to the row with a bull- tongue or small sweep, plow out the middles, and lastly, plow out all the soil between the rows.

Tangipahoa: Usually the small solid sweep, buzzard wing, and five- toothed cultivator are used ; the kind of cultivation depends

upon the kind of soil, and the progress the grass may have made.

De Soto: The turn plow, sweep, and hoe are used ; weeds and grass are kept out of the row with the hoe. The final plowing is with the sweep and as shallow as it can be done.

Bossier: The row is first barred off with a turn plow or scraper, then thinned out, then dirted by the shovel plow, and again plowed and hoed, and finally the solid sweep is used until August to keep down weeds, especially tie-vines, in the bottom.

Red River: First, hoe, sweep, and plow ; second, plow, sweep, and hoe ; third, sweep, hoe, and plow ; and pull out tie-vines in August with the hands, and again when picking.

Sabine: Throw dirt to the row with the turning plow ; hoe once and use an 18-inch sweep generally twice.

Franklin: The row is barred off, scraped, and partially thinned, and should then have a shallow furrow thrown to it from each side, for a support to the plants, and to cover what little grass may have been left by the hoes, etc.

Other parishes also use these methods of cultivation.

20. What is the height usually attained by your cotton before blooming ?

Caldwell, Catahoula, and *Franklin:* 10 to 14 inches. *Morehouse, Madison, Concordia, Sabine,* and *Bienville:* 24 to 36 inches.

Other parishes : 18 to 24 inches.

21. When do you usually see the first blooms ?

1 *Rapides* and *Saint Landry:* May 20 to June. *Concordia, Vernon, Natchitoches, Winn, Saint Helena, De Soto, Red River,* and *Union:* June 1 to 5. *Seven parishes :* June 5 to 10. *More-*

house, 2 *Rapides, Saint Tammany, Claiborne:* June 10 to 15. *Bossier :* June 20. *Bienville:* June 30. *Union :* July 1 to 10.

22. When do the bolls first open ?

De Soto: 40 to 60 days after the first blooms open. 1 *Rapides, Caldwell:* July 1 to 4. *Catahoula, Madison, Saint Landry, Natchitoches, Sabine:* July 10 to 20. *Concordia,* 2 *Rapides, Claiborne, Franklin:* Late in July. *West Feliciana, Winn, Saint Helena,*

Tangipahoa, Saint Tammany, Bossier, Red River : August 1 to 10. *Morehouse,* 3 *Bossier, Bienville, Union:* August 15 to 20. *Vernon :* Late in August.

23. When do you begin your first picking ?

Caldwell, Catahoula, Madison, Concordia, 1 *Rapides, Saint Landry, Natchitoches, Sabine:* August 1 to 10. 2 *Rapides, West Felici- ana, Tangipahoa, Saint Tammany, De Soto, Red River, Clai-*

borne, and *Franklin:* August 15 to 20. *Morehouse, Bossier :* Late in August. *Other parishes :* September 1 to 15.

24. How many pickings do you usually make, and when ?

Morehouse, Madison, Bienville: Two, in September and November. *Saint Helena, Saint Tammany, Union:* Four, in August, Sep- tember, October, and November. *Other parishes :* Three, in September, October, and November, or as fast as it can be

picked over. *Bossier, Red River :* Picking is continuous, without regard to number of times. *Claiborne:* Beginning as soon as a hand can pick 100 pounds.

25. Do you ordinarily pick all your cotton ?   At what date does picking ordinarily close ?

Cotton is all, or nearly all, picked in all of the parishes except Red River. The season usually closes December 25 or January 1, or, in De Soto, as late as February. In Caldwell, Saint

Landry, Winn, Tangipohoa, Vernon, and Claiborne, early in December or last of November.

26. At what time do you expect the first " black frost" ?

Morehouse, September 15; *Concordia,* 1 *Tangipahoa,* October 28 and 26; in most of the parishes, from November 1 to 15; 2

Tangipahoa, December 25.

27. Do you pen your seed-cotton in the field, or gin as picking progresses ?

It is usually ginned as picking progresses. *Catahoula:* Small farmers house it until enough for several bales are picked. *Morehouse, Vernon, Winn, Claiborne, Saint Tammany :* Pen in the field. *Red River:* Pen it, and let much of it rot, in wet weather. *Bienville:* If crop is heavy, pen in the field ; if light, gin as picked. *Bossier:* Both ; generally each tenant has a pen near his house,

or sometimes uses a division of the gin-house; when he has gathered enough for several bales he gins. Men who have no gins pen it near their houses. *De Soto* and *Franklin:* The best planters gin as picking progresses, or put in a good cotton-house; others sometimes leave it on the ground in the field or in rail pens exposed to the weather.

GINNING, BALING, AND SHIPPING.

28. What gin do you prefer? How many saws? What motive power? If draft animals, which mechanical "power" arrangement do you prefer? How much clean lint do you make in a day's run of 10 hours?

Brown's gin is mentioned in four parishes:
With 50 saws, run by 4 mules, it makes from 1,700 to 2,200 pounds lint.
With 60 saws, run by 4 mules, it makes 4,000 pounds of lint.
With 80 saws, run by steam-engines, it makes from 3,000 to 4,500 pounds of lint.

Gullett's gin, in eight parishes:
With 60 saws, run by steam-engines or 4 mules, it makes 2,700 to 3,000 pounds.
With 70 saws, run by water-power, 2,500 pounds.
With 60 saws, run by water-power, 2,250 pounds.

The Eagle gin, in five parishes:
With 70 saws, run by steam-engine, makes 2,500 pounds.
With 60 saws, run by steam-engine, makes 1,000 pounds.

Pratt's gin, in seven parishes:
With 60 saws, run by 10 to 15 horse-power steam-engine, about 3,000 pounds.
With 75 saws, run by 20 horse-power steam engine, about 4,000 pounds.

With 75 saws, run by 10 horse-power steam-engine, about 4,000 pounds.
Revolving-head gin, 80 saws, run by 12 horse-power steam-engine or 4 mules, about 6,500 pounds.
With 50 saws, run by water-power, 1,660 pounds.

McCurdy gin, in one parish:
With 40 saws, run by mules, 600 to 1,000 pounds.

The *Griswold gin*, in one parish:
With 50 saws, run by horses or mules, 1,660 pounds.

The *Carver gin*, in one parish:
45 to 80 saws, run by 4 mules, 2,500 to 3,000 pounds.

Catahoula: Brown's stand is the lightest. *Saint Helena*: Farms in this county are mostly small, and a few Gullett gins gin the crop of the community for one-fifteenth of the amount ginned. *Sabine*: Water-power is most generally used. *West Feliciana, Bossier, Red River*: The old-fashioned big wheel, with iron segments and pinion and band-wheel, is preferred.

29. How much seed-cotton is required for a 475-pound bale of lint?

Saint Landry, Vernon, Saint Tammany, Bienville, Union: 1,425 pounds. *Winn*: 1,450 pounds. *Morehouse*: 1,425 to 1,775. *West Feliciana*: 1,425 to 1,660 pounds. *Caldwell, Natchitoches, Tangipahoa, De Soto, Red River*: 1,540 pounds. *Bossier*: 1,540 pounds when first picked, 1,425 after being housed some weeks. *Concordia*: 1,540 to 1,720 pounds. *Madison, Franklin*: 1,600 pounds. *Catahoula*: 1,660 pounds. *Rapides*: 1,630 to 1,720 pounds. *Saint Helena, Sabine*: 1,485 pounds.

30. What press do you use for baling? What press is generally used in your region? What is its capacity?

Southern standard press, in one parish.
With 5 men and 2 mules, capacity is 20 bales per day.

Brooks press, in three parishes:
With 5 men and 2 mules, 20 bales per day or 3 bales per hour.

Lewis press, in one county:
"Has a capacity of 40 bales per day if properly worked" (*Madison*).

Coleman's press, in three parishes.
With horses, 15 bales per day.

Newell press, in four parishes:
25 to 30 bales per day.

McComb press, in one parish:
25 to 30 bales per day.

Reynolds press, in two parishes:
3 bales per hour.

Ingersoll press, in one parish.

Gullett's press, in two parishes:
By steam- or horse-power, 20 bales per day.

Albertson press or "Compass lever", in two parishes:
10 to 15 bales per day; "30 bales have been packed here in a day with it" (*Union*).

Wooden screw-press, in seven parishes:
Mostly home-made, and make from 10 to 25 bales per day. *Bossier*: The home-made wooden screw-press is used almost exclusively; it will easily pack a 500-pound bale in half an hour—often in twenty minutes—when run by four men and a horse or mule. There is here an abundance of fine post oak and pine, of which good presses can cheaply be made; when housed they last twenty years, and are more efficient than any patent press. With these, one little mule presses a 500-pound bale with ease. The big river planters send as far as fifteen miles to the hills to obtain timber for such presses.

31. Do you use rope or iron ties for baling? If the latter, what fastening do you prefer? What kind of bagging is used?

Iron ties are used exclusively throughout the state. The arrow fastening also is in general use; the buckle and alligator or lightning fastening in one parish each. Jute bagging is very generally used with some gunny bagging and hemp.

32. What weight do you aim to give your bales? Have transportation companies imposed any conditions in this respect?

400 pounds in Franklin; 450 pounds in four parishes; 500 pounds in eight parishes; 550 pounds in Natchitoches and Red River parishes. In other parishes the weight varies from 450 to 500 pounds. No conditions are imposed except in Bossier, where bales of less than 450 pounds are subject to some extra charges. Cotton is mostly carried per bale regardless of weight.

DISEASES, INSECT ENEMIES, ETC.

33. By what accidents of weather, diseases, or insect pests is your cotton crop most liable to be injured—caterpillar, boll-worm, shedding, rot of bolls, rust, blight? At what dates do these several pests or diseases usually make their appearance, and to what cause is the trouble attributed by your farmers?

Morehouse: Too much rain at fruiting time causes shedding, running to weed, rot of bolls, and rust; the caterpillar is troublesome, and appears late in July, and the boll-worm seems to be an annual visitor to the plant; no cause for it is offered.

Caldwell: By very wet springs, or very dry summers; a very wet July is generally followed by the caterpillar, the forerunners of which usually appear about July 15; by rust, which generally appears on old lands, and by boll-worm, boll-rot, and shedding.

Catahoula: Cold, wet weather causes "sore shin" and aphides; moles run under the plants, and locusts or cut-worms cut off the plant just below the leaves; some caterpillars appear annually, and the boll-worm is very destructive; morning rains cause shedding, and continued rains cause rot of bolls; any soil is liable to rust. The plant is never, at any stage, entirely free from some pest. Farmers attribute these things to seasons less favorable to cotton than to its enemies. The worms are attributed to too much rain late in June or July.

Madison: Extremely wet or dry weather; the evil effects of the first are attributed, in some degree, to lack of drainage; both occur in July and August. In this region the overflows of the Mississippi river are dreaded more than all else.

1. *Concordia:* Storms, aphides, caterpillars, boll-worms, shedding, rot of bolls, rust, and blight; they are assigned to many different causes.

2. *Concordia:* Storms, very dry weather, excessive rains in spring or fall are bad; worms in July and August, shedding in August; some attribute worms, rust, and blight to excessively hot weather and rains, others believe them to be due to some deficiency of soil ingredients.

1. *Rapides:* By too much wind and rain, the caterpillar, boll-worm, shedding, rot of bolls, and blight; they appear from June 15 to the end of the season.

2. *Rapides:* By frosts, "sore shin," rust, blight, locusts, and shedding, when the plant is young; and later, by caterpillar, boll-worm, and boll-rot. They are chiefly attributed to wet weather.

Saint Landry: By the caterpillar in some seasons; very little by boll-worm or rust, some shedding and rot of bolls; these appear August 1 to September 15, and none can tell the cause.

Vernon and West Feliciana: By the caterpillar in August and September.

Natchitoches: By wet weather, caterpillar, boll-worm, shedding, boll-rot, and rust. They appear about July 1, and are all attributed to an excess of rain.

Winn: By excessively wet weather, and by the caterpillar about September 1; also by boll-warm, shedding, rot of bolls, rust, and blight; they are attributed to succession of cotton on the same land.

Saint Helena: By extremes of wet and hot weather, caterpillar, boll-worm, boll-rot, shedding, and rust, in July and August. They are attributed to warm winters and wet springs.

Tangipahoa: By rust, by shedding when wet weather is followed by dry weather, by rot of bolls when rains are excessive; not often by caterpillar or boll-worm. They appear in July. Shedding is attributed to shallow tillage, excessive rains, and poverty of soil. Low-lying fields are damaged first and most by the caterpillar.

Saint Tammany: By storms and excessive rains; by caterpillar and boll-worm in August.

De Soto: Chiefly by caterpillar, boll-worm, and shedding; also by rust and blight. The boll-worm appears in July; the caterpillar is injurious late in August and early in September. Shedding is attributed to extreme states of wet or dry weather; cause of rust and blight is not known.

1. *Bossier:* By wet weather (dry weather has never been injurious); by caterpillar, August 20 to September 30; very little by rust and blight; by boll-worm, boll-rot, and shedding in July and August. Wet weather causes the worms; very wet

weather causes boll-rot, and wet following dry weather causes shedding.

2. *Bossier:* By caterpillar, August 25 to September 30; drought in June; rust in September; and boll-worm and shedding in July and August. Shedding is attributed to wet following dry weather; rot of bolls is attributed to wet weather; causes of other things are not known. In dry seasons the caterpillar, boll-worm, or boll-rot do not appear; in wet seasons there is no shedding. Not more than half the crop is ever lost by all these things combined.

3. *Bossier:* By rust in the middle of July, caterpillar late in August, boll-worm all along, shedding in dry weather, or wet after dry weather; causes are not known; a total failure of a cotton crop has never been known here.

4. *Bossier:* By extremely wet or dry weather, late and early frosts; by the caterpillar, August 20 to September 30; boll-worm all along; shedding in July and August, and caused by wet following dry weather; rot of bolls in August and September, attributed to too much wet weather; rust in September, and blight all along.

Red River: By wet weather, "sore shin" in spring, yellow rust in summer, boll-worm in August, rot of bolls in wet weather, blight, shedding, and the caterpillar.

Close observation for fifteen years has led the writer to believe that the caterpillar will damage the crop every year in which there is a scarcity of ants. In wet seasons the ants cannot become sufficiently great in numbers to destroy the caterpillar; hence the abundance of the latter in such seasons, of which 1880 was an example. In 1879 there were in his field of 1,000 acres as many caterpillars as cotton plants; and on the 15th of August each plant had on it about thirty ants per leaf, and the writer is most positively certain that these little ants saved his crop from the most determined onset of caterpillars he ever saw. The caterpillars were routed, killed, and eaten by the ants. The latter were so thick that the hoers could not stand still without getting their feet covered with them.

It appears that the moth of the cotton-caterpillar remains in hiding places all winter, coming out occasionally in warm weather. Writer captured one attracted by the light on the night of February 7, 1881.

Sabine: By aphides in wet, late springs, about May 1; by the caterpillar about August 1; by rust in September, and by shedding. Aphides are attributed to cold weather, shedding and rust to wet weather; cause of caterpillar is not known.

Bienville: By drought, caterpillar, boll-worm, and shedding; from July 1 to September 30. They are not accounted for, and frequently come when least expected.

Claiborne: By the boll-worm in July and caterpillar in August, and by wet weather, shedding, and blight. The farmers do not know their causes.

Union: By caterpillars in July, and by the boll-worm, and occasionally rust; their causes are not known.

Franklin: By cold, damp springs; dry, hot summers; cut-worms; by "sore shin" in early spring, which seems to be caused by cold, damp atmosphere; by rust in July or August; by caterpillar, boll-worm, and boll-rot about September 1; their causes are undetermined.

34. What efforts have been made to obviate the trouble? With what success?

None in most of the parishes.

Caldwell: The best remedy against the caterpillar is to plant as early as possible; two-thirds of the crop will then mature before it destroys the plant. 1. *Bossier:* None; in the necessary late sweepings for tearing out tie-vines, many limbs are broken, allowing better circulation of air and access of sunlight; rot of bolls is thus prevented. 2, 4. *Bossier:* Rank cotton rots sometimes; mules are then driven between rows, break-

ing off limbs and allowing a better circulation of air, which stops the rot. During the last twenty-seven years there has not been a failure of the cotton crop, even from all causes combined. *Sabine:* None so far as known, except that, against the caterpillar, some farmers top their cotton to hasten its maturity. Paris green is also used when the caterpillar appears.

35. Is rust or blight prevalent chiefly on heavy or ill-drained soils? Do they prevail chiefly in wet or dry, cool or hot seasons? On which soil described by you are they most common?

Usually on ill-drained soils in most of the parishes. *Morehouse:* In wet, hot seasons; most common on the gum and prairie lands, especially on the latter. *Caldwell:* Chiefly on old lands, in dry seasons, and most common on the sandy soils. *Catahoula:* Rust is not a respecter of soils; it prevails chiefly in wet and cool seasons; if the weather is favorable to it, the richest soil of the Mississippi bottom, and the poorest soil of the pine hills, are alike subject to rust. *Madison:* In wet seasons, and most common on the sandy loam. Since the war not one plantation in this region has been well ditched. *Concordia:* To some extent both on heavy and ill-drained soils, in wet, or dry, hot seasons, and most common on the sandy soils. *Rapides:* In wet and cool seasons. *West Feliciana:* On ill-drained soils, in wet, hot seasons. *Saint Landry:* There is very little rust in this region; it occurs on various soils, most common on the sandy soil. *Vernon:* In wet and

hot seasons; most common on the bottom lands. *Natchitoches:* Chiefly in wet seasons. *Winn:* Chiefly on old soils, in wet and cool seasons; most common on the sandy upland. *Saint Helena:* Chiefly on heavy soils, in wet and hot seasons; most common on the heavy, clayey loam. *Tangipahoa:* Chiefly on heavy soils, in wet seasons, most common on table-lands. *De Soto:* On heavy soils, in wet seasons, and most common on bottom lands. *Bossier:* Chiefly on dry and light soils. *Red River:* Chiefly on heavy soils, in wet and cool seasons; most common on the wet sandy land. *Sabine:* Chiefly on heavy calcareous (?) soils, in wet and hot seasons; all the lands here are more or less subject to them, but chiefly the calcareous (?) soils of the low bottoms. *Union:* Both on light and heavy soils; worse, as a rule, in wet than in dry seasons, most common on light, sandy knolls. *Franklin:* On any kind of soil, without any perceptible preference.

36. Is Paris green used as a remedy against the caterpillar? If so, how; and with what effect?

It is not used in *Morehouse, Caldwell, Madison, West Feliciana, Saint Helena, Tangipahoa, Saint Tammany, Bienville, Claiborne,* and *Franklin.* To some extent in other counties.
Catahoula: The trouble is, the worms come too suddenly; by the time Paris green is applied, the plant is already much damaged; it is a question whether the crop is damaged or not by Paris green itself. *Rapides:* With flour and water; with moderate success; in solution of one pound in thirty gallons of water; with good effect, as some believe. *De Soto:* A little; dissolved in water and sprinkled, or mixed with flour

and dusted on the plants; some claim success, others condemn the poison. *Bossier:* It was used a little years ago; results do not pay the cost, risk, and trouble. How to get the worm to eat it is the question; it would doubtless kill him if he ate it. *Red River:* Yes; with only tolerable success. If an early rain comes, it is washed off; if not, it kills the worm. *Sabine:* Occasionally; dissolved in water and sprinkled on the plant; it usually kills the caterpillar. *Union:* Yes; it has been used mixed with flour and plaster; it killed the worm, and, in some instances, also the plant.

LABOR AND SYSTEM OF FARMING.

37. What is the average size of farms or plantations in your region?

Twenty to 50 acres in *Catahoula, West Feliciana, Winn, Tangipahoa, Saint Tammany,* and *Franklin,* 100 acres and less in *Vernon, Saint Helena, Sabine,* and *Bienville,* 30 to 300 acres in *Caldwell,* 320 in *Union,* 150 to 400 in *Madison, Bossier,* and *Rapides,* as

high as 500 in *Morehouse, Saint Landry, Natchitoches, De Soto,* and *Claiborne,* 500 to 800 in *Concordia,* and 50 to 2,000 in *Red River.*

38. Is the prevalent practice "mixed farming" or "planting"?

Planting in *West Feliciana, Natchitoches, Bossier, Claiborne,* and *Franklin;* "mixed farming" in other parishes.

39. Are supplies raised at home or imported; and if the latter, where from? Is the tendency toward the raising of home supplies increasing or decreasing?

Supplies are generally raised at home in *Vernon, Winn, Catahoula, Saint Tammany,* and *Sabine.* Corn and some meat are generally raised at home in *Caldwell, Natchitoches, Claiborne,* and *Union.* In other parishes much, especially corn, is raised at home, but the markets of Saint Louis and New Orleans are depended upon for a large part of the supplies.

The tendency toward raising home supplies is decreasing in *Morehouse* and *Madison,* on account of the practice among the negroes of stealing swine; unvarying in *West Feliciana* and *Franklin,* and increasing in all other parishes.

40. Who are your laborers chiefly; whites (of what nationality), negroes, or Chinese? How are their wages paid; by the year, month, or day? At what rates? When payable?

Chiefly whites in *Catahoula, Vernon, Winn, Saint Tammany,* and *Sabine;* whites and negroes in *Saint Helena, De Soto, Bossier, Red River, Claiborne, Union,* and *Franklin.* Chiefly negroes in all other parishes.
Wages are from $6 to $10 per month in *Saint Helena, De Soto, Bossier,* and *Union,* and from $10 to $15 in other parishes. Daily wages are usually 50 cents, with board, or 75 cents to $1 without board.

In *Catahoula* yearly wages are $140 to $200; in other parishes the laborer usually takes a part of the crop when working by the year.
Wages are paid according to contract, either monthly, or sometimes one-half monthly. Daily wages are paid at the end of the day or week.
Supplies are furnished at the expense of the laborer; in *Tangipahoa,* at about 35 per cent. profit to the employer.

41. Are cotton farms worked on shares? On what terms? Are any supplies furnished by the owners?

The share system prevails in all of the parishes except Saint Tammany, and to some extent only in Bienville and Franklin.
When the owner furnishes land, teams, and implements the crop is evenly divided between laborer and owner. For the land alone the owner receives usually one-fourth of the crop.

Should board also be furnished with implements and land, the owner receives two-thirds of the crop. Supplies furnished laborers are usually charged against them and deducted from their share of the crop at the end of the year.

42. Does your system give satisfaction? How does it affect the quality of the staple? Does the soil deteriorate or improve under it?

The share system gives satisfaction only in Concordia, West Feliciana, Vernon, Natchitoches, Winn, Saint Helena, Bossier, Sabine, and Bienville. In others it does not; "prices and seasons are too uncertain," and "on account of the indolence of the negro".

The quality of the staple is not affected except in Saint Helena, Red River, and probably in Franklin.
The soil deteriorates, except in Saint Landry, 2 Rapides, 1 Tangipahoa, and Saint Tammany (by wages).

43. Which system (wages or share) is the better for the laborer, and why?

The share system in ten parishes, and for the following reasons:
Morehouse: The negro likes it best, because it allows him more time for idleness and to enjoy his freedom. *Caldwell, Saint Helena,* and *Rapides:* He spends wages as fast as earned. *Concordia:* They are interested in the work; wages are best for the improvident. *Natchitoches:* It keeps him busy for only half of his time. *Winn:* Is more encouraging to the laborer. *Tangipahoa:* Can make more if industrious, though makes no progress under either system. *Saint Tammany:* Encourages him to be careful. *Bossier:* Money he spends; his share of corn he keeps, or is apt to do so; out of his cotton share he may buy a mule, and in the following year become a tenant farmer.

Wages system in other parishes. *Catahoula:* The planter's instruction makes work easier, and the laborer is sure of his pay. *Madison:* He cannot go in debt at the country stores. *Sabine:* No risks; knows what he is going to get. *Claiborne:* Rations are furnished. *Union:* Labor can be more successfully controlled by it. *Bienville:* Because under the share system he makes calculations and obtains property which he can neither carry nor pay for unless he has a heavy crop, which, of course, is uncertain. *Franklin:* Wages; they receive rations with wages, and not with shares; deduct from the value of the share the cost of rations, and it will fall far short of the wages the laborer might receive.

44. What is the condition of the laborers?

Good and comfortable and prosperous in all of the parishes except Red River, where it is "bad". *Claiborne:* They have good clothes, cabins, and food. *Franklin:* Fair, when they are industrious and economical; the reverse when indolent and improvident. *Vernon:* They are dependent on their employers.

45. What proportion of negro laborers own land or the houses in which they live?

Saint Landry, Winn, 1 *Tangipahoa:* About one-half. *Catahoula* and *Sabine:* One in three. 2 *Tangipahoa, Saint Helena, Saint Tammany,* and *Bienville:* One in ten or fifteen. *De Soto, Union,* and *Franklin:* One in twenty. *Bossier* and *Claiborne:* One in twenty-five or fifty heads of families. *Other parishes:* Very few.

46. What is the market value of the land described in your region? What rent is paid for such land?

Morehouse: Per acre, $10 for unimproved, or $30 for improved lands; rents, $5 to $8.
Caldwell: Per acre, $5 to $10; rents, $3 to $5.
Catahoula: Per acre, for public lands, $1 25; for improved lands, $15 to $20; rents, $3 to $6.
Madison: Per acre, cultivated land, $25; rents, $6 to $10.
Concordia: Per acre, cultivated lands, $35 to $50; rents, $5 to $7.
1. *Rapides:* Per acre, $20 to $50; rents, $3 to $5.
2. *Rapides:* Per acre, $15; rents, $3 to $5.
West Feliciana: It has hardly any value; rent, a bale of cotton for 10 to 12 acres.
Saint Landry: Per acre, $8 to $15; rents, $2 to $4.
Vernon: Per acre, $2 50; rents consist of shares of crops.
Natchitoches: Per acre, $20; rents, $5 to $10.
Winn: Per acre, $2 50; rents, $6 to $5.
Saint Helena: Per acre, $3 to $8; rent, one-fourth the crops.
Tangipahoa: Per acre, $5 to $10 to $20; rent, about $4, land being furnished cabin to live in.

Saint Tammany: Per acre, improved land, $1 to $5; rent, one-fourth the crop.
De Soto: Per acre, improved and unimproved together, $2 to $20; rents, $2 to $5.
1. *Bossier:* Per acre, $30 for whole plantations; rents, $8 to $10. Per acre, $3 to $5 for tracts including improved, unimproved, and wastes; rent, $2 per acre.
Red River: Per acre, $1 to $100; rents, all the way to $10.
Sabine: Per acre, $5 to $8; rent, $4.
Bienville: Per acre, 10 cents to $10; rents, one-third or one-fourth of the crop.
Claiborne: Per acre, $10; rents consist of shares of crops.
Union: Per acre, $1 50 to $10; if shares, one-third of corn and one-fourth of the cotton raised.
Franklin: Per acre, $2 50 for unimproved, $5 for cultivated lands; rents, $2 to $3.

47. How many acres, or 450-pound bales "per hand", is your customary estimate?

Morehouse, Caldwell, Catahoula, Madison, Concordia, 1 *Tangipahoa, Bossier, Sabine, Union:* 5 or 6 bales, or 10 acres. *Rapides, Saint Landry:* 7 or 8 bales. *Winn:* 10 bales, or 15 acres. *De Soto:* 10 acres in cotton, or 3 to 6 bales. *Other counties:* 3 to 5 bales, with corn.
2, 3, 4. *Bossier:* 4 bales raised on 8 acres; each man generally has three hands—himself, wife, and two half-hands; these produce what one good slave formerly did.
Red River: 1½ bales in 1880, and 5 bales in 1879; it is very uncertain and various.
Sabine: 5 bales, or 14 acres, 6 of which are in cotton, the balance in corn, etc.

48. To what extent does the system of credits or advances upon the growing cotton crop prevail in your region?

The system prevails very generally throughout the state.
Rapides: To a considerable extent. The merchants (the chief of which are Jews) have heretofore got about all the negro made, whether that was one bale or ten. *Catahoula:* Country merchants furnish small farmers or new beginners a reasonable amount of goods for themselves and families for the year, taking a mortgage on the crop, which must be delivered to the merchant at the end of the year. Four-fifths of the farmers deal in this way. *De Soto:* It is almost universal; very few planters pay cash for everything, and almost no laborers do. *Bossier:* It is universal, and is our greatest evil. The law giving privilege for supplies has done more injury to agriculture, both before and since the war, than could well be calculated, yet all classes favor it. *Red River:* To an alarming extent after a good season; but a bad season checks the system.

49. At what stage of its production is the cotton crop usually covered by insurance? Is such practice general?

Concordia, Rapides, Vernon, Bossier: Not until in the gin-house.

Morehouse: Not until ginning commences, and then only a small part of the cotton in addition to the house and gin; the practice is not general.

Other counties: Cotton is not insured until shipped.

50. What are the merchants' commissions and charges for storing, handling, shipping, insurance, etc., to which your crop is subject? What is the total amount of these charges against the farmer per pound or bale?

Morehouse: 25 cents per bale for shipping, $2\frac{1}{2}$ per cent. for selling, $\frac{1}{2}$ per cent. for river and fire insurance, and 1 per cent. for drayage and storage. A great deal of the crop is bought by country merchants in the little town of Bastrop, and some is taken to Monroe, about twenty-five miles distant, and sold. Total charges are about $4 50 per bale.

Caldwell: The total for shipping, selling, etc., amounts to about $3 50 per bale.

Catahoula: Freight varies from $1 to $2; other charges amount to $4 per bale; total, $5 to $6.

Madison: Total charges are about 1 cent per pound, or $4 50 per bale.

1. *Concordia:* $2\frac{1}{2}$ per cent. commission; 75 cents per bale for storing, handling, and shipping, and $\frac{3}{8}$ per cent. for insurance; total about $\frac{3}{8}$ to $\frac{1}{2}$ of a cent. per pound.

2. *Concordia:* Total charges amount to about $3 50 per bale.

1. *Rapides:* Freight, $1 50 per bale; commission, $2\frac{1}{2}$ per cent.; storing and handling, 75 cents per bale; insurance, $\frac{1}{2}$ per cent. The total amounts to 1 to $1\frac{1}{4}$ cent per pound.

2. *Rapides:* The total is about $7 per bale.

West Feliciana: $2\frac{1}{2}$ per cent. commission; 75 cents per bale for weighing, drayage, and labor. The total amounts to about $\frac{3}{4}$ of a cent per pound.

Saint Landry: Regular New Orleans rates are charged; freight charges depend upon the stage of water.

Natchitoches: About $3 50 per bale.

Winn: Not more than $2 per bale.

Saint Helena: About $4 25 per bale.

1. *Tangipahoa:* About $4 per bale, including freights. The crop is generally sold to local merchants.

2. *Tangipahoa:* Freight, $1 50; insurance, 30 cents; storage, weighing, and labor, 75 cents; brokerage, 12 cents per bale; commission, $2\frac{1}{2}$ per cent. Total charges amount to $3 85 per bale.

Saint Tammany: No charges; ship direct.

De Soto: Warehouse charges are 50 to 75 cents per bale; insurance, 1 per cent.; commission, $2\frac{1}{2}$ per cent.

1. *Bossier:* Insurance—river, 50 cents per bale; fire, $\frac{3}{8}$ per cent.; freight, $1 50 per bale; storage in New Orleans, 75 cents; brokerage, 35 cents; commission, $2\frac{1}{2}$ per cent. Total charges, $3 50 per bale.

2, 3, 4. *Bossier:* In Shreveport, per bale, storage, 50 cents; fire insurance, 35 cents per month; drayage, 10 cents. If shipped to New Orleans, river insurance, 50 cents; freight, $1 50; storage, 75 cents; brokerage, 35 cents per bale; fire insurance, $\frac{3}{8}$ per cent.; commission for selling, $2\frac{1}{2}$ per cent. Total, $5 $42\frac{1}{2}$ per bale.

Red River: $2\frac{1}{2}$ per cent. for commission, 75 cents per bale for handling, and $1 for insurance; total, including freight, $4 per bale.

Sabine: The hauling to the shipping point included, it usually costs $1\frac{3}{4}$ cents per pound to sell cotton in New Orleans.

Bienville: About $5 per bale.

Claiborne: The cost of shipping from here and selling cotton in New Orleans is about 2 cents per pound, or $9 per 450-pound bale.

Union: Commission, $2\frac{1}{2}$ per cent.; storing and shipping, 25 cents per bale; insurance, $1\frac{1}{4}$ per cent.; storage after shipping, per month, about $\frac{1}{2}$ per cent. Total charges vary from $4 to $10 per bale.

Franklin: Charges for freight, drayage, storage, labor, weighing, river and fire insurance, and commission, amount to about $4 25 per bale.

51. What is your estimate of the cost of production in your region, exclusive of such charges, and with fair soil and management?

2 *Concordia, Saint Tammany, Saint Helena, Sabine,* 2 *Rapides:* 5 or 6 cents per pound. *Madison, Franklin,* and *Natchitoches:* 7 cents. *Caldwell,* 1 *Rapides, Saint Landry, Winn, Tangipahoa, De Soto,* and *Claiborne:* 8 cents per pound. *Morehouse,* 8 to 10 cents. 1 *Concordia:* $7\frac{1}{2}$ to $8\frac{1}{2}$ cents. *Catahoula:* 10 cents, when raised alone; 9 cents if raised as a surplus crop. *Union:* Under close management, 6 to 8 cents per pound. *Red River:* 5 cents per pound in good seasons; in bad seasons, 25 cents per pound.

Bossier: Under the share system, $4\frac{1}{4}$ cents per pound to the owner for his half, and 7 cents to the laborer for his half. There has been no greater error than the general understanding of the cost of producing cotton. Time and again have I seen the cost put nearly equal to the selling price. Under the share system the planter always makes a profit, and the laborer, if he gets his dues, always gets due pay for labor. Since the war the whole cotton country has become pessimistic and has forgotten how to reason. If cotton be low, rent, labor, stock, and implements are low, or ought to be. So, when cotton is at 6 cents, we ought to calculate by lower prices for rents, labor, etc. *This is my calculation on 30 acres of upland:*

Rent	$60	Produce:	
Rent of mule	25	Pounds clean cotton	6,000
Wear and tear of tools	10	Pounds, planter's half	3,000
Cost of ginning	10		
Pro rata for overseer	25	Value at gin, @ 10 cts. per lb	$300
Total cost	130	Cost of production	130
		Profit to planter	170

Planter's outlay divided by the pounds of cotton he makes, gives $4\frac{1}{4}$ cents as the cost to him of his cotton per pound. Beyond this, he makes a profit on the cotton he takes, a profit on the advances to the laborer, and has the seed besides, worth $16. The baling is got back in the sale as cotton. The ginning and packing is done by the laborers, and so hire of gin only is counted. Because in slavery times he made three times this amount of money on the same land, the planter is dissatisfied, forgetting always that *then* he had three times the capital invested.

INDEX TO COTTON PRODUCTION IN LOUISIANA.

100

REPORT

ON THE

COTTON PRODUCTION OF THE STATE OF MISSISSIPPI,

WITH A DISCUSSION OF

THE GENERAL AGRICULTURAL FEATURES OF THE STATE.

BY

EUGENE W. HILGARD, Ph. D.,

PROFESSOR OF AGRICULTURE AT THE UNIVERSITY OF CALIFORNIA, FORMERLY AT THE UNIVERSITY OF MISSISSIPPI, AND STATE GEOLOGIST OF MISSISSIPPI,

SPECIAL CENSUS AGENT.

TABLE OF CONTENTS.

LETTER OF TRANSMITTAL.

Hon. C. W. SEATON,
Superintendent of Census.

DEAR SIR: I have the honor to transmit herewith a report on the cotton production of the state of Mississippi, with a general description of its physico-geographical and agricultural features, special descriptions of the several counties, and cultural and economic details of cotton production, with discussion thereof.

In the elaboration of this report I have conformed to the general plan originally suggested by Superintendent Walker and subsequently arranged in detail by myself, which has been substantially adhered to in the series of reports of which this forms a part, covering the whole of the cotton-producing area of the United States.

The sources of information upon which I have chiefly drawn for the substance of this report, aside from the census returns, are the published reports and unpublished records of the geological and agricultural survey of the state and the answers to schedule questions received from 42 out of the 74 counties in the state.

The published reports alluded to are the following:

I. *First Report of the Geological and Agricultural Survey of Mississippi, by B. L. C. Wailes, Jackson, 1854.*—This report contains a good deal of historic and general descriptive matter, including a chapter on culture, illustrated by plates, some general facts as to the geological formations of the state, as well as plates of fossils from the Jackson shell-beds, but without descriptions of the same.

II. *Preliminary Report on the Geology and Agriculture of Mississippi, by L. Harper, Jackson, 1857.*—This is somewhat of an oddity, both in a literary and scientific point of view, among the reports of American state surveys. It gives an account of the author's own observations on several excursions, and what purports to be a report and elaborations of the observations made by myself during a season's work in the Cretaceous, Tertiary, and Drift area of northeastern Mississippi in the capacity of assistant. The author's peculiar bias has, however, so far overshadowed both the facts and the theories that I cannot recognize either as my own work. I have subsequently fully covered again all the ground gone over by him.

III. *Report on the Geology and Agriculture of Mississippi, by E. W. Hilgard, Jackson, 1860.*—This report covers the field-work of three seasons, as also the laboratory and palæontological work done by myself personally up to the time of publication, including also, so far as relevant and reliable, the observations of my predecessors in the office of state geologist. Though printed in 1860, the intervention of the civil war prevented its actual publication and distribution until late in 1865.

By an act of the legislature, passed in 1861, the state survey was continued with a small appropriation during the war, and upon the cessation of hostilities placed *ipso facto* upon its former footing. Little progress could, of course, be made during that stormy period, but between 1866 and 1872 the field and laboratory work was continued at intervals by myself and assistants, Dr. E. A. Smith, now state geologist of Alabama, and Dr. R. H. Loughridge, since special agent of the census; also, for a short time, by Dr. George Little, late state geologist of Georgia. The work was stopped in 1872, and no publication of the field and laboratory work (mostly done by Dr. Smith) has until now been made.

IV. The MS. notes and reports of Dr. Smith, together with the laboratory record books and my own original field notes, were courteously loaned to the Census Office by consent of the board of trustees of the University of Mississippi (under whose charge these records had passed) through the chancellor, Rev. Alexander T. Stewart, and all have been freely drawn upon for the purposes of the present report. It should be stated that of the unpublished field-work the explorations of the Mississippi bottom region, as well as of the counties lying just north of the "Central prairie region" (the territory of the Buhrstone or "Siliceous Claiborne" geological group), were made by Dr. Smith, who also made the bulk of the soil and marl analyses not given in the last published report, but here inserted. (a) A summary of his observations in the Yazoo bottom was, however, published in the proceedings of the American Association for the Advancement of Science for 1871, page 252.

Having made a close and detailed study of the soils of the state for many years, with a special view to the deduction and verification of the practical indications furnished by a study of their chemical composition and of all physical characters, these are naturally dwelt upon more in detail, and perhaps more with a view to showing the practical bearings of such investigations than is the case in other reports of this series, in which the subject is only casually brought up, and with respect to a few of the most characteristic and widely different soils. I trust that these discussions, as well as the report at large, may prove useful in making better known the great agricultural resources of Mississippi, and in enlisting still further the interest of her farmers on behalf of improved and progressive agriculture.

All of which is respectfully submitted.

EUG. W. HILGARD, *Special Agent.*

a Of the 120 chemical soil analyses here reported, 22 only appear in my report of 1860, with 14 of marls and greensands, the number of which now on record is 54, although only some representative ones are here introduced. No additional full analyses have been made under the auspices of the Census Office, but the determinations of humus here communicated, as well as some of hygroscopic coefficients, have been so added.

202

TABULATED RESULTS OF THE ENUMERATION.

TABLE I.—AREA, POPULATION, TILLED LANDS, AND COTTON PRODUCTION.

Counties.	Land area.	POPULATION.					Average per square mile.	TILLED LANDS.		Per cent. of tilled land.	COTTON PRODUCTION.		Average per acre.			Cotton acreage per square mile.	Bales per square mile.
		Total.	Male.	Female.	White.	Color'd.		Acres.	Per cent. of area.		Acres.	Bales.	Rais.	Seed cotton.	Lint.		
	Sq. mis.												Lbs.	Lbs.			
The State	46,340	1,131,597	567,177	564,430	479,398	652,199	24.4	4,997,561	16.6	42.7	2,106,214	963,111	0.46	687	219	45.5	20.8
NORTHEASTERN PRAIRIE REGION.																	
Prairie belt.																	
Alcorn	400	14,272	7,095	7,177	9,862	4,409	35.7	82,966	20.5	25.9	18,362	7,477	0.40	570	190	47.2	18.7
Prentiss	410	12,158	6,041	6,117	9,727	2,431	29.7	59,788	22.8	31.2	18,610	7,307	0.39	555	185	45.4	17.6
Lee	440	20,470	10,231	10,149	13,656	7,814	27.0	101,822	29.5	37.9	38,378	14,406	0.37	538	176	71.4	26.7
Chickasaw	500	17,905	8,925	8,980	7,696	10,209	35.8	97,323	30.4	39.6	38,477	12,861	0.33	471	157	77.0	25.7
Monroe	790	28,553	13,991	14,562	10,551	18,002	36.1	155,308	30.3	45.8	71,402	23,530	0.33	471	157	90.4	30.3
Clay	400	17,367	8,504	8,862	5,255	12,112	43.4	81,441	31.8	51.1	41,966	13,137	0.32	456	152	104.1	32.8
Oktibbeha	420	15,973	7,857	8,121	5,109	10,389	37.2	65,365	22.8	45.4	29,679	9,929	0.33	471	157	68.0	23.1
Lowndes	500	28,244	13,961	14,283	5,588	22,656	56.5	128,312	39.5	51.2	64,670	21,586	0.34	486	162	129.3	43.8
Noxubee	620	29,874	14,906	15,066	5,302	24,572	43.9	151,704	34.9	54.4	83,483	25,294	0.31	441	147	131.8	27.2
Total	4,650	184,621	91,503	93,918	71,737	113,064	39.7	891,989	30.0	45.3	404,418	136,027	0.34	486	162	87.0	26.3
Pontotoc ridge.																	
Tippah	450	12,967	6,227	6,540	9,902	3,065	28.6	55,092	19.1	34.0	18,756	7,434	0.40	570	190	41.7	16.5
Union	360	13,030	6,416	6,614	9,922	3,606	36.2	56,999	24.7	37.8	21,255	8,250	0.39	555	185	59.0	22.9
Pontotoc	530	13,858	6,932	6,926	9,509	4,349	26.1	73,848	21.5	29.4	21,443	8,085	0.38	542	181	40.5	15.3
Total	1,340	39,755	19,675	20,080	29,343	10,412	29.7	184,939	21.6	33.2	61,461	23,766	0.39	555	185	45.9	17.7
YELLOW LOAM REGION.																	
Brown loam table-lands.																	
Benton	260	11,023	5,577	5,446	5,777	5,246	30.6	55,501	24.1	40.4	23,401	8,123	0.36	513	171	62.2	22.6
Marshall	720	29,330	14,612	14,718	10,992	18,338	40.7	161,091	34.9	41.9	97,411	26,441	0.39	555	185	91.6	36.7
De Soto	680	23,994	11,613	11,811	7,561	15,343	49.3	118,343	40.1	51.1	80,488	28,480	0.47	669	223	131.5	61.9
Tate	390	18,721	9,557	9,164	9,094	9,627	48.0	124,980	50.1	58.6	48,345	22,653	0.47	669	223	124.7	58.1
Panola	680	28,353	14,253	14,100	9,521	18,831	41.7	168,445	34.1	45.2	67,060	30,055	0.45	642	214	98.6	44.2
La Fayette	720	21,671	10,962	10,709	11,385	10,286	30.1	88,423	12.8	40.8	35,300	15,214	0.43	612	204	49.0	21.1
Yalobusha	400	15,649	7,865	7,784	7,532	8,116	34.0	1,850	34.4	42.7	30,396	12,969	0.43	612	204	66.1	28.2
Grenada	440	12,071	5,990	6,062	5,236	6,835	27.4	49,600	17.6	51.2	25,390	10,225	0.40	570	190	57.7	23.2
Carroll	640	17,795	8,901	8,804	7,691	9,964	27.8	98,730	21.2	43.8	37,957	17,422	0.46	657	219	59.3	27.2
Holmes	750	27,164	13,568	13,598	6,911	20,953	36.1	204,993	42.7	50.5	62,558	30,463	0.46	660	239	83.4	40.6
Total	5,620	204,700	102,965	101,715	79,861	134,839	38.4	1,107,944	30.8	41.3	487,215	202,058	0.44	627	209	81.4	34.0
Short-leaf pine and oak upland region.																	
Tishomingo	450	8,774	4,350	4,424	7,611	1,163	19.5	28,419	13.3	19.7	7,556	2,672	0.35	498	166	16.8	5.9
Itawamba	550	10,663	5,391	5,372	9,555	1,168	19.4	51,615	14.6	28.9	14,861	5,113	0.34	486	162	27.0	9.3
Calhoun	580	13,492	6,781	6,711	10,191	3,301	23.3	60,576	16.3	31.4	19,028	9,596	0.50	714	238	32.8	16.4
Montgomery	430	13,348	6,652	6,696	6,671	6,677	31.0	60,398	21.9	40.9	24,636	10,541	0.43	612	204	57.3	24.0
Sumner	400	9,534	4,749	4,785	7,239	2,295	23.5	40,701	15.9	23.4	13,012	5,226	0.46	657	219	34.0	13.6
Choctaw	270	9,086	4,510	4,826	5,697	3,489	33.5	43,779	34.8	31.6	13,497	5,737	0.43	612	204	50.0	21.3
Winston	690	10,087	5,043	5,044	6,113	3,974	14.6	45,091	10.2	23.4	15,081	5,864	0.29	555	185	21.9	8.5
Attala	720	19,868	9,988	10,000	11,653	8,335	27.6	93,084	20.2	28.6	35,986	15,296	0.43	612	204	48.9	97.3
Leake	580	13,146	6,648	6,498	8,104	5,042	22.7	52,460	15.8	41.0	21,016	8,330	0.43	649	181	21.6	13.8
Neshoba	580	8,741	4,300	4,418	5,583	3,158	15.1	44,983	25.4	...	11,927	4,677	0.32	486	152	24.2	7.7
Kemper	720	15,719	7,931	...	7,119	8,610	21.6	78,315	18.3	36.1	28,360	9,426	0.30	429	143	27.7	11.2
Newton	580	15,486	6,785	6,701	8,428	5,008	23.2	55,019	15.6	32.8	19,589	6,341	0.32	456	152	32.8	10.9
Total	6,580	143,984	72,804	72,070	95,737	50,307	22.3	673,091	16.0	34.2	230,090	89,354	0.39	555	185	35.0	13.6

TABLE I.—AREA, POPULATION, TILLED LANDS, AND COTTON PRODUCTION—Continued.

Counties.	Land area.	POPULATION.						TILLED LANDS.			COTTON PRODUCTION.					Cotton acreage per square mile.	Bales per square mile.
		Total.	Male.	Female.	White.	Color'd.	Average per square mile.	Acres.	Per cent. of area.	Per cent. of tilled lands.	Acres.	Bales.	Average per acre.				
													Bale.	Seed cotton.	Lint.		
CANE HILLS.	*Sq. mls.*													*Lbs.*	*Lbs.*		
Warren	580	21,288	15,542	15,596	5,717	22,531	52.1	60,631	15.6	56.8	34,127	22,950	0.67	954	318	56.9	38.3
Claiborne	460	16,768	8,228	8,540	3,910	12,856	36.5	97,175	33.0	34.1	33,121	18,518	0.56	798	266	72.0	40.3
Jefferson	510	17,314	8,473	8,841	4,260	13,054	33.9	62,218	19.1	51.7	32,141	18,512	0.58	829	276	63.0	36.3
Adams	410	22,649	10,673	11,976	4,796	17,853	55.2	67,853	25.9	47.3	32,117	19,026	0.59	840	280	78.3	46.4
Wilkinson	650	17,815	8,648	9,167	3,570	14,245	27.4	62,065	14.9	54.3	33,720	16,620	0.49	699	233	51.9	25.6
Total	2,630	105,784	51,584	54,420	25,253	80,531	40.2	349,342	20.8	47.8	165,226	95,626	0.58	828	276	62.8	36.4
MISSISSIPPI ALLUVIAL REGION.																	
Tunica	440	8,461	4,628	3,833	1,256	7,205	19.2	30,318	14.0	76.0	29,681	18,008	0.60	855	285	67.9	40.9
Coahoma	500	13,568	7,368	6,200	2,412	11,156	27.1	51,741	16.2	62.7	32,984	26,287	0.80	1,140	380	65.9	52.6
Quitman	400	1,407	784	623	592	815	3.5	5,714	2.2	59.9	3,420	2,327	0.68	969	323	8.6	5.8
Tallahatchie	540	10,926	5,605	5,321	4,168	6,758	17.1	42,501	10.4	52.9	22,462	11,570	0.52	741	247	35.1	18.1
Le Flore	610	10,246	5,419	4,827	2,230	8,016	16.6	40,156	10.3	44.2	17,790	11,925	0.67	954	318	29.1	18.5
Sunflower	720	4,661	2,542	2,119	1,764	2,897	6.5	13,968	3.0	50.8	7,107	5,707	0.80	1,140	380	9.9	7.9
Bolivar	900	18,652	10,105	8,547	2,694	15,958	20.7	73,467	12.6	59.0	48,330	36,419	0.84	1,197	399	48.1	40.5
Washington	900	25,367	13,371	11,996	3,478	21,889	28.2	95,893	16.6	66.1	63,400	54,873	0.87	1,229	413	70.5	61.0
Yazoo	1,000	33,845	17,354	16,591	8,498	25,347	33.8	156,223	26.4	52.2	83,184	46,321	0.58	826	276	83.2	48.3
Sharkey	540	6,306	3,406	2,900	1,405	4,901	11.7	23,328	6.8	72.0	17,041	14,162	0.83	1,182	394	31.6	26.2
Issaquena	390	10,004	5,291	4,713	826	9,178	25.7	37,639	13.1	56.0	18,293	16,150	0.88	1,254	418	46.9	41.4
Total	7,040	143,443	75,773	67,670	29,923	114,120	20.4	574,985	12.8	58.9	288,622	245,750	0.72	1,041	347	43.1	34.9
CENTRAL PRAIRIE REGION.																	
Madison	720	25,866	12,665	13,201	5,946	19,920	35.9	127,504	27.7	44.2	56,390	21,538	0.38	543	181	78.3	29.9
Hinds	860	43,958	22,176	21,782	11,675	32,283	54.9	184,607	36.1	42.3	80,013	36,684	0.46	657	219	100.0	45.9
Rankin	800	16,752	8,192	8,560	7,198	9,559	20.9	69,518	13.6	43.4	30,151	11,775	0.39	555	185	37.7	14.7
Scott	560	10,845	5,369	5,476	6,633	4,212	18.7	30,711	10.7	41.0	15,282	6,227	0.38	543	181	28.1	10.7
Jasper	680	12,126	6,048	6,078	6,344	5,882	17.8	56,213	13.4	34.8	20,905	6,228	0.31	441	147	29.9	9.2
Clarke	650	15,021	7,371	7,650	7,181	7,840	23.1	45,888	11.0	34.7	15,986	4,623	0.29	414	138	24.5	7.2
Wayne	790	8,741	4,320	4,421	4,971	3,770	11.1	20,977	4.1	36.0	7,369	1,979	0.26	372	124	9.6	2.5
Total	5,620	133,309	66,141	67,168	49,843	83,466	26.6	546,611	17.0	41.5	226,629	89,124	0.39	555	185	45.1	17.9
LONG-LEAF PINE AND COAST REGION.																	
Long-leaf pine, oak, and hickory uplands.																	
Copiah	750	27,552	13,605	13,947	13,101	14,451	36.7	119,366	25.0	45.6	54,816	23,736	0.43	612	204	72.8	31.6
Lincoln	580	13,547	6,846	6,701	7,701	5,846	23.4	55,409	14.9	31.8	17,272	6,296	0.36	512	171	29.8	10.8
Pike	730	16,688	8,374	8,314	5,572	8,116	22.3	53,803	11.7	36.9	19,842	6,507	0.33	471	157	27.6	9.0
Franklin	560	9,729	4,791	4,938	4,852	4,877	17.4	37,580	10.5	48.3	16,211	6,042	0.44	627	209	32.5	10.7
Amite	720	14,004	6,906	7,098	5,494	8,510	19.5	62,095	13.5	44.7	27,740	9,953	0.36	513	171	38.5	13.8
Lawrence	690	9,430	4,809	4,611	4,967	4,469	18.2	47,220	11.9	27.6	17,806	5,967	0.34	486	162	28.7	9.6
Simpson	580	8,008	4,025	3,983	4,994	3,014	13.8	31,479	8.5	28.1	8,855	3,501	0.40	570	190	15.3	6.0
Smith	600	8,088	4,053	4,025	6,452	1,636	13.5	32,155	8.4	32.8	10,543	3,721	0.35	498	166	17.6	6.2
Lauderdale	680	21,501	10,608	10,893	9,959	11,542	31.6	70,249	16.1	46.1	32,972	9,350	0.29	414	138	47.6	13.8
Total	5,810	128,537	64,097	64,450	66,062	62,475	22.1	510,056	13.7	40.6	207,266	77,053	0.37	528	176	35.7	13.3
Long-leaf pine hills and flats.																	
Covington	560	5,993	3,006	2,987	4,034	1,959	10.8	30,390	8.2	22.9	6,968	2,071	0.30	429	143	12.0	3.6
Jones	700	3,826	1,874	1,954	3,480	350	5.5	12,822	2.9	21.8	2,794	624	0.22	315	105	4.0	0.9
Marion	1,500	6,901	3,439	3,462	4,450	2,451	4.6	18,080	1.9	26.1	4,717	1,579	0.33	471	157	3.1	1.1
Perry	1,000	3,427	1,732	1,695	2,357	1,070	3.4	10,081	1.6	5.3	537	146	0.27	384	128	0.5	......
Greene	790	3,194	1,605	1,589	2,381	813	4.0	5,997	1.2	......	35	12	0.34	486	162	......	......
Jackson	1,140	7,607	3,905	3,702	5,124	2,483	6.7	4,186	0.6	......	......	......	......	......	......	......	......
Harrison	1,000	7,895	3,948	3,947	5,749	2,146	7.9	2,849	0.4	......	20	11	0.42	600	200	......	......
Hancock	940	6,439	3,246	3,193	4,635	1,804	6.9	4,390	0.7	......	......	......	......	......	......	......	......
Total	7,650	45,284	22,755	22,529	32,190	13,085	5.9	88,604	1.8	17.0	15,077	4,443	0.29	414	138	2.0	0.5

II.—ACREAGE AND PRODUCTION OF THE CHIEF CROPS OF THE STATE.

Counties.	COTTON.		INDIAN CORN.		OATS.		WHEAT.		SWEET POTATOES.	
	Acres.	Bales.	Acres.	Bushels.	Acres.	Bushels.	Acres.	Bushels.	Acres.	Bushels.
Total for the State	2,106,214	963,111	1,570,550	2 1,340,800	196,497	1,959,620	43,534	218,580	41,874	3,610,600
NORTHEASTERN PRAIRIE REGION.										
1. Prairies.										
Alcorn	18,862	7,477	22,589	381,365	2,356	31,989	1,072	5,070	224	16,714
Prentiss	18,610	7,307	23,018	368,777	2,806	35,534	893	4,798	364	31,466
Lee	33,378	14,406	36,073	596,899	4,676	48,047	1,480	7,387	643	49,702
Chickasaw	36,477	13,861	34,358	512,005	3,725	49,627	1,415	9,933	692	55,265
Monroe	71,402	23,880	53,421	700,967	7,278	76,270	4,114	16,396	1,217	100,540
Clay	41,556	18,137	26,295	400,397	3,117	35,592	431	2,137	514	46,533
Oktibbeha	38,579	9,929	25,261	306,558	3,386	39,063	1,068	6,078	611	54,681
Lowndes	64,570	21,698	43,055	562,726	3,784	41,230	1,618	8,060	515	33,873
Noxubee	82,463	25,394	50,904	741,542	5,429	74,165	29	186	825	70,446
Total	404,413	136,027	314,674	4,074,251	33,471	431,467	12,176	61,056	5,605	464,192
2. Pontotoc ridge.										
Tippah	18,758	7,434	33,348	385,623	3,814	36,435	3,587	17,941	375	24,853
Union	21,255	8,259	35,884	429,040	2,695	26,413	2,426	13,355	456	33,218
Pontotoc	21,448	8,085	26,588	414,335	2,169	18,826	2,751	14,692	500	42,028
Total	61,461	23,768	75,810	1,228,998	8,678	81,674	8,764	45,888	1,331	100,099
YELLOW LOAM REGION.										
1. Brown loam table-lands.										
Benton	23,401	8,123	22,977	330,689	1,735	15,846	1,285	6,073	245	15,313
Marshall	67,411	26,441	50,140	684,062	3,130	26,646	3,094	14,605	669	43,373
De Soto	60,488	26,489	37,452	561,272	1,688	18,008	1,236	7,283	493	46,399
Tate	48,245	22,653	33,321	467,144	1,762	17,628	1,100	6,496	286	22,735
Panola	67,080	30,055	43,091	531,193	2,119	22,016	1,602	9,351	526	45,399
La Fayette	35,309	15,214	35,809	498,614	4,091	36,375	2,052	9,222	401	31,200
Yalobusha	36,398	12,989	23,609	275,309	1,728	17,479	594	2,961	517	42,843
Grenada	23,390	10,225	15,906	163,580	568	6,238	6	68	364	27,142
Holmes	62,556	30,463	37,355	468,614	1,297	17,441	50	488	822	60,906
Carroll	37,957	17,428	30,019	315,722	1,977	22,134	337	1,972	479	43,297
Total	457,215	202,068	339,579	4,297,195	16,996	206,816	11,968	58,534	4,797	377,676
2. Short-leaf pine and oak upland region.										
Tishomingo	7,555	2,672	15,965	280,654	3,327	25,362	702	3,904	332	25,047
Itawamba	14,851	5,112	22,955	304,682	3,154	21,772	1,918	8,580	252	32,029
Calhoun	19,028	9,886	22,414	358,919	4,464	44,080	908	4,753	982	43,178
Montgomery	24,696	10,541	17,765	200,650	3,178	31,275	148	630	420	32,076
Sumner	18,613	6,226	18,900	287,962	3,269	29,544	1,874	8,379	487	37,544
Choctaw	13,497	5,787	18,139	243,287	3,931	38,706	2,215	9,413	436	34,197
Winston	15,081	5,864	17,181	217,796	4,170	37,075	902	4,580	451	43,787
Attala	35,950	15,265	33,784	413,532	6,688	66,106	1,400	6,921	819	68,722
Leake	24,000	9,016	21,390	256,331	4,749	44,070	294	1,537	498	41,504
Neshoba	14,621	4,477	15,752	207,784	3,512	26,810	222	1,215	609	36,861
Kemper	26,280	8,430	28,346	347,258	5,706	37,599	56	255	839	76,566
Newton	19,589	6,941	20,636	281,307	6,716	56,336	127	858	675	64,601
Total	226,990	90,254	253,192	3,373,822	50,954	460,587	10,767	49,990	6,617	539,107
CANE HILLS.										
Warren	24,13?	12,353	10,871	109,537	90	1,043			366	19,394
Claiborne	55,141	18,018	15,744	197,565	82	1,290			457	46,281
Jefferson	33,141	18,513	16,365	261,536	212	3,195			750	66,179
Adams	32,117	19,026	9,027	126,647	57	900			1,043	57,489
Wilkinson	33,720	16,620	15,068	206,986	304	3,035			743	56,347
Total	165,226	95,626	66,565	973,353	724	9,474			3,279	256,690
MISSISSIPPI ALLUVIAL REGION.										
Tunica	29,681	18,008	9,447	196,352	127	2,350			38	4,797
Coahoma	53,964	36,397	14,297	328,054	138	2,340	76	832	105	7,035
Quitman	5,420	3,327	1,477	34,510	24	580				
Tallahatchie	22,463	11,370	16,169	260,719	772	9,282	108	870	172	18,506
Le Flore	17,730	11,925	10,965	144,378	76	1,351			53	5,400
Sunflower	7,107	5,797	3,730	61,398	80	1,315			103	9,740

II.—ACREAGE AND PRODUCTION OF THE CHIEF CROPS OF THE STATE—Continued.

Counties.	COTTON.		INDIAN CORN.		OATS.		WHEAT.		SWEET POTATOES.	
	Acres.	Bales.	Acres.	Bushels.	Acres.	Bushels.	Acres.	Bushels.	Acres.	Bushels.
MISSISSIPPI ALLUVIAL REGION—continued.										
Bolivar	43,390	36,419	18,624	388,466	187	5,254			406	23,415
Washington	63,409	54,873	16,515	400,418	65	680			266	27,450
Yazoo	88,184	48,321	38,207	534,615	454	5,824			1,343	94,850
Sharkey	17,041	14,162	7,540	169,130	36	350			1	50
Issaquena	18,208	16,150	3,849	89,620	17	260			62	5,005
Total	235,822	245,750	198,820	2,548,460	1,965	23,392	184	1,802	2,449	196,496
CENTRAL PRAIRIE REGION.										
Madison	56,393	21,538	97,089	381,297	1,490	21,107	22	221	1,128	105,406
Hinds	80,013	36,684	47,810	532,086	1,962	26,380	16	130	1,368	132,920
Rankin	30,181	11,775	23,450	271,996	5,781	55,450	4	45	1,009	98,482
Scott	16,292	6,227	15,664	193,013	5,129	50,370	111	729	493	47,604
Jasper	20,305	6,226	19,594	202,643	5,467	36,590	5	100	790	70,313
Clarke	15,905	4,603	17,336	174,712	3,193	30,101			683	54,078
Wayne	7,550	1,979	10,411	95,890	1,608	13,044	7	43	738	43,305
Total	226,630	86,124	172,296	1,850,187	24,630	255,532	165	1,267	6,229	582,091
LONG-LEAF PINE, OAK, AND HICKORY UPLANDS.										
Copiah	54,616	23,736	38,292	447,197	5,920	50,021			1,339	156,580
Lincoln	17,272	6,286	19,843	209,747	5,704	49,924			908	67,344
Pike	19,543	6,507	19,248	200,810	6,003	55,909	8	60	979	74,838
Franklin	16,211	5,042	12,045	145,581	1,012	9,021			655	62,486
Amite	27,749	9,962	22,589	262,352	3,184	27,180			947	80,806
Lawrence	17,866	5,967	20,758	217,041	4,845	41,809	6	25	965	89,679
Simpson	8,855	3,501	14,165	147,672	4,211	34,837	5	40	435	50,623
Smith	10,543	3,721	14,614	156,922	5,009	46,959	78	478	504	65,681
Lauderdale	33,373	9,850	23,345	254,798	5,907	57,843	5	50	1,212	103,095
Total	207,286	77,052	184,890	2,048,150	41,255	382,472	102	653	8,024	751,191
Long-leaf pine hills and flats.										
Covington	6,968	2,071	10,682	115,088	3,553	25,215			508	50,575
Jones	2,794	824	5,664	47,269	3,451	30,592			369	41,580
Marion	4,717	1,979	9,087	99,941	1,348	12,302			726	55,630
Perry	527	146	4,466	38,446	2,615	20,308			465	43,165
Greene	35	12	3,563	27,271	891	5,790			477	33,095
Jackson			128	1,826	5	90			43	4,090
Harrison	36	11	1,064	15,130	142	2,110			241	23,163
Hancock			41	410	20	5,800			632	113,630
Total	15,077	4,443	34,705	345,381	12,064	106,906			3,544	360,117

PART I.

PHYSICO-GEOGRAPHICAL AND AGRICULTURAL FEATURES

OF THE

STATE OF MISSISSIPPI.

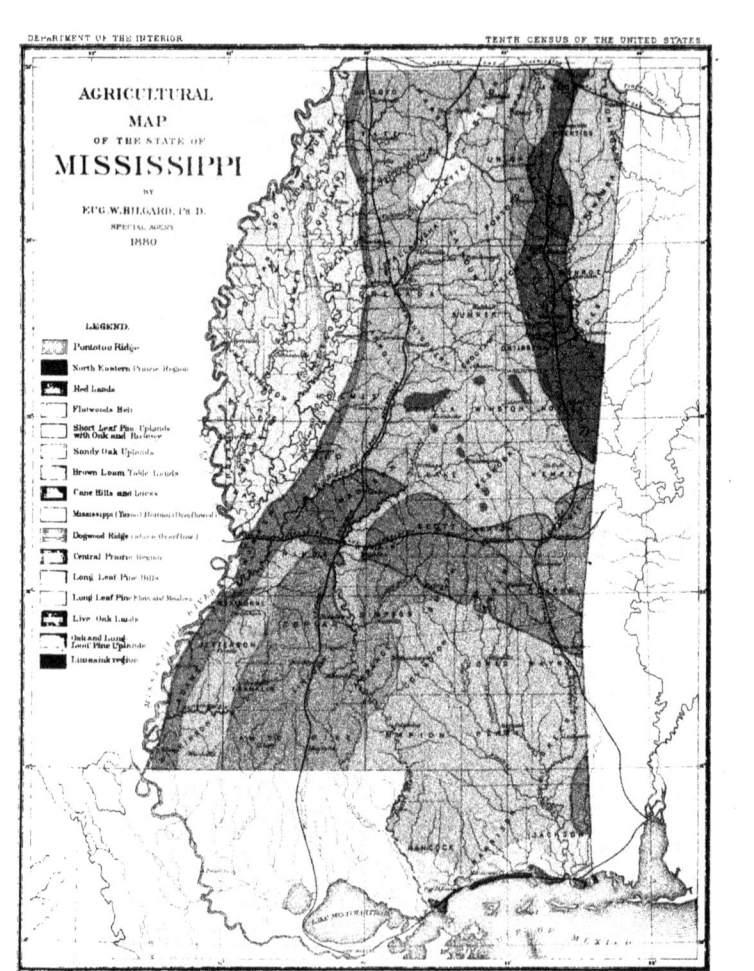

AGRICULTURAL
MAP
OF THE STATE OF
MISSISSIPPI
BY
EUG. W. HILGARD, Ph. D.
SPECIAL AGENT
1880

LEGEND.

Pontotoc Ridge

North Eastern Prairie Region

Red Lands

Flatwoods Belt

Short Leaf Pine Uplands
with Oak and Hickory

Sandy Oak Uplands

Brown Loam Table Lands

Cane Hills and Loess

Mississippi (Yazoo) Bottom (Bayou Deserted)

Dogwood Ridge (where flooded)

Central Prairie Region

Long Leaf Pine Hills

Long Leaf Pine Flats and Swamps

Live Oak Lands

Oak and Long
Leaf Pine Uplands

Limesink region

Scale

OUTLINE OF THE PHYSICAL GEOGRAPHY

STATE OF MISSISSIPPI.

Mississippi lies between the meridians of 88° 6′ and 91° 37′ of west longitude, and between the parallels of 30° 11′ and 35° north latitude. The greatest dimensions of the state are 331 miles north and south and 188 miles east and west. The total area (including half of the boundary portions of Mississippi and Pearl rivers and Bay Saint Louis) is 46,810 square miles, of which 470 square miles is water surface. About 7,460 square miles are lowlands of the Mississippi bottom. Of this area, 7,100 belong to the "Yazoo bottom" plain. The rest, or five-sixths of the state's area, is rolling, hilly, or sometimes almost level timbered uplands.

CLIMATE.—The climate of Mississippi is a "warm temperate" one in the literal sense of the term, the extremes of temperature prevailing farther north being tempered materially by the influence of the winds blowing from the Gulf of Mexico. The extreme cold of winter sometimes occurring in the northern part of the state (at Oxford and Holly Springs, where ordinarily the winter minimum is from 15° to 20° F.) is 10° F., sufficient to kill fig trees six years old; but at Grenada, on the Yalobusha river, the fig rarely suffers. At Vicksburg and Natchez the extreme cold thus far observed is 17° F.; inland, at Jackson, several degrees lower. It is only near the sea-coast that the orange and lemon can ordinarily be grown without winter protection in the open air. A warm belt extends along the Mississippi river, but, unlike that of the coast, it is liable to "cold snaps" from the influence of northwest winds, which render the outdoor culture of the subtropical fruits precarious even as far south as Baton Rouge. Cool belts or regions are formed by the elevated ridge lands at the heads of the larger rivers of the state. The summers are long, practically including May and September. During this time the weather is warm (the usual range of the thermometer being from 70° to 90° F.), but excessive heat and sultriness, such as prevails so commonly during the shorter summers in the middle and northern states, is rare, and sunstroke is almost unknown.

The following table (extracted from those published by the Smithsonian Institution in 1876) gives the mean temperatures for each of the four seasons for some of the prominent points in the state where observations have been made. Where these were deficient, those for points lying near the line in Tennessee and Louisiana have been introduced:

	Spring.	Summer.	Autumn.	Winter.	Year.
INTERIOR STATIONS.					
La Grange, Tennessee	62.2	79.4	62.6	43.2	61.7
Grenada, Mississippi	61.4	78.6	63.9	46.2	62.6
Columbus, Mississippi	62.2	78.9	63.2	45.6	62.2
Jackson, Mississippi	65.6	78.7	64.6	49.3	64.4
Brookhaven, Mississippi	64.4	78.1	63.5	46.7	62.9
Paulding, Mississippi	66.9	81.2	67.2	50.9	66.6
RIVER AND COAST.					
Memphis, Tennessee	60.9	79.5	60.8	42.1	60.7
Vicksburg, Mississippi	65.8	80.5	65.6	50.6	65.6
Natchez, Mississippi	65.5	79.8	65.5	50.4	65.3
Baton Rouge, Louisiana	68.9	81.4	68.1	54.9	68.2
Pass Christian, Mississippi		82.7			

It will be noted that, with one exception, the average temperatures given for interior stations are decidedly lower than for stations on the Mississippi river in corresponding latitudes. Compare in this respect Vicksburg with Jackson and Natchez with Brookhaven. In the case of Memphis and La Grange, however, the relation is reversed, from causes not thus far understood, but evidently operating so

0

211

as to cause exceptional cold waves reaching Memphis to be felt more severely in a southeasterly direction to a distance of from 50 to 70 miles inland, in the northwestern corner of Mississippi, than at similar distances due east in Tennessee. Still farther inland, at Columbus, the autumn and winter temperatures are found to be lower than at Grenada, nearly one-third of a degree farther to the north.

The observations thus far available are not sufficiently numerous to trace very accurately the limits of the several climatic divisions of the state; but the discussion of those made, as laid down in the maps of the Smithsonian Institution, may be summarized as follows: The isothermal line indicating a mean annual temperature of 64° F. crosses the state almost centrally from east to west. Southward, the line of 68° traverses it a short distance inland from the gulf shore, while to the northward the line of the annual mean of 60° meanders near the state line. Roughly speaking, then, these lines, indicating differences of 4° in the annual mean, lie about 150 miles apart inland and south, so that, on the average, there is a change of 1° in the annual mean for every 31 miles. But these general features are materially modified in many regions. The influence of elevation in reducing the temperatures both of winter and summer makes itself felt in the northeastern portion of the state, on the headwaters of the larger rivers, the Hatchie, Tallahatchie, and Tombigbee, and more or less on those of the Yalobusha, Big Black, and Pearl rivers; likewise in the ridge lands traversed by the Great Northern railroad between Jackson and New Orleans, in the counties of Copiah, Lincoln, Amite, and Pike. There is a warm belt along the Mississippi river, and a region of warm summers, especially on the waters of Pearl and Leaf rivers, in the southeastern portion of the state; on the other hand, a region of occasional low winter minima extends from Vicksburg southward along the river to Baton Rouge, apparently the eastern edge of the "Texas northers".

Late frosts sometimes injure the early vegetables, and more frequently the early blooming fruits, among which the peach and apricot are so liable to damage in the northern part of the state as to induce a horticultural convention, held at Memphis, to decide that these fruits could not be recommended as a money-crop for market purposes. Among the many varieties of peaches in cultivation, however, some always escape injury, and apples, pears, and cherries rarely suffer at all. In one case, even the half-grown foliage of the forest trees has been killed northward of Grenada late in April by a northwest storm following a rain from the west.

WINDS AND RAINFALL.—During the summer the winds are altogether predominantly from the south, and blow quite steadily and gently, greatly relieving the sun's heat and allowing sultriness only for short periods. Between southeast and due south these winds bring clear, warm weather; but as they veer toward southwest the sky clouds over, and between southwest and due west lie the winds that bring warm, steady rains, usually without any severe electrical excitement. The winds between due west and northwest in summer bring the violent thunder-storms, coming suddenly, and sometimes rising to the violence and cyclonic character of tornadoes. In winter the northwest winds bring the severe "cold snaps", usually of only a few days' duration, and accompanied by but a slight precipitation, so that snow rarely falls to the depth of more than a few inches even in the northern part of the state, and is quickly melted by the south and southwest winds with warm rains. As the wind rarely lies for any length of time between northwest, east, and southwest, either in summer or winter, the change from a cold and dry northwest wind, with snow flurries, to warm south and southwest winds, laden with moisture, is frequent and rapid in winter, giving that season a character of rather unenjoyable dampness overhead and slushiness under foot, which are, however, offset by its brevity, for the temperate and beautiful autumn often extends into the latter half of December, and the middle of February usually finds the early vegetables fairly up in the gardens, even in the northern part of the state.

The subjoined table exhibits the amount of rainfall (including snow) for some principal points at which observations have been made for a sufficient length of time to give reliable averages:

	Spring.	Summer.	Autumn.	Winter.	Year.
INTERIOR STATIONS.					
La Grange, Tennessee	18.2	10.9	8.0	11.7	45.8
Grenada, Mississippi	19.4	10.3	8.3	17.3	55.3
Columbus, Mississippi	15.7	12.0	10.3	17.5	55.5
Jackson, Mississippi	11.5	14.2	10.3	18.6	54.6
Brookhaven, Mississippi	20.0	15.5	10.7	17.7	63.9
Paulding, Mississippi	14.6	12.9	8.4	15.4	51.3
RIVER AND COAST.					
Memphis, Tennessee	13.7	9.1	9.0	12.7	44.5
Vicksburg, Mississippi	14.6	11.8	10.3	15.1	51.3
Natchez, Mississippi	14.5	12.4	11.4	16.1	54.4
Baton Rouge, Louisiana	14.1	18.6	12.5	15.3	60.5
Pass Christian, Mississippi	4.6	14.0	17.3	....	....

It will be noted that within the state there is quite a wide range even of these averages, from a minimum less than 50 inches in the extreme northern part of the state to nearly 65 inches near the coast and in the southwestern part as far north as Jackson. Even the minimum may be considered an abundance for agricultural purposes, and the maximum is not excessive, in view of the (on the whole) remarkably uniform distribution through the seasons; the minimum occurring throughout the autumn (the season for cotton picking), while winter and spring together sometimes include nearly two-thirds of the entire amount, but always leave a fair proportion of precipitation to occur in summer. While the spring rains are at times, and in certain localities especially, so abundant and continuous as to interfere somewhat with the proper after-cultivation of cotton (which occasionally "gets into the grass" in wet seasons), the summer showers, usually of short duration, are considered as especially conducive to the welfare and abundant fruiting of the cotton-plant. Once in a series of years excessive and long-continued rains in August may cause the "shedding of the bolls" by starting a new growth, which then comes too late to ripen its own crop.

Especially in the southern part of the state the variations in the amount of rainfall in different years is also very great. The subjoined table strikingly illustrates such variations for a number of prominent localities:

Table of maxima and minima of rainfall.

Locality.	Number of years covered by observations.	Maximum.	Minimum.
INLAND STATIONS.			
La Grange, Tennessee............................	3	53.3	41.0
Grenada, Mississippi	4	68.3	40.0
Columbus, Mississippi	15	56.4	45.3
Brookhaven, Mississippi..........................	6	80.3	57.9
RIVER STATIONS.			
Memphis, Tennessee.............................	7	57.0	44.1
Vicksburg, Mississippi	20	70.1	37.2
Natchez, Mississippi.............................	19	75.7	31.6
Baton Rouge, Louisiana	10	114.4	41.3

While it is true that the greater number of years covered by the observations at the river stations tend to show a greater contrast between extreme maxima and minima, yet the general outcome of the comparison is sufficiently obvious to show the much greater difference between the maxima and minima at the southern river stations than at those situated inland. The average difference in the case of the latter, as well as at Memphis, is about 50 per cent., or 1 : 1½; at Vicksburg the ratio is slightly below, and at Natchez somewhat above, that of 1 : 2; while at Baton Rouge it rises to nearly 1 : 4. It should not, however, be inferred that the greater rainfall, whether by averages or by maxima and minima, necessarily implies a correspondingly greater number of rainy days. In the southern region the rain is more apt to fall in torrents several inches during comparatively brief "spells", while the time actually occupied in falling may be the same as for a more northerly station with a much smaller total rainfall.

TOPOGRAPHY AND DRAINAGE SYSTEMS.—Outside of the plain of the Mississippi or Yazoo bottom, and of the prairies and "flatwoods" of northeastern Mississippi, the surface of the state is rolling or sometimes hilly and even broken upland, with a general surface-slope from the northeast to the southwest, or in the eastern portion of the state nearly due south, as is indicated by the course of the rivers in both cases. There is no axis of elevation within the state, all the ridges of the present time owing their existence to the erosion by water of a substantially plane surface inclining away, westward to southward, from the last spurs of the Cumberland range, which just touch the northeast corner of the state. The highest elevations lie in the region dividing the waters of the Hatchie, Tallahatchie, and Tombigbee, in Tippah and Union counties, where some ridges rise to a height of between 800 and 1,000 feet above the sea, the adjacent "table-lands" of western Tennessee range themselves on the state line as much as 500 feet above sea-level. Another region of high, broken ridge lands lies on the heads of the Pearl river, in Neshoba and Winston counties, but although sometimes as high above the drainage as the "Hatchie hills" their absolute elevation is much less. The same may be said of the high ridges skirting the Pearl river in Lawrence and Marion counties, of the "Devil's backbone" skirting the Homochitto on the south, and of the broken "cane hills" bordering the Mississippi river from Vicksburg to the Louisiana line. Elsewhere in the state also high and narrow ridges occasionally form the main divides, but as a rule the ridges are broad and rounded, ranging from 50 to 120 feet only above the smaller creeks. In the southern part of the state the streams are separated largely by undulating plateau lands, covered by long-leaf pine forest.

Not all the ridges in the state, however, form water divides, nor are all the water divides ridges in the ordinary sense of the term. Thus the "Pontotoc ridge" in its northern portion is a true divide between the waters of the Tallahatchie on the west and those of the Tombigbee on the east; but farther south many of the western tributaries of the Tombigbee break through the ridge, heading in the level "flatwoods" region, where their headwaters interlace with those of the Yalobusha, Big Black, and Pearl rivers. This anomaly is especially striking in southern Pontotoc and northern Chickasaw, where the sluggish creeks of the level flatwoods are seen to flow on either side into a hilly country, to which the traveler makes a rather abrupt ascent. Farther south, the Noxubee river crosses the flatwoods belt from the hilly country on the west, but the divide still runs close to the western edge. The cause of this state of things is obviously the slight westerly dip of the hard and tough "flatwoods clay", which here overlaps the older (Cretaceous) formation (see "Geological features", page 12).

In the central portion of the state the divide between the Pearl and Big Black rivers, Madison and Hinds counties, is a region of gently rolling uplands, 15 to 25 miles wide, dotted with small prairies, whose general slope is toward the Big Black, the tributaries of which head close to the main Pearl river, while farther south high and mostly sandy pine ridges divide the waters of the Mississippi from those of Pearl river and lake Pontchartrain. The same is true of the divides between the waters of the Pascagoula on the one hand and those of the Tombigbee and Pearl on the other.

The general hilly character of the uplands continues to within a short distance of the Gulf coast, where the sandy pine hills flatten out into the "pine meadows". These in their turn abut on the coast of the Sound in a terrace 20 to 30 feet above sea-level. Toward the Mississippi river the uplands fall off pretty abruptly from 250 to 400 feet into the Yazoo bottom plain, or, southward of Vicksburg, into the Mississippi river itself, which washes the foot of the bluffs at Vicksburg, Grand Gulf, Rodney, Natchez, Fort Adams, and several intermediate points.

GEOLOGICAL FEATURES.—As remarked on page 11, the last undulations of the Cumberland range extend into the northeast corner of the state, and here we find (in Tishomingo county) a small area underlaid by the limestones, sandstones, and cherts of the Carboniferous formation. No true coal, however, exists within the state.

Around the mountain spur referred to, and inclining away from it in a direction varying from due west near the Tennessee line to nearly due south in the southeast part of the state, lie successively the several stages (*Eutaw, Rotten limestone,* and *Ripley* groups) of the Cretaceous formation; above, and therefore west and southward of these, and with dips similar in direction but smaller in amount, are the several stages of the Tertiary, which are exposed on the break of the Mississippi bluff from Memphis to Fort Adams. Above all these older formations, and mostly covering them to depths varying from a few to as much as 200 feet, lies the southern stratified drift, or "orange sand", a formation of *Quaternary* age, consisting chiefly of well-rounded, mostly ferruginous sand, and in certain belts of extensive beds of rolled gravel, with occasional, but mostly quite limited, beds of variously colored pipe-clays, that usually lie in proximity to clay strata of the older formations. Outside of the Yazoo bottom, the cane-hills belt, the prairies and flatwoods of northeast Mississippi, and the coast flats, the orange sand in its various modifications shapes the surface of the state. It forms the upper portion of nearly all ridges, and largely their body as well; and throughout the northern part of the state, at least, every higher ridge or point is capped by more or less extensive deposits of a peculiar ferruginous sandstone, formed by the cementation of the sand by means of limonite or brown iron ore, more rarely by silex. These caps of brown sandstone are sometimes several feet (as much as eight) in thickness, and have of course served to prevent the washing away of the underlying sand, into which elsewhere the present valleys have been excavated. Frequently this rock has taken fantastic shapes, such as tubes, plates, etc.; and sometimes, though rarely within the state, it is sufficiently rich to serve as an iron ore. Into this sand formation most of the wells are dug down to the underlying older and denser materials, which also usually shed the water, forming springs, by which the line between the two formations may often be traced for miles along the ridges. Wells and springs, with abundant water, can rarely be obtained within the orange sand, and in southern Mississippi extensive tracts, underlaid by these sands to a great depth, are destitute of springs, which only appear, sometimes with enormous volume, in the deeper valleys below the limit of this thirsty formation that has no regular stratification but the "flow-and-plunge" structure indicative of its deposition in violently flowing water coming from the northward.

These arid sands are almost everywhere overlaid by from 3 to 20 feet of a yellow or brownish loam, such as forms the subsoil of by far the greater portion of the state, varying greatly in productiveness according to the nature of the underlying formation, whose character it shares more or less. This loam is devoid of any stratification, usually increases in thickness as the larger water-courses are approached, and is absent only from the highest ridges, while covering pretty uniformly, like a blanket, the undulating uplands. It forms the basis and the subsoil of all the better class of uplands in the state.

The Tertiary strata underlie all but that portion of the state lying east of the flatwoods belt (see map), and have dips varying from less than 5 feet per mile west in the northern part of the state to 10 feet per mile south-southwest at Vicksburg and Jackson. From the Tennessee line south to Attala and Holmes counties the materials of the formation are dark-colored clays and sands, with occasional beds of lignite, that locally assume economic importance (Northern lignitic); while the clay beds furnish excellent potters' clays; but wells dug into these strata mostly have ill-tasting and sometimes mineral water. From Holmes and Carroll southeastward to Lauderdale sandstones alternate with the clays, and occasionally there occur agriculturally valuable beds of greensand ("Buhrstone" and "Claiborne" groups). Southward of this belt, the Tertiary beds are chiefly calcareous marls and partly limestones ("Jackson" and "Vicksburg" groups), with abundance of oyster and other sea-shells, and sometimes huge bones of extinct sea-monsters (Zeuglodon). These beds underlie the "Central prairie region" (see map), a country partly undulating, partly hilly, dotted with small prairies of varying character, but mostly with a stiff, black, and very fertile soil. Southward of this there is a rather sudden ascent into sandy ridge lands, covered with long-leaf pine forest and underlaid by the sandstones, claystones, and clays of the uppermost Tertiary ("Grand Gulf" group), which thence extends to within a short distance of the coast. The dip of this formation is very slightly to the southward. The coast flats themselves are underlaid by gray clays of *Quaternary* age (the "Port Hudson" group), more extensively developed in Louisiana and Texas. The same formation also underlies the Mississippi bottom, sometimes near the surface and forming soils ("Buckshot clay"), or else buried at a greater or less depth beneath the more recent alluvium. Along the edge of the Mississippi bottom, and especially from Yazoo City southward, there lies above the Port Hudson clays the curious deposit of calcareous silt now generally known as the loess, forming the "cane-hills" belt, and characterized by fossil land snails and bones of the mastodon, tapir, etc.

The portion of the state lying east of the flatwoods belt (see map) is mainly underlaid by the strata of the *Cretaceous* formation, of which the calcareous stages form the "Pontotoc ridge" and the "prairie belt". The former, rising suddenly from the flatwoods, is underlaid by the limestones and the shell marls of the "Ripley group". From this ridge there is an abrupt descent into the level or gently rolling and often treeless country, underlaid by the soft, whitish, or bluish "rotten limestone" and characterized by the black "prairie" soil. From this rich agricultural region we ascend again, on the east, into a hilly country, timbered with pine and oaks, and having a sandy and inferior soil outside of the valleys. This region, reaching to the Alabama line, is underlaid by the sandy and clayey strata of the "Eutaw" group, devoid of lime and shells, but containing occasional beds of lignite of no economic value.

The Pontotoc ridge terminates near Houston, Chickasaw county; so that in the southern part of the Cretaceous region the flatwoods adjoin directly the black prairie region.

The Cretaceous strata dip nearly due west near the Tennessee line about 20 feet to the mile. Southward the direction of dip gradually changes to southwest, and the amount to 25 feet per mile. This structure renders artesian wells, or at least bored wells, successful in this territory, a point of especial importance in the prairie country, which has no springs or flowing streams in summer. The water is found beneath the impervious "rotten limestone", the thickness of which varies from 300 to 1,100 feet within the state. The water is hard, but otherwise pure and palatable, and usually rises within easy reach of, or frequently above, the surface, forming flowing wells. In a portion of the Tertiary region also such bored wells are practicable.

AGRICULTURAL SUBDIVISIONS OR REGIONS.—In accordance with the general features outlined above, the state may, for the purposes of description, conveniently be considered under the following heads and subheads:

I.—*Northeastern prairie region.*
   1. Rotten limestone or black prairies.
   2. Pontotoc ridge.
II.—*Flatwoods region.*
   1. Post-oak flatwoods.
   2. White-oak flatwoods.
III.—*Yellow loam or oak uplands region.*
   1. Flatwoods hills.
   2. Short-leaf pine and oak uplands.
   3. The red lands.
   4. The sandy oak uplands.
   5. The brown loam table-lands.
IV.—*Mississippi bottom region.*
V.—*Cane hills region.*
VI.—*Central prairie region.*
VII.—*Long-leaf pine region.*
   1. Long-leaf pine hills { Long- and short-leaf pine and oak lands. / Sandy pine hills.
   2. Pine flats and coast region.

Each of these regions and subdivisions is described, with analyses of its soils, in the following pages.

I.—THE NORTHEASTERN PRAIRIE REGION.

This division, characterized by the more or less general occurrence of heavy, calcareous clay soils (popularly called prairie soils even when fully timbered), formed wholly or partially from the materials of the Cretaceous formation, presents two very strongly defined features, the one being largely level calcareous prairie, the other a rolling and mostly well-timbered upland region. Together they constitute one of the most important cotton-growing districts of the state, producing, in average seasons, about 17 per cent. of the crop, with a staple of very high quality.

ROTTEN LIMESTONE PRAIRIE REGION.

The rotten limestone prairie region, or (in its northern part) "white lime country", forms a belt varying in width from 6 to 25 miles, which enters the state near its northeastern corner, in Alcorn county, and, widening to the southward, after traversing Prentiss county occupies large portions of the counties of Lee, Chickasaw, Monroe, Clay, Oktibbeha, Lowndes, and Noxubee, and finally passes southeastward into Alabama through the extreme northeast portion of Kemper. Its maximum length within the state is thus 196 miles, with a total area of about 1,535 square miles.

Black prairie.—Of this area probably two-thirds is occupied by the black prairie soil in its several varieties, although not nearly as much was originally treeless. In fact, by far the greater part of the black prairie soil was simply sparsely timbered, clumps of crab and plum thickets dotting the prairie proper, while the general surface was more or less sparsely occupied by oaks, mingled with honey-locust and other lime-loving trees. Among these, both on the open and timbered prairie, the cedar (*Juniperus Virginiana*) was not uncommon. These features are spoken of in the past tense, because the prairie lands of northeastern Mississippi were among the earliest occupied by settlers, both on account of their great fertility and the comparative facility with which they could be taken into cultivation; and at the present time open fields, cultivated or "turned out", form the landscape, varied only by the scattered homesteads or poorer, sandy ridges, timbered with oaks, that occur more or less throughout the region.

The oaks most prevalent on the black soils are the black-jack and post oak, trees elsewhere known as characterizing inferior soils. They have here, however, so far changed their form that many imagine them to be different species from those occupying the poor sandy ridges or intractable gray clay soils elsewhere. The trunks of both are sturdy and undivided, that of the post oak rapidly tapering, and when tall almost always curving to one side, while the short and crooked branches, running out squarely from the trunk, form a dense, leafy top, reaching low down. The black-jack forms an equally compact but low and rounded top, giving it the appearance of an apple tree, a habit assumed by it on all heavy soils, whether fertile or not.

The streams of the prairie region proper have no bottoms. The channels of the minor ones are mere depressions in the general surface (like the "coulées" of Louisiana) and have running water only during the rainy season, since, owing to the geological structure of the country, there are no springs. In the case of the larger streams there is sometimes a longer slope; at others the prairie abuts directly on the banks of the channel. Near the water-courses, as well as sometimes in the level prairie, the black soil sometimes reaches to a depth of 3 feet, while ordinarily it is from 15 to 18 inches deep, and is then underlaid by a yellow (or rather greenish-yellow) subsoil. Below the latter, usually at a depth of from 7 to 10 feet, lies the white or bluish, soft "rotten" limestone, which is the country rock, and varies in thickness from 250 in the northern to 1,100 feet in the southern portion of the belt. No veins of water can be found within it, but artesian water rises from beneath it when penetrated, either above or within available distance of the surface. North of Lee county "rotten limestone" is frequently so clayey and soft as to be simply a very calcareous clay or clay marl, while farther south it is generally more solid and chalk-like, though nowhere capable of making a chalk mark. The soils formed from it of course vary accordingly.

Black-jack prairie.—From the points of greatest thickness the black soil often thins out more or less rapidly until the yellow subsoil lies at or near the surface over considerable tracts. These constitute the "black-jack prairie", possessing a soil whose tenacity as well as color, when wet, justifies the title of "waxy" commonly allotted to it. When well cultivated it yields good returns in fair seasons, though much inferior to the black prairie in thriftiness.

"*Bald prairie.*"—A subordinate but very characteristic feature, occurring more or less throughout the prairie region, is the "bald prairie", so called from its being mostly destitute of any tree growth save small clumps of crab, plum, or persimmon. These are formed wherever the "rotten limestone" lies within about 3 feet or less of the surface and has contributed essentially to the formation of the soil, as is sometimes apparent from its whitish tint. This naturally happens most frequently in the more undulating northern portions of the prairie belt, in Alcorn, Prentiss, and Lee counties. Here we often find on the slopes of the loam uplands limited patches of "black" or "bald" prairie soil, passing on the one hand, by intermixture with the reddish loam, into the highly esteemed "mahogany" soils, and on the other into the very stiff, greenish-yellow clay of the black-jack prairie, here designated as "beeswax hummocks", and often too intractable for cultivation. They are more or less directly derived from the underlying stiff clay marls, which there, to a large extent, replace the harder and more chalky "rotten" limestone of the southern part of the prairie belt. In the latter region the admixture of this rock does not necessarily render the soils very heavy. This may be noted in the "Chickasaw Old Fields", a name applied to a group of small prairies in the southern part of Lee county, where the soil is often so shallow that the plow scrapes the rock.

From either the black-jack or the black prairie there may be a transition to the soils of higher ridges, which often form the divides between water-courses or the head regions of prairie streams. We then see the upland oaks gradually intermingling with those inhabiting the prairie, and in the northern portion of the belt such soils, timbered with tall, sturdy black, Spanish, and post oaks, are very prevalent and sometimes very fertile; but in the southern portion, as in Chickasaw and Clay counties, these ridges have a pale-yellow, sandy loam soil of little fertility, as is at once evidenced by their undersized growth of oaks, among which the scarlet oak (*Q. coccinea*) is very prominent.

COMPOSITION OF PRAIRIE SOILS.—The following analyses afford an insight into the characteristics of the prairie soils of this region:

Nos. 175 and 176. *Soil and subsoil* from Sec. 16, T. 5, R. 7 E., near Booneville, Prentiss county. Black soil 8 to 10 inches deep, very heavy, but crumbling in drying. Subsoil a pale greenish-yellow clay ("joint clay" from the manner in which it cracks on drying), with an obvious increase of lime as we descend, passing into a whitish marl. This is a fair representative of the "bald" prairie spots of the region, with scattered groups of crab, wild plum, and black-jack oak on the edges, where the black soil becomes thin or is wanting; a very productive soil in favorable seasons, but difficult to till, and subject to injury from drought.

Nos. 172 and 173. *Surface soil* (0 to 15 inches) and *underclay* (24 to 36 inches), taken in the main prairie belt on the Buena Vista and Aberdeen road, Sec. 20, T. 14, R. 6 E., Monroe county. Timber: black-jack oak, widely scattered. The black surface soil varies in depth from 8 to 15 inches, when there is a change of color to a brownish subsoil, reaching down to about 2 feet, and, in drying, cleaving into vertically prismatic fragments. Both contain numerous (2 to 6 per cent.) particles of globular concretions of brown iron ore, varying from the size of poppy seed to that of pease and of a reddish tint in the upper portion, olive tint in the underclay. These lands hardly deteriorate perceptibly during twenty years' exhaustive culture in corn and cotton, having yielded from 1,200 to 1,500 pounds of seed-cotton per acre, the staple rating very high in the market. The black soil has here in the highest degree the peculiarity of crumbling in drying from its water-soaked condition, so that in case of need it is even plowed while wet without materially injuring its tilth during the season, but in so doing heavy draft is required. The mud formed on the roads is tenacious and adhesive in the highest degree.

No. 125. *Black prairie soil* from J. D. Hollimon's land, near Buena Vista, Chickasaw county. A dark-gray heavy soil, nearly black when moist. Depth and subsoil not known accurately. The soil is stated to be very productive in favorable seasons, but to rust (or " blight ") the cotton very badly when the seasons are at all unfavorable, especially when wet. This defect is clearly not the fault of the chemical composition, which is excellent, being superior to that of the Monroe prairie (No. 172), but is doubtless due to imperfect drainage, whereby the tap-root of the cotton plant is killed by drowning so soon as it reaches a certain depth.

No. 170. *Noxubee prairie soil* from near Macon, T. 15, R. 12 E., Noxubee county. Brownish black to mahogany, and heavy ; depth, 12 to 15 inches. Subsoil, tawny to reddish. Timber, scattered post oak 'and hickory. Average product, 1,000 pounds of seed-cotton when fresh. Staple rates good middling.

No. 139. *Hillside prairie soil* from Sec. 12, T. 12, R. 18 E., J. J. Pettus' land, Kemper county. Occupies limited areas on hillsides below points where the rotten limestone appears. Black, rather sandy, 10 to 12 inches deep. An excellent soil for wheat and corn, but liable to rust cotton.

Analyses of soils and subsoils in the northeastern prairie region.

	PRENTISS COUNTY, BOONEVILLE.		MONROE COUNTY (SEC. 20, T. 14, R. 6 E).		CHICKASAW COUNTY, NEAR BUENA VISTA.	NOXUBEE COUNTY, MACON.	KEMPER COUNTY, RIDGE PRAIRIE.
	Soil.	Subsoil.	Soil.	Subsoil.	Soil.	Soil.	Soil.
	No. 175.	No. 176.	No. 172.	No. 173.	No. 125.	No. 170.	No. 139.
Insoluble matter	64.816 } 68.411 8.695 }	43.955	75.292	71.589	84.644 } 75.704 11.060 }		67.078
Soluble silica							
Potash	0.362	0.352	0.833	0.542	0.484	0.396	0.099
Soda	0.129	0.134	0.060	0.290	0.098	0.074	0.136
Lime	0.987	12.101	1.367	1.075	0.966	1.354	1.371
Magnesia	0.777	0.191	0.962	0.771	0.227	0.718	1.003
Brown oxide of manganese	0.045	0.076	0.143	0.046	0.138	0.118	0.345
Peroxide of iron	7.851	6.917 } 14.294 {		5.419	5.510	0.567	6.748
Alumina	14.365	5.978 }		13.155	11.155	6.918	13.068
Phosphoric acid	0.157	0.229	0.104	0.051	0.267	0.068	0.032
Sulphuric acid	0.610	0.065	0.034	0.086	0.027	trace.	0.077
Carbonic acid		11.892					
Water and organic matter	7.065	12.150	5.747	6.992	7.151	8.466	9.453
Total	100.459	100.000	100.688	99.854	100.035	100.341	99.911
Humus			1.995		1.418		1.277
Available inorganic			4.394		1.788		1.084
Hygroscopic moisture	13.07	12.08	13.83	1.85	10.90	14.39	11.45
absorbed at	18 C.°	18 C.°	19 C.°	9 C.°	16 C.°	20 C.°	8 C.°

The only mechanical analysis thus far made of soils of this region is that of No. 173, the yellow subsoil of the Monroe prairie, perhaps a somewhat extreme representative in the direction of heaviness. To the southward the soils appear on the whole to become lighter in texture.

Monroe county prairie subsoil.

	Subsoil.
	No. 173.
MECHANICAL ANALYSIS.	
Weight of gravel over 1.2mm diameter.	
Weight of gravel between 1.2 and 1mm	
Weight of gravel between 1 and 0.5mm (limonite)	2.1
Fine earth	97.9
Total	100.0
MECHANICAL ANALYSIS OF FINE EARTH.	
Clay	54.1
Sediment of <0.25mm hydraulic value	26.2
Sediment of 0.25mm	5.1
Sediment of 0.5mm	2.0
Sediment of 1.0mm	7.6
Sediment of 2.0mm	2.9
Sediment of 4.0mm	1.2
Sediment of 8.0mm	0.2
Sediment of 16.0mm	
Sediment of 32.0mm	} 0.6
Sediment of 64.0mm	
Total	100.0

This is quite a heavy clay soil, with but a very small proportion of the coarser sediments to relieve its closeness; but to some extent it shares the peculiarity of its surface soil to pulverize of its own accord in drying, somewhat like the buckshot soil of the Yazoo bottom, and so is not as intractable under tillage as might be imagined. Moreover, the numerous fine fissures so formed give passage to the roots of cotton to the depth of several feet.

The most obvious chemical feature of all the soils analyzed is the large percentage of lime, ranging within a few tenths of 1 per cent., or nearly four times as much as is usually present in good upland soils. With this fact, leading us to class them all as calcareous, their dark tint is intimately correlated. It may be broadly stated that, as a rule, an exceptionally dark tint in any well-drained soil is a mark of the presence of a large supply of lime. This tint (so generally associated with the instinctive estimate of a soil's fertility) is always indicative of a large supply of humus, as is apparent from the figures given, the amount ordinarily contained in upland soils being about three-quarters of 1 per cent. only. Many soils possessing a much larger supply do not show the shade and depth of tint observed in highly calcareous soils. Manifestly this tint is due in a measure to the kind or quality of the humus formed under the influence of a large supply of lime, and it is at least probable that such humus possesses in the highest degree the important properties which render its presence in the soil so essential to profitable culture, viz: that of serving as a vehicle for the soil's mineral ingredients to the plant. This, added to the well-known action of lime in rendering available the inert plant-food in the soil, explains sufficiently the uniformly high productiveness of the prairie soils, notwithstanding serious differences in their ultimate percentages of plant-food. It will be noted that the potash percentage ranges from one-third to nearly nine-tenths of 1 per cent., while the phosphoric acid is even more variable, and would in the case of the Kemper (if correctly determined) and Noxubee soils be accounted deficient, while in the soils from Prentiss and Chickasaw it is quite high. It is, however, to be expected that in the former soils the supply would soon become deficient by exhaustive culture and will have to be replaced by the use of commercial phosphates. It will be seen by reference to the statements made in regard to it that, unlike the prairie lands farther north, its cotton product is reduced from 1,000 to 600 pounds in the course of five years' cultivation. The good effect of phosphate manures in these lands is already being experienced.

An important feature of all these soils is their high capacity for absorbing moisture, varying from 10.3 to 14.3 per cent., and averaging in the soils analyzed 12 per cent. This property belongs to clay soils generally, but is always heightened by the presence of a large supply of lime, and especially by that of much humus. It is important in preventing the acquisition of too high a temperature by the soil during hot and dry weather, and is therefore a factor in preventing injury from drought. So, also, is the great depth of the prairie soils; and it is curious to note that, notwithstanding their heaviness, the cotton roots penetrate them to great depths.

Ridge soils.—On the higher ridges in the more hilly prairie region of Kemper there occurs another soil equally stiff, but differing materially in composition from the prairie soil below it, its color being orange-red instead of black, although its iron percentage is but little greater. It is, of course, comparatively poor in humus, and its red tint scarcely varies down to 12 inches depth. The rotten limestone usually underlies at 2 to 6 feet. It produces fine wheat, and also cotton, whose growth is short, but well bolled. Where this soil mixes with the black prairie (on hillsides) the latter does not rust cotton. This red soil is manifestly related to the "red lands" farther west and north, and resembles in aspect, as well as in composition and tilling qualities, the "red hills" soil of western Attala. Its analysis gave the following results (the prairie soil is placed along side for comparison).

No. 141. *Red ridge soil* from Sec. 12, T. 12, R. 18 E., J. J. Pettus' land, Kemper county :

Ridge lands.

	Red ridge soil.	Hillside prairie soil.
	No. 141.	No. 139.
Insoluble matter	54.565 } 67.784	67.076
Soluble silica	13.219	
Potash	0.431	0.609
Soda	0.277	0.136
Lime	0.540	1.371
Magnesia	0.536	1.003
Brown oxide of manganese	0.079	0.345
Peroxide of iron	7.089	6.748
Alumina	16.971	13.068
Phosphoric acid	0.187	0.036
Sulphuric acid	0.009	0.077
Volatile matter	6.923	9.453
Total	100.225	99.978
Humus	0.781	1.277
Available inorganic	3.256	1.086
Hygroscopic moisture	13.07	11.45
absorbed at	11 C.°	8 C.°

The main differences between this soil and the prairie soil lying at lower levels (No. 139) are its smaller percentages of potash, lime, magnesia, and organic matter and higher amounts of phosphoric acid and alumina. These facts agree with the tendency to small development of stalk and heavy fruiting which characterize the red soil. The admixture of more vegetable matter by green manuring would seem to be the improvement most immediately suggested by the analysis.

Hickory hummocks.—In southwestern Tippah the Pontotoc ridge flattens into gently-rolling woodland, from which there is a gradual transition into the flatwoods proper by a change of soil and timber. Along the edge of the flatwoods there is thus a belt of land known as "hickory hummocks", from their being largely timbered with hickory, intermingled with post and Spanish oak, black gum, and some pine. The analysis of a specimen of this soil, which is fairly productive when well tilled, is given below.

No. 273. *Soil of hickory hummock* from Sec. 31, T. 4, R. 3 E., Tippah county. Timber as above stated; hickory (*Carya tomentosa*) mostly quite young. Soil grayish, not very heavy; depth, 5 inches.

No. 275. Subsoil of above. Color dun, heavier than soil; taken 5 to 12 inches deep.

Hickory hummock land of Tippah county.

	Soil.	Subsoil.
	No. 273.	No. 275.
Insoluble matter	81.176 } 87.134	78.083 } 86.048
Soluble silica	5.958	7.965
Potash	0.217	0.217
Soda	0.068	0.067
Lime	0.350	0.380
Magnesia	0.559	0.567
Brown oxide of manganese	0.292	0.127
Peroxide of iron	3.431	4.859
Alumina	3.436	4.678
Phosphoric acid	0.163	0.096
Sulphuric acid	0.016	0.006
Water and organic matter	4.396	3.315
Total	99.871	100.050
Hygroscopic moisture	6.86	9.03
absorbed at	11 C.°	11 C.°

The high lime percentage of this soil, indicating the nearness of the marl strata (although it lies within the flatwoods), ought to insure its thriftiness with deep tillage and good drainage. The latter appears to be the point of difficulty, since the stiff clay, underlying at no great depth, prevents the rapid drainage of water. The phosphoric acid percentage is fair; that of potash rather low, but doubtless adequate for the present. The greensand marls of the adjoining Pontotoc ridge afford ready means for the improvement of the soil in this respect.

Sandy upland ridges.—Of the pale-yellow, sandy loam lands forming ridges between the prairie belts but one specimen has been analyzed. It has been stated that these lands are generally of quite an inferior quality, at least for cotton culture. Their best adaptation appears to be for wheat and sweet potatoes, the better class of lands yielding, when fresh, from 20 to 25 bushels of the former to the acre; but they become exhausted in the course of a few years, after which it requires manure to make them produce. The more clayey varieties are also benefited by fallowing. On these the post, Spanish, and scarlet oaks (*Q. stellata, Q. falcata, Q. coccinea*) prevail, the development of the timber growth indicating very accurately their agricultural value, being generally the more vigorous on the darker tinted (yellow or orange) subsoil. The surface soil is generally so shallow that the subsoil forms the main mass of the cultivated surface. At times, especially in the lower ridges, the soil is whitish, and a poor stunted growth of scarlet and willow oaks (*Q. coccinea, Q. Phellos*) prevails. Such tracts are practically too poor for cultivation.

The specimen analyzed (No. 164) was taken in the belt of such uplands forming the divide between Houlka and Suckatonche creeks near Pikeville, northeast quarter of T. 14, R. 5 E., Chickasaw county. It is here about 4 miles wide, and on each side slopes off gradually into prairie belts, which border both streams. Timber: post, Spanish, and some scarlet oak, rather undersized; surface soil whitish, scarcely exceeding 2 inches in depth; subsoil a pale-yellow, fine sandy loam. Specimen taken to 10 inches depth.

Pikeville upland soil of Chickasaw county.

	Soil.
	No. 164.
Insoluble matter	93. 628 } 94. 978
Soluble silica	1. 356
Potash	0. 093
Soda	0. 065
Lime..	0. 069
Magnesia	0. 126
Brown oxide of manganese	0. 022
Peroxide of iron	1. 690
Alumina	1. 472
Phosphoric acid...	0. 032
Sulphuric acid..	0. 005
Water and organic matter	1. 990
Total	99. 944
Hygroscopic moisture	1. 80
absorbed at..	11 C.°

The cause of the poverty and want of durability of this soil is sufficiently obvious from the analysis. It is notably deficient in all the elements of mineral plant-food, even in potash, and nothing short of manure, in the widest sense of the word, can keep it productive when once its first supply is exhausted.

Bottom soils.—Ordinarily the bottom soils of the prairie region differ in no material point from those of the higher prairies. The formation of the black soil is, as a rule, determined by the nearness of the "rotten limestone" to the surface, and hence it is almost always found near the streams, which mostly have little or no definite flood plain.

Where, however, these streams traverse or head in uplands of the character just described we generally find a definite bottom, and even the timber of the uplands is present on a somewhat improved scale. Yet, even though it may have a dark tint, it is not necessarily fertile, that fact being commonly indicated by a timber growth of indifferent willow and water oaks (*Q. Phellos aquatica*). So soon, however, as the admixture of lime becomes considerable the black and white oak, tulip tree, sweet gum, etc., mingle with the two oaks mentioned, and the fresh soil, at least, is very productive. The following analyses illustrates one of these cases, which occur rather frequently near the western edge of the prairie region:

No. 177. *Black hummock soil* from the flats or second bottom (above any ordinary overflows) on Coonewah creek, Sec. 15, T. 9, R. 5'E. Timber as last mentioned above. Soil black, but only to the depth of 3 to 5 inches; heavy and putty-like when wet, although not very clayey.

No. 178. Subsoil of above, taken 5 to 15 inches deep. Color, pale yellow; a rather sandy loam, quite similar in appearance to No. 164. This land is said to produce, when fresh, 70 to 80 bushels of corn and 1,000 to 1,200 pounds of seed-cotton per acre, and in favorable seasons even more. The analysis resulted as follows:

Coonewah hummock land of Lee county.

	Soil.	Subsoil.
	No. 177.	No. 178.
Insoluble matter	86. 160 } 89. 964	90. 688 } 93. 430
Soluble silica..................................	3. 804	2. 742
Potash...	0. 207	0. 173
Soda...	0. 171	0. 151
Lime...	0. 247	0. 102
Magnesia......................................	0. 283	0. 218
Brown oxide of manganese	0. 045	0. 058
Peroxide of iron...............................	1. 587	1. 542
Alumina.......................................	3. 022	2. 638
Phosphoric acid...........	0. 066	0. 115
Sulphuric acid.................................	-0. 046	0. 048
Water and organic matter.....	4. 761	1. 636
Total	100. 304	100. 304
Hygroscopic moisture..........................	3. 38	3. 51
absorbed at	9 C.°	9 C.°

In this case the texture of the soil, as well as the alumina percentage and the hygroscopic coefficient, shows the surface soil to be more clayey than the subsoil, as is not unfrequently the case in alluvial soils. The potash percentage, though nearly twice that of the Pikeville soil, is still low; the same is true of the phosphoric acid. The latter, however, is nearly doubled in the subsoil, while the lime percentage in the soil is quite high, and thus explains its thriftiness. It is not likely, however, to be very durable in its productiveness.

THE PONTOTOC RIDGE.

The Pontotoc ridge is a belt of ridgy, sometimes rolling, sometimes hilly, oak uplands, whose main body lies between Ripley, Tippah county, and Houston, Chickasaw county, a distance of about 60 miles north and south, with a width varying from 5 to 15 miles, and averaging from 9 to 10 miles east and west. Northward of Ripley it forms a narrow strip only 1 to 2 miles wide, and is but faintly represented beyond the state line.

As the white "rotten limestone" formation underlying the prairie country determines its main features, so those of the Pontotoc ridge are largely determined by the alternating strata of hard, granular limestone and soft, bluish marls of the Upper Cretaceous formation that constitute the body of the hills, though often covered to a considerable depth by the orange or "red" sands that form so conspicuous a feature of the surface of the whole state (see "Geological features", page 10). Where this is the case, the soils and timber growth are very similar to those of the oak uplands region farther west; and, as in the case of the latter, long spurs of piny ridges extend in places into the body of the ridge land. As a rule, however, the influence of the underlying calcareous strata manifests itself very distinctly in the appearance of the soils, especially in their deep red tint and in the frequent presence, to a very large extent, of smooth and mostly globular concretions of brown iron ore (limonite), varying from the size of fine bird-shot to that of a fist. In the timber growth the presence of lime is also observable in the frequent appearance of the black walnut, tulip tree ("poplar"), black locust (*Robinia*), and cucumber trees (*Magnolia auriculata*) among the prevailing growth of oaks and hickories, as well as in the absence of the scarlet oak (*Q. coccinea*), whose prevalence is almost everywhere the proof of a comparatively unthrifty soil, poor in lime.

In consequence of the dip of the limestone strata toward the west the ascent to the ridge lands from the west is very gentle, although its limits are in general very distinctly marked by the contrast with the level, gray clay lands of the flatwoods region. Toward the east, on the contrary, there is usually a steep and well-marked descent of from 150 to 200 feet from the jutting edges of the hard limestone forming the crest of the ridge, into the level prairie or "white lime country". In the northern portion of the belt this crest forms the divide between the waters of the Tombigbee and Tallahatchie, but in the southern portion it is traversed by the tributaries of the Tombigbee, the divide lying in the flatwoods. In Tippah county, however, the Pontotoc ridge lands do not reach the edge of the prairie country, but pass insensibly to the eastward into the hilly pine country known as the "Hatchie hills".

Unlike the prairies, the Pontotoc ridge is well watered by streams fed by living springs, which flow partly from the red sandy surface strata and partly from between the limestone ledges, alternating with sandy marls. Well water also is usually obtainable at moderate depths, and is good, though mostly hard.

The soils of the Pontotoc ridge vary considerably, as may be expected from the variety of materials which, as above mentioned, form the body of its ridges. They may be classified as follows:

1. *Pale-yellow loam uplands*, timbered with a moderately strong oak growth, among which the post oak and black-jack form a considerable ingredient, and which, through a gradual increase of sand, accompanied by an admixture of scarlet oak, chestnut, and finally short-leaf pine, forms the transition toward the pine hills and the sandy ridges of the prairie country. It forms gently rolling plateau tracts, interspersed more or less throughout the eastern portion of the ridge belt, and is only moderately productive, yielding, when fresh, from 600 to 700 pounds of seed-cotton per acre, and wearing out in the course of from eight to twelve years.

2. The opposite extreme of the above is the soil of the "*Beeswax hummocks*"—a very heavy, greenish-yellow, intractable soil, appearing on hilltops and slopes where clayey marls (greatly resembling those of some parts of the prairie country) come to or near the surface and have mainly formed the soil. Thus are formed either true "bald prairies" or "black-jack prairie", on which the prevailing tree is itself reduced to a height of from 10 to 18 feet, with the compact habit peculiar to it on such soils, while the ground is in some cases almost bare of grass or any other undergrowth. This soil is rarely cultivated, and the roads on which it prevails are the dread of teamsters. Not unfrequently, however, it passes, as in the prairie region, into a true black and very fertile "prairie soil", which forms limited belts and patches on the hillsides.

From the intermixture of the black prairie, black-jack prairie, or "beeswax" soil with the sandy soils mentioned under No. 1 there results the most highly esteemed soil of the Pontotoc ridge, viz:

3. The *mahogany* (or *mulatto*) *soil*, in which the native fertility of its clayey ingredient is made available by the admixture of sufficient sandy loam to produce an easily tilled, durable, and highly productive soil. It usually occupies the lower slopes of ridges and the smaller valleys in irregular tracts.

4. The "*red lands*" and "*buncombe*" soils. These occur especially where the sandy marls and limestones come to or near the surface and have become mixed with the yellow loam or formed the soil altogether. They are distinguished by the deep red or orange color of the subsoil at least, and sometimes of the surface soil itself. The "red lands" proper are of a clay-loam character, and occur most characteristically to the southward of the town of

Pontotoc. They are full of small rounded concretions of brown iron ore, and the loam subsoil upon which they rest is sometimes from 7 to 10 feet in thickness. The "buncombe" soil is of a lighter character, and is evidently formed almost directly from the marls of the Cretaceous formation. The regions where it prevails (chiefly in eastern Union, on the heads of the Oconstyhatchie, and near the southern end of the ridge, in Chickasaw, on the extreme heads of the Houlka and Suckatonche) are everywhere characterized by an extraordinary predominance of smooth brown iron-ore pebbles (or, more properly, concretions) up to the size of a fist, which often impart to the land a most unpromising aspect; but it wears well, and, with little trouble, produces from 60 to 80 bushels of corn per acre and up to 1,600 pounds of seed-cotton. Here, as in the red lands of Louisiana, the broken surface, and not unfrequently the rocky nature of the soil, interfere somewhat with tillage.

By the occasional intermixture of the red lands soil with that of the "beeswax hummock" a heavier and somewhat less thrifty but very durable red soil is produced, while from the intermixture of the red soil with the yellow loam (No. 1) there results another kind of "mahogany" or "mulatto" soil, which occupies considerable tracts on the western side of the Pontotoc ridge especially, and is highly esteemed for its productiveness and easy tillage, its quality varying sensibly in accordance with the depth of its color.

The following analysis of one of this kind of "mulatto" soils is probably fairly representative of their character:

No. 226. *Mulatto soil* from Mr. Stephen Dagett's land, R. 3 E., T. 10, Sec. 33, Pontotoc county. Timber growth: Black, Spanish ("red"), and post oak, and hickory, all large, stout trees; some sweet and black gum and walnut toward lower ground. Depth of soil taken, 10 inches; a light chocolate tint when moist, mellow, and easily tilled. Average product, 1,000 pounds of seed-cotton per acre.

No. 122. Subsoil of the preceding, taken from 10 to 18 inches depth; of a pale-yellowish tint above, but deepens in color to that of the "red lands" below.

Mulatto land of Pontotoc ridge, Pontotoc county.

	Soil.	Subsoil.
	No. 226.	No. 122.
Insoluble matter..............................	·83. 270 } 88. 836	79. 280 } 87. 743
Soluble silica................................	5. 566	8. 463
Potash.....................................	0. 274	0. 414
Soda	0. 219	0. 229
Lime......................................	0. 362	0. 221
Magnesia	0. 234	0. 469
Brown oxide of manganese....................	0. 276	0. 142
Peroxide of iron	2. 350	4. 625
Alumina	4. 511	4. 345
Phosphoric acid.............................	0. 082	0. 295
Sulphuric acid	0. 017	0. 066
Water and organic matter	3. 106	2. 199
Total	100. 295	100. 498
Hygroscopic moisture........................	4. 076	5. 60
absorbed at	11 C.°	16 C.°

The prominent features of this soil are the high percentages of lime in both the soil and subsoil and the large amount of phosphoric acid in the subsoil, while that in the surface soil is quite moderate. The potash percentages in both are fair, though not large, and there seems to be but little difference in the mechanical constitution of the soil and subsoil, the former being deficient in vegetable matter. The latter circumstance partially explains why a soil of such excellent chemical and physical qualities produces only 1,000 pounds of seed-cotton, when soils otherwise similarly constituted, but richer in organic matter, as a rule produce a 400-pound bale per acre. The most important direct mode of improvement (by green manuring) is thus at once indicated, while for the maintenance of fertility in the future the marl beds of the region furnish excellent material.

The following analysis of a hillside or "hummock" soil from Sec. 34, T. 12, R. 3 E., Chickasaw county, shows the character of the soil near the southern end of the ridge, where it flattens and forms a gradual transition to the pale ridge lands of the prairie country.

The timber here is mainly black oak and hickory, with some chestnut-white, water, and scarlet oaks, and dogwood; in the lower land, also, some ash, wild plum, and cottonwood, indicating the presence of lime.

No. 346. The soil is a light loam, mouse color, to the depth of 6 to 9 inches, according to its position on the hillside. The subsoil (No. 347) is somewhat heavier, of a yellow or light orange tint, taken to the depth of 18 inches.

Pontotoc ridge hummock land, Chickasaw county.

•	Soil.	Subsoil.
	No. 346.	No. 347.
Insoluble matter..........................	87.044 } 90.169	70.697 } 77.266
Soluble silica	3.125	6.569
Potash...................................	0.153	0.263
Soda....................................	0.085	0.105
Lime....................................	0.168	0.263
Magnesia	0.215	0.420
Brown oxide of manganese	0.106	0.134
Peroxide of iron	2.758	5.521
Alumina.................................	3.581	11.228
Phosphoric acid	0.113	0.094
Sulphuric acid...........................	0.018	0.022
Water and organic matter..., ...	3.096	4.796
Total	100.432	100.111
Hygroscopic moisture	4.06	9.01
absorbed at	19 C.°	19 C.°

It thus appears that this soil is materially less rich in mineral plant-food (potash and phosphoric acid) than the "mulatto soil" of Dagett's neighborhood, and it will doubtless be found to be less durable. But in present productiveness it is (according to the testimony of the inhabitants) quite equal to the former, owing doubtless to the greater amount of organic matter present, while its large lime percentage for a soil of its kind explains its present thriftiness in accordance with the indications of its timber growth.

Natural fertilizers of the northeastern prairie region.—Among the materials of the (Cretaceous) formation underlying the region there is quite a variety of marls of excellent quality for soil improvement, beside enormous deposits of limestones, which, by burning, will furnish lime for agricultural as well as other purposes: A number of analyses of such materials are given in the table on page 22.

The best natural marls, as well as the purest limestones, occur on the Pontotoc ridge. The best marls are of bluish tint. They mostly contain greensand or glauconite grains, and usually also a certain (not inconsiderable) percentage of phosphoric acid, rising as high as a quarter of 1 per cent. and even more. The potash percentage of some rises as high as 1¾ per cent., but is more frequently near three-fourths in the soft marls. The harder ones are not so rich in greensand. The lime percentage of the blue marls is, on the whole, rather low, and from half to three-fourths of their mass is commonly inert matter. They do not, therefore, as a rule, bear transportation far from the points where they occur. The inert portion is mostly sandy, and hence it will sometimes pay to use them on heavy soils needing to be rendered lighter. This is especially true of the heavy clay soil of the adjoining "flatwoods", the effect of marling upon which is abundantly apparent at the foot of the marl hills, where the two materials have naturally mingled.

In the black prairie belt the underlying whitish marly materials are mostly of a clayey character, and their chief useful ingredient is, in most cases, the lime, with small percentages of potash and phosphoric acid. The prevalent "rotten limestone" has taken part in the formation of the black prairie soils naturally; yet it has been found that when these have become "tired" a dressing even of the raw but pulverized rock is helpful, and still more helpful is a dressing of the lime made from it. This will doubtless be extensively used in the future, especially on the less thrifty soils of the "post-oak prairie" and on the sandy upland ridges dividing the prairie belts proper. At many points the limestone is very clayey and easily disintegrated, as in the case of the marl from near Chewalla, and can then, of course, be more easily applied to the fields.

In the southern portion of the region along the Tombigbee river there are extensive outcrops of greenish sands, usually glistening with mica, and often more or less indurate, frequently full of shells. The analyses made of these (see table on page 20) do not place them very high as fertilizing materials, as they contain from 80 to 90 per cent. of inert matter and only from 1 to 6 per cent. of lime, with usually little else of agricultural importance. In some cases, as in that of No. 2226, there is enough of glauconite in the mass to render it available, at least where it is convenient for application to needy soils.

No. 338. *Greensand shell marl* from Sec. 22, T. 4., R. 3 E., 2 miles west of Ripley, Tippah county (Vernor's place). Crops out in the bed of a small creek about 2 feet thick, and is full of soft, rounded grains of greensand and broken shells.

No. 708. *Blue marl* from the well of Judge O. Davis, in the town of Ripley, Tippah county. Sandier than No. 338, and greensand grains smaller and less abundant. Similar marl crops out in the bed of Town creek, just south of the town, and at numerous other localities in the region.

No. 318. *Indurate blue marl*, or marlstone, from Braddock's place, Sec. 21, T. 3, R. 4 E., Tippah county. Somewhat difficult to crumble, and for use would require to be exposed to the weather for some length of time. No greensand grains visible.

No. 271. *Blue marl* from Nabor's place, southeast of Ripley, exact locality not given. Bluish, soft, full of mica scales, somewhat clayey, with a few shells. This marl represents most of those occurring in the eastern part of the marl region of Tippah and Union, and contains, as will be noted, a good deal of inert matter, and only about 6½ per cent. of lime. The marl occurring on Owl creek is quite similar to this.

No. 123. *Bluish greensand marl* from an outcrop 1 mile south of the town of Pontotoc, Pontotoc county. Several feet in thickness, with visible greensand grains. Easily accessible, and rich in lime and potash.

No. (?) "*Rotten limestone*" from near Okolona, Chickasaw county. This is a fair sample of the " white prairie rock", and it makes fair lime for building purposes. At some points it pulverizes by exposure, and can be thus obtained for agricultural use.

No. 2221. *Yellowish clay marl* from a railroad cut southeast of Chewalla station, in Alcorn county. Quite heavy and tough when wet, but cracking and pulverizing readily in drying; similar to the subsoil of some prairie spots and materials found near Corinth and Booneville, Prentiss county.

No. 2226. *Greenish micaceous sand* from a bluff on the Tombigbee river near Dr. Tyndall's place, near Aberdeen, Monroe county. A sandy mass of light olive tint, easily pulverized; crops out abundantly on the several bluff banks on the river near and south of Aberdeen. This sand should not be confounded with the non-calcareous and agriculturally worthless loose yellowish sands that underlie it.

No. 327. *Greenish micaceous sand* from the bluff on the Tombigbee river near Waverly, Lowndes county. Abundant, and some portions consolidated into ledges showing impressions of large shells. Quite rich in phosphoric acid, but poor both in lime and potash, and therefore hardly available for hauling to any distance. The material in the bluff at Columbus is poorer than this.

Marls of the northeastern prairie region.

	BLUE OR GREENSAND MARLS.				WHITISH CLAY MARLS.			GREENISH SANDS.	
	TIPPAH COUNTY.			PONTOTOC COUNTY.	CHICKASAW COUNTY.	ALCORN COUNTY.	MONROE COUNTY.	LOWNDES COUNTY.	
	Marl two miles west of Ripley.	Ripley marl.	Braddock's indurate marl.	Nabor's shell marl.	One mile south of Pontotoc, blue marl.	Okolona rotten lime-stone.	Chewalla marl.	Tyndall's Tombigbee sand.	Waverly greenish mi-caceous sand.
	No. 256.	No. 708.	No. 318.	No. 271.	No. 123.	No. 1	No. 2221.	No. 2226.	No. 327.
Insoluble matter	48.819	62.441	40.854	78.242	49.054	10.908	55.524	81.224	86.702
Potash	1.342	0.708	0.154	0.797	1.701	0.248	0.587	0.785	0.304
Soda	0.122	0.272	0.030	0.611	0.156	0.896	0.275	0.117	0.190
Lime	12.228	7.902	21.396	6.874	16.247	45.791	12.297	4.926	1.851
Magnesia	2.823	1.560	0.910	1.445	1.091	0.877	1.214	0.824	0.722
Brown oxide of manganese	0.142	0.160	0.093	0.204	0.070		0.050	0.040	
Peroxide of iron	} 12.512	{ 11.849	11.108	8.027	8.696	1.421	4.766	3.695	} 5.596
Alumina		5.665	1.250	2.591	7.359	1.967	8.444	8.677	
Phosphoric acid		0.396	0.299	0.186	0.199		0.144	0.131	0.826
Sulphuric acid	Fe. S. 0.949		0.185	0.184	0.007		0.212	0.063	0.013
Carbonic acid	11.903	} 9.909	21.425	2.944	11.704	35.723	10.222	1.845	0.472
Water and organic matter	4.449		2.675	1.430	2.701	2.540	4.841	2.862	2.203
Total	100.206	100.977	100.341	99.819	100.075	100.082	99.676	99.869	99.584

II.—THE FLATWOODS REGION.

The flatwoods region constitutes a belt of level land, varying from 6 to 12 miles in width and averaging about 8 miles, which borders on the west the northeastern prairie region, and traverses the western portions of the counties of Tippah, Union, Pontotoc, Chickasaw, Clay, Oktibbeha, Noxubee, and tracts in northeastern Winston and Kemper counties, continuing into Alabama. In its northern portion its eastern outline is sharply defined by an ascent into the red lands of the Pontotoc ridge, while southward of Houston it merges rather imperceptibly into the equally level prairie lands. From these, however, it is distinguished by its timber growth, which differs not so much in the species of the prevailing trees as in their form and development. On the west their outline is also often marked by an abrupt ascent into the hills of the adjacent Yellow loam region, notwithstanding the fact that (as appears from an inspection of the map) the divide between the waters of the Tombigbee and Mississippi lies largely within or on the western border of the flatwoods belt.

The region is throughout underlaid by strata of heavy, gray clay belonging to the older Tertiary formation, from which its prevalent soil is almost directly derived, and into which the transition is often almost insensible within a few feet of the surface. The gray, heavy, intractable soil bears almost throughout a moderately dense growth of post oak, interspersed with short-leaf pine and black gum, and varied with occasional belts or tracts of small-sized, round-headed black-jack, where the soil is excessively heavy. The post oak, unlike that of the prairies, is of a lank, thin growth, with long, rod-like branches pointing upward, and frequently clothed with short, tuft-like, leafy boughs. Near the streams the growth becomes more sturdy, and hickory as well as oaks appear to some extent. The streams, however, have scarcely any true bottoms, their shallow, crooked channels being simply cut into the general level descending slightly toward them. The drainage is therefore exceedingly slow, and during the winter rains the country over large areas is covered with a shallow, slow-moving sheet of muddy water. This, together with the tenacity and depth of the mud, renders the flatwoods belt an almost impassable barrier to teams in winter and far into the spring. For a like reason, the soil frequently remains untillable until the planting season is nearly over, and thus subjects the crop to the uncertain chances of a short growing-season; yet in favorable years, when the water subsides early and the plowing can be done when the soil is just in the right condition, very good crops of corn and cotton are made.

The analyses below show the composition of a specimen of this soil, and of the material from which it was originally derived:

No. 230. *Heavy flatwoods soil* from Sec. 4, T. 10, R. 2 E., Pontotoc county. Timber, post oak and short-leaf pine. No perceptible difference between surface soil and subsoil; specimen taken to 12 inches depth. A yellowish-gray, massy clay, with yellowish cleavage planes.

No. 288. *Flatwoods clay* from an outcrop on same section as above. A roundish nodular, slightly indurated clay, a little lighter in color than the soil, and not plastic until worked for some time, underlies the soil at a depth varying from 0 to 4 feet.

Lands of the flatwoods region.

	Heavy flat-woods soil.	Flatwoods clay.
	No. 230.	No. 288.
Insoluble matter	77. 854 }	68. 099 } 74. 115
Soluble silica		5. 016
Potash	0. 753	0. 797
Soda	0. 106	0. 360
Lime	0. 178	0. 490
Magnesia	0. 691	1. 787
Brown oxide of manganese	0. 167	0. 078
Peroxide of iron	5. 899	7. 123
Alumina	10. 302	11. 322
Phosphoric acid	0. 052	0. 004
Sulphuric acid	0. 032	0. 002
Water and organic matter	3. 680	4. 429
Total	99. 653	100. 471
Humus	0. 306	
Available inorganic	1. 806	
Hygroscopic moisture	9. 33	10. 4
absorbed at	22 C.°	16 C.°

A comparison of the chemical composition of the soil and clay material shows a very close agreement, outside of such differences as are referable to the processes of soil formation, viz, a partial leaching out of lime, magnesia, and soda and an increase of the elements of plant-food that are specially deficient in the clay (viz, phosphoric and sulphuric acids), probably as the result of the additions annually made by the decaying vegetation. But as it is, the soil, though rich in potash, is extremely deficient in phosphates, and, as its color proves, is almost totally devoid of vegetable matter. In consequence, the soil is unthrifty in a marked degree, and the addition of vegetable matter, as well as the use of phosphate manures, is indicated as of first necessity in taking it into cultivation.

Another kind of soil, the extreme opposite of the one described, occupies considerable tracts in northern Pontotoc and northern Chickasaw counties. This soil is in the main a fine, almost pulverulent sand or silt, of a gray tint, with ferruginous dots, the latter in the subsoils sometimes developing into grains of bog ore or "black gravel". It shows but little change from the surface downward, even sometimes to the depth of 20 feet, except when (as is frequently the case) it is underlaid by the heavy soil or clay, in which it seems to form irregular, lake-like basins or channels. Except in the bottoms of the streams in and below the flatwoods we rarely find the two soils naturally intermingled; and while the one is remarkable for its heaviness and imperviousness, the other is equally noted for being so light and leachy that it will hold neither moisture nor manure enough for ordinary crops. Its composition is shown in the analysis on page 24.

15 C P

No. 165. *Light flatwoods soil* from Sec. 36, T. 10, R. 2 E., Chickasaw county. Timber almost exclusively post oak, very little Spanish ("red") oak (*Q. falcata*); huckleberry bushes in depressions. A pale-gray, powdery soil, full of ferruginous dots, increasing downward. No perceptible difference between soil and subsoil; specimen taken to the depth of 12 inches.

Light flatwoods soil.

	Soil.
	No. 165.
Insoluble matter	} 90.375
Soluble silica	
Potash	0.254
Soda	0.068
Lime..	0.082
Magnesia	0.175
Brown oxide of manganese	0.111
Peroxide of iron	1.445
Alumina	3.805
Phosphoric acid................................	trace.
Sulphuric acid	0.008
Water and organic matter	1.333
Total	98.654
Humus	0.801
Available inorganic.............................	4.064
Hygroscopic moisture (air-dried)...............	} 1.70 / 2.05

The mechanical analysis of the two soils (Nos. 230 and 165) resulted as follows:

Mechanical analysis of flatwoods lands.

	PONTOTOC COUNTY.	CHICKASAW COUNTY.
	Heavy flatwoods soil.	Light flatwoods soil.
	No. 230.	No. 165.
Weight of gravel over 1.2^{mm} diameter	....	....
Weight of gravel between 1.2 and 1^{mm}.........	0.3	2.9
Weight of gravel between 1 and 0.6^{mm}........	0.4	7.0
Fine earth	99.3	90.1
Total....................................	100.0	100.0
MECHANICAL ANALYSIS OF FINE EARTH.		
Clay	36.7	9.0
Sediment of < 0.25^{mm} hydraulic value..........	32.7	17.3
Sediment of 0.25^{mm}	36.5	34.5
Sediment of 0.5^{mm}	9.1	13.6
Sediment of 1.0^{mm}	2.7	16.8
Sediment of 2.0^{mm}	1.6	4.0
Sediment of 4.0^{mm}	0.3	2.3
Sediment of 8.0^{mm}	0.3	2.0
Sediment of 16.0^{mm}	....	3.1
Sediment of 32.0^{mm}	....	4.3
Sediment of 64.0^{mm}	....	2.6
Total....................................	98.9	98.8

These analyses show the two soils to be even more unlike in their mechanical than in their chemical composition. The extremely small proportion of the coarser sediments in No. 230, with the high clay percentage, shows good cause for the excessive heaviness. That this can be measurably relieved by the use of the marls which abound on the Pontotoc ridge is shown by the experience had in their actual use, as well as by the great improvement of this soil when lying near the foot of the ridge and receiving its washings. The phosphates and lime carried by these marls of coarse take a share in this improvement.

The clay percentage of No. 165 is larger than would have been supposed from its appearance, but its sediments are so proportioned as to render it powerless toward retentiveness.

While extremely unlike in mechanical composition, the two chief varieties of flatwoods soil agree very nearly in their main deficiencies, viz, in phosphates; and apparently also in sulphuric acid; the percentage of potash in the light soil is not too small for so deep a soil, but lime is quite low, and humus fair, while very deficient in No. 230.

The mode of improvement indicated is thus nearly the same for both soils, viz: green manuring and liming to increase the vegetable matter and to render the light soil more retentive, the heavy one lighter; for the same end intermixture of the two soils wherever this can be done by deep plowing or diversion of drainage; use of the marls of the adjacent Pontotoc ridge for a supply of lime and phosphates; on the small scale, use of bone meal on the light soil, and the same, or superphosphate, on the heavy one.

It has been found that here, as in the gray silt prairies of Louisiana, the treading of cattle improves the light soil for cultivation. In any case, however, it is far inferior to the heavy soil in durability; the latter, in fact, could readily be rendered similar to the prairie soil by the liberal use of marls and green manuring. This may sometimes be noted where it lies at the foot of the ridge and receives the washings of the marl beds; and a similar improvement is noted wherever either the plow or nature has intermingled it with the red ridge soil.

In fair seasons the cotton product averages about 500 or 600 pounds of seed-cotton on the light and 800 or 900 pounds on the heavy soil, when fresh.

WHITE-OAK FLATWOODS.

This kind of land forms belts of one-quarter to several miles in width intervening between the post-oak flatwoods and the hills on the west in southern Chickasaw and southward in Sumner and northern Oktibbeha. Here, as we traverse the flatwoods from east to west, we find the dead gray of the post-oak soil gradually changing toward the yellow, with an increasing amount of sand. The pine and post-oak becomes of sturdier growth, and the Spanish instead of the black-jack oak mingles with them. As we advance the hickory and white oak appear, and near the hills become quite prevalent. The surface of the ground also, instead of being almost bare, as in the post-oak flatwoods, is here covered with a fine growth of grass.

The soil is a rather sandy loam, with a tendency to "working like putty" and adhering strongly to the plow when wet. This is apt to occur in consequence of its being underlaid at the depth of 3 or 4 feet by a stratum of solid, impervious clay, which compels all water to drain slowly sideways. Drainage is therefore the first condition for its profitable cultivation; but the fact that its iron has not been accumulated into bog-ore grains proves that this can be easily done. In favorable seasons it yields even now very fair crops. The soil is best adapted to corn and sweet potatoes, but will make from 500 to 600 pounds of seed-cotton per acre. Its analysis resulted as follows:

No. 147: *White-oak flatwoods soil* from Sec. 33, T. 14, R. 2 E., Chickasaw county. Vegetation as described above; depth taken, 6 inches. A fine sandy loam, pale-yellow tint, drying into hard clods when taken wet.

No. 144. Subsoil of above, 6 to 18 inches. Somewhat heavier than the surface soil, but of the same tint, a little more reddish; was fairly afloat with soil water at 18 inches at the time when taken (April 11).

White-oak flatwoods.

	CHICKASAW COUNTY.	
	Soil.	Subsoil.
	No. 147.	No. 144.
Insoluble matter	89.802 } 92.458	83.040 } 88.730
Soluble silica	2.656	5.690
Potash	0.127	0.171
Soda	0.109	0.152
Lime	0.060	0.148
Magnesia	0.147	0.119
Brown oxide of manganese	0.067	0.051
Peroxide of iron	3.057	3.936
Alumina	1.778	4.627
Phosphoric acid	0.106	0.206
Sulphuric acid	0.013	0.007
Water and organic matter	1.908	2.290
Total	99.945	100.379
Hygroscopic moisture	3.24	7.45
absorbed at	21 C.°	18 C.°

A comparison of this soil with the light soil (No. 165), which it resembles in many respects, shows it to contain less potash but considerably more phosphoric acid, and doubtless more vegetable mold. It also contains more iron, and that in a finely divided condition (in which it renders the soil more absorbent of moisture and heat), instead of being in the shape of bog-ore spots. In the subsoil the only notable difference is that the amounts of lime and phosphoric acid are notably greater than in the latter surface soil, and the percentage of the latter ingredient is especially quite high. This, added to the greater retentiveness of the subsoil, as indicated by the high percentage of alumina, renders its superior productiveness quite intelligible. After the primary requirement of drainage, that of potash manures (for which the greensand marls of the Pontotoc ridge are available) will probably soonest be felt.

BOTTOMS OF THE FLATWOODS REGION.—Where the heavy soil prevails exclusively the streams, as stated, have no bottom properly so called, and the soil near them is practically the same as elsewhere; but where the water-courses traverse belts of the several different kinds the alluvial soils resulting from their intermixture are often of an excellent mechanical constitution and possess considerable fertility, as indicated by their timber growth. Among the latter the chestnut-white oak is almost always prominent, and large black and sweet gums, shellbark hickory, and willow oak are rarely wanting. Ash, elm, and tulip tree ("poplar") also occur with frequency. Notwithstanding their fertility, these bottoms are as yet but little settled, on account of their undrained condition, which makes crops late, and also renders them unhealthy.

The numerous streams heading in the flatwoods region generally preserve their characteristics for a considerable distance beyond its limits, and this is especially the case with those flowing westward toward the Yalobusha and Yockeney, whose heavily timbered bottoms become and remain submerged and impassable simultaneously with the flatwoods proper, and for that reason, and also in a measure on account of the heavy expense of clearing them, are as yet but little settled. Wherever reclaimed, these soils have proved very fertile; no analyses have yet been made of them.

The following analyses of bottom soils, taken within the hilly region adjoining the flatwoods on the west and deriving their soils from them, serve to exemplify some of their characters:

No. 180. *Bottom soil* from Potlockney creek, Sec. 15, T. 10, R. 2 W., La Fayette county. Very heavily timbered as above stated, with the addition of beech and white oak on the higher portions. Soil closely resembling that of the white-oak flatwoods (see page 23), rather sandy, and when wet "working like putty", but very productive when well cultivated and drained. Soil taken to 8 inches depth, of a tawny tint.

No. 299. Subsoil of above, 8 to 18 inches. Pale yellow, and when taken wet "working like putty" and then hardening into a rock-like mass.

No. 369. *Soil of bottom of Loosha-Scoona river* from Sec. 12, T. 13, R. 2 W., Calhoun county. Timber, the bottom oaks, tulip trees, beech, elm, and hornbeam, with some maple and ash. Soil, mouse-color when wet, whitish when dry; some ferruginous spots.

No. 370. Subsoil of above, 10 to 18 inches, and whitish, putty-like, with spots and concretions of bog ore.

Bottom lands of the Flatwoods region.

	La Fayette County (R. 2 W., T. 10, S. 15).		Calhoun County (R. 2 W., T. 13, S. 12).	
	POTLOCKNEY BOTTOM.		LOOSHA-SCOONA BOTTOM.	
	Soil.	Subsoil.	Soil.	Subsoil.
	No. 180.	No. 299.	No. 369.	No. 370.
Insoluble matter............................	87.880 } 89.370	88.472 } 90.640	77.539 } 84.866	81.920 } 89.148
Soluble silica..............................	1.490	2.168	7.327	7.228
Potash....................................	0.180	0.392	0.494	0.392
Soda......................................	0.090	0.083	0.410	0.165
Lime......................................	0.156	0.089	0.295	0.122
Magnesia..................................	0.277	0.394	0.442	0.306
Brown oxide of manganese..................	0.264	0.106	0.088	0.106
Peroxide of iron...........................	2.725	2.956	3.057	2.579
Alumina..................................	2.792	3.115	3.896	5.485
Phosphoric acid...........................	0.115	0.075	0.176	0.055
Sulphuric acid.............................	0.014	0.006	0.004	0.005
Water and organic matter..................	4.446	2.686	7.839	2.349
Total.................................	100.368	100.434	100.499	100.214
Hygroscopic moisture......................	6.81	6.00	6.81	5.56
absorbed at...............................	11 C.°	11 C.°	15 C.°	16 C.°

According to these analyses these bottom soils differ from the two principal flatwoods soils essentially in their considerably greater percentage of potash, and phosphoric acid, which in both, moreover, is larger in the surface soil than in the subsoil. This fact is doubtless connected with the more or less continuous formation of bog ore, by which the subsoil is being depleted of phosphates through a kind of leaching process. In the white-oak flatwoods, where this process does not occur, the phosphates in the subsoil are nearly double those in the surface soil.

The high percentages of potash, lime, and phosphoric acid in the Loosha-Scoona soil, coupled with the large amount of soluble silica (indicating a corresponding availability of the plant-food) and a desirable moisture coefficient, indicate that this soil, when reclaimed by drainage, will be highly productive and very durable. In the latter respect the Potlockney surface soil is likely to be greatly inferior, but this may be balanced by the large phosphate percentage in the subsoil.

III.—YELLOW LOAM OR OAK UPLANDS REGION.

The main body of the lands classed under this head lie in northern Mississippi between the flatwoods on the east and the Mississippi bottom on the west and north of the "Central prairie region". Minor bodies of similar lands, however, occur in the southern part of the state, as shown by the coloring on the map; and as there are all degrees of transition from its soils to those of the adjoining regions its limits cannot be very accurately defined.

The general characteristics of its soils may be thus stated: Those of the better class of uplands are formed by a yellow or brownish loam, varying greatly in thickness from a few inches to as much as 20 feet, but averaging

238

from 3 to 4 feet, and forming mostly light or only moderately heavy soils, underlaid at the depth stated by either hard-pan or loose sand of the Drift formation. On the poorer uplands this loam subsoil is thin or sometimes entirely wanting, so that the Drift materials themselves, or their intermixtures with the loam, form sandy soils, which, though sometimes quite productive at first, wear out very rapidly.

TIMBER TREES.—The former class of soils is timbered essentially with Spanish, black, and large, sturdy post oak (*Q. falcata, tinctoria, stellata*), and more or less hickory, to which, in case either of unusual heaviness or sandiness, the black-jack oak (*Q. nigra*) is commonly added. The scarlet oak (locally also called "Spanish", *Q. coccinea*) also occurs more or less scattered among the predominant growth mentioned, its appearance being considered a sure indication of a comparatively inferior soil, merging into the "black-jack ridge" and "pine-hill" soils of northern Mississippi. A frequent admixture of hickory, on the contrary, is as surely deemed an indication of improvement and of a strong soil, the "hickory hummocks" forming the slopes toward the streams in the hill lands being, as a rule, the best.

The appearance of the short-leaf pine (*Pinus mitis*) among the timber growth is always an indication of inferior durability of the soil, which is mostly a pale-yellow, sandy loam, bearing, in addition to the pine, post and black-jack oaks, or, in case of extreme sandiness, the latter alone, forming the hopelessly barren "black-jack ridges". An admixture of hickory indicates the existence of a more or less retentive and fertile subsoil, and commonly varies inversely as the pine, so that we usually find the latter disappearing on the lower slopes, while scarlet, Spanish, and finally the black oak set in as the bottoms are approached. The latter are, as a rule, the lands chiefly cultivated in the short-leaf pine region.

It is very essential, however, in judging by its timber-growth the position of any of these soils in the scale of comparison, to take into account not only the kind (species) of the trees, but also their mode of growth. The black-jack and post oak especially, as species, characterize the poorest as well as the richest upland soils, both of this region and of the southwestern states generally, but their mode of development is very different in each case. So of the Spanish oak (*Q. falcata*), whose range of soils is almost equally wide, and whose different forms it is not at all easy to distinguish.

A good-sized post oak of sturdy, thick-set growth, with stout, short, crooked, and rapidly tapering branches and a dense, well-shaped top, will never be found on a poor or easily exhausted soil; but let it be small and scrubby, with numerous small branches and a sparse, tattered top, or its trunk tall, thin, and tapering, with long, rod-like branches, themselves often clothed with short, leafy twigs, forming an open, irregular, tattered top, and little is to be expected of the soil's productiveness.

With the black-jack oak the characteristics are somewhat different. The short and knotty black-jack, whose trunk will sometimes scarcely yield a straight piece long enough for a fence-post and generally places the purchaser of cord-wood under a grievous disadvantage, which possesses short and very crooked branches and a tattered, open top, is characteristic of the poor "black-jack ridges", and, when very small beside, denotes the very poorest soil. Dense, rounded tops, with rather low, but straight trunks, belong to the heavy prairie soils of northeastern and central Mississippi, and, on the other hand, to the fertile but extremely sandy ridge soils of southern Noxubee, Kemper, Landerdale, and Jasper; while on the fertile yellow loam soils of northern Marshall, Yalobusha, Holmes, and Yazoo the black-jack forms large, well-shaped, spreading trees, sometimes 50 feet and more in height, with trunks comparatively straight, or at least not whimsically knotted, like those of the pine hills, but generally leaning over to one side with a regular curve and without straggling branches on the trunk below the top.

The Spanish ("red") oak (*Q. falcata*) does not frequent soils of any extreme physical or chemical character. Soils where this tree prevails are generally easily tilled, but are yet not liable to suffer from drought. As to their quality, a great deal depends upon the size of the tree. If it be rather stout; if the main branches grow out at a large angle (more or less squarely), so as to form a rounded top, closed on all sides, the soil is sure to be a strong one; but if the trunk be lank, slender, and of a whitish hue, forking into straight, slender branches, tending upward (somewhat in the shape of a broom) and presenting a tattered top, open below, but little can be expected of the soil.

The same, though on a higher grade of soil, applies to the black oak. The white oak (*Q. alba*), when of a sturdy growth and with rounded top, belongs to the best of "hummock" soils, but is not a safe mark of strong land when it is lank and tall with a very long top. It is, of course, not only the mode of growth, but also, and very essentially, the size of the trees, that requires to be considered in judging of land by its timber growth. Very large trees of any kind will rarely be found on a poor soil. Nor will the individual trees of any region necessarily exhibit the same type throughout. It is the average or predominant form and size that must be taken as a guide; and it must not be forgotten that where the growth is crowded all peculiarities of form must be greatly modified, or even entirely lost.

Small trees of the black gum (*Nyssa multiflora*) are usually an unwelcome indication in the uplands, and the chestnut, though not always considered as characterizing a poor soil, is found almost universally in large, scattered individuals in the pine lands of northern Mississippi.

FLATWOODS HILLS.

It has been stated (page 20) that the western limit of the post-oak flatwoods is often sharply defined by a sudden descent from the hilly country of the region now under consideration. Sometimes the transition is then very sudden from a very sandy ridge to the stiff gray flatwoods clay soil. But this is by no means always the case; and even when the transition from hill to level is abrupt we not uncommonly find the lower portion of the hills continue the flatwoods character far inland, while sandy knolls cap the crests of the ridges. The transition region thus formed I shall designate as the Flatwoods hills. This feature is especially developed in ranges 1 E. and 1 W., in La Fayette and Calhoun counties, where numerous strips and escalops on the heavy clay soils, with the timber growth of the flatwoods, extend westward into the hill country. North of the Tallahatchie river, in Tippah county, we also meet this feature more or less, the flatwoods belt itself, as previously stated, being there rather undulating. But inasmuch as the materials of the underlying strata are there largely sandy, the resulting soils are, as a rule, much less heavy than is the case farther south. Here, as we approach this region from the west, the change from the sandy soils of the pine hills is indicated in the shape and development of the post, Spanish, and scarlet oaks, previously referred to. These trees become lank and thin, with long branches forming open tops, and have whitish barks. The soil, instead of washing badly, as is the case elsewhere in the yellow-loam region, remains firm, and simply cracks open in summer, while in winter it forms redoubtable muddy hillsides, of bad repute with teamsters. Where the sandy strata overlying the clay are of some thickness springs usually flow from the upper surface of the latter, which can often be readily traced by the terraces running along the hillsides.

The soils formed from the heavy clays in these hills are, on the whole, safer in cultivation than those of the level flatwoods, being better drained; but they are not thrifty, and, unless well and deeply tilled, as a rule yield but poor returns. Hence here also it is the lower hillsides and bottoms of streams that are chiefly cultivated, and their soils being an intermixture of the two extremes they are mostly very productive.

In the portion of this region adjacent to the white-oak flatwoods the white oak is usually found on the hills also, and where this is the case the soil is less extreme in character, more tractable, and generally more productive. Such is the case in southeastern Calhoun and the adjacent portion of Sumner county.

Farther south the clay soils of the flatwoods hills are generally of a more reddish cast, less refractory in tillage, and more productive, as in Sumner and Choctaw counties, where they yield as much as 800 pounds of seed-cotton per acre and hold out remarkably well. In Winston county we find the "Noxubee hills", with their productive red clay soils, bordering the flatwoods on the west as far south as Winstonville. Beyond this point, in Noxubee and northern Kemper, very sandy ridges form the western limit of the flatwoods; but in eastern Kemper, on the Bodka, where the flatwoods terminate, we once more find "flatwoods hills" like those of La Fayette and Calhoun.

The following analyses of soils from this region indicate their general character:

No. 119. Soil from Sec. 25, T. 9, R. 1. W., just west of McLaurin's creek, La Fayette county. Timber, mainly post oak, with black-jack and pine, a few scattered Spanish, and sometimes a scarlet oak. Specimen taken to the depth of 6 inches; color, yellowish-buff, moderately heavy. Beneath, a very stiff, yellow or light orange tinted subsoil.

No. 374. Soil from upland near Benela, just south of the main Yalobusha, Sec. 27, T. 14, R. 1. W., Calhoun county. Timber, short-leaf pine, Spanish, black, and post oak, more or less hickory, and black gum. Trees mostly of good size, often bearing grape-vines. A fair upland soil, yielding from 700 to 800 pounds of seed-cotton per acre. Color, gray; depth, 6 to 8 inches; not heavy.

No. 367. Subsoil of the above, 8 to 18 inches. Color, dark orange; quite heavy in tillage.

No. 160. *Noxubee hills subsoil* from Sec. 7, T. 15, R. 13 E., Winston county. Timber, white and black oak and hickory; on lower hillsides, some tulip tree ("poplar", *Liriodendron*). The soil here is quite dark tinted, but is only a few inches deep. The subsoil analyzed was taken from 3 to 10 inches depth, and thus represents more nearly the arable soil, which is quite durable, and yields from 800 to 1,000 pounds of seed-cotton per acre when well cultivated. This is one of the "red lands" soils to be hereafter considered more in detail.

Lands of the flatwoods hills.

	LA FAYETTE COUNTY, M'LAURIN'S CREEK.	CALHOUN COUNTY, BENELA UPLANDS.		WINSTON COUNTY, NOXUBEE HILLS.
	Soil.	Soil.	Subsoil.	Subsoil.
	No. 119.	No. 374.	No. 367.	No. 160.
Insoluble matter............................	92.872 } 94.504	91.498 } 98.220	83.900	88.390 } 86.006
Soluble silica................................	1.632	1.722		2.609
Potash..	0.152	0.127	0.855	0.196
Soda..	0.058	0.094	0.097	0.096
Lime..	0.144	0.172	0.197	0.092
Magnesia......................................	0.130	0.203	0.502	0.215
Brown oxide of manganese................	0.065	0.095	0.708	0.063
Peroxide of iron.............................	1.631	1.872	4.628	3.570
Alumina.......................................	1.274	1.822	6.943	4.770
Phosphoric acid.............................	0.040	0.088	0.080	0.271
Sulphuric acid...............................	0.036	....	....	0.014
Water and organic matter.................	3.350	3.304	3.280	4.873
Total.....................................	100.384	100.229	100.255	100.154
Hygroscopic moisture......................	3.71	3.96	7.73	10.38
absorbed at..............................	18 C.°	11 C.°	11 C.°	17 C.°

It will be noted that, while the two soils agree very nearly in their composition, they differ widely from the two subsoils analyzed. As is in fact apparent from inspection, as well as from the statement made by those cultivating them, "the quality of their land depends more upon the subsoil than the surface soil." Deep tillage is therefore the first point indicated for profitable cultivation and improvement.

The soil from McLaurin's creek is manifestly the poorer, both in phosphoric acid and lime as well as in vegetable matter, and quite unretentive of moisture; hence subject to drought unless tillage reaches into the subsoil. The Benela soil and subsoil are twice as rich in phosphates, though even there the amount is not large, and will soon require to be supplied, while in the subsoil potash is quite abundant, though low in both surface soils. The superior fertility of the Noxubee hills subsoil is obviously due to the unusually large amount of phosphoric acid, which makes up for its deficiency in lime. The latter is comparatively abundant in the soils from La Fayette and Calhoun, but more would be beneficial, and can be added with advantage. Both subsoils have a high moisture coefficient, and thus resist drought: a property probably largely aided by the iron (ferric hydrate) with which they are tinted.

SHORT-LEAF PINE AND OAK UPLANDS.

The short-leaf pine (*Pinus mitis*) rarely occupies the ground exclusively within the state, as in Louisiana. It generally occurs intermixed to a greater or less degree with oaks, and its admixture to the oak growth is, as a rule, considered an indication of a poorer or at least a less durable soil than that which is timbered with the same oaks alone, unless, indeed, it be in the case of the sandy "black-jack ridges". The oaks usually accompanying it are the post and black-jack. Some small hickory and black gum is rarely wanting, and large chestnut trees occur scattered throughout even the poorest pine hills.

The pine is generally most abundant on the crests of the ridges, and is more and more displaced by the oaks as we descend from them. Concurrently, the scarlet and Spanish oak, and often the black oak, make their appearance, and finally prevail, with hickory in the smaller bottoms and lower slopes of the region. The latter form the bulk of the cultivated lands within the short-leaf pine districts. Where the latter border upon the oak uplands or table-lands the outposts of the pine may be seen afar in small groups, occupying high crests or knolls, usually rooted among piles of ferruginous sandstone, which caps the higher points almost throughout the hill region of northern and middle Mississippi.

Apart from such spots the soil occupied by the pine is mostly very light, often sandy, of a tawny tint, and underlaid at a few inches depth by a pale-yellow sandy subsoil. This may pass farther down into a pure sand, and then little can be done with the soil; or it may be underlaid by a sandy or more or less clayey loam or hard-pan, forming a good foundation capable of bearing any improvement. These variations, while of course more or less noticeable in the growth of the pine itself, are most strikingly indicated by the changes in the concomitant trees. Pine hill plateaus, with a vigorous growth of the tree, are often quite profitably cultivated for from four to eight years in corn and cotton, yielding from 500 to 800 pounds of the latter per acre, after which the land is usually "turned out" and a fresh tract cleared. The first, after three or four years' rest, may yield a few more crops, provided all its soil has not in the meantime been washed away or cut up by gullying, but after that manure alone will enable it to produce profitable crops. What effect the simple return of the cottonseed made from the outset would produce can only be conjectured as yet, as commercial fertilizers have probably never yet touched such lands within the state.

While, however, the lands of a large portion of the area shown on the map by the pale-red tint are of this character, and are in part so broken as to be unavailable for cultivation on that account, there are frequently interspersed upland tracts, more or less extensive, where the pine forms only a subordinate ingredient among the timber, and where the Spanish, post, scarlet, with some white or black oak, really form the characteristic growth, and for short distances the pine may be entirely absent. Such tracts occur especially on the headwaters of the Big Black and Yalobusha rivers, in southern Calhoun, in Sumner, and in Choctaw counties, and such lands, with thorough culture, will produce for eight to ten years from 800 to as much as 1,000 pounds of seed-cotton per acre. The creek bottoms in this region are wide and especially fine for cotton, and are generally very heavily timbered. Similar lands occur in the western portion of the area laid down, as well as in western La Fayette, southern Benton, eastern Tippah, and generally in the region lying east of the prairies in northeastern Mississippi. On the whole, however, it is a country of small farms, where corn, sweet potatoes, and cereals dispute the ground with cotton, and should probably over a large portion of the area replace it altogether. Where communications permit, sawing the pine into lumber forms a lucrative business.

The short-leaf pine country of southern Mississippi differs in some respects from that lying north of the "Central prairie region". Ridges timbered with short-leaf pine and oak occur interspersed more or less throughout the northern long-leaf pine region and form its best upland soils, and are usually the sites for villages. But it would be difficult to map them out in detail. A large continuous tract in eastern Rankin is, however, laid down on the map, and will be more specially mentioned hereafter.

In southwestern Mississippi there lies between the long-leaf pine region on the east and the "Cane hills" on the west a belt of hilly medium quality uplands bearing a mixed growth of oaks and short-leaf (with occasional strips of long-leaf) pine, and also interspersed with more or less extensive tracts, whose gently undulating surface and better soil have caused them to be taken into cultivation by preference, as in portions of Franklin and Claiborne counties. These lands will be again noticed in the description of the bordering regions.

SOILS OF THE SHORT-LEAF PINE AND OAK LANDS.—The following analyses of soils from the short-leaf pine and oak districts, though few in regard to the large surface to be covered, probably convey a pretty correct idea of this class of soils:

No. 142. *Oak upland soils* from Sec. 22, T. 20, R. 9 E. (about half-way between Bellefontaine and Greensboro'), Sumner county. Gently rolling; timber, almost exclusively Spanish oak (*Q. falcata*), with some post oak and hickory. Soil yellowish-buff, rather light; taken to 6 inches depth. Produces 700 to 900 pounds of seed-cotton per acre when fresh.

No. 145. Subsoil of the above. 6 to 15 inches depth; yellow, clayey.

No. 37. *Pine upland soil* from Marion, Lauderdale county. Surface somewhat hilly; timber, post oak, short-leaf pine, sturdy trees prevalent, intermixed with more or less hickory, Spanish, and some black oak and black gum. Soil down to 12 inches of a buff color, sandy, and easily tilled.

No. 118. Subsoil of the above. A yellow, sandy loam to 2 feet depth. This soil produces fairly from 600 to 700 pounds of seed-cotton per acre, and is interesting because the culture of the Catawba grape has succeeded well in the neighborhood, the soil having been worked to the depth of 2 feet.

No. 71. *Soil from "Hamburg hills"*, Sec. 11, T. 7, R. 1 E., 1 mile north of the town, Franklin county. From the level top of the ridge the country is somewhat broken. Timber, Spanish, black-jack, black and white oaks, hickory, magnolia, black gum, sweet gum, some short-leaf pine, and muscadine vines. Color, dun down to 7 inches; a medium light loam.

No. 73. Subsoil of the above, 7 to 20 inches depth, and apparently unchanged for 3 feet. This soil is said to be very durable, and when fresh produces from 700 to 900 pounds of seed-cotton per acre.

No. 108. *Upland soil* from Sec. 47, T. 13, R. 4 E. (Mr. J. F. Brock's land), near Rocky springs, Claiborne county. Ridgy upland near the western edge of the long-leaf pine region; timber, largely beech and large Spanish oak, also white and chestnut-white (or basket) oaks, much holly, small magnolias in heads of hollows, and some short-leaf pine. Soil, pale dun color, somewhat ashy down to 10 inches depth.

No. 112. Subsoil of the above, taken 10 to 18 inches deep. A moderately clayey loam, yellow to brownish, much heavier than the surface soil. The latter produces well only peanuts and sweet potatoes, and manure remains unaltered in it for a long time. It is evidently very unretentive.

Short-leaf pine and oak uplands.

	SUMNER COUNTY, NORTH OF GREENSBORO'.		LAUDERDALE COUNTY, MARION.		FRANKLIN COUNTY, HAMBURG HILLS.		CLAIBORNE COUNTY, BROCK'S PLANTATION.	
	Soil.	Subsoil.	Soil.	Subsoil.	Soil.	Subsoil.	Soil.	Subsoil
	No. 142.	No. 145.	No. 37.	No. 118.	No. 71.	No. 73.	No. 108.	No. 112.
Insoluble matter	90.296 } 92.556	76.925 } 83.658	95.702 } 93.576	83.212 } 88.596	88.750 } 90.560	74.894 } 84.368	78.992 } 86.422	78.804 } 86.714
Soluble silica	2.324	7.533	1.874	5.386	1.810	9.474	7.430	7.910
Potash	0.236	0.359	0.093	0.227	0.140	0.286	0.318	0.296
Soda	0.085	0.103	0.021	0.082	0.090	0.104	0.087	0.084
Lime	0.092	0.067	0.047	0.089	0.070	0.127	0.137	0.090
Magnesia	0.196	0.381	0.116	0.227	0.185	0.599	0.800	0.492
Brown oxide of manganese	0.072	0.071	0.021	0.037	0.075	0.144	0.072	0.032
Peroxide of iron	1.830	5.151	0.966	3.330	2.405	5.672	4.970	4.613
Alumina	1.886	7.079	1.031	4.337	2.098	6.106	5.061	5.277
Phosphoric acid	0.081	0.070	0.019	0.061	0.077	0.050	0.025	0.042
Sulphuric acid	0.007	0.008	0.005	0.007	0.005	0.006	0.007	0.056
Water and organic matter	2.834	3.321	1.651	2.728	4.310	2.659	2.477	2.767
Total	98.868	100.282	99.547	99.763	100.015	100.163	100.178	100.343
Hygroscopic moisture absorbed at	3.57	3.59	1.56	5.81	4.40	3.81	3.64	7.61
	11 C.°	11 C.°	16 C.°	16 C.°	22 C.°	22 C.°	18 C.°	18 C.°

The soil from Sumner county is probably a fair representative of the best class of upland soils occurring within the short-leaf pine region of northern Mississippi, forming tracts a few miles in extent where the pine is scarce or entirely absent. It is to be regretted that we have no analyses of some pine soil of the same region, but on comparison with the poorer (though by no means the poorest) soil from Marion we find a wide difference between them as regards potash, lime, and phosphoric acid, in all of which the Marion soil is several times poorer. But the subsoils are not unlike in the two localities, though a slight advantage still remains with the Sumner subsoil. The Hamburg hills soil stands intermediate between the two former in regard to the main points, potash and phosphates, but is somewhat richer in lime, and hence is more thrifty. Brock's soil shows a considerable amount of potash, but is, on the other hand, so poor in phosphates and so unretentive of moisture that the faults complained of in regard to it are at once explained. A dressing of bone-meal and green manuring are the improvements indicated in this case.

Throughout the whole set we find that the percentage of phosphoric acid is low, the highest being 0.091, the lowest 0.019 in the soils. The average in the soils is 0.053; in the subsoils, 0.056. There can thus be little doubt that phosphatic fertilizers will be found most efficacious in sustaining their productiveness, and that deep tillage, increasing the retentiveness of the soil and its supply of potash, will be serviceable in all cases where the subsoil is not sandy. The use of lime or marl also would seem to be specially called for in order to render active, and thus available for crops, such supply of plant-food as the soil contains.

THE RED LANDS.

Interspersed among the pine lands of central Mississippi, in Attala, Winston, Leake, Neshoba, and part of Kemper and Newton counties, there occur limited areas of generally clayey land, whose deep orange tint stands in strong contrast to the peculiarly pale yellow of the prevailing pine-woods soils. The origin of these red lands is best observed in northwestern Attala, where regular strata of similar material crop out on the banks of the Big Black river and its tributaries. There, as well as in the adjacent portion of Holmes county, the orange-colored clay and sand not unfrequently contain abundant grains of greensand, so that in places a greensand fertilizer of great value can be obtained. It is doubtless this circumstance that in a large degree gives rise to the lasting fertility of these soils, which is keenly appreciated by the inhabitants throughout their region of occurrence. From the fact that the red-clay stratum is neither very thick nor always continuous, it will be readily inferred that in a hilly country it must appear sporadically in limited patches along hillsides or forming the tops of ridges or a terrace along streams, according to the level at which it may accidentally appear on the surface.

The two largest bodies of these red lands occur, respectively, in northwestern Attala, on Zilfa and Poukta creeks, and in northeastern Winston, where they form the "Noxubee hills", already referred to in connection with the "Flatwoods hills". The two bodies are connected by numerous patches lying between and not easy to map out; the characteristic features of the soil are best developed in Attala. The country occupied by it is always broken (as is the case with the red lands of Louisiana), and the creek bottoms are very narrow, but extremely fertile, and bear a very heavy growth of timber. On the hills also the timber is unusually large, and consists of white, post, and black oak, hickory, tulip tree ("poplar"), and sometimes sweet gum, always with an admixture of short-leaf pine. Sometimes the light pine-woods soil overlies the red soil for a few inches, but where the latter alone prevails there seems to be little difference between soil and subsoil, all being of a deep orange tint and quite heavy. It is not, however, very difficult to till when taken at the right time. Where instead of the clay the simflarly-colored sandy strata come to the surface the soil is often scarcely distinguishable from that of the ordinary pine woods save by its timber growth. Such is largely the case in the country lying between Zilfa creek and the Big Black river.

The Noxubee hills, on the southern heads of the Noxubee river, in Winston county, greatly resemble in general character and timber growth the country on the Poukta—the surface broken, bottoms of the streams narrow but fertile, the country well settled with small farms; and the soil with very imperfect tillage produces from 800 to 1,000 pounds of seed-cotton per acre and is very durable, in strong contrast to the pale and sandy pine-woods soil, which produces from 400 to 600 pounds for a few years and is then exhausted.

The following analyses exhibit the composition of some of these soils. One of them (No. 141) has already been mentioned in connection with the prairie soils, to which it evidently bears a close relation on one hand, while on the other it manifestly, from its nature, position, and behavior in cultivation, belongs to the class of "red lands".

No. 246. *Red hills soil* from Sec. 4, T. 14, R. 7 E., about 3 miles north of Kosciusko, Attala county. Timber, white, post, black, and Spanish oaks, hickory, and some short-leaf pine. A deep orange, rather heavy clay, gritty with sharp sand grains, taken to 12 inches depth; no perceptible difference between surface soil and subsoil.

No. 141. *Red ridge soil* from Sec. 12, T. 12, R. 18 E., Kemper county. (See "Northeastern prairie region".)

No. 160. *Noxubee hills subsoil*, Sec. 7, T. 15, R. 13 E., Winston county. (See "Northeastern prairie region".) This soil likewise does not represent the best of its kind.

Red lands.

	ATTALA COUNTY, NORTH OF KOSCIUSKO.	KEMPER COUNTY, PETTUS' PLANTATION.	WINSTON COUNTY. NOXUBEE HILLS.	CARROLL COUNTY, VAIDEN GREENSANDS.	
	Soil.	Soil.	Subsoil.	Sandy.	Clayey.
	No. 246.	No. 141.	No. 160.	No. 265.	No. 266.
Insoluble matter	61.971	84.969 } 87.781 / 11.819	85.899 } 88.898 / 3.099	89.105	72.272
Soluble silica	8.795	0.431	0.196	1.604	0.945
Potash	0.297	0.277	0.068	0.945	0.401
Soda	0.920	0.540	0.082	0.186	0.164
Lime	1.463	6.836	0.318	1.630	1.129
Magnesia	0.129	0.079	0.082		0.177
Brown oxide of manganese	10.500	7.080	3.570 } 84.347 /	3.435
Peroxide of iron	17.500	16.071	4.770		4.440
Alumina					
Phosphoric acid	0.012	0.187	0.271	trace.	trace.
Sulphuric acid		0.009	0.014	0.129	0.001
Water and organic matter	6.580	6.922	4.873	7.013	4.790
Total	100.006	100.225	100.184	100.638	100.442
Humus		0.781			
Available inorganic		3.286			
Hygroscopic moisture	16.59	13.07	10.88		
absorbed at	8 C.°	11 C.°	17 C.°		

A mechanical analysis of the Attala red hills soil, No. 246, resulted as follows:

Attala county red hills soil.

	Subsoil.
	No. 246.
MECHANICAL ANALYSIS.	
Weight of gravel over 1.2ᵐᵐ diameter....................	....
Weight of gravel between 1 2 and 1ᵐᵐ.................... }	2.0
Weight of gravel between 1 and 0.6ᵐᵐ.................... }	
Fine earth	98.0
Total	100.0
MECHANICAL ANALYSIS OF FINE EARTH.	
Clay	41.2
Sediment of < 0.25ᵐᵐ hydraulic value..................	25.8
Sediment of 0.25ᵐᵐ..............................	18.6
Sediment of 0 5ᵐᵐ..............................	2.8
Sediment of 1.0ᵐᵐ...........................A.	3.7
Sediment of 2.0ᵐᵐ..............................	1.8
Sediment of 4.0ᵐᵐ..............................	1.8
Sediment of 8.0ᵐᵐ..............................	0.7
Sediment of 16.0ᵐᵐ..............................	3.1
Sediment of 32.0ᵐᵐ..............................	2.4
Sediment of 64.0ᵐᵐ..............................	0.7
Total	96.1

The apparent excessive amount of clay in this soil, as shown above, is, in part, to be charged to the large percentage of iron (ferric oxide) contained in it, and nearly all of which in this case accumulates in the finest portion of the soil. The ferric oxide in the entire soil amounts to 10.5 per cent., and probably at least 9 per cent. of that amount is included in the 41.2 per cent. of "clay", of which, therefore, only about 32 per cent. should be counted, adding the 9 per cent. to the finest sediment. This brings the red soil nearly to the same composition as the Monroe prairie subsoil, with which it has many points in common.

The Attala soil, by its unusually large percentage of alkalies, shows the presence of small grains of greensand. Its lime percentage is nearly as high as that of some prairie soils; its iron and alumina extraordinarily high; and the former is so finely diffused and so highly colored as to impart to the soil a very unusual character, especially as to its hygroscopic power, which is greater than that of any soil that has come under my observation, save only peat soils. The extremely low percentage of phosphoric acid is very unexpected, and I am inclined to believe it incorrect, both on account of its actual fertility and of the high percentage of the other soils of the same class. In more than one respect this peculiar soil deserves farther investigation.

Except as to phosphates, the characters of No. 141 are similar, but less pronounced.

Apart from its large amount of phosphates there is little to distinguish the Noxubee hills soil from other clay loam soils, and its heaviness is rather surprising, as is its deep tint, with an iron percentage no greater than is found in common yellow loams.

As an example of the materials from which these soils are mainly formed, I give the analysis of a coarse, sandy mass, bearing abundant greensand grains, which occurs in the railroad cut near Vaiden station, Carroll county, and has been used with advantage on other soils; also that of a stiff, gritty clay occurring near the same place and on the banks of the Big Black river opposite, forming strata of considerable thickness. Extensive deposits of these materials exist, especially in northeastern Attala, and will doubtless in the future be utilized as fertilizers.

The striking scarcity of phosphates in these materials may explain sufficiently the corresponding feature in the soil more or less directly derived from them. In all other respects the Attala red lands soil are so promising that beyond a doubt the use of phosphatic fertilizers on them would be followed by a greatly increased productiveness.

THE SANDY OAK UPLANDS.

These are ridgy lands, often intervening between the short-leaf pine country and the "table-lands" proper, or extending in ridges into them or into the prairie region of central Mississippi. They differ from the pine country in the absence of the pine sand in the alternation of often sharp and sandy ridges, with broader and lower ones covered with a loam stratum resembling that of the table-lands, but more sandy, and, in most cases, inferior to them in fertility. These bear a fair growth of upland oaks, among which the Spanish oak (*Q. falcata*, "red" oak of the natives) is perhaps the most prominent, mingled more or less with black, scarlet, and post oak, and, as the soil grows sandier, with the black-jack. On the sandy ridges the latter reigns supreme, low trees, with a few long, crooked, and spreading branches, forming an open, "sprangling," tattered top, and is accompanied by huckleberry bushes. Tall, compact-topped, black-jack trees, on the contrary, denote the best class of upland soils in this region.

234

◄

the soil being in that case somewhat heavier than that occupied by the other oaks mentioned. Hickory is also a common ingredient of the timber of the better class of soils, sometimes forming extensive "hickory hummock" tracts of excellent soil.

This description applies more especially to the eastern border of the table-lands of northern Mississippi, and is most extensively developed in Marshall and La Fayette counties, as shown on the map by a light-yellow color. It would scarcely be possible, or even useful, to map out in detail elsewhere this transition phase between the short-leaf pine hills and table-lands bordering the Mississippi bottom.

The subjoined analyses afford an insight into the nature of the soils of this region:

No. 228. *Oak uplands soil* from southeast ¼ T. 7, R. 3 W. (Alex. Pegues' place), La Fayette county. Face of country, rolling; timber, Spanish, black, some black-jack and post oak, and hickory; large and compact trees. Soil, dun color, light, 5 inches deep, and liable to damage by washing. Cotton product, 800 to 1,000 pounds per acre when land is fresh.

No. 221. Subsoil of above. Brownish-yellow, heavier than surface soil, taken to 18 inches depth. Total thickness, 4 to 7 feet to hard-pan or sand.

No. 345. *Black-jack ridge soil* from ridge one-half mile west of the campus of the University of Mississippi, Oxford, La Fayette county. Country somewhat broken; timber on ridge, small black-jack oaks, huckleberry bushes. Taken to the depth of 6 inches a pale-dun tint, and quite light and sandy.

Sandy oak uplands of La Fayette county.

	OAK UPLANDS.		BLACK-JACK RIDGE.
	Soil.	Subsoil.	Soil.
	No. 228.	No. 221.	No. 345.
Insoluble matter.............................	90.150 } 91.786		
Soluble silica	1.636 }	8.677	97.092
Potash	0.119	0.364	0.078
Soda	0.119	0.135	0.029
Lime	0.147	0.358	0.142
Magnesia	0.532	0.272	0.109
Brown oxide of manganese...................	0.176	0.450	
Peroxide of iron	2.532	2.428	0.907
Alumina	2.602	4.526	0.646
Phosphoric acid...............................	0.154	0.045	
Sulphuric acid.................................	0.007	0.069	0.062
Water and organic matter	2.217	3.467	0.911
Total..........................	100.392	100.726	99.887
Hygroscopic moisture.........................	4.60	4.68	1.20
absorbed at........................	11 C.°	10 C.°	14 C.°

A comparison of the soil and subsoil Nos. 220 and 221 with those from Sumner county (Nos. 142 and 145) shows that they differ in the main as to their lime percentage, which is considerably greater in both of the La Fayette soils; hence the absence of pine. The subsoils are alike as to potash. The distribution of the phosphates is also alike, and averages about the same amount in both, while in neither is it very large, and will therefore soon require replacement.

The Black-jack ridge soil is wretchedly poor in every ingredient except lime, of which it has still a better supply than the average pine-woods soils; but its potash and phosphates are very deficient, and it is droughty beside, even more so than the pine soil.

As compared with the adjacent brown-loam table-lands, the sandy oak uplands differ in that their subsoils are generally inclined to be sandy instead of heavier than the surface soils, and also poorer in phosphates. Hence, although deep tillage is desirable, it will not be as much of an improvement as in the case of the table-lands, nor are the soils as durable under exhaustive cultivation.

THE BROWN-LOAM TABLE-LANDS.

This rolling or gently undulating upland region, producing a large proportion (about 30 per cent.) of the best upland cotton grown in the state of Mississippi, forms a belt running more or less parallel to the "bluff" of the Mississippi bottom, which bounds it on the west, while on the east it is bordered by the pine and oak uplands previously described. In western Tennessee, and down to the latitude of Ashland, about 12 miles south of the state line of Mississippi, its width east and west is from 60 to 65 miles; but it thence rapidly contracts to about 20 miles near Panola, and maintains about that width for a hundred miles to the southward (to the line of Yazoo county), where it again widens to about 40 miles, so as to reach Pearl river in the counties of Madison and Hinds, about 50 miles southward. Here it abuts against the pine hills of Copiah, while its most westerly portion, modified by the "bluff or loess" formation which here underlies it, continues skirting the Mississippi bluff, with a width varying from 15 to 6 miles, to the Louisiana line. Its total area thus outlined is about 5,800 square miles; but the broken country lying along the river bluff from Yazoo city southward will be separately described under the designation of "the Cane hills", embracing about 1,800 square miles of the above area.

Excluding these from consideration, the character of the main body may be thus summed up:

The soil-forming material is a stratum of brown or yellowish-brown loam, usually from 6 to 8 feet thick, but sometimes as much as 20 feet or as little as 3 feet. It is commonly underlaid by sand of various colors, from white to red, more or less cemented, and sometimes entirely loose, belonging to the stratified "Drift" formation. The timber consists essentially of oaks and hickories. Of the former, the post oak is perhaps the tree most universally present. On the heavier soils it is largely accompanied by the black-jack oak (*Q. ferruginea*); on the lighter more prevalently by Spanish and black oak (*Q. falcata* and *Q. tinctoria*). The sturdy and vigorous growth of the post oak and the corresponding forms of the other trees, denoting a soil of great fertility, are very strikingly developed here. Near the eastern border of the region, often not very well defined, we often find sandy ridges extending in from the adjacent hilly lands or forming isolated outliers, whether of oak alone or mingled with short-leaved pine. From the country of the latter character the transition to the table-lands proper is generally quite sudden, while that to the sandy oak hills is often quite insensible, as in northwestern La Fayette. On the western border the gradual admixture of tulip tree ("poplar", *Liriodendron*), sweet gum, and sometimes ash and sassafras with the other timber forms a transition to the lands of the immediate Mississippi bluff. Originally all this region had the appearance of a natural park, being an open forest with little undergrowth, but waving with long grass and brilliant flowers. The ranging of cattle and the indiscriminate and injudicious firing of the dry leaves and grass have sadly changed the aspect even of such tracts as have remained uncultivated, the washing away of the surface soil and the formation of deep gullies having frequently not only rendered the fair face of the country unsightly, but also seriously impaired its agricultural value. Elsewhere the open woods have to a great extent been marred by the springing up of a thick undergrowth of young saplings, which of yore were kept down in favor of the grass pasture by the regular and judiciously-timed burning practiced by the Indians.

The surface soil as at present existing is not generally rich in vegetable matter, and often differs but little in aspect from the subsoil found at a depth of 2 or 3 feet; yet usually the surface layer to the depth of 10 or 12 inches is darker and more mellow in cultivation than the deeper layers, having at least a shade of "mulatto" tint added to the reddish brown of the subsoil. The latter is mostly a "clay loam", with a tendency to increasing heaviness as we approach the edge of the "bottom" and the reverse as we near its eastern border.

The following analyses of soils and subsoils from different portions of the table-land region illustrate their composition, although they leave unrepresented the large counties from Marshall and De Soto to Carroll. The specimens analyzed, however, agree so nearly in regard to the main points that it is fair to presume that the part of the region lying intermediate between them would not differ materially from them as to their general nature:

No. 216. *Soil from the table-lands* on the divide between Coldwater and Wolf rivers, near Lamar, Benton county, Sec. 30, T. 2, R. 1 W. (Clayton's plantation), from a level tract below the summit ridge. Timber, black-jack, post oak, and hickory, with some sweet gum and a few Spanish oaks (*Q. falcata*); all large and well-formed compact-topped trees. Depth taken, 10 inches; quite mellow, and of a "mulatto" tint.

No. 235. Subsoil of the above; depth, 10 to 20 inches—a pretty solid, brownish loam, heavier than the soil.

No. 219. Subsoil from same section of land, but taken on the summit ridge itself. Same depth as last, and altogether resembling it.

No. 53. *Soil of loam uplands* from near Richland, Holmes county, Sec. 23, T. 13, R. 5 E. (Mr. Elias Taylor's land). Gently rolling surface; timber, post and Spanish oak, large, and ground covered with fine grass. Taken 8 inches deep. When fresh yields 1,200 pounds of seed-cotton per acre; after 10 years, still 750 pounds.

No. 56. Subsoil of above, but taken in a gully some distance off, at the depth of 3 feet, the loam appearing perfectly uniform for from 6 to 15 feet, and sometimes more.

No. 55. *Cultivated soil* from same locality, taken to 6 inches depth. Has been cultivated exhaustively, all but one year of fallow, for twenty-one years in corn and cotton. Yields about 500 pounds of seed-cotton per acre.

No. 298. *Loam upland subsoil* from Dr. T. J. Catchings' place, Sec. 2, T. 4, R. 3 W., Hinds county. Gently undulating; timber, black-jack, post, and Spanish oaks, all large and sturdy, with well-formed tops; some tall hickory; undergrowth of dogwood and persimmon. Depth taken, 9 to 20 inches. A light porous loam, easily tilled; color, brownish yellow. Seed-cotton product, about 1,200 pounds per acre when fresh.

No. 348. *Loam upland soil* from H. O. Dixon's place, Sec. 26, T. 6, R. 1 W. (about half way between Clinton and Jackson), Hinds county. Gently undulating; timber, Spanish, post, and black-jack oaks, hickory, some walnut and mulberry. Depth taken, 8 inches; easily tilled, pervious enough for drainage. Yields from 1,000 to 1,500 pounds of seed-cotton per acre; after eight years' culture, 600 to 1,000.

No. 349. Subsoil of the above taken 8 to 20 inches deep. Color, yellow to red; heavier than the surface soil.

No. 232. *Brown loam upland soil* from James Watson's place, 5½ miles northeast of Port Gibson, Claiborne county. This is in the "Cane hills" region, as previously stated, and is a continuation of the loam stratum of the table-lands, but is modified by the underlying formation. Face of the country, hilly; specimen taken from level summit of ridge; timber, white, chestnut white, black and some Spanish oaks, beech, hickory, sweet and black gum, linden, sassafras, elm, some magnolia. Soil taken to 8 inches depth; rather light, of a buff tint; fine.

No. 233. Subsoil of the above. Depth taken, 8 to 20 inches. A yellowish-brown loam, much heavier than the surface soil.

Brown-loam table-lands.

	BENTON COUNTY.			HOLMES COUNTY.			HINDS COUNTY.				CLAIBORNE COUNTY.	
	TABLE-LANDS.			RICHLAND.	UPLAND.		UPLAND LOAM.	UPLAND.			UPLAND LOAM.	
				Virgin.	Cultivated.							
	Soil.	Subsoil.	Ridge subsoil.	Soil.	Subsoil.	Soil.	Subsoil.	Soil.	Subsoil.		Soil.	Subsoil.
	No 216.	No. 235.	No. 219.	No. 53.	No. 56.	No. 55.	No. 296.	No. 348.	No. 349.		No. 232.	No. 233.
Insoluble matter........	} 83.347	83.990	{70.530}{12.300} 83.830	89.509	85.462	92.254} 94.145 1.891}	80.788	82.198} 92.746 0.548}	74.179} 66.796 10.617}		97.573	79.477
Soluble silica............												
Potash...................	0.549	0.700	0.690	0.304	0.762	0.129	0.624	0.417	0.519	}	0.458	0.761
Soda....................	0.082	0.041	0.090	0.054	0.175	0.043	0.185	0.042	0.131		0.124	0.248
Lime....................	0.245	0.139	0.270	0.250	0.392	0.159	0.296	0.156	0.204		0.244	0.228
Magnesia...............	0.479	0.597	0.450	0.307	0.756	0.351	1.059	0.140	0.626		0.545	0.690
Br. oxide of manganese .	0.760	0.933	0.960	0.374	0.256	0.141	0.180	0.067	0.039		0.205	0.346
Peroxide of iron........	4.796	3.562	5.110	2.136	4.297	1.627	4.927	1.903	4.100		2.231	3.655
Alumina................	5.292	7.729	5.090	3.554	5.787	1.703	5.940	3.157	6.747		4.642	5.849
Phosphoric acid........	0.068	0.206	0.210	0.074	0.087	0.071	0.151	0.038	0.050		0.103	0.092
Sulphuric acid..........	0.062	0.054	0.020	0.018	0.049	0.012	0.076	0.019	0.029		0.028	trace.
Water and organic matter.	4.195	2.716	3.140	3.557	2.345	2.019	3.239	2.364	3.039		3.073	3.496
Total	100.567	100.820	100.900	100.237	100.696	100.300	100.294	100.550	100.280		100.438	99.952
Humus...	0.767										0.718	
Available inorganic.	0.668										0.718	
Hygroscopic moisture ...	6.84	7.42		4.70	5.84	2.43	5.54	4.26	7.23		5.18	5.88
absorbed at...........	17 C.°	17 C.°		17 C.°	9 C.°	11 C.°	17 C.°	9 C.°	10 C.°		21 C.°	8 C.°

The following are the mechanical analyses of soils from the oak uplands region thus far made. No. 397 is from the portion of the "sandy oak uplands" lying nearest the table-land area, while No. 219 is representative of the table-lands of Marshall and Benton counties. See the descriptive notes preceding the table.

	LA FAYETTE COUNTY.	BENTON COUNTY.
	Upland subsoil.	Table-land subsoil.
	No. 397.	No. 219.
MECHANICAL ANALYSIS.		
Weight of gravel over 1.2ᵐᵐ diameter........		
Weight of gravel between 1.2 and 1ᵐᵐ........		} 0.2
Weight of gravel between 1 and 0.6ᵐᵐ........		
Fine earth..............................	100.0	99.8
Total..............................	100.0	100.0
MECHANICAL ANALYSIS OF FINE EARTH.		
Clay..................................	17.9	19.2
Sediment of 0.25ᵐᵐ hydraulic value..........	15.9	22.7
Sediment of 0.5ᵐᵐ	27.5	15.1
Sediment of 0.5ᵐᵐ........................	16.6	13.1
Sediment of 1.0ᵐᵐ........................	13.1	7.3
Sediment of 2.0ᵐᵐ........................	5.6	9.9
Sediment of 4.0ᵐᵐ........................	0.8	6.8
Sediment of 8.0ᵐᵐ........................	0.2	0.8
Sediment of 16.0ᵐᵐ........................		{1.2
Sediment of 32.0ᵐᵐ........................	} 0.8	{2.5
Sediment of 64.0ᵐᵐ........................		{1.5
Total..............................	98.5	97.8

These analyses place both subsoils into the heavier class of loams, while the surface soils of both are considerably lighter. Both soils and subsoils have, when exposed to rain and followed by sunshine, the disagreeable peculiarity of forming a hard surface crust, which should be broken whenever formed, as it is a serious hinderance to the success of crops in critical seasons.

The common chemical characteristics of these soils, and especially of their subsoils, are high percentages of potash and lime, with usually a large supply of phosphoric acid in the subsoil, at least of the heavier lands; while in the case of the lighter soils, such as that of the Richland neighborhood, as well as in that from southern Hinds, the phosphates are rather low, even deficient in the latter case. The great depth and perviousness of the arable layer in these cases makes up for the smaller proportion of phosphates, but there can be no doubt that the want of these will be the first felt when the soil becomes "tired", and that supplying them will greatly increase the crops, as has in fact already been demonstrated in many cases. Potash is not likely to become deficient in the subsoils at least; but the supply of humus is not large (as is evident from inspection), and green manuring is one of the most important improvements indicated. Originally this was not the case, for the surface soils were, and in protected spots still are, dark-colored to almost black when wet; but the washing away of the surface and the burning of the woods have served to deplete the surface of this and other important ingredients, so that over a large portion of the region it is the subsoil, and not the surface soil, as given in the analysis, that the farmer has to deal with. In this case the addition of vegetable matter is, of course, doubly important, and green manuring of denuded tracts with cow-pease is one of the most convenient, as it has proved to be one of the best, means of improvement. The analyses show that so long as the subsoil remains the question of restoration of a "tired" soil is simply one of time and judicious management. But unfortunately there has been a great deal of almost irretrievable damage done to these lands by allowing them to be washed and finally gullied by the rains, the water ultimately cutting into the underlying sand, and thereafter undermining the soil stratum and converting the hill lands into unavailable sand-hills, while the valleys also have been filled up with a mixture of sand and soil, the former usually predominating, rendering them almost as unavailable for cultivation as the hills. Considering that these lands are doubly valuable from being naturally underdrained by the underlying sand and gravel, this dilapidation is doubly to be deplored. In the eastern portion of the table-land belt, especially in the counties of Benton, Marshall, western La Fayette, and southward, where the surface is somewhat rolling, the amount of injury thus done is of wide extent, and, when once begun, difficult to check. It usually originates in the practice of plowing up and down hill instead of horizontally, the plewing being very shallow at that. Deep tillage and "horizontalizing" of the hillsides are therefore the first and most indispensable measures to be taken against this evil. It is of little avail to manure the soil so long as its best portion is allowed to wash away. The unsightly red-scarred slopes, so lamentably abundant along the line of the Central railroad, can with proper management be mostly restored to productiveness; but every year the evil increases in a geometrical ratio, and if unchecked must result in the serious and permanent injury to the agricultural interests of one of the fairest and naturally most highly favored portions of the state.

BOTTOM SOILS OF THE YELLOW-LOAM REGION.—The bottom soils of the yellow-loam region are quite variable, according to the location and size of the water-courses and the direction in which they flow. The bottom soils of the smaller streams heading and emptying within the region are usually quite light, and sometimes even very sandy where ravines have been cut into the drift sands, in consequence of neglect of old fields. The same is generally true of streams flowing nearly north and south, while those having (as is mostly the case) a southwesterly course, and heading in the clay hills bordering the flatwoods on the west or in the flatwoods themselves, have heavy bottom soils, at least in the upper part of their course. Such is the case especially with the Loosha-Scoona and Yockeney-Patafa, and to a greater or less degree also with the Tallahatchie and Yalobusha rivers, while the Big Black and Pearl, whose heads remain almost entirely west of the flatwoods territory, have almost throughout light bottom soils.

The second bottoms, or "hummocks", usually elevated from 2 to as much as 5 feet above the first bottom and seldom reached by high water now, are almost throughout lighter than the corresponding first-bottom soils, and are, on the whole, considered to be less durable. They are frequently "white" or light-gray silts, with a subsoil of similar character, and usually contain more or less bog-ore spots or grains, proving that at some time they were subject to long-continued submergence or at least to drenching with water.

The following analyses, though not as numerous as could be desired for the representation of all the different classes of bottom and "hummock" soils in the region, will convey some general idea of their character:

No. 365. *Soil of the first bottom of the Tallahatchie river*, taken near the town of Panola, R. 7 W., T. 9, Sec. 6, Panola county. This is just at the point where the river bottom begins to widen out preparatory to entering the great Yazoo bottom plain. It is very heavily timbered, and is traversed by numerous cypress sloughs. The prominent trees are sweet gum, tulip tree (very large), hickories, ash, chestnut-white and water oaks, walnut, much holly, hornbeam, etc. The soil is dark-colored, rather light, and the same to the depth of 18 inches or more. Depth of the sample taken, 12 inches. A highly productive soil, but subject to annual overflows.

No. 369. *Soil of the bottom of the Loosha-Scoona river*, R. 1 W., T. 14, Sec. 4, on the Pittaborough and Sarepta road, Calhoun county. The timber is beech, sweet and black gum, ash, chestnut-white and water oaks, shellbark and other bottom hickories, hornbeam, elm, maple, holly, and box elder. Trees mostly tall and vigorous. The soil is remarkably shallow for a bottom soil. being only about 6 inches deep, and when dry does not appear to be very heavy, though when wet it forms extremely tough mud, and is heavy in tillage. The subsoil is gray, with brown dots when wet, very pale gray when dry, and pulverizes readily on exposure to the weather. Being annually overflowed until late in the season, it has hardly as yet been tried in cultivation.

No. 370. Subsoil of the above, taken 6 to 18 inches deep. Somewhat heavier than the surface soil.

No. 180. *Soil from the bottom of Potlockney creek,* R. 2 W., T. 10, Sec. 10, La Fayette county. Very heavily timbered, so as to render clearing very costly. Beech very prevalent on the higher "ridges", less so in the lower ground; white oak very prevalent; also chestnut-white oak, sweet gum, tulip tree or poplar, shellbark hickory, black gum, holly, ironwood, cucumber tree (*Magnolia acuminata*), snowdrop tree (*Halesia tetraptera*), dogwood, red-bud, ash, and maple. The soil is a fine-grained loam of a mouse color to the depth of about 15 inches; tills like putty when too wet, which is apt to be the case pretty late in spring, but is very productive in good seasons.

No. 299. Subsoil of the above, 12 to 20 inches in depth. Pale yellow, fine, sandy, disposed to be wet, putty-like. In low places becomes pale-bluish, and full of bog-ore spots.

No. 135. *Soil from the bottom of Besachitto creek,* R. 10 E., T. 19, Sec. 11, Choctaw county. Timber, beech, ash, shellbark hickory, and others, chestnut-white, water and willow, and bottom scarlet oaks (*Q. coccinea*), sweet gum, tulip tree, ironwood, holly; timber mostly large. Soil, a light loam, blackish, color nearly the same for 2 feet, when it becomes heavier and of a paler tint. Very productive. This may be considered as a type of good bottom soils of the smaller streams in the yellow-loam region.

On the Big Black river and its tributaries the hummock or second bottom lands are usually quite extensive, and lie conveniently for cultivation. The following analyses convey a general view of their composition:

No. 156. *Hummock soil* from the second bottom of the Big Black river at the crossing of the Greensborough and Bankston road, R. 9 E., T. 19, Sec. 33, Sumner county. A mellow, chocolate-colored soil, occupying a bench only 3 to 4 feet above the first bottom, about 1 mile wide, and well settled here. Sample taken to the depth of 12 inches. Timber, beech, hickory, elm, ash, ironwood, red-bud, etc. The first bottom here is so much subject to overflow as to have hardly been tried, but the soil resembles that of the hummock.

No. 58. *Hummock soil* from the flat bordering the Big Black river on the Benton-Canton road on the south side for several miles width. A light gray, sometimes white, powdery soil, taken to the depth of 6 inches; timber, a rather undersized growth of post, willow, and some black-jack oaks of the low, spreading type. The land is not very productive, and is liable to injury from drought, but is nevertheless largely in cultivation.

No. 57. Subsoil of the above taken from 6 to 12 inches depth. Nearly of the same tint as the subsoil, but somewhat stiffer, putty-like when wet, and with occasional spots of bog ore, indicating lack of drainage. Lower down the subsoil becomes somewhat darker and stiffer, and is full of bog-ore gravel.

No. 48. *Hummock soil* from the flat intervening between the uplands and the bottom of the Big Black river near Vaiden station, R. 6 E., T. 17, Sec. 17, Carroll county. A light, silty soil, of a dark-gray tint for about 12 inches depth. It is mainly treeless, but has occasional clumps of moderate-sized post oaks, and occasionally some small sweet gum. This soil when fresh produces good Irish potatoes and cereals (small grain), but is not suited to corn or cotton; is somewhat liable to injury from drought.

No. 52. Subsoil of the above, a fine, slightly clayey sand of a pale-yellow tint, very pervious. Seems to continue with little change to a depth of about 15 feet, where water is found in wells.

No. 50. *Yockanookana hummock soil,* from the lower slope of the uplands toward the Yockanookana river, R. 6 E., T. 12, Sec. 13 (John T. Denald's land), Leake county. Soil apparently the same to the depth of 18 inches; sample taken to the depth of 12 inches. It is gray, ashy, full of bog-ore spots; well timbered with mockernut hickory, white, black, scarlet, and Spanish oaks, elm, beech, and bottom pine, all moderately-sized trees. The soil produces fairly well.

Bottom lands of the Yellow-loam region.

	PANOLA COUNTY (R. 7 W., T. 9, S. 6).	CALHOUN COUNTY (R. 1 W., T. 14, S. 4).		LA FAYETTE COUNTY (R. 2 W., T. 10, S. 10).		CHOCTAW COUNTY (R. 10 E., T. 19, S. 11).
	TALLAHATCHIE.	LOOSHA-SCOONA BOTTOM.		POTLOCKNEY BOTTOM.		BESACHITTO BOTTOM.
	Bottom soil.	Soil.	Subsoil.	Soil.	Subsoil.	Soil.
	No. 365.	No. 369.	No. 276.	No. 180.	No. 299.	No. 135.
Insoluble matter	81.368 } 86.466	77.033 } 84.466	81.600 } 86.148	83.276 } 90.840	88.134 } 90.784
Soluble silica	5.888	7.577	7.220	1.600 } 82.070	2.168 } 2.698
Potash	0.788	0.494	0.292	0.186	0.292	0.238
Soda	0.234	0.410	0.165	0.209	0.063	0.638
Lime	0.365	0.235	0.122	0.156	0.090	0.076
Magnesia	0.928	0.442	0.306	0.277	0.394	0.297
Brown oxide of manganese	0.113	0.069	0.168	0.294	0.108	0.142
Peroxide of iron	2.075	2.037	2.079	2.725	2.935	1.871
Alumina	4.087	3.536	5.085	2.702	3.115	2.906
Phosphoric acid	0.125	0.178	0.055	0.115	0.075	0.063
Sulphuric acid	0.035	0.004	0.055	0.014	0.006	0.009
Water and organic matter	3.601	7.839	2.849	4.446	2.656	3.639
Total	100.751	100.409	100.214	100.2.8	100.434	100.475
Hygroscopic moisture	6.12	6.61	5.56	6.81	6.69	5.52
absorbed at	11 C.°	15 C.°	18 C.°	11 C.°	11 C.°	18 C.°

COTTON PRODUCTION IN MISSISSIPPI.

Bottom lands of the Yellow-loam region—Continued.

	SUMNER COUNTY (R. 9 E., T. 10, S. 22).	MADISON COUNTY (R. 11 E., T. 10, S. 24).		CARROLL COUNTY (R. 6 E., T. 17, S. 17).		LEAKE COUNTY (R. 9 E., T. 12, S. 13).
	BIG BLACK HUMMOCK.	BIG BLACK HUMMOCK.		POST-OAK HUMMOCK.		YOCKANOOKANA HUMMOCK.
	Soil.	Soil.	Subsoil.	Soil.	Subsoil.	Soil.
	No. 156.	No. 56.	No. 57.	No. 48.	No. 52.	No. 50.
Insoluble matter	85.692 } 89.834	90.847	88.342 } 93.226	89.391	86.080 } 90.230	93.232
Soluble silica	3.642 }		4.964 }		4.150 }	
Potash	0.172	0.341	0.142	0.192	0.212	0.207
Soda	0.064	0.044	0.063	0.060	0.076	0.042
Lime	0.092	0.163	0.063	0.075	0.059	0.132
Magnesia	0.250	0.153	0.131	0.087	0.238	0.104
Brown oxide of manganese	0.450	0.231	0.034	0.117	0.127	0.123
Peroxide of iron	2.873	1.014	1.668	1.214	3.921	0.983
Alumina	3.470	2.102	2.980	4.373	3.350	1.036
Phosphoric acid	0.175	0.079	0.004	0.054	0.076	0.041
Sulphuric acid	0.007	0.028	0.005	0.046	0.008	0.026
Water and organic matter	2.969	1.892	1.760	4.093	2.573	2.230
Total	90.877	96.894	100.250	99.702	100.780	100.005
Hygroscopic moisture	4.65	1.20	4.54	4.66	5.11	3.25
absorbed at	11 C.°	8 C.°	22 C.°	11 C.°	21 C.°	6 C.°

A prominent and coincident feature of all these bottom soils is their lightness, as indicated by the high insoluble residues, ranging from 86.6 to 90.8, and their nearly uniform moisture coefficient, ranging between 5.5 and 6.8, enhanced, no doubt, by a considerable percentage of humus. The supply of lime in the surface soils is larger than in the corresponding soils of the adjacent uplands (see previous table), and is also uniformly larger in the surface than in the subsoils. The phosphoric acid appears to follow a similar law as between soil and subsoil, but is evidently not always increased as compared with the corresponding upland soils. The potash percentages are at least not materially higher than in the uplands. It is evidently the greater depth of the soil layer proper, its easy tillage and more uniform moisture throughout the growing season, that causes the preference shown to bottom soils by cultivators.

The second bottom soils are more siliceous in character on the average, and their potash percentages are, on the whole, remarkably low, not only in this region, but elsewhere, as compared with the corresponding upland soils. This ingredient will therefore probably have to be supplied soon. The lime percentages are at least not increased, and the same is true of the phosphates, even as determined in the analyses, which includes that contained in the almost universally present bog-ore grains. The gray hummock soils are probably in the great majority of cases deficient in both lime and phosphates, as they nearly always are in humus, and their easy and convenient tillability renders their improvement by green manuring and the use of bone-meal or superphosphates specially advisable. No. 156 is exceptional in its supply of phosphates, which renders it very productive when fresh. It does not, however, lie entirely above the reach of present overflows, and differs little from the first-bottom soil. The soil from Vaiden seems to be in great need of more lime, which would probably correct its behavior toward corn and cotton crops. The low moisture absorption of No. 58 explains the droughtiness, and its color, as well as the small percentage of volatile matter, shows it to be in need of a supply of vegetable matter by green manuring.

NATURAL FERTILIZERS IN THE YELLOW LOAM REGION.—The formation underlying the greater part of the region ("northern lignitic" Tertiary) furnishes no materials of any fertilizing qualities. In its southern portion, however, adjoining the "Central prairie" region, not only are the marls of that country accessible for use, but there also occur within the limits of the Short-leaf pine and oak uplands, at a number of points somewhat irregularly distributed, deposits of sandy or clayey materials rich in greensand or glauconite grains, which are rich in potash in a very available form. Similar materials occur in New Jersey and elsewhere, and are used with great advantage on lands exhausted by cultivation, in vegetable gardens, etc. When concentrated by washing, the greensand will bear shipment by rail. The occurrence of greensands near Vaiden, Carroll county, has been mentioned in the description of the red lands, where also analyses are given. Materials not quite so rich occur in the banks of the Chickasawhay river, at and near Enterprise, Clarke county, and thence northwestward are often found in outcropping in Clarke and Newton counties. Their agricultural value may be pretty correctly estimated from the amount of soft greenish grains contained in the mass, which, when cut wet, make green streaks on the smooth surface. They sometimes contain a little lime, but rarely any considerable amount of phosphoric acid.

240

IV.—THE ALLUVIAL REGION OF THE MISSISSIPPI.

The portion of the alluvial plain of the Mississippi river lying within the state, and popularly known as the " Yazoo bottom", forms a lozenge-shaped body of 7,200 square miles between the eastward sweep of the bluff and a corresponding westward curve of the river, at whose head lies the city of Memphis, and which terminates southward at the high ridge (the " Walnut hills") which abuts upon the river at Vicksburg. The area thus outlined has a maximum length a little west of south of about 190 miles, while its greatest width, almost at its geometrical center, is 70 miles. Southward of Vicksburg the river keeps close to the eastern highland, whose base it frequently washes (see " Cane hills region"), and between which only small and isolated alluvial areas (aggregating to a total of about 250 square miles) are found within the state. The main area includes the following counties and parts of counties: all of Tunica, Quitman, Coahoma, Bolivar, Sunflower, Le Flore, Washington, Sharkey, and Issaquena, the western portions of De Soto, Panola, Tallahatchie, Grenada, Holmes, Yazoo, and Warren.

TOPOGRAPHY.—The Mississippi river receives scarcely any of the drainage of the bottom plain until it has all accumulated in the Yazoo. This, as has been previously explained (see " general features of the alluvial plain", etc., above), arises from the fact that the main river occupies a ridge forming the highest portion of a cross section of the alluvial plain, so that its overflow at any given point will find the lowest portion at the foot of the eastern and western bluff (the Yazoo or Washita) and will tend to flood the entire intervening regions. Originally several natural channels formed outlets toward either side, in Mississippi especially, the Yazoo pass diverging from the main river at Moon lake above Friar's point and connecting with the Coldwater river about 18 miles to the eastward. But the attempt to prevent the flooding of the back country by means of levees on the main river involved the closing of these lateral outlets—a policy that has given rise to much bitter local controversy.

The surface of the entire region is apparently level, but each stream or " bayou" repeats on a small scale the feature of the main river just referred to, viz, it is bordered by a ridge formed of its own deposits, higher than the " back country" intervening between it and its next neighbor, which is usually, in part at least, occupied by low swamps. The variations of surface level do not usually exceed 15 feet, and the entire region presents a network of meandering bayous, creeks, and rivers, and is dotted with innumerable small lakes, mostly representing deserted " bends" of water-courses.

There are three chief drainage systems, parallel with each other, through which the waters find their way slowly and sluggishly southward, where they finally unite with the main Yazoo and empty into the Mississippi river. These are the *Coldwater and Yazoo basin* on the extreme east, from the Tennessee line southward; the *Sunflower basin* and its tributaries, occupying a large region centrally from Friar's point southward to the Yazoo; and the *Deer creek basin* on the southwest, a narrow but important region, nearly adjoining the Mississippi river, from Washington county southward to the Yazoo. Within these several regions the lands are so low that the bayous often form connecting links between the waters of the streams without affecting their general southward course.

The timber growth of the swamps is mostly cypress, sometimes hung with long moss (*Tillandsia usneoides*), and sometimes having an undergrowth of greenbrier, etc., though mostly open. On either side, and reaching to the ridges, the forest growth is more dense, often accompanied by a heavy undergrowth of cane (canebrakes), and comprises a great variety of trees, according as the land is of the rich buckshot character of the Deer creek region, the " white land" variety of the Sunflower basin, or of the dark loam of the Yazoo. The ridges themselves also are heavily timbered with sweet gum, oak, maple, etc.

The larger proportion of the population and of the lands under cultivation within the region is found along the highlands that border the Mississippi river and along Deer creek. Here, too, are the great cotton plantations, where the largest part of the cotton is produced, its acreage comprising from 15 to 20 per cent., or even more, of its total area. Cotton is the chief crop of the region, its product being about 30 per cent. of that of the entire state. Its average yield per acre is 984 pounds of seed-cotton, the maximum of 1,272 pounds being reached in Issaquena county.

Water for domestic purposes is throughout the bottom obtained either from shallow wells or by means of iron tubes driven into the ground, the water always rising to within 30 feet of the surface, so that even where the tubes are driven 60 or 80 feet the water can easily be drawn up with pumps. It sometimes even happens that the water approaches to within 2 feet of the surface. In some parts of the region the people prefer to use the water from the bayous. This, however, during the summer months, and when the bayous are shallow, is of a greenish tint and " very hard", i. e., calcareous, and charged with vegetable matter, causing malarious diseases.

SOIL VARIETIES.—The lands of the alluvial region embrace several distinct varieties, which are thus given by Professor Smith :

1. A *dark-gray sandy loam*, forming the front-land of many of the creeks and bayous of the bottom. The timber growth is chiefly honey-locust, hackberry, and sweet gum. The soil of the Dogwood ridge and the front-lands of the Mississippi in most places are of this class.

16 C P

2. *A light-gray sandy loam*, with yellowish and orange streaks. This loam is sometimes of a light-yellow color, forms the front-land of Sunflower and Tchula lake (Holmes county), and occurs frequently elsewhere. The growth is sweet gum, maple, water and willow oaks, elm, and hackberry.

3. *A light-colored sandy "clay"*, or fine sediment, of close texture, with a few yellow spots. The growth is chiefly swamp chestnut, oak, and sweet gum, with some ash, maple, and willow oak. This is the soil of the "white lands", which occurs chiefly on Silver creek and on the bayous on both sides of the Sunflower river westward to about half way between the Sunflower river and Deer creek, while northward it is found to some extent on the east side of the Dogwood ridge, in Tallahatchie county. ·

4. *A light-gray tenacious "buckshot" clay*, traversed by cracks, streaked with ferruginous coloring matter, and crumbling upon exposure to the weather into angular fragments—"buckshot." This occurs chiefly in the northern part of the region.

5. *A stiff, dark-gray "buckshot" clay*, sometimes nearly black, traversed in all directions by cracks, and full of streaks and dots of ferruginous matter. This is the "buckshot" clay *par excellence*, and forms the most fertile soil in the bottom. The territory of which it forms the surface soil is generally subject to overflow, but there is usually a strip from one-half to three-fourths of a mile wide back from the banks of the streams under cultivation. The growth is sweet gum, overcup, willow and water oaks, hackberry, and pecan; near the banks of the streams an undergrowth of cane, and in the low swamps no cane, but an open cypress glade.

For convenience in a more detailed description of the alluvial region the three separate drainage systems or basins and the Dogwood ridge given above will be treated of as distinct divisions, each of which is pretty well characterized by its peculiar soil varieties.

The Yazoo basin.—The belt of country thus designated lies in the eastern portion of the alluvial region, reaching from the Tennessee line southward to Vicksburg, and is included between the "Dogwood ridge" on the west and the bluff or upland region on the east. It covers an area of about 2,600 square miles, and is drained on the north by the Coldwater river, and south by the Yazoo, the name given to the former after its junction with the Tallahatchie. These rivers have numerous tributaries, the largest and most important of which enter the alluvial region from the highlands of the east. Its surface is also interspersed with many lakes, creeks, and bayous, which often cross-connect the larger streams. The greater part of the belt is a dense swamp of low overflowed lands, the higher lands occurring only along the streams themselves in strips from one-half to a mile wide, and comprising the only areas at present under cultivation or inhabited. The soil of the lowlands in the upper half of the belt is mostly a black loam, very rich and productive when it can be cultivated. Near the junction of the Coldwater and the Tallahatchie rivers there is some "white land" having a yellowish sandy soil a few inches deep and a white clay subsoil, probably the most northerly occurrence of that variety which so largely characterizes the Sunflower river section. Its timber growth here embraces sweet gum, swamp chestnut oak, with some white oak and hickory. The bottoms of the east side of the Tallahatchie have a light yellowish-sandy loam soil, and a growth of sweet gum, swamp chestnut oak, with a few white oaks, holly, and an undergrowth of cane. The banks of the Coldwater river are high and more or less sandy, and are largely under cultivation to within 4 miles of the junction, yielding very fine crops of cotton.

The southern half of this Yazoo belt is more swampy in character than the northern, the low, overflowed swamps being wider and more extensive. In other respects the two are very similar, and we here find only close to the streams lands high enough above overflow to warrant cultivation, while the low swamps occupy the interior with their dark loam or "greenish-yellow, hard-baked" soils (as near the mouth of the Sunflower river), largely covered with an abundant growth of pecan, also red and willow oaks, large and symmetrical, a few water oaks, honey-locust, sycamore, sweet gum, and hackberry. At the foot of the bluff on the east the lands embrace a dark sandy loam, very rich and productive, formed to a large extent by the washings from the loess hills.

A feature of the southern half of the Yazoo river region is the occurrence of a number of so-called "prairies" upon the higher portions of the bottom lands. They have none of the characteristics of the prairies of other parts of the state, except that they were destitute of large trees when first found. They are probably simply the "clearings" made by the Indians, as shell heaps and Indian mounds usually are found near them. Their soil is apparently the same as that of the surrounding bottoms, and they are now occupied by plantations.

Honey island, in the western part of Holmes county, is formed by the Yazoo river on the west and Tchula lake and creek on the east, the latter being simply an old bed or "cut-off" of the river. The island is narrow, interspersed with lakes, the higher and tillable lands lying chiefly along the river and around the lake, and comprising the somewhat sandy, light-grayish "front-land" soils. The immediate western border of the lake is 5 or 6 feet lower than the ridge, and has a soil less sandy, breaking up into clods similar to the buckshot clay. Both ridge and lower lands have ferruginous streaks, and are timbered with overcup and very large willow oaks, sweet gum, and hackberry. On the immediate border of the lake there are large cypress trees.

242

At the northern end of Honey island, on the banks of the bayou connecting Tchula lake with the Yazoo river, there is a bluff bank, showing at a low stage of water a section of over 22 feet, which exhibits strikingly the structure of the beds underlying the bottom lands. These are here chiefly dark-colored clays with ferruginous concretions.

The following is an analysis of a bottom soil of the Tallahatchie river in the northern part of the basin:

No. 354. *Light sandy loam*, Tallahatchie river bottom, Tallahatchie county.

Bottom land of Tallahatchie river, Tallahatchie county.

	Soil.
	No. 354.
Insoluble matter	87.146 } 91.944
Soluble silica	4.798 }
Potash	0.301
Soda	0.084
Lime	0.301
Magnesia	0.385
Brown oxide of manganese	0.156
Peroxide of iron	2.120
Alumina	2.151
Phosphoric acid	0.112
Sulphuric acid	0.005
Water and organic matter	2.644
Total	100.205
Hygroscopic moisture	4.79
absorbed at	22 C.°

Dogwood ridge.—The divide between the drainage system of the Yazoo and Sunflower rivers is a low sandy ridge, or rather a series of ridges, above overflow, reaching from near the Mississippi river a few miles north of Friar's point, in Coahoma county, southward and slightly eastward to the Yazoo river, in Holmes county. The irregular outline, as determined by the United States delta survey and marked out on the map accompanying this report, places this ridge in the eastern part of Coahoma, the southwestern corner of Tallahatchie, and the central (north and south) part of Le Flore, the widths varying from about 3 miles in the north and central portions to from 6 to 9 miles in Le Flore county, the entire area being a little more than 300 square miles. It is well settled, especially in its northern part.

This ridge is a marked feature of the Alluvial region, and is doubtless the continuation of the very similar Crowley's ridge of the Arkansas region, which passes southward from the northeastern part of the state, with finally an eastern bend to Helena, on the river, and nearly opposite Friar's point. Here the river has apparently cut through it, but in Mississippi, after continuing this course for a few miles, the ridge turns southward. The soils of the two nearly adjoining portions of the ridges are very similar to each other in character; the growth also is similar, except that poplar characterizes the one and dogwood the other. It is interesting to note that the white clays of the bluffs of Crowley's ridge are in Mississippi apparently spread out over the bottoms and form the "white lands" of the bayous and creeks of the Sunflower region west of the Dogwood ridge.

The chief characteristics of the ridge are light, slightly yellowish, sandy loam soils, showing no change at a depth of 2 feet, and timbered with a growth of dogwood, sweet gum, holly, ash, sassafras, and a kind of prickly pear. The soil is as productive as that of the river-front lands, which it resembles, except in being lighter in color, is easily tilled, and when turned up and exposed to the sun and weather it turns dark, like the other soils. The lower lands or depressions in this belt have light yellowish buckshot clays similar to the clays on the bank of the Sunflower river.

The following analyses show the composition of these two soils:

No. 395. *Light sandy loam soil of the Dogwood ridge*, taken between Swan lake and Cypress bayou, from the plantation of Governor J. L. Alcorn, Coahoma county; vegetation, dogwood, sweet gum, holly, ash, and sassafras; depth taken, 2 feet.

No. 396. *Light yellow buckshot clay* from the edge of a depression or pond on the ridge near the above soil; growth, as above; depth taken, 8 inches.

Dogwood ridge soils.

	DOGWOOD RIDGE SOILS, COAHOMA COUNTY.		CROWLEY'S RIDGE, LEE COUNTY, ARKANSAS.
	Sandy loam ridge soil.	Buckshot clay bottom soil.	Sandy loam soil.
	No. 395.	No. 396.	No. 430.
Insoluble matter.....................................	83.886 } 90.908	75.519 } 86.408	89.415
Soluble silica..........	7.022	10.889	0.386
Potash.......	0.392	0.606	0.084
Soda..........................	0.084	0.146	0.135
Lime..	0.250	0.380	0.831
Magnesia..	0.596	0.972	0.345
Brown oxide of manganese........................	0.086	0.133	1.965
Peroxide of iron...........	2.691	2.804	....
Alumina...............	3.509	4.457	3.027
Phosphoric acid...................................	0.143	0.278	0.221
Sulphuric acid..........	0.010	0.007	....
Water and organic matter......	2.007	4.401	3.465
Total.......	100.770	100.596	99.722
Hygroscopic moisture.............................	3.95	6.04	2.55
absorbed at...............................	10 C.°	12 C.°	Air-dried.

The ridge soil, sandy as it is, shows good fertility in its percentages of potash and phosphoric acid and its abundance of lime and magnesia, while the buckshot clay in a like manner upholds the high reputation of that class of lands in other parts of this state and Arkansas. A comparison of the sandy loam ridge soil with that of Crowley's ridge of Arkansas (taken in Lee county, on the southern part of the ridge, and where the growth is nearly the same) shows marked similarity in composition, and points to a probable common origin and time of deposition.

The Sunflower basin.—The Sunflower river and its chief tributary, the bayou Phalia, drain that part of the alluvial region lying westward from the Dogwood ridge to Deer creek, and covers about 3,000 square miles. The river rises near Friar's point, in Coahoma county, and flows southward with a sluggish motion to the Yazoo. The bayou Phalia, rising in the western part of Bolivar county, unites with it in Washington county, while on the south Silver creek, Little Sunflower, and other streams aid in draining that section. The surface of the entire country is very level, well timbered, and very largely swampy, with innumerable lakes and bayous, and is subject to overflows from the Mississippi river. The only high lands occur along the larger streams or at a very short distance from them, the surface thus being shaped into parallel troughs, whose edges border the streams, and whose lowest portions, midway between, are marked by dense cypress swamps, matted with bamboo brier. The lands of the region may be classed as *front-land*, *back-land*, and *swamps*. The former, or *front-lands*, comprise the higher lands or low ridges along the streams, and, with their light-gray, sandy loam soils, are the chief farming lands of the region. The banks of the Lower Sunflower are not high, the sandy front-land soils that overlie the clays of the bottoms being only from 4 to 6 feet thick in many localities, and, being subject to overflow, are therefore not very largely under cultivation. The timber growth is mostly sweet gum, maple, water and willow oaks, elm, and hackberry. These soils, with their yellowish and orange streaks, resemble those of Tchula lake and of Honey island, Holmes county.

The lands of Indian bayou, in Sharkey county, seem to be the highest of the region, and for many miles are under cultivation. The soil of both this and Straight's bayou, as well as of Silver creek on the south, belong to that class known as *white lands*, being underlaid by a white "clay" and timbered with swamp chestnut-oak and sweet gum, some hickory, holly, water and willow oaks, dogwood, etc., and often with an undergrowth of cane.

Bayou Phalia is in a swamp, and seems not to have any ridge lands along its border.

The back-lands of the Sunflower region, viz, those of the lowlands back from the streams, are mostly stiff clays, embracing the two varieties known as *white lands* and *buckshot clays*. The former occupy nearly if not all of the region east of the Sunflower river, and 6 miles west of it, in Sharkey county, being overlaid as they approach Deer creek by the black buckshot clays. They are most extensive in the southern half of the Sunflower region, and have as a characteristic growth sweet gum and swamp chestnut oak. The white lands are not prized very highly in comparison with others of the alluvial region, though they are said to yield very largely in seed-cotton per acre.

The buckshot clays of the back-lands in the northern part of the region are light gray in color and tenacious, traversed with ferruginous coloring matter, and crumble, upon exposure to the weather, into angular fragments. (See analysis in the description of Dogwood ridge.)

In the southern part we find the dark gray or sometimes nearly black and richer variety belonging to the Deer creek region (under which it is more fully described) overlying the "white lands" of the Sunflower region just mentioned.

The following analyses are given to show the composition of the lands of the Sunflower region:

No. 394. *Sunflower river front-land soil* from a ridge on the bank of the river at Buck's ferry, Issaquena county. Depth taken, about 12 inches; a light-gray sandy loam, with a growth of sweet gum, maple, willow oak, elm, and hackberry.

No. 376. "*White land*" *soil* of Indian bayou front-land, taken near C. Gillespie's, Sunflower county. Depth, 5 inches; growth, sweet gum, swamp chestnut oak, hickory, holly, water, willow, and red oaks, dogwood, some maple and ash, with an undergrowth of cane. Soil is grayish, and somewhat sandy.

No. 377. Subsoil of the above. A whitish, close clay, with reddish flecks, and somewhat "jointy". Depth taken, 5 to 18 inches.

Front-lands of the Sunflower river region.

	ISSAQUENA COUNTY.	SUNFLOWER COUNTY.	
	SUNFLOWER RIVER SANDY RIDGE.	INDIAN BAYOU WHITE LAND.	
	Soil.	Soil.	Subsoil.
	No. 394.	No. 376.	No. 377.
Insoluble matter	71.164 } 84.670	87.898 } 91.984	87.898 } 91.714
Soluble silica	13.506	4.086	3.816
Potash	0.401	0.226	0.205
Soda	0.191	0.118	0.079
Lime	0.406	0.153	0.147
Magnesia	0.696	0.256	0.392
Brown oxide of manganese	0.011	0.048	0.050
Peroxide of iron	3.845	1.848	2.812
Alumina	6.689	2.585	2.998
Phosphoric acid	0.165	0.182	0.283
Sulphuric acid	0.018	0.043	....
Water and organic matter	2.748	3.012	1.499
Total	100.088	100.363	99.779
Hygroscopic moisture	7.39	4.07	5.63
absorbed at	15 C.°	14 C.°	16 C.°

The sandy ridge soil of the Sunflower river, No. 394, is far more clayey than its name would indicate, and resembles rather the light buckshot soils of the northern part of the region both in this and the amounts of potash, phosphoric acid, lime, and magnesia. Were it higher above overflow it would be classed as the most valuable of the ridge or uplands. Its high lime percentage accounts for its superiority over the white lands. The soil and subsoil of Indian bayou show a strong resemblance to each other, the latter naturally being a little richer in its important elements, but showing little of the clayey characteristic to be expected from its popular name, "white clay lands." It is rather a fine white sediment, very close-textured, so as to appear as clay. Both soil and subsoil are fairly supplied with all of the elements of fertility, and strongly resemble in their composition the soil of the Dogwood ridge. The high phosphoric acid percentage in the subsoil suggests that its want of thriftiness may be attributable to physical defects, among which probably is want of adequate drainage for so close a soil. It could also probably be hereafter improved by liming.

The Deer Creek region.—This region embraces a narrow belt on the west between the Sunflower and the Mississippi rivers, from the southwestern part of Bolivar county south to the Yazoo river—in all not more than 1,300 square miles in area. Deer creek is the most important stream, and with its tributaries, Black and Steel's bayous, drains the country southward into the Yazoo. As in the other regions, its level surface is dotted with lakes, and has a network of bayous, which often interconnect the sluggish waters of the larger streams. The higher lands, as usual, lie along the stream, falling inland toward the low swamps, that for the most part are under water or are too boggy for cultivation, being also subject to overflows from the Mississippi river. The river lands are high and not subject to inundation, and, extending back some distance inland, embrace the chiefly settled portion as well as the largest plantations of the region. The soil of this high land is a dark alluvial loam, very rich and productive. The timber growth along the immediate river bank (often very sandy) is mostly cottonwood, while inland it embraces honey-locust, hackberry, and sweet gum.

On the immediate banks of Deer creek and Steel's bayou, as well as on Black bayou, there are low ridges of dark-gray sandy loam, some 200 yards in width, above ordinary overflows, timbered with honey-locust in great abundance; also pecan, water and willow oaks, and sweet gum. In the upper Deer Creek region these ridges are higher and largely under cultivation.

The Deer creek region is, however, especially noted for its extremely rich "buckshot" soils, that occur very extensively, and, taken as a whole, are in their percentages of plant-food the richest yet found. The "Buckshot" occupies the lowlands of the country, and is subject to overflow, levees having been constructed for protection, and is usually densely timbered with a growth of sweet gum, pecan, willow and water oaks, hackberry, and honey-locust near the streams and an undergrowth of cane. The soil is a stiff, dark clay, traversed by cracks, and mottled with spots of ferruginous matter. Upon drying it breaks up into little angular fragments, giving rise to the popular name. Another of its characteristics is the formation of hillocks or small ridges wherever it forms the surface soil, the result of its bulging upward when drying and crumbling. There is no change in its character for several feet in depth. In the lower swamps the growth is mostly cypress, more open, the trees often being covered with long moss (*Tillandsia usneoides*). The following analysis shows the chemical composition of a fair sample of this soil:

No. 390. *Dark, stiff buckshot soil* of Deer creek back-land from the plantation of J. D. Hill, Issaquena county. Depth taken, 12 inches; growth, sweet gum, hackberry, honey-locust, pecan, willow and water oaks, with an undergrowth of cane.

Deer creek buckshot soil, Issaquena county.

	Soil. No. 390.
Insoluble matter	51.063 } 71.767
Soluble silica	20.704 }
Potash	1.104
Soda	0.295
Lime	1.349
Magnesia	1.665
Brown oxide of manganese	0.119
Peroxide of iron	5.818
Alumina	10.539
Phosphoric acid	0.304
Sulphuric acid	0.024
Water and organic matter	7.369
Total	100.383
Hygroscopic moisture	14.31
absorbed at	15 C.°

Taken as a whole, the plant-food percentages in this soil are probably unexcelled by any soil in the world thus far examined.

Cotton on this buckshot land grows to the height of 10 or 15 feet, and is said to yield as much as 1,000 pounds of cotton lint per acre. Much of the land is under cultivation, and to its high product per acre is doubtless due the high rank of Issaquena in this regard among the counties of the cotton states.

Cotton seems to produce best on that portion partly covered with the loam of the higher lands, thus indicating, perhaps, all that is required to make it a soil of maximum fertility.

Mechanical composition of the bottom soils.—The following analyses are of interest as showing the wide differences in the mechanical composition of some of these soils, more especially of those which may be considered as modern deposits as compared with those of more ancient origin, represented by the buckshot soil:

	PANOLA COUNTY.	SUNFLOWER COUNTY.	COAHOMA COUNTY.	ISSAQUENA COUNTY.
	Tallahatchie bottom soil.	White land sub-soil.	Dogwood-ridge soil.	Buckshot soil.
	No. 365.	No. 377.	No. 395.	No. 390.
MECHANICAL ANALYSIS.				
Weight of gravel over 1.2mm diameter				0.1
Weight of gravel between 1.2 and 1mm				
Weight of gravel between 1 and 0.5mm }	0.1			0.1
Fine earth	99.9	100.0	100.0	99.8
Total	100.0	100.0	100.0	100.0
MECHANICAL ANALYSIS OF FINE EARTH.				
Clay	9.6	8.5	10.4	44.4
Sediment of <0.25mm hydraulic value	25.4	50.2	8.7	35.2
Sediment of 0.25mm	19.8	2.0	9.6	9.0
Sediment of 0.5mm	20.4	4.2	9.9	2.7
Sediment of 1.0mm	8.9	12.9	14.0	2.2
Sediment of 2.0mm	9.4	18.9	21.8	1.6
Sediment of 4.0mm	2.7	16.9	21.5	0.3
Sediment of 8.0mm	1.3	2.4	3.7	0.3
Sediment of 16.0mm	0.2	3.0		
Sediment of 32.0mm	0.1 }	0.9	0.2 }	0.4
Sediment of 64.0mm	0.1 }			
Total	98.9	98.8	99.8	100.1

The buckshot soil, with its 44.4 per cent. of clay and 47.2 of the two finest sediments, contrasts strongly with the modern alluvial soils with from 5 to 10 per cent. of clay and 18 to 45 of the sediments. The Dogwood ridge soil, taken alone, contrasts even more strongly, there being a great predominance of the coarser silts.

The above results, however, do not adequately explain the singular property of the buckshot, which causes it to disintegrate with great energy on drying even when it has been worked wet. The same property is manifested, though to less degree, by the black prairie soils of the northeastern region, and is doubtless connected with the calcareous nature of both materials.

V.—THE CANE-HILLS REGION.

Along the edge of the Mississippi bottom above Vicksburg, and below that point along the river itself, we find a narrow belt of ridgy, often broken land, from 3 to 10 and in places up to 15 miles wide, rising abruptly from the bottom or river level not unfrequently to a height of from 400 to 500 feet, and probably more at the most elevated points, which seem to lie on either side of the line between the states of Mississippi and Louisiana, forming from some points of view a wilderness of veritable peaks. Thence southward the level gradually sinks, and the sharp ridges flatten out into the gently undulating plateau country on which Port Hudson and Baton Rouge are situated. The latter city stands on the last spur of the uplands, which thence fall off rapidly into the great delta plain. (See map and text, La. Rep., p. 21.)

The peculiar surface features of this bordering belt are in the main due to the presence, either at or near the surface, of a deposit of fine calcareous silt, which at one time obviously covered the entire bottom plain, but is now represented only by the belt in question, and on the Louisiana side by a few isolated patches lying on top of the hill-tops in the Washita country (see La. Rep., p. 23). It is substantially the same deposit that forms the "bluffs" of the upper Mississippi and lower Missouri, and is hence known as the "bluff" or (from its German congener) the "loess" formation, evidently deposited in fresh-water lakes or gently-flowing broad rivers. It is characterized by containing numerous oddly-shaped concretions of carbonate of lime ("tufa"), and near the landward edge by abundance of shells of land snails as well as bones of large land animals.

The loess material, though but slightly cemented and easily crushed by the hand or plow, is remarkable for its resistance to denudation or washing away by water. Hence the valleys are mostly narrow, V-shaped troughs, separated by sharp-backed ridges wherever the same material forms the surface. But very frequently there lies above the silt, and sharply defined from it, a stratum 4 to 8 feet thick of a yellow, clayey loam, similar to that of the "table-lands" above described, and forming tracts of level, high plateau land quite closely resembling that of northern Mississippi and western Tennessee, of which it is in fact the continuation. It is mainly timbered with oaks, white, chestnut-white, black, and some Spanish, with more or less hickory, sweet and black gum, and where the silt does not lie very deep (as on the brows of the hills) or mingles with the loam (as on the slopes) there is an increasing admixture of holly, linn or basswood, elm, large sassafras, tulip tree, hornbeam, and some magnolia. The "bottom" character of this timber growth is supplemented and in places protected from cattle by a dense growth of cane, covering the hills from base to top. This was originally the case all over this region, which is hence to this day designated as "the cane hills". The approach of the calcareous silt to the surface is indicated by the accession or predominance of lime-loving trees, such as "poplar" or tulip trees, mulberry, honey-locust, and, lower down, crab-apple, red haw, and sycamore. The beech is found more or less throughout. The greater part of the ridges formed of the loess alone are at this time, however, altogether treeless.

Springs are rare in the cane hills, since the water percolates into the silt very rapidly. Streams heading within the region mostly go dry in summer, and their water, as well as that of wells, is hard and limy. The larger streams traversing the region—the Big Black river, Bayou Pierre, and the Homochitto and Buffalo rivers—have rather narrow valleys within it, and the flood-plains are mostly above ordinary overflow, while the beds are very wide, often very sandy, and in them the stream meanders to and fro and sometimes loses itself in the dry season.

This having been one of the earliest settled portions of the state, but little land susceptible of cultivation has remained untouched; and the cultivated lands, originally highly productive, have by the usual process of exhaustive cultivation, turning out, and washing away of the surface soil been greatly reduced in fertility. The Bermuda grass has almost throughout taken possession of the slopes, preventing their washing and affording pasturage for cattle.

The soils of the Cane-hills region are not very much varied. Outside of the bottoms only two materials, each of nearly uniform composition, contribute to their formation, viz, the calcareous silt and the yellow or brown loam of the hill-tops, which intermingle in varying proportions on the slopes. The following analyses convey a fair idea of the characteristics of these materials:

No. 232. *Loam upland soil* from James Watson's place, 5½ miles northeast of Port Gibson, Claiborne county. Timber growth, mainly oaks, as enumerated above; sample, taken to the depth of 8 inches, of a buff color, and considerably lighter in working than the loam subsoil.

No. 233. *Brown loam subsoil* of the above, taken from 8 to 20 inches depth. A moderately clayey loam, about 7 feet in thickness, overlying the calcareous silt in the level hill-tops.

No. 113. *Magnolia upland soil* from a hilly tract on Widow's branch of the Bayou Pierre, about Sec. 8, T. 11, R. 11 E., 4 miles southwest of Port Gibson, Claiborne county. Vegetation, magnolia and cucumber tree

(*M. grandiflora* and *macrophylla*) and cane. This tract is only a few miles in extent, on which the large-leaved magnolia thrives; a tree it has been found difficult to grow in other localities of apparently similar soil and climate, e. g., Natchez. The soil is a light chocolate-colored loam taken to the depth of 10 inches.

No. 114. *Subsoil of the above.* Yellowish-brown loam, heavier than the surface soil, taken from 10 to 24 inches depth.

Cane-hills lands, Claiborne county.

	WATSON'S LOAM.		MAGNOLIA UPLAND.	
	Soil.	Subsoil.	Soil.	Subsoil.
	No. 222.	No. 223.	No. 113.	No. 114.
Insoluble matter .... }	87.973	79.477	86.304 } 90.996 4.694 }	72.348 } 81.838 9.490 }
Soluble silica .... }				
Potash	0.458	0.741	0.290	0.448
Soda	0.134	0.248	0.042	0.078
Lime	0.344	0.238	0.279	0.381
Magnesia	0.545	0.880	0.290	0.705
Brown oxide of manganese	0.205	0.346	0.137	0.081
Peroxide of iron	3.201	5.656	2.298	4.950
Alumina	4.842	5.849	3.345	7.694
Phosphoric acid	0.105	0.092	0.128	0.082
Sulphuric acid	0.022	trace.	0.018	0.088
Water and organic matter	3.073	3.486	3.941	3.819
Total	100.429	99.962	100.542	99.761
Humus	0.713	....	....	....
Available inorganic	0.713	....	....	....
Hygroscopic moisture	6.518	8.00	2.36	7.53
absorbed at	21 C.°	8 C.°	....	21 C.°

It will be seen that these soils differ from the better class of soils in the northerly portion of the yellow loam region only by a somewhat greater proportion of lime (which is especially noticeable in the magnolia soil) and a smaller supply of phosphoric acid. When fresh, they yielded a 400-pound bale, or 1,200 to 1,300 pounds of seed-cotton per acre, and some of these soils yield even now, after long exhaustive cultivation, from 900 to 1,000 pounds of the same. The perviousness of the underlying loess material, and the resistance of the latter to washing away, has greatly restricted the damage to the land, so grievously apparent in northeastern Mississippi.

The composition of the calcareous silt is shown in the following analyses:

No. 237. *Calcareous silt or loess* from a hillside cut near James Watson's place, Claiborne county (see table), about 10 feet below its highest level at this point. Vegetation, the lime-loving trees mentioned, with some oaks. A yellowish-buff, fine silt, mostly impalpable, somewhat coherent, floury to the touch; contains more or less calcareous concretions of various sizes and snail shells.

No. 116. *Loess material* from the "magnolia upland" near Widow's branch, Claiborne county (see table); resembles the preceding; a little more grayish.

Loess lands, Claiborne county.

	Near J. Watson's.	Magnolia upland.
	No. 237.	No. 116.
Insoluble matter .... }	78.344	64.590 } 71.035 6.445 }
Soluble silica .... }		
Potash	0.211	0.260
Soda	0.115	0.199
Lime	5.921	7.572
Magnesia	3.278	4.507
Brown oxide of manganese	0.252	0.146
Peroxide of iron	3.273	2.947
Alumina	2.628	2.512
Phosphoric acid	0.143	0.188
Sulphuric acid	0.060	0.149
Carbonic acid	5.729	10.004
Water	1.231	0.654
Total	99.079	100.227
Hygroscopic moisture	4.13	2.74
absorbed at	20 C.°	26 C.°

The mechanical analysis of No. 237 resulted as follows:

Loess, Claiborne county.

	Near J. Watson's.
	No. 237.
MECHANICAL ANALYSIS.	
Weight of gravel over 1.2ᵐᵐ diameter	
Weight of gravel between 1.2 and 1ᵐᵐ .... }	0.2
Weight of gravel between 1 and 0.6ᵐᵐ .... }	
Fine earth	99.8
Total	100.0
MECHANICAL ANALYSIS OF FINE EARTH.	
Clay	2.5
Sediment of <0.25ᵐᵐ hydraulic value	33.6
Sediment of 0.25ᵐᵐ	5.6
Sediment of 0.5ᵐᵐ	20.1
Sediment of 1.0ᵐᵐ	16.2
Sediment of 2.0ᵐᵐ	14.3
Sediment of 4.0ᵐᵐ	2.0
Sediment of 8.0ᵐᵐ	1.7
Sediment of 16.0ᵐᵐ	0.9
Sediment of 32.0ᵐᵐ	0.6
Sediment of 64.0ᵐᵐ	0.4
Total	97.9

The large amounts of carbonates of lime and magnesia and small percentage of alumina and combined water are the prominent features of this material here as elsewhere in the world. The amounts of potash and phosphates are quite large in presence of so high a lime percentage, in view of which they must be accounted as being largely in an available condition.

The examination of the sediments obtained in the mechanical analysis shows that nearly the whole of the particles above 0.25ᵐᵐ diameter hydraulic value are concretions cemented by carbonates of lime and magnesia. On treatment with acids the latter dissolve and leave the residue in an impalpable condition, showing a remarkably uniform fineness of the deposit as originally formed. The subsequent formation of the concretions, acting in lieu of sand, imparts to this material the quality of remarkably easy tillage, while at the same time, in the absence of any large amount of clay, it is thus rendered somewhat leachy. Being identical in composition from top to bottom for from 5 to 50 feet, it will not hold manure well; and the rapid percolation of the rain-water, followed by air, keeps it depleted of vegetable matter also. While, therefore, the pure loess soils were at the outset very productive after the removal of their covering of cane, from which vegetable mold had accumulated for centuries, culture, with tillage and exposure to the air in the warm summers, soon allowed the vegetable mold to be burnt out, to the great damage of the soil's retentiveness and resistance to drought. This is now the capital fault of the pure loess soils, which is severely felt even by gardeners. Deep-rooted plants, whose terminal rootlets may be found at great depths in this pervious material, are best adapted to it.

While this is true of those ridges in which the calcareous silt alone prevails, those that are, or originally were, capped with the stratum of brown loam have on their slopes soils formed by the intermixture of the two materials lighter and more calcareous than the brown loam and not so leachy as the silt, and highly productive, the latter acting as a true marl. While, therefore, for obvious reasons, it may not be desirable to allow the level loam plateaus to be washed down, this washing is really not so serious a damage as elsewhere; in fact, where all the loam has been removed from the summits and the loess itself appears on the backs of the ridges its washing down upon the loam hillsides is a positive advantage. In many cases this intermixture can be effected or favored by plowing or scraping, especially in small scale cultivation, and it invariably results in an improvement of productiveness.

BOTTOM OR VALLEY SOILS OF THE CANE-HILLS REGION.—Since the streams of the cane hills run so as to cross it in the course of a few miles, the bottoms are but little influenced by their materials, which moreover do not wash down very freely. The valley soils therefore bear, as a rule, the character of the regions lying to the eastward, viz, the long-leaf pine region and the border belt of oak uplands described on page 48. Where the latter belt is very narrow, as in Claiborne and part of Warren counties, the bottoms have light sandy or silt soils of little durability, such as characterize the adjacent long-leaf pine region. Farther south, where the oak upland belt is broader and the streams largely head within it, the bottom soils are of better and partly of excellent quality. The following analyses exemplify this state of things:

· No. 117. *Bottom soil* from higher ground in bottom of bayou Pierre, on Mr. J. C. Humphreys' land, near Port Gibson, Claiborne county. A light, fine sandy soil, grayish buff, to the depth of 9 inches; bears naturally but a small growth of oaks (water and post), black gum, etc.

No. 115. *Subsoil* of the above, 9 to 18 inches in depth; very sandy, and lighter colored than the soil.

249

No. 110. *Coles' creek bottom* (or *hummock*) *soil*, from Sec. 13, T. 9, R. 2 E., Jefferson county. Timber growth, sweet gum, sycamore, hornbeam, walnut, honey-locust, white, chestnut-white, and Spanish oaks; much cane. A gray, rather light loam, varying little to the depth of 2 feet; specimen taken to 12 inches depth.

Bottom soils of the Cane-hill region.

	CLAIBORNE COUNTY.		JEFFERSON COUNTY.
	BAYOU PIERRE.		COLES' CREEK.
	Soil.	Subsoil.	Bottom soil.
	No. 117.	No. 115.	No. 110.
Insoluble matter	93. 627 } 95. 189	96. 108 } 97. 279	73. 856 } 83. 983
Soluble silica	2. 562	1. 171	10. 127
Potash	0. 133	0. 119	0. 240
Soda	0. 020	0. 081	0. 824
Lime..	0. 101	0. 338	0. 140
Magnesia	0. 167	0. 095	0. 355
Brown oxide of manganese....................	0. 125	0. 074	0. 362
Peroxide of iron.............................	1. 004	0. 765	3. 135
Alumina......................................	1. 390	0. 150	6. 238
Phosphoric acid...........................,..	0. 067	0. 126	0. 056
Sulphuric acid	0. 045	0. 064	0. 096
Water and organic matter	2. 092	1. 116	5. 532
Total	100. 346	100. 217	100. 401
Hygroscopic moisture.........................	2. 25	1. 60	6. 65
absorbed at	14 C.°	12 C.°	12 C.°

The Bayou Pierre soil has a remarkably low potash percentage, which is not offset by any large supply either of lime or phosphoric acid. Both the latter are more abundant in the subsoil, but potash is on the decrease, and the absurdly low percentage of alumina speaks of the increasing want of retentiveness, also indicated by the low moisture absorption, the soil having, in popular parlance, "no foundation." It will, when fresh, yield a crop of 700 to 800 pounds of seed-cotton per acre for a few years; after that it will make paying crops of corn only. In most of these points, therefore, it is a "pine-woods soil".

The Coles' creek soil, derived in the main from the loess region itself, is a light loam, retentive of moisture, with a fair supply of potash and lime, and is of great depth. It produces from 1,100 to 1,200 pounds of seed-cotton when fresh; but it is evident that its supply of phosphates will soon require to be replaced, and marling with the loess materials of the hills above it would not come amiss.

The oak uplands belt, intervening between the cane hills and the long-leaf pine region in southwestern Mississippi, has already been referred to in general in connection with the corresponding region of the northern part of the state. (See page 47.) Since, however, it offers many peculiarities, and is in some respects intimately connected with the cane hills, some details regarding it will be given here.

The face of the country is prevalently hilly, though usually not as abruptly so as either in the cane or long-leaf pine hills. The timber is a mixture of oaks (prevalently black-jack and post, with some Spanish and white oak) and hickory, with the short-leaf pine. The latter is sometimes rather predominant near the eastern edge of the region, while toward its western limit its gradual disappearance and the predominance of the oaks and the appearance of the chestnut-white oak and sweet gum among them announce the approach of the loess region. On the lower hillsides and in the valleys the beech is of very frequent occurrence.

The subsoil of the region varies from a yellow sandy loam on its eastern portion to a brownish or orange-colored clay loam in the western, the latter passing insensibly into the rich brown loam of the cane hills. Ridges of the two extreme kinds of soil, with their corresponding vegetation, extend from both sides into this border region.

In northeastern Claiborne the transition from the one to the other is quite sudden, so that we find, *e. g.*, on Little Sand creek, near Rocky Spring, the pine-hills soil overlying a good, brown-loam subsoil, as is shown by the timber growth.

Farther south, in Jefferson county, we find around and northward of Fayette a gently rolling tract of brown loam uplands from which the pine is absent. It is 8 to 10 miles long (northeast and southwest) by a few miles wide, being bordered by the cane hills on the west and rising into hilly short-leaf pine and oak uplands on the east and south. An analysis of the brown loam subsoil of this tract is given on page 49 (No. 109).

Still farther south, in the northern part of Franklin county, we find the "Hamburg hills", a somewhat broken tract of oak uplands with a yellow loam subsoil of fair fertility, producing from 700 to 900 pounds of seed-cotton per acre and quite durable. A good deal of hickory and magnolia mingles here with the oaks.

The country between the forks and south of the Homochitto, in Franklin county, is quite hilly ("Homochitto hills"), so that its brokenness is an obstacle to cultivation. The soil, though quite sandy, is deep, and bears a timber growth of oaks and hickory, laden with long moss, giving evidence of considerable fertility. Hence the bottoms, though rather narrow and their soils quite sandy in most cases, are very productive. Analyses of some of the bottom soils of this region are given below.

Of the upland soils of the region the following analyses, already given in a previous table (see Oak Uplands region), furnish examples. They do not differ materially from those of the more northerly portion of the short-leaf pine and oak uplands, and their cotton product ranges from 700 to 1,000 pounds of seed-cotton per acre when fresh. It is noteworthy that the region around Fayette, of which No. 109 represents the subsoil, has been remarkably durable in its cotton production, more so than would be expected from its composition, which may not be altogether a fair sample. The circumstance may, however, be due to the considerable depth and easy penetrability of this underlying loam and to the levelness of the region, whereby little damage has resulted from washing away of the soil.

No. 108. *Upland soil* from hillside land on Mr. J. F. Brock's place, R. 4 E., T. 13, Sec. 47, near Rocky Spring, Claiborne county. A light gray, somewhat ashy soil, with occasional bog-ore spots to the depth of 10 inches. Timber, prevalently beech, with some large oaks (Spanish white and chestnut white), much holly, and some small magnolias in the heads of hollows. With all these there mingles more or less of short-leaf pine. Mr. Brock complains that this land is unthrifty and will not be benefited by manure, which remains undecomposed in the soil. Peanuts and field pease are about the only successful crops.

No. 112. Subsoil of the above. A brown loam similar to that of the cane-hills country; begins to mingle with the soil at 10 inches, and fairly sets in at 12. Depth taken, 12 to 20 inches.

No. 109. *Brown loam subsoil* from the level region near Fayette, Jefferson county. The loam stratum here is from 10 to 15 feet in thickness, with apparently little change from top to bottom. Sample taken from 12 to 18 inches depth. A brownish-orange, moderately light loam forms the subsoil of the region, which is well settled and has been long under cultivation, and when fresh yielded from 1,000 to 1,100 pounds of seed-cotton per acre, now diminished to from 700 to 800 pounds, even in favorable seasons.

No. 71. *Soil of Hamburg hills*, taken on the ridge about 1 mile northeast of Hamburg, Franklin county. This is rather a broken country with steep ridges. The crests of the ridges, however, are broad enough to give room for fine farms. The surface soil is of a tawny tint and rather light to the average depth of 7 inches, to which the sample was taken. The timber is Spanish, black, red, and white oaks, pignut hickory, magnolia, large-leaved magnolia, black and sweet gum. Small pines form the undergrowth. Down the hillsides white oak and sweet and black gum become more abundant, sometimes prevalent.

No. 73. Subsoil of the above taken from 7 to 20 inches depth. A brownish-orange colored loam, medium heavy from 18 to 36 inches in thickness, then becoming whitish, and gradually passing into the sandy materials of the drift

Lands of the belt of oak uplands.

	CLAIBORNE COUNTY.		JEFFERSON COUNTY.	FRANKLIN COUNTY.	
	R. 4 E., T. 13, S. 47.		Near Fayette, brown loam.	Hamburg hills.	
	Soil.	Subsoil.	Subsoil.	Soil.	Subsoil.
	No. 108.	No. 112.	No. 109.	No. 71.	No. 73.
Insoluble matter	78.992 } 86.422	78.804 } 86.714	81.287 } 84.787	88.750 } 90.560	74.804 } 84.358
Soluble silica	7.430	7.910	3.500	1.810	9.474
Potash	0.318	0.286	0.164	0.140	0.286
Soda	0.087	0.064	0.100	0.090	0.104
Lime	0.127	0.090	0.084	0.070	0.127
Magnesia	0.800	0.492	0.704	0.185	0.509
Brown oxide of manganese	0.072	0.022	0.136	0.075	0.144
Peroxide of iron	4.970	4.613	5.303	2.405	5.672
Alumina	5.061	5.377	5.162	2.096	6.106
Phosphoric acid	0.026	0.042	0.040	0.077	0.060
Sulphuric acid	0.007	0.016	0.011	0.333	0.088
Water and organic matter	9.477	3.161	3.238	4.310	3.699
Total	100.176	100.543	99.920	100.015	100.163
Hygroscopic moisture	3.64	7.61	3.70	4.40	3.81
absorbed at	18 C.°	18 C.°	12 C.°	22 C.°	22 C.°

The insignificant proportion of phosphoric acid in No. 108, together with its ashy character, explains sufficiently the faults complained of in its cultivation. It is too light to assimilate any but well-rotted manure or commercial fertilizers, and of the latter superphosphate would be best adapted to the case. The supply of potash is fair in both soil and subsoil, while that of lime is only moderate, and humus is sadly wanting. Phosphoric acid is also very low in the subsoil. The tree growth, however, seems to show that deep-rooted crops would, with deep tillage, succeed on this soil.

The subsoil from near Fayette likewise does not promise much durability, except it be on account of its great depth and easy penetrability, it being low both in potash and phosphates.

The Hamburg hills soil is the most promising of the three, as its subsoil contains fair supplies both of potash and lime, and the surface soil a larger proportion of phosphoric acid than either of the others. But for its brokenness this region would be a very desirable farming country.

The bottom soils of this border region are generally quite sandy and of considerable depth, are of a dark tint, and are especially adapted to the cultivation of cotton, producing a 400-pound bale, or from 1,200 to 1,500 pounds of seed-cotton per acre, with only little diminution of the product in the course of time. Among their timber the lowland oaks, beech, and magnolia are most prominent, the latter three attaining enormous dimensions, especially in the Homochitto region, noted for the fine cotton grown on its bottom lands. Analyses Nos. 68 and 64 furnish examples of the soils of the latter. No. 66, from the bottom of the West Amite, near Liberty, Amite county, as well as Nos. 67 and 70, from the same locality, are examples of the soils occurring nearer to or within the limit of the long-leaf pine region, and differ materially from those of the Homochitto.

Level "hummocks", or second bottoms, elevated from 4 to 6 feet above the first bottoms, often intervene between the latter and the hills, and sometimes extend to the banks of the streams. The soils of these hummocks are moderately light, of a buff tint, 9 to 12 inches in depth, and are then underlaid by a pale-yellow light loam, the timber being beech, white oak, hickory, sweet gum, holly, cherry, etc., but little or no magnolia. These soils also mostly produce good cotton (1,200 to 1,300 pounds per acre), but not so uniformly as the bottoms, while all produce good corn. None of the hummock soils have as yet been analyzed.

No. 68. *Bottom soil* from the middle fork of the Homochitto, Sec. 16, T. 6, R. 3 E., Franklin county. Timber, chiefly large magnolias and beech; also chestnut-white oak, sweet gum, poplar, and maple, all very large. Specimen taken to the depth of 12 inches, but no material change of tint was perceptible to the depth of 32 inches. This soil is of a light-chocolate tint when damp and very sandy, and is said to be the best cotton soil of the region and to produce indefinitely.

No. 64. Subsoil of the above, taken from 12 to 32 inches depth, nearly the same in tint as the soil, but perhaps a little sandier.

No. 66. *Dark bottom soil* from the West Amite, near Liberty, Amite county. Timber, large magnolias and holly, beech, chestnut-white oak, white oak, some large ash and sweet gum, and some poplar. The soil is a brownish loam, unchanged in color to a depth of 2 feet. Specimen taken to the depth of 12 inches; very productive, but does not occur in very large bodies.

No. 67. *White bottom soil* from the west fork of the Amite near Liberty, Sec. 36, T. 5, R. 4 E., not far from No. 66. Timber, bottom pine, chestnut-white, white and water oak, hornbeam, sweet gum, some small hickory, and black and red oak. The timber is rather under size and lank. Soil, grayish white, ashy; produces fair cotton, not large, but well bolled, and yields from 700 to 900 pounds per acre. On account of bad drainage it is difficult to obtain a full stand. Depth taken, 10 inches.

No. 70. Subsoil of the above, taken from 10 to 20 inches depth, ashy above, more clayey and adhesive below; "crawfishy," and with more or less "black pebble" or bog ore.

The above two kinds of bottom soil occur alternately in patches, the proportion of the dark soil increasing as the stream is descended.

Bottom lands of the oak uplands belt.

	FRANKLIN COUNTY.		WEST AMITE, DARK BOTTOM.	AMITE COUNTY.	
	MIDDLE HOMOCHITTO BOTTOM.			WEST AMITE, WHITE BOTTOM.	
	Soil.	Subsoil.	Soil.	Soil.	Subsoil.
	No. 68.	No. 64.	No. 66.	No. 67.	No. 70.
Insoluble matter	92. 164	88. 780 } 91. 970	87. 543	91. 834	90. 490 } 93. 872
Soluble silica		3. 190 }			3. 382 }
Potash	0. 148	0. 140	0. 486	0. 270	0. 150
Soda	0. 044	0. 087	0. 054	0. 102	0. 045
Lime	0. 123	0. 084	0. 215	0. 134	0. 055
Magnesia	0. 212	0. 280	0. 354	0. 197	0. 190
Brown oxide of manganese	0. 204	0. 084	0. 690	0. 141	0. 085
Peroxide of iron	1. 183	2. 058	5. 028	1. 241	1. 771
Alumina	3. 219	2. 780	2. 407	3. 878	2. 542
Phosphoric acid	0. 079	0. 035	0. 100	0. 149	0. 045
Sulphuric acid	0. 045	0. 006	0. 048	0. 022	0. 005
Water and organic matter	2. 697	1. 847	3. 507	2. 961	1. 635
Total	100. 197	99. 361	100. 982	100. 270	100. 223
Humus				0. 717	
Available inorganic				1. 003	
Hygroscopic moisture absorbed at	4. 06	3. 55	5. 52	2. 48	3. 77
	8 C.°	21 C.°	6 C.°	20 C.°	22 C.°

The soil and subsoil Nos. 68 and 64 are striking examples of the inadequacy of mere chemical analyses and percentage statements for a correct apprehension of the productive capacity of soils. On such a basis they would be pronounced to be absolutely poor and unfit for profitable cultivation; but when it is known that, instead of the usual 6 or 8 inches, nearly 3 feet of well-drained and aerated soil is at the command of the plant, the matter assumes a very different aspect, for the percentages of the plant-food ingredients will then appear multiplied by three or four each and show very advantageous proportions.

In the dark soil of the West Amite bottom a considerable depth of soil is combined with high percentages of potash and lime, a fair supply of phosphates, and both humus and clay enough to render it retentive. The white soil is much shallower, and has less of potash, lime, and humus and a poor, ill-drained subsoil. A comparatively high percentage of phosphates explains the free bolling of the cotton grown on this soil, whose want of retentiveness and whose depth need to be corrected by green manuring, deep tillage, and drainage.

VI.—CENTRAL PRAIRIE REGION.

The region I thus designate traverses the state near its center in a northwestern and southeastern direction as a wedge-shaped belt, varying in width from about 45 miles from Vicksburg northward to 18 miles on the Alabama line northward of Winchester, Wayne county.

Within the area thus roughly outlined prairies do not generally form the prevalent surface feature, not even to the extent to which this is the case in the "northeastern prairie region". The black prairie soil occupies bodies of land, from a fraction of an acre to several thousands in extent, intervening between more or less elevated ridges, the latter formed either of the sandy materials of the stratified drift, covered by the soils similar to those of the adjacent yellow loam and long-leaf pine regions, or consisting of the clayey and non-calcareous materials of the Tertiary, and forming the heavy and intractable pale-yellow soils popularly designated as "hog-bed" or "hog-wallow" prairie. The latter occur more especially in the eastern portion of the belt, where the fertile black prairie soil is mostly confined to the lower slopes and to the bottoms of the streams, and is contradistinguished from the unproductive clay soils of the ridges by the designation of "shell prairie", fossil shells and bones being abundantly scattered over their natural surface. These prairie soils are, of course, derived from the lower calcareous strata of the Tertiary, which are found directly underlying them. It is only in the extreme east, in Clarke and Wayne counties, that the black prairie soil occupies the ridges to any extent. It is everywhere highly productive, though from causes not well understood it is not always adapted to the culture of cotton, the latter being liable to "rust" in the low ground. The "hog-wallow" soil is thus far held in very low esteem; for although moderately productive in favorable seasons, it is too liable to injury from both wet and dry seasons, and is unthrifty and hard to till.

West of Pearl river the true "prairie" feature is but very little developed. The surface features of the upland portions of the counties of Warren and Yazoo are, in the main, those of the cane hills and adjacent table-land regions, although small patches of black prairie occur even at the Vicksburg bluff and more or less all along the Yazoo bluff, and landward up to the line of Holmes county. East of the Big Black river, in Madison and Hinds, we have a gently undulating farming region, mostly with a yellow loam soil resembling that of the table-lands farther north, but showing evidences of more lime in the soil by its tree and herbaceous growth, while occasional patches of black prairie soil, with its peculiar greenish-yellow clay subsoil and groves of crab-apple and honey-locust, show the nearer approach of the calcareous strata to the surface. At Jackson the clay marls that appear everywhere in the banks of Pearl river so far predominate as a soil ingredient that its tendency to crack and cleave during changes from wet to dry interferes somewhat with the maintenance of the foundations of houses and of cisterns, the latter being chiefly used on account of the mineral character of the well waters, when these can be obtained at all.

The soils of the bottom of Pearl River near Jackson are only locally of a "prairie" character, and no prairie soil appears to the eastward until after crossing a belt of sandy oak uplands, which here skirts the hummock of Pearl river at a distance of 3 miles from the river, and is itself about 5 miles wide. Beyond we again find gently rolling uplands with a clay loam soil and occasional black prairie spots, as well as tracts of the "hog-wallow" character, caused by the approach to the surface of the heavy gypseous clays, which are frequently seen in the banks of the stream. These "gypseous prairies" are not very productive. Their surface soil is rather light and silty, from a dun to a chocolate tint, and is underlaid by a heavy, tawny yellow subsoil, often filled with crystals of gypsum. Sometimes the heavy subsoil itself forms the surface, and it is then covered with a sparse growth of scrubby black-jack and water oak and stunted red elm. Such soils will, when well tilled, produce good corn, but invariably rust or blight cotton. But the mixed or "mahogany" soils, formed by the intermixture of this material, as well as of the black prairie soil, with the yellow upland loam (which impart to freshly-plowed slopes a very variegated appearance), are excellent cotton soils, producing a plant of rather short growth, but very heavily bolled, as is usually the case in calcareous soils.

These features—oak upland ridges with a yellow loam soil, sometimes with more or less pine, and alternating with more or less of the black and "hog-wallow" soils on the plateaus, slopes, or in the valleys—characterize the northern portions of Rankin and Smith, the southern part of Scott, and the southwest corner of Newton county. West of the head of Leaf river, in eastern Smith, pine mingles largely with the oak growth on the ridges, and the prairie soils are quite subordinate.

Beyond Leaf river, in Smith, as well as in northwest Jasper, the arrangement of soils is a very uniform one. The bottoms of the larger streams, the Hatchusbe, the Tallahalas, Tallahoma, and their larger confluents, as well as sometimes them the lower portions of the slopes toward them, are of the black prairie character. Above these, forming level or gently undulating upland tracts, appears the hog-wallow or hog-bed prairie soil, timbered chiefly with post oak of a lank, tattered growth, or sometimes with black-jack and short-leaf pine similarly circumstanced. When the ridges are much higher than 25 or 30 feet above the streams named their crests are formed by sandy knolls or ridges perched on the "hog-wallow" plateau and bearing a growth of pine or oaks. Sometimes the soft white-shell limestone is quite near the surface, forming "bald prairies", on which cotton is apt to blight, and here the huge bones of the zeuglodon (see "Geology") are frequently found lying about or are upturned by the plow. These, as well as the oyster shells, have been burned for lime.

In southwestern Clarke and northeastern Wayne the black prairie soil generally lies higher on the hills, forming considerable tracts, of which the smaller part only is really bare of timber, with clumps of honey-locust and crab-apple. Such tracts generally have rather a light soil, while that timbered with sturdy post oak and short-leaf pine, thickly hung with long moss and with an undergrowth of plum, crab-apple, etc., forms the larger portion, and has a heavy black or mahogany-colored soil, with a subsoil of a deep-orange tint at the depth of from 6 to 12 inches, this in its turn being underlaid at from 3 to 10 feet by more or less calcareous clays. These soils are intermediate between the black and "hog-wallow" soil, and are not as safe as those of the open prairie, but are very productive in favorable seasons.

In Wayne county the prairies are in smaller tracts, and are generally of a lighter character. On plowed hillsides the great variety of tints indicates great and frequent variations. The country is here more broken and the bottoms of streams quite narrow, but the bottom soils are very productive, formed as they are by the intermixture of so great a variety of soils and continually fertilized by the marls washed down from the hillsides.

The greatest drawback to the settlement of a large portion of the fertile tracts of the central prairie region of Mississippi is the difficulty of obtaining good water. This difficulty does not exist where sandy ridges give rise to springs; but in the more level portions well-water can sometimes be obtained only by means of the artesian auger, and is even then mostly very hard, and sometimes fetid. The use of cisterns for household purposes is therefore very common.

SOILS OF THE CENTRAL PRAIRIE REGION.

The soils of the level or gently undulating yellow loam or table-land region west of the Pearl river have been described above in connection with the closely related ones of the "table-lands" proper, from which they differ only locally by the admixture of the underlying calcareous clays.

The following analyses represent pretty fairly the chief characteristic soils of the variegated region lying east of the Pearl river to the Alabama line.

1.—Black prairie soils.

No. 188. *Black prairie soil* from R. 4 E., T. 6, Sec. 20, Mr. John Parker's land, Rankin county. This soil forms a spot not exceeding an acre on a hillside; is coal-black when wet to the depth of about 12 inches, when it passes into a yellow clay subsoil, and is timbered with young sweet gum, lately grown up, mingled with cherry, mulberry, wild plum, crab-apple, muscadine, etc.; scarcely any grass on the surface. Higher up on the plateau, and occupying the plateau on top, lies a "hog-wallow" subsoil, gaping into wide cracks in summer, the surface soil varying from yellow loam to a gray-ashy character, the latter of little value for cultivation. As usual, black-jack and post oaks occupy these soils almost exclusively. Black prairie spots of the character above given are interspersed with the other soils on hillsides, and produce fine corn, but rust cotton very badly, unless intermixed with the other soils to form the "mahogany".

No. 210. *Black prairie soil* from R. 7 E., T. 3, Sec. 22, Smith county, Mr. L. E. Crook's place, from a tract skirting the bottom of Okahay creek. A black, stiff soil, overgrown with a thick growth of small sweet gum, some ash and mulberry, with here and there a red elm. It was originally almost treeless. The land produces splendid corn, but rusts cotton incorrigibly. Toward the uplands this land gradually passes into a true "hog-wallow" soil, or into one similar to that of Hudnall's prairie (Nos. 187 and 301).

No. 203. *Ridge prairie soil* from north slope of the dividing ridge between Shongalo and Bowland's creek, R. 8 E., T. 3, Sec. 32 (?), Smith county. The crest of the ridge is sandy, and the prairie soil forms a shelf or terrace about half way up. The surface soil, only a few inches in depth, is black or grayish, with little grass, but has the usual growth of hawthorn, crab-apple, etc. None of this soil is under cultivation so far as noted.

No. 207. Subsoil of No. 203. Very stiff, of a deep-orange tint, opening into wide cracks in summer.

No. 199. *Bottom prairie soil* from near the crossing of Leaf river, on the Raleigh and Garlandsville road, Jasper county, R. 9 E., T. 3, about Sec. 6. A deep black soil, cracking and crumbling in drying, underlaid at about 20 inches by a yellow clay subsoil. Soil taken to the depth of 12 inches. Timber, honey-locust, crab-apple, wild plum, and red haw. Not cultivated here, but farther above; said to grow splendid corn, but to rust cotton.

No. 195. *Bottom prairie soil* from Suanlovey creek, near Garlandsville, Jasper county, from the land of Mr. Elias Brown, Sec. 8, T. 4, R. 12 E. Deep black, 2 to 3 feet in depth; timbered prevalently with large sweet gum, and ash, elm, cottonwood, water oak, mulberry, sycamore, and maple. But little of this soil is in cultivation as yet, it being very stiff, dry, and hard and full of gaping cracks. Whether or not it rusts cotton could not be definitely ascertained. It produces splendid corn.

No. 44. *Upland prairie soil* from General W. B. Trotter's plantation, Clarke county, R. 7 W., T. 10, Sec. 3, taken from a hillside belt of black soil to the depth of 15 inches, there being no change of color for at least two feet; stiff, deep, black, and shining; growth of grasses and clumps of crab-apple and red haw. Produces excellent cotton.

No. 40. *Bald prairie soil* from same section as 44. Soil whitish, passing insensibly into a marly mass at 8 to 10 inches depth, and is sandy rather than clayey. No timber growth; scant grass and some verbenas. None cultivated.

No. 363. *Under-subsoil of black prairie* from R. 9 E., T. 4, Sec. 15, Nichols' place, Smith county. This is a small prairie tract bordered by low hills, with a stiff (hog-wallow) soil, timbered with short-leaf pine, post and black jack oak. Near the edge of the prairie the pine disappears and red and Spanish oak come in. The black soil is shallow, and only occurs in spots; frequently the pale, greenish-yellow subsoil forms the surface, and continues with little change to from 3 to 5 feet. It is a heavy, greenish-yellow clay without definite structure, and smooth, shining cleavage, showing some ferruginous concretions and crystals of gypsum, and effervesces strongly with acids. It is full of the bones of the zeuglodon, but little petrified, and in consequence of the tendency of the mass to crack into wide fissures when drying gullies are washed into it in many places, and in these the bones are abundant. The soil in favorable seasons will grow good corn, but invariably rusts cotton so much that the plant will not even reach the time of blooming. The sample analyzed was taken at the depth of 3 feet from the side of a gully. It may be considered as forming a transition between the black and the hog-wallow prairie materials.

2.—*Gypseous and hog-wallow prairie soils.*

No. 187. *Soil of McRae's or Hudnall's prairie,* R. 4 E., T. 6, Sec. 17, Rankin county. This is a gently rolling, treeless tract, with a growth of stunted persimmon, sumach, and short grass. The soil to the depth of 8 inches is rather light and silty, of a brownish-buff tint, and tills easily. It becomes heavier lower down, and is underlaid at the depth of from 1 to about 3 feet by the heavy clay subsoil No. 301. It is said to be very droughty, and apparently the spatters of rain on the leaves of cotton seem to corrode them.

No. 301. *Under subsoil* of the preceding, taken at 3 feet depth. A greenish-gray, heavy clay, with numerous small white specks (of gypsum) and some round, smooth concretions of limonite; cleaves into prismatic fragments in drying. The gypseous prairies are generally bordered by a low, dense-topped growth of black-jack oak, from which there is a transition into oak upland, with short-leaf pine, having a light, ashy surface soil and a heavy, droughty subsoil, cracking open in summer.

No. 242. *Hog-wallow prairie soil* from the level region east of West Tallahala creek, R. 10 E., T. 3, about Sec. 2, Jasper county. A brownish-gray, very stiff soil, dotted with minute, dark-brown spots of bog-iron ore, which, when washed out, forms irregularly shaped grains with a rough surface, mostly soft enough to be crushed with the finger-nail. Depth, 6 inches, underlaid by a yellow clay subsoil; cracks open into wide gaping fissures in summer, the lumps being of stony hardness and having, when cut, a shining surface. The soil will hardly produce corn, but in good seasons, and when plowed just in the right condition, will make a fair crop of cotton. The timber where this soil was taken is slender post oak, with tattered, open tops, short-leaf pine, and here and there a Spanish oak. When lying higher on the hills it is usually timbered with black-jack.

No. 38. *Hog-wallow upland soil* from Clarke county, R. 7 W., T. 10, Sec. 3. Level plateau land, timbered with slender pine, sturdy but very leafy post oak, some black-jack and hickory. Soil, pale-yellow, and stiff to the depth of about 8 inches; then stiff clay, speckled yellow and orange; at the lower levels on the hillsides, black prairie. This soil is droughty and unfit for corn, but brings a short, fairly bolled cotton stalk when the season is favorable.

No. 33. Subsoil of the above, 8 to 18 inches depth. A heavy, tawny-yellow clay, mottled with orange.

COTTON PRODUCTION IN MISSISSIPPI.

LANDS OF THE CENTRAL PRAIRIE REGION.

1.—Black prairie soils.

	RANKIN COUNTY.	SMITH COUNTY.			JASPER COUNTY.		CLARKE COUNTY.	
	R. 4, T. 6, S. 20.	R. 7 R., T. 2, S. 22.	R. 8 R., T. 3, S. 22, Rowland's creek.		R. 9 R., T. 3, S. 4, Leaf River, near Pineville.	R. 12 R., T. 4, S. 5, Suanlovey creek, near Garlandsville.	R. 7 W., T. 10, S. 3, Trotter's plantation.	
	Black prairie.	Post-oak prairie.	Ridge prairie.		Bottom prairie.	Bottom prairie.	Upland prairie.	Bald prairie.
	Soil.	Soil.	Soil.	Subsoil.	Soil.	Soil.	Soil.	Soil.
	No. 188.	No. 210.	No. 203.	No. 207.	No. 199.	No. 195.	No. 44.	No. 40.
Insoluble matter	99.949 } 74.404	90.264	51.749	43.523} 48.120 6.597	52.435	67.562}77.488 9.926	43.615}60.710 16.095	31.504}40.330 7.826
Soluble silica	4.455							
Potash	0.904	0.573	0.534	0.288	0.796	0.384	0.686	0.589
Soda	0.344	0.114	0.230	0.385	0.137	0.059	0.227	0.223
Lime	1.040	0.966	0.484	0.796	1.815	1.726	2.017	22.870
Magnesia	0.910	0.529	1.005	1.621	1.112	0.861	1.227	1.094
Brown oxide of manganese	0.130	0.392	0.098	0.035	0.479	0.128	0.152	0.111
Peroxide of iron	4.762 } 10.961		23.796	20.790	6.996	3.809	7.341	4.094
Alumina	7.360		10.354	17.660	16.696	7.680	17.829	7.446
Phosphoric acid	0.466	0.128	0.151	0.050	0.232	0.104	0.115	0.102
Sulphuric acid	0.150	0.035	0.022	0.021	0.085	0.005	0.112	0.246
Carbonic acid								17.411
Water and organic matter	10.799	6.798	11.385	9.966	9.028	7.772	10.726	6.779
Total	101.000	100.000	100.268	100.743	100.000	100.128	100.252	99.905
Humus	1.971				1.809			
Available inorganic	0.982				0.743			
Hygroscopic moisture	16.21	11.14	19.79	23.13	20.92	13.78	18.08	12.10
absorbed at	14 C.°	20 C.°	17 C.°	19 C.°	23 C.°	16 C.°	9 C.°	11 C.°

2.—Gypseous and hog-wallow prairie soils.

	RANKIN COUNTY.		SMITH COUNTY.		CLARKE COUNTY.	
	McRae's prairie, R. 4 R., T. 6, S. 17.		Tallahala creek waters, R. 10 R., T. 3, S. 2.	R. 9 R., T. 4, S. 15.	General W. R. Trotter's plantation, R. 7 W., T. 10, S. 3.	
	Gypseous prairie.	Gypseous underclay.	Hog-wallow.	Gypseous underclay.	Hog-wallow.	Upland.
	Soil.	Subsoil.	Prairie soil.	Soil.	Soil.	Subsoil.
	No. 197.	No. 201.	No. 242.	No. 363.	No. 36.	No. 33.
Insoluble matter	} 82.556	67.027	76.788	43.589	76.518 } 85.228 9.710	70.982
Soluble silica						
Potash	0.339	0.518	0.525	0.638	0.382	0.309
Soda	0.023	0.414	0.190	0.136	0.199	0.127
Lime	0.432	5.696	0.424	14.967	0.138	0.188
Magnesia	0.513	1.233	0.674	1.004	0.274	0.149
Brown oxide of manganese	0.092	0.509	0.550	0.238	0.040	0.074
Peroxide of iron	3.064	4.344	4.121 } 17.086		3.951	23.040
Alumina	7.434	10.751	10.059		6.387	
Phosphoric acid	0.076		0.063	0.139	0.039	0.100
Sulphuric acid	0.068	5.751	0.050	7.784	0.018	0.050
Carbonic acid		1.018		7.466		
Water and organic matter	5.322	2.740	5.723	7.174	2.806	5.146
Total	99.921	100.000	99.165	100.000	100.418	100.147
Humus			0.729			
Available inorganic			2.166			
Hygroscopic moisture	5.43		6.82	16.71	6.40	15.90
absorbed at	air-dried.		air-dried.	20 C.°	11 C.°	18 C.°

Of the preceding soils only the "Hog-wallow", No. 196, has thus far been mechanically analyzed, with the following result:

Jasper county Hog-wallow subsoil.

	No. 196.
MECHANICAL ANALYSIS.	
Weight of gravel over 1.5^{mm} diameter	8.5
Weight of gravel between 1.5 and 1^{mm}	1.3
Weight of gravel between 1 and 0.5^{mm}	86.0
Fine earth	
Total	100.0
MECHANICAL ANALYSIS OF FINE EARTH.	
Clay	48.0
Sediment of < 0.25^{mm} hydraulic value	24.7
Sediment of 0.25^{mm}	26.6
Sediment of 0.5^{mm}	3.3
Sediment of 1.0^{mm}	6.7
Sediment of 2.0^{mm}	3.5
Sediment of 4.0^{mm}	6.3
Sediment of 8.0^{mm}	6.3
Sediment of 16.0^{mm}	5.0
Sediment of 32.0^{mm}	1.6
Sediment of 64.0^{mm}	2.0
Total	100.1

The 48 per cent. of clay in this soil is the highest figure for that substance that has thus far come under my observation, and it is no wonder that the soil is found excessively refractory in tillage, as it lacks entirely the quality of many of the black prairie soils of "slaking" or pulverizing in passing from the wet to the dry condition. In that process it simply cracks open into widely gaping fissures, and is wetted with difficulty. When wet, it becomes excessively tenacious; still, when taken under the plow in just the right condition, it assumes very fair tilth, and in good seasons yields fair crops. Deep and very thorough tillage is evidently of first necessity.

The obvious characteristic of the black prairie soils here is, as in the case of the Northeastern prairie region, a large lime percentage, ranging from somewhat less than 1 to 2 per cent. and over. The potash percentage is also high, ranging between one-half and nearly 1 per cent. The phosphoric acid varies greatly, from one-tenth to over four and a half tenths per cent. (in No. 188). The humus is probably, in all cases above 1 per cent. A notable feature, doubtless connected with the latter substance, is the extraordinarily high absorption of moisture, exceeding 10 per cent. in all cases, and rising as high as 21 per cent. in No. 199. The alumina is in some cases very high (as in Nos. 203 and 199), but in others no greater than in many loam soils (as in Nos. 188 and 195), and on comparison of the two last-named with No. 44 it seems as though there was little direct relation between the alumina percentage obtained in analysis and the moisture coefficient. On the other hand, the effect of the presence of ferric oxide upon the absorption of moisture is very strikingly illustrated in the case of Nos. 203 and 207, the latter, containing scarcely any humus, having nevertheless the highest moisture coefficient, obviously on account of the great iron percentage of nearly 21.

In view of the great depth and somewhat extreme character of the black prairie soils, rendering them liable to injury from drought, deep and thorough preparation of the soil, as well as good drainage, cannot be too strongly recommended. When "tired", phosphate manures will probably be the first called for to restore productiveness.

In the hog-wallow soils the lime percentage is uniformly lower, falling below five-tenths—from 0.12 to 0.43. The latter, however, is itself by no means a low amount. The phosphoric acid is low; the humus a little over half of that in the black prairie soils, and about the same as in other good upland soils.

The obvious inference is that in order to render the hog-wallow soils more similar, chemically, to the black prairie soils they should be supplied with more lime, which, with green manuring, would soon supply the deficient humus, and that phosphates should be used as manures.

It is quite obvious, however, that the mechanical condition of the hog-wallow soils stands chiefly in the way of their productiveness. This also would in a measure be remedied by the application of lime and vegetable matter, but, in addition, thorough tillage and good drainage are indicated as first essentials. It is probable that simple underdrainage and use of lime would render these soils fairly and uniformly productive.

17 C P

A difficult question arises in regard to the tendency of the black prairie soils to "rust" cotton. It is probable that in many cases what is commonly called rust in this region is in reality simply blight, caused primarily by a faulty condition of the soil in respect to moisture and aeration; in other words, by an impervious and ill-drained subsoil, such as commonly underlies the black prairie soils. This indication is confirmed by the fact that the small prairie tracts lying on hillsides (such as No. 44 and others occurring near the southern limit of the prairie region) do not produce the blighting, but bear excellent crops, and also by the fact that corn, a shallow-rooted crop, does excellently well on the "rust soils".

It would, however, remain to be explained why it is that the heavy and ill-drained "hog-wallow" soils are not charged with rusting cotton, but on the contrary are reputed as bearing moderately good crops in favorable seasons. The facts well observed are perhaps hardly sufficient to determine the point, for, as has been stated, the hog-wallow lands lie mostly on higher levels, and may be better drained than the black-bottom prairie, reputed as rusting cotton. It may also be that the greater thriftiness imparted to the plant by the rich soil of the latter turns the scale to its disadvantage whenever the check of the tap root in the subsoil occurs. The entire subject is greatly in need of much closer study than has heretofore been bestowed upon it, for the area of land for cotton culture in this region would be more than trebled if the rich bottom prairie and the hog-wallow uplands could be rendered available.

SANDY RIDGE LANDS.—The non-calcareous sandy soils which form the higher portions of the dividing ridges in the central prairie region differ but little from the lands similarly situated northward and southward of the prairie belt. In the eastern portion of the region these ridge lands usually bear the long-leaf pine, with a transition belt of oak between them and the hog-wallow lands, while in the western portion the short-leaf pine plays a similar part. In northern Rankin there are some quite extensive tracts of gently undulating oak lands, with a yellow non-calcareous yellow loam soil, and low ridges of a similar character are found in Scott county. Some of these ridges are directly connected with the regions on either side, but many are insular outliers.

The bottom soils of the central prairie region, as has been stated, are largely themselves of a "prairie" character, especially in the eastern portion of the belt. Elsewhere they relate more or less directly to the soils of the country lying to the northward. West of Pearl river especially the soils are often light and very productive, while the hummocks have prevalently the gray silty type.

MARLS OF THE CENTRAL PRAIRIE REGION.—Marls of various kinds and agricultural value underlie the greater portion of the region as outlined on the map, and they frequently crop out on the banks of streams and on hillsides. Not unfrequently they can be reached by digging pits in the fields themselves, so that on the whole they are very generally available for soil improvement. The important results achieved by the use of the same class of fertilizers in Virginia and the Carolinas render a brief description of the chief varieties a matter of direct interest to the agricultural system of Mississippi. Some of these marls are purely calcareous so far as their useful ingredients are concerned; in other words, they are a mass of soft carbonate of lime, mixed with more or less sand and clay, as the case may be. These are very widely diffused, and often pass insensibly into hard limestone on the one hand and into subsoils and soils on the other. The clayey varieties of these marls occur chiefly in the northern portion of the Central prairie region ("Jackson" Tertiary), and are often characterized by the huge bones of the zeuglodon, while the sandy or purely calcareous varieties lie more generally near the southern edge of the region adjacent to the northern limits of the long-leaf pine ("Vicksburg" Tertiary). Their tints are usually white or yellowish-white. The following analyses show the composition of some representative samples:

No. 1794. *Yellowish clay marl* from the banks of the Chickasawhay river, near Dr. Ogburn's, R. 16 E., T. 1, Sec. 21, about 30 feet in thickness, underlaid by brown and reddish clay.

No. 336. *Yellowish clay marl* from Moody's branch, near Jackson, Hinds county, sometimes forming a soft marlstone. Varies in the neighborhood of Jackson from 20 to 45 feet in thickness, and is usually underlaid by a blue shell marl, often too sandy for profitable use.

No. 335. *White marl* from the farm of Dr. Quin, 4 miles southeast of Brandon, Rankin county; a rather friable mass, easily pulverized; forms a stratum 15 to 20 feet in thickness in bluff banks above the drainage.

No. 39. *Yellowish, friable marl* from General W. B. Trotter's plantation, on Chickasawhay river, R. 7. W., T. 10, Sec. 3. Occurs in strata of variable thickness up to 10 feet between limestone ledges on the hillsides and in the river banks. Some is much less pure than the sample analyzed, containing as much as 60 per cent. and over of sand.

White and yellowish marls of central prairie region.

	CLARKE COUNTY.	HINDS COUNTY.	RANKIN COUNTY.	CLARKE COUNTY.
	Dr. Ogburn's clay marl.	Moody's branch, clay marl.	Dr. Quin's place, white marl.	Trotter's plantation, yellowish marl.
	No. 1794.	No. 236.	No. 235.	No. 39.
Insoluble matter..............................	39.110	27.400	13.074	17.972
Potash.......................................	0.436	0.445	0.265	0.221
Soda...	0.103	0.206	0.031	0.292
Lime...	25.235	28.621	46.223	29.003
Magnesia.....................................	1.601	1.467	0.614	0.940
Brown oxide of manganese	0.043	....	0.067	0.111
Alumina.................................... }	3.506	} 5.133	2.723 }	2.475
Peroxide of iron.............................	6.269			6.296
Phosphoric acid..............................	(?)	0.256	trace.	0.223
Sulphuric acid...............................	0.085	....	0.053	0.035
Carbonic acid................................	19.203	23.064	34.754	20.766
Water and organic matter.....................	4.061	3.346	2.050	2.017
Total....................................	100.454	100.000	99.857	100.455

It will be noted that these marls, aside from the carbonate of lime, contain from one-fourth to one-half per cent. of potash, and some as high as one-fourth per cent. of phosphoric acid also. The decided effect produced by a dressing of these marls, diminishing after eight or ten years, long before the lime introduced can have been sensibly diminished, proves that the above ingredients are present in an available form, although the mass contains no visible greensand grains. Dressings may profitably range from 200 to 500 bushels per acre.

The white marls are usually richest in phosphoric acid where the large zeuglodon bones occur within them, but in some cases they are too clayey to be profitably used (as is the case especially in the extreme northern belt of the region) with the stiff subsoil of the black prairies in Madison, Smith, and Scott counties.

The blue marls are more commonly sandy than clayey, and mostly contain well-preserved shells ("shell marls") and some grains of greensand or glauconite, which are rich in available potash. When not too sandy for profitable use (that is, on account of handling too much inert material) they usually contain from one-half to as much as one per cent. and over of available potash, with usually a notable amount of phosphoric acid. On the whole, then, the blue marls are richer in potash and phosphoric acid than the white marls, but also very commonly poorer in lime, because of containing more inert matter.

The following analyses exemplify the composition of some representative samples of blue marls:

Blue greensand marls Nos. 314 and 2224 occur together in the bank of Garland's creek, on Sec. 21, R. 16 E., T. 1, Clarke county. No. 4314 overlies, with a thickness of about 2 feet, the bed represented by No. 2224, with a visible thickness of 5 feet. The first is a greensand shell marl of extraordinary richness both in potash and phosphoric acid; the second, while still having a fair amount of potash, is almost destitute of phosphates, showing how widely and essentially such materials may differ in value even at the same locality. Almost a precisely parallel case occurs in the banks of Pearl river near Byram station, Hinds county.

No. 2232. *Blue marl* from Smith's bridge, Warren county. Details not known.

No. 337. *Blue shell marl* from the bluff at Vicksburg, about midway down the face, about 5 feet thick between ledges of limestone. Somewhat compact, clayey, with visible grains of greensand, and numerous shells not well preserved.

No. 2231. *Blue marl* from the bed of Chickasawhay river, at the mouth of Limestone creek, Wayne county. A rather sandy marl, of which about 2 feet is visible at low water, underlying a heavy bed of white marl similar to that from Quin's (see above, No. 235).

No. 304. *Blue shell marl* from the bed of Shongalo creek, near Austin's mill, about 2 miles north of Raleigh, Smith county. Rather clayey, and somewhat compact.

Analyses of blue greensand marls.

	CLARKE COUNTY.		WARREN COUNTY.		WAYNE COUNTY.	SMITH COUNTY.
	Garland's creek greensand shell marl.		Smith's bridge, greensand marl.	Vicksburg blue shell marl.	Limestone creek, greensand marl.	Austin's mill blue shell marl.
	No. 214.	No. 2234.	No. 2282.	No. 237.	No. 2281.	No. 204.
Insoluble matter................................	45.881	29.733 } 3.497 } 38.230	21.464 } 9.751 } 31.215	29.997	52.136 } 2.661 } 56.787	62.221
Soluble silica................................						
Potash..	1.717	6.973	0.836	0.753	0.399	0.170
Soda...	0.405	0.166	0.193	0.283	0.173	0.066
Lime...	14.785	26.197	30.194	27.543	30.796	13.906
Magnesia.......................................	2.476	1.482	1.704	2.062	0.530	2.856
Brown oxide of manganese.....................	0.402	0.050	0.084	....	0.083	0.040
Peroxide of iron..............................	13.090	5.696	4.661	4.732	1.926	2.410
Alumina..	7.761	2.602	2.850		0.956	2.085
Phosphoric acid...............................	0.237	0.069	0.033	0.135	0.131	0.130
Sulphuric acid................................	0.506	0.005	0.320	....	0.085	1.338
Carbonic acid.................................	13.492	20.019	23.318	30.635	16.273	12.356
Water and organic matter.....................	....	2.569	4.415	2.607	1.100	2.176
Total.....................................	99.883	99.962	99.750	99.590	99.851	99.936

It will be noted that the Warren county marls, while not as rich in potash as those from Clarke, are richer in lime; moreover, other samples analyzed from the neighborhood of Vicksburg show over a fourth of one per cent. of phosphoric acid. As they contain but a moderate amount of inert matter, they may be considered of very good quality. Almost precisely the same kind of marl occurs in the banks of Pearl river at Byram station, and doubtless at many intermediate points in Hinds and Warren, as well as in Rankin.

The marls from Wayne and Smith counties represent the poorer qualities of blue marls, containing too much inert matter for transportation to any distance, but still useful when they can be applied near at hand, especially on the adjacent pine lands. But where the white marls are equally accessible they should be given the preference, on account of their higher percentage of lime.

These marls are especially useful on the "sour" lands of the pine region south of their localities of occurrence, where the gallberry takes possession of the valleys and level lands generally, and they would be eminently useful in the marshes of the coast if they could be cheaply conveyed, as e. g., by floating down the Chickasawhay, Pascagoula, and Pearl rivers.

VII.—LONG-LEAF PINE REGION.

The long-leaf pine region embraces about one-third of the area of the state, viz, 14,800 square miles. It comprehends nearly the entire portion lying south of the "central prairie" belt, and a triangular area north of the same adjoining the Alabama line, which may be roughly circumscribed by lines drawn through Gainesville junction to Lake station, in Scott county, thence to the southeast corner of Clarke county, and thence back to the initial point. On the west, it reaches to within 20 or 30 miles of the Mississippi river, where a belt of loam uplands, timbered with oaks and short-leaf pine, forms a transition to the cane hills that skirt the Mississippi on the east. (See "Oak Uplands Region.")

Within this wide area there is, on the whole, a remarkable uniformity of general character, broken most obviously near the Gulf coast by a narrow belt of land similar to the "pine flats" of Louisiana. The rest of the region is popularly known as the "pine-hills country", with little discrimination as to the quality of the land. A closer discussion, however, both of the timber growth, the soil, and the average product of cotton per acre, as shown by the census returns, justifies a subdivision, as given on the map, of the northern and western part of the region, with its stronger soils and partial oak and hickory tree-growth, from the southeastern portion, where the long-leaf pine prevails almost exclusively, even in the bottoms, where the soil is very sandy, and produces even in the creek bottoms not more than an average of one-fourth of a bale of cotton per acre, as against about one-third in the counties embraced within the division marked by the yellowish-green color on the map. The two divisions, however, grade off into each other so insensibly, and have so much in common, that they are best described together, with special references to the differences in particular localities.

THE LONG-LEAF PINE HILLS.

The surface of the long-leaf pine hills country is generally undulating or rolling, but sometimes it is hilly, especially where the uplands fall off toward the larger water-courses. Between these we frequently find dividing plateaus, which are gently undulating or almost level, this being especially the case where the strata of the drift formation (which underlies the whole region) consist of pervious sands without water-shedding layers. Here the rain-water sinks into the ground, instead of washing out deep valleys and ravines (as is mostly the case in northern Mississippi), and then reappears at or near the drainage level in the form of copious springs.

The surface soil of the uplands is almost throughout quite sandy, partly pebbly or intermixed with coarse sand, as is commonly the case west of Pearl river, or more generally a fine, grayish-white, ashy material, very siliceous, light, and unretentive. On the larger dividing plateaus the depth of this soil varies from 10 to 18 inches, at which depth it is mostly underlaid by a yellow sandy loam; but sometimes the soil passes directly into the sand strata of the drift, and is then very poor, and scarcely capable of successful cultivation.

The prominent forest tree of the region is the long-leaf pine (*Pinus australis*, Michx.), which near the northern and western border occupies only the higher ridges, but gradually, as we progress southward and eastward, descends, until we find it on the very verge of the bottoms, although it rarely occupies the latter themselves. (a) In the uplands it is accompanied by more or less of the black-jack and post oaks, and almost invariably, especially on the hill sides, by some black gum (*Nyssa multiflora*), generally also dogwood (*Cornus Florida*), and, where the soil is stronger, small or medium-sized hickory.

The frequency, size, and shape of these accompanying trees (as well as, less markedly, that of the long-leaf pine itself) mark the variations in the fertility of the soil where, as in the most southerly portion, the short-leaf pine (*P. mitis*) is rare or absent. In the northern and western portions, however, the partial or complete replacement on the ridges of the long-leaf pine by the short-leaf species is the most common intimation of an improvement of the soil. This generally consists of the nearer approach to the surface of the sandy loam subsoil already referred to and its increased clayeyness. In this case also the black-jack and post oak increase in frequency and improve in aspect and the Spanish and scarlet oaks make their appearance. It is chiefly in patches of this character, varying in extent from a few acres to several sections, that the uplands are cultivated to any considerable extent in this region.

Where the long-leaf pine alone prevails the soil is generally so poor that cultivation is altogether confined to the lower hillsides and bottoms. The latter are mostly quite narrow, those of Leaf river and Okatoma and Okahay creeks, in southern Smith county, for instance, rarely exceeding a quarter of a mile. On the larger streams (as on Pearl, Lower Leaf, and Pascagoula rivers) they are often skirted by a second bottom or hummock of equal or greater width, ordinarily inferior in fertility to the first bottoms, but still in general superior to the uplands. The soil of both bottoms and hummocks are of course mostly quite light, but the former especially are quite productive, probably on account of the great depth to which the roots of crops can go. Those of the streams heading in the prairie region, such as Leaf river, the Tallahalas, etc., are of very high quality for some distance below the line of that region from the intermixture of the heavy "bottom prairie" soils with the lighter materials of the pine country. Among the timber of the bottoms the beech generally forms a very prominent ingredient; besides the magnolia, the bottom pine (*P. Tæda*) and black gum are rarely wanting, while the undergrowth is formed by the witch-hazel, calico bush, star anise (*Illicium Floridanum*, here popularly known as "stinking bush"), various species of black haw (*Viburnum nudum*, *V. dentatum*, etc.), bay (*Magnolia glauca*), bay galls (*Laurus Carolinensis*), various species of Andromeda, Leucothoë, Vaccinium or low huckleberry, and especially to the southward the ink-berry (*Prinos glaber*), buckwheat tree or ti-ti (*Mylocarium*), *Cyrilla*, and others.

The herbaceous vegetation and undergrowth of the long-leaf pine uplands is scarcely less characteristic than the timber growth. Wherever the regular burning of the woods, as practiced by the Indians, has not been superseded by the irregular and wasteful practice of the white settlers, the pine forest is almost destitute of undergrowth and appears like a park, whose long grass is beautifully interspersed with bright-tinted flowers. The prevailing grasses are of the broom-sedge tribe (*Andropogon, Erianthus*), and next to these those of the millet relationship (*Paspalum, Panicum*) in numerous species. The "wire-grass" of Alabama and Georgia is represented only by *Agrostis juncea*, to which the name is here applied; in the southern portions, the curious toothache grass (*Monocera aromatica*) is abundant. Among the flowers there are conspicuous in spring the New Jersey tea (*Ceanothus Americanus*), devil's shoestring (*Tephrosia Virginica*), which in southern Mississippi rarely bears perfect flowers, *Phlox pilosa, Hedyotis purpurea, Rudbeckia hirta, Coreopsis lanceolata, Silene Virginica* (crimson catch-fly), *Viola palmata* (wild pansy), *Delphinium exaltatum* (the bright blue larkspur), *Pentstemon pubescens*, and the beautiful *Malva papaver*, whose flowers resemble closely those of the red poppy. Somewhat later, two small species of cassia (*C. nictitans* and *C. Chamæcrista*, sometimes called sensitive plants), *Lobelia glandulosa, L. puberula*, two species of Saint Andrew's cross (*Ascyrum Crux-Andreæ* and *A. stans*), the white morning-glory (*Ipomœa pandurata*), and a kind of wild lettuce (*Hieracium Gronovii*), also *Pycnanthemum linifolium* (fine-leaved horsemint), become very prominent. Thereafter the autumnal flora consists of many plants of the sunflower family: of true sunflowers, *Helianthus angustifolius, H. occidentalis*, and *Chrysopsis sericea, Mariana*; of golden rods, *Solidago odora, S. altissima, S. leptocephala*, many species of aster, among which *A. concola* is characteristic; also *Sericocarpus tortifolius, Diplopappus ericoides, Eupatorium rotundifolium* (wild hoarhound), *parviflorum*, and in the bottoms several species of *Stevia*. Several species of *Liatris*, as *L. odoratissima* (vanilla plant), *L. pycnostachya, L. gracilis, L. squarrosa, L. scariosa* (rattlesnake's master), *Gnaphalium margaritaceum* (wild everlasting), and many other *compositæ*. Of the mint tribe, *Monarda punctata* (horsemint), *Hyptis capitata*, and *Pycnanthemum incanum* are prominent, while *Gerardia pedicularis, Herpestis nigrescens*, and sometimes *Gerardia purpurea* represent the Scrophularineæ.

The farther we advance southward the more numerously various species of huckleberry and whortleberry (*Vaccinium*), most of which flower in spring, are represented among the undergrowth; and similarly the gallberry (*Prinos glaber*) and candleberry (*Myrica cerifera* and *M. Carolinensis*) increase in a southward direction, until, near the sea-coast, they become very abundant.

---

a This fact should exclude from use, as misleading and contrary to facts, the earlier name of "*Palustris*", applied to the species by Linnæus.

Where strata not pervious to water underlie the soil at no great depth wet places, terminating in little branchlets, which afterward often sink into the sand, are formed. In these "pine hollows" we find a flora somewhat resembling that of the "pine meadows" of the coast, such as the candleberry, cord-rush (*Eriocaulon decangulare, E. villosum*), the yellow star grass (*Aletris aurea*), the *Xyris, Pinguicula*, sundew (*Drosera brevifolia*), the *Mitreola sessiliflora, Rhexia ciliosa, Eryngium virgatum*, and in the more southern portion the pitcher-plants (*Sarracenia variolaris, S. Psittacina*) and gallberry. The dark-colored soil, or muck, of these pine hollows is not unfrequently used for the improvement of garden plots, and where they are not too wet the hollows themselves are cultivated by preference.

Such being with considerable uniformity the character of the bulk of the long-leaf pine region, its description requires the mention of the exceptions rather than of the rule.

Along the northern limit of the region as far east as Raleigh, Smith county, we generally find some rather abrupt rocky ridges overlooking the prairie country to northward. The body of these ridges is formed by the white or gray "Grand Gulf sandstone" (see Geological features), often capped on top with some of the brown sand-rock of the drift. Southward the sandstone is gradually replaced by blue and green clays, which, east of Pearl river, lie mostly low down on the hillsides or in the valleys, covered by sometimes as much as 200 feet of sands of the stratified drift. Hence the region east of Pearl river is more of a plateau character, while on the west, where the white sand-rock extends as far south as the Louisiana line, it is frequently broken into abrupt ridges or "backbones". Such is the case especially in Copiah and in portions of Lincoln and Franklin, extending into Wilkinson, and to a less degree in the region intervening between the pine hills and the Mississippi river. A corresponding state of things exists in the upland portion of Louisiana lying opposite (see description of Louisiana, p. 20).

As in Louisiana, we occasionally meet in the pine hills of Mississippi isolated bodies of more fertile soil, where the long-leaf pine is partially or wholly replaced by the short-leaf species, or even altogether by oaks. One of the largest of such "coves" lies in Covington county, south of Mount Carmel, on the waters of White Sand creek (see analysis below), occupying several sections, and similar ones are met with more or less in the northern and western long-leaf pine region, where they are usually marked by flourishing settlements. Elsewhere, the fact that cultivation is restricted to the narrow bottoms of necessity causes the inhabitants to be much scattered along the streams.

Broadly speaking, the soils in the county lying east of Pearl river are more sandy than those to the westward, where, as we advance toward the Mississippi, the retentive subsoil comes nearer the surface, and thus gives rise to soils which, if not naturally thrifty, are at least susceptible of ready and permanent improvement, having a good foundation of loam subsoil of considerable depth. At the same time the bottom soils are correspondingly stronger. Such is the case in Copiah, Lincoln, Pike, and adjacent counties, while from Jones and Marion counties, east and southward, the soils of both uplands and lowlands become in general lighter and less retentive. As a matter of course, the bottoms of the larger streams, such as the Chickasawhay, Pascagoula, and in part Leaf river and its larger tributaries, are frequently of great fertility.

SOILS OF THE LONG-LEAF PINE REGION.—No. 205. *Soil* from the dividing ridge between the waters of Strong river and Silver creek, R. 19 W., T. 10, about Sec. 9, 2 miles east of Westville, Simpson county. This is one of the ridges timbered with short-leaf pine and oaks, post, Spanish, scarlet, and some black oak, and more or less hickory. The undergrowth is mainly copal sumach (*Rhus copallina*). This is substantially the same kind of land as that on which the town of Westville stands. The soil is gray and very ashy or sandy for an inch from the surface, then becomes of a dun color and more compact for about 6 inches, when it merges into the subsoil.

No. 192. *Subsoil of the above*, taken from 6 to 15 inches depth. A coarse, sandy loam, of a deep yellow or orange tint.

No. 206. *Soil from the long-leaf pine plateau* forming the divide between Okatoma and Okahay creeks, in the north half of T. 10, R. 16 W., Smith county. This is an open, long-leaf, pine country, with here and there a post oak, and more rarely a medium-sized black-jack, black gum, or hickory, the ground being covered with broom-sedge (*Andropogon*), devil's shoestring (*Tephrosia*), etc. Soil, about 5 inches; an ashy, yellowish-white material, with very little coarse sand.

Subsoil of the above, from 5 to 12 inches depth. A pale yellow, sandy loam. Not analyzed.

No. 209. Under subsoil of the above, dark yellow or orange loam, much stiffer than the subsoil. Specimen taken from the depth of 12 to 18 inches, but continues to 25 inches and more, when it is underlaid in its turn by stratified sand.

No. 292. *Subsoil of level oak uplands* on the waters of White Sand creek, R. 19 W., T. 7, Lawrence county. The soil here is a red or orange loam, mixed with much coarse sand, and produces good cotton and excellent corn. The subsoil, taken at 8 to 18 inches depth, is a kind of coarse, sandy hard-pan of a deep orange tint.

No. 249. *Subsoil loam* from the landward edge of the hummock of the Bogue Chitto river, R. 9 E., T. 3, S. 26, H. M. Quin's land. A yellow, rather light loam, resembling the subsoil of the pine woods, but here forming a deposit about 23 feet thick, skirting the bottom to the hills. Timber, oak and hickory; soil little different from the subsoil, which was taken at the depth of 10 to 18 inches.

No. 218. *Pine land soil* from near Summit station, on the Chicago, Saint Louis, and New Orleans railroad, Pike county, on the dividing ridge between the Bogue Chitto and the Tangipahoa rivers, 480 feet above tide-water. A rolling or sometimes hilly country, timbered in the main with long-leaf pine, with which the short-leaf species occasionally mingles; also more or less of oaks, as black-jack, post, black, and Spanish. The ashy surface soil is generally much more shallow here than farther eastward, and is frequently replaced by the sandy loam that elsewhere forms the subsoil. The sample analyzed was taken to the depth of 9 inches, and is a sandy loam of a buff tint.

No. 222. Subsoil of the above, taken from 9 to 20 inches depth. An orange yellow, rather sandy loam.

Long-leaf pine lands.

	SIMPSON COUNTY.		SMITH COUNTY.		LAWRENCE COUNTY.		PIKE COUNTY.		
	Dividing ridge between Strong river and Silver creek (R. 13 W., T. 10, S. 9).		Dividing ridge between Okatoma and Okahay creeks (R. 16 W., T. 10, N. ½).		White Sand creek, level oak uplands (R. 19 W., T. 7 S.).		R. 9 E., T. 3, S. 26.	Summit station (R. 6 E., T. 4, S. 25).	
	Pine ridge.		Pine hills.				Bogue Chitto underclay.		
	Soil.	Subsoil.	Soil.	Under subsoil.	Red subsoil loam.			Soil.	Pine land subsoil.
	No. 206.	No. 192.	No. 206.	No. 209.	No. 292.	No. 249.		No. 218.	No. 222.
Insoluble matter	92.826 } 94.850 2.024	96.756 } 91.534 4.778	98.257	82.080	81.229 } 87.918 6.689	87.144 } 96.968 8.824		89.501	77.981
Soluble silica									
Potash	0.076	0.160	0.256	0.486	0.269	0.160		0.218	0.296
Soda	0.046	0.034	0.065	0.061	0.195	0.075		0.078	0.073
Lime	0.061	0.038	0.139	0.073	0.059	0.059		0.034	0.133
Magnesia	0.112	0.229	0.180	0.519	0.343	0.145		0.306	0.262
Brown oxide of manganese	0.117	0.114	0.146	0.153	0.046	0.050		0.072	0.085
Peroxide of iron	1.262	2.210	1.251	4.145	3.647	2.744		2.402	4.456
Alumina	1.475	2.600	2.356	3.893	5.114	3.795		3.783	11.570
Phosphoric acid	0.069	0.041	0.090	0.022	0.101	0.065		0.033	0.042
Sulphuric acid	0.004	0.004	0.034	0.021	0.133	0.306		0.036	0.085
Water and organic matter	2.075	1.643	2.330	3.117	2.691	2.191		3.446	3.961
Total	99.948	99.627	100.027	100.519	100.921	100.478		100.212	99.593
Hygroscopic moisture	2.19	4.04	2.48	7.69	6.66	2.90		4.11	10.00
absorbed at	22 C.°	22 C.°	18 C.°	19 C.°	18 C.°	18 C.°		21 C.°	21 C.°

The mechanical analysis of a representative soil and its subsoil gave the following results:

Smith County pine hills.

	Soil.	Subsoil.
	No. 206.	No. 209.
MECHANICAL ANALYSIS.		
Weight of gravel over 1.2^{mm} diameter		
Weight of gravel between 1.2 and 1^{mm}	0.4	0.4
Weight of gravel between 1 and 0.6^{mm}	3.0	0.8
Fine earth	96.6	98.8
Total	100.1	100.0
MECHANICAL ANALYSIS OF FINE EARTH.		
Clay	4.6	10.9
Sediment of <0.25^{mm} hydraulic value	30.7	35.3
Sediment of 0.25^{mm}	14.8	17.0
Sediment of 0.5^{mm}	14.6	7.9
Sediment of 1.0^{mm}	6.5	5.4
Sediment of 2.0^{mm}	3.6	2.6
Sediment of 4.0^{mm}	1.2	0.6
Sediment of 8.0^{mm}	1.6	1.5
Sediment of 16.0^{mm}	3.0	3.9
Sediment of 32.0^{mm}	3.1	3.4
Sediment of 64.0^{mm}	6.9	6.5
Total	90.9	97.5

A comparison of the composition of these soils with that of the soils analyzed from the short-leaf pine and oak uplands of northern Mississippi does not show any wide divergence. As regards the physical properties, it appears from the hygroscopic coefficients that the long-leaf pine surface soils are, on the whole, less retentive, being more sandy than the latter, and continuing so to a greater depth, viz., from 8 to 12 inches, while in the northern Mississippi soils the more retentive and fertile subsoil lies generally within from 5 to 7 inches of the surface, and can readily be made to form a part of the tilled soil. Hence the long-leaf pine soils are generally more droughty, as even their subsoil is usually underlaid at no great depth by loose sand; otherwise the mechanical analyses given show for the latter subsoil a composition of a light but adequately retentive loam, whose intermixture with the soil by means of deep tillage should be accomplished whenever practicable.

In regard to chemical composition, a low percentage of phosphoric acid seems to prevail throughout, ranging between 0.020 and 0.040 of 1 per cent., while in the short-leaf pine soils the average is above 0.050. The average potash percentage ranges between 0.250 and 0.300 in both regions, and may be considered adequate, but is doubtless to a great extent unavailable in the absence of a sufficient supply of lime. An application of lime, here as elsewhere, at once causes a disappearance of the pine growth and its replacement by oaks, as is abundantly shown near the edge of the pine region lying toward lime formations.

Summarily, deep tillage and the use of lime and phosphates are indicated as the proper or at least the most direct, and therefore cheapest, means of improving the upland soils of the long-leaf pine region wherever a reasonably thick layer of loam subsoil underlies. Where this is wanting the soil is hardly susceptible of profitable improvement for general culture for many years to come. It is scarcely fair, however, to gauge the possible utility of these soils by the results obtained in the culture of cotton and corn, almost the only crops ordinarily attempted. There are many crops specially adapted to soils of this character which will in time find their way into practice. Prominent among these is the peanut or goober pea. Among forage plants the lupins and others of the pea family grown in the dry regions of southern Europe should command attention.

The marls of the adjacent "prairie region" will doubtless in time be extensively used for the improvement of the pine lands, and will relieve one of the great obstacles to thriftiness: deficiency in lime. There is another resource available to a considerable extent, and even now utilized by thrifty farmers in this region, viz., the fallen leaves or straw of the pines themselves. This can be obtained in enormous quantities at the proper season at very little expense, and this practice should altogether replace the wasteful and irrational one of burning the woods every autumn, whereby not only the pine straw, but also the roots of the pasture grasses, have been almost destroyed, converting the park-like slopes of the long-leaf pine forest into a dreary waste of useless weeds and blackened trunks and seriously injuring the pine timber, especially where it has been used for the gathering of turpentine. In this case the annual fires soon destroy the trees, smeared as they are with the combustible pitch; and it is thus that many entire townships of once splendid forest now stand almost valueless for any present purpose, and with little prospect of practical utility for many years to come unless restocked with pasture grasses by artificial means.

PINE STRAW.—As regards the possible utility of "pine straw" for soil improvement, the following analysis will give some light.

The leaves were collected, freshly fallen, about October 1, 1858, in southern Smith county, on the plateau land where the soil samples Nos. 206 and 209 were taken. The air-dried "straw", carefully freed from adhering impurities, yielded 2.5 per cent. of ash. The composition of the latter (calculated exclusive of about 6.5 per cent. of carbonic acid) was found to be as follows:

Ash of long-leaf pine straw.

	Per cent.
Silica	65.343
Potash	5.550
Soda	0.416
Lime	13.800
Magnesia	5.206
Brown oxide of manganese	1.681
Peroxide of iron	0.141
Alumina	4.530
Phosphoric acid	1.154
Sulphuric acid	0.890
Potassium chloride	1.479
Total	100.089

Notwithstanding the unusually low percentage of phosphoric acid shown by this analysis, the composition of this straw is such that about 1,400 pounds of it would amply replace the drain upon the soil caused by the growing of one bale of cotton lint, provided the seed was also returned.

In the sandy, unretentive soils of the region, however, the pine straw turned under by the plow directly will sometimes not decay for one or two seasons, and thus renders the soil too open for cultivation in the interval. It should therefore be first used as a material for composting, whether with earth, muck, stable manure, or marls, bone-meal, etc., as the case may be, and only applied to the land after it is decayed. This practice is already pursued in the older states with excellent results.

It is thus possible to concentrate the fertility of a large area of pine land upon a small portion kept in a high state of culture, instead of, as heretofore, laboriously clearing large areas, whose profitable fertility lasts only a few years and then suddenly " gives out", in consequence, probably, of the exhaustion of the plant-food, accumulated near the surface during many years by the decay of the pine leaves. Whether it will be best to apply this system to the production of cotton on these pine lands, or whether other branches of husbandry could, on the whole, be more profitably pursued, is a question that must be largely determined by local and commercial conditions. Since cotton, so long as the seed is regularly returned to the soil, is probably the least exhaustive crop known, its culture would seem to be specially adapted to lands of limited natural resources under an intelligent system of farming.

BOTTOM SOILS OF THE LONG-LEAF PINE REGION.—The bottom soils of the long-leaf pine region are usually, of course, very light, often positively sandy, and in that case often not very durable. This condition of things is, however, measurably varied and relieved by the circumstance that over a large portion of the area the streams cut into the clayey strata underlying the drift sand prevailing on the hills, and thus, by an intermixture of the two materials, the alluvial soils of the larger streams especially are rendered much stronger and more thrifty than is the case with those derived alone from the washings of the uplands. Moreover (as has already been mentioned), the streams heading northward of the pine region, in the heavy clay areas of the "central prairie region", carry the character of the latter down with them for some distance into the pine hills.

It thus happens that the character and productiveness of the bottoms of this region vary very greatly from one stream to another, and cannot be defined in a general manner. In some cases, the older and the newer deposits of the same stream (the "first" and "second" bottoms) differ to an extreme degree, proving a progressive, but occasionally a very abrupt, change of conditions in respect to the sources from which the alluvial soils were derived.

These variations are exemplified in the subjoined analyses of soils from the various portions of this extensive region, although not nearly all the practically important differences are here represented.

No. 361. *Soil from the hummock of bayou Pierre*, R. 2 W., T. 14 N., Copiah county. The exact locality from which this soil was taken is not known. The timber was mainly beech, and the soil was originally very fairly productive, but is becoming exhausted. It is a gray, rather silty or powdery soil, moderately retentive, and is very easily worked.

No. 360. *Subsoil of the above.* Whitish-gray, lighter colored than the surface soil, and containing more or less of small, roughish bog-ore concretions; a shade more sandy or silty than the soil.

No. 343. *Soil from the hummock or second bottom of Bahala creek*, R. 9 E., T. 9, Copiah county. Very similar in appearance to No. 361; whitish, silty, with but little coarse sand. Taken to 10 inches depth.

No. 344. *Subsoil of the above*, taken from 10 to 20 inches depth. Quite similar to No. 360.

No. 67. *Bottom soil from the west fork of Amite river*, R. 4 E., T. 5, Sec. 36, Franklin county, land of Mr. Joseph R. Coten. White, "crawfishy;" timber, bottom pine (*P. Tæda*), chestnut-white, white, and water oaks, some black and red (?) oaks, ironwood, sweet gum, some small hickory, holly, and red haw. The soil at the surface is ashy, but becomes more clayey downward. Samples taken to the depth of 10 inches. It produces good cotton, a small stalk, but well bolled; corn does not succeed. Being low and ill-drained, it is difficult to obtain a stand. This soil does not occur in large bodies here, most of the bottom being of the character of No. 66, but is more prevalent lower down on the stream. A soil similar in appearance to this, but much poorer, and characterized by post oak and huckleberry, occurs in the "upland ponds" of this region.

No. 70. *Subsoil of the above*, taken to the depth of 10 to 20 inches. Apparently less retentive than the surface soil and lighter tinted, but containing small grains of bog ore intermixed.

No. 66. *Dark bottom soil from the west fork of the Amite*, same locality as the preceding, and but a short distance from the spot. Dark brownish black, without change for 2 feet; a moderately clayey loam. Timber, large magnolias and hollies, beech, chestnut-white and white oaks, some ash, sweet gum, and poplar (tulip tree), all very large; a highly productive soil, making a 400-pound bale of cotton per acre, but not occurring in large tracts, and scarcer farther down the stream. Its timber is tall and stout, in contrast with the comparatively thin and lank growth on the white soil.

No. 80. *Second bottom or hummock soil* from Bogue Chitto creek, R. 9 E., T. 3, Sec. 17, H. M. Quin's land, Pike county. Timber growth, magnolia, sweet gum, "poplar," sassafras, hickory, all very large; some beech (chiefly on the bank itself and in sandy spots), white oak, chestnut-white oak, hornbeam, ironwood, holly, black or stag-horn sumach (*Rhus typhina*, here called "white sumach", a name elsewhere given to *Rhus venenata*, or varnish tree). The soil is a dark-colored, light loam, scarcely varying to the depth of 30 inches; sample taken to that of 12 inches. It is a highly esteemed soil, very productive when fresh, and has scarcely diminished its product in six years.

No. 194. *Bottom soil from the first bottom of Okahay creek*, R. 15 W., T. 10, about S. 21, Smith county. A brownish-gray, light loam, bearing a heavy growth of white and chestnut-white oak, as well as hickory and beech ;

also water and willow oaks, black and sweet gum, etc., and, close to the stream, large magnolias. Very productive, but very limited in area, the bottom being scarcely over one-fourth of a mile wide, but well settled.

No. 11. *Bottom soil from the bottom of Buckatunna creek*, Wayne county, near the crossing of the Mobile and Ohio railroad, south side. This soil is rather heavy, of a brownish tint for 10 inches, then getting heavier and of a lighter tint to 20 inches depth. The timber is sweet gum and bottom pine (*P. Tœda*). Near the creek, where the soil is somewhat lighter, large magnolias occur. The soil of the second bottom (about 3 feet higher and more extensive than the first, which is subject to overflow) is nearly the same, and ought to be profitable in cultivation.

No. 19. *Bottom soil from the first bottom of Chickasawhay river*, near Mr. W. P. Avera's, R. 6 W., T. 5, Sec. 36, Greene county. A high bottom, rarely overflowed; soil light "mulatto" color, of variable depth, underlaid partly by sand and partly by orange-colored clay. Timber mostly very large, consisting of ash, red elm, willow and Spanish oak, sweet gum, magnolia, tulip tree, and some very large black gum; undergrowth, buckeye (*Æsculus discolor*), *Illicium Floridanum* (star anise), and red-bud. Yields about 30 bushels of corn; cotton not tried. There is not much of this high bottom land; most of it is low and sloughy, but the character of the soil is about the same.

No. 8. *Soil from the first bottom of Pascagoula river*, R. 7 W., T. 2, Sec. 6, Jackson county. A dark-colored, heavy soil (hence is designated as "bottom prairie") down to 9 inches depth, where it is underlaid by a heavy gray clay subsoil to 30 inches depth. Timber, prevalently chestnut white oak, sweet gum, holly, Spanish oak (*Q. falcata*), magnolia (*grandiflora*), all very large trees; also some water and willow oak, a good deal of hornbeam, some mulberry, and staghorn sumac, and a little bottom white pine. This soil produces fine corn when not overflowed too late; cotton not yet tried.

No. 18. *Soil from second bottom or hummock of Pascagoula river*, same locality as the preceding, but lying from 4 to 6 feet higher than the first bottom, and not subject to overflow. Timber, white oak, bottom white pine, magnolia, water oak, chincapin, some holly and ironwood, and a good deal of very large staghorn or black sumach. The soil is of a dark chocolate tint and quite light, underlaid at 10 inches depth by a very sandy, yellow subsoil. This soil is also very productive, and, being much safer than that of the first bottom, is chiefly cultivated in the region. Cotton is hardly grown here; has a disposition to run to weed.

No. 25. *Subsoil of the above*, 10 to 20 inches depth.

Bottom and hummock lands of the long-leaf pine region.

	COPIAH COUNTY.				FRANKLIN COUNTY.		
	R. 2 W., T. 14, Bayou Pierre hummock.		R. 9 R., T. 9, Bahala second bottom.		R. 4 E., T. 5, S. 36, West Amite white bottom.		R. 4 E., T. 5, S. 36, West Amite.
	Soil.	Subsoil.	Soil.	Subsoil.	Soil.	Subsoil.	Bottom soil (dark).
	No. 361.	No. 360.	No. 343.	No. 344.	No. 67.	No. 70.	No. 66.
Insoluble matter	86.169	86.511	91.870 } 4.003 } 85.873	81.420 } 3.925 } 85.345	91.334	96.490 } 2.382 } 93.872	87.542
Soluble silica							
Potash	0.253	0.333	0.499	0.357	0.270	0.150	0.486
Soda	0.050	0.067	0.257	0.208	0.103	0.045	0.054
Lime	0.121	0.125	0.090	0.120	0.134	0.055	0.215
Magnesia	0.180	0.277	0.546	0.277	0.197	0.120	0.334
Brown oxide of manganese	0.245	0.342	0.041	0.089	0.141	0.085	0.690
Peroxide of iron	3.700	3.969	2.293	3.409	1.341	1.771	5.528
Alumina	5.301	6.106	5.182	6.385	3.729	2.542	2.407
Phosphoric acid	0.100	0.087	0.047	0.091	0.149	0.048	0.100
Sulphuric acid	trace	0.049	0.035	0.009	0.022	0.005	0.048
Water and organic matter	4.177	2.516	3.788	3.354	2.961	1.628	3.507
Total	100.296	100.782	100.291	100.253	100.221	100.321	100.962
Humus						0.717	
Available inorganic						1.608	
Hygroscopic moisture	5.80	5.32	6.74	6.18	3.93	3.77	5.52
absorbed at	19 C.°	26 C.°	6 C.°	4 C.°	20 C.°	22 C.°	6 C.°

Bottom and hummock lands of the long-leaf pine region—Continued.

	PIKE COUNTY.	SMITH COUNTY.	WAYNE COUNTY.	GREENE COUNTY.	JACKSON COUNTY.		
	R. 9 E., T. 5, S. 17, Bogue Chitto.	R. 15 W.. T. 10, S. 21, Okahay.	R. 5. W., T. 9, S. 8., Buckatunna.	Avera's place, R. 6 W., T. 5, S. 30, Chickasawhay.	R. 7 W., T. 2, S. 6, Pascagoula.	R. 7 W., T. 2, S. 6, Pascagoula hummock.	
	Second bottom soil.	Bottom soil.	Bottom soil.	Bottom soil.	"Prairie" bottom soil.	Soil.	Subsoil.
	No. 80.	No. 194.	No. 11.	No. 19.	No. 8.	No. 18.	No. 22.
Insoluble matter	85.376 } 89.178	84.699 } 87.736	71.382 } 80.653	91.816 } 93.540	71.066 } 79.796	94.200 } 94.941	90.336 } 92.186
Soluble silica	3.802	3.037	9.221	1.724	8.729	0.741	1.850
Potash	0.126	0.149	0.211	0.123	0.312	0.115	0.173
Soda	0.060	0.078	0.130	0.076	0.097	0.095	0.055
Lime	0.090	0.413	0.197	0.094	0.062	0.076	0.132
Magnesia	0.136	0.069	0.493	0.142	0.221	0.081	0.153
Brown oxide of manganese	6.150	0.262	0.915	0.095	0.140	0.029	0.063
Peroxide of iron	1.821	2.107	4.580	1.210	4.638	0.604	1.373
Alumina	3.497	2.107	5.526	1.372	6.856	1.158	1.941
Phosphoric acid	0.063	0.149	0.132	0.060	0.042	0.066	0.057
Sulphuric acid	?	0.007	trace	0.005	0.008	trace	trace
Water and organic matter	4.971	6.619	7.372	2.307	7.904	2.777	4.496
Total	99.754	99.731	102.475	99.961	100.160	99.892	100.639
Hygroscopic moisture	4.72	6.61	3.01	4.39	11.96	2.14	4.15
absorbed at	18 C.°	22 C.°	10 C.°	22 C.°	22 C.°	22 C.°	22 C.°

As might be expected, these soils are extremely variable in composition, according to location. The greatest differences are manifestly due to the derivation of the soils from sources lying outside of the pine region, especially in the case of such as head among the rich, heavy clays of the central prairie region, like the Okahay and Buckatunna. The character of a great majority of these soils is that of a light sandy loam of no great depth, and, in view of that fact, very deficient in lime and phosphoric acid and not rich in potash, as might be expected from the character of the uplands from whose washings they have been derived. In the more southern portion of the region, where heavy, impervious clays underlie everywhere at no great depth, the subsoil, though itself still light, is frequently ill-drained, and remains water-soaked until late in the season: a condition of things usually made manifest by the prevalence of the ink-berry or gallberry, wax myrtle, and other plants of like habit. These disappear very strikingly as we approach the calcareous regions on either side, and equally striking is the increased thriftiness of the soils, concurrently with the increase of their lime percentage, even while that of the phosphates and potash percentage remains small. The natural inference is that among the most important improvements to be made within the long-leaf pine region, both on uplands and lowlands, is the use of lime or of the calcareous marls so abundantly present in the "central prairie region". Phosphate manures are indicated as next in importance by the uniformly small amounts of these substances shown by the analysis. In this, as in other respects, it is interesting to compare the analyses of the two kinds of bottom soils occurring on the west fork of the Amite in Franklin county. The two lie nearly at the same level in immediate proximity, and must have been originally of the same composition; but the white soil and subsoil (Nos. 67 and 70) have been subjected to the leaching action of stagnant water in consequence of imperviousness of the underlying hard-pan. Perhaps these very leachings have contributed to the high percentages of potash and lime found in the dark soil (No. 66), which is little inferior in quality as well as in depth to the bottom soils of the Tallahatchie river (see Mississippi bottom region). Nos. 194 and 11, though somewhat deficient in potash, show good cause for their exceptional thriftiness in the proportions of lime and phosphoric acid, which are considerably above the average.

The white hummock soils from Cuplah rank as of medium quality only, that of Bayou Pierre being superior to the Buhain soil both as regards lime and phosphates, the more so as a portion of the phosphoric acid shown for the subsoil is doubtless contained in the unavailable form of bog ore. Both would be materially improved by the use of the marls occurring on Pearl river, not far away; but bone-meal or superphosphate will be wanted on them before long.

The second bottom soil of Bogue Chitto, No. 80, is rather a remarkable case as showing high fertility, both from its timber and from the results of cultivation, and yet containing low percentages of all the chief ingredients of plant-food. But the fact that it is almost the same to the depth of 3 feet, and pervious and well-drained, explains the apparent anomaly. It is a parallel to the esteemed cotton soil of the middle Homochitto, No. 68, which would be thought a poor soil from its low percentage of plant-food, but makes up for this deficiency by its extraordinary depth of from 3 to 4 feet. (See cane hills region under head "Oak Uplands Belt".)

A similar saving clause applies to the Chickasawhay bottom soil, No. 19, almost identical in composition with the Bogue Chitto soil just referred to, but not quite so deep nor so well drained, and hence less productive.

The analyses of the Pascagoula soils are also very instructive. The prairie bottom soil, No. 8, looks by far most promising, but until late in the season it is very heavy and ill-drained. Hence in cultivation the hummock soil, No. 18, is preferred, which has not only the advantage of a larger supply of phosphates, though less of potash, but is well drained, and is of considerable depth. It would require heavy dressings of lime or marls and the use of phosphate manures to render No. 8 at all available for profitable culture, because in it the roots can only penetrate to one-third or one-half the depth that is easily reached in the lighter hummock soil.

PEARL RIVER SOILS.—Almost throughout its course Pearl river is bordered by comparatively narrow bottoms and rather wide second bottoms or hummocks. At Jackson, for instance, the first bottom is about half a mile in width, and beyond it lies an almost level second terrace, 5 to 6 feet above the flood-plain, 2½ to 3 miles wide, and differing widely both in soil and timber from the first bottom. Southward this feature becomes perhaps even more pronounced, the first bottom being often of insignificant width only in the long-leaf pine region, while the second bottom, or "flat", as it is there commonly called, is from one mile to several miles wide. It thus forms an important portion of the readily available arable area of the region, and numerous soil specimens representing these lands have been collected at different points. The following are the only analyses thus far made, but they afford an insight into the general character of these lands:

No. 181. *Hummock soil* from the flat of Pearl river, R. 21 W., T. 7, Sec. 23, opposite Monticello, Lawrence county. The level country here is from 1 to 1½ miles wide and is well cultivated. The land is timbered with bottom pine (*P. Tæda*), sweet and black gum, water and willow oaks, etc. The soil is of a pale mouse-color, quite light, and rather silty to about 6 inches depth.

No. 182. Subsoil of the above, taken from 6 to 18 inches depth. This soil is a little heavier than the surface soil, so as to retain manure, and is of a pale-yellow tint. Below the depth mentioned the material becomes gradually lighter, and finally white and more sandy, with numerous brown spots of bog ore, occasionally washed out as "black pebble". The surface of the flat is about 20 feet above low-water level.

No. 61. *Hummock soil* from the flat of Pearl river, R. 18 W., T. 2 N., Sec. 26 (?), 3 miles below the mouth of South Little river, Marion county. Soil light, rather silty, and of a mouse color; taken to the depth of 6 inches. Timber: bottom pine prevalent; water, willow, white, and Spanish oaks, not large; small sweet gum, some small sassafras, staghorn sumac, dogwood, Spanish mulberry (*Callicarpa*), grape-vines, and huckleberry. No settlements near, but a similar soil at Spring Cottage post-office yields fair crops.

No. 62. Subsoil of the above, taken from 6 to 20 inches depth. Pale yellow, more retentive than the surface soil, and apparently more so than No. 182.

No. 60. *Bottom soil* of Pearl river, from R. 17 W., T. 1 N., Sec. 6, Mr. Ford's land. Soil blackish, apparently rather heavy, cracking open in the dry season. Taken to the depth of 10 inches. Timber mostly very large, especially the sweet gum, which is very prevalent; pignut hickory, water, Spanish, basket, and black oaks, hornbeam, ironwood, snowdrop tree, styrax, some mulberry, beech in low places, grape-vines (*V. æstivalis*), cissus, hop tree (*Ptelea*), staghorn sumac, and but little magnolia. The timber denotes a strong soil, which produces very well and tills easily, but the late overflows often belate the crops.

No. 63. Subsoil of the above, taken from 10 to 20 inches depth. Differs little from the surface soil in aspect, and seems to continue unchanged to a greater depth.

Pearl River hummock and bottom lands.

	LAWRENCE COUNTY.		MARION COUNTY.			
	R. 21 W., T. 7, S. 23.		R. 18 W., T. 2 N., S. 26 (?).		R. 17 W., T. 1 N., S. 6.	
	Hummock.		Hummock.		Bottom.	
	Soil.	Subsoil.	Soil.	Subsoil.	Soil.	Subsoil.
	No. 181.	No. 182.	No. 61.	No. 62.	No. 60.	No. 63.
Insoluble matter	94.384 } 96.122	89.008 } 93.502	87.520 } 90.216	85.354 } 90.178	87.024 } 87.826	85.213 } 89.204
Soluble silica	1.738	4.494	2.696	4.824	0.802	3.993
Potash	0.107	0.155	0.134	0.160	0.174	0.212
Soda	0.053	0.077	0.088	0.076	0.060	0.051
Lime	0.060	0.056	0.113	0.054	0.078	0.072
Magnesia	0.083	0.107	0.141	0.212	0.275	0.107
Brown oxide of manganese	0.005	0.077	0.134	0.065	0.078	0.050
Peroxide of iron	0.612	1.990	1.990	2.774	2.511	2.021
Alumina	0.613	2.127	3.326	4.134	2.674	4.054
Phosphoric acid	0.014	0.130	0.060	0.059	0.146	0.100
Sulphuric acid	0.005	0.006	0.016	0.005	0.006	0.005
Water and organic matter	2.182	1.729	4.951	2.820	5.941	3.562
Total	100.100	98.742	100.778	100.046	98.782	100.380
Hygroscopic moisture	2.35	4.15	4.41	5.67	5.49	3.60
absorbed at	19 C.°	19 C.°	21 C.°	....	23 C.°	22 C.°

On the whole, the composition of these soils agrees with that of corresponding soils in the rest of the long-leaf pine region. The low potash percentage of the hummock soils is quite striking, and the same feature is apparent in the bottom soil. No. 181 is in fact throughout a very inferior soil in every respect, but is somewhat redeemed by the high phosphate percentage of its subsoil. Both are poor in lime, and little durability can be expected of them. When "tired", the land will require complete manures to restore profitable productiveness. Nos. 61 and 62 reflect the better quality of the timber in their composition, especially in the higher percentages of potash and lime, to which is added a greater depth of the more substantial subsoil. Still these soils cannot be durable in their natural productiveness, and manuring must soon be resorted to by those cultivating them.

The bottom soil, Nos. 60 and 63, differs materially by the higher percentages of phosphoric acid in both soil and subsoil, with likewise a somewhat larger amount of potash. In lime it is still low, and the use of marl would doubtless be one of the most important improvements in its cultivation. The large timber seems to indicate that some important supplies of plant-food come from a greater depth than the 20 inches represented above, whose composition does not, apparently, justify either the character of the natural growth or the good reports from its cultivation. As compared with the hummock soils, it has, of course, the advantage of abundant moisture, for the crop failures in the "flat" are largely due to droughts, which quickly injure such leachy lands.

THE PINE FLATS REGION.

The "pine flats" are not as extensively represented in Mississippi as in Louisiana. At several points (as near bay Saint Louis) the long-leaf pine ridges, with their characteristic soil and vegetation, reach almost to the Gulf coast. Unlike the marshy belt that fringes the Louisiana coast, the shore-line of Mississippi sound is almost throughout characterized by a bluff bank 10 to 25 feet high, consisting of sandy materials in its upper portion at least, while near the water's edge there appear not unfrequently gray or black clays, with cypress stumps, precisely as is the case at Côte Blanche, Petit Anse, and Grande Côte, in Louisiana. The marshes are small and local, so as to scarcely deserve representation on the map until the mouth of Pearl river is approached. Here also, however, all but a small area of marsh falls within the limits of the state of Louisiana.

Almost throughout this region thus far agriculture is practiced only on a very limited scale, chiefly along the coast and on the higher lands lying along some of the bayous. The raising of stock on the natural pastures, lumbering, and charcoal burning constitute the chief pursuits in the back country, while immediately along the coast there lie numerous towns, settlements, and residences, occupied mainly as places of summer resort, and to a limited extent by manufacturing establishments, connected closely by rail as well as by steamers with the cities of New Orleans and Mobile.

In approaching the coast from the interior the transition from the pine hills proper is at first announced by the appearance, on the very summits of the pine ridges, of marshy flats or shallow ponds, occupied by a peculiar vegetation, partly of rushes and sedges and partly of pitcher-plants (*Sarracenia*), long-leaved sundew (*Drosera filiformis*), cord rush (*Eriocaulon*), bright colored orchids, etc. As we advance southward this feature becomes more prevalent. The tall and stout pines become small and lanky and widely scattered, and among them appears on the very uplands an equally diminutive and sparse growth of cypress. These incongruous trees, sadly worsted apparently by their mutual concessions of natural habit, here rarely exceed 25 feet in height. The undergrowth is formed by low but closely packed and profusely flowering and fruiting bushes of the gallberry (*Prinos glaber*), and the shallow depressions through which the surplus water of these bogs finds outlets are skirted, or at times completely overgrown, with low thickets of bay (*Magnolia glauca*), the Carolina laurel or bay galls (*Laurus Carolinensis*), the candleberry or bayberry (*Myrica*), and a few others, frequently interspersed with tracts of dwarf palmetto (*Sabal minimus*). The latter, with some oaks, likewise form the chief growth of the very sandy bottoms of the larger streams (such as Red and Black creeks), and along these streams the bluff banks exhibit the explanation of the state of things on the surface. The uppermost 2 or 3 feet of the profile show almost pure sand; but at the depth of 4 or 5 feet there underlie heavy, impervious gray or yellowish clays, which shed all the water falling on the surface. The latter is therefore compelled to drain slowly sideways through the sand to the larger channels that at long intervals intersect this plateau land. In so doing it converts the entire surface into a bog, and becomes so impregnated with vegetable matter that the water of the streams appears of a coffee color, although perfectly clear and transparent, showing distinctly every object on the bottom, including the magnificent trout that abounds in these deep channels.

Occasionally, especially near the streams, we find low ridges, on whose flanks there appears a yellow loam subsoil, stretching in from the pine hills and creating a distinction between upland and lowland, both in soil and vegetation; but in the more southerly portion (such as that lying on Bluff creek) the landscape appears like a level park or meadow land, whose sparse growth of diminutive pine and cypress scarcely interferes with the view—the ground covered with bright flowers in spring, but with no other inhabitants than the prairie lark. The soil is a grayish-white sand, water-sodden, and hopeless for cultivation, though doubtless to a great extent available as a pasture ground for cattle.

The "pine meadow" character continues usually to within one or two miles of the beach, with little change, save near the larger streams, where the "loam ridges" come in. In the belt immediately along the coast the drainage is better, probably in consequence of a more rapid slope of the clay stratum toward the sea. The cypress disappears, the long-leaf pine improves in stature and appearance, and there mingles with it another pine, commonly called pitch-pine, and frequent all along the sound and on the islands. It has of late been recognized as distinct, and is described by Dr. George Engelmann, under the name of Elliott's pine (*P. Elliottii*).(a) It is very resinous, and is used to some extent as firewood. Together with the live-oak, it is characteristic of the "sand hummocks" of the coast.

The soil of the "sand hummocks" is little else than sand, though near the surface it has sufficient substance to bear crops for a few years, and frequently has a more compact subsoil, allowing of the profitable use of manure. As the roots can penetrate to great depths, tap-rooted crops do not suffer from drought as much as might be anticipated.

At many points the sand hummocks abut directly upon the beach. Frequently, however, their character is materially changed by the presence on the surface of the "shell-heaps", which have given rise to so much speculation all along the Gulf coast. Where these masses of shells (mainly, in most cases almost exclusively, the gnathodon or common "clam" of the Gulf) have occupied the ground for any considerable length of time the loose yellow sand has been converted into a dark, sometimes black, sandy soil, containing a large amount of vegetable mold and bearing a vigorous growth of bottom timber, mingled with the live-oak, while the pitch-pine is altogether absent. The soil of these "shell hummocks" is highly productive, and is everywhere occupied either by residences, market gardens, or plantations. Like the shell heaps themselves, it forms only limited patches, but it is by far the best soil of the coast.

THE COAST MARSHES.

The "sand hummocks" of the coast form strips or bands from one-eighth to one-half mile in width, separated from one another by small marshes, formed by short water-courses which empty directly into the Gulf. Beside these, all the larger streams, such as the Pascagoula, Tshula Cahawfa, Biloxi, Wolf, Jourdan, and Pearl, form more or less extensive marshes at their mouths and for some distance inland, the largest bodies being those belonging to the first and last named. The main body of the Pearl river marsh, however, lies on the Louisiana side, leaving on the east side only a narrow strip between Mulatto bayou and the main river south of Pearlington.

The soil of the marshes derived from the short streams heading in the sand hummocks or meadow lands is usually very sandy, so far as it has any solid basis at all. Sometimes the soil is represented only by a semi-fluid, almost gelatinous mass of black, fetid muck, into which a pole may easily be pushed down to a depth of 8 or 10 feet. Such marshes are occupied mainly by the "cutting rush", a sedge grass (*Cyperus*) with triangular stems and formidably sharp, saw-toothed leaves, which the visitor soon learns to hold in awe. Where the soil is more solid, the prevailing growth is the "round rush" (*Scirpus lacustris*), with its round, soft, pithy stem. With it there usually grows the marsh milkweed (*Asclepias paupercula*), the large arrowhead (*Sagittaria lancifolia*), and the pickerel weed (*Pontederia cordata*). In both kinds of marsh we frequently see stunted bushes of bay (*Magnolia glauca*), bay galls (*Laurus Carolinensis*), and candleberry (*Myrica Carolinensis*). Stunted pine, cypress, maple, black gum, etc., are occasionally seen.

In the marshes belonging to the larger streams, such as the Wolf, Pascagoula, and Pearl, there is generally near the main stream a belt of heavy clay soil, covered by from 10 to 18 inches of matted "grass roots". Farther away the soil is usually more sandy, and the "cutting rush" more abundant.

Attempts to reclaim the marshes for cultivation have as yet been made on a small scale only by throwing up the soil from a portion, so as to form ridges above the level of the overflow or to serve as levees around the areas intended to be reclaimed. When freshly dug up all these soils are very fetid. On the whole, they are not very strongly impregnated with salt, and samphire and other salt growth is seen mainly near the beach. It is noteworthy that, notwithstanding this, the region is remarkably healthy, and the presence of the mosquito in large numbers is the only drawback to its pleasantness as a health resort from the cities.

SOILS OF THE PINE FLATS AND COAST REGION.—The soils of the immediate coast and those of the pine flats inland are so intimately correlated that the two are best considered together, the more as the areas covered by the coast soils are very limited.

· No. 214. *Soil of pine meadow lands* from R. 7 W., T. 6, south of Little Bluff creek, Jackson county. Perfectly level, timbered with the scattered growth of stunted pine and cypress, and the ground covered with a dense turf of small sedges, cord-rush (*Eriocaulon*), xyris, short-leaved sundew (*Drosera brevifolia*), etc. The soil here appears to be uniform to the depth of 12 inches, being gray, very sandy, and unretentive; lower down pale-yellow sand at the time (May), drenched with water.

No. 17. *Soil of "shell hummock"* from the land of Mrs. McRae, at West Pascagoula, Jackson county. Timber, large live-oak, red cedar, magnolia, bay galls (unusually large here), Spanish oak (*Q. falcata*), water oak, holly, dogwood, sweet gum, pitch-pine, wild plum (*Prunus Americana*), ironwood, prickly ash (*Xanthoxylon Carolinianum*), Hercules club (*Aralia spinosa*, commonly called "prickly ash" in the interior of Mississippi), muscadine (*V. rotundifolia*), frost grape (*V. cordifolia*); of smaller shrubs, cassine (*Ilex Cassine*), French mulberry (*Callicarpa Americana*); also very abundantly an *Actinomeris*, (†) called by the Creoles "l'herbe a trois quarts", and considered an indication of an excellent soil. It will be noted that with a few exceptions this growth is characteristic of calcareous soils elsewhere. Soil almost black, very sandy, with shells intermixed.

No. 15. *Subsoil of the above*, taken from 6 to 12 inches depth, somewhat lighter in color, and very sandy.

a It is probably the same as *P. Cubensis*, Griseb.

No. 88. *Soil of shell hummock on Mulatto bayou*, R. 16 W., T. 10, Hancock county, from the sea island cotton plantations. The timber is almost precisely the same as that recorded above as occupying the shell hummock at West Pascagoula, with the addition of a good deal of hickory and of the laurel-leaved oak (*Q. laurifolia*) and sassafras. The soil is very light, and is of a dark "mulatto" or chocolate tint, unvarying for about 20 inches, at which depth there underlies a pale-yellow sand, highly productive, yielding 40 bushels of corn or a bale of cotton per acre, very light and easily worked. Prior to the war this tract was almost exclusively occupied by the culture of long-staple cotton. Its greatest width is about one-third of a mile, and it extends along the bayou with a varying width for 4 or 5 miles. Shell heaps, consisting of oysters and clams, form long levee-like ridges along both the present and older channels. Soil sample taken to 12 inches depth.

No. 90. *Subsoil of the above*, 12 to 20 inches depth.

No. 241. *Soil from the marsh of Pearl river*, Hancock county, taken about 30 yards from the river bank, near Mr. Brown's mill; thrown up from a ditch 3 feet deep, the first 12 inches being a matted mass of grass roots. The chief growth of this marsh along the banks of the river and its bayous is a tall "round rush" (*Scirpus lacustris*) 6 to 10 feet high, with an undergrowth of arrow-head, pickerel weed, and lizard's tail (*Saururus cernuus*). The cutting rush also occurs apparently in the more elevated places, and with it the marsh milkweed. The only shrub to be seen on the green plain, extending westward as far as the eye can reach, is the wax myrtle (*Myrica Carolinensis*), growing to a height of 8 to 14 feet, and at intervals a solitary bush of the bay (*Magnolia glauca*). The soil near the river bank is simply a stiff, bluish-gray clay, apparently with but little vegetable matter. Farther inland it becomes darker, and where the sample was taken it was black when moist and of a slate color when dry. It contains very little sand, cuts with a shining surface, and is variegated with irregular dark-colored veins and specks, which, on exposure to air, become yellow or rust color.

It is stated that this soil when laid dry (which can readily be done, since it forms firm levees) is easily worked and produces fine vegetables, such as peas, beans, cabbage, etc., but is specially adapted to water- and musk-melons. None of these plants showed any disposition to wither, as was the case with the Pascagoula marsh soil. Near Pearlington, where the soil is the same, an experiment was made with rice. The crop was very abundant and of fine quality.

No. 215. *Marsh soil*, thrown up to the depth of about 3 feet, in a small "cutting-rush" marsh adjoining the premises of Alfred Lewis, West Pascagoula, Jackson county. This is one of the small marshes formed by branchlets heading in the meadows or "gallberry flats", or in the sand hummocks. The portion in which the soil was thrown up adjoins the beach. When in its natural condition a pole could be pushed down some 8 feet into it. The soil is almost black when wet, dark gray when dry, and to the eye appears like a mere mixture of sand and marsh muck. In attempting to cultivate this soil Mr. Lewis found that both corn and rice thrive finely up to a certain age, producing a large crop of leaves. When both were about 15 inches high the leaves began to turn yellow, and the corn soon died out altogether; the rice "spindled up" into a weakly stem, some of which even bloomed, but failed to fructify. The application of shell quicklime produced no sensible difference in the result in the season following its application in spring.

No. 220. *Marsh muck*, taken from the same marsh farther inland, dark brown and spongy, with more or less of undecomposed vegetable matter; thin and mushy when fresh, and fetid.

Soils of the coast region.

	UPLAND OR HUMMOCK SOILS.						MARSH SOILS.	
	JACKSON COUNTY.			HANCOCK COUNTY.			JACKSON COUNTY.	
	R. 7 W., T. 7, pine meadow.	R. 6 W., T. 8, 8, 7, shell hummock, West Pascagoula.		R. 16 W., T. 10, Sea island cotton land.		R. 16 W., T. 8, S. 30, (?) Pearl river.	R. 6 W., T. 8, S 7, West Pascagoula.	
	Soil.	Soil.	Subsoil.	Soil.	Subsoil.	Marsh soil.	Marsh soil.	Marsh muck.
	No. 314.	No. 17.	No. 15.	No. 88.	No. 90.	No. 241.	No. 215.	No. 220.
Insoluble matter .... }{ Soluble silica	44.802	86.609) 94.880 0.680)	90.742) 97.707 0.512)	95.084) 98.082 2.448)	95.870	74.150	70.183	25.235
Potash	0.061	0.065	0.015	0.045	0.080	1.002	0.550	
Soda	0.050	0.046	Not detr.	0.057	0.045	0.970	0.967	
Lime	0.052	0.223	0.072	0.096	0.115	0.182	0.160	
Magnesia	0.089	0.101	0.080	0.114	0.065	1.004	0.742	
Brown oxide of manganese	0.045	0.016	0.042	0.058	0.035	0.065	0.007	5.556
Peroxide of iron	0.650	0.433	0.404	0.516	0.324	2.330	1.171	
Alumina	0.348	0.585	0.322	0.484	0.322	10.045	5.504	
Phosphoric acid	0.031	0.104	0.148	0.097	0.107	0.188	0.111	
Sulphuric acid	trace.	0.004	0.018	trace.		0.658	0.176	0.247
Water and organic matter ...	2.277	2.561	1.019	3.618	1.821	5.890	18.626	66.079
Total	98.445	100.016	98.920	100.544	99.484	100.212	99.796	100.000
Hygroscopic moisture	....	2.06	0.98	2.52	2.04	7.94	15.44	21.49
absorbed at	....	10 C.°	10 C.°	22 C.°	22 C.°	Air-dried.	22 C.°	21 C.°

No. 214, the pine meadow soil, shows throughout such low percentages of the important ingredients of plant-food that its sterility does not appear surprising. Yet, when we compare it with the highly productive shell hummock soils from two widely separated localities, we find that these differ from the other, so far as the mineral ingredients are concerned, in only two material points, viz, amounts of lime and of phosphoric acid, from four to six times greater. (a) The shell hummock soils are even poorer in potash than the meadow soil, but doubtless contain a good deal more of true humus, the vegetable matter of the meadow and marsh soils being in a sour and soluble condition, in which it does not serve the nutrition of the ordinary culture plants.

But apart from these important chemical differences there is a most important physical one. The shell hummock soils are several feet deep and are well drained, permitting the roots to penetrate to great depths, and thus to utilize the plant-food of a very large soil mass. In the case of the meadow soil, as has been stated, the subsoil is water-soaked at the depth of 10 to 12 inches, and thus effectually precludes the penetration of roots to any greater depth. Hence we find on it only fibrous-rooted plants or very small tap-rooted ones, and of all these the seeds are exceedingly small, conforming to the very small amount of phosphates available.

Undoubtedly the original material of the shell hummocks was the same as that of the sand hummocks, gallberry flats, and meadows. The change has been brought about by the long-continued action of the disintegrating shells. It is not difficult to see how these acted. While furnishing slight amounts of phosphates and nitrogen compounds directly, the chief effect has been to retain and accumulate near the surface all the plant-food absorbed by successive crops of vegetation by virtue of the effect of lime in rendering humus insoluble and preventing its waste, and with it that of the accompanying available plant-food. In the meadow soils the dark-colored drainage-water speaks plainly enough of the acid condition of the humus, as manifested by the growth of "sour" grasses. A dressing of lime would promptly relieve this condition, as is actually sometimes done for a few years after the burning of the dry grasses (by their ashes); but so long as the land is left undrained the continued formation of more acid in the soil soon destroys this effect.

Drainage first, and then the use of lime, are therefore the first steps to be taken in the reclamation of the ill-drained "meadow" soils wherever the value of land may be such as to justify such treatment of a soil of such slender natural resources. Doubtless the broadcast sowing of lime on meadow pastures would soon create a great improvement, even without drainage, rendering it possible to replace the sedges by sweeter grasses. As to the sand hummocks, which are well drained, but are too poor and unretentive for profitable culture, it would seem probable that they could be made available for market-garden purposes at least by the combined use of dressings of lime and marsh muck; a treatment which would result in the production of a soil similar to the "shell hummocks", produced by the action of the shell lime, which has continued for many centuries. The muck will carry with it both plant-food and the property of retentiveness to the soil, which will thus ultimately be made capable of retaining manure.

As to the marsh soils, it is clear that those occurring along the channels of the larger streams, such as No. 241, require only drainage and aeration to render them profusely productive. They are, in fact, little more than rich, heavy bottom soils, with high percentages of every mineral ingredient of plant-food; but they are in a condition in which they contain compounds positively poisonous to plant growth, such as the soluble salts of iron, and in the case before us of sulphate of magnesia or epsom salt, which has doubtless been derived from the sea-water. From the experience had, it would seem that simple aeration, after leveeing, enables these soils to bear ordinary crops; but it cannot be doubted that even with them the use of some lime to favor the aeration process and to decompose the poisonous epsom salt would be found highly advantageous.

As regards the soil and muck of the "cutting-rush" marsh, as exemplified in Nos. 215 and 220, the best use of the latter would doubtless for the present be the improvement of the sand hummocks near the coast, in conjunction with lime, as above stated. Where such marshes can be drained, such soils as No. 215 would offer considerable inducements for cultivation, since it is not only reasonably rich in plant-food, but is also rather unexpectedly retentive and otherwise qualified for culture by its not inconsiderable percentage of clay. The withering of the crops tried by Mr. Lewis, as above stated, was undoubtedly due to the contact of the roots with the acid, and to them in many respects poisonous, water of the adjoining marsh, charged with soluble iron salts and (as shown by the odor alone) sulphureted hydrogen. It will not do simply to throw up the soil in ridges, but the marsh must cease to exist as such immediately around it.

NATURAL FERTILIZERS OF THE LONG-LEAF PINE REGION.—Apart from the pine straw, which at present is the most generally available material for the production of manure (see page 58, under the head of "Soils of the long-leaf pine region"), and from the marls available to the portion of the region adjacent to the central prairie region, there are within it but few naturally occurring materials of much value as fertilizers. The green and gray clays cropping out in the beds of streams are often taken for marls, and are usually without agricultural value. In a few localities these clays contain enough of lime and other ingredients of plant-food to be useful as fertilizers. Analyses of three such are given on page 71.

---

a The high lime percentage of No. 17 is probably partly due to shell particles mechanically scattered in the mass, and not wholly to the chemically diffused substance.

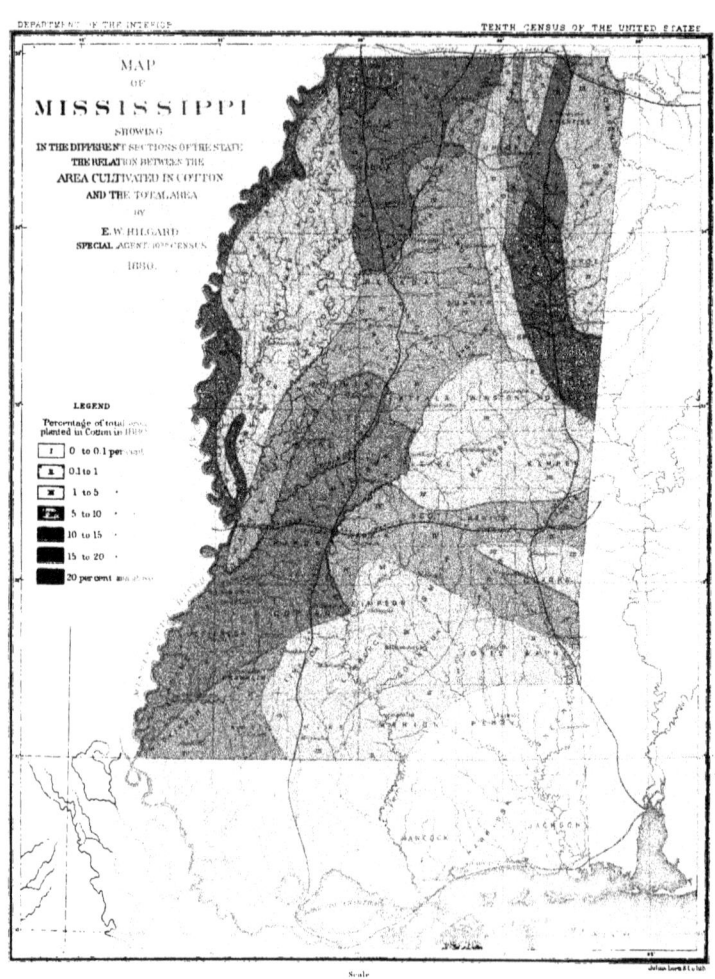

MAP
OF
MISSISSIPPI
SHOWING
IN THE DIFFERENT SECTIONS OF THE STATE
THE RELATION BETWEEN THE
AREA CULTIVATED IN COTTON
AND THE TOTAL AREA
BY
E. W. HILGARD
SPECIAL AGENT 10TH CENSUS
1880.

LEGEND

Percentage of total area
planted in Cotton in 1879

0 to 0.1 per cent
0.1 to 1
1 to 5
5 to 10
10 to 15
15 to 20
20 per cent and above

Scale

It should be recollected that, as stated, lime is notably deficient in all lands bearing the long-leaf pine as their exclusive growth; hence its addition is the most needful improvement, as what other plant-food is contained in the soils will thus be made more available. Of commercial fertilizers bone-meal, which supplies both lime and phosphoric acid, will probably be found the most immediately profitable. Were Pearl and Chickasawhay rivers to be made navigable for flats at least, the lime and marls of the prairie region would become sufficiently accessible for use along these streams. But, above all, those growing cotton should keep in mind that they cannot afford to lose any portion of the plant-food contained in their cotton-seed. All this should be either directly and indirectly, but fully and faithfully, returned to the cotton-fields, for in losing its substance the very life essence of cotton culture is lost.

No. 261. *Red clay marl* from a hilltop on Sec. 1, T. 6, R. 3 E., on the south fork of the Homochitto (Judge Cassady's land), Franklin county. A stiff, dark orange-colored clay, with calcareous concretions (not included in the analysis); once a "prairie spot" covered with strawberry bushes; black soil, now washed away.

No. 293. *Gray clay marl* from a high bluff, on Pearl river, on Secs. 2 and 35, T. 4 and 5, R. 12 E., Marion county. Forms a stratum about 6 feet thick in the face of the bluff some 30 feet above the river level.

No. 267. *Green loam* from Burnett's bluff, on Lower Pearl river, near Spring Cottage post-office, Marion county. Forms a stratum 5 feet thick above low water of the river. A greenish, loose, loamy mass.

The two first are fairly good marls, especially for the sandy lands of the region in which they occur. No. 267 would hardly pay for hauling to any distance, being too poor in lime, but might be available for the somewhat stiff bottom lands of the neighborhood.

	FRANKLIN COUNTY.	MARION COUNTY.		SMITH COUNTY.
	Cassady red clay marl.	Barnes' bluff gray clay marl.	Burnett's bluff green loam.	Long-leaf pine straw.
	No. 261.	No. 293.	No. 267.	
Insoluble matter	49.475	77.438	83.691	65.242
Potash	1.342	0.709	0.827	5.830
Soda	0.153	0.101	0.368	0.416
Lime	13.190	4.800	0.793	13.860
Magnesia	1.825	1.248	1.053	5.208
Brown oxide of manganese	0.366	0.316	0.223	1.661
Peroxide of iron	5.586	2.989	4.394	0.341
Alumina	12.587	6.449	6.947	4.589
Phosphoric acid	0.192	0.111	0.148	1.154
Sulphuric acid	0.083	Trace.	0.023	0.899
Carbonic acid	9.555	3.372 ⎱ Not determined.		
Water	5.875	2.554 ⎰		1.479
Potassium chloride				
Total	99.870	100.087	99.766	100.089

GENERAL FEATURES OF COTTON PRODUCTION IN THE STATE OF MISSISSIPPI.

The map exhibiting graphically the relation between cotton acreage and the total areas in the several portions of the state shows very striking inequalities of distribution; and this inequality would be even more pronounced if, instead of the acreage, the product in bales of cotton had been made the basis of the delineation.

The broadly obvious fact shown by the map, as well as by the tables, is that by far the greater portion of the area planted in cotton lies in the northern and western part of the state, while in the extreme south there is an area where cotton culture is either very subordinate or practically non-existent. This area continues into the adjacent portion of eastern Louisiana, and it is the region where lumbering, turpentine making, and cattle raising form thus far the predominant industries of the sparse population.

The most abrupt inequalities are met with when traversing the state from east to west about latitude 34° 45′ north. Here we meet no fewer than eight alternate belts of low and high intensity. A glance at the soil map of the state shows that these belts correspond closely with the soil regions there laid down. Southward, the variations become less extreme and the areas of similar intensity broader.

Unlike the case of Louisiana, the decrease of cotton culture in the southeastern part of Mississippi is not accompanied by a corresponding increase of some other staple production. It is primarily due to the inferior quality of the soils in that section, improving steadily, however, as we advance westward to the Mississippi river.

18 C P

TABLE III.—POPULATION AND COTTON PRODUCTION IN EACH AGRICULTURAL REGION OF THE STATE.

Agricultural region.	Area.	POPULATION.			COTTON PRODUCTION.								
		Total.	White.	Colored.	Acres.	Bales.	Average per acre.			Total in tons.		Per-centage of the state's total production.	Cotton acreage per sqr. mile.
							Bales. 475 lb.	Seed cotton. ton.	Lint.	Seed.	Lint.	Seed.		
The State	Square miles. 46,340	1,131,597	479,398	652,199	2,196,214	963,111	0.44	Lbs. 857	Lbs. 219	Lbs. 436	228,739	457,478	100.0	43.5
Table-lands	5,020	204,700	70,361	134,339	437,215	202,058	0.44	627	209	418	47,960	95,978	21.0	81.4
Oak and short-leaf pine uplands	6,580	145,964	95,757	50,207	290,000	89,254	0.39	555	185	370	21,198	42,396	9.2	35.0
Northeast prairie region	4,550	184,821	71,757	113,064	404,418	138,027	0.34	486	162	324	32,306	64,012	14.1	87.0
Pontotoc ridge	1,840	59,755	29,343	10,412	61,461	23,768	0.39	555	185	370	5,645	11,290	2.5	45.9
Central prairie	5,030	133,309	49,343	83,466	236,620	89,134	0.39	555	185	370	21,187	42,234	9.3	45.1
Cane hills	2,850	106,784	25,253	80,531	165,226	95,626	0.56	828	276	552	22,711	45,422	9.9	52.6
Mississippi alluvial	7,040	148,443	29,323	114,120	338,622	245,750	0.73	1,041	347	694	58,968	116,726	25.5	48.1
Long-leaf pine, oak, and hickory uplands	5,810	138,537	66,062	62,475	207,365	77,052	0.37	528	176	352	18,390	36,800	8.0	35.7
Long-leaf pine hills and flats	7,550	45,204	32,199	13,085	15,077	4,443	0.29	414	138	276	1,055	2,110	0.5	2.0

TABLE IV.—COUNTIES IN EACH REGION HAVING THE HIGHEST PRODUCTION.

REGIONS, ACCORDING TO AVERAGE PRODUCT PER ACRE.		COUNTIES HAVING HIGHEST TOTAL PRODUCTION.					COUNTIES HAVING HIGHEST PRODUCT PER ACRE.				
Name.	Average product per acre.	Counties.	Rank in total production in state.	Acres.	Bales.	Product per acre.	Rank in product per acre in state.	Counties.	Rank in total production in state.	Acres.	Bales.	Product per acre.	Rank in product per acre in state.
Mississippi alluvial	0.73	Washington	1	63,409	54,873	0.87	2	Issaquena	22	18,298	16,150	0.88	1
Cane hills	0.56	Warren	13	34,127	22,950	0.67	9	Warren	13	34,127	22,950	0.67	9
Table-lands	0.44	Holmes	5	62,556	30,463	0.49	18	Holmes	5	62,556	30,463	0.49	18
Oak and short-leaf pine uplands	0.39	Attala	20	25,960	13,285	0.43	30	Calhoun	38	19,028	9,538	0.50	16
Pontotoc ridge	0.39	Union	43	21,356	8,250	0.39	37	Tippah	47	18,753	7,424	0.40	33
Central prairie	0.39	Hinds	3	80,013	36,894	0.46	22	Hinds	3	80,013	36,894	0.46	22
Long-leaf pine, oak, and hickory uplands	0.37	Copiah	12	54,616	23,736	0.43	26	Franklin	45	15,211	6,542	0.64	26
Northeast prairie region	0.34	Noxubee	16	82,463	26,294	0.31	57	Alcorn	46	15,862	7,477	0.40	38
								Prentiss	48	15,610	7,207	0.39	33
Long-leaf pine hills and flats	0.29	Covington	68	5,968	2,071	0.30	56	Marion	60	4,717	1,879	0.32	51

County in the state having the highest total production : Washington, 54,873 bales.
County in the state having the highest average product per acre : Issaquena, 1,354 pounds seed-cotton.
County in the state having the greatest cotton acreage per square mile (see Table I) : De Soto, 181.5 acres.

DISTRIBUTION OF COTTON PRODUCTION AMONG THE SEVERAL AGRICULTURAL REGIONS.

Table III shows the total products, in bales of 475 pounds, of each region, as resulting from the summation by counties. The county lines having no relation to the natural divisions, these summations can only be rough approximations; but the form of the census returns does not admit of a complete segregation of the product of each natural division, and the outlines of the several shades on the acreage map are, to a considerable extent, shaped in accordance with information derived partly from the answers to schedules and partly from outside information and personal knowledge of the actual distribution of production. Similar corrections must, of course, be applied in the discussion of the subject.

Perhaps the most unexpected fact to the generality of readers would be the relatively small proportion of the cotton product of the state coming from the lowlands of the Mississippi, for it has been customary to consider the pre-eminence of Mississippi as a cotton-producing state to be due mainly to the "rich lowlands". On the contrary, it appears that only a little over one-quarter (25.5 per cent.) of that product is derived from the Mississippi and Yazoo bottoms, while over 30 per cent. is produced in the yellow loam or oak and short-leaf pine uplands region and table-lands north of the central prairie belt. At the same time, the long-leaf pine region of the south, exceeding the oak uplands region in area by over a thousand square miles, produces only 8.5 per cent. of the total product.

THE YAZOO BOTTOM.—The relatively low total product of the.lowlands is at once explained by reference to the column giving the percentage of tilled lands, which is only 12.8 per cent. for the region as a whole, and even this is too high a figure, from the introduction into the summation of the uplands of Yazoo and Tallahatchie counties, which are well settled. The scanty population and the low percentages of tilled lands in the interior counties, such as Quitman and Sunflower, show that large portions of the bottom are almost without settlements, while the higher percentages of the counties fronting on the Mississippi river are equally eloquent in the opposite direction. In this case the difference is not merely due only to the facilities for shipment offered by the great river, but largely to the greater danger of inundation in the interior and, therefore, lower portions of the bottom plain. Until this danger is measurably removed this state of things is not likely to change materially, and production will remain concentrated on the higher lands fronting the Mississippi, Yazoo, and a few other streams. It has not been practicable to obtain any detailed outlining of the areas of intense production existing on the Yazoo and the Tallahatchie rivers.

Of the tilled area in the great bottom as a whole, nearly 59 per cent. is occupied by cotton; in the counties of Tunica and Sharkey the percentage rises to 76 and 73 respectively. These are the highest figures reported from the state for any region or county, showing the marked preference given to cotton in these lowlands.

YELLOW-LOAM REGION.—The returns from the two divisions of this region show a striking difference in the product, the larger one, exceeding the other by nearly a thousand square miles, yielding only 9.3 per cent. of the state's product, against 20.9 furnished by the other, viz, the table-lands division. Parallel with this is the showing of the respective percentages of tilled lands, viz, 16 of the area of the oak and short-leaf pine region, against 30.7 in the table-lands, or again approximately as 1 to 2. But in the latter region 41.3 per cent. of the tilled lands is given to cotton culture, as against 34.2 in the short-leaf pine country. While in the oak and short-leaf pine region the whites exceed the negro population in the proportion of nearly two to one, the reverse occurs in the table-lands, the whites counting only two to every three negroes. As regards density of population, the two divisions are related nearly as 2 to 3.

In the table-lands the area of highest intensity of production lies in the counties of De Soto and Tate, with cotton acreages respectively of 131.5 and 123.7 per square mile. While this may, in part, be due to proximity to the great cotton mart of Memphis and the excellent facilities for transportation, inspection of the table shows that a special adaptation of the soil must be called in to account for the high production, which, in the case of Tate at least, is to be credited exclusively to the uplands, i. e., outside of the Yazoo bottom. No other portion of the state shows such a combination of high figures, both as regards the density of rural population, the percentage of total area under cultivation, and of tilled lands given to cotton culture, the cotton acreage per square mile, and the product per acre; so that this portion of Mississippi seems to constitute (in common probably with the adjacent portion of Tennessee) the *center of maximum cotton production in the uplands*. In Tate, notwithstanding this high position as a cotton-growing county, the white and colored population are nearly equal in numbers.

In the upland short-leaf pine and oak region a corresponding position may be assigned to Montgomery county, which, however, lies partly within the table-lands region. Excluding it from comparison, Attala and Choctaw would seem to compete for the next rank upon a combination of the several points.

The density of the population in the short-leaf pine division being not quite two-thirds of that in the table-land counties (22.2 to 36.4), and the proportion of the total area under tillage nearly as 1 to 2 (16 to 30.8), it would seem that less land suffices for each inhabitant in the pine division, and the reason for this is obvious upon a reference to Table II; for while in the latter division corn occupies one-tenth more land than cotton, in the table-lands region the proportion is more than reversed, corn being given only three-fourths as much land as cotton, and of course a corresponding amount of provisions must be there purchased from outside sources. Concurrently, we find that in the table-lands division the negroes outnumber the whites in the ratio of 100 to 64, while in the pine country the ratio is 100 to 190.7, or nearly two whites to one negro. In the matter of product per acre, the pine country, of course, falls behind the table-lands (0.39 against 0.44 bale), but here the figure is still higher than that of the southern portion of the prairie belt (0.33 bale per acre), where again the negro population is in an overwhelming majority.. It is true that in the pine region a large proportion of the tilled lands, especially of those given to cotton, is creek bottom land.

The *Cane-hills region* is best considered in connection with the table-lands, to which it partially belongs, and with which its statistics of production most nearly correspond. It will be noted that, with approximately half the area of the table-lands, the cane-hills region produces also very nearly half the amount of cotton, viz, 9.9 per cent. of the state's total, against 21 in the former region. When, however, we consider that in each of the counties of the group a not inconsiderable proportion of Mississippi alluvium contributes to the results as shown in the tables (such as the average product per acre and the proportion of tilled lands occupied by cotton), it becomes obvious that in the details of production there are not inconsiderable differences. Remembering that these counties belong to the first settled regions of the state, the low percentage of tilled lands in the case of Warren and Wilkinson (15.6 and 14.9), placing them in this respect on a level with such counties as Lauderdale, Newton, and Winston, and below Copiah (25 per cent.), which is by them regarded as a pine-hills country, is very striking. In connection with this, the fact that nearly one-half (47.3 per cent.) of the tilled lands is, on the average, given to cotton, and that the negro population exceeds the white in the proportion of over three to one (80,531 to 25,253 whites), the economic picture presented is somewhat puzzling and not altogether flattering. In the case of Claiborne, Jefferson, and

Wilkinson about half as much as the cotton area is devoted to corn, while in Warren and Adams not as much as one-third of the amount of land given to cotton culture is devoted to the production of corn. The area given to other cultures is insignificant.

It thus appears that, unlike other regions, where in the course of time there comes an adjustment favoring a self-sustaining policy in farming, these counties have either remained fixed in the policy of cotton-growing, regardless of provisions, or have lapsed from a better condition toward this undesirable state of things which involves the importation of the bulk of the necessaries of life.

. The country, when "fresh", was occupied by large plantations, and the black deep loam soil, enriched by the cane growth, yielded crops scarcely inferior to those now obtained in the bottom lands. These original plantations have nearly all disappeared, their owners generally removing their working force and appliances to the Tensas bottom, opposite, while mostly retaining their residence in the hills; but their hill lands were to a large extent "turned out", and, as is natural in a hilly country, had their soil washed away to a great extent, deep gullies and ravines forming across the once cultivated fields, making their cultivation progressively more difficult and less profitable. In other words, the plantation system has passed away, leaving large areas apparently barren and wasted; and the small farmers that are to reclaim them by careful culture and thrift have not yet come in to any great extent. Hence one may travel in the uplands of Warren, for example, for miles together without seeing what appears to be a prosperous farm outside of the valleys; the country surrounding Vicksburg thus forming a striking contrast to that near Memphis, where the density of rural population and that of cotton culture jointly reach their maxima within the state.

By reference to the descriptions of the cane-hills region at large and of its individual counties, it will, however, be seen that this state of things is not a necessary consequence of natural conditions, and that its still rich and easily reclaimed soils offer great inducements to industrious small farmers. The satisfactory results of such a system may be best seen in Claiborne county, where the large tilled area is more generally subdivided into small holdings.

NORTHEASTERN PRAIRIE REGION.—The cotton product of this region, forming in the aggregate 16.6 per cent. of the state's total, is quite unevenly distributed among its several portions. The culture is most intense in the southern portion of the prairie region proper, where we have in Lowndes and Noxubee counties the highest percentage of tilled lands (39.5 and 34.9), the largest proportion of the same in cotton (51.2 and 54.4), the highest acreage per square mile (129.3 and 121.3), and the largest number of bales per square mile (43.8 and 37.2). To this is to be added the densest population, viz, 56.5 and 43.9 per square mile, respectively, the figures in the case of Lowndes being disproportionately high on account of including the city of Columbus. It is significant that this predominance of cotton culture is here again associated with the greatest predominance of the black over the white population, being between four and five negroes to one white.   •

Leaving out of consideration Oktibbeha, a large portion of which lies outside of the prairie belt, we find to the northward a pretty regular decrease of " bales per square mile", and, concurrently, of the percentage of tilled lands and of the proportion of these given to cotton. Parallel with these the proportion between the white and colored population changes, until it is completely inverted in Prentiss, where the whites outnumber the negroes in the ratio of between four and five to one. At the same time the product per acre has risen from 0.31 bale in Noxubee to an average of 0.39 bale in Prentiss.

The three counties embracing the greater portion of the Pontotoc ridge (Tippah, Union, and Pontotoc), furnishing 2.5 per cent. of the state's cotton crop, are a good deal varied in their surface. The flatwoods belt forms a very considerable but very sparingly cultivated portion of their area, to which in Tippah is added the broken and sandy and also very sparsely settled valley of the Hatchie; hence in the latter case the surprisingly low percentage of the tilled lands as compared with the total area, while as a matter of fact the Pontotoc ridge portion of the county is probably among the most densely settled portions of the state. Union, also, has a large slice of thinly-settled and scantily-producing flatwoods, but on the other hand embraces a tract of fertile black prairie country, as well as some of the choicest portions of the "ridge"; hence, of the three counties, it has the largest percentage of lands under cultivation, the largest proportion of these in cotton, the maximum cotton acreage, and the highest number of bales per square mile. It has also the densest population, but the whites outnumber the negroes more than three to one, as in Tippah. Pontotoc stands lowest of the three in most of the points mentioned under the combined influence of the flatwoods belt and of the lower productiveness of a portion of its ridge lands. Unlike the prairie counties, those of the ridge give a large portion of their land to corn and small grain, these being given an area over one-half greater than that assigned to cotton (93,242 acres, against 61,461 in cotton), while in the prairie belt the total of cereal area is about one-tenth less than that given to cotton (365,321, against 404,418).

In other words, the returns show the Pontotoc ridge country to be one of a more or less varied and self-sustaining culture, with a white population of small farmers outnumbering the colored nearly three to one, while in the prairie belt there prevails the old system of cotton plantations purchasing supplies from the outside and employing chiefly negro laborers, who accordingly outnumber the whites nearly two to one (113,064 negroes, against 71,757 whites). Concurrently, the average product per acre is considerably less in the rich prairie belt than in the hill country. The contrasts become much more striking when, as may properly be done, the counties of Prentiss and Alcorn are either eliminated from the comparison or joined with the ridge counties, to which, in some respects, they more properly belong, being largely upland, and greatly varied in their agricultural features. The average product per acre of the prairie counties is then reduced to 0.33 bale, against nearly 0.40 in the northern counties, where the staple is chiefly produced by white labor.

The *flatwoods region* cannot be separately considered upon the basis of the census returns, but only upon that of a general knowledge of its agricultural condition and capacities. It is almost throughout very thinly settled, and that by small farmers, whose means do not allow them to purchase lands held in higher estimation. As has been stated in the original description (see Part I), the soil, while not intrinsically poor in the ingredients of plant-food, is difficult of cultivation, being mostly very heavy, and the entire region is ill-drained and liable to remain wet until late in the season. It will require intelligence and thrift to render their cultivation profitable, but this is feasible, as it has been done locally. With systematic drainage of the region will come not only easier tillage and more certain crops, but also improved health. In its southern portion, in Oktibbeha, Noxubee, and Kemper, the character of the soil is less extreme, and settlements are more abundant.

The counties belonging to the *central prairie region*, growing altogether nearly one-tenth of the state's cotton crop, are so much varied in their surface features and soils that few general statements can be made that will hold for all of them. Thus, Madison and Hinds, furnishing two-thirds of the product of the entire central belt, agree in most points with the table-lands section in percentage of area under tillage, the predominance of cotton culture as shown in percentage of tilled lands in cotton, cotton acreage per square mile, etc., as well as in the large predominance of negro population over the white (nearly 3.1); and thus what has been said in the discussion of the table-lands will substantially apply here. In the counties east of Pearl river we at once have a reduction of the percentage of tilled area of one-third of the average on the west side (31.9: 10.6), due to the fact that large portions of these counties belong to the adjacent long- and short-leaf pine regions, while the form of the census returns does not permit the segregation of the product of each division. At the same time, the average proportion between the white and colored population approaches equality, but this average is in part the result of considerable variations in opposite directions. Wherever the rich black prairie lands are available for cotton growing (which is not always the case, on account of "rust", see regional description) the negro population is in the majority, as in northern Rankin, southwestern Scott, and northeastern Jasper. But Smith county, notwithstanding the large part of its area on which prairie soils do occasionally occur, is statistically clearly within the long-leaf pine region, most of the "prairie" soil being unavailable for cotton culture on account of a tendency to "rust". Wayne might be similarly classed but for the fact that practically nearly all its cotton product comes from the northeastern portion within the prairie belt, and in view of this fact the low product per acre (0.26 bale) is somewhat surprising. Here, as well as in Clarke and Smith, a more painstaking system of culture would result in a material improvement of the quantity and quality of the cotton product, for not only are there large tracts of intrinsically very productive soils now almost untouched on account of difficult tillage, but the marls occurring so abundantly in the region allow of indefinite and exceptionally cheap improvement of the soils. (See regional description.)

THE LONG-LEAF PINE REGION, embracing over one-fourth of the area of the state, furnishes only a little over one-twelfth of the total product (8.5 per cent.). Of this contingent, moreover, over 94 per cent. is produced in the northern and western counties of the region, where oaks and short-leaf pine, at least in the bottoms, mingle with the long-leaf species, while the balance is produced scatteringly within the long-leaf pine division proper, where this tree descends even to the sandy bottoms or bordering flats, in which the ti-ti, gallberry, star anise, and similar shrubs are its associates. Outside of these bottoms there is practically, as yet, no cultivation, except along the immediate sea-coast and in the western portion of Covington county, that county having the largest proportion of tilled lands and producing nearly half of the cotton of the group; so that its figures might, with almost equal propriety, place it with the western group of counties, where oaks and hickory accompany the pine. As a whole, the long-leaf pine region is characterized by the sparseness of its population, among which the whites exceed the negroes in the proportion of 13 to 10, by the small average percentage of tilled lands (7.4 per cent. of the area), and the correspondingly small cotton acreage per square mile (16.5), and nearly an equal amount of land given to corn. It is curious that, considering the remoteness of a large portion of the region from markets, so large a share of the cultivated area should be given to cotton. The good roads, so easily maintained on the sandy soils, have their share in encouraging this state of things, hauling being habitually done to great distances. Thus this region would, as a whole, seem to be less nearly self-sustaining than is the short-leaf pine area.

Copiah stands at the head of the western group, having the largest proportion of tilled area (25 per cent.) and the highest aggregate production, exceeding that of Madison (the two counties having nearly the same total area) on a somewhat smaller area given to cotton, and therefore with a higher average product per acre (0.43 bale against 0.38 in Madison); certainly an excellent showing for a "pine-woods" county which has been long settled. Its numerous and well-watered valleys, occupied by small farms largely worked by whites (the latter nearly equaling the negroes in number), appear to prove more than a match for the large upland plantations of the former county, where the negroes outnumber the whites more than three to one. The acreage given to corn also differs by only a few hundred acres, while the corn product of Copiah exceeds that of Madison by over 66,000 bushels. The result of the comparison is certainly a remarkable one, and probably unexpected to both counties concerned.

Proceeding southward from Copiah, we find in Lincoln, Pike, and Franklin counties a rapid falling off of the percentage of lands under tillage (10.5 in the latter county), indicating an increasing restriction of the cultivation to the bottoms of the streams, the surface of the country being rather broken. The percentage rises again in Amite and Lawrence, under the influence of considerable bottom areas, but falls again as we cross Pearl river eastward, in Simpson and Smith, where only 8.4 per cent. of the total area is under tillage. The proportion of the tilled lands given to cotton seems in all these cases to be largely controlled by the facilities for communication with a market, the remoter portions growing more corn in proportion. The high average product per acre, exceeding that of the black prairie region of Lowndes and Monroe in most cases, testifies to the use of bottom lands for cotton. Lauderdale stands somewhat apart from the rest of the group in its statistics as well as in geographical position. Its higher percentage of tilled area (16.2), and the fact that as much as 46 per cent. of that area is given to cotton culture, are doubtless due to its railroad facilities; for the figure given for product per acre (0.29 bale) proves that the soil is not more productive, and that uplands are contributing to the general average. Concurrent with the high proportion of lands devoted to cotton the negro population is seen to exceed the white (11.5 : 10), and the same relation is noticeable in Amite (8.5 : 5.5). In the rest this proportion ranges from near equality to (in the case of Smith) 4 whites to 1 negro.

In the southeastern group of counties, the especial home of the long-leaf pine, pure and simple, the sparseness of the population (5.9 to the square mile), the low percentage of tilled lands (average, 1.8 per cent.), and the low cotton product per acre (0.29 bale), all speak of the comparative poverty of the soil, which in its natural condition is not adapted to the profitable production of the staple. Pasturage and lumbering will be profitable for some time to come. Better tillage of smaller areas and the use of fertilizers have improved similar soil regions farther east, in Georgia and the Carolinas.

No sea-island or long-staple cotton was reported from Mississippi for the census year. Prior to the war it was profitably grown on a limited area near the coast, on the deep, sandy "shell hummock" soils of Mulatto bayou, in Hancock county. In due time this culture will doubtless be renewed, and by an artificial application of the process by which nature and man have combined to form, in course of time, the "shell hummocks", the long-staple cotton may yet occupy an important place in the products of the Gulf-shore region.

RELATIONS OF THE TWO RACES TO COTTON CULTURE AND PRODUCTION.

These have been cursorily alluded to in the discussion of the several regions, but it may be well to summarize the conclusions more definitely here. Broadly speaking, it is obvious that the bulk of the cotton is produced where the bulk of the negro population is found in the state as a whole. A glance at the column giving the proportion of the tilled lands occupied by cotton shows that, on the whole, this percentage is greatest where the negro race predominates most, viz, in the great Yazoo bottom, where, with an average predominance of the negro race over the white in the ratio of nearly four to one (3.9 : 1), we find also the maximum percentage of the tilled lands in cotton (58.9). Still, in detail this general rule does not hold good, for we see in Issaquena the greatest disproportion between the two races (11.1 negroes to 1 white, almost the same as the parish of East Carroll, opposite), yet the proportion of tilled lands in cotton is only 56 per cent., being less than the average, while the maximum percentage of total area in cotton is found in Tunica, where the whites are nearly twice as numerous (5.8 negroes to 1 white). Among the upland regions the greatest overbalancing of the negro race is found in the cane hills (3.2 : 1), with the next greatest percentage of lands in cotton (47.3), and here the greatest percentage of tilled lands in cotton agrees with the greatest overbalancing of the colored race in Wilkinson county (Warren being largely lowland, and containing a large city, cannot enter into the comparison). The northeastern prairie region and the table-lands division of the yellow-loam region show almost the same proportion between the two races (1.58 and 1.56 negroes to 1 white, respectively), while the respective percentages of tilled lands in cotton are 45.3 and 41.3, again showing a slight preponderance of cotton area where the negro population is most predominant. In the case of the prairie region this becomes much more obvious when we segregate the "black prairie counties" of the south from the group formed by Lee, Prentiss, and Alcorn (see discussion of the prairie region). In the southern group, Noxubee, with nearly 4 negroes to 1 white, has also the maximum percentage of tilled lands in cotton (54.4). In the rest of the state, apart from the local influence of great centers, there is a more or less obvious inverse ratio between the predominance of the negro population and the percentage of lands occupied by cotton. But the relation between the product per acre and that predominance is equally marked, and here the ratio is as obviously an inverse one when the natural productive capacities of the several soils occupied is taken into consideration. The best possible comparison is that made above between the northern and the southern groups of the northeastern prairie region, where the best soil under negro predominance, and in the very center of the cotton belt, yields only an average of 0.33 bale per acre, while northward, under the influence of a predominance of the whites and a consequent subdivision into small farms, the product per acre rises to an average of nearly 0.40 bale. Under the same influences the average product of the Pontotoc ridge, with inferior soils on the whole, exceeds by 4 per cent. that of the black prairie region. Similar relations are abundantly exemplified among the counties of the yellow-loam region.

The bottom region forms only an apparent exception; for while its lands under the greatest negro predominance among the regions shows also the highest production per acre, this is manifestly due to the great native fertility of the soil, which, under favorable circumstances, will produce as much as 2 bales per acre. Instead of this, these lands actually yield only an average of 0.73 bale, and the highest product reached, even in the profusely fertile buckshot lands of Issaquena, is 0.88 bale per acre. Here also, with an overwhelming negro predominance, out of over 22,000 acres of land under tillage, only 3,849 are given to corn, although that crop, as will be noted, actually yielded during the census year the surprising average of over 100 bushels per acre. In the face of such advantages, nearly all the subsistence and supplies are purchased from the outside. Whether or not this is due to free choice on the part of the colored race or to the prevailing plantation system is not apparent from the returns; but be that as it may, the concurrence of the two factors is none the less significant. The negro population seeks the rich lands, especially the lowlands, and at present tends to continue there a system of agriculture which involves as direct results indifferent culture, exhaustion of the soil, and a continued indebtedness incurred for the purchase of the prime necessaries of life, which these very soils are so eminently adapted to produce advantageously at home.

AGRICULTURAL METHODS IN THE PRODUCTION OF COTTON.

The view afforded by the schedule replies of the methods and condition of agriculture in the state shows that it is largely in the first and partly in the transition stage, resulting from a partial exhaustion of the soil beginning to direct attention to the best and cheapest methods of resuscitation. The almost universally shallow tillage, the rare use of the subsoil plow, together with the variety of opinions expressed as to the merits whether of deep plowing or subsoiling proper, the turning out of "tired" land, while fresh portions are cleared and brought under the same primitive system of cultivation, and the fact that the use of fertilizers is exceptional, are all characteristic of the advance of the settler into the wilderness, from Alabama and Wisconsin to the Pacific coast. Generally, however, the reduction of the soil's production under this treatment is only temporary, and yields to intelligent culture by the more permanent successor of the pioneer farmer.

RESULTS OF IMPERFECT TILLAGE.—Mississippi has the unenviable privilege of an exception in the latter respect, her copious rainfall and peculiarity of soils having combined to render her uplands, and among them the very best, liable to great and permanent damage from the effects of shallow plowing and "turning-out" of "tired" land. The causes and details of this state of things have been discussed, in treating of the yellow-loam uplands region, from the point of view afforded from personal observations, and are further illustrated by the abstracts of reports received from the counties concerned. But the actual extent of the damage done by this washing and final gullying of the hillside slopes, with the final undercutting into the underlying sands and the bodily descent of the upland soil into the valleys, mingling with a flood of sand, which renders useless alike the hills and the valleys, must be seen to be appreciated. While "horizontalizing" and hillside ditching is now being made in a measure to prevent these inroads, yet the shallow plowing does not give a sufficient depth of tilled soil to hold the heavy downpours of water that occur more or less every year, so that the hillside furrows are broken sideways. The difficulty of making the unintelligent laborers, prevalently employed, follow the prescribed hillside levels, instead of plowing up and down hill, as customary, makes it more difficult to preserve any improvements made in this respect. But however difficult, no more pressing problem than this comes before the cultivators of the uplands of northern and western Mississippi; for, quite apart from such serious and almost irremediable injury as is caused by gullying, there is primarily involved the washing away of the best portion of their surface soil. Even the use of a subsoil plow every alternate year would go far to prevent this grave evil.

ROTATION AND FALLOW.—Next in importance among the means of maintaining productiveness is a proper system of rotation and fallowing, or, what amounts to the same thing, a proper diversity of crops. That this cannot be maintained where half or more of the tilled area is given to cotton is obvious; yet this state of things exists in a large number of counties, as will be noted by reference to Table I, where it will be seen that in very few counties only does cotton occupy less than one-third of the tilled area, the average for the state being 42.7 per cent. While the answers show that a conviction of the benefits of rotation is gaining ground, this is obviously the case mainly in the more remote regions, where circumstances compel a greater diversity of crops. But it is plain that in the great cotton-growing counties the tilled area is practically divided between corn and cotton only; and even this alternation is very commonly only begun and maintained after the cotton product of the land bearing it year after year has seriously diminished. This has been especially the history of the northeastern prairie country, where one bale to the acre was at first the regular crop, which has now diminished to an average of about one-third (0.33). But it is expressly stated by several respondents that this succession is far from satisfactory, and that the intervention of at least one additional crop (field pease) secures far better results. A four-year rotation, including sweet potatoes, is strongly recommended by some; but when we compare the areas given to that crop (one of the common necessaries of life) with that given to other crops it is quite evident that there would not be months enough to consume the product of one-fourth of the tilled area. There is a fifth alternative, practicable to any extent, viz, the fallow; but it must be such fallow as tills the land not planted, instead of letting it go to waste by washing, as now happens when land is "turned out". The great difficulty lies in convincing the negro, and even a portion of the white population, that tillage bestowed on land not planted is not thrown away. When land turned out lies level and "grows up in briers", as is quaintly stated in the answers, it means, of course, that it does not wash away, and from this a benefit is uniformly reported; but when it means only the absence of tillage and the washing away of the soil, joined perhaps to the treading of ranging cattle in wet weather, it is no wonder that "lying out" is not found to benefit the land, as is so frequently stated. Few cotton-growers in the state appreciate adequately the injury done to their fields by the practice of letting the cattle pick up what they can through the winter, the forage thus utilized being dearly paid for by the cloddiness and lack of tilth found in the spring plowing, the difficulties of after-cultivation, and the quick "burning up" of the crop under the influence of dry weather.

FALL PLOWING.—The difference of opinion regarding the utility of fall plowing, with perhaps a leaning against it, is perhaps, in a measure, justified by the necessity existing in any case, of repeated surface tillage. The soil thus receives on the whole a very fair amount of stirring, and to this extent the never-ending fight against "the grass" is a benefit.

WEEDS.—By the wholesale ripening of the weed seeds in the cornfields the fight is made to be a life and death question for the crop whenever a wet season occurs. The most universally troublesome weed—the crab-grass—makes excellent hay. The reason given for letting this matter go by default each season is that *the hands are too busy picking cotton*, which must ever be true so long as two-fifths or more of all tilled land is occupied by that crop. It is clear, then, that so long as this is the case no sound or permanently practicable system of farming can exist. Hay, corn, and bacon will have to be purchased from the outside, and the energies of the cotton-planter must continue to be given to "fighting crab-grass".

PLANTING IN RIDGES.—The universal practice of planting cotton in ridges is intimately connected with shallow tillage. The reason assigned is that when cultivated level cotton is liable to be "drowned out" by heavy rains, and that the greater depth of surface soil so secured is an advantage. The experience of the older states has shown that deep preparation and level cultivation is by far the safer method, for by it security against drought, as well as wet, is gained, and of late the droughts have proved, on the whole, the more fatal to success. In view of the adaptation of the implements now in use to ridge culture, it will probably continue to hold its own for some time, especially where negro labor is in the ascendant. The skill attained in the use of these implements is really remarkable.

FERTILIZATION — USE OF COTTON-SEED.—The answers concerning fertilization are also pregnant with information as to the prevailing ideas and practice. It is only from regions where the soil is naturally of inferior productiveness that we hear of the use of commercial fertilizers; elsewhere they have scarcely been thought of, and even stable manure and cotton-seed, and composts made of them, are used only by "small farmers". Green manuring is chiefly practiced by turning in cow-peas, but large planters only turn in crops of weeds. The discussion as to whether cotton can be profitably grown on a large scale by the aid of fertilizers is still actively going on, the tendency still being to increase production by cultivating more land in the old way, rather than to intensify production on small areas. Cotton-seed is generally recognized as a good fertilizer, and in some regions it is used systematically; but a great deal of it is still lost by being allowed to rot in neglected piles. Some is fed to cattle, whose manure is then scattered in the woods. From Sharkey its use for fuel in making steam for gins is reported. The grievous loss incurred from the wasteful practice of the past is beginning to be appreciated; but now comes the temptation to sell the seed to the oil-mills for cash, with little thought of getting back the seed-cake. As a hopeful symptom, Lowndes and Prentiss report an occasional exchange of the raw cotton-seed for its equivalent, approximately, in seed-cake meal. The seed-cake, or its substance in the guise of the manure of cattle fed with it, should be returned to the soil. (See on this subject the article on "Cotton-seed and its uses" in the general report.) Thus far this essence of fertility is chiefly shipped from the mills to Old and New England.

"INTENSE CULTURE."—The experiments repeatedly made in the eastern cotton states, more especially in Georgia, by Mr. Dickson, and later by Judge Furman, showing plainly and irrefragably the profitableness of intense production on small areas by the use of fertilizers, cannot be too strongly commended to the attention of the cotton-growers of Mississippi. The habit of scattering the energies of the working force over large surfaces, producing only a fraction of a bale per acre, with great risks in case of an unfavorable season, is a proceeding that evidently cannot be long continued, if only on account of its depleting effects on the soil; and it perpetuates the pernicious system of credits and advances upon crops for provisions which could be more cheaply produced at home.

LABOR SYSTEM.—A system of intense culture is incompatible with the now most generally prevailing practice of planting on shares with the laborers or renting land to tenants for a certain portion of the crop. Under either arrangement there is no prospect of the maintenance or improvement of the soil, since the laborer or tenant-at-will is nowise interested in anything except "skimming the soil" to the utmost, and is generally too ill-informed to appreciate the advantages of intense culture, even if he was sure that he would enjoy the results of what improvements he makes. The wage system, placing the plantation under a central, intelligent management, is obviously the only one under which improved methods of agriculture are possible; and even under this system it is not easy to overcome the old slovenly habits and the easy-going ways of the colored race.

GENERAL CONCLUSIONS.—In comparison with the need of greater attention and a steady change in respect to the matters above noted all questions of detail sink into insignificance. Taking the state as a whole, few of the cotton states can compare with Mississippi as to the extent of area occupied by first-class soils, such as those of the Yazoo bottom, table-lands, and prairies, the like of which cannot be found, save in very small bodies, in the Atlantic states. Even of the lands now considered too poor for profitable cotton culture a large proportion only await rational treatment to rise to a level with the good average uplands of Georgia and the Carolinas. The climate is pre-eminently adapted to the culture not only of cotton, but of most of the other products of the warm temperate zone, and in the uplands at least is certainly more conducive to the health of the white race than the prairies of Illinois and Missouri. The rare invasions of the yellow fever, as experience has shown, can be controlled by rational and strict sanitary regulations. The great bottoms are, as yet, during the summer, a safe abiding-place only for the colored race and a small proportion of acclimated whites; but with the exclusion or regulation of overflows, and greater care especially in the matter of the drinking-water used, there will be a great improvement in the sanitary condition of the lowlands, together with possibilities of production, of which the rough, wholesale treatment these lands have thus far experienced can only give a remote idea. It is true that for the census year all replies state that all the cotton has been picked; but it is notorious that many times heretofore, when exceptionally favorable seasons realized the conditions of high and intense culture, the ordinary force of the plantations has been inadequate to pick nearly all the crop, of which, in some cases, as much as one-third has been estimated to have remained in the field on the buckshot lands, the portion actually picked amounting to two (400 pound) bales; so that the product per acre must in these cases have been between 1,100 and 1,200 pounds of lint per acre, or the same result that, in the Georgia experiments, was produced by the highest culture and abundant manuring on worn-out land. The virgin soils of the black prairies of northeastern Mississippi, when first occupied, produced frequently a 400 pound bale and a half; the table-lands of the western part did nearly as well, and, as the replies show, are still credited with the ability to do so, although the statistical evidence shows the rarity of that result at the present time. Since, as a matter of fact, all these lands have merely been "skinned" with tillage a few inches in depth, there can be no question that their resuscitation and restoration to their original production is merely a question of time and good husbandry, and not nearly as much dependent upon actual manuring as is the case in the worn soils of the Atlantic states, whose original store of plant-food was much smaller. There is, then, no natural cause why Mississippi should ever cease to be what she has been for some time past, the banner state for cotton production. Texas, with its immense area, may soon surpass Mississippi in total product by force of numbers, as it were; but it would be difficult to cut out of that state an area equal to that of Mississippi which would equal the latter state as a whole in capacity of production. But it is certain that in order to maintain this pre-eminent position the state must speedily adopt material changes from the old methods of wastefulness, especially as regards the "turning-out" of her "tired" uplands and failure to return the cotton-seed to the cotton-fields, directly or indirectly.

The statistical facts brought out in the preceding tables and their discussion show very clearly some of the leading points to be noted in bringing about this improved state of things. It appears, as a rule, that as yet the regions producing the largest proportion of the cotton product of the state have also the largest negro population. Inspection of the census table giving the size of farms also shows that in such regions the system of large plantations is still in the ascendant, and the system of planting on shares definite or contingent. The effect upon the crop is most noticeable in the columns giving "product per acre", which, other things being equal, seems to be in nearly an inverse ratio to the excess of negroes over whites and to the size of the farms or plantations. Any one familiar with the subject will not need the figures to prove this, but to the world at large they will make the most convincing showing. In the course of the preceding discussion this point of view has been brought forward repeatedly. It is perhaps best exemplified in the comparison between the northern and southern counties of the northeastern prairie region, but with a different form of statistical returns it would be equally apparent in many other cases. When we find that the average product of the Yazoo bottom counties is not quite three-quarters of a bale per acre, instead of an easily possible two bales, as shown in numerous cases of careful culture, the showing becomes quite as cogent in their case as in that of the prairie counties. It is quite clear, then, that a subdivision of the land into smaller holdings, in whose maintenance the owner is personally interested, and, concurrently, the substitution of the wage system for that of shares, at least so far as the negro laborer is concerned, are conditions-precedent of the introduction of a rational and permanently possible agricultural system, not only in Mississippi, but wherever in the cotton states a similar condition of things still prevails; for while the white farmer is far from appreciating, as he should, the advantages of rational agriculture, yet as a matter of fact he is incomparably more accessible to the influence of progress than the negro race, whose excessive conservatism in respect to habits once formed will need the time of several generations to be overcome and replaced by more thrifty methods and ideas.

Analyses of soils, subsoils, and clays of Mississippi.

Number	Description	Locality	County	Vegetation
	NORTHEASTERN PRAIRIE REGION.			
173	Prairie soil.	Booneville prairie.	Tishomingo.	
176	Prairie subsoil.	do.	do.	
172	Prairie soil.	Monroe prairie.	Monroe.	
1/2	Prairie underclay.	do.	do.	Black-jack oak, widely scattered.
185	Cedar-rearing soil.	Hoffman's place.	Chickasaw.	
179	Prairie soil.	Houston prairie.	Houston.	Scattered post oak and hickory.
139	Hillside prairie soil.	Petина' place.	Kemper.	
341	Heavy clay soil.	do.	do.	Hickory.
59	Dark loam hummock soil.	do.	Tippah.	
175	Subsoil.	Pikeville.	Chickasaw.	Scarlet, post, and Spanish oaks.
94	Pale loam upland soil.			
177	Heavy clay soil.	Ocmawah creek.	Pontotoc.	Willow and water oaks, etc.
178	Heavy clay subsoil.	do.	do.	
258	Dark loam soil.	Dugger's place.	Pontotoc.	Black, black-jack, post, and Spanish oaks.
22	Subsoil.	do.	do.	
87	Dark loam soil.	School.	Chickasaw.	Black oak, hickory, some water oak, etc.
260	Heavy clay soil, pale in color.	Flatwoods.	Pontotoc.	Post oak and pine.
254	Clay.	do.	do.	
142	Light sandy soil.		Chickasaw.	Post oak chiefly.
	Bottom lands of Ashwood region.			
147	Heavy siliceous soil.	White-oak flatwoods.	Chickasaw.	Post and Spanish oaks and pine.
144	Heavy siliceous subsoil.	do.	do.	Chestnut-white and willow oaks, grass, hickory, ash, and elm.
140	Heavy siliceous soil.	Pollocking bottom.	La Fayette.	
200	Heavy siliceous subsoil.	Lonoke-Siouan bottom.	Calhoun.	Oaks, beech, elm, and hornbeam.
30	Heavy siliceous subsoil.	do.		
119	YELLOW LOAM REGION. Heavy clay upland subsoil, of a pale color.	Mataschie's creek.	La Fayette.	Post oak, black-jack, and pine.

Analyses of soils, subsoils, and clays of Mississippi—Continued.

Number	Description.	Locality.	County.	Vegetation.	Depth.	Insoluble matter.	Soluble silica.	Insoluble matter and soluble silica.	Potash.	Soda.	Lime.	Magnesia.	Brown oxide of manganese.	Peroxide of iron.	Alumina.	Phosphoric acid.	Sulphuric acid.	Carbonic acid.	Water and organic matter.	Total.	Hygroscopic moisture.	Temperature of absorption C.°	Humus.
	CANE HILLS—continued.																						
357	Loess	Mrs. J. Watson's.	Claiborne	Oaks and poplar																			
116	Upland loam	Magnolia hills	do	do																			
137	Thin hammock soil	Bayou Pierre	do	Water and post oaks, black gum, etc.																			
315	Thin hammock subsoil	do	do	do																			
310	Brown loam soil	Cole's creek, near Fay. ette.	Jefferson	Sweet gum, sycamore, walnut, locust, oak, and cane.																			
109	Brown loam subsoil	do	do	do																			
	Bottom lands of cane land.																						
65	Sandy soil	Middle Homochitto creek bottom.	Franklin	Magnolia, beech, oak, gum, poplar, and maple.																			
64	Subsoil	do	do	do																			
66	Dark soil	West Amite bottom	do	do																			
67	White soil	do	do	do																			
70	White subsoil	do	do	Pine, oaks, gum, hickory, and sweet gum.																			
	MISSISSIPPI ALLUVIAL REGION.																						
305	Light bottom soil	Dogwood ridge	Coahoma	Dogwood, sweet gum, holly, ash, and magnolia.																			
306	Light-colored buckshot loam.	do	do	do																			
304	Light bottom soil	Tallahatchie	Tallahatchie	do																			
375	Light front-land soil	Indian bayou	Sunflower	Sweet gum, oak, hickory, holly, and dogwood.																			
376	Subsoil	do	do	do																			
384	Light front-land soil	Sunflower river	Issaquena	Sweet gum, maple, oak, elm, and sassafras.																			
300	Heavy clay buckshot soil	Deer creek	do	Sweet gum, hackberry, locust, pecan, oak, and cane.																			
	CENTRAL PRAIRIE REGION (Tertiary).																						
198	Black prairie loam soil	Parker's place	Rankin	Sweet gum, wild cherry, plum, and mulberry.																			
219	Post-oak prairie soil	Crook's place	Smith	Small sweet gum and oak.																			
207	Ridge prairie soil	Newbold's capot	do	do																			
199	Prairie soil	Leaf river	Jasper	Locust, crab-apple, etc.																			
195	do	Strawberry creek bottom	Clarke	Sweet gum, ash, elm, cottonwood, oaks, and maple.																			
44	Upland prairie soil	Trotter's plantation	do	Sour crab-apple and haw.																			
49	Bald prairie soil	Nichols' place	Smith																				
263	Gypseous underclay																						
	a. Hog-wallow and apparent prairie.																						
187	Gypseous prairie soil	McEae's prairie	Rankin																				
401	Gypseous prairie under-clay.	do	do																				

PART II.

AGRICULTURAL DESCRIPTIONS

OF THE

COUNTIES OF MISSISSIPPI.

AGRICULTURAL DESCRIPTIONS

OF THE

COUNTIES OF MISSISSIPPI.

The counties are here grouped under the heads of the several agricultural regions, previously described, to which each predominantly belongs, or, in some cases, under that to which it is popularly assigned. Each county is described as a whole. When its territory is covered in part by several adjacent soil regions, its name will be found under each of the several regional heads in which it is concerned, with a reference to the one under which it is actually described. In the lists of counties placed at the head of each group the names of those described elsewhere are marked with an asterisk, (*) and the reference to the head under which these are described will be found in its place in the order of the list in the text itself.

The regional groups of counties are placed in the same order as that in which the regional descriptions themselves are given.

The statements of areas of woodland, prairie, etc., refer to the original state of things, irrespective of tilled or otherwise improved lands.

Appended to the description of each county from which a report or reports have been received is an abstract of the main points of such reports, so far as they refer to natural features, production, and communication. Those portions of the reports referring to agricultural and commercial practice have been summarized and placed in a separate division (Part III), following that of county descriptions. In making the abstracts of reports it has been necessary in most cases to change somewhat the language of the reporter, while preserving the sense. In some cases statements palpably incorrect or overdrawn have been altogether omitted, while explanatory words have been added, placed in parentheses.

NORTHEASTERN PRAIRIE REGION.

This embraces the following counties and parts of counties: Alcorn, Tippah, Prentiss, Union, Lee, Pontotoc, Chickasaw, Monroe, Clay, Oktibbeha, Lowndes, Noxubee, and Kemper.* The counties of Tippah, Union, and Pontotoc are largely embraced within what is known as the Pontotoc ridge, which is described as a separate region in the general part of the report.

ALCORN.

Population : 14,272.—White, 9,863; colored, 4,409.
Area : 400 square miles.—Short-leaf pine and oak uplands, 245 square miles; prairie belt, 155 square miles.
Tilled lands : 52,566 acres.—Area planted in cotton, 18,863 acres; in corn, 22,589 acres; in oats, 3,358 acres; in wheat, 1,078 acres.
Cotton production : 7,477 bales; average cotton product per acre, 0.40 bale, 570 pounds seed-cotton, or 190 pounds cotton lint.

Alcorn county, formed since the war from portions of Tippah and Tishomingo counties, is traversed almost centrally by the "prairie belt", here averaging about 10 miles in width, while in the rest of its area, east and west of that belt, sandy, short-leaf pine hills form the prevailing feature. The western pine-hill region belongs to the Hatchie valley; the rest of the county is drained by the Tuscumbia and its branches, excepting the heads of creeks tributary to the Tennessee, on the extreme east.

The "prairie belt" here has scarcely any open prairie land, except small "bald" prairies here and there. The white limestone, however, underlies it everywhere at no great depth, and materially influences the quality of the soil, even where it does not produce the black prairie soil. The surface is mostly gently undulating, and is timbered with oaks (post, black, Spanish, and black-jack), with more or less hickory, according to the proximity of the calcareous strata to the surface, and, in the higher ridges, is occasionally mingled with pine, the subsoil being a yellow loam. Where the rock lies nearer the surface we have either black or bald prairie or "mahogany" soil, and sometimes even the "beeswax". The yellow loam soils predominate more and more as we approach the Tennessee line, forming near Farmington, and Corinth especially, an excellent farming country.

The tilled lands of Alcorn county constitute 20.5 per cent. of the total area. Of these lands 35.9 per cent. is given to cotton culture, while about 43 per cent. of the same is devoted to corn, the latter having an unusually large proportion for a region possessing such facilities for communication. The cotton acreage per square mile is 47.2, and the average product per acre 0.40 bale, showing that the best lands are selected for cotton.

At Corinth, the county-seat, the Memphis and Charleston and the Mobile and Ohio railroads cross, affording excellent opportunities for communication. Cotton is shipped by either route as fast as baled to Mobile or New Orleans at the rate of $3 per bale.

ABSTRACT OF THE REPORT OF W. L. WILLIAMS, RIENZI.

The upland is hilly and rolling; the lowland consists of first and second bottoms of Tuscumbia creek.

The soil is a light, fine sandy loam of a brown color, 4 inches deep; the subsoil is a red clay. This soil is early, well-drained, and easily tilled. Its natural growth is red, Spanish, black, and post oaks, chestnut, pine, etc. It covers all of this, and extends into other counties.

The chief crops are cotton, corn, and oats; but the soil is apparently best adapted to cotton, and three-fifths of the cultivated area is planted with the same. The plant grows from 2 to 3 feet high; is most productive at 2 feet. In wet seasons, or on soils rich in vegetable matter, it inclines to run to weed; but potash added to the soil restrains it and favors bolling. The seed-cotton product per acre of fresh land is 800 pounds; 1,780 pounds make a 475-pound bale of first-class lint. After two years' cultivation (unmanured) the product is 1,000 pounds, and the ratio of seed to lint remains the same. One-fourth of such land originally cultivated now lies "turned out", and when again cultivated it produces well after the first year. Weeds are numerous. Slopes are seriously injured by washing and gullying, and the valleys are injured by being covered with sand. No efforts have been made to check these damages.

Cotton is shipped, as fast as gathered, by rail to Mobile, Memphis and New Orleans, at $3 per bale.

ABSTRACT OF THE REPORT OF J. M. TAYLOR, M. D., CORINTH.

(The region described embraces about 106 square miles, or T. 1, 2, 3, R. 7 E.)

The surface of this part of the county is rolling; the ridges between the creeks and branches are light and thin, but in the lowlands the soil is rich, black, and loamy. Cotton is cultivated on three classes of land, viz, 1. *Gray upland*, with sandy branch bottoms. 2. *Black hammock* and alluvial bottoms. 3. "*Beeswax*" ridges.

The *gray uplands* are most extensive, and have a timber growth of red, post, and white oaks, and hickory; on the bottoms are poplar, sweet and black gums, walnut, elm, dogwood, cherry, beech, birch, maple, red-bud, sycamore, willow, hazel, sumach, and an undergrowth of grape-vines. The soil is a fine sandy loam, 3 or 4 inches deep, merging insensibly into the subsoil, which is a pale-red or yellowish clay. 10 to 20 feet thick, the lower part being known as "joint clay". Blue marl underlies this clay. The land is early, warm, and ill-drained, and produces all the crops. Cotton comprises from one-third to one-half of the tilled land, grows 2 to 5 feet high, and yields an average of 800 pounds of seed-cotton per acre both on fresh and old land. Crab-grass is the most troublesome weed. Very little of the land lies turned out; washes readily on slopes, but does no damage.

The *black or hammock land* occurs only in small areas in this region, but southward becomes the prevailing soil of the prairies. Its growth is white oak, walnut, red-bud, wild plum, buckeye, and grape-vines. The soil is a heavy loam, black and very tenacious, about 3 feet thick, and is difficult to till in all seasons when not broken early and in proper cultivation. It is best adapted to corn, and a less proportion is planted in cotton than on the gray lands. Cotton grows from 6 to 7 feet high, and runs to weed when gentle rains fall in July and August, though restrained by thorough drainage and barnyard manure. The yield per acre is from 1,000 to 2,000 pounds of seed-cotton, making one-fourth its weight of middling lint. Deeper plowing renews the soil when "tired". Cocklebur and morning-glory vines are most troublesome.

The *beeswax* soil also occurs only in small amount, and has a growth of post oak, hickory, wild plum, and black-jack. It is a heavy, putty-like clay, orange-red in color, difficult to till, and best adapted to cotton. The amount given to cotton, and the growth and yield per acre of cotton, is the same as on the gray land. A larger proportion of this land lies turned out, and does not recuperate as quickly as either of the other two classes of land.

While this region is a little north of the true cotton belt, and its capacity is not quite equal to lands farther south and west, yet the crop is more uniform and reliable, and is less liable to injury from diseases and insect enemies than in the true cotton belt. The average yield, therefore, for a series of years will quite equal that of the cotton belt, though the staple may not be quite as high.

TIPPAH.

Population : 12,867.—White, 9,802; colored, 3,065.

Area: 450 square miles.—Short-leaf pine and oak uplands, 140 square miles; brown-loam table-land, 115 square miles; flatwoods, 165 square miles; red land, 130 square miles; all woodland.

Tilled lands: 55,092 acres.—Area planted in cotton, 18,758 acres; in corn, 23,388 acres; in oats, 3,814 acres; in wheat, 3,587 acres.

Cotton production: 7,424 bales; average cotton product per acre, 0.40 bale, 570 pounds seed-cotton, or 190 pounds cotton lint.

In Tippah county three principal features are represented. In the central portion we find the continuation of the Pontotoc ridge, which to the northward narrows down to a mile or two in width, and presents only to a limited extent the "red-land" character. On the west the ridge country passes rather gradually into the post-oak flatwoods, which also in a measure lose their normal character and become undulating, and even hilly, in their northern portion. On the east the headwaters of the Hatchie occupy a sandy pine-hill country, rather broken, and with narrow valleys..

The Tippah flatwoods are, on the whole, less extreme in the character of their soils than those of Pontotoc and Chickasaw, and settlements are more numerous, the soil being fairly productive in most seasons. In the overflowed bottoms, however (as in that of Muddy creek), the soil is excessively heavy, ill-drained, and late for crops.

The Pontotoc ridge lands slope gently down into the flatwoods, and on the slope lie some of the largest bodies of cotton lands. The ridge lands themselves are less hilly than farther south. "Mulatto" soils are prevalent, and the extreme "red-land" character, as well as that of the intractable "beeswax hummock", is less common. Long spurs of pine ridges occasionally reach into the region from the Hatchie country, where, in the extreme southeastern corner of the county, some of the highest land in the state forms the divide between the Hatchie, Tallahatchie, and Tombigbee rivers.

Northward of Ripley the fertile ridge land falls off steeply into the bottom of Muddy creek on the one hand, while on the other it slopes off gently into the Hatchie valley. Jonesborough and Ruckersville lie within this narrow fertile belt.

Since the war Tippah has become more and more a region of small farms; the negro population has greatly diminished as compared with the white, and corn has taken precedence of cotton in acreage. The tilled lands of Tippah amount to 19.1 per cent. of the total area, and 34 per-cent., or over one-third of these lands, is given to cotton culture, while 42.4 per cent. is occupied by corn. The cotton acreage per square mile is 41.7, and the average product per acre 0.40 bale.

Shipments are chiefly made from Ripley, the county-seat, by a branch of the Mobile and Ohio railroad, Memphis and Charleston railroad to New Orleans via Memphis, or to Mobile, at $3 per bale.

ABSTRACT OF THE REPORT OF J. A. KIMBROUGH, RIPLEY.

Of the cultivated lands of this county the low bottoms along the water-courses comprise about one-tenth, the blackish and black clay loam upland one-third, and the yellowish-red and mahogany, fine sandy and gravelly clay upland forms one-fourth. Cotton and corn are the chief crops.

The bottoms bear a natural growth of beech, ash, hickory, and oak. The soil is a black and blackish, putty-like clay loam, 1 to 3 feet thick. The subsoil is clay, underlaid by rotten limestone at 10 feet. Tillage is difficult in wet seasons. The soil is late, cold, and ill-drained, is best adapted to cotton, and one-half its area is planted with the same. The plant grows from 5 to 6 feet high, but is most productive at 5 feet. In moderately wet seasons it inclines to run to weed, but this may be remedied by planting closely in rows farther apart. The seed-cotton product per acre of fresh land is 1,800 pounds; 1,485 pounds make a 475-pound bale of lint. The staple from all fresh lands here rates high. After five years' cultivation (unmanured) the product is 1,500 pounds, and 1,425 pounds make a bale of better lint. Cockleburs are the most troublesome weeds. Not more than one-twentieth of such land lies "turned out". A rest of one or two years improves its yield.

The clay-loam upland extends beyond the county limits. Its natural growth is nearly all oak. Its soil is 6 to 12 inches deep, and rests upon yellowish clay, which is underlaid by rock at 10 to 20 feet. The soil is early, warm, easily tilled, but ill-drained. Two-thirds of it is planted with cotton. The plant grows from 3 to 3½ feet high, the latter being most productive. It rarely runs to weed; if so, in very wet seasons it may be checked by topping. The seed-cotton product per acre of fresh land is from 800 to 1,000 pounds; 1,425 pounds make a 475-pound bale of lint. After five years' cultivation (unmanured) the product is from 600 to 800 pounds, and 1,485 pounds then make a bale of lint differing but little from that of fresh land. The Spanish needle is the most troublesome weed. One-tenth of such land lies "turned out", and produces only tolerably when again cultivated.

The red-clay soil also extends beyond the county limits, and bears a natural growth of short oaks. Its soil is 6 inches deep, and rests upon a heavier, tenacious, and impervious clay, containing flinty, white, angular pebbles, underlaid by gravel and rock at 4 to 10 feet. The soil is late, cold, ill-drained, easily tilled in dry seasons, and one-tenth of its area is planted with cotton. The plant usually grows 18 to 24 inches high, but is most productive at 24, and never runs to weed. The seed-cotton product per acre of fresh land is 600 pounds; 1,425 pounds make a 475-pound bale of lint. Six years' cultivation (unmanured) reduces the yield to one-half, and 1,545 pounds then make a bale of inferior lint.

Rag-weed is the most troublesome. One-half of such cultivated land lies "turned out", and not much has ever been tried again. Slopes anywhere on the uplands wash and gully readily, and are thus seriously damaged. Some injury is also done the valleys by the washings, and to check the damage hillside ditching has been practiced with moderate success.

Cotton is shipped from the 1st of November to the last of December, by rail to Memphis and New Orleans, at $3 per bale.

PRENTISS.

Population : 12,158.—White, 9,737; colored, 2,421.

Area : 410 square miles.—Woodland, all short-leaf pine and oak uplands, 290 square miles; prairie belt, 120 square miles.

Tilled lands : 50,738 acres.—Area planted in cotton, 16,610 acres; in corn, 23,018 acres; in oats, 3,806 acres; in wheat, 993 acres.

Cotton production : 7,207 bales; average cotton product per acre, 0.39 bale, 555 pounds seed-cotton, or 185 pounds cotton lint.

Prentiss county is divided by the Mobile and Ohio railroad into two unequal parts, the western and smaller one forming part of the "prairie belt", here generally known as the "white lime country" (excepting a small area in the northwest corner of the county belonging to the "Hatchie hills"). The portion lying east of the railroad, embracing the extreme heads of the Tuscumbia at the north and of the Tombigbee at the south, is, on the whole, a region of sandy pine hills, but with many wide and fertile bottoms and undulating tracts of loam uplands, particularly in its southern part, on Big and Little Brown's creeks, where excellent crops are made.

In the "white lime country" we find large tracts of black prairie soil, especially along the streams, mostly, however, timbered with oak and hickory, with which the honey-locust, mulberry, wild plum, sycamore, ash, black walnut, and tulip tree, or poplar, mingle the more the nearer the limestone is to the surface. Carrollville and Blackland are centers of "black prairie" tracts; Booneville, the county-seat, lies on the edge of the hills on the railroad.

The streams of the "white lime region" (tributaries of the Tuscumbia river in the northern part, and of Twenty-mile creek and the Tombigbee river in the southern) mostly head within it, and, not being fed by springs, mostly go dry in summer. The water supply is derived from deep wells or cisterns.

The tilled lands of Prentiss county amount to 22.8 of the total area, and 31.2 per cent. of such lands is occupied by cotton culture, while 38.5 per cent. is given to corn. The average cotton acreage per square mile is 45.4, and the average product per acre 0.39 bale.

Shipments are made by the Mobile and Ohio railroad mostly to Mobile direct, or via Memphis to New Orleans, at the rate of $3 75 per bale.

ABSTRACT OF THE REPORT OF B. B. BOONE, BOONEVILLE.

East of the Mobile and Ohio railroad the lands are rolling and covered by sandy loam chiefly, with some patches of black prairie on the western edge. West of the railroad are the gray and black hummock lands, and along the streams are rich bottoms.

The prairie soil is a blackish and black, clayey loam, 18 inches deep, and covers one-eighth of this county, extending south to near the middle of the state and north to the state line. The subsoil is a heavy, stiff clay, retentive of moisture, which bakes hard on exposure if wet, but on continued exposure to freezes and air crumbles and is easily worked. It contains shells entire or decomposed, and is underlaid at from 3 to 10 feet by hard blue clay. The soil is early when well-drained, and is easily tilled, except when too wet; it is then too sticky, and weeds grow too rapidly. Of field crops, this soil is best adapted to cotton, the same being depended upon as the only source of cash returns. One-half the cultivated portion of this soil (also of the other uplands) is planted with cotton. The plant grows from 3 to 5 feet high, the medium being most productive. An abundance of animal and vegetable matter in the soil inclines the plant to run to weed; the remedy consists in the free use of mineral fertilizers. The seed-cotton product per acre of fresh land is from 800 to 1,200 pounds in good seasons; 1,425 pounds (from any soil in this region) make a 475-pound bale of good middling lint. After two or three years' cultivation (unmanured) production gradually decreases until it ceases to be profitable. The ratio of seed to lint and quality of staple are about the same as on fresh land. The same is true of the other soils here. All upland slopes wash and gully readily, and are thus seriously damaged. The washings seriously injure narrow valleys, but improve broad valleys. Only a few attempts have been made to check these damages, only with partial success, owing chiefly to imperfect execution of the work.

The timbered land surrounding these prairies bears a natural growth of most of the oaks, hickory, sycamore, ash, poplar, walnut, chestnut, pine, elm, gum, mulberry, persimmon, maple, catalpa, etc., and a great variety of undergrowth.

The creek bottoms occupy about one-fiftieth of the county area, and bear a natural growth of various oaks, walnut, hickory, chestnut, poplar, cottonwood, etc. The character of this land applies to all creek bottoms coextensive with the prairies just described. The soil is a black, alluvial clay loam, 2 to 6 feet deep, contains hard "black gravel" in many places, and is underlaid by blue rock at 15 feet. Tillage is difficult in wet, but rather easy in dry seasons. The soil is late, is cold and ill-drained, and is best adapted to corn, but in dry seasons produces the best cotton crops. One-third of its cultivated area is planted in cotton. The plant grows from 4 to 5 feet high, but is most productive at 4 feet. It inclines to run to weed on this and the soil next described in wet seasons and when deeply cultivated. Shallow cultivation is the best remedy.

The seed-cotton product per acre of fresh land is 1,000 pounds. This land deteriorates but little even after many years' cultivation (unmanured). Crab-grass and morning-glories are the most troublesome weeds.

The gray and black sandy lands occupy about two-thirds of this region, and are common over the state. Their natural growth is oaks, hickory, pine, and chestnut in the uplands, and maple, poplar, walnut, etc., in the bottoms. The soil varies from a fine sandy loam to a clay loam, and averages 10 inches deep. The heavier subsoil is a mulatto-colored clay, considerably mixed with sand, and sometimes containing "black gravel". It is underlaid by sand or blue clay at 15 to 20 feet. The soil is easily tilled, is early, warm, and ill-drained, and is best adapted to cotton. The plant grows from 3 to 4 feet high, and the seed-cotton product per acre of fresh land is 800 pounds. After four years' cultivation (unmanured) the product is 500 pounds. Crab-grass is the most troublesome weed. One-twentieth of such cultivated land lies "turned out"; when again cultivated it produces poorly, unless fertilized.

This location is near the northern limit of the cotton belt. The cotton crop suffers much from backward springs, does not start up vigorously, and is liable to be seriously affected by early frosts. Our northern location exempts us from the ravages of insects, and generally gives us a healthy plant, which in a great measure counteracts the disadvantages of the cold weather.

UNION.

Population: 13,030.—White, 9,932; colored, 3,098.

Area: 360 square miles.—Short-leaf pine and oak uplands, 55 square miles; prairie belt, 40 square miles; flatwoods, 95 square miles; red land, 170 square miles; all woodland.

Tilled lands: 56,999 acres.—Area planted in cotton, 21,255 acres; in corn, 25,834 acres; in oats, 2,695 acres; in wheat, 2,426 acres.

Cotton production: 8,259 bales; average cotton product per acre, 0.39 bale, 555 pounds seed-cotton, or 185 pounds cotton lint.

The agricultural features of Union county are very similar to those of Pontotoc, of which the southern half was originally a part. The Pontotoc ridge and the post-oak flatwoods form the two main features, occupying the middle of the county. A tract of sandy, short-leaf pine hills covers the extreme western portion, while on the east of the Pontotoc ridge there is a steep descent into the level black prairie country around Ellistown. The Tallahatchie and its tributaries drain almost the whole of the county, and have running water throughout the year.

A peculiar feature of the Pontotoc ridge lands occurs northeast of New Albany, the county-seat, viz, of a tract of ridge lands of most unpromising aspect at first sight, yet accounted among the most fertile uplands of the state, popularly designated the "Buncombes". The soil is deeply tinted with iron, light and loamy, and is filled with smooth concretionary pebbles of brown iron ore from the size of a pea to that of a fist, rendering tillage somewhat troublesome, but nevertheless very remunerative. It may be considered as land thoroughly marled by the underlying strata of sandy marls and limestones rich in greensand grains, and kept so by the continual disintegration of these materials and their admixture with the tilled soils. It is a good example of what can be done for most of the lands throughout the ridge by a free use of the marls by which it is underlaid.

The bottoms of the Tallahatchie and of tributary streams are very fertile. The former, however, are largely liable to overflows, and hence are not very extensively cultivated as yet. The second bottoms, or hummocks, are preferred for safety, and are almost equally productive. They are timbered chiefly with oaks, hickory, walnut, and poplar.

The tilled lands of Union county amount to 24.7 per cent. of the total area, and of these lands somewhat over one-third (37.3 per cent.) is given to cotton culture and a considerably larger proportion (over 45 per cent.) to corn. The average cotton acreage per square mile is 59, and the average product per acre 0.39 bale—a remarkably good showing for an upland county, which places it alongside of Marshall and Prentiss counties.

Communication is mainly with the Mobile and Ohio railroad, from the several stations of which (especially Baldwin) cotton is shipped, usually as fast as ginned, to Mobile, at the rate of $4 25 per bale. The flatwoods being almost impassable for teams in winter, cotton is hauled westward to the New Orleans and Chicago railroad only from the country lying west of the flatwoods belt.

LEE.

Population : 20,470.—White, 12,656 ; colored, 7,814.

Area : 540 square miles.—Oak uplands, 35 square miles; prairie lands, 495 square miles ; red land, 10 square miles; all woodland.

Tilled lands : 101,822 acres.—Area planted in cotton, 38,578 acres ; in corn, 36,073 acres ; in oats, 4,676 acres ; in wheat, 1,400 acres.

Cotton production : 14,406 bales ; average cotton product per acre, 0.37 bale, 528 pounds seed-cotton, or 176 pounds cotton lint.

Lee county lies wholly within the prairie belt, the chief exception being a small area in the northeast corner, where undulating oak uplands, with a sandy loam soil, form a gradual transition toward the prairie belt proper. The latter is mainly drained by Old Town creek and its branches, of which the Coonewah and Chirrapa are the chief, and, heading in the Pontotoc ridge, carry more or less water throughout the year.

Of the tilled area of this county (29.5 per cent.) but little was originally open prairie, interspersed in small bodies among the woodlands. Among these the "Chickasaw old fields" were the most notable. This tract, about 8 miles long by 2 wide, lies between Coonewah and Old Town creeks, west of Tupelo and Verona stations, and consists partly of black and partly of "bald" prairie, the soil on the latter being often so thin as to expose the white rock. Clumps of crab-apple and plum are their only growth. South of Chiwapa creek also small bodies of similar prairies exist.

The bottoms of the creeks, as well as the adjacent uplands, are also largely occupied by black prairie soil, the former heavily timbered, the latter more or less sparsely so, with an oak and hickory growth varying in character, as in approaching the low dividing ridges we meet the "black-jack" prairie and sometimes a lighter loam soil on the summits.

Lee county is well settled, and although long and exhaustively cultivated the predominance of the black prairie soil leaves its product per acre (0.37 bale) the highest of the prairie counties proper. Of the tilled area 37.9 per cent. is given to cotton culture and nearly an equal area to corn. The average cotton acreage per square mile is 71.4.

The Mobile and Ohio railroad traverses the county centrally from north to south, and its numerous stations afford ample facilities for shipments, which are mostly made to Mobile as fast as the cotton is ginned.

ABSTRACT OF THE REPORT OP H. L. HOLLAND, GUNTOWN, LEE COUNTY.

(Refers to a portion of the black prairie region 10 miles north and south of Sec. 35, T. 6, R. 5 E.)

The best soil for cotton is that of the old bottoms and second bottoms of creeks. These cover one-third of this region, and have a natural growth of white, red, black, and Spanish oaks, white and black walnut, hickory, ash, poplar, elm, dogwood, red-bud, cucumber, sassafras, sycamore, gums, beech, holly, ironwood, and grapes in abundance.

The soil is a blackish sandy loam, 12 to 36 inches thick in bottoms and 8 to 10 in second bottoms. The subsoil is a deep yellow or pale red clay, underlaid by marl at 8 to 10 feet. The soil is moderately early and warm when well drained, is easily tilled, and is well adapted to cotton, corn, and potatoes. These, with wheat and oats, are the chief crops of this region. Cotton occupies one-third of the cultivated part of this soil, and grows from 4 to 8 feet high, but is most productive at 4 feet. Wet seasons and deep culture incline it to run to weed ; heavy manuring is the remedy.

The seed-cotton product per acre of fresh land varies from 1,000 to 1,500 pounds ; 1,425 pounds make a 475-pound bale of fair lint. After twenty years' cultivation (unmanured) the product varies from 800 to 1,000 pounds, the ratio of seed to lint and quality being about the same. Cocklebur and smartweed are most troublesome weeds.

Another third of this region, designated as hillside land, is coextensive with the bottoms, and bears a natural growth of white, red, black, and Spanish oaks, elm, red-bud, mulberry, wild cherry, poplar, grape, brier, bramble, etc. The soil varies from fine sandy to clayey loam, is dark gray in color, and is from 3 to 8 inches thick. The subsoil is like that of the bottoms, but the underlying marl is 4 or 5 feet deeper. This soil is moderately early and warm when well drained, is easily tilled, and is best adapted to cotton and wheat, cotton occupying two thirds of the cultivated portion. The plant attains a height of from 2 to 4 feet, but is most productive at 4 feet. It inclines to run to weed in wet seasons, but this can be remedied by topping and manuring.

The seed-cotton product per acre of fresh land varies from 500 to 700 pounds, but twenty years' cultivation (unmanured) reduces the yield from 200 to 400 pounds. The ratio of seed to lint and quality of the staple are about as on the bottoms. About half of such originally cultivated land has been "turned out" and not again cultivated. The most troublesome weeds are crab-grass and hog-weed.

The remaining third of the region is designated poor beeswax ridge land. It is coextensive with the other kinds, and bears a natural growth of black-jack, some post and black oaks, hickory, and huckleberry. The soil is a beeswaxy or putty-like yellow clay ; the similar subsoil is heavier, occasionally contains sand-rock, and is underlaid by sand, gravel, and marl at 20 to 25 feet. Tillage is very difficult, and the soil is best adapted to growing sedge-grass and sheep pasturage. Cotton is rarely planted on it. Cotton will grow 10 to 20 inches high, and produce from 100 to 300 pounds of seed-cotton per acre on fresh land, and none after twenty years' cultivation without manure. The ratio of seed to lint and quality are as on the other lands. All of such originally cultivated land now lies "turned out".

Slopes readily wash, and in a few cases are seriously damaged ; the valleys also are to a small extent damaged by the washings. To check this a little hillside ditching has been done, generally inefficient, but it is successful when well done. In wet seasons cotton grows too tall, and, in consequence of luxurious foliage, does not open well. Cotton is shipped, as fast as ready, by rail to Mobile, at $4 25 per bale.

PONTOTOC.

Population: 13,859.—White, 9,609; colored, 4,249.

Area: 530 square miles.—Woodland, all; short-leaf pine and oak uplands, 80 square miles; prairie belt, 15 square miles; flatwoods, 230 square miles; red land, 205 square miles.

Tilled lands : 72,848 acres.—Area planted in cotton, 21,448 acres; in corn, 26,588 acres; in oats, 2,169 acres; in wheat, 2,751 acres.

Cotton production: 8,085 bales; average cotton product per acre, 0.38 bale, 543 pounds seed-cotton, or 181 pounds cotton lint.

The two prominent agricultural features of Pontotoc county are the Pontotoc ridge (see p. 17), which, with a little black prairie, occupies the eastern half of the county, and the post-oak flatwoods (see p. 20), which, with a narrow strip of the adjacent uplands, occupies the western half.

The flatwoods are here at their maximum width of 10 miles, and are very characteristically developed, both as to the feature of the light, silty, whitish soil and that derived from the heavy flatwoods clay. Although settled to some extent by small farmers, and in favorable seasons yielding fair crops, especially near the foot of the ridge, the flatwoods contribute but little to the cotton production of the county. The cotton acreage shown by the returns may therefore be considered as belonging almost entirely to the eastern half of the county, the generous soils of the ridge showing their quality by the relatively high product per acre of nearly four-tenths of a bale. Considering that the Pontotoc ridge is one of the oldest settled regions of northern Mississippi, the fact that in this county, as well as in those of Union and Tippah, the average product per acre is higher than in the black prairie counties is quite remarkable. This is partly, no doubt, attributable to the prevalence of mixed farming, as shown in the large acreage of corn and other cereals, while in the prairie counties the cotton acreage mostly exceeds that of all the cereals combined.

The Pontotoc ridge is, properly speaking, a broad belt of rolling or hilly timbered uplands, to which there is a gradual ascent from the flatwoods on the west, while on the east there is quite an abrupt descent into the level prairie country. The subsoil is prevalently an orange-colored or "red" loam, mostly light enough to be easily tilled, rarely sandy, but in all cases thrifty ("red lands"), passing, on the one hand, into a pale-yellow, silty subsoil (somewhat resembling that of the ridges separating that of the black prairies), which occasionally occupies level upland tracts, and on the other through the "mahogany" or "mulatto" soils (generally lying on the slopes of ridges, and esteemed the best of all) into a true black prairie soil, or the heavy, intractable, greenish-yellow clay of the "beeswax hummocks". The whole country is underlaid by strata of sandy shell marls and limestones, to whose presence the thriftiness of the land is doubtless due, and the use of which on "tired" land is always followed by the best results.

The timber is a fine growth of oaks, black, Spanish, post, and, on the heavier soils, black-jack, with much hickory, and on the best lands black walnut, a tree not common elsewhere in the state; also, a good deal of tulip tree, or "poplar", especially in the valleys. On the inferior soils the scarlet oak is common.

The tilled lands of the county amount to 21.5 per cent. of the area. Of these lands, 29.4 per cent. is given to cotton and 36.5 to corn. The cotton acreage per square mile is 40.5, and the average product per acre is 38, being somewhat below Tippah and Union counties.

Communication is chiefly with stations on the Mobile and Ohio railroad, the flatwoods being impassable for teams during the winter months, when cotton is commonly shipped, chiefly to Mobile, at the rate of $4 per bale.

ABSTRACT OF THE REPORT OF R. C. CALLAWAY, ALGOMA.

The east side of the county is hummock land; the west side is clayey land, and is the best for cotton. Its natural growth is oak, pine, gum, hickory, etc. The soil is quite various in color and constitution, and is from 2 to 4 inches deep to change of color. It is underlaid by sand, gravel, and rock at 1 to 10 feet, and is ill-drained, difficult to till when wet, but easy when dry. The chief crops of this region are corn, cotton, and potatoes. The soil is equally well adapted to all, but one-half its cultivated area is planted in cotton. The plant attains a height of from 2 to 3 feet, and inclines to run to weed in wet weather, which is remedied by topping. The seed-cotton product per acre of fresh land varies from 600 to 1,000 pounds; 1,600 pounds make a 475-pound bale of good lint. Old land produces from 400 to 800 pounds; the staple is then a little shorter. Hog-weed and crab-grass are most troublesome.

Slopes are seriously damaged by washing and gullying, and the valleys are injured to the extent of 10 per cent. by the washings. To check these horizontalizing and hillside ditching have been successfully practiced.

CHICKASAW.

Population : 17,905.—White, 7,696; colored, 10,209.

Area : 500 square miles.—Short-leaf pine and oak uplands, 30 square miles; prairie belt, 215 square miles; flatwoods, 180 square miles; red land, 75 square miles; all woodland.

Tilled lands : 97,233 acres.—Area planted in cotton, 38,477 acres; in corn, 34,258 acres; in oats, 3,735 acres; in wheat, 1,415 acres.

Cotton production: 12,861 bales; average cotton product per acre, 0.33 bale, 471 pounds seed-cotton, or 157 pounds cotton lint.

Chickasaw county is quite varied in the character of its surface and soils. Its eastern portion, embracing about two-fifths of its area and traversed by Suckatonche and Houlka creeks, lies within the prairie belt, and was originally spotted with numerous bodies of open prairie, separated by low woodland ridges. The lower slopes of these, as well as the bottoms of the streams, have almost the same soil as the prairies. Somewhat higher up lies the "mulatto" or yellow "black-jack prairie", of varying width, timbered with short, sturdy black-jack and post oaks; then on the plateaus or ridge tops a pale grayish soil, underlaid by a silty loam subsoil and of inferior quality, timbered with a somewhat scrubby growth of scarlet, post, and Spanish oaks, with some black-jack. The prairie

294

country is well settled, but much land has been thrown out of cultivation on account of exhaustion by improvident culture. As in the other prairie counties, the average product per acre has fallen from 1,200 to less than 500 pounds of seed-cotton per acre. The region around Okalona has, in times past, been especially noted for its high production of high-grade cotton, and there can be no doubt that this state of things can easily be restored.

Northward of Houston there reaches into the county the southern extremity of the Pontotoc ridge, with an average width of about 6 miles, forming a wedge between the prairie country on the east and the flatwoods belt on the west. The red loam soils of these somewhat broken lands are highly productive. They are timbered with a good growth of oaks, hickories, etc., mixed with black walnut and tulip tree ("poplar"), and produce excellent cotton.

The Pontotoc ridge flattens out and loses its peculiar character near Houston; but a belt of rolling oak uplands continues southeastward, and rises into a high ridge, sandy on its western slope, in the northwestern part of Clay.

The extreme western portion of the county is formed by the flatwoods belt, here 6 to 7 miles in width and of the usual character in its northern portion, where both the heavy and the light silty soils occur (see regional description, p. 21), and which is but very little settled. In the southern portion of the belt the peculiar soils of the "white-oak flatwoods" are quite extensively represented (see p. 23), and cultivation is more successful. The level region near Sparta forms a transition between the flatwoods proper and the wooded prairie country, which is more prominent in Clay and Oktibbeha.

The tilled lands of Chickasaw constitute 30.4 per cent. of the total area. Of these lands, 39.6 per cent. are given to cotton culture and about 35 per cent. to corn. The average cotton acreage per square mile is 77, and the average product per acre 0.33 bale, as in Monroe and Oktibbeha.

Cotton is shipped from Okalona, Egypt, and other stations on the Mobile and Ohio railroad, chiefly to Mobile

MONROE.

Population : 28,553.—White, 10,551; colored, 18,002.
Area : 790 square miles.—Short-leaf pine and oak uplands, 525 square miles; prairie belt, 265 square miles.
Tilled lands: 155,808 acres.—Area planted in cotton, 71,402 acres; in corn, 53,431 acres; in oats, 7,278 acres; in wheat, 4,114 acres.
Cotton production : 23,830 bales; average cotton product per acre, 0.33 bale, 471 pounds seed-cotton, or 157 pounds cotton lint.

Monroe county is divided by the Tombigbee river, which traverses it from north to south, into two unequal portions, of which the eastern one, a region of sandy uplands, timbered with short-leaf pine and oaks, has about twice the area of the western portion. The latter, however, possesses by far the richer soils, and the bulk of the population as well as of cotton production. A large proportion of its area (probably over one-third) was originally treeless (or almost treeless) black prairie, forming a belt from 3 to 5 miles wide, trending a little east of south, bordered by tracts bearing a timber growth of oaks and hickory and soils partly like that of the prairie itself, partly of a "mulatto" or yellow tint and much less thrifty, but still of such quality that nearly the whole of this western division is, or has been, under cultivation for many years, and has been claimed as being the best upland cotton region of the eastern part of the state. The fact shown by the returns that the present average production per acre is only one-third of a bale is due to long-continued exhaustive cultivation, whereby the product has fallen from about 1,300 pounds of seed-cotton to less than 500; yet the soil is so rich naturally, and so deep, that with better methods of culture the original productiveness can undoubtedly be restored in this as in the rest of the prairie country. The black prairie belt is traversed almost centrally by the Mobile and Ohio railroad.

The Tombigbee river is bordered on the east throughout the county by a flat varying from 4 to 6 miles in width, of which the portion nearest the river has the character of a bottom, is more or less liable to overflow, and bears a heavy growth of timber, indicative of a rich soil, while the inland portion, especially in the northern part, is timbered with upland oaks, with a large admixture of bottom pine. The soil is gray, the subsoil a pale yellow silty loam, and is fairly productive of both cotton and corn. Water is found 15 to 18 feet beneath the surface, and is brought up by sweeps. This country is as yet but little settled, partly, it is said, on account of unhealthfulness, due perhaps to the quality of the water. This could doubtless be obviated by the use of artesian wells.

Eastward of the flat the country rises into a sandy hill region, partly of the usual character of the "short-leaf pine hills", but also (as near Athens and on the dividing ridge between the Buttahatchie and Tombigbee generally) in part of a plateau character, with a good loam subsoil timbered with oak and hickory, and forming a fine upland farming country. The bottoms of the streams (Buttahatchie and Sipsie) are wide and fertile, and, with their tributaries, possess a large area of good valley land.

The tilled lands of Monroe county constitute 30.8 per cent. of the county area, and 45.8 per cent. of these lands is given to cotton culture, against 34.2 devoted to corn. The average cotton acreage per square mile is 90.4, and the average product per acre 0.33 bale.

Cotton is hauled from all parts of the county to the Mobile and Ohio railroad for shipment, chiefly to Aberdeen, which is also the head of navigation on the Tombigbee, though steamers now rarely ascend beyond Columbus.

CLAY.

Population : 17,367.—White, 5,255; colored, 12,112.
Area : 400 square miles.—Short-leaf pine and oak uplands, 15 square miles; prairie belt, 320 square miles; flatwoods, 65 square miles.
Tilled lands: 81,441 acres.—Area planted in cotton, 41,656 acres; in corn, 26,295 acres; in oats, 3,117 acres; in wheat, 431 acres.
Cotton production : 13,137 bales; average cotton product per acre, 0.32 bale, 456 pounds seed-cotton, or 152 pounds cotton lint.

Clay is essentially a prairie county, although only a small portion of its area was originally open prairie, viz, one body northward of Palo Alto, on Houlka creek, and two in the eastern portion of the county, north and northeast of West Point. A large proportion of the woodland, however, has almost the same black soil as the prairie, especially near the streams, and has long been cleared and put into cultivation. On the higher portions of the rolling uplands, however, we find, first, the "mulatto" black-jack prairie skirting the black soil, and òn the summits of the ridges the pale, silty loam, of inferior fertility, and bearing a rather indifferent growth of post, Spanish, scarlet, and some black-jack oaks.

A belt of rolling oak uplands, rising in the flatwoods northwest of Houston, Chickasaw county, and running thence southeastward, rises into a high sandy ridge in the northwestern border of the county. This ridge falls off steeply on the east, showing outcropping white limestone, but gradually flattens out to the southward, terminating in the fork of the Suckatonchee and the Tibbee.

As in the other prairie counties, the rich soils have been depleted by improvident cropping, without returns or rotation; but their restoration, by a suitable rational system of culture, will be an easy task.

In its extreme western portion the county embraces a strip of the flatwoods belt from 4 to 6 miles wide, and of the usual character as given in the regional description, passing rather gradually from the whitish clay soil of the flatwoods to the black or yellow "prairie" soil, which is timbered with nearly the same kind of trees (with the exception of the pine), but of larger size and different type, sturdy and dense-topped, instead of lank and sparsely branched, and associated more or less with the plum and crab-apple.

The tilled lands of Clay county amount to 31.8 per cent. of the total area, and 51.1 per cent. of these lands is devoted to cotton culture, against 32.3 given to corn, a proportion of three to two. The average cotton acreage per square mile is 104.1, placing the county fifth (De Soto, Lowndes, Noxubee, and Tate taking precedence) in the state in this respect. The average cotton product per acre, however, is only 0.32 bale, the same as Newton and Neshoba counties.

Cotton is shipped, as fast as baled, from Muldoon, West Point, Tibbee, and other stations to Mobile.

OKTIBBEHA.

Population : 15,978.—White, 5,109; colored, 10,869.

Area : 430 square miles.—Short-leaf pine and oak uplands, 40 square miles; prairie belt, 190 square miles; flatwoods, 200 square miles.

Tilled lands : 65,365 acres.—Area planted in cotton, 29,679 acres; in corn, 25,251 acres; in oats, 3,288 acres; in wheat, 1,088 acres.

Cotton production : 9,929 bales; average cotton product per acre, 0.33 bale, 471 pounds seed-cotton, or 157 pounds cotton lint.

Oktibbeha county embraces three well-defined agricultural features. Its eastern portion (somewhat less than half of the total area) belongs to the prairie region, and is quite similar to the adjacent portions of Lowndes and Clay. Prairie tracts, interspersed with oak woodlands, of which some have the black prairie soil also, while others have either the less thrifty "post-oak prairie" soil, or, less frequently, the pale-yellow upland loam, are timbered with post, Spanish, scarlet, and other oaks, rather undersized. To the westward the level or gently undulating woodlands pass rather insensibly, in most cases, into the level post-oak flatwoods belt, which traverses the county in a southeastern direction from its northwestern corner with a width varying from 8 to 10 miles. The flatwoods here do not differ materially from the more northern portion of the belt and are little settled. Trim Cane creek drains the northern part, while the Noxubee and its various branches traverse the southern portion of the county, crossing both the flatwoods and the prairie region. In the southwestern corner the county embraces a small area of sandy hill lands, timbered with short-leaf pine and oaks. The streams heading in this region (like the Noxubee river itself) maintain a flow of water during the summer; those heading within the flatwoods or the prairie region are usually dry during the summer months.

The tilled lands of Oktibbeha county amount to 23.8 per cent. of the total area. Of these lands 45.4 per cent. is given to cotton and 38.6 to corn culture, showing an advantage in this regard over the neighboring county of Noxubee. The average cotton acreage per square mile is 69, and the average cotton product per acre 0.33 bale, about one-tenth higher than Noxubee.

Starkville, the county-seat (where the state agricultural college is located), is connected by a branch road with the Mobile and Ohio railroad at Artesia station, and cotton is shipped by rail to Mobile. The cotton product of the county is derived almost entirely from the prairie belt.

LOWNDES.

Population : 28,244.—White, 5,588; colored, 22,656.

Area : 500 square miles.—Short-leaf pine and oak uplands, 220 square miles; prairie belt, 280 square miles.

Tilled lands : 126,312 acres.—Area planted in cotton, 64,670 acres; in corn, 42,855 acres; in oats, 3,784 acres; in wheat, 1,618 acres.

Cotton production : 21,886 bales; average cotton product per acre, 0.34 bale, 486 pounds seed-cotton, or 162 pounds cotton lint.

Lowndes county is naturally subdivided into two strongly contrasted portions: the southern, characterized by tracts of black prairie, interspersed with more or less rolling oak uplands, and the northern (east of the Tombigbee river), which is hilly and sandy, and is timbered with oaks, intermingled with short-leaf pine. The river is skirted on the west by a narrow belt of hilly country, sometimes abutting on the stream in abrupt bluffs, back of which lies the prairie country proper, while on the east side there is a flat six or seven miles wide, of which only the portion nearest the river is subject to overflow and traversed by sloughs, the greater part being above high water, with a gradual ascent toward the base of the pine hills. This eastern portion is rather thinly settled, the bulk of the population, as well as of cotton cultivation, being found in the prairie country.

Of the latter probably about one-third or less was originally treeless or very sparsely timbered black prairie, with a heavy, "waxy" soil several feet in depth. Between the prairie tracts or belts there lie (generally at a somewhat higher level, plateau-like) slightly rolling lands, timbered more or less with post, Spanish, black-jack, and sometimes black oaks and hickory; the soil being a clay or clay loam, varying from black to "mulatto" or mahogany tint, with yellow subsoil. This "post-oak land" is less productive and durable than the black prairie proper, but is much superior to the light loamy or silty ridges separating the prairies of Chickasaw, and is extensively cultivated in cotton. Considering the excellent quality of the lands chiefly cultivated, the low average per acre given by the enumeration is to be explained by the long practice of exhaustive culture without rotation or return to the soil, Lowndes being among the regions longest settled in the state. With rational culture, however, these prairie soils can probably be readily restored to their original productiveness.

The bottoms of the streams are narrow, and the soil, usually somewhat lighter than that of the prairie proper, is very productive in good seasons. All the streams heading within the prairie region go dry during the summer, and the water supply is dependent upon bored wells, from which it frequently rises above the surface, the depths varying from 250 to 400 feet.

East of the river, and northward of Columbus, cotton culture is not very extensive. The soil of the river flat is better adapted to sweet potatoes and grain than to cotton, being rather light, and is underlaid by gravel at 4 to 8 feet and timbered largely with water and willow oak, with occasionally some short-leaf pine. Water is found at 18 to 20 feet, and sweeps are largely used. In the hilly country the soil of the uplands is rather thin and sandy, and the valleys are chiefly cultivated by small farmers.

The tilled lands of Lowndes amount to 39.5 per cent. of the county area. Of these lands 51.2 per cent. is devoted to cotton culture, against 34 per cent. given to corn. The average cotton acreage per square mile is 129.3, placing it second in the state to De Soto. The average product per acre is, however, only 0.34 bale, against 0.47 in De Soto. Originally the product of the prairie country was the higher of the two.

Cotton is usually shipped as soon as baled from Columbus and the several stations of the Mobile and Ohio railroad to Mobile, New Orleans, and direct to eastern manufacturers at Fall River and Providence, and sometimes in winter by steamers to Mobile.

ABSTRACTS OF THE REPORTS OF JAMES O. BANKS, COLUMBUS, AND R. W. BANKS, COBB'S SWITCH.

The uplands consist of black and mulatto post-oak table-lands and gently rolling prairies. The lowlands are the first and second bottoms of creeks. The kinds of soil are rolling prairie, alluvial and hummock, and post-oak soils.

The prairie is the chief one, and includes about 70 per cent. of the cultivated land of this region. It extends about 50 miles north, 25 south, thence southeasterly to Montgomery, Alabama. The name is sometimes indiscriminately applied to all lime lands in what is known as the "prairie belt". The soil is a clay loam, waxy and putty-like, blackish and yellowish-black, and is from 2 to 6 feet thick. The underlying material is heavier, gradually becoming like the surface by exposure, is quite impervious, can easily be made to hold water for stock the year round, contains in places smooth brownish and whitish pebbles (the latter having a worm-eaten appearance), and is underlaid by blue joint-clay, and this by limestone, which crops out in some places and is 20 feet below the surface in others. The soil is early when well-drained, is easily tilled, except when too wet, and is best adapted to corn. But one-half of its cultivated area is planted in cotton. Corn and cotton are the chief crops of this region.

The usual and most productive height of the cotton-plant on the prairies is from 3½ to 4 feet. Excess of rain, especially in July and August, and the boll-worm's depredations incline the plant to run to weed on all soils here, and to restrain it topping is sometimes practiced, but is not always satisfactory. Early planting favors early bolling. The seed-cotton product per acre of fresh land varies from 1,200 to 1,400 pounds; in the average season 1,600 pounds make a 475-pound bale of middling to good middling lint. After ten years' cultivation (unmanured) the product varies from 400 to 1,000 pounds, according to season and kind of cultivation; from 1,665 to 1,720 pounds then make a bale of lint not so strong or so long as that from fresh land.

About 5 or 6 per cent. of such originally cultivated land lies "turned out", and when again cultivated it produces a small crop the first year, but improves after that. It is usual to plant corn on such land the first year. The troublesome weeds are crab-grass and morning-glory.

In addition to the above, Mr. J. O. Banks describes the following soils:

The alluvial creek bottom and hummock land has a natural growth of oak, hickory, gum, ash, mulberry, wild plum, etc. The soil is a blackish clayey loam from 2 to 4 feet thick. The underlying material is heavier, but rather similar to a considerable depth, rather leachy, and is underlaid by limestone at 10 to 12 feet. Tillage is generally easy, but is not so easy in wet as in dry seasons. The soil is later than the prairie, but is generally well-drained on the surface. It is best adapted to cotton after the first year's cultivation, and about 80 per cent. of the cultivated area is planted with it. The plant attains a height of from 4 to 6 feet, but is most productive at 5 feet. The seed-cotton product per acre of fresh land varies from 1,200 to 1,600 pounds, and about 1,620 pounds make a 475-pound bale of middling to good middling lint. After ten years' cultivation (unmanured) the product is from 500 to 1,000 pounds; the ratio of seed to lint is about the same, but the staple is a little shorter and weaker. Crab-grass, morning-glory, and purslane are the troublesome weeds. None of such land has been "turned out".

The black and mulatto post-oak land borders the prairies, is coextensive with them, and has a natural growth almost entirely of oak. The soil is a putty-like and waxy clay loam, varying in color from yellow to mulatto, blackish and black, and is 12 to 36 inches deep. The subsoil is heavier, but gradually becomes like the surface when turned up. It is impervious, packs like the prairie subsoil, and is underlaid by limestone at 18 to 24 feet. Tillage is difficult when the soil is wet, but easier when it is dry, and on the whole is more difficult than the other soils. The soil is early, well-drained, and is best adapted to cotton, nine-tenths or more of the cultivated part being planted with the same.

The plant grows from 4 to 4½ feet high on fresh land and 2 to 4 on old land, and is less inclined to weed than on other soils. The seed-cotton product of fresh lands varies from 1,200 to 1,500 pounds; 1,600 to 1,665 ounds make a 475-pound bale of middling to good middling lint. After five years' cultivation (unmanured) the product varies from 400 to 800 pounds, and from 1,660 to 1,720 pounds then make a bale of lint, neither so long nor so strong as that from fresh land. This land deteriorates more rapidly than the other kinds. Five to 8 per cent. of it lies "turned out", and yields rather poorly when again cultivated. Crab-grass is the most troublesome weed. Slopes readily wash and gully, and are occasionally seriously damaged; but this may be easily checked if done in time, for which purpose horizontalizing and hillside ditching are successfully practiced.

On the lowlands cotton does best in dry, hot seasons, for in wet seasons it runs too much to weed and bears little fruit.

The yield of lint cotton depends more upon the seasons and the variety of seed than upon the soil. The stronger and fresher soil yields more seed than the poorer soils, but in 1878 all soils gave a poor yield, requiring about 3½ pounds of seed-cotton to give one of lint. The crop of 1879 gave one of lint for 3¼ to 3½ pounds of seed-cotton.

Cotton is shipped as soon as baled by rail or river from Columbus to Mobile and New Orleans, and to eastern manufacturers at Fall River and Providence. Rates of freight are 90 cents to $1 per 100 pounds to the east, $1 50 to $2 per bale to Mobile, and $2 50 to $3 per bale by river and rail to New Orleans.

NOXUBEE.

Population: 29,874.—White, 5,302; colored, 24,572.

Area: 680 square miles.—Short-leaf pine and oak uplands, 55 square miles; prairie belt, 495 square miles; flatwoods, 130 square miles.

Tilled lands: 151,704 acres.—Area planted in cotton, 82,483 acres; in corn, 50,904 acres; in oats, 5,429 acres; in wheat, 39 acres.

Cotton production: 25,294 bales; average cotton product per acre, 0.31 bale, 441 pounds seed-cotton, or 147 pounds cotton lint.

Of Noxubee county by far the greater portion (about five-sevenths) lies within the prairie belt. A large body of originally open prairie lies northward of Macon, the county-seat, and smaller bodies of such prairie are found all over the county. All have long since passed into cultivation, and partly out of it again, and, as much of the woodland possesses the same soil, it is not now easy to circumscribe these open prairie tracts. Most of the area within the prairie belt is more or less timbered (post-oak prairie), and ridges of a sandy loam soil, timbered with a variety of oaks, form the divides between many of the streams.

The post-oak prairie land in this county, as well as in Kemper, has not unfrequently a dark-orange or red subsoil, differing from that of the more northern portion of the prairie belt, and giving rise to a very varied coloring of the plowed fields, ranging from gray, through mahogany, to orange and black. It will be noted that the average product per acre in this county is somewhat less than in the other prairie counties, owing partly to the more limited proportion of true black prairie and partly, no doubt, to the fact noted in the general description and discussion of soils (see page 14) that the proportion of phosphates in the prairie soil itself is less than in those of Monroe and Lowndes. The use of phosphate manures will probably be followed by a very great increase in productiveness.

Westward of the prairie country we find, as elsewhere, the flatwoods belt narrowing here to only 4 or 5 miles in the southern part of the county. Its agricultural and surface features are the same as in Oktibbeha, the soil perhaps a shade less heavy, but yet very refractory and unthrifty in cultivation, and hence the region is but little settled. It is drained by numerous creeks tributary to the Noxubee river, but, in the absence of springs, is mostly dry during the summer.

In the southwest corner of the county there is a small area of very sandy uplands, timbered partly with short-leaf pine forest and partly with oaks only, fairly productive, as in the Gholson neighborhood. From these sandy hill lands there is an abrupt descent into the flatwoods, and from these again there is an almost equally abrupt ascent into the high prairie plateau of Kemper.

The tilled lands of Noxubee form 34.9 per cent. of the area, and 54.4 per cent., or over one-half of these lands, is given to cotton culture, while only 33.5 per cent., or one-third, is given to corn. The cotton acreage per square mile is 121.3, the county standing fourth (to Tate, Lowndes, and De Soto) in this respect in the state. The average product per acre is, however, only 0.31 bale—a remarkable comment upon the exhaustive methods of culture that have depressed this ratio to a level with that of the adjoining county of Kemper, and nearly to that of the "pine hills" counties generally.

Almost all the cotton of the county is grown within the prairie belt, and is shipped via Macon and other stations on the Mobile and Ohio railroad, which traverses the county nearly centrally from north to south, keeping within the prairie belt. Cotton is shipped as soon as baled by rail to Mobile at $4 per bale.

ABSTRACT OF THE REPORT OF F. R. W. BOCK, MACON.

The uplands are generally rolling, not hilly, and some are level table-lands. They consist of post-oak prairies and timbered lands in the ratio of two to one.

The prairies bear a scattered growth of post-oak and hickory. The soil is a clay loam, varying in color from gray to mahogany, orange, red, and blackish, and is underlaid at 18 inches by a subsoil of heavier buff and brick-red, hard and leachy material, which is again underlaid by limestone at 12 feet.

Such land extends east and west about 3 miles and through the entire townships north and south, with small portions of sandy lands. The soil is early, ill-drained, easily tilled, except when it is too wet, and is best adapted to cotton, three-fourths of its cultivated area being planted with the same. The plant grows from 3 to 4 feet high, and inclines to run to weed when the seasons are too wet and the stand is too much crowded and shaded. The remedy is topping in early August.

The average seed-cotton product per acre of fresh land is 1,000 pounds; 1,665 pounds make a 475-pound bale of good middling lint. After five years' cultivation (unmanured) the product is 600 pounds, and 2,135 pounds make a 475-pound bale of inferior and shorter lint. The most troublesome weeds are wild indigo, prairie weed, and vines. One-tenth of such cultivated land (also of that next described) lies "turned out". It produces well for three years when again cultivated, and then deteriorates. Slopes do not readily wash and gully.

The timbered land bears a natural growth chiefly of pine, white oak, red oak, hickory, etc., and occurs in bodies of 100 to 5,000 acres. The soil is a gray and blackish-gray, fine and coarse sandy loam, 12 inches thick. The subsoil is heavier, is of a dirty-yellow color, readily becomes very hard on exposure, and is underlaid by sand and limestone at from 4 to 15 feet. Tillage is easy, the soil being early and warm in some places, late and cold in others, and is generally ill-drained. Two-thirds of its cultivated area is planted in cotton, to which the soil is apparently best adapted. The plant grows from 2 to 4 feet high, but is most productive at 4 feet, and runs to weed, etc., as on the prairie. The seed-cotton product per acre of fresh land is 900 pounds; 1,780 pounds make a 475-pound bale of good middling lint. Five years' cultivation (unmanured) reduces the product to 500 pounds, and from 1,900 to 2,130 pounds make a 475-pound bale of lint, which rates two points below the staple from fresh land. Wild indigo is the most troublesome weed.

Slopes wash and gully readily, but are not generally seriously damaged, the washings injuring the valleys, but to no great extent. Horizontalizing and hillside ditching are practiced, and pretty generally check the damage. The chief crops here are cotton, corn, oats, sweet potatoes, and peas. From April 15 to November 1 the weather is generally very warm and very favorable to cotton raising. The cotton-plant grows and matures very rapidly here, more especially on the prairie (termed here post-oak prairie) than on the sandy lands, and produces more fruit to the stalk on such lands than on sandy.

KEMPER.

(See "Short-leaf pine and oak uplands region".)

FLATWOODS REGION.

This embraces the following parts of counties, all of which are described under other regional heads: Tippah, Union, Pontotoc, Chickasaw, Oktibbeha, and Noxubee.

TIPPAH.

(See "Northeastern prairie region".)

UNION.

(See "Northeastern prairie region".)

PONTOTOC.

(See "Northeastern prairie region".)

CHICKASAW.

(See "Northeastern prairie region".)

OKTIBBEHA.

(See "Northeastern prairie region".)

NOXUBEE.

(See "Northeastern prairie region".)

SHORT-LEAF PINE AND OAK UPLANDS REGION.

(Embraces the following counties and parts of counties: East of the prairie region—Tishomingo, Alcorn,* Prentiss,* Tippah,* Itawamba, Lee,* Monroe,* and Lowndes;* west of the prairie region—Benton,* Union,* La Fayette,* Pontotoc,* Calhoun, Yalobusha,* Grenada,* Montgomery, Sumner, Choctaw, Oktibbeha,* Winston, Attala, Leake, Neshoba, Kemper, Lauderdale,* Newton, Scott,* Rankin,* Simpson,* Hinds,* Claiborne,* Jefferson,* Franklin,* Adams,* and Wilkinson.*)

TISHOMINGO.

Population : 8,774.—White, 7,611 ; colored, 1,163.
Area : 450 square miles.—Woodland, all; all short-leaf pine and oak uplands.
Tilled lands : 38,419 acres.—Area planted in cotton, 7,555 acres; in corn, 15,965 acres; in oats, 3,237 acres; in wheat, 702 acres.
Cotton production : 9,079 bales; average cotton product per acre, 0.35 bale, 498 pounds seed-cotton, or 166 pounds cotton lint.

Tishomingo county differs from all other parts of the state in its features, from the fact that it is underlaid by rocks not represented elsewhere in the state, though covering a large portion of northern Alabama, whence the sandstones and limestones of the coal formation extend into this county. They are prominent on the waters of Big Bear creek, which drains all the eastern part of the county, and likewise exist on Mackay's creek, a tributary of the Tombigbee, and on the other creeks directly tributary to the Tennessee, such as Yellow and Indian creeks.

The region underlaid by these rocks is generally gently undulating; the surface is gravelly, rather than sandy, at least on the lower slopes. The lands of the immediate valley of Bear creek are fine, and produce abundant crops of corn and cotton They are largely "hummocks" or second bottoms, elevated 20 to 40 feet above the streams, and their timber is singularly various—Spanish, black, post, water, willow, chestnut-white, white, and black-jack oaks, hickory, sweet gum, pine, dogwood, walnut, tulip tree, and some red cedar—varying according as the underlying rocks are sandstones or calcareous shales. On the former the timber (post oak, black-jack, and pine) is remarkably sparse and quite small, as in the "barrens" of Alabama.

The Tennessee river has little or no bottom on the Mississippi side, the pine hills coming up pretty close to the bank, which is timbered with walnut and sycamore. Yellow creek, which at its head has remarkably wide bottoms, has but a very narrow one in the lower part of its course. On the bordering hills shaly hydraulic limestone often lies close to the surface, while elsewhere gravel beds form the higher portion of the ridges.

The tilled lands of Tishomingo form 13.3 per cent. of the area.

Small farming is the rule in Tishomingo. Cotton occupies but one-fifth of the cultivated area, while somewhat less than half of the same is given to corn, it being the predominant crop. The cotton product per acre is relatively high (0.35 bale), most of it being grown in bottom lands.

Cotton shipments are made either by the Memphis and Charleston railroad to New Orleans or Mobile, or by steamer from Eastport, on the Tennessee river.

ABSTRACT OF THE REPORT OF J. M. D. MILLER, IUKA.

The uplands are hilly and rolling, and have a variety of soils and some patches of muck, but chiefly a thin, light sandy soil, on which cotton is liable to suffer from drought.

The lowlands consist of first and second bottoms of creeks; they are narrow, sometimes overflow, and are subject to early frosts.

Sandy and clay uplands and bottom soils are cultivated in cotton. The upland soils are chiefly cultivated, and constitute seven-tenths of the county's area. The same kinds extend 21 miles north, 40 south, 4 east, and 20 west. They bear a natural growth of red, post, black-jack, and Spanish oaks, and gum. The soils vary in color from whitish-gray to buff, yellow, brown, orange, red, and blackish, and are 2 to 6 inches thick, the chief variety being coarse, sandy, and gravelly. The subsoil is generally heavier and leachy, and consists of tougher reddish clay, with coarser gravel, or, in places, with whitish sand, underlaid by sand and gravel. The chief crops of the region are cotton and corn. The soil is early, warm, well-drained, always easily tilled, and is best adapted to cotton, three-fourths of the cultivated area being planted with the same. The plant grows from 12 to 24 inches high, but is most productive at 18, and is a little inclined to run to weed in wet weather. The product per acre of fresh land is about 800 pounds of seed-cotton; 1,425 pounds make a 475-pound bale of middling to good middling lint. After three years' cultivation (unmanured) the product is about 300 pounds; 1,545 pounds then make a bale of shorter lint. One-half or more of such originally cultivated land lies "turned out," which produces very well when again cultivated if the soil has not been washed away by rains. There is some crab-grass, but the soil is generally too poor for other weeds. Slopes wash and gully readily, but are not yet seriously damaged; perhaps 1 per cent. of the valleys have been injured by the washings. Horizontalizing has been practiced with fair success in checking the damage.

Cotton is shipped in November and December by rail to Memphis at $2 15 per bale.

ALCORN.
(See "Northeastern prairie region".)

PRENTISS.
(See "Northeastern prairie region".)

TIPPAH.
(See "Northeastern prairie region".)

ITAWAMBA.

Population : 10,663.—White, 9,555; colored, 1,108.

Area : 550 square miles.—All short-leaf pine and oak uplands.

Tilled lands : 51,415 acres.—Area planted in cotton, 14,851 acres; in corn, 22,055 acres; in oats, 3,134 acres; in wheat, 1,918 acres.

Cotton production : 5,113 bales; average cotton product per acre, 0.34 bale, 486 pounds seed-cotton, or 162 pounds cotton lint.

Itawamba county is a region of rolling or sometimes hilly uplands, usually with sandy loam soils, timbered with oaks and pine, more or less mingled with hickory, according to the higher or lower grade of the soil. On the southwest a portion of these uplands bears more or less the character of the prairie belt. The main Tombigbee traverses the western part from north to south, receiving numerous tributaries from either side. Among these the Bull Mountain drains the eastern half of the county, joining the Tombigbee river just at the southern county line. In the fork there is an upland tract of fertile red loam soil, timbered with Spanish, scarlet, black, and white oaks, hickory, and some sturdy pine. Similar tracts occur at other points, as near Yocony. The bottoms of Bull Mountain, Hurricane, and other larger creeks are wide, heavily timbered, and very fertile; those of the smaller streams rather narrow, but with much good land on the lower slopes. The bottom of the Tombigbee within the county is from 1 to 1½ miles wide, and is very productive, but unfortunately it is subject to annual overflows. The wide flat skirting the Tombigbee on the east in Monroe and Lowndes counties begins just south of Bull Mountain creek.

Itawamba county is a region of small farms, the culture of corn occupying an area one-half larger than that of cotton, although the latter is universally grown as a "money crop". The tilled lands of Itawamba constitute 14.6 per cent. of the county area, and 28.9 per cent. of these is given to cotton. The cotton product per acre (0.34 bale) gives Itawamba a fair position among the counties of the short-leaf pine and oak upland region. Shipments are made from stations on the Mobile and Ohio railroad, to which cotton is hauled, chiefly in December.

LEE.
(See "Northeastern prairie region".)

MONROE.
(See "Northeastern prairie region".)

LOWNDES.
(See " Northeastern prairie region".)

BENTON.
(See " Brown-loam table-lands".)

UNION.
(See " Northeastern prairie region".)

LA FAYETTE.
(See " Brown-loam table-lands".)

PONTOTOC.
(See " Northeastern prairie region".)

CALHOUN.

Population : 13,492.—White, 10,191; colored, 3,301.
Area : 580 square miles.—Short-leaf pine and oak uplands, 570 square miles; flatwoods, 10 square miles.
Tilled lands : 60,576 acres.—Area planted in cotton, 19,028 acres; in corn, 22,414 acres; in oats, 4,464 acres; in wheat, 908 acres.
Cotton production : 9,536 bales; average cotton product per acre, 0.50 bale, 714 pounds seed-cotton, or 238 pounds cotton lint.

Calhoun county is, generally speaking, a region of hilly or ridgy and sometimes even broken upland, timbered with a mixture of short-leaf pine and oaks, among which the black-jack and post oak predominate on the higher ridges, but on the lower slopes and broader ridges are largely replaced by black and Spanish oaks. The Loosha-Scoona and Yalobusha rivers, traversing the county in a southwesterly direction, divide it into three nearly equal portions, all copiously watered by numerous creeks, to the bottoms of which the cultivation, especially of cotton, is chiefly confined in the two northern divisions, while in the portion lying south of the Yalobusha river, and especially on the waters of Tapashaw creek, the upland ridges are broader and lower, the bottoms wider, and cultivation and settlement more general.

The bottoms of the two main streams are wide (1½ to 2 miles), and, judging by their large and heavy timber, have productive soils, but are liable to late annual overflows, which render crops precarious, particularly on the heavy soils of the Loosha-Scoona (derived from the flatwoods), which render its bottom impassable until late in the season. It is, however, bordered by a gently-sloping hummock, timbered with oaks and hickory, forming large bodies of good farming land but little settled as yet.

The eastern portion of the county adjoining the flatwoods has predominantly heavy upland soils, largely timbered with post oak (see regional description, page 26), while in the western portion the crests of the ridges are prevalently sandy, with a large proportion of black-jack oak.

Only a little over 16 per cent. of the area of the county is under tillage, and the lands cultivated lying chiefly in the creek bottoms, it will be noted that the average product per acre is remarkably high, making Calhoun county stand sixth in this respect among the upland counties of the state, while the cotton acreage per square mile is 32.8. As usual in regions of small farms, the area planted in cereals exceeds that in cotton by nearly one-half, and the white population outnumbers the colored in the proportion of nearly 3 to 1.

The communication of the county is chiefly with stations on the New Orleans and Chicago railroad, the flatwoods impeding communication eastward during the winter and spring months. The numerous streams render the maintenance of good wagon-roads somewhat difficult and expensive.

YALOBUSHA.
(See " Brown-loam table lands ")

GRENADA.
(See " Brown-loam table-lands".)

MONTGOMERY.

Population : 13,348.—White, 6,671; colored, 6,677.
Area : 430 square miles.—Short-leaf pine and oak uplands, 350 square miles; brown-loam table-lands, 80 square miles; all woodland.
Tilled lands : 60,293 acres.—Area planted in cotton, 24,636 acres; in corn, 17,768 acres; in oats 3,178 acres; in wheat, 148 acres.
Cotton production : 10,541 bales; average cotton product per acre, 0.43 bale, 612 pounds seed-cotton, or 204 pounds cotton lint.

Montgomery county embraces rolling, and in its northern portion, in part, quite hilly and broken uplands, timbered mostly with oaks, mingled more or less with short-leaf pine on the higher and more sandy ridges, on which also the black-jack and post oaks prevail; while on the lower and broader ones the post oak is largely accompanied by the black, Spanish, and especially the scarlet oak, indicating a soil of fair fertility, which is said to last remarkably well. The scarlet oak is especially abundant on a very pale yellow loam soil, which appears southward of the Duck Hill ridge and prevails in the southern part of the county, extending thence southeastward into Attala, Winston, Leake, and Neshoba, where it contrasts strongly, both in its color and its lightness, with the heavy "red hills" soils interspersed within it. These uplands, which produce from 800 to 1,000 pounds of seed-cotton per acre when fresh, slope off rather gently toward the Big Black river, the main body of which lies on the eastern side of the stream, while on the western side there is usually a strip of hammock or second bottom, timbered with post, water, and some willow oaks, and only moderately productive. The two last-named oaks are also very prevalent in the river bottom itself, which has rather a light soil, exceedingly productive, but unfortunately is much subject to overflows.

The tilled lands of Montgomery county constitute nearly 22 per cent. of its area, and of this amount nearly 41 per cent. is given to cotton culture, against about three-fourths as much devoted to corn. The average cotton product per acre is 0.43 bale, and the cotton acreage per square mile 57.3, slightly less than in Grenada.

Cotton shipments are made by the New Orleans and Chicago railroad, either direct to New Orleans or via Vicksburg and the Mississippi river steamers.

SUMNER.

Population: 9,534.—White, 7,239; colored 2,295.

Area: 400 square miles.—Short-leaf pine and oak uplands, 360 square miles; flatwoods, 40 square miles.

Tilled lands: 40,701 acres.—Area planted in cotton, 13,613 acres; in corn, 18,900 acres; in oats, 3,269 acres; in wheat, 1,374 acres.

Cotton production: 6,226 bales; average cotton product per acre, 0.46 per bale, 657 pounds seed-cotton, or 219 pounds cotton lint.

Sumner county is a region of undulating or sometimes hilly uplands, higher sandy or clayey ridges, timbered with short-leaf pine, black jack and post oak, alternating with rolling land bearing a growth of black, Spanish, post, and other oaks, mixed with hickory, and possessing a good, moderately heavy loam soil. The central portion of the county east and west is mainly of the latter character, while in the northern and southern portions pine ridges are more frequently seen. A broad belt of oak and hickory land borders the Big Black river on the north, while pine ridges prevail immediately south of the same.

The first bottom of the Big Black, about 1 mile wide, is so much subject to overflow that it has scarcely been settled as yet, though evidently very fertile and heavily timbered. It is bordered by a second bottom, 3 or 4 feet above the first, which is well settled and possesses a deep chocolate-colored mellow soil, timbered with beech, hickory, elm, ash, and lowland oaks, and is very productive. (For analysis, see general part.)

Cotton is grown on the uplands to some extent; and this, with a smaller area of bottom lands, depresses the average cotton product per acre (0.46) somewhat below that of Calhoun (0.50 bale), while the cotton acreage per square mile is slightly higher. The best uplands, when fresh, are stated to produce from 800 to 1,000 pounds of seed-cotton. The total area of tilled lands is a trifle less than 16 per cent. of the whole, divided chiefly among small farms. The area of corn culture is nearly one-half greater than that given to cotton.

Sumner, like Calhoun, communicates chiefly with stations on the New Orleans and Chicago railroad and partially, roads permitting, with the Starkville branch of the Mobile and Ohio railroad.

CHOCTAW.

Population: 9,036.—White, 6,537; colored, 2,499.

Area: 270 square miles.—All short-leaf pine and oak uplands.

Tilled lands: 42,779 acres.—Area planted in cotton, 13,497 acres; in corn, 18,139 acres; in oats, 3,931 acres; in wheat, 2,215 acres.

Cotton production: 5,757 bales; average cotton product per acre, 0.43 bale, 612 pounds seed-cotton, or 204 pounds cotton lint.

Choctaw county greatly resembles Sumner in its general features, being rolling or moderately hilly, without very high ridges, and also, except along the streams, without large continuous tracts of very productive soil. The higher ridges are characterized by the presence of the short-leaf pine, and are sandy in the western and rather clayey in the eastern portion of the county, while the lower ridges, or rolling lands, have an oak and hickory growth, with a soil varying from a light, pale-yellow loam in the western to a somewhat clayey loam in the eastern portion. Fine bodies of farming upland exist, especially in the southwestern portion, on the waters of McCurten's creek.

Choctaw is drained by numerous creeks, with fertile valley lands, flowing in three directions, viz, to Big Black, Pearl, and Noxubee rivers.

Nearly one-fourth (24.8 per cent.) of the county area is under tillage, the average product per acre being a little below that of Sumner county, probably because of a somewhat more extensive cultivation of the uplands. The cotton acreage per square mile (50) is greater than that of Sumner in the ratio of 3 to 2. The corn acreage exceeds that of cotton by nearly one-half.

Choctaw is about equidistant from both the great trunk railroad lines of the state, and communicates partly with either, according to the season and the state of the roads.

ABSTRACT OF THE REPORT OF R. H. BIGGES, CHESTER.

(Refers to T. 16, 17, 18, and 19, R. 9, 10, 11, and 12.)

The lowlands are first and second bottoms of creeks; the uplands are hilly and sandy, but vary but little, and are in some localities extensively cultivated.

Cotton on the lowlands can generally be planted early, and in that case they yield more than the uplands.

The bottoms chiefly are cultivated, and the best soil for cotton is that of the second bottoms. This is the prevailing kind in this region, and it is a black, coarse sandy loam, 2 to 6 inches deep to change of color. The subsoil is heavy and white, and bakes on exposure, but becomes like the surface by cultivation. It contains flinty, rounded white gravel, and is underlaid by sand and gravel. The natural growth is chiefly oak, hickory, and gum. The chief crops of this region are cotton and corn. Tillage of this soil is not usually troublesome, but is difficult in wet seasons; the soil is early when well drained, and is best adapted to cotton, with which one-half its cultivated area is planted. The usual and most productive height of the plant is 4 feet; in wet weather it inclines to run to weed. Frequent plowing will restrain it and favor bolling. The seed-cotton product per acre of fresh land is 1,200 pounds; 1,545 pounds make a 475-pound bale of good middling lint. After five years' cultivation (unmanured) the product is 800 pounds; 1,665 pounds then make a bale of lint rating lower than that from fresh land. One-half of such originally cultivated land lies "turned out", and does not produce very well when again cultivated.

The upland soil washes and gullies readily, seriously damaging the slopes, and to some extent the valleys, by the washings. Some, with more or less success, have practiced hillside ditching to check these damages.

Cotton is shipped during fall, winter, and spring by rail, chiefly to New Orleans, at $1 50 per bale.

OKTIBBEHA.

(See "Northeastern prairie region".)

WINSTON.

Population: 10,087.—White, 6,113; colored, 3,974.
Area: 690 square miles.—Woodland, all; short-leaf pine and oak uplands, 510 square miles; flatwoods, 50 square miles; red land, 130 square miles.
Tilled lands: 45,091 acres.—Area planted in cotton, 15,081 acres; in corn, 17,131 acres; in oats, 4,170 acres; in wheat, 902 acres.
Cotton production: 5,864 bales; average cotton product per acre, 0.39 bale, 555 pounds seed-cotton, or 185 pounds cotton lint.

Winston county embraces two chief varieties of uplands, which are throughout rolling, or sometimes hilly and broken. In the western and southern portion the uplands have a shallow, pale-tinted soil and a pale yellow, rather sandy, loam subsoil, the former often, the latter always, containing more or less concretions of bog ore ("black pebble"). This soil is timbered with short-leaf pine, post, Spanish, and scarlet oaks, generally accompanied with some hickory, black gum, and maple. The whole growth is disposed to be somewhat scrubby and the soil of inferior fertility, the creek bottoms forming the bulk of the land under cultivation. The central portion, near Louisville, and westward on the divide between the Big Black and Pearl rivers, is rather gently undulating or rolling, but in the southwest corner we find between the heads of Pearl river high, rocky ridges, strewn with sandstone blocks, which continue into the adjacent portion of Neshoba county, forming the highest and most broken land in the state south of the Hatchie hills, in Tippah county. In the southeastern portion the surface is less broken and the soil somewhat more coarsely sandy, occupied at times almost exclusively by the short-leaf pine. In the northern and northeastern portion of the county, and to within 3 miles of Louisville on the east, there prevails a heavy clay soil, generally only a few inches in depth, underlaid by a sometimes glaringly red clay subsoil, similar to that of the "red hills" of Attala. (See regional description, page 29.) The country it occupies is considerably broken and the hillsides are steep, and on them, as well as in the gullies, the "poplar" and ash occur. Occasionally on higher ridges we find sandy soils, ferruginous sandstone, etc., with scrubby black-jack and post oaks; but mainly the red soil prevails, and, whenever a space is afforded, settlements and plantations show the good estimation in which the land is held. The "Noxubee hills", on the extreme heads of the Noxubee and Pearl rivers, comprise the main body of these red lands, but smaller tracts occur on the them, as well as in the Yockanookana, in the northern part of the county. These uplands yield, when fresh, from 800 to 1,000 pounds of seed-cotton per acre, and are very durable. From the "Noxubee hills" there is on the east a sudden and steep descent into the post-oak flatwoods, which occupy the northeastern corner of the county and possess the usual heavy, gray, clay soil.

The tilled lands of Winston constitute only 10 per cent. of its area, and about one-third of them is devoted to cotton culture, or 21 acres per square mile. As this culture is restricted mainly to the bottom lands, the average product per acre (0.39 bale) is equal to that of the table-land counties. Winston communicates chiefly with stations on the Mobile and Ohio railroad; its western portion also with the Kosciusko branch of the New Orleans and Chicago railroad.

ABSTRACT OF THE REPORT OF WILLIAM T. LEWIS, LOUISVILLE.

The uplands are hilly and rolling, and have some prairies; the lowlands are on the first bottoms of rivers and creeks. The bottoms are very rich and productive, but cotton on such runs too much to weed, and suffers from rot of bolls in wet seasons if not picked out early. It is also liable to be prematurely frost-killed, while on the high, sandy ridges cotton has been seen in January with blooms uninjured by frost.

The chief crops of this region are cotton and corn; oats, sorghum, potatoes, and wheat are also raised. Wheat is very uncertain, but succeeds best on fresh or manured lands. About one-third of the cultivated area is planted with cotton.

The lands of the county comprise *black sandy bottoms* or *moderately undulating, light sandy* or *mulatto lands,* and *whitish* or *ash-colored,* rather stiff or heavy.

The chief soil, viz, the black sandy land, occupies about 30 per cent. of the county's area, and includes the bottoms. Its natural growth is oaks, chestnut, pine, poplar, gum, and hickory. The soil varies from coarse sandy to clayey loam, brown, mahogany, or blackish in color, and averages 12 inches deep. The subsoil is heavier, generally reddish or ash-colored clay, contains hard, rounded "black gravel", and is underlaid by sand, gravel, and sand-rock at 1 to 20 feet. Tillage is generally easy, excepting in wet seasons. The soil is early, warm, well drained, and is best adapted to cotton, corn, oats, sorghum, and potatoes. The usual and most productive height of the cotton-plant is from 3 to 4 feet. The seed-cotton product per acre of fresh land varies from 1,200 to 1,600 pounds; 1,425 make a 475-pound bale of lint. Old land yields from 400 to 550 pounds of seed-cotton per acre. The weeds of this region are crab-grass, hog-weed, ragweed, cocklebur, Spanish needle, and broom-sedge. About one-tenth of this and the next soil described lies "turned out"; it produces very well for a few years when again cultivated.

About 50 per cent. of the county's area is chiefly a light sandy, mulatto-colored soil, but it is varied with more or less gravelly and clayey soils of brown, orange, red, and blackish colors from 8 to 10 and in places 24 inches deep. The subsoil is in all respects similar to that of the first-described soil, and is underlaid by sand and soft rock at 5 feet and less. Its growth is oaks, pine, hickory, dogwood, maple, walnut, beech, chestnut, gum, cypress, poplar, hornbeam, etc. One-tenth of this land is prairie. The soil is early, warm, well drained, and is easily tilled, except in wet weather. The usual height of the plant is from 3 to 4 feet, but it is most productive at 4 feet. The seed-cotton product per acre of fresh land is from 1,200 to 1,300 pounds; 1,425 pounds make a 475-pound bale of lint. Old land (unmanured) produces from 300 to 400 pounds of seed-cotton per acre. The remaining 20 per cent. of the county's area is distributed in the form of ridges, which have a growth of post, red, and black-jack oaks, pine, persimmon, sourwood, etc. The soil varies from fine sandy to gravelly and clay, and is whitish, brown, and orange-red in color, and from 3 to 6 inches deep. The subsoil is heavier, leachy, whitish or ash-colored, contains hard, rounded white and black gravel, and is underlaid by sand and gravel and some rock at 1 to 6 feet. Soil is early, warm, and well drained. Tillage is easy, except in wet weather. Cotton grows on this soil 2 to 3 feet high, but it is most productive at 3 feet. The seed-cotton product per acre is from 700 to 800 pounds on fresh land or 200 to 300 pounds on old (unmanured) land; 1,425 pounds from fresh or 1,545 from old land make a 475-pound bale of lint, that from old land being the shorter. About one-fifth of such originally cultivated land lies "turned out", but when again cultivated the yields are small and the soil does not long endure.

Sandy slopes are damaged to a serious extent by washing and gullying. Low and marshy valleys are improved by the washings; others are damaged to the extent of 25 per cent. of their value. To check the damage, felling timber into the gullies and hillside ditching are practiced. They succeed very well if done in time, before the gullies get too deep. Their depths sometimes equal 20 feet, the sides exhibiting white sand.

The generally prevalent subsoil is clay, and in wells it extends 15 to 20 feet below the surface, and at 30 feet water is found in white sand. In some parts of the county water is 80 to 90 feet below the surface.

Cotton is hauled from October to December by wagon to railroad towns at 50 cents per 100 pounds in summer and 75 cents in winter.

ATTALA.

Population : 19,988.—White, 11,653; colored, 8,335.

Area : 720 square miles.—Woodland, all. Short-leaf pine uplands, 645 square miles; red land, 75 square miles.

Tilled lands : 93,034 acres.—Area planted in cotton, 35,950 acres; in corn, 33,784 acres; in oats, 6,888 acres; in wheat, 1,400 acres.

Cotton production : 15,285 bales; average cotton product per acre, 0.43 bale, 612 pounds seed-cotton, or 204 pounds cotton lint.

Attala county forms part of the hilly, sometimes broken, oak and short-leaf pine uplands region, whose character is very little varied within the limits of the counties of Attala, Winston, Leake, and Neshoba. With the exception of the "red land" areas, these uplands are in general not naturally very productive, though mostly capable of good improvement by the use of fertilizers. The bottoms of the numerous streams, however, form the larger part of the area planted in cotton, which is about one-third of the entire area of tilled lands in the county. Hence the cotton product per acre is comparatively high. These bottom soils are mostly light and easily tilled, and are very productive when fresh, as is indicated by the large size of their timber trees. The latter are largely bottom oaks, such as white, chestnut-white or basket, overcup, and bottom scarlet oak (a), hickories, and sweet gum, with more or less of the "poplar" or tulip tree, which appears especially where the greensand and red-clay strata of the Tertiary are not far off. The same oak growth ascends more or less the hillsides, and even forms a large proportion of the hill growth where these strata are near the surface. The higher and sandier ridges have a pale-yellow, sandy loam soil, bearing a growth of post and scarlet oaks, with more or less of the short-leaf pine, according to quality.

The country lying between the Yockanookany and the Big Black, in the southwestern portion of the county, a less hilly than is the case farther east and north. A broad belt of good farming land, gently rolling, and timbered with oaks and hickory, with but little pine, slopes gently down to the Yockanookany. The latter is bordered by a hummock or second bottom averaging half a mile in width, having a gray, ashy, but quite productive soil. The bottom itself has a light sandy soil, largely timbered with beech. Its timber growth shows it to be productive, but overflows have thus far prevented its cultivation.

In the northern and eastern portions of the county especially there are isolated or more or less continuous and extensive tracts of "red lands" (see p. 29), formed by the approach to the surface of the orange-colored, greensand-bearing clays above referred to. It is prominent in the country lying between the two prongs of Poukta creek and south of the same to within a short distance of Kosciusko, and thence in a more or less continuous body northeastward, on the divide between the Poukta and the Yockanookany. The soil is popularly known as that of the "red hills", and occasionally appears suddenly, occupying a short ridge among the sandy hills, contrasting by the glaringly "red" color of its soil and the prevalence of the white and black oak, with hickory, over the pine and post oak. Such localities are usually marked by upland farms, producing as much as half a bale of cotton per acre when the land is fresh and well tilled, which, on account of its stiffness, is very essential to success. It produces good oats and fair corn, but is too heavy for potatoes.

The greensand manures occurring at many points in the northern part of the county will serve to maintain and improve the fertility of the uplands especially.

One-fifth of the area of Attala is reported as under tillage. Of this amount over one-third (38.6 per cent.) is given to cotton culture, and somewhat less to corn. The average product per acre is high, 0.43 bale, the best lands being given to this culture. The cotton acreage per square mile is 49.9.

Cotton shipments are made by rail via the branch road connecting Kosciusko with the New Orleans and Chicago railroad. Freight to New Orleans, $3 50 per bale.

---

a An apparently undescribed variety, (?) with the leaves and habit of Q. ▨▨▨▨▨ ▨ ▨ ▨▨ ▨▨▨▨ habitat; not uncommon in southern Mississippi.

ABSTRACT OF THE REPORT OF A. TUR, FRENCH CAMP.

About two-tenths of the county area consists of bottoms of creeks and smaller streams. These have the best soil, and this varies considerably, and is best where there is a good supply of lime. (a) It lies along the streams all over this and the adjoining counties. Its growth is gum, hickory, beech, cypress, poplar, holly, dogwood, etc. The soil is a blackish and black, fine sandy loam, which changes color at 2 or 3 inches below the surface. The subsoil is mostly clayey, the most of it pervious, and some impervious. It contains hard black and other gravel in places, and is underlaid by sand and sand-rock at 5 to 10 feet.

The chief crops of the region are cotton, corn, oats, and wheat, but the latter sometimes fails. The soil is early and warm when well-drained, and is rather difficult to till when too wet; but generally tillage is easy, and the soil is evidently best adapted to cotton, though good crops of corn and oats are also raised. More than half of all the cultivated lands here are planted in cotton. The height attained by the plant varies from 1 to 3 or 4 feet, but produces best at from 2 to 3 feet. The seed-cotton product per acre of fresh land varies from 800 to 1,000 pounds; 1,425 pounds make a 475-pound bale of good middling lint. After 6 to 8 years' cultivation (unmanured) the product varies from 400 to 800 pounds, and about 1,485 pounds then make a bale of lint about a grade below that of fresh land. Crab-grass is the most troublesome weed. About one-half of such land earliest cleared and cultivated now lies "turned out"; but its soil has been washed off by overflows, and when again cultivated it produces poorly.

The second quality of land occupies about one-half the area of the county, and is distributed all over this and adjoining counties. The greater part of its timber is pine, interspersed with black-jack and other oaks and some hickory. The soil consists of fine silt, and is gravelly in some places and black sandy in others. Its general surface color is whitish-gray, which changes at 1 to 2 inches below the surface. The subsoil is generally heavier, and varies from entirely sand in some spots to entirely clay—from leachy to impervious hard-pan. In places it contains hard, "black gravel," sometimes angular, underlaid by sand at 10 to 30 feet. The soil is early and warm when well-drained, is easily tilled, and is best adapted to corn and cotton. The cotton-plant grows from 18 to 24 inches high, and the seed-cotton product per acre of fresh land varies from 500 to 800 pounds, about 1,485 pounds making a 475-pound bale of low middling lint. After five years' cultivation the product varies from 300 to 500 pounds, 1,545 pounds then making a bale, the staple being equal to that of fresh land if picked when the bolls first open. Crab-grass is the farmer's great pest here. At least nine-tenths of that part of this land which was the earliest cleared and cultivated now lies "turned out", and when again cultivated it produces poorly.

About three-tenths of the county area consists of ridge tops, as widely distributed as the preceding soils, and bear a growth of black-jack and other oaks, scrubby pine, and an occasional switch hickory. The soil is a whitish-gray, fine sandy and gravelly loam, its surface color reaching no more than one-quarter or one-half an inch below. The subsoil is a grayish clay, largely mixed with whitish sand, often leachy, and sometimes impervious. It contains soft, white, angular pebbles, and is underlaid by sand and gravel and in places by rock, often at a few feet below the surface. The soil is early and warm when well-drained, is easily tilled, and is best adapted to oats and sweet potatoes. The cotton-plant attains a height of 10 to 12 inches on this soil. The seed-cotton product per acre of fresh land varies from 200 to 400 pounds, and about 1,485 pounds make a 475-pound bale of lint. The staple rates as that of the soil last described. After eight to ten years' cultivation the soil becomes unprofitable and is usually "turned out". None that was originally cultivated is now cultivated, as it is only suitable for sedge-grass and Lespedeza or Japan clover. Slopes wash and gully readily, and are in most cases seriously and often irreparably damaged. In some cases the valleys are badly injured by the washings, but where the latter is deposited in low, wet places it is beneficial. Horizontalizing and hillside ditching have been practiced, but have usually failed to check the damage, because the work was not properly attended to. The ditches were allowed to fill up after a few years, the heavy spring rains broke ever, and gullies resulted.

The growth of cotton here is often checked by cool nights in April and May, but it usually recovers from their effects in the warm months of June and July.

LEAKE.

Population : 13,146.—White, 8,104; colored, 5,042.
Area : 580 square miles.—Short-leaf pine and oak uplands, 570 square miles; table-lands, 10 square miles.
Tilled lands : 58,469 acres.—Area planted in cotton, 24,000 acres; in corn, 21,390 acres; in oats, 4,749 acres; in wheat, 294 acres.
Cotton production : 9,016 bales ; average cotton product per acre, 0.38 bale, 543 pounds seed-cotton, or 181 pounds cotton lint.

Leake county is traversed diagonally by Pearl river, with two chief tributaries on either side, viz: from the north, the Labutcha and the Yockanookany; from the south, the Standing and the Tuscalamite or Young Warrior.

The eastern portion, like the adjoining part of Neshoba, is mainly hilly and sometimes broken upland, timbered with short-leaf pine, intermixed with oaks, whose species, together with a greater or less admixture of hickory, indicate the varying fertility of the ridges, some of them possessing to a considerable extent the red-hills character, with walnut and "poplar" ascending into the hill lands. The western portion of the county is less hilly or only rolling, and west of the Yockanookany is undulating, passing gradually into the table lands country westward. The largest tracts of good farming land found in this western portion are on the eastward slopes toward the Yockanookany, gradually passing into the wide second bottom of that stream; and throughout the county the second bottom terraces of the larger streams, timbered with oaks, hickory, bottom pine, and usually with some beech, are largely occupied by settlements. Their soil is usually whitish and silty, underlaid by a pale-yellow loam subsoil, with more or less bog ore or "black gravel". (See analysis, p. 36.) The soils of the first bottoms are somewhat similar in aspect, but generally somewhat darker and heavier, and are often underlaid at from 18 to 24 inches by "black gravel", which in its turn rests on gray clay. The timber is Spanish, white, and water oaks, hickory, and pine. These bottom soils are designated as "hot" by the inhabitants, being very droughty and easily exhausted. Hence the bottoms of small streams are cultivated by preference. They frequently widen out into bodies of canebrake swamps, similar to those occurring in Neshoba and equally fertile when drained, so as to constitute an important factor in the production of the county.

a Referring probably to the bottoms passing through "red land" areas, lime being popularly, though erroneously, supposed to render soils heavy. In the present case the remark is, however, actually correct. (See analysis, p. 29.)

The tilled lands of Leake county constitute 15.8 per cent. of its area, and the cotton acreage slightly exceeds that devoted to corn, amounting to 41.4 acres per square mile. Owing to the predominant cultivation of bottom lands, the average cotton product per acre (0.38 bale) is equal to that of Madison and Pontotoc counties.

The communication of Leake county is partly with stations on the New Orleans and Chicago railroad and Kosciusko and partly to Meridian, on the Mobile and Ohio railroad. From these places it is shipped chiefly to New Orleans by rail or river at from $2 to $4 50 per bale.

ABSTRACTS OF THE REPORTS OF JOSEPH D. EADS, CARTHAGE, AND THOMAS C. SPENCER, LAUREL HILL.

About two-thirds of the county is upland, hilly, rolling, or level, bearing a growth of black-jack and other oaks, hickory, pines, etc. This upland soil is a fine sandy loam, reaching 6 inches below the surface. The subsoil is heavier, orange in color, contains soft red and rounded gravel, and is underlaid by gravel and sometimes by rock at 16 feet.

The chief crops of this region are cotton, corn, wheat, oats, and potatoes. The soil is early, warm, and well drained, is always easily tilled, and is best adapted to cotton, half of the cultivated area being planted with it.

The plant usually grows from 3 to 4 feet high, is most productive at 3½ feet, and inclines to run to weed on all the lands of this region in wet and sultry seasons, which may be restrained by topping late in July and plowing rapidly. The seed-cotton product per acre of fresh land is 1,000 pounds; 1,425 pounds make a 475-pound bale of good middling lint. After two years' cultivation (unmanured) the yield declines yearly, the ratio of seed to lint remaining the same, and the staple becomes shorter, but is otherwise considered superior to that from fresh land. At least one-third of such originally cultivated land lies "turned out", but if it rest long enough to have a considerable growth of scrub pine and briers it will produce as well as ever. The troublesome weeds are hog-weed, butter-weed, smart-weed, and Spanish needle. Slopes are seriously damaged by washing and gullying, and at least one-fifth of the valley lands are rendered worthless by the washings. Successful efforts have been made to check the damage by horizontalizing and hillside ditching.

The red or mulatto soil covers about one-sixth of the county. There is a strip of this about 2 miles wide running from east to west about 20 miles. The natural growth is post and black oaks, hickory, pine, walnut, and poplar. The soil is a gravelly, heavy clay, orange-red in color, and about 8 inches deep. The subsoil is heavier than the soil, is waxy, and is inclined to adhere tenaciously. It contains hard "black gravel", underlaid by sand and rock at 6 to 8 feet. The soil is difficult to work in wet seasons, but easy in dry; is early, warm, and well drained, and is apparently best adapted to wheat and cotton, about 50 per cent. of the land being devoted to the latter crop. The usual and most productive height of cotton is 4 feet. It inclines to run to weed in wet weather, and may be restrained by topping the plant and working the soil rapidly. The seed-cotton product on fresh land is 1,200 pounds, and 1,425 pounds make a 475-pound bale of good middling lint. The seed-cotton product after three years' cultivation is reduced to 1,000 pounds, and then 1,425 pounds of seed-cotton make a 475-pound bale of lint, which rates favorably with that from fresh land. The troublesome weeds are the same as on the black, sandy land; crab-grass is, however, worse on this land. About one-third such land originally cultivated now lies "turned out", is growing up in pines, and produces well when again brought under cultivation if it is not too badly washed or gullied. This soil does not wash or gully as badly on the slopes as the black sandy soil; but little damage has been done, and the valleys are injured some (about one-eighth their value) by the washings. Horizontal ditching has been tried with success to remedy damages.

About one-sixth of the county area consists of creek bottoms, and bears a growth of many kinds of oak, pine, hickory, maple, sweet gum, cypress, etc. The soil is a black or blackish loam, has much vegetable matter, and averages 8 inches in thickness. The subsoil is heavier and more or less impervious. The soil is early, very easily cultivated except when too wet, is best adapted to cotton, corn, oats, and wheat, and about two-thirds of its cultivated area is planted with cotton. The plant attains a height of from 3 to 5 feet, and yields from 500 to 1,000 pounds of seed-cotton per acre. Crab-grass is a most troublesome weed. Very little of such land lies "turned out," and when again cultivated produces very well for a few years, especially if overgrown by briers during the rest.

There are in the county two other kinds of land: low, flat land of Pearl river bottom and reed-brake land. These are not adapted to raising cotton. The first occurs along the Pearl river and its larger tributaries, and bears large oaks, pine, sweet gum, and occasionally poplar, beech, etc. The soil is a fine black or blackish sandy loam, 12 to 24 inches deep. The leachy subsoil is similar, except in color, and the soil, in consequence, is "hot" in character. The soil is early, warm, well drained, easily tilled at any time, and is best adapted to those crops that mature early in the season, as peace, early corn, and the small cereals.

The reed-brake land includes about one-tenth of the cultivated soil of the county. It occurs about the heads of small streams, and bears a growth of green-bay, holly, tupelo gum, briers, and reeds. The soil is a putty-like black loam, 4 to 6 feet thick, has a small proportion of coarse sand, and is underlaid by sand and gravel.

Tillage is easy in dry but difficult in wet seasons. The soil is late and in need of artificial drainage. It is best adapted to corn and oats, producing of either from 50 to 100 bushels per acre. It costs from $25 to $30 per acre to drain such land, after which, when in cultivation, it is worth from $50 to $100 per acre.

NESHOBA.

Population: 8,741.—White, 6,555; colored, 2,186.
Area: 580 square miles.—Woodland, all. Short-leaf pine and oak uplands, all.
Tilled lands: 45,979 acres.—Area planted in cotton, 14,021 acres; in corn, 16,752 acres; in oats, 3,512 acres; in wheat, 223 acres.
Cotton production: 4,477 bales; average cotton product per acre, 0.32 bale, 456 pounds seed-cotton, or 152 pounds cotton lint.

Neshoba county is drained almost wholly by Pearl river (which traverses its northern portion) and its tributaries, the extreme heads of the Chickasawhay reaching into its southeastern corner. In the western portion of the county the surface is quite broken, the ridges being sometimes steep and rocky and of considerable elevation, so that cultivation is mainly restricted to the bottoms, except where tracts of the red-clay soil occur. Apart from these, the soil is chiefly of the pale-yellow, sandy loam character so prevalent in Winston and Leake. The timber is short-leaf pine, mixed with oaks, prevalently the black-jack and post, with more or less of scarlet and Spanish oaks where the soil improves. The surface of the eastern portion of the county is less hilly, sometimes only undulating, and the black-jack and barren scrub oak prevail largely on the uplands, which are but little cultivated. The bottom of Pearl river is about 1½ miles wide near the western line, is liable to overflow, and is very boggy during the rainy seasons, rendering the roads impassable. While the main bottom is therefore but little cultivated, there are often found in the bottoms of small tributary creeks on both sides dense swamps, timbered prevalently with sour gum and bay, some maple and sweet gum, with a dense undergrowth of cane. These swamps, which are quite numerous, have a very black soil when wet, but light gray when dry, which is a sort of swamp muck, sometimes 4 to 5 feet thick. When drained they are the most fertile, durable, and the best farming spots in the whole country. These glades are said to produce as much as 80 bushels of corn per acre. Cotton does not do so well, being apt to run to weed.

One-eighth of the area of Neshoba county is reported to be under tillage, and corn culture predominates somewhat over cotton, which occupies 36 per cent. of the tilled lands. The average cotton product per acre (0.32 bale) is considerably below that of Winston and Leake counties.

Communication is divided between the three railroads east, south, and west, whose nearest points are about equidistant—"a three days' haul."

KEMPER.

Population : 15,719.—White, 7,100; colored, 8,619.

Area : 750 square miles.—Woodland, 720 square miles; short-leaf pine and oak uplands, 520 square miles; long-leaf pine hills, 90 square miles; prairie belt, 80 square miles; flatwoods, 60 square miles.

Tilled lands : 78,316 acres.—Area planted in cotton, 28,269 acres; in corn, 28,246 acres; in oats, 3,706 acres; in wheat, 56 acres.

Cotton production : 8,426 bales; average cotton product per acre, 0.30 bale, 429 pounds seed-cotton, or 143 pounds cotton lint.

· Fully five-sevenths of the area of Kemper county is occupied by sandy uplands, timbered with short-leaf pine and oaks. The southeast corner embraces a few townships of long-leaf pine woods, which here attain their most northern point in the state. In the northeast corner lies the most fertile portion of the county, the extreme southern point of the prairie belt in the state, bordered on the west, as usual, by the flatwoods belt, here only about 3 miles wide. The ridge skirting the flatwoods on the west forms the divide between the waters of the Noxubee river (Scooba creek) and Turkey creek, one of the chief tributaries of the Sucarnochee, which drains the rest of the county. The flatwoods being narrow, and therefore considerably modified by the adjacent regions, are not quite so extreme in character as farther north. On the east they pass insensibly into the level "prairie" country on Wahalack creek; but east of that stream the country rises into a ridge of white prairie limestone, about 200 feet above the drainage, forming a kind of prairie plateau, which slopes off gently toward the Alabama line. The true black prairie is found only in small bodies on this plateau and in the valleys of the streams, where the limestone approaches the surface. The general level land of the region is timbered with large post and Spanish oaks and hickory, and has a loam soil, with a yellow loam subsoil—a fair soil for cereals. On the higher ridges there lies a heavy red clay soil, usually underlaid by limestone at no great depth, which produces small but heavily bolled cotton and good wheat. Timber, sturdy black-jack and post oaks. The black prairie soil is found in patches and bands at lower levels; it is not very heavy, and produces good corn, but is apt to rust cotton where not intermingled with the red soil. That lying near the streams and in the level region west of Wahalack creek is less liable to rust cotton, and is very productive.

The flatwoods soil is said to produce well here in favorable seasons. Of the hilly pine and oak uplands a portion (as on the ridge on which De Kalb, the county-seat, is located) is very sandy, but the soil is not unproductive, being very deep, and sometimes oak and hickory prevail, to the exclusion of the pines. Cultivation is, however, mostly confined to the numerous creek bottoms. These have very sandy soils in the southern part of the county, while the ridges, on the contrary, become more clayey, and show, by their large oak and pine timber, a better promise for the farmer than the sandy ones timbered with black-jack and post oak, with which they are interspersed.

The tilled lands of Kemper county constitute 16.3 per cent. of the total area. Of these lands 36.1 per cent. is given to cotton culture and an equal area to corn. The average cotton acreage is 37.7, and the average product per acre 0.30 bale, rather remarkably low.

Cotton is hauled from the interior, as well as from the prairie country, to stations on the Mobile and Ohio railroad, which traverses the eastern half of the county from north to south. Freight to Mobile is $3 25 per bale from Scooba, one of the chief shipping points.

ABSTRACT OF THE REPORT OF JOHN A. MINNIECE, SCOOBA.

Heavy yellow clay soil predominates, covering most of this township, and post-oak ridges and black prairie slopes (nearly level) are frequent. The lowlands consist of creek bottoms, having a productive soil, which averages 250 pounds of cotton lint per acre, but is not entirely above overflow. The bald prairie lying on the east is used mostly for corn; it is also well adapted to oak. The flatwoods lie on the west. Cotton, corn, and oats are the chief crops raised here. About half of all the cultivated lands are planted with cotton. The average product per acre of fresh land is 1,000 pounds of seed-cotton, and from 1,545 to 1,665 pounds make a 475-pound bale of middling lint. After five years' cultivation (unmanured) the average product is 600 pounds. Crab-grass is the most troublesome weed. The natural growth is post and red oaks on the uplands, and gum, white oak, hickory, and ash on the bottoms.

The soils vary in depth from 3 to 36 inches, and are mostly underlaid by yellow clay, under which, at 5 to 10 feet, is the impervious rotten limestone. The soil is late, cold, and ill-drained, but is easily tilled, except when wet. The cotton-plant grows about 3 feet high on the uplands and 4 feet on the lowlands. In wet, warm weather it inclines to run to weed, for which the correspondent knows no remedy that would not injure the crop. More than one-half the upland originally cultivated now lies "turned out", and, where it has not been too badly washed, if plowed in the fall produces very well when again cultivated. Slopes are seriously damaged by washing and gullying, and when the uplands are sandy the lowlands are much damaged. Horizontalizing and hillside ditching are practiced to some extent, and when properly done they successfully check the damage. The climate is favorable to cotton production.

The rich bottom lands are most productive, and average half a bale of 500 pounds of lint per acre. The uplands are thin and worn, and with no fertilizers produce about 600 pounds of seed-cotton.

LAUDERDALE.
(See "Long-leaf pine region".)

NEWTON.

Population: 13,436.—White, 8,428 ; colored, 5,008.

Area: 580 square miles.—Short-leaf pine and oak uplands, 225 square miles; long-leaf pine hills, 300 square miles; central prairie, 55 square miles.

Tilled lands: 58,019 acres.—Area planted in cotton, 19,589 acres; in corn, 20,638 acres; in oats, 6,716 acres; in wheat, 127 acres.

Cotton production: 6,341 bales; average cotton product per acre, 0.32 bale, 456 pounds seed-cotton, or 152 pounds cotton lint.

Newton county is drained chiefly by Chunky creek (the west fork of the Chickasawhay river) and its numerous tributaries, the bottoms of which constitute the bulk of the farming lands.

The uplands are mainly hilly, sometimes broken. In the southern part of the county the long-leaf pine forms the predominant timber, more or less mixed with oaks, according to the quality of the soil. In the northern portion the short-leaf pine, with oaks, prevails. In both sections there occur occasionally hills and ridges of the red-land character (see page 29), where the pine is subordinate or absent, and which give rise to upland farms of fair productiveness. Aside from these, but little cotton is grown in the sandy pine uplands. In the southwestern corner of the county, on the headwaters of Tallahala creek (a tributary of the Leaf river), the uplands have more or less the character of the "Central prairie region" (see regional description, page 50), the ridges being less abrupt, and in their lower portion sometimes showing the heavy clay soils, popularly known as "hog-wallow" or post-oak prairie. Occasionally, in the deeper bottoms, the soils approximate to the black-prairie character, which is more abundantly developed in the adjacent part of Jasper county.

The tilled lands amount to 15.6 per cent. of the area, the cotton acreage being somewhat below that given to corn, and amounting to 33.8 acres per square mile. The average cotton product per acre (0.32 bale) is equal to that of Clay and Neshoba counties.

The Vicksburg and Meridian railroad traverses the southern portion of the county, and communication is mainly with stations on that road, from which cotton is shipped either to New Orleans or Mobile.

SCOTT.
(See "Central prairie region".)

RANKIN.
(See "Central prairie region".)

SIMPSON.
(See "Long-leaf pine region".)

HINDS.
(See "Central prairie region".)

CLAIBORNE.
(See "Cane-hills region".)

JEFFERSON.
(See "Cane-hills region".)

FRANKLIN.
(See "Long-leaf pine region".)

ADAMS.
(See "Cane-hills region".)

WILKINSON.
(See "Cane hills region".)

BROWN-LOAM TABLE-LANDS.

(The region embraces the following counties and parts of counties: Benton, Marshall, De Soto, Tate, Panola, La Fayette, Yalobusha, Tallahatchie,* Grenada, Montgomery,* Carroll, Holmes, Yazoo,* and Madison.*)

BENTON.

Population: .11,023.—White, 5,777; colored, 5,246.

Area: 360 square miles.—Woodland, all. Short-leaf pine and oak uplands, 125 square miles; brown loam table-lands, 145 square miles; flatwoods, 20 square miles; sandy oak uplands, 70 square miles.

Tilled lands: 55,501 acres.—Area planted in cotton, 22,401 acres; in corn, 22,877 acres; in oats, 1,735 acres; in wheat, 1,285 acres.

Cotton production: 8,123 bales; average cotton product per acre, 0.36 bale, 513 pounds seed-cotton, or 171 pounds cotton lint.

The northern part of Benton county (around and north of Ashland, the county-seat) is a gently undulating plateau region of the "table-lands" character (see regional description, p. 31), timbered with a fine growth of upland oaks (black, Spanish, sturdy post, and black-jack) and hickory, naturally very productive, and quite thickly settled. This portion of the county is drained by Wolf river and its tributaries, and its features remain the same to the southward until the headwaters of Tippah creek are reached, which in its turn (with Ocklimita creek, its largest tributary) drains the southern portion. Here we find, first, a transition zone of more or less hilly and sandy loam uplands, timbered with oaks and hickory, occupying the country between the dividing ridge and Tippah creek, and continuing southwestward into Marshall and La Fayette counties (see description of "Sandy oak uplands", p. 30). Here the creek bottoms and lower slopes of the ridges are chiefly cultivated. Beyond Tippah creek and southward to the county-line the country is hilly and sandy, and outside of the bottoms is timbered with short-leaf pine and oaks, with more or less hickory on the hillsides, while the bottoms (e. g., that of the Ocklimita near Hickory flat) are quite extensive and very productive and constitute the bulk of the land under cultivation. In the southeastern corner of the county a portion of the post-oak flatwoods reaches in from the main body in western Tippah.

It is doubtless the comparative inferiority of the lands in the southern part of the county that renders the average product per acre of Benton the lowest among the table-land counties (0.36 bale), though still above the average of the prairie counties, of which only three rank above it.

The tilled lands of Benton county constitute 24.1 per cent. of the total area. Of these lands nearly 41 per cent. are given to cotton, and a slightly greater area to corn. The cotton acreage per square mile is 62.2.

Cotton shipments are mostly made by the New Orleans and Chicago and Memphis and Charleston railroads to Memphis, either by the producers or mostly by merchants who buy the cotton from them. Freight from Lamar station to Memphis is about $1 75 per bale.

ABSTRACT OF THE REPORT OF H. T. LIPFORD, ASHLAND.

All the lands of this county produce cotton well. The bottoms do not usually dry early enough to admit of early planting, but when early planted they yield as well as uplands. Cotton on the bottoms, being usually planted late, opens late and not well.

The lowlands consist of the first and second bottoms of Wolf and Tippah rivers. About one-third of the county uplands are level, and the remainder hilly.

The chief soil is a *dark loam*, extending throughout the county and occupying about half its area. It becomes lighter and less productive in the southern part. Its natural growth is black-jack and other oaks and hickory. The soil varies from a fine sandy to a clayey loam, black, blackish, or lighter colored, and averages 6 inches thick; in some parts 2 inches. The heavier subsoil is generally a red or lighter colored clay, sometimes quite sandy. It generally absorbs much water, contains pebbles about upland ponds, and is underlaid by sand at 10 to 15 feet. The chief crops of this region are cotton, corn, potatoes, sorghum, wheat, oats, and rye. The soil is early when well drained, is always easily tilled, is best adapted to cotton and corn, and about two-thirds of its cultivated area is planted with cotton, but this proportion is diminishing. Potatoes do well; wheat tolerably. The cotton-plant grows from 2 to 4 feet high, but is most productive at 3 feet. It inclines to run to weed in wet weather, but this depends much upon the system of cultivation. As a remedy the crop should be cultivated judiciously. Some succeed by topping. The seed-cotton product per acre of fresh land varies from 1,000 to 9,000 pounds, 1,545 pounds making a 475-pound bale of lint. The yields gradually decline after five years' cultivation (unmanured), but the ratio of seed to lint and the quality of the staple remain as on fresh land, and may be improved by manuring. Nearly one-third of such originally cultivated land lies "turned out"; but when again cultivated it produces very well if it has soil enough left to produce sedge-grass. The most troublesome weeds are smart-weed and crab-grass. The latter is its great enemy, growing so rapidly as to ruin it even when the crop has the advantage of one working.

About a sixth or an eighth of the county is a *black, fine, sandy loam,* 6 to 8 inches thick. It generally occurs on slopes facing southward, and makes gradual transitions into other varieties. The subsoil is generally a red clay, as under the first described soil, but in some parts it is only sand. It contains pebbles, and is underlaid by sand at 8 to 10 feet. The soil is early, well-drained, always easily tilled, and is best adapted to cotton and potatoes. Two-thirds of the cultivated area is devoted to cotton. The seed-cotton product per acre varies from 800 to 2,000 pounds. It is hard to restore such land to fertility when once exhausted. Smart-weed is most troublesome. The sand washings are hard to control, and do great damage.

Another sixth or eighth of the county area consists of *bottoms of creeks and rivers.* Its growth is beech, white oak, maple, and walnut. The soil is a clayey loam, 2 to 8 inches thick, varying in color from gray to black. The heavier subsoil is generally a grayish clay, more or less leachy, containing soft, white, and frequently other pebbles, and is underlaid by clay to an unknown depth. Tillage is easy, except when the soil is too wet. The soil is late, cold, ill-drained, and best adapted to corn, and if well-drained to cotton. Cotton occupies about half the cultivated area. The plant grows from 3 to 5 feet high, inclines to run to weed under all circumstances, and may be restrained by judicious cultivation, not more than is absolutely necessary. The product per acre of fresh land varies from 600 to 1,600 pounds of seed-cotton, 1,665 pounds making a 475-pound bale of lint. After five years' cultivation yields generally decline. About one-tenth of such originally cultivated land lies "turned out"; but a sufficiently long rest restores fertility. Smart-weed is most troublesome, and the washings of the slopes have done immense damage to many valleys. Many partially successful efforts have been made to check the damage by horizontalizing and hillside ditching.

Cotton is sold to merchants who ship during picking season to Memphis; freight per bale from Lamar, $1 75.

MARSHALL.

Population: 29,330.—White, 10,992; colored, 18,338.

Area: 720 square miles.—Woodland, all. Short-leaf pine and oak uplands, 20 square miles; brown-loam table-lands, 590 square miles; sandy oak uplands, 110 square miles.

. *Tilled lands:* 161,001 acres.—Area planted in cotton, 67,411 acres; in corn, 50,140 acres; in oats, 3,130 acres; in wheat, 3,094 acres.

Cotton production: 26,441 bales; average cotton product per acre, 0.39 bale, 555 pounds seed-cotton, or 185 pounds cotton lint.

By far the greater portion of Marshall county lies within the belt of "table-lands" with a brown-loam subsoil which extends through western Tennessee, gradually narrowing as far south as Baton Rouge, Louisiana (see p. 31). These lands are most characteristically developed in the northern part of the county, on the headwaters of Coldwater river, and on the northern confluents of Pigeon Roost creek. Here the country is gently undulating, and is scarcely more uneven than in the prairie country of eastern Mississippi, except where it breaks off into creek bottoms. It is, however (or rather was), uniformly, but somewhat sparsely, timbered with oaks and hickory. Among the former the black, Spanish, and black-jack oaks, with some post oak, predominate, the hickory being most abundant on the lower slopes, and hence these slopes are often designated as "hickory hummocks". On the southern branches of Pigeon Roost creek, and especially on the creeks directly tributary to the Tallahatchie river, the country is more undulating, somewhat abruptly so on the edge of the Tallahatchie bottom, and sandier ridges are more or less interspersed with the table-lands, forming a gradual transition to the "Sandy oak uplands" of La Fayette county.

The bottoms of the larger streams, and especially of the Tallahatchie, are not extensively cultivated, though very fertile, on account of their liability to overflows. In the smaller bottoms much cotton is grown, but they, as well as the adjacent uplands, are liable to grievous damage from the cutting of gullies into the hillsides, undercutting the subsoil, and causing it, with the underlying sand, to be washed into the valleys, in some of which the original flood-plain is now covered with from 15 to 20 feet of sand, in which only willows, briers, and Bermuda grass find a congenial existence.

Prior to its subdivision in the formation of Benton and Tate counties, Marshall was considered (next to Hinds) the banner upland county for cotton production, the crop being less liable to failure from extreme seasons than in the competing counties of the prairie region. As now circumscribed, it stands foremost in cotton acreage, Hinds, Noxubee, and Monroe ranking above it in this respect, while in total production it stands third to Hinds and De Soto among the upland counties, while in product per acre it ranks nearly even with the highest of the prairie counties. Its cotton area is still over one-fourth greater than that planted in corn.

Cotton is shipped during the picking season by rail from Holly Springs and other stations of the New Orleans and Chicago railroad at from $2 to $3 per bale to Memphis, $3 75 to New Orleans, or at from $5 to $7 per bale to eastern cities.

ABSTRACT OF THE REPORTS OF A. J. WITHERS AND F. B. SHUFORD, HOLLY SPRINGS.

The chief crops are cotton, corn, oats, wheat, sweet and Irish potatoes, and pease. The certainty of a cotton yield, and of realizing reasonable returns for the same, and the cheaper transportation of it than other crops that might be raised, cause cotton to keep its place as the exclusive export product. Fully one-half of all the arable land of the county is planted with cotton, although it is equally well adapted to all of the chief crops mentioned.

The river bottoms are usually too wet, and therefore but little cultivated. The level and rolling uplands, valleys, and creek bottoms are cultivated chiefly. They occupy about three-fourths of the county area, and bear a natural growth of post, red, white, and black-jack oaks and hickory, generally on ridges, and poplar, ash, hickory, and gum in the valleys. The soil presents much variation of constitution and color, but differs little in productiveness, and is 3 to 12 inches deep. The subsoil is most generally a sticky, red clay, often a mahogany-colored, impervious hard-pan, containing iron. It is underlaid by sand, gravel, and flat rock at 2 to 6 feet. Tillage is easy, and the soil early, warm, and generally well drained. The usual and most productive height attained by the cotton plant is 3 feet. On fresh land, and in wet seasons, it inclines to run to weed. Good and shallow cultivation is the remedy. The seed-cotton product per acre of fresh land varies from 800 to 1,800 pounds, according to soil and season. The higher lands are more certain, while the valleys give the greater yields. About 1,650 pounds make a 475-pound bale of good lint. After five years' cultivation (unmanured) the yields perceptibly decline, and the staple is coarser and shorter. About 1,720 pounds then make a bale. Crab-grass and smart-weed, iron and hog-weed, cocklebur and foxtail, and crow-foot and tickle-grass are troublesome. One-fourth of the originally-cultivated land is now "turned out". It is improved 10 per cent. by rest when not washed, gullied, or covered with sand deposits. Nearly everywhere slopes are seriously damaged by washings and gullying, and the lowlands (on larger streams especially) are also badly injured by the washings. Many valleys are now submerged by sand and clay and abandoned to willows and briers. To save the soils, horizontalizing and hillside ditching have been practiced. The former has been in some cases satisfactorily successful, but both methods have, in the majority of cases, failed, and so have other means.

Cotton is shipped during the picking season, by rail, from $2 to $3 per bale to Memphis, or $3 75 to New Orleans, and to eastern cities at from $5 to $7 per bale.

DE SOTO.

Population: 22,924.—White, 7,581; colored, 15,343.

Area: 460 square miles.—Mississippi bottom, 65 square miles; cane hills, 45 square miles; brown-loam table-lands, 350 square miles; all woodland.

Tilled lands: 118,342 acres.—Area planted in cotton, 60,488 acres; in corn, 37,452 acres; in oats, 1,688 acres; in wheat, 1,236 acres.

Cotton production : 28,469 bales; average cotton product per acre, 0.47 bale, 660 pounds seed-cotton, or 223 pounds cotton lint.

De Soto county, occupying the northwestern corner of the state, and fronting on the Mississippi river for about 9 miles, has about one-seventh of its area in the bottom of the latter river, the rest being brown-loam "table-lands" of the best quality, with a belt of "bluff" lands, several miles in width, skirting the bottom.

The Mississippi state line strikes Horn lake nearly at its vertex, leaving about half of it in Tennessee. Horn Lake pass issues from the lake not far below the state line and flows near the foot of the bluff, joining Coldwater river, which forms the southern line of the county, near the southwestern corner. The upland drainage is divided between the tributaries of Coldwater river and Horn lake.

The upland soils of De Soto are, on the whole, somewhat heavier than those of Marshall, which they otherwise resemble in "lay" and in timber, especially in the eastern portion. In the western a good deal of sweet gum, tulip tree or "poplar", and walnut commingles with the oak and hickory, increasing as the bluff is approached. The uplands generally slope off gently into the creek bottoms, forming extensive second bottoms or "hummocks", which are highly esteemed both for productiveness and the quality of the staple grown on them.

De Soto county is quite thickly settled, standing third (to Tate and Holmes) in the state as to the percentage of its total area under tillage (40 per cent.), and, notwithstanding its smaller area, third (to Hinds and Madison) among the upland counties for total production. In product per acre it stands even with its neighboring county, Tate (0.47 bale), a fact showing that the average product is not materially influenced by that of the lowland plantations on Horn lake and pass, however excellent. The above figure is next to the highest among the upland counties (Calhoun showing 0.50, or half a bale per acre, the cotton being there, however, chiefly grown on bottom lands). De Soto stands second only to Noxubee in the percentage of the tilled area occupied by cotton (51 per cent.), and the area in corn is only three-fifths of the latter. It is thus evident that the growing of home supplies is little practiced, the nearness to the Memphis market presenting a great temptation to buy supplies. The Mississippi and Tennessee railroad traverses the county centrally from north to south, and cotton is shipped, as ginned, to Memphis at the rate of $1 40 per bale, and thence from 75 cents to $1 to New Orleans.

ABSTRACT OF THE REPORT OF T. C. DOCKERY, LOVE STATION.

The county has every variety of soil, chief among which are alluvium of Mississippi bottom, the loams along creeks and smaller streams (which produces our best staple, and often a 500-pound bale per acre), and the red and yellow stiff clay soils of the uplands. The latter class occupies three-fifths of the county area, extending 16 miles east and 18 miles west; its chief growth is oak, hickory, and poplar. The surface color, which is gray, reaches 3 inches below to yellow clay, which extends 5 feet downward, then becoming a shade lighter. About 20 feet below the surface sand, hard pan, and pipe-clay in strata are encountered. About one-tenth of this kind of soil originally cultivated now lies "turned out". When again cultivated it produces finely for two or three years. Slopes wash and gully readily, and are seriously damaged in this way. The washings also injure the valley lands. To check the damage, horizontalizing and hillside ditching are practiced, and when such work is well done the results are entirely satisfactory.

TATE.

Population : 18,721.—White, 9,094; colored, 9,627.

Area : 390 square miles.—Woodland, all. Mississippi bottom, 15 square miles; cane hills, 35 square miles; brown-loam table-land, 340 square miles.

Tilled lands : 124,980 acres.—Area planted in cotton, 48,245 acres; in corn, 33,321 acres; in oats, 1,763 acres; in wheat, 1,100 acres.

Cotton production : 22,653 bales; average cotton product per acre, 0.47 bale, 669 pounds seed-cotton, or 223 pounds cotton lint.

The surface and agricultural features of Tate county are substantially the same as those above given for De Soto: undulating table-lands sparsely timbered, with oaks and hickory, and with a deep subsoil of brown loam of high fertility, and hence more largely under cultivation than the uplands of any other county in the state, viz, one-half of the total area, Holmes standing next and De Soto third. The county is drained by the tributaries of Coldwater river (which forms part of its northern boundary), chief of which are Bear Tail, Hickahala, and Arkabutla, their fertile first and second bottoms contributing largely to the cultivated area and total production.

As in De Soto and Panola, the soil and subsoil within a few miles of the edge of the bluff are similar to those prevailing near Memphis, being formed of the calcareous silt of the bluff or loess formation, and bearing a corresponding timber growth, among which sweet gum, tulip tree, and others indicative of a calcareous soil, are prominent.

One-half of the county area is actually under tillage, the county standing first in the state in this respect, and of these lands 38.6 per cent. is given to cotton. Tate county stands third (to Lowndes and De Soto) in the proportion of its area cultivated in cotton, viz, 123.7 acres per square mile, corn occupying only about two-thirds as much.

In view of the nearly equal division of the population between the white and colored races the high and predominant production of cotton is remarkable.

Cotton shipments are made chiefly to Memphis by rail, or direct to New Orleans via Granada.

PANOLA.

Population : 28,352.—White, 9,521; colored, 18,831.

Area : 680 square miles.—Woodland, all; Mississippi bottom, 140 square miles; cane hills, 85 square miles; brown-loam table-land, 455 square miles.

Tilled lands : 148,445 acres.—Area planted in cotton, 67,060 acres; in corn, 43,091 acres; in oats, 2,119 acres; in wheat, 1,603 acres.

Cotton production : 30,055 bales; average cotton product per acre, 0.45 bale, 642 pounds seed-cotton, or 214 pounds cotton lint.

The greater portion of Panola county is of the "table-land" character (see p. 32), modified in the southeastern portion especially by more or less sandy ridges extending in from the neighboring portion of La Fayette county. The county is timbered, as in Marshall, with oaks and hickory, to which, as the edge of the bottom or "bluff" is approached, the sweet gum, ash, and the tulip tree ("poplar") are more and more frequently added, the former especially sometimes becoming predominant. Within from 1 to 3 miles of the bluff the subsoil and underlying material are largely of the character of the calcareous silt or "loess" which prevails more extensively in the river counties south of Vicksburg as well as in Tennessee, the surface being somewhat broken, but the soil very productive. Farther inland gravel beds underlie to a considerable extent and at varying depths, sometimes contributing largely to the soil and subsoil.

The extreme western portion of the county lies within the Yazoo bottom plains (here designated as the Cold-water and Tallahatchie bottoms), which form a deep embayment into the uplands at the entrance of the Tallahatchie river. The latter traverses the northern part of the county from northeast to southwest. Though liable to overflow, and apparently not quite as productive as the more southerly portions of the great plains, these bottoms are quite as extensively under cultivation; but as their product has not been segregated in the returns from these of the uplands its influence upon the total production and products per acre in the county cannot be determined. The product per acre of the uplands is evidently somewhat below that of Tate, though probably higher than that of Marshall. As in the last-named county, the cotton acreage exceeds considerably that planted in corn, and is 44 per cent. of the total of tilled lands.

Panola stands second among the upland counties in total production, and sixth in cotton acreage per square mile. Outside of the bottoms the county is well settled, especially along the Mississippi and Tennessee railroad (from Memphis to Grenada), which traverses the county from north to south.

Cotton shipments are made on this road, from October to July, to Memphis at $3.75, or to New Orleans at $4, per bale.

There are three kinds of soil cultivated in cotton: the shelly and gravelly loam of the bottoms, the "buckshot" and crawfishy land, and the upland. The first includes about one-fourth of the river and creek bottoms of the county, and bears a natural growth of oak, poplar, ash, gum, hickory, cypress, and maple. The soil is about 2 feet thick, is generally dark colored, and is underlaid by rock and gravel at 3 to 4 feet. The chief crops of this region are cotton and corn; some wheat, oats, potatoes, onions, fruits, etc., are also raised. The soil is easily tilled, except when too wet. It is best adapted to cotton and corn, and about three-fourths of the cultivated part is planted with cotton. The plant grows from 3 to 6 feet high, but is most productive at 4 feet. It inclines to run to weed on very rich, fresh land in wet seasons, which is restrained by topping and shallow cultivation. The seed-cotton product per acre of fresh land varies from 1,000 to 1,500 pounds; 1,780 pounds make a 475-pound bale of middling lint. After four years' cultivation the product is no less in good seasons. The most troublesome weeds are smart-weed and crab-grass. Very little of the land lies turned out. The "buckshot" and crawfishy land occupies in some localities about half the acreage, and occurs in bodies of one to several miles in extent along the rivers. The soil is a marshy, crawfishy, and sandy loam, containing fine sand, varying in color from gray to yellow, brown, blackish, and black, and is 2 feet deep. The subsoil, often lighter, contains hard, rounded "black gravel", sometimes pebbles as large as eggs and is underlaid by sand, gravel, and rock at 3 to 4 feet. The soil is early, warm, and well drained, and when not too wet is easily tilled. About three-fourths of its cultivated area is planted with cotton. The plant often grows from 7 to 8 feet high, but is most productive at 3 to 4 feet. Topping and late cultivation restrain it from growing as high as it otherwise would in wet seasons. The seed-cotton product per acre of fresh land varies from 800 to 1,200 pounds, and after several years from 1,000 to 1,500 pounds, 1,780 pounds making a 475-pound bale of middling lint. Smart-weed is most troublesome.

The upland soil occupies about half the county area, and bears a natural growth of oak, poplar, sweet gum, ash, and hickory. The soil is a coarse, sandy, and gravelly loam, of buff, yellow, brown, and mahogany colors, is 12 inches deep, and is underlaid by sand and gravel at 3 feet. The soil is early, easily tilled, and three-fourths of its cultivated area is planted with cotton. The usual and most productive height of the plant is 3 to 4 feet. The seed-cotton product per acre of fresh land varies from 800 to 1,000 pounds, and the ratio of lint to lint and quality of staple (land fresh or old) are the same as on other lands described. The most troublesome weeds of this region are smart-weed and crab-grass. About 2,500 acres lie "turned out" in this county, which, when again cultivated, produces as well as when freshly cleared. Slopes wash and gully readily, but the extent of damage is not serious; the valleys are also to a slight extent injured by the washings. Horizontalizing and hillside ditching have been successfully practiced in checking the damage. When the seasons are too wet cotton runs to weed, producing large stalks and small bolls, which open late.

Cotton shipments are made, from October to July, to Memphis at $3 75, or to New Orleans at $4 per bale.

LA FAYETTE.

Population: 21,671.—White, 11,385; colored, 10,286.
Area: 720 square miles.—Short-leaf pine and oak uplands, 280 square miles; brown-loam table-lands, 115 square miles; sandy oak uplands, 325 square miles; all woodland.
Tilled lands: 86,493 acres.—Area planted in cotton, 35,309 acres; in corn, 35,809 acres; in oats, 4,091 acres; in wheat, 2,052 acres.
Cotton production: 15,214 bales; average cotton product per acre, 0.43 bale, 612 pounds seed-cotton, or 204 pounds cotton lint.

La Fayette county exhibits quite characteristically the several features of the yellow-loam uplands. It is traversed diagonally from northeast to southwest by the broad dividing ridge between the streams flowing directly into the Tallahatchie river and those tributary to the Yockeney-Patafa. In its higher portions this ridge is prevalently sandy, and is timbered with black-jack oak of the "sprangling" type, especially where the brown sandstone of the stratified drift caps the summits, and the soil is unproductive (see analysis, p. 31, No. 148); while in the lower and broader portions the sand is covered by the more or less fertile varieties of the yellow or brown loam to the depth of 3 to 4 feet. Southeast of the main divide and of the line running from the mouth of Pouskous creek up to the head of Yellow Leaf creek, and down that creek to its mouth, the short-leaf pine and post oak prevail mainly on

312

the ridges, with black and Spanish oaks and hickory in the valleys; and as we progress eastward the soil gradually becomes heavier and assumes the character of the "flatwoods hills". A large amount of excellent creek-bottom land, originally heavily timbered, is cultivated in cotton. The fertile bottom of the Yockeney is unfortunately subject to almost annual overflows.

Northwest of the main divide the ridges gradually flatten down, the sandy knolls become more rare, and the loam subsoil layer deeper and darker colored, bearing a timber growth prevalently of black and Spanish oaks and hickories, with large and compact black-jack and post oaks, thus forming a gradual transition from the ridgy country of the "Sandy oak uplands" to the gently undulating character of the "table-lands". The latter are quite characteristically developed in the northwestern corner of the county, on Toby-Tubby and Clear creeks, and at several points reach and even cross the railroad near Abbeville. These fertile and well-settled uplands fall off with a gentle slope toward the Tallahatchie River bottom. The latter is itself profusely fertile and about a mile in width, but is so much subject to overflows that but little of it is in regular cultivation.

Much and often irreparable damage has been done to the uplands as well as to the valleys of this part of the county by hillside washes, which soon cut through the loam subsoil into the underlying sand, baring the latter on the hills and deluging the valleys with it.

The tilled lands of La Fayette constitute 18.8 per cent. of the total area, standing in this respect between Tippah and Grenada counties. Of the tilled lands, 40.8 per cent. is given to cotton production, while an equal amount is devoted to corn. The average cotton product per acre is 0.43 bale, being the same as in Montgomery, Choctaw, and Yalobusha counties. The cotton acreage per square mile is 49.

Shipments are made by the New Orleans and Chicago railroad, either direct to New Orleans or northern markets, or largely to Memphis, which is the chief market of northern Mississippi. Freight to New Orleans, $3 75 per bale.

ABSTRACTS OF THE REPORTS OF P. FERNANDEZ, P. H. SKIPWITH, AND S. W. E. PEGUES, OXFORD.

Tallahatchie and Yockeney rivers are in this county about 14 miles apart, and pass through it southwesterly. They have wide, flat, alluvial bottoms, needing drainage in some places. The higher portions alone are cultivated, and are very productive. From these bottoms the hills rise with gentle slopes and form the uplands, which are hilly, rolling, and level, and comprise four-fifths of the cultivated land of this county.

The *light sandy loam* of the table-lands, etc., is the chief cotton-producing soil, and covers about two-thirds of the county. It extends eastward 10, south 25, west 25, and north 20 miles, interrupted occasionally by lowlands and swamps, having a growth of red, post, and black-jack oaks, dogwood, gum, etc. The soil is generally 5 to 6 inches thick and blackish in color. The subsoil is a red clay, underlaid by sand at 5 to 10 feet, sometimes less. The soil is a little tenacious when too wet, but tills quite easily otherwise; it is early, warm, and well-drained naturally. The chief crops of this region are cotton, corn, oats, wheat, sorghum, and sweet potatoes; but the soil is best adapted to cotton, and five-eighths of it is planted with the same. The usual and most productive height of the plant is from 3½ to 4 feet; the extremes are 2 and 6 feet. Deep cultivation and wet seasons incline the plant to run to weed, and to restrain it shallow tillage, early planting, and topping are practiced. The seed-cotton product per acre of fresh land varies from 600 to 1,000 pounds, 1,545 pounds of September picking or 1,425 pounds of December picking making a 475-pound bale of lint. After ten years' cultivation, when the land is kept from washing, the product is 800 pounds, the ratio of seed to lint is the same, and the quality of the staple is not known to differ from that of fresh land. About one-tenth of such land lies "turned out", and when again cultivated it produces well if it is not washed and gullied and has borne sedge-grass seven or eight years. Crab-grass, smart-weed, and hog-weed are most troublesome on this soil.

The *sandy hillside* soil comprises about one-eighth of the lands of this region, occurs in small areas, and has a growth of black-jack and some Spanish and post oaks. The soil is a fine sandy loam of a gray to brown color, in some places black before cultivation, and 1 to 2 inches deep to change of color. The lighter subsoil consists of sand, with strata of white clay, contains sand-rock occasionally, and is underlaid by sand and white clay. The soil is early, warm, well drained, easily tilled, and is best adapted to sweet potatoes and watermelons, but five-eighths of its cultivated area is planted with cotton. The plant attains a height of 3 feet for five or six years only. The seed-cotton product per acre of fresh land is 800 pounds; after five years' cultivation (unmanured) the product is 400 pounds. More than one-half such land lies "turned out" and cannot be reclaimed. Hog-weed and mullein are most troublesome as weeds. The uplands wash readily, doing serious damage. The valleys joining such land are narrow and sandy, and the sand constantly encroaches. Hillside ditching is only temporarily successful; the best plan is either not to clear these slopes adjoining the valleys or to stop cultivating where there is soil enough to grow broom-sedge.

ABSTRACT OF REPORT OF IRA B. ORR, WATER VALLEY (SOUTHWESTERN PART OF THE COUNTY).

The *black or dark sandy loams* occur on dry branches in bodies of from 10 to 50 acres each, and comprise one-half of the cultivated land of the county. They have a natural timber growth of all the oaks, hickory, walnut, dogwood, ash, gum, beech, elm, sumach, and hazel-nut. The soil is a light, fine, sandy clay loam from brown to black in color and from 1 to 14 inches deep. The subsoil is heavier than the soil, is a yellow and red clay, sometimes whitish, and is beneficial when mixed with the surface soil. The soil is early, warm, and ill-drained, and is apparently best adapted to cotton and corn. Cotton forms two-thirds of the crops cultivated. It usually is from 2 to 7 feet high, is most productive at 3 feet, and inclines to run to weed if planted close and well cultivated or in wet seasons, and may be restrained by giving distance to plants and topping during the last of July. The seed-cotton product per acre on fresh land is from 1,200 to 2,000 pounds in good seasons; 1,545 pounds are necessary for a 475-pound bale, which rates as good as any. After twenty years' cultivation the yield is from 500 to 1,000 pounds per acre; about the same amount is necessary for a bale as from fresh land, and the staple is the same. The troublesome weeds are crab-grass and careless and hog-weeds. About one-sixth of such lands now lie "turned out". They do well when again cultivated, but not so well as fresh lands. These soils wash very much on the slopes, and are damaged beyond estimate. The valleys are greatly injured by the washings of the slopes, but horizontalizing and hillside ditching have been a successful check to such injuries.

The upland soils vary greatly from one ridge to another, being in tillable areas of from one-half to 20 acres each.

The *black, loose, sandy land* comprises about seven-eighths of the lands of the township on the south side of the Yockeney and Patapha creeks and to the southern limit.

The natural timber growth is white, red, and post oaks, hickory, pine, and chestnut. The soil is a fine sandy clay loam, gray to black in color, and 8 inches deep. The subsoil is a heavy, tough, bluish-yellow clay, baking hard when exposed, but gradually becoming like the surface soil by continued exposure to the air. It is impervious when undisturbed, and is underlaid by a grayish, gravelly pipe-clay at from 2 to 3 feet. The soil is rather difficult to till in wet seasons, though not usually troublesome, and is early when well drained. It is best adapted to cotton, although all the crops of this region do well; also the grasses and red clover. Over one-half of the cultivated land is devoted to cotton, which is usually 3½ feet high, and produces best at that height. Fresh land, wet seasons, and late planting incline the plant to run to weed, but this is remedied by early planting on older land and shallow cultivation. The seed-cotton product per acre on fresh land is 1,000 pounds, and 1,425 pounds are required to make a 475-pound bale of lint; but on land after fifteen years' cultivation 800 pounds is the yield under ordinary rotation of crops. The staple from old land is not as good as that from fresh land. The troublesome weeds are smart, cocklebur, and morning-glory; crab-grass is the greatest trouble. Probably about 10 per cent. of such lands lie "turned out", and they produce well when again cultivated. The slopes wash and gully readily, are seriously damaged, but the valleys are not injured. Horizontalizing has been practiced to prevent this, and has been successful until neglected.

At various places in the valleys of running streams occur bodies of land designated *swamp* or *crawfish land*. Its growth is white oak, gum, and cypress, and its soil is a heavy clay loam of a whitish-gray color. The impervious subsoil is heavier, whiter, and sometimes gravelly; otherwise it is similar to surface. After cultivation white gravel appears in it, which is underlaid by sand at from 5 to 20 feet. The soil is tilled with difficulty either in wet or dry seasons, and is late, cold, ill-drained, and best adapted to corn planted in June. Cotton is rarely planted on it. Its troublesome weeds are ox, bear, and crab grasses. Very fine soil is being made by running the washings from uplands into this land. Cotton matures well in this region after the soil has been cultivated one or two years. Uplands are earlier and more easily cultivated, and the bolls open earlier than on the lowlands. Cotton is liable to be late and prematurely frost-killed on the lowlands; hence some prefer uplands. When lowlands are well cultivated they endure drought well, and the plant has a steady growth and sheds less than on the uplands. Soil and work being equal, the yields of uplands and lowlands will be about the same.

Cotton is sold during the picking season at railroad stations, whence it is shipped mostly to New Orleans at $3 75 from Oxford.

YALOBUSHA.

Population: 15,649.—White, 7,533; colored, 8,116.

Area: 460 square miles.—Short-leaf pine and oak uplands, 160 square miles; brown-loam table-lands, 290 square miles; sandy oak uplands, 10 square miles; all woodland.

Tilled lands: 71,850 acres.—Area planted in cotton, 30,398 acres; in corn, 23,609 acres; in oats, 1,728 acres; in wheat, 594 acres.

Cotton production: 12,989 bales; average cotton product per acre, 0.43 bale, 612 pounds seed-cotton, or 204 pounds cotton lint.

Yalobusha county is divided into two somewhat unequal portions by the Great Northern railroad, which traverses it from north-northeast to south-southwest. Most of the country lying east of the railroad is ridgy and sandy, and is timbered mainly with short-leaf pine and black-jack and post oaks, many high rocky knolls crowning the abrupt ridges and the narrow creek bottoms being almost alone in cultivation. West of the railroad the country bears mostly the character of the brown-loam table-lands, and is very productive, cotton being altogether the prevalent crop. The divide between the waters of Yockeney and Loosha-Scoona, running almost east and west across the county, is a gently undulating country, with only a few knolls of sandy land. The uplands fall off gently into the bottoms of the two main streams, these bottoms being densely timbered and profusely fertile, but subject to annual overflows, rendering their cultivation precarious. They are bordered by a second-bottom terrace of varying width, having a pale yellow loam subsoil and a timber growth of willow and water oaks. Where these are large the soil is very productive, but where the growth is small it is ill-drained and of a whitish tint, and is of inferior productiveness.

The cotton of Yalobusha county (which then included the adjacent portion of Grenada county) was of old reputed to be the best upland cotton grown in the market. The deterioration of the soils by improvident culture and washing away of the surface has somewhat diminished both in quantity and quality, but improved methods of culture can probably restore these lands to their old standing in both respects.

TALLAHATCHIE.
(See "Mississippi alluvial region".)

GRENADA.

Population: 12,071.—White, 3,236; colored, 8,835.

Area: 440 square miles.—Short-leaf pine uplands, 165 square miles; Mississippi bottom, 75 square miles; cane hills, 10 square miles; brown-loam table-lands, 190 square miles; all woodland.

Tilled lands: 49,600 acres.—Area planted in cotton, 25,390 acres; in corn, 15,906 acres; in oats, 568 acres; in wheat, 6 acres.

Cotton production: 10,228 bales; average cotton product per acre, 0.40 bale, 570 pounds seed-cotton, or 190 pounds cotton lint.

Grenada county, like Yalobusha, is approximately divided by the Great Northern railroad into a hilly and sandy eastern portion, where sandy ridges, timbered with short-leaf pine, black-jack and post oaks, form the prevailing feature, and a western one, which in the upland and larger portion is of the "table-lands" character, while the most westerly part lies within the Mississippi bottom plain. The county is traversed near its middle, from east to west, by the Yalobusha river, whose extensive "second-bottom" plain, gradually rising to the level of the table-lands proper, forms a large proportion of the best and most thickly-settled farming lands. Of these those lying south and west of the town of Grenada are held in especial esteem.

Down to its junction with the Loosha-Scoona the Yalobusha river has a bottom from 1½ to 2 miles in width, bordered by abrupt pine ridges and subject to annual overflow. The same is true of the Loosha-Scoona, but the bottom soils of the two streams differ materially; those of the latter being very heavy and "sobby", while those of the Yalobusha are rather light and more easily tilled (see analyses, p. 35), and its channel near Grenada is obstructed by sand-bars. The joint bottom of the two streams is 2 miles in width, and is traversed by numerous and very large sloughs, rendering it difficult of access in all but the lowest stages of water. Being subject to annual overflows, but little of this profusely fertile and densely-timbered plain is in cultivation. The second-bottom terrace, varying from 1 to 3 miles in width, and lying from 5 to 10 feet above the level of the bottom, hence above overflow, is also highly productive. Its timber is mainly willow, water, and chestnut-white oaks, with which, near the margin, much post and white oaks mingle. The soil is a pale-yellow loam, easily tilled, and mostly well drained. It is occasionally traversed by low, sandy ridges, with a poor soil bearing an inferior growth of black-jack, post, and Spanish oaks. This second-bottom land constitutes a large body of the densely-settled farming land south and southwest of the town of Grenada, on the waters of Beadupanbogue and Perry's creeks, passing into gently undulating loam uplands on the water-shed between these streams and those flowing directly toward the great bottom plain. The lands on the immediate "bluff" of the latter are somewhat broken, and their soil differs from those farther inland by an admixture of the calcareous loam of the "loess" formation (see analyses, p. 31), which manifests itself by the appearance of such lime-loving trees as the tulip tree, or "poplar", the linden, sweet gum, sassafras, etc., among the oaks.

The tilled lands of Grenada county constitute 17.6 per cent. of its area, and a little over half of this amount (51.2 per cent.) is given to cotton culture, while only two-thirds as much is devoted to corn. The cotton acreage per square mile is 57.7. The cotton product per acre (0.40 bale) is slightly less than that of Yalobusha and Montgomery, the adjoining counties.

ABSTRACT OF THE REPORT OF J. D. LEFLORE, GRENADA.

The chief soil is that of the black sandy bottoms of all the creeks for 10 miles around, which bears a natural growth of many kinds of oak, hickory, walnut, poplar, sweet gum, and ash. The soil is a blackish and black sandy loam 2 feet deep; the subsoil a yellow clay, not very hard, and becomes like the surface when turned up. It is underlaid by sand at 5 to 10 feet. The soil is early when well drained, always easily tilled, and is best adapted to cotton and corn, the chief crops of this region, and one-half its cultivated area is planted with cotton. The plant grows from 5 to 8 feet high, but is most productive at 5 feet. It inclines to run to weed in wet weather. The remedy consists in barring off to check growth. The seed-cotton product per acre of fresh land varies from 1,800 to 2,200 pounds; 1,425 pounds make a 475-pound bale of lint. After ten years' cultivation the product is from 800 to 1,000 pounds, 1,545 pounds being then needed for a bale, and the staple is much shorter than that from fresh land. Cocklebur and crab-grass are the troublesome weeds. Not much of such land lies "turned out", and it produces very well when again cultivated.

At the foot of the hills, in the western part of the county, lies the Yalobusha valley, which extends many miles up and down along the hills. The soil is a blackish and black loam 1 to 2 feet deep, generally alike for hundreds of miles, being varied only by bodies more sandy and gravelly and by bodies of clayey prairie. Its natural growth is oak, gum, hickory, walnut, poplar, cypress, and in some places pine, etc. The subsoil is yellow clay, not very hard when turned up. It contains white gravel in places, and is underlaid by sand or gravel at 5 to 10 feet. Tillage is not very difficult in wet seasons, and very easy in dry seasons. The soil is early when well drained, well adapted to cotton and corn, and one-half its cultivated area is planted with cotton. The plant attains the height of from 4 to 6 feet, but is most productive at 4½ to 5 feet. The seed-cotton product per acre of fresh land varies from 1,800 to 2,200 pounds; 1,425 pounds make a 475-pound bale of good middling lint. After ten years' cultivation the product varies from 800 to 1,500 pounds, and 1,545 pounds then make a 475-pound bale of lint inferior to that of fresh land. Other details are as on land previously described.

The uplands are no less productive than the lowlands, and occur in bodies of several hundred acres, bearing chiefly pine; also hickory and oak. The soil is a blackish and black clay loam, 1 to 2 feet thick, with a yellow clay subsoil, underlaid by sand at 5 to 10 feet. Some of this land has been cultivated over forty years. Morning-glory, cocklebur, and crab-grass are the troublesome weeds. The remaining details are as given for the lowlands. Slopes are seriously damaged by washings and gullying, and the valleys are, to some extent, injured by the washings. To check the damage hillside ditching is practiced in some places, and with success when attended to.

Shipments are made, as soon as cotton is ginned, by rail from Grenada to New Orleans at $3 50, or by river at $2 50 per bale.

ABSTRACT OF THE REPORT OF M. K. MISTER, GRENADA.

About one-fourth of the cultivated soil of this region is the *black, light, sandy soil* of the second bottoms of the Yalobusha river and tributaries. It often occurs in bodies of thousands of acres, and bears a natural growth of hickory, poplar, and white and black oaks. The depth of soil to change of color is, in many localities, 30 inches. The subsoil is much heavier, more clayey, and of lighter color, but it is very productive if not too dry. The soil is moderately well drained, always easily tilled, and is well adapted to cotton, corn, oats, sweet and Irish potatoes, and a great variety of vegetables. These are the chief crops of the region. Wheat is also raised, but is not so certain to succeed. About two-thirds of the cultivated area is planted with cotton. The plant grows from 3 to 4 feet high, and when early summer is too dry and late summer is too wet the plant inclines to run to weed, for which there is no remedy whatever. Fresh land produces 1,200 pounds of seed-cotton per acre; 1,425 pounds make a 475-pound bale of No. 1 lint. After six to eight years' cultivation (unmanured) the cotton yield declines with constant tillage at the rate of 2 per cent. per annum, and 1,545 pounds then make a 475-pound bale. The lint is generally inferior, but that depends on the season. Crab-grass is the most troublesome weed. About one-sixth of such cultivated land lies "turned out", but produces pretty well when again properly cultivated. Slopes wash very badly, and are thus seriously damaged; but the washings do little or no damage to the valley lands. Efforts to check this damage have been entirely neglected lately, but were formerly made to great advantage.

The uplands are rather level, and embrace the second quality of soil. There are also white, clayey, rolling lands, whose soil is inferior. The bottoms are very rich, but are liable to be overflowed once or twice annually. They produce abundantly when cultivated, but the cotton crop is liable to be late, and is sometimes injured by early frosts.

Many sell their crop as soon as it is baled, a large proportion of which is sold at Grenada, from which place it is shipped to New Orleans at $3 50 per bale.

MONTGOMERY.

(See "Short-leaf pine and oak uplands region".)

CARROLL.

Population: 17,795.—White, 7,831; colored, 9,964.

Area: 640 square miles.—Short-leaf pine and oak uplands, 190 square miles; Mississippi bottom, 50 square miles; cane-hills, 80 square miles; brown-loam table-lands, 320 square miles; all woodland.

Tilled lands: 86,739 acres.—Area planted in cotton, 37,957 acres; in corn, 30,019 acres; in oats, 1,877 acres; in wheat, 337 acres.

Cotton production: 17,423 bales; average cotton product per acre, 0.46 bale, 657 pounds seed-cotton, or 219 pounds cotton lint.

Carroll county, since the formation of Le Flore in 1871, comprehends but a small area of the Mississippi bottom plain, and its uplands are mostly undulating "table-lands", somewhat broken near the edge of the "bluff" and in the eastern and central portions, where the continuation of the "Duck hill" ridge from the adjacent county of Montgomery forms the divide between the waters of the Big Black and Yazoo rivers. The latter is sandy and timbered with black-jack and post oaks, mingled with short-leaf pine, while the "bluff" lands show the usual marks of increased fertility through the admixture of the calcareous "loess" in the mingling of the poplar, linden, sweet gum, large sassafras, and sometimes walnut, with the upland oaks. The valleys of the numerous streams are wide, and are very productive where the washing of the uplands has not been allowed to damage them.

In the southeastern portion of the county, near Vaiden especially, the pale-yellow loam of the more northerly region becomes of a deeper tint, evidently from the admixture of the orange-red, clayey soil of the "red hills" character, which is prominent at the town of Vaiden. Here in the railroad cuts there appears one of the beds of "greensand", to the admixture of which with the soils the high productiveness of the "red lands" is mainly due. (See p. 29.)

The uplands in this region often come down to the bottom of the Big Black with a decided slope, but in places there intervene tracts of level hummock or second bottom, lying 3 to 4 feet above the first bottom, and of very variable fertility. These are nearly or quite destitute of timber, excepting small groups of post oak, and, in low spots, scrubby sweet gum. The soil is a light, gray silt, unretentive, suitable for good wheat and sweet potatoes, but unsuited to cotton and corn (see analysis of this soil, p. 36). The main body of the first bottom in this region lies on the east side of the river.

HOLMES.

Population: 27,164.—White, 6,911; colored, 20,253.

Area: 750 square miles.—Woodland, all; Mississippi bottom, 205 square miles; cane hills, 60 square miles; brown-loam table-lands, 485 square miles.

Tilled lands: 204,993 acres.—Area planted in cotton, 62,556 acres; in corn, 37,355 acres; in oats, 1,237 acres; in wheat, 59 acres.

Cotton production: 30,463 bales; average cotton product per acre, 0.49 bale; 699 pounds seed-cotton, or 233 pounds cotton lint.

The features of the upland portion of Holmes county are very similar to those of Carroll (see above), save that in general the surface is more gently undulating and the loam soil is, on the whole, somewhat heavier and deeper, acquiring in the southern part of the county a thickness of as much as 18 and even 20 feet. The Big Black river is mostly bordered on the west by a "hummock" belt from one-half to one mile wide, timbered with post oak, willow, and water oak and some short-leaf pine. From this there is a gradual ascent into a gently-undulating oak upland region a few miles in width, beyond which, on the divide, the country becomes more hilly, and, in consequence, less convenient for cultivation, though apparently not less fertile, the timber being the same, viz, large post, Spanish, and scarlet oaks, with an occasional large black-jack and hickory. The short-leaf pine appears on the higher portions of the dividing ridge in the northern part of the county; and the southern, the fine agricultural region about Richland, though lying on the Big Black side, is separated from the Big Black hummock by a strip of hilly country in which the pine is occasionally seen. The upland soils, when fresh, produce from 1,200 to 1,300 pounds of seed-cotton per acre, and are very durable when washing away is prevented.

The lowland portion of Holmes county embraces the wonderfully productive portion of the Yazoo bottom known as Honey island, famed equally for the quality and quantity of its cotton product, and hence quite extensively in cultivation; the proprietors, however, residing mostly in the uplands, on account of the peculiarly insidious malaria, attributed to the island formed by the forking of the Yazoo river near the northern line of the county and the reunion of the two streams on the southern. It seems that the best quality of the "buckshot soil" (see pp. 38 and 42) prevails over the larger portion of this area.

The tilled lands of Holmes county constitute 42.8 per cent. of the total area, the county standing second in this respect in the state; 30.5 per cent. of these lands is devoted to cotton. The cotton acreage per square mile is 83.4, and the average cotton product per acre, 0.49, Holmes standing eighth in this respect among the upland counties in the state; but, considering the influence of the Honey Island (Yazoo bottom) region upon this average, that of the uplands alone must be very much less.

The cotton product of this lowland region is shipped by water to Yazoo City or Vicksburg, while that of the upland portion of the county is mainly transported on the Great Northern railroad, which here closely skirts the Big Black river.

ABSTRACT OF THE REPORT OF CHARLES C. THORNTON, M. D., CHEW'S LANDING.

The lands are a little undulating, though frequently in large areas, with little or no fall; but as a general rule there is sufficient fall for drainage. Two-thirds of the cultivated land is blackish and black loam, composed of fine silt, sand, and clay. It is commonly designated black loam. The same extends 5 to 8 miles east, 10 to 20 south, 15 to 20 north, and to the Mississippi river 75 to 100 miles west. Its natural growth is oaks, gum, elms, sassafras, walnut, holly, red-bud, cypress, pecan, ash, ironwood, and palmetto. The soil is from 3 to 5 feet deep. The darker soils have a lighter subsoil, while the clayey soils have a waxier and heavier subsoil, which is very hard when dry. The underlying material at 20 to 30 feet is quicksand. In good seasons the dark and sandy lands work like an ash-bed, but the clayey lands are easy to till in wet seasons, especially when in crops like tobacco. These soils are early and warm when well drained.

The chief crops of the region are cotton, corn, potatoes, pease, pumpkins, tobacco, and vegetables; anything that will grow elsewhere will grow in the Yazoo bottom. The soil is equally well adapted to all. Corn will grow almost without culture, but about two-thirds of the cultivated part of this land is planted with cotton. With rows 4½ to 5 feet apart, the plant is most productive at 5 feet high, though it frequently grows to 10 feet. The height makes little difference if it has sufficient space. The plant inclines to run to weed when it has not space enough, or when the weather is excessively wet and when planted late or cultivated too much on fresh land. The remedy consists in allowing ample space between the rows and drills, laying by early, cultivating little while the plant grows rapidly, and keeping weeds down with hoes and shallow-plowing sweeps.

The seed-cotton product per acre of fresh land varies from 1,200 to 5,000 pounds with proper cultivation, and from 1,425 to 1,665 pounds make a 475-pound bale of lint. After three years' cultivation the product varies from one to three bales (400 pounds each) or 600 to 800 pounds of lint if properly cultivated. The staple is a little inferior, if at all different, and perhaps is not quite so silky and a little coarser, though much of this is due to neglect in the selection of seed. Cocklebur is the greatest pest; other weeds are crab-grass, morning-glories, hog-weeds, careless-weeds, purslane, and wild tea that pulls like twine. Nearly one-fourth of the best lands are now idle; and, considering the small yields that are gathered from some of the best lands in the county, much more might as well lie idle. When again cultivated such lands produce from 1,000 to 1,500 pounds of seed-cotton, and with early breaking and good cultivation they sometimes come fully up to their original standard. Lands suffer from washings only near the foot of the hills, where several large plantations have been nearly or quite ruined. Horizontalizing has not been successful as a check.

One-sixth of the cultivated land has a surface soil of *fine silt and sandy loam* of a gray and yellow color. It is coextensive with the black loam, has the same depth (3 to 5 feet) and about the same kind of growth, with perhaps more pecan, hickory, and oaks, and less gum. The underlying material is sand. When too wet, the soil is mucky; when dry, it tills like an ash-bed. It is early and warm when well drained, and is best adapted to corn and potatoes, but is also good for cotton, and the latter occupies from five- to seven-eighths of its cultivated area. The seed-cotton product of fresh land per acre varies from 800 to 1,200 pounds, and usually 1,665, or in dry seasons 1,425 pounds, make a 475-pound bale of lint. After three years' cultivation the product varies from 1,200 to 2,000 pounds, and frequently 3,000 pounds are raised. The ratio of seed to lint remains the same, but the staple is not so soft nor so silky as that from fresh land. The weeds are the same in kind, but fewer and less luxuriant than on the black land. About one-fourth of such originally cultivated land lies "turned out". When again taken into cultivation the land does not produce as well unless broken early.

The remaining sixth of the cultivated land, or much more than one-third of the unimproved, consists of *low wet lands, palmetto flats,* and *white-oak ridges.* It is commonly designated white "buckshot" soil, and occurs more or less on each plantation, and bears a natural growth of white oak, hickory, ironwood, elm, bitter pecan, palmetto, grape, bamboo, briers, and vines generally. The soil is a whitish-gray, stiff clay, 12 inches thick; the subsoil is a stiff waxy, mottled clay, hard and impervious, which breaks into gravel-like fragments. At 2 feet it is underlaid by a stiff mucky clay. Tillage is easy if the soil is not too wet; if dry, it is almost impossible to break it, except in clods as large as one's head. The soil is late and cold when well drained, and is best adapted to cotton and pease. Cotton does not shed its fruit as on other land, and is not, like them, subject to drought. Nearly all the cultivated portion is planted with cotton, as it is fit for little else. The plant grows from 3 to 4 feet high, and is most productive at that. It does not run to weed nor shed its fruit, nor does it suffer from drought as on other lands. The seed-cotton product per acre varies from 400 to 1,000 pounds; 1,665 pounds make a 475-pound bale. After three years' cultivation the product varies from 200 to 800 pounds. The ratio of seed to lint remains the same, but the staple is coarser than that of fresh lands, and generally coarser than that of other lands. The cocklebur is the most troublesome weed; it grows where nothing else will.

Nearly one-half of such land originally cultivated has been "turned out". It produces but little better after rest, and the first five years of cultivation generally exhausts it. This land resists washing as would a rock, and would be benefited by the intermixture of an ocean of sand.

Cotton on the lowlands or flats where there is great moisture suffers from rust and sheds greatly, and is perhaps more affected by early frosts than on uplands; but the correspondent concludes, from his twenty years' experience as an experimental farmer and cotton planter, that the most serious hinderances to profitable cotton culture are due more to the methods of cultivation than to soil or climate. Alternations of wet and dry extremes cause shedding of forms, squares, and blooms; but this, he believes, would not be so did not that partial hard-pan formed by the plow-soles repeatedly running at the same depth prevent the roots from descending far enough to be beyond the reach of, and unaffected by, those sudden surface changes. With suitable treatment these lands are not excelled in yields by any in the world. Cotton shipments continue from October to March, by steamboat generally, to New Orleans, at $1 50 per bale; also, to Yazoo City at 75 cents, and to Vicksburg at $1 per bale.

ABSTRACT OF THE REPORT OF J. W. C. SMITH, BENTON.

The lowlands of the county comprise the first and second bottoms of the creeks. The soil of the first bottom is a black alluvial, with much decayed vegetable matter. The growth is walnut, hickory, pecan, magnolia, beech, holly, water, live, and white oaks, buckeye, cucumber tree, etc. The subsoil is a yellowish or bluish clay, nearly impervious to water unless disturbed.

The chief soil of the county is the hilly uplands, which comprises about 80 per cent. of the area, and has a timber growth of white, red, black, and overcup oaks, hickory, poplar, and dogwood. The subsoil is a yellowish clay at from 3 to 6 inches from the surface. Tillage is difficult in wet seasons, but easy in dry. The soil is early when well drained, is best adapted to cotton, and seven-tenths of its cultivated area is planted with the same. The usual and most productive height of the plant is 4½ to 5 feet. Frequent light surface cultivation in moist, warm weather inclines the plant to run to weed. The remedy is deep cultivation to cut the lateral roots and check the plant's growth while the moisture continues, and this is not likely to cause shedding of young bolls. The seed-cotton product per acre of fresh land varies with the land from 1,200 to 3,060 pounds; 1,665 to 1,780 pounds make a 475-pound bale of fair lint if free of trash. After two years' cultivation the product is from 5 to 10 per cent. more, and a little less is needed to make a bale. Crab-grass, purslane, and kellis are the most troublesome, and where there is a sod of Bermuda grass cotton cannot be cultivated. About one-fourth of the originally cultivated lands here now lie "turned out", and produce very well when again cultivated. Slopes are seriously damaged by washings and gullying, especially when not cultivated, and valley lands are injured to the extent of 30 to 50 per cent. by the washings. Very little effort to check the damage is made, and some efforts at hillside ditching have met with poor success. Most of the lands here are rented, and tenants do not keep such ditches open.

Wet weather accompanies overflows of the Mississippi river; for during such overflows the prevailing winds are from the west-southwest and are heavily laden with moisture, which is precipitated every time there comes a cold breeze from the north. The chief crops are cotton, corn, sorghum, and pease. Cotton is shipped in November and December, by steamboat, to New Orleans at $1 25 per bale.

YAZOO.
(See "Mississippi alluvial region".)

MADISON.
(See "Central prairie region".)

MISSISSIPPI ALLUVIAL REGION.

(Embraces the following counties and parts of counties: North of Vicksburg—Tunica, De Soto,* Coahoma, Quitman, Panola,* Tallahatchie, Grenada,* Le Flore, Sunflower, Bolivar, Washington, Holmes,* Yazoo, Sharkey, Issaquena, and Warren;* south of Vicksburg—Claiborne,* Jefferson,* Adams,* and Wilkinson.*)

The counties of this region are very similar in their topographical and agricultural features, and, in order to avoid a very large amount of unnecessary repetition, their descriptions are made as short as possible, and the reader is referred to the more general description in the first part of this report.

TUNICA.

Population: 8,461.—White, 1,256; colored, 7,205.
Area: 440 square miles.—All Mississippi bottom; wooded.
Tilled lands: 39,318 acres.—Area planted in cotton, 29,881 acres; in corn, 9,447 acres; in oats, 137 acres.
Cotton production: 18,008 bales; average cotton product per acre, 0.60 bale, 855 pounds seed-cotton, or 285 pounds cotton lint.

Tunica is the most northerly of the alluvial counties, and is bordered on the west by the Mississippi river, while on the east the cane hills lie along a portion of the border. The surface is very level. Its eastern portion is drained southward by the Coldwater river, a tributary of the Yazoo, and interspersed with numerous lakes and bayous. The entire country is heavily timbered with the usual bottom growth, and is sparsely settled, except along the immediate Mississippi river front, where also lie the large cotton plantations. The average of tilled lands for the county at large is 89.3 acres per square mile, and of these 67.9 acres are given to the cultivation of cotton.

DE SOTO.
(See "Brown-loam table-lands".)

COAHOMA.

Population: 13,568.—White, 2,412; colored, 11,156.
Area: 500 square miles.—Mississippi bottom, 416 square miles; dogwood ridge, 84 square miles; woodland.
Tilled lands: 51,741 acres.—Area planted in cotton, 32,964 acres; in corn, 14,297 acres; in oats, 138 acres; in wheat, 76 acres.
Cotton production: 26,287 bales; average cotton product per acre, 0.80 bale, 1,140 pounds seed-cotton, or 380 pounds cotton lint.

Coahoma is one of the river counties of this region, and is interspersed with lakes, bayous, and creeks, which mostly flow southward and are tributary to the Yazoo river. Of these streams the Sunflower river is the largest.

The surface of the county is level, with the exception of Dogwood ridge, on the east, is subject to overflow when not protected by levees, and is heavily timbered with the usual swamp growth. The lands comprise the alluvial loams and buckshot soils described in the general part of the report, and along the river front are largely under cultivation, cotton comprising the chief crop. The Dogwood ridge alluded to is a low ridge above overflow, trending in an irregular course north and south, with a width varying from 2 to 5 miles, and having a light sandy and deep soil, timbered with a growth of dogwood, sweet gum, holly, ash, sassafras, and prickly pear. The lands under cultivation average 103.4 acres per square mile for the county at large, and of this number 65.9 acres are given to cotton. The large plantations, however, lie along the river front, convenient to shipping facilities.

QUITMAN.

Population: 1,407.—White, 592; colored, 815.
Area: 400 square miles.—Mississippi bottom, 395 square miles; dogwood ridge, 5 square miles; woodland.
Tilled lands: 5,714 acres.—Area planted in cotton, 3,420 acres; in corn, 1,477 acres; in oats, 24 acres.
Cotton production: 2,337 bales; average cotton product per acre, 0.68 bale, 969 pounds seed-cotton, or 323 pounds cotton lint.

Quitman county borders Coahoma on the east, its eastern boundary-line reaching to within a few miles of the bluff region. The surface is very level, is drained by the Coldwater river, which flows southward, and by its numerous creeks and bayous, and is heavily timbered with a swamp growth of sweet gum, swamp-chestnut oak, some white oak, holly, and an undergrowth of cane. While most of the county is subject to overflow, there is a great deal of high and sandy land along the streams, nearly all of which is under cultivation, yielding large crops of cotton. The lowlands are chiefly dark loams or buckshot clays, and are very highly productive when properly drained. "White land" also occurs in some localities, having a sweet gum and swamp-chestnut oak growth. Along the Tallahatchie river the bottom lands are from 10 to 15 miles wide, and have a light yellowish sandy loam soil. The average of lands under tillage for the county at large is 14.2 acres per square mile, and of these 8.5 acres are given to the culture of cotton.

PANOLA.

(See " Brown-loam table-lands".)

TALLAHATCHIE.

Population: 10,926.—White, 4,168; colored, 6,758.
Area: 640 square miles.—Mississippi bottom, 549 square miles; cane hills, 53 square miles; dogwood ridge, 38 square miles; all woodland:
Tilled lands: 42,501 acres.—Area planted in cotton, 22,463 acres; in corn, 16,169 acres; in oats, 772 acres; in wheat, 108 acres.
Cotton production: 11,570 bales; average cotton product per acre, 0.52 bale, 741 pounds seed-cotton, or 247 pounds cotton lint.

Tallahatchie county, lying in the eastern part of the region, includes within its limits a large area of the high bluff lands described in the general part of this report. By far the greater part of the county, however, is covered by the level and heavily-timbered swamp lands of the alluvial region with the exception of the narrow and sandy Dogwood ridge which crosses the southwest corner. The county is drained southward by the Coldwater river and its several tributaries.

The lands under cultivation are found chiefly on the bluff uplands, and here, too, the greater part of the population reside. It is thought that about 15 per cent. of the total area of this bluff section and from 1 to 5 per cent. of the alluvial region is planted in cotton.

The average of tilled lands for the county at large is 66.4 acres per square mile, of which 35.1 acres are in cotton.

GRENADA.

(See "Brown-loam table-lands".)

LE FLORE.

Population: 10,246.—White, 2,230; colored, 8,016.
Area: 610 square miles.—Mississippi bottom, 434 square miles; dogwood ridge, 176 square miles; woodland.
Tilled lands: 40,158 acres.—Area planted in cotton, 17,730 acres; in corn, 10,965 acres; in oats, 76 acres.
Cotton production: 11,925 bales; average cotton product per acre, 0.67 bale, 954 pounds seed-cotton, or 318 pounds cotton lint.

Le Flore county, lying in the eastern part of the alluvial region, is entirely included in it, though bordered on the east by the bluff region. The Dogwood ridge, here reaching its maximum width of from 5 to 8 miles, passes north and south through the county, is low, and has a sandy loam soil timbered with dogwood, sweet gum, holly, ash, sassafras, etc.

The rest of the county is low and swampy, is heavily timbered except in small spots or "prairies" (which seem to be old Indian mounds and "clearings"), and is subject to overflow.

The county is sparsely settled with an average of 16.8 persons per square mile, the average of tilled lands being 65.8 acres per square mile. Cotton is the chief crop, its average being 29.1 acres per square mile.

ABSTRACT OF THE REPORT OF JOHN A. AVENT, GREENWOOD.

The lands of the county comprise two varieties of soil, *a black sandy loam* and *heavy clay putty-like soil* (second class). The *black sandy soil* is chiefly cultivated. The same extends 50 miles west, 20 east, and about 100 north and south, and covers three-fourths of this region. Its natural growth is gum, oak, hickory, cottonwood, ash, box-elder, ironwood, and cane. The soil is a black, fine sandy and gravelly loam 30 inches deep. The subsoil is an impervious, putty-like clay, contains white gravel, and is underlaid by sand at 10 feet. The chief crops of this region are cotton and corn. The soil is easily tilled, except when too wet. It is ill-drained, but early and warm, and is best adapted to cotton, three-fourths of its cultivated area being planted with the same. The usual and most productive height of the plant is from 4 to 5 feet, and it inclines to run to weed when rains are excessive in August. The product per acre of fresh land is 2,000 pounds of seed-cotton; 1,200 pounds make a 475-pound bale of good middling lint. After ten years' cultivation (unmanured) the product is 1,500 pounds, and 1,780 pounds then make a bale of lint slightly superior to that of fresh land. One-tenth of such originally cultivated land has been "turned out", but produces well when again cultivated. The most troublesome weed is crab-grass. The soil washes and gullies readily on slopes, but they are not seriously damaged yet; neither are the valleys by washings.

Cotton is shipped during the picking season by steamboat, generally to New Orleans, at $1 50 per bale.

SUNFLOWER.

Population: 4,661.—White, 1,764; colored, 2,897.
Area: 720 square miles.—Mississippi bottom, 708 square miles; dogwood ridge, 12 square miles; woodland.
Tilled lands: 13,998 acres.—Area planted in cotton, 7,107 acres; in corn, 3,730 acres; in oats, 80 acres.
Cotton production: 5,707 bales; average cotton product per acre, 0.80 bale, 1,140 pounds seed-cotton, or 380 pounds cotton lint.

Sunflower is a narrow but long county lying in the central part of the alluvial region. Its surface is very level, with some higher lands along the larger streams; the lowlands are subject to overflow. The county is drained southward by the Sunflower river and its tributaries, though the greater part is low and swampy and is interspersed with many lakes. The lands of the swamps are what are termed "white lands", the soil being somewhat sandy, of a grayish color, and underlaid by a whitish close-textured clay, with reddish ferruginous spots, and its vegetation comprises sweet gum and swamp-chestnut oak. The front-lands along the streams also comprise "white lands", perhaps a little more sandy, having an additional timber growth of hickory, holly, willow oaks, dogwood, some ash, and an undergrowth of cane. These front-lands only are under cultivation, the swamps being too low and subject to overflow.

The county is sparsely settled, the average of population being 6.5 persons and that of tilled land 19.4 acres per square-mile. The lands in cotton average but 9.9 acres per square mile. The northern half of the county is hardly inhabited.

BOLIVAR.

Population: 18,652.—White, 2,694; colored, 15,958.
Area: 900 square miles.—All Mississippi bottom; wooded.
Tilled lands: 73,467 acres.—Area planted in cotton, 43,330 acres; in corn, 16,624 acres; in oats, 187 acres.
Cotton production: 36,419 bales; average cotton product per acre, 0.84 bale, 1,197 pounds seed-cotton, or 399 pounds cotton lint.

Bolivar county lies along the eastern side of the Mississippi river, and is entirely included within the alluvial region. Its surface is very level, with higher lands along the river, and is heavily timbered with the usual swamp growth. Sunflower river enters the county a short distance on the east in its southward course, while in the central portion are the headwaters of Deer creek, which flows parallel with the Mississippi river through several counties on the south. A few small bayous enter the latter river, but the drainage is mostly to the south. The entire county is dotted over with small lakes, especially in the eastern half, which is little else than a great swamp, scarcely inhabited, and subject to overflows. The lands of the county largely embrace buckshot clays in the lowlands, covered on the higher portions along the river by light alluvial loams from 6 to 8 feet thick.

The lands under cultivation for the county at large average 81.6 acres per square mile, and of these 48.1 acres are given to the culture of cotton. The cotton plantations, however, lie chiefly adjoining the Mississippi river, convenient to transportation.

ABSTRACT OF THE REPORT OF G. W. WISE, CONCORDIA.

As far as productiveness is concerned, it is hard to tell which is better, the black sandy loam or the black "buckshot" soil, as neither can be excelled. These together constitute about four-fifths of this region and extend from 50 to 75 miles up and down the Mississippi river and about 10 miles east of it. Its natural growth is chiefly sweet gum and hackberry, and some elm, oak, ash, cottonwood, etc. Both soils are black or blackish; one is fine sandy loam, the other is a stiff, clayey loam. Their depths vary from 1½ to 9 feet. The subsoil is apparently heavier, but when exposed to the sun and air it becomes like the surface soil. They are underlaid by sand or clay. The heavier soil contains black pebble.

Tillage is always easy except in wet seasons. The soil is early and warm when well drained, but most of it is ill-drained. Cotton and corn are the chief crops. Both do well, but the soil seems best adapted to cotton, and five-sixths of its cultivated area (the same is true of other soils here) is planted with cotton. The plant usually attains the height of 4 to 5 feet on the "buckshot", 6 to 7 feet on the black sandy soil, and 3½ to 4½ feet on the white sandy soil. It inclines to run to weed on fresh land or when July and August are very rainy. No remedy has here been tried except shallow cultivation, and this is believed to be the best remedy. The seed-cotton product per acre of fresh land is 1,500 pounds (gathered), but sometimes a part is destroyed by rains or by early frosts; from 1,545 to 2,135 pounds make a 475-pound bale of lint. After twenty years' cultivation (unmanured) the product varies from 1,300 to 1,800 pounds, and about 1,780 pounds then make a bale of lint slightly better than that from fresh land. Yellow-top and the morning-glory are the most troublesome weeds, the latter being worst on the sandy land. Perhaps one-twentieth of such land originally cultivated now lies "turned out", but it produces just as well as ever, excepting the first crop, which is uncertain.

About one-fifth of this region along the river consists of a whitish-gray or muddy-yellow fine sandy loam. This reaches up and down as far as the land last described, but does not extend so far east or back from the river. Its growth is cottonwood, hackberry, ash, elm, and cane. This soil varies from 2 to 10 feet in depth. When 10 feet deep, it is generally followed by quicksand; when 2 feet, it is underlaid by a clayey subsoil; and in either case quicksand prevails at 10 to 20 feet. The soil is easily tilled, is early, warm, generally well drained, and is best adapted to cotton. The plant usually grows about 5 feet high, but is most productive at 4½ feet. The seed-cotton product per acre of fresh land, or after twenty years' cultivation, varies from 1,200 to 1,500 pounds, according to seasons. The morning-glory is the troublesome weed. Not much of this land is "turned out". Other details are as on the soils before described.

There is considerable swamp, white oak, and hickory land occurring in bodies from 10 miles east of the river to the uplands. Its chief growth is swamp, white oak, hickory, elm, and some red oak, gum, pecan, and cane. The soil is a sandy loam of a whitish-gray color, 8 inches thick. The subsoil is lighter in color and material, and is underlaid by white or yellowish sandy clay.

Tillage is easy, more so when dry than wet. The soil is early and warm, but ill-drained, and is best adapted to cotton and vegetables. The usual and most productive height attained by the cotton-plant is from 3½ to 4 feet. The seed-cotton product per acre of fresh land is about 1,500 pounds; 1,780 pounds make a 475-pound bale of lint. After ten years' cultivation the product varies from 1,000 to 1,500 pounds. A little less is needed to make a bale, and the staple is a little better. Crab-grass is the troublesome weed. Not more than one-fortieth of such land originally cultivated now lies "turned out"; it improves by rest, producing better for the first two or three years. In the ordinary good season the sandy soils produce best, but they cannot endure drought as the "buckshot" soil, and in very wet seasons the plant sometimes takes the second growth. Therefore the "buckshot" soil is best in either extremes of wet or dry seasons.

Cotton is shipped at all times, by river chiefly, to New Orleans, at 75 cents to $1 25 per bale.

3.0

WASHINGTON.

Population: 25,367.—White, 3,478; colored, 21,889.
Area: 900 square miles.—All Mississippi bottom; wooded.
Tilled lands: 95,893 acres.—Area planted in cotton, 60,409 acres; in corn, 16,515 acres; in oats, 65 acres.
Cotton production: 54,873 bales; average cotton product per acre, 0.87 bale, 1,239 pounds seed-cotton, or 413, pounds cotton lint.

Washington county extends eastward from the Mississippi river to the Yazoo, the greater part, however, bordering the former river. It is entirely included within the alluvial region, and is watered by the Big Sunflower river, Deer creek, and Black bayou, all flowing southward into the Yazoo river. The Mississippi river receives scarcely any drainage water from the country direct, the lands along its border being higher than elsewhere. The general surface of the county is very level and heavily timbered with bottom growth. In the eastern part of the county, from about half way between Deer creek and Sunflower river, the variety of land known as white land prevails. The soil is mostly rather sandy, but is underlaid by a stiff, white clay, and has a growth of sweet gum and swamp-chestnut oak. The banks of the Sunflower are low, and have a sandy loam soil. To the westward the buckshot clays are found overlying this clay, and, with the still higher alluvial loams of the streams, are the chief lands under cultivation. The lowest lands are cypress swamps. Cotton is the principal crop of the county, its acreage on the west embracing from 15 to 20 per cent. of the total area of that section. For the county at large the average is 79.5 acres per square mile out of an average of 106.5 acres of tilled lands. Washington is the second "banner county" of the state in its average product per acre, and ranks as fourth among the counties of all the cotton states.

HOLMES.

(See "Brown-loam table-lands".)

YAZOO.

Population: 33,845.—White, 8,498; colored, 25,347.
Area: 1,000 square miles.—Mississippi bottom, 430 square miles; cane hills, 260 square miles; brown-loam table-lands, 310 square miles; all woodland.
Tilled lands: 156,228 acres.—Area planted in cotton, 83,184 acres; in corn, 38,207 acres; in oats, 454 acres.
Cotton production: 48,321 bales; average cotton product per acre, 0.58 bale, 828 pounds seed-cotton, or 276 pounds cotton lint.

Yazoo county is almost evenly divided between the uplands and the lowlands traversed by the Yazoo and lower portion of the Big Sunflower river, the fertility of which is scarcely less noted than that of Honey island. The uplands are of two chief types. In the eastern and northeastern part there are brown-loam "table-lands", traversed more or less by higher ridges, on which the loam stratum is thin, and therefore liable to damage by hillside washes cutting into the underlying sand. On the westward slope of the divide between the Yazoo and the Big Black these are timbered with black-jack and post oaks, with occasional pines, while on the lower slopes and broader ridges the black, Spanish, and scarlet oaks, with hickory, predominate. Toward the westward slope of the divide between the Yazoo and Big Black rivers, in the western and southern parts of the county, the influence of the calcareous silt of the "cane hills" becomes perceptible in the admixture of lime-loving trees with the oak timber (see Holmes county), and the country assumes the character of the "walnut-hills" region near Vicksburg. (See description of cane-hills region and of Warren county.)

The tilled lands of Yazoo amount to 24.4 per cent. of the total area. The form of the returns does not admit of the segregation of the lowlands from the uplands, and hence it is not possible to draw definite conclusions regarding the relative statistics of production. The high cotton product per acre (0.58 bale) as compared with the adjoining county of Madison (0.38 bale) shows the influence of the lowland plantations upon this factor; and as the uplands are apparently as well settled as are those of Holmes, adjoining on the north, the remarkable difference in the proportion of tilled lands, as compared with Holmes, seems to be attributable to the thinly-settled lowlands. Over one-half of the tilled area (53.2 per cent.) is occupied by cotton, against only 30.5 in Holmes, and less than one-half as much is given to the production of corn. The cotton acreage per square mile is, however, essentially the same in both counties (83.2 and 83.4).

Cotton shipments are made chiefly by steamers down the Yazoo river to Vicksburg or New Orleans, and some cotton is sold to commission merchants at Yazoo City. Freight per bale to New Orleans, $1 25.

ABSTRACT OF REPORT OF J. W. C. SMITH, BENTON.

The uplands of the county are hilly and rolling and well timbered, having a growth of white, black, red, and overcup oaks, hickory, poplar, and dogwood.

The lowlands of the county comprise the first and second bottoms of Spring creek, the former having a black sandy alluvial soil, the second bottom, or table-lands, having a yellow loam subsoil, with 3 to 6 inches of black humus on the surface. These bottoms have a growth of walnut, hickory, magnolia, beech, pecan, holly, buckeye, cucumber tree, and water, live, and white oaks.

The *table-lands and hills* having the black vegetable mold soil and yellow-loam subsoil are the chief lands devoted to cotton culture, and comprise 80 per cent. of the county area, embracing all of the lands except the swamps of the creeks and Big Black river. The soil is a buff-colored, coarse sandy or clayey loam, 8 inches in depth, with a heavier yellowish clay subsoil nearly impervious to water unless disturbed by the plow, contains hard, white and reddish pebbles, frequently mixed with shells on creek bluffs, and is underlaid by sand and gravel. The soil is easily tilled if dry, difficult if wet; is early when well drained, and is best adapted to cotton. About 70 per cent. of

21 C P

the cultivated land is devoted to cotton, which is usually from 4½ to 5 feet high, and is most productive at that height. The plant, inclined to run to weed in moist, warm weather, and with frequent light surface plowing, may be sustained by deep plowing, to cut the roots and check growth while moisture continues, and is not likely to shed young bolls, even though the roots be injured.

The seed-cotton product per acre from fresh land is from 1,200 to 3,000 pounds; from 1,720 to 1,780 pounds are required to make a 475-pound bale of middling lint. After two years' cultivation the product of seed-cotton is from 5 to 10 per cent. better than the first year, and from 1,600 to 1,865 pounds (in wet season, when the seeds are large) are then required to make a 475-pound bale of lint, which does not rate any better than first year's crop. Careless, purslane, silk, and crab-grass are the most troublesome weeds, and where there is a mat or turf of Bermuda grass cotton cannot be cultivated. Probably about 25 per cent. of such land originally cultivated now lies "turned out", and produces excellently when again brought under tillage. The slopes wash very much where not cultivated, and are damaged seriously. The valleys are injured to from 30 to 50 per cent. of their value, but very little has been done to check the damage, as the renters do not keep the sidehill ditches open.

The chief crops of the county are cotton, corn, sorghum, and peas. No circumstances of "local climate" influence the cotton crop, except in years when the Mississippi river overflows the swamp; then, as our spring and summer winds are west-southwest, the atmosphere being heavily laden with moisture, every chilly wave from the cold regions causes a shower and makes the overflow springs in the Mississippi bottoms and causes wet springs in the adjacent uplands.

Shipments are made in November and December by steamboat to New Orleans at $1 25 per bale.

SHARKEY.

Population: 6,306.—White, 1,405; colored, 4,901.
Area: 540 square miles.—All Mississippi bottom; wooded.
Tilled lands: 23,328 acres.—Area planted in cotton, 17,041 acres; in corn, 7,540 acres; in oats, 35 acres.
Cotton production: 14,162 bales; average cotton product per acre, 0.83 bale, 1,182 pounds seed-cotton, or 394 pounds cotton lint.

Sharkey, an inland alluvial county, is separated from the Mississippi river by the county of Issaquena. Its surface is very level, is well timbered with bottom growth, and is drained southward by the Little Sunflower river and Deer creek. The lands of the eastern half of the county seem to be of the low and swampy "white land" variety, comprising rather sandy soils and white clay subsoils, with a growth of sweet gum, swamp-chestnut, oak, etc. The banks of the Sunflower are rather low, and have a light-gray sandy loam soil and a growth of sweet gum, maple, elm, and hackberry. In the western half, along Deer creek, the lands are chiefly buckshot clays, covered with sandy soils near some of the streams. The prevailing growth on this land is sweet gum, hackberry, and cottonwood, with an undergrowth of cane and bamboo. On the sandy portions there is honey-locust, sycamore, and cottonwood, with a less amount of cane.

The buckshot lands along Deer creek comprise the principal cotton lands of the county, and above Rolling Fork are wide and generally in cultivation. The lands under cultivation for the county at large average 43.2 acres per square mile, and of these 31.6 acres are given to cotton.

ABSTRACT OF THE REPORT OF THOMAS P. SCOTT, ROLLING FORK.

Two-thirds of the land is sandy alluvial, one-fourth is alluvial "buckshot," and one-twelfth is waxy or putty-like prairie. The *sandy alluvial* occupying the margins of streams is called front-land, and has a natural growth (as have the other soils) of four species of oak, ash, pecan, cypress, and hackberry. The soil is a fine silt and sandy loam of a brown and black color from 2 to 20 feet deep, and the underlying material is scarcely different, except that it has more or less stratified pipe-clay. The chief crops of this region are cotton, corn, rice, and sorghum. This soil is early, warm, well drained, easily tilled, and is best adapted to cotton and corn, but the other crops can be satisfactorily and profitably produced.

Two-thirds of its cultivated area is planted with cotton. On all lands here the plant usually attains the height of 6 to 8 feet (the maximum is 10), but is most productive at from 5 to 6 feet. In very moist or moderately wet seasons, and with clean cultivation, the plant inclines to run to weed. On this and the next soil described it can be remedied by running one furrow with a subsoil colter midway between rows and cutting lateral roots. The seed-cotton product per acre of fresh land varies from 2,500 to 4,000 pounds; 1,545 pounds (on all soils here) make a 475-pound bale of lint. After twenty years' cultivation (unmanured) the yields vary from 2,000 to 2,600 pounds, and 1,485 pounds (on all old soils here) make a 475-pound bale of lint which rates a grade below that of fresh land, except in case of the third-named soil, where it equals that of fresh land. The difference is in the length of the staple. The troublesome weeds are crab-grass, rag-weed, and hog-weed. One-twentieth of such cultivated land is at present used for summer pasturage. It yields 2,500 pounds of seed-cotton when again cultivated.

The *alluvial buckshot soil* comprises one-third of the county area, extending to its limits. Its growth is similar to that of the soil already described. The soil is a mahogany, blackish, and black-clay loam, 5 feet thick, underlaid by pipe-clay. The soil is late, warm, well drained, is easily tilled except in wet seasons, and is best adapted to cotton and corn. Four-fifths of its cultivated area is planted in cotton. The seed-cotton product per acre of fresh land is 2,500 pounds; after twenty years' cultivation it is 2,000 pounds. As weeds and cockleburs are most troublesome, none of this land lies "turned out", but it improves, when rested, about 25 per cent.

The *black waxy or putty-like prairie* has 12 to 24 inches of soil resting upon a leachy, sandy mold. The soil is late, cold, ill-drained, and difficult to plow when too wet. It is best adapted to cotton and corn, and all that is cultivated is planted with cotton. The plant grows to a height of 6 or 8 feet, and is most productive at 5 to 6 feet. The product per acre is equal to that of the soil last described, but this soil does not deteriorate during twenty years' cultivation, and the staples from fresh and old land are equal in quality. Beggar lice and cockleburs are most troublesome as weeds. One-half of this land originally cultivated now lies "turned out".

The climate is favorable to cotton growing. During the fruiting season a damp atmosphere prevails during evening, night, and early morning, the rest of the 24 hours being arid sunshine or dry and parching heat, that is absolutely necessary to the successful production of cotton. The county has two streams navigable during the year. Cotton is shipped by water, from December to June, to New Orleans, at $2 75 per bale; also to Vicksburg.

ISSAQUENA.

Population: 10,004.—White, 826; colored, 9,178.
Area: 390 square miles.—All Mississippi bottom.
Tilled lands: 32,639 acres.—Area planted in cotton, 18,293 acres; in corn, 3,849 acres; in oats, 17 acres.
Cotton production: 16,150 bales; average cotton product per acre, 0.88 bale, 1,254 pounds seed-cotton, or 418 pounds cotton lint.

Issaquena is a narrow river county, having the shape of the letter L, the foot reaching eastward to the Yazoo river. The surface of the county is level and subject to overflow, against which a system of levees have been built. The drainage is southward through Steel's bayou, Deer creek, and their tributaries. Numerous lakes occur in the lowlands. The lands embrace a front-land along the streams of light sandy or loam soils, and a back-land of stiff buckshot clays occupy the lowland away from the streams. The growth here is sweet gum and Spanish oak, with a dense undergrowth of cane. The soil along the Mississippi is a dark, sandy loam, 1 or 2 miles wide, mostly cultivated. The immediate banks are sandy, and have an almost exclusive growth of cottonwood trees.

The lands under cultivation average 83.7 acres per square mile, and of these 46.9 acres are given to the culture of cotton. The cotton plantations lie chiefly along the river, covering from 15 to 20 per cent. of the total area of that section. In average product per acre Issaquena ranks as first in the state and third among the cotton counties of all the cotton states.

ABSTRACT FROM THE REPORT OF W. E. COLLINS, MAYERSVILLE.

The lands embraced in this description are of the alluvial plain of the Mississippi river, and extend back from the river for 4 miles to Steele bayou. They embrace black buckshot and sandy loams of the river bank. The chief one is the *black buckshot*, which occupies fully two-thirds of the region, extending from the upper line of Bolivar to the lower line of Issaquena county. The soil is black when first turned up, changing to light gray, and is about 20 inches deep; the subsoil, to a depth of 4 feet resembling red clay, is the buckshot proper, crumbling into small pieces about the size of buckshot after being exposed to the sun and air. This is underlaid by fine sand to a depth of 6 feet, and then by blue mud. The timber growth is cottonwood, sweet gum, ash, oak, hickory, elm, box-elder, holly, sycamore, cypress, and many other trees, with an undergrowth of wild grapes and cane.

The soil is early and warm when well drained, always easily tilled, and is best adapted to cotton. It produces from 2,000 to 3,000 pounds of seed-cotton per acre of fresh land, and just as much after fifteen years' cultivation (unmanured). The plant grows from 5 to 7 feet high. In townships 11 and 12 about 600 acres lie "turned out". When again cultivated it produces nearly the original yields. The most troublesome weeds are hog-weed, morning-glory, and cocklebur.

The *sandy land*, with its growth of cottonwood, sweet gum, hackberry, etc., has a light, sandy, gray soil 10 feet deep, ill-drained, but early, easily tilled at any time, and is best adapted to cotton and corn. The cotton-plant grows from 3 to 5 feet high, but is most productive at 4 feet. The seed-cotton product per acre of fresh land varies from 1,200 to 1,400 pounds (400 of lint); old land produces about as much. Very little of such land lies "turned out", and it produces finely when again cultivated. Crab and Bermuda grasses are most troublesome as weeds.

Cotton is shipped chiefly in November by river to New Orleans at from 75 cents to $1 per bale.

WARREN.

(See "Cane-hills region".)

CLAIBORNE.

(See "Cane-hills region".)

JEFFERSON.

(See "Cane-hills region".)

ADAMS.

(See "Cane-hills region".)

WILKINSON.

(See "Cane-hills region".)

CANE-HILLS REGION.

(It embraces the following counties and parts of counties: Warren, Yazoo,* Hinds,* Claiborne, Jefferson, Adams, and Wilkinson.)

WARREN.

Population: 31,238.—White, 8,717; colored, 22,521.
Area: 600 square miles.—Mississippi bottom, 240 square miles; cane hills, 360 square miles; woodland.
Tilled lands: 60,031 acres.—Area planted in cotton, 34,127 acres; in corn, 10,371 acres; in oats, 69 acres.
Cotton production: 22,950 bales; average cotton product per acre, 0.67 bale, 954 pounds seed-cotton, or 318 pounds cotton lint.

Warren is emphatically a "river county", fronting on the Mississippi for about 60 miles of its course. The Yazoo enters the county from the north and empties into the great river a few miles above Vicksburg. The eastern and southern boundary is formed by the Big Black river, which joins the Mississippi a little beyond the southern end of the county.

All the uplands west of the Big Black are characteristically of the cane-hills character, if we except a few spots of heavy black prairie soil which appear on the hills near the city of Vicksburg, where the cane hills fall off abruptly toward the river, which encroaches upon their base. From about a mile above to some 9 miles below the city, at Haynes' bluff, 12 miles above Vicksburg, the Yazoo river strikes the bluff and continues from its base to its mouth. This bordering ridge, originally heavily timbered, has long been known as the "Walnut hills". Like the rest of the cane-hills country, it is now mostly treeless, the slopes being covered with Bermuda grass, and the original large upland plantations are giving way to smaller holdings, although here, as in Claiborne county, the damage from washing away of the soil is much less than farther south, the country being less deeply broken. A great deal of the upland lies "turned out". In the valley lands cultivation has steadily continued, but the land is in small bodies, though very productive. The bottom or hummock lands of the Big Black river are largely on the Hinds county side.

In the portion of the county lying within the Mississippi bottom the excellent cotton-producing lands on Steel's bayou and Deer creek are especially noted. There are many lakes in the region, and its location at the confluence of the Mississippi and the Yazoo renders it especially liable to overflow in its present unprotected condition. In favorable seasons it is profusely productive.

The tilled lands of Warren in 1879 amounted to only 15.6 per cent. of the total area; a remarkable contrast with the neighboring counties of Claiborne, Copiah, Hinds, and Yazoo, in which that percentage ranges from 24.4 per cent. in Yazoo to 36 per cent. in Hinds. We have a parallel case of depression in consequence of abandonment of cultivated lands in the old county of Wilkinson (14.9 per cent.). Of the tilled area of Warren, 56 per cent. is given to cotton culture, and less than one-third as much to corn. The average cotton product per acre is 0.67 bale, a figure indicating plainly the influence of the high production on the plantations of the Mississippi lowland.

The communication in Warren county is mainly by rail and steamer with the city of Vicksburg, and thence to New Orleans, chiefly by river, at $1 per bale.

YAZOO.
(See "Mississippi alluvial region".)

HINDS.
(See "Central prairie region".)

CLAIBORNE.

Population: 16,768.—White, 3,910; colored, 12,858.

Area: 460 square miles.—Short-leaf pine and oak uplands, 195 square miles; Mississippi bottom, 25 square miles; cane hills, 240 square miles; all woodland.

Tilled lands: 97,175 acres.—Area planted in cotton, 33,121 acres; in corn, 15,744 acres; in oats, 82 acres.

Cotton production: 18,518 bales; average cotton product per acre, 0.56 bale, 798 pounds seed-cotton, or 266 pounds cotton lint.

Claiborne county is drained centrally to westward by the north and south forks of bayou Pierre. A few short creeks are tributary to the Big Black river, which forms most of its northern-boundary and joins the Mississippi a few miles above Grand Gulf. At the latter point, as well as at Bruinsburg, 10 miles below, the Mississippi river washes the foot of high bluffs; elsewhere bodies of bottom land intervene between the river and the cane hills. The latter are, on the whole, less broken in Claiborne than farther south, and the damage done by the washing away of the soil and gullying of the hillsides is less extensive, though still quite serious. In some tracts in the southwestern part of the county the hills are timbered almost exclusively with magnolia of large size, the soil being a dark-colored, deep, and easily-tilled loam. Elsewhere oaks (among which the chestnut-white oak is prominent), sweet gum, tulip tree, linden, walnut, etc., form the upland timber, while beech is abundant on the lower hillsides and in the valleys. With ordinary care to prevent damage by washing, and small farms instead of the plantation system, a large proportion of the cane-hills lands of Claiborne can be cultivated to great advantage. (For analyses of Claiborne upland soils, see regional description, p. 44.)

To the eastward the cane-hill ridges interlace with those of the sandy uplands, with which they contrast quite strongly both as to soil and as to the sudden appearance of short-leaf pine, copiously intermingled, even on the hills, with beech and magnolia. The surface here appears to be that of the pine hills, while the subsoil in which the trees have their roots is a fertile brown loam (for analyses and discussion, see regional description, page 47). In this eastern portion of the county the hummocks of the valleys and the lower hillsides are chiefly cultivated. The streams frequently meander in wide sandy beds with little or no first bottom.

Within the cane-hill region the bayou Pierre flows in a deep channel bordered by a hummock above ordinary overflows. Near the river the soil is sometimes light and silty, and bears a growth of water and post oak; farther back, beech, black walnut, sycamore, etc., prevail, and the soil is very productive.

The tilled lands of Claiborne county constitute one-third (33 per cent.) of its area. One-third (34.1 per cent.) of the tilled lands is devoted to cotton, and about one-half as much to corn.

The average cotton product per acre is 0.56 bale, and the average cotton acreage per square mile is 72.

The communication of Claiborne county is chiefly with Port Gibson, and thence by narrow-gauge railroad to Grand Gulf; thence by river steamers to New Orleans, at the rate of $1 25 per bale. From the northern part of the county some hauling is done to Vicksburg, or to stations on the Vicksburg and Meridian railroad.

ABSTRACT OF THE REPORT OF GEORGE P. M'LEAN, ROCKY SPRING.

The soils of this region are the light, buff-colored, calcareous loam of the cane-hills region and brown and blackish, clayey loam, lying just east of and adjoining that region. The two belts extend along the Mississippi river from Louisiana to Vicksburg (and farther), and are together about 25 miles wide. Their natural growth is oak, beech, poplar, magnolia, sweet gum, and some hickory. The soils are 2 to 3 feet; the subsoils are of like material to 8 feet at least.

The chief crops are cotton, corn, cow-peas, and sweet potatoes. The soil is naturally well drained, always easily tilled, is best adapted to cotton, and about three-fourths of its area is planted with the same. The plant usually grows 3 feet high, but inclines to run to weed in wet weather, which cannot be remedied if such weather long continues. The seed-cotton product per acre of fresh land varies from 1,000 to 2,000 pounds, but thirty years' cultivation (unmanured) reduces the yield to about 1,000 pounds; 1,300 to 1,660 pounds make a 475-pound bale of middling lint (whether from fresh or old land). Hog-weed, cocklebur, Spanish needle, and crab-grass are the troublesome weeds. At least one-third of such cultivated land lies "turned out", and when again cultivated produces almost as well as when fresh.

Slopes are seriously damaged by washings and gullying of their surfaces, but valleys are improved by the washings, because the subsoil is very rich. Horizontalizing and hillside ditching have been practiced, and successfully check the damage.

JEFFERSON.

Population : 17,314.—White, 4,260; colored, 13,054.
Area : 510 square miles.—Short-leaf pine and oak uplands, 250 square miles; long-leaf pine hills, 50 square miles; Mississippi bottom, 50 square miles; cane hills, 160 square miles; all woodland.
Tilled lands : 62,218 acres.—Area planted in cotton, 32,141 acres; in corn, 16,365 acres; in oats, 312 acres.
Cotton production : 18,512 bales; average cotton product per acre, 0.58 bale, 828 pounds seed-cotton, or 276 pounds cotton lint.

Jefferson county is drained centrally to westward by the two forks of Cole's creek, its eastern portion being partly drained to the northward by creeks tributary to the south fork of bayou Pierre and partly to the southward by the headwaters of the Homochitto. The county presents four different surface features. The southeastern corner, with drainage toward the main Homochitto, forms part of the broken "Homochitto hills" country, with long-leaf pine and the sandy soil on the higher ridges. To the westward the long-leaf pine is replaced by the short-leaf species, more and more mingled with oak and hickory as we progress westward. Beyond the divide between the Homochitto and Cole's creek the ridges flatten and the country becomes rolling or gently undulating, the yellow-loam subsoil, similar to that of the Hamburg hills (see description of Franklin county), being gradually replaced by the umber-colored loam of the fine agricultural upland region, in which Fayette, the county-seat, is located. Thence westward there is a gradual transition to the character of the cane hills. The latter are of the usual character (see regional description, page 43) and fall off steeply into the Mississippi bottom, or at Rodney and at the mouth of Cole's creek, into the river itself, which washes the base of the bluff. The area of Mississippi bottom land within the county is small, but very productive.

The valley of Cole's creek within the cane hills is rather narrow and of a hummock character. Among its timber black walnut, sycamore, and honey-locust are very prominent, and the soil is especially well adapted to corn. Higher up, the valleys of the streams are usually divided between first and second bottom, prevalently timbered with beech and oaks, with more or less magnolia. They are productive, easily tilled, and form a large proportion of the cultivated area of the region.

The tilled lands of Jefferson constitute 19.1 per cent. of its area. Somewhat more than one-half of such lands (51.7 per cent.) is occupied by cotton, against about one-half as much given to corn culture, showing here also a great deficiency in the home production of supplies. The average cotton product per acre is 0.58 bale, while the average cotton acreage per square mile is 63.

The communication of Jefferson county is chiefly via Fayette and other stations of the Jackson and Natchez railroad with Natchez, and thence by river steamers with New Orleans. The freight from Natchez to New Orleans is 75 cents per bale; from Fayette to Natchez, by rail, $1 10.

ABSTRACT OF THE REPORT OF J. W. BURCH, FAYETTE.

The west half of the county comprises bluff lands, hilly and very fertile; the east half is rolling, with light sandy soils.

The soils cultivated in cotton are on the rolling uplands of the east half of the county, the second bottoms of creeks above overflow, and the Mississippi bottom.

The *upland soil* extends into other counties, covers five-eighths of this region, and bears a natural growth of hickory, gum, magnolia, beech, pine, various oaks, poplar, etc. The soil is a fine sandy loam of brown, mahogany, and blackish colors, and is 10 inches deep. The subsoil is a heavier, brown clay loam, very productive when manured or mixed with surface soil. It contains hard, rounded, and angular pebbles, and is underlaid by orange sand and sand-rock at 5 to 10 feet. The soil is early, warm, well drained, easily tilled, and is best adapted to cotton, which occupies three-fourths of its cultivated area. The other chief crop is corn. The usual and most productive height of the cotton-plant on this soil is 4½ feet. In warm, wet weather it inclines to run to weed, but this may be remedied by shallow cultivation. The seed-cotton product per acre of fresh land is 1,000 pounds; 1,600 pounds make a 475-pound bale of lint. After ten years' cultivation (unmanured) the product is 500 pounds, and the ratio of seed to lint and quality of staple are the same as on fresh land. One-half of such originally cultivated land lies "turned out", but when well turfed it again produces a few good crops. Cocklebur, purslane, crab, and Bermuda grasses are the troublesome weeds. The slopes wash very fast, and do serious damage, except to the valleys, which are rather benefited. Horizontalizing makes the lands last twice as long.

The *second bottoms of creeks* occupy about one-fourth of the county area, and have a natural growth much like that of the uplands. The soil is a brown, blackish, and black loam, 12 inches deep. The subsoil is a dark-brown and yellow clay, containing hard, rounded, and angular pebbles, underlaid by blue potters' clay at 10 feet. The soil is early, warm, well drained, easily tilled, except when too wet, and is best adapted to cotton, with which three-fourths of its cultivated area is planted. The plant's usual and most productive height ls 5 to 6 feet. The seed-cotton product per acre of fresh land is 1,600 pounds, or a 475-pound bale of lint, in quality equal to that of uplands. After 10 years' cultivation the product is 1,000 pounds of seed-cotton. Very little of such land lies "turned out"; it recuperates rapidly, and produces as well as ever. The troublesome weeds are rag, carrot, and smart weeds, cocklebur, crab and Bermuda grasses.

The remaining soil, designated *Mississippi swamp land*, consists of a narrow belt along the river, extends through the county, and contains only a few plantations. Its natural growth is cypress, gum, cottonwood, hackberry, and willow. The soil is a black alluvium, 10 feet thick, underlaid by sand. Tillage is generally easy, but is difficult when the soil is either too wet or too dry. The soil is early and warm when well-drained; it however needs ditching. It is best adapted to cotton and corn, and nine-tenths of its cultivated part is planted with cotton. The usual and best height of the plant is 6 feet. The seed-cotton product per acre of fresh or old land is 1,500 pounds; 1,780 pounds make a 475-pound bale of lint. Ten years' cultivation have made no difference in the quantity or the quality of yields. The cocklebur is the most troublesome weed.

ADAMS.

Population: 22,649.—White, 4,796; colored, 17,853.

Area: 410 square miles.—Short-leaf pine and oak uplands, 110 square miles; Mississippi bottom, 125 square miles; cane hills, 175 square miles; all woodland.

Tilled lands: 67,853 acres.—Area planted in cotton, 32,117 acres; in corn, 9,037 acres; in oats, 57 acres.

Cotton production: 19,026 bales; average cotton product per acre, 0.59 bale, 840 pounds seed-cotton, or 280 pounds cotton lint.

Adams was the first county organized within the present limits of the state, and Natchez, the county-seat, is, next to New Orleans, the oldest town on the lower Mississippi. The county fronts on the Mississippi river for over 70 miles, and about one-third of its area is bottom land, lying in the bends of the river, which, though long cultivated, is still very productive. From the bottom level there is rather an abrupt ascent into the cane-hills country. The base of the bluff, however, is washed by the river at Natchez and at Saint Catherine's bend (Ellis' cliffs), about 10 miles below; also at Rifle point, 6 miles above. Natchez is located on a plateau level about 200 (?) feet above the river.

The southern part of the county is drained by short creeks tributary to the Homochitto river, of which Second and Sandy creeks are the chief. The middle portion, back of Natchez, is traversed by Saint Catherine's creek, along the course of which deep and steep ravines have been cut into the soft material of the cane hills. The latter are of the usual character (see regional description, page 43), and long cultivation, with shallow tillage, has greatly reduced the area of uplands not too broken for convenient culture. With proper treatment, nevertheless, good crops are still grown on these lands.

The country east of the cane hills is undulating or rolling land, originally timbered with oak and hickory, and on the ridges with short-leaf pine, or in part with oaks only, the subsoil being an umber-colored loam, similar to that overlying the calcareous silt of the cane hills, and forming a durable and originally very productive soil, of which, however, a not inconsiderable proportion has been thrown out of cultivation.

The tilled lands of Adams county amount to somewhat over one-quarter (25.9 per cent.) of the total area, and nearly one-half (47.3 per cent.) of such lands is given to cotton, while only 13.3 per cent. are planted in corn, showing a remarkable deficiency in the home production of supplies. The average cotton product per acre is 0.59 bale; the average cotton acreage per square mile is 78.3.

The communication of Adams county is altogether with Natchez, and thence by river steamers with New Orleans.

WILKINSON.

Population: 17,815.—White, 3,570; colored, 14,245.

Area: 650 square miles.—Short-leaf pine and oak uplands, 395 square miles; Mississippi bottom, 70 square miles; cane hills, 185 square miles; all woodland.

Tilled lands: 64,065 acres.—Area planted in cotton, 33,720 acres; in corn, 15,068 acres; in oats, 204 acres.

Cotton production: 16,620 bales; average cotton product per acre, 0.49 bale, 699 pounds seed-cotton, or 233 pounds cotton lint.

Wilkinson county is one of the oldest in the state, having been organized in 1802, and is second only to Adams county. This county fronts on the Mississippi river for about 20 miles, its northern line being formed by the Homochitto river. The central portion is drained by the Buffalo river and the southern by Bayou Sara and Thompson's creek. The county embraces three chief surface features, viz, on the east, rolling and more or less sandy and gravelly upland, timbered with oak, hickory, and short-leaf pine, which extends westward a few miles beyond Woodville, the county-seat. Here the country assumes rather suddenly the character of the cane hills (see regional description, page 43): steep and mostly sharp-backed ridges, separated by deep and narrow valleys, now mostly bare of timber, but originally bearing a heavy growth of cane and timbered with oaks (among which the chestnut-white oak is prominent), poplar, sweet gum, magnolia, linden, sassafras, etc. This belt has a width varying from 6 to 12 miles, skirting the Mississippi bottom, into which the hills fall off steeply, the river washing at Fort Adams the base of ridges which rise abruptly to over 300 feet above low-water mark. The bottom here is low and subject to overflow, and is studded with lakes, but contains some excellent plantations.

The cane-hills lands, originally covered with a deep black mold soil and highly productive, have been grievously damaged by long, shallow, and exhaustive cultivation. The surface soil has, to a great extent, been washed off, and large bodies of the uplands, originally constituting level or gently undulating plateaus, have been deeply scored with gullies and ravines, impeding and restricting cultivation, the slopes being mostly too steep for tillage and sometimes forming almost vertical caving walls, supported by loose sand and gravel. The Bermuda grass, which has taken possession of almost the entire region, now acts in a measure as a preventative of farther inroads and affords pasturage to cattle. But the large upland plantations are, of necessity, giving way to small farms, which by more careful husbandry can restore to cultivation the "worn-out" lands.

In the eastern portion of the county the bottoms and hummocks of the streams form the bulk of the cultivated lands, especially in the somewhat broken country on the Homochitto, which is a continuation of the "Devil's Backbone", a sandstone ridge which, beginning in the southwest corner of Copiah, is more or less distinctly traceable through Franklin and Wilkinson counties to fort Adams.

The tilled lands of Wilkinson county constitute at present only 14.9 per cent. of its area, but they have doubtless greatly diminished since 1860. More than one-half of these lands is given to cotton; less than one-quarter to corn. The cotton area per square mile is 51.9, with the high average product of 0.49 per acre, due doubtless in part to the bottom plantations.

The communication of Wilkinson county is partly with landings on the Mississippi river, partly by railroad from Woodville to Bayou Sara, and thence by steamer to New Orleans; freight on cotton is $1 per bale.

ABSTRACT OF THE REPORT OF D. L. PHARES, A. M., M. D., WOODVILLE.

Nearly all the soil here, both on the rolling uplands and the bottoms, was originally a black or dark loam ; now only one-third of the cultivated land is of this kind, the balance, having changed its character by being allowed to have its soil washed off, being now yellow and brown clay. The same kind of black land occurs 20 miles east, 8 north, and 20 west and south. Its natural growth is tulip tree, linden, magnolia grandiflora, holly, sweet and black gums, beech, six species of oak, and many other trees.

The soil varies in depth from 4 inches to 10 feet. The subsoil is a tenacious yellow and brown clay with considerable sand, and in some places gravel. It is slowly pervious to water, contains hard rounded gravel, and is underlaid by yellow or red sandstone at 1 to 20 feet. Tillage is easy in dry and difficult in wet seasons. The soil is early on well-drained slopes facing the east and south, and is adapted, in the order named (best first), to clover, grasses, pease, potatoes, cotton, sorghum, sugar-cane, oats, and corn. These are the chief crops of this region. Two-thirds of its area is planted with cotton. The plant usually grows from 5 to 8 feet high on fresh soil, and from 3 to 5 feet on worn soil ; but the most productive height is from 4 to 6 feet. It inclines to run to weed on rich, fresh land when there is much rain and little root pruning. When the soil is not too wet and heavy, this is prevented by deep plowing, so as to restrain root and stem growth until fruiting time. The seed-cotton product per acre of fresh land varies from 2,000 to 2,500 pounds, about 1,460 pounds making a 475-pound bale of good middling lint. After forty years' cultivation (unmanured) the yield varies from 600 to 1,200 pounds, according to the extent the soil has been washed off. About 1,520 pounds then make a 475-pound bale of lint, the staple of which is much shorter, and rates two or three grades lower than that of fresh land.

The troublesome weeds are several species of crab-grass, two of water-grass, crowfoot-grass, in many places Bermuda grass, and the cocklebur. One-third of such land originally cultivated now lies "turned out"; when again cultivated it often produces from 30 to 100 per cent. better than when first "turned out". The soil on slopes washes and gullies readily only where marked by a plow, wagon rut, or path, and many slopes are thus seriously damaged, and the washings cover many parts of the valleys to the extent of 6 to 48 inches deep. Horizontalizing and hillside ditching are practiced and completely check the damage.

Very little clay land occurs in this county, none originally, and now produced by bad management of other lands, in allowing the original soils to be washed off. Its depth varies from 2 to 10 inches, and it bears a growth of pine trees more commonly than the original land.

Most of the above statements apply to the whole of township —, range 1 west, and sections 19, 20, 21, and 31, all parts of which are well supplied with streams, making up east and middle Thompson creeks. Proper cultivation here has always brought good yields of cotton, except perhaps in 1846, when it rained almost daily throughout the planting and growing season and the caterpillar came early and in large numbers.

Cotton is shipped as fast as it is baled, by river and rail, to New Orleans, at $1 per bale.

CENTRAL PRAIRIE REGION.

(Embraces the following counties and parts of counties: Madison, Hinds, Rankin, Scott, Newton,* Smith,* Jasper, Clarke, and Wayne.)

MADISON.

Population ; 25,866.—White, 5,946; colored, 19,920.

Area : 720 square miles.—Short leaf pine and oak uplands, 5 square miles ; cane hills, 5 square miles ; central prairie, 530 square miles ; brown-loam table-lands, 180 square miles ; oil woodland.

Tilled lands : 127,594 acres.—Area planted in cotton, 56,393 acres ; in corn, 37,000 acres ; in oats, 1,498 acres ; in wheat, 22 acres.

Cotton production : 21,538 bales ; average cotton product per acre, 0.38 bale, 543 pounds seed-cotton, or 181 pounds cotton lint.

Madison county presents almost throughout a gently undulating surface, similar to that of the table-lands farther north.

Lying between the Pearl and Big Black rivers, which, flowing nearly parallel, approach to within 15 miles of each other, its drainage and slope are almost entirely toward the Big Black, the dividing ridge running within a few miles west of the Pearl river. The northeastern part of the county, as far south as Doak's creek, is of the table-land character, and is similar to the adjoining portion of the Yazoo. A few sandy ridges, with pine, appear at the extreme northeast. Southward the table-land character continues as to the general aspect of the country, but the soil is to a great extent materially modified by the influence of the stiff calcareous clays of the Tertiary formation, which manifests itself partly in the presence of a stiff, greenish-yellow subsoil and frequently in the occurrence of spots and smaller or larger bodies of black-prairie soil, accompanied by the appearance of lime-loving trees, such as honey-locust, wild plum, haw, crab-apple, walnut, etc. The prairie lands, as well as the general face of the country, are generally sparsely timbered with oaks (among which stout black-jack and post oaks, with more or less of the black and Spanish oaks, are conspicuous) and hickory. The uplands slope gently toward the creek bottoms, or flats, and the soils of these vary materially with the location and length of the streams. In the northern part of the county they are mostly of a whitish, silty character, and are underlaid by impervious bog ore, thus forming many "crawfishy" tracts, ill-drained and little cultivated, timbered chiefly with water oak and sweet gum. Such is also, in part, the character of the Big Black bottom, which is moreover subject to overflow, and is but little cultivated. The bottom of the Pearl river, on the contrary, has prevalently a sandy soil, alternating in the southern portion with tracts and "ridges" of tough clay soil of greater fertility, but difficult to till. The soils of the creek bottoms of the southern part of the county are more similar to those of the adjoining uplands, are very productive, and are largely under cultivation.

Madison is an old and well-settled county, and its present area of tilled lands, as given in the returns (27.7 per cent.), does not adequately represent its position in respect to improvements among the counties of the state. It has been pre-eminently a region of large upland plantations of great productiveness; but its soil has been so severely drawn upon by heavy cropping, without returns or rotation, that large tracts once cultivated in cotton have passed out of cultivation, only awaiting, however, a rational system of small farming to restore the productiveness. The cotton acreage, nevertheless, still exceeds that of corn in the ratio of 4 to 3, and the average product per acre (0.38 bale) is but slightly below that of the northern table-land counties. In cotton acreage per square mile (72.5 acres) Madison stands fourteenth in the state.

The New Orleans and Chicago railroad, which traverses the county centrally, carries cotton to New Orleans either directly or via Jackson and Vicksburg and river steamers.

HINDS.

Population: 43,958.—White, 11,675; colored, 32,283.

Area: 800 square miles.—Short-leaf pine and oak uplands, 175 square miles; long-leaf pine hills, 245 square miles; cane hills, 125 square miles; central prairie, 255 square miles; all woodland.

Tilled lands: 184,607 acres.—Area planted in cotton, 80,013 acres; in corn, 47,510 acres; in oats, 1,962 acres; in wheat, 16 acres.

Cotton production: 36,684 bales; average cotton product per acre, 0.46 bale, 657 pounds seed-cotton, or 219 pounds cotton lint.

Hinds county is one of the largest and the most populous counties in the state, and contains the state capital, Jackson, with 5,204 inhabitants. Its drainage is in three directions, the largest area being occupied by streams tributary to the Big Black, a region of gently undulating table-lands similar to those of southern Madison, the same being true of the narrow belt of country drained by the numerous short streams tributary to the Pearl river. The southern part of the county around the heads of the bayou Pierre is a region of high sandy ridges, timbered with long-leaf pine and more or less oaks, interspersed with lower and broader ridge lands of fair productiveness. The country immediately contiguous to the Big Black river is somewhat ridgy and at times broken, and in timber and soil is similar to the adjoining upland portion of Warren county, viz, more or less of the bluff or cane-hills character.

The prairie character of the soil is, on the whole, much less frequent in Hinds than in Madison county, and is most pronounced on the Pearl river slope, the soil of northern Hinds being more strictly of the table-land character, easily tilled, and originally very productive—in aspect a very attractive farming country. Near Jackson the heavy "black-jack prairie" soil is quite prominent in the uplands, though frequently overlaid by the lighter and more easily tilled table-land soil. The characteristic cracking and fissuring of the tenacious subsoil during the dry season not unfrequently interferes with the stability of foundations and cistern walls, and on steep slopes (as where the uplands break off into Pearl river bottom) sometimes give rise to land-slides. Here also heavy clay soils predominate in the river bottom, which is subject to overflow, the main portion of it, however, lying on the opposite side. (See description of Rankin county.)

Agriculturally, Hinds is situated very nearly like Madison. It has been, and is still to some extent, a region of large upland-cotton plantations, upon many of which the soil has materially deteriorated by long and exhaustive culture; yet the average cotton product per acre (0.46) is materially higher than that of Madison (0.38), as is also its cotton acreage per square mile (100), both together placing it first on the list of total production among the upland counties of the state. This, unfortunately, is offset by an inadequate production of corn, the acreage of the latter being to that of cotton as 3 to 5.

The abundance of excellent marls, easily accessible in a large part of the county (as mentioned in the regional description, page 54), will greatly facilitate the maintenance of fertility of lands in Hinds county whenever a rational system of small farming shall replace the improvident practice of the past.

The New Orleans and Chicago and the Vicksburg and Meridian railroads both traverse the county, intersecting at Jackson, and cotton is shipped either direct or via Vicksburg and the river to New Orleans at $2 75 per bale, most of it being marketed by the producers at Jackson.

ABSTRACT OF THE REPORT OF H. O. DIXON, JACKSON.

Much the greater part of the soil of the county is an upland clay loam, yellow, brown, and blackish, 8 inches thick, with a heavier subsoil of yellow and red clay, 3 to 5 feet thick, underlaid by gypsum and white clay at 15 to 20 feet. The red subsoil is pervious to water and indicates the best land. Such land extends 40 miles north, 8 to 10 south, 5 east, and 30 miles west, and has a natural growth of post, red, and black-jack oaks, hickory, walnut, and mulberry.

The chief crops are cotton, corn, pease, oats, and sweet potatoes. The soil is early, warm, well drained, is well adapted to the chief crops named and to clover and many varieties of cultivated grapes, but three-fourths of its cultivated area is planted with cotton. The plant grows from 2 to 4 feet high, but is most productive at 3 feet, and inclines to run to weed in wet seasons on fresh land or when planted late; the remedy consists in early planting and frequent deep plowing. The seed-cotton product per acre is from 1,000 to 1,500 pounds on fresh land, or 600 to 1,000 pounds after eight years' cultivation on level or unwashed land. In either case about 1,485 pounds make a 475-pound bale of lint. The seeds are lighter on old land. The fresh-land staple rates as middling; that of old land differs but little. Old land is more easily affected by unfavorable seasons. One-half of such originally cultivated land lies "turned out"; when grown up with broom-sedge it produces nearly as well as originally. The old fields are generally burnt off each year, but the great need of such land is vegetable matter.

Slopes are damaged to a serious extent by washings and gullying of the soil, and the valleys are injured to a slight extent by the washings. To check the damage hillside ditching is practiced, and is successful when properly done.

The farmer or planter in this section, however great his desire may be for improvement in modes of cultivation or treatment of his soil, finds himself checked by the uncertain and uncontrollable labor he has to depend on.

Cotton culture, to be remunerative, requires unceasing attention for twelve months, and the work must be properly done and at the right time. Intelligent experience alone can meet these imperative demands under the many contingencies which are certain to occur through the season. Hence it is that cotton cannot be produced as cheaply with the present free labor as with that of the slaves, it being both ignorant and uncertain as well as unmanageable as to both the quantity and the quality of the work, resulting in producing less and costing more.

RANKIN.

Population: 16,752.—White, 7,193; colored, 9,559.

Area: 800 square miles.—Short-leaf pine and oak uplands, 360 square miles; long-leaf pine hills, 155 square miles; central prairie, 285 square miles.

Tilled lands: 69,516 acres.—Area planted in cotton, 30,151 acres; in corn, 23,450 acres; in oats, 5,781 acres; in wheat, 4 acres.

Cotton production: 11,775 bales; average cotton product per acre, 0.39 bale, 555 pounds seed-cotton, or 185 pounds cotton lint.

The surface of Rankin county is a good deal diversified, but may be classed under three chief heads, to wit: Skirting Pearl river on the east, a broad but more or less interrupted belt, timbered with oak and in part with short-leaf pine, and possessing a light loam soil, sometimes deeply colored with iron. It is about 4 miles wide, well settled, and is drained mainly by short creeks directly tributary to the Pearl river. East of this belt, and interlacing with it, we have in the northern portion of the county an undulating or rolling oak upland region, interspersed with spots and bodies of black calcareous as well as post oak and gypseous prairies, the former being found chiefly in the valleys and the latter on the hillsides and lower ridges, while the higher portions of ridges are frequently sandy, sometimes with an admixture of pine to the oak growth. This region is drained by the heads of Funnegusha and Pelahatchie creeks and a few tributaries of Strong river. The southeastern portion of the county, drained by Sander's, Dobb's, Campbell's, and other creeks tributary to Strong river, is a sandy long-leaf pine region, which rises abruptly from the prairie belt into high ridges of sand and clay stones, but becomes gently undulating to the southward. In this region, as usual, the valleys and their slopes are alone cultivated, and it is but thinly settled. The level country extends westward to within a few miles of Pearl river, the long-leaf pine stopping at the divide between Strong river and Steel's creek. On the waters of the latter there is quite a variety of upland soils, partly sandy loam ridges, partly bearing a "flatwoods" aspect, with heavy, gray clay soils, which in places are productive and well settled, in others quite poor. Their timber varies accordingly, from black and Spanish oaks, with hickory, to short leaf pine, with scrubby black-jack. Between this country and Pearl river there intervene the red-ridge lands previously mentioned.

The part of the county lying within the prairie belt is agriculturally the richest portion, but its soils are so variable within small areas as to render it difficult to give an average estimate of its productiveness. The black prairie soil is profusely fertile, but is not always adapted to the cultivation of cotton, which is liable to rust, probably on account of the stiff, clay subsoil, which the tap-root cannot penetrate. Such soils (naturally timbered with sweet gum, mulberry, crab-apple, and honey-locust) produce heavy crops of corn. The same is true more or less of the post-oak prairie, especially in the low land. The best cotton is grown where the lighter upland soils are naturally or artificially marled by the prevailing materials of the Tertiary formation, which offer an inexhaustible store of natural fertilizers for the improvement and restoration of the fertility of the lands of this region. (See regional description, page 54.) The gypseous prairies are, perhaps, the least promising, on account of their intractable clay subsoil.

The first bottom of Pearl river, which lies chiefly on the Rankin side, is little cultivated, on account of overflow, although the soil is very fertile. It is from one-half to three-quarters of a mile wide. From it there is an ascent of 5 or 6 feet into a flat or second bottom, timbered with post, willow, and water oaks, bottom pine, some hickory, and magnolia. The soil is gray and silty, with a pale yellow loam subsoil, not very productive, and but little settled.

The tilled lands of Rankin county are reported to be but 13.6 per cent. of its large area, the cotton acreage per square mile being 37.7. The average product per acre is 0.39 of a bale, ranking in this respect with Marshall and Union counties, and slightly above Madison. The corn acreage is slightly below that devoted to cotton.

The communication of Rankin is partly with stations on the Vicksburg and Meridian railroad, especially with Brandon, where much of the crop is marketed, and partly across Pearl river, with stations on the New Orleans and Chicago railroad. The freight to New Orleans is about $3 per bale.

ABSTRACT OF REPORT OF E. JACK, BRANDON.

The uplands of the county comprise three-fourths of its area, and on the north are hilly, with sandy soils and clay subsoils, interspersed with prairies of different sizes having stiff clayey soils. In the southern part of the county the lands are loose and sandy.

The usual depth of the upland soils is from 3 to 6 inches, and the timber growth comprises pine, oak, hickory, gums, dogwood, black-jack, elm, etc. The subsoils are usually clay, having a small proportion of sand. Very little hard-pan occurs, and a few small patches are impervious to water. Some parts are underlaid by sand at 6 to 10 feet. The upland soils are tilled with moderate ease, excepting the prairies, which are difficult to till in wet weather, but easy to till in dry seasons after being once broken up.

Cotton, corn, and oats are the chief crops of this region, and during later years making molasses from sorghum and Louisiana cane has received some attention. The soil seems best adapted to cotton, about one-half the cultivated area being planted with the same. The plant inclines to run to weed in wet seasons, and as a restraining remedy some suggest running a center furrow in bedding up. The seed-cotton product per acre of fresh land is 1,000 pounds, or 800 pounds after ten years' cultivation; 1,425 pounds make a 475-pound bale of lint. The staple from fresh land is the better, but by a little manuring old land can be kept equal to fresh, both in quantity and quality of the cotton product. Hog-weed and crab-grass are the most troublesome. About one-fifth of such originally cultivated upland lies "turned out". The soil on slopes washes and gullies, but not so much but that it can be remedied, for which purpose horizontalizing and hillside ditching are successfully practiced. The washings improve the valley soils.

The lowlands embrace the first and second bottom lands of the Pearl river and its tributaries. They have a loose, sandy soil and sufficient fall for good drainage.

The cultivated portion of the lowlands consists of dry ridges about 2 feet above high water. Between these are cold, wet sloughs, which can be drained and cultivated, but they remain stiff and cold in spring. It is generally believed that the river bottoms are better suited to cotton production than the uplands.

Cotton is shipped as fast as baled, by rail and river, to New Orleans, at about $3 per bale.

SCOTT.

Population: 10,845.—White, 6,633; colored, 4,212.

Area: 580 square miles.—Short leaf pine and oak uplands, 150 square miles; central prairie, 430 square miles.

Tilled lands: 39,711 acres.—Area planted in cotton, 16,282 acres; in corn, 15,664 acres; in oats, 5,129 acres; in wheat, 111 acres.

Cotton production: 6,227 bales; average cotton product per acre, 0.38 bale, 543 pounds seed-cotton, or 181 pounds cotton lint.

The greater part of Scott county is similar to eastern Rankin in its surface features. The undulating and sometimes hilly uplands are timbered partly with oaks and hickory only and partly with the same trees mingled more or less with pine (short-leaf in the northern and long-leaf in the southern portion), such admixture indicating always an increasing sandiness of the soil, and occurring mostly on the higher dividing ridges. Other and usually lower ridges, as well as the lower portions of the more elevated ones, exhibit the post oak or "hog-wallow" prairie character; while in the deeper valleys, according to elevation and position, either the same or the black-prairie soil prevails (see regional description, page 50), forming rich bodies of several square miles' area. The feature of the gypseous prairie is less frequent than in Rankin, and much of the black prairie yields excellent crops of cotton; but here also the heavy black or chocolate-colored bottom prairie is liable to blight or rust cotton, though producing abundant crops of corn.

The northeastern portion of Scott county, traversed by the Tuskalamite and its tributaries, is a sandy hill country, timbered with short-leaf pine and oaks, and resembles the adjacent part of Leake county.

The tilled lands of Scott amount to 10.7 per cent. of its area, and 41 per cent. of these lands are cultivated in cotton, and nearly an equal amount in corn. The cotton acreage per square mile is 28.1, being below that of Rankin (37.7). The average product per acre is 543 pounds of seed-cotton.

The communication of Scott is with Forest and other stations on the Vicksburg and Meridian railroad, which traverses the county almost centrally from west to east. Cotton is shipped to New Orleans at from $3 50 to $4 per bale.

ABSTRACT OF THE REPORT OF W. T. ROBERTSON, FOREST.

The chief soil is the *black upland prairie.* It covers one-eighth of the county, occurs in spots of 5 to 150 acres, is 2 to 3 feet thick, and bears a scattered, natural growth of post oak, hickory, ash, plum, and haw. The subsoil is a tough, yellow, waxy clay, which bakes very hard on exposure to sun, but after a rain becomes mellow. It contains soft, white, limy, angular gravel, and some large pebbles. The soil is early, but ill-drained, and is rather difficult to till in wet seasons. It is best adapted to cotton, and half its cultivated area is planted with the same. The height attained by the plant varies with seasons from 3 to 5 feet, and it inclines to run to weed on any soil here when the same is fresh and rich, for which the correspondent knows no remedy. The seed-cotton product per acre varies from 800 to 1,800 pounds; 1,425 pounds from fresh or 1,485 pounds from old land make a 475-pound bale of lint. The same is true of the two remaining kinds of land. After eight years' cultivation (unmanured) the yield varies from 400 to 800 pounds. Staple from fresh land rates as good middling; that from old land differs very little. The troublesome weeds on this and the next soil to be described are crab-grass, morning-glory, cocklebur, and tea-weed. Very little of this land lies "turned out", but it improves by rest.

The *black-prairie creek bottoms* form one-sixth of the county area. They are from one-half to 1 mile wide, and occur in bodies of 1 to 5 miles long. They are subject to overflows. Where timber occurs, it consists of red and white oaks, hickory, ash, poplar, elms, and many others. The soil is 2 to 5 feet deep, rests upon a stiff, yellowish clay, which bakes very hard when first exposed, but pulverizes after a rain. It contains limy pebbles. Tillage is difficult only in wet seasons. The soil is late, cold, and ill-drained, but produces corn and cotton well. One-half its area is planted with cotton. The plant usually attains a height of from 4 to 8 feet, but is most productive at from 4 to 5 feet. The seed-cotton product per acre is from 1,000 to 1,800 pounds, and the staple rates as good middling. After fifteen years' cultivation (unmanured) the product is 800 pounds with good tillage. The staple is not very different from that of fresh land. A great deal of this kind of land has not yet been brought into cultivation.

A small proportion of the cotton land consists of *dark sandy hummock soil,* in spots of from one-half to three-fourths of a mile in extent. Its growth is hickory, ash, dogwood, mulberry, walnut, poplar, and various oaks. The soil is a brown and mahogany-colored coarse sandy loam 2 feet thick; the subsoil is a light, reddish clay, easily worked, and becomes like the surface on exposure. It contains soft, angular "black gravel". The soil is early, warm, well-drained, easily tilled in all seasons, and is very well adapted to cotton, corn, peas, and almost any southern crop. About one-half its area is planted in cotton. The plant grows from 4 to 6 feet high, and is most productive at 4 feet.

The seed-cotton product per acre of fresh land averages 1,200 pounds; the staple is the best produced here. Ten years' cultivation (without manure) reduces the yield to 600 pounds, and the staple becomes inferior. Crab-grass is the troublesome weed. None of this land has been "turned out", and some has never been improved. The soil washes and gullies readily and seriously damages the slopes. Horizontalizing and hillside ditching are successfully practiced, and are the only means of saving the soil of the slopes. Bottom lands are also sometimes damaged by deposits of clay from overflowing waters. Ditches are cut to facilitate the passage of such waters and prevent such deposits. The chief crops of this region are cotton, corn, oats, sweet potatoes, and sugar-cane.

NEWTON.
(See "Short-leaf pine and oak uplands region".)

SMITH.
(See "Long-leaf pine region".)

JASPER.

Population: 12,126.—White, 6,244; colored, 5,882.
Area: 680 square miles.—Long-leaf pine hills, 220 square miles; central prairie, 460 square miles.
Tilled lands: 58,318 acres.—Area planted in cotton, 20,305 acres; in corn, 19,934 acres; in oats, 5,467 acres; in wheat, 5 acres.
Cotton production: 6,228 bales; average cotton product per acre, 0.31 bale, 441 pounds seed-cotton, or 147 pounds cotton lint.

Jasper county, drained chiefly by confluents of the Leaf river (the east and west Tallahala, Tallahoma, and others, flowing southward), is traversed almost centrally from northwest to southeast by the prairie belt, leaving the northeast and southwest corners occupied by sandy, hilly uplands, timbered with long-leaf pine and more or less of oaks and hickory. From these sandy pine ridges extend more or less into the central belt, which is itself a country of ridges interspersed with valleys, on the slopes or in the bottoms of which the "hog-wallow" and black prairie soils appear to a greater or less extent. Thus on the west Tallahala and its tributaries, in the northwestern part of the county, we find the extreme of heavy "hog-wallow" soil, timbered with scrubby black-jack and post oaks, forming the lower ridges and the lower portion of the higher ones, often leaving narrow crests or isolated knolls of sandy land, with oak and pine growth, perched on a broader plateau of the tough, brown-clay soil, while in the bottoms of the streams we find either the same, somewhat modified and often covered with a gray ashy surface soil, or else the calcareous black prairie soil appears. These extreme clay soils contrast oddly with those of the opposite character, which form the body, *e. g.*, the ridge intervening between the west Tallahala and the Tallahoma, west of Garlandsville. This ridge is timbered only with oaks and hickory, and the soil is very productive, but is so extremely sandy that its best portions are liable to be blown away by the wind when plowed dry (see page 54). Similar ridges form the higher divides elsewhere in the county, Paulding, the county-seat, being located on one of them, the soil, however, being inferior to that of the Tallahoma ridge.

The black prairie feature is somewhat extensively developed near Garlandsville, on Suanlovey creek, some of it being of the "bald" character, the white marl coming to the surface. The bottom soil, also of the black prairie character, is profusely fertile, but is liable to rust or blight cotton (see analysis and discussion, page 52). A similar state of things exists more or less southeastward across the county.

In the southern part of the prairie belt the features are somewhat similar, but the "hog-wallow" feature is less pronounced, and the black prairie soil less heavy, as, *e. g.*, in the neighborhood of Claiborne. Limestone hills replace in a measure those formed of the heavy clays, and small bodies of black prairie soil, often only a few acres or even less in extent, are found on the hillsides or on the lower ridges.

Besides the more extreme types of soil, there are, especially in the northern portion of the county, tracts of gently rolling oak uplands with a loam soil, quite productive and easily tilled, and on that account often preferred to the heavier though more fertile soils.

The tilled lands of Jasper county amount to 13.4 per cent. of its total area, being about the same as that of Rankin. About one-third of these, or 29.9 acres per square mile, are in cotton, the corn acreage being about the same. The average product per acre is 0.31 of a bale; somewhat low, owing, doubtless, to the growing of corn in the richest bottom lands.

The communication of Jasper county is partly with stations on the Vicksburg and Meridian railroad, in Newton, or with those on the Mobile and Ohio railroad, in Clarke county, both of which approach within 6 miles of the county line.

ABSTRACT OF THE REPORT OF S. G. LOUGHRIDGE, M. D., GARLANDSVILLE.

In the order of their productiveness the three kinds of soils cultivated in cotton are, according to their common designations, first, black slough prairie; second, black, "hog-wallow," and shell prairie, with sandy hummock land along creeks; third, sand hills and waxy prairie. The *first and second* are continuous, and occur in bodies of 50 to 1,000 acres throughout the county. Their soils are 18 to 24 inches deep. The subsoil is in either case a tough, yellow, hard, impervious clay, which takes hard on first exposure, but becomes by cultivation like surface soil. It contains soft, limy, white, rounded, and angular pebbles, and the second more shells than the first, and is underlaid by rotten lime-rock at 10 feet. The first is late and ill-drained, but is easily cultivated when broken deep. The second is early when well drained, and is difficult to till when too wet, but easy when dry, if well drained. Both soils are best adapted to cotton, corn, oats, rye, and sugar-cane. About one-half their cultivated area is planted in cotton. On the first the plant grows usually 4 feet high, and is most productive at from 4 to 5 feet. The seed-cotton product per acre of fresh land varies from 1,000 to 2,000 pounds; from 1,425 to 1,545 pounds from any fresh soil here make a 475-pound bale of lint, which commands the highest price. This soil deteriorates but little in ten years of good deep cultivation (unmanured); 1,425 pounds from old land make a bale of lint inferior to that of fresh land. Crab-grass, morning-glory, and a kind of water-grass are the most troublesome weeds.

On the second quality of soil the usual and most productive height of the plant is 3 feet. The seed-cotton product per acre of fresh land varies from 1,050 to 1,200 pounds; but after ten years' cultivation (unmanured) it is from 800 to 1,000 pounds, and the staple is coarser. Crab-grass, morning-glory, purslane, and careless-weed are most troublesome. About one-third of such land lies "turned out"; in the second year after it is again taken in it produces as fresh land. The upland growth outside of the prairies is hackberry, ash, hickory, oak, red-bud, red haw and plums. The hummocks have hickory, oak, pine, dogwood, and grape-vines. The lands wash readily, doing much damage, and the valleys are injured by the washings when the hills are poor. But little is done to check the damage.

The *sand-hills and waxy prairie* occupy about one-half of the area of this region. They occur in patches, and vary greatly from ridge to ridge, their timber being pine and post oak. The soil is 8 to 10 inches thick; the subsoil is heavier, and is underlaid by rather soft limestone at 5 to 20 feet. The soil is early, well drained, difficult to till in wet, but generally easy in dry seasons. It is best adapted to cotton, and about two-thirds of its cultivated area is planted with the same. The plant usually grows about 2 feet high. The seed-cotton product per acre of fresh land is from 600 to 800 pounds, but after ten years' cultivation (unmanured) it is from 400 to 600 pounds. The staple is then inferior, and it takes a little more seed-cotton to make a bale. Crab-grass is the most troublesome weed. About one-half such land originally cultivated lies "turned out". The plant inclines to run to weed on fresh land (of any kind described) in wet seasons, and drainage and deep plowing constitute the remedy. The uplands wash readily, and the valleys are somewhat injured. Clean staple sells for much more than the same quality not clean. The prairies that are black produce best in dry seasons; the sandy soils require most rain.

All creeks running east or west have poor sandy soil on the north side and rich black prairie on the south. The chief crops of this region are cotton, corn, rice, sugar, sorghum, oats, peas, and sweet potatoes.

Cotton is shipped as soon as baled, by rail, to Mobile, at $3 per bale.

CLARKE.

Population: 15,921.—White, 7,181; colored, 7,840.
Area: 650 square miles.—Long-leaf pine hills, 425 square miles; central prairie, 225 square miles.
Tilled lands: 45,888 acres.—Area planted in cotton, 15,936 acres; in corn, 17,333 acres; in oats, 3,193 acres.
Cotton production: 4,693 bales; average cotton product per acre, 0.29 bale, 414 pounds seed-cotton, or 138 pounds cotton lint.

Clarke county is drained to the southward by the Chickasawhay river and its tributaries, of which Chunkey, Okatibbee, and Buckatunna are the chief. The northern portion is a region of rolling or hilly long-leaf pine lands, whose quality varies in accordance with a greater or less admixture of oaks and hickory, cultivation being, however, thus far mainly restricted to the lowlands. Of these the wide "hummock" of the Chickasawhay, with a good sandy loam soil, forms an important part, the more so as beds of greensand and marls occurring at and below the town of Enterprise afford an important means of improving and maintaining the fertility of the soil. A line drawn from northwest to southeast through De Soto marks the northern limit of the prairie belt proper, although the influence of the marly beds which crop out in the creeks appears in the valleys as far north as Quitman in the occurrence of the tulip tree, walnut, ash, etc.

The prairies of southern Clarke form plateaus between the streams and differ in several respects from those farther west, the extreme hog-wallow character being less pronounced. There are few treeless tracts. The prevalent timber is sturdy post oak and short-leaf pine, thickly hung with long moss, and accompanied by an undergrowth of crab-apple, wild plum, honey-locust, etc. It is a very heavy soil, producing in rainy times a fearfully tenacious mud. The black surface soil is from 6 to 12 inches deep, below which lies an equally heavy, deep orange-tinted subsoil, and beneath this, at from 3 to 10 feet, there are yellowish clay marls. The open prairie tracts, with occasional clumps of crab-apple and honey-locust, have a much lighter soil, sometimes whitish from the admixture of the underlying marl. Both soils produce cotton finely, but the open prairie is the safer and more easily tilled, the heavy black soil standing intermediate in character between the intractable hog-wallow of Smith and Jasper and the true black prairie soil. Besides this, we find to the southward a belt about 3 miles wide of a tawny-colored soil, more of the true "hog-wallow" type, timbered with lank post oak and short-leaf pine and black gum, which has not thus far been brought into cultivation. Southward of this belt there are, in the southwest corner of Clarke and in the adjacent parts of Wayne county, ridgy lands, with small upland prairies, similar to those of southern Jasper. The Chickasawhay river here runs between rocky banks in a deep channel.

Most of the cotton grown in the county is from this southern prairie region and the Chickasawhay flat.

The percentage of tilled lands is 11, and the cotton acreage is one-seventh less than that devoted to corn, making it 24.5 per square mile. The cotton product per acre is 0.29, being somewhat below that of Jasper county, and the same as in Lauderdale.

The Mobile and Ohio railroad traverses the western part of the county from north to south and affords ample opportunity for shipment and communication. Freight to Mobile, $3 per bale.

ABSTRACT OF THE REPORT OF W. SPILLMAN, M. D., ENTERPRISE.

(Refers to T. 4, R. 14 east, the northwestern corner of the county.)

The best land is that of the *bottoms of the Chunkey and the Chickasawhay rivers*, which occupies about one-sixth of the township and extends through the county. Its growth is magnolia, maple, beech, bay, swamp oak, sycamore, and a few cottonwoods. The soil is a fine, sandy loam of a gray, buff, and blackish color, and varying depths. The subsoil is leachy, and is underlaid by sand-rock at 15 to 20 feet. The soil is early, warm, well drained, always easily tilled, is best adapted to cotton, and three-fourths of the cultivated area is planted with the same. The usual and most productive height attained by the plant is from 3½ to 4 feet. In wet seasons it inclines to run to weed on all soils here, and the remedy consists in topping at about 3 feet.

The seed-cotton product per acre of fresh land varies from 800 to 1,000 pounds, and from 1,425 to 1,545 pounds make a 475-pound bale of lint. After five years' cultivation the product varies from 400 to 600 pounds seed-cotton. Crab-grass is the most troublesome of all weeds.

About one-fifth of the township consists of *cane-brake or hummock land*, and its chief natural growth is walnut, poplar, sweet gum, water oak, and maple. The soil is a deep blackish and black loam. Tillage is difficult in wet seasons, but easy in dry. The soil is well drained, but late and cold. It is best adapted to corn and cotton, and three-fourths of its cultivated area is planted with cotton. The plant grows from 4 to 6 feet high, but is most productive at 4 feet. The seed-cotton product per acre of fresh land varies from 1,000 to 1,500 pounds; 1,425 pounds make a 475-pound bale of lint. After five years' cultivation the product varies from 800 to 1,000 pounds. The cocklebur is the most troublesome weed.

The remainder, or nearly two-thirds of the township, is *hilly upland*, which extends 11 miles west, 30 east, and from 20 to 30 north, and bears a natural growth of pine chiefly; also hickory, dogwood, black-jack, and other oaks. The soil is formed of clay and fine sand, is whitish, gray, and brown in color, and from 4 to 6 inches deep; the subsoil is impervious red and yellow clay, with a large proportion of sand. The soil is early, warm, always easily tilled, does not endure drought well, is best adapted to oats and cotton, and three-fourths of its cultivated area is planted with cotton. The plant rarely exceeds 3 feet in height. The seed-cotton product per acre varies from 400 to 500 pounds on fresh land; 1,425 pounds make a 475-pound bale of lint. After five years' cultivation the product varies from 300 to 400 pounds. The most troublesome weed is crab-grass. About one-fourth of such land originally cultivated now lies "turned out". The slopes are seriously damaged by washing and gullying, but the valleys are not much injured by the washings. To check the damage a little horizontalizing and hillside ditching have been practiced with good success.

The chief crops are cotton, corn, oats, potatoes, and cow-peas. Cool nights in May retard the growth of cotton, and aphides just then kill a large portion of it, causing thin stands.

The southern portion of the county (about one-third) consists of very productive calcareous prairie land. It produces 40 bushels of corn or from 1,000 to 1,500 pounds of seed-cotton per acre in favorable seasons and deteriorates but slightly.

Cotton is shipped, as soon as ready, by rail from Enterprise to Mobile at $3 per bale.

ABSTRACT OF THE REPORTS OF JOHN A. BASS, CHARLES W. MOODY, AND J. E. WELBORN, SHUBUTA.

(Refers to T. 10, R. 6, 7, 8, and 9.)

The lands of the county comprise the black and yellow prairies and stiff bottoms, the sandy pine hills, hummocks, and level creek bottoms, and the light sandy bottoms of Chickasawhay river and Shubuta and Dry creeks.

The chief cotton-producing soil is the *black and yellow prairies* of the level and rolling uplands, occurring in bodies of from 50 to 1,000 acres. One-half or more of the cultivated soil of this region is of this kind. Its chief growth is ash, red elm, hickory, post, black-jack, and some white and red oaks. The soil is a clayey loam 6 to 30 inches deep; the subsoil is heavier, but otherwise similar, and is putty-like and adhesive when wet. It contains flinty, brownish pebbles, with shells and bones, and is underlaid by sand, gravel, and soft rock at 18 inches or more. When once broken, the soil is generally easily tilled; but it is difficult to till when too wet, especially if level. The rolling portions are early and well-drained; the level parts are late and ill-drained. The soil is equally well adapted to all of the chief crops of this region, viz, corn, cotton, oats, peas, potatoes, and sugar-cane, and the shelly lands are especially well adapted to corn and oats. About one-half of the cultivated area is planted with cotton. The plant attains heights of from 3 to 7 feet, but is most productive at from 4 to 5 feet. It inclines to run to weed in excessive rainy seasons, especially when the clay is at a depth of from 2 to 3 feet, but in stiff yellow or black prairies it scarcely ever goes too much to weed. Early planting and proper or uniform cultivation has generally succeeded in preventing too great a growth and has induced bolling. The seed-cotton product per acre of fresh land varies from 800 to 1,000 pounds; 1,660 pounds make a 475-pound bale of middling lint. The soil being fresh and all things favorable, 3 pounds of seed-cotton usually yield 1 pound of lint. After twenty-five years' cultivation (unmanured) the product varies from 500 to 600 pounds, and ratio of seed to lint remains the same, but the staple is inferior. About one-half of such originally cultivated land lies "turned out", and when again cultivated it produces well after the first year, but little in that year. The troublesome weeds are crab-grass, morning-glory, coffee-weed, tea-weed, and purslane.

The *sandy lands* cover one-half of the county area, though occurring only in spots. Its natural growth is short-leaf pine, chinoapin, red and black-jack oaks, black and sweet gums, hickory, some ash, chestnut, dogwood, etc. The soil is various, and besides the generally prevailing coarse, sandy loam there are gravelly and clayey loams, the colors of which are whitish-gray, buff, and yellow, the depth averaging 18 inches. The heavier subsoil is yellowish and red clay, and contains small pebbles. The soil is early, well drained, easily tilled, and one-half to three-fourths of its cultivated area is planted with cotton. The usual and most productive height of the plant is from 3 to 4 feet, and when showery weather continues for a time it inclines to run to weed. The seed-cotton product per acre of fresh land varies from 800 to 1,200 pounds; 1,660 pounds make a 475-pound bale of low middling to good middling lint, according to seasons, etc. Ten years' cultivation (unmanured) causes a decline in yields of from 33 to 50 per cent., and about 1,935 pounds then make a 475-pound bale of lint rating one or two grades below that of fresh land. A small amount of this land has been "turned out", but after ten or fifteen years' rest it produces as well as originally. Slopes in some localities are seriously damaged by washings and gullying of the soil. Valleys are usually so much benefited by the washings as to double their yields; but if the valley lands and the hillside washings are both stiff and clayey they are damaged. A little hillside ditching has been done, and the damage successfully checked to that extent.

North of the locations described are extensive areas of "*poor pine land*", timbered chiefly with long-leaf pine, with occasionally some post, red, and black-jack oaks, and hickory. The soil is a gray clay loam 18 to 24 inches thick; the subsoil is similar to that of the bottoms last described, and is underlaid at from 15 to 20 feet by blue marl. The soil is easily cultivated, early, warm, and well drained, but only a small proportion of it is cultivated.

Cotton on the uplands may be planted earlier and matures earlier than on the lowlands, even if planted at the same time. It is rarely frost-killed in this region.

Cotton is shipped during all the picking season chiefly to Mobile, by rail, at $3 per bale; distance, 96 miles.

WAYNE.

Population: 8,741 —White, 4,971; colored, 3,770.

Area: 790 square miles.—Long-leaf pine hills, 490 square miles; central prairie, 300 square miles.

Tilled lands: 20,977 acres.—Area planted in cotton, 7,550 acres; in corn, 10,411 acres; in oats, 1,408 acres; in wheat, 7 acres.

Cotton production: 1,979 bales; average cotton product per acre, 0.26 bale, 372 pounds seed-cotton, or 124 pounds cotton lint.

Wayne county is traversed in a southerly direction by the Chickasawhay river, and in the east by Buckatunna creek, both crossing the prairie belt, which may be defined as lying north of a line passing a short distance south of Waynesboro', in a northwestern and southeastern direction. South of this line lie hilly or rolling lands, heavily timbered with long-leaf pine, which are thinly settled, cultivation being restricted to the narrow bottoms.

The uplands and bottoms of the northern part of the county, lying within the prairie belt, produce the bulk of the cotton grown. The surface features of this region are a counterpart of southern Clarke county (see page 130), the largest tracts of heavy upland prairie occurring in the northern portion, while in the southern (as on Yellow and Limestone creeks) are rolling or hilly lands with a loam soil, timbered with oak and more or less pine, interspersed with small tracts and patches of black upland prairie, with here and there a tract of the hog-wallow soil.

From the county-line to near Waynesboro' the Chickasawhay river flows in a deep channel cut into limestone strata, which it rarely fills, the bordering hummock or flat being practically above overflow and cultivated to advantage. The same is true more or less of the tributary creeks within the limestone region. Southward, in the pine region, the river channel is more shallow, and its bottom liable to overflow.

Winchester, in this county, was one of the early settlements in this part of the state, and at one time was quite a thriving town, with brick houses and other improvements and some social reputation. It was until lately the county-seat, now removed to Waynesboro'.

At present the cultivated lands of Wayne amount to only 4.1 per cent. of its area, the cotton acreage being 9.6 per square mile, against one-third more given to corn. The average cotton product per acre is 0.26 bale.

The Mobile and Ohio railroad follows the Chickasawhay river nearly through the county, leaving it and the state at its southeast corner. Shipments go by this road to Mobile.

LONG-LEAF PINE REGION.

(It embraces the following counties and parts of counties: Copiah, Claiborne,* Jefferson,* Hinds,* Lincoln, Pike, Franklin, Amite, Lawrence, Simpson, Rankin,* Smith, Jasper,* Newton,* Lauderdale, Clarke,* Wayne,* Covington, Jones, Marion, Perry, Greene, Jackson, Harrison, and Hancock.)

COPIAH.

Population: 27,552.—White, 13,101; colored, 14,451.
Area: 750 square miles.—Short-leaf pine and oak uplands, 60 square miles; long-leaf pine hills, 690 square miles.
Tilled lands: 119,866 acres.—Area planted in cotton, 54,616 acres; in corn, 38,292 acres; in oats, 5,320 acres.
Cotton production: 23,726 bales; average cotton product per acre, 0.43 bale, 612 pounds seed-cotton, or 204 pounds cotton lint.

The greater part of Copiah county is drained by bayou Pierre and its tributaries, and on the east by creeks flowing toward Pearl river, of which Copiah and Big Bahala creeks are the chief. The heads of the Homochitto reach into the southwest corner.

The surface of Copiah is rolling or hilly, sometimes broken, with sharp sandstone ridges, especially in the southwestern part, long-leaf pine prevailing on all the higher ridges, interspersed more or less on their flanks and on the lower ridges with the oaks and short-leaf pine, which are there predominant. The upland soil is sometimes very sandy, but chiefly a light brownish yellow loam, underlaid by yellow or orange loam subsoil, forming a good foundation for improvement. These oak and pine uplands are moderately productive, and are cultivated to a considerable extent; but the numerous valleys are the preferred culture lands. These valleys are usually wide and largely of a hummock or second-bottom character, the first bottoms being mostly narrow and sometimes altogether wanting, when the streams often meander in wide sandy beds. The hummock soils are usually gray or whitish and rather fine, silty, and sometimes sandy and gravelly, according to the nature of the adjacent uplands, which are often traversed by gravelly ridges. The timber of these hummocks usually consists of oaks and bottom pine, mingled with more or less of hickory, magnolia, holly, and, when sandy, a good deal of beech. (For analyses of these hummock soils, see regional description, page 62.)

In the northwest corner of Copiah the long-leaf pine is absent, while oaks, hickory, and short-leaf pine, with more or less beech and magnolia on the slopes, constitute the timber of the rolling country. On the Pearl river side also there is a belt of country, from which the long-leaf pine is absent, skirting the river valley, which is here formed of a wide hummock timbered with large bottom pine, post, scarlet, and Spanish oaks, hickory, and, near the river, with water and willow oaks and a good deal of hickory and sweet gum. This is excellent cotton land, but the creek bottoms adjacent are even more highly esteemed.

Copiah county is a region of small farms, was early settled, and stands ninth in population among the counties of the state, and in density of population is next above Monroe county. The tilled lands amount to one-fourth of the total area. Not quite one-half of them are devoted to cotton culture, and a little over two-thirds as much to corn. The average cotton acreage per square mile is 72.8, and the average product per acre is 0.43 bale. This is a remarkable showing for what is popularly classed as a pine-hills county.

The communication of Copiah is chiefly with Hazlehurst and other stations on the New Orleans and Chicago railroad, which traverses the eastern part of the county from north to south on the dividing ridge between bayou Pierre and Pearl river. To avoid the hilly roads the western portion communicates partly with Port Gibson and Grand Gulf landing, whence cotton is shipped by steamer to New Orleans.

CLAIBORNE.
(See "Cane hills region".)

JEFFERSON.
(See "Cane hills region".)

HINDS.
(See "Central prairie region.")

LINCOLN.

Population: 13,547.—White, 7,701; colored, 5,846.
Area: 580 square miles.—Woodland, all; long-leaf pine hills, all.
Tilled lands: 55,409 acres.—Area planted in cotton, 17,272 acres; in corn, 19,843 acres; in oats, 5,704 acres.
Cotton production: 6,286 bales; average cotton product per acre, 0.36 bale, 513 pounds seed-cotton, or 171 pounds cotton lint.

Lincoln county is drained by streams flowing in five different directions, viz: Centrally and chiefly by the Bogue Chitto and its tributaries; in the northeastern portion by Fair river and Bahala creek, tributary to Pearl river; in the northern part by the extreme heads of bayou Pierre; in the northwestern by those of the Homochitto river; and in the southwestern by the east fork of the Amite, tributary to lake Pontchartrain. It is naturally, therefore, a region of rolling, hilly, and sometimes broken uplands (rising to the elevation of 480 feet at Brookhaven), which are timbered chiefly with long-leaf pine, largely interspersed, especially in the western part, with oaks and hickory, indicating a corresponding improvement in the soil as we approach the oak and short-leaf pine belt bordering the cane hills (see regional description, page 56). The numerous bottoms afford equally numerous though usually small bodies of good farming land, on which the cotton produced is chiefly grown. The uplands are as yet cultivated on a small scale only, having thus far been given to the lumbering industry, which has been extensively developed since the establishment of railroad communication.

The tilled lands of Lincoln constitute nearly 15 per cent. of its area, over one-quarter of them (31.2 per cent.) being given to cotton, and nearly one-third more (35 per cent.) to corn. The average cotton product per acre is 0.36 bale, with an average of 29.8 acres per square mile.

The communication of Lincoln county is by way of the New Orleans and Chicago railroad, which traverses it centrally, chiefly with New Orleans.

PIKE.

Population: 16,688.—White, 8,572; colored, 8,116.
Area: 720 square miles.—Woodland, all; long-leaf pine hills, all.
Tilled lands: 53,803 acres.—Area planted in cotton, 19,842 acres; in corn, 19,248 acres; in oats, 6,003 acres; in wheat, 8 acres.
Cotton production: 6,507 bales; average cotton product per acre, 0.33 bale, 471 pounds seed-cotton, or 157 pounds cotton lint.

Pike county is covered throughout with a heavy forest of long-leaf pine. The Bogue Chitto river traverses it in a northwestern and southeastern direction, and the country eastward of that stream is drained by its tributaries, of which Magee's and Tapashaw creeks are the chief. West of the Bogue Chitto the dividing ridge between it and Tangipahoa comes in so closely as to leave room only for short creeks, so that the country to the westward is drained almost wholly by the tributaries of the last-named stream, nearly all of which carry running water throughout the season.

The northern portion of Pike county is hilly or rolling pine land. In its eastern portion it is quite sandy, but as the Bogue Chitto is approached the increasing admixture and the appearance of black-jack oaks indicates the approach to the surface of a brown-loam subsoil, which becomes more and more prevalent to the westward, and forms a good foundation for the cultivation and improvement of the uplands, which thus far has not been inaugurated to any great extent, but on a small scale has been quite successful. (For analysis and discussion of this soil, see regional description, page 59.)

In the southern portion of the county, within 10 miles of the Louisiana line, the level of the country (which at Summit station reaches the height of 425 feet) sinks visibly, the surface becoming gently undulating, still, however, underlaid by sand and gravel at the depth of a few feet. In the northern part of the county, where the upland has been denuded of its timber or thrown out of cultivation, the existence of these substrata gives rise to deep hillside washes or ravines. At some points the soil itself is very gravelly.

The immediate valley of the Bogue Chitto varies from 1 to 2 miles in width. The bottom proper, usually not very wide, has rather a light soil, which is timbered with beech, magnolia, bottom white pine, elm, and some black and sweet gums, and is productive, but subject to overflow. The soil of the second bottom is generally preferred for cultivation. It is a dark-colored loam, sometimes as much as 2½ feet in depth, more or less traversed by sandier "beech ridges," and the usual timber, which is very large, is magnolia, sweet gum, poplar, hickory, sassafras, and some beech; also chestnut white oak and holly. It is a very fine and durable soil. The soils and timber on the smaller streams are quite similar in character.

The tilled lands of Pike county constitute 11.7 per cent. of its area. Of these over one-third (36.9 per cent.) is devoted to cotton culture, with an average product of 0.33 bale per acre, the cotton acreage being 27.6 per square mile. The corn acreage is a trifle less than that of cotton.

The lumber industry has been extensively developed in this county since the completion of the New Orleans and Chicago railroad, utilizing not only the long-leaf pine, but also the large "poplar" (white-wood) and magnolia and other timber of the bottoms. Other manufacturing industries have been started at stations on the line of the railroad, such as a cotton-mill, factories of agricultural implements, etc. Magnolia and stations south of the same also serve as summer resorts for health and pleasure for the population of New Orleans.

Cotton is shipped, as fast as baled, to New Orleans, at $2 30 per bale.

ABSTRACT OF THE REPORT OF W. W. VAUGHT, MAGNOLIA.

The surface of the country is rolling, the uplands comprising pine hills, covered with a dense pine growth. The first and second bottoms of creeks and rivers is the chief cotton-producing soil. It occupies about one-fifth of the area of this region, and extends about 25 miles west, to the state line east and south, and to Crystal Springs, 50 miles north. The land is somewhat subject to overflow, and has a natural growth of oak, gum, poplar, beech, hickory, etc.

The soil is a fine sandy loam of blackish and black colors, extending 4 to 8 inches below the surface. The subsoil is rather sandy and leechy, and is underlaid by sand. The soil is early and warm when well drained, and is generally easily tilled, except in wet weather. The chief crops of this region are cotton, corn, oats, sweet potatoes, and sugar-cane, and the soil seems best adapted to these crops. It yields from 30 to 50 bushels of corn. About half its cultivated area is planted with cotton. The usually attained height of the cotton-plant is from 3 to 5 feet; at greater heights it is less productive. It inclines to run to weed in wet seasons and on fresh land, and the remedy consists in applying phosphates or bone-meal to the soil, and thus favors bolling. The seed-cotton product per acre of fresh land varies from 1,200 to 1,800 pounds, or, after ten years' cultivation (unmanured), from 300 to 500 pounds; in either case 1,425 to 1,545 pounds make a 475-pound bale of lint. The quality of staple from old land is but little different from that of fresh land. All the cotton from this region rates generally as middling. About one-fourth of such land lies "turned out", but by deep plowing and systematic manuring it can be made to produce as well as ever. Crab-grass is the only troublesome weed, hog and rag weeds giving but little trouble.

The *pine hills* are but little in cultivation, but about two-fifths of the area being suitable for tillage when cleared. Besides its natural growth of pine, it has more or less oak, hickory, and gum, and it is coextensive with the lowland described. The soil is a yellow, sandy loam, 4 to 8 inches thick; the subsoil a heavy red clay, 1 to 3 feet thick, containing some fine sand and a variety of gravel, underlaid by sand and gravel. The soil is early, warm, well drained, and easily tilled, producing about 500 pounds of seed-cotton per acre from fresh lands and 300 pounds after ten years' cultivation.

Slopes are seriously injured by washings and gullying of the soil, the washings to some extent damaging the valleys. To check the damage considerable horizontalizing and hillside ditching have been done, and where the work has been well done this has been successful. When droughts occur here it is rarely before July 15, when the plant is so nearly matured as not to suffer.

FRANKLIN.

Population: 9,729.—White, 4,852; colored, 4,877.

Area: 560 square miles.—Short-leaf pine and oak uplands, 250 square miles; long-leaf pine hills, 310 square miles; all woodland.

Tilled lands: 37,680 acres.—Area planted in cotton, 18,211 acres; in corn, 12,045 acres; in oats, 1,012 acres.

Cotton production: 8,042 bales; average cotton product per acre, 0.44 bale, 627 pounds seed-cotton, or 209 pounds cotton lint.

The greater part of Franklin county is drained by the Homochitto river, which traverses diagonally the eastern half of the county and is joined by numerous creeks from both sides. The surface is throughout hilly, especially along the main Homochitto, where the "Homochitto hills" constitute a country of narrow and steep, sometimes rocky, ridges, the uplands being largely too broken for cultivation. The county is nearly equally divided into an eastern portion, timbered with long-leaf pine, more or less mingled with oaks, hickory, and short-leaf pine on the slopes and lower ridges, and a western one, in which oaks, hickory, and short-leaf pine alone prevail, save occasionally on higher ridges extending in from the east. In both sections the bulk of the cultivated lands lies in the valleys of the streams, in which (as is generally the case in southwestern Mississippi) the second bottom or hummock lands predominate over the first bottoms, and are most generally under cultivation.

The soils of the Homochitto hills and of the eastern portion of the county generally are mostly quite sandy, yet not infertile, as is shown by the vigorous growth of oaks and hickory laden with long moss. The poorer and excessively sandy tracts are characterized by the presence of the upland willow, oak, or narrow-leaf black-jack among the post, Spanish, and white oaks, resembling exceedingly the sandy ridge lands of Smith and Jasper counties. The soils of the first bottoms in this region are correspondingly sandy, and so continue almost to the mouth of the Homochitto river. Their depth, however, compensates so far for the excess of sand that some of these bottom lands (e. g., on the middle fork of the Homochitto) are reputed to be among the most durable and productive cotton lands of the state. (For details regarding these soils, see regional description, p. 63.) The beech and magnolia are the most prominent timber trees of these bottoms, together with the chestnut-white oak, sweet gum, poplar, maple, etc. The hummock soils of this region, elevated from 2 to as much as 6 feet above the first bottom, are only moderately light, of a buff color, underlaid by a pale-yellow loam, the timber of which is the beech, white oak, hickory, holly, sweet gum, cherry, sourwood, etc. Some of these hummock soils produce from 1,200 to 1,300 pounds of seed-cotton per acre. While the average width of the valleys in this region is the same as elsewhere, the wide, shallow, sandy beds which the streams excavate for themselves in flood-time often diminish seriously the amount of valley land suitable for cultivation, the smaller streams especially sometimes occupying in this way the entire width of their valleys. The uplands of the western section of the county are much less sandy, and the bottom lands correspond in this respect, especially in the northwestern portion, on the heads of Well's creek and Morgan's fork. Here the "Hamburg hills" form a body of rolling or ridgy uplands, partly of a plateau character, having an excellent subsoil of light-brown loam, which makes itself felt by the scarcity of the pine, hickory, white, Spanish, and black oaks, together with the large-leaved magnolia, occupying the ridges, while on the slopes the sweet gum, ash, and poplar, or tulip tree, are also found. The uplands are quite productive, and the valley lands are excellent.

In the southwestern part of the county the Homochitto hills continue to form a ridgy, broken country, of which the portion lying between Well's creek and the Homochitto is known as "The Devil's Backbone", so called among teamsters from the unenviable reputation of its clayey slopes. The summits of the ridges, however, are sandy and partly rocky.

The table-lands of Franklin county constitute 10.5 per cent. of its area. Of these nearly one-half is occupied by cotton, only two-thirds as much being given to corn. The average cotton product per acre is 0.44 bale, a trifle less than that of Panola county. The communication of Franklin county is chiefly with Natchez, whence cotton is shipped to New Orleans. The eastern portion also communicates with stations on the New Orleans and Chicago railroad.

AMITE.

Population: 14,004.—White, 5,494; colored, 8,510.
Area: 720 square miles.—Short-leaf pine and oak uplands, 85 square miles; long-leaf pine hills, 635 square miles; woodland.
Tilled lands: 62,095 acres.—Area planted in cotton, 27,749 acres; in corn, 22,589 acres; in oats, 3,184 acres.
Cotton production: 9,952 bales; average cotton product per acre, 0.36 bale, 513 pounds seed-cotton, or 171 pounds cotton lint.

The greater part of Amite county resembles closely in its surface features the portion of Pike county lying west of the Bogue Chitto, and is drained centrally and chiefly by the several forks and tributary creeks of the Amite river. In the northwest corner some of the tributaries of the Homochitto interlock with the Amite, and the southeast corner is drained by the heads of the Tickfaw river.

The bulk of the cultivated lands of Amite county still lies in the bottoms and hummocks of the streams. Outside of these, in the rolling and hilly uplands, the long-leaf pine forest prevails over all but the extreme western portion of the county, where short-leaf pine and oaks take possession first of the flanks, and then of the summits of the ridges, being more or less commingled with the long-leaf pine throughout. The upland soil, when dry, is of a pale brownish-yellow tint with an orange loam subsoil, which, besides common gravel, usually contains more or less of black pebble. In level places, where huckleberry bushes prevail, it is sometimes white, and is also underlaid by the yellow subsoil. It is fairly productive. In the northwestern portion the Homochitto hills form a belt of broken ridge lands, mostly sandy, occupied by oaks and hickory, heavily curtained with long moss, the pine being quite subordinate; but these hill lands, though having a productive soil, are almost too broken for cultivation. The southern part of Amite county, like the corresponding part of Pike, is a more gently rolling, sometimes almost level, pine-woods region.

The valleys of the various forks and tributaries of the Amite river, though not usually very wide (1 to 2 miles on the main Amite), contain bodies of excellent farming land, chiefly on the second bottom level. These bodies alternate more or less with apparently ill-drained tracts of a white, "crawfishy" soil, underlaid by black pebbles, which increase proportionally as we descend the streams. Such tracts are characterized by a growth of bottom pine and a great deal of water oak among the timber, which is otherwise the same in species as that of the better class of bottom lands, but is rather under size. In the well-drained portions of the bottoms the soil is a dark or mulatto-colored loam from 1½ to 2 feet in depth, with a large timber growth of magnolia, holly, white and chestnut-white oaks, ash, sweet gum, beech, and some poplar. The soil is very productive, though crops are liable to damage from overflows.

The tilled lands of Amite county amount to 13.5 per cent. of the total area, placing the county in this respect above Pike and Franklin, but below Lincoln (14.9 per cent.), and nearly on a level with Rankin. The cotton acreage exceeds that of corn by one-fourth, and the average product per acre is the same as that of Benton county (0.36 bale).

The communication of Amite county is chiefly with stations on the New Orleans and Chicago railroad, or via the Clinton narrow-gauge railroad to Bayou Sara, and by steamer to New Orleans. Freight on cotton, $2 to $2 25 per bale.

ABSTRACT OF THE REPORTS OF J. R. GALTNEY AND GEORGE F. WEBB, LIBERTY.

By long experience planters have found it safest to plant the rolling uplands in cotton and the lowlands in corn. The bottoms of creeks and smaller streams are, in comparison with river bottoms, easily tilled, and, being the safest for all crops, they are regarded by most farmers as the best lands in the region. The river bottoms are subject to overflows, and cotton is liable to be prematurely frost-killed, besides suffering more from insect pests than on other lands. The chief crops of this region are cotton, corn, sugar-cane, oats, field pease, sweet potatoes, and sorghum.

All the soils are apparently best adapted to cotton, although the other crops succeed well, and more than half the cultivated land is planted with that staple. The chief soil is a *brown or mahogany upland loam*, 5 inches thick, with a subsoil of red, clayey loam, rather impervious, containing a variety of gravel, large and small, and underlaid by sand and gravel. Three-fourths of the cultivated land of the county is of this kind. Its natural growth is red, white, and black oaks, chincapin, long-leaf pine, sweet gum, cherry, sassafras, etc. The soil is early, warm, and well-drained, and the cotton-plant usually grows from 2½ to 3½ feet high. On this, as well as on all other lands described, it inclines to run to weed in wet seasons, but may be restrained by using the hoe instead of the plow in after-cultivation. The seed-cotton product per acre of fresh land is from 700 to 800 pounds, 1,445 pounds (or 1,425 late in the season) making a 475-pound bale of lint. After five years' cultivation (unmanured) the product is from 500 to 600 pounds, and then from 1,455 to 1,485 pounds make a bale of lint shorter and weaker than that from fresh land. The troublesome weeds on all of the lands are crab-grass, cocklebur, and morning-glory. About one-half of such originally cultivated land lies "turned out"; when it is overgrown with briers, it again produces as well as originally, but not so well if overgrown with sedge and pine.

A comparatively small part of this region consists of *second bottom or hummock land*, which occurs in strips less than half a mile in average width, next to parallel and continuous with the swamp or river bottom lands. Its growth is oak (red, white, and black), pine, beech, hickory, ash, gum, holly, poplar, magnolia, etc. The soil is a loam varying from clayey to fine sandy, and in color from mahogany to black, and is 6 to 12 inches deep; the subsoil is clayey, tough, hard, and impervious, but by cultivation and exposure it gradually becomes like the surface soil. It contains a variety of gravel, and is underlaid by sand and gravel and sometimes large pebbles. The soil is early and warm when well-drained, and the cotton-plant grows from 3 to 5 feet high, but is most productive at 5 feet. The seed-cotton product per acre of fresh land is about 1,000 pounds; 1,600 pounds make a 475-pound bale of lint. After five years' cultivation (unmanured) the product is 800 pounds, and 1,630 pounds then make a bale. About one-third of such originally cultivated land lies "turned out"; when again cultivated, it produces about the same.

The remaining kind is usually designated *swamp land*, and includes river and creek bottoms, the greater part of it lying along the Amite river, where its width is about 2 miles. Its growth is red, white, water, and pin oaks, beech, poplar, ash, hickory, magnolia, sweet and black gums, cypress, holly, etc. The soil is a loam of a mahogany, blackish and black color, 1 to 3 feet deep; the subsoil is a compact, impervious hard-pan while undisturbed, which bakes very hard when first exposed, but gradually becomes like the surface by tillage. It is underlaid by sand in some places; in others by clay. The plant grows from 3 to 6 feet high, but is most productive at 4 feet. The product per

22 C P

acre of fresh land is from 1,000 to 1,500 pounds of seed-cotton, 1,580 pounds making a 475-pound bale. After five years' cultivation (unmanured) the product is from 600 to 1,000 pounds, about 1,545 pounds then making a bale. Nearly half of such land originally cultivated now lies "turned out", and the longer it rests the more it yields when again cultivated.

When slopes are sandy they are seriously damaged by washings and gullying, and the washings injure the valleys to the extent of reducing their yields from one-fourth to one-third. To check the damage many efforts have been made by filling the gullies with cotton stalks, etc., and by horizontalizing and hillside ditching. The success has been sufficient to justify the labor and expense involved.

Cotton is shipped, as soon as ready, by rail from Osyka, 88 miles, to New Orleans, at $2 90 per bale, or at $2 per bale from Clinton, Louisiana, by rail and river.

LAWRENCE.

Population: 9,422.—White, 4,937; colored, 4,485.
Area: 620 square miles.—All long-leaf pine hills.
Tilled lands: 47,320 acres.—Area planted in cotton, 17,996 acres; in corn, 20,758 acres; in oats, 4,845 acres; in wheat, 6 acres.
Cotton production: 5,967 bales; average cotton product per acre, 0.34 bale, 486 pounds seed-cotton, or 162 pounds cotton lint.

Lawrence county is a region of rolling, hilly or sometimes broken, and mostly sandy uplands, heavily timbered with long-leaf pine, the flanks of some, and sometimes entire ridges, being occupied by the short-leaf pine, mingled more or less with post and black-jack oaks and hickory. The western portion of the county is traversed in a southern direction by Pearl river. Its valley being rather deeply and abruptly impressed into the surface, the bordering hills, composed of soft sandstones and sandy clay materials, have a tendency to form steep slopes or high bluffs, which sometimes offer the unusual spectacle of waterfalls. Through these hills the tributary streams, which carry running water throughout the season, have worn narrow valleys with steep sides, so that outside of the main valley the larger bodies of cultivated creek-bottom land are chiefly found in the upper course of the streams. Of these, Silver, White Sand, and Green's creeks are the chief on the east and Fair river and Hall's creek on the west side of the valley.

Pearl river has but little bottom proper, and its hummock or second bottom is timbered with bottom pine, sweet and black gum, water and willow oaks, elm, etc. Its soil is productive, and is of a pale gray tint, but possesses a heavier whitish or yellowish subsoil, which will retain manure, underlaid at 15 to 24 inches from the surface by a loose whitish sandy material with spots of bog ore, and beneath this by tenacious gray clay, which sometimes causes a lack of proper drainage, and thus gives rise to "crawfishy" spots and tracts. Between Silver and Green's creeks the drainage of the hummock is less defective.

On the heads of White Sand creek, in the eastern portion of the county, there is a gently undulating upland tract, timbered to a considerable extent with oaks and hickory, and possessing a subsoil of a deep orange-red, sandy hard-pan several feet in thickness. This soil produces good cotton and very fine corn, and lasts well. In the long-leaf pine hills themselves we not unfrequently find a good loam subsoil at a depth of 8 to 12 inches.

The tilled lands of Lawrence amount to nearly 12 per cent. of its area. Of these over one-third (37.2 per cent.) is given to cotton, making an average cotton acreage of 29.7 per square mile, with an average product of 0.34 bale per acre. The corn acreage exceeds that of cotton about one-sixth.

The communication of Lawrence county is westward to stations of the New Orleans and Chicago railroad in Lincoln and Copiah counties.

SIMPSON.

Population: 8,005.—White, 4,993; colored, 3,012.
Area: 580 square miles.—Woodland, all. Short-leaf pine and oak uplands, 80 square miles; long-leaf pine hills, 500 square miles.
Tilled lands: 31,479 acres.—Area planted in cotton, 8,855 acres; in corn, 14,165 acres; in oats, 4,211 acres; in wheat, 5 acres.
Cotton production: 3,501 bales; average cotton product per acre, 0.40 bale, 570 pounds seed-cotton, or 190 pounds cotton lint.

The greater part of Simpson county is a region of long-leaf pine hills, interspersed with more or less ridges of short-leaf pine and oak. This pine region is drained chiefly by Strong river and its tributaries, and in their eastern part by the headwaters of Okahay, Okatoma, and Bouie creeks. The western and smaller portions, drained by the smaller creeks directly tributary to Pearl river, is timbered with oaks and short-leaf pine, and its soils and surface conformation resemble that of Rankin county, immediately north. This belt of oak lands continues with a width of several miles as far south as the mouth of Strong river. Beyond, it gradually loses its character, becoming merged with the hummock of Pearl river. It is chiefly in this belt that the uplands are cultivated to any considerable extent in Simpson county, while the bottom lands are excellent. East of the dividing ridge between Pearl and Strong rivers the soil becomes more and more sandy, and the bodies of good valley land are small, though sometimes very productive. Strong river usually runs in a deep channel, and has little or no first bottom subject to overflow. Its valley or hummock is from 1 to 2 miles wide, and near Westville is timbered prevalently with bottom pine and post oak, with some Spanish, scarlet, and black oaks and hickory. Its soil is generally light gray, with a pale-yellow loam subsoil, and is particularly well adapted to sweet potatoes, but produces good crops of corn and cotton also, especially in the portion nearest Pearl river. In the eastern part of the county, on the headwaters of Bonie and Okatoma creeks, oaks and hickory sometimes become quite prevalent among the pine, indicating a good brown-loam subsoil and generally wider valleys of good productiveness. The dividing ridge between these streams and Strong river is a very sandy plateau, on which the water quickly sinks, so as to form few definite channels, but only shallow, rounded troughs, while springs of great volume gush out at the levels where impervious strata shed the water, thus suddenly forming creeks of considerable size and of the clearest and purest water.

In the southwestern portion of Simpson, on Silver and Crooked creeks, the country is somewhat ridgy and broken, and the sandy pine hills are interrupted by ridges, along the slopes of which, and sometimes on the summits, heavy gray clays, alternating with sandstone ledges, form level terraces covered with long grass and stunted pine, and a different class of soils occur more frequently on the west side of Pearl river. When not too heavy they are more productive than the pine-hill soils. The hilly country breaks off rather abruptly into Pearl river hummock, the soil of the latter partaking more or less of the character of the uplands so modified.

The tilled lands of Simpson constitute 8.4 per cent. of its area, being the same as in Smith and a trifle more than in the case of Covington. Of these lands nearly 28 per cent. is planted in cotton. The area given to corn is somewhat less than double. The average cotton product per acre is quite high (0.40 bale), showing the productiveness of the bottoms in which the staple is mainly grown.

The communication of Simpson is partly with Brandon, on the Vicksburg and Meridian railroad, and partly with Hazlehurst and other stations on the New Orleans and Chicago railroad.

ABSTRACT OF THE REPORT OF J. C. M'LAURIN, MOUNT ZION.

The chief soil devoted to cotton is that of *creek bottoms* above overflow, which includes one-tenth of the cultivated land of this region. The soil is a black, coarse sandy and gravelly loam 4 to 6 inches thick. The impervious subsoil is a very hard red clay in some places, and a mixture of yellow sand and clay in others. It contains a variety of pebbles, and in some places large quantities of black iron-rock, and is underlaid by sand. The chief crops of this region are corn, oats, and cotton. The soil is tilled with difficulty if too wet, is not troublesome when dry, and is generally easy when once well broken. It is early when well drained, and is best adapted to corn. About 45 per cent. of it is planted with cotton. The plant grows from 4 to 6 feet high, but is generally most productive at 4 feet. It inclines to run to weed in wet seasons and on low, wet lands; but early planting, early cultivation, and the application to the soil of well-rotted leaves and straw, with barn-yard manure, will restrain it and favor boiling. The seed-cotton product per acre of fresh land varies from 500 to 1,500 pounds, 1,545 to 1,665 pounds making a 475-pound bale of middling lint. After ten years' cultivation (unmanured) the product varies from 400 to 700 pounds, and 1,665 to 1,780 pounds then make a bale of lint inferior to that from fresh land. Three-tenths of such land originally cultivated lies "turned out", but if nearly level it produces very well when again cultivated. The troublesome weeds of this region are red-joint, careless, and pepper weed, crab-grass, etc.

The second quality of soil is that of the dark uplands or second bottoms, comparatively level. About 45 per cent. of it is planted with cotton, and its yields equal those of first soil described.

The third quality is the *light sandy soil* of Pearl and Strong river bottoms, 30 per cent. of which is planted with cotton; its yields are 80 per cent. of those of the chief soil. The details of these second and third qualities are in all respects but slightly different from those of the first quality. Slopes wash and gully readily, and, unless very carefully prevented, those which have not a clay subsoil are seriously damaged. The valleys are injured to the extent of from 5 to 20 per cent. by the washings. Efforts have been made to check the damage by circling and hillside ditching, and with success when made in time.

Cotton is hauled by ox-wagons to Beauregard, Hazlehurst, Jackson, and Brandon at 75 cents per hundred pounds.

RANKIN.

(See "Central prairie region".)

SMITH.

Population: 8,084.—White, 6,452; colored, 1,632.

Area: 600 square miles.—Long-leaf pine hills, 325 square miles; central prairie, 275 square miles; wooded.

Tilled lands: 32,155 acres.—Area planted in cotton, 10,543 acres; in corn, 14,614 acres; in oats, 5,009 acres; in wheat, 78 acres.

Cotton production: 3,721 bales; average cotton product per acre, 0.35 bale, 498 pounds seed-cotton, or 166 pounds cotton lint.

Smith county is nearly evenly divided between two surface features by a line traversing the county centrally in a northwestern and southeastern direction. South of this line we find hilly or undulating, sometimes almost level, sandy upland, covered by heavy forests of long-leaf pine, with occasional ridges, where a more generous and retentive soil bears the short-leaf pine, mingled with oaks. The region is thinly settled, the narrow bottoms being alone under cultivation.

In the northern part of the county the surface features resemble those of Scott in the alternation of ridges timbered with oaks, or oaks and short-leaf or long-leaf pine, with tracts having more or less of the "hog-wallow", and in the valleys and bottoms the black-prairie character. The latter feature is less prominent than in Scott county; the bodies of the prairie being smaller and less frequent in the uplands at least, while in the bottoms, especially in the eastern part of the county, the heavy black prairie and "hog wallow" soils predominate, not only within the region of occurrence in the uplands, but for a considerable distance below the line above mentioned. These profusely rich bottoms, now subject to overflow, have hardly been touched by cultivation as yet, for the reason, it is stated, that cotton rusts or blights when grown on them. In any case, however, they would produce abundance of corn and other crops adapted to such soils. (For analysis and discussion of the latter, see regional description, p. 63.) Among the oak ridges and prairie bottoms skirting the creeks tributary to the heads of Leaf river and West Tallahala many extensive and attractive sites for settlements lie untouched.

The tilled lands of Smith county amount to only 8.4 per cent. of its area, the cotton acreage per square mile being 12.6, about half as much as is given to corn. The average cotton product per acre, however, is 0.34 of a bale, being equal to that of Lowndes in consequence of the predominant cultivation of creek bottoms and prairie spots.

The communication of Smith county is chiefly with stations on the Vicksburg and Meridian railroad; in its southern part with the Mobile and Ohio railroad, in Clarke county.

ABSTRACT FROM THE REPORT OF A. S. BAUGH, POLKVILLE.

About one-eighth of the county area is black sandy hummock, two-eighths swamp, and five-eighths hill or upland. The natural growth consists of black-jack and other oaks and pine on the uplands, and poplar, gum, hickory, cypress, beech, sycamore, and walnut on the bottoms. The soils vary greatly in depth, the best class being underlaid by red clay subsoils, loose and porous for 8 to 12 inches, then very hard and firm for 6 to 10 feet, and underlaid in turn by red sand 20 to 30 feet thick. The inferior soils have a yellowish white sand subsoil. Tillage is generally easy; the clayey land is sticky when too wet, and when too dry is cloddy unless well broken in early spring. The chief crops of the county are corn, cotton, oats, rice, potatoes, sugar, and sorghum-cane, and all do well. From one-fourth to one-third of the cultivated lands are planted in cotton. The plant attains a height of 4 to 8 feet, but is most productive at 5 feet. It inclines to run to weed in wet weather, but is remedied by topping early in August. The seed-cotton product per acre of fresh land is 700 pounds; 1,425 pounds make a 475-pound bale of strict middling lint. After six years' cultivation (unmanured) the product is 500 pounds of seed-cotton, when 1,485 pounds make a bale of lint rating one grade lower. Hog-weed, butter-weed, crab-grass, and cockleburs are most troublesome.

One-fifth or more of the land originally cultivated now lies "turned out". When again cultivated, it produces 12 to 25 per cent. less than fresh land. Slopes are seriously damaged by washings and gullying, and when the *débris* is carried upon the valleys it damages them to the extent of one-tenth their value. Horizontalizing and hillside ditching are practiced, and successfully check the damage.

Cotton is shipped to New Orleans in November at $3 50 per bale.

JASPER.
(See "Central prairie region".)

NEWTON.
(See "Short-leaf pine and oak uplands region".)

LAUDERDALE.

Population : 21,501.—White, 9,960 ; colored, 11,541.

Area : 680 square miles.—Short-leaf pine and oak uplands, 105 square miles ; long-leaf pine hills, 575 square miles ; all woodland.

Tilled lands : 70,249 acres.—Area planted in cotton, 32,872 acres ; in corn, 23,345 acres ; in oats, 5,967 acres ; in wheat, 5 acres.

Cotton production : 9,350 bales ; average cotton product per acre, 0.29 bale, 414 pounds seed-cotton, or 138 pounds cotton lint.

Lauderdale county is drained mainly by small creeks forming the heads of the Chickasawhay river, of which Okatibee, in the western part, is the largest. In the eastern a few streams flow toward the Tombigbee. The surface is mostly hilly, and, except in the northwestern part, the long-leaf pine is altogether the predominant tree, mingled more or less, however, with oaks, and interspersed with ridges of oak and short-leaf pine, which in the northwestern portion predominate and constitute a region of good upland farms having a moderately light-brown loam subsoil, such as in the south Atlantic states would be considered very desirable, and is well adapted to improvement. The country rock (sandstone) comes near the surface in some of the ridges, which are strewn with blocks and fragments of the same, rendering tillage somewhat troublesome. In the southern part of the county the valleys form the body of the cultivated lands and yield well, the ridge soils being more sandy and less durable than in the northern part.

Settlement and good cultivation have been greatly stimulated in Lauderdale county by the facilities of communication and transportation afforded by the two railroads, the Vicksburg and Meridian (continued eastward in the Alabama and Great Northern) and the Mobile and Ohio railroad, which intersect at Meridian, and have made that town an important railroad and manufacturing center, with a rapidly increasing population. The southeastern part of the county, on the heads of the Buckatunna, is the most thinly settled, and appears to be the least fertile. The Lauderdale springs, in the northeastern part, have long been a popular place of resort; the water is a chalybeate sulphur, and is highly esteemed for its curative effects.

The lands under tillage constitute 16.2 per cent. of the total area, of which somewhat less than half is given to cotton, while the acreage given to corn is but a little over one-third of that devoted to cotton, doubtless in consequence of the ready communication with the markets. The cotton acreage per square mile is 48.5, and the average product per acre is 0.29 per bale, the same as Clarke and a little less than Kemper county (0.30).

The cotton produced is mostly sold at Meridian, and thence shipped to Mobile.

ABSTRACT OF REPORT OF J. J. SHANNON, MERIDIAN.

The uplands of the county are rolling and sometimes level. They vary greatly in quality, and are best near small branches or in valleys between hills.

The *lowlands* comprise the first bottoms of Sowashee creek and Chickasawhay river and of small branches leading into the former, in which there is a low alluvial soil.

The *uplands* are generally regarded as the best and most certain for cotton cultivation. It is difficult to get a good "stand" in the bottoms, and in wet summer seasons the stalks go to weed too much and the bolls rot. The uplands comprise from 70 to 80 per cent. of the county area, and prevail throughout eastern Mississippi. They have a timber growth of post and red oaks, pine, hickory, gum, dogwood, and chestnut, though the first five predominate. The soil varies from a fine sandy to a clayey loam, has gray, brown, and blackish colors, and is 5 to 12 inches thick. The subsoil is various, mostly a hard, orange-red clay, which is considered the best; and in some places it is whitish and sandy. In places it contains various kinds of gravel, underlaid by clay marl at 3 to 5 feet. The chief crops of this region are cotton, corn, oats, sweet and Irish potatoes, sorghum, and sugar-cane. The soil is early, naturally and generally well-drained, easily tilled, except when too wet, and apparently is equally well adapted to cotton, oats, sweet potatoes, and sorghum. From 50 to 60 per cent. of its cultivated area is planted with cotton. The plant grows from 2½ to 5 feet high, but is most productive at 4 feet, and inclines to run to weed during excessively rainy weather, for which there is no remedy. The seed-cotton product per acre of fresh land varies from 500 to 1,000 pounds; 1,485 pounds make a 475-pound bale of lint, as good as any in market if well handled. Five years' cultivation (unmanured) reduces the yield one-fifth, or much more if the soil washes or gullies in the meantime. Cotton is rarely the first crop raised on new land. After the first year there is very little observed difference between fresh and old land in respect to the ratio of seed to lint and quality of the staple. From 15 to 20 per cent. of this land lies "turned out", and if the soil is not washed away it produces well when again cultivated. Crab-grass is the greatest enemy to cotton, but sometimes cocklebur and morning-glory are troublesome. The lands wash and gully readily on slopes, doing sometimes serious damage, though not generally to the lowlands. Hillside ditching is practiced with success.

One-fourth of the cotton crop is raised on *creek bottoms*. These have a natural growth of gum, oak, beech, pine, hickory, ash, and poplar. The soil is a black and blackish clay loam, more or less sandy, and 7 to 15 inches thick; the subsoil is heavier, often whitish clay, sometimes like that of the hill land. It is a hard-pan, generally impervious, contains flinty, angular, and sometimes rounded white gravel, in some places none, and is underlaid by clay marl at 3 to 5 feet. Tillage is generally easy, except in wet seasons, and the soil is later than upland unless well drained. It is apparently best adapted to corn and sugar-cane. In dry seasons it produces very good cotton, but it is planted mostly with corn. The most productive height of the cotton-plant is about 5 feet; it inclines to run to weed in rainy seasons, for which there is no remedy.

The seed-cotton product per acre of fresh land varies from 800 to 1,000 pounds. More is needed to make a bale of lint than on the uplands, and the staple is of average quality. The yield is but little less after ten years' cultivation; 1,485 pounds then make a 475-pound bale of lint equal to that of fresh land. Scarcely any of such land lies "turned out", and it produces as well as ever when again cultivated. The troublesome weeds of this region are crab-grass, cocklebur, and morning-glory.

Farmers sell their cotton in Meridian as soon as it is baled.

CLARKE.
(See " Central prairie region ".)

WAYNE.
(See " Central prairie region ".)

COVINGTON.

Population: 5,993.—White, 3,991; colored, 2,002.
Area: 580 square miles.—All long-leaf pine hills.
Tilled lands: 30,390 acres.—Area planted in cotton, 6,968 acres; in corn, 10,682 acres; in oats, 3,553 acres.
Cotton production: 2,071 bales; average cotton product per acre, 0.30 bale, 429 pounds seed-cotton, or 143 pounds cotton lint.

The surface of Covington is rolling, occasionally hilly, traversed in a northwestern and southeastern direction by the Okahay, Okatoma, and Bouie, with numerous tributary creeks, while Leaf river passes through the northeast corner, and Holliday's creek, tributary to the Pearl river, heads in the southwestern corner. In the larger part of the county the long-leaf pine, with its sandy and comparatively inferior soils, prevails; but there are numerous ridges timbered exclusively or on their flanks with oaks and short-leaf pine, possessing a good, brown-loam soil, and usually falling off into valleys, with gentler slopes and wider bottoms than is the case with the long-leaf pine ridges. This is more especially true of the eastern part of the county, on the waters of Bouie and White Sand creeks. On the latter, partly in Covington and partly in Lawrence county, there is a tract of oak uplands with a deep red-loam subsoil where the pine is scarcely seen. (See analysis, p. 59.) On the whole, however, the bottoms are chiefly cultivated, the dwellings being located on the adjacent hills. The bottom soils are almost all light and easily cultivated, but the frequency with which bog ore occurs in their subsoil shows the need of drainage. Some of these bottoms are very productive.

There is a great deal of excellent pine timber in Covington, but its remoteness from market and transportation routes has caused lumbering to be neglected. The streams have running water throughout the season, but, on account of the slow drainage from the sandy uplands, are not well adapted to logging.

The tilled lands of Covington constitute 8.1 per cent. of the total area, being slightly less than that of Smith and Simpson counties. Somewhat less than one-fourth of these lands is devoted to cotton and about three-eighths to corn, the average cotton product per acre being 0.30 bale, the same as in Kemper and Jasper counties.

The communication of Covington is chiefly westward to the New Orleans and Chicago railroad (Brookhaven and Hazlehurst); in time of high water in Pearl river, to stations on the Mobile and Ohio railroad.

ABSTRACT OF THE REPORT OF C. WELCH, STATION CREEK.

The uplands are level and rolling; the lowlands consist of second bottoms of creeks; the first bottoms are not cultivated. The kinds of land are hummock and pine land in the southern and "hollow" lands in the northern half of the county.

The *sandy pine lands* include most of the cultivated soil, and extend 100 miles west, 50 east, 30 south, and 20 miles north, with a natural growth of pine (long- and short-leaf), red, white, and post oaks, hickory, gums, and dogwood. The soil is a coarse sandy loam, whitish-gray, brown, and blackish in color, and 3 to 4 inches deep. The subsoil is a yellowish sandy loam, contains white gravel, and is underlaid by sandy clay. The soil is early, warm, well-drained, always easily tilled, and is probably best adapted to corn and oats; but cotton occupies about one-third of its cultivated area. The other important crops are corn, oats, and sweet potatoes. The cotton-plant grows from 2½ to 4 feet high, but is most productive at about 3 feet. It inclines to run to weed in excessively wet weather and on some fresh lands, for which a dressing of lime might be beneficial.

The seed-cotton product per acre of fresh land is from 500 to 600 pounds, and 1,545 pounds make a 475-pound bale of low middling lint. After five years' cultivation (unmanured) the product is from 400 to 500 pounds, and a little more is needed for a bale and the staple is perceptibly inferior. From one-half to three-fourths of such originally cultivated land lies "turned out", and it is said to produce about half the original yields when again cultivated. The hog-weed, red careless-weed, and butter-weed are troublesome on some varieties of soil, but crab-grass is the most so. The slopes wash readily, doing some damage, but the valleys are not injured very greatly. Horizontalizing and hillside ditching retards, but does not entirely prevent, the damage.

The "hollows" or small valleys include about one-fourth of the cultivated soil of the northern half of the county. Their natural growth is oak of several species, some pine, hickory, poplar, and sweet gum. The soil is a fine sandy loam of gray, brown, and black colors, 3 to 10 inches deep; the subsoil is a dense red or yellowish-red clay loam, contains "black gravel" in some places, and is underlaid by sand and some gravel. The soil is easily tilled, except where too wet; is early and best adapted to corn, cotton, and oats, and about 35 per cent. of its cultivated area is planted with cotton. The usual and most productive height of the plant is from 3 to 4 feet.

The seed-cotton product per acre of fresh land is about 800 pounds; 1,485 pounds make a 475-pound bale of lint. After five years' cultivation the product is from 600 to 700 pounds, but the staple is said to be shorter than that from fresh land. About one-half such originally cultivated land lies "turned out"; when again cultivated, it produces about half its original yields. Crab-grass and cocklebur are the most troublesome weeds.

The cotton crop suffers from cool rains and chilly, dry north winds in spring and heavy rains and protracted moist weather in summer; frequently also from severe drought in August and September, while cotton is maturing.

Cotton is hauled by wagon, in December and January, to railroad stations, at $2 to $2 50 per bale.

JONES.

Population: 3,828.—White, 3,469; colored, 359.
Area: 700 square miles.—All long-leaf pine hills.
Tilled lands: 12,822 acres.—Area planted in cotton, 2,794 acres; in corn, 5,664 acres; in oats, 3,481 acres.
Cotton production: 624 bales; average cotton product per acre, 0.22 bale, 315 pounds seed-cotton, or 105 pounds cotton lint.

The whole of Jones county is covered with long-leaf pine forest, and is traversed in its northern and southern directions by the Bogue Homo, Tallahala, Tallahomo, and Leaf rivers, with their tributaries. The northern part of the county is the more populous and productive, the bottoms of the larger streams preserving in a measure the fertility brought down from the prairie region, while in the southern portion these bottoms possess sandy and more or less acid and ill-drained soils, as is evidenced by their growth of gallberry, wax myrtle, and similar shrubs. The uplands are little cultivated, except where the sandy soil of the long-leaf pine is underlaid by the brown loam, of which the presence is ordinarily indicated by the prevalence of the short-leaf pine, mixed with oaks. It is on ridges of such character, commonly skirted by broader valleys or bottoms, that settlements are generally located. Lumbering and turpentine-making might, with better means of communication, occupy a considerable population, as they now do a portion of the inhabitants.

Not quite 3 per cent. of the area of Jones county is under tillage, and somewhat over one-fourth of this is in cotton, with an average yield of 0.22 of a bale per acre. The corn acreage is double that of cotton.

Communication is with stations on the Mobile and Ohio railroad in Wayne and Clarke counties, and thence with Mobile.

MARION.

Population: 6,901.—White, 4,451; colored, 2,450.
Area: 1,500 square miles.—All long-leaf pine hills.
Tilled lands: 18,080 acres.—Area planted in cotton, 4,717 acres; in corn, 9,087 acres; in oats, 1,348 acres.
Cotton production: 1,579 bales; average cotton product per acre, 0.33 bale, 471 pounds seed-cotton, or 157 pounds cotton lint.

Marion, the largest county in the state, is traversed by Pearl river in its western portion, and is drained by its tributaries and by the heads of Black and Red creeks on the east and by those of the Wolf and Habolo Chitto rivers on the south. It is throughout a region of long-leaf pine hills and plateaus with narrow sandy valleys and sandy soils, which, though mostly possessing a loam subsoil, renders them capable of improvement; are naturally of inferior productiveness and durability; and partly because of its remoteness from lines of communication Marion county is very thinly settled, the population being but 4.6 persons per square mile, second in this respect in the state, Perry being the most thinly settled. The chief settlements are in the belt of country adjoining Pearl river and on its smaller tributaries. Within the county the bottom proper, subject to the overflow of Pearl river, is rather narrow, save in the extreme southern part, where it widens to as much as 2 miles, and is timbered with a very large growth of sweet gum, shellbark hickory, water, Spanish, chestnut, white, and black oaks, holly, ironwood, some mulberry, and magnolia. The soil is quite heavy, but is not as difficult to till as might be supposed. It is very productive, but crops are often belated by overflows. In this region the long-leaf pine descends into the river hummock. Farther north (as at Spring Cottage post-office) there intervenes between the pine uplands and the river a narrow belt of sandy land, timbered with tall, graceful willow oaks, with some Spanish, red, and black oaks, and hickory. The soil is very fertile, but does not last long. Similar belts and patches also occur higher up, but usually a hummock, varying from 1½ to 3 miles, with a light, whitish, often sandy and sometimes ill-drained soil, timbered generally with bottom pine, water, willow, Spanish and post oaks, and more or less sweet gum and hickory, according to the quality of the lands. Near the river bank the beech is sometimes abundant. The greater part of the hummock or flat is here usually on the east side of the river, and breaks off into its channel in very sandy bluff bank, underlaid by solid, green and blue clays. On the west bank of Pearl river, in the northwestern part of the county, the hills frequently approach close to the channel, forming high and precipitous bluffs, or, when receding, slopes timbered with oak or oak mixed with short-leaf pine, in striking contrast to the heavy long-leaf pine forest which crowns the summit, from which extensive and beautiful views of the Pearl river country can be obtained.

342

The lumber resources of Marion county are very great, and have hardly been developed to any notable extent. At some points turpentine-making is extensively carried on. The tilled lands of Marion are reported at 8.9 per cent. of the area, of which one-fourth is devoted to cotton, producing on an average 0.33, or one-third of a bale per acre. The cotton acreage per square mile is 2.9.

The communication of Marion county is mostly with stations on the New Orleans and Chicago railroad in Pike county, and to some extent, in times of high water, down Pearl river in flats or small steamers to Shieldsborough.

PERRY.

Population: 3,427.—White, 2,357; colored, 1,070.
Area: 1,000 square miles.—All long-leaf pine hills.
Tilled lands: 10,081 acres.—Area planted in cotton, 537 acres; in corn, 4,466 acres; in oats, 2,615 acres.
Cotton production: 146 bales; average cotton product per acre, 0.27 bale, 384 pounds seed-cotton, or 128 pounds cotton lint.

Perry county is, throughout a region of sandy, long-leaf pine uplands, traversed by numerous streams, mostly with narrow, sandy valleys. The northern portion is drained by Leaf river, which is here joined by its largest tributaries—the Okatoma, Tallahala, Boguehomo, Thompson's, and Gaines creeks, while Black creek, with its numerous branches, drains the southwestern portion. Perry is as a whole the most thinly inhabited county of the state, there being only 3.4 inhabitants per square mile, while the tilled lands amount to 1.6 per cent. of its area, being in this respect ahead of Greene, Hancock, Jackson, and Harrison counties.

The bottoms as well as the uplands of Perry are timbered with a heavy growth of long-leaf pine, proving that the soil, though sandy, is not devoid of productiveness even in the uplands. Some saw-logs are rafted down Leaf river, and turpentine orchards have from time to time been run on a large scale in this county; but its remoteness from lines of communication has prevented any extensive development of either industry.

GREENE.

Population: 3,194.—White, 2,382; colored, 812.
Area: 790 square miles.—All long-leaf pine hills.
Tilled lands: 5,997 acres.—Area planted in cotton, 35 acres; in corn, 3,563 acres; in oats, 891 acres.
Cotton production: 12 bales; average cotton product per acre, 0.29 bale, 414 pounds seed-cotton, or 138 pounds cotton lint.

Greene county is almost throughout a region of undulating and sometimes hilly, sandy uplands, covered with a heavy forest of long-leaf pine. It is very thinly settled, and only along the water-courses, of which the Chickasawhay and Leaf rivers, uniting on the southern line of the county to form the Pascagoula, are the chief. Rogers and Big creeks, the latter traversing the county almost centrally from north to south, are the chief tributaries.

The immediate valley of the Chickasawhay, from 1 to 3 miles in width, is formed chiefly by a high hummock or second bottom above overflow, the first bottom being usually quite narrow, but possessing rather heavy and fertile soils heavily timbered. Occasionally there are tracts of high bottom land of a sandy character, but very productive. The second bottom proper has mostly silty or sandy, whitish soils, ill-drained, as shown by the growth of gallberry appearing in all low spots, which, with the long-leaf pine, constitutes almost its exclusive growth in the middle and southern parts of the county. The same is true of the hummock of Leaf river within the county.

In the uplands east of the Chickasawhay, in the southern part of the county, the feature prevailing in the adjacent portion of Alabama, viz, a loam subsoil, bearing a growth chiefly of oaks and hickory, sparingly mingled with pine and with tulip tree and magnolia on the hillsides, is more or less prevalent, giving rise to some upland settlements.

The tilled lands of Greene county form but 1.2 per cent. of its area, and but 11 acres were reported as having been planted in cotton in 1879, producing 4 bales; 3,563 acres of corn were planted. The chief products of the county, however, are lumber and turpentine.

ABSTRACT OF THE REPORT OF J. H. M'CLEAN, ADAMSVILLE.

The lowlands consist of first and second bottoms of the Chickasawhay river. The country is moderately undulating, and has no very high hills nor impenetrable swamps. The soils are mostly sandy, are based on the orange-sand formation, and are naturally well drained.

Labor is engaged chiefly in producing turpentine and pine lumber. Cotton is raised only to a small extent, and is planted chiefly on the uplands. The lowlands are very liable to overflow, and are therefore rarely planted. The natural growth of the upland is chiefly long-leaf pine.

The soil is a coarse sandy loam of an orange-red color about an inch deep. The lighter subsoil consists mostly of sand to considerable depth. The soil is early, warm, easily tilled, and equally well adapted to corn, potatoes, winter oats, and sugar-cane, which, with rice on the lowlands, constitute the chief crops of the region.

A very small proportion of cotton is planted, which grows to a height of 3 feet and produces 800 pounds of seed-cotton per acre of fresh land, 1,425 pounds making a 475-pound bale of lint. After the first year (without manure) the yield increases and the staple improves. Three-fourths of such land, originally cultivated, now lies "turned out", and in four or five years it again produces very well. White clover is the most troublesome weed.

Slopes and valleys are damaged to a serious extent by the washing of the soil from the former down upon the latter, and where the lowland is covered by the washings it is entirely ruined. No efforts have been made to check the damage.

Cotton is shipped in December by rail to State Line station at $2 25 per bale.

JACKSON.

Population: 7,607.—White, 5,122; colored, 2,485.
Area: 1,140 square miles.—Long-leaf pine hills, 550 square miles; pine flats, 590 square miles.
Tilled lands: 4,195 acres.—Area planted in cotton, none; in corn, 138 acres; in oats, 5 acres.

Jackson county forms the southeastern corner of the state and fronts on the Gulf of Mexico, and includes also a number of sandy islands, of which Horn island is the largest, and forms part of the outer reef of Mississippi sound. The northern part of the county is rolling pine uplands with a pale-tinted sandy soil, mostly of very inferior quality, especially where underlaid by impervious clay, which is frequently the case on the very summits of ridges and plateaus, where bogs covered with sour grasses and rushes appear. The ridges flatten out to the southward, and pass insensibly into a gently undulating or level country, sparsely timbered with stunted long-leaf pine and cypress, forming an open, park-like landscape. This "pine-meadow" country extends to within a few miles of the sea-shore, where it passes into the sand hummocks of the coast.

The soil of the pine-meadow country is scarcely fit for cultivation, and in its natural condition affords but scanty pasturage, the only use to which thus far it has been put. It is little else but a white sand or silt, which at the depth of from 2 to 3 feet is underlaid by impervious gray clay; hence it remains water-soaked until late in the season, the drainage progressing slowly toward the flat, shallow channels of the streams, which carry clear, coffee-colored water. The bottom lands of the larger streams, such as Black and Red creeks, are almost too sandy for cultivation, but they are sometimes bordered by ridge lands possessing a yellow sandy loam subsoil above the impervious clay, and are thus rendered cultivable. Such lands extend, for example, along the south fork of Bluff creek, and bear a fair though not heavy growth of long-leaf pine timber.

Few settlements exist in the country west of the Pascagoula river, save on the bluff immediately overlooking its valley, the inhabitants, however, cultivating the valley lands almost exclusively. These are quite productive (see analysis and discussion in the regional description, p. 63). The heavy, fertile bottom soil is, however, mostly liable to overflow, and hence the lighter soil of the second bottom, 2 or 3 feet above the first, is chiefly cultivated. No cotton, and but little corn, was grown in the county in 1879, and the tilled lands are reported as constituting but 0.6 per cent. of the total area.

The chief industries of the county are the raising of cattle and sheep on the natural pastures, charcoal-burning, and the cutting and sawing of lumber, with headquarters at Scranton (the county-seat) and east Pascagoula, whence shipments are made by rail or schooner to New Orleans and Mobile. The logs are floated down the Pascagoula and its tributaries from the pine lands of the interior.

The towns mentioned, as well as Ocean Springs and, more or less, the entire coast, are places of summer resort for Mobile and New Orleans. The sandy coast belt, elevated usually from 18 to 25 feet above the beach and timbered with live-oak and pitch pine, affords fine sites for residences, and sometimes, where shell-heaps exist or have existed, there is a light but very fertile soil for gardens and small fields (see in regional description "shell hummock soil", p. 67). The small streams emptying into the sound are usually bordered by small marshes. The coast is, however, exceedingly healthy.

HARRISON.

Population: 7,895.—White, 5,746; colored, 2,149.
Area: 1,000 square miles.—Long-leaf pine hills, 735 square miles; pine flats, 265 square miles.
Tilled lands: 2,649 acres.—Area planted in cotton, 26 acres; in corn, 1,064 acres; in oats, 142 acres.
Cotton production: 11 bales; average cotton product per acre, 0.42 bale, 600 pounds seed-cotton, or 200 pounds cotton lint.

Harrison, the middle one of the three counties bordering on the Gulf, is very similar to Jackson in its general features, the northern part, a rolling pine hills country, being drained chiefly by Red creek. It is very thinly settled, and is occupied chiefly by stock-raisers and lumbermen. The southern part, drained by Wolf river and the streams emptying into Biloxi bay, is largely of the pine-meadow character within from 7 to 12 miles of the coast, but lower ridges, possessing a moderately fertile yellow-loam subsoil, accompany most of the streams, and give rise to some cultivation inland. The upper portion of the streams mentioned lies within the sandy rolling pine country, the resort of the stock and lumbermen and charcoal-burners.

Mississippi City, on Pass Christian, and other points on the coast, through which passes the New Orleans and Mobile railroad, are well-known places of summer resort and points of shipment for lumber, charcoal, wool, stock, and turpentine. Handsborough is a manufacturing town.

Only 0.4 per cent. of the area of Harrison county is reported as being under tillage, the smallest proportion of any county in the state. Only 18 acres were planted in cotton in 1879, producing 9 bales (probably of sea-island cotton, 250 to 300 pounds to the bale), the soil cultivated being probably of the shell-hummock character. Low ridges, possessing a yellow-loam subsoil, approach the sea-shore at several points, as, e. g., near Pass Christian, affording opportunity for cultivation.

HANCOCK.

Population: 6,460.—White, 4,643; colored, 1,817.
Area: 940 square miles.—Long-leaf pine hills, 610 square miles; pine flats, 330 square miles.
Tilled lands: 4,390 acres.—Area planted in corn, 41 acres; in oats, 29 acres.

The northern and greater part of Hancock county is a rolling, more rarely hilly, upland region, heavily timbered with long-leaf pine, and traversed by numerous streams with narrow sandy valleys. On the east this rolling country reaches the head of bay Saint Louis, while in the Pearl river country it terminates southward at the junction of the eastern and western prongs of the Habolo Chitto. In this region there is little cultivation away from Pearl river valley (the river bottom, however, lies almost wholly on the Louisiana side), and lumbering, tar- and charcoal-making, and stock-raising are the chief occupations of the inhabitants, settlements being very sparse. The soil of the pine country is light and of little productiveness, but the yellow or reddish subsoil of light sandy loam renders it quite capable of improvement by fertilizers. Within a few miles east of Pearl river, especially near the smaller tributary creeks, there is a gently undulating country—a kind of high hummock or second bottom of Pearl river—where there is a large admixture of oaks among the pine, and the soil, though still very light, has a substantial subsoil, fairly productive, and settlements are more numerous.

South of the Habolo Chitto a level country extends to the coast. It corresponds in many respects to the pine-meadow country farther east, and open meadow lands, with stunted pine growth as well as boggy spots, occur to a greater or less extent throughout. The greater part of the area, however, is occupied by pine timber, though less heavily than on the rolling lands, and the trees are rather lank in growth. The entire region appears to be underlaid, usually at a depth of from 2 to 3 feet, but sometimes much nearer to and even at the surface, by the same heavy gray clay which forms the pine glades of Jackson county. This clay and the overlying whitish, putty-like subsoil is frequently brought up by the crawfish, which inhabit the lower lands in great numbers. But the soil is less sandy, more substantial, and better drained. Its best quality is found on the western heads of Mulatto bayou, being there occupied chiefly by a growth of post, Spanish, water, and live oaks. The subsoil, a pale yellow loam, is evidently well drained. The high hummock of Pearl river, northward from Pearlington to the Habolo Chitto, averages about half a mile in width, and is timbered with large bottom pine, sweet gum, and fine water, willow, and white oaks. It has a pale yellow loam subsoil (a good brick-clay), and is fairly productive.

Along the coast we find the bluff bank, on the whole, less elevated than in Jackson and Harrison counties—say from 10 to 15 feet—and not so much of the sand-hummock character, sometimes consisting of yellow loam or brick-clay. A great abundance of shell heaps has largely transformed the sterile sandy soil into "shell hummocks" (see regional description, p. 66), which occur scatteringly along the coast line, and along lower Mulatto bayou extend some distance inland, forming a body of several hundred acres between the marsh and the pine woods. Here before the war the sea-island or long-staple cotton was cultivated with considerable success; but this industry has not been resumed since, and no cotton is reported as having been grown in this county in 1879. The cultivated lands of Hancock amount to 0.75 per cent. of its area, of which 41 acres were in corn, producing 10 bushels per acre. Apart from the town of Shieldsborough, which is a favorite place of summer resort, the whole coast of Hancock county is largely occupied by residences and smaller places of resort, which are easily reached by rail or steamer from New Orleans. The marsh at the mouth of Pearl river lies chiefly on the Louisiana side, forming part of the great Pontchartrain marsh plain in the adjoining parishes of Saint Bernard and Saint Tammany; but it, as well as the smaller marshes bordering bay Saint Louis, does not appear to affect injuriously the health of the region.

Communication with the interior is greatly facilitated throughout the level region by the deep canal-like channels of the tide-water bayous, some of which are navigable for sloops and schooners nearly to their heads, greatly to the surprise of the cross-country traveler, who finds no bridges and cannot ford the streams.

ABSTRACT OF THE REPORT OF BEN. LANE POSEY, BAY SAINT LOUIS.

The uplands consist of gently undulating table-lands (the hills are few and small), occupying the northern half of the county and extending to within 20 miles of the coast. The lowlands consist of bottoms and hummocks of Pearl and Jourdan rivers and of tide-water marshes along the coast and streams. The mild sea-coast climate is favorable to the production of the sea-island or long-staple cotton. In 1860, 80 bales of it were produced in this county, but since the war no cotton of any kind has been raised. Sea-island cotton might be raised with profit; so might rice and sugar, the production of which is small, but annually increasing. The soil is poor, but the elements of fertility are abundant, and it costs only care and labor to utilize them.

The industry and small capital are devoted to the preferred pursuits of rearing cattle and sheep and in producing lumber, wood, charcoal, and turpentine, and some are engaged in the coast fisheries and small coastwise commerce.

The lowland and richest soil of this region is a *fine black alluvial mud or muck* of the tide-water marshes, frequently overflowed, and well adapted to rice culture. Its natural growth is live and water oaks, cypress, hickory, cedar, magnolia, and bay; a few small prairies occur on it.

The *second quality of soil* occurs on the low flat lands in the southern half of the county, and occupies one-third its area. It is a whitish-gray, fine sandy soil, 2¼ feet thick, and rests on pipe-clay which makes good brick. Its tillage is always easy. The natural growth is pine, cedar, oaks, hickory, cypress, magnolia, and bay. The remaining kind of soil covers the uplands of the north half of the county, and extends 50 miles north, 100 east, and 30 west. Its growth is pine exclusively. The soil is light, varies from fine to coarse sandy, is gray, and 3 feet thick; the subsoil is a leachy red clay. The soil is early, warm, well drained, and easily tilled. One-tenth of such originally cultivated soil lies "turned out"; it produces but poorly until fertilized.

The soil on cultivated or "turned out" slopes washes and gullies readily, but the damage to slopes or adjoining lower lands is not serious, and no efforts have been made to check it. This soil is well adapted to sea-island cotton, sugar-cane, sweet potatoes, small fruits, and vegetables generally. Some cotton is raised for domestic use, but not a bale in the county is raised for export. The soil is poor, and especially deficient in lime, but sea-shells and other natural fertilizers in abundance are near at hand.

PART III.

CULTURAL AND ECONOMIC DETAILS

OF

COTTON PRODUCTION.

REFERENCE LIST

OF

NAMES AND ADDRESSES OF CORRESPONDENTS.

NORTHEASTERN PRAIRIE REGION.

Alcorn.—W. L. WILLIAMS, Rienzi, December 19, 1879; J. M. TAYLOR, M. D., Corinth, October 27, 1880.
Prentiss.—B. B. BOONE, Booneville, January 25, 1880.
Tippah.—J. A. KIMBROUGH, Ripley, January 8, 1880.
Lee.—H. L. HOLLAND, Guntown, March 16, 1880.
Pontotoc.—E. C. CALLAWAY, Algoma, March 1880.
Lowndes.—JAMES O. BANKS, Columbus, March 18, 1880; R. W. BANKS, Cobb's Switch, March 16, 1880.
Noxubee.—F. R. W. BOCK, Macon, January 25, 1880.

SHORT-LEAF PINE AND OAK UPLANDS REGION.

Tishomingo.—J. M. D. MILLER, Iuka, December 22, 1879.
Choctaw.—R. H. BIGGES, Chester, February 28, 1880.
Winston.—W. T. LEWIS, Louisville.
Attgla.—A. TUR, French Camp, January 24, 1880.
Leake.—J. D. EADS, Carthage, March 26, 1880; T. C. SPENCER, Laurel Hill.
Kemper.—J. A. MINNIECE, Scooba, February 3, 1880.

BROWN-LOAM TABLE-LANDS.

Benton.—H. T. LIPFORD, Ashland, February 27, 1880.
Marshall.—F. B. SHUFORD, Holly Springs, February 24, 1880; A. J. WITHERS, Holly Springs, January 4, 1880.
De Soto.—T. C. DOCKERY, Love Station, March 24, 1880.
Panola.—D. B. STEWART, Courtland, April 28, 1880.
La Fayette.—S. W. E. PEGUES, Oxford, March 10, 1880; IRA B. ORR, Water Valley, April 1, 1880; S. E. RAGLAND, De Lay, May 1, 1880 ; P. H. SKIPWITH, Oxford, March 6, 1880; P. FERNANDEZ, Oxford, March 8, 1880.
Grenada.—M. K. MISTER, Grenada, February 5, 1880; J. D. LE FLORE, Grenada, April 1, 1880.
Holmes.—CHARLES C. THORNTON, M. D., Chew's Landing, February 1, 1880; J. W. C. SMITH, Benton.

CANE-HILLS REGION.

Warren.—L. WAILES, Vicksburg, March 10, 1880.
Claiborne.—G. P. MCLEAN, Rocky Springs, March 10, 1880.
Jefferson.—J. W. BURCH, Fayette, January 12, 1880.
Wilkinson.—D. L. PHARES, M. D., Woodville.

MISSISSIPPI ALLUVIAL REGION.

Le Flore.—JOHN A. AVENT, Greenwood, March 1, 1880.
Bolivar.—G. W. WISE, Concordia, March 8, 1880.
Yazoo.—J. W. C. SMITH, Benton, January 2, 1880.
Sharkey.—T. F. SCOTT, Rolling Fork, December 30, 1879.
Issaquena.—W. E. COLLINS, Mayersville, July 3, 1880.

CENTRAL PRAIRIE REGION.

Hinds.—H. O. DIXON, Jackson, March 31, 1880.
Rankin.—E. JACK, Brandon, March, 1880.
Scott.—W. T. ROBERTSON, Forest, January 10, 1880.
Jasper.—S. G. LOUGHRIDGE, M. D., Garlandsville.
Clarke.—JOHN A. BASS, C. W. MOODY, J. E. WELBORN, Shubuta, April 20, 1880; W. SPILLMAN, M. D., Enterprise, February 4, 1880.

LONG-LEAF PINE REGION.

Lauderdale.—J. J. SHANNON, Meridian, February 21, 1880
Greene.—J. H. MCCLEAN, Adamsville, January 27, 1880.
Hancock.—BEN. LANE POSEY, Bay Saint Louis, June 16, 1880.
Covington.—C. WELCH, Station Creek, March 11, 1880.
Simpson.—J. C. MCLAURIN, Mount Zion, March 5, 1880.
Smith.—A. S. BAUGH, Polkville, January 1, 1880.
Pike.—W. W. VAUGHT, Magnolia, March 15, 1880.
Amite.—J. R. GALTNEY, Liberty, April 8, 1880 ; GEORGE F. WEBB, Liberty, January 2, 1880.

SUMMARY OF ANSWERS TO SCHEDULE QUESTIONS.

[Special answers, when given, are either preceded by the name of the county (from which it is taken) in italics alone, or followed by that name in italics and parentheses.]

TILLAGE, IMPROVEMENT, ETC.

1. Usual depth of tillage (measured on land-side of furrow). What draft employed in breaking up?

NORTHEASTERN PRAIRIE REGION: From 3 to 6 inches, and with two mules in all of the counties except Tippah and Pontotoc, in which from 1 to 3 inches, with one mule only, is reported.

YELLOW-LOAM REGION: Usually 2 to 4 inches; sometimes 5, or even 8 and 9, in all of the counties. The draft employed is one mule, though sometimes two.

MISSISSIPPI BOTTOM REGION: In three counties, 2 to 3 inches; in the rest, 4 and 5 inches. The draft is one mule or horse in three counties and two mules in two counties.

CANE-HILLS REGION: Depth, 2 to 3 inches; draft, one mule or horse in Wilkinson; two mules usually in the other counties.

CENTRAL PRAIRIE REGION: From 3 to 5 inches, with one or two mules or horses.

LONG-LEAF PINE REGION: From 2 to 4 inches in five counties; 4 to 6 in Pike and Amite, and 8 in Hancock. Draft, usually one horse or mule.

2. Is subsoiling practiced? If so, with what implements, and with what results?

NORTHEASTERN PRAIRIE REGION: Very rarely. The bull-tongue follows the turn-plow. Results are good where the subsoil is a red clay (*Alcorn*). Subsoiling would be decidedly beneficial if done in the fall, when the ground is dry, but not so if done when the ground is wet (*Prentiss*).

YELLOW-LOAM REGION: But little in any of the counties, except Benton, where with subsoil plows "it is beneficial to clay lands, and but little to the sandy". The subsoil plow is used in five counties, while in others one plow is usually made to follow another in the same row. Results always good, except in La Fayette, where "it is a disadvantage, unless the soil be heavily manured".

MISSISSIPPI BOTTOM REGION: Only in Holmes county, one plow following another in the same row. In Sharkey "it is unnecessary, the soil being sandy".

CANE-HILLS REGION: Only a little in Wilkinson, with Brinley's or Murfee's subsoil plow. The result is excellent if the subsoil is dry; otherwise, damaging.

CENTRAL PRAIRIE REGION: To some extent only in Rankin, with Murfee's subsoiler, with satisfactory results. In Hinds "it has been found to be useless, and sometimes injurious".

LONG-LEAF PINE REGION: A little in Clarke, Pike, Lauderdale, Simpson, Amite, and Covington, subsoil plows and scooters being used, and usually with good results. In Pike county "the subsoil packs again, so that the process should be repeated".

3. Is fall plowing practiced, and with what results?

NORTHEASTERN PRAIRIE REGION: To some extent in all the counties except Tippah and Noxubee, and with beneficial results. *Prentiss:* By turning under stubble, and if done while vegetation is green, it is decidedly beneficial; but if after frost, it is damaging.

YELLOW-LOAM REGION: Yes; in Panola and Choctaw; very little in six counties, and not at all in four. *Marshall:* When stubble and green vegetation are turned under in such manner and at such time that they will rot rather than dry. *Benton:* The practice would result well if it did not facilitate washing and gullying, to which the sandy soil here is much inclined.

Winston and *Leake:* The soil is again packed by the heavy winter rains.

MISSISSIPPI BOTTOM AND CANE-HILLS REGION: Very little in Holmes; a much better and more easily cultivable condition of the soil is the result.

CENTRAL PRAIRIE REGION: A very little, only in Hinds and Rankin. "It benefits soil not cultivated during the summer, but it is injurious to those cultivated" (*Hinds*).

LONG-LEAF PINE REGION: A little only in five counties; opinions as to results differ. "If vegetation be well turned under the results are very good" (*Amite*).

4. Is fallowing practiced? Is the land tilled while lying fallow, or only "turned out"? With what results in either case?

NORTHEASTERN PRAIRIE REGION: Fallowing is not practiced. The land is only "turned out" when rest is necessary. *Lee:* It grows up in briers and sedge-grass, and the slopes wash and gully. *Noxubee:* When pastured it slowly improves.

YELLOW-LOAM REGION: Fallowing is generally practiced in Attala; but little in two other counties, and not in the rest. *Winston, Attala,* and *Panola:* Land is generally tilled while lying fallow, and is much improved if green vegetation be turned under, without which tillage is of no benefit. *Leake and Benton:* It is rarely tilled while lying fallow, but improves in a short time if allowed to grow up in briers. *De Soto:* The land is damaged by treading of stock; it also washes and gullies much worse without than with tillage while fallow. *Marshall:* Some improve the fallow soil by green manuring in the meantime with cow-pease and weeds.

MISSISSIPPI BOTTOM AND CANE-HILLS REGION: Lands are only turned out in these counties. *Holmes:* It is sometimes turned out just for one year, because the grass has formed a sod which cannot easily be plowed or hoed; a grass pasture results, but the grass is usually turned off preparatory to plowing, so that no benefit results from the vegetation. *Wilkinson:* The soil becomes mellower, easier to cultivate, and richer in vegetable matter. *Warren:* It is only "turned out" for want of labor to cultivate it; the result is washing and gullying.

CENTRAL PRAIRIE REGION: Land is only turned out for rest. In Hinds a great quantity has thus grown up in sedge, briers, and weeds, which, when turned under and left undisturbed a year, much improves the land.

LONG-LEAF PINE REGION: Lands are usually only "turned out", and are much improved by rest. In Covington some is tilled while lying fallow, increasing the yields for a year or two.

5. Is rotation of crops practiced? If so, of how many years' course, in what order of crops, and with what results?

NORTHEASTERN PRAIRIE REGION: To a limited extent only in the counties, and usually of three years' course with cotton, corn, and oats or pease. *Alcorn:* Rotation is indispensable with either corn or cotton to insure good crops.

YELLOW-LOAM REGION: It is practiced in seven counties, and very little or not at all in the rest. No regular order is observed, except that cotton never follows immediately after corn; the course is usually three or four years with cotton, corn, and small grain. *Yazoo:* Each change results well; pease especially leave the soil much better. *Leake:* Cotton is often planted for five consecutive years on the same land; so is corn on the bottoms and reed-brakes. Results of rotation are good. *Benton:* Yields invariably decline without manuring.

MISSISSIPPI BOTTOM AND CANE-HILLS REGIONS: In Bolivar cotton only has been planted for the last forty years. In other

counties rotation is practiced to some extent with cotton and corn, and sometimes sweet potatoes and oats, and with good results; and in Issaquena, material improvement both to soil and crop. Fresh land will produce fine crops of cotton for several years without change.

CENTRAL PRAIRIE REGION: To some extent in this region corn and small grain or sweet potatoes usually following cotton. *Hinds:* Result is an exhaustion of the vegetable matter and consequent washing and gullying of the soil. *Scott:* Without rotation the soil would soon fail to produce any other crop.

LONG-LEAF PINE REGION: Yes, in Covington, Pike, and Amite, and to some extent in other counties. In Pike and Amite the order is cotton, corn, oats, etc. In some counties cotton and corn alternate, while in others sweet potatoes are also brought in. Results are said to be good.

6. What fertilizers or other direct means of improving the soil are used in your region? Is green manuring practiced? With what results in either case?

NORTHEASTERN PRAIRIE REGION: No commercial fertilizers are used in the region. Composts of stable manure and cotton-seed are often applied to lands with good results, increasing the yields one-fourth. Green manuring is practiced by but very few farmers; cow-pease, weeds, and stubble turned under produce good results. In Alcorn, pease are generally planted with corn at second plowing for pasturage when the crop is gathered.

YELLOW-LOAM REGION: Commercial fertilizers are scarcely used in the region; composts of stable manure, cotton-seed, etc., used only by small planters in some of the counties. *Winston:* Cotton-seed renders the least and bone-dust the most permanent improvement to the soil. *De Soto:* Cotton-seed almost doubles the grain crops. *La Fayette:* With barnyard manure and cotton-seed crops may be doubled, except in very dry seasons. *Yazoo:* Barnyard manure increases the yields one-fourth. Green manuring is practiced in some of the counties with good results and improvement of the soil. *Marshall:* It is regarded as the best and cheapest means of restoring fertility to the soil on the large scale. *Yazoo:* Cow-pease are best, as they grow luxuriantly on the poorest soil and increase crops from 3 to 6 per cent. The large planters only turn under dry weeds, grass, etc.

MISSISSIPPI BOTTOM: Neither fertilizing or green manuring are generally practiced in the region. *Sharkey:* Some apply cotton-seed to corn land, and thus increase the yields 30 to 50 per cent. *Grenada:* Cotton-seed is put into the center furrow if

sound, or spread broadcast if rotted; its good results may be observed for several years. In Holmes county green manuring has been tried on very stiff lands and found to be satisfactory.

CANE-HILLS REGION: Both fertilizing and green manuring are practiced to some extent; cotton-seed and stable manure are used either alone or with leaves, straw, etc., in compost, and in Jefferson county double the crop. In Wilkinson the corn crop is sometimes increased 50 per cent. by green manuring.

CENTRAL PRAIRIE REGION: Some commercial fertilizers are used in some of the counties, but composts of cotton-seed, barnyard manure, etc., are most common. *Scott:* Sandy soils cannot be made to produce without these. *Clarke:* They pay well on these lands. *Jasper:* They add 300 pounds of seed-cotton to the yield per acre. *Rankin:* A crop of cow-pease will improve the soil, even if the pease are gathered and the vines eaten by stock.

LONG-LEAF PINE REGION: Very little commercial fertilizers is used in the region. Composts of cotton-seed, stable manure, with sometimes swamp muck, ashes, etc., are applied to lands with excellent results. Hancock and Simpson alone report the use of pine straw with manure and leaves. *Simpson:* The general practice is to keep the floors of stock-yards and stables covered with pine straw and remove it every two months; this makes a good fertilizer. Green manuring is but little practiced in any of the counties.

7. How is cotton-seed disposed of? If sold, on what terms or at what price?

NORTHEASTERN PRAIRIE REGION: It is largely fed to cows and sheep in most of the counties, and in all of the counties is used more or less as a fertilizer. Its price is usually from 8 to 10 cents per bushel; in Lowndes, Alcorn, and Prentiss some is sold to oil-mills at from 10 to 15 cents (or $6 per ton), delivered at railroad stations, or exchanged at the rate of one ton of seed for 700 pounds of seed-cake meal.

YELLOW-LOAM REGION: It is fed to stock or used as manure in most of the counties. The usual price is from 8 to 10 cents, and in but few of the counties it is sold to oil-mills.

MISSISSIPPI BOTTOM: It is seldom returned to the soil, but mostly sold to oil-mills, delivered at the river landings at from $4 50 to $7 per ton. In Sharkey it is chiefly burned in plantation

furnaces. *Issaquena:* Before a combination was effected between oil-mill companies the price was $15 per ton.

CANE-HILLS REGION: It is partly fed to cattle, partly returned to the soil in Jefferson and Wilkinson, partly wasted in Claiborne, or sold at the river stations or factory at from $2 to $5 per ton.

CENTRAL PRAIRIE REGION: It is used as feed for cattle and as manure in all of the region; where convenient for shipment in Hinds and Clarke, it is mostly sold to oil-mills at from 8 or 10 cents per bushel.

LONG-LEAF PINE REGION: It is fed to stock or used as manure in all of the region, but little going out of its county. Its price, when sold, is from 10 to 15 cents per bushel.

8. Is cotton-seed cake used for feed? Is it used for manure?

NORTHEASTERN PRAIRIE REGION: Very little is used in the region either for feed or manure; in the former case it is always mixed with other food, as cattle do not like it alone.

YELLOW-LOAM REGION: In seven counties it is not used at all for either food or manure. In other counties it is used to a slight extent for both purposes. *Grenada:* Some is used as stock feed, is valuable as such, and is much wanted; some is used

as manure, generally alone, and when properly applied is very effective.

MISSISSIPPI BOTTOM: But two counties in this region report its use either as food or as manure.

CANE-HILLS REGION: Not used in Warren and Claiborne. In Jefferson a little is fed to milch cows, and it is coming into use as a manure for cotton and corn. In Wilkinson a little is fed to stock, and it is used rarely as manure alone or mixed with stable manure and phosphates for cotton and corn.

CENTRAL PRAIRIE REGION: Not at all in three counties, and but little in the others either as food or as manure.

LONG-LEAF PINE REGION: Not in Simpson, Covington, and Hancock; in the others both as manure and as food for stock to some extent. In Amite, when cheap or when damaged, it is used as food for cows and sheep, for which it is highly approved.

PLANTING AND CULTIVATION OF COTTON.

9. What preparation is usually given to cotton land before bedding up?

Throughout the state no other preparation is given to the land other than knocking down (sometimes burning) and plowing under the cotton stalks of the previous year, though this spring plowing is not done in very many of the counties. Stubble land, when intended for planting, is usually plowed in the fall season.

10. Do you plant in ridges, and how far apart?

It is almost the universal practice throughout the state to plant in ridges. In the bottom lands of the Mississippi river the distance between rows is from 4 to 5 feet, though Issaquena and Sharkey report as much as 6 and 7 feet. In the upland counties, Noxubee reports from 1½ to 2 feet, while in all the rest the distances are from 3 to 4 feet on the sandy lands and from 4 to 5 feet on the richer; in Wilkinson and Warren, from 5 to 7 feet on the rich and fresh lands.

11. What is the usual planting time?

The earliest date given is March 20, in Claiborne and Jefferson counties, of the cane-hills region (southwestern part of the state); March 25 in Warren and Lowndes, lying respectively in the western and eastern center of the state. In all other upland counties the earliest dates given are the 1st of April in the southern and middle counties, with Tippah and La Fayette on the north, and from the 10th to the 15th of April in other of the northern counties. Planting time closes in the state about the middle of May. In the Mississippi bottom the time is from the 1st the 10th of April, the season closing as late as May 31 in Bolivar.

12. What variety of cotton is preferred?

Of the many short-staple varieties named often two and more from a single county. The Dixon is more generally reported throughout the state, or from three counties in each region, except the yellow loam, in which it is mentioned once. The Peeler variety comes next from nine counties, the Petit Gulf from eight counties, the Herlong from five, Boyd's Prolific from four, Cheatham two, and the other varieties once or twice each; these comprise the Baggarly, Brook, Callahan, Edwards, Browns, Golden Prolific, Magnolia, Java, Chambers South American, Chaplin, etc. In Hancock county the sea-island or long-staple cotton is planted. Grenada, La Fayette, Sharkey: Dixon for quantity, and Peeler for fine staple. Wilkinson: Dixon prolific for poor soil, and Chambers South American for rich soils.

13. How much seed is used per acre?

Twenty-eight counties report from 1 to 3 bushels per acre, while in the rest from 1 to 5, 6, and 10 bushels are given. One bushel is the minimum given in nearly all of the counties.

14. What implements are used in planting?

In all of the regions a narrow instrument or plow, either a drill or bull-tongue, is used to open the furrow. The seed is then usually dropped by hand and covered with a harrow or by means of a block or board attached to a shovel-plow stock.

15. Are cotton-seed planters used? What opinion is held of their efficacy or convenience?

NORTHEASTERN PRAIRIE REGION: They are used in the northern counties, and approved; in Noxubee and Kemper the old method of planting is preferred.

YELLOW-LOAM REGION: Not used in Tishomingo, but in other counties are considered efficient and satisfactory so far as tried; in La Fayette said to be "not worth their cost".

MISSISSIPPI BOTTOM: They are used to a greater or less extent in the region, but are considered unnecessary in Bolivar, and are not popular in Le Flore. In Issaquena "they are held in high esteem as a labor-saving implement, and one by which crops can be more cheaply and evenly tilled; but here our lands are tenanted by a class who adhere strictly to the old idea generated during slavery, and which will never be eradicated; hence cotton and corn planters are never used on our plantations".

CANE-HILLS REGION: Not in Warren and Claiborne, "because they require better preparation of the soil and more labor, for which there is no compensation; and the negroes will not use improvements." In other counties they are used, but not extensively. Wilkinson: "They do better work and save half the labor of the old way."

CENTRAL PRAIRIE REGION: They are not used in Clarke; in Jasper some are found to be advantageous; in Scott are the only means of planting regularly; in Hinds they are a convenience, though farmers sometimes fail to get a "stand" with them, while in Rankin most farmers reject them.

LONG-LEAF PINE REGION: They are used in Lauderdale and a little in Pike, where they do well on land freshly plowed and clear of rubbish. In other counties they are not much used or liked.

16. How long usually before the seed comes up?

The least time given is three days in the yellow-loam region, four in the Mississippi bottom, cane-hills, and long-leaf pine regions, and five in the central and northeastern prairies. In some of the counties ten days is given as the least time. Unfavorable circumstances, such as depth to which the seed has been planted, the temperature and moisture of the soil, etc., may lengthen the time to an unusual extreme, reported as ten days in the cane-hills, fifteen in the central and northeastern prairie regions, twenty days in the yellow-loam and long-leaf pine regions, and twenty-eight in the Mississippi bottom. An average of all the reports in each region would give the probable usual time as seven days for the cane-hills region, eight days for the central and northeastern prairie regions, nine for the long-leaf pine, ten for the yellow-loam region, and eleven days for the Mississippi bottom. Holmes: If seed is planted by machine, and, therefore, at uniform depths, the "stand" is all up in from seven to ten days; otherwise, it takes from fourteen to twenty-eight days to get a "stand".

17. At what stage of growth do you thin out the stand, and how far apart?

Throughout the state the practice is general to thin out the plants when they are from 6 to 10 inches high, at which time they are two or more weeks old and have put out three or four leaves. They are then chopped out with a hoe, leaving one or two plants at distances of from 8 to 12 inches, except on the very rich lands, where as much as 18 or 20 inches space is given. In Issaquena county the thinning is postponed till all danger of frost is past. *Leake:* Thinning should not be completed before May 15. *Benton:* In cold, backward seasons it is well to leave several plants in a hill for a while.

18. Is the cotton liable to suffer from "sore shin"?

Not at all in three counties; to a greater or less extent in the rest of the state, and mostly during cool, wet spring weather, or when bruised in hoeing. *Holmes:* It is caused by bruising the plant with the hoe, and by allowing it to stand too long after scraping and hoeing before throwing the soil back to it, thus permitting the soil to dry and contract around the plant, so as to interfere with circulation of moisture and air.

19. What after-cultivation do you give, and with what implements?

NORTHEASTERN PRAIRIE AND FLATWOODS REGION: *Tippah* and *Alcorn:* Usually two shallow plowings are given with broad shovel plows and rows kept clean with hoes. *Kemper:* Sweeps and hoes are used constantly until August 1; crab-grass is not troublesome later. *Prentiss:* After scraping and thinning to a stand, solid sweeps and cultivators are run through as often as once in fifteen days. *Lee:* Scrape or harrow, hoe and thin out, and run through with a 20-inch cultivator about every ten days till July 15 to 30. *Lowndes:* Deep plowing while the plants are small; after thinning out, the sweep is run 1 to 1½ inches deep; when there is rather much rain and crab-grass the turn plow is used.

YELLOW-LOAM REGION: *De Soto* and *Panola:* First use the turn plow or scraper, afterward the shovel plow or cultivator. *Tishomingo:* Bar off, throw dirt back to the row with the bull-tongue plow, and afterward use light sweeps. *Benton:* Bar off or scrape, then use an 8-inch, next a 12-inch, and finally a 16-inch shovel plow; some use large shovels or sweeps exclusively. *Marshall:* Usually scrape, sometimes bar off with turn plow or harrow with side harrows; after this the crop is plowed successively with larger shovels or sweeps, throwing the soil about the plants; the middles are sometimes turned out with the turn plow. *La Fayette:* Bar off or scrape, thin to a stand and hoe, throw dirt to the plants with a shovel plow, then use a larger shovel plow, and at the same time an 18-inch sweep for the middles; finally throw dirt to the row successively with 16- and 18- or 20-inch sweeps or cultivators, or in wet seasons with turn plows. Weeds are chopped out with hoes three times. *Winston:* Bar off,g enerally with the scraper, sometimes with turn plow; next thin to a stand, hill up with shovel or turn plow, then cultivate as corn; harrows and sweeps are used by some. *Yazoo:* Scrape, hoe to a stand, hill up, and plow the middles; if the soil was at first well broken, cultivation is shallow; otherwise, it is deep, and the turning plow is used for the purpose. *Leake:* After barring off, the crop is generally hoed, then, until late in summer; two or three hoeings and as many plowings are given with large sweeps.

MISSISSIPPI BOTTOM: 2. *Grenada:* Scrape out and then use shovel plows and sweeps. *Le Flore:* Generally bar off, run scrapers and 18- or 20-inch sweeps, respectively. *Sharkey:* The majority give shallow cultivation with sweeps; some plow deep, and such are always in debt. *Issaquena:* Bar off, hoe to a stand, throw dirt to the row, then cultivate with plow, and sweep till the crop is laid by. *Holmes:* After scraping and hoeing the crop the soil should, if possible, be thrown back and well up around the plant the same day by a sweep, shovel, or turn plow, so as to lap in the drill from both sides Correspondent,always observes this, and his cotton never dies out, nor has the "sore-shin", except when the plants are barked or bruised by hoes, or suddenly bent at right angles against the baked crust of the bed.

CANE-HILLS REGION: *Jefferson:* The plow, harrow, and all sorts of cultivators are used. *Wilkinson:* The crop is sometimes harrowed; various hoeings and plowings are given and repeated, as required; cultivation must vary with soil and season. *Warren:* Two thorough plowings and hoeings; three are better for the crop. *Claiborne:* After thinning out, the soil is twice molded up to the row with sweeps and the middles are broken out with plows, and the crop is hoed as often.

CENTRAL PRAIRIE REGION: *Smith* and *Scott:* Cultivating is done chiefly with steel sweeps, but may be done almost wholly with plows. *Rankin:* Bar off with turn plow or scraper; next use sweeps and hoe about twice. *Hinds:* Scrape, hoe, plow the soil to the row, plow the middles again thoroughly, after which plow and hoe when necessary. 1. *Clarke:* Bar off, hoe to a stand, throw soil gently back to the row with a small sweep, and continue by cultivating the crop every ten to fifteen days until it is laid by.

LONG-LEAF PINE REGION: *Greene:* Bar off, thin to a stand, then plow with solid sweeps. *Pike:* Bar off and scrape, throw soil to the row, plow and hoe, then run through once or twice with sweep, side harrow, or cultivator. *Simpson:* After thinning out and throwing soil to the row with a half shovel the crop is cultivated with sweeps about three times. *Covington:* Run a furrow on each side of the row with the scooter, next use a half shovel, and when the crop is too large for close plowing use sweeps. *Lauderdale* and 2. *Clarke:* Three or four plowings and two or three hoeings are generally necessary to produce a crop; the sweep or wide shovel is used almost exclusively; the crop is often injured by plowing. *Amite:* Bar off with a turn plow or scrape, thin to a double stand, throw soil to the row, thin to stand, break out middles with a turn plow, then use sweeps until the crop is laid by.

20. What is the height usually attained by cotton before blooming?

NORTHEASTERN PRAIRIE REGION: 24 to 36 inches in Alcorn, Tippah, and Kemper; 12 to 18 inches in the other counties.

YELLOW-LOAM REGION: 24 to 30 inches in six counties; 12 to 20 inches in the others.

MISSISSIPPI BOTTOM: 12 in Issaquena, 15 to 20 in Sharkey, and 30 to 36 in other counties.

CANE-HILLS REGION: *Jefferson*, 18 inches; 24 to 36 inches in the rest.

CENTRAL PRAIRIE REGION: *Scott*, 24 to 36 inches; in the other counties, 12 to 18 inches.

LONG-LEAF PINE REGION: 24 inches in Lauderdale and Pike; 12 to 18 inches in other counties.

21. When do you usually see the first blooms?

May 20 in Pontotoc county; from the 1st to the 10th of June in the cane-hills region, and in Holmes, Bolivar, and Issaquena counties, and several counties of the long-leaf pine region. In the rest of the state the time varies from the middle of June to the 10th of July.

22. When do the bolls first open?

From six to eight weeks after blooming. About the last of July in five counties of the yellow-loam region, and in Noxubee and Jasper counties. From the 1st to the middle of August in four counties of the northeastern prairie region, five of the yellow-loam region, four in Mississippi bottom, three of the cane-hills region, and three of the long-leaf pine region. In other counties the latest time given is October 1, in Alcorn county.

23. When do you begin your first picking?

About August 15 in Noxubee, Grenada, Le Flore, Jasper, and Clarke; August 25 in Lowndes, Kemper, De Soto, Panola, Yazoo, Sharkey, Issaquena, and Jefferson. Of the other counties, nineteen report September 1, eight September 15, and the rest from that time to October 15, Alcorn and Lee giving the latest dates.

24. How many pickings do you usually make, and when?

NORTHEASTERN PRAIRIE REGION: Three pickings usually in October, November, and December. *Lowndes:* Farmers strive to gather as fast as the cotton is ready, beginning when 25 or 30 pounds per hand can be picked, and ending when the winter rains begin.

YELLOW-LOAM REGION: Three pickings usually; a light one in September, second and chief one in October, and often only gleanings in November and December.

MISSISSIPPI BOTTOM AND CANE-HILLS REGIONS: Usually three or four. *Holmes:* The first, in August and September, rarely amount to 200 pounds per acre; the chief pickings are in October, November, and December.

CENTRAL PRAIRIE REGION: Three pickings as rapidly as possible,

usually in September, October, and November. *Hinds:* As many as possible with the force at command; the sooner cotton is picked the cleaner and better the staple and the less the waste in the field or at the gin. *Clarke:* The top crop is never all open until a killing frost, after which picking soon ends.

LONG-LEAF PINE REGION: Three pickings usually as fast as cotton opens sufficiently to admit of a fair day's gathering. *Amite:* First when one or two bolls per plant are open, second when most of them are open, and third when all are open; but the number and times depend upon the yield, weather, and the picking force employed. Picking is continuous and as rapid as possible.

25. Do you ordinarily pick all your cotton?

It is very generally all gathered throughout the state, excepting of course that lost by bad weather and live-stock. *Holmes:* Sometimes when the price is low it does not pay to glean the fields. *Lee:* Owing to indolence, some cotton is not gathered.

Winston: Some farmers, however, have been observed to plow their stalks under with cotton on them, having failed to pick it in time for plowing the next crop.

26. At what date does picking usually close?

The last of November in Noxubee, Winston, and Pike; in December in twenty-nine counties, comprising the cane-hills, central prairie, long-leaf pine, and most of the yellow-loam regions;

in January and later in the other counties; the latest date is that of March 31, in Sharkey county.

27. At what date do you expect the first black frost?

The earliest date is from the 20th to the 30th of September in Prentiss and Tippah counties. October 1 to 15 in eight counties, viz, Alcorn, Pontotoc, De Soto, Choctaw, Winston,

Claiborne, Clarke, and Amite. From the 15th to the 30th of October in twenty-two counties, while in other counties it is expected from the first to the last of November.

28. Do you pen your seed-cotton in the field, or gin as picking progresses?

Both are practiced in all the counties. On the small upland farms it is usually customary to pen in the field near the tenants' houses until enough is gathered to justify ginning. If there is a gin on the plantation, it is usually run as picking progresses. *Clarke* and *Amite:* The larger farmers gin as they pick; others generally house their cotton for safe-keeping and finish picking before they gin. Private gins have been superseded by neighborhood gins in Amite county. On the

bottom lands "it is impossible to gin as fast as it is picked; it is therefore penned and afterward hauled to the gin". In Holmes it is generally kept near the tenants' dwellings in houses or pens, or sometimes left in heaps in the field exposed to rains and storms. *Issaquena:* House it at each tenant's cotton-house; never pen it in the field, as the handling would be double.

GINNING, BALING, AND SHIPPING.

29. What gin do you use? How many saws, and what motive-power? How much clean lint do you make in a day's run of ten hours?

There are fourteen different gins mentioned in the state, one county often reporting the use of two or more patents, while others simply state that several are used.

Pratt's gin is mentioned by sixteen counties; Gullett's by thirteen counties; Brown's by five counties; Carver's by four counties; the Eagle gin by three counties. The following are each mentioned once: Atwood, Hurt, Manuel, Cunningham, Eclipse, Emery, Dubois, and Avery. Their ginning capacity in ten hours' run may be summed up from the different reports as follows:

Pratt's gin: 60 saws, run by steam-power, 3,500 to 5,000 pounds of lint; by mules, 2,000 pounds; 50 saws, by mules, 1,500 to 1,800 pounds, and by water 2,000 pounds; 45 saws, by steam, 2,000 pounds of lint.

Gullett's gin: 60 saws, by steam, from 2,500 to 3,500 pounds; by mules, 2,000 pounds; 50 saws, by steam, 1,750 pounds; 45 saws, by mules, 1,000 to 1,200 pounds.

Brown's gin: 80 saws, by steam, 5,000 pounds; 50 saws, by steam, 2,500 to 3,000 pounds; 45 saws, by mules, 1,000 to 1,500 pounds.

Carver's gin: 75 saws, by steam, 4,000 to 4,500 pounds.

Eagle gin: 60 saws, by mules, 1,400 pounds; 40 saws, by mules, 1,000 pounds.

Atwood gin: 50 saws, by mules, 900 pounds of lint (*Amite*).

Hurt gin: 50 saws, by mules, 1,275 pounds of lint (*La Fayette*).

Eclipse gin: 70 saws, by steam, 3,500 pounds of lint (*Bolivar*).

Dubois gin: 50 saws, by mules, 1,300 pounds of lint (*Hinds*).

The capacity of other gins are not given.

"With a gin of 100 saws 6,000 pounds of lint are made in a run of ten hours with a steam-engine of 20 to 40 horse-power" (*Sharkey*). "The steam-engine is far more economical than mule power even for a small planter; it is less expensive in every particular; the risk of fire is less than that of the mortality of stock" (*Holmes*). "Steam-engines would be preferred if they were not so expensive; the county is well supplied with water-power, but has not the capital to utilize it" (*Leake*).

30. What mechanical "power" arrangement is preferred when horses or mules are used?

Tippah county: Schofield's. *Noxubee:* Peacock's iron "horse-power" from Selma, Alabama. *Lauderdale* and *Sharkey:* The Faust Deering power of Louisville, Kentucky. *Benton:* The 12-foot cogwheel and treadwheel. *Marshall:* Segment and pinion power; an 8-foot band wheel and 10- or 12-foot master wheel,

with horizontal lever, to each end of which a team is hitched. In many other counties the old-style power is preferred, the old wooden screw, with two mules and one or two men, turning out 8 bales per day; the old style compress with eight men and two mules, making from 20 to 25 bales.

23 C P

31. How many pounds of seed-cotton, on an average, is required for a 475-pound bale of lint?

Claiborne: 1,306 to 1,665, according to kind of seed. *Prentiss, Lee, De Soto, Winston, Attala, Jefferson, Rankin, Scott,* and *Pike:* 1,435. *Leake* and *Grenada:* 1,425 to 1,545. *Pontotoc, La Fayette,* and *Amite:* 1,425 to 1,600. *Clarke:* 1,425 to 1,665. *Smith:* 1,455. *Wilkinson, Hinds,* and *Jasper:* 1,485. *Lauderdale:* 1,485 to 1,545. *Tippah, Benton, Tishomingo, Sharkey,* and *Covington:* 1,545. *Lowndes:* 1,545 to 1,600. *Kemper:* 1,545 to 1,665. *Choctaw, Warren,* and *Simpson:* 1,660. *Marshall, Yazoo, Holmes,* and *Issaquena:* 1,665. *Alcorn, Panola, Le Flore, Bolivar,* and *Greene:* 1,780. *Noxubee:* 1,900.

32. What press is generally used in your region, and what is its capacity per day?

There are eighteen different presses mentioned among the counties as being in use, and very often several patents are found in one county.

Brooks' press is mentioned in eight counties. Its capacity, with six men and one mule, is 25 bales per day; with four men and one mule, 12 bales, or as fast as ginned. "It will press in one day all that two 80-saw stands can gin in a week" (*Issaquena*).

Scofield's iron-screw press from 3 counties; with two men and one mule a day's ginning can be baled.

Paul Williams' press from 3 counties; with one mule, 10 bales.

Paul Pitman's press from 3 counties; with four men and one mule, 90 bales.

Southern standard; with four men and one mule, 10 to 20 bales.

Way's hand-lever press; with six men, 15 bales.

Lewis' press, by hand, 12 bales.

The following is a list of the other presses named, and their capacity is about that of those already given: Provost, Wright's, Churchill's, Reynold's, Simmonds, Wilson's, Shaw's, Ku-Klux, Newel's, Grasshopper, and Nesbit's. They are mentioned but once or twice each among all the counties.

33. Do you use rope or iron ties for baling? If the latter, what fastening do you prefer?

Iron ties are used exclusively throughout the state. The arrow fastening is preferred in 21 counties; the buckle in 10 counties.

Among the other counties, the Wallis, button, Harper, and Root fastenings are mentioned.

34. What kind of bagging is used in your region?

Chiefly jute in 16 counties; chiefly hemp in 9 counties; while in the rest the gins are given without choice.

35. What weight do you aim to give your bales? Have transportation companies imposed any conditions in this respect?

Farmers in Claiborne and Wilkinson aim to make the weight of bales 400 pounds; in Holmes, 400 to 500 pounds; 450 pounds in 8 counties; 500 pounds in 24 counties, and 600 pounds in Sharkey. The freight charges are usually by the bale, regardless of weight, except, perhaps, to the eastern and northern cities. The bales are required to be well covered. *Amite:* A bale under 300 pounds' weight is not considered merchantable, the freight being by bale. In a number of counties buyers deduct $1 from the price of bales under 400 pounds' weight. *Holmes:* Transportation companies usually agree to deliver a 450-pound bale at contract prices, and frequently specify that they will charge for each additional 100 pounds, but rarely do so on boats. Taking advantage of this, merchants urge producers to make bales of 500 and 600 pounds. Insurance companies specify and hold themselves accountable only for 450-pound bales.

DISEASES, INSECT ENEMIES, ETC.

36. By what accidents of weather, diseases, or insect pests is your cotton crop most liable to be injured? At what dates do these several pests or diseases usually make their appearance? To what cause is the trouble attributed by your farmers?

NORTHEASTERN PRAIRIE REGION: The caterpillar appears in Lowndes county in July, in Lee in September, and in Kemper and Noxubee. The boll-worm appears in August and September in most of the counties. Shedding and rust also do much damage when dry weather follows an excessively wet season. Boll-rot and blight are reported only in Noxubee, Lee, Lowndes, and Pontotoc counties, and are supposed to be due to wet weather. Aphides are reported in Lowndes and Tippah in June on isolated spots, and are attributed to cold nights.

YELLOW-LOAM REGION: The caterpillar appears in Marshall, Choctaw, Yazoo, and Leake, and sometimes in De Soto, Panola, Attala, and La Fayette, "though rarely, and has not hurt this region in twelve years." The boll-worm occurs in most of the counties in July or August, while boll-rot, rust, and shedding also do much damage, and is attributed to weather extremes, either wet or dry. Blight is reported in seven of the counties, though rarely in most of these.

MISSISSIPPI BOTTOM: The caterpillar appears in Grenada in August, in Holmes in September and October, and in Sharkey and Issaquena. The boll-worm appears throughout the region, and usually a month earlier. Boll-rot occurs to some extent, and in Bolivar is attributed to the overgrowth of the plant. Blight in June, rust in July and August, and shedding in July to September also occur to some extent, and are usually attributed to weather extremes. *Holmes:* They are due to plowing too near and disturbing the roots of the plants.

Issaquena: Diseases and insects generally attack cotton on sandy soils first.

CANE-HILLS REGION: The caterpillar usually appears in Warren county "in numbers about July, the earlier the most destructive, but most so in September", at which time it is reported in other counties. The boll-worm appears in July and August, or sometimes much later. Shedding, boll-rot, blight, and rust also occur.

CENTRAL PRAIRIE REGION: The caterpillar appears in Hinds, Scott, and Clarke late in August. The boll-worm does some damage in all of the counties, while excessive rains and extreme dry weather cause boll-rot and shedding and rust. In Jasper the latter is attributed to shallow plowing and lack of vegetable matter in the soil. Aphides appear in Clarke as soon as cotton is up.

LONG-LEAF PINE REGION: The boll-worm in July and August, the caterpillar in August and September, are reported in this region. Aphides appear on the plants in the spring in Covington county. Boll-rot and shedding are thought to be respectively produced by wet and dry weather, and occur throughout the region. Boll-rot in Covington is attributed to insects, rust to stagnant water near the roots of the plants, and shedding to irregularity of seasons or injudicious tillage. In Amite all diseases are thought to be due to improper cultivation, while in Simpson rust is attributed to insect life.

37. What efforts have been made to obviate these diseases and pests? With what success?

Throughout the state but few efforts have been made, and these with indifferent success. *Holmes:* It is considered dangerous to use destroyers for insects; those who cultivate cotton with care have less of these evils. *Bolivar* and *Sharkey:* A favorable dry season at the time of these pests and good cultivation always insure greater yields than can be gathered by the cultivating force. *Wilkinson:* Early planting, so as to favor early fruiting, has met with but little success. *Lowndes:* Early planting and thorough cultivation have been successful. *Panola:* Change of crop and culture have been successful against rust and blight. *Grenada:* A plenty of manure is considered to be the best remedy for rust, blight, shedding, and boll-rot. *Rankin* and *Hinds:* Attraction of the moths by lights at night and catching them in some liquid has been only partially successful. *Lauderdale:* Shedding may be partly prevented in some seasons by shallow plowing, but not wholly

in very wet or dry weather. *Amite:* Deep preparatory plowing of the soil and after-cultivation adapted to the varying conditions of the weather and soil. The first generation of worms is destroyed by hand; at the second coming of the moth it is decoyed by lights at night; when the third generation of worms appears all is lost. These methods have not proved successful.

38. Is rust or blight prevalent chiefly on heavy or ill-drained soils? Do they prevail chiefly in wet or dry, cool or hot seasons? On what soil described by you are they most common?

NORTHEASTERN PRAIRIE REGION. They prevail mostly on the black and stiff and ill-drained lands of this region, and on the hummock lands and light, shelly prairie-ridge soils of Pontotoc county. They occur chiefly in wet and cold seasons in three counties, in dry seasons after much rain in two counties, and in cold seasons, whether wet or dry, in Pontotoc county. In Lee rust prevails chiefly on dry lands in dry seasons, and commonly on the uplands; blight chiefly on wet lands in wet seasons, and commonly on the bottoms. In Alcorn rust is limited to small spots, and is supposed to be due to microscopic parasites.

YELLOW-LOAM REGION: They prevail in wet and cool seasons on heavy and ill-drained soils in De Soto, Panola, Winston, and Attala; on loose, sandy, or fresh soils in Benton; on black, sandy loam in Leake; on white, cold clay soil in any season in Grenada; on heavy, ill-drained soils having the largest gravel and lightest colored subsoil, and are worse on the gray gravelly or buckshot soil in Yazoo county; on heavy and ill-drained soils in Marshall county. "The red rust chiefly in dry seasons on dry, rich, alluvial and mellow soils, sometimes extending, as the season advances, to clayey soils, in which it is not liable to start, and if it does will not spread rapidly. Blight prevails chiefly in wet seasons." Rust on light, sandy

soils, and blight on heavy and ill-drained soils and in wet seasons in La Fayette. "Close observers have noticed them most frequently in fresh soils of any kind that have borne cotton for three or four consecutive years" (*La Fayette*).

MISSISSIPPI BOTTOM: They prevail on light and sandy soils in most of the counties; in cool and wet seasons in three counties; in hot periods, preceded by excessive rains, in Holmes, and in any season in other counties. In Bolivar, on rich loams where the severest cases of blight are generally connected with late plowing, which is very likely to disturb the roots of the plants.

CANE-HILLS REGION: Chiefly on wet and ill-drained soils; in all seasons in Claiborne, and in wet and hot seasons in other counties.

CENTRAL PRAIRIE REGION: On heavy and ill-drained soils in Rankin and Scott; on all soils in Hinds and Jasper, and on light, shelly soil in Clarke; in cool weather in Jasper; in extreme states of weather in the other counties.

LONG-LEAF PINE REGION: On ill-drained, sometimes sandy and sometimes heavy, soils. Chiefly on the bottom lands in four counties; in wet and cool seasons in Greene, and hot and wet seasons in Simpson and Amite.

39. Is Paris green used as a remedy against the caterpillar? If so, how, and with what effect?

It is not used in 31 of the counties from which reports have come. *Noxubee:* When properly used it has generally saved seven-eighths of the crop. *Marshall:* The worm generally begins in the center of the field, but in a few days is all over it, stripping the plants. Paris green would undoubtedly destroy it, but the damage is great before it is discovered. *Grenada:* Its efficacy is not doubted, but its use is entirely neglected. *Holmes:* Its use would prevent keeping of calves in the cotton-fields, and it is, besides, regarded as far too troublesome to apply this poison. 1. *Clarke:* It destroys both worm and

plant, and has been abandoned in the last two years. 2. *Clarke:* Mixed with flour and land plaster it generally kills the caterpillar, but his place is soon taken by another generation. *Amite:* Its solution has been sprinkled and its powder dusted on the plants while wet with dew, and has done but little good. *Scott:* It has been sprinkled on the plant with water, and is pronounced a failure. *Yazoo:* By sifting it upon the leaves while wet with dew, if commenced in time, it will materially check the ravages of the caterpillar.

LABOR AND SYSTEM OF FARMING.

40. What is the average size of farms or plantations in your region?

UPLAND COUNTIES: Less than 100 acres in 11 counties; from 100 to 200 acres in 6 counties; 200 to 300 acres in 5 counties; 300 to 500 acres in 6 counties. In the cane-hills region, and in a few counties of the yellow-loam and northeastern prairie regions, some of the farms have as much as 1,000 to 3,000 acres, and in Rankin county, of the central prairie region, a maximum

of 6,000 acres. In Amite plantations vary from 500 to 3,000 acres, and are divided into farms of 40 and 120 acres, which are rented to families.

MISSISSIPPI BOTTOM REGION: There are a few small farms of less than 300 acres, but mostly large plantations of from 500 to 3,000 acres.

41. Is the prevalent practice "mixed farming" or "planting"?

UPLAND COUNTIES: Mixed farming in 22 counties, and planting in 11 counties.

MISSISSIPPI BOTTOM AND CANE-HILLS REGIONS; Planting exclusively.

42. Are supplies raised at home or imported? If the latter, where from? Is the tendency toward raising them at home increasing or decreasing?

NORTHEASTERN PRAIRIE REGION: In 4 counties supplies are wholly imported; in the others a portion only is imported, from Saint Louis, Louisville, and Cincinnati, and in 1 county in part from Mobile.

YELLOW-LOAM REGION: In all of the counties a portion of the supplies, comprising the meat, flour, and part of the corn, is obtained from Memphis and the cities of the western states.

MISSISSIPPI BOTTOM AND CANE-HILLS REGIONS: Supplies are chiefly imported from the north and west in all of the counties except Grenada, in which the corn is mostly raised at home. In Holmes some of the supplies are brought from New Orleans.

CENTRAL PRAIRIE REGION: Largely imported in 4 counties from

the northern cities; corn from Tennessee and Kentucky. In Hinds many raise all of their supplies, some a part, and others none at all. In Rankin supplies are chiefly raised at home; sugar and coffee from New Orleans.

LONG-LEAF PINE REGION: Mostly imported in all of the counties from New Orleans and the northern cities; a part from Tennessee, Kentucky, Missouri, and Ohio.

The tendency toward raising home supplies is said to be increasing in all of the counties of the state except five, in which there is no perceptible change in either direction, and in Le Flore, in which it is decreasing.

43. Who are the laborers chiefly?

Negroes, chiefly, in 25 counties, embracing the cane-hills and the Mississippi bottom regions, and some of the upland counties. Whites chiefly in 7 counties, while in the other counties of the state the two races are about equally divided. The nation-alities represented are some Germans and Irish in Winston, and various in Holmes, Tippah, and Rankin counties; otherwise, all Americans.

44. How and at what rates are their wages paid, and when payable?

Daily wages are very generally 50 cents with board and 75 cents without board, usually at the end of the week. In Clarke, 30 cents to women and 40 cents to men, with board in each case, are paid. Monthly wages are usually from $6 to $12 throughout the state with a few exceptions, while to yearly laborers from $100 to $150, at the end of the year, or when needed, are paid to men, and a less amount to women and boys. A house and sometimes rations are also given to the yearly laborer. In many of the counties, however, the laborers work on shares in preference to regular wages. Monthly wages are paid when the time of service ends, or at the end of the season, when crops are sold, in most of the counties. Monthly payments are made in a few counties, while in many cases a portion is paid as it is needed by the laborer.

45. Are cotton farms worked on shares? If so, on what terms?

The share system prevails very generally throughout the state, though in a few counties the farms are rented, the renter paying 400 pounds of lint per 10 or 15 acres for the use of land, houses, and utensils. The terms vary but little in all of the counties. If the land-owner furnishes the land, implements, and teams, he receives one-half of the crop; otherwise for the land alone he receives one-fourth to one-third of the cotton, and one-third of the corn, if any is produced. In some counties the owner furnishes the ginning and ginning material instead of the farming implements. When the laborer is boarded, and has everything else furnished to him, the owner receives three-fourths of the crop.

46. Does the share system give satisfaction? How does it affect the quality of the staple? Does the soil deteriorate or improve under it?

In ten of the counties the system does not give satisfaction, but in the rest of the state there is but little complaint. In Marshall one or the other party complains every year. When the crop is not promising, or too liberal advances have been made to the laborer, he is likely to become dissatisfied, quit working his own crop, and hire out by the day to other farms. The staple is thought to be injured by the share system in 11 of the counties; in a few of the others it is said to improve, while in the rest of the state no change is apparent. In Holmes the negroes are very careless and indifferent as to gathering and housing their cotton; they allow a great deal of it to rot. In Sharkey the staple is two grades below that of 1860 from the same soil. In Tishomingo and Covington the staple is shorter. In Amite the laborer is usually more careful in picking when he owns a share. In almost all of the counties the soils are thought to deteriorate, in some very rapidly, unless manures are used or rotation practiced. *Issaquena:* The best cotton is grown by the "one-half-crop" system, for then the owner or his agent sees that the crop is properly tilled.

47. Which system (wages or share) is the better for the laborer? Why?

The share system is thought to be the best in 19 counties of the state. *Lowndes:* "The negro, being thriftless and improvident, will by no other system have so much for his family at the end of the year." The following summary of reasons are given: He can make more money; have garden land free of rent; can double his wages and have all the extra time to himself; he becomes interested in the results of his labor; he is more industrious and improves his habits; the entire family can be employed. In the other counties of the state the wages system is thought better. *Hinds:* "He is sure of a living, while under the share system the shiftless laborer often obtains credits to the extent of his interest in the crop and has nothing in the end. When under control, he makes more, spends less, and has a surplus of cash at the end of the year. There are exceptions, of course." The following summary of reasons are also given: He is certain of his earnings, and takes no risks of failures of crops; supplies consume his profits under the share system; he works better, and always has money. He receives his money more certainly and at shorter intervals. They cannot receive credit beyond their wages; he must work for wages, while under the share system he is indolent and careless. *Issaquena:* He is assured a livelihood as long as willing to work, his labor being in demand at good prices from January to January, at 75 cents to $1 per day. Under any other system shiftlessness prevails to a more or less extent with serious neglect of crops. Renters average three bales of cotton per hand, while with wages eight or ten will be produced, the latter thus bringing into circulation more money and creating a greater demand for the laborer's services.

48. What is the condition of the laborer?

In the river counties their condition is generally good, except in Le Flore and Bolivar, where "it might be good if they were more industrious". *Holmes:* They are usually able to pay their merchants and have some money besides. *Issaquena:* "They generally own their teams, have cows, hogs, etc., and are usually supplied with money to meet all necessary wants. A beggar was never known here, except in that characteristic habit of our colored friends to beg tobacco." In 18 upland counties the condition of the negro laborer is said to be good where industrious; but in many other counties they are in rather a destitute condition, due to improvidence and indolence. White laborers are usually in good circumstances. In Claiborne and Rankin "the laborers are fat and lazy".

49. What proportion of the negro laborers own land or the houses in which they live?

In seventeen counties, not 1 in 100; in twelve counties, not one in 20, and often not one in 50. In twelve other counties, a larger proportion own their lands and houses. In Claiborne they seem to have no desire to own lands. In Wilkinson and Winston they are securing homesteads on government land.

50. What is the market value of land in your region? What rent is paid for such land?

In the *Mississippi bottom counties* the prices vary from $2.50 to $10 for unimproved and $25 to $50 for improved. The rent is from $5 to $10 per acre or one-third of the crop raised, or 85 to 100 pounds of lint per acre.

UPLAND COUNTIES: In sixteen counties the prices are from $5 to $10 or $15 and even $25 for improved lands; in the remaining counties the prices are from $1 to $3, and even as low as 25 or 50 cents for poorer lands in some regions. Rents are from $2 to $5 for the best classes of land, or are one-fourth of the cotton produced on it, or 30 or 40 pounds of lint per acre.

51. How many acres or bales of cotton, per hand, is your customary estimate?

NORTHEASTERN PRAIRIE REGION: About 10 acres, or 3 bales with supplies and 5 bales without supplies. *Lee:* A good hand can cultivate 12 or 15 acres. *Kemper:* 9 acres of cotton and 6 of corn per hand. *Alcorn:* 7 or 8 acres of cotton and corn each. YELLOW-LOAM REGION: 12 to 15 acres of land per hand, yielding from 4 to 6 bales. *La Fayette:* Two hands with one mule raise about 4 bales of cotton and 100 bushels of corn. MISSISSIPPI BOTTOM: Usually 10 or 12 acres of from 3 to 5 bales. *Issaquena:* A steady worker who gives his fields proper attention frequently produces from 10 to 18 bales. *Holmes:* Man

and wife 20 acres, from which they frequently gather 12 to 20 bales and raise one-fourth to one-third more than they gather. CANE-HILLS REGION: Usually 15 acres of cotton and corn or 3 bales of cotton. *Warren:* The negro produces from 1 to 4 bales, formerly 6 to 8 bales. *Wilkinson:* 6 acres or 2 bales; good hands can cultivate and raise four times as much. CENTRAL PRAIRIE REGION: 2 to 3 bales in four counties; 6 to 8 bales from 15 acres in Scott. LONG-LEAF PINE REGION: Usually 3 bales, with some corn. "White laborers have made 6 bales, besides corn", etc.

52. To what extent does the system of credits or advances upon the growing cotton crop prevail in your region?

MISSISSIPPI BOTTOM: It prevails very generally throughout the region and to the extent of the whole or three-fourths of the growing crop. In Holmes, it is exceptional that any one, white or black, pays cash for an article. Deeds of trust are the rule. In Issaquena, frequently the tenants (all negroes), when they have sufficient money and are able to pay cash as they go, prefer to keep their money and exhaust their credit. UPLAND COUNTIES: The system prevails generally throughout the region and in most of the counties to the extent of one-half or more of the prospective value of the crop. It is not prevalent in Greene and Hancock counties, while in Benton, Grenada, Clarke, Covington, and Amite the practice of getting advances is declining. *Alcorn:* Hands occasionally desert the crop after getting all the advances they can. *Marshall:* At least one-half of the crop is virtually raised on credit at ruinous rates.

Noxubee, Pike, and *Simpson:* But few laborers can get along without credit. *Hinds:* It is due to this that land has no market value and that labor is taken from the land-owner's control and forced into cotton production exclusively. *Scott:* It is one of the farmer's misfortunes that he is in debt and at the mercy of the merchant. *Simpson:* It is one great cause of the laborer's extravagance and wastefulness. *Leake:* Necessitates the exclusive production of cotton; the land-owner advances provisions, clothing, etc., to the laborer at such ruinous profits as to absorb his share. *Amite:* Especially among the negroes, most of whom are very extravagant and greatly abuse the credit which this system gives them; the system is now less prevalent and more restricted than formerly. Both farmers and merchants were once bankrupted by it and have learned to be cautious.

53. At what stage of production is the cotton crop usually covered by insurance?

BOTTOM COUNTIES: Not at all in Grenada and Sharkey, and rarely in Bolivar. When on the steamboat, Le Flore. When gathered in the gin-houses in Issaquena and Holmes. The practice is general only in two counties.

UPLAND COUNTIES: Not practiced in 14 counties. Sometimes, when picking begins, in Wilkinson. When put in the gin-house in Clarke and Pike. When in market, in five counties. It is practiced also in eight other counties.

54. What are the merchants' commissions and charges for storing, handling, shipping, insurance, etc., to which your crop is subject? What is the total amount of these charges against the farmer per pound or per bale?

Commissions throughout the state are usually 2½ per cent. on gross sales; storage, drayage, and weighing, 75 cents per bale, or 50 cents for storage for the first month and 25 cents for each additional month. For shipping, 25 cents per bale. Brokerage, one-fourth per cent. Insurance, fire, three eighths per cent.; river, one-fourth to one-half per cent, and railroad, one-fourth per cent. In many of the counties the crop is sold to local buyers at a little below New Orleans quotations, the farmer paying 20 cents a bale for weighing. *Winston:* 75 cents per 100 pounds for hauling to a shipping point, $5 per bale for shipping; adding to this storage, commission, etc., the total is about $20 per bale.

The total per bale exclusive of freight is $1 80 to $2 40 in Lowndes, about $2 25 in Amite, and $3 25, with some loss of weight while stored, in Hinds. Including freight charges the total amounts from $2 to $5 in Pontotoc; $4 to $6 in Warren, Issaquena, and Claiborne (with some loss of weight while stored); about $4 15 in Wilkinson; about $4 50 in Attala; $4 75 in Alcorn, Benton, Yazoo, Lauderdale, Simpson, and Pike; $5 in Panola, Tishomingo, Rankin, Jasper, and Clarke; $5 to $6 in Grenada; $5 40 in Prentiss; $5 50 in Lee; $5 50 to $6 in Holmes (if shipped to New Orleans); $5 60 in Kemper; $6 in Noxubee, Bolivar, and Jefferson; $7 in Scott and Sharkey.

55. What is your estimate of the cost of production per pound in your region, exclusive of such charges and with fair soil and management?

In fourteen counties, about 8 cents; in seven counties, about 7 cents; in seven counties, about 10 cents; in four counties, from 5 to 6 cents; in Sharkey, 9 cents; in Attala, 4½ cents; in other counties the number given is indefinite, but between these extremes. *Panola:* About one-fourth of its market value. *Pontotoc:* About one-half its market value. *Warren* and *Clai-*

borne: 10 cents where supplies are bought. *Wilkinson:* 8 cents ordinarily, but 5 cents with hired labor and good management. *Hinds:* 10 to 12 cents, according to season, wear and tear of implements, taxes, and interest on investment. *Issaquena:* About $25 per bale.

56. What is usually paid for extra work in picking cotton? How much seed-cotton is ordinarily picked in a day?

Holmes: "Fifty to 65 cents per 100 pounds of seed-cotton, without board, and 40 to 50 cents with board." In all other counties 75 cents without or 50 cents with board is usually paid. In some counties the pickers are sometimes paid daily wages, at $1 per day without or 50 cents with board. *Jasper:* Ordinary hands usually pick from 40 to 100 pounds of seed-cotton, and will not pick "by the 100 pounds", but are paid wages. The best hands pick an average of 300 pounds, and

will only pick by the 100 pounds. *Tippah:* "Ordinary hands pick 200 to 250 pounds per day." In other counties the amount is usually 175 pounds in full crops, and 150 when the crop is light. On the richer lands, the best hands pick from 500 to 600 pounds per day in full crops. Some have even reached 750 pounds, with a boy to wait on them, empty the sacks, and bring them water and food.

INDEX TO COTTON PRODUCTION IN MISSISSIPPI.

REPORT

ON THE

COTTON PRODUCTION OF THE STATE OF TENNESSEE,

WITH A DISCUSSION OF

ITS GENERAL AGRICULTURAL FEATURES,

AND A NOTE ON

COTTON PRODUCTION IN THE STATE OF KENTUCKY.

BY

JAMES M. SAFFORD, A. M., Ph. D., M. D.,

STATE GEOLOGIST OF TENNESSEE, PROFESSOR OF GEOLOGY AND NATURAL HISTORY IN VANDERBILT UNIVERSITY,

AND

SPECIAL CENSUS AGENT.

TABLE OF CONTENTS.

24 C P

iv   •   TABLE OF CONTENTS.

LETTERS OF TRANSMITTAL.

BERKELEY, CALIFORNIA, *June* 1, 1883.

The SUPERINTENDENT OF CENSUS.

DEAR SIR: I have the honor to transmit herewith a report on the cotton production and agricultural features of the state of Tennessee by Professor James M. Safford, of Vanderbilt University, and state geologist, acting as special agent for the census.

Professor Safford's previous publications and reports on the geology and agriculture of Tennessee are well known to the public, and his labors in that connection have rendered his co-operation in the present series of reports doubly important and acceptable. While much of the subject-matter may be found in former publications, the compact form in which it is here presented, in connection with the predominant productive industry of the western slope, renders it interesting and available to a wider circle of readers, and will convey even to the specialist a more graphic conception of the varied features of the state than he has heretofore been enabled to compile from data scattered through various works. Agriculturally, politically, and geologically, the cross-section of the eastern valley of the Mississippi here afforded by Tennessee is extremely interesting and instructive.

Very respectfully,

E. W. HILGARD,
Special Agent in charge of Cotton Production.

NASHVILLE, TENNESSEE, *May* 1, 1883.

Professor EUGENE W. HILGARD,
Special Agent in charge of Cotton Production.

SIR: I have the honor to submit herewith a report on cotton production in the state of Tennessee, with a discussion of the general natural features of the state, so far as they may be related to cotton culture; also a note on cotton production in Kentucky. I have endeavored, in the preparation of the report, to follow out your instructions as to plan and matter, and trust you may find its contents, for the most part at least, in accordance therewith. Had it been allowed to give the report greater length, much more might have been said, omissions supplied, and some of the more practical parts expanded. It may be better, however, as it is.

So little of Kentucky is within the cotton region proper that it has not been considered desirable or pertinent to give any extended notice of that state as a whole in its relation to cotton culture. Such notice would be quite appropriate were tobacco the subject-matter in question. A narrow area, however, in the southwestern part of the state, contiguous to Tennessee, and forming the extreme northern limit of the cotton-growing region of the eastern Mississippi valley, has received due attention.

In the preparation of the report, the chief sources of information, besides the data supplied by the Census Office and the answers and notes of correspondents in the returned schedules, have been my own reports on the geology of Tennessee and personal knowledge of the state outside of these, the geological reports of Kentucky, and your own reports and papers on the geology of Mississippi and neighboring states.

In conclusion, I desire to express my obligations to yourself, Dr. R. H. Loughridge, Dr. Eugene A. Smith, of the University of Alabama, and Messrs. John R. Proctor and W. M. Linney, of the Kentucky geological survey, for special favors received.

Very respectfully, your obedient servant,

JAMES M. SAFFORD.

TABULATED RESULTS OF THE ENUMERATION.

TABLE I.—AREA, POPULATION, TILLED LAND, AND COTTON PRODUCTION.

TABLE II.—ACREAGE AND PRODUCTION OF LEADING CROPS.

TABLE I.—AREA, POPULATION, TILLED LAND, AND COTTON PRODUCTION.

Counties.	Land area.	POPULATION.						TILLED LAND.		COTTON PRODUCTION.						
		Total.	Male.	Female.	White.	Color'd.	Average per square mile.	Acres.	Percentage of area.	Percentage of tilled lands devoted to cotton.	Acres.	Bales.	Bale.	Seed-cotton.	Lint.	Cotton average per square mile.
	Sq. mls.													Lbs.	Lbs.	
The State	41,750	1,542,359	769,277	773,082	1,138,831	403,528	36.9	7,700,041	28.82	9.38	722,589	390,621	0.46	551	217	17.2
ALLUVIAL PLAIN OF THE MISSISSIPPI RIVER.																
Lake	210	3,969	2,145	1,828	3,274	604	18.9	34,056	25.79	9.37	3,240	2,412	0.74	1,059	353	15.5
ALLUVIAL PLAIN OF THE MISSISSIPPI RIVER AND PLATEAU SLOPE OR WEST TENNESSEE.																
a. Alluvial plain and bluff.																
Dyer	570	15,118	7,774	7,344	11,206	3,912	26.5	76,194	20.89	19.21	14,627	5,364	0.59	834	278	25.7
Lauderdale	410	14,918	7,627	7,391	9,081	5,837	36.4	56,010	22.11	41.83	34,063	18,350	0.55	783	261	56.7
Tipton	330	21,033	10,816	10,217	10,482	10,561	63.7	100,696	47.06	36.17	36,429	21,415	0.59	795	265	116.5
Shelby	600	78,430	38,856	39,574	34,508	43,922	113.7	195,726	44.92	47.33	92,620	46,386	0.50	714	238	134.2
Obion	540	22,912	11,875	11,037	18,841	4,071	42.4	109,527	31.79	6.61	7,259	4,225	0.58	828	278	13.4
Total	2,540	152,411	76,948	75,463	84,118	68,293	60.0	540,453	33.25	32.76	177,028	93,842	0.53	756	252	69.7
b. Brown-loam table-lands, midland counties.																
Fayette	640	31,871	15,941	15,930	9,633	22,238	49.8	197,516	46.22	46.70	92,231	39,221	0.43	606	202	144.1
Hardeman	610	22,921	11,491	11,430	13,312	9,008	37.6	130,437	30.85	37.27	44,885	18,987	0.42	600	200	73.6
Haywood	570	26,053	12,014	13,139	8,497	17,556	45.7	137,155	37.60	36.40	49,919	23,093	0.46	660	220	87.6
Madison	580	30,874	15,355	15,519	15,406	15,468	53.2	125,693	33.86	36.46	45,825	19,257	0.42	600	200	78.0
Crockett	260	14,109	7,081	7,028	10,493	3,616	54.2	65,428	39.32	27.22	17,807	9,230	0.52	747	249	68.5
Gibson	550	32,685	16,671	16,014	23,540	9,145	59.4	146,163	41.52	25.19	36,830	19,272	0.52	747	249	56.9
Weakley	620	34,588	12,454	12,064	20,125	4,418	39.6	159,075	32.53	11.94	15,406	7,576	0.49	702	234	24.8
Total	3,830	193,061	91,907	91,144	101,007	82,044	47.8	921,487	37.59	32.87	302,893	136,675	0.45	642	214	74.1
c. Summit region of watershed.																
Henry	550	22,162	11,018	11,124	15,486	6,654	40.3	148,392	37.90	9.88	13,186	5,516	0.42	597	199	24.0
Carroll	550	22,103	11,014	11,089	16,534	5,579	40.2	120,321	34.16	20.55	24,711	10,505	0.43	600	200	38.5
Henderson	530	17,430	8,671	8,759	14,414	3,016	30.1	93,341	25.12	23.96	22,344	9,419	0.42	600	200	36.5
McNairy	590	17,271	8,605	8,666	14,845	2,426	25.0	73,800	17.84	30.36	23,135	9,419	0.41	570	193	32.5
Total	2,370	78,946	39,308	39,688	61,271	17,675	33.3	435,064	28.06	19.59	83,376	34,859	0.42	597	199	36.2
WESTERN VALLEY OF TENNESSEE RIVER.																
Benton	350	9,780	4,880	4,900	9,147	633	25.7	46,425	19.09	10.60	4,923	1,801	0.37	522	174	12.0
Decatur	310	8,498	4,171	4,327	7,276	1,222	27.4	37,981	19.08	14.77	5,561	2,189	0.39	552	184	18.0
Hardin	610	14,793	7,394	7,459	12,775	2,018	24.3	72,446	18.56	17.75	12,859	5,345	0.42	591	197	21.1
Perry	400	7,174	3,630	3,544	6,609	565	17.9	35,423	14.79	1.26	452	196	0.43	618	206	1.1
Humphreys	480	11,379	5,746	5,633	9,708	1,671	25.3	53,938	18.73	0.29	155	90	0.58	828	276	0.3
Houston	260	4,295	2,181	2,114	3,487	808	16.5	21,253	12.77	0.40	8	4	0.50	711	237	
Stewart	500	12,890	6,392	6,198	9,333	3,787	25.4	58,864	16.68	0.06	40	15	0.33	474	158	0.1
Total	2,910	68,809	34,494	34,115	58,935	9,874	28.6	331,270	17.55	7.48	24,098	9,630	0.40	579	199	8.2
THE HIGHLANDS, OR HIGHLAND RIM OF MIDDLE TENNESSEE.																
a. Western subdivision.																
Montgomery	540	28,481	14,103	14,378	14,786	13,695	52.7	135,666	39.26			2	1.00	1,425	475	
Robertson	500	18,861	9,565	9,296	13,242	5,619	37.7	157,644	49.26							
Cheatham	370	7,958	4,073	3,885	6,296	1,661	21.5	43,366	17.90	0.01	5	2	0.40	570	190	
Dickson	530	13,460	6,365	6,095	10,229	2,231	18.3	50,651	14.79	0.05	21	13	0.62	897	199	
Hickman	610	12,095	6,047	6,048	9,849	2,246	18.8	71,970	18.43	4.35	3,138	1,803	0.43	564	198	5.1
Lewis	360	2,181	1,092	1,089	1,963	218	6.1	11,854	5.06	1.96	229	102	0.45	636	212	0.6
Wayne	710	11,301	5,543	5,758	10,232	1,069	15.9	56,456	12.42	5.78	3,265	1,307	0.37	529	176	4.6
Lawrence	590	10,383	5,188	5,195	9,599	784	17.6	47,855	12.67	5.32	1,830	702	0.38	546	182	2.1
Total	4,810	105,718	51,966	51,782	76,195	27,523	24.1	588,398	21.15	1.46	8,490	3,230	0.39	558	186	2.0

COTTON PRODUCTION IN TENNESSEE.

TABLE I.—AREA, POPULATION, TILLED LAND, AND COTTON PRODUCTION—Continued.

Counties.	Land area.	POPULATION.						TILLED LAND.		Percentage of tilled lands devoted to cotton.	COTTON PRODUCTION.					Cotton acreage per square mile.
		Total.	Male.	Female.	White.	Color'd.	Average per square mile.	Acres.	Percentage of area.		Acres.	Bales.	Average per acre.			
													Bale.	Seed-cotton.	Lint.	
THE HIGHLANDS, OR HIGHLAND RIM OF MIDDLE TENNESSEE —continued.	Sq. mls.													Lbs.	Lbs.	
b. Eastern subdivision.																
Macon	280	9,321	4,687	4,634	8,429	892	33.3	53,438	29.82	0.01	4	1	0.25	357	119	......
Clay	260	6,987	3,508	3,479	6,588	399	26.9	41,880	25.17	......	2	1	0.50	711	237	......
Overton	540	12,153	5,980	6,173	11,811	342	25.5	73,0.2	21.13	0.13	95	41	0.43	615	205	0.2
Jackson	280	12,008	5,980	6,028	11,575	433	42.9	56,122	31.32	0.10	56	28	0.50	711	237	0.2
Putnam	400	11,501	5,744	5,757	10,903	598	25.0	60,817	29.06	0.02	14	4	0.29	408	136	......
De Kalb	300	14,813	7,438	7,375	13,660	1,153	49.4	67,846	35.56	0.01	26	12	0.46	657	219	0.1
White	440	11,176	5,820	5,636	10,173	1,003	25.4	69,349	24.63	0.49	338	139	0.41	585	195	0.8
Warren	440	14,979	6,915	7,164	11,801	2,278	32.0	85,854	30.50	0.24	206	96	0.47	663	221	0.5
Coffee	300	12,894	6,327	6,567	11,164	1,730	43.0	71,051	37.01	0.08	55	20	0.36	519	173	0.2
Franklin	500	17,178	8,551	8,627	13,646	3,532	29.1	92,752	34.86	0.43	414	171	0.41	588	196	0.7
Total	3,890	122,110	60,660	61,450	109,750	12,360	31.4	672,213	27.00	0.18	1,210	513	0.42	603	201	0.3
CENTRAL BASIN.																
Giles	500	36,014	18,039	17,975	21,824	14,190	61.0	170,599	45.18	18.42	31,416	13,802	0.44	627	209	53.2
Lincoln	540	26,960	13,402	13,498	20,643	6,317	49.9	146,276	42.84	6.06	8,862	3,486	0.39	561	187	16.4
Moore	270	6,223	3,169	3,064	5,448	735	23.1	38,937	22.53	0.05	20	7	0.35	498	166	0.1
Bedford	520	26,025	12,934	13,091	18,536	7,489	50.0	184,800	49.52	1.36	2,289	940	0.42	597	199	4.3
Marshall	350	19,259	9,652	9,607	14,429	4,830	55.0	117,005	52.23	4.01	4,697	1,722	0.37	572	174	13.4
Maury	590	39,904	19,690	20,214	21,721	18,173	67.6	216,095	57.22	16.07	21,748	8,912	0.41	585	195	36.9
Williamson	540	28,313	14,065	14,248	15,922	12,391	52.4	158,970	44.00	7.46	11,850	4,538	0.38	546	182	72.0
Rutherford	500	36,741	18,136	18,605	20,248	16,493	62.3	200,049	52.98	16.22	32,637	12,414	0.38	543	181	55.4
Cannon	226	11,850	5,905	5,954	10,696	1,169	53.9	64,965	46.14	0.12	77	85	0.45	648	216	0.3
Davidson	500	79,026	38,923	40,103	47,678	31,348	158.1	139,186	42.49	2.31	3,234	1,393	0.41	588	196	6.4
Wilson	410	28,747	14,221	14,526	20,292	8,455	70.1	170,229	64.87	1.87	3,191	1,272	0.40	587	189	7.8
Smith	360	17,799	8,971	8,828	14,215	3,584	49.4	100,855	43.77	......	......	......	......	......	......	......
Sumner	580	23,625	11,751	11,874	16,294	7,331	44.6	139,960	41.27	0.52	782	317	0.48	618	206	1.4
Trousdale	180	6,646	3,334	3,312	4,505	2,141	36.9	55,817	31.09	......	1	1	1.00	1,425	475	......
Total	6,190	367,151	192,252	194,890	252,461	134,690	62.5	1,863,764	47.05	6.46	120,729	48,773	0.40	576	192	19.5
CUMBERLAND TABLE-LAND.																
Fentress	500	5,941	3,017	2,924	5,838	103	11.9	35,067	11.24	0.02	6	2	0.33	476	158	......
Scott	640	6,021	3,081	2,940	5,884	137	9.4	28,946	7.07	0.01	3	2	0.67	951	317	......
Morgan	400	5,156	2,722	2,434	4,967	292	12.9	19,845	7.75	0.02	4	1	0.25	357	119	......
Cumberland	690	4,538	2,291	2,247	4,496	42	6.6	15,196	3.44	......	......	......	......	......	......	......
Van Buren	340	2,933	1,481	1,452	2,747	186	8.6	17,976	8.26	0.49	88	29	0.33	471	157	0.3
Grundy	400	4,592	2,518	2,074	4,154	438	11.5	14,899	5.80	0.22	32	21	0.66	998	312	0.1
Total	2,970	29,181	15,110	14,071	27,986	1,215	9.8	132,771	6.90	0.10	133	55	0.41	586	196	
CUMBERLAND TABLE-LAND, VALLEY OF EAST-TENNESSEE, AND UNAKA MOUNTAIN REGION.																
a. Table-land and valley.																
Marion	500	10,910	5,485	5,425	9,541	1,369	21.8	47,640	14.89	0.19	89	33	0.39	561	187	0.2
Sequatchie	220	2,565	1,396	1,369	2,509	56	11.7	17,087	12.14	......	......	......	......	......	......	......
Bledsoe	280	5,617	2,848	2,769	4,838	779	20.1	40,915	22.83	......	......	......	......	......	......	......
Hamilton	370	23,642	12,025	11,617	16,230	7,405	63.9	53,030	31.97	0.95	496	143	0.29	420	140	1.3
Rhea	340	7,073	3,550	3,514	6,300	773	20.8	40,956	18.83	0.02	9	4	0.44	633	211	......
Anderson	440	10,820	5,441	5,379	9,917	903	24.6	56,628	20.82	0.10	80	38	0.48	903	301	0.1
Campbell	400	10,005	4,989	7,016	9,571	434	25.0	53,730	20.60	0.01	6	1	0.25	357	119	......
Claiborne	340	13,273	6,684	6,689	12,484	789	39.0	64,420	29.60	0.02	13	5	0.33	549	183	......
Total	2,890	84,005	42,327	41,678	71,489	12,506	29.1	375,400	20.30	0.18	661	226	0.34	496	162	0.2
b. Valley.																
James	200	5,187	2,580	2,607	4,478	709	25.9	32,565	25.39	......	......	......	......	......	......	......
Bradley	340	12,124	5,894	6,230	10,258	1,866	35.7	71,396	32.76	0.07	31	15	0.39	420	140	0.2
McMinn	430	15,064	7,261	7,803	12,718	2,346	31.4	104,174	33.91	0.08	30	22	0.27	393	131	0.2

TABLE I.—AREA, POPULATION, TILLED LAND, AND COTTON PRODUCTION—Continued.

Counties	Land area.	POPULATION.						TILLED LAND.		Percentage of Tilled lands devoted to cotton.	COTTON PRODUCTION.					Cotton acreage per square mile.
		Total.	Male.	Female.	White.	Color'd.	Average per square mile.	Acres.	Percentage of area.		Acres.	Bales.	Average per acre.			
													Bale.	Seed-cotton. Lbs.	Lint. Lbs.	
CUMBERLAND TABLE-LAND, ETC.—continued.																
b. Valley—continued.	Sq. mls.															
Meigs	300	7,117	3,584	3,533	6,303	814	23.7	49,124	25.50	0.07	96	14	0.39	555	185	0.1
London	280	9,148	4,564	4,584	7,382	1,766	39.8	68,532	46.55	0.01	8	4	0.50	711	237	.....
Roane	450	15,237	7,649	7,588	13,310	1,927	33.9	72,596	25.21	0.05	35	18	0.51	732	244	0.1
Knox	500	39,124	19,099	20,025	31,880	7,244	78.2	154,188	48.18	0.01	11	7	0.64	906	302	.....
Jefferson	320	15,846	7,781	8,065	13,339	2,507	49.5	89,764	43.83	.*	....	....	....	....	....	....
Union	220	10,260	5,087	5,173	10,042	218	46.6	54,311	38.57	....	3	1	0.50	711	237	....
Grainger	320	12,384	6,043	6,341	11,555	829	38.7	76,299	37.30	0.06	50	36	0.61	870	290	0.2
Hamblen	150	10,187	4,990	5,197	8,481	1,706	67.9	45,872	47.78	0.03	12	2	0.17	237	79	0.1
Hancock	340	9,098	4,466	4,632	8,616	482	26.8	45,847	21.53	....						
Hawkins	570	20,610	10,066	10,544	17,956	2,654	36.2	124,295	34.07	....	2	2	1.00	1,435	478	....
Washington	350	16,181	7,921	8,260	14,604	1,577	46.2	109,500	48.88	....						
Sullivan	400	18,321	9,015	9,306	17,011	1,310	45.8	112,537	43.95	....						
Total	5,170	215,886	106,000	109,886	187,933	27,955	41.7	1,211,911	36.63	0.02	296	121	0.40	582	194	0.1
c. Valley and Unaka.																
Polk	400	7,269	3,525	3,744	6,893	376	18.2	36,316	14.19	0.32	115	36	0.31	441	147	0.3
Monroe	500	14,383	7,080	7,303	12,991	1,392	28.6	94,211	29.44	0.14	120	72	0.56	798	265	0.3
Blount	770	15,985	8,039	7,946	14,273	1,712	20.8	92,860	18.84	0.21	198	70	0.35	504	168	0.3
Sevier	520	15,541	7,707	7,834	14,845	668	29.9	79,463	23.86	0.01	10	6	0.60	856	285	.....
Cocke	540	14,808	7,278	7,530	13,361	1,447	27.4	70,189	20.31	0.01	8	5	0.62	891	297	.....
Greene	530	24,005	11,808	12,197	21,850	2,155	45.3	148,065	43.89	....	3	1	0.33	474	158	.....
Union	480	3,645	1,826	1,819	3,526	119	7.6	16,269	5.30	....						
Carter	340	10,019	5,013	5,006	9,585	434	29.5	42,979	19.75	....						
Johnson	390	7,766	3,884	3,882	7,295	471	19.9	36,218	14.51	....						
Total	4,470	113,321	56,160	57,161	104,422	8,899	25.4	617,161	21.07	0.06	454	190	0.41	565	195	0.1

COTTON PRODUCTION IN TENNESSEE.

TABLE II.—ACREAGE AND PRODUCTION OF THE LEADING CROPS.

Counties.	COTTON.		INDIAN CORN.		OATS.		WHEAT.	
	Acres.	Bales.	Acres.	Bushels.	Acres.	Bushels.	Acres.	Bushels.
The State.................	722,562	330,621	¹ 2,904,873	62,764,429	488,566	4,722,190	1,196,563	7,931,358
ALLUVIAL PLAIN OF THE MISSISSIPPI RIVER.								
Lake...	3,349	2,412	14,780	536,265	108	4,266	1,608	24,293
ALLUVIAL PLAIN OF THE MISSISSIPPI RIVER AND PLATEAU SLOPE OF WEST TENNESSEE.								
a. Alluvial plain and bluff.								
Dyer.............................	14,637	8,564	27,820	900,776	1,961	27,271	11,620	101,823
Lauderdale...	24,063	13,250	22,580	580,707	1,875	17,266	3,589	24,983
Tipton..	38,429	21,415	33,378	762,731	2,431	34,096	7,363	55,137
Shelby..	92,650	46,888	55,260	906,210	5,216	72,674	2,564	23,437
Obion..	7,250	4,225	45,005	1,501,581	2,105	35,098	25,868	236,243
Total...	177,028	93,842	183,044	4,742,345	13,088	196,637	52,004	436,293
b. Brown-loam table-lands, midland counties.								
Fayette..	92,291	36,721	63,419	1,030,505	3,661	58,129	3,737	18,004
Hardeman..	44,855	18,937	45,307	787,294	2,554	30,907	4,758	23,991
Haywood...	49,919	25,092	39,373	730,949	2,978	29,299	5,326	29,278
Madison..	45,825	19,237	46,585	906,255	3,187	31,542	9,623	50,918
Crockett...	17,807	9,220	25,650	626,762	1,501	16,171	9,869	54,431
Gibson..	36,620	19,272	57,838	1,449,633	3,978	44,282	26,016	182,477
Weakley..	15,406	7,576	50,001	1,307,873	1,795	22,583	25,479	171,835
Total...	302,293	136,675	328,878	6,819,301	19,622	202,813	84,822	510,934
c. Summit region of water-shed.								
Henry...	13,186	5,316	51,852	1,128,660	3,171	35,407	20,853	124,537
Carroll...	24,711	10,505	46,076	1,018,415	3,413	37,694	17,354	88,396
Henderson..	22,344	9,419	37,734	862,349	4,543	42,176	9,791	48,941
McNairy..	23,135	9,419	33,501	678,059	5,093	47,559	6,736	38,678
Total...	83,376	34,659	169,163	3,687,383	16,220	162,836	54,734	290,552
WESTERN VALLEY OF TENNESSEE RIVER.								
Benton..	4,922	1,801	24,786	562,354	2,368	26,832	4,600	19,785
Decatur...	5,591	2,169	19,958	473,924	2,701	26,399	3,829	14,911
Hardin..	12,859	5,345	30,909	790,739	3,387	35,620	5,445	29,248
Perry..	452	196	15,007	423,461	1,461	23,274	2,113	16,031
Humphreys..	155	90	26,387	825,941	1,988	24,521	5,436	25,371
Houston..	8	4	8,974	231,311	841	13,846	1,864	9,092
Stewart...	45	15	28,007	778,404	2,070	26,639	5,620	34,855
Total...	24,083	9,620	155,007	4,096,134	14,816	177,731	29,897	149,283
THE HIGHLANDS, OR HIGHLAND RIM OF MIDDLE TENNESSEE.								
a. Western subdivision.								
Montgomery..	2	2	49,852	1,236,561	7,368	86,098	17,122	148,534
Robertson...			45,468	793,702	9,679	115,678	21,912	134,426
Cheatham...	5	2	19,718	437,189	3,309	42,297	3,368	18,036
Dickson..	31	13	28,351	518,422	4,200	50,735	6,518	45,318
Hickman...	3,128	1,302	30,716	826,117	2,896	42,488	7,874	37,491
Lewis...	229	102	5,272	114,010	339	4,308	1,189	4,834
Wayne..	3,265	1,207	25,674	563,305	2,100	27,442	8,791	40,038
Lawrence..	1,890	702	21,673	484,215	2,813	30,097	8,053	43,331
Total...	8,490	3,330	224,545	5,063,521	32,801	399,571	76,777	471,908
b. Eastern subdivision.								
Macon..	4	1	21,296	486,904	3,676	34,581	6,461	31,495
Clay..	2	1	20,010	412,287	1,955	15,205	4,790	24,424
Overton..	95	41	30,336	550,091	4,193	32,953	9,609	40,015
Jackson..	56	28	27,448	663,019	3,596	28,714	6,825	40,294
Putnam...	14	4	25,510	511,610	2,919	34,160	5,726	43,033
De Kalb..	26	12	31,004	863,307	2,275	21,202	12,416	75,303
White..	238	139	34,670	637,143	2,775	24,811	11,354	44,653

378

TABLE II.—ACREAGE AND PRODUCTION OF THE LEADING CROPS—Continued.

Counties.	COTTON.		INDIAN CORN.		OATS.		WHEAT.	
	Acres.	Bales.	Acres.	Bushels.	Acres.	Bushels.	Acres.	Bushels.
THE HIGHLANDS, OR HIGHLAND RIM OF MIDDLE TENNESSEE—continued.								
b. Eastern subdivision—continued.								
Warren	206	96	26, 456	670, 848	5, 612	51, 613	15, 888	66, 163
Coffee	55	20	27, 962	656, 296	3, 127	34, 180	9, 574	56, 155
Franklin	614	171	41, 560	745, 298	5, 350	71, 960	20, 178	135, 816
Total	1, 210	518	296, 211	6, 186, 595	30, 389	339, 379	106, 621	558, 831
CENTRAL BASIN.								
Giles	31, 416	13, 802	67, 756	1, 545, 605	3, 592	33, 289	30, 796	190, 205
Lincoln	8, 868	3, 486	57, 460	1, 232, 915	3, 968	37, 309	37, 279	278, 452
Moore	20	7	14, 329	327, 956	1, 050	14, 729	8, 659	66, 806
Bedford	3, 329	940	55, 492	1, 682, 358	6, 270	57, 408	29, 580	287, 425
Marshall	4, 697	1, 721	47, 997	1, 176, 536	4, 675	59, 567	30, 484	179, 1.
Maury	21, 748	8, 912	85, 496	2, 177, 071	6, 063	91, 452	43, 510	271, 58.
Williamson	11, 850	4, 586	61, 122	1, 469, 446	5, 912	55, 522	38, 685	315, 966
Rutherford	33, 657	13, 414	75, 753	1, 590, 855	6, 452	74, 794	29, 256	173, 997
Cannon	77	35	27, 812	521, 012	1, 962	23, 802	12, 991	94, 150
Davidson	3, 234	1, 333	52, 764	1, 436, 582	8, 141	133, 907	15, 651	157, 530
Wilson	8, 191	1, 272	63, 468	1, 806, 262	9, 978	123, 506	32, 963	188, 540
Smith			37, 166	1, 071, 050	3, 734	47, 340	17, 645	104, 945
Sumner	732	317	49, 345	917, 940	6, 188	95, 081	30, 445	140, 595
Trousdale	1	1	15, 373	396, 384	3, 297	36, 197	6, 620	37, 284
Total	120, 729	48, 778	739, 225	17, 641, 971	71, 323	941, 713	366, 596	2, 446, 432
CUMBERLAND TABLE-LAND.								
Fentress	6	3	14, 591	210, 418	2, 483	15, 824	2, 705	11, 092
Scott	3	2	13, 586	185, 646	3, 506	23, 060	447	3, 297
Morgan	4	1	7, 889	115, 329	2, 660	19, 490	686	3, 832
Cumberland			5, 453	127, 636	1, 366	10, 826	517	2, 797
Van Buren	88	29	7, 771	139, 070	784	4, 008	2, 954	13, 007
Grundy	32	21	6, 564	114, 758	889	3, 507	1, 753	7, 855
Total	133	55	57, 853	892, 853	11, 787	83, 445	9, 043	39, 880
CUMBERLAND TABLE-LAND, VALLEY OF EAST TENNESSEE, AND UNAKA MOUNTAIN REGION.								
a. Table-land and valley.								
Marion	89	35	21, 965	474, 115	4, 240	54, 582	2, 684	18, 275
Sequatchie			8, 267	145, 532	709	5, 337	1, 068	6, 735
Bledsoe			17, 474	342, 340	2, 748	21, 382	3, 546	18, 106
Hamilton	486	148	23, 337	461, 070	4, 771	45, 378	7, 618	45, 925
Rhea	9	4	16, 45C	362, 801	3, 848	33, 650	4, 764	31, 290
Anderson	60	38	21, 047	359, 063	10, 330	86, 195	7, 843	44, 609
Campbell	4	1	22, 135	341, 945	8, 100	68, 534	4, 518	25, 549
Claiborne	12	5	28, 475	496, 262	9, 186	74, 921	9, 128	44, 192
Total	661	226	159, 176	2, 968, 923	43, 782	396, 182	40, 619	234, 681
b. Valley.								
Hamilton			14, 418	222, 791	7, 316	15, 146	6, 680	34, 67
Bradley	31	15	33, 794	587, 143	4, 922	33, 613	18, 819	84, 56
McMinn	50	22	35, 312	430, 396	9, 365	78, 972	20, 196	116, 97.
Meigs	36	14	21, 812	444, 103	5, 367	45, 124	8, 141	47, 797
London	3	4	22, 512	319, 263	10, 027	91, 296	14, 490	90, 555
Roane	35	18	33, 261	697, 787	13, 305	130, 821	19, 415	54, 276
Knox	11	7	44, 129	762, 559	23, 068	228, 796	34, 417	227, 705
Jefferson			39, 317	506, 592	9, 448	83, 035	21, 261	125, 849
Union	2	1	19, 844	319, 702	7, 524	62, 223	8, 015	39, 208
Grainger	50	36	25, 532	356, 128	10, 366	83, 075	12, 896	61, 563
Hamblen	12	3	16, 143	231, 184	6, 731	51, 270	11, 085	68, 007
Hancock			17, 132	292, 195	5, 673	41, 626	6, 162	32, 189
Hawkins	2	2	35, 791	706, 806	12, 686	117, 575	30, 143	115, 636
Washington			20, 154	407, 622	11, 394	106, 979	23, 740	159, 394
Sullivan			25, 477	550, 374	13, 473	111, 963	21, 330	131, 319
Total	296	131	384, 924	6, 626, 484	146, 514	1, 275, 281	296, 097	1, 388, 549

TABLE II.—ACREAGE AND PRODUCTION OF THE LEADING CROPS—Continued.

Counties.	COTTON.		INDIAN CORN.		OATS.		WHEAT.	
	Acres.	Bales.	Acres.	Bushels.	Acres.	Bushels.	Acres.	Bushels.
CUMBERLAND TABLE-LAND, VALLEY OF EAST TENNESSEE, AND UNAKA MOUNTAIN REGION—continued.								
c. *Valley and Unaka.*								
Polk	116	36	16, 009	299, 224	1, 827	10, 506	7, 133	97, 126
Monroe	129	72	33, 928	566, 356	10, 116	90, 793	19, 773	114, 884
Blount	196	70	31, 680	450, 011	12, 888	95, 367	20, 588	110, 196
Sevier	10	6	27, 761	488, 685	5, 923	53, 274	17, 450	89, 429
Cocke	8	5	38, 366	588, 567	5, 767	50, 165	16, 680	94, 763
Greene	3	1	39, 484	719, 455	16, 507	136, 134	36, 250	227, 302
Unicoi			5, 049	81, 852	2, 309	22, 501	1, 840	9, 365
Carter			12, 403	243, 906	5, 046	51, 141	8, 226	55, 150
Johnson			7, 555	147, 368	3, 364	33, 496	4, 488	31, 022
Total	464	196	202, 217	3, 496, 664	63, 827	543, 276	195, 417	779, 367

PART I.

PHYSICO-GEOGRAPHICAL AND AGRICULTURAL FEATURES

OF THE

STATE OF TENNESSEE.

7

AGRICULTURAL
MAP
OF
KENTUCKY & TENNESSEE

, COMPILED FROM MAPS
PUBLISHED REPORTS AND MS NOTES
BY
JAMES M. SAFFORD, PH D, M D
SPECIAL AGENT

·1883·

LEGEND

OUTLINES OF THE PHYSICAL GEOGRAPHY ·
OF THE

STATE OF TENNESSEE.

The southern boundary of Tennessee coincides mostly with the parallel of latitude 35° north; its northern limit is a broken line lying between the parallels of 36° 29′ and 36° 41′. In general outline the state has approximately the figure of a long rhomboid. Its mean length from east to west is about 385 miles, while its mean breadth cannot be much over 109 miles. Its land area is estimated to be 41,750 square miles; its water surface, 300 square miles.

VARIETY IN NATURAL FEATURES.—The length of the state, and the fact that it reaches, in its ribbon-like form, from the crest of a great mountain range on the east to the very low alluvial plain of the Mississippi on the west, through a varied territory, gives to Tennessee its most prominent characteristic, to wit, *great variety.* This is seen in its topography, geology, soil, climate, agriculture, and we may say in the character and habits of its population. As I have said elsewhere, (a) nearly all the important physical and geological features of the states around it are represented more or less (grouped as if for contrast) within its borders. Tennessee has, for example, on the one hand, some of the greatest mountain ridges of the Appalachians, with their "bald" summits and ancient rocks; on the other, the low land, cypress swamps, and alluvial beds of the Mississippi river. It has also well represented the singular parallel valleys and ridges of middle Virginia, the highlands, the "barrens", and the rich limestone lands of Kentucky, and the orange-colored sand-hills, the Cretaceous beds, and cotton soils of northern Mississippi. The same variety and contrasts exist in the matter of climate, especially as to summer temperatures.

GENERAL TOPOGRAPHY AND ELEVATION.—To aid in understanding the topography of the state it will be well to assume and have in mind a great horizontal plane, having an elevation of 900 feet above the sea, with which to compare the *general surface.* Throwing out of view for the moment some of the local geographical features, that is to say, the mountain ranges of the eastern portion and the basins and valleys of the western, the general surface coincides more or less with this plane. I say more or less, for the surface is in a degree a warped one, coinciding at very many points with the plane, but at others either rising above or sinking below it. Reference may here be made to the diagram below, which is intended to show the great natural divisions of the state, there being eight of them:

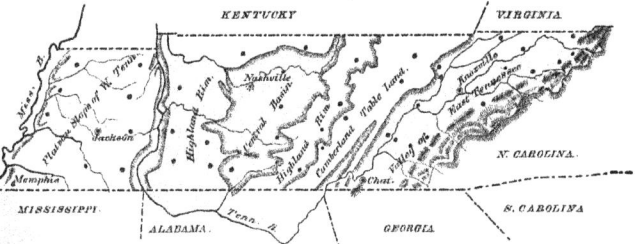

The following divisions are not named in the diagram: The *Unaka Mountain region,* in the extreme eastern part of the state; the *Western Valley,* through which the Tennessee river flows northerly into Kentucky; and the *Mississippi Bottom region,* in the extreme western part of the state

---

a *Geology of Tennessee,* 1869, p. 10.

The parts of the state approximately coinciding with our assumed plane of 900 feet elevation, or at least directly referable to it, are the great divisions named: the *plateau slope of West Tennessee*, the *highland rim of Middle Tennessee*, and the *valley of East Tennessee*.

The valley of East Tennessee is in its upper or northern part a few hundred feet above the plane, while in its central and southern parts it at first coincides and then very gradually falls below it. The highlands of Middle Tennessee in some counties, as in Lawrence and Wayne, present a flat surface 100 feet higher than our assumed reference plane, while in Montgomery and adjoining counties the corresponding highlands are considerably lower. The "ridge" in West Tennessee dividing the waters of the Tennessee and the Mississippi rivers, and including the summit-line of the great plateau slope, must at some points be nearly, if not quite, as high as the plane. Westward, however, the general surface sloping off toward the Mississippi falls considerably below, and may be regarded as terminating at an average elevation of not far from 400 feet along the edge of the bluff escarpment which faces the alluvial plane of the great river.

Upon the surface, as described, rest the mountains of the state, the most important being the great ranges of the Unaka region and the Cumberland table-land. Cut out of it and below it are the central basin of Middle Tennessee, the western valley of the Tennessee river, and the Mississippi bottom region.

Politically, the state is divided into three large divisions, namely, West Tennessee, Middle Tennessee, and East Tennessee. The first embraces all the counties between the Mississippi and Tennessee rivers, including the whole of Hardin county, altogether less than one-third of the state; the second the counties between the Tennessee river and a line approximately dividing longitudinally the Cumberland table-land, the largest division; and the third all the remaining counties in the eastern end of the state.

CLIMATE.—As already stated, in climate, as in other natural features, the state presents a marked variety. This is especially true of summer temperatures. The valley lands of upper East Tennessee have the summers of Ohio and New Jersey; the lowlands of Middle Tennessee have the summers of the northern part of Georgia; while West Tennessee is warmed by the summer of the central parts of Georgia and South Carolina. And further, there is, as will be seen hereafter, an extended line of high points on the eastern border of the state which have the cool breezes of a Canadian summer, and are, to some extent, clothed with a Canadian flora.

The climate of the state, exclusive of its mountains, is in general midway in character between that of a temperate and that of a subtropical region, or rather it combines the milder features of the two. In common with a large part of the valley of the Mississippi, the climate is subject to comparatively great extremes; yet these extremes never reach the excessive cold of the northern states or the highest temperature of the tropics.

Herbage is often green throughout the year, and cattle can generally graze, with but little interruption from cold or snow, during all the months of winter. Many shrubs which in states farther north lose their leaves during the winter, here not unfrequently retain them the year round. The daily changes of temperature are considerable, and, in common with a large area of the Mississippi valley, the state has a full share of humidity and sufficient rains. It is a part of the region of which it is said "cotton, Indian corn, and the cane find their natural climate here, but not elsewhere in any considerable degree beyond the tropics".

The *annual mean temperature* along a parallel running longitudinally through the middle of the state is, according to the best observations and estimates, about 60.5° for West Tennessee, 58.5° for Middle Tennessee on the meridian of Nashville, and 57.5° for the valley of East Tennessee. For the annual means of parts of West and Middle Tennessee near the northern boundary of the state one degree may be subtracted from each of the above numbers respectively, and for parts near the southern boundary one degree added. In East Tennessee two degrees must be added and subtracted respectively for the northern and southern means. These approximations are the best that can be made at present. In making them, the temperatures of the mountain divisions, namely, the Cumberland table-land and the Unaka region, have not been considered.

The *length of the period between the last killing frost of spring and the first killing frost of autumn* is to the agriculturist an important element of climate. It is the measure of the growing season, at least so far as the cotton-plant is concerned. Not including the mountains, the average time for the last killing frost of spring is the middle of April in the northern counties of the state, excepting in those of upper East Tennessee, where it occurs a few days later. In the southern part of the state it is a week sooner. The average time of the first killing frost of autumn in the northern counties is the middle of October. It occurs a few days earlier in upper East Tennessee, and a week later in the southern counties of the state. The number of days between these frosts, that of spring and that of autumn, averages 189 for the northern part of the state and 203 for the southern. Frosts of course may occur respectively before or after the times specified, but the probabilities are against it. Early frosts begin to be a source of apprehension before the last of September, especially in the more northern portions of the state, and the cotton crop often suffers more or less from them.

The latitude of Tennessee is such that a fall of two degrees of temperature in the northern part of the state might cause a killing frost, resulting in the destruction of the cotton-plants, while the same fall in the southern part would leave them intact. The length of the growing season for cotton is, at the best, short enough in the southern part of the state, and where so slight a change of temperature produces such results we can readily see how, in the northern part, it may be generally too short for full crops, which in reality it is. It amounts nearly to the same thing to say that the margin of the cotton-growing section of the country runs through Tennessee.

In an inspection of the map showing percentage of aggregate areas in cotton, as compared with the entire area of any given region, it is seen that the counties in Tennessee which plant and produce the most cotton are strikingly the most southerly ones, and that from these the production decreases almost uniformly as we go north. This is especially so in West Tennessee. Now, in explanation of this, in great part at least, it is to be noted that the isotherms, or lines of equal temperature, for spring and fall extend west-northwest through the state, say parallel with a line running through Chattanooga and Trenton or thereabout. This shows the southwestern corner to be the warmest, and here is our greatest center of cotton culture. The greater warmth stimulates the cotton, and by throwing back the killing frosts increases the length of the growing season. The soils have their influence, but that they are not dominant in this distribution of percentage culture is shown by the fact that as we go north the decrease occurs, though the soils and elevation remain essentially the same. It is also noteworthy that as we go eastward from each of the two centers of cotton culture (the southwesterly corner of the state and the southern part of the central basin) the percentage of cotton culture rapidly decreases. The temperature and higher elevation obviously have much to do with this decrease.

The *rainfall* for seven years (1873-1879) was: at Memphis, 54.40 inches; at Nashville, 51.98 inches; and at Knoxville, 54.52 inches, giving a mean of 53.60 inches. Our data indicate that we have the least rain in autumn and the most in winter and spring, yet so distributed through the months as to prevent any marked distinction into wet and dry seasons. The most favorable seasons are those in which the rainfall is about a mean, provided it is suitably distributed among the months. It is more frequently too dry than too wet during the summer.

THE ROCKS AND SOILS IN GENERAL.—The varied character of the natural features of Tennessee, both geological and agricultural, have already been referred to. As to the latter, this variety is marked, and will appear farther on. From the North Carolina boundary to a line nearly coincident with that part of the Tennessee river which flows northwestward across the state from Mississippi to Kentucky the strata underlying the soils, excepting the limited river bottoms, are everywhere *hard rocks* of many varieties: gneissoid and half metamorphic conglomerates, slates, and sandstones of the mountains to begin with; then calcareous shales, dolomites, and limestones of the valleys and calcareo-siliceous rocks of certain flat highlands. Much the greater part of the state, including the whole of Middle and East Tennessee, is made up of these hard rocks. Passing the line referred to, a wonderful change takes place. The hard rocks suddenly disappear, beveled off as if it was once a coast-line washed by the waves, and abutting against their beveled edges begin strata, little indurated, of clays, sands, and other material, which spread over nearly the whole of West Tennessee. The latter strata, which we call, by way of contrast, *soft rocks*, are of much later geological age than the former, and give to West Tennessee characteristic features.

The strata of the state, be they soft or hard rocks, are approximately horizontal in position, excepting those of the valley of East Tennessee and the Unaka mountains, which are generally tilted, dipping to the southwest, often at a high angle, with their edges outcropping at the surface in long lines running northeast and southwest. The position of the strata has much to do with the topography of a country and with the extent and shape of its agricultural areas. Owing to the outcropping of the tilted strata of East Tennessee in long lines, it is a *fluted* country, made up of closely packed long and narrow valleys and ridges, all running in straight courses to the northeast and southwest. Its best soils and agricultural areas occur, therefore, in long, narrow strips or belts separated by ridges. No such parallelism of valley and ridge is to be seen in the other parts of the state.

The soils are classified for the most part by the rocks, and it is the decay and disintegration of the latter which supply the inorganic materials. In Middle and East Tennessee, where, with unimportant exceptions, superficial drift formations are absent, the connection between the limestones, sandstones, shales, etc., and the overlying soils is very apparent. There being many kinds of rocks, there will be many kinds of soil, and the most important in the divisions just named are the calcareous soils; that is, those of the limestones, dolomites, and calcareous shales. With the exception of the limited alluvial areas of certain streams the cotton of Middle and East Tennessee is produced, substantially, on calcareous soils.

The most important cotton soils of Middle Tennessee belong to two horizons of the Trenton limestone period, namely, the upper part of the Hudson river (Nashville) rocks, and certain beds of the lower part (the Central or Murfreesborough limestone).

In East Tennessee the little cotton cultivated is mostly found on the calcareous shale and dolomites of the Quebec (Knox) division of the Canadian period.

In West Tennessee the soils are chiefly based on sands, sandy clays, loess (calcareo-siliceous earths), and alluvial deposits. They are for the most part mellow, warm, and well adapted to the growth of corn, cotton, and tobacco.

THE NATURAL DIVISIONS OF THE STATE.—These have already been referred to, and are here briefly characterized. They are well defined, and will be taken as a basis in the arrangement of the matter of this report.

1. *The Mississippi bottom region*, embracing the Tennessee portion of the great alluvial and low plain in which the Mississippi river has its tortuous bed; area, approximately, 900 square miles; average elevation above tide, about 260 feet.

25 C P

2. *The upland or plateau slope of West Tennessee*, including the entire area between the low bottoms of the Mississippi and the Tennessee valley next mentioned. It begins with the line of bold bluffs or escarpments overlooking the bottoms, and gradually ascends eastward, embracing the ridge dividing the waters of the Mississippi and the Tennessee rivers, respectively, and the highlands immediately beyond.. Average elevation, 560 feet; area, 8,850 square miles, equal to one-fifth of the state.

3. *The western valley of the Tennessee river*, a comparatively narrow, broken area, through which the Tennessee river flows in its direct northward course from the state of Mississippi to Kentucky. The valley is crowded between the breaks and slopes of two plateaus, the one just mentioned and the Highland Rim, lying next to the east. Average elevation, 360 feet; area, 1,200 square miles.

4. *The highland rim, or rim highlands* of Middle Tennessee, encircling, terrace-like, a basin of rich lowlands in the very center of the state. From the valley last mentioned eastward to the western foot of the Cumberland table-land, a distance of more than 100 miles, there lies a nearly square portion of the state. This area is a plateau having an average elevation of 1,000 feet above tide, out of the middle of which has been excavated a basin, named below the *central basin.* The part left intact is the rim, a complete circle of flat highlands, with an area of 9,320 square miles, nearly two-ninths of the state.

5. *The central basin.*—The basin surrounded by the rim is thus designated. It is the central part of Tennessee, supplies the site for its capital, and is the garden of the state. It is oval in form, with longer and shorter diameters, respectively, of about 120 and 55 miles. Average elevation above the sea, 600 feet; area, 5,450 square miles, more than one-eighth of the state.

6. *The Cumberland table-land, usually known as Cumberland mountain*, is a plateau with broad and generally level top, and stands in bold relief above the lowlands on each side. It is capped with sandstone, and is the Tennessee coal-field. Elevation, 2,000 feet; area, 5,100 square miles.

7. *The valley of East Tennessee.*—The great valley of which Knoxville is the metropolis is a fluted region or succession of parallel minor valleys and ridges, and is one of the most beautiful and populous portions of Tennessee. It extends obliquely through the state, and is bounded on the west and northwest by the eastern escarpment of the Cumberland table-land, and on the southeast by the Unaka chain. Average elevation, 1,000 feet; area, 9,200 square miles, exceeding one-fifth of the surface of the state.

8. *The Unaka region* comprises an area of bold mountain ridges, more or less parallel, having a general northeast and southwest trend and inclosing many valleys and coves, and is the eastern mountain border of the state. The line separating Tennessee from North Carolina is, for the most part, the crest of the most easterly and highest ridge. Average elevation of summit, 5,000 feet above the sea; area, excluding the interlocked valleys and coves, about 2,000 square miles.

THE MISSISSIPPI BOTTOM REGION.

That portion of the great alluvial plain of the Mississippi river pertaining to Tennessee, or, I might say, to Kentucky and Tennessee, is comparatively small. The course of the river is such on the western border of these states as to divide the plain very unequally, throwing much the greater part, popularly known as the Saint Francis bottom, into Missouri and Arkansas, and leaving a narrow interrupted strip in Kentucky and Tennessee.

In the latter states, as indeed farther south, the alluvial plain is bounded on the east by a sharply defined line of bold bluffs, or a bluff escarpment, the edge of the flat uplands which extend off eastward. This bluff escarpment, or edge, reaches in a nearly straight line from Kentucky, through Tennessee, to Mississippi. We shall call it the bluff. The strip of the great plain belonging to Kentucky and Tennessee is interrupted and cut into a number of sections by the repeated bending in of the river to the bluff. The river thus strikes the uplands at the following points: Columbus and Hickman, in Kentucky, and Fulton, Randolph, and Memphis, in Tennessee. (a) The largest of the sections, and the most important so far as Tennessee is concerned, lies between Hickman and Fulton. This includes Madrid bend and an area in Kentucky south of Hickman, but the main part is in Tennessee. The next most important section stretches from Randolph to Memphis. The section between Randolph and Fulton is inconsiderable, the points being but a few miles apart. Below Memphis begins the large division of the great plain known in Mississippi as the "Yazoo bottom". This belongs to the latter state, excepting the extreme northern end, which is in Tennessee. It is to be added that there is a number of cultivated islands in the Mississippi river which must be included in the Kentucky and Tennessee portion of the plain.

The alluvial plain in Tennessee has about the same general features as elsewhere. It is, or has been, forest-covered, much of it heavily so, and many parts are subject to overflow. It has its bayous, lakes, and cypress swamps. The highest land, and that chiefly under cultivation, often called "front-land", is generally a raised, wide bank or belt bordering the river, and formed by the deposition of alluvial matter in great overflows of the past, the overflowing water having lost the bulk of its earthy load as it first escaped from the deep and swift channel

a Formerly the river washed the uplands at another point, "Old river," as now known by some, in the southern part of Tipton county. The four points, Fulton, Randolph, "Old river," and Memphis, were once known as the four "Chickasaw bluffs", Fulton being the first and Memphis the fourth.

current. Going from the river and this higher land, the surface generally slopes off into lower " back-lands", with "buckshot" clays and soils, finally ending, it may be, in a lake or a cypress swamp. Such at least are the typical features. This division embraces the whole of Lake county, about one-third each of Dyer and Lauderdale counties, and a fraction each of Tipton and Shelby. It also embraces Reelfoot lake and limited lands in Obion county. The entire area has been estimated to be 900 square miles, but this is probably an overestimate. The blue tint on the colored map indicates this division. The cultivated land forms for the most part an interrupted belt along the Mississippi river, and has a width ranging from the fraction of a mile to two miles or more. The greatest single body of such land lies in the middle and northern parts of Lake county, where the proportion in cultivation is estimated to be at least two-thirds of the area. In the southern part of Lake the proportion is not more than one-fourth; half of which is along the river. There is much timber land, and large bodies are subject to overflow. South of Lake county the proportion of land in cultivation is still less. In Dyer county the cleared land is a more or less broken strip bordering the river from half a mile to 2 miles wide, with an average width of 1 mile. There are, however, in this county many thousand acres fit for farming purposes as yet uncleared.

The following extracts from letters of correspondents refer to the Mississippi bottom region in Lauderdale county. The characteristics given, however, may in the main be taken as illustrative of the general features of the entire division in Tennessee. Mr. J. L. Lea, of Fulton, writes:

A slip of cultivated land runs along the Mississippi river, and but little lies back from the river. The best and highest land is always along the river. The bottom about the mouth of the Hatchie is small. Hatchie bottom proper is about 1 mile or 2 miles wide, and has a slough of cypress timber and some tupelo-gum swamps. There is not much cultivation until you strike the second bottom along the foot of the hills.

The main Mississippi bottom region of this county is the area lying between Coal creek, Forked Deer river, and Mississippi river, an area, say, 8 to 10 miles wide and 15 or 20 long, and including 100,000 acres. I believe that in extreme high water every spot of this has been covered, unless it be certain Indian mounds.

There are farms in the bottom bordering the Mississippi river, but not along Coal creek or Forked Deer river. It is 3 or 4 miles above the mouth of Coal creek before the farms begin. I suppose 6,000 or 8,000 acres would cover all the cultivated land of the bottom. Cypress swamps exist all through the area, say 25 per cent. of the whole. I do not know that there are any tupelo-gum swamps in it; do not remember to have seen or heard of any. This bottom would be a magnificent tract of land were it not for the interference of the water. There is a disposition to bring it into use notwithstanding, and some persons are clearing more deeply overflowed lands than had been thought available. I have cleared some land having 10 or 12 feet overflow and make corn on it almost every year. I plant in June, and secure 40 or 50 bushels of hard corn per acre. It is safer from overflow in summer than any creek or river bottom in hilly or mountainous countries. I suppose 25 per cent. of this bottom overflows 2 feet or less, 25 per cent. 5 feet or less, 25 per cent. 10 feet deep or less, and the balance is made up of lakes and sloughs. Two-thirds of the cultivated land is in cotton. There is no road along the bank of the Mississippi river across the mouth of Coal creek, and none, I think, across the mouth of old Forked Deer river, except perhaps in low water. Roads are found in all the farming areas. These statements are necessarily imperfect, and in some points may be incorrect.

Mr. J. C. Marley, of Ripley, writes :

According to the best statements I can make, there are about 100,000 acres of land between the bluff and the Mississippi river termed bottom or overflowed land. This is equal to about one-third of the area of the county. Of this there is in cultivation about 8,000 acres, of which about 5,000 are in cotton. Most of the cultivated land is near the river, and lies in a broken belt along its banks. There are a few patches of cultivated land out back from the river; and other land is also susceptible of improvement, some near the bluff or highlands. Very little of this bottom land is entirely above extreme high water, but there is much of it on which the overflow is slight. I would estimate that on one-third of the land the water never gets more than 2 feet deep, and that on one-half it never exceeds 4 feet. It is thought by our best farmers on the river that a slight overflow is advantageous. The difficulty in cultivating land subjected to deep overflows is that the fences float away. There is no land in our county that produces so well as this bottom. A friend of mine near Hale's Point tells me that he has for the last eight years cultivated about 50 acres in cotton, and that it averaged each year 500 pounds of lint to the acre.

The bottom in Tipton is estimated to average 4 miles in width. Farms occur at intervals all along the river, but none back until the bluff is reached. This country includes also four islands, containing in the aggregate 17,000 acres, 2,500 of which are under cultivation. The bottom continues into Shelby, with the same general features as heretofore described.

The soils may be grouped into two classes, the loams and the " buckshot " clays. The loams prevail, and are dark and exceedingly fertile, at times clayey and stiff, and then sandy and mellow, sometimes becoming too sandy. The buckshot soils are subordinate. Mr. Lea says :

The term " buckshot " is applied to certain stiff black soils which break up into small fragments when cultivated. These soils are not uniform in kind, and vary a little in color and in other characteristics. They are not generally found in very large bodies, as the overflows deposit sandy and loamy lighter soils at intervals upon them.

These buckshot soils are derived from a stratum of dark clay which extends throughout the bottom, and upon which, as a floor, the high waters deposit their alluvial load.

No analyses have been made of samples of the soils of this division taken from Tennessee. Analyses, however, have been made of the corresponding soils in other parts of the Mississippi plain which fairly represent the composition of those of Tennessee.

We select as typical the following analyses, the soil being found in the Yazoo bottom in Mississippi. They are extracted from Professor E. W. Hilgard's report on the cotton production of Mississippi:

No. 354. *Dark-colored, rather light loam*, from Tallahatchie county, Mississippi, a good representative of the "front-land" soils.

No. 376. *Grayish, rather sandy soil*, from Sunflower county, Mississippi. This land is reported as not much esteemed by farmers.

No. 394. *Stiff, pale gray loam*, with yellowish or orange flecks, so that when worked up the soil is somewhat yellow. This soil is from Issaquena county, Mississippi.

No. 396. *Light "buckshot" clay*, taken from the edge of a depression or pond, Coahoma county, Mississippi.

No. 390. *"Buckshot" soil* of Deer Creek back-land, Issaquena county, Mississippi. It is a stiff, dark-colored clay soil, traversed by numerous cracks, and mottled with spots of ferruginous matter. Upon drying, it breaks up into little angular fragments. It is exceedingly fertile.

Mississippi river bottom soils, Mississippi.

	TALLAHATCHIE COUNTY.	SUNFLOWER COUNTY.	ISSAQUENA COUNTY.	COAHOMA COUNTY.	ISSAQUENA COUNTY.
	Tallahatchie bottom soil.	Indian Bayou front-land soil.	Sunflower River front-land soil.	Light colored buckshot clay.	Deer Creek buckshot soil.
	No. 354.	No. 376.	No. 394.	No. 396.	No. 390.
Insoluble matter	87.146 }91.944	87.868 }91.954	71.164 }84.670	75.513 }86.408	51.063 }71.767
Soluble silica	4.798	4.036	13.506	10.895	20.704
Potash	0.301	0.226	0.401	0.506	1.294
Soda	0.084	0.116	0.191	0.146	0.325
Lime	0.301	0.153	0.406	0.386	1.349
Magnesia	0.385	0.256	0.696	0.972	1.665
Brown oxide of manganese	0.156	0.048	0.011	0.133	0.119
Peroxide of iron	2.120	1.848	3.845	2.804	5.818
Alumina	2.121	2.965	0.689	4.487	10.599
Phosphoric acid	0.112	0.102	0.165	0.278	0.304
Sulphuric acid	0.005	0.042	0.016	0.007	0.094
Water and organic matter	2.644	3.013	2.748	4.401	7.369
Total	100.205	100.363	100.036	100.598	100.982
Hygroscopic moisture	4.79	4.07	7.39	6.04	14.31
absorbed at	22 C.°	14 C.°	15 C.°	12 C.°	15 C.°

In giving these analyses, Professor Hilgard makes the following remarks:

These soils are types of the prominent soil-varieties occurring equally on both sides of the Mississippi north of the mouth of Red river. Without entering into a detailed discussion of these soils in this place, it is important to call attention to the fact that in its store of plant-food of all kinds the "buckshot" soil stands pre-eminent above all the rest, and well justifies its reputation of being the most productive and durable soil of the great bottom. Unlike most other clay soils, it may be tilled at almost any time when the plow can be propelled through it, because, on drying, it crumbles spontaneously into a loose mass of better tilth than many an elaborately tilled upland soil. It is of such depth that the deepest tillage, even by the steam-plow, would not reach beyond the true soil material, and its high absorptive power secures crops against injury from drought. At the same time (owing doubtless to its being traversed by innumerable fine cracks and being underlaid by gravel and sand) it drains quite readily. In good seasons a large part of the cotton crop grown on this soil has often been left unpicked for want of labor after taking off from 1,500 to 1,800 pounds of seed-cotton to the acre. Two bales of lint per acre can undoubtedly be produced on such soils with fair culture and good seasons.

THE UPLAND OR PLATEAU SLOPE OF WEST TENNESSEE.

This large and important division is pre-eminently the cotton region of the state. Leaving the great bottom at any point, we ascend the bluff to an average elevation of about 130 feet and find ourselves upon a flat and wide-spreading plateau. From the bluff the plateau extends eastward, gradually rising to the Tennessee ridge, by which name the high belt of country which lies on both sides of the actual summit of the water-shed dividing, respectively, the waters of the Mississippi and Tennessee rivers, and chiefly within the counties of Henry, Carroll, Henderson, and McNairy, has been designated. The plateau, or plateau slope, has from its western to its eastern limit a mean length of about 84 miles. Its form is nearly rhombic, and its area 8,850 square miles. It is a section of a greater plateau lying in Kentucky, Tennessee, and northern Mississippi, between the bottoms of the Mississippi river on the one hand and the valley of the Tennessee on the other, and embraces in its area the following counties and parts of counties: All of Weakley, Gibson, Carroll, Crockett, Haywood, Madison, Henderson, Fayette, and Hardeman; much the greater parts of Henry, McNairy, Shelby, Tipton, Lauderdale, and Obion, and smaller parts of Hardin, Decatur, Benton, and Dyer.

The division is well supplied with water-courses. The summit of the water-shed is so near the Tennessee river that much the longer slope is on the Mississippi side. On this side, therefore, the rivers are most characteristic. They are numerous and long for their water volume, and run in nearly parallel courses, from the Tennessee ridge northwestward, until they intersect or nearly reach the line of the bluff, when they turn southwestward through the bottoms of the Mississippi river. These rivers have sluggish currents, and usually a wide flat bottom on both sides, bearing a heavy forest growth, and are often swampy and subject to overflow. Back from the immediate bottoms the surface often rises in "second bottoms", supplying arable lands of good quality.

The following data indicate the general elevation of the plateau slope. The Tennessee ridge, or belt of highlands referred to, has in the southeastern part of the division, in McNairy and Henderson counties, an elevation above tide of from 500 to 600 feet. Some points exceed this, probably reaching as much as 800 feet. From Jackson northward the elevation ranges from 400 to 500 feet, and going toward Memphis the elevation falls considerably below 400 feet. The bluff has a mean elevation of about 400 feet. At Memphis its height is below the average both as to the sea and as to the Mississippi; at Randolph its height above both is an average. Passing northward, its elevation above tide becomes greater, but remains about the same as to the Mississippi.

We divide the plateau slope into three subdivisions, as follows:

1. *The bluff region.*
2. *The brown-loam table-lands.*
3. *The summit region of the water-shed.*

THE BLUFF REGION.

The bluff region (orange color on map) includes nearly the whole of Obion county and the larger parts of Dyer, Lauderdale, Tipton, and Shelby counties. It is a belt of country from 20 to 25 miles wide extending from Kentucky to the state of Mississippi, and lies east of and adjoining the Mississippi bottom. Its eastern limit is approximately coincident with that of the tier of counties mentioned. Its soil is a calcareo-siliceous loam, often called clay, based on yellowish-gray or often an ashen-colored loess, more or less calcareous.(a) The loess itself rests on a bed of gravel and orange sand, which sometimes appears at the surface, especially near the eastern margin of the belt, in washed places and road-cuts. The upland soil is the prevalent one, and varies in color from a gray or ashen to a brown or dark loam, is deep and mellow, in fine pulverulent condition, easily tilled, contains more calcareous matter than is ordinarily met with in the soils of this part of the state, and is altogether a superior upland soil. It is easily washed, and needs judicious tillage. It is remarkable for its forest growth. In some sections it supplies the largest trees to be found in the state, great "poplars" (tulip-trees), oaks, sweet gums, elms, hickories, walnuts, sassafras (growing up like great pine trees, with long trunks), beeches, and other trees reaching dimensions much above the average. In favorable seasons from 1,500 to 1,800 pounds of seed-cotton are often raised per acre upon the best of this land. Shelby, the most southerly county of the belt, produced in the main upon this soil in the census year more cotton than any other county of the state, besides making good crops of Indian corn and oats. Owing to long or improvident culture the soil in some sections is more or less exhausted. It and its substratum, however, are strong in the elements of fertility, so much so that, unless badly cut up by washes, it is susceptible, when impoverished, of great improvement, or even restoration.

In addition to the uplands, the second bottoms of the streams, both of creeks and rivers, supply a large aggregate of arable land of good quality, the soils being strong loams or mixed soils composed of ingredients from the loess and subjacent strata. And further, the alluvial dark bottom lands of the creeks, if escaping ordinary overflows, are often very fertile and durable. As a general thing, the bottoms of the rivers are clayey and cold, but they sometimes present areas prized for their fertility.

The following analyses are given of a representative soil and subsoil and loess of this region. The specimens were taken and averaged with care in accordance with directions given by Professor E. W. Hilgard:

No. 15. *Upland soil* from a poplar grove at Gill's station, 2½ miles east from Memphis, Shelby county. Depth, 6.2 inches; timber growth, chiefly "poplar" (tulip-tree), sweet gum, and hickory; also sugar maple, red, and other oaks, red bud, and dogwood. The soil, after drying, has a light brownish gray or ashen color.

No. 16. *Upland subsoil,* taken below the above soil. Its appearance, with the exception of a yellowish cast, does not differ very much from the soil.

These analyses have representative value, but it will require the analysis of many such specimens, selected from all the counties of the belt, to give true averages of the composition of this upland soil and of its most important varieties.

No. 17. *Loess* from the river bluff at Memphis, Shelby county, taken at 12 inches. This specimen was selected by J. G. Snedecor, esq., of Memphis.

---

a This formation, the loess, can be satisfactorily studied in the bluff at Memphis. All the material of the bluff here above high-water mark belongs to it. The cuts made for the streets and railroads expose it well. The gravel and sands underlying the loess at this point can only be seen at low water.

Lands of the bluff and loess region, Shelby county.

	GILL'S STATION.		MEMPHIS BLUFF.
	Upland soil.	Upland subsoil.	Loess.
	No. 15.	No. 16.	No. 17.
Insoluble matter	84.646 } 88.112	83.138 } 86.961	73.113 } 76.503
Soluble silica	4.466	3.853	3.390
Potash..	0.322	0.399	0.433
Soda..	0.065	0.131	0.120
Lime..	0.343	0.343	3.967
Magnesia.......................................	0.677	0.436	3.291
Brown oxide of manganese................	0.030	0.042	0.094
Ferric oxide....................................	2.416	3.064	4.697
Alumina..	2.233	3.025	3.103
Phosphoric acid	0.063	0.084	0.319
Sulphuric acid.................................	0.030	0.010	0.050
Carbonic acid..................................			5.561
Water and organic matter	4.150	2.680	1.730
Total	99.555	99.663	99.927
Hygroscopic moisture	5.00	6.31	4.67
absorbed at.........	16 C.°	17 C.°	16 C.°
Humus..	1.062		
Inorganic matter	0.972		
Available silica................................	0.473		
Available phosphoric acid	0.049		

[The soil and subsoil from Gill's station, while having a fair amount of potash and lime, are deficient in phosphoric acid. More than one-half of the latter is in an available form in the soil, as shown in the humus determination. The loess, much less sandy than the other soil, is also richer in potash, and contains large percentages of lime and phosphoric acid, as well as of magnesia. Its organic matter is low.—R. H. L.]

The following abstracts from the reports of correspondents bear more or less upon the features of the subdivision in general, and will be in place here. The name and the county of the correspondent are given in each case: (a)

JOHN H. McDOWELL, OBION COUNTY: The kinds of soils cultivated in cotton are: (1) Light, easily tilled, easily drained blackish uplands, having very little sand and a clay subsoil; (2) black, loamy lowlands, with heavy gray and cold subsoils; (3) light-brown surface soil, with a yellow subsoil. The chief soil is the blackish level upland. It comprises one-fourth of the land in this region, and extends 12 miles north and south and 10 miles east and west, with the exception of the small intervening creek bottoms. The native growth is hickory, oak, ash, linden, sugar-maple, beech, gum, walnut, "poplar," box-elder, hornbeam, and others.

B. W. HERRING, OBION COUNTY: The soils put in cotton are: (1) That of the uplands, which is best and most used, light clay, mixed with some sand, ashen colored or gray; (2) waxy bottom lands. Three-fourths of the land is of the first kind. The growth is oak, hickory, poplar, ash, and walnut.

LOUIS M. WILLIAMS, DYER COUNTY: The soils are: (1) Rolling or hilly land, a clay loam with yellow clay subsoil; (2) valley and creek bottom, black loam land; (3) flat land, crawfishy or whitish-gray. The best is the clay loam, comprising about two-thirds of this region, and embracing all rolling land; its depth is from 6 to 24 inches, and it extends east 10 miles, west 8, north 4, and south 7 miles. The soil to the east becomes more sandy. The growth is principally poplar, intermixed with gum, white oak, maple, and sugar-tree. The subsoil is yellowish in most places, in others reddish and very tenacious. On being turned up to the sun and frost it pulverizes and becomes very fine, incorporating readily with the soil. It is impervious to water in many places. Underdraining remedies many evils to which our soil is subject. Rounded pebbles occur at a depth of from 16 to 18 feet; also sand and thin sand-rock at from 20 to 25 feet.

FRANK T. RICE, LAUDERDALE COUNTY: The soils used for cotton are: (1) Dark upland, much worn and turning rapidly to red clay; depth on the hills, 4 inches; (2) dark loam soil of Lagoon and Williams' creeks; (3) dark loam, occurring on the Hatchie river. The best is the hill or upland soil, covering three-fourths of this region, and extending 30 miles north, 40 south, 50 east, and 25 west. The growth is white, black, and red oaks, poplar, sweet and black gums, elm, maple, hickory, ash, dogwood, sassafras, and others. The subsoil is a tough red clay, baking hard when exposed. The soil is not very productive.

J. H. SHINAULT, TIPTON COUNTY: The soils cultivated in cotton are: (1) Black upland soil, lying mostly in patches of from 10 to 50 acres; (2) dark alluvial soil, lying near creeks and branches, of which there is but little; (3) heavy buckshot of mixed dark and light colors. The chief soil is the black upland, covering about half of the surface here, and extending north 10 miles, east 15, south 30, and west 8 miles. Thickness, 10 inches. There is now, however, a great difference in the productive qualities of this soil, some of it being worn out. The principal growth is oak, poplar, and gum, with ash, elm, and maple. The subsoil is a light mahogany, soft for subsoil, which becomes like the surface soil by cultivation; it is not entirely impervious to water when undisturbed, and is underlaid by red sand at 25 feet.

H. L. DOUGLASS, SHELBY COUNTY: Cotton is cultivated upon the following soils: (1) light gray, and (2) dark gray. The chief soil is the light gray, a fine silty loam, sometimes brownish, and from 3 to 8 inches thick. Cotton matures earlier upon it. This soil extends north 50 or 60 miles, west 6 or 8, south 20 or 25, and east 20 or 25 miles. The growth is white and red oaks, sweet and black gums, walnut, honey-locust, mulberry, and maple. The subsoil is a tough red or yellow clay, crumbling when exposed, underlaid by sand and blue clay at from 10 to 30 f

a For the post-offices of correspondents and the particular region of each, see the list on pages 94-96, Part III.

W. H. NELSON, SHELBY COUNTY: The cotton soils are: (1) a clay loam, and (2) alluvial bottom soil. The chief soil is the clay loam, which occurs over three-fourths of this region, and extends northward through two or more counties and southward into Mississippi, 8 miles west and 20 east. This soil is brown, becoming lighter after long cultivation; thickness, 5 inches. The growth is oak, hickory, "poplar," maple, gum, dogwood, elm, ash, walnut, beech, and cottonwood. The subsoil is a yellow brick clay about 25 feet in depth, without sand or gravel, except in some places along the brows of hills, not impervious to water, and contains hard, rounded pebbles and sand at 25 or 30 feet.

THE BROWN-LOAM TABLE-LANDS.

The region of the brown-loam table-lands (light orange color on map) constitutes the largest and most important agricultural subdivision of the plateau slope. These table-lands present a belt-like area, extending through the state, twice as broad as that of the bluff region, and embraces the following counties, which we may call the *midland counties* of the plateau slope: Fayette, Hardeman, Haywood, Madison, Crockett, Gibson, and Weakley, together with large parts of Carroll and Henry and small parts of other counties. Its area is about 4,450 square miles, or about half that of the entire plateau slope.

Of the counties mentioned, the first seven only are considered in the remarks immediately below, Carroll and Henry being included in the third subdivision and the fractional parts of the others in the first and third. The subdivision, as thus limited, supplies about five-twelfths of the entire cotton product of the state, besides being surpassed by only two sections in the yield, respectively, of Indian corn and tobacco (the central basin in corn and the western subdivision of the highland rim in tobacco, both sections of Middle Tennessee). On the map showing percentage of acres in cotton as compared with the whole number of acres in any given district it will be seen that the color area indicating the highest percentage lies, as already observed, in the southwestern corner of the state. This area is confined to the southern parts of the bluff region and the subdivision under consideration, and lies in the counties of Shelby, Tipton, Fayette, Haywood, Hardeman, and Madison, the first two being counties of the bluff region. From this, in every direction within the state, the relative proportion of cotton planted decreases, until, to the east only, we reach the central basin, in the southern part of which is a second but subordinate center of cotton culture.

The table-lands subdivision as shown upon the map, and including the counties and parts of counties first enumerated, is a plateau region of moderately rolling uplands cut into sections by the numerous rivers and their tributaries. The formation underlying the soils and subsoils is the orange sand of the drift. The orange, yellow, and sometimes gray sands of this formation are often seen in the railroad cuts, in gullies, and in bluffs on the rivers, at depths below the subsoil of from 3 to 10 feet or more. The soil of the uplands is, of course, the prevailing one. It is a brown, or, when moist, blackish, warm, siliceous loam, noted for its mellowness, and on slopes is easily washed, and therefore requires careful handling. The subsoil is reddish-brown and more clayey than the surface soil. The soil is well suited to the culture of cotton, especially in a region like that of West Tennessee, where the shortness of the growing season (the period between killing frosts) makes early maturity desirable. The same belt of country and soil extends far into Mississippi, where it contributes largely to the production of the best upland cotton in that state. The soil is tolerably uniform in character, though here and there sections occur which, by their more stunted natural growth, show them to be below the average fertility. (a) In many districts the soil has been more or less injured by bad or improvident culture, and can no longer yield as formerly. In this way lands once of first grade have been reduced to the second or even third grade. Where it is not too late it should be looked to that no further deterioration of this kind shall occur, and that the soils which have suffered shall be brought back to something like their primitive strength and fertility.

The characteristic native growth of the soil is oak—white, red, black, Spanish, post, and black-jack oaks. Hickories are common, with "poplars"; also some walnuts, maples, chestnuts, dogwood, hazel-nut, and many other trees and shrubs. Rarely patches of poorer sandy spots are met with having a growth of pine trees.

The soils of the second bottoms, though generally not the best for cotton, may be richer than those of the uplands. When mellow and gravelly, they are often in dry seasons the best for cotton. The bottoms above overflow have sometimes a very fertile soil. Then again, they are too clayey and crawfishy.

No analyses have been made of samples of soils from this subdivision in Tennessee. Fortunately, however, the belt extends into the state of Mississippi, and the analyses of its soils there will, doubtless, fairly represent their composition here. The following analyses are taken from Professor E. W. Hilgard's report on cotton culture in Mississippi:

No. 216. *Soil from the table-lands* on the divide between Coldwater and Wolf rivers, near Lamar, Benton county, from a level tract below Summit ridge. Timber, black-jack, post oak, and hickory, with some sweet gum and a few Spanish oaks. Depth taken, 10 inches; quite mellow, and of a "mulatto" tint.

No. 235. *Subsoil* of the above, 10 to 20 inches.

No. 219. *Subsoil* from same section of land, but taken on the Summit ridge itself; resembles the last.

---

a It may be remarked here that the upland soil of this subdivision merges insensibly into that of the bluff region. Both are mellow, siliceous soils, and in their best condition are very fertile. The line separating them has their been accurately traced out, and the one on the map is simply an approximation. Many of the correspondents treat the soils of the two subdivisions as one, and so speak of them in their reports. The underlying loess of the bluff thins out eastwardly to a feather edge overlapping the orange sand, the two often, doubtless, contributing to the formation of the same subsoil.

Brown-loam table-lands of Mississippi.

	Soil.	Subsoil.	Ridge subsoil.
	No. 216.	No. 235.	No. 219.
Insoluble matter	83.347	83.993	82.830
Potash	0.549	0.700	0.630
Soda	0.082	0.041	0.096
Lime	0.245	0.139	0.270
Magnesia	0.479	0.597	0.450
Brown oxide of manganese	0.700	0.332	0.080
Peroxide of iron	4.798	3.982	5.110
Alumina	4.682	7.728	8.090
Phosphoric acid	0.068	0.236	0.210
Sulphuric acid	0.082	0.054	0.020
Water and organic matter	4.195	2.714	3.140
Total	100.867	100.399	100.900
Humus	0.797		
Available inorganic	0.068		
Hygroscopic moisture	6.84	7.42	
absorbed at	17 C.°	17 C.°	

Professor Hilgard thus discusses these analyses:

The common chemical characteristics of these soils, and especially of their subsoils, are high percentages of potash and lime, with usually a large supply of phosphoric acid in the subsoil, at least of the heavier lands. Potash is not likely to become deficient in the subsoils at least; but the supply of humus is not large (as in fact is evident from inspection), and green-manuring is one of the most important improvements indicated. Originally this was not the case, for the surface soils were, and in protected spots still are, dark-colored to almost black when wet; but the washing away of the surface and the burning of the woods have served to deplete the surface of this and other important ingredients, so that over a large portion of the region it is the subsoil, and not the surface soil, as given in the analysis, that the farmer has to deal with. In this case the addition of vegetable matter is, of course, doubly important; and green-manuring of denuded tracts with cowpeas is one of the most convenient, as it has proved to be one of the best, means of improvement. The analyses show that so long as the subsoil remains the question of restoration of a "tired" soil is simply one of time and judicious management.

The following are abstracts from the reports of correspondents bearing upon the features of this subdivision:

GILBERT PATTERSON, WEAKLEY COUNTY: Cotton grows well on any of our heavy clay loams. The second bottoms are better for cotton, excepting that while fresh it grows too rank. On the partly black, hilly lands cotton grows well. The black level or rolling upland soil, covering three-fourths of the county, is the chief one. It extends from the south line of this county to the Kentucky line, and from the east line of Weakley county to the Mississippi bottom. Its growth is white and black oak, "poplar," beech, hickory, and black and white gum.

JOHN C. LIPSCOMB, WEAKLEY COUNTY: The soil cultivated in cotton is the black upland, lying mostly in good-sized bodies of level land. It is a fine silty and clay loam about 12 inches thick, and is found on one-half the area of the county. No cotton is raised on second-class lands. The growth is beech, "poplar," ash, oak, and some walnut.

E. T. BOHANNON, CARROLL COUNTY: The soils cultivated in cotton are: (1) good upland with black sandy soil; (2) bottom land with black sandy soil; (3) hill land with a light gray soil. The black sandy upland is the best, and embraces about one-half of the lands here. It extends north 30 miles, west 50, and south 35 miles. To the east the country is broken and varied to the Tennessee river. The growth is oak, hickory, "poplar," gum, ash, and walnut. The soil has a clay foundation, which is underlaid by sand at from 15 to 30 feet.

Z. BRYANT, SR., GIBSON COUNTY: The cotton soils are largely upland. Here and for 40 miles north, 100 miles south, as far as the Tennessee river east, and for 50 miles west the soil is inclined to be sandy, with some gravel. The native growth is white, red, and black-jack oaks, hickory, gum, dogwood, walnut, poplar, beech, ash, chestnut, etc.

A. D. HURT, MADISON COUNTY: The kinds of soils cultivated in cotton are: (1) dark sandy upland and second bottom; (2) black-jack oak land or light sandy ridges, requiring constant attention to prevent washing; (3) buckshot, containing small whitish gravel. The chief soil is the upland or table-land. It covers perhaps three-fifths of this county, and extends west many miles and north to the state line. The growth is mostly undisturbed, and underlaid by sand at from 6 to 12 feet, impervious when undisturbed, and underlaid by sand at from 6 to 12 feet.

J. B. BRANTLY, HAYWOOD COUNTY: The kinds of soils are: (1) level or gently rolling upland and second bottom—a dark brown soil with some sand; (2) soil similar, of less depth and more rolling; (3) that of overflowed bottom land, greenbrier land, and cypress swamps. The chief soil is the first, the dark brown sandy. One-half of this region is of this kind. It occurs over the entire county, and on the west and south into the adjoining counties. Its native growth is oak of different varieties, hickory, poplar, ash, walnut, dogwood, papaw, hazel-nut, and sumac. The subsoil is mostly a red or yellow clay, with some little sand; also some white clay, which is occasionally gravelly, underlaid by sand and gravel, or pipe-clay, at from 6 to 15 feet.

AARON WALKER, HAYWOOD COUNTY: The soils cultivated in cotton are: (1) Black upland loam in large bodies when properly cared for and not exhausted; (2) soils somewhat worn and mixed with clay; (3) worn soil, washed and exhausted. The land here before being worn is all of the first class, and is reduced to the second and third classes by bad cultivation. The character of the soil is only changed by being mixed with clay. I describe the land of Haywood county, which is all of the same character, excepting the overflowed or swamp lands of the river bottoms. All the soil, with the exceptions just stated, was originally black upland loam. Its extent was west 40 miles to the bottoms of the Mississippi, north to Kentucky, east 20 miles, and south 20 miles to the sandy soil of Fayette county. Its growth is poplar (*Liriodendron*), black oak, hickory, and gum. Thickness, from 4 to 6 inches usually. The subsoil is a tough red clay, baking hard when first exposed to the sun, but gradually becoming like the surface soil, underlaid by sand at from 20 to 30 feet.

H. M. POLK, HARDEMAN COUNTY: The kinds of soils cultivated in cotton are: (1) The siliceous and dark ashen-colored soil of the uplands, lying in long rolling slopes and in level plateaus, extending to many hundred acres in one body; (2) the somewhat heavier soils of Spring and Pleasant creeks; (3) the heavy soil of Hatchie river, mostly above overflow. With the exception of some pine land on the north of Hatchie river and in a portion of the southeastern corner of the county, the dark ashen-colored upland extends over nearly the whole county. Beyond this the soil spreads over Fayette, Haywood, Madison, Gibson, and Weakley, and parts of Shelby, Tipton, and Henderson counties. Its native growth is red, post, and white oaks, hickory, dogwood, red-bud, walnut, sassafras, and wild cherry. Average thickness, about 12 inches. The subsoil in Hardeman is a deep red rich clay, extending down from 10 to 18 feet. When turned up to the action of the sun and frosts it produces well. It contains no gravel, and water does not percolate easily through it. The soil yields from 1,000 to 1,800 pounds of seed-cotton on fresh land, or from 800 to 1,000 pounds after 20 years' cultivation.

THE SUMMIT REGION OF THE WATER-SHED.

This is the part of the upland or plateau slope through which the Tennessee ridge extends in its nearly south and north course from the state of Mississippi to Kentucky. The summit line of this ridge, dividing the waters of the Mississippi from those of the Tennessee, passes through the counties of McNairy, Henderson, Carroll, and Henry, and the region is made to include the counties of McNairy and Henderson, the eastern parts of Henry and Carroll, and the western parts of Hardin, Decatur, and Benton. On the west it merges gradually into the second subdivision, the brown-loam table-lands, and on the east reaches the breaks of the highlands, finally sinking away into the western valley of the Tennessee river. Its breadth along the Mississippi state line is 35 or 40 miles; but it grows narrower as we go north, until along the Kentucky line the breadth is reduced to 8 or 10 miles. The area is about 2,830 square miles. Though containing tracts of level lands, it is, as a whole, very broken. In some of the counties, as in McNairy and Henderson, the ridges are high and bold, presenting many wild and picturesque sections. In the northern part of the area the valley of the Big Sandy traverses it longitudinally and modifies to some extent the roughness of its features. The mean elevation of the water-shed and the heights of the ridges were referred to in discussing the elevation of the entire plateau slope.

The streams are generally small, those on the western side of the summit-line being merely headwaters of rivers flowing into the Mississippi, while those on the eastern side are necessarily small, on account of the proximity of the summit to the Tennessee river. The Big Sandy has such a course as to make it exceptionally large and long. Beech river, rising in Henderson and crossing Decatur county, is the next most important stream. The other streams consist of creeks and branches, some of the former being of noteworthy size.

The soil most frequently met with is a sandy loam derived from both the orange sand and older sandy strata. There is, however, a great variety of soils, the subdivision embracing, to a great extent provisionally, belts of country having different soils with different formations underlying them. Approaching the Mississippi state line, this variety is more marked, the area becoming easily separable into belts, each with a soil and a surface more or less distinct. Just within Mississippi, where they have been much more thoroughly studied than in Tennessee, they are named as follows, commencing with the most westerly: The *Flatwoods* belt, the *Pontotoc ridge*, the *Short-leaf pine and oak sandy uplands*, the *Black prairie belt*, and lastly the *Short-leaf pine and oak sandy uplands* again.

FLATWOODS BELT.—The *Flatwoods belt* extends through Tennessee, though its name is not especially descriptive of its surface or topography here, for it is often broken and hilly. Its characteristic underlying strata are beds of laminated or slaty clays, of dark color when wet, but light gray when dry, and varying in thickness from an inch to a hundred feet or more. With these are interstratified more or less sand. Often, however, these strata are covered and concealed from view by the deposits of the orange-sand formation. The soils are of two general classes, the clayey and heavy and the sandy and light, in accordance with the character of the strata upon which they rest. The superficial orange sand contributes a large proportion of its mellow light soil.

SANDY PINE AND OAK UPLANDS.—The *sandy pine and oak uplands* occur in two belts. We consider the more westerly first. The *Pontotoc ridge* area extends from Mississippi into Tennessee, but soon runs out, and is lost in the sandy pine and oak uplands. This area brings with it calcareous strata, limestone even, while a little to the west of it occurs "green (glauconitic) sand", much like the "greensand" of the black prairie belt, to be described. Such formations exist in the southeastern corner of Hardeman county. With them, however, are many beds of interstratified sand, showing often interlaminated clayey leaves. Going north, the calcareous and glauconitic materials disappear and give place to laminated sands; but as with the flatwoods, so here the orange sand has spread its material over a great part of the belt, concealing the older beds, and in many sections giving character to the agricultural features of the surface. As provisionally given upon the map, including the area made by the projection of the Pontotoc ridge belt into the state, the sandy pine and oak uplands form the largest of the belts of the summit region, reaching throughout the state. On the Mississippi state line it is 15 miles wide, but has a less average width, and it is exceedingly varied in agricultural features. It has areas of poor pine uplands, but these make in the aggregate little of its surface; it is in the main rough and broken, yet there are numerous large bodies of arable land, which lie well and are productive. Some of these are uplands, others valley lands, of which those of the Big Sandy are to be noted.

BLACK PRAIRIE BELT.—The *black prairie belt* adjoins on the east the region just described. It is well known in Tennessee as a distinct area, but the designation *black prairie* is more generally applicable in Mississippi than in Tennessee. The characteristic underlying formation is known as "greensand", and farther south as "rotten limestone". It is a great bed, at some points 300 feet deep, of clayey sand, highly calcareous, containing green grains of a soft substance (glauconite), and at many points abounds in fossil sea-shells, among which are huge oyster shells. The belt thus characterized has, commencing with the Mississippi line, an average width of about 8 miles for at least half way through the state. Farther north it becomes inconspicuous, and its limits in this direction have not been satisfactorily made out. It extends through the eastern parts of McNairy and Henderson counties and the northwestern corners of Hardin and Decatur. Much of it is very hilly and rough.

The soils of the belt, where resting upon the greensand, and normally formed from them, are more clayey and calcareous than is usual in West Tennessee. We would naturally look also for a greater percentage of potash in them, as the substance of the "green grains" contains this constituent in its composition. Where the land lies well this soil is often strong and fertile, and on ridges it is usually sandy and thin. The subsoil derived from the greensand is from 2 or 3 to 20 feet in depth. It is a grayish or dirty buff, tenacious material, locally called "joint clay", from its tendency to cleave when drying in irregular block-like masses.

At numerous points in McNairy and Henderson counties the greensand comes to the surface, forming "glades" or "bald places", spotted over with a stunted growth of trees or shrubs. In these places the formation often presents a gray marly surface, with little or no depth of soil or subsoil.

It is to be observed, however, that a large proportion of the soils of the belt are not those of the greensand. As in the belts described, over much of the area the orange sand covers and conceals all else, supplying on level or rolling spots its mellow, fertile soil, or on rugged places a sandy and gravelly one, of little or no fertility.

EASTERN SANDY PINE AND OAK UPLANDS.—The last belt of the summit region is the eastern belt of the *sandy pine and oak uplands*. This in its underlying formations and soils is much like the first belt of this name. Much of it is covered with the orange sand, which here often includes beds of gravel. It occupies a belt of country varying from 2 to 8 miles in width, and extends northward more than half way through the state. In Hardin county it reaches the Tennessee river, and here forms a part of the immediate valley of the river. This part is only included in the plateau slope of West Tennessee, for the reason that its formation, a sandy one, naturally belongs to this division of the state; and the same may be said of that part of the black prairie belt lying in the western part of Hardin and the eastern part of McNairy counties.

The following abstracts from reports of correspondents illustrate the features of the summit region:

W. P. SMALLWOOD, HENRY COUNTY : The cotton soils in this county are as follows: (1) Dark upland clay loam; (2) whitish clay of flat lands away from water-courses ; (3) sandy loam of hazel hollows and branch bottoms. The chief soil is the dark upland loam, which constitutes about one-fifth of all, occurring sometimes in bodies of 1,000 acres or more. Its thickness is from 6 to 8 inches. The growth is black oak, hickory, black gum, grape-vine, etc. The subsoil is a red clay, mixed with white sand, is slightly leachy, usually well drained, and is underlaid by sand at from 8 to 10 feet.

D. L. WILLETT, HENRY COUNTY : The lands of the waters of the Big Sandy and the West Sandy rivers are referred to. The soils cultivated in cotton are: (1) Fine sandy loam of uplands, gray or dark, and in some places gravelly ; (2) black sandy soil of lowlands, rather heavy, and in places rather wet, comprising the bottom soils of the territory between the Big Sandy and the West Sandy rivers; (3) second bottom rolling lands, clayey and gravelly. The chief soil is that of the uplands, extending to the bottoms and bordering the rivers, and has a depth of 6 inches. The growth is "poplar", hickory, grape-vine, chestnut, white oak, some ash and walnut, with some "post-oak glades" in the eastern part of the twenty-fourth civil district. The subsoil is a heavy red sand, containing soft black gravel, but not much rock, and is underlaid by sand at from 6 to 10 feet. The growth of soil No. 2 is beech, white oak, red gum, maple, poplar, and "water oak". The growth of soil No. 3 is like the last, excepting beech and adding papaw. There is less of soil No. 3 than of No. 2.

J. H. JORDAN, CARROLL COUNTY : The first and second bottoms of Hollow Rock creek, and also the hilly, rolling, and level uplands, are referred to. The following are the soils cultivated in cotton: (1) Coarse sandy clay loam, with red clay subsoil, of flat portions of the uplands; (2) black sandy soil, with clay subsoil, on hilly lands; (3) blackish soil of bottom land. The most important is the first-named, of which the proportion is one-third. It is 8 inches thick, and extends north 8 miles, east 4 miles, south 20 miles, and west 2 miles. The principal growth is red, white, and post oak, poplar, cherry, and hickory.

W. C. TRICE, HENDERSON COUNTY : The uplands, or the hilly, rolling, and level table-lands of the waters of Forked Deer river, are referred to. The chief soil is a sandy loam, with some red-clay loam. Three-fourths of the soils are of this kind. It is a fine sandy loam of a mahogany and orange-red color, is 4 inches thick, and extends 10 miles east, 100 west, 50 north, and 100 south. The growth is chiefly black, red, and post oak, and hickory. The subsoil is leachy.

E. W. CUNNINGHAM, HENDERSON COUNTY : The region, which includes the waters of Beech, Big Sandy, and Forked Deer rivers, is considered. The soils cultivated in cotton are: (1) That of second bottoms, mixed clay and sand, above overflow ; (2) dark sandy soils of hilly and rolling uplands ; these vary greatly, the south sides of slopes being sandy, the north sides usually a clay with little sand; (3) soil of lowlands, liable to overflow, which yield well in some seasons when frost is late. The chief kind is that of the second bottoms. It is one-fifth of the whole, and is from 12 to 24 inches thick. This soil extends back from the overflowed area for a distance of from 100 yards to 1 mile or more. In its growth are found red oak, poplar, dogwood, sumac, and ash. The subsoil is generally a yellow or reddish-yellow and leachy clay. It contains gravel, and sometimes pebbles. Soil No. 2 forms about two-thirds of the whole, and lies in patches all over the county. Its growth includes red, post, and black-jack oak, and hickory. The soil of the lowlands, No. 3, is about one-tenth of the whole, and lines the rivers on both sides, with widths varying from 100 yards to half a mile or more. Its growth is generally white oak, poplar, gum, and elm, and sometimes beech.

T. M. STUBBLEFIELD, HENDERSON COUNTY : Refers to the southeastern part of the county, including the first and second bottoms of Cane, Flat, and Middleton creeks, which are waters of the Beech and Tennessee rivers, as well as to the hilly, rolling, and level table-lands between them. The soils cultivated in cotton are: (1) Black soil, mixed with sand, in the valleys; (2) gray sandy soils, on flat highlands, with sand or gravel underneath; (3) clay lands, with very little soil on the hills, having a "joint-clay" foundation. The first and third soils lie over a heavy stratum of "black dirt" (greensand) filled with shells and from 6 to 100 feet in depth, which extends north and south through the county, and is in some places 15 miles wide. The unchanged black dirt is about 16 feet below the surface, and is a good fertilizer. The changed part (the subsoil) is called "joint-clay". The chief soil is the first given—the black, mixed with sand. It forms about one-eighth of all, is 6 inches deep, and extends north 20 miles, east 4 miles, south 10 miles, and west 4 miles. Its growth is poplar, beech, hickory, white and black oak, gum, and some walnut. In addition to this soil, there is a stiff land on the hills that produces cotton very well.

SYDNEY PLUNK AND F. E. MILLER, McNAIRY COUNTY: Our location is near the dividing ridge of the Mississippi and Tennessee rivers, on the waters of Sweet Lips creek, a tributary of the Forked Deer river. The chief soils cultivated in cotton are: (1) Black, fine sandy loam, found principally in small valleys; (2) well-drained second bottom or branch bottom lands, a black, loose sandy loam; (3) fresh uplands, with clay subsoil. The first named is the chief soil, a black sandy loam, which includes one-half the land in cultivation. The growth in the bottoms is hickory, dogwood, maple, gum, and white oak; in the second and branch bottoms, red, post, black, and white oaks, poplar, beech, red-bud, papaw, and buckeye; on the high uplands, black-jack, red, black, post, and Spanish oaks, and scrubby hickories. There are three kinds of land in this county, which change but little in different localities, namely, the black sand, the yellow sand, and the gray clay land.

W. J. SUTTON, McNAIRY COUNTY: The locality is on the waters of Owl creek, of the Tennessee river, and on the east side of the water-shed of West Tennessee. The soils cultivated in cotton are: (1) Soils of the first and second bottoms, black and mixed with calcareous matter, the subsoil being a marl or "joint-clay"; (2) second bottom black loam, with some sand, much like No. 1, and subsoil the same; (3) quite a variety, mostly upland, yellow, sticky clay, some as dark as the bottoms; also the "bald knobs" and shell beds. The first and second bottoms make up about one-fourth of this region, and extend north to Owl creek, and then, interspersed with shells and sand, far north and south, east nearly to the Tennessee river, and west to the top of the water-shed. The timber on the bottom lands is poplar, gum, hickory, elm, walnut, box-elder, etc. The soil is a fine sandy loam, some of it putty-like, and called beeswax, of a blackish color, and averages from 4 to 9 inches, though sometimes 2 feet deep. The subsoil includes the jointed clay, which reaches down to the marl or greensand. The soil is easily tilled in wet or dry weather, but more easily when moderately wet or dry. The third class of soils makes up about one-half this region. Their growth is black-jack, post, red, and Spanish oak, dogwood, and hickory. The thickness is from 2 to 4 inches, and when the subsoil is present it is a sticky, yellow clay. The underlying formation is "greensand".

THE WESTERN VALLEY OF THE TENNESSEE RIVER.

This division has been briefly characterized before. As compared with the plateau slope just described, it shows a marked falling off in the percentage of land in cotton. (See map showing relations between area and cotton acreage.) The northeastern part of the division, that east of the Tennessee and north of Duck river, is in the "penumbral region" of cotton culture, very little cotton being produced. Passing from this to the southwestern part, the percentage rises, until in the western portion of Hardin county and on the eastern border of McNairy it reaches the maximum for this division.

The Western valley, as already stated, is a long, narrow, and comparatively broken area crowded between the spurs and breaks of two plateaus, one on the west and the other on the east side of the Tennessee river. Its limits on both sides may be taken to be the lines respectively along which the highlands for the most part break away. As thus limited, it has an average width of not more than 10 or 11 miles, with an area, say, of 1,200 square miles (a small portion of the state), and embraces the greater parts each of Benton, Decatur, and Hardin counties, much of Henry, a little of McNairy, the western portions of Stewart, Houston, Humphreys, and Perry, and the northwestern corner of Wayne. The bounding highlands on both sides are fringed with numerous spurs, many of which run within 2 or 3 miles of the river, and some quite to it. Interlocked with the spurs, the valley sends out many ramifications, among which are the narrow valleys of the tributaries of the Tennessee river, not a few of which run back 10 or 15 miles and some 20 or more before they terminate. Some of the creek valleys of Hardin and Wayne are among the longest ramifications. These are serpentine and narrow, averaging not more than a mile in width, but at many points are very fertile. The spurs separating them are high, flat-topped arms of the highlands, like most of the spurs on this side of the valley. Buffalo river, with the lower part of Duck river, in Wayne, Perry, and Humphreys counties, presents in its valley an important ramification. This, however, and the upper parts of the long creek valleys mentioned, are to be regarded as deep cuts in the division next considered, the Highland Rim. The valley of the Big Sandy is a ramification on the western side of the division.

Taking the high-water elevation of the Tennessee river as the floor of the valley under consideration, its average elevation above tide is about 360 feet. The depth of the valley below the highlands that bound it on the east is, say, 500 feet, and below those on the west not far from 350 or 400 feet.

The formations of the division are of many kinds. We have, in our progress eastward, the last of the sandy and clayey strata of West Tennessee and the first of the hard strata, the limestones and siliceo-calcareous strata of Middle Tennessee. It thus includes the junction of the soft rocks of the one with the hard rocks of the other—a junction which appears to mark the position of the ancient coast-line referred to on a previous page. Here and there also, overlying the formations on each side of the junction, and indeed on both sides of the Tennessee river, are patches of sandy material and gravel pertaining to the eastern margin of the orange-sand drift.

In the more southern counties (Decatur, Perry, and the eastern part of Hardin and Wayne) numerous "glades" are met with—gravelly, marly places, resulting from the appearance at the surface of a gray, often shaly, limestone, with but little or no covering of soil. With the exception of patches of bushes or shrubby cedars, these places are nearly naked. These glades are sometimes several acres in extent, and make in the aggregate a large area, occurring usually on hillsides and slopes, but often forming the surface of isolated and low knobs, and are wholly different from those before spoken of as characteristic of the "black prairie belt". In another section of the valley, however, the western part of Hardin and the eastern part of McNairy, many of the glades of the black prairie belt do occur, which have been already noticed in connection with the belt to which they belong.

Alluvial bottoms occur alternately on the two sides of the river. These are not often more than a mile wide; yet their aggregate area is very considerable. The bottoms usually have high "front-land" along the river and lower "back-land" away from it, the latter sometimes running into swamps, often cypress swamps. The bottoms of the tributary creeks also are to be taken into account, as they make an important addition to the agricultural capabilities of the valley.

This variety in formation gives a great variety of surface and soil. The alluvial lands are generally very productive, and yield abundant crops of Indian corn, the chief product. Much of the second bottom and arable sloping lands of this division and of the ramifications running out from it, especially on the eastern side of the river, are made gravelly by the angular flinty *débris* from the siliceous rocks of the ridges, and where not worn too much are generally very mellow, productive lands. Some of the limestone lands also are gravelly, from the liberation and shivering of the flinty seams contained in the underlying rocks. To these may be added patches of gravelly land resting on the water-worn gravel of the drift. Areas of flatwoods land occasionally occur, as in Hardin county.

The chief products of the valley are, in the order of greatest importance, Indian corn, wheat, cotton, oats and tobacco. With these also must be given peanuts, a crop of no little importance in some sections. While most of the cotton is the product of the southern part of the division, most of the tobacco comes from the northern part.

The following abstracts from the reports of correspondents refer chiefly to lands in the western valley:

A. C. PRESSON, BENTON COUNTY: For 40 miles along the eastern boundary of the county the river has a line of bottoms averaging about 1 mile in width, the soil of which is excellent for cotton. The bottoms are overflowed in very high freshets, making it sometimes 'too late for planting. The Tennessee river hills, back of thebottoms, are rocky, and generally do not produce cotton well. There is a dividing ridge between the waters of the Tennessee and Sandy rivers for three-fourths of the length of the county, the eastern side of which is mostly rocky and gravelly, and is not so good for cotton; but the western side is mostly sandy, and is good cotton land. Nearly all the lands of Sandy river in this county produce the staple well, excepting its first bottoms, which are too wet. Some of the hilly lands of Sandy river wash badly. The bottoms of the county, when not too wet, average more per acre than the uplands; yet there is more cotton grown on the uplands, for the reason that they are more easily worked. The kinds of soil cultivated in cotton are: (1) Bottom lands, black sandy soils with clay subsoils, such as those of the Tennessee river and of Birdsong, Cypress, and Rushings creeks; (2) uplands, also black sandy soils with clay subsoils; (3) yellow sandy soil. The chief soils are those of the bottoms. They form one-ninth or one-tenth of the whole, and are found on creeks and along the whole length of the Tennessee river; thickness, about 12 inches. The growth is elm, poplar, hickory, hackberry, sugar-maple, oaks, cypress, etc. The clay subsoil is at first yellow and hard, but upon cultivation becomes more like the soil, and is underlaid by sand or rock at various depths. Soils of the second class are found on the uplands, and make about 5 per cent. of the whole, extending pretty much through the length and breadth of the county. The growth is oak, hickory, poplar, chestnut, etc. The third class includes rolling sandy lands, which aggregate one-third or more of the whole, with a thickness of soil of about 5 inches. These lands within the county extend 10 miles north from Camden, south 20, east 5, and west 3 miles, but within the state 50 miles both south and west. Growth, much the same as that of the second class. The soil is from 3 to 5 inches deep, and is easily cultivated, whether wet or dry.

JOHN McMILLAN, DECATUR COUNTY: There is a variety of lands in this county, the most of which are cultivated in cotton, excepting those that are low and marshy. They comprise: (1) Fresh sandy lands; (2) clay lands, manured; (3) common flat lands. The chief soil is the fresh sandy land. One-third of the county has a sandy soil, and this is true of the country as far west as the Mississippi river. The growth is various, but is chiefly of species of oaks. The chief crops are corn, cotton, wheat, oats, and peanuts. The land is apparently best adapted to the first two. Cotton comprises about one-fourth of the crops.

JOHN H. PEARCY, DECATUR: The lands of the waters of Turkey creek and Beech river cultivated in cotton are principally: (1) The second bottom and ridge lands, and (2) the common ridge lands. The chief lands are the first mentioned, and about two-thirds in this region are of this kind. They extend in each direction from 5 to 10 miles, and their growth is beech, walnut, hickory, and various oaks. They are generally blackish gravelly loams with a thickness of 8 or 10 inches. The subsoil is yellow or red, and is underlaid by sand, gravel, or rock at 5 feet. The chief crops are corn, cotton, oats, wheat, potatoes, and sorghum-cane. This land is best suited to corn and cotton, and about one-third is planted in the latter. The land of the second class, the common ridge land, forms about one-third of the cultivated land, and extends 10 or 12 miles in each direction. Upon it grow hickory, dogwood, post, and other oaks. Its soil is about 4 inches thick, resting upon a subsoil, which is underlaid by sand and gravel, and is best adapted to cotton and small grain. About one- of the tilled land is in cotton. chief

L. D. CRAWLEY AND J. G. YARBOROUGH, DECATUR COUNTY: This report refers to the lands of White's creek and the Tennessee river. The bottoms of the Tennessee are tolerably wide, and the lands on the west side, in Decatur county, are much better for cotton than those on the opposite side, in Perry. Fronting the river the soil is black and sandy, but back of it the soil has a mahogany color. The soils cultivated in cotton are as follows: (1) Yellowish sandy soils of the second bottom of the Tennessee river lying in ridges or swells parallel with the course of the river; (2) upland dark soil, with clay subsoil; (3) dark gravelly slopes or points of hills that approach the bottoms. Cotton on the lowlands matures as early as it does on the higher lands, excepting in some very low flats lying between the swells or ridges in the bottoms. In these the cotton is later and liable to be caught by frost, but when frost is late the flats yield well. The upland soils are good, excepting portions including limestone breaks. The chief of these, the yellowish sandy soils of the higher parts of the bottoms, are fine sandy loams from 8 to 10 inches thick. In this vicinity they make a strip half a mile wide and 10 miles long. Similar strips are met with at intervals for 10 miles down the river. The growth is beech, poplar, sugar-tree, sweet and black gum, hickory, white oak, elm, and ash. The subsoil is light clay with a good deal of sand, and sometimes hard-pan with no sand, and is underlaid by sand and gravel at 50 feet. Cotton and corn are the chief crops, the proportion in cotton being about two-thirds. On the uplands the subsoil is a deep red clay, which becomes lighter on exposure.

J. C. MITCHELL, HARDIN COUNTY (west of the Tennessee river): The remarks apply to the region drained by White Oak creek and its tributary, Hurricane creek, the Tennessee river lying on the east, and includes first and second bottoms and hilly and rolling uplands. The upland soil is generally in small bodies, and produces well for a few years, but soon washes into gullies, and is abandoned. The soil is pretty uniformly good in the valleys, but poor on the hills. The overflows from the Tennessee river in the spring back the water over the creek bottoms, often delaying planting, so that cotton does not mature before frost. With late frosts fine crops are made in the bottoms, especially if the season is rather dry. The uplands are, upon the whole, much more reliable than the bottoms. The cotton soils are: (1) Black upland soil, lying mostly on the hillsides and branch bottoms; (2) dark-loam soil of the Tennessee river bottom, generally subject to overflow; (3) rich sandy bottom near the river bank. The chief soil is the black-hazel upland, which forms one-half of the cultivated land, and extends west 15 miles, north and south 25 or 30 miles, and east but a few miles. There is little of such land east of the Tennessee river. Its average thickness is 12 inches in the bottoms and 3 on the hillsides, and its natural timber is white and black oak, hickory, ash, walnut, red elm, sweet gum, and post oak. The subsoil in the bottoms is a tough, yellow clay; on the hillsides it is mixed with gravel. The land is difficult to till in wet weather, but easy in dry, and is early when well drained. The chief crops are cotton and corn, the soil being best adapted to the latter. At least one-half of this land is put in cotton. Soil No. 2 belongs to a narrow belt from 1 mile to 5 miles wide, running along the river and through the county. It is, however, not continuous, being interrupted at intervals by the higher lands coming in to the river. Upon this flourish poplar, gum, elm, ash, walnut, red-bud, linden, and dogwood. It is a fine sandy and clay loam with a thickness of from 2 to 3 inches. Its subsoil is underlaid by rock at from 12 to 20 feet. Very little cotton is planted upon it, corn being the principal crop. Soil No. 3, sandy bottom, lies in very narrow strips along the river, so far as I am acquainted, say 30 or 40 miles. Its timber is cottonwood, ash, red-bud, birch, and walnut. This soil is a coarse sandy loam, and is easily tilled at all times. Its subsoil is a clay, generally dark, but sometimes bluish, underlaid by rock at 1½ feet, and is best adapted to cotton, with which three-fourths of it is planted.

J. W. IRWIN (east side of the river): The region is drained by the waters of Horse and Turkey creeks, with the Tennessee river on the west. It includes first and second bottoms and varied uplands of the creeks, with the bottoms of the river, and embraces front- and back-lands and cypress swamps.

In this district are uplands and some ridges, but principally level lands, susceptible of cultivation, and flatwoods. The soils planted in cotton are: (1) The black sandy soil of the creek and river bottoms; (2) second bottoms and highlands contiguous to creeks; (3) flatwoods. The chief soil is the black sandy loam with a grayish clay foundation. About one-fourth of the land is of this kind, and occurs in an area of 8 by 2 miles in this district. The timber is white oak, scaly-bark hickory, box-elder, ash, hackberry, mulberry, gum, poplar, and other kinds. The soil is dark silt and sandy loam, and near the river it is 3 feet thick, but 2 miles back it is reduced to 1 foot. It contains no pebbles of any kind, is easily tilled when seasonable, but becomes too hard to plow when very dry. The soil is early when well drained. The chief crops produced are corn and cotton, yielding from 40 to 60 bushels of corn, or from 800 to 1,500 pounds of seed-cotton per acre. About a fifth part of the river bottom is put in cotton. Soil No. 2 is designated "ridge land", although much of it is level. There is about one-fifth of this. Its growth includes red, white, and post oaks, hickory, and dogwood. It is a fine sandy, gravelly, and blackish loam with a clay foundation, and has an average thickness of from 4 to 8 inches.

The subsoil in second bottoms is a grayish clay; on upland, a red clay. It contains gravel and pebbles, and is underlaid by sand and gravel, and at some places by limestone, at a depth of from 2 to 4 feet. The soil is easily tilled in dry seasons, and is warm, producing early crops if well drained. It is best adapted to cotton, corn, and vegetables. About one-fifth of it is in cotton. Soil No. 3 is that of the flatwoods, and about three-fifths of the land is of this kind. Its extent is about 8 by 2 miles. The timber is post and red oaks, with black and red oak undergrowth. It is a fine sandy loam, grayish and mahogany colored, and has a thickness of from 2 to 6 inches. The subsoil is gravelly, and is underlaid by sand and gravel at from 3 to 20 feet. It tills easily in dry seasons, is warm when well drained, and is best adapted to corn and vegetables. About one-tenth part is put in cotton.

W. J. WHITE, HUMPHREYS COUNTY (southwestern part): The region includes the first and second bottoms and highlands of the Buffalo and Tennessee rivers. Most of the cotton produced last year (1879) was cultivated in the valley of the Buffalo river. There is but little cotton raised, the season being rather short. The Tennessee river bottoms, when put in cotton, yield generally 1,000 pounds of seed-cotton to the acre. The land of the creeks making into the Tennessee river is well suited to the culture of peanuts, and this is the most profitable crop; it is also very good for corn. The Duck river lands equal the best for corn. The Buffalo river lands have a rich soil, 3 to 4 inches deep, with a clay foundation, and are adapted to the raising of most any kind of crop. The valleys are broad and level, and the Buffalo is a beautifully clear stream. The soils may be classified as follows: (1) Sandy; (2) black land; (3) soil with a clay foundation. The river lands have mostly black soil; that of the creeks are gravelly and clayey. It generally rest upon limestone or flinty rocks, and often upon a soft weathered rock that can be cut with an ax and is used for building chimneys. Upon the best of the soils the growth is poplar, walnut, gum, hickory, white, red, and black oaks, with other timber.

THE HIGHLAND RIM.

The general topographical characteristics and the limits and area of the Highland Rim have been briefly given (see also diagram). It is a great rim of flat highlands, within which lies the Central Basin. I have divided e area, for convenience, into two subdivisions: the western and the eastern. The first includes the following counts and parts of counties: Montgomery, Robertson, Dickson, Hickman, Lewis, Wayne, Lawrence, the greater parts Perry, Humphreys, and Stewart, considerable portions of Giles, Hardin, Williamson, Cheatham, and Sumner, and small parts of Maury and Davidson. The second includes the greater parts of Macon, Clay, Overton, Putnam, De Kalb, White, Warren, Coffee, and Franklin, considerable parts of Jackson, Cannon, Moore, and Lincoln, and small portions of Smith, Bedford, Van Buren, and Grundy

As a cotton area the Highland Rim is of little importance, the most of it being referable to the "penumbral" region of cotton culture. It did not in all produce in 1879 more than 4,000 bales, and of this five-sixths was reported as the product of three counties, Hickman, Wayne, and Lawrence. The cotton yield of the entire division was not during the same year a third of that of Rutherford, a county of the Central Basin. And further, most of the cotton accredited to the three counties mentioned was not raised upon the highlands, but in the deep valleys traversing them—valleys which, with their soils and rocks (those at least of Hickman and Wayne), can be regarded as ramifications either of the Central Basin on the one hand or of the Western Tennessee valley on the other. Thus, but little cotton came from the highlands proper. The exceptions are certain southern parts of Wayne and Lawrence and the cotton-producing land of the eastern subdivision, most of the latter being on the highlands. An inspection of the cotton-percentage map will give information as to where cotton is cultivated in this division, and in what relative proportion. It may be observed that the low percentage colors separating the two chief cotton regions of Tennessee lie in the western subdivision of the rim.

In this large division the depth of the soils, together with the underlying earth or *débris* down to the rocks, is often very great. This is seen in digging wells, in the railroad cuts, and in the great excavations made at the iron-ore banks, nearly all of which west of the Cumberland table-land are within the area of the rim. For the most part, the soils and all the earthy matter below them have been derived from the decay of the underlying solid rocks in place. The exceptions are due to the occurrence here and there, often on the highest flats or summits, of spots in which the soils rest upon water-worn gravel, the latter being outlying patches of the orange-sand drift. Often the worn gravel is mixed with the angular cherty *débris* which has never been transported.

There are two chief soils in this division, as shown on the agricultural map, the *siliceous* (No. 11 of the map) and the *calcareous red clay* (No. 7b).

SILICEOUS LANDS.—The siliceous soil is thin, often light-colored, and rests upon a yellowish, sometimes reddish clay-subsoil. It is, as a rule, gravelly, made so by the angular flinty *débris* of layers of the underlying formation, the latter in general a siliceo-calcareous rock, but often varying from a limestone in one locality to beds of massive chert in another. So far as the rocks and soils are concerned, extensive portions of the area of the siliceous soils, especially portions bordering the Central Basin, may be said to be "leached" sections of country; that is to say, sections more or less deprived of calcareous matter by the action of water. They are now regions of freestone water, and as such, in connection with their elevation and the fact that they often supply springs of sparkling sulphur water, present acceptable sites for summer retreats, both for invalids and for pleasure-seekers. The leached condition is indicated by the freestone water, the poverty of the soil, and the frequent occurrence of massive layers and bluffs of chert once interstratified with or containing calcareous matter.

The land in general is arable, yet sparsely cultivated, most of that in cultivation pertaining properly to the area of this soil lying in the shallow valleys of the smaller streams. The chief products are Indian corn, wheat, oats, and tobacco. Much of the area is in woods, presenting, indeed, in many parts, extensive flatwoods with open growth, chiefly oaks of moderate size. Many such sections are known as "the barrens". In dry places black-jack and scrubby red, Spanish, and black oaks are met with; in swampy areas, willow and water oaks; then again a better class of timber occurs, especially on slopes, such as white oaks, hickories, chestnut, poplar, and sourwood.

It may be added that within the limits of the siliceous soil, as given upon the map, there are certain regions of variable extent whose soils approach in agricultural characteristics the calcareous red clay next described, and make indeed a transition from the siliceous to the red clay. In these transition areas the rocks making the red clay soil begin to appear. The areas may be found in both subdivisions of the rim, but occur most extensively on the midway highlands between the Central Basin and the western valley of the Tennessee river. But in these, as elsewhere within the limits of the siliceous soil, the lands mostly in cultivation are those of the valleys.

CALCAREOUS RED CLAY.—The calcareous red clay is one of the strong, fertile, and durable soils of the state, ranking in many sections next to the blue-grass soils of Kentucky and Tennessee. It is a great tobacco, corn and wheat soil in both the states mentioned and a good cotton soil in Alabama, and nearly one-third of the entire tobacco crop of Kentucky was produced in 1879 upon this soil. Montgomery and Robertson, the leading tobacco counties of Tennessee, have this for their chief soil. It is warm, mellow, and easily tilled, much of which is due to its being tempered with the fine gravel and siliceous grains of crumbling chert. When first broken it is a brown loam from 4 to 6 inches deep, which changes to red by cultivation, becoming mixed with the red clay subsoil.

The rocks underlying the red clay soil belong to the Saint Louis group of geologists. They are generally pale-blue fossiliferous limestones, containing often cherty layers or nodules. By disintegration and decay these rocks supply, more or less abundantly, masses of leached spongy fossiliferous chert, which are scattered over the surface and through the earthy matter below, becoming, indeed, everywhere characteristic of this soil area. The red color of the subsoil is due to iron oxide liberated by the halfway decay or leaching of the chert layers or of flints, which originally in the limestones were rich in iron.

A marked feature of the area of the calcareous red clay, and one well-nigh universal, is the presence at the surface of hopper-shaped sink-holes. These are very numerous in the rim and highland regions of both Tennessee and Kentucky. They communicate with caves below, through which flow subterranean streams, the whole making an underground system of drainage of great extent.

The geographical range of the red clay is best seen upon the map. A large section lies in Kentucky and Tennessee, chiefly within the great bend of the Cumberland river. Much of this in the southwestern part of Kentucky, and reaching a little way into Tennessee, was formerly known as the "Barrens", and has a curious history. The following is from the first volume of Owen's *Geological Report of Kentucky*:

In the early settlement of Kentucky the belt of country over which it [the red clay soil] extended was shunned and stamped with the appellation of "Barrens". This arose in part from the numerous cherty masses which locally incumbered the ground, in part from the absence of timber over large tracts, and in consequence of the few trees which here and there sprung up, being altogether a stunted growth of black-jack oak [black], red and white oaks. The value of the red calcareous soil of the "Barrens" is now (1856) beginning to be appreciated, so that lands which formerly were considered hardly worth locating are now held at $25, $30, and, in the neighborhood of some towns, even as high as $50 an acre. At the present time the so-called "Barrens" of Kentucky are, to a considerable extent, timbered with the above varieties of oak, hickory, and occasionally butternut, black walnut, dogwood, and sugar-tree. The old inhabitants of that part of Kentucky all declare that, when the country was first settled, it was for the most part an open prairie district, with hardly a stick of timber sufficient to make a rail, as far as the eye could reach, where now forests exist of trees of medium growth obstructing entirely the view.

Another large and important section lies in a belt immediately west of the Cumberland table-land. This belt extends in both directions through Tennessee, northward into Kentucky and southward into Alabama. A limited and isolated area in Cannon and De Kalb counties occurs around the base of the Short mountains.

The growth of the red soil is chiefly oak; that of the "Barrens" is spoken of in the quotation given. Omitting the black-jack oak, many flat portions of the area of this soil in Tennessee, outside of the region referred to, have a similar growth. In sections with a rolling surface, on slopes and in the valleys, the timber is often heavy. Good-sized oaks, white, black, and red, abound, with more or less poplar, ash, black gum, walnut, and in places wild-cherry and sugar-tree.

As in the case of the other divisions, we append here for further illustration the following abstracts from reports of correspondents:

J. M. GRAHAM, HICKMAN COUNTY: The first and second bottoms of Piney creek and Duck river, as well as the hilly, gravelly uplands of the same streams, are referred to. The hills planted in cotton are those running up from the second bottoms to the tops of ridges. Cotton is liable to be caught by early frosts, especially in the bottoms and on the most fertile lands. A dry September is preferred, as it hastens the plant to maturity. The soils cultivated in cotton are: (1) Bench or second bottom lands, a grayish or gravelly loam; (2) hillside lands, when fresh, also grayish and gravelly; (3) lands on the tops of ridges. The chief soil is that of the second bottoms, which comprises about one-fiftieth of the lands, and occurs throughout the county. Its growth is black walnut, ash, poplar, white oak, elm, beech, and ironwood. It is a fine sandy loam with an average thickness of 10 inches, and has a stiff red clay subsoil, which indeed is true of all the lands excepting those of the first bottoms. The whole is underlaid by gravel and gray limestone at from 3 to 20 feet. This soil is cold and late as compared with the black limestone lands of the Central Basin. Its crops are Indian corn, peanuts, cotton, wheat, oats, rye, cow-peas, sorghum, clover, and grasses, but it is best adapted to corn, cotton, and peanuts. The proportion of cotton planted is about one-twentieth.

The hillside lands or uplands constitute about three-fourths of all and extend throughout the county. Its timber is poplar, different oaks, dogwood, and hickory, with occasionally ash and walnut. The soil is a gravelly, brown clay loam, 2 inches thick, and lies either upon red clay or red clay mixed with gravel. The underlying rock is limestone. This land is easily tilled in wet or dry seasons, and has a good surface drainage, but is late and cold. It is best adapted to the cereals. I estimate one-thirtieth of the crops to be cotton.

The ridge lands constitute about one-fifth of all, and are also found in all parts of the county. Their timber is black, white, red, post, chestnut, and black-jack oaks, dogwood, hickory, and occasionally poplar. The soil, about 2 inches thick, is a light gravelly or a heavy clay loam. The subsoil is usually clay, but may be red, whitish, or yellow, in the latter two cases being leachy, in the other impervious. It contains white gravel and rounded pebbles in places, and rests upon gravel at from 1 to 4 feet. The soil is not easily tilled in wet weather. Like the others, it is late and cold, but is usually well drained, and is best suited to peanuts and cereals. Cotton comprises not more than a twenty-fifth part of the crops planted.

N. M. HOLLIS, LAWRENCE COUNTY: The county has a number of creeks which are tributaries of Shoal and other creeks and of Buffalo river, streams which empty into the Tennessee river. The lands may be classed under six heads, as follows: first bottoms, second bottoms, rich hills near the creeks, the less productive hills further back, the first quality of table-land, and the second quality of table-land, or the "barrens". Neither climate nor soils in this county are so adapted to cotton as to make it a profitable crop, though there is about one-tenth of the land, in the southern half of the county, devoted to this staple. The soils in cotton are: (1) Second bottoms; (2) southeast and west hillsides, or third bottoms; (3) tops of hills or highlands. The chief soil, a gravelly blackish loam, making about one-tenth of the lands, has no great extent in any one body. The numerous creeks run nearly parallel with each other, and the hills and table-lands between them cut up the lands into the different varieties enumerated. The natural timber is hickory, walnut, poplar, chestnut, five or six kinds of oak, beech, persimmon, sugar-tree, gum, elm, and hackberry. The soil is a gravelly and clay loam of a brown and yellowish color, having a thickness of from 4 to 24 inches. The subsoils in the county are gray, yellow, and orange-red, containing angular gravel, and underlaid by rock at 3 feet. The land is easily tilled in suitable seasons, producing corn, wheat, oats, rye, and cotton, the latter forming about one-tenth part of the crops. The soil is best adapted to corn and vegetables, and clover and grasses grow well. The second soil, that of the hillsides, makes a small part of the area. Its growth is poplar, chestnut, hickory, persimmon, and sassafras, and several kinds of oak. The soil is a gravelly clay loam from 3 to 12 inches deep, and the subsoil is underlaid by rock at 3 feet. The land is easily tilled, and about one-tenth of the crops is cotton. The soil or soils of the highland make more than half the area of the county, spreading widely out in all directions, with a native growth of chestnut, several kinds of oak, poplar, hickory, dogwood, and black gum. It is a gray and yellow clay loam, its subsoil containing angular and sometimes rounded gravel, with the rock at 2 feet below. The soil is early and warm, is naturally well drained, and is best adapted to wheat and corn. About one-fifteenth part is planted in cotton.

M. F. WEST, MACON COUNTY: The lowlands and the rolling and level uplands referred to are drained by the waters of the Barren river. Cotton with us is liable to be damaged by frosts in the fall; in fact, it is only raised in the county in patches for domestic purposes. No baling is done. Our soils may be described as gravelly soils, brown when fresh and yellow when worn, with a yellow and sometimes red clay subsoil, which work freely. The subsoil is often close, more or less impervious, and is underlaid by clay at 18 or 20 inches. The lands are early and warm when well drained and fertilized, producing as chief crops corn, wheat, oats, and rye; but they are, perhaps, best adapted to wheat and rye.

R. S. CLARK, GRUNDY COUNTY: Our lands are on Prairie creek, a tributary of Elk river, and consist of first and second bottoms and uplands. Cotton is cultivated only to a limited extent. I have a gin which is patronised from parts of three counties, Franklin, Coffee, and Grundy. The soils vary considerably in this locality. The chief one is the upland soil, which makes the greater part of the lands in this region. Its growth is hickory, walnut, and black and post oaks. In the creek bottom we find elm, ash, sweet and black gum, and white oak. The thickness of the soil of the uplands is from 4 to 12 inches; that of the bottoms 24 inches. The chief crops of the region are corn, wheat, oats, and potatoes, the soil being best adapted to the first three. The proportion of cotton planted is about 2½ per cent.

JOHN F. ANDERSON, FRANKLIN COUNTY: The report is confined to the valley of Crow creek, a tributary of the Tennessee river, which is hemmed in on both sides by high ridges or arms of the Cumberland table-land. Occasionally cotton is injured by late northwest winds and cold, the latter giving it the rust or sore-shin. We are, however, so well protected by the mountains that cotton is seldom damaged. Vegetation is two weeks earlier here than elsewhere in the county. The soils cultivated in cotton are: (1) The alluvial soil lying on each side of Crow creek, which differs greatly in character along the creek; (2) a fertile yellowish or sometimes brown soil, which is calcareous, like the underlying formation; (3) the soil of the mountain side, very rocky, thin, and not much cultivated. The chief land is the alluvial soil along the creek, constituting two-thirds of the lands in this region, and extending north and south from 12 to 14 miles, with a width of from one-fourth to half a mile. Its growth is sycamore, willow, beech, sugar-tree, black walnut, ash, hackberry, red elm, and linden. This soil is a dark clay loam. That immediately on the creek is somewhat sandy, and has a thickness of from 3 to 24 inches. The subsoil is yellowish, compact, coarse, gravelly, rocky, and rests mostly on limestone at a depth of from 2 to 24 feet. Its tilling qualities are usually good. The chief crops are corn and cotton, the soil being best adapted to the first ; but one-fourth of the total acreage is planted in cotton. The second or calcareous soil makes about one-third of our lands, and extends in narrow strips, like the alluvial lands, lengthwise through the valley. These strips average hardly a half mile in width. The timber is cedar, white oak, beech, yellow poplar, hickory, black walnut, elm, linden, and hackberry. The soil is clay loam, very fertile, 9 inches thick, brown when fresh, but sometimes becoming reddish. The subsoil contains sand, gravel, and pebbles, and is underlaid by limestone at from 1 foot to 10 feet. The soil is easily tilled and is well adapted to cotton. The third soil, or that of the mountain side, is thin and light, but does not here occur in bodies to any extent. The rocky mountain sides make fully one-half the lands, and are covered with all kinds of timber. The soil is well adapted to corn, vegetables, and fruit. No cotton is planted.

THE CENTRAL BASIN.

The form and area of this important division, as well as its relation to the Highland Rim, have been given on page 14. Its contour and central position are shown both in the diagram on page 11 and on the agricultural map, the color area, 8b, of the latter indicating the extent and place of the basin as well as its soil. This division is the most populous portion of Tennessee, and is the center of wealth and political influence, and in its varied agricultural capabilities is the garden spot of the state. It supplies, as before stated (page 19), one of the centers of cotton production; a fact well brought out on the map showing percentages of area in cotton. The soils are suited to the production of all the great leading crops. Indian corn is the chief product, and in this the basin is much ahead of any other division. Then, in the order of acreage cultivated, follow wheat, cotton, oats, rye, and tobacco. Furthermore, in many sections pasture-lands abound, carpeted richly with "blue-grass" (Poa pratensis) and other nutritive grasses, on which live-stock of all kinds graze and mature.

The basin is mostly well defined on all sides by the steep escarpments of the highlands which surround it and rise from 300 to 500 feet above its floor. Their tops reach approximately the same general elevation, that of the Highland Rim making a high border, which, from favorable points within the basin, presents itself to the eye as a level wide-reaching horizon. The border, however, is a fringed one, made so by the multitude of ridges and spurs jutting in from the encircling rim.

The division is crossed by three rivers, the Cumberland, the Duck, and the Elk, which descend from the eastern side of the rim, flow in a more or less westerly direction, and finally escape from the basin through comparatively narrow and often rugged valleys cut severally through the northwestern, western, and southwestern sides of the rim.

It will aid in understanding the topography of the basin to state that if the narrow valleys or outlets through which the three rivers mentioned make their escape were filled up to the general level of the highlands the entire basin would fill with water and become a lake 120 miles long and 50 miles wide. At Nashville the water would be 300' or 400 feet deep, and one might sail over the city and never recognize its site. The summits of the highest hills in the basin would appear above the water as low, scattered islands.

The following counties and parts of counties lie within the division: All of Trousdale, Wilson, Rutherford, and Marshall; nearly all of Smith, Davidson, and Bedford; the greater parts of Sumner, Williamson, Maury, Giles, Lincoln, and Moore; large parts of Jackson, Cheatham, and Cannon, and small parts of Macon, De Kalb, Putnam, and Coffee.

The surface of the basin is in the main rolling, but level tracts abound. Here and there, especially as summit lines, separating the areas drained respectively by the different rivers and creeks, ridges more or less conspicuous start up, whose slopes are green with grasses, or, when in the wild state, are heavy with timber. Then again, limited sections are met with which are hilly or made wild with groups of interlocking ridges. There is one great ridge, known as Elk ridge, which is remarkable, and merits notice. It is, in fact, an almost unbroken though narrow arm, running entirely across from one side of the Highland Rim to the other, and cutting off, as a well-marked division, the southern end of the basin. In general, it has about the elevation of the highlands, and presents in its course but very few low gaps. It is the summit of the water-shed between the Duck and Elk rivers. On its northern side Elk ridge has but few spurs, and these are short. Its northern aspect faces the level or gently rolling regions of Maury, Marshall, and Bedford, regions checkered with alternating cotton lands and cedar glades. On its southern side, however, it is different. Here, running out southerly toward Elk river and southwesterly toward Richland creek for 5, 10, and 20 miles, are grand sprays of bold ridges, which have exceedingly rich slopes, and were covered originally with heavy forests. The valleys between the ridges, like the greater valleys of the two streams mentioned, are noted for the strength and fertility of their soils. The subdivision south of Elk ridge embraces all of Giles, Lincoln, and Moore counties within the basin, together with the southern end of Marshall. This whole region (not omitting the south and west sides respectively of the valleys of Elk river and Richland creek) is remarkable for the multiplicity of its ridges and for its fertile and beautiful valleys, the latter often wide and open, supplying great bodies of first-class land.

Originally most of the area of the basin was covered with cane, and even now this grows spontaneously in open woods when protected from cattle. Large oaks, poplar, sweet gum, walnut, hickories, hackberry, black locust, honey-locust, ash, elms, beech, sugar-maple, linden, dogwood, and red-bud abound. The "cedar glades", a characteristic feature of the land, are areas more or less detached or scattered, upon which grow or have grown great cedar

400

forests. They may be estimated to have covered in the aggregate 300 square miles. The soil of the glades is often black or dark colored, with a reddish-yellow subsoil, frequently thin and much mixed with fragments of thin flaggy limestone, or the soil may be confined to the joint fissures (widened by erosion) of outcropping limestone in place, the bare rock making most of the surface. The true glades uniformly occur upon the outcrops of a particular bed of rock known as the "glade limestone", a thin-bedded, flaggy limestone with clay partings having a maximum thickness of 120 feet and belonging to the Trenton period. Where the soil is of sufficient depth the cedars grow tall, straight, and of great size for the species (*Juniperus Virginiana*), now and then reaching 80 or 90 feet in height, with a diameter of 3 or 3½ feet, and fair trees grow in soil among the loose rocks or in the earth of the fissures. Cedar timber standing in the woods has often been sold for $100 per acre. The trade in cedar logs and lumber has been for many years, and is now, one of great interest in the Central Basin.

A great ring or belt of the cedar glades is found in Rutherford county. This belt incloses an oval area of red cotton lands which is 24 miles long and 12 miles wide. The line of the Nashville and Chattanooga railway lies nearly lengthwise across this oval, cutting the belt of glades on opposite sides. Murfreesborough is in the included area a short distance east of the center. In Wilson county, and along Duck river in Bedford, Marshall, and Maury counties, are many glades, which cover large tracts. These occur also in Williamson and Davidson counties. The glades very generally either surround or lie contiguous to one of two kinds of cotton lands, sometimes, indeed, lying between bodies of the two kinds. One of these is represented by the red soil of Rutherford. Both will be considered hereafter.

The soils of the Central Basin, and the earthy layer of *débris* upon which they rest, have been in the main derived from the decay and disintegration of underlying rocks in place. The chief exceptions are the alluvial soils, which, however, may not aggregate the thousandth part of the whole. Exceptions also are found in the case of certain steep slopes, where *débris* from above has been washed or otherwise brought down upon the lower lands; but the exceptions are inconsiderable, and may here be passed over. The rocks underlying and giving origin to the soils (limestone of the Trenton period) are rich in fossil remains of plants and animals and in the materials of fertile soils. Locally, the strata appear to be horizontal or undulating; but complete sections across the basin show that they rise or swell up in a great dome, the top of which is in the central region of Rutherford county. From this central region the strata have been removed by denudation and the dome has been decapitated, thus exposing the lowest rocks (limestones) of the basin. Here, then, the latter are to be seen and studied. Passing from this central area in any direction the approximately concentric belts of other outcropping limestones are successfully encountered.

The limestones of the basin have in the aggregate a thickness of 1,000 feet, but the strata differ in certain particulars. All have impurities; some have an excess of sandy, others of clayey material in their composition; some abound in flints or chert, or in organic remains; one is thick-bedded, another thin-bedded; some disintegrate slowly, others rapidly. They are therefore grouped into subdivisions or kinds, each kind supplying a more or less characteristic soil. The kinds are enumerated below, beginning with the lowest, with notes.

1. CENTRAL LIMESTONE DIVISION.—A series of limestones, 225 feet thick, chiefly heavy-bedded. They are light-blue or dove-colored rocks, fossiliferous, containing black or dark flints, especially the lower ones. The soil formed is a warm clay loam, brown when fresh, but becoming red (chocolate or copper-colored), like the subsoil, after several years' cultivation, and is known as a red soil. The subsoil is generally deep, and rests often upon a gray, clayey bed, the rock following below at depths varying from 1 foot to 20 feet, with an average depth of about 10 feet. All the earthy matter above the limestone very generally contains fragments of decomposing flints. The soil and subsoil are mellowed by siliceous grains and gravel from this source, their color being derived from the iron of the flints. The native growth, representing well that of the entire basin, indicates strong land, this red soil being one of the best in Middle Tennessee for the culture of cotton. Lands having it, which we may call the "central lands", occur chiefly in Rutherford, Bedford, and Marshall, and to a limited extent in Wilson and Maury counties, and generally lie well. The largest single body of such land is in Rutherford, and is the oval area inclosed in a belt of cedar glades already spoken of. Fine level areas, the lands alternating with cedar glades, are found throughout Marshall and in the northwesterly part of Bedford. The following analyses are given of samples of soils of the central limestones that were never in cultivation. The region from which they were taken is gently rolling, and, where trees do not interfere, a slight elevation is sufficient to give the eye a range over a great extent of country. The depth of soils in this region varies from nothing, on rocky spots, to 15 or 20 feet, with an average depth of about 10 feet (C. F. Vanderford). The red subsoil varies from 2 to 5 feet in thickness. Under this we have a bottom bed of a more plastic light yellow or gray clay containing more or less angular flinty gravel or decaying chert, often easily cut with the spade.

No. 1. *Red clay soil*, taken from a wood-lot near Florence station, Nashville and Chattanooga railroad, a little less than 7 miles northwest of Murfreesborough, Rutherford county. Depth taken, 7 inches; growth, species of hickory, red, white, and post oaks, elms, ash, honey-locust, black walnut, wild-cherry, sugar-trees, poplar, hackberry, red-bud, dogwood, and papaw. Originally covered with cane.

No. 2. *Subsoil* of the above, taken at a depth of from 7 to 15 inches.

Nos. 3 and 4 are a *soil* and *subsoil* from near the same locality.

26 C P

No. 7. *Red clay soil* from J. W. Burton's place, 3 miles north of Murfreesborough, Rutherford county, taken 7 inches deep. The vegetation is about as that given above.

No. 8. *Subsoil* of the above, taken at a depth of from 7 to 15 inches.

Red clay lands of the Central Basin, Rutherford county.

	SEVEN MILES NORTHWEST OF MURFREESBOROUGH.				THREE MILES NORTH OF MURFREESBOROUGH.	
	Soil.	Subsoil.	Soil.	Subsoil.	Soil.	Subsoil.
	No. 1.	No. 2.	No. 3.	No. 4.	No. 7.	No. 8.
Insoluble matter	79.580 } 83.208	66.092 } 77.789	80.850 } 86.116	81.670 } 87.750	73.850 } 82.660	76.470 } 82.480
Soluble silica	3.628	11.697	5.266	6.080	7.319	6.010
Potash	0.150	0.508	0.140	0.211	0.255	0.251
Soda	0.065	0.088	0.034	0.033	0.258	0.036
Lime	3.054	0.119	0.510	0.151	0.340	0.142
Magnesia	0.029	0.204	0.094	0.301	0.296	0.074
Brown oxide of manganese	0.195	0.273	0.175	0.157	0.038	0.149
Peroxide of iron	3.420	6.837	3.709	3.613	5.184	4.773
Alumina	4.988	10.199	4.173	5.220	5.567	7.774
Phosphoric acid	0.242	0.305	0.207	0.056	0.079	0.056
Sulphuric acid	0.089	0.079	0.192	0.008	0.079	0.072
Water and organic matter	4.962	3.728	4.784	1.956	4.902	4.230
Total	100.402	100.228	99.972	100.476	99.718	100.051
Hygroscopic moisture	8.64	8.84	7.23	5.59	7.29	7.93
absorbed at	22.9 C.°	17.2 C.°	22.9 C.°	17.2 C.°	22.2 C.°	22.2 C.°

[In the above analyses the first two soils (Nos. 1 and 3) resemble each other very strongly in every regard except their large lime percentages, which may be due in the case of No. 1 to some local circumstance, such as undecomposed particles of limestone, the country rock. Both soils may be considered as being fairly supplied with potash and heavily so with phosphoric acid, and, in the presence of so much lime, should be exceedingly thrifty. There is, however, a great difference in their subsoils. soil No. 1 being supported by a heavy clay, rich in phosphoric acid, extremely so in potash, though having a small and insufficient amount of lime. Soil No. 3, on the other hand, rests upon a subsoil less clayey in character, containing a fair percentage of potash, but very deficient in phosphoric acid, an unusual thing for clay subsoils. The deficiency in lime in both subsoils is accompanied by increased percentages of magnesia, which, in the surface soils, is extraordinarily low. In volatile matter and hygroscopic moisture the difference between the two subsoils is due to their clayeyness, and throughout are satisfactory. The soil and subsoil from nearer Murfreesborough both fall very short in their percentages of phosphoric acid, though they are fairly supplied with other necessary constituents.—E. W. H.]

2. CEDAR GLADE LANDS.—Next above the central limestones follow the thin-bedded flaggy limestones, making the *cedar glades* already spoken of. The soils of this division have been noticed. Where these are deep enough, and the cedar stumps and loose flags permit it, the land in the middle and southern portions of the basin is often cultivated in cotton. In general, however, comparatively little of it is produced upon the areas of the "glade-limestones".

3. CARTER'S CREEK LIMESTONE LANDS.—Resting upon the flaggy limestones next comes a heavy-bedded rock, which, owing to its conspicuous outcrops on Carter's creek, in Maury county, I have called the *Carter's Creek limestone*. It is also known as the *Woodbury limestone*, this county town being built upon it. The rock is light blue in color, containing siliceous fossils and more or less chert, and is in all nearly 100 feet in thickness. Where the surface lies well, and is level or gently rolling or sloping, this rock often supplies a good agricultural country. Areas underlaid by it occur in all the counties within the basin, and it underlies much of the surface outside of the "cedar glades" in the counties of Wilson, Rutherford, Bedford, Marshall, Maury, and Williamson. Excepting a few limited and unimportant spots, it is the lowest rock appearing at the surface in Smith, Trousdale, Sumner, Davidson, De Kalb, Cannon, Lincoln, and Giles counties. The soil above it is, when fresh, brown or dark; the subsoil is yellowish or reddish-yellow, rather clayey, and contains gravelly chert. It has not the markedly red color of the subsoils and warm soils of the central limestones. In the main, the lands of the Carter's Creek limestones, as compared with the central limestones, are second class. They do not generally lie so well, are often hilly, and are more frequently broken by rough, rocky places ("rocky roughs"), upon some of which cedars grow, making outliers of the true glades. Yet there are many sections where, topography being equal, they are little inferior to the central lands in tilling qualities and fertility. Both kinds of lands are often confounded with the true glade lands, all being designated "cedar lands". This is due to the fact that the central and Carter's creek areas adjoin the glades, the first concentrically within and the second without, or are locally and irregularly interlocked with them. A considerable proportion of the best of them, commencing with Wilson county and going southward, are cultivated in cotton with fair results.

402

4. ORTHIS LIMESTONE LANDS.—A series of sandy limestones from 70 to 100 feet in thickness, which we shall call the *Orthis bed*, follows in ascending order. In certain sections of the basin, as about Nashville, the upper portion of this series is a remarkably laminated current-formed rock of about 25 feet in thickness, made up in general of comminuted shells or "shell sand". The grains are generally calcareous, but are much mixed with siliceous grains. This portion has been named the *Capitol limestone*, as it supplied the stone for the capitol at Nashville. The lower and much the greater portion, as well as the persistent portion (being found in its geological horizon throughout the basin), is the *Orthis bed proper*, so named because at most points it is well filled with individuals of a fossil shell having about the diameter of a dime, known to geologists as *Orthis testudinaria*. The bed is, in general, a sandy or siliceous, often shaly, calcareous rock, and when freshly quarried is light blue in color; but upon thorough weathering it becomes a yellowish sandy shale or a porous sandstone, and blocks of the latter are often met with on slopes. Sometimes these blocks, when broken, show a blue unchanged nucleus within. The usual thickness is from 50 to 75 feet. In the eastern part of Williamson county, however, as about Triune, there is a local thickening of the bed, it becoming 150 feet thick or more. Owing to its sandy or siliceous nature, the rock has a degree of weather-resisting power, and hence contributes local plateaus and terrace and level lands to the topography of the basin. These local features are best seen west of the central areas of the basin in Wilson, Sumner, Davidson, Williamson, and Maury counties, and include some of the fairest and best farming tracts in Middle Tennessee. The soil, when first cultivated, is a rich brown loam, with a subsoil usually yellow, but sometimes reddish-yellow. The latter also is often made more or less gravelly by thin, sandy fragments, the *débris* of the disintegrated rocks. This soil is mellow, warm, well drained, and easily cultivated—characteristics which make it a favorite cotton soil—and its areas are generally known as poplar lands, the so-called "poplar" (*Liriodendron*) being, or having been, a very characteristic tree of its forests. Its growth, besides poplar, includes beech in places, especially on the slopes and in the heads of hollows, ash, sugar-tree, oaks, elms, dogwood, hickories, hackberry, black walnut, linden, box-elder, and other species, the variety being remarkably great. It must be stated, however, that the lands of this bed are not uniformly good, for tracts occur, especially on the slopes and ridges, where the soil has been washed or leached or otherwise impoverished, and the lands reduced to third rate, supporting an uninviting native growth. In cultivated fields in rolling or hilly regions, especially if old, it is no uncommon thing to see naked, badly washed, and "scalded" places with soil all gone, spotting at intervals along the slopes the horizontal line of the outcrop of the bed. These bare places are made so by careless cultivation and inattention.

The following analyses are given of lands of this region, the samples being obtained from localities lying well, and among the best and most beautiful agricultural sections in the state:

No. 11. "*Poplar*" *land soil* from Vanleer Polk's place, Maury county. Depth taken, 11 inches; timber growth, "poplar", sweet gum, walnut, oak, ash, elm, hackberry, honey-locust, and dogwood. Originally covered with cane.

No. 12. *Subsoil* of the above, taken at a depth of from 11 to 23 inches.

No. 13. "*Poplar*" *land soil* from the Hermitage, Davidson county. Depth taken, 10 inches ; timber growth about the same as that of soil No. 11.

No. 14. *Subsoil* of the above, taken at a depth of from 10 to 22 inches.

Poplar lands of the Central Basin.

	MAURY COUNTY.		DAVIDSON COUNTY.	
	VANLEER POLK'S PLACE.		HERMITAGE.	
	Soil.	Subsoil.	Soil.	Subsoil.
	No. 11.	No. 12.	No. 13.	No. 14.
Insoluble matter	79.270 } 84.742	73.340 } 84.871	78.800 } 85.760	75.100 } 84.080
Soluble silica	5.472 }	8.531 }	8.900 }	8.930 }
Potash	0.310	0.377	0.098	0.084
Soda	0.858	0.556	0.047	0.114
Lime	0.515	0.547	0.378	0.468
Magnesia	0.342	0.358	0.308	0.444
Brown oxide of manganese	0.040	0.088	0.003	0.054
Peroxide of iron	3.663	3.283	2.627	3.692
Alumina	5.594	7.120	6.060	6.970
Phosphoric acid	0.349	0.342	0.255	0.318
Sulphuric acid	0.192	0.107	0.085	0.056
Water and organic matter	4.749	3.872	4.498	2.483
Total	100.084	99.497	100.415	99.729
Hygroscopic moisture	8.02	11.43	16.02	16.00
absorbed at	29 C.°	29 C.°	26.2 C.°	26.2 C.°

[The common and prominent characteristics of all of these poplar soils is a very unusually high percentage of phosphoric acid, accompanied by a large supply of lime,—two prime conditions of thriftiness and durability. The supply of potash also is ample, and with a high hygroscopic power and easy tillage shows them to be altogether excellent soils.—E. W. H.]

5. MULATTO LANDS OF THE NASHVILLE SERIES.—In this subdivision we include all the remaining Silurian limestones above the Orthis bed. The series in the northern part of the basin is from 400 to 500 feet in thickness, but in the southern and southwestern part its thickness is much reduced. Here, too, its lowest layers often contribute to the topmost of the Orthis bed in making the underlying rock of many nearly level and superior agricultural tracts. It is in the main a sandy or earthy highly fossiliferous limestone, containing in its composition all the inorganic and some of the organic elements of exceedingly fertile and mellow soils. It is named, by way of distinction, the *Nashville series*, being well displayed about the city, especially on the higher grounds. The area of the outcrop of these rocks, and hence the area of the soils derived from them, sweeps around the basin in a ring or circular belt outside of the concentric outcrops and soils of the limestones already mentioned. This ring is much the wider on the western and southern sides, and supplies large and valuable tracts of land in the counties of Trousdale, Sumner, Davidson, Williamson, Maury, Giles, Lincoln, and Moore. The surface is in places level or gently rolling; then it becomes hilly, especially as we go westward toward the limit of the basin. On the eastern side, in Smith, De Kalb, the southeastern part of Wilson, Cannon, the southern part of Rutherford, and the eastern part of Bedford, the ring is not so wide. Here, however, numerous beautiful valleys and tracts occur, many of which, as we approach the eastern side of the basin, are separated by high ridges with exceedingly rich and fertile slopes. In fact, the sides of the basin all around are fringed with bold spurs, whose limestone slopes have unsurpassed fertility of soil. With these may be included the slopes of such high knobs and ridges as exist within the basin. Of the latter, Elk ridge, already spoken of, with its northern face and declivities in the southern parts of Maury, Marshall, and Bedford, and its southern ramifications in Giles, Lincoln, and Moore, is a noted example. Altogether, the aggregate area of the lands of the Nashville series must be one-half or more of the entire area of the basin. The soils are mulatto-colored loams with yellow subsoils, the latter tempered with cherty gravel and siliceous remains of fossils. Approaching the spurs and ridges, we often find the soils and subsoils of the slopes much mixed with gravelly *débris* that has been washed down or otherwise brought down from the siliceous sub-Carboniferous rocks that cap these jetting arms of the highlands. The growth presents a rich flora, including many species, among which may be mentioned great bur or overcup oaks, elms, ash, hickories, linden, black walnut, cucumber-tree, mulberry, cherry, and, on hill sides, yellow wood, coffee trees, butternut, and black locusts. Excepting in the more southern counties of the basin, the soils of the series are not considered as among the best for cotton, as the plant grows too luxuriantly, and does not mature in season. In Giles and Lincoln, however, they are, with the creek and river bottoms, chiefly relied upon for the production of cotton. In the southern part of Marshall, and in some parts of Maury and Williamson also, a good share of their areas is devoted to cotton culture. The following analyses are given of samples of this land:

No. 9. *Mulatto clay soil* from Belle Meade, a few miles west of Nashville, Davidson county. Depth taken, 8 inches; timber growth, oaks, elm, hickory, ash, linden, sugar maple, hornbeam, walnut, cherry, dogwood, and red-bud. Originally with an undergrowth of cane.

No. 10. *Subsoil* of the above. Depth taken, 8 to 20 inches.

No. 6. *Subsoil* from near the above. Depth taken, 8 to 20 inches.

Mulatto clay lands of Nashville, Davidson county.

	Soil. No. 9.	Subsoil. No. 10.	Subsoil. No. 6.
Insoluble matter	56.540 } 63.380	47.950 } 58.960	54.932 } 65.472
Soluble silica	8.840	11.010	10.540
Potash	0.408	0.732	0.242
Soda	0.108	0.174	0.054
Lime	6.540	8.362	3.015
Magnesia	0.509	0.615	0.673
Brown oxide of manganese.................	0.187	0.091	0.192
Peroxide of iron	7.286	9.584	9.761
Alumina.	12.419	17.303	15.272
Phosphoric acid	0.563	0.335	0.175
Sulphuric acid	0 156	0.188	0.119
Water and organic matter	6.214	3.501	4.268
Total	99.994	99.905	100.145
Humus	1.676	....	....
Available phosphoric acid	0.179	....	....
Hygroscopic moisture	10.55	11.01	9.70
absorbed at	26.6 C.°	26.6 C.°	17.8 C.°

[The extraordinary percentage of phosphoric acid in soil No. 9 and its subsoil (the former exceeding all others heretofore analyzed), together with the unusual predominance of lime and large supply of potash, shows sufficient cause for the high estimate placed upon their productiveness, and gives promise of almost indefinite durability.— E. W. H.]

The following mechanical analysis has been made of the mulatto clay subsoil No. 10, of Belle Meade, near Nashville, by M. E. Jaffa, of the University of California:

Per cent.

Clay	27. 930
Sediment of < 0.25ᵐᵐ by hydraulic value	29. 203
Sediment of < 0.25ᵐᵐ by hydraulic value	4. 315
Sediment of < 0.50ᵐᵐ by hydraulic value	6. 799
Sediment of < 1.00ᵐᵐ by hydraulic value	5. 802
Sediment of < 2.00ᵐᵐ by hydraulic value	3. 390
Sediment of < 4.00ᵐᵐ by hydraulic value	2. 994
Sediment of < 8.00ᵐᵐ by hydraulic value	6. 967
Sediment of <16.00ᵐᵐ by hydraulic value	3. 936
Sediment of <32.00ᵐᵐ by hydraulic value	5. 096
Sediment of <64.00ᵐᵐ by hydraulic value	0. 495
Total	96. 927

The following abstracts are given in further illustration of the general features of the basin:

CHARLES F. VANDERFORD, RUTHERFORD COUNTY (central limestone area): The country around Florence station is referred to, which includes the first and second bottoms of Overall creek and Stone's river, together with the more extensive moderately rolling uplands. The region is nearly or quite surrounded by ridges and knobs from 50 to 100 feet high, which are mostly covered with a forest growth of cedar ("glades"). These cedar-covered ridges influence the winds and give us a local climate nearly as equable and quite as warm as that of the Tennessee valley in Madison and Limestone counties of Alabama. The kinds of soil cultivated in cotton are: (1) Red clay loam brown when fresh) on uplands and slopes; (2) second bottoms, found at the bases of slopes; (3) river or creek bottoms, excellent for cotton when well drained. The chief soil is the brown or red clay loam, about three-fifths of the land being of this kind, which extends over an area embracing something more than 110 square miles. The native growth is white, black, red, and post oaks, elms, poplar, black walnut, hickories, wild cherry, black locust, and honey-locust. The soil is from 6 to 20 inches in thickness; the subsoil is a rather stiff clay, for the most part mixed with rotten and comminuted limestone and chert, which changes by weathering so as to become nearly as fertile as the surface soil. Clay thrown from railroad cuts or from wells, after exposure for a few months, will produce almost any crop, and such clays are used with very satisfactory results as a top-dressing for certain of our black soils. The subsoil is underlaid by limestone at from 8 to 20 feet. Our cotton lands are very retentive, and are easily worked when in proper condition; but they are much injured if worked when too wet, for then in dry weather they become very hard and difficult to manage. Properly handled, however, the most retentive soils work easily and withstand drought as well as if thoroughly underdrained. This peculiarity is due to the large proportion of fragmentary chert which is found intermixed with all the undersoils of this region. The chief crops are cotton, corn, wheat, oats, and clover, the uplands and second bottoms being best for cotton, wheat, and oats, and the second and first bottoms for corn and cotton. About one-third of the land is put in cotton.

DR. J. W. DAVIS, RUTHERFORD COUNTY (central limestone area): The region of Stewart's creek and lands thereabout, embracing a part of Stone's river, includes first and second bottoms and uplands. The upland soil is generally good. In the bottoms cotton is late and is sometimes injured by frost. After several years' cultivation, however, and in dry seasons, the bottoms make the heaviest crops. The soils cultivated in cotton are: (1) Brown upland, with red clay subsoil; (2) dark sandy land of Stewart's creek bottom above overflow; (3) light sandy bottoms of Stone's river. Of these the brown upland is the chief, making three-fourths of the whole. The extent of this soil is, across the streams, from 4 to 6 miles; with them, from 20 to 30 miles. Its growth is poplar, ash, walnut, oak, elm, sugar-tree, dogwood, and ironwood. Its depth ranges from 4 to 12 inches. Under the best lands the subsoil is a fine red clay, containing sometimes flinty gravel, and is underlaid by limestone at from 1 foot to 20 feet. The land is tilled with difficulty in wet weather, but easily in dry weather if not too dry. The chief crops are cotton, corn, oats, rye, wheat, and clover. The soil is best adapted to corn and cotton, though clover and wheat do well. From one-third to one-half is planted in cotton.

REV. M. F. THOMPSON AND B. F. RANSOM, BEDFORD COUNTY (central limestone area): The lands are those of Fall creek and the north fork of Duck river. They are in bodies of from 5 to 50 acres or more. The only circumstance of "local climate" influencing cotton growing is the shortness of the season, as the cotton is liable to be late and prematurely frost-bitten. The chief soil is the red upland, lying in level or rolling bodies, known as red land, and forms about one-fifth of the area of the region referred to. It extends 10 miles east and west, and as many miles north and south, and has a growth of hickory, dogwood, and walnut. It is a light clay loam with an average thickness of about 8 inches. The subsoil is a tough red clay, which bakes hard when exposed, but generally becomes by cultivation like the surface soil. It is not impervious, contains small angular gravel, and is underlaid by limestone at from 5 to 10 feet. In tilling qualities the soil is fair, and is early when well drained. Its chief crops are corn, grass, and wheat, below apparently best adapted to the first two. A small proportion of cotton is planted. The uplands are, however, various, their bodies of cultivated soil alternating with "cedar roughs", or rocky, glady places. Bedford, as a whole, cannot be considered a cotton-growing area, all the cotton produced being raised in the northwestern quarter of the county. We have no cotton plantations proper. With the exception of one crop of 60 acres, I know of no other crop of over 20 acres. Two-thirds of the cotton raised is from patches of less than 5 acres.

J. B. EZELL, MARSHALL COUNTY: The first and second bottoms and the generally level uplands of Spring creek and Duck river are the lands reported upon. The soils cultivated in cotton are brown and black upland soils, occurring mostly in fields of from 10 to 30 acres. Three-fourths of the lands in this region are of this kind, and extend 10 miles to the east, west, and south, and 4 miles north. The growth is red and black oak, ash, elm, and dogwood. The soils are a clay loam from 4 to 6 inches thick; the subsoils are gravelly. Limestone lies from 2 to 5 feet from the surface. The soils are very difficult to till in wet seasons, but easy in dry. Their crops are corn, oats, wheat, and cotton, but they are best suited to the first two. Cotton makes about 20 per cent. of the crops. There is very little difference in our upland soils.

E. H. THORNTON, WILSON COUNTY: The lands cultivated in cotton in Wilson are mostly on Hurricane, Sugg's, and Sinking creeks. Some is also raised near Lagnardo, and on Barton's and Cedar creeks. None is raised in the eastern part of the county. The lowlands are creek bottoms, generally with a black loam soil; and some lands on the banks of the Cumberland river are sandy. The uplands consist of the lands of Poplar ridge, and also of red cedar lands in the southern part of the county. The season is hardly long enough for cotton to mature; the greatest danger being the autumn frost. The soils cultivated in cotton are: (1) The poplar ridge lands (chiefly soils of the Orthis bed) in the middle part of the county; (2) the red cedar lands (of the central, glade, and Carter's Creek limestones) in the southern part of the county. These include all our cotton lands. The poplar ridge lands extend 10 miles in a northern and southern direction, and 20 miles in an eastern and western direction. The red cedar lands extend 12 miles in a northern and southern direction, and 10 or 12 miles east and west. The growth of the first kind is poplar, hickory, and oak; that of the second, oak, hickory, ash, and cedar, the latter chiefly in the glades. The crops produced are principally corn, oats, wheat, cotton, tobacco, and vegetables. The soil is apparently best adapted to corn and hay. The cotton planted forms about 4 per cent. of the crops.

S. R. DOXEY, SUMNER COUNTY (Orthis bed): Lands of the waters of Drake's creek and Cumberland river. The first and second bottoms are cultivated principally in corn. The uplands only are used for cotton. It will not open in the lowlands before frost. Soil No. 1 is about two weeks earlier than No. 2. The former is sandy and warm; the latter, more clayey, retains water longer, and is cooler. The soils are: (1) Yellow poplar land, lying on plains, ridges, and slopes; (2) dark loam, known as blue-grass land. There is but little of the yellow poplar land, which lies not far from the creek and river and runs along the north side of the latter in a strip for 5 miles or more. Its growth is poplar, gum, hickory, maple, ash, elm, walnut, some beech, dogwood, and ironwood. The soil is a fine sandy friable loam, brown and yellow, with a thickness of from 6 to 20 inches; the subsoil a deep yellow clay, containing more or less small gravel, underlaid by clay and rock at from 2 to 10 feet. It is not worked in wet weather, and is easily tilled in dry. The chief crops produced are cotton, corn, wheat, oats, potatoes, and grasses. In the particular region described the proportion of cotton planted is from one-fourth to one-half of all.

B. GRAY, DAVIDSON COUNTY: Hilly and level uplands of Hurricane creek, a tributary of Stone's river. The soils cultivated in cotton are: (1) Red clay lands, strongly calcareous, reaching from this point eastward and extensively into Rutherford county; (2) black loam, with yellowish clay subsoil, extending west, and also south into Williamson and north into Wilson county. The chief soils are the red clay lands. These are gently undulating, not hilly, and make about one-third of the lands in this region. The growth is poplar, oak, ash, some sugar-tree, elm, and hickory. These lands adjoin or alternate with "cedar glades". The soil is from 8 to 10 inches thick, and is early, warm, and naturally well drained. The chief crops are cotton, corn, and wheat, with also German millet for seed. Over one-half of the land is devoted to cotton, the lands appearing best adapted to this staple. The black loam, amounting to about two-thirds of the lands, extends north, south, and west for at least 15 miles. Its growth is poplar, oak, elm, ash, sugar-tree, beech, walnut, ironwood, dogwood, with here and there a patch of cedar on rocky places. The soil is from 8 to 12 inches thick, is easily tilled in dry weather, and is best adapted to corn. About one-sixth is planted in cotton.

J. M. TURNER, EDGEFIELD JUNCTION, DAVIDSON COUNTY: The first and second bottoms of the Cumberland river have a freestone (Orthis bed) soil, generally sandy, with, say, one-sixth part of a blackish mucky nature. These are the cotton soils: the first mahogany and gravelly, and the second sandy. The yellow mahogany is the chief soil, and forms three-fourths of the lands of this region. It extends northward about 15 miles, eastward 4 miles, southward 20 miles or more, and westward 4 miles. Its growth is elm, ash, poplar, hackberry, walnut, and sugar-tree. This soil has a depth of from 2 to 6 inches, a subsoil of yellow, heavy, stiff clay, often impervious to water, and is underlaid by limestone at from 1 foot to 20 feet. The land is easily tilled, and is early, warm, and well drained. It is not so well adapted to cotton as to other crops, though farmers raise more cotton than anything else, because it brings more ready money. About one-half is planted in cotton. The second or sandy soil forms about one-eighth of our lands, and has limited extent. Among its trees are sweet and black gum, oak, poplar, and beech. It is a fine sandy loam, 10 inches thick. The land is warm, easily tilled, and is best adapted to cotton, two-thirds of it being planted with this staple.

JOHN S. CLAYBROOKE AND S. A. POINTER, WILLIAMSON COUNTY: The lands of Aenon, Wilson's, and Harpeth creeks and the bottoms of Duck and Big Harpeth rivers are referred to. Duck River ridge, dividing the waters of Duck river from those of Big Harpeth, runs northeastward and southwestward through my place, "Wheatland." The uplands are rolling and level on the waters of the creeks mentioned. The shortness of the growing season forces us to put our best lands in cotton and work well. so as to push the plant and make it mature and open early. The writer has contended for many years that Williamson, Maury, and Giles counties afford, perhaps, the best cotton land in the south, and that, taking a number of years together, it would produce (not being subject to overflows, etc.) more to the acre than any section south of us. The cotton soils are: (1) Mulatto soil, on which grow white oak and white poplar, and, as we approach the hills, black soil with yellow poplar, large beech, and gum; (2) light sandy, white-oak soil, washing badly; (3) red soil (of Carter's Creek limestone) near and in the cedars. The chief one is the white poplar mulatto soil, embracing, while confined to Williamson and Maury counties, nearly all the lands for seventy miles on both sides of Duck and Big Harpeth rivers. In general, they extend from Brentwood to Mount Pleasant, an area of 50 miles in length and 10 miles in breadth. The mulatto soil is about 1 foot deep, with a clay foundation; the black from 1 foot to 3 feet, without clay foundation, the soil generally extending down to the rock. This is superior corn land. The mulatto and black soils contain but little gravel, and are underlaid by limestone at from 2 to 10 feet. We frequently cultivate from 8 to 10 acres to the hand. As to crops, wheat predominates; but cotton and corn are raised largely, with some barley and oats. The land is best adapted to cotton and wheat. About one-third of the land is put in cotton. The second kind of soil, the light sandy, occurs in small proportion in this region, and is met with for 4 or 5 miles east of the Columbia pike. A strip 30 miles long and 5 miles wide lies in the eastern part of Williamson and Maury. Much of this land is second rate, and produces little cotton. The third kind, red soil, near or in the cedars, occurs in large areas in the eastern parts of Maury and Williamson, and extends into Marshall and Rutherford counties. Like the last mentioned, much of it is second rate.

W. O. GORDON, MAURY COUNTY: The lands of the waters of Carter's creek embrace rich bottoms, second bottoms, rolling and hilly uplands, with respectively black, mulatto, and gravelly soils. The lands cultivated in cotton are: (1) The mulatto or poplar lands, supplying the best and surest yield; (2) the high gravelly hills or ridges, which are next preferred; (3) bottom lands, good if the fall is late, but not so reliable. The chief kind is the poplar uplands with mulatto soil. About one-third of the land is of this kind. They extend 30 miles northward and southward, but the best quality predominates from Ewell's southward to Mount Pleasant. It is a light sandy clay loam, about 9 inches deep, with a clay subsoil of stronger color, mixed more or less with gravel, and resting on rock at 4 feet. The soil is easily tilled in dry weather, and is early, warm, and well drained. It produces chiefly corn, wheat, and cotton; also oats, rye, and Irish and sweet potatoes, but is best suited to corn. About 30 per cent. of cotton is planted. Of the second kind, high gravelly lands, we have about 25 per cent., which lie on the tops and slopes of the highest ridges, the spurs of the highlands west of us, and the dividing ridges, like Elk ridge. The soil is gravelly, light, and loose, with gravelly subsoil. It is more easily tilled in wet weather, is early, warm, and well drained, and is best adapted to corn, cotton, and wheat. Allowing for roughness, these lands are the surest for the crops just mentioned. About 5 per cent. of cotton is planted, but more would be were it not for the rough hoeing. Of the third kind, bottom lands, we have about 40 per cent. They are best adapted to corn and hay. The cotton cultivated amounts to about 10 per cent. of the crops.

L. E. POLK, MAURY COUNTY: The lands referred to are the rolling and level uplands of the waters of Duck river. The soils cultivated in cotton are: (1) The yellow-poplar soil, or highlands, with chocolate-colored soil and yellow subsoil; (2) black sandy soil. The first is the chief soil, and 85 per cent. of the lands are of this kind. They have a wide extent within the basin of Middle

Tennessee. The growth is remarkable for its variety. Among the trees we have the large elm, oaks, poplar, sugar-tree, ash, beech in places, hickories, walnut, cherry, linden, box-elder, hackberry, and the black locust. The soil is a gravelly loam, alternating with a clay loam. The subsoil is gravelly, with good drainage capacity, and when exposed to the sun and air produces well. It is underlaid by limestone at from 6 to 20 feet. The soil is easily tilled in wet or dry seasons. The crops produced are corn, wheat, oats, and cotton, but the soil is apparently best adapted to corn and grass. About 15 per cent. of the tilled land is put in cotton. The second kind, the black sandy soil, making about 15 per cent. of the lands, alternates with the other over much of the basin. Its growth is much like that of the first, excepting that poplar is rarely seen. It is a deep soil in low places and branch bottoms with gravelly subsoil, which rests upon gravel and rock at from 2 to 6 feet from the surface. It is early, warm, and well drained. Cotton is cultivated upon 25 per cent. of this land.

LEON FRIERSON, MAURY COUNTY: First and second bottoms and rolling uplands of the Big Bigby river. The rolling land was originally rich brown loam, interspersed with black spots, but is now in many places much worn. We have, strictly speaking, no uplands, as this portion of the county lies within the Central Basin; so we use the term relatively. The soils cultivated in cotton are: (1) "Mulatto lands," or dark loam; (2) black porous soil, very loose (corn planted in it "frenches"); (3) gravelly soil, of which there is very little. The mulatto or dark loam lands are the chief, three-fourths being of this kind. The soil is from 12 to 18 inches thick, with a stiff clay subsoil, which changes to soil after it freezes and thaws. In some places the soil is mixed with coarse gravel. Limestone is met with at from 5 to 10 feet from the surface. The soil is best adapted to cotton and corn. One-third is planted in cotton. The second, the black, porous soil, forms a fourth of our lands. It is generally interspersed with the first all through this section of country, is 24 inches thick, and has a yellow, sticky clay for its subsoil, which is impervious to water if undisturbed. It contains gravel, and is underlaid by limestone at a depth of from 3 to 6 feet from the surface. This land is best adapted to wheat and oats. But little cotton is planted.

J. E. ABERNATHY, W. RIVERS, AND D. T. REYNOLDS, GILES COUNTY: These lands comprise the first and second bottoms and the rolling and hilly uplands of Big and Richland creeks. The uplands to a certain altitude are underlaid by limestone; above that by a flinty rock. All are rich and productive. Cotton in the lowlands is liable to be late and to be killed by frost, and is also more subject to rust. These lands, when fresh, with abundant vegetable matter and in favorable seasons, are very productive. We now prefer the uplands. The lands cultivated in cotton are: (1) Second bottoms above overflow; (2) uplands below the level of the flint formation; (3) uplands on the flint formation. The chief soil is that of the second bottoms, forming one-fourth of our soil and extending over a good part of the basin of Middle Tennessee. It is a mahogany colored clay loam with a hard clay subsoil, pulverizing readily. It is easily cultivated when well drained, is early and warm, and produces cotton, corn, and wheat, but is best adapted to corn, though all grow well. The cotton planted is about one-third of the crops. The second kind, uplands below the flints, comprise about one-third of the lands. These occur on the slopes of the ridges throughout the county, and are in native growth, color of soil, character of crops, and proportion of cotton planted much like the second bottoms. The third kind, the uplands on the flint, occur near and on the summits of the ridges throughout the county. Their timber is yellow and white poplar, beech, oaks, chestnut, hickory, ash, sassafras, and elm. It is a gravelly clay loam, but flint and gravel make it dark gray. Its subsoil is yellow clay, mixed with gravel. It is best for corn, though all crops grow well. Very little cotton is planted. Cultivation is more difficult than in the case of other lands, on account of the excess of coarse gravel present.

J. D. TILLMAN, LINCOLN COUNTY: The first and second bottoms of Elk river are considered. Cotton is liable to be killed by frost. The lands cultivated in cotton are: (1) The alluvial bottoms of Elk river, containing sand; (2) uplands of mellow formation, breaking up without clods or lumps. The chief kinds are called "cotton lands", which form about one-twentieth of our tillable areas, and extend from the headwaters of the Elk river to its mouth. Their growth is hickory, oak, poplar, sycamore, black locust, and honey-locust. The soil is fine silt and sandy, gravelly loam of a brown or dark color, with a clay subsoil; sand, gravel, or limestone lie below at from 3 to 20 feet. This soil is easily tilled in dry weather, and produces corn, oats, clover, wheat, and cotton, but is best adapted to the first three. About one-twentieth of all the land planted is in cotton.

THE CUMBERLAND TABLE-LAND.

Leaving the Central Basin, and crossing the eastern division of the Highland Rim, we reach the foot of the western escarpment of the Cumberland table-land, an elevated and sharply outlined division of the state. This is usually called Cumberland mountain, but it is better designated as table-land. It is, as already said, a plateau with broad and generally level top, standing in bold relief above the lowlands on each side, the rim lands on the west and the East Tennessee-valley lands on the east rising up, in round numbers, 1,000 feet above these and 2,000 feet above the sea. It is the Tennessee coal-field, and embraces an area of 5,100 square miles—about one-eighth of the state. The form, relative size, and oblique northeasterly and southwesterly position of the table-land are seen upon the agricultural map, and is the portion marked 12a, and colored. (See also diagram.) Within its limits are included Scott, Morgan, and Cumberland counties, and the greater parts, severally, of Fentress, Van Buren, Grundy, Bledsoe, Sequatchie, and Marion, with considerable portions of Overton, Putnam, White, Warren, Coffee, and Franklin on the west, and of Claiborne, Campbell, Anderson, Rhea, and Hamilton on the east. The western edge of the division is notched and escaloped by deep coves and valleys, which are separated by finger like spurs pointing westward, while its eastern edge is a nearly direct or gracefully curving line. At almost all points, on both sides, the surface suddenly breaks off in sandstone cliffs from 20 to 200 feet in height, giving everywhere a sharp and prominent margin or brow to the division. Commencing in the very body of the division, near the middle of the state, and extending southwestward into Alabama, the table-land is completely split longitudinally in two by the deep Sequatchie valley, a narrow, straight trough, 60 miles long, and averaging not more than 4 miles in width, if as much. Of the two arms thus formed, that to the west of the valley mentioned retains the name Cumberland, while that to the east is known as Walden's ridge.

The surface of the table-land is often flat for miles, with an open growth, mostly of oaks; then again it is rolling and diversified with hills and shallow valleys. In the northeastern part are high ridges, which may be regarded as mountains on the table-land. The division is very generally capped with sandstone, and shales are sometimes met with. The soils are thin, sandy, and porous, and are decidedly poor as compared with the limestone regions we have considered. In some sections they afford a pasturage of wild grasses. Apples and grapes often do well, and so do garden vegetables and Irish potatoes with plenty of manure. Here and there, on slopes at the foot of knobs or ridges and along streams, more fertile areas are found, where land is cultivated, but in the aggregate farming operations on the table-land amount to very little. In general, the population is sparse, and wide regions without an inhabitant are traversed. The mountain, however, has attractions outside of its agricultural features which have drawn to certain localities many enterprising men, resulting in the building up of towns and intelligent communities. A very great accession is the establishment of the University of the South at Sewanee. By reference to the percentage map of acreage in cotton it will be seen that this division has no value as a cotton-producing area. Now and then little patches are seen in which some cotton is raised for domestic purposes, but the cotton reported in Table I as produced by this division was almost wholly raised on the lowland portions of the counties enumerated. Very little, in any case, is to be referred to the table-land proper.

We pass now from the sandy top of the table-land to the rich limestone declivities which make its sides. Below the great cap of the mountain—a cap made up of sandstones, shales, and coal-beds interstratified—there is everywhere a great limestone bed, known as "mountain limestone", whose strata outcrop on all sides. The outcrops along the western side or slopes, which have more agricultural importance than the eastern, make at least two-thirds of the ascent from the base up. The surface is generally rocky, with very little soil. At intervals, however, bodies of land are met with which are rich and fertile. Not much of this land has been brought into cultivation, but now and then a small farm or a field shows itself as an open spot among the trees on the face of the ascent as one travels the lowland roads parallel with the mountain. The slopes are in the main covered with heavy forests, the trees, often of large size—poplar, black and white walnut, white oak, linden, mulberry, hackberry, species of ash, cherry-tree, together with the cucumber-tree, the great-leaf magnolia, papaw, and others—making a rich forest flora.

North of McMinnville a bench or terrace is very generally to be seen running along the slopes of the table-land and about half-way up. This comes from a thin sandstone, which in this region is interpolated in the series of mountain limestones. Immediately west of the main mountain and its outliers are many flat-topped ridges and "little mountains", which have the same height as the benches, and are capped with the same sandstone. The flat summits of all of these have a rich, mellow soil, often sandy, upon which corn and wheat grow luxuriantly, and present favorite areas for orchards. Cotton, which is now occasionally seen in "patches", would, in a more southern climate, do well upon them. We add that at the foot of the main mountain, as well as around the outliers, there is often much good land. This is especially true of the coves, some of which are noted for rich and beautiful farming areas. Going westward, these soils soon run into the red clay soils of the Highland Rim; in fact, they, as well as the soils of the steep mountain slopes, might have been considered consecutively after the red soils of the rim, since their underlying limestones belong to the same group, the sub-Carboniferous. In the southern part of the state cotton was formerly cultivated to a considerable extent in the coves and elsewhere along the base of the mountain, but now but little of it is raised. Below is an abstract from a report on lands in a mountain-hemmed valley, which may be regarded as a long cove in the table-land, having the same limestones as those referred to for its floor, and bearing the same relation to the mountain sides :

JOHN F. ANDERSON, FRANKLIN COUNTY: The district is bounded on the south by the Alabama line. The first and second bottoms of Crow creek, a tributary of the Tennessee river, are considered, together with the mountain slopes on each side of the Crow Creek valley. Occasionally cotton is injured by late northwest winds, and cold rains cause rust or "sore-shin"; but we are so protected by the mountains that such damage is rare. I consider this the best part of Franklin for cotton. All vegetables are two weeks earlier here than elsewhere in the county. The kinds of soil cultivated in cotton are: (1) Alluvial soils, differing greatly in character along the creek; (2) yellowish or reddish lands, sometimes black, based on limestone, and fertile; (3) mountain side, very rocky, soil thin, and not much cultivated. The chief lands are the alluvial or bottom lands. Two-thirds of the cultivated areas are of this kind, and extend along the valley for 12 or 14 miles with a width of from a fourth to half a mile. The growth is sycamore, willow, beech, sugar-tree, black walnut, ash, hackberry, elm, and linden. The soil is 24 to 30 inches deep. The subsoil is compact, coarse, gravelly, and rests upon limestone, the latter lying at from 2 to 24 feet below the surface. The land is usually tilled with little trouble, is early when well drained, and produces as chief crops corn and cotton; but it is best adapted to corn. One-fourth of the total acreage is put in cotton. The second kind of soil, the yellowish or reddish land, makes a third of our tillable areas, and extends through the valley in narrow strips outside of the alluvial lands. Its growth is cedar, white oak, beech, yellow poplar, hickory, black walnut, elm, linden, and hackberry. The subsoil contains much flinty gravel. The limestone lies below the surface at from 1 foot to 10 feet. The soil is easy to cultivate and produces well, and is best adapted to cotton, which forms about a fourth of the crops. The lands of the mountain sides are fully equal in area to the tillable lands below. The growth is made up of a great variety of timber. It is best adapted to corn, vegetables, and fruits. No cotton is raised upon it. The lands on the top of the mountain are good for tobacco, Irish potatoes, and fruit of all kinds.

THE VALLEY OF EAST TENNESSEE.

Passing in our course eastward the Cumberland table-land, with its flat areas, oak woods, and sandy soils, we find ourselves in the great and populous valley of East Tennessee, with its diversified rocks, soil, and scenery.(a) This division has been briefly characterized on a former page. Within it is embraced nearly all the

___

a It may be noted that the Cumberland table-land, rising so boldly above the general level of the state, separates two of the great sections of Tennessee—sections great in area, wealth, and population : the Central Basin, with the best of the rim uplands around it, on the west, and the valley of East Tennessee on the east. The comparatively barren table-land has always been a serious obstacle in the way of free intercourse between these sections. Even now no railroad crosses it within the state. To pass from Nashville to Knoxville it is necessary to make a great detour to the south through Alabama.

agricultural wealth which is usually accredited to the civil division we call East Tennessee. Its oblique position relative to the northern and southern boundaries of the state and its shape are seen in the cut on page 11, as well as on the agricultural map. Its area extends through the state from Virginia to Georgia, and is included between the Cumberland table-land on the west and the Unaka mountains on the east or southeast, its lateral limits being clearly defined by these mountains. (a) It includes the following counties and parts of counties: The whole of James, Bradley, McMinn, Meigs, Loudon, Roane, Knox, Jefferson, Union, Grainger, Hamblen, Hancock, Hawkins, Washington, and Sullivan, parts of Marion, Sequatchie, Bledsoe, Hamilton, Rhea, Anderson, Campbell, and Claiborne (the other parts of these being on the table-land), and parts of Polk, Monroe, Blount, Sevier, Cocke, Greene, Unicoi, Carter, and Johnson (the remaining portions of the latter making up the area of the Unakas). Measured directly across in the northern part of the state, the area is 55 miles wide or thereabout. Toward the south the mountain barriers approach each other, and the width is reduced approximately to 34 miles, not including the outlier, Sequatchie valley. As seen from the high points of the Unaka mountains the valley of East Tennessee presents a wide-spreading floor—a vast, nearly level plain, limited on the west in the distance by the wall-like eastern escarpment of the Cumberland, and having but a few isolated ridges, like long narrow islands, projecting above the general surface. But when we descend from the mountains and travel across this floor it is anything but a level-plain, the whole becoming an area fluted with a multitude of smaller valleys and ridges—a furrowed field on a Titanic scale. The valleys and ridges are crowded together, and extend in parallel lines to the northeast and southwest, the prevailing directions in the valley of East Tennessee. The smaller streams take, in the main, either the one or the other course. The rivers flow to the southwest, or, in the case of those from North Carolina, make their way across the country by the shortest routes through gaps and breaks of the ridges to those that flow to the southwest. The railroads and other chief lines of travel and commerce run with the valleys. This northeasterly and southwesterly striation, if I may use the word, of the great valley, so far as its natural and many of its artificial characteristics are concerned, is strikingly seen on the geological and topographical as well as agricultural maps of the state. This is all due primarily to the fact that the rocky strata are greatly inclined or tilted so that their edges outcrop along the surface, which they do in northeasterly and southwesterly lines. Thus the rocks present themselves at the surface in long, narrow, parallel strips or belts with the trend indicated. The hard strata-like sandstones and cherty dolomites make the ridges; the soft, like limestones and shales, the valleys. The several soils of the valleys and ridges necessarily occur in strips as represented on the agricultural map. Some of the valleys, or valley ranges, though averaging hardly a mile in width, may be traced, or indeed traveled in, from Virginia to Georgia, a distance of 150 miles, to say nothing of their extension either way beyond the limits of the state. Certain ridges, straight or slightly curving, are equally long, and most of them may be followed for scores of miles. Some ridges are narrow and sharp, like a steep roof; others are wide, broadly rounded on top, and of far greater importance, of which Copper, Chestnut, and Missionary ridges are types. These are dolomite ridges, and their surfaces are strewed with cherty masses and gravel. The ridge upon which Knoxville is built is one of the latter, a range originating in the northern part of Knox county and traceable into the state of Georgia. Ridges of this type occasionally flatten out, giving us plateau areas of great agricultural value, such, for example, as the body of land traversed by the East Tennessee and Virginia railroad in Jefferson and Hamblen counties, or break up more or less into wide belts of cherty knobs, as those in Hamilton and Rhea, between the Tennessee river and the Cincinnati railroad, or those in Hamilton and James east of Missionary ridge, and crossed by the Chattanooga and Cleveland railroad. But these cherty dolomite knobs are not the only ones. The kinds of knobs characterizing the two areas designated respectively as the "red belt" (7c) and the "gray belt" (8c) on the map differ materially from those mentioned, and differ in a degree from each other. The red belt begins in Jefferson county, has its greatest width in Knox and Blount, and continues southwestward through other counties to the Georgia state line. (See map.) This area is remarkable for its long lines of red knobs and red lands. With the lines of knobs are intervening broken valleys. The soils are based upon calcareous shales, with which are interstratified very ferruginous sandy limestones, flaggy limestones, and red marbles. They are often very mellow and fertile, as upon the slopes of the knobs. The gray belt, so named from the prevalence of gray lands and earthy gray rocks, lies further to the eastward. It is a great club-shaped area commencing on the Virginia line and extending southwestward to the Hiawassee river, reaching, indeed, nearly through the state. (See map.) Its characteristic feature is found in its isolated and often crowded knobs, which beset the surface like monster ant-hills. Many portions of the belt are spoken of locally as "the knobs". These are conical hills of all heights, from 100 to 500 feet, and sometimes they are more or less elongated, forming short ridges; and in some regions, where closely set, they make a wild country traversed by narrow labyrinthine valleys. The formation of the area is a heavy body of sky-blue, calcareous, and often sandy shales, weathering to yellowish-gray or buff, and containing occasionally thin

a I include in this division, as outliers, the interesting valleys and coves which are more or less interlocked with the ridges of the mountains on each side. One of these, Sequatchie valley, splitting the southern portion of the table-land, has been spoken of. On the eastern side there are many, some of them noted for the attractiveness of their natural features. The cultivated part of one county, Johnson, in the northeastern part of the state, is a mountain-hemmed cove, with no way of getting in or out except by scaling mountains or by passing through dark and rocky water-gaps. Other interesting coves are Wear's, in Sevier county, and Tuckaleechee and Cade's, in Blount county.

flaggy limestones, and at some points thin sandstones. The belt often possesses a dark rich soil, supporting a growth of white oak, poplar, and hickory, and some portions abound in small farms between the knobs and on their slopes. In such regions we have what has been called "the poor man's rich land".

If we draw a line from Virginia to Georgia lengthwise through the middle of the great valley, splitting it into halves, the knobby belts we have just described will lie in the eastern or southeastern half. Besides these, there are in this part many ridges and valleys based on other rocks.. It is, however, in the other half of the valley, on the northwestern side of the median line, that we have the most characteristic display of the wonderfully long, yet narrow, parallel, and alternating valleys and ridges. The length of these has already been referred to. I add a word more as to the valleys. These are troughs between the ridges, and are wide or narrow in proportion to the separation of the latter. They vary in width from the fraction of a mile to 1 mile or 2 miles, not often more than this, and most of them are attractive and fertile. Some of the narrow ones are cold and unproductive. There are two principal classes, as will be hereafter noticed, the limestone valleys and the shale valleys, and both kinds in general are amply watered by streams abundantly supplied with free-flowing springs, well populated, abounding in arable fields. Each valley is a kingdom in itself, communities being separated from each other by the intervening ridges. Most of the population live in the valleys, though houses and farms are occasionally seen upon some of the ridges of the Copper Ridge type. For the most part, the ridges are the wooded portions of the country. Seen from a distance, they are marked out by lines of forests crowning the summits, which heighten the contrast between ridge and valley. The fields of the valleys often creep a long way up the slopes to the line of the trees.

For present purposes enough has been said as to the general character of the valley of East Tennessee. To go into detail, enumerating and describing all its numerous and varied features of structure and surface, would carry us far beyond reasonable limits. (a) Such detail can be dispensed with the better since the valley is not a cotton region proper. It belongs at most to the *penumbral region* of cotton culture. The whole yield reported for the census year, including also the little cotton raised in the mountain parts of such of its counties as reach out, respectively, upon the table-land and the Unakas, is only 537 bales, and of this more than 400 bales were raised in the valley portions of counties south of the latitude of Knoxville. (See percentage map of cotton culture.) In nearly all the counties quarter-acre or half-acre patches are occasionally met with, in which a little cotton is cultivated for home use.

The soils indicated upon the map and named in the legend have in part been noticed. The "*red belt*" (7c) and the "*gray belt*" (8c) have been sufficiently spoken of. The "*limestone lands of certain valleys in East Tennessee*" (8b) make some of the best agricultural belts of the division. They have blue limestone soils, the equivalents of the soils in the Central Basin, and nearly all the important valley ranges on the western or northwestern side of the median line of the division have these soils. Such are the valleys known as Powell's, Beaver creek, Raccoon, Hickory, Savannah, and others. They make the long valley ranges to which attention has been called, and are everywhere in cultivation and dotted with farm-houses. Toward the south, and before reaching the Georgia line, most of these valleys are pinched out, giving way to shale valley ranges or to ridges. On the east or southeast side of the median line there are very few of these, and they are unimportant. The "*calcareous shale and valley lands*" (9a) belong to a group of valleys equal in importance to those just mentioned. The rocks which supply the soils are variegated, chestnut-colored, greenish and buff shales, generally calcareous, and show now and then an interstratified layer of dolomite or limestone. This series is called the *Knox shale*. Many of the valleys are very desirable agricultural belts. In the southern part of the division especially a number of them are wide, gently rolling or level, and afford tracts of highly fertile land, often in a good state of cultivation. It is one of the important soils upon which cotton is cultivated. The soils are clayey, but are mellowed by the *débris* of thin sandy layers and by calcareous matter. On the west side of the median line the shale valleys, or valley ranges, when followed northeastward up the country, become very much narrowed, losing their importance. This is also the case to some extent on the eastern side of the valley. The "*magnesian limestone lands*" (10a) are those of level or rolling plateau belts, or of moderate slopes based on dolomites, and such as that above-mentioned traversed by the railroad in Jefferson and Hamblen counties. There are but few of these areas, and these are chiefly in the upper end of the valley. These soils are strong and fertile, and under cultivation. The subsoils are deep yellowish or reddish, and contain cherty gravel and masses of chert. These areas I have spoken of as dolomite ridges flattened out into plateau land. The "*ridge and cherty lands*" (10b) are those of many wide and rounded dolomite ridges in the valley, of which Copper, Chestnut, and Missionary ridges, before mentioned, are good examples. In these the rocky strata are usually concealed by a great depth of clayey, reddish subsoil, in which there is much chert and cherty gravel intermixed. The surface of the ridges is often so covered with flinty gravel as to supply natural macadam road-beds, over which it is pleasant to drive. The wooded summits, the encroachments of the cultivated fields upon the slopes, and the presence occasionally of houses and farms upon the ridges, have been referred to. In regard to alluvial lands, bottoms occur at intervals along the streams, there being noted ones on the French Broad, the Holston, Tennessee, and other rivers. The aggregate of such land, however, though very considerable, is limited in this division as compared with what we have in the western part of the state.

---

a For further information as to the physical and agricultural features of this division, see the writer's *Geology of Tennessee.*

Sequatchie valley is the most important outlier of the valley of East Tennessee. Its relation to the Cumberland table-land or mountain has been given in Part I under the head of that division. As there stated, it is a narrow, straight trough, 60 miles long, with an average width of not more than 4 miles, and lies compressed between the steep and parallel walls or edges of the table-land, which rise on both sides to an elevation of 1,000 feet and overshadow its area. Looking from these heights down upon the valley below, we see first a central, depressed, wide, and wooded ridge, running as far as the eye can reach lengthwise through the valley, and constituting the greater part of its surface, and then two cultivated valleys, one on each side of the ridge, between it and the foot of the mountain slopes. The rocks of the central ridge are dolomites, like those of Copper and Chestnut ridges in the main valley to the east, to which class of ridges it belongs, the cherty lands, native growth, etc., being similar. The valleys have strong soils based on blue limestones, and give a large aggregate of good farming lands. That on the eastern side, in its rocks and soils, is to be referred to the class of valleys, including Powell's, Beaver creek, Raccoon, and others, before mentioned. That on the west side has frequently more cherty limestones (mountain or Saint Louis) for its underlying rocks. The Tennessee river, breaking through the eastern arm of the mountain, enters the southern end of the valley and then flows in the extended course of the latter far into Alabama. Sequatchie river runs through the whole length of the valley, winding along for the most part, very curiously, in the ridge area, breaking up the latter here and there into hills and knobs.

But three reports have been received from counties in the valley of East Tennessee, abstracts of which are given in Part II, on page 92. As to the first, it may be noted that Chickamauga is near the Georgia line. Dolomite cherty ranges, as well as a valley of the Knox shales, pass through this region.

THE UNAKA MOUNTAIN REGION.

We have now reached the last of the eight natural divisions of Tennessee, the *Unaka Mountain region*. The general character of the division, its position, elevation, and area, are briefly given on page 14. It embraces the mountainous parts of Polk, Monroe, Blount, Sevier, Cocke, Greene, Unicoi, Carter, and Johnson counties. Including interlocked valleys and coves, the region is a long belt, with a width of about 13 miles, lying contiguous to the state of North Carolina, and reaching from Virginia to Georgia. (See 13 on the agricultural map.) It gives to the eastern end of Tennessee a greatly raised, cloud-capped border, strikingly in contrast with the low and often flooded plains of the western end. The included valleys and coves having been referred to and treated as outliers of the division last described, we are concerned here mainly with the mountains proper. The great ridges embraced in the division, and often named the Unakas, are arranged approximately in two principal chains, which are more or less crowded together in parallel lines. The chains are not continuous. The main one, the axis of the group (of which Catface mountain, the Yellow, the Roan, the various "Balds", the Great Smoky, and the Frog are some of the prominent points), is cut directly across by rivers, seven in number, which flow from the western slope of the Blue Ridge in North Carolina northwestward into Tennessee, passing the great axis in deep and magnificent water-gaps. The most westerly chain, of less average height (to which belong Star's, English's, Chilhowee Creek, Holston, and other mountains), was elevated by the original geological forces in detached ridges, often many miles apart, but arranged lengthwise, end facing end. Nevertheless, some of the isolated mountains—Star's and Chilhowee, for example—are cut in two by water-gaps. The portion of the main axis between the French Broad and Little Tennessee presents in its length of 65 miles a series of peaks but a few feet lower than the highest of the Black mountains in North Carolina. Many of these exceed 6,000 feet. Altogether, we have here without exception the boldest and greatest mountain mass to be found anywhere east of the Mississippi river, known as the Great Smoky. Farther to the northeast, in the section between the Watauga and Nolichucky, are several great ridges, among which we may mention the Roan. This, though not having the highest peaks, is in some respects the grandest mountain of the Unakas. Its summit, presenting a number of peaks more than 6,000 feet high, is in many places destitute of trees, owing to the low temperature of the heights. These are called "balds". On the Roan there is a succession of them, giving the broad summit at intervals a meadow-like aspect. Such places we have seen in the summer time alive with stock of all kinds, feeding and fattening upon the rich herbage. The "balds" are not confined to the Roan, but occur at many points along the summits of the main Unakas. As a rule, the ridges are clothed with forests. When, however, a height of about 5,000 feet above tide is reached, the deciduous trees—beeches, oaks, and maples—become more or less dwarfed, and often in ascending farther entirely disappear, the summit then becoming a "bald". Some of the highest points, instead of being bald, are dark, with a heavy balsam and evergreen growth.

The rocks of the Unakas are micaceous and hornblendic gneisses, granites, slates, semi-metamorphic conglomerates, and sandstones, the strata of which are upturned and dip at high angles. The ridges are cold, steep, and rocky, and, in the main, have thin, sandy soils. Nevertheless, on the tops of the highest ridges are tracts, like those of the "balds", prairie-like, black, and rich. Places of considerable fertility are rarely met with on wooded slopes supporting a growth of walnut, beech, poplar, wild cherry, and the like, but at long intervals a cleared spot may be discerned. The mountains proper can hardly be said to be inhabited, and it is rare to meet with a true mountaineer. The chief settlements are below in the valleys and coves. Occasionally, cabins and small

411

cultivated fields may be found along a stream in a depression of the high mountains. But we have already dwelt longer than necessary upon the characteristics of this division. As a section for the growing of cotton it has no interest. Of that reported in Table II as the product of certain counties partly pertaining to the division perhaps not as much as a bale was raised upon the Unaka ridges proper. The mountains, so far as utilized, have been in the main grazing grounds for cattle.

REMARKS ON COTTON ACREAGE AND PRODUCTION IN TENNESSEE.

An inspection of the map of relative acreage, as well as of the tables, shows at first glance that the cotton-producing areas of Tennessee lie substantially in the western half of the state. It is also seen that there are two chief regions of production, the one mostly within the great plateau slope of West Tennessee, and the other in the Central Basin; and furthermore that these regions are united by an area of low production lying within the limits of the highlands, in the western part of Middle Tennessee. The western chief region is much the more important of the two. Its area of greatest acreage in cotton, and the greatest occurring in Tennessee (15 per cent. and above), lies in the southwestern corner of the state. Passing from this outward, northerly to Kentucky or easterly toward the highlands before referred to, areas of less and less acreage are successively crossed. The eastern chief region, that in the basin, has no one center of greatest acreage. The highest reached is 10 to 15 per cent., and this is found in detached belts or sections in different parts of the basin inclosed by areas of lower acreage. We add that as in going northward the cotton product diminishes the tobacco product, in general, takes its place and increases.

It is to be noted that the northern edge of the cotton-producing portion of Tennessee and of a small strip of western Kentucky between the Mississippi and Tennessee rivers is, for the inland section east of the Mississippi river, the extreme northern limit of the cotton region of the south. (a)

The chief circumstance which determines this limit is the low temperature of the climate, or, as we may put it, the shortness of the growing season; that is to say, the season between frosts. This matter has already been discussed in this report (page 13). It is there shown that the isotherms, or lines of equal heat, of spring and fall for the non-mountainous parts extend diagonally through the state, or, say, parallel to a line running from its southeastern to its northwestern corner. In accordance therewith, the limit of the cotton region, as seen in Tennessee and Kentucky, is approximately parallel to such a line, or would be, excepting that at one point the exceptionally warm and mellow lands of the Central Basin prevail and carry the limit beyond the normal line. And further, in harmony with the direction of the isotherms, the extreme southwestern corner of the state is the warmest and has the longest growing season, and here we have the area of greatest production. Cultivators of cotton in all parts of the state, even in the warmest portion just referred to, fear the late frosts of spring and the first killing frosts of autumn, and are often driven from the rich but colder alluvial bottoms to the warmer, early-maturing uplands.

TABLE III.—POPULATION AND COTTON PRODUCTION IN EACH AGRICULTURAL REGION IN THE STATE.

Agricultural regions, arranged according to product per acre.	Land area.	POPULATION.			COTTON PRODUCTION.										
		Total.	White.	Colored.	Acres.	Bales.	Product per acre.				Total in tons.			Percentage of state's total production.	Cotton acreage per square mile.	Bales per square mile.
							Bale.	Seed-cotton.	Lint.	Seed.	Lint.	Seed.			
	Sq. mis.							*Lbs.*	*Lbs.*	*Lbs.*					
The State	41,750	1,542,359	1,138,831	403,528	722,562	330,621	0.46	651	217	434	78,522	157,044	100.0	17.3	7.9
Lake county (Mississippi river alluvium).	210	3,968	3,274	694	3,349	2,413	0.74	1,059	353	706	573	1,146	0.7	15.5	11.4
Mississippi river alluvial and bluff region.	2,540	152,411	84,116	68,293	177,028	93,843	0.53	756	252	504	22,287	44,574	28.4	69.7	36.9
Brown loam table-lands *	6,590	261,067	162,278	99,719	386,209	171,594	0.44	621	207	414	40,739	81,478	51.9	63.3	27.7
Western valley of Tennessee river	3,918	68,609	58,935	9,674	24,062	9,629	0.40	570	190	380	2,285	4,570	2.9	6.3	3.3
Highland Rim	8,590	295,628	265,945	29,683	9,799	3,843	0.41	582	194	388	913	1,826	1.2	1.2	0.5
Central Basin	6,190	387,151	252,461	134,690	120,729	48,778	0.40	576	192	384	11,585	23,170	14.7	19.5	7.9
Cumberland table-lands †	2,970	29,181	27,966	1,215	133	55	0.41	586	196	392	13	26	.....	.....	.....
East Tennessee	12,530	413,214	363,854	49,360	1,421	537	0.35	552	184	368	127	264	0.2	0.1	.....

* Including summit region of water-shed. † Cotton produced mostly on rim lands or valley lands of the table-lands proper.

a We do not regard the penumbral regions of cotton culture in Tennessee and Kentucky. What we find there only proves that under unusually favorable circumstances, or in special cases, cotton may be cultivated out of its proper domain, within which only fair and constant mean results are attainable.

8

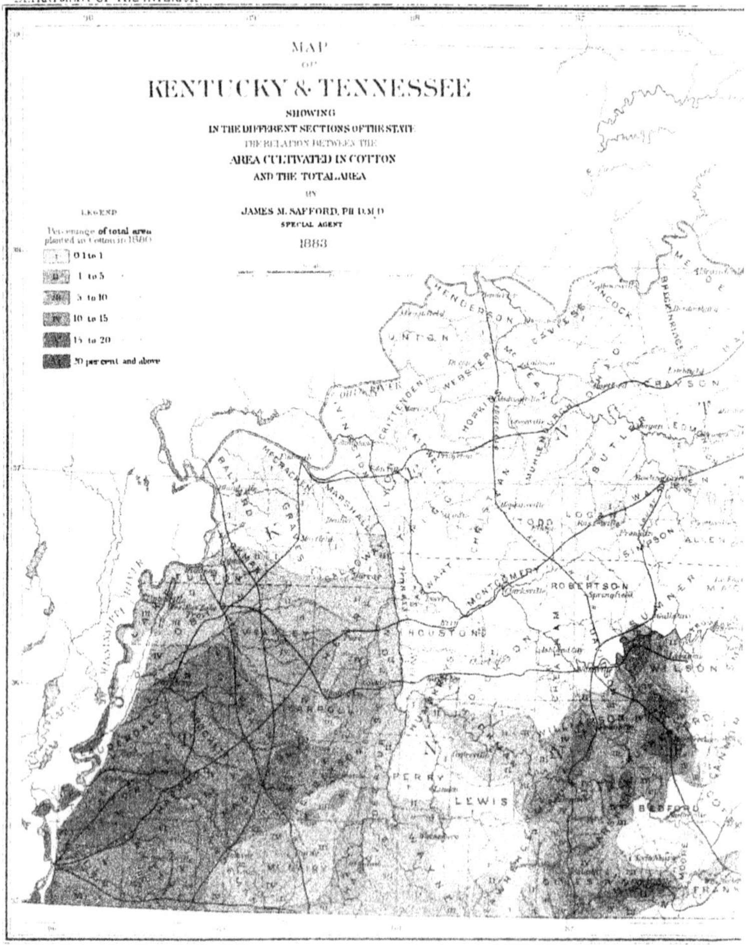

MAP
OF
KENTUCKY & TENNESSEE
SHOWING
IN THE DIFFERENT SECTIONS OF THE STATE
THE RELATION BETWEEN THE
AREA CULTIVATED IN COTTON
AND THE TOTAL AREA
BY
JAMES M. SAFFORD, PH.D. M.D.
SPECIAL AGENT
1883
LEGEND
Percentage of total area planted in Cotton in 1880
0 to 1
1 to 5
5 to 10
10 to 15
15 to 20
20 per cent and above
HENDERSON
UNION
WEBSTER
CRITTENDEN
HOPKINS
BUTLER
GRAYSON
HANCOCK
BRECKINRIDGE
TODD
LOGAN
SIMPSON
ALLEN
MONTGOMERY
ROBERTSON
HOUSTON
WILSON
PERRY
LEWIS
BEDFORD
MISSISSIPPI RIVER

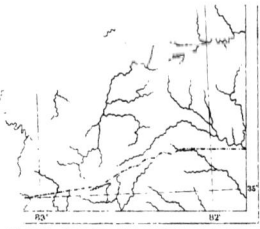

TABLE IV.—BANNER COUNTIES, AS REGARDS TOTAL PRODUCTION AND PRODUCT PER ACRE, IN EACH AGRICULTURAL REGION.

Regions according to product per acre	Average product per acre	COUNTY HAVING HIGHEST TOTAL PRODUCTION.					COUNTY HAVING HIGHEST PRODUCT PER ACRE.					
		Name.	Rank in product per acre in state.	Acres.	Bales.	Product per acre.	Name.	Rank in production in state.	Acres.	Bales.	Product per acre.	Rank in product per acre in state.
	Bale.					Bale.					Bale.	
Lake county (Mississippi river alluvium)	0.74	Lake	1	3,249	2,412	0.74	Lake	23	3,249	2,412	0.74	1
Mississippi river alluvial and Bluff region	0.53	Shelby	8	92,620	46,388	0.50	Dyer	16	14,687	8,564	0.50	2
							Obion	21	7,950	4,235	0.55	3
Brown-loam table-lands ‡	0.44	Fayette	13	92,281	39,221	0.43	Crockett	14	17,307	9,230	0.52	6
							Gibson	5	36,520	19,272	0.52	7
Cumberland table-lands ‡	0.41	Van Buren		82	29	0.33	Scott	60	3	2	0.67	
Western valley of Tennessee river	0.40	Hardin	23	13,859	5,845	0.42	Humphreys	40	155	90	0.58	
Highland Rim	0.40	Hickman	22	3,128	1,362	0.43	Montgomery	60	3	2	1.00	
Central Basin	0.40	Giles	12	31,416	13,902	0.44	Trousdale	75	1	1	1.00	
East Tennessee	0.36	Hamilton	38	486	142	0.29	Hawkins	74	2	2	1.00	

* Omitting those whose production is less than 100 bales.
† Including summit region of water-shed.
‡ Cotton produced mostly on rim lands or valley lands of the table-lands proper.

County in the state having highest total production, Shelby, 46,388 bales. County in the state having highest product per acre, Lake, 1,059 pounds of seed-cotton. County in the state having highest cotton acreage per square mile, Fayette, 144 acres. County in the state having highest percentage of tilled land in cotton, Shelby, 47.3 per cent.

In the tables the aggregate number of bales produced in each natural division is approximately given. Many counties have portions in two contiguous divisions, which circumstance has caused more or less embarrassment in the attempt to classify the counties with reference to the divisions. For this reason the aggregates are approximations only. The defect, however, has been rectified to a considerable extent in the descriptions of the divisions given in the report. The map of relative acreage also will serve as a check in this direction.

The *Mississippi bottom region*, the smallest of our natural divisions, has the distinction of containing lands which produce the most cotton to the acre. This, however, is only an inference based on general information, as, throwing out Lake county, which is wholly within the bottom, the data were not at hand necessary for the separation of the products of the bottoms from those of the uplands. Lake county reports less than 10 per cent. of its tilled land in cotton, which is much below the average of the river lands south of this county. The yield per acre in Lake was 0.74 of a bale of 475 pounds, the greatest yield recorded for any county.

The great *plateau-slope region of West Tennessee* stands pre-eminent within the state in cotton culture, its great expanse of level or gently undulating brown loams, together with the warmer climate, giving it this position. Its first subdivision (a) on the west, the bluff region, had in 1879 a fraction less than 33 per cent. of its tilled lands in cotton. The yield per acre was 0.53 of a 475-pound bale, the highest rate attained, excepting that for the single county of Lake. The latter result is doubtless attributable in part to the character of the plateau areas of fine siliceous and limy loess soils of the subdivision. The Mississippi lands within these counties may help to exalt the rate, but they are too limited, comparatively, to affect it materially. The second subdivision (b), the brown-loam table-lands, had also a fraction less than 33 per cent. of its tilled lands in cotton, but its rate of yield per acre was less, being 0.45 of a 475-pound bale. If on the acreage map the color area of highest percentage of total area, a section lying in the southern parts of the two subdivisions (a and b), alone be taken, the percentage of tilled land in cotton was 41.5, the greatest proportion in this particular that has been reached, and the rate per acre 0.47 of the standard bale of 475 pounds. In the third subdivision, the summit region of the water-shed (c), there is a material falling off in the proportion of tilled land in cotton, it being 19.4 per cent. The yield per acre was 0.42 of the standard bale.

In the *western valley of the Tennessee river* the percentage of cotton production, as seen on the acreage map, is much reduced, especially in the northern part of the state. On the eastern side of the Tennessee, north of Duck river, it is, excepting a spot in Stewart county, practically nothing. Within the cotton-producing portion of this valley the percentage of tilled land in cotton was not quite 7 per cent. The yield per acre was 0.40 of a bale.

Next follows the *western subdivision of the great Highland Rim*. This high "barreny" belt of country, with areas of lowest production alternating, could they be shown, with areas of non-production, lies between the two chief regions of cotton culture, and almost makes a break in the continuity of the cotton-belt as a whole. What cotton is put to its credit was mostly raised in the deep valleys intersecting the belt.

The *Central Basin* as a cotton-producing area rates pretty well in the number of bales and in the percentage of the total acreage with that part of West Tennessee, nearly half, which embraces, with Benton, the two northern tiers of counties. Including as a part of the basin area the valley of Duck river, in Hickman, the West Tennessee fraction had the better of it by about 1,000 bales. In the basin, as a whole, the proportion of tilled lands in cotton was 6.4 per cent.; in a number of the northern counties, however, little or no cotton was planted, tobacco taking its place. If the non-cotton counties and parts of counties could be thrown out the proportion of tilled land in cotton would be much greater. For Giles county, as the case stands, it is 18 per cent.; for Rutherford, 16; for Maury, 10; for Williamson, 7. The yield per acre for the cotton area proper of the basin is 0.40 of a 475-pound bale. Giles goes above this, the yield being 0.44 of a bale. Rutherford and Williamson fall to 0.38 of a bale. It is not clear, from a study of the column of "bales per acre" in Table I, that there is any relation between the figures there given for the counties of the basin and the capacities of the soils concerned, though in the case of Giles the rate would appear to be significant.

East of the basin the two mountainous divisions, the *Cumberland table-land* and the *Unaka Mountain region*, are non-producing as to cotton. The remainder of this part of the state, the *eastern subdivision of the Highland Rim* and the *valley of East Tennessee*, is in the penumbral region of cotton-growing. It would appear that the culture of cotton in the valley of East Tennessee had been advancing to some extent northward for a few years previous to 1880.

RELATIONS OF COTTON PRODUCTION TO THE RACES.—As to the relations of whites and negroes to cotton culture and production, Table I authorizes the broad statement that where the greatest aggregate of cotton is produced there is, other things being equal, the greatest negro population; and, further, that as the one decreases in the several belts the other does also, though not necessarily at the same rate. Take, for example, the group of six counties in West Tennessee (Shelby, Fayette, Hardeman, Tipton, Haywood, and Madison), producing the most cotton and embracing on the acreage map the color area of the greatest acreage in cotton (15 per cent. and above), and we find that they contain nearly one-third (30 per cent.) of the entire negro population of the state, although their aggregate area is a little less than one-twelfth (about 8 per cent.) of the area of the state. And it makes little difference in this estimate if Shelby, with Memphis, be thrown out of the calculation. In this same group of counties the negro population is 57 per cent. of the total population. Similar calculations as to the production and population of the other color areas on the acreage map, especially in West Tennessee, will bear out, in general, both statements made. In the Central Basin the relations cannot be made so apparent, chiefly because the color areas are small and broken and the data are not at hand for making out the negro population of each separately. A real aberration, however, in the force of the statement is caused by the fact that some of the very rich counties, either in whole or in part, especially in the northern portion of the basin, find profitable employment for negro labor other than in the raising of cotton. Another circumstance to be considered, both as to West and to Middle Tennessee, is the presence of large and prosperous towns or cities in which negroes congregate, and which cannot always be eliminated in the calculations. We add that the negro population of the cotton region as a whole is approximately 68 per cent. of the entire negro population of the state, while its area is only about 48 per cent. of that of the state.

It must also be stated that while the greatest number of negroes are found in areas of greatest aggregate production, yet it does not follow that in such areas the most cotton is produced per acre. In the six counties referred to, in the southwestern corner of the state, we have, area for area, the most cotton produced and the highest percentage of negro population, with an average yield per acre of 0.46½ of a 475-pound bale, while in another group of counties in the northwestern corner of the state (Lake, Obion, Dyer, Lauderdale, Gibson, and Crockett), where the relative production and percentages of negro population are much less, we have an average yield per acre of 0.58½ of the standard bale—a wide difference. This is in the case before us due much, but not altogether, to the differences in the qualities of the soils concerned. How far the kind of labor as to race enters as a factor in such results is a question for consideration.

METHODS OF COTTON CULTURE.—A few general notes are appended as to the agricultural methods employed in the cultivation of cotton within the state.

Fallowing is practiced in all the divisions, but only to a limited extent, and rarely in the alluvial region of the Mississippi. Land lying fallow within the area of the plateau slope of West Tennessee and of the western valley of the Tennessee river is sometimes tilled, sometimes only turned out. Weeds are often turned under and the land sown in field-pease, or in grain in place of pease, or sometimes in clover or grass. In the Central Basin the land is in a majority of cases only turned out; sometimes sown in clover, grass, or wheat. The results in both cases are generally reported as good.

Rotation of crops is generally practiced, but with little system. Cotton, corn and wheat, or corn, cotton and wheat, are made to follow each other in courses of three to four and five years. In the place of wheat, oats or clover, or sometimes pease, sweet potatoes, or even in certain counties peanuts, are substituted. On strong land the courses are sometimes reduced to two years, cotton and corn alternating, wheat or oats occasionally taking the place of the latter. It is the rule perhaps to change yearly, but there are many exceptions to this, the same crop, as cotton or corn, being raised on the same land for a series of years, covering sometimes a period of five or even ten or more years. The general testimony is, as we might have anticipated, that rotation relieves the land and is of material benefit.

Fall plowing is done to a greater or less extent in all parts of the cotton region, more generally in the Mississippi bottom and the bluff region and in the Central Basin, and less so within the limits of the brown-loam table-lands of West Tennessee. It is often done for wheat alone, and the results are very generally reported as good. Subsoil plowing amounts to but little in any of the divisions. When done, a bull-tongue is generally run in the furrow after a turning-plow.

Outside of a scanty supply of stable manure the fertilizers used amount to but little. Land plaster to a small extent and less guano are applied in the midland counties of West Tennessee. Some plaster is likewise used in the Central Basin, together with a limited amount of manufactured fertilizers. Cotton-seed, especially away from cottonseed-oil mills, is thus in part disposed of. In addition, compost material, straw, cornstalks, ashes, etc., are utilized by provident cultivators. The lands are further often improved by the plowing under of clover, pease, and weeds. The cotton lands of Tennessee are in the main still quite productive as compared with many sections in other states, and there does not exist the same necessity for the use of fertilizers; nevertheless there are areas with us which would be greatly benefited by a judicious application of artificial or other fertilizers, and which, in truth, need them if good crops are to be expected.

Cotton-seed, in addition to its use as manure, is largely employed as a food for cattle, especially in regions remote from cottonseed-oil mills. When transportation to the mills is easy, much of it goes in that direction.

The most troublesome weed in all the cotton region is crab-grass. This is characterized as "most fatal", "great trouble," "pest," "worst enemy," etc. Cocklebur ranks second and careless-weed or smart-weed third as "pests" in all parts except the Central Basin, where careless-weed is second and cocklebur third. Other more prominent weeds are foxtail grass, rag-weed, purslane, and hog-weed.

The farms or plantations in the cotton region, as a whole, vary from 5 to 2,000 acres, rarely 3,000. The largest are in the alluvial region of the Mississippi, the midland counties of West Tennessee, and the Central Basin. It is impossible to make out the average size of farms from the answers in the schedules with even an approximation to correctness, either for the whole area or any of its leading subdivisions.

Mixed farming is general throughout the entire region.

Supplies are everywhere chiefly raised at home. In West Tennessee some are imported from Saint Louis. Memphis, Cincinnati, Louisville, and Nashville, the point from which they are imported depending upon the facility of transportation. The tendency of raising supplies at home is evidently increasing.

Taking the whole cotton region into consideration, the chief laborers are negroes, and landlords often express a decided preference for them. There are no Chinese, and but few foreigners of any kind. In some parts of the region the proportion of white as compared with negro laborers is considerable. In the extreme northwestern counties the proportion is large, more than half, and in the summit region of the water-shed it is about half; but in the western valley of the Tennessee river and in the western subdivision of the highlands the whites predominate.

The wages paid will average throughout the area about $10 per month, including board. In the extreme western part the rates appear to be higher, averaging $12. In most cases the wages are due at the end of the year, though money and provisions may be advanced at any time. Many are hired by the month, and even by the day. Farms are often worked on shares. In such cases the landlords furnish for the most part all implements and the means necessary for the support of hands and for carrying on the farm work. In general, the system gives satisfaction, though occasionally objections are recorded against it.

The proportion of negroes owning houses or land is small, approximately 5 per cent for the whole region. In the bluff and midland counties of West Tennessee and in the Central Basin the proportion is, according to reports, from 4 to 5 per cent. In the section lying between these, where the negro population is comparatively small (the Tennessee Ridge region, the western valley of the Tennessee, and the highlands), the proportion is greater, ranging from 8 to 13 per cent. The reports vary much as to the condition of the negroes, the general inference to be drawn being that the frugal and industrious—and there are not a few of this class—are prosperous, improving, and in general doing well, but that the improvident and indolent, of whom there are too many, are poor and uncomfortable, and likely to remain so. There is a general disposition to treat them fairly and kindly, though in rare cases doubtless they are imposed upon by selfish and designing men.

A remark further is added as to the increase in the total cotton product of 1879 over that of 1860, as shown by the census reports. Taking the whole state, and allowing for manifest errors in the report of 1870, and making the proper reductions, the total product of 1869 becomes 147,824 bales of 475 pounds each, and the total for 1879 is 330,621 bales, an increase of 124 per cent. over the product of 1869. The main increase was in West Tennessee. In the Central Basin it amounted to 47 per cent. In East Tennessee it was greater than elsewhere, though here but comparatively little cotton is raised.

Table of analyses of Tennessee soils and subsoils.

Number.	Name.	Locality.	County.	Vegetation.	Depth in inches.	Insoluble residue.	Soluble silica.	Total insoluble res. due and sand.	Potash.	Soda.	Lime.	Magnesia.	Brown oxide of manganese.	Ferric oxide.	Alumina.	Phosphoric acid.	Sulphuric acid.	Carbonic acid.	Volatile matter.	Total.	Hygroscopic moisture.	Temperature C° of absorption of ab.	Analyst.
1	Red clay soil	Florence station	Rutherford	Species of hickory, red, white, and post oaks, elm, ash, honey-locust, black walnut, wild cherry, sugar-tree, poplar, hackberry, red-bud, dogwood, and pawpaw. Originally covered with cane.																			Durrett.
2	Red clay subsoil	do	do																				McCauley.
3	Red clay soil	do	do																				Durrett.
4	Red clay subsoil	do	do																				Corp.
7	Red clay soil	J. F. W. Barrow's (3 miles north of Murfreesborough)	do	About as above.																			Do.
8	Red clay subsoil	do	do																				Do.
9	Red clay soil	W. G. Harding's (Belle Meade)	Davidson	Oaks, elms, hickories, ash, linden, sugar-maple, hornbeam, walnut, cherry, dogwood, and red-bud. Originally in cane.																			Do.
10	Red clay subsoil	do	do																				Do.
6	Red clay subsoil	do	do																				Do.
11	Poplar soil	Vanleer Polk's	Maury	Poplar abundant, sweet gum, also fragrant, walnut, oak, ash, elm, hackberry, honey-locust, and dogwood. Originally covered with cane.																			Do.
12	Poplar subsoil	do	do																				Do.
13	Poplar soil	Hermitage	Davidson	About the same as 11 and 12.																			Do.
14	Poplar subsoil	do	do																				Do.
15	Upland soil	Gill's station	Shelby	Poplar, sweet gum, and hickories; oaks, red-bud, and dogwood. Originally.																			Colby.
16	Upland subsoil	do	do																				Do.
17	Cane soil	Memphis Bluff	do																				Do.

NOTE.—With the exception of Nos. 3, 4, 7, and 8, the soils and subsoils analyzed were each an average sample obtained by thoroughly mixing samples taken in the same lot from three or four excavations or holes dug for the purpose. Nos. 3 and 4 were obtained from a single hole, and are not averages. Nos. 7 and 8 are each an average of four samples from as many holes. In every case the lands supplying the samples have never been cultivated or entirely cleared. All are pasture grounds, with more or less of the native growth remaining.

PART II.

AGRICULTURAL DESCRIPTIONS

OF THE

COTTON-PRODUCING COUNTIES

OF

TENNESSEE.

AGRICULTURAL DESCRIPTIONS

COTTON-PRODUCING COUNTIES OF TENNESSEE.

In the descriptions which follow, the counties are arranged in groups according to the natural divisions to which they severally, either wholly or predominantly, belong. Each county is noticed separately and as a whole. Where a county lies in two divisions, its name is given in both; but it is described under the head of the division to which it chiefly belongs, and reference is made to this. The asterisk (*) indicates that the description of the county to which it is attached appears under some other regional head. It may be stated here that in Part I of this report many counties have been incidentally noticed or partially described. To such notices or descriptions references are made whenever it may be deemed desirable. Under each county head the statement of woodland refers to the original condition of the land before it was cleared and brought into cultivation.

· Following the descriptive notices of the several counties are abstracts from such parts of the reports of correspondents as refer to natural features and production. In many instances abstracts from two or more persons who describe the same region have been combined. The substance of the remainder of the reports, referring to agricultural and commercial practice, will be found in Part III, at the beginning of which is also a complete list of correspondents, with their post-offices, and the names or location of the particular regions which they severally discuss.

ALLUVIAL PLAIN OF THE MISSISSIPPI RIVER.

This region embraces the whole of Lake, large parts of Dyer * and Lauderdale,* and small parts of Tipton* and Shelby* counties.

LAKE.

Population: 3,968.—White, 3,274; colored, 694.
Area: 210 square miles.—Woodland, all.
Tilled lands: 34,666 acres.—Area planted in cotton, 3,249 acres; in corn, 14,730 acres; in wheat, 1,608 acres; in oats, 108 acres; in tobacco, 5 acres.
Cotton production: 2,412 bales; average cotton product per acre, 0.74 bale, 1,059 pounds seed-cotton, or 353 pounds cotton lint.

Lake is the only county in Tennessee wholly within the alluvial plain of the Mississippi river. It lies compressed between the Mississippi on the west and Reelfoot lake on the east. Its area is long and narrow, having a length of 23 or 24 miles and a width varying from 3 to 11 miles. There are no uplands proper, but as a general thing the lands are higher along the Mississippi, becoming lower as we approach the lake. About one-third of the county is entirely above overflow from the river. Of the remainder, one-third seldom overflows, and only in very high water, and this is said to be the most productive part. The northern third of the county, the wider and better part, is mostly above overflow and nearly all under cultivation. Two-thirds of the middle part is also under cultivation, there being good sections of land both on the Mississippi and the Reelfoot sides. Alternating belts of timber and cultivated lands extend longitudinally through the southern part, and a cultivated strip is usually found near the river and parallel with it. Much of the southern end, comparatively, is subject to overflow. The same may be said of a strip along Reelfoot lake in the northeastern corner of the county. (See also description of the region.)

The soils are described as black and yellow, alluvial, and sandy and mixed loams. Alternating with these are buckshot clays. The general growth is cottonwood, sweet gum, ash, oak, hickory, pecan, elm, hackberry, walnut, box-elder, red maple, mulberry, and cypress, with papaw and spicewood undergrowth. Shipments are made to Memphis, New Orleans, or Saint Louis, by steamboat, at from $1 to $1 50 per bale.

C. M. PEACOCK AND DAVID WAGONER.—The soils of the county are the (1) black alluvial; (2) the black sandy loam; (3) the buckshot and light sandy. The first is the chief soil, forming one-fifth of the land, and occurs at intervals over the county. It is from 1 foot to 10 feet in thickness, very porous, readily drains itself, and is easily cultivated. The crops produced are cotton, corn, wheat, oats, Irish and sweet potatoes, and peanuts, to all of which the soil is well adapted. One-fifth of the tilled land is planted in cotton. Plants grow to a height of from 4 to 8 feet, that not exceeding 5 feet being the best. Wet seasons and too much plowing cause the plant to run to weed. The remedy is less and shallow plowing. The product of seed-cotton per acre on fresh land is from 1,200 to 1,500 pounds, 1,720 pounds being required for a 475-pound bale. Staple, good ordinary. After twelve years' cultivation the yield is from 2,000 to 2,500 pounds, requiring 1,660 pounds for a bale, and the staple is much better than that from fresh land. The troublesome weeds are cocklebur, smart- and careless-weeds, and crab-grass. No land of this kind lies turned out.

The *black sandy loam* aggregates one-third of our lands, and occurs scattered over the county, and at a depth of 3 feet is black dirt or white sand. One-fifth of the cultivated land is in cotton, which grows to a height of from 5 to 10 feet, the lower the better. In wet weather the plants are kept down by plowing but little and by cultivating with the hoe. Seed-cotton product on fresh land is from 500 to 800 pounds per acre, requiring 1,900 pounds for a 475-pound bale, rating as good ordinary. After twelve years' cultivation the yield is from 1,800 to 2,000 pounds, of which 1,660 pounds are required for a bale, the staple being much better than that from fresh land. Weeds same as above.

The *buckshot soil* constitutes one-fifth of the lands, and exists in small spots over the county; thickness, 5 feet. This soil is not easily tilled in wet seasons, and is hard to manage in dry. It is best adapted to corn, and very little cotton is planted. Cotton attains a height of from 2 to 4 feet, the latter being the most productive. The seed-cotton product on fresh land is from 800 to 1,000 pounds, and after ten years' cultivation 1,500 pounds. The weeds are foxtail and cocklebur.

R. S. BRADFORD.—The uplands are very level and rich, and almost all are fit for cultivation. The chief cotton soil is a black, moderately stiff soil, which comprises from one-half to two-thirds of white sand, the remainder being clay. Pebbles are met with at a depth of 36 feet. The chief crops are corn and cotton, about one-twentieth being planted in the latter, but it is well adapted to either. The yellow sandy soil is about one-fifteenth of our lands, and occurs throughout the county. One-twentieth is planted in cotton, to which it is well adapted, as also to corn. The buckshot clay forms about one-fourth of the lands, and occurs throughout the county. It is best adapted to cotton, in which one-twentieth is planted. All these soils have the same growth of timber.

R. M. DARNALL (northwestern part of the county).—This region is continuous with Madrid Bend, in Kentucky. The higher lands are alluvial, and are elevated above overflow. They are so surrounded by the river that cotton is often protected from frost when in other localities, even farther south, it is killed. The kinds of soils are: (1) White sandy; (2) yellow sandy; (3) putty or buckshot clay. The chief is the white [gray] sandy soil. One-twentieth of our land is of this kind, and occurs from Cairo, Illinois, to Memphis. Three-fourths of the subsoil of Lake county is underlaid, in some places at 15 feet, by gravel. The soil is easily cultivated in wet or dry seasons, and two-thirds of it is planted in cotton, the other chief crops being corn and wheat, but it is well adapted to any crop. Cotton grows from 3 to 7 feet high, but is best at 5 feet. On fresh land, unless the season is dry, the plant goes to weed. It produces about 1,200 pounds of seed-cotton, requiring 1,900 pounds for a 475-pound bale. Land twenty years old produces a bale of lint to the acre. The lands are level, and there is no washing.

L. DONALDSON (Mississippi bottom, near the margin of Reelfoot lake).—The black clay (buckshot) with a substratum of sand forms one-half of our lands, and extends 2 and 3 miles in each direction. The subsoil is either a brown sand or black putty clay, not impervious. Tillage is generally easy, but difficult after wet springs followed by dry seasons. Crops are various. The land is best adapted to corn and cotton, and one-fourth of it is planted with the latter. The seed-cotton product on fresh land is 1,900 pounds per acre, 1,630 being required for a 475-pound bale. It rates as low middling and good ordinary. After ten years the product per acre is 1,600 pounds. On the mixed sand the product, after the same time, is 1,500, and on the sandy land 1,200 pounds per acre, the staple being the same as before. One-half per cent. only is turned out. Such land taken in again is better by 25 per cent.

J. W. FOWLER (between Reelfoot lake and the river).—The report agrees substantially with that of L. Donaldson.

DYER.
(See "The Bluff region".)

LAUDERDALE.
(See "The Bluff region".)

TIPTON.
(See "The Bluff region".)

SHELBY.
(See "The Bluff region".)

MISSISSIPPI ALLUVIUM (in part) AND BLUFF REGION.

This region includes nearly all of Obion county, and the larger parts of Dyer, Lauderdale, Tipton, and Shelby.

OBION.

Population: 22,912.—White, 18,841; colored, 4,071.
Area: 540 square miles.—Woodland, nearly all, excepting the area of Reelfoot lake.
Tilled lands: 100,857 acres.—Area planted in cotton, 7,259 acres; in corn, 45,005 acres; in wheat, 25,368 acres; in oats, 2,105 acres; in tobacco, 1,432 acres.
Cotton production: 4,225 bales; average cotton product per acre, 0.58 bale, 828 pounds seed-cotton, or 276 pounds cotton lint.

Previous to 1870 Obion was the most northwesterly county of the state. In the year mentioned a large part, all west of Reelfoot lake, was cut off to make Lake county, the old county thereby losing well-nigh all of its share of the Mississippi bottom, and its best lands. The lake was retained.

The county is in the main one of our most fertile areas. Uplands predominate, and their soils are based chiefly upon the formation we have called the loess. The description given of this formation and of the soils of the Bluff region on page 17 of this report applies to this county, and the reader is referred to what is there said. I note here that the loess is underlaid by gravel and sand, and these again by clayey beds. Hence it happens that the subsoils of the uplands are often underlaid, at greater or less depths, by gravel or sand, or both, and further, that the lower lands often have a clay basis. The very fine ashen or yellowish loess is frequently considered popularly as clayey matter, and is so called.

The uplands are often rolling, but supply extensive level tracts. Approaching the bluffs in the western part of the county they become more or less hilly. A narrow alluvial tract lies along the eastern border of Reelfoot lake, between the lake and the foot of the bluffs. This land is rich and fertile, and some of it is subject to overflow. That above overflow yields good crops of cotton, and upon all of it farmers manage to raise heavy crops of corn. The timber is cypress, ash, walnut, and cottonwood, with an undergrowth of cane. Alluvial lands or bottoms, subject to overflow, occur on both sides along the Obion river and its forks, which traverse the southern part of the county. The bottoms often extend out a mile or two from the river. The soils are a thin, crawfishy clay, and support chiefly a growth of beech and cypress, with an undergrowth of cane. Outside of these are the second bottoms, above overflow, often supplying a level country with a rich and productive soil. The second bottoms rise gradually into uplands, together giving a belt of country of great fertility, and once remarkable for its heavy timber, great "poplars" and oaks, gum, beech, sugar-tree, and hickory, with cane and papaw beneath.

ABSTRACTS FROM REPORTS.

J. H. McDOWELL (continuation of abstract in Part I, region of Hoosier creek).—The lowlands are very level for 10 miles east and west by 8 miles north and south, and the soil is better adapted to cotton culture than is usual with sections so far north. While the seasons are short for cotton, the yield will compare well with points much farther south. The nature of the soil is such, especially on the uplands, as to force and hasten maturity. Yet this cannot properly be considered a cotton-producing region. Cotton in the bottoms runs too much to weed, and is often cut short by frost.

The chief soil, the light blackish upland, rests upon a heavy gray to light brownish-gray subsoil, which in turn is underlaid by sand and gravel at from 10 to 20 feet. The land is easily tilled, especially after the first breaking and harrowing. It is looser in dry seasons, and, if well drained, is early and warm. The chief crops are cotton and corn on the uplands, and corn, wheat, and tobacco in the lowlands, corn best suiting the soil. Cotton is planted in the proportion of one-sixth for the uplands and one-twentieth for the lowlands. The height attained is 4 feet, the most productive. It runs to weed in low wet lands. The seed-cotton product on fresh land is from 600 to 800 pounds, of which 1,660 pounds are needed for a 475-pound bale. After five years' cultivation the land (unmanured) yields from 800 to 1,200 pounds, requiring 1,545 pounds for a bale. The staple from the old land brings from one-fourth to one-half cent more, but there is no positive rule as to this. Some fresh lands yield a staple equal to that from old lands, while others in the same locality supply an inferior article. As to the yield per acre, I may state that it was last season (1879) far above the figures given in this report, the second-class lands running as high as 1,500 pounds, and the first, in favorable locations, occasionally as high as 1,800 pounds. The weeds are crab-grass and cocklebur in bottoms, crab-grass and smart-weed on uplands. About one-hundredth part of the uplands are "turned out"; none of the lowlands. Rest helps comparatively level land. The slopes are injured by washing, but the valleys are improved by the material thus brought upon them. A good deal of ditching has been done, the lands thereby becoming drier and warmer.

The black loamy lowland forms four-fifths of the lands in this region, and occurs over an area 0 by 10 miles in extent. Its growth is hickory, ash, gum, sassafras, walnut, red, white, black, and turkey oaks, hornbeam, hornbeam, boxelder, beech, and maple. It rests upon a gray clayey subsoil containing brownish gravel, underlaid by sand at from 10 to 20 feet, and readily drained. The land is easily tilled in wet or dry seasons, is late and cold, and is best adapted to corn, wheat, and tobacco. Only about one-fortieth part is planted in cotton.

B. W. HERRING (western part of the county).—The upland, the best for cotton and most used, is a light clay, mixed with some sand, ashen-colored or gray, making three-fourths of the lands. Its timber is oak, hickory, poplar, ash, and walnut. The soil, 12 inches thick, is underlaid by a light yellowish subsoil. The land is easy to till in dry weather, but difficult in wet. Its chief crops are corn, wheat, tobacco, and grasses. Not more than one-tenth part is planted in cotton. The weeds are rag-weed, cocklebur, white-top, and crab-grass.

J. S. MURPHY (northeastern part of the county).—The land in this section is termed ridge land, and is situated between Harris' fork and Obion river. We have substantially but one soil, known as gray soil. The entire section, excepting a small amount of glade, is of this kind. It extends 8 miles to the south and west and 15 or 20 miles to the north and east. Its growth is oak, hickory, dogwood, walnut, poplar, gum, elm, red-bud, and hazel. It is from 4 to 6 inches thick, and rests upon yellow clay. The land is productive, any kind of crop growing well. One-fifth of the land is planted in cotton, which grows from 2½ to 3 feet high, the latter giving the best yield. The seed-cotton product per acre is from 1,200 to 1,800 pounds, 1,600 pounds being required for a 475-pound bale. The staple rates as middling. I have gathered 1,600 pounds per acre from land after six years' cultivation. The staple from the older land is shorter and not so good. The weeds are hog-weed and crab-grass. I do not know that an acre of this land is "turned out".

DYER.

Population: 15,118.—White, 11,206; colored, 3,912.
Area: 570 square miles.—Woodland, all, excepting a few small lakes in the bottoms.
Tilled lands: 76,194 acres.—Area planted in cotton, 14,637 acres; in corn, 27,820 acres; in wheat, 11,820 acres; in oats, 1,961 acres; in tobacco, 364 acres.
Cotton production: 8,564 bales; average cotton product per acre, 0.59 bale, 834 pounds seed-cotton, or 278 pounds cotton lint.

Dyer county is not far from being equally divided between bottom lands and uplands. The western part lies in the alluvial plain of the Mississippi, while the eastern is high land pertaining to the bluff region. The reader is referred to what is said under these heads on page 15 for general characteristics. The Mississippi bottom is traversed by the Obion river, and as a whole is thinly settled. The interrupted strip of cultivated land along the Mississippi river has been referred to in Part I. Within the bottom the Forked Deer river, which runs westward into the Mississippi, is the boundary between Dyer and Lauderdale counties. Leaving the bottom of the Mississippi and entering the bottom lands proper of the Forked Deer, in Dyer county, the latter are found to have a sandy loam of great fertility, giving some of the best cotton-producing areas in the county. Other good alluvial lands are found along the tributaries of Forked Deer and Obion rivers. Bottoms, however, occur which are clayey, cold, and subject to overflow.

The highlands have a general elevation of from 100 to 150 feet above the Mississippi bottoms. They are frequently level, often undulating, but become broken when approaching the bluffs, where they end abruptly in a steep escarpment overlooking the great alluvial area to the west. The soil is a rich brown loam, based on loess, having had a native growth, as in Obion, of very heavy timber, poplar, gum, white oak, sugar-tree, ash, walnut, elm, and dogwood, with species of a smaller growth. These lands present an agricultural region of great interest, and among the best in the state.

Cotton is shipped to Memphis, New Orleans, or Cincinnati at $2 50 to $3, and by rail or by water to Memphis at $1 per bale.

ABSTRACTS FROM REPORTS.

(An abstract from L. M. Williams' report has already been given.)

C. H. Pate.—The alluvial and cultivated belt along the Mississippi river is interrupted at intervals, but extends for 75 miles up and down the river. It is a sandy soil from 18 to 20 inches thick, with a growth of cottonwood and sycamore. The subsoil with very few exceptions is sandy. The crops are cotton and corn, the soil suiting both. One-half the lands are put in cotton. The plants grow to 5 feet in height, and at that are most productive. Bolling is favored by topping or removing the bud in July. The seed-cotton product is 1,800 pounds per acre, requiring 1,600 pounds for a 475-pound bale. The product is about the same on old land, requiring 1,545 pounds for a bale. In the latter case the staple is one grade better. A vine known as the devil's shoe-string is a troublesome weed. No land is turned out.

A. Harris (east and northeast of Dyersburg).—We have two kinds of soils or lands: (1) dark loamy uplands, mostly cultivated in cotton, and presenting great uniformity; (2) light sandy soil of the bottoms, not so great in area, but better for cotton. The first and chief soil makes three-fourths of our lands, and occurs out of bottoms all over the county. It is from 6 to 12 inches in thickness, and rests upon a subsoil of reddish clay, which crumbles in water, and is liable to wash on slopes. The subsoil contains small pebbles in places, and is underlaid by sand. The soil is easily tilled, and is early, warm, and usually well drained. The crops are corn, cotton, tobacco, wheat, oats, clover, timothy, and red-top, all of which grow well. About one-fourth is planted in cotton. Cotton reaches a height of 4 feet, and is then most productive. It runs to weed in warm, wet weather, and through continuous cultivation. Plowing close to the cotton and throwing the dirt from the roots check the growth. The seed-cotton product is from 1,200 to 1,500 pounds, requiring 1,780 pounds for a 475-pound bale. The staple rates as low middling to middling. After ten years the product is from 800 to 1,200 pounds, requiring 1,900 pounds for a bale, the staple being shorter but finer. Weeds are cocklebur and careless-weed. Very little land lies "turned out". Such land, when manured and clovered, produces as well as ever. The soils wash on slopes unless prevented by circling. Some ditching has been done with good results.

The sandy soils of the bottoms make about one-tenth of the lands in cultivation. The growth is oak, hackberry, box-elder, gum, ash, and maple. The soil is best adapted to corn and cotton, one-third being planted in the latter. The cotton grows to a height of 4 or 5 feet, and at this is most productive. The seed-cotton product is from 1,500 to 2,000 pounds per acre, 1,780 pounds being needed for a bale. The change in the land and in the cotton produced is very small after a number of years.

D. C. Churchman and Smith Parks (northeastern part of the county, covering about 10 miles square between the Obion and Forked Deer rivers, and waters of Reed's and other creeks).—But little of the bottom land is in cultivation. The uplands are undulating, from 6 to 12 inches deep, resting on a red clay subsoil, and are much alike in productiveness. The soil is poplar, oak, ash, and elm. Twice within my recollection has the cotton all been killed by frost on the 18th of September. The yield per acre depends much as to whether killing frosts come early or late in October. Our soils are a clay loam with some sand in them, and present no noteworthy differences. They are dark in color, and sometimes yellowish, and are underlaid by sand at various depths. The crops produced are corn, wheat, cotton, tobacco, and clover, with various grasses for hay. About a fourth of the land is put in cotton. It grows from 2 to 6 feet in height; 3 feet is a good height. Too much rain in July and August causes it to run to weed. To remedy this and to favor bolling some practice topping; others plow, throwing the dirt from the cotton. The seed-cotton produced on fresh land varies from 800 to 1,600 pounds per acre, of which about 1,780 pounds will pay toll and make a bale. The staple rates as low middling and middling. After five years' cultivation the land produces as well as at first if well circled. The troublesome weeds are cockleburs and crab-grass. Very little of the land lies turned out.

LAUDERDALE.

Population: 14,918.—White, 9,081; colored, 5,837.
Area: 410 square miles.—Woodland, all, excepting a few small lakes in the Mississippi bottom.
Tilled lands: 58,010 acres.—Area planted in cotton, 24,083 acres; in corn, 22,580 acres; in wheat, 3,889 acres; in oats, 1,375 acres; in tobacco, 58 acres.
Cotton production: 13,250 bales; average cotton product per acre, 0.55 bale, 783 pounds seed-cotton, or 261 pounds cotton lint.

Lauderdale county is nearly a square, and lies between the Forked Deer river on the north and the Hatchie river on the south. Like Dyer, it is nearly equally divided between bottom lands and uplands. On the west we have the alluvial plain of the Mississippi; on the east, the high plateau lands of the bluff region. The line of bluffs, the abrupt western limit of the high or plateau lands, runs in a nearly northeasterly and southwesterly direction through the middle of the county, dividing it as stated. The Mississippi alluvial portion has been sufficiently described by Mr. J. L. Lea, of Fulton, and Mr. J. C. Marley, of Ripley, on page 15 of this report, under the head of the Mississippi bottom region. The growth of the bottoms is cypress, gums, oak, sassafras, hickories, pecan, mulberry, hackberry, coffee-nut, walnut, cottonwood, willow, sycamore, and cane. Low bottoms or first bottoms, often cold and swampy, are found very generally along Forked Deer and Hatchie rivers.

The upland portion has the general features of the bluff region (page 17), and is of course much like the plateau portions of Obion and Dyer counties. It is limited on the north and south, respectively, by the bottom lands of Forked Deer and Hatchie rivers, and is traversed by a number of creeks, the most important of which are Cane, Coal, and Knob creeks. Between the streams are extensive tracts, both level and rolling, occasionally becoming hilly. Fertile second bottoms succeed these as we approach the first bottoms. The uplands were originally very productive and were preferred for cotton on account of its maturing earlier, and in many sections, where not too much worn, are still preferred. The second bottoms and the sandy first bottoms are usually rich and yield well, better than the uplands, but their crops are more in danger from early frosts. The native growth of the uplands is poplar, oaks, hickories, ash, beech, sassafras, some chestnut, and sweet and black gum.

Cotton is shipped by water to Memphis at 75 cents, to New Orleans at $1 25, and to Saint Louis at $1 per bale.

ABSTRACTS FROM REPORTS.

(Items from the report of F. T. Rice, of Durhamville, have been given under the head of "the Bluff region", in Part I.)

J. F. YOUNG (county generally).—Cotton on sandy lowlands matures as early as on the uplands, and since the uplands, though very productive when fresh, deteriorate greatly, the lowlands, even without sand, are more desirable for cotton and much more so for corn. We have two qualities of uplands, poplar predominating on the one and oak on the other. Both are productive when fresh. The poplar lands are considered the best. The kinds of soil under cultivation are: (1) Light mulatto soil on uplands or slopes; (2) dark loams of the second bottoms of the rivers and creeks; (3) sandy bottom soils of the Mississippi. The chief soil is the mulatto upland. About one-half of Lauderdale county is of this kind. It covers an area 20 miles long by 10 wide, varying in thickness from 6 to 12 inches. Its subsoil is tough yellow clay, baking hard when wet and exposed to the sun. By cultivation it gradually becomes like the soil, but is not so friable. It is nearly impervious when undisturbed; is underlaid by sand and gravel at from 10 to 20 feet, and is generally easily cultivated, except when wet. The chief crops are corn, cotton, wheat, and oats. Nearly one-half the land is planted in cotton, growing on comparatively fresh land to 4 and 5 feet, and at this height is most productive. Cotton runs to weed on rich and wet lands in wet seasons. Very shallow tillage may restrain the plant and favor bolling a little, but very little. The seed-cotton product per acre on fresh land is 1,000 pounds, requiring 1,660 pounds for a 475-pound bale. The staple is very good. After ten years' cultivation the product is from 700 to 1,200 pounds if the land is kept from washing by horizontalizing. In this case 1,660 pounds are also required for a bale, and the staple is about the same as the other, excepting on very poor land, when it is shorter. The weeds are crab-grass and cocklebur. Very little of the land lies turned out. Hilly or broken lands, when turned out, wash so badly that their restoration costs more than they are worth. The slopes wash readily, causing serious damage. The valleys are not injured much thereby, there being little sand in the washings. Considerable horizontalizing and hillside ditching have been tried, with satisfactory results when well done.

The *dark loams of the second bottoms* of Forked Deer and Hatchie rivers form a fifth of the lands, occurring in areas from a fourth to 1 mile or 2 miles in width, and from 5 to 10 miles in length. The natural timber is poplar, ash, red and white oaks, beech, hickory, hackberry, sweet gum, and dogwood. The soil is from 8 to 12, or in places 4 to 5 inches thick, and has for the most part a subsoil resembling that of the uplands, which is underlaid by sand and gravel at from 10 to 15 feet. It is later and colder than the uplands, especially where not well drained. The soil is best adapted to corn and cotton, and when thoroughly drained produces wheat well. One-half of it is put in cotton, which grows to a height of 5 or 6 feet. The seed-cotton product on fresh land is from 1,200 to 1,800 pounds, according to season, requiring 1,660 pounds for a 475-pound bale. The staple is equal to any. After ten years' cultivation the product is nearly as good as at first, and the staple about the same. The weeds on this soil are crab-grass, smart-weed, and cocklebur. None of it, to my knowledge, lies turned out. This land is generally nearly level, and does not wash badly. Some of it is rolling enough to be benefited by horizontalizing, but does not need hillside ditching. Parts of it would be benefited by underdraining, but very little of this is done.

The following special descriptions are given by other correspondents, in addition to the soils described above:

P. T. GLASS AND JOE L. LEA.—Cotton on the margins of rivers and lakes is protected from frost in the spring and fall by the waters. The first bottom soils of the Hatchie are clayey and cold; the second make a rank growth of cotton. The lands of this and the Mississippi river embrace clay and sandy loams and stiff buckshot clays.

E. R. OLDHAM AND I. A. LACKEY (eastern part of county).—The uplands of Cane creek and its tributaries are undulating and rather hilly, but the soils are very productive. The bottom soil forms about one-fifth of the lands, and lies along the creek in strips half a mile wide. About half is planted in cotton, which grows to a height of from 4 to 5 feet, producing most when highest. The seed-cotton product on fresh land is about 1,400 pounds, and about the same after four years' cultivation.

F. T. RICE AND J. J. ANDERSON.—The chief soil of the southeastern and southern parts of the county is the dark or mulatto upland, which is best adapted to cotton, yielding about 1,400 pounds of seed-cotton per acre on fresh land, or 500 pounds after ten years' cultivation. The troublesome weeds are crab-grass, purslane, Jamestown weed, cocklebur, and hog-weed. The dark loam soil of Lagoon and Williams' creeks, or second bottom, makes one-fourth of our lands. It reaches out 25 or 30 miles. The timber growth is tupelo-gum and cane. The subsoil is red clay, baking hard when exposed, and is underlaid by some sand-rock at from 20 to 35 feet. The tilling qualities of the land are tolerably good in dry seasons, but not good in wet. It is early and warm if well drained, and is best adapted to cotton, three-fifths of the land being planted in this staple. The height usually attained is 5 feet, the best at 6 feet. The seed-cotton product on fresh land is 1,600 pounds, 1,545 pounds making a 475-pound bale. It rates as middling. After ten years' culture the product is 700 pounds, the staple being slightly better. The weeds are cocklebur, purslane, and hog-weed. None of this land lies turned out.

The Hatchie bottom soil forms one-twentieth of our lands. It is a strip 2 miles wide and very long. The soil is 3 feet thick, with a red subsoil, under which is sand at from 15 to 20 feet. It is early and warm if well drained, and is best adapted to cotton, two-thirds of the land being planted in this staple. Cotton grows to a height of 5 feet, but is best at 6½ feet. The product on fresh land and the staple are as in the second bottom. After ten years' cultivation it yields 1,000 pounds per acre.

(J. H. Flowers, W. W. Hurt, R. L. Halliburton, and J. C. Marley.—Their reports of the uplands and bottom lands are similar to those given.)

423

TIPTON.

Population: 21,033.—White, 10,482; colored, 10,551.
Area: 330 square miles.—Woodland, all.
Tilled lands: 100,666 acres.—Area planted in cotton, 38,429 acres; in corn, 32,379 acres; in wheat, 7,363 acres; in oats, 2,431 acres; in tobacco, 46 acres.
Cotton production: 21,415 bales; average cotton product per acre, 0.56 bale, 795 pounds seed-cotton, or 265 pounds cotton lint.

The greater part of Tipton county is upland, and is included in the bluff region belt. The line of bluffs forming the western termination of the uplands or plateau highlands strikes the Mississippi river below the mouth of the Hatchie, and, after bordering the river for several miles, and forming what is known as the second Chickasaw bluff, bears off toward Memphis, leaving a comparatively narrow strip of bottom, which has been estimated to average 4 miles in width. This, together with four islands, Nos. 35, 36, 37, and the one named Centennial, makes up the part of the Mississippi alluvial plain pertaining to Tipton. The parts of the islands in cultivation, presenting superior cotton lands, aggregate something more than one-seventh of their area (see page 14). The limited cultivated lands along the east bank of the Mississippi occur chiefly in two separate strips. Much of the alluvial plain within the county, as well as of the first bottoms of the Hatchie river, is subject to overflow.

The surface of the upland portion of Tipton county might be inferred by one knowing the characteristics of the bluff region belt. It is in general an undulating table-land, traversed here and there by creek valleys. In some parts it becomes hilly, especially as we go westward and meet the breaks of the bluffs. The fresh soils are generally dark brown, rich and productive, resting upon a yellowish or reddish, siliceous, and often compact subsoil. Dark alluvial soils lie at intervals along the creeks and branches. The second bottoms and gently sloping lands between the streams and the highlands present very fertile and important agricultural areas. Nearly all the lands in Tipton, except those of the low bottoms subject to deep overflow and some steep hills, are suitable for cotton culture. As compared with the total area, the southeastern part of the county lies in the belt of highest percentage of acreage in cotton.

Cotton is shipped to Memphis by rail at $1 75, and by water to Saint Louis or New Orleans at $1 per bale.

ABSTRACTS FROM REPORTS.

Dr. W. H. Hill, S. P. Driver, and J. U. Green.—The upland soil of Town creek and Big Hatchie river is a black loam. Some of the flats near the creeks and large branches have patches of a white gravelly soil; the balance is a rich loam. Cotton in the valleys and lowlands is liable to injury by frost. The land is too rich and the cotton runs too much to weed. Our remedy is to plant early, and generally to top the cotton, checking the growth. The uplands are preferred for cotton, as they are more easily cultivated, are better drained, which is a great item, and the crop matures earlier. The kinds of soils are: (1) Clay loam uplands; (2) black loam of Town creek and Hatchie river above overflow; (3) whitish gray or crawfishy. The chief soil is the clay loam, forming three-fifths of our lands, and extending in every direction to the confines of the county. Its growth is white and black oaks, poplar, hickory, black and white walnuts, sugar-maple, and other varieties. In the main, the subsoil is a rich, red clay, which under the microscope shows fine particles of sand, and is easily gullied. It is underlaid by sand and gravel at from 10 to 20 feet. The chief crops are corn, cotton, wheat, oats, potatoes, and sorghum, the soil being well adapted to these. Over one-half is planted in cotton, which grows to a height of from 3 to 5 feet, and is most productive at 4 feet. To restrain the plant and favor bolling we plant early, run no center furrow when bedding, bar off while cultivating, and top. On fresh land the seed-cotton product per acre is from 1,000 to 1,500 pounds, 1,780 pounds being required for a 475-pound bale. The staple is from low middling to middling. After fifteen years' cultivation the product is on fair upland, which has been rotated, 800 pounds. The texture is as good, though probably not so long in fiber. The weeds troubling us are careless-weed, purslane, and crab-grass. In the southeastern portion of the county one-eighth of this land lies turned out; in other parts, none. By putting in clover or peas such land in a few years can be made to yield good crops. The soil washes readily on slopes, and the valleys are injured at least 33 per cent. Hillside ditching to a small extent and horizontalizing have been tried with the best results. It is to be regretted that it was not commenced sooner.

The *black loam* forms nearly two-fifths of our land, and generally exists in large bodies. It occurs in every part of the county, and embraces nearly all of the branch, creek, and river bottoms. Its timber is black oak, the finest in the world, red gum, ash, hickory, hackberry, walnut, mulberry, dogwood, papaw, hornbeam, and hazel-nut. Its thickness is from 1 foot to 15 feet. The subsoil is generally a red or yellow clay, which is underlaid by sand at from 20 to 30 feet. The land is easily tilled, unless suffered to bake in dry seasons before being plowed. It is best adapted to corn, cotton, wheat, and oats, and will make from 2 to 4 tons of timothy or clover per acre. All well-drained portions are planted in cotton. It grows from 6 to 10 feet high, but is best at 5 feet. In seasonable years it will yield from 1,200 to 1,500 pounds of seed-cotton, which rates as low middling. After fifteen years' cultivation its product is from 1,000 to 1,300 pounds, the staple not being quite so good. The weeds are cocklebur, careless-weed, and sometimes crab-grass. None of it is turned out. It does not wear out, though it may become exhausted by continuing in one crop. This land is level, and does not wash.

The *whitish-gray or crawfishy* soil forms less than one-fifth of the lands, and can be found in every part of the county at the foot of hills, in depressions on uplands, and in creek and branch bottoms. Cotton is seldom planted on such land.

J. H. Shinault (see abstract, Bluff region, Part I) and Dr. T. W. Roane (southern part of the county).—On the lands of Beaver Dam creek cotton is seldom injured by frost. We prefer upland that is fresh or has been well taken care of.

Upland gray loam forms seven-eighths of our land, and, excepting valley lands, prevails throughout the county. Its thickness is 5 inches or more. The subsoil varies from a pale yellow, crumbling clay to a deep yellow or orange tenacious clay, and is underlaid by sand and gravel (rarely by calcareous layers) at from 20 to 50 feet. The timber growth is hickory, post, white, and red oaks, poplar, and dogwood. When new and fresh the soil is best adapted to corn and oats; when several years old and well preserved, to cotton. Sixty per cent. is put in cotton. Weeds are restrained and bolling favored by very early planting, rapid culture, early laying by, and also by the application of well-rotted manure. The seed-cotton product on fresh land is from 600 to 1,000 pounds, 1,650 pounds being required for a 475-pound bale. After ten years' cultivation the product is from 400 to 1,200 pounds, according to preservation, exposure, and previous tillage. The staple from this is finer, longer, and of a richer color than that from fresh land. Crab-grass is the worst enemy the cotton-plant has. In some localities 5 per cent. of this land lies turned out; in others, from 30 to 50 per cent. If not washed badly, it will, when cultivated again, produce well. For twenty-five years horizontalizing has been done, and where well done the washing is but slight.

The, *black alluvial* of the bottoms forms 20 per cent. of our lands, there being, however, not more than 8 per cent. of this land in cultivation. One-half the cleared portion is put in cotton. The seed-cotton product on fresh land is 1,000 pounds per acre, but the yield increases as the land gets older.

The crops of the black upland soil are cotton, corn, wheat, oats, and clover. About three-fifths of this soil is planted in cotton, which grows to a height of 4 feet. The seed-cotton product per acre on fresh land is 1,000 pounds, 1,660 pounds being required to make a bale of 475 pounds. After fifteen years' cultivation the soil will produce 800 pounds if well cared for. The troublesome weeds are crab-grass, smart-weed, rag-weed, and cocklebur. One-tenth of this land lies turned out, but most of it can be reclaimed.

The *gray buckshot soil* is that of branch bottoms, and makes about one-eighth of our soil. It is good for herd's-grass, but not for cotton. The heavy buckshot or bottom land is suited for cotton, and also produces fine herd's-grass.

A. W. SMITH (northwestern part of the county, Indian Creek lands).—The seasons often prove too short for full maturity of the crops. One-half of our cultivated land is put in cotton. The soils are gray uplands and bottom lands above overflow. The latter is a rich loam, mixed with some sand, very productive, and will make under good tillage 1,500 pounds of seed-cotton per acre. It is designated as alluvial, and aggregates a fourth of the land, and occurs near the streams all over the county. Its growth is walnut, hickory, sassafras of large size, beech, gums, cottonwood, black and white oaks, pecan, dogwood, and papaw. There is also a cold gray soil good only for grass; but there is very little of it, and it is not cultivated.

SHELBY.

Population: 78,430.—White, 34,508; colored, 43,922.
Area: 690 square miles.—Woodland, all, excepting small lake areas in the Mississippi bottom.
Tilled lands: 195,726 acres.—Area planted in cotton, 92,020 acres; in corn, 55,260 acres; in oats, 5,216 acres; in wheat, 3,564 acres; in rye, 378 acres; in tobacco, 41 acres.
Cotton production: 46,388 bales; average cotton product per acre, 0.50 bale, 714 pounds seed-cotton, or 238 pounds cotton lint.

Shelby is the most southern of the tier of counties bordering the Mississippi river; a tier which, if Lake and Obion be made one, as they were of old, includes both the whole of the Tennessee portion of the Mississippi bottom and very nearly all of the bluff region belt. Shelby county has comparatively little of the Mississippi alluvium. The line of bluffs strikes the river at Memphis, and is not at any point many miles from it. The comparatively narrow intervening bottoms usually have their higher "front-lands" along the river, supplying cultivated strips at intervals, and lower "back-lands", often swampy, toward the bluffs. Cotton is a chief crop in the cultivated areas.

Disregarding the limited Mississippi alluvium, the county is an undulating upland plateau lying in the bluff region belt. It is abundantly supplied with streams, and the Loosahatchee and Wolf rivers traverse it. Among its creeks Big creek and Nonconnah run through large sections. The chief soil is that of the upland. This, where fresh, is a light-brown loam resting upon an ashen-gray, often yellowish or reddish-yellow, siliceous subsoil, containing more or less of both clayey and calcareous matter. The subsoil in the reports is called clay, a name not expressing its nature. It comes chiefly from the underlying formation of fine siliceous silt or earth called loess, or often, on the slopes, from a mixture of loess with material (sand, gravel, and clay) from strata underlying the loess in turn. (See further under "Bluff region", on page 17, an analysis of the soil and one of the subsoils being there given.) The lands are very fertile and vary little in character. The forest growth is heavy and varied, and consists of white and red oaks, hickories, poplar, sweet and black gums, elm, maple, cottonwood, ash, walnut, beech, honey-locust, mulberry, red-bud, dogwood, occasionally holly, and others. When first cleared the lands produced large crops for half a lifetime, but by bad culture have been in some regions much worn; yet when properly treated they may be restored to almost their original fertility. Cotton is the great staple. The county stands at the head of the list in number of bales produced, and also ranks high in the percentage of bales to the acre. About one-half of the tilled lands of the county is planted in cotton. In some parts the proportion is two-thirds or three-fourths. The bottoms of the Wolf and the Loosahatchee rivers and of the larger creeks supply in the aggregate much rich and available land. As compared, however, with the uplands it has small importance.

Shipments are made to Memphis at 65 or 70 cents per bale.

ABSTRACTS FROM REPORTS.

(Abstracts from the reports, respectively, of H. L. Douglas and W. H. Nelson have been given on pages 18 and 19, under "Bluff region".)

JAMES STEWART (county generally).—The upland varies little, and the level and plateau-like portions are as fine as need be. Rolling lands require to be protected by circling, plowing, and ditching. The low areas are extremely rich. All kinds of soils are put in cotton, which is cultivated all over the county. The original soil is 12 inches or more in thickness, resting upon a yellow, heavy clay loam, averaging 4 feet in depth, very rich and fertile when broken up, sometimes leachy and sometimes impervious. The subsoil is underlaid by sand and gravel. The land is easily tilled at all times, and is well adapted, with fair culture and attention, to any crop suited to the climate. About one-half of the aggregate crop of the county is cotton. The plant grows from 1 foot to 5 feet, the higher the better. The seed-cotton product per acre on fresh land is from 1,000 to 1,700 pounds, 1,760 pounds being required for a 475-pound bale. The staple is first class. On our worst land the product per acre is 350 pounds, requiring five times that much for a bale. The staple is short and inferior. We have no weeds worth noticing. Two-thirds of the land lies turned out; but such land produces as well as ever when it regains freshness, but it is often allowed to go into gullies. The soil washes badly on slopes—to the improvement, however, of the valleys. Efforts are made to check the drainage by horizontalizing and hillside ditching, and is our only chance for working rolling land.

Dr. S. HAMMONTREE AND Dr. W. D. TUCKER (civil district No. 4, lands of Big creek).—The soils cultivated in cotton are the clay loam of the uplands and the alluvial. The clay loam is found on all the uplands, and forms about two-thirds of the lands. It extends west to the Mississippi bottom, east 10 miles, and has a thickness of from 6 to 8 inches. Sand and gravel occur at from 30 to 60 feet below the surface. The soil is easily tilled in dry weather, and is early and warm when well drained. It is apparently best adapted to cotton, in which two-thirds of it is planted. Cotton attains a height of from 2 to 5 feet, 3 and 4 feet being the most productive. To favor bolling some farmers remove the dirt, and some top the plant. The seed-cotton product per acre is from 1,000 to 1,500 pounds, about 1,500 pounds being needed for a 475-pound bale; average cotton lint rates as middling. After ten years' cultivation level lands (unmanured) will make from 1,000 to 1,200 pounds, about the same as before being required for a bale. The staple on fresh land is longer and coarser; on old land shorter and finer. Very little land lies turned out. In the southeastern portion of the county, however, that turned out amounts to from 10 to 20 per cent. Such land, if again cultivated, produces very well. The soil washes seriously on slopes, very much to the injury of the valleys. Circling has been done to check the damage, with very good results.

THE BROWN-LOAM TABLE-LANDS.

This subdivision includes the following counties: Fayette, Hardeman, Haywood, Madison, Crockett, Gibson, and Weakley, together with large parts of Henry* and Carroll,* and very small parts of the counties mentioned below. The first seven only, called "midland counties", are considered here. Carroll and Henry are referred to in the next group. On the west the southeastern corners of Obion, Tipton, and Shelby, and on the east the northwestern corners of Henderson and McNairy, project into this area, but the parts thus included are inconsiderable.

FAYETTE.

Population: 31,871.—White, 9,633; colored, 22,238.
Area: 640 square miles.—Woodland, all.
Tilled lands: 197,516 acres.—Area planted in cotton, 92,231 acres; in corn, 63,419 acres; in wheat, 3,737 acres; in oats, 3,661 acres; in tobacco, 66 acres.
Cotton production: 39,221 bales; average cotton product per acre, 0.43 bale, 606 pounds seed-cotton, or 202 pounds cotton lint.

Fayette county ranks next to Shelby in the number of bales of cotton produced in 1879, both being much ahead of any other county, and makes the best showing of all upon the map of acreage in cotton. The large tract of upland country in the southeastern corner of the state, bounded on the north and east by the Big Hatchie river, is noted for its great fertility. Of this area, Fayette county is nearly the central as well as an important part. The county is traversed by the Loosahatchee and Wolf rivers, and is well supplied with smaller streams. Much of the surface is level or moderately undulating. The western part is inclined to be hilly, with extended plateaus; the southeastern portion is more hilly, but with fertile valleys. In the southern portion the valley of Wolf river affords much alluvial land in its extended bottoms.

The formation underlying, and in great part giving character to the soils and subsoils of the uplands, is the orange-sand drift, a series of sands, clays, and sometimes gravel. Below the drift are strata more clayey, which, when the former is absent, yield stiffer soils with less sand. The soil of the higher lands is a mellow, warm, siliceous, or sandy loam, well suited to a variety of crops. It is readily washed on the slopes, and requires judicious management. The valleys supply a fair proportion of alluvial lands. The forest growth of the uplands is oak, walnut, poplar, and hickory, often of great size; of the bottoms, white and overcup oaks, beech, red and black gum, birch, and, along the streams, cypress. Shipments are made to Memphis at from $1 50 to $2 25 per bale.

The reports obtained from the county refer chiefly to particular regions, and two are confined to the Wolf river country. No report containing an adequate description of the upland soils in general was received. The characteristics of these, however, are much the same as those of the upland soils of the parts of Hardeman and Haywood counties contiguous.

ABSTRACTS FROM REPORTS.

J. B. THORNTON AND A. L. PEARSON (southwestern corner of the county, creeks of Wolf river).—The uplands in this region are rolling, and are locally known as "ridge land", little of them being sufficiently level to be called table-land. The soils cultivated in cotton are: (1) Creek bottoms; (2) ridge land; (3) "buckshot" clay land. The chief soil is the creek bottom, which forms one-half of the lands, occurring with little variation in all directions. It is generally a yellowish, sometimes dark, sandy loam, about 8 inches thick, and rests upon a sandy yellow clay, which changes to a lighter color upon exposure to the air, and is in most places leachy. Strata of sand are met with at from 20 to 60 feet. The soil is easily tilled at all times, and is early, warm, and well drained. The crops produced are cotton and corn, two-thirds of the land being planted in the former, which grows to a height of from 3 to 3½ feet, but corn is the most productive crop. Cotton runs to weed in wet weather, which can be remedied by throwing dirt from the roots or "barring off". On fresh land the seed-cotton product is 800 pounds per acre, requiring 1,600 pounds for a 475-pound bale, which rates as middling. After three years' cultivation the product is 750 pounds, the same amount being required for a bale. The troublesome weeds are cocklebur and morning-glory vines. But little of the land lies turned out, and such land produces as well as ever when cultivated again.

The "ridge land" or upland soil makes one-half of our lands, and extends off indefinitely in all directions. The growth is oak, gum, hickory, poplar, etc. It is a sandy clay from 4 to 5 inches thick, resting upon a yellow clay subsoil, with sand below at from 20 to 40 feet. The soil is easily tilled in all seasons, but is sometimes inclined to run together and bake. It is early, warm, naturally well drained, and is best adapted to cotton, in which two-thirds is planted. The cotton grows to a height of 2 feet, and at this is most productive. When fresh, it produces 750 pounds of seed-cotton per acre, 1,600 pounds being required for a bale of 475 pounds. After three years' cultivation it produces from 500 to 750 pounds, the same amount making a bale. The weeds are crab-grass and fox-tail. One-fourth of the land lies turned out, and is owing more to want of hands than to anything else. Such land produces well when again cultivated. It washes seriously on slopes, much to the damage of the lower grounds. Some hillside ditching has been done with good success.

Of the "buckshot" *clay loam* there is but little. It is white or gray, with an impervious clay subsoil, contains soft gravel-like particles, and in dry seasons produces cotton well.

A. D. LEWIS (southeastern part of the county, Wolf river lands).—On the west of Wolf river are the fine alluvial lands, but they are low and late, and their crops are liable to be caught by frost. The best cotton land is the black sandy upland—a prairie soil lying mostly on second bottoms and slopes. It forms one-fourth of our lands, and occurs on creeks and along rivers in long strips a fourth to half a mile wide. Its subsoil is sandy and leachy. Two-thirds of the land is planted in cotton, which grows to a height of 3 and 4 feet, the latter being the most productive. On fresh land the seed-cotton product is from 1,000 to 1,200 pounds per acre, and after eight years' cultivation from 600 to 800 pounds. On bottoms, after eight years, the product is from 1,000 to 1,200 pounds. Twenty-five per cent. of this land lies turned out. Such land, when again cultivated, does well for two or three years. On our flat lands we have a white pipe-clay, which is impervious to water.

J. M. GALLAWAY (northwestern part of the county, Cane Creek alluvial region).—The soils are the black alluvial, with here and there crawfishy lands, the latter a white gravelly kind. These make up all our lands. Similar lands are found elsewhere in Fayette, and also in Tipton and Shelby counties. The growth is poplar, oak, gum, hickory, ash, walnut, elm, and dogwood. The soil is a loam with but little clay. One-half the land is planted in cotton, of which the tallest, though not always the most productive height, is 5 feet. The seed-cotton product on fresh land is 1,000 pounds per acre, requiring 1,545 pounds for a 475-pound bale, which rates as middling and fair. After ten years' cultivation we can see but little difference. Cotton is generally better on lands that have been cultivated for three or four years. About 10 per cent. of the land lies turned out.

HARDEMAN.

Population : 22,921.—White, 13,313 ; colored, 9,608.
Area : 610 square miles.—Woodland, all.
Tilled lands : 120,437 acres.—Area planted in cotton, 44,885 acres ; in corn, 45,207 acres ; in wheat, 4,758 acres ; in oats, 2,554 acres ; in tobacco, 84 acres.
Cotton production : 18,937 bales ; average cotton product per acre, 0.42 bale, 600 pounds seed-cotton, or 200 pounds cotton lint.

Hardeman is one of the southern tier of counties, and lies immediately east of Fayette. Its central and western portions are generally level or moderately rolling. The northern part is more broken, but includes many level areas. The eastern and southern portions are more or less hilly, but include many good farming sections. The county is remarkably well and symmetrically watered. The Big Hatchie flows diagonally through it from the southeastern corner to the northwestern, splitting the county into two triangular sections. Into the Hatchie, as the main channel, the numerous tributary creeks, with coarses mostly at right angles to the river, pour their contents. Thus the two parts of the county, separated by the valley of the Hatchie, are each cut up into sections by the parallel valleys of the creeks. The streams afford along their borders a large aggregate of rich alluvial land, with which, at intervals, stiff crawfishy areas occur.

The prevailing upland soil, the most important in the county, is a rich, mellow, siliceous loam, warm and early, resting upon a reddish yellow, sandy clay, the underlying formation being the orange sand. It is found all over the county, but spreads out most uniformly in the western and northwestern parts—parts which belong to the area of the highest percentage yield of cotton. In the eastern and southeastern sections of the county, in addition to lands such as have been noticed, are others more clayey and some quite calcareous. These are based upon the outcrops of formations below the orange sand.

The growth of the chief soil, the siliceous loam of the uplands, is in the more level parts of Hardeman red, white, and post oaks, hickory, walnut, wild cherry, dogwood, red-bud, and in the western part black-jack oak. In the more hilly portions, the southwestern, southern, and northeastern, black-jack and Spanish oaks and chestnut are found. The growth of the lowlands is beech, white and red oaks, sweet and black gums, poplar, hackberry, red-bud, cane, and others. Areas of yellow pine occur in the northeastern and eastern portions. Cypress is met with along the streams. Shipments of cotton are made to Memphis at $2 and $2 10 per bale.

ABSTRACTS FROM REPORTS.

H. M. POLK (lowlands and uplands of Spring creek and Hatchie river).—Our uplands vary but little, often affording thousands of acres suitable for cultivation. On account of late and early frosts the uplands are preferred for cotton. The counties in the southwestern part of Tennessee, having generally a soil of rich siliceous loam, are the best for cotton. The soil, which is warm and matures the crop earlier than elsewhere in the state, has been described in Part I. Probably one-fourth of the land once cultivated lies turned out. Time, aided by weeds, broom-grass, *Lespedeza striata*, etc., restores its capacity for half a crop. It washes and matures very easily, and on slopes seriously, to the injury of the valleys. Horizontalizing and hillside ditching have been practiced by all farmers for the saving of the soil.

The siliceous or the sandy loam of the bottoms of Spring and Pleasant Run creeks form about a twentieth of the lands, and occurs throughout the valleys of the two streams named. Its timber is white and red oaks, beech, red-bud, hackberry, etc. It is of gray, buff, and brown colors, 12 inches thick, resting upon a subsoil of yellowish clay, thought not to be so rich as the red clay subsoil of uplands. It is easily cultivated in dry seasons, is late and well drained, and is best adapted to corn. One-fourth is planted in cotton, which grows to a height of 3 or 4 feet. The plant inclines to run to weed in warm, wet seasons, when the land is fresh. The remedy is shallow cultivation after deep breaking of the soil in the spring. The seed-cotton product on fresh land is from 600 to 700 pounds, requiring from 1,545 to 1,750 pounds for a 475-pound bale. The staple rates high. After twenty years' cultivation the yield is about the same, the staple being shorter. Crab-grass is troublesome. Very little of this land lies turned out. Rest improves all land.

The heavy loam of Hatchie river, mostly above overflow, is a sandy loam similar to that of the uplands, but colder, and makes about a twentieth of our lands. Its timber is white oak, beech, gum, and cane. The soil is a brown or blackish clay loam, 24 inches thick, and rests upon a subsoil of yellowish clay, containing fine white sand. In tilling qualities, crops, proportion, and yield of cotton, as well as in seed-cotton product, it is much like the soil described.

O. B. POLK (western part of the county).—The soils cultivated in cotton are: (1) Mellow siliceous upland loam, varying but little; (2) sandy loam bottom lands of Dry creek; (3) gravelly land in small spots of 1 or 0 acres. The chief is the mellow siliceous soil, comprising three-fourths of the lands. It extends north 8 miles to Whiteville, south 15 miles to the state line, west 2 miles to Fayette county, and east 5 miles to Spring creek. Its growth is red, black-jack, post oaks, and hickory. It is a fine sandy dark-colored loam 5 inches thick, resting upon red clay, which, when mixed with the soil, produces well. Sand is met with at from 6 to 10 feet. It is easily tilled in wet or dry seasons, and is early, warm, and well drained. Its chief crops are cotton and corn, but it is best adapted to cotton, three-fourths of the land being planted with this staple. The plant grows to 3 feet, its most productive height. The seed-cotton product per acre on fresh land is 1,250 pounds; on land cultivated for ten years, from 600 to 700 pounds. In the first case, 1,660 pounds are generally required for a 475-pound bale; in the second, 1,780 pounds. Cotton marketed at home is not sold on the basis of staple, but as to cleanliness and freedom from trash. Crab-grass is our enemy. But little of the land lies turned out, say one-fifteenth. Such land, when taken in again, produces well for three or four years. On slopes the soil washes seriously, to the injury of the valleys.

The sandy loam of Dry creek forms only one twenty-fifth of our lands. It occurs throughout the area embracing the first soil. Its growth is red oak and hickory. One-third of it is planted in cotton, which attains a height of 4 feet.

The gravelly land, of which there is about 1 per cent., occurs in small spots, containing an acre or two each, scattered through the area indicated above for the others. Its growth is persimmon, Spanish oak, and sweet gum. It produces fine cotton when properly drained.

427

J. A. MANSON AND E. E. LOW (southwestern corner of the county).—The kinds of soils cultivated in cotton are: (1) Mahogany clay (siliceous) loam; (2) black sandy loam; (3) light sandy loam. The chief soil is the mahogany clay soil, which forms four-fifths of the land in this region. Its timber is oak of many kinds, hickory, and chestnut. On the lowlands are poplar, beech, and sweet and black gums. (Description agrees with that given by O. B. Polk.)

The *black sandy loam* constitutes a fifth of our lands. Cotton is planted on two-thirds of this soil, yielding from 1,000 to 1,500 pounds of seed-cotton per acre. The staple rates first class.

The *light sandy loam* forms a twentieth of the lands in this region. Six miles to the northeast and southeast there is much of it. Its growth is black-jack, scrub oak, scrub hickory, and chestnut. It rests upon a subsoil of gray clay, mixed with sand. One-half is planted in cotton, which grows from half a foot to 2 feet in height, yielding from 400 to 600 pounds of seed-cotton per acre. The staple is first class. Two-thirds of the land lies turned out. It washes seriously, to the great injury of the valleys.

WILLIAM RUSH (region northeast from Bolivar, Piney Creek lands).—The upland soils, in patches of from 1 acre to 10 acres, vary greatly from ridge to ridge as to kind and productiveness. The bottoms also vary much. In wet seasons the cotton in bottoms is too late; in dry, it does well; but good upland is considered the best. The soils in cotton are: (1) Black sandy and clay upland; (2) piny bottom land above overflow; (3) crawfishy or white gravelly bottom land. The principal soil is the black sandy and clay upland, about one-fifth of the tillable land, and occurs in patches from the headwaters of Piney creek to the Hatchie river. Its growth is red, black, and Spanish oaks, walnut, and in places yellow pine. It is a fine sandy loam 5 inches thick, and rests upon a yellow clay subsoil, which is mixed with sand, and works well after exposure. Sand is met with at 10 feet. The soil works more easily in wet seasons than that of any other land. Its crops are corn, cotton, wheat, and oats, to all of which it is well adapted. About one-fourth is planted in cotton, the plant growing to 3½ feet. The seed-cotton product per acre is 1,000 pounds, requiring 1,485 pounds for a 475-pound bale; it rates as middling. After ten years' cultivation, if the land is kept from washing, the yield is 800 pounds. Of this 1,545 pounds are required for a bale, the staple differing little. The weeds are cocklebur and crab-grass. One-fourth of the land lies turned out, but little of it being cultivated again. It washes readily on slopes, but has not as yet seriously injured the valleys. Horizontalizing and hillside ditching have been practiced, and with good results where kept up.

The *piny bottom land* forms about one-half of the tillable land, and occurs throughout the length of the valley of Piney creek. Its growth is white oak, gum, beech, poplar, and ash. It is a sandy clay loam, early and warm when well drained, 8 inches thick, with a yellow clay subsoil. It is tilled with difficulty in wet seasons, but very easily in dry. It is best adapted to corn and cotton. About one-fourth is planted in cotton, which grows to 4 feet. Too much rain inclines the plant to run to weed. Our remedy is to turn out the middles with the turning-plow. The seed-cotton product on fresh land is 1,000 pounds per acre; on land worked for twenty-five years it is 800 pounds in good seasons. The staple in both cases rates middling. The weeds are cocklebur, smart-weed, rag-weed, and crab-grass. None of this land lies turned out.

The third soil, the crawfishy, forms about a fourth of the bottom lands. It occurs throughout the valley of Piney creek, and there is hardly a 10-acre field but that has some of it. Its timber is gum, maple, beech, etc. It is a gravelly, whitish to blackish clay loam, sometimes putty-like, 5 inches thick, with a subsoil of a lighter color. The subsoil, when at the surface, is nearly white; is impervious when undisturbed. The soil is late, cold, and ill drained, tolerably well adapted to cotton, in which one-fourth is planted. The plant usually grows to 3½ feet; in wet seasons to 5 feet. The seed-cotton product on fresh land is about 800 pounds per acre; on land worked for fifteen years, 700 pounds. In both cases it rates middling, and 1,545 pounds are required for a bale. The weeds are smart-weed, rag-weed, and cocklebur. None of this land lies turned out.

HAYWOOD.

Population: 26,053.—White, 8,497; colored, 17,556.

Area: 570 square miles.—Woodland, all, excepting a few small lakes in the Hatchie river bottom.

Tilled lands: 137,155 acres.—Area planted in cotton, 49,919 acres; in corn, 39,878 acres; in wheat, 5,326 acres; in oats, 2,976 acres; in tobacco, 62 acres.

Cotton production: 23,092 bales; average cotton product per acre, 0.46 bale, 660 pounds seed-cotton, or 220 pounds cotton lint.

Haywood county ranks third in the number of bales of cotton produced in 1879. Two-thirds of the county lies in the area having the greatest percentage of acreage in cotton. Little variety comparatively is presented in its surface and soil. It is a plateau region, traversed in its southern part by the Hatchie river, and having the South Forked Deer along its northern boundary. These rivers have numerous tributary creeks well distributed through the county. Much of Haywood is a water-shed lying between the Hatchie and South Forked Deer, with gentle slopes, yet embracing large areas of level lands. The chief soil is that of the uplands, a fine, dark, siliceous loam, warm, easily tilled, and extending pretty well over the county. It is mellow, readily washed, and requires careful culture. In some sections the land has been overworked or carelessly worked, and is badly worn or washed. The subsoil is usually a reddish clay, below which lie, at various depths, strata of sand, interstratified occasionally with beds of clay. The growth is white, red, and black oak, poplar, walnut, hickory, ash, dogwood, with papaw and hazel-nut. The creek valleys and the second bottoms of the rivers afford many tracts of valuable land. The second bottoms, lying on the north side of the Hatchie, are noted for their productiveness. The first bottoms of the rivers, as well as of many creeks, making in the aggregate a large area, are subject to annual overflows. Cotton is shipped by rail to Memphis at $2 25 per bale, or by water at $1 50; to Jackson, $1 per bale.

ABSTRACTS FROM REPORTS.

AARON WALKER (county generally).—The soil of the uplands was originally a black, light loam, and all of it was tillable. The first river bottoms are subject to overflow, and are not in cultivation. Cotton on lowlands and on fresh, rich soil is liable to be caught by early frost. We prefer good upland. (For kinds, extent, growth, etc., of soil, as reported, see Part I.) The first, the *black upland loam*, is usually not troublesome either in wet or dry seasons. Cotton is the chief crop, but corn and wheat are raised, with some clover and oats. The soil is adapted to any of these when well managed. From one-half to two-thirds of the land is planted in cotton, which attains a height on the first soil of 4 or 5 feet, and on the second and third soils of 1½ to 3 feet; it is most productive at 4 feet. The plant inclines to run to weed on fresh land in wet seasons. There is no certain remedy; early planting should be practiced. The seed-cotton product on fresh land is from 1,200 to 1,500 pounds, 1,545 pounds being required for a 475-pound bale. Staple rates with the best. After five years' cultivation the product is from 1,000 to 1,200 pounds, but much depends upon the season and cultivation. The staple compares favorably with that of fresh land. Crab-grass and careless-weed are the most troublesome. One-tenth of the land lies turned out. Such land, after a crop of pease, and when well circled, will produce well when again cultivated. It washes readily on slopes, the valleys being rather benefited thereby. Horizontalizing and hillside ditching have been practiced with good results where well done and when in time.

F. A. LORD, J. W. KERR, AND DR. H. C. ANDERSON (central, western, and northwestern parts of the county).—The lands of this region in their virgin state were covered with the wild pea-vine and but few bushes. The soils cultivated in cotton are: (1) Upland soil, a light sandy loam, with a clay foundation, very tender and easily washed, not showing sand in excess, as in Madison county; (2) bottom soil, a heavy mixture of loam and sand when good; when not so good, pipe-clay and gravelly loam; (3) the poorest, a stiff white clay, but productive when well drained. The first, the *upland soil* or *loam*, is the chief soil, and forms about two-thirds of the upland, or, including the bottoms of the Hatchie and Forked Deer, one-half the lands. The growth on the best cotton land is black oak, hickory, a few poplars, and some white oak; near the rivers, on second bottoms, poplars and large red oaks predominate. The soil is dark colored, and contains small and soft blackish pebbles, which crush easily. At 40 feet a stiff clay is met with, then sand or white and yellow gravel and hard and smooth sandstone. The chief crops are cotton, corn, wheat, sorghum, Irish and sweet potatoes, oats, etc. The soil suits all of them. About four-sevenths of the land is planted in cotton. The seed-cotton product is from 1,000 to 1,600 pounds per acre, of which from 1,485 to 1,840 pounds, depending partly upon the year, are required for a 475-pound bale. After twenty-five years' cultivation the product is from 250 to 350 pounds, but with a little manure it may be doubled. Crab-grass is our worst enemy. Three-tenths of the land lies turned out so far as I can judge. Such land taken in again is the very best for cotton when well managed, but does not held out more than two years. It washes badly, the great trouble in West Tennessee. The valleys are not always injured thereby. We check the damage mostly by circling, with sufficient fall. It requires thought and tact to do it well, but the results are the very best.

The *glady soil*, of which there is but little, has a growth of white and post oak. Cotton is generally planted upon it, but the yield is uncertain. The land is flat, and does not wash.

HENRY WILLIAMS (northwestern part of the county).—The soils cultivated in cotton are: (1) Black soil with little sand, loose and soft; rolling upland; (2) black, with small black gravel; no sand; (3) level, white gravelly land, cold, wet, and late. The first is the chief soil. One-half of the land is of this kind. It is suited to corn and cotton, two-thirds being planted in the latter. The soil is from 4 to 1½ inches thick, and rests upon a hard, rather sticky red clay subsoil. The seed-cotton product is from 800 to 1,200 pounds, requiring from 1,425 to 1,780 pounds for a 475-pound bale. The second soil is somewhat rolling, add forms about one-third of the lands. It is much like the first soil. About one-half is planted in cotton. The third soil forms about one-sixth of the lands, its chief growth being the post oak, and nearly all of it is planted in cotton, which grows to a height of from 3½ to 4 feet. The seed-cotton product per acre is from 500 to 1,000 pounds. The land remains the same for years. There are no slopes, and hence there is no washing.

H. M. CLARKE AND J. B. BRANTLY (eastern part of the county, between the Hatchie and Forked Deer rivers).—The soils cultivated in cotton are: (1) Fine sandy loam, easily cultivated, and if well circled will not gully badly; (2) a deep, dark, slightly sandy loam of creek bottoms; on this, unless old, cotton grows too rank and matures too slowly; (3) soil mixed with pipe-clay, also of the bottoms; very tenacious, and when wet, very wet; when dry, hard, tough and lumpy in breaking up; drained and broken up, will make the very best cotton in a dry year. The first is the chief kind, forming three-fourths of our ridge land. It extends 5 miles to the west, and from the Forked Deer river, through Madison and Hardeman, to Bolivar county. It is 3 inches thick, and is underlaid by reddish, more tenacious clay, and contains some gravel. Gravel and rock are found at from 5 to 10 feet. Nearly one-half the land is put in cotton, which grows to 3 feet, the most productive height. Cotton runs to weed when not brought to a stand early and is too wet and badly cultivated. Our remedy is early thinning, good cultivation, and shallow plowing. The seed-cotton product is 1,400 pounds per acre, 1,960 pounds making a bale of 400 pounds. On land worked for twenty-five years the product is 600 pounds, 1,300 pounds making a bale. The staple on the old land is slightly better. The only weed seriously troubling us is crab-grass. About one-fourth of the land lies turned out. It produces finely when taken in again, if properly cared for and green manure is turned under before seeding.

The *bottom* or *swamp lands* are in small proportion. The bottom of the Forked Deer river averages a mile in width. Some of this land lies on creeks. The soil is blackish, a part whitish or gray, from 6 inches to several feet in thickness. The subsoil is generally sandy clay; in places clay and gravel. But very little of this land is cultivated. When protected from overflow the land produces corn, cotton, and grasses well.

J. M. SHAW AND PROFESSOR JOSEPH NELSON (eastern part of the county).—Our soils are: (1) The chocolate-colored, undulating hazel-nut plains, the most important and best; (2) white clay loam, adjoining uncultivated bottoms. The soil of the plains or gently rolling uplands form three-fourths of our tillable area, including all the more valuable lands. It extends widely over West Tennessee. The subsoil under the hazel lands is clayey and easily gullied, and contains frequently water-worn pebbles. About three-fourths of the land is planted in cotton. The best height of the plant is 4 feet, which it usually attains. The slopes wash seriously. Horizontalizing is practiced with marked success. In certain more rolling sections one-tenth lies turned out.

The *white clay loam* occurs along all our streams, and, excepting in Hardeman county, where there is more sand, along all the streams in this end of the state. Post oak is the unfailing characteristic growth. The soil is a clay intermixed with buckshot gravel. Cultivation has disclosed no difference between soil and subsoil, save its hard-pan and impervious character. Not much of it is planted in cotton. The plant grows to 3 feet in height. The seed-cotton product is about 1,500 pounds per acre, which is greater after a few years' cultivation, but never equals that of the uplands. Washes from the slopes improve this land.

There is much of the impoverished hazel plains. In Haywood the clay washes easily, and is wasting. The timber was taken off long ago. The negro hands go over it and raise a little low cotton. It never goes to weed; we would that it might.

MADISON.

Population: 30,874.—White, 15,406; colored, 15,468.
Area: 580 square miles.—Woodland, all.
Tilled lands: 125,693 acres.—Area planted in cotton, 45,825 acres; in corn, 46,885 acres; in wheat, 9,623 acres; in oats, 3,157 acres; in tobacco, 67 acres.
Cotton production: 19,257 bales; average cotton product per acre, 0.42 bale, 600 pounds seed-cotton, or 200 pounds cotton lint.

Madison is one of the four counties forming the central area of West Tennessee, the others being Haywood, Crockett, and Gibson. It is nearly square in shape, and, like Hardeman, is cut diagonally by a river into two triangular sections. These sections are nearly equal. The river is the South Fork of the Forked Deer river, running northwestward from the southeastern to the northwestern corner of the county. The Middle Fork of the Forked Deer river runs through and drains the extreme northern portion of the county, while the creeks of the Big Hatchie drain the southwestern. For the greater part the drainage of the surface is into the valley of the South Fork. From the disposition of the waters of the three rivers, the area of the county is made to consist generally of two wide dividing belts of uplands, with the South Fork between and the two slopes of the other streams to the north and the southwest respectively. There are many creeks, some of which are of large size, such as Little Middle Fork, Johnson's, and Cypress. In the main, the surface is a level or undulating table-land. The eastern and southern portions, however, have very rolling or hilly sections. Low ridges, with thinner soils, are sometimes met with on the table-lands.

The deepest strata are beds of usually dark stratified sands and clays. These are mostly covered and concealed by the more superficial deposits of the orange sand. Some of the underlying clays outcrop in the eastern and southeastern parts of the county, giving origin to strips of stiff argillaceous soils. The soil of the uplands is very generally a mellow siliceous or sandy loam, brown when fresh, early, warm, and well suited to cotton culture. It is based on a reddish or sometimes yellowish sandy clay subsoil. The gentle slopes, bottoms of the smaller streams and second bottoms of the larger, afford much good land. The bottoms of the rivers are low, flat, in great part subject to overflow, and are unfit for cultivation. The growth of the uplands includes white, Spanish, black, red, and post oaks, hickories, ash, poplar, mulberry, dogwood, walnut, beech, and in different sections a smaller growth of papaw and hazel-nut. On the poorer ridges are black-jack, post oak, hickory, and some chestnut. The valleys of the branches and the second bottoms of the larger streams supply "poplar", sweet gum, red and white oaks, hickories, maple, walnut, mulberry, ash, sassafras, dogwood, and papaw; and the river bottoms beech, sweet gum, overcup and other oaks, ironwood, hornbeam, shell-bark hickory, maple, poplar, cypress, holly, and tupelo-gum. Cotton is the great crop. Most of the county lies within the greatest percentage belt of acres in cotton, there being 15 per cent. or more of the total area planted in cotton. The remainder of the county (strips to the northwest and southeast) has from 10 to 15 per cent. in cotton. Cotton is shipped by rail to Memphis or Mobile at about $3 per bale.

ABSTRACTS FROM REPORTS.

G. C. BUTLER AND S. M. OSIER (southeastern part of the county, lands of the Forked Deer and its branches).—The uplands vary from slightly rolling to hilly. The soil is in patches of a few acres to 40 and 50 acres. Uplands are preferred, on account of early frosts. The soils planted in cotton are: (1) Dark upland, on ridges, slopes, and level fields; (2) dark sandy soil of the valleys of the Forked Deer river and the branches above overflow; (3) black, muddy, and sandy soils of these streams. The dark upland is the chief soil. Three-fourths of the cotton is raised on such land, a fine sandy loam from 3 to 5 inches thick, and early in dry springs when well drained. The chief crops are corn and cotton first; then wheat, oats, rye, and peas; but the soil is best adapted to corn and peas, though other crops do well. Cotton comprises about three-fifths of the crops, and grows to 2 or 5 feet, but is most productive at 3 or 4 feet. The plant inclines to run to weed on rich, fresh lands when the late summer is wet. Manure favors bolling. The seed-cotton product per acre on fresh land is from 800 to 1,200 pounds, 1,600 pounds being required for a 475-pound bale. The staple is middling and low middling. After twenty years' cultivation the product is from 300 to 1,000 pounds, and the staple about the same. Smart-weed and others abound on good land, but grass is the worst. One-fourth of the land lies turned out, and when taken in again does tolerably well if level and not washed in gullies. The soil washes seriously on slopes, often to the injury of the valleys. Horizontalizing has been practiced with good success where well done.

The dark sandy soil of the valleys varies in places and on different sides of the streams. It is from 6 to 8 inches thick. Two-thirds is planted in cotton, which grows to a height of 4 or 6 feet, but is best at 4 or 5 feet. The seed-cotton product per acre on fresh land is from 800 to 1,200 pounds, 1,660 pounds making a 475-pound bale. Staple is middling. After twenty years' cultivation the product and staple are about the same. The weeds are smart-weed, cocklebur, and other kinds. Very little lies turned out, and where taken in again it has done well. The washing of the soil, the damage done, and the remedy applied are the same as with the first soil.

The black sandy soil of the bottoms forms about one-fourth of our lands, and varies on different sides of the streams like soil 2. It is in the main a fine sandy loam, dark grayish in places, sometimes gravelly, with here and there a clay loam. Cotton grows to 5 or 6 feet. Seed-cotton product per acre on fresh land is from 1,000 to 1,200 pounds when favorable. The staple is middling and low middling. The product on land after twenty years' cultivation is nearly as much as on fresh land.

JOHN Y. KEITH, JOHN J. BOON, AND THOMAS INGRAM (lands of creeks and Forked Deer river).—Early frost is our most serious trouble. A variety of cotton maturing a month earlier than what we have would increase the crop at least one-third. The soils cultivated in cotton are: (1) The table or upland, most reliable, but differing in short distances; (2) creek and branch bottoms; (3) river bottoms. The chief soil is the upland, forming perhaps nine-tenths of our land, and extending, with considerable variation, through most of the county. It is a dark loam, with a little sand, is from 4 to 10 inches thick, and rests upon a sandy, generally yellow, sometimes reddish, clay subsoil. The subsoil is occasionally gravelly or mixed with coarse sand. If hard-pan, it is marked by pools of waters. Tillage is more difficult in wet than in dry seasons.

The soil is best adapted to corn, but produces cotton, wheat, oats, rye, peas, potatoes, peanuts, clover, etc. About one-half the crop is cotton, which grows to 3 and 4 feet, but is best at 3½ feet. We restrain the plant by topping it about the 12th of August. The seed-cotton product per acre on fresh land is from 800 to 1,000 pounds, from 1,485 to 1,660 pounds making a bale of 475 pounds. It rates as other cotton. On land worked for thirty years the product is from 500 to 700 pounds, a bale requiring the same as before, with no difference in staple. The weeds are crab- and foxtail-grasses, rag-weed, cocklebur, smart-weed, iron-weed, white bloom, golden rod, and others. Ten per cent., perhaps, lies turned out; but where taken in again, unless injured by washing or the tramping of stock, it has produced well. It washes seriously on slopes, many fields being nearly ruined and the valleys injured. Horizontalizing and hillside ditching have been practiced, but not with uniform success, as great rains break over and flood the lower lands, doing great damage.

A. D. HURT (western part of the county, lands of Johnson's and Cub creeks and Forked Deer river).—The area reported covers a space 3 miles wide and 6 miles long, on which more cotton is raised than in any other section of the county. For cotton growing we need a dry June; then some rain from the 1st to the 15th of July; then mostly dry weather for a month for blooming and fruiting. The chief soil, black sandy upland and second bottom, commonly designated "table-land", and covering three-fourths of the county, is early, warm, and well drained. Its crops are cotton, corn, wheat, etc. Cotton forms about three-fifths of the crops, and attains a height of 4 or 5 feet; warm rains and keeping the crop clear of grass incline the plant to run to weed. We restrain this by throwing dirt from the roots with a small shovel-plow, care being taken not to check too suddenly. The seed-cotton product per acre on fresh land is, in good seasons, from 1,000 to 1,500 pounds, from 1,485 to 1,780 pounds being required for a bale of 475 pounds. Staple rates good middling. After ten year's cultivation, if crops have been properly alternated, the land will produce as good cotton, if not better, than when fresh. Crab-grass is the troublesome weed. I know of none of this land turned out. The washing on slopes is not serious, ... Horizontalizing and hillside ditching have been practiced with favorable results.

430

The *black-jack ridges*, occurring to the east and southeast, form about a fifth of the lands. The soil is from 1½ to 2 inches thick, and rests upon a red clay containing more or less sand. Below this again is sand at from 15 to 40 feet. The soil is best adapted to cotton, in which about two-fifths is planted. The cotton attains a height of 3 feet, and rarely runs to weed. The seed-cotton product per acre on fresh land is from 350 to 700 pounds, of which from 1,600 to 1,800 pounds are required for a 475-pound bale. After ten years' cultivation the product amounts to little or nothing. One-third lies turned out, and such land is seldom taken in again. It washes seriously, to the injury of lower lands. Horizontalizing and hillside ditching have been tried with unsatisfactory results, the land not justifying the labor.

The *buckshot and crawfishy soil* forms about one-fifth of the lands. It is about 3 inches thick, rests upon a whitish clay subsoil with little sand, which becomes hard upon exposure to the sun; is impervious, contains some gravel, and is underlaid by sand at from 25 to 40 feet. The land is best adapted to grasses. One-tenth is planted in cotton, yielding from 350 to 500 pounds of seed-cotton per acre. Cultivation for a number of years increases the yield.

E. C. Harbert and T. C. Long (western part of the county, lands of Cypress and Johnson's creeks and Forked Deer river).— This region is one of the best for varied crops. With fertilizers and proper cultivation we can make a bale of cotton of 500 pounds to the acre, the only drawback being the shortness of the season. The soils are: (1) The brown, fine, loamy soil of the second bottoms and table-lands, the most reliable; (2) soil of hill or ridge land, as productive as the first, of the same color, but more worn; (3) bottom and swamp land and greenbrier glades, of little value except for timber. The chief soil is the first mentioned, which comprises one-third of the lands and extends through Madison and other counties, and rests upon a subsoil which changes to a deep yellow or red clay at a depth of from 4 to 5 feet. Its crops are corn and cotton, but it is best adapted to corn. More than one-half is planted in cotton, which attains a height of from 2 to 5 feet; but 3 or 4 feet is the best. The seed-cotton product per acre on fresh land is from 1,200 to 1,500 pounds, 1,780 pounds making a bale of 475 pounds. On land worked for ten years the product is from 800 to 1,000 pounds. It rates middling in both cases. Over one-third of the land is turned out. Such land taken in again produces well after the first year. It washes seriously on slopes, sometimes to the ruin of the valleys. Not much horizontalizing has been done since the war. When properly done the results are good. The second soil forms more than a third of the land, and like the first spreads over several counties. It is from 6 to 10 inches thick, and rests upon a subsoil which is yellow at first and then changes to red. Some of the subsoil is impervious; sand lies below at from 10 to 15 feet. The soil is best adapted to corn, cotton, and sweet potatoes.

Cotton forms over one-half of the crops, and grows from 1 foot to 4 feet high, 2½ to 3 feet being the best. The seed-cotton product is from 800 to 1,200 pounds, 1,660 to 1,780 pounds making a bale. After fifteen years' cultivation the product is from 700 to 800 pounds, the same as before being required for a bale, and the staple rating the same. As to washing and the remedy, see under first soil. The third soil or land forms one-third of all, and occurs along all the rivers from head to mouth. Cotton is very rarely planted upon it.

M. V. B. Exum (northwestern part of the county, lands of Cane and Dyer creeks and Middle Fork of Forked Deer river).—About one-fourth of these lands consist of *black buckshot*, rather wet, with a hard-pan subsoil. The second bottoms are richer than the uplands, and, where sandy enough, are preferred; but where sand does not predominate, the uplands or hill lands are preferred. The chief soil is the sandy loam of the second bottoms and some adjacent uplands, which occurs in different directions for 6 miles, and has a red clay subsoil, with more or less sand. The tillage is easy in dry seasons; less so in wet. After heavy rains the soil becomes hard. It is best adapted to cotton, corn, and clover. More than one-half is planted in cotton, which attains a height of from 4 to 5 feet, 3 feet being the best. Wet and warm weather in July and August incline the plant to run to weed, for which topping and taking the dirt from the roots are the remedies. The seed-cotton product per acre on fresh land is from 1,000 to 1,500 pounds, 1,615 pounds making a bale of 475 pounds. On land worked for ten years the product is from 800 to 1,000 pounds, a little less being needed for a bale. The staple then rates as middling to good middling. The weeds are crab-grass, foxtail, rag-weed, purslane, smart-weed, etc. Very little of the land lies turned out, say one-twentieth, and such land, when taken in again, if not too much in gullies, produces fairly well. The slopes wash seriously, to the injury of the valleys, and some few farms have been ruined. Horizontalizing and hillside ditching have been practiced—the only salvation for hilly lands.

J. D. Pearson (northeastern part of county).—The soils are: (1) Black clay loam, mixed with sand, second bottom, and upland; (2) alluvial, above overflow or drained; (3) light sandy upland, subject to drought. The first is the chief soil, and forms a fourth of our lands. It extends north from 6 to 20 miles, west 40, south 40, and east 2 miles, and is 10 inches thick. The subsoil is yellow or red, baking hard on exposure, but under cultivation gradually becoming like the soil, though requiring manure to make it fertile. It is underlaid by sand at from 12 to 15 feet. The land is generally easily tilled, and produces corn, cotton, wheat, and some oats. It is best adapted to corn and cotton, one-third being planted in the latter. The plant grows to 2 or 4 feet, 3½ feet being the best. The seed-cotton product per acre on fresh land is 1,000 pounds, 1,485 pounds being required for a bale of 475 pounds. The staple is as good as any. After eight years the product is about 600 pounds, 1,545 pounds then being required for a bale. About one-tenth of the land lies turned out, and where taken in again it does well if not too badly washed. The soil washes seriously in many places, in some localities to the injury of the valleys. Some hillside ditching has been done with success.

The second soil, the *alluvial*, forms one-fourth of the lands. It is best adapted to corn and wheat. Not much is planted in cotton. In dry seasons, on fresh land, it produces 1,200 pounds of seed-cotton to the acre.

The third soil, the *light sandy*, forms half the lands, with the same extent as the first soil. It is 4 inches thick, and rests upon a sandy subsoil, and is best adapted to sweet potatoes, peanuts, and melons. It is difficult to estimate the proportion of cotton planted, as it lies in patches; but when fresh it yields 600 pounds of seed-cotton product to the acre, and after six years' cultivation 400 pounds.

M. P. Collins (northeast from Jackson).—The soils vary little. Cotton is always shut in growing on account of cold nights in late spring and early summer. Much is killed, and the stand is often ruined. Then again the fall frosts often damage the cotton in the boll. The soils are all sandy, and extend for miles on every side. The subsoil is a sandy clay. Sand and gravel lie below at from 5 to 10 feet. The soil is easy to till in dry weather, but difficult in wet. It is late and cold, but well drained. The crops are cotton, corn, wheat, oats, potatoes, and clover. This soil is perhaps best adapted to corn; but nearly one-half of it is planted in cotton, which grows from 3 to 6 feet high, 4 feet being the best. The plant may run to weed on fresh ground in wet weather. To restrain it we use Peruvian guano or stable manure. The seed-cotton product on fresh land is 1,000 pounds per acre, 1,660 pounds making a 475-pound bale. The staple rates as good middling. On land worked ten years the product is 800 pounds per acre, 1,600 pounds then making a bale, the staple being somewhat shorter. Hog-weed and smart-weed are the most common pests. About 1 per cent. of the land lies turned out, and where taken in again, if manured and clovered, produces excellently. The soil washes seriously on slopes, sometimes covering the valleys with sand. Horizontalizing and hillside ditching have been practiced, and with very great success where well done.

D. R. Allison (southeast from Jackson, lowland).—The soil cultivated in cotton in this section is *gray gravelly land*, which lies near water-courses and contains gray gravel. This soil, when rained upon after being plowed, looks white. Its timber is beech and elm. One-half of it is planted in cotton, which attains a height of 3 feet. The seed-cotton product on fresh land is from 800 to 1,000 pounds per acre. Of this 1,485 pounds are needed for a 475-pound bale. On land worked for four years the product is the same. The weeds are crab-grass, cocklebur, and smart-weed. The wash from slopes has ruined some of the valley lands. Horizontalizing and hillside ditching have been practiced with good results in some cases.

CROCKETT.

Population: 14,109.—White, 10,493 ; colored, 3,616.
Area: 260 square miles.—Woodland, all.
Tilled lands: 63,428 acres.—Area planted in cotton, 17,807 acres ; in corn, 25,650 acres ; in wheat, 9,883 acres ; in oats, 1,501 acres ; in tobacco, 35 acres.
Cotton production: 9,320 bales ; average cotton product per acre, 0.52 bale, 747 pounds seed-cotton, or 249 pounds cotton lint.

Crockett county, claimed by some to be the best body of land for its dimensions in the state, lies lengthwise and asymmetrically, in a northwest and southeast direction between two of the forks of the Forked Deer river—the Middle Fork on the northeast and the South Fork on the southwest. Excepting two small segments on the northeastern and southwestern sides, respectively, the one belonging to Gibson and the other to Haywood, the county occupies all the space from fork to fork. Its surface, therefore, is a water-shed, extending longitudinally through the county, with general drainage from a central and higher belt. To the northwest, however, the higher belt is split nearly equally in two by the valley of Pond creek, which rises near the county-seat, Alamo, and runs northwestward out of the county. The surface is further cut by Cypress, Black, and other smaller creeks. In general the county is an upland plateau region, modified by the streams as above indicated. It has many level areas. Sections more or less hilly occur in the western, northwestern, and eastern portions. There is comparatively little of low bottom land ; but the second bottoms afford much land, which of late years has been cultivated in cotton with fair success.

The soils out of the low bottoms are very generally fine siliceous or sandy loams based on yellowish or reddish sandy clays, the underlying formation being chiefly the orange sand, and they all produce cotton. The area planted in cotton is from 10 to 15 per cent. of the total area of the county. In considering the soils, Crockett may be divided lengthwise into three nearly equal belts, two lateral or outside, bordering the rivers respectively on the northeast and southwest, and a middle one between. The two lateral belts, supplying the best and strongest lands, are heavily timbered with large white and red oaks, yellow poplar, hickory, ash, elm, maple, beech, gum, walnut, dogwood, papaw, etc. The middle belt has a thinner, lighter soil, is higher and more rolling, and is covered with a dense growth of small black oaks, white "poplar", hickory, etc. In dry, favorable seasons the lateral belts produce the most cotton ; in wet seasons, the middle belt. Taking the years together, they all yield about the same average. The staple of cotton raised on the middle belt is finer than that of the others. Cotton is shipped to Memphis by rail at $2 50 per bale.

ABSTRACTS FROM REPORTS.

P. M. NEAL (western part of the county, waters of Black creek and South Forked Deer river).—The soils cultivated in cotton are : (1) Dark clay loam of the uplands; (2) a light and fine gray soil, intermixed with brownish gravel and a little fine whitish sand, lowland; in the main above overflow; (3) light brownish soil. The first is the chief soil, and forms one-fifth of this civil district, or, taking the whole county, one-twelfth of the lands. It occurs in spots mostly on the highland belts adjacent to the river valleys, and is from 10 to 12 inches thick. The subsoil is a light and tough yellow clay, baking hard when exposed, and quite impervious to water. It contains more or less hard, yellowish gravel, and is underlaid by sand at from 5 to 6 feet. The land is tilled with difficulty in wet or very dry seasons, but with ease if the ground is in good condition. It is warm when well drained, producing chiefly corn, cotton, and wheat, but is best adapted to the first two. About one-fifth is planted in cotton, which grows from 3½ to 5 feet high. The plant inclines to run to weed in wet weather, and the only remedy known to me is to drain and cultivate lightly. The seed-cotton product on fresh land is 800 pounds per acre, 1,780 pounds making a bale of 475 pounds. After fifteen or twenty years' cultivation the product is about 600 pounds if the land is not washed and not too far exhausted. Of this 1,545 pounds make a bale. The staple of old land is considered better than that of the fresh, and the best cotton is made on such land. Cocklebur, crab-grass, and foxtail are the pests. Not more than one-thirtieth of this land is turned out. Such land taken in again produces well if the soil is not washed away, especially if broken up the previous fall. Soil washes readily on slopes, causing damage in places. Some valleys are injured, but not seriously. Horizontalizing and hillside ditching have been practiced, but to no great extent. Where done well, the results are very good.

T. J. WOOD (county generally).—Our soils are: (1) Black poplar, second bottom, and upland; (2) clay soil, worn out or poor lands, and plenty of it; (3) buckshot, or white crawfish, low for cultivation and poor. The first is the chief soil, forming one-third or more of the lands. It is from 3 to 5 inches thick, is difficult to till in wet weather, but easy in dry. The crops are corn, cotton, wheat, and oats, the soil being best adapted to corn. About one-fourth is planted in cotton, which grows from 3 to 3½ feet high, 3 feet being the best. The plant tends to run to weed on fresh ground and in very wet weather, and the remedy is topping. The seed-cotton product on fresh land is 800 pounds, 1,650 pounds making a bale. The staple rates as middling. After five years' cultivation the product is from 400 to 500 pounds, and the staple is shorter and a shade under middling. Crab-grass is troublesome. Very little of this land lies turned out, and when taken in again does well if seeded to clover or sown in peas. The soil washes seriously on slopes if not attended to, but the valleys are rather benefited. Horizontalizing and hillside ditching have been practiced with very good results.

E. J. READ, sn. (lowland of Black creek and uplands generally).—The soils cultivated in cotton are: (1) Black poplar, creek, valley, and upland; (2) second river bottom; (3) thin red clay. The first is the chief soil, forming one-half of the lands, and extending off from 10 to 20 miles. This soil is 8 inches thick. The subsoil is tough reddish clay, baking hard, but gradually forming soil by cultivation, which contains some gravel, and is underlaid by sand at from 10 to 20 feet. The land is easily tilled in dry weather, but is difficult in wet, and about equally adapted to the crops produced. About half the crops is cotton, which averages 2½ feet in height, 3 feet being most productive. If necessary, topping in August restrains the plant. The seed-cotton product on fresh land is 1,200 pounds, 1,900 pounds making a bale of 475 pounds. Staple rates as middling. On land worked for six years the product is 800 pounds, 1,780 pounds then making a bale, and the staple is better. Crab-grass is the pest. About one-tenth of this land lies turned out, and when taken in again produces well for several years. The soil washes readily on slopes, but the damage is not serious, the valleys being greatly improved thereby.

The *second river bottom* forms about one-third of the lands. It is a clay loam, 8 inches thick, with a subsoil like that of the first soil. About two-thirds of this land is planted in cotton. The seed-cotton product on fresh land is from 1,200 to 1,500 pounds per acre. About one-twentieth lies turned out. In other respects it is like first soil.

The *thin red clay* forms one-fifteenth of the lands, and is 2 or 3 inches thick. The subsoil is a red clay, but is not fertile. The land is early, warm, well drained, and best adapted to cotton, which forms two-thirds of the crops. The seed-cotton product is 800 pounds per acre, the staple rating middling. On land worked four years the yield is 400 pounds per acre, the staple being better

GIBSON.

Population: 32,685.—White, 23,540; colored, 9,145.
Area: 550 square miles.—Woodland, all.
Tilled lands: 146,163 acres.—Area planted in cotton, 36,820 acres; in corn, 57,838 acres; in wheat, 26,016 acres; in oats, 3,378 acres; in tobacco, 56 acres.
Cotton production: 19,272 bales; average cotton product per acre, 0.52 bale, 747 pounds seed-cotton, or 249 pounds cotton lint.

Gibson county lies chiefly between the South Fork of the Obion river on the northeast and the Middle Fork of the Forked Deer on the southwest. To this must be added a small segment cut off by a bend in the latter river, and lying on the Crockett county side. The longest line that could be drawn in Gibson would lie in a northwesterly and southeasterly direction about midway between the rivers mentioned, and would connect the northwestern and southeastern corners of the county. Rutherford Fork of the Obion river traverses the northeastern part of the county. Little North Fork of the Forked Deer is an important stream. Besides these, there are many creeks draining all parts of the surface. Gibson county is a part of the great plateau region of West Tennessee, and is the most northerly of four counties constituting a central group in West Tennessee, the others being Crockett, Haywood, and Madison. The surface of the county is generally level, though cut up or made more or less rolling by the valleys of the streams. South and east from Trenton, the county-seat, the county is more hilly than in other sections. The prevailing soil is uplands, a sandy, fertile, and mellow clay loam with sandy clay subsoil, the latter generally resting upon strata of the orange sand. The parts of the bottoms of the rivers and larger streams above overflow afford a comparatively small proportion of the lands. Some of these are dark and rich, others (and no inconsiderable part of the whole) are light colored and crawfishy. The growth of the uplands are "poplar", white, red, and black-jack oaks, sweet and black gum, ash, elm, hickory, walnut, beech, chestnut, dogwood, papaw, hazel, etc.; that of the bottoms or second bottoms, oak, hickory, beech, sweet gum, ash, and some papaw. The lands are well suited to the growth of cotton, and this is the principal crop. But for the shortness of the season the yield, acre for acre, would be equal to that of some of the best lands much farther south. With the exception of the northeastern corner of the county, the relative proportion of the area planted in cotton is from 10 to 15 per cent. of the total area. In the part excepted it is from 5 to 10 per cent. Cotton is shipped by rail to Memphis at from $2 to $2 25, and to New Orleans at $3 25 per bale.

ABSTRACTS FROM REPORTS.

L. P. McMURRY AND J. W. HAYS (southwestern part of county, Big Creek and Forked Deer River lands).—Creeks flowing into the Forked Deer have low, wet bottoms, subject to overflow, and mostly unfit for cultivation. Uplands vary greatly from clay loam to "buckshot". Rains often prevent early planting, and early frosts often injure the plant before maturing, especially on fresh land and lowlands. The soils cultivated in cotton are: (1) Clay loam on level and rolling uplands; (2) dark and gray loam soil of the Forked Deer river and its tributaries above overflow; (3) "buckshot" upland, containing small ore-like gravel—a cold land. The *clay loam* is the chief soil, forming about 85 per cent. of our lands, and occurring throughout the county. It is yellow clay loam from 8 to 12 inches thick. The subsoil is a tough yellow clay, with more or less sand, baking when exposed, and by culture becoming like the soil; lessely on the slopes, impervious when undisturbed, and underlaid by sand at from 15 to 25 feet. Tillage of the land rather difficult when wet, but generally not troublesome. Early when well drained. The crops are corn, wheat, oats, cotton, red clover, timothy, and herd's-grass. The soil is well suited to all. One-third of the tillable land is planted in cotton. Deep plowing and much vegetable mold cause the plant to run to weed; shallow plowing, with stable manure and superphosphates, restrain it. The seed-cotton product on fresh land is 1,000 pounds per acre, 1,790 pounds making a 475-pound bale. Staple rates as middling. On land worked ten years the product in ordinary seasons is from 800 to 900 pounds, 1,800 pounds making a bale, but the staple is not so long as on fresh land. The weeds are crab-grass, foxtail, smart-weed, and cocklebur. About 2 per cent. of the land lies turned out. A little has been reclaimed, but does not produce well. Soil washes seriously on hilly land, and sometimes ruins the lower lands. Horizontalizing and hillside ditching have been practiced with good results.

The *dark and gray loam* of the lowlands, forming about 5 per cent. of the lands in this region, occurs along the river and larger creeks throughout the county. The subsoil is a tough bluish clay, baking hard, but by cultivation becoming like the soil. It is impervious when undisturbed, and is underlaid by sand at various depths. Tillage is not difficult unless when wet. The soil is generally late, and is best adapted to corn and sorghum; but much of it is planted in cotton, the latter growing to 4 and 7 feet, a medium most productive. Wet weather inclines the plant to go to weed. The seed-cotton product is about 1,200 pounds per acre, 1,790 pounds making a bale of 475 pounds. Staple is middling. After ten years' cultivation the product ranges from 800 to 1,000 pounds, with the staple about the same. The weeds are smart-weed, cocklebur, crab-grass, and foxtail. Little of the land has been turned out. Some injury is caused by washes from upland.

J. M. SENTER AND Z. BRYANT, SR. (county generally).—The soils of the county are: (1) Dark-brown clay loam; (2) Dark sandy loam in small proportion. The first is the prevailing soil of the county. The subsoil is a yellow clay, underlaid by sand at 15 feet. The crops are cotton, corn, clover, wheat, oats, and grasses. The soil is best adapted to the first three, but one-half of it is planted in cotton, which attains a height of from 3 to 6 feet. Topping is practiced to restrain the plant from going to weed on fresh land. The seed-cotton product on fresh land is 1,000 pounds per acre, 1,780 pounds making a bale of 475 pounds. After four years' cultivation the product is from 1,000 to 1,200 pounds. The staple is middling in both cases. None of the land lies turned out. The slopes wash seriously, and the valleys are also injured thereby. Hillside ditching has been practiced with good results.

The second soil is met with over the county. The subsoil is a reddish-yellow clay. Cotton grows from 2 to 3 feet, 2½ feet being the best. The seed-cotton product on fresh land is from 600 to 800 pounds, 1,780 pounds making a 475-pound bale. On land worked for four years the product is 700 pounds. The staple is middling in both cases. Little of the land lies turned out, and when taken in again produces well after pease or clover. The washing of slopes, etc., as under the first soil.

WEAKLEY.

Population: 24,538.—White, 20,125; colored, 4,413.
Area: 620 square miles.—Woodland, all.
Tilled lands: 129,075 acres.—Area planted in cotton, 15,406 acres; in corn, 50,001 acres; in wheat, 25,479 acres; in tobacco, 4,770 acres; in oats, 1,795 acres.
Cotton production: 7,576 bales; average cotton product per acre, 0.49 bale, 702 pounds seed-cotton, or 234 pounds cotton lint.

28 C P

Weakley is one of the northern tier of counties adjoining the state of Kentucky, and is well supplied with water-courses, which flow very generally in a westerly direction. Two of the large forks of the Obion river, the North Fork in the northern part of the county and the Middle Fork in the southern, pass entirely through its area. On the southwest the South Fork of the Obion separates the county from Crockett. The creeks tributary to these are very numerous, and some of them are large. The county is a typical part of the plateau slope of West Tennessee. Its surface is generally level, but more or less broken areas occur, as around Dresden, the county-seat. The northeastern part inclines to be hilly. The formation underlying the subsoil is chiefly the orange-sand drift; but occasionally, in banks along streams outcropping from beneath this, the dark laminated sands and clays of a lower formation are seen. The prevailing soil, that of uplands and sloping lands, is generally a brown, siliceous loam, more or less clayey, fertile, and suited to corn, wheat, cotton, tobacco, oats, potatoes, grasses, and indeed any crop of the latitude. The growth is black and other oaks, poplar, beech, hickory, black and sweet gum, black walnut, dogwood, and hazel-nut. In parts of the county, as east of Dresden, are areas denominated "barrens", which are of different kinds, the "hickory, dogwood, and black gum barrens" affording good land, the "post-oak barrens", with land of second quality, and the "black-jack barrens", with poor land. The streams of the county are, for the most part, sluggish, and their bottoms low, more or less subject to overflow, and comparatively of little agricultural value. The parts above overflow, however, supply good land. On the map showing percentage areas of cotton it is seen that in about two-thirds of the county, including the southern and southwestern portions, the relative per cent. of acreage in cotton to total acreage for the census year was from 5 to 10; in most of the remainder from 1 to 5 per cent. In the extreme northeastern part it was 0.1 to 1. Cotton is shipped by rail to Nashville at from $1 to $1 25, and to New Orleans at $3 25 per bale.

ABSTRACTS FROM REPORTS.

J. C. LIPSCOMB, G. PATTERSON, AND E. D. TANSILL (southwestern part of the county, Mud creek and Obion River lands).—The uplands vary. Some are white-oak highlands, with hickory and poplar, and the most productive; some have a red oak growth; but others are post-oak glady lands. The uplands are preferred for cotton on account of shortness of season; but with a late fall, as in 1879, bottom lands make the best crops. The soils put in cotton are: (1) The white-oak and hickory highlands and the post-oak ridge; (2) branch bottom and second bottom of the smaller rivers. The first is the chief soil, and forms about one-third of the area, or half the lands in cultivation. The soil is a clay loam (the white oak part brown, the glady part whitish) from 3 to 8 inches thick. The subsoil is a yellow clay, washing easily, but rather impervious. Land is easily cultivated in dry seasons, but not in wet, and is early when well drained. All our crops do well on it. One-third of the crops in this section is cotton, which averages about 3 feet in height. The seed-cotton product on fresh land is about 1,000 pounds, from 1,660 to 1,780 pounds making a bale of 475 pounds; on land five years in cultivation the product is from 800 to 1,000 pounds. The staple is much the same in both cases. Crab-grass, with some foxtail, is troublesome. About 8 or 10 per cent. of the land lies turned out. Such land when taken in again does poorly unless manured. Hillsides are rarely reclaimed. The slopes wash seriously, but the valleys are not much injured thereby. Little if any effort is made to check the damage.

A. M. SMYTH (southern part of county, Spring Creek and Obion River lands).—As a general thing none but the first quality of lands are cultivated in cotton. The soils are: (1) Brown sandy of table-land and second bottoms; (2) gray or mulatto, undulating; (3) poor and broken. The first is the chief soil, and forms about one-third of our lands. Thickness, 6 inches. Subsoil is light, loamy, and gray. Tillage is easy in dry seasons, but less so in wet. Land is best adapted to cereals and grasses. One-fourth is planted in cotton, which grows to 3 and 4 feet in height. Plants are restrained by barring off with turning-plow and by topping. The cotton-seed product on fresh land is from 1,000 to 1,200 pounds per acre, from 1,485 to 1,500 pounds making a 475-pound bale; on land worked for ten years the product is from 600 to 1,000 pounds, the staple on fresh land being the best. Crab-grass is the troublesome weed. But little land in my section is turned out, and that generally is damaged by the tramping of stock. Slopes wash seriously, but the valleys are not much injured thereby. Ditching has been done with success.

T. D. MARTIN, G. W. ISBELL, AND S. C. CRAVENS (northwest from Dresden).—The soils cultivated in cotton are: (1) Upland; (2) bottom. The chief soil is the upland, forming four-fifths of the lands. It is a clay loam, mahogany and black alternating, and 5 inches thick. The subsoil is a tough, yellow clay, impervious when undisturbed. Ten per cent. of cotton is planted. Plant is restrained by topping. The seed-cotton product on fresh land is 1,200 pounds per acre, 1,660 pounds making a 475-pound bale; on land in cultivation for ten years from 800 to 900 pounds, from 1,544 to 1,800 pounds making a bale. Staple on fresh land is a little longer. Crab-grass is the most troublesome.

The bottom land is about one-fifth of the lands. It is a black loam 12 inches thick. The subsoil is a tough whitish clay, baking hard on exposure, but becoming like the surface soil. Tillage is not usually troublesome. The soil is early when well drained. Cotton grows from 4 to 6 feet high. Topping is resorted to when necessary. The seed-cotton product is from 1,200 to 1,500 pounds, according to season, about 1,660 pounds making a 475-pound bale.

HENRY.
(See "Summit region of the water-shed".)

CARROLL.
(See "Summit region of the water-shed".)

OBION.
(See "The Bluff region".)

TIPTON.
(See "The Bluff region".)

SHELBY.
(See "The Bluff region".)

HENDERSON.
(See "Summit region of the water-shed".)

McNAIRY.
(See "Summit region of the water-shed".)

THE SUMMIT REGION OF THE WATER-SHED.

In this region are included the middle part of Henry county, the eastern part of Carroll, nearly all of Henderson and McNairy, and the western margins of Hardin,* Decatur,* and Benton.* The southeastern corners, respectively, of Hardeman* and Madison* project into the area of this subdivision. The two latter counties have been described under "Brown-loam table-lands". Further, the northwestern corner of Henderson is cut off to the table-lands, and the northeastern part of Henry to the western valley of the Tennessee river.

HENRY.

Population: 22,142.—White, 15,488; colored, 6,654.
Area: 550 square miles.—Woodland, all.
Tilled lands: 133,392 acres.—Area planted in cotton, 13,186 acres; in corn, 51,852 acres; in wheat, 20,853 acres; in oats, 3,171 acres; in tobacco, 2,726 acres.
Cotton production: 5,516 bales; average cotton product per acre, 0.42 bale, 597 pounds seed-cotton, or 199 pounds cotton lint.

Henry is the most northeasterly county of West Tennessee. Its northeastern corner reaches to the Tennessee river, and its northern boundary coincides with the Kentucky line. It is near the northern border of the cotton-growing region. The northeastern half of the county had on an average in the census year less than 1 per cent. of its area planted in cotton, the southwestern and the southeastern corners from 5 to 10 per cent., and the remainder of the county from 1 to 5 per cent. The summit-line dividing the waters of the Mississippi from those of the Tennessee runs in a direction a little north of east through the center of the county. Along this line or "divide" are strips of ridgy land with sandy soil, easily washed, but producing fair crops of corn, wheat, and cotton. To the west of the line the county slopes at first gently away, then becomes level, supplying large sections of fine farming lands, the whole well watered by a great spray of branches and creeks, the headwaters of the middle and north forks of the Obion river. To the east of the summit-line the general slope to the Big Sandy and Tennessee rivers is greater, and the country more broken; nevertheless, extensive areas of level and nearly level productive lands occur. The eastern slope is broken chiefly by West Sandy river and its tributaries.

The prevailing soil of this county is a brown siliceous or sandy loam, found on uplands and slopes and in the valleys of the smaller streams, upon which corn, wheat, cotton, oats, and tobacco grow well and are the leading crops. The subsoils are yellowish or reddish clays, more or less sandy. The timber is white and black oaks, poplar, hickory, and dogwood; also, interspersed with these, are elm, walnut, ash, mulberry, red-bud, etc. On the higher lands, with a thinner soil, are red, post, and sometimes black-jack oaks, chestnut, etc. There is no great extent of tillable bottom land along the larger streams. Second bottoms are often desirable tracts. The growth of the bottoms consists of beech, white and water oaks, sweet gum, poplar, maple, and cypress; that of the second bottoms is much the same, excepting cypress.

The underlying formations are various. In the middle and western portions are great strata of laminated sands and clays, and in the extreme eastern and northeastern portions are beds of limestone and cherty rocks. All these, however, are generally concealed by the beds of the orange sand, the latter giving origin to the sandy soils. Cotton is shipped by rail to Memphis or Saint Louis at from $2 to $3 per bale.

ABSTRACTS FROM REPORTS.

S. C. DOBBINS (southern and southwestern part of the county).—Rolling and level table-land. The black sandy soil, which forms one-fourth of the lands, is preferred for cotton, and extends 12 miles south of Paris, where most of the cotton of the county is raised. Thickness, 6 inches. The subsoil is generally clay, underlaid by sand at from 10 to 15 feet. Tillage is easy in all seasons. One-tenth of the crops consists of cotton. To restrain the plant and favor bolling some farmers top, but I doubt the advantage. The seed-cotton product on fresh land is 1,000 pounds per acre, 1,545 pounds making a 475-pound bale; on land worked a number of years the product is from 600 to 800 pounds, the staple middling in both cases. The weeds are rag-weed and cocklebur. I cannot say how much land is turned out, but when taken in again, if sown in peas, it would be improved. Slopes wash seriously, and valleys are much injured.

J. F. CAVITT (western part of the county, waters of the forks of the Obion river).—The black sandy loam of hazel-nut valleys and ridges in the northwestern part of the county is the chief soil, making one-tenth of the lands, in bodies of from 50 to 1,000 acres or more, and from 5 to 8 inches thick. The subsoil is brownish-red, leachy, and is considered injurious when mixed with the soil. Tillage is easy in dry seasons, but is not very troublesome in wet. Land is early and warm when well drained, and is best adapted to corn, tobacco, wheat, and cotton, in the order named. About one-tenth of crops is cotton, which reaches 3½ feet. The plant is restrained, when necessary, by topping from the 1st to the 10th of August. The seed-cotton product on fresh land is from 700 to 1,200 pounds per acre, 1,660 pounds making a 475-pound bale; after ten years' cultivation, if the land is cared for, from 600 to 800 pounds, from 1,660 to 1,780 pounds making a bale. Staple of fresh land is middling upland; that of old land hardly so long. Only grasses are troublesome. Much of the land is turned out, and is not improved thereby. The slopes sometimes wash seriously; some valleys are thus injured, others not. Some horizontalizing and hillside ditching are done, with very good results.

The blackish clay or black table-land of the southwest, forming one-fifteenth of the lands, is found in large tracts, and is from 5 to 8 inches thick. Subsoil is brownish-red sandy clay. Tillage is rather difficult in wet seasons, and the land is early. Cotton forms one-fifteenth of the crops, which grows to a height of 3½ feet. Seed-cotton product on fresh lands is from 800 to 1,000 pounds per acre, 1,660 pounds making a 475-pound bale. Staple is middling upland. On land ten years old, if preserved, the product is from 700 to 1,000 pounds per acre. Grasses only are troublesome. Washing of soil, the damage and remedy, are as under first soil.

The clay or ridge land of the southwest, forming one-tenth of the lands, occurs in large tracts, with red and post oak growth; thickness, from 2 to 3 inches. Subsoil, pale yellow clay, underlaid by sand at some depth. Land is late and cold when well drained, and is best for corn and grasses. Cotton forms one-fifth of the crops, which grows to 2½ feet. The seed-cotton product on fresh land is from 400 to 700 pounds, requiring from 1,660 to 1,780 pounds a 475-pound bale. Staple rates middling upland. On land worked for ten years, if preserved, the product is 300 pounds, and it then requires from 1,780 to 1,900 pounds for a bale. The staple is shorter. Not much washing occurs on slopes, but the valleys are injured thereby. Horizontalizing and hillside ditching have been practiced with moderate success.

A. ROBINS (south of east from Paris, land of Gin branch and Big Sandy river).—The soils are much the same, and are: (1) U.ac. sandy, level; (2) gray sandy, rolling; (3) pipe-clay of creek bottoms. The *black sandy* is the chief soil, forming a third of the lands, and extends 2 miles northeast and 6 miles southwest. It is a sandy loam from 8 to 10 inches deep. The subsoil is a yellow sandy clay, productive when exposed for a time, and underlaid by sand at from 10 to 20 feet. The chief crops are corn, cotton, and tobacco, one-third being cotton, which grows from 3 to 3½ feet. Seed-cotton product on fresh land is from 1,000 to 1,200 pounds per acre, 1,485 pounds making a bale The staple rates well. After thirty years' cultivation the product is from 500 to 800 pounds per acre, the staple and amount required for a bale being as before. The weeds are cocklebur and careless-weed. None of the land lies turned out. Slopes wash seriously if neglected, and horizontalizing and hillside ditching have been tried with considerable success.

D. L. WILLETT (southeastern part of the county, in the angle between the Big and West Sandy rivers).—The crops of the *upland sandy loam* are cotton, corn, tobacco, wheat, oats, pease, peanuts, potatoes, and sorghum; but the lands are best suited to cotton and peanuts. Post-oak glades make fair cotton. Cotton forms three-fourths of the entire crop, and grows from 3 to 4 feet high. Topping about the middle of August restrains the plant from growing rank on fresh ground or in wet seasons. The seed-cotton product on fresh land is from 1,000 to 1,500 pounds, from 1,660 to 1,900 pounds making a bale of 475 pounds. Staple rates good ordinary. The product on old land falls off with loss of soil, and staple loses length and fineness. Weeds are crab-grass, cocklebur, foxtail, and purslane.

The *black sandy bottom* forms about a sixth of the lands. Very little of it is planted in cotton. The plant grows from 2 to 5 feet in height; a medium is most productive. Seed-cotton product on fresh land is from 500 to 1,200 pounds per acre, but after five years' cultivation the crop is better. One-fifteenth lies turned out.

The *rolling second bottom* forms about a tenth of the lands. One-fifth is planted in cotton, which grows from 2 to 4 feet high, but is best at 3 feet. One-tenth lies turned out. Slopes wash badly, valleys being injured thereby. Horizontalizing and hillside ditching have been tried with only moderate success.

J. R. WILLIAMS, B. D. BOWDEN, W. P. SMALLWOOD, AND DR. W. S. FRYER (county generally).—The soils cultivated in cotton are : (1) Black sandy loam on flat and productive highlands, also in bottoms of the Obion and Sandy rivers; (2) gray sandy, moderately light soil, ridgy or hilly ; (3) light poor soil, upland and hilly ; (4) whitish clay of flatlands. The *black sandy loam* forms about a fourth of our lands, embracing much of the southern portion of the county, and is from 6 to 15 inches thick. Subsoil is red clay. This land is best adapted to corn, wheat, rye, and sorghum. About one-fourth of the crops is cotton. The plant grows from 2 to 4 feet, the latter the best, which can be restrained, if necessary, by topping in August. Seed-cotton product on fresh land per acre is from 800 to 1,500 pounds, about 1,900 pounds making a 475-pound bale. On land worked five years the product is from 400 to 800 pounds. The weeds are crab-grass, cocklebur, and hog-weed. About one-third of this land lies turned out, and if taken in again would do fairly if not gullied. Slopes wash seriously, but valleys are not much injured thereby. Some horizontalizing and hillside ditching have been done, though not generally with good results.

The *gray sandy* forms a fourth or more of our lands, extending pretty well over the county, with a thickness of from 4 to 6 inches. The subsoil is a reddish clay. Land is early and warm, and is best adapted to cotton. The largest proportion of crops is cotton. Plant grows from 1½ to 3 feet, the latter the best. Seed-cotton product on fresh land is from 500 to 1,000 pounds per acre, 1,900 pounds being required for a 475-pound bale. Staple is second class. On land cultivated five years the product is from 400 to 700 pounds, and the same is required for a bale. Staple is a shade better. The weeds are as on first soil. One-half of this land lies turned out, but where taken in again it does fairly if not washed. Washing on slopes, etc., as under first soil.

The *light poor soil* occurs in small proportion over the county, and has a growth of oaks of different kinds, post, black, red, and black-jack; thickness from 2 to 4 inches, and is best adapted to grass. Very little is planted in cotton. Plants grow from 1 foot to 2 feet, the latter being the best. Seed-cotton product on fresh land is from 200 to 400 pounds per acre, 2,010 pounds making a bale of 475 pounds. Staple is only common. Crab-grass is troublesome.

The *whitish clay of flatlands* forms about a tenth of cultivated lands. Growth, post and white oaks, shell-bark hickory, etc. The subsoil is whitish clay, becoming soil on exposure, quite impervious, and underlaid by sand at from 8 to 15 feet. Land is late ; generally too wet, and is best adapted to grass and corn. About one-fourth is planted in cotton, which grows to 3 feet. The seed-cotton product on fresh land is from 800 to 1,000 pounds per acre, 1,800 pounds being required for a 475-pound bale. Staple, middling upland. On land worked ten years and cared for the product is from 600 to 800 pounds. Crab-grass only is troublesome. Very little land is turned out, and is level and does not wash.

A *sandy loam of hazel hollows and branch bottoms*, much less in extent than the others, occurs in tracts of from 100 to 500 acres. Growth, black oak, hickory, and black-jack. The soil is fine sandy loam, 8 inches thick. The subsoil is sandy, leachy, and underlaid by sand at from 3 to 10 feet. Tobacco grows finely upon it. One-fourth of the crops is cotton, which grows to 3½ feet, the best height. Seed-cotton product per acre on fresh land is from 1,200 to 1,500 pounds, 2,140 pounds making a bale of 475 pounds. Staple rates middling upland. After ten years' cultivation the product is reduced to 800 or 1,000 pounds per acre. Crab-grass is troublesome. Washing of land is as under first soil.

CARROLL.

Population : 22,103.—White, 16,524; colored, 5,579.

Area : 550 square miles.—Woodland, all.

Tilled lands : 120,231 acres.—Area planted in cotton, 24,711 acres; in corn, 46,076 acres; in wheat, 17,354 acres; in oats, 3,413 acres; in tobacco, 100 acres.

Cotton production : 10,505 bales; average cotton product per acre, 0.43 bale, 606 pounds seed-cotton, or 202 pounds cotton lint.

The greater part of Carroll (more than two-thirds) is drained by the head streams of two forks of the Obion river, South Fork and Rutherford's Fork. The remainder of the county, the eastern end, is drained by the Big Sandy river, which traverses the county, passing out at the northeastern corner. To the west of the Big Sandy, and crowding upon its valley, is the belt of highlands dividing the waters of the Mississippi from those of the Tennessee. Regarding the county from this "divide," we have to the west a plateau slope embracing the middle and western parts, and to the east a valley (though no very deep one) constitutes the remaining part. The middle part is much broken. There are two small areas, corners of the county, not included above: the extreme southwestern, crossed and drained by the Middle Fork of the Forked Deer river, and the extreme southeastern, lying on the divide between the Big Sandy and the Tennessee.

The northern and western portions of the county present many level areas; but the middle, southern, and eastern portions are often broken, and the latter are sometimes hilly. The prevailing soils of the county are brown and grayish loams, more or less sandy, found on uplands and in the valleys of branches and small streams, with reddish and yellow and reddish clayey subsoil, the whole underlaid usually by sand, but in some localities within a belt running north and south through the middle of the county by laminated clay (soap-stone). The growth includes hickory, poplar, post, red, and black oaks, and gum, and, locally, ash, walnut, cherry, and chestnut. The principal crops are corn, cotton, wheat, oats, pease, sorghum, tobacco, sweet and Irish potatoes, clover, and grasses. The lands appear to be best adapted to corn and cotton. On the map of relative acreage in cotton it is seen that the county had, with the exception of two portions, from 5 to 10 per cent. of its area in cotton. The exceptions are: the southwestern corner, in which the percentage was greater, from 10 to 15, and a peninsula-like portion running down from Henry, nearly through the middle of the county, in which it was less, from 1 to 5 per cent. Cotton is shipped by rail at $2 75 to Memphis and $3 25 to New Orleans and Mobile.

ABSTRACTS FROM REPORTS.

A. R. CARNES AND T. N. LANKFORD (northern and northwestern part of the county, Obion uplands).—Bottoms do not produce cotton in this region. The soil cultivated in cotton is the light sandy loam of the uplands, forming about 40 per cent. of our lands, and extending off 20 miles in every direction. About one-fourth is planted in cotton, which grows to a height of 3½ feet, the best for a good yield. Warm, wet, and cloudy August incline plants to run to weed, for which no remedy is known here. Seed-cotton product per acre on fresh land is from 600 to 1,000 pounds, 1,545 pounds making a bale. After fifteen years' cultivation the product is 600 pounds, but varies greatly, according to the care taken. The staple is best on old land, seed lighter, and lint longer. The weeds are careless-weed, cocklebur, crab-grass, and foxtail. One-tenth of the land is turned out; if taken in again would produce well if not gullied. Slopes wash seriously; some valleys are injured thereby. Hillside ditching has been done with success.

E. T. BOHANNON AND B. T. HILSMAN (western part of the county, lands of Lick and Reedy creeks and Obion river).—Cotton is cultivated on good upland and on black sandy bottom land. The chief soil is good upland, forming one-half of our lands, and extends many miles north, west, and south. The country to the east is broken and varied to the Tennessee river. The soil is blackish, and is from 6 to 12 inches thick. Subsoil, a red and yellow clay, underlaid by sand at from 15 to 20 feet. Tillage is easy in dry, but difficult in wet seasons. The chief crops are corn, wheat, and cotton. One-fourth of the crops is cotton, which grows from 9½ to 5 feet high, but is best at 4 feet. Seed-cotton yield per acre on fresh land is from 1,000 to 1,500 pounds, 1,545 pounds making a bale of 475 pounds, the staple rating as good middling. On land worked 10 years the product is from 700 to 1,000 pounds; amount for bale and staple as before. Weeds are crab-grass and cocklebur. Five per cent. of the land lies turned out, and if not washed would produce well again for a few years. Slopes wash readily, and valleys are more or less injured.

J. F. SLOAN (western part of the county, Obion lands).—The black sandy soil of the "hickory barrens" is our best cotton soil, and will make fair cotton every year, wet or dry. Yellow sandy soil fires in dry seasons, causing squares to wad. Dry branch bottoms and old bottoms manured will bring good cotton, maturing early and opening well. On rich bottoms cotton grows too tall and shades itself, causing the bolls to rot and not to open. On gravel or clay land it is difficult to get a stand. The chief crop is cotton, the soil being best adapted to this and corn. One-half or more of the crops is cotton. The plant grows to 4 feet, which can be restrained, if need be, by close cultivation or throwing dirt from the plant to destroy fibrous roots. Seed-cotton product per acre on fresh lands is from 1,000 to 1,200 pounds, 1,425 pounds being required for a 475-pound bale. The weeds are crab-grass, cocklebur, and smart-weed. Very little of the land lies turned out. On such land, when taken in again, crops are generally light. Slopes wash seriously if neglected; valleys are also injured. In some places hillside ditching has been done with very good results.

J. H. JORDAN (northeastern part of the county, lands of Hollow-rock creek and the Big Sandy river).—The chief soil is the sandy clay loam of the flat uplands. Its crops are corn, wheat, oats, and cotton, but the land is best adapted to corn. One-third of the crops is cotton. The plant grows to 4 feet, 3½ feet being the best. Topping is used to restrain plant, if need be. Seed-cotton product per acre on fresh land is 1,000 pounds, 1,545 pounds making a 475-pound bale, the staple rating as good middling. The weed is cocklebur. No land lies turned out. Sandy slopes wash readily, but the damage is not great. Horizontalizing and hillside ditching have been done with good results.

Of the black hilly uplands there are 1,000 acres in this region. The soil is 8 inches thick, and is best adapted to corn. One-third of the crops is cotton. Seed-cotton product on fresh land is 1,000 pounds per acre, 1,545 pounds making a bale; staple rates as good middling. None of the land lies turned out.

The black bottom soil forms a third or less of our lands, and is best adapted to corn. One-third of the crops is cotton. Plant grows to 4 feet, most productive at 3 feet; restrained, when need be, in wet weather by topping. Seed-cotton product is 1,000 pounds per acre, 1,545 pounds making a bale; staple rates as good middling. Cocklebur is the troublesome weed. No land lies turned out.

WILLIAM JOHNSON (southeastern part of the county, Roane's Creek and Big Sandy River lands).—The lands cultivated in cotton are: (1) Coarse black sandy, lying up; (2) fine red sandy; (3) pale yellow clay land. The coarse black sandy forms one-tenth of our lands, and occurs in tracts of 10 and 20 acres, alternating with the red sandy for miles. It is a sandy loam 8 inches thick. The subsoil is yellowish, getting white on going down, and underlaid by sand at about 6 feet. Tillage is easy in dry seasons, but difficult in wet. The land is early, warm, and well drained, and is best adapted to cotton, corn, and grass. One-third of the crops is cotton, which usually grows to 2½ feet, but is best at 2½ feet. Warm, wet weather inclines the plant to run to weed, which is restrained only by dry weather and ceasing to plow. The seed-cotton product on fresh land is from 800 to 1,000 pounds per acre, 1,545 pounds being required for a 475-pound bale. On land worked ten years the product is from 500 to 800 pounds, and 1,660 pounds are then required for a bale; staple is better than on fresh land. The weeds are cocklebur and careless-weed. One-fifth of the land lies turned out; if taken in again and not washed it would produce well. Slopes frequently wash seriously, and the valleys are more or less injured. Horizontalizing and hillside ditching have been done with good results.

The red sandy soil forms also a tenth of the lands; thickness, 5 inches. Subsoil yellow for 6 feet down, then whiter, and underlaid by white sand. One-third of the crops is cotton, the latter usually growing 3 feet high. Seed-cotton product on fresh land is from 700 to 900 pounds, and 1,720 pounds are needed for a bale. On land worked eight years the product is from 400 to 700 pounds, 1,660 pounds making a bale; staple better than on fresh land. Weeds as under first soil. One-tenth of this land is turned out; if taken in again and not gullied would produce very well for a short time. Washing on slopes damages as under first soil.

The pale yellow clay soil forms about one-third of the cotton lands, and occurs in bodies of from 20 to 40 acres for long distances. Growth, red and post oaks and some dogwood. Thickness, 3 inches. Subsoil deeper yellow than the soil, and underlaid by gravel at 2 or 3 feet. Tillage is difficult in wet weather; less so in dry. The soil is late, cold, and ill-drained, and is best adapted to corn and grass. One-third of the crops is cotton, the latter growing usually to 18 inches; best at 3 feet. Seed-cotton product on fresh land is from 600 to 800 pounds, 1,690 pounds being needed for a bale; after ten years' cultivation the product is from 400 to 500 pounds. One-sixth of this land is turned out; if not washed, and taken in again, it would produce well for a time.

HENDERSON.

Population: 17,430.—White, 14,414; colored, 3,016.
Area: 580 square miles.—Woodland, all.
Tilled lands: 93,241 acres.—Area planted in cotton, 22,344 acres; in corn, 37,734 acres; in wheat, 9,791 acres; in oats, 4,543 acres; in rye, 238 acres; in tobacco, 123 acres.
Cotton production: 9,419 bales; average cotton product per acre, 0.42 bale, 000 pounds seed-cotton, or 200 pounds cotton lint.

Henderson is pre-eminently the summit county of the water-shed. From its high table-lands and ridges the Middle and South Forks of Forked Deer, Big Sandy, Beech, and White Oak rivers all take their rise, flowing off severally to all points of the compass. The forks of Forked Deer gather waters for the Mississippi; the other rivers are tributary to the Tennessee. Beech river has its head streams in the central portion of the county, flows eastward, receives tributary creeks from most of the eastern portion, and finally entering and crossing Decatur county empties into the Tennessee river. With many level areas, much of Henderson is rough and hilly. This is especially true of parts of the highlands which divide the western and eastern waters. Going both westward and eastward from this, the surface is less hilly, becoming finally, to the west especially, simply undulating.

The soils are the brown sandy loams of the uplands, rolling lands, branch and second bottoms, and the darker loam of creek bottoms. In the western parts of the county the sandy uplands and rolling lands are generally preferred for cotton; in the eastern and southeastern the second bottoms and bottoms are considered best. The deep formations are strata of laminated clays and sands, and to the east and southeast a greenish marly, more or less clayey, material, loaded with fossil shells, called greensand, or rotten limestone. The latter outcrops at intervals in the eastern and southeastern parts of the county, giving a rich dark soil and a stiff subsoil, often called "joint clay". (See page 21, under "Black Prairie Belt".) The deep formations, however, are often concealed by the beds of sand (and sometimes gravel) of the orange sand, which supply, in the main, the characteristic soils of sandy loam. In the growth of the higher lands red, post, and black oaks, and hickory are common, with black-jack oak and chestnut on the thinner lands. The chief crops are corn, cotton, wheat, oats, and potatoes. The growth on second and first bottoms includes white oak, sweet gum, beech, poplar, and hickory, with walnut, sugar-tree, etc. On the map showing for 1879 percentage of acres in cotton in given areas, it is seen that, with the exception of a strip in the northeastern corner, the percentage of the northwestern half of the county was from 10 to 15, and of the southeastern half from 1 to 5. In the part excepted it was intermediate, from 5 to 10. Cotton is shipped by water to Cincinnati at $1 25, or to Mobile and New Orleans and Cincinnati at $3 25 per bale.

ABSTRACTS FROM REPORTS.

E. W. CUNNINGHAM (county generally).—The soils vary greatly, the southern sides of slopes being often sandy, while the northern sides are more clayey. Cotton on lowlands with deep soil inclines to run to weed, and sometimes is caught by early frost. Second bottoms are most reliable. Fresh black sandy uplands are well adapted to cotton, but burn in midsummer, causing the dropping of squares. The second bottom soil is cultivated easily in dry seasons, and is early, warm, and generally well drained. One-third of the crops is cotton; plants grow from 3 to 5 feet, the medium height best. The seed-cotton product per acre on fresh land is 800 pounds, 1,545 pounds making a bale of 475 pounds; staple rates middling. On land worked for three years the product is 500 pounds, 1,545 pounds making a bale; staple a shade inferior. The weeds are hog-weed, careless-weed, purslane, and crab-grass. Little of the land lies turned out, and is easily kept up. Such land taken in again produces too much weed the first year. Slopes wash seriously; valleys are much injured. Little horizontalizing and hillside ditching as yet, but so far as done the results are good.

The soil of hilly and rolling uplands is from 1 inch to 6 inches deep. Subsoil is coarse sandy. Land easily cultivated, and early and warm. One-third of the crops is cotton. The seed-cotton product per acre on fresh land is from 700 to 800 pounds, from 1,495 to 1,545 pounds making a 475-pound bale; staple is middling. After three years' cultivation the product is from 400 to 500 pounds per acre. One-fifth of the land lies turned out, and would produce well again if manured. Horizontalizing and hillside ditching are done with good results.

The brown clay loam of lowlands has a lighter clay subsoil. Tillage is easy in dry seasons, but difficult in wet. One-tenth of the crops is cotton, which grows from 4 to 6 feet high. Warm, wet weather inclines the plant to run to weed, which is restrained by throwing dirt off with a turning-plow. The seed-cotton product per acre on fresh land in dry seasons is from 600 to 1,000 pounds, 1,600 pounds making a bale. Staple rates well, being heavy. The land remains productive for years, and when overflow is escaped it makes the best cotton. The weeds are Spanish needle, butter-weed, etc. One-tenth of the land lies turned out, but it would produce well again if broken up deeply in the fall or winter.

W. C. TRICE (southwestern part of the county, uplands of Forked Deer headwaters).—The chief soil, the sandy loam, makes three-fourths of our lands. It is a mahogany, sometimes reddish clay loam, 4 inches thick, with a leachy subsoil. It is easily tilled in dry seasons, and is early, warm, and well drained. One-half of the crops is cotton, plants growing to 3 feet. Late planting and wet seasons cause the plant to run to weed, which is restrained by early planting and on hard beds. Seed-cotton product per acre on fresh land is 1,000 pounds, 1,600 pounds making a 475-pound bale. The staple rates as good middling. After five years' cultivation the product is 900 pounds, and after ten years' cultivation 700 pounds, in the latter case 1,660 pounds making a bale. Staple is one grade lower, or middling. Crab-grass and foxtail are troublesome. One-tenth of the land for from 6 to 10 miles in each direction lies turned out. Such land, if kept inclosed, improves; otherwise not. Slopes wash seriously; valleys much injured. A little hillside ditching is done with tolerable success.

JOHN PEARSON AND C. M. DAVIS (eastern part of the county, Beech river lands).—Hillsides are sandy and very productive. The lands lying between the hills cover from 20 to 200 acres in a body. The uplands are generally black sandy, with red clay subsoil, and are easily cultivated in cotton. With good seed it never fails to have a stand. Fresh land will make three-fourths of a bale to the acre. Cotton on lowland generally matures, but sometimes the last-formed bolls are killed by frost. The soils are: (1) Upland black sandy, with red clay subsoil, best adapted to cotton; (2) second bottom, best adapted to corn. The first, the upland black sandy, is 6 inches thick. Tillage is easy in wet and dry seasons. The land is early, warm, and well drained. The chief crops are corn and cotton. One-half is planted in cotton. Plants grow to 3 and 4 feet, 4 feet being the best, and are restrained in a wet August by topping. The seed-cotton product per acre on fresh land is 1,000 pounds, 1,600 pounds being required for a 475-pound bale; staple rates well. After four years' cultivation the product is 800 pounds, the same as above making a bale; staple not quite so good. The weeds are crab-grass and foxtail. One-fourth of the land lies turned out. When not gullied, would produce well again if manured. ▓▓ ▓ ▓▓▓▓▓▓ ▓ ▓▓▓ ▓▓▓▓▓▓▓▓ ▓▓ ▓ ▓▓ ▓ ▓▓▓▓▓▓▓ ▓▓▓ ▓▓▓▓▓▓ ▓▓▓▓▓▓▓ have been done with complete success.

433

T. M. STUBBLEFIELD AND R. J. DYER (southeast from Lexington Cane Creek lands).—The soils cultivated in cotton are: (1) Black bottom, the best cotton land; (2) second bottom, good for cotton; (3) dark uplands with more or less clay. The black bottom soil is the chief, forming one-half of our lands, and occurring 5 miles east and west and 15 or 20 miles north and south. It is a fine, sandy clay loam, 12 inches thick, early, warm, and well drained, and about one-third is planted in cotton. Plants grow to 4 and 5 feet, and if too rank in wet weather in July and August they are restrained by topping and running around with a suitable plow. Seed-cotton product per acre on fresh land is from 1,100 to 1,500 pounds, 1,545 pounds making a 475-pound bale. Staple rates as good middling. The weeds are grass and cocklebur. About one-twentieth of the land is turned out, which would produce as other poor lands after the first year if taken in again. Soil washes on slopes, but not seriously; valleys injured thereby but little. Horizontalizing and hillside ditching have been done with good success.

F. G. ROGERS (southeastern part of county, lands of Cane and Flat creeks, waters of Beech river).—The soils cultivated in cotton are: (1) Light sandy of creek bottoms, above overflow; (2) yellow sandy upland on slopes, from 20 to 30 acres in places; (3) light sandy of Beech river. The chief soil, the light sandy of the bottoms, is in large proportion. The soil of the uplands is much the same, and has an average thickness of from 4 to 5 inches. The subsoil is a yellowish, sandy clay, which crumbles on exposure and mixes kindly with the soil, underlaid in places by sand or gravel, or rock, at 4 and 5 feet. Tillage of lower lands is difficult in wet seasons. Second bottoms are best for cotton. Plants grow to 3 and 5 feet, and topping is resorted to in wet seasons if necessary. Seed-cotton product on fresh second bottoms 1,300 pounds per acre, 1,495 pounds making a bale; staple first quality. After four years' cultivation the product is from 800 to 1,000 pounds per acre if gathered early, and the staple is better. The weeds are crab-grass and cocklebur. Not much of this land lies turned out; and when taken in again, it would produce from 500 to 700 pounds per acre.

P. B. MCNATT AND A. H. FARNSWORTH (southeastern part of the county, lands of Hurricane and Middleton creeks, waters of the Tennessee river).—Cotton on the lowlands of Hurricane creek, based on greensand, is later and liable to be caught by frost; on the more sandy lands of Middleton creek it is earlier. Sandy bottoms are generally preferred; but if devoted to cotton, corn will have to be bought. The soils cultivated in cotton are: (1) Dark shell soil of Hurricane bottoms above overflow; (2) red upland, mostly in patches on slopes; (3) light and gray sandy bottom of Middleton creek. The first, the dark shell soil, forms about one-half of our lands on both lowland and upland, and occurs a long way north and south. White oak is a common growth. Thickness 10 inches. Subsoil, a tough red clay, which bakes hard when exposed, but crumbles to soil on cultivation. This soil is impervious when undisturbed, and contains fossil shells in places. Tillage is difficult in wet seasons, but not in dry. The soil is early, warm, and well drained. The crops are corn and cotton, some oats, and little wheat. The land is best adapted to corn, but makes fair cotton; and wheat does well when sown early. Nearly one-half of the crops is cotton. The plant grows to 3 and 5 feet, the latter the best. I know no remedy for plants going to weed. Seed-cotton product per acre on fresh land is from 500 to 700 pounds, 1,545 pounds making a bale of 475 pounds; staple good ordinary. On land cultivated for three years the product is from 800 to 1,000 pounds; the staple is then from one-half to a grade better, due to handling. The weeds are horse-weed and cocklebur. One-twentieth of the land lies turned out; if taken in again, produces according to wear and management. The slopes wash to some extent, and valleys are injured thereby 50 per cent. Annual efforts are made at horizontalizing and hillside ditching with moderate success.

The red upland soil, forming about one-third of cultivated lands, is a clay loam with little sand, 2 inches thick, which reddens with wear. The subsoil hardens in the sun, but mixes slowly with the soil; impervious when dry, and contains gravel in some places. Tillage is difficult in wet seasons, but easy in dry. Land is early when well drained, and is best adapted to cotton. About two-thirds of the crops are cotton. Plants grow to 1 foot and 2 feet high. Seed-cotton product per acre on fresh land is from 300 to 500 pounds, and about 1,545 pounds are needed for a 475-pound bale; staple good ordinary. On land cultivated three years the product per acre is from 500 to 700 pounds, 1,545 pounds, as before, making a bale; staple generally better. Weeds are rag-weed, crab-grass, and some cocklebur. One-third of the land lies turned out and is not reclaimed. Slopes wash seriously in places to the ruin of the valleys.

The gray sandy soil of Middleton creek forms about one-fourth of our lands, and occurs in a belt 2 miles wide along the course of the creek for a long distance; thickness 10 inches. Subsoil does not bake so hard, and mixes readily with the soil; contains some pebbles in places. Tillage is easier than in case of other soils. Land is early and well drained, and is best adapted to corn. About one-third of the crops is cotton. The weeds are smart-weed, cocklebur, and crab-grass. In other respects this soil is like the first.

McNAIRY.

Population: 17,271.—White, 14,845; colored, 2,426.

Area: 690 square miles.—Woodland, all, excepting an inconsiderable aggregate of marly and glady places; "bald knobs" in the southern and eastern parts of the county.

Tilled lands: 78,800 acres.—Area planted in cotton, 23,135 acres; in corn, 33,501 acres; in wheat, 6,726 acres; in oats, 5,093 acres; in tobacco, 95 acres.

Cotton production: 9,419 bales; average cotton product per acre, 0.41 bale, 579 pounds seed-cotton, or 193 pounds cotton lint.

McNairy is the most southerly of the summit counties, and is one of the southern tier lying contiguous to the state of Mississippi. It is rectangular and regular in form, its longer dimension extending north and south. The ridge or belt of highlands dividing the waters of the Mississippi from those of the Tennessee runs nearly straight, north and south, through the county, and has such a position as to throw the county into two very unequal portions, a larger and western one, drained by tributaries of the former river, and an eastern one, supplying headwaters for creeks emptying into the latter. The western slope affords much level or undulating table-land. To the southwest it is dissected and made more or less rolling or hilly by tributaries of the Hatchie river. Around Purdy, the county-seat, the country is more or less hilly. This town is on the border of an elevated area of the county northwest of the center, within which are the beginnings of many streams flowing off severally in opposite directions: to the northwest, waters of the South Fork of the Forked Deer; to the southwest, those of the Hatchie; to the east, those of the Tennessee.

The soils of the western portion are generally brown, siliceous, or sandy loams, mellow and productive, and well suited to the culture of cotton and corn. Fine level tracts, with numerous and fertile branch bottoms and gentle slopes, desirable farming regions, occur in the more western, northern, and southern parts of the county. Then again, at intervals, are sections of thinner uplands, denominated "barrens", with a growth of small oaks and hickories. Sandy lands make also a part of the eastern portion, and with them are many areas of darker and stiffer soils, based on the so-called "joint clay". The latter occur, too, on the dividing highlands in the southern part of the county. The belt of country including the stiffer soils begins with the Mississippi line, covering there the eastern half of the county, and extends a little east of north, through McNairy and the northwestern part of Hardin, into Henderson county.

439

Taking the whole county, the deep formations are mostly strata of sands, or of sands finely laminated with thin papery layers of clay, the whole often dark with fossil leaves or plant remains. Below these is the great stratum of "greensand", outcropping (where not covered by the superficial drift mentioned below) throughout the belt of the darker and stiffer soils referred to above, and supplying by natural changes the "joint clay" subsoil upon which they rest, and, where soils are absent, the "shell glades" and "bald knobs" of the southeastern and eastern parts of the county. (See also under Black Prairie Belt, page 21.) The deep formations, however, are often covered and concealed by the sands and sometimes gravel of the orange-sand drift. The mellow siliceous soils come chiefly from the latter. The "greensand" is less covered than the others, and is the surface stratum in many sections. The growth of best uplands and second bottoms includes white, red, and black oaks, hickory, dogwood, poplar, and beech, with elm, ash, papaw, red-bud, and some walnut, buckeye, and others. White, black, post, and black-jack oaks, with scrubby hickories, are common on the thinner uplands. The chief crops are corn, cotton, wheat, and oats. together with some rye, sweet and Irish potatoes, tobacco, and grasses. Most of the area of the county had in 1879 from 1 to 5 per cent. of total acreage planted in cotton. Much of the western and northwestern parts, and a strip running across the southern part, have more than this, from 5 to 10 per cent. Cotton is shipped by rail to Mobile and other places at from $2 50 to $3 per bale.

ABSTRACTS FROM REPORTS.

A. W. STOVALL (county generally).—The soils cultivated in cotton are: (1) Brown sandy, in hickory and hazel branch valleys, on slopes, etc.; (2) second bottom; (3) creek bottom. The *brown sandy soil* forms one-third of the cotton lands, is varied in character, and occurs in all sections of the county, excepting to the southeast. The growth is hickory, black-jack and black oaks, etc. The chief crops are cotton and corn, but the land is best adapted to cotton, which forms about one-half of the crops, but the plants hardly average 3 feet in height. The seed-cotton product per acre on fresh land is 1,000 pounds, from 1,465 to 1,500 pounds, with toll paid, making a bale; staple middling. After a few years' cultivation the product is greater, and the staple rates as good middling. Much of the hillsides lies turned out, and only last eight or ten years if not protected. (None of first and second bottoms are turned out.) Land turned out, if allowed to improve, does well; and if manured, does as well as ever. The soil washes considerably on the hillsides, but the valleys are not much injured. Hillside ditching is practiced successfully.

The *second bottom soil* exists in considerable amount, though the aggregate is small in proportion, being confined to a few sections of the county. The growth is white oak, hickory, beech, etc. Tillage is difficult in wet seasons, but less so in dry. The land is tolerably early; partly well drained, partly not. Cotton forms about one-fourth of the crops. Plants grow to 3 and 5 feet high. Topping is done by some when necessary. Seed-cotton product per acre on fresh land is from 1,000 to 1,200 pounds, the same quantity as before making a bale.

The *creek bottom soil* exists in considerable amount, but cotton is not generally raised upon it. The growth is white oak, gum, beech, etc.

W. J. SUTTON AND J. G. COMBS (southeastern part of the county and east of Purdy).—The larger portion of cotton is grown on lowlands, which yield greater than other lands, though frost sometimes is damaging. The soils cultivated in cotton are: (1) Black limy (greensand soil) bottom land, lying, respectively, south of Snake creek and east of Lick creek; (2) dark gray bottom lands of the same creeks, north of the former and east of the latter; (3) brown sandy loam of uplands. The *black limy bottom land* occurs in small proportion, extending 3 miles east and 6 miles north. The growth is gum, ash, hickory, poplar, black oak, and papaw. The soil is black and putty-like when wet, and the subsoil is a tough, dark yellow clay, which becomes like the soil on exposure, is impervious when undisturbed, and contains limy matter and fossil sea-shells, underlaid by sand at 30 feet. Tillage is rather difficult in wet seasons, but less so in dry. The chief crops are cotton, corn, wheat, oats, sweet and Irish potatoes, sorghum, clover, and grasses. The soil does well for all excepting sweet potatoes. Cotton forms one-fourth of the crops. Plants grow to 5 and 6 feet, but are best at 4 feet. They grow rank when wet and the land is too fresh, and are restrained by topping in July and August. The seed-cotton product per acre on fresh land is from 1,000 to 1,200 pounds, 1,425 pounds making a bale of 475 pounds; staple middling. On land cultivated for ten years the product is from 900 to 1,000 pounds per acre, 1,545 pounds making a bale; staple not so long. The weeds are cocklebur and smart-weed. Very little land lies turned out, but such land would produce well again.

The *dark gray soil* forms about one-third of the lands. The growth is gum, beech, white, and black oaks, hickory, and poplar. The soil is a gray loam, with some sand, from 3 to 10 inches thick; the subsoil a light yellow clay, impervious when undisturbed, and underlaid by clay at 5 feet. The land is best adapted to corn, cotton, and grasses. One-fourth of the crops is cotton. Seed-cotton product per acre is less by 200 pounds than on the first soil.

The *brown sandy loam* of the uplands described above forms the larger proportion, and the growth is chiefly black-jack, white, black, and post oaks, hickory, poplar, and hazel; thickness from 3 to 8 inches. The subsoil is a red sandy clay, underlaid by sand and some gravel at 20 feet. One-fifth of the crops is cotton. The seed-cotton product on fresh land is from 900 to 1,000 pounds per acre, 1,425 pounds making a bale of 475 pounds. Staple is middling. Slopes wash seriously, and the valleys are damaged thereby. Horizontalizing and hillside ditching are practiced with success.

J. H. MEEKS (eastern part of the county generally).—Farmers chiefly fear early frost in the fall, which, however, rarely occurs. The soils cultivated in cotton are: (1) Dark brown alluvial, mixed with sand of first bottoms, very productive; (2) lighter brown of second bottoms, less productive; (3) light gray, with sand of uplands or "barrens", productive when fresh. The *dark brown alluvial* is the chief soil, and forms one-fourth of the first and second bottoms. It extends north many miles, east to the Tennessee, south 12 miles to the state line, and west 2 or 3 miles. The growth is oak, poplar, gum, maple, beech, ash, walnut, mulberry, red-bud, dogwood, etc. The soil is a fine sandy clay loam, 7 inches thick. The subsoil is light yellow and friable, intermixed with fine sand, and underlaid by gravel at 18 feet. The land is early and warm, partly well and partly ill drained, and is best adapted to corn. Two-thirds of the crops is cotton. Plants average 3½ feet in height, and when growing rank are restrained by shallow and little plowing. The seed-cotton product per acre on fresh land is 1,200 pounds, 1,545 pounds or less making a 475-pound bale. All our cotton rates well when clean. On land cultivated for five years the product is less by 200 pounds per acre, 1,485 pounds making a bale; staple is better, when there is any difference. Crab-grass is the pest of the cotton-growers. One-twentieth of the land lies turned out, but not so much so as formerly. Considerable has been taken in, which produces well at first too much exhausted. Slopes do not wash badly. Some little hillside ditching is done with good success.

The *second soil* is a fine sandy loam of a lighter color from 3 to 6 inches in depth, and having the same extent as the first soil. The subsoil is a reddish clay, mixed with fine sand, friable, and underlaid by sand and gravel at 18 feet. Land is easily worked until very old, and is best adapted to two-thirds cotton grows well. Cotton forms two-thirds of the crops. Plants grow to an average height of 2½ feet, and this is the best. The seed-cotton product per acre on fresh land is 1,000 pounds, 1,425 pounds making a bale of 475 pounds, and the staple rates well. On land cultivated five years the product is 900 pounds per acre.

The *light gray soil* of the "barrens" makes 1 . . . . and extends throughout the county. The growth is black-jack, black, ... and post oaks, hickory, dogwood, etc. The soil is from 2 to 4 inches deep. The subsoil is reddish and friable, contains sand, and is underlaid by sand and gravel at 16 feet. The land is best adapted to corn. Cotton form two-thirds of crops, and grows to a height of 2 feet. The seed-cotton product per acre on fresh land is from 500 to 700 pounds, and the staple is as good as any. Slopes have not washed to any serious extent.

B. M. TILLMAN, J. H. ROWSEY, S. PLUNK, AND F. E. MILLER (northwestern and northern part of the county, Sweet-lips creek and waters of the Forked Deer river).—The climate is not so well adapted to cotton as the land, as the seasons are often too short. The black fine sand is the chief cotton soil. One-half its crops is cotton. Plants grow to 3 and 4 feet in height, 3 feet being the best. The seed-cotton product per acre on fresh land is 1,000 pounds, 1,435 pounds making a bale of 475 pounds; staple middling. On land cultivated ten years the product is 600 pounds; but if manured the product may be from 1,600 to 1,800 pounds per acre. Crab-grass and foxtail are the only seriously troublesome weeds. A small proportion of the land lies turned out. Soils wash seriously on slopes, and the valleys are more or less injured. We check it by plowing on a dead level; have no hillside ditches.

The second soil, that of well-drained second and branch bottoms, produce per acre, when fresh, 800 pounds of seed-cotton, 1,425 pounds making a 475-pound bale; staple rates middling. After ten years' cultivation the land produces 600 pounds, but if manured, from 1,000 to 1,500 pounds; staple better, if there is any difference.

The gray uplands form the greatest portion, if woodlands are included. Black-jack, red, post, black, and Spanish oaks, and scrub hickory are common on these lands. The soil is 3 inches thick. One-half of the crops is cotton. The seed-cotton product per acre on fresh land is from 600 to 800 pounds per acre, 1,425 pounds making a 475-pound bale. On land cultivated ten years the product is from 600 to 800 pounds per acre. One-fourth of the land lies turned out, and is seldom taken in again unless lying well.

R. D. ANDERSON (south west from Purdy; Oxford's creek, waters of Hatchie river).—Our best lands are branch and small valley lands on creeks. Hill land is being abandoned. Bottoms are preferred for cotton, and with a fair season will produce per acre three times as much as hillsides; yet the latter will make some cotton, even in wet weather. I may note as a fact that open blooms, wet by rain in the morning, never mature. The important cotton-soils are those of bottoms or valleys, as follows: (1) Mulatto, sandy front-lands; (2) gravelly or buckshot back-lands. The *mulatto front-lands* is the chief soil, forming half the bottoms, the buckshot being the other half, and both together form an area three-fourths of a mile wide and 5 miles long. The soils of both average about 6 inches in depth. The subsoil of the first is sandy, leachy, and a brighter mulatto than the soil. The first soil is easily tilled in dry seasons, and in wet if well drained, and should be plowed when dry, but before becoming top dry; is late, but warm if well drained. The chief crops on both soils are corn, cotton, wheat, and oats, with some clover, millet, and herd's-grass. From one-third to one-half is planted in cotton. On first soil, the most productive, cotton grows to 4 feet. Plants become rank if wet in July and August, and there is no remedy. The seed-cotton product per acre on fresh land is 1,000 pounds, 1,545 pounds making a 475-pound bale, including 24 pounds for bagging and ties; the staple is very fine. On land worked ten years the product is 800 pounds, 1,425 pounds making a bale; staple not quite so good. The weeds are crab-grass, cocklebur, and smart-weed. None of the valley land lies turned out. Land is sometimes seriously injured by washings from slopes. All thrifty farmers practice horizontalizing and hillside ditching, with satisfactory results.

The *gravelly or buckshot* soil rests upon a gravelly subsoil, continuing down much the same for from 2 to 6 feet, and is then generally hard-pan and impervious. Excepting for weeds, tillage is easy in wet and dry seasons.

HARDIN.
(See "Western valley of the Tennessee river".)

DECATUR.
(See "Western valley of the Tennessee river".)

BENTON.
(See "Western valley of the Tennessee river".)

HARDEMAN.
(See "Brown-loam table-lands".)

MADISON.
(See "Brown-loam table-lands".)

WESTERN VALLEY OF THE TENNESSEE RIVER.

This natural division, as limited in Part I, embraces much of Henry,* the greater parts severally of Benton, Decatur, and Hardin counties, a little of McNairy,* the northwestern corner of Wayne,* and the western parts of Perry, Humphreys, Houston, and Stewart. Stewart and Houston are outside of the cotton region proper, and are not described. Stewart reported fifteen bales as the cotton product of 1879, and Houston four bales; but most of the cotton raised in Stewart, and all of that in Houston, was from parts of the counties within the limits of the Highland Rim to the east. For statistics of these counties see tables I and II, in Part I.

HENRY.
(See "Summit region of water-shed".)

BENTON.

Population: 9,780.—White, 9,147; colored, 633.
Area: 380 square miles.—Woodland, all.
Tilled lands: 46,425 acres.—Area planted in cotton, 4,923 acres; in corn, 24,788 acres; in wheat, 4,600 acres; in oats, 2,368 acres; in tobacco, 389 acres.
Cotton production: 1,801 bales; average cotton product, per acre, 0.37 bale, 522 pounds seed-cotton, or 174 pounds cotton lint.

The Big Sandy and the Tennessee rivers both flow in northerly directions, gradually approaching, until they meet at an acute angle not far south of the Kentucky line. In the angle thus formed the long and narrow county of Benton is situated, placed, as if thrust in from the south, with its sharp northern end foremost. The Tennessee bounds it on the east and the Big Sandy for much of the distance on the west. It thus happens that Benton is chiefly a water-shed between two rivers. Its eastern margin, having a length along the river of 50 miles or more, is mostly made up of the rich alluvial bottoms of the Tennessee, averaging for the entire length nearly a mile in width. On the other side, for half the length of the western boundary, the bottoms of the Big Sandy make the western margin. The remainder of this boundary is a straight line running from a point on the Big Sandy directly south. The southwestern corner of the county is thus thrown out of the valley of the Big Sandy, and exceptionally upon the uplands of the water-shed.

The upland belt between the rivers has a varied surface, much of which is sandy, undulating, moderately fertile, and hilly. It is traversed by a multitude of creeks, some of large size, their valleys affording in the aggregate a great amount of good land. It must be noted that the "old shore" line spoken of on previous pages, or the junction of the hard rocks of Middle Tennessee with the soft strata of West Tennessee, passes through Benton. (See page 13, under "Outline of physical geography", and also under "Western valley of Tennessee river".) The eastern part of the county, therefore, including its northern end, is based on hard rocks, flinty, silicco-calcareous rocks, and limestones, which often show themselves in bluffs and in the beds of creeks. The western part, on the other hand, has to a great extent a basis of laminated clays and sands. Over nearly all, however, excluding the alluvium of the Tennessee and other large streams, are strewed, sometimes thinly, the sands, and often the gravels, of the orange-sand drift. Going toward the valley of the Big Sandy sandy rolling lands predominate. Approaching the bottoms of the Tennessee the country breaks away in bluffs and spurs, often with cherty, gravelly surfaces and soils.

The soils on the uplands are comparatively thin, but areas of rich brown loams occur. The growth is hickory, poplar, chestnut, black-jack, black, white, and other small oaks. The most important soils are those of the first and second bottoms and gentle slopes. The black alluvial lands of the Tennessee are very productive, and would be first-class cotton lands were it not for overflows in spring, which often seriously delay planting. The first bottoms of the Big Sandy are low and wet, but the second bottoms and "long slopes", with their brown, mellow, sandy loams, are favorite grounds for cotton-growers. The numerous creek and branch valleys contribute largely to the aggregate of cotton lands. The growth of valley land is elm, poplar, hickory, hackberry, black, and white oaks, sugar-tree, beech, papaw, and, in the bottoms of the larger streams, cypress.

Benton is on the margin of the cotton region. On the map showing acreage in cotton it is divided nearly north and south into three belts. The western belt, in the southwestern part of the county, had in 1879 from 5 to 10 per cent. of its total area in cotton; the middle belt, a narrow one reaching farther north, from 1 to 5 per cent.; and the eastern, the larger part, extending through the entire length of the county, from 0.1 to 1 per cent. Cotton is shipped by rail to Nashville at $1 or to Louisville at $2 per bale.

ABSTRACT FROM REPORTS.

J. H. BRIDGES, W. F. MAIDEN, A. E. SWINDLE, AND P. M. MELTON (middle and northern parts of the county).—The soils cultivated in cotton are: (1) Dark gray of gently sloping upland; (2) dark loam of Sandy and Tennessee river bottoms; (3) flat-land soil, light-colored, and inclined to be stiff. The *dark gray soil* forms one-fifth of our lands. It is a clayey loam 5 inches thick. The subsoil bakes in the sun, but crumbles and mixes readily with the soil; is impervious when undisturbed, contains gravel, and is underlaid by sand, gravel, or rock at from 1 foot to 3 feet. The land is early, warm, and well drained. The chief crops are corn, wheat, oats, cotton, tobacco, and potatoes, but the land is best adapted to corn and oats. One-fifth of the crops is cotton. Plants in places reach a height of 6 feet, but produce best at 3½ to 4 feet. They may overgrow when planted late and the season is wet, for which topping is advocated by some as a remedy. The seed-cotton product per acre on fresh land is 600 pounds, 1,660 pounds being required for a 475-pound bale; staple is ordinary. On land cultivated five years the product is 400 pounds; staple heavier, though shorter. The weeds are hog-weed, rag-weed, and crab-grass in wet weather. One-fifth of the land lies turned out, and if taken in again would produce well if manured. Slopes wash seriously in places; the valleys are not generally injured thereby, but very often are improved. Some horizontalizing and hillside ditching are done, with good results.

A. C. PRESSON (county generally.—For kinds of soils, etc., see page 24, Part I, under "Western valley of the Tennessee river").—The first soil, the *black sandy* of bottoms, is easily tilled in dry seasons, but with difficulty in wet. The crops are corn, wheat, cotton, tobacco, oats, potatoes, and peanuts. The land is best adapted to corn, cotton, and tobacco. About 2 per cent. of the cleared land is planted in cotton. Plants grow to 3½ feet, and are best at that. Cotton on fresh land in wet seasons may run to weed, and some restrain it by topping. The seed-cotton product per acre on fresh land is 1,000 pounds, 1,570 pounds making a bale of 475 pounds; staple rates good. On land in cultivation ten years the product is 500 pounds per acre, 1,580 pounds making a bale; staple a little different. The weeds are crab-grass and cocklebur. No land lies turned out.

The second soil, the *black sandy of level uplands*, is a sandy clay loam 5 inches thick, easily tilled in dry and wet seasons; is early, warm, well drained, and is planted in cotton to the extent of 20 per cent. Plants grow to 3 feet, and are best at that. Seed-cotton product on fresh land is a little less than on first soils. Other points are as under third soil.

The third soil is the *yellow sandy* of rolling uplands. Subsoil on hillsides is sand; on tops of hills and level portions, yellow clay. The land is early, warm, and well drained. Most of the crops are cotton. Plants grow from 2½ to 3 feet high, the latter the best. The seed-cotton product per acre on fresh land is 800 pounds, 1,575 pounds making a 475-pound bale; staple rates well. On land worked six years the product is 500 pounds, 1,580 pounds making a bale. Chief weed, crab-grass. One-fourth of the land is turned out. Hilly lands, when once turned out, are never taken in again. Slopes wash seriously, but the valleys are but little damaged thereby. Horizontalizing and hillside ditching are practiced with very good results.

DECATUR.

Population: 8,498.—White, 7,276; colored, 1,222.

Area: 310 square miles.—Woodland, all, excepting a limited aggregate of marly limestone glades.

Tilled lands: 37,861 acres.—Area planted in cotton, 5,591 acres; in corn, 19,985 acres; in wheat, 3,829 acres; in oats, 2,701 acres; in tobacco, 59 acres.

Cotton production: 2,169 bales; average cotton product per acre, 0.39 bale, 552 pounds seed-cotton, or 184 pounds cotton lint.

442

Decatur county has a long, narrow, rectangular form, its length being more than three times its width. It lies lengthwise north and south, and is bounded on two sides (the eastern and southern) by the Tennessee river. The "old shore" line, or the junction of the soft strata of West Tennessee with the hard rocks of Middle Tennessee (see page 13, under "Outline of physical geography", and also under "Western valley of the Tennessee river"), runs longitudinally through the county, splitting it into a western, sandy, and higher belt, and an eastern, rocky, and lower one. The western belt is indeed the eastern border of the great sandy plateau slope of West Tennessee. Its high areas, table-lands, rolling lands, and hills supply the headwaters of many creeks flowing into the Beech and the Tennessee rivers. The Beech itself, rising farther west, flows eastward directly across both belts of the county. The rocky, or eastern, belt falls away to the bottoms of the Tennessee, though ridges continuous with the western highlands often run eastward a long way toward the river. The prevailing rocks off the ridges are limestones, often cherty, several beds of them marly, and forming at numerous points marly, glady places, destitute, or nearly destitute, of native growth. At the tops of the ridges are layers of flinty and calcareo-siliceous rocks, such as cap the high flat table-lands of Middle Tennessee east of the Tennessee river. Over all the strata of the county, alluvial bottoms excepted, the sands and gravels of the orange-sand drift have been deposited more or less continuously. In the western belt its sands prevail and cover the deeper strata to great extent; in the eastern, gravel is common, and the deposits are broken and occur at intervals. Here on high ridges beds of gravel, sand, and *débris* are met with. In such masses, at a number of localities, exist accumulations of iron ore of economic interest.

The chief soils may be grouped as follows: First, the dark alluvial of the rivers and larger creeks, of which there is a full show, with a native growth of white oak, poplar, hickory, ash, sweet and black gum, beech, walnut, sugar-tree, and elm, with cypress in the swampy back-lands; secondly, the brown sandy loams of the second bottoms, slopes, and branch valleys, with sandy or gravelly, or clayey subsoils, and a growth of oaks chiefly, with beech, hickory, walnut, and gum; and lastly, the thinner sandy soils of flat and hilly highlands, on which grow hickory, post and other oaks, and sometimes chestnut. Calcareous, clayey soils, based on limestones, are found in the eastern and southern portions. The Tennessee river washes the borders of the county for nearly 50 miles, and the bottoms occur along much of this distance. These bottoms are often more than a mile wide, and sometimes extend back 2 miles from the river. Then again they are narrowed and cut off by the running in of the highlands. Many of them present the characteristic features of "front-lands" and of lower, swampy, and cypress "back-lands". They must average for the whole length of the river not much, if any, less than 1 mile, the "front-lands" supplying an exceedingly valuable body of land.

The crops are those given at the head of this description, together with sorghum, peanuts, rye, pease, grasses, and potatoes. All the lands, excepting marshy lands, are cultivated more or less in corn and cotton, to which they are best adapted. The larger part of the county had in 1879 from 1 to 5 per cent. of its total area planted in cotton; but a strip in the southwestern part of the county, contiguous to the western boundary, had more, from 5 to 10 per cent., and the northeastern corner less, from 0.1 to 1 per cent. (See map of relative acreage in cotton.) Cotton is shipped, by river or rail, to Louisville or Cincinnati at from $1 to $1 50 per bale.

ABSTRACTS FROM REPORTS.

J. H. PEARCY, L. D. CRAWLEY, AND J. McMILLAN (county generally).—Cotton is a sure crop, and brings ready money. Women and children can work at it, which is a consideration. (For kinds of soil, etc., see Part I, under "Western valley of the Tennessee river".) The subsoil of the fresh sandy land is yellowish and reddish. On this soil plants grow to 3 feet, the best height. Topping about the 1st of August is practiced when plants run to weed on fresh land in wet weather. The seed-cotton product per acre on fresh land is 800 pounds, 1,485 pounds making a 475-pound bale; staple rates middling. On land worked five years the product is from 500 to 600 pounds for a few years, 1,600 pounds making a bale; staple not quite so good. Crab-grass is the pest. Ten per cent. of the land lies turned out. Horizontalizing and hillside ditching have been done with success in most cases.

On the *black sandy soil* on the river cotton grows from 2 to 6 feet in height, the highest being the most productive. Wet seasons incline the plant to become weedy, which is restrained by topping by the last of July or in August. The seed-cotton product per acre on fresh land is 1,000 pounds, 1,600 pounds making a 475-pound bale; staple brought last season (1879) 12 cents. After the first year's cultivation the product is about the same; staple somewhat better. The weeds are crab-grass and cocklebur. Very little land, say one-thirtieth, lies turned out. The slopes wash seriously, and the valleys are injured thereby 5 per cent. Very little is done to check the damage.

The *black and clayey soil* on the creeks is early, warm, and tolerably well drained. Cotton grows to 2 and 5 feet, but is best at 3 feet. The seed-cotton product on fresh land is the same as on first soil; staple middling. On land cultivated six years the product is 800 pounds per acre, 1,545 pounds making a bale; staple good ordinary. The valleys are injured by washing of slopes 25 per cent. Either items as under first soil.

On the *hilly, clay loam* the growth is oak and hickory; depth of soil, 4 inches. Cotton grows to 2 feet. The seed-cotton product per acre on fresh land is 500 pounds, 1,660 pounds making a bale; staple good ordinary. After four years' cultivation the product is 400 pounds; staple not so good. Crab-grass is troublesome. One-fourth of the land lies turned out, and if taken in again would produce very poorly. Valleys are injured 25 per cent. by the washing of slopes. Other items as above.

W. H. BOGGAN, J. F., W. R., AND R. J. AKIN, AND R. T. SIMMONS (southern part of the county, Stewman's Creek and Tennessee River lands).—Uplands vary in areas from 1 acre to 100 acres. Cotton in low, wet lands is late in spring, becomes lousy, and is often caught by early fall frost. The soils cultivated in cotton are: (1) Black bottom lands, in bodies of from 10 to 100 acres, partly subject to overflow; (2) upland, mulatto or yellow, above overflow; (3) hill- and table-land, sandy soil in patches. The *black bottom lands* form 40 per cent. of all, and occur 10 miles east, 12 west, 3 north, and 6 miles south. It is a sandy clay loam (putty-like in small patches) of alternating black, brown, and yellow colors. The subsoil is a tough yellow, dark red, and white clay, gradually becoming like the soil upon cultivation, is impervious when undisturbed, often contains gravel, and is underlaid by sand, gravel, or limestone (cement-rock) at from 2 to 12 feet. The land is easily tilled in dry seasons, but with some difficulty in wet, and is best adapted to corn and cotton. Fifteen per cent. of crops are cotton. Plants grow from 2½ to 6 feet; are best at 3 feet. Bolling is favored by the use of fertilizers. The seed-cotton product per acre on fresh land is 800 pounds, 1,720 pounds making a 475-pound bale; staple middling to middling fair. On land worked five years the product is 700 pounds, and if well manured 2,000 pounds, 1,600 pounds making a bale; staple not so long or fine. The weeds are crab-grass, cocklebur, smart-weed, and careless-weed. No land lies turned out. The slopes wash to no great extent. Some hillside ditching has been done with good success.

The *upland*, above overflow, which forms half the lands, extends off 8 or 12 miles in each direction, and is a clayey, often gravelly loam 6 inches deep. The subsoil is underlaid by sand or gravel, or limestone (cement-rock), at from 1 foot to 30 feet. Tillage is not usually troublesome in dry seasons, but is rather difficult in wet. (In other respects this soil is like first, with the exceptions below.) The seed-cotton product per acre on fresh land is 700 pounds; staple middling. On land worked five years the product is 650 pounds; if well manured, 2,000 pounds per acre. Two per cent. of the land lies turned out, and would produce, if taken in again, 600 pounds per acre.

The *hill- and table-land* forms 10 or 12 per cent. of the lands, and extends from 12 to 16 miles, bordering on heads of creeks and sand-hills. The growth is oak, hickory, poplar, chestnut, black gum, and sourwood. The soil is a sandy, gravelly clay loam of gray, yellow, or brown color, from 3 to 6 inches deep. The subsoil contains gravel at points of the hills, and is underlaid by sand and gravel and sand-rock at from 2 to 4 feet. The land is early, warm, and well drained, and is best adapted to cotton, which makes 4 per cent. of the crops. Plants grow to 18 and 20 inches, the latter the best. The seed-cotton product per acre on fresh land is from 400 to 600 pounds, 1,660 pounds making a 475-pound bale; staple middling. On land worked five years the product is from 300 to 450 pounds, 1,500 pounds making a bale; staple less fine and long, with a heavier coat on seed. Grass is the most troublesome. Five per cent. of the land lies turned out, and would produce from 250 to 500 pounds per acre if taken in again. The slopes do not wash badly, and the valleys are not injured.

D. M. SCOTT AND J. G. YARBOROUGH.—The yellowish, sandy soil of swells in the bottoms has a subsoil underlaid by sand and gravel at 50 feet. The tillage of soil in wet seasons is rather difficult, but is very easy in dry. The land is early when well drained. Cotton grows to 2 and 5 feet and higher; is best at 3 feet. Wet weather in July and August inclines the plants to run to weed, for which I know of no remedy. The seed-cotton product per acre on fresh land is from 1,000 to 1,500 pounds, 1,485 to 1,550 pounds, including bags and ties, making a 475-pound bale; staple good middling. On land under cultivation fifteen years the product is from 500 to 1,500 pounds, if manured to some extent; staple not differing essentially. The weeds are crab-grass, careless-weed and buffalo- or pig-weed. No land lies turned out.

HARDIN.

Population: 14,793.—White, 12,775; colored, 2,018.
Area: 610 square miles.—Woodland, all, excepting a limited aggregate of marly limestone glades.
Tilled lands: 72,446 acres.—Area planted in cotton, 12,859 acres; in corn, 30,909 acres; in wheat, 5,445 acres ; in oats, 3,387 acres; in tobacco, 88 acres.
Cotton production: 5,345 bales; average cotton product per acre, 0.42 bale, 591 pounds seed-cotton, or 197 pounds cotton lint.

Hardin is the only county in the western part of the state that lies on both sides of the Tennessee river. The states of Mississippi and Alabama corner on its southern boundary at a point nearly bisecting the boundary, and where, too, the Tennessee river enters the state of Tennessee. The county is rectangular in form, its longer dimension lying north and south, and is greatly varied in its topography, rocks, and soils. Lying on both sides of the river, it presents, indeed, characteristics of both Western and Middle Tennessee. If we divide the county into four approximately equal belts by lines running north and south, the western belt or quarter will have for its geological basis stratified sands and the "greensand" stratum pertaining to McNairy and other western counties, while the other belts will be based on solid rocks, limestones, shales, and flinty strata, representing a number of much older formations. The line cutting off the western quarter thus coincides with, and indeed is, the "old shore line", of which I have before spoken. (See page 13, under "Outline of physical geography", and also under the "Western shore line of the Tennessee river".) The Tennessee river coincides for a good part of its course with the same "shore line". Entering the county, with hard rocks on both sides, the river curves to the west until it reaches the "shore line", and then flows northward, with sandy bluffs on the western side and rocky ones on the eastern. At a point about two-thirds of the way through the county the river, bending to the northeast, leaves the "shore line" and enters the area of the hard rocks, escaping finally from the sandy strata at its northeastern corner. It thus happens that limestones are found in the extreme northern and southern parts of the county west of the Tennessee. In any section of Hardin, even upon the highest ridges of the eastern portion, scattered patches of the sand and gravel of the orange-sand drift may be met with resting upon all the deeper strata and rocks mentioned.

The Tennessee river, in bending as it does through the county, has a long immediate valley. This includes many rich bottoms, but is in the main rougher than we would look for in the valley of so great a stream. Going west from the river bottoms through the country, though broken, has level areas interspersed, which rise into ridges between the creek valleys as we approach the western boundary. The soils west of the "shore line" are sandy, often mellow and fertile, and, in the northwestern part of the county especially, alternate more or less with the stiffer soils of the "greensand" formation. Going east from the river the country presents varied features, and in the southern part of the county the high table-lands of the Highland Rim are soon met with. East of Savannah there is an area of post-oak flatwoods resting upon sand and gravel.

Most of the northeastern part of Hardin is a rolling limestone region, supplying more or less good land, and in places marly glades, nearly naked, or spotted with clumps of small cedars. Within this section are several large creeks, with valleys of good land. East and southeast of the central portion are heavy, often flat-topped ridges, interlocked with narrow valleys. Farther to the southeast the country is chiefly high table-land, resting upon the great Highland Rim, with calcareo-siliceous, flinty, and sometimes cherty limestone rocks. The soils are thin, though better areas on the branches are interspersed. The main rim sweeps around from the Highland Rim, in the southern part of the county, northeasterly into Wayne. Many ridges in the northeastern part of Hardin are but spurs, in places reduced to lines of hills, running out westerly and northwesterly from the rim.

The chief crops are corn and cotton. For most of the county the acreage planted in cotton in 1879, as compared with total area, was from 1 to 5 per cent.; for the western third of the county, excepting a fraction at the southern end, it was more—from 5 to 10 per cent. Cotton is shipped to Cincinnati and Louisville at $1 50 per bale.

ABSTRACTS FROM REPORTS.

J. C. MITCHELL (northwestern part of the county, west of Tennessee river.—For remarks, kinds of soils, etc., see pages 24, 25).—On the first soil, black upland, lying on hillsides and branch bottoms, cotton grows to 2 and 5 feet in height, but is best at 3 feet. Wet seasons incline the plant to run to weed; topping is often done, and is said to be beneficial. Seed-cotton product per acre on fresh land is 700 pounds, 1,660 pounds making a 475-pound bale; staple low middling. On land cultivated five years the product on upland is from 300 to

400 pounds, and on bottoms 600 pounds, 1,545 pounds making a bale; staple about the same. The weeds are crab-grass and cocklebur. One-third of the land lies turned out, but if taken in again it would produce well. Slopes wash seriously, and valleys are considerably damaged thereby. Horizontalizing is done to a limited extent, and with good success so far as tried.

On the dark loam of the Tennessee River bottom cotton grows to 5 and 10 feet. The seed-cotton product per acre on fresh land is from 500 to 1,500 pounds, 2,140 pounds making a 475-pound bale; staple good ordinary. On land cultivated for five years the product is about the same, 2,010 pounds making a bale; staple of some rates low middling. The weeds are cocklebur and crab-grass. Land is only turned out when overflows wash it into gullies.

On the sandy bottom soil, near the river bank, cotton grows to a height of 5 or 10 feet. The seed-cotton product per acre on fresh land is from 1,000 to 1,800 pounds, 1,900 pounds making a bale of 475 pounds; staple middling. On land cultivated fifteen years the product and the staple are the same as on fresh land. Cocklebur is the troublesome weed. No land lies turned out unless gullied. Slopes gully readily, but nothing is done to check the damage.

J. W. IRWIN (central part of the county, east of Tennessee river).—On the black sandy soil of creek and river bottoms cotton grows to a height of from 3 to 7 feet, 5 feet being the best. To check growth in wet seasons thinning and topping are resorted to. Seed-cotton product per acre on fresh land is from 1,000 to 1,200 pounds, 1,660 pounds making a 475-pound bale; staple low middling. On land worked five years the product is about the same, as the roots are killed by that time, 1,600 pounds making a bale; staple finer but shorter. The weeds are island-weed, morning-glory, and cocklebur. Land is only turned out when washed. Slopes wash readily, but the damage is not serious, and is checked by permitting small undergrowth to take the land.

On the soil of second bottoms and slopes (so-called "ridge land") cotton grows to 2½ and 4 feet. Plants grow rank only in very wet seasons, and topping is rarely necessary on upland. The seed-cotton product per acre on fresh land is from 800 to 1,000 pounds, 1,660 pounds making a bale of 475 pounds; staple middling. On land cultivated five years, the product is from 400 to 750 pounds, 1,600 pounds making a bale; staple finer. One-third of the land lies turned out; but if taken in again, and not washed, would produce well. The slopes wash seriously, and the valleys are injured thereby 25 per cent. Very little is done to check damage, our people not yet realizing the importance of saving and restoring land.

On the soil of the flatwoods cotton grows from 2 to 3½ feet, and rarely needs topping. The seed-cotton product per acre on fresh land is from 600 to 800 pounds, 1,600 pounds making a 475-pound bale; staple middling. On land worked five years the product is 400 pounds; staple finer. Weed crab-grass. One-half this land lies turned out; but if taken in again it would produce nearly as well as at first. Slopes wash seriously, and little is done to check the damage.

McNAIRY.

(See " Summit region of the water-shed".)

WAYNE.

(See " The Highland Rim".)

PERRY.

Population: 7,174.—White, 6,609; colored, 565.

Area: 400 square miles.—Woodland, all, excepting a small aggregate of marly limestone glades.

Tilled lands: 35,422 acres.—Area planted in cotton, 452 acres; in corn, 15,007 acres; in wheat, 3,113 acres; in oats, 1,461 acres; in tobacco, 29 acres.

Cotton production: 196 bales; average cotton product per acre, 0.43 bale, 618 pounds seed-cotton, or 206 pounds cotton lint.

Perry and the county contiguous on the north (Humphreys) contribute a long central portion to the eastern slope of the western valley of the Tennessee. Both counties have the Tennessee for their western boundary. Perry has Wayne to the south of it and Hardin to the southwest. The diagonal corners of Perry and Hardin would nearly touch but for the northwestern corner of Wayne, which is thrust between them and borders the Tennessee for a number of miles. Perry is approximately rectangular in form, nearly twice as long as wide, with the longer dimension north and south. Its topography is easily understood. Parallel with the Tennessee river, and running in the same direction to the north through the eastern part of the county, is Buffalo river, with a well-marked valley. Conceiving the county to be split into four equal belts by three lines running north and south, the most easterly line will mark the place of Buffalo river, throwing one-fourth of the county to the east of that stream, and the middle line will nearly coincide with a high ridge 300 or 400 feet above adjacent valleys, a "divide" between the waters of Buffalo river and the Tennessee. We say "nearly coincide", for the course of the divide lies a little east of the line and crowds upon the Buffalo valley, greatly narrowing its western slope. Half or more of the county forms a belt west of the divide. The county as a whole is thus seen to consist of parallel and unequal sections lying lengthwise within its bounds. The divide sends off numerous spurs westward toward the Tennessee river, arranged quite regularly, like teeth in a comb. Between these are many creek valleys, based on limestone, which widen as we descend toward the river, supplying many rich bottoms, with fair second bottoms and slopes. Reaching the river, we find at intervals along its course the characteristic alluvial lands, though the aggregate of these is less than on the western bank.

The western slope of the Buffalo valley, from the river to the divide, is narrow, with short, swift streams. The eastern slope is quite different. Within the limits of Perry, outside of the river bottoms, it shows the ends of many spurs jutting into the county from the east, and between them the lower parts of as many creeks flowing into the Buffalo. Curiously, the ends of the spurs are the ends of the teeth of another comby topography such as we have in the western half of Perry. The back of the second comb, or the second "divide", lies in sections of Hickman and Lewis, contiguous to Perry, and from it spurs (broad and flat-topped here for much of their course) extend off westward toward the Buffalo, as in the other case they do toward the Tennessee. Between these are many valleys, a good part based on limestone, which widen and supply bottoms and other good lands until the immediate valley of the Buffalo is reached. Both combs lie with their teeth in the same direction and their backs nearly parallel.

Buffalo and the creeks of the eastern portion all have valleys with a fair proportion of rich, mellow bottom lands. The slopes are generally in cultivation, supplying often very desirable farming tracts, with siliceous or calcareous soils, based on clayey subsoils. The ridges are capped with siliceous rocks, the soils of which are thin and unproductive. As in other counties of this part of the state, patches of gravel of the orange-sand drift are occasionally met with.

The chief crops of Perry are corn, wheat, oats, and peanuts, with some cotton, potatoes, and tobacco. Cotton was once more largely cultivated than now. The census of 1870 gave 495 bales (400 pounds each) as the product of 1869; we have reported only 196 bales (475 pounds each). This falling off, amounting to 220 standard bales of 475 pounds each, is in good part due to the substitution of the culture of peanuts for that of cotton. On the map of acreage in cotton it is seen that three-fourths of the county had in 1879 less than 0.1 per cent. of total area in cotton. Most of the cotton was raised in the southern part. A strip on the southern boundary shows from 1 to 5 per cent.; another, next north, from 1 to 0.1 per cent.

HUMPHREYS.

Population: 11,379.—White, 9,708; colored, 1,671.
Area: 450 square miles.—Woodland, all.
Tilled lands: 53,938 acres.—Area planted in cotton, 155 acres; in corn, 26,387 acres; in wheat, 5,426 acres; in oats, 1,988 acres; in tobacco, 33 acres.
Cotton production: 90 bales; average cotton product per acre, 0.58 bale, 828 pounds seed-cotton, or 276 pounds cotton lint.

It is only the southern part of Humphreys county that can lay any claim, so far as actual products are concerned, to be within the cotton-growing region, and the claim for this part is a feeble one. The county lies north of Perry, and with it contributes, as stated in the description of the latter county, a long central portion to the eastern slope of the western valley of the Tennessee river. The Tennessee bounds it on the west. Its middle and eastern parts are mainly high table-lands, forming a section of the great Highland Rim of Middle Tennessee. We may say, in fact, that the whole county is an elevated table-land, sloping off on the west as it approaches the lowlands of the Tennessee river, and is channeled throughout by water-courses running more or less westerly. Its southern part is cut across by the curving valley of Duck river, with which, coming from the south, Buffalo valley unites. Large creeks rise in the eastern and northeastern parts of the county and beyond the boundary, in the margin of Dickson county, next east, of which some flow south-westward into Duck river, and others westward into the Tennessee. The latter widen as they approach the river.

The valleys supply substantially the productive lands. The bottoms and gentle slopes of the creeks, based on calcareo-siliceous rocks, sometimes on limestones, and often on cherty gravel, are usually mellow siliceous loams, and are everywhere in cultivation. The valleys of Duck and Buffalo rivers, in which most of the cotton is raised, have bottoms, some of large size, noted for their mellowness and fertility. In addition, the Tennessee river, washing the western side of the county for 30 miles, contributes a large and important quota of dark sandy alluvium. The native growth of the valleys is heavy, and includes many species, among which white, black, and red oaks, poplar, walnut, sweet gum, hickory, ash, and beech may be mentioned. The leading crops are corn, peanuts, wheat, and oats, but some attention is given to rye, tobacco, potatoes, clover, and grasses. Peanuts take the place of cotton as a ready-money product. The table-lands are chiefly in open woods, often denominated "barrens", and are very sparsely settled—for miles not at all. They have thin soils, little productive. The growth is black, red, white, post, and Spanish oaks, hickory, dogwood, and black gum, with sometimes black-jack, chestnut, and occasionally poplar. On the map of relative acreage planted in cotton in 1879 the southern part only is regarded, and there the acreage in cotton is represented as less than one-thousandth of the total area. Cotton is shipped to Cincinnati at $1 50 per bale.

ABSTRACTS FROM REPORTS.

W. J. WHITE AND W. D. KING (southern part of the county).—But little cotton is planted. The peanut crop is the most important, farmers resorting to it after enough corn and wheat are planted to supply bread. The kinds of soil cultivated in cotton are: (1) Bottom; (2) upland and second bottom. One-third of all our lands is good for cotton. On the first soil cotton grows to 3 and 6 feet high, but is best at 4 feet. Wet seasons and soils too rich cause plants to grow rank, for which I know of no remedy. The seed-cotton product per acre on fresh land is from 800 to 1,500 pounds, 1,780 pounds making a 475-pound bale. Staple rates low middling to middling. Culture of cotton injures the land but little. The weeds are rag-weed, smart-weed, purslane, careless-weed, and crab-grass. Little, if any, of this land lies turned out.

The upland and second bottom soil forms one-half the cultivated lands, and occurs up and down the valleys of Duck and Buffalo rivers. It is a fine sandy and gravelly loam of a gray, yellowish, or blackish color, from 3 to 12 inches thick. Cotton grows upon it 3 and 6 feet high, 4 feet being the best. The seed-cotton product per acre on fresh land is 1,000 pounds, 1,780 pounds making a bale of 475 pounds; staple rates as low middling. No land worth noting lies turned out. The slopes do not wash seriously, and not much effort is made to check the damage.

THE HIGHLANDS, OR HIGHLAND RIM OF MIDDLE TENNESSEE.

In Part I, under the head of "The Highland Rim", this natural division is considered to consist of two parts, a western and an eastern, and the counties included, or partly included, in each were enumerated. Under the same head the character of the division as a cotton-producing area is noticed.

HIGHLAND RIM (WESTERN SUBDIVISION).

This subdivision embraces all or parts of Hardin,* Wayne, Lawrence, Lewis, Perry,* Hickman, Humphreys,* Dickson, Cheatham, Robertson, Montgomery, Stewart, Giles,* Maury,* Williamson,* Sumner,* and Davidson.* The counties of Dickson, Cheatham, Robertson, Montgomery, and Stewart are outside of the cotton region proper, or in the "penumbral region" of cotton culture. Montgomery and Cheatham produced in 1879 but 2 bales each, Dickson 31 bales, and Robertson none. The cotton reported from Houston, 4 bales, and much of that from Stewart, 15 bales, was from lands within this subdivision. (For the statistics of these counties see Tables I and II in Part I.) These "penumbral" counties are not separately described, and the reader is referred to the general descriptions of the regions represented in each.

HARDIN.

(See "Western valley of the Tennessee river".)

WAYNE.

Population: 11,301.—White, 10,232; colored, 1,069.
Area: 710 square miles.—Woodland, all.
Tilled lands: 56,456 acres.—Area planted in cotton, 3,265 acres; in corn, 25,674 acres; in wheat, 8,791 acres; in oats, 2,109 acres; in rye, 505 acres; in tobacco, 63 acres.
Cotton production: 1,207 bales; average cotton product per acre, 0.37 bale, 528 pounds seed-cotton, or 176 pounds cotton lint.

Wayne county, resting upon the southern boundary of the state, is a characteristic county of the Highland Rim, to which division it all belongs, excepting its northwestern corner. The part excepted is washed by the Tennessee river for 10 miles or more, and contains a fair proportion of alluvial lands, and back of the bottoms there is much rolling limestone, often glady land. In the main the county is a high, flat table-land from 800 to 1,000 feet above the sea. Within its central portions are the headwaters of numerous creeks, which flow in all directions. The northwestern portion breaks down into the rolling and glady limestone lands referred to, and constitutes the section of the county belonging to the western valley of the Tennessee river. Within it are a few long spurs from the highlands reaching out far toward the river. The northeastern portion crowds upon the valley of Buffalo river, the limit in that direction. Many of the creeks, before passing the boundaries of the county, become considerable streams, and cut deeply into the table-land down to underlying limestone rocks, thereby supplying long, narrow valleys of strong, arable lands.

Indian and Hardin's creeks, flowing westward and then northwestward through Hardin county into the Tennessee, have valleys especially deep. Many others are but little less so.

The rocks of the county are first, at top, siliceous or calcareo-siliceous beds, surmounted in some regions with cherty limestones, making the floor of the highlands; and, secondly, below these, grayish and reddish marly limestone, outcropping in the valleys and on the lower slopes of the northeastern portion. As in other counties bordering on the Tennessee river, the marly limestones outcrop here and there, forming glades, bespotted with clumps of cedars. Upon any of the strata of the county, high or low, it is no unusual thing to meet with patches of gravel, outliers of the orange-sand drift.

The soils of the highlands are poor and thin, and miles may be traveled through the woods without meeting with a house or a hut. Oaks of moderate size prevail (white, black, chestnut, black-jack, post, and others), and with these are poplar, chestnut, and, in the southern part of the county especially, yellow pine. The timber on rolling lands is better than that of the flatwoods. The farming lands are substantially confined to the valleys, the lands of which are often rich, the soils mellow, and subsoils clayey and gravelly, producing corn, cotton, wheat, oats, rye, sorghum, peanuts, tobacco, and hay. The cotton product in 1000, according to census reports, was 1,101 bales of 400 pounds each, as against 1,207 bales of 475 pounds each in 1879. The map of relative acreage in cotton shows that the western and southern portions had in 1879 the greatest per cent. of area in cotton, namely, from 1 to 5 per cent., and the northwestern part the least, below one-tenth of 1 per cent., while an intermediate strip had from one-tenth to 1 per cent.

LAWRENCE.

Population: 10,383.—White, 9,599; colored, 784.
Area: 590 square miles.—Woodland, all.
Tilled lands: 47,855 acres.—Area planted in cotton, 1,830 acres; in corn, 21,673 acres; in wheat, 8,053 acres; in oats, 2,812 acres; in rye, 357 acres; in tobacco, 31 acres.
Cotton production: 702 bales; average cotton product per acre, 0.38 bale, 546 pounds seed-cotton, or 182 pounds cotton lint.

Lawrence is one of the southern tier of counties, and rests upon the Alabama line, and is the second county west of the longitude of Nashville. It is a typical area of the Highland Rim. The wooded flatlands and rolling

447

surfaces are often more than 1,000 feet above the sea, and from 300 to 400 feet above the floor of the Central Basin to the east. From a belt lying east and west, north of the center, some of the branches and creeks run northward to form Buffalo river, and others southward to form the most important stream of the county, Shoal creek. The latter flows diagonally through the larger portion of the county, escaping at the southwestern corner. Sugar and Blue Water are other creeks in the southeastern and southern portions. High table-lands prevail in the county, supporting a growth of black, red, white, post, chestnut, and black-jack oaks, chestnut, black gum, dogwood, and occasionally hickories and poplars. More favored areas, however, occur with a stronger soil and timber of a better class. The northern part is made rolling or hilly by the tributaries of Buffalo river, while the southern part is cut deeply into by the rapid creeks of that section, and the continuity of the table-lands is much broken by the valleys, often wide and fertile, of these streams. The formations of the highlands are those characteristic of the Highland Rim, calcareo-siliceous rocks, with which are limestones more or less cherty. The deepest valleys in the southern portion of the county are cut down through these, exposing the lower gray and blue limestones. The lands of the county have been classified as follows: Bottoms and second bottoms; rich hill lands near the creeks; less productive hill lands farther from the creeks; first quality of table-land, second quality of table-land, or the " barrens". The crops are given above. For most of the county the percentage of total area planted in cotton was in 1879 less than 0.1; in the southwestern and southeastern corners it was greatest, from 1 to 5.

ABSTRACT FROM REPORT.

N. M. HOLLIS (southwestern part of the county, waters of Shoal creek).—Neither soil nor climate is well suited to cotton. The soils cultivated in cotton are: (1) Second bottom; (2) third bottoms, southeastern and western hillsides; (3) hill-top. The *second bottom soil* is a gravelly dark loam, forming about one-tenth of our lands. It does not occur in great bodies, and is confined to creek valleys, which are separated by hills and table-lands. The growth is hickory, walnut, poplar, chestnut, ash, a variety of oaks, beech, persimmon, sugar-tree, gum, elm, and hackberry. The subsoil contains angular gravel, and is underlaid by gravel or rocks at 3 feet. The land is naturally well drained, and is best adapted to corn, vegetables, clover, and grasses. About one-tenth of the crops is cotton. Plants grow from 2 to 6 feet high, but are best at from 3 to 3½ feet. Late rains and too late cultivation incline the plants to run to weed. The use of fertilizers, early and good cultivation, and topping in August are the remedies. The seed-cotton product per acre on fresh land is from 800 to 1,000 pounds, 1,425 pounds making a 475-pound bale; staple good ordinary. After twenty years' cultivation the seed-cotton product per acre is from 500 to 600 pounds, and with manure 1,000 pounds, 1,485 pounds then making a bale; staple same as before. The weeds are cocklebur, crab-grass, and ground ivy. None or but little of the land lies turned out. Slopes do not wash seriously. Little is done to check the damage.

The *third bottom or hillside soil* exists in small proportion and over short distances. Growth, small kinds of oaks, poplar, chestnut, hickory, persimmon, and sassafras. The soil is a gravelly clay loam from 3 to 12 inches thick. The subsoil is more or less impervious, contains angular gravel, and is underlaid by gravel and rock at 3 feet. The land is easily tilled in dry weather, and one-tenth of the crops is cotton. Plants grow to 2½ and 3 feet. The seed-cotton product per acre on fresh land is from 600 to 700 pounds, 1,425 pounds making a 475-pound bale; staple good ordinary. After fifteen years' cultivation the product is from 300 to 500 pounds, and with manure from 600 to 700 pounds; staple about the same. Crab-grass is troublesome. One-tenth of the land lies turned out, and would produce well again if manured. The slopes in some instances wash seriously, but the valleys are little injured by it. Some little horizontalizing is done, with moderate results.

The *hill-top or highland soil* makes over half the lands, and extends widely in all directions. It is a gray or yellowish loam. The subsoil contains gray, angular gravel, with rock or gravel below. The land is nearly well drained, and is best adapted to wheat and corn. One-fifteenth of the crops is cotton. Plants grow from 2 to 2½ feet high. The seed-cotton product per acre on fresh land is from 300 to 400 pounds, 1,425 pounds making a 475-pound bale; staple good middling. After ten years' cultivation the product is from 200 to 400 pounds, or with manure from 400 to 500, 1,485 pounds then making a bale; staple about the same. The weeds are grass and rag-weed. One-fifth of the land lies turned out, and very of little such land is taken in again. Slopes wash seriously, but the valleys are not much injured. Little is done to check the damage.

LEWIS.

Population : 2,181.—White, 1,963; colored, 218.
Area : 360 square miles.—Woodland, all.
Tilled lands : 11,654 acres.—Area planted in cotton, 229 acres; in corn, 5,272 acres; in wheat, 1,139 acres; in oats, 339 acres; in tobacco, 7 acres.
Cotton production : 102 bales; average cotton product per acre, 0.45 bale, 636 pounds seed-cotton, or 212 pounds cotton lint.

Lewis county occupies a central position in that section of the Highland Rim which lies between the valley of Duck river and the Alabama line. It is one of the small counties of the state, is twice as long as it is wide, and lies lengthwise east and west between Hickman on the north and Wayne and Lawrence on the south. It is a high, wooded table-land with thin soils, bearing a growth of red and black oaks, chestnut, tough poplars, called "blue poplars", small hickories, and other similar growth. Long distances may be passed without the sight of a field or a human habitation, and such is the county in the main. The table-land, however, is traversed by the valleys of many creeks, in which the cultivated land lies and the people live. The population of the county is very small, and less than that of any other county in the state. There are but six inhabitants to the square mile, while Maury, lying next east, in the Central Basin, has nearly sixty-eight to the mile. The wildness of the uplands becomes apparent when it is considered that the scanty population is substantially confined to these valleys. Buffalo river lies to the south, in a portion of its course flowing westward through an angle of the county, and in another portion making a part of the southern boundary. This river, flowing to the west beyond the county for 5 miles or thereabout, turns squarely to the north and runs through Perry county, thus becoming parallel, though not contiguous, to the western boundary of Lewis. We may say that Lewis, with a small rectangular section of Perry, lies in the great angle of Buffalo river. The central highlands of the county embrace the headwaters of numerous creeks, flowing off severally in all directions. Swan creek, having the heads of its chief tributaries in the eastern and northern portions, flows northward and empties into Duck river in Hickman county. Cane creek rises in the northern portion, flows northwestward through a corner of Hickman, and unites with the Buffalo in Perry. Smaller creeks rise on the highlands of the western margin, and flow westward to the Buffalo in the same county. Trace, Big Rock House, and

Grinder's creeks, mostly with fertile valleys, rise in the central portions and flow southward into the Buffalo. In the small fraction on the south side of the Buffalo, cut off by the river, are lower parts of other creeks heading in Lawrence.

The rocks of the highlands consist of calcareo-siliceous beds, with here and there limestones, generally cherty. Below these lie gray limestones of an older age. Black and greenish shales often separate the two series. Resting upon these in the highlands or in the valleys one may occasionally meet with outlying patches of the orange-sand drift—gravel beds, in which at some points iron ore has accumulated in sufficient quantity to make an "ore bank" of value. The deepest portions of the creek valleys reach down to the gray limestones, and these supply a moderate proportion of the soils of the second bottoms or sloping lands. Much of the valley land, however, is based on the higher beds. The soils may be classified as follows: The alluvial of the bottoms, the gravelly soils of slopes and rolling lands, and the thin soils of the highlands. The first are very rich, and the second often mellow and productive. The chief crops are corn, wheat, peanuts, oats, and cotton, with some rye and barley. On the map of relative acreage in cotton the county is seen to have had in 1879 less than 0.1 per cent. of its total area in cotton.

PERRY.

(See "Western valley of the Tennessee river".)

HICKMAN.

Population: 12,095.—White, 9,849; colored, 2,246.
Area: 610 square miles.—Woodland, all.
Tilled lands: 71,970 acres.—Area planted in cotton, 3,128 acres; in corn, 30,716 acres; in wheat, 7,874 acres; in oats, 2,896 acres; in rye, 225 acres; in tobacco, 51 acres.
Cotton production: 1,302 bales; average cotton product per acre, 0.42 bale, 594 pounds seed-cotton, or 198 pounds cotton lint.

Hickman is the central county of the western subdivision of the Highland Rim. It is nearly square in form, and is set a little obliquely to the cardinal points, its eastern and western sides ranging east of north. The county, as a whole, is a table-land nearly 1,000 feet above the sea. It is, however, so seriously cut into by the valleys of rivers and a score of creeks that its characteristics as a table-land are not always recognizable. It is cut up rather asymmetrically by the streams. The tortuous Duck river, flowing north of west through the county, cuts it into two nearly equal parts. Piney river, Lick creek, and other creeks, tributaries of the Duck river, with their sprays of smaller streams, divide the northern part into varied sections, wide plateau areas or flat-topped ridges, or, it may be, render the surface rolling and hilly, and Swan and Beaver Dam creeks, with their sprays of streams, do the same thing for the southern part. High flat lands abound in the extreme northern and southern portions of the county.

The strata of the highlands and ridges are calcareo-siliceous rocks and cherty limestones, yielding a thin, poorly remunerative soil, with a growth characterized by red, black, chestnut, post, and black-jack oaks, with hickories, chestnut, and some poplars. Much of the county is of this character, and long stretches of country occur without inhabitants; yet there are large exceptional areas with rolling surface, in which the lands are much better, the timber heavier and of a better class, and the soils, especially along the streams, under cultivation.

The deep valleys, cut down from 300 to 500 feet below the general level of the highlands, expose the strata underlying the rocks of the latter, chiefly gray and blue limestones. These limestones, with the alluvial bottoms, supply the best and the main producing lands of Hickman. They have their greatest outcrop in the eastern part of the county, where the Duck River valley and the creek valleys, such as those of Swan and Lick creeks, are the widest.(a) In the western part of the county their outcrop (owing to a local dip of strata to the west) is confined to the lowland levels of the Duck river. Rich alluvial and fair sloping lands, however, occur at intervals along the whole length of the river to the western boundary. Piney valley is chiefly (due to the westerly dip) in the silieceo-calcareous and cherty limestone strata noticed as pertaining to the highlands, and does not cut down to the gray and blue limestones until within a few miles of the Duck river. It is, however, often wide, with many rich and desirable farming sections, embracing bottoms and sloping lands. Its soils are generally very gravelly, made so by angular, cherty gravel from the hills, which indeed is true of most of the soils of the county, though the limestone soils of the more open valleys are less so than others. The creek valleys, generally of the western portion of the county, are based on the same siliceous strata of the highlands, their lands being poor and thinly settled. The valleys of the southwestern portion, however, must be excepted. Here the strata are more elevated and the beds of the larger creeks, as that of Cane creek, in gray limestones, their valley areas often wide, well settled, and productive. The timber of the better valleys is poplar, beech, maple, ash, hackberry, white ash, walnut, butternut, red-bud, elm, ironwood, etc.

The crops of the county include, in addition to those given at the head of the description, peanuts, one of the chief crops, barley, buckwheat, cow-pease, sorghum, clover, and grasses. In 1869 the cotton product was 755 bales (400 pounds each), equal to about 636 475-pound bales of cotton, as against 1,302 bales (475 pounds each) in 1879, a marked increase. On the map of relative acreage planted in cotton in 1879 it is seen that in a central belt, lying on both sides of the Duck river, and widening toward the east, the percentage was the greatest, from 1 to 5; in belts outside of this, one on each side, from 0.1 to 1; while in the extreme northern and southern portions it was the least, less than 0.1.

---

a The Duck River valley is here indeed the beginning of the great Central Basin to the east, to which the blue limestone especially pertains.

ABSTRACT FROM REPORT.

J. M. GRAHAM (lands of Piney and Duck rivers.—For kinds of soils, etc., see page 27).—On the first soil, bench or second bottom land, cotton grows from 3 to 5 feet, 3 feet being the best. Wet seasons, in July or August, incline the plant to run to weed, for which topping is the remedy. The seed-cotton product per acre on fresh land is 1,000 pounds, 1,735 pounds making a bale of 475 pounds; staple middling. On land tilled ten years the product is 800 pounds per acre. The troublesome weeds are in the order named: Morning-glory, smart-weed, cocklebur, careless-weed, and lamb's-quarter; also crab-grass, rag-weed, and purslane. None of the land lies turned out. The slopes wash seriously, the valleys being injured thereby but little.

On the fresh hillside or uplands cotton grows to 18 inches. Seed-cotton product per acre on fresh land is from 750 to 800 pounds, 1,735 pounds making a 475-pound bale. On land tilled ten years the product is from 500 to 600 pounds. The weeds are crab-grass, rag-weed, and careless-weed. One-twentieth of the land lies turned out. Such land taken in again is generally much improved, depending upon the time it has been idle. The slopes wash seriously, the valleys being injured but little. Nothing is done to check damage.

On the land on the ridges cotton grows 10 and 18 inches high. The seed-cotton product per acre on fresh land is from 600 to 700 pounds, 1,735 pounds making a 475-pound bale; staple middling. On land tilled ten years the product is from 300 to 600 pounds. The weeds are crab-grass, foxtail, rag-weed, and purslane. One-twentieth of the land lies turned out, and if let alone for ten or fifteen years it is much improved. The slopes wash seriously, but the valleys are little injured. Cotton is shipped by wagon to Nashville or to Pinewood, where the Nashville price is paid for it.

HUMPHREYS.
(See "Western valley of the Tennessee river".)

GILES.
(See "Central Basin".)

MAURY.
(See "Central Basin".)

WILLIAMSON.
(See "Central Basin".)

SUMNER.
(See "Central Basin".)

DAVIDSON.
(See "Central Basin".)

Giles, Maury, Williamson, and Davidson counties have western portions, and Sumner a northern portion on the western subdivision of the Highland Rim, within the limits of which some cotton was raised. From the rim lands of Sumner, however, two bales only were reported.

HIGHLAND RIM (EASTERN SUBDIVISION).

This subdivision embraces the greater parts of the counties of Franklin, Coffee, Warren, White, De Kalb, Putnam, Overton, Clay, and Macon, considerable parts of Jackson, Cannon,* Moore,* and Lincoln,* and small parts of Bedford,* Grundy, Van Buren, and Smith.*

This entire subdivision must be referred to the "penumbral region" of cotton culture. As a cotton-producing district, however, it makes a better showing outside of the cotton belt proper than any other of equal extent in Tennessee. The counties embraced, with the cotton produced in 1879 and arranged in the order of greatest production, are as follows: Franklin, 171 bales; White, 139; Warren, 96; Overton, 41; Jackson, 28; Coffee, 20; De Kalb, 12; Putnam, 4; Macon, 1; and Clay 1. With these must be included the northwestern part of Van Buren and the southwestern part of Grundy counties, chiefly pertaining to the Cumberland table-land, but having the parts given resting upon the lower Highland Rim, where, substantially, all the cotton reported from the counties, 29 bales from Van Buren and 21 from Grundy, was raised.

On the map of relative acreage in cotton the cotton areas of the eastern subdivision (usually with less than one acre in a hundred in cotton) are well seen. With inconsiderable exceptions, they are upon the Highland Rim and in parts of counties lying along the western foot of the Cumberland table-land. (a) The largest area is in White, Van Buren, and Warren, the next in importance in Grundy and Franklin, and a third in Overton. The chief soil of the areas is the calcareous red clay of the Saint Louis limestone, brown when fresh, becoming red by cultivation, the soil mixing with the underlying red clay subsoils. (See Part I, under the Highland Rim.)

One county only of the subdivision is described. This may be taken as a type of the counties in the tier that includes the chief cotton areas, the tier extending in a direction east of north through the state, with its western part on the Highland Rim and its eastern on the more elevated table-land. For description of the areas of non-cotton producing counties, see general regional descriptions.

a The small areas in Jackson, Putnam, and De Kalb are the exceptional ones. They are chiefly on the rim, miles away from the table-land, but in some parts (in Jackson especially) extend down into valleys referable to the Central Basin.

FRANKLIN.

Population: 17,178.—White, 13,646; colored, 3,532.
Area: 590 square miles.—Woodland, all.
Tilled lands: 92,753 acres.—Area planted in cotton, 414 acres; in corn, 41,560 acres; in wheat, 20,178 acres; in oats, 5,959 acres; in rye, 204 acres; in tobacco, 61 acres.
Cotton production: 171 bales; average cotton product per acre, 0.41 bale, 588 pounds seed-cotton, or 196 pounds cotton lint.

Franklin is the most southeasterly county of the Highland Rim. Its form is polygonal, approaching that of a semi-ellipse, with the base resting upon the Alabama line, and having a position east of the longitude of Nashville. The county is divided into two nearly equal parts: the northwestern, on the Highland Rim, with an average elevation not much if any less than 1,000 feet above the sea, and the eastern and southeastern, on the Cumberland table-land, 1,000 feet higher, or 2,000 feet above the sea. Neither part is unbroken. The Highland Rim west of the county-seat (Winchester) has the immediate valley of Elk river, 300 or 400 feet deep, eroded out of it, the latter supplying an area of rich blue limestone slopes and river lands like those of the great Central Basin. The area is indeed an inlet of the basin reaching eastward into the highlands. The table-land, on the other hand, is deeply cut in two its eastern part by the narrow valley of Crow creek, a stream heading·in the mountains and running southward to the Tennessee river. It is further cut along its Alabama margin by creeks rising within its limits and running into that state. There are also great openings within the area of the table-land, "inland coves" we may call them, such as Lost cove, Sinking cove, Round cove, and others.

The Highland·Rim portion, making the great body of land in cultivation, includes a wide belt of strong red clayey lands, both level and undulating, extending northeastward and southwestward through the county parallel to the general direction of the Cumberland table-land. The belt spreads out laterally toward the table-land, and embraces the rich coves at its foot. Like the belt, too, in soils and rocks, are the valley of Crow creek and the lower parts of the "inland" coves of the mountain. On the northwest the belt gives place to the "barrens", with gray and thinner soils and a growth chiefly of half-size black and red oaks. · The soil of the red lands, when fresh, is brown, with a red clay subsoil. The plow, however, after a few years' cultivation, mixes the two, and the red prevails. The underlying rocks are cherty limestones (Saint Louis), the liberated chert rendering the subsoils and soils gravelly with angular flinty or siliceous *débris*. Many streams traverse this portion of the county, their valleys contributing rich bottoms and arable slopes. Elk river flows for many miles over its rocks in the northern part of the county before descending into the "inlet" spoken of.

The lands of the table-land or mountain are based on sandstones and shales. They are thin and sandy, with an open growth of oaks, and have, with one noted and honorable exception, a scanty population, or none at all. The exception is that portion in the northeastern part of the county upon which the University of the South and its surroundings are located. The western, or rather northwestern, edge of the table-land is greatly indented with escalops and notches, and sheltered in these are the coves, some of large size, lying at its foot, the rich lands of the latter being greatly in contrast with the barren-like lands of the mountain. The edge of the mountain commands a most extensive view to the northwest. At the foot are the coves; beyond these, spreading out almost indefinitely, are the great plains of the Highland Rim, and in the dim distance, hardly discernible, the breaks marking the beginnings of the lowlands of the Central Basin. (For a notice of the steep slopes of the mountain, see page 35, under "The Cumberland table land.")

The native growth of the red lands, especially near creeks, and that of the coves and of the slopes of the table-land, includes many species, white and other oaks, poplar, black and white walnut, hickory, elm, linden, beech, ash, locust, etc. The timber is heaviest near the foot and on the slopes of the mountain. Away from the mountain and out of the valleys the growth is less heavy, black and red oaks abounding, with hickory and dogwood. Reaching the "barrens", black-jack, with its usual associates, appears. The chief crops are given above. Additional products are barley, buckwheat, potatoes, pease, and sorghum. Franklin in 1869 produced 289 bales of cotton (400 pounds each), and in 1879, 171 bales (475 pounds each), a falling off equal to 72 standard bales of 475 pounds each. The areas of the county in which the staple is cultivated, and also the relative acreage planted in each, may be seen on the map.

ABSTRACT FROM REPORT.

John F. Anderson (southeastern corner of the county, Crow Creek valley.—For a notice of valley, kinds of soils, etc., see page 27). On the first soil, the alluvial, cotton plants grow from 3 to 6 feet in height, and are most productive at 4 feet. They incline to run to weed where left too thick and are not properly worked. The remedy is to top in August. The seed-cotton product per acre on fresh land is 1,500 pounds, 1,700 pounds making a 475-pound bale; staple good ordinary. After ten years' cultivation the product is 800 pounds, 1,545 pounds making a bale; staple low middling. The weeds are run wild, cocklebur, lamb's-quarter, and a little crab-grass. One-tenth of the land lies turned out, and if taken in again would produce as well as at first.

Of the yellowish and calcareous soil about one-fourth is planted in cotton. Plants grow to 3 and 4 feet, 3 feet being the best. The seed-cotton product per acre on fresh land is from 1,000 to 1,200 pounds, 1,860 pounds making a 475-pound bale; staple good ordinary. After eight years' cultivation the product is from 600 to 700 pounds per acre, 1,545 pounds making a bale; staple much better; the older the land the better the cotton. The weeds are Spanish needles, cocklebur, smart-weed, and dog-fennel. Very little of the land lies turned out, and produces about as well after a rest of a year or two. Very little washing occurs on slopes. No cotton is raised on the soil of the rocky mountain side.

Cotton is shipped to Nashville at $1 40 per bale, or to Cincinnati.

CANNON.

(See "Central Basin".)

MOORE.

(See "Central Basin".)

LINCOLN.

(See " Central Basin ".)

BEDFORD.

(See " Central Basin ".)

SMITH.

(See " Central Basin ".)

THE CENTRAL BASIN.

This embraces the whole or parts of the following counties: The greater part or all of Giles, Lincoln, Moore, Bedford, Marshall, Maury, Williamson, Rutherford, Davidson, Wilson, Sumner, Trousdale, and Smith; large parts of Cheatham,* Jackson,* and Cannon; and small parts of Macon,* Putnam,* De Kalb,* and Coffee.* The counties of the basin wholly within the cotton region proper are : Giles, Lincoln, Bedford, Marshall, Maury, Williamson, Rutherford, Davidson, Wilson, and Sumner. These are described below. Of the remaining counties, as named in Tables I and II, Moore reported, as the product of 1879, 7 bales; Cannon, 35; Smith, 9; and Trousdale, 1 (see also note at foot of page 11). The location of the cotton-producing section of the basin, with its areas of greatest and least production, may be seen to advantage on the map of relative acreage in cotton. This map may be compared with the diagram of the state on page 11. Lawrence and Lewis are entirely west of the basin. Much the greater part of Hickman is also, but the portion of the valley of Duck river in the eastern part of this county is properly referred, through its topography, rocks, and soils, to the basin. It is an inlet of the latter, reaching westward into the highlands. Not much, if any, less than two-thirds of the cotton product of Hickman must be accredited to the basin.

The Central Basin supplies, as stated on page 19, a subordinate center of cotton culture. In 1879 it produced 50,000 bales in round numbers, equal approximately to 15 per cent. of the entire yield of the state. The increased yield of the basin over that reported in the census of 1870 is, allowing for difference in weight of bales, 47 per cent.

GILES.

Population: 36,014.—White, 21,824; colored, 14,190.

Area: 590 square miles.—Woodland, all.

Tilled lands: 170,599 acres.—Area planted in cotton, 31,416 acres; in corn, 67,758 acres; in wheat, 30,795 acres; in oats, 2,592 acres; in rye, 1,124 acres; in tobacco, 66 acres.

Cotton production: 13,802 bales; average cotton product per acre, 0.44 bale, 627 pounds seed-cotton, or 209 pounds cotton lint.

Giles takes the lead of the counties of the basin in cotton production. This county was originally nearly a rectangle in form, with its longer dimension extending north and south. In 1870 its northeastern corner was cut off to Marshall. It is one of the southern tier of counties, and rests upon the Alabama line in a position immediately west of the meridian of Nashville. Elk river and its tributary, Richland creek, are the chief streams. The first crosses the southeastern corner of the county, and the second, the most important, traverses much of the interior. Both have wide valleys with exceedingly fertile bottoms and slopes. Besides, there are numerous tributary creeks, all with bodies of choice lands. The county is made up of rich valleys and bold, though usually narrow ridges. The prominent ridges rise to the level of the Highland Rim surrounding the basin, and are capped off with its characteristic rocks. We may suppose indeed the flat highlands to have extended once unbroken over the whole area of the county, and that the waters, assisted by atmospheric agencies, have since scooped and worn out the valleys, leaving remnants of the highlands to stand as ridges.

With the exception of the western margin of the county, which rests mostly upon the Highland Rim, the area of Giles county is within the basin. It is one of the group of counties lying south of Elk ridge and spoken of on page 28, to which the reader is referred. The lands of the valleys and their slopes, excepting alluvial bottoms, are based on Silurian limestones, and mainly upon the Nashville series. (See page 30.) In some parts of the valley of Richland creek and its tributary, Big creek, the lowlands rest in places upon rocks of the Orthis bed, and even upon the Carter's Creek limestones. The limestone lands are everywhere naturally strong clay loams, mellow, often tempered with small cherty gravel, very fertile, and are found on second bottoms, moderate slopes, and steep declivities of the ridges. The lands of the ridge tops rest on siliceous or flinty and calcareo-siliceous rocks. Their soils are charged with flinty *débris*, and are but moderately fertile. A part of the gravel of the lower limestone lands comes from the ridge tops, though much is from the chert and siliceous fossils of the limestone in place. As to native growth, reference must be made to the abstracts of correspondents. The map of relative acreage in cotton will exhibit the belts of greatest and least production. On this the immediate valleys of Elk river and Richland creek hold the first place as cotton-producing areas. Cotton is shipped to Nashville by rail at $1 75 per bale, or is sold at home.

452

D. T. REYNOLDS AND T. O. ABERNATHY (northern part of the county, waters of Richland creek).—The soils cultivated in cotton are: (1) Dark and brown loam of bottoms, with dark clay subsoils; (2) lighter loam, with reddish clay subsoils (uplands below flint lands); (3) gravelly or flint upland (near tops of ridges). The first, the loam of the second bottoms, is the chief soil, which forms about one-fourth of the lands, and occurs in a belt varying from 2 to 4 miles wide on either side of Richland creek, with a length of 30 miles. The chief timber is beech, elm, sugar-tree, black walnut, ash, and poplar. The soil is 10 inches thick, of a mahogany color, and rests upon a hard-pan or red clay and gravel mixed, all underlaid by rock at from 2 to 10 feet. The land is easily tilled in wet or dry seasons if not too wet in spring for preparation, and is best adapted to corn and cotton, the latter forming one-half of the crops. Cool weather in July inclines the plant to run to weed, the remedy for which is early and deep preparation and shallow cultivation. The seed-cotton product per acre on fresh land is from 1,200 to 1,750 pounds, 1,545 pounds (allowing 25 pounds for bagging and ties) making a 475-pound bale; staple rates as middling. On land cultivated for thirty years from 1,200 to 1,600 pounds of seed-cotton per acre were produced in 1879 on many farms, 100 pounds making from 29 to 31 pounds of lint; staple from one to two grades better than that from fresh land if the autumn was dry. The weeds are crab-grass and careless-weed. No land lies turned out. Slopes wash seriously if not well managed, the valleys being benefited thereby unless too much clay is washed down. Hillside ditching and level culture are done with good success.

The upland soil below the flint lands makes one-half of the lands. The growth is beech, poplar, oak, elm, and hickory. The soil, a clay mahogany loam, is from 4 to 10 inches thick. The subsoil, a tough reddish-yellow clay, is usually free from gravel, and is underlaid by limestone and sandy rock at from 4 to 6 feet. The land is easily tilled in wet and dry seasons, is early, warm, and well drained, and is best adapted to cotton, corn, and peas.

The flint upland soil makes about one-fourth of the lands, and is found on all the hills of the county. The growth is oak, hickory, elm, and walnut. The soil is a brown clay and gravel mixed, and is from 3 to 10 inches thick. The subsoil contains gravel, and is underlaid by limestone at from 4 to 10 feet. Land is easily tilled in all seasons, is early and warm, and is best adapted to corn, wheat, oats, and rye.

J. E. ABERNATHY AND SAMUEL YOKLEY (northwestern part of the county, waters of Big creek.—For kinds of soils, etc., see page 35).— On the second bottom mulatto soil cotton grows to 3 feet, and is best at that. The plant inclines to grow to weed on fresh soil after clover and after excessive rain in August. The remedies are cultivating thick in the drill, shallow plowing, and sometimes topping. The seed-cotton product per acre on fresh land is from 800 to 1,200 pounds, 1,545 pounds making a 475-pound bale, the staple rating low middling. On land cultivated ten years, rotating with corn and wheat, the product is from 600 to 800 pounds per acre, 1,660 pounds being needed for a bale, the staple being shorter. Weeds on fresh land are cocklebur and Spanish needles; afterward, careless-weed and lamb's-quarter. On the creek very little land lies turned out. Slopes wash only on badly managed farms. Horizontalizing and hillside ditching are done, with good success.

On the gravelly hillside soil cotton grows to 3 feet, and is best at that. Seed-cotton product per acre on fresh land is from 800 to 1,000 pounds. This land deteriorates by constant cultivation in cotton.

On the ridge land soil cotton grows to 2 feet. Seed-cotton product per acre on fresh land is 800 pounds, 1,545 pounds making a 475-pound bale. The staple is the best produced on our soils. The land does not bear continued cultivation in cotton.

JIM RIVERS AND NEWTON WHITE (waters of Richland creek).—There are some very coarse sandy lands on the high banks of Richland creek from 2 to 5 miles from its junction with Elk river. Such lands are not often seen in Tennessee. The lowlands are not as reliable as the uplands, but when the season suits they make more lint, but of poorer quality. Hillsides exposed to the south are always best for cultivation, opening, and quality of lint, but require manure and rest. The soils cultivated in cotton are: (1) Coarse sandy, surest for a crop, and makes the best staple; (2) poplar soil, mulatto or brown, with yellowish-red subsoil; (3) bottom or black soil.

The coarse sandy soil forms a fourth or less of our lands, and extends from 1 mile north to 3 miles south in patches along the creek and river. The growth is poplar, beech, and hickory. Cotton forms two-thirds of the crops. The seed-cotton product per acre on fresh land is 1,000 pounds.

The poplar or mulatto soil comprises one-half the cotton lands, and is found generally over the county from the Alabama line northward in tracts of from 1,000 to 10,000 acres, nearly all of which is planted in cotton. The growth is poplar, beech, ash, some hickory, and elm. The seed-cotton product per acre on fresh land is from 700 to 1,200 pounds.

The bottom or black soil makes one-third of the lands planted in cotton, and is found all over the county in creek bottoms. The growth is sweet gum, beech, and elm. Cotton forms about one-half the crops. The seed-cotton product per acre on fresh land is from 200 to 1,500 pounds.

J. N. PATTESON AND W. RIVERS (waters of Richland creek and Elk river).—The uplands contain flinty gravel, are fertile, easily cultivated, endure drought, suffer less from wet weather, and are the most reliable farming lands in the county. The kinds of soils cultivated in cotton are: (1) Brown and mahogany clay loam or yellow poplar soil; (2) black soil on most of the small creeks of the county. The brown and mahogany clay loam forms three-fourths of the lands, and occurs throughout the eastern, over three-fourths of the southern, half of the northern, and one-third of the western portions of the county. The growth is black walnut, beech, yellow poplar, sugar-tree, hickory, linden, buckeye, and oaks. The subsoil is a tough clay that will hold moisture and retain manure. The land is well adapted to cotton, corn, wheat, potatoes, rye, sorghum, grasses, etc. About one-fourth of the land is planted in cotton. The seed-cotton product per acre on fresh land is from 1,000 to 1,800 pounds; on good land cultivated for twenty years with alternation of crops, from 800 to 1,200 pounds.

The black soil forms one-fourth of the lands. The growth is sweet gum, oak, box-elder, maple, etc. The land is best adapted to corn. About one-half of the crops is cotton. Seed-cotton product per acre on fresh land is from 1,200 to 1,600 pounds; after twenty years' cultivation, from 800 to 1,200 pounds.

J. J. LINDSAY (waters of Egnew's creek, west of Pulaski).—Our hill soils produce cotton about as well as the lowlands, stand long droughts better, and, owing to the gravel present, never bake. The soils cultivated in cotton are: (1) Brown, with very little gravel, or beech and poplar land, making about one-half the lands that occur along Egnew's and Richland creeks, about one-half of which is planted in cotton; (2) hill-land soil, dark, with flinty gravel, making nearly half the lands, one-third of which is planted in cotton; and (3) clay ridge soil, worthless except for chestnut timber.

J. S. EDMONSON, J. F. PARKER, AND J. G. MASON (Civil District No. 2, Jenkins', Ford's, and Richland creeks, southwestern part of county).—The soils do not vary much from hill to hill, all being well adapted to cotton-growing. The growing season is too short to risk the first bottoms. The soils are: (1) Hill or upland on brooks or on the river, making 60 per cent. of the lands; (2) mahogany second bottom; (3) first bottom. The first is found 10 miles off in every direction. It rests upon a clayey subsoil, running down into coarse gravel and flinty masses, with limestone at from 3 to 15 feet.

J. K. P. BLACKBURN (lands of Richland and Bradshaw creeks, eastern part of the county).—The uplands vary from rather elevated undulating table-lands to steep slopes and rugged hills. The soils cultivated in cotton are: (1) Brown or mahogany lands, lying well, with undulating surface, known to us as sand-rock land, which constitutes one-half of the lands, and occurs from 12 to 15 miles north, west, and south, and 6 miles east of this locality; is a quick, lively soil, from 3 to 12 inches thick, and has a subsoil of stiff, yellowish or reddish clay, getting harder on long cultivation, and underlaid by limestone at from 1 foot to 10 feet, with one-third to one-half planted in cotton; (2) second bottom soil, occurring along Richland creek for 25 miles; (3) steep hillside and ridge top, from one-third to one-half of the lands. (Further details much as in other reports.)

T. B. WADE (lands of Pigeon Roost and Richland creeks, north of Pulaski).—Upland soils generally mixed with sharp, angular, flinty gravel. Some soils are free from gravel. Cotton is cultivated on southern hillsides, but will not mature on northern hillsides. On the black creek bottoms cotton is subject to rust, and the young fruit falls off. When the black soil is covered by a heavy deposit from a recent overflow of creek or river cotton grows well, and land subject to occasional overflow is the best for constant cultivation. The soils are: (1) Mahogany upland on southern slopes and in coves or valleys between the hills, making two-thirds of the lands, or the greater portion of uplands in the county, with nearly all that is suitable planted in cotton; (2) bottom soil above overflow, though bottoms with occasional overflows, as stated above, are better; (3) bottom with light deposit, the cotton on which is subject to rust. The general growth is beech and poplar on the hills and slopes, sugar-tree, elm, and some oak in the coves, and wild cherry, beech, walnut, and oaks in the bottoms. (Further details much the same as in reports.)

LINCOLN.

Population: 26,960.—White, 20,643; colored, 6,317.
Area: 540 square miles.—Woodland, all.
Tilled lands: 146,326 acres.—Area planted in cotton, 8,868 acres; in corn, 57,460 acres; in wheat, 37,279 acres; in oats, 2,993 acres; in rye, 268 acres; in tobacco, 39 acres.
Cotton production: 3,486 bales; average cotton product per acre, 0.39 bale, 561 pounds seed-cotton, or 187 pounds cotton lint.

The area of Lincoln was once nearly square. The establishment in later years of two counties, Marshall and Moore, deprived it respectively of its northwestern and northeastern corners, so that its northern boundary is now approximately circular or rounded. The county has a wide base resting on the Alabama line. The meridian of Nashville cuts off a slice of the western portion, throwing the body of the county to the east of this line. A controlling topographical feature is the immediate valley of Elk river. This stream runs nearly west through the middle of the county, its valley dividing the latter into two portions nearly equal in area, but very unequal in population and agricultural importance. To the south lie elevated flatwoods "barrens", pertaining to the Highland Rim. North of the valley the whole country is made up of a multitude of long and rich creek valleys, with intervening ridges. In many parts of the county, especially northward, the ridges are numerous and bold, rising to the height of the Highland Rim, and showing its siliceous strata as capping rocks. Approaching the Elk river from the north, the ridges tend to run out, and the valleys widen, often unite, and finally open into the greater valley of the river. The ridges are spurs of Elk ridge, which for a short distance is a part of the northern boundary of the county, and make a portion of the sprays of ridges spoken of on page 28, under the Central Basin.

The lands of Lincoln of most interest are the alluvial bottoms of the river and creeks, the lands of second bottoms, moderate slopes, and steep ridge sides, all of which are based on the blue limestones of the Nashville series, and are remarkable for their fertility. (See part of report just cited.) These make up much the greater part of the northern portion of the county. The ridges have a gravelly, thinner soil, but a better one than that of the unbroken "barrens" south of the Elk River valley. Their growth includes great "poplars", chestnuts, oaks, and elms. The high "barrens" to the south have great extent. The soils are thin and the growth half-size oaks. Approaching the Alabama line, the lands improve, and areas of brown lands, with red subsoils, resting upon Saint Louis limestones, are met with. Creeks also occur with valley lands of better quality.

The distribution of the percentage belts of cotton culture and their relation to the Elk River valley are exhibited upon the map of relative acreage in cotton. This county lies at the eastern limit of the cotton-growing region proper.

ABSTRACTS FROM REPORTS.

M. D. HAMPTON AND J. D. TILLMAN (lands of the Elk river).—The uplands are gravelly, with a dark yellow soil. Springs are sometimes too late, and frosts too early. The Elk River lands constitute two-thirds of all the lands cultivated in cotton. Their growth is oak, hickory, beech, poplar, gum, ash, etc. The soils are fine, sandy, and sometimes gravelly loam and heavy clay loam of gray, yellow, and blackish colors; the subsoil a reddish-yellow clay, mixed below with whitish gravel and pebbles, which becomes like the surface soil by cultivation, and is impervious when unbroken. Limestone rock occurs at from 10 to 30 feet. The land is easily tilled. The crops comprise all the grains and grasses, and some cotton. About one-half of the crops is cotton. Plants grow about waist-high in good seasons, but not so high in dry. The seed-cotton product per acre on fresh land is from 600 to 1,200 pounds, 1,860 pounds making a 475-pound bale; staple rates as middling. After a number of years' cultivation the product is from 400 to 800 pounds, 1,660 pounds making a bale, and the staple differing little. Crab-grass is troublesome. Very little land lies turned out and recuperates rapidly. Slopes do not wash seriously. Hillside ditching has been done with good success.

Cotton is shipped by rail to Nashville at $2 per bale.

BEDFORD.

Population: 26,025.—White, 18,536; colored, 7,489.
Area: 520 square miles.—Woodland, all.
Tilled lands: 164,800 acres.—Area planted in cotton, 2,239 acres; in corn, 68,492 acres; in wheat, 39,589 acres; in oats, 6,270 acres; in rye, 806 acres; in tobacco, 51 acres.
Cotton production: 940 bales; average cotton product per acre, 0.42 bale, 597 pounds seed-cotton, or 199 pounds cotton lint.

Bedford, nearly square in form, lies immediately north of Rutherford, the central county of middle Tennessee, and is walled in on the north and south by the steep slopes of the Highland Rim and Elk ridge. Spurs from these highlands encroach upon its area, but to no great extent, before breaking away into rolling lands or lines of hills between the streams. Hence the eastern and extreme southern portions of the county are undulating or hilly. They include, however, many beautiful and productive valleys and level areas.

West, northwest, and north from Shelbyville the surface is far less rolling, level or flat lands, indeed, predominating. This is the great cedar section of the county, and patches and belts of cedar glades are scattered all over it. It is, too, especially the more northwesterly part, the cotton section of the county. Cotton-growing lands, sometimes occurring in large bodies, alternate with cedar glades. Tracts are met with completely encircled by belts of these glades. The soil chiefly producing cotton is identical with the warm red soil of the cotton region of Rutherford county and rests upon the "central limestones", the lowest rocks geologically appearing at the surface within the basin. Above these, and resting upon them, often in low ridges, come the flaggy limestones of the cedar glades. These different limestones, with their soils and the character of the cedar glades, have been discussed on page 29 under the Central Basin.

All the Silurian limestones enumerated in the part of the report just referred to occur in Bedford, each supplying its characteristic lands and its characteristic topography. Leaving the checkered cedar and cotton section as a lower area, and proceeding backward either toward the eastern or southern boundaries of the county, we cross the successive belts of the outcropping limestones, ascending in the mean time until we land above the latter on the elevated and flinty lands of the Highland Rim or Elk ridge. The ascent is long, gradual, and irregular until the foot of the highlands is reached, when it becomes rapid. The whole, could we look from an elevated point in the northern section, would be a sort of grand topographical and agricultural amphitheater, but an exceedingly broken and interrupted 'one. These lands, though often very productive, are not cultivated in cotton to any noteworthy extent.

On the map of relative acreage in cotton it is seen that the northwestern corner only of Bedford lies within the cotton-producing region.

ABSTRACTS FROM REPORTS.

B. F. RANSOM, W. R. RANSOM, REV. M. F. THOMPSON, R. C. ALLISON, AND B. F. JARRELL (northwestern part of the county).—The chief soil is the dark red of the more elevated level land, making from one-half to two-thirds of the lands. The growth is ,black oak, dogwood, ash, walnut, hickory, and elm. The land is underlaid by limestone at from 2 to 6 feet, easily tilled in dry seasons, but is difficult when wet; it is early, warm, and well drained, and is well adapted to corn, wheat, oats, and clover. Not more than one-sixth of the crops is cotton. Plants grow to 4 feet, and are best at this height. They incline to run to weed when cultivated too loose in or near the drill, which can be remedied by running the mold-board of the Carey plow near the cotton. The seed-cotton product per acre on fresh land is from 700 to 1,000 pounds, about 1,660 pounds making a 475-pound bale; the staple rating well. After five years' cultivation the product is from 600 to 800 pounds per acre; staple not so good. The weeds are foxtail and crab-grass. Not more than 5 per cent. of the land lies turned out; but such land, if bushes are kept down and washes prevented, would produce well again. The soil washes on slopes; damage, 2 per cent. of value; valleys are not injured.

The *dark creek loam* makes about one-sixth of the lands in this section, and is best adapted to corn, wheat, and oats. Not more than 3 per cent. is planted in cotton in this section. The seed-cotton product per acre on fresh land is 800 pounds, 1,545 pounds making a bale. After twenty years' cultivation, if well managed, the product is as much as when fresh.

The *red gravelly clay* soil makes a tenth of the lands, and occurs in spots all over the region. The growth is poplar, ash, oak, etc. Very little land is planted in cotton. The seed-cotton product per acre is 400 to 500 pounds.

Cotton is shipped by rail and wagon to Nashville at from $1 to $2 per bale.

MARSHALL.

Population: 19,259.—White, 14,429; colored, 4,830.

Area: 350 square miles.—Woodland, all.

Tilled lands: 117,005 acres.—Area planted in cotton, 4,697 acres; in corn, 47,927 acres; in wheat, 30,484 acres; in oats, 4,675 acres; in rye, 392 acres; in tobacco, 47 acres.

Cotton production: 1,721 bales; average cotton product per acre, 0.37 bale, 522 pounds seed-cotton, or 174 pounds cotton lint.

Marshall is a hatchet-shaped county, with its broad edge turned southward and resting upon Giles and Lincoln. The meridian of Nashville passes lengthwise through the county, nearly bisecting its area. North of a line running east and west through Lewisburg, the county-seat, the county is level or moderately rolling. This part is a great checkered area, made so by alternating bodies of red cotton- and corn-producing land and cedar glades. The red lands (brown when fresh) are based on the "central limestones", and the glades, sometimes called significantly "cedar roughs," on the flaggy rocks of the "glade limestone". (See page 29, under the Central Basin.) It may aid in the understanding of this part of Marshall to assume the limestone of the red lands to be the floor or basis of the whole region, and that there have been squatted upon these at intervals belts and areas of cedar glades, from one mile to many square miles in extent, with their flaggy rocks and cedar timber. In harmony with this assumption, the belts and areas are often raised in low ridges and tables above the level of the red lands, like low islands above the sea. The aggregate areas of the red and cedar lands respectively are about equal. Chapel Hill is in a great body of the red lands noted for its beautifully lying and fertile farming tracts, and reaching from the northern boundary of the county across the Duck river to Farmington. The Spring Creek lands in the northeastern portion of the county are a part of this belt. Caney Spring and Verona are in another range. The greatest body of cedar land is in the northwestern corner of the county.

The southern portion of Marshall differs wholly from that north of Lewisburg. It is a great water-shed having Elk ridge, a backbone to the region, extending in an eastern and western course through its widest and middle part. The ridge is a bold summit which divides the waters of Duck river on the north from the waters of Richland creek on the south. It has numerous spurs. These are short on the north side, soon breaking up into foot-hills and productive rolling lands, with intervening fertile coves and valleys or broad level tracts. On the southern side the spurs are much longer, extending, where not cut off by coalescing valleys, far to the south. The valleys between them are mostly of unsurpassed fertility, and here and there open out into areas of the very best farming lands.

455

The soils of the valleys and slopes in the vicinity of Elk ridge, on both sides, are based on blue limestones of the Nashville series. They are brown and mulatto-colored, more or less gravelly, with heavy and varied native growth, warm, mellow, easily tilled, and suited to many crops. On the south side we have the head of the valley of Richland creek, so famous in Giles county as a productive area. Passing to the other side of the ridge, and proceeding northward toward the region of the cedar glades, belts of lands are successively crossed based on the sandy limestones of the Orthis bed and the pure lighter-colored ones of the Carter's creek group. Taking the whole county, it is seen that all of the subdivisions of the Silurian limestones outcrop within its limits and supply, ridge tops excepted, the aggregate of its soils. Elk ridge and its leading spurs mount to the level of the Highland Rim. The rocks of the crests are siliceous or flinty. The soils are gravelly, friable, of easy tillage, draining quickly, and moderately productive.

The growth of the county is heavy and rich, especially in the region of Elk ridge, including great oaks, poplar, elm, beech, sugar-tree, ash, linden, walnut, cherry, hackberry, locust, buckeye, and, on the ridges, chestnut. In addition, the glades supply the best of cedar timber. On the map of relative acreage in cotton the northern end and the southwestern corner of the county are seen to have had in 1879 the greater number of acres in cotton. The southeastern corner is the only part without the cotton-producing region. Cotton is shipped to Nashville by rail at $1 50 or by wagon at $2 per bale.

ABSTRACTS FROM REPORTS

J. B. EZELL (Spring Creek and Duck River lands, northeastern part of the county.—For soils cultivated in cotton, etc., see page 33).— Cotton grows from 2 to 4 feet high, 4 feet being the best. Continued wet weather inclines the plants to run to weed, for which the remedy is topping. Seed-cotton product per acre on fresh land is from 800 to 1,000 pounds, 1,660 pounds making a bale of 475 pounds, but the staple does not rate as high as old-land cotton. After two years' cultivation the product is 1,000 pounds, 1,600 pounds making a bale. Rag-weed is troublesome. One-fiftieth of the land lies turned out, and would produce well if taken in again. Slopes wash some, but not seriously.

J. F. BRITTAIN (northeastern part of the county).—We select ground, old and new, having as much sand as possible. The chief soil makes up two-thirds of the lands, and extends off 25 miles in different directions. The growth is beech, poplar, and walnut. The chief crops are corn, cotton, wheat, and oats. The land is best adapted to corn and wheat. Cotton forms one-fourth of the crops. The remedy for running to weed is deep plowing near the stalk. The seed-cotton product per acre on fresh land is 800 pounds, 1,545 pounds making a 475-pound bale; staple rates as low middling. After six years' cultivation the product is 600 pounds, 1,485 or 1,545 pounds making a bale; seed lighter, with more lint than on new ground. Weeds are rag-weed, foxtail, and crab-grass. Very little land lies turned out, and would produce well if taken in again. Washing has been checked by sowing grasses, also by horizontalizing and hillside ditching, with good success.

W. B. GLENN (northeastern part of the county).—The lands are generally level for miles around, and the soil of the uplands is much alike. The chief soil cultivated in cotton is the richest upland, making about two-thirds of the lands. The growth is white and black oaks, ash, hickory, sugar-tree, dogwood, and some poplar. Cotton forms about 20 per cent. of the crops. Seed-cotton product per acre, in good seasons, on fresh land, is from 1,000 to 1,200 pounds, 1,660 pounds making a 475-pound bale; staple rates low middling.

MAURY.

Population: 39,904.—White, 21,731 ; colored, 18,173.
Area: 590 square miles.—Woodland, all.
Tilled lands: 216,066 acres.—Area planted in cotton, 21,748 acres; in corn, 85,496 acres; in wheat, 43,510 acres; in oats, 6,068 acres ; in rye, 286 acres; in tobacco, 72 acres.
Cotton production: 8,912 bales; average cotton product per acre, 0.41 bale, 585 pounds seed-cotton, or 195 pounds cotton lint.

Maury ranks third among the counties of the basin in amount of cotton produced in 1879. Every civil district contributed to the aggregate. The county has a general pentagonal form, with its base resting upon Giles and Lawrence (mostly upon the former) and its center lying in a line running south-southwest from Nashville. The great cultivated area of the county, and the greater body of it, is walled in on the south, west, and northwest by a complete semicircle of bold highlands—Elk ridge on the south, and the edges and spurs of the Highland Rim on the west and northwest. Could one be sufficiently elevated above Columbia, the bold semicircle would come in view, sweeping more than half way round the horizon. To the west-northwest might be discovered a gap made for the egress of Duck river. To the west and southwest the eye, before reaching the distant ridges, would range over a wide, nearly level expanse of one of the grandest bodies of farming lands in the state. To the northwest the ridges would be nearer and more distinct, the cultivated lands being more encroached upon here by the highlands than elsewhere.

Turning about and directing the eye to the northeast, east, and southeast, the view changes. The ridges are absent, and the country becomes undulating or, in the distance, level to the very borders of the county.

The extreme eastern section of the county, in the region of Duck river, abounds in cedar glades, among which are limited areas of red lands, such as occur in Marshall and Rutherford. The rocks underlying the red lands are the "central limestones", the lowest geologically found in the basin. Then above these come the flaggy rocks of the cedar glades. Starting with this section of red lands and the more extensive glades as a central area, and proceeding radially over the county to the semicircle of highlands on the borders, belts of lands will be passed over corresponding to concentric outcrops of all the remaining subdivisions of Silurian limestones enumerated on page 29, under the Central Basin. Outside of the red lands and cedar glades is first a wide belt of the lands based on the Carter's Creek limestones. The belt extends to Columbia, and southward toward Culleoka. It supplies many good farming areas, and many upon which the thick-bedded and light-colored limestones crop out in blocks and ledges. Outside of this again come benches and tables of sandy lands, resting upon the sandy limestones of the Orthis bed. The latter graduate without any special line of demarkation into the highly fertile lands of the lower layers of the Nashville series. And here we find the broad expanses of undulating and level "poplar" lands, like those of the Polk and Frierson settlements and Big Bigby creek, which have given so much character to the southwestern part of Maury as an agricultural region. North of Duck river and west of Columbia, and also in the southern part of the county, this belt is more rolling, often becoming hilly. Proceeding to the foot of the semicircle of highlands, the country becomes at all points broken and hilly, and valleys and coves, interlocked with ridges, especially on the northern side of Duck river, are met with, but all are based on the rocks of the Nashville series, and are rich nearly to the tops of the ridges. The ridges are capped with siliceous and flinty strata. Their soils are gravelly and mellow, though thin and but moderately productive.

I have said nothing of bottom lands. I can only add that Maury has a fair quota of these along Duck river and the numerous creeks, adding much to the agricultural capacity of the county.

The native growth and crops are given in the abstracts of correspondents. On the map of relative acreage in cotton the belt of greatest area planted in cotton runs through the middle of the county. It is chiefly located on the soils of the Nashville limestones. Cotton is hauled to Columbia in wagons at 50 cents per bale, or shipped to Nashville at $1 per bale.

ABSTRACTS FROM REPORTS.

D. F. WATKINS AND L. E. POLK (Big Bigby lands, western and southwestern part of the county).—On new land cotton is liable to be too late unless the fall is very dry. Old lands are preferred. The soils cultivated in cotton are: (1) Yellow or poplar; (2) lowland, mostly black. The yellow or poplar is the chief soil, forming two-thirds of our lands, and extending from 5 to 15 miles in different directions. The growth is poplar, beech, oak, ash, walnut, sugar-tree, hickory, cherry, linden, with a dogwood and hornbeam undergrowth. The soil is a gravelly clay loam; the subsoil, a tough yellow clay, which bakes when exposed, but by cultivation becomes like the surface soil, and is underlaid by limestone at from 1 foot to 15 feet. Tillage is not troublesome in dry seasons, but rather difficult in wet. The chief crops are corn, cotton, and wheat, but the soil is best adapted to corn. About one-fourth of the crops is cotton. Plants grow to 3 and 6 feet, but are best at 3 feet, and incline to run to weed in wet seasons on rich, new (or bottom) lands, which is restrained by constant work to the last of July. The seed-cotton product per acre on fresh land is from 500 to 1,500 pounds, 1,780 pounds making a 475-pound bale; staple rates middling. The weeds are crab-grass, hog-weed, and purslane. No land lies turned out, but is generally seeded to wheat, oats, or barley, followed by clover, when it produces finely. The slopes do not wash seriously.

J. W. FRIERSON AND LEON FRIERSON (Big Bigby lands, southwestern part of the county).—For general statements, kinds of soils, etc., see page 35).—On the mulatto or dark loam soils cotton grows to 2 and 3 feet, 3 feet being the best. Some topping is done to restrain the plants. The seed-cotton product per acre on fresh land is from 1,000 to 1,500 pounds, 1,900 pounds making a 475-pound bale; staple rates low middling. After twenty years' cultivation the product is from 500 to 800 pounds per acre, according to the care taken of the land, 2,140 pounds making a bale. The weeds are careless-weed, smart-weed, cocklebur, and rag-weed. Very little land lies turned out; need never be turned out. Slopes wash on old thin lands. Horizontalizing and hillside ditching have been done, with indifferent success in most cases.

On the black porous soil the cotton raised is very productive at 4 feet, but the crop is uncertain. (Seed-cotton product and other details as under first soil.)

The gravelly soil occurs in a few spots, and has a growth of white and pin oaks and a few poplars. It is a gravelly yellow loam with a stiff clay. The subsoil is underlaid by gravel and limestone at from 3 to 6 feet. About one-fourth is planted in cotton. The seed-cotton product on fresh land is 1,000 pounds, 2,010 pounds making a bale; staple rates low middling. After twenty years' cultivation the product is from 300 to 500 pounds. (Other details as above.)

J. B. WILKES (Fountain Creek lands, southeastern corner of the county).—The lands vary; some yellow sandstone (Orthis bed) lands, some dark limestone. From 5 to 100 acres in places are tillable, and all are planted in cotton. The growth is poplar, oak, ash, beech, elm, sugar-tree, hickory, etc. The soils contain sometimes flinty gravel, are easily tilled in wet or dry seasons, and are early and warm when well drained. The chief crops are cotton, wheat, oats, barley, and corn, the soils being well adapted to all. Plants are restrained when necessary by topping. The seed-cotton product per acre on fresh land is from 800 to 1,900 pounds, 1,545 pounds making a 475-pound bale; staple rates low middling. Weeds are careless-weed and crab-grass. Very little land lies turned out. Such land, when taken in again, would produce well. Slopes wash seriously in some localities, but the valleys are not injured.

W. O. GORDON (lands of Carter's creek, north of Columbia).—On the mulatto or poplar uplands cotton grows to 3 feet. In warm, rainy seasons plants incline to run to weed, for which no remedy is used. The seed-cotton product per acre on fresh land is 800 pounds, 1,780 pounds making a 475-pound bale; staple rates good ordinary. After five years' cultivation the product is 600 pounds per acre, 1,760 pounds making a bale; staple rates as low middling. The weeds are rag-weed, crab-grass, and foxtail. Ten per cent. of the land lies turned out. If taken in again it would require green fertilizers for its restoration. Slopes wash seriously, but the valleys are injured thereby to no great extent. Efforts are made to check the damage by horizontalizing, hillside ditching, and the use of wheat straw, and increased acreage of wheat is sown for this purpose.

On the gravelly hill land the growth is black gum, beech, hickory, elm, sugar-tree, walnut, and in some places black locust. Cotton grows to 3½ feet, and frequently remains green two or three weeks longer than that on the first soil. Seed-cotton product per acre on fresh land is 1,000 pounds, 1,990 pounds making a 475-pound bale; staple rates low middling. After five years' cultivation the product is 800 pounds.

On the creek bottom soil the growth is beech, oak, box-elder, hackberry, sycamore, and elm. It is a fine black loam, and is best adapted to corn and grasses. Cotton forms 10 per cent. of the crops. Plants grow to 3 feet, but get too weedy in wet seasons, for which no remedy is used. Seed-cotton product per acre on fresh land is rarely 1,200 pounds; the average is 500 pounds for all seasons, 1,840 pounds making a 475-pound bale. The weeds are morning-glory, smart-weed, rich-weed, and white-top.

WILLIAMSON.

Population: 28,313.—White, 15,922; colored, 12,391.
Area: 540 square miles.—Woodland, all.
Tilled lands: 158,970 acres.—Area planted in cotton, 11,859 acres; in corn, 61,122 acres; in wheat, 39,685 acres; in oats, 5,912 acres; in rye, 413 acres; in tobacco, 197 acres.
Cotton production: 4,538 bales; average cotton product per acre, 0.38 bale, 546 pounds seed-cotton, or 182 pounds cotton lint.

Among the counties of the basin Williamson ranked fourth in 1879 as a cotton-producing county. Its product was hardly a third of that of Giles. The county lies immediately west of Rutherford, the central county of Middle

Tennessee, and south of Davidson county. It has an ill-shaped area. If the northwestern corner were rounded off, its form would approach that of a semicircle, with its base tilted to the southeast, resting aslant against a sloping side of Maury.

The western end, including nearly or quite a third of the county, is on the Highland Rim, the remaining two-thirds being within the Central Basin. Although Williamson is among the richest counties of Middle Tennessee, and has many broad plateau belts and valleys of land inferior to none, yet it is, taken as a whole, a greatly broken county. Great ridges traverse many parts of it, and high hills are rarely out of view. Big Harpeth river is the trunk stream, into which all others, with inconsiderable exceptions, pour their waters. This river, rising just without the eastern boundary of Williamson county, enters the county near its southeastern corner and flows northwestward entirely through its area. Little Harpeth, in the northern part of the county, and West Harpeth, to the west of Franklin, the county-seat, the first flowing westerly and the second northerly, are important tributaries of the Big Harpeth. All these have unsurpassed farming lands along their courses and a great aggregate of them. The hills even bordering their valleys are rich to the tops. In the eastern part of the county the Big Harpeth has its bed chiefly in the Carter's Creek limestone, and at a few points in the lower glade limestone. With this exception the rocks of the Harpeth valleys belong to the Orthis bed and Nashville limestones, whose strata are so rich in all the elements that make a fertile soil. (See page 31, under the Central Basin.) On the same rocks rest the fine undulating lands south of Franklin, and indeed most of the best lands of the county.

In the eastern part of Williamson, over a considerable area, as at Triune, the Orthis bed has an unusual development. Its sandy layers (so-called sandstones) and shales are greatly thickened, and make the underlying rocks of table-areas upon which cotton is cultivated. The sandy, mellow, and poplar lands of these rocks make much of the upland country from Nolensville to Triune and southward to the beautiful valley of Grove creek. They occur in sections between the creeks, the immediate valleys of the latter usually cutting down to the heavy-bedded, light-colored limestones of the Carter's creek subdivision.

In the eastern end of the fourteenth district, about half way between Triune and Franklin, and touched on the south by Big Harpeth river, is a spot of cedar glades two miles or more across. It has all the characteristics—flaggy limestones, cedar timber, and black and reddish-yellow soils—of a Rutherford county glade. (a) In describing the lands of Williamson we might have begun with this spot as a geological and agricultural center and proceeded outward, for its rocks belong to the lowest subdivision outcropping in the county. First, without completely surrounding the cedar center and making much of the territory of the fourteenth district and of contiguous parts of districts to the south, is an irregular belt of country resting upon the Carter's Creek limestones, containing many upland areas of fair land, but much interspersed with tracts spotted and slopes terraced with naked rocks. Outside of this again come the sandy benches of the Orthis bed, the lands of which, often thin at first, run back, especially to the north, west, and southwest, and blend with those of the Nashville series, giving the grand bodies of farming lands, valley plateau, and hill lands we have already noticed, the aggregate of which is equal to half the county. To these again in the west (west of West Harpeth) succeed the lands of the elevated Highland Rim, with its great expanse of "barreny" flatwoods cut into sections by mountain streams, some of which, like South Harpeth, have narrow and rugged but very rich valleys.

The growth and crops of the county are given in the abstracts of correspondents. On the map of relative acreage in cotton the belt of greatest percentage is a continuation of that in Maury, the whole belt lying mostly on the lands of the Orthis bed and the Nashville limestones. Cotton is shipped, by rail or wagons, to Nashville at from 75 cents to $1 per bale.

ABSTRACTS FROM REPORTS.

SAMUEL PERKINS (lands of Nelson's, Wilson's, and Arrington's creeks, eastern part of the county).—These lands alternate with ridges of light loam and dark limestone land. The particular lands of this region are considered unusually well adapted to cotton, and have a well-drained and warm soil. The lighter sandy loam produces a taller stalk, matures early, and is less inclined to blight. High on the hills the surface is covered with yellowish sandstone, blocks detached from a stratum underneath the soils. On hills higher than the sandstones blue limestones are seen, and on slopes below it are lighter colored limestones.

The soils cultivated in cotton are: (1) Brown light loam inclined to be sandy, with a yellow or red clay subsoil, mixed with sandy gravel and underlaid usually with sandstone at from 6 to 10 feet; (2) dark or black limestone, containing flinty gravel, and a subsoil of stiff yellow clay. The chief soil is the brown loam, making not quite half the lands. The ridges of this soil extend eastward 2 miles, ending in a limestone ridge. The growth is white and yellow poplar, black gum, ash, dogwood, white and red elm, white and black walnut, white and red oaks. The land is easily tilled in wet or dry seasons. Cotton grows to 2 and 4 feet; best at 2½ and 3 feet. Seed-cotton product per acre on fresh land is from 800 to 1,200 pounds; on land cultivated twenty years, if rolling, or slopes, and neglected, from 250 to 500 pounds, or if well cultivated from 500 to 1,000 pounds. Very little land lies turned out.

The dark limestone soil makes about 60 per cent. of the lands, and occurs generally throughout the county. The growth is sugar-tree, white ash, box-elder, black walnut, red elm, and red oak. The seed-cotton product per acre on fresh land is from 600 to 1,000 pounds.

J. S. CLAYBROOKE, H. B. HYDE, AND W. L. JOHNSON (lands of Wilson's creek and Harpeth river).—Uplands are quick, especially the black, flinty, rolling lands, and bolls mature early. The bottoms are generally narrow, and cotton on them grows too much to stalk and is liable to be killed by frost. When, however, the frost is late and the fall is warm and dry the bottoms will yield nearly a bale to the acre. The soils cultivated in cotton are: (1) Black gravelly upland, limestone land; (2) sandy upland, sandstone and limestone land, with poplar as the prevailing growth; (3) black bottoms, on which cotton does not open. (Details much as in preceding abstract.)

T. F. P. ALLISON (lands of Grove creek, southeastern part of the county).—There are many kinds of soils in this district. The flinty gravel and yellow sandstone soils are the best both for cotton and wheat; the black loam is best for corn. These make about 80 per cent. of the lands. The growth generally is beech, elm, sugar-tree, poplar, white oak, walnut, and, on the high lands, chestnut. The chief crops are wheat and corn. The soil is adapted to a variety of crops. One-sixth of the crops is cotton. The seed-cotton product per acre on fresh land is 1,800 pounds, 1,780 pounds making a 475-pound bale. The staple on old land is the best. One-tenth of the land lies turned out. If taken in again and broken in the fall, and rebroken in the spring, it would produce good corn, but not cotton the first year.

a A spot of cedar timber and glade limestone occurs in the extreme eastern angle of the county as we enter Rutherford, and another about Nolensville, on Mill creek, in the northwestern corner of the county.

8. A. POINTER (lands of Aenon and Harpeth creeks and of Duck and Big Harpeth rivers, southern part of the county.—For remarks and kinds of soils, see page 34).—On the mulatto poplar soil cotton grows from knee to shoulder high; waist high is the best. To prevent plants from going to weed, wet and roll the seed in plaster, plant early, and top the stalks in August. The seed-cotton product per acre on fresh land is from 700 to 1,500 pounds, 1,660 pounds making a 475-pound bale; staple rates middling. After fifteen years' cultivation the product is 500 pounds per acre, and even lower; yet if not plowed too wet it is injured less than any other crop; have known it planted in the same field for forty years. Staple on old land is somewhat shorter, but the yield is about the same. Foxtail and crab-grass are the most troublesome weeds. Little or no land lies turned out. Land that has been lying out, if not too badly washed, produces finely. Land lying out washes badly, and valleys are injured very little, if at all. Hillside ditches are often cut, with good success.

The light sandy soil lasts but a few years, even where cultivated carefully. Very little cotton is planted. Seed-cotton product per acre on fresh land is from 500 to 800 pounds, 1,660 pounds making a 475-pound bale; staple rates low middling. After fifteen years it would not sprout pease, and is too poor to grow weeds. Grasses alone are troublesome.

BROADWELL BROTHERS (northeast of Franklin).—The mulatto or poplar soil is the one almost universal here, and has a growth of poplar, black walnut, sugar-maple, and beech, with an undergrowth of papaw. The soil is a light gravel-clay loam of a mahogany color from 6 to 12 inches thick. The subsoil, a gravelly clay, becomes loose when exposed to the air and frost, and is underlaid by limestone at from 2 to 20 feet. The crops are cotton, corn, and wheat. The soil is best adapted to the last two. Cotton forms one-sixth of the crops. Plants grow to 3 feet; best at that. Topping is used to restrain the plants if need be, but is of no benefit unless followed by dry weather. The seed-cotton product per acre on fresh land is from 1,200 to 1,500 pounds, 1,840 or 1,900 pounds making a 475-pound bale; staple rates middling. After thirteen years' cultivation the product is 600 pounds per acre, 1,840 pounds making a bale; staple is shorter and finer, but thicker on the seed, and the seed lighter. Very little land lies turned out, and if taken in again would produce well. Slopes wash to some extent. A little horizontalizing and hillside ditching is done, with good success.

RUTHERFORD.

Population : 36,741.—White, 20,248 ; colored, 16,493.
Area : 590 square miles.—Woodland, all.
Tilled lands : 200,049 acres.—Area planted in cotton, 32,657 acres; in corn, 75,753 acres; in wheat, 29,250 acres; in oats, 6,482 acres; in rye, 483 acres; in tobacco, 47 acres.
Cotton production : 12,414 bales; average cotton product per acre, 0.38 bale, 543 pounds seed-cotton, or 181 pounds cotton lint.

Rutherford, one of the counties of the basin, stands second only to Giles in the number of bales produced in 1879. It is first in number of acres planted in cotton ; a fact which, taken in connection with the above statement, is more to the credit of Giles than of Rutherford. Both in these respects are much ahead of any other in the basin, only one county indeed, Maury, making a distant approximation to them. The county would be roughly square in form and with the cardinal points if the sharp northwestern corner were cut off to the north. It is the central county of Middle Tennessee, and indeed of the state. The central part of the basin lies within its area a few miles to the west of Murfreesborough.

The agricultural areas of Rutherford are arranged quite symmetrically. We have first a large level or undulating area of red cotton lands, elliptical in form, lying centrally and diagonally within the county. The town of Smyrna is near its northern end, Murfreesborough a few miles east of its center, and Christiana (points on the Nashville and Chattanooga railroad) at the southern end. The area along its principal axis is 24 miles in length and 12 in width, and is equal in square miles to a third of the county. The soil, when fresh, is a brown-clay loam, becoming red after several years' cultivation, owing to an admixture of the red clay subsoil. It is mellowed by flinty grains and gravel from the chert of the underlying rocks. The latter are called the "central limestones", and are the lowest rocks exposed in the basin. (See page 29, under the Central Basin.) The native growth of these lands, which we may call "central lands", is a species of hickory, large red and white oaks, common locust, honey-locust, black walnut, cherry, post oak, sugar-tree, poplar, box-elder, mulberry, and hackberry, with dogwood, red-bud, hornbeam, and cane.

Then, secondly, around the central area is a remarkable belt of cedar glades, inclosing it (quoting from a previous page) as a frame its picture. (a) These glades are in the aggregate equal to another third of the surface of the county. They often rise in low ridges above the central lands. The rocks which make them are known as glade limestones. The glades have little value outside of the great cedar timber they supply. (See page 29.)

The glade belt extends out to the northern boundary of the county, and even beyond it into Wilson. It also reaches the western boundary at certain points. In all other directions, after passing the glade area, we intersect within the county the lands of a second great belt or ring, that based on the Carter's Creek limestones. This belt is complete in itself, but the northern portion is thrown into Wilson county, and much of its western portion into Davidson and Williamson by the extension of the glades in those directions. The lands, though in the main of second class, supply, when lying well, very desirable farming regions and cotton soils. They are, however, often hilly and rough from outcropping rocks. In Part I of the report (place referred to above) they are more fully described.

The lands of the second belt constitute most of the county remaining outside of the cedars. In the southeastern corner, however, there succeed bodies of the mulatto lands of the Orthis and Nashville limestones. This part is rolling, at points hilly, and includes several large ridges. Within the area of the second belt, at different points in the county, isolated hills or groups of hills, like Versailles knob, in the southwestern part of the county, rise up, whose slopes show Orthis and Nashville rocks and their characteristic soils. Finally, beyond all, a section of the eastern boundary a little north of the southeastern corner rests upon the high edge of the Highland Rim.

On the map of acreage the central lands are prominent as to percentage of land in cotton. Table I shows a great increase in the product of 1879 over that of 1869. Allowing for difference in weight of bales, the increase is 76 per cent.

Cotton is shipped, by rail or wagon, to Nashville at from 50 cents to $1 50 per bale.

---

a A little north of Florence station a low ridge of cedars extends across the central lands, cutting off really the northern end. This is not regarded in the general account above.

C. F. VANDERFORD, W. N. MASON, J. S. GOOCH, AND DR. R. B. HARRIS (lands of Overall's and Stewart's creek and east and west forks of Stone's river, northwestern part of the county).—The uplands of these streams are our best. Cotton lands do not vary much, as the country is generally level. The soils cultivated in cotton are: (1) Yellow (red) loam, with stiff clay subsoil; (2) yellow gravelly soil, with the same subsoil; (3) black coarse soil, not often used. The first, *the yellow (or red) loam*, makes more than half the lands. The subsoil contains flinty gravel, underlaid first by gravel and then by limestone at from 3 to 10 feet. Land is not easily tilled in wet weather; more easily in dry. The chief crops are cotton, corn, and wheat; also sorghum-cane, oats, and potatoes to a limited extent. One-fourth of the farming land is put in cotton. Plants grow to a height of 3 feet; this is the best. Wet weather inclines the plants to run to weed, which is restrained sometimes by reducing the ridge. Seed-cotton product per acre on fresh land is from 800 to 1,000 pounds, 1,660 pounds making a 475-pound bale; staple rates low middling. After twenty years' cultivation the product is from 600 to 800 pounds, 1,780 pounds then making a bale; staple rates inferior. The weeds are crab-grass and foxtail. None of the land lies turned out, but is put in clover. Slopes wash, but are easily checked. In a few instances horizontalizing has been done, with good success.

The *yellow gravelly soil* makes one-fourth of the lands. One-fourth of this soil is planted in cotton. Plants average 2 feet. The seed-cotton product per acre on fresh land is from 400 to 600 pounds, 1,425 pounds making a 475-pound bale; staple rates low middling. After fifteen years' cultivation the product is from 200 to 300 pounds. Crab-grass is troublesome. One-half or more of the land is in clover.

The *black coarse soil* comprises about a fourth of the lands, and is mostly cultivated in corn.

J. W. SMITH, DR. J. W. DAVIS, ROBERT BRUCE, W. S. BATTEN, D. M. NELSON, AND A. H. SANDERS (land of Stewart's creek and Stone's river.—For remarks, kinds of soils, etc., see page 33).—On the brown upland soil with red clay subsoil cotton grows from 2 to 4 feet high; best at 3 feet. A wet autumn, after a dry summer and deep cultivation, incline the plant to run to weed, for which shallow plowing is the remedy. The seed-cotton product per acre on fresh land is from 800 to 1,300 pounds, 1,680 pounds making a 475-pound bale; staple rates well. After twenty years' cultivation the product is from 600 to 800 pounds; staple compares well with that of fresh land. The weeds are crab-grass and morning-glory. About one-fifteenth of the land lies turned out; taken in again it would produce well if not washed. Slopes wash seriously in some places, but can be restored; valleys are sometimes injured, but to no great extent. Horizontalizing and throwing brush in the gullies have been practiced with benefit. The second soil does not differ enough from the first to make a description necessary. There is very little of the third soil.

A. M. McELROY (county generally).—In 1867–'68 I was the cotton weigher for Rutherford county. The crop of 1867 was the largest ever made in the county. My books show that I weighed for that year over 20,000 bales. The cotton lands lie on the water-courses, the three prongs of Stone's river being the principal ones. The soils cultivated in cotton are: (1) Dark mulatto, one-tenth of the land in cultivation, from 6 to 10 inches thick, with a subsoil of yellow clay; (2) lighter yellow—more of this than of any other kind; (3) red, like the second in productive capacity.

DAVIDSON.

Population: 79,026.—White, 47,678; colored, 31,348.
Area: 500 square miles.—Woodland, all.
Tilled lands: 139,166 acres.—Area planted in cotton, 3,224 acres; in corn, 52,764 acres; in wheat, 18,651 acres; in oats, 8,141 acres; in rye, 379 acres; in tobacco, 41 acres.
Cotton production: 1,333 bales; average cotton product per acre, 0.41 bale, 588 pounds seed-cotton, or 196 pounds cotton lint.

Davidson claims distinction inasmuch as the capital stands within its area. The county is pyramidal in shape, with a concave base, and it may be compared to a military cap seen in profile, with its sharp southwestern corner as the visor. The Cumberland river, with a general course to the west-southwest, winds through its area in a remarkably serpentine manner, the huge folds inclosing alternately on the two sides large and rich bodies of land. Such are Jones', Neely's, McSpadden's, Cockrill's, White's, and Bell's bends, the first being the most easterly and the last the most westerly. The surface of the county is in general rolling, with many rich valleys and plateau areas. Some parts are hilly; others almost mountainous, with high ridges.

The greater part of the county is within the area of the basin. The western part, equal to one-third or more of the whole, is properly on or within the range of the Highland Rim. We may, indeed, refer all of the county west of the valleys of White's creek, on the north side of the Cumberland river, and Richland creek on the south side, to the rim. But this great belt is not a continuous flat highland. Its southern part is intersected by the valleys of the Cumberland, Harpeth, and West Harpeth rivers, and is otherwise badly cut up by the valleys of creeks. North of the valley of the Cumberland the high belt is little dissected, and presents here a large block of flatwoods and rolling highlands, with the characteristic half-size oak growth and thin soils. Many spurs start out eastward from the highlands and interlock with scores of exceedingly fertile valleys. These, with but few exceptions, soon break down into lines of rich hills and then into level or rolling uplands. One of the exceptions is the prominent ridge dividing the waters of the Cumberland and Harpeth rivers.

Reaching in a direction nearly north and south through the middle of the county, between the valleys of White's and Richland creeks on the west and the Louisville and Nashville and the Nashville and Decatur railroads on the east, is a central belt of the county, averaging 5 or 6 miles in width, that is unsurpassed in fertility, and is the pride of the county. The land has the characteristic mulatto soil of the Nashville limestone, with a varied, heavy native growth. (See page 32, under the Central Basin.) But little cotton is raised upon it.

The part of the county east of the railroads mentioned, and extending to within a few miles of the Rutherford line and a corner of Wilson county, may be regarded, in general, as a wide-spreading table upland area with mellow, warm, and early lands based on sandy limestones. It is on this upland that most of the cotton of the county is raised. Within it are Jones' bend, the Hermitage, and the uplands along the Murfreesborough and Nolensville turnpikes. The rocks determining its table topography and giving character to it as an agricultural region are in the main the sandy strata of the Orthis bed. (See page 31.) Here and there swells and hills rise up above the plateau and locally contribute rocks and soils of the overlying Nashville series. The great table is cut into sections by the valleys of the Cumberland and Stone's river and Mill creek, and their most important tributaries. These streams have cut through the capping sandy rocks and made their beds in the light-colored and heavy-bedded limestones of the Carter's creek subdivision. This conformation and arrangement of formations and surface, so different from that west of Nashville, is made possible by the gradual rising of the strata as we go eastward. Westward the Orthis bed sinks below the river.

In the extreme eastern part of the county, contiguous to the Rutherford line and a corner of Wilson, the part excepted above, the sandy lands grow thin and break away, giving place to those of the Carter's Creek limestones, which become predominant. At a few points the county even touches the great cedar-glade belt of Rutherford.

A reference to the map of relative acreage will show that part of Davidson in which cotton is cultivated. The northeastern part is the area of greatest production. The product of 1879 was but little greater, 12 per cent., than that reported for 1869. In 1879 the product of Davidson was only one-twelfth of that of Rutherford.

Cotton is shipped to Nashville at 50 cents per bale.

ABSTRACTS FROM REPORTS.

W. WEAVER, W. A. DONELSON, AND J. M. TURNER (lands of Cumberland river, northeastern part of the county).—The soils cultivated in cotton are: (1) Brown clay loam; (2) light sandy loam; (3) black loam with little sand. The *brown clay loam* forms one-half of the lands, and has a growth of oak, hickory, ash, walnut, beech, hackberry, maple, elm, and gum. Subsoil, clayey and gravelly, which turns to a top soil when thrown up, produces a growth of weeds the first year and makes fine summer turnips, and is underlaid by limestone at from 1 foot to 10 feet. The soil is early and warm, and is best adapted to grain. Cotton forms one-fifth of the crops, and grows to a height of 3½ feet. New or strong land and wet weather cause overgrowth. The seed-cotton product per acre on fresh land is 1,200 pounds, 1,520 pounds making a 475-pound bale; staple not so good as on old land. After thirty-nine years' cultivation the product is 800 pounds per acre; if the land does not wash, it ought to improve; 1,520 pounds make a bale; staple finer but shorter. Weeds are morning-glory, cocklebur, and rag-weed. One-tenth of the land lies turned out, and is generally worn to the rocks; if not, it could soon be revived by clover. Slopes wash seriously. We try to prevent it by horizontalizing, with moderate success. The *light sandy soil* forms one-fourth of our lands, extending half a mile in each direction. The growth is small swamp oak, holly, and beech. The soil is late and cold. One-third of the crops is cotton. The seed-cotton product per acre is one-half bale. The black limestone land is unfit for anything.

W. S. DONELSON (Hermitage, Cumberland River lands, northeastern part of the county).—The soils cultivated in cotton are the red clay and black limestone, forming three-fourths of the lands. One-tenth of the crops is cotton. The seed-cotton product per acre on fresh land is from 800 to 1,200 pounds, 1,680 pounds making a 475-pound bale; staple rates low middling. After twenty years' cultivation the product is from 300 to 500 pounds per acre; staple is better. The weeds are careless-weed and crab-grass.

PHILIP EARHEART (Stoner's Creek lands, northeastern part of the county).—The soils cultivated in cotton are: (1) Black sandy; (2) flat lowland, partly overflowed; (3) light yellow sandy, ridge land. The *black sandy upland* is the best, and forms half the lands. Its growth is poplar, ash, oak, hickory, dogwood, elm, and papaw. One-third of the crops is cotton. The seed-cotton product per acre on fresh lands is from 1,000 to 1,200 pounds.

The *flat lowland* soil occurs up and down Stone's river and Stoner's creek. Its growth is overcup oak, hackberry, box-elder, sugar-tree, maple, willow, cottonwood, some hickory, and ash. Very little cotton is planted.

The *light sandy* soil forms one-fourth of the lands, and is productive, especially for cotton. Its growth is white and black oaks, some poplar, persimmon, dogwood, black haw, hickory, and ash. One-fourth of the crops is cotton. The seed-cotton product per acre on fresh land is from 500 to 600 pounds.

M. M. LEEK (Mill Creek lands, east of Nashville).—Our lands produce corn, wheat, clover, and some cotton, and are adapted to almost any crop. The seed-cotton product per acre on fresh land is from 800 to 1,000 pounds, 1,545 to 1,780 pounds making a 475-pound bale; staple rates low middling. After five years' cultivation the product is from 600 to 800 pounds per acre; staple is good ordinary. Crab-grass is troublesome.

B. GRAY (Hurricane creek, southeastern corner of the county.—For kinds of soils cultivated in cotton, etc., see page 34).—On the red clay soil cotton grows to a height of from 1 foot to 4 feet; best at from 2½ to 3 feet. Wet seasons or very rich land incline cotton to run to weed; topping is the only remedy used, and this is a doubtful one. The seed-cotton product per acre on fresh land, if the season is suitable, is 1,000 pounds, 1,545 pounds making a bale of 475 pounds. After ten years' cultivation the product is from 500 to 800 pounds per acre. Foxtail and crab-grass are most troublesome. Very little land lies turned out. The second soil is the black loam land. (Details much the same as above.)

WILSON.

Population: 28,747.—White, 20,292; colored, 8,455.

Area: 410 square miles.—Woodland, all.

Tilled lands: 170,229 acres.—Area planted in cotton, 3,191 acres; in corn, 68,468 acres; in wheat, 32,983 acres; in oats, 9,078 acres; in rye, 852 acres; in tobacco, 361 acres.

Cotton production: 1,072 bales; average cotton product per acre, 0.40 bale, 567 pounds seed-cotton, or 189 pounds cotton lint.

Wilson lies north of Rutherford and west of Davidson county. Its northern boundary is for the most part the Cumberland river, and the county would be nearly rhombic in shape were not the southwestern corner cut largely away to Rutherford. The surface of the county is greatly varied. Alluvial lands occur at intervals along the streams, and rolling lands alternate with plateau areas and benches or great cedar glades. Some parts are hilly, and high, bold ridges are met with in the eastern and southeastern parts of the county.

The cedar glades are a marked feature in this county, as in Rutherford, Bedford, and Marshall. They are based on thin, flaggy limestones, cover many square miles, and have supplied a vast amount of superior cedar logs and timber. A great belt of glades, 10 miles or more across, comes out of Rutherford and extends, though with contracting width, northward through the central part of Wilson to Lebanon, the county-seat. Glades of limited extent, alternating with other areas, occur north and northwest and also east from Lebanon, and in the cedar regions patches of arable lands, with black and brown soils, are met with. The latter, with gravelly yellowish or reddish-yellow subsoils, are the most important, and are sometimes cultivated in cotton, especially in the southern part of the county. (a) The flaggy limestones of the cedars belong to the subdivision of the Silurian limestones I have denominated "glade limestones". (See page 30, under the Central Basin.)

a Occasionally spots of the red lands of the Central limestones, so extensively developed in Rutherford, are discovered. Their aggregate area, however, is very limited.

Next outside of the glades we have everywhere lands in valleys, belts, or sections of greater or less size, based on the heavy-bedded and light bluish-gray limestone, named "Carter's Creek limestone". (See page 30.) There is much of this in the angle of the county to the southwest of Lebanon, and many wide desirable valleys to the northwest of the same place, all within the cotton-producing portion of the county. The same lands occur in valleys to the north, east, and southeast from Lebanon; in fact, summarily, pretty well over the county. The alluvial and second bottom or gently sloping lands of these valleys, taken together, give to the county many superb farms noted for strength of soil and productiveness.

Again, in most of the county, highlands occur between the valley areas. These are often mere dividing ridges or lines of hills. In many portions, however, they are flat-topped ridges or plateau areas of greater or less extent. Their soils are sandy, and rest upon the sandy limestones (blending upward sometimes with the bottom layers of the Nashville limestones) belonging to the subdivision named on page 31 the "Orthis bed". The Lebanon and Nashville turnpike crosses such ranges, as at Silver Springs and Greenhill, and just without the county in Davidson, at the Hermitage. Others occur north and south of this line. They are known as poplar or hickory ridges, and they supply in this part of the county favorite cotton-growing tracts. (a)   In the eastern part of the county they are also present. In this direction, however, many of the high ridges rise above the "Orthis bed" and contribute to the agricultural wealth of the county rich slopes of the mulatto lands characteristic of the Nashville limestones.

On the map of relative acreage in cotton it is seen that the cotton-producing portion of Wilson lies chiefly in the southwestern and western portion of the county; and further, that this portion is for the most part the northern end of the cotton-growing region of Middle Tennessee. Cotton is shipped to Nashville at from $1 to $1 50 per bale.

ABSTRACTS FROM REPORTS.

E. H. Thornton (southwestern part of the county.—For remarks and kinds of soils cultivated in cotton, see page 33).—On the soils named cotton grows from 1 foot to 4 feet high, 3 feet being the best. Wet weather in August inclines the plant to run to weed, for which topping is the remedy. The seed-cotton product per acre on fresh land is 600 pounds, 1,660 pounds making a 475-pound bale; staple is coarse. After four years' cultivation the product is from 200 to 400 pounds, 1,545 pounds making a bale; staple is shorter but finer, and seed lighter. Crab-grass is troublesome. But little land lies turned out. Slopes wash seriously, but the valleys are not injured thereby until the soil on the uplands is exhausted. Horizontalizing has been tried with good success.

W. C. Davis and Turner Vaughan (lands of Spencer's creek and Cumberland river, northwestern part of the county).—The Cumberland River uplands cannot properly be considered hilly until we get east of the cotton region of this section. The soils cultivated in cotton are: (1) Brown poplar ridge, lying mostly on slopes; (2) red or limestone, mostly on level or gradually sloping plains; (3) yellow or red sandstone land. The chief soil, "poplar" ridge, makes about one-fifth of the lands, and occurs to the east, south, southeast, and southwest for 15 miles, but is largely broken up by other varieties. Its growth is poplar, walnut, dogwood, mulberry, oak, etc. Tillage is easy in wet or dry seasons, and the soil is early, warm, and well drained. The chief crops are corn, cotton, oats, wheat, and clover; but one-twentieth of the land is planted in cotton. Plants grow to a height of from 1½ to 2 feet. Excessive rain and thick planting may cause them to run to weed, but this may be restrained by early planting. The seed-cotton product per acre on fresh land is 1,000 pounds, 1,600 pounds making a 475-pound bale; staple rates good ordinary. After ten years' cultivation the product is 750 pounds, 1,000 pounds making a bale; staple not so good or fine. The weeds are smart-weed and crow-foot grass. Very little land lies turned out; if taken in again it would produce finely, and is easily restored, only requiring time. Steep slopes alone wash; valleys are injured more or less in proportion to the clay washed down. Little is done properly to check damage.

The red or limestone soil is perhaps not more than one-twentieth of the lands of this region. It occurs to the east, 10 miles; south and southeast, 20; southwest, 12. Any crop does well on this. (Other details as above.)

The yellow or red soil of sandstone land forms not more than one-fiftieth of our lands. One-twentieth of this land is planted in cotton. Under no circumstances does cotton incline to run to weed. (Details as under first soil.)

SUMNER.

Population: 23,625.—White, 16,294; colored, 7,331.
Area: 530 square miles.—Woodland, all.
Tilled lands: 139,980 acres.—Area planted in cotton, 732 acres; in corn, 49,245 acres; in wheat, 20,445 acres; in oats, 9,188 acres; in rye, 779 acres; in tobacco, 495 acres.
Cotton production: 317 bales; average cotton product per acre, 0.43 bale, 618 pounds seed-cotton, or 206 pounds cotton lint.

Sumner lies north of Wilson and Davidson counties, between the Cumberland river and the Kentucky line. Its area has nearly the form of a square, excepting that the southwestern corner protrudes to the west and the southeastern is encroached upon by Trousdale. The topography of the county is simple and its belts of land compact and easily comprehended. The northern portion of the county is on the Highland Rim, and the southern portion within the basin, the area being about equally divided between the two. The northern half is therefore elevated. Its lands, between the shallow valleys of the streams, are flat and "barreny", the timber small oaks and hickories, with chestnut, and the soils are thin and poor. Toward Kentucky the lands improve as the red soils of the Saint Louis limestones are approached.

South of the edge of the highland, or of "the ridge", as they call it in Sumner, to within a mile of the river, is a belt of mulatto lands averaging 5 miles or thereabout in width and extending eastward and westward through the county, the like of which is to be seen only in the grand belt, of which it is a part, lying along the foot and in front of the edge of the Highland Rim in Williamson and Maury counties. On the north side the lands of this belt are made hilly or rolling by spurs jutting out from the highland. Going toward the river, the county becomes less rolling, and often spreads out into the most beautiful farming tracts. These lands are based on Nashville limestones and rocks of the "Orthis bed". Nearest the river the sandy lands of the latter rocks generally predominate, and it was on these, in the southwestern corner of the county, that most of the cotton accredited to Sumner was raised.

a Often on the steeper slopes, where these lands break away as we pass to those of the Carter's Creek limestones below, the soil is very thin and poor, frequently presenting bare or "scalded" places along the hillsides.

Within a mile of the Cumberland, more or less, the lands we have noticed break away and give place to the immediate valley of the river. This valley supplies another but narrow and often rough belt of lands based chiefly on the Carter's Creek limestones. At a few points the sandy lands of the "Orthis bed" sink down to the level of the river. Rich alluvial bottoms occur at intervals along the river, and a fair proportion of them along the creeks of the county.

On the map of relative percentage the location of the cotton-producing lands is seen. It is a small area, and is at the extreme northern end of the cotton region of Middle Tennessee. Cotton is hauled to Nashville at 50 cents per bale.

ABSTRACTS FROM REPORTS.

J. G. MARTIN AND S. R. DOXEY (lands of Drake's creek and Cumberland river, southwestern part of the county).—On the yellow poplar soil cotton grows to a height of 3 or 4 feet, and at this height is most productive. In wet seasons plants incline to grow to weed, for which we know no remedy. Cotton is not planted on fresh land. After five or six years' cultivation the seed-cotton product per acre is from 1,000 to 1,200 pounds with good attention, from 1,600 to 1,780 pounds making a 475-pound bale; staple very fine. Crab-grass and foxtail alone are troublesome. No land lies turned out, but is sometimes clovered and grassed and then put in cotton. There is very little washing on slopes. Nothing of consequence is done to check it.

The second soil, dark loam or blue-grass soil, forms about half of our lands, and occurs for 5 or 10 miles in small and large farms. Growth, walnut, ash, oak, locust, and the like. The soil is a brown clay loam with a deep yellow clay subsoil; thickness, 6 to 8 inches. The subsoil is friable when exposed, becoming like the surface soil, and is underlaid by clay and rock at from 1 foot to 4 feet. The land is easily tilled, though not so easily as the first soil; is later than the first, and is well drained naturally. The soil is best adapted to blue grass and other grasses, corn, potatoes, and then cotton. Very little is planted in cotton. Plants grow to 18 and 30 inches, the last the best. Fresh land is not put in cotton. After five or six years the product per acre is from 800 to 1,000 pounds, 1,660 to 1,780 pounds making 475-pound bale. Grasses alone are troublesome. None of the land lies turned out, but all is planted in grass or clover. Very little washing occurs on slopes, and scarcely anything is done to check it.

HARRY SMITH AND J. G. MARTIN (lands of Drake's creek and Cumberland river).—There are a number of farms in this immediate vicinity having a red or yellow sandy soil adapted to cotton. Cotton is more successfully raised here than elsewhere in the county, due to a greater proportion of sand in the soil. The soils are: (1) Red or yellow sandy upland, either on level land or slopes; (2) brown-loam or blue-grass soil, suited to corn and grain; (3) black buckshot, very sleek in wet weather. The chief soil for cotton is the red or yellow sandy, making three-fourths of the land in this vicinity, and extending a mile and a half north, 3 miles east and west, and bounded on the south by the Cumberland river. Its growth is poplar, ash, oak, elm, walnut, some beech, dogwood, ironwood, etc. The soil is a fine sandy loam 6 inches thick. The subsoil is a yellow clay, which crumbles in the sun, but is almost impervious when undisturbed, and is underlaid by limestone at from 5 to 20 feet. The land is early and well drained. Cotton is the money crop, and the soil is best adapted to the staple. One-third of the crops is cotton. Plants grow to 2¼ and 3 feet. Soil too rich or containing too much calcareous matter inclines the plants to run to weed, which some restrain by topping; but my plan is to use the hoe. The seed-cotton product per acre on fresh land is from 500 to 1,500 pounds, 1,780 to 1,900 pounds making a 475-pound bale; staple is best from old land. After forty years' cultivation the product on the farm I work is from 500 to 1,000 pounds, the same quantity making a bale. Crab-grass is very troublesome from the middle of June until fall. Very little land lies turned out. Cotton cultivation does not exhaust the land, excepting on slopes which wash. Slopes wash seriously in some places, but the valleys are rather improved thereby. Horizontalizing has been done with very good success.

CHEATHAM.
(See "Highland Rim, western subdivision".)

JACKSON.
(See "Highland Rim, eastern subdivision".)

MACON.
(See "Highland Rim, eastern subdivision".)

PUTNAM.
(See "Highland Rim, eastern subdivision".)

DE KALB.
(See "Highland Rim, eastern subdivision".)

COFFEE.
(See "Highland Rim, eastern subdivision".)

THE CUMBERLAND TABLE-LAND, THE VALLEY OF EAST TENNESSEE, AND THE UNAKA MOUNTAIN REGION.

These regions respectively embrace the following counties:

TABLE-LAND.—Fentress, Scott, Morgan, Cumberland, Van Buren, and Grundy.

TABLE-LAND AND VALLEY.—Marion, Sequatchie, Bledsoe, Hamilton, Rhea, Anderson, Campbell, and Claiborne.

VALLEY.—James, Bradley, McMinn, Meigs, Loudon, Roane, Knox, Jefferson, Union, Grainger, Hamblen, Hancock, Hawkins, Washington, and Sullivan.

VALLEY AND UNAKA.—Polk, Monroe, Blount, Sevier, Cocke, Greene, Unicoi, Carter, and Johnson.

The leading topographical and agricultural features of these great natural divisions of the state have been given in Part I of this report. They lie within the penumbral region of cotton culture; or, strictly, the valley of East Tennessee is a " penumbral region", while the other two, the Cumberland table-land and the Unaka Mountain region, both mountainous divisions, lay so feeble a claim to the designation that we may throw them out as non-producing areas. Their relations to cotton production are sufficiently given in the respective accounts given of them in Part I.

In the valley of East Tennessee, though the division has no county in which cotton can be considered as one of the chief crops, there are many isolated areas, especially in the southern and middle portions of the valley, in which from 1 bale to 70 bales were produced. One county, indeed (Hamilton), reports the respectable number of 143 bales. The distribution of these areas is best learned by a reference to the map of relative acreage. The entire constellation of colored spots and patches seen on this map, and lying east of the counties of Franklin, Grundy, Bledsoe, Cumberland, Morgan, and Fentress, is within the valley. The colored area in Marion is in Sequatchie valley, but Sequatchie belongs properly to the great valley. In Table I the product of the several counties from Marion, producing 35 bales, to Johnson, producing nothing, is given, and need not be repeated here. (a) The total production of the entire valley was in 1879 only 537 bales, an aggregate product less than that of the limited cotton-producing corner of Sumner county within the basin.

The soils of the valley have been noticed in the description of the division in Part I of the report. In many sections they would produce cotton well if the growing season were long enough to be relied upon. The cotton actually produced was cultivated upon a variety of them; but the yield, in the aggregate, was so small, and the areas concerned so scattered, that even if we had the proper data but little practically would come from a discussion of the relations. It will be observed upon the map that there is a general increase in cotton culture as we approach Georgia and Alabama. The valley is indeed "penumbral" to areas of higher percentage production in these states. An examination of Table I brings out the fact (allowing for errors in the column of cotton bales for 1870) that there was comparatively a great increase in the product of 1879 over that of 1869.

ABSTRACTS FROM REPORTS.

HAMILTON COUNTY, J. M. Ellis: The first and second bottoms and uplands of Chickamauga creek are considered. Cotton-growing, tried here for five years, seems satisfactory on the first and second soils. On low, rich bottoms there is too much weed, and bolls do not open. The soils used for cotton are: (1) Red soil, lying high and fair to the sun; (2) cherty gray soil, lying high; (3) bottom lands, not often planted in cotton. The chief soil is the dark red soil, and about half of our land consists of this kind. The growth includes oak, hickory, poplar, and ash. The soil is about 12 inches thick, but often less, and is underlaid by gravel and limestone (dolomite) at from 1 foot to 10 feet. The chief crops are corn, oats, clover, red-top, and wheat, all of which, excepting wheat, do well. About two acres in a hundred are planted in cotton, the plants attaining a height of 2½ feet. Wet weather and deep plowing promote the growth of weeds, which is restrained by shallow plowing and the free use of some good fertilizer. The yield of seed-cotton on fresh land is from 600 to 800 pounds per acre, of which it requires 1,485 pounds for a 475 pound bale, the staple rating as good ordinary. On land that has been in cultivation the product is from 400 to 600 pounds, requiring the same number of pounds as on fresh land for a bale, the staple comparing favorably with that of the first soil. Rag-weed and crab-grass are most troublesome. The second soil, the gray cherty, forms a fourth of the lands. Its growth is oak and hickory principally. It is a sandy, gravelly, grayish loam, sometimes black, 2 or 3 inches thick, underlaid by limestone (dolomite) at from 1 foot to 5 feet. It is tilled more easily in wet seasons than in dry. The subsoil is heavy, with angular gravel. The soil is best adapted to corn and clover, but about 2 per cent. of it is planted in cotton, which grows 2½ feet high. The seed-cotton yield is from 400 to 600 pounds per acre, requiring the same as that on the first soil for a bale, the staple rating as low middling. After two years' cultivation the land produces from 600 to 800 pounds per acre, the staple being the same. The weeds are rag-weed and crab-grass. About 5 per cent. or less now lies turned out. Such land tends to wash, and hence does not do so well when again cultivated. No efforts have been made to prevent washing.

JAMES COUNTY, J. A. Green: The first and second bottoms and uplands of Ooltewah creek and of the Tennessee river are referred to. The climate here is too cold and generally too wet for cotton. It does well occasionally on the mulatto uplands when the fall is dry. The soils cultivated in cotton are: (1) The mulatto uplands; (2) gray sandy land, or black gravelly upland; (3) black land. The first kind makes the largest proportion of the lands. Its growth is hickory, oak, and poplar, with occasionally pine forests. The chief crops produced are corn, wheat, oats, potatoes, and vegetables. Not more than one-twentieth is put in cotton. About 1,425 pounds of seed-cotton are required for a 475-pound bale, the staple rating as fair in the market. The most troublesome weeds are rag-weed, cockleburs, and Spanish needles.

POLK COUNTY, Erly Boyd: Cotton has but recently been cultivated in this county, but to no great extent. It is planted in the light sandy bottoms of the Hiawassee and Oconee rivers and in lands of Conasauga creek. The lands are best adapted to corn. Cotton grows from 2 to 4 feet in height. From 1,000 to 1,200 pounds of seed-cotton are produced per acre, of which from 1,600 to 1,900 pounds are required for a 475-pound bale. The staple rates as good. The troublesome weeds are rag-weed, crab-grass, and morning-glory.

---

a In the study of this table, and also of Table II, the general heading must not mislead. So far as cotton is concerned, all reported from Marion, inclusive, to the end pertains, as stated substantially above, to the valley of East Tennessee.

PART III.

CULTURAL AND ECONOMIC DETAILS

OF

COTTON PRODUCTION.

ALLUVIAL PLAIN OF THE MISSISSIPPI RIVER.

(Received during 1880.)

Lake.—(1) W. H. ANDERSON, Tiptonville, July 10; refers to county generally. (2) C. M. PEACOCK, Tiptonville, June 28; civil district No. 4, on eastern side of county. (3) D. WAGONER, Tiptonville, May 31; county generally. (4) R. S. BRADFORD, Tiptonville, May 15; county generally. (5) L. DONALDSON, Tiptonville, July 21; Mississippi alluvium, margin of Reelfoot lake. (6) J. W. FOWLER, Tenbrook, July 1; civil district No. 3. (7) R. M. DARNALL, Marr's Landing, April 2; civil district No. 1, northwestern part of county. *Dyer and Lauderdale.*—(8) C. H. PATE, Cottonwood Point, Missouri, July; alluvial and cultivated belt along the Mississippi.

ALLUVIAL PLAIN OF THE MISSISSIPPI RIVER AND PLATEAU SLOPE OF WEST TENNESSEE.

Lauderdale.—(9) JOE L. LEA, Fulton, May 3; civil district No. 4, southwestern corner of county; Mississippi and Hatchie alluvium; Hatchie second bottoms; uplands of Tipton and Cane creeks and of the Hatchie. (10) I. A. LACKEY, Ripley, April 21; Cane creek and river lands. (11) J. F. YOUNG, Double Bridges, April 22; county generally. (12) J. J. ALSTON, Glimpville, June 1; southern part of county. (13) P. T. GLASS, Ripley, April 9; civil district No. 1, southeastern part of county; Hatchie lands and Mississippi alluvium.

PLATEAU SLOPE OF WEST TENNESSEE.

Lauderdale.—(14) R. L. HALLIBURTON AND J. C. MARLEY, Ripley, April 1; civil district No. 2, eastern part of county. (15) E. R. OLDHAM, Ripley, May 1; civil district No. 2, eastern part of county; lands of Cane creek. (16) F. T. KICE, Durhamville, April 1, southeastern part of county; waters of Hatchie river. (17) J. H. FLOWERS, Henning, July 12; civil district No. 3, southeastern part of county. (18) W. W. HURT, Double Bridges, August 1; northeastern part of county.
Dyer.—(19) D. C. CHURCHMAN, Newbern, June 19; civil district No. 6, northeastern part of county. (20) SMITH PARKS, Newbern, April 3; northeastern part of county. (21) L. M. WILLIAMS, Newbern, March 25; northeastern part of county, between the Obion and Forked Deer rivers. (22) A. HARRIS, Newbern, January 3; northeastern part of county.
Tipton.—(23) Dr. W. H. HILL, Covington, April 19; civil district No. 1, northern part of county. (24) J. U. GREEN, Covington, April 14; civil district No. 1, northern part of county. (25) S. P. DRIVER, Covington, June 28; civil district No. 1, northern part of county. (26) Dr. T. W. ROANE, Covington, April 30; lands of Beaver Dam creek and of Big Hatchie. (27) J. H. SHINAULT, Mason, April 12; civil districts Nos. 8 and 9, southern part of county. (28) A. W. SMITH, Brighton, April 22; central and northwestern parts of county, Indian creek lands.
Shelby.—(29) DR. W. D. TUCKER, Lucy, April 17; civil district No. 3, northern part of county; Big creek lands. (30) H. L. DOUGLASS, Woodstock, April 26; northwestern part of county, lands of Big creek and Loosahatchie. (31) Dr. S. HAMMONTREE, Woodstock, April 1; civil district No. 4, lands of Big creek. (32) JAMES STEWART, Memphis, March; county generally. (33) W. H. NELSON, White Haven, April 16; part of county south of Memphis, Nonconnah and Hurricane lands and Mississippi alluvium.
Obion.—(34) J. H. McDOWELL, Union City, May 1; civil districts Nos. 10 and 13, north of Troy; Hoosier creek lands. (35) B. W. HERRING, Union City, July 1; uplands, western part of county. (36) J. S. MURPHY, Harris Station, April 17; northeastern part of county, between Obion river and Harris' Fork.
Fayette.—(37) J. B. THORNTON and A. L. PEARSON, Roseville, June 25; civil district No. 16, southwest corner of county and northeast part of district. (38) A. D. LEWIS, La Grange, March 25; southeastern part of county, Wolf river lands. (39) J. M. GALLAWAY, Gallaway, January 2.
Hardeman.—(40) WILLIAM RUSH, Pine Top, April 15; a part of county northeast from Bolivar, Piney creek lands. (41) E. E. LOW, Saulsbury, April; civil district No. 1, southwestern corner of county; Spring creek lands. (42) J. A. MANSON, Saulsbury, March 31; civil districts Nos. 1 and 10, southwestern corner of county. (43) O. B. POLK, Hickory Valley, April 30; civil districts Nos. 2 and 3, western part of county. (44) H. M. POLK, Bolivar, March 29; lowlands and uplands of Spring creek and Hatchie river.
Haywood.—(45) AARON WALKER, Brownsville, April 15; county generally. (46) F. A. LORD, Brownsville, March 1; civil district No. 7, center of county. (47) J. W. KERR, Brownsville, May 27; civil district No. 9, western part of county. (48) H. WILLIAMS, Brownsville, May 1; northwest part of county. (49) J. B. BRANTLY, Wellwood, April 10; civil districts Nos. 4 and 5, eastern part of county. (50) H. M. CLARKE, Wellwood, April 5; eastern part of county, between Forked Deer and Hatchie rivers. (51) Dr. H. C. ANDERSON, Carolina, March 29; western and northwestern parts of county. (52) J. M. SHAW, Brownsville, and Professor J. NELSON, Dancyville, April 15; civil district No. 4, eastern part of county.

Madison.—(53) D. R. ALLISON, Stephenson, June 30; eastern part of county. (54) J. D. PEARSON, Clay Brook, June 28; civil district No. 12, northeastern part of county. (55) S. M. OSIER, Pinson, May 1; southeastern part of county. (56) THOMAS INGRAM, Andrew Chapel, May 1; civil district No. 7, western part of county; Panther creek and Forked Deer lands. (57) E. C. HABBERT, Andrew Chapel, July 9; lands of Cypress and Johnson's creeks, western part of county. (58) J. Y. KEITH, Jackson, April 28; lands of Johnson's creek and Forked Deer river, western part of county. (59) J. J. BOON, Jackson, April 21; civil district No. 8, southwest of Jackson; Hopper's creek and Forked Deer lands. (60) T. C. LONG, Jackson, April 10; western part of county, Johnson's creek lands. (61) A. D. HURT, Jackson, July 1; western part of county, Johnson's and Cub creek lands. (62) M. V. B. EXUM, Carroll, June; northwestern part of county, Cane and Dyer Creek lands. (63) M. P. COLLINS, Carroll, April 3; civil district No. 11, northeast from Jackson.. (64) G. C. BUTLER, Medon, June 25; southern part of county, Clover creek lands.

Crockett.—(65) T. J. WOOD, Bell's Depot, November 19; county generally. (66) E. J. READ, sr., Bell's Depot, March 22; lowlands of Black creek; uplands generally. (67) P. M. NEAL, Maury City, July 10; civil district No. 10, western part of county.

Gibson.—(68) J. M. SENTER, Trenton, July 15; county generally. (69) J. W. HAYS, Trenton, June 24; Cane creek lands, south of Trenton. (70) L. P. McMURRY, Trenton, July; southwestern part of county, Big creek and Forked Deer lands. (71) ZACK BRYANT, sr., Milan, April 3; southeastern part of county, waters of the Obion and Forked Deer rivers.

Weakley.—(72) E. D. TANSIL, Sharon, May 1; southwestern part of county, lands of Mud creek and Obion river. (73) A. M. SMYTH, Gleason, April 20; southern part of county, lands of Spring creek and Obion river. (74) G. W. ISRELL, Gardner's Station, April 24; northwest from Dresden. (75) S. C. CRAVENS, Gardner's Station, April 22; northwest from Dresden. (76) J. C. LIPSCOMB, Greenfield, April 17; southwestern part of county, lands of the three forks of the Obion river. (77) GILBERT PATTERSON, Greenfield, July; southwestern part of county. (78) T. D. MARTIN, Martin, April 3; northwest from Dresden.

Henry.—(79) W. P. SMALLWOOD, Paris, July 5; county generally. (80) S. C. DOBBINS, Paris, April 19; south and southwest parts of county. (81) J. F. CAVITT, Paris, January 2; northwestern and southwestern parts of county, waters of the forks of the Obion river. (82) B. D. BOWDEN, Cottage Grove, July 23; county generally. (83) J. E. WILLIAMS, Henry Station, April 22; county generally. (84) Dr. W. S. FRYER, Paris, July 3; county generally. (85) A. ROBINS, Manlyville, April 26; waters of Gin branch and Big Sandy river, southeast from Paris. (86) D. L. WILLETT, Springville, July 15; civil districts Nos. 7 and 24, southeastern part of county.

Carroll.—(87) E. T. BOHANNON, Trezevant, April 20; western part of county, waters of Lick creek and Obion river. (88) B. T. HILSMAN, Trezevant, April 20; western part of county, waters of Reedy creek and Obion river. (89) A. R. CARNS, Caruaville, July; northern part of county, waters of Crooked creek. (90) T. N. LANKFORD, McKenzie, April 1; northwestern part of county, Obion uplands. (91) J. F. SLOAN, Milan, Gibson county, August 4; northwestern part of county, Obion lands. (92) J. H. JORDAN, Hollow Rock, June 18; northeastern part of county, lands of Hollow Rock creek. (93) WILLIAM JOHNSON, Clarksburg, July 1; southeastern part of county, Roane's creek and Big Sandy lands.

Henderson.—(94) W. C. TRICE, Henderson, Madison county, April 8; southwestern part of county, uplands of Forked Deer river. (95) E. W. CUNNINGHAM, Lexington, March 1; county generally. (96) JOHN PEARSON, Lexington, June 3; eastern part of county, Beech river lands. (97) N. C. ESSARY, Lone Elm, July; county generally. (98) C. M. DAVIS, Lone Elm, June 22; eastern part of county, Beech river lands. (99) T. M. STUBBLEFIELD, Shady Hill, July 10; southeast from Lexington. (100) R. J. DYER, Shady Hill, April 1; civil district No. 14, southeast from Lexington. (101) F. G. ROGERS, Scott's Hill, April 20; southeast corner of county, lands of Cane and Flat creeks and Beech river. (102) A. H. FARNSWORTH, Centre Point, May 1; civil districts Nos. 12 and 13, southeastern part of county. (103) P. B. McNATT, Centre Point, March 4; southeastern part of county, Middleton creek lands.

McNairy.—(104) B. M. TILLMAN, Henderson, Madison county, January 8; civil districts Nos. 4 and 14, northwestern part of county, (105) A. W. STOVALL, Bethel Springs, June 29; county generally, waters of the Hatchie and Tennessee rivers. (106) J. H. ROWSEY, McNairy Station, July; northwest from Purdy, waters of the Hatchie. (107) R. D. ANDERSON, Falcon, April 10; southwest from Purdy, Oxford's creek, waters of the Hatchie river. (108) SYDNEY PLUNK, Tinsley, and F. E. MILLER, Sweet Lips, April 13; northern part of county, waters of the Forked Deer. (109) J. G. COMBS, Purdy, April 15; parts of districts Nos. 15, 7, 10, and 11, east of Purdy. (110) J. H. MEEKS, Stantonville, April 9; civil districts Nos. 5, 9, and 10, southeastern part of county; also much of eastern part. (111) W. J. SUTTON, Corinth, Mississippi, April 15; southeastern part of county, Owl creek lands.

WESTERN VALLEY OF THE TENNESSEE RIVER.

Benton.—(112) A. C. PRESSON, Camden, July; county generally. (113) P. M. MELTON, Big Sandy, April 9; northern part of county. (114) J. H. BRIDGES, Camden, April 5; middle of county, Cypress creek, waters of the Tennessee. (115) A. E. SWINDLE, Camden, March 20; lands on Tennessee river side. (116) W. F. MAIDEN, Camden, April 15; lands on Tennessee river side.

Decatur.—(117) J. H. PEARCY, Decaturville, June 20; lands of Turkey creek, west of Decaturville. (118) D. M. SCOTT, Decaturville, April 10; middle and southern parts of county. (119) JOHN McMILLAN, Decaturville, January 22; county generally. (120) R. T. SIMMONS, Swallow Bluff, June 24; southern part of county. (121) W. R. and R. J. AKIN, Swallow Bluff, April 20; southern part of county, Stewman's creek lands. (122) J. G. YARBOROUGH, Peter's Landing, Perry county, July 6; civil district No. 2, southeastern part of county, along the Tennessee. (123) W. M. DOGGAN, Bath Springs, June 23; southern part of county, Turnbow's creek lands. (124) J. F. AKIN, Bath Springs, April 20; southern part of county, Turnbow's creek lands. (125) L. D. CRAWLEY, Peter's Landing, Perry county, April 7; south of Decaturville, White's creek lands.

Hardin.—(126) J. C. MITCHELL, Saltillo, June 10; northwestern part of county. (127) J. W. IRWIN, Savannah, June 26; civil district No. 4, central part of county.

Humphreys.—(128) W. J. WHITE, Fowler's Landing, July 20; southern part of county. (129) W. D. KING, Buffalo, July 20; southern part of county.

THE HIGHLANDS, OR HIGHLAND RIM OF MIDDLE TENNESSEE.

Hickman.—(130) J. M. GRAHAM, Pine Wood, July 30; lands of Piney and Duck rivers.

Lawrence.—(131) N. M. HOLLIS, West Point, July 20; southwestern part of county.

Franklin.—(132) J. F. ANDERSON, Anderson, January 26; civil district No. 12, southeastern corner of county; Crow creek valley.

CENTRAL BASIN OF MIDDLE TENNESSEE.

Giles.—(133) D. T. REYNOLDS, Buford, February 12; northern part of county, waters of Richland creek. (134) T. O. ABERNATHY, Buford, April 1; northern part of county, waters of Richland creek. (135) J. E. ABERNATHY, Buford, April 10; civil district No. 13, northern part of county; waters of Big creek. (136) NEWTON WHITE, Pulaski, February 26; waters of Richland creek. (137) JIM RIVERS, Pulaski, February 10; waters of Richland creek. (138) J. N. PATTERSON, Pulaski, February 10; waters of Richland creek and Elk river. (139) W. RIVERS, Pulaski, February 15; waters of Richland creek and Elk river. (140) J. J. LINDSAY, Pulaski, March 10; waters of Egnew's creek, west of Pulaski. (141) J. G. MASON, Prospect, February 13; civil district No. 2, southern part of county. (142) J. S. EDMONDSON, Bethel, January 21; southern part of county, Jenkin's creek lands. (143) J. F. PARKER, Bethel, February 14; civil districts Nos. 3 and 4, southwestern part of county. (144) J. K. P. BLACKBURN, Brick Church, March 27; eastern part of county, lands of Richland and Bradshaw creeks. (145) SAMUEL YOKLEY, Campbellsville, April 12; northwestern part of county, lands of Big creek. (146) T. B. WADE, Wales Station, February 4; lands of Pigeon Roost and Richland creeks, north of Pulaski.

Lincoln.—(147) M. D. HAMPTON, Fayetteville, June 28; lands of Elk river. (148) J. D. TILLMAN, Fayetteville, February 4; lands of Elk river.

Moore.—(149) E. Y. SALMON and others, Lynchburg, July 23; lands of Mulberry creek and Elk river.

Bedford.—(150) B. F. RANSOM, Fosterville, July 26; civil districts Nos. 5, 6, 8, and 11, northwestern part of county. (151) W. R. RANSOM, Shelbyville, July 19; lands of Fall creek, northwestern part of county. (152) Rev. M. F. THOMPSON, Unionville, July 22; civil district No. 11, northwestern part of county. (153) B. F. JARRELL, Rover, July 17; civil district No. 10, northwestern corner of county. (154) R. C. ALLISON, Rover, July 6; civil district No. 10, northwestern corner of county.

Marshall.—(155) J. F. BRITTAIN, Holt's Corners, February 10; northeastern part of county, Spring creek lands. (156) J. B. EZELL, Chapel Hill, July 1; Spring creek and Duck river lands, northeastern part of county. (157) W. B. GLENN, Chapel Hill, July 3; civil district No. 8, northeastern corner of county.

Maury.—(158) L. E. POLK, Columbia, July 10; civil district No. 11, southwestern part of county. (159) D. F. WATKINS, Columbia, February 4; western part of county, Big Bigby lands. (160) LEON FRIERSON, Columbia, February 14; civil districts Nos. 13 and 14, western part of county; Big Bigby lands. (161) J. W. FRIERSON, Columbia, February 14; civil districts Nos. 13 and 14. (162) J. B. WILKES, Culleoka, February 10; civil district No. 6, Fountain creek lands; southeastern part of county. (163) W. O. GORDON Dark's Mills, March 22; lands of Carter's creek, north of Columbia.

Williamson.—(164) BROADWELL BROS., Franklin, May 10; civil district No. 8, north of Franklin; lands of Big Harpeth. (165) W. L. JOHNSON, Franklin, February 12; lands of Big Harpeth. (166) J. S. CLAYBROOKE, Trinne, February 10; civil district No. 18, eastern part of county; lands of Wilson's creek and Harpeth river. (167) Dr. H. B. HYDE, Trinne, January 25; lands of Wilson's creek and Harpeth river. (168) SAMUEL PERKINS, Trinne, July 18; civil district No. 18, lands of Wilson's, Nelson's, and Arrington creeks. (169) S. A. POINTER, Thompson's Station, February 20; lands of Aenon and Harpeth creeks, and of Duck and Big Harpeth rivers. (170) T. F. P. ALLISON, College Grove, July; civil district No. 21, southeastern part of county.

Rutherford.—(171) ROBERT BRUCE, Murfreesborough, May 15; waters of Stone's river. (172) C. F. VANDERFORD, Florence Station, February 27; civil district No. 6, northwest from Murfreesborough. (173) Dr. R. B. HARRIS, Jefferson, February 29; northwestern part of county, Stewart's creek lands. (174) W. N. MASON, La Vergne, February; northwestern part of county, Stewart's and Overall creek lands. (175) A. M. McELROY, Fosterville, February 7; county generally. (176) W. S. BATTEN, Fosterville, February 6; southern part of county, lands of west fork of Stone's river. (177) J. W. SMITH, Smyrna, February 9; northwestern part of county, lands of Stewart's creek and of Stone's river. (178) A. H. SANDERS, Smyrna, February 5; Stone's river lands. (179) J. S. GOOCH, Smyrna, February 13; lands of Stewart's creek and Stone's river. (180) Dr. J. W. DAVIS, Smyrna, February 13; lands of Stewart's creek and Stone's river. (181) D. M. NELSON, Smyrna, February 10; lands of Stewart's creek and Stone's river.

Davidson.—(182) W. WEAVER, Edgefield Junction, June 28; northern part of county, lands of Cumberland river. (183) J. M. TURNER, Edgefield Junction, February 6; northern part of county, lands of Cumberland river. (184) W. A. DONELSON, Hermitage, July 13; northeastern part of county. (185) PHILIP EARHEART, Hermitage, February 2; northeastern part of county, Stoner's creek lands. (186) W. S. DONELSON, Hermitage, June 28; northeastern part of county, Cumberland river lands. (187) B. GRAY, La Vergne, Rutherford county, February 20; civil district No. 6, southeastern part of county. (188) M. M. LEEK, Donelson, July; east of Nashville, Mill creek lands.

Wilson.—(189) E. H. THORNTON, Gladeville, June 26; southwestern part of county. (190) TURNER VAUGHAN, Laguardo, June; lands of Spencer's creek and Cumberland river, northwestern part of county. (191) W. C. DAVIS, Laguardo, July 8; lands of Spencer's creek and Cumberland river, northwestern part of county.

Sumner.—(192) J. G. MARTIN, Hendersonville, July 9; southwestern part of county; Drake's creek and Cumberland river lands. (193) HARRY SMITH, Hendersonville, June 20; southwestern part of county; Drake's creek and Cumberland river lands. (194) S. R. DOXEY, Hendersonville, January 24; civil district No. 5; Drake's creek and Cumberland river lands.

VALLEY OF EAST TENNESSEE.

Hamilton.—(195) J. M. ELLIS, Chickamauga, June 24; southeastern corner of county.

Polk.—(196) EBLY BOYD, Benton, September 2; lands of Conasauga creek and of the Oconee and Hiawassee rivers, western part of county.

OTHER CORRESPONDENTS.

Grundy.—R. S. CLARK, Pelham, March 15.

James.—J. A. GREEN, Ooltewah, July 1.

Macon.—M. F. WEST, Walnut Shade. January 30.

SUMMARY OF ANSWERS TO SCHEDULE QUESTIONS.

[In the following pages the numbers placed before the county names are for reference to the table of correspondents.]

TILLAGE, IMPROVEMENT, ETC.

1. Usual depth of tillage (measured on land-side of furrow): What draft employed in breaking up?

MISSISSIPPI BOTTOM: From 4 to 6 inches, and usually with two mules or horses.

PLATEAU SLOPE OF WEST TENNESSEE: 3 or 4 and sometimes, though rarely, 6 and 8 inches; usually with one mule or horse. (51) *Haywood:* "Our freedmen, if left to themselves, will not go deeper than 1½ to 2 inches, while good farmers plow from 5 to 6 inches deep."

In *Gibson, Weakley,* and *Henry* counties the depth is 4 to 6 inches with double teams.

In the valley of the Tennessee, the Central Basin, and East Tennessee regions the usual depth is 4 to 8 inches, with double teams.

2. Is subsoiling practiced? If so, with what implements, and with what results?

To a very limited extent throughout the state. The implements used are Blount's sulkies, Hughes', Avery's, Oliver's, and Dunn's plows; Brinley's and Murfee's subsoil plows. In many counties a bull-tongue is made to follow immediately behind a turn-plow. A majority give the results as good. (93) *Carroll:* Improves the yield the first year, but after that is of no benefit. (25) *Tipton:* No improvement the first year, but after that is beneficial. (45) *Haywood:* "When the land is subsoiled the clay retains the moisture only; no food for the plant. When the soil is turned under

deeply the moisture, in a dry season, will draw the roots of the plant to the bottom, where they find food alone." (52) *Haywood:* Best for corn and cotton. (59) *Madison:* Especially good on old and worn-out land. (62) *Madison:* Diminishes the washing, increases the production, and lessens the effect of drought. (66) *Williamson:* Also increases the product in all seasons. (168) *Williamson:* Decided benefit if done in the fall; if in the spring, first crop is not so good.

3. Is fall-plowing practiced? With what results?

It is practiced to some extent throughout the state, chiefly on corn, wheat, or other cereal lands, or after a pasturing season. The picking season of cotton crops usually comes too late to permit the practice.

The results are usually good, the lands generally being more easily tilled after fall plowing, and yield better crops.

(7) *Lake:* Insects killed and clay land pulverized. (14) *Lauderdale:* Fall-plowing does no good on land that has been cultivated, but on sod-land it is very beneficial. (33) *Shelby:* The

lands are more liable to injury after washing rains, but otherwise results are good. (45) *Haywood:* In preparing the land for cotton after a wheat crop fall-plowing should be done; after corn or cotton it is not necessary. (91) *Carroll:* The results are not good; lands run together, and become hard and cloddy in spring. (134) *Giles:* It helps to protect lands against the washings of winter rains, and when green vegetable matter is turned under makes a better crop.

4. Is fallowing practiced? Is the land tilled while lying fallow, or only "turned out"? With what results in either case?

To a small extent in all of the counties, but is not general, the lands being "turned out" for rest when becoming exhausted. (41) *Lauderdale:* If the land is very rolling or hilly when left out it washes or gullies badly. If plowed deeply, turning under a green crop with all the litter, it does not wash. (26) *Tipton:* A few plow up; most turn out to weeds or clover; always beneficial, provided the land is protected from washing, and not tramped by stock. In clover the benefit is 100 per cent. (33) *Shelby:* Only by necessity when exhausted; is not tilled except it is sometimes sown in pease or planted in sweet potatoes without cultivation. To till without some crop to shade the soil is injurious; to "turn out" is of little benefit temporarily, and none permanently. (38) *Fayette:* Sometimes tilled, but never permanently turned out; the result is good when tilled, but better when turned out for twelve months; then subsoil and plant.

(51) *Haywood:* Some sow pease, which, when done in July, are turned under in September; but more "turn out" than otherwise. To let land lie out and permit the weeds to mature is, in my opinion, a great folly. Thus to mature seed by the million, with the expectation of improvement, is, I think, non-sense. I have urged farmers to turn weeds under and plant pease, or, if nothing better, to turn weeds under when green. (60) *Madison:* Summer fallowing is usually followed with fine results. (67) *Crockett:* To till the land impoverishes the soil; to "turn out" restores it. (145) *Giles:* After lying in clover or grasses for four or five years a good crop is expected. (169) *Williamson:* "Turning out" improves land if level and not tramped by stock; if rolling, it is injured more by washing than benefited by rest. (188) *Davidson:* Only turned out for persimmon orchards; good persimmons, fat opossums, and happy negroes.

5. Is rotation of crops practiced? If so, of how many years' course, in what order of crops, and with what results?

Rotation is practiced quite generally throughout the state, and especially on farms where but little cotton is raised. Cotton is frequently planted for years in succession before being relieved

by other crops. There is, as a rule, no regular order of succession. Corn usually is planted after cotton, and often followed in turn by small grain and clover, sometimes pease. Results are always

97

469

excellent. The following extracts are given from reports: (4) *Lake:* Corn usually three to five years, cotton four to five years, wheat two to three years, clover two years. Results, increased production of 20 to 33 per cent. (11) *Lauderdale:* Cotton is usually succeeded the next year by corn, wheat, or oats, and cotton again the following year. (26) *Tipton:* Generally corn follows cotton, and *vice versa;* cotton on wheat stubble is the rule, and is highly beneficial where the land is fed by clover, pease, etc. Corn, cotton, and wheat rotated will impoverish the land. (45) *Haywood:* Cotton should not be planted the first year after clover; a crop of pease is a fine preparation for cotton. We find it best to rotate every year. (50) *Haywood:* Cotton is a great exhauster, and by rotation we save our lands and make better crops. (51) *Haywood:* Cotton, corn, wheat, and clover, with a mixture of herd's-grass and orchard grass, and let lie, including the wheat year, three years. Best results. I can then haul out manure in July, August, and September, and spread on the grass all the winter. Grass protects the manure in warm weather from the burning sun, and gives a firm track for the wagon in muddy winter weather. (84) *Henry:* Alternate years, corn followed by wheat, cotton by wheat, and then corn; beneficial. (115) *Benton:* In planting cotton longer than two years on the same soil it don't open as well, neither does the lint grow so long. (120) *Decatur:* We sow oats and clover when the lands get too poor to make 500 pounds of seed-cotton. (135) *Giles:* Corn after clover, and sometimes wheat after clover; corn after wheat, and then allow to stand two years for grazing or mowing; land is kept in good condition by this rotation. Cotton-planters generally practice wheat rotation. (141) *Giles:* When cleared, corn is planted for three years, afterward cotton for four or six years, then small grain. (144) *Giles:* Sometimes the same crop is planted for ten years without change. (169) *Williamson:* Cotton, then wheat, then corn; then in wheat or oats, or clover, and then back into wheat or cotton. Land makes larger yields and improves daily.

6. What fertilizers or other direct means of improving the soil are used by you, or in your region? With what results? Is green-manuring practiced? With what results?

Commercial fertilizers are very rarely used in the state. Barn-yard and stable manure, or composts with these and cotton-seed, leaves, etc., comprise the fertilizers applied to lands, and are generally in use to their full extent in all of the counties. Land plaster also is frequently applied to clover lands, and sometimes when cotton is planted. (3) *Lake:* Only knew of one man hauling out manure from his barn, which he did to banish fleas. Our lands are too rich for fertilizers, but they would pay well on black land. (19) *Dyer:* When used, we make one-third more cotton. (26) *Tipton:* Sheep penned on poor spots. (34) *Obion:* Stable manures usually hauled out and spread broadcast in the spring; increased production in proportion to amount used. Most of the cotton-seed in this county is fed to cattle and sheep through the winter and returned to the soil in the form of manure, especially in the uplands. The bottom lands, being rich, are seldom fertilized, though when done they have bountifully repaid the cost with an increased yield and earlier maturity, and with a better fiber. (51) *Haywood:* Put all the old leaves, straw, corn-stalks, etc., into my barn-yard to let it absorb all the liquids possible, and when rotted haul out at leisure times. Scattered on poor clover land, bare spots, makes it better than the best. (57) *Madison:* Cotton-seed is one of the best fertilizers; its quick action as plant-food and its light weight to handle makes it preferable to anything else. All we need is something to kill the germ or grind the seed into meal while in the sound state, the meal, hulls and all, to be applied. It is thought by our best farmers that this would increase the crop 50 per cent. and improve the land every year. I think the seed is injured by heating or throwing into pens to rot. The meal from the oil-mills has double the strength. Very good results. (152) *Bedford:* The usual practice here is to plant small patches, from 1 to 5 acres, and manure well with barn-yard manure. By this, 1,200, 1,500, and sometimes 1,800 pounds of seed-cotton per acre are raised. (169) *Williamson:* "I use Virginia plaster in great quantities, and with very satisfactory results. The best method is to soak the seed in water and then roll them well in plaster before planting. Make as much plaster stick on as possible. Treated in this way, the seed come up sooner and grow off more rapidly. The bugs, so troublesome on young cotton, seem to leave the plants raised this way earlier. The above is the most important application of plaster, yet it ought to be sowed on in addition after the cotton is thinned to a stand and when the dew is on the leaf. I recommend the thorough trial of plastering in this way. The benefits resulting are not so apparent in wet weather as in dry. The plaster adds 50 per cent. to clover and 33½ per cent. to cotton.

GREEN-MANURING is practiced to quite an extent in all of the counties; with pease and clover in all of the regions except the Central Basin, where clover is most popular. Results always excellent.

(11) *Lauderdale:* We regard red clover as the best fertilizer we have on a large scale. (45) *Haywood:* One good crop of clover restores the land almost to its original state. The cheapest and most certain way to improve our land is with pease when it is too thin for clover; yet when a stand of clover can be obtained by the use of land plaster, the land can be made in a few years as good or better than ever and pay in the meantime as a pasturage. (62) *Madison:* Soil is made deeper, lighter, and more easy to till. (160) *Maury:* With clover generally; pease are becoming popular as a fertilizer, and are sown more and more every year. All lands produce better after them. (169) *Williamson:* With clover, the land adds 33 to 50 per cent. to the cotton yield.

7. How is cotton-seed disposed of? If sold, on what terms, or at what price?

It is largely sold to the oil-mills of Memphis, Jackson, and Nashville, except in the counties of the Highland Rim, western valley of the Tennessee, and valley of East Tennessee, prices being an average of about 10 cents per bushel, or \$7 to \$10 per ton. The seed is also largely used for fertilizers, and for feed to cattle and sheep during winter months.

(30) *Shelby:* All sold to oil-mills, which pay to the gins of Memphis, and within a radius of 5 miles, \$10 50 per ton; to others, \$9 per ton. (33) *Shelby:* Price is fixed by combination of oil-factories, with a forfeit of \$100 for any one paying more than the agreed price. (51, 52) *Madison:* Good farmers rot them and spread them on the land; negroes sell all they can and beg seed the next spring for planting.

8. Is cottonseed-cake used with you for feed? Is it used for manure?

Except in the immediate neighborhood of the mills, the cake is scarcely used for any purpose. In the towns it is sometimes fed to cattle, mixed with other food. (29) *Shelby:* We have to pay \$22 per ton, while New England farmers pay from \$15 to \$18 per ton. (33) *Shelby:* For feed, the price of the meal is too high. Near Memphis it is used in market gardens for manure. (42) *Hardeman:* For milch cows, mixed with bran; for dry cows it is fed alone. As manure for any crops. (70) *Gibson:* For feeding cattle, only mixed with wheat, bran, or corn-meal. (109) *McNairy:* Just being introduced; too rich for feed alone; as manure for vegetables, but not for cotton. (166) *Williamson:* By dairymen for increase of milk and butter; also used to fatten beeves. (191) *Wilson:* To some extent as manure.

PLANTING AND CULTIVATION OF COTTON.

9. What preparation is usually given to cotton land before bedding up?

Fall plowing is very seldom done, except on stubble fields. If the land was in cotton the previous year, it is almost the universal practice to simply "bed up" between the former cotton rows, the old stalks being knocked down and plowed under.

(29) *Shelby:* Cotton is never picked out in time for fall plowing. (50) *Haywood:* Listing is done as early in the spring as possible; that is, throw two furrows up, let it stand until time for planting, when "bedding up" is done. (51) *Haywood:* Fall or winter plowing is pursued by good farmers; spring plowing by those who

are always in a hurry, and who do everything out of time. (107) *McNairy:* If the ground is rough, it is either broken broadcast or rebedded in spring. Shallow plowing is gaining favor among our farmers and is now almost universally adopted, no center furrow even being run for the bed. The plant, when young, does much better in ground that is well settled together than in loose soil. (151) *Bedford:* A thorough breaking of the soil is made; best if done in the fall and bedded in spring just before planting.

10. Do you plant in ridges? How far apart? What is your usual planting time?

It is the universal custom to plant in ridges, the distance apart being from 3 to 4 feet, occasionally 2½ feet. This distance is great-

est on bottom lands. Planting time is from the 10th of April to the 1st of May.

11. What variety do you prefer? How much seed is used per acre?

Seventeen varieties of seed are named by correspondents, the "green-seed" being the most popular. A number of answers are to the effect that after two or three years all the varieties become "green-seed". In many cases no special variety is chosen, the seed being mixed.

The following varieties are given by correspondents: Java Prolific, 16 correspondents; Sugar-loaf and Dixon, 9 each; Taylor, 8; Petit Gulf and Peeler, 7 each; Boyd Prolific, 5; Cluster, 4; Matagorda Silk, 3; Williams (N. C.) Prolific, 2. The following 1 each: Johnson, Schneider, Triple Twin, Golden Prolific, Arkansas Silk, Cheatham Prolific, and Tennessee Green-seed.

(9.) *Lauderdale:* The Taylor or Matagorda Silk is a good long staple. Dixon or any short staple lint and white seed is better than green-seed. (22) *Dyer:* Southern seed preferred here; after a few years' cultivation the seed becomes green and the lint

shorter. (51) *Haywood:* Sugar-loaf degenerating into "green-seed" is the best where large crops are planted, as it will wait on the picker without falling out. Taylor cotton (Matagorda Silk?) has the longest staple and sells from ⅓ to 1¼ cents more per pound. Java Prolific and Boyd's Extra Prolific grows in bunches, and if early would suit new land the best. (62) *Crockett:* No variety does well under four or five years' planting unless imported from the north of us. (158) *Marshall:* Our seasons are short, and many of the varieties that can be used south will not mature here; hence the Petit Gulf or regular green-seed is preferred. (175) *Rutherford:* The seed from the more southern states yield plants that run to weed and do not boll.

Two to four bushels are usually used per acre; sometimes a great deal more.

12. What implements do you use in planting? Are "cotton-seed planters" used in your region? What opinion is held of their efficacy or convenience?

Some farmers use plows to open the rows; the seed is planted by hand and covered with a harrow or board. Cotton-seed "planters" (largely home-made) are, however, mostly in use in all of the counties in the western part of the state where the lands are suitable, and to some extent in the central and eastern counties. The complaint in Lauderdale is that they cover the seed too shallow, and thus in dry weather it is very difficult to obtain a stand; otherwise they are highly esteemed in all of the counties by the majority of those who use them. (7) *Lake:* They are

indispensable to large planters. (9) *Lauderdale:* Good, if properly managed, especially for early planting; they save much work, and put in the seed better than hand-planting. (34) *Obion:* Save seed, and save work in chopping out. (44) *Hardeman:* Save seed, put it in thin, and in a very straight drill, which is advantageous. (145) *Giles:* Convenient if the seed are rolled. (146) *Giles:* Good for intelligent labor, generally a nuisance. (153) *Bedford:* Are looked upon with suspicion. (194) *Sumner:* Convenient, but "stands" are bad.

13. How long, usually, before your seed comes up? and how far apart? **At what stage of growth do you thin out your stand,**

The time given varies very greatly, and is dependent on weather. In good seasons the plant makes its appearance in about a week or ten days; in wet weather earlier, and in dry sometimes as late as two or three weeks. When it has attained a growth of several inches, or has put out three or four leaves, it is thinned out, usually leaving several plants in a place at distances of from 15 or 18 inches on bottom lands and from 9 to

12 on the uplands. Afterward these plants are again thinned, leaving one or two in a hill, though many planters thin to this at the first. The first thinning is by many done as soon as possible after the crop is well up, so that a "scraper" can be used. (69) *Gibson:* When the land is damp, the plant appears in six days; when dry, in two weeks.

14. Is your cotton liable to suffer from "sore-shin"?

"Sore-shin" attacks the young plants to some extent throughout the state, and is attributed by planters to a number of causes, but mostly to cool and wet weather in the spring months and to injury by hoes.

(9) *Lauderdale:* When wet and cold, especially if the ground is not

bedded up in time to let it settle before the plant comes up. (31) *Shelby:* In cold, wet weather if the dirt is thrown to it. (44) *Hardeman:* In very windy weather when very young. (160) *Maury:* On old cotton land. (169) *Williamson:* If worked too soon and not plowed immediately after the hoes.

15. What after-cultivation do you give, and with what implements?

(1) *Lake:* Scrape, hoe, and plow with a small shovel plow, and then run close to the cotton with double-shovel and sweep. (9) *Lauderdale:* Scrape, hoe, sweep; scrape again, hoe, and sweep, and sometimes scrape the third time if the grass is bad, and follow with hoe and sweep. Generally go over the crop three times. Many use the scraper only once, but I find scraping saves much hoeing, and is cheaper. (31) *Shelby:* In old land

plow deep with shovel plows; in fresh land, shallow, with a 20-inch shovel plow. (43) *Hardeman:* Scrape and thin to a stand; then run two furrows with 16-inch shovel plow and hoe again; then two furrows with turning plow if wet or with 18-inch shovel plow if dry; plow again with turning plow and hoe again. (51) *Haywood:* Light harrowing and shallow culture toward the last; the side harrow is a great leading implement in dry weather. Cotton is a plant that will wait upon the lazy producer and seemingly be as good in his fields as in others, but at gathering time the tale is told. (53) *Madison:* Small shovel *once;* large shovel, get further off and shallower as the plant grows larger. (57) *Madison:* I first scrape down and pass the hoes through it, leaving it in bunches, say four or five stalks in a bunch. Then I follow the hoes with a turning plow, and thus keep a good bed to the cotton. I think the cotton grows best in the good beds. Should I be pressed with the grass or any other trouble, this culture gives me the advantage. I can scrape it down again, and the hoes can cut it to a stand, leaving one or two stalks every 8 or 10 inches. Then follow the hoes again with the turning plow to keep the middles clean. Cotton should be thinned to a stand by the 20th of June, and should be in clean and good fix; otherwise we cannot expect it to pay us for our trouble. (167) *Williamson:* Bull-tongue and shovel plows; then Carey plows next the cotton; split the middles out with shovels or sweep, Carey or Avery plow. (169) *Williamson:* Continue to use the hoe and to plow with small turning plows or bull-tongues with small sweeps attached behind them. Close and deep plowing after the 15th of June is very injurious if dry. In cultivating cotton the land should be broken up early and deeply in the springs, say to a depth of 6 to 10 inches. (It is

better to break in the fall and rebreak in the spring.) In bedding, the plows should be sharp and put in the ground as deeply as the teams can pull them. In giving the cotton the first plowing it is well enough to let the plow into the ground deeply, but after the 15th day of June deep plowing is injurious. After the 15th of July, and I might say perhaps after the 10th of July, deep plowing is ruinous, and the worse if done in dry weather. By using plaster freely both before and after planting and working the ground once in every twelve days, running further from the cotton each time and seeing that your laborers at the last plowing almost take their plows out of the ground, I will insure 1,000 pounds of cotton to the acre on all good land in Williamson, Maury, or Giles, providing the season is a fair one for cotton culture. (172) *Rutherford:* The scraper is first used for the double purpose of destroying young grass and weeds and to straighten and trim the row of plants to a thin line. Plants are "chopped" with the hoe to a stand. Subsequent cultivation with the plow, so done as to keep the bed and middles clear of grass and weeds and to promote vigorous "stocky" growth. (183) *Davidson:* With plows or shovels keep it hilled up so it will not fall down, and keep it chopped clean in the drill. It will depend upon the seasons how often it is worked.

16. What is the height usually attained by your cotton before blooming? When do you usually see the first blooms?

In the Mississippi bottom region plants usually reach a height of from 18 to 30 inches; throughout the rest of the state it varies greatly, even in the same counties, but is usually 12 to 18 inches, sometimes but 6, and sometimes 24 inches.

The earliest date given in which the first blooms appear is the 10th of June, in Madison county (62). In Lake, Lauderdale, and Dyer the last of June or 20th to 30th. Throughout the rest of the state, July 1 to July 10.

17. When do the bolls first open?

"Latter part of July:" (3) *Lake,* (29) *Shelby,* (73) *Weakley,* (142) *Giles,* and (190) *Wilson.*

"August 1 to 15:" (7) *Lake,* (9) *Lauderdale,* (21) *Dyer,* (33) *Shelby,* (44) *Hardeman,* (46) *Haywood,* (50) *Madison,* (82, 84) *Henry,* (93) *Carroll,* (95, 103) *Henderson,* (110) *McNairy,* (112) *Benton,* (119)

Decatur, (127) *Hardin,* (133, 137) *Giles,* (151) *Bedford,* (162) *Maury,* (165) *Williamson,* (174, 176) *Rutherford, Hamilton,* and *Polk.*

In other counties, from the 15th of August to the 1st and 10th of September.

18. When do you begin your first picking? How many pickings do you usually make?

Picking begins as soon as there is enough cotton open to make a day's work (50 or 75 pounds); the usual time is from the 1st to the 10th or as late as the 15th of September, though in the western part of the state some picking is done a little earlier. (4, 7) *Lake:* 15th of August to 1st of September. (14) *Lauderdale* and

(34) *Obion:* 20th and 25th of August. Two and three pickings are usually made, the crop being picked over as rapidly as possible, and as often as necessary to gather all the cotton. Sometimes the seasons are late, and only one picking is made.

19. Do you ordinarily pick all your cotton? At what date does picking usually close?

All of the cotton is very generally gathered throughout the state, excepting of course that which falls to the ground before the picker reaches it. Help is usually employed in gathering the crop, and is paid by the 100 pounds of seed-cotton. In the western part of the state picking usually closes about the 25th of

December, though it is frequently continued to the 1st of February, and even March, when the crops are large. In the Highland Rim, the Central Basin, and East Tennessee regions it closes by the 25th of December, and sometimes earlier.

20. At what time do you expect the first "black frost"?

Usually about the 10th or 20th of October. Some reports give an earlier and some a much later date. (52) *Haywood:* The last of September. (6) *Lake:* Middle of November. (31) *Shelby:* Usually November 1, though I have had cotton killed in September. (54) *Madison:* December 1. (66) *Crockett:* 15th of November.

(106) *McNairy:* Latter part of November. (131) *Lawrence:* Freezing weather November 1 to 10. (136, 138, 140) *Giles:* White frost 15th to 20th October. (159) *Maury:* November 15. (165) *Williamson:* November 20. (183) *Davidson:* Cotton and bolls killed October 15. (185) *Davidson:* About middle of September.

21. Do you pen your seed-cotton in the field, or gin as the picking progresses?

Both methods are practiced, according as the crop is large or small. Cotton is usually penned in the field if crops are large and sent to gin as fast as possible, the latter being kept running all the time. On small farms the seed-cotton is usually housed at home and sent to gin as soon as a bale is gathered. (33) *Shelby:* Never

pen in field, as country stores would get much of it. (51) *Haywood:* Make rail pens and line the inside with boards, perpendicularly placed. In this way, with a good cover, the cotton is kept dry, and much labor and time are saved.

GINNING, BALING, AND SHIPPING.

22. What gin do you use? How many saws? What motive power? If draft animals, which mechanical "power" arrangement do you prefer? How much clean lint do you make in a day's run of 10 hours?

Gins of twenty-four different names or patents are mentioned by correspondents, as shown below. Number of saws vary from 40 to 80. Both steam-engines and draft animals are used as a motive power. With the latter the inclined tread-wheel is quite popular in some of the counties.

(20) *Dyer:* Prefer steam first, then inclined wheel, then lever power. (43) *Hardeman:* Old-fashioned gin-gearing, spur-wheel, and band-wheel. (51) *Haywood:* Gins of eighty saws are being used all over the county by men who do nothing but gin for the public. Steam gins are preferable, but farmers who have many mules are glad to have them at work. This ginning is hard on the mule. (134) *Giles:* The "Robinson Bevel Gearing" makes the lightest draft for the amount of speed given the gin. (135) *Giles:* The old-style large wooden driving-wheel with cast segments and cast pinion. (172) *Rutherford:* The sweep power, with 12-foot main driving-wheel, with band-wheel 6 to 8 feet diameter, driven by pinion from main wheel, gin-pulley usually 8 inches diameter.

CAPACITY OF GINS AS GIVEN BY CORRESPONDENTS.

PRATT'S GIN, mentioned in 18 counties:

	Pounds.
60 saws, by steam-engine	2,300 to 4,000
60 saws, by 4 horses or mules	1,800 to 2,000
50 saws, by steam-engine	2,500 to 3,300
50 saws, by 4 horses or mules	1,000 to 1,800
50 saws, by 6 horses or mules	2,000
50 saws, by tread-wheel	1,000 to 1,500
45 saws, by horse-power	1,500

CAROW GIN, mentioned in 15 counties:

80 saws, by 10 horse-power steam-engine	2,500 to 3,000
70 saws, by mules (draft-wheel)	800 to 1,000
60 saws, by steam-engine	2,750
60 saws, by 45 horse-power steam-engine	3,750
60 saws, by 6 or 8 mules on inclined wheel	1,000 to 1,500
50 saws, by 16 horse-power steam-engine	2,625

GULLETT GIN, mentioned in 14 counties:

80 saws, by steam-engine	3,200
60 saws, by 12 horse-power steam-engine	3,500
50 saws, by 16 horse-power steam-engine	2,625
50 saws, by 8 horse-power steam-engine	3,200
50 saws, by tread-wheel	1,200 to 1,500

BROWN'S GIN, mentioned in 10 counties:

80 saws, by steam-engine	4,000 to 6,000
60 saws, by tread-wheel	1,850
50 saws, by mules and tread-wheel	1,200 to 1,500
50 saws, by mules or horses	1,350 to 2,000
50 saws, by water-power	1,700 to 2,000
40 saws, by mules	900

EAGLE GIN, mentioned in 9 counties:

80 saws, by 20 horse-power steam-engine	4,000
50 saws, by 10 horse-power steam-engine	3,000

50 saws, by 4 mules	1,000 to 1,700
40 saws, by mules on inclined wheel	900

SMITH'S GIN, mentioned in 6 counties:

70 saws, by steam-engine	4,000 to 5,000
60 saws, by steam-engine	3,000
60 to 80 saws, by inclined wheel and mules	2,000
50 saws, by mules	1,500

HICK'S GIN, mentioned in 6 counties:

70 saws, by steam-engine	2,000 to 3,000
50 saws, by mules	1,500
45 saws, by mules	1,000

WINSHIP GIN, mentioned in 4 counties:

60 saws, by 12 horse-power steam-engine	3,750 to 5,080
50 to 60 saws, by inclined wheel and mules	1,500
40 saws, by steam-engine	1,850
50 saws, by mules	1,200

NEEDLE GIN, mentioned in 4 counties:

80 saws, by 12 horse-power steam-engine	7,000
50 to 60 saws, by horses or mules	1,500

ROBINSON GIN, mentioned in 4 counties:

50 to 60 saws, by horses or mules	1,500

NANCE GIN, mentioned in 3 counties:

60 saws, by inclined wheel and mules	1,150
55 saws, by mules	1,500

EMERY GIN, mentioned in 3 counties:

50 saws, by horses	1,200
45 saws, by horses (lever power)	1,500

STAR GIN, mentioned in 3 counties:

50 saws	1,500

MAGNOLIA GIN, mentioned in 2 counties:

80 saws, by steam	3,200

GEORGIA GIN, mentioned in 2 counties:

60 to 80 saws	2,000
50 saws	960 to 1,100

The following gins in 1 county each:

Kingsland, Fergerson & Co., 50 to 80 saws, by horse-power	2,000
Chafin (home-made), 50 saws, mules	1,500
Phœnix, 50 saws, 6 mules	1,700
Latham, 60 to 60 saws, mules	1,500
Webb, 50 saws, mules	1,500
Wilkerson, 50 saws, mules	1,500
Elliott (home-made), 60 saws, tread-wheel	1,500
Hall and Sattern's gins (capacity not given).	

23. How much seed-cotton, on an average, is required for a 475-pound bale of lint?

The estimate varies very greatly even in the same county, and is between 1,545 and 1,660, or even 1,780 pounds, without regard to regions. The number of pounds required is, as stated by one of the correspondents (16 Lauderdale), early, 2,140, late, 1,545,

dependent upon the time that elapses between picking and ginning; the earlier the greater the weight.

Very few estimates are as low as 1,425, the general average being about 1,600 pounds.

24. What press do you use for baling? What press is generally used in your region? What is its capacity?

There are 25 patented iron-screw presses reported in the state, while in many of the counties the old style home-made wooden press is still in use. The capacity of the iron-screw presses with sev-

eral men and one mule is from 10 to 15 bales per day. Some report Brooks' as much as 20 bales. The following list embraces those reported: Wilson press in 8 counties; Brooks' and

.473

Scofield's presses in 7 counties each: Arrow and Reynolds' in 5 counties each; Finley and Cheek in 4 each; Deering in 3 counties; Southern Standard, Nesbit, Collins, and Fergerson presses in 2 each. The following in 1 county each: Caruthers, Crenshaw, McDermott, Reeder, Winship, Lewis, Russell, Rutherford county press, Spread Eagle, Shearer, Jackson, and Janney's. "The old wooden press is clumsy and slow;" with 2 men and 1 mule it will press about 4 bales per day. (51) *Haywood:* Reynolds' revolving press. There is no lifting of cotton in this press; it is rolled in by men and boys. It can't be used by steam as yet. With men, boys, and 1 mule it will make 1 bale every 45 minutes. Nesbit's press, by steam, will press a bale every 30 minutes. (175) *Rutherford:* With two horses or mules we can make a bale of 600 pounds with the old wooden-screw press. The box or hay press works by lever power, and 2 strong men can make a 500-pound bale. The patent iron-screw presses are superior to the others.

25. Do you use rope or iron ties for baling? If the latter, what fastening do you prefer? What kind of bagging is used in your region?

Iron ties are used exclusively in all of the counties, except Polk, in the valley of East Tennessee, where rope is used. The fastening embraces three kinds, the arrow, the buckle, and the button or Beard tie, and are about equally preferred. Jute, hemp, and flax 2-pound bagging are used, the first two, and especially hemp, having the preference.

26. What weight do you aim to give your bales? Have transportation companies imposed any conditions in this respect?

A weight of 500 pounds is aimed at almost universally, freight being charged per bale regardless of weight. A requirement is made that each bale must be over 400 pounds; otherwise a deduction of $1 or more is made from its price by merchants. (37) *Fayette:* Bales under 350 pounds are not merchantable. Whether this regulation is laid down by railroad companies or boards of trade I do not know. (172) *Rutherford:* The railroad companies make no distinction as to weight of bales, the sizes being nearly the same, whether light or heavy. About 24 bales of uncompressed cotton will fill an average car; the freight charges are therefore based upon bulk rather than upon weight.

DISEASES, INSECT ENEMIES, ETC.

27. By what accidents of weather, diseases, or insect pests, is your cotton crop most liable to be injured? At what dates do they usually make their appearance?

Caterpillars have only appeared, though very rarely, in the counties of Lauderdale, Tipton, Shelby, Fayette, Hardeman, Haywood, Madison, Weakley, Henry, Franklin, Giles, Lincoln, Maury, Williamson, Rutherford, Davidson, Wilson, and Sumner. They are by some considered a benefit to the cotton crop. The *bollworm* has sometimes appeared in these counties, and also in Carroll, McNairy, Benton, Decatur, and Moore. The *cut-worm* in a few counties in the western part of the state appears early in May and does some damage. *Lice (Aphides)* are quite a common enemy to the plant in May, except in East Tennessee, where no mention is made of them.

The diseases incident to the weather, such as shedding, rot of bolls, rust, blight, etc., are prevalent in all of the counties to a greater or less degree and in summer months. (9) *Lauderdale:* The caterpillar has never come early enough to do any serious damage, but sometimes does good by stripping leaves off. Lice in May and June do much damage by retarding growth and sometimes kills young plants. (51) *Haywood:* In cold, rainy, sunless weather cotton suffers greatly, first, from a general shrinkage of the stalk, sore-shin, and black leaf, and then death, or a shock from which it very slowly recovers. Then lice prey upon it until the 25th of June, but if the weather is hot no injury is done.

28. To what cause is the trouble attributed by your farmers?

The various diseases are commonly attributed to extreme changes of weather. The following extracts are made: (49, 50) *Haywood:* Rust is considered an insect originating from old stumps and decaying wood, and appears most frequently in new ground. (51) *Haywood:* Blight or blasting rust, as some call it, often in dry spells of weather late in August. Rust and shedding of bolls are among our great evils. What causes rust I do not think is well known; what it does we know well. It is an insect, like the rust of the raspberry leaves, wheat, oats, etc. It comes generally on new land, and mostly around hickory stumps, but often not a stump of any kind is visible. Rain often arrests it. I tried salt last year, throwing it over the stalks and suffering much of it to settle around the stem at the ground. My field of 15 acres which was attacked was saved, but I cannot say the salt did it, for a rain came in a few days, and this might have arrested it. Rust is not to be confounded with what is termed blasting, which is a species of rust caused by extreme dry weather, and will spread over a field in a day or two; this is worse on old land than on new. As to the shedding of bolls, if even one-third of those that fall could be made to stick and do the work nature seems to have intended for them we could raise a bale of cotton (500 pounds) every year to the acre. To prevent shedding, the best plan, I think, to be pursued is to subsoil the row over which the cotton stalks grow; that is, after fallowing deeply, say in February or March, when the rows are to be laid off, run in this furrow a subsoil plow, then bed on this. The cotton plant, having a long tap-root, can get down easily to moisture, and if any good fertilizer suitable for cotton is there this tap-root certainly would have plant-food far removed from the blasting influence of a drought. I have tried this on a small scale, and the cotton raised did not shed the bolls half so much. (110) *McNairy:* Red rust is more prevalent during very dry weather; the black rust is caused by excessively wet weather, and both are thought to be parasitic. (121) *Decatur:* Black rust on wet land to wet weather; on uplands, the red rust to dry weather. (133) *Giles:* Blight is caused by applying the soil to the plant too freely in dry weather and rain following in less than five days: shedding is caused by deep culture and want of moisture; rust is caused by excess of lime in soil and deep culture, followed by dry weather, checking the growth suddenly, and to the peculiarity of season and improper culture.

29. What efforts have been made to obviate it against the caterpillar? With what success? Is Paris green used as a remedy

As a rule no efforts have been made against insects or diseases; Paris green has not been used. (11) *Lauderdale:* None that I know of, except to burn the old stumps and trees in the field where it usually prevails; it almost always begins near one of these, and is generally recognized as an insect. It is hard to tell as to success, as rust may be very injurious to the crop one season and may not appear even in the same field the next. (14) *Lauderdale:* I try to obviate the rust by plowing with a light plow, so as not to disturb the roots of the cotton. I think it is benefited, but don't know to what extent (08) *Tipton:* None except not to use crops and turning under vegetable matter. A few claim that lime broadcast prevents rust and blight. Some farmers of good sense ascribe rust to the presence or near vicinity of the poke-root. Rotation appears to relieve rust. We have never been troubled with worms. A variety of caterpillar occasionally strips off all the leaves the last of August. This stripping has always proved to be of service by hastening the maturity and opening. (42) *Hardeman:* Shedding in dry weather stopped to some extent by continued plowing; rust, pull up first stalks and burn or bury; this often stops it from spreading. (44) *Hardeman:* We have begun to practice rotation and putting our land in better condition. Marked improvement. Paris green not used. It is said to be a remedy, but is too poisonous to be handled. Let the birds live and they go as far in destroying the caterpillar as nostrums now used. (51) *Haywood:* Some have burned up every hickory stump and tree in the field, but shallow culture with broad shovel and side harrow, and never plowing when the land is

wet, has been our best protection. (57) *Madison:* None but to pull up the plant affected and carry it out of the field. I have stopped the red rust in that way in its early stage. The black rust seems to spread so fast that it is useless to try to stop it. (107) *McNairy:* Have known common salt sown when the plant was wet with rain or dew, which was thought to check it. (108) *McNairy:* Success is attained only on well drained and well-cultivated lands. (190) *Decatur:* Light harrowing is good after the plowing is done in dry weather to prevent the droppings. One furrow in the middle is good to keep it from baking if likely to be too wet. (169) *Williamson:* Plaster is used to drive off the bugs; running the plow far off and plowing shallow will prevent red rust; change of weather from wet to dry alone will stop black rust and August shedding. Good success.

30. Is rust or blight prevalent chiefly on heavy or ill-drained soils? Do they prevail chiefly in wet or dry, cool or hot seasons? On which soil described by you are they most common?

Blight is prevalent chiefly on ill-drained soils, in extremes of weather, and on either heavy or light soils.

Rust appears, apparently regardless of weather or character of lands, as seen in some of the following replies:

(9) *Lauderdale:* Blight does not appear uniformly on heavy and ill-drained soils; in some cases land that had been formerly planted in corn escaped blight, when dry cotton land in the same field suffered. Blight is more frequent on wet lands and bottoms. (12) *Lauderdale:* Rust on high land, blight on low; prevails in extremes of weather. Rust on mulatto and blight on black sandy land. (14) *Lauderdale:* Light soils suffer more from rust, new land more than old. Wet, damp weather for blight; cool, dry seasons for rust. The blight on heavy soil, and the rust on new or that recently put in cultivation. (23) *Tipton:* Very seldom on old lands; always in violent changes of temperature. (31) *Shelby:* In all extremes of weather; red rust is more common on light soils in hot, dry weather; black rust on heavy soil in cool, wet weather. (37) *Fayette:* Eccentric and sporadic, but this law of generation don't seem connected much with soils. (49, 51) *Haywood:* It seems worse on loose, black, friable soils. Dry and hot weather. On a black, porous, mellow, friable soil rust seems to do its worst. Hickory land is thought to be more subject to it than other classes of timbered land, yet I have seen it on purely poplar land. (57, 59) *Madison:* Hot and dry, often too much wet weather. On uplands, first appearing around or near stumps or dead trees and near the fence, especially if poke-stalks grow about them.

(104) *McNairy:* On uplands as bad, if not worse, than on bottoms. The kind of season does not seem to affect it. No soil is exempt; bottom lands are cleanest, and fresh uplands most subject to it. (107) *McNairy:* Buckshot land does not have rust. Loose hazel soil is most subject, and in cool seasons. Rust does not damage cotton on wet, heavy soils. (109) *McNairy:* Wet, hot seasons. Red rust on very loose, loamy soil, with gray subsoil containing black, angular gravel; black rust on yellow-gray soil; subsoil same as above. (110) *McNairy:* Red rust is prevalent on well-drained land; black rust on any. Red rust in dry, black rust in wet seasons. On our black sandy loam, hazel-nut and poplar lands we have red rust if the weather is very dry; the black rust is common to any soil. (122) *Decatur:* Light soils. Dry, hot seasons; some spots of black land in wet seasons on dry, high sandy soils. Rust is unknown on clay soils in this vicinity. (146 and others) *Giles:* On black soils, extreme wet or dry weather. Black rust on black soil, red rust on any soil, by sudden checking of growth, caused by deep culture or dry weather. (158) *Marshall:* Blight is very rare here; is produced by wet weather; rust by dry weather; gravelly lands most subject to it. (169) *Williamson:* Red rust is worst on poor land; black rust in wet weather, on low, rich bottom land; red rust in dry weather on poor upland. (190) *Wilson:* Heavy soils, wet and cool weather, on low and wet lands. Wood-ashes and lime greatly counteract this disease in the cotton-plant. (194) *Sumner:* Dark loam land, known as blue-grass land, is most liable to rust.

LABOR AND SYSTEM OF FARMING.

31. What is the average size of farms or plantations in your region? Is the prevalent practice "mixed farming" or "planting"?

In the Mississippi river bottom region there are many small farms of from 10 to 50 acres. Other farms contain 100 to 300 acres, and some as much as 800 to 1,000 and 1,500 acres. In the counties of the adjoining region of West Tennessee the size of farms vary very greatly, from 50, 100, to 500 acres, and more in a very few instances: (38, 39) *Fayette:* 640 to 3,000. (51) *Haywood:* 500 to 2,000. (104) *McNairy:* 100 to 1,000. In the western valley of the Tennessee the farms contain mostly 100 acres and less, a larger number seldom being reported, and then in no instance more than 500. In the Highland Rim region 100, 150, to 200 acres are given as averages. In the Central Basin the same

variation occurs as in West Tennessee, the greater number of average estimates falling below 500 acres, and mostly from 100 to 300. The following extreme sizes are given, but not as an average of the county: (137, 138) *Giles:* 1,000 and 1,800 acres. (166, 168) *Marshall:* 1,000 acres. (167, 169, 171) *Williamson:* 800 and 2,000 acres. (178) *Rutherford:* 1,000 acres. (185) *Davidson:* 1,700 acres. (192) *Sumner:* 3,000 acres. In the valley of East Tennessee the average of 200 acres is given.

Mixed farming is the prevalent practice throughout the state, though some planting is done in Lake, Lauderdale, Tipton, Fayette, Hardeman, Haywood, Madison, and McNairy.

32. Are supplies raised at home or imported, and if the latter, where from? Is the tendency toward the raising of home supplies increasing or decreasing?

In all of the counties but Shelby, and largely in Hardeman, the greater part of the supplies are raised at home, only a comparatively small portion being brought from Saint Louis or New Orleans. (30) *Shelby:* Very few are self-sustaining; most everything, from a pin to a steamboat, is brought from Memphis. (32) *Shelby:* Our good farmers raise their own; others raise cotton only, and buy supplies. (43) *Hardeman:* The greater part of

the meat and all of the flour for laborers and landlord are imported from Saint Louis and Cairo.

All of the correspondents report the tendency toward raising supplies as increasing, or in some cases as stationary, except (46) *Haywood,* (99, 103) *Henderson,* (137) *Giles,* (184) *Davidson,* (33) *Shelby;* with whites, increasing; with negroes, decreasing.

33. Who are your laborers chiefly? whites, of what nationality? How are their wages paid—by the year, month, or day, and at what rates? When payable?

Mostly negroes in West Tennessee, while in the western valley of the Tennessee and regions eastward the whites predominate, among whom are very few foreigners, a few Swedes in Tipton, and Germans in Decatur. Wages are mostly paid by the month at from $8 to $12, payable at the end of the month. Yearly wages are from $100 to $125, payable as needed or when due. Daily wages are from 50 to 75 cents and $1, payable at the end of the day or week. Board is included usually with monthly and yearly wages. Women receive lower wages than men.

34. Are cotton farms worked on shares? On what terms? Are any supplies furnished by the owners?

The share system is prevalent throughout the state, supplies being often furnished by the owner. When the owner furnishes land only, the laborer delivers to him one-third of the crop or one-fourth the cotton and one-third the corn. When supplies, such as teams, implements, seed, etc., are furnished by the owner, the crop is evenly divided. There is but little, if any, deviation from this rule in any of the counties.

35. Does your system give satisfaction? How does it affect the quality of the staple? Does the soil deteriorate or improve under it?

With but few exceptions the system seems to give satisfaction throughout the state. Nearly all of the replies indicate no material change in quality of staple, but a great deterioration in soils. In some an improvement in both staple and soil is noted. (1) *Lake:* Makes staple trashy, and leaves soil foul and hard to cultivate. (19) *Dyer:* Change in soil depends upon the attention of the owner. (29) *Shelby:* Poor cultivation makes poor staple, and vice versa. (43) *Hardeman:* A disadvantage to staple; with hired labor the owner can direct how and when to gather.

(44) *Hardeman:* Whites lose by farming on shares. Negroes are unwilling to manure the land because of extra work. (110, 111) *McNairy:* Staple injured by careless and late picking; hilly land deteriorates, level land does not. (172) *Rutherford:* Staple not so good nor lint so clean as when by hired labor under control of owner. Most negroes are averse to hiring for wages, because of an idea that croppers have greater privileges. (192) *Sumner:* Satisfaction given unless negroes get too many orders for dry goods and groceries.

36. Which system (wages or share) is the better for the laborer?

The advocates for shares and wages are about equally divided in number. Their reasons may be summed up as follows:

SHARES: In the end brings him twice the amount of money. He gets some hogs and cattle of his own, if at all thrifty; is interested, does more, and does it better. The incentive to work is greater. With good judgment and a family he does best on shares, because the children, 10 to 15 years old, are just as efficient with the cotton hoe and as pickers as a German worth $20 per month if the father and mother will attend to them. He has a home where he can raise his own supplies, is more independent, and a better citizen. They are too much inclined to spend their wages.

WAGES: Runs no risk and makes mere money. He gets his money, spends it, and don't conclude that he has been swindled because he has no money at the end of the year. Because of his disposition to neglect the crop when not under control he is kept at work, and avoids temptation to crime and vice. He gets the benefit of the owner's experience and direction, and pays cash for supplies, and at cheaper rates.

37. What is the condition of the laborers? What proportion of negro laborers own land, or the houses in which they live?

The condition of the laborer throughout the state is generally either good or moderately so, especially among the industrious classes; and though often "poor" and dependent, but few are in actual want.

A very small part of the negroes own land, or even the houses in which they live.

(67) *Crockett:* They are mostly self-sustaining. In this part of the county the more thrifty colored people, those who own horses and mules and have their own provisions, as a general thing are renters. They pay so much rent and run the farms themselves. The share croppers, as a general rule, are those who own no stock; have no provisions at all, or only in part. This class does not make much advance.

38. What is the market value of the land described in your region? What rent is paid for such land?

The prices naturally vary very greatly, according to amount of improvements. In the alluvial region of the Mississippi, from $5 to $50, and rents from $3 to $5 per acre. In the counties of West Tennessee and valley of the Tennessee, from $5 to $25, and rents from $3 to $5 per acre. On the Highland Rim they are valued at $15, $20, and $60, and rent for $5 per acre. In the Central Basin prices vary from $5 and $10 to $40, $50, and even $100 per acre; rents, from $1 to $5 per acre. In the valley of East Tennessee, values from $5 to $50 per acre.

39. How many acres, or 400-pound bales, per "hand" is your customary estimate?

On Mississippi river alluvial lands, 10 acres and 10 bales; sometimes much more is made. On the uplands of the rest of the state the usual estimate and average is about 4 bales with other crops, or 6 or 8 bales if cotton alone is planted.

40. To what extent does the system of credits or advances upon the growing cotton crop prevail in your region?

It prevails to a considerable extent throughout the state (often to three-fourths the value of the crop), except in the counties of *Madison, Henry, Benton, Hickman, Lincoln, Moore, Marshall, Williamson, Davidson,* and *Polk,* where but a small portion of the laborers require advances, unless it be improvident negroes.

(11) *Lauderdale* and (24) *Tipton:* To negroes and small farmers; the former are supplied usually by the employer or on their own responsibility. (28) *Tipton:* It has been general, but we are having better times, and the people are getting out of debt and are more self-sustaining. (29) *Shelby:* All share hands go on credit; their crops are consumed before made. Improvidence, idleness, and whisky does this, and landlords are compelled to advance to them from the beginning. (46) *Haywood:* Has pre-vailed to a great extent; more cash in the county now and credit not so much desired. (108) *McNairy:* The owner of the land gets a lien on the growing crop for supplies furnished. (132) *Franklin:* It is the custom of merchants to advance supplies to two-thirds the value of the growing crop. (168) *Williamson:* Is given only to the negro laborer have enough to clothe and feed him comfortably; with whites, but little required. (172) *Rutherford:* Since 1875 the system has been greatly curtailed. The loss of credit resulting from a series of poor crops from 1872 to 1876, and the financial troubles of these years, have had an excellent effect upon the management of farm affairs.

41. At what stage of its production is the cotton crop usually covered by insurance? Is such practice general?

Cotton is not insured until ready for shipment and at the depot.

(76) *Weakley:* All the crop is not usually covered by insurance.

(108) *McNairy:* As soon as planted, if there are debts over the laborer.

476

42. What are the merchants' commissions and charges for storing, handling, shipping, insurance, etc., to which your crop is subject? What is the total amount of these charges against the farmer per pound, or 400-pound bale?

Commissions, 2½ per cent. Shipping, 25 cents per bale. Storage per month, 50 cents in Memphis and 25 cents per bale in Jackson and other places. Drayage, 25 cents per bale. Weighing, 10 cents per bale. The total cost is, with transportation, from $3 to $5 per bale, or three-fourths to 1 cent per pound. Cotton is, however, mostly sold from the wagon to merchants at home and these costs avoided. (9) *Lauderdale:* Fire insurance, 0.2 per cent.; river insurance, 0.4 per cent. per month. Total, five-eighths cent to Memphis and Saint Louis, three-fourths cent to

New Orleans, if sold soon; if kept longer, insurance is added. (21) *Dyer:* 0.75 per cent. marine insurance; 1 per cent. fire insurance; total, including freight, etc., $5 32 per bale, as shown by my accounts. It will average $5. (59) *Madison:* Railroad and fire insurance, each 0.35 per cent. Total charges per bale to New Orleans, $6 to $7. (105) *McNairy:* Mobile merchants handle and pay freight at a cost of about 1 cent per pound. (177) *Rutherford:* 2 pounds dockage per bale; insurance, 25 cents.

43. What is your estimate of the cost of production in your region, exclusive of such charges and with fair soil and management?

The usual estimate is from 7 to 10 cents per pound; a few correspondents place it higher, others much lower. Some probably include all charges.

(14, 16) *Lauderdale,* (78) *Weakley,* (178) *Rutherford:* 2¼ to 3 cents per pound. (2, 7) *Lake,* (8, 18) *Lauderdale,* (25) *Tipton,* (31) *Shelby,* (67) *Crockett,* (75) *Weakley,* (84) *Henry,* (96) *Henderson,* (113, 114, 116) *Benton,* (117, 123) *Decatur,* (146) *Giles,* (151, 152, 153) *Bedford,* (162) *Maury,* (167) *Williamson,* (171, 177) *Rutherford,* (187) *Davidson:* 4 to 5 cents per pound. A few estimate it at 6 cents per pound.

(51) *Haywood:* About $15 to $19 to make a bale of cotton, and about $5 to $6 to cultivate an acre of corn. (115) *Benton:* A good hand will make and gather 4 bales for about $80. (116) *Benton:* The cost of producing 800 pounds seed-cotton (yield of one acre), including wear of land, taxes, wear of tools, labor, etc., is about $8, which, at 2½ cents per pound for seed-cotton, leaves a profit of $12 per acre. If the land were manured the profit would be greater.

COST OF EACH ITEM OF LABOR AND MATERIAL EXPENDED IN THE CULTIVATION OF AN ACRE OF COTTON.

Items.	J. L. Lea, Lauderdale	B. L. Halliburton, Lauderdale county.	A. L. Pearson, Fayette county.	Aaron Walker, Haywood county.	B. D. Hurt, Madison county.	W. C. Trice, Henderson county.	W. D. King, Humphreys county.	J. F. Anderson, Franklin county.	T. O. Abernathy, Giles county.	Rev. M. F. Thompson, Bedford county.	B. F. Jarrell, Bedford county.
Total	$16 90	$11 15	$13 83	$6 65	$12 76	$14 12	$4 06	$9 10	$10 95	$12 20	$11 00
Rent	6 00	4 00	2 75	4 00	....	4 00	3 00	4 50	5 00	3 00	5 00
Fencing, repairs, and interest on	50	25	1 00	25	25	04	....	....	58	1 75	50
Knocking stalks	20	10	10	....	10	03	05	....	10	10	....
Balling and burning stalks	60	....	....	....	....	06	20	....	....	....	....
Other cleaning up	....	10	21	....	....	05	....	....	....	....	10
Listing	50	35	....	....	25	....	....	....	20	....	14
Breaking up	....	20	1 25	60	....	1 00	75	....	....	1 00	....
Harrowing	....	15	25	....	....	20	10	....	10	10	....
Barring old beds	....	....	....	....	....	20	....	1 00	....	....	....
Splitting middles........A	50	15	21	....	13	20	....	....	20	....	25
Reversing	75	....	42	....	....	....	....	....	....	....	....
Laying off	35	17	10	....	13	20	10	....	10	20	07
Manuring, home-made	....	....	....	....	5 00	....	....	....	....	....	....
Applying manures	....	....	....	....	1 00	2 50	....	1 00	....	....	....
Bedding up	....	....	....	50	50	1 00	....	....	....	30	....
Splitting middles	....	15	....	....	....	....	....	....	....	....	....
Knocking off beds	20	....	....	10	....	20	....	....	....	....	....
Planting:											
Opening	20	10	10	15	} 33	....	45	....	10	20	12
Dropping	15	15	10	} 1 00		....		....	08	15	15
Covering	20	06	11	....		....		....	15	10	18
Seed	40	20	30	20	30	25	....	20	30	30	15
Thinning	60	75	75	1 00	50	1 20	....	50	....	....	50
Number of plowings	2 75	3 00	1 50	1 35	3 00	40	....	50	1 40	2 00	1 25
Number of hoeings	2 25	....	2 50	....	1 00	50	....	50	1 10	1 50	2 25
Hauling to gin	75	30	75	50	10	75	....	25	05	1 00	50
Management	....	1 00	1 40	....	....	1 00	....	....	1 50	....	....
Not included in the above estimate:											
Picking, per hundred-weight	75	80	75	50	50	60	....	45	50	50	50
Ginning, per hundred-weight	1 00	18	70	1 00	80	25	....	40	22	20	20

REMARKS.—*J. L. Lea:* Cost of cultivating an acre of cotton, including team, feed, and tools, is about $8. Some was cultivated at $6. Average yield over half a bale of 500 pounds lint per acre. Cultivation of cotton has increased a little in ten years in excess of the amount of new clearing. *A. L. Pearson:* The original cost of fencing is about $2 50 per acre. The above estimate is on the basis of one-half bale of 500 pounds lint per acre and a selling price of 10½ cents per pound. The cultivation of cotton has increased in average and amount produced, owing to a vast increase of the number of white laborers entering the field.

477

NOTE

ON THE

COTTON PRODUCTION OF THE STATE OF KENTUCKY.

TABLE I.—AREA, POPULATION, AND COTTON PRODUCTION OF THE COTTON-PRODUCING COUNTIES OF KENTUCKY.

Cotton counties.	Land area.	POPULATION.						TILLED LAND.		COTTON PRODUCTION.					Cotton acreage per square mile.
		Total.	Male.	Female.	White.	Colored.	Average per square mile.	Acres.	Per cent. of area.	Acres.	Bales.	Product per acre.			
												Bale.	Seed-cotton.	Lint.	
	Sq. mile.												Lbs.	Lbs.	
Total for entire State...	40,080	1,648,690	833,590	815,100	1,377,179	271,511	41.2	8,387,910	22.7	....	....	....	....	....	....
Total for cotton counties.	13,910	655,557	329,349	326,208	546,575	108,982	47.1	3,036,894	34.1	2,697	1,367	0.51	729	243	0.2
CHIEF COTTON-PRODUCING COUNTIES.															
Calloway	450	13,295	6,617	6,678	12,080	1,215	29.5	75,450	26.2	318	165	0.52	744	248	0.7
Graves	590	24,138	12,359	11,779	21,287	2,851	40.9	143,037	37.9	869	417	0.48	684	228	1.5
Hickman	240	10,651	5,433	5,218	8,687	1,964	44.8	62,963	41.0	451	254	0.56	864	288	1.9
Fulton	200	7,977	4,076	3,901	6,371	1,606	39.9	43,584	34.0	549	300	0.55	780	260	2.7
Total	1,480	56,061	28,485	27,575	48,425	7,636	37.9	225,023	34.3	2,185	1,136	0.52	741	247	1.5
OTHER COTTON-PRODUCING COUNTIES.															
Allen	300	12,089	6,125	5,964	11,020	1,069	40.2	66,876	30.9	3	2	0.67	961	317	....
Ballard	430	14,378	7,824	6,554	12,653	1,725	34.2	95,300	35.5	31	15	0.48	690	230	0.1
Barren	500	22,321	11,295	11,026	17,380	4,941	44.6	140,420	43.9	16	7	0.44	694	208	....
Bell	190	6,055	3,073	2,982	5,874	181	31.9	24,480	20.1	2	1	0.50	714	238	....
Bracken	200	13,509	6,966	6,543	12,693	816	67.5	86,716	68.3	10	5	0.50	714	238	0.1
Butler	270	12,161	6,163	6,018	11,361	820	22.9	76,290	32.3	2	1	0.50	714	238	....
Christian	590	31,682	16,144	15,538	17,043	14,639	52.7	190,431	50.4	2	1	0.50	714	238	....
Crittenden	420	11,688	5,906	5,782	10,537	1,151	27.8	77,265	28.7	11	4	0.36	519	173	....
Daviess	450	27,730	14,230	13,500	22,876	4,854	61.6	154,698	53.7	8	9	1.13	1,602	534	....
Edmonson	280	7,222	3,637	3,585	6,667	555	25.8	42,965	24.5	8	4	0.50	714	238	....
Estill	300	9,860	4,989	4,871	9,349	511	25.6	35,765	18.6	3	2	0.35	387	119	....
Floyd	500	10,176	5,112	5,064	9,977	199	20.4	40,069	12.5	12	2	0.17	227	79	....
Green	300	11,871	5,966	5,885	9,463	2,408	39.6	70,585	36.9	2	1	0.50	714	238	....
Henderson	450	24,515	12,646	11,869	16,943	7,572	54.4	135,723	47.0	21	9	0.43	612	204	....
Jefferson	430	145,019	70,685	73,325	130,408	25,602	336.6	143,387	52.1	110	48	0.44	621	207	0.2
Laurel	620	9,131	4,595	4,536	8,864	267	14.7	48,140	12.1	2	1	0.33	474	158	....
Letcher	300	6,601	3,405	3,196	6,459	142	22.0	28,561	14.9	2	2	1.00	1,425	475	....
Livingston	280	9,165	4,672	4,493	8,130	1,035	22.7	69,465	36.8	2	1	0.50	714	238	....
Logan	590	24,358	12,262	12,096	16,977	7,381	41.3	178,967	46.1	22	11	0.50	714	238	....
McCracken	330	16,362	8,095	8,227	11,878	4,884	49.3	42,901	20.3	33	18	0.55	777	250	0.1
Magoffin	300	6,944	3,540	3,404	6,794	150	23.1	35,915	18.7	4	4	1.00	1,425	475	....
Marshall	350	9,647	4,870	4,777	9,207	440	27.6	59,306	26.5	23	10	0.43	621	207	0.1
Muhlenburgh	600	15,096	7,788	7,360	13,020	2,078	25.2	75,655	20.5	4	4	1.00	1,425	475	....
Pendleton	400	16,702	8,580	8,122	15,922	780	41.8	88,697	35.0	13	9	0.75	1,068	356	....
Pike	140	13,001	6,696	6,305	12,826	175	92.9	46,812	52.2	16	9	0.56	801	267	0.1
Pulaski	120	21,318	10,733	10,585	20,122	1,196	177.7	118,027	152.7	2	1	0.50	714	238	....
Simpson	400	10,641	5,356	5,285	7,844	2,797	26.6	74,880	29.2	5	3	0.60	855	285	....
Trigg	420	14,489	7,392	7,097	10,449	4,040	34.5	96,822	27.1	8	6	0.75	1,068	356	....
Trimble	150	7,171	3,727	3,444	6,594	577	47.8	33,112	34.8	30	15	0.50	714	238	0.1
Warren	550	27,531	13,783	13,748	19,892	7,639	50.1	164,023	46.6	31	19	0.62	459	153	0.1
Wayne	430	12,512	6,156	6,356	11,512	999	29.1	81,013	29.4	96	16	0.39	555	185	0.1
Whitley	500	12,060	6,019	5,961	11,752	248	21.4	51,296	14.8	1	1	1.00	1,425	475	....
Wolfe	190	6,698	3,896	3,512	5,563	75	20.7	30,810	25.1	2	1	0.50	714	238	....
Total	12,430	599,496	300,064	299,602	498,150	101,346	45.2	2,711,871	34.1	487	231	0.48	684	227	....

TABLE II.—ACREAGE AND PRODUCTION OF THE LEADING CROPS IN THE COTTON COUNTIES OF KENTUCKY.

Counties.	COTTON.		INDIAN CORN.		OATS.		WHEAT.		TOBACCO.	
	Acres.	Bales.	Acres.	Bushels.	Acres.	Bushels.	Acres.	Bushels.	Acres.	Pounds.
Total for entire State	2,087	1,307	3,621,176	72,852,263	403,416	4,580,736	1,160,106	11,556,113	226,100	171,120,784
Total for cotton counties	2,687	1,307	1,152,506	25,955,700	156,584	1,730,481	436,062	3,436,448	154,477	91,794,750
CHIEF COTTON-PRODUCING COUNTIES.										
Calloway	316	185	35,209	780,639	3,420	38,050	8,076	47,890	5,035	3,477,320
Graves	809	417	59,359	1,540,345	4,546	52,876	23,379	147,925	11,318	8,961,434
Hickman	451	254	28,306	784,826	889	12,857	14,296	107,006	658	481,946
Fulton	549	300	19,755	617,202	631	10,835	10,978	98,795	537	410,287
Total	2,185	1,196	142,631	3,723,114	9,466	110,618	56,729	396,616	17,548	13,351,237
OTHER COTTON-PRODUCING COUNTIES.										
Allen	3	2	31,578	401,279	6,309	56,821	10,505	46,648	283	160,255
Ballard	31	15	36,451	951,357	1,696	20,962	21,166	161,843	5,195	3,706,747
Barren	16	7	50,291	850,338	13,897	130,904	17,819	139,775	3,120	3,303,586
Bell	2	1	11,558	201,777	1,521	11,091	518	2,794	34	4,567
Bracken	10	5	21,023	562,550	705	9,715	13,435	178,979	7,159	6,126,635
Butler	2	1	34,579	651,593	7,271	88,543	5,860	32,813	1,652	1,020,029
Christian	2	1	60,724	1,430,154	4,961	64,341	40,347	437,698	16,475	12,577,574
Crittenden	11	4	27,706	848,900	3,608	37,022	7,395	48,221	2,988	1,947,936
Daviess	8	9	53,321	1,392,599	4,678	79,946	13,313	147,303	13,390	9,523,451
Edmonson	8	4	10,082	208,150	1,738	13,457	4,040	23,858	727	450,676
Estill	8	2	18,430	207,952	1,840	16,027	8,400	32,617	58	18,886
Floyd	12	3	21,351	429,286	2,501	15,072	2,750	18,356	73	12,845
Green	3	1	20,085	411,278	3,279	24,843	8,672	57,537	2,345	1,417,070
Henderson	21	9	55,038	1,680,007	1,781	27,589	9,832	124,391	12,468	10,312,451
Jefferson	110	48	38,757	1,056,209	8,056	114,793	15,825	186,212	26	11,532
Laurel	3	1	17,962	278,074	2,933	26,378	4,550	22,528	68	23,302
Letcher	3	2	11,175	215,547	1,141	8,904	1,640	10,622	23	2,907
Livingston	2	1	29,981	740,746	2,469	23,072	7,296	63,465	1,127	769,574
Logan	22	11	54,988	1,181,600	8,932	130,639	36,898	340,362	8,104	6,059,983
McCracken	38	18	20,543	483,776	3,856	30,677	8,614	64,549	3,377	2,419,985
Magoffin	4	4	13,751	267,726	3,004	20,843	3,166	14,861	73	11,484
Marshall	23	10	28,379	602,913	3,410	33,014	9,766	47,755	3,065	1,411,662
Muhlenburgh	4	4	33,798	652,279	7,814	100,340	9,688	65,874	3,856	2,731,716
Pendleton	12	9	28,813	792,695	1,536	20,694	14,740	181,845	5,302	4,072,291
Pike	16	9	26,505	543,463	3,402	24,186	3,052	18,207	100	18,048
Pulaski	3	1	42,955	612,388	31,186	76,150	16,287	80,636	106	50,516
Simpson	5	3	20,778	579,055	6,122	88,700	18,287	117,010	2,340	1,068,055
Trigg	8	6	32,919	796,954	1,219	14,879	9,789	94,516	8,481	5,987,143
Trimble	30	15	13,135	281,183	2,199	22,599	5,505	60,427	2,070	1,654,307
Warren	31	10	47,177	1,495,419	14,448	204,000	31,173	150,750	3,565	2,605,588
Wayne	36	14	37,774	465,994	3,235	24,137	10,945	56,574	50	20,364
Whitley	1	1	24,802	300,429	3,001	30,417	4,472	17,984	19	3,496
Wolfe	3	1	12,756	261,896	2,745	18,518	2,514	16,985	50	29,820
Total	482	231	1,028,875	22,223,586	147,186	1,619,863	862,350	3,038,822	106,929	78,548,513

COTTON PRODUCTION IN KENTUCKY.

Excepting a narrow strip of country in the western part of the state contiguous to Tennessee, Kentucky is hardly entitled to notice as a cotton-producing region. Tobacco takes the place of cotton, and is a leading crop, and even the area excepted might be claimed as naturally a part of Tennessee. This area lies between the Mississippi and the Tennessee rivers, in Fulton and the southern parts of Hickman, Graves, and Calloway counties, in an offset made at the expense of the sister state of Tennessee by the abrupt dropping southward between the rivers of the line separating the two states. Indeed, if, after reaching the Tennessee river in its course from the east, the boundary-line had continued directly on to the Mississippi, the cotton-producing strip would be a part of Tennessee and the latter state would have no notch in its northwestern corner to mar its symmetry. An inspection of the acreage map will show how this is. The relative importance of the fraction referred to as an area contributing to the total cotton product of Kentucky in 1879 is strikingly brought out when it is stated that of the total for the state, 1,367 bales, 1,136 were raised within this area, leaving only 231 to be accounted for. This strip indeed is the extreme northern limit of the cotton region in the eastern part of the Mississippi valley, the whole state of Kentucky, excepting this small fraction, being thrown into the penumbral region of cotton culture.

The entire area in Kentucky between the Mississippi and the Tennessee rivers, containing about 2,500 square miles, with an elevation above the sea of 280 feet along the river bottoms and 350 to 450 feet on the uplands, is based on strata of sands, calcareo-silice us and loamy earths, with limited beds of clay and gravel, all but little consolidated, and belonging to geological formations (the uplands Quaternary and the lowlands "Recent") of comparatively modern age. These strata may be called "soft rocks", the Tennessee river being their eastern limit. Beyond this very different strata abruptly set in, "hard rocks" of solid limestone and other kinds, members chiefly of the far older sub-Carboniferous division of geologists.

The area in Kentucky between the rivers is but the northern end of a great belt of country, famous for its mellow, rich lands and as a cotton-producing region, that lies immediately east of the Mississippi river, mainly in the states of Mississippi and Tennessee. The belt begins on the west with the alluvial bottoms of the Mississippi (1 on the agricultural map). Proceeding eastward, and crossing the bottoms at any point, we are suddenly confronted with a bold, steep escarpment, or the "bluff", which, like a wall, reaches from southern Mississippi, through Tennessee, far into Kentucky. The bluff is touched by the Mississippi river at but few points: in Tennessee, at Memphis, Randolph, and Fulton; in Kentucky, at Hickman and Columbus. Ascending to the top of the bluff, 100 to 200 feet or more above the bottoms, we find ourselves upon a plateau country (2–6 on the agricultural map) which extends eastward for a long distance. This plateau country is the greater part of the belt. Its surface in Tennessee is divided longitudinally into three long sections or smaller belts: one on the west, with the bluff as its western limit; another to the east, rising up into a dividing summit between the waters of the Mississippi and the Tennessee rivers; and a third intermediate and wider one. These sections extend into Kentucky with their characteristic strata and soils, the western and middle (2 and 3 on the map) the more extensively. The western section is from 10 to 30 miles wide. Its soils are based upon a remarkable bed of very fine siliceous earth, containing more or less calcareous matter, and called, in the language of geologists, loess. There is much of this formation in Fulton, Hickman, Ballard, and other counties in the part of Kentucky west of the Tennessee river. The middle section or sub-belt has in Tennessee brown, loamy, mellow soils, based on sandy strata, fertile and important, which also occur in Kentucky. These, with the soils of the loess, spread over the region between the rivers, and together make the warm lands—of easy tillage, highly productive of tobacco, and enticing cotton culture, in spite of climate—within their area. The loess of this region is thus spoken of by D. D. Owen in one of his first reports on the geology of Kentucky:

The most conspicuous and frequently occurring beds of the Quaternary is a very fine calcareo-siliceous earth of pale reddish-gray or ashen-flesh tint. This imparts character to the soil where the Quaternary formations exist more frequently than any of the other beds, and it gives rise to some of the best tobacco land. Its usual constituents may be seen from the following chemical analysis of a specimen taken from the great cut of the Mobile and Ohio Railroad near Columbus, in Hickman county:

	Per cent
Combined moisture	1.35
Organic matter soluble in water	0.30
Insoluble silicates	73.30
Carbonic acid	10.00
Lime	6.80
Magnesia	3.78
Alumina and peroxide of iron	2.80
Chlorine	0.12
Loss, and alkalies not determined	1.55
	100.00

Analysis of the insoluble silicates.

	Per cent
Silica	60.6
Alumina	7.4
Lime	1.1
Magnesia	0.4
Loss, alkalies and trace of iron not estimated	3.8
	73.3

Its calcareous matter is derived, in a great measure, from the land and fresh-water shells, often abundantly disseminated through it, sometimes in a good state of preservation, but oftener in a very soft and tender condition, so that they crumble to pieces as soon as touched. Calcareous concretions are not unfrequently disseminated through this earth in considerable abundance, formed by the percolation of water charged with carbonic acid, which, dissolving the calcareous matter in the upper part of the deposit, carries it by filtration to the lower part of the bed, redepositing it in the form of hard masses, which not unfrequently envelop the same shells in a very perfect condition. This is also the most superficial bed of the Quaternary deposits, as it is generally reached immediately after passing through the subsoil. It has a thickness of from 30 to 40 feet, and rests generally in southwestern Kentucky on gravel chiefly composed of brown hornstone and chert, derived from the sub-Carboniferous strata.

The reader, desiring further information as to loess soils, is referred to the report on Mississippi, in which there is a discussion of them by Professor Hilgard.

The alluvial belt of the Mississippi river supplies fine areas of tillable lands, in some parts of which, in Fulton county especially, cotton is cultivated to a greater or less extent. Such are the lands of Madrid Bend and the "front-lands", extending for miles along the river from the town of Hickman to the Tennessee line. Cotton, however, is chiefly raised upon the uplands.

Table I gives the population and the cotton production of the counties designated as cotton-producing, and in which, substantially, the cotton reported as the yield of the state in 1879 was raised. Their total product is 1,136 bales of 475 pounds each. The yield per acre is high—0.52 per cent. of a 475-pound bale, or 741 pounds of seed-cotton. The increase in total products over that of 1869 is, after making the proper reduction, 67½ per cent. The negroes form about 14 per cent. of the total population.

Of the other counties in the Quaternary region, Ballard produced, in 1879, 15 bales; McCracken, 18; and Marshall, 10; making for the entire region 1,179 bales, and leaving only 188 bales for the remainder of the state.

In the counties east of the Tennessee river the cotton patches of 1879 were scattered in a remarkable manner over its area, as may be seen on the acreage map. Some of them occupy anomalous positions. One occurs in Bracken county and two in Trimble county, in the northern part of the state, and not far from Cincinnati. Jefferson reports a product of no less than 48 bales. Thirty-one counties east of the Tennessee produced varying amounts, none reporting less than a bale being included.

With such a scanty product of cotton as we have in this part of Kentucky, any discussion of the soils with reference to cotton-growing would not be pertinent, and could have no practical bearing. It is especially in relation to tobacco-growing that such discussions would be in place.

INDEX TO COTTON PRODUCTION IN TENNESSEE AND KENTUCKY.

REPORT

ON

COTTON PRODUCTION IN THE STATE OF MISSOURI,

WITH A BRIEF DESCRIPTION OF

THE AGRICULTURAL FEATURES OF THE STATE IN GENERAL, AND ESPECIALLY
OF THE COTTON-PRODUCING COUNTIES.

BY

R. H. LOUGHRIDGE, Ph. D.,
SPECIAL AGENT.

1
493

TABLE OF CONTENTS.

LETTERS OF TRANSMITTAL.

BERKELEY, CALIFORNIA, *June* 1, 1883.

To the SUPERINTENDENT OF CENSUS.

DEAR SIR: I transmit herewith a report on cotton production in the state of Missouri, with a description of the agricultural features of the cotton-growing counties of the state, by Dr. R. H. Loughridge.

The information on the latter subject, having been derived entirely from correspondence and the somewhat scattered data contained in published reports, is not as full as could be desired, or as it has been possible to make it in other cotton-growing states. The obvious fact that, in order to compete with the cotton belt proper, the culture of the staple in Missouri is being more and more confined to the early and highly-productive bottom lands of the southeastern extremity, renders the minor details of less importance in this case, the cotton-producing area being altogether similar in its surface features to the northeastern corner of Arkansas.

Very respectfully,

E. W. HILGARD,
Special Agent in charge of Cotton Production.

BERKELEY, CALIFORNIA, *May* 1, 1883.

Professor E. W. HILGARD,
Special Agent in charge of Cotton Production.

DEAR SIR: I have the honor to submit herewith my report on cotton production in the state of Missouri. The acreage of cotton within the state is limited to so small an area that it was not thought necessary to give more than a very brief description of the agricultural and physical features of the state, and for the same reasons the county descriptions are limited to the few on the south which produce more than 100 bales each. I have followed in this report the plan proposed by you and followed in other state reports, viz, placing the subject-matter in the following divisions, preceded by the tabulated enumeration results for the cotton-producing counties:

Part I. General (though brief) description of the physical features of the state and of each agricultural region.

Part II. Descriptions of the chief cotton-producing counties, accompanied by abstracts from such answers to question schedules as have been received from correspondents.

Part III. Cultural details of cotton production, as embraced in the answers to the schedules.

I have been compelled to depend entirely upon the *Hand-book of Missouri*, issued by the state board of immigration in 1880, the published reports of the state geological survey (especially that of 1873-'74), and the state agricultural report of 1878, as well as upon the answered question schedules mentioned above, for the data contained in this report, and regret that more detailed descriptions could not be given.

Very respectfully,

R. H. LOUGHRIDGE.

TABULATED RESULTS OF THE ENUMERATION.

TABLE I.—AREA, POPULATION, TILLED LAND, AND COTTON PRODUCTION.
TABLE II.—ACREAGE AND PRODUCTION OF LEADING CROPS.

TABLE I.—AREA, POPULATION, TILLED LAND, AND COTTON PRODUCTION.

COUNTIES HAVING 100 ACRES AND OVER IN COTTON.

Counties.	Area.	POPULATION.						TILLED LAND.		COTTON PRODUCTION.							
		Total.	Male.	Female.	White.	Color'd	Average per square mile.	Acres.	Per cent. of area.	Per cent. of tilled lands.	Acres.	Bales. 500 lbs.	Fraction of bale.	Seed-cotton.	Lint.	Acres per square mile.	Bales per square mile.
	Sq. mls.													Lbs.	Lbs.		
The State	68,735	2,168,380	1,127,167	1,041,193	2,022,826	145,554	31.5	13,266,756	30.0	0.2	33,116	20,518	0.62	945	315	0.5	0.3
Cotton counties	8,240	94,499	49,942	44,557	89,140	5,350	11.5	467,358	8.9	6.8	31,947	20,226	0.63	945	315	3.9	2.5
ALLUVIAL REGION.																	
Pemiscot	480	4,299	2,300	1,999	4,031	268	9.0	19,810	6.4	19.1	3,787	2,848	0.75	1,135	375	7.9	5.9
Dunklin	500	9,604	5,162	4,442	9,440	164	19.2	42,648	13.3	26.0	11,100	7,361	0.66	990	330	22.2	14.7
New Madrid	620	7,694	4,145	3,549	5,813	1,881	12.4	49,326	12.4	5.1	2,518	1,649	0.65	975	325	4.1	2.7
Mississippi	430	9,270	5,130	4,140	7,116	2,154	21.6	63,092	22.9	0.3	213	182	0.62	930	310	0.5	0.3
Scott	440	8,587	4,631	3,956	8,036	551	19.5	57,103	20.3	0.5	294	165	0.56	840	280	0.7	0.4
Stoddard	850	13,431	6,923	6,508	13,396	35	15.8	61,516	11.3	9.1	5,676	3,202	0.57	855	285	6.7	3.8
Butler	580	6,011	3,221	2,790	5,871	140	10.4	20,475	5.5	2.2	446	235	0.53	795	265	0.8	0.4
Total	3,900	58,896	31,512	27,384	53,703	5,193	15.1	313,962	12.6	7.6	23,933	15,502	0.65	975	325	6.1	4.0
UPLAND COUNTIES.																	
Ripley	620	5,377	2,803	2,574	5,367	10	8.7	23,181	5.8	3.7	866	471	0.54	810	270	1.4	0.8
Oregon	740	5,791	2,995	2,796	5,773	18	7.8	27,672	5.8	6.7	1,848	1,126	0.61	915	305	2.5	1.5
Howell	920	8,814	4,495	4,319	8,723	91	9.6	40,065	6.6	4.5	1,800	1,075	0.60	900	300	2.0	1.2
Ozark	740	5,618	2,919	2,699	5,604	14	7.6	18,588	3.9	8.1	1,500	800	0.53	795	265	2.0	1.0
Taney	800	5,599	2,897	2,702	5,594	5	7.0	34,584	4.8	5.3	1,300	760	0.58	870	290	1.6	0.9
Stone	520	4,404	2,321	2,083	4,376	28	8.5	20,396	6.0	2.5	700	400	0.57	855	285	1.3	0.7
Total	4,340	35,603	18,430	17,173	35,437	166	8.2	163,376	5.5	5.2	8,014	4,634	0.58	870	300	1.8	1.1

COUNTIES HAVING LESS THAN 100 ACRES IN COTTON.

Counties.	Acres.	Bales.	Counties.	Acres.	Bales.	Counties.	Acres.	Bales.
Barry	4	2	Douglas	12	5	Reynolds	1	1
Dollinger	29	20	Hickory	9	5	Washington	10	6
Carter	2	1	Laclede	46	20	Wayne	19	13
Cedar	2	2	Miller	5	2	Wright	8	5
Christian	5	2	Osage	10	5			
Dallas	4	2	Perry	2	1	Total	169	92

COTTON PRODUCTION IN MISSOURI.

TABLE II.—ACREAGE AND PRODUCTION OF LEADING CROPS.

COUNTIES HAVING 100 ACRES AND OVER IN COTTON.

Counties.	COTTON.		INDIAN CORN.		WHEAT.		OATS.	
	Acres.	Bales.	Acres.	Bushels.	Acres.	Bushels.	Acres.	Bushels.
The State	33,116	20,318	5,588,305	202,414,413	2,074,394	34,906,627	966,473	20,670,956
Cotton counties	31,947	20,226	256,301	7,875,327	63,726	663,386	20,541	280,213
ALLUVIAL REGION.								
Pemiscot	3,797	2,848	11,896	406,999	208	3,029	80	1,013
Dunklin	11,106	7,361	20,121	608,909	2,905	24,160	1,066	19,689
New Madrid	2,878	1,649	37,462	1,116,696	4,226	49,273	691	11,345
Mississippi	212	122	42,296	1,506,055	8,276	110,448	1,190	24,420
Scott	394	165	34,453	721,366	14,227	209,876	1,119	19,639
Stoddard	5,076	3,202	28,815	917,604	11,875	97,611	3,196	26,734
Butler	445	235	11,825	281,770	1,604	10,925	1,696	23,283
Total	23,933	15,592	176,911	7,557,489	45,421	496,013	8,916	148,898
UPLAND COUNTIES.								
Ripley	886	471	26,140	317,140	1,745	12,190	1,709	14,984
Oregon	848	1,128	12,749	338,539	2,053	16,296	1,115	13,027
Howell	1,800	1,075	21,486	576,332	5,441	87,067	3,846	46,229
Ozark	1,500	800	10,445	296,572	2,133	17,908	1,547	19,919
Taney	1,800	760	11,627	294,602	3,196	19,943	1,729	29,678
Stone	700	400	9,943	254,663	3,737	38,284	978	14,492
Total	8,014	4,634	79,390	2,017,848	18,305	197,973	10,925	140,220

PART I.

PHYSICAL AND AGRICULTURAL DESCRIPTION

OF THE

COTTON-PRODUCING REGION

OF

MISSOURI.

OUTLINE OF THE PHYSICAL GEOGRAPHY

STATE OF MISSOURI.

The state of Missouri covers an area of about 69,415 square miles, of which 68,735 is land surface. This is divided into 114 counties with areas varying from 280 to 1,145 square miles. The state is bordered on the east by the Mississippi river, while the Missouri river, entering at the northwest corner, flows in an irregular course southeastward to the former, and is the chief recipient of the waters of the state. The Osage river on the west, one of the largest tributaries of the Missouri, flows eastward and unites with it near the center of the state. On the extreme south, Saint Francis and White rivers and tributaries carry off into Arkansas the waters from an area of about 12,000 square miles, the Ozark mountains forming the water divide between this basin and that of the Missouri. The state is naturally divided into two separate and distinct physical divisions, viz, open prairies and timbered lands. The former embrace all that part of the state lying north of the Missouri river, excepting the timbered belts along the Missouri, the Mississippi, and other streams; also that part lying west of a line from Jefferson City, the capital, to Stone county, on the Arkansas line, though this is interspersed with much timber. The remainder of the state, or that part on the southeast, comprises the timbered division, having a heavy growth of oaks, hickory, and, on the south, short-leaf pine, each variety irregularly distributed.

The general character of the country north of the Missouri is that of a broad, undulating plain, rising northwestward from 428 feet to an elevation of about 1,200 feet above the sea. It is somewhat hilly and broken midway across the northern part of the state, and bluffs also occur along the largest streams. The most of this territory, as well as that between the Missouri and the Osage rivers on the west, is an open prairie, interrupted now and then with timbered lands. On the south of the Missouri and the Osage rivers the country is more hilly and broken, the Ozark range of mountains forming a water divide between the tributaries of the Missouri and those of the White river. This range is thus described:

From the state of Kansas this important range enters Missouri in Barton county and traverses the state in a course slightly north of east, reaching the Mississippi river in Perry county opposite Grand Tower. In Kansas this ridge divides, and the northern branch passes into Missouri in Cass county, and soon disappears near the headwaters of La Mine river. From Barton county on the west, for nearly three-fourths of the distance across the state, the Ozarks widen out into broad, arable plateaus, and are best described as a series of high table-lands, possessing none of the essential characteristics of a range of mountains. The highest point in this part of the state is at Marshfield, Webster county, where an elevation of 1,475 feet above the sea is reached. Advancing eastwardly the ridges become more narrow, irregular, and precipitous, and abound in isolated hills and knobs, the highest of which, Pilot Knob, Iron county, is 1,490 feet. South of the Ozark divide, from Springfield, Greene county, on the west, to about Marble Hill, Bollinger county, on the east, extending to the Arkansas line, the country presents a series of alternating ridges and valleys. Below Cape Girardeau the alluvial bottom lands become very extensive and embrace several counties on or near the Mississippi, with the lowest elevation in New Madrid county, about 250 feet above the sea-level.

This region south of the Osage and the Missouri rivers is very generally well timbered.

CLIMATE.—A long series of observations taken at Saint Louis shows the average yearly temperature of that part of the state to be about 55°. The mean winter temperature is 33°, varying from 26° in the coldest to 40° in the mildest winters. The temperature occasionally falls to 20° and 24° below zero. The mean summer temperature is 76°, varying from 72° in the coldest to 80° in the warmest summers. An extreme of 100° to 104° has sometimes occurred. The average annual rainfall in Saint Louis is about 41 inches, varying in different years from 25 to 55 inches. The chief rainfall and also the greatest number of thunder-storms occur between the last of April and the first of July.

The south and southeast winds are the prevailing ones, especially in the warmer seasons; in winter they are as often west and northwest winds. These winds are usually brisk, but rarely very high; but occasionally tornadoes are formed and devastate narrow strips of country, invariably taking a southwest to northeast course.

The climate of southern Missouri is a dry one. In the spring heavy rains fall, and in the latter part of that season the state is visited by continuous showers, known to farmers as "the long season in May". In June summer showers fall, but not in excess, seldom lasting longer than a few hours. The average rainfall in southern Missouri is 41 inches; in the southeast larger; in the northwest less. The rains come generally from the southwest. The amount of fair weather is very large, and, while a few of the summer days are excessively hot, an electrical disturbance generally occurs, and a thunder-storm and a copious shower bring a refreshing change of temperature. Killing frosts occur, on an average, on the 10th of October, and late frosts on the 7th of April.—*Agr. Report.*

Snow rarely falls, and then to an average depth of 2½ inches, and disappears in a day or two. The winters are short and pleasant.

TIMBER GROWTH.—Most of northern Missouri and of the western counties consists of prairie. The prairies, during the spring and summer seasons, are covered with a natural and luxuriant growth of many different species of grasses and other plants, many of them having beautiful flowers. These counties have generally belts of timber extending along the streams, affording a sufficient supply for fuel and other neighborhood uses. The Missouri bottoms are generally heavily timbered with cottonwood, hickory, walnut, hackberry, and bur and red oaks. The counties along the Missouri, from the Platte eastward, often have heavy bodies of fine timber; but, until Howard county is reached, these are interspersed with occasional extensive bottom prairies. Howard and the counties eastward have timbered belts of from 10 to 20 miles wide, extending parallel to the Missouri river, which include the finest varieties of hard-wood timber, such as ash, oak, walnut, sugar-tree, hackberry, hickory, elm, etc. A similar belt, from 15 to 20 miles wide, lies parallel to the Mississippi, while along the Osage are heavy bodies of excellent timber. All the counties to the south contain large tracts of good timber, chiefly oak. Yellow poplar and sweet gum are common in the counties south of Madison. The swamps abound in cypress, oak, catalpa, tupelo gum, walnut, and sycamore.

In southern Missouri open prairies are rare, except on the extreme southwest; but in their stead are occasional tracts of barrens, or hilly districts covered with tall grass, on which are scattering, stunted oaks, including black-jack and post oaks and black hickory.

UPLAND AGRICULTURAL REGIONS.

The geological survey of the state has recognized and described (a) the following upland agricultural regions in addition to the bottom lands:

First class.—Black calcareous prairies of the northwest.
Second class.—Sandy prairies and timbered lands.
Third class.—Gravelly and red-clay prairies.
Fourth class.—Timbered magnesian-limestone lands and barrens.

BLACK CALCAREOUS PRAIRIES.

These, the richest uplands of the state, lie in northwestern Missouri, and consist mostly of prairie, and are underlaid by the Upper Coal Measures, with the Middle Measures beneath and appearing along its southeast and eastern margin. A line entering the state from the northwest, in the northwestern part of Vernon county, passing north and east through the western part of Bates, thence eastwardly through the southern part of Cass, northeastwardly to the central part of Johnson county, eastwardly through La Fayette and Saline, thence northwardly to Chariton in the direction of Salisbury, and a little west of north to the northern boundary of the state in Mercer county, will include, on the west, the richest farming land in Missouri. There are, of course, occasional tracts of inferior land included within these limits, but the soil is generally of uncommon fertility. The soil is generally based on a deep bluff deposit or on limestone, and is, for the most part, calcareous. It is generally at least a foot thick and quite black, yielding good crops of corn, grass, pumpkins, squashes, potatoes, turnips, etc. The yield of corn will average from 50 to 75 bushels per acre with ordinary cultivation, and lands that have been in cultivation thirty years yield as abundantly as when first cultivated. Blue-grass grows well when the prairies have been grazed down. This is probably no better for wheat than the lands in eastern Missouri; in fact, during similar seasons, the yield is not always as large per acre, but fine crops of wheat are often raised, frequently 25 bushels per acre, the general yield being from 15 to 25 bushels. Apples and some small fruits succeed very well, and occasionally there is a good crop of peaches. There seems to be no better soil for the gooseberry, and the cultivated grape becomes of a large size, but the vines grow too luxuriantly.

SANDY PRAIRIES AND TIMBERED LANDS.

This region lies just east and south of the first named. Its southern and eastern boundary passes through Barton into the western part of Cedar, thence through Saint Clair, Benton, the northwest part of Morgan, through Cooper, the southern part of Boone and Callaway, and eastward, parallel to and within 10 miles of the Missouri river, to a point opposite the central part of Saint Louis county. This district may also include extensive areas of the other counties lying southward along the Mississippi river.

a *Geol. Surv. Mo.* 1873–'74, page 42.

586

There are several well-marked varieties among the soils of this district. That in the western and northern portions consists chiefly of prairie, often spreading out, in·north Missouri, into flat prairies. That in the southwest is a rolling country, with generally a sandy soil. The yield is usually from 30 to 50 bushels of corn per acre. The timbered lands in eastern Missouri and in the counties along the Missouri river produce very fine crops of wheat, sometimes yielding over 25 bushels per acre.

GRAVELLY AND RED-CLAY PRAIRIES.

This class occurs chiefly in southwest Missouri, becoming a narrow belt to the northeast, barely dividing the second from the fourth. It may include part of McDonald, Barry, Lawrence, Christian, Greene, Polk, Dade, Jasper, Barton, Cedar, Hickory, Saint Clair, Benton, Morgan, Cole, Moniteau, Osage, Gasconade, Franklin, Saint Louis, and Jefferson counties, and a band passing southwardly. Some of the lands in Jasper, Lawrence, and Greene are as good as those of the second class. The soil is generally somewhat gravelly and often mingled with red clay. Good crops of wheat and corn and fine crops of fruit are produced, especially in those counties along the Missouri river, whose hills yield fine peach and grape crops every year.

TIMBERED MAGNESIAN-LIMESTONE LANDS AND BARRENS, OR UPLAND COTTON REGION.

This class includes the main body of southern Missouri, excepting the swamp counties of the southeast and the other counties above named. It constitutes an extensive tract elevated higher than other parts of the state (plateau lands of the Ozark range), it being from 1,200 to 1,500 feet above the sea. It is underlaid by the primordial sandstones and magnesian limestones, with an occasional elevation or peak of porphyry or granite in the eastern part. The country is broken by stream channels cutting down from 200 to 300 feet below the tops of the bluffs, with valleys often as much as 400 feet below the main distant ridges. Near the streams it is generally very rugged, with either abrupt or long, steep ascent to the hills. When the main streams are wide apart the country spreads back into a flat land with light-colored soil, supporting chiefly a growth of post oak; when a little more hilly, black oak and black hickory are common. With more soil there is often a fine growth of white oak mingled with sassafras, dogwood, etc. South of the main Ozark ridge, where the hills are either covered with sandstones or chert fragments, we find but little soil, and often a heavy growth of pine. On the slopes from the magnesian limestones are often seen fine cedar groves. There are extensive tracts within this district where the soil is either too thin or too rocky to admit of present cultivation; but all these lands will grow the grape. Corn yields from 20 to 35 bushels per acre, and wheat from 15 to 20 bushels. The valleys along the streams near the south line produce fine crops of corn and cotton.

The extreme southern part of this region is the upland cotton region of the state, and, together with the alluvial region of the Mississippi river, is that which is of greatest interest in this report. It occupies the southern slope of the Ozark water-shed, whose width varies from about 40 miles on the west to more than 75 miles on the east. The streams, therefore, that flow southward have as yet attained no great width, and while the greater number are tributary to White river of Arkansas, those on the east of Saint Francis river, including that stream, enter the Mississippi alluvial region.

In its general features the surface of the country is very similar to the adjoining portions of Arkansas. On the east and west the upland surface is made hilly and broken by the numerous streams that find their way southward; and narrow gravelly and rocky ridges with a black-jack-oak growth are a feature of the country. The same is partly true of the southern parts of the central counties of Howell and Oregon, while the northern portions of all the counties have more of the character of broad table-lands, from 200 to 500 feet above the larger streams, their surfaces undulating and largely timbered with forests of short-leaf pine and other growth. On the extreme west the country opens out into the more level red-clay prairies of the third class of lands already mentioned. The lands of these uplands may be classed in three groups: 1. Pine lands of the table lands, already mentioned, resting upon sandstone, and timbered with a growth of short-leaf pine, post, white, and red oaks, hickory, and sassafras. The soil is a sandy loam, best adapted to grain crops, though not much in cultivation. 2. Black-jack lands upon the narrow and rocky ridges; these have a stunted growth of black-jack and post oaks. 3. White and post oak lands derived chiefly from the magnesian limestone; they occupy the valleys and gradually sloping hillsides, and are dark in color, light and warm in character, with red-clay subsoils. They are well timbered with oaks, hickory, and other growth, and are the principal farming lands of the region. Cotton is grown only on these valley lands, and, in spite of the disadvantages of the high latitude and consequent short seasons, yields an average of about 900 pounds of seed-cotton per acre. That this high average is not due to the experimental culture of the crop is shown by the fact that the upland county having the highest cotton acreage (Oregon, 1,848 acres) has also the highest product per acre—915 pounds of seed-cotton; the two counties next in acreage being also next in product per acre.

Small open prairies occur in the southern part of Howell county, the soil of which is a black, tenacious clay, impervious, and needing drainage to insure fertility.

10 COTTON PRODUCTION IN MISSOURI.

MISSISSIPPI ALLUVIAL REGION.

The most prominent as well as most important region of southeast Missouri is the broad alluvial plain that reaches in length from the Arkansas line to Cape Girardeau, and in width from the Mississippi river westward beyond the Saint Francis river, a distance of from 50 to 75 miles or more. It covers an area of about 3,500 square miles, and is the northern portion of the great alluvial region that borders the Mississippi river southward to Helena and thence to the Gulf. In this state it includes all of the counties of Pemiscot, Dunklin, New Madrid, Mississippi, Scott, Stoddard, and a large part of Butler. The surface is undulating and interspersed with low sandy ridges and flat and open prairies, and on the south and east with bayous and lakes. A portion of the lands is said to be liable to overflow. The prairies are silty in character, and seem to be similar to those of the Crowley's Ridge region of Arkansas and still southward in Louisiana. The ridges are from 10 to 15 feet above the swamp, and are continuations of Crowley's ridge of Arkansas; they vary in width, sometimes being 2 or 3 miles wide. The principal ridge is that on which Charleston is situated, and which extends for 90 miles through Dunklin and Stoddard counties.

In Stoddard county there are said to be numerous island-like tracts or so-called "hills", having circumferences varying from 10 to 25 miles. Hillocks and solitary hills covering several hundred acres also rise abruptly to a height of 100 or 200 feet above the swamps.

The region is traversed by the Saint Francis, the Castor, the Whitewater, the Black, the Little Black, and other smaller rivers and many creeks, all of which are said to have ample fall, when not obstructed by decayed timber and rafts, to carry away the water rapidly, except in a few very low portions of the country, which can be easily drained.

The soil is a black loam, rich in decayed vegetation, easily tilled, and capable of yielding, under cultivation, fine crops of cotton, corn, potatoes, and small grain. The region is, however, sparsely settled, and but 12.5 per cent. of its lands are in cultivation.

The following subdivisions have been thus described by Professor G. C. Swallow, of the agricultural college of Missouri, in the *Agricultural Report* for 1878:

The bottom has several natural divisions, well recognized by the people of the country, and designated as *high bottoms, low bottoms* or *swamp*, and *cypress*.

High bottoms have a deep, porous, and rich sandy soil, which produces a gigantic growth of elm, sugar maple, white ash, cherry, locust, linden, sweet gum, buckeye, bur, red, Spanish, swamp, and scarlet oaks, thick shellbark hickory, hackberry, pecan, black walnut, plum, catalpa, and mulberry. Grape-vines, trumpet and Virginia creepers, poison oak, and wistarea climb the highest trees and mingle their scarlet and purple flowers and fruits with their highest foliage.

Low bottoms have a soil similar to the high bottoms, but they are so low as to be covered by water at ordinary overflow. Sycamore, cottonwood, white maple, box-elder, red birch, buckeye, hackberry, willow, river and frost grapes, and poison ivy are the most common vegetation. The overflows render these lands useless for farming purposes, but when the floods are kept out by levees they are most productive and valuable.

Swamp or *wet bottoms* are terms usually applied to a variety of bottom lands very similar to the two preceding, but differing in being so located as to be saturated with or nearly covered by water. They sustain a heavy growth of pin, swamp, and red oak, holly, spice bush, white and black ash, red birch, box-elder, button bush, sycamore, cottonwood, wahoo, elm, sweet gum, water locust, white and red maple, poison oak, frost and river grapes. The name "*cypress*" is given to low bottoms which are covered with standing water for a large part of the year. The decomposition of vegetable matter in these waters adds a new deposit of vegetable mold annually to their rich soil, which sustains a very heavy growth of cypress, tupelo, sour gum, water locust, white and red maple, pin and Spanish oaks. These cypresses are numerous and very extensive in southeast Missouri. Buffalo cypress and honey cypress are good examples. The central and wettest portions of them usually have deposits of bog ore. These soils are useless for ordinary farming purposes, but their timber is unique, abundant, and most valuable.

The ridge lands within this region have sandy soils with clay subsoils and a timber growth of oaks and hickory, and are said to be very productive under tillage. The same ridge lands (or Crowley's ridge) in Arkansas yield about 800 pounds of seed-cotton per acre.

The prairies are quite level, and with their excellent grasses afford fine pasturage for stock.

REMARKS ON COTTON PRODUCTION IN MISSOURI.

As a cotton-producing state Missouri may be classed with Kentucky and Virginia, which have been styled "penumbral", from the scattered and isolated areas in which that crop is planted.

The maximum of production thus far reached was in the years preceding the late civil war, the crop of 1859, according to the Eighth Census, being 41,188 bales. Various causes have contributed to very greatly reduce this production, and we find that cotton is not so prominent a crop now as then. Among these causes may be mentioned the disturbed condition of the state during the war, the demoralization of the negroes (almost the only cotton-field laborers) consequent upon freedom, the intensity of cotton production in the southern states, and the low market prices which made other products far more profitable. The area over which cotton cultivation is extended embraces a far less territory now than in 1859, for in that year cotton was planted in a few counties as far north as the Iowa state line, while in 1879 the Missouri river formed its northern limit.

The census of 1870 showed a very great falling off in the production—from 41,188 bales in 1859 to 1,270 bales in 1869—though its territory still extended to the northern boundary-line of the state (in Scotland and Harrison counties, 7 bales). In that year cotton was reported in thirty-three counties, seven of which are north of the Missouri river. The greatest production was naturally on the southeast, Stoddard county reporting 487 bales, and the entire alluvial region 948 bales. Twenty-four counties produced less than 10 bales each, two from 10 to 50, four from 50 to 100, and three counties above 100 bales each.

In 1879, as shown by the Tenth Census, the yield again increased to 20,318 bales, though the area of production was greatly lessened and embraced twenty-nine counties, all of which are south of the Missouri river. Of these but thirteen, along the Arkansas line, can properly be called cotton counties, as the others have a production of less than 25 bales each (thirteen less than 10 bales each), and form simply an outlying region. A few are entirely separated from the cotton region, and cotton is planted either as an experiment or for domestic uses alone.

The cotton region proper embraces portions of two agricultural regions of the state, viz, the Mississippi alluvial lands and the uplands of the magnesian-limestone region, and the former, naturally the richest, not only gives the greatest yield per acre, 975 pounds of seed-cotton, but has the greatest acreage in cotton, 23,933 acres. The uplands, or rather the valley lands of the upland counties, give remarkably high averages in products per acre (from 795 to 915 pounds of seed-cotton) for so high a latitude, where the seasons are necessarily short; and these counties excel the greater number of those of other states more favored in this regard.

The high products of seed-cotton per acre in both the alluvial lands and the valley lands of the uplands has placed Missouri at the head of all of the cotton states in general average of product per acre.

The cotton-growing region embraces the following counties: Pemiscot, Dunklin, New Madrid, Mississippi, Scott, Stoddard, Butler, Ripley, Oregon, Howell, Ozark, Taney, and Stone. The counties that border this region report a small cotton acreage, but not sufficient to entitle them to be called cotton counties. Dunklin stands at the head of the list of counties with regard to cotton acreage and production, Stoddard and Pemiscot following; but Pemiscot ranks first in product per acre, its average being 1,125 pounds of seed-cotton. Of the upland counties, Oregon is first both in production and in average product per acre.

PART II.

AGRICULTURAL DESCRIPTIONS

OF THE

COTTON-PRODUCING COUNTIES

OF

MISSOURI.

AGRICULTURAL DESCRIPTIONS

OF THE

COTTON COUNTIES OF MISSOURI.

The cotton counties of the state are embraced within two agricultural divisions, and they are here grouped under these heads and arranged as nearly geographically as possible. When a county embraces within its area portions of each of the regions its description will be found under that to which it predominantly belongs, while its name only will appear in the proper place in the other region. In the list of counties at the head of each division an asterisk (*) placed after a county shows that its description will be found in the other region.

Abstracts from answered schedules from correspondents will be found appended to their respective counties. They are made to embrace only matter descriptive of the qualities of the lands and the character of the country. Those parts referring to cultural details will be found in Part III of this report.

The statistics at the head of each county are made up from reports in the Census Office, and are the results of the work of the Tenth Census.

Those counties whose total yield for 1879 was less than 100 bales each are not included in these descriptions.

MISSISSIPPI ALLUVIAL REGION.

(Includes the counties of Pemiscot, Dunklin, New Madrid, Mississippi, Scott, Stoddard, and Butler.)

PEMISCOT.

Population: 4,299.—White, 4,031; colored, 268.

Area: 480 square miles.—Woodland, all.

Tilled lands: 19,810 acres.—Area planted in cotton, 3,787 acres; in corn, 11,936 acres; in wheat, 208 acres; in oats, 80 acres.

Cotton production: 2,848 bales; average cotton product per acre, 0.75 bale, 1,125 pounds seed-cotton, or 375 pounds cotton lint.

Pemiscot, the extreme southeastern county of the state, and in what is known as the "Panhandle", has a level surface, bordered on the east by the Mississippi river, and is entirely included in the alluvial plain of that stream. Portions of the county are subject to overflow; lakes and bayous occur extensively, but the greater part of the country is said to be easily drained to the Saint Francis and reclaimed from its present swampy character, the fall being 6 inches per mile from east to west, and 7 inches from north to south. The lands are heavily timbered with black, red, overcup, and willow oaks, cypress, ash, walnut, cottonwood, persimmon, elm, sycamore, black and sweet gums, black and honey locusts, maple, hickory, hackberry, mulberry, pecan, and catalpa, with an undergrowth of dogwood, spicewood, ironwood, etc.

The soils are those characteristic of the Mississippi alluvial region, and embrace the yellowish or reddish silty loams along the front-lands of the river and dark or black loams farther back, both very rich and productive when in cultivation.

The county is sparsely settled, and has 41.3 acres of land under cultivation per square mile. Corn, wheat, and cotton are the chief crops. As a cotton county it ranks third in total acreage, though second in the number of acres (7.9) per square mile, and also second in the percentage of tilled lands in cotton, viz, 19.1 per cent.

The lands, with fair cultivation and good seasons, are capable of yielding as much as 1¼ bales of lint per acre, though a 500-pound bale of lint, or 1,500 pounds of seed-cotton, is said to be the usual yield, above the average for the county for 1879.

ABSTRACT OF THE REPORT OF ROBERT G. FRANKLIN, OF BRAGGADOCIO.

All of this county is a rich sandy deposit from former overflows of the Mississippi river and Pemiscot bayou. The uplands are level table-lands, some above the overflow along the waters of the bayous and some in places along the river.

The chief crops of the region are corn, all the grasses, wheat, oats, potatoes, and cotton. The soils cultivated in cotton are the sandy loam, lying along the borders of bayous and lakes, and the black buckshot. There are also some hard, stiff spots too difficult to cultivate. The most important land is the cottonwood bottoms above overflow, comprising about three-fourths of the area of the county, and extending from the foot of the hills in Scott county to the Arkansas line, taking in Mississippi, New Madrid, Pemiscot, Dunklin, and a part of Scott counties.

The timber growth is black walnut, hickory, elm, cottonwood, sycamore, oak, ash, mulberry, and sassafras. The soil varies, but is mostly a black sandy loam, from 3 to 10 feet deep, and is underlaid by sand and gravel. The soil is easy to till if the weather is not wet, and is variable as regards warmth and drainage. It is apparently best adapted to corn, cotton, wheat, and grasses; three-fourths of the crops are in cotton. The plant is usually 3½ feet high, sometimes 10 feet, inclining to run to weed on new land or during wet weather; shallow tillage and early topping restrain it. The seed-cotton product from fresh land is from 600 to 1,000 pounds; 1,520 pounds make a 475-pound bale of lint which does not rate well. After four years the product per acre is less on account of the land becoming richer. Sometimes 1,615 pounds make a 475-pound bale of lint which rates better than that from fresh land, for the older the land the better the staple. Crab-grass, cockleburs, wild cucumbers, and morning-glories are the most troublesome weeds. None of this land lies turned out except for want of labor; it has to be grown in corn a while to wear it a little.

An early, dry, and warm spring is best for cotton culture here. Twenty years ago cotton was never planted before the 1st to the 10th of May, but we now plant from the 1st of April to the 10th of May. Sometimes it happens that the Mississippi river overflows, and if the water goes off by the 1st or 10th of May a fair crop is expected. On the black buckshot land it is hard to get a stand of cotton, but a large yield of from 1,500 to 2,100 pounds of seed-cotton per acre is certain if a stand is obtained.

Cotton is shipped, as fast as it is ginned, by river to Memphis, Saint Louis, or New Orleans, at from 75 cents to $1 per bale.

DUNKLIN.

Population : 9,604.—White, 9,440; colored, 164.
Area : 500 square miles.—Woodland, nearly all.
Tilled lands : 42,648 acres.—Area planted in cotton, 11,100 acres; in corn, 20,121 acres; in wheat, 2,905 acres; in oats, 1,066 acres.
Cotton production : 7,361 bales; average cotton product per acre, 0.66 bale, 990 pounds seed-cotton, or 330 pounds cotton lint.

Dunklin, one of the Panhandle counties of the southeastern part of the state, is bordered on the west by the Saint Francis river. A large proportion of the county is included in the alluvial region of that river, and is well timbered with ash, walnut, oak, hickory, etc. These lands have mostly a dark loam soil, capable of yielding a bale of cotton per acre when properly cultivated. In the eastern part of the county there is a narrow belt of open upland with sandy soils and a growth of oak and hickory. Open prairies occur on the southwest, Grand Prairie, in which the village of Cotton Plant is situated, being the most important. On the northwest Crowley's ridge passes northward from Chalk bluff into Stoddard county; it has the sandy lands and poplar growth, with oak and hickory, that characterize it in Arkansas.

Dunklin county has an average of 85.3 acres of lands in cultivation per square mile. The crops comprise corn, wheat, cotton, etc. It is the chief cotton county of the state, the average being 22.2 acres and 14.7 bales per square mile; 26 per cent. of its tilled lands is devoted to cotton culture.

ABSTRACT OF THE REPORT OF E. J. LANGDON, OF COTTON PLANT.

The lowlands of the county are the bottoms of the Saint Francis and Little rivers, Buffalo creek, and Honey Cypress, Kinemore Seneca, and Ragland sloughs, and are generally called sunken or overflowed lands. They were caused by the earthquakes of 1811, and are too low to be available for cultivation without a general system of drainage by clearing out the bogs and sand-bars in the old channels of the rivers and creeks.

The uplands are mostly timbered, level table-lands and some prairie lying in large tracts between the above-named rivers and creeks, varying in width from 1 mile to 4 miles, with a uniform soil. Although these lands are above the overflow, in wet seasons they are sometimes covered with water and it is late before the lowest upland can be planted. A general system of drainage would be very beneficial; it has been tried, locally, with success.

Sand-blows on our uplands were caused by the earthquake of 1811 forcing water and sand up through the subsoil to the surface. Some of them can be plowed through and the surface soil turned up; others are deeper, and in order to be reclaimed must be scraped off upon the surrounding soil. These sand-blows are very scarce on new lands; on others, as many as ten to fifteen per acre.

The chief crops of the county are corn and cotton; sweet and Irish potatoes, oats, and wheat are also raised. The most important cotton land is that with dark prairie soil, uniform in timber and prairie land; it comprises all of the area of the region excepting small patches of clay soil in low places, and the sandy soil of the sand-blows. This land extends south into Arkansas, west to Saint Francis river, north into Stoddard county, and east nearly to the Mississippi river, with the exception of changing to a lighter color in some parts after going north 6 miles. The timber growth is sassafras, black walnut, cottonwood, hackberry, black, red, overcup, and white oaks, dogwood, hickory, mulberry, pecan, and a large amount of sweet gum.

The soil is a fine sandy loam, with some clay, brown and black, and alternating or mixed in color, with a depth of 22 inches. The subsoil is a heavy, yellow, brittle clay, occasionally mixed with sand, and is leachy when undisturbed; it mixes easily with the surface soil. The soil is easy to till in wet or dry seasons, is early, warm when well drained, and is best adapted to corn and sweet potatoes; cotton comes next after these. One-third of the cultivated land is in cotton; the plant grows from 3½ to 6 feet high, and is most productive at from 4 to 5 feet. On all new or highly-manured land the plant inclines to run to weed; topping in August does very little good toward restraining the plant; it is preferable to plant on medium soil. From 600 to 1,200 pounds, according to the season, is the seed-cotton product per acre from fresh land; 1,580 pounds make a 475-pound bale of low to middling lint. After five years' cultivation the product is from 1,200 to 2,000 pounds, according to the season, and 1,580 pounds make a 475-pound bale of lint, generally one grade better because a large portion of the crop is well matured. Crab-grass is the most troublesome weed. None of this land lies turned out now; but after the land has been cultivated, say twenty years, two years' rest will increase the crop one-fourth.

The growing and maturing seasons for cotton are too short in this latitude. On new or very rich land, in wet seasons, it grows too large, keeps green, and early frost overtakes it with very few bolls open or matured. We prefer to plant on land that has been in cultivation from five to ten years. The production of cotton has increased fully one-third in the last ten years; this is mostly due to emigration and increase in acreage.

Cotton is shipped throughout the season, by water and by rail, mostly to Saint Louis, at $2 25 for hauling and $2 for freight per bale

This county is specially adapted to cotton-raising. Frosts seldom come early enough to injure the crop, and we have been remarkably exempt from the boll-worm and other injurious insects. Close investigation will show that we can successfully compete, in the cultivation of this staple, with any part of the south. The soil, for the most part, is a sandy loam, most of the clay land being found on the islands formed by the Saint Francis and its tributaries. But comparatively little of the county is in cultivation. The yield is good, the average being three-quarters of a bale per acre, and, when picked early and handled well, classes as good middling. Since I commenced business here in 1865 the staple has gradually improved, and there is no doubt that the introduction of improved machinery and closer cultivation would increase both quality and quantity of staple. The system of cultivation employed is rude, and vast improvements can and will undoubtedly be made in this direction.

NEW MADRID.

Population: 7,694.—White, 5,813; colored, 1,881.
Area: 620 square miles.—Woodland, nearly all.
Tilled lands: 49,338 acres.—Area planted in cotton, 2,518 acres; in corn, 37,463 acres; in wheat, 4,326 acres; in oats, 691 acres.
Cotton production: 1,649 bales; average cotton product per acre, 0.65 bale, 975 pounds seed-cotton, or 325 pounds cotton lint.

The surface of New Madrid county is quite level, with but a gentle slope southward, and is diversified with broad alluvial lands along the Mississippi river, and timbered uplands interspersed with small and open prairies in the northern and central parts of the county. The soil of the Mississippi alluvial region is a dark loam, from 1 foot to 5 feet deep, and heavily timbered with a large variety of growth. These soils are very highly productive, and yield, with cultivation, over three-fifths of a bale of cotton per acre. They extend westward from the Mississippi to the sunk lands of Little river, which are subject to overflow. A large region of the northeastern part of the county also suffers from yearly inundation. The prairies that occur in the rest of the county seem to be quite similar in character to those of the Crowley Ridge region of Arkansas, of which these uplands are but a continuation. Their soils are light or silty in character, overlie an impervious clay, and are easily tilled. The timbered uplands have sandy soils with clay subsoils, and are generally preferred to the prairies as farming lands.

Of tilled lands there are 79.6 acres per square mile. Corn and cotton and small grain are the chief crops. Cotton has an average of 4.1 acres and 2.7 bales per square mile, the county ranking as fourth in the state. Its comparatively high yield per acre is attributable to the large proportion of alluvial lands, which can produce as much as a bale per acre. The yield of the uplands is from 600 to 800 pounds per acre.

MISSISSIPPI.

Population: 9,270.—White, 7,116; colored, 2,154.
Area: 430 square miles.—Woodland, nearly all.
Tilled lands: 63,092 acres.—Area planted in cotton, 213 acres; in corn, 42,298 acres; in wheat, 8,276 acres; in oats, 1,130 acres.
Cotton production: 132 bales; average cotton product per acre, 0.62 bale, 930 pounds seed-cotton, or 310 pounds cotton lint.

The surface of Mississippi county is very level; it is bordered on the east by Mississippi river, and is nearly all included within the alluvial lands of that stream. Three small open prairies occur in the county, Mathews, Long, and East prairies, each with an area of from 4 to 6 square miles, and occasionally interspersed with small groves of timber.

The soil of the county is mostly a dark alluvial loam, several feet in depth and heavily timbered. Cottonwood, walnut, locust, white, red, black, overcup, and post oaks, maple, mulberry, sweet and black gums, persimmon, dogwood, and papaw. Along the water-courses cypress is very abundant. The lands are very productive, yielding, it is said, from 40 to 130 bushels of corn, 20 to 40 of oats, 20 to 55 of wheat, 200 to 500 of potatoes, and from 1,200 to 1,500 pounds of seed-cotton per acre. Fruits also do well.

The average of lands under cultivation is 146.7 per square mile, the highest average in the region. Cotton has an average of but half an acre per square mile.

SCOTT.

Population: 8,587.—White, 8 036; colored, 551.
Area: 440 square miles.—Woodland, all.
Tilled lands: 57,103 acres.—Area planted in cotton, 294 acres; in corn, 24,453 acres; in wheat, 10,227 acres; in oats, 1,119 acres.
Cotton production: 165 bales; average cotton product per acre, 0.56 bale, 840 pounds seed-cotton, or 280 pounds cotton lint.

Scott county is bordered on the east by the Mississippi river and on the west by Little river. The northern part of the county is hilly, and broken by a spur of the Ozark Mountain range; its soil is a clayey loam, well adapted to wheat. The eastern portions south of the hills, and the western portion along Little river, are rich, wide, and productive river bottoms, embracing black alluvial loam soils of the Mississippi River region.

The southern and central parts of the county have sandy loam soils, easily cultivated, well timbered, and very productive, yielding about 1,000 pounds of seed-cotton per acre.

The average of tilled lands is 129.8 acres per square mile. The crops embrace corn, small grain, potatoes, and cotton. The acreage of the latter is, however, very small, averaging six-tenths of an acre per square mile.

ABSTRACT OF THE REPORT OF B. DICKERSON, OF BLODGETT.

This county is nearly square and about 30 miles each way. The northern part is hilly and well adapted to grain, grass, and fruit. The western part is watered by Little river, and has swamp and rich black alluvial soil. The eastern portion has the black loamy lands of the Mississippi river, excellent land for grain and grass. In the southern and central part of the county is the cotton region. This region seems to have been produced by some great convulsion of nature; it is unique, being surrounded on all sides by an entirely different soil.

The chief crops of the region are wheat, corn, oats, barley, cotton, clover, hay, watermelons, and peas. The land is low and level, and the soil cultivated in cotton is sandy, from whitish to blackish in color. It comprises about three-fourths of the area of the region, extending 20 miles one way and 15 miles the other, with a timber growth of sumac, hickory, ash, hazel, papaw, oak, and dogwood.

The soil is a fine and coarse sandy loam, from 4 to 10 inches deep, sometimes 2 feet, with a heavy, coarse, yellow sandy subsoil sometimes mixed with clay. The soil is easy to till in wet or dry seasons, is early, warm, and generally well drained, and well adapted to all of the crops of the county. One-twentieth of the tilled lands is devoted to the culture of cotton, which usually grows from 3 to 6 feet in height, but is most productive at from 3 to 4 feet, inclining to run to weed during very wet weather, and is restrained by topping. From 1,000 to 1,500 pounds is the seed-cotton product from fresh land; 1,900 pounds make a 475-pound bale of low middling lint. After five years' cultivation the product is not reduced more than one-fourth, and the same amount is necessary for a 475-pound bale of lint, which is somewhat shorter and not so white as that from fresh land. Burs, rag-weed, nettle, and grass are the troublesome weeds. Very little of this land lies turned out, but it produces well when again cultivated. The slopes wash, but not seriously.

The great warmth of the land causes cotton to mature much sooner than it otherwise would. This county is north of the cotton region proper, some 2 degrees at least.

Cotton is shipped, as soon as it is ginned, by railroad to Saint Louis at $1 per bale.

STODDARD.

Population: 13,431.—White, 13,396; colored, 35.
Area: 850 square miles.—Woodland, nearly all.
Tilled lands: 61,516 acres.—Area planted in cotton, 5,576 acres; in corn, 28,815 acres; in wheat, 11,875 acres; in oats, 3,135 acres.
Cotton production: 3,302 bales; average cotton product per acre, 0.57 bale, 855 pounds seed-cotton, or 285 pounds cotton lint.

Stoddard county lies between two streams, Whitewater on the east and Saint Francis on the west, along whose borders are broad and heavily-timbered bottom lands. The surface of the rest of the county is rolling or hilly and somewhat broken, and is a continuation of Crowley's ridge of Arkansas. The soil of this ridge is a sandy loam over clayey subsoils, and is well timbered. It is said to be best adapted to wheat and other grain. The bottom lands with their dark loam soils are highly productive, yielding an average of from 1,200 to 1,500 pounds of seed-cotton with fair seasons and good cultivation. The average for all the lands of the county, 855 pounds of seed-cotton, is quite high. The timber growth of these lands comprises oak, hickory, gum, maple, ash, and cypress, some walnut, elm, catalpa, etc.

The county has an average of nearly sixteen persons per square mile, and of tilled lands an average of 72.4 acres per square mile. In total cotton acreage the county ranks as second in the state, but in the average of that crop per square mile, 6.7 acres, it ranks third, or below Dunklin and Pemiscot.

ABSTRACT OF THE REPORT OF JAMES P. WALKER, OF DEXTER CITY.

The lowlands of the county are the first bottoms of the Castor river, comprising alluvial plain, front-land, and cypress swamp. The uplands are hilly and rolling, with prairies in the southern part of the county. The hill land is very productive. Corn, cotton, and wheat are the chief crops of the region. The soils cultivated in cotton are the black sandy loam and the clay.

The most important soil is the swamp land, comprising two-thirds of the county area, extending for a distance of 100 miles with a width of 12 miles. The natural timber growth is all kinds of oaks, sweet gum, ash, and walnut. The soil is a fine sandy clay loam, mostly black colored, with a depth of 2 feet. The subsoil is heavier than the soil. The soil is very easy to till in all seasons, is early and ill drained, and well adapted to all of the crops of the region. About one-fourth of the crops is of cotton, which usually grows 4 feet high and is most productive at that height. Wet weather inclines the plant to run to weed; topping restrains it. One thousand eight hundred pounds is the seed-cotton product per acre both from fresh land and land that has been cultivated ten years; 1,600 pounds make a 475-pound bale of good middling lint. Cockleburs are the most troublesome weeds. None of this land lies turned out.

The hill land comprises one-third of the area of the county, extending for 100 miles with a width of 6 miles, and having a timber growth of oak, hickory, ash, and poplar. The soil is a blackish, heavy clay loam, 6 inches deep, with a heavier clay hard-pan subsoil containing pebbles, and underlaid by sand and gravel. The soil is easy to till, is early, warm, well drained, and best adapted to cotton, wheat, and tobacco. One-fourth of the crops is of cotton; the usual and most productive height of the plant is 3 feet. When the land is very fresh the plant runs to weed. It is best to raise corn for two years and then plant cotton. The seed-cotton product from fresh land is 1,200 pounds; about 1,660 pounds make a 475-pound bale of good middling lint. Ten years' cultivation only reduces the seed-cotton product to 1,100 pounds, and the amount necessary for a bale, and the rating is the same as that from fresh land. Crab-grass is the most troublesome weed. None of this land to amount to anything lies turned out. It washes readily on the slopes, but not seriously; neither are the valleys injured by the washings. No efforts have been made to check the washings. Early frost occasionally injures the cotton crop.

Cotton is shipped as soon as it is ready, by the Iron Mountain railroad, to Saint Louis, at $2 50 per bale.

BUTLER.

Population: 6,011.—White, 5,871; colored, 140.
Area: 580 square miles.—Woodland, all.
Tilled lands: 20,475 acres.—Area planted in cotton, 445 acres; in corn, 11,825 acres; in wheat, 1,604 acres; in oats, 1,695 acres.
Cotton production: 235 bales; average cotton product per acre, 0.53 bale, 795 pounds seed-cotton, or 265 pounds cotton lint.

The surface of Butler county is hilly and broken, and is well watered by numerous streams flowing nearly due south, and tributary to Black and White rivers. Saint Francis river forms the eastern boundary of the county, but is turned eastward by Crowley's ridge. The county is well timbered with a large variety of growth. The streams are bordered by bottom lands, embracing a first bottom, or low cypress swamp, and a second bottom, or bench, with very productive loam soils. The timber growth is poplar, walnut, maple, ash, gum, etc. The uplands comprise the flatwoods, or barrens, and hills of the magnesian-limestone region, which covers nearly all of southern Missouri. The barrens are usually timbered with a scrub growth of oaks and hickory, the hills, when sandy, often having a predominance of short-leaf pine, accompanied by a heavy growth of oaks.

The county is comparatively sparsely settled, with an average of about ten persons per square mile. The average of tilled lands is 35.3 acres per square mile. The crops are corn, wheat, and cotton, the acreage of the latter being very small—its average eight-tenths of an acre per square mile. The average yield is about 800 pounds of seed-cotton per acre.

UPLAND COTTON COUNTIES.

(Includes the cotton counties of Butler,* Ripley, Oregon, Howell, Ozark, Taney, and Stone, besides border counties not described.

BUTLER.

(See "Mississippi alluvial region".)

RIPLEY.

Population: 5,377.—White, 5,367; colored, 10.
Area: 620 square miles.—Woodland, all.
Tilled lands: 23,181 acres.—Area planted in cotton, 866 acres; in corn, 13,140 acres; in wheat, 1,745 acres; in oats, 1,700 acres.
Cotton production: 471 bales; average cotton product per acre, 0.54 bale, 810 pounds seed-cotton, or 270 pounds cotton lint.

The surface of Ripley county is partly gently undulating, and in part rough, hilly, and rocky, especially along and near the large streams, and is well timbered with red, post, and other oaks and a variety of other growth. It is well watered by the Current river and other streams, all flowing south and tributary to the White river of Arkansas.

The lands of the uplands are derived from the sandstones and magnesian limestones of the region, and are therefore varied in character, presenting sandy or clayey soils, some suitable chiefly for grazing purposes, and others well adapted for cultivation, producing good crops of grain, though best for fruit-growing and especially for grapes. The bottom lands are rather narrow, but have very productive soils, and are the lands chiefly cultivated. They are the cotton lands of the county, yielding an average in good seasons of nearly 1,000 pounds of seed-cotton per acre. The county is sparsely populated, with an average of not quite nine persons per square mile. The lands under cultivation comprise 5.8 per cent. of the area, and average 37.4 acres per square mile. The cotton crop averages but 1.4 acres per square mile.

OREGON.

Population: 5,791. White, 5,773; colored, 18.
Area: 740 square miles.—Woodland, all.
Tilled lands: 27,672 acres.—Area planted in cotton, 1,848 acres; in corn, 12,749 acres; in wheat, 2,053 acres; in oats, 1,118 acres.
Cotton production: 1,128 bales; average cotton product per acre, 0.61 bale, 915 pounds seed-cotton, or 305 pounds cotton lint.

The surface of Oregon county is rolling and hilly, well timbered, and well watered by the Eleven Points river and other smaller tributaries of the White river. The lands of the county are derived from the sandstones and magnesian limestones of the region, and have soils varying from sandy to clayey in character. The northern and northeastern part is a high and rolling plateau, principally covered with pine forests. In the southern and southwestern part the greater portion of the land is arable and fitted for cultivation, the timber consisting mostly of hickory and oak, and the soil being a rich sandy loam. South of the Eleven Points river there is a vast amount of valley and uplands or hickory flats, all of which is good farming land and easily cultivated.

The county is sparsely populated with an average of about eight persons per square mile. The lands under cultivation comprise 5.8 per cent. of the area, and average 37.4 acres per square mile. The cotton crop of 1879 had an average of 2.5 acres per square mile.

HOWELL.

Population: 8,814.—White, 8,723; colored, 91.
Area: 920 square miles.—Woodland, nearly all.
Tilled lands: 40,065 acres.—Area planted in cotton, 1,800 acres; in corn, 21,486 acres; in wheat, 5,441 acres; in oats, 3,840 acres.
Cotton production: 1,075 bales; average cotton product per acre, 0.60 bale, 900 pounds seed-cotton, or 300 pounds cotton lint.

The surface of Howell county is rolling, and along the streams broken, and is embraced in the region of sandstones and magnesian limestones; small prairies occur in the southern portion of the county. The hills are irregular in their direction and cannot be said to lie in ranges; their elevation is gradual from the valleys at their base to their summits. Irregular valleys, some of which have streams of water, lie among the hills; others are dry, though containing springs whose waters run a few rods away and disappear in the subterraneous passages. The soil of the county is varied, and might properly be classified as follows:

1. *Pine lands* with a sandy loam, which occupy the most broken part of the county on the north and northwest, underlaid by the sandstone of the magnesian-limestone series. These lands produce well in wheat, corn, rye, and tame grasses. The timber is pine, post, white, and red oaks, black hickory, with sassafras and summer grapes.

2. *White and post oak soil* covers a large territory. Its character is dark, warm, and light, and in the valleys it is very productive; on the slopes it is lighter in quality and not so productive for the heavier crops. The subsoil of these lands is often richer than the surface, and consists of dark red clay. Some of the lands are covered with flint and conglomerate, and in many places where these occur the soil is the most productive.

3. *Black-jack soil* is generally the poorest of all; it covers the narrow and rocky ridges, and has a stunted growth of black-jack and post oaks. The soil is dark in color, thin and cold, and is underlaid with pale yellow or slate-colored clay.

4. The soil of the *black prairies* in the southern part of the county is black, tenacious, and rich, but lacks drainage to produce well. The lowlands are said to be gradually closing in with a thrifty growth of black elm, hickory, ash, water oak, walnut, sycamore, and hazel. The valley lands are the most productive in the county, and in these the cotton is produced.

The average population is 9.6 persons; tilled lands, 43.5 acres per square mile. Cotton has an average of 2 acres per square mile.

OZARK.

Population: 5,618.—White, 5,604; colored, 14.
Area: 740 square miles.—Woodland, nearly all.
Tilled lands: 18,538 acres.—Area planted in cotton, 1,500 acres; in corn, 10,445 acres; in wheat, 2,133 acres; in oats, 1,547 acres.
Cotton production: 800 bales; average cotton product per acre, 0.60 bale, 900 pounds seed-cotton, or 300 pounds cotton lint.

The surface of Ozark county is hilly, with large areas of gently rolling country. The dividing ridges between the larger streams have a general elevation of from 150 to 200 feet, though some rise as high as 500 feet. The county is well watered by many streams which are tributary to the White river on the south in Arkansas.

The county is included in the region of magnesian-limestone lands and barrens, the sandstones and limestones of which give variety to its lands and general features. In some localities where the surface rock is sandstone or one of the limestone series (third), the lands are too rough and rocky and the soil too thin and light to be well fitted for cultivation.

The surface of the county is well timbered, mostly with a growth of white, red, post, and black-jack oaks, and in the northern and northeastern parts with short-leaf pine. The lands under cultivation are confined chiefly to the bottoms along the streams, though these are generally very narrow, averaging not more than 300 or 400 yards, and sometimes half a mile. These lands are very productive and are timbered with water oak, walnut, cypress, elm, etc.

The average population of the county is 7.6 persons, and the average of tilled lands 25 acres per square mile. The cotton crop averages only 2 acres per square mile.

TANEY.

Population: 5,599.—White, 5,594; colored, 5.
Area: 800 square miles.—Woodland, nearly all.
Tilled lands: 24,384 acres.—Area planted in cotton, 1,300 acres; in corn, 11,627 acres; in wheat, 3,196 acres; in oats, 1,729 acres.
Cotton production: 760 bales; average cotton product per acre, 0.58 bale, 870 pounds seed-cotton, or 290 pounds cotton lint.

The surface of Taney county is broken and hilly, with small valley lands, and is well watered by White river and its tributaries. The lands are well timbered and varied in character, and are derived from the sandstones and magnesian limestones that occur throughout the county. The former rock usually caps the hills and table-lands, producing a rough and broken surface, with sandy soils best adapted to fruit and grape culture, though to some extent planted in cereals and tobacco. The valley lands, with their excellent loamy soils, are those chiefly in cultivation, producing wheat, corn, cotton, and oats.

The county is sparsely populated, with an average of seven persons per square mile. The lands under cultivation comprise but 4.8 per cent. of the county area, and average 30.5 acres per square mile. This is one of the chief upland cotton counties of the state, though that crop only averages 1.6 acres per square mile, or 5.3 per cent. of the tilled lands. The comparatively high product per acre indicates that it is grown only in the better class of valley lands.

STONE.

Population: 4,404.—White, 4,376; colored, 28.
Area: 520 square miles.—Woodland, all.
Tilled lands: 20,036 acres.—Area planted in cotton, 700 acres; in corn, 9,943 acres; in wheat, 3,737 acres; in oats, 976 acres.
Cotton production: 400 bales; average cotton product per acre, 0.57 bale, 855 pounds seed-cotton, or 285 pounds cotton lint.

The surface of Stone county is hilly and broken, timbered throughout, and watered by White river and James fork, and tributaries. The lands of the uplands are rocky and but little under cultivation, and are now covered with wild grape-vines. The soil of the extreme northern part is said to be light and ashy, but underlaid at a few inches by a red loam, which in other portions of the county is the prevailing soil. On the south the soil is dark, the red loam appearing only at a depth of 30 or 40 feet, and short-leaf pine becomes a prominent growth. It is said that there are no prairie lands in the county, though in the northern part there are level or gently-undulating stretches of land that seem as if they might have been prairies at some former period, but are now covered with a growth of scrub oak, black-jack, and dwarf hickory. The crops of the county are corn, wheat, rye, oats, and some hay. Corn averages from 30 to 40 bushels per acre, wheat and rye about 15 bushels each, and oats about 30 bushels. Some cotton is also produced, the acreage being small, averaging 1.3 acres per square mile.

The country is sparsely populated, with an average of 8.5 persons per square mile, and has an average of 38.5 acres of tilled lands per square mile.

PART III.

CULTURAL AND ECONOMIC DETAILS

OF

COTTON PRODUCTION.

REFERENCE TABLE

OF

REPORTS RECEIVED FROM MISSOURI COUNTIES.

ALL OF THE MISSISSIPPI ALLUVIAL REGION.

Dunklin.—E. J. LANGDON, Cotton Plant, December 21, 1880; W. F. SHELTON, Kennett, November 26, 1880.
Pemiscot.—ROBERT G. FRANKLIN, Braggadocio, July 22, 1881.
Scott.—B. DICKERSON, Blodgett, July 26, 1881.
Stoddard.—JAS. P. WALKER, Dexter City, December 29, 1880.

24

522

ANSWERS TO SCHEDULE QUESTIONS.

The following answers are taken from schedules of questions on cotton culture sent to parties in the cotton counties. The alluvial region only has been heard from, and therefore these answers refer only to that part of the state.

TILLAGE, IMPROVEMENT, ETC.

1. Usual depth of tillage (measured on land side of furrow).

Stoddard county reports 3 inches. *Pemiscot:* 4 inches. *Scott:* From 5 to 7 inches. *Dunklin:* 6 inches.

2. What draft is employed in breaking up? Is subsoiling practiced?

Stoddard: One horse. *Dunklin:* One or two horses, according to the size of the plow. *Scott:* Usually two horses; sometimes one. *Pemiscot:* One or two horses or mules. Subsoiling is not practiced in any of these counties.

3. Is fall plowing practiced? With what results?

Scott: Yes, with fine results. *Stoddard:* Only when sowing wheat. *Pemiscot:* Not for cotton, although it is supposed to prevent the cut-worm from attacking the young plants in the spring. *Dunklin:* No; but it would be beneficial on stubble land.

4. Is fallowing practiced? Is the land tilled while lying fallow, or only turned out? With what results in either case?

Scott: Not to any extent; the land is only turned out. *Dunklin:* It is not practiced. In some years owners of large plantations fail to rent all of their land; it is then customary to leave the oldest and least productive portion idle. The effect on future crops is good, but it would be much better if the vegetation were plowed under before the frost appears. *Pemiscot* and *Stoddard:* No.

5. Is rotation of crops practiced? If so, of how many years' course, and in what order of crops? With what results?

Stoddard: Yes; with corn, sweet potatoes, oats, and wheat; results are good. *Scott:* With corn, wheat, oats, clover, and pease; there is no regular system, but the practice is attended with good results. *Dunklin:* Very little; with corn, oats, and wheat; no regular order of crops. *Pemiscot:* Rotation of crops is not practiced; cotton has been planted on the same land for many years; there is some land on which corn has been planted for forty years, which will now produce 35 bushels to the acre.

6. What fertilizers, or other direct means of improving the soil, are used by you, or in your region? With what results? Is green-manuring practiced? With what results?

Dunklin: Very few farmers use any fertilizers; I use cotton-seed, barn-yard manure, and, on very old land, occasionally some ashes; the results are good. All, or nearly all, the attention that has been paid to keeping up the land has been by using stalk-cutters on both corn and cotton fields, and then plowing in; the land improves under such treatment. *Stoddard:* A little cotton-seed is used, with good results. *Pemiscot:* No fertilizers are used. Green-manuring is practiced in *Scott* county, with clover, grass, pease to some extent, weeds, stubble, etc.

7. How is cotton-seed disposed of? If sold, on what terms, or at what price? Is cottonseed-cake used for feed or manure?

Dunklin: Cotton-seed is used mostly as feed for cattle; to some extent as fuel for gins running by steam-power; and the surplus, if any, is used as a fertilizer on old land. If not put on too thick it has a good effect on the crops for three or four years; but if used too freely it causes the ensuing crop to "fire". It is not salable in this district, as there are no shipping facilities. *Stoddard:* It is mostly shipped to Saint Louis, at $6 50 per ton; a little is used as feed. *Pemiscot:* Partly fed to stock and partly sold to the oil-mills at $9 per ton. Cottonseed-cake is not used in any of the counties.

PLANTING AND CULTIVATION OF COTTON.

8. What preparation is usually given to cotton land before bedding up?

Dunklin: Spring plowing is practiced by some planters; others bed directly by turning the old bed to the center. *Scott* and *Stoddard:* Sometimes spring plowing, but generally no preparation is given. *Pemiscot:* The old stalks are removed.

9. Do you plant in ridges? How far apart?

Planting in ridges is the practice in all of the counties. *Dunklin:* From 3 to 4 feet; prefers 4. *Stoddard:* Three and a half feet. *Scott:* From 3½ to 4 feet. *Pemiscot:* Four feet.

10. What is your usual planting time?

Pemiscot: From April 1 to May 10. *Dunklin:* From April 10 to May 1. *Stoddard:* From April 15 to May 1. *Scott:* Early in May.

11. What variety do you prefer?

Pemiscot: White seed. *Stoddard:* Green seed. *Dunklin:* Matagorda. *Scott:* Petit Gulf, or green seed.

12. How much seed is used per acre?

Dunklin: 1½ to 2 bushels. *Stoddard* and *Pemiscot:* 3 bushels. *Scott:* 3 to 4 bushels.

13. What implements do you use in planting? Are "cotton-seed planters" used in your region? What opinion is held of their efficacy or convenience?

Dunklin: The keg "cotton-seed planter", which gives perfect satisfaction, is the only one used. It consists of a perforated keg set in a frame so that it will revolve and allow the seed to drop out. Attached to the frame, in front, is a cultivator, toothed or crooked stick to open with; and, at the back, a board to cover with. *Stoddard:* "Cotton-seed planters" are used, but hand planting is considered the better. *Pemiscot:* Hand planting is mostly practiced; a few use the "cotton-seed planters", but they do not give satisfaction. *Scott:* A small plow and coverer. The "planters" are used, but the opinion held of them is not favorable.

14. How long usually before your seed comes up?

Dunklin: Five to seven days. *Pemiscot:* Five to ten days. *Scott:* Six to ten days. *Stoddard:* Eight days.

15. At what stage of growth do you thin out your stand, and how far apart?

Pemiscot: Thin out, when fourth leaf appears, to distance apart equal to the width of a wide hoe. *Scott:* When the plant is about 6 inches high, and from 8 to 12 inches apart. *Dunklin:* Chop out with a hoe as soon as it is fairly up; bring to a stand when 6 inches high, and from 10 to 15 inches apart. *Stoddard:* At the second hoeing, and 8 inches apart.

16. Is your cotton liable to suffer from sore shin?

Pemiscot: In wet weather. *Dunklin:* Not unless the weather is cold and wet, when the cotton is small. *Stoddard:* Yes, if the spring is cold. *Scott:* No.

17. What after-cultivation do you give, and with what implements?

Stoddard: The dirt is kept to the plant, and the weeds down, by using the double-shovel plows. *Scott:* After-cultivation is given with hoe, plow, and sweep. *Pemiscot:* The scraper, hoe, and sweep. *Dunklin:* Generally use scrapers and hoe twice, finishing by throwing dirt to the plant with sweep or shovel. Some finish with double-shovel, others with sweep.

18. What is the height usually attained by your cotton before blooming, and when do you see the first blooms?

Stoddard: 18 inches. *Scott* and *Dunklin:* 2 feet. *Pemiscot:* 3 feet. The first blooms are seen about the 20th of June in Dunklin; 24th of June in Pemiscot; 1st of July in Stoddard, and about the 4th of July in Scott.

19. When do the bolls first open?

Dunklin: Late in July or early in August. *Stoddard:* About the 10th of August. *Pemiscot:* The middle of August. *Scott:* The last of August.

20. When do you begin your first picking, and how many pickings do you usually make?

Dunklin: The first picking is begun between August 20 and September 1, and lasts until October 15, when the second picking commences; this continues until the crop is gathered. *Stoddard:* September 15, between which date and January 1 two pickings are made. *Pemiscot:* In September, if not too hot. Three pickings are made, being continuous. *Scott:* The first picking is made in September, the second in October.

21. Do you ordinarily pick all your cotton, and at what date does picking usually close? How much is paid for picking 100 pounds of seed-cotton?

Cotton is all picked in *Scott*, *Stoddard*, and *Dunklin* counties, but not in *Pemiscot*. Picking closes in November in *Scott*; on January 1 in *Stoddard*, and on the 1st of April in *Dunklin*. *Dunklin:* Seventy-five cents with board or $1 without board is paid for picking. At this price there is very little margin for profit left to the owner when picked by hired labor. *Pemiscot:* Seventy-five cents to $1 per day with board is paid. As soon as frost falls the natives go coon-hunting, and then picking stops until cold weather drives the men out of the woods, and the crops are ruined.

22. At what time do you expect the first "black frost"?

Scott: October 10. *Dunklin:* From the 10th to the 20th of October. *Pemiscot:* The 15th of October. *Stoddard:* November 1.

23. Do you pen your seed-cotton in the field, or gin as the picking progresses?

Pemiscot, *Stoddard*, and *Dunklin:* Pen in the field and haul from pen to gin as picking progresses, or at any convenient time. *Scott:* Seed-cotton is housed.

GINNING, BALING, AND SHIPPING.

24. What gin do you use; how many saws? What motive power; steam- or horse-power? How much clean lint do you make in a day's run of ten hours?

Stoddard: Phœnix's and Pratt's gins of from 60 to 80 saws, run by steam-power; making 4,000 pounds of clean lint. *Dunklin:* Pratt's gin of 80 saws, run by steam, will make 4,000 pounds of lint. The Eagle, Carver, and other gins of from 50 to 80 saws, with, in most cases, steam-power, are also in use in this county. *Scott:* The Eagle gin, of 60 saws, when run by horse-power, makes 1,250 pounds of lint; with steam, 2,500 pounds. *Pemiscot:* The old-fashioned gin of 80 saws with steam-power, making 2,500 pounds of lint.

25. How much seed-cotton, on an average, is required for a 475-pound bale of lint?

Pemiscot: 1,610 pounds. *Dunklin:* 1,520 pounds. *Stoddard:* 1,660 pounds. *Scott:* 1,800 pounds.

26. What press do you use for baling? What press is generally used in your region? What is its capacity per day?

Dunklin: Lever beam and arrow beam press (with a wooden screw), when run by two men and one mule, will pack ten 500-pound bales. The hand lever, old-fashioned screw, and iron screw presses are also in use, there being no preference for any one kind. *Pemiscot:* The old-fashioned lever packs 5 bales. *Stoddard:* Nearly all kinds are used.

27. Do you use rope or iron ties for baling? If the latter, what fastening do you prefer?

Scott and *Stoddard:* Iron ties. *Dunklin* and *Pemiscot:* Iron ties and buckle fastening.

28. What kind of bagging is used in your region?

Stoddard: Jute, 2 pounds to the yard. *Scott:* Mainly jute. *Dunklin:* Jute. *Pemiscot:* Kentucky hemp.

29. What weight do you aim to give your bales? Have transportation companies imposed any conditions in this respect?

Scott: 450 pounds. *Pemiscot:* 500 pounds. *Dunklin:* From 500 to 550 pounds. *Stoddard:* 550 pounds. None of the above counties report transportation companies as having imposed any conditions.

DISEASES, INSECT ENEMIES, ETC.

30. By what accidents of weather, diseases, or insect pests is your cotton crop most liable to be injured? At what dates do the several diseases or pests usually make their appearance? To what cause is the trouble attributed by your farmers? What efforts have been made to obviate it, and with what success?

Dunklin: Shedding from July 20 to August 20, attributable to drought; rot of bolls late in the seasons, caused by too much wet weather; and rust in August, the cause of which is unknown. Rust seldom injures the crop in this locality. When it does, it is in small patches scattered over the field, or sometimes in one corner or at one side. *Pemiscot:* Shedding; rot of bolls in wet weather; rust, blight, and severe storms. *Scott:* The cotton crop is subject to few injuries of any kind. *Stoddard:* Rust in August, attributable to the weather changing from an extremely wet state to a very dry one.

31. Is rust or blight prevalent chiefly on heavy or ill-drained soils? Do they prevail chiefly in wet or dry, cool or hot seasons? On which soil described by you are they most common?

Pemiscot: They occur on all soils, but are prevalent chiefly on heavy ones, and in both cool and hot seasons. *Dunklin:* Rust prevails chiefly on light, dry soils, in seasons with sudden changes. It is more common on lands which have been under cultivation for twenty years than on new lands. *Stoddard:* Rust is prevalent chiefly on ill-drained soils, in hot seasons. It is most common on the sandy prairie lands.

LABOR AND SYSTEM OF FARMING.

32. What is the average size of farms or plantations in your region? Is the prevalent practice mixed farming or planting?

Stoddard: 40 acres. *Pemiscot:* From 40 to 100 acres. *Scott:* From 40 to 400 acres. *Dunklin:* 80 acres. There are some larger farms, from 100 to 1,000 acres, but they are generally rented in subdivisions of from 20 to 100 acres each. Mixed farming is the prevalent practice in all of these counties.

33. Are supplies raised at home or imported; and if the latter, where from? Is the tendency toward the raising of home supplies increasing or decreasing?

Stoddard and *Pemiscot:* Supplies are raised at home. *Scott:* All except groceries are raised at home. *Dunklin:* Mostly at home; some flour and bacon are occasionally imported from Saint Louis. The tendency toward the raising of home supplies is increasing in all of the above-named counties.

34. Who are your laborers chiefly?

Laborers are Americans chiefly in all the counties. Negroes are reported as working on the rivers in *Pemiscot;* there are a few negroes in *Scott;* very few in *Dunklin;* none are reported in *Stoddard.*

35. How are wages paid? At what rates? When payable?

Pemiscot: Wages are from $12 to $15 per month; payable at the end of the month. *Dunklin:* $12.50 to $15 per month or 75 cents per day with board, and from $20 to $25 per month or $1 per day without board. Wages are generally paid as the work progresses. *Scott:* From $15 to $20 per month or from 50 cents to $1 per day; payable when the work is done. *Stoddard:* $20 per month; payable at the end of each month.

36. Are cotton farms worked on shares? Are any supplies furnished by the owners?

Cotton farms are worked on shares; the owner furnishing teams, feed for same, and all necessary implements for making and gathering the crop, and receiving one-half the crop, in *Stoddard*, and one-third, delivered at the gin, in *Dunklin*. The share system is practiced to some extent, the owner furnishing teams and all implements, excepting gin and press, in *Pemiscot*. In *Scott* county the cotton farms are not worked on shares, but generally by hired labor.

37. Does your system give satisfaction? How does it affect the quality of the staple? Does the soil deteriorate or improve under it?

Stoddard: The share system gives satisfaction, and lowlands seem to improve under it. *Scott:* The share system is satisfactory, having no effect on the quality of the staple, but the soil deteriorates. *Dunklin:* The share system is being replaced by the renting system. Under the share system the quality of the staple is not affected, and the soil maintains its fertility. *Pemiscot:* If the crop is gathered early and dry, a staple of good quality results; but if late, a low quality of the staple is obtained. The soil improves.

38. Which system (wages or share) is the better for the laborer?

Scott: The share system, because it stimulates the laborer to greater diligence. *Dunklin:* Under the share system the laborer can make more than under the wages system. *Stoddard:* The share system is better, because under it good crops are usually made. *Pemiscot:* The wages system, as he then receives more than he earns.

39. What is the condition of the laborers?

Stoddard: Fair. *Scott:* Generally comfortable. *Dunklin:* All conditions are represented; good, indifferent, and bad. *Pemiscot:* Their life is easier than that of the farmer.

40. What proportion of negro laborers own land, or the houses in which they live?

Negroes are reported as not owning land or houses in any of the counties.

41. What is the market value of the land described in your region? and what rent is paid for such land?

Pemiscot: Price—From $5 to $25 per acre. *Scott:* From $8 to $30 per acre. *Dunklin:* From $10 to $20, according to improvements. *Stoddard:* $15 per acre. *Scott:* Rent—$2 50 to $3 per acre. *Pemiscot:* $2 50 to $5 per acre. *Stoddard:* $3 per acre. *Dunklin:* $3 50 to $4 per acre.

42. How many acres, or 500-pound bales, per hand is your customary estimate?

Pemiscot: 10 acres; from which, in 1880, I made 8 bales and raised 300 bushels of corn. *Stoddard:* When cotton alone is tended 15 bales is the estimate. *Scott:* There is no regular estimate, as cotton is not the leading business. *Dunklin:* A mixed crop is raised; no definite estimate can be given.

43. To what extent does the system of credits or advances upon the growing cotton crop prevail in your region?

Scott: To a very small extent. *Stoddard:* About one-half the farmer's supplies are advanced. *Dunklin:* Merchants make liberal advances; often to too great an extent for the good of all parties concerned. *Pemiscot:* Generally; when it is done it is ruinous both to the merchant and laborer, as the latter buys more than he can pay for.

44. At what stage of its production is the cotton crop usually covered by insurance?

Dunklin, Scott, and *Stoddard:* The cotton crop is not insured at any stage of its production. *Pemiscot:* When it is shipped; the practice is general.

45. What are the merchants' commissions and charges for storing, handling, shipping, insurance, etc., to which your crop is subject? What is the total amount of these charges against the farmer, per pound, or 500-pound bale?

Stoddard: 2½ per cent. commission by Saint Louis merchants; county merchants charge nothing. The total charges are about $4 25. *Dunklin:* No charges are made, except for actual expense incurred, by home merchants. It costs about $4 50, including marine insurance, to place a bale in Saint Louis, Memphis, or Cincinnati. The total amount of charges, including commission on sales, is about $7 per bale. *Pemiscot:* The charges are about $5 25 per bale.

46. What is your estimate of the cost of production in your region, exclusive of such charges, and with fair management?

Scott: About $12 50 per bale of 500 pounds. *Stoddard:* $23 per bale. *Dunklin:* $30. *Pemiscot:* $39 50 per bale, as follows: Picking, $20; ginning and hauling, $10; rent of land, $3 50; cost of cultivation, $6. This does not include wear of tools and expense of teams. Laborers are greatly needed here.

REPORT

ON THE

COTTON PRODUCTION OF THE STATE OF ARKANSAS,

WITH A DISCUSSION OF

THE GENERAL AGRICULTURAL FEATURES OF THE STATE.

BY

R. H. LOUGHRIDGE, Ph. D.,
SPECIAL AGENT TENTH CENSUS.

1

531

TABLE OF CONTENTS.

TABLE OF CONTENTS.

LETTERS OF TRANSMITTAL.

BERKELEY, CALIFORNIA, *July* 1, 1882.

The SUPERINTENDENT OF CENSUS.

DEAR SIR: I transmit herewith a report on the cotton production and agricultural features of the state of Arkansas, by Dr. R. H. Loughridge, special agent.

This report is written on the general plan heretofore outlined by me and adopted in its essential features by the special agents in charge of the other cotton states. It differs from all the other reports in that it is not based upon any personal observation within the state, but has been compiled from all available sources of information, including, of course, the answers to the schedule questions on cotton culture sent out by this office. It is a matter of regret that these answers in the present instance have been but very few in number. For the rest, the omission of any field exploration of the state seemed to be justified by the existence of the valuable and elaborate reports of the survey of Arkansas by Dr. D. D. Owen and his assistants, in which not only the geological but also the agricultural features were closely observed and recorded. Dr. Owen was foremost among those who believed that agriculture should receive at least as much attention from state surveys as is usually, and too often almost exclusively, given to those features relating to mining and other industries; and, had he lived, an agricultural description of Arkansas substantially like the one herewith transmitted would probably have been issued by himself. His early death left a large amount of material unelaborated, and, although published, its form has stood in the way of its usefulness and of the recognition of the practical value of the work done. That this has been so cannot be surprising, in view of the amount of labor it has cost us to eliminate, segregate, and arrange the materials scattered through the volumes of the Arkansas reports into one connected and systematic whole. The same labor would have had to be performed to a greater or less extent by any one desiring to utilize these data for the understanding or description of any particular portion of the state; and that the task has been thought too hard is obvious from the very meager descriptions, filled up with vague generalities, that have been issued at various times by immigration societies, railroad companies, and other sources, as a guide to immigrants. The present case is but one of many similar ones, in which the reports of surveys, both state and national, are practically useless to the agricultural immigrant, because, instead of presenting to him an intelligible and well-digested summary of the agricultural features, he is usually left to the weary search for scattered data through ponderous volumes, the result being that he is almost as much thrown upon the reports and representations of interested parties as though no effort had been made by the government to make known the resources of the country.

The numerous soil analyses made in connection with the Arkansas survey by Dr. Robert Peter acquire double interest in the grouping now given them under the respective regional heads, and supply many striking proofs of the ability of soil analysis to furnish such definite indications of the general quality, peculiarities, and cheapest mode of improvement of soils, as will, when properly interpreted, serve as a sound basis for practical agriculture. The record is, however, defective as regards the specific statement of the depths to which the soil samples were taken, and also in that the determinations of the hygroscopic moisture were not made under definite conditions, but from "air-dried" material.

Considering the circumstances under which the present report has been written, it is quite probable that it is not in all respects as complete and accurate as might have been desirable, or as may be the case with those on

535

LETTERS OF TRANSMITTAL.

other states in which personal researches have served as the basis for the description. To those who may note such imperfections, it can only be said that Dr. Loughridge has fully and faithfully utilized all available sources of information, and, with myself, can but regret that they have not been more complete.

Very respectfully,

EUG. W. HILGARD,
Chief Special Agent in charge of Cotton Production.

BERKELEY, CALIFORNIA, *May* 31, 1882.

Professor E. W. HILGARD,
Special Agent in charge of Cotton Production.

DEAR SIR: I have the honor to transmit herewith the report on cotton production in the state of Arkansas, embracing also, in accordance with your instructions, a description of its agricultural and such other features as affect the culture of this, one of the chief crops of the state.

The report embraces the following general divisions, preceded by statistical tables of population, cotton production, and the acreage and yield of other chief crops.

PART I. The general description of the state and its agricultural regions.

PART II. Short descriptions of counties, arranged according to regions, and embracing also abstracts of schedule reports.

PART III. Details of cotton culture in the counties of the state, as compiled briefly from the answered schedules of correspondents.

In preparing this report I have been compelled to draw almost entirely upon the publications of the state geological survey by Dr. D. D. Owen, and upon a pamphlet by James P. Henry, entitled "Resources of the state of Arkansas", and upon such other information as I could gather by correspondents and the answered question schedules on cotton culture sent out from this office to parties in each county. I very much regret that I had not the advantage of a personal visit to the several sections of the state, which would doubtless have enabled me to present its agricultural resources in a much more clear and satisfactory manner. I have, however, found Dr. Owen's report invaluable, for, although not generalized, being rather, for the most part, a description of some of the counties, it embraces a brief mention of some of the agricultural features of each county passed over by the survey corps. From this scattered material, incomplete in many particulars (probably because of the death of Dr. Owen), I have been enabled to arrange and describe the several agricultural regions with sufficient clearness and accuracy, I hope, to give any one a correct idea of the state.

The soil analyses found throughout the report are also from the work alluded to, and were made by Dr. Robert Peter, of Kentucky. The methods of analysis used were very much the same as have since been adopted by yourself, thus rendering comparable the chemical composition of the soils of this and other states. The map which accompanies the report does not pretend to give more than a general outline of the chief regions, as it was found impossible under the circumstances to obtain the details of the areas embraced in each. The colors used in designating the regions are, as far as possible, made to agree with those of similar regions in the other states under your charge, and also with the general map. The outlines of the alluvial region of the Mississippi river are from the report of Humphreys and Abbott, while those of the Arkansas, below Little Rock, were given by the correspondent from Prairie county.

Very respectfully,

R. H. LOUGHRIDGE.

TABULATED RESULTS OF THE ENUMERATION.

TABLE I.—AREA, POPULATION, TILLED LAND, AND COTTON PRODUCTON.

Counties.	Land area.	POPULATION.						TILLED LAND.			COTTON PRODUCTION.		Average per acre.				
		Total.	Male.	Female.	White.	Color'd.	Average per square mile.	Acres.	Per cent. of	Per cent. of tilled lands devoted to cotton.	Acres.	Bales.	Bale.	Seed cotton.	Lint.	Cotton acreage per square mile.	Bales per square mile.
	Sq. mls.												Lbs.	Lbs.			
The State	53,045	802,525	416,279	386,246	591,531	210,994	15.1	8,483,900	10.1	20.4	1,043,976	608,256	0.56	870	290	19.7	11.5
ALLUVIAL REGION.																	
Mississippi bottom lands.																	
Chicot	840	10,117	5,321	4,796	1,563	8,554	12.0	26,666	7.2	66.7	26,941	25,338	0.94	1,410	470	33.1	30.2
Desha	730	8,973	4,877	4,096	2,452	6,521	12.3	43,643	9.1	48.6	21,130	15,103	0.86	1,290	430	29.0	34.8
Crittenden	660	9,415	5,034	4,381	1,899	7,516	14.3	43,646	10.2	56.9	24,413	16,039	0.65	980	330	37.0	24.3
Mississippi	810	7,322	4,006	3,336	4,671	2,951	9.1	20,320	5.7	48.5	13,326	10,430	0.78	1,170	390	16.5	12.9
Total	8,040	35,827	19,238	16,599	10,585	25,282	11.8	134,276	7.9	55.6	85,839	66,910	0.81	1,215	405	28.2	23.0
Crowley's ridge.																	
Phillips	630	21,262	11,085	10,177	5,444	15,818	33.7	78,916	19.6	54.1	43,654	29,070	0.68	1,020	340	67.7	46.1
Monroe	660	9,574	5,104	4,470	4,365	5,209	14.5	50,372	11.9	43.7	22,017	14,106	0.64	960	320	33.4	21.4
Lee	580	13,288	7,121	6,167	4,138	9,150	22.9	61,307	14.5	53.8	33,000	21,147	0.64	960	330	56.9	36.5
Woodruff	580	8,646	4,502	4,143	4,163	4,483	14.9	37,880	10.2	47.8	18,134	12,311	0.68	1,020	340	31.3	21.2
Saint Francis	620	8,389	4,518	3,871	4,921	3,468	13.5	35,406	8.9	33.5	11,857	5,906	0.50	750	250	19.1	9.6
Cross	620	5,050	2,693	2,357	3,261	1,789	8.1	19,225	4.8	39.6	7,507	4,769	0.63	945	315	12.3	7.7
Poinsett	760	2,192	1,140	1,052	1,902	290	2.9	7,712	1.6	30.8	2,373	1,514	0.64	960	320	5.1	2.0
Jackson	620	10,877	5,771	5,106	8,112	2,784	17.5	46,488	11.7	46.7	21,718	13,895	0.64	960	320	35.0	23.4
Lawrence	690	8,782	4,645	4,137	8,315	467	14.6	43,806	11.4	24.6	10,708	6,450	0.60	900	300	17.9	10.3
Craighead	730	7,037	3,645	3,392	6,776	261	9.6	35,814	7.6	20.4	7,946	4,374	0.60	900	300	9.9	6.0
Greene	640	7,480	3,944	3,536	7,405	75	11.7	29,109	7.1	23.7	6,896	3,711	0.54	810	270	10.8	5.8
Clay	580	7,213	3,814	3,399	7,191	22	12.4	26,327	7.1	16.1	4,289	2,307	0.54	810	270	7.3	4.0
Total	7,620	109,790	57,963	51,807	65,994	43,796	14.4	472,075	9.7	39.9	188,498	119,649	0.63	945	315	24.7	15.7
GRAY SILT PRAIRIE REGION.																	
Arkansas	1,000	8,038	4,236	3,802	4,971	3,067	8.0	35,128	5.5	35.9	12,611	8,506	0.67	1,005	335	12.6	8.5
Prairie	710	8,435	4,455	3,980	5,691	2,744	11.9	35,033	7.7	34.6	12,134	6,977	0.58	870	290	17.1	9.8
Lonoke	760	12,146	6,523	5,623	8,143	4,003	16.0	63,653	13.1	33.9	20,910	11,704	0.56	840	280	27.5	15.4
Total	2,470	28,619	15,214	13,405	18,805	9,814	11.6	133,812	8.4	34.1	45,845	27,189	0.60	900	300	18.5	11.0
YELLOW-LOAM REGION.																	
Ashley	950	10,156	5,096	5,061	5,026	5,130	10.7	48,455	8.0	40.4	19,555	11,271	0.58	870	290	20.6	12.0
Union	1,000	13,419	6,830	6,789	6,985	6,434	13.4	60,472	10.9	43.4	30,136	11,613	0.37	555	185	30.1	11.0
Columbia	860	14,090	7,078	7,012	8,587	5,503	16.4	80,309	14.8	40.4	23,427	13,020	0.40	600	300	37.7	15.2
La Fayette	490	5,730	2,931	2,799	2,116	3,614	11.7	27,361	8.7	38.6	10,611	6,339	0.60	900	300	21.7	12.9
Miller	690	9,919	5,226	4,693	5,324	4,595	14.4	46,038	10.4	41.5	19,111	11,643	0.61	915	305	27.7	16.9
Little River	530	6,404	3,378	3,026	3,064	3,340	12.1	27,082	8.0	38.3	10,368	7,116	0.69	1,035	345	19.6	13.4
Sevier	550	6,192	3,178	3,016	5,088	1,104	11.3	25,448	7.2	28.6	7,283	4,075	0.56	840	280	13.2	7.4
Howard	630	9,917	5,105	4,812	7,409	2,508	15.7	44,812	11.1	27.4	12,259	7,051	0.58	870	290	19.5	11.2
Hempstead	730	19,015	9,728	9,287	9,593	9,422	26.1	76,537	16.4	35.5	27,142	13,965	0.52	780	260	37.1	19.2
Nevada	670	12,959	6,665	6,294	9,236	3,723	19.3	70,858	16.5	33.6	23,925	10,529	0.44	660	220	35.7	15.7
Ouachita	730	11,758	5,886	5,872	5,504	6,254	16.1	85,733	14.1	34.3	79,855	8,849	0.27	855	185	32.7	12.1
Calhoun	810	5,671	2,926	2,745	3,583	2,088	9.2	32,391	8.6	46.1	13,377	5,376	0.40	690	200	21.9	8.8
Bradley	700	6,285	3,158	3,127	4,075	2,210	9.0	34,068	7.6	35.9	12,221	4,900	0.40	600	200	17.5	7.0
Drew	860	13,281	6,118	6,115	6,672	5,759	14.6	55,537	10.0	40.7	31,796	9,964	0.40	690	230	25.9	11.9
Lincoln	600	8,548	1,193	4,355	6,643	3,971	14.3	38,491	11.1	43.0	17,819	11,569	0.68	690	234	31.4	
Dorsey	600	8,370	4,330	4,040	6,041	2,329	13.9	42,564	11.1	38.3	16,643	8,146	0.49	690	230	27.7	13.5
Dallas	660	6,505	3,288	3,217	4,299	2,206	9.9	25,505	8.4	40.3	14,306	6,157	0.43	645	215	21.7	9.3
Clark	950	15,771	8,191	7,580	10,567	5,204	16.6	67,529	11.1	37.2	25,092	12,924	0.55	825	275	26.4	14.7
Grant	650	6,186	3,211	2,974	5,629	556	9.5	29,844	7.2	32.4	9,680	5,000	0.41	615	203	14.9	6.3
Jefferson	670	22,386	11,716	10,679	5,331	17,055	25.7	72,141	12.0	63.0	45,426	34,588	0.76	1,140	380	52.2	39.8
Total	14,250	212,218	108,606	102,562	118,141	94,077	14.9	969,706	10.8	39.6	391,551	201,512	0.51	765	255	14.1	
RED-LOAM REGION.																	
Pike	620	6,345	3,248	3,097	5,951	394	10.2	26,628	6.7	27.6	7,341	3,787	0.52	780	260	11.8	6.1
Polk	945	5,857	3,011	2,846	5,792	65	6.2	23,815	3.9	17.8	4,230	2,061	0.49	735	245	4.5	2.2
Montgomery	840	5,729	3,039	2,690	5,471	258	6.8	19,086	3.7	17.9	3,512	1,819	0.52	780	260	4.2	2.2
Hot Spring	690	7,775	4,002	3,773	7,030	745	11.3	30,327	6.9	24.4	8,068	3,755	0.47	705	235	11.7	5.4
Garland	580	9,023	4,761	4,262	7,437	1,586	15.6	16,748	4.5	5.9	993	534	0.54	810	270	1.7	0.9
Saline	690	8,958	4,625	4,338	7,596	1,367	13.0	35,604	5.1	24.8	8,846	5,075	0.57	855	285	12.8	7.4

COTTON PRODUCTION IN ARKANSAS.

TABLE I.—AREA, POPULATION, TILLED LAND, AND COTTON PRODUCTION—Continued.

Counties.	Land area.	POPULATION.						TILLED LAND.		Per cent. of tilled lands devoted to cotton.	COTTON PRODUCTION.					Cotton acreage per square mile.	Bales per square mile.
		Total.	Male.	Female.	White.	Color'd.	Average per square mile.	Acres.	Per cent. of area.		Acres.	Bales.	Average per acre.				
													Bale.	Seed-cotton.	Lint.		
RED-LOAM REGION—continued.	*Sq. mls.*													*Lbs.*	*Lbs.*		
Pulaski	810	32,616	17,294	15,322	17,667	14,949	40.3	78,019	14.1	30.9	20,697	20,439	0.70	1,050	350	35.9	25.2
Perry	580	3,672	2,010	1,862	3,072	800	6.7	13,706	4.2	32.4	5,063	3,314	0.65	975	325	8.6	5.7
Yell	900	13,852	7,193	6,659	12,733	1,119	15.4	55,220	9.6	30.1	16,596	10,428	0.63	945	315	18.4	11.6
Scott	920	9,174	4,706	4,468	9,135	89	10.0	30,631	5.2	29.0	8,867	4,826	0.54	810	270	9.6	5.2
Sebastian	570	19,560	10,123	9,437	17,970	1,590	34.3	68,596	18.6	28.8	19,722	11,113	0.56	840	280	34.6	19.5
Logan	670	14,885	7,763	7,122	13,901	984	25.3	65,794	15.3	24.9	16,377	9,753	0.60	900	300	24.4	14.6
Conway	540	12,755	6,787	5,968	9,546	3,209	23.6	51,967	15.0	29.7	15,434	9,096	0.59	885	295	28.6	16.3
Faulkner	650	12,786	6,735	6,051	11,368	1,418	19.7	52,515	12.6	30.0	15,749	8,692	0.55	825	275	24.2	13.4
White	1,100	17,794	9,237	8,537	15,761	2,033	16.2	79,827	11.3	29.2	23,304	11,921	0.51	765	255	21.2	10.7
Van Buren	1,100	9,565	4,858	4,707	9,447	118	8.7	28,905	5.5	18.2	7,034	3,277	0.48	720	240	6.4	3.1
Pope	800	14,822	7,871	6,951	13,413	909	17.9	63,312	12.4	23.8	15,062	8,700	0.58	870	290	18.8	10.9
Johnson	800	11,565	5,944	5,621	11,073	492	17.5	48,153	11.4	25.4	12,217	7,760	0.64	960	320	18.5	11.8
Franklin	700	14,951	7,861	7,090	14,455	496	21.4	58,175	13.0	27.9	16,295	9,268	0.57	855	285	23.2	13.2
Crawford	620	14,740	7,607	7,133	13,323	1,408	23.8	54,714	12.8	31.8	15,145	5,980	0.56	840	280	26.0	14.5
Washington	940	23,844	12,112	11,732	22,894	950	25.4	116,871	19.4	0.3	302	133	0.44	680	220	0.3	0.1
Benton	880	20,328	10,383	9,945	20,147	181	23.1	111,279	19.8	0.2	296	136	0.44	680	220	0.3	0.1
Total	16,805	296,291	150,670	139,621	255,171	35,201	17.3	1,133,681	10.5	22.1	250,511	144,864	0.58	870	290	14.9	8.6
NORTHERN BARRENS AND HILLS.																	
Madison	860	11,455	5,747	5,708	11,331	124	13.0	67,740	11.0	0.4	255	129	0.51	765	255	0.3	0.1
Newton	810	6,120	3,143	2,977	6,115	5	7.6	34,333	4.7	16.7	2,602	1,466	0.54	810	270	3.2	1.7
Searcy	700	7,278	3,720	3,558	7,262	16	10.4	28,581	6.4	15.1	4,390	2,464	0.57	865	285	6.2	3.5
Stone	840	5,089	2,593	2,496	4,984	105	8.0	20,906	5.1	17.5	3,656	2,049	0.56	840	280	5.7	3.2
Independence	580	16,086	9,313	8,773	16,703	1,383	30.6	81,230	14.4	24.1	19,602	11,156	0.57	855	285	22.5	12.7
Randolph	640	11,724	6,113	5,611	11,097	627	18.3	53,016	12.9	20.8	11,628	6,548	0.57	855	285	17.2	9.9
Sharp	580	9,047	4,623	4,424	8,871	176	15.3	43,191	11.4	15.6	8,435	4,350	0.51	765	255	14.3	7.4
Izard	580	10,857	5,625	5,332	10,635	222	16.7	54,705	14.7	16.5	9,029	4,800	0.53	795	265	15.6	8.3
Fulton	668	8,730	3,508	3,212	6,694	36	10.2	34,239	5.7	16.5	3,994	2,438	0.61	915	305	4.1	3.7
Baxter	500	6,004	3,131	2,873	5,959	45	12.0	27,564	8.6	17.4	4,798	2,879	0.60	900	300	9.6	5.9
Marion	640	7,907	4,019	3,888	7,864	43	10.8	28,673	7.0	24.8	7,116	3,925	0.55	825	275	11.1	6.1
Boone	640	12,146	6,104	6,042	12,058	88	19.0	36,883	13.9	9.0	5,095	2,686	0.53	795	265	8.0	4.2
Carroll	700	13,397	6,979	6,358	13,272	65	19.1	43,903	9.8	2.2	962	502	0.51	765	255	1.4	0.7
Total	8,880	125,770	64,518	61,282	122,855	2,905	14.2	545,930	9.7	14.7	80,923	45,632	0.56	840	280	9.1	5.1

TABLE II.—ACREAGE AND PRODUCTION OF LEADING CROPS.

Counties.	COTTON.		INDIAN CORN.		OATS.		WHEAT.	
	Acres.	Bales.	Acres.	Bushels.	Acres.	Bushels.	Acres.	Bushels.
The State	1,042,976	608,256	1,208,810	24,156,417	106,513	2,216,822	204,064	1,208,715
ALLUVIAL REGION.								
Mississippi bottom lands.								
Chicot	26,941	25,335	7,209	117,391	86	972		
Desha	21,150	18,106	9,819	186,177	169	2,139	18	171
Crittenden	24,413	16,029	8,610	216,194	73	1,128	20	200
Mississippi	13,236	10,430	9,858	214,116	181	4,340	68	655
Total	85,520	69,910	36,796	837,878	502	8,879	106	1,026
Crowley's ridge.								
Phillips	42,464	29,070	19,695	323,565	834	13,410	94	867
Monroe	22,017	14,106	12,945	206,067	764	13,996	80	200
Lee	23,009	21,147	16,124	271,650	806	13,067	83	620
Woodruff	18,124	12,311	11,146	229,962	497	9,908	307	1,307
Saint Francis	11,897	5,968	9,934	197,061	706	8,849	364	1,825
Cross	7,607	4,768	6,985	138,614	838	11,131	471	2,648
Poinsett	2,372	1,514	3,907	87,183	258	3,490	297	1,537
Jackson	21,718	13,895	17,361	384,398	500	6,399	910	7,413
Lawrence	10,768	6,480	19,902	523,720	3,356	40,851	2,361	12,662
Craighead	7,346	4,374	15,623	367,451	1,874	20,360	2,794	16,552
Greene	6,886	3,711	14,068	347,926	1,902	29,110	1,702	10,475
Clay	4,239	2,307	13,879	343,836	977	13,406	2,340	13,406
Total	188,496	119,649	161,559	3,432,003	13,409	181,848	11,725	74,373
GRAY SILT PRAIRIE REGION.								
Arkansas	12,611	6,508	16,242	136,272	685	16,350	48	539
Prairie	12,124	6,977	16,112	135,462	2,191	31,944	457	2,214
Lonoke	20,910	13,704	17,502	249,724	3,310	43,074	1,181	5,562
Total	45,645	27,189	37,862	521,456	6,186	91,372	1,686	8,316
YELLOW-LOAM REGION.								
Ashley	19,555	11,371	15,228	182,299	1,411	12,218	14	86
Union	20,196	11,012	27,796	171,779	1,349	6,405	103	543
Columbia	22,427	13,039	25,868	226,376	3,341	22,545	1,019	5,548
La Fayette	19,611	6,320	8,286	97,271	140	1,262	13	77
Miller	19,111	11,642	16,673	232,726	391	6,796		
Little River	10,358	7,116	8,141	66,819	563	8,520	118	774
Sevier	7,283	4,575	16,557	158,839	1,045	12,603	1,012	4,740
Howard	12,359	7,051	17,071	272,635	2,486	20,409	3,867	12,618
Hempstead	27,142	13,985	30,394	418,897	3,489	42,678	1,289	6,702
Nevada	23,925	10,570	23,173	253,222	1,329	11,861	635	2,807
Ouachita	23,855	8,849	21,994	186,655	567	2,921	164	692
Calhoun	13,277	5,370	12,910	150,688	673	5,839	129	653
Bradley	13,221	4,900	12,330	97,241	1,073	8,316	236	1,309
Drew	21,796	9,964	20,506	145,461	1,488	11,521	280	1,344
Lincoln	17,819	11,563	12,547	144,068	1,400	15,310	185	1,021
Dorsey	15,462	6,146	14,787	113,690	1,777	18,967	980	3,218
Dallas	14,305	6,197	13,330	136,790	894	3,749	443	3,010
Clark	88,601	13,968	37,806	470,852	3,121	36,965	2,515	11,962
Cleve	9,889	4,—	13,799	149,654	1,364	10,488	878	3,016
Grant								
Jefferson	45,436	34,588	16,839	299,566				878
Total	391,561	201,612	352,254	3,964,062	27,496	292,976	13,876	57,689
RED-LOAM REGION.								
Pike	7,841	3,787	11,604	186,256	1,382	11,043	2,023	8,898
Polk	4,230	2,061	10,616	179,400	1,616	15,816	3,454	12,096
Montgomery	3,513	1,819	5,920	187,991	825	9,000	3,029	16,766
Hot Spring	8,068	3,735	13,802	263,650	910	11,191	1,377	7,384
Garland	982	534	8,785	153,434	1,381	17,9056	1,445	7,442
Saline	8,846	5,075	15,821	392,628	2,802	38,046	1,454	7,589
Pulaski	20,097	20,430	20,843	349,911	2,199	32,976	1,078	6,623
Perry	5,023	3,314	6,469	134,995	843	11,119	561	2,861
Yell	16,496	10,428	22,791	426,138	2,654	42,430	3,954	22,678
Scott	5,897	4,826	15,438	279,532	2,945	29,661	1,955	7,957
Sebastian	10,722	11,113	25,382	558,512	4,278	53,976	6,095	32,107

COTTON PRODUCTION IN ARKANSAS.

TABLE II.—ACREAGE AND PRODUCTION OF LEADING CROPS—Continued.

Counties.	COTTON.		INDIAN CORN.		OATS.		WHEAT.	
	Acres.	Bales.	Acres.	Bushels.	Acres.	Bushels.	Acres.	Bushels.
RED-LOAM REGION—continued.								
Logan	16,277	9,752	34,136	481,536	3,543	46,916	4,376	20,213
Conway	15,436	9,696	15,809	369,394	1,685	34,674	1,778	9,345
Faulkner	15,749	8,605	19,867	347,965	3,796	39,347	3,360	16,197
White	22,304	11,621	28,148	444,885	6,967	96,250	3,560	17,330
Van Buren	7,034	3,677	17,545	345,915	3,037	31,606	3,256	15,323
Pope	15,062	8,700	34,736	494,778	3,622	36,741	7,773	34,460
Johnson	13,217	7,769	20,606	483,486	2,783	34,686	3,509	18,466
Franklin	16,206	9,268	22,034	547,723	3,353	53,609	6,017	31,500
Crawford	16,145	8,980	19,777	405,356	2,360	38,216	5,347	31,040
Washington	302	133	58,063	1,226,557	18,103	220,437	20,507	234,060
Benton	296	130	40,138	1,116,234	13,012	245,362	21,462	186,067
Total	260,511	144,364	460,074	9,396,210	76,707	1,127,966	116,296	718,212
NORTHERN BARRENS AND HILLS.								
Madison	255	139	29,514	730,432	4,382	75,068	13,318	85,414
Newton	2,002	1,406	12,217	297,609	1,906	28,810	2,341	14,302
Searcy	4,230	3,484	14,399	362,328	1,901	34,776	3,665	19,179
Stone	3,656	2,949	9,156	200,275	1,420	19,297	2,006	13,387
Independence	19,602	11,156	31,114	691,188	5,100	61,300	3,055	37,160
Randolph	11,098	6,368	27,313	726,469	3,902	58,187	4,016	31,344
Sharp	5,435	4,350	18,506	432,570	4,411	53,361	3,176	18,903
Izard	9,030	4,800	21,728	451,064	4,913	40,362	4,320	35,902
Fulton	3,594	3,438	11,636	280,020	1,693	30,637	1,692	10,934
Baxter	4,798	3,879	10,804	261,537	2,054	21,673	1,776	9,985
Marion	7,116	3,935	13,664	320,305	1,956	26,704	2,494	13,834
Boone	5,095	3,666	26,712	655,945	5,733	92,273	5,480	56,581
Carroll	982	502	23,379	563,734	4,696	64,461	7,343	51,932
Total	80,922	48,022	248,164	6,613,216	42,010	596,162	61,442	408,859

PART I.

PHYSICO-GEOGRAPHICAL AND AGRICULTURAL FEATURES

OF THE

STATE OF ARKANSAS.

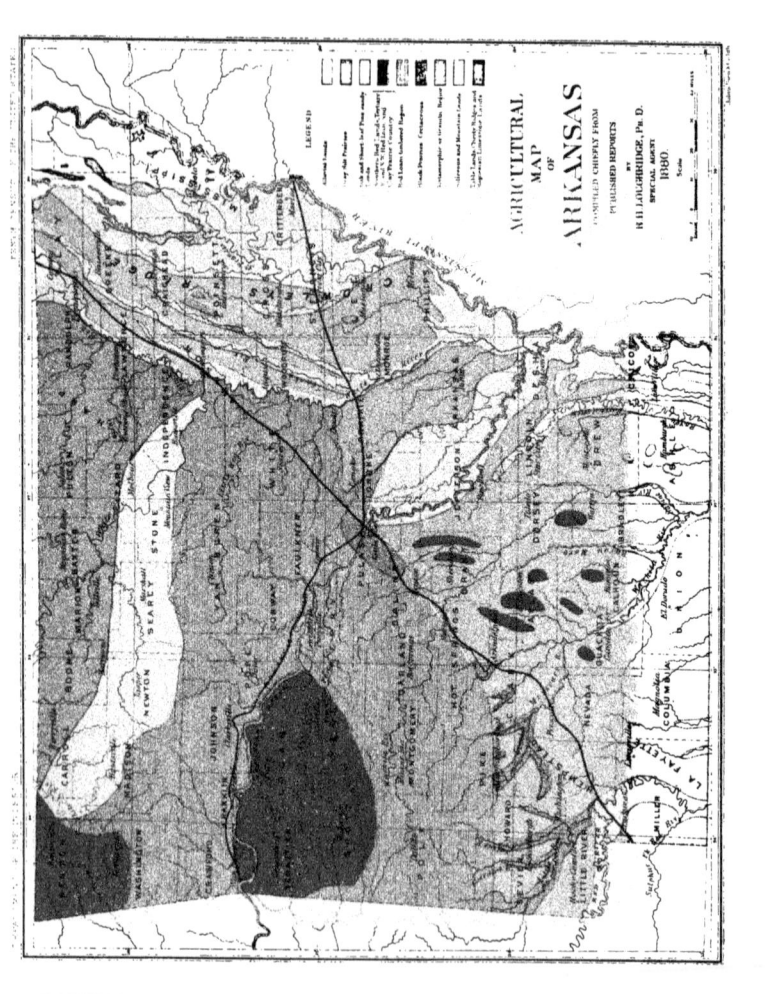

LEGEND

AGRICULTURAL
MAP
OF
ARKANSAS

COMPILED CHIEFLY FROM
PUBLISHED REPORTS
BY
H. H. LOUGHRIDGE, Ph. D.
SPECIAL AGENT
1880
Scale

PHYSICAL AND AGRICULTURAL FEATURES OF THE STATE OF ARKANSAS.

The state of Arkansas (a) lies between parallels 33° and 36° 30′ north latitude, while the extreme limits east and west are 89° 40′ and 94° 42′ west longitude. It covers altogether 53,850 square miles, including about 805 miles of water surface, and is divided into 74 counties, whose land areas vary in size from 490 to 1,100 square miles, according to the determinations made by Mr. Henry Gannett, of the Census Office. Nearly the entire surface of the state is well timbered with a large variety of growth.

SURFACE FEATURES.—The Mississippi river borders the state on the east, its broad bottom lands on the north reaching far westward from the river, some 60 miles, to the foot of Crowley's ridge, beyond the Saint Francis river. On the south these lands are narrower, and near the Louisiana line they are interspersed with ridges and upland peninsulas. Crowley's ridge is one of the most prominent features in this region. Lying between the White and the Mississippi rivers, this ridge, extending from the extreme northeastern part of the state southward to Helena, in Phillips county, with an elevation of from 100 to 150 feet, forms a sudden termination to the low swamps of the Mississippi and Saint Francis bottoms; but this elevation rapidly diminishes westward, with flat lands, prairies, and low sandy ridges, to White river, at the border of the hilly and mountainous region of northern Arkansas and the prairies of the south. Another broad alluvial region, bordering the Arkansas river on the north side, extends from near Little Rock (on the line of the rocky and hilly region) southeastward, and, embracing all the country lying between the river and bayou Meta, becomes again narrow at the junction of the two streams. Its width in one place is said to be as much as 30 miles, and the region presents very much the same features as that of the Mississippi. Broad alluvial bottom lands also border that portion of the Red river embraced in this state and the southern portion of Ouachita county near the state line.

A view of the state northward from the line of Louisiana to Missouri presents the following general topographical features in addition to those already given: Along the southern border the country is undulating and somewhat hilly, and is timbered with a prominent growth of short-leaf pine, with oak and hickory—the continuation of the Tertiary yellow-loam region of Louisiana and Texas. Northward the surface becomes more and more hilly, and is interspersed with red lands and Tertiary iron-ore hills. On the northeast of these, after passing the wide bottom plain lying between the Arkansas river and bayou Meta, we reach a large area of silty prairies, which separate this region from the Mississippi alluvial and Crowley's Ridge regions; while on the southwest there is a region, interspersed with small black Cretaceous prairies, which occupies the lowlands along the streams and at the foot of the pine ridges. The line marking the limit of this pine-hill country would pass from near Des Arc, on White river, in Prairie county, nearly westward to Little Rock, thence southwest to Arkadelphia, in Clark county, and westward through the middle of Sevier county into the Indian territory.

Northward from this line we enter upon a hilly and broken country, with a few ranges of high hills and mountains composed of sandstones and mill-stone grit, the valley lands being derived from the associated red shales. The surface of the country is well timbered with oak and hickory as far north as the range of mountains lying between Polk and Scott counties on the west. Open and level prairies are found interspersed throughout the region northward to the Arkansas river in the counties of Scott, Sebastian, Logan, and Yell, but occur chiefly in the first two. North of the river, after passing a timbered belt of country similar to that on the south, we reach the Ozark Mountain region of high hills and ridges, which increase in altitude from but a few hundred feet on the south to 1,000 or 1,500 feet above the general level of the country on the northwest, where they leave the state. This country is well timbered with a great variety of growth, except on some of the highest ridges, where the poor sandy

---

a The proper pronunciation of this name is doubtless that of the Indian tribal name from which it was originally derived, viz, *Akansa* or *Arkansa*, the first and last syllables being alike, with the accent on the first. A tribe of Indians of this name was found in this country by La Salle in 1680, and is mentioned in the account of his expedition. After the French took possession of this territory their writers quite naturally added the present final letter "s" to the name. At the present time the old pronunciation is still given to it, not only throughout the adjoining states, but by the Indians on the west, through whose territory the river of the same name runs.

and cherty soil will support little else than grasses, weeds, and stunted oaks. Little or no limestone has been observed southward from the Louisiana line to these mountains, but it now appears at the foot and on the sides of the hills, producing lands of richness and fertility. The hilly and broken character of the country continues to the Missouri line, and in the extreme northern tier of counties we find a region of cherty limestone hills and small open prairies and barrens, the latter having often a soil rich in potash, lime, and phosphoric acid. In the middle of this region the prairies are less extensive than on the extreme west, where, in Benton county, they open out into the broad and more level prairie region of the Indian territory. The hills are from 400 to 600 feet high, and are largely timbered, with pine and other growth, except in places where the soil is too thin for anything else than scrub oaks.

CLIMATE.—The records of the Smithsonian Institution for a period of many years, as summed up in the *Smithsonian Contribution to Knowledge*, volume XXI, place the annual mean temperature of that part of the state lying south of the Ozark mountains (or a line from the junction of White and Black rivers, in Independence county, westward to Fayetteville, in Washington county) at from 60° to 64°, and thence to the Missouri line at 56° F. For the winter months during this time the average temperature in the northern counties was from 28° to 40°, and in the southern counties from 40° to 52°. The annual mean at Helena, in Phillips county, was 61.1°; at Little Rock, 62.3°; Fort Smith, 60.1°, and at Washington, on the southwest, 61.5°. For the summer months the mean temperature for the time mentioned was from 76° to 80° over all of the state, except in the extreme southeastern counties, where the mean was from 80° to 88°. July is generally the hottest month, the thermometer sometimes rising as high as 100°. The nights are said to begin to grow cool about the middle of August, and the first "black" frost appears about the last of October.

Rainfall.—The prevailing winds are from the south, and, charged as they are with the vapors of the Gulf, we find the greatest condensation or rainfall in the southern half of the state. As the result of many years of observation the following facts have been brought out by Mr. Schott in a late publication of the Smithsonian Institution: The average number of rainy days in each year for fifteen years has been 75. The highest annual rainfall occurs in the southwestern counties, and averages 56 inches. From Louisiana northward to a limit marked by a line from the northeastern corner in Mississippi county to the lower part of Sebastian county, on the west, an average of from 44 to 56 inches falls yearly, while northward over the rest of the state a 38-inch fall is reported.

During the winter months the greatest fall (16 inches) occurred in the southwestern counties and along the Mississippi river from the mouth of the Arkansas river northward to Cross and Crittenden counties. There was a fall of 12 to 15 inches in the southeastern region, which may be bounded west by a line from the lower part of Poinsett county to Jacksonport, at the bend of White river; thence southward with a curve passing south of Little Rock, west to Mount Ida, Montgomery county, and south to Red river. Over the rest of the state on the north and west the rainfall for the winter was from 6 to 8 inches. These estimates include the snow that falls during these months, sometimes to a depth of several inches. During the spring months the southern counties were favored with over 15 inches of rain, while north of a line from Sevier county to Little Rock, Arkansas, and Memphis, Tennessee, the fall was from 12 to 15 inches, except on the extreme northwest, where it was less than 12 inches.

During the summer months the rainfall was more evenly distributed over the state, and averaged from 10 to 14 inches, a maximum of 18 inches occurring at Helena, in Phillips county, on the Mississippi river, and a minimum of less than 10 inches in the northwestern counties of the state. The autumn months were drier, the heaviest rains, more than 12 inches, occurring along the Red river, on the southwest. From 10 to 12 inches was reported over the rest of the state, except on the northwest and in the Saint Francis bottom lands, on the northeast, where it was less than 10 inches.

DRAINAGE.—Apart from the Mississippi and Saint Francis rivers on the east and northeast, the northern part of the state is drained by White river, the middle by the Arkansas, the south by the Ouachita, and the southwest by Red river.

Arkansas river, which is next in size to the Mississippi, divides the state into two almost equal parts. Entering on the west from the Indian territory, its course is very irregular, at first mostly eastward, and then, turning to the southeast, its waters flow into the Mississippi in Desha county. Its basin, covering an area of 11,270 square miles, is bounded on the north by the Ozark mountains, and has an average width of from 20 to 30 miles. On the south its width along the line of the Indian territory is about 50 miles, bounded by the range of Rich and Fourche La Fave mountains, which have an east and west trend, and approach near the river in Perry county. Thence southeastward the river basin becomes quite narrow, its southern rim lying very near the river.

White river is the most important stream in the northern part of Arkansas, draining, with its tributaries, about 17,400 square miles; an area greater than that of any other river within the state. This river rises in the southern part of Washington county, flows northward into Missouri, whence it soon turns southeastward to the lowlands of the Mississippi river, where, after its junction with the waters of the Black river from the north, it continues southward, and unites with the Arkansas river near its junction with the Mississippi. (*a*)

---

a In former times the mouth of the Arkansas river was at Napoleon, but so near that the mouth of White river to the Mississippi that its waters during high-water floods usually found their way direct to the latter river independent of the Arkansas. A permanent change took place, and the Arkansas river has since then followed the old White river cut-off, emptying its waters into the Mississippi several miles north of Napoleon.

The Ouachita river basin includes very nearly the entire country south of the Arkansas basin, an area of about 11,804 square miles, while that of Red river, on the southwest, has only an area of about 4,590 square miles.

GEOLOGY.—The oldest occurring rocks of the state are probably those of the Lower Silurian age in the northern counties, embracing a few outcrops of the Potsdam sandstone and large areas of later cherty magnesian limestones. With a broad base resting against Black river north of its junction with White river, covered eastward by Quaternary deposits, the triangular area of this formation extends westward, with narrowing limits in this state, until it passes out near the western boundary. Dipping toward the south, it is overlaid by the sub-Carboniferous Archimedes limestones, chert, and sandstones, which form the southern border of the Ozark mountains in the northern portions of Stone, Searcy, Newton, Madison, and Carroll counties. So far as known, the Upper Silurian and the Devonian formations are not represented in the state, except perhaps in very small areas. A southern dip carries the sub-Carboniferous under the Coal Measures, which constitute the most extensively developed geological region in the state. This is represented by the sandstones and red shales of the millstone grit, which form the hills and high ridges, its shales also underlying much of the valley land. Coal-beds appear in many of the counties. The rock strata are generally regular, except in the lower part of the region, where the effects of granitic disturbance are seen in upturnings and contortions and the presence of many mineral veins.

The next older formation represented is the Cretaceous, and this occurs in the southwestern part of the state. It enters the state from the Indian territory with a width of about 30 miles, reaching from Ultima Thule, in Sevier county, to Red river, but gradually narrows eastward to a point at Arkadelphia, on the Ouachita river, in Clark county. Characteristic fossils of this formation are abundant in localities, and are probably of the rotten-limestone group. This is the northeastern termination of the great Cretaceous belt, that, extending westward through the southern part of the Indian territory, turns southward through the central part of Texas to the southern foot of the table-lands and the Llano Estacado, which are also but a continuation of the same formation northwestward into New Mexico.

The black, waxy, and open prairies, that form so prominent a feature of the formation elsewhere, are in this state found only in small patches in the lowlands, the formation being covered in the uplands by the Quaternary sands and clays, which form hills bearing a short-leaf pine and other timber growth. Salt-licks are a feature of the Cretaceous lands of this state, especially in Sevier county (as well as of Louisiana).

During or immediately after the Cretaceous period there seems to have occurred a great disturbance or upheaval, bringing to the surface the granitic and metamorphic rocks, which cover large areas of country in Saline and Pulaski counties, with also a small outcrop in Hempstead county. At the same time the shales and sandstones of the region southwestward in Garland, Hot Spring, Pike, Polk, and the northern portion of Sevier counties were upturned, contorted, and, in some instances, broken and altered. (a)

On the northwest of Little Rock the continuation of the line of disturbance is observed in the upturned or folded strata of the Ozark mountains, which pass into Missouri from Carroll county. Argentiferous galena ores, in veins, are an accompaniment of this formation in Arkansas, the Kellogg silver mines, a few miles north of Little Rock, being the most noted occurrence. Novaculite (whetstone) and sandstone, filled with crystals of quartz, are among the most commonly occurring metamorphic rocks, the former being found in abundance chiefly around the celebrated Hot Springs, in Garland county.

The Tertiary formation is represented in this state only by the marl-beds and limestones of the Eocene, which extends southward into Louisiana. Marl-beds, with characteristic Tertiary fossils, occur at the foot of Crowley's ridge, in Saint Francis county, and also in the counties lying south of Little Rock. Thick and extensive beds of lignite are said to be found in Ashley, Union, Bradley, and Calhoun counties, exposed in the banks of the streams. The Tertiary is all overlaid by beds of Quaternary sands, pebbles, and clays, which, by erosion, have been left as irregular hills and ridges, capped with ferruginous sandstone formed from these materials. Crowley's ridge, which forms so prominent a feature of the country lying between the Mississippi and the White rivers, is made up almost entirely of the material of this last group nearly to its entire height of from 100 to 150 feet, and throughout nearly the whole of its length, from the Chalk bluffs of Saint Francis river, in the extreme northeastern corner of the state, to Helena, on the Mississippi river, it is underlaid by Silurian and Carboniferous beds on the north and by Tertiary marls and limestones on the south.

AGRICULTURAL FEATURES.—The lands of the state may be grouped in two grand divisions, separated by a line from the western part of Clay county, on the northeast, along Black and White rivers to Des Arc, in Prairie county, and thence to Little Rock and Arkadelphia, on the southwest; thence west to Ultima Thule, on the line of the Indian territory, in Sevier county. Westward and northward of this line lie the rocky, hilly, and mountainous lands, or "up country"; but on the east and south the lands are more generally rolling, or level, sandy, and sometimes gravelly in character, and almost entirely free from rocks on the surface, excepting some scattered pieces of

a This granitic axis is very extensive, reaching westward into the Indian territory, with granite outcrops (penetrated by trap) at Boggy depot and Tishomingo, in the Chickasaw Nation, and other places; thence it turns southward into Texas, a large area of granite occurring in Llano and in Gillespie county, and passes southwestward into Mexico, as shown by several basaltic hills in Frio and Uvalde counties, as well as by the metamorphosed condition of the Cretaceous limestone beds in Kinney county, on the Rio Grande, and by the disturbed strata and the old volcanic cones at the Santa Rosa mountains in Mexico. (See *Mexican Boundary Survey Report*.)

ferruginous sandstone. This southern region also includes those river alluvial lands whose extensive areas make them of great agricultural value. The two divisions may be subdivided into other regions, whose lands differ from each other in some general and soil features, topographical position, etc., each region in turn having its soil varieties.

The prairies of the state.—The greater part of Arkansas is a well-timbered country, but there are several large regions of open prairies, each region differing from the others in topographical and geological features and elevation, as well as in the character of the lands. They may be separated into the following classes, and will be thus described:

1. Eastern Tertiary gray silt prairies, occurring chiefly in Lonoke, Prairie, and Arkansas counties, and in smaller areas in Lincoln, Drew, and Ashley on the south, and between White river and Crowley's ridge northward as far as Craighead county.

2. Black Cretaceous prairies, occurring in small bodies in the lowlands of the southwestern part of the state.

3. Reddish-loam prairies of the west, lying south of the Arkansas river. These lands overlie the coal-beds of the Carboniferous formation.

4. Sandy prairies in the northern part of the state, in the extreme tier of counties, underlaid by cherty sub-Carboniferous limestones. They are small in all of the counties except Benton, where commence the broad and open prairies of the Ozark region, extending into the Indian territory westward. These will be included in the description of the northern region.

AGRICULTURAL REGIONS.—The following is a list of the agricultural regions as at present determined, which will be separately described in the report:

1. Alluvial lands.
   a. Bottom lands of the Mississippi, Arkansas, and Red rivers, and their larger tributaries.
   b. Crowley's ridge of the Mississippi plain.
2. Gray silt prairies of eastern Arkansas.
3. Yellow-loam and sandy pine-hills region.
   a. Red hills.
   b. Sandy pine hills.
   c. Flat sandy and pine lands.
4. Black lands of the southwest, prairie in part.
5. Red-loam region, shaly, rocky, and hill lands.
   a. Timbered lands.
   b. Prairie lands.
   c. Northwestern prairie region.
   d. Metamorphic lands.
6. Northern barrens, hills, prairies, and siliceous lands.
   a. Siliceous lands of chert, sandstone, and limestone.
   b. Barrens and cherty and magnesian limestone lands.

These regions are mostly continuations of similar regions in the adjoining states on the north and south, some of them terminating abruptly against the broad alluvial region of the Mississippi river. No single region is continuous through the state, even the Mississippi alluvial being interrupted by the high Crowley's ridge, which reaches to the river itself. The outlines, as defined on the map accompanying this report, are merely general, as absolute correctness would require a very detailed survey of the border of each region.

STATISTICS.—*Population.*—The number of inhabitants of the state in 1880 was 802,525, and these, if evenly distributed, would average a little more than fifteen persons per square mile. We find, however, that the most populous counties are those along the Arkansas river, and that, together with Phillips on the east (in which the large town of Helena is located), Hempstead on the southwest, and Washington and Benton on the northwest, they include all of those counties whose average is more than twenty persons per square mile, their combined population also comprising three-eighths of that of the state. That this should be the case is not surprising, for the river has long afforded excellent facilities for the transportation of supplies and produce, and a railroad along its northern banks has aided in the settlement of the country. The two grand divisions of the state, the rocky and mountainous on the northwest and the sandy and rolling lower lands of the southeast and east, each comprising about one-half of the area of the state, have about the same population. The relative proportion of whites to negroes is nearly three of the former to one of the latter, the whites comprising 73.7 per cent. of the entire population; but the two races are not evenly distributed between the two divisions of the state given above. The well-known preference of the negro for the easily cultivated and sandy "low country" is as well shown in Arkansas as in any other southern state, and the line marking the separation of the two agricultural divisions may also be properly called the "color line" between a region with comparatively few negroes and another in which the two races are nearly evenly represented, the whites predominating. Of the entire negro population, 18 per cent. only is found in the "up country", or northern division, which embraces the mineral region, while 82 per cent. belong to the "low country", comprising the sand and pine hills of the south, Crowley's ridge and the eastern sandy prairies, and the alluvial lands of the Mississippi, Arkansas, Red, and other streams. On the contrary, 64 per cent. of the white population is found on the north and but 36 per cent. in the low country. In the counties of Chicot, Desha, Ashley, Lincoln, Jefferson, Phillips, Monroe, Lee, Woodruff, and Crittenden, which are largely alluvial bottoms, the negro population is predominant (with an aggregate ratio of 100 white to 218 colored), the malaria of these lowlands affecting them much less than it does the whites. The counties of La Fayette, Little River, and Ouachita on the southwest have also a predominant negro population, also due probably to the large amount of bottom lands which are in cultivation.

LANDS UNDER CULTIVATION.—The total land area of Arkansas has been approximately given at 33,948,800 acres. Of this only about one-tenth is under cultivation, averaging a little more than 64 acres per square mile. The remaining 90 per cent. is still in its original virgin condition, mostly covered with a forest growth, and much of it is either too swampy or too hilly and broken for successful tillage. A large proportion of the alluvial lands of the Mississippi and Arkansas rivers are of this swampy overflowed character, and can be made fit for cultivation only by a system of levees. The region most generally settled and under tillage is that of the extreme northern and northwestern counties, the average being 90 acres per square mile, Benton county, with its average of 126 acres, ranking as first in the state. The yellow loam and sandy pine-hills of the south are next, with an average of 69.1 acres. Other regions average from 50 to 60 acres, the Mississippi alluvial naturally being lowest, because of its lands being subject to overflow. Phillips county, fronting on the Mississippi river, but having a large proportion of ridge lands, ranks as second in its average of tilled area, 125.3 acres; Washington third, with its average of 120 acres. Poinsett, though crossed by Crowley's ridge, has the least average of tilled lands, 10.1, and ranks as lowest in the state in this regard, while the upland counties of Montgomery, Polk, Perry, and Garland have only from 23 to 28 acres per square mile.

There are but seven counties whose average is as much as 100 acres per square mile, while in sixteen the average is between 75 and 100 acres, and in twenty-six between 50 and 75 acres, all others being below 50 acres to the mile.

ALLUVIAL LANDS.

THE MISSISSIPPI AND SAINT FRANCIS ALLUVIAL REGION.—The alluvial or bottom lands that border the Mississippi river on the west are most extensive northward from the junction of the Saint Francis river, and have the greatest width in this state, 50 or more miles, opposite the northern line of Craighead county. The region extends westward beyond Saint Francis river to the foot of the high ridge known as Crowley's ridge, which forms the western border southward to Helena, in Phillips county, on the Mississippi river, and covers an area of about 4,220 square miles, exclusive of Crowley's Ridge region. The surface of the country is rather level, diversified with low ridges, lakes, sloughs, bayous, and streams, mostly tributary to the Saint Francis river, and is well timbered with a growth of walnut, cottonwood, ash, elm, hickory, sweet and black gums, dogwood, hackberry, sycamore, honey-locust, white oak, pecan, black and red haw, box-elder, sassafras, beech, and maple on the higher lands, usually above overflow; sweet and black gums, oak, hackberry, hickory, etc., on the lands subject to annual overflow; and ash, elm, hickory, cypress, water oak, and willow in the deep swamps. The highest lands of the bottoms are those that border the Mississippi river, known as front-lands, and are formed from the more recent alluvial deposits, consisting of fine loams and silts, extremely

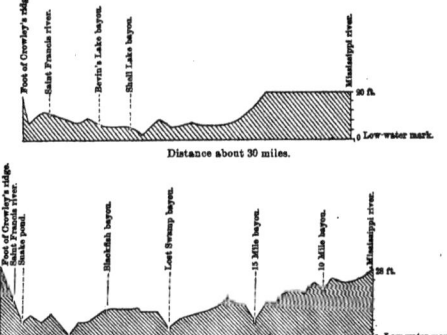

Sections showing the surface of the Saint Francis or Mississippi river bottom from the levees near Memphis westward to Crowley's ridge, from report on the Mississippi river, by Humphreys and Abbot, 1861.

rich and productive under cultivation. Westward to Crowley's ridge there is a rapid descent in the surface of the bottoms, and, as shown in the following sections, their general level is from 10 to 20 feet below the Mississippi front-lands. The banks of the Saint Francis and the various bayous are also much lower than those of the Mississippi, and, like the latter, have been formed from alluvial deposits, the beds of the streams gradually filling up, until they have become in most instances higher than the intermediate swamps and lowlands.

The greater part of the bottom lands are subject to overflow, the mean depths in the great flood years being estimated by the United States engineer corps to be about 3 feet, exclusive of the ridge lands. In the northern part of the region there is a large area of what is known as "sunk land" now covered by large lakes. The sudden sinking of the surface occurred during the New Madrid earthquake of 1811, and the lands are now 15 or 20 feet below flood levels.

The lands of this region comprise light sandy alluvial soils along the front-land of the Mississippi and on the low ridges of the interior and a heavy and stiff black buckshot soil on the overflowed lands, the latter soil deriving its name from a tendency to crumble into grains or small irregular balls on drying after being disturbed. This soil becomes hard and is difficult to plow if allowed to dry before tillage. Both this and the alluvial sandy loam of the ridges are very productive under proper cultivation, yielding from one to two bales of cotton lint or 70 to 80 bushels of corn per acre. Still southward on the Louisiana line the bottoms of the Mississippi river and bayous Bartholomew and Maçon preserve the same character of soil and growth as already given. The region is, however, penetrated by oak and short-leaf pine peninsulas from the interior with their sandy and gravelly upland soils, and isolated ridges of the same separate the three streams from each other. The bottom lands in this part of the region are about the only lands under cultivation, the uplands being too poor.

The following analyses are given to show the chemical composition of the lands of this region:

No. 217. *Black sand bottom land*, foot of Crowley's ridge, Greene county. Timber growth, gum, walnut, and poplar; undergrowth, papaw and spicewood; Quaternary deposits. The dried soil is of a light umber color, sandy, containing much clear and some reddish rounded grains.

No. 219. *Sandy subsoil* of the above. Sandy, and dirty-gray buff colored.

No. 228. *Genuine black sand land*, Greene county. Growth, poplar, gum, and oak; undergrowth, papaw and spicebush; Quaternary deposits. The dried soil is of an umber color. Some small rounded pebbles were sifted out of it with the coarse sieve.

No. 230. *Red underclay* of the above. Light brick-red color.

No. 419. *Saint Francis bottom soil*, Craighead county. Growth, gum, elm, white oak, black hickory, and hackberry. The dried soil is of a light mouse-color, in very tenacious lumps, and contains vegetable twigs, remains of leaves, etc.

No. 422. "*Gum soil*," Saint Francis River bottom, Crittenden county. Dried soil of a light mouse-color, in very tenacious lumps.

No. 420. *Bottom land* near No. 422. Growth, large oaks; dried soil is of a light mouse-color, in quite tenacious lumps.

No. 423. *Genuine buckshot land*, bottom land, Sec. 15, T. 7 S., R. 4 W., Crittenden county. Dried soil is mouse-colored, in very tenacious lumps.

Saint Francis bottom lands.

	GREENE COUNTY.				CRAIGHEAD COUNTY.	CRITTENDEN COUNTY.		
	BLACK SANDY LANDS.					BUCKSHOT CLAY LANDS.		
	Soil.	Subsoil.	Soil.	Red underclay.	Soil.	Gum soil.	Oak land soil.	Buckshot soil.
	No. 217.	No. 219.	No. 228.	No. 230.	No. 419.	No. 422.	No. 420.	No. 423.
Insoluble matter	90.045	97.995	90.696	79.485	72.915	73.645	71.095	70.270
Potash	0.183	0.132	0.183	0.396	0.454	0.758	0.721	0.654
Soda	0.050	0.048	0.058	0.055	0.143	0.232	0.139	0.084
Lime	0.225	0.054	0.221	0.067	0.403	0.655	0.641	0.901
Magnesia	0.252	0.193	0.296	0.400	5.745	1.155	1.070	1.237
Brown oxide of manganese	0.190	0.020	0.245		0.345	0.320	0.295	0.170
Peroxide of iron	1.185	1.010	1.485	15.335	4.940	5.340	6.890	6.765
Alumina	0.570	0.295	1.490		7.485	8.685	10.485	10.185
Phosphoric acid	0.183	0.078	0.250	0.288	0.250	0.294	0.347	0.367
Sulphuric acid			0.088	0.021	0.110	0.067	0.101	0.101
Water and organic matter	6.243	1.233	4.825	4.013	12.728	6.590	9.319	9.527
Total	98.135	101.158	99.781	100.007	100.128	90.650	100.592	101.131
Hygroscopic moisture, air-dried	3.300	0.650	2.065	4.950	8.750	8.475	8.990	9.475

The black sandy soils contain over 90 per cent. of sand, and are black, with a large percentage of vegetable matter. They also contain fair percentages of potash and large proportions of lime and phosphoric acid, explaining their thriftiness under cultivation.

The heavy buckshot lands, with their large amounts of iron, alumina, and magnesia, have high percentages of potash, phosphoric acid, vegetable matter, and lime, and altogether show a high and lasting productive power under proper cultivation. The results of the analysis exhibit a remarkable agreement with those from other states, and add testimony to their being the richest lands of the river region.

ARKANSAS RIVER BOTTOM LANDS.—The bottom lands of the Arkansas river, from the line of the Indian territory to Little Rock, are usually narrow and irregularly distributed, though in places they afford large areas of tillable lands, the hills, through which the river has found its way, often approaching to near the water's edge. The lands embrace two terraces or bottoms, the first, or lowest, having a reddish, sandy, alluvial soil, timbered with cottonwood, maple, willows, etc., and mostly subject to overflows. The second bottom, about 15 feet higher, has soils of a dark sandy loam, timbered with red, pin, and chestnut oaks, black walnut, sweet gum, mulberry, and linden, with an undergrowth of papaw, sassafras, greenbriers, brambles, alder bushes, and grape-vines. This bottom is very productive, yielding from 1,500 to 2,000 pounds of seed-cotton or 50 bushels of corn per acre.

At Little Rock the river enters the sands, gravel, and clays of the southern pine-hills, and thence to its junction with the Mississippi river the bottom lands are mostly continuous on both sides of the river, covering in all about 1,200 square miles. On the south side the alluvial lands are comparatively narrow, the river sometimes flowing at the foot of the uplands; on the north they are very extensive, and, according to the correspondent from Prairie county, reach as far as bayou Meta, a distance in one place of about 30 miles. Below the mouth of the bayou the bottoms become more narrow, and the open prairies of the southern part of Arkansas county approach to within one mile of the river. The lands are well timbered with the growth already given, and comprise a red sandy, sometimes clayey loam—forming a front-land along the river, derived from the red sediment brought down during high water—and black sandy and black tenacious buckshot lands, forming the back-lands of the bottoms. The buckshot soils are, as in other bottoms described, usually wet and ill-drained, difficult to till, unless plowed before they become dry and hard, and are very productive. The region is interspersed with lakes, sloughs, and bayous, is largely subject to overflows, and levees have been constructed on portions of the river banks for protection. The lands are the chief cotton lands of this part of the state, and when under cultivation yield from 2,000 to 3,000 pounds of seed-cotton or from 50 to 70 bushels of corn per acre. The following analyses are given to show their composition:

No. 273. *Arkansas bottom waste land*, near Van Buren, Crawford county. Alluvium at the base of millstone grit. The dried soil is of a mouse-color, derived doubtless, in part, from the red sediment of the ferruginous shales of the Cherokee country.

No. 275. *Subsoil* from the same; dried, is a light-chocolate color.

No. 282. *Sandy loam*, Arkansas bottom land, near Van Buren, Crawford county. Millstone grit formation. The dried soil is of a brownish-umber color.

No. 284. *Subsoil* from the same. Dull light brick-dust color.

No. 385. *Bottom soil*, Sec. 10, T. 5, R. 18 west, Conway county. Timber growth, white, red, and black oaks, sweet gum, black hickory, and walnut; derived from millstone grit formation. The dried soil is of a light gray-brown color, and contains shot iron ore and fragments of deep ferruginous sandstone.

No. 387. *Subsoil* of the above. Gray buff colored.

No. 388. *Arkansas bottom land*, foot of Petit Jean mountain, Perry county. Nearest rock formation, millstone grit. The dried soil is of a gray-brown color, and contains much fine sand in clear grains.

No. 390. *Subsoil* of the above, taken 9 to 12 inches below the surface.

No. 424. *Soil* from a new field, Sec. 19, T. 5 S., R. 7 W., Jefferson county. Dried soil, mouse-colored, with a tint of umber.

No. 425. *Subsoil* from trench at the mill-seat near No. 424. Dried soil of a light brick-dust color.

No. 426. *Polished buckshot, or stiff red or chocolate-colored land*, from Sec. 9, T. 6 S., R. 7 W., Jefferson county (cuts like cheese or soap). The dried soil is of a powdered chocolate color, in very tenacious lumps.

No. 427. *Subsoil of a stiff red or chocolate-colored* land, three years in cultivation, near No. 426, Jefferson county. Dried soil like the preceding.

No. 428. *Black elm, ash, oak, and hickory land*, Sec. 20, T. 5 S., R. 7 W., Jefferson county. The dried soil is of a powdered chocolate color, having tenacious lumps.

No. 429. *Cotton soil* that polishes with the plow, taken 6 inches below the surface; same locality as No. 428, Jefferson county. Dried soil like the preceding.

No. 411. Sample of the so-called *buckshot land*, Sec. 16, T. 6 S., R. 6 W., Arkansas county. Timber growth, gum, hackberry, box-elder, etc. Dried soil, in very tough lumps, of a chocolate, dark-gray color. The infusion of the soil in carbonated water had a fetid smell, which was the case with some other soils of this kind.

No. 412. *Under or iron-shot clay*, taken from ravines at Arkansas Post, Arkansas county. It contains moderately friable rounded lumps of dark-brown oxide of iron, and is of a light-drab color.

No. 414. *Arkansas River bottom soil*, T. 7, R. 4 W., Arkansas county. A sandy soil, containing minute specks of mica, of a warm brownish-gray color.

No. 416. *Subsoil* of above. Lighter colored, and not so sandy.

No. 333. *Bottom soil*, Moton's plantation, Arkansas county. The dried soil is of a light, dirty, brownish color.

Arkansas river bottom lands.

NARROW LANDS ABOVE LITTLE ROCK.

	CRAWFORD COUNTY.				CONWAY COUNTY.		PERRY COUNTY.	
	Waste alluvial land.		Sandy loam.		Sandy loam.		Sandy.	
	Soil.	Subsoil.	Soil.	Subsoil.	Soil.	Subsoil.	Soil.	Subsoil.
	No. 273.	No. 275.	No. 283.	No. 284.	No. 285.	No. 287.	No. 288.	No. 290.
Insoluble matter	84.720	80.595	88.520	89.895	88.915	90.940	94.565	98.515
Potash	0.435	0.579	0.246	0.307	0.149	0.140	6.148	0.206
Soda	0.153	0.136	0.059	0.059	0.034	0.050	0.048	0.038
Lime	0.450	0.039	0.124	0.165	0.241	0.053	0.403	0.221
Magnesia	1.170	0.436	0.880	0.781	0.658	0.306	0.415	0.628
Brown oxide of manganese	0.145		0.095	0.220	0.345	0.220	0.080	0.120
Peroxide of iron	2.390	11.342	2.185	2.900	2.840	2.365	1.200	1.536
Alumina	8.815		1.600	3.090	2.310	2.985	1.485	0.810
Phosphoric acid	0.184	0.212	0.063	0.167	0.178	0.150	0.191	0.179
Sulphuric acid	0.050	0.052	0.083	0.094	0.067	0.045	0.036	0.041
Water and organic matter	7.896	6.562	4.791	2.467	4.505	3.056	1.747	2.050
Total	100.007	100.485	98.636	99.485	100.142	100.319	100.363	99.148
Hygroscopic moisture, air-dried	2.975	4.835	2.425	1.735	2.900	2.000	1.250	2.050

BROAD LANDS BELOW LITTLE ROCK.

	JEFFERSON COUNTY.						ARKANSAS COUNTY.				
	Black sandy soil.	Clayey subsoil.	Red buckshot.		Stiff clayey soil.	Polished cotton soil.	Buckshot soil.	Under-clay.	Cotton.		Soil.
			Soil.	Subsoil.					Sandy soil.	Clayey subsoil.	
	No. 434.	No. 425.	No. 426.	No. 427.	No. 428.	No. 429.	No. 411.	No. 412.	No. 414.	No. 416.	No. 333.
Insoluble matter	88.545	85.745	71.980	71.185	70.340	78.990	75.740	88.615	93.418	81.340	78.388
Potash	0.502	0.641	0.899	1.013	0.941	0.710	0.642	0.212	0.201	0.714	0.352
Soda	0.111	0.107	0.149	0.175	0.125	0.147	0.204	0.153	0.100	0.080	0.062
Lime	1.297	0.185	0.780	0.753	0.550	0.613	0.941	0.263	0.212	0.543	0.222
Magnesia	0.939	1.100	2.871	2.513	2.577	1.292	2.301	0.876	0.737	1.555	0.845
Brown oxide of manganese	0.295	0.006	0.145	0.345	0.195	1.170	0.310	0.170	0.170	0.245	0.165
Peroxide of iron	1.940	3.490	5.985	7.000	6.815	4.615	3.750	3.513	1.740	4.640	8.050
Alumina	1.410	6.050	9.995	10.835	11.360	6.560	5.410	5.885	2.185	6.065	
Phosphoric acid	0.301	0.194	0.351	0.457	0.238	0.258	0.257	0.130	0.127	0.221	0.250
Sulphuric acid	0.110	0.041	0.050	0.067	0.135	Not estim'd	0.101	0.041	0.050	0.084	0.067
Carbonic acid	0.988										
Water and organic matter	6.568	2.384	7.879	5.511	7.879	8.750	7.880	2.470	1.803	5.021	9.342
Total	99.956	99.821	100.543	99.334	101.154	101.105	99.536	99.980	100.740	100.486	99.892
Hygroscopic moisture, air-dried	3.225	3.550	7.850	3.350	3.435	5.200	3.000	4.250	1.550	4.925	3.975

Little Rock, which marks a point on the dividing line between the sandy pine-hills of the south and the rocky and red-loam lands of the north and west, is also about the point of separation between the sandy bottom lands of the upper portion of the river and the rich and broad lands of the lower. The lands above Little Rock are very generally the same in character throughout, the exception being in the "waste land" of Crawford county. Why this latter should be so called does not appear in Owen's report, as the soil is richer than the sandy loams in all the elements of fertility, and, unless unfavorably situated, is evidently more productive. The analysis of soil from an old field of the same thirty years in cultivation shows no material diminution, the elements being replaced probably either by subsoiling or by sediment from overflows. This waste land resembles very much the rich bottoms below Little Rock in its large amounts of potash, lime, and phosphoric acid. In the other sandy lands these elements are in fair amounts, except in that of Crawford, where the phosphoric acid is deficient.

The lands below Little Rock are among the richest in the state, and contain large percentages of potash, lime, magnesia, and phosphoric acid, the buckshot lands of Jefferson being especially rich in these as well as in vegetable matter, the latter doubtless rendering readily available much of the phosphoric acid. The magnesia, so abundant in all of the river soils, is probably derived chiefly from the magnesian limestones found along its banks and those of its tributaries in the Indian territory.

THE LANDS OF WHITE RIVER AND ITS TRIBUTARIES.—White river, in its course from Benton county, on the northwest, northward into Missouri, and thence southeastward to Jackson county, where it reaches the Crowley's Ridge region, has comparatively little bottom land. The stream has cut its way through and among the hills and mountains of the northern counties, and is bordered by upland valleys and sloping hillsides, or often by high and precipitous bluffs of limestone or sandstone. The lands of this part of the river are very fertile and productive when in sufficient tracts for cultivation. In Independence county, on the south side of the river, there is a large tract, known as the "oil-trough bottom", having a length of 15 miles, and bordered by high hills of limestone and sandstone, the principal timber growth of which is pin, red, and water oaks, elm, pecan, black walnut, sweet gum, hackberry, and buckeye, with an undergrowth of very large papaw, cane, grape-vines, and a little spicewood. The soil is a dark sandy loam, the subsoil being more tenacious, though black, to a depth of several feet. The land under cultivation is capable of yielding 50 bushels of corn or 30 bushels of wheat per acre.

From Jackson county southward to the junction with Arkansas river the bottom lands of the river vary in width from 1 mile to 5 miles or more, and lie apparently chiefly on the eastern side of the river, the western being bordered by the hills of Independence and White and the prairies of Prairie and Arkansas counties. The principal tributaries on the east are the Black and Cache rivers, lying parallel with each other, and separated by low sandy and gravelly ridges, 10 or 15 feet above overflow. The lands of White river are chiefly black sandy loams, well timbered with oak, ash, hickory, walnut, sweet gum, etc., and capable of yielding, when cultivated, from 1,200 to 1,500 pounds of seed-cotton or 50 bushels of corn per acre. These lands, however, are largely subject to overflow, and are interspersed with marshes and ponds.

South of the termination of Crowley's ridge, in Phillips county, there is a broad region of bottom land lying between the White and the Mississippi rivers, well timbered, and interspersed with lakes, sloughs, bayous, and a few low ridges, the latter above overflow. The lands comprise the black and light sandy loams of the ridge front-lands along the river and the stiff buckshot lands of the low bottoms.

BLACK RIVER LANDS.—Black river borders Crowley's ridge on the west, its course from the Missouri line being slightly southwestward to its junction with White river at the right angle bend of that stream at Jacksonport. The alluvial lands proper, low and mostly subject to overflow, are interspersed with sloughs and lakes, and are well timbered with a large growth of white, red, black, and post oaks, gum, elm, hickory, and black walnut. Magnesian limestone hills and bluffs occur on the west of the river, while on the east the low ridges are formed of Quaternary deposits of sand, gravel, and clay. The soil is a black sandy loam, easily cultivated, and where above overflow has a yellow clay subsoil; it yields under cultivation from 50 to 70 bushels of corn per acre.

CACHE RIVER LANDS.—Cache river cuts a long groove, as it were, in the broad region of Crowley's ridge (on the west of the main ridge), extending from the Missouri line slightly southwestward to Clarendon, on White river, in Monroe county, a distance of more than 150 miles in a direct course, its broad bottom lands lying some 15 or 20 feet below the summits of the adjoining ridges, and having widths varying from 3 to 10 miles. This river runs parallel with White river, but has no "cut-off" connections with it. The lands embrace three chief varieties, viz: black sandy lands, post-oak lands, and black spice lands. The latter two are usually too wet for successful cultivation. The black spice lands support a timber growth of gum, ash, pin oak, and hackberry, besides the black spice. The growth of the black sandy lands is, as in the Saint Francis bottoms, sweet gum, hickory, walnut, poplar, dogwood, and hackberry, with an undergrowth of papaw and large grape-vines. These lands, when above overflow, are rich and productive, yielding under cultivation about a bale of cotton lint or from 50 to 70 bushels of corn per acre.

The following analyses are given of the lands of White river and its tributaries:

No. 244. *Oil-trough bottom soil*, Independence county. Timber growth, pin, red, and water oaks, elm, pecan, black walnut, sweet gum, hackberry, and buckeye, with an undergrowth of very large papaw, grape-vines, and a little spicewood. The dried soil is of an umber color.

No. 246. *Subsoil* of 244. Lighter colored.

No. 379. *White river bottom soil* near hills 1 mile above Batesville, Independence county. Growth, elm, hackberry, scaly-bark hickory, Spanish oak, walnut (near the river), and box-elder; nearest formation sub-Carboniferous. The dried soil is of an umber color, the lumps somewhat tenacious.

No. 381. *Subsoil* of the above. Lighter and more yellowish; lumps tenacious.

No. 382. *Bottom soil* close to river bank, 1 mile above Batesville, Independence county. Nearest formation is sub-Carboniferous. Dried soil is of a gray-umber color, more sandy and not so dark colored as preceding soil, and the lumps less tenacious. Effervesces slightly with acids.

No. 384. *Subsoil* near No. 382. Lighter and more yellowish; lumps very tenacious.

No. 324. *Black river bottom soil* near Parroquet bluff, Independence county. Dried soil is umber-gray in color, with some darker particles intermixed.

No. 436. *Clay soil* from what is called "buckshot land", low bottom, Sec. 6, T. 3 S., R 5 E., Phillips county. Principal growth, cottonwood, sycamore, ash, elm, and mulberry; said to be the most productive land in the county. Dried soil is mouse-colored, in very tenacious lumps.

No. 438. *Subsoil* near No. 436. Ash-gray in color.

No. 439. *Sandy loam soil*, high (sugar-tree) ridge on Long lake, from same locality as No. 436, Phillips county. Growth, sweet gum, red elm, sugar-tree, hackberry, box-elder, white elm, large red oak, papaw, black walnut, sassafras, muscadine and other grape-vines; soil light-umber color when dry.

No. 441. *Subsoil* near the above. Lighter colored and yellowish.

No. 231. *Cache River bottom land*, black sandy soil, Jackson county. Growth, sweet gum and elm, with an undergrowth of slippery elm and dogwood.

No. 233. *Subsoil* near the above. Lighter colored and more yellowish.

No. 243. *Cache River swamp*, post-oak and hickory soil, Poinsett county. Dried soil is of a buff-gray color, and in a very fine state of division.

Lands of White river and its tributaries.

	INDEPENDENCE COUNTY.						BLACK RIVER BOTTOM.	PHILLIPS COUNTY.					JACKSON COUNTY.		POINSETT COUNTY.
	WHITE RIVER.							BUCKSHOT.		HIGH RIDGE.			CACHE RIVER.		CACHE RIVER.
	Oil trough.		Soil.	Subsoil.	Sandy soil.	Subsoil.	Soil.	Soil.	Subsoil.	Soil.	Subsoil.		Black soil.	Sandy subsoil.	Silty soil.
	Soil.	Subsoil.													
	No. 244.	No. 245.	No. 279.	No. 381.	No. 382.	No. 384.	No. 224.	No. 436.	No. 438.	No. 439.	No. 441.		No. 231.	No. 233.	No. 243.
Insoluble matter	79.970	83.790	80.205	83.975	87.215	91.590	84.080	67.542	73.220	84.840	90.400		88.620	91.626	90.865
Potash	0.565	0.440	0.406	0.376	0.227	0.297	0.145	0.493	0.777	0.347	0.904		0.396	0.296	0.108
Soda	0.202	0.150	0.111	0.095	0.088	0.104	0.156	0.168	0.244	0.168	0.156		0.035	0.056	0.108
Lime	0.515	0.362	0.683	0.389	1.439	0.193	0.198	1.332	0.919	0.590	0.473		0.263	0.165	0.101
Magnesia	0.504	0.614	0.539	0.521	0.967	0.356	0.250	1.721	1.703	2.097	0.746		0.466	0.425	0.233
Brown oxide of manganese	0.230	1.495	0.090	0.190	0.180	0.113	1.270	0.200	0.220	0.220	0.220		0.230	0.145	0.095
Peroxide of iron	3.385	3.310	3.140	4.350	2.490	2.115	0.140	5.485	5.840	2.065	2.710		1.305	2.063	3.290
Alumina	5.390	5.290	5.610	4.460	2.310	2.810	3.615	6.502	6.600	3.670	3.385		2.725	2.190	3.265
Phosphoric acid	0.222	0.222	0.973	0.298	0.193	0.209	0.282	0.303	0.314	0.297	0.259		0.294	0.192	0.104
Sulphuric acid	0.042	0.042	0.110	0.058	0.072	0.050	0.066	0.165	0.084	0.075	0.650		0.033	0.045	0.042
Carbonic acid							1.131			1.016	0.701	0.465	0.372		
Water and organic matter	6.672	5.516	6.242	4.421	3.463	1.914	3.353	14.390	5.378	5.556	1.859		4.759	1.963	2.679
Total	96.897	101.180	96.569	99.133	98.505	99.663	99.555	99.587	100.200	101.380	100.764		99.628	99.193	100.919
Hygroscopic moisture, air-dried	4.475	3.025	6.275	4.450	2.400	2.075	4.565	11.225	9.475	4.150	3.225		2.975	1.700	1.000

The richest lands of the above group are the buckshot clays of Phillips county, the clayey loams of Oil Trough bottom, and Nos. 379 and 381, all of which are rich in important elements and show high fertility and durability. The other bottom lands of Independence county, while rich in phosphoric acid, have small amounts of lime, the Black river soil being also low in potash. The sandy lands of the high ridge, and of Cache river, in Jackson, rank high in their potash and phosphoric acid percentages, but are low in lime, while the soil of Poinsett county is comparatively poor in all.

BOTTOM LANDS OF THE OUACHITA RIVER AND ITS TRIBUTARIES.—The bottom lands of the Ouachita river north of its junction with bayou Moro are extensive, and are heavily timbered with a growth of white and water oaks, large pines, beech, hickory, dogwood, and ash, and an undergrowth of cane. The soil is mostly a dark sandy loam, rich and very productive, and yields from 40 to 50 bushels of corn, or from 1,500 to 2,000 pounds of seed-cotton per acre. South of the mouth of bayou Moro the lands become broader and more subject to overflows. The first or low bottoms have in places a whitish clay soil, cold, wet, and slushy, with an abundant growth of palmetto, and overlie beds of lignite, which often outcrop on the banks of the river. The second bottoms or hummocks are usually dark and sandy, and are preferred for cultivation to either the uplands or low bottoms. They yield from 1,000 to 1,500 pounds of seed-cotton or from 30 to 35 bushels of corn per acre, and have a timber growth of hickory, pine, and oaks, and an undergrowth of witch-hazel and sumac.

The lands of Saline river are very similar to those of the Ouachita, and some of its bottoms are high and the soils more clayey than the hummocks, but yield under cultivation about the same. In Saline county, near the headwaters of the river, the lands embrace a first and second bottom, the soil of the latter being a dark sandy loam, timbered with large white, red, and black oaks, sweet and black gums, elm, hickory, and some sycamore.

The following analyses are given to show the composition of the lands of these streams:

No. 378. *Ouachita bottom soil* from Sec. 30, T. 12, R. 18, Ouachita county. Timber growth, white and water oaks, large pines, beech, hickory, dogwood, and ash; undergrowth, cane and yellow basswood. The soil is of a dirty-gray buff color.

No. 335. *Second-bottom soil* of the north fork of the Saline river, Sec. 16, T. 1 S., R. 15 W., Saline county. Timber growth, large red, white, and black oaks, sweet and black gums, elm, hickory, and some buttonwood. The dried soil is of a dark dirty-buff color.

No. 337. *Subsoil* of the same color as the soil, taken near the same place.

Bottom lands of the Ouachita and Saline rivers.

	OUACHITA COUNTY.	SALINE COUNTY.	
	OUACHITA RIVER.	SALINE RIVER.	
	Soil.	Soil.	Subsoil.
	No. 378.	No. 335.	No. 337.
Insoluble matter	80.040	85.940	89.990
Potash	0.207	0.309	0.212
Soda	0.078	0.076	0.073
Lime	0.087	0.246	0.092
Magnesia	0.519	0.817	0.482
Brown oxide of manganese	0.395	0.240	0.270
Peroxide of iron	3.415	2.490	5.265
Alumina	6.065	3.535	1.185
Phosphoric acid	0.282	0.163	0.182
Sulphuric acid	0.075	0.134	0.046
Water and org.nic matter	8.232	5.460	2.451
Total	99.365	99.400	100.240
Hygroscopic moisture, air-dried	4.650	3.850	2.100

These soils contain fair amounts of potash and phosphoric acid, though for river lands they fall far below the usual standard for other rivers of the state, resembling rather some of the upland soils. There is a great deficiency in lime in the Ouachita soil and the subsoil of Saline river, while the vegetable matter is present in fair quantities.

The soils of the two rivers cannot with these two analyses be properly compared with each other, for the reason that the Ouachita specimen was taken not very far from the junction of the two streams, while the Saline specimen came from the headwaters of that stream, in the region of the millstone grit and metamorphic rocks. The former would probably be a representative of the lower Saline river lands.

RED RIVER BOTTOM LANDS.—Red river, in its eastern course along the line of Texas and Arkansas, and thence southward into Louisiana, is bordered by wide and level bottom lands, interspersed with small lakes and sloughs and intersected by other streams, and covers a probable area of 560 square miles. These lands attain their greatest width of 10 to 15 miles within the bend of the river, in the northeastern part of Miller county, becoming narrower where the course of the river is regular.

The lands are mostly well timbered with pin, willow, and over-cup oaks, ash, walnut, pecan, gum, cottonwood, dogwood, cypress, and elm, and are often bordered by open black sandy prairies. One of these prairies, lying in the southern part of La Fayette county, is about 10 miles long and from 1 to 2 miles wide, and is bordered on the east by black hog-wallow lands. The river bottoms embrace two chief varieties of lands, a black sandy loam, occupying usually the second bottom or terrace, easily tilled, and yielding from 1,500 to 2,000 pounds of seed-cotton per acre, and a red, sticky clay, sandy in places, and probably the most prominent soil of the river. This soil is derived in part from the red sediment brought down by the waters of the river and in part from the red clay beds that are exposed in the banks, and is considered the richest land in the bottom. It is covered with a dense cane undergrowth, and when under cultivation is said to yield sometimes as much as two bales of cotton lint per acre.

The following analyses show the average composition of these bottom lands:

Nos. 329 and 331. *Black sandy prairie bottom soil and subsoil,* near Lanesport, Sevier county.

No. 332. *Red cotton land,* Red river bottom, near Lanesport, Sevier county. Produces best in dry seasons.

No. 357. *Genuine red or chocolate-colored, stiff cane, cotton, Red river bottom land;* edge of Lost prairie, but in timbered land, Miller county. This is one of the varieties of the celebrated cotton lands of the Red river bottom.

No. 359. *Subsoil* near the above, and lighter colored.

No. 354. *Black sandy soil* of Red river bottom, T. 14, R. 26, Miller county. Contains much fine sand.

No. 356. *Subsoil* taken near the above. Umber colored, lighter, and with a reddish tint.

Bottom lands of Red river.

	SEVIER COUNTY.			MILLER COUNTY.			
	BOTTOM PRAIRIE LAND.		RED COTTON LANDS.	RED CANE AND COTTON LAND.		BLACK SANDY LAND.	
	Soil.	Subsoil.	Soil.	Soil.	Subsoil.	Soil.	Subsoil.
	No. 329.	No. 331.	No. 332.	No. 357.	No. 359.	No. 354.	No. 356.
Insoluble matter	84.540	89.040	78.290	74.740	79.415	93.990	92.990
Potash	0.413	0.352	0.679	0.657	0.526	0.214	0.164
Soda	0.077	0.088	0.122	0.191	0.155	0.053	0.062
Lime	0.669	0.185	2.682	2.542	2.248	0.120	0.064
Magnesia	0.691	0.624	0.685	2.839	2.209	0.463	0.556
Brown oxide of manganese	0.156	0.165	0.265	0.140	0.115	0.115	0.065
Peroxide of iron	2.090	3.940 } 10.940		4.990	4.715	1.346	1.540
Alumina	3.310	2.710 }		5.590	4.840	1.285	1.840
Phosphoric acid	0.130	0.256	0.162	0.162	0.162	0.176	0.126
Sulphuric acid	0.084	0.062	0.067	0.064	0.041	0.062	0.058
Carbonic acid	0.526	....	2.106	1.998	1.767	....	....
Water and organic matter	6.627	2.631	4.616	5.527	3.289	2.309	1.822
Total ... A	99.312	99.453	100.027	100.540	99.683	100.127	100.187
Hygroscopic moisture, air-dried	3.875	7.750	6.150	5.135	3.475	1.475	1.225

The red and stiff lands are seen by these analyses to be rich in the elements of fertility. The percentages of potash, lime, and magnesia are very high, while that of phosphoric acid is good, and sufficient for very many years' fertility.

The black bottom prairie lands rank next in fertility and in richness of soils. The percentages of potash, phosphoric acid, lime, and vegetable matter are good in the soil, and also, with the exception of lime, in the subsoil. The black sandy lands, while having an abundance of phosphoric acid and potash, are deficient in lime.

CROWLEY'S RIDGE, OR POPLAR RIDGE LANDS EAST OF WHITE RIVER.

On the east of the White and Black rivers, which form a continuous water-course north and south from Missouri to the Arkansas river, there is a region of low ridges, flat lands, and small prairies, bordered on the east by a high and prominent ridge, known as Crowley's ridge, the summit being from 125 to 150 feet above the bottom lands. The region embraces the counties of Clay and Greene, the eastern half of Lawrence, the western halves of Craighead, Poinsett, Cross, Saint Francis, and Lee, and nearly all of Jackson, Woodruff, Monroe, and Phillips, with small areas in Randolph and Prairie counties, covering in all about 5,250 square miles. A prominent feature is the wide prevalence of the tulip tree, popularly called poplar (*Liriodendron tulipifera*), and this is said to be the only region of the state where this tree is found growing.

Crowley's ridge proper forms at Chalk bluff, on Saint Francis river, in Clay county, on the Missouri line, a high bluff, a vertical section of which shows the following strata of Quaternary and Tertiary material below the soil and subsoil:

	Feet.
Chert and hornstone gravel	25
Pink and variegated sand locally indurated into a soft crumbling sandstone	96
White silicous clay shale or marly earth	24
Fine white potters' clay to water's edge	6

Southward the ridge extends through the central parts of Greene, Craighead, Poinsett, Cross, Saint Francis, and Lee counties, reaches the Mississippi river at Helena, in Phillips county, and is there composed of the same materials. Its width varies from 1 to 6 miles, and is narrowest in Craighead county; it maintains about the same height throughout its length, but is broken into hills from the point where it touches the Saint Francis river in Cross county, southward to the Mississippi, and at Helena it slopes gradually to the river.

The following section is given from this latter point:

Yellow silicous clay	feet.	6
Yellow and orange sand and gravel	feet.	20
Gravel	inches	6
Reddish clay	feet.	9
Plastic clay (potters'), local	inches	6
Yellowish and white sand, with some gravel	feet.	5
Sand and gravel	feet.	15
Space concealed to bed of slough	feet.	12

The summit of the ridge in the several counties is usually sandy and gravelly, with a large growth of tulip tree and beech, red, Spanish, and white oaks, hickory, sweet and black gums, black walnut, butternut, sugar. tree, honey-locust, and sometimes an undergrowth of cane. The lands are said to stand drought well, and to yield from 30 to 40 bushels of corn, 20 to 30 bushels of wheat, or 800 pounds of seed-cotton per acre.

In Phillips county the ridge spreads out into a comparatively level table-land, watered by Big creek, and has a deep-yellow or mulatto soil, with now and then small spots of an ashen color, probably the former beds of small, dried up ponds. "The chief growth is sweet gum, but on the most elevated portion of this land, where the soil for analysis was collected, the growth is beech, tulip tree, red and white elm, mulberry, sweet gum, white oak, black walnut, dogwood, sassafras, and red maple." This table-land is said to yield an average of 1,000 pounds of seed-cotton, 25 to 30 bushels of corn, or 20 bushels of wheat.

West of Crowley's ridge and the table-land to White river the country declines in elevation, and is composed of low ridges, with intervening white-clay flats, interspersed with occasional wet or glady prairies. The latter extend as far north as Craighead county, no mention being made of their occurrence in the counties of Greene and Clay. In the northeastern corner of Monroe county are Big and Little prairies. The latter appears to have been the bed of a dried up swamp. The soil and subsoil in this prairie are an ash-colored clay, charged with small iron gravel, having a depth of from 2 to 2½ feet, and resting on a substratum of red clay. These prairies require drainage for successful cultivation.

The country lying west of the ridge in Woodruff and the counties northward is not more than 10 or 15 feet above high water, and is much cut up by Cache river and many smaller streams. The low ridges are covered with sands and gravel, and are very similar in character and productiveness to the uplands already described.

The following analyses of the several varieties of land in this region are given:

No. 220. *Sandy soil* from the hickory and oak land of Crowley's ridge, Greene county. The dried soil is of a dirty-gray buff color.

No. 222. *Subsoil* of above.

No. 225. *Soil* from Sec. 11, T. 16, R. 4 E., Greene county.

No. 227. *Subsoil* of same, and buff-colored.

No. 445. *Hill land*, southern termination of Crowley's ridge, Phillips county. Derived from the clay and sand above the gravel bed. Principal growth, large poplar, beech, black walnut, white walnut, sweet gum, red, black, white, Spanish, and post oaks, and sugar tree. The soil is of a dark-drab color.

No. 447. *Subsoil* of the same. The dried soil is of a buff-gray or drab color; lighter than the preceding.

No. 442. *Table-land soil* from Sec. 5, T. 2 S., R. 4 E., Phillips county. Growth, beech, sweet and red gum, poplar, red oak, white and Spanish oaks, elm, ash, mulberry, black walnut, sassafras, red-bud, box-elder, honey-locust, and some black gum. It is at the foot of Crowley's ridge, and is derived from the Quaternary. The soil is of a dark ash-gray color.

No. 417. *Mamelle prairie soil*, edge of the "sunk land", Craighead county. Derived from the Quaternary. The dried soil is of a light-umber color, and contains small, clear, rounded grains of sand.

No. 433. *Little Prairie soil*, near Moreau post-office, Lee county. Growth, coarse grass, wild indigo, and sassafras shrubs in places. Dried soil is of an umber-gray color.

No. 434. *Subsoil* of the same. Dried; is ash-gray in color.

No. 435. *Red underclay*, from the same. Taken about 2½ feet below the surface.

No. 223. *Soil* from oak and pine ridge land 4 miles south of Gainesville, Greene county. Dried soil is of a buff-gray color.

No. 297. *Ridge soil*, Sec. 25, T. 1 N., R. 3 W., Monroe county. Growth, sweet gum, dogwood, and elm; some hickory and oak. Dried, is of a light-umber color; contains much fine, clear sand.

No. 430. *Ridge soil* from Sec. 11, T. 2 N., R. 1 E., Lee county. Growth, white, red, and post oaks, hickory, dogwood, black and sweet gum, and sassafras. Dried soil of a gray-buff color.

No. 449. *Ridge soil* from Governor Izzard's land, on the west side of Crowley's ridge, Saint Francis county. Growth, sweet gum, hickory, poplar, walnut, dogwood, red-bud, black ash, elm, muscadine, and other grape-vines. The dried soil is light mouse-colored.

No. 450. *Soil* of the same, cultivated thirty years.

No. 234. *Sandy soil* from 2 miles north of Jacksonport, Jackson county. Growth, black and white oaks; some hickory and sweet gum; Quaternary deposit. The dried soil is of a light-umber color.

No. 237. *Sandy soil*, Sec. 32, T. 14, R. 2 W., Jackson county. Growth, black and some white oaks, hickory, and sweet gum; Quaternary period. The dried soil is of a gray-brown color, and contains a large proportion of fine sand, composed of clear, rounded grains.

Lands of Crowley's Ridge region.

	CROWLEY'S RIDGE LANDS.						TABLE-LANDS.	PRAIRIES.			
	GREENE COUNTY.				PHILLIPS COUNTY.		PHILLIPS COUNTY.	CRAIGHEAD COUNTY.	LEE COUNTY.		
	Soil.	Subsoil.	Soil.	Subsoil.	Soil.	Subsoil.	Soil.	Soil.	Soil.	Subsoil.	Under clay.
	No. 220.	No. 222.	No. 225.	No. 227.	No. 445.	No. 447.	No. 442.	No. 417.	No. 433.	No. 434.	No. 435.
Insoluble matter	96.695	91.870	89.220	89.593	90.790	91.700	88.450	89.455	88.490	88.295	78.495
Potash	0.188	0.207	0.162	0.304	0.246	0.168	0.220	0.256	0.217	0.290	0.336
Soda	0.067	0.065	0.049	0.100	0.117	0.012	0.004	0.216	0.069	0.075	0.158
Lime	0.166	0.152	0.211	0.064	0.185	0.249	0.333	0.193	0.109	Trace.	0.081
Magnesia	0.225	0.412	0.490	0.537	0.618	0.357	0.356	0.504	1.263	0.504	2.235
Brown oxide of manganese	0.245	0.195	0.281	0.721	0.425	0.290	0.365	0.270	0.245	0.195	0.170
Peroxide of iron	1.080	1.080	1.602	2.085	1.950	2.290	1.640	2.370	2.465	2.790	5.315
Alumina	1.745	1.370	2.065	2.340	2.735	2.360	2.070	2.110	2.435	4.685	9.829
Phosphoric acid	0.250	0.117	0.111	0.341	0.242	0.193	0.444	0.151	0.165	0.129	0.251
Sulphuric acid	0.026	0.041	0.050	0.041	0.050	0.080	0.079	0.062	0.075	0.060	0.066
Water and organic matter	4.000	2.329	5.080	2.301	3.148	1.719	5.300	3.778	3.768	2.374	4.296
Total	99.278	98.518	98.899	99.019	100.506	100.528	100.194	99.475	100.381	99.697	99.814
Hygroscopic moisture, air-dried	1.725	1.275	2.365	1.815	2.175	2.000	3.425	2.725	3.300	3.125	5.750

	OTHER RIDGE LANDS.						
	GREENE COUNTY.	MONROE COUNTY.	LEE COUNTY.	SAINT FRANCIS COUNTY.		JACKSON COUNTY.	
	Soil.	Soil.	Soil.	Soil.	Soil cultivated 30 years.	Soil.	Soil.
	No. 223.	No. 297.	No. 430.	No. 449.	No. 450.	No. 234.	No. 237.
Insoluble matter	90.934	93.970	89.415	83.390	89.790	94.045	92.995
Potash	0.147	0.143	0.386	0.246	0.261	0.140	0.120
Soda	0.061	0.082	0.054	0.022	0.046	0.042	
Lime	0.129	0.081	0.125	0.753	0.252	0.109	0.138
Magnesia	0.205	0.256	0.631	0.494	0.502	0.308	0.065
Brown oxide of manganese	0.171	0.170	0.245	0.370	0.390	0.220	0.070
Peroxide of iron	1.610	1.100	1.065	2.125	2.340	1.190	1.365
Alumina	1.015	4.740	3.037	3.535	3.035	1.940	0.800
Phosphoric acid	0.112	0.090	0.221	0.535	0.210	0.094	0.110
Sulphuric acid	0.050	0.045		0.084	0.067	0.033	0.022
Water and organic matter	5.464	2.192	3.483	8.555	3.619	1.796	1.992
Total	99.898	100.820	99.723	100.439	100.543	99.917	98.966
Hygroscopic moisture, air-dried	2.365	1.525	2.550	5.225	2.600	1.175	0.935

From these analyses it appears that there is comparatively little difference in the soils of Crowley's ridge and other ridges in the same localities, and that there is a very marked increase in richness in the lands of the southern part of the region over those of the northern. In the soils of Greene county (on the north) the analyses show a medium percentage of potash and a fair amount of phosphoric acid, except in No. 220, where it is much better. The lime is hardly sufficient to insure durability in the fertility of the soils. In Phillips county there is a large increase in the percentage of potash, the phosphoric acid also being large. The lime is insufficient, and an application of that element would doubtless prove beneficial.

The ridge lands of Lee and Saint Francis counties are well supplied with potash and phosphoric acid, the percentage of both phosphoric acid and lime being very high in the latter county, and resembling more the bottom lands of the river, if indeed it is not such. A soil (No. 450) from the same land under cultivation thirty years is seen by the analysis to have lost much of its phosphoric acid, lime, and vegetable matter, while the potash has remained about the same. Notwithstanding this diminution in important elements, the land was said to still yield a bale of cotton lint, 40 to 50 bushels of corn, or 15 bushels of wheat per acre.

The lands of the low ridges of Monroe county are very sandy and deficient in both phosphoric acid, vegetable matter, and lime, and have a fair amount of potash and magnesia. The table-lands of Phillips county produced by the flattening out of Crowley's ridge are very rich in phosphoric acid and vegetable matter, with a fair amount of potash and lime. The latter, however, is not sufficient for long continued thriftiness, and liming would soon have to be resorted to.

The prairie lands of both the north and south of the region have very nearly the same percentages of important elements, their differences being mostly in the amounts of soda and magnesia, the latter being very high in the soil from Lee county. This is also the case in the red underclay, though not in the subsoil. These prairies, with sufficient drainage and the application of lime, should produce fairly, as there are fair amounts of potash and phosphoric acid present for the needs of a crop.

The iron and alumina in all of the soils above analyzed are rather low, while the insoluble residue of sand is mostly high, thus indicating easy tillage. The magnesia is comparatively high throughout, and is no doubt derived from the large region of magnesian limestones in the adjoining portions of Arkansas and Missouri.

GRAY SILT PRAIRIES OF THE EAST.

The country lying in the sharp angle formed by the White river on the east and the bottom lands of the Arkansas river and bayou Meto on the west, the point of junction being on the southeast, is very generally an open prairie, its surface being slightly rolling, and drained by many small streams, which unite to form two larger ones flowing southward parallel with White river. The region embraces nearly the whole of Arkansas and Prairie counties and a large portion of the southern half of Lonoke, the northern limit passing 3 miles west and south of the county seat of Lonoke and 2 miles south of Des Arc, the county-seat of Prairie county. On the east the prairies approach very nearly, if not immediately to, the banks of the White river, while on the south they are within 1 mile of the Arkansas river. The region embraces an area of about 1,535 square miles, and is dotted with small settlements, the average population being nearly twelve persons per square mile. The soil of the prairies is a sandy loam, with a depth of from 8 to 12 inches to a whitish and impervious clay subsoil, is ill-drained, and in low places is wet, spouty, and crawfishy; the higher portions are more sandy. In the northern part of the region the prairies are interspersed with timbered lands, underlaid by the material of the millstone-grit formation. The lands of the southern and greater part are underlaid by Tertiary clays, and probably by marls.

Going southward from this main region, we find occasionally small open prairies in Drew and Ashley counties, as well as still southward in Louisiana, on the same upland peninsula that is included between the Ouachita river and bayou Bartholomew, viz, prairies Mer Rouge and Jefferson. These prairies in the two states seem to be similar to each other, as well as to those of Arkansas and Prairie counties, with this exception: that those of Ashley and Drew are interspersed with small mound-like elevations, and are bordered with oak openings having the same feature. The lands of the latter prairies are usually flat and ill-drained, and are not as much in cultivation as those in Louisiana.

Crossing White river on the northeast side of the main prairie region we enter a region interspersed with bayous, small open prairies, and low ridges, which extends to Crowley's ridge, and is included in the description of Crowley's Ridge region. The prairies are usually flat, ill-drained, and wet, and not in cultivation. Little Prairie, in the western part of Lee county, appears to have been the bed of a dried-up swamp. The soil and subsoil are an ash-colored clay, charged with small iron gravel, having a depth of 2 to 2½ feet, and resting on a substratum of red clay. The northern limit of these prairies, as far as reported, is in Craighead county, and, as on the south, is composed of Quaternary clays and sand, forming a loamy soil with an impervious clay subsoil, wet and ill-drained, and not in cultivation.

The following analyses show the average composition of these prairie lands:

No. 321. *Soil of Grand Prairie*, 7 miles east of Brownsville, Prairie county. Millstone-grit formation, locally covered with Quaternary. Soil is of a light-umber color.

No. 323. *Subsoil* taken near the above.

No. 406. *Soil of the prairie* adjoining the Spanish grant on Sec. 18, T. 7 S., R. 3 W. An average of the prairie land of Arkansas county. Dried soil is of a light-umber color.

No. 408. *Subsoil* of the above.

No. 400. *Prairie soil* from the highest of the prairie, on Sec. 17, T. 7 S., R. 3 W., Arkansas county. Drier and looser than No. 406.

No. 410. *Upland woodland soil* adjoining the prairie land of the Spanish grant, T. 7 S. R. 4 W., Arkansas county.

No. 412. *Under (or iron-shot) clay* taken from ravines washed out at Arkansas Post, Arkansas county. This kind of clay underlies the prairie soil near Arkansas Post.

COTTON PRODUCTION IN ARKANSAS.

Gray silt prairie lands.

	PRAIRIE COUNTY.		ARKANSAS COUNTY.				
	GRAND PRAIRIE.		PRAIRIE.		HIGH PRAIRIE.	WOODLAND.	PRAIRIE.
	Soil.	Subsoil.	Soil.	Subsoil.	Soil.	Soil.	Underclay.
	No. 221.	No. 223.	No. 406.	No. 408.	No. 409.	No. 410.	No. 412.
Insoluble matter...................	90.920	92.390	88.465	86.460	88.865	87.965	86.815
Potash...........................	0.053	8.127	0.183	0.169	0.103	0.174	0.212
Soda	0.035	0.026	0.050	0.044	0.072	0.055	0.103
Lime	0.026	0.026	0.053	0.058	0.081	0.087	0.263
Magnesia.........................	0.290	0.265	0.482	0.526	0.475	0.519	0.876
Brown oxide of manganese	0.295	0.196	0.245	0.345	0.229	0.260	0.170
Peroxide of iron..................	1.885	2.015	2.740	2.965	2.140	3.015	2.515
Alumina..........................	1.735	1.515	2.535	4.910	2.960	3.635	5.235
Phosphoric acid	0.146	0.129	0.212	0.118	0.153	0.179	0.130
Sulphuric acid	0.055	0.041	0.071	0.067	0.101	0.067	0.041
Water and organic matter	4.653	2.138	4.094	3.506	4.998	3.814	3.470
Total	98.953	98.806	99.130	100.163	99.878	99.742	99.980
Hygroscopic moisture, air-dried......	3.300	1.925	3.690	3.750	3.950	3.390	4.250

These analyses show low percentages of potash in all of the soils and subsoils, with a deficiency in the Grand Prairie soil. The proportions of phosphoric acid, magnesia, and organic matter are fair, but the lime is extremely deficient. The underclay, No. 412, would apparently be of little advantage to the soil if commingled with it, as it contains less phosphoric acid, though more potash and lime than the latter.

The soil of Grand prairie is said to produce from 20 to 30 bushels of corn, or 30 bushels of wheat per acre.

Comparing these prairies with those of Crowley's Ridge region, on page 22, we find them to have larger percentages of potash, magnesia, and lime, with about the same percentage of phosphoric acid.

For comparison with the soil of prairie Mer Rouge, of Morehouse parish, Louisiana, the characteristic soils of the three groups are placed together.

	LEE COUNTY.		ARKANSAS COUNTY.		MOREHOUSE PARISH, LOUISIANA.	
	LITTLE PRAIRIE, OF CROWLEY'S RIDGE.		GRAY SILT PRAIRIE.		PRAIRIE MER ROUGE.	
	Soil.	Subsoil.	Soil.	Subsoil.	Soil.	Subsoil.
	No. 433.	No. 434.	No. 406.	No. 408.	No. 234.	No. 235.
Insoluble matter...................................	88.490	88.395	88.465	86.460	93.196	94.088
Potash..	0.217	0.290	0.183	0.169	0.131	0.155
Soda..	0.069	0.075	0.050	0.044	0.066	0.085
Lime..	0.109	Trace.	0.053	0.058	0.156	0.127
Magnesia..	1.263	0.504	0.482	0.526	0.070	0.225
Brown oxide of manganese..........................	0.245	0.195	0.245	0.345	0.066	0.135
Peroxide of iron...................................	2.465	2.790	2.740	2.965	1.370	1.731
Alumina...	3.435	4.885	2.535	4.910	1.080	1.798
Phosphoric acid	0.185	0.179	0.212	0.118	0.178	0.093
Sulphuric acid....................................	0.075	0.060	0.071	0.067	0.061	0.210
Water and organic matter	3.748	2.374	4.094	3.506	3.297	1.608
Total	100.281	99.697	99.130	100.163	99.670	100.284

The following conclusions may be reached from this comparison:

The subsoil in each region is poorer, though more clayey than the soil.

The lands of prairie Mer Rouge are more sandy and less ferruginous than those of the other prairies.

There is a decrease in the percentage of potash in the prairies from Craighead county southward into Louisiana.

The percentages of phosphoric acid and organic matter are about the same throughout, the highest being in Arkansas county.

YELLOW LOAM, OR OAK, HICKORY, AND SHORT-LEAF PINE UPLANDS.

The large region thus designated occupies the larger part of the southern portion of the state, and is the continuation northward of the similar regions in Texas and Louisiana. It embraces in Arkansas all or parts of twenty counties, viz: all of Ashley, Union, Columbia, La Fayette, Miller, southern part of Hempstead; nearly all of Nevada; all of Ouachita, Calhoun, Bradley, Drew, Lincoln, Dorsey, Dallas; the southern part of Clark; the southeastern part of Hot Spring; all of Grant; all of Jefferson, except the alluvial of the Arkansas river; and a small part of Saline and Pulaski counties, covering in all about 12,720 square miles. The high uplands of Little River, the northern part of Hempstead, the middle of Clark, and of the southern part of Sevier and Howard, lying above the black prairies, belong also properly to this region. It is bordered on the east by the alluvial lands of the Mississippi and the Arkansas rivers, and on the north by the red-loam lands of central Arkansas. In its western part the ridges are interspersed with small black prairie lowlands of the Cretaceous formation; the rest of the region covers the Tertiary.

The surface of the country is usually rolling and hilly, most so toward the north, where the hills are from 100 to 150 feet above the streams, that of the south being more level and undulating, especially along the Louisiana line. It is generally well timbered with short-leaf pine, red, post, white, and black oaks, hickory, dogwood, holly, and beech. The latter growth, said by Dr. Owen not to occur north of this region, is first seen below Rockport, on the banks of the Ouachita river, and southward becomes more and more common, till it is the prevailing growth, or even covers by itself alone low hills of the Tertiary or Cretaceous formations. The region is well watered by many streams flowing southward. Of these, Red river on the west, Ouachita and Saline in the center, and bayou Bartholomew on the east are most important, the Ouachita, with its tributaries, draining the greater part. The lands are underlaid chiefly by the clays, gravel beds, etc., of the Quaternary and Tertiary periods, while ferruginous sandstones, conglomerates, and iron ores cap many of the hills in the northern counties of the region. Gravel beds are very extensive, the stones varying from a few ounces to as much as 20 pounds in weight. Tertiary limestone underlies the lands in Clark, Dallas, and Grant counties, and beds of gypseous marls are reported in the southwest the part of Bradley. In the southern counties bordering the Ouachita river thick beds of lignite are found at depths of from 15 to 30 feet.

This yellow-loam region is not as thickly settled as others in the state, though the average is nearly fifteen persons per square mile. The greatest average is found in the counties of Hempstead, Jefferson, and Nevada, the first and last having also the greatest average acreage of tilled lands. A little more than one-tenth of the area of the region is under cultivation, a proportion about equal to that of the other regions of the state. The chief crops comprise cotton, corn, wheat, oats, and sweet potatoes. Cotton has the largest acreage. The corn produced in 1879 would average about 18.6 bushels per inhabitant: an amount not nearly sufficient for the full supply for man and working stock.

The lands of the region derived from or made up of such a variety of material are themselves naturally varied in character and composition, without any regular relationship with reference to each other. They occur in small and large tracts, and may, in general, be classed as red lands, gray sandy loams, prairies, and flats.

RED LANDS.—The largest and most prominent of occurrences of the red lands of this region are in the counties of Grant, Dallas, Bradley, Dorsey, Calhoun, and Ouachita, with smaller areas elsewhere. These lands are either the clay subsoils which underlie a great part of the sandy soils of the region and here approach to the surface, or are sandy in character, and derived from the ferruginous sandstones, limonite, or other forms of Tertiary iron ore that occur in the hills or on their summits. Occasionally the commingling of the red clays with sands from the hillsides produces a chocolate-colored or mulatto loam, easier to till, and often as productive as the former.

The red clay that borders the Red river bottom in La Fayette and Miller counties, as well as that found in other counties, has a deep red color, and is said to be suitable for paint, if well washed.

The timber growth is generally elm, mulberry, prickly ash, red oak, and a few white oaks and hickory, with an undergrowth of dogwood, muscadine and other grape-vines in great abundance. The lands are said to produce an average of from 800 to 1,000 pounds of seed-cotton, 40 bushels of corn, or 15 bushels of wheat per acre.

The following analysis gives the composition of perhaps a fair sample of these lands:

No. 375. *Genuine red soil* from the northeast corner of Sec. 4, T. 11, R. 11, in the southern part of Dorsey county. The dried soil is of a reddish chocolate-brown color.

Red lands soil of Dorsey county.

	No. 375
Insoluble matter	66.600
Potash	0.338
Soda	Not det'd.
Lime	0.285
Magnesia	0.413
Brown oxide of manganese	0.745
Peroxide of iron	15.930
Alumina	5.966
Phosphoric acid	0.231
Sulphuric acid	0.075
Water and organic matter	6.806
Total	100.587
Hygroscopic moisture	4.500

This analysis shows the presence of very high percentages of iron and manganese and a fair one of alumina. The phosphoric acid percentage is high, with scarcely enough lime to render it fully available. Its thriftiness would be greatly increased and tillage improved by the addition of the latter. There are fair amounts of potash and magnesia present, and apparently of organic matter.

GRAY SANDY LANDS.—The greater part of the yellow-loam region is covered with a sandy soil, often very gravelly, timbered with a growth of oak, hickory, and short-leaf pine, the latter being very prominent and characteristic of these lands. This is especially the case as regards the higher uplands, which are frequently known as pine hills. The subsoils vary in character from a yellowish to a deep-red clay, more or less impervious, and at depths of from 6 to 12 or 18 inches below the surface. In the hilly lands of the northern counties of the region the red-clay subsoils are most prominent, being exposed in ditches and on the roadside, as well as forming large areas of red lands by the removal of the sandy soil by denudation.

In the southern counties the subsoils seem more generally to be a yellowish sand or clay, and the lands are about as productive as the others, yielding from 600 to 800 pounds of seed-cotton, 25 bushels of corn, or 15 bushels of wheat to the acre when in cultivation. Both are easily tilled and generally well drained.

The following analyses are given to show the composition of these soils:

No. 348. *Sandy soil*, taken near Lisbon, northwestern part of Union county. The dried soil is ash-gray or umber-gray colored. It contains much sand and some rounded quartzose pebbles.

No. 350. *Subsoil* from the same locality, taken at 10 inches depth from the surface. Contains some rounded quartzose pebbles.

No. 369. *Sandy soil* from E. T. Franklin's yard, Sec. 22, T. 12, R. 10, 2½ miles northwest of Warren, Bradley county. The dried soil is of a dirty yellowish-gray color. Rounded quartz pebbles of various sizes were sifted out of it by the coarse sieve, of 150 apertures to the inch.

Gray sandy uplands, or pine-hill soils.

	UNION COUNTY.		BRADLEY COUNTY.
	Soil.	Subsoil.	Soil.
	No. 348.	No. 350.	No. 369.
Insoluble matter	95.800	92.115	90.905
Potash.................................	0.029	0.096	0.121
Soda.................................	0.095	0.026	0.006
Lime.............................	0.413	0.089	0.218
Magnesia	0.301	0.898	0.446
Brown oxide of manganese	0.140	0.185	0.185
Peroxide of iron.................................	0.965	1.865	2.740
Alumina	0.385	2.995	2.490
Phosphoric acid.............................	0.052	0.062	0.066
Sulphuric acid.............................	0.027	0.033	0.041
Carbonic acid	....	....	....
Water and organic matter................	1.898	1.674	3.207
Total	99.689	99.903	99.888
Hygroscopic moisture, air-dried	0.950	1.435	2.068

The above sample of soil from Union county may, from its analysis, be said to be poor in everything except sand, magnesia, and manganese. The essential elements of fertility are lacking both in the soil and subsoil. The soil from Bradley county is somewhat better, though still deficient in potash and phosphoric acid. The effect of a greater percentage of iron and of alumina is seen in the increased moisture coefficient. These soils, though producing a fair crop when fresh, would soon fail, and if they were not supported by a good subsoil would need the aid of fertilizers for productiveness.

PINE FLATS, GLADY LANDS, AND OAK FLATS.—Along the borders of the creek and river bottoms in a number of the counties, especially on the south, there frequently occur low and flat lands, wet and glady in character, and considered of no value agriculturally, the soil of which is generally a white siliceous clay, impervious and ill-drained. These localities are timbered with an almost exclusive pine or oak growth, sometimes associated with other trees, and seem to be similar in many respects to the clay flats occurring in the region between the White river and Crowley's ridge, on the east, in Phillips, Monroe, and other counties.

In Union county and the southern part of Calhoun there are tracts of the glady pine flats, with crawfishy, white clay soils, an analysis of which is given below. In Columbia county, along bayou Dorchite, these flats have an oak growth, the soil being apparently the same in character. They are bordered by sandy land, elevated but a few feet above high water. On Big creek flats, in the same county, the soil is a white clay with a growth of pine, holly, and beech. The flats of Ouachita county, with their wet pipe-clay soil, when properly drained, have yielded under cultivation as much as 1,200 pounds of seed-cotton per acre. In wet seasons neither cotton nor corn yield good crops.

No. 340. *Camp creek glady soil*, near Lisbon, Union county. The dried soil is mouse-colored. When calcined and the organic matter is burnt out, it is of a light-gray color, indicating the almost entire absence of oxide of iron.

Glady pine flat lands of Union county.

	Soils
	No. 340.
Insoluble matter...	90.715
Potash..	0.055
Soda...	0.036
Lime...	0.078
Magnesia...	0.206
Brown oxide of manganese	Trace.
Peroxide of iron	Trace.
Alumina..	2.735
Phosphoric acid...	0.006
Sulphuric acid...	0.062
Water and organic matter	6.613
Total	101.583
Hygroscopic moisture, air-dried........................	3.675

This soil is deficient in every element of fertility except organic matter and magnesia. Even for the small percentage of phosphoric acid present there is not sufficient lime to render it available. The analysis shows that the native resources of the land are not such as to invite its reclamation.

PRAIRIES.—In the counties of Ashley, Drew, and Lincoln, especially in the former two, some prairies are found interspersed throughout the uplands, producing a feature different from the rest of the yellow-loam region. These prairies are usually small and open, and appear to be but a continuation southward of the prairies lying between the Arkansas and White rivers and along the western border of Crowley's ridge, still northward on the east of White river. They seem also to correspond to the lowland prairies of Dubate, Seymore, Mer Rouge, and Jefferson, immediately south, in Louisiana, though differing somewhat in character. These prairies in Arkansas are very level, and are usually bordered on all sides by a scattering growth of post oak, known as oak openings. Their elevation is probably not more than 12 or 15 feet above the water-level of the streams, at which depth water is obtained in wells. Their surface, as well as that of the oak openings, is dotted over with small mound-like elevations. The soil is a "close-textured siliceous clay", underlaid by an impervious clay, and consequently the land is ill-drained and not much in cultivation. Sand is said to underlie the prairies at a reasonable depth for successful ditching, which would probably render these soils fairly productive.

BLACK PRAIRIES OF THE SOUTHWEST.—A region of black prairies occurs in the southwestern part of the state, with a width of about 30 miles, from Red river, northward on the line of the Indian territory, to Ultima Thule, about half way through Sevier county. Eastward the region becomes more and more narrow, until it culminates in a point at Arkadelphia, on the Ouachita river, in Clark county, and embraces the county of Little River, half of Sevier and Howard, and a small part of Pike, the northern part of Hempstead, the northwestern corner of Nevada, and the central part of Clark, an area of about 1,950 square miles. The region may be considered as the initial point of that great black prairie region that, passing into the southern part of the Indian territory, and turning southwestward through Texas to San Antonio and westward to the foot of the table-lands (if not including also these and the Llano Estacado again northward), forms one of the most prominent and most important topographical and agricultural features of that country.

In Arkansas, as well as in the eastern part of the Indian territory, the region is represented, not, as in Texas, by large and continuous prairies, open and almost entirely without timber growth, but by very small prairies (if, indeed, they can be called such), occupying the lowlands along the borders of the creek bottoms and lying at the foot of the sandy pine ridges that form the water divide of all the streams of the region. These lowlands usually have a more or less abundant timber growth of bois d'arc (also called Osage orange), haw, hickory, and sumac, and an undergrowth of scrubby swamp dogwood, indicating the low character of the land. The bois d'arc seems to be the characteristic growth of the black prairies, both in this state and in northeastern Texas (as observed near Clarksville), "attaining considerable size, and flourishing everywhere, even on the bare Cretaceous beds."

This region is underlaid throughout by the Cretaceous formation, the scattered prairies resting directly upon its beds of limestone, marls, and clays, while the ridges are composed of later material. These marls and limestones contain large percentages of carbonate of lime, which give to the prairie lands a highly calcareous character.

In Sevier county salt-licks and flats occur in the vicinity of Graham. The black lands of this region are more or less clayey in character, usually calcareous, and are very productive, and are said to yield from 35 to 50 bushels of corn, 20 bushels of wheat, or from 1,000 to 1,500 pounds of seed-cotton per acre.

The black sandy lands of Red river, though overlying Cretaceous beds, are not properly Cretaceous soils, as they differ very materially in composition, and especially in that they contain but a small percentage of lime. Prairies of this character occur on the borders of the bottom lands, and are described elsewhere as bottom prairies of Red river. The following analyses are given of these soils:

No. 341. *Genuine black sticky, waxy soil,* taken from Sec. 19, T. 8, R. 19, Clark county. Timber growth, sweet gum, mulberry, and walnut.

No. 343. *Genuine Cretaceous soil,* Sec. 28, T. 17, R. 20, collected adjacent to a marl bluff on Decipher creek, Clark county. Growth, gum, hickory, pin and Spanish oaks, ash and sea-ash.

No. 326. *Soil* from Sec. 7, T. 11, R. 25, Hempstead county. Usually 'limited prairies, surrounded with pine, hickory, ash, and bois d'arc (Osage orange). Undergrowth, spice bush, papaw, swamp dogwood, and buckeye; overlies marly limestone.

No. 328. *Subsoil,* taken near the same. Mostly disintegrated shell marl with vegetable matter. Its soil contained much limestone in fragments.

No. 339. *Genuine Cretaceous soil* from Sec. 2, Fr. T. 10, R. 30 W., west part of Sevier county.

No. 366. *Black soil* from Sec. 12, T. 13, R. 32, Sevier county. Timber growth, hickory, scrub haw, and Osage orange; undergrowth, swamp scrub dogwood. It contains small whitish particles, which decrepitate when the soil is heated.

No. 368. *Subsoil,* taken near the above.

No. 372. *Soil* from Sec. 4, T. 8, R. 26, on a branch of Bacon creek, Pike county, over the Cretaceous formation, with small spiral shells. Principal growth, white oak; some large rounded quartzose pebbles were removed from the soil.

No. 374. *Pebbly subsoil* from near the same place.

Lands of the black calcareous prairies.

	CLARK COUNTY.		HEMPSTEAD COUNTY.		SEVIER COUNTY.			PIKE COUNTY.	
	Waxy soil.	Soil.	Soil.	Subsoil.	Soil.	Soil.	Subsoil.	Soil.	Subsoil.
	No. 341.	No. 343.	No. 326.	No. 328.	No. 339.	No. 366.	No. 368.	No. 372.	No. 374.
Insoluble matter	68.315	64.015	77.740	35.140	73.115	27.990	10.915	85.915	92.795
Potash	0.583	0.351	0.314	0.314	0.432	0.382	0.135	0.155	0.130
Soda	0.111	0.090	0.015	0.095	0.125	0.146	0.099	0.035	0.087
Lime	1.478	1.890	1.332	20.134	1.086	20.389	44.385	0.360	0.056
Magnesia	1.797	1.044	1.142	1.213	0.490	2.279	0.702	0.562	0.282
Brown oxide of manganese	0.370	0.545	0.290	0.340	0.251	0.290	0.140	0.205	0.270
Peroxide of iron	6.350	5.015	4.295	3.535	3.780	4.415	1.615	1.495	2.015
Alumina	12.910	8.935	8.236	5.285	9.027	6.165	2.740	2.735	2.560
Phosphoric acid	0.302	0.185	0.191	0.087	0.282	0.366	0.152	0.152	0.115
Sulphuric acid	0.075	0.144	0.087	0.066	0.077	0.247	0.115	0.092	0.041
Carbonic acid	1.182	1.488	1.068	22.106	0.852	16.051	34.873	....	....
Water and organic matter	8.216	16.852	5.882	8.387	5.583	3.213	12.005	8.444	1.775
Total	101.589	100.081	100.081	100.978	99.612	100.077	100.415	100.253	100.157
Hygroscopic moisture, air-dried	11.650	11.029	4.975	4.800	7.475	9.675	2.775	4.100	1.435

These analyses show the presence of an abundance of potash, magnesia, and lime in all of the soils except from Pike county, while the phosphoric acid is high in Nos. 341 and 366, with fair percentages in the others. The subsoil No. 368 is but little else than impure carbonate of lime, Nos. 328 and 366 also having very high percentages.

The soil from Pike county, while overlying limestone, is sandy and has but comparatively little lime. Its vegetable matter is high.

THE CENTRAL RED LOAM, OR SHALE AND SANDSTONE REGION.

The region thus designated has a greater extent of territory than any other region of the state. It occupies a central north and south position, and its boundaries may be in general marked by the following outlines: From the line of the Indian territory, on the west, eastward through the middle of Sevier and Howard counties, the south of Pike, and thence quite direct to Little Rock, on the Arkansas river, and to a point on White river two miles south of Des Arc, in the northern part of Prairie county. This line also marks the northern limit of the black prairies, sandy pine-hills, and the large prairie silt region between the two rivers mentioned. From Des Arc to

Jacksonport, in Jackson county, White river forms the eastern border of the region, separating it from the lowlands of Crowley's ridge. From Jacksonport westward its northern limit passes through the southern portions of Independence, Stone, Searcy, and Newton and the middle of Madison counties, and northward through the eastern part of Benton county to the line of Missouri. The region embraces altogether seventeen entire and parts of fourteen counties, and covers about 15,680 square miles. The Arkansas river divides the region into two unequal portions, its basin draining the greater area on either side. On the northwest the headwaters of White river flow northward, and the northeast tributaries of the same flow eastward, while the southern part of the region is drained by the heads of the Ouachita and tributaries of the Red river.

The general surface of the country is hilly and broken, with high and prominent mountain ridges from 500 to 1,000 feet above the general level. It is generally well timbered, with the exception of a large region of prairies in the counties of Sebastian, Scott, Logan, and Yell, and in Washington and Benton on the northwest, and its lands are derived almost exclusively from the sandstones, shales, etc., of the Carboniferous formation, the shales usually underlying the prairies in the southern part of the region. There are areas of granite and other metamorphic rocks, forming, where extensive, lands different in character from those of the main region.

The following agricultural divisions are recognized in the region, and will be considered separately :

1. The gray and red-loam timbered region.
2. The central and western red-loam prairies.
3. Northwestern red-loam prairies.
4. The granitic or metamorphic region.

This region is more thickly populated than any other in the state, the average being a little more than seventeen persons per square mile. Pulaski and Sebastian counties, in which are located Little Rock and Fort Smith, are naturally at the head of the list, Crawford and Washington being next. The lands under cultivation comprise 10.5 per cent. of the entire area, with an average of 67.5 acres per square mile. In Washington, Benton, and Sebastian counties this acreage is nearly doubled, and in Logan and Conway it is respectively 98 and 96 acres per square mile. Benton county, on the northwest, has a maximum of 126 acres per square mile, and is thus at the head of all of the counties of the state in this regard, while at the same time it is lowest in acreage devoted to the culture of cotton. The counties of Montgomery, Polk, Garland, Perry, Scott, and Van Buren have the smallest percentage of tilled lands in the region.

The chief crops of the region are corn, cotton, wheat, oats, and sweet potatoes. The acreage of cotton was 22.1 per cent. of the lands under cultivation, or an average of 14.9 acres per square mile. A little more than half a bale of lint, or 870 pounds of seed-cotton, was produced per acre in 1879. The acreage of corn was the greatest, comprising 40.6 per cent. of the tilled lands, or about 27.4 acres per square mile. The yield for 1879, 9,398,210 bushels, was an average of 8.3 bushels per acre, or 32.4 bushels per capita.

GRAY AND RED LOAM TIMBERED REGION.

The two parts of this region lying on either side of the Arkansas river differ from each other to some extent in their topographical and lithological features, though both belong to the same geological formation. These differences are produced by the general dip of the rock strata toward the south, where the sandstone, shales, etc., have a great thickness, causing a gradual thinning out on the north and the bringing up of the limestones of the lower formation, whose material enters more or less into the composition of the soils. This is especially the case in Washington, Crawford, and Franklin counties, the other counties resembling those on the south of the river. Taking the Arkansas river as a line of division, the two parts will, for convenience, be described separately.

COUNTRY SOUTH OF THE ARKANSAS RIVER.—The general character of this country is that of a rolling and broken region, having hills and ridges ranging from 350 to 600 feet high, and a few mountain chains having elevations of from 1,000 to 1,400 feet above the surrounding valleys, with trends nearly east and west.

The surface of the country on the southwest, in the counties of Sevier and Howard, is more level than in the other counties, and gradually rises northward to the foot of the Cossatot range, near Dallas, in Polk county. Its sandstones and shales are, to some extent, metamorphosed under the influence of the same causes that have produced the granites and metamorphic rocks of Saline, Pulaski, Hot Spring, and other counties, and mineral veins are said to exist in several localities. In Pike, Montgomery, and counties eastward the surface of the country is very hilly and broken, with high ridges of sandstone, which rock is sometimes changed into novaculite or is studded with magnificent quartz crystals.

The Cossatot mountain range, passing east and west through the central part of Polk county near Dallas, has an elevation of about 1,000 feet, and is composed of the upturned and broken strata of sandstone and shales. The next range of mountains on the north is the Fourche La Fave, whose summit, 1,000 feet above the valley, forms the line between Polk and Scott counties. Its trend is irregularly east and west to the edge of Montgomery county, when it turns slightly northeastward into Yell, in which county its height is said to be 800 feet.

In Sebastian county there are a number of high ridges and mountain peaks, that of Sugar Loaf having an elevation of from 1,200 to 1,400 feet.

The Petit Jean mountain, in the northern part of Perry county, has an elevation of from 450 to 500 feet, which gradually declines to the westward, until it loses itself as a conspicuous landmark near the confines of Perry and Yell, and a gradual improvement is visible in the soil of the country. The Magazine mountains lie still northward of these, forming a prominent range, which terminates in a headland on the Arkansas river near the town of Dardanelle.

These ranges of mountains are composed almost entirely of sandstones and shales, the former usually forming the summit, one of its beds appearing as a prominent escarpment, running like a battlement along the brow of the mountain. Some of these mountains and high ridges have a timber growth of pine, oak, and hickory, indicating loose sandy and unproductive soils, such as would result from the disintegration of the sandstones.

The lands of this region, derived from the sandstones and shales as these materials are commingled, and may in general be classed as gray sandy soils and reddish loams or clay soils.

The gray sandy lands, occurring usually on the table-lands or at the foot of the sandstone ridges, are loose and easily tilled, and at a depth of a few inches (when in the valleys) are underlaid by reddish clay subsoils. These lands have a timber growth of pine, oak, and hickory, and, it is estimated, yield from 25 to 30 bushels of corn or about 800 pounds of seed-cotton per acre.

The reddish loam or red clayey lands are considered the best agricultural lands of the region, and are derived from the shales that usually immediately underlie them. These lands have a timber growth of red, black, white, and post oaks, dogwood, hickory, etc., and are very productive, yielding about 1,000 pounds of seed-cotton or from 30 to 35 bushels of corn per acre.

The following analyses are given:

No. 312. *Sandy soil*, taken 8 miles north of Little Rock, Pulaski county. Timber growth, black and post oaks and some hickory.

No. 314. *Subsoil*, containing some small ferruginous concretions, taken near the above.

No. 363. *Soil of red land* from Sec. 33, T. 2 S., R. 30 W., Polk county. Timber growth, red, black, white, and post oaks, dogwood, black walnut, wild cherry, pine, red elm, and hickory. The soil is composed of millstone grit, crystalline sandstones and shales, with bands of black flint.

No. 365. *Subsoil*, taken near the above; contains fragments of chert.

No. 360. *Yellowish brown soil*, taken 1 mile north of Waldron, Scott county. Timber growth, red, white, black, and post oaks, black ash, elm, cherry, black walnut, and dogwood; undergrowth, white and black sumac.

No. 362. *Subsoil*, taken near the above. Dried, is of a gray-buff color.

No. 391. *Brownish-gray soil*, Sec. 18, T. 6, R. 21 W., Yell county.

No. 393. *Subsoil*, taken near the above. Dried, is of a gray-buff color.

No. 394. *Reddish ferruginous soil* from Sec. 2, T. 7, R. 25, Logan county. Timber growth, beech, oak, hickory, and post oak, with sumac undergrowth; derived from shales. Some ferruginous concretions separated from it before analysis.

No. 396. *Subsoil*, taken near the above. Contains a few small sandy, ferruginous concretions.

Lands of the shale and sandstone region south of the Arkansas river.

	SANDSTONE LANDS.		SHALE LANDS.							
	PULASKI COUNTY.		POLK COUNTY.		SCOTT COUNTY.		YELL COUNTY.		LOGAN COUNTY.	
	Soil.	Subsoil.	Soil.	Subsoil.	Soil.	Subsoil.	Soil.	Subsoil.	Soil.	Subsoil.
	No. 312.	No. 314.	No. 363.	No. 365.	No. 360.	No. 362.	No. 391.	No. 393.	No. 394.	No. 396.
Insoluble matter	95.445	90.910	83.785	84.990	87.340	88.215	90.985	90.840	92.340	91.415
Potash	0.086	0.092	0.196	0.232	0.193	0.227	0.149	0.162	0.106	0.200
Soda	0.045	0.081	0.023	0.080	0.037	0.065	0.021	0.072	0.065	0.058
Lime	0.090	0.012	0.134	0.081	0.106	0.106	0.106	0.024	0.112	0.069
Magnesia	0.219	0.253	0.419	0.573	0.316	0.359	0.005	0.339	0.546	0.314
Brown oxide of manganese	0.145	0.096	0.220	0.396	0.145	0.195	0.195	0.115	0.100	0.190
Peroxide of iron	3.190	2.205	3.515	3.890	3.065	4.750	1.740	2.940	1.715	3.190
Alumina	1.273	3.455	5.200	5.110	4.085	5.585	3.165	3.190	1.340	1.840
Phosphoric acid	0.063	0.063	0.247	0.194	0.361	0.138	0.161	0.208	0.206	0.142
Sulphuric acid	0.027	0.032	0.062	0.058	0.050	0.042	0.056	0.052	0.058	0.053
Water and organic matter	2.761	2.354	6.343	3.323	4.763	2.873	4.556	1.960	3.354	2.094
Total	100.269	99.621	100.121	99.809	100.361	100.545	100.142	96.879	99.704	99.496
Hygroscopic moisture, air-dried	2.275	1.068	4.225	2.995	3.225	2.475	2.225	1.600	1.675	1.675

The lands derived from sandstone are shown by the analyses to be deficient in potash, lime, and phosphoric acid, the elements necessary for continued fertility. Magnesia is present in fair quantity.

The lands from the red shales show fair amounts of potash and lime and a good percentage of phosphoric acid and magnesia. They should be very durable, especially if lime be applied after a few years' cultivation.

COUNTRY NORTH OF THE ARKANSAS RIVER.—The surface of this part of the region is generally hilly and broken, and is timbered to the Ozark range of mountains along the northern border. These highlands are composed of the usual sandstones and shales of the millstone grit formation, which, by their inclination toward the south, have allowed the underlying limestone to come to the surface or be exposed in the sides of the hills.

In White county, on the east, the sandstone and millstone grit form high and prominent table-lands and cliffs, especially along the bluffs of Little river, imparting wild and romantic scenery to the country for many miles along the banks of that stream. The table-lands on the borders of this and Van Buren county are about 400 feet high, have sandy soils, and are timbered with a forest growth of pine. The northern part of Conway and western portion of Van Buren are mountainous, the mountains north of Clinton attaining an elevation of more than 1,200 feet. These continue through the northern parts of Pope, Johnson, Franklin, and Crawford and southern parts of Madison and Washington counties, while southward the country is less hilly, and affords a greater proportion of tillable lands. The Boston mountains, a high and broken range, occur in the adjoining parts of Crawford and Washington counties. The limestone appears more generally in these western counties than on the east, outcropping at the foot of the hills, and sometimes entering into the composition of the lands. Open, marshy prairies also occur occasionally in these counties in localities where the underlying impermeable shales or clays present large flat areas. In Washington county only some of these prairies, underlaid by red shales, have a soil more permeable to water, which is partly cultivated. The lands are similar to those on the south of the river already described, except in localities where the limestone can effect a difference in composition and, consequently, in fertility. The gray sandy lands from sandstone disintegration occupy chiefly the table- and hill-lands, and present tillable areas only where the surface is sufficiently flat to avoid washing away and where water does not find an easy course down the declivities and is retained, moistening the ground by percolating through it. The timber growth is usually Spanish, black-jack, post, white, black, and red oaks, pine, chestnut, chincapin, and persimmon. On some of the table-lands pine is most prominent, forming large forests, as in the southeastern part of Van Buren county; on others black-jack oak, or stunted oak and hickory, is the chief growth, especially on gravelly ridges. These lands are not very durable, though producing good crops for a few years. Their yield is said to be about 800 pounds of seed-cotton, 25 bushels of corn, or 12 bushels of wheat per acre.

The red loams or clayey lands derived from the shales are the best and most productive uplands of the region. These are found in the valleys, and at the foot of the ridges are usually covered by or commingled with the sand washings. The red lands, when not open prairies or post-oak flats, are timbered with red, scarlet, black, and chestnut oaks, sweet and black gums, wild black cherry, hickory, etc.

A large area of lands of this character occurs in White and Van Buren counties, and are supposed to cover about 360 square miles, or 30 miles east and west and 12 north and south. The red soil of these level farming lands is quite productive, yielding good crops of cotton, corn, wheat, and the finest oats in ordinary seasons, viz, 800 to 1,500 pounds of seed-cotton, 20 to 25 bushels of wheat, or 40 to 60 bushels of oats per acre, when there are seasonable rains. This soil, an analysis of which is given (No. 279), is probably a fair representative of the red lands of the entire region where they are not underlaid by tenacious clays or shales, which tend to render them stiff and marshy. The banks or bottoms of water-courses running between the high hills are generally narrow and rocky, and do not afford large tillable areas; but in the more level country along the Arkansas river they are wider, and in some of the counties are broad, flat, and marshy, with a growth of water, willow, and pin oaks, interspersed with a few very small prairies.

The following analyses indicate the character of the gray sandy and red clayey soils of this region:

No. 318. *Gray sandy soil*, taken 1½ miles east of Clarksville, Johnson county. Principal growth, post, black, and black-jack oaks, persimmon, and sumac. This soil contains a considerable quantity of iron gravel and fragments of ferruginous sandstone.

No. 320. *Brownish orange-colored subsoil*, with a little iron gravel, taken near the above.

No. 315. *Gray sandy soil* from six miles north of Dover, Pope county. Large timber growth of post, black, red, and white oaks, and some hickory.

No. 317. *Subsoil*, taken near the above. Contains also a few fragments of ferruginous sandstone.

No. 309. *Brownish upland soil*, taken 1 mile from Van Buren, Crawford county. Derived in part from the shales. This soil contained one-fourth its weight of ferruginous sandstone in fragments, which were separated before analysis.

No. 311. *Subsoil*, taken near the above.

No. 288. *Reddish soil* from T. 5, R. 14, Faulkner county, derived from the shales. Timber growth, black oak, hickory, and some white and black-jack oaks. Some fragments of ferruginous sandstone were removed from it before analysis.

No. 290. *Subsoil*, taken near the above.

No. 279. *Reddish soil* of true oak land from Sec. 13, T. 9 N., R. 12 W., in the southeastern part of Van Buren county. Timber growth, black and post oaks, with sumac undergrowth.

No. 281. *Subsoil*, taken near the above.

No. 300. *Red ferruginous soil* from 8 miles west of Searcy, White county. Timber growth, black, red, and black-jack oaks and hickory. This soil is derived from the ferruginous shales, fragments of which were separated from it before analysis.

No. 302. *Subsoil*, taken near the above. Dried, is of a brick-dust color.

No. 276. *Red upland soil*, overlying the Archimedes limestone in the central part of Washington county. Timber growth, white and overcup oaks, hickory, hackberry, walnut, slippery elm, ash, dogwood, and locust, with an undergrowth of papaw, spice, and large grape-vines.

No. 278. *Red subsoil* from near the same place.

Red lands region north of the Arkansas river.

	GRAY LANDS.						RED LANDS.							
	JOHNSON COUNTY.		POPE COUNTY.		CRAWFORD COUNTY.		FAULKNER COUNTY.		VAN BUREN COUNTY.		WHITE COUNTY.		WASHINGTON COUNTY.	
	Soil.	Subsoil.	Soil.	Subsoil.	Soil.	Subsoil.	Soil.	Subsoil.	Soil.	Subsoil.	Soil.	Subsoil.	Soil.	Subsoil.
	No. 313.	No. 320.	No. 315.	No. 317.	No. 309.	No. 311.	No. 268.	No. 290.	No. 279.	No. 281.	No. 300.	No. 302.	No. 276.	No. 278.
Insoluble matter	90.545	86.857	90.295	90.810	90.795	80.770	91.145	92.695	86.800	92.120	87.880	86.545	85.820	86.795
Potash	0.092	0.273	0.116	0.149	0.101	0.161	0.116	0.140	0.150	0.096	0.121	0.187	0.482	0.111
Soda	0.034	0.014	0.022	0.047	0.039	0.006	0.024	0.042	0.007	0.025	0.018	0.087	0.168	0.025
Lime	0.025	0.089	0.067	0.061	0.095	0.080	0.087	0.053	0.109	0.067	0.122	0.053	0.207	0.129
Magnesia	0.250	0.362	0.306	0.362	0.362	0.395	0.371	0.296	1.360	0.208	0.418	0.297	0.457	0.392
Brown oxide of manganese	0.145	0.270	0.145	0.195	0.135	0.170	0.270	0.170	0.245	0.245	0.220	0.245	0.295	0.495
Peroxide of iron	3.050	3.390	1.680	2.050	2.490	2.490	2.210	2.010	3.695	1.920	2.935	2.985	3.085	3.135
Alumina	1.910	3.110	2.865	3.060	1.990	2.115	2.695	3.113	3.440	2.515	2.915	4.975	3.015	1.545
Phosphoric acid	0.174	0.095	0.113	0.178	0.176	0.128	0.137	0.105	0.597	0.097	0.142	0.184	0.217	0.118
Sulphuric acid	0.063	0.083	0.041	0.083	0.041	0.013	0.060	0.016	0.038	0.083	0.055	0.083	0.050	0.050
Water and organic matter	3.216	4.147	4.212	2.898	2.176	2.271	3.207	1.469	5.592	2.407	4.989	3.714	4.325	4.871
Total	99.573	100.550	100.382	99.789	100.001	99.489	100.212	100.021	101.033	99.729	99.187	99.905	100.073	98.476
Hygroscopic moisture, air-dried	2.000	2.000	2.675	2.075	1.625	2.025	1.800	1.200	2.550	1.225	2.800	2.850	2.725	2.100

The richest soil in the list just given is that of Washington county, which contains fair percentages of phosphoric acid, potash, and magnesia. The lime is rather low, but, aided as it probably is by the magnesia, is in sufficient quantity for a short term of high productiveness, after which it must be applied to the soil. This soil is said to yield 800 pounds of seed-cotton, 25 bushels of corn, and 15 bushels of wheat per acre, and is especially adapted to oats. All of the other soils of the group, while mostly containing good percentages of phosphoric acid and small amounts of potash, are deficient in lime, the only exception being the red soil of White county, which surpasses all the others in this respect. As a consequence, it has a higher productive capacity, the yield being estimated at 1,500 pounds of seed-cotton per acre, against from 800 to 1,000 bushels per acre on the other soils.

WESTERN AND CENTRAL RED-LOAM PRAIRIE REGION.

In the counties of Sebastian, Logan, Yell, and Scott there are many open prairies interspersed throughout an area covering about 2,840 square miles, and lying between the Arkansas river and Fourche la Fave mountain chain. These prairie soils are underlaid by the reddish shales of the millstone grit or Carboniferous formation, and seem to occur always when an extensive area of the shales are level and flat. They are thus described by Professor Lesquereux:

The prairies of the Carboniferous shales are generally flat, surrounded by hills, or at least by a higher border, which gives them the appearance of the bottom of drained lakes. These prairies are of various extent, and, although they may overlie different kinds of ground or geological formation, in Arkansas they are generally underlaid by Carboniferous fire-clay or shales. In the spring they are covered with water, which cannot percolate, and, becoming true marshes for a time, have the vegetation of marshes—the rushes and the sedges. This semi-aquatic vegetation gives, according to the nature of the underlying strata, either a hard, compact, cold soil, by decomposition of shales or clay. A few trees—the water and pin oaks and honey-locust—grow along the creeks which meander in their middle. The soil is, in its natural state, mostly covered with the great composite of the prairies and the hard grasses, species of beard-grass and broom-corn (*sedge, Andropogon*). The prairies are most extensive in Sebastian county. Their surface is often somewhat rolling, with occasional elevated ridges and spurs and peaks of the mountain chains, and each is usually designated by some special name. They are not much in cultivation, but are chiefly devoted to the grazing of stock.

Grand prairie, of Franklin county, is underlaid by ferruginous black shales, or sometimes by the fire-clay of the coal. A few low hills are still left in the middle of it, with the original stratification of the measures to which they belong, a succession of shales and fire-clay. Some hills like these, but more abrupt and higher, look like Indian mounds on the flat surface of Long prairie, in Sebastian county. Neither humidity or a peculiar nature of the ground can account for the barrenness of these hills, on which there only grows the same species of herbaceous plants as those of the prairie.

The following analyses show the composition of these prairie lands:

No. 351. *Red sumac prairie soil*, Hodge's prairie, Sec. 12, T. 5, R. 31, Sebastian county, based on the shales over the coal. The dried soil is of a brown color, and contains some fragments of ferruginous sandstone.

No. 353. *Reddish subsoil*, taken near the above.

Reddish loam prairies, Sebastian county.

	Soil.	Subsoil.
	No. 351.	No. 353.
Insoluble matter........................	86.900	82.340
Potash.................................	0.294	0.214
Soda..................................	0.047	0.050
Lime..................................	0.081	8.073
Magnesia..............................	0.420	0.306
Brown oxide of manganese...............	0.175	0.165
Peroxide of iron.......................	4.890	6.940
Alumina...............................	1.235	4.510
Phosphoric acid........................	0.175	0.209
Sulphuric acid.........................	0.058	0.050
Water and organic matter...............	3.675	4.347
Total........................	99.740	100.015
Hygroscopic moisture, air-dried..........	2.025	2.300

The above soil and subsoil are very deficient in lime, but possess a sufficiency of other elements of plant-food to insure excellent fertility if other circumstances, such as depth and drainage, were favorable.

NORTHWESTERN RED PRAIRIES.

Reference has already been made to the small prairies that occur between the ridges in Fulton county and that cap some of the ridges in Carroll and adjoining counties. Besides these, there are larger and more extensive ones in Carroll, the southern part of Boone, and more especially on the west of White river, in Benton and Washington counties, which extend westward and northward out of the state.

Marshall prairie, near the corner of the counties of Newton, Searcy, and Boone, is bordered on the south by mountain peaks rising more than 800 feet above its level, and the grayish loam soil of both this and Huzza prairie is derived in part from the sub-Carboniferous limestone, sandstones, and shale, and in part from the cherty limestone which underlies it. The surface is rolling and well drained; the soil is deep and very fertile, yielding, in good seasons, 50 to 60 bushels of corn and an average of 15 or 20 bushels of wheat.

The prairies of Benton and Washington counties are quite level, but the lowest portions are marshy and somewhat difficult to drain. They are thus described by Professor Lesquereux in the Arkansas report:

In the spring the low grounds are covered by 3 feet of water. When the drainage has been attended to, the prairie soil produces, on an average, 40 bushels of corn, 15 or 20 bushels of wheat, or from 1,000 to 1,500 pounds of tobacco per acre. The lands between White river and Bentonville are mostly oak barrens interspersed with prairies. West of Bentonville there is a mulatto soil, somewhat different in its character from that immediately around town, which is very productive.

Beatie's prairie, in the northwestern part of the county, has a gently undulating surface, fringed with groves of oak and small hickory and dotted with low mounds, bearing tufts of rank weeds, and made up of isolated heaps of chert gravel. The soil is underlaid by red clay.

The limestone prairies of northern Arkansas are singular in this fact, that their surface is not always flat, and that they are mostly placed on the soft declivities or coves along or between the ridges. They are mostly of small extent, and are surrounded by thickets of low trees. The compact or somewhat porous sub-Carboniferous limestone which they cover does not absorb water with rapidity. Hence, in the spring water percolates slowly along the slope, taking with it the detritus of the slope and depositing it where its course is either stopped or slackened. A scant swamp vegetation springs up there; its decomposed remains are mixed with the original deposit, which, bye and by, augments in thickness under the action of water and vegetation. This soil is naturally spongy, preserves water for a part of the year, like the peat which it resembles, and thus cannot sustain trees. They establish themselves on a firmer ground all around. When by successive contributions of limestone deposited by water and of particles of humus received from the plants this soil has become thick enough it is, when drained by a few ditches (serving as channels for the water of the rainy season), a fertile and easily cultivated ground. The channels of drainage are generally formed by a natural depression, the depth of which varies with the thickness of the soil of each prairie. In this case, as the coarser materials are of course heaped on the banks of these creeks, a few trees grow along them. They are mostly stunted specimens of the post and rock-chestnut oaks, persimmon, juniper, and a shrub, *Bumelia lanuginosa*, Pers. The characteristic herbaceous plants of these limestone prairies are especially *Ambrosia polystachya*, *Kuhnia eupatorioides*, *Aster sericeus*, *Croton capitatum*, *Grindelia lanceolata*, *Palafoxia callosa*, *Oxybaphus albidus*, etc., species which are not found on the prairies of other formations. Besides these, they are covered with a great number of species belonging to the prairies in general.

The following analyses only have been made of the prairie lands of this region:

No. 252. *Prairie soil* from land on Sugar Loaf creek, Marion county. Some fragments of decomposing chert were removed from it.

No. 254. *Subsoil*, taken near the above.

Prairie land of Marion county.

	Soil.	Subsoil.
	No. 253.	No. 254.
Insoluble matter	82.520	88.980
Potash	0.301	0.204
Soda	0.152	0.084
Lime	0.068	0.168
Magnesia	0.473	0.217
Brown oxide of manganese	} 3.465	2.065
Peroxide of iron		
Alumina	5.276	3.340
Phosphoric acid	0.230	0.137
Sulphuric acid	0.067	0.038
Water and organic matter	7.729	3.534
Total	100.205	99.727
Hygroscopic moisture, air-dried	4.365	1.950

This land, while well supplied with potash, magnesia, and phosphoric acid, is deficient in lime. Vegetable matter is present in the soil in large amounts. Under favorable circumstances, and with the application of lime, this soil should be highly productive.

METAMORPHIC REGION.

This region is represented by granites and other eruptive rocks, chiefly in Pulaski, Saline, Garland, and Hot Spring counties, with a small area also in Pike, and by metamorphosed shales and sandstones of the millstone grit in Polk county, where it forms the Cossatot range of mountains, lying south of Dallas and extending east and west.

The granitic regions are usually broken and hilly, the ridges sometimes forming coves, in which tillable lands are occasionally found. Of these, Magnet cove, on the line of Garland and Hot Spring counties, and Fourche cove, south of Little Rock, in Pulaski county, are the most prominent. The lands of the latter are, however, composed chiefly of the sands, clays, etc., of the Tertiary pine-hills of the southern part of the state, though hemmed in by granitic ridges. Northward from the ridges are areas of tillable granitic lands, embracing mostly sandy and gravelly soils, with a timber growth of red, black, and white oaks, black and pig-nut hickory, dogwood and maple. When under cultivation these lands are said to produce 30 bushels of wheat or 25 bushels of corn per acre. One of the greatest disadvantages of this soil is its disposition to produce a spontaneous growth of persimmon sprouts, which are very difficult to eradicate. There are said to be some fine lands in Magnet cove. The granites, dykes, and metamorphosed rocks of other localities appear in such small areas that their material from disintegration does not affect the lands to any obvious extent, and they are therefore included in the more general region of the red lands of the millstone grit. The following analyses are given:

No. 400. *Granite soil* near the eastern slope of the granite range of Fourche cove, near the north line of Sec. 4, T. 1 S., R. 12 W., Pulaski county. Timber growth, red and white oaks, dogwood, black and pig-nut hickory, and maple; soil, dried, is of a light gray umber color, with small fragments of decomposing granite.

No. 402. *Brownish gray* subsoil, taken near the above.

No. 403. *Under clay* of the above. Light brick-dust color, and contains spangles of mica.

Granite lands, Pulaski county.

	Soil.	Subsoil.	Underclay.
	No. 400.	No. 402.	No. 403.
Insoluble matter	85.811	87.940	60.515
Potash	0.306	0.227	0.347
Soda	0.065	0.061	0.394
Lime	0.315	0.128	0.383
Magnesia	0.436	0.439	1.266
Brown oxide of manganese	0.243	0.140	0.140
Peroxide of iron	4.300	4.290	7.650
Alumina	3.860	4.635	21.365
Phosphoric acid	0.138	0.143	0.189
Sulphuric acid	0.055	0.041	0.045
Water and organic matter	4.877	2.524	8.396
Total	99.916	100.113	100.350
Hygroscopic moisture, air-dried	2.775	1.950	5.675

This land, while sandy in character, has a fair proportion of potash, phosphoric acid, and lime, as well as of magnesia. There is comparatively little difference between the soil and subsoil, but the underclay is much richer in potash and phosphoric acid, and has a very large amount of alumina, which also holds much water. The depth to this clay from the surface is not given.

NORTHERN BARRENS AND HILLS REGION.

The region thus designated, occupying the extreme northern part of the state, is bounded by Missouri on the north and Crowley's ridge and the alluvial region on the east, while the southern boundary is marked rather indefinitely by a line extending from the great bend of White river, at the mouth of Black river, in Independence county, westward through the southern part of Stone, Searcy, and Newton and the middle of Madison, and northward through east Benton, to the Missouri line. The region thus embraces nine entire counties and parts of six counties, and covers an area of nearly 9,000 square miles.

White river, rising in the western part, flowing at first with a northern course into Missouri, and soon turning southeastward through the central part, drains with its many tributaries the entire region. The surface of the country is generally very hilly and broken, the highest ridges and mountains occurring in Newton county, where the Boston mountains rise to an elevation of about 1,000 feet above the lowlands. This region of high hills extends northward into the southern part of Boone and Carroll counties, where some of the peaks are more than 1,200 feet above the streams. In other counties the ridges are from 150 to 300 feet high, except on the southeast, where some of them are as much as 500 feet high. The surface of the counties that lie on the east and south as far west as Washington is well timbered both on the hills and in the valleys, while in Fulton, Baxter, Marion, Boone, and Carroll the timbered lands are interspersed with small prairie barrens, that increase in extent westward from Fulton, until at Bentonville, in Benton county, the country opens out into the broad open prairies of the west. The highest ridges, where covered with cherty and siliceous soils, whether derived from the cherty rocks of the sub-Carboniferous of the first group or those of the Lower Silurian of the prairie counties, are usually timbered with a growth of pine.

Two general subdivisions may be recognized in this region, viz:

1. Cherty and siliceous hills, with heavy beds of sandstones, forming mostly sandy and well-timbered lands.
2. Cherty and magnesian limestone hills, forming barrens, prairies, and sandy lands.

The entire region has a population averaging nearly fifteen persons per square mile, unequally distributed in the counties. Independence, on the east, and Carroll, on the west, have the highest averages, while Newton and Stone, in the center, have the lowest, due no doubt to the hilly and broken character of the country. The average of cotton is 9.1 acres per square mile for the region, and that of all lands under cultivation is 61.9 acres per square mile.

Independence county has the largest cotton acreage, but Marion has the highest percentage of tilled lands (24.8) devoted to the culture of that crop. As a cotton-producing region this naturally ranks low (14.7 per cent. of tilled land), because of its high latitude, though in several of the counties of the extreme north that crop embraces a greater percentage of the lands under cultivation than in some counties one or two degrees further south. The average product per acre is quite high (840 pounds of seed-cotton).

The greatest proportion of cotton is produced in the counties on the east; their average acreage being from 14 to 21 acres per square mile, this average decreasing westward, until in Madison it is but the fraction of an acre and in Carroll 1.4 acres per square mile.

SANDY AND CHERTY LANDS OF THE SANDSTONE REGION.

This division embraces chiefly the counties of Independence, Stone, Searcy, Newton, Madison, the northern part of Carroll, the southern part of Izard, and parts of other counties, and comprises perhaps the most hilly portion of the northern region. The hills are composed mostly of the sandstone and barren limestone of the sub-Carboniferous formation, often capped with heavy beds of chert, and the soils, sandy and gravelly in character, have a timber growth either of pine, or when thin, of a low scrub oak, and are termed "oak barrens". Though producing perhaps well for a few years, these soils are not durable, and the elements of fertility soon become exhausted. Analysis No. 285 shows the small percentages of important elements in a soil of this character in Benton county. The productiveness of the virgin soil is not given, but an old field soil, taken near the same place and twenty-three years under cultivation, is said to yield about 35 bushels of oats per acre; its analysis, however, shows it to have been of a better class than the oak barrens proper. The limestone that underlies these cherty and sandstone beds, when coming near the surface on the lower ridges or when outcropping on the sides of the hills, produces, by the commingling of its limy materials with the sands, a rich and highly productive soil. Such lands are found throughout the entire region in the valleys and on the hillsides, whose slope is so gradual as to prevent the washing away of the soil. A characteristic sample of these lands is given in No. 240, from Izard county. This land has a timber growth of post and white oaks, hickory, persimmon, and dogwood, and in some localities black-jack oak and sassafras are abundant. The subsoil is usually a dark yellowish clay, and the lands are said to

COTTON PRODUCTION IN ARKANSAS.

produce 30 bushels of wheat, 40 to 50 of corn, 20 to 25 of oats, and about 800 pounds of seed-cotton per acre. From Long creek to King's river, along the Bentonville road westward, there is a succession of low hills, formed of alternate strata of cherty limestone and of sandstone, which are generally cultivated, except on some of the most rocky and dry places. The highest ridges are still covered with beautiful prairies of the same nature, which have the same fertility and the same vegetation as Huzza prairie, on the southeast. The dividing ridges in the northwestern part of Madison county are formed partly of sandstone and partly of cherty limestone, and are barren and dry when high, steep, and narrow, but are fertile when low, with gentle slopes, and thus keep on their summit or their declivities the decomposed particles of limestone, which, on steep and narrow ridges, are easily washed down by the rain. The divide between War Eagle creek and White river, in this county, is timbered with pine, chincapin, chestnut, and post, black-jack, and chestnut oaks. Another rocky divide lies on the west of White river and at the edge of the prairie region that extends westward.

The following soils, whose analyses are given, are probably fair samples of the lands thus briefly described :

No. 285. *Sandy soil*, taken east of Bentonville, Benton county. Timber growth, black hickory; undergrowth, sumac and hazel.

No. 287. *Subsoil*, taken near the above.

No. 306. *Brush creek barrens soil* from the northwestern part of Madison county. Growth, black-jack oak and hickory. This soil contains fragments of decomposing chert.

No. 308. *Subsoil* from near the above.

No. 291. *Light umber-colored soil*, taken near Jasper, Newton county. Timber growth, black, white, red, and water oaks, black and sweet gums. Ferruginous and cherty fragments were separated from it.

No. 293. *Brownish, buff-colored subsoil*, taken near the above.

No. 294. *Soil* from near the mouth of Dry Fork of Clear creek, northwest part of Searcy county.

No. 296. *Subsoil*, taken near the above.

No. 240. *Uplands soil*, lot 25, T. 15, R. 8 W., Izard county. Timber growth, post and white oaks, hickory, dogwood, and persimmon. This soil contains some clear grains of sand and fragments of decomposing chert.

No. 242. *Brownish-colored subsoil*, taken near the above.

No. 303. *Soil*, taken two miles west from Batesville, Independence county. Growth, hickory, oaks, etc.

No. 305. *Yellowish brown subsoil* from near the above.

Sandstone and barren limestone lands.

	BENTON COUNTY.		MADISON COUNTY.			NEWTON COUNTY.		SEARCY COUNTY.		IZARD COUNTY.		INDEPENDENCE COUNTY.	
				BARRENS LAND.									
	Soil.	Subsoil.	Soil.	Soil.	Subsoil.	Soil.	Subsoil.	Soil.	Subsoil.	Soil.	Subsoil.	Soil.	Subsoil.
	No. 285.	No. 287.	No. 306.	No. 306.	No. 308.	No. 291.	No. 293.	No. 294.	No. 296.	No. 240.	No. 242.	No. 303.	No. 305.
Insoluble matter	92.290	92.195	88.945	91.945		84.945	90.845	92.695	88.445	81.720	85.080	86.920	90.130
Potash	0.125	0.193	0.137	0.130		0.137	0.170	0.164	0.150	0.405	0.973	0.205	0.297
Soda	0.025	0.087		0.015		0.054	0.054	0.007	0.067	0.111	0.105		0.004
Lime	0.053	0.026	0.110	0.067		0.418	0.109	0.836	0.112	0.283	0.137	0.137	6.095
Magnesia	0.364	0.976	0.230	0.579		0.318	0.347	0.184	0.364	0.403	0.561	0.292	0.260
Brown oxide of manganese	0.145	0.170	0.245	0.320		0.445	0.470	0.195	0.470	0.130	0.130	0.345	0.205
Peroxide of iron	2.000	2.580	1.885	2.180		2.110	2.460	1.820	2.410	4.270	4.455	1.985	2.310
Alumina	0.840	1.190	2.715	2.325		2.090	2.140	1.140	3.475	5.440	4.790	3.320	2.315
Phosphoric acid	0.078	0.040	0.195	0.193		0.151	0.084	0.078	0.151	0.239	0.193	0.162	0.145
Sulphuric acid	0.034	0.016	0.041	0.022		0.060	0.042	0.043	0.023	0.045	0.042	0.043	0.012
Water and organic matter	2.818	1.401	4.853	2.114		7.722	3.302	2.933	2.919	6.874	3.343	4.204	2.788
Total	98.792	98.807	100.156	99.779		98.415	100.024	99.094	99.586	100.060	99.238	98.620	98.581
Hygroscopic moisture, air-dried	1.550	1.225	2.750	1.875		4.500	2.075	2.000	2.435	3.025	3.050	3.075	2.275

The soils taken from Benton and Madison counties are said to be derived chiefly from sandstones; hence their high percentages of sand and insoluble matter. That from the former county is deficient in phosphoric acid and lime, while having also a low percentage of potash. In the soil from Madison the percentage of phosphoric acid is good, that of lime fair, while that of potash is low. The other soils of the division are partly derived from limestone of the hills, as shown by an increased amount of lime, and this should add much to their thriftiness. Otherwise, with the exception of that from Izard county, they do not differ materially from the first-named group.

The percentages of potash and of phosphoric acid are high in the limestone soil of Izard, and it contains much more clay than is found in the other samples. The vegetable matter in this as well as in the Newton county soil is high, and must exert an important influence toward their high productiveness.

CHERTY MAGNESIAN LIMESTONE HILLS, BARRENS, AND PRAIRIES.

This region embraces most of the counties along the northern boundary-line, with parts of Independence, Izard, and Lawrence on the east, and Newton and Carroll on the west, and is marked or underlaid mostly by the Lower Silurian cherty magnesian limestones, etc. On the east, along Black river, and extending back several miles, the hills are capped with Quaternary gravel, pebbles, and ferruginous sandstone, and have a timber growth of small oaks and hickory. Westward the summits of the ridges are mostly cherty and gravelly, timbered in some cases with pine and in others with only a low and scrubby growth of oak. Small prairies are interspersed throughout the region westward from Fulton county, occupying mostly the valleys between the hills.

The following description of these northern counties is taken from Professor Lesquereux in the Arkansas survey report:

The geographical character of the country is that of a plateau divided into a series of successive ridges by numerous clear creeks, mostly running southward or northward to White river, or by some of its forks. When the ridges are composed of compact, hard magnesian limestone, they are nearly barren, the top only being covered with a scanty vegetation. When the limestone is somewhat porous and retentive of water, the flat surfaces of the tops, or even the declivities of the ridges, are covered with prairies. Where the rock is soft and easily disaggregated it is mostly covered with trees. In the eastern part of Fulton county the ridges, mostly of cherty limestone, are rocky, but are, nevertheless, covered with trees of small size, the mockernut hickory and the black-jack and post oaks. The top of these ridges is clothed by a luxuriant vegetation of grasses and numerous species of herbaceous plants, thus furnishing a good and abundant pasture for cattle, especially for sheep. The slopes are gentle and covered with humus, or with a soil of greater fertility than might be supposed from the stunted growth of the trees. It is the hickory or mulatto barren soil, soft, permeable, of a grayish color, producing abundant crops of corn (50 to 60 bushels to the acre in favorable situations), and especially wheat (25 to 35 bushels). The trees growing on this kind of ground are scattered or distant, and are of the same species as those on the ridges, with the red, black, and white oaks. The Spanish oak is also mixed with this vegetation, but it is scarce, and of the remarkable variety *Quercus tridentata*, Englemann. On the hickory barrens the trees are generally of small size and the forests without underwood; a phenomenon which may be caused either by the hardness of the rock, which cannot be easily penetrated by the roots, or by fire, which ought to be active on such a rocky light soil. Between these low cherty ridges the flats or bottoms along the creeks are mostly half-prairies, covered with shrubs, green briers, Indian currant, two species of sumac, the kinnikinnik, and sassafras. The soil is black, deep, somewhat cold and clayey, and apparently less fertile than the soil of the slopes. It produces on an average 40 to 50 bushels of corn, and is too compact and too strong for wheat. As these half-prairies form the banks of streams, of which the beds are generally deeply cut, it would be easy to drain them, and thus they would be better for agricultural purposes than the upper mulatto land, because they are formed of the same rock, have the same elements, and have also a far greater nutritive power.

Be.ween Salem and Benetz bayou (westward) the sub-Carboniferous sandstone crops out and constitutes some hills, and its vegetation shows a difference first in the size of the trees, which become larger and of a more healthy growth. With the mockernut, the black-jack and post oaks in the most barren places, this sandstone has the chincapin, or dwarf chestnut, which sometimes descends the declivities to the base of the hills; upon the gentle slopes the black, red, scarlet, white, and Spanish oaks (this last becoming of great size), and the black gum, which does not like the limestone. The underwood is pretty thick in places, formed of sumac, hazel, and especially of the farkleberry, also a species characteristic of the sandstone. Where the underwood is wanting, three or four species of bush clover, a beautiful blue gentian (*Gentiana puberula*), three species of gerardia, some asters, especially *Diplopappus linariifolius*, and the dittany, all, except the last, showy and richly-colored flowers, clothe the rocky ground. Though this sandstone is more favorable for the vegetation of trees than the cherty limestone, the agricultural value of the soil derived from it is far from being as great. The decomposed parts of the rocks, though pulverized and mixed with the decayed remains of plants, preserve their nature of sand.

The Rap and Talbot barrens, in Baxter county, have a soil about like that of the half-prairies of Fulton county. Where thick enough it is said to produce 40 or 50 bushels of corn per acre. It is too strong for wheat, and would require to be drained, or at least deeply plowed, to show its full value. Naturally irrigated every year by water running from the ridges of soft porous limestone, they are continually furnished with the nutritive elements of a rich soil.

In the central part of Marion county magnesian limestone crops out and forms higher, more abrupt, and entirely barren ridges. Trees are scarce there. Only a few stunted specimens of the rock-chestnut oak, juniper, persimmon, and winged elm grow in the cracks of humid decomposing rocks. Some species of herbaceous plants, the ragweed (*Ambrosia polystachya*), the flocculent and whitish *Croton capitatum*, the pretty *Stenosyphon virgatum*, and the hard and long-beard grasses help to cover the barrenness of this formation. These ridges produce nothing. The patches of thin yellow soil, which are here and there attached to places where the water cannot attain them and carry them away, look like half-burnt pieces of brick, which can scarcely be attacked by any kind of vegetation. On the way from Yellville to Carrollton, in Carroll county, the alternation of high, steep, and sterile hills of the magnesian limestone with low and undulating ridges of fertile cherty limestone show a remarkable contrast in the vegetation, and consequently in the fertility of both formations. The highest ridges of Marion county are overlaid by sub-Carboniferous sandstone, sometimes covered with pines.

The chemical composition of these barren and siliceous lands is shown in the following analyses of samples taken in several of the counties:

No. 264. *Barrens soil* from Sec. 31, T. 18, R. 17 W., Fulton county. Timber growth, a few scrub hickories, oaks, and walnuts.

No. 266. *Subsoil*, taken near the above. Contains fragments of chert.

No. 261. *Barrens soil* from Sec. 23, T. 19, R. 14 W., Baxter county. Growth, rosin-weed and grass. Some fragments of chert were taken from it.

No. 263. *Yellowish subsoil*, taken near the above.

No. 255. *Upland siliceous soil* from near the waters of Big creek, Marion county. Growth, big-bud hickory and black-jack and red oaks. A few small fragments of ferruginous chert were removed from it.

No. 257. *Subsoil* from near the above.

No. 267. *Second upland siliceous soil*, Fulton county. Growth, white oak and hickory.

No. 269. *Subsoil* from near the above.

No. 248. *Upland siliceous soil*, taken a few miles west of Powhatan, Lawrence county. Growth, black-jack and post oaks and small hickory. This soil contains ferruginous chert.

No. 250. *Subsoil* from near the above.

No. 270. *Pine upland soil*, one mile from Calico, Izard county. Growth, black oak, hickory, and pine. This soil contains a large proportion of fine, clear, rounded grains of sand. Some fragments of chert were removed from it.

No. 272. *Sandy subsoil* from near the above.

Barrens and cherty and siliceous lands.

	BARRENS.				CHERTY AND SILICEOUS LANDS.							
	FULTON COUNTY, TIMBERED.		BAXTER COUNTY, PRAIRIE.		MARION COUNTY.		FULTON COUNTY.		LAWRENCE COUNTY.		IZARD COUNTY, PINE HILL.	
	Soil.	Subsoil.	Soil.	Subsoil.	Soil.	Subsoil.	Soil.	Subsoil.	Soil.	Subsoil.	Soil.	Subsoil.
	No. 264.	No. 266.	No. 261.	No. 263.	No. 255.	No. 257.	No. 267.	No. 269.	No. 248.	No. 250.	No. 270.	No. 272.
Insoluble matter	79.430	77.345	78.296	83.220	86.920	90.796	88.070	91.345	92.830	91.270	91.345	98.880
Potash	0.686	0.790	0.698	0.530	0.296	0.349	0.232	0.265	0.184	0.238	0.186	0.198
Soda	0.061	0.101	0.583	0.117	0.129	0.141	0.481	0.016	0.084	0.115	0.055	0.019
Lime	0.380	0.243	0.384	0.190	0.196	0.109	0.234	0.089	0.100	0.109	0.089	0.086
Magnesia	0.341	0.383	0.815	0.586	0.304	0.290	0.388	0.371	0.387	0.245	0.285	0.306
Brown oxide of manganese	0.220	0.370	0.296	0.295	2.165	2.065	0.320	0.270	0.120	5.890	0.070	0.145
Peroxide of iron	4.110	5.360	5.810	3.350			1.960	2.680	0.576		1.390	1.165
Alumina	5.165	7.340	5.015	3.700	2.616	3.840	1.815	3.965	3.115		3.985	2.290
Phosphoric acid	0.164	0.165	0.147	0.162	0.193	0.117	0.162	0.078	0.095	0.078	0.104	0.095
Sulphuric acid	0.084	0.069	0.084		0.028	0.025	0.050	0.050	0.028	0.083	0.024	0.011
Water and organic matter	7.575	6.341	11.011	6.133	4.808	2.389	5.793	1.794	2.970	1.979	3.673	1.705
Total	98.206	98.787	99.113	98.219	100.065	100.130	99.040	100.353	99.388	100.047	99.606	99.900
Hygroscopic moisture, air-dried	3.875	4.200	4.650	2.825	1.850	1.900	2.475	1.100	1.325	1.650	1.465	0.872

The barren lands do not deserve their name if we are to judge them entirely by their chemical composition, for they contain very high percentages of potash, with fair amounts of phosphoric acid and lime. The vegetable matter is also very high, with probably a corresponding high humus percentage, carrying with it a large amount of available phosphoric acid. Everything indicates a high productive power under favorable mechanical conditions. The red clays of the hills seem to be especially rich in potash, an analysis of a sample from Marion county showing the presence of 0.921 per cent. with 0.453 of soda. This was found underlying the magnesian limestone and sandstone, forming a stratum 6 to 8 inches thick.

The cherty and siliceous lands show their sandy character by high percentages of insoluble matter and rather low amounts of potash and lime, with, however, fair amounts of phosphoric acid. In Lawrence county, and in the pine lands of Izard, the phosphoric-acid percentage is too low for what might be considered a fertile soil.

GENERAL REMARKS ON COTTON PRODUCTION.

There is no record at hand showing the early history of cotton production in Arkansas, but it is more than probable that cotton formed one of the crops long before its admission as a state into the Union in 1836. From the several census reports the following statistics have been obtained : The first record, that of the census of 1840, shows a production of 15,072 bales of 400 pounds weight, which was an average of a bale to every six persons then in the state. In 1850 the population had a little more than doubled, while the production of cotton was more than four times as great as that of the previous census. Of the fifty-one counties of the state, seventeen produced each more than 1,000 bales, Chicot being first, with 12,192 bales, and Union second, with 7,037 bales. Nine counties produced each from 500 to 1,000 bales, eleven counties from 100 to 500, and nine below 100 bales, Randolph and Washington having one bale each. The counties of Benton, Carroll, Newton, Perry, and Searcy reported no yield. The census of 1860 showed another doubling of the population over that of 1850, while the yield in cotton had increased five and one-half times, the ratio then being a little more than eight-tenths of a bale to each person.

The census of 1870 showed that the laboring classes, and especially the negroes, had not recovered from the demoralization consequent upon the civil war, for although the population had increased 11.3 per cent., the amount of land under cultivation had fallen off to but 67.5 per cent. of what it was in 1860, and cotton production averaged but half a bale per capita. Jefferson county had the greatest yield and Phillips the next; six counties had each a yield of over 10,000 bales; thirty-eight from 1,000 to 10,000; twelve from 100 to 1,000; while four had a less number than 100, and one had none.

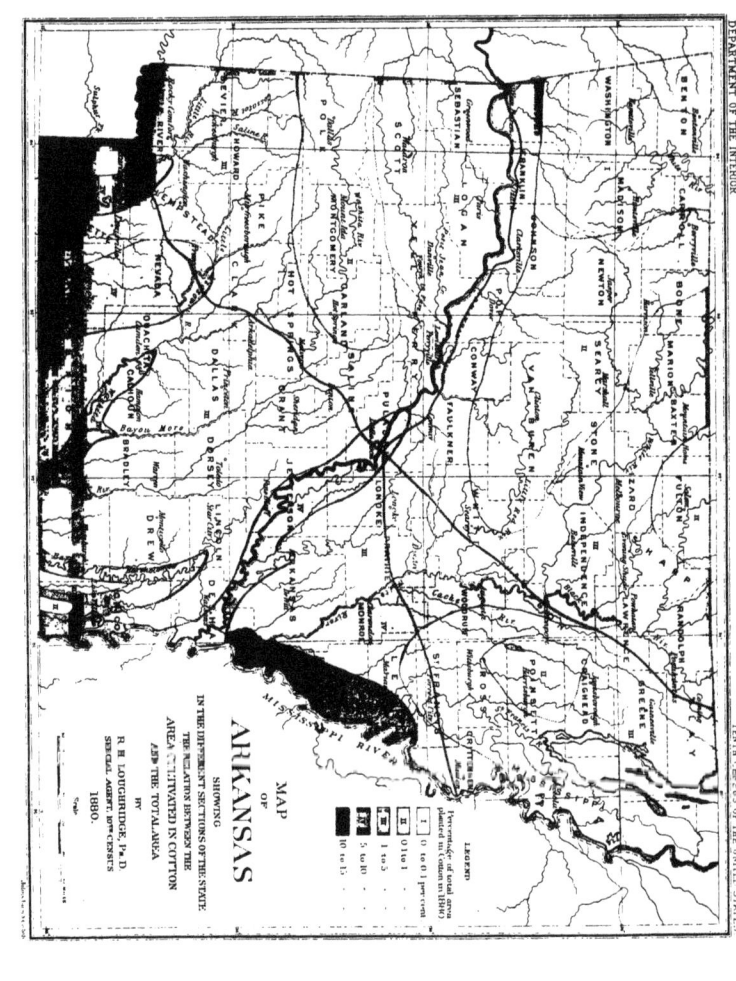

MAP
OF
ARKANSAS
SHOWING
IN THE DIFFERENT SECTIONS OF THE STATE
THE RELATION BETWEEN THE
AREA CULTIVATED IN COTTON
AND THE TOTAL AREA

BY
R. H. LOUGHRIDGE, PH. D.
SPECIAL AGENT, 10TH CENSUS
1880.

LEGEND

Percentage of total area
planted in Cotton in 1880

0 to 0.1 per cent
0.1 to 1 . . .
1 to 3 . . .
3 to 5 . . .
5 to 10 . . .
10 to 15 . . .

By the census of 1880 we find that the population of the state has increased a little more than 65 per cent. over that of 1870, and the lands under cultivation 84.5 per cent.; while the number of bales has been much more than doubled, being now an average of seven-tenths of a bale per capita.

STATISTICAL RESULTS OF THE TENTH CENSUS.—Arkansas in 1879 produced 608,256 bales of cotton from 1,042,976 acres, as shown by the statistical tables ·at the beginning of this report, and ranked as fifth in total production among the cotton-producing states, though sixth as regards the number of acres devoted to its culture. This crop is produced to a greater or less extent in all of the seventy-four counties, and although the latitude of the northern part of the state causes a short season, yet fair crops are produced, the average product per acre gathered being more than half a bale, or from 750 to 850 pounds of seed-cotton, even in the hilly counties far removed from the rich bottom lands of the Mississippi river. This high yield, brought about probably by careful culture by white labor, has, together with increased facilities for transportation, been the cause of an increased average in the past few years in these northern counties. Where, in 1870, scarcely any cotton was planted, census statistics for 1879 show that, while for the state at large the acreage of corn is much greater than that of cotton, there are twenty-nine counties in which the reverse is true, the acreage of cotton in some instances far exceeding that of any other crop. These comprise the southern portion of the Mississippi alluvial region and Crowley's ridge, all of the eastern prairie region, and all of the southern pine-hills region except the counties of Sevier, Howard, Hempstead, Bradley, Clark, and Grant. Pulaski county also has a greater cotton than corn acreage. That cotton should be the chief crop of these counties is not surprising when it is remembered that not only does the tillable area embrace a large proportion of rich river bottom lands so specially adapted to cotton culture, but that the laborers are chiefly negroes, who, from a lifetime association with that crop, seem wedded to it, so much so that they can hardly be induced to raise even the necessaries of life. To them "cotton is king" most emphatically, presenting its golden visions of *cash in hand* when the crop shall be gathered, preceding the Christmas and New Year festivities. At this time old debts to merchants are to be paid and new arrangements made for the coming year. Cotton is also almost the only crop on which merchants and others will advance the necessary supplies for subsistence during the year, and new obligations are usually assumed by the laborer (an item of no small importance in the domestic economy of each family of this race), a cotton crop of a certain number of acres being pledged.

ACREAGE.—For the state at large the acreage devoted to cotton embraces 30.4 per cent. of all the lands under cultivation, or 3 per cent. of the total area of the state, and if evenly distributed would average 19.7 acres per square mile. We find, however, a greater acreage on the south, and of all the counties Phillips is foremost, with 42,650 acres, or an average of 67.7 acres per square mile. Lee and Jefferson have, respectively, 56.9 and 52.2 acres per square mile, these three counties being the only ones with an average higher than 38. In thirteen counties the average is between 30 and 38; in seventeen between 20 and 30; and in all others below that. With the exception of White county, the eighteen counties of the state whose acreage is above 20,000 lie south of the line from White river through Little Rock that marks the northern limit of the pine-hills region.

PERCENTAGE OF TILLED LANDS IN COTTON.—Chicot stands at the head of the counties in the proportion of cultivated lands devoted to cotton culture, viz, 69 per cent. Other counties above 50 per cent. are Jefferson, Crittenden, Phillips, and Lee. In thirteen counties the percentage is between 40 and 50; in twelve other counties one-third is devoted to cotton; in six the percentage is below 10, and in Benton, Washington, and Madison, in the extreme northwestern part of the state, less than one-half of 1 per cent. is given to cotton.

PRODUCTION.—About 69 per cent. of the state's production is raised in the counties south of the northeast and southwest diagonal line from Des Arc, on White river, through Little Rock, to the northern line of Sevier county; and in but five of the thirty-five counties north of the line is the yield greater than 10,000 bales, and in nine others greater than 5,000 bales. Benton, Madison, and Washington each produced, respectively, 126, 129, and 133 bales. On the south, Jefferson has 34,588 bales, the highest number in the state; Phillips 29,070, and Chicot 25,338 bales. Of the thirty-nine counties four have a production of more than 20,000 bales, two others more than 15,000, thirteen more than 10,000, and twelve more than 5,000 bales.

PRODUCT PER ACRE.—The general average product per acre for the state, as shown by census statistics for the year 1879, was a little more than half a bale (0.58); and, assuming that the average weight of bales was 500 pounds of lint (a weight given by correspondents from different parts of the state), we find the average product to have been 870 pounds of seed-cotton or 290 of lint. Arkansas thus ranks as third among the cotton states.

The richest and most productive lands are those of the Mississippi alluvial region, and here the yield was 1,215 pounds of seed-cotton per acre. Crowley's ridge, which properly belongs to the region, though embracing sandy uplands, has the next highest average, 945 pounds, a product higher than such lands alone would give, and representing rather a combination of the sandy uplands and alluvial lands which are found in these counties. The same is probably true of the eastern silt prairies, which adjoin these lands and have a productiveness of 900 pounds, thus ranking third in the list of regions.

The productiveness of the western red loam (870 pounds), as well as that of the northern barrens regions (840 pounds), is higher than that of the yellow loam and pine hills region (765 pounds), because of better lands and probably better culture by white labor.

575

COUNTIES.—Chicot county, on the southeast, ranks first in the state in product per acre (1,410 pounds of seed-cotton), and is second in the entire list of counties of the cotton states, East Carroll, Louisiana, being first. It is one of a group of three counties in adjoining states and also adjoining each other (East Carroll, of Louisiana, Chicot, of Arkansas, and Issaquena, of Mississippi) that "form the center of maximum cotton production per acre on natural soils in the United States, and probably in the world". (Census Bulletin 251). Desha county is next to Chicot in yield per acre (1,290 pounds), while Mississippi and Jefferson rank as third and fourth.

Nine counties in the state have a yield per acre of more than 1,000 pounds of seed-cotton per acre; seventeen others, 900 to 1,000; twenty-three, found almost exclusively in the central and northern parts of the state, 800 to 900; thirteen counties, also in the same regions, from 700 to 800; ten counties, from 600 to 700 pounds, and the remaining two, Ouachita and Union, 555 pounds of seed-cotton per acre.

REGION COMPARISONS.—The following tables have been prepared to give at a glance a comparative view of the production of each region in the state, and also of the counties of each which rank as first in total number of bales produced and the yield per acre:

TABLE III.—SHOWING POPULATION AND COTTON PRODUCTION IN EACH AGRICULTURAL REGION OF THE STATE.

Agricultural region.	Area.	POPULATION.			COTTON PRODUCTION.											
		Total.	White.	Colored.	Acres.	Bales.	Average per acre.				Total in tons.		Percentage of the state's total production.	Cotton acreage per sqr. mile.	Bales per sqr. mile.
							Bales 500 lbs.	Seed-cot-ton.	Lint.	Seed.	Lint.	Seed.			
	Square miles.								Lbs.	Lbs.	Lbs.					
The State	53,045	802,525	591,531	210,994	1,042,976	608,256	0.58	870	290	580	152,064	304,128	100.0	19.7	11.5
Mississippi alluvial	3,045	36,837	10,585	25,252	85,889	68,910	0.81	1,215	405	810	17,478	34,966	11.5	28.2	22.0
Crowley's ridges	7,820	109,720	65,994	43,706	138,406	119,640	0.83	945	315	630	29,912	59,826	19.7	34.7	15.7
Gray silt prairie	3,470	26,619	18,805	9,814	43,645	27,189	0.60	900	300	600	6,797	13,594	4.5	18.5	11.0
Yellow loam	14,250	212,218	118,141	94,077	391,551	201,612	0.51	765	256	510	50,402	100,804	33.1	27.5	14.1
Western red loam	16,505	290,291	255,171	35,120	250,511	144,864	0.58	870	290	580	36,216	72,422	23.8	14.9	8.6
Northern barrens and hills	8,980	125,770	122,835	2,935	80,922	45,022	0.56	840	280	560	11,258	22,516	7.4	9.1	5.1

TABLE IV.—SHOWING "BANNER COUNTIES" AS REGARDS PRODUCTION AND PRODUCT PER ACRE IN THE VARIOUS AGRICULTURAL REGIONS OF THE STATE.

Regions according to product per acre.	Average product per acre.	COUNTY IN EACH REGION HAVING HIGHEST TOTAL PRODUCTION.					COUNTY IN EACH REGION HAVING HIGHEST PRODUCT PER ACRE.					
		Name.	Rank in product per acre in the state.	Cotton acreage.	Total production, bales.	Product per acre.	Name.	Rank in total production in the state.	Cotton acreage.	Total production.	Product per acre.	Rank in product per acre in the state.
Mississippi alluvial	0.81	Chicot	1	26,941	25,338	0.94	Chicot	3	26,941	25,338	0.94	1
Crowley's ridges	0.83	Phillips	7	42,054	29,070	0.69	Phillips	2	42,054	29,070	0.69	7
Gray silt prairie	0.60	Lonoke	19	20,910	11,704	0.56	Arkansas	33	12,611	5,908	0.47	9
Western red loam	0.58	Pulaski	6	29,077	20,439	0.70	Pulaski	5	29,077	20,439	0.70	6
Northern barrens and hills	0.56	Independence	35	19,602	11,156	0.57	Fulton	61	3,904	2,433	0.61	20
Yellow loam	0.51	Jefferson	4	45,426	34,588	0.76	Jefferson	1	45,426	34,588	0.76	4

As "banner counties" of the state, Jefferson ranks first in the total number of bales produced, 34,588; Chicot first as regards the percentage of tilled lands devoted to the culture of cotton and the product per acre, while Phillips has a higher cotton acreage per square mile than any other county in the state.

The counties of the *yellow-loam region*, with a combined area of 14,250 square miles, or nearly 27 per cent. of that of the state, produced in 1879, from 391,551 acres, 201,612 bales, or 33 per cent. of the total yield. Its cotton acreage per square mile was 27.5, yielding 14.1 bales, and comprising 39.6 per cent. of the lands under cultivation. The yield per acre was 0.51 of a bale or 765 pounds of seed-cotton, and was lower than in any other region of the state. Jefferson county produced the highest number of bales in this region (34,588), as well as in the state, its product per acre (1,140 pounds of seed-cotton) being also the highest in the region and fourth in the state.

The counties of the *western red-loam region*, covering an area of about 16,805 square miles, comprising 31.7 per cent. of that of the state, and of which 10.5 per cent. was in cultivation, had a cotton acreage of 250,511 acres, yielding 144,864 bales; this was 23.8 per cent. of the total production. The average per square mile was 14.9 acres and 8.6 bales, with a product of 0.58 of a bale or 870 pounds of seed-cotton per acre, the region thus ranking above the yellow loam or sand and pine-hills region. The county having the highest total yield was Pulaski, 20,439 bales, its product per acre, 1,050 pounds of seed-cotton, also being higher than that of any other county of the region. It ranks as fifth in the state in the latter regard.

Crowley's ridge region produced the third highest percentage, 19.7 of the total production of the state. It has an area of 7,620 square miles, or 14.3 per cent. of that of the state. In 1879, from 188,498 acres, the yield was 119,649 bales, an average of 945 pounds of seed-cotton per acre, thus ranking second. Its cotton acreage comprised 39.9 per cent. of its tilled land, and averaged 24.7 acres per square mile. Of the twelve counties comprising the region, Phillips ranks first, both in total number of bales and in product per acre. All of the counties had an average of more than 900 pounds of seed-cotton per acre, except Saint Francis, Greene, and Clay, and in these the yield was from 750 to 810 pounds. Poinsett has a sparser population and consequently a less acreage of tilled land and cotton than even the two counties on the extreme north.

The *Mississippi alluvial counties*, standing highest in product per acre, have an area of 3,040 square miles, comprising 5.7 per cent. of that of the state. Hardly 8 per cent. of this is in cultivation, and of such lands 55.6 per cent. is devoted to the culture of cotton, its acreage being 28.2 per square mile. In 1879 this region produced 11.5 per cent. of the state's production, or 69,910 bales of cotton from 85,839 acres, the average product being 1,215 pounds of seed-cotton or 405 pounds of lint per acre. Chicot county ranks first in this region in the number of bales produced, and first both in the region and state in its product per acre, 1,410 pounds of seed-cotton or 470 of lint. The other three counties have a high total production and product per acre.

The *northern barrens and hill lands* in 1879 produced 7.4 per cent. of the state's total production, although its cotton acreage was but 9.1 acres per square mile. The area of the counties comprising the region is 8,860 square miles, or 16.7 per cent. of the state's area. But 9.7 per cent. of this area is under cultivation, 14.7 per cent. of that being devoted to the culture of cotton. The product per acre was 840 pounds of seed-cotton. Independence county produced the greater number of bales, and nearly twice that of any other county of the region. In but two of the counties the number of bales was less than 1,000. Fulton, an upland county, has the highest product per acre in the region, 915 pounds of seed-cotton, and is nearly equaled by the adjoining county of Baxter. The average of all the counties is high, there being none having less than half a bale per acre.

The *gray silt prairies*, in the eastern part of the state, embracing but three counties, with an area of but 2,470 square miles, or 4.6 per cent. of the state's area, produced 4.5 per cent. of the cotton for 1879 from an acreage which averaged 18.5 acres per square mile. But 8.4 per cent. of its area was in cultivation, and of this 34.1 per cent. was devoted to the culture of cotton. Lonoke produced the greater number of bales, 11,704, the other two counties falling much below. Arkansas had the highest product per acre, 1,005 pounds of seed-cotton, the other counties averaging 840 and 870 pounds.

TRANSPORTATION FACILITIES.—*Rivers.*—The two large rivers, the Mississippi and the Arkansas, are navigable for steamboats throughout their limits within the state, while White river is open only as far north as Jacksonport, where it emerges into the alluvial plain from the rocky hills and mountains of the northern part of the state. The Ouachita is said to be navigable for a great distance, and the Red river, on the southwest, is open to boats throughout its course between the lines of Louisiana and the Indian territory. These streams thus afford facilities for easy transportation direct to New Orleans, Memphis, or northern ports, not only for the thirty-six counties that immediately border them, but for many others within easy hauling distance, an aggregate area of two-thirds or more of the state.

Railroads.—Little Rock is the center of the railroad system of the state, and from it railway lines reach westward along the Arkansas river border to Fort Smith, northeast to Saint Louis, southeastward to Texas, and eastward to Memphis, together with short lines elsewhere on the southeast, affording greater and quicker transportation facilities and with competitive rates from those portions of the state already having river routes. The people of the northern and western counties remote from the Arkansas and the navigable portion of White river are dependent entirely upon wagon transportation for the removal of their farm products to market, and under the circumstances it is somewhat surprising that cotton should form so large a part of the crops in the extreme north.

Rates.—The rates of transportation for cotton are fixed per bale for all bales of less than 600 pounds weight, and it thus happens that merchants and other buyers require that the minimum weight of all offered for sale shall be 400 or 450 pounds. On bales below that weight there is usually charged a forfeit of $1, payable by the producer. Shipments are made from Little Rock to New Orleans at $2, and to New York at $5 a bale. · Rates from particular counties are given with the county descriptions, Part II of this report.

Analyses of soils and subsoils (air-dried), made by Dr. Robert Peter.

[Arranged from the Geological Survey Report of Arkansas, 1888.]

Description	Locality	County	Vegetation
ALLUVIAL LANDS.			
1. Saint Francis and Mississippi river bottoms.			
Black sandy soil	Fork of Crowley's ridge	Greene	Gum, walnut, and poplar
Gray sandy subsoil	do	do	
Black sandy soil	do	do	Poplar, gum, and oak
Red and stiff malacolay	do	do	
Light soil	Saint Francis river bottom	Craighead	Gum, elm, white oak, black hickory, and hackberry
"Gum soil"	do	Crittenden	
Light tenacious soil	Near No. 422	do	Large oaks
Backland soil	Sec. 16, T. 7 S., R. 4 W	do	
2. Arkansas river bottom.			
Waste land soil	Near Van Buren	Crawford	
Light chocolate-colored subsoil	do	do	
Brownish sandy loam soil	do	do	
Subsoil	Sec. 19, T. 8, R. 19 W	do	
Light grayish-brown soil	Foot of Petit Jean mountain	Conway	White, red, and black oaks, sweet gum, black hickory, and walnut
Subsoil	do	Perry	
Subsoil	Sec. 19, T. 8 S., R. 7 W	Jefferson	
Subsoil	Sec. 8, T. 8 S., R. 7 W	do	
Stiff red subsoil	Sec. 30, T. 8 S., R. 7 W	do	Black elm, oak, oak, and hickory
Chocolate-colored and tenacious soil	do	do	
Garden soil	Sec. 14, T. 8 S., R. 4 W	Arkansas	Gum, hackberry, box-elder, etc.
Black-land soil	Enviaen at Arkansas Post	do	
Underclay	T. 1, R. 4 W	do	
Sandy bottom cotton soil	do	do	
Subsoil	Melon's plantation	Independence	Pine, red and water oaks, elm, pecan, black walnut, sweet gum, hackberry, and buckeye.
3. White river bottom.			
Soil	Oil-trough bottom		

Analyses of soils and subsoils (air-dried) made by Dr. Robert Peter.—Continued.

Number.	Description.	Locality.	County.	Vegetation.	Insoluble matter.	Potash.	Soda.	Lime.	Magnesia.	Brown oxide of manganese.	Peroxide of iron.	Alumina.	Phosphoric acid.	Sulphuric acid.	Carbonic acid.	Water and organic matter.	Total.	Hygroscopic moisture (air-dried).
	CROWLEY'S RIDGE REGION—continued.																	
430	Gray soil	Sec. 11, T. 2 N., R. 1 E.	do	White, red, and post oaks, hickory, dogwood, black and sweet gum, and sassafras.														2.500
297	Soil	Sec. 26, T. 1 N., R. 3 W.	Monroe	Sweet gum, dogwood, and elm, some hickory and ash.														1.825
449	Light soil	Governor Izzard's land, west side of Crowley's ridge.	Saint Francis	Sweet gum, hickory, poplar, walnut, dogwood, red bud, black ash, elm, muscadine and other grape-vines.														
524	Light sandy soil	Two miles north of Jacksonport	Jackson	Blue's and white oak, some hickory, and sweet gum.														1.175
527	Sandy soil	Sec. 32, T. 14, R. 2 W	do	Black and some white oaks, hickory, and sweet gum.														0.925
	GRAY SILT PRAIRIE.																	
31	Light soil	Grand prairie, 7 miles east of Brownsville.	Prairie															2.300
222	Subsoil of No. 229	do																1.825
406	Light prairie soil	Adjoining Spanish grant, Sec. 18, T. 7 S., R 3 W.	Arkansas															1.690
408	Subsoil of No. 406	do	do															1.730
409	Soil	From the highest prairies on Sec. 17, T. 7 S., R. 3 W.	do															1.850
410	Upland woodland soil	Adjoining the prairie land of the Spanish grant, T. 7 W., R. 3 W.	do															3.299
	YELLOW-LOAM REGION.																	
273	Red soil	Southern part of county	Dorsey															4.500
246	Sandy soil	Near Lisbon	Union															3.500
340	Subsoil of No. 346	do	do															1.425
342	Gladdy soil	Camp creek, near Lisbon.	Union															1.675
390	Sandy soil	3½ miles northwest of Warren	Bradley															2.085
	BLACK CRETACEOUS LANDS OF SOUTHWEST PRAIRIE REGION.																	
21	Black waxy soil	Sec. 19, T. 8, R 19	Clark	Sweet gum, mulberry, and walnut.														3.650
13	Cretaceous soil	Adjacent lime marl bluff on Dœdpher creek, Sec. 22, T. 7, R 23.	Hempstead	Gum, hickory, oaks, and ash														4.675
228	Black soil	Sec. 7, 11, R 28	do	Usually limited prairies, surrounded with pine, hickory, ash, and Osage orange.														
229	Subsoil	do	do															4.900
329	Cretaceous soil	Sec. 5, fractional T. 10, R. 20 W	Sevier															7.475
366	Black soil	Sec. 13, T. 13, R. 22	do	Hickory, scrub haw, and Osage orange.														9.675
368	Subsoil	Taken near the above	do															2.775
372	Pebbly soil	Sec. 4, T. 8, R. 26, on a branch of Bacon creek.	Pike															3.100
374	Pebbly subsoil	From near above place	do	Chiefly white oak														1.423

580

No.	Locality	County	Growth
RED LOAM (SHALE) UPLANDS.			
Lands south of Arkansas river.			
313 Sandy soil	8 miles north of Little Rock	Pulaski	Black and post oaks, and some hickory.
314 Subsoil	do	do	
365 Red soil	Section T. 2 S., R. 20 W	Polk	Red, black, white, and post oaks, dogwood, black walnut, wild cherry, plum, red oak, and hickory.
395 Subsoil	do	do	
360 Yellowish-brown soil	One mile north of Waldron	Scott	Red, black, white, and post oaks, black oak, elm, cherry, black walnut, and dogwood.
363 Gray subsoil	do	Scott	
361 Brownish gray soil	Sec. 26, T. 2 R. 21 W	Yell	
362 Gray subsoil	Sec. 9, T. 7, R. 25	Logan	Beech, oak, hickory, and post oak, with some undergrowth.
364 Red ferruginous soil	do	do	
396 Subsoil			
RED LOAM PRAIRIES.			
331 Red some prairie soil	Haller's prairie, Sec. 12, T. 4, R. 21	Sebastian	
332 Reddish subsoil	do	do	
Lands north of Arkansas river.			
333 Gray sandy soil	3½ mile west of Clarksville	Johnson	Post, black, and black-jack oaks, persimmon, and sumac.
320 Subsoil of No. 333			
315 Gray sandy soil	8 miles north of Dover	Pope	Post, black, red, and white oaks, and some hickory.
317 Subsoil	do		
349 Brownish upland soil	1 mile from Van Buren	Crawford	
311 Subsoil	do		
350 Reddish soil	T. 3, R. 14	Faulkner	Black oak, hickory, and some white and black-jack oaks.
399 Subsoil	do	do	
379 Reddish soil	Southeastern part of county	Van Buren	Black and post oaks.
281 Subsoil	do	do	
300 Red ferruginous soil	3 miles west of Searcy	White	Black, red, and black-jack oaks, and hickory.
302 Subsoil	do	do	
278 Red upland soil	Central part of county	Washington	White and greenup oaks, hickory, hackberry, walnut, elm, ash, dogwood, and locust.
279 Red subsoil	do		
Granitic lands.			
409 Light gray soil	Near the eastern slope of granite range of Fourche cove	Pulaski	Red and white oaks, dogwood, hickory, and maple.
463 Brownish-gray subsoil	Allum near the above	do	
603 Micaceous underclay	do	do	
NORTHERN BARRENS AND HILLS			
1. Barrens and magnesian limestone lands.			
295 Sandy soil	Near Bentonville	Benton	Black hickory.
297 Subsoil	do	do	
306 Brush creek barrens soil	Northwest part of county	Madison	Black-jack oak and hickory.

Analyses of soils and subsoils (air-dried) made by Dr. Robert Peter—Continued.

Number.	Description.	Locality.	County.	Vegetation.	Insoluble matter.	Potash.	Soda.	Lime.	Magnesia.	Brown oxide of manganese.	Peroxide of iron.	Alumina.	Phosphoric acid.	Sulphuric acid.	Carbonic acid.	Water and organic matter.	Total.	Hygroscopic moisture (air-dried).
	NORTHERN BARRENS AND HILLS—cont'd.																	
380	Brush creek barrens subsoil	Northwest part of county	Madison	Black, white, red, and water oaks, black and sweet gums.														
381	Light soil	Near Jasper	Newton															
382	Subsoil	do	do															
383	Soil	Near the mouth of Dry fork of Clear creek	Searcy															
384	Subsoil	do	do															
385	Upland clayey soil	Lot 26, T. 13, R. 3 W	Izard	Post and white oaks, hickory, dogwood, and persimmon.														
386	Brownish colored subsoil	do	do															
387	Soil	2 miles west of Batesville	Independence	Hickory, oaks, etc														
	Yellowish-brown subsoil	do	do															
	2. Clayey and siliceous lands.																	
388	Barrens soil	Sec. 31, T. 18, R. 17 W	Fulton	A few scrub hickories, oaks, and walnuts.														
389	Subsoil	do	do															
390	Barrens soil	Sec. 26, T. 18, R. 16 W	Baxter	Basinwood and grass														
	Yellowish subsoil	do	do															
	Upland siliceous soil	From near waters of Big creek	Marion	Big-bud hickory, black-jack, and red oaks.														
	Subsoil	do	do															
	Siliceous soil of second uplands	do	Fulton	White oak and hickory														
	Subsoil	do	do															
	Upland siliceous soil	A few miles west of Powhattan	Lawrence	Black-jack and post oaks and small hickory.														
	Subsoil	do	do															
	Fine upland soil	1 mile from Calico	Izard	Black oak, hickory, and pine														
	Sandy subsoil	do	do															
	3. Prairie.																	
	Soil	Sugar Loaf creek	Marion															
	Subsoil	do	do															

PART II.

AGRICULTURAL DESCRIPTIONS

OF THE

COUNTIES OF ARKANSAS.

AGRICULTURAL DESCRIPTIONS

OF THE

COUNTIES OF ARKANSAS.

The counties are grouped under the several agricultural regions, and each is described as a whole under that to which it predominantly belongs, its name alone being given with an asterisk (*) in the county list of any other region which may include a minor part of its area, a reference also being made to that region in which it is described.

The statistical matter given at the head of each county description is derived from the Tenth Census reports; and there are also added abstracts from such answers to schedules of questions as have been received from correspondents in the 38 counties heard from.

The county descriptions, because of the large number of counties in the state, are necessarily short; and in order to keep the report within properly prescribed limits only general descriptions are given.

MISSISSIPPI ALLUVIAL REGION.

(Includes parts of Chicot, Desha, Phillips,* Lee,* Saint Francis,* Cross,* Poinsett,* Craighead,* Greene,* and Clay,* and the whole of Crittenden and Mississippi counties.)

CHICOT.

Population: 10,117.—White, 1,563; colored, 8,554.
Area: 840 square miles.—Woodland, all; yellow-loam region, 205 square miles; alluvial, 635 square miles.
Tilled lands: 38,658 acres.—Area planted in cotton, 26,941 acres; in corn, 7,309 acres; in oats, 80 acres.
Cotton production: 25,338 bales; average cotton product per acre, 0.94 bale, 1,410 pounds seed-cotton, or 470 pounds cotton lint.

Chicot county is included almost entirely within the low and level alluvial lands of the Mississippi river, which forms its eastern boundary, and those of bayous Maçon, Bœuff, and Bartholomew (on the north) and Big Bayou. These lands comprise the front or higher lands along the borders of the river and the large bayous, the back-lands away from the streams, cypress swamps, and canebrakes, and some high ridge or sandy pine uplands on the south and north, but not in the middle of the county.

The soil of the front-lands is a fine sandy loam, quite deep, and well-timbered with cottonwood, gum, walnut, etc. The lands of the river are celebrated for their productiveness, the yield being about two bales of cotton per acre. The back-lands have a stiff clayey buckshot soil, and are not as productive as those of the front-lands. This land is said to suffer from drought and to produce best in a tolerably wet summer. Cypress brakes occur frequently throughout their extent. The tilled lands comprise 7.2 per cent. of the county area, and of these 69.7 per cent. are devoted to the culture of cotton. The averages per square mile are 46 acres of tilled lands and 32.1 of cotton, the county ranking as fourteenth in the latter regard. In cotton yield per acre it is first in the state and second in the United States.

ABSTRACT OF THE REPORT OF DANIEL B. BRAWNER, LUNA LANDING.

The lowlands comprise the first and second bottom of Bayou Maçon, and the front-land, back-land, and cypress swamps of the Mississippi river. The uplands consist of the level table-lands drained by the Mississippi river, Chicot lake, and bayou Maçon.

The soils cultivated in cotton are the black sandy soil of the river bottom, the clay loam of bayou Maçon, and their intermixtures.

The most important of these is the black sandy land of the river bottom, covering about two-thirds of the surface of the county, and extending in the direction of the river about 50 miles. Almost every variety of timber can be found in this county. The soil is light, and is from 4 to 5 feet in depth. Sand is found at 6 feet. The land is easily cultivated in dry seasons, is early and well drained, and is best adapted to cotton and corn, which are the only crops raised in this county. About nine-tenths of the cultivated area is devoted to cotton, which grows to a height of about 5 feet, but inclines to run to weed on all lands of the county in wet seasons, no remedy as yet having been found to restrain it.

From fresh land, or from land after ten years' cultivation, the product per acre in seed-cotton is from 1,400 to 2,800 pounds; from very old land about 1,400 pounds, 1,665 pounds being required for 475 pounds of lint, rating from fresh land as good ordinary, and from old land not quite so high, as it has not the glossy color or silky feeling. Cocoa, crab, and several other grasses are quite troublesome. One-fourth of the land lies "turned out", producing, when again cultivated, as well as fresh land.

The clay loam, constituting about one-tenth of the tillable area, extends about 15 miles along bayou Maçon, and is many miles wide. The soil is a heavy clay loam, 2 feet deep, having a variety of colors, being yellow, brown, orange-red, and blackish in different places. It is heavy in breaking up, but becomes fine as it is cultivated. The subsoil is heavier than the surface soil, and is underlaid by clay at 17 feet. The land is easily tilled in dry seasons, is early and warm when well drained, and is best adapted to cotton and corn, the former comprising about nine-tenths of the crops planted. The plant usually attains a height of from 3 to 4 feet. About 1,200 pounds of seed-cotton per acre are obtained from fresh land, but after ten years' cultivation only one-half the above amount. In either case 1,425 pounds are required for a 475-pound bale of good ordinary lint. Crab, cocoa, and Bermuda grasses are the most troublesome weeds. About one-fourth of the land lies "turned out", producing, when again cultivated, only about three-fourths of its original yield.

The climate must be very warm when the seed is planted, and the most productive cotton crops are raised when there is very little rain. When there is much rain the plant runs to weed. Owing to the long seasons in this part of the county there is no trouble from frost.

Cotton is shipped, from the middle of September until December, by river to New Orleans, at the rate of $1 per bale.

DESHA.

Population : 8,973.—White, 2,452; colored, 6,531.

Area : 730 square miles.—Woodland, all; yellow-loam region, 285 square miles; eastern prairie region, 55 square miles; alluvial, 390 square miles.

Tilled lands : 42,642 acres; area planted in cotton, 21,159 acres; in corn, 9,819 acres; in oats, 169 acres; in wheat, 18 acres.

Cotton production : 18,103 bales; average cotton product per acre, 0.86 bale, 1,290 pounds seed-cotton, or 430 pounds cotton lint.

Desha county, bordered on the east by the Mississippi river, is divided into two parts by the Arkansas, which flows southeastward, and the northern part is again divided by the White river, flowing southward into the Arkansas. The lands of the county, therefore, belong mostly to the level and flat alluvial region. In the southern portion of the county, and lying between the Arkansas river and bayou Bartholomew, there are some oak and pine uplands with sandy soils. The alluvial lands are the richest and best cotton lands, and embrace the usual front or high lands bordering the rivers, having dark sandy loams, capable of producing two bales of cotton per acre, and the back-lands away from the river, with their stiff black waxy and oftentimes ill-drained land, less productive and interspersed with cypress brakes. The lands are, for the most part, subject to overflow in high-water seasons, and levees have been constructed along the Arkansas and the Mississippi rivers for protection. The lands under cultivation in Desha county comprise 9.1 per cent. of the entire area, or an average of 58.4 acres per square mile. Of the latter, 29 acres are devoted to cotton, the county thus ranking as seventeenth in the state. In cotton yield per acre it ranks as second, or next to the adjoining county of Chicot.

ABSTRACT OF THE REPORT OF JAMES MURPHY, NAPOLEON.

The lowlands of the county comprise the first bottoms of the Arkansas river. The chief crops of the region are cotton, corn, vegetables of all kinds, and sweet and Irish potatoes. The soil does not seem to be well adapted to small grain.

The chief soils devoted to cotton are the sandy alluvial on the front of bayous, rivers, etc., and the clammy buckshot on back-land.

The *sandy alluvial* soil comprises the larger part of the Arkansas river valley. This soil is a fine silty loam, yellow or blackish colored, 2½ feet in depth, with a light yellowish sandy subsoil, underlaid by sand at 2½ feet, and is easy to cultivate in all seasons, being early, warm, well drained, and best adapted to cotton. From two-thirds to three-fourths of the crops cultivated are in cotton. The plant usually grows about 5½ feet high, and is most productive at that height. It inclines to run to weed when there is too much rain, which may be remedied by throwing the dirt from the plant, and also by topping in August. The seed-cotton product per acre for fresh land is 1,800 pounds, and in October 1,780 pounds make a 475-pound bale of lint; later it takes less to make the same bale, the staple rating from middling to low middling. After ten years' cultivation the yield is 2,500 pounds of seed-cotton, when 1,660 pounds are necessary for a 475-pound bale of lint superior to that from fresh land. Cockleburs, careless and iron weeds, crab-grass, and morning-glory vines are most troublesome. About one-half of these lands lie idle for want of labor and not from poverty of soil, and produce much better for not being in constant cultivation.

Cotton is shipped after 16th of October by steamboat to Memphis and New Orleans at $1 per bale.

PHILLIPS.
(See "Crowley's Ridge region".)

LEE.
(See "Crowley's Ridge region".)

SAINT FRANCIS.
(See "Crowley's Ridge region".)

CROSS.
(See "Crowley's Ridge region".)

POINSETT.
(See "Crowley's Ridge region".)

CRAIGHEAD.
(See "Crowley's Ridge region".)

GREENE.
(See "Crowley's Ridge region".)

CLAY.
(See "Crowley's Ridge region".)

CRITTENDEN.

Population : 9,415.—White, 1,899; colored, 7,516.
Area : 660 square miles.—Woodlands, all; all Mississippi alluvial.
Tilled lands : 43,646 acres.—Area planted in cotton, 24,413 acres; in corn, 9,810 acres; in oats, 73 acres; in wheat, 20 acres.
Cotton production : 16,039 bales; average cotton product per acre, 0.66 bale, 990 pounds seed-cotton, or 330 pounds cotton lint.

The surface of Crittenden county is level, and is bounded on the east by the Mississippi river, other smaller streams flowing westward into the Saint Francis river. The county is entirely included in the alluvial region of the Mississippi, and is heavily timbered with an undergrowth of cane. The lands that border the river and cover one-half of the county are dark sandy loams, which are easily tilled and very productive, yielding from 70 to 80 bushels of corn or 1,500 pounds of seed-cotton per acre. Interspersed with this land, and lying mostly on the west at a lower level. are stiff black and clayey buckshot lands with a timber growth of cypress, cottonwood, and water oak. These soils are ill-drained and cold, and are not apparently desirable for the cultivation of corn, as cotton is said to be the exclusive crop. They are said to yield 1,500 pounds of seed-cotton per acre.

There are many small lakes and bayous interspersed throughout the interior of this county. The lands under cultivation comprise 10.3 per cent. of the area, an average of 66.1 acres per square mile. Of the latter, 37 acres are devoted to the culture of cotton, placing the county as sixth in the state in the amount of its cotton lands. In cotton yield per acre it is eleventh in the state and seventh in the number of bales. The greater part of the cotton is produced in the southern half of the county.

ABSTRACT OF THE REPORT OF A. C. BREWER, SCANLONS.

The lowlands of the county are the first bottom or front-land of the Mississippi river, the chief crops of which are cotton and corn. The soils cultivated in cotton are the flat, black sandy land, the dark loam soil, and the black buckshot soil subject to overflow. The chief soil is the *black sandy*, which comprises one-half of the county area, and extends from Missouri to the Gulf of Mexico, following the course of the Mississippi river. This soil is a fine sandy loam, blackish in color, 3 feet in depth, with a lighter, coarse white sandy subsoil. It is difficult to till in wet seasons, but easy when dry, and is early, warm, well drained, and best adapted to cotton, to which four-fifths of it is devoted. The usual and most productive height of the cotton plant is 5 feet. It inclines to run to weed in wet weather and on very rich land, for which baring off and topping are the remedies.

The yield of seed-cotton per acre from fresh land is 1,000 pounds; 1,680 pounds make a 475-pound bale of lint, which is long, strong, and first rate. After ten years' cultivation the yield is better than from fresh land, 1,500 pounds being then produced per acre, and 1,780 pounds making a 475-pound bale, the lint of which is not so long as that from fresh land, but is equally as strong. The troublesome weeds are cocklebur, tie-vines, and morning-glory. None of these lands lie "turned out".

The *dark loam* land comprises one-fourth of the county area, and extends throughout the Mississippi bottoms, with a timber growth of cottonwood, oak, pecan, dogwood, hackberry, box-elder, and honey-locust. This soil is a heavy clay loam, putty-like, with a brown or mahogany color, and is from 4 to 5 feet deep, the subsoil being lighter than the surface soil. The soil is difficult to till in wet seasons, but easy when dry ; is early, warm, ill-drained, and best adapted to cotton, to which four-fifths of it is devoted. Five feet is the usual and most productive height of the plant, which runs to weed in wet weather. In other particulars the soil is like the first described, with the exception that the staple from older cultivated lands is not so good or so long as that from fresh land.

The *black buckshot* land comprises one-fourth of the area of the county, extending throughout the bottoms, and has a timber growth of cypress, cottonwood, and water oak. This soil, putty-like and black, 7 feet deep, with a lighter, coarse, white, sandy subsoil, is best adapted to cotton, to which it is all devoted. The plant usually is 3 feet high, and is longest and most productive in dry weather. The seed-cotton product per acre from fresh land is 900 pounds; 1,000 pounds make a 475-pound bale of good lint. After ten years the yield increases to 1,500 pounds of seed cotton, when 1,780 pounds make a 475-pound bale of lint, comparing well with that from fresh land. The troublesome weeds are burs. None of this land lies "turned out".

The cotton is best with a small amount of rain and warm, sunny weather. What is most wished for is a dry spring, wet July, dry August and September, and a late frost.

Cotton is shipped, as soon as ginned, by steamboat to New Orleans at $1 per bale.

MISSISSIPPI.

Population : 7,332.—White, 4,671; colored, 2,661.
Area : 810 square miles.—Woodland, all; all Mississippi alluvial.
Tilled lands : 29,330 acres.—Area planted in cotton, 13,326 acres; in corn, 9,858 acres; in oats, 181 acres; in wheat, 68 acres.
Cotton production : 10,430 bales; average cotton product per acre, 0.78 bale, 1,170 pounds seed-cotton, or 390 pounds cotton lint.

Mississippi county, which occupies one of the northeastern corners of the state, is bordered on the east by the Mississippi river, and is entirely included in its alluvial region. That part lying along the river embraces dark sandy loam lands, higher than the lands of the interior, which are easily tilled and very productive, yielding from 1,500 to 1,700 pounds of seed-cotton or 70 to 80 bushels of corn per acre.

The interior and western portions of the county are interspersed with lakes, bayous, sloughs, and cypress swamps, the soils of which are mostly stiff and clayey or buckshot in character. They are also ill-drained and cold, though, when properly cultivated, they are said to yield as much as 1,500 pounds of seed-cotton per acre. Their timber growth is cypress, cottonwood, and water oak. Comparatively little of the land of this county is in cultivation, the average being only 36.2 acres per square mile. Of these 16.5 acres are devoted to cotton, the yield of that crop being greater than in any other county except Chicot and Desha.

ABSTRACT OF THE REPORT OF HARRY S. WILLIAMS, OSCEOLA.

The lowlands of the county consist of the first bottom and alluvial plain of the Mississippi river, embracing front-land, back-land, and cypress swamps. The lands devoted to the cultivation of cotton comprise dark buckshot and white chalky crawfish and light sandy and dark loam soils of the Mississippi river bottom. The most important is the *dark sandy loam* of the river bottom, which covers about three-fourths of the surface of the county, and extends, with the exception of the Saint Francis river bottom, from the Mississippi river to Crowley's ridge, a distance of about 40 miles, and has a natural timber growth of oak, cypress, sweet gum, cottonwood, elm, hickory, ash, maple, some dogwood, etc. Its soil, clayey and putty-like in places, varies in color from gray to mahogany or black, and is 5 feet deep. The tillage is not usually difficult. Cotton and corn constitute the chief crops of the region, corn being best adapted to the soil.

About three-fourths of the crops are of cotton, which usually attains a height of from 4 to 5 feet, runs to weed when the soil is too fresh, and yields from fresh land 1,400 pounds of seed-cotton per acre, 1,700 pounds being the product after three years' cultivation (unmanured); 1,900 pounds are required from fresh land, and about the same quantity from old land, for a 475-pound bale of middling lint, that from old land being a little shorter. Hog-weed and crab-grass are the most troublesome weeds. No land lies "turned out". On account of the early frost cotton is liable to be cut short, unless farmers can plant their crops early in the spring.

Cotton is shipped throughout the season, by river, to Memphis and to Saint Louis at the rate of 75 cents per bale.

CROWLEY'S RIDGE REGION.

(Includes all or parts of Phillips, Monroe, Lee, Prairie,* Woodruff, Saint Francis, Cross, Poinsett, Jackson Lawrence, Craighead, Greene, Clay, and Randolph.*)

PHILLIPS.

Population: 21,262.—White, 5,444; colored, 15,818.

Area: 630 square miles.—Woodland, all; Crowley's ridge, 410 square miles; Mississippi alluvial, 220 square miles.

Tilled lands: 78,916 acres.—Area planted in cotton, 42,654 acres; in corn, 19,685 acres; in oats, 834 acres; in wheat, 36 acres.

Cotton production: 29,070 bales; average cotton product per acre, 0.68 bale, 1,020 pounds seed-cotton, or 340 pounds cotton lint.

Phillips county, bordered on the east by the Mississippi river, has a generally level surface, with the exception of that portion occupied by Crowley's ridge. This ridge, which reaches the river at or near Helena, the county-seat, is composed of sands, clays, and gravel of the Quaternary period, and is well timbered. The soil is sandy, red or yellow in color, with a clay subsoil, and is said to stand droughts well, producing 40 to 45 bushels of corn, 20 to 30 bushels of wheat, or 800 pounds of seed-cotton per acre. The ridge flattens out westward, forming large bodies of level land, which is watered by Big creek, and has for the most part a deep yellow or mulatto soil, with now and then small spots of an ashen color, probably the former beds of small ponds. These lands will produce on an average 1,000 pounds of seed-cotton, 25 to 30 bushels of corn, or 20 bushels of wheat per acre. The principal growth is sweet gum; but on the most elevated portions the growth is beech, poplar, red and white elm, mulberry, sweet gum, ash, white oak, black walnut, dogwood, sassafras, and red maple. Still westward the country is traversed by low ridges, with intervening clay flats and occasionally wet prairies. These ridges have, for the most part, a reddish, sandy clay soil, and occasionally a gray sandy loam.

In the southern part of the county are the broad bottom lands of the Mississippi river, interspersed with small old river lakes and bayous. Low ridges of a dark loam soil occur elevated a few feet above overflow, and these have a timber growth of sugar trees, large black walnut, red oak, persimmon, white and red elm, sweet gum, mulberry, large sassafras, papaw, and grape-vines. The buckshot lands of the low bottoms of lakes and sloughs lie 10 or 15 feet lower than the ridges, and the principal growth is large cottonwood, buttonwood, and blue ash, with occasionally overcup oak and mulberry. One bale of lint cotton, or 50 to 70 bushels of corn, may be raised per acre. The alluvial land immediately adjoining the Mississippi river is a sandy loam, easily cultivated, and very fertile, producing one bale of cotton per acre.

Phillips county is one of the principal agricultural counties of the state, its lands under cultivation comprising 19.6 per cent. of the total area, and averaging 125.3 acres per square mile, Benton alone having a higher number. It also ranks first in acreage per square mile devoted to the culture of that crop, 67.7 acres. Though second in total cotton acreage and total number of bales, its rank in product per acre in the state is seventh; and in its average population, 33.7 persons per square mile, it is surpassed only by Pulaski and Sebastian counties, in which are located the cities of Little Rock and Fort Smith.

Shipments of cotton are made by river boats either to New Orleans or Memphis.

MONROE.

Population: 9,574.—White. 4,365; colored, 5,209.

Area: 660 square miles.—Woodland, nearly all; Crowley's ridge, 600 square miles; Mississippi alluvial, 60 square miles.

Tilled lands: 50,372 acres.—Area planted in cotton, 22,017 acres; in corn, 12,945 acres; in oats, 764 acres; in wheat, 60 acres.

Cotton production: 14,106 bales; average cotton product per acre, 0.64 bale, 960 pounds seed-cotton, or 320 pounds cotton lint.

The surface of Monroe county is level, and is bounded on the west by the White river. The bottom lands of this stream are broad, well timbered, and have dark sandy soils, rich and productive, yielding from 1,200 to 1,500 pounds of seed-cotton per acre when above overflow and properly cultivated. The rest of the county on the east, higher than the bottom lands, is cut up by sloughs and flats, and occasionally by a wet prairie, and has a sandy soil, similar to that of the uplands of Phillips county, having a timber growth of white, red, and post oaks, hickory, dogwood, sassafras, and some sweet gum. In the northeastern part of the county are the Big and Little prairies. The latter appears to have been the bed of a swamp. The soil and subsoil in this prairie are an ash-colored clay charged with small iron gravel, having a depth of two to two and a half feet, and resting on a substratum of red clay. To be suitable for cultivation these prairies require drainage.

The average population of Monroe county is a little more than 14 persons per square mile; its tilled lands, 76.3 acres, or 11.9 per cent. of the total area. Its cotton acreage is greater than that of any other crop, being an average of 33.4 acres per square mile, ranking in this regard eleventh in the state. In cotton product per acre it ranks as thirteenth.

Shipments of cotton are made either by rail eastward to Memphis, or by boat down the White and Mississippi rivers to New Orleans or Memphis.

LEE.

Population: 13,288.—White, 4,138; colored, 9,150.

Area: 580 square miles.—Woodland, nearly all; Crowley's ridge, 405 square miles; Mississippi alluvial, 175 square miles.

Tilled lands: 61,307 acres.—Area planted in cotton, 33,009 acres; in corn, 16,124 acres; in oats, 806 acres; in wheat, 83 acre

Cotton production: 21,147 bales; average cotton product per acre, 0.64 bale, 960 pounds seed-cotton, or 320 pounds cotton lint.

Lee county, bordered on the east by the Mississippi river, is also traversed on the east by the Saint Francis and the L'Anguille rivers. That portion of the county between these streams is a level bottom land, embracing the sandy alluvial loams adjoining the rivers above overflow, and the stiff black buckshot soils a few feet lower, and more or less subject to overflow. The bottoms are heavily timbered, and the soils, when under cultivation, yield from 1,500 to 2,000 pounds of seed-cotton or from 50 to 70 bushels of corn per acre. Immediately on the west of L'Anguille river Crowley's ridge has a width of from 2 to 4 miles, which is timbered with oaks, large poplars, hickory, gum, ash, dogwood, etc. Its soils are sandy, from red to gray in color, with clay subsoils, and yield, when cultivated, about 800 pounds of seed-cotton or 30 to 40 bushels of corn per acre. West of the ridge the lands are almost level, watered by a number of small streams, and embrace low sandy ridges, with intervening clay flats and occasional wet prairies.

Lee county is one of the chief agricultural counties in the state, its lands under cultivation averaging 105.7 acres per square mile, or 16.5 per cent. of its area; and in this regard it is surpassed by only five counties. It is also among the best cotton counties, the acreage of that crop being 56.9 acres per square mile, the second highest number in the state; the bales, 36.5 per square mile, the third in the state. In product per acre it is, however, surpassed by thirteen counties.

ABSTRACT OF THE REPORT OF J. A. GAINES, ASKEW.

The lands along the rivers are substantially the same in character. Immediately on the banks the soils are, as a general thing, light sandy loams, subject to overflow. The rich tough clayey land, called "buckshot", is generally higher above water, but back from the river this in a great measure is replaced by a tough clammy soil, sometimes sticky, like putty, which is called "crawfishy", and is unfit for cultivation and very low, being always under water in the winter and spring. Many ridges reach from river to river, the soil of which is black sandy or loam approaching to buckshot.

The lands of the L'Anguille river are entirely different from the others mentioned, not receiving any of the fertilizing deposits from the Mississippi overflows, and are almost universally clammy, hard, and cold. East from the base of Crowley's ridge the "flatwoods" extend the whole length of the county, the soil of which is a black loam, frequently sandy, with a clay subsoil. West of Crowley's ridge (2 to 4 miles wide) is a country almost level, having a variety of soils, from light sandy to the black buckshot, all rich, and needing a great deal of ditching.

The description of one portion will, as a general thing, answer for the whole of the county. The chief crops are cotton, corn, oats, and millet.

The important soils on which cotton is cultivated are the Mississippi and Saint Francis river lands, comprising black buckshot, light yellow sandy, and black sandy soils; the black (loam) or stiff land and light clay, sometimes black sandy, of Crowley's ridge; and the black yellow loam, in swamps, and occasional buckshot on L'Anguille river. The black and yellow loam of the river bottoms covers a large part of the county. The natural timber growth is oak, ash, hickory, gum, pecan, hackberry, elm, walnut, cypress, papaw, etc. The soil is putty-like in a few places, and is from 2 to 4 feet in depth. The subsoil, lighter than the soil, is sandy, and very rarely contains pebbles. The soil is easy to till in dry seasons, is early and warm when well drained, and is well adapted to all of the crops of the county. About four-sevenths of this land is devoted to cotton culture, the plant usually attaining a height of 6 feet, but is most productive at 4 feet. Wet seasons and new land inclines the plant to run to weed, and nothing restrains it. The seed-cotton product per acre from fresh land is 2,000 pounds, 1,545 pounds and more in the early part of the season making a 475-pound bale of lint, which rates the same as upland lint. After ten years' cultivation there is but little difference in productiveness, etc. The most troublesome weed is crab-grass. About 3 per cent. of these lands lie "turned out", which produce very well when again brought under cultivation.

On Crowley's ridge and west of that ridge the hills are not much cultivated. The black loam soil is about 8 inches in depth. The subsoil is a light clay, easily managed, as it readily pulverizes when turned over, is slightly impervious, and contains in places yellow and white sand, underlaid by clay and sand. The soil is early and warm when well drained, and is best adapted to cotton, one-half being devoted to that crop, which usually grows to a height of 3½ feet, 3 feet being the most productive. During extreme wet seasons, and when planted on new soil, the plant inclines to run to weed, and nothing remedies this unless the rows are wide on fresh soil. From 1,000 to 1,500 pounds is the seed-cotton product from fresh land, 1,545 pounds of which, in November, make a 475-pound bale of lint, which rates about the same as that from other lands. After ten years' cultivation the product per acre is 1,000 pounds on this land and about 1,500 pounds on best land in good seasons; but the staple is much shorter, and will not bring the same price as that from fresh land. Crab-grass, careless weeds, and many others, if land has "laid out", trouble this soil. A very small portion of land lies "turned out", and when again cultivated it is hard to get a stand from it the first year, but it yields well the second year. The soils of the slopes of the flatwoods of Crowley's ridge do not wash readily, and the valleys at the foot of the ridge are but slightly injured by the washings.

Cotton on the river lowlands is not as liable to be killed by frost as in the uplands east of the L'Anguille and Saint Francis rivers. These soils are richer and warmer, and more easily cultivated, and are more remunerative to the planter than the uplands.

The acreage of cotton is on the increase: first, because there are more whites working their own crop; second, because there are many who have moved to the cotton belt from northern and western states and from foreign countries who have bought or rented land, which they plant in cotton; third, because the negroes are becoming more thrifty, and depend more upon themselves than formerly, and, being ambitious to rise in the world, plant largely in cotton.

Cotton is shipped, as soon as ready, by river, and some by railroad, to Memphis, Helena, and New Orleans at $1 per bale.

PRAIRIE.
(See "Gray silt prairie region".)

WOODRUFF.

Population: 8,646.—White, 4,163; colored, 4,483.
Area: 580 square miles.—Woodland, nearly all; all Crowley's Ridge region.
Tilled lands: 37,889 acres.—Area planted in cotton, 18,124 acres; in corn, 11,146 acres; in oats, 497 acres; in wheat, 307 acres.
Cotton production: 12,311 bales; average cotton product per acre, 0.68 bale, 1,020 pounds seed-cotton, or 340 pounds cotton lint.

The surface of Woodruff county is level or undulating, and is bounded on the west by White river and traversed from north to south by Cache river. Other small streams aid in draining the county. Along the rivers the lands are low and flat, more or less subject to overflow, while further back they have an elevation above overflow. The latter have sandy soils, a timber growth of oak, hickory, walnut, etc., and are capable of yielding from 1,200 to 1,500 pounds of seed cotton per acre. The lower lands have usually a black sandy loam soil, deep, rich, and very productive, interspersed with small uncultivated areas of a stiff buckshot character. These lands are easily tilled, are well timbered with black, white, and other oaks, hickory, poplar, cypress, dogwood, elm, ash, etc., and an undergrowth of papaw and vines, and are said to yield from 1,500 to 2,000 pounds of seed-cotton per acre.

Woodruff has a population that averages about 15 persons per square mile. The tilled lands comprise 10.2 per cent. of the area, or 65.2 acres per square mile, of which 31.2 acres are devoted to cotton culture. In the latter regard it ranks as fifteenth in the state. In cotton product per acre the county ranks as eighth.

ABSTRACT OF THE REPORT OF J. B. DENT, AUGUSTA.

The lowlands of the county comprise the first and second bottoms of White and Cache rivers and the alluvial plain lying between. The chief crop is cotton, the other crops being corn, Irish and sweet potatoes, sorghum, wheat, and clover. Corn yields 40 bushels per acre, and last year, with heavy cotton-seed fertilizer, 40 bushels of wheat per acre were raised, while the ordinary crop is only from 16 to 20 bushels. From 200 to 300 bushels is the yield of potatoes. The soils cultivated in cotton are the gum land, or a sort of "made earth", or dark sandy loam, the fine light sandy, and the "buckshot".

The *dark sandy loam* soil, or "gum land", as it is called, comprises two-thirds of the area of the county, extending throughout all of the White river valley, over 100 miles in length and from 20 to 40 miles in width. The timber growth is gum, all kinds of oak, dogwood, poplar, soft maple, papaw, cypress, etc. The soil is a blackish and rich dark brown loam, 14 inches in depth, with a heavy reddish-brown clay subsoil, known as mulatto, almost impervious. It is easy to cultivate, is early and warm, but ill-drained, and is well adapted to all of the crops of the region. One-half of this land is devoted to cotton, the usual height of the plant being 5 feet. It inclines to run to weed in wet seasons or on new land, which cutting off the top in August helps somewhat to restrain. The seed-cotton product per acre from fresh land is 1,500 pounds, and from 1,425 to 1,545 pounds make a 475-pound bale of middling lint. After ten years' cultivation the product is from 1,500 to 2,000 pounds, and 1,480 pounds make a 475-pound bale of lint, which is but little different from that of fresh land. The most troublesome weed is crab-grass; there is also some careless weed. None of this land lies "turned out".

The *fine sandy land* comprises nearly one-third of the county area, extending the whole distance of White River valley, and alternating with the gum land. The timber growth is oak, hickory, walnut, elm, and gum. The soil is fine and sandy, brown colored, and 12 inches deep, with a heavier brown or iron-rust colored clay subsoil, which is sticky when wet and is nearly impervious. The soil is early, warm, and well-drained, is easy to till, and is best adapted to cotton, sweet potatoes, and ground-peas. One-half of it is devoted to cotton, which usually grows to about 4 feet high, and only runs to weed on very new land. Topping restrains the plant. Fifteen hundred pounds of seed-cotton is the product per acre, of which 1,480 or 1,545 make a 475-pound bale of middling lint. After ten years the product of seed-cotton is 1,200 pounds, and there is but little difference, if any, in the amount necessary for a 475-pound bale of lint, or in the rating between this and that from fresh land. Weeds scarcely trouble this soil, although crab-grass grows rapidly. None of this land lies "turned out".

The *buckshot* or white land is not cultivated, except in small patches, which are inclosed by the soils already described. It is always found in the swales or low places in the field, and is cultivated as other land. It makes the best grass and wheat land. Shipments are made, from October to April, by steamer to Memphis at $1 25, and to New Orleans at $2 per bale.

SAINT FRANCIS.

Population : 8,389.—White, 4,921 ; colored, 3,468.
Area: 620 square miles.—Woodland, nearly all; Crowley's ridge, 370 square miles; Mississippi and Saint Francis alluvial, 250 square miles.
Tilled lands : 35,406 acres.—Area planted in cotton, 11,857 acres ; in corn, 9,934 acres ; in oats, 706 acres ; in wheat, 354 acres.
Cotton production : 5,966 bales; average cotton product per acre, 0.50 bale, 750 pounds seed-cotton, or 250 pounds cotton lint.

The surface of Saint Francis county is quite level, with the exception of Crowley's ridge, which lies from north to south through the center of the county, and along the west side of the Saint Francis river. This ridge is here from 2 to 6 miles in width and is well timbered, and its soils produce, when well cultivated, from 1,000 to 1,200 pounds of seed-cotton or 30 to 40 bushels of corn per acre.

On the east of the ridge is the broad region of alluvial lands of the White and the Mississippi rivers. They comprise dark sandy loam and stiff buckshot lands, are heavily timbered with oaks, walnut, hickory, ash, cypress, elm, gum, etc., and where cultivated produce from 1,500 to 1,800 pounds of seed-cotton or 60 bushels of corn per acre. There is a marl bed near Madison (with very large fossil oyster shells) many feet thick, containing over 40 per cent. of lime, which would form a valuable fertilizer on the sandy lands of the ridge.

Crowley's ridge is much broken into hills, but westward the surface of the country is characterized by low sandy and clay ridges, with intervening flat clay land, the latter, for the most part wet and spouty and without drainage, being unfit for cultivation.

The county has a population averaging a little more than 13 persons per square mile; and tilled land 57.1 acres, or 8.9 per cent. of the total area. Cotton comprises about one-third of the lands under cultivation, and averages 19.1 acres per square mile. The average product per acre in 1879 was but half a bale of lint cotton, or 750 pounds in the seed.

ABSTRACT OF THE REPORT OF THOMAS B. HOY, MILLBROOK.

The lowlands consist of the second bottoms and alluvial planes of the L'Anguille and Saint Francis rivers.

The uplands are the level table-lands of Crowley's ridge; the west side of which slopes off into a beautiful level plain about three miles in width, and is very productive. The lands devoted to the cultivation of cotton comprise the gray loam of Crowley's ridge and some white buckshot in the sinks and the lowlands, varying in color from gray to nearly black, extending about 40 miles north, the same south, having a width of about 4 miles, a timber growth of white and black oaks, gum, elm, poplar, walnut, hackberry, dogwood, and papaw, and running parallel to Crowley's ridge. The most important is *the gray loam,* which occupies an area of 18 square miles, and has a natural timber growth of white and black oaks, poplar, sweet gum, hackberry, box-elder, and papaw. The soil is a fine sandy loam, from gray to blackish in color, and 6 inches deep. Its subsoil is a light leachy clay, which, when taken from ditches 2 feet deep and mixed with the soil, benefits it. Sand and gravel are found at 30 feet. The land is rather difficult to till in wet seasons, but not unusually troublesome ; it is early when well drained, and is best adapted to cotton. The chief crops of the region are cotton and corn ; sweet and Irish potatoes, peas, beans, etc., are also raised. Three-fourths of the cultivated area is devoted to cotton, which grows to a height of from 2 to 5 feet, being most productive at 4 feet. It inclines to run to weed in the fresher lands, which is obviated by planting the smaller varieties of cotton. About 1,500 pounds of seed-cotton per acre are produced from fresh lands, and 1,200 pounds after twenty-five years' cultivation (unmanured); 1,785 pounds are required from fresh land and 1,425 from old lands for 475 pounds of lint, rating in the former case from middling to good middling, and in the latter strict middling, if well handled. Crab-grass, cocklebur, careless weed, and morning-glory vines are the most troublesome weeds.

The soil washes readily on the few slopes there are in this region, doing serious damage, but only injuring the valleys to a very slight extent. Very little of the land lies turned out, and that only on the spurs of Crowley's ridge. Very little effort has been made to check the damage.

Shipments of cotton are made, in November and December, by railroad, from Forest City to Memphis, at the rate of $1 65 per bale.

CROSS.

Population : 5,050.—White, 3,261 ; colored, 1,789.
Area: 620 square miles.—Woodland, nearly all; Crowley's ridge, 425 square miles; Mississippi alluvial, 195 square miles.
Tilled lands : 19,225 acres.—Area planted in cotton, 7,607 acres ; in corn, 6,985 acres ; in oats, 805 acres ; in wheat, 171 acres.
Cotton production : 4,768 bales; average cotton product per acre, 0.63 bale, 945 pounds seed-cotton, or 315 pounds cotton lint.

Cross county is watered by the Saint Francis river on the east and L'Anguille river on the west. The most prominent topographical feature between these two streams is Crowley's ridge, with a width of from 2 to 6 miles and a height of from 100 to 150 feet, which on the south is much broken into ridges. The timber growth comprises oaks, hickory, poplar, dogwood, and some pine, and its soils yield from 30 to 40 bushels of corn or 600 to 800 pounds of seed-cotton per acre. The rest of the county is quite level and flat; and on the west the ridge, flattening out, is cut up by numerous small streams and interspersed with small open prairies. The soils of this western part are sandy, varying in color from gray to red, and are quite productive. The Saint Francis river bottom lands are mostly black and sandy in character, and are heavily timbered. The lands are very rich and productive, yielding from 1,200 to 1,500 pounds of seed-cotton or 80 bushels of corn per acre. In the northeastern part of the county there are stiff or waxy black lands (similar to the buckshot lands of counties southward), which are said to yield from 50 to 70 bushels of corn per acre. The county is very sparsely settled, the average being about eight persons per square mile. The lands under cultivation average only 31 acres per square mile, of which 12.3 acres are devoted to cotton. In cotton product per acre the county ranks as nineteenth.

591

ABSTRACT OF THE REPORT OF W. C. MALONE, WITTSBURG.

The lowlands are those of the Saint Francis river, and consist of bottom, alluvial, front-land, back-land, cypress swamp, etc. The uplands are rolling timbered land. The land in the eastern portion of the county is a level valley, in the middle portion rolling, and in the west flat and even. The chief crops are cotton, corn, oats, potatoes, and all kinds of vegetables. The cotton soils are the reddish, gray, and black sandy soil of the hills and valleys, and the kind known as buckshot soil, not so good as the former.

The *black sandy* or alluvial soil comprises the larger part of the county, extending east 16 miles, south 5 miles, north 17 miles, and in the west is mixed with other soils. The timber growth is poplar, gum, ash, pine, hackberry, haw, oak, elm, etc. The soil varies from fine sandy to gravelly loam, with some heavy clay loam. The color varies exceedingly, and the depth is from 3 inches to 10 feet. The color of the subsoil varies, being in some places light, in others dark; is partly leachy and partly impervious, and contains gravel, pebbles, etc., according to locality, underlaid by sand-rock at 10 feet. The soil is difficult to till in wet seasons, easy when dry, and is not well drained.

Cotton forms about one-half of the crops, the usual height of the plant being from 4 to 8 feet; but 6 feet is the most productive height. On low, wet land the plant inclines to run to weed; but early topping in some years and late culture in others restrains the plant. After three years' cultivation the seed-cotton product per acre is from 800 to 2,000 pounds; 1,780 or 1,900 pounds make a 475-pound bale of lint, which rates nearly the same as that from fresh land, depending on the season. Cocklebur, careless weed, and crab-grass are the most troublesome weeds. Very little of this land lies "turned out". When again cultivated it does not do as well as fresh land. The soil washes and gullies seriously on the slopes; but the valleys are not much injured, and in some instances are bettered by the washings. But little has been done to check the damage.

Cotton grows well on all the land when well cultivated; and in almost every season, with proper culture, it will make from 800 to 1,500 pounds of seed-cotton per acre. Cotton grows and matures best on the black loamy land. The implements used are not of the best quality, but the county is improving in this respect.

Shipments are made during the fall and winter by river to Memphis or New Orleans at $1 50 per bale.

POINSETT.

Population: 2,192.—White, 1,902; colored, 290.

Area: 760 square miles.—Woodland, nearly all; Crowley's ridge, 360 square miles; Mississippi alluvial, 400 square miles.

Tilled lands: 7,712 acres.—Area planted in cotton, 2,373 acres; in corn, 3,907 acres; in oats, 258 acres; in wheat, 237 acres.

Cotton production: 1,514 bales; average cotton product per acre, 0.64 bale, 960 pounds seed-cotton, or 320 pounds cotton lint.

The surface of Poinsett county is generally level, with the exception of Crowley's ridge, which occupies a central position north and south. This ridge, lying between the bottom lands of the Saint Francis and L'Anguille rivers, is high, and is timbered with black and white oaks, poplar, and some pine. These lands are drained by numerous branches, and have a growth of poplar, gum, ash, elm, and dogwood. The soils produce from 30 to 40 bushels of corn per acre.

On the west of the ridge is a level prairie region, comprising about one-tenth of the county area, the soil of which is sandy, with a clay subsoil, producing 40 to 50 bushels of corn per acre. The bottom land of L'Anguille river is mostly a bluish clay, and has a timber growth of red and white oaks and small scattering sweet gum, with some post oak on the "post-oak land." On the east of Crowley's ridge low, flat, bottom lands extend through the county, comprising mostly a black sandy soil, timbered with poplar, walnut, hickory, sweet gum, and dogwood, with an undergrowth of papaw, spicewood, and large grape-vines, and yielding from 1,200 to 1,500 pounds of seed-cotton or 80 to 100 bushels of corn per acre.

There is an area of black waxy lands in the southern part of the Saint Francis bottom, on the west side of the river, formerly overflowed by the back-water of the Mississippi, which is of extraordinary fertility, and yields from 50 to 75 bushels of corn per acre.

Poinsett is the most thinly populated county in the state, the average being only about three persons to each square mile. The lands under cultivation comprise but 1.6 per cent. of the total area, or 10.1 acres per square mile, of which 3.1 acres are devoted to the culture of cotton. The acreage in corn is the larger. In cotton product per acre the county ranks sixteenth in the state.

Shipments of cotton are made mostly by river.

JACKSON.

Population: 10,877.—White, 8,113; colored, 2,764.

Area : 629 square miles.—Woodland, all; red-loam region, 110 square miles; Crowley's ridge, 510 square miles.

Tilled lands: 46,483 acres.—Area planted in cotton, 21,718 acres; in corn, 17,861 acres; in oats, 500 acres; in wheat, 910 acres.

Cotton production: 13,895 bales; average cotton product per acre, 0.64 bale, 960 pounds seed-cotton, or 320 pounds cotton lint.

Jackson county is very largely alluvial in character, the only hill land embraced within its limits being on the southwest. White and Black rivers form the western border of the lowlands, and Cache river and Village creek on the east flow southward almost parallel with Black river, and are tributary to White river. Between these streams the lands are elevated 6 or 8 feet above the overflowed bottoms and flats, and at a depth of 7 feet are underlaid by a tough yellow clay for 18 feet, and then by sand. They have a sandy soil, a timber growth of black, white, and post oaks, sweet gum, poplar, black walnut, and some hickory, and are capable of yielding an average of 800 pounds of seed-cotton per acre for many successive years. The spice-land of Cache river is very rich when drained and reclaimed, but in its natural state it is wet and miry. It supports a growth of large timber, viz, gum, ash, pin oak, and hackberry, besides the black spice. The average population of Jackson is not quite 18 persons, and its tilled lands 75 acres per square mile. Of the latter 35 acres are given to cotton, the county ranking ninth in this regard. In cotton product per acre it ranks fifteenth in the state.

Shipments of cotton are made either by rail to Little Rock and Saint Louis, or by river boats to New Orleans and Memphis.

LAWRENCE.

Population: 8,782.—White. 8,315; colored, 467.

Area: 600 square miles.—Woodland, all; northern barrens, 300 square miles; Crowley's Ridge region, 300 square miles.

Tilled lands: 43,895 acres.—Area planted in cotton, 10,768 acres; in corn, 19,902 acres; in oats, 3,256 acres; in wheat, 2,591 acres.

Cotton production: 6,480 bales; average cotton product per acre, 0.60 bale, 900 pounds seed-cotton, or 300 pounds cotton lint.

Lawrence county is about equally divided by Black river. The portion east of the river is an almost level alluvial plain, belonging to the general division of the Crowley's Ridge region. The soil is a black loam, largely subject to overflow, and well timbered with oaks, elm, ash, walnut, gum, and hickory. This soil is easily cultivated, has a yellow clay subsoil, and is very productive, yielding from 50 to 60 bushels of corn or 1,200 to 1,500 pounds of seed-cotton per acre. Some portions of the bottoms are much above overflow and are termed ridges, the chief one being "Buncombe ridge".

On the west of Black river the surface of the county is hilly and broken, comprising sandstones and cherty limestones, these being capped with ferruginous sandstone, clays, and gravel of the Quaternary period. They have a timber growth of black-jack and post oaks, and small hickory, with pine. The lands, when tillable, are sandy and gravelly, with subsoils somewhat clayey, and capable of yielding good crops for a few years.

The county has a population averaging about 15 persons, and tilled lands averaging 73 acres per square mile. As in other counties in the northeast part of the state, corn is the chief crop, cotton being next, with an average of 17.9 acres per square mile. In cotton product per acre the county ranks with Craighead on the east, Lafayette on the southwest, and Baxter and Logan on the north and west of the state.

CRAIGHEAD.

Population: 7,037.—White, 6,776; colored, 261.

Area: 730 square miles.—Woodland, nearly all; Crowley's ridge, 410 square miles; Mississippi alluvial, 320 square miles.

Tilled lands: 35,514 acres.—Area planted in cotton, 7,246 acres; in corn, 15,023 acres; in oats, 1,374 acres; in wheat, 2,734 acres.

Cotton production: 4,374 bales; average cotton product per acre, 0.50 bale, 900 pounds seed-cotton, or 300 pounds cotton lint.

Craighead county is largely included within the alluvial region of the Saint Francis river, which lies on the east. The distance from the river westward to the uplands of Crowley's ridge is said to be 20 miles, and this portion of the county is low, heavily timbered with walnut, poplar, dogwood, sweet gum, hickory, and hackberry, and an undergrowth of spicewood, papaw, and grape-vines, and is generally subject to overflow. The higher and tillable portions of these lands have a black sandy soil, which is easily tilled, and produce from one to two bales of lint cotton or 80 to 100 bushels of corn per acre. The upland known as Crowley's ridge has a width of about 10 miles. The lands have occasionally some pine, with the usual hard woods. The surface is undulating, sometimes broken, and is watered by small streams. On the southwest there are some open prairies with sandy soils, which yield, it is said, from 30 to 40 bushels of corn per acre.

The bottom lands of Cache river are broad, and comprise black sandy soils, similar to those of the Saint Francis river, and what are termed "post-oak lands", with wet and ill-drained soils, and are not much in cultivation. The population of this county is sparse, the average being about ten persons, while that of the lands under cultivation is 48.6 acres per square mile. The county is situated in the northeastern part of the state, and we naturally find that the acreage in cotton, only 9.9 acres per square mile, is much smaller than that of corn. The product per acre compares favorably with other counties of this region.

ABSTRACT OF THE REPORT OR J. W. RANSOM, JONESBORO'.

The land of Crowley's ridge is finely timbered and watered by creeks and river branches, which have first-class bottom soils, generally black sandy, on which, in a good season, a 500-pound bale of lint per acre is sure. Any land of the county, if not too broken or wet, will produce cotton, corn, wheat, oats, sorghum, and buckwheat. On the east of this ridge a low, heavily-timbered rich bottom country begins and continues for 20 miles to the Saint Francis river, and from here to the Mississippi river the soil is a fine black sandy one, and the country is a little more elevated, but level and richly timbered.

On the west of Crowley's ridge begins the Cache river bottoms, extending about 15 miles to the river, a considerable portion of which cannot be cultivated with profit unless drained, though some of the land makes a 500-pound bale of lint or 60 bushels of corn to the acre. West of Cache river the country is more elevated, but is level to the White river.

In the western part of the county a prairie, with an average width of 3 miles, begins, extending 30 miles, which is chiefly devoted to stock raising.

The most important cotton soil is the *dark mulatto* uplands, comprising two-thirds of the cultivated lands of the county, extending from the Saint Francis to the Cache river bottoms, with a plentiful miscellaneous timber growth. The soil is a fine sandy and gravelly loam, with some prairie, the color of which varies; the depth is from 1 to 3 feet. The subsoil is a heavy yellow clay, underlaid by sand and gravel. This soil is difficult to till when wet, but quite easy when dry, and is well adapted to all of the crops of the region.

38 c P

Cotton forms about one-half of the crops, which grows usually from 3 to 6 feet in height, and runs to weed on very rich land and during wet seasons, the remedy for which is to bar off, throwing the soil from the cotton plants. The seed-cotton product per acre is about 1,500 pounds, making one-third of its weight of lint. After 30 years' cultivation the seed-cotton product per acre and the proportion of seed-cotton to lint is about the same as on fresh land. The troublesome weeds are white and careless and cockleburs. No very large amount of this land lies "turned out", and when properly plowed it produces very well. The slopes wash, but not very seriously, if injudiciously plowed. To some extent the valleys are injured by washings of slopes. Very little has been done to check the damage.

Shipments are made, chiefly in May, to Newport, Louisville, and Saint Louis, at from $2 50 to $5 per bale.

GREENE.

Population: 7,480.—White, 7,405; colored, 75.

Area: 640 square miles.—Woodland, all; Crowley's ridge, 480 square miles; Mississippi alluvial, 160 square miles.

Tilled lands: 29,109 acres.—Area planted in cotton, 6,886 acres; in corn, 14,068 acres; in oats, 1,802 acres; in wheat, 1,702 acres.

Cotton production: 3,711 bales; average cotton product per acre, 0.54 bale, 810 pounds seed-cotton, or 270 pounds cotton lint.

Greene county is bordered on the east by the Saint Francis river and on the west partly by the Cache river. Between these two streams Crowley's ridge, with its sandy lands, occupies the greater part of the county, and is timbered with black oak, hickory, black and white walnut, and large poplar. Where gravelly the growth is principally post oak and pine. The ridge lands yield an average of 40 to 50 bushels of corn and 20 to 30 bushels of wheat per acre.

The flat Cache river lands comprise black sandy lands and post-oak flats, the latter too wet for cultivation unless well drained. The black sandy lands of both this river and the Saint Francis are deep and rich, and are said to yield from 80 to 100 bushels of corn or from 1,000 to 2,000 pounds of seed-cotton per acre. The timber growth is poplar, walnut, gum, dogwood, and oaks, with an undergrowth of spicewood, papaw, and grape-vines.

This county has an average population of nearly 12 persons and 45.5 acres of tilled lands per square mile. Corn is the chief crop. The acreage of cotton is greater than in the more southerly counties of Craighead and Poinsett, and averages 10.8 acres per square mile, or 23.7 per cent. of the tilled lands. The product per acre is also greater than that of Saint Francis county, which is more favorably situated.

Comparatively little cotton is produced in the lowlands of the Saint Francis river on the east, while in the small townships of Poland and Saint Francis, in the southern part of the county, the average acreage is greatest.

CLAY.

Population: 7,213.—White, 7,191; colored, 22.

Area: 580 square miles.—Woodland, all; Crowley's ridge, 330 square miles; Mississippi alluvial, 235 square miles; northern barrens, 15 square miles.

Tilled lands: 26,337 acres.—Area planted in cotton, 4,239 acres; in corn, 13,979 acres; in oats, 977 acres; in wheat, 2,240 acres.

Cotton production: 2,307 bales; average cotton product per acre, 0.54 bale, 810 pounds seed-cotton, or 270 pounds cotton lint.

Clay, the extreme northeastern county of the state, is comparatively level, and is drained by the Saint Francis river on the east, Cache river in the center, and Black river on the west. These rivers are bordered by low, flat bottom lands, heavily timbered, and subject to overflow. Between the Black and the Cache rivers there is a low ridge, which extends southwestward through several counties. Between the Cache and Saint Francis rivers there is a still more prominent and wider ridge, which is the beginning of what is known as Crowley's ridge. Chalk bluff, where it abuts against the Saint Francis river, has an elevation of 135 feet above the river, and, as its name implies, is formed largely of white siliceous or potters' clay, overlaid by heavy beds of sand and gravel. The surface of the ridge is undulating and the soils sandy, covered with a timber growth of black oak, hickory, black and white walnut, and large poplar. In the southern part of the county there is a large area of gravelly lands, whose growth is mostly a barren oak.

The better class of these ridge lands are said to produce from 40 to 50 bushels of corn and 20 to 30 bushels of wheat per acre. About two-thirds of the Cache lands are black sandy lands and one-third post-oak lands. The latter are too wet for cultivation without a complete system of drainage. The black sandy soils of both this and the region east of Crowley's ridge are deep and rich, and are said to be warm and to stand both dry and wet seasons well, yielding from 80 to 100 bushels of corn per acre. The timber growth is sweet gum, hickory, walnut, poplar, dogwood, and occasionally hackberry and box-elder; undergrowth, papaw, spicewood, and large grape-vines.

Clay county has a somewhat larger average population than either Greene or Craighead, over 12 persons per square mile. The average of tilled lands is 45.4 acres per square mile, but of these only 7.3 acres are devoted to the culture of cotton. The product per acre is also the same as in Greene, and in Newton, Scott, and Garland counties of the western uplands of the state.

RANDOLPH.

(See "Northern barrens and hill region".)

GRAY SILT PRAIRIES.

(Includes the northwest corner of Desha,* most of Arkansas and Prairie, and the southern part of Lonoke counties.)

DESHA.

(See "Mississippi alluvial region".)

ARKANSAS.

Population: 8,038.—White, 4,971; colored, 3,067.

Area: 1,000 square miles.—Woodland, one-third; eastern prairie, 760 square miles; alluvial, 240 square miles.

Tilled lands: 35,128 acres.—Area planted in cotton, 12,611 acres; in corn, 10,248 acres; in oats, 685 acres; in wheat, 48 acres.

Cotton production: 8,508 bales; average cotton product per acre, 0.67 bale, 1,005 pounds seed-cotton, or 335 pounds cotton lint.

Arkansas county is bordered on the south by the Arkansas river and on the east by White river. The surface of the country is mostly undulating or gently rolling and open prairie land, with timber growth along the streams. The soil of these prairies is rather clayey, and is underlaid by a yellow impervious clay, which renders it difficult to cultivate in wet seasons. The woodlands are preferred for tillage, and are said to yield 1,000 pounds of seed-cotton or 30 bushels of corn per acre.

The river lands are broad, and have dark sandy loam soils, heavily timbered with cottonwood, gum, cypress, etc., and are very highly productive. Their average yield is said to be 1,500 pounds of seed-cotton per acre.

This county has a smaller population than either of the other counties of the region, the average being 8 persons per square mile. The lands under cultivation also average but 35.1 acres per square mile, or 5.5 per cent. of the county area, and are nearly equally divided between corn and cotton, the acreage of the latter being the greatest, 12.6 acres per square mile. In product per acre the county ranks as ninth in the state.

ABSTRACT OF THE REPORT OF JAMES A. GIBSON, DE WITT.

The uplands consist of prairie and timbered lands, and are drained by Lagrue bayou. The lands devoted to cotton culture are the rich black loam of the Arkansas river and the uplands.

The most important is the *upland clay loam*, the soil of which is about 8 inches in depth, with an impervious yellow clay or hard-pan subsoil, underlaid by sand at 8 feet. This land is easily tilled in dry seasons, but quite the reverse in wet ones, and is late, cold, ill-drained, and best adapted to cotton and sweet potatoes. The chief crops of the region are cotton, corn, sweet potatoes, peas, and all kinds of vines. About three-fourths of the tilled area is devoted to cotton, which grows to a height of 3½ feet, running to weed on fresh land, either bottom or upland, when there is too much cultivation, or in wet seasons. Shallow cultivation is the remedy applied. The yield per acre from fresh land in seed-cotton is 1,000 pounds; after ten years this is reduced one-third; but in either case 1,425 pounds are necessary for 475 pounds of middling lint. Crab and cocoa grass and cocklebur are the most troublesome weeds. No land lies "turned out". The soil washes on slopes, but the damage done is not of serious extent, and no efforts have been made to check it.

The *black loam* of the bottoms is about 6 miles wide, and extends the whole length of the county along the Arkansas river. This soil is 6 to 8 feet in depth, and is underlaid by sand. It is easily cultivated in all seasons; is early, warm, and well drained, and is best adapted to cotton, to which about four-fifths of the cultivated area is devoted. The plant usually attains a height of about 5 feet. The product per acre from fresh land in seed-cotton is about 1,500 pounds; after ten years of cultivation the yield and rating of the staple are about the same; 1,425 pounds are requisite for a 475-pound bale of lint, rating as middling. Cocklebur and cocoa grass are the most troublesome weeds. No land lies "turned out", because of exhaustion. Drought or too much rain are about the only sources of injury to the cotton crop in this county.

Shipments of cotton are made as fast as it is ginned by river to Memphis, freight being $1 25 per bale.

PRAIRIE.

Population: 8,435.—White, 5,691; colored, 2,744.

Area: 710 square miles.—Woodland, probably one-half; eastern prairie region, 535 square miles; red-loam region, 175 square miles.

Tilled lands: 35,032 acres.—Area planted in cotton, 12,124 acres; in corn, 10,113 acres; in oats, 2,191 acres; in wheat, 457 acres.

Cotton production: 6,977 bales; average cotton product per acre, 0.58 bale, 870 pounds seed-cotton, or 290 pounds cotton lint.

The surface of Prairie county is undulating or slightly rolling, and is bordered on the east by White river, by whose tributaries it is mostly watered.

The uplands of the county are mostly open prairies, especially in the central and southern portions, interspersed with areas timbered with red, post, black-jack, white and Spanish oaks, and hickory. The land of the prairies is clayey in character, underlaid by a yellow impervious clay subsoil, and, being difficult to till in wet seasons and ill-drained, is mostly devoted to grazing purposes. The timbered lands are sandy to a depth of several feet, and are underlaid by clays. While yielding well at first, they are said to deteriorate rapidly under cultivation, and after 20 years produce but 300 pounds of seed-cotton per acre. The bottom lands of the river and larger streams comprise the usual front-land of sandy loams and back-lands of stiffer soils, sometimes buckshot in character. These have a timber growth of white and black oaks, elm, walnut, ash, sweet gum, hickory, etc., and yield from 1,500 to 1,800 pounds of seed-cotton per acre.

The extreme northern part of the county is underlaid by material of the millstone grit formation, and is well timbered with the growth of that region. The prairies reach to within two or three miles of Des Arc from the south, their northern limit extending westward into Lonoke county.

Prairie county has an average population of nearly 12 persons, and 7.7 acres of tilled lands per square mile. The acreage of corn and cotton is nearly the same, that of the latter being the greatest, with an average of 17.1 acres per square mile. In product per acre the county ranks much below Arkansas, but equal with a number of counties of the red-loam region. The greater part of that crop is produced in the northern or timbered portion. A small part of the county area—that east of White river—is covered by the sands and clays of Crowley's Ridge region, and is not only largely planted in cotton (producing more than one-fourth of the total yield of the county), but has a higher product per acre—1,010 pounds of seed-cotton.

ABSTRACT OF THE REPORT OF R. CARL LEE, DEVALL'S BLUFF.

The low lands comprise the first and second bottoms, front- and back-lands of White river. The uplands are level table-lands, partly black when first cultivated, watered by White river and many of its tributaries. These lands vary greatly, and many flats occur of from 5 to 50 acres in area, which are marked by the timber growth.

The soils cultivated in cotton are the very porous light black sandy bottom loams, mostly above overflow, and those comprising the hill, branch bottoms, and prairie land. The bottom land covers one-half the area of the county, extending east to the Cache river and west to the White river. The soil is a light, fine sandy loam, mahogany to black-colored, 18 inches in depth, with a heavier but light and sandy subsoil. The chief crops are corn and cotton, the soil being best adapted to the latter crop, to which from one-third to one-half of it is devoted. The usual height of cotton is from 6 to 8 feet. The plant inclines to run to weed in wet weather, and nothing restrains it; however, some farmers top it.

The seed-cotton product per acre from fresh land is 1,800 pounds, 1,660 pounds of the first picking or 1,425 after frost making a 475-pound bale of middling to fancy lint. After twenty years' cultivation 1,500 pounds is the seed-cotton product, and the same amount is necessary for a 475-pound bale of lint as from fresh land. On new land cotton does not open as well as on old land. Crab-grass and careless and rag weeds are most troublesome on this soil. None of this land lies "turned out".

The hill and prairie lands cover one-half the county, extending east to White river and west to bayou Meta, with a timber growth of post, black, white, Spanish, willow, and black-jack oaks, and hickory.

The soil of the upland is a fine sandy loam; that of the prairies clayey; and the color varies from whitish and gray to blackish, with a depth of 3 inches. The subsoil is yellow and sandy, gradually changing into clay at a depth of 2½ feet, then to hard-pan, which is impervious. The soil is easy to till when dry, but difficult when wet, and is cold and ill-drained, and best adapted to cotton, sweet potatoes, and peas. About one-half of this land is devoted to the cultivation of cotton, which usually grows from 3 to 6 feet in height. Wet weather inclines the plant to run to weed, and nothing restrains it. The seed-cotton product per acre from fresh land is 1,200 pounds, but after twenty years' cultivation it is 300 pounds per acre, 1,545 pounds from both fresh and old lands making a 475-pound bale of middling lint. Crab-grass is the most troublesome weed. One per cent. of this land lies "turned out". The soil washes readily on the slopes, doing serious damage to them and to the valleys, which, on the average, are injured 25 per cent. No efforts have been made to check this damage.

Shipments are made, from October to May, by rail and by boat to Saint Louis at $2, to Memphis at $1, and to New Orleans at $1 50 per bale.

LONOKE.

Population : 12,146.—White, 8,143; colored, 4,003.

Area : 760 square miles.— Woodland, two-thirds or more; red-loam region, 295 square miles; alluvial, 280 square miles; eastern prairie region, 185 square miles.

Tilled lands : 63,652 acres.—Area planted in cotton, 20,910 acres; in corn, 17,502 acres; in oats, 3,310 acres; in wheat, 1,131 acres.

Cotton production : 11,704 bales; average cotton product per acre, 0.56 bale, 840 pounds seed-cotton, or 280 pounds cotton lint.

The surface of Lonoke county is rolling, and is mostly timbered, open prairies being a prominent feature on the east. The northern part of the county is somewhat hilly and the soils sandy, varying in color from gray to red, with reddish clay subsoils and underlying shales and sandstones of the millstone-grit formation.

The prairies, as in the counties on the east, are clayey in character, and at depths of a few inches are underlaid by light-colored and impervious clays, which renders artificial drainage a matter of some importance in the cultivation of the land.

On the south there is, according to Mr. Lee, the correspondent from Prairie county, a large region of swamp lands covering all that part of the county except a belt of prairies extending southeast from Lonoke, the county-seat, along bayou Two Prairies. The lands of this region have a dark sandy loam soil several feet deep and a timber growth of sweet gum, walnut, oaks, hickory, elm, ash, etc. They are very productive and durable, yielding an average, from one season to another, of nearly 1,000 pounds of seed-cotton per acre. Lonoke, with its average of 16 persons per square mile, is more thickly populated than either of the other counties of the region, the lands under cultivation also averaging 83.8 acres.

Cotton is the chief crop, with an acreage not much above that of corn, and averaging 27.5 acres per square mile. As in Prairie county, cotton is planted chiefly in the timbered portion of the county, and comparatively little in the prairies. As a whole, Lonoke ranks with Sevier on the southwest, Crawford on the west, and Stone on the north in product per acre. There is, however, a very great difference in the respective lands within the county in this regard, and we find from the statistics that the richest are those of the alluvial lands of the southwest, their yield being 1,165 pounds of seed-cotton per acre, while that of the north is from 675 to 750 pounds.

YELLOW-LOAM REGION.

(Including also the region of black Cretaceous prairies on the southwest. It embraces the whole or parts of the counties of Ashley, Union, Columbia, Lafayette, Miller, Little River, Sevier, Howard, Pike,* Hempstead, Nevada, Ouachita, Calhoun, Bradley, Drew, Chicot,* Desha,* Lincoln, Dorsey, Dallas, Clark, Hot Spring,* Saline,* Pulaski,* Grant, and Jefferson.)

ASHLEY.

Population: 10,156.—White, 5,026; colored, 5,130.

Area: 950 square miles.—Woodland, nearly all; yellow loam region, 700 square miles; alluvial, 250 square miles.

Tilled lands: 48,455 acres.—Area planted in cotton, 19,555 acres; in corn, 15,335 acres; in oats, 1,411 acres; in wheat, 14 acres.

Cotton production: 11,371 bales; average cotton product per acre, 0.58 bale, 870 pounds seed-cotton, or 290 pounds cotton lint.

The surface of Ashley county is undulating, and is watered by numerous streams that are tributary to the Saline and the Ouachita rivers on the west, or by bayou Bartholomew in the eastern part.

The uplands are well timbered, and are interspersed with small open prairies, bordered with a scattered growth of oak, known as "oak openings". Both of the latter are dotted over with small mound-like elevations composed of materials that have for a greater time resisted denudation. These prairies are not under cultivation, their soils being stiff and poorly drained and underlaid by impervious clays. The timbered uplands have usually gray sandy soils and red or yellow clay subsoils, and are easily tilled, the best producing from 25 to 30 bushels of corn and about 1,000 pounds of seed-cotton per acre. The western part of the county is rolling, and the soil contains more gravel. The highest and most broken part is on Beech creek. East of the prairies and toward Holly Point there is a ridge of good land, on which gum trees are the principal growth.

The bottom lands are the best adapted to cotton, and are the richest lands of the county. Those of the river and bayou Bartholomew comprise front-lands of gray alluvial loam soils along the river fronts and back-lands of clayey or buckshot soils. The bottoms have often a width of several miles, with a timber growth of oak, gum, hickory, ash, elm, dogwood, holly, etc., and are above overflow. They are largely in cultivation, and produce from one to two bales of cotton per acre.

The population of Ashley county averages more than 10 persons, and the tilled lands 51 acres per square mile. Cotton and corn are the chief crops, the former predominating, with an average of 20.6 acres per square mile.

ABSTRACT OF THE REPORT OF J. P. HARBISON, HAMBURG.

The lowlands consist of the first and second bottoms of Saline river, bayou Bartholomew, and their tributaries. The uplands are level table-lands, lying in areas of from 10 to 200 acres, with some uncultivated prairie. The lands devoted to the culture of cotton are the gray alluvial front-lands and the buckshot soils of the back-land of the bottoms of the large streams, the light sandy soils of the pine table-lands mixed with enough loam to make them productive, and the reddish clay soils of the oak uplands. The chief crops of the county are cotton, which is the staple product, corn, oats, pease, and potatoes, which are not produced in sufficient quantity for home consumption.

The *gray alluvial* land on bayous and creeks has a timber growth of oak, gum, hickory, ash, elm, dogwood, and holly, and has a fine sandy clay loam soil, gray in color, with a depth of 2½ feet. The subsoil is a very hard white clay, quite impervious when not disturbed, and contains white gravel and angular pebbles, underlaid by clay at 1 to 3 feet. The soil is difficult to till in wet seasons, is early, warm, and ill-drained, and apparently is best adapted to cotton. Oats, pease, and potatoes yield good crops, while corn yields poorly. Cotton forms one-half of the crops, and usually grows to a height of 5 feet. It inclines to run to weed in wet seasons, and many farmers practice topping during the last of July to restrain the plant and favor bolling. The seed-cotton product per acre on fresh land is from 2,000 to 2,400 pounds, 1,425 pounds making a 475-pound bale of lint, which brings from 1 to 1¼ cents per pound more than that from old land. After ten years' cultivation the product is from 1,000 to 1,500 pounds of seed-cotton, 1,545 pounds making a 475-pound bale of lint, which is about 10 per cent. poorer than that from fresh land. Crab-grass is the worst enemy cotton-planters have to contend with here, as it cannot be killed in wet weather unless it is covered up. Burs are quite troublesome on low land. But very little bottom land lies turned out.

The *light sandy* alluvial soil of the uplands, with a timber growth of pine, oak, hickory, and dogwood, is gray in color and from 6 to 10 inches deep, with a hard yellow subsoil, inclined to be red, mixed with gravel and underlaid by clay at 1 to 3 feet. The soil is easily tilled, and one-half of its tilled area is devoted to cotton, which usually reaches 3 feet in height. The seed-cotton product per acre of fresh land is from 1,000 to 2,000 pounds, but after ten years' cultivation the product is reduced 500 to 700 pounds. Two-thirds of this land lies turned out, and when allowed to grow up in briers and pine for twelve or fifteen years it produces nearly as well as when first brought into cultivation. The slopes wash and gully seriously, and the valleys are injured to about 10 per cent. of their value by the washings. Some horizontalizing and hillside ditching has been practiced with success.

The *gray sandy* land, comprising about one-fourth of the uplands, and the black sandy and alluvial land, comprising about one-eighth of the bottoms, are very much alike in general character. The soil varies in color from whitish and gray to black, with a depth of 2 feet; but the subsoil is heavier, and contains hard white gravel and angular pebbles, underlaid by gravel and rock at from 1 to 2 feet. The soil is difficult to till in wet seasons, is early, warm, and ill-drained, and apparently is best adapted to cotton, oats, and potatoes. About 50 per cent. of the crops are cotton, which reaches 3 to 4 feet in height, runs to weed in wet weather, and is topped to restrain it and favor bolling.

The seed-cotton product per acre of fresh land is from 1,200 to 1,500 pounds, 1,425 pounds of which make a 475-pound bale of lint. After ten years the product is from 700 to 900 pounds, and 1,545 pounds are then necessary to make a 475-pound bale of lint, which rates 10 per cent. less than that from fresh land. The troublesome weeds are crab-grass and hog-weed. About one-third of this land lies turned out, and after resting ten years produces nearly as well as at first. The soil of the uplands washes seriously, and the valleys are injured from 10 to 20 per cent. Very little has been done to check the damage, but horizontalizing and hillside ditching are successful. We seldom have cotton injured by frost. The lands on bayou Bartholomew are very rich, producing from 1 to 2 bales of lint per acre.

Cotton is shipped, during December, January, and February, by steamboat, chiefly to New Orleans, at $2 per bale. Considerable has been hauled this season to the railroad and shipped to Saint Louis.

UNION.

Population: 13,419.—White, 6,985; colored, 6,434.

Area: 1,000 square miles.—Woodland, all; yellow-loam region, 895 square miles; alluvial, 105 square miles.

Tilled lands: 69,472 acres.—Area planted in cotton, 30,136 acres; in corn, 27,795 acres; in oats, 1,249 acres; in wheat, 103 acres.

Cotton production: 11,013 bales; average cotton product per acre, 0.37 bale, 555 pounds seed-cotton, or 185 pounds cotton lint.

The surface of Union county is mostly rolling, with areas of level and flat lands. Ouachita river forms the eastern boundary, and a dividing ridge passes east and west through the county, throwing the waters of the small streams of the north 'into Smackovert creek, a tributary of the Ouachita, those of the south flowing southward into Louisiana before reaching the Ouachita.

The country is well timbered, and comprises three varieties of soils on the uplands: 1. Yellow siliceous or sandy soil, on which the principal growth is beech, oak, gum, holly, pine, maple, and ironwood, with an undergrowth of hazel. This is the most productive soil in the county, and prevails in the northwestern and southeastern parts. It yields 800 pounds of seed-cotton, 20 bushels of corn, or 10 bushels of wheat per acre under proper cultivation. 2. Light sandy land, which occupies a belt in the center of the county, the line running from northeast to southwest a little south of Lisbon. This soil is based on the orange-colored sand and clay lying just above the gravel, and will produce on an average from 600 to 800 pounds of seed-cotton or 15 to 25 bushels of corn per acre. 3. White crawfish land, flat pine, or glady pine land. This soil is not much cultivated, and is generally considered worthless. There is no genuine red land in this county, but there are some small tracts of chocolate or mulatto-colored soil.

The country is broken around El Dorado, and the orange sand and clay which underlie soil No. 2 has a thickness of 40 or 50 feet. Ferruginous sandstone occurs in considerable amounts in the central part of the county, and lignite is said to underlie the whole country on the southeast.

The average of population in this county is a little more than 13 persons, and that of lands under cultivation 69.5 acres per square mile. Cotton and corn are the chief crops, the former predominating, with an average of 30.1 acres per square mile, the county ranking sixteenth in the state in the latter regard. Though fifth in the state in total acreage in cotton, Union is lowest in the average product per acre.

ABSTRACT OF THE REPORT OF H. L. CHANDLER, EL DORADO.

The lowlands of the county are the second bottoms and hummocks of Ouachita river and Smackovert creek. The uplands are rolling and level, and are well drained. Crops other than cotton, corn, and sweet and Irish potatoes receive very little attention.

The soils cultivated in cotton are the light hummock or loams along the margins of creeks, the red sandy soil, and the light or gray clay and sandy soil. The *creek hummocks* form the chief cotton land, comprising about one-twentieth of the area, extending throughout the county. The soil is a fine sandy loam, whitish or gray colored, 3 to 10 feet deep, with a heavier yellow clay subsoil, underlaid by rock at 10 to 12 feet. It is easily tilled in either wet or dry seasons, is early when well drained, and is best adapted to cotton, to which one-half of its tilled area is devoted. Three feet is the average and most productive height of the cotton-plant, which inclines to run to weed in excessive wet weather, for which there is no remedy. The seed-cotton product from fresh land is from 1,000 to 2,000 pounds per acre, 1,425 pounds being required to make a 475-pound bale of low-middling lint. After eight years' cultivation the product is 700 pounds; after 12 years 500 pounds; the same amount being necessary for a 475-pound bale of lint, which rates one grade lower than that from fresh land. With the exception of rag-weed, there are but few troublesome weeds. About one-third of this land lies "turned out", which, when again cultivated, produces about two-thirds as well as when first cleared. The slopes wash readily, but are not seriously injured, the creek lands being always improved by washings from the hills.

The *red sandy* soil, comprising a very small proportion of the county area, is 2 to 5 feet deep, with a heavier clay subsoil filled with pebbles and underlaid by sand and gravel at 10 to 30 feet. This soil is easy to till both in wet and in dry seasons, is early, warm, and well drained, and is best adapted to cotton. In other respects it is like the hummock land.

The *light or gray clay and sand* soil of the uplands, comprising about four-fifths of the county, is a fine, sandy, gravelly white clay, somewhat putty like, whitish to gray in color, and from 6 inches to 3 feet deep. The subsoil is heavier, and is inclined to be impervious, and contains pebbles, underlaid by red clay at from 6 inches to 3 feet. This soil is more difficult to till than either of the preceding soils described, as it is late and cold when ill-drained, and is apparently best adapted to cotton. In other respects it is like the hummock soil.

The cotton crop is here much influenced by wet or dry seasons, a wet season subjecting the crop to many risks, such as rust, boll-worm, caterpillar, rain blight, boll-rot, late picking, etc. Dry seasons are conducive to a healthy crop with but few disasters.

Cotton is shipped, from December to March, by river to New Orleans at $1 25 per bale.

COLUMBIA.

Population: 14,090.—White, 8,587; colored, 5,503.

Area: 860 square miles.—Woodland, all; all yellow-loam region.

Tilled lands: 80,309 acres.—Area planted in cotton, 32,427 acres; in corn, 28,868 acres; in oats, 3,241 acres; in wheat, 1,019 acres.

Cotton production: 13,039 bales; average cotton product per acre, 0.40 bale, 600 pounds seed-cotton, or 200 pounds cotton lint.

The northern part of Columbia county is rolling, with mostly gray, sandy, and gravelly lands, underlaid by reddish sandy subsoils and clays, and chiefly timbered with a growth of pine and oak. The southern part is more level, with sandy and gravelly lands, yielding about 1,000 pounds of seed-cotton per acre. On King's creek the country is generally a level black sandy land; on Big creek flats the soil is a white clay, and the growth holly, beech, and pine. In the western part of the county, on the oak flats of bayou Dorcheat, the soil is a siliceous clay, bordered by sandy lands elevated a few feet above high water; at a still higher level the sand and gravel beds alternate with dark sands and red siliceous clays. The crops of the country are cotton, corn, rye, and potatoes, and fruits.

The average of the population of this county is a little more than 16 persons, and that of lands under cultivation 93.4 acres per square mile. Of the chief crops cotton has the largest acreage, its average of 37.7 acres per square mile placing the county fourth in the state, Phillips, Lee, and Jefferson alone surpassing it. In product per acre it is, on the other hand, among the six lowest in the state.

ABSTRACT OF THE REPORT OF J. D. ZACHRY, MAGNOLIA.

Columbia county is on the dividing ridge between the Ouachita and Red rivers. The land is rolling and very productive, and nearly all the crops adapted to this latitude can be raised successfully. Sugar-cane does very well, 400 to 500 gallons of sirup per acre having been produced. There is but little difference in the productiveness of the several soils of this county. The quality of the cotton raised on different soils does not vary perceptibly, as the lands seem better adapted to it than to any other crop.

The soils devoted to the cultivation of cotton are the dark sandy land, the red sandy and red clay land, and the light sandy and flat moist land. The dark sandy land, extending throughout the county, has a natural timber growth of white, red, black, and post oaks and pine. The soil is a light sandy clay loam 1 to 2 feet deep, with color varying from gray to blackish, which contains white pebbles in patches, underlaid by sand and gravel at from 10 to 20 feet. This soil is easily tilled, and is well adapted to all of the crops of the region. Three-fifths of this land under cultivation is devoted to cotton, which is usually about 3 feet high. It inclines to run to weed on fresh land or when planted late and the season is wet, which is remedied by allowing the cotton to remain thick in the drill and plowing the dirt from it. The product of seed-cotton is from 1,000 to 1,500 pounds per acre.

When negro laborers are employed not more than 500 pounds of seed-cotton can be raised; 1,495 pounds are necessary to make a 475-pound bale of lint, which rates as good middling. Six hundred pounds of seed-cotton is the yield after seven years' cultivation, the same amount being needed for a 475-pound bale of low middling lint as from fresh land. Crab-grass is the most troublesome weed. About 20 per cent. of this land lies "turned out", and after fifteen or twenty years it produces the same as fresh land. The soil washes to some extent on the slopes, but the valleys are not injured by the washings. Horizontalizing and hillside ditching have proved successful checks when properly done. Cotton does best in a warm and tolerably dry season, and such seasons we generally have.

Shipments are made, from September to April, by railroad and river to Saint Louis at $3, and to New Orleans at $1 50 per bale.

LA FAYETTE.

Population : 5,730.—White, 2,116 ; colored, 3,614.

Area : 490 square miles.—Woodland, nearly all ; yellow-loam region, 400 square miles ; alluvial, 90 square miles.

Tilled lands : 27,361 acres.—Area planted in cotton, 10,611 acres ; in corn, 8,366 acres ; in oats, 140 acres ; in wheat, 13 acres.

Cotton production : 6,339 bales ; average cotton product per acre, 0.60 bale, 900 pounds seed-cotton, or 300 pounds cotton lint.

La Fayette county is bordered on the west by Red river, while bayou Badeau waters the eastern side, both flowing southward, and having broad bottom lands. The surface of the county is rolling, and the ridges and hills between the numerous water-courses attain an elevation of from 100 to 130 feet, and for the most part are composed of white and gray sand, orange-colored sand, ferruginous sand, and conglomerate and sandy iron ore. These, alternating with red clay and gravel, give character to a variety of upland soil which will yield from 800 to 1,000 pounds of seed-cotton per acre. The county is well timbered. There are some prairies in the northern part with black sandy soils.

The river bottoms have mostly soils of this black character, varied with red sandy or clayey lands, and a timber growth of black, pin, willow, and overcup oaks, hickory, ash, gum, pecan, walnut, cottonwood, cypress, and elm. The lands are very productive, yielding from 2,000 to 2,500 pounds of seed-cotton per acre. Ascending from these bottoms to the Lewisville road, both the clay and the sand are very red ; and some of it, if washed, might be suitable for a paint.

The average of the population of La Fayette is more than 11 persons per square mile, and of tilled lands 55.8 acres per square mile. While cotton and corn comprise the chief crops of the county, the former has the largest acreage, its average being 21.7 acres per square mile, or 38.8 per cent. of the tilled lands. The rich bottom lands of Red river have, by their high yields, placed the county high in the list as regards product per acre, the uplands belonging to that class having an average of less than half a bale.

Shipments are made, by rail and river, to Saint Louis and New Orleans.

MILLER.

Population : 9,919.—White, 5,324 ; colored, 4,595.

Area : 690 square miles.—Woodland, nearly all ; yellow-loam region, 370 square miles ; alluvial, 320 square miles.

Tilled lands : 46,038 acres.—Area planted in cotton, 19,111 acres ; in corn, 16,672 acres ; in oats, 691 acres.

Cotton production : 11,643 bales ; average cotton product per acre, 0.61 bale, 915 pounds seed-cotton, or 305 pounds cotton lint.

Miller is the extreme southwestern county of the state, and Red river forms the eastern and northern boundaries. Texarkana, the county-seat, is located on the state line, which passes along one of the principal streets. The uplands of the county are rolling, and, with the exception of a few small prairies, are well timbered. The soil is sandy and, in a few places, gravelly, the subsoil being a reddish loam, which yields from 500 to 800 pounds of seed-cotton per acre with fair cultivation.

The river bottoms, lying about 100 feet below the uplands, are many miles in width, and for the most part are well timbered. The soils vary from a dark sandy loam to a red or chocolate-colored clay several feet deep, and are the chief cotton lands of the county, producing from 1,800 to 2,500 pounds of seed-cotton per acre in good seasons. It is said that as much as 3,500 pounds have been produced on a single acre. Some open prairie lands occur in these bottoms.

The population of Miller county averages a little more than 14 persons per square mile, and the tilled lands 66.7 acres per square mile. Cotton has a greater acreage than corn, and comprises 41.5 per cent. of the lands under cultivation, with an average of 27.7 acres per square mile. The broad alluvial lands of Red river places the average product per acre a little above La Fayette, or twenty-first in the state, the uplands having the same productiveness as Columbia and Union.

ABSTRACT OF THE REPORT OF E. T. DALE, TEXARKANA.

The lowlands consist of the first and second bottoms of McKinney bayou and the front-land, back-land, and cypress swamp of Red river. The uplands are mostly rolling, only a small part being prairie, and are watered by Nix and Dag's creeks. The lands cultivated in cotton comprise black sandy loam lying along the rivers and bayou, sandy loam lying on the creek bottoms, and light sandy soils of the uplands.

The most important is the *black sandy lands* of the river bottoms, constituting about one-third of the area of the county, extending the entire length of the Red and Sulphur rivers, and having a natural timber growth of hickory, ash, walnut, pecan, gum, cottonwood, dogwood, cypress, elm, red cedar, and pin, black, willow, and overcup oaks. The soil is a light, fine sandy loam, from dark red to black in color, and from 2 to 3 feet in depth. Its subsoil is heavier and leachy, and consists of a mixture of sand and clay reddish in color, especially along the borders of Red river, and is underlaid by sand. This land is cultivated with difficulty in wet seasons, but is very easily tilled in dry ones, and is early, warm, ill-drained, and best adapted to cotton. Corn and cotton are the chief crops of the region. About three-fourths of the crops planted are in cotton, which grows to a height of from 4 to 6 feet, but is most productive at 4½ feet, and yields on fresh land from 1,800 to 2,500 pounds of seed-cotton per acre, 1,425 of which are required for a 475-pound bale of middling lint. After ten years' cultivation (unmanured) the yield is about 1,700 pounds, and in some instances this year (1880) 3,500 pounds of seed-cotton per acre, from 1,425 to 1,665 pounds being necessary for 475 pounds of lint, rating fully as well and often better than that from fresh land. The plant inclines to run to weed in wet weather, for which thorough cultivation and topping are the remedies resorted to. Rag-weed, crab-grass, and cocklebur are the most troublesome weeds. About one-fourth of the land lies "turned out", producing, when again cultivated, as well as it did originally.

The *creek bottom lands*, covering about one-sixth of the surface, and occurring in small bodies scattered throughout the county, have a natural timber growth of white, post, black, and willow oaks, elm, gum, willow, dogwood, holly, birch, hickory, and soft maple. The soil is a fine sandy loam, gray, brown, or black in color, and 18 inches deep. Its subsoil is heavier and leachy, consisting of reddish clay and sand, and contains hard white gravel and rounded pebbles, underlaid by sand. The land is easily tilled in all seasons, is early, warm, and well-drained, and is best adapted to cotton, to which about one-half the cultivated area is devoted. It grows to a height of from 3 to 4 feet, the former being the most productive, and inclines to run to weed in wet seasons, the remedies applied being drainage and cultivation. Twelve hundred pounds from fresh land and 600 pounds from land after five years' cultivation (unmanured) are the products per acre in seed-cotton. From 1,425 to 1,665 pounds from fresh and 1,665 from old lands are required for 475 pounds of lint, rating in the former case as low middling. In the latter case the staple is poorer and shorter. Crab-grass is the most troublesome weed. About one-eighth of the land lies "turned out", which produces poorly when again cultivated, but when manured yields as well as ever.

The *light sandy soil* of the uplands comprises about one-half of the tillable lands, and is found in all parts of the county except on the borders of the river. The natural timber growth is mostly yellow pine, with some black and post oaks and dogwood. The soil is sandy, in some few places gravelly, and varies greatly in color, being gray, yellow, brown, or sometimes orange red, and is 6 inches deep. Its subsoil is heavier and leachy, and consists of a mixture of sand and reddish clay, underlaid by sand. The land is easily cultivated in all seasons, is early, warm, and well drained, and is best adapted to cotton, which forms about one-half the crop planted. The plant usually attains a height of from 1 to 3 feet, being most productive at the latter, and never runs to weed on this land. The yield per acre in seed-cotton from fresh land is from 800 to 1,200 pounds, and from 400 to 800 pounds after five years' cultivation (unmanured). From fresh land 1,425 and from old lands 1,665 pounds are requisite for a 475-pound bale of lint in the former case as low middling; but in the latter case the staple is poorer and shorter. Crab-grass is the most troublesome weed. One-eighth of the land lies "turned out", producing poorly when again cultivated if not manured, but as well as ever if manured. The soil washes on slopes, doing considerable damage and injuring the valleys sometimes to the extent of one-half their value. Horizontalizing and hillside ditching are practiced to a slight extent, but with good success. The climate of both uplands and lowlands is very favorable for the growth of cotton; occasionally, however, a wet spring delays planting in the bottoms.

Cotton is shipped, as fast as baled, by railroad and river to Saint Louis and New Orleans, at the rate of $3 50 per bale of 500 pounds.

LITTLE RIVER.

Population: 6,404.—White, 3,064; colored, 3,340.

Area: 530 square miles.—Woodland, nearly all; yellow-loam region, 425 square miles; Red river alluvial, 105 square miles.

Tilled lands: 27,083 acres.—Area planted in cotton, 10,368 acres; in corn, 9,141 acres; in oats, 582 acres; in wheat, 118 acres.

Cotton production: 7,116 bales; average cotton product per acre, 0.69 bale, 1,035 pounds seed-cotton, or 345 pounds cotton lint.

Little River county, in the southwestern part of the state, lies in the fork formed by the junction of Little river with Red river. A well-timbered dividing ridge, about 250 feet above the bottom lands, and lying in the middle of the county, separates the tributaries of the two streams. In the western part of the county this ridge is 4 or 5 miles wide and 6 or 8 long, and has chiefly a post-oak growth. Its surface is level and the soil cold and wet. To the eastward or northeast from Rocky Comfort this dividing ridge has a coarse, sandy, and gravelly soil, with chiefly an oak growth on the southern side, and then pine and oak prevails. Six or seven miles from Rocky Comfort, in the same course, the lands are heavy sand beds with a stunted growth of oak and pine. Along the slopes of these ridges there are red or chocolate-colored clays, with a little fine gravel. The rest of the uplands of the county are interspersed with small prairies of black sandy lands, having a stiff clayey subsoil, underlaid by Cretaceous limestones.

The river lands are broad, and comprise the black sandy soils of the second bottom and the red sandy or clayey soils of the first bottom or terrace. The bottom timber growth is cottonwood, ash, pecan, walnut, etc., with a cane undergrowth. The lands yield from 1 to 2 bales of cotton per acre, and are very durable. Salt-licks are found in the northwestern part of the county.

The county has an average population of about 12 persons per square mile, while that of the lands under cultivation is 51.1 acres per square mile, or 8 per cent. of the county area. As in the other counties of this region thus far described, cotton is the chief crop, its acreage comprising 38.3 per cent. of the tilled lands, and averaging 19.6 acres per square mile. The large proportion of alluvial lands under cultivation add greatly to the average product per acre.
Cotton is shipped, by rail or river, to Saint Louis or New Orleans.

SEVIER.

Population: 6,192.—White, 5,088; colored, 1,104.
Area: 550 square miles.—Woodland, some prairies; red-loam lands, 160 square miles; yellow-loam region, 390 square miles.
Tilled lands: 25,448 acres.—Area planted in cotton, 7,283 acres; in corn, 10,557 acres; in oats, 1,045 acres; in wheat, 1,012 acres.
Cotton production: 4,075 bales; average cotton product per acre, 0.56 bale, 840 pounds seed-cotton, or 280 pounds cotton lint.
Sevier county is bordered on the south by Little river. That portion north of a line eastward from Ultima Thule is hilly and broken, with narrow valleys between the hills. Outcrops of metamorphic rocks occur, and this part of the county is embraced in the mineral belt that extends from Little Rock into the Indian territory. Its soils are sandy, timbered with oak and hickory. The southern part of the county is more level, and is interspersed with large tracts of black sandy soils, underlaid by the limestones and marls of the Cretaceous formation. Sandy oak and pine ridges occur between the streams, their gray or red gravelly soils being underlaid with red clay subsoils. Some ferruginous conglomerate appears on the pine ridges on the southeast, 250 feet above Little river. The bottom lands of the river are very broad, have a dark sandy loam soil, are well timbered with oak, pine, ash, walnut, and elm, and have an undergrowth of cane. Salt-licks are found on the west and east within this black land region, and salt works were at one time in operation near Ultima Thule. The population of this county has an average of about 11 persons, while the lands under cultivation average only 46.3 acres per square mile, or 7.2 per cent. of the total area. It is one of the few counties of the region in which the acreage of corn is greater than that of cotton, the latter embracing 28.6 per cent. of the tilled lands and averaging 13.2 acres per square mile.

ABSTRACT OF THE REPORT OF M. W. LOCKE, LOCKESBURG.

The lowlands comprise the first and second bottom of Cossetot creek and the waters and alluvial plain of Little river. The uplands consist of gently rolling table-land, finely timbered. The lands devoted to the cultivation of cotton are the red, black, and gray sandy.
The *red gravelly land* covers about one-fourth of the surface, and is found more or less throughout the county. Its natural timber growth is black, post, and white oaks, hickory, and pine. The soil is a heavy clay loam, orange-red in color, and from 18 inches to 2 feet in depth, with a heavier subsoil, consisting of a deep red stiff clay or hard-pan, containing pebbles and "black gravel", and overlying gravel at 6 feet. The land is easily tilled in all seasons, is early and warm when well drained, and is best adapted to cotton and sorghum. The chief crops of the region are cotton, corn, wheat, oats, sorghum, and potatoes. About one-half the crops planted are in cotton, which grows to a height of from 3 to 3½ feet, and tends to run to weed in July and August, when there is too much rain, topping being the remedy applied to restrain it. From 1,200 to 1,500 pounds is the seed-cotton product per acre from fresh land, and from 800 to 1,000 pounds after 40 years' cultivation, 1,605 pounds being required for 475 pounds of lint, rating as first class from fresh land but not so high from old lands, the lint being shorter. Cocklebur, hog-weed, purslane, and crab-grass are the most troublesome weeds. About one-twentieth of the land lies "turned out", producing very well when again cultivated. The soil does not wash readily on the slopes.
The *black land*, comprising about one-fifth of the cultivated area, extends in each direction about seven miles, and has a natural timber growth of hackberry, ash, oak, elm, hickory, and walnut. Its soil is black and waxy, 2 feet in depth, overlying a hard-pan, which is impervious when undisturbed, and contains shells. Limestone is found at 10 feet. The land is quite difficult to till in wet, but quite easy in dry seasons. It is early and warm, when well drained, and is best adapted to cotton, which constitutes about one-half the crops. The plant usually attains a height of 4 feet, but inclines to run to weed in the latter part of summer if the weather is very wet, no remedy being applied to restrain it. From fresh land 1,500 pounds of seed-cotton are produced per acre, 1,605 of which are necessary for 475 pounds of lint, rating as first class. Some of this land has been cultivated from thirty to forty years without manure, the amount required for a 475-pound bale of lint being the same as in case of fresh land, but the staple is a little shorter. Burs, purslane, and hog-weeds are the most troublesome weeds. About one-tenth of this land lies "turned out", which, when again cultivated, produces very well. The soil washes on slopes, damaging some old fields. but improving the valleys; but no efforts have been made to check the damage.
The *gray sandy lands* cover about one-fourth of the surface of and extend throughout the county. The natural timber growth is pine, hickory, dogwood, sumac, walnut, and all varieties of oaks. The soil is a fine sandy loam, clayey in places, gray or ash-like in color, and from 1 to 2 feet in depth. Its subsoil is heavier, and consists of a deep red clay, impervious when undisturbed, which contains rounded pebbles, and is underlaid by sand at 4 feet. The land is sandy, tilled in all seasons, is early and warm when well drained, and is best adapted to small grain and cotton, the latter forming one-half the crops planted. The plant usually attains a height of 4 feet. Fresh land produces from 1,200 to 1,500 pounds of seed-cotton per acre, 1,600 pounds being requisite for 475 pounds of lint, rating first-class. This land will fail after ten years' cultivation unmanured. Crab-grass and purslane are the most troublesome weeds. About one-twentieth of the land lies "turned out", yielding fair crops when again cultivated. There is very little washing of the soil on slopes. Cotton matures either on bottoms or uplands, but the bottoms are more liable to rust.
Shipments of cotton are made, about Christmas time, by railroad and steamboat to New Orleans and Saint Louis. The rates of freight are, by wagon, $1 50 per bale to the river landing, or $3 to the railroad; thence to market, $1.

HOWARD.

Population: 9,917.—White, 7,409; colored, 2,508.
Area: 630 square miles.—Woodland, nearly all; red-loam lands, 305 square miles; yellow-loam region, 325 square miles.
Tilled lands: 44,812 acres.—Area planted in cotton, 12,259 acres; in corn, 17,671 acres; in oats, 2,486 acres; in wheat, 3,357 acres.

Cotton production : 7,051 bales; average cotton product per acre, 0.58 bale, 870 pounds seed-cotton, or 290 pounds cotton lint.

The surface of Howard county is rolling on the south and hilly and broken on the north. Some of the hills are very high, and belong to the mountainous and mineral or metamorphic region of the interior. From a few miles north of Center Point, the county-seat, southward through the county, the country is included in the belt of black lands that are underlaid by Cretaceous limestones and marls. These lands are bordered by timbered uplands, or gray and red sandy, gravelly soils, which seem to constitute the chief cotton lands of the county, and yield an average of 800 pounds of seed-cotton per acre. The soils of the northern part of the county are mostly rocky and sandy, gray in color, except from the headwaters of Muddy creek westward to Saline river, where red lands prevail. The population of the county averages nearly 16 persons to the square mile, and its tilled lands 71.1 acres per square mile. Corn is the chief crop, and the county has the largest wheat acreage in the region. Cotton has an average of 19.5 acres per square mile, and the county ranks with Ashley and Prairie in product per acre.

ABSTRACT OF THE REPORT OF J. A. THOMAS, CENTRE POINT.

The uplands of the county consist of rolling and level table-land, and are watered by the Saline river and smaller creeks. There is but little bottom land in this vicinity. The soils devoted to the cultivation of cotton are the red gravelly, the dark sandy, and the black waxy lands. The chief soil is the red gravelly, which comprises three-fourths or more of the area of the county and extends 60 miles east and west and 6 to 10 miles north and south, and has a timber growth of post, black and white oaks, pine, walnut, and ash. The soil is a coarse sandy and gravelly loam, orange red in color, 12 to 20 inches deep, with a heavy clay subsoil, containing hard white gravel, underlaid by sand, gravel, and rock at from 2 to 3 feet. The chief crops of the region are corn, wheat, oats, and cotton. The soil is difficult to till in dry seasons, is early, warm, and well drained, and is best adapted to cotton, to which one-third of it is devoted. The plant usually grows from 3 to 6 feet high; is most productive at from 3½ to 4 feet, inclining to run to weed in wet seasons if the land is too deeply plowed, which can be remedied by shallow cultivation. The seed-cotton product per acre from fresh land is from 1,000 to 1,200 pounds, from 1,480 to 1,510 pounds being necessary for a 475-pound bale of lint, which brings from one-fourth to one-half a cent more than that from old land. After ten years' cultivation the product per acre is reduced to 700 or 800 pounds, from 1,425 to 1,450 pounds making a 475-pound bale of lint, which is shorter than that from fresh land, but the seed is smaller and lighter. Not more than one-fourth of this land lies "turned out", and when cultivated again it produces cotton best the first year, as it matures better than on other land. The slopes do not wash to any extent, as the soil is a heavy clay; the valleys are but very little injured by the washings. There has been but one instance of hillside ditching to check damages from washing, and that was successful. We would prefer lowland for cotton, although good fresh upland is well adapted to it.

Cotton is shipped, from October 1 to March, by railroad to Saint Louis at $6 50 per bale, which includes both freight and charges.

PIKE.
(See " Red-loam region ".)

HEMPSTEAD.

Population : 19,015.—White, 9,593; colored, 9,422.

Area: 730 square miles.—Woodland, the greater part; yellow-loam region, 685 square miles; alluvial, 45 square miles.

Tilled land : 76,537 acres.—Area planted in cotton, 27,142 acres; in corn, 30,284 acres; in oats, 3,489 acres; in wheat, 1,289 acres.

Cotton production : 13,985 bales; average cotton product per acre, 0.52 bale, 780 pounds seed-cotton, or 260 pounds cotton lint.

Hempstead county is bordered on the southwest by Red and Little rivers, though their bottom lands comprise but a small percentage of the county area. The larger portion of the county is watered by tributaries of the Ouachita river, flowing in a northeast and easterly direction. The surface is generally undulating or rolling, and from Washington northward comprises small open prairies of black sandy calcareous lands, interspersed among sandy and gravelly hills, and underlaid by limestones of Cretaceous age. The prairies are said to cover one-sixth of the county area. Fossil shells and remains have been found in great abundance near Washington and in other places. Bois d'arc, or Osage orange, is the characteristic timber growth of these black lands, which are surrounded by pine, ash, and hickory, and have an undergrowth of spice-bush, papaw, dogwood, and buckeye. Southward from Washington, after leaving the sand, there occur dark and stiff tenacious soils, underlaid by blue marly Tertiary clays, which extend 3 or 4 miles south of Spring Hill, near the county-line, where they are covered by the sandy and gravelly soils and clayey subsoils of the pine ridges. Ferruginous conglomerate and sandstones are found on these hills. The uplands of the county are said to produce about 800 pounds of seed-cotton or 30 bushels of corn per acre, while the dark alluvial lands of the streams yield 1,500 pounds of seed-cotton or 50 bushels of corn. This is the most thickly populated county in the region, and in this regard is surpassed but by three in the state, Pulaski, Sebastian, and Phillips, its average being about 26 persons per square mile. The average of lands under cultivation is 104.8 acres per square mile, the counties of Benton, Phillips, Washington, Sebastian, Nevada, and Lee alone having a greater average. While the acreage of corn is greater than that of cotton, the county ranks as seventh in the state in the total acreage of cotton and fifth in the average number of acres (37.2) of that crop per square mile. Cotton is shipped, by rail and river, to Saint Louis or New Orleans.

NEVADA.

Population: 12,959.—White, 9,236; colored, 3,723.

Area: 670 square miles.—Woodland, all; all yellow-loam region.

Tilled lands: 70,858 acres.—Area planted in cotton, 23,925 acres; in corn, 23,173 acres; in oats, 1,329 acres; in wheat, 635 acres.

Cotton production: 10,520 bales; average cotton product per acre, 0.44 bale, 660 pounds seed-cotton, or 220 pounds cotton lint.

The surface of Nevada county is rolling and well timbered with pine, oak. and hickory. Little Missouri river borders it on the north, and most of the streams are tributary to it, flowing northward. The river lauds have dark alluvial soils and are very productive. The uplands are mostly sandy, with red or yellow subsoils, producing from 800 to 1,000 pounds of seed-cotton per acre. The crops of the county are cotton, corn, and small grain. The acreages of corn and cotton are nearly the same, the latter predominating.

The county has an average population of about 19 persons per square mile, which is greater than any other county of this region except Jefferson and Hempstead. The lands under cultivation embrace 16.5 per cent. of its area, averaging 105.8 acres per square mile, and placing the county fifth in the state in this regard, Benton, Phillips, Washington, and Sebastian alone ranking above it. Of this average of tilled lands 35.7 acres are devoted to the culture of cotton, seven counties alone in the state having a greater number, Phillips, Lee, Jefferson, Columbia, Hempstead, Crittenden, and Pulaski. In product per acre the county stands very low, only eight counties in the state having each a less average yield. Shipments are made by rail mostly to Little Rock or Saint Louis.

OUACHITA.

Population: 11,758.—White, 5,504; colored, 6,254.
Area: 730 square miles.—Woodland, all; yellow-loam region, 675 square miles; alluvial, 55 square miles.
Tilled lands: 65,733 acres.—Area planted in cotton, 23,855 acres; in corn, 21,924 acres; in oats, 567 acres; in wheat, 164 acres.
Cotton production: 8,849 bales; average cotton product. per acre, 0.37 bale, 555 pounds seed-cotton, or 185 pounds cotton lint.

Ouachita county has a rolling surface with areas of level uplands, and is well timbered with short-leaf pine, red and white oaks, hickory, etc. Ouachita river flows through it in a southeasterly course and receives all the drainage of the county on either side. The bottom lands of the river are from 2 to 4 miles wide, with buff-colored sandy soils and a timber growth of white and water oaks, large pines, beech, hickory, dogwood, and ash, and an undergrowth of cane, etc. This land is said to produce a bale of cotton or 40 to 50 bushels of corn per acre under fair cultivation. The light hummock lands along the creeks are also fine cotton lands, yielding from 1,000 to 1,500 pounds of seed-cotton per acre.

The uplands embrace several varieties of soils, gray and red sandy and gravelly lands and pine flats or glady lands. The latter occur only in certain localities, and are not considered worthy of cultivation. They are underlaid by pipe-clay, and, in wet seasons, water remains on them for some time. The gray sandy lands cover the greater part of the county, interspersed with large areas of red sandy soils, and underlaid by red sands and clays to a depth of many feet. Their average yield is said to be from 500 to 800 pounds of seed-cotton per acre. Red lands occur throughout the county, and are associated with ferruginous or iron-stone pebbles and gravel. Toward the northeastern part of the county the gravel is said to increase and the land to become redder. Along the Calhoun county-line, however, the county becomes level, and the sands are not deep. The red lands are not so productive as the gray, except in wet seasons, when they are more productive. Lignite is abundant in the vicinity of the river. Cotton and corn are the chief crops, and, as in the adjoining counties, the former has the largest acreage. The population averages about sixteen persons per square mile, and 14.1 per cent. of the county area is in cultivation, with an average of 90 acres per square mile. Of the latter 32.7 acres are devoted to cotton, placing the county twelfth in the state. Though having so large an acreage, the product per acre is lower than that of any other county except Union, which has the same.

Shipments of cotton are made by wagon to the nearest railroad station.

CALHOUN.

Population: 5,671.—White, 3,583; colored, 2,088.
Area: 610 square miles.—Woodland, all; yellow-loam region, 515 square miles; alluvial, 95 square miles.
Tilled lands: 33,391 acres.—Area planted in cotton, 13,377 acres; in corn, 12,910 acres; in oats, 873 acres; in wheat, 128 acres.
Cotton production: 5,370 bales; average cotton product per acre, 0.40 bale, 600 pounds seed-cotton, or 200 pounds cotton lint.

Calhoun county is bordered on the east by bayou Moro, and on the south by the Ouachita river, other streams mostly flowing southward into the latter. Ten miles north of Hampton there is a ridge 140 feet high covered with gravel, and in the vicinity are others less prominent; but otherwise the surface of the county is said to be generally level and well timbered. In the southern and western parts of the county the lands are sandy. East of Champagnole creek the land is low and flat and the soil sandy, but contains more clay than on the west side of the creek, in some places being inclined to be crawfishy and spouty.

The greater part of the northern area of the county is covered with gray sandy soils and reddish clay subsoils, having a timber growth of white, red, and post oaks, and pine, with an undergrowth of chincapin. This soil is said to produce from 800 to 1,000 pounds of seed-cotton per acre. The principal red lands of the county occur north of Hampton, the county-seat, beginning at 2½ miles and extending to within 10 miles of the foot of the gravel ridge. On Moro river the soil is of a rich chocolate color, with some red sand and loam. Sandstone, ferruginous conglomerate, and sandy iron ore form occasional beds north of Hampton.

The crops of the county are cotton, corn, oats, potatoes, and some wheat, the acreage of the former being somewhat greater than that of corn, and averaging 21.9 acres per square mile. The county is sparsely populated, with an average of about 9 persons per square mile, while the lands under cultivation comprise 8.6 per cent. of the area, or 54.7 acres per square mile. In product per acre the county is but little better than Ouachita and Union, the counties ranking lowest in the state in this regard.

BRADLEY.

Population: 6,285.—White, 4,075; colored, 2,210.

Area: 700 square miles.—Woodland, all; yellow-loam region, 580 square miles; alluvial, 120 square miles.

Tilled lands: 34,068 acres.—Area planted in cotton, 12,221 acres; in corn, 12,330 acres; in oats, 1,073 acres; in wheat, 336 acres.

Cotton production: 4,900 bales; average cotton product per acre, 0.40 bale, 600 pounds seed-cotton, or 200 pounds cotton lint.

The surface of Bradley county is mostly rolling, and is well timbered with short-leaf pine, oak, and hickory. The lands of the uplands of the southern part of this county comprise chiefly gray sandy soils from 6 to 10 inches deep, with yellow clay subsoils, which are inclined to be gravelly. Patches of ferruginous conglomerate occur in some places, and lignite is also found in great abundance. In the northern part the soils of the uplands are largely chocolate in color, from the Tertiary iron ores that are found in the adjoining county of Dorsey, and have red clay subsoils. These uplands, as well as those of the south, are said to produce, when properly cultivated, from 800 to 1,000 pounds of seed-cotton or 25 to 30 bushels of corn per acre. Saline river on the east, Ouachita river on the south, and bayou Moro on the west, give to the county a large area of bottom lands. The low bottom lands of these streams on the south are said to be a white clay, cold, wet, and slushy, with an abundant growth of low palmetto. The high bottom lands of the Saline are of much better quality, yielding 1,500 pounds of seed-cotton per acre. The second bottoms, or hummocks, are sandy in character and very productive, yielding from 1,600 to 1,500 pounds of seed-cotton and about 30 bushels of corn per acre. The crops of this county are cotton, corn, potatoes, and oats, with a small acreage in wheat, and it is one of the few counties of this region that has a larger acreage of corn than of cotton, though the difference is very small. The average population per square mile (9 persons) is smaller than in any other county of the region, while that of lands under cultivation (48.7 acres) is greater than in Grant and Sevier only, and of these 17.5 acres are devoted to the culture of cotton. From the census reports it seems that the greater part of the crop is produced in the northern half of the county. In product per acre the county ranks among the four lowest in the state.

DREW.

Population: 12,231.—White, 6,472; colored, 5,759.

Area: 840 square miles.—Woodland, all; yellow-loam region, 735 square miles; alluvial, 105 square miles.

Tilled lands: 53,537 acres.—Area planted in cotton, 21,796 acres; in corn, 20,005 acres; in oats, 1,488 acres: in wheat, 280 acres.

Cotton production: 9,964 bales; average cotton product per acre, 0.46 bale, 690 pounds seed-cotton, or 230 pounds cotton lint.

The surface of the eastern and western parts of Drew county is generally level, while through the center, from north to south, the country is rolling, and the dividing ridge between the waters of Saline river and bayou Bartholomew is said to be very prominent. Around Monticello the soil is gravelly, with a subsoil of red or yellow clay and a timber growth of red and other oaks and short-leaf pine. The ridges in the vicinity of Lacey, on the south, are about 65 feet above the bottoms, and are composed of red and yellow clay and gravel. In the western part of the county the highest land is about 140 feet above the bed of Saline river, the soil of which is a sandy loam, more or less gravelly, with a yellow siliceous clay subsoil, which is said to produce about 800 pounds of seed-cotton per acre in fair seasons. Its timber growth is mostly pine. There are a number of small prairies in this county, Long prairie, 10 or 12 miles south of Monticello, being partly in cultivation. The bottoms of bayou Bartholomew are from 3 to 6 miles wide, and consist of a front-land along the stream with a fine silty or sandy loam soil, and a back-land of a stiffer character and a heavy impervious subsoil. Cypress brakes occur throughout the bottoms, which have a deep black mucky soil, said to be well adapted to cotton and very durable, producing, both when fresh and after 40 years' cultivation, as much as 2,500 pounds of seed-cotton per acre. The crops comprise cotton, corn, wheat, oats, potatoes, and tobacco, and fruits are said to be abundant. Cotton is the chief crop, with an acreage of 25.9 acres per square mile. The lands under cultivation embrace 10 per cent. of the total area, with an average of 63.7 acres per square mile, an amount much less than that of most of the other counties of the region. In product per acre it ranks quite low in the state, there being but eleven counties each with a less average.

ABSTRACT OF THE REPORT OF S. A. DUKE, BAXTER.

The lowlands of the county comprise the front-land, the back-land, and the cypress swamps of bayou Bartholomew. The chief crops of the county are cotton and corn. The lands devoted to the culture of cotton are the bayou Bartholomew alluvial lands, comprising one-half of the tilled lands of the county, and having an average width of 8 miles, with a natural timber growth of many varieties of oak, cypress, gum, cottonwood, linden, ash holly, black walnut, dogwood, papaw, and prickly ash.

The soil is a fine sandy clay loam brown, mahogany, or blackish in color, with an average depth of 1 foot. The subsoil on the front-land is heavier than the soil, and is a fine sandy loam (quicksand), with occasional spots (generally a little back) of tenacious waxy yellow clay. It is slightly leachy, and is underlaid by very fine quicksand at 22 feet. The soil is easy to till in all seasons, is easily drained, and is best adapted to cotton, to which about two-thirds of its tilled area is devoted, its usual height being 5 feet. The plant runs to weed in wet weather and in such weather as produces the best corn crops. Light surface culture with hoes or "buzzard-wing Dickson sweeps" restrains the plant. The seed-cotton product per acre from fresh land in two test cases, 1875 and 1879, was 2,102 pounds, 1,490 pounds making a 475-pound bale of lint, which rates No. 1. After forty years' cultivation the estimated product is 1,600 pounds on best land, the amount necessary to make a 475-pound bale of lint, and the staple is the same as that from fresh land. Crab-grass, cocklebur, and careless weeds are the most troublesome. One-tenth of these lands lie "turned out", which produce about the same as at first when again cultivated if broom-sedge grass is thoroughly gotten rid of.

The back-lands or flats, comprising about three-eighths of the county area, occur in spots all along the bayous, and have a timber growth of hickory, elm, and hackberry. The soil is 6 inches deep, with a subsoil of heavier yellow clay hard-pan, impervious, and underlaid by

,aand at 22 feet. This soil is late and cold, whether well or ill drained, and is apparently best adapted to cotton, two-thirds of its cultivated portion being devoted to this crop. Four and one-half feet is the usual and most productive height attained by the cotton-plant, which does not run to weed on this soil. The seed-cotton product from fresh land is 1,250 pounds, the amount necessary to make a 475-pound bale, and the rating is the same as in the last described soil. After forty years' cultivation the yield of seed-cotton is 500 pounds per acre.

The *cypress brake* land comprises about one-eighth of the county, and occurs at intervals along the whole course of the bayou. The soil is mucky and black, and its depth is unknown. It is easily tilled in wet weather after it is broken, cotton roots penetrating to a great depth. The soil is late and warm when well drained, and is best adapted to cotton, but raises good corn and rice. Nearly all the tilled area of this land is devoted to cotton, which grows 6 feet high and runs to weed under any circumstances, which is remedied by shallow culture. The seed-cotton product for fresh land is 2,500 pounds, the same amount being necessary for a 475-pound bale of excellent lint as on other lands of the county. After forty years' cultivation the product and the rating are the same as on fresh land. The most troublesome weed is the tie-vine (morning-glory). One-tenth of these lands lie "turned out", and when again cultivated produce as well as at first.

Shipments are made, as soon as the cotton is baled, by rail to the Mississippi river, and via Arkapolis to New Orleans, at $2 75 per bale.

CHICOT.
(See "Mississippi alluvial region".)

DESHA.
(See "Mississippi alluvial region".)

LINCOLN.

Population: 9,255.—White, 4,212; colored, 5,043.

Area: 540 square miles.—Woodland, nearly all; yellow-loam region, 400 square miles; alluvial, 140 square miles.

Tilled lands: 38,421 acres.—Area planted in cotton, 17,519 acres; in corn, 12,547 acres; in oats, 1,400 acres; in wheat, 185 acres.

Cotton production: 11,563 bales; average cotton product per acre, 0.66 bale, 990 pounds seed-cotton, or 330 pounds cotton lint.

The surface of Lincoln county is slightly rolling and mostly well timbered, and is interspersed with some open prairies. Bayou Bartholomew flows through the middle of the county, while the Arkansas river forms the northeast boundary. Both of these streams have wide and rich bottom lands. The soils are alluvial loams, varying from dark to reddish sands and clays, yielding from 2,000 to 3,000 pounds of seed-cotton per acre.

Lawyer's prairie, in the southern part of the county, is surrounded by large oak timber, and is very productive. The average of lands under cultivation is 71.1 acres per square mile, and the crops are cotton, corn, oats, potatoes, and some wheat. Cotton is the chief crop, its acreage being the greatest, comprising 45.6 per cent. of the tilled lands, and averaging 32.4 acres per square mile, in which it ranks as thirteenth in the state. The rich bottom lands along the Arkansas river and bayou Bartholomew give to the county a high product per acre, and place it as tenth in rank in the state. The average product of the pine-hills, in the southwestern corner of the county, is 630 pounds of seed-cotton per acre; the average of the rest of the county is 1,035 pounds, or as that of Little River county. In the small township of Kimborough, lying on the Arkansas river on the north, we find the average to be 460 pounds of lint or 1,380 pounds of seed-cotton—an average nearly equal to that of Chicot, the banner county of the state.

ABSTRACT OF THE REPORT OF CHARLES V. DIXON, AUBURN.

The lands devoted to the cultivation of cotton comprise light sandy, buckshot, and black sandy soils. The most important is the light sandy loam, covering about three-fifths of the surface of the county, and extending from Pine Bluff to Napoleon, along the banks of the Arkansas river, a distance of about 90 miles. It is from one-half to a mile wide, and has a natural timber growth of cottonwood, willow, box-elder, honey-locust, elms, oaks of different varieties, and sycamore. The soil is a light fine silty or clay loam, blackish in color, and about 2 feet deep; the subsoil, which is lighter, is generally fine white sand, but occasionally clay of a reddish or blackish color. The land is easily cultivated in dry weather, but is tilled with difficulty in wet seasons. It is late, warm, and well drained, and is best adapted to cotton. The chief crops of the region are cotton, corn, and German millet. About four-fifths of the cultivated area is devoted to cotton, which grows to a height of from 4 to 5 feet, and inclines to run to weed in wet seasons when cultivated with the turning plow, for which plowing lightly and topping are the remedies. When the land is fresh the product in seed-cotton per acre is from 1,500 to 1,800 pounds, and 1,500 pounds after 20 years if the land is well cultivated, 1,425 to 1,585 pounds being the amount required, either from fresh or old lands, for a 475 pound bale of lint, rating in the former case as low middling, and in the latter somewhat better, the fiber being stronger. Cocklebur, morning-glory vines, and especially crab-grass, are the most troublesome weeds. About one-eighth of the land lies "turned out", producing, when again taken into cultivation, better than originally, but being harder to cultivate. The lands wash readily on slopes, but the damage to them, or to the lowlands, is not serious, except in the hill country, 10 or 15 miles back. Any damage is checked by horizontalizing or hillside ditching.

Shipments of cotton are made, in December, by steamer to Memphis and New Orleans; freight to Memphis $1 50, and to New Orleans at from $2 to $3 per bale.

DORSEY.

Population: 8,370.—White, 6,041; colored, 2,329.

Area: 600 square miles.—Woodland, all; all yellow-loam region.

Tilled lands: 42,564 acres.—Area planted in cotton, 15,462 acres; in corn, 14,737 acres; in oats, 1,777 acres; in wheat, 660 acres.

Cotton production: 6,146 bales; average cotton product per acre, 0.40 bale, 600 pounds seed-cotton, or 200 pounds cotton lint.

The surface of Dorsey county is undulating, with occasional ridges, and is watered by a number of streams tributary to the Saline river, which flows through its center. Bayou Moro forms the western boundary, the water divide between it and Saline river passing very near it. The bottom lands of these streams, and especially of Saline river, are broad and well timbered. The alluvial soils are very productive, yielding, it is claimed, from 40 to 50 bushels of corn and a bale of cotton per acre under cultivation.

The uplands are mostly gray and sandy, interspersed with red lands, and have a yellow or reddish sandy loam subsoil. Red lands occur chiefly in the southern part of the county, associated with an abundance of Tertiary iron ore. The characteristic timber growth is elm, mulberry, prickly ash, red oaks, and a few white oaks and hickory; the undergrowth is dogwood and muscadine and other grape-vines in great abundance. The average yield is 800 pounds of seed-cotton, 40 bushels of corn, or 15 bushels of wheat per acre. Gypsum, gypseous marl, and Tertiary shell marl are found in the southwestern part of the county. The average of the lands under cultivation is 70.9 acres per square mile, and the chief crops are cotton, corn, oats, potatoes, and some wheat. Cotton is the chief crop, comprising 36.3 per cent. of the tilled lands, and averaging 25.8 acres per square mile. In product per acre the county ranks among the three lowest in the state. Cotton is hauled in wagons to the nearest landing on the Arkansas river, and thence shipped by boat to New Orleans or Memphis.

DALLAS.

Population: 6,505.—White, 4,299; colored, 2,206.
Area: 660 square miles.—Woodland, all; all yellow-loam region.
Tilled lands: 35,505 acres.—Area planted in cotton, 14,306 acres; in corn, 13,330 acres; in oats, 894 acres; in wheat, 443 acres.
Cotton production: 6,157 bales; average cotton product per acre, 0.43 bale, 645 pounds seed-cotton, or 215 pounds cotton lint.

The surface of Dallas county is rolling and well timbered. The Ouachita river forms the western boundary, and, with its tributaries, drains the greater portion of the county. Bayou Moro flows along the eastern border. The uplands comprise both red and gray sandy lands, chiefly the former. The subsoils are mostly reddish clays. The lands yield at first about 800 pounds of seed-cotton per acre, but only 400 pounds after 30 years' cultivation.

The river bottom lands embrace two terraces, or first and second bottoms. The first or lowest bottoms have mostly red alluvial soils, usually subject to overflows, which produce from 1,000 to 1,500 pounds of seed-cotton and 50 bushels of corn per acre.

The soil of the second or upper bottoms is a dark loam more or less sandy, which produces an average of 20 bushels of corn, 10 bushels of wheat, and 800 pounds of seed-cotton per acre. The timber growth of the Ouachita bottom is red, pin, swamp chestnut, swamp white, willow, and water oaks, beech, pecan, sweet gum, magnolia, and holly, and a dense undergrowth of vines, briers, and cane. The lowest bottoms have a cypress and tupelo growth.

The average of lands under cultivation is 53.8 acres per square mile, or 8.4 per cent. of its area. The chief crops are cotton, corn, and potatoes, with some oats and wheat. The acreage of cotton is the greatest, comprising 40.3 per cent. of tilled lands, and averaging 21.7 acres per square mile. In product per acre it ranks low in the state, there being but seven counties below it, due to the fact that it is almost exclusively an upland county.

ABSTRACT OF THE REPORT OF W. H. YOUNG, TULIP.

The lands devoted to cotton culture comprise the dark red gravelly and light rolling sandy soils of the uplands and dark sandy soils of the creek bottoms. The chief soil is the *red gravelly land*, constituting about three-fifths of the surface of the county, which extends about 25 miles north and south, and, omitting several creek bottoms, the same distance east and west. The natural timber growth is white post, black, and red oaks, pine, hickory, gum, dogwood, and many other varieties, with common wild grapes. The soil is 5 inches in depth. The subsoil is a yellowish or reddish leachy clay, containing water-worn pebbles, which is underlaid by a bed of closely packed gravel, very deep in places. The land is difficult to till in dry seasons, but easy in wet ones, is early, warm, and well drained, and is best adapted to corn and fruits. The chief crops of the region are cotton, corn, potatoes, peas, and fine fruits of almost all kinds. Cotton forms one-half the crops planted, and grows to a height of from 3 to 4 feet, the taller the better, and yields on fresh land from 700 to 1,200 pounds of seed-cotton per acre. From 1,300 to 1,545 pounds are required, either from old or from fresh land, for a 475-pound bale of good middling lint. After thirty years' cultivation (unmanured) the yield is reduced to 400 pounds per acre, the fiber being then shorter perhaps, but not weaker than that from fresh land. Too much moisture and plowing has a tendency to incline the plant to run to weed on all lands of this county. Shallow plowing and cutting off the tops about the 5th of August are the remedies applied to restrain it. Rag-weed and hog-weed cause trouble, but the planters dread only crab-grass. About one-third of all the cultivated lands of the county have been "turned out" since the war, not so much from exhaustion as from scarcity of labor. When again cultivated, such land produces a little better than that which has had no rest. Old fields pastured and then burned over every year do not grow rich.

The *dark sandy creek bottoms* cover about one-fifth of the surface of the county, and have a natural timber growth of pine, hickory, gum, ash, hornbeam, ironwood, hazel, all the varieties of oak, walnut, cane, etc. The soil is about 6 inches in depth, with a heavier yellow clay subsoil, underlaid by sand and gravel, is easily tilled in all seasons, is early, warm, and ill-drained, and is best adapted to corn. About one-half the cultivated area is devoted to cotton, which grows to a height of from 3 to 5 feet, the latter being the most productive. The yield per acre in seed-cotton from fresh land is from 1,200 to 1,300 pounds, and 600 pounds after twenty years' cultivation (unmanured). In either case 1,300 pounds are necessary for a 475-pound bale of good middling lint, the fiber from old lands being shorter, but as salable when clean. Crab-grass and cocklebur are the most troublesome weeds.

The *sandy uplands* comprise one-fifth of the cultivated area, and extend 40 miles north and south and 20 east and west. The natural timber growth is the same as that of the red lands, with the addition of chincapin. The soil is 5 inches deep, varying in character from fine to coarse, and in color from gray to blackish. The subsoil, heavier than the soil, is leachy, and consists in some places of yellowish clay, and in others of a mixture of clay and sand. Sand and rock are found at from 5 to 10 feet. The soil is easily tilled in either wet or dry weather, is early, warm, and ill-drained, and is best adapted to corn. Cotton, which constitutes one-half of the crops planted, grows to a height of from 3 to 4 feet, and yields on fresh land from 600 to 800 pounds of seed-cotton per acre and 400 pounds after twenty years' cultivation (unmanured); 1,300 pounds, either from fresh or old lands, makes a 475-pound bale of good middling lint, the staple from old lands being as little shorter. Crab-grass and burs are the most troublesome weeds, though none cause much trouble. The soil washes considerably on slopes, doing serious damage, but the valleys, as yet, have not been injured. Occasionally a farmer plows around a hill instead of going over it. Hillside ditching is practiced with good results if the furrows do not fill up with grass and cause a break.

Cotton is hauled, as fast as ginned, by wagon to Malvern, and thence by railroad to Saint Louis.

CLARK.

Population: 15,771.—White, 10,567; colored, 5,204.

Area: 950 square miles.—Woodland, all; yellow-loam region, 670 square miles; red-loam region, 280 square miles.

Tilled lands: 67,529 acres.—Area planted in cotton, 25,092 acres; in corn, 27,005 acres; in oats, 2,121 acres; in wheat, 2,515 acres.

Cotton production: 13,924 bales; average cotton product per acre, 0.55 bale, 825 pounds seed-cotton, or 275 pounds cotton lint.

The surface of Clark county, which is rolling and mostly well timbered, is well watered by the Ouachita river on the east, the Little Missouri river on the west, and Terre Noir in the center of the county, all flowing southwardly and forming a junction on the southeast. These streams have wide bottom lands, heavily timbered with red, pin, swamp chestnut, white, willow, water, and overcup oaks, pecan, beech, walnut, hickory, sweet gum, magnolia, etc., with a dense undergrowth of vines, cane, and greenbriers. The deepest part of the marshy bottoms have a growth of cypress and tupelo gum. The first or lowest bottom has a reddish alluvial soil, more or less subject to overflow, which, when in cultivation, yields from 1,500 to 2,000 pounds of seed-cotton or 50 to 80 bushels of corn per acre. The second bottom or upper terrace has a dark, sandy, alluvial soil, easily tilled, and yields from 800 to 1,000 pounds of seed-cotton or 20 bushels of corn per acre.

The uplands of the southern and northern parts of the county are mostly sandy, with underlying red sands and clays, and have a timber growth of pine, oak, and hickory. In the central part of the county, from a point 15 miles south of Arkadelphia to that town, the soils vary greatly, comprising black sandy, black and stiff waxy buckshot lands on the lowlands, and gray sandy lands on the hills. Cretaceous limestones and marls are found underlying the surface of the country, and are, so far as known, the most easterly outcrop of that formation which forms so important a feature of the state of Texas. The black sandy and stiff clayey lands peculiar to that formation are, however, found occupying the valleys, and are covered on the higher uplands by the sands, gravel, and clays of later formations. The timber growth of these lands, as given in the abstract below, is characteristic of them.

The chief and most productive cotton lands are the black lands, yielding from 800 to 1,000 pounds of seed-cotton per acre. The sandy hill lands, next in importance and productiveness, have a yield of from 600 to 800 pounds per acre, while the stiff buckshot lands are said to yield but 400 to 500 pounds. The lands of the northern part of the county are rocky, gravelly, and sandy, and belong to the metamorphic and sandstone region, which extends westward from Little Rock to the Indian territory.

The average of lands under cultivation is 71.1 acres per square mile, or 11.1 per cent. of the county area. The crops embrace cotton, corn, oats, potatoes, and quite an acreage in wheat. This is one of the six counties in the region whose acreage of corn is greater than that of cotton, the latter crop averaging 26.4 acres per square mile, and comprising 37.2 per cent. of the tilled lands. Its product per acre is below the average for the state at large, but higher than that of the majority of the counties of this region.

ABSTRACT OF THE REPORT OF THOMAS H. MOREHEAD, ARKADELPHIA.

The uplands of this county vary much in character. The lowlands consist of the first and second bottoms of Caddo creek and the Ouachita river.

The lands devoted to the cultivation of cotton comprise the black sandy, the light sandy on the hills, and the buckshot on the flats. The most important is the *black sandy land*, covering about two-fifths of the surface of the county, and extending about 25 miles west and 15 miles south. Its natural timber growth is hickory, oak, ash, walnut, and sweet gum. The soil is about 32 inches in depth; and the subsoil, somewhat lighter colored, is very sticky when wet, and contains "black gravel" and pebbles, underlaid by gravel at 20 feet. This land is difficult to cultivate in wet, but very easy in dry seasons, is early when well drained, and is best adapted to cotton. The chief crops of the region are cotton, corn, wheat, sweet potatoes, and sorghum, cotton forming about one-third of the crops planted. The plant usually attains a height of 4½ feet, but is most productive at 4 feet, and inclines to run to weed in warm, showery weather, for which topping is the remedy applied. The product per acre of seed-cotton from fresh land is 1,000 pounds; from land eight years under cultivation (unmanured), 800 pounds. From fresh land 1,545, and from old land 1,425 pounds, are necessary for a 475-pound bale of lint. From fresh land 1,545, and from old land 1,425 pounds, are necessary for a 475-pound bale of lint. After the land has been under cultivation eight years the product per acre is reduced to 600 pounds, which is increased by the use of manure, and 1,425 pounds are necessary for a 475-pound bale of lint, which rates one grade higher than that from fresh land. Careless-weed and crab-grass are the most troublesome weeds. About 20 per cent. of this land lies "turned out", producing very well when again cultivated. The soil washes on slopes to some extent, but not enough to do any serious damage.

The *buckshot* land occurs in spots, constitutes about one-fifth of the county area, and has a natural timber growth of post and red oaks. The soil is gray, chalky, putty-like, 26 inches deep, with a heavy, sticky, hard-pan subsoil, containing soft, rounded pebbles. Gravel and rock are found at 26 feet. The soil is difficult to till in wet seasons, is late and cold, and is best adapted to grasses. About one-

6:7

fifth of the crops planted is in cotton, which usually attains a height of 2½ feet, being most productive at 3 feet. Cotton does not run to weed on this soil. The yield from fresh land per acre in seed-cotton is 500 pounds; after eight years cultivation (unmanured) 40J pounds. From fresh land 1,545 and from old land 1,425 pounds are required for 475 pounds of ordinary lint. Crab-grass is the troublesome weed. About four-fifths of this land lies "turned out". The uplands are considered the safest for cotton, as on the lowlands the crop is very apt to be injured by rust.

　　Shipments of cotton are made, by rail, in December, to Saint Louis at the rate of $2 50 per bale.

HOT SPRING.

(See "Red-loam region".)

SALINE.

(See "Red-loam region".)

PULASKI.

(See "Red-loam region".)

GRANT.

　　Population: 6,185.—White, 5,629; colored, 556.
　　Area: 650 square miles.—Woodland, all; yellow-loam region, 645 square miles; red-loam region, 5 square miles.
　　Tilled lands: 29,844 acres.—Area planted in cotton, 9,080 acres; in corn, 12,765 acres; in oats, 1,244 acres; in wheat, 573 acres.
　　Cotton production: 3,999 bales; average cotton product per acre, 0.41 bale, 615 pounds seed-cotton, or 205 pounds cotton lint.
　　The surface of Grant county is rolling and well timbered. Saline river passes through the western part, and with its wide bottom lands occupies comparatively a large area, though the land is not much in cultivation. The soil is a dark sandy loam, heavily timbered with cottonwood, ash, walnut, gum, etc. The lands of the uplands belong to the oak, hickory, and pine region, and comprise mostly red sandy soils, interspersed with gray sandy pine areas, both underlaid with red and yellow clays. The timber growth of the red lands is chiefly oak and hickory, with some pine, that of the gray being mostly short-leaf pine. The two varieties of land are said to yield respectively 750 and 700 pounds of seed-cotton when fresh, and 300 and 200 pounds after ten years' cultivation.
　　The county is sparsely populated, the average being a little more than 9 persons, and that of tilled lands 45.9 acres per square mile. The chief crops are corn, cotton, oats, potatoes, and some wheat, the acreage of corn being greatest, that of cotton comprising 32.4 per cent. of the lands in cultivation, and averaging but 14.9 acres per square mile. In product per acre the county is among the lowest in rank in the state.

ABSTRACT OF THE REPORTS OF T. W. QUINN, PRATTSVILLE, AND W. N. CLEVELAND, DOGWOOD.

　　The uplands comprise rolling or level table-lands, and the lowlands consist of the sandy loam second bottoms of the Saline river. The lands cultivated in cotton are the red hickory soils, with a clay subsoil and a sandy loam, mixed with gravel of the uplands, and sandy land of the creek and river bottoms. The *red land*, covering about 70 per cent. of the surface of the county, extends 15 miles north, 20 east, 10 south, and 1 mile west, and has a natural timber growth of oak, hickory, ash, dogwood, and pine. The soil is a heavy, gravelly loam, mixed with clay, orange red—in some places gray—in color, and 6 inches deep. The subsoil is heavier, and consists of clay, frequently mixed with gravel, and contains pebbles, underlaid by gravel and small rocks at from 9 to 10 feet. The land is easily cultivated in either wet or dry seasons, is early, warm, and well drained, produces finely, and is best adapted to cotton, though sweet potatoes do remarkably well.
　　The chief crops of the region are corn, cotton, wheat, oats, potatoes of both kinds, and sometimes sorghum. Cotton forms from one-third to one-half the crops planted, and grows to a height of from 3 to 4 feet, being most productive at 3½ feet. In wet seasons, followed by warm and sultry weather, the plant inclines to run to weed, for which topping is the remedy. From fresh land the yield per acre in seed-cotton is from 750 to 1,000 pounds, from 800 to 1,300 pounds after two and 300 pounds after ten years' cultivation (unmanured), 1,000 pounds, allowing one-tenth for toll, being required, either from fresh or old lands, for a 475-pound bale of lint, rating in the former case as good, and in the latter as middling. Hog-weed, crab-grass, and sometimes careless weed, are most troublesome. About 15 per cent. of the land lies "turned out", producing, when again cultivated, about three-fourths of its original yield. The soil washes readily on slopes, doing serious damage, which is increasing in extent. Narrow valleys are seriously injured by the washings. Horizontalizing is practiced with considerable success to check the damage.
　　The *sandy and gravelly land* of the uplands comprises about 15 per cent. of the tillable area, generally occurring in the pine lands, the natural timber growth being almost exclusively pine. The soil is 2½ inches deep, with a heavier leachy subsoil, becoming lighter in color as the depth increases, often mixed with gravel and pebbles. Sand, gravel, and rock are found at 1 foot. The land is easily cultivated in dry seasons, but is late, cold, and ill-drained. About three-fifths of the tilled area is devoted to cotton, which is most productive at a height of 2 feet. The plant inclines to run to weed in wet, warm weather with warm nights, and no remedy has been applied to restrain it. Seven hundred pounds from fresh land, and from 200 to 250 pounds from land which has been under cultivation (unmanured) for ten years, is the product per acre in seed-cotton; in either case, 1,600 pounds are required for 475 pounds of good lint. Crab-grass is the most troublesome weed. About 10 per cent. of the land lies "turned out", yielding, when again cultivated, about one-half as much as it did originally. The soil washes on slopes, doing serious damage to the uplands, but not injuring to any great extent, as yet, the valleys. Horizontalizing has been practiced with moderate success.

The *sandy loam* of the creek bottoms, constituting about 5 per cent. of the cultivated area, occurs in several localities, and has a natural timber growth of oak, hickory, ash, linn, etc. The soil is a sandy loam, blackish to black in color, and from 1 to 2 feet in depth. Its subsoil is heavier, and in some places increases in richness with the depth; in others, it comes in contact with an impervious hard-pan, and contains soft, white gravel and rounded and angular pebbles, underlaid by sand. The land is easily cultivated in dry seasons, and is early when well drained. Cotton comprises about one-half the crops planted, and usually attains a height of 5 feet, but it inclines to run to weed in wet weather, no remedy being applied. From 1,100 to 1,200 pounds is the yield per acre in seed-cotton from fresh lands, and 500 pounds from that which has been under cultivation (unmanured) for ten years. In either case 1,545 pounds are necessary for 475 pounds of lint, rating from fresh land as first-class, but not so high from old land. Burs and hog-weed are the most troublesome weeds. No land lies "turned out".

The *sandy loam* of the river bottom covers about 10 per cent. of the surface of the county, and extends in each direction from 20 to 30 miles. The soil is 10 to 12 inches in depth, underlaid by a very deep red-clay subsoil. It is easily tilled in dry seasons, and is early and warm. Cotton comprises about one-half the crops planted, and grows to a height of from 4 to 5 feet, being most productive at 4 or 4½ feet. The plant inclines to run to weed in wet seasons, which is to some extent restrained by topping. From 1,000 to 1,500 pounds is the product per acre in seed-cotton from fresh land, or that which has been under cultivation (unmanured) for 2 years, at which time it is in its best stage. About 1,485 pounds from fresh land are required for a 475-pound bale of lint; but not quite so much from the old land, the staple rating better. Purslane, crab-grass, and cocklebur are the most troublesome weeds. Very little land lies "turned out". When again cultivated, after a few years rest, it produces almost as well as ever. About once in every five years the cotton crop is liable to be injured by the excessive rainfall in April and May. The very dry and hot weather which frequently happens in August and September also damages the cotton. Shipments of cotton are made from October to December, by railroad, to Little Rock at $2 per bale, and by water to New Orleans.

JEFFERSON.

Population: 22,386.—White, 5,331; colored, 17,055.
Area: 870 square miles.—Woodland, all; yellow-loam region, 425 square miles; alluvial, 445 square miles.
Tilled lands: 72,141 acres.—Area planted in cotton, 45,426 acres; in corn, 16,839 acres; in oats, 398 acres; in wheat, 32 acres.
Cotton production: 31,588 bales; average cotton product per acre, 0.76 bale, 1,140 pounds seed-cotton, or 380 pounds cotton lint.

The Arkansas river divides Jefferson county into two parts, and its broad bottom lands, with those of the creeks and bayous, occupy a large proportion of the area. The surface of the uplands is rather level, well timbered chiefly with pine, and is designated as pine-hill lands. Oak and hickory form a part of the timber growth. These uplands, covered with a sandy soil about 6 inches deep, are usually dark gray in color, underlaid by a red clay subsoil. They lie on both sides of the river bottoms, and do not seem to be very productive, yielding 600 pounds of seed-cotton when fresh, and less after several years' cultivation.

The river bottom lands are among the richest in the state, and comprise dark alluvial loams of great depth, stiff reddish or chocolate-colored clays or "buckshot" lands, and what is known as oak and sweet-gum lands, differing from the latter in being lighter colored, more porous, and less tenacious, warmer, inducing a more rapid growth, and when plowed not forming clods. This light-colored soil is underlaid by red ferruginous clay. There are also extensive canebrakes along the river. The bottom lands are said to produce an average of 2,000 pounds of seed-cotton or 50 to 70 bushels of corn per acre. The average of the lands in cultivation is 82.9 acres per square mile. The chief crops are cotton, corn, potatoes, and a small acreage in oats and wheat. The acreage in cotton is greater than in any other county of the state, and comprises 63 per cent. of the tilled lands, with an average of 52.2 acres per square mile, ranking third in the state, or below Phillips and Lee. Phillips county alone produced in 1879 a greater number of bales, but in product per acre Jefferson is below Chicot, Desha, and Mississippi counties, or fourth in the state.

ABSTRACT OF THE REPORTS OF THOMAS DUNNINGTON AND S. H. COCKRELL, PINE BLUFF.

The Arkansas river runs through Jefferson county, alluvial bottom lands lying on both sides of the river. The lands embrace sandy soils, buckshot clays, and a compound of the two. The creeks are called bayous here, and have narrow but very productive bottom lands. They give value to the hill lands. The uplands are hilly and rolling, and are watered by numerous creeks. Corn, cotton, and vegetables are the principal crops of the region.

The chief soils devoted to the cultivation of cotton are: 1. The river bottoms, which are alluvial, 20 feet in depth, and very productive; 2. The bayou bottoms, back from the river, narrow, occurring in small bodies, and 12 feet in depth; 3. The rolling hill lands, with clayey and sandy soil, from 3 to 15 inches deep.

The *alluvial bottoms*, comprising about one-third of the county area, extend east and west the whole length of the county and north and south about one-fourth of the distance. The timber growth is cottonwood, cypress, pine, oak, gum, ash, and hickory. The soil is fine and coarse sandy loam, grayish to blackish in color, with a heavier subsoil. It is easy to till in any season, in both well- and ill-drained, and is best adapted to cotton, which is usually from 3 to 6 feet in height, but is most productive at from 3 to 4 feet. When the season is very wet, the plant inclines to run to weed, for which there is no effective remedy, although cutting the side roots with a plow and topping help to restrain it. The seed-cotton product from fresh land is 2,000 pounds; 1,545 pounds in dry and 1,720 pounds in wet seasons make a 475-pound bale of lint, which rates No. 1, and has no superior. After twenty years' cultivation the seed-cotton product per acre is from 1,200 to 1,500 pounds, 1,600 pounds of which make a 475-pound bale of lint. The buckshot land has no weeds or grass; sandy land is most troubled with crab-grass and tie-vine (morning-glory). About one-fourth of this land lies "turned out", and produces very well when again cultivated.

The *hill land* (or *pine woods*), comprising from one-half to two-thirds of the county's area, is rolling, and occurs on all sides of the alluvial land. This land has a natural timber growth of pine, oak, ash, hickory, and elm. The soil is sandy, with a depth of from 4 to 6 inches; the subsoil is a yellow and red clay. The soil is not difficult to till when wet, but when dry is not easy, is late, cold, and ill-drained, and is well adapted to corn, oats, peas, vegetables, and sweet potatoes. Manuring with lot manure and cotton-seed has an excellent effect. About one-fourth of the crops is cotton, which grows usually from 2½ to 3 feet in height. The plant is not much inclined to run to weed on this soil, although very wet seasons and manuring will cause it to do so. The seed-cotton product from fresh land is from 500 to 600 pounds, and from 1,720 to 1,785 pounds make a 475-pound bale of lint, which rates very well. After six years the product declines, and the amount necessary for a 475-pound bale of lint increases a little, the staple comparing very well with that from fresh land. Hog-weed, rag-weed, and grass are the most troublesome. About one-sixth of these lands lie "turned out", which produce very well when again cultivated. The lands do not wash readily on the slopes. This county is too far north for the caterpillar, is above the overflow, and away from the Gulf storms. Frost in April and in October allows six months generally, and often seven months, for the cotton-plant to grow and mature. The hill lands and bayou bottoms are well adapted to the white race.

Shipments are made, during October, November, and December, by railroad and river, to New Orleans at $1 50 and to Memphis at $1 25 per bale.

Remarks by Sterling H. Cockrell.—The Arkansas valley is a fine cotton region, having a railroad from its mouth to the Indian territory. The river and bayou bottoms are very productive, and the rolling hill lands grow grass for stock. These are termed pine hills, to distinguish them from the bottoms. The hills are best for whites because of malaria. Negroes are not affected by such diseases, and consequently live comfortably on the bottoms.

RED-LOAM REGION.

(Includes part of the counties of Pike, Sevier,* Howard,* Clark,* all of Polk, Montgomery, Garland, part of Hot Springs, Saline, Pulaski, all of Perry, Yell, Scott, Sebastian, Logan, Conway, Faulkner, White, part of Lonoke,* Prairie,* Jackson,* and Independence,* all of Van Buren, Pope, Johnson, Franklin, Crawford, Washington, nearly all of Benton, and a part of Madison,* Newton,* Searcy,* and Stone.*)

PIKE.

Population: 6,345.—White, 5,951; colored, 394.
Area: 620 square miles.—Woodland, all; red-loam region, 415 square miles; yellow-loam region, 205 square miles.
Tilled lands: 26,628 acres.—Area planted in cotton, 7,341 acres; in corn, 11,604 acres; in oats, 1,232 acres; in wheat, 2,032 acres.
Cotton production: 3,787 bales; average cotton product per acre, 0.52 bale, 780 pounds seed-cotton, or 260 pounds cotton lint.

The northern part of Pike county, from a few miles north of Murfreesboro', is hilly and somewhat mountainous, the rocks being mostly sandstones and millstone grit, interspersed with areas of metamorphic rocks. The southern part is more level, and comprises the rolling table-lands of the region of the Cretaceous limestones and marls, with their black sandy and stiff calcareous soils.

The soils of the northern part are rocky and sandy, interspersed with large tracts of red lands at the head of Antoine creek, on the northeast, and north of Bear Creek mountain, extending west to the Little Missouri, Muddy river, and the Saline in Howard county. At Plaster bluff, on the Little Missouri, on sections 29 and 30, township 8 south, range 25 west, are valuable beds of gypsum from 15 inches to 15 feet in thickness, associated with limestone and red clays. South of Murfreesboro' there is another small tract of metamorphic rocks.

The Cretaceous rocks of the southern part of the county are largely covered with clays, gravel, and sand of later formations, the characteristic black calcareous lands appearing only in limited areas. Pine and oak form the prevailing timber growth of this region. The soils are underlaid by red clay subsoils, and yield an average of from 700 to 800 pounds of seed-cotton per acre. The Cretaceous marls that are found here would probably serve as valuable stimulants and aids to increased productiveness on these sandy lands, containing, as they do, over 20 per cent. of carbonate of lime.

Cultivated lands average 42.9 acres per square mile, or 6.7 per cent. of the area. The crops comprise corn, cotton, oats, wheat, and potatoes, the acreage of corn being the greatest. The acreage of cotton is 27.6 per cent. of the lands under cultivation, and averages 11.8 acres per square mile, and much less than in some of the northern counties of the state. Its product per acre is less than that of the state at large.

SEVIER.
(See " Yellow-loam region ".)

HOWARD.
(See " Yellow-loam region ".)

CLARK.
(See " Yellow-loam region.")

POLK.

Population: 5,857.—White, 5,792; colored, 65.
Area: 945 square miles.—Woodland, nearly all; all red-loam region.
Tilled lands: 23,815 acres.—Area planted in cotton, 4,230 acres; in corn, 10,616 acres; in oats, 1,416 acres; in wheat, 2,424 acres.
Cotton production: 2,061 bales; average cotton product per acre, 0.49 bale, 735 pounds seed-cotton, or 245 pounds cotton lint.

Polk county, bordered on the west by the Indian territory, is exceedingly mountainous on the north and hilly and broken over the rest of its surface. The northern boundary is marked by a high range of mountains, while south of Dallas, the county-seat, the Cossitot chain traverses the county. These mountains are formed largely of metamorphic strata, very much upturned, and have altitudes reaching to 1,000 feet or more. In the ascent of Hanna mountain immense parallel walls of quartzite and chalcedonic chert and dull, milky, cherty quartz, etc., may be followed running up the flanks of the mountain, with deep ravines of loose, crumbled, incoherent shales between, which are almost inaccessible. These shales, disintegrating rapidly, are finding their way from the higher situations into the valleys. On the south the ridges of sandstone and millstone grit are of less elevation than in the center of the county.

The lands of the county vary from gray and gravelly to red sandy and clayey. The latter are derived from the red shales, and have a timber growth of red, black, white, and post oaks, dogwood, walnut, wild cherry, elm, pine, and hickory. The average population of the county is about six persons, and that of tilled lands 25.2 acres per square mile, the latter being a less number than in any other county of the state, except Montgomery and Poinsett. Corn, cotton, wheat, oats, and potatoes are the chief crops, the acreage of corn being greatest, that of cotton comprising 17.8 per cent. of the lands under cultivation, and averaging only 4.5 acres per square mile.

MONTGOMERY.

Population : 5,729.—White, 5,471; colored, 258.
Area : 840 square miles.—Woodland, nearly all; all red-loam region.
Tilled lands : 19,656 acres.—Area planted in cotton, 3,512 acres; in corn, 9,629 acres; in oats, 825 acres; in wheat, 3,023 acres.
Cotton production : 1,819 bales; average cotton product per acre, 0.52 bale, 780 pounds seed-cotton, or 260 pounds cotton lint.

The surface of Montgomery county is hilly and mountainous, and is well timbered. The Ouachita river flows through the northern part in an easterly course, while Caddo creek and other tributaries water the southern portion.

The range of Crystal mountains lies east and west, south of Mount Ida, the county-seat, and is formed of sandstones. "Almost every fissure of this vast sandstone formation for a distance of 1 to 2 miles in length and from three-quarters to 1 mile in width is lined with these crystal brilliants (quartz), which, exposed in bursting open the crevices of the rock, glitter and flash in the sun's rays like a diadem" (*Owen*).

There are areas of metamorphic rocks in the county comprising chloritic slates, etc., and some minerals have been found. The upland soils are mostly dark sandy loams, somewhat gravelly, with red-clay subsoils. The timber growth is pine, red oak, hickory, dogwood, sassafras, etc. The soil is durable, and yields an average of 1,000 pounds of seed-cotton per acre. The most fertile portion of the county is said to be in Caddo cove, on the southwest, where much limestone appears.

The surface of the county is sparsely populated, with an average of nearly 7 persons per square mile. Its average of tilled lands is less than in any other county in the state except Poinsett, comprising 3.7 per cent. of the area, and averaging 23.4 acres per square mile. The crops are corn, cotton, wheat, oats, and potatoes, the first named having the largest acreage. Cotton comprises 17.9 per cent. of the lands in cultivation, and averages but 4.2 acres per square mile. The product per acre is less than that of the state at large.

ABSTRACT OF THE REPORT OF G. WHITTINGTON, MOUNT IDA.

The lowlands consist of first bottom lands of South Fork creek and the Ouachita river. The uplands are rolling and level table-lands well timbered.

The lands devoted to the cultivation of cotton are the mahogany uplands, mostly level, the black loam of the south fork of the Ouachita river, and the light upland timbered lands. The most important is the *mahogany or hickory upland*, extending in each direction about 25 miles, and having a natural timber growth of pine, hickory, red oak, ash, walnut, dogwood, and sassafras.

The soil is a silty and gravelly loam, clayey in places, varying in color from brown or mahogany to blackish or black, and is 18 inches in depth. The subsoil is heavier than the soil, with which it assimilates when turned up. It is red in color, mixed with gravel, contains hard white gravel and angular and rounded pebbles, and is underlaid by gravel and slate rock at 6 feet. The soil is cultivated with difficulty in all seasons, is early and warm, and is best adapted to corn and wheat. The chief crops of the region are cotton, corn, wheat, and oats. One-tenth of the tillable area is devoted to cotton, which grows to a height of 4 feet and runs to weed on all lands of the county in long-continued wet weather, no remedy being known that will restrain it. The yield from fresh land, or from that which has been under cultivation (unmanured) for twenty years, is 1,000 pounds of seed-cotton per acre. Fourteen hundred and twenty-five pounds are required, either from fresh or old lands, for 475 pounds of good ordinary lint. Crab-grass and cocklebur are the most troublesome weeds on all lands of the county. None of the land lies "turned out". The soil washes slightly on slopes, but the damage done is not of a serious nature; neither are the valleys injured by the washings.

The *Ouachita river bottom lands* extend east and west about 20 miles, and have a natural timber growth of water, overcup, and bur oaks, walnut, elm, ash, and mulberry. The soil is a sandy loam, clayey in places, blackish to black in color, and 4 feet in depth. The subsoil, which is heavier than the surface soil, consists of a yellowish, impervious clay hard-pan, containing rounded and angular pebbles, and overlies gravel and slate rock at 10 feet. The land is easily tilled in all seasons, is early, warm, and well-drained, and is best adapted to corn. Cotton, forming one-fifth of the crops planted, grows to a height of 5 feet, and yields from fresh land 1,200 pounds, and from land after twenty years' cultivation (unmanured) from 1,000 to 1,200 pounds of seed-cotton per acre, 1,435 pounds being required, either from fresh or old lands, for a 475-pound bale of lint rating as good ordinary.

The *light-timbered upland* and *second-bottom lands* have a natural timber growth of white and post oaks, pine, elm, and sweet gum. The soil is a fine sandy, gravelly loam, clayey and putty-like in places, which varies in color from whitish or gray to orange-red, and is from 1 to 2 feet in depth. The subsoil varies very much in character, is heavier than the soil, and consists, in different places, of a stiff, yellow, impervious clay, a white clay, and a gravelly cement which usually makes a kind of hard-pan, or it is rocky. Gravel and rock are found at from 2 to 6 feet. The land is difficult to till in all seasons, is late and cold, and, when fresh, is best adapted to cotton, corn, and wheat, but when old best adapted to cotton only. About one-fourth of the crops planted is in cotton, which grows to a height of 3 feet.

611

The yield per acre in seed-cotton from fresh land is 800 pounds, and 600 pounds after twenty years' cultivation (unmanured), 1,425 pounds being necessary for 475 pounds of good ordinary lint, either from fresh or old lands. There is considerable washing of the soil on slopes, doing no serious damage, and benefiting the valleys.

The cotton crop is badly injured by early frosts after a wet, late season, especially in the rich bottom lands.

Cotton is shipped to Hot Springs, and thence by rail to market.

GARLAND.

Population: 9,023.—White, 7,457; colored, 1,566.

Area: 580 square miles.—Woodland all; all red-loam region.

Tilled lands: 16,748 acres.—Area planted in cotton, 993 acres; in corn, 8,785 acres; in oats, 1,281 acres; in wheat, 1,445 acres.

Cotton production: 534 bales; average cotton product per acre, 0.54 bale, 810 pounds seed-cotton, or 270 pounds cotton lint.

Garland county has a rough and broken surface, which is hilly or mountainous in places and well timbered. The celebrated place of resort, the Hot Springs, is situated in this county, in a valley on the south side of Whetstone mountain. These springs come from the sides of the mountain, and have temperatures varying from 100° to 147° F., the greater number being above 120°. The mountain is composed mostly of different varieties of novaculite rock, which is quarried extensively for whetstones. The height of the mountain is about 500 feet above the valley, with a trend very nearly northeast and southwest, and is covered with a timber growth of pine, oak, hickory, and dogwood. On the south side of the Ouachita river there is a complete labyrinth of high ridges, composed of quartz and novaculite. The county is watered by the tributaries of Saline river on the northeast, and by the Ouachita river and its tributaries in the central and southern portions. The lands of the east and south are mostly light and sandy, while those of the north and west are said to be darker and stiff, with more clay in their composition. The yield of seed-cotton per acre averages about 800 pounds. The average of tilled lands is 28.9 acres per square mile, less than in any other county except Perry, Polk, Montgomery, and Poinsett. The chief crops are corn, oats, wheat, and cotton, the acreage of cotton being less than that of any one of the others, and also less than in any of the other counties of the region except Washington and Benton. The average of that crop is only 1.7 acres per square mile, while its product per acre is less than for the state at large.

ABSTRACT OF THE REPORT OF JOHN J. SUMPTER, HOT SPRINGS.

The lowlands consist of the first and second bottoms of various small creeks, front-land, back-land, and hummocks, and of the Ouachita and Saline rivers. All varieties of uplands are found in this county, except prairies.

The lands devoted to cotton culture comprise the black sandy loam, the light sandy, the mulatto, and the clay lands. The chief land is the *light sandy,* constituting about two-thirds of the tillable area, extending east and south for many miles; but north and west the soil becomes tough and tight with dark color, and there are indications of rock near the surface. The natural timber growth is hickory, ash, cherry, walnut, black locust, linn, gum, pine, and various kinds of oaks. The soil is a light sandy loam, clayey in places, 10 feet deep in the lowlands and 18 inches in the uplands; and as the land is nearly all new, there is very little subsoiling done, but when reached it presents a dark appearance, and inclines to crumble and become very hard when exposed to the sun. This soil is underlaid by gravel and large rocks at from 2 to 6 feet. The soil is easily cultivated in all seasons, is early when well drained, and is best adapted to corn and cotton. The chief crops of the region are corn, cotton, cereals generally, and grapes.

About one-third of the cultivated area is devoted to cotton, which grows to a height of 4 feet on the uplands, and from 5 to 7 feet on the lowlands. In wet seasons and on new lands the plant inclines to run to weed, for which topping or clipping the top branches in August is the remedy. Fifteen hundred pounds of seed-cotton is the yield per acre from fresh land, 1,545 of which are necessary for a 475-pound bale of lint. After the land has been under cultivation (unmanured) for five years the yield is reduced in the uplands to 800 pounds and in lowlands to 1,200 pounds per acre. The same amount is necessary for a 475-pound bale of lint as in case of fresh land, but the staple rates one grade lower. Crab-grass is the only troublesome weed. About 1 per cent. of the land lies "turned out", being greatly improved by the rest; but it would require many years to restore the soil to its original strength and power of production. The soil washes on slopes, seriously injuring the uplands, but improving the valleys to the extent of the amount washed down. Very little effort has been made to check the damage, though those efforts have been attended with success.

Occasionally heavy rains in the spring prevent early planting and the crop is injured by frost. This applies to all lands of the county, but more particularly to the lowlands and lands having very rich soils, as the richer the soil the larger the weed and the later the crop is maturing.

Cotton is sold as fast as baled to home merchants, and they ship it to Saint Louis, Memphis, New Orleans, and New York.

HOT SPRING.

Population: 7,775.—White, 7,030; colored, 745.

Area: 690 square miles.—Woodland, all; red-loam region, 550 square miles; yellow-loam region, 140 square miles.

Tilled lands: 30,537 acres.—Area planted in cotton, 8,008 acres; in corn, 13,002 acres; in oats, 910 acres; in wheat, 1,377 acres.

Cotton production: 3,755 bales; average cotton product per acre, 0.47 bale, 705 pounds seed-cotton, or 235 pounds cotton lint.

Hot Spring county is mostly a rolling and hilly county, well timbered, and is watered almost entirely by the Ouachita river and its tributaries. The southeastern part, included in the yellow-loam region of the southern part of the state, has its sandy soils, varying from gray to red, underlaid by red subsoils and the clays and sands of the Tertiary formation, and is well timbered. This region extends a few miles beyond Malvern, the county-seat.

Northward, the rest of the county is included in the sandstone and metamorphic region of the state, and the rocks of the latter formation seem to form a more prominent feature than in some of the counties adjoining. The lands are sandy and gravelly, with red clays on the slopes, and are said to be underlaid largely by novaculite and other rocks. The uplands are timbered with white, red, post, and black oaks, pine, hickory, gums, etc., and are said to produce about 800 pounds of seed-cotton per acre.

Magnet cove, in the extreme northern part of the county, is a notable place. "This cove, though the area is not very extensive nor yet very elevated, seems to be the center of the igneous action of Hot Spring and Garland counties. The igneous rocks occupy the depressed portions of the cove and the lower subordinate ridges. The higher ridges, by which the cove is bounded on the north, are composed, in great part, of novaculite rock. South of the cove a great wall of true novaculite runs into the Ouachita river" (Owen). There is probably no portion of Arkansas that affords a greater variety of minerals. The center and southern part of the cove is said to be a fine agricultural region.

The average of the lands in cultivation is 44.3 acres per square mile, or 6.9 per cent. of the area. Of the crops corn has the largest acreage, cotton being second, with an average of 11.7 acres per square mile, and comprising 26.4 per cent. of the tilled lands. There are but twelve counties in the state having a less product per acre.

The lowlands consist of the alluvial plain of Saline river and the back-land, cypress swamps, pine flats, and hummocks of the Ouachita river. The uplands vary greatly in character, and occur in bodies of from 20 to 150 acres.

The soils devoted to the cultivation of cotton comprise the black sandy and the red clay soils lying on slopes and enriched by washes, the deep black bottom of the Ouachita river not always above overflow, and the light sandy and gravelly soil, adapted to fruits, grasses, etc. The chief soil is the black sandy and red clay upland, which extends in each direction about 5 or 6 miles, and has a natural timber growth of yellow pine, white, red, black, and post oaks, hickory, and sweet and black gum. The soil is a fine sandy, gravelly loam, clayey in places, which varies greatly in color and is 18 inches deep. Its subsoil is heavier and leachy, and when first exposed bakes hard, but becomes pliable after cultivation, and contains yellow gravel and pebbles, underlaid by sand, gravel, and rock at 15 feet.

The land is easily tilled in dry seasons, is early, warm, and well drained, and is best adapted to cotton and corn, which, with oats and sweet potatoes, constitute the chief crops of the region. About one-half the cultivated area is devoted to cotton, which grows to a height of 3 feet, being most productive at 2½ feet. When planted late, and in very wet weather, the plant inclines to run to weed, for which topping about 6 inches in August is the remedy. The product per acre in seed-cotton from fresh land is 800 pounds, and 750 pounds after three years' cultivation (unmanured); 1,485 pounds from fresh lands are required for 475 pounds of low middling lint, and 1,425 pounds from old lands, and the lint rates better. Crab-grass and hog-weed are the most troublesome weeds. No land lies "turned out". The soil washes on slopes, but the damage is not of a serious nature, and the valleys are made 50 per cent. richer by the washing. Horizontalizing and hillside ditching are practiced, and are attended with very good success.

The gravelly and clay lands, covering about two-thirds of the surface of the county, occur in each direction from 2 to 20 miles, and have a natural timber growth of pine and oak. The soil is gravelly or clay loam, adobe in places, is yellow, brown, or mahogany in color, and 1 foot in depth. The subsoil is heavier than the surface soil, is leachy, and consists of a loose clay mixed with pebbles, and also contains hard white gravel. Sand, gravel, and rock are found at 5 feet. The land is difficult to till at all times, and is early and well drained. Cotton forms about one-half of the crops planted, which grows to a height of from 2 to 3 feet, but is most productive at 2½ feet. The plant inclines to run to weed where the land is fresh and the weather is wet, and is prevented by "bedding" high. The yield per acre from fresh land in seed-cotton is 700 pounds, 1,425 of which are necessary for 475 pounds of low middling lint. After three years' cultivation (unmanured) the product is 600 pounds per acre; from 1,425 to 1,545 pounds are then required for a 475-pound bale of lint, which rates better than that from fresh land. Very little land lies "turned out". After two or three years' rest it is much improved. There is no washing of the soil on slopes, as there is too much gravel on them.

The low black and bottom lands comprise about one-eighth of the cultivated area, and extend in each direction from 1 to 15 miles. The natural timber growth is oak and sweet and black gums. The soil is gravelly or clayey in places, from brown to blackish or black in color, and 6 inches deep. The subsoil is heavier, of a deep black color, baking hard until exposed to the air. Sand is found at 12 feet. The land is tilled with difficulty in dry seasons, is early, and in some portions is well drained, in others ill-drained. Only a small part of the cultivated area is devoted to cotton, which attains a height of from 4 to 7 feet, running to weed in wet weather. Planting early is practiced to prevent it. From 1,500 to 1,700 pounds is the product per acre in seed-cotton either from fresh land or from land after three years' cultivation (unmanured), 1,485 pounds from fresh and 1,425 pounds from old lands being required for 475 pounds of lint, rating as middling in the former case and higher in the latter. Rag-, hog-, and horse-weeds and crab-grass are the most troublesome weeds on this soil. No land lies "turned out". The medium uplands are preferred for cotton, though the lowlands produce very well, especially if the season is late, so that the bolls are not injured by the frost. Within the last few years the county has greatly improved in the way of farming, as there seems to be greater interest taken in the manner of cultivating the soil, so as to obtain the best results. Old farms are better cultivated, and new ones are being dotted all over the county.

Cotton is shipped, in October, November, and December, by railroad to Saint Louis at the rate of $2 50 per bale.

SALINE.

Population: 8,953.—White, 7,586; colored, 1,367.

Area: 690 square miles.—Woodland, all; red-loam region, 540 square miles; yellow-loam region, 150 square miles.

Tilled lands: 35,604 acres.—Area planted in cotton, 8,846 acres; in corn, 15,821 acres; in oats, 2,802 acres; in wheat, 1,454 acres.

Cotton production: 5,075 bales; average cotton product per acre, 0.57 bale, 855 pounds seed-cotton, or 285 pounds cotton lint.

Saline county includes the greater part of the headwaters of Saline river, which flows in a southeast course. The surface of the country is rolling and hilly, and is well timbered. The southern yellow-loam and pine region, with its red and gray sandy soils, Tertiary clays, conglomerates, sandstones, and underlying lignites, is represented in a small area on the extreme south. Its growth is chiefly pine, oak, and hickory.

Northwestward through the county there are small areas occupied by crystalline or metamorphic rocks among the limestones and rocks of other formations. A granite outcrop appears near the center of the county, bearing northeast and southwest, with a width of about 1 mile and a length of 4 miles. Sandstone, with veins of white quartz, dikes, or walls of quartz several feet thick, talcose and chloritic slates, alum slates, etc., are found in various parts of the county.

The lowlands, or first and second bottoms of Saline river and tributaries, are broad, and comprise a large part of the area of the county. The soil is chiefly a dark sandy loam, well supplied with potash, lime, and phosphoric acid, and has a timber growth of large white, red, and black oaks, sweet and black gum, elm, hickory, etc. These lands yield about 1,500 pounds of seed-cotton per acre.

The average of lands under cultivation is 51.6 acres per square mile, or 8.1 per cent. of the county area. Corn is the chief crop. Cotton has an acreage embracing 24.8 per cent. of the tilled lands, and averaging 12.8 acres per square mile. In product per acre it has almost the average for the state at large.

Cotton is shipped, by rail or river, to Memphis, Saint Louis, or New Orleans.

PULASKI.

Population: 32,616.—White, 17,667; colored, 14,949.

Area: 810 square miles.—Woodland, all; red-loam region, 580 square miles; yellow-loam region, 110 square miles; alluvial, 120 square miles.

Tilled lands: 73,019 acres.—Area planted in cotton, 29,097 acres; in corn, 20,843 acres; in oats, 2,199 acres; in wheat, 1,076 acres.

Cotton production: 20,439 bales; average cotton product per acre, 0.70 bale, 1,050 pounds seed-cotton, or 350 pounds cotton lint.

The surface of Pulaski county is hilly and broken, well timbered, and watered by the Arkansas river and its tributaries. One of the highest points of the county is a conical peak known as "the Pinnacle", with a height of 770 feet above the Arkansas river, the summit of which is of hard sandstone of the millstone-grit formation. On the extreme southeast there is a small area covered with the sands, clays, and rocks of the southern yellow-loam region, with its growth of short-leaf pine, oak, and hickory, and with beds of Tertiary marls and limestones. The rest of the county is largely metamorphic in character, areas of granite and other rocks being interspersed among those of the millstone-grit formation. Valuable minerals are found in the county, the most important workings being the Kellogg silver-lead mines, 10 miles north of Little Rock, in which are associated argentiferous galena, copper pyrites, spathic iron, zincblende, etc. The veins of these minerals are said to occupy a belt of country from north to south of more than half a mile, and the whole system of quartz veins and tilted strata of which they form a part must have a width in the same direction exceeding 12 miles. Several assays of the ore proved it to be very rich in silver.

The uplands of the county have mostly dark sandy soils and subsoils and a timber growth of black and post oaks and hickory. The granitic lands south of Little Rock are light gray in color, and have a timber growth of red, black, and white oaks, black and pig-nut hickories, dogwood, and maple. They are said to produce an average of 25 bushels of corn and 30 bushels of wheat per acre.

The chief agricultural lands of the county are the bottoms of the Arkansas river, which comprise a first or front-land bottom of the river sandy loam along the borders of the river and a second bottom or back-land of stiffer and black buckshot loam, lying back from the river. The timber growth of these bottoms is cottonwood, hackberry, elm, sweet gum, ash, hickory, etc. The lands yield from 1,500 to 2,500 pounds of seed-cotton per acre. The tilled lands average 90.1 acres per square mile, the county ranking thirteenth in the state. Cotton is the chief crop, with an acreage larger than corn, averaging 35.9 acres per square mile, and is surpassed by but six counties in the state. Its average product per acre is also greater than in any county except Chicot, Desha, Mississippi, and Jefferson.

ABSTRACT OF THE REPORT OF WALTER WITTENBERG, LITTLE ROCK.

The lowlands of the county, comprising the first and second alluvial bottoms and cypress swamps of the Arkansas river, are from 1 to 20 miles wide. The soil of the front-land is sandy loam; that of the back-land a buckshot clay. The uplands, with a peaty and mulatto soil, are hilly and rolling, and vary from one hill to another; the bottoms of small streams are from one-fourth to three-fourths of a mile wide; the valleys vary in area from 20 to 500 acres. The chief crops of the region are cotton, corn, oats, hay, potatoes, and grapes.

The soils cultivated in cotton are the river bottoms, producing from one to two bales of lint per acre, the uplands producing from one-half to three-fourths of a bale, and the creek bottoms about the same yield as the uplands.

The river bottoms comprise about one-third of the area of the county, and extend along the Arkansas river, from the Indian territory to its mouth. The timber growth is cottonwood, hackberry, elm, sweet gum, oak, hickory, etc. The soil varies from a fine sandy loam to a coarse sandy and gravelly; the color is gray to black, with an average depth of 3 feet. The alluvial river bottoms are from 10 to 100 feet in depth. The subsoil is clay, containing flint and rocks and "black gravel" and other pebbles, underlaid by rock at from 3 to 100 feet. The soil is easy to till in all seasons, and is best adapted to cotton, corn, and potatoes. About three-fourths of such land is planted in cotton, which usually grows 5 feet in height, and runs to weed in extremely wet weather. The product is from one to two bales per acre, 1,660 pounds of seed-cotton making a 475-pound bale of lint, rating No. 1, or Orleans best. After fifty years the yield is one bale, which rates the same as that from fresh land; 1,780 pounds seed-cotton then make a 475-pound bale of lint. Cocklebur and careless weeds are the most troublesome on this soil. None of this land lies "turned out". Underdraining is beneficial.

Our heavy crops are raised on river lands, and with plenty of rain we have no cause for failure of a cotton crop.

Cotton is shipped, during the whole of the year, by rail and boat, to New York at $5, and to New Orleans at $2 per bale.

PERRY.

Population: 3,872.—White, 3,072; colored, 800.

Area: 580 square miles.—Woodland, nearly all; all red-loam region.

Tilled land: 15,706 acres.—Area planted in cotton, 5,082 acres; in corn, 6,469 acres; in oats, 842 acres; in wheat, 561 acres.

Cotton production: 3,314 bales; average cotton product per acre, 0.65 bale, 975 pounds seed-cotton, or 325 pounds cotton lint.

614

The surface of Perry county is hilly, somewhat mountainous and broken, and is largely timbered. Open prairies occur occasionally, interspersed with prominent hills and skirts of timber. Arkansas river forms the northeastern boundary of the county, while the Fourche la Fave traverses the middle portion from west to east. The Petit Jean range of mountains, in the northern part of the county, has an elevation of from 500 to 800 feet above the general level of the country, gradually declining westward into Yell county, where it loses itself as a conspicuous landmark. The summits of the mountains and hills are formed of sandstones, underlaid by shales, etc., and have a timber growth of pine. The timbered lands of the county have usually sandy soils, with reddish clay subsoils, and have a growth of red, post, black, and other oaks, hickory, etc. The prairies are small and their soils stiff, and are underlaid by red, impervious clays, derived from the shales. The bottom lands of both the Arkansas and Fourche la Fave are broad, and are heavily timbered with walnut, ash, cottonwood, hickory, hackberry, etc., and very productive, yielding from 1,500 to 2,000 pounds of seed-cotton per acre. An almost unbroken pinery stretches along the latter stream to the hills. The county is sparsely populated, with an average of nearly 7 persons per square mile, the tilled lands averaging 27.1 acres, Polk, Montgomery, and Poinsett alone having a less number. Corn is the chief crop. Cotton has an average of 8.8 acres only per square mile, but its rank in product per acre in the state is twelfth.

YELL.

Population: 13,852.—White, 12,733; colored, 1,119.
Area: 900 square miles.—Woodland and prairies; all red-loam region.
Tilled lands: 55,229 acres.—Area planted in cotton, 16,598 acres; in corn, 22,791 acres; in oats, 2,654 acres; in wheat, 5,954 acres.
Cotton production: 10,428 bales; average cotton product per acre, 0.63 bale, 945 pounds seed-cotton, or 315 pounds cotton lint.

The surface of Yell county is hilly and broken, comprising both timbered and open prairie lands, and is bordered on the northeast by the Arkansas river. There are several mountain ranges traversing the county from west to east, the summits of which are composed of the sandstones of the millstone-grit formation, underlaid by shales, which give character to the greater part of the soils. The general level of the mountains is over 500 feet above that of the surrounding country, and some points are over 800 feet, the highest summits being covered with a pine growth. The lands of the county are generally sandy, with reddish clay subsoils, timbered with red, post, and other oaks, hickory, etc. The better class of these lands are said to yield from 600 to 800 pounds of seed-cotton per acre.

The prairie lands are usually stiff, and are underlaid by red impervious clays, derived from the shales, but are not much in cultivation.

The river lands are broad, and are the most productive in the county. They comprise the usual red and dark loams of the first and second bottoms, respectively, and have a timber growth of walnut, pecan, ash, cottonwood, hackberry, etc., and are said to yield from one to two bales of cotton lint, or 1,500 to 2,000 pounds of seed-cotton per acre.

The average of lands under cultivation is 61.4 acres, or 9.6 per cent. of the county area. Corn, cotton, wheat, oats, etc., are the chief crops, corn having the largest acreage. The area devoted to the culture of cotton is 18.4 acres per square mile, the county ranking eleventh in the region, or in its total acreage fourth in the region. Three counties of the region each produce a greater number of bales. Seventeen counties in the state have each a higher average product per acre than Yell.

SCOTT.

Population: 9,174.—White, 9,085; colored, 89.
Area: 920 square miles.—Woodland and prairies; all red-loam region.
Tilled lands: 30,621 acres.—Area planted in cotton, 8,867 acres; in corn, 15,435 acres; in oats, 2,345 acres; in wheat, 1,956 acres.
Cotton production: 4,826 bales; average cotton product per acre, 0.54 bale, 810 pounds seed-cotton, or 270 pounds cotton lint.

The surface of Scott county is rolling and broken, with mountain chains on the north and south. A dividing ridge passes through from northeast to southwest, the streams on the northwest flowing into the Indian territory, those on the southeast being tributaries of the Arkansas river and flowing eastward.

There are open prairies on the northeast, with red-loam lands; but otherwise the county is reported to be well timbered with black, red, and post oaks, hickory, etc. The soils of the uplands are mostly sandy, mulatto, or chocolate in color, underlaid by clays, and are chiefly derived from the shales, etc., of the millstone grit formation. The lands are very productive, yielding from 1,200 to 1,500 pounds of seed-cotton per acre. The prairie lands above mentioned belong to the western red-loam region.

The average of tilled lands is 33.3 acres per square mile, or but 5.2 per cent. of the area. The crops are corn, cotton, oats, wheat, etc., the average of corn being the greatest. Cotton averages but 9.6 acres per square mile (as in Baxter county, on the Missouri line), and the average yield per acre is much below that of the state at large.

ABSTRACT OF THE REPORT OF WILLIAM B. TURMAN, WALDRON.

The lowlands of the county comprise the first bottom or front-land of the Arkansas and Potean rivers and creeks, and are sandy alluvial plains. The uplands are rolling table-lands.

The chief crops of the region are corn, cotton, wheat, and rye. The chief cotton soils are the sandy bottom, the sandy upland, and the clayey bottom land of creeks.

The *upland or mulatto soil* comprises two-thirds of the county, extending 4 miles north, 8 miles east, 3 miles south, and 20 miles west, and has a growth of black, red, and post oaks, hickory, ash, walnut, hackberry, linden, and cherry. The soil is a fine sandy or clayey loam, yellow, brown, or black in color, 15 inches deep, with a heavier gravelly and clayey yellow and orange-red subsoil, which contains soft "black gravel" and rounded pebbles, underlaid by gravel and rock at 10 feet. The soil is moderately easy to till in wet seasons, easy and pleasant when dry; is early, warm, and well-drained, and best adapted to corn, cotton, and rye. One-half of it is devoted to cotton, which usually is from 3 to 6 feet in height, but is most productive at from 4 to 4½ feet. Late rains and late plowing inclines the plant to run to weed, for which topping early in August is the remedy. The seed-cotton product per acre from fresh land is 1,500 pounds, 1,480 pounds of which are necessary for a 475-pound bale of good middling lint. After three years' cultivation the yield is 1,200 pounds; about the same amount is necessary to make a 475-pound bale of lint, which rates equal to that from fresh land. Careless weed, cockleburs, and crab-grass are the troublesome weeds. A very small amount of this land lies "turned out", and, when again cultivated produces good crops. These lands do not wash on the slopes.

The *red clay or mahogany soil* comprises one-fourth of the area of the region, and occurs, intermixed with the mulatto and bottom land, in Poteau valley, a distance from east to west of 24 miles, and from north to south of 6 to 10 miles. The natural timber growth is red and black oaks, black hickory, dogwood, and black ash. The soil is a gravelly loam, brown to red in color, and 10 inches deep. The subsoil is a heavier red leachy clay, which contains soft "black gravel", rounded sandstone pebbles, and is underlaid by clay, gravel, and slate rock at 12 feet. The soil is easy to till in all seasons, is early and warm if well drained, and is best adapted to wheat, corn, and cotton, about one-fourth being devoted to the latter crop. The usual and most productive height is 3 feet. Late cultivation, with late rains, inclines the plant to run to weed, which is remedied by topping and shallow cultivation. The product of seed-cotton per acre from fresh land is 1,200 pounds, 1,545 pounds making a 475-pound bale of middling upland lint. After four years the seed-cotton product is about 1,000 pounds per acre, and 1,480 pounds are then necessary for a 475-pound bale of lint, which is not quite equal to that from fresh land. Cockleburs, careless weed, crab-grass, and hog-weed are the most troublesome weeds. A very small amount of this land lies "turned out", and, when again cultivated, is for two years equal to fresh land. These lands do not wash readily on slopes.

The *post oak land* covers about one-tenth of the region, and appears throughout the county in small tracts near the small natural drains, with a timber growth of post oak, ash, elm, and haw. The soil is a gravelly, heavy clay, putty-like, whitish yellow in color, with a depth of 3½ inches. The subsoil is heavier than the soil, is leachy, contains soft "black gravel" and rounded iron-ore pebbles, underlaid by slate rock at 5½ feet. The soil is difficult to till in wet seasons, easy when dry, is late and cold, and is best adapted to oats and rye. Cotton grows usually from 4 to 5 feet in height on this land, runs to weed in a dry summer with good cultivation, which is restrained by topping early in August. The seed-cotton product from fresh land is 750 pounds; 1,790 pounds make a 475-pound bale of lint. After four years the product is reduced from 300 to 500 pounds, and 1,860 pounds make a 475-pound bale of lint equal to that from fresh land. Rag-weed and grass are the troublesome weeds. About one-half of this land lies "turned out", and when again cultivated is not as good as fresh land. The slopes do not wash. Ditching drains this land and increases its productiveness.

Strong, new land causes the cotton plant to grow a greater length of time, thereby subjecting the crop more to early frosts; consequently old bottom or strong upland is chosen for cotton growing.

Shipments are made, as fast as cotton is ginned, by wagon to Fort Smith, Arkansas, at $2 50 per bale.

SEBASTIAN.

Population: 19,560.—White, 17,970; colored, 1,590.
Area: 570 square miles.—Woodland and prairies; all red-loam region.
Tilled lands: 68,595 acres.—Area planted in cotton, 19,722 acres; in corn, 28,283 acres; in oats, 4,378 acres; in wheat, 6,095 acres.
Cotton production: 11,112 bales; average cotton product per acre, 0.56 bale, 840 pounds seed-cotton, or 280 pounds cotton lint.

The surface of Sebastian county is rolling and hilly, and comprises open prairies and tracts of timbered lands, interspersed with high hills destitute of timber growth. A range of mountains borders the county on the south, the Arkansas river forming the northern boundary.

The hills and ridges are mostly formed from the sandstones of the millstone-grit formation, underlaid by the reddish shales, etc., of the Coal Measures. These shales naturally produce reddish, clayey lands, and with the sands from the hills form the brown and red loams of the prairies, underlaid by red clays.

A general feature of the many ridges, as stated in the abstract below, is that, while they are steep on the north side, they have a gradual slope and are well timbered on the south, affording, with their sandy soils and protected position, the chief cotton lands of the county.

The river bottom lands, embracing reddish loam first bottoms and dark loam second bottoms, are broad, and have a timber growth of cottonwood, walnut, pecan, ash, hackberry, oak, hickory, etc., and are said to yield from 1 to 2 bales of lint cotton per acre.

The average of lands under cultivation is 120.3 acres per square mile, a number exceeded only by the counties of Benton, Phillips, and Washington. The acreages of corn, cotton, oats, and wheat are quite large, the first, however, predominating. Cotton has an average of 34.6 acres per square mile, which places the county tenth in the state in this regard, while its product per acre is lower than that of the state at large.

ABSTRACT OF THE REPORT OF T. C. MILLER, DAYTON.

The uplands of the county are rolling and level table-land, part prairie with dark loam soil, watered by the small creeks and tributaries of the Arkansas river. The timbered soil is of a light sandy nature, especially on the south side of ridges, while on the north side the soil is darker and richer in surface deposit.

The chief crops are corn, cotton, oats, millet, wheat, sweet and Irish potatoes, and sorghum. The principal part of the cotton crop of the county is planted on sandy upland lying mostly on the south side of ridges; the remainder is planted on prairie land, and does well, but is a little later.

The chief soil is the sandy upland of slopes, comprising one-third of the cultivated farms, occurring on all the ridges of the county; the north side of these ridges is generally steep, and is heavily timbered with a growth of red and post oaks and hickory.

The soil is fine sandy and coarse gravelly loam, 12 inches deep, with a clay subsoil and hard-pan or gravel bed at from 2 to 3 feet. It contains hard, white, rounded pebbles, and is underlaid by rock at 6 feet. The soil is difficult to till in wet weather, but if the land is stirred it remains mellow. All of the crops of the county do well on this soil, but almost half of it is devoted to cotton, which usually grows 3 or 4 feet high. Wet weather inclines the plant to run to weed, which topping and shallow cultivation restrains. From 800 to 1,200 pounds is the seed-cotton product per acre from fresh land, 1,425 pounds of which make a 475-pound bale of good ordinary lint. After five years' cultivation the yield is 800 pounds per acre, and 1,545 pounds make a 475-pound bale of lint, which rates one grade lower than that from fresh land, as the staple is a little shorter. Crab-grass is the only troublesome weed. None of this land lies "turned out ", as every foot of worn-out land is kept up by manuring. The soil on the slopes does not wash badly, and the valleys are always improved by the washings. Many places in the low land have been raised 3 feet by the washings, and are of excellent character. Many farmers practice plowing horizontally, thereby preventing the washing of the slopes.

Cotton planted on the upland generally matures before frost, except when planted late and on new land. None of the land is here subject to overflow. The streams are small, with narrow, rich productive bottom lands, well adapted to all crops, and yielding from 1,200 to 1,500 pounds of seed-cotton.

Shipments are made, from November to January, by rail to Saint Louis at $1 50 per bale.

LOGAN.

Population : 14,885.—White, 13,901 ; colored, 984.
Area : 670 square miles.—Woodland and prairies; all red-loam region.
Tilled lands: 65,784 acres.—Area planted in cotton, 16,377 acres; in corn, 24,136 acres ; in oats, 3,543 acres; in wheat, 4,376 acres.
Cotton production : 9,752 bales; average cotton product per acre, 0.60 bale, 900 pounds seed-cotton, or 300 pounds cotton lint.

The surface of Logan county is rolling, broken, and somewhat hilly, partly timbered and partly prairie, and is bounded on the north by the Arkansas river. Sandstones cap the hills, and are underlaid by the shales of the millstone grit. The soils of the highlands are sandy, while those of the timbered valleys are reddish loams with red clay subsoils, and have a timber growth of several varieties of oak, hickory, etc. The prairie lands are stiffer in character, with impervious red clay subsoils, and are usually ill-drained. "Haguewood prairie, which skirts the river bottom from the base of the two short mountains southward, is broken, rolling, and fertile, covered with luxuriant grasses and prairie growth, with springs occasionally gushing out, and is underlaid throughout by coal. A large pinery extends from the mouth of Shoal creek to Dardanelle Rock (Yell county), some 18 miles, from 5 to 8 miles wide, and lies immediately along the river all the way" (*Henry*).

The bottom lands of the Arkansas river are the same as given in other counties, viz: Reddish loams along the river and dark sandy loams back from the river, occupying a second terrace or bottom. The timber growth is cottonwood, walnut, ash, pecan, hackberry, oak, etc. The lands are said to yield from one to two bales of cotton lint per acre.

The average of lands in cultivation is 98.2 acres per square mile, the county ranking eighth in the state. Of the crops, corn has the largest acreage, the average of cotton being 24.4 acres per square mile. The product per acre of cotton is much above that of the state at large.

CONWAY.

Population: 12,755.—White, 9,546; colored, 3,209.
Area : 540 square miles.—Woodland, nearly all; all red-loam region.
Tilled lands: 51,967 acres.—Area planted in cotton, 15,424 acres; in corn, 15,959 acres; in oats, 1,685 acres; in wheat, 1,778 acres.
Cotton production: 9,096 bales; average cotton product per acre, 0.59 bale, 885 pounds seed-cotton, or 295 pounds cotton lint.

Conway county is bordered on the south by the Arkansas river, into which all the other streams that water the county flow. The northern part of the county is hilly and broken, and the summits of the hills, formed from the sandstones of the millstone-grit formation, are underlaid very much in the southern part of the county, seldom exceeding 300 feet, and are composed mostly of thin-bedded sandstones, underlaid by reddish siliceous and dark argillaceous shales. In the northeast veins of quartz, talc, etc., traverse the shales from northeast to southwest for several miles.

The lands of the county are derived mostly from the sandstones and shales, these producing sandy soils and reddish clay lands, respectively, the subsoils being usually red clays. The timber growth is red, white, post, and black oaks, hickory, etc. The most important tracts of arable uplands are said to occur in the southern part of the county.

The river bottom lands are several miles wide, and comprise a first bottom of sandy loam soils and a second bottom of a stiffer buckshot character, both said to be equally productive. The timber growth is cottonwood, ash, pecan, walnut, sweet gum, etc., and the lands are said to yield from 2,000 to 3,000 pounds of seed-cotton per acre.

The average of tilled lands is 96.2 acres per square mile, there being but eight counties in the state having a greater number. The acreage of corn and cotton is nearly the same, the former predominating. As in most of the river counties, the acreage of cotton is quite large, the average being 28.6 acres per square mile, the county ranking eighteenth in the state. The average cotton yield per acre is above that of the state at large.

ABSTRACT OF THE REPORT OF W. C. STOUT, HAWKSTONE.

The lowlands of the county comprise the creek bottoms and the front- and back-lands of the Arkansas river, and are entirely alluvial in character.

The *river bottom lands* consist of soils from sandy to very stiff silts, and, though quite different in composition, their productiveness is nearly equal. Their depth is unknown, but wells have been sunk 50 and 60 feet without reaching the limit. The highest surface is about 35 feet above low-water mark of the river, and most of these lands are subject to overflow at long intervals. There has been no general overflow since 1844. Banks, bars, and shores are subject to change. The average width of these very fertile lands is, from Little Rock to the western border of the state, 4 to 5 miles; from Little Rock to the mouth of the Arkansas river, 10 to 15 miles. These lands produce cotton, corn, wheat, tobacco, and indeed everything that has been tried, and the percolation of the soils by the waters of the river enables them to maintain their fertility and renders them practically inexhaustible. These bottom lands are the chief cotton soils of the county, comprising, perhaps, one-tenth its area. The natural timber growth is oaks, cottonwood, ash, sweet gum, pecan, walnut, cane, and many other varieties. The soil is a light sandy "buckshot" alluvium from yellowish or chocolate to blackish in color. It is equally fertile when taken from any depth. Some very heavy silts are improved by culture. The soil is underlaid by sand, gravel, or rock, and is easy to cultivate, and if broken early there is no choice between dry and wet seasons. It is early, warm, naturally well drained, and equally well adapted to all the crops of the region, which are corn, cotton, tobacco, wheat, sorghum, and a large number of other products. Perhaps one-half of this land is devoted to cotton, which grows from 4 to 5 feet high. It is most productive at the latter height, and inclines to run to weed under late culture and too much rain in August, and cannot be restrained. Early cotton laid by from 15th to 20th of July hardly ever fails.

The seed-cotton product for fresh land is from 2,000 to 3,000 pounds, 1,545 pounds of which are necessary for a 475-pound bale of first-rate lint. After twenty years' cultivation the yield and also the staple are the same. The troublesome weeds are cockleburs, crab-grass, careless weed, morning-glory, dewberry vines, etc. None of this land has ever been "turned out".

The creek bottoms are very fertile, and although very different in character they produce very nearly the same amount throughout. On these lands there are some very beautiful farms. The washings from the hills and an occasional overflow add to their fertility. There is generally a second bottom or bench-land lying between bottoms, strictly speaking, and the hills, which is classed with the creek bottoms, both because it makes up a portion of most creek-bottom farms and because it is derived from the same source, viz., the denudation and washing down of the hills and mountains and decomposition of the shales, clays, and stones of which they are composed. From this source the lowlands are receiving an increase of fertility and an enlargement of the area of arable land. These lands comprise, perhaps, one-tenth of the county area, occurring for 100 miles on all the tributaries and creeks of the Arkansas, White, Saline, Ouachita, and Red rivers, and have a growth of oaks, hickory, walnut, gum, ash, elm, hackberry, and many others. The soil is mixed with vegetable matter, and is variable in color and consistence. The depth of the soil depends on culture, which blackens and deepens it. The subsoil is lighter in color, and in some places is leachy hard-pan, sometimes an impervious clay, which contains either hard or soft "black gravel", and sometimes pebbles and undecomposed shales, underlaid by loose gravel and small rocks at from 5 to 15 feet.

The soil is easily tilled, but difficult both in wet or dry seasons if not broken well or if permitted to bake, and is variable as regards warmth and drainage. About one-half of this land is devoted to cotton, which is usually from 3 to 4 feet in height, sometimes 5, and inclines to run to weed in wet seasons and with late plowing. This is remedied by early culture and drainage. The seed-cotton product per acre from fresh land is from 900 to 1,500 pounds, 1,545 pounds of seed-cotton making a 475-pound bale of first-rate lint. For five years the product remains the same; after that time it falls off in some degree. The troublesome weeds are cockleburs, careless weed, crab-grass, and numerous others. None of this land lies "turned out".

The uplands of this region are extensive and generally wooded, and furnish a good soil for all the cereals, cotton, and tobacco. These lands, generally occupied by farmers who own their homes, and, in the aggregate, producing most of the crops of the county, are not so fertile as the creek and river bottoms, but being cheaper and easier to clear they attract poor men. This is the character of all lands that are not bottom, and comprise the greater part of central Arkansas. The timber growth is white, red, black, and post oaks, hickory, black gum, ash, elm, walnut, etc.

The soils of the uplands are of great variety: light, fine, silty loams, yellow, gray soils, to heavy clay loams and "buckshot". The depth is usually 9½ feet, but after being cultivated is much greater. The subsoil, heavier than the soil, blackens on exposure to the air, and is changed by deep culture to soil; in places it is hard-pan, a little leachy, sometimes impervious, but not often, and contains some hard and soft "black gravel", white gravel, and rounded and angular pebbles, more generally undecomposed shales, and is underlaid by some gravel and shale or rock at from 3 to 6 feet. The soil is usually easy to till in both wet and dry seasons, but varies sometimes, and is early, cold, and ill-drained, and suffers from drought. One-third of such land is devoted to cotton. The usual height of the plant is from 2½ to 4 feet, but it is most productive at 4 feet. The seed-cotton product per acre on fresh land is from 600 to 1,000 pounds, 1,545 pounds making a 475-pound bale of lint, which rates favorably with that from other land. After five years the product falls off, and the staple is not so long as that from fresh lands. Crab-grass is the most troublesome weed; there are, however, many other varieties of weeds. Some of this land lies turned out, but produces well when again cultivated and plowed deep. The soil washes on the slopes, in some places seriously, and the valleys are improved by the washings. Nothing has been done to check the injuries.

The seasons are favorable to cotton culture: a sufficiency of rain until after the summer solstice, then a dry month, followed by August rains, and usually a dry autumn. The proximity of the river and shelter of the mountains with the sea breeze from the Gulf of Mexico modify the temperature of both winter and summer and favor the cultivation of cotton.

Cotton culture has increased in this section in the last ten years. There is not so much produced on the large plantations, but generally more on the small farms, especially in the uplands. The reasons are these: First, there is a considerable increase in population and in upland farms; second, cotton is the most certain money-crop that can be produced; third, it is most easily marketed in proportion to value; and fourth, it is a crop in which all the children and women of the family can earn their own support at home without undue exposure or hard labor. In this whole region four-fifths of the cotton is produced by white people, chiefly on small farms.

Cotton is shipped, by river or rail, to Memphis, New Orleans, or Saint Louis at about $3 50 per bale.

FAULKNER.

Population: 12,786.—White, 11,368; colored, 1,418.

Area: 650 square miles.—Woodland, nearly all; all red-loam region.

Tilled land: 52,515 acres.—Area planted in cotton, 15,749 acres; in corn, 19,647 acres; in oats, 2,793 acres; in wheat, 3,300 acres.

Cotton production: 8,692 bales; average cotton product per acre, 0.55 bale, 825 pounds seed-cotton, or 275 pounds cotton lint.

The surface of Faulkner county is rolling and hilly, and is well watered by numerous streams flowing into Arkansas river, which forms a part of the western boundary. The country is mostly well timbered, open prairies occurring in some portions.

The northern part of the county is skirted by a continuation of the chain of mountains that form a prominent feature in the counties on the west, the summits of the hills being composed of sandstones of the millstone grit, underlaid by reddish siliceous and dark argillaceous shales. The lands are formed from these rocks, the sandstones producing sandy soils, while from the shales are derived the red clay lands, the subsoils of both being usually reddish clays. Large areas of the latter soil, with a timber growth, of oak and hickory, are found on the east extending into White county. They are said to yield from 600 to 800 pounds of seed-cotton per acre.

The river bottom lands, several miles in width, comprise the usual first and second bottoms of dark loams, with a timber growth of cottonwood, cypress, oaks, walnut, gum, hackberry, etc. They are said to produce 1,000 pounds of seed-cotton per acre, and are the chief cotton lands of the county, though that crop matures later than on the uplands.

The average of the lands in cultivation is 80.3 acres per square mile. The acreage of corn is larger than that of cotton, the latter averaging 24.2 acres per square mile. The product per acre is smaller than that of the state at large.

ABSTRACT OF THE REPORT OF W. C. WATKINS, CONWAY.

The lowlands comprise the first and second bottoms of the Arkansas river. The uplands are hilly and rolling, with level prairie, and are watered by Cadean creek and the Arkansas river. The soils devoted to the cultivation of cotton are the bottom lands, the prairie lands, and the uplands.

The chief soil is that of the *river bottoms*, comprising one-half of the county, extending 10 miles, with a width of 2 miles, and has a natural timber growth of cypress, oak, cottonwood, walnut, gum, hackberry, and hickory.

The soil has an average depth of 10 feet, and is underlaid by sand at 10 feet. The soil is difficult to till in either wet or dry seasons. It is both early and late, also warm, cold, and ill-drained, and is best adapted to cotton, which is the chief crop of the county. About three-fourths of this soil is devoted to the crop, which grows usually from 6 to 8 feet high, but is most productive at 6 feet. Inclining to run to weed on new land and in wet weather, topping is the remedy. The seed-cotton product per acre from fresh land is 1,000 pounds, 1,960 pounds making a 475-pound bale of middling lint. After two years' cultivation the product of seed-cotton is from 1,200 to 1,500 pounds, and 1,425 pounds are then necessary to make a 475-pound bale of lint, one grade better than that from fresh land. Rag-weed, burs, and morning-glory vines are the troublesome weeds. None of this land lies "turned out".

The *black upland prairie* soil comprises one-fourth of the area of the region, extending about 4 miles, with a timber growth of oak. The soil is a light fine sandy or heavy clay loam, yellow to black in color, and has a depth of 6 inches. The subsoil is heavier than the surface soil, contains hard "black gravel", rounded and angular pebbles, and is underlaid by rock at 6 to 10 feet. The soil is early, warm, and well drained, and is best adapted to cotton, to which two-thirds of it is devoted. The usual height attained by the plant is 3 to 4 feet. It is most productive at 3 feet, and inclines to run to weed on fresh land and during very wet weather; topping restrains the plant. From 600 to 700 pounds is the seed-cotton product per acre from fresh land, 1,960 pounds making a 475-pound bale of middling lint. After two years' cultivation the product of seed-cotton is from 800 to 1,000 pounds, and 1,425 pounds then make a 475-pound bale of lint, which rates one grade better than that from fresh land. Hog-weed and crab-grass are the troublesome weeds. None of this land lies "turned out". The soil does not wash or gully on slopes.

The *black and red uplands* cover one-fourth of the county, extending four miles, with a growth of oak and hickory. The soil is a fine sandy and gravelly clay loam, gray to black in color, and 6 inches deep. The subsoil is heavier than the soil, contains "black gravel" and pebbles, and is underlaid by slate rock at from 4 to 8 feet. The soil is easy to till, is early, warm, well drained, and best adapted to cotton, to which two-thirds of it is devoted. The usual height of the plant is 3 to 4 feet, is most productive at 3 feet, and runs to weed in wet weather, which is restrained by topping.

The seed-cotton product per acre from fresh land is 500 to 600 pounds; 1,660 are required for a 475-pound bale of middling lint. After two years' cultivation the product is 600 to 800 pounds, and 1,425 pounds make a 475-pound bale of lint, rating one grade higher than that from fresh land. Crab-grass is the most troublesome weed. None of this land lies "turned out".

Cotton in the lowlands is liable to be late and frost-bitten. The crop on the uplands always matures before the frost.

Shipments are made, as soon as picked, by rail to Saint Louis and Memphis at $2 50 per bale.

WHITE.

Population: 17,794.—White, 15,761; colored, 2,033.
Area: 1,100 square miles.—Woodland, all; all red-loam region.
Tilled land: 79,327 acres.—Area planted in cotton, 23,304 acres; in corn, 29,148 acres; in oats, 6,957 acres; in wheat, 3,509 acres.
Cotton production: 11,821 bales; average cotton product per acre, 0.51 bale, 765 pounds seed-cotton, or 255 pounds cotton lint.

White county is bordered on the east by White river, and is also watered by Little Red river and many other streams and bayous. The surface of the county is hilly and broken on the west, but more level on the east, and is well timbered. The prevailing rocks of the county are sandstones, conglomerates, and shales of the millstone grit formation, the former on the west forming high and prominent cliffs, especially along the bluffs of Little Red river.

The soils are mostly sandy in localities where the sandstone forms the chief rock, their subsoils being red clays, giving to the soil strength and durability. The shales of the formation produce by disintegration a red clayey soil and subsoil, and in this county covers a large area on the west of Searcy, the county-seat, and smaller spots in other places. The former is said to extend north and south 10 or 12 miles and 30 miles east and west, and to produce an average of 800 to 1,500 pounds of seed-cotton, 20 to 25 bushels of wheat, or 40 to 60 bushels of oats per acre.

The bottom lands, occurring chiefly on the streams in the eastern part of the county, consist of sandy and clayey loams, and have a timber growth of oak, gum, hickory, walnut, etc. The average of lands in cultivation is 72.6 acres per square mile. Of the various crops corn has the highest acreage, an average of 26.5 acres per square mile, that of cotton being 21.2 acres. In this region, Pulaski county alone produces a greater number of bales than White, or has a larger total acreage. The cotton product per acre of White is much below that of the state at large.

The lowlands of the county are the first and second bottoms of White and Little Red rivers and Departee creek, comprising front-land, back-land, and cypress swamps. The uplands are hilly and rolling, with gravelly and rocky soil. The chief crops of the county are cotton, corn, wheat, oats, sweet and Irish potatoes. The soils cultivated in cotton are the sandy loam, the sandy, and the clay mixed with some sand.

The chief soil is the *black sandy loam*, which comprises one-fourth of the area of the county, occurring in patches and spots for many miles, interspersed with clay lands. The natural timber growth is gum, oak, hickory, black walnut, and a great variety of others. The soil is fine, somewhat rocky, 10 inches to 2 feet deep, with a tough clay subsoil, which bakes very hard when exposed to the sun, but gradually becomes like the soil. It is quite impervious when undisturbed, contains soft "black gravel" and angular and large pebbles, and is underlaid by sand-rock at from 2 to 5 feet. The soil is not difficult to till, is early and warm when well drained, and is apparently best adapted to cotton, corn, and sweet potatoes. About 50 per cent. of this land is planted in cotton, the usual height of the plant being from 3 to 5 feet, but it is most productive at 4 feet. On fresh land or in wet seasons the plant inclines to run to weed, and topping is preferred by some as a restraint.

The seed-cotton from fresh land is from 500 to 1,500 pounds per acre, 1,545 pounds making a 475-pound bale of lint, rating the same on all lands; 700 to 1,800 pounds is the product after four years' cultivation, 1,425 pounds making a 475-pound bale of lint, which some think is of a better quality than that from fresh land. Crab-grass and burs are the troublesome weeds. About 5 per cent. of these lands lie "turned out", and when again cultivated produce a little better than when turned out. The soil on the slopes washes but little, and the valleys are not injured by the washings.

The *black or dark clay land*, comprising about one-third of the county area, occurs in spots for many miles, and has a growth of gum, cypress, ash, hickory, and oak. About 50 per cent. of this land is planted in cotton, which usually grows from 3 to 5 feet in height. Wet weather inclines the plant to run to weed, which is restrained by topping. From 500 to 1,000 pounds is the seed-cotton product from fresh land, 1,425 to 1,650 pounds making a 475-pound bale of lint, which rates the same for all of the land. After six years' cultivation the product of seed-cotton is from 500 to 1,500 pounds, when 1,425 pounds make a 475-pound bale of lint, rating about the same as that from new land. Crab-grass is the most troublesome weed. About 10 per cent. of these lands lie "turned out", and when again cultivated produce about the same.

On the low or bottom lands cotton is more liable to rot and not to mature than on the uplands; consequently, the uplands are preferred for cotton.

Cotton is shipped, from October 1 to December 1, by river and railroad to Memphis, Saint Louis, and New Orleans, at from $2 to $3 per bale.

LONOKE.
(See "Gray silt prairies".)

PRAIRIE.
(See "Gray silt prairies".)

JACKSON.
(See "Crowley's ridge region".)

INDEPENDENCE.
(See "Northern barrens and hills region".)

VAN BUREN.

Population: 9,565.—White, 9,447; colored, 118.

Area: 1,100 square miles.—Woodland, all; red-loam region, 1,065 square miles; siliceous lands, 35 square miles.

Tilled lands: 38,905 acres.—Area planted in cotton, 7,084 acres; in corn, 17,548 acres; in oats, 2,627 acres; in wheat, 3,325 acres.

Cotton production: 3,377 bales; average cotton product per acre, 0.48 bale, 720 pounds seed-cotton, or 240 pounds cotton lint.

The surface of Van Buren county is hilly and broken, well timbered, and watered by the many streams forming the headwaters of Little Red river, which flows southeastward, and is one of the tributaries of White river.

The lands of the county are derived from the sandstones, shales, etc., of the millstone-grit formation, which form the hills and ridges and vary in character from gray and red sandy to clayey. In localities where sandstone prevails the lands are sandy and support a timber growth chiefly of pine with black-jack and scrubby oaks. In the southern part of the county there is a table-land of this character 400 feet above the general drainage. The valley lands, mostly derived from the red shales underlying the sandstone, are reddish in color, and have red clay subsoils. They are very fertile, stand drought well, and produce 20 or 25 bushels of corn and 15 of wheat, or from 600 to 800 pounds of seed-cotton per acre. The valley of the Little Red river, said to be the richest in the county, has a growth of ash, elm, maple, gum, oak, and hackberry and an undergrowth of papaw, spicewood, and leatherwood. A few miles north of Clinton, the county-seat, a ridge rises to an elevation of 1,200 feet above the town, north of which appear the limestones and other rocks of the formation characterizing the northern part of the state. The county is sparsely populated, with an average of about 9 persons per square mile, its tilled lands averaging 35.4 acres, or 5.5 per cent. of the area. Corn is the chief crop, averaging 15.9 acres, that of cotton being but 6.4 acres per square mile. Its average product per acre is also very low.

POPE.

Population: 14,322.—White, 13,413; colored, 900.
Area: 800 square miles.—Woodland, all; all red-loam region.
Tilled lands: 63,312 acres.—Area planted in cotton, 15,062 acres; in corn, 24,736 acres; in oats, 2,688 acres; in wheat, 7,772 acres.
Cotton production: 8,700 bales; average cotton product per acre, 0.58 bale, 870 pounds seed-cotton, or 290 pounds cotton lint.

The surface of Pope county is well timbered, and is watered by numerous streams that flow south into the Arkansas river, the southern boundary. "The northern part is broken and mountainous; the mountains are composed of massive sandstones, belonging to the millstone-grit formation at the summit, and thin bedded and shaly sandstones at the base. On Indian creek the sub-Carboniferous limestone appears beneath these rocks. South of Dover, between Illinois bayou and Galley creek, and south of Carrion Crow mountains, the country is comparatively level" (*Owen*).

The uplands of the county comprise sandy and gravelly soils and red clay lands, derived respectively from the sandstones and reddish shales, the subsoil being usually red clay. The cultivated lands lie chiefly in the south, the yellowish or reddish loams predominating. The timber growth is oak and hickory.

The river bottom lands are several miles wide, and embrace dark loam first bottom soils and stiffer buckshot second bottoms, and yield from 2,000 to 2,500 pounds of seed-cotton per acre. The timber growth is cottonwood, ash, pecan, walnut, hickory, etc. The average population of the county is nearly 18 persons, and the average tilled lands 79.1 acres per square mile. Corn averages 30.9 and cotton 18.8 acres per square mile, while the product per acre is the same as that of the state at large.

ABSTRACT OF THE REPORT OF T. S. EDWARDS, GUM LOG.

The lowlands comprise the first and second bottoms of Illinois bayou, which rises in Boston mountain. The uplands are rolling, and are partly sandy and partly clayey.

The lands devoted to the cultivation of cotton comprise the black sandy creek bottoms, the sand and clay uplands, frequently with a clay subsoil, and the red clay lands, which are considered the best wheat lands. The most important is the *black sandy soil*. It covers one-half the surface of the county, extends in each direction from 8 to 10 miles, and has a natural timber growth of gum, hickory, ash, walnut, mulberry, and different varieties of oaks. The soil is sandy and gravelly, and in places is a mixture of clay and sand. It is yellow in color, and varies in depth from 6 to 30 inches. The subsoil is heavier than the soil, more compact, less mixed with gravel, to some extent impervious, and contains soft "black gravel" and small rounded pebbles. Very hard sand rock is found at from 8 to 10 feet. The land is not difficult to cultivate in wet seasons, is early, warm, and well drained, and is best adapted to cotton.

The chief crops of the region are cotton, corn, wheat, and oats. One-half the lands planted are in cotton, which grows to a height of from 3 to 5 feet, being most productive at 5 if well bolled. The plant runs to weed in very wet summers, for which topping in July is the remedy. The product per acre in seed-cotton from fresh land is from 1,000 to 2,500 pounds, 1,665 pounds being necessary for a 475-pound bale of lint. After ten years' cultivation (unmanured) the yield is from 500 to 700 pounds, provided the season is favorable, and 1,425 pounds are then required for a 475-pound bale of lint, which rates higher than that from fresh land, in being finer and softer.

Crab-grass and poor weed (so called in this country) are the most troublesome weeds. Only a very small portion of the land lies "turned out", which produces, when again cultivated, as well as it did originally. The land washes readily on slopes, doing no serious damage. The valleys are improved by the washings, and after a few years the yield is greater than at first. Very feeble efforts have been made to check this washing, horizontalizing giving good results.

Cotton on the creek bottoms grows higher and heavier than on the second bottom or on the uplands, though the latter are preferred by many for the cultivation of cotton because it matures earlier. Cotton is rarely injured by frost in this climate.

Cotton is shipped, as fast as baled, by railroad to Saint Louis at the rate of $2 50 per bale.

JOHNSON.

Population: 11,565.—White, 11,073; colored, 492.
Area: 660 square miles.—Woodland, nearly all; all red-loam region.
Tilled lands: 48,153 acres.—Area planted in cotton, 12,217 acres; in corn, 20,603 acres; in oats, 2,763 acres; in wheat, 3,509 acres.
Cotton production: 7,769 bales; average cotton product per acre, 0.64 bale, 960 pounds seed-cotton, or 320 pounds cotton lint.

The surface of Johnson county is hilly and mountainous on the north, but more level on the south, and is well timbered and watered by the tributaries of the Arkansas river, which forms the southern boundary. Sandstone of the millstone-grit formation is the principal rock of the hills, producing a sandy soil, which supports a growth of large pines. The red shales which lie below the sandstone occur chiefly on the south, and from them are derived the uplands of the county that are under cultivation. They furnish a reddish clay soil, more or less sandy from accompanying rocks, and have a timber growth of post, black, and black-jack oaks, persimmon, sumac, some hickory, etc. They are said to produce from 600 to 800 pounds of seed-cotton per acre.

The river bottom lands are broad, and comprise a first bottom of dark loam and a second bottom of a stiffer buckshot soil, and are well timbered with cottonwood, pecan, walnut, ash, elm, oaks, etc. The lands yield from 2,000 to 2,500 pounds of seed-cotton per acre.

The average of tilled lands is 73 acres per square mile. The average of corn is 34.3 and of cotton 18.5 acres per square mile; the product per acre is far above that of the state, the county ranking as seventeenth.

Transportation is by river or by railroad to Little Rock.

021

FRANKLIN.

Population: 14,951.—White, 14,455; colored, 496.
Area: 700 square miles.—Woodland, with some prairies; all red-loam region.
Tilled lands: 58,175 acres.—Area planted in cotton, 16,205 acres; in corn, 23,024 acres; in oats, 3,383 acres; in wheat, 6,017 acres.
Cotton production: 9,268 bales; average cotton product per acre, 0.57 bale, 855 pounds seed-cotton, or 285 pounds cotton lint.

Franklin county is divided into two parts by the Arkansas river. The northern part is hilly, and on the extreme north mountainous, from a spur of Boston mountain which enters from the west. Sandstone of the millstone-grit formation is the prevailing rock of the hills, underlaid by reddish shales, which produce, by disintegration, the red and yellow clay lands of the valleys, made more or less sandy from the former rock. The country north of the river is well timbered with white, red, post, black, and black-jack oaks, hickory, and sweet and black gums.

A large part of the southern part of the county is occupied by open and rather level prairies, underlaid by clay and shales; a few low hills are seen occasionally in Grand prairie. The soil is yellow or red in color and very similar to that of the timbered red lands, yielding from 800 to 1,000 pounds of seed-cotton per acre.

The river bottom lands have soils varying from dark to orange-red loams, with a timber growth of cottonwood, walnut, oaks, ash, pecan, gum, hickory, etc. They yield an average of 1,600 pounds of seed-cotton per acre.

The average of tilled lands is 83.1 acres per square mile, the county ranking seventeenth in the state. The acreage of corn averages 32.9 acres, and that of cotton 23.2 acres per square mile. The product per acre is a little below that of the state at large.

ABSTRACT OF THE REPORT OF J. M. PETTIGREW, CHARLESTON.

The lowlands of the county comprise the first and second bottoms of the Arkansas river and Mulberry creek. The bottoms of the creeks are generally quite level, and are free from swamp; the river bottoms are level and very rich, with little swamp. The uplands are hilly and level table-lands, with some open prairies. The chief crops are corn, cotton, wheat, and oats. The lands cultivated in cotton are the uplands, the creek bottoms, and Arkansas river bottom land.

The *yellowish-red* soil of the uplands comprises about nine-tenths of the area of the county, and extends all along the valley of the Arkansas river, and both north and south of it, for 30 miles. The natural timber growth consists of black-jack and other kinds of oak and hickory. The soil is fine, sandy, and gravelly, orange-red to blackish in color, and 18 inches deep. The subsoil is heavier than the soil, and in a large portion of the county is a light-red clay, which is underlaid by shale. In the prairie the subsoil is sometimes a hard-pan, which is impervious.

The soil is easy to till in dry seasons but difficult in wet, is early, warm, and well drained, and best adapted to corn and cotton. About one-fourth of this land is devoted to cotton, which usually reaches 3 feet in height, and runs to weed in wet seasons and with rapid tillage; topping and stopping work prevents and remedies this.

The seed-cotton product from fresh land is 1,000 pounds, 1,600 pounds making a 475-pound bale of low-middling lint. After ten years' cultivation the yield is 800 pounds on average land, and about the same amount of seed-cotton is necessary to make a 475-pound bale of lint, which rates about the same as that from fresh land. Cockleburs and crab-grass are the most troublesome weeds. But little land in this county is "turned out"; but after lying out some ten years it produces nearly as well as at first. The soil does not wash readily on the slopes. Valley land is generally improved by the washings. Horizontalizing is a good check to the washing of the slopes when practiced.

The *lowlands* of river and creek bottoms comprise nearly 7 per cent. of the region, and have a natural timber growth of walnut, hackberry, sweet gum, cottonwood, hickory, box-elder, cherry, pecan, papaw, etc. The soil is a fine sandy loam, orange-red and black colored, 20 feet deep in river bottoms and 18 inches in creek bottoms, with a sand and gravel subsoil, underlaid by sand and gravel at from 4 to 20 feet. The soil is easy to till in dry seasons, is early and warm, and in some parts is well drained, in others ill-drained. Nearly one-half of this land is planted in cotton, which usually is 5 feet high, and is most productive at that height. It inclines to run to weed if there is too much rain in late summer, which is remedied by topping and "laying by" early. The product of seed-cotton from fresh land is 1,600 pounds per acre, or a 475-pound bale of low to strict middling lint. The product of seed-cotton, after twenty years' cultivation, is from 1,000 to 1,400 pounds. Cockleburs are the most troublesome weeds.

Frost is more severe in the lowlands, especially when the soil is of a stiff clayey nature; consequently the planting of such land is deferred somewhat later than that of the more sandy and loamy soils.

Cotton is shipped, during the picking season, by rail and water to New Orleans, Memphis, and Saint Louis.

CRAWFORD.

Population: 14,740.—White, 13,332; colored, 1,408.
Area: 620 square miles.—Woodland, nearly all; all red-loam region.
Tilled lands: 50,714 acres.—Area planted in cotton, 10,145 acres; in corn, 19,777 acres; in oats, 2,369 acres; in wheat, 5,347 acres.
Cotton production: 8,980 bales; average cotton product per acre, 0.56 bale, 840 pounds seed-cotton, or 280 pounds cotton lint.

Crawford county, bounded on the west by the Indian territory and on the south by the Arkansas river, is a mountainous, broken, and well timbered county. The Boston Mountain range lies along the northern edge. The hills are composed of sandstones of the millstone grit, their summits being usually sandy, dry, and sterile, and not cultivated. They have a timber growth of pine, several varieties of oak, chestnut, etc. The valley lands, formed mostly from the underlying red shales, are those chiefly in cultivation. Their soils are reddish loams, more or less sandy, with red-clay subsoils, and a timber growth of red, black, and post oaks, hickory, etc. "In the southern part of the county the land becomes flat and the soil more sandy. It is arable, but of middle quality, and is especially characterized by the Spanish oak, which there forms by itself whole forests. Between Van Buren and Frog bayou there are extensive, somewhat marshy, sandy, and argillaceous flats, where this oak constitutes nearly the whole vegetation. Small prairies, apparently barren, inclosed in this forest are surrounded by a beautiful hawthorn" (*Lesquereux*).

The river bottoms are broad, and comprise the usual first bottom of a reddish alluvial loam and a second bottom of a dark and stiff buckshot loam, both very productive and well timbered. The yield is said to be from one to two bales of lint per acre.

The average of lands in cultivation is 81.8 acres per square mile. Corn has an average of 31.9 and cotton 26 acres. There are but twenty-one counties having each a higher cotton average, but the county has a lower product per acre than for the state at large.

The lowlands of the county comprise the first and second bottoms of the Arkansas river and a number of creeks. The uplands are partly hilly, but mostly level table-lands, with very little prairie. The soils devoted to the cultivation of cotton are the river and creek bottoms, comprising the black sandy, which is regarded as the best, the buckshot land, and the stronger or waxy land, which is the most difficult to work when entirely dry or lumpy, the upland loams, and the flat oak lands with whitish subsoil.

The chief crops are cotton, corn, wheat, and potatoes. The yield of corn is from 20 to 75 bushels per acre, according to the amount of cultivation given and the character of the land. On poorer, old upland 20 bushels to the acre is all that is sometimes obtained, but the same land will yield in a good season half a bale of cotton to the acre. Wheat is an uncertain crop in this county. Sometimes on old bottoms the yield has been 25 bushels, but on common uplands 6 to 15 bushels is the yield per acre. Oats are very little sown, and never pay; sweet potatoes yield 200 bushels per acre. Irish potatoes are only planted here for summer use, because the hot summer and autumn spoils them before digging; however, on top of Boston mountain 200 bushels of good potatoes to the acre are produced.

The chief soil is the river and creek *bottom land*, which comprises about one-fourth of the area of the county, extending east and west on Arkansas river the whole width, and north and south on the creeks the entire length of the county, and has a timber growth of ash, walnut, oaks, gum, hackberry, cottonwood, and sycamore. The soil is a fine sandy or clay loam, varying in color from whitish and gray to black, having a depth of from 2 to 20 feet, with sometimes substrata of sand and clay, and the humus or black color almost always extends as far down as the soil is cultivated. The soil is seldom too dry to plow or work, and is equally well adapted to cotton and to corn; but about three-fourths of its area is devoted to cotton. The plant is usually 5 feet or more in height, and inclines to run to weed on new land; but deep plowing against the roots, thus breaking them, and then throwing the soil back again, restrains the plant. The seed-cotton product per acre on fresh land is from 1,200 to 2,500 pounds. After several years' cultivation the yield is 1,500 pounds, and from 1,425 to 1,545 pounds of seed-cotton make a 475-pound bale of lint. The most troublesome weed is the cocklebur. None of this land lies "turned out", though it is done with advantage to the soil.

The *upland loam* soil comprises about three-fourths of the area of the county, and is timbered principally with oaks. This soil is grayish and sandy, with generally a reddish clay subsoil, which holds manure well; otherwise, it is a whitish clay, and in places a coarse gravel, and is underlaid by rock at from 3 to 90 feet. This soil is better for cotton than for corn, particularly such lands as have been worn out. About three-fourths of this land is planted in cotton, which usually grows from 3 to 5 feet high. After several years' cultivation the product per acre of seed-cotton is 500 pounds. The most troublesome weed on this soil is the horse-nettle. Where this land is sandy it washes on the slopes, but this does not injure either the slopes or the valleys. Horizontalizing has been practiced, and always with success.

Our staple is regarded as superior. The only drawback is that sometimes, but not oftener than one year in ten, the frost comes a little too early.

Cotton is generally sold to merchants as fast as ginned. Sometimes they hold it, but usually it is shipped at once to Saint Louis at $3, or to New Orleans at $3 75, a bale.

WASHINGTON.

Population: 23,844.—White, 22,894; colored, 950.

Area: 940 square miles.—Woodland and prairies; red-loam region, 750 square miles; northwestern prairies, 190 square miles.

Tilled lands: 116,871 acres.—Area planted in cotton, 302 acres; in corn, 53,083 acres; in oats, 13,103 acres; in wheat, 28,507 acres.

Cotton production: 133 bales; average cotton product per acre, 0.44 bale, 660 pounds seed-cotton, or 220 pounds cotton lint.

The surface of Washington county is broken and mountainous on the south and east, the Boston range of mountains lying along the southern boundary. The northern part is rolling and well timbered, and is interspersed with prairies, while around Fayetteville and on the west there are several large prairies. These prairies, usually level, are underlaid by the red shales. The soil is mostly reddish, and has a natural growth of sumacs, hawthorn, bramble, etc.

The hills of the county are high and steep, and their summits, capped with sandstone of the millstone-grit formation, have a timber growth of Spanish, black-jack, post, white, red, and chestnut oaks, yellow pine, chestnut, persimmon, etc. The soil is sandy and deep, and, where level enough to retain water and moisture, is said to be productive, yielding from 25 to 30 bushels of corn or 15 to 20 bushels of wheat per acre. It is, however, soon exhausted.

On the east, between White river and Lee's creek, there is a high sandstone ridge, 600 feet above the river, supporting a luxuriant growth of timber. "The trees grow here at an equal distance from each other, just as though they had been planted by hand, raising their straight, large trunks to a height of 60 or 80 feet, and supporting immense pyramids of branches, forming an arch of plashing boughs" (*Lesquereux*). The valleys or uplands between these hills, when not so near the hills as to be rendered sandy from the washings, are usually red, from the shales. The shales are red, scarlet, black, and chestnut oaks, sweet and black gum, wild cherry, and hickory. These soils are the most productive of the county, yielding excellent crops of corn, wheat, etc., and fruit of many kinds. The lands in cultivation embrace 19.4 per cent. of the county area, and average 124.3 acres per square mile, a number exceeded in the state only by Benton and Phillips. Corn, wheat, and oats are the principal crops, the average of corn being 56.5 acres, and that of wheat 30.3 acres per square mile. The area in cotton is very small, with only three-tenths of an acre per square mile, this being the lowest in the state. The product per acre is also comparatively very low.

BENTON.

Population: 20,328.—White, 20,167; colored, 161.
Area: 880 square miles.—Woodland and prairies; northwestern prairies, 830 square miles; red-loam region, 50 square miles.
Tilled lands: 111,279 acres.—Area planted in cotton, 286 acres; in corn, 49,135 acres; in oats, 13,912 acres; in wheat, 21,461 acres.
Cotton production: 126 bales; average cotton product per acre, 0.44 bale, 660 pounds seed-cotton, or 220 pounds cotton lint.

Benton, the extreme northwesterly county of the state, is represented as a high and level plateau, with small streams flowing outward from the center in every direction, except on the east, where White river has a northward and very irregular course through the county. The most prominent feature in its surface is the broad and extensive prairies that occur especially on the west of Bentonville, the county-seat, and which are the beginning of the great prairie region that covers the northern part of the Indian territory, and are similar in character to the smaller ones found in the counties eastward and southward from the White river. On the east there is an ascent of 310 feet to the summit of a ridge, and thence to Bentonville the lands are mostly oak barrens, interspersed with prairies. The prairies are represented to be flat and of wide extent, and the lowest parts of the surface marshy and somewhat difficult to drain. In the spring the low grounds are covered by three feet of water. The soil is a sandy loam, overlying limestone and sometimes sandstone, and when well drained is said to produce 40 bushels of corn, 15 to 20 bushels of wheat, or from 1,000 to 1,500 pounds of tobacco per acre.

The gently undulating surface of Beatty's prairie, northeast of Maysville, is fringed with groves of small oak and small hickory, and dotted with low mounds, bearing tufts of rank weeds, and made up of isolated heaps of chert gravel. Red clay underlies these prairies, as also in Missouri, on the north.

The average of lands in cultivation is 126.5 acres per square mile, a number greater than that of any other county of the state. Corn and wheat are the chief crops, the former averaging 55.8 acres and wheat 24.4 acres per square mile. The acreage of oats is also larger than in any other county in the state. Comparatively little cotton is planted, the average being but three-tenths of an acre per square mile, as in Washington county. The product per acre, the same as in Washington, is very low in comparison with the majority of counties.

MADISON.
(See "Northern barrens and hills region".)

NEWTON.
(See "Northern barrens and hills region".)

SEARCY.
(See "Northern barrens and hills region".)

STONE.
(See "Northern barrens and hills region".)

NORTHERN BARRENS AND HILLS REGION.

(Includes the greater parts of Madison, Newton, Searcy, Stone, Independence, part of Lawrence,* and all of Randolph, Sharp, Izard, Fulton, Baxter, Marion, Boone, and Carroll; also a small part of Benton.*)

MADISON.

Population: 11,455.—White, 11,331; colored, 124.
Area: 880 square miles.—Woodland, nearly all; siliceous lands, 280 square miles; red-loam region, 600 square miles.
Tilled lands: 61,746 acres.—Area planted in cotton, 255 acres; in corn, 29,514 acres; in oats, 4,368 acres; in wheat, 12,318 acres.
Cotton production: 129 bales; average cotton product per acre, 0.51 bale, 765 pounds seed-cotton, or 255 pounds cotton lint.

The surface of Madison county is very hilly and broken, and is watered by tributaries of White river flowing northwestward. There are some prairies, but the greater part of the county is timbered with oak, hickory, and pine. The hills are composed mostly of cherty limestones, sandstones, and other material, and when high and narrow are dry and barren. Some of the cherty hills have a scanty growth of post and black-jack oaks; others

a growth of chestnut, post, and black-jack oaks, chincapin, and yellow pine. The tillable lands are found chiefly on the prairies and lowlands, and on those hills whose slopes are so gentle that the washing away of the soils can easily be prevented. The soil is a sandy and gravelly loam, often with a reddish clay subsoil, and is very productive.
The average of tilled lands is 70.1 acres per square mile. Corn, wheat, and oats are the chief crops, the first two averaging, respectively, 33.5 and 14 acres per square mile. Very little cotton is planted, the acreage of that crop averaging but three-tenths of an acre per square mile, as in the counties of Benton and Washington. The average product per acre is a little more than half a bale, or less than the average of the state at large.

NEWTON.

Population: 6,120.—White, 6,115; colored, 5.
Area: 810 square miles.—Woodland, nearly all; siliceous lands, 630 square miles; red-loam region, 180 square miles.
Tilled lands: 24,333 acres.—Area planted in cotton, 2,602 acres; in corn, 12,217 acres; in oats, 1,906 acres; in wheat, 2,241 acres.
Cotton production: 1,406 bales; average cotton product per acre, 0.54 bale, 810 pounds seed-cotton, or 270 pounds cotton lint.
Newton is said to be one of the most mountainous counties in the state, some of the peaks belonging to the Boston range attaining an elevation of more than 1,000 feet above the general level of the country. The surface is well timbered, and is mostly watered by the Buffalo fork of White river, which flows eastward, while on the extreme south the streams flow into the Arkansas river. The chief timber growth is black, white, red, and post oaks, pine, and hickory. The lands of the county, derived from the sandstones, limestones, and other rocks of the region, are sandy and gravelly, though yielding very good crops of corn, wheat, etc. There are some prairies on the north and northeast having grayish-loam soils and clay subsoils that yield from 30 to 50 bushels of corn per acre.
The county is sparsely populated with an average of only about 8 persons per square mile, and the average of the lands in cultivation is only 30 acres per square mile, the county ranking among the six lowest in the state in this regard. Of the crops corn predominates, cotton being next, with an acreage ten times greater than in Madison, and averaging 3.2 acres per square mile. Wheat and oats are also prominent crops. The cotton product per acre is much less than that for the state at large.

SEARCY.

Population: 7,278.—White, 7,262; colored, 16.
Area: 700 square miles.—Woodland, nearly all; siliceous lands, 695 square miles; red-loam region, 5 square miles.
Tilled lands: 28,581 acres.—Area planted in cotton, 4,320 acres; in corn, 14,399 acres; in oats, 1,901 acres; in wheat, 3,085 acres.
Cotton production: 2,464 bales; average cotton product per acre, 0.57 bale, 855 pounds seed-cotton, or 285 pounds cotton lint.
Searcy is a hilly and broken county, mostly timbered with oak, pine, and hickory, and watered by the Buffalo fork of White river and its tributaries. The hills and ridges are usually several hundred feet in height above the waters of the streams, and are formed of sandstones, limestones, etc. The lands are gravelly and sandy, dark in color, and have clayey subsoils. They yield from 30 to 50 bushels of corn or 25 bushels of oats per acre. The seed-cotton yield will average probably 700 pounds per acre.
The average of the lands in cultivation is 40.8 acres per square mile. The chief crops are corn, cotton, wheat, and oats, corn predominating, with an average of 20.6 acres per square mile; that of cotton is 6.2 acres. Its cotton product per acre is nearly equal to that of the state at large.

STONE.

Population: 5,089.—White, 4,984; colored, 105.
Area: 640 square miles.—Woodland, all; siliceous lands, 540 square miles; red-loam region, 95 square miles; northern barrens, 5 square miles.
Tilled lands: 20,906 acres.—Area planted in cotton, 3,666 acres; in corn, 9,156 acres; in oats, 1,439 acres; in wheat, 1,066 acres.
Cotton production: 2,049 bales; average cotton product per acre, 0.56 bale, 840 pounds seed-cotton, or 280 pounds cotton lint.
Stone county is bordered on the northeast by White river, to which all the streams that water the county are tributary. The surface is hilly and broken, with high ridges or mountains formed of sandstones, limestones, etc., having an elevation of from 350 to 500 feet above the general level of the country. The southwestern part of the county is watered by Little Red river, a tributary of White river, but flowing southeast through several counties.
The lands of the county are sandy, and more or less gravelly loams, with clayey subsoils and a timber growth of oaks, hickory, and some pine. The latter occurs chiefly on some of the high ridges on the north. The lands yield from 30 to 50 bushels of corn or 600 to 800 pounds of seed-cotton per acre.
The average population of this county is 8 persons, and that of lands in cultivation is only 32.7 acres per square mile, or 5.1 per cent. of the area. The usual crops of the region are produced in the county, the acreage of corn being the greatest, with an average of 14.3 acres per square mile. The acreage of cotton averages but 5.7 acres per square mile, the product per acre being less than for the state at large.

INDEPENDENCE.

Population: 18,086.—White, 16,703; colored, 1,383.

Area: 880 square miles.—Woodland, all; red-loam region, 360 square miles; siliceous lands, 275 square miles; northern barrens, 245 square miles.

Tilled lands: 81,220 acres.—Area planted in cotton, 19,602 acres; in corn, 31,114 acres; in oats, 5,100 acres; in wheat, 8,055 acres.

Cotton production: 11,156 bales; average cotton product per acre, 0.57 bale, 855 pounds seed-cotton, or 285 pounds cotton lint.

The surface of Independence county, hilly and broken, is divided by White river, which receives the waters of many small tributaries both from the north and south. The ridges are high, especially on the west and north, and are composed of sandstone and limestone. There are extensive areas of table-lands on the north of White river underlaid by the cherty limestones that form the fertile barrens of the northern part of the state. Their soils overlie red clays, are retentive and durable, and have a timber growth of black-jack and other oaks, hickory, sassafras, and persimmon. The lands throughout the county vary greatly, being derived from the rocks that predominate in the several portions. On the south are the red clay and gray sandy lands, formed from the rocks and shales of the millstone-grit formation, while on the north from Batesville the cherty limestone and its associated rocks forms the table-lands alluded to, and finally caps the ridges, producing gravelly and sandy soils with red clay subsoils. There are some extensive bottom lands along the rivers with dark loamy soils and a timber growth of oaks, ash, hickory, walnut, elm, etc., which yield from 1,000 to 1,200 pounds of seed-cotton per acre; the uplands not as much.

The Oil-trough bottom is a noted tract of very rich alluvial land lying on the southwest side of White river, in the southeast part of the county. It is about 15 miles long, and is bordered on the north and west by ridges of limestone 150 feet high. The soil is very dark colored even to the depth of 5 or 6 feet, the subsoil being nearly as black as the soil, but more tenacious. The principal timber growth is pin, red, and water oaks, elm, pecan, black walnut, sweet gum, hackberry, and buckeye, with an undergrowth of very large papaw, cane, grape-vines, and a little spicewood.

The average lands under cultivation is 92.3 acres per square mile, or 14.4 per cent. of the area. In this average the county ranks twelfth in the state.

Of the various crops of the county corn has the highest acreage, averaging 35.4 acres per square mile, cotton being next, with an average of 22.3 acres. The product per acre is somewhat less than for the entire state at large.

Shipments are made by river from Jacksonport.

LAWRENCE.

(See "Crowley's Ridge region".)

RANDOLPH.

Population: 11,724.—White, 11,097; colored, 627.

Area: 640 square miles.—Woodland, all; northern barrens, 535 square miles; Crowley's ridge, 75 square miles; Mississippi alluvial, 30 square miles.

Tilled land: 53,016 acres.—Area planted in cotton, 11,028 acres; in corn, 27,312 acres; in oats, 2,903 acres; in wheat, 4,016 acres.

Cotton production: 6,248 bales; average cotton product per acre, 0.57 bale, 855 pounds seed-cotton, or 285 pounds cotton lint.

Randolph county, bordered on the east by Black river and the alluvial region of the Mississippi, has a rolling and hilly surface, well timbered and watered by numerous streams. The ridges are 250 to 300 feet in height, their summits, formed of the clays, ferruginous sandstones, and gravel of the Quaternary period, overlying cherty magnesian limestones, and having a timber growth of small oaks and hickory. The valley and bottom lands are those chiefly in cultivation, their soils being dark and rich, and yielding from 600 to 800 pounds of seed-cotton per acre. The bottom lands of Black river have a timber growth of black, post, and red oaks, hickory, elm, walnut, ash, etc., and are said to yield a bale of cotton lint or 50 bushels of corn per acre.

Lands under cultivation average 82.8 acres per square mile, or 12.9 per cent. of the area. Of the various crops corn has the greatest acreage, averaging 42.7 acres per square mile, while that of cotton is 17.2 acres, a number greater than in 32 counties, some of them located, too, in the middle of the state. In cotton yield per acre the county ranks comparatively high, though its average is a little less than that of the state at large.

SHARP.

Population: 9,047.—White, 8,871; colored, 176.

Area: 590 square miles.—Woodland, all; all northern barrens.

Tilled lands: 43,191 acres.—Area planted in cotton, 8,455 acres; in corn, 18,508 acres; in oats, 4,411 acres; in wheat, 3,178 acres.

Cotton production: 4,350 bales; average cotton product per acre, 0.51 bale, 765 pounds seed-cotton, or 255 pounds cotton lint.

The surface of Sharp county is hilly and broken, and is watered by Strawberry and other streams flowing into Black river. The ridges, from 200 to 300 feet high, are composed of sandstones or cherty limestones, and are timbered with a growth of scrubby oak and hickory. Where sandstone forms the summit, pine is the prevailing growth. The valley lands derived from these rocks, especially the cherty limestones, are dark loams, very rich and productive.

and are usually drained by small streams. They yield from 600 to 800 pounds of seed-cotton per acre, and comprise the chief lands under cultivation in the county. The timber growth of the creek bottoms is ash, walnut, elm, mulberry, etc.

The average of the lands under cultivation is 73.2 acres per square mile, or 11.4 per cent. of its area. As in the other counties of this part of the state, corn is the chief crop, its acreage averaging 31.4 acres per square mile. As a cotton county Sharp ranks fourth in the region, with an average of 14.3 acres per square mile, or 19.6 per cent. of the tilled lands. In this average it is also ahead of 27 counties in the state, most of them much farther south.

IZARD.

Population: 10,857.—White, 10,635; colored, 222.
Area: 580 square miles.—Woodland, all; northern barrens, 345 square miles; siliceous lands, 235 square miles.
Tilled lands: 54,705 acres.—Area planted in cotton, 9,029 acres; in corn, 21,728 acres; in oats, 4,913 acres; in wheat, 4,830 acres.
Cotton production: 4,800 bales; average cotton product per acre, 0.53 bale, 795 pounds seed-cotton, or 265 pounds cotton lint.

Izard county is bordered on the southwest by White river, the streams on the east being mostly tributary to Black river. The surface of the county is varied with high ridges and hills, rolling and broken valleys, and narrow bottom lands, and is well timbered with oaks, hickory, etc. Some of the high ridges are from 350 to 500 feet in elevation, and are covered with a growth of pine. The lands comprise chiefly sandy or gravelly soils with clayey subsoils, are easily tilled, and yield from 30 to 40 bushels of corn or 600 to 800 pounds of seed-cotton per acre.

The average of tilled lands is 94.3 acres per square mile, or 14.7 per cent. of the area. In the state there are but nine counties whose average of tilled lands is each greater. Of the crops corn has an average of 37.5 acres and cotton 15.6 acres per square mile; 29 counties in the state have each a less cotton average and 24 a less cotton product per acre.

FULTON.

Population: 6,720.—White, 6,684; colored, 36.
Area: 660 square miles.—Woodland, nearly all; all northern barrens.
Tilled lands: 24,259 acres.—Area planted in cotton, 3,994 acres; in corn, 11,686 acres; in oats, 1,692 acres; in wheat, 1,602 acres.
Cotton production: 2,438 bales; average cotton product per acre, 0.61 bale, 915 pounds seed-cotton, or 305 pounds cotton lint.

Fulton, one of the extreme northern tier of counties, has a rolling and hilly surface, with cherty ridges from 200 to 300 feet above the streams. Pilot Knob, near Salem, the county-seat, has an elevation of 445 feet above the town, and is capped with a reddish sandstone. The hills and ridges are usually timbered with black-jack and black oaks and hickory, and are formed of siliceous or cherty limestones and other rocks of the "barrens". The soils are rocky, covered with fragments of chert. Where these hills are overlaid by sandstones, as in the southern and northwestern parts of the county, the timber growth is pine. In the valleys or coves between the ridges are meadow lands or prairies with dark soils, derived mostly from a white, earthy limestone, and drained by small streams. These are the chief agricultural lands of the county, and produce about 800 pounds of seed-cotton per acre.

The average of lands under cultivation is 36.8 acres per square mile. Of the latter corn has an average of 17.7 acres and cotton 6.1 acres per square mile, there being but 10 counties in the state with a less cotton average. In the cotton yield per acre there are but 19 counties in the state that rank above Fulton, and of these 16 embrace broad river alluvial lands within their borders.

ABSTRACT OF THE REPORT OF S. W. COCHRAN, UNION.

The lowlands of the county comprise the first and second bottoms of Strawberry creek and semi-prairie or branch bottoms, with hazel growths. The upland soils are red and gray in color, with a growth of oak and hickory. All the lands are classed as cotton lands.

The chief soil is the *dark sandy alluvial* bottom land, embracing one-fifth of the area of the county, which extends the whole distance of the creek or river, and is covered with a growth of oak, hickory, walnut, birch; undergrowth, red-bud, hazel, etc. The soil is a light, fine sandy clay, varying in color from buff to black, and has a depth of from 1 to 2 feet. The subsoil is generally a heavy red clay, in some places whitish, which is impervious, and is underlaid by lime rock. These, with wheat and hay, are the chief crops of the county. About one-eighth of the crops is cotton, which usually grows from 2½ to 5 feet in height, but is most productive at from 3 to 4 feet. Cotton plants incline to run to weed on fresh land or new ground in wet seasons, which may be restrained by shallow cultivation. The seed-cotton product per acre of fresh land is from 800 to 1,200 pounds, 1,545 pounds of which make a 475-pound bale, after paying the toll for ginning. The staple rates as good ordinary. After two years' cultivation the yield is from 900 to 1,300 pounds of seed-cotton, 1,545 pounds making a 475-pound bale of lint, which rates about the same as that from fresh land. The troublesome weeds are hog-weed and a kind of careless weed. None of this land has ever been "turned out".

The *red upland* soil comprises about one-sixth of this region, and extends west probably 150 miles, east 50 miles to the bottoms, with a natural timber growth of black-jack and other oaks, hickory, etc. The soil is loamy, varying in color from gray to black, and is from 1 to 2 feet in depth. The subsoil is generally a red impervious clay, containing soft, white gravel, and in places some rock, and is underlaid by sandstone, gravel, and limy rock at 6 feet. The soil varies as regards warmth, is ill-drained, and is best adapted to corn, wheat, oats, and cotton in the order given. One-eighth of the crops is of cotton, which is usually 2½ to 4 feet in height, but is most productive at from 2½ to 3½ feet. Wet weather inclines the plant to run to weed, which shallow cultivation restrains. The seed-cotton product per acre of fresh land is from 700 to 1,100 pounds, 1,425 pounds making a 475-pound bale of good ordinary lint. After two years' cultivation the product of seed-cotton is from 750 to 1,200 pounds, and the same amount is necessary for a 475-pound bale of lint, which rates the same as that from fresh land. The troublesome weeds are careless weed and crab-grass. None of this land lies "turned out", and but very little washing is done on the slopes; but no injury is done by the washings.

The *gray oak and hickory uplands* comprise one-fourth of the county area. The soil is a sandy loam of a gray or blackish color, and its depth is 6 inches. The subsoil is a yellowish clay, cracking when exposed, leachy, and contains flinty angular pebbles, and is underlaid by sandstone, gravel, and lime-rock at 2 to 6 feet. It is variable as regards warmth, is ill-drained, and is best adapted to corn, oats, cotton, and wheat, in the order mentioned.

About one-eighth of the crops on this land is cotton, which reaches from 2 to 4 feet in height, and is most productive at 3 feet. From 800 to 1,000 pounds of seed-cotton is the yield per acre, 1,425 pounds making a 475-pound bale of lint, rating from ordinary to good ordinary. The second crop is in all respects like the first. Crab-grass is the most troublesome weed. None of this land lies turned out, nor do the slopes wash much, and very little injury is done by the washings.

There is but little difference between the uplands and bottom lands in the maturing of cotton. We have a black land from the cherty hills on which cotton inclines to run too much to weed, and is slow in maturing.

Cotton is shipped by wagon to Batesville and Newport at from $3 to $4 per bale.

BAXTER.

Population: 6,004.—White, 5,959; colored, 45.
Area: 500 square miles.—Woodland, nearly all; northern barrens, 415 square miles; siliceous lands, 85 square miles.
Tilled lands: 27,564 acres.—Area planted in cotton, 4,798 acres; in corn, 10,804 acres; in oats, 2,024 acres; in wheat, 1,776 acres.
Cotton production: 2,879 bales; average cotton product per acre, 0.60 bale, 900 pounds seed-cotton, or 300 pounds cotton lint.

Baxter county has a rolling and hilly surface, mostly timbered and watered by the White river and its tributaries. Prairie barrens, with their black, deep, somewhat cold and clayey soils and underlying limestone, are scattered over the country, and are partly in cultivation, yielding from 40 to 50 bushels of corn per acre. Artificial drainage is necessary to some extent. Rocky ridges of cherty limestone occur occasionally, lying higher than the prairies, but are not in cultivation. They are usually timbered with a growth of black-jack and other oaks and hickory. From the top of the limestone cliffs of the north fork of White river the view from the hills on both sides of the river is said to be truly beautiful. The country around looks like an undulating sea of green forests alternating with small prairies, which appear like clearings or patches of cultivated fields.

The average of tilled lands is 55.1 acres per square mile, 21.6 acres of which are devoted to corn, and 9.6 acres to cotton. There are but 25 counties in the state whose cotton yield per acre is greater than that of Baxter.

ABSTRACT OF THE REPORT OF O. L. DODD, MOUNTAIN HOME.

The lowlands of the county consist of the first and second bottoms of White river and its tributaries. The land on Bennett's bayou has a very rich, black sandy soil. As much as 2,000 pounds of seed-cotton or 60 bushels of corn to the acre are produced on the bottom lands. The uplands are rolling and level, and are watered by White river and Bennett's creek. The chief crops of the county are corn, wheat, oats, and cotton, the latter rapidly increasing in amount.

The soils which are devoted to the cultivation of cotton are the upland, known as barren land, with dark yellow soil, and the black river bottom land.

The *upland barren land* is the chief cotton soil, comprising about nine-tenths of the county area, and extending 100 miles east, 125 west, and 50 miles south, with a timber growth of black, white, and post oaks, hickory, black walnut, and a large amount of pine. The soil is a dark yellow gravelly clay loam, sometimes black and mulatto in color, with a depth of 1 foot. The subsoil is a heavy, light red-colored clay, which, when broken in the fall, produces well, and is underlaid by rock in places at from 3 to 10 feet. The soil is easily tilled unless when very wet, it being then extremely hard to break. It is well drained and best adapted to corn and cotton; but the climate is more favorable to corn, the latitude being 36.5° north. One-third of this land is cultivated in cotton, which usually attains a height of 3 to 4 feet. It inclines to run to weed on fresh land and during wet seasons, and is restrained by topping. The yield of seed-cotton per acre is 1,400 pounds from fresh land, 1,425 pounds being necessary for a 475-pound bale of lint, which rates very well. The yield after five years is reduced to from 600 to 800 pounds of seed-cotton, and 1,545 pounds are required for a 475-pound bale of lint, which does not rate as well as that from fresh land, the staple being rather shorter. Crab-grass does the most injury to cotton when the crop is small. None of this land is "turned out", but a large amount of fresh land is cleared every year. The slopes do not wash very much, and the valleys are but little injured by the washings. Hillside ditching prevents a large flow of water in the bottoms.

The *river and creek bottom land*, which covers about one-tenth of the county, extends for 50 miles north and south on the water-courses, and has a timber growth of all varieties of oak, walnut, hackberry, and white and red hickory. The soil is a black, heavy loam, very productive, 3 feet in depth, and has a heavy black subsoil mixed with sand and some clay. The subsoil contains soft, "black gravel," and is underlaid by sand. The soil is sticky and very difficult to till in wet weather, is early, warm, and ill-drained, and apparently is best adapted to corn and cotton. One-half of this land is devoted to the latter crop. The plant usually is from 5 to 6 feet high, but is most productive at 5 feet. The seed-cotton product from fresh land is 2,000 pounds per acre, 1,300 pounds making a 475-pound bale of lint, rating very well. After ten years' cultivation 1,500 pounds of seed-cotton is the average yield, and 1,495 pounds are required for a 475-pound bale of lint, which does not rate as well as that from fresh land, as the staple is somewhat shorter. The troublesome weeds are cocklebur and Spanish needles.

About one-tenth of the county is *very broken, rocky*, and *hilly upland* extending north 50 miles, east, west, and south about the same distance, having a timber growth of black-jack and other oaks and hickory, and is but little cultivated. The soil is a gravelly red clay 3 to 4 inches deep, with a heavy, very red subsoil, containing some flinty pebbles and white gravel, underlaid by gravel and rock. The soil is too rocky to be cultivated.

Early frosts in some seasons injure the cotton crop, as we are a little too far north. Boll-worm and other insects never trouble our crops. Before the war there was not one bale of cotton raised in this county.

Cotton is shipped, as soon as baled, by wagon and railroad to Springfield, Missouri, and Saint Louis, at from $5 to $7 per bale.

MARION.

Population: 7,907.—White, 7,864; colored. 43.

Area: 640 square miles.—Woodland, nearly all; northern barrens, 335 square miles; siliceous lands, 305 square miles.

Tilled lands: 28,673 acres.—Area planted in cotton, 7,116 acres; in corn, 13,034 acres; in oats, 1,985 acres; in wheat, 2,494 acres.

Cotton production: 3,925 bales; average cotton product per acre, 0.55 bale, 825 pounds seed-cotton, or 275 pounds cotton lint.

The surface of Marion county is broken and hilly, the hills having usually an altitude of several hundred feet above the general level of the country. White river traverses the northern and eastern parts of the county, and to it the other streams are tributary.

The lands north of Crooked creek embrace gravelly hill lands, small prairies, barrens, and what are termed hickory barrens. The latter are ridge lands, having a growth of hickory and oak and a dark loam soil, capable of producing 40 to 50 bushels of corn or 25 bushels of wheat per acre. The prairie barrens have a dark and somewhat clayey soil, which is very productive when well drained.

In the central part of the county magnesian limestone crops out and forms higher, more abrupt, and entirely barren ridges, on which trees are scarce. Only a few stunted specimens of the rock-chestnut oak, the juniper, the persimmon, etc., grow in the cracks of humid, decomposing rocks. These ridges produce nothing. On the way from Yellville to Carrollton (west) the alternation of high, steep, and sterile hills of the magnesian limestone with low, undulating ridges of fertile cherty limestone shows a remarkable contrast in the vegetation, and consequently in the fertility of both formations. The highest ridges of the county are overlaid by sub-Carboniferous sandstone, and are sometimes covered with pines.—*Lesquereux.*

The lands of the southern part of the county are said to have mostly dark sandy loam soils and a timber growth of white, post, and black-jack oaks, hickory, etc. The soil is easily cultivated, and yields, it is said, an average of about 1,000 pounds of seed-cotton per acre.

The average of lands under cultivation is 44.8 acres per square mile. There are but sixteen counties in the state whose average acreage is each lower. Of the tilled lands 20.4 acres per square mile are devoted to corn and 11.1 acres to cotton. The cotton yield per acre is less than that of the state at large.

ABSTRACT OF THE REPORT OF W. B. FLIPPIN, YELLVILLE.

The lowlands of the county comprise the dark sandy loam first bottoms of White river and Crooked creek; the uplands the mountain and prairie barrens between the waters of Crooked creek and White river. White river enters the county near the northwest, and runs near the line to the northeastern part of the county, where Crooked creek empties into it. Crooked creek divides the county from west to northeast; south of this creek the soil is generally dark sandy, easily cultivated, and is well adapted to cotton. Northeast of the creek the soil is dark "hickory barrens", with small patches of prairie. The hill land has a gravelly clay soil. In extremely wet, cold seasons cotton does best on the sandy lands, but when the season is moderately dry it does well on the barrens, running to weed on the prairie barrens. Early frosts materially injure the cotton on the barrens, more so than on the sandy land, for on this the plant does not grow so tall, and matures earlier. On an average these sections produce about the same amount. The chief crops are corn, cotton, wheat, oats, rye, potatoes, sorghum, and tobacco.

The soils cultivated in cotton are the black sandy bottom or upland, the prairie barrens and clay upland, the mountain rocky or gravelly land, and, in fact, all the soils of the county.

Nearly one-half of the county is black sandy loam, having a timber growth of hickory, ash, walnut, locust, pine, and white, post, and black-jack oaks. All lands are difficult to cultivate in cotton in wet seasons. The soil is best adapted to corn and cotton, and in some localities to tobacco; one-third of it is devoted to cotton. The usual and most productive height is 2½ feet, as at a greater height the boll does not open well. Wet seasons incline the plant to run to weed, which plowing the roots in August helps to restrain. One thousand pounds is the average seed-cotton product per acre from fresh land, 1,660 pounds making a 475-pound bale of good middling lint; about 800 pounds of seed-cotton is the product after five years' cultivation, and 1,780 pounds make a 475-pound bale of good ordinary lint. Crab-grass is the most troublesome weed. None of this land lies "turned out".

The soil does not wash very much on the slopes, and the valleys are improved from 25 to 50 per cent. by the washings. Early frost in the fall is the greatest drawback to the cotton crop.

Cotton is shipped, after January, by wagon to Springfield, Missouri, and thence by railroad to Saint Louis, at $6, or by steamboat to Newport, and thence on the Iron Mountain railroad to Saint Louis, at $5 per bale.

BOONE.

Population: 12,146.—White, 12,058; colored, 88.

Area: 640 square miles.—Woodland, nearly all; northern barrens, 345 square miles; siliceous lands, 295 square miles.

Tilled lands: 56,883 acres.—Area planted in cotton, 5,095 acres; in corn, 26,713 acres; in oats, 5,752 acres; in wheat, 8,499 acres.

Cotton production: 2,686 bales; average cotton product per acre, 0.53 bale, 795 pounds seed-cotton, or 265 pounds cotton lint.

Boone county has a hilly and broken surface, with partly timbered and partly prairie lands, and is watered by streams that flow northward into White river. The rocks comprise sandstones, cherty limestones, shales, etc., and give character to the various lands of the county. Hills having an altitude of 1,000 feet or more above the streams are conspicuous on the southeast, bordering Marshall's prairie, and are formed of conglomerates, sandstones, and underlying limestones. The prairies lie several hundred feet above the waters of the streams, and their soils, derived from these formations, are grayish, sandy loams, with clay subsoils, underlaid by limestone. They are said to be very fertile, yielding from 35 to 50 bushels of corn or 15 bushels of wheat per acre.

94 COTTON PRODUCTION IN ARKANSAS.

Other upland soils are sandy or gravelly, and have a timber growth of post and other oaks, hickory, and some pine. The crops of the county are corn, cotton, wheat, and other grain, grasses, and fruits. Corn has an average acreage of 41.7 acres, and cotton 8 acres per square mile. The entire lands under cultivation average 88.9 acres per square mile, there being but 14 counties in the state with a greater number. The cotton product per acre is less than that of the state at large.

ABSTRACT OF THE REPORT OF H. A. CRANDELL, HARRISON.

The lowlands comprise the first and second alluvial bottoms of White river and Crooked creek. The uplands are rolling table-lands and occasional prairies. Boone county is bounded on the south by the Boston mountains, on the east by a high range of Gaither mountains, and on the west by the White river range, or Ozark mountains. The chief crops of the county are wheat, corn, cotton, vegetables, and fruit, the last always very fine, and a sure crop.

The soils cultivated in cotton are the blackish gravelly loam, with occasional patches of red clay and sandy clay loam, the clay sandy loam ridge or post-oak land, and the brown clay loam.

The chief soil is the *black gravelly* loam, which comprises 70 per cent. of the lands under cultivation. Not more than one-half of the lands of the county lie uncultivated. This soil extends south 12 miles, west 9 miles, and north 20 miles, with occasional patches of very rocky and red clay land, and has a timber growth of black-jack oak, hickory, elm, walnut, sycamore, and pine. The soil is a coarse sandy, gravelly loam, blackish in color, 4 to 12 inches deep, with a brownish clay subsoil, which changes to dark red clay at from 4 to 6 feet below the surface, and contains rock at unequal depths. The soil tills easily, is partly well drained, and is well adapted to all the crops of the region. Only about from one-eighth to one-tenth of it is planted in cotton, which usually grows 2 to 3 feet high, and produces best at about 2½ feet. The plant inclines to run to weed in damp, cloudy autumn days, and topping is frequently beneficial in favoring bolling. Twelve hundred pounds is the product of seed-cotton from fresh land, 1,425 pounds of which make a 475-pound bale of middling lint. The product is about the same, and also the rating, after four years' cultivation. Cocklebur, careless weed, crab-grass, and Spanish needle are the most troublesome weeds, crab-grass being the most injurious, as its growth is late and rapid. The soil very seldom washes on the slopes, and when it does the washings improve the valleys a little. Nothing has been done to check this. None of the lands of the county lie turned out.

The circumstances favorable to the culture of cotton are the uniform seasons, this region never having been subjected to excessive drought or continuous rains. Late spring or early autumn frosts very seldom seriously injure the crop, and there is no doubt but that the winters in this climate destroy the larvæ of the boll-worm and caterpillar to a great extent. The unfavorable circumstances are that the seasons are too short for cotton to reach its full growth and maturity.

Cotton is shipped, from October 1 to April 30, by wagon to Springfield, Missouri, at $3 75 per bale.

CARROLL.

Population: 13,337.—White, 13,272; colored, 65.

Area: 700 square miles.—Woodland, nearly all; siliceous lands, 355 square miles; northern barrens, 200 square miles; northwestern prairies, 145 square miles.

Tilled lands: 43,903 acres.—Area planted in cotton, 982 acres; in corn, 22,979 acres; in oats, 4,626 acres; in wheat, 7,343 acres.

Cotton production: 502 bales; average cotton product per acre, 0.51 bale, 765 pounds seed-cotton, or 255 pounds cotton lint.

The surface of Carroll county is hilly and broken, partly prairie, but mostly timbered, and is watered by streams which flow northward into White river. The hills are formed of alternating strata of limestone and sandstone, and the highest are covered with fertile prairies having a deep grayish soil and clayey subsoil and underlying limestone. These prairies are said to produce 35 bushels of corn or 20 bushels of wheat per acre. Some of the ridges are rocky, barren, and dry when they are high, steep, and narrow, but where low, with gentle slopes, they are fertile. Pine forms the prominent growth on the high and barren ridges near King's river.

The average of lands under cultivation is 62.7 acres per square mile. Of these, 32.8 acres are given to corn, while but 1.4 acres per square mile are in cotton. Madison, Washington, and Benton alone in the state have each a less cotton average.

630

BENTON.
(See "Red-loam region".)

PART III.

CULTURAL AND ECONOMIC DETAILS

OF

COTTON PRODUCTION.

REFERENCE TABLE

OF

NAMES AND ADDRESSES OF CORRESPONDENTS.

MISSISSIPPI ALLUVIAL REGION.

Chicot.—DANIEL B. BRAWNER, Luna Landing, April 15, 1881.
Desha.—JAMES MURPHY, Napoleon, January 5, 1880.
Crittenden.—A. C. BREWER, Scanlona, November 17, 1880.
Mississippi.—HARRY S. WILLIAMS, Osceola, April 29, 1881.
Lee.—J. A. GAINES, Askew, May 8, 1881.
Woodruff.—JAMES B. DENT, Augusta, March 21, 1881.
Saint Francis.—THOMAS B. HOY, Millbrook, February 6, 1880.
Cross.—W. C. MALONE, Wittsburg, April 27, ——.
Craighead.—J. W. RANSOM, Jonesboro', April 15, 1880.

GRAY SILT PRAIRIE REGION.

Arkansas.—JAMES A. GIBSON, De Witt, November 23, 1880.
Prairie.—R. CARL LEE, Devall's Bluff, December 15, 1879.

YELLOW-LOAM REGION.

Ashley.—J. P. HARBISON, Hamburg, January 1, 1880.
Union.—H. L. CHANDLER, El Dorado, ——.
Columbia.—J. D. ZACHRY, Magnolia, December 25, 1880.
Miller.—E. T. DALE, Texarkana, January 6, 1880.
Sevier.—M. W. LOCKE, Lockesburg, January 20, 1880.
Howard.—J. A. THOMAS, Centre Point, January 17, 1881.
Drew.—S. A. DUKE, Baxter, December 21, 1879.
Lincoln.—CHARLES V. DIXON, Auburn, May 7, 1881.
Dallas.—W. H. YOUNG, Tulip, ——.
Clark.—THOMAS H. MOREHEAD, Arkadelphia, December 30, 1880.
Grant.—W. N. CLEVELAND, Dogwood, November 9, 1880 ; T. W. QUINN, Prattsville, December 23, ——.
Jefferson.—THOMAS DUNNINGTON, Pine Bluff, March 10, 1880 ; S. H. COCKRELL, Pine Bluff, March 10, 1880.

RED-LOAM REGION.

Montgomery.—G. WHITTINGTON, Mount Ida, March 23, 1880.
Garland.—JOHN J. SUMPTER, Hot Springs, January 11, 1881.
Hot Spring.—E. HUGH VANCE, jr., Malvern, May 3, 1881 ; W. D. LEIPER, Malvern, May 3, 1881.
Pulaski.—WALTER WITTENBERG, Little Rock, January 5, 1880.
Scott.—WILLIAM B. TURMAN, Waldron, December 29, 1879.
Sebastian.—T. C. MILLER, Dayton, June 19, ——.
Conway.—W. C. STOUT, Hawkstone, November 10, 1880.
Faulkner.—W. C. WATKINS, Conway, December 27, 1879.
White.—L. ORTO, Searcy, May 25, ——.
Pope.—T. S. EDWARDS, Gum Log, January 31, 1880.
Franklin.—J. M. PETTIGREW, Charleston, March 22, 1880.
Crawford.—L. C. WHITE, Van Buren, March 24, 1881.
Fulton.—S. W. COCHRAN, Union, January 1, 1880.
Baxter.—O. L. DODD, Mountain Home, January 15, 1880.
Marion.—W. B. FLIPPEN, Yellville, April 15, ——.
Boone.—H. A. CRANDELL, Harrison, ——, 1880.

96

SUMMARY OF ANSWERS TO SCHEDULE QUESTIONS.

The answers from the thirty-eight counties heard from are combined, as far as possible, under the head of each of the natural divisions of the state, the name of each county giving such answer being added or prefixed.

In nearly all cases where a correspondent has expressed himself more fully than others on a subject of interest his answer is given in full. By a glance at the reference table the name of the writer will always be found.

TILLAGE, IMPROVEMENT, ETC.

1. What is the usual depth of tillage (measured on land side of furrow)?

UPLANDS.—Ten counties report from 3 to 7 inches; eight, 4 inches. *Prairie, Pulaski*, and *Scott* each report 5 inches. *Franklin, Garland*, and *Montgomery*, each 6 inches. *Drew* and *Columbia*, 3 inches. *Union* and *Howard*, from 2 to 4 inches. *Pope* and *Sebastian*, from 6 to 10 inches.

MISSISSIPPI RIVER ALLUVIAL REGION.—*Saint Francis* and *Cross*, 3 inches. *Craighead*, from 3 to 8 inches. *Desha* and *Crittenden*, 4 inches. *Woodruff*, 5 inches. *Lee* and *Chicot*, 6 inches. *Mississippi*, 8 inches.

2. What draft is employed in breaking up?

UPLANDS.—Eleven counties report the use of two horses or mules; ten counties, one or two horses or mules; six, one horse or mule. *Arkansas*: one, two, or three horses. *Pope*: two horses, mules, or oxen.

MISSISSIPPI RIVER ALLUVIAL REGION.—*Crittenden, Desha, Chicot*, and *Mississippi*: Two horses or mules. *Craighead, Cross, Lee*, and *Saint Francis*: One or two horses or mules. *Woodruff*: Usually one mule.

3. Is subsoiling practiced? If so, with what implements, and with what results?

UPLANDS.—It is reported as not practiced in 19 counties, and to some extent only in 10 counties, with various subsoil plows, and with good results. *Howard*: Yes, with Brinley and other subsoil plows; results are paying, if done in the fall or early winter. *Miller*: Crops are increased at least one-half and old lands made equal to fresh. *Dallas*: The chief results are that the land is easier of cultivation, resists drought longer, and even when unusually wet produces better crops. *Pope*: Not justifi-

able except in a very dry year. *Baxter*: Results good when practiced in the fall season. *Grant*: Results good after freezing and thawing.

MISSISSIPPI RIVER ALLUVIAL REGION.—It is reported as not practiced in *Crittenden, Desha, Saint Francis, Chicot, Mississippi, Woodruff, Craighead,* and *Cross* counties. *Lee*: Very little, with good results.

4. Is fall plowing practiced? With what results?

UPLANDS.—Yes, in seven counties; to some extent in nine; rarely in *Sevier* and *Grant* (where it is practiced by a few farmers for corn), and not at all in twelve counties. Results in nearly all reported cases are good. *Clark*: Crops are increased 25 per cent. *Pope*: In some years the results are good; in others no benefit is derived from the practice. *Franklin*: It tends to improve the land by giving vegetation time to rot. *Boone*: It invariably

insures an early stand. *Howard*: Besides benefiting the soil, it tends to destroy insects.

MISSISSIPPI RIVER ALLUVIAL REGION.—It is not practiced in *Crittenden, Desha, Chicot, Mississippi, Woodruff, Craighead,* and *Lee* counties. *Saint Francis*: Very little, but with good results.

5. Is fallowing practiced? Is the land tilled while lying fallow or only "turned out"? With what results in either case?

UPLANDS.—Yes, in *Pulaski* and *Sevier* counties, with good results, the land being tilled while lying fallow; not at all in twenty counties, and to a limited extent, with good results, in the remaining counties. *Conway*: Land sometimes lies out for want of labor. *Columbia* and *Howard*: The land is only "turned out"; results are good. *Miller*: The land is "turned out" and grows up very quickly with trees, requiring to be again cleared. *Grant*: Sometimes the land is sown in peas; the results are excellent. *Franklin*: Land fallowed, when deeply plowed, in the fall, before vegetation is killed by frost, is greatly increased in fertility.

MISSISSIPPI RIVER ALLUVIAL REGION.—It is not practiced in *Lee, Crittenden, Desha, Saint Francis, Woodruff,* and *Mississippi* counties. *Cross*: To some extent, with good results; the land is tilled while lying fallow. *Craighead*: Sometimes the land is greatly improved. *Saint Francis*: Yes; and the results are good. *Chicot*: Land when cultivated, after having been turned out for five or six years for pasturing purposes, is equal to fresh land. *Lee*: When the land is "turned out" it grows up in crab-grass and other weeds so thoroughly that it is hard work for a year or two to get rid of them.

6. Is rotation of crops practiced? If so, of how many years' course, and in what order of crops?

UPLANDS.—It is practiced in seventeen counties; to a limited extent in nine counties, and not at all in *Lincoln, Faulkner, Arkansas,* and *Prairie.* Cotton, corn, and wheat or oats are alternated in twelve counties; cotton and corn in *Pulaski, Hot Spring, Dallas, Union,* and to some extent in *Sevier* and *Miller;* but generally the land is planted in cotton for from ten to twenty years, and then "turned out"; on uplands from three to five years. Cotton two years, and corn, wheat, or oats one year, is the order in *Ashley, Drew,* and *Crawford.* Cotton for five or ten years, then corn or small grain, in *White.*

MISSISSIPPI RIVER ALLUVIAL REGION.—It is practiced in *Mississippi, Woodruff,* and *Lee,* on the uplands of Crowley's ridge; to some extent in *Craighead, Cross, Saint Francis,* and *Desha,* and not at all in *Chicot* and *Crittenden.* Cotton and corn alternate in *Desha, Craighead, Woodruff,* and *Mississippi.* Cotton, corn, wheat, oats, or millet alternate in *Lee* and *Saint Francis.* Corn, sweet potatoes, and oats in *Cross.* *Crittenden:* Corn grows best after cotton, though cotton does not do so well after corn. It grows better year after year in the same ground.

7. What results follow from the rotation of crops?

UPLANDS.—*White, Fulton, Hot Spring, Pulaski, Montgomery, Sebastian, Union, Drew, Miller,* and *Columbia:* The results are good. *Dallas:* The lands grow poorer with every crop. *Ashley:* Cotton does best when planted on corn or oat land, as it is then not so liable to suffer from shedding, but is more difficult to cultivate. *Grant:* Corn yields 10 per cent. more after cotton; so do wheat and oats. Any crop does well after cotton. *Franklin* and *Pope:* The average yield is kept up without the aid of fertilizers. *Scott:* Ten per cent. gain. *Garland:* Good for all crops, but particularly so for cotton planted after wheat if the stubble is turned

under in the fall. *Howard:* Beneficial, as a continuous planting of corn impoverishes the land more than any other crop. *Crawford:* Results are always marked. *Baxter:* Improves the crops and the land. *Sevier:* Those who have open land enough to rotate make better crops by it. *Conway:* The laborer takes all he can from, and returns nothing to, the soil.

MISSISSIPPI RIVER ALLUVIAL REGION.—*Saint Francis:* Cotton will grow better, and not be so liable to disease, if planted after corn, wheat, or oats. *Desha:* Results are excellent for either cotton or corn. *Cross* and *Lee:* Results are good.

8. What fertilizers or other direct means of improving the soil are used by you, or in your region? With what results? Is green manuring practiced? With what results?

UPLANDS.—*Crawford, Baxter, Sevier, Pulaski, Sebastian, Dallas, Columbia, Jefferson,* and *Union* counties report the use of barnyard manure and cotton-seed. *Ashley, Hot Spring, Grant, Fulton, Franklin,* and *Scott:* Barnyard manure and such other fertilizers as are made on the farm, consisting of compost heaps, leaf manure, ashes, etc.; sometimes cotton-seed for small grain in *Grant.* *Garland:* Stable manure, cotton-seed, and occasionally ashes. *Pope:* Same as in *Garland,* with the addition of rotted straw and logs. *Howard:* This county being comparatively new, nothing is used except barnyard manure, and that only to a limited extent. *Conway:* In a few cases the stalks are plowed under and the surplus cotton-seed returned to the soil. *Miller:* Animal manure, and occasionally cotton-seed on garden patches of uplands only. *Boone:* Nothing except animal manure on meadows, orchards, and vegetable gardens. *Lincoln:* Cotton-seed on light spots. The results are excellent in all cases. *Sevier, Sebastian,* and *Scott:* From 50 to 100 per cent. gain. *Franklin:* A small amount of any fertilizer pays largely.

Green manuring is practiced in six counties; to some extent in nine, and not at all in fifteen. Results are good in all cases. *Crawford:* With cow-peas on old uplands it is one of the best fertilizers.

Arkansas: With cow-peas it increases the crops about 25 per cent. *Sebastian:* It consists of plowing under weeds, grass, and stubble; tends to destroy next year's crop of weeds, and is of benefit to the land. *Sevier, Garland, Howard, Baxter,* and *Franklin:* The productiveness is increased by turning under stubble, grass, and weeds. *Pope:* Sometimes with oats and rye; but the best results are obtained from the use of cow-peas.

MISSISSIPPI RIVER ALLUVIAL REGION.—*Lee* and *Craighead:* Barnyard manure and cotton-seed to some extent, and with excellent results. *Chicot* and *Woodruff:* Occasionally cotton-seed, and with the best results. *Cross:* Compost and stable manure. *Chicot:* The yield is increased about 25 per cent. *Cross:* The results are good. *Crittenden:* The lands of this county are new, and fertilizers are not needed. It is found that the oldest fields yield the most cotton, as the plant is inclined to run to weed too much on new land, which also would result from fertilizing the old land, the joints of the plant becoming long and the bolls scattering.

Green manuring with cow-peas is practiced to some extent, and with good results, in *Cross* and *Saint Francis,* and rarely in *Lee.* In the remaining counties it is hardly thought of.

9. How is cotton-seed disposed of? If sold, on what terms, or at what price?

UPLANDS.—Ten counties report it as partly sold and partly fed to cattle; thirteen as partly sold, partly used as a manure, and partly fed to cattle. *Lincoln, Pulaski, Sebastian,* and *Jefferson:* Part sold to oil-mills, and remainder used as a fertilizer. *Prairie* and *White:* Sold to the oil companies. *Drew:* Partly sold, partly fed to cattle and sheep, and partly wasted. The prices obtained from the sale of it are: in fourteen counties, 10 cents per bushel; in nine, from 5 to 10 cents per bushel. *Pulaski, Prairie,* and *Clark:* 25 per ton. *Conway* and *Miller:* 25 per ton. *Drew:* 24 per ton. *Hot Spring:* From 10 to 15 cents per bushel.

MISSISSIPPI RIVER ALLUVIAL REGION.—*Cross, Chicot, Crittenden, Desha, Saint Francis,* and *Mississippi* counties report it as sold at prices ranging from 24 to 29 per ton. *Craighead:* It is used as food, being hardly ever sold. *Lee:* Partly as a fertilizer, but the greater part is sold at 29, and sometimes more, per ton. It is the opinion that it would pay better to use it all as a manure than to sell it. *Woodruff:* A small portion is sold at 24 50 per ton; the remainder is used as a feed for cattle.

10. Where is the nearest cottonseed-oil factory?

The oil-mills most convenient, both in and out of the state, are located in Little Rock and Pine Bluff, Arkansas, Memphis, Tennessee, Greenville, Mississippi, and New Orleans and

Shreveport, Louisiana. That of Little Rock is most convenient to the greatest number of counties.

11. Is cottonseed-cake used with you for feed or manure?

UPLANDS.—It is reported as not used at all in twenty-four counties. As a manure alone in *White;* to some extent, for cotton and corn, in *Crawford;* and very little, for corn, in *Baxter.* As a feed for cows, in *Pulaski,* and, to a limited extent, in *Franklin.* In *Jefferson* it is used to some extent both as a feed and as a manure, but the greater part is shipped to Europe.

MISSISSIPPI RIVER ALLUVIAL REGION.—It is reported as not used at all in *Mississippi, Desha, Saint Francis, Crittenden,* and *Craighead.* As a manure alone for corn, in *Woodruff* and *Chicot.* To some extent, both as feed for cattle and as a manure, in *Cross* and *Lee.*

PLANTING AND CULTIVATION OF COTTON.

12. What preparation is usually given to cotton land before bedding up?

UPLANDS.—Nine counties report no preparation given; eight, the clearing off of stalks, and, in most cases, the burning of them. *Baxter, Fulton, Franklin,* and *Garland:* The land is well broken up before bedding. *Grant:* The stalks, if large, are pulled up and burnt, and the land is sometimes broken up. *Sebastian, Clark, Marion, Scott,* and *Pulaski:* Fall plowing to some extent,

but usually spring plowing only. *Jefferson* and *Howard:* Spring plowing only. *Crawford:* The best farmers plow twice in the spring.

MISSISSIPPI RIVER ALLUVIAL REGION.—*Cross, Crittenden, Craighead, Saint Francis, Mississippi,* and *Woodruff* counties report no preparation. *Chicot, Desha,* and *Lee:* Removal of old stalks.

13. Do you plant in ridges? How far apart?

UPLANDS.—Planting in ridges is universal in all counties reported, sixteen of which report the ridges from 2½ to 4 feet apart. *Faulkner, Miller, Drew, Pulaski, Sevier,* and *Jefferson:* From 3 to 6 feet apart. *Baxter, Columbia, Marion,* and *Union:* 3 feet. *Ashley:* From 4½ to 6 feet on bottoms; from 3 to 3½ feet on uplands. *Garland:* On poor soil, 3 feet; rich soil, from 4 to 6 feet. *Arkansas:* 4 feet on bottoms, 3 feet on uplands.

MISSISSIPPI RIVER ALLUVIAL REGION.—In *Cross, Mississippi,* and *Woodruff* counties the ridges are from 3 to 4 feet apart. *Desha, Saint Francis,* and *Crittenden:* 4 feet. *Craighead:* From 3 to 5 feet. *Lee:* From 4 to 4½ feet on bottoms; en uplands, from 3 to 3½ feet.

14. What is your usual planting time?

In the southern counties the earliest time is that reported from *Ashley,* being from the 1st to the 20th of April; the latest, from April 20 to May 20, from *Miller.*

In the middle counties (east to west) the earliest time is the first week in April, reported from *Sevier;* the latest, May 20, from *Scott.*

In the northern counties the time varies from April 10 to the last of May. The earlier time is reported from *Boone* and *Cross,* and the later from *Crittenden.*

15. What variety of cotton do you prefer?

UPLANDS.—The prolific varieties are preferred in seven counties, Boyd's being mentioned twice. Dixon's alone in *Arkansas* and *Drew,* with other varieties of cluster cotton in *Union,* and with Petit Gulf in *Faulkner.* Short-limbed cotton alone in *Miller,* with Java Prolific in *Grant* and *Dallas,* where the short-limbed is thought to be best for poor uplands. Early Johnston (a mixture of Green-seed and Prolific), Bagley, Green-seed, Multi-boll and Multi-lock, and Peeler varieties, each are mentioned once. Taylor's silk cotton and Bagley are reported as preferred in *Prairie* county, Peeler or Prolific in

White. Bagley Improved or Petit Gulf in *Sevier.* In *Ashley,* the African variety, because it yields the best, and the price of lint is from 1 to 2 cents more per pound than other varieties.

MISSISSIPPI RIVER ALLUVIAL REGION.—The Peeler variety is reported as preferred in *Desha,* with Boyd's Prolific in *Chicot.* Petit Gulf alone in *Craighead,* in connection with Green-seed in *Mississippi,* Taylor's silk or Java Prolific in *Saint Francis,* Matagorda silk in *Cross,* Boyd's Prolific, Dixon's and Taylor's in *Lee,* Green-seed in *Crittenden,* and any short-limbed in *Woodruff* county.

16. How much seed is used per acre?

UPLANDS.—Seven counties report from 1 to 2 bushels, seven counties 2 bushels. *Miller:* From one-half to 1 bushel. *Crawford* and *Scott:* Each 1 bushel. *Sevier:* From 1 to 3 bushels. *Jefferson* and *Dallas:* From 1 to 4 bushels. *Prairie* and *Pope:* From 2 to 5 bushels. *Pulaski:* 3 bushels. *Drew:* From 3 to 5 bushels.

MISSISSIPPI RIVER ALLUVIAL REGION.—*Desha:* 1 bushel. *Craighead:* 1¼ bushels. *Mississippi:* By hand, 2 bushels; by machine, 1 bushel. *Lee:* With planters, from 1 to 2 bushels; by hand, 3 bushels. *Woodruff:* From 2 to 4 bushels. *Cross:* From 2 to 5 bushels. *Saint Francis:* 4 bushels with planters. *Chicot:* 5 bushels. *Crittenden:* 150 pounds.

17. What implements do you use in planting?

UPLANDS.—Twelve counties report the use of a small plow to open with, and a harrow, board, or block to cover with. Nine counties report the use of the cotton-planter only. *Hot Spring, Drew, Grant,* and *Scott:* Plow to open with, and harrow, board, or block to cover with, and also cotton-planters. *Franklin* and *Boone:* The revolving planter. *Howard:* Various implements of home construction.

MISSISSIPPI RIVER ALLUVIAL REGION.—*Lee* and *Mississippi:* Ordinary farming implements. *Woodruff:* An opener and block or planter. *Cross:* Wooden planters. *Crittenden, Saint Francis,* and *Craighead:* Cotton-planters. *Chicot:* Drill the seed by hand.

18. Are cotton-seed planters used in your region?

UPLANDS.—Seventeen counties report their extensive use; eight counties to some extent, and five report them as not being used. The general opinion is very favorable, they being valued as great savers of time and labor. *Jefferson:* Not satisfactory; they are only used 6 or 8 days in a year. *Pope* and *Union:* Not much appreciated. *Sebastian:* If the spring is dry, planting by hand is the best.

19. How long usually before your seed comes up?

The time depends upon the condition of the weather and soil. The minimum time is that reported from *Desha* county, being twenty-four hours after a rain. The maximum, from 10 to 20 days, is reported from *Pulaski* and *Sevier.* Eight counties report the time as being from 5 to 10 days. *Dallas:* 8 to 20 days.

What opinion is held of their efficacy or convenience?

MISSISSIPPI RIVER ALLUVIAL REGION.—They are reported as used, more or less, in all the counties of the region, and in most cases are liked very much. *Crittenden* and *Desha:* Opinion is divided; some like them, others do not. *Cross:* In wet seasons they do well, but fail in dry ones.

Drew, Prairie, and *Mississippi:* From 3 to 10 days. *Faulkner, Craighead,* and *Grant:* From 8 to 10 days. *Lincoln, Saint Francis,* and *Woodruff:* About 10 days. Eleven counties: From 4 to 6 days. Seven counties: From 6 to 16 days.

20. At what stage of growth do you thin out your stand, and how far apart?

Prairie and *Scott* counties report the thinning of the crop to a stand when the second leaf appears. Seven counties: When the third leaf appears. Six counties report thinning out as soon as four leaves are formed. *Lee:* Delay in thinning out, after the third leaf appears, injures the crop. *Faulkner:* When the plant has from three to four leaves. *Columbia:* When the fourth or fifth leaf appears. *Cross:* When the bud leaf puts forth, and the top root sends out fibers. *Pope:* When one week old. *Ashley* and *Chicot:* From 10 to 15 days after coming up. *Marion* and *Grant:* When the plant is from three to four weeks old. *Mississippi, Lincoln, Baxter,* and *Desha:* When the plant is 3 or 4 inches above ground. *Jefferson* and *Sebastian:* From 3 to 6 inches. *White, Fulton,* and *Dallas:* As soon as it comes up. *Clark:* As soon as possible after the stalk appears. *Howard:* As first working, from May 15 to June 1.

The distances apart are, in *Jefferson* and *Ashley*, from 6 to 12 inches. Five counties: From 8 to 12 inches. *Franklin, Baxter, Montgomery,* and *Marion:* 1 foot. Seven counties: From 10 to 15 inches. Eleven: From 10 to 20 inches. *Prairie* and *Garland:* From 10 to 24 inches. *Miller:* From 18 to 25 inches. *Hot Spring* and *Arkansas:* 12 inches on upland and 18 on bottoms. In the bottom lands the distances are from 15 to 24 inches.

21. Is your cotton liable to suffer from sore-shin?

UPLANDS.—In *Arkansas, Garland,* and *Prairie* counties the disease occurs quite extensively; occasionally or to some extent in ten counties. In nine counties the cotton suffers from it when the weather in spring is wet and cold, or if the nights are cold. *Union:* On old lands and in wet seasons. *Conway:* When planted too thick. *Drew* and *Dallas:* If the young plants are injured by the hoe. *Jefferson:* Not if hilled up. *Pulaski, Boone,* and *Fulton:* Does not occur at all.

MISSISSIPPI RIVER ALLUVIAL REGION.—*Desha* and *Cross* counties report it as occurring in cold, wet seasons. *Lee, Saint Francis, Mississippi,* and *Woodruff:* To a limited extent only. *Crittenden:* Not if uninjured in hoeing. *Chicot* and *Craighead:* Not at all.

22. What after-cultivation do you give, and with what implements?

UPLANDS.—*Garland:* First use the harrow as the cotton cracks the ground, then the scraper; thin out the plants and throw dirt from the row with a small plow; then hoe and throw dirt to the plants with larger plow, after which give two good, thorough plowings with large cotton sweeps. *Dallas:* First bar off with turning plow, then hoe out grass, thinning out at the same time; next throw up dirt with shovel-plow, and repeat every ten days until August 1; then break the middles with sweep. *Union:* Plowing with scooter and the heel-sweep attached on same stock (about the same as a Dixon sweep). *Drew:* Bar off and scrape (of late improved scrapers do the work without barring); use small shovel-plow to throw soil up to cotton; then cultivate about three times with bar or shovel-plows or sweeps. *Howard:* Use wide shovels or sweeps three or four times, according to seasons, and hoe once or twice. *Fulton:* Use scraper, cultivator, and bull-tongue plow, etc. No two farms are alike or have tools alike. *Jefferson:* Scrape or harrow first; then follow, on the same day, with the sweep. If the ground is hard, repeat this two or three times, then clean the middles with sweeps. *Boone:* Four plowings and three hoeings. *Pope:* Four plowings after scraping and hoeing, first with a small shovel, and the other rows with different-sized sweeps. After-cultivation is given by first barring off with turning-plow, or using scraper; then throwing dirt to cotton with sweep; in *Miller* and *Montgomery,* where the sweep is not used for a week or ten days after scraping, then repeating the process; and in *Ashley,* where the sweep is in constant use until the crop is laid by, although some finish with turning-plow. The grass and weeds are kept out by hoes, and the ground is well stirred with sweeps, in *Marion, Scott, Clark,* and *Columbia.* The shovel-plow, either double or single, is used after scraping or hoeing, then the sweep until crop is laid by, in *White, Prairie,* and *Sebastian;* plowing with sweeps from one to four times is done in *Faulkner, Lincoln, Pulaski* (scraper also in use), and *Sevier,* where broad shovels are also used. The various implements mentioned are in use also in all of the other upland counties, and the methods are very various.

MISSISSIPPI RIVER ALLUVIAL REGION.—*Saint Francis:* Sweeps of various sizes and sometimes turning-plows; the land is generally plowed four times and hoed twice after it has been brought to a stand. *Mississippi:* Bar off with a common scraper, then throw up with single shovel, and cultivate with a sweep and turning-plow; some use a side-harrow. *Lee:* The shovel and side-harrow are used in any season, but if there is much wet weather the grass will take such hold as to render plowing necessary. *Craighead:* Scrapers, plows, and harrows are used. *Desha:* Scrapers, hoes, sweeps, and turning-plow. In other counties the implements are the same as given above, and the methods as various, except in Chicot, where the correspondent says that no after-cultivation is given.

23. What is the height usually attained by your cotton before blooming?

UPLANDS.—Six counties report the height as being from 10 to 18 inches. *Jefferson:* From 8 to 15 inches. Eight counties: From 15 to 20 inches. *Pope* and *Prairie:* From 12 to 24 inches. *Conway* and *Hot Spring:* From 18 to 24 inches. *Ashley:* From 18 to 30 inches. *Marion* and *Pulaski:* 2 feet. *Arkansas:* 1 foot on uplands; 2 feet on bottoms. *Montgomery, Baxter, Howard,* and *Crawford:* From 2 to 3 feet. *Sebastian, Drew,* and *Lincoln:* 3 feet.

MISSISSIPPI RIVER ALLUVIAL REGION.—*Saint Francis:* 12 inches *Woodruff:* Generally 15 inches. *Cross:* From 15 to 18 inches. *Chicot* and *Crittenden:* 18 inches. *Desha:* From 18 to 20 inches. *Mississippi* and *Lee:* 2 feet. *Craighead:* 2½ feet.

24. When do you usually see the first blooms?

In the southern counties the earliest time, from the 1st to the 10th of June, is reported from *Union;* the latest, July 1, from *Miller.* *Drew:* The average time from planting, according to a record of six years, is 63½ days, the earlier plantings being longer before blooming. In 1874 cotton planted April 6 bloomed the 26th of June; cotton planted May 6 bloomed the 28th of June. In 1875 cotton planted April 30 bloomed the 24th of June; in 1876 cotton planted May 10 bloomed the 5th of July; in 1877 cotton planted April 25 bloomed the 28th of June; in 1878 cotton planted May 10 bloomed the 1st of July; in 1879 cotton planted April 1 bloomed the 19th of June; cotton planted April 15 bloomed the 22d of June; cotton planted April 21 bloomed the 24th of June.

In the middle counties the two extremes are from the 15th to the 25th of June in *Howard* and the 10th of July in *Arkansas.*

In the northern counties the earliest time, from the 16th to the 20th of June, is reported from *Franklin;* the latest, from *Craighead* and *Marion,* being about the 4th of July.

25. When do the bolls first open?

In the southern counties the earliest time at which the bolls first open is the 1st of August, reported from *Columbia;* the latest, from the 10th to the 20th of August, from *Miller.* Four counties give the middle of August.

In the middle counties July 30, the earliest time, is reported from *Pulaski;* the latest, September 1, from *Sebastian.* Most of the counties report from the middle to the latter part of August.

In the northern counties the extremes are from August 10 to 15, reported from *Baxter,* and from September 15 to 20 in *Boone.* Five counties report about the middle, and six the latter part of August.

26. When do you begin your first picking, and how many pickings do you usually make?

SOUTHERN COUNTIES.—*Ashley:* From the 20th to the 25th of August in dry and 1st of September in seasonable years. *Columbia, Lincoln,* and *Chicot:* September 1. *Drew, Union,* and *Desha:* The early part of September. *Miller:* Usually in September. Three pickings are made in all counties except *Miller* and *Drew,* where two are usually made.

MIDDLE COUNTIES.—*Pulaski:* August 20. *Howard, Saint Francis,* and *Jefferson:* The latter part of August. *Clark, Prairie, Cross,* and *Garland:* September 1. *Pope, Arkansas, Hot Spring,* and *Sebastian:* The early part of September. *Montgomery:* From the 1st to the 15th of September. In the remaining counties usually

in September. One or two pickings are made in *White.* Two pickings are made in eleven counties, two or three in *Grant, Lee,* and *Jefferson,* two to four in *Pulaski,* and three in *Garland* and *Montgomery.*

NORTHERN COUNTIES.—*Mississippi:* The latter part of August. *Crawford, Marion, Baxter,* and *Crittenden:* September 1. *Faulkner, Conway,* and *Woodruff:* From first to middle of September. *Franklin* and *Fulton:* The middle of September. *Boone:* October 12. From one to two pickings are made in *Craighead,* two in nine counties, from two to three in *Crawford,* and three in *Crittenden.*

27. Do you ordinarily pick all your cotton?

UPLANDS.—*Lincoln:* Hardly ever. *Miller* and *Faulkner:* No. *Conway:* Scarcely more than half. *Ashley:* All is picked except that which is wasted by storms. *Arkansas* and *Prairie:* There is some loss on bottom lands. *Grant:* Yes, except when an overcrop is made.

In the remaining counties all the crop is said to be picked.

MISSISSIPPI RIVER ALLUVIAL REGION.—*Craighead, Crittenden,* and *Cross:* No. *Lee:* A great deal is lost in some seasons. *Mississippi:* Considerable is left on the ground. *Chicot, Desha, Woodruff,* and *Saint Francis:* Yes.

28. At what date does picking usually close?

SOUTHERN COUNTIES.—Picking closes in November in *Columbia;* about the 25th of December in *Union* and *Desha* (though often prolonged to late in January) and on uplands in *Ashley,* the date for bottoms being from the 1st to the 10th of February, January 1, but sometimes continues to March 10, in *Drew,* February 1 in Lincoln, and February 28 in *Miller.*

MIDDLE COUNTIES.—October 25 in *Pulaski.* From the 1st to the 10th of December in *Grant;* December 15 in *Howard.* The last of

December in eight counties. January 1 in *Montgomery* and *Garland.* About the 1st of February in *Sevier.*

NORTHERN COUNTIES.—Picking closes November 30 in *Boone.* From first to middle of December in *Fulton.* From December 1 to last of January in *Baxter.* December 15 in *Franklin.* About the 25th of December in *Crawford.* January 25 in *Marion.* Usually in December, but sometimes continues till March in *Conway.* February 1 in *Crittenden.* At planting time in Craighead.

29. What is the rate paid for picking?

The rate reported from different parts of the state is 75 cents per 100

pounds of seed-cotton. In *Boone* county the rate is 50 cents.

30. At what time do you expect the first "black frost"?

SOUTHERN COUNTIES.—The earliest time, from the 10th to the 20th of October, is reported from *Union;* the latest, from December 1 to 15, from *Ashley.* *Columbia,* November 15. In the remaining counties from October 17 to 25.

MIDDLE COUNTIES.—*Cross* and *Garland* report October 10. Five counties: the middle of October. Eight: From the middle to the last of October. *Lee:* From October 20 to November 15. *Scott:* In November. *Pope:* From November 24 to December 4.

NORTHERN COUNTIES.—*Marion:* October 12. *Crawford:* October 15. Five counties report from the 20th to the 27th of October. *Faulkner:* November 1. *Crittenden:* November 5. *Fulton* and *Woodruff:* From the 10th to the 15th of November. *Craighead:* November 20, which is the latest date.

November is reported from a greater number of counties in this, than in either of the middle or northern counties.

31. Do you pen your seed-cotton in the field, or gin as the picking progresses?

UPLANDS.—Fourteen counties report the seed-cotton as penned in the field. *Boone:* Usually pen in the field, covering to keep dry. *Pope* and *Fulton:* Usually pen, unless more convenient to gin. *Jefferson* and *Lincoln:* Generally pen; in some cases ginning and picking are carried on together. *Franklin:* Pen it, and, when a few bales are out, have it ginned. *Baxter, Conway,* and *Crawford:* It is usually penned in the field a short time before ginning. *Pulaski:* Gin as fast as picking progresses. *Ashley:* As much ginned as possible, the remainder penned to await ginning. *Grant:* Sometimes it is penned, so as to allow it to shrink before ginning; but frequently ginned as fast as picked. *Ark-*

ansas and *Prairie:* Both plans are adopted. *Dallas:* Gathered and placed in good house, and ginned in wet weather.

MISSISSIPPI RIVER ALLUVIAL REGION.—*Cross, Desha, Chicot, Mississippi,* and *Craighead* counties report both methods as practiced, some first pen and then haul to gin, others gin as picking progresses. *Woodruff:* Pen in the field. *Crittenden:* Gin as picking progresses. *Lee:* Sometimes share-hands prefer to pen their cotton under lock in the field, but usually it is hauled to the gin. *Saint Francis:* It is first penned; ginning commencing after several bales have been picked.

GINNING AND BALING.

32. What gin do you use? How many saws? What motive power, steam, horses, or mules?

Pratt's gin, with from 35 to 80 saws, is reported in thirteen counties; Hall's, with from 50 to 80, in seven; Brown's, with from 50 to 80, in six; the Eagle and Emery gins, with from 50 to 80 saws, each in three; the Carver, with from 35 to 80 saws, in four; the Winship, with from 50 to 80, and the Champion, with from 50 to 70,

each in two. The Gullet of 80 saws, the Pine Bluff with 60, the Clemmens with from 50 to 60, Chaffin, 35 to 80, the Dubois of 60, and Phœnix of 40 saws, each in one county. The use of steam power is reported in fifteen counties, steam- and horsepower in thirteen, and horse- or mule-power in ten.

33. How much clean lint do you make in a day's run of ten hours?

Pratt's gin of 80 saws, with steam-power, will make 5,000 pounds (*Mississippi*); with steam- and horse-power, 4,000 pounds (*Franklin*); with horse-power, 1,500 pounds (*Arkansas*); 60 saws, steam-power, 5,000 pounds (*Scott*); 4,000 pounds (*Lincoln*); 60 saws, steam- and horse-power, from 3,000 to 3,500 pounds (*Pulaski*); from 50 to 80 saws, with steam- or horse-power, 1,875 pounds (*Hot Spring*); horse-power, 1,800 to 2,000 pounds (*Saint*

Francis); from 50 to 60 saws, with steam- and horse power, from 1,500 to 2,000 pounds (*Lee*); from 45 to 60 saws, steam-power, 2,000 pounds, and horse-power, 1,000 pounds (*Union*); from 40 to 60 saws, with steam, 4,000 pounds, and horse-power, 2,000 pounds (*Baxter*); from 35 to 80 saws, horse-power, 1,600 pounds (*Jefferson*).

Hall's gin of 80 saws, steam-power, 5,000 pounds (*Faulkner*); 4,500 pounds (*Woodruff*); 60 saws, steam, 4,000 pounds (*Pope*); steam- and horse-power, 3,000 to 3,500 pounds (*Pulaski*); horse power, 1,500 pounds (*Grant*); from 50 to 60 saws, with steam-power, 2,000 pounds (*Drew*); one bale of 500 pounds for each 10 saws (*Crawford*).

Brown's gin of 70 saws, with steam- and water-power, will make 4,500 pounds (*Marion*); 60 saws, with steam-power, 5,000 pounds (*Scott*); with steam- and horse-power, 3,000 to 3,500 pounds (*Pulaski*); 50 saws, steam-power, 2,000 pounds (*Columbia*).

Gullett's gin of 80 saws, with steam-power, will make 4,000 pounds (*Conway*).

The Eagle gin of 80 saws, with steam-power, 4,000 pounds (*Chicot*); 50 saws mule-power, 900 pounds (*Desha*).

The Carver gin, 80 saws, with steam-power, 5,000 pounds (*Mississippi*); 60 saws, steam-power, 6,000 pounds (*Crittenden*).

Emery's gin of 50 saws, horse- or mule-power, will make 1,500 pounds (*Clark*); 1,200 pounds (*Garland*).

The Champion gin of 60 saws, steam-power, 6,000 pounds (*Crittenden*).

The Dubois gin of 60 saws, steam-power, 5,000 pounds (*Scott*).

The Pine Bluff gin of 60 saws, steam-power, 3,000 to 4,000 pounds (*Dallas*).

The Phœnix gin of 40 saws, with steam-power, will make 1,000 pounds (*Boone*).

34. How much seed-cotton, on an average, is required for a 475-pound bale of lint?

UPLANDS.—1,425 pounds is reported in ten counties; 1,485 in *Scott*, *Crawford*, *Prairie*, and *Howard*; 1,485 to 1,605 in *Grant*; 1,545 in *Conway*, *Garland*, *Lincoln*, *Pope*, and *Franklin*; 1,580 in *Drew*; 1,605 in *Clark*, *Pulaski*, and *Sevier*; 1,605 to 1,665 in *Jefferson*; 1,665 in *Miller*; 1,425 to 1,785 in *White*; 1,785 in *Marion*.

MISSISSIPPI RIVER ALLUVIAL REGION.—1,485 pounds is reported in *Woodruff*; 1,545 late, and 2,375 early in the season, in *Lee*; 1,665 in *Chicot*; 1,665 to 1,785 in *Desha*; 1,665 to 1,900 in *Saint Francis*; 1,795 in *Crittenden*; 1,785 in *Cross*; 1,840 to 1,900 in *Mississippi*.

In answering the above, some of the correspondents have doubtless added the toll of one tenth or twelfth for ginning; if ginning is done immediately after picking, and while the seed is green, more is required for a bale of lint than when the seed is dry. On rich bottom lands, the seed is heavier than on the uplands, and therefore more seed-cotton is required to make the same amount of lint. The common rule is that "cotton will third itself", or yield one-third of its weight of lint.

35. What press do you use for baling? What press is generally used in your region? What is its capacity per day?

No preference for any particular press is reported in ten counties. The wooden screw press is reported in seven; the iron screw in six; the Arrow in five; Brooks' in four; Deering's and home-made, each in three; the Compass, Albertson, and Planters', each in two; the Eclipse, Lewis, Lever, Check, Grasshopper, revolving wooden, McDermott, Utley's, Reynolds' Centennial, Newell's, and Provost, each in one county.

The Albertson press, with four men and two mules, will pack 25 bales (*Drew*); with three men and three mules, 12 bales (*Jefferson*); the Arrow press, with five men and two horses, will pack from 10 to 20 bales (*Jefferson*); 10 to 450 pound bales in ten hours (*Desha*); with three men and one horse, 10 bales (*Crittenden*); with two men and one horse, 8 bales (*Arkansas*). The Grass-

hopper press will pack 20 bales (*Faulkner*); the Deering press will pack ten 450-pound bales (*Desha*); with two men and two horses, 16 bales (*Pope*); Brooks' press will pack 8 bales (*Mississippi*); with two men and one mule, 8 bales (*Saint Francis*); with two men and four horses, 6 bales (*Scott*); the Eclipse and Planters' presses, with three men and three mules, each 12 bales (*Pulaski*); Reynolds' and Utley's presses, with four men and one horse, 15 bales (*Lee*); the Compass press will pack 6 bales (*Howard*); with two men and one horse, from 4 to 6 bales (*Union*); the wooden screw press will pack 4 bales (*Hot Spring*); the iron screw press with one man and one mule, 10 bales (*Grant*); with three men and one horse or mule, 7 bales (*Marion*); the home-made press will pack from 6 to 10 bales (*Baxter*).

36. Do you use rope or iron ties for baling? If the latter, what fastening do you prefer?

The use of iron ties is universal throughout the state, the old method of baling with rope having disappeared. The preference for the arrow or buckle fastening is reported in 27 counties. Some

in *Cross* prefer the buckle, others the loop. Iron loop or ring in *Union*. English buckle and tie in *Marion*. No preference or choice is reported in *White* and *Conway*.

37. What kind of bagging is issued in your region?

The use of jute bagging is reported in eleven counties; hemp and jute in seven; hemp in six; jute, hemp, and flax in *Conway*; hemp and flax in *Lee*; India or jute in *Franklin*; India or hemp

in *Union*; Greenleaf or jute in *Prairie*; Greenleaf in *Marion*, and gunny, in *Miller*. The merchants furnish the cheapest in *Craighead*.

38. What weight do you aim to give your bales? Have transportation companies imposed any conditions in this respect?

Twenty-five counties report 500 pounds. *Arkansas*, *Chicot*, *Desha*, *Jefferson*, and *Union*: 450 pounds. *Hot Spring*, *Dallas*, and *Grant*: From 450 to 500 pounds. *Crawford* and *Lee*: From 400 to 595 pounds. *Prairie*: From 500 to 550 pounds. *Baxter*: From 500 to 600 pounds. Nineteen counties report that transportation companies impose no conditions whatever. *Hot Spring*, *Faulkner*, *Lincoln*, *Jefferson*, and *Pope*: Freight charges are per bale, regardless of weight. *Franklin*: Large bales of 500 pounds and upward are preferred. *Lee*: Railroad charges are by the pound; steamer, by the bale. *Pulaski*: Railroad charges are per 100 pounds; no

conditions by steamer, the freight being per bale. *Scott*: Bales are averaged at 450 pounds. *Saint Francis*: If a bale weighs more than 600 pounds it is charged extra. *Miller*: A bale weighing less than 500 pounds is discounted; if less than 450 pounds, it is not merchantable. Bales weighing less than 400 pounds are discounted, by merchants, $3 in *Howard*, $1 in *Dallas*, and are not considered merchantable in *Sevier*. Bales weighing less than 300 pounds are discounted $2 in *Dallas*, $1 in *Cross*, and are not merchantable in *Conway*, where, also, some regulations have been attempted in regard to wrapping.

DISEASES, INSECT ENEMIES, ETC.

39. By what accidents of weather, diseases, or insect pests is your cotton crop most liable to be injured? Caterpillar, boll-worm, shedding, rot of bolls, rust, blight? At what dates do these several pests or diseases usually make their appearance, and to what cause is the trouble attributed by your farmers?

UPLANDS.—The caterpillar and boll-worm are both of common occurrence in *Columbia*, *Union*, *Pope*, *Garland*, *Drew*, *Grant*, and *Hot Spring*; sometimes found in *Crawford*, *Dallas*, and *Scott*, and

not at all in *Fulton*, *Miller*, *Faulkner*, *Pulaski*, *Baxter*, *Prairie*, *Sebastian*, *Clark*, and *White*. The time of their appearance varies from early in the summer until late in the autumn. The caterpillar alone is found extensively in *Lincoln* and *Arkansas;* to some extent in *Boone;* in some seasons in *Howard;* and not at all in *Conway, Franklin, Montgomery, Marion,* and *Sevier.* In *Jefferson* it comes too late to do any harm to the cotton. The boll-worm alone is common in *Franklin, Boone, Howard,* and *Sevier;* occurs to some extent in *Lincoln, Conway, Marion, Jefferson,* and *Montgomery,* and not at all in *Arkansas.* It injures the crops more than anything else in *Pope.*

Aphides occur generally in *Lincoln, Prairie, Sebastian, Montgomery,* and *Pulaski,* and sometimes in *Conway.* They are attributable to cold, wet springs.

The army-worm is found in *Hot Spring* and *Jefferson,* where, with the ant, it is more dreaded than the caterpillar.

Shedding is of common occurrence in all the counties of this region excepting *Boone, Jefferson, Baxter,* and *Conway,* where it only occurs to a limited extent. It is generally attributed to extreme states of the weather, either wet or dry, and appears about the middle of summer or early part of autumn. It is also caused in *Jefferson* by bad cultivation.

Rot of bolls and rust are common in *Lincoln, Faulkner, Pope, Columbia* (rust on old lands), *Arkansas, Union* (rust is black), *Garland, Drew, White, Pulaski, Miller, Grant, Clark,* and *Howard;* are found somewhat in *Jefferson, Boone, Fulton,* and *Conway,* rarely in *Crawford,* and not at all in *Franklin, Dallas,* and *Sebastian.* Rot of bolls occurs generally in wet weather.

Rust is the worst trouble in *Boone;* it also occurs quite extensively in *Woodruff, Sevier,* and *Montgomery,* owing to sudden changes of weather; in *Hot Spring,* due to cool weather; to some extent in *Prairie, Baxter,* and *Marion.* The time of occurrence is from July to September.

Blight is quite general in fourteen counties, and to some extent occurs in *Conway* and *Jefferson.*

Excessive wet weather and drought are great causes of trouble in many of the counties. Warm winters and southwesterly winds in spring damage the crop in *Lee.* The bottoms in dry seasons always yield large crops, averaging a bale or more to the acre

in *Jefferson.* Cold summers, rains, and cool, damp nights cause trouble in *Boone.*

In *Conway* there are very few pests, none ever destroying a crop. A minute insect, common to the poke-weed, is thought to produce red rust. Black rust or blight appears in spots, and either kills or causes shedding.

Early frosts injure the crop in *Baxter* and *Clark.* Drought only is feared in *Dallas.*

MISSISSIPPI RIVER ALLUVIAL REGION.—The caterpillar, in the latter part of summer, is the only source of injury in *Chicot;* it is also found in *Lee* and *Crittenden.*

The boll-worm appears in *Mississippi,* and to a slight extent in *Lee.* Shedding occurs quite extensively in *Crittenden, Lee, Mississippi,* and *Woodruff,* due to extreme states of the weather. In *Craighead* and *Desha* it is the only thing to be feared.

Rot of bolls and rust are common in *Crittenden, Mississippi,* and *Lee.* Rust also occurs in *Woodruff* and *Cross.*

Blight appears in *Crittenden, Cross, Lee, Mississippi, Saint Francis* (in July), and *Woodruff.*

The cut-worm in spring injures the crop in *Crittenden;* it is also a source of trouble in *Woodruff;* aphides in *Mississippi.* Drought occurs in August in *Saint Francis.*

The time of appearance of the various pests and diseases varies from late in the spring till fall. The cause is generally attributed to the weather, it being either too wet or too dry. *Lee:* In the same field there will be spots of diseased plants, the balance perfectly healthy. Insects cause very little uneasiness. *Crittenden:* We have suffered more with blight during the last four years than with all the other diseases together. In June, when the crop looks the best, it is attacked by blight, the most vigorous plants being attacked, causing them to wither, and nothing but the stalk remains, which slowly buds again, and finally regains its lost foliage, but never in time to make fruit before frost. The cause is unknown. *Desha:* The caterpillar does not attack the crop until too late to do harm; in fact, it is rather beneficial in stripping off the leaves.

40. What efforts have been made to obviate these pests and diseases, and with what success? Is Paris green used as a remedy against the caterpillar?

UPLANDS.—Twenty-two counties report that no efforts have been made. *Conway:* None worthy of notice. *Hot Spring:* Judicious cultivation is in some degree beneficial, and is attended with fair success. *Howard:* Very little, if any. *Grant:* None in this county as yet, though farmers are trying, with limited success, devices which may be suggested by experience and observation. *Pope:* Several patent remedies have been applied, but very little benefit has been derived from the use of them. *Garland:* But little, except to create moisture by thorough plowing during shedding; the success is good. If it is not done, the first rain will cause the "squares" to fall off. *Pulaski:*

Very little success has attended the use of everything that money could buy or brains could think of.

MISSISSIPPI RIVER ALLUVIAL REGION.—*Crittenden, Craighead, Desha, Mississippi, Saint Francis,* and *Woodruff* report that no efforts have been made. *Chicot:* Paris green and London purple have been tried with good success, provided there is no rain to wash them off after their application. *Cross:* But very little. Some advocate deep plowing, and others shallow culture. *Lee:* The worm may be killed, but there is no way to treat the rust and blight.

41. Is rust or blight prevalent chiefly on heavy or ill-drained soils? Do they prevail chiefly in wet or dry, cool or hot seasons? On which soil described by you are they most common?

They are prevalent on ill-drained soils in cool weather, either wet or dry, on low lands in *Cross,* in wet and dry weather in *Miller,* and on black, sticky land in *Faulkner;* on light sandy land, when very hot weather follows rain, in *Garland* and *Drew;* in wet and cool weather on gray and black soils in *Fulton;* on lowlands in *Hot Spring, Desha,* and *Howard;* and on sandy lands in *Lincoln.* On heavy soils in wet and cool weather, most common on clay sandy loam or post-oak land in *Boone;* on black land in *Marion;* and on sandy land in *Sebastian.*

On heavy and ill-drained soils, in wet and cool seasons, in *Franklin;* most common on sandy creek bottoms in *Dallas;* on sandy and crawfishy land in *Mississippi;* in wet seasons on sandy land in *Lee;* on clay land in *White;* on low and old lands in *Grant;* in cold seasons, on bottoms in *Clark;* and on old lands that are not fertilized in *Columbia.* They appear on all soils, and in all

seasons in *Arkansas* and *Prairie,* more especially on old lands long planted in cotton; in wet and cool seasons in *Union,* and in wet seasons in *Sevier;* in hot and wet seasons they have been known to spread over an entire field during the night, in *Pope.* They prevail chiefly in hot and dry seasons, and are most common on river bottoms in *Pulaski* and on loamy bottoms in *Scott;* in cool weather and on every sandy soil in *Chicot.* In very dry seasons the light sandy soil suffers most; in wet, the other kinds, in *Woodruff.* In hot seasons on the highest, and also on walnut land in *Saint Francis.* Red rust in dry, and blight in wet seasons, appear to some extent on all soils in *Conway.* In *Crawford* the soils are so uniformly good that the matter has not received much attention. When they appear, which is very seldom, they are found on heavy and ill-drained soils, in wet and cool seasons.

LABOR AND SYSTEM OF FARMING.

42. What is the average size of farms or plantations in your region?

Pope and *Cross* counties: From 10 to 500 acres. *Sebastian*: From 20 to 60 acres. *Union*: From 20 to 200 acres. *Crawford*: From 30 to 100 acres; some few farms of 350 acres. *Grant*: From 40 to 100 acres. *Baxter* and *Conway*: From 50 to 100 acres. *Marion*: 40 acres. *Faulkner, Boone, Franklin, Garland, Montgomery,* and *Scott*: 50 acres. *Fulton*: From 50 to 150 acres. *Arkansas*: From 50 to 500 acres. *Pulaski*: From 50 to 1,200 acres. *Columbia* and *Prairie*: 60 acres. *White*: 80 acres. *Clark*: 100 acres. *Hot Spring*: From 100 to 250 acres. *Craighead*: From 100 to 300 acres. *Lee*: From 120 to 600 acres. *Desha*: 150 acres. *Saint Francis* and *Dallas*: 160 acres. *Drew*: 200 acres. *Mississippi*: 250 acres. *Lincoln* and *Miller*: 300 acres. *Howard*: 320 acres. *Jefferson*: 450 acres. *Crittenden* and *Chicot*: 500 acres. *Sevier*: The majority of the farms are small.

43. Is the prevalent practice "mixed farming" or "planting"?

Mixed farming is reported as practiced on large farms in *Sevier*; to some extent in *White*; and as being the prevalent practice in twenty-eight counties. Mixed farming, cotton predominating, is practiced in *Crawford*. "Planting" is the prevalent practice in *Clark, Crittenden, Jefferson, Lincoln,* and *Miller*.

44. Are supplies raised at home or imported, if the latter, where from?

UPLANDS.—Supplies are raised at home in *Marion, Scott, Montgomery, Hot Spring,* and *Boone*. The bulk is raised at home in *Franklin*. In *Columbia* abundant supplies can be raised, but a large amount is imported from Saint Louis. In *Dallas* hogs and cattle are raised, and many raise all their supplies; negroes obtain a great deal from the woods; importations are from St. Louis. In *White* about one-half are raised at home, the balance being imported from Saint Louis and Memphis. In *Drew* the importations are made from Saint Louis; pork and corn are raised, but not in sufficient quantities. In *Union* about one-half the meat and nearly all the corn are raised at home, the balance of supplies being imported from Saint Louis and New Orleans. Six counties report the greater part of the supplies raised at home, the importations being as follows: From Saint Louis, in *Pope, Clark,* and *Miller*; from Saint Louis and Memphis in *Conway, Faulkner,* and *Prairie*, where some supplies are also obtained from New Orleans; flour and bacon from Missouri in *Fulton*; flour and pork in *Sebastian* and *Baxter*, from Springfield, Missouri. Partly raised at home and partly imported from Saint Louis in *Howard, Pulaski, Crawford, Garland,* and *Grant*, where importations are also made from Cincinnati. Supplies are imported from Louisville, Memphis, Saint Louis, and Cincinnati in *Arkansas*; from Saint Louis and New Orleans in *Sevier*; from Saint Louis, Memphis, and New Orleans in *Lincoln* and *Jefferson*.

MISSISSIPPI RIVER ALLUVIAL REGION.—In *Craighead* enough can be raised at home, but it is cheaper to obtain some from Saint Louis. In *Lee*, sometimes, corn has to be bought from Memphis, owing to there having been too much cotton planted. In *Woodruff* pork and flour are, to some extent, imported from the north. In *Desha* about two-thirds of the supplies are raised at home, the remainder being imported from Memphis and Saint Louis. In *Saint Francis*, partly raised at home and partly imported from Memphis. In *Cross*, some raise their supplies, others import from northwestern markets. Supplies are imported from Saint Louis and New Orleans in *Chicot*, and from Saint Louis and Memphis in *Mississippi* and *Crittenden*.

45. Is the tendency toward the raising of home supplies increasing or decreasing?

The tendency is reported as decreasing in *Chicot*, and this year (1880) in *White*; as neither increasing nor decreasing in *Montgomery, Boone,* and *Mississippi*; as increasing to some extent in *Jefferson*; and as increasing in thirty-one counties.

46. Who are your laborers chiefly?

UPLANDS.—Whites chiefly in *Boone, Baxter, Fulton, Conway, Montgomery, Hot Spring, Scott, Franklin, Sevier* (negroes mostly on large farms), and *Marion*. Partly whites and partly negroes in *Grant, White, Pope, Dallas, Columbia, Garland, Crawford, Pulaski, Howard, Clark, Faulkner,* and *Prairie*. The laborers are chiefly negroes in *Lincoln, Arkansas, Miller, Union, Drew,* and *Jefferson*. A few Chinamen are also reported in the last county. In *Sebastian* negroes generally own their farms.

MISSISSIPPI RIVER ALLUVIAL REGION.—The laborers are chiefly Americans in *Craighead*, Americans and negroes in *Woodruff*. Whites of various nationalities and negroes in *Lee* and *Cross*. Negroes and a few Chinese in *Chicot*, and chiefly negroes in *Desha, Mississippi, Saint Francis,* and *Crittenden*.

47. How are wages paid—by the year, month, or day? At what rates, and where payable?

Wages are paid daily, weekly, or monthly in *Desha, Lee, Mississippi, Crawford,* and *Drew*; in the latter county yearly hands generally contract to leave part of their wages unpaid until the end of the year. Weekly in *Crittenden* and *Pulaski*. Monthly in *Baxter, Clark, Saint Francis, Marion,* and *Miller*. Monthly or yearly in *Columbia* and *Grant*. Yearly in *Hot Spring* and *Sevier*. On demand in *Montgomery, Prairie,* and *Scott*. At the gathering or laying by of the crop in *Cross, Pope, Franklin,* and *Dallas*. In the latter county laborers can, if they wish, obtain their wages as needed. When the work is done, or at the end of the time contracted for, in *Boone, Fulton, Garland, Howard, Union, White,* and *Woodruff*. In *Lincoln* one-half is paid monthly, balance on the 1st of August. A share of the crop constitutes the wages, payable when it is gathered, in *Faulkner, Chicot, Arkansas,* and *Conway*. In the latter county very little hiring is done. In *Jefferson* one-half is cash, payable weekly or monthly; the remainder, a share in the crop, is paid in December.

The rates are: 50 cents per day in *Scott*; 50 to 75 cents in *Dallas* and *Grant*; 60 cents to $1 in *Lee*; 75 cents in *Desha, Crittenden, Jefferson, Mississippi,* and *Prairie*; 75 cents to $1 in *Crawford* and *Howard*; 75 cents to $1 50 in *Union*; 90 cents in *Drew*. From $6 to $12 per month, board included, in *Marion* and *Pope*; $10 in *Columbia, Miller,* and *Jefferson*; $10 to $13 in *Dallas* and *Grant*; $10 to $15 in *Hot Spring* and *Montgomery*; $10 to $18 in *Crawford*, and including board, in *Prairie*; $11 in *Franklin*; $12 in *Saint Francis, Fulton* (or $15 without board), and *Clark* ($16 without board); $12 50 in *Scott* and *Howard*; $12 to $15 in *Desha*, and, including board during crop season, in *Baxter*; $12 to $20 in *Lincoln*; $14 in *Woodruff*; $15 in *Mississippi* and *Cross*; $15 to $20 in *Union*; $16 66 in *Drew*; $120 per year in *Scott*, and $150 in *Drew, Howard,* and *Union*.

640

48. Are cotton farms worked on shares? Are any supplies furnished by owners?

In *Montgomery* there are no exclusive cotton farms. In *Hot Spring* cotton farms are worked on shares to some extent only; in all other reported counties they are worked or rented on shares. The owner furnishes supplies and working implements (2 plows, 1 basket, and 1 horse or mule to every 15 or 20 acres), and receives, as his share, one-half the crop; in *Arkansas, Craighead, Cross, Crittenden, Desha, Garland, Pulaski, Lee, Mississippi, Union,* and *Miller* counties, in the latter 2 plows, 1 cotton-basket, and 1 horse or mule are furnished for each 15 or 20 acres. Likewise in *Sevier, Pope,* and *Columbia,* excepting that the laborer furnishes his own supplies or pays for them out of his share of the crop. The tenant boards himself and provides the gin and press; the owner furnishes all other implements, and receives one-half the crop in *Saint Francis, Clark, Conway,* and *Franklin.*

If the tenant provides himself with all supplies and implements he retains three-fourths, or, if the owner furnishes everything, one-half of the crop, in *Dallas, White, Woodruff,* and *Hot Spring;* also in *Chicot, Prairie,* and *Scott,* excepting that the owner does not furnish provisions. In *Hot Spring* and *Prairie* one-third of the corn is also included in the rent of the land. The owner receives one-third or one-fourth of the crop as rent for the land, or, if he furnishes everything except gin and press, one-half of the crop, in *Grant, Marion. Faulkner, Howard,* and *Crawford.* The tenant delivers to the owner, as rent, one-third of the crop in the field or one-fourth at the gin, in *Sebastian, Boone, Fulton,* and *Baxter.* In *Jefferson* the owner furnishes everything but board and receives one-half the crop; gardens are given to the negroes rent free.

49. Does your system give satisfaction? How does it affect the quality of the staple? Does the soil deteriorate or improve under it?

Nineteen counties report the share system as giving entire satisfaction. In *Hot Spring* and *Miller* they give general satisfaction. In *Columbia, Franklin, Arkansas,* and *Conway* they are not altogether satisfactory. In *Cross, Scott,* and *Marion* they are not always satisfactory to the planter. In *Drew* they give satisfaction when the crops are good. In *Grant, White,* and *Crittenden,* when the work is well performed. In *Dallas, Desha,* and *Saint Francis* they do not give satisfaction.

Eighteen counties report the system as having no effect on the quality of the staple. *Prairie:* The quality is not so good as when the owner picks his own crop. *Dallas:* The effect is very bad; cotton rarely classes as low middling under the share system. *Conway:* Unfavorably; the staple does not rate as high by two degrees as it did in "olden times". *Columbia:* The quality is lowered by the laborers not taking proper care. *Franklin, Desha, Grant,* and *Clark:* It deteriorates under the tenant system.

Cross: The quality is not affected to any extent. *Pope:* The staple is good if gathered at the right time and care taken with it. *Howard* and *Pulaski:* The quality of the staple is improved. *Jefferson:* The one-half share system makes the best crops in quantity and quality. *Lee* and *Chicot:* The share hands are more careful in gathering the cotton than hired pickers, and hence a higher quality of staple is obtained, commanding a better price.

In twenty-five counties the soil is reported as deteriorating under the share system. *Desha:* It deteriorates because the injurious grasses and weeds are not destroyed. *Howard:* From lack of skill in cultivating it. *Garland:* Deteriorates unless manured. *Faulkner* and *Mississippi:* The soil deteriorates to some extent. *Crawford, Boone, Lincoln, Pope, Chicot,* and *Scott:* The soil maintains its fertility. *Craighead:* It improves.

50. Which system (wages or share) is the better for the laborer? Why?

UPLANDS.—The *wage system* is thought to be better in *Dallas;* also in *Scott, Drew, Prairie, Howard, Garland,* and *White,* because the laborer is sure of his money and takes no risk of crop failures; in *Lincoln,* because, under the share system, they are inclined to be extravagant, and if they fail to come out ahead they are apt to blame the employer; in *Pope,* because until this year the price of cotton has been so low; in *Columbia* and *Clark,* because the laborer puts in more time.

The *share system* is reported to be better for the laborer in *Baxter, Sebastian, Fulton, Arkansas, Franklin,* and *Marion,* because, if he is industrious, he can realise more than under the wage system; in *Union,* because the share system prevents him from spending the value of his crop before it is made; in *Miller,* because he can make two or three times as much as under the wage system; in *Faulkner,* because as a general thing good crops are raised; in *Ashley,* because he only works five months to make a crop, and four or five to gather it in; in *Boone,* because it is a greater incentive to industry; in *Crawford,* because he can save enough in a few years to buy a farm of his own; in *Jefferson,* because the teams, tools, and supplies are certain and good. *Hot Spring:* Both systems are good. *Conway:* Doubtful; a share in the crop makes the laborer improvident. *Sevier:* If he is economical he can do well under either system. In *Grant* and *Pulaski* both systems are practiced.

MISSISSIPPI RIVER ALLUVIAL REGION.—The *share system* is the bet-

ter in *Lee, Desha,* and *Woodruff,* because the laborer is not as likely to run about and spend all he makes as under the wage system, for he cannot obtain money, except for clothes, rations, etc., until the crop is gathered; in *Craighead,* because everything is supplied, and the laborer gets half the crop; in *Chicot,* because they take more interest in the production and gathering of the crop; in *Saint Francis,* because they are more contented; in *Crittenden* it is better for both owner and laborer when the contract is faithfully carried out. The negro has his home, garden "patch", and fuel free of charge; has the loan of a cow, if he does not own one. He generally raises pigs (all his own), and his house is situated "away" from the "quarter". These conditions engender feelings of respectability and pride at home, a laudable ambition to excel in farming, and to a great extent obviates the necessity of overseeing on the part of the owner. The best class of colored citizens work this way, and prefer it. Only a portion of the land is able to be worked in this manner. When hired labor is employed, the hands are irresponsible, lazy, and vicious, and require wages every Saturday; when paid they leave for the city; when "broke" they return and work another week: are inveterate gamblers, and are called "roustabouts". The wage system is thought to be better in *Mississippi,* because the employer gets more work done and the laborer more money; in *Cross,* because each knows what to do.

51. What is the condition of the laborers?

UPLANDS.—The condition of the laborer is good in *Fulton, Franklin, Miller, Faulkner, Boone, Hot Spring, Pope,* and *Drew* counties; generally good in *Grant* and *Crawford;* mostly comfortable in *Sevier;* negroes very comfortable in *Jefferson;* good and comfortable when wages are paid in *Prairie;* good when they are steady and industrious in *White, Garland,* and *Conway;* very good, being better clothed than formerly, and all have a little cash in *Ashley;* cheerful and easy in *Howard;* the majority of whites are prosperous in *Columbia;* laborers are independent, because

they are scarce in *Dallas* and *Scott.* The condition of the laborers is improving in *Pulaski;* contented, but usually very poor in *Union;* bad generally in *Arkansas;* poor in *Baxter, Lincoln,* and *Marion;* and very poor in *Clark.*

MISSISSIPPI RIVER ALLUVIAL REGION.—The condition of the laborer is good in *Lee* and *Craighead;* generally good in *Chicot, Woodruff,* and *Mississippi;* very good in *Saint Francis;* and not very good in *Cross.* The condition of the laborers has been improving during the last few years in *Desha.*

41 C P

52. What proportion of negro laborers own land or the houses in which they live ?

In *Arkansas, Clark, White,* and *Saint Francis,* 1 per cent. ; in *Prairie,* 4 per cent. ; in *Jefferson, Lincoln,* and *Pulaski,* 5 per cent. ; in *Sevier, Ashley, Columbia, Drew,* and *Woodruff,* 10 per cent. ; in *Grant,* 12½ per cent. ; in *Cross, Crawford,* and *Union,* 20 per cent. ; in *Garland,* 25 per cent. ; in *Dallas,* 50 per cent.; in *Sebastian,* 66⅔ per cent. ; in *Boone, Scott,* and *Montgomery,* 75 per cent. In *Craighead* nearly all negroes own their houses. In *Hot Spring* some of them own land and houses; in *Desha, Miller, Mississippi, Chicot, Pope, Conway,* and *Howard* only a very few ; in *Faulkner* and *Crittenden* none; in *Lee* they are buying land and setting up for themselves; in *Baxter* and *Marion* there are very few negroes, and in *Fulton* there are none.

53. What is the market value of the land described in your region ?

UPLANDS.—In *Union* the value is from 50 cents to $5 per acre; in *Dallas* from $1 to $5; in *Prairie* from $1 to $50; in *Fulton* and *Grant* from $2 to $10; in *Columbia,* $2 to $10; in *Hot Spring* from $2 50 to $20; in *Marion* ffom $3 to $10; in *Pope* from $3 to $20; in *Howard,* $5; in *Clark* from $5 to $8; in *Baxter, Scott, White,* and *Sevier* from $5 to $10; in *Garland* from $5 to $20; in *Crawford* from $5 to $25; in *Conway,* $5 to $30 (cleared); in *Sebastian,* $7 to $10; in *Miller,* $10 to $12; in *Arkansas* and *Lincoln,* $10 to $20; in *Pulaski,* $10 to $30; in *Boone,* $15; in *Faulkner,* $25 to $50; in *Ashley,* $3 to $6 for uplands, and $10 to $20 for bottoms, three-fourths of which is woodland; in *Jefferson* before the war the bottoms were from $25 to $50, and the uplands $5 to $10 per acre; in *Drew* the market value is nominal. MISSISSIPPI RIVER ALLUVIAL REGION.—In *Desha* the value varies, as the land is subject to overflows; in *Cross* it is from $1 to $10; in *Craighead,* $5 to $10 for improved land; *Lee,* $10 to $25 for improved land; in *Saint Francis,* $12; in *Crittenden,* $20; *Mississippi,* $40 to $50; *Chicot,* $50.

54. What rent is paid for such land ?

UPLANDS.—One to two dollars per acre, or one-fourth the cotton and one-third the grain, in *Grant ;* from $1 50 to $2 per acre in *Dallas ;* $2 to $5 in *Pope* and *Garland ;* $2 to $6 in *Conway ;* $2 to $8 in *Prairie ;* $2 to $10 in *Hot Spring ;* $2 50 to $3 in *Boone* and *Howard ;* $2 50 to $4 in *White* and *Sevier ;* $3 to $4 in *Miller ;* $3 to $5 in *Drew ;* $5 in *Scott ;* $5 to 10 in *Pulaski ;* $6 to $10 in *Lincoln* and *Faulkner ;* $3 to $3 50 for uplands and from $5 to $6 for bottom land in *Ashley* and *Crawford.* Land is scarcely ever rented for cash in *Marion* and *Sebastian.* The rent paid in *Jefferson* is from 50 to 100 pounds lint per acre; one-fourth of the crop in *Union* and *Clark ;* one-fourth of the cotton and one-third of the corn in *Columbia* and *Arkansas ;* one-fourth of the cotton and one-third of all cereals in *Franklin, Fulton,* and *Baxter.* MISSISSIPPI RIVER ALLUVIAL REGION.—*Uross :* From $2 to $5 per acre in *Cross ;* $3 to $6 in *Lee ;* $4 in *Woodruff ;* $5 in *Saint Francis* and *Crittenden ;* $5 to $8 in *Mississippi* and *Desha,* or in the latter county from 60 to 100 pounds of lint per acre; sometimes $10 per acre, but generally one-fourth of the crop when the tenant furnishes everything, in *Chicot ;* one-fourth of the cotton and one-third of the grain in *Craighead.*

55. How many acres or bales per "hand" is your customary estimate ?

UPLANDS.—*Howard :* 3 bales is a good average. *Clark :* 3 bales of cotton, or 6 acres in cotton and 6 in corn. *Fulton* and *Franklin :* 3 bales with other crops. *Grant :* 3 to 4 bales, including other crops. *Union :* 15 acres, or 3 to 6 bales, depending upon disasters. *Miller* and *White :* 4 to 8 bales. *Lincoln, Arkansas,* and *Prairie :* 5 bales. *Jefferson :* 8 acres in cotton, or 6 to 7 bales. *Scott* and *Sevier :* 8 bales, or in the latter county 15 acres. *Faulkner :* 10 bales. *Crawford :* 10 to 15 acres or 10 bales. *Hot Spring* and *Pope :* 10 acres in cotton and from 5 to 7 in corn. *Pulaski, Sebastian, Boone,* and *Garland :* 10 acres. *Columbia :* 15 acres in cotton, or 12 in cotton and 6 in corn. *Baxter :* 16 acres in cotton, or 5 in cotton and 15 in corn. *Ashley :* From 5 to 6 bales on uplands, and 8 to 10 on bottoms. *Conway :* 4 bales is an average, but it ought to be 10 to a good hand. *Dallas :* If white labor is employed, 4 bales ; if negro labor, 3 bales. MISSISSIPPI RIVER ALLUVIAL REGION.—*Uross :* From 4 to 6 bales. *Desha :* 5 to 6 bales, or 10 acres. *Woodruff :* 7 bales. *Saint Francis :* 6 bales, or 8 acres. *Chicot :* In good seasons 8 bales ; otherwise 3 or 4. *Mississippi :* 10 bales. *Crittenden :* 12 acres, or 12 bales. *Lee :* From 6 to 15 bales, according to location, or 10 acres. *Craighead :* 16 acres of either corn or cotton.

56. To what extent does the system of credits or advances on the growing cotton crop prevail in your region ?

UPLANDS.—*Fulton :* It prevails to a small extent; none of the farmers are rich, and they pay cash for what they buy. *Miller* and *Boone :* The system is quite general. *Arkansas, Jefferson,* and *Grant :* It prevails to a very large extent. *Columbia :* To a ruinous extent. Nearly all the hired laborers are negroes, who obtain their supplies from the merchants, the farmers having no control over their labor. *Marion :* Farmers frequently have to mortgage to merchants at very high rates of interest. *Conway :* It prevails to a large and ruinous extent, and induces laborers to spend their year's wages in advance, and leads to lawsuits. *White, Pope,* and *Franklin :* To a very serious extent, so much so that in many cases the credit given is equal to the full value of the crop. *Dallas* and *Garland :* To an alarming extent; in the latter county the condition of things is improving. *Baxter* and *Drew :* Largely, and to its fullest extent; generally a planter is credited for the full amount of the crop, and in some instances to a greater amount. *Faulkner, Sevier, Lincoln,* and *Union :* The system is almost universal. *Sebastian :* The poorer class of farmers secure the advances they need by mortgaging a few acres of the growing crop; the better class obtain credit without mortgage. *Hot Spring :* Farmers obtain credit to the extent of about two-thirds the value of the prospective crop. *Ashley :* Three-fourths of those renting and one-half of those owning land obtain advances from merchants. *Pulaski :* About 20 per cent. of the farmers obtain advances. *Scott :* About 35 per cent. *Crawford :* Probably 60 per cent. *Clark :* 66⅔ per cent. *Prairie :* 90 per cent. *Howard :* Credit is given to the amount of at least one-half of the bacon consumed; breadstuffs are raised at home. MISSISSIPPI RIVER ALLUVIAL REGION.—*Cross* and *Mississippi :* The system prevails to a great extent. There are but very few who run their farms upon a credit system. *Chicot :* The crop is made entirely on a credit system, as the negroes give a mortgage before the crop is planted for all supplies, to enable them to make and gather it. *Lee :* Nine-tenths of the white and all the colored planters give mortgages to merchants for their supplies. *Crittenden :* Nine-tenths of the crops are made by money advanced by merchants of Memphis and New Orleans. *Desha, Woodruff,* and *Saint Francis :* The credit system is almost universal. *Craighead :* Farmers buy more than they can pay for, but that don't hurt their feelings one particle.

57. At what stage of its production is the cotton crop usually covered by insurance ?

In a large number of counties the crop is not insured at any stage before shipment. The crop is generally insured when in the gin-house in *Crittenden, Pulaski, Jefferson,* and *Lincoln,* or in the last county when on the boat; sometimes when in the gin-house in *Clark.* It is insured after baling in *Miller ;* as soon as bolling commences in *Grant ;* generally as soon as planted in *Woodruff ;* when picking commences, and also when in the gin-house, in *Lee.*

58. What are the merchants' commissions and charges for storing, handling, shipping, insurance, etc., to which your crop is subject? What is the total amount of these charges against the farmer per pound or bale?

The usual rates of commissions are 2½ per cent. on sales; in *Scott*, 1½ per cent.; in *Howard*, 1 per cent. Drayage, usually 25 cents; *storage*, 50 cents per bale per month; insurance, 25 to 50 cents, and shipping in *Mississippi* county, 75 cents per bale. The total amount of these charges are $3 per bale in *Mississippi* county; $3 25 in *Lee*; $3 50 in *Grant, Desha*, and *Miller*; $3 75 in *Pope, Boone*, and *Faulkner*; $3 85 in *Arkansas*; $4 in *Drew, Lincoln, Saint Francis*, and *Howard*; $4 50 in *Franklin*; $5 in *Chicot, White, Crittenden, Cross, Columbia, Conway* (most of the cotton is sold in local markets), and *Union*; $6 50 in *Clark*; $8 75 in *Prairie*; $10 in *Sevier* and *Scott*; $10 to $15 in *Fulton*; $1 50 to $2, exclusive of freight, in *Hot Spring*. *Dallas*: The charges

amount to about $4 per bale, but usually cotton is sold from the wagons, as the farmers who are under mortgage are not allowed to ship, and the others have no confidence in the merchants. *Jefferson*: The charges are from 1 to 1½ cents per pound; when the spindles are working in Little Rock, two yards of cloth are obtained for one pound of cotton. *Craighead*: Merchants buy cotton at the gin, paying about $13 a bale. *Pulaski, Baxter*, and *Garland*: The usual practice is to sell to local merchants. *Crawford* and *Woodruff*: At home no charge is made for handling and shipping; the expense begins at the depot, and depends on the market to which it is shipped; in the former county it varies from 1 to 1½ cents per pound.

59. What is your estimate per pound of the cost of production in your region, exclusive of such charges, and with fair soil and management?

UPLANDS.—*Clark*: 4 cents. *Lincoln*: 4 to 5 cents. *White, Conway,* and *Drew*: 5 cents. In *Drew* it is at 2 cents less this year (1879) than it was last. *Prairie*: On bottom lands, 5½ cents; on uplands, 7 cents. *Scott, Sevier,* and *Hot Spring*: 6 cents. *Union*: 6 to 7 cents. *Miller, Faulkner, Garland,* and *Boone*: 7 cents. *Arkansas*: 7½ cents. *Baxter, Crawford,* and *Pulaski*: 8 cents. *Pope* and *Howard*: 8½ cents. *Dallas*: 9 cents. The cost is about 33½ per cent. of the value of the crop in *Columbia*, 55 per cent. in *Franklin*, and 85 per cent. in *Grant*. *Jefferson*: $5 per acre is about the cost. *Sebastian*: $10 per acre. *Conway*: The

cost is about 5 cents per pound, or $25 per bale. In this estimate regard is had to its production in an ordinary family, owning the land and doing their own work. When produced on rented land by hired labor the cost is uncertain and very variable. If a family produces cotton, that production ought always to be more profitable than any other, none being realized from a year's labor.

MISSISSIPPI RIVER ALLUVIAL REGION.—*Chicot*: 4 cents. *Lee*: 4½ to 5½ cents. *Mississippi*: 5 cents. *Crittenden* and *Woodruff*: 7 cents. *Saint Francis*: 9 cents. *Desha*: 10 cents.

Cost of each item of labor and material expended in the cultivation of an acre of cotton.

Items.	Conway.	Crittenden.	Boone.	Garland.	Grant.
Rent..	$4 00	$5 00	$3 00	$8 00	....
Fencing, repairs, and interest on	50	2 00	20	1 00	....
Knocking stalks.............................	50	25		50	....
Pulling and burning stalks.................	1 00	....	40	50	....
Listing		25	75		....
Breaking up	2 00		1 00		....
Harrowing	25	20	20		....
Barring old beds............................	25				....
Splitting middles	25		20		....
Reversing	1 00				....
Laying off	10		15		....
Bedding up	1 00	50		1 50	....
Splitting middles	25	....		50	....
Knocking off beds	10				....
Planting:					
Opening	10		15		....
Dropping	10	50	15	50	....
Covering	10		20		....
Replanting			15		....
Seed	30	50	20	25	....
Thinning	50	75	75	1 50	....
Number of plowings.........................	2 00	2 50	5 00	5 00	....
Number of hoeings	2 00	3 00	3 10	3 00	....
Wear and tear of implements................	50	....	75		....
Management	....	....	....	....	$11 50
Team use	3 50				
Forage, per acre	1 25				1 25
Making rail pen			50		....
Cabins and fuel	1 00				....
Board for hands					1 50
For hoes			50		....
Waste and damage..........................	1 00				....
Total	22 55	15, 45	16 85	17 25	14 25
Picking, per hundred-weight	75	75	50	75	23½
Hauling to gin	2 00	25	1 00	2 00	....
Ginning, per hundred-weight	30	75		25	....
Bagging and ties............................			2 00		....

NOTES ON THE PRECEDING TABLE.

CONWAY COUNTY.—The rent for bottom lands is from $5 to $6; for uplands, from $2 to $3 per acre. It is quite hard to fix the cost of fencing, repairs, etc. Other cleaning up, besides pulling and burning of stalks, depends upon the condition of the field. Cotton land in good culture is usually only bedded up, opened, and planted; reversing is seldom done. If a cotton-planter is used, the whole cost of planting is about 10 cents per acre. Thirty cents allows for 3 bushels of seed; 1 bushel may do. The ginning is done for one-twelfth toll. The cost of management depends upon the size of the farm. The number of plowings is four; of hoeings, three. All the items above enumerated are not always chargeable to a crop, and others may be. The whole cost of producing a bale of 400 pounds of lint may be placed at $25 when labor and forage are cheap, but often the cost will be $40, and sometimes much more than the cotton is worth.

CRITTENDEN COUNTY.—Knocking down is done by one man, with two mules hitched to a log. This is also done instead of harrowing. Pulling and burning stalks has not been done for ten years past.

BOONE COUNTY.—The cost of ginning is from one-twelfth to one-fifteenth of the cotton as toll.

GARLAND COUNTY.—With the above-mentioned cost, the usual yield of one acre of the best bottom land is 1,600 pounds of seed-cotton, which will pay for ginning (one-tenth toll) and make a 500-pound bale of lint for the producer.

GRANT COUNTY.—One-tenth is the toll for ginning, including wrapping and ties.

644

INDEX TO COTTON PRODUCTION IN ARKANSAS.

REPORT

ON THE

COTTON PRODUCTION OF THE STATE OF TEXAS,

WITH A DISCUSSION OF

THE GENERAL AGRICULTURAL FEATURES OF THE STATE.

BY

R. H. LOUGHRIDGE, Ph. D.,
SPECIAL AGENT.

TABLE OF CONTENTS.

iii

LETTERS OF TRANSMITTAL.

BERKELEY, CALIFORNIA, *June* 1, 1882.

To the SUPERINTENDENT OF CENSUS.

DEAR SIR: I transmit herewith a report on the cotton production and agricultural features of the state of Texas, with illustrative maps, by Dr. R. H. Loughridge, special agent.

The data upon which this report and map are based are derived partly from personal observations by Dr. Loughridge (himself a former resident of the state), made during a three months' rapid reconnaissance under the auspices of the Census Office, and partly from personal correspondence and answers to schedules, as well as from all other available published sources. I thus feel assured that the information here conveyed may fairly claim to be, both as to correctness and completeness, considerably in advance of any former publications.

It will be noted that the map differs materially from that given by Mr. Roessler in 1874, nor do the descriptions given in the text agree altogether with those published by Mr. Oscar Loew about the same time; but being based upon closer and wider observations by one well qualified for the task, I think they will be found measurably in accordance with the facts, so far as the immense area of the state has permitted their ascertainment. A much more minute agricultural survey is, of course, eminently desirable.

Very respectfully,

E. W. HILGARD,
Special Agent in charge of Cotton Production.

Professor E. W. HILGARD,
Special Agent in charge of Cotton Production.

DEAR SIR: I have the honor to transmit to you the accompanying report on cotton production in Texas, embracing also a description of the agricultural features of the state, with other information that bears either directly or indirectly upon that great industry. In this report I have followed the plan adopted by you for use in all of the states under your charge, comprising—

Part I. The general description of the state, its separation into agricultural regions, and their respective descriptions.

Part II. Brief county descriptions, with abstracts from the reports of correspondents.

Part III. Details of cotton culture and production, as summarized exclusively from schedules of questions, answered by correspondents in each county.

Comparative tables of population, production of cotton, corn, and other crops, returned by the Tenth Census, as well as tables of chemical analyses made of characteristic soils of the state, accompany the report. The chemical analytical work was done at the laboratory of the University of Alabama, in Tuscaloosa, by Messrs. Henry McCalley, assistant in chemistry, University of Alabama; J. B. Durrett, of Tuscaloosa; Chappell Cory, of Selma, Alabama, and myself, the necessary supplies being furnished by the Census Office. Special determinations of humus and other elements have since been made under your instructions by Mr. George Colby, at the University of California, in Berkeley.

42 C P

The material from which this report is compiled was obtained in part from data gathered in a general and hasty trip by myself in 1879 (from the 15th of August to the 25th of December) over parts of the state, visiting the chief points along the lines of travel from the east as far west as Graham, Breckenridge, Brownwood, San Saba, Austin, San Antonio, Cuero, and Indianola; in part from a previous residence in the southern portion of the state, and also from various publications at my command.

Early in 1880 printed schedules of questions on cotton culture were addressed to parties in each organized county of the state. Answers have been received from the greater number of the counties, and abstracts will be found in Parts II and III.

The paragraph on the geology of the state is perhaps more lengthy than the subject of the report would seem to justify; but as all the geological data exist only in detached portions in various publications (which are out of print), and as the rock structure of a country bears an important relation to its lands, I have, at your suggestion, given a general outline of the geological formations as far as was possible from the information at my command. The outlines of the Cretaceous and later formations were mostly obtained from personal observations.

Two maps accompany the report, one representing as nearly as possible the general outlines of the chief agricultural divisions of the state without giving the details and irregularities, which could only be obtained by a long term of examinations; the other showing the relative percentages of total area and cotton acreage. I have endeavored to keep the report within proper limits, and hence much is omitted that to some persons may appear to be important. This is especially so in Part II, where the county descriptions are made as concise as possible, though giving the chief agricultural features, and are limited to those counties in which cotton is produced.

The names of parties who have furnished important information, either by schedule or by letter, will be found in Part III. I would add that the postmasters in many of the counties have responded promptly to any notes of inquiry that I may have addressed them. Among the publications of more or less service to me were Thrall's *History of Texas, Description of Southwestern Texas*, reports of the United States topographical engineers, Pacific railroad reports, and Roessler's map of Texas.

Very respectfully,

B. H. LOUGHRIDGE,
Special Agent.

TABULATED RESULTS OF THE ENUMERATION.

TABLE I.—AREA, POPULATION, TILLED LAND, AND COTTON PRODUCTION.
TABLE II.—ACREAGE AND PRODUCTION OF LEADING CROPS.

TABLE I.—AREA, POPULATION, TILLED LAND, AND COTTON PRODUCTION.

COTTON-PRODUCING COUNTIES.

Counties.	Land area.	POPULATION.						TILLED LAND.			COTTON PRODUCTION.				Product per acre.			Cotton average per square mile.	Bales per square mile.
		Total.	Male.	Female.	White.	Color'd.	Average per square mile.	Acres.	Per cent. of area.	Per cent. of tilled land.	Acres.	Bales.	Fraction of bale.	Seed-cotton.	Lint.				
The State	*265,290	1,591,749	827,840	755,909	1,197,237	394,513	6.1	7,025,536	4.5					500 lbs.	Lbs.	Lbs.			
Cotton counties	128,430	1,526,075	799,480	726,595	1,135,021	391,054	12.1	7,564,456	8.2	26.7	3,178,435	906,284	0.37	555	185	17.2	6.4		
Other counties, mostly western arid lands.	135,860	65,674	38,360	27,314	62,216	3,458	0.5	64,080	0.1										

OAK, HICKORY, AND PINE UPLANDS, WITH SOME PRAIRIES.

Cass	950	16,734	8,657	8,067	10,274	6,460	17.6	33,069	13.7	41.9	34,622	16,181	0.46	690	230	36.7	17.0		
Morris	260	5,023	2,626	2,406	2,988	2,044	19.4	29,160	17.5	36.5	10,650	4,880	0.46	690	230	41.0	18.8		
Titus	420	5,950	3,080	2,879	4,600	1,350	14.2	30,507	11.3	30.8	9,395	4,923	0.52	780	260	22.4	11.7		
Franklin	300	5,280	2,719	2,561	4,666	614	17.6	26,539	13.2	33.9	5,680	4,048	0.47	705	235	36.9	13.6		
Hopkins	750	15,461	8,052	7,409	13,306	2,155	20.6	85,799	17.9	22.4	19,342	8,379	0.48	645	215	25.7	11.0		
Rains	270	3,035	1,586	1,449	2,785	250	11.2	16,127	9.3	27.3	4,300	1,915	0.44	660	220	16.3	7.1		
Wood	700	11,212	5,879	5,323	6,653	2,559	16.0	48,786	10.9	31.7	13,406	7,881	0.48	720	240	22.1	10.3		
Camp	205	3,921	2,051	1,870	2,035	1,946	29.7	33,367	27.0	34.5	11,473	5,659	0.50	750	260	27.4	28.4		
Marion	430	10,983	5,590	5,393	3,750	7,234	36.2	36,978	13.2	46.2	17,102	7,815	0.44	640	220	40.7	17.9		
Upshur	530	10,966	5,396	4,971	6,884	3,982	19.7	58,063	17.4	33.4	19,418	8,022	0.41	615	205	37.3	15.4		
Gregg	280	6,530	4,409	4,121	3,817	4,713	30.5	38,585	21.5	35.7	13,767	4,590	0.33	495	165	49.2	16.4		
Harrison	900	25,177	12,753	12,424	7,976	17,201	26.0	126,462	22.0	36.9	46,614	17,619	0.38	570	190	51.8	19.6		
Panola	800	13,219	6,296	5,923	7,234	4,985	15.2	71,946	14.1	29.6	28,430	10,844	0.36	540	180	35.6	12.9		
Rusk	920	18,966	9,678	9,306	10,307	8,179	20.6	90,714	16.9	28.4	38,226	11,145	0.29	435	145	41.7	12.1		
Smith	920	21,863	10,992	10,871	11,506	10,357	22.8	139,918	19.7	27.8	45,705	16,325	0.36	540	180	47.6	17.0		
Van Zandt	840	13,619	6,601	6,018	11,456	1,163	16.0	63,507	11.6	28.1	17,879	6,967	0.40	600	200	20.9	8.3		
Henderson	960	9,735	5,221	4,514	7,641	2,094	10.1	45,641	7.9	22.4	15,768	6,159	0.39	585	195	16.4	6.4		
Navarro	1,040	21,702	11,544	10,158	16,356	5,346	20.9	138,069	20.4	32.6	45,716	23,066	0.26	435	145	44.0	12.2		
Limestone	970	16,246	8,448	7,798	13,075	3,171	16.7	84,309	13.6	43.1	36,539	9,057	0.25	375	125	36.6	9.3		
Freestone	880	14,921	7,656	7,325	8,402	6,453	17.0	100,662	17.9	31.2	31,373	8,182	0.26	390	130	35.7	9.3		
Anderson	1,000	17,395	9,052	8,343	9,619	7,776	17.4	78,514	13.3	30.1	23,735	7,646	0.32	480	160	23.7	7.5		
Cherokee	1,000	16,723	8,442	8,281	11,014	5,709	16.7	90,430	14.1	32.8	29,706	9,013	0.33	495	165	29.7	9.0		
Nacogdoches	970	11,590	5,960	5,630	6,550	5,040	11.9	66,863	10.8	25.1	14,762	4,791	0.29	435	145	17.3	4.9		
Shelby	800	9,523	4,919	4,613	7,369	2,154	11.9	44,764	8.7	26.0	15,136	6,171	0.33	570	190	26.2	7.7		
Sabine	570	4,161	2,106	2,055	3,168	993	7.3	13,631	4.3	22.6	5,323	1,706	0.32	480	160	9.3	3.0		
San Augustine	560	5,084	2,617	2,467	3,169	1,915	9.1	25,120	7.0	28.7	7,219	2,797	0.38	570	190	12.9	4.9		
Angelina	850	5,239	2,660	2,579	4,665	584	6.0	19,729	3.5	28.8	5,621	2,219	0.41	615	205	6.5	2.6		
Trinity	750	4,915	2,496	2,419	3,753	1,162	6.6	23,421	3.3	30.6	4,909	2,666	0.39	585	195	6.5	3.5		
Polk	1,150	7,189	3,611	3,578	4,842	2,347	6.5	28,955	3.4	30.3	7,339	3,689	0.50	750	250	6.4	3.2		
Houston	1,170	16,702	8,586	8,116	9,465	7,237	14.3	73,854	9.9	36.8	26,519	9,720	0.36	540	180	22.0	8.3		
Leon	1,000	12,817	6,624	6,193	7,707	5,110	13.8	68,078	10.6	34.6	23,372	7,960	0.31	465	155	23.6	7.9		
Robertson	870	22,383	11,821	10,562	11,386	10,997	25.7	117,990	21.2	42.2	49,854	16,980	0.34	540	180	57.3	20.8		
Madison	480	5,283	2,765	2,620	3,603	1,702	11.7	34,268	8.3	37.7	9,133	3,656	0.29	435	145	19.9	8.8		
Walker	780	13,094	6,732	5,291	5,787	15.3	51,129	10.5	39.4	20,162	6,441	0.32	480	160	26.5	8.5			
Grimes	780	18,003	9,487	9,186	8,320	10,290	22.9	79,877	16.0	45.0	35,984	11,701	0.32	495	165	46.1	15.0		
Brazos	520	13,576	7,132	6,444	7,235	6,261	26.1	61,603	18.6	45.4	26,044	9,748	0.35	525	175	52.9	18.7		
Burleson	650	9,242	4,966	4,345	5,356	3,897	14.2	47,190	11.3	32.4	15,296	5,065	0.39	585	195	23.5	9.2		
Milam	960	15,650	8,750	6,909	14,732	2,995	16.5	61,023	14.4	41.3	37,473	10,944	0.29	435	145	27.8	11.0		
Lee	600	8,487	4,466	4,096	6,991	1,896	14.6	48,961	11.6	27.0	13,963	5,358	0.40	600	200	35.1	8.9		
Bastrop	900	17,215	9,000	8,215	11,202	7,123	18.1	66,190	10,114	0.41	615	205	35.7	10.3					
Gonzales	1,070	14,840	7,687	7,153	9,974	4,866	13.9	88,536	12.9	25.7	22,729	7,511	0.33	495	165	21.2	7.0		
Wilson	760	7,118	3,783	3,335	6,197	921	9.0	33,542	6.7	17.3	5,814	1,874	0.32	480	160	7.4	2.4		
Total	31,490	511,212	264,786	246,426	320,881	190,321	16.2	2,561,485	12.9	35.2	914,305	325,854	0.36	540	180	29.0	10.3		

LONG-LEAF PINE REGION.

Newton	670	4,359	2,223	2,136	2,852	1,507	5.0	13,450	2.4	26.1	3,510	1,393	0.28	570	190	4.0	1.5		
Jasper	970	5,779	2,919	2,860	3,241	2,538	6.0	17,304	2.8	25.7	4,456	1,410	0.32	480	160	4.6	1.5		
Orange	390	2,938	1,610	1,328	2,475	463	7.5	2,023	0.8	3.3	56	22	0.38	495	165	0.2	0.1		
Hardin	850	1,870	987	883	1,634	236	2.2	3,368	0.6	7.8	264	103	0.39	585	195	0.3	0.1		
Tyler	920	5,825	2,921	2,904	4,323	1,502	6.3	19,371	3.3	28.9	3,543	1,348	0.40	600	200	6.0	2.0		
Liberty	1,170	4,999	2,615	2,384	2,565	2,434	4.3	13,027	1.7	28.9	3,788	1,852	0.49	735	245	3.2	1.6		
Total	5,140	25,770	13,225	12,545	17,090	8,680	5.0	68,543	2.1	25.6	17,587	7,362	0.41	615	205	3.4	1.4		

* The additional water area is 2,490 square miles, comprising coast waters (bays, gulfs, etc.), 2,510 square miles; rivers, 800 square miles; lakes and ponds, 180 square miles.

TABLE I.—AREA, POPULATION, TILLED LAND, AND COTTON PRODUCTION—Continued.

COTTON-PRODUCING COUNTIES—Continued.

Counties.	Land area.	POPULATION.						TILLED LAND.			COTTON PRODUCTION.		Product per acre.			Cotton acreage per square mile.	Bales per square mile.
		Total.	Male.	Female.	White.	Color'd.	Average per square mile.	Acres.	Per cent. of area.	Per cent. of tilled land.	Acres.	Bales.	Fraction of bale.	Seed-cotton.	Lbs.		
														Lbs.	Lbs.		
SOUTHERN AND COAST PRAIRIE REGION.													500 lbs.				
Region east of the Brazos river.	*Sq. mis.*																
San Jacinto	640	6,186	3,100	3,077	2,851	3,335	9.7	26,660	6.2	36.3	9,840	5,364	0.54	810	270	15.4	8.4
Montgomery	1,050	10,154	5,248	4,906	4,926	5,228	9.7	54,785	8.2	24.9	12,311	4,093	0.31	465	156	12.7	3.9
Waller	500	9,024	4,649	4,975	3,192	5,832	18.0	31,665	9.9	31.9	10,704	3,923	0.39	585	195	20.2	7.8
Harris	1,800	27,985	14,074	13,911	17,160	10,825	15.5	25,122	2.2	17.7	4,446	1,892	0.42	645	215	3.3	3.3
Galveston	670	24,121	12,099	12,022	16,454	5,667	36.0	2,790	0.7	10.4	289	136	0.47	705	235	0.4	0.2
Chambers	350	2,187	1,180	1,007	1,494	693	3.6	3,306	0.6	4.2	140	91	0.65	975	325	0.2	0.1
Jefferson	1,000	3,489	1,896	1,563	2,290	1,199	3.5	4,796	0.7	2.8	133	77	0.58	870	290	0.1	0.1
Total	6,510	82,146	42,195	40,941	50,367	32,779	12.8	148,155	3.6	25.8	86,237	15,565	0.41	615	205	5.9	2.4
Region west of the Brazos river.																	
Washington	609	27,565	14,028	13,537	13,345	14,720	45.9	138,712	36.3	42.0	58,705	20,692	0.35	525	175	97.8	34.5
Austin	700	14,429	7,419	7,010	10,490	3,939	20.6	73,426	16.4	42.6	31,921	13,135	0.43	630	210	44.7	18.8
Fayette	950	27,996	14,487	13,509	19,167	8,829	29.3	187,318	22.3	43.5	58,352	24,706	0.43	630	210	60.8	25.8
Colorado	900	16,673	8,476	8,197	7,686	8,987	18.5	96,865	16.8	34.1	32,994	15,582	0.47	705	235	36.7	17.3
Lavaca	1,000	13,641	6,965	6,676	10,221	3,420	13.6	94,970	14.8	27.1	25,728	9,976	0.39	580	196	25.7	10.0
De Witt	900	10,082	5,141	4,941	7,344	2,963	11.2	41,792	7.3	18.2	7,635	3,183	0.39	495	145	8.5	2.4
Victoria	880	6,289	3,105	3,184	3,883	2,406	7.1	34,895	4.3	7.1	1,739	730	0.42	630	210	2.0	0.8
Jackson	900	2,723	1,393	1,330	1,310	1,413	3.0	8,829	1.5	7.3	645	202	0.31	465	155	0.7	0.2
Matagorda	1,400	3,940	2,055	1,885	1,416	2,524	2.8	17,917	2.0	19.2	3,435	2,095	0.61	915	305	2.5	1.5
Calhoun	905	1,739	869	870	1,192	547	1.8	778	0.1								
Karnes	720	3,270	1,742	1,528	2,780	490	4.5	51,398	11.0	3.1	1,607	288	0.18	270	90	2.2	0.4
Atascosa	1,300	4,217	2,279	1,938	3,930	279	3.5	14,744	1.9	9.6	1,432	450	0.32	495	165	1.3	0.4
Frio	1,000	2,130	1,199	931	2,065	65	2.1	5,822	0.9	9.7	543	156	0.29	435	145	0.5	0.2
Live Oak	1,100	1,994	1,057	937	1,918	76	1.8	3,846	0.5	0.5	16	4	0.35	375	125		
Bee	890	2,296	1,231	1,067	2,145	153	2.6	7,188	1.3	0.6	44	9	0.30	300	100		
Goliad	820	5,832	2,998	2,834	4,166	1,666	7.1	30,547	5.8	5.8	1,779	728	0.41	615	205	2.2	0.9
Refugio	850	1,585	833	752	1,349	236	1.9	2,955	0.6	1.2	36	15	0.42	630	210		
San Patricio	730	1,010	535	475	936	74	1.4	1,809	0.3	0.3	6	2	0.32	495	165		
Total	16,530	147,413	75,812	71,601	95,893	51,561	8.9	755,272	7.1	30.0	226,001	91,048	0.40	600	200	13.7	5.5
CENTRAL BLACK PRAIRIE REGION.																	
Cooke	900	20,391	10,888	9,503	19,560	831	22.7	98,180	17.0	28.3	27,795	11,547	0.42	630	210	30.9	12.8
Montague	890	11,257	6,076	5,181	11,210	47	12.6	48,834	8.6	22.4	10,947	4,172	0.38	570	190	12.3	4.7
Wise	900	16,601	8,871	7,790	16,436	165	18.4	84,081	14.6	25.4	21,352	7,521	0.34	510	170	23.7	8.0
Denton	900	18,143	9,730	8,413	17,071	1,072	20.2	110,220	19.1	27.0	29,785	11,568	0.29	585	196	33.1	12.9
Collin	900	25,983	14,100	11,883	24,008	1,980	28.5	170,577	30.3	26.2	48,236	22,145	0.46	690	230	54.8	24.3
Hunt	870	17,230	9,184	8,046	16,015	1,215	19.8	111,797	20.1	23.2	36,906	10,905	0.43	630	210	39.8	12.4
Delta	200	5,597	2,961	2,636	4,990	686	21.5	28,389	17.7	30.4	9,640	4,911	0.55	825	275	34.4	16.9
Kaufman	880	15,448	8,191	7,257	13,471	1,977	18.6	84,317	15.9	31.6	26,659	10,686	0.40	600	200	33.1	13.9
Rockwall	150	2,984	1,615	1,369	2,896	86	18.9	36,443	27.5	31.9	5,786	2,630	0.45	675	225	36.6	17.5
Dallas	900	33,488	18,079	15,409	28,580	4,958	37.3	190,543	33.1	22.3	44,377	21,469	0.52	780	260	49.3	23.9
Tarrant	900	24,671	13,292	11,379	23,488	2,183	27.4	143,440	24.9	19.4	27,621	10,950	0.39	585	195	30.9	13.2
Parker	900	15,870	8,673	7,197	15,350	520	17.6	78,707	13.7	19.1	15,086	4,454	0.30	450	150	16.7	4.9
Hood	490	6,125	3,217	2,908	5,927	198	12.5	34,819	11.1	20.5	7,139	1,966	0.28	430	140	14.6	4.0
Erath	1,000	11,796	6,222	5,574	11,539	257	11.8	61,647	9.6	23.1	14,320	3,857	0.30	300	100	14.3	3.9
Somervell	200	2,649	1,396	1,253	2,631	18	13.3	15,600	12.2	25.8	4,030	1,096	0.26	390	130	20.2	5.3
Johnson	900	17,911	9,529	8,382	17,387	574	20.0	134,842	30.5	30.0	40,446	13,778	0.34	510	170	58.0	20.0
Ellis	900	21,294	11,320	9,974	18,755	2,539	22.1	172,084	28.3	30.3	52,172	18,808	0.36	540	180	54.9	20.0
Hill	1,000	16,554	8,872	7,682	15,356	1,298	16.6	135,331	21.2	28.5	38,585	8,860	0.22	330	110	38.5	8.4
Bosque	1,000	11,917	6,056	5,150	10,718	499	11.2	68,981	10.8	28.5	19,624	8,653	0.20	300	100	19.6	8.8
Hamilton	900	6,365	3,395	3,000	6,341	34	6.5	35,604	5.7	19.2	6,840	1,147	0.17	355	85	7.6	1.2
Lampasas	850	5,421	2,842	2,579	5,248	173	6.4	25,435	5.2	15.6	626	0.14	210	70	5.4	0.7
Coryell	950	10,924	5,677	5,247	10,539	385	11.5	78,763	13.0	25.0	19,886	3,321	0.17	355	85	20.7	3.5
McLennan	1,000	26,934	14,001	12,933	19,276	7,658	24.9	203,882	30.5	26.2	58,394	12,777	0.34	390	130	49.4	11.8
Falls	730	16,240	8,524	7,716	9,565	6,675	20.8	114,987	22.0	34.5	39,669	12,496	0.32	480	160	50.9	16.0
Bell	1,000	20,518	10,706	9,812	18,783	1,735	20.8	139,039	30.2	24.6	37,826	9,217	0.34	360	120	37.8	9.2
Williamson	1,100	15,155	8,054	7,101	13,520	1,635	13.8	141,362	30.2	18.1	18,528	4,217	0.23	345	115	16.8	3.8
Travis	1,000	27,028	14,166	12,862	18,410	8,618	27.0	86,734	13.0	34.0	29,500	9,271	0.31	465	155	28.5	9.2
...	1,000	...	...	...	18,410	...	...	54,914	15.9	34.4	15,209	7,009	0.49	690	200	35.0	14.1

TABLE L.—AREA, POPULATION, TILLED LAND, AND COTTON PRODUCTION—Continued.

COTTON-PRODUCING COUNTIES—Continued.

Counties.	Land area.	POPULATION.					Average per square mile.	Per cent of col'd.	TILLED LAND.	Per cent of tilled land.	COTTON PRODUCTION.		Product per acre.			Cotton acreage per square mile.	Bales per square mile.
		Total.	Male.	Female.	White.	Color'd.			Acres.		Acres.	Bales.	Fraction of bale.	Seed-cotton lbs.	Lint lbs.		
CENTRAL BLACK PRAIRIE REGION—continued.	Sq. mls.												500 lbs.	Lbs.	Lbs.		
Hayes..................	680	7,555	4,069	3,486	6,076	1,479	11.1	32,711	7.5	30.2	9,868	3,441	0.35	525	175	14.5	5.1
Blanco..................	710	3,583	1,948	1,635	3,415	168	5.0	16,090	3.5	18.9	3,039	690	0.23	345	115	4.3	1.0
Gillespie..............	980	5,228	2,764	2,464	5,096	132	5.3	10,127	1.6	40.2	4,082	767	0.19	285	95	4.2	0.8
Kerr	1,100	2,168	1,145	1,023	2,075	93	2.0	9,481	1.3	4.9	460	72	0.15	233	75	0.4	0.1
Kendall..............	670	2,763	1,492	1,271	2,588	175	4.1	9,410	2.2	19.2	1,808	285	0.16	240	80	2.7	0.4
Comal..................	670	5,546	2,864	2,682	5,276	270	8.3	32,414	7.8	17.5	5,800	2,102	0.36	540	180	8.7	1.1
Guadalupe............	710	12,202	6,375	5,822	8,747	3,455	17.2	69,660	15.3	23.6	16,469	6,521	0.40	600	200	23.2	9.2
Bexar..................	1,190	30,470	16,083	14,387	26,603	3,867	25.8	54,200	7.2	7.9	4,273	1,543	0.36	540	180	3.6	1.3
Medina................	1,300	4,492	2,396	2,096	4,209	283	3.5	16,967	2.0	4.0	685	239	0.43	630	210	0.5	0.2
Bandera	1,000	2,158	1,116	1,042	2,127	31	2.2	11,636	1.6	1.9	223	53	0.23	345	115	0.2	0.1
Uvalde................	1,550	2,541	1,425	1,116	2,478	63	1.6	3,466	0.9	4.1	141	58	0.36	570	190	0.1	......
Total..............	38,440	514,387	273,371	240,886	452,179	62,078	15.4	2,941,154	13.7	25.3	744,085	249,892	0.34	510	170	22.3	7.5
NORTHWESTERN RED-LOAM PRAIRIE REGION.																	
Clay..................	1,100	5,045	2,764	2,281	5,019	26	4.6	24,586	3.5	13.4	3,289	1,155	0.35	525	175	3.0	1.1
Wichita	590	433	298	185	416	17	0.7	2,478	0.7	4.2	103	43	0.42	630	210	0.2	......
Baylor	900	715	435	280	709	6	0.8	3,480	0.4	12.1	326	83	0.25	375	125	0.4	0.1
Archer................	900	596	354	242	589	7	0.7	3,614	0.6	2.9	104	43	0.41	615	205	0.1	......
Jack..................	870	6,626	3,574	3,052	6,508	118	7.6	29,338	3.5	16.2	4,751	1,444	0.30	450	150	5.5	1.7
Young................	900	4,726	2,538	2,188	4,709	17	5.3	23,122	4.0	8.9	2,049	554	0.27	405	135	2.3	0.6
Throckmorton	900	711	413	296	699	12	0.8	3,741	0.6	1.4	51	10	0.20	300	100	0.1	......
Jones	900	546	320	226	542	4	0.6	1,191	0.2	6.8	81	19	0.23	345	115	0.1	......
Shackelford	900	2,037	1,199	838	1,781	256	2.3	2,307	0.4	1.0	23	5	0.23	330	110	......	......
Stephens	900	4,725	2,566	3,180	4,700	25	5.3	18,042	3.1	3.6	686	187	0.30	300	100	0.8	0.2
Palo Pinto............	960	5,885	3,530	3,355	5,797	28	6.1	24,463	4.0	17.5	4,362	865	0.21	315	105	4.5	0.9
Eastland..............	900	4,855	2,681	2,174	4,827	13	5.4	19,722	3.4	14.5	3,284	743	0.33	345	115	3.6	0.8
Callahan	900	3,453	2,028	1,425	3,419	34	3.6	8,471	1.6	5.1	434	86	0.20	300	100	0.5	0.1
Coleman..............	1,340	5,603	2,028	1,575	5,568	35	2.9	17,017	2.1	4.7	796	243	0.31	465	155	0.6	0.2
Brown................	1,200	5,414	4,480	3,934	5,291	123	7.0	45,655	5.9	9.3	4,254	998	0.23	345	115	3.5	0.8
Comanche	930	8,608	4,560	4,048	8,529	79	9.3	44,191	7.4	21.0	9,361	2,098	0.23	345	115	10.0	2.3
San Saba..............	1,130	5,234	2,758	2,566	5,183	141	4.7	21,075	2.9	13.4	2,819	400	0.14	210	70	2.5	0.4
McCulloch............	1,000	1,533	869	664	1,511	22	1.5	2,866	0.4	5.1	145	54	0.37	555	185	0.1	0.1
Mason	900	2,655	1,452	1,198	2,614	41	3.0	17,224	3.0	1.5	262	64	0.24	360	120	0.3	0.1
Llano	900	4,962	2,636	2,326	4,896	66	5.5	17,558	3.0	12.5	3,247	489	0.31	315	105	2.5	0.5
Burnet................	1,000	6,855	3,621	3,234	6,607	248	6.9	37,188	5.6	18.2	7,024	1,399	0.20	300	100	7.0	1.4
Total..............	19,920	82,307	44,905	37,402	80,924	1,383	4.1	306,195	2.9	12.6	46,301	10,981	0.34	360	190	2.3	0.5
RED RIVER ALLUVIAL COUNTIES.																	
Bowie	900	10,965	5,817	5,148	6,628	4,337	12.2	36,576	6.7	30.1	11,599	7,956	0.69	1,035	345	12.9	8.8
Red River	1,080	17,194	8,961	8,233	10,912	6,282	16.2	83,005	12.2	27.7	31,291	17,669	0.56	840	280	29.5	16.7
Lamar	900	27,193	14,139	13,054	20,445	6,748	30.3	123,533	21.4	33.7	40,390	24,672	0.61	915	305	44.9	27.4
Fannin	890	25,501	13,697	11,804	22,081	3,420	28.7	106,735	27.5	29.6	44,813	22,386	0.50	750	250	50.4	25.2
Grayson	960	38,108	20,069	18,039	33,549	4,559	39.7	185,522	30.2	23.2	41,339	19,166	0.46	690	230	43.1	20.0
Total..................	4,710	118,961	62,698	56,278	93,619	25,366	25.3	535,371	19.5	28.2	169,133	91,849	0.54	810	270	35.9	19.5
BRAZOS ALLUVIAL OR SUGAR-BOWL REGION.																	
Fort Bend	880	9,380	4,946	4,434	1,871	7,509	10.7	38,379	6.8	28.3	10,673	6,431	0.59	885	295	12.4	7.3
Wharton	1,070	4,549	2,295	2,264	917	3,632	4.3	22,735	3.3	24.5	5,563	3,182	0.57	855	285	5.2	3.0
Brazoria	1,400	9,774	5,145	4,629	2,280	7,594	7.0	28,415	3.2	19.0	5,402	3,484	0.64	960	320	3.9	2.5
Total	3,350	23,703	12,376	11,327	5,082	18,665	7.1	89,529	4.2	24.4	21,638	13,097	0.60	900	300	6.5	3.9
RIO GRANDE VALLEY.																	
Cameron..............	3,000	14,959	7,865	7,094	14,842	117	5.0	15,909	0.8	0.2	25	23	0.92	1,380	460	......	......
Hidalgo	2,350	4,347	2,272	2,075	4,233	114	1.8	2,843	0.2	0.8	24	9	0.36	570	190	......	......
	5,350	19,306	10,137	9,169	19,075	231	3.6	18,752	0.5	0.3	49	32	0.65	975	325	......	......

TABLE I.—AREA, POPULATION, TILLED LAND, AND COTTON PRODUCTION—Continued.

NON-COTTON-PRODUCING COUNTIES.

Counties.	Land area.	POPULATION.					TILLED LAND.
		Total.	Male.	Female.	White.	Colored.	Acres.
	Square miles.						
Total	82,370	62,759	36,914	26,845	60,376	3,383	64,090
Aransas	440	996	508	488	917	79	229
Concho	950	800	504	296	723	17	123
Crockett	2,500	· 127	76	51	127	....	148
Crosby	900	82	77	5	81	1	45
Dimmit	1,000	665	390	275	649	16	584
Donley	900	160	136	24	150	1	214
Duval	1,700	5,732	3,173	2,559	5,687	45	3,956
Edwards	950	266	155	111	265	1	284
El Paso	8,000	3,845	1,954	1,891	3,598	247	10,587
Encinal	1,700	1,902	1,123	779	1,901	1	12
Fisher	900	136	94	43	135	1	35
Gray	900	56	50	6	55	1	50
Hardeman	1,130	50	43	8	48	1	72
Haskell	900	48	43	5	46	2	55
Hemphill	900	149	95	54	148	2	365
Kimble	1,300	· 1,343	737	606	1,335	8	1,447
Kinney	1,700	4,487	2,801	1,686	4,006	481	4,231
Knox	900	77	55	22	74	3	120
La Salle	1,500	789	507	282	775	14	555
Lipscomb	900	69	59	10	67	2	24
McMullen	1,180	701	450	251	654	47	455
Maverick	1,300	2,967	1,685	1,282	2,873	94	937
Menard	920	1,280	800	480	1,202	27	788
Nolan	· 900	640	371	269	685	5	856
Nueces	2,500	7,673	4,328	3,345	7,044	629	5,406
Pecos	11,000	1,807	1,064	743	1,680	127	4,105
Presidio	12,500	2,873	1,761	1,113	2,444	429	5,687
Runnels*	900	980	600	380	967	13	....
Starr	2,500	8,304	4,689	3,665	8,098	211	1,391
Taylor	900	1,736	978	758	1,728	8	2,794
Tom Green	12,500	5,615	3,343	1,272	3,966	649	1,065
Webb	1,500	5,273	3,015	2,258	5,089	184	1,179
Wilbarger	940	126	86	40	126	....	976
Zapata	1,300	3,636	1,897	1,639	3,620	16	3,209
Zavalla	1,300	410	210	200	400	10	12,194

* Organized 1880.

POPULATION OF THE COUNTIES.

	Total.	Male.	Female.	White.	Colored.		Total.	Male.	Female.	White.	Colored.
Total	1,215	1,446	469	1,840	75	Childress and Collingsworth	81	80	1	27	4
						Cottle, Dickens, King, and Motley	116	92	24	115	1
Andrews, Dawson, Gaines, Martin, Terry, and Yoakum ...	44	37	7	43	1	Floyd, Garza, and Lynn	48	40	8	47	1
Armstrong, Briscoe, Randall, and Swisher	50	43	8	49	1	Hall	36	29	7	35	1
Bailey, Cockran, Hale, Hockley, Lamb, and Lubbock	25	25	....	25	....	Scurry	103	73	29	94	8
Borden, Howard, and Mitchell	202	152	50	195	7	Hansford, Ochiltree, and Sherman	18	16	2	18	....
Carson, Hutchinson, Moore, Potter, and Roberts	110	88	22	108	2	Wheeler	512	363	159	477	35
Castro, Dallam, Deaf Smith, Hartley, Oldham, and Parmer.	425	279	146	424	1	Kent and Stonewall	196	160	36	183	13

AREAS OF UNORGANIZED COUNTIES.

Counties.	Area.	Counties.	Area.	Counties.	Area.	Counties.	Area.	Counties.	Area.
Total	46,490	Cockran	820	Hale	1,100	Lubbock	900	Randall	900
		Collingsworth	900	Hall	900	Lynn	900	Roberts	900
Andrews	1,500	Cottle	1,100	Hansford	910	Martin	900	Sherman	910
Armstrong	900	Dallam	1,400	Hartley	1,470	Mitchell	900	Scurry	900
Bailey	1,050	Dawson	900	Hockley	900	Moore	900	Stonewall	900
Borden	900	Deaf Smith	1,400	Howard	900	Motley	1,140	Swisher	900
Briscoe	900	Dickens	900	Hutchinson	900	Ochiltree	900	Terry	900
Carson	900	Floyd	1,100	Kent	900	Oldham	1,470	Wheeler*	900
Castro	900	Gaines	1,500	King	900	Parmer	850	Yoakum	820
Childress	750	Garza	900	Lamb	1,100	Potter	900		

* Organized 1879.

TABLE II.—ACREAGE AND PRODUCTION OF LEADING CROPS.

COTTON-PRODUCING COUNTIES.

Counties.	COTTON.		INDIAN CORN.		OATS.		WHEAT.		SWEET POTATOES.	
	Acres.	Bales.	Acres.	Bushels.	Acres.	Bushels.	Acres.	Bushels.	Acres.	Bushels.
Total for the State	2,178,435	805,284	2,468,567	29,065,172	286,010	4,893,930	273,570	2,567,737	19,580	1,460,979
OAK, HICKORY, AND PINE UPLANDS.										
Cass	34,822	16,181	34,410	427,683	3,188	35,150	363	1,651	434	46,041
Morris	10,650	4,880	11,062	144,914	1,256	15,706	275	1,398	150	12,524
Titus	9,896	4,923	11,370	179,550	1,997	30,045	372	1,926	110	10,660
Franklin	8,080	4,048	9,804	144,297	1,519	28,986	489	2,448	52	4,495
Hopkins	19,343	8,279	25,573	818,214	7,974	157,162	3,804	20,644	256	14,756
Rains	4,390	1,915	5,477	75,555	1,055	25,351	552	4,226	81	7,609
Wood	15,486	7,381	18,685	355,079	2,801	40,729	2,932	16,644	168	13,080
Camp	11,473	5,689	11,360	153,467	1,544	22,077	334	3,361	78	8,347
Marion	17,102	7,515	13,554	137,006	565	6,562	13	30	169	15,023
Upshur	19,418	8,023	20,728	246,117	2,517	36,067	1,425	5,838	294	26,139
Gregg	13,787	4,500	13,411	120,819	827	7,161	22	702	145	11,611
Harrison	46,614	17,619	38,508	278,961	765	7,542	18	147	588	47,520
Panola	29,480	10,944	27,452	192,090	1,525	18,749	44	205	292	27,764
Rusk	38,226	11,145	39,744	267,706	2,965	30,953	128	506	418	33,386
Smith	43,703	16,285	43,631	515,515	4,633	54,005	549	3,229	387	25,823
Van Zandt	17,573	5,957	21,635	302,427	4,084	76,744	1,506	8,221	187	14,496
Henderson	15,762	6,158	18,607	254,828	2,490	38,907	179	959	165	12,050
Navarro	46,716	12,958	40,133	521,462	4,288	131,548	2,872	25,180	96	6,125
Limestone	35,519	9,097	32,981	336,620	2,497	60,035	1,269	13,887	156	12,974
Freestone	31,372	8,182	29,242	253,742	1,462	32,623	151	1,947	290	14,032
Anderson	23,725	7,548	29,652	306,722	2,780	38,510	17	119	229	15,172
Cherokee	29,706	9,813	37,344	450,573	4,312	54,483	210	1,358	296	21,894
Nacogdoches	16,762	4,791	25,102	218,205	896	9,600	....	....	294	21,968
Shelby	16,136	5,171	20,965	185,484	1,900	13,356	201	849	310	22,489
Sabine	5,252	1,706	5,522	66,362	296	2,618	....	....	183	13,334
San Augustine	7,219	2,737	11,443	80,422	561	7,827	....	....	172	13,624
Angelina	5,681	2,319	8,987	77,656	156	1,507	....	....	190	18,063
Trinity	6,902	2,656	9,184	96,564	159	1,671	....	....	80	7,041
Polk	7,229	3,689	10,807	121,355	296	3,396	....	....	101	10,485
Houston	26,519	9,730	28,966	283,402	617	9,947	20	281	178	13,490
Leon	28,578	7,900	25,490	229,555	735	9,806	....	....	167	9,021
Robertson	40,554	18,080	34,355	422,889	1,407	36,873	67	560	147	10,973
Madison	9,158	2,656	9,694	74,350	322	4,803	....	....	43	2,923
Walker	20,162	6,441	17,512	153,726	387	6,645	15	125	245	11,689
Grimes	35,994	11,701	29,072	296,969	555	10,011	70	615	150	7,432
Brazos	26,044	9,743	15,543	165,100	626	14,435	8	35	130	7,496
Burleson	15,396	5,965	14,692	171,552	320	7,549	113	567	50	3,922
Milam	27,473	10,944	32,735	396,792	1,942	50,168	508	3,341	123	6,163
Lee	15,662	5,596	14,396	146,271	745	16,432	196	795	60	4,334
Bastrop	35,730	14,714	31,786	401,999	1,845	38,704	853	4,929	158	11,543
Gonzales	23,729	7,511	30,964	227,501	767	13,811	646	4,480	60	4,572
Wilson	5,814	1,874	7,699	57,447	42	320	96	355	60	4,513
Total	914,305	325,854	923,986	8,928,079	70,654	1,184,947	20,291	122,646	7,893	620,635
LONG-LEAF PINE REGION.										
Newton	5,510	1,322	7,508	69,842	512	4,946	....	....	312	35,150
Jasper	4,455	1,418	9,768	97,396	1,097	10,194	....	....	940	81,785
Orange	92	88	1,697	18,913	....	....	....	....	119	8,541
Hardin	254	103	2,461	21,589	194	1,395	....	....	188	15,155
Tyler	5,504	2,543	11,055	122,837	1,343	11,744	5	25	358	31,957
Liberty	3,768	1,852	6,102	91,998	40	215	....	....	168	13,781
Total	17,567	7,262	38,156	424,701	3,197	28,568	5	25	1,457	137,738
SOUTHERN AND COAST PRAIRIE REGION.										
Region east of the Brazos river.										
San Jacinto	9,940	5,354	9,494	102,853	163	2,127	....	....	86	5,127
Montgomery	13,311	4,692	13,702	115,017	88	800	....	....	171	17,749
Waller	16,104	8,923	10,350	132,661	126	2,185	....	....	213	14,560
Harris	4,440	1,892	9,895	136,933	172	7,165	....	....	905	67,532
Galveston	289	136	655	16,367	44	1,115	....	....	253	16,302
Chambers	140	91	1,839	30,214	....	....	....	....	289	37,384
Jefferson	133	77	1,758	24,169	....	....	....	....	121	10,914
Total	38,257	15,565	47,693	560,644	593	13,392	....	....	2,038	160,968

TABLE II.—ACREAGE AND PRODUCTION OF LEADING CROPS—Continued.

COTTON-PRODUCING COUNTIES—Continued.

Counties.	COTTON.		INDIAN CORN.		OATS.		WHEAT.		SWEET POTATOES.	
	Acres.	Bales.	Acres.	Bushels.	Acres.	Bushels.	Acres.	Bushels.	Acres.	Bushels.
SOUTHERN AND COAST PRAIRIE REGION—cont'd.										
Region west of the Brazos river.										
Washington	56,706	20,692	43,610	571,662	776	22,727	49	234	244	9,029
Austin	31,321	13,165	26,810	448,481	519	13,584	22	161	210	19,274
Fayette	56,353	24,766	47,770	604,862	1,028	28,645	265	1,622	414	20,706
Colorado	32,994	15,552	29,711	532,486	227	5,446	......	......	174	16,962
Lavaca	25,726	9,978	28,474	377,914	789	14,316	94	704	215	27,396
De Witt	7,625	2,183	19,148	135,016	629	6,188	500	1,942	181	6,835
Victoria	1,729	730	6,258	90,210	174	3,418	28	280	141	6,791
Jackson	648	202	2,767	37,175	45	580	......	......	144	7,948
Matagorda	5,435	2,096	4,747	74,563	14	580	......	......	197	17,732
Calhoun	......	......	366	2,072	......	......	......	......	15	917
Karnes	1,007	283	5,184	13,115	44	507	52	132	8	230
Atascosa	1,422	480	4,475	20,992	93	840	......	......	82	6,494
Frio	543	156	1,574	7,449	......	......	8	40	27	1,372
Live Oak	16	4	456	2,120	......	......	......	......	13	438
Bee	44	9	2,966	18,192	......	......	......	......	23	1,026
Goliad	1,779	728	9,050	87,305	273	3,600	272	1,264	94	4,216
Refugio	36	15	3,238	27,975	......	......	......	......	15	291
San Patricio	6	2	1,219	4,358	14	70	......	......	11	265
Total	226,061	91,068	287,747	3,145,962	4,634	90,864	1,321	6,110	2,377	147,225
CENTRAL BLACK PRAIRIE REGION.										
Cooke	27,796	11,547	32,353	514,439	4,388	73,506	7,900	62,306	94	6,107
Montague	10,947	4,172	15,871	196,584	1,012	13,202	3,101	14,958	109	1,494
Wise	21,352	7,321	27,400	307,494	3,307	43,963	4,121	26,749	101	3,650
Denton	29,785	11,568	35,296	531,637	6,232	112,681	13,103	73,413	280	13,265
Collins	48,236	23,145	52,285	1,016,140	10,694	238,419	34,342	152,702	277	17,481
Hunt	25,906	10,805	39,127	965,004	6,214	154,617	7,205	43,533	179	10,361
Delta	6,940	4,911	9,190	130,061	1,905	39,349	1,406	7,673	51	4,147
Kaufman	26,650	10,963	34,598	354,781	4,522	113,215	8,921	70,701	163	12,620
Rockwall	5,786	2,630	6,715	88,713	981	26,305	3,515	20,966	8	225
Dallas	44,377	21,469	44,004	575,667	8,306	200,281	26,854	195,460	295	17,724
Tarrant	27,821	10,950	33,496	429,118	7,055	155,671	26,481	198,673	181	5,363
Parker	15,026	4,454	24,987	248,245	3,253	30,561	13,306	61,688	86	5,326
Hood	7,129	1,966	10,437	72,927	608	12,907	4,356	21,519	15	404
Erath	14,230	2,897	19,702	108,888	1,622	22,950	5,832	26,397	46	1,408
Somervell	4,020	1,066	5,620	56,236	238	3,793	1,508	13,256	11	562
Johnson	46,442	18,772	38,131	413,940	5,828	134,566	14,339	96,299	90	6,064
Ellis	52,172	18,963	43,680	577,131	5,528	153,527	15,500	176,215	96	4,528
Hill	38,535	8,969	32,013	327,484	4,476	143,144	6,533	51,743	15	1,090
Bosque	19,694	3,833	23,491	203,645	2,279	33,980	9,305	74,704	30	1,779
Hamilton	6,840	1,147	13,941	73,052	723	12,550	3,773	24,184	15	441
Lampasas	4,611	628	9,156	49,402	760	10,747	3,628	17,690	20	2,174
Coryell	19,698	3,381	22,363	196,713	2,733	60,498	8,506	55,919	26	1,562
McLennan	58,294	13,777	48,357	515,648	9,091	267,545	18,982	197,520	77	3,454
Falls	39,069	13,496	29,943	376,555	1,200	30,567	953	6,636	150	8,682
Bell	37,626	9,217	40,475	402,929	5,169	161,324	10,923	84,267	54	2,344
Williamson	18,528	4,217	26,225	208,711	8,694	195,490	7,901	56,695	82	8,900
Travis	28,500	9,371	20,632	264,675	4,779	105,106	4,048	24,033	148	9,773
Caldwell	18,006	7,609	18,393	190,646	1,364	33,333	3,085	11,036	130	7,947
Hays	9,968	3,441	10,749	99,096	3,223	86,251	3,789	16,690	49	2,506
Blanco	3,039	691	6,382	38,380	597	8,963	3,106	6,931	26	1,427
Gillespie	4,062	767	5,397	13,965	827	5,327	3,533	13,396	66	2,762
Kerr	469	73	1,345	6,456	185	1,168	1,134	2,726	25	2,730
Kendall	1,206	286	2,537	5,852	655	3,502	1,187	1,850	34	1,494
Comal	5,060	2,102	6,900	39,086	861	10,717	2,896	13,414	50	2,940
Guadalupe	16,469	6,521	28,501	101,390	3,260	53,216	4,463	21,194	102	6,513
Bexar	4,273	1,543	14,601	98,841	2,150	26,136	1,597	7,678	220	10,910
Medina	655	289	11,000	50,164	1,069	6,016	1,008	3,116	13	488
Bandera	222	82	3,641	13,506	259	3,764	1,200	3,223	14	863
Uvalde	141	59	1,345	10,234	91	963	407	967	7	785
Total	744,685	240,588	840,684	9,373,676	131,966	2,856,914	280,969	2,008,072	3,435	195,647

TABLE II.—ACREAGE AND PRODUCTION OF LEADING CROPS—Continued.

COTTON-PRODUCING COUNTIES—Continued.

Counties.	COTTON.		INDIAN CORN.		OATS.		WHEAT.		SWEET POTATOES.	
	Acres.	Bales.	Acres.	Bushels.	Acres.	Bushels.	Acres.	Bushels.	Acres.	Bushels.
WESTERN RED-LOAM PRAIRIE REGION.										
Clay	3,280	1,155	8,778	98,766	1,343	11,959	2,283	16,851	70	5,009
Wichita	103	43	1,361	18,625	10	70	50	582	10	358
Baylor	326	83	1,308	13,407	45	377	113	567	2	190
Archer	104	43	404	4,095	33	510	50	371	7	240
Jack	4,751	1,444	10,990	115,761	230	5,117	1,966	10,899	81	4,447
Young	2,049	564	9,181	96,561	114	1,319	1,047	12,197	8	788
Throckmorton	81	10	397	8,197			605	3,944	3	250
Jones	81	19	409	4,110	54	1,193	91	509	1	35
Shackelford	23	5	699	3,916	18	290	238	1,407	5	75
Stephens	686	137	3,324	26,974	354	3,081	3,137	11,191	5	170
Palo Pinto	4,292	865	9,301	60,626	305	5,416	2,435	11,844	50	958
Eastland	3,304	742	5,867	25,479	89	1,123	1,941	7,069	1	25
Callahan	434	98	2,245	14,059	56	569	1,091	5,078	43	858
Coleman	796	243	4,333	19,855	90	1,430	1,568	11,938	2	95
Brown	4,254	998	12,408	55,194	516	8,457	7,814	38,743	26	1,200
Comanche	9,301	2,508	14,297	85,454	400	6,839	5,074	29,141	82	2,878
San Saba	3,819	400	8,921	41,079	678	9,068	3,145	12,731	40	2,755
McCulloch	145	34	1,006	6,625	108	765	463	3,131	5	700
Mason	262	64	3,082	8,923	89	1,014	958	4,492	12	483
Llano	2,347	469	7,700	60,300	209	2,805	1,145	4,209	5	332
Burnet	7,034	1,599	14,187	133,506	1,997	30,136	5,173	26,071	42	1,722
Total	46,301	10,931	130,466	895,563	6,675	190,955	40,227	215,626	480	23,005
RED RIVER ALLUVIAL COUNTIES.										
Bowie	11,509	7,058	13,129	194,782	600	6,895	7	20	136	14,819
Red River	31,391	17,068	32,896	694,490	2,970	52,453	1,044	7,678	150	11,434
Lamar	40,390	24,628	40,617	817,864	5,851	131,967	3,047	18,963	226	15,862
Fannin	44,613	23,386	48,134	922,788	9,698	205,680	7,758	54,504	188	12,253
Grayson	41,339	19,166	56,544	976,731	10,009	188,138	15,736	95,740	315	21,414
Total	169,432	91,302	191,132	3,546,505	28,928	584,524	27,587	177,905	1,015	75,762
BRAZOS ALLUVIAL OR "SUGAR-BOWL" REGION.										
Fort Bend	10,873	6,491	14,710	226,648	384	4,940			343	21,756
Wharton	5,568	3,182	9,477	245,717	5	50	5	25	50	6,225
Brazoria	5,402	3,464	13,044	234,950	348	5,235			400	43,884
Total	21,836	13,097	39,231	807,315	697	9,625	5	25	702	71,867
RIO GRANDE VALLEY.										
Cameron	25	23	9,526	187,695	25	135				
Hidalgo	24	9	2,117	43,465					8	430
Total	49	32	11,643	230,160	25	135			8	430

COTTON PRODUCTION IN TEXAS.

TABLE II.—ACREAGE AND PRODUCTION OF LEADING CROPS—Continued.

NON-COTTON-PRODUCING COUNTIES.

Counties.	INDIAN CORN.		OATS.		WHEAT.		SWEET POTATOES.	
	Acres.	Bushels.	Acres.	Bushels.	Acres.	Bushels.	Acres.	Bushels.
Total	17,979	256,066	811	12,765	3,755	43,126	176	14,802
Aransas	104	800	9	100			11	800
Concho	40	900						
Dimmit	80	215					4	600
Dooley	126	565						
Duval	456	1,117	25	250				
Edwards	102	605			14	84	2	150
El Paso	688	4,419	5	130	2,534	26,911		
Encinal	28	500						
Gray	40	500						
Kimble	152	1,155	10	110	5	90	10	2,062
Kinney	1,575	26,940	255	5,700			8	2,500
Knox	60	1,500						
La Salle	26	250						
McMullen			80	1,200				
Maverick	686	7,434						
Menard	72	690					15	3,270
Nolan	64	230						
Nueces	3,165	60,615	13	160			127	6,100
Pecos	2,533	16,572	7	125	20	120		
Presidio	3,213	35,450	208	1,850	1,025	11,423		
Starr	894	16,805						
Taylor	72	1,009			157	1,610		
Tom Green	488	7,095	106	1,900				
Webb	626	5,594						
Wilbarger	226	3,600					1	76
Zapata	3,135	62,940	15	600				
Zavalla	149	1,535	51	680				

700

PART I.

PHYSICO-GEOGRAPHICAL AND AGRICULTURAL FEATURES

OF THE

STATE OF TEXAS.

r

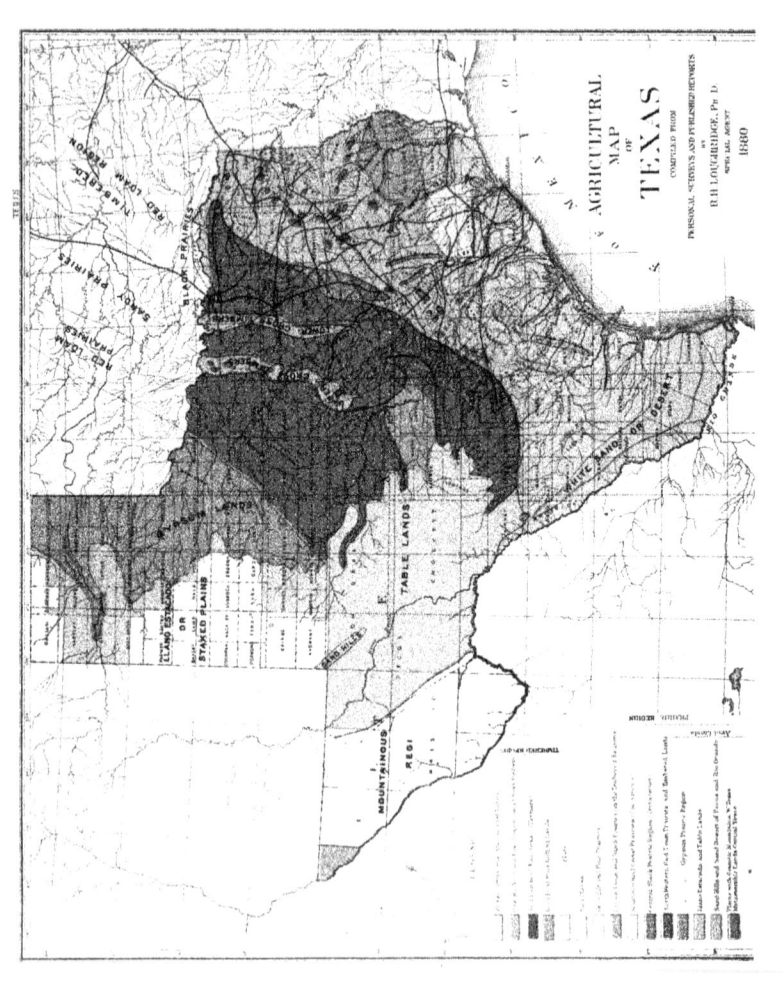

AGRICULTURAL
MAP
OF
TEXAS

COMPILED FROM

PERSONAL SURVEYS AND PUBLISHED REPORTS

BY

R H LOUGHRIDGE, PH. D.

SPEC. LOC. AGENT

1880

GENERAL DESCRIPTION OF THE STATE OF TEXAS.

Texas is the extreme southwestern state of the Union, the Rio Grande separating it from Mexico and the meridian of 103° forming the line between it and New Mexico. On the north the boundary is marked by the Red river from Louisiana to the meridian of 100°, thence northward of that meridian to its intersection with the parallel of 36° 30′ north latitude, and thence west to the meridian of 103°. There are two hundred and twenty-five counties in the state, seventy-two of which are still unorganized, and they vary in area from 150 to 12,000 square miles, the large counties lying in the uninhabited portion of the state on the west.

The entire area, as estimated by Mr. Henry Gannett, geographer of the Tenth Census, is 265,780 square miles, which includes 3,490 square miles of water area, comprising coast bays and gulfs, rivers, and lakes, leaving 262,290 square miles of land surface alone.

The area of Texas, therefore, comprises 8.7 per cent. of the entire area of the United States and territories (3,025,600 square miles), and, comparing it with other states, we find it to be nearly as large as the combined areas of Louisiana, Mississippi, Alabama, Georgia, and Florida, or of that of the New England and middle states, with Ohio and Illinois, all combined. In comparison with the countries of Europe, we find that Texas is larger than either the Austrian or the German empire, France, or the islands of Great Britain.

It is estimated by Mr. Gannett that of the entire area of the state 129,200 square miles comprise the inhabited portion, with a population of 1,591,749, giving an average of a little more than twelve persons per square mile. The remaining 133,090 square miles (land area) include the southwestern prairies and the plains and gypsum lands of the west and northwest.

Between the extreme east and west points of the state there are about 13 degrees of longitude, or a little more than 900 miles; from north to south there are included about 10.75 degrees of latitude, or nearly 750 miles.

TOPOGRAPHY AND GENERAL FEATURES.—In the state of Texas we find combined a great diversity in both soil and topography, the former passing from the extreme of fertility on the Red river on the north, the Brazos in the middle, and the Rio Grande on the extreme south, to the extreme of sterility in the sand desert of the south; in topography, from the extreme of low and flat prairie lands and a very little marsh along the coast, by gradual transitions and elevations, to the chains and peaks of mountains on the far west, whose summits are 5,000 feet or more above the sea.

To these extremes may be added that of population, for we find on the east and central (north and south) parts of the state comparatively thickly-settled counties and large and flourishing towns and cities, while on the west emigration and settlements have scarcely yet reached the foot of the plateau of the great plains.

To complete the picture of extremes, as it were, we find that several of the great agricultural regions that form so prominent a feature in the other southern states have their termini in Texas, and are cut off on the southwest either by the prairies of the coast or by the great mesquite and cactus chaparral prairies of the Rio Grande region, or they abut against the eastern bluffs of the plains.

The coast of Texas presents features different from those of any other state; for while in other states the mainland coast is greatly cut up into large bays, extending many miles inland, it is here bordered by an almost continuous chain of islands and peninsulas (the latter having the same trend as the islands). The Gulf border of this chain is a very regular line southwest from the mouth of the Sabine river or lake to near Corpus Christi, which occupies the highest point on the entire coast, and thence turns with a regular curve south and slightly southeast to Mexico. The islands and peninsulas, which are separated from the mainland by distances of from 10 to 20 miles, more or less, are covered with heavy belts of sand and sand dunes, rising 10 or 20 feet above the beach. The latter skirt the shore-line for many miles, and, as on Galveston island, are usually broad, and offer many inducements to pleasure-seekers. The longest of these islands is Padre island, which extends from Corpus Christi bay to near the mouth of the Rio Grande, a distance of more than 100 miles. The large estuaries that have been formed at the mouths of the streams, except the Sabine, the Rio Grande, and those of the Brazos section, form another feature peculiar to the Texas coast. The border lands of these estuaries are usually high, their almost vertical clay bluffs being washed by the waters of the bay, and the open prairies of the uplands often extend to their very edge.

Mr. Gannett estimates the water area of the coast bays, gulfs, etc., to be 2,510 square miles, and that of the rivers and lesser streams at about 800 square miles.

A general view of the state, as presented in two cross-sections, presents the following features:

1. *Along the Louisiana line.*—From the mouth of Sabine river northward we find at first a small area of marsh lands, terminating the marsh region of Louisiana, and not occurring to any extent westward. Passing these, we come to the long-leaf pine flats, extending westward only to the Trinity river, and being also the western terminus of the belt that extends across all of the Gulf states, the lower part of Florida, and along the Atlantic coast through North Carolina. Its surface in Texas is quite level northward for about 50 miles, when the more undulating or rolling pine hills are reached, which also form a border to the pine flats just mentioned across the southern Gulf states. Thence northward to Red river the country is rolling and hilly, and is covered with oak, hickory, and short-leaf pine—a region that extends eastward through Louisiana, Arkansas, and the northern part of Mississippi into Tennessee. This region passes southwestward, becoming more and more narrow, until it tapers off to a point 100 miles from the Rio Grande, and also includes the belt of red Tertiary hills of the other states, that probably terminates on the southwest in Guadalupe county.

2. *From the coast in a northwest and west direction.*—The mainland coast of Texas presents a very irregular outline with its many bays, peninsulas, and islands, and but a small proportion of the mainland reaches the waters of the Gulf. As before stated, there is scarcely any marsh land on the coast west of the Sabine marshes.

For a distance of from 50 to 100 miles inland from the coast the country is very level, with open prairies, whose continuity is broken only by the timbered streams, with occasional strips or "motts" or clumps of timber, and by the broad and heavily timbered alluvial or "sugar-bowl" region of the Brazos.

The rise, slight and very gradual inland from the coast, is almost imperceptible for many miles, when the country becomes undulating and then rolling, and the prairies give way to the more or less broken and hilly oak and pine uplands, which cover all of the northeastern part of the state, as already mentioned. The country rises rapidly to the north and northwest, reaching an elevation of several hundred feet along the western edge of the timbered region, and is interspersed throughout with small "brown-loam prairies". Leaving the timber lands, and continuing northwest, we find a region of "black waxy prairies", underlaid by the Cretaceous "rotten limestone", extending southwest to San Antonio, and thence west to the foot of the plains. Northward this region passes through the southern part of the Indian territory into Arkansas. These prairies are at first, on the east, rather level, or at most undulating, with an altitude of 500 or 600 feet, but westward become more rolling, hilly, and broken, until finally, on their western limits, high and bald hills and peaks stand out in bold relief at an elevation of nearly 1,000 feet above the sea. The monotony of these interior prairies is broken by the timbered streams and on the north by the wide belt of "lower cross timbers", which reaches from the Red river to the Brazos in an almost due south course. Otherwise there is very little timber to be seen.

At the western edge of the northern half of the black prairie region there is another belt of "cross timbers", interspersed with small black Cretaceous prairies, very irregular in outline and in width, and beyond it is the broad red-loam and partly timbered region, comprising high ridges, mesquite prairie valleys, and broad table-lands, the country gradually rising to the foot of the high plateau of the Llano Estacado, several thousand feet above the level of the sea. This region terminates on the southwest against the bluffs of the plains south of the Llano Estacado, and a large area penetrates southeastwardly almost across the black prairie region.

On the northwest there is a large, extensive region, lying wedge-shaped, with its point south, between the red-loam lands and the Llano Estacado, and comprising the great gypsum lands of the state, with high and rolling prairies, whose uplands are largely destitute of timber.

To the westward the broad, level, and bare plains of the Llano Estacado occupy a terrace with abrupt bluffs on the north some 200 feet above these regions, and with a gentle rise pass out of the state into New Mexico on the west and to the mountains on the southwest. Deep cañons have been cut into the eastern part of this plateau by the headwaters of the large rivers of the state, but to the west there is only a vast, treeless plain, more or less undulating, with a few low but prominent sand hills and ridges.

On the extreme west, between the Pecos and the Rio Grande, the country reaches its maximum height, with several chains of almost treeless mountains rising several thousand feet above the general level, and separated from each other by broad and level plains 20 or 30 miles in width and almost destitute of vegetation. These mountain ranges enter the state from New Mexico. Southward the plains extend along the Rio Grande to a point a little south of its junction with the Pecos. Thence to the Gulf are broad and high prairies, broken by deep arroyos or ravines, and with little growth other than occasional live-oak trees and great chaparrals or thickets of thorny shrubs.

TIMBER GROWTH.—The upland timber growth most general throughout the state is post and black-jack oaks. These occur on all of the sandy timbered lands that cover so large a region on the east from Red river southward and southwestward to the Nueces river, are the chief growth of the upper and lower cross timbers, and are found on the hills of the eastern part of the northwestern red-loam region and on the borders of the bottom lands of the streams of the central black prairie region. They are associated more or less throughout the state with scarlet, black, white, and other oaks and hickory, and in eastern Texas with short-leaf pine, dogwood, persimmon, sassafras, etc.

The short-leaf pine is most prominent in the extreme northeastern and southern parts of the eastern timbered region, while the long-leaf species is found only on the southeast, between Trinity and Sabine rivers, being the almost exclusive growth over a large part of the region, which covers an area of about 5,312 square miles.

Live oak is a prominent tree in the coast region, appearing in motts or clumps on its prairies, in the valleys of the Brazos, the Colorado, and other rivers, and in the counties bordering the great plains. The widely extending branches of the tree are on the south usually festooned with long moss (*Tillandsia usneoides*), and the tree affords a pleasant retreat on the prairies during the heat of a summer day.

The mesquite (*Prosopis juliflora*) may be considered a prairie growth, though having usually the size of a small tree, and is not found, so far as I am aware, east of the ninety-fifth meridian. It occurs at first on the east rather sparsely in motts in low places on the prairies, but westward it is more and more abundant, and on the southwest, to the Rio Grande and to the foot of the Llano Estacado, it becomes almost the exclusive upland growth, and with the "wesatche" (probably a variety) and the cactus forms the great chaparrals of the west. On the plains its buried stocks or roots afford almost the only fuel; nothing but a twig of the stock appears above ground, its growth no doubt being prevented by the severe winds that sweep over the plains, the dwarfed cedars of the bluffs only remaining, because protected.

BOTTOM GROWTH.—Elm, hackberry, and pecan occur more generally than any other trees throughout the bottom lands of the state, and on the large rivers in the timbered region they are associated with walnut, ash, several varieties of oaks, hickory, sweet and black gums, wild peach, etc., and on the extreme east with some cypress and magnolia (*M. grandiflora*). The latter growth is not reported west of the pine region. The bottom lands of the region are heavily timbered, and elm, cottonwood, hackberry, mesquite, and some pecan are found along the banks of the streams to their headwaters at the foot of the Llano Estacado. The Pecos and the Rio Grande north of Hidalgo have little or no timber growth.

CLIMATE.—*Temperature.*—The large territory occupied by the state naturally presents a variety of climate, and we find from the reports of the United States signal stations for 1880 (a statement of which has been furnished me from the chief office at Washington) that while the coast counties are warmed by the sea breezes during the winter months and have a mean temperature of 53° in December, the northern counties suffer severer weather, the temperature of Denison for the same month being 41°. The minimum and maximum extremes during December were at Galveston 18° and 72°, and at Denison 2° and 76°. At Corsicana, an intermediate point, the extremes were 6° and 80°, with a mean of 47.4°. Brownsville, situated more than three degrees south of Galveston, has for the same month the same minimum (18°) and a higher maximum (83°).

During the summer months the northern counties of the settled portion of the state enjoy cooler nights and hotter days than those of the coast, though the mean temperature was the highest on the coast by several degrees. July at Galveston, and August at Denison, were the hottest months, the average temperatures being respectively 83° and 80°, with maximums of 93° and 101°.

Eagle Pass, on the Rio Grande, seems to be the hottest place in the state, its maximums for the months from the first of March to the last of July being greater than was recorded at any other point during the same time, and that for the months of June and July, 108°, being also the highest in the state for the year.

At Rio Grande City a maximum temperature of 105° was recorded in April and June, and at Fort Stockton, in Pecos county, 106° in June. At Brownsville and San Antonio the highest temperature, 96° and 98° respectively, was reached in July.

Fort Elliott, in the northwestern part, or Panhandle, of the state, enjoys the coolest summers, the thermometer for the three months not rising above 86.7°.

One of the most prominent features of Texas climate is what is commonly termed "the Texas norther", a sudden and extreme change of temperature produced by a rush of cold wind from the north, usually coming unannounced, though sometimes indicated by a haziness in the northern sky. The northers are usually preceded by a warm spell of twenty-four hours, more or less, and the change of temperature is very great, sometimes in the winter months falling as much as 30° or 40°, though usually much less. They continue about three days, the second being the coldest, and are succeeded by warm weather, though sometimes the northers follow each other so closely as to produce eight or ten days of cold. They may be expected at all times of the year, and it is customary for travelers to be provided with blankets even for a trip of a few days. These northers are sometimes accompanied by rain, and are classed as *dry* or *wet* northers. The summer northers are not as frequent as the winter ones nor as marked, sometimes being oppressively close and warm, instead of cold.

43 C P   673

Thunder-storms occur during the year throughout the state, and severe winds and tornadoes sometimes sweep over sections of the country. The latter are, however, of far less frequency than in the northwestern states.

Rainfall and water supply.—The winds that bring rain and thunder-storms usually come from the southwest, those from the north being mostly dry. From the records of the United States signal office it seems that during 1880 the greatest amount of rain-fell at Galveston, amounting to 50.1 inches, and at Denison 46.3 inches, while at Corsicana, San Antonio, Fredericksburg, and Brackettsville, lying in a northeast and southwest course from each other, the precipitation was over 40 inches. The least amount of rainfall (from 16 to 24 inches) was reported from Fort Elliott, in the Panhandle, Fort Davis, west of the Pecos river, and Rio Grande City, in Webb county, on the southwest, while at several other points on the west and along the Rio Grande it was less than 30 inches.

With regard to the seasons, it seems that the winter months are the driest of the year very generally throughout the state, the precipitation varying from 3 to 7 inches, and much less in Denton county and several points on the west and southwest. During the spring months the rainfall was greatest in the eastern counties, amounting to from 12 to 13 inches. At all other points, except San Antonio, Mason, Fredericksburg, and Fort Griffin, less than 9 inches was obtained, the country west of the Pecos river being very dry.

During the summer months the country around Corsicana suffered greatest from droughts, while Denison, San Antonio, and other places over the west and southwest enjoyed their greatest rainfall for the year, the maximum for any one month in the year throughout the state (21 inches) having been reached at Brownsville in August.

The fall months vary but little from those of summer, except that there is more rain in the eastern counties. From the reports given, San Antonio seems to enjoy the greatest regularity in its monthly rainfalls, there being but one month when it was less than 2 inches, while its maximum for any month of the year was 8.6 inches. The record of Corsicana shows very nearly the same regularity, a maximum of 7.7 inches.

The country west and southwest of the black prairie region is visited by rains, chiefly between the first of May and the last of September. These rains come suddenly, and, while lasting but a few hours, are drenching in character, flooding the country, and hence probably producing the great ravines or *arroyos* that form a prominent feature of the southwest. The water soon disappears; the small streams are dry throughout the greater part of the year, and dependence is put chiefly upon the larger ones that have their sources from springs at the foot of the great plains. In the red-loam region, on the north, parties have sometimes been successful in digging wells that afford a supply of water for a portion of the summer; and when near a village or town such wells, or even streams of water, are a source of revenue to the owners. Attention is now being turned to the sinking of artesian wells, but I know not with what success their efforts have been met.

In the black prairie region, occupying the central portion of the state, the various small streams usually become dry during the summer, and some trouble is experienced in obtaining a sufficient supply for general purposes. Wells cannot be relied upon, and their water is so strongly saturated with lime from the rotten limestone rock (Cretaceous) as to be almost unfit for domestic uses, thus compelling families either to build cisterns or to haul water in casks and barrels from some neighboring stream, sometimes several miles distant. In the large cities water is furnished from artesian wells 700 feet or more in depth, the supply coming from beneath the rotten limestone formation.

The timbered region of eastern Texas is better supplied with water than any other part of the state. Springs of good freestone water are found in almost every county, and wells furnish an abundant supply for domestic purposes. The small streams usually become dry during the summer months, and artificial reservoirs, or simple earth embankments, collect a sufficient amount of water during the rainy seasons for farm and stock purposes.

RIVER SYSTEMS AND DRAINAGE.—Since the entire country is little else than a vast plain, gradually rising from the coast to the northwest, the drainage is naturally southeast to the Gulf, and the many rivers of the state cut their way in almost parallel courses to the coast. The Red, Brazos, and Colorado rivers all have their sources at the foot of the eastern bluffs of the Llano Estacado, whence they flow eastward through the red-clay lands to the black prairies, and, with the exception of the first, then turn southeast to the Gulf.

Red river maintains its eastern course along the entire northern border of the state, and turns south only after it enters the state of Arkansas. It drains an area of about 29,000 square miles in Texas alone. From the red clays these streams of the northwest derive that red color which characterizes their waters throughout their course, and which has given Red and Colorado rivers their names. The waters of Canadian river, on the northwest, are similar in character, and to this is due the mistakes of the earlier military surveying parties in their location of the sources of the Red river.

The waters of the Brazos and Red rivers, passing as they do through the gypsum beds of the northwest, have dissolved much of that mineral, and for many miles after leaving the beds are salty and disagreeable to the taste and scarcely fit for use. Captain Marcy found that this was due entirely to this gypsum formation, and that the sources of the streams, when westward of that region, comprised springs of pure and excellent water.

The streams, in their passage through the soft materials that enter into the formations of the western region, have cut their way to great depths, forming great narrow and steep cañons, with gradually widening valleys to the eastward. Quicksands characterize the river beds, and during seasons when the waters are low and the sand banks become dry great sand clouds are raised by the winds and borne here and there. The banks of Red river are high, and the stream is navigable for a great distance during high water.

Sabine river has its source in northeastern Texas, and forms the eastern boundary of the state from the thirty-second parallel of latitude to the Gulf. It is navigable during high water for a distance of 300 miles from its mouth. The Texas side of the basin, drained by the Sabine and its tributaries, comprises about 17,100 square miles.

Trinity river rises a short distance west of the central black prairie region, and has a general southeast course to the Gulf. It is not very wide, and the water has a great depth in wet seasons. It is a very crooked stream, but boats have ascended from its mouth to Dallas, a distance of 900 miles. It drains, with its tributaries, about 16,600 square miles.

Brazos river drains a larger territory than any other stream, about 35,000 square miles, and it is looked upon as the most important river of the state. Its basin is very wide on the northwest, comprising various forks and tributaries, viz, Elm, Double Mountain, Salt forks, and Leona rivers. Below the mouth of the latter the river basin becomes very narrow, the level lands of the "sugar-bowl" allowing the small streams that lie within three or four miles of the river to find their way independently to the Gulf. Boats are said to have ascended the river to the falls near Marlin, in Falls county, a distance of 600 miles.

The *Colorado river* rises at the south of the gypsum formation, and its waters escape its influence. It is bordered in many places by high bluffs, but much of its bottom land is subject to overflow during high water. It is said to be closed to navigation by a sand-bar at its mouth and a raft in its channel. Its basin comprises about 24,700 square miles.

The *San Antonio* and *Guadalupe* rivers, formed by the union of other streams, are not as long as the other rivers described, but drain a territory of about 10,000 square miles.

The *Nueces* rises near the northern border of the plains, and has a very irregular course, flowing for a long distance in a northeasterly course. It is joined by the Frio and the Leona, and with them drains a territory of about 15,300 square miles.

The *Rio Grande* finds its way to the Gulf from the mountains of the northwest through cañons and high banks, and is only navigable to Camargo, about 500 miles from the Gulf. Its tributaries on the Texas side are mostly short, and its drainage system south of the Pecos covers but about 9,300 square miles. Quicksands form a prominent feature of the river bed.

The *Pecos river* is described as being a narrow stream of muddy water flowing rapidly between high and vertical banks, on which there is little or no vegetation to mark its course.

GEOLOGY.—The geological features of the state are as yet but comparatively little known, the state surveys that have been inaugurated having been in existence but a short time before support was withdrawn by the legislature and when the results of the work were but partially published. In view of this fact, and covering, as the state does, such a vast territory, it has been thought best to give a rather full description of its more general geological features, as gathered from available sources and personal observation.

Azoic.—The Azoic series of rocks, represented chiefly by granites, is found most generally in two regions, viz, in the mountainous region west of the Rio Pecos, and in the counties of Gillespie, Llano, Burnet, and San Saba, in the central part of the state. So far as known, they do not occur in broad areas, as in some of the other states, but in rather isolated spots, surrounded by or associated with later Palæozoic and Mesozoic formations.

On the west of the Pecos the several chains of mountains (Guadalupe, Sacramento, and Organ) that rise several thousand feet above the intermediate and level plains are largely granitic, with accompanying sandstones and limestones. In some of the mountains characteristic eruptive rocks are reported as penetrating the later formations and rising above them in huge masses, or forming vertical columns, as in the Organ range, near El Paso.

The *easterly granitic region* lies south of San Saba river, its southern limit being 17 miles north of Fredericksburg, in Gillespie county. Its eastern limit follows the Colorado river, and its western extends into Mason county. The rocks are mostly of the pink feldspathic variety, resist disintegration, and form high and prominent points or hills throughout the region. One of these hills, the Enchanted Rock, 18 miles north of Fredericksburg, is thus described in Thrall's *History* :

It is a huge granite and iron formation, about 800 feet high, covering at its base several acres of space, its top being about 400 yards square. Its name is derived from its magnificent appearance, for when the sun shines upon it in the morning and at evening it resembles a huge mass of burnished gold.

These hills are surrounded on all sides by a comparatively level country, and their rocks are overlaid by later formations.

Northward from the outcrops of Llano county granite has not been observed in Texas, but it occurs extensively in the Wichita mountains north of Red river, and I found it in a recent trip at Tishomingo and Boggy Depot, Indian territory, near the line of the Choctaw and the Chickasaw nations, where it was massive in form and consisted largely of pink feldspar, and was penetrated by seams of bluish trap-rock.

These granites seem to be a part of an eruptive dike that passes through the state from the Santa Rosa mountains, in Mexico, northeastward into the Chickasaw nation, and terminate in the eruptive rocks of Missouri and

Arkansas. (a) In the region of these mountains in Mexico are the cones of extinct volcanoes, while the associated limestones are highly metalliferous, with disturbed and even vertical strata. The face of the country from the mountain to the mouth of Elm creek, on the Rio Grande, is said to be "broken, while the flat, long stretching ranges of hills are frequently overthrown".

On the Texan side, the first marks of volcanic action are to be seen at the head of Leona river. Here a solitary hill of 60 or 70 feet in height occurs, formed entirely of dark green basalt, which is closely allied to that of the Santa Rosa mountains, containing much hornblende and olivine. In the vicinity of Fort Inge, and also near the head of Las Moras, are several hills of the same nature. The road from Leona to the first crossing of Devil's river leads over several places indicating volcanic action. The west bank of the Rio Frio at the crossing is formed of a solid mass of basaltic rock, which undoubtedly belongs to the dike alluded to as having its origin in the Santa Rosa mountains, and here crossing the Cretaceous formation. (b)

Palæozoic.—The formations referred to this age enter the state from the north and extend south through the Azoic region, in Gillespie county. They are bordered by the Cretaceous formation on the east, the line marking the limit passing from Montague county southward to a point 15 miles west of Weatherford, in Parker county, thence through Erath and Comanche to the western part of Lampasas county at Senterfitt, and into Burnet county, where they become associated with the Azoic rocks. The western limit of the region is as yet indefinitely known, though probably marked by the eastern boundary of the gypsum formation, extending from near the mouth of the Big Wichita river southwest to the headwaters of the Colorado.

It has not been ascertained to what extent the different formations of the Palæozoic are represented in the state; but Silurian sandstones and limestones are reported in Llano, Burnet, and San Saba counties, while the northern and greater part of the region seems to be Carboniferous. Beds of coal (probably of the Upper Coal Measures), varying from a few inches to several feet in thickness, occur in Stephens, Young, and several other counties, while conglomerates, sandstones, and limestones, accompanied by Carboniferous fossils, are found in abundance. The hills are usually capped by a reddish sandstone (probably Permian) several feet thick, and its materials, which are devoid of fossils, vary from fine to coarse sand, and are accompanied sometimes by fragments of iron ore.

Palæozoic rocks are reported in the mountains west of the Pecos river, and include representatives of each of the formations except Devonian (which has not been recognized in Texas), sometimes with uptilted strata, resting upon granites and surrounded in the valleys by horizontal Cretaceous beds. The Permian rocks are extensively developed in the Guadalupe range (according to Dr. Shumard), (c) and so far as known this is the only occurrence of this formation in Texas.

Triassic and Jurassic.—The extensive gypsum and red-clay beds of the northwest have been referred to these formations by some geologists. They extend westward to the foot of the great plains, and consist of alternating strata of red clays and gypsum, overlaid sometimes by sandstone and conglomerate. Dr. Shumard observed them underlying the bluffs of the Llano Estacado, a Cretaceous formation.

Cretaceous.—The most prominent geological as well as agricultural division of the state is the Cretaceous, its broad area of white rotten limestones and black waxy prairie lands occupying a central position in the state east and south of the region just mentioned, and extending westward to El Paso, including the great plains. The most eastern exposure of the rocks of the formation which I observed was at a point not far below the mouth of Kiamitia creek, which enters Red river from the Indian territory. Cretaceous fossils (among them *Ostrea quadriplicata*) are here found in a bluish calcareous marl and sandstone several feet in thickness, overlying a softer sandstone, which in the river beds has been worn, into a variety of fantastic forms. To the southward the Cretaceous beds are covered by the sands and clays of the Tertiary uplands, which extend from the east to within three miles of Clarksville, where are found the great outcrops of rotten limestone—a soft, chalky rock, white for the first few feet from the surface, but bluish below. It is the rock so extensively developed all over this central black prairie region, and which is in localities so rich in huge ammonites, gryphæa, and other fossils.

The line marking the eastern limit of the formation passes from Clarksville, Red River county, southwestward to Terrell, where in the railroad cut I observed an outcrop of a hard fossiliferous limestone, resembling in character that of the Ripley group of Mississippi, and with blackened fossil fragments as in the Cretaceous beds north of Lumpkin, in Stewart county, Georgia. Among the fossils recognized were *Turritella, Exogyra, Belemnites,* and *Cardium Ripleyensis.* Farther southward the most easterly Cretaceous outcrops are four miles west of Corsicana, in Navarro county, a few miles east and south of Marlin, in Falls county, at Cameron, in Milam county, a mile or two west of Elgin or near the western line of Bastrop county, at Seguin, in Guadalupe, and thence the line passes through the northwest corner of Atascosa, and westward south of the mouth of the Pecos river, on the Rio Grande.

The territory occupied by the Cretaceous formation is very large, comprising the broad eastern and southern region whose limits have just been given and the great plains of the Llano Estacado, and extending far beyond to

a The line of outcrop, in its nearly westward course from Little Rock, Arkansas, through the Indian territory, to the Wichita mountains, thence southward to Gillespie county, and again southwestward into Mexico, coincides with the strikes of the metamorphic strata of eastern Georgia, as well as with the trendings of the chain of metamorphic mountains that borders the same region on the northwest (the Salacoa, Pine Log, Dug Down, *et al.*). (See report on Georgia, page 12, this series.)

b Mexican Boundary Survey, vol. I.

c Trans. Acad. Sci. of Saint Louis, vol. I.

the northwest. The rocks of the eastern prong of this formation, or "the central prairie region", as it has been agriculturally termed, have been estimated by Dr. Shumard to have a thickness of about 1,500 feet, with the following subdivisions and characteristics, as given by him in the *Trans. Acad. Sci. of Saint Louis*, vol. I, part 4 :

Section of Cretaceous strata in Texas.

Divisions.	Subdivisions.	Feet.	Characteristic fossils.
UPPER CRETACEOUS OR CALCAREOUS.	Caprina limestone........................	60	
	Comanche Peak group................	300 to 400	Exogyra Texana, Gryphæa Pitcheri, Janira occidentalis, Cardium multistriatum, Lima Waconensis, Ammonites Pedernalis, Natica Pedernalis, Heteraster Texanus, Holectypus planatus, Cyphosoma Texana, and Diadema Texana.
	Austin limestone......................	100 to 200	Gryphæa vesicularis, Exogyra costata, Radiolites Austinensis, Nautilus Dekayi, Baculites anceps.
	Fish-bed.............................		Fish remains—Mosasaurus.
	Indurated blue marl..................	60	Exogyra arietina, Dentalia.
	Washita limestone...................	100 to 120	Gryphæa pitcheri, var. Trecumcarei, Ostrea subovata (O. Marshii Marc.), O. carinata, Inoceramus problematicus, Hamites Fremonti.
	Blue marl............................	50	Inoceramus problematicus, Ostrea, etc.
	Caprotina limestone.................	55	Orbitolina Texana, Caprotina Texana, Natica acutispira.
LOWER CRETACEOUS.	Arenaceous group .... }	80	{ Ostrea bellarugosa. Cyprina (?). Fish remains.
	Fish-bed............................ }		
	Marly clay or Red river group........	150	Ammonites Swallovii, A. Mackianus, Ancyloceras annulatus, Scaphites vermiculus, Baculites, gracilis, Gervilia gregaria, Inoceramus capulus, fossil wood.

I.—UPPER CRETACEOUS OR CALCAREOUS REGION.

This division, in the eastern or settled portion of the state, attains a thickness of from 800 to 1,000 feet, but in its western extension reaches a much greater development. It presents the following subdivisions, from above downward : *Caprina limestone, Comanche Peak group, Austin limestone, Exogyra arietina marls, Washita limestone, Inoceramus problematicus beds,* and *Caprotina limestone.*

CAPRINA LIMESTONE (thickness, 60 feet).—This is the uppermost recognized member of the series, and, although of no great thickness, has a somewhat extended geographical range. It is a yellowish-white limestone, sometimes of a finely granular texture, and sometimes made up of rather coarse, subcrystalline grains, cemented with a chalky paste. It generally occurs in thick, massive beds, and is capable of withstanding the action of the weather to a greater extent than most of the members of the Cretaceous system.

This formation is usually found capping the highest elevations, and its presence may be nearly always recognized, even at a distance, by the peculiar flat-topped and castellated appearance it imparts to the hills.

According to Dr. Riddell, it is finely displayed along the bluffs of Brazos river, in Bosque, McLennan, and Hill counties; also along the Leon and Bosque rivers. The summits of the remarkable elevation known as Comanche peak, in Johnson county, and that of Shovel mountain, in Burnet county, consist of this rock. The fossils are chiefly *caprina, cytherea,* and *ammonites* of undetermined species.

COMANCHE PEAK GROUP (thickness, from 300 to 400 feet).—The Comanche Peak group, which next succeeds in descending order, is an important member of the series, and presents a greater development, both horizontally and vertically, than either of the others. It is made up of soft yellowish and whitish chalky limestone and buff and cream-colored limestones of greater or less compactness. The best exhibitions of this formation that we have seen are at Comanche peak, Shovel mountain, and at mount Bonnell, near Austin.

AUSTIN LIMESTONE (thickness, from 100 to 200 feet).—This subdivision consists of cream-colored and bluish limestone, and resembles in lithological features portions of the preceding group, but contains quite a different assemblage of organic remains. Some of the beds are soft, and crumble readily upon exposure, while others are moderately hard, and furnish a handsome building rock, which may be cut into almost any required shape with a common hand-saw. The state-house and several of the public buildings at Austin are constructed of this stone. This formation occurs at Austin, and near San Antonio and New Braunfels. Dr. Riddell also recognized it in McLennan and Bosque counties, and Dr. G. G. Shumard in Grayson county.

The greatest thickness observed is in the vicinity of Austin, where the beds are exposed to the height of about 100 feet.

EXOGYRA ARIETINA MARL (thickness, 60 feet).—This is an indurated blue and yellow marl, with occasional bands of gray sandstone and thin seams of selenite interstratified. It contains iron pyrites in the form of small spherical masses, and the fossils are also frequently studded with brilliant crystals of this substance. It is well exposed toward the base of mount Bonnell, near Austin, where it presents a thickness of about 60 feet. It may also be seen to advantage near New Braunfels, in Comal county, at various points in Bell county, and Dr. G. G. Shumard found it resting upon the limestone of Fort Washita, in Arkansas.

Fossils.—Exogyra arietina, Gryphæa pitcheri, Janira Texana, and a small undescribed species of *Dentaria.* On Shoal creek, near Austin, *Exogyra arietina* occurs in the greatest profusion, the surface of the ground being sometimes literally covered with them.

WASHITA LIMESTONE (thickness, from 100 to 120 feet).—This important member of our Cretaceous system is made up of a nearly white, yellow, gray, and blue limestone, some of the layers being moderately hard, while others disintegrate rapidly upon exposure. This formation is exhibited at many locations in the state. Good exposures occur near Austin, and in Grayson, Fannin, and Red River counties. According to Dr. G. G. Shumard, it is finely developed near Fort Washita.

BLUE MARL (thickness, 50 feet).—This member was examined in Grayson county by Dr. G. G. Shumard, who describes it as an indurated arenaceous marl of a schistose structure, with small nodules of iron pyrites and irregular masses of lignite disseminated through it. It has not been recognized south of Grayson county. This subdivision should, perhaps, be grouped with the preceding. It corresponds with No. 2 of the Nebraska section.

CAPROTINA LIMESTONE (thickness, 50 feet).—The *Caprotina limestone*, which follows in descending order, forms the base of the upper Cretaceous, and is composed of light gray and yellowish gray earthy limestone, with intercalated bands of yellow marl and sometimes flint. It is exposed at the base of the hills near Comanche peak, and is seen underlying the Washita limestone near the Colorado, at the foot of mount Bonnell.

II.—LOWER CRETACEOUS.

For a knowledge of this division of our Cretaceous system I am indebted to Dr. G. G. Shumard, who has had excellent opportunities for examining it. He describes it as being composed of sandstones and gypseous and marly clays, the latter containing numerous septaria, filled with fossils. It is separable into two groups, namely, *Arenaceous* and *marly clay* or *Red river* group.

ARENACEOUS GROUP (thickness, 90 feet).—This member consists of light yellow and blue sandstone and beds of sandy clay, with crystals of selenite and some lignite. Its characters may be understood from the following section, taken by Dr. G. G. Shumard on Post Oak creek, in Grayson county:

	Feet.
No. 1. Soft, fine-grained, yellow sandstone	10
No. 2. Hard, fine-grained, blue sandstone, becoming yellow upon exposure, and sometimes passing into gritstone and fine conglomerate	5
No. 3. Yellow sandstone, same as No. 1	10
No. 4. Indurated, blue, slaty clay, with crystals of selenite	20
No. 5. Thinly laminated layers, same as No. 2	3

With regard to the Nebraska equivalent of our Arenaceous group, I think there can scarcely be a doubt that it represents No. 1 (perhaps the upper part) of the section of Messrs. Hall, Meek, and Hayden.

MARLY CLAY, OR RED RIVER GROUP (thickness, 150 feet).—This member immediately underlies the fish-bed of the Arenaceous group, and is described by Dr. G. G. Shumard as a blue marly clay, occasionally variegated with red and brown, and with thin bands of sandstone interstratified. The clay contains crystals of selenite, flattened nodules of compact brown and blue limestone, and septaria of compact blue limestone, reticulated with brown, yellow, and purple spar. The nodules occur in the upper, and the septaria toward the base of the formation. The best exposures of the group are in Grayson, on Post Oak, Choctaw, and Big Mineral creeks, where sections of from 50 to 60 feet have been measured. It occurs also on Red river in Fannin and Lamar counties. The estimated thickness of the group in this part of the state is about 150 feet; but we have not seen the base of the formation.

The age of the Llano Estacado or the Great Plains has been definitely determined as Cretaceous, from the occurrence of numerous characteristic fossils on the Pecos, and also at El Paso. The rotten limestone that outcrops throughout the southern portion of the plains and at the headwaters of the Colorado river seems to thin out or disappear toward the north, and the sections given in Captain Marcy's report on Red river represent the bluffs at the head of the south fork of Red river as "600 feet high, and composed of horizontal layers of drift and sandstone, interstratified with white limestone (5 feet), the inferior strata, or those between the base of the bluffs and the river, having been ascertained from numerous observations to consist of gypsum and red clay". No fossils are mentioned as occurring on the north. W. P. Jenney gives the following section of the bluff at Castle cañon, near Horsehead crossing, on the Pecos: (a)

The strata, beginning at the base, are arranged as follows:

1. A coarse red sandstone, without fossils, but probably of the Triassic age, 50 feet exposed.
2. Soft calcareous brown sandstone, with fragments of fossil shells. This bed is 50 feet in thickness, and probably of Cretaceous age.
3. Soft yellow limestone, 450 feet in thickness, containing an abundance of well-known Cretaceous fossils, including *Gryphæa pitcheri*, *Exogyra Texana*, *E. arietina*, etc.
4. Compact yellow limestone, 30 feet or more in thickness, wanting at Castle cañon, but forming the tops of the highest hills on the Llano, and also found on the tops of the mountains in Jones county.

The characteristic fossil of this bed is the *Caprina crassifibra*, which is very abundant.

The Cretaceous beds on the banks of the Rio Grande at El Paso contain fossils identical with those from bed 3.

The most southerly outcrop of the Cretaceous formation on the Rio Grande is probably at the mouth of the Las Moras creek, north of Eagle Pass, at which place were found the last Cretaceous fossils mentioned in the report of Arthur Schott, of the Mexican boundary survey commission. Southward from this the greensand rocks, blue clays, lignitic beds, and the white bluffs, 20 miles south of Eagle Pass, are doubtless Tertiary, the first-named being perhaps the continuation of similar rocks which I found in Lee county, on the northeast, and which overlie blue marls filled with Tertiary fossils.

The following description is given by Mr. Schott of the limestone south of the mouth of San Pedro river and north of Eagle Pass:

The limestone does not form such solid masses as that above the mouth of the river. The high table-lands change into a more rolling, sometimes broken country. The lithological characters of the rock becomes more earthy; its fracture sharper. That embraced in the section of country lying between the mouths of San Pedro and Las Moras, like that above, seems to be metamorphic; it, however, differs from that, in indication of having been subjected to the action of a higher temperature. The fossils occurring in these localities are of the Cretaceous age. As an essential characteristic, we cite here strata and shoals, consisting almost solely of entire and fragmentary pieces of *exogyra* and *arietina*. They appear either in a state of perfect preservation or as a real breccia, the cement of which is mostly an ochre-colored sand or clay.

---

a Amer. Jour. Science and Art, 1874.

He ascribes this change or metamorphism of the beds to their position on the axis of that eruption which apparently resulted in the hills of dark green basalt at the head of Leona river and on the west bank of the Frio, and which seems to have had its origin in Santa Rosa mountain, in Mexico. (a)

Salines.—In several counties of the timbered region in the northeastern part of the state there are salines or salt-works lying in a northerly and southerly course from each other. The salt is obtained from a stratum in wells 15 to 25 feet in depth, and limestone is said to be found in the localities. That these salines are but outliers of the Cretaceous formation there can be but little doubt, resembling, as they do, the salines of Louisiana, which have been recognized as Cretaceous by Professor E. W. Hilgard.

Tertiary.—The Eocene, or lowest division of the Tertiary, occupies all the northeastern part of the state between the Cretaceous and the eastern boundary, and extends south along the Louisiana line to the southeastern corner of Sabine county. A line marking approximately its southern limit would pass west from this point to Trinity, in Trinity county, to Burton, in the western part of Washington county (where the belt becomes narrow), and southwestward into the southern part of Gonzales county, and to Rio Grande City.

To what extent the Mississippi subdivisions of the Eocene are represented in Texas is not definitely known, but it seems probable that the lignitic covers the greater part of the region, its beds of lignite being found in many of the counties, both on the east and on the Rio Grande. In Lee, Nacogdoches, and Caldwell counties limestones, beds of fossils, and blue fossiliferous marls and greensand rock are reported, but their age has not been determined. The line of low hills at the eastern edge of the black Cretaceous prairie region in Limestone and Falls counties, known as the Tehuacana hills and Blue ridge, are composed of Tertiary rocks, with a few fossils, *Venericardia planicosta*, etc.; while northward, at Corsicana and Wills' point (in Van Zandt county), as well as on the southwest, near Bremond, are soft sandstones, with Tertiary fossil casts overlying lignite beds at 40 feet or more below the surface. The Claiborne group of white limestones and fossils has not been recognized in Texas.

On the Rio Grande the glauconitic sandstones, mentioned by Mr. Schott (b) as occurring along the river from the Cretaceous rocks at the mouth of Las Moras creek, north of Eagle Pass, southward to Roma, near Rio Grande City, are doubtless of Tertiary age and the continuation of the sandstone in Lee county, which overlies a bed of blue clayey marl rich in Eocene fossils. Their Tertiary position is corroborated by the fact that at Roma and vicinity Mr. Schott reports beds of fossil shell and large ostreas (*O. Georgiana*) as occurring in abundance. Lignite is abundant throughout this greensand region in beds sometimes 3 and 4 feet thick, and was found to contain monocotyledonous and dicotyledonous leaves and plants.

This extensive bed of greensand is of great value agriculturally, containing probably a large percentage of potash. It is this bed that contributes so greatly to the high fertility of the lands of the lower Rio Grande and gives to it the extreme amount of potash. It is not known to what extent the greensand rocks occur in the eastern counties, the outcrop in Lee being the only one observed. There are, however, in the counties of the timbered region of east Texas, and notably in San Augustine, Nacogdoches, and neighboring counties, beds of shell marl that might be advantageously used on the sandy lands of the region.

Immediately south of the Eocene there is a belt of sandstone extending across the state, that has been referred to the Grand Gulf, of probably Miocene age. Its northern limit enters the state at the lower part of Sabine county, and outcrops on the Trinity river near Trinity station, in Trinity county, forming a bluff of about 100 feet in thickness. In Washington county, near Chapel Hill and Burton, the sandstone appears near the surface exposed in the railroad cuts; in Fayette county, at La Grange, it forms a bluff over 100 feet high on the south side of the river; in De Witt county it outcrops in the high hills on the north and in the bed of the river at Hellgate ferry, near Cuero. Still southwest, from all that can be ascertained from reports and other sources, the upper limit of this group forms a line of hills via Oakville, Live Oak county, southwestward through Duval county to the Rio Grande, at Rio Grande City.

The width of the formation is not great, being covered with the Port Hudson clays on the south along the entire coast. On the east it probably includes the long-leaf pine' region, while on the Rio Grande it does not, so far as known, approach nearer to the coast than Hidalgo, where the first line of sandstone hills comes to the river. The rock is usually very coarse in character, and rather a conglomerate, in which a coarse quartz grit is combined with a white siliceous clay as a cementing material. Sometimes it is massive in structure, and often thinly laminated and fine grained.

These sandstones contain no fossils so far as known, and identification of the group is dependent wholly upon the position and character of its rocks.

Quaternary, or stratified drift.—The superficial deposit of rounded sands, grit, and water-worn pebbles that represent the drift formation in other southern states is also found in Texas, and is confined chiefly to the Eocene and Grand Gulf groups, the timbered uplands of the streams, and the upper and lower cross timbers, the territory being overlaid to the seaward by the Port Hudson clays.

These deposits are very irregularly distributed, sometimes forming low hills or ridges of large pebbles and sand, as near La Grange, Bastrop, Gonzales, and many other places, or deep sand beds, that are found almost everywhere in the region mentioned north of the Grand Gulf. Agates and variously colored quartz pebbles are usually abundant in the drift beds, and silicified wood, in small and large fragments, is found in very many of the counties.

From Rio Grande City, Starr county, to the mouth of the Pecos and beyond rounded pebbles are said to cover the ground nearly everywhere, and among them are found some very fine agates.

Port Hudson.—The group in Louisiana to which the name of Port Hudson has been given by Professor E. W. Hilgard is described by him as consisting of a—

Blue-clay stratum, usually containing stumps or trunks of the cypress or other lowland trees, and extends not only over the entire alluvial plain of the Mississippi as high as Memphis at least, of Red river as high as Shreveport, and correspondingly in other larger tributaries, both of these rivers and of the Gulf of Mexico, but also over the entire coast region of Texas, Louisiana, Mississippi, and Alabama from the Rio Grande to the Escambia, and doubtless farther along the coast of Florida. It forms along these coasts the "blue-clay bottom" so well known to navigators, that generally, at a distance varying from 7 to 20 miles out from the mainland, breaks off into deep water.

In the bluff at Port Hudson, Louisiana, whence the group derives its name, these blue clays are overlaid by or associated with strata of gravel and sand in irregular bands, which contain leaves, wood, and mastodon bones. Overlying this is a stratum of yellow hard-pan from 18 to 25 feet thick, in turn underlying a yellow surface loam 4 to 10 feet thick. West of Port Hudson few outcrops or well profiles in the Opelousas and Anacoco prairies, from bayou Cocodrie to the Calcasieu river, reach below what are doubtless the equivalents of the upper portion of the Port Hudson bluff, viz, gray, yellow, or mottled siliceous silts or loams. * * * Near the latitude of lake Charles the soil of the Calcasieu prairie is directly derived from the stiff clay, with calcareous nodules, that crops out in the beds of streams.

In Texas these prairies continue westward to the Rio Grande, overlying the sandstones of the Grand Gulf and drift, and usually extending to the mainland coast. The silty soils or loams are prominent from the Sabine to the Brazos delta, but beyond that the formation is prominently represented by heavy yellow and dark colored gypseous or calcareous clays, inclosing white calcareous concretions and some limestone beds, and in it have been found (at Lavaca) the fossil bones and teeth of mammoth quadrupeds. These clays, when not covered by later sand deposits, form the heavy, black, waxy and hog-wallow prairie lands of the southern prairie region.

The immediate coast and islands of the Gulf are low and covered with sand beds and shells, but inland a mile, and often less, the surface of the country is 15 or 20 feet above the water, the stiff clays forming perpendicular bluffs along the bays and bayous. The formation is limited or covered on the southwest of Corpus Christi by the sands of what is termed "the desert" to within 50 miles of Brownsville, where are found again its characteristic stiff lands.

Other deposits.—The islands and the immediate coast are covered by beds and hills of sand, or "sand dunes", which are being constantly blown here and there by the winds; but the most prominent bed of sand in the state is perhaps that of "the desert" of the southwest, already alluded to. With its base reaching from the valley of the Rio Grande, 50 miles north of Brownsville, along the coast to within a few miles of Corpus Christi, it reaches inland or northwest, becoming more narrow near Laredo, and finally forms merely a broad dividing ridge 35 or 40 miles southeast of Eagle Pass. The sand-hills of the plains along the Pecos river are doubtless but a continuation of this desert belt. Rev. Mr. Hall, of Brownsville, describes this region as being "composed of pure white sand, studded over with live oaks, festooned with long moss".

The northern portion of the Llano Estacado is covered by a horizontal bed of drift material varying from 10 to 15 feet in thickness beneath the surface covering of soil. Dr. Shumard reports this sand as differing from that of the regular stratified drift, in being angular instead of rounded by attrition with water. The same is also said of the sands that form the hills, so prominent on the plains. From the drift bed Dr. Shumard obtained specimens of chalcedony, jasper, granite, obsidian, agates, and fossil wood.

AGRICULTURAL FEATURES.—The state of Texas, with its immense territory, naturally presents agricultural features greater in variety, perhaps, than those of any other state in the Union. Its position at the southwestern extreme of the agricultural regions of the south gives to a part of the state features similar in most respects to other southern states. Including, as it does, the southeastern borders of the great western plains, the lands of the western part of the state resemble those of New Mexico. Those of the gypsum formation and of the red-loam region seem only to extend northward into the Indian territory. The following agricultural regions may be conveniently distinguished:

1. Timbered upland region of east and central Texas:
    Oak, hickory, and pine uplands.
    Short-leaf pine region or pineries.
    Red hill lands.
    Brown and sandy loam prairies.
    Long-leaf pine hills and flats.
    Upper and lower cross timbers.
2. Southern and coast prairie region:
    Country east of the Brazos.
    Country west of the Brazos to the Nueces and Frio rivers.
    Southwestern prairies and sandy "desert".
3. Central black prairie region.
4. Northwestern red-loam lands.
5. Western and northwestern uninhabited region:
    Gypsum lands.
    Llano Estacado or the Great Plains.
    The mountain region.
6. River alluvial lands, including the Brazos delta, or "sugar-bowl".

THE TIMBERED UPLAND REGION OF TEXAS.

The timbered region, which name is popularly applied to all that part of the state lying east of the central prairies and southward to the coast prairies, and which here is made to include also "the cross timbers" of the former, embraces an area of 45,995 square miles. It covers the eastern part of the state from Red river southward to the marshes of the Sabine river, and extends southwestward, becoming more and more narrow, until it nearly reaches the Frio river, about 100 miles from the Rio Grande, where it ends.

The area, exclusive of the cross timbers, is 40,685 square miles, or greater than that of either Kentucky, Indiana, or Virginia. It includes all or the greater part of about 50 counties.

TOPOGRAPHY.—The surface of the country is more or less rolling throughout, while in the counties of Panola, Rusk, and in others in the central region, and in Lee and Bastrop on the southwest, there are prominent hills of Tertiary iron and ferruginous sandstone, forming a belt of interrupted red lands across the state in a northeast and southwest course. The entire country, with the exception of a few small prairies here and there, is well timbered with black, red, post, and black-jack oaks, hickory, and some short-leaf pine. In the extreme eastern counties, along the Louisiana line, and in the counties bordering the pineries, the short-leaf pine (*Pinus mitis*) is a very prominent growth, but in border counties along the black prairie it appears only sparsely.

Small insular brown-loam prairies are a prominent feature of the western side of the region along its entire length as far north as Red river. They also occur on the east around Boston, Bowie county, and in Cherokee county, and will be described among the special features of the region.

The region is crossed by all of the largest streams of the state, except the Nueces and Rio Grande rivers. They flow in a great measure parallel with each other southeast to the Gulf, each with its many small tributaries forming a separate drainage system. Water of excellent quality is abundant throughout the year from springs, wells, and the various larger streams. Summer rains are more frequent than in the regions westward, and crops do not usually suffer materially from droughts.

In the timbered uplands that border the bottom lands of Red river and southward for some distance in Red River county (as well as in the adjoining portions of Louisiana) are innumerable small mounds 3 or 4 feet high, and having diameters varying from 10 to 25 or 30 feet. They usually bear the growth of grass, shrubs, and trees that are found on these uplands, while in the depressions lying between the mounds there is little else than grass or weeds, growing on an impervious clay, and sometimes containing water, milky in appearance from suspended white clay. When exposed by the railroad excavations, the mounds are seen to have the same structure of sandy-loam soils and yellowish sandy subsoils that are observed in the pine lands of Bowie county.

The country is properly divided into three general divisions, *the oak, hickory, and short-leaf pine uplands, the long-leaf pine hills and flats*, and *the prairies*, which are interspersed throughout the former. In addition to these *the bottom lands* of the entire region will be separately described, those of Red river forming a division on page 41.

OAK, HICKORY, AND SHORT-LEAF PINE UPLANDS.

This group, as will be seen by the map, occupies nearly the entire area of the timbered lands southward to the southern part of Sabine, San Augustine, Polk, and San Jacinto counties, or 35,350 square miles. Its surface presents three general features, which are best described separately, viz: a region of prominent *short-leaf pine growth* on the east and southeast, known as "the pineries"; a belt of *red hill lands* occupying the central portion southwestward; and the *oak and hickory lands* proper, with some short-leaf pine growth. This region is more thickly populated than any other in the state, the average being a little more than 16 persons per square mile. The proportion of lands under cultivation (13.2 per cent.) is a very little less than that of the central prairie region, while the percentage of these devoted to the culture of cotton is 34.4, a far greater proportion than is found in any other part of the state. The cotton acreage per square mile is 28.4 per cent., corn being the chief crop of the region.

The short-leaf pine region.

This region, thus designated because of the prevalence of this short-leaf species of pine, embraces the eastern part of the county of Bowie, a large part of Cass, and portions of the counties south bordering the long-leaf pine region, and also extends in belts along the Nueces river, in Cherokee and Anderson counties, constituting what are often called "pineries".

The lands are generally but slightly rolling, and have light sandy or silty soils from 10 to 12 inches deep, a yellowish sandy subsoil two or more feet deep, and a red underclay. These depths vary greatly, the clay often coming near to the surface. The pine is interspersed more or less with oaks and hickory, and the bottom lands of the creeks that flow through the region have a growth of sweet gum, elm, oak, etc. The sandy nature of the land makes tillage easy. Drainage is good, and it is claimed that the lands will produce an average of 800 pounds of seed-cotton per acre in favorable seasons without the aid of fertilizers.

The following analyses are given to show the composition of the lands of the pine region:

No. 1. *Gray sandy soil* from Bowie county, near Texarkana, Arkansas. Depth taken, 12 inches; growth, oak, hickory, and short-leaf pine.

No. 2. *Yellow sandy subsoil* of the above, taken at from 12 to 20 inches.

Short-leaf pine lands, Bowie county.

	Soil.	Subsoil.
	No. 1.	No. 2.
Insoluble matter	95.197 } 96.174	88.802 } 92.339
Soluble silica	0.977 }	3.537 }
Potash	0.047	0.046
Soda	0.096	0.069
Lime	0.274	0.228
Magnesia	0.162	0.164
Brown oxide of manganese	0.075	0.019
Peroxide of iron	1.035	2.171
Alumina	0.382	3.040
Phosphoric acid	0.090	0.000
Sulphuric acid	0.015	0.022
Water and organic matter	1.456	2.074
	99.646	100.233
Available inorganic	0.540	
Available phosphoric acid	0.027	
Humus	0.410	
Hygroscopic moisture	1.780	3.990
absorbed at	18 C.°	18 C.°

The above analyses show that both the soil and subsoil are greatly deficient in potash, with low percentage of phosphoric acid, as well as vegetable matter, while a relatively large percentage of lime explains their present thriftiness. A fair yield in seed-cotton would probably be realized for two or three years, as the lime is sufficient, to make available the little phosphoric acid that the lands contain, but durability cannot be expected.

The red hills.

Hills of ferruginous sandstone and concretionary iron ore occur in a number of the counties of eastern Texas, and notably in Cherokee, Cass, Marion, and Rusk. Southwestward the belt of iron ore and red lands extends beyond the Guadalupe river, but, with the exception of a few isolated hills, the country is not so broken, the rocks rather forming beds below the soils. The iron hills of Cherokee county are from 150 to 200 feet above the general level of the country, and are in some cases broad on their tops, while on the sides masses of iron ore outcrop in large and small fragments. The soil of the valley lands between these hills is full of ferruginous pebbles, making them, as is claimed by the farmers, more liable to drought.

The iron ore of these counties is usually a brown hematite or Tertiary ironstone, more or less concretionary in form, with often a matrix of ocherous clay, rich in iron. Furnaces were at one time in operation in a number of the counties, but have been either abandoned or destroyed. An interesting feature of these iron hills in the extreme eastern counties is their occurrence as isolated spots, surrounded by the forests of short-leaf pine and by poor sandy lands, except in their immediate neighborhood.

Red sandy and clayey lands occur in most of the counties of the oak and hickory region to a greater or less extent, but chiefly, so far as known, in Cass, Morris, Marion, Harrison, Smith, Cherokee, Rusk, Nacogdoches, San Augustine, Sabine, Houston, Anderson, Lee, and Caldwell. These red lands are considered best for corn and small grain, though cotton grows well and produces from 600 to 800 pounds of seed-cotton per acre. In Lee and some other counties the lands are enriched by a glauconitic limestone (Tertiary), which lies in fragments on the surface. The timber growth of the red lands is hickory, red and post oaks, sweet and black gums, and elm.

The following analyses show the composition of the red lands:

No. 4. A *dark loamy soil* near Palestine, Anderson county, taken 8 inches deep. Growth, hickory, white and black-jack oaks. Though the soil is more sandy than is the case perhaps elsewhere, both soil and subsoil may be taken as an average of the whole, the lands all being more or less sandy.

No. 5. *Red clayey subsoil* of the above, taken from 8 to 12 inches.

No. 6. *Red glauconitic soil* from the place of Mrs. E. R. Wilson, 6 miles north of Lexington, Lee county. Depth, 12 inches.

No. 35. *Red pebbly clay soil* from Harwood, Gonzales county, taken 10 inches. Timber growth, oak and hickory.

Red lands of the timbered region.

	ANDERSON COUNTY.		LEE COUNTY.	GONZALES COUNTY.
	Soil.	Subsoil.	Soil.	Soil.
	No. 4.	No. 5.	No. 6.	No. 35.
Insoluble matter	92.943 } 93.952	79.954 } 81.205	74.963 } 78.868	60.770 } 74.370
Soluble silica	1.009	1.251	3.905	13.600
Potash	0.111	0.067	0.713	0.445
Soda	0.093	0.060	0.131	0.077
Lime	0.147	0.188	0.288	0.389
Magnesia	0.077	0.012	0.530	0.209
Brown oxide of manganese	0.051	0.170	0.032	0.043
Peroxide of iron	1.814	2.478	9.883	9.622
Alumina	1.470	6.078	5.801	7.944
Phosphoric acid	0.198	0.194	0.102	0.282
Sulphuric acid	0.090	0.006	0.029	0.106
Water and organic matter	2.301	4.109	4.717	5.093
Total	99.929	100.547	100.018	99.583
Available inorganic			1.472	
Available phosphoric acid			0.085	
Humus			0.740	
Hygroscopic moisture	8.781	11.655	7.883	9.758
absorbed at	14 C.°	15 C.°	12 C.°	10° C.

The sandy soil and clayey subsoil of Anderson county are both deficient in potash, though they have fair percentages of phosphoric acid and lime.

The Lee county soil in its high percentage of potash shows the influence of the glauconite (greensand) that occurs in the rocks found on its surface. The amount of phosphoric acid, however, is rather low for a soil containing such high percentages of iron and alumina, and after a few years' cultivation the application of phosphatic manures to the soil are found to be necessary to insure its full productiveness. There are fair percentages of lime and of humus.

The Gonzales county soil is rich in all of its important elements, and should be highly productive and durable. It lies almost within the belt of iron-ore hills mentioned above.

The oak and hickory uplands.

The timbered uplands, in whose growth pine is almost entirely absent, covers the largest part of this division of the state, and lies between the central black prairie region on the west and the pineries and southern coast prairie region on the east and south. The region has a southwesterly course, reaching from the Red river on the northeast nearly to the Nueces river on the southwest, and while wide at first (from 60 to 100 miles), becomes narrow at the Brazos river, and is to the southwest interspersed with and penetrated by the southern prairies, the latter feature giving the appearance of long arms or peninsulas of timber extending out from the main region.

The oak and hickory lands proper present very much the same characters and productiveness throughout. Here and there we find such local exceptions as "post-oak flats", "sand flats," etc., which, however, will be mentioned only in the description of counties in which they occur.

The surface of the country is generally rolling, sometimes hilly; the soil sandy to a depth of about 12 inches, and is very generally underlaid by a good clay subsoil, usually red in color. Decayed leaves and other vegetation has given to the surface soil a dark color an inch or two deep, adding much to its productiveness.

The general timber growth of these lands is red, black, post, and black-jack oaks, and hickory, with a thick scrubby undergrowth, and some short-leaf pine. The crops of the region are cotton, corn, wheat, oats, sugar and sorghum-cane, pease, and upland rice. The uplands are best adapted to cotton, which comprises a large proportion of the crops. It usually grows to a height of 3 feet in dry and 5 or 6 feet in wet seasons, producing, it is claimed, from 500 to 1,000 pounds of seed-cotton per acre when fresh, and from 600 to 800 pounds after many years' cultivation. The lands wash readily when allowed to lie idle any length of time, but as yet any effort to prevent this is exceptional.

The following analyses are given to show the composition of these lands:

No. 3. *Sandy upland soil*, taken near Mineola, Wood county. Depth, 24 inches; timber growth, post, red, and black-jack oaks, hickory, and sumac.

No. 30. *Light sandy soil* from near Troup, Smith county, taken 12 inches deep. Timber growth, hickory, and post, red, and black-jack oaks.

No. 31. *Light yellow subsoil* of the above, taken from 12 to 18 inches. Overlies a yellow shaly sandstone.

No. 21. *Sandy upland soil* from McDade, Bastrop county, taken 12 inches. Timber growth, post oak. Ferruginous sandstone and pebbles occur on the surface.

Oak and hickory uplands.

	WOOD COUNTY.	SMITH COUNTY.		BASTROP COUNTY.
	Soil.	Soil.	Subsoil.	Soil.
	No. 2.	No. 30.	No. 31.	No. 21.
Insoluble matter	92.051 } 96.415	94.350 } 94.275	93.458 } 96.278	92.835 } 95.041
Soluble silica	2.364 }	0.925 }	1.820 }	2.206 }
Potash	0.114	0.111	0.148	0.195
Soda	0.074	0.105	0.080	0.095
Lime	0.081	0.076	0.090	0.172
Magnesia	0.061	0.061	0.081	0.113
Brown oxide of manganese	0.111	0.040	0.121	0.097
Peroxide of iron	0.611	2.062	2.397	1.145
Alumina	0.908	0.303	0.779	0.504
Phosphoric acid	0.169	0.227	0.296	0.186
Sulphuric acid	0.013	0.031	0.105	0.020
Water and organic matter	0.611	2.035	0.911	1.687
Total	99.117	99.936	100.175	99.173
Hygroscopic moisture	0.74	1.671	1.80	1.687
absorbed at	12 C.°	12 C.°	12 C.°	17 C.°

From these analyses it appears that all of the soils have a low percentage of potash and a rather large one of phosphoric acid (accounting for durability), the latter being greatest in the soil from Smith county. There is not, however, a sufficiency of lime to render the phosphoric acid available to any extent, except perhaps in No. 2, where it is a minimum quantity. The soils are quite durable, but liming or marling will doubtless render them more productive.

PRAIRIES OF THE EASTERN TIMBERED REGION.

SANDY PRAIRIES.—The prairies of the region differ from each other in character, those on the west partaking largely of the black waxy nature of the central prairies, while those on the east are lighter and sandy. In Cherokee county the latter are known as "brush prairies", from the fact that they are rapidly being covered with a low scrubby growth of red, post, and black-jack oaks. The past eight years is said to have witnessed a great change in this respect, and is attributed to the fact that they are not now usually burned off, as formerly was the case.

The soils of both these and the Boston prairies, in Bowie county, are light sandy or silty, and are not considered as productive as the adjoining timbered sandy uplands, the cotton-plant not growing as high, and yielding only from 500 to 700 pounds of seed-cotton per acre when fresh. The prairies are very level, those of the Boston being about a mile in diameter, and interspersed with clumps of trees.

BROWN-LOAM PRAIRIES.—In the counties of Navarro, Limestone, Grimes, Brazos, Burleson, and Lee there are high, rolling, and open prairies having a brown-loam soil a foot or two in depth and an underlying heavy clay, which in the prairie valleys or lowlands forms very heavy waxy lands, similar in every respect to the black prairies of the west. The largest of these brown-loam prairies covers a large part of the two first counties named, and lies along the eastern edge of the black prairie region, extending on the north and south into the adjoining counties, and covering an area of about 1,825 square miles.

In Limestone county and southward the western line of these prairies is marked by a low range of hills, treeless, and formed by a hard Tertiary limestone, which is in places fossiliferous, and forms rocky ledges along the summit.

The first of these hills, in the northern part of Limestone county, is known as "the Tehuacana hills", here rather abrupt in character, but forming broad table-lands northward toward Corsicana. On the south the Navasota river cuts through the hills, the southern end then receiving the name of "Honest ridge". The next in the line of ridges is "Horn hill", about three miles in length; then "Big bill", one mile long. "Buffalo Mop", four miles southwest of the latter, is a small but prominent elevation, forming a connecting link with the "Blue ridge", the last of the chain of hills, and terminating, after a length of 10 miles, between Big creek and Little Brazos river, in Falls county, on the southwest. The entire range is of very much the same character throughout, is most abrupt on the western side, while on the east there is a broad and almost even prairie, extending with a slight slope to the timbered lands, and having in localities a low growth of mesquite trees (*Prosopis juliflora*).

In Navarro county the prairies are higher, and are rendered more broken by numerous streams, which have cut their way into them, and which now have heavily timbered and black bottom lands, with occasional oak and hickory uplands along their border, as along Chambers creek, east of Corsicana.

On the west and north of Corsicana are found Tertiary fossiliferous rocks, both in the banks of the streams, and lying in fragments on the prairie, while on the east of Chambers creek the prairie lands have much quartz gravel of all colors, large and small.

The lands of these prairies have a rich brown-loam soil from 12 to 24 inches in depth and a heavy reddish, clay subsoil. Mesquite growth is plentiful. The lands yield well, and are said to be very durable. Cotton grows well, often to a height of 4 or 5 feet, producing an average of about 800 pounds of seed-cotton per acre. It is stated, that very little of this land that has been long under cultivation now lies turned out for rest, its productiveness being as yet but slightly diminished. A large proportion of these prairie lands has never been under cultivation, and still is used for pasturage.

The "San Antonio prairies" of Burleson, and those of Brazos and Grimes counties, are similar in character to these described, and the same and even greater productiveness is claimed for them.

The following analyses show the composition of the prairie lands:

No. 7. *Sandy prairie soil*, taken near Tehuacana, Limestone county. Depth, 12 inches; a little mesquite growth.

No. 34. *Dark sandy prairie soil*, taken 2 miles west of Corsicana, Navarro county. Depth, 10 inches; no timber growth.

Brown-loam prairie soils.

	LIMESTONE COUNTY.	NAVARRO COUNTY.
	No. 7.	No. 34.
Insoluble matter	92.949 } 94.370	87.557 } 92.740
Soluble silica	1.421	5.188
Potash	0.140	0.117
Soda	0.096	0.070
Lime	0.194	0.220
Magnesia	0.059	0.181
Brown oxide of manganese	0.032	0.062
Peroxide of iron	1.438	1.625
Alumina	0.907	2.204
Phosphoric acid	0.368	0.229
Sulphuric acid	0.681	0.110
Water and organic matter	2.134	2.623
Total	99.632	100.515
Hygroscopic moisture	5.490	4.756
absorbed at	19 C.°	19 C.°

These two soils each have a low percentage of potash. That from Limestone county, while rich in phosphoric acid, is rather deficient in the lime necessary to render it fully available. The Navarro soil, on the contrary, has a sufficiency of lime to render available for a time the fair amount of phosphoric acid it contains. Both soils are sandy, and lack vegetable matter.

SALINES.—Salines occur in several of the counties of these eastern timbered regions. The largest of these is in Van Zandt county, and covers several hundred acres of land. Much salt has been obtained from the water of the wells at a depth of 18 or 20 feet. Much smaller salines occur in Smith county. They cover but a few acres, and are reported to be surrounded by hills, in which is found limestone (probably Cretaceous, as in the salines of Louisiana).

BOTTOM LANDS OF THE TIMBERED REGION.—Under this head are included only the lands of the smaller streams, those of the large rivers comprising a separate division, viz, alluvial lands, which will be found on page 41.

Sulphur Fork river lies mostly within this region on the northeast, and is parallel with Red river, to which it is tributary, and flows almost due east. Its bottom lands, as well as those of the neighboring White Oak and Big Cypress creeks, have a dark and heavy loam soil, quite deep, and overlying a stiff bluish clay. They have a timber growth of hickory, pecan, ash, walnut, and white oak, with pin, burr, overcup, and Spanish oaks. Cotton is very much inclined to run to weed on these lands, and is represented as producing as much as 1,500 pounds of seed-cotton per acre in favorable seasons.

Angelina and Neches rivers, in their separate courses, belong to this division, uniting soon after they enter the pineries. Their bottom lands are from one-fourth of a mile to 1 mile in width, and have a timber growth of oak, elm, hickory, beech, and walnut, with an undergrowth of cane, bamboo, muscadine, and wild peach. The soil is a black loam from 2 to 4 feet deep, over a heavy clay subsoil. Cotton grows to a height of 5 feet, and is said to yield, when fresh, as much as 1,500 pounds of seed-cotton, or from 800 to 1,000 pounds after five years' cultivation. The hummock lands that border these bottoms have a width of from one-fourth to 1½ miles, and a timber growth of pine, oak, hickory, and ash. The soil is said to be a heavy whitish-brown clayey loam from 12 to 24 inches deep, underlaid by a heavier subsoil and by gravel at a depth of 6 or 8 feet. It yields, when fresh, from 500 to 800 pounds of seed-cotton, or from 400 to 700 pounds after five years' cultivation.

Navasota river bottom is said to have very much the same character of soil and growth as that of the Brazos, to which its waters are tributary. A very high yield is claimed for both, viz, over a bale per acre.

The bottom lands of the *Yeguas* (creeks lying between the Brazos and Colorado rivers) are not much under cultivation, as they are subject to overflow. They have a timber growth of pin oak, pecan, elm, ash, and hackberry. When cultivated they yield, it is said, about 1,400 pounds of seed-cotton per acre. The bottom lands of the *Guadalupe river* are subject to overflow, and therefore are not under cultivation. Its valley lands are rich and productive, having a dark loamy or often a black prairie soil, 2 or 3 feet deep, over a gray clayey subsoil, and at 10 feet a bed of sand and gravel. Cotton grows usually from 5 to 8 feet in height, and yields about 1,400 pounds of seed-cotton per acre.

LAKE BOTTOM LANDS.—The bottom lands of Little Cypress river and Caddo lake, in Harrison county, are from 2 to 3 miles in width, and have a timber growth of pin and overcup oaks and pine, cypress in the marshes, and blue-jack oak and myrtle thickets along the borders of the lake. The soil is black and stiff, and water stands on it during half of the year. The creek bottoms in the same county have a growth of red oak, sweet gum, hickory, red elm, chincapin, and bitter pecan. These lands are not extensive, and are little in cultivation.

On the Sabine river, in Rusk county, there are some cypress swamps. The creeks of the county have a bottom growth of white, red, post, and overcup oaks, ash, maple, and hickory, and a fine sandy soil 18 inches in depth, overlying a compact clay, and said to produce from 1,000 to 1,200 pounds of seed-cotton per acre.

THE LONG-LEAF PINE REGION.

The region thus designated does not include all of that part of the state in which the long-leaf pine is found, but, as in Georgia and other states, is meant to represent only lands that are so sandy as to support a timber growth of little else than this species of pine.

In Sabine, Panola, and other counties there are large areas covered with a prominent growth of this timber, associated with such hard woods as oak and hickory, and having clay subsoils. They thus differ from the lands in the more southern counties, and are properly classed with the oak, hickory, and pine region. .

The poorer lands, or the long-leaf pine region proper, merge into the better class so gradually that it has been found impossible with the information at hand to define their limits with extreme accuracy, and therefore the outlines as given on the map must be considered simply as general.

The long-leaf pine region, or "pineries" as it is called, comprises both hills and flats, and embraces the counties of Newton, Jasper, Tyler, Orange, and Hardin, the southern parts of Sabine, Angelina, Trinity, San Augustine, and Nacogdoches, the eastern and southern part of Polk, and probably the southeastern part of San Jacinto, as well as areas in Shelby and Panola and elsewhere. It covers an area of about 6,000 square miles. The "flats" are found in the southern part of the region between the Trinity and Sabine rivers, and form the western limit of the pine flats of Louisiana and other states. The rest of the region is more rolling and well timbered, chiefly with long-leaf pine, and forms the western extreme of that great belt of pine timber so prominent from Texas to the Atlantic coast.

The northern part of the pine region in Texas is interspersed with open prairies having a variety of soils, from sandy to stiff black loams and clays, and is similar in position and other features to the Anacoco prairie of Louisiana. The timbered uplands have but little else than dark or gray sandy soils, with mostly sandy subsoils, sometimes to a depth of several feet, and are not considered very productive. The country is sparsely settled, with an average of about five persons per square mile. The chief industry of the people is the cutting and shipment of lumber.

The lands under cultivation are chiefly the hummocks that lie along the creeks and larger streams. Their soils are sandy to a depth of many inches, and have a growth of oaks, hickory, beech, walnut, magnolia, etc. It is claimed that these lands will produce as much as 1,500 pounds per acre when fresh and 800 pounds after eight years' cultivation; 2.1 per cent. only of the area of the region is under cultivation, and that is mostly devoted to corn. The cotton average is 3.4 acres per square mile, comprising 25.6 per cent. of the tilled lands, with an average yield of 615 pounds of seed-cotton per acre.

THE CROSS TIMBERS.

The name of "cross timbers" is popularly given to two wide belts of timbered lands that extend southward from Red river; the one, or "lower", in the central part of the black prairie region; the other, or "upper", on the west of the prairie, or between it and the red lands. These belts resemble each other very much in their general features.

The belt of the "*lower cross timbers*" enters the state from the Indian territory immediately to the east of the big bend of the river north of Gainesville, Cooke county, the stream having apparently been turned north by the belt.

Southward it has an average width of from 10 to 15 miles, extends to the Brazos river, in McLennan county, a distance of 135 miles, and covers an area of about 1,720 square miles. Its western edge is marked by the towns of Gainsville, Denton, and Cleburne, while Fort Worth is within a few miles to the west of this limit. The belt is thickly timbered with a growth of post and black-jack oaks, and has a deep sandy soil. Its surface is rolling, and there is a line of low hills of gray and ferruginous sandstone and conglomerate along its center, and quantities of small and brown ferruginous gravel cover the surface in many localities. On either side of the belt the sandstone seems to thin out, the underlying limestone and fossil beds of the prairies sometimes appearing near the surface. Wells have been dug to a depth of 40 feet in the belt through sands and clays without reaching the rotten limestone that characterizes the adjoining prairies. Some lignite is reported on the north. In many points along its course the general surface of the belt is lower than the adjoining prairies, and the general features of the lower cross timbers almost lead to the conclusion that at some time a deep trough-like valley connected Red (perhaps the Canadian) and Brazos rivers, probably forming the bed of the former river and conveying its waters to the Gulf through the present channel of the Brazos, and that by some agency this valley was filled with clays and sands and the present channel of the river formed.

The soils of the uplands are generally very sandy for a foot or more in depth, and are not considered valuable. Along the streams and in the lowlands the soil is a dark sandy loam with a clay subsoil, rich and productive. On it cotton grows 4 or 5 feet high, and, it is claimed, yields as much as 1,500 pounds of seed-cotton per acre even on lands that have been several years under cultivation.

The "upper cross timbers" also leave Red river at the foot of a long southeast bend, and pass south through the middle of the county of Montague with a width of 10 or 15 miles, covering probably 3,500 square miles. At the lower edge of the county it divides, the eastern portion passing south through Wise and Parker to the Brazos river; the other a little westward, and more interrupted in its character, extending far south into Erath county, and forming, as it were, a line of separation between the black prairie and the western red-loam regions in this part of the state.

Between these two prongs in Parker county there are high and bald hills of rotten limestone of the black prairies, and on emerging suddenly at their feet from the thickly-timbered and quite level belt that lies between them and the Brazos on the west a person is struck with their prominence. To the south can be seen the high points of Comanche and other peaks rising above the line of ridges. The belt is throughout its length and breadth interspersed with small and open prairies. The lands are the same in character as those of the lower cross timbers, the uplands, with their deep sandy soil (often little else than pure white and deep sand), having a timber growth of scrubby post and black-jack oaks, and the lowlands, with their dark loam soils and growth of ash, cottonwood, pecan, and hackberry, producing an average of 1,000 pounds of seed-cotton per acre.

The following analyses show the composition of the soils of these two belts:

No. 17. *Sandy soil* of the "lower cross timbers" from near Arlington, Tarrant county, the eastern edge of the belt, taken 8 inches deep. Timber growth, post and red oaks. This is a representative of the better class of level lands of the region.

No. 26. *Sandy upland soils* of the "upper cross timbers" from near the stage crossing of Leon river, Comanche county, taken 12 inches deep. Timber growth, post oak almost exclusively.

Lower and upper cross timbers soils.

	TARRANT COUNTY.	COMANCHE COUNTY.
	Lower cross timbers.	Upper cross timbers.
	No. 17.	No. 26.
Insoluble matter	88.092	98.789
Soluble silica	8.812	1.179
Potash	0.218	0.209
Soda	0.079	0.058
Lime	0.242	0.088
Magnesia	0.174	8.206
Brown oxide of manganese	0.016	0.061
Peroxide of iron	2.486	0.497
Alumina	2.672	0.671
Phosphoric acid	0.098	0.121
Sulphuric acid	0.045	0.080
Water and organic matter	2.785	0.889
	99.886	100.286
Hygroscopic moisture	4.485	1.028
absorbed at	13 C.°	13 C.°

These two soils, while containing very nearly the same proportions of potash and phosphoric acid, respectively, differ greatly in several other particulars, the advantages being with that of the lower belt, No. 17. This soil is less sandy, has much more of iron and alumina, and, what is better still, a fair amount of vegetable matter and a large percentage of lime. The latter is amply sufficient to render available the small percentage of phosphoric acid. There is a deficiency in the lime percentage in No. 26, but the potash in both soils is present in fair proportions.

SOUTHERN COAST PRAIRIES.

The coast of Texas is bordered by a low and level prairie, reaching from the marshes of Sabine Pass westward to the densely timbered Brazos alluvial basin, and thence westward, with scarcely any interruption, to the Rio Grande, excepting the narrow timbered lands of a few streams. While there is a similarity in some of its features throughout its length, yet certain portions of the coast have such marked peculiarities as to merit a division into three groups for purposes of description. These are *the prairie region east of the Brazos alluvial, the prairie region west of the Brazos alluvial*, extending to the Nueces river, and *the southwestern prairie region*, lying between the Nueces and Frio rivers to the Rio Grande. The entire region embraced is about 47,080 square miles, which is about the area of the state of Mississippi.

EAST OF THE BRAZOS ALLUVIAL REGION.—In the southeastern part of the state, lying between the Brazos and the Trinity rivers, and extending eastward to the Neches, there is a large region of level prairie lands, having large areas each of *gray silty* and *black waxy* soils, interspersed with "motts" of pine or oak, and intersected by timbered streams. The region extends from the coast inland into the counties of Waller, Montgomery, and San Jacinto, and includes besides these all or portions of Jefferson, Liberty, Chambers, Galveston, Brazoria (eastern part), and Harris.

The prairies of the northeastern part of the division usually have gray silty soils, and deserve more properly the name of "pine prairies"; but where the underlying Port Hudson clays approach the surface the result is a black waxy soil. On the northwest of the city of Houston, and extending nearly to Hempstead, in Waller county, there is but little to break the monotony of a level and open prairie. Southward to the coast the prairies extend almost uninterruptedly, covering areas of from 20 to 30 miles in breadth, and are characterized by the absence of all growth other than grasses and occasional motts of large live-oak trees. Along Buffalo bayou and other streams the uplands are well timbered with oak and pine, and in the immediate vicinity of the streams the magnolia (*Magnolia grandiflora*) is a large and prominent growth. The trees, and especially the live oaks, are very generally festooned with the greatest abundance of the long moss (*Tillandsia usneoides*) so common in the coast region of all of the southern states. The surface of the entire region is very level and even, with a descent to the coast so gradual as to afford no drainage to the soils, and, as a natural consequence, water remains in pools upon the prairies of the region until removed by evaporation.

The immediate coast lands from the marshes of Sabine river westward to the Brazos alluvial are almost entirely open prairies with a light sandy soil, becoming darker inland, and underlaid by a white concretionary clay. This latter comes to the surface near Clear Creek station, 19 miles from the shore-line. Small natural mounds from 10 to 20 feet in diameter and several feet high cover some parts of this coast region. At Allen's station, about 40 miles from the coast, the subsoil changes to a yellow clay with calcareous concretions.

The soil of the region is very generally a light sandy loam, underlaid at varying depths by heavy impervious clays. Large areas of black clayey lands occur along the border of the Brazos alluvial, and eastward to Harrisburg and beyond the Trinity river, which are very similar to those described on the west of the Brazos.

As shown by the analyses given below, the loam prairie lands of the region are well supplied with the mineral elements necessary for fertility, but from their want of proper drainage are not under cultivation. They are given up entirely to grazing purposes and the production of hay, for which the thick carpet of grass that covers them is admirably suited. The farms of the region are found in the timbered uplands that border Buffalo bayou and some of the streams.

No. 9. *Grayish sandy prairie soil* from near Pierce's junction, 5 miles south of Houston, Harris county; taken 8 inches deep.

Sandy pratrie loam soil, Harris county.

	No. 9.
Insoluble matter	80.360 } 83.973
Soluble silica	3.613 }
Potash	0.291
Soda	0.197
Lime	0.653
Magnesia	0.272
Brown oxide of manganese	0.174
Peroxide of iron	3.461
Alumina	4.978
Phosphoric acid	0.156
Sulphuric acid	0.075
Water and organic matter	5.213
Total	99.584
Available inorganic	1.491
Available phosphoric acid	0.034
Humus	3.132
Hygroscopic moisture	10.688
absorbed at	12 C.°

This soil has a fair amount of potash and of phosphoric acid and a large percentage of lime, which would render them both productive and durable. The absorptive power is also great.

WEST OF THE BRAZOS.—One of the prominent features of the southern and coast prairie region is the large area of *black and stiff or waxy lands* that occupies a central position between the Sabine and Rio Grande rivers and reaches from the coast northward into Washington county. In the counties of Calhoun, Victoria, Jackson, and the western parts of Matagorda and Wharton these prairies are very broad and extensive, with a gradual rise from the coast inland for 20 or 30 miles, and then become slightly rolling, the view interrupted here and there by the timber growth of the streams or "motts" of mesquite and live oak. On Lavaca bay there is much Mexican scarlet bean (*Erythrina*) and a few "Brazil-wood" trees. Northward, in the counties of De Witt, Lavaca, Colorado, Fayette, Washington, and Austin, the prairies are smaller, and are interspersed with sandy and timbered uplands and sandy prairies. In adjoining portions of Gonzales and De Witt counties there are high and rolling sandy prairies, underlaid by sandstone (Grand Gulf). In the lowlands and flats of these the soil is often a heavy black clay. On either side of the alluvial lands of the Brazos and adjoining streams, in Fort Bend and Brazoria counties, or the "sugar-bowl", there are other strips of black prairies.

As far inland as Clinton, in De Witt county, and Columbus, Colorado county, the prairies are underlaid by heavy light and blue-colored clays (Port Hudson) full of calcareous concretions, and often containing crystals of gypsum. They form bluffs from 15 to 25 feet high around Lavaca bay and the inland lakes, and in them have been found large fragments of the bones of extinct mammoth animals. Limestone also occurs to some extent in these beds. Excellent grass covers the lands of the region, and the prairies are almost entirely devoted to the grazing of stock, the sandy timbered lands of the streams being used for farming purposes. The entire country is very sparsely settled, "nearest neighbors" being generally many miles apart. But little cotton is produced in the counties along the coast, but as we advance inland we find that crop receiving more attention, over one-third of the tilled land of the upper counties of the region being devoted to cotton culture.

The soil of these prairies is black waxy or adobe in character, tenacious, and very difficult to till in wet seasons, while in dry weather it becomes hard, and shrinks, forming deep and wide cracks—traps, as it were, for the feet of the unwary beast. Hog-wallow lands are found in localities throughout the region, a feature resulting from the shrinkage and subsequent swelling and bulging out of the underclay upon access of water through the cracks when the winter rains come. The soil has a depth of from 12 to 24 inches, and overlies a lighter-colored and stiff clay, which sometimes contains gravel. The lands are thought to be best adapted to corn. Cotton grows to a height of from 3 to 5 feet, the yield being variously estimated to be from 600 to 1,000 pounds of seed-cotton per acre when fresh and after long cultivation. Some planters place the estimate much higher.

The following analyses show the composition of these prairie lands in several sections of the region:

No. 8. *Black prairie soil* from Schulenberg, Fayette county, taken 12 inches deep.

No. 10. *Black waxy prairie soil* from near Victoria, Victoria county, taken 12 inches deep.

No. 11. *Black prairie upland soil* from Chapel Hill, Washington county, taken 12 inches deep.

44 C P

COTTON PRODUCTION IN TEXAS.

Southern black prairie soils.

	FAYETTE COUNTY.	VICTORIA COUNTY.	WASHINGTON COUNTY.
	Soil.	Soil.	Soil.
	No. 8.	No. 10.	No. 11.
Insoluble matter	74.172 } 82.398	55.436 } 77.851	75.530 } 87.713
Soluble silica	8.726	22.415	12.183
Potash	0.274	0.420	0.235
Soda	0.309	0.218	0.145
Lime	0.965	1.050	0.948
Magnesia	0.968	1.092	0.477
Brown oxide of manganese	0.182	0.064	0.056
Peroxide of iron	3.802	11.280	2.296
Alumina	4.620	1.265	4.161
Phosphoric acid	0.162	0.063	0.168
Sulphuric acid	0.332	0.280	0.075
Water and organic matter	5.572	5.914	3.741
Total	99.564	99.511	99.925
Available inorganic		4.002	
Available phosphoric acid		0.036	
Humus		2.754	
Hygroscopic moisture	11.730	14.110	7.862
absorbed at	16 C.°	17 C.°	17 C.°

These soils are well supplied with every element of fertility except phosphoric acid, which should be larger in such lands. Of the latter, the Fayette county soil contains an amount that may be considered a little more than a minimum for high productiveness and durability.

THE SOUTHWESTERN PRAIRIE REGION.—The southwestern part of the state lying west of the Nueces and Frio rivers is almost entirely a prairie region, and includes the agricultural counties of Frio, McMullen, and Duval, and the counties of Maverick, Zavalla, Dimmit, La Salle, Webb, Encinal, Zapata, Starr, Hidalgo, and Cameron, (the latter two, however, having large areas of river lands, described on page 46), which properly may be included in what is termed "the desert".

The entire country is very sparsely settled and almost exclusively devoted to stock raising. Mesquite and a scrubby chaparral variety, with occasional live-oak trees and cacti, are almost the only growth, giving to the region a barren and desolate appearance. "The desert" is a broad area of white sand lying along the border of the Laguna de la Madre from a few miles south of Corpus Christi to the Rio Grande alluvial lands at the mouth of the Sal Colorado, and extending back (westward) to within a few miles of the Rio Grande, and up that stream to near Eagle Pass, as reported by Rev. Mr. Hall, of Brownsville.

The following is taken from a description of this region (in the *Texas Almanac* of 1868) by Ex-Governor E. J. Davis:

At Corpus Christi bay the high lands of the interior come down to the bay, and part of the town of this name is built upon a bluff nearly 50 feet above the water-level. I believe this is the highest land anywhere on the Gulf coast within the territories of the United States.

About 20 miles southwest of Corpus Christi commence the famous sands which border the Laguna Madre down to the Sal Colorado. These sands are quite remarkable. Extending in a northwesterly direction from the coast, they reach within 20 miles of the Rio Grande. They lie across the country in a wedge shape, of which the base lies on the Laguna. In many places these sands form bare hills, rising from 50 to 100 feet above the grassy plains, and being of a light-yellow color are landmarks of the country and visible at great distances. The sands have evidently been formed by the prevalent southeasterly winds, which have blown them across from Padre Island. Like similar formations in England and other parts of the world, where history aids the observer in accounting for them, it is likely that they constantly progress inland under the influence of the southeast wind, and will probably reach or cross the Rio Grande in course of time.

This district, after leaving the coast country just described, becomes rolling and gradually hilly. On the extreme northwest it borders on the outlying hills or mountains of the "Staked Plain" (*Llano Estacado*), but within its limits there are no very high elevations, though the general level of the northwestern part is nearly 1,000 feet above the sea.

There is a distinctly marked range of hills crossing the territory from northeast to southwest which deserves special notice, not only because it presents an interesting natural feature of the country, but because of the indications of valuable minerals found in the range. * * * This range commences in the western side of Karnes county, at the place called "Rocky". It passes across the Nueces a short distance above Oakville, and strikes the Rio Grande a few miles below Carriza, Zapata county. The "Zancaujo" hill (or mountain), in Duval county, is part of the range; and in the southern part of that county, and in Zapata county, it presents quite a marked feature, and is called by the Mexicans "La Sierra".

On the Rio Grande, from the commencement of the hills, the country is much more broken than anywhere east of it. From Rio Grande City (Ringgold) up to Eagle Pass, as the road winds along the river, high mountains, the offshoots of the Sierra Madre of Mexico, are never out of sight on the western horizon. This is not an agricultural region. In nothing is the increasing dryness of the climate as you proceed west and south more noticeable than in the growth of vegetation. The cypress, magnolia, dogwood, and other trees of a moist and temperate climate, common in eastern Texas, pretty much disappear on the Colorado. The pine reaches the river near Bastrop, and the cedar is seen on the hills north of San Antonio. But none of these trees are found in the country I am describing. Post oaks and live oaks are found between the San Antonio and Nueces rivers, and the latter is common in the "sands" south of Corpus Christi, but they go no farther southwest. I believe the only trees on the Rio Grande which are indigenous to eastern Texas are the ash, elm, cottonwood, and hackberry. The eastern man who goes southwest will find another system of vegetation gradually supplanting that to which he has been accustomed. The mesquite tree, which is in the desert, can send its roots far down in search of moisture, and with its bright pea-green leaves becomes a prominent feature of the landscape. The "Spanish bayonet", an endless variety of the cactus, and a dozen or more species of scrubby, thorny shrubs, known under the general designation of "chaparral", the product of a climate of great droughts, form in many parts an almost impenetrable jungle. On the Rio Grande the ebony tree becomes common, and is a handsome tree when full grown. There is also found a very ornamental and graceful tree called the "Tepajaque", which is nowhere found north of the Rio Grande valley.

All the trees and vegetation, and even the native animals, birds, and insects, seem especially adapted to a dry climate.

But if this country is too dry for planting purposes we are compensated in another way. Many years' experience has shown that Texas is the best stock-raising state in the Union, and for the same business this country is certainly the best part of Texas. The very dryness of the climate, in preventing the growth of trees to shade the soil, enables fine and nutritious grasses to abound. It is the paradise of horses, sheep, and cattle.

The following descriptions have been taken from the reports of surveying expeditions. The first is from Lieutenant T. N. Michler, (a) and describes the country from Corpus Christi northwest along the Nueces, Frio, and Leona rivers to the foot of the plains:

To San Patricio the road is over a high rolling prairie, with the exception of two sand flats, each two or three miles in length. The prairie is covered with fine mesquite grass and interspersed with mesquite trees and motts of live oaks. Sand-hills occur near the river south of San Patricio. At the Nueces river, 70 miles from Corpus Christi, the prairies come to the river. Limestone forms the bed of the stream, and cottonwood, elm, and oaks are found on its border.

Northwest, along the Frio, the high rolling prairies continue with mesquite trees and grass. Some parts of the river are timbered with growth given above, and, from one to two miles out, a thick growth of chaparral, with mesquite and cactus of every description. The first "mountains occur about 15 miles from the junction with the Nueces"; they set into the river in a direction perpendicular to its course. The distance between them is generally about a mile from base to base, extending but a short distance back into the country, and then gradually merging into the high prairies between the rivers. They approach to within a mile of the river, and then abruptly break off in the form of a pair of steps, and are covered with loose stone and almost impassable chaparral. As a general thing the lands on both the Frio and the Leona may be divided into four parallel strips; the first, next to the river, consisting of heavy timber and a heavy black soil; the second, a mesquite flat, of small width, and the soil of a lighter nature, and very fertile; the third, a range of low hills covered with loose stone and thick chaparral; the fourth, a wide open prairie, the soil generally very dry, but covered with excellent grass, which generally is very scarce close to the river; sometimes a second line of chaparral hills is found beyond the prairie land. Each of these strips is distinct, and parallel to the general course of the river.

Along the Frio, northward to its junction with the Leona, there are dense chaparrals a mile or two in width, but westward there are high and rolling prairies, extending as far as the eye can reach. Along the Leona northward the valley for the first 10 miles is about a mile wide, and bounded by low chaparral hills, difficult to penetrate, and extending from the ford to the head-waters of the river. After 14 miles the valley widens to 16 miles, and gradually becoming more elevated, it spreads out into a high flat prairie, and extends on unbroken until it rises into the range of hills which stretch across from the Frio—miles above the head springs of the Leona. This prairie (black Cretaceous) is very heavy in wet weather.

The following is made up from extracts selected from the report of Major Emory of the Mexican boundary survey, and describes the country along the Rio Grande:

West of the Nueces, and between that river and the Rio Bravo [Rio Grande], the want of rain makes agriculture a very uncertain business, and as we approach the last named river this aridity becomes more marked, and the vegetation assumes a spinose stunted character—indeed, so marked is the change, that when we get within a few miles of the river the vegetation is a complete chaparral. West and south of the Nueces the country is sometimes exposed to excessive and long continued droughts, and it is doubtful if agriculture can be made profitable without irrigation. All the region between that river and the Rio Bravo is, however, a fine grazing country.

This section of country is traversed by deep gullies, called arroyos, sometimes difficult to pass in wagons. These arroyos are natural consequences of the unequal manner in which the rain falls throughout the year. Sometimes not a drop falls for several months; again it pours down in a perfect deluge, washing deep beds in the unresisting soil, leaving behind the appearance of the deserted bed of a great river. The streams which are found in this country have their rise in limestone regions, and the water is very unwholesome even when the stream is flowing; but usually the beds of the streams are partly dry, and the water is found standing in holes. Superadded to its noxious mineral ingredients, it holds in solution offensive vegetable matter, and is disgusting to drink.

As we ascend above the alluvial lands within the water level (bottoms) become more frequent and extended, and at many places cultivated fields form a prominent feature in the landscape. Up as high as Reynosa the belt of alluvial soil subject to the influence of the moisture from the river is very considerable in width, and, in addition to corn, the sugar-cane is seen planted with success. The foliage on this portion of the river indicates a richer soil, and the trees assume very much the dimensions of those on the alluvial bottoms of the Mississippi.

Reynosa is built on a low Cretaceous (b) ridge, and it is here the first rocks above the surface are seen; yet none appear on the immediate banks of the river until we reach Las Cuevas, some distance above, where we find a stratum of Cretaceous (b) sandstone 10 or 15 feet thick. At the last-named point, and thence up the river, there is also a marked diminution in the quantity of bottom land susceptible of cultivation, and vegetation changes its character, becoming more dwarfed and spinose. The uplands on either side impinge closely upon the river, and the vegetation is principally mesquite and cactus. On the Texas side, as we recede from the river, the chaparral gives place to the open prairie, covered with luxuriant grass. This character of the river lands extends, with little variation, up to Ringgold barracks.

a Reconnaissance New Mexico and Texas.   _b Probably Tertiary, instead of Cretaceous.—R. H. L._

The beautiful town of Roma, 16½ miles above Ringgold barracks, is the present head of steamboat navigation; it is built upon a high bluff of yellowish sandstone, containing ferruginous nodules.

Just above Roma, at the foot of the island of Las Adjuntas, and at several other localities in the neighborhood, are banks of fossil oyster-shells of great size, some of them measuring 18 inches in length. (a)

I have noted at Roma the occurrence of sandstone studded with nodules of ferruginous composition. Throughout the section between the San Juan river and Laredo septaria and strata of yellowish and green sandstone frequently occur. Often the nodules of more durable substance project beyond the weather-worn surface of the softer sandstone, producing picturesque appearances.

The land from Belleville to Laredo is not altogether barren; there are many flats on which the water of the river could be brought for the purposes of irrigation.

The country around Laredo is much the same as that described about Ringgold barracks, but is more elevated and more frequently intersected by dry arroyos, which give evidence of more frequent and copious falls of rain.

From Eagle Pass upward, extending along the river 70 miles, until within 5 or 10 miles of the mouth of the San Pedro, or Devil's river, the country is the most fertile and desirable portion of the whole Rio Bravo for settlement. On the Texas side it is watered by the beautiful, limpid streams of Las Moras, Piedras Pintas, Zocaté, and San Felipe, which come into the Rio Bravo at right angles and at equal intervals. A very extensive region of land is here within the water-level, and can be successfully irrigated.

On the mesas, or table-lands, which are unsuited to the purposes of cultivation, many plants are found growing useful in medicine and dyeing, and various yuccas, dasylirions, and agaves, genera well known for their useful fibers. There are also extensive growths of shrubs and trees of the leguminous order, furnishing gums, tannin, and nutritious pods, highly relished by the herbivorous animals, wild and domestic.

Ascending beyond the mouth of the San Pedro, or Devil's river, the whole character of the country changes. The bed of the river becomes hemmed in by rocky mural banks, the tops of which are beyond the reach of irrigation; and, from the aridity of the climate, they can never be made subservient to the purposes of agriculture. The general formation of the country is limestone, deposited in strata perfectly horizontal, and, where the river has washed its way through the banks, presents the appearance of gigantic walls of dry-laid masonry. The course of the river from this point up to Fort Teton, near the Presidio del Norte, a distance of 387 miles, is almost one continuous cañon, utterly unsuited to navigation, and, with a few exceptions, unsuited for settlement. Occasionally this limestone formation, over 1,000 feet in depth, is broken through and upturned by igneous irruptions from below, forming stupendous mountains and gorges of frightful sublimity.

THE CENTRAL BLACK PRAIRIE REGION.

One of the most prominent features of the state is the broad region of high, rolling, and black waxy prairie lands, lying in the central part of the state, from Red river on the north south-southwest to San Antonio, and thence westward. A line marking the eastern limit of the region would begin on the east of Paris, in Lamar county, at the southern edge of the timbered river uplands, pass in a southwest direction to the east of Terrell, in Kaufman county, and 4 miles west of Corsicana, in Navarro county; thence south to Cameron, in Milam county, southwest to a point a few miles south of San Antonio, and westward to the edge of the great plains of the west. The western limit of the region has not been fully determined, except that it passes from Montague south through the counties of Wise, Parker, Erath, Comanche, Lampasas, Burnet, and Blanco; thence west through Gillespie and Kimble. The region has a width of about 140 miles on the north, 100 in the middle, and is quite narrow on the south, not more than 50 or 60 miles. It embraces twenty-three and parts of twenty-six counties, covering in all about 26,050 square miles. A white rotten limestone (Cretaceous) underlies the entire region, and often appears on the surface. The eastern part of the region throughout its length is composed of prairies, slightly rolling, and interrupted by frequent streams, which are bordered with narrow timbered valleys. In its central part is the broad belt of "lower cross timbers", extending southward from the Red river to the Brazos, near Waco, in McLennan county, and which has been described elsewhere (see page 28). To the west the country is more and more rolling and broken, the bald hills on the extreme west standing out in bold relief as isolated peaks and prominent ridges, with high and abrupt sides facing the broad prairie valleys. Rotten limestone, accompanied by beds of Cretaceous fossils, outcrops everywhere on the sides of the hills, in the valleys, and in the beds of the streams. On analysis by M. E. Jaffa (University of California), it was found to contain:

	Per cent.
Insoluble residue	11.451
Iron and alumina	3.648
Carbonate of lime	82.512
Carbonate of magnesia	1.189
Total (b)	98.800

Some 7 miles on the west of Weatherford, Parker county, the prairies come to a sudden and abrupt termination, and the stage road descends 100 or 200 feet into a broad and level timbered post oak and black-jack region·several miles in width, which forms a part of the "upper cross timbers belt", and reaches to the Brazos river, in Palo Pinto county. From this high prairie point a fine view is obtained over the timbers westward for 20 or 30 miles to the hills of the northwest red-loam region, while southward the bald hills, including Comanche peak, in Hood county, are plainly visible, though many miles away.

On the north of Weatherford, 12 or 15 miles, another high prairie occurs within the belt of cross timbers, and the road to Jacksboro', after passing over a high plateau of a gryphæa conglomerate, suddenly descends into the timbered lands of the northwestern red-loam region.

---

a Probable Oster Gesnidges of the Tertiary (Vicksburg).—R. H. L.
b Water and alkalies not determined.

On the south, after crossing the Brazos river, the transition from the central black prairies is not so abrupt, and while high and bold limestone ridges, with almost perpendicular sides, occur near the border, yet the prairie valleys are more gradually merged into the mixed prairies and timbered lands of the west.

In Lampasas county there is but a narrow strip of sandy timbered lands lying between the black prairies and Colorado river, while immediately on the west bank of the river the high red sandstone hills rise abruptly 100 feet or more above the valley.

In its general level the country rapidly rises from the east toward the west, the altitude of Dallas being 481 feet; Fort Worth, 30 miles westward, 629 feet; Weatherford, 35 miles still westward, 1,000 feet. The latter place is near the western border of the region. On the south Austin has an elevation of 650 feet, San Antonio 575 feet, while Fredericksburg, 60 or 70 miles to the west, has an altitude of 1,614 feet above the sea. From San Antonio northwest to Cibolo the country is a rolling prairie, becoming more and more hilly, and covered with clumps of live oak and other timber. Thence to the Guadalupe river the hills increase in height, with alternating rolling prairies and flats. Limestone is abundant all the way to Fredericksburg. The country northward is well wooded, and granite begins at 17 miles.

The following is taken from Captain French's report (a) on a route westward from San Antonio to the Rio Grande:

The road to Castroville runs through a generally level prairie, covered with a luxuriant growth of grass; the soil is good and well adapted to cultivation and grazing. The Medina is here a clear, bold, and rapid stream, about 30 yards wide, flowing between banks that rise near 50 feet in height on either side. From Castroville the road leads over some gentle hills, and thence through a tract of land pretty well timbered, until it opens out into what is known here as a hog-wallow prairie. Beyond this prairie is an elevated ridge, from the top of which spread out before him the traveler sees the beautiful valleys of Quihi and Hondo, pent in by the blue hills in the distance. The valley of Quihi is sparsely covered with timber, chiefly mesquite and oak.

From the Hondo the road stretches over a prairie country to the Seco, crossing a hog-wallow that, owing to late rains, we found nearly impassable. Thence westward the country is undulating for several miles; then opens out into a level prairie, which continues to Ranchero creek, 8 miles distant. The Sabinal is bordered with large trees, and westward to the Frio the country is more rolling and diversified; the growth of small mesquite bushes begins to take the place of the open prairie. The banks of the Rio Frio are high, presenting in places a wall of limestone of considerable height. Its bed is covered with well-attritioned limestone, and its edges are bordered in many places with oaks of large growth. Prairies extend westward to Leona river, a stream having a dense forest along its banks, on either side a quarter of a mile in width. The Nueces is bordered with a sandy bottom land nearly a half-mile in width, and heavily timbered with large trees. Beyond the river the country becomes slightly hilly; limestone rocks are abundant, the hills are stony and barren, and the rich loam soils are found only in the valleys.

Mesquite is a common growth of all the prairies of the central prairie region, but especially in the south, where, with a height of from 10 to 15 feet, it forms rather dense thickets. The "chaparrals" of this part of the state are formed mostly of a low thorny growth of what is known as "wesatche", belonging probably to the mesquite family.

SOILS OF THE PRAIRIE REGION.—The lands comprise three varieties, viz: Black waxy prairie, or "adobe", covering the greater part of the region; black sandy, occurring in localities along the borders of the former, and forming a transition to the sandy lands that border the streams; besides these are the bottom lands, the most important of which are described under the head of "river lands". The first of these varieties, or the *black waxy lands*, are what their name would indicate—a heavy, deep black, and tenacious clay, possessing a very high absorptive power (14 to 17 per cent.). Their extreme tenacity is illustrated and appreciated by the luckless teamster who has to drive his wagon across one of these prairies during a wet season. The black mud adheres in great masses to the wheels, filling up the spaces between the spokes and spreading out on either side, thus making an empty vehicle a load in itself for a team. The mud sticks in masses to the feet of those attempting to walk over these lands in wet weather. In dry weather the prairies assume altogether a different aspect; the roads become very hard and comparatively smooth, and the soil cracks open in every direction.

Hog-wallow lands.—The underlying rock of the region, rotten limestone, comes to the surface very often, though chiefly on the high uplands, being covered to a greater depth by the soils in the lowlands. The soils have a general depth of from 12 to 24 inches, the only perceptible difference in the subsoil being a change in color from a black to a lighter yellow or drab-colored clay.

The lands are very productive and durable, yielding about 800 pounds of seed-cotton per acre, both when fresh and after long cultivation. Many farmers claim a greater yield, but this is exceptional. The plant grows to a height of from 4 to 6 feet, and is very often troubled with blight, or "dying in spots" in the dry seasons at a time when it has about begun to bloom.

Black sandy prairie lands.—These are formed by the commingling of the black waxy just mentioned and the sands of the upland timbered lands, which are usually adjoining. They are generally underlaid by the heavy clay subsoils of the prairies. These lands are comparatively easy to till, and are fully as productive as the waxy lands of the prairies. The plant grows 3 or 4 feet high, yielding from 800 to 1,000 pounds of seed-cotton per acre. These prairies are usually level, and present excellent farming lands.

The timbered uplands that border the streams in narrow belts have gray sandy soils, 10 or 12 inches deep, and a yellowish clay subsoil. They are usually called "post-oak lands", from the predominance of that timber growth.

a Reports of Secretary of War, with reconnaissance of routes from San Antonio to El Paso.

Hickory, elm, and mesquite trees are also common. The lands are easily tilled, well drained, and produce well, and are therefore most preferred for agricultural purposes. Cotton grows to a height of from 2 to 3 feet, and it is claimed that it will produce as much as 800 pounds of seed-cotton in good seasons.

The bottom lands of the creeks are narrow and hardly worthy of mention, those of the rivers and large streams only being under cultivation. The timber growth of all of the bottoms is live and pin oak, elm, pecan, hackberry, etc. The lands are described under the general division of "river lands". (See page 41.)

The following analyses are given to show the composition of the lands of the region:

No. 27. *Black sandy soil,* Wills' Point, Van Zandt county, taken 10 inches.

No. 12. *Black sandy prairie soil* from 1 mile south of Ennis, Ellis county, taken 10 inches deep.

No. 15. *Black prairie soil* from 6 miles northeast of McKinney, Collin county, taken 12 inches deep.

No. 14. *Black waxy prairie soil* from 2 miles west of Cleburne, Johnson county, taken 12 inches.

No. 13. *Black waxy prairie soil* from 8 miles northeast of Marlin, Falls county, taken 12 inches.

No. 33. *Black waxy prairie soil* from 8 miles southwest of Waco, McLennan county, taken 12 inches. This soil is said to be a typical sample of the best class of these prairie lands.

No. 36. *Black prairie soil* from near Lampasas Springs, Lampasas county, taken 12 inches.

Black prairie lands.

	VAN ZANDT COUNTY.	ELLIS COUNTY.	COLLIN COUNTY.	JOHNSON COUNTY.	M'LENNAN COUNTY.	FALLS COUNTY.	LAMPASAS COUNTY.
	Black sandy soil.	Black sandy soil.	Black waxy soil.	Black waxy soil.	Black waxy soil.	Black waxy soil.	Black waxy soil.
	No. 27.	No. 12.	No. 15.	No. 14.	No. 33.	No. 13.	No. 36.
Insoluble matter	77.582 } 87.762	82.513 } 86.200	46.145 } 63.386	60.854 } 65.917	34.082 } 53.426	51.797 } 73.153	50.330 } 57.520
Soluble silica	10.180	3.687	17.941	5.563	19.844	21.356	7.190
Potash	0.285	0.291	0.619	0.365	0.447	0.718	0.365
Soda	0.130	0.182	0.186	Trace.	0.120	0.309	0.155
Lime	0.223	0.569	7.464	3.790	15.552	2.643	13.070
Magnesia	0.257	0.391	0.620	0.708	1.230	1.594	0.102
Brown oxide of manganese	0.042	0.056	0.409	0.030	0.050	0.020	0.255
Peroxide of iron	2.802	1.788	4.216	5.345	4.226	2.683	4.092
Alumina	4.433	4.008	11.078	5.748	5.990	4.392	0.643
Phosphoric acid	0.115	0.062	0.151	0.178	0.580	0.455	0.387
Sulphuric acid	0.156	0.144	0.104	0.047	0.080	0.644	0.102
Carbonic acid	....	....	1.875	6.594	10.388	1.082	9.550
Water and organic matter	3.808	6.237	9.510	5.895	7.592	5.896	6.900
Total	99.973	98.808	98.882	90.968	98.478	99.780	98.715
Humus	....	2.950	....	....	2.304	....	....
Available inorganic	....	2.010	....	....	1.906	....	....
Available phosphoric acid	....	0.040	....	....	0.089	....	....
Hygroscopic moisture	5.986	5.988	17.613	11.600	14.536	16.340	12.130
absorbed at	14 C.°	13 C.°	13 C.°	13 C.°	13 C.°	13 C.°	39 C.°

These analyses show a percentage of potash from medium to large in all of the black prairie soils; also of lime in all. Phosphoric acid is deficient in the first two given, has a minimum percentage for high fertility and durability in the third, while in the last three the proportions are large, showing soils of high productiveness and durability. The amounts of organic matter are also high, and in No. 33 show the presence of much humus. The percentages of magnesia in the soils are also high, except in No. 36.

The central prairie region is but sparsely settled outside of the towns and cities. The houses and farms are mostly situated in or near the timbered uplands, the prairies, with their excellent grasses, being reserved almost exclusively for the grazing of cattle. The level nature of the land, and the comparative freedom from rocks, render it especially well adapted to the use of improved cultivators and other agricultural implements. The seasons of summer and fall are always very dry, which, though sometimes cutting off the cotton crop as much as one-third, never produce a total failure. The droughts are felt most by other crops, and in the scanty supply of water for stock and for domestic uses. Creeks and branches become dry, and the dependence is upon "tanks" or artificial ponds and cisterns filled by the winter and spring rains. Wells are unreliable, and their waters are to such an extent impregnated with lime and other salts from the rotten limestone as to make them unfit for domestic purposes.

Within the past few years much interest has been taken in artesian wells, and a number have been bored in Dallas and Fort Worth, from which a bountiful supply of good water is obtained at a depth of 300 or 400 feet in the former and 700 feet in the latter place, or below the rotten limestone. They are probably practicable throughout this region at a depth of not exceeding 1,000 feet.

NORTHWESTERN RED-LOAM REGION.

West of the upper cross timbers and the black prairie region there is a large region embracing what is known as the red lands of the northwest. It enters the state from the Indian territory, and extends westward and southward to the gypsum formation and the plains, while a large section passes southeast nearly to Austin and Fredericksburg. In this latter portion of the belt the red lands are not as prominent as farther north and west, and are associated with gray sandy soils, from the granites and other rocks that occur to a large extent. The entire region covers an area of about 27,012 square miles, and embraces twenty-five organized counties, besides those that have as yet been only outlined and named.

The surface of the eastern counties of the region is hilly or "mountainous" and broken, and is well supplied with timber. These hills are usually long, high, and narrow ridges or divides, generally not more than 100 feet high, with rather abrupt sides, are covered with a heavy growth of post and black-jack oaks, and have a sandy soil. Sometimes, as in the southern part of Brown county, the summit is broad and comparatively level, with only a low and stunted oak growth. The valley lands between these hills are broad and open prairies, with red soils and occasional clumps of mesquite bushes, interspersed with motts of live oak. In the low flats, where limestone is often found outcropping, the soil is a dark stiff or waxy clay, very productive.

The surface of the country in the western part of the region is little else than a high rolling prairie, somewhat hilly on the north, but more and more level on the southwest, where, with a gradual rise, it merges into the Great Plains, or southern part of the Llano Estacado. The surface is covered with grass and frequent chaparrals, and in localities with mesquite trees and motts of live oak. Red sandstone is perhaps the most prominent rock of the region (except on the south), and is found capping the great majority of the hills in ledges and broken masses of sometimes many feet thickness. Blue crystalline limestones (Palæozoic) also occur abundantly.

SOILS.—On the prairies and in the valleys the greater part of the lands of the region are of a red loam character, more or less sandy, and quite deep. In some of the low mesquite flats in Brown, San Saba, Stephens, and other counties on the east are found areas of stiff black clays with a growth of live oak, while the summits of the hills are sandy and often covered with a low scrubby undergrowth. The streams are usually bordered with a timber growth of elm, pecan, cottonwood, etc.; their valleys on the west are very narrow, but widen eastward to some extent, and are covered with rich and productive soils from the red-clay hills of the gypsum formation and bluffs of the Llano Estacado.

The following analysis has been made of a sample of the red upland soil:

No. 16. *Red loam soil*, prairie near Jacksboro', Jack county, taken 10 inches deep. Covered with a growth of mesquite bushes.

Red loam soil, Jack county.

	No. 16.
Insoluble matter	74.945 } 83.596
Soluble silica	8.651 }
Potash	0.435
Soda	0.108
Lime	0.135
Magnesia	0.882
Brown oxide of manganese	0.150
Peroxide of iron	5.050
Alumina	5.076
Phosphoric acid	0.095
Sulphuric acid	0.047
Water and organic matter	4.805
Total	100.594
Available inorganic	0.460
Available phosphoric acid	0.014
Humus	0.106
Hygroscopic moisture	10.840
absorbed at	18 C.°

This analysis shows the presence of a large amount of potash, a fair percentage of lime and magnesia, and a low percentage of phosphoric acid. The yield of fresh lands is about 800 pounds of seed-cotton per acre, but durability can hardly be expected in these uplands without the application of phosphates after a few years.

The region is almost exclusively devoted to stock raising, for which purpose the excellent grasses are well adapted. The long droughts, and consequent lack of water in the streams and wells, is the chief evil to contend with in all the various interests in which the people are engaged; but with an increased population and a development of the resources of the country this lack in water supply will, in part, probably be overcome. At present cotton culture, and in fact every agricultural pursuit, is confined almost altogether to those counties on the extreme east most accessible to markets, though the extreme limit of production in this census year is in the county of Jones, more than 100 miles west of the black prairie region.

It is only in the last few years that the western tide of immigration has reached the most eastern of these counties, and five years ago the Indians roamed over a large part of the region and made their raids as far east as Hood county, in the black prairie country. Even the most eastern counties are still very sparsely settled, the county-seats usually containing the bulk of the population.

Of the valley lands of the western part of this country, at the headwaters of the Colorado river, Captain Marcy says:

> Immediately after we descended from the high table-lands we struck upon an entirely different country from the one we had been passing over before. We found a smooth road over a gently undulating country of prairies and timber, and abounding with numerous clear spring branches for 200 miles, and in many places covered with a large growth of mesquite timber, which makes the best of fuel. The soil cannot be surpassed for fertility; the grass remains green during the entire winter, and the climate is salubrious and healthy; indeed, it possesses all the requisites that can be desired for making a fine agricultural country.

The following is taken from the report of Lieutenant F. T. Bryan on a route from San Antonio to El Paso, (a) via Fredericksburg, and is descriptive of the southern part of the region:

> The first granite outcrops were seen 18 miles north of Fredericksburg; sandstone also appears, and the country is covered with a reddish sandy soil. Northward to the Llano river the prairies and timber lands are found alternating; some portions of it are hilly, large granite outcrops are found occasionally, and the soils are light and sandy, and sometimes red in color. To the San Saba the country continues rolling and hilly; some of the hills are rocky and precipitous, and when within 3 miles of the river large slabs of limestone appear, both on the hills and in the bed of the stream. Still northward to Brady's creek the country continues hilly; "rotten limestone" occurs on the hills, and the prairies are covered with mesquite bushes and grass. Westward to Kickapoo creek the country is a level and open prairie, with mesquite wood sufficient only for cooking purposes. The timber on this and other creeks consists of live oak and pecan, of large size. Still westward the prairies becomes hilly, stony, and barren, being a succession of gentle undulations and depressions covered with broken pieces of limestone. There is an absence of anything like timber on these prairies. This continues to Green Mounds near the head of south Concho river, where the broad and level prairies are entered.

WESTERN AND NORTHWESTERN TEXAS.

The country lying west and southwest of the northwestern red-loam region, and forming the unpopulated portion of the state, is as yet comparatively unknown, especially so with regard to its agricultural features. It embraces sixty-three counties (unorganized), which, though having a name, have virtually no inhabitants, and lie in a wild and desolate region, including what is known as the Panhandle of Texas. The great extent of its territory, the lack of water and fuel on the plains, and the many other difficulties attending travel and explorations, make its examination a matter of much time and expense, as well as danger. At present we are largely dependent upon the reports of the United States exploring expeditions, made many years ago, for the little that is known regarding the great western plains.

Three important divisions are represented in this region, viz, the gypsum formation of the northwest and the plains, including the celebrated Llano Estacado or Staked Plain, the southern plain, and the mountainous region west of the Pecos, embracing in all 111,500 square miles, or 42.51 per cent. of the area of the state. The three divisions will be considered separately.

GYPSUM REGION.

One of the most interesting as well as valuable features of the western region is the great area of gypsum lands, covering in Texas, as far as can be determined, about 17,500 square miles. Dr. George G. Shumard, who explored this region with Captain Pope, reports that on Red river the gypsum beds are from a few inches to 30 feet thick. On Delaware creek, a few miles below its source, they are 60 feet, while between the Big Wichita and Brazos rivers there are hills nearly 700 feet high, composed almost entirely of this material. It occurs in its many different forms of granular, massive, fibrous, and in large plates of transparent selenites, and is associated with heavy beds of red clays, and overlaid by sandstones and drift deposits. The exact limits of the region have not as yet been determined. The best source of information are United States Pacific railroad survey reports.

The following is taken from Marcy's *Red River Report of* 1853, page 163:

> I have traced this gypsum belt from the Canadian river in a southwest direction to near the Rio-Grande in New Mexico. It is about 50 miles wide upon the Canadian, and is embraced within the ninety-ninth and one hundredth degrees of west longitude. Upon the north, middle, and south forks of Red river it is found, and upon the latter is about 100 miles wide, and embraced within the one hundred and first and one hundred and third degrees of longitude. I have also met with the same formation upon the Brazos river, as also upon the Colorado and Pecos rivers, but did not ascertain its width. The point where I struck it upon the Pecos was in longitude 104½° west.

---

a Reports of Secretary of War on routes from Fort Smith to Santa Fé and from San Antonio to El Paso.

In the same report (page 184) Dr. Shumard, in his notes 'under date of July 22, makes the last mention of gypsum outcrops. The survey party were then returning eastward, and on the divide between Beaver and Rush creeks, just east of the ninety-eighth degree of longitude and south of the thirty-fifth parallel, in the Indian territory. In Texas gypsum is reported (in Thrall's *History of Texas*) as occurring in Hardeman, northwest Baylor, Haskell, and Knox counties, and also on the headwaters of the Colorado river. A line, therefore, connecting these points would probably mark the true easterly limit of the formation. The bluffs of the Llano Estacado form the western border of the region northward across the headwaters of the Brazos and south fork of Red river, and along the one hundredth degree of longitude to the Canadian river.

The surface of the country is represented to be a vast open and rolling prairie, somewhat broken on the east, with abrupt hills or large mounds of gypsum and red clay 50 feet high and a gradually increasing elevation westward to the foot of the plains, where the beds of gypsum are observed only in ravines and cañons. The soil of the uplands is thin and sandy, supporting a growth of gramma grasses only; that along the streams and in the valleys is a reddish loam, thought to be very productive with irrigation, and south in some localities with fine grasses. A few cottonwood trees are found along some of the large streams, with occasional pecan, elm, and hackberry, while on the bluffs are brakes of stunted red cedar (*Juniperus Virginiana*). Wild grape-vines 4 feet high were observed on Red river The streams are usually very narrow, and their beds are mostly composed of quicksands. The water is largely impregnated with salts from the gypsum beds, except where the source of the river is westward of the formation, as Captain Marcy found to be the case with regard to the south fork of Red river.

In the Red river section of the region belts of sand-hills, with a width of many miles in places, border the river. These hills are about 30 feet high, rounded in form, and without vegetation, except occasional dwarf-oak bushes, wild onions, and grasses.

THE LLANO ESTACADO, OR THE STAKED PLAIN.

The northwestern and the extreme western part of the state is part of what is known as the "Llano Estacado", or the "Staked Plain", the name being given to it from the tradition "that in 1734, when the fathers from Santa Fé visited San Saba to establish a fort and a mission, they set up stakes with buffalo heads on them, so that others might follow their route". The name is usually given only to that portion lying east of the river Pecos, in both Texas and New Mexico, but the plains proper extend westward to the Rio Grande. From the northern limit of the state it reaches southward nearly to the twenty-ninth parallel, its eastern border lying along the 101st meridian, through five degrees of latitude, thence turns eastward to McCulloch county, and south to Bandera. The area embraced in Texas is about 74,500 square miles, or about 28 per cent. of the entire area of the state. On the north the eastern limits of the plains are strongly defined, and, according to Captain Marcy, are marked by vertical bluffs about 800 feet above the country or gypsum formation on the east. These bluffs consist of red and yellow clays, overlaid by 10 or 15 feet of sandstone, and a heavy deposit of drift pebbles, the whole capped by a sandy soil and subsoil. Southward, at the headwaters of the Colorado, the bluffs are not so high, a descent of only 50 feet being noted by Captain Marcy, and limestone (probably Cretaceous) is found at its foot. This rock, as reported, seems to underlie the entire plains south of the thirty-second parallel, and is almost absent in the Panhandle region, appearing only in thin seams in beds of sandstone. Throughout the rest of the border on the east and south the line marking the limit between the plains and the regions east can hardly be defined; the country is broken and hilly, with valleys, cañofis, and isolated ridges, in which rotten limestone (Cretaceous) occurs abundantly.

The surface of the plains presents a vast and level prairie, "as smooth and firm as marble," apparently boundless; the soil is chiefly a brown loam, sometimes sandy, and with no vegetation other than gramma and mesquite grasses and small mesquite shrubs, which appear a few inches above the surface and serve the purpose of a guide to the large roots below—the firewood of the plains. Alkali ponds or lakes occur frequently, especially in the southern half, and also a number of springs whose waters are suitable for use. Some gypsum is said to occur around the edges of the lakes. The height of the eastern part of the plains was estimated by Captain Marcy to be 2,450 feet above the sea. Westward the country gradually rises 200 feet, and reaches its maximum near the one hundred and third degree of longitude.

On this line, near the southwest corner of the Panhandle, there is a range of sand-hills rising from 20 to 100 feet above the plain, occupying a region 50 miles long (north and south) and about 15 miles wide. The hills are conical in shape and utterly destitute of vegetation, and the section, because of the deep beds of sand, is hardly passable with wagons.

From this point westward the country falls some 200 feet to the Pecos, whose banks are without timber growth. A person may come very near to the edge of the gorge without becoming aware of its presence. From the river still westward to the foot of the Guadalupe mountains the country rises 200 feet, and thence to the Rio Grande, at El Paso, again gradually falls.

Country from the mouth of the Wichita river southwestward across the plains to the Pecos.

[Extracts taken from the report of Lieutenant N. H. Michler; *Reconnaissance in New Mexico and Texas.*]

The distance from the Red river to the main fork of the Brazos is about 96 miles. The route for this entire distance lay upon the divide between the Big and Little Wichita, with the exception of the last 10 miles, which crossed the divide between the Wichitas and the Brazos. It passes over a slightly rolling prairie, with intervals for miles of perfect dead level flats. A more beautiful country for roads of any kind cannot be found. Near the Red river the soil is slightly sandy, and you meet with a few post-oak motts. It then becomes a fine mesquite country, well timbered with mesquite, and for miles perfectly level, and even when a rolling prairie the elevations and depressions are small. The grass at first is principally gramma and the ordinary sedge and their species, but then comes the fine early mesquite and the winter mesquite. The whole extent was well watered by numerous branches of the two Wichitas. Most of the streams possessed a slightly brackish taste; all of them were well timbered.

Crossing the divide, you travel over a continuation of the mesquite range, and come to the Brazos river without the slightest indication of its presence. No timber along its banks as far as the eye can see, you stumble upon it without any forewarning. High bluff banks along its very edge conceal it until you reach the top of them. Its channel is about 50 yards in width, and bounded by a small strip of bottom land. Owing to its red sandy bottom the waters have a reddish appearance, though clear and free from mud. The Indians call this stream the Colorado, and much more deservedly than the one bearing that name on the map of Texas. The water is exceedingly brackish. Small streams of fresh water are found emptying into it, which will serve every purpose. In the bottom was good grazing of sedge and water-grass, and on the top of the bluffs again spread out the mesquite flats. Near the Red river the formation seemed to be sandstone, but on the Brazos we found some beautiful limestone. The bluffs were white with the large limestone rocks that lay strewn on their surface.

On rising the bluffs of the main fork of the Brazos we again found a continuation of the mesquite flats, over which we traveled until we reached the head of the Double Mountain fork of the Brazos. Day after day the country was almost perfectly level. One exception alone can be made; a distance of 4 or 5 miles over some high sand-hills, perfectly destitute of grass, and covered with a low scrub oak, the rest was either mesquite flats or a very slightly rolling mesquite country. There was but little timber upon the streams after leaving the main fork of the river, but the farther we advanced the more we found, elm being the principal growth. The whole country was timbered with mesquite. Double Mountain fork has a gravelly bottom, and in a few places a hard limestone bottom; the banks are generally high, the prairies extending to the edge of them. For 70 miles westward from the Brazos the country is mountainous, but now assumes new features. High mounds and low ridges come in sight, being a succession of spurs or oblong mounds overlapping each other, separated by deep ravines and gullies. Two high peaks form prominent landmarks near the head of Double Mountain fork; limestone abounds on them, and live oak and cedar are first seen.

Westward from the Brazos and Colorado divide the country undergoes a complete change; we meet with high and rolling prairies, arid, destitute of timber, and with scarcely any grass but of the most miserable kind. Occasionally we cross low sand-hills containing some low cedar and scrubby oak. This country extends to the "Big springs of Colorado", which are very large, covering a space of about 20 feet square, and in some places 15 feet deep. They are walled in by a ledge of conglomerate limestone, formed by numerous shells, united by a siliceous cement. The surface of the ground around is covered with angular fragments of limestone; the soil is chiefly sand. Westward the road lay over a high, arid plain, perfectly destitute of timber, scarcely a sprig of mesquite, except in the neighborhood of water-holes. For miles the country would be a perfect level, and then a slightly rolling prairie; it seemed destitute of all growth of any kind, and nothing was to be seen upon it excepting the antelope, wolf, and prairie-dog town. Occasionally a small spot of mesquite was found. This continued to the commencement of the low sand-hills, a distance from the "Big springs" of 76 miles. The Mustang springs, 21 miles from Big springs, are in a low prairie of about 100 acres in extent, in form nearly circular, and bounded by low bluffs, principally of white limestone.

The sand-hills for the first 12 miles are low ridges of sand running parallel with each other, plains of the same kind interspersed between them, with small hillocks. The sand was here of a black color. Then come the white sand-hills, which are really an object of curiosity. They are a perfect miniature Alps of sand, the latter perfectly white and clean; in the midst of them you see summit after summit spreading out in every direction, not a sign of vegetation upon them, nothing but sand piled upon sand. They form a belt 2 or 3 miles in width, and extend many miles in a northwest direction. Large water-holes are found at the base of the hills; large, deep, and contain most excellent water, cool, clear, and pleasant, and is permanent. A great deal of vegetable matter and young willow trees are found on their banks.

Westward to the Pecos, 29 miles, the first two miles was over the sand-hills, then a slightly rolling prairie, with a hard and sandy soil, covered with a thick growth of chaparral to the river. The Pecos is a rolling mass of red mud, with nothing to indicate its presence but a line of high reeds growing upon its banks. Along its banks are numerous lakes, the water of which is still more brackish than that of the river.

From the Nueces river northwest along the Pecos nearly to Horsehead crossing, and thence westward through the central part of the region to the mountains.

[From the report of Capt. S. G. French; *Reconnaissance in New Mexico and Texas.*]

Leaving the Nueces the country becomes slightly hilly; the hills rise to a considerable elevation, are stony and barren, with limestone on the surface. The rich loamy soils are found only in the valleys. The valley at the head of Turkey creek is of large extent and fertile, and is covered with a large growth of mesquite. The banks of the creek are bordered with live and post oaks. Westward to the Las Moras the country is more rolling and more open. That stream flows over a bed of limestone, and trees line its banks as far as the eye can reach. To the Rio Grande the country is open, with only here and there a few mesquite trees, except along the streams. North of the Arroyo Pedro the soil becomes barren, and is covered with cactus and dwarf chaparral as far as the San Felipe, a stream shaded at its mouth with large groves of pecan, maple, elm, and mulberry trees. Thence the country rises northward to the San Pedro, where the table-lands of the plains are entered. Limestone forms the bed of this stream, while the valley is bordered by mountains, in which limestone appears with horizontal strata. Thence to the Pecos the plain is traversed with valleys extending out from the streams, from which others branch off to the right and left, ramifying the country in every direction; and near the Pecos these valleys head in innumerable chasms and cañons, with rocky sides so high and steep as to form impassable barriers.

The Pecos is a remarkable stream, narrow and deep, extremely crooked in its course and rapid in its current; its waters are turbid and bitter, its banks are steep, and in the course of 240 miles there are but few places where an animal can approach them with safety. Not a tree or bush marks its course. Its average width is about 60 feet, and its depth 8 feet.

Leaving the Pecos, 30 miles south of Horsehead crossing, the road turns directly to the west up a wide valley or plain, with hills in broken ridges on both sides. As the distance increases the soil becomes more and more sterile, without grass, and yielding support to nothing but dwarf bushes, Spanish bayonets, and stunted cactus. For about 35 miles the country remains about the same to Comanche spring. The hills now gradually disappear, and the country becomes open. The soil is light, and, on being trodden up by the animals, was wafted by the strong wind over the plain, covering the bushes and grass for miles. Thence to the Sierra Diablo the road passes over a dreary and barren country, without timber or grass.

THE MOUNTAINOUS REGION.

Westward from the Pecos river to the Rio Grande the broad undulating plains continue, not continuously as on the east, but interrupted by several high and broken ranges of mountains, rising suddenly several thousand feet above the general surface. The plains, having widths of 20 or 30 miles between these mountains, are covered largely with mesquite bushes, cactus, and thorny chaparrals, and are interspersed with large salty depressions. Gramma grass occurs in localities, sometimes plentifully; but water suitable to drink is very scarce. The soil is usually very sandy and often covered with incrustations of salt. The area comprised in this region is about 19,500 square miles.

The Sierra Blanco mountains on the south, near the Rio Grande, is near the point of union of the Southern Pacific and Texas Pacific railroads, and is said to be the highest point in the state, the plains themselves being about 4,500 feet above the sea. Along the route of the former, northward to El Paso, wells have been sunk by the railroad company to a depth as great as 400 feet, and I have been informed by one of the engineers that the water even at that depth is too salty for use.

The following description of these mountains is taken from the report of Captain Marcy:

It appears that there are three distinct ranges of mountains traversing the country east of El Paso in a north and south direction from New Mexico into Texas; the first, the Organ range, 20 miles east of the Rio Grande; the Sacramento range, 30 miles east of this, the continuation of which, about 50 miles north of Doña Ana, is called the Sierra Blanco, and has perpetual snow upon its summit; the third, the Guadalupe, 50 miles east of the Sacramento range.

The Organ range takes its name from the supposed similarity of the high pointed peaks to the pipes of an organ. They are a trap formation, and somewhat columnar in structure, with the columns standing vertically, and in some cases rising to a height of 1,000 feet, and terminating in sharp points.

Captain French thus describes the country from Horsehead crossing westward to the Rio Grande across the central portion of the region (*Reconnaissance in New Mexico and Texas*):

Mountains rise on the right and left; the limestone formation has generally disappeared, and the hills wear a somber appearance from the dark rocks of the primitive formation. The country is beautiful; and the mountains, covered with green grass to their summits, present a pleasing appearance. The mountains of the Sierra Diablo do not form a single continuous ridge, but rise in irregular order, mountain on mountain and peak on peak, covering an immense extent of country, forming innumerable small shaded valleys, deep cañons, and ravines that wind in a circuitous course around their base. Columnar basaltic rocks that rise one behind the other to many feet in altitude form the sides of some of the cañons. But few places can present anything more lovely than Wild-Rose pass, surrounded as it appears to be by a wall of vertical rocks, rising a thousand feet in altitude, these rocks partly forming the sides of mountains that rise still higher and overlook the valley from every point. Northwestward other mountains appear of igneous origin, forming a lofty and continuous ridge, and presenting an extremely jagged and serrated crest. Near their tops forests of pine are visible. Westward to the mountains that border the Rio Grande the country is mostly an elevated plain, and also beyond these mountains to the river. The bottom lands of the river on the American side to the lower end of the island, a distance of 50 miles, are in many places very fertile. Timber is thinly scattered over the whole extent. The country around El Paso, excepting the bottom lands of the river, is sandy and covered with a dwarf growth of bushes.

ALLUVIAL OR RIVER LANDS.

The river lands form an important division in the agricultural features of the state, more from their richness, and consequent high productiveness, than from the area comprised by them. They are all but lightly timbered on the west of the central black prairie region, but thence to the coast the timber growth becomes larger, more dense, and of greater variety. The bottom lands also widen out inward the coast. The most important of the rivers described are the Red and the Brazos, and with the latter are the smaller streams, Oyster and Caney creeks, which are included in the region of its "sugar-bowl" or delta lands. These are looked upon as representing the highest type of fertility, and but for the malarial character of the densely timbered portions would be mostly under cultivation and more highly valued. The lands of the rivers are considered separately.

RED RIVER LANDS.—Red river forms in part the boundary between Texas and the Indian territory. Its course is eastward, for the most part across the head of the other large rivers of the state, until it passes into Louisiana. The following description of the upper portion of the river is made up of extracts from the report of Captain Pope:

Red river, rising among the cañons and bluffs of the Llano Estacado, has at first but little alluvial lands, but eastward through the gypsum region the valley widens out irregularly; the north fork has a sandy soil; the south fork a red loam; both streams having a growth of grass and some mesquite, etc. Along the immediate banks of the streams there is sometimes a timber growth of hackberry and very large cottonwood, principally the latter.

The gramma and mesquite grasses, which cover the entire surface, are short and early, growing very thickly and almost matted, and form a firm, spongy sod. They do not dry up and lose their strength and nutriment during the winter, as is the case with the grasses further east, but actually "cure" where they grow, like hay which has been prepared by the farmer.

The valley is 14 miles in width from the point at which the route of survey intersected its first tributary to the crossing of the river at Preston.(a) About four-fifths is covered with large timber, a few patches of prairie of limited extent only sufficing to interrupt its continuity. The immediate valley of the river is about 100 feet below the gently receding bluffs which border it, and is overgrown by timber of the largest size and best quality—oak, pecan, hickory, elm, etc.

The valley of the river between the thirty-second and thirty-fourth parallels of latitude (from Natchitoches, Louisiana, to Preston) is a thickly timbered region of fertile soil, well watered, and possessing a mild and healthy climate. It produces abundantly all the cereals, and is admirably adapted to the cultivation of cotton. The pasturage is very fine, and is only interrupted by the seasons for two or three months of the year.

Soon after leaving the plains the valley of the north fork of Red river assumes the terrace feature that is maintained eastward through the state. In the agricultural regions the terraces are known as the first and second bottoms. Captain Marcy thus describes them as they appear in the gypsum formation:

The first terrace rises from 2 to 6 feet above the stream, is in places subject to inundation, and generally is from 50 to 200 yards wide. The second is from 10 to 20 feet high, is never submerged, and is from 200 to 1,500 yards wide. The third, which forms the high bluff bordering the valley of the river, is from 50 to 100 feet high, and bounds the prairie.

The following description of the river bottoms near the eastern limit of the red-loam region is taken from the report of Lieutenant N. H Michler:

The regular channel of the river at the ford is about 100 yards wide. There is at first a sand flat, the bed of the river in high water, with nothing upon it but large quantities of drift, and about one-fourth of a mile wide from the water's edge to the first bottom. The latter contains a rich alluvial soil, sand mixed with red clay, and timbered along the edge near the flat with young cottonwood and willows. This bottom bears evidence of being frequently overflowed. Then comes the second bottom, separated from the first generally by a steep bluff bank, the latter intersected by gullies and ravines, impassable at most places for wagons. High sand-hills are found on the edge of this bottom. At the foot of the bluffs are fine springs and lakes, well timbered, and with good grass along them. This bottom is also subject to overflows. The width of the valley from bluff to bluff is about 1¼ miles, and the open prairies (uplands) extend southward from their borders.

In the Black prairie region the valley of the river is very narrow, the high limestone bluffs often approaching near the water's edge. In Cooke county these bluffs are 275 feet high, and are formed of the rotten limestone (Cretaceous) of the central prairie region. On the north side of the river, in the Indian territory, the river lands are broader, and are partly under cultivation by whites; but to the west, on either side of the river, scarcely any cultivated lands are found. From the "lower cross timbers", in the eastern part of Cooke county, eastward to the Louisiana line, the bottom lands increase in width, and are among the richest in the state. They are heavily timbered with cottonwood, pecan, walnut, black oak, hackberry, mulberry, and white hickory, and have a dense undergrowth of cane.

Besides the low sandy overflowed lands, there are two general classes comprising the bottoms and occupying terraces above each other, viz: First bottom of red sandy or clayey land, and second bottom of dark or black loam, lying about 10 feet above the first and at the foot of the bluff or uplands. These two bottoms are peculiar only to those Texan rivers whose sources are in the region of the Llano Estacado on the northwest, viz, Colorado, Brazos, and Red rivers, as well as the Canadian, North Fork, and Arkansas rivers of the Indian territory. The soil characters mentioned by Michler continue down the river, the red sands and clays of the first bottom being derived from the red sandstones and red lands of the northwest region. This first bottom soil is of two varieties: a deep red sandy loam, overlying a red-clay subsoil, and a red waxy clay, with a subsoil of the same character. Both are highly productive, and subject to occasional overflow, being from 10 to 20 feet above low water. This red-land terrace is at first rather narrow, but becomes wider toward the eastern boundary of the state.

The black-loam terrace, about 10 feet above the first, is known as the second bottom, and is very level. Its soil is of a light and loose nature, rather silty, and darkened by the long accumulation of decayed vegetation. At the foot of the limestone bluff, in Grayson county, it is stiff and rather waxy, but this is a local feature only. The entire bottom of the river is from 1 to 2 miles in width, and, though comprising some of the finest lands of the state, a large proportion is still covered with its original timber growth. Cotton is one of the chief crops, growing from 4 to 6 feet in height, and yielding, under proper management, a bale of 500 pounds of lint per acre, even after many years' cultivation.

The following analyses show the composition of the soils of different parts of the valley:

No. 38. *Red clay soil* of the "first bottom", opposite Cooke county, taken 12 inches deep. Growth, cottonwood and hackberry.

No. 39. *Red waxy clay soil* of the first bottom from near the mouth of Kiamitia creek, opposite Lamar county, in the Choctaw nation, taken 12 inches deep. Growth, cottonwood, hackberry, etc.

No. 40. *Dark sandy loam soil* of the second bottom, at the same place as No. 39, depth taken 12 inches. Growth, ash and elm.

a *Pacific Railroad Survey*, vol. II. Captain Pope was traveling eastward to Preston, a point on the river nearly north of Sherman, Texas.

Red river soils.

	NORTH OF COOKE COUNTY.	NORTH OF LAMAR COUNTY.	
	First bottom.	First bottom.	Second bottom.
	No. 38.	No. 39.	No. 40.
Insoluble matter	65.765 } 72.363	68.050 } 77.913	76.560 } 85.660
Soluble silica	6.618	9.863	9.100
Potash	0.405	0.345	0.404
Soda	0.030	0.005	0.089
Lime	2.933	1.116	0.456
Magnesia	2.623	1.217	0.619
Brown oxide of manganese	0.085	6.136	6.189
Peroxide of iron	4.681	5.274	6 2.296
Alumina	5.561	5.367	3.346
Phosphoric acid	0.156	0.209	0.163
Sulphuric acid	0.020	0.086	0.077
Carbonic acid	1.707	0.953	....
Water and organic matter	6.998	4.906	5.758
Total	100.352	100.521	99.947
Available inorganic	....	1.450	0.732
Available phosphoric acid	....	0.051	0.066
Humus	....	0.882	1.000
Hygroscopic moisture	2.962	2.566	6.777
absorbed at	28 C.°	28 C.°	27 C.°

In the above analyses the percentage of potash is adequate for high fertility. There is a fair proportion of phosphoric acid, with an amount of lime more than sufficient for full thriftiness. In the three soils the differences lie chiefly in the lime and magnesia, which in the first bottom exist as carbonates, and are rather excessive in quantity, and in the fact that the second bottom soils are more sandy. These analyses corroborate the statements that the valley lands of Red river yield yearly an average of a bale (1,500 pounds of seed-cotton) per acre.

SABINE RIVER LANDS.—The bottom lands of Sabine river, from its headwaters as far east as Cass county, are of a dark and heavy waxy nature, quite wide and well-timbered, but subject to overflow, and are not under cultivation. Thence to its mouth this waxy feature is destroyed by the intermixture of sand, a dark sandy loam covering the wide undulating bottoms, which are here above overflow, and are timbered with post oak and short-leaf pine. Cotton is largely planted on these lands (except in the extreme southern counties), grows to a height of from 5 to 7 feet, and yields, it is claimed, 1,500 pounds of seed-cotton per acre.

TRINITY RIVER LANDS.—The extreme headwaters of the Trinity river are in Jack county, but a short distance west of the central black prairie region. The lands of the river bottoms are therefore derived chiefly from the sandy uplands adjoining the streams, and are of a dark loamy or silty character until near the eastern limit of the black prairies, from which point southward there is a thick deposit of black waxy clay over the silt. The bottoms of the upper division of the river are well timbered with oak, elm, pecan, black walnut, bois d'arc (known also as Osage orange), honey-locust, hackberry, and cottonwood.

The lands are rich, as shown by the analysis of a sample as given in the table on page 44, but are not very generally under cultivation, being more or less subject to overflow. They are said to produce in ordinary seasons 1,000 pounds of seed-cotton per acre.

In this part of the state there are broad prairie valley lands on either side of the Trinity bottom several miles in width, bounded by the high bluffs of rotten limestone. At the foot of the ridges the soil is usually stiff and waxy, but becomes more and more sandy toward the river, with heavy beds of sand in some places. The valley lies beautifully for agricultural purposes, is gently undulating, and is apparently easy of cultivation. A growth of mesquite occurs occasionally on the prairie. Very little of the valley is in actual cultivation.

The bottoms of the middle and southern portions of the river have widths varying from 1 to 5 miles, and are heavily timbered with red, burr, and pin oaks, pecan, ash, and cottonwood, with cypress on the south.

The lands immediately adjoining the river are light and silty in character, but further back they are a heavy and waxy black clay, several feet in depth, and are underlaid usually by sand. They are very difficult to till in wet weather, and produce excellent crops of corn, cotton, and sugar-cane. Cotton grows 6 or 8 feet high, and, it is claimed, produces from 1,500 to 2,000 pounds of seed-cotton per acre.

The following analysis gives the composition of the valley land of the upper part of the Trinity:

No. 25. *Dark sandy loam* from 2 miles west of Dallas, in Dallas county, taken 10 inches deep. Timber growth, oak, elm, and hickory.

Trinity river valley soil, Dallas county.

	No. 26.
Insoluble matter	36.065 } 52.618
Soluble silica	16.858
Potash	0.560
Soda	0.226
Lime	16.344
Magnesia	1.602
Brown oxide of manganese	0.054
Peroxide of iron	3.897
Alumina	5.306
Phosphoric acid	0.123
Sulphuric acid	0.158
Carbonic acid	12.008
Water and organic matter	6.270
Total	**99.002**
Hygroscopic moisture	10.620
absorbed at	14 C.°

The prominent feature of this soil is the very large percentage of carbonate of lime, the latter from the adjoining hills of rotten limestone. There is a considerable percentage of potash and a fair amount of phosphoric acid, which, in presence of so much lime, is readily available, and makes the soil highly productive.

BRAZOS RIVER LANDS.—The lands of the Brazos river are considered the best and most valuable in the state, and are the most extensive of the river lands. The source of the river is at the foot of the Llano Estacado, and for a distance of 300 or 400 miles the river cuts its way among the gypsum beds, sandstones, and limestones of the northwestern region, carrying down with its waters the red sands and clays which go to form the first bottom lands along its entire course to the coast.

The bottom lands, before the river enters the black prairie region, are rather narrow, the bluffs often coming to the bank of the stream. They are not generally heavily timbered, mesquite trees being the prevailing growth in many places. The soil is a red sandy loam, except near the gypsum beds, where it is said to be whitish in color. The water of the river in this northwest region is somewhat salty, and salt incrustations are frequently found on some of the rocks in the streams.

VALLEY OF THE BRAZOS.—Separated by a very gentle dividing ridge, we find the valley of the Brazos extending 150 miles westward to the summit between its waters and those of the Colorado. It is in all respects similar in character and natural features to the valley of the Trinity, but rather more heavily timbered to a point near the head of the Clear fork.

The gently rolling country east and west dips with a gradual slope, in most cases of about 50 feet, to the immediate bottom lands along the river, which do not exceed a mile in width.

As we proceed to the west from the Clear fork, the oak and ash timber become much scarcer, until near the last tributary of the Double Mountain fork of the river we lose it entirely. It is then replaced by dense groves of large mesquite, which cover at least two-thirds of the country to a point a few miles east of the dividing ridge of the waters of the Brazos and those of the Colorado.

The country drained by the Brazos and its tributaries is more uneven in its surface and more densely timbered than either the Trinity to the east or the Colorado to the west, and with a climate in all respects delightful; it is a very fertile region, eminently adapted to agricultural purposes.—*Captain Pope.*

The bottom lands of the river, after leaving this region, may for description be conveniently divided into two sections, the first extending to Richmond, in Fort Bend county, the second thence to the coast, and known as "the sugar-bowl".

The bottoms of the first division have a width of from one-half to 2 miles, and are covered with a heavy timber growth of cottonwood, poplar, black walnut, pecan, and elm, and a dense undergrowth of cane, etc. The soil of the first bottom is a red alluvial loam, quite deep, overlying a red clay. At 30 feet a bed of "white and round quartz pebbles" occurs. That of the second bottom is usually a dark sandy loam.

In some of the counties the red lands of the first bottom are most prominent and extensive, but both seem to be equally productive, and are considered the best cotton lands of the state. A large proportion of these bottoms is under cultivation, but their unhealthfulness hinders their settlement. Cotton grows to a height of from 6 to 8 feet, yielding about a bale of lint or 1,500 pounds of seed-cotton per acre. Corn also is very productive, yielding, it is claimed, as much as 40 or 60 bushels per acre.

BRAZOS DELTA, OR "THE SUGAR-BOWL".—The lower division of these alluvial lands is the sugar-producing region of the state. It covers an area of about 900 square miles, and embraces, besides the lands of the Brazos, those of Oyster and San Bernard creeks on either side.

The region is perfectly level, heavily timbered, has a dense undergrowth, and lies from 20 to 30 feet above the common water-level of the river.

The soils of the region present three different varieties, viz, the red alluvial loam, immediately adjoining the river and the two creeks; ash and elm flats lying next to this, and finally the black wild peach lands.

The red-loam lands are considered the best, because of their excellent drainage, easy tillage, and great fertility. They occur in belts from one-half to a mile in width, or in bodies containing from 100 to 1,000 acres each. They have a depth of about 30 feet, the color of the soil changing somewhat at 18 inches.

Canebrakes cover the land, the timber growth being cottonwood, ash, elm, pecan, sycamore, hackberry, and a variety of oaks. Cotton grows to a height of from 5 to 10 feet, and yields about 2,000 pounds of seed-cotton per acre, both when fresh and after fifty years' cultivation.

The ash and elm lands have a stiff black soil, and are 18 inches deep, with a dark subsoil not so stiff. The timber growth is principally elm and ash. The lands are flat and poorly drained, and do not seem to be much under cultivation, though producing, it is claimed, as much as 1,500 pounds of seed-cotton per acre.

The black peach lands, while black in color, are sandy in character, and occur interspersed in small areas. They have a soil 18 inches in depth, and a lighter subsoil, and are easily tilled and best adapted to sugar-cane. They have a growth of wild peach, pecan, live oak, and hackberry, and are in part prairie. Cotton grows very high on these lands, and it is claimed will produce as much as 2,500 pounds of seed-cotton per acre.

Sugar is the chief production of the sugar-bowl region, the yield upon 5,340 acres for the year 1879, according to the census returns, being 4,443 hogsheads, with 355,573 gallons of molasses. The average yield per acre was eight-tenths of one hogshead of sugar and 66.5 gallons of molasses.

The following analyses show the composition of the various soils of the Brazos bottom, and are taken from different sections:

No. 19. *Brazos river red soil* from Granbury, Hood county, taken 12 inches deep. Timber growth, live and post oaks, pecan, and sumac.

No. 20. *Red clay subsoil* of the above, taken from 12 to 20 inches.

No. 18. *Brazos bottom red-loam soil* from 4 miles west of Hearne, Robertson county, taken 10 inches deep. Timber growth, pin oak, ash, walnut, and pecan.

No. 29. *Oyster creek red soil*, Brazoria county, taken 12 inches deep. Timber growth, live and other oaks, elm, ash, hackberry, pecan, etc. Cane undergrowth.

No. 32. *Black peach soil* of San Bernard river, near Columbia, Brazoria county. Depth taken, 12 inches, by David Nation, of Columbia; timber growth, pecan, live oak, hackberry, mulberry, and wild peach.

Brazos river bottom land.

	UPPER VALLEY LAND.			BRAZOS DELTA, OR SUGAR-BOWL.	
	HOOD COUNTY.		ROBERTSON COUNTY.	BRAZORIA COUNTY.	
	Brazos river second bottom.		Brazos bottom.	Oyster creek.	San Bernard river.
	Red soil.	Subsoil.	Red soil.	Red soil.	Black peach soil.
	No. 19.	No. 20.	No. 18.	No. 29.	No. 32.
Insoluble matter	88.177 } 90.328	75.570 } 80.066	69.291 } 80.682	66.441 } 80.411	80.806 } 87.009
Soluble silica	2.151	4.496	11.391	13.950	6.203
Potash	0.296	0.582	0.256	0.781	0.441
Soda	0.081	0.217	0.084	0.226	0.055
Lime	0.413	0.326	2.050	1.876	0.596
Magnesia	0.345	0.680	0.604	1.307	0.607
Brown oxide of manganese	0.040	0.010	0.100	0.013	0.098
Peroxide of iron	2.076	2.873	2.484	4.987	2.878
Alumina	2.006	10.988	6.989	4.030	2.885
Phosphoric acid	0.000	0.109	0.270	0.148	0.055
Sulphuric acid	0.020	0.056	0.290	0.094	0.080
Carbonic acid			1.047	1.961	
Water and organic matter	2.735	2.676	6.890	4.042	5.748
Total	98.956	100.155	99.297	99.116	100.504
Available inorganic			0.740	0.585	1.226
Available phosphoric acid			0.035	0.094	0.055
Humus			1.018	5.714	2.656
Hygroscopic moisture	6.026	11.219	5.835	5.430	5.980
absorbed at	12 C.°	16 C.°	16 C.°	13 C.°	13 C.°

In the soil and subsoil from Hood county the most prominent feature developed by the analyses is the low percentage of phosphoric acid, a minimum quantity. It is, however, made available by the abundance of lime present. The percentage of potash is large in the subsoil, and in sufficient quantity in the soil for thrifty land.

In the sample from Robertson county a much larger amount of lime is present, derived probably from the rotten limestone through which the river and its tributaries have cut their way. The percentage of. phosphoric acid also is extraordinarily high, with a fair amount of potash, thus making the alluvial land of the river in this place much richer than in Hood county. This increased fertility is also seen in the higher yield of cotton per acre.

The lands of the sugar-bowl of the Brazos alluvial are noted for their fertility, yielding usuallv from 1 500 to 2,000 pounds of seed-cotton per acre. In the above analyses the soil from Oyster creek is richer in mineral ingredients than that from the San Bernard river, containing larger percentages of potash, lime, and phosphoric acid, and resembles very much the red lands of the Brazos river.

The black peach land contains a larger amount of humus, and it will be seen that all of the phosphoric acid in the soil is available.

COLORADO RIVER LANDS.—The sources of the Colorado and of its western tributary, the Concho, are among the western hills and broad plains and table-lands of the Llano Estacado. For a distance of several hundred miles its waters flow among the sandstones and limestones of the western region with an easterly course to the black prairie region, then turn southward along its border to the lower edge of Burnet county, and thence east-southeast to the coast.

The bottom lands of the river, from its source to the black prairie region, are narrow, with many and frequent high bluffs near the stream.

COLORADO VALLEY.—Passing the dividing ridge of Brazos, we descend upon the tributaries of the Colorado, about 27 miles from the main stream. This valley, from the summit of the dividing ridge to the eastern base of the Llano Estacado, is about 67 miles in width, and is intersected in that distance by many small running streams tributary to the Colorado, and from 2 to 6 miles apart. The east side of the valley is about equally divided into prairie and forests of mesquite timber, and is much less undulating in surface than the country to the east. The mesquite becomes less abundant on the west side of the river, probably not occupying more than one-fourth of the country, until at the base of the Staked Plain it disappears altogether. The soil of the valley of the Colorado is good, but less moist and fertile than that of the valley of the Brazos. The rain is not so abundant as in the valleys of the streams to the east, but falls in sufficient quantity to obviate the necessity of irrigation, as was sufficiently evinced in the fact that although we traversed it at the very driest season of the year most of the small tributaries of the river were running streams, and few were without water. The Colorado itself was about 40 feet in width, and with a rapid current traversed its valley from side to side in a very tortuous course. The low and gently sloping ridges on each side were faced with red sandstone, and the soil was a rich red loam, which, although light, was very fertile. Limestone and other building material, with the exception of mesquite timber large enough for joists and planking, are readily obtained at any point of the valley, and its agricultural features, although not so eminently favorable as those of the country to the east, are nevertheless good. The mesquite, a hard and durable wood, grows in extensive forests, is about 30 feet high and from 4 to 10 inches in diameter.—*Captain Pope.*

On entering the more level lands of the prairies the bottom lands become wider, and thence to the coast have widths varying from one-half to a mile or more. This includes the valley or second bottom lands, the first, or bottoms proper, being narrow and more or less subject to overflow in high-water seasons. The bottoms have a large timber growth of white and pin oaks, elm, ash, cottonwood, sycamore, pecan, and hackberry, with usually a dense undergrowth of cane, etc. The lands are for the most part a reddish loam or silt several feet in depth, underlaid by clay. Near the uplands on either side the lands are darker, and in the black prairie region stiffer and more clayey in character. South of Columbus, in Colorado county, they resemble the lands of the sugar-bowl or Brazos alluvium, and properly belong to it. Cotton is the chief crop on the bottom lands of the river, the stalk growing from 5 to 7 feet high, and yielding from 1,500 to 2,000 pounds of seed-cotton per acre.

SAN SABA RIVER LANDS.—The lands of the San Saba, a tributary of the Colorado, comprise narrow and timbered bottoms along the banks of the stream, mesquite valleys, with both red gravelly soils and black loamy and clayey soils, reaching back to the hills. These valleys afford the chief farming lands of that section. (See description of San Saba county.)

GUADALUPE RIVER LANDS.—The bottom lands of the Guadalupe river are not very extensive or wide, and have a timber growth of cottonwood, pecan, ash, oaks, mulberry, and hackberry, with a variety of undergrowth. The soil is mostly a sandy loam from 10 to 15 inches deep; the subsoil a yellow clay, sometimes jointed in character. The valley lands are in some places broad and open, with a mesquite growth and a dark calcareous soil. Cotton grows from 5 to 7 feet high, and yields about 1,500 pounds of seed-cotton per acre.

SAN ANTONIO RIVER LANDS.—The bottom lands of the San Antonio river are narrow and unimportant. Its valleys have in some counties a width of 1½ miles and a growth (in Wilson county) of elm, hackberry, pecan, ash, and mesquite. In the counties near the coast the river flows between high banks of white clay-stone, or adobe, along which there is usually a growth of pecan trees and mesquite.

NUECES RIVER LANDS.—The Nueces river is mainly confined to the thinly inhabited southwestern section of the state. In San Patricio county its bottoms have a growth of live oak, cottonwood, ash, elm, hackberry, and willow, and a black alluvial soil. Its valley lands seem to be preferred; they have a growth of mesquite and "wesatche", and a light sandy soil, which is easily tilled.

RIO GRANDE RIVER LANDS.—The bottom and valley lands of the Rio Grande river from its headwaters southward to Edinburg, Hidalgo county, are narrow, and, so far as known, are unimportant, the hills of the uplands coming to the river banks very often. From Edinburg to the mouth of the river these lands widen out rapidly, and embrace those of the Sal Colorado, which stream is said to be but an outlet of the Rio Grande in high water, and runs off almost at right angles to it.

The entrance to the mouth of the Rio Grande is over a bar of soft mud varying from 4 to 6 feet deep, and the river within a few hundred yards of its mouth is not more than 1,000 feet wide. The shore-line of the coast, scarcely broken by the action of the river, is formed of a series of low shifting sand-hills, with a scanty herbage. Inside these hills are numerous salt marshes and lagoons, separated by low belts of calcareous clay, but a few feet above the sea, and subject to overflow. The first high land is 10 miles from the mouth.

Northward to Brownsville the lands on each side of the river are level and covered with a dense growth of mesquite. The margin of the river, which is exposed to overflow, abounds in reed, canebrake, palmetto, willow, and water plants.—*Mex. Bound. Survey*, vol. I.

The valley from Brownsville northward has a width of 50 miles. The following information is from Rev. J. G. Hall, of Brownsville:

The growth of these lands is mesquite and ebony, though there are many other scrubby varieties. In many places, too, the undergrowth is very heavy, forming chaparrals. For the first 50 or 60 miles up the river the valley loses itself in the plain; farther up it becomes narrower, until at little over 100 miles it becomes almost nothing. The land along the lower river is in belts of black waxy and of sandy soils, both being very fertile, but the former more so than the latter. Neither has a clay subsoil. With rains these lands are wonderfully productive, and now that the border has been comparatively quiet for some years the agricultural interests are rapidly advancing. These belts of land are sometimes 8 or 10 miles wide and sometimes 2 or 3 miles. The timber is not very heavy anywhere, but is heaviest along the river.

Up to this time there has been very little cotton planted, but the people are beginning to turn their attention more to its cultivation.

The following analyses are given to show the composition of the valley lands of two of these rivers:

No. 22. *Colorado river valley loam soil* from Bastrop, Bastrop county, taken 10 inches deep. No growth where taken.

No. 23. *Colorado valley loam soil* from 4 miles east of Austin, Travis county, taken 10 inches deep. Timber growth, pecan, elm, oak, and hackberry.

No. 24. *Soil* taken 8 inches deep from a field near the above that has been under cultivation more than forty years.

No. 28. *San Saba river red valley soil* from north of San Saba, San Saba county, taken 10 inches deep. Timber growth, mostly mesquite.

No. 37. *Rio Grande valley soil* from near Brownsville, taken 12 inches deep, and sent by Rev. J. G. Hall. Growth, mesquite and ebony.

River valley lands.

	COLORADO RIVER VALLEY.			SAN SABA RIVER.	RIO GRANDE VALLEY.
	BASTROP COUNTY.	TRAVIS COUNTY.		SAN SABA COUNTY.	CAMERON COUNTY.
	Soil.	Soil.	Cultivated soil.	Red loam soil.	Dark loam soil.
	No. 22.	No. 23.	No. 24.	No. 28.	No. 37.
Insoluble matter	71.062 } 83.337	62.306 } 72.063	87.068 } 91.742	77.617 } 82.164	36.041 } 53.296
Soluble silica	12.275	10.207	4.654	4.547	17.255
Potash	0.444	0.581	0.398	0.507	1.305
Soda	0.166	0.118	0.077	0.197	0.218
Lime	0.675	7.793	0.459	3.971	14.433
Magnesia	0.090	1.879	0.447	0.990	1.532
Brown oxide of manganese	0.183	0.126	0.106	0.075	0.069
Peroxide of iron	3.058	2.934	2.065	2.340	4.085
Alumina	5.291	2.388	3.043	2.665	0.114
Phosphoric acid	0.258	0.207	0.096	0.281	0.304
Sulphuric acid	0.208	0.680	0.038	0.067	0.041
Carbonic acid		8.673	Traces.	2.256	8.912
Water and organic matter	3.335	3.035	2.876	4.412	6.006
Total	99.730	99.225	99.834	100.687	100.230
Available inorganic		1.879			1.465
Available phosphoric acid		0.041			0.951
Humus		1.866			
Hygroscopic moisture	3.164	7.570	3.700	7.280	13.754
absorbed at	14 C.°	10 C.°	18 C.°	13 C.°	12 C.°

These soils show large percentages of potash, with a sufficiency of lime for the large amounts of phosphoric acid that are present. There is a comparatively large amount of humus in the Travis county soil.

The analysis of the cultivated soil is instructive in showing large reductions in all of the essential ingredients, viz, potash, lime, magnesia, phosphoric acid, and organic matter. It is evident that the addition of phosphate manures to this land will soon be necessary to maintain its fertility.

45 c p

The soil of San Saba river valley is rich in all of the elements necessary to fertility and durability, viz, potash, phosphoric acid, and lime. It is light and sandy, and yields abundant crops.

The soil of the Rio Grande valley contains an extraordinary percentage of potash, a large amount of phosphoric acid, and a very large amount of carbonate of lime. The percentage of humus is also great, and the soil has a large retentive power for moisture. Altogether, this soil, which is easily tilled, seems to be nearer what may be thought to be a "perfect soil" than any other in the state.

The following description by Captain Pope (a) regarding the valley lands of the Rio Grande from El Paso southward is given at length, because of the little that is generally known concerning a region in which these valleys offer almost the only tillable lands:

VALLEY OF THE RIO GRANDE.—At Frontera, about 5 miles above El Paso, the Rio Grande commences to make its passage through the chain of mountains which intersect its course, and to a point immediately in the neighborhood of Molino it is bordered closely on both sides by a range of high and rugged mountains. At Frontera, four miles above, the range on the west side subsides into the vast level table-lands which extend, with little interruption, many miles to the westward; but on the east side the mountains gradually depart from the river, becoming more rugged and lofty, until they unite on the "Jornada del Muerto" with the continuous ridges of the Rocky mountains. The river cuts through them between Frontera and Molino by a succession of rapids, and at one place by a perpendicular fall of 2 or 3 feet, and this passage has, from the period of its discovery by the Spaniards, been known as El Paso. The Mexican town of that name is about 2 miles below the debouchure of the river from the mountains. With the exception of the limited strip between Frontera and Molino, the immediate valley of the Rio Grande is from 2 to 5 miles in width and perfectly level, and the river traverses it from side to side in many sinuosities. These level bottom lands can be readily irrigated from the river, and possess a soil which, although not deep, and containing rather too large a proportion of sand for the notions of farmers in the United States, is nevertheless extremely fertile, and well adapted to the production of all the cereal grains.

The system of irrigation renews the fertility of the soil by spreading over it every year a fat deposit several inches in thickness, which is brought down in suspension by the river, and to this deposit is undoubtedly due the fact that the Mexicans for so many successive years have been able to continue the same crops upon the land. The soil is only about 4 or 5 inches deep, and for cultivating it the Mexican implements have been conclusively shown, by experience of several years, to be the best. The wooden plow which they use barely enters the earth sufficiently to turn up 3 or 4 inches in depth, and they thus never pass below the yearly deposits of the river. The iron plow, on the contrary, passes several inches below this, and turns up a soil more than four-fifths of which is sand, and consequently of little productiveness. As an evidence of the results, it will suffice to say that of two fields of the same size contiguous to each other and identical in soil, the one cultivated with great care by the government, after the American fashion, the other the property of an old Mexican, who cultivated it himself without assistance, the products were little or nothing for the first and a crop averaging from 30 to 40 bushels of corn to the acre for the last. The immediate valley of the river between Dona Aña and Frontera contains about 128,000 acres of arable land.

The most valuable feature, however, of the valley of the Rio Grande is yet but partially developed; and as it ministers to the luxuries rather than to the necessities of life, it cannot, in the absence of demand for such things, occupy a very important place in the present wealth of New Mexico. I refer to the peculiar adaptation of the valley to the culture of the grape. The east side of the Rio Grande is faced by chains of lofty mountains at an average distance from the river of 15 miles, which, at San Felipe at the north and El Paso at the south, impinge directly upon the banks. A semicircular sweep of country is thus inclosed from the northern and eastern winds, and in consequence we find within it a very mild and equable climate, little subjected to the change of the seasons. The river having a general course to the southeast, and the ranges of mountains on the east side being nearly parallel to it, the whole of this area has a southern and western exposure, and, with a soil sufficiently fertile and of great warmth, it is most wonderfully adapted to the culture of the grape.

SURVEYS AND MEASUREMENTS IN TEXAS.—The system of surveying lands is not that common in other western states, viz, that of dividing it into townships, sections, and numbered subdivisions; but the Spanish land measure in use when the state was a separate republic, and in which the original land grants were expressed, is the legal measure. The divisions are varas, labors, and leagues, and distances are at present given in linear varas, instead of in chains and feet.

Spanish land measure.

1 vara	33⅓ inches.
1 acre	5,846 square varas = 4,840 square yards.
1 labor	1,000,000 square varas = 177 acres.
⅓ league	8,333,333 square varas = 1,476 acres.
1 league	25,000,000 square varas = 4,428 acres.
1 league and labor	26,000,000 square varas = 4,605 acres.

To find the number of acres in a given number of square varas, divide by 5,846—fractions rejected.

REMARKS ON COTTON PRODUCTION IN TEXAS.

In Thrall's *History of Texas* it is stated that cotton-seed was brought to the Brazos river in Texas in 1821 by Colonel Jared E. Grace, one of the earliest settlers, and that in 1825 he erected the first cotton-gin in the state. The next year the Austins built one on the west side of the Brazos about 10 miles north of Columbia. This was subsequently burned, and the place has been known as the Burnt Gin place. About the same time another gin was built on Old Caney, in Matagorda county. The staple at that time was packed in bales of 50 and 100 pounds weight and transported to the Rio Grande on mules, 250 pounds constituting a mule-load. In 1831 Edwin Waller sent a schooner-load of cotton from the mouth of the Brazos to Matamoras, and sold it for 62½ cents per pound.

---

a Report to Captain A. A. Humphreys, in charge of the office of explorations and surveys, on "artesian well experiments".

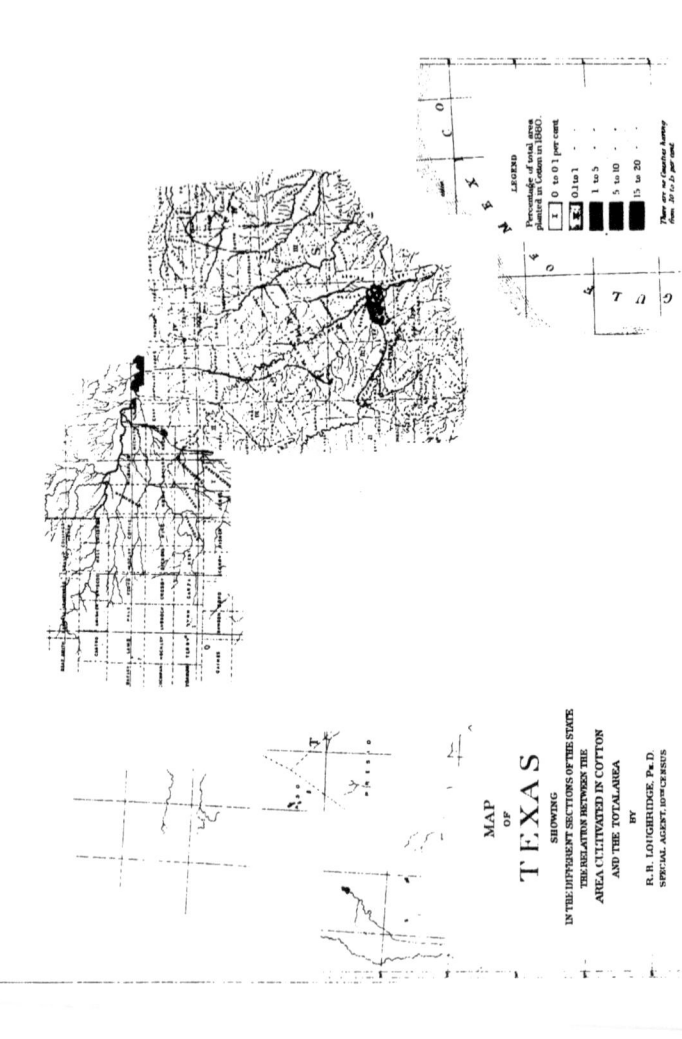

MAP
OF
TEXAS

SHOWING

IN THE DIFFERENT SECTIONS OF THE STATE
THE RELATION BETWEEN THE
AREA CULTIVATED IN COTTON
AND THE TOTAL AREA

BY

R. H. LOUGHRIDGE, Ph. D.
SPECIAL AGENT, 10th CENSUS

LEGEND

Percentage of total area
planted in Cotton in 1880.

	0 to 0.1 per cent
	0.1 to 1
	1 to 5
	5 to 10
	15 to 20

There are no Counties having
from .10 to .5 per cent.

In 1834 the cotton crop was estimated to be worth $600,000.

In 1848 the crop amounted to 39,774 bales of 500 pounds weight, and in successive census years, according to the returns, as follows: In 1850, 58,072 bales; in 1860, 431,463; and in 1870, 350,628 bales. For the census year 1880 the returns show 805,284 bales, an increase of 454,656 since 1870, or more than double the production of that year, the state ranking as third in cotton product, raising 13.7 per cent. of the entire crop of the country.

Area.—In 1869 the region of cotton cultivation extended nearly half-way across the state from east to west, and embraced in its limits about 108,000 square miles, or about 41 per cent. of the land area. A line marking its western limit would pass southward from Red river, through the counties of Montague, Wise, Parker, Erath, and Hamilton, to Atascosa, and thence eastward to Matagorda county.

A line marking the limit for 1879 would pass from Red river, into Wichita county, southwest into Jones and Taylor, and south through Coleman, McCulloch, Mason, Kerr, Bandera, and Uvalde to the Nueces river, which it would follow nearly to the Gulf, thence turning northwest to the northwest corner of Calhoun county. Small spots of cotton production (49 acres altogether) occur also on the Rio Grande in Cameron and Hidalgo counties. The entire region of production includes an area of about 126,000 square miles, or not one-half of the land area of the state, and extends nearly 100 miles farther west and embraces 18,430 square miles more than in 1869.

The building of the new lines of railroad westward will probably be instrumental in extending the region of cotton production to the Llano Estacado long before the census year of 1890.

Taking the combined area of what may be termed the agricultural portion of Texas, viz, the oak, hickory, and pine region, the central black prairies, the northwest red-loam lands, and a part of the coast prairies, we find it to be in round numbers about 102,000 square miles, or 65,280,000 acres.

Texas is chiefly a corn-producing state, that crop occupying 2,468,587 acres, or 32 per cent. of the lands under cultivation, and exceeding the area of cotton by 130,017 acres. The number of bushels of corn produced was 29,065,172, the average production for the state being, for 1879, 11.7 bushels per acre. Cotton is the second crop of the state as regards acreage (2,178,435), wheat being third (373,570 acres), their percentages of tilled lands being respectively 28.5 and 4.8.

Of the organized counties, one hundred and thirty-nine report their acreages of corn to be greater than that of any other crop; twenty-eight counties produce no cotton at all, but are chiefly devoted to stock-raising, leaving one hundred and forty-two that may be called cotton counties.

By reference to the tables at the beginning of this report, it will be seen that in thirty-one counties alone does the cotton acreage exceed that of corn. These are embraced mostly in the central part of the state northward from Washington and Fayette counties, and include the following: Cass, Camp, Marion, Gregg, Harrison, Panola, Smith, Navarro, Limestone, Freestone, Robertson, Walker, Grimes, Brazos, Burleson, Milam, Lee, Bastrop, Kaufman, Dallas, Johnson, Ellis, Hill, McLennan, Falls, Caldwell, San Jacinto, Washington, Austin, Fayette, and Colorado.

Thirty-four counties of the state have one-third or more of their tilled lands in cotton; in eleven of these the percentage is over 40. Marion county ranks highest, the percentage being 46.2 of the tilled lands; Grimes and Brazos follow with 45 and 45.4 per cent.

TABLE III.—SHOWING POPULATION AND COTTON PRODUCTION IN EACH AGRICULTURAL REGION OF THE STATE.

Agricultural regions.	Area.	POPULATION.			COTTON PRODUCTION.										
		Total.	White.	Color'd.	Acres.	Bales.	Fraction of bale (500 lbs.).	Average per acre.			Total in tons.		Percentage of the state's total production.	Cotton acreage per square mile.	Bales per square mile.
								Seed-cotton.	Lint.	Seed.	Lint.	Seed.			
	Sq. mis.							*Lbs.*	*Lbs.*	*Lbs.*					
Total for the State	262,290	1,591,749	1,197,237	394,512	2,178,435	805,284	0.37	555	185	370	201,321	402,642	100.0	17.2	6.4
Red River alluvial	4,710	118,961	93,615	25,346	169,432	91,802	0.54	810	270	540	22,951	45,902	11.4	36.0	19.5
Oak, hickory, and pine uplands	31,400	511,213	320,681	190,531	914,305	223,054	0.36	540	180	360	81,414	162,828	40.4	29.0	10.2
Long-leaf pine	5,140	25,770	17,090	8,680	17,567	7,262	0.41	615	205	410	1,816	3,632	0.9	3.4	1.4
Central black prairie	33,440	514,257	452,179	62,078	744,585	249,883	0.34	510	170	340	62,473	124,946	31.0	22.3	7.5
Northwestern red-loam prairie	19,920	82,307	80,924	1,383	46,201	10,931	0.24	360	130	260	2,732	5,464	1.4	2.3	0.5
Southern and coast prairie	22,020	230,559	146,219	84,340	264,258	100,613	0.40	600	200	400	26,653	53,306	12.3	11.5	4.6
Brazos alluvial, or sugar-bowl	3,350	23,703	5,038	18,665	21,838	13,097	0.60	900	300	600	3,274	6,548	1.6	6.5	3.9
Rio Grande valley	5,350	19,306	19,075	231	49	32	0.65	975	325	650	8	16			
Other counties	135,960	65,674	62,216	3,458											

TABLE IV.—SHOWING "BANNER COUNTIES" AS REGARDS PRODUCTION AND PRODUCT PER ACRE IN THE VARIOUS AGRICULTURAL REGIONS OF THE STATE.

REGIONS ACCORDING TO PRODUCT PER ACRE.		COUNTY IN EACH REGION HAVING HIGHEST TOTAL PRODUCTION.					COUNTY IN EACH REGION HAVING HIGHEST PRODUCT PER ACRE.					
Name.	Average product per acre, (fraction of a bale).	Name.	Rank in product per acre in the state.	Cotton acreage.	Total production (bales).	Product per acre, fraction of bale.	Name.	Rank in total production in the state.	Cotton acreage.	Total production (bales).	Product per acre.	Rank in product per acre in the state.
Rio Grande valley	0.65	Cameron	1	25	28	0.92	Cameron	133	25	28	0.92	1
Brazos alluvial, or sugar-bowl	0.60	Fort Bend	7	10,873	6,451	0.59	Brazoria	73	5,402	3,484	0.64	4
Red River alluvial	0.54	Lamar	6	46,890	24,623	0.61	Bowie	41	11,699	7,955	0.69	3
Long-leaf pine	0.41	Tyler	19	5,904	2,548	0.46	Liberty	91	3,785	1,859	0.49	19
Southern and coast prairie	0.40	Fayette	33	58,353	24,766	0.43	Chambers	122	140	91	0.65	8
Oak, hickory, and pine uplands	0.36	Robertson	56	49,654	18,080	0.36	Titus	50	9,395	4,923	0.52	12
Central black prairie	0.34	Collin	26	48,296	22,145	0.46	Delta	60	8,940	4,911	0.55	11
Northwestern red-loam prairie	0.24	Comanche	123	9,301	2,096	0.23	Wichita	131	103	43	0.42	37

Banner county of the state as regards total production: Fayette, 24,766 bales; banner county (a) of the state as regards product per acre: Bowie, 1,035 pounds seed-cotton; banner county of the state as regards percentage of tilled lands in cotton: Marion, 46.2 per cent.; banner county of the state as regards cotton acreage per square mile: Washington, 97.3 acres per square mile.

COMPARISON OF AGRICULTURAL REGIONS.—The Brazos alluvial region, which ranks as first among the cotton-producing regions (b) in average product per acre (900 pounds), has, on the other hand, but an average of 6.5 cotton acres per square mile, a large part of the region being at present unfit for cotton cultivation, because of its heavy, undrained soils. Fort Bend county produces the greatest number of bales, but Brazoria has the highest product per acre, 960 pounds. Since 1870 cotton production has increased with greater rapidity than the population, the percentages of increase being respectively 58 and 32, or as 1.8 to 1.

The Red river counties are next in product per acre, and the yield, 810 pounds, would no doubt be equal to that of the Brazos alluvial but for the large area of cultivated uplands, which reduces the general average of the region. The average cotton acreage per square mile, 36.1, is greater than that of any other region, and its production is 11.4 per cent. of the total for the state. Lamar county produces the largest number of bales, but Bowie ranks first, both in the region and state, as regards product per acre (excepting those counties whose production is less than 100 bales). In 1870 this region produced but 5.2 per cent. of the state's entire yield, but since then it has more than doubled its population and almost quadrupled its cotton production, the ratio of increase being as 1 of the former to 3.8 of the latter.

The long-leaf pine region, in the southeastern part of the state, while ranking next as regards product per acre, has but a very small area in cotton cultivation, the average being 3.4 acres per square mile, and this is confined mostly to the better class of bottom lands. Tyler county produces the greatest number of bales, but Liberty ranks first in the region in productiveness, viz, 735 pounds per acre.

The southern and coast prairie region both east and west of the Brazos river produces 13.3 per cent. of the cotton of the state, and the average product per acre is 608 pounds. The acreage of that crop on the east is but 5.9 per square mile, while on the west it is 13.7, but in the entire region it is confined to counties inland from the coast. Fayette county has the highest total production both in the region and in the state, while Chambers, with its very small cotton acreage, has the highest product per acre in the region. Since 1870 the increase in cotton production and population on the east has been very great.

The oak, hickory, and pine uplands, with an area greater than any other agricultural region, produces 40.4 per cent. of the cotton yield of the state, and has an average product per acre of 540 pounds of seed-cotton. The average cotton acreage per square mile is 0.29, that of population being 16.2. Robertson county produces the greatest number of bales, and Titus has the highest product per acre (780 pounds) in the region.

The central black prairie region now produces 31 per cent. of the state's entire yield, upon an average of 22.3 acres per square mile. The average yield per acre is 510 pounds of seed-cotton, Kaufman county ranking first in this regard, with an average of 880 pounds per acre. Sixteen of the thirty-nine counties forming this division each have an average of less than 450 pounds, that of ten counties lying mostly in the northern part of the region being above 600 pounds. Collin county produces the largest number of bales, an average of 690 pounds per acre, and ranks twenty-sixth in this regard among the counties of the state.

a Omitting those whose production is less than 100 bales. b The Rio Grande valley is not included among these.
7Ud

The red-loam prairie region of the northwest has but a comparatively small area under cotton cultivation, confined chiefly to those counties on the east that border the black prairies. The average product per acre is 360 pounds, an average less than in any other region. Comanche county produces the largest number of bales, and Wichita has the greatest product per acre (630 pounds). This and Archer county are the only ones of the region whose product is 600 pounds per acre.

ACREAGE PER SQUARE MILE.—The cotton acreage of Washington county averages 97.8 acres per square mile, the county ranking highest in the state. Fayette follows with 60.8 acres, then Johnson with 58.6 acres. Eight other counties, viz, Camp, Robertson, Ellis, Collin, Brazos, Harrison, Falls, and Fannin, have an average each of 50 acres and above; twelve counties average from 40 to 50 acres; seventeen counties from 30 to 40; twenty-three from 20 to 30; seventeen from 10 to 20; thirty-four from 1 to 10, and the other twenty-nine counties below 1 acre per square mile.

DISTRIBUTION OF PRODUCTION.—The county reporting the highest number of bales is Fayette, one of the southern prairie counties, and there are five others having a yield of above 20,000 bales each. These are Lamar and Fannin, on Red river; Collin and Dallas, of the northern part of the black prairie region, and Washington, adjoining Fayette. Eight counties have each a yield of from 15,000 to 20,000 bales, viz, Red River, Grayson, Cass, Harrison, Smith, Robertson, Ellis, and Colorado. Fifteen counties report from 10,000 to 15,000 bales, and all other counties below that number. Washington county has an average yield of 34.5 bales per square mile; a number far greater than in any other county of the state. Fayette county, which adjoins it, has a yield of 25.8 bales; Camp, in the northeast part of the state, 28.4 bales, and a few other counties above 24 bales per square mile, but all others are much below.

A region of low production is comprised in the counties of the long-leaf pineries and coast prairies east of the Brazos, the average number of bales being about 1.4 per square mile, though unequally distributed. Northward from this region to the Red river the average is much greater, about 10 bales per square mile. The greatest part of the cotton of the state is produced in the region west of the ninety-sixth degree of longitude, and includes the counties south from Fannin, Grayson, and Cook counties to Washington, Fayette, and Colorado, inclusive. The counties along the Red river have a yield equal to any except the very highest.

By reference to the cotton acreage map it will be seen that a region of intense cotton culture (from 15 to 20 per cent. of the total area) lies in Washington county; that a region of from 5 to 10 per cent. of the total occupies a very large area from the Red river southward in the central part of the state to the parallel of latitude 29.5, and another of the same percentage embraces a number of counties in the northeast; and that southward to the coast and eastward the relative acreage diminishes in broad belts.

PRODUCT PER ACRE.—In 1879 there were produced 805,284 bales of cotton upon 2,178,435 acres, which gives an average of 0.37 of a bale per acre. Assuming that the average bale contained 500 pounds of lint (as reported by correspondents), the yield per acre is found to be 185 pounds of lint, or 555 pounds of seed-cotton. The secretary of the cotton exchange at Galveston, however, reports that the average of all the bales received at that port in the season of 1879–'80 was about 513 pounds, which, if an average for the state also, would make a yield per acre of 189 pounds of lint.

The ratio between seed-cotton and lint varies greatly with the character of the land and the time of ginning. On rich lands the seeds are heavier, and therefore for a given amount of lint a greater weight of seed-cotton is required. The same is true as regards ginning, a larger amount of seed-cotton being required immediately after picking (the seeds being greener) than if allowed to dry before being ginned. The usual and accepted ratio between seed-cotton and the lint that can be obtained from it is as 3 to 1. The variations from this ratio are mentioned in the county descriptions. The above is an excellent average of natural productiveness if we take into consideration the fact that the year 1879 was an exceedingly dry one (it being claimed that the crop was reduced one-third), and that, with few exceptions, the lands are unaided by the use of fertilizers.

The chief cotton lands comprise the rich bottoms of Red and Brazos rivers and the uplands of the state. The former, therefore, would naturally yield the highest returns, and we find the "banner county" of the state to be Bowie, on the extreme northeast; a county in which the uplands consist of deep sandy soils, with a prominent growth of short leaf pine, and on whose red river bottom lands cotton is chiefly produced, with an average yield of 1,035 pounds of seed-cotton per acre.

Cameron, on the Rio Grande, surpasses Bowie in yield per acre, but only 25 acres have been under cultivation in that county, and it should be properly omitted from the list of cotton counties.

Chambers county, on the lower Trinity, with its 140 acres of cotton, lying mostly in the river bottoms, ranks next to Bowie, its average yield being 975 pounds of seed-cotton. Brazoria, one of the Brazos or "sugar-bowl" counties, ranks third, with a yield of 960 pounds per acre. Thus with Cameron on the extreme southwest, Bowie on the extreme northeast, and Chambers and Brazoria on the south, we have the maxima of cotton productions at directly opposite parts of the state, and on each of the four great alluvial or river belts. Besides these, Matagorda and Lamar counties, whose cotton lands are located chiefly on river bottom lands, have each a yield of from 900 to 915 pounds of seed-cotton per acre.

Eleven counties of the state have average yields of from 750 to 900 pounds, viz, Polk, San Jacinto, Jefferson, Fort Bend, Wharton, Delta, Red River, Fannin, Titus, Dallas, and Camp; thirty-two counties have an average of from 600 to 750 pounds, and forty-nine from 450 to 600 pounds; all others below that amount.

SHIPMENTS.—Farmers usually haul their cotton to the nearest market as soon as a few bales have been ginned, and, if pressed for supplies, they sell immediately. It is the general custom to sell to cotton buyers at these markets, and thus avoid the troubles of transportation, commissions, etc., though the larger planters prefer to ship to the commission merchants in the cities. Some of the eastern mills have adopted the plan of sending buyers into the country towns, and thus get their supplies direct from the farmers, paying the quotation prices, less the cost of transportation.

Galveston and Houston are the chief points from which shipments of cotton are made to New York and other markets of the United States, as well as to those of foreign countries. From Galveston the exports are mostly to foreign markets direct, the greater part going to Great Britain. New York receives the next largest bulk of the cotton, about one-fifth of the whole shipments being almost entirely by ocean routes.

Houston, though properly an inland city, is connected with the Gulf by Buffalo bayou, whose channel has been deepened and straightened sufficient to afford water passage for Morgan's Gulf steamers to within a few miles of the city, a short railroad completing the connection. Cotton is mostly shipped direct to New Orleans by this route, that intended for foreign markets going to Galveston by rail. A line of railway also connects Houston with New Orleans direct. The cotton bales are reduced to one-third of their bulk, preparatory to shipment, by steam compresses located in each of these cities, the cost being borne by the transportation companies.

The rates of transportation to New York were (in 1879) about 65 cents by rail, 50 cents by steamship, and a little less by sail per 100 pounds. To Liverpool the rates were $\frac{1}{4}d.$ by steamship and $\frac{1}{8}d.$ by sail per pound.

The following statement regarding receipts and exports for 1879–'80 have been furnished by the cotton exchange of Galveston. The season is from September 1, 1879, to August 31, 1880:

Comparative statement of cotton shipments from Galveston.

	Bales.
Net receipts	480,352
Receipts from New Orleans (a)	933
Receipts from Indianola	4,290
Gross receipts	485,575
Exports to Great Britain	213,243
Exports to France	23,831
Exports to the continent	49,679
Exports to channel ports	9,282
Total foreign	296,035
Exports to New York	116,466
Exports to Morgan City	49,574
Exports to other United States ports	14,163
Exports north by railroad	9,058
Total coastwise	189,261
Total exports	485,296
Average weight	501 15–100
Date of first bale	July 12
Where from	Yorktown, De Witt county.

In the northern part of the state cotton is largely shipped by rail to Saint Louis at about 90 cents (from Dallas), or to New York at $1 34 per 100 pounds. If intended for foreign markets, it is sent to Galveston, at $4 50 per bale. The rates of transportation from minor points are given in each county description.

ANALYSES OF THE SOILS OF THE STATE.

The table on pages 54 and 55 comprises the analyses that have been made of the soils of the state. The specimens taken represent as nearly as possible the most important regions, and were mostly collected by myself. The most important results of these analyses, as regards percentages of each of the chief elements of plant-food, viz, potash, phosphoric acid, lime, and vegetable matter, may be thus briefly summarized:

Potash.—In the light sandy soils of the northeastern counties of the timbered lands potash is somewhat deficient. While the minimum percentage is reached in the Bowie county uplands (0.047), the maximum in the region (0.195) is found to be in the most southwestern soil analyzed, viz, that from Bastrop county. The soils of the cross timbers have still higher percentages.

The soils of the red lands of the region show the same maximum on the southwest (0.718 in Lee county), due probably to the presence of Tertiary greensand rock in the neighborhood.

---

a From the wreck of a vessel called the Reform.

In the central black prairie the percentages of potash are large, especially in the soils from Collin on the north and McLennan and Falls counties in the center, representatives of the best class of black waxy lands of the state. That from Falls is surpassed but by two soils of the state in its potash percentage, viz, those of the Rio Grande valley and Oyster creek, in the Brazos delta. These prairie lands are stiff and difficult to till, while the black sandy soils of the same region are easy, and have also a sufficiency of potash.

The lands of the southern prairies, as well as those of the northwestern red-loam region, are adequately supplied, while those of the various alluvial regions surpass, as a whole, any of the soils of the state in their percentages of potash. The Rio Grande valley is remarkable in this regard, its proportion of 1.308 being the greatest of any soil within the state, due probably to extensive beds of greensand along the river, northward from Rio Grande City, there being also but few tributary streams to dilute with sands and clays the washings from these beds.

Phosphoric acid.—This most important fertilizing element is present in minimum quantities in the upland soils of Bowie county, on the northeast, and of the upper and lower cross timbers, as well as in the subsoil of the former. In the other soils of the timbered region, both gray and red, and the brown-loam prairies that are interspersed in it throughout many of the counties, there is a fair percentage, except in Smith county, where it is unusually high. The black lands of the central prairies vary greatly, the percentages of phosphoric acid ranging from low to inadequacy in the black sandy prairies of Ellis and the black waxy soils of Collin, to fair in the soil from Van Zandt and Johnson, and extraordinarily high in McLennan, Falls, and Lampasas. These latter are the highest for the state, and phosphate manures will manifestly not be required in a very long time for soils of such high percentages.

The southern and coast prairies, though consisting largely of black, tenacious, and calcareous soils, are comparatively deficient in phosphoric acid in Washington, rather low in Victoria, and fair in the other counties. These prairies will soon require phosphate manures in cultivation.

The river lands of the state, while, as a rule, having a fair amount, cannot be said to be rich in this element, with the exception of the Brazos bottom, southward from Hearne, whose alluvium contains the unusually high percentage of 0.370, thus ranking third in the state. The same land on the northwest is rather deficient in phosphoric acid, probably due to the fact that the valley is there narrow and more sandy from the washings of the bordering sandy uplands, as is also shown by the high per cent. of insoluble residue. The percentages are high in the San Saba river soil, and large in the Colorado soils at Austin and in that of the Rio Grande near Brownsville; the rest are generally from fair to low.

Lime.—As a stimulator and agent in rendering available the mineral elements above mentioned lime acts an important part, and, with humus, is a very essential ingredient in the soil. Based upon the estimate of Professor E. W. Hilgard (*American Journal of Science and Arts*, 1881) that the minimum amount of lime necessary to insure productiveness should not be less than one-tenth of 1 per cent., the soils of Texas, with a few exceptions, may be considered as rich in lime. Concurrently with large lime percentages we find large amounts of dissolved alumina and soluble silica, and, so far as a few determinations go, of humus, which is corroborated by the dark tint of the prairie soils. The red color of the alluvial soils would naturally lead us suspect a large percentage of iron, but this does not appear from the analyses, the color resulting from the diffusion of the iron, imparting to the soil important physical advantages. We are reminded of the existence of the great gypsum beds at the headwaters of the rivers by the high percentages of sulphuric acid in the soils, especially in the alluvial lands.

Blight.—Much trouble is experienced by farmers throughout the state with what is termed "dying in spots", a blight that attacks all crops having long tap-roots. Cotton on such land suddenly dies in spots, or in areas varying from a few feet to as much as 50 feet or more in diameter, at a time when the plant has reached its usual height for fruiting and when the blooms are about to appear. Sometimes but a single plant dies in this manner, the others on all sides being healthy and vigorous. The decay begins usually at the lower extremity of the tap-root, proceeding upward to the surface of the ground, the growing plant showing no signs of trouble until the lateral roots are unable to furnish sufficient moisture. While this evil occurs on all lands throughout the state to a greater or less extent, it seems to be most prevalent in the heavy clay soils of the central black prairie region, which is underlaid by the compact and heavy-bedded rotten limestone.

Many theories have been advanced by farmers as to the cause of this decay, some claiming that "it is due to too much lime in the soil", an idea originating in the very general impression that all heavy soils are limy, because those of the black prairies contain much lime. That it cannot be due to this cause is apparent by the fact that cotton may often be seen growing well on lands full of fragments of rotten limestone, while dying on lands having very little lime in their composition.

That some plants are killed by other means, such as diseases and insects, is doubtless true; but from all the facts gathered on this subject, there is much more reason to believe that this dying in spots is chiefly produced either by ill drainage or by some cause that arrests the extension of the tap-root downward in its search for water and moisture. The tap-root of the cotton-plant is known to penetrate many feet into the earth, and it is not at all improbable that an impervious stratum of clay, or of the limestone, may be reached by a large number of the plant-roots, or that a rock may be in the way of a single root, thus producing the decay of a large area of plants or of the single plant.

COTTON PRODUCTION IN TEXAS.

Analyses of the soils and subsoils of Texas.

Number	Name	Locality	County	Vegetation	Depth	...	Analyst
	OAK, HICKORY, AND PINE UPLANDS. 1. Gray sandy lands.						
1	Sandy soil	Near Texarkana	Bowie	Pine, oak, and hickory			R. H. Loughridge.
2	Yellow sandy subsoil	do	do	do			Do.
3	Sandy upland soil	Minesh.	Wood	do			J. R. Dorrett.
8	Light sandy soil	Near Troop	Smith	do			Do.
12	Light sandy subsoil	do	do	do			Do.
13	Sandy soil	McDade.	Bastrop	Post oak and hickory			H. McCalley.
17	Sandy upland soil	Cross timbers, Arlington.	Tarrant	Post and black-jack oak.			Do.
20	2. Red lands. Dark loamy subsoil	Upper cross timbers, Leon river.	Comanche	Red oak and hickory			J. R. Dorrett.
4	Red sandy subsoil	Palestine	Anderson	do			Do.
5	Red sandy soil	3 miles north of Luling.	Lee	No timber growth where taken.			G. E. Colby.
25	Dark pebbly soil.	Elmwood	Gonzales	Post oak and hickory			C. Cory.
24	BROWN AND BLACK LOAM PRAIRIE. Dark sandy prairie soil	2 miles west of Corsicana	Navarro	Open prairie.			C. Cory.
7	CENTRAL BLACK WAXY PRAIRIE. Black waxy soil	Near Tehuacana	Limestone	Open prairie.			J. R. Dorrett.
16	Black waxy subsoil	6 miles north of McKinney	Collin	do			H. McCalley.
27	Black sandy prairie soil	Wills' Point.	Van Zandt	do			R. H. Loughridge.
14	Black waxy prairie soil	1 mile west of Rusk.		do			H. McCalley.
15	do	South from Lampasas	Lampasas	do			R. H. Loughridge.
23	do	3 miles southwest of Waco.	McLennan	do			J. R. Dorrett.
22	SOUTHERN PRAIRIE REGION. Black prairie upland soil	8 miles northeast of Marlin.	Falls	Open prairie.			Do.
11	Black prairie soil	Chapel Hill	Washington	do			H. McCalley.
9	Sandy prairie soil.	Schulenberg.	Fayette	do			J. R. Dorrett.
10	Black waxy prairie soil.	Victoria.	Victoria	do			R. H. Loughridge.

	NORTHWESTERN RED LOAM REGION.																					
16	Red sandy soil	Jacksboro'	Jack	Mesquite prairie	10	74.945	8.651	83.596	0.425	0.103	0.125	0.882	0.150	5.050	5.076	0.095	0.047	......	*4.805	100.354	10.840	18 R. H. Loughridge.
	ALLUVIAL LANDS.																					
38	Red clay, first bottom soil.	Red river north of Cooke county.	Indian territory.	Cottonwood and hackberry.	12	63.765	6.618	72.383	0.405	0.030	2.933	2.623	0.085	4.681	8.361	0.156	0.020	1.707	6.998	100.282	9.982	28 J. B. Durrett.
39	......do	Red river north of Lamar county.	...do	......do	12	68.050	9.863	77.913	0.345	0.066	1.116	1.217	0.126	5.274	8.367	0.209	0.030	0.952	*4.906	100.521	9.566	28 Do.
40	Dark loam, second bottom soil.	.... do	...do	Ash and elm	12	76.580	9.100	85.680	0.404	0.069	0.466	0.619	0.169	3.296	3.246	0.163	0.077	......	*5.758	99.947	6.777	27 C. Cory.
25	Dark Trinity valley soil	2 miles west of Dallas	Dallas	Oaks, elm, and hickory	10	36.065	16.553	52.618	0.509	0.225	16.344	1.602	0.054	2.857	5.205	0.152	0.158	12.006	6.270	99.002	10.630	14 R. H. Loughridge.
19	Brazos valley soil	Granbury	Hood	Live and post oaks, pecan and sumac.	12	88.177	2.151	90.328	0.296	0.061	0.413	0.342	0.040	2.076	2.508	0.094	0.020	......	2.735	98.996	6.026	12 H. McCalley.
20	Brazos valley subsoil	......do	...do		12–20	75.570	4.496	80.068	0.582	0.217	0.326	0.669	0.010	2.873	10.580	0.109	0.056	......	3.676	100.155	11.219	10 Do.
18	Brazos bottom soil	4 miles west of Hearne	Robertson	Pin oak, ash, walnut and pecan.	10	69.391	11.291	80.682	0.258	0.084	2.050	0.604	0.100	3.454	3.589	0.370	0.290	1.047	*6.800	99.337	8.835	10 J. B. Durrett.
29	Red-loam soil	Oyster creek, east of Columbia.	Brazoria	Live oaks, elm, ash, hackberry, pecan, etc.	12	66.461	13.950	80.411	0.781	0.226	1.876	1.907	0.012	3.697	4.020	0.148	0.034	1.961	*4.042	99.116	8.420	12 R. H. Loughridge.
32	Black peach soil	San Bernard river, Columbia.	...do	Pecan, hackberry, live-oak, mulberry, and wild peach.	12	80.806	6.203	87.009	0.441	0.065	0.596	0.807	0.069	2.179	3.685	0.055	0.030	......	*5.748	100.504	5.980	13 Do.
28	Red valley soil	San Saba river	San Saba	Mesquite trees	10	77.617	4.547	82.[illegible]	0.507	0.197	3.971	0.990	0.078	2.949	2.665	0.281	0.067	2.356	4.412	100.637	7.290	12 Do.
23	Colorado valley soil	4 miles east of Austin	Travis	Pecan, elm, oak, and hackberry.	10	62.306	10.357	72.663	0.581	0.118	7.793	1.379	0.126	2.934	3.288	0.207	0.033	5.075	*5.028	99.225	7.570	10 Do.
24	Colorado valley cultivated soil.†	......do	...do	......do	8	87.088	4.654	91.742	0.393	0.077	0.459	0.447	0.106	2.068	2.042	0.086	0.026	Trace	2.376	99.824	3.700	18 Do.
22	Colorado valley virgin soil.	Bastrop	Bastrop	Open valley	10	71.082	12.275	83.357	0.444	0.168	0.675	0.090	0.152	3.068	6.291	0.258	0.208	......	5.028	99.730	9.164	14 J. B. Durrett.
37	Rio Grande valley soil	Near Brownsville	Cameron	Mesquite; few live-oaks	12	36.041	17.255	53.296	1.306	0.218	14.433	1.532	0.069	4.065	9.114	0.204	0.041	9.912	*6.008	100.229	12.754	12 G. E. Colby.

* See Humus table.

† Cultivated 40 years.

Determinations of humus and the available ingredients in some of the above soils (percentages referred to soils), by G. E. Colby, University of California.

Number.	Name.	Locality.	County.	Humus.	AVAILABLE— Inorganic.	Phosphoric acid.	Silica.
1	Sandy soil	Near Texarkana	Bowie	0.410	0.640	0.017	0.216
6	Red sandy soil	Six miles north of Lexington	Lee	0.740	1.472	0.036	0.640
12	Black sandy prairie soil	One mile south of Ennis	Ellis	2.250	2.010	0.040	1.184
33	Black waxy prairie soil	Eight miles southwest of Waco	McLennan	2.304	1.906	0.039	1.276
9	Sandy prairie soil	Pierce's junction	Harris	2.132	1.691	0.024	1.286
10	Black waxy prairie soil	Victoria	Victoria	2.754	4.002	0.036	2.844
16	Red sandy soil	Jacksboro'	Jack	0.898	0.460	0.014	0.208
39	Red clay, first bottom soil	Red river, north of Lamar county	Indian territory	0.982	1.450	0.051	0.682
40	Dark loam, second bottom soil	...do	...do	1.099	0.732	0.056	0.308
18	Valley soil	Brazos river, Granbury	Hood	1.016	0.740	0.035	0.485
29	Red-loam soil	Oyster creek, east of Columbia	Brazoria	0.714	0.585	0.034	0.214
32	Black peach soil	San Bernard river, Columbia	...do	2.658	1.226	0.055	....
23	Valley soil	Colorado river, east of Austin	Travis	1.688	1.579	0.041	0.592
37	Valley soil	Rio Grande river, Brownsville	Cameron	1.465	0.951	....	0.659

PART II.

AGRICULTURAL DESCRIPTIONS

OF THE

COUNTIES OF TEXAS.

AGRICULTURAL DESCRIPTIONS

OF THE

COUNTIES OF TEXAS.

The counties are described as a whole, and are grouped under the head of the agricultural regions to which each predominantly belongs with regard to the lands under cultivation. The regions naturally embrace small portions of many counties whose description properly belongs elsewhere, and in such cases the name of the county is given in the head list for each region, and marked with an asterisk (*), and is also given in the regular order in the text, with a reference to the region where its description may be found.

The arrangement of counties in each region is, as nearly as possible, in geographical order, beginning with the most northern; and this order is also maintained in the preliminary list for each region. The data at the head of each county description are derived from the reports of the present census.

Abstracts from reports of correspondents are appended to the description of each county from which such reports have been received. These give the more important data regarding the nature and productiveness of each soil of the county. Other information concerning the counties may be found in the tables at the beginning of this report.

RED RIVER ALLUVIAL COUNTIES.

(Comprise parts of Bowie, Red River, Lamar, Fannin, and Grayson.)

BOWIE.

Population: 10,965.—White, 6,628; colored, 4,337.
Area: 900 square miles.—Woodland, nearly all; Red river alluvial, all.
Tilled lands: 38,576 acres.—Area planted in cotton, 11,599 acres; in corn, 13,199 acres; in oats, 600 acres; in wheat, 7 acres.
Cotton production: 7,958 bales; average cotton product per acre, 0.69 bale, 1,035 pounds seed-cotton, or 345 pounds cotton lint.

Bowie, the extreme northeastern county of the state, is bounded by the Red river on the north and the Sulphur Fork on the south. Its surface is more or less rolling, and is well timbered with red, post, and black-jack oaks, hickory, and short-leaf pine on the uplands, interspersed with small open prairies in the central and western parts of the county. These prairies are very level, have a width of a mile or more and a stiff silty soil, and are not considered well adapted to cotton culture. Small clumps of trees appear on the prairies, and, together with those along the borders, are usually of low and stunted growth.

The soils of the timbered section are gray and sandy, and are from 12 to 18 inches in depth, underlaid by red and yellowish sandy subsoils (see analyses, page 24). These lands are not very much under cultivation, but yield when fresh about 800 pounds of seed-cotton per acre. In the western part of the county small mounds occur over the surface of the uplands, and mounds are also observed on the river uplands in the counties west, and in Galveston county, near the Gulf coast. In this county the mounds have the structure of the timbered uplands, viz, sandy soils and yellowish subsoils, and are from 15 to 20 feet in diameter, usually supporting the undergrowth of the region. The depressions between these mounds have a depth of several feet, with little or no shrubby growth, and are underlaid by an impervious clay. Water, when standing in these depressions, holds a white clay in suspension, thus assuming a white milky appearance.

The river lands are said to be several miles in width, have a red sandy or often clayey loam soil, and are somewhat subject to overflow in high water seasons. The timber grown comprises walnut, pecan, hackberry, ash, sweet gum, burr and red oaks, elm, cottonwood, cypress, dogwood, bois d'arc, wild plum, etc. The county is sparsely settled, and but a little more than 6.7 per cent. of the area is under cultivation, averaging 42.9 acres per square mile. Cotton acreage comprises 30.1 per cent. of the tilled lands, or 12.9 acres per square mile, and its yield per acre, 1,035 pounds, is greater than in any other county of the state except Cameron, due chiefly to the river bottom lands. A cotton-compress is located in Texarkana.

The chief soils of the county are those of the first and second bottoms of the Red river, the sandy timbered land of the uplands, and black prairies, and they are known to extend 60 miles east and west and more than the width of the county south of the Red river. The natural growth of this region on uplands is pine, red oak, hickory, black-jack, and post oak, and on creeks and rivers white oak, hackberry, swamp dogwood, and elm.

On the *uplands* the gray, coarse sandy and gravelly loam, 18 inches deep, alternates with bodies of stiff black prairie soil. Both kinds are early, warm, and well drained, but a little more difficult to cultivate in wet than in dry seasons. Cotton and corn are the chief crops of the region. Cotton is planted on one-half of the cultivated area, and usually attains a height of 3 feet, at which it is most productive; it inclines to run to weed in wet seasons, but may be restrained and boiling be favored by running a furrow by the side of the row. The seed-cotton product per acre of fresh land in an average season is 1,200 pounds, 1,545 pounds making a 475-pound bale of lint. After five years of cultivation the product per acre, ratio of seed to lint, and quality of the staple are about the same as at first, but the lands are most productive in the third year. Careless-weed and crab-grass are most troublesome as weeds here. Thirty per cent. of the lands first cultivated in this region now lie "turned out", and produce well only for one or two years when again cultivated. The soil washes and gullies readily on slopes, but no serious amount of damage is done to them, while the valleys are considerably improved by the washings. No efforts have been made to check the damage.

Farmers haul their cotton by wagon to Texarkana, at a cost of 75 cents per bale.

RED RIVER.

Population: 17,194.—White, 10,912; colored, 6,282.
Area: 1,060 square miles.—Woodland, greater part; oak, hickory, and pine region, 860 square miles; central black prairie, 200 square miles.
Tilled lands: 83,005 acres.—Area planted in cotton, 31,291 acres; in corn, 32,898 acres; in oats, 2,970 acres; in wheat, 1,044 acres.
Cotton production: 17,669 bales; average cotton product per acre, 0.56 bale, 840 pounds seed-cotton, or 280 pounds cotton lint.

Red River county lies between the Red river on the north and the Sulphur Fork on the south. Its surface is rolling, and comprises the black waxy and Cretaceous prairies on the south and timbered oak and hickory uplands thence to the bottom lands of the Red river. The prairie portion of the county is underlaid by white rotten limestone, the most easterly outcrop of which is seen about 4 miles east of Clarksville, the county-seat. There is an outcrop of Cretaceous marl and sand-rock at Kiamitia, on the Red River.

The bottom lands of the river consist of a "first bottom" of red sandy and clayey alluvial soil, about 10 or 15 feet above the overflowed bottom, and a much broader second bottom of a dark sandy loam 10 or 15 feet above the other. These lands have a large timber growth of walnut, ash, elm, etc., and a dense undergrowth of cane, etc. The river uplands form a broad belt of lands timbered with post oak and hickory, and have a gray sandy soil and clay subsoil. The belt is rolling, and apparently much higher than the prairies on the south, and reaches in width from the river to within 5 miles of Clarksville.

In the eastern part of the county, on the border of the prairies, the black and stiff clays that form the soils of the latter are covered by the sands and gravel of the timbered region, thus becoming the subsoils or underclays; a feature observed in the cuts in the railroad for some distance.

Of the area of the county 12.2 per cent. is under cultivation, with an average of 78.3 acres per square mile, the remainder being still unimproved. Corn is the chief crop. Cotton acreage comprises 37.7 per cent. of the tilled lands, or an average of 29.5 acres per square mile. Its yield per acre is much above that of the state at large. The rich bottom lands of the Red river, which yield an average of a bale per acre, are probably the cause of this result.

The lowlands consist of the alluvial plains of the first and second bottoms of the Red river, and the uplands of stiff black prairie and sandy timbered lands.

The chief soil is the *black upland prairie*. It covers one-third of the uplands of the county, and is a stiff black clayey loam from 1 foot to 20 feet below the surface. The chief crops of the region are cotton and corn; but the soil is best adapted to cotton, to which one-third of the cultivated portion is devoted. The usual and most productive height attained by the cotton-plant is 4 feet, but excessive rains on all soils here incline the plant to run to weed, for which there is no remedy. The average seed-cotton product per acre is 1,200 pounds, 1,720 pounds making a 475-pound bale of lint, which rates in the market as middling. After five years' cultivation there is no change in the amount per acre or the quality of the product. The most troublesome weeds are cocklebur, crab-grass, and morning-glories. Very little of any of the lands once cultivated now lie "turned out". A few years' rest make it almost as good as when fresh. The slopes of all the uplands are liable to serious damage by the washing and gullying of their soils, but the washing does not injure the valleys, and no efforts have been made to check it.

The soil of *Red river bottom* is a fine and coarse sandy, reddish loam, bearing a growth of oak, pecan, cottonwood, bois d'arc, walnut, and willow. Its color extends from 6 inches to 10 feet below the surface, and at that depth it is underlaid by clay. This soil is easily tilled in any season, and when well drained is early and warm. It is apparently best adapted to corn and cotton, and half of its cultivated area is planted in cotton. The plant attains a height of from 5 to 10 feet. The product per acre of fresh land is from 1,400 to 2,000 pounds of seed-cotton, the ratio of seed to lint and quality of the staple being the same as on the upland soils, and alike on fresh or old land. After five years' cultivation the product is 1,600 pounds of seed-cotton per acre. Crab-grass is the most troublesome weed.

The soil of the *timbered upland* embraces about two-thirds of the uplands of the county, and is covered with a timber growth of oak and hickory. It is a sandy and gravelly loam 4 inches deep, underlaid by clay, which in turn is underlaid by sand and gravel. Tillage is always easy, and the soil being early, warm, and well drained, is apparently best adapted to potatoes, fruits, and vegetables. One-fourth of it is planted in cotton. The plant attains a height of 5 feet, at which it is usually most productive. The seed-cotton product per acre is from 700 to 1,200 pounds, and after five years' cultivation it is from 300 to 800 pounds. The troublesome weed is crab-grass.

Most of the cotton of this county is raised on Red river bottom lands and on black prairie lands. The best crops are made on these lands in the driest seasons we have. The black uplands need more rain.

Cotton is shipped, as baled, to Saint Louis, New Orleans, or Galveston, at $4 25 to $4 50 per bale.

LAMAR.

Population: 27,193.—White, 20,445; colored, 6,748.
Area: 900 square miles.—Woodland, nearly one-half; oak, hickory, and pine region, 400 square miles; central black prairie, 500 square miles.
Tilled lands: 123,533 acres.—Area planted in cotton, 40,390 acres; in corn, 40,617 acres; in oats, 5,651 acres; in wheat, 3,047 acres.
Cotton production: 24,623 bales; average cotton product per acre, 0.61 bale, 915 pounds seed-cotton, or 305 pounds cotton lint.

Lamar county is bounded on the north by the Red river and on the south by the north prong of the Sulphur Fork, the Texas and Pacific railroad marking the divide between their tributaries. The surface is rolling, and, as in other counties of the belt, comprises three classes of land—Red river bottoms, sandy timbered uplands along both rivers, and the black prairies of the central prairie region on the south of Paris. The river lands are broad, and include the first and second bottoms as already described in Red River and Bowie counties. (See analyses, page 43.)

The uplands of Red river have a width of 10 or 15 miles, are high and rolling, and are timbered with a growth of post and black-jack oaks, hickory, etc. The soil is sandy and underlaid by clayey subsoils, and is locally known as "wire-grass lands". The timbered lands of Sulphur Fork have a width of 5 or 6 miles. The prairies cover a large part of the county with their heavy, black waxy, and hog-wallow soils, and are generally devoted to stock-grazing, the light and easily tilled sandy lands being preferred for farming purposes.

About 21.4 per cent. of the county area is under cultivation, giving an average of 137.3 acres per square mile. The crops are chiefly corn, cotton, rye, oats, wheat, vegetables, and fruit. Cotton has the largest acreage, and comprises 32.7 per cent. of the tilled lands, or 44.9 acres per square mile. Its yield per acre in 1879 was exceeded only by two counties in the state (among those whose production is more than 100 bales), viz, Bowie and Brazoria. The average yield of corn is said to be 30 bushels per acre, and of wheat 20 bushels. Fruits do well in the timbered uplands on the north.

Farmers usually sell their products to buyers in Paris, the county-seat, who ship it thence by railroad to other markets.

FANNIN.

Population: 25,501.—White, 22,081; colored, 3,420.
Area: 890 square miles.—Woodland, about one-fourth; oak, hickory, and pine region, 230 square miles; central black prairie, 660 square miles.
Tilled lands: 156,725 acres.—Area planted in cotton, 44,813 acres; in corn, 48,124 acres; in oats, 9,698 acres; in wheat, 7,753 acres.
Cotton production: 22,386 bales; average cotton product per acre, 0.50 bale, 750 pounds seed-cotton, or 250 pounds cotton lint.

The surface of Fannin county is undulating, and is watered by numerous small streams, the tributaries of Red river, Sulphur Fork on the north and east, and of the Trinity river on the south. About one-third of its area is timbered with walnut, post oak, elm, ash, bois d'arc, etc., the rest being an undulating prairie, with black waxy and sandy lands, and having no timber growth except a few scattering oaks. On the north of the county the first and second bottoms of Red river have a width of from 1 mile to 2 miles and a heavy timber growth of walnut, pecan, ash, hackberry, mulberry, cottonwood, etc., the first having a deep soil of a red waxy nature, or a red sand in localities, and the second or hummock land, 10 or 15 feet higher, having a dark loam soil and a greater width. Adjoining these bottoms on the south are high uplands from 10 to 15 miles wide, timbered with oak and hickory, and having a sandy soil and clayey subsoil, with white quartz gravel and pebbles. There is a little open and sandy prairie on these uplands. These lands are called "wire-grass lands". South from this are the open prairies and black lands of the central prairie region. Immediately adjoining the timbered lands the prairie soils are dark sandy, but the subsoils are the usual stiff clays of the region.

A little more than one-fourth of the area of this county is under cultivation, the average being about 176.1 acres per square mile. The remainder of the county is in its original condition. Corn is the chief crop of the county, cotton being next, with an average of 50.4 acres per square mile, or 28.6 per cent. of the tilled lands. The average yield per acre for the county was in 1879 quite high. Corn on the lowlands is said to yield as much as 50 bushels per acre; on the uplands from 15 to 25 bushels; wheat 15, and oats from 40 to 50 bushels per acre.

ABSTRACTS FROM THE REPORTS OF JOHN L. BLAIR, OF HONEY GROVE, AND THOMAS LIGHTFOOT, OF BONHAM.

The soils of this region endure either wet or dry seasons very well. The climate is favorable, the seasons are sufficiently long, and the region is not liable to insect pests. The most unfavorable circumstance is a very wet season. The largest yields of cotton are produced in dry, hot summers. The river bottoms are planted in cotton almost exclusively, and are owned by "planters"; for small cereals they are too low.

The kinds of soil cultivated in cotton are black waxy prairie, black coarse sandy loam, and light, fine sandy soil, timbered and prairie.

The *black waxy prairie* extends 13 miles north and south and 30 miles east and west, and along the streams are narrow belts of timber, consisting of bois d'arc, elm, ash, and hickory. The soil maintains its color to depths varying from 2 to 10 feet, about one-half of which rests upon a soft white stone, down to which there is no change in its quality, the other half having a subsoil of heavy red clay that is seldom touched by the plow. The soil is warm, generally well drained, easily cultivated, and apparently best adapted to corn, cotton, and oats; wheat is also one of the crops of the county. Cotton occupies three-tenths of the cultivated portion of this soil. The plant usually attains a height of 4 feet, but is most productive at 3 feet. When allowed too much space, and in wet seasons, the plant inclines to run to weed, but may be restrained by topping and by drawing the soil from the plant. The seed-cotton product per acre of fresh

719

land is 1,000 pounds, 2,100 pounds making a 475-pound bale of lint, which rates in the market as ordinary. After ten years' cultivation the product is from 800 to 900 pounds per acre, and 2,140 pounds make a 475-pound bale. Buyers here make no distinction as to quality of staple. The most troublesome weeds on this land are cocklebur and crab-grass.

The *black sandy loam soil* covers one-fifth of the county, and lies on either side of the black waxy soil for a width of 3 miles and through the length of the county. It has a natural growth of bois d'arc, post oak, hickory, pecan, and elm. The soil changes color at 2 inches from the surface; the subsoil is a buff-colored leachy clay, containing rounded pebbles, underlaid by sand and gravel at 3 feet. The soil is early, warm, and well drained, easy to cultivate at any time, and is apparently best adapted to cotton, which comprises one-half the cultivated area. The plant usually attains the height of 5 feet, but is most productive at 4 feet. The seed-cotton product per acre of fresh land is 1,900 pounds, 1,650 pounds making a 475-pound bale of lint. After ten years' cultivation the product is 600 pounds, and 1,780 pounds then make a 475-pound bale of lint, which rates much lower than that from fresh land. The worst weed is crab-grass. About one-twentieth of this land originally cultivated now lies "turned out"; it is very much improved by rest. The soil on slopes washes and gullies readily, and serious damage results to them, but not to the valleys. Successful efforts are made to check the damage by hillside ditching and horizontalizing.

The *light sandy soil* covers three-tenths of the county, and embraces a tract 9 miles wide and 30 miles long. Its natural growth is post and black oaks and wild grape-vines. The soil is 10 inches deep; the subsoil is heavier but leachy, and contains hard white gravel pebbles, underlaid by gravel at 3 feet. The soil is well drained and easily tilled, but is late and cold, and is apparently best adapted to orchards and grasses. One-tenth of it is planted in cotton, the plant usually attaining a height of 2 feet. The seed-cotton product per acre is 300 pounds when the land is fresh, but after ten years' cultivation the soil is exhausted. Nineteen hundred pounds make a 475-pound bale of lint. Crab-grass, the most troublesome weed, grows luxuriantly on this soil, one-fourth of which has been exhausted, "turned out," and not again cultivated. The slopes are seriously damaged by washing and gullying; the valleys are not injured. Unsatisfactory attempts have been made to check the damage by horizontalizing and hillside ditching.

Cotton is shipped in December, by rail, to Saint Louis and Galveston, at $4 50 per bale.

ABSTRACT FROM THE REPORT OF GIDEON SMITH, OF BONHAM.

The lands of the county embrace the first and second bottoms of Red river and hummocks of the lowlands, and sandy timbered lands and black waxy prairies of the uplands. There is still another variety of upland, known as "wire-grass" lands, a medium between black waxy and sandy, combining the bad qualities of both and not much of their good ones. The Red river bottom lands, both waxy and sandy, comprise about one-half of the lands of this region. Their natural growth is cottonwood, pecan, black walnut, hackberry, mulberry, and white hickory.

The chief crops of this county are cotton, corn, and all the small cereals. All fruits, especially apples, do well.

The soils of the *bottoms* comprise both light sandy and heavy clay loams about 10 feet in depth. The lands are easily tilled, and are best adapted to cotton, which covers about one-fourth of the land under cultivation. The plant grows to a height of 6 feet, and runs to weed in wet seasons, which can be prevented by frequent plowing. The seed-cotton product per acre is from 1,000 to 2,000 pounds both on the fresh land and after twenty-five years' cultivation. The staple from old lands is not quite so silky or long, and is a little rougher to the touch than that from fresh lands. The troublesome weeds are all the varieties of careless-weed, purslane, hog-weed, and bur-grass. None of the lands lie "turned out", as they are thought to improve by continued culture, especially if the stalks, etc., are not burned. This applies also to other lands of the county.

The "*wire-grass*" lands, covering about one-third of the area of the county, comprise both a high and low grade of farming land, and have a natural growth of post, black-jack, and red oaks, elm, some hickory, hackberry, etc. The soil is a gray sandy loam, 6 inches or more in depth. The subsoil is generally lighter in color and heavier than the surface soil. The larger portion has no subsoil, there being only a gradual fading of color; some is leachy, but the greater part is impervious. It contains white gravel and rounded angular pebbles. The subsoil is underlaid by sand, gravel, and occasionally by rock at from 1 foot to 10 feet. The soil is usually easily tilled, and is best adapted to corn and cotton, and one-sixth of the land under cultivation is devoted to the latter crop. Cotton usually attains a height of from 2 to 5 feet, being most productive at from 3 to 4 feet. Running to weed is prevented by thorough draining and frequent plowing. The seed-cotton product per acre is from 800 to 1,200 pounds, and from 1,425 to 2,400 pounds make 475 pounds of middling lint. The weeds troublesome on this soil are careless, purslane, hog, wild flax, and yellow-blossom. A very small amount of this land lies "turned out". The soil washes considerably on the slopes, and is becoming seriously damaged; but the valleys are not yet injured by the washings, and but little has been done to check it.

The "*wire-grass*" and *post-oak flats* (lime points) comprise about one-tenth of the county, and considerable of it is of a high grade and is fair farming land; most of it, however, is more valuable for grazing than for anything else. The natural growth is post, black-jack, and some red oaks and elm. The soil is heavy, soapy, and putty-like, varying in depth from 1 inch to 24 inches. The subsoil is lighter in color and more tenacious than the soil, some of it leachy and much of it impervious, and contains hard and soft black gravel on the high points, where it is somewhat limy, underlaid by sand and gravel, and occasionally by rock. The land is easily tilled in wet weather, but in dry seasons it bakes hard. It is early, warm, and much of it is well drained, and it is better adapted to cotton than to any other crop. About one-twentieth of the land is devoted to cotton, which usually attains a height from 1 foot to 2 feet, but produces best at 18 inches. The seed-cotton product per acre is from 300 to 1,000 pounds, and from 1,540 to 1,800 pounds make a 475-pound bale. The staple from fresh soil rates as low middling in the market. Regular and moderate seasons suit the crop best; if too wet or too dry the plant is injured. Much of the land improves with cultivation. The weeds troublesome to this soil are wild flax, yellow-blossom, and crab-grass. A considerable amount of this land lies "turned out". The soil washes or gullies readily on the slopes, and this is considered rather an advantage, by affording drainage. Much of this land is known as flatwoods, flat post-oak land, and flat prairie. Cattle, horses, and hogs do well on it.

The climate is most favorable to cotton production. Crops are not liable to be troubled by insects, boll-worms, and caterpillars, and yet there is sufficient time for maturity. Much of the soil is favorable to extreme wet or dry seasons, as all the river lands, though level, possess a large absorbing power, holding all the water which falls on them, and still are free from swamp or seepy land. The same may be said of the uplands where undulating, especially of the black and waxy, of which there is a large percentage. We succeed now in raising quite abundant crops—from 40 to 60 bushels of corn and generally 500 pounds of cotton lint, and occasionally as much as 1,000 pounds of lint are the yields per acre; but these yields can be increased by planting every third or fourth row of the cotton crop in corn; if every third row, the corn will bear crowding to the extent of holding as much in one row as is ordinarily here put in three.

GRAYSON.

Population: 38,108.—White, 33,549; colored, 4,559.

Area: 960 square miles.—Woodland, about one-third; oak, hickory, and pine region, 140 square miles; central black prairie, 660 square miles; lower cross timbers, 160 square miles.

Tilled lands: 185,532 acres.—Area planted in cotton, 41,339 acres; in corn, 56,344 acres; in oats, 10,009 acres; in wheat, 15,736 acres.

Cotton production: 19,166 bales; average cotton product per acre, 0.46 bale, 690 pounds seed-cotton, or 230 pounds cotton lint.

Grayson county comprises open black prairie, timbered uplands, and Red river alluvium. The general level of the country is about 700 feet above the sea; its surface is undulating, and is almost entirely susceptible of tillage.

The southern part of the county, comprising perhaps three-fourths of its area, is an open prairie, broad and undulating, without timber, except on the streams, which are not numerous. The soil is of the black waxy nature peculiar to the central prairie region, except near the timbered lands, where it is more sandy. These prairies are mostly given up to stock-grazing, with only occasional farms.

Immediately north of the prairies there is a belt of timbered uplands lying along and parallel with the river bottoms and having a growth of post, red, and black oaks, hickory, etc. The soil is sandy, with some ferruginous gravel and a yellowish sandy subsoil, and is underlaid by a hard limestone at a depth of a few feet.

The river bottoms north of Denison are 1 mile wide, and are composed of a first bottom of a deep red sandy soil, heavily timbered, and a second bottom, or hummock, of a dark sandy loam, extending back to the foot of the bluff, where it becomes black and somewhat waxy and calcareous, from the rotten limestone that outcrops in the abrupt bluffs. The timber growth is cottonwood, elm, ash, walnut, pecan, hackberry, etc. These lands are rich and productive, yielding, it is claimed, fully a bale per acre. In this county the uplands seem to be preferred. Rotten limestone is the prevailing rock throughout the county, and Cretaceous fossils are abundant in many localities.

The lands under cultivation comprise 30.2 per cent. of the county area, averaging 193.3 acres per square mile; but four counties in the state have a greater percentage. Corn is the chief crop of the county, its acreage being greater than that of any other, cotton ranking next, with an average of 43.1 acres per square mile, or 22.3 per cent. of tilled lands. The average yield of crops other than cotton on the river bottoms is: corn, from 25 to 40 bushels; wheat, 18 to 20 bushels; oats, 50 bushels per acre.

ABSTRACTS FROM THE REPORTS OF M. T. BRACKETT AND J. P. HOPSON, OF SHERMAN.

The lands are very fertile, and we have the long and sunny months, so necessary for the production of cotton. The first bottom of Red river is a red sandy loam from 6 to 10 feet deep. Cotton is raised chiefly on the uplands, which consist of the black waxy prairie soil and black, fine sandy and gravelly loam.

The *black waxy soil* covers from one-half to two-thirds the area of this region, and extends 100 miles east, 150 west, 60 south, and 10 miles north. It is chiefly prairie, bearing only grass. The depth from the surface to the change of color in the soil varies from 6 to 48 inches. The subsoil is a yellowish clay, mixed with white limestone gravel, and occasionally with pebbles. It is an impervious hard-pan, and is underlaid by blue and white rock at from 5 to 20 feet. Tillage is difficult in wet but easy in dry seasons; the soil is early, cold, and well drained, and endures drought well. The chief crops produced in this region are cotton, corn, wheat, oats, barley, sweet potatoes, and sorghum; but the soil is apparently best adapted to cotton, wheat, sorghum, and oats. One-fourth of the cultivated area is planted in cotton, the usual and most productive height attained by the plant being 5 feet. In very wet seasons, especially in July and August, the plant inclines to run to weed, which may be restrained by taking off the top bud when a sufficient height is attained. The average product of seed-cotton per acre is 1,200 pounds, and 1,775 pounds make a 475-pound bale of lint, which rates in the market as middling. After ten years' cultivation the product is about 800 pounds per acre, the ratio of seed to lint being the same and the staple finer and stronger, but not so long as that from fresh land. The most troublesome weeds are the Canadian thistle, crab-grass, careless-, and rag-weeds. No land that has been cultivated lies "turned out". The soil washes and gullies but little on slopes, but they are not yet seriously damaged, nor are the lower lands much injured by the washings.

The *fine sandy and gravelly loam* covers one-fourth the area of this region, but occurs in rather small bodies, and bears a natural growth of post, red, and black oaks, hickory, hackberry, ash, pecan, and walnut. The soil is dark, 12 inches thick, and its yellow subsoil is an impervious hard-pan, containing soft, white, angular fragments, underlaid by yellow sand and gravel and white rock at 6 feet. The soil is early, warm, well drained, and easily tilled in any season, and one-half of its area is devoted to cotton. The usual and most productive height of the plant is 3 feet. The seed-cotton product per acre is about 1,250 pounds, equal to about 400 pounds of lint, which rates in the market as middling. The staple from old land is finer, if anything, but the ratio of seed to lint is the same as in the case of fresh land. The most troublesome weeds are cockleburs and crab-grass. The surfaces of slopes readily wash into gullies, but no serious damage is done, and no efforts are made to check it.

Cold rains in the early part of the season check the growth of cotton on the bottom land and sometimes give it the sore-shin; but this is not common unless planted early.

Cotton is shipped as soon as baled, by rail, to New York at $5 per bale, and to Galveston at $4.

OAK, HICKORY, AND SHORT-LEAF PINE REGION.

(Comprises all or parts of the counties of Bowie,* Red River,* Lamar,* Fannin,* Cass, Morris, Titus, Franklin,. Hopkins, Rains, Wood, Camp, Marion, Upshur, Gregg, Harrison, Panola, Rusk, Smith, Van Zandt, Kaufman,* Henderson, Navarro, Limestone, Freestone, Anderson, Cherokee, Nacogdoches, Shelby, Sabine, San Augustine, Angelina, Trinity, Polk, Houston, Leon, Falls,* Robertson, Madison, Walker, San Jacinto,* Grimes, Waller,* Brazos, Burleson, Milam, Lee, Bastrop, Caldwell,* Fayette,* Washington,* Austin,* Colorado,* Lavaca,* Gonzales, Guadalupe,* Bexar,* Wilson, De Witt,* Goliad,* Bee,* Karnes,* Atascosa,* Frio,* and Medina.* *Lower cross timbers.*—Cooke,* Grayson,* Denton,* Tarrant,* Dallas,* Johnson,* Hill,* and McLennan.* *Upper cross timbers.*—Montague,* Wise,* Parker,* Palo Pinto,* Hood,* Erath,* Comanche,* and Hamilton.* All of the above cross timbers counties, except Comanche, are described in the central black prairie region; Comanche,. in the northwestern red-loam region.)

BOWIE.
(See " Red river alluvial region".)

RED RIVER.
(See " Red river alluvial region".)

LAMAR.
(See " Red river alluvial region ".)

FANNIN.
(See " Red river alluvial region".)

CASS.

Population: 16,724.—White, 10,274 ; colored, 6,450.
Area: 950 square miles.—Woodland, all; oak, hickory, and pine region, all.
Tilled lands: 83,069 acres.—Area planted in cotton, 34,822 acres; in corn, 34,410 acres; in oats, 3,188 acres; in wheat, 363 acres.
Cotton production: 16,181 bales; average cotton product per acre, 0.46 bale, 690 pounds seed-cotton, or 230 pounds cotton lint.

The surface of Cass county is somewhat rolling and broken. It is bounded on the north by the Sulphur Fork, flowing eastward, and, with its small tributaries, watering that part of the county. The streams on the south flow southeast into Caddo lake. Tertiary iron-ore hills are reported to be numerous, especially on the south of Linden, the county-seat, where much of the country is too broken for cultivation.

The soils of the uplands vary from the gray to red sandy, with areas of white sands, underlaid very generally by red sandy or, in places, by clayey subsoils. Cass county is well timbered with oak, hickory, and short-leaf pine, and while principally an agricultural county, only about 13.7 per cent. of its area is under cultivation, averaging 87.4 acres per square mile. Cotton and corn are the chief crops, the acreage of the former being somewhat the larger, comprising 41.9 per cent. of the tilled lands, or 36.7 acres per square mile. The seed-cotton yield per acre in 1879. was much above the average of the state, and compares very favorably with the best of the upland counties-

ABSTRACT FROM THE REPORT OF J. J. FOWLER, OF LINDEN.

The surface of the county is quite varied, comprising hilly, rolling, and level lands. The uplands occur in tracts containing from 50· to 1,000 acres each. The soils devoted to the cultivation of cotton may be classed as red lands (forming about one-half of the area of the county), the gray lands, and the white sandy lands.

The timber growth of the *red lands* is pine, black and white oaks, and dogwood, and the depth of the soil varies from 18 inches to 4 feet. The subsoil is similar to the surface soil, but somewhat heavier. The land is easily cultivated, and is early, warm, and well drained. Cotton, corn, sweet potatoes, pease, and pinders (peanuts) constitute the chief crops. About three-fourths of the land is devoted to cotton, which varies in height from 3 to 6 feet; the best yield is obtained at 4½ feet. There is in wet seasons a tendency of the plant to run to weed, which can be restrained by cultivation. On fresh land from 1,000 to 1,500 pounds of seed-cotton may be produced per acre; after ten years' cultivation this yield is reduced to from 500 to 1,000 pounds, the staple remaining the same as when the land was fresh. The most troublesome weed on this soil is crab-grass. One-fifteenth of this land lies "turned out", producing good crops when again cultivated. The valleys are improved by the washing of the soil on slopes, and the uplands are not injured.

The *gray lands* are devoted to cotton and corn, and the timber growth is pine and dogwood. The soil, a gray sandy loam, covering about one-fifth of the surface of the county, is from 3 to 5 feet deep, overlying a red sandy subsoil. It is easily cultivated, is early, warm, and well drained, and best adapted to cotton, which forms three-fourths of the entire crops. The height of the plant ranges from 3 to 5 feet, the latter being the most productive. In production, etc., this soil is similar to the one just described.

About one-sixth of the tillable area is composed of the *white sandy soil*, having a depth of from 6 to 10 feet, with a light red subsoil, the natural growth being pine and black-jack oak. It is easily tilled, is early, warm, and well drained, and best adapted to cotton. Cotton comprises three-fourths of the crops, which attains a height of from 3 to 5 feet, the latter being preferred. The yield from fresh land is from 1,000 to 1,800 pounds. The production of this soil, after ten years' cultivation, is similar to that of soils previously mentioned. Crab-grass is the most troublesome weed. The soil washes readily on slopes, doing serious damage, but the valleys are not injured. About one twentieth of this land lies "turned out", producing very well when again cultivated.

Shipments are usually made in October by railroad to Galveston and Saint Louis.

MORRIS.

Population: 5,032.—White, 2,988; colored, 2,044.
Area: 260 square miles.—Woodland, all; oak, hickory, and pine region, all.
Tilled lands: 29,160 acres.—Area planted in cotton, 10,650 acres; in corn, 11,082 acres; in oats, 1,256 acres; in wheat, 275 acres.
Cotton production: 4,880 bales; average cotton product per acre, 0.46 bale, 690 pounds seed-cotton, or 230 pounds cotton lint.

Morris is one of the smallest counties of the state, and is bounded on the north by the Sulphur river, while the small streams of the southern portion flow eastward into Caddo lake. The surface of the country is more or less rolling and well timbered with oak, hickory, and short-leaf pine, the latter growth prevailing chiefly on the south of the county-seat. The uplands are sandy and gravelly, with some red clayey soils, and are underlaid usually by red clays. The bottom lands are stiff and dark, partly subject to overflow, and have a timber growth of white oak, walnut, sweet gum, etc. Morris is chiefly an agricultural county, the lands under tillage comprising 17.5 per cent. of its entire area, and averaging 112.2 acres per square mile. Corn and cotton are the principal crops, the acreage of the latter being the smallest, viz, 41 acres per square mile, or 36.5 per cent. of the tilled lands. The average yield per acre in seed-cotton in 1879 was 690 pounds, which was surpassed by only a few counties in the state.

ABSTRACT FROM THE REPORT OF JAMES M. BAKER, OF WHEATVILLE.

Crops rarely fail in this region; but cotton is sometimes injured by excessive rains in July and August, causing it to shed its forms, and by cool nights in April, May, and June.

The chief soil cultivated in cotton is a *dark red, sandy and gravelly, rolling, timbered upland*, and embraces very nearly the southern half of the county. Its natural growth is red, black-jack, white, and post oaks, hickory, sumac, and some pine south and east of Daingerfield. The soil is 2 feet deep; the subsoil is a very red, firm, impervious clay, sometimes yellowish, with white streaks, termed "calico clay". It contains hard, rough, "black gravel" (rich red iron ore), underlaid in the northern part of the county by hard limestone at from 1 foot to 12 feet. Tillage is very easy in dry and very difficult in wet seasons, and the soil is in most localities well drained and apparently well adapted to corn, cotton, potatoes, pease, peanuts, chufas, watermelons, and squashes, these, excepting the two last named, with sugar-cane, constituting the chief crops of this region. One-half the cultivated area is planted in cotton, which usually attains a height of 4 feet, at which it is most productive; but it inclines to run to weed in wet weather and when cultivated with the turning plow, to restrain which and favor bolling plowing should be stopped and the hoe freely used. The seed-cotton product per acre is from 1,000 to 1,200 pounds, the staple rating as low middling. After ten years' cultivation the product per acre is from 800 to 1,000 pounds, and 1,545 pounds then make a 475-pound bale of lint, the staple being generally shorter than that from fresh land. Hog-weeds, red careless-weeds, and a large weed resembling the rag-weed are the most troublesome. Very little of such land originally cultivated now lies "turned out", and for a while it is as good as fresh when again cultivated. Slopes are damaged to a serious extent by washing and gullying, and the valleys are sometimes seriously damaged by the washings. Efforts have been made to check the damage, and with success when continued.

The *bottom lands* of White Oak river, comprising about one-fourth of the cultivated area, subject to overflow in spring and considered unhealthy, are covered with a natural growth of white, post, and overcup oaks, hickory, black walnut, and sweet gum. The soil is black, stiff, and tenacious when wet, and from 10 to 15 feet deep. The subsoil is heavier, of a grayish color, inclined to be chalky, and is underlaid by limestone at from 6 to 20 feet. Tillage is generally difficult in wet or dry seasons. The soil is late and cold, and most always ill drained, and is apparently best adapted to cotton, corn, and sugar-cane, about two-thirds of its cultivated area being devoted to cotton. The plant usually attains a height of from 5 to 8 feet, but is most productive at 5 or 6 feet, and inclines to run to weed in dry and hot weather. The seed-cotton product per acre is from 1,500 to 2,000 pounds, rating low middling; after ten years' cultivation the product varies from 1,800 to 2,500 pounds, and the staple is then about the same as that from fresh land. The cocklebur and sheep-sorrel are the troublesome weeds. Very little of such land lies "turned out"; it is improved 25 per cent. by washings from the slopes.

Cotton is shipped chiefly in December, by rail, to Texarkana and Jefferson at $1 25 per bale.

TITUS.

Population: 5,959.—White, 4,609; colored, 1,350.
Area: 420 square miles.—Woodland, nearly all; oak, hickory, and pine region, all.
Tilled lands: 30,507 acres.—Area planted in cotton, 9,395 acres; in corn, 11,379 acres; in oats, 1,997 acres; in wheat, 372 acres.
Cotton production: 4,923 bales; average cotton product per acre, 0.52 bale, 780 pounds seed-cotton, or 260 pounds cotton lint.

Titus county is very similar in many of its features to the counties adjoining it on the east. The difference is chiefly in the absence of a pine growth and the occurrence on the northwest of the first of the dark-loam prairies that are found interspersed throughout the timbered lands near the border of the central black prairie region.

Sulphur Fork forms the northern and Big Cypress creek the southern boundary of the county, while White Oak creek flows parallel to the former on the north. The uplands are rather level, and, except near the streams, have a dark sandy soil, and are well timbered with oaks and hickory. The alluvial lands of the streams have a timber growth of elm, sycamore, birch, sweet gum, etc. Titus is chiefly an agricultural county, the lands under tillage comprising about 11.3 per cent. of its entire area, averaging 72.6 acres per square mile. Of these 30.8 per cent., or 22.4 acres, is devoted to the culture of cotton, and 37.3 acres to that of corn.

The average yield in seed-cotton for 1879 was 780 pounds, an amount exceeded by only 12 counties in the state, and 7 of those have each a production of less than 100 bales.

ABSTRACT FROM THE REPORT OF J. W. JACKSON, OF MOUNT PLEASANT.

The lowlands consist of the first and second bottoms of creeks and rivers; the uplands of large bodies of level timbered lands (a little broken near streams), generally all tillable. The growth of cotton is sometimes hindered on lowlands by excessive rains in spring, and sometimes the crop is prematurely frost-killed on such land in the fall.

The chief cotton-producing soil is the *black sandy upland*, which embraces three-fifths of the lands at present cultivated in this county, and extends over the entire county, excepting a small strip of black prairie in the northwestern corner. Its natural timber is hickory, and red, black, post, and black-jack oaks. The soil is a blackish and black fine sandy loam 8 or 10 inches thick; the subsoil is a tenacious dark red clay, which bakes if moved while wet, but pulverizes and mixes beneficially with the soil if plowed while moderately dry, and contains soft "black gravel", underlaid by gravel and sometimes by rock at the depth of 2 feet. Tillage is always easy, and the soil is early and warm when well drained and deeply plowed. The chief crops of this region are corn, cotton, wheat, oats, potatoes, sugar-cane, sorghum, tobacco, rice, and pease. The soil is equally well adapted to all, but cotton occupies from one-third to one-half of this soil. The plant attains a height of from 4 to 6½ feet, but is most productive at from 4 to 5 feet when proper distances are allowed between plants. If the soil has not been stirred well until the plant is far advanced, and the rainfall then becomes excessive, the plant is inclined to run to weed. To prevent this and to favor bolling the soil should be well tilled; then, if the season becomes wet, break the roots on one side of each row with a scooter-plow, and five or six days later break those on the other side. The product per acre of seed-cotton is from 1,000 to 1,200 pounds, 1,500 pounds making a 475-pound bale of lint, which rates as first class in market. After ten years' cultivation the product is from 800 to 1,000 pounds, and to make a 475-pound bale of lint then requires 1,465 in a dry season or 1,495 pounds in a wet season, and the staple is a little shorter and coarser than that from fresh land. The most troublesome weeds on all soils of this region are cocklebur, careless-weed, rag-weed, hog-weed, and crab-grass. About one forty-fifth of this land once cultivated now lies "turned out", and this is on hillsides, where the soil has been washed away; but from one-half to two-thirds of a crop may be raised from such lands if in the preceding fall a green crop be turned under. Slopes wash and gully readily where the subsoil consists of joint clay or sand; but as sands are very deep, the damage is very trifling to slopes, and very little damage, if any, is done to the valleys. Hillside ditches have occasionally been made to check such washings, and with complete success. The same is true of slopes of the remaining two kinds of land.

The *bottom land of the small streams* is a dark sandy loam, a little heavy, and having a growth of hickory, pecan, birch, white, pin, and burr oaks, walnut, and gum. The soil is a black loam, somewhat heavy, from 12 to 24 inches deep. The subsoil is stiff, impervious when undisturbed, very tenacious, varying in color from brownish to bluish-gray, containing soft, rounded "black gravel", and is further underlaid by grayish-blue clay. Tillage is easy when dry, somewhat difficult when too wet, but when broken early is quite easy and pleasant. The soil is early and warm when well drained and deeply plowed, and is best adapted to cotton, corn, small cereals, sugar-cane, and pease. From one-third to one-half the soil is occupied by cotton. The plant attains the height of from 5 to 7 feet, and is most productive at from 4 to 5 feet if proper distance is allowed between the rows. If the soil be well prepared and after-cultivation be thorough, the plant inclines to run to weed in June during good seasons; this is restrained as on the soil last described. The seed-cotton product per acre is from 1,200 to 1,800 pounds; after ten years' cultivation (unmanured) the product is from 1,000 to 1,500 pounds, or more if rotation of crops has been regularly practiced. The ratio of seed to lint and quality of the staple are as on the soil last described.

The *bottom lands of the larger streams*, viz, White Oak, Cypress, and Sulphur creeks, lie in scattered bodies throughout the county, including some prairie and low bottom soils. Its growth is white, post, burr, and pin oaks, hickory, walnut, elm, gum, linden, and mulberry. The soil is a rather dark, stiff clayey loam from 12 to 24 inches thick, and is underlaid by a heavier subsoil of bluish-yellow, tenacious clay, usually fine and waxy, and impervious when undisturbed; it contains "black gravel" nearly as soft as the subsoil itself, and is underlaid by a clay resembling soapstone. This soil is easily tilled in dry seasons if broken deep and early, but with some difficulty in wet seasons; if well drained it is early and warm, but if ill drained it is late and cold, and is best adapted to corn, cotton, and pease. The proportion planted, height attained, circumstances of running to weed, etc., are the same as on the other bottom land described. The seed-cotton product per acre is from 1,000 to 1,500 pounds, 1,500 pounds making a 475-pound bale of lint, which rates as first class. After ten years' cultivation the product is from 1,000 to 1,200 pounds, and 1,550 pounds make a 475-pound bale of second-class lint, the same being shorter and coarser than that from fresh land. None of this soil lies "turned out".

Merchants ship cotton by rail to Galveston at $3 50, to Saint Louis at $4, or to New Orleans by water at $1 50 per bale.

FRANKLIN.

Population: 5,280.—White, 4,666; colored, 614.
Area: 300 square miles.—Woodland, all; all oak, hickory, and pine region.
Tilled lands: 25,528 acres.—Area planted in cotton, 8,660 acres; in corn, 9,804 acres; in oats, 1,519 acres; in wheat, 489 acres.
Cotton production: 4,048 bales; average cotton product per acre, 0.47 bale, 705 pounds seed-cotton, or 235 pounds cotton lint.

Franklin is one of the tier of counties that are bounded on the north by the Sulphur Fork and watered by White Oak and Big Cypress creeks. Its surface is rather level, except near the streams, where it becomes more or less rolling and broken. The uplands are timbered with red, post, and black-jack oaks. hickory, etc., and have a dark sandy soil, underlaid by heavy clay subsoils. The bottom lands are dark and stiff in character, and have a timber growth of white oak, walnut, ash, elm, pecan, etc. The crops of the county are corn, cotton, small grain, and potatoes. Lands in cultivation comprise 13.3 per cent. of the county area, or 85.1 acres per square mile.

Corn is the chief crop of the county, its acreage being larger than that of cotton, and its average yield from 15 to 20 bushels per acre.

Cotton comprises about one-third of the tilled lands, and averages 28.9 acres per square mile. The general character and productiveness of the lands, the methods of tillage, etc., are the same as described by the correspondents for Titus and Hopkins counties.

Shipments are made by wagon to the nearest railroad stations.

HOPKINS.

Population: 15,461.—White, 13,306; colored, 2,155.

Area: 750 square miles.—Woodland, about three-fourths; oak, hickory, and pine region, 620 square miles; central black prairie region, 130 square miles.

Tilled lands: 85,792 acres.—Area planted in cotton, 19,242 acres; in corn, 25,573 acres; in oats, 7,974 acres; in wheat, 3,804 acres.

Cotton production: 8,279 bales; average cotton product per acre, 0.43 bale, 645 pounds seed-cotton, or 215 pounds cotton lint.

Hopkins county is about equally divided between prairie and timbered lands, the latter occupying the eastern half. The surface of the prairie lands is undulating, while that of the rest is rather rolling.

The water-divide between the tributaries of the Red and those of the Sabine river passes through this county in an easterly course. These tributaries furnish an abundant supply of water to portions of the county, the south prong of the Sulphur Fork forming the northern boundary.

The prairie lands seem to be devoted to grazing purposes, although they have partly the rich black clayey soil of the central prairie region. Their difficult tillage probably makes them less desirable than the sandy lands of the timbers. Other parts of these prairies have a stiff, gray land, not well adapted to tillage.

The timbered lands have a grayish sandy soil, easily cultivated and very productive, yielding about 700 pounds of seed-cotton per acre. Corn is the chief crop of the county, its yield being an average of 12 bushels per acre; that of oats is 20 bushels, and of wheat 5 bushels per acre.

The county is rather sparsely settled, the average being about 20.6 persons and 114.4 acres of tilled lands per square mile. The cotton acreage per square mile is about 25.7, or 22.4 per cent. of the tilled lands, and is confined chiefly to the sandy timbered lands.

ABSTRACT FROM THE REPORT OF B. M. CAMP, OF SULPHUR SPRINGS.

One-half the county consists of stiff, gray, rolling prairie land. The timbered half has a deep, gray, sandy, alluvial soil, and embraces mostly the uplands, together with the bottoms of small streams. It is commonly designated *deep sandy land*, and is the chief soil cultivated in cotton. Two thirds of the cultivated land is of this kind, and it extends 25 miles east, 50 miles south, and half-way across the county to the north and west. Its natural growth is post, red, and black-jack oaks, and briery underbrush. The soil is from 6 to 12 inches deep. The subsoil is lighter, contains a few pebbles in places, and is underlaid by sand, gravel, or rock at various depths. The soil is early, warm, well drained, easily cultivated, and is well adapted to cotton, oats, and vegetables. The other important crops of this region are corn, wheat, sweet potatoes, Irish potatoes, rye, barley, peas, melons, etc. Cotton occupies one-third of the cultivated portion of this soil. Good stands of cotton are obtained, and the soil is earlier and endures drought better than the prairie. The cotton-plant grows from 4 to 5 feet high, but is more productive at 4 feet. It inclines to run to weed in wet weather, the remedy for which consists in dwarfing the plant by deep, close plowing, so as to cut off side roots. On fresh land the seed-cotton product per acre is from 800 to 900 pounds, and 1,650 pounds make a 475-pound bale of lint, which rates in market as middling or good middling. After ten years' cultivation the product is from 700 to 800 pounds, and 1,550 pounds make a bale. The staple from old land is shorter in dry seasons, but the same in wet seasons as from fresh land. The most troublesome weed is crab-grass. None of this land lies "turned out". The soil on slopes washes and gullies readily, but no serious damage is yet done, and no efforts have been made to check the washings, which greatly benefit the lower lands.

The *black waxy prairies*, covering one-half of the county, usually suffer from drought. They have a hard and close soil, and are late, cold, and difficult to till. They produce about 800 pounds of seed-cotton per acre.

Cotton is shipped by rail as fast as baled to Galveston at $4, or to Saint Louis and New Orleans at $4 75.

RAINS.

Population: 3,035.—White, 2,785; colored, 250.

Area: 270 square miles.—Woodland, greater part; oak, hickory, and pine region, 200 square miles; central black prairie region, 70 square miles.

Tilled lands: 16,137 acres.—Area planted in cotton, 4,399 acres; in corn, 5,477 acres; in oats, 1,055 acres; in wheat, 553 acres.

Cotton production: 1,915 bales; average cotton product per acre, 0.44 bale, 660 pounds seed-cotton, or 220 pounds cotton lint.

Rains county has a rolling surface, well timbered with oak and hickory, and is bounded on the south by the Sabine river. The Lake fork of the river flows eastward in the northern part of the county.

The uplands are mostly sandy, with clayey subsoils, and are interspersed on the eastern border of the central black prairie region.

The bottom lands of the river are heavy and stiff waxy clays, heavily timbered with ash, walnut, white oak, etc. They are very difficult to till, somewhat liable to overflow, and are not much under cultivation. The uplands are easily tilled, and yield from 700 to 800 pounds of seed-cotton per acre, the average for 1879 being greater than that of the state at large.

Nearly one-tenth of the county area is under cultivation, the average being 59.7 acres per square mile. Of this latter 16.3 acres are devoted to the culture of cotton. The crops of the county are corn, cotton, oats, wheat, potatoes, etc., the first having the largest acreage, and yielding from 12 to 15 bushels per acre. The methods of cotton culture, improvement of lands, etc., are the same as described in the adjoining counties.

Cotton is shipped by wagon to the nearest railroad station, and thence to markets, or is sold to local buyers.

WOOD.

Population: 11,212.—White, 8,653; colored, 2,559.

Area: 700 square miles.—Woodland, all; all oak, hickory, and pine region.

Tilled lands: 48,786 acres.—Area planted in cotton, 15,486 acres; in corn, 18,635 acres; in oats, 2,801 acres; in wheat, 2,282 acres.

Cotton production: 7,381 bales; average cotton product per acre, 0.48 bale, 720 pounds seed-cotton, or 240 pounds cotton lint.

Wood county lies on the north side of the Sabine river, and is watered by its tributaries, except on the extreme north, where the streams flow northeast and form Big Cypress creek.

The surface of the country is quite level and well timbered, embracing several kinds of land. On the east the soil is gray and sandy, with yellow sandy subsoil, the short-leaf pine being the most prominent growth. On the north there are areas of red or chocolate-colored sandy lands, with clay subsoils, and this is said to be the best farming section of the county. (See analyses, page 26.) Sabine river, on the south, has wide bottom lands of stiff waxy clays, heavily timbered, and subject to overflow. There are second bottom lands in some localities, covered with a dense cane growth, that are above overflow and very productive.

These river lands are bordered on the east by a belt of level uplands of unproductive lands known as glades. They consist of a fine silty, impervious material, of much depth, in whose depressions ponds of water stand for a large part of the year. They have a timber growth chiefly of post oak. This belt is from 10 to 100 yards in width, and extends from 15 to 20 miles along the river. The uplands of this part of the county are level and covered with a deep sandy soil, and have a timber growth of post, red, and black-jack oaks, hickory, and sumac.

Wood is an agricultural county, and 10.9 per cent. of its area is under cultivation, with an average of 69.7 acres per square miles; of the latter 22.1 acres are devoted to the culture of cotton.

The average yield per acre in seed-cotton for the county was in 1879 much greater than that for the state at large.

ABSTRACT FROM THE REPORT OF J. H. NEWSOM, OF MINEOLA.

The lands devoted to the cultivation of cotton comprise the light gray ashy soil and a dark loam of the second bottom of the creeks, red gravelly loam mostly on the divides or high lands, and the coarse white sandy soils.

About two-thirds of the surface of the county is covered by a *light gray ashy soil*. It has a depth of 18 inches, and is underlaid by a yellowish clay. This bakes when turned up wet and exposed to the sun, but if stirred up when moist it becomes like the surface soil. It contains some pebbles and white gravel. The natural growth of this land is hickory, smooth-leaf black-jack, and thin-bark post oaks. It is early and warm when well drained, and not difficult to cultivate, being best adapted to cotton, though producing cotton, corn, and oats. About four-tenths of the land is devoted to the first named, which grows to a height of from 3 to 6 feet, being most productive at 4 feet. Topping is the remedy applied to restrain the plant from running to weed, which happens in June and July, when the season is very wet. The yield of seed-cotton per acre is, when the land is fresh, 1,600 pounds; three years' cultivation reduces this product to 1,200 pounds, and the staple is not quite as good; 1,775 pounds from fresh and 1,550 from old lands make 475 pounds of lint. Crab-grass, associated with lamb's-quarter and careless- and rag-weeds, gives much trouble. About 5 per cent. of this land now lies "turned out", but it is almost as good as fresh when again taken in. The washing from the slopes is prevented to some extent by hillside ditching and by underdraining.

The *red lands* have a growth of black-jack and rough hickory and a depth of 1 foot, and are underlaid by lighter subsoil, free from gravel, overlying red sandstone at 4 feet. These lands constitute about one-sixth of the cultivated lands of the county, and are early, warm, well drained, and easily cultivated. The soil is best adapted to corn and wheat, though one-third of the crops consists of cotton. This grows to a height of 4 feet, yielding 2,000 pounds of seed-cotton when the land is fresh and 1,600 pounds after three years' cultivation, 1,650 pounds being requisite for a 475-pound bale. The staple from old land rates better than that from fresh, the amount then needed for 475 pounds of lint being 1,600 pounds. The most troublesome weeds on this land are cocklebur and lamb's-quarter. The land washes readily, doing serious damage to the slopes, but not to the valleys.

The *coarse, white, sandy soils* have a growth of red-leaf black-jack, blue-jack, and post oak, and grape-vines, and a depth of .10 feet. The subsoil is heavier, and is mixed with a yellow clay. The soil is late, cold, and well drained. It is best adapted to oats, pease, and watermelons, very little cotton being produced. Twelve hundred pounds of seed-cotton per acre may be obtained when the land is fresh, and 500 after three years' cultivation, 1,550 pounds from fresh and 1,300 from old lands being needed for 475 pounds of lint, the staple remaining the same. Owing to the above decrease in the yield after cultivation one-half of the land lies "turned out". The most troublesome weeds are bear-grass, yellow-bloom, mullen, and bull-nettle.

The uplands are generally preferred to the lowlands, because on the latter there is a greater tendency of the cotton-plant to run to weed, thus causing rot in the bottom fruit; also, the worm attacks the bottom lands first. The timber growth on bottoms is white hickory, walnut, cherry, etc.

Shipments are made, as soon as the cotton is baled, by rail from Mineola to New York, freight being $5 75 per bale.

CAMP.

Population: 5,931.—White, 3,085; colored, 2,846.

Area: 200 square miles.—Woodland, all; all oak, hickory, and pine region.

Tilled lands: 33,257 acres.—Area planted in cotton, 11,473 acres; in corn, 11,369 acres; in oats, 1,544 acres; in wheat, 824 acres.

Cotton production: 5,689 bales; average cotton product per acre, 0.50 bale, 750 pounds seed-cotton, or 250 pounds cotton lint.

Camp is one of the smallest counties in the state. Its surface is rolling and well timbered with oak, short-leaf pine, and some hickory. It is watered by Big Cypress creek and small tributaries flowing east into Caddo lake, on the Louisiana line.

The lands are a sandy loam, dark from decayed vegetation, and having red and yellow subsoils more or less sandy. The county is well populated, and a little more than a fourth of its area is under cultivation. Of the latter 57.4 acres are devoted to the culture of cotton. But three counties surpass it in cotton acreage per square mile, Washington, Fayette, and Johnson. The crops of the county are cotton, corn, oats, cane, etc. The lands are

easily tilled and produce well, yielding from 750 to 900 pounds of seed-cotton, 15 to 20 bushels of corn, or 18 to 20 bushels of oats per acre. That of cotton for 1879 was much greater than the average for the state. The methods of culture do not differ materially from those in practice in the adjoining counties.
The railroads afford easy transportation to markets, though the cotton is mostly sold to local buyers.

MARION.

Population: 10,983.—White, 3,759; colored, 7,224.
Area: 420 square miles.—Woodland all; all oak, hickory, and pine region.
Tilled lands: 36,978 acres.—Area planted in cotton, 17,102 acres; in corn, 13,554 acres; in oats, 565 acres; in wheat, 13 acres.
Cotton production: 7,515 bales; average cotton product per acre, 0.44 bale, 660 pounds seed-cotton, or 220 pounds cotton lint.
The county of Marion borders Louisiana on the east. Its surface is rolling, and is well timbered with short-leaf pine, oak, and hickory. The bottom lands of the streams, and those that border Caddo lake, have a timber growth of cypress, ash, walnut, cedar, etc.
Iron ore occurs in some of the hills, and furnaces were at one time erected for its reduction. The lands of the county comprise the dark sandy loams of the lowlands and the gray sandy soils of the uplands, interspersed with large bodies of red land, derived from iron ore and ferruginous sandstone. The subsoils of most of the soils consist of red or yellow clays, more or less sandy, and at depths of from 6 to 10 inches from the surface. The lands of the bottoms yield from 1,000 to 1,200 pounds of seed-cotton per acre. Those under cultivation comprise 13.8 per cent. of the county area, and average 88 acres per square mile. They are easily tilled, and produce good crops of corn, oats, cotton, sugar-cane, potatoes, fruits, and vegetables. Cotton is the chief crop of the county, with an average of 40.7 acres per square mile, or 46.2 per cent. of the tilled lands, and an average yield in good seasons of from 600 to 800 pounds in the seed per acre. Its yield for the dry year of 1879 was 660 pounds.
Jefferson, the county-seat, affords a market for cotton, whence it is shipped by rail to Saint Louis, Houston, or Galveston, or by boat to Shreveport and New Orleans.

UPSHUR.

Population: 10,266.—White, 6,884; colored, 3,382.
Area: 520 square miles.—Woodland all; all oak, hickory, and pine region.
Tilled lands: 58,063 acres.—Area planted in cotton, 19,418 acres; in corn, 20,728 acres; in oats, 2,517 acres; in wheat, 1,425 acres.
Cotton production: 8,023 bales; average cotton product per acre, 0.41 bale, 615 pounds seed-cotton, or 205 pounds cotton lint.
The surface of Upshur county is rolling and well timbered, and is watered by the Sabine river on the south and by other streams that flow eastward into Caddo lake. Tertiary iron ores and sandstones occur in some parts of the county, forming a part of the belt that passes southwest toward San Antonio. Two ranges of hills, separated by the waters of Little Cypress creek, a tributary of Caddo lake, are said to extend from the center to the boundary-line of Harrison county. The soils of the upland are mostly gray sandy loams, interspersed with red sandy lands, and underlaid by reddish clays. Their timber growth is principally red, black, and black-jack oaks, hickory, and short-leaf pine. The bottom lands consist of loamy soils, black with decayed vegetation, very fertile, and having a heavy timber growth of walnut, elm, pin oak, and sweet gum. The uplands seem to be preferred for cotton, because of the greater ease in tillage and the more rapid maturity of the crop.
The tilled lands of the county comprise about 17.4 per cent. of its area, or 111.7 acres per square mile, and of this about one-third, or an average of 37.3 acres per square mile, is devoted to cotton culture. The yield per acre of this crop is a little over the average for the state. Corn is the chief crop of the county, and yields an average of from 12 to 15 bushels per acre; wheat, 7 to 10 bushels per acre.

ABSTRACT FROM THE REPORT OF J. M. GLASCO, OF GILMER.

The surface of the county is rolling, and is covered with a growth of pine, red, black, black-jack, and post oaks, and hickory. The only soil fit for cultivation is a *dark fine sandy loam*, 18 inches deep, underlaid by a dark red clay, changing to a light red. Under this at from 10 to 20 feet is a clay stratum impervious to water. These sandy uplands cover about two-thirds of the county, the rest being low hills, with stiff unproductive land, called "clay-galls". The chief crops of the county are corn, cotton, oats, sweet potatoes, and peas. About one-half of the land under cultivation is devoted to cotton. Its usual height is 3½ feet, running to weed when the season is showery and warm without heavy rains. Topping and close plowing are the remedies applied to restrain it. The product of seed-cotton per acre from fresh land is 1,000 pounds, 1,500 pounds making 475 pounds of lint, which rates as low middling. Eight years' cultivation reduces the yield to 600 pounds per acre, the staple then rating as good ordinary. Crab-grass is the only weed that occasions trouble. No land lies "turned out"; it washes readily on slopes, doing serious damage unless care is taken to prevent it.
Saint Louis is the usual shipping point, to which the cotton is sent in December and January, the rate being $4 50 per bale.

GREGG.

Population: 8,530.—White, 3,817; colored, 4,713.
Area: 280 square miles.—Woodland, all; all oak, hickory, and pine region.
Tilled lands: 38,585 acres.—Area planted in cotton, 13,767 acres; in corn, 13,411 acres; in oats, 827 acres; in wheat, 22 acres.
Cotton production: 4,590 bales; average cotton product per acre, 0.33 bale, 495 pounds seed-cotton, or 165 pounds cotton lint.

The surface of Gregg county is rolling, and is well timbered with short-leaf pine and oak on the uplands and sweet gum, walnut, ash, white oak, etc., on the streams. Sabine river flows with an easterly course through the southern part of the county, and has but a few small tributaries.

The lands of the uplands are gray and sandy, with red and yellow sandy and clayey subsoils. They are easily tilled, and produce an average of from 500 to 700 pounds of seed-cotton per acre. Their pine growth is largely utilized for lumber by the many saw-mills of the county.

The bottoms of the Sabine river are a stiff, waxy clay soil, very difficult to till, heavily timbered, and mostly subject to overflow.

The lands of the county under cultivation comprise 21.5 per cent. of its area, an average of 137.8 acres per square mile, the principal crops being cotton, corn, oats, vegetables, etc. Cotton has the largest acreage, the average being 49.2 per square mile, or 35.7 per cent. of the tilled lands.

The methods of culture, etc., do not differ materially from those used in the adjoining counties.

Shipments are made by railroad to the north or south.

HARRISON.

Population: 25,177.—White, 7,976; colored, 17,201.
Area: 900 square miles.—Woodland, all; all oak, hickory, and pine region.
Tilled lands: 126,462 acres.—Area planted in cotton, 46,614 acres; in corn, 38,808 acres; in oats, 765 acres; in wheat, 18 acres.
Cotton production: 17,619 bales; average cotton product per acre, 0.38 bale, 570 pounds seed-cotton, or 190 pounds cotton lint.

The surface of Harrison county is rather rolling, and in some places broken. On the south it is watered by Sabine river and its small tributaries, while on the north a number of streams flow into Caddo lake.

The soils of the county are mostly gray sandy loams, varied occasionally with red and gravelly lands, and well timbered with post, red, and black-jack oaks, hickory, and short-leaf pine. The subsoils are sometimes heavy red clays, though more generally a yellowish sand.

Sandstones and brown coals or lignites are reported as underlying the lands of the county at depths of from 20 to 40 feet.

The bottom lands of Little Cypress creek and Caddo lake are said to be from 2 to 3 miles wide, and are mostly marshes, on which water stands for half of the year. Their soils are black and stiff, and they have a timber growth of pin and overcup oaks, short-leaf pine, and cypress. Along the borders of the lake are found "blue-jack" oaks and myrtle thickets.

The uplands of the county are the chief cotton lands, and a yield of 800 pounds of seed-cotton per acre is claimed for them. In fair seasons and with proper cultivation this is probably correct, as the average yield for the entire county in the droughty year of 1879 was 570 pounds, an average much below that of the adjoining counties for the same year. Harrison is principally an agricultural county, nearly 22 per cent. of its area, or 140.5 acres per square mile, being under tillage. The crops consist of corn, cotton, small grain, tobacco, vegetables, fruits, and grapes. Cotton is the chief of these, its acreage comprising 36.9 per cent. of the lands under cultivation, and averaging 51.8 acres per square mile, a number exceeded by only seven counties in the state.

ABSTRACTS FROM THE REPORTS OF W. T. WARE AND H. V. SENTELL, OF JEFFERSON, W. J. CAVEN, OF MARSHALL, AND THOMAS STEELE, OF ELYSIAN FIELDS.

When the lowlands or river and creek bottoms are well drained they are preferred for cotton, because they endure drought better and produce more per acre. They are, however, generally late, and ill drained, and far more expensive to reduce to a tillable state than is the case with uplands. Cotton on the lowlands is also liable to be prematurely frost-killed. The uplands are therefore preferred, and they produce abundant returns for the labor bestowed upon them. The climate here is well suited to cotton production.

The uplands vary from level to broken, and from red gravelly to gray soils of varying depths, and occur in available spots of from 10 to 50 acres. The chief soils cultivated in cotton are the uplands; next to these are the creek bottoms, the lower and broader bottoms of the larger streams being overflowed much of the time.

The *gray sandy lands*, lying mostly in the northern part of the county, have a natural growth of pine, post, red, black-jack, and black oaks, and hickory. The soil is a fine gray sandy loam from 1 foot to 2 feet in depth. The subsoil in some places is red clay, in others a mixture of red and yellow clay, and sometimes yellow sand; and where clay is the subsoil sand is found at from 10 to 40 feet, replaced sometimes by a variety of lignite. The land is easy to till at all times, and is early, warm, and well drained.

Cotton and corn, some oats, pease, and potatoes constitute the chief crops of the county, the soil being best adapted to cotton, which occupies about two-thirds of the tillable area, the plant averaging about 4 feet in height; on fresh land from 5 to 7 feet is attained. The most productive height is from 2½ to 3 feet, as there are then more bolls in proportion to the height. In excessive wet seasons there is a tendency of the plant to run to weed; also, when closely crowded in drills and rows. In the former case topping and good cultivation are the remedies resorted to to restrain the running to weed; in the latter case, allowing greater distance between the rows and keeping the land well drained. On fresh land the product per acre in seed-cotton is from 1,000 to 1,200 pounds; after ten years' cultivation, where the land is level, 800 pounds; where rolling, 600 pounds, and from 400 to 600 pounds after the land has been under cultivation for thirty-five years. The rating of the staple from fresh land is from good middling to fair, that from old land being one grade lower, the fiber being shorter. The seed is smaller on old land. Crab-grass and cockleburs are the most troublesome weeds of any importance. From 15 to 33 per cent. of the land lies "turned out", growing up in scrub or old-field pine and persimmon. It is improved by rest, and sometimes produces as much as 700 or 800 pounds per acre, especially when not badly washed. The soil washes to some extent, doing serious damage in some places. Low marshy valleys are very greatly improved by the washings, sometimes doubling their original value. In some places the valleys are injured as much as 15 or 20 per cent. No appreciable efforts have been made to prevent the washing of the soil, and the ditches soon fill up with sand.

The *red gravelly lands* have a natural timber growth of red, post, white, and black-jack oaks, hickory, persimmon, walnut, buckeye, and numerous other varieties. The soil is a heavy gravelly clay loam, about 6 inches deep, with a heavier subsoil, mixed with sand in places; also found very stiff and almost impervious in others. The subsoil contains hard "black gravel", and is underlaid by sand, gravel, and rock at a depth of from 1 foot to 5 feet. In wet seasons there is no difficulty in tillage, but when seasons are dry it becomes hard. The soil is best adapted to cotton, which occupies one-half the cultivated area. Corn is also quite productive on fresh land, which often yields as much as 25 bushels per acre. Cotton is usually from 3 to 4 feet in height, producing best at about 3 feet. The plant inclines to run to weed if too closely crowded in drills and rows, and if the soil is too wet this may be remedied by giving a greater distance in drill and rows and by keeping the land well drained. The seed-cotton product per acre on fresh soil is from 1,000 to 1,200 pounds. The lint rates as good middling. After ten years' cultivation the seed-cotton product per acre is from 800 to 900 pounds, about 1,355 pounds then making a 475-pound bale of lint, and the staple is shorter and seed not so large as that from fresh land. Crab-grass is the most troublesome weed on this soil. About one-tenth of such land originally cultivated now lies "turned out", and where the top soil has not been entirely washed off it makes fair crops. The soil washes and gullies readily on the slopes, and in places is injured, and the valleys are sometimes injured to the extent of perhaps 10 per cent. Very little has been done to check this damage, but the success was good as long as it was practiced.

The soil of *bottoms of creeks* and smaller streams is a blackish clayey loam, having an average of 24 inches in depth, and resting upon a subsoil in various places of blue, yellowish, light brown, and red clays, adhesive, close, and impervious when undisturbed, and free from rock of any kind. Tillage is difficult in wet seasons, but easy in dry if well broken before the ground is too dry. This soil covers about an eighth of the county, and bears a natural growth of white, red, water, post, and pin oaks, sweet and black gums, bitter pecan, hickory, red elm, chincapin, maple, and papaw. The greater part of such soil is late, cold, and ill drained. When well drained, it is well adapted to growing corn, cotton, and sugar-cane. Cotton is planted on two-thirds of the cultivated part of this land. The usual height attained by the plant is from 6 to 8 feet, but it is most productive at from 5 to 6 feet. (The inclination to weed and the remedy are as on soil first described.) The seed-cotton product per acre is 1,500 pounds, about 1,485 pounds being required for a 475-pound bale of lint rating as strictly good middling. After ten years' cultivation the product varies from 1,300 to 1,500 pounds, 1,495 pounds then making a bale of 475 pounds; the staple is very little shorter and the seed is smaller. The troublesome weeds are crab-grass and cocklebur, the latter growing very rapidly. None of this land lies "turned out" for the usual cause, but some parts are sometimes abandoned because they are flooded, and these floodings sometimes damage fields by leaving deposits of sand.

The *bottom lands* of the lake and larger streams are from 2 to 3 miles wide, and have a growth of pin and overcup oaks, pine, and cypress in the marshes, and blue-jack and myrtle thickets along the borders of Caddo lake. The soil is partly a black, stiff clay loam, very little of which is cultivated, being under water half the year. There are spots of from 1 acre to 10 acres each of blackish, sandy land, more or less wet, which has been drained and leveed, and is fine for cultivation. The soil has a depth of about 10 feet, with a clay subsoil, and is best adapted to cotton. The yield is from 700 to 800 pounds of seed-cotton per acre, and from 500 to 600 pounds after ten years' cultivation. The most troublesome weeds are crab-grass and bull-nettles.

Farmers usually haul their cotton to Jefferson or Shreveport, from whence it is shipped to New Orleans, via Red river, at $2 per bale.

PANOLA.

Population: 12,219.—White, 7,284; colored, 4,935.
Area: 800 square miles.—Woodland, all; all oak, hickory, and pine region.
Tilled lands: 71,946 acres.—Area planted in cotton, 28,480 acres; in corn, 27,452 acres; in oats, 1,825 acres; in wheat, 44 acres.
Cotton production: 10,344 bales; average cotton product per acre, 0.36 bale, 540 pounds seed-cotton, or 180 pounds cotton lint.

Panola county is divided into two parts by the Sabine river, which flows in an irregular southeast course. Its surface is gently rolling or undulating and well drained by numerous small streams tributary to the river. The lands are mostly gray sandy loam soils on the uplands, with yellowish and red clayey subsoils, and are well timbered with short-leaf pine, oak, and hickory, the former predominating. Extensive long-leaf pineries occur in the county, interspersed with hard timber growth.

The bottoms have a stiff black soil and subsoil and a growth of ash, elm, sweet gum, walnut, cypress, and magnolia. They are more or less subject to overflow, and are not much under cultivation.

The tilled lands of the county comprise about 14.1 per cent. of its area, or 89.9 acres per square mile, and of all the crops corn has the largest acreage, and has an average yield of 7 bushels per acre; wheat, 10 bushels. The cotton acreage is 39.6 per cent. of the tilled lands, or an average of 35.6 acres per square mile.

The river is navigable for small boats during a part of the year, and shipments can be made south to Beaumont, and thence either by boat or railroad to New Orleans or Galveston.

ABSTRACT FROM THE REPORT OF H. FYKE, OF CARTHAGE.

The uplands are rather undulating, comprising both level and rolling lands. The greater part of the agricultural region is composed of a light gray, fine sandy loam, 8 inches deep, overlying a yellowish, leachy, clayey subsoil. The natural growth is red, post, and black oaks, hickory, and pine. The soil is late, warm, well drained, and easily cultivated at all times. The chief productions are cotton and corn, the former being best adapted to the soil. About three-fifths of the crops is in cotton, which usually attains a height of 3½ feet, too much moisture tending to cause it to run to weed. When the land is fresh, 800 pounds of seed-cotton can be produced per acre; 500 pounds after sixteen years' cultivation. The lint rates as good middling, the rating of the staple from old land being one grade lower. The most troublesome weed is crab-grass. There is not enough land "turned out" to be estimated. The soil washes to some extent, but occasions no serious damage.

Cotton is sold to local merchants.

RUSK.

Population: 18,986.—White. 10,807; colored, 8,179.
Area: 920 square miles.—Woodland, all; all oak, hickory, and pine region.
Tilled lands: 99,714 acres.—Area planted in cotton, 38,326 acres; in corn, 39,744 acres; in oats, 2,965 acres; in wheat, 123 acres.
Cotton production: 11,145 bales.—Average cotton product per acre, 0.29 bale, 435 pounds seed-cotton, or 145 pounds cotton lint.

The surface of Rusk county is rolling and hilly, and is well timbered with oak, hickory, and short-leaf pine. The mast, which is very abundant, serves largely for food for hogs.

On the north the county is watered by the tributaries of the Sabine river, while on the south the small streams flow into the Angelina river.

The soils are gray, sandy, and more or less gravelly, interspersed with bodies of red clay lands, all having a red or yellowish clay subsoil. Some of the hills have large deposits of Tertiary iron ores and sandstones, and a good quality of lignite or brown coal is reported as occurring 10 feet below the surface near Henderson, the county-seat.

Rusk is an agricultural county chiefly, its tilled lands comprising about 16.9 per cent. of its entire area, or 108.4 acres per square mile, while corn has a larger acreage than any other crop. Cotton ranks next, with an average of 41.7 acres per square mile, or 38.4 per cent. of the lands under cultivation. There are only 13 counties in the state having each a greater cotton acreage in proportion to its area. Its product per acre for 1879 was very small, 435 pounds of seed-cotton.

ABSTRACTS FROM THE REPORTS OF C. B. RICHARDSON, OF HENDERSON, AND J. D. WOODWARD, M. D., OF OVERTON.

The soils of the county comprise gray and red sandy uplands and the dark first and second bottom of the streams.

The *light, fine sandy, gray loam* covers about half the area of the uplands, and lies chiefly in the northeastern half of the county. Its chief natural growth is white, red, post, and black-jack oaks, pine, chincapin, dogwood, and gum. The soil is from 12 to 18 inches thick, and has a subsoil of hard yellow clay, which stands in the wall of a well without curbing of any kind. It is further underlaid in the vicinity of Henderson by potter's clay, and still further by sand at 18 feet in some localities. Tillage is easy in all seasons, and the soil is early, warm, and well drained. The chief crops of this region are cotton, corn, small cereals, Irish and sweet potatoes, sugar-cane, pease, and a great variety of fruits and vegetables. All succeed well on this soil, but about one-half its cultivated area is planted in cotton. The usual and most productive height attained by the plant is 3½ feet. If planted late, it is inclined to run to weed in wet seasons, the remedy for which consists in planting early and throwing dirt from the row when wet periods begin. The seed-cotton product per acre varies from 800 to 1,200 pounds, from 1,425 to 1,485 pounds making a 475-pound bale of middling to good middling lint. After five years' cultivation (unmanured) the product varies from 600 to 1,000 pounds, the ratio of seed to lint and the quality of staple, which depends upon the manner of handling, being about the same. Crab-grass and cockleburs are the most troublesome In 1865 one-third of this land lay "turned out"; it is now all fenced, and new land in addition. Land lying out does not improve when closely grazed, but does if kept under fence. Slopes are damaged to a serious extent by washing and gullying. In some cases the washings carried down upon the lowlands damage them to the extent of from one-third to one-half their value. New land is so cheap that very little effort is made to save the old; it is customary, however, to make hillside rows horizontal.

The *yellow and orange red gravelly loam*, chiefly in the southwestern half of the county, is 15 inches deep. This soil is more difficult to cultivate in wet seasons, and endures cultivation longer. In all other details it is like the soil last described.

The soil of the *bottom lands* of the Sabine river and creeks includes about one-fourth of the county area. Its natural growth is white, red, post, and overcup oaks, hickory, ash, maple, and muscadine vines. The soil is a fine, sandy, gray and blackish loam, 18 inches deep, underlaid by a compact yellow clay subsoil. Tillage is easy in dry but difficult in wet seasons, and the soil is late, cold, and ill drained in its natural condition. It is apparently best adapted to corn and cotton, and one-half of its improved area is planted in cotton. The usual and most productive height of the plant is 4 feet. The seed-cotton product per acre of fresh land is 1,200 pounds, or 1,100 pounds after five years' cultivation. This soil deteriorates less rapidly than the others mentioned, and sometimes such land is damaged by the washing away of the banks of creeks, or by the deposit of washings from overflowing waters. Straightening of the creek beds by cutting large ditches has been a successful remedy. Bur- and crab-grass are the most troublesome weeds.

Warm, dry springs are favorable, and wet, cool springs and hot, dry weather in July and August are disastrous to both corn and cotton crops.

Cotton is shipped, when baled to Houston, at $3 75 per bale, or to Galveston, New Orleans, or Saint Louis at $4 50.

SMITH.

Population: 21,863.—White, 11,506; colored, 10,357.

Area: 960 square miles.—Woodland, all; all oak, hickory, and pine region.

Tilled lands: 120,916 acres.—Area planted in cotton, 45,703 acres; in corn, 43,631 acres; in oats, 4,633 acres; in wheat, 589 acres.

Cotton production: 16,285 bales; average cotton product per acre, 0.36 bale, 540 pounds seed-cotton, or 180 pounds cotton lint.

Smith county is watered on the north by the Sabine river and a few small tributaries, and on the west and south by the headwaters of the Neches and Angelina rivers. Its surface is rolling and somewhat hilly, and is well timbered with oak, hickory, and short-leaf pine. Tyler, the county-seat, is situated in a valley between parallel chains of iron-ore hills on the east and west that are distant about 12 miles from each other, and have a northeast and southwest trend. There are several large salines on the north and southwest of Tyler that during the late civil war furnished large quantities of salt. Limestone is reported near them, and is probably of Cretaceous age.

The uplands of the county vary from gray to red sandy or clayey loams, are easily tilled, and produce from 550 to 700 pounds of seed-cotton per acre. The sandy soils are best suited to cotton, the red and mulatto to grain. (See analyses, page 26.) The bottom lands of the river are stiff and waxy in character, and, while highly productive, are very difficult to till, and are not much under cultivation, being also more or less subject to overflow. They are heavily timbered with ash, walnut, oak, etc.

Smith is an agricultural county, 19.7 per cent. of its area being under cultivation, the average being 126 acres per square mile. The principal crops are corn, cotton, oats, wheat, rye, etc., with a yield of from 12 to 18 bushels of corn and from 15 to 20 bushels of oats. Cotton is the chief crop, its acreage per square mile being 47.6, or 37.8 per cent. of the tilled lands.

The methods of cotton culture and the improvement and tillage of the lands are the same as those of the counties above described.

The county is connected by railroad with each of the two great railway trunk lines from the cities on the west and south to northern markets.

VAN ZANDT.

Population: 12,619.—White, 11,456; colored, 1,163.
Area: 840 square miles.—Woodland, about three-fourths; oak, hickory, and pine region, 650 square miles; central black prairie, 150 square miles; brown-loam prairie region, 40 square miles.
Tilled lands: 62,597 acres.—Area planted in cotton, 17,579 acres; in corn, 21,635 acres; in oats, 4,034 acres; in wheat, 1,506 acres.
Cotton production: 6,957 bales; average cotton product per acre, 0.40 bale, 600 pounds seed-cotton, or 200 pounds cotton lint.

Van Zandt county lies on the border between the central black prairie region and the timbered uplands of the eastern part of the state. That portion lying west of Wills' Point is included in the belt of brown-loam prairies (or intermixture of brown-loam and black prairie) that is found between the two regions. Mesquite is a prominent growth. The remainder and largest part of the county is covered with a timber growth of oak, hickory, and some short-leaf pine; its surface is somewhat rolling, and its soil a light gray sandy loam with a yellowish clay subsoil.

Near Grand Saline, on the northeast, the country is hilly, with an abundance of concretionary iron-ore nodules (which shale off on their surface) and underlying strata of light sands and micaceous clays having salt incrustations. Jordan's saline is said to cover several hundred acres, and to have yielded at one time a thousand sacks of salt daily. The water is obtained at a depth of 18 feet.

The county is watered on the north by the tributaries of the Sabine, which river forms the northeast boundary, by those of the Neches on the southeast, and by those of the Trinity on the southwest.

While the county is chiefly an agricultural one, nearly if not fully four-fifths of its lands are as yet undisturbed. Corn is the chief crop, cotton averaging 20.9 acres per square mile, or 28.1 per cent. of the tilled lands.

ABSTRACT FROM THE REPORT OF G. J. CLOUGH, OF BEN WHEELER.

The uplands of this county, consisting partly of rolling and in part of level lands, are considered very well adapted to the growth of cotton. The only cotton-producing soil of any importance is the sandy land of the uplands and second bottom. The depth is 3 feet, and the natural growth oak, hickory, and pine. They cover the greater part of the county.

The crops grown are cotton, corn, oats, wheat, and sugar-cane; but cotton, which constitutes one-third of the crops grown, seems best adapted to the soil. It varies in height from 2½ to 5 feet, being most productive at 3 feet, but tends to run to weed in wet seasons, which can be restrained by close plowing when growing too fast. From 1,000 to 1,400 pounds of seed-cotton per acre can be produced on fresh land; 1,600 pounds are needed for a 475-pound bale, the lint of which rates as strict middling. After several years' cultivation the yield is diminished and the rating lowered. Crab-grass is the most injurious weed. No land lies "turned out". To prevent the washing of the soil horizontalizing and hillside ditching are practiced, and are attended with good results.

Cotton is shipped by wagon to Wills' Point at $2 per bale, the time depending on the price of the staple.

KAUFMAN.
(See "Central black prairie region".)

HENDERSON.

Population: 9,735.—White, 7,641; colored, 2,094.
Area: 960 square miles.—Woodland, greater part; oak, hickory, and pine region, 870 square miles; black prairie region, 20 square miles; brown-loam prairie region, 70 square miles.
Tilled lands: 48,641 acres.—Area planted in cotton, 15,763 acres; in corn, 18,607 acres; in oats, 2,490 acres; in wheat, 179 acres.
Cotton production: 6,159 bales; average cotton product per acre, 0.39 bale, 585 pounds seed-cotton, or 195 pounds cotton lint.

Henderson county lies between the Neches and Trinity rivers, the dividing upland passing in a southeast course through near the center. The surface of the county is slightly rolling, and is very generally timbered with the oak and hickory growth of the region. The soil of the uplands is a light sandy loam with a clayey subsoil, and is interspersed in some parts of the county with red lands and deep sands.

The bottom lands of the streams are narrow, but with their dark soils, rich in decayed vegetation, seem to be preferred for tillage. They have a timber growth of ash, elm, pecan, hackberry, etc.

The county is not as well populated as the others of this region, and its tilled lands comprise only 7.9 per cent. of the county area, and average 50.7 acres per square mile. Of these 16.4 acres (or 32.4 per cent.) are devoted to the culture of cotton. Corn is the chief crop, and yields from 10 to 20 bushels per acre.

ABSTRACT FROM THE REPORT OF N. P. COLEMAN, OF ATHENS.

The soils comprise the dark sandy land, lying mostly on slopes; the light sandy and mulatto, covering one-half of the surface of the county, and forming the soil of the slightly rolling uplands; and the very deep light sandy land. The best soil as regards the cultivation of cotton is the dark sandy second bottom, which forms a very small portion of the tillable area. The light sandy mulatto, the next in importance, is the most largely cultivated. The timber of the bottom lands is oak, ash, hickory, gum, elm, etc.

The soil of the *uplands* is fine and sandy, dark gray to mulatto in color, from 6 inches to 2 feet in depth, with a yellow-clay subsoil impervious to water; that of the red lands contains soft red ironstone pebbles. It is early, warm, well drained, and easily cultivated, producing corn and cotton; but it is best adapted to the latter, which varies in height from 2½ to 5 feet, seldom growing to weed. The yield of seed-cotton per acre is from 800 to 1,200 pounds, 1,485 pounds being required for 475 pounds of lint, which rates as low middling. The plant on the lowlands inclines to run to weed in wet seasons, for which no remedy is applied. About one-third of the land is devoted to cotton, to the successful raising of which drought is the great obstacle. The most troublesome weeds are crab-grass, lamb's-quarter, and careless-weed. Late crops are occasionally damaged by the army-worm. and during protracted wet seasons by the boll-worm. Very little land lies "turned out", but the rest which it thus has is very beneficial, as is shown by the yield when the land is again cultivated. The soil on the slopes washes quite readily, doing, in some instances, serious damage, especially when neglected. Hillside ditching, when effectually accomplished, is attended with satisfactory results.

Cotton is shipped, when the price suits, to Palestine by wagon, and thence by rail to Galveston. Rate of freight is $3 75 per bale.

NAVARRO.

Population : 21,702.—White, 16,356; colored, 5,346.
Area : 1,040 square miles.—Woodland, small part; oak, hickory, and pine region, 150 square miles; central black prairie region, 240 square miles; brown-loam prairie region, 650 square miles.
Tilled lands : 136,099 acres,—Area planted in cotton, 45,716 acres; in corn, 40,133 acres; in oats, 4,288 acres; in wheat, 2,872 acres.
Cotton production : 12,958 bales; average cotton product per acre, 0.28 bale, 420 pounds seed-cotton, or 140 pounds cotton lint.

Navarro county is bounded on the east by the Trinity river, into which flow Chambers and Richland creeks, with their numerous tributaries.

The surface of the county is almost entirely an open prairie, with the exception of narrow timbered areas along some of the streams and a large region on the east, which are timbered with a growth of post and black-jack oaks and hickory. These latter lands have usually gray sandy soils, with red or yellow clay subsoils, and often extend to the immediate banks of the river, forming high bluffs, in one of which, near Rural Shade, the following section was obtained :

Soil and gravel	feet..	4
Sandstone	foot..	1
White laminated joint clay with leaf impressions	feet..	20
Ferruginous sandstone and lignite	inches..	6
Sand	feet..	3
Sandstone and a seam of lignite	feet..	2
Yellow micaceous sand	feet..	10
Thinly-laminated sandstone, exposed above water	feet..	3

On the west of these uplands, and occupying the central portion of the county, are broad and almost level brown-loam and sandy prairies, with beds of variously colored quartz, pebbles, and stiff clayey subsoils, which resemble in every respect those of the black central prairie region. In the lowlands and flats of this part of the county this subsoil seems to become the soil—a black, waxy, hog-wallow clay, that cracks open in dry seasons and is covered with a mesquite growth. The continuity of these prairies is broken only by the timbered lands of the streams, the belt passing through the county from north to south, and reaching in width several miles west of Corsicana to the black waxy lands of the central prairie region. (See analysis, page 27.) Near Corsicana are found fossiliferous sandstones of the Tertiary, the uplands being apparently the continuation of the more prominent Tehuacana hills of Limestone county on the south.

The black, waxy, central prairie lands cover all of the western part of the county, are level, somewhat sandy, and underlaid by the soft rotten limestone of the Cretaceous.

Navarro is one of the principal agricultural counties of the state. The lands under cultivation average 130 acres per square mile, or 20.9 per cent. of the county area. One-third of these tilled lands is devoted to the culture of cotton, the chief crop, which has an average of 44 acres per square mile.

ABSTRACTS FROM THE REPORTS OF M. DRANE AND JAMES N. BRACEWELL, OF CORSICANA, AND W. INGRAM, OF RURAL SHADE.

One-half of the area of the county is covered by *black, stiff, clayey soil,* wooded only where it extends into the bottoms of larger streams or along the margins of the creeks passing through it. The timber then consists of ash, elm, pecan, Spanish oak, and hackberry. The soil varies from 2 to 5 feet in depth. The subsoil is a tough, light yellow joint clay down to 15 or 20 feet, and hard-pan farther down to 50 feet. This latter is as impervious to water as are cisterns. The deeper down, the harder and more impervious to water it becomes, but it is productive after being exposed awhile on the surface. The subsoil contains occasionally flinty, rounded, black pebbles and angular fragments of rotten limestone. It is hard to reduce this soil to a state of easy tillage, but after it is done there is no difficulty with it, except when too wet. It is early, warm, generally well drained, and best adapted to corn, wheat, and oats, these, with cotton, barley, sorghum, millet, rye, and Irish and sweet potatoes, constituting the chief crops of the region.

From one-third to two-fifths of this soil is planted in cotton. The plant grows usually 2½ feet high, is most productive at 3, and inclines to run to weed (also on the sandy prairie next described) in wet seasons, which is remedied by topping or plowing and by early "laying by" when the falls are not wet. When the lands are fresh the average product per acre is 500 pounds of seed-cotton, 1,545 pounds making a 475-pound bale of second-rate lint. This soil yields more after six or ten years' cultivation than at first, and it has not been known to decline in cotton yield, which averages from 1,000 to 1,200 pounds per acre. The land having no sand or dust, the staple from it is in better condition than that from other soils. The most troublesome weeds are cocklebur, sunflower, careless-weed, and purslane. Slopes are all prevented from washing by horizontalizing.

Additional abstracts from the reports of Messrs. Drane and Ingram.

Three-eighths of the county area is covered by fine and coarse *sandy, gray and blackish loam prairie land,* which occurs in belts of from 3 to 6 miles wide, reaching across the county in some cases and into the adjoining counties in other cases. Along the borders of the streams there is a growth of post and black-jack oaks and hickory. The soil is from 6 to 24 inches deep, and rests upon a leachy subsoil of clay, varying from red to yellow in different localities, containing hard, rounded, and angular white and black gravel, which inclines to bake, but gradually becomes like the surface soil when cultivated. It is underlaid by sand at from 10 to 20 feet. Tillage is easy in wet seasons; but in dry seasons the soil is hard, and cuts the implements like a grindstone. The soil is early, warm, well drained, and best adapted first to corn, second to cotton, third to potatoes, and last to small cereals. From one-third to one-half of the cultivated area is planted in cotton. The plant usually grows from 3 to 5 feet high, but is most productive at 3½ or 4 feet. The maximum seed-cotton product per acre of fresh land is 1,500 pounds, the average 550 pounds, and 1,485 pounds make a 475-pound bale of middling lint. After four years' cultivation (unmanured) the average product is from 600 to 700 pounds; after six to ten years, from 500 to 600 pounds; 1,665 pounds then make a 475-pound bale of inferior staple. The troublesome weeds are chiefly crab, nut, and fox-tail grasses. Very little, if any, of this land lies "turned out"; it improves a little if allowed to rest. The soil washes and gullies, seriously damaging steep slopes; but the washings rather improve the valleys. Horizontalizing and hillside ditching have been practiced, and are fairly successful in checking the damage.

The *bottom lands* of the Trinity river and of Richland, Chambers, and other creeks occupy one-eighth of the county, and have a growth of burr, Spanish, and water oaks, cedar, pecan, elm, ash, and hackberry. The soil of those is a heavy, coarse sandy, gray, blackish, and black loam from 2 to 5 feet thick. The subsoils are clays, some hard-pans, some leachy, and contain hard rounded black and white gravel, underlaid by sand, gravel, and rarely by rock at from 10 to 20 feet. Tillage is easy in dry but difficult in wet seasons, and the soil is late, cold, and ill drained. It is best adapted first to cotton, second to corn, and third to sorghum and ribbon-cane. From one-half to three-fourths of this land is planted in cotton. The plant grows from 4 to 7 feet high, is most productive at 6, and inclines to run to weed when showers are frequent (not necessarily excessive), the remedy consisting in topping and rapid cultivation. The maximum seed-cotton product per acre of fresh land is from 1,500 to 1,800 pounds, the average 800 pounds, 1,545 pounds making a 475-pound bale of first-rate lint. After four years' cultivation, in fair seasons, rather dry for uplands, the average product is from 1,000 to 1,300 pounds, without change in the ratio of seed to lint and in quality of staple. Horse-weeds, sunflowers, burs, etc., are most troublesome. Such land does not lie idle, except when overflowed or when fencing is washed away. Frosts often occur in the vicinity as late as April 20 sufficient to destroy all cotton then above ground. In autumn in the timbered uplands and creek or branch bottoms the cotton is killed, much earlier than on the high, rolling prairies, and vegetation is killed later in the spring. The drought generally commences in July, and causes cotton to shed its forms and young bolls to a serious extent in August. This county is north of the usual limit of the caterpillar depredations. Occasionally, however, they strip the plants of their leaves, but this is only in wet seasons, at which time the maturing of the boll is promoted by stripping off the foliage and allowing the sun to strike in upon the bolls, which otherwise would rot from shade and moisture.

According to Mr. Drane, the cotton products of the county for the years 1863 and 1864 were respectively 30 and 40 bales. The present annual export is 20,000 bales. The increase is due chiefly to immigration and to the development of the resources of the county.

Additional abstract from the report of Mr. Ingram.

The *light sandy soil* of the timbered upland along the streams has a natural growth of post and black-jack oaks and hickory, and is 18 inches deep. The subsoil is a heavy, tough, reddish-yellow clay, containing white gravel and rounded pebbles, and is underlaid by sand. The land is easily tilled, is late and well drained, and about one-half of such land is planted in cotton. The plant usually attains a height of 4 feet, at which it is most productive. The seed-cotton product per acre on fresh land is 1,000 pounds, about 1,550 pounds being necessary for a 475-pound bale of lint, which rates as good ordinary. After four years' cultivation (unmanured) the product per acre is 700 pounds, and 1,550 pounds are required for a 475-pound bale of lint, which is shorter than that raised on fresh land. The most troublesome weeds on this land are cocklebur and careless-weed. The soil washes on the slopes and serious damage is done to them. The valleys are injured by the washings; very little has been done to check the injury.

Cotton is shipped, from September to December, by rail from Corsicana to Galveston at $4 50 per bale; also to Houston and to New York.

LIMESTONE.

Population: 16,246.—White, 13,075; colored, 3,171.

Area: 970 square miles.—Woodland, greater part; oak, hickory, and pine region, 140 square miles; central black prairie region, 170 square miles; brown-loam prairie region, 660 square miles.

Tilled lands: 84,299 acres.—Area planted in cotton, 35,519 acres; in corn, 32,988 acres; in oats, 2,497 acres; in wheat, 1,269 acres.

Cotton production: 9,037 bales; average cotton product per acre, 0.25 bale, 375 pounds seed-cotton, or 125 pounds cotton lint.

The surface of Limestone county is somewhat rolling, and is drained by the headwaters of Navasota river, which flow in a southerly course. It is almost entirely an open prairie, with skirts of timber along the streams and covering the eastern corner of the county. A line of low hills passes in a southerly course a few miles west of the railroad, which receive the name of "Tehuacana hills", and are a part of the "Blue Ridge" chain, already mentioned in the general description. These are formed from Tertiary sandstone, fossiliferous in places, and very nearly mark the dividing line not only between the Tertiary and the Cretaceous formations, but also that between the black waxy prairies of the central region and the brown loam prairies that border it on the east.

Three general classes of lands are found in this county, viz:

(1) The black prairies on the west of the hills, with their stiff calcareous soils and still stiffer underclays. They are underlaid by white and soft or rotten limestones (Cretaceous), which often come to the surface. These lands are difficult to till, but are very productive, yielding from 800 to 1,000 pounds of seed-cotton per acre.

(2) The brown-loam prairies (Tertiary), with a soil rather stiff, a surface quite level, and partly covered with a growth of mesquite. The lands are easily tilled, and are very productive. (See analysis, page 27.)

(3) The timbered lands (Tertiary), with their gray sandy soils and clay subsoils, which occupy the eastern corner of the county. The timber growth is post, live, and black oaks and hickory, etc., as in the large region of which it is a part. The streams have a growth of elm, hackberry, ash, etc.

Limestone is largely an agricultural county, the tilled lands comprising 13.5 per cent. of its area, or 86.9 acres per square mile. Cotton is the chief crop, the average being 36.6 acres per square mile, or 42.1 per cent. of the tilled lands.

ABSTRACT FROM THE REPORT OF C. M. BELL, M. D., OF TEHUACANA.

The chief cotton-producing soils are the *brown and black sandy loams of the upland prairies*, interspersed with small patches of heavy, black waxy soil. The same extend to the sandy timbered uplands on the southeast, about 3 miles from this place, and from 20 to 30 miles in other directions. Such is about three-fourths of the area of this region. The prairie bears a scattered growth of mesquite; along its water-courses are ash, elm, and hackberry. The *timbered uplands* have a growth of post oak and hickory. These soils are about 15 inches deep. The sandy soil rests upon a subsoil of tough ferruginous and impervious clay, and the black waxy upon grayish impervious joint clay; they are underlaid by sand at 4 feet. The soils are early, warm, well drained, and easily tilled (except the black waxy in wet weather), and are well adapted to cotton and corn, and the waxy to small grains. About one-third of the cultivated land is planted in cotton. The plant usually grows 3 feet high, is most productive at 4 feet, and inclines to run to weed when showers are too frequent. Could the farmer know that the season was to be wet, the remedy would consist of topping and root pruning. The seed-cotton product per acre of fresh land is 1,200 pounds, 1,600 pounds making a 475-pound bale of lint. After ten years' cultivation (unmanured) the product per acre is about 1,000 pounds, and after twenty years 800 pounds, the ratio of seed to lint and the quality of staple remaining about the same. The most troublesome weeds are crab-grass on the sandy and cockleburs on the waxy soil. Very little of such land lies "turned out", and it produces as well as originally when again cultivated. Slopes readily wash and gully, but are not seriously damaged, nor are the valleys injured by the washings. Slight but successful efforts have been made to check the gullying by horizontalizing.

There is a general lack of rain in June and July. Wet summers are always followed by caterpillars in the cotton of timbered lands, but they rarely do much damage on the prairies.

Cotton is shipped about Christmas, by rail, to Galveston at $4 50 per bale.

ABSTRACT FORM THE REPORT OF J. Z. ADAMS, OF KOSSE.

The sandy prairie land is best adapted to corn, though much of the land in cultivation is given to cotton. Cotton grows to a height of 4 feet, is inclined to run to weed, and produces about a bale (500 pounds) of lint on every three acres. About 1,700 pounds of seed-cotton are required to make 475 pounds of lint. The lands wash readily when rolling.

FREESTONE.

Population: 14,921.—White, 8,269; colored, 6,652.
Area: 880 square miles.—Woodland, about seven-eighths; oak, hickory, and pine region, 780 square miles; brown-loam prairie region, 100 square miles.
Tilled lands: 100,693 acres.—Area planted in cotton, 31,372 acres; in corn, 29,242 acres; in oats, 1,462 acres; in wheat, 151 acres.
Cotton production: 8,182 bales; average cotton product per acre, 0.26 bale, 390 pounds seed-cotton, or 130 pounds cotton lint.

The surface of Freestone county is somewhat rolling and well timbered, except on the west, where the corner reaches into the broad brown-loam prairie region that is so prominent in Navarro and Limestone counties. The eastern part of the county is watered by the Trinity river and its tributaries; the western by some of the headwaters of the Navasota river.

The prairies have soils varying from dark loam to black waxy in character, and are underlaid by heavy clay subsoils, similar to those of the black prairie region. The rest of the county is covered with sandy lands having clay subsoils, and has a timber growth of post and black-jack oaks, hickory, and short-leaf pine. Cypress and cedar trees occur occasionally.

The bottom lands of the river are usually stiff and waxy in character, have a tall timber growth of oaks, ash, pecan, etc., and are more or less subject to overflow. The cultivated lands of Freestone county comprise 17.9 per cent. of its area, with an average of 114 acres per square mile. The acreage of cotton is larger than that of any other crop, but does not comprise one-third of the tilled lands; its average is 35.7 acres. In the average of population and cotton acreage per square mile, as well as in the seed-cotton product per acre, it is almost exactly similar to Limestone county.

ABSTRACT FROM THE REPORT OF H. MANNING, OF BUTLER.

About four-fifths of the county is upland, one-tenth valley land and creek bottoms, and one-tenth is embraced in Trinity river bottom and prairie on the uplands of the western part of the county. The chief crops of this region are cotton and corn.

The *uplands* bear a natural growth of post and black-jack oaks, hickory, a little sumac, and a thick growth of underbrush generally. The soil is a brown, fine sandy (gravelly in places) loam, 12 inches thick. The subsoil is heavier, contains some pebbles, and is generally underlaid by clay. The soil is early, warm, well drained, and easily tilled, except in wet seasons, when crab-grass makes tillage difficult. It is best adapted to cotton, with which two-fifths of its area is planted. In wet seasons (on this and the soil next described) the plant is inclined to run to weed; topping sometimes causes the plant to commence bolling. Usually the plant grows from 3 to 4 feet high. The seed-cotton product per acre of fresh land is from 1,200 to 1,300 pounds, about 1,455 pounds making a 475-pound bale of lint. After ten or fifteen years' cultivation (unmanured) the product per acre is from >900 to 1,000 pounds, about 1,515 pounds then making a bale of lint a shade inferior (shorter) than that from fresh land. The most troublesome weed is crab-grass. One-eighth of such land lies "turned out", and when again cultivated it produces well for a few seasons. These lands wash readily on slopes, doing serious damage; the valleys are also injured to some extent, sometimes covering them with sand in spots of 1 or 2 acres. No efforts have been made to check the damage.

The valley and creek *bottom lands* have a natural growth of red and pin oaks, sweet gum, a little walnut, and linden, and brier thickets. The soil is a blackish, fine sandy loam, 2 feet deep. The subsoil is lighter, and is underlaid by sand, sometimes by clay. Tillage is easy if not too wet, and the soil is early and warm if well drained, for which purpose ditches are often necessary. The soil is best adapted to cotton, though corn does well on it. Cotton occupies one-half the cultivated area, and usually grows from 5 to 6 feet high. The seed-cotton product per acre of fresh land varies from 1,500 to 2,000 pounds, 1,455 pounds making a 475-pound bale of very long lint. After ten or fifteen years' cultivation (unmanured) the product varies from 1,200 to 1,500 pounds, 1,515 pounds then making a bale of shorter lint. Crab-grass and burs are troublesome weeds. Very little of such land lies "turned out".

The *Trinity bottom* land bears a natural growth of red, pin, and burr oaks, pecan, and ash. The soil is black, adhesive, putty-like, and several feet deep; the subsoil is like it, excepting its light color. Tillage is difficult when too wet or too dry; the soil is early, warm, and to some extent naturally well drained, though some ditching is necessary. The soil is equally well adapted to corn and cotton, and one-half of its cultivated area is planted in the latter. The plant grows from 5 to 6 feet high. The seed-cotton product per acre of fresh land varies from 1,200 to 1,500 pounds, 1,485 pounds making a 475-pound bale of very good lint. Ten years' cultivation (unmanured) makes but little difference in the quantity or the quality of the cotton product. Cockleburs are the most troublesome weeds. Very little of this land lies "turned out".

Cotton is shipped in November and December, by rail, to Galveston at $4 a bale.

ANDERSON.

Population: 17,395.—White, 9,619; colored, 7,776.
Area: 1,000 square miles.—Woodland, nearly all; all oak, hickory, and pine region.
Tilled lands: 78,814 acres.—Area planted in cotton, 23,725 acres; in corn, 29,852 acres; in oats, 2,780 acres; in wheat, 17 acres.
Cotton production: 7,548 bales; average cotton product per acre, 0.32 bale, 480 pounds seed-cotton, or 160 pounds cotton lint.

Anderson county is bounded on the east and west by the Neches and Trinity rivers, Palestine, the county-seat, being situated on the divide between their tributaries. The surface of the county is rolling, and very generally timbered with post and black-jack oaks, hickory, and short-leaf pine. In the eastern part of the county the latter largely predominates, and furnishes a large supply of lumber for the many mills that are located in that region. There are a few prairies on the north and west, but their combined areas do not probably exceed one-fifth that of the county. Beds of concretionary iron ore (Tertiary) are found at Palestine and northward half-way between the Neches and Trinity rivers.

The uplands consist of gray sandy soils in the pineries of the east and intermixtures of areas of gray sandy and red-loam soils over the remainder of the county, which are underlaid very generally by red or yellow clayey subsoils. The surface soil is usually quite dark from decayed vegetation. (See analysis, page 25.) Besides these, there are small bodies of poor and unproductive lands, the soils of which are little else than sand, nearly a foot in depth, and whose subsoils, also poor, do not supply their deficiency in the elements of plant-food.

The bottom lands of the rivers are in some places quite wide, and have a black and stiff clayey soil, large timber growth of oaks, ash, etc., and are more or less subject to overflow. All of these lands are described in the abstracts given below.

Anderson is chiefly an agricultural county, though rather sparsely populated outside of the towns. The lands under cultivation average about 79 acres per square mile, or 12.3 per cent. of the entire area. The acreage of corn is greater than that of cotton, the latter, averaging 23.7 acres per square mile, comprising only 30.2 per cent. of the tilled lands.

ABSTRACTS FROM THE REPORTS OF W. H. TUCKER, OF PALESTINE, AND DR. WILLIAM HAMLETT, SR., OF BEAVER.

The lands of the county, according to Dr. Hamlett, comprise 33 per cent. of upland clayey loam, varying in color from yellow to black, and commonly designated chocolate soil; 33 per cent. of black upland sandy loam; and 15 per cent., of commonly-designated sand flats, composed of fine and coarse whitish sand.

The *upland clayey loam* is the preferable soil for cotton, and is from 3 to 5 (frequently 10) feet deep. The underlying material is a hard-pan, generally impervious; otherwise similar to the surface soil. The soil is always easily tilled, except when extremely wet, is early and well drained, and bears a natural growth of hickory, black-jack, post oak, and a great variety of other timber. The chief crops of this region are corn, cotton, potatoes, ribbon- and sugar-cane, etc. The soil is apparently best adapted to cotton and small grains; other crops do well, however. One-half the cultivated area of this soil is planted in cotton, the average and most productive height being 5 feet. Deep cultivation inclines the crop to run to weed, for which topping early in August is the remedy. The average seed-cotton product per acre of fresh land is 1,200 pounds; lint rates as middling. After five years' cultivation (unmanured) the average product is 900 pounds; the staple then rates as low middling. Cockleburs and hog-weeds are the most troublesome. About one-twentieth of such land lies "turned out", and produces a little better when again cultivated. The soil on slopes washes and gullies, injuring the land to the extent of 5 per cent. in ten years. Valleys are rarely injured by the washings; sometimes they are improved by it. Some efforts to check the damage by horizontalizing and hillside ditching have been made with success.

The *black upland sandy soil* is 30 inches deep, and naturally bears hickory and a great variety of oaks and other timber. The subsoil is heavier but lighter in color, and is hard pan, underlaid by sand at 10 feet. Tillage is always easy, and the soil is early, warm, and well drained, and perhaps best adapted to cotton, to which one-half its cultivated area is devoted. The plant attains the height of 2½ or 3 feet; is most productive at 2½ feet. Wet weather and deep cultivation incline it to run to weed, the remedy for which is topping early in August. The seed-cotton product per acre on fresh land is 1,000 pounds; lint rates as middling. Three years' cultivation without manure reduces the product to 750 pounds, and the staple deteriorates to low middling. The hog-weed is most troublesome. One-tenth of such land lies "turned out", and when again cultivated it produces from 600 to 800 pounds of seed-cotton or 20 bushels of corn per acre. Slopes wash and gully as on land previously described.

The "*sand flats*" occur in bodies of from 10 to 1,000 acres, and bear a natural growth of scrub oaks, hackberry, hickory, etc. The soil is 10 inches deep, with a subsoil similar in appearance to leached ashes compressed into hard lumps; it is leachy, and is underlaid by sand and occasionally rock at varying depths. The soil is easily tilled at all seasons, and is early, warm, well drained, and is apparently best adapted to cow-peas. About one-twentieth of the cultivated part of such land is planted with cotton only because small bodies of it occur in cotton-fields. It grows from 8 to 12 inches high, yielding on fresh land from 100 to 200 pounds of seed-cotton, making good ordinary lint; the seed is very light. Weeds are not troublesome. One-half of such land lies "turned out"; none has again been cultivated. Slopes are promptly and fatally damaged by washing and gullying of the soil, and the valleys are damaged in places to the extent of one-fourth their value. No efforts to check the damage have been made.

Additional abstract from the report of W. H. Tucker.

The *lowlands* consist of the black, stiff, buckshot soil of the Trinity river bottom and the black and brown sandy soils of tributary streams, covered with a growth of overcup, pin, and burr oaks, and ash; pecan occurs on the upland prairies. The Trinity bottom soil is from 2 to 8 feet deep; the subsoil is heavier, has more or less red clay, which bakes hard when exposed, but gradually becomes like the surface soil, is impervious when undisturbed, and contains soft yellow gravel, underlaid by gravel and solid rock at from 12 to 15 feet. Tillage is rather difficult. The soil is early when well drained, but late as it is now cultivated. Cotton must be planted from ten to fifteen days later than on the uplands; and for this reason the crop is late in the fall, and is liable to be prematurely frost-killed. Some of the best yields on lowlands are from cotton planted in May. The soil is best adapted to cotton and corn, and cotton is raised on about half its cultivated area. The plant grows from 4 to 8 feet high, but is most productive at 4 or 5 feet. On fresh land, in wet seasons, it inclines to run to weed, which is remedied by topping and thinning out. The seed-cotton product per acre of fresh land varies from 900 to 1,800 pounds, one-third of which is lint, rating as good ordinary to good middling. The quantity of product does not decline during the first three years, and fresh lands produce the best staple. Crab-grass and cockleburs are the most troublesome weeds on this and other lowlands. Very little improved land of this kind lies uncultivated, which improves by rest. The washings from upland slopes are not damaging to lowlands unless they consist wholly or largely of sand. Efforts have been made to check such damages by horizontalizing, hillside ditching, and embanking, and generally with very good results.

The *black and brown sandy soils* of smaller streams are from 1 to 4 feet deep, and have a growth of overcup and post oaks, hickory, dogwood, birch, and sumac. The subsoil is heavier, more or less mixed with red clay, impervious in places, contains soft yellow angular gravel, and sometimes, near water-courses, large pebbles, inclosing sea-shells. It is underlaid by rather soft lime-rock at from 4 to 10 feet. The soil is usually easily tilled in wet or dry seasons, is early when well drained, and is best adapted to cotton and corn. About half its cultivated area is generally planted in cotton. The plant usually grows from 3 to 6 feet high, yields most at from 3 to 5 feet, and inclines to run to weed when land is fresh and seasons unusually wet, which is remedied by topping and thinning out. The seed-cotton product per acre of fresh land varies from 700 to 1,500 pounds.

Cotton is shipped, as soon as baled, from Palestine to Houston at $3, or chiefly to Galveston at $3 75 per bale.

CHEROKEE.

Population: 16,723.—White, 11,014; colored, 5,709.
Area: 1,000 square miles.—Woodland, nearly all; all oak, hickory, and pine region.
Tilled lands: 90,480 acres.—Area planted in cotton, 29,708 acres ; in corn, 37,244 acres; in oats, 4,312 acres; in wheat, 210 acres.
Cotton production: 9,813 bales.—Average cotton product per acre, 0.33 bale, 495 pounds seed-cotton, or 165 pounds cotton lint.

Cherokee county is separated from the counties on the west by the Neches river, while Angelina river forms a part of the eastern boundary. The tributaries of these two streams in this county are very short. The northern part is undulating and partly timbered with oak, hickory, and short-leaf pine, and is partly small open prairie land, known as brush prairies. These prairies are rapidly being covered with a low growth of red, post, and black-jack oaks, attributable, it is thought, to the discontinuance of the custom of burning off the grasses for many years past.

Two miles south of Jacksonville we come to a region of iron-ore hills that occupies the central portion of the county southward to 4 miles beyond Rusk, the county-seat. The highest of these hills is found near Rusk, and is called the mountain, because of its prominence. It has a height of 175 feet above the valley, or 125 feet above the town, and its abrupt sides are covered with masses of ore and ferruginous sandstone. Its summit, nearly 2 miles in width, has a deep, white sand over most of its surface, and a growth of oak and hickory. The ore is said to be rich, and was at one time utilized. The southern part of the county, and a belt from 3 to 10 miles along the river on the west of the hills, is more level, and has a timber growth, in which pine is most prominent, which is said to be very dense 12 miles south of Rusk.

The lands of the northern and central portions of the county are mostly gray and sandy, interspersed with numerous areas of red soils, and usually filled with ferruginous gravel, which is said to render them drouthy. The subsoils are generally heavy clays. The lands of the pineries on the west and south are sandy, and, excepting those in the immediate vicinity (bottoms) of the rivers, which are black and stiff, are considered poor. The lands under cultivation in the county comprise about 14.1 per cent. of its area, the remainder being still in their original condition. Of the various crops corn is the chief, the acreage of cotton being less than one-third of the tilled lands, with an average of 29.7 acres per square mile.

ABSTRACTS FROM THE REPORTS OF J. T. WALKER, OF ETNA (SMITH COUNTY), AND W. F. THOMPSON, OF JACKSONVILLE.

Cotton is raised chiefly on the uplands, which embrace three kinds of soils, viz, mulatto, gray sandy, and red.

The *fine sandy and gravelly, mahogany-colored loam* comprises fully one-half of the county, and extends north about 7 or 8 miles, south 15 or 16, east 9 or 10, and west 25 or 30 miles. It bears a natural growth of red, post, and black-jack oaks, and hickory. The soil is 6 inches deep, with a subsoil heavier in character, lighter in color, and freely mixed with sand. It contains "black gravel", and is underlaid by red and yellow clay at from 1 to 3 feet. Tillage is easy in wet or dry seasons, and the soil is early, warm, and generally well drained. The chief crops are cotton, corn, oats, potatoes, and sorghum, but the soil is apparently best adapted to cotton. All the crops named, as well as vegetables in great variety, do well here.

One-half the cultivated area is planted in cotton, the usual height of which is 4 feet, but the yield is greatest at 5 feet. When there is too much rain, the plant inclines to run to weed on this and other soils, to restrain which some farmers pinch off the top bud when from 3 to 4 feet high. The seed-cotton product per acre of fresh land in an average season is 1,000 pounds, 1,545 pounds making a 475-pound bale of middling lint. After fifteen years' cultivation (unmanured) the product per acre, well cultivated, is 700 pounds, and about 30 pounds less is required to make a bale, and the staple is shorter. Rag-weed, careless-weed, and cocklebur, especially crab-grass, are the most troublesome weeds. About one-twentieth of this land originally cultivated now lies "turned out", but after several years' rest it produces two or three crops almost equal to those of fresh land unless the soil has been washed away. Slopes are damaged to a serious extent by washing and gullying of the soil, and valleys are also slightly damaged by the washings, to prevent which horizontalizing has been practiced, but with little success.

The *gray sandy loam*, embracing 35 per cent. of the uplands, has a natural growth of red black-jack, with occasional post oaks and hickory. The soil is 5 inches deep; the lighter subsoil is sandy, and is underlaid by clay at 2½ feet. Tillage is always easy, except when the ground is extremely wet, when for a short time it is too soft. One-half its cultivated area is planted in cotton, to which it is apparently best adapted. The plant usually attains the height of 4½ feet, but is more productive at from 5 to 5½ feet. The seed-cotton product per acre of fresh land is 1,100 pounds, 1,545 pounds making a 475-pound bale of middling lint. After fifteen years, with good cultivation (unmanured), the product per acre is 500 pounds, 1,485 pounds then making a bale of lint, which is then inferior, because the staple is shorter. The amount of such land "turned out", etc., is as that of soil first described. The slopes are seriously damaged by washing, and the valleys are damaged to a great extent. No efforts have been made to check it.

The *red lands* embrace about 15 per cent. of the uplands, and are a deep red, putty-like, clayey loam, 18 inches deep, with a heavier subsoil, containing occasionally hard "black gravel" (but generally free from gravel of any kind), and underlaid by red clay at from 5 to 12 feet. They have a natural timber growth of red oak and hickory, and occasionally post oak. Tillage is difficult in wet or dry seasons. The soil is early and warm, and is apparently best adapted to corn, oats, and wheat. A small proportion of its cultivated area is planted in cotton. The plant usually attains the height of 3 feet, is most productive at 4½ feet, and yields 900 pounds of seed-cotton per acre on fresh land, 1,545 pounds making a 475-pound bale of low middling lint. After fifteen years' cultivation the product is from 750 to 800 pounds; it takes 90 pounds less to make a bale, and the lint is shorter. The objection to such land for cotton is that the cotton is stained by the red clay. The troublesome weeds are rag-weed, careless-weed, cocklebur, and a little crab-grass. Perhaps 1 per cent. of such land lies "turned out", and is worthless. Excepting wet springs and dry summers, the climate is generally all that could be desired for cotton production. On bottom lands crops are later in spring because of bad drainage, but such lands yield more cotton or corn per acre than the uplands. The red or brown lands are highest, and crops upon them advance most rapidly in spring. The gray, sandy upland endures drought better than the red or brown soil, but the crop is later.

Cotton is shipped as fast as bailed to Galveston at $3 75, and to New Orleans at $5 10 per bale.

NACOGDOCHES.

Population: 11,590.—White, 8,550; colored, 3,040.
Area: 970 square miles.—Woodland all; all oak, hickory, and pine region.
Tilled lands: 66,863 acres.—Area planted in cotton, 16,762 acres; in corn, 25,102 acres; in oats, 886 acres.
Cotton production: 4,791 bales; average cotton product per acre, 0.29 bale, 435 pounds seed-cotton, or 145 pounds cotton lint.

Nacogdoches county is triangular in shape, and lies within the angle formed by the junction of Attoyac creek with Angelina river. The surface of the county is rolling and somewhat hilly, and well watered by numerous creeks, tributaries of the streams mentioned. It is well timbered with long- and short-leaf pines, post and black-jack oaks, hickory, etc. The mast furnishes subsistence for the hogs. The soils of the uplands are gray and sandy, interspersed with large areas of red clayey loams, and underlaid by red and yellow clays. The bottom lands have soils varying from sandy alluvial to stiff and black clays.

Blue fossiliferous marls and limestones are said to occur in various parts of the county, and blue clays at from 20 to 50 feet. The lands under cultivation average 68.9 acres per square mile, and comprise 10.8 per cent. of the county area. Cotton has an average of only 17.3 acres per square mile, that of corn being 25.8 acres. The product per acre for 1879 was far below the general average for the state. The utilization of the marls by application to the lands would prove of great benefit.

ABSTRACT FROM THE REPORT OF R. P. WHITE, OF NACOGDOCHES.

The soils are quite variable in eastern Texas. Limestone is abundant, and blue clay is found in wells at from 20 to 50 feet. The gray and red sandy soils are preferred for cotton, the red clayey soil being subject to rust, and liable to stain the staple. On the black land cotton grows too rank, and much of the so-called first crop, i. e., the earlier bolls, is destroyed by the rot.

The *gray and dark and red sandy soil* embraces about half the area of the county, and is interspersed to some extent with other kinds. It has a natural growth of various oaks, hickory, pine, black-jack oak, mulberry, walnut, dogwood, and buckeye. The soil varies in depth from 1 foot to 5 feet. The subsoil is a tough clay, much of which is yellow, and some orange red, containing soft calcareous and rounded red gravel and layers of limestone. Sand, gravel, and rock are found at various places and at different depths below the surface. Tillage is generally easy, and the soil is best adapted to cotton and peas, cotton occupying at least two-fifths of the cultivated lands. The other chief crops produced here are corn, oats, potatoes, and vegetables, and tobacco does well. The cotton-plant attains a height of from 4 to 7 feet; the medium is most productive. On any soil in this region it inclines to run to weed when the weather is too wet, the remedy for which is drainage and topping in August. The seed-cotton product per acre of fresh land is from 1,000 to 1,900 pounds, 1,545 pounds making a 475-pound bale of middling lint. After twelve years' cultivation the product is from 600 to 900 pounds, 1,570 pounds then making a 475-pound bale of low middling lint. Careless-weed, cocklebur, and crab-grass (the latter on the gray sandy soil) are the most troublesome. Very little of this land lies "turned out". When again cultivated the red sandy produces well, the gray sandy not so well. All cultivated slopes, except those of black, tough soils, are inclined to wash and gully, and the damage is sometimes serious. The washings make the valley soils tough, injuring some parts and slightly improving others, to check which horizontalizing and hillside ditching have been practiced with success.

The *stiff, red clayey soil* embraces about three-tenths of the county area, bears a natural growth of black-jack and other oaks, some dogwood, sweet gum, buckeye, etc., and is from 6 to 18 inches deep. The heavier subsoil is an impervious red clay, containing soft, red, and some large rounded pebbles, and is underlaid by gravel and limestone at varying depths. The soil is early and warm, but ill-drained, and difficult to till, and it is best adapted to corn and oats, but two-fifths of its area is planted in cotton, which attains a height of from 3 to 5 feet. The seed-cotton product per acre of fresh land is from 800 to 1,500 pounds, 1,570 pounds making a bale of low middling lint. After twelve years' cultivation the product is from 500 to 800 pounds, 1,600 pounds then making a bale of lint shorter than that of fresh land. Cocklebur is the most troublesome weed. About 4 per cent. of such land lies "turned out", and produces tolerably well when again cultivated.

The *black prairie soil* covers about one-tenth of the county area, and occurs in widely distributed spots. The bordering timber consists of hickory, ash, white oak, and sweet and black gums. The soil is a blackish and black, slightly waxy, tough clayey loam from 1 to 5 feet thick. The subsoil is an impervious mulatto-colored clay, immediately underlaid by limestone, at some points only 1 foot

4⁷ C P

below the surface. Tillage is difficult in very wet or dry weather, and plowing must be done while the soil is near the medium moist condition. The soil is late, cold, ill-drained, and is best adapted to corn and oats, but two-fifths of its cultivated area is planted in cotton. The height attained by the plant varies from 4 to 7 feet, the medium being most productive. The seed-cotton product per acre of fresh land varies from 1,000 to 2,000 pounds, 1,545 pounds making a 475-pound bale of middling lint. After twelve years' cultivation the product is from 800 to 1,500 pounds, and 1,570 pounds make a bale of low middling lint. Cocklebur is the most troublesome weed. Very little of this land lies "turned out"; it produces very well when again cultivated.

Cotton is shipped from September to January, by wagons, at 50 cents per 100 pounds to Henderson, and $1 per 100 pounds to Shreveport, Louisiana.

SHELBY.

Population: 9,523.—White, 7,369; colored, 2,154.
Area: 800 square miles.—Woodland, all; all oak, hickory, and pine region.
Tilled lands: 44,764 acres.—Area planted in cotton, 16,136 acres; in corn, 20,985 acres; in oats, 1,200 acres; in wheat, 201 acres.
Cotton production: 6,171 bales; average cotton product per acre, 0.38 bale, 570 pounds seed-cotton, or 190 pounds cotton lint.

Shelby county lies between the Sabine river on the east and Attoyac creek on the west. Its surface is more or less rolling, and is timbered with long- and short-leaf pine, red, post, and black-jack oaks, hickory, etc. The soil of the uplands is mostly a gray sandy loam 12 to 18 inches deep, with a sandy subsoil, and is underlaid by clay at a depth of several feet.

The bottom lands of the larger streams have a dark loam soil, very rich, and a large and varied growth, as shown in the abstract below.

The tilled lands of the county comprise one-eleventh of its area. The crops are corn, cotton, sugar-cane, sweet potatoes, wheat, rye, oats, rice, vegetables, and fruits. Cotton has an average of 20.2 acres per square mile, or 36 per cent. of the lands under cultivation, and its yield is a little above the average for the state.

The Sabine river affords a means of shipment by small steamboats to Beaumont, and thence by railroad or boat to New Orleans or to Galveston.

ABSTRACT FROM THE REPORT OF JOHN HOLT, OF CENTER.

There may be distinguished in this county three varieties of lands: (1) The black sandy loam and black waxy. (2) Hummock lands of a mulatto color, with some black waxy. (3) The gray and black sandy, constituting the soil of the uplands, which comprise both rolling and level lands. Both the uplands and the lowlands are well adapted to the growth and maturity of cotton. The lowlands, notwithstanding that they are more difficult to cultivate, are generally preferred to the uplands, owing to the more luxuriant growth, especially on fresh or manured land, and the greater yield per acre of the plant.

The most important soil is the *black sandy loam* of the bottom lands, which covers about 5 per cent. of the surface of the county, and has a natural growth of pine, hickory, ash, walnut, sweet and black gum, dogwood, chincapin, cherry, birch, magnolia, tupelo-gum, and white, red, post and pin oaks. The depth of the soil is 18 inches, and it is easily tilled and early when well drained. Its chief productions are cotton, potatoes, and sugar-cane.

Cotton forms 30 per cent. of the entire crops planted, and reaches a height of 6 feet, at which it is most productive. It inclines to run to weed in wet seasons, to obviate which topping is resorted to. The yield per acre of seed-cotton is 2,000 pounds on fresh land; 1,800 pounds after ten years' cultivation. In either case 1,545 pounds are required for 475 pounds of lint, which rates as good middling when from fresh land, but from the cultivated land the rating is not so good. The most injurious weeds are cocklebur and crab-grass.

The second-best soil of this county is a *dark sandy loam*, comprising 40 per cent. of the tillable area. It is 18 inches deep, and has a timber growth of hickory, pine, dogwood, sweet gum, red, black, and post oaks. It is easily cultivated, is early, warm, and well drained, and produces cotton, sugar-cane, and potatoes. One-third of the crops is in cotton, which attains a height of 4 feet, at which it is very productive; but it runs to weed in wet seasons, the remedy being underdraining. When the land is fresh 1,000 pounds of seed-cotton per acre can be produced, but this amount is diminished to 800 pounds after ten years' cultivation, 1,545 pounds being necessary for a 475-pound bale of lint in either case, rating as good middling. A very small amount of this land lies "turned out", and the yield when it is again "taken in" is as good as that from fresh land.

The *gray sandy lands* form about 50 per cent. of the county, and have a timber growth of pine, hickory, black- and white-jacks, black, red, and post oaks. The chief crops of this soil are cotton and potatoes, the former amounting to 50 per cent. of the crops planted. The soil is 6 inches deep, with a red-clay subsoil, is early, warm, and well drained, and is easily cultivated. Cotton does not run to weed on this soil; but it yields 800 pounds of seed-cotton per acre, of which 1,485 pounds are needed to make a bale, which rates as middling. After ten years' cultivation the yield decreases to 600 pounds, the staple remaining the same as when the land was fresh. Careless- and hog-weeds are the most troublesome on this soil. None of the land lies "turned out". Wheat, being liable to rust, is not sown. Sugar-cane will yield on good bottom or uplands 300 gallons of sirup per acre.

Shipping commences as soon as the cotton is baled, and is sent by wagon to Shreveport, Louisiana, at the rate of $4 per bale.

SABINE.

Population: 4,161.—White, 3,168; colored, 993.
Area: 570 square miles.—Woodland, all; oak, hickory, and pine region, 400 square miles; long-leaf pine region, 170 square miles.
Tilled lands: 15,631 acres.—Area planted in cotton, 5,252 acres; in corn, 8,322 acres; in oats, 295 acres.
Cotton production: 1,705 bales; average cotton product per acre, 0.32 bale, 480 pounds seed-cotton, or 160 pounds cotton lint.

The surface of Sabine county is rolling and well timbered with post and black-jack oaks, hickory, and pine, and is watered by the Sabine river and its tributaries.

Long-leaf pineries occur in the southern part of the county, beginning 20 miles south of Milam; sandstone (of the Grand Gulf formation) is also said to occur. The upland soils are gray and sandy, interspersed with

738

large areas of red lands, while the soils of the bottoms are dark sandy loams, very productive. The red lands are said to occur chiefly on the northwest, and to form a belt from 3 to 10 miles wide and 100 miles long, extending into Nacogdoches county. They have a timber growth of post and black-jack oaks.

Lumbering is the chief industry, the river affording a ready means of transportation to market.

The county is sparsely settled, and the lands under cultivation comprise but 4.3 per cent. of its area, averaging 27.4 acres per square mile. Of these about one-third is devoted to cotton culture, the average being about 9.2 acres per square mile. Live-stock comprises 6,404 head of cattle, 821 sheep, and 13,617 hogs.

The best cotton lands are the bottoms of small streams. They often produce a bale (475 pounds) per acre.

The uplands consist of light gray and chocolate-colored sandy soils and red soil. The sandy is the second quality of cotton land, and comprises two-thirds of the area of the county; but the red soil is better adapted to corn and oats, and often produces 35 and 40 bushels of corn (50 bushels are said to have been gathered) per acre. The sandy soils produce when fresh from 600 to 1,000 pounds of seed-cotton per acre, but when exhausted by cultivation not more than one-half that amount. The natural drainage is generally good. Horizontalizing and hillside ditching are practiced, and are necessary to protect the washing of slopes. Valleys are nearly ruined where the soil is covered by washings from upland slopes. Tillage is easy, except when the soil is too wet, and weeds grow rapidly. This entire region is nearly all underlaid by a heavy, stiff clay.

About Milam the red land predominates, and is part of a belt from 3 to 10 miles wide and 100 or more miles long, with a scrub timber growth. It is more or less interrupted by spots of gray loam, red and brown sandy soils, and creek bottoms, and all these spots are good for cotton. The red soil does not easily wash into gullies on slopes, and is not easily exhausted. Some of the old fields of it here are said to have been cultivated fifty years without manure or rest. Its timber is generally inferior.

Cotton production has increased in the ten years past, but not so rapidly as other branches of agriculture. A great deal of the land originally cultivated in cotton by large planters by means of slave labor is now lying out, and is covered with pines, its slopes being washed into gullies. Farming is now done chiefly by white men on a small scale. Not more than one-fourth of the available land in this region is cleared and cultivated.

Cotton is shipped from November to March, by wagon, to Shreveport at $5, or by steamboat to Galveston at $3 per bale.

SAN AUGUSTINE.

Population: 5,084.—White, 3,169; colored, 1,915.

Area: 560 square miles.—Woodland, all; oak, hickory, and pine region, 520 square miles; long-leaf pine region, 40 square miles.

Tilled lands: 25,130 acres.—Area planted in cotton, 7,219 acres; in corn, 11,442 acres; in oats, 561 acres.

Cotton production: 2,757 bales; average cotton product per acre, 0.38 bale, 570 pounds seed-cotton, or 190 pounds cotton lint.

The surface of San Augustine county is rather broken, and is well timbered with long- and short-leaf pine. It is watered by Attoyac and other creeks, all tributary to Angelina river, on the south. The lands vary from gray and sandy to a red loam; the latter is found in large areas in the northern part of the county, and is also said to cover the upland ridge in the central part. It has a timber growth of oak and hickory. The bottom lands of the streams, with widths of from 100 to 1,000 yards, have dark sandy soils, which are very productive, and a timber growth of cypress, magnolia, hickory, oak, walnut, wild cherry, sumac, and an undergrowth of cane.

Lumbering is said to be the chief industry of the county, the pine logs being rafted down the river to the mills at Beaumont, whence the sawed lumber finds its way to market by railroad.

The lands under cultivation comprise 7 per cent. of the county area, or an average of 44.9 acres per square mile. The chief crops are corn, cotton, oats, potatoes, vegetables, etc. The lands are easily tilled, and yield from 500 to 800 pounds of seed-cotton per acre. The area devoted to it has an average of 12.9 acres per square mile.

The methods of tillage, etc., are the same as given in the adjoining counties.

Shipments of cotton are made by wagon to the nearest railroad station.

ANGELINA.

Population: 5,239.—White, 4,405; colored, 834.

Area: 880 square miles.—Woodland, nearly all; one-half oak, hickory, and pine region; one-half long-leaf pine region.

Tilled lands: 19,729 acres.—Area planted in cotton, 5,681 acres; in corn, 8,957 acres; in oats, 156 acres.

Cotton production: 2,319 bales; average cotton product per acre, 0.41 bale, 615 pounds seed-cotton, or 205 pounds cotton lint.

Angelina county lies between Angelina river on the east and Neches on the west. Its surface is rolling, the uplands being mostly covered with a growth of short- and long-leaf pine, interspersed with oak and hickory, and the bottom lands with beech, magnolia, ash, walnut, etc. Prairies occur occasionally. The county is watered by the tributaries of the rivers mentioned and by numerous springs. The long-leaf pine region covers most of the southern half of the county, and that growth also occurs occasionally on the north. The lands comprise the dark loams of the bottoms, the bordering hummocks, and the sandy uplands.

The county is sparsely populated, and the lands under cultivation average but 22.4 acres per square mile, or 3.5 per cent. of the entire area. Of these cotton receives a fair percentage, 6.5 acres per square mile, though it is not the chief crop. The average yield of the county in seed-cotton per acre is greater than that of the state.

ABSTRACT FROM THE REPORT OF E. L. ROBB, OF HOMER.

The lowlands consist of the first and second bottoms of Shawnee and other creeks. The first, or cane bottoms, are from one-quarter of a mile to one mile wide, and the second bottoms, or hummocks, lie above and along each side generally, and at the head of the first bottoms, and are from one-quarter of a mile to one mile and a half wide. The uplands embrace partly gray sandy prairie lands and partly stiff, brown, and black timbered land. The chief crops here are corn, cotton, and sugar-cane.

The *bottom lands* bear a natural growth of oak, elm, hickory, beech, walnut, bamboo, cane, muscadine vine, wild peach, etc. The soil is a black and blackish alluvial loam from 2 to 4 feet deep; the subsoil is heavier, and is underlaid by sand and gravel. Tillage is easy, and the soil is early, and alike well adapted to each of the chief crops produced. One-third of its cultivated area is planted in cotton. The plant's usual and most productive height is 4 or 5 feet. Too much rain and too rich a soil incline the plant to run to weed, for which topping is believed to be a good remedy. The seed-cotton product per acre of fresh land is 1,600 pounds, 1,545 pounds making a 475-pound bale of middling lint. After five years' cultivation the product is from 850 to 1,100 pounds, 1,600 pounds making a bale of lint inferior to that of fresh land. Cocklebur, hog-weed, and coffee-weed are most troublesome. Very little of this land lies "turned out", but it is almost equal to fresh land when again cultivated.

The *hummock lands* bear a natural growth of pine, black-jack, and other oaks, hickory, ash, etc. The soil is a stiff, brown, clayey loam, from 12 to 30 inches deep. The subsoil is heavier, rather hard, and is underlaid by gravel at from 6 to 8 feet. The soil is late, easily tilled after being once thoroughly broken up, and is best adapted to cotton, with which one-third of its cultivated area is planted. The plant grows from 3 to 5 feet high, and yields from 500 to 800 pounds of seed-cotton per acre, 1,665 pounds making a 475-pound bale of lint. After five years' cultivation the product is from 400 to 700 pounds; and the ratio of seed to lint is the same, the staple being but little different from that of fresh land. Cocklebur and crab-grass are the most troublesome weeds. Very little of this land lies "turned out", and it produces very well when again cultivated.

The *timbered uplands* bear a natural growth chiefly of long and short-leaf pine, but also of considerable hickory and red and post oaks. The soil is from 12 to 24 inches deep; the subsoil is generally heavier, but sometimes light, sandy, and quicksandy. The soil is early, warm, easily tilled, and best adapted to cotton, and one-third of its area is planted with the same. The plant grows from 2 to 4 feet high. The seed-cotton product per acre of fresh land is from 600 to 1,000 pounds, 1,665 pounds making a bale of good ordinary to middling lint. After five years' cultivation (unmanured) the product is from 300 to 700 pounds, 1,780 pounds making a bale of lint a little inferior to that from fresh land. Several years' rest improves this land considerably. Crab-grass and coffee-weed are most troublesome. Slopes wash and gully readily in some places, and are seldom seriously damaged, no efforts having been made to check it. The valleys are not injured by the washings. Rather a dry season is best adapted to cotton, as too much wet weather causes shedding on all the lands and rust on the prairie and stiff, timbered lands.

Cotton is shipped in January to Galveston by the Angelina river; rates per bale, $3 75 by flatboat, $4 25 by steamboat.

TRINITY.

Population: 4,915.—White, 3,753; colored, 1,162.
Area : 710 square miles.—Woodland, nearly all; all oak, hickory, and pine region.
Tilled lands: 23,491 acres.—Area planted in cotton, 6,802 acres; in corn, 9,184 acres; in oats, 159 acres.
Cotton production: 2,666 bales.—Average cotton product per acre, 0.39 bale, 585 pounds seed-cotton, or 195 pounds cotton lint.

Trinity county lies between Neches river on the east and Trinity on the west, the upland that separates the tributaries of each being about midway. The surface is somewhat rolling, and consists of lands timbered on the west with short- and long-leaf pine, red and white oaks, and hickory, interspersed with small bodies of open prairies, while on the east are the long-leaf pine forests of the lumber region. The southern part of the county is underlaid by the coarse sandstone of the Grand Gulf age, which comes to the surface near Trinity station, and is exposed in the river banks, and also forms a high bluff at Riverside, on the south. The lands of the timbered uplands usually comprise sandy soils and subsoils, and are underlaid by sands and gravel, though stiff clays are found in some localities. The prairies have mostly brownish, sandy, or loamy soils, and are quite level. Near the Trinity river, and occupying what may be termed the second bottom, are small bodies of black, waxy prairies, with no timber growth except here and there a single oak, pecan, or elm tree.

The river bottom lands have a dark sandy loam soil, deep and covered with a heavy timbered growth of walnut, pecan, ash, etc. These lands are broad in some places, but are more or less liable to overflow, and are not much under cultivation.

The county is rather sparsely settled, and the tilled lands comprise but little more than 5 per cent. of its entire area. The principal crops are corn, cotton, oats, rye, vegetables, and fruits. It is claimed that the bottom lands will produce from 40 to 50, and the uplands from 20 to 30 bushels of corn per acre. The average for the entire county in 1879 (a dry year) was a little more than 10 bushels.

Cotton comprises but 29 per cent. of the lands under cultivation, or an average of 9.6 acres per square mile.

ABSTRACTS FROM THE REPORTS OF SAMUEL T. ROBB AND W. R. SHEFFIELD, OF TRINITY, AND J. W. HAMILTON, OF CENTRALIA.

The *cane bottoms* of rivers and creeks form about one-tenth of the area, and are the best cotton lands in the county. They have a width of one mile on each side of the streams, and have a natural growth of oak, gum, ash, walnut, pecan, elm, hickory, short-leaf pine, and cane. The soil is a fine sandy loam of whitish-gray and black colors, and 2 feet deep; the subsoil is heavier, but otherwise changes but little from the surface downward. It is underlaid in some parts by sand-rock at 10 feet. Tillage is easy in wet or dry seasons, and the soil is early, warm, and well drained.

The chief crops of this region are corn, cotton, sugar-cane, and a great variety of vegetables. The soil is apparently equally well adapted to all of them, but cotton occupies two-thirds of the cultivated area. The plant attains a height of from 7 to 10 feet, and in rainy weather inclines to run to weed, which may be checked by topping. The seed-cotton product per acre is from 1,500 to 1,700 pounds. After twenty-years' cultivation creek and river bottoms and hummocks and prairie lands yield as much as when fresh; but it takes less of seed-cotton to make a bale, because the seed is smaller and lighter and the staple shorter, and therefore inferior to that from fresh land. Crab-grass is the most troublesome weed.

The remainder of the county, excepting numerous small spots of black sandy and black waxy prairies, is all upland of *light gray sandy loams*, bearing a natural growth of pine, red and white oaks, sweet and black gum, and numerous kinds of vines. The soil is about 22 inches deep; the subsoil is heavier, and is underlaid by sand and gravel generally. Tillage is always easy. The land lies rather level, and is apparently best adapted to cotton or sweet potatoes. About one-half its cultivated area is planted in cotton, its most productive height varying from 2 to 4 feet. The seed-cotton product per acre is about 800 pounds, from 1,425 to 1,540 pounds making a 475-pound bale, the staple rating as good ordinary. Old land is more difficult to keep clear of weeds, and produces slightly inferior staple. Crab-grass is the most troublesome weed. About one-tenth of this land lies "turned out", but it produces very well after a rest if it has not been too badly washed. In some localities slopes are seriously damaged by washing of the soil, but these washings improve some lower lands and damage others. As there is yet plenty of new land to be had, farmers do not try to save their old fields from ruin by such washing and gullying.

The *black prairie lands* lie along the Trinity river uplands, and contain only about 1,000 acres in all. The growth is scattering oak, pecan, and elm. The soil is a black, waxy clay, having a depth of from 3 to 8 feet, and is underlaid by the sandstone at 10 or 20 feet. It is very difficult to till in wet weather, and in dry seasons it cracks open. About one-half of the crops planted on it consists of cotton, though it is best adapted to corn. Cotton grows to a height of from 2 to 4 feet, producing about 1,000 pounds of seed-cotton per acre on fresh land, 1,650 pounds being required for 475 pounds of lint. Cultivation of a few years improves it, making the yield from 1,200 to 1,400 pounds, with a longer staple. In this portion of Texas the warm and moist climate makes cotton grow rapidly.

Shipments are made in November and December, by rail, to Houston at $2 15 and to Galveston at from $2 90 to $3 75 per bale.

POLK.

Population: 7,189.—White, 4,342; colored, 2,847.

Area: 1,100 square miles.—Woodland, nearly all; oak, hickory, and pine region, 430 square miles; long-leaf pine region, 670 square miles.

Tilled lands: 23,865 acres.—Area planted in cotton, 7,229 acres; in corn, 10,937 acres; in oats, 298 acres.

Cotton production: 3,629 bales; average cotton product per acre, 0.50 bale, 750 pounds seed-cotton, or 250 pounds cotton lint.

Polk county lies on the east side of Trinity river, and is watered both by its tributaries and by those of the Neches on the east. The southern portion of its surface is level, and is covered with a timber growth of long-leaf pine, which also extends into the eastern and northern part of the county, and is included in the pineries of southeastern Texas. This region is sparsely populated, and its soils are sandy and not much under cultivation. The northern and western parts of the county are more rolling in character, and consist of oak and pine lands (long and short leaf), mostly interspersed with prairies, having soils varying from black and hog-wallow to sandy. It is estimated that these prairies cover about one-tenth of the area of the county.

The bottom lands of the rivers are usually broad, and have soils varying from reddish sandy to heavy black loams, which are heavily timbered with elm, maple, walnut, cypress, cottonwood, beech, etc. The second bottoms, or valleys, are mostly black, waxy prairies, similar to those in Trinity county. The timber of the county is utilized by a large number of saw-mills, and lumbering forms a prominent industry. The two rivers are navigable during a large part of the year, and afford easy transportation to the Gulf. The East and West Texas Narrow-Gauge railroad also connects the county with Houston.

Polk county is not thickly populated, and but 3.4 per cent. of its area is under cultivation, with an average of 21.7 acres per square mile. Of the latter 6.6 acres is devoted to cotton, and its average yield in seed-cotton (750 pounds) places the county among the first fifteen in the state in product per acre.

ABSTRACT FROM THE REPORT OF J. P. KALE, OF LIVINGSTON.

The soils cultivated in cotton are the brown, blackish, and black stiff lands of the bottoms of the Neches and the Trinity rivers and all their tributaries, and black stiff upland, partly timbered and partly prairie, occurring in belts, one of which extends through the county. The uplands contain good prairie land in patches of from 20 to 200 acres, a part of which is "hog-wallow" in character. The remainder of the county is sandy upland, generally poor, and bearing pine timber. Cotton and corn are the chief crops of this region.

The *bottoms* contain about one-fourth the cultivated lands of the county, and bear a growth of various oaks, hickory, ash, gum, and elm. The soil is 30 inches deep; the subsoil is heavier and generally impervious, and is underlaid by sand. Tillage is always easy, except in wet seasons, and the soil is early, warm, and well drained; and best adapted to cotton, with which rather less half the cultivated area is planted. The plant grows to various heights, but is most productive at 5 feet; in wet seasons (on this and other soils) it inclines to run to weed, for which no remedy is known. The seed-cotton product per acre of fresh land is 2,000 pounds, 1,545 pounds making a 475-pound bale of middling lint. In four years' cultivation there is no decline in the quantity or quality of the cotton yield per acre, and little change is perceptible in twenty years. The same is true of the black upland next to be described. The cocklebur is the most troublesome weed on the black upland soil.

The *black, mostly prairie, upland* includes another fourth of all the cultivated area, the timbered part bearing a growth of gum, pine, and post oak. The largest prairie runs parallel with the Trinity river between Long King and Kickapoo creeks, in a northwest direction; it is very irregular and narrow in places, though sometimes 3 miles in width. The subsoil is a heavier hard-pan, generally impervious, and is underlaid by clay at various depths. Tillage is easy, except when the soil is too wet. The soil is early, warm, and well drained, and best adapted to corn; but one-half its cultivated area is planted in cotton. Three feet is the usual and most productive height attained by the plant, which does not run to weed on this soil. The seed-cotton product per acre of fresh land is 1,600 pounds, 1,665 pounds making a 475-pound bale of low middling lint. There is no perceptible decrease after twenty years' cultivation. The uplands wash readily, doing some damage, except to the lowlands.

The *sandy pine land*, covering one-half of the county (growth generally pine), has a soil 6 inches deep, a heavier but leachy subsoil, and is underlaid by clay and rock in a few localities. Some hard, white, rounded pebbles are on the surface. The soil is easily tilled in any season, is early, warm, and well drained, and best adapted to cotton, one-half its area being planted with the same. It varies in height, and is most productive at 3 feet. The seed-cotton product per acre is from 800 to 1,000 pounds, 1,780 pounds making a bale of low middling

711

741

lint. After ten years' cultivation the product per acre is 400 pounds of seed-cotton. Cocklebur and hog-weed are troublesome, but crab-grass is the worst. About 15 per cent. of this land lies "turned out"; but when out four or five years it generally produces as well as originally. Slopes are seriously damaged by the washing and gullying of the soil, and the washings, if sand, damage good valley land by covering it. A little hillside ditching has been practiced, which successfully checks the damage. This is a good cotton region, neither low nor upland having the preference, and each has peculiar advantages. Some laborers have this season (1879) produced 10 bales each. Could the cotton-worm, worse than all other drawbacks, be gotten rid of, there would be very little uncertainty of crops on account of droughts.

Cotton is shipped in December to Galveston, by wagon and rail,.at $3 75 per bale.

HOUSTON.

Population: 16,702.—White, 9,465; colored, 7,237.
Area: 1,170 square miles.—Woodland, nearly all; all oak, hickory, and pine region.
Tilled lands: 73,884 acres.—Area planted in cotton, 26,819 acres; in corn, 28,966 acres; in oats, 617 acres; in wheat, 29 acres.
Cotton production: 9,730 bales; average cotton product per acre, 0.36 bale, 540 pounds seed-cotton, or 18 pounds cotton lint.

Houston county lies between the Neches and Trinity rivers, which form respectively the east and west boundaries. Its surface is rolling and mostly well timbered, having small prairies interspersed throughout, and comprising about one-tenth of its area. In the eastern part of the county short- and long-leaf pine is said to predominate, while post, red, and black-jack oaks, hickory, etc., form the prevailing timber growth of the remaining portion of the uplands. On the bottom lands of the streams the growth is white and water oaks, elm, walnut, mulberry, etc.

The county surveyor, B. F. Duren, writes as follows regarding the pine region of the county:

The pineries in the eastern portion of Houston county comprise both the short- and the long-leaf species, though mostly the former. The belt extends northward along the Neches river as far as Anderson county; is about 10 miles in breadth on the east, but narrows down to three at the Anderson county-line. The timber in this belt north of what is known as the old San Antonio road is not considered valuable.

The prairies are small, and belong to the brown-loam class that occurs in so many of the counties of this part of the state. The timbered uplands have a predominance of gray sandy lands, throughout which are interspersed bodies of red loams, underlaid by red or yellow clay subsoils. The cultivated lands of Houston county comprise 9.9 per cent. of its area, and average 63.2 acres per square mile. The acreage of cotton comprises 36.3 per cent. of these, with an average of 22.9 acres per square mile, but that of corn is still greater.

ABSTRACT FROM THE REPORT OF C. E. DOUGLAS, OF CROCKETT.

The kinds of land are: (1) gray and red uplands, lying in patches and occasional large bodies of 1,000 acres or more, forming the divides between the rivers and large creeks, and constituting about 65 per cent. of the county area; (2) dark loam of the bottoms and second bottoms of the Trinity and Neches rivers and tributaries (which are numerous), occupying about 25 per cent. of the area; (3) about 10 per cent. of dark-colored prairie soil scattered over the county. The chief crops are cotton, corn, potatoes, oats, sorghum, and West India sugar-cane.

The *gray and red upland soil* bears a natural growth of red, post, and black oaks, hickory, mulberry, dogwood, sumac, etc. The soil is from 4 to 18 inches deep; the subsoil is heavier, generally a yellow clay, though frequently a stiff, impervious red clay, containing hard "black gravel", and underlaid by clay, sometimes rock. Tillage is easy in dry, and not difficult in wet seasons. The soil is early and warm, and for the most part naturally well drained, and is apparently best adapted to cotton, although with sufficient moisture all the chief crops succeed well.

More than three-fifths of its cultivated area is planted in cotton. The plant usually grows 4 feet high, but on fresh land and in very wet seasons it inclines to run to weed. In the first case early planting and topping is the remedy; there is no remedy for the second. The seed-cotton product per acre on fresh lands varies from 800 to 1,500 pounds, from 1,425 to 1,545 pounds making a 475-pound bale of lint, which frequently rates highest in the market. After ten years' cultivation (unmanured) the product varies from 500 to 1,200 pounds, 1,425 pounds then making a 475-pound bale of lint that is shorter than that from fresh land, but is bright in color and classes well. Some of these lands continue their original yields for twenty years (unmanured). The iron-weed (perennial) is most troublesome, but does not occur on all parts. About 1 per cent. of such land lies "turned out"; it grows up in weeds, and is expected after a rest to produce very well. Lands wash readily when improperly plowed, but very little damage is done to either slopes or valleys.

The soil of the *bottoms* is a mellow loam, varying in color from brown to black, and is 5 feet deep. The subsoil is a heavier bluish and yellowish clay, containing soft "black gravel", and is underlaid by clay and marl. The soil is easily tilled where drained; it is early or late, warm or cold, according to seasons, and is well drained. Its natural growth is white and water oaks, elm, black walnut, mulberry, etc. It is best adapted to cotton, corn, and sugar-cane, and three-fourths of its cultivated area is planted in cotton. The plant attains a height of from 6 to 12 feet, the medium most productive. Fresh land, wet seasons, and late planting incline it to run to weed, and early planting and thorough tillage constitute the remedy. The seed-cotton product per acre of fresh land varies from 1,200 to 2,200 pounds,· about 1,545 pounds making a 475-pound bale of good lint. After ten years' cultivation (unmanured) there is little apparent deterioration if rotation of crops has been practiced, 1,425 pounds then making a bale of lint as good as that from fresh land. Very little of such land lies "turned out", and it produces very well when again cultivated. Hog-weed, butter-weed, etc., grow very rank, but are less troublesome than old stalks.

The *prairie soil* varies from a sandy to a clayey loam, and from gray to brown, mahogany and blackish in color, and is from 2 to 3 feet deep. The subsoil is heavier, rarely impervious, contains hard, soft, and angular "black gravel", and sometimes pebbles, and is underlaid by gravel and rock. When the soil has once been pulverized, it is easily tilled in dry seasons, but with difficulty in wet seasons. The soil is early, warm, generally well drained, and best adapted to cotton and small cereals, and one-fourth of its cultivated area is planted in cotton. The plant grows from 3 to 5 feet high, is most productive at 5 feet, and is rarely inclined to run to weed. The seed-cotton product per acre of fresh land is from 500 to 1,000 pounds, 1,425 pounds making a 475-pound bale of good lint. After ten years' cultivation (unmanured) the product is from 300 to 800 pounds, the ratio of seed to lint and quality of staple being about the same as on new land. Iron-weed is most troublesome. Very little of this land lies "turned out,", which produces well when again cultivated. When improperly plowed, slopes wash and gully readily, but are not seriously damaged, nor are the valleys materially injured. To prevent such damage nothing but judicious plowing is practiced. An occasional drought and a wet spring are, perhaps, the only circumstances adverse to the cotton-grower here.

Cotton is shipped during the gathering season, by rail, chiefly to Galveston at $3 50 per bale; also to Houston at $3, and to New Orleans.

LEON.

Population: 12,817.—White, 7,707; colored, 5,110.
Area: 1,000 square miles.—Woodland, nearly all; all oak, hickory, and pine region.
Tilled lands: 68,073 acres.—Area planted in cotton, 23,578 acres; in corn, 25,490 acres; in oats, 725 acres.
Cotton production: 7,360 bales; average cotton product per acre, 0.31 bale, 465 pounds seed-cotton, or 155 pounds cotton lint.

Leon county is bounded on the east and west by the Trinity and Navasota rivers, the divide between their respective tributaries being on the west near the latter. The surface of the county is somewhat rolling, and is well timbered with post and black-jack oaks and pine and hickory on the uplands, and cottonwood, elm, walnut, hackberry, etc., on the streams. The uplands are interspersed with brown-loam prairies, their combined area covering, it is estimated, about 100 square miles. These prairies are well supplied with grasses, and are very generally devoted to the grazing of stock. The timbered uplands have usually gray sandy loam soils with subsoils more or less clayey; those of the bottom lands are a black loam, quite deep, and rather subject to overflow.

Leon county is sparsely settled. The lands under cultivation comprise 10.6 per cent. of the county area, and average 68.1 acres per square mile. The crops of the county are corn, cotton, sugar-cane, small grain, fruits, and vegetables. Cotton, comprising 34.6 per cent. of county area, has an acreage of 23.6 per square mile, its growth and yield per acre, and the methods of its culture, etc., being the same as in the adjoining counties.

FALLS.

(See "Central black prairie region".)

ROBERTSON.

Population: 22,383.—White, 11,386; colored, 10,997.
Area: 870 square miles.—Woodland, nearly all; oak, hickory, and pine region, 840 square miles; brown-loam prairie region, 30 square miles.
Tilled lands: 117,990 acres.—Area planted in cotton, 49,854 acres; in corn, 34,255 acres; in oats, 1,407 acres; in wheat, 67 acres.
Cotton production: 18,080 bales; average cotton product per acre, 0.36 bale, 540 pounds seed-cotton, or 180 pounds cotton lint.

Robertson county lies between the Navasota and Brazos rivers, which form respectively the east and west boundaries, Calvert, the county-seat, being situated on the divide between their tributaries. Its surface is undulating, with a small area of mesquite prairies on the north around Bremond and on the southwest near Hearne. The rest of the county uplands are well timbered with post and black-jack oaks and hickory, and have a gray sandy soil (in places little else than deep white sand) and a red or yellow clayey subsoil. Between Hearne and Bremond there is seen the red ferruginous sandstone strata belonging to that belt which passes from the northeastern part of the state southwest into Guadalupe county. The red iron-ore hills that characterize this belt in other counties are not so prominent here. Brown coal or lignite (Tertiary) is found beneath these lands at a depth of 30 or 40 feet, and is said to be of good quality. The prairies are scarcely under cultivation. They have rather a stiff loamy soil, sandy near the timbers, and are largely covered with a low mesquite growth. They belong to the brown-loam belt that borders the central black prairie region in the counties north of Robertson.

The river lands are broad, timbered with walnut, pecan, ash, elm, etc., and have reddish loam soils of great depth and productiveness. It is claimed that they will produce an average of 40 or 50 bushels of corn and 1,500 or 2,000 pounds of seed-cotton per acre in fair seasons. The county is very well populated, and the lands under cultivation average 135.6 acres per square mile, or 21.2 per cent. of its entire area. Cotton is the chief crop, comprising 42.3 per cent. of tilled lands, and averaging 57.3 acres per square mile, there being but five counties with a greater proportion of tilled lands devoted to its culture, and but three having a greater acreage of cotton per square mile, viz, Washington, Fayette, and Johnson.

ABSTRACT FROM THE REPORT OF H. D. PENDERGAST, OF CALVERT.

Bottom land includes one-fourth of all that is cultivated in the county. The soil is an alluvium, from 2 to 10 feet deep, varying from gray sandy to red and black waxy. Its growth is pin oak, ash, walnut, and pecan. The subsoil is frequently sandy, and sometimes clayey. Tillage is easy where sandy, but difficult in wet seasons where the soil is clayey or waxy. The soil is well drained, and is equally well adapted to cotton and corn, which are the chief crops of the region. More than one-half the cultivated area is planted in cotton, the height attained by the plant varying from 4 to 7 feet, but it is most productive at 5 feet. In wet seasons it inclines to run to weed on any soil here, which may be checked by ceasing to cultivate, and might be prevented, if the wet weather could be foreknown, by shallow cultivation. The seed-cotton product per acre of fresh land is 1,125 pounds. By ten to twenty years' cultivation (without manure) production has declined about one-fifth on the sandy and not any on the clayey soils, nor has the staple visibly changed in quality. Crab-grass, cocklebur, and dewberry-vines are the most troublesome as weeds. The lowlands are slightly damaged in some places by washings from the uplands. The upland slopes, however, do not readily wash and gully anywhere in this region. No efforts have been made to check the slight damage on the lowlands.

The *upland cotton-growing soil* is gray or chocolate colored, from 5 to 12 inches deep, has a red-clay subsoil, and bears a growth chiefly of post and black-jack oaks. About half its cultivated area is planted in cotton. The plant usually grows 3 feet high, or from 5 to 6 feet in wet seasons, the higher the more productive. The seed-cotton product per acre of fresh land is from 800 to 1,200 pounds, with the general ratio of 3 pounds of seed-cotton for 1 of lint, rating as low middling. The production declines about one-fifth in ten years' cultivation (unmanured), but the ratio of seed to lint and quality of staple do not apparently vary. This region is too far north to suffer from the caterpillar, and is not often affected by drought.

Cotton is shipped from October to February, about one-fourth of which goes to Galveston at about $3 75 ber bale, the balance to New York, or to the mills, at about $8 per bale.

MADISON.

Population: 5,395.—White, 3,693; colored, 1,702.
Area: 460 square miles.—Woodland, nearly all; all oak, hickory, and pine region.
Tilled lands: 24,268 acres.—Area planted in cotton, 9,158 acres; in corn, 9,694 acres; in oats, 322 acres.
Cotton production: 2,656 bales; average cotton product per acre, 0.29 bale, 435 pounds seed-cotton, or 145 pounds cotton lint.

Madison, a narrow county lying between Trinity river on the east and Navasota on the west, has a somewhat rolling surface, partly of open prairies and partly of timbered post-oak uplands, and is watered chiefly by the tributaries of the Trinity, the divide being in the western part of the county. The streams have a dark-loam soil, are well timbered with oak, hickory, pecan, ash, and walnut, and are subject to overflow. The rivers are bordered by low prairie valley lands or "second bottoms", with little or no timber growth, and have a black waxy soil, similar in character to the black upland prairies.

The upland prairies cover a large part of the county, and have soils varying from black waxy or clayey to brown loams, as is usual with the prairies of this portion of the state. They are interspersed with sandy post and black-jack oak uplands, the soils of which are from 6 to 10 inches deep, with clayey subsoils. One of these prairies is said to extend east and west through the county with a width of 10 or 15 miles. The lands under cultivation average 52.8 acres per square mile, or 8.2 per cent. of the entire area of the county, while 37.7 per cent. of these lands (or 19.9 acres per square mile) is devoted to the culture of cotton. The acreage of corn is the greatest. The average yield per acre of seed-cotton was in 1869 very much below that for the state.

ABSTRACT FROM THE REPORT OF P. K. GOREE, OF MIDWAY.

The lowlands consist of the bottoms of several creeks and of Trinity river, and also of black prairie second bottoms lying along the river, interspersed with sand ridges and pecan groves. Two-thirds of the upland is prairie, with a blackish, gravelly loam soil, and one-third is woodland, chiefly with a whitish, coarse sandy loam, in places sandy, in others more clayey. The uplands are rolling, and the slopes are inclined to wash and gully, but are not yet seriously damaged. Nor are the valleys materially injured by the washings, but are as often improved. Very little effort is made to check the damage.

The *prairie soil* is from 8 to 20 inches thick; the subsoil is a putty-like, impervious clay, containing hard "iron gravel" and some other pebbles. Tillage is easy, except when very wet or very dry; in the latter case the soil becomes very hard. The soil is early, warm, and portions are well drained. The chief crops are corn, cotton, and oats, from one-half to three-fifths of the cultivated part of this land being planted in cotton. The plant grows from 3 to 4 feet high, but is most productive at 4 feet. It inclines to run to weed during wet seasons, and should not ordinarily be restrained, but bolling should be favored by cultivation. The seed-cotton product per acre of fresh land is from 800 to 1,050 pounds, 1,600 pounds making a 475-pound bale of low middling to middling lint. During twenty years' cultivation (unmanured) the lands improve each year. After that time 1,545 pounds make a bale of lint, which is perhaps not perceptibly different from that of fresh land. Crab-grass is most troublesome on this and the soil next to be described. None of this land lies "turned out", but a vast amount is being brought under cultivation.

The *woodland* lies chiefly along the small streams which drain the prairies. The soil is 3 feet deep. The subsoil is an impervious yellowish and sometimes blackish clay, containing variously colored, hard, rounded, and angular pebbles. The soil is early and warm when well drained, and is easily tilled, except in wet seasons. One-half of its cultivated area is usually planted in cotton. The plant grows from 4 to 5 feet high, and inclines to run to weed in very wet seasons; but topping would remedy this if done at 4 feet high. The seed-cotton product per acre of fresh land is from 400 to 1,000 pounds; of old land, from 400 to 800 pounds, the staple being first-class alike from old or fresh land. A very small proportion of this land lies "turned out", and is somewhat improved by rest. On the river bottom crops are much more liable to be injured by excessive rains and backward springs than on the uplands.

Cotton is shipped as soon as baled by wagon to Huntsville, and thence by rail to Houston or Galveston, at a cost of from $5 to $6 per bale.

WALKER.

Population: 12,024.—White, 5,257; colored, 6,767.
Area: 760 square miles.—Woodland, nearly all; all oak, hickory, and pine region.
Tilled lands: 51,129 acres.—Area planted in cotton, 20,162 acres; in corn, 17,512 acres; in oats, 387 acres; in wheat, 15 acres.
Cotton production: 6,441 bales; average cotton product per acre, 0.32 bale, 480 pounds seed-cotton, or 160 pounds cotton lint.

The surface of Walker county is more or less rolling, and is mostly covered with a timber growth of long-leaf pine, red, post, and black-jack oaks, and hickory on the uplands, and interspersed with brown-loam prairies on the west. It is watered chiefly by the Trinity river and its tributaries on the north, and a few small streams on the south which flow into the San Jacinto river. The lands are sandy loams, with red and yellow clay subsoils overlying concretionary clays and sandstones (Grand Gulf).

A large bluff of the latter occurs on the Trinity river at Riverside, and is quarried for small buildings and other purposes. It has an exposed thickness of about 75 feet, is coarse and gritty, and lies in layers of varying thicknesses, with occasional strata of clay-stone. The rock itself also sometimes incloses white clayey concretions.

744

The river bottom lands have dark-loam soils, with the usual bottom timber growth, and is bordered by small black prairie valley lands, or "second bottoms". The lands under cultivation in this county comprise 10.5 per cent. of its area, with an average of 67.3 acres per square mile. The crops are corn, cotton, oats, sugar-cane, vegetables, and some fruits. Very little wheat is planted. Cotton growth, yield, methods of culture, etc., are very much the same as described in Madison county.

SAN JACINTO.

(See "Southern prairie region".)

GRIMES.

Population: 18,603.—White, 8,323; colored, 10,280.
Area: 780 square miles.—Woodland, seven-eighths; all oak, hickory, and pine region.
Tilled lands: 79,877 acres.—Area planted in cotton, 35,984 acres; in corn, 29,072 acres; in oats, 555 acres; in wheat, 70 acres.
Cotton production: 11,701 bales; average cotton product per acre, 0.33 bale, 495 pounds seed-cotton, or 165 pounds cotton lint.

The surface of Grimes county is rolling, about one-eighth being prairie, and the remainder being timbered with post and black-jack oaks, hickory, short-leaf pine, dogwood, etc. A low-water divide passes north and south through the county, and on the west, forming one of the boundaries, is the Navasota river (with short tributary streams), which unites with the Brazos near the southwestern corner. On the east the county is watered partly by some of the headwaters of the San Jacinto and partly by tributaries of the Trinity river.

The prairies occur in areas of from 50 to 100 or more acres throughout the county. Their soils are mostly of the stiff, black, waxy character of the southern prairie region, underlaid by the calcareous concretionary clays of the Port Hudson age. They are not much under cultivation.

The timbered lands comprise two classes, which are intermixed, viz, the post oak and the black-jack pine lands. The former is considered the best, and has a depth of a few inches to a clayey subsoil, while the black-jack lands are sandy to a depth of several feet. A high yield is claimed for both varieties.

The river bottom lands, with their dark and reddish alluvial soils, are the richest and most productive. They extend through the county with a width of 1 or 2 miles, and are heavily timbered with walnut, pecan, ash, etc. Grimes is principally an agricultural county, though but 16 per cent. of its area is under cultivation, averaging 102.4 acres per square mile. It is one of the chief cotton counties of the state, that crop averaging 46.1 acres per square mile, or 45 per cent. of the tilled lands.

Corn is the second crop with regard to acreage, and has an average yield of from 9 to 15 bushels per acre.

In addition to the abstract given below, Mr. Blackshear has sent the following in regard to the features of the county:

Navasota river has a bottom of from one-fourth to 1½ miles in width, with a belt of sandy, timbered upland about one-fourth of a mile wide, bordered by a prairie which gradually rises for 200 yards to a rocky bluff from 10 to 15 feet high, almost parallel with the river for many miles. Large prairies extend from this bluff to the middle of the county, becoming smaller eastward. Brazos river has a bottom proper, varying from 1 to 3 miles in width, with a belt of sandy upland from 1 to 2 miles wide, interspersed with small meadow prairies, level and flat, rather sandy, and usually wet. Sandy post-oak lands lie in the eastern and northern parts of the county; pine lands also in the eastern portion.

ABSTRACTS FROM THE REPORTS OF P. D. SAUNDERS, OF GIBBONS CREEK, AND OF ROBERT D. BLACKSHEAR, C. H. EHINGER, AND A. R. KILPATRICK, OF NAVASOTA.

The kinds of soils cultivated in cotton are: Bottom lands of the Brazos and Navasota rivers and a few large creeks, the blackish prairies, both sandy and stiff hog-wallow lands, and the light soil of the gray, sandy, hilly, timbered lands.

The *bottom* land embraces one-fourth the area of the county, but not one-half of it is cultivated. The soil is an alluvium, with varying proportions of sand, orange-red to dark chocolate in color. The subsoil is lighter in color, until at a depth of from 5 to 25 feet it is composed of sand, associated with white, black, and reddish pebbles. When this soil is broken in winter or spring tillage is easy throughout the year, and the soil is early and well drained by natural ravines. The natural timber growth is pecan, elm, hackberry, ash, hickory, and black, red, and post oaks. It is apparently best adapted to cotton, corn, and oats, but with proper cultivation is also produces potatoes and peas successfully.

Two-thirds of the cultivated portion is planted in cotton. The plant attains a height usually of from 3 to 7 feet, but is most productive at 1. It inclines to run to weed in wet weather, which is remedied by topping. The seed-cotton product per acre is from 1,800 to 2,500 pounds, from 1,545 to 1,780 pounds making a 475-pound bale of lint, which rates as good middling to fair. If rotation of crops is practiced, twenty years' cultivation shows no decline in the quantity of production and very little change in the quality of staple. Cocklebur, tie-vines, and careless-weeds are most troublesome. Very little of such land lies "turned out", and rest improves its yield, but increases the labor in getting rid of sprouts. It is slightly improved in some places by material washed from upland slopes.

The *prairies* comprise two varieties, viz, black sandy prairie and black hog-wallow prairie. The first is a fine and coarse sandy loam; the second is a tenacious, adhesive, clayey loam. They vary in depth from a few inches to 4 or 5 feet, and occur in all directions for 20 miles in spots of from 50 to 500 acres or more. The timbered lands, alternating with these prairies, bear a natural growth of elm, ash, pecan, and post, pin, and black-jack oaks. The prairie subsoil is a heavy clay, varying in color from red to yellow, and is sometimes a joint clay, underlaid by strata of sand and gravel in some parts, and in others by limestone, varying from 1 foot to 20 feet in thickness. The prairie soils, unless baked too hard, are easily tilled in dry weather, but are difficult to till in wet weather. They are early and warm when well drained, and are well adapted to all of the crops produced here.

From one-half to two-thirds of the cultivated area is planted with cotton, and the plant usually attains a height of from 3 to 5 feet, but is most productive at 3 feet. In favorable growing weather, with good tillage, and in wet weather, the plant inclines to run to weed, which is remedied by throwing the dirt from the row and by topping the plant. The seed-cotton product per acre varies from 1,000 to 1,800 pounds, from 1,425 to 1,655 pounds from both fresh and long-cultivated land making a bale of middling lint. If rotation is practiced, production does not decline in quantity after twenty years' cultivation. As the soil gets thinner, the stand of cotton is left closer or thicker and the width of the row is diminished, so that the production holds out. None of this land lies "turned out", but it improves by rest, and is not much injured by weeds in the interval. The most troublesome weeds on this soil are blood, careless, bur, and purslane, besides all weeds which infest southern farms; grasses do not give much trouble. Serious damage is done to slopes by washing and gullying of the soil, but the washings improve the valley lands and render them mellow and easy of tillage. To check the damage some farmers practice horizontalizing with success.

The *fine gray sandy loam* is from 5 to 18 inches thick, and comprises one-half the area of the county and seven-eighths of the land under cultivation. It has a subsoil of red and yellow clay, impervious in places, which becomes very hard when dried in the sun. It contains occasionally black and white pebbles, and is underlaid by sand, gravel, hard sandstone, and limestone in various localities, and at depths varying from 3 to 10 feet. Tillage is generally easy at any time, and the soil is early, warm, and well-drained. Its natural growth is ash, hickory, dogwood, French mulberry, some short-leaf pine, and post, black-jack, and many other oaks. It is apparently best adapted to cotton and sweet potatoes, and one-half its cultivated area is planted in cotton. The plant attains a height of from 2 to 4 feet. In wet weather plants are inclined to run to weed, which is remedied by topping and by frequent stirring of the soil. The seed-cotton product per acre varies from 600 to 1,000 pounds, 1,545 pounds making a 475-pound bale of lint, the staple rating as middling. Five years' cultivation reduces the product per acre to nearly one-half, requiring a very little less to make a bale, and the staple is a grade lower because shorter. Crab and crow-foot grasses, cocklebur, careless-weed, and May-pop vines are the most troublesome as weeds. None of this land has yet been "turned out", except that which was abandoned when laborers emigrated to Kansas. It improves much by rest and green-manuring. Many slopes are seriously damaged by washing and gullying of the soil, but the valleys are improved by the washings. Some horizontalizing and hillside ditching have been done, which check the damage except during heavy rains, when the water breaks over the dams.

The cotton crop is sometimes damaged by late and by early frosts. If planted early, and the spring be wet and the nights cool, the crop is likely to suffer from "red or sore shin" and aphides. The best time for planting here is from April 1 to 15. The crop also sometimes suffers from drought, but that cotton can grow with very little moisture was shown by the production of one-fourth of a crop in 1879 in this locality, when no rain fell between April 23 and November. Scarcely 2 bushels of corn were raised per acre. It is thought by the best farmers that a wet or very rainy May is conducive to the early appearance of the cotton-worm, whereas if we have a dry May the worm does not destroy the cotton before September or October. As evidence of this, in 1846, the first year that the cotton-worm appeared in this county, it rained the entire month of May, and the cotton crop was destroyed by the 15th or 25th of July. The yield for that year was about a 500-pound bale to 40 acres.

Cotton is shipped in November and December, or as fast as ginned, from Navasota to Houston and Galveston at from $1 75 to $2 50 per bale, respectively.

WALLER.
(See "Southern prairie region".)

BRAZOS.

Population: 13,576.—White, 7,325; colored, 6,251.
Area: 520 square miles.—Woodland, probably one-half; all oak, hickory, and pine region and prairies.
Tilled lands: 61,803 acres.—Area planted in cotton, 28,044 acres; in corn, 16,542 acres; in oats, 626 acres; in wheat, 8 acres.
Cotton production: 9,743 bales; average cotton product per acre, 0.35 bale, 525 pounds seed-cotton, or 175 pounds cotton lint.

Brazos county is triangular in shape, and lies within the angle formed by the junction of the Brazos and Navasota rivers, the west and east boundaries. The surface of the country is undulating, and about equally divided between prairies and timbered lands. The bottom lands of the rivers, and especially of the Brazos, are broad, and well timbered with a large growth of ash, pecan, elm, cottonwood, pin oak, hackberry, etc. The soil of the Brazos consists of the usual red loam that occurs in other counties along the river, and is very highly productive and largely under cultivation. A yield of 40 or 50 bushels of corn and 2,000 pounds of seed-cotton per acre is claimed for them. The upland prairie lands have a brownish loam soil more or less sandy, interspersed with areas of a black waxy nature, and underlaid by clays.

The timbered uplands have a timber growth of post and black-jack oaks and hickory, and a sandy and gravelly soil, quite deep, with a red or yellow clay subsoil. These lands are easily cultivated, and with the prairies yield about 800 pounds of seed-cotton per acre in fair seasons.

Brazos is better populated than most of the counties of the state, and is chiefly an agricultural county. The lands under cultivation average 118.9 acres per square mile, or 18.6 per cent. of its area.

Cotton is the principal crop of the county, comprising 45.4 per cent. of the tilled lands, with an average of 53.9 acres per square mile, a number exceeded by only six counties in the state.

ABSTRACT FROM THE REPORT OF J. W. BICKHAM, OF BRYAN.

Cotton here is a sure crop, but on account of accidents of weather and insect pests, etc., is not always a full crop. All the uplands, including creek bottoms, are well adapted to cotton, and embrace a variety of soils, including the *prairie*, which is a mixture of the black sandy and waxy soils. The timbered part is also sandy, and equal in area to the prairie, and bears a natural growth of post and black-jack oaks and hickory. The bottoms have a growth of pecan, ash, and hackberry. These kinds of soil prevail in all the upland counties of this region. Depths of soils vary from 6 to 30 inches. Tillage is easy, except when some parts are too wet. The soil is early, warm, and well drained, and best adapted to cotton, and at least one half the land is planted in the latter. The other chief crops are corn, potatoes, and hay.

The cotton-plant attains a height of from 3 to 6 feet, but is most productive at 4, and inclines to run to weed in wet seasons, or when stripped by the boll-worm. No remedy is known here. The seed-cotton product per acre of fresh land is from 1,000 to 1,200 pounds, 1,600 pounds making a 475-pound bale of low middling lint. After twenty years' cultivation the product is from 800 to 1,000 pounds, 1,545 pounds then making a bale of lint, equal in quality to that from fresh land. No land here is "turned out", but some of it would improve by a few years' rest. Slopes do not readily wash and gully, and valleys are not injured but improved by the washings.

Cotton, as soon as ready, is sold in Bryan and shipped to Galveston.

BURLESON.

Population: 9,243.—White, 5,356; colored, 3,887.
Area: 650 square miles.—Woodland, three-fourths; all oak, hickory, and pine region.
Tilled lands: 47,190 acres.—Area planted in cotton, 15,298 acres; in corn, 14,692 acres; in oats, 320 acres; in wheat, 118 acres.
Cotton production: 5,965 bales; average cotton product per acre, 0.39 bale, 585 pounds seed-cotton, or 195 pounds cotton lint.

Burleson county, lying in the angle formed by the junction of the Yegua river with the Brazos, has an undulating surface, generally well timbered, and interspersed with the brown-loam prairies that occur in these central counties. It is estimated that the prairies cover about one-fourth of the county area, and have soils varying from black to reddish or brownish and sandy, with stiff clayey subsoils. These prairies are open, without any timber growth, and are well covered with grasses. The largest, varying in width from 1 to 4 miles, are known as the San Antonio and String prairies, and are thought to be better adapted to grain than to cotton. They are said to extend 50 miles northeast and many miles southwest of Caldwell, the county-seat.

The timbered lands have usually gray sandy soils, with clayey subsoils, and are timbered with a growth of post and black-jack oaks and hickory, the former predominating, and hence giving its name to the lands. The Brazos bottom lands, with a width of from 3 to 4 miles, have dark loamy and reddish clayey soils and a timber growth of pecan, cottonwood, hackberry, etc. They are the best cotton lands in the county, and are largely under cultivation, yielding over a bale of lint per acre. The tilled lands of the county comprise 11.3 per cent. of its area, and average 72.6 acres per square mile. Cotton is the chief crop, with an average of 23.5 acres per square mile, or 32.4 per cent. of the tilled land.

ABSTRACT FROM THE REPORT OF HILLARY RYAN, OF CALDWELL.

There are in this county, besides the Brazos bottom, 190 square miles of black prairie, 65 square miles of red prairie, 50 square miles of sandy black-jack oak land, and 300 square miles of sandy post-oak land.

The *Brazos bottom land* covers nearly one-fourth of the county area, and extends 200 miles up and 190 miles down the river. Its chief timber is cottonwood, pecan, and box-elder. The soil is a red alluvium, 30 feet deep, becoming more and more gravelly, and at from 30 to 40 feet is underlaid by gravel, in which water is found. This soil is easily tilled, except in wet seasons, and is best adapted to corn and cotton, which are the chief crops produced here. One-half of its cultivated area is planted in cotton. The plant grows from 8 to 12 feet high, but is most productive at 10. It inclines to run to weed in wet seasons and on new land, for which no remedy is used. The seed-cotton product per acre of fresh land is 2,000 pounds, 1,665 pounds making a 475-pound bale of middling lint. After forty years' cultivation the product is 1,400 pounds, the ratio of seed to lint remaining the same, but the staple a little shorter. Cockleburs are the troublesome weeds.

The *red and black prairies* cover one-fourth of the area of the county, and also extend 50 miles northeast and 300 miles southwest. The soils are 12 inches deep, underlaid by heavier but leachy yellow clay, containing "black" gravel, and at 40 feet the whole is underlaid by rock. The soil is early, warm, and easily tilled, except in wet seasons, and is best adapted to corn, but one-half of its cultivated area is planted in cotton. The plant usually grows 4 feet high, the higher the more productive. The seed-cotton product per acre of fresh land is 1,200 pounds, 1,600 pounds making a bale of low middling lint. · Twenty years' cultivation (unmanured) causes no decline in the quantity or quality of cotton produced. Crab-grass is the most troublesome. Slopes, alike on this and the post-oak lands, readily wash and gully, but are not seriously damaged, nor are the valleys by the washings.

· Three-sevenths of the county area is *post-oak land*, the soil of which varies from a fine sandy to clay loam, and in color from gray to dark brown, and is 12 inches deep. The subsoil is a heavy adhesive clay, underlaid at 4 feet by pipe-clay. The soil is early, warm, easily tilled, and best adapted to cotton, with which one-half its cultivated area is planted. The plant usually grows 6 or 8 feet high, but is most productive at 8 feet. The seed-cotton product per acre on fresh land is 1,500 pounds, and after twenty years' cultivation (unmanured) the product and its quality are about the same. All other details are as given for the prairies last described. The cotton crop is closely dependent on the amount of rain. Seasons are usually fair, but droughts are likely to occur in July and cause shedding to a serious extent. Everything is favorable to cotton production.

Cotton is shipped in October and November, by rail, to Galveston at $3 50 per bale.

MILAM.

Population: 18,659.—White, 14,723; colored, 3,936.
Area: 990 square miles.—Woodland, greater part; oak, hickory, and pine region, 800 square miles; central black prairie region, 170 square miles.
Tilled lands: 91,032 acres.—Area planted in cotton, 37,473 acres; in corn, 32,725 acres; in oats, 1,946 acres; in wheat, 593 acres.
Cotton production: 10,844 bales; average cotton product per acre, 0.29 bale, 435 pounds seed-cotton, or 145 pounds cotton lint.

The surface of Milam county is rolling and somewhat hilly, and is watered by Little river and smaller streams, all tributary to the Brazos, which form the eastern boundary. Nearly one-half of the county on the northwest is included in the central prairie region, its eastern limit passing northeast and southwest. Near Cameron, the county-seat, the soils are usually black, waxy, and calcareous in character, underlaid by heavy clays and Cretaceous rotten limestone, and interspersed with black sandy and brown-loam prairies, with bodies of timbered uplands along the streams. The southeast half of the county is well timbered with post and black-jack oaks, hickory, etc., on the uplands, and its lands are sandy, with red and yellow clayey subsoils. Beds of deep white sand, and areas of red land and ferruginous sandstone are found on the south. The Brazos river is bordered in this county by its usual wide bottom lands of stiff reddish clays and loams and large timber growth of oaks, elm, ash, pecan, etc.

The lands under cultivation average 92 acres per square mile, and comprise 14.4 per cent. of the county area. Cotton is the chief crop, with an average of 37.8 acres per square mile, or 41.2 per cent. of the tilled lands. The prairies are mostly devoted to stock grazing.

The soils cultivated in cotton are those of the black and sandy rolling upland prairies, the blackish and black alluvial bottoms of Little and San Gabriel rivers and Elm and Pond creeks, and the post-oak uplands.

More than one-half of the county is *prairie*. The soil is black and waxy, light brown and sandy, and is 30 inches deep. The subsoil is a red and yellow clay under the sandy, and dark colored (rarely whitish) heavy clay under the black prairie land. The soil is early, easily tilled, and best adapted to cotton; other crops also do well on it. The chief crops of this region are cotton, corn, oats, rye, barley, millet, potatoes, and onions. One-third the cultivated acreage is planted in cotton, the average and most productive height of which is 4 feet. It inclines to run to weed in wet seasons on fresh land, the remedy, if any, consisting in shallow cultivation. The seed-cotton product per acre of fresh land is from 800 to 1,000 pounds, with the usual 3 pounds of seed-cotton for one of lint from any soil, fresh or old. After three years' cultivation (unmanured) the product is from 1,200 to 1,400 pounds. (My average for ten years on this land has been 1,300 pounds of seed-cotton per acre.) The staple from old land is about equal to that from new. The most troublesome weeds are crab-grass on the sandy soil, and cocklebur, lamb's-quarter, and morning-glory on the black waxy prairie soil. There is very little or no washing of slopes.

The *bottom lands* occupy one-tenth of the area of the county. The chief growth is elm, ash, white and burr oaks, hackberry, etc. The soil is about 6 feet deep, and is underlaid by an impervious joint clay. The soil is early and easily tilled, except in wet seasons, when it is adhesive, and it is best adapted to cotton, with which two-thirds of its cultivated area is planted. The plant grows from 5 to 7 feet high, and inclines to run to weed in wet seasons, for which no remedy is used. The seed-cotton product per acre is 1,000 pounds on fresh land, or 1,500 pounds after three years' cultivation (unmanured). The troublesome weeds are cocklebur and morning-glory. (Other details of this land are as already given in the description of the prairie preceding.)

The *post oak or sandy upland* comprises about one-third the county area. The soil is 12 inches deep, presents much variety in composition and color, and has a subsoil of impervious red and joint clays containing black and white gravel. The soil is early, easily tilled, best adapted to cotton and potatoes, and one-half its cultivated area is planted in cotton. The plant usually grows from 3 to 4 feet high. The seed-cotton product per acre is from 800 to 1,000 pounds on fresh land, or from 600 to 1,000 pounds after ten years' cultivation (unmanured). (Other details as given in preceding descriptions.) The troublesome weeds are crab-grass, careless-weed, and cocklebur. Very little of this land lies "turned out". Slopes wash and gully very little, and the valleys are to some extent injured by the washings; but very little effort is made to check the damage. The river bottom lands are the richest in Texas, and are especially adapted to cotton. The uplands are more easily cultivated, healthier, and better adapted to the white race.

As soon as it is baled cotton is carried by wagons to Calvert and Rockdale, then shipped by rail to Houston or to Galveston at $1 25 per bale.

LEE.

Population: 8,937.—White, 6,981; colored, 1,956.

Area: 600 square miles.—Woodland, nearly all; all oak, hickory, and pine region.

Tilled lands: 42,331 acres.—Area planted in cotton, 15,662 acres; in corn, 14,396 acres; in oats, 745 acres; in wheat, 136 acres.

Cotton production: 5,526 bales; average cotton product per acre, 0.35 bale, 525 pounds seed-cotton, or 175 pounds cotton lint.

The surface of Lee county is more or less rolling, with timbered post-oak lands, interspersed with brown-loam and black prairies over the entire area. It is watered by the several prongs of the Yegua creeks on the north and the tributaries of the Colorado river on the south. The Tertiary sandstone and iron-ore belt crosses the northwestern part of the county, and bodies of red lands occur in a number of places.

Near Lexington, the county-seat, beds of fossiliferous blue marl (Jackson) are frequently found in wells at depths of a few feet from the surface, and glauconitic sandstone occurs in some of the red lands of that section, giving to them a high percentage of potash (see analysis, page 25). The post-oak lands comprise the principal uplands of the county, and have a gray sandy soil, with red or yellowish clay subsoil. Heavy beds of white sand are often found associated with them.

Eleven per cent. of the area of the county is under cultivation, averaging 70.6 acres per square mile. Cotton is the chief crop, comprising 37 per cent. of the tilled lands, or an average of 26.1 acres per square mile.

The lands cultivated in cotton are the gray, sandy, post-oak lands, bearing a natural timber growth of post and black-jack oaks and hickory; yellow, red, brown, and black prairies, with heavier subsoils; and creek bottoms, one-fourth of a mile to 2 miles wide, having a natural timber growth of wild peach, elm, pin oak, ash, pecan, mulberry, hackberry, and an undergrowth of sumac on the second bottoms. The chief crops of this region are cotton, corn, oats, wheat, millet, sorghum, sugar-cane, and sweet and Irish potatoes.

The chief soil of the county is the *fine, sandy, gravelly loam* first mentioned. It is 6 inches in depth, and has a lighter subsoil, underlaid by a yellow and red clay at from 1 foot to 4 feet. The land is early, warm, well drained, and easily tilled, and is best adapted to cotton, but produces the other crops very well. From one-half to two-thirds of its cultivated area is planted in cotton. The height attained by the plant varies from 2 to 6 feet in wet seasons, and from 1 to 4 feet in dry seasons, but it is most productive at from 2 to 4 feet. In warm, wet seasons, and when stands are too thick, the plant inclines to run to weed on all cotton lands here, the remedy, according to some farmers, consisting in giving a sufficient distance between the rows and by topping in August. The seed-cotton product per acre of fresh land is from 1,000 to 1,200 pounds, about 1,545 pounds making a 475-pound bale of lint, the staple rating as good middling. After fifteen years' cultivation the product is from 500 to 800 pounds, 1,065 pounds making a 475-pound bale, and the staple is shorter and coarser. Crab-grass and cocklebur are the most troublesome weeds.

The *prairie soils* are best adapted to small grains. There is a scattering growth of post, black-jack, pin, or water oaks, elm, hickory, and mesquite. The soil is about 30 inches deep, and is underlaid by red and joint clays, with some yellow, blue, and whitish clays in places. It is difficult to till in wet and dry seasons, and is early, warm, and well drained.

The *bottom lands* comprise the hickory and sumac second bottom, and the sandy peach and elm bottoms. The former, covering about 20 per cent. of this region, occurs in available bodies of from 1 acre to 100 acres, and has a timber growth of hickory, black-jack, and post oaks, and mulberry. The soil is a sandy loam, 2 feet in depth, with a yellow-clay subsoil, which contains some lime pebbles, and is underlaid by sand-rock at from 5 to 10 feet. It is tilled with difficulty in wet or dry seasons, is naturally well drained, and is best adapted to cotton, corn, oats, and potatoes. One-half of its cultivated area is planted in cotton. The plant usually attains a height of 6 feet, but is most productive at 5 feet. The seed-cotton product per acre varies from 1,200 to 1,600 pounds, about 1,545 pounds making a 475-pound bale, and the staple is of the first quality. After fifteen years' cultivation the product is from 1,000 to 1,400 pounds, and about 1,630 pounds make a bale, the staple being coarser than that from fresh land. Crab-grass is the most troublesome weed.

The *sandy peach and grayish elm bottom lands* cover not more than 5 per cent. of the county, the bottoms ranging from one-fourth of a mile to 2 miles wide, and extending unbroken for several miles along the creeks. The natural timber growth is wild peach, elm, ash, pecan, mulberry, hackberry, and pin oak, with smaller undergrowth. The soil is a fine sandy loam 3 feet in depth, with a heavier and tougher subsoil, consisting of grayish or blackish sandy clay, and underlaid by sand. The soil is late, warm, and well drained, and is best adapted to corn. Cotton does equally as well, though uplands are preferred. One-third of the cultivated area is devoted to cotton, which grows to a height of from 3 to 8 feet, being most productive at 6 feet. Too much rain in conjunction with warm weather inclines the plant to run to weed, and in some cases topping is the remedy applied. The product per acre of seed-cotton from fresh land is 1,400 pounds, and after ten years' cultivation the yield is 2,000 pounds per acre, 1,425 pounds from fresh and 1,545 pounds from old land being requisite for 475 pounds of first-rate lint. A very small portion of this land lies "turned out", and when again "taken in" the land produces very well. Cocklebur, crab-grass, and careless-weed are the most troublesome weeds.

On account of their liability to overflows and to late and early frosts bottom lands are but little cultivated. They produce large yields, however, in favorable seasons. The under-bolls are liable to rot in summer and fall if there is much rain. Dry and hot weather in the spring months is favorable to cotton; cold and wet springs are detrimental. The advance of the crop is more rapid on the uplands than on the bottoms. The gray, sandy, prairie land requires the least rain to produce a crop; the red prairie more, and the mesquite prairie most rain.

Shipments are made to Galveston at the rate of $3 50 per bale.

BASTROP.

Population: 17,215.—White, 9,909; colored, 7,306.

Area: 900 square miles.—Woodland, nearly all; nearly all oak, hickory, and pine region.

Tilled lands: 85,732 acres.—Area planted in cotton, 35,730 acres; in corn, 31,786 acres; in oats, 1,345 acres; in wheat, 852 acres.

Cotton production: 14,714 bales; average cotton product per acre, 0.41 bale, 615 pounds seed-cotton, or 205 pounds cotton lint.

The surface of Bastrop county is more or less rolling, and is very generally timbered with post and live oaks, hickory, pine, etc. Small prairies are found in the eastern part of the county, their combined area covering, it is estimated, about one-third its entire area. The county is divided into two parts by the Colorado river, which flows in a southeasterly course, and to which all the streams on either side are tributary.

The valley lands of the river are usually broad, and consist of a dark reddish loam soil and a clayey subsoil, very productive, and very generally under cultivation. The timber growth of the river lands is walnut, pecan, ash, elm, etc., with several varieties of oaks.

The uplands that border the valley present broken bluffs or cedar brakes near Bastrop covered with drift sand, gravel, and rounded quartz pebbles, and almost devoid of any vegetation other than dwarf cedars. To the north and west the uplands are sandy, with a prominent growth of post and black-jack oaks, interspersed with areas of red sandy loams, ferruginous pebbles, etc. (See analysis of soils, page 26.)

There are a few prominent hills of Tertiary iron ore in this section, a part of the belt from the northeastern counties. Beds of lignite of good quality are exposed in the banks of the river above the town of Bastrop.

In the eastern and southern parts of the county there are a number of open prairies, with soils varying from sandy to black and hog-wallow in character, and having an occasional growth of mesquite and live-oak trees. Passing southward from Bastrop to Lockhart, in Caldwell county, there is at first some timbered land for 16 miles, then open black prairies, with belts of timber and some mesquite trees, for 15 miles more. Shippo lake, on the southeast, is said to have an extent of 5 miles in length, and to be from one-fourth to one and one-half miles in width.

Bastrop is an agricultural county, 14.9 per cent. of its area being under cultivation, making an average of about 95.3 acres per square mile. Cotton is the principal crop, its acreage being 41.7 per cent. of the tilled lands, or an average of 39.7 acres per square mile. Its yield per acre is above that of the adjoining counties, and also of that of the state.

ABSTRACT FROM THE REPORTS OF JOHN FAWCETT, OF SMITHVILLE, AND W. A. HIGHSMITH, OF SNAKE PRAIRIE.

The chief soils of this county are those of the river bottom, the sandy post-oak uplands, and the sandy and waxy prairies.

The *bottom lands* of the Colorado river has a less area than either of the other kinds of land, but it embraces three-fourths of all the soil at present cultivated in the county, and extends from Austin to the mouth of the river, about 300 miles. Its natural growth is post, black-jack, burr, and pin oaks, pecan, cedar, elm, and hackberry, and there are spots of prairie in it. The soil is a clay loam, putty-like in spots, varying in color from brown to black, and is from 3 to 10 feet deep. The subsoil is of a mahogany color, tough and unproductive, and is underlaid by gravel at 25 feet. The soil is easily tilled, excepting tough spots in wet weather, is early and tolerably well drained, and is apparently best adapted to cotton, to which one-half the cultivated area is devoted. Corn and cotton are the chief crops of this region. The plant grows from 4 to 7 feet high, and yields most at 5 feet, but inclines to run to weed on any soil here in long-continued wet seasons, for which topping is sometimes practiced as a remedy. The seed-cotton product per acre of fresh land is 2,500 pounds, 1,665 pounds making a 475-pound bale of good middling lint. Forty years' cultivation reduces the production to about one-half the original, 1,450 pounds of seed-cotton being needed for a bale, and the staple being finer and shorter. Cocklebur is the most troublesome weed. Very little damage is done this soil by washings from upland slopes.

The *black mesquite prairies* are the second quality of cotton land. The soil is tough and adhesive, and occurs from 20 to 30 miles in all directions, interspersed with patches of fine sandy, gray, yellow, and blackish post-oak land. The soil is 2 feet deep; the subsoil is a tough yellow clay, baking very hard when exposed to the sun, and contains flinty pebbles and small shells, underlaid by gravel at 10 feet. Tillage is difficult in wet weather, and not very easy in dry seasons. The soil is late, cold, well drained, and best adapted to cotton, with which one-third of the cultivated portion is planted. The usual and most productive height of the plant is 4 feet. The seed-cotton product per acre of fresh land is 1,000 pounds, 1,600 pounds making a 475-pound bale of good middling lint. Five years' cultivation (unmanured) does not diminish the product, while the staple becomes finer and longer. None of such land lies "turned out". Careless-weed is the most troublesome. Slopes are damaged to a serious extent by washing and gullying, and no efforts have been made to check the damage. The valleys are not injured by the washings.

The fine sandy, gray, yellow, and blackish *post-oak timbered lands* occur in bodies alternating with the prairies. The soil is from 3 to 6 inches deep; the subsoil is heavier, a red clay in some places and bluish joint clay in others, and is impervious, the former containing flinty rounded "black gravel". Both are underlaid by gravel in places at 15 feet. The soil is easily tilled in any season, is early, warm, and generally well drained, and is best adapted to cotton, the same occupying two-thirds of the cultivated portion. The plant attains a height of from 2 to 4 feet, and the seed-cotton product per acre of fresh land is 800 pounds, 1,545 pounds making a bale of strictly good middling lint. Twenty years' cultivation reduces the product to 500 pounds, and the ratio of seed to lint remains the same, but the staple is shorter. Crab-grass is the most troublesome weed. One-fifth of such land has been "turned out". Slopes wash and gully slightly, and valleys are damaged to a small extent by the washing. Horizontalizing and hillside ditching are very successfully practiced to check the damage.

Cotton is shipped by rail to Galveston, as soon as it is ready, at $3 40 to $5 25 per bale.

CALDWELL.
(See "Central black prairie region".)

FAYETTE.
(See "Southern prairie region".)

WASHINGTON.
(See "Southern prairie region".)

AUSTIN.
(See "Southern prairie region".)

COLORADO.
(See "Southern prairie region".)

LAVACA.
(See "Southern prairie region".)

GONZALES.

Population : 14,840.—White, 9,974; colored, 4,866.
Area : 1,070 square miles.—Woodland, greater part; oak, hickory, and pine region, 820 square miles; southern prairie region, 250 square miles.
Tilled lands : 88,538 acres.—Area planted in cotton, 22,729 acres; in corn, 30,984 acres; in oats, 767 acres; in wheat, 646 acres.
Cotton production : 7,511 bales; average cotton product per acre, 0.33 bale, 495 pounds seed-cotton, or 165 pounds cotton lint.

The surface of Gonzales county is rolling, and in places somewhat broken, and is watered by the Guadalupe and San Marcos rivers, which unite near the county-seat.

The northern, western, and southwestern parts of the county are well timbered with post and other oaks and hickory. The lands are diversified with gray sandy and red loam soils and sandy post-oak flats, and in places contain much ferruginous gravel. (See analysis, page 25.)

In the eastern and southern parts of the county there are open and rolling prairies, interspersed throughout the uplands, with soils varying from black to sandy, and having some mesquite growth. They also form some of the valley lands of the large streams. In the uplands of the southern part there are low ridges covered with much flinty gravel, variously colored quartz pebbles, and silicified wood (Quaternary), with also occasional outcrops of the soft Grand Gulf sandstone.

The lands of the rivers are dark loams, very productive, with a timber growth of black walnut, burr and Spanish oaks, pecan, ash, cottonwood, elm, willow, sycamore, etc., and a dense undergrowth of black and red haw, dogwood, buckeye, wild plum, and vines.

Gonzales is an agricultural county, though sparsely populated. The lands under cultivation average about 82.7 acres per square mile, or 12.7 per cent. of the entire area. Cotton comprises but 25.7 per cent. of the tilled lands, or an average of 21.2 acres per square mile.

ABSTRACT FROM THE REPORT OF B. W. BROTHERS, OF HARWOOD STATION.

San Marcos river bottom comprises one-fourth of the cultivated land of the county, the balance consisting of "hog-wallow" prairie and timbered sandy upland.

The *bottom land,* which is preferred for cotton, is of uniform quality throughout the county, and its chief growth is pecan, elm, cottonwood, and box-elder. The soil is a black loam, 30 inches deep; the subsoil is a heavier, more clayey loam, and is hard. It is underlaid by sand and gravel at 10 feet. The soil is early, warm, well drained, and equally well adapted to cotton, corn, oats, and potatoes, which are the chief crops produced here. One-third of the cultivated area is planted in cotton. The height attained by the plant reaches from 5 to 9 feet, the higher the more productive. In very wet seasons the plant inclines to run to weed, for which topping is said to be a good remedy. The seed-cotton product per acre is about 1,400 pounds. Cocklebur and morning-glory are the most troublesome weeds. Where upland slopes are sandy they are seriously damaged by washing and gullying, which is checked by horizontalizing the rows. The valleys have not been injured by the washings. Cotton requires more time for maturing on the bottoms, but is not liable to be frost-killed.

Cotton is shipped in October and November, by rail, from Harwood to Galveston at $4 50 per bale.

GUADALUPE.

(See "Central black prairie region".)

BEXAR.

(See "Central black prairie region".)

WILSON.

Population: 7,118.—White, 6,197; colored, 921.
Area: 790 square miles.—Woodland, little more than half; oak, hickory, and pine region, 450 square miles; southern prairie region, 340 square miles.
Tilled lands: 33,642 acres.—Area planted in cotton, 5,814 acres; in corn, 7,999 acres; in oats, 43 acres; in wheat, 96 acres.
Cotton production: 1,874 bales; average cotton product per acre, 0.32 bale, 480 pounds seed-cotton, or 160 pounds cotton lint.

The surface of Wilson county is undulating, and is watered by the San Antonio river and its tributary streams. The county is situated at the southwestern terminus of the large oak and hickory region of eastern Texas, Floresville, the county-seat, being nearly on the limit, though narrow prongs or offshoots, as it were, extend south and southwestward. Two agricultural regions are therefore here represented, viz, the post-oak uplands, covering most of the northern part, and the southwestern prairie region on the south. The former has some live-oak growth, and a soil varying from a dark to gray and sandy loam, underlaid by clays and sandstone.

The prairies on the south have partly a mesquite growth and scattered or isolated live- and post-oak trees. They have a sandy loam soil, well covered with grasses, and are usually used as grazing lands for stock.

The valley lands of the rivers, with their stiff black soils and growth of pecan, elm, ash, etc., are very wide, and seem to be the chief lands under cultivation, yielding fine crops of cotton and corn. The county is rather sparsely populated, and stock raising forms one of the chief industries. Of its area but 6.7 per cent. is under cultivation, with an average of 42.6 acres per square mile.

Cotton is as yet but a secondary crop, averaging 7.4 acres per square mile, or 17.3 per cent. of the tilled lands.

ABSTRACT FROM THE REPORT OF J. W. ANDERSON, OF SUTHERLAND SPRINGS.

The lands of the county are those of the bottoms of San Antonio river and Cibolo creek, the rolling and level post-oak uplands, and the upland prairies.

The *valley soils* are the black, shelly, and waxy loams on Cibolo creek and ash-colored alluvial loam on San Antonio river. These extend no more than 1½ miles on either side of the streams, and include one-fifth of the cultivated area of the county, being the chief cotton lands. Their natural growth is elm, hackberry, pecan, ash, and mesquite. The soil is from 2 to 8 feet deep, and is underlaid by a lighter clay, rather more impervious than the soil, the whole being underlaid by sand, gravel, and sand-rock at from 20 to 50 feet. Tillage is easy, except in wet weather, or when a real drought prevails, and in many places the soil is late, cold, and ill-drained. The chief crops of this region are corn, cotton, oats, wheat, and sweet potatoes. This soil is best adapted to cotton and corn, and two-fifths of its area is planted in cotton. The plant grows from 4 to 5 feet high, the medium being the most productive. It inclines to run to weed when excessive rains follow thorough cultivation, the remedy for which is to throw dirt from the row. The seed-cotton product per acre of fresh land is from 1,200 to 2,000 pounds, about 1,485 pounds making a 475-pound bale of lint. Ten years' cultivation (unmanured) causes no perceptible decline in the yield; a very little less is needed for a bale, and the staple is a little shorter. The cocklebur and careless-weed are most troublesome. A small percentage of such land, consisting of abandoned farms, is now lying out. When again cultivated it produces as well or better than ever.

The *post-oak land* includes one-third of the tilled lands of the county, and has a growth of post, black-jack, and some live oaks, hickory, and some bastard oak (a variety of white oak). The soil is a brown (black in some parts), fine sandy loam, from 1½ to 8 feet thick, and rests upon a lighter clayey loam, which is again underlaid by sand and sand-rock at from 15 to 40 feet. The soil is early, warm, and well drained, always easily tilled, and is best adapted to cotton, three-fifths of its cultivated area being planted with the same. The plant grows from 3 to 7 feet high, is most productive at 4 or 4½, and is inclined to run to weed as on the bottoms last described. The seed-cotton product per acre of fresh land varies from 1,200 to 2,800 and sometimes 3,000 pounds, 1,485 pounds making a 475-pound bale of low middling to middling lint. After ten years' cultivation (unmanured) the product varies from 1,000 to 2,000 pounds, and 1,625 pounds make a 475-pound bale of lint not perceptibly different from that on fresh land. Old land improves by rest, but none is known to have been "turned out". Slopes do not wash or gully badly, unless the soil is very deep, in which case the damage is very effectually checked by filling the gullies with straw or brush.

One-fourth of the county area is *upland mesquite prairie*. The soil is a varying loam (sandy, fine and coarse), gravelly, gray, red, brown, and in low places black, and is from 1½ to 5 feet thick. The subsoil is a clayey loam, pervious to water, and underlaid by sand and sand-rock at 12 to 20 feet. The soil is early, warm, generally well drained, easy to till in wet seasons, but becomes hard in dry seasons unless plowed after a rain, and is best adapted to corn, cotton, and wheat. Nearly one-half its cultivated area is planted in cotton. The plant grows about 4½ feet high, the higher the more productive. It is rarely inclined to run to weed. The seed-cotton product per acre of fresh land is from 1,200 to 1,400 pounds, 1,545 pounds making a 475-pound bale of good ordinary to low middling lint. After ten years' cultivation (unmanured) there is no perceptible decline in the quality or the quantity of cotton produced per acre. The broom-weed and dwarf careless-weed are most troublesome.

Cotton is shipped as fast as baled, by wagon, to Cuero (De Witt county) or Marion (Guadalupe county), and thence to Galveston; rate per bale via Marion, $5 75.

DE WITT.
(See "Southern prairie region".)

GOLIAD.
(See "Southern prairie region".)

BEE.
(See "Southern prairie region".)

KARNES.
(See "Southern prairie region".)

ATASCOSA.
(See "Southern prairie region".)

FRIO.
(See "Southern prairie region".)

MEDINA.
(See "Central black prairie region".)

LONG-LEAF PINE REGION.

(It comprises all or parts of the counties of Sabine,* San Augustine,* Angelina,* Trinity,* Polk,* San Jacinto,* Liberty, Hardin, Tyler, Jasper, Newton, Orange, and Jefferson.*)

SABINE.
(See "Oak, hickory, and pine region".)

SAN AUGUSTINE.
(See "Oak, hickory, and pine region".)

ANGELINA.
(See "Oak, hickory, and pine region".)

TRINITY.
(See "Oak, hickory, and pine region".)

POLK.
(See "Oak, hickory, and pine region".)

SAN JACINTO.
(See "Southern prairie region".)

LIBERTY.

Population: 4,999.—White, 2,565; colored, 2,434.

Area: 1,170 square miles.—Woodland, nearly all; all long-leaf pine region.

Tilled lands: 13,027 acres.—Area planted in cotton, 3,768 acres; in corn, 6,102 acres; in oats, 40 acres.

Cotton production: 1,852 bales; average cotton product per acre, 0.49 bale, 735 pounds seed-cotton, or 245 pounds cotton lint.

The surface of Liberty county is quite level. The uplands of the eastern and northern parts are well timbered with long-leaf pine and some oak, hickory, and ash; the rest, comprising, it is thought, about three-fifths of the area, has a growth of short-leaf pine, interspersed with open prairies. The Trinity river divides the county into two parts, each of which is watered by small streams that flow independently to Galveston bay. The lands of the river bottom are broad, and have a reddish loam soil, very rich and productive, and a timber growth of cypress, magnolia, ash, walnut, etc. It is claimed that this land will produce an average of a bale of cotton per acre. The prairie second bottoms, from one-half of a mile to 2 miles wide, are said to produce as well. The timbered uplands have a 'sandy soil, while the lands of the prairies vary from a light sandy loam or silt to a black and stiff clay, underlaid by heavy clay subsoils.

These prairies afford fine pasturage for stock, and are mostly used for that purpose. Tarkinton's prairie is said to cover about 100 square miles. The county is sparsely populated, and but 1.7 per cent. of the lands are in cultivation, giving an average of 11.1 acres per square mile. The chief crops are corn, cotton, sugar-cane, potatoes, rice, and vegetables. Comparatively little cotton is planted (3.2 acres per square mile, or 28.9 per cent. of the tilled lands), and that only on the best lands. It grows from 3 to 5 feet high, and yields an average for the county of 735 pounds in the seed; a product higher than in any other county in southeastern Texas, and higher than the average for the state.

Shipments of produce are made by railroad either to Houston, Galveston, or New Orleans.

HARDIN.

Population: 1,870.—White, 1,634; colored, 236.
Area: 820 square miles.—Woodland, nearly all; all long-leaf pine region.
Tilled lands: 3,368 acres.—Area planted in cotton, 264 acres; in corn, 2,491 acres; in oats, 194 acres.
Cotton production: 103 bales; average cotton product per acre, 0.39 bale, 585 pounds seed-cotton, or 195 pounds cotton lint.

The surface of Hardin county is quite level, and is watered by the Neches river and its numerous tributaries. With the exception of a small extent of prairie lands on the southwest, the county is heavily timbered with long-leaf pine on the uplands, and oak, beech, walnut, holly, magnolia, etc., on the bottoms.

The lands of the pineries have gray sandy soils from 12 to 18 inches deep and yellowish subsoils, and are scarcely at all under cultivation.

The hummocks comprise the farming lands of the county, the prairies, with their dark sandy soils and excellent grasses, being used for grazing purposes. Sour lake, on the southwest, is much resorted to by invalids. It is said to have an area of about 2 acres.

The population of the county is very sparse, the average being about two persons per square mile. Lumbering is the chief industry, the river affording easy shipment to Beaumont. The lands under cultivation comprise but six-tenths of 1 per cent. of the area, or 41.1 acres per square mile, and are mostly devoted to corn. Very little cotton is planted.

ABSTRACT FROM THE REPORT OF P. S. WATTS, OF HARDIN.

We have only the level, fine sandy, gray hummock land in this county, the soil of which is 7 inches deep to change of color. Tillage is easy, and the soil is early, and best adapted to cotton and oats, which, with corn and sweet potatoes, constitute the chief crops of the county. One-fourth of the cultivated area is planted in cotton. The plant grows from 3 to 4 feet high, is most productive at 3 feet, and is inclined to run to weed in wet seasons, for which no remedy has been tried. The seed-cotton product per acre of fresh land is 1,500 pounds, and 1,780 pounds are required to make a 475-pound bale of lint. After eight years' cultivation (unmanured) the product is 800 pounds, and 1,900 pounds make a 475-pound bale. The staple from fresh land is best. When old land rests for a few years it only produces about two-thirds of the original yield. The most troublesome weed is crab-grass.

Cotton is shipped, chiefly in February and March, by rail to Galveston at $2 per bale.

TYLER.

Population: 5,825.—White, 4,323; colored, 1,502.
Area: 920 square miles.—Woodland, nearly all; oak, hickory, and pine region, 110 square miles; long-leaf pine region, 810 square miles.
Tilled lands: 19.371 acres.—Area planted in cotton, 5,504 acres; in corn, 11,055 acres; in oats, 1,343 acres; in wheat, 5 acres.
Cotton production: 2,543 bales; average cotton product per acre, 0.46 bale, 690 pounds seed-cotton, or 230 pounds cotton lint.

The surface of Tyler county is undulating, and is mostly well timbered, with long-leaf pine on the uplands and cypress, ash, magnolia, beech, and walnut on the streams. The county is watered by the Neches river and its tributaries, whose bottom lands are dark sandy loams, deeply colored with decayed vegetation. The county is sparsely settled. The uplands of the lower half of the county have light sandy soils, are easily cultivated, but are not very productive. Those on the north are more thickly populated, have a better class of soils, with clayey subsoils, and are interspersed with a few prairies. The latter are considered better for grazing than for farming purposes, and are not under cultivation.

The chief crops of the county are corn, cotton, oats, potatoes, and sugar-cane, and 3.3 per cent. of its area is under cultivation, with an average of 21.1 acres per square mile. Corn has twice the acreage of cotton, yielding from 10 to 15 bushels per acre.

The lands devoted to the culture of cotton comprise 28.4 per cent. of the tilled lands, averaging about 6 acres per square mile. The yield in seed-cotton is, with the exception of Liberty, much greater than in any of the counties in this part of the state, and is also greater than the general average for the state itself. The methods of tillage, improvement, etc., are the same as in the adjoining counties.

Shipments are made either by wagon to the narrow-gauge railroad in Polk county, and thence to Houston, or by boat down the river to Beaumont, and thence by railroad to Houston and to New Orleans.

48 C P

JASPER.

Population : 5,779.—White, 3,241 ; colored, 2,538.
Area : 970 square miles.—Woodland, all ; all long-leaf pine region.
Tilled lands : 17,304 acres.—Area planted in cotton, 4,455 acres ; in corn, 9,763 acres ; in oats, 1,097 acres.
Cotton production : 1,410 bales ; average cotton product per acre, 0.32 bale, 480 pounds seed-cotton, or 160 pounds
cotton lint.

The surface of Jasper county is undulating and heavily timbered, long-leaf pine comprising the almost exclusive
growth on the uplands. It is watered by the Neches river and its tributaries on the west, and those of the Sabine
on the east, the water-divide passing north and south through the center. The lands are sandy in character, but
in the bottoms along the streams they are dark, from decayed vegetation, and have a timber growth of oak, ash,
magnolia, beech, holly, etc. The county is very sparsely settled, and lumbering is the principal industry, the pine
rafts being usually floated down the river to the saw-mills at Beaumont. The tilled lands comprise but about 2.8
per cent. of the county area, and average 17.8 acres per square mile. Corn is the chief crop, and yields from 10 to
15 bushels per acre. Of the lands under cultivation 25.7 per cent. is devoted to cotton, or 4.6 acres per square mile.

ABSTRACT FROM THE REPORT OF L. C. WHITE, OF JASPER.

There is here some bottom land and some heavy black loam on the uplands, but nine-tenths of the soil is *gray, sandy upland.* This
soil is generally poor, but is better suited for cotton than for corn, and oats rapidly exhaust it. It extends about 100 miles in all directions,
its growth being chiefly pine on the uplands, with oak, ash, hickory, gum, magnolia, and beech on the bottoms. The soil is 4 inches
deep, and the subsoil is generally lighter, whiter, and sandier. It is clayey in a few places, and contains some pebbles ; rock underlies
some of it in the northern part of the county. Tillage is easy, except when too wet, the chief crops being corn, cotton, a little sugar-
cane, and rice. Cotton occupies about one-half of the tilled lands. The plant grows usually 3 feet high, but produces most at 4 feet.
In long wet periods it inclines to run to weed, and is restrained by topping all stalks, suckers, and long limbs.

The seed-cotton product per acre on fresh land is about 800 pounds, the lint rating good ordinary to middling. Old lands produce
about 300 pounds of seed-cotton per acre, and 1,545 pounds from such land make a 475-pound bale of ordinary to low ordinary lint. The
most troublesome weeds are cocklebur, hog-weed, and purslane. About one-half of such land lies "turned out", and after three years"
rest produces well, but not as originally. Slopes are very seriously damaged by washing and gullying, but in some localities much of it is
checked by horizontalizing, hillside ditching, and underdraining. The valleys are improved to the extent of 50 per cent. by the washings.
This cannot be regarded as a good farming county on account of sudden changes of weather and liability to droughts. Corn does very
well, but fails when hot weather begins. Cotton is liable to be mildewed, and when thus affected is sure to be attacked by worms,
especially in showery weather. This is a good fruit-producing county, and apples, grapes, peaches, pears, etc., do well.

Cotton is hauled off as soon as baled ; in winter, to Bevilport, at $1 per bale ; in summer, to Weiss Bluff, at $3 per bale.

NEWTON.

Population : 4,359.—White, 2,852 ; colored, 1,507.
Area : 870 square miles.—Woodland, all ; all long-leaf pine region.
Tilled lands : 13,450 acres.—Area planted in cotton, 3,510 acres ; in corn, 7,508 acres ; in oats, 513 acres.
Cotton production : 1,332 bales ; average cotton product per acre, 0.38 bale, 570 pounds seed-cotton, or 190 pounds
cotton lint.

Newton county is separated from Louisiana on the east by the Sabine river. Its surface is quite level and low,
and is well timbered with long-leaf pine on the uplands, with cypress, magnolia, etc., on the bottom lands. The
county is watered by small streams flowing into the Sabine. It is sparsely populated, and the principal industry
is lumbering, the timber being floated down the river to the saw-mills at Orange.

The soils of the uplands are light and sandy ; those of the bottoms are dark loams, deeply colored with decayed
vegetation. The lands under cultivation average but 15.4 acres per square mile, or 2.4 per cent. of the county area.
The chief crops of the county are corn, cotton, oats, and vegetables. Cotton is a secondary crop, with an average
of but 4 acres per square mile ; but its yield in fair seasons is from 500 to 800 pounds in the seed per acre.

The methods of tillage, improvement of the lands, etc., practiced in this county are the same as given by
correspondents in the adjoining counties.

Shipments are made usually by boat down the river to Orange, and thence to other markets.

ORANGE.

Population : 2,938.—White, 2,475 ; colored, 463.
Area : 390 square miles.—Woodland, nearly one-half ; southern prairie region, 290 square miles ; long-leaf pine
region, 100 square miles.
Tilled lands : 2,023 acres.—Area planted in cotton, 66 acres ; in corn, 1,237 acres.
Cotton production : 22 bales ; average cotton product per acre, 0.33 bale, 495 pounds seed-cotton, or 165 pounds
cotton lint.

Orange county is about evenly divided between prairies and woodland. The former occupies the lower portion,
and has a level surface and gray silty soils, and is devoted only to stock grazing. The northern portion of the county
is heavily timbered with long-leaf pine, which is largely utilized for lumber and in the production of cross-ties for
the railroads. The hummock lands are low, and are suitable only for the cultivation of rice.

There is but little cotton raised in this part of the county. The lands consist of large bodies of hummocks and cypress swamps, while the largest part of the county is covered with a growth of long-leaf pine. The hummocks have a growth of short-leaf pine, oak, hickory, and magnolia. The soil is light and sandy, and is capable of producing from 500 to 1,000 pounds of seed-cotton or from 20 to 30 bushels of corn per acre.

JEFFERSON.
(See "Southern prairie region.")

SOUTHERN COAST AND PRAIRIE REGION.

East of the Brazos river: Comprises all or parts of the counties of San Jacinto, Montgomery, Waller, Harris, Liberty,* Jefferson, Orange,* Chambers, Galveston, Fort Bend,* and Brazoria.*

West of the Brazos: Washington, Austin, Fayette, Colorado, Lavaca, Gonzales,* DeWitt, Wharton,* Victoria, Jackson, Matagorda, Karnes, Wilson,* Atascosa, Frio, Medina,* Uvalde,* and Goliad.

Border counties producing but little cotton, or none at all, whose descriptions are very briefly given: Calhoun, Aransas, Refugio, San Patricio, Nueces, Duval, Bee, Live Oak, Hidalgo, and Cameron.

SAN JACINTO.

Population: 6,186.—White, 2,851; colored, 3,335.

Area: 640 square miles.—Woodland, greater part; oak, hickory, and pine region, 450 square miles; southern prairie region, 190 square miles.

Tilled lands: 25,560 acres.—Area planted in cotton, 9,840 acres; in corn, 9,494 acres; in oats, 163 acres.

Cotton production: 5,354 bales; average cotton product per acre, 0.54 bale, 810 pounds seed-cotton, or 270 pounds cotton lint.

San Jacinto county has for its eastern boundary the Trinity river, while on the southwest are the headwaters of the San Jacinto river, flowing southward.

The surface of the county is undulating, and very generally timbered with long- and short-leaf pine and some oak. On the southwest there are some prairies, with soils varying from black to gray and sandy, which are very productive. These soils are underlaid by the concretionary clays of this southern prairie region. The timbered uplands, with their predominating pine growth, have sandy soils and subsoils, and are not much under cultivation, being more valuable for their lumber.

The river lands, sometimes several miles in width, are heavily timbered with oaks, cottonwood, cypress, ash, magnolia, etc., and have soils varying from heavy black clays to the red alluvium or silt of the immediate banks of the stream. They are very difficult to till, and are considered best suited to sugar-cane and cotton.

The lands under cultivation in this county average 39.9 acres per square mile, or 6.3 per cent. of its area. Cotton is the chief crop, the average being 15.4 acres per square mile, or 38.3 per cent. of the tilled lands, and having a yield per acre exceeded by but eleven counties in the state.

The uplands comprise black and rolling prairies, light gray and black hummocks, wild peach, and poor pine lands, all of which are more or less devoted to cotton. The richest lands are those of the bottoms of rivers and creeks, constituting one-sixth of the county's area. River bottoms are from 3 to 5 miles wide; the creek bottoms from one-fourth of a mile to 1 mile. They bear a growth of oaks, cottonwood, cypress, hickory, ash, wild peach, beech, pine, and every kind peculiar to the heavily timbered land of this country.

The *bottom soil* is a black, stiff alluvium. Both prairie and bottom soils are 2 feet deep. The subsoils contain hard, limy clay, and are underlaid by sand, gravel, and rock. The soils are early and tillage is easy, excepting the stiff alluvium, which is difficult either when too wet or too dry. The chief crops of this region are corn, cotton, sugar-cane, sweet and Irish potatoes, vegetables, fruit, etc., the bottom lands being best adapted to sugar-cane and cotton, the prairies to corn. One-third of the cultivated area is planted in cotton. The plant grows from 2 to 6 feet high on the upland, and from 5 to 8 feet on the bottoms; it is more productive on the bottoms. On any land here the plant inclines to run to weed in wet seasons, the only remedy being to pinch off the top bud. The seed-cotton product per acre of fresh lands varies from 1,500 to 2,000 pounds, 3½ pounds yielding a pound of good lint. After ten years' cultivation (unmanured) the product of the upland is 1,000 pounds, and of the bottom from 1,500 to 2,500 pounds per acre, 3½ pounds yielding a pound of lint, about equal to that from fresh land. One-tenth of such land lies "turned out", but produces very well when again cultivated. The most troublesome weeds are morning-glory, cocklebur, and crab-grass.

About three-fifths of the county's area is occupied by *sandy land*, including the *hummock, wild peach,* and *pine lands;* they also bear oaks. These soils are from 10 to 12 inches deep. They have rarely a good clay subsoil; but where there is clay, it is chiefly pipe-clay. The subsoils contain white, rounded pebbles, and are underlaid by sand. The soils are early, easily tilled, and best adapted to corn, pease, and potatoes. One-third of their cultivated area is planted in cotton, the plants growing from 3 to 4 feet high. The seed-cotton product per acre is from 800 to 1,000 pounds, 3½ pounds making 1 pound of good ordinary to middling lint. After ten years' cultivation (unmanured) the product is about 600 pounds, 3½ pounds making 1 pound of inferior lint. Crab-grass is most troublesome. One-tenth of this land lies "turned out", and produces poorly when again cultivated.

Cotton does well on all lands in this region. Some prefer the rich river and creek bottoms, others the rich rolling upland prairies, and each has its advantage. The negro laborer prefers the bottom, endures its climate, and is not affected by malarial fever, as the whites are.

Cotton is hauled by wagon to Shepherd as soon as it is baled, and thence by rail to Galveston at $2 per bale.

MONTGOMERY.

Population : 10,154.—White, 4,926; colored, 5,228.
Area : 1,050 square miles.—Woodland, large part; oak, hickory, and pine region, 70 square miles; southern prairie, 980 square miles.
Tilled lands : 54,785 acres.—Area planted in cotton, 13,311 acres ; in corn, 13,702 acres ; in oats, 88 acres.
Cotton production : 4,092 bales; average cotton product per acre, 0.31 bale, 465 pounds seed-cotton, or 155 pounds cotton lint.

Montgomery is an undulating county, and is situated upon the divide between the Brazos and the Trinity rivers, but its streams find their way independently of these rivers to Galveston bay. The surface of the county is mostly timbered with a short-leaf pine and a scrubby growth of other timber on the uplands, with larger timber on the bottoms. The southern part of the county is dotted over with small prairies having a light silty soil and a sandy subsoil, the surface sometimes being dark from decayed vegetation. They are covered with grass, and are best adapted to grazing purposes. The country changes a short distance south of Willis, becoming slightly rolling, and under the sandy soil appears a mottled clay, associated with small yellow ferruginous concretions or pebbles. Thence northward the character of the country improves, the growth being more largely oak and hickory ; the lands have a yellow or red subsoil, and are more generally under cultivation, yielding from 500 to 800 pounds of seed-cotton per acre. The crops of the county are corn, cotton, potatoes, etc. Lands under cultivation comprise 8.2 per cent. of the county area, and average 52.2 acres per square mile. Corn has a somewhat larger acreage than cotton, and yields from 8 to 15 bushels per acre. Cotton has an average of only 12.7 acres per square mile, comprising 24.3 per cent. of the tilled lands. Shipments are made by railroad either to Houston and Galveston, or to points northward.

WALLER.

Population : 9,024.—White, 3,192; colored, 5,832.
Area : 500 square miles.—Woodland, some; oak, hickory, and pine region, 290 square miles; southern prairies, 210 square miles.
Tilled lands : 31,665 acres.—Area planted in cotton, 10,104 acres ; in corn, 10,350 acres ; in oats, 126 acres.
Cotton production : 3,923 bales; average cotton product per acre, 0.39 bale, 585 pounds seed-cotton, or 195 pounds cotton lint.

The surface of Waller county is quite level, and consists almost entirely of open prairies, timber only occurring along the Brazos river, which forms the western boundary, and on some of the small streams. The eastern rim of the river basin is here very narrow, the divide between its waters and those of other streams on the east lying not very far from it, and the county is itself very narrow. This divide is, however, scarcely perceptible to the eye, the surface of the country being only undulating.

The prairie lands are about equally divided between the black waxy and the sandy silt or loam, the latter occupying the broad open country on the east, the former comprising a belt near the river bottoms and smaller streams. Both varieties are covered with grasses, and are devoted mostly to stock grazing.

The bottom lands of the Brazos river are broad, and are considered the best lands of the county, but are subject more or less to malarial diseases. Their soil is a reddish clayey loam, very deep, heavily timbered with walnut, elm, pecan, ash, etc.

The lands of the county under cultivation comprise nearly 9.9 per cent. of its area, or 63.3 acres per square mile. Cotton is one of the principal crops, its acreage being but little less than that of corn, with an average of about 20.2 acres per square mile, or 31.9 per cent. of the tilled lands.

ABSTRACT FROM THE REPORT OF P. S. CLARKE, OF HEMPSTEAD.

The uplands vary much in character, and consist partly of level black and hog-wallow prairies, but mostly of light sandy loam.

The *Brazos bottom land* above overflow, covering about one-eighth of the surface of the county, is the chief soil devoted to cotton. It has a very rich soil, some of it known as buckshot, varying in color from gray to mahogany, and is about 10 feet in depth, with a timber growth of black walnut, ash, elm, hackberry, red oak, pecan, hickory, etc. It is easily cultivated, is early, warm, and naturally well drained, and produces cotton and corn. Fifty-five per cent. of the tilled land is in cotton, which attains a height of from 5 to 8 feet, the former being the better for productiveness. When too thick, or in rainy seasons, the plant inclines to run to weed, the remedy for which is thinning out and topping the plant. The yield per acre in seed-cotton is 1,400 pounds, 1,545 pounds of which are needed for 475 pounds of lint. Three years' cultivation increases the above product to 1,800 pounds, the same amount as before being necessary for a bale. Cocklebur and crab-grass form the most troublesome weeds. Very little land lies "turned out", but when again cultivated it shows the benefit of rest.

About three-eighths of the county is of the *black upland prairie land,* the soil of which is 1 foot in depth, with a subsoil of yellow clay which by cultivation becomes thoroughly mixed with the surface soil. Sand is found at 1½ feet. The soil is early, warm, naturally well drained, and easily tilled in dry seasons. The chief production is cotton, yielding 800 pounds of seed-cotton per acre, 1,545 pounds being required for a 475-pound bale, and the same after three years' cultivation of the land. The height usually attained by the plant is 4 feet. Topping restrains the tendency to run to weed, which occurs in rainy summers. When cotton is planted at the proper time it will grow to perfection without any local hinderance. The steady cotton growth in dry summers is attributed to the effects of the breeze from the Gulf, which brings moisture. The yield when again "taken in" is not materially different from that of fresh land.

The *light sandy prairies* comprise about one-half of the tillable area of the county, black-jack oak, which occurs in spots, being the natural timber growth. The soil is from 6 to 24 inches deep, and has a heavy yellow clay subsoil, sometimes approaching the surface, and containing in places white gravel ; it overlies sand at from 10 to 12 feet. This soil is easily cultivated in all seasons, is early, warm, and well drained, and is best adapted to cotton and sweet potatoes, the former growing to a height of 3½ feet, and yielding 600 pounds of seed-cotton per acre, 1,545 pounds being requisite for 475 pounds of lint. Many years' cultivation does not decrease the yield. As in the last soil, so in this, crab-grass is the only troublesome weed.

Shipments are made as soon as baled, by rail, to Houston and Galveston, the rates per bale being respectively $1 50 and $2 25.

HARRIS.

Population: 27,985.—White, 17,160; colored, 10,825.
Area: 1,800 square miles.—Woodland, a fair proportion; southern prairie region, all.
Tilled lands: 25,123 acres.—Area planted in cotton, 4,440 acres; in corn, 9,895 acres; in oats, 172 acres.
Cotton production: 1,892 bales; average cotton product per acre, 0.43 bale, 645 pounds seed-cotton, or 215 pounds cotton lint.

The surface of Harris county is generally level, with broad open prairies, interspersed with small timbered areas in "motts" and along the streams. This is especially the case in the western part, while in the extreme east, along the San Jacinto river and Spring creek, there is a well-timbered long-leaf pine region, in which are located many saw-mills. A prominent feature of the growth is the great abundance of the *Magnolia grandiflora*. It is estimated that three-fourths of the county area is open prairie, with mixed black waxy and sandy lands, the latter, however, apparently predominating. (See analysis, page 31.)

The prairies on the west, with their excellent grasses, are mostly devoted to stock-grazing, while the farming lands are situated nearer the streams.

A stiff concretionary clay (Port Hudson) underlies the greater part of the county, making proper drainage a matter of difficulty. But 2.2 per cent. of the county area is under tillage, with an average of 13.9 acres per square mile. The acreage of cotton comprises 17.7 per cent. of the tilled lands of the county, and has an average of 2.5 acres per square mile. Its product per acre for 1879 was considerably over the average for the entire state.

The city of Houston is connected with the Gulf by rail and by the waters of Buffalo bayou, which has been made navigable for ocean steamers to within a few miles of the city. It is the great railway center of southeastern Texas, and shipments can be made direct to the principal markets. Several cotton compresses are here.

The rolling black upland prairies along Burnet's bay, with timbered land along the San Jacinto river, comprise the uplands of the county. All along the bay front the land is good for cotton and corn.

The *black rolling prairies* are stiff, and comprise one-third of the land of the county, extending for 30 miles up and down the bay, and lying from 1 mile to 4 miles from the river. The soil is 2 feet deep, with a subsoil of tenacious grayish clay, containing hard "black gravel". It is early, warm, and well drained, and is not easily cultivated until well broken up; but when that is properly done there is no trouble. Cotton and corn constitute the chief productions, one-half the crops being in cotton, which grows to a height of 4½ feet, and tends to run to weed in wet weather. The yield per acre in seed-cotton from fresh land or from land that has been under cultivation ten years is about 1,400 pounds, which, early in the season, is the amount needed for 400 pounds of lint, rating low middling to middling. Late in the season but 1,300 pounds are required for 400 pounds of lint. Burs and crab-grass are the only weeds which have to be contended with.

The *post-oak land*, with its growth of post and pin oaks, occurs in spots along the edge of the prairies on each side of small streams throughout the county. It has a gray clay loam soil, from 8 inches to 1 foot in depth, over a subsoil of yellow, stiff clay, is early, warm, and well drained, and difficult of cultivation, and is best adapted to cotton. Corn does not yield so well. The cotton-plant usually attains a height of from 4½ to 5 feet, yielding about 1,400 pounds of seed-cotton per acre, 1,665 pounds early in the season and 1,545 pounds later being requisite for a 475-pound bale. After nine years' cultivation the above figures are not changed. The troublesome weeds on this soil are the same as those of the black prairie.

The *sandy flat-lands* extend for miles along the edge of the prairie, reaching into the river. The growth is principally pine, with pin oak and some timber of nearly every species. The soil is very thin, with a heavier subsoil, which in the wood is inclined to bog when wet. This land is timbered, and none of it is cultivated, but serves as a winter range for cattle. We have a very mild climate, oranges growing finely; and cotton, when well cultivated and the season is suitable, produces finely. Sea-island cotton grows well, and is very productive.

The lands devoted to cotton comprise (1) the hummock lands, lying on creeks and bayous, with a timber growth of six varieties of oaks, pine, cedar, gum, and various small growth, and (2) the stiff prairie lands.

The soil of the *hummock land*, which covers about 1 per cent. of the county, is 2 feet 6 inches in depth, overlying clay, which varies in depth according to location, the soil being deeper on the bottom lands than on the prairies. The chief crops are cotton and corn for the market and a small amount of sugar-cane for home use. Cotton grows to a height of 5 feet, yielding 1,200 pounds of seed-cotton per acre, which is the amount needed for 400 pounds of lint, rating good middling. Only about 75 per cent. of the above yield is obtained after the land has been six years under cultivation, in which case the rating is one grade lower than that of fresh land. About five-eighths of the land is devoted to cotton, very little lying "turned out", and that, when turned, may yield one-half as much as it did when fresh. Cockleburs, the vine, crab-grass, and careless-weed form the most troublesome weeds.

Shipments are made early in the season, by rail or wagon, to Houston at from 50 cents to $1 per bale.

LIBERTY.

(See "Long-leaf pine region".)

JEFFERSON.

Population: 3,489.—White, 2,290; colored, 1,199.
Area: 1,000 square miles.—Woodland, small part; long-leaf pine region, 270 square miles; marshes and southern prairie region, 730 square miles.
Tilled lands: 4,796 acres.—Area planted in cotton, 133 acres; in corn, 1,758 acres; in rice, 16 acres.
Cotton production: 77 bales; average cotton product per acre, 0.58 bale, 870 pounds seed-cotton, or 290 pounds cotton lint.

Jefferson, the extreme southeastern county of the state, has a surface quite level, and is watered by the Neches river and a number of small streams emptying into Sabine lake.

The northwestern part of the county has a sandy soil, and is timbered with the long-leaf pine of the lumber region, with some oak, hickory, magnolia, cypress, etc., on the streams. The rest is mostly an open prairie, with a few small patches of timber. The lands comprise both the black waxy and dark sandy soils, with underlying heavy concretionary clays of the Port Hudson age. These prairies are poorly drained and difficult to till, and are not much under cultivation. They are best adapted to stock-raising, being covered with excellent grasses.

Along the Gulf shore the lands are sandy, with some marshes on the east, bordering Sabine lake.

ABSTRACT FROM THE REPORT OF W. M. CAMPBELL, OF BEAUMONT.

The uplands comprise mostly level prairies, interspersed with small bodies of timber, consisting of hickory, elm, and hackberry. The lands devoted to the cultivation of cotton are the black waxy prairie, the black sandy, and the light or gray sandy soils. The most important is the *black waxy prairie*, which covers about one-half of the surface of the county; its soil is about 3 feet deep, over a yellow clay subsoil. It is difficult to till in wet seasons, is late and ill-drained, and produces corn, cotton, cane, and rice, the chief crop being corn. Cotton, forming about one-fourth of the entire crops planted, grows to a height of 3½ feet, and yields from 1,800 to 2,400 pounds of seed-cotton per acre, even after twenty years' cultivation. There is no tendency of the plant to run to weed. About one-half the land lies "turned out", and produces as well as it did originally when again taken into cultivation.

The *black sandy lands* constitute about one-third of the tillable area of the county, and the natural timber growth is post and black-jack oaks in spots, most of the land being prairie. The land is very easily cultivated in all seasons. The depth of the soil is 2 feet, with a compact yellow clay subsoil. Its productions are corn, cotton, cane, potatoes, rice, and fruits. It is early, warm, and partly well and partly ill drained. One-fourth of the crops is in cotton, which grows to a height of 3½ feet, yielding from 1,800 to 2,000 pounds of seed-cotton per acre. After ten years' cultivation the yield is reduced, being from 1,200 to 1,800 pounds, the rating being the same as before. One-half of the land lies "turned out", producing, when again cultivated, better than fresh lands.

The timber of the *light gray sandy lands*, which cover about one-twentieth of the county, is hackberry, gum, pin oak, ash, elm, bay, and magnolia. The soil is from 1 foot to 3 feet deep, and the subsoil is mostly a mixture of red sand and clay, though in some places it is similar to the surface soil. It is early, warm, and, like the previous soil, partly well and partly ill drained, producing corn, cotton, cane, rice, oranges, and grapes. About one-fifth of the cultivated land is devoted to cotton, which usually attains a height of from 3 to 8 feet, being most productive at 3 feet. In moderately wet seasons there is a tendency to run to weed, which is restrained by either topping the plant or by stopping the cultivation. The yield per acre of seed-cotton is from 1,200 to 2,400 pounds, which yield is reduced about one-third after the land has been cultivated for ten years. One-fourth of the land lies "turned out", the yield of which when again cultivated is equal to that from fresh land.

Shipments are made about the 1st of January by rail to Galveston, the rate being $1 50 per bale.

ORANGE.

(See "Long-leaf pine region".)

CHAMBERS.

Population: 2,187.—White, 1,494; colored, 693.
Area: 850 square miles.—Woodland, very little.
Tilled lands: 3,336 acres.—Area planted in cotton, 140 acres; in corn, 1,839 acres.
Cotton production: 91 bales; average cotton product per acre, 0.65 bale, 975 pounds seed-cotton, or 325 pounds cotton lint.

Chambers, one of the Gulf counties, has a level and mostly open prairie surface, and is watered by Trinity river and several small streams, all emptying into Galveston bay. In the southern part of the county the soil is of a dark silty character, sandy along the coast, underlaid by heavy clays with calcareous concretions (Port Hudson). In the northern part these clays come near the surface, forming black waxy lands, intermixed with areas of sands; they are difficult to till, poorly drained, and are not much under cultivation. The alluvial lands of the river are rich and well timbered, but rather subject to overflow.

ABSTRACT FROM THE REPORT OF M. BYERLY, OF WALLISVILLE.

The uplands consist of prairie and timber lands. The black sandy land of Trinity bottom above overflow is the chief land of the county, the next in importance being the black prairie.

The *black sandy land*, covering about one-half of the county area, has a natural timber growth of pine, different kinds of oaks, hickory, and magnolia, and is underlaid by yellow, sticky clay at a depth of 3 feet. It produces corn, cotton, potatoes, and sugar-cane, though it is best adapted to cotton and cane. The black waxy soil is difficult and the black soil easy to till in wet weather, but all are easily tilled in dry seasons. The soils are early, warm, and badly drained. About one-quarter of the land is devoted to cotton, which grows to a height of about 4 feet, at which it is the most productive. Cotton inclines to run to weed in wet weather, topping being the remedy applied. The average product per acre in seed-cotton is 1,900 pounds, 1,780 pounds being required for a 475-pound bale of lint rating as middling. After one year's cultivation the yield is increased to 1,400 pounds per acre, but there is no difference in the quality of the staple. There is no danger from frosts in this county, as it is too far south. Bur and tie-vine are the weeds which occasion the greatest amount of trouble. No land lies "turned out".

GALVESTON.

Population: 24,121.—White, 18,454; colored, 5,667.
Area: 670 square miles.—Woodland, very little; all southern prairies.
Tilled lands: 2,790 acres.—Area planted in cotton, 289 acres; in corn, 655 acres; in oats, 44 acres.
Cotton production: 136 bales; average cotton product per acre, 0.47 bale, 705 pounds seed-cotton, or 235 pounds cotton lint.

Galveston, one of the Gulf counties, comprises the island of that name and a large area of the mainland. The surface of the country is very level, with a gradually ascending elevation inland from the shore. The county is almost entirely an open prairie, with a dark silty soil, except along the coast and on the island, where the surface is little less than a white sand. The lands are underlaid by a heavy clay containing white calcareous concretions (Port Hudson), which comes to the surface near Clear creek, the northern boundary of the county.

There is very little drainage to the lands, the water standing in pools on the surface during the rainy seasons, unable either to flow off or to find an underground passage through the impervious clays. For this reason the county, outside of the city of Galveston, is mostly devoted to stock-raising, and the grasses of the prairies are converted into hay. Along the streams there are some tillable lands having a black sandy loam soil and a growth of mesquite, pine, magnolia, etc.

The island of Galveston is about 32 miles long, with an average width of from 2 to 5 miles. Its surface is very level and sandy, with an elevation of from 2 to 10 feet above tide-water. But very little of the county is under cultivation, that is chiefly around the city of Galveston.

ABSTRACT FROM THE REPORTS OF SIDNEY SCUDDER AND WILLIAM J. JONES, OF GALVESTON.

The various lands devoted to the cultivation of cotton comprise buff-colored sandy loam on Galveston island, black sandy loam on the mainland prairies, and heavy black soil on the river banks.

The *black sandy loam* of the prairies is the most important, occupying about 80 per cent. of the county area, the natural timber growth being mesquite, magnolia, oak, cedar, pine, ash, and hackberry, lying mostly along the rivers. The soil is 3 feet 8 inches thick, with a subsoil consisting almost entirely of light sand, which extends to a depth of several feet. It produces cotton, sugar-cane, and potatoes, both Irish and sweet, is early, warm, and ill-drained, and is easily cultivated in all seasons. Cotton grows to a height of from 3 to 5 feet, yielding from 1,200 to 1,500 pounds of seed-cotton per acre. After five years' cultivation, unmanured and without rotation, there is a diminution of one-third in the yield. The fiber of the cotton grown on the coast is classed as being of a firmer and softer texture than that of inland counties, and matures very early. This is probably owing to a saline atmosphere and earlier seasons, the weather being essentially modified by the sea breezes. Sea-island cotton shows this more decidedly. In rainy seasons, more particularly in what is termed showery weather, the plant tends to run to weed, which may be restrained by topping. There are very few weeds of any description, crab-grass being the most troublesome. Very little land lies "turned out".

Shipments of cotton are made as soon as ginned, by wagon, to the nearest railroad station, and thence to the best markets, the rates depending on the distance.

FORT BEND.
(See "Brazos alluvial region".)

BRAZORIA.
(See "Brazos alluvial region".)

WASHINGTON.

Population: 27,565.—White, 12,845; colored, 14,720.

Area: 600 square miles.—Woodland and prairies; oak, hickory, and pine region, 200 square miles; southern prairies, 400 square miles.

Tilled lands: 139,712 acres.—Area planted in cotton, 58,705 acres; in corn, 43,610 acres; in oats, 776 acres; in wheat, 49 acres.

Cotton production: 20,692 bales; average cotton product per acre, 0.35 bale, 525 pounds seed-cotton, or 175 pounds cotton lint.

Washington county is bounded on the east by the Brazos river, to which most of the other and smaller streams are tributary. The surface of the county is rolling, its eastern and southern portions being mostly open prairies, which extend west to 3 miles beyond Burton, a railroad station, interspersed with timbered lands, that are also found on the north and west, and border the river bottoms. These prairies have soils varying from black waxy and hog-wallow clays to dark and brown sandy loams, and are underlaid by heavy clays with calcareous concretions, these, in turn, overlying the soft sandstones, as seen outcropping in the ravines and railroad cuts, and that prevail southward. The lands are rich and productive, though tilled with difficulty, and yield from 700 to 900 pounds of seed-cotton per acre. (See analyses, page 32.)

The timbered lands of the west and north belong to the large region of oak and hickory uplands that forms a diagonal belt nearly across the state from northeast to southwest. These lands are sandy and pebbly, with usually clay subsoils, and have a timber growth of post and black-jack oaks, and, with the timbered lands that skirt the streams, cover, it is estimated, about one-half the area of the county. The Brazos bottoms are wide and heavily timbered with walnut, ash, elm, pecan, etc., and have stiff red clay and loam soils. The undergrowth is usually very dense. The banks are said to be from 15 to 30 feet high and above the ordinary rise of the waters of the river. The lands are considered the best in the county, producing immense corn crops, and from 1,500 to 2,000 pounds of seed-cotton per acre.

Washington is well populated, and is the chief agricultural county in the state, its tilled lands covering 36.3 per cent. of its area, with an average of 232.8 acres per square mile. Its acreage devoted to cotton is also greater than that of any other county (97.8 per square mile), but in the number of bales produced it ranks as sixth in the state.

ABSTRACT FROM THE REPORT OF O. H. P. GARRETT, OF BRENHAM.

About two-thirds of the uplands of the county is perhaps prairie, reasonably good and productive, and with long and sufficiently rolling slopes. The lands devoted to cotton comprise Brazos bottoms, with red or chocolate-colored soils, and a timber growth of hackberry, ash, pecan, elm, walnut, cedar, and mulberry; black hog-wallow prairies, waxy and stiff, and dark, fine sandy loam.

The sandy loam is pleasant to till, and is the most desirable, covering more than one-fourth of the surface of the county. The soil is from 6 inches to 2 feet in depth, with a subsoil somewhat heavier, the chief crops being corn, cotton, oats, wheat, potatoes, and sorghum. About two-fifths of the tillable area is devoted to cotton, yielding from 1,000 to 2,000 pounds of seed-cotton per acre from fresh land. After several years' cultivation the yield is reduced to from 400 to 800 pounds. In the former case 1,545 pounds, and in the latter 1,600 pounds, are required for 475 pounds of lint, but the staple is not so good, being shorter from the long cultivated lands. In wet weather there is a tendency of the plant to run to weed, which is restrained by topping. Very little land lies "turned out", and when again cultivated, if well fertilized, it produces moderately well. There is considerable washing of the soil on slopes, which sometimes does serious injury to the uplands, but improves the valleys. Hillside ditching and horizontalizing are practiced, and are attended with beneficial results. Cocklebur is the most troublesome weed.

The soil of the *black waxy prairie* or hog-wallow and black sandy land is about 18 inches deep. Cotton constitutes about one-half of the crops planted, and usually attains a height of from 4 to 6 feet. In wet weather there is a tendency of the plant to run to weed; topping is the remedy applied. The yield per acre of seed-cotton from fresh land is from 1,000 to 1,600 pounds, 1,545 pounds of which are required for a 475-pound bale, which rates as middling. Very little land lies "turned out". The cocklebur is the most troublesome weed.

Shipments are made from the middle of September to the middle of February, by rail, to Galveston and Houston.

AUSTIN.

Population: 14,429.—White, 10,490; colored, 3,939.

Area: 700 square miles.—Woodland, greater part; oak, hickory, and pine region, 170 square miles; southern prairies, 530 square miles.

Tilled lands: 73,492 acres.—Area planted in cotton, 31,321 acres; in corn, 26,810 acres; in oats, 519 acres; in wheat, 23 acres.

Cotton production: 13,185 bales; average cotton product per acre, 0.42 bale, 630 pounds seed-cotton, or 210 pounds cotton lint.

Austin county is bounded on the east by the Brazos river, and on the southwest by the San Bernard. Its surface is rolling, the northern part consisting mostly of open prairies, and the southern of timbered post and black-jack oak lands. The former comprises lands of a black and stiff clayey character, interspersed with brown sandy loams, and underlaid by heavy clay subsoils and sandstones (Grand Gulf). They are the chief cotton lands of the county, and cover, it is estimated, one-half of its area. The timbered region, or post-oak lands, lying south of Bellville, the county-seat, have gray sandy soils over heavy clay subsoils at 2 feet, similar in character to those of the prairies. They seem to be but little under cultivation.

The Brazos river bottom lands, several miles in width, are heavily timbered with ash, elm, pecan, walnut, etc., and have the usual red alluvial soils that are found throughout its length. The land under cultivation comprises 16.4 per cent. of the area of the county, and averages about 105 acres per square mile. Corn is the chief crop, with an average yield of from 15 to 20 bushels per acre.

Cotton, comprising 42.6 per cent. of the tilled lands, has an average of 44.7 acres per square mile, and its yield per acre is greater than that for the state at large.

ABSTRACTS FROM THE REPORTS OF MARTIN M. KENNEY, OF BELLVILLE, AND J. H. KRAUCHER, OF MILLHEIM.

The uplands of the county are rolling, and comprise black and sandy prairies on the north and timbered lands on the south. The sandy lands are usually on the tops of hills, and have a red subsoil, but the black lands of the valleys vary from black sandy to black waxy. The black waxy soil of Mill Creek bottom, because of overflow, is not much under cultivation.

The *black waxy prairie* is the chief cotton soil. It is a perfectly black, stiff clay, and when burnt forms a yellow brick. It changes to the less sandy and more sandy varieties in various localities, and occupies, with few exceptions, all of the northern and western parts of the county, or about one-half of its area. The natural growth of the prairie is grass, with a few scattering post and live oaks. The soil is from 1 foot to 6 feet, or on an average 2 feet deep. The subsoil is a gray or whitish clay, sometimes yellowish, with chalky gravel and thin strata of sandstone, or it is a red loam, which is the best. The gray or whitish clay contains great numbers of fossil bones, chiefly of a small animal of the horse kind. In some places the subsoil is leachy; in others it is an impervious hard-pan. The soil is difficult to cultivate when too wet or too dry, but easy in intermediate states. It is early, warm, and generally well drained, is best adapted to corn, cotton, and sugar-cane, and from one-half to three-fourths of its cultivated area is planted in cotton. The plant grows from 3 to 6 feet high, but is most productive at 4 or 5 feet. On rich or heavily-manured land (of this or other kinds) in wet seasons the plant inclines to run to weed, the remedy for which consists in close planting and topping about the first week in July. The seed-cotton product per acre of fresh land varies from 500 to 2,000 pounds, but the average is about 1,200 pounds, from 1,425 to 1,665 pounds making a 475-pound bale of low to good middling lint. After twenty years' cultivation (unmanured) the quantity and quality of the cotton product is the same. The troublesome weeds are cocklebur, careless-weed, crab-grass, wild hemp, and morning-glories. Slopes in old fields are seriously damaged by washing and gullying of the soils, and if these are sandy, and the material is washed down upon better valley lands, the latter are damaged by being overlaid with a poorer soil. To check these damages horizontalizing is practiced, which succeeds in some cases, but not always. The rains are so violent as often to break over the ridges and do more damage than if the rows were sloped.

The *sandy upland prairies* occur in irregular areas from latitude 30° to the Gulf, and from the Trinity to the Rio Grande rivers, occupying about one-fourth of the county area. The soil is a fine sandy loam of a reddish color, 24 inches thick, resting upon a hard, red clay subsoil, which becomes white at 30 feet deep, and is commonly called joint clay. It contains soft, white, angular, chalky gravel. In some places there is a stratum of water-worn quartz pebbles on this subsoil. Sand-rock underlies this clay. The soil is early, warm, well drained, easily tilled, and well adapted to almost all southern crops; it is enduring, and gives liberal returns for manuring. Some fields have been constantly cultivated for thirty years, and are still good. One-half the cultivated part of this land is planted in cotton, and the plant is most productive at its usual height of 3 feet. The seed-cotton product per acre of fresh land is 1,000 pounds in good seasons, 1,665 pounds making a 475-pound bale of low middling lint. Ten years' cultivation (unmanured) causes no decline in the quantity or quality of the product. Very little of this land lies "turned out", and it does not improve by fallowing, but grows up in sunflowers, nettles, and crab-grass, the two latter being the most troublesome weeds here.

The *sandy post-oak uplands* comprise about one-eighth of the county area, the other growth being black-jack, hickory, and some live-oak. Spots of it occur north of Bellville scattered over the sandy prairie, and the greater portion of the south and southeast part of the county is covered by it. The soil is mostly sandy, with gravel, the color varying from whitish to gray, buff, yellow, and orange-red, but lighter colors prevail. The depth is 2 feet. The subsoil is generally yellow or red loam or clay, always heavier than the surface soil, and mostly impervious when undisturbed. It contains a variety of gravel, and sometimes "iron pebble" and small shells, and is underlaid by sand, gravel, ironstone, and hard sandstone at 6 feet and less. Tillage is generally easy, but in wet seasons the soil is frequently boggy, and in dry seasons it becomes hard in many places. The soil is late, warm when well drained, and best adapted to sweet potatoes and cotton. Three-fourths of its cultivated area is planted in cotton. The plant grows from 2 to 4, or, if well manured, from 6 to 7 feet high, but inclines to run to weed in good seasons on heavily-manured land, which may be prevented by close planting and topping. The seed-cotton product per acre of fresh land varies from 400 to 1,000 pounds, from 1,545 to 1,665 pounds making a 475-pound bale of middling to good ordinary lint. Two years' cultivation (unmanured) causes a decline of 50 per cent. in the cotton yield; more is needed to make a bale, and the staple is inferior, generally very short, and without the fine gloss. Crab-grass, morning-glory, crowfoot, etc., are the troublesome weeds. But a small amount of such land lies "turned out", but by manuring it can be made to equal or even exceed its original yields.

The *Brazos bottom* occupies about one-eighth of the county area, and from four- to five-tenths of its cultivated area is planted in cotton. The bottom averages 3 miles, sometimes 5 or 6 miles wide, and its red-clay alluvium, brought from the Staked Plain, is 50 feet deep and very rich, producing an average of 2,000 pounds of seed-cotton per acre, and more in some places, or 40 bushels of corn. All southern crops grow luxuriantly upon it. The soil is light, warm, early, usually well drained, and easily cultivated, and cotton does not die out upon it. These 50 feet of alluvium rest upon a mixture of clay and coarse sand, gray in color, containing skeletons of the mammoth in great numbers. The bottom has a great variety of natural growth, among which are oaks, ash, walnut, mulberry, pecan, elm, hackberry, etc. The troublesome weeds are wild hemp and other tall growers.

The seasons are irregular as to the amount and time of rainfall, and this is perplexing to the planter. On the uplands the rows are made 4½ feet apart and the plants 18 inches apart in the drill. If the season happens to be dry, the plants are too thin on the ground; if wet, they are too thick; but these conditions cannot be known until the after-cultivation is nearly completed. The climate is generally favorable to the production of all upland varieties of cotton. To produce the best crop of the best staple not much rain is needed, the average summer, with just enough rain to keep the plant in a growing condition, being sufficient. The chief crops of this region are cotton, corn, sweet potatoes, sorghum, and ribbon cane.

Cotton is shipped during picking time, by rail, chiefly to Galveston, at $1 40 per bale from Millheim, or $2 from Bellville.

FAYETTE.

Population: 27,996.—White, 19,167; colored, 8,829.

Area: 960 square miles.—Woodland, greater part; oak, hickory, and pine uplands, 750 square miles; southern prairie, 210 square miles.

Tilled lands: 137,218 acres.—Area planted in cotton, 58,353 acres; in corn, 47,770 acres; in oats, 1,023 acres; in wheat, 265 acres.

Cotton production: 24,766 bales; average cotton product per acre, 0.42 bale, 630 pounds seed-cotton, or 210 pounds cotton lint.

The surface of Fayette county is rolling, nearly equally divided between prairies and timbered lands, and is watered by many streams, most of which are tributary to the Colorado river, which flows through the central part of the county in a northwest and southeast course. The river is bordered by wide bottom lands, heavily timbered with cottonwood, ash, walnut, elm, etc., and have soils varying from reddish sandy to dark alluvial loams, underlaid by beds of concretionary clays, that outcrop occasionally on the banks. These lands are very productive, and are largely under cultivation.

The uplands are high and rolling, and comprise broad skirts of post-oak timber along the river and creek bottoms, large and open prairies on the north and south, and other post-oak lands on the north and northwest, interspersed in smaller areas throughout the county. (See analysis, page 32.)

The lands of the timbered region are sandy and often gravelly, and are filled with variously colored and rounded quartz and agate pebbles. They, as also the prairies, are underlaid by concretionary clays and sandstones, that are frequently found outcropping in the banks of ravines. A high sandstone bluff occurs on the river opposite the town of La Grange, the county-seat. These lands are easily tilled and quite productive, except where the concretionary clays come near the surface, rendering drainage poor, and causing cotton and deep-rooted crops to die, even when near maturity. They have a growth of post and black-jack oaks, pine, hickory, etc., and in places the former is open and almost the exclusive tree.

The prairies have soils varying from black waxy and hog-wallow clays to brown, sandy loams, with underlying heavy clays and sandstones. While very productive, they are generally preferred for grazing purposes. (See analysis, page 32.)

The county has 22.3 per cent. of its area under cultivation, with an average of 142.9 acres per square mile. Of the latter, 60.8 acres are devoted to cotton, the chief crop of the county.

ABSTRACT FROM THE REPORT OF HENRY B. RICHARDS, OF LA GRANGE.

The uplands of the county are rolling, and comprise black prairies and sandy timbered lands; but the latter, with thin, poor soils, are not well adapted to cotton. The cotton lands comprise the shelly bottom lands of the Colorado river and creeks, the black hog-wallow prairie uplands, and the black sandy prairies. The chief crops of this region are cotton, corn, and sweet potatoes.

The *bottom lands*, embracing about 30 per cent. of the cultivated area, have a natural timber growth of live, pin, and white oaks, elm, ash, box-elder, red cedar, cottonwood, sycamore, pecan, etc. The soil is a brown and blackish, fine silty loam containing small shells, and is 30 inches thick. The underlying material is gravel, large and small, with cobblestones down to 30 or 35 feet, where it rests upon a stiff, impervious clay. The soil is early, warm, and well drained, always easily tilled, and is best adapted to cotton. One-half of its cultivated area is planted with the same. The cotton-plant usually grows from 4½ to 5 feet high. In wet seasons (on other good soils as well) the plant inclines to run to weed, which is remedied by topping in mid-season or when 2 or 2½ feet high. The average seed-cotton product per acre of fresh land is from 600 to 800 pounds, 1,600 pounds making a 475-pound bale of low middling lint. Fifteen years of good cultivation (unmanured) make no difference in the average quantity or quality of the cotton product. Cocklebur and morning-glory vines are the most troublesome weeds. No such land lies "turned out" at present.

761

The "*hog-wallow*" *prairies* occur in large bodies, and comprise one-half the cultivated area. Their natural growth is grass. The soil is a blackish and black clayey loam, putty-like when wet, from 2 to 4 feet thick; the subsoil a reddish clay, in some places gravelly (white, rounded, angular, hard, and soft), and is always underlaid by clays at from 25 to 30 feet. The soil is late, cold, ill-drained, and tillage is difficult when it is wet, but easy when dry. With good cultivation it yields best in dry seasons. It is best adapted to corn and cotton, and these alone are planted, one-third of the cultivated area being in cotton. The plant grows from 2 to 5 feet high, and is most productive at 5 feet. After ten years' good cultivation (unmanured) the average seed-cotton product per acre is from 400 to 600 pounds, 1,600 pounds making a 475-pound bale of low middling lint, whether from fresh or old land. The product per acre of fresh is less than that from old land of this kind. No land lies "turned out". Cockleburs and morning-glory vines are the troublesome weeds.

The *sandy prairie* and *post-oak lands* occur sometimes in long, narrow belts, and sometimes in large bodies, several miles in diameter, and comprise 20 per cent. of the tillable area. The timbered portion bears live and other oaks; the prairie is covered with considerable grass. The soil is various—fine and coarse sandy or gravelly and whitish-gray, buff, or mahogany in color. It is 6 inches thick, and is underlaid by leachy sand and gravel in variety, and these again by pipe-clay and rock at from 1 foot to 10 feet. This soil is early, warm, and well drained, and always easily tilled. It is not productive farming land, although one-half its cultivated area is planted in cotton, and the other half in corn and potatoes. The cotton-plant grows from 1 foot to 3 feet high, but is most productive at 3 feet. The seed-cotton product per acre of fresh land is from 300 to 600 pounds, 1,600 pounds making a 475-pound bale of low middling lint. After ten years' cultivation (unmanured) the product is about 100 pounds. None of this land lies "turned out". Crab-grass is the troublesome weed. The slopes are seriously damaged by washing and gullying, but the washings do not injure the valleys. No efforts are made to check the damage.

The earliest planting produces the largest yields in favorable seasons, but early planting is liable to be killed by late frosts. These are more disastrous to the crop than anything else.

Cotton is shipped as fast as it is baled, by wagon, to the railroad station at $1 per bale, thence to Houston at $2 25, or to Galveston at $3 per bale.

COLORADO.

Population: 16,673.—White, 8,987; colored, 7,686.

Area: 900 square miles.—Woodland, about one-third; oak, hickory, and pine region, 230 square miles; southern prairie, 670 square miles.

Tilled lands: 96,865 acres.—Area planted in cotton, 32,994 acres; in corn, 29,711 acres; in oats, 227 acres; in sugar-cane, 161 acres.

Cotton production: 15,552 bales; average cotton product per acre, 0.47 bale, 705 pounds seed-cotton, or 235 pounds cotton lint.

Colorado county is divided into two parts by the Colorado river, and Big Bernard creek forms the eastern boundary. The surface of the county is undulating, with a gradual fall toward the south, and the larger streams on the east, middle, and west pursue their way independently to the coast. Eagle lake, in the southeastern part of the county, has a surface of about 4,000 acres. The river lands are broad, well timbered with live oak, pecan, ash, walnut, hackberry, etc., and have a dark alluvial soil about 2 feet in depth, underlaid by clay loams and clays, and at 12 feet by sandstone. These lands are largely under cultivation, and yield from 800 to 1,200 pounds of seed-cotton per acre.

The uplands of the county are mostly open prairies, diversified with skirts of timbered lands, and have soils varying from black waxy and hog-wallow clays to black and gray sandy loams of both prairies and timbers. They are underlaid by heavy concretionary clays and sandstones, and beds of variously colored quartz pebbles frequently appear near the surface. The black prairies occupy the highest lands, while on the lowlands the soils are sandy, probably from the sandstone under the clays, and are timbered with a post- and live-oak growth.

The prairies are mostly given up to purposes of stock-grazing, for which they are admirably suited. The river lands are, to some extent, devoted to the culture of sugar-cane, the predominant crop of all of the alluvial lands of the Colorado and Brazos rivers on the south.

The population of the county is largely composed of Germans, an industrious and thrifty people, who immediately adopt the usual methods of farming—at first renting the land, and very soon buying for themselves.

The lands of the county under cultivation comprise 16.8 per cent. of its area, or an average of 107.3 acres per square mile. Cotton is the chief crop, with an average of 36.7 acres per square mile, or 34.1 per cent. of tilled lands, and its yield per acre is greater than in most of the counties in the southern prairie region. That of corn is from 18 to 25 bushels, and of oats from 25 to 30 bushels per acre.

ABSTRACTS FROM THE REPORTS OF W. T. M'LEARY, M. D., JOHN KNIPSCHEER, AND F. BOETTCHER, OF WEIMAR, AND OF W. H. CARLTON, OF COLUMBUS.

The uplands of the county are rolling and level, comprising timbered lands and prairies, and have soils varying from gray sandy to black waxy. The lowlands comprise the first and second bottoms, and also the bottom prairies adjacent to Colorado and Navidad rivers and other streams.

The *Colorado river bottoms* are the best and most productive lands, and comprise both sandy and black clayey and reddish clay loams. They bear a natural timber growth of cottonwood, ash, hackberry, elm, pecan, walnut, and wild peach. The soil is 5 or more feet deep; the subsoil is a black clay, called joint clay. Tillage is a little hard when the soil is wet, but otherwise very easy. The soil is early, warm, and naturally well drained, and is best adapted to cotton, corn, sugar-cane, oats, and sweet and Irish potatoes. From one-half to two-thirds of its cultivated area is planted in cotton. The plant grows from 5 to 7 feet high, and inclines to run to weed in wet seasons and when too closely planted; topping will check its growth and cause it to limb heavily. The seed-cotton product per acre of fresh land or after six years' cultivation (unmanured), the soil being in good condition, is from 1,500 to 1,800 pounds, 1,485 pounds making a 475-pound bale of lint, the staple being as good as any. The cocklebur is the most troublesome weed. Very little of this land is "lying out", and it recovers to some extent from the effects of bad farming and again produces very well if well managed.

The *black prairie* occupies about one-third of the county area. The soil is from 2 to 5 feet deep; the subsoil is heavier, a clay hard-pan, somewhat leachy, underlaid by sand and rock at from 10 to 20 feet. Tillage is difficult only when the soil is very wet or dry. The soil is early, warm, and well drained, and is best adapted to cotton, corn, and potatoes. One-third of its cultivated area is planted in cotton, which grows 4 or 5 feet high. The seed-cotton product per acre during the first six years of cultivation is 1,600 pounds if the ground is in good condition, 1,545 pounds making a 475-pound bale of middling lint from the fresh or of good middling from the old land, the staple being longer in the latter case. The troublesome weeds are careless-weed, and in old fields cocklebur and sometimes morning-glories.

The *sandy prairie* occupies about two-fifths of the county area. Distributed over it are bodies of timber, consisting of post, black-jack, and a few live oaks, with soils like the prairie. The color of the soil extends from 4 to 12 inches below the surface; the subsoil is heavier bu. leachy, and is underlaid at 20 feet by sand, gravel, and rock. Tillage is always easy, the soil being early and warm, but not always well drained. The soil is best adapted to corn, cotton, and potatoes, but one-half of its cultivated area is planted in cotton. The plant grows from 2 to 4 feet high, but is most productive at 4 feet. The average seed-cotton product per acre is from 600 to 700 pounds on fresh land, 1,665 pounds making a 475-pound bale of good ordinary lint. After six years' cultivation (unmanured) the product is scant 600 pounds, and 1,780 pounds make a 475-pound bale of somewhat inferior lint. Crab-grass and, in some places, bur-grass are the troublesome weeds. Very little of such land lies "turned out", and does not appear to have improved by resting.

This land is thickly settled, and endures drought well. A few years ago it was considered worthless; now some of the best farmers make a 500-pound bale per acre. By careless management slopes are allowed to become seriously damaged by washing and gullying, and horizontalizing is practiced with success, but it is troublesome. "Hillside ditching should be begun immediately, and for that purpose I have had the first level in this country constructed, and will set the example to save our lands. In Tennessee before the war all of our slopes were successfully protected against such damages by hillside ditching" (*McLeary*).

The washings improve *valley lands*, except when it consists of sand; it then ruins such lands in many cases. The chief crops of this region are corn, cotton, oats, potatoes, peaches, pecans, pumpkins, melons, and other early garden products of good quality, and in abundance.

The climate is generally favorable to cotton growing; but there is an occasional cold, wet spring, when rust and aphides appear, and sultry, showery weather in May and June, which are likely to be followed by the caterpillar. Dry seasons are best for cotton on the river bottom, and even on the prairies moderately dry is best. There are occasionally frosts as late as April, which kill cotton and corn; and dry weather is apt to check the growth of late corn.

Cotton is shipped from September to March, by rail, from Weimar to Galveston at $3 25, or to Houston at $2 50 per bale. Thence it sometimes goes to New York.

LAVACA.

Population: 13,641.—White, 10,221; colored, 3,420.
Area: 1,000 square miles.—Woodland, little less than one-half; oak, hickory, and pine region, 480 square miles; southern prairie, 520 square miles.
Tilled lands: 94,970 acres.—Area planted in cotton, 25,728 acres; in corn, 28,474 acres; in oats, 789 acres; in wheat, 94 acres.
Cotton production: 9,976 bales; average cotton product per acre, 0.39 bale, 585 pounds seed-cotton, or 195 pounds cotton lint.

The surface of Lavaca county is undulating, with a gradual fall southward, and about one-half is timbered with post and black-jack oaks, the rest being mostly open prairies.

The various streams flow south and southeastward, and are timbered with elm, cottonwood, hackberry, etc. Their bottom lands are subject to overflow, and are not under cultivation; but their second bottoms or valley lands have a dark alluvial soil, and are highly productive.

The prairie uplands lie chiefly in the northern part of the county, and extend west to the Guadalupe river, though the timbers of the south are somewhat interspersed with them. Their soils vary from black waxy clays to dark sandy loams, and are underlaid by the heavy concretionary clays and sandstones that characterize the southern prairie region.

The timbered lands have usually an open growth of post and black-jack oaks and a sandy, sometimes pebbly soil and clayey subsoil, with the underclays that underlie the prairies. They are easily tilled, and produce an average of about 500 pounds of seed-cotton per acre. The pecan tree is a prominent growth of the uplands of the county, and furnishes a large supply of this nut to the markets.

Lavaca is an agricultural county, 14.8 per cent. of its area being under cultivation, with an average of 95 acres per square mile. Of the latter, 25.7 acres are given to the culture of cotton. Corn is, however, the chief crop of the county.

ABSTRACTS FROM THE REPORTS OF JOHN WILLIAMS, OF WILLIAMSBURG, AND HENRY K. JUDD, OF HALLETTSVILLE.

The surface of the county is rolling, and consists of sandy, timbered post-oak lands and the open prairies. The latter comprise stiff hog-wallow and black sandy soils. The lowlands consist of the first and second bottoms of Navidad and Lavaca rivers and have rich black and yellow sandy soils, well adapted to the cultivation of cotton and corn. The river bottoms are not used, on account of overflow.

The soil of the bottom lands is prevalently a black, alluvial loam, with a depth of from 10 to 48 inches. Its area forms one-eighth of the county, and its growth is pecan, elm, cottonwood, hickory, live, post, and burr oaks, hackberry, mulberry, wild peach, and a variety of undergrowth. The subsoil is a heavy limy or chalky clay. This land is best adapted to corn, cotton, oats, and ribbon-cane; but about one-half of its cultivated area is planted in cotton. The plant grows from 3 to 5 feet high, but is most productive at 4 feet. It inclines to run to weed in warm, wet weather, the only remedy used being cutting off the top bud. The seed-cotton product per acre of fresh land varies from 900 to 1,500 pounds, 1,545 pounds making a 475-pound bale of middling lint. The cotton product is, after ten years' cultivation (unmanured), reduced to one-half. The lint is shorter, and 3½ pounds of seed-cotton make 1 of lint. Cockleburs, crab-grass, morning-glory, and careless-weeds are most troublesome.

The *prairie uplands* occur in bodies of from 10 to 100 acres or more. The northern part of the county is chiefly prairie. The prairie area occupies about one-half of the county. The soil is chiefly black "hog-wallow", with more or less brown sandy soil, and is from 14 to 60 inches deep, generally resting on soft limestone or chalk. The soil is difficult to till in extremes of wet or dry weather, but ordinarily it is easy to till. It is early, warm, and well drained, and best adapted to corn and the smaller cereals, but one-half of the area is planted in cotton. The plant grows from 2 to 3 feet high. The seed-cotton product per acre of fresh land, or that cultivated twenty years (unmanured), is alike from 900 to 1,500 pounds, and in either case 1,665 pounds make a 475-pound bale of middling lint. Cockleburs are the most troublesome weeds.

The light sandy *post-oak uplands* are distributed in bodies among the prairies, and occupy about one-fourth of the county area. The natural growth is post and black-jack oaks. The soil is from 6 to 24 inches deep, and the subsoil is a heavy clay. Tillage is always easy. The soil is early, warm, well drained, and best adapted to cotton, and one-half its cultivated area (which is small) is planted with the same. The plant grows from 1 to 3 feet high. The seed-cotton product per acre of fresh land is from 500 to 1,000 pounds, 1,545 pounds making a 475-pound bale of middling lint, either from fresh or old land. The most troublesome weed is crab-grass. Such lands are now attracting more attention, as they are considered to be excellent cotton lands. The soils (especially subsoils) of slopes wash and gully to some extent, but no serious damage has yet resulted, and no efforts have been made to check the same. The washings rather improve than injure the valleys.

The chief crops of this region are cotton, corn, oats, rye, barley, sweet and Irish potatoes, millet, ribbon-cane, and sorghum; wheat occasionally succeeds.

As soon as baled cotton is hauled to the nearest railroad station, at $1 per bale, and sold; thence shipped to Galveston at $3 per bale.

GONZALES.
(See "Oak, hickory, and pine region".)

DE WITT.

Population: 10,082.—White, 7,144; colored, 2,938.
Area: 900 square miles.—Woodland, about one-third; oak, hickory, and pine region, 300 square miles; southern prairie, 600 square miles.
Tilled lands: 41,792 acres.—Area planted in cotton, 7,625 acres; in corn, 19,148 acres; in oats, 639 acres; in wheat, 500 acres.
Cotton production: 2,183 bales; average cotton product per acre, 0.29 bale, 435 pounds seed-cotton, or 145 pounds cotton lint.

De Witt county has a surface of partly rolling and partly level prairie and timbered lands, and is divided by the Guadalupe river, which flows in a southeastern course.

The extreme northern part of the county is composed of high and rolling prairies, with rocky sandstone knobs (Grand Gulf) and usually gray and sandy soils. Southward toward Cuero, the county-seat, the surface of the country falls, and at Hellgate ferry, 4 miles north of the town, the last outcrop of the sandstone is seen, with an exposure 10 feet in thickness, through which the waters of the river have cut a passage.

Still southward appear the black hog-wallow prairies, that extend to the coast and are underlaid by concretionary clays (Port Hudson). This part of the county is more level, but has a gradual fall toward the coast.

Post-oak sandy lands occur in large areas throughout the county, and heavy beds of sand are found in some localities, especially near the river between Cuero and Clinton. The prairies are largely devoted to stock-raising.

ABSTRACT FROM THE REPORT OF A. G. STEVENS, OF CONCRETE.

About one-half of the uplands is prairie. The lands devoted to the cultivation of cotton comprise the black waxy and black sandy prairie, the light sandy loam, and the very light sandy timbered lands. The timbered uplands have a growth of post oak. The bottom lands have a width of from one-half mile to 2 miles, and a growth of elm, hackberry, burr oak, pecan, and cottonwood.

The *black sandy prairie* is preferred for cotton. The soil is from 3 to 5 feet in depth, and its chief crops are corn, cotton, and oats. About one-third of the tilled land is in cotton, which grows to a height of 4½ feet, and yields 1,500 pounds of seed-cotton per acre, 1,665 pounds making 475 pounds of middling to good middling lint. After ten years' cultivation no material change is noticed in the yield, but the rating of the staple is one grade lower. The most troublesome weeds are cocklebur and blood-weed. The late frosts often do injury to the cotton. Very little land lies "turned out".

The *light sandy loam*, covering about one-fourth of the county, has a natural timber growth of mesquite and post oak. The soil is from 8 to 15 inches deep, with a subsoil of red and joint clay, and the yield is from 1,000 to 1,200 pounds of seed-cotton per acre after ten years' cultivation.

Shipments are made by railroad from Cuero to Galveston and New York, the rate to the latter place being $5 per bale.

WHARTON.
(See "Brazos alluvial region".)

VICTORIA.

Population: 6,289.—White, 3,883; colored, 2,406.
Area: 880 square miles.—Woodland, but little; all southern prairies.
Tilled lands: 24,395 acres.—Area planted in cotton, 1,739 acres; in corn, 6,253 acres; in oats, 174 acres; in wheat, 28 acres.
Cotton production: 730 bales; average cotton product per acre, 0.42 bale, 630 pounds seed-cotton, or 210 pounds cotton lint.

The surface of Victoria county is undulating on the north, becoming quite level southward, and is watered by the Guadalupe and San Antonio rivers and a number of large creeks, some of which flow independently into Lavaca bay. Black and sandy prairies cover the greater part of the county, and are very generally devoted to the grazing of stock. (See analysis, page 32.) They are underlaid by the heavy concretionary clays of this region. The streams are bordered by narrow sandy uplands, timbered with post and live oaks or by mesquite prairie flats, which have a deep black waxy soil.

The bottom lands of the rivers are narrow and heavily timbered with pecan, ash, oaks, hackberry, mulberry, etc., and have a dark sandy alluvial soil, rich and very productive. The lands under cultivation comprise but 4.3 per cent. of the county area, and but a small part of these is devoted to the culture of cotton. The average yield of this crop is above that of the state. The farmers are chiefly Germans, who have devoted most of their tilled lands to crops other than corn and cotton.

ABSTRACT FROM THE REPORT OF THOMAS R. COCKE, M. D., OF VICTORIA.

The uplands consist of black hog-wallow prairie and rolling lands, mostly the former, which constitutes the most important land devoted to the cultivation of cotton. The gray shelly lands of the river bottoms above overflow, the light sandy near the creek, and the post-oak land form the remainder of the lands so applied.

The *black hog-wallow* and *black sandy prairie lands* cover about five-eighths of the county; continuous hog-wallow tracts of 8 or 10 miles is very usual in this region, the intermediate soil being sandy. The soil is a black sandy loam, varying in depth from 2½ to 5 feet, with a subsoil of yellow joint clay, replaced in some cases by shell and marl. If the land is well broken up in the winter or fall, it is very easily cultivated, producing corn, sugar-cane, and cotton. Small grain crops are being tried; oats do well. Owing to labor being so unreliable, only one-tenth of these lands is in cotton, which grows to a height of 4 feet, though when well branched it attains 5 or 6 feet, the last being the most productive. The yield is 1,800 pounds of seed-cotton per acre, and 1,900 pounds are required for 475 pounds of lint, which rates as middling. Thirty years' cultivation causes no change in the yield, but the staple is shorter, stronger, and heavier. Wet weather causes the plant to run to weed, which to some extent is restrained by topping. About five-eighths of the land lies "turned out", grazing being substituted for cultivation. Crab-grass, careless-weed, and cocklebur are the most troublesome weeds, the first being the worst enemy to cotton planting.

The lands adjoining the river, as well as those of the river bottoms, differ very materially from those of the creeks, the former being gray and black alluvium, from 6 to 8 feet deep, the latter a light sandy soil, either yellow or gray, on a red-clay subsoil. The cotton on the low lands free from overflow grows much higher and produces from 25 to 33 per cent. more to the acre; it is not injured by the winds, and the fiber, though not quite so fine, is stronger and longer than on the uplands.

The *gray shelly lands* of the river bottoms cover about one-eighth of the county, and have a timber growth of buckeye, white oak, and pecan, and an undergrowth of grape and other vines. The soil is a gray sandy loam, 10 feet deep, over yellow joint clay from 4 to 8 feet in depth. It is early, warm, well drained, easily tilled in all seasons, and well adapted to cotton, corn, and sugar-cane, one-tenth of the area planted being devoted to cotton, which yields from 1,800 to 2,500 pounds of seed-cotton per acre, 1,305 pounds being necessary for 475 pounds of lint, which rates as middling. It usually attains a height of 5 or 6 feet. The yield is not altered after the land has been under cultivation for thirty years. About four-fifths of the land lies "turned out". Wet seasons on the lowlands are the cause of mildew, which may be obviated by planting farther apart; topping is applied to restrain the running to weed, which occurs when there is too much rain. The most troublesome weeds on this soil are cocklebur, careless-, and blood-weed.

The *light sandy soil* lying along the creeks comprises about one-fourth of the tillable area, and has a timbered growth of post, black-jack, and live oaks. The soil is a grayish, fine, or coarse sandy loam, 15 inches in depth, with a red-clay subsoil occasionally mixed with clay or marl, contains ferruginous pebbles, and is underlaid by sand or gravel. The soil is early, warm, well drained, easily tilled in dry seasons, and best adapted to cotton, tobacco, potatoes, and fruit. One-sixteenth of the entire crops is cotton, which grows to a height of 3 feet in good seasons, and yields 1,000 pounds of seed-cotton per acre, 2,140 pounds being requisite for 475 pounds of good middling lint. After three years' cultivation the yield is sensibly diminished, as is also the rating of the staple, and 2,380 pounds are necessary for 475 pounds of lint. One-quarter of the land lies "turned out", and when again cultivated produces about 87½ per cent. of the original product. This character of soil has never been extensively cultivated. The soil washes on the slopes, doing considerable damage to the valleys, and horizontalizing is practiced with fair success to check the damage. Crab-grass is the most troublesome weed.

Cotton is hauled by wagon as soon as baled to Victoria.

JACKSON.

Population : 2,723.—White, 1,310; colored, 1,413.
Area : 900 square miles.—Woodland, probably one-third; all southern prairies.
Tilled lands : 8,829 acres.—Area planted in cotton, 648 acres; in corn, 3,787 acres; in oats, 45 acres.
Cotton production : 202 bales; average cotton product per acre, 0.31 bale, 465 pounds seed-cotton, or 155 pounds cotton lint.

The surface of Jackson county is undulating, and is watered by numerous streams flowing southward into Lavaca and other bays. These streams are timbered with oak, elm, ash, pecan, hackberry, wild peach, some hickory, etc. The rest of the county is mostly open prairies, and comprises, it is thought, two-thirds of the entire area. The lands of the timbered areas are sandy, those of the prairies varying from black, waxy clays to dark, sandy loams. The crops of the county are corn, cotton, oats, vegetables, etc. Jackson is principally a stock-raising county, and but 1.5 per cent. of its area is under tillage, the average being 9.8 acres per square mile.

Corn is the chief crop, with a yield of from 10 to 20 bushels per acre. Very little cotton is produced. Wild mustang grapes are said to be abundant. The methods of cotton culture are the same as in the adjoining counties. Shipments are made by boat down the bay to Indianola, and thence by steamer to Galveston.

ABSTRACT FROM THE REPORT OF GEORGE F. HORTON, OF TEXANA.

The soils of the county are very equally divided between sandy and black waxy. Five living streams water the county, passing through its entire length, and about 8 miles apart; they are well timbered on either side from one-fourth of a mile to 2 miles. The sandy lands occur in this timbered portion, while the black, waxy lands occupy the open intermediate prairies.

MATAGORDA.

Population : 3,940.—White, 1,416; colored, 2,524.
Area : 1,400 square miles.—Woodland, very little; southern prairie loam, 1,380 square miles; alluvial, 20 square miles.
Tilled lands : 17,917 acres.—Area planted in cotton, 3,435 acres; in corn, 4,747 acres; in oats, 14 acres; in sugar-cane, 300 acres.
Cotton production : 2,096 bales; average cotton product per acre, 0.61 bale, 915 pounds seed-cotton, or 305 pounds cotton lint.

Matagorda is one of the coast counties, and its surface is quite level, comprising mostly open prairies, with timbered lands along the Colorado river, Cany creek, and other streams that flow south into Matagorda bay. The lands of the prairies present the variety of black waxy and hog-wallow clays to dark sandy loams usual to the southern prairie region, and are underlaid by heavy concretionary clays. They are almost exclusively given up to grazing purposes.

The lands of the Colorado river and Cany creek are several miles in width, and are heavily timbered with cottonwood, pecan, elm, ash, mulberry, hackberry, etc., and noted for their richness and high productiveness. Their soils are mostly red and black alluvial loams, capable of producing from 1,500 to 2,000 pounds of seed-cotton per acre. Sugar-cane is one of the chief crops of these lands, and in 1879 yielded 270 hogsheads of sugar and 20,000 gallons of molasses from 300 acres.

Matagorda is a sparsely populated county, and but a small part (2 per cent.) of its lands is under cultivation, the average being 12.8 acres per square mile. Its cotton acreage is comparatively small, though in product per acre it ranks as fifth in the state. The methods of cotton culture are the same as practiced in the adjoining counties. Shipments are made by steamer from the port of Matagorda to Galveston and other points.

KARNES.

Population : 3,270.—White, 2,780; colored, 490.
Area : 730 square miles.—Woodland, about one-half; oak, hickory, and pine region, 330 square miles; southern prairie, 400 square miles.
Tilled lands : 51,393 acres.—Area planted in cotton, 1,607 acres; in corn, 5,184 acres; in oats, 48 acres; in wheat, 52 acres.
Cotton production : 283 bales; average cotton product per acre, 0.18 bale, 270 pounds seed-cotton, or 90 pounds cotton lint.

Karnes, though included among the prairie counties of southern Texas, is largely covered with the timber of the oak and hickory uplands of the eastern part of the state, which terminates here, and is associated with a mesquite growth. South and east of Helena, the county-seat, there are chiefly prairies, with soils varying from the black calcareous and hog-wallow to the dark sandy, and underlaid by heavy clays. The timbered lands are mostly sandy, and have a growth of post oak. The surface of the county is generally level or undulating, and is watered by the Medina river and its tributaries, which flow in a southeasterly course. It is sparsely settled, and the people are largely engaged in stock-raising.

A small proportion of the lands under cultivation is devoted to the culture of cotton, and the yield for 1879 was very low, viz, 270 pounds of seed-cotton per acre. The methods of tillage, etc., are the same as practiced in the adjoining counties. Cuero, in De Witt county, is the nearest market, to which place cotton is hauled on wagons, and thence shipped, via Indianola and the Gulf, to Galveston and other points.

ABSTRACT FROM THE REPORT OF THOMAS BUCKMAN, OF HELENA.

The surface of the county is rolling, partly prairie and partly timbered. The most important soil is a *black, stiff prairie,* partly hog-wallow, covering one-fifth of the county, the latter occurring in spots all over the county, the natural timber growth being a scattering one of post and live oaks and mesquite. Hackberry, pecan, cottonwood, and mulberry lie on the bottoms. The soil is 2 or 3 feet deep, with a heavy blue-clay subsoil. It is early, warm, well drained, easily cultivated, and produces chiefly corn and cotton. About one-quarter of the farming land is devoted to cotton, which attains a height of from 4 to 6 feet, inclines to run to weed in wet seasons, and yields 1,200 pounds of seed-cotton per acre, 1,520 pounds being necessary for 475 pounds of lint, which rates as low middling. No land lies "turned out". Sometimes the plant continues to yield until near Christmas. In rainy seasons it is troubled with web-worms, which web up and hatch out every six weeks, increasing with every hatching. Cultivation of the land does not seem to diminish the yield of seed-cotton. The climate is well adapted to the growth of cotton, because of long seasons and not too much rain. Shipments are made in winter by railroad from the nearest station to Galveston at $2 25 per bale.

WILSON.

(See "Oak, hickory, and pine region".)

ATASCOSA.

Population : 4,217.—White, 3,938; colored, 279.
Area : 1,200 square miles.—Woodland, little more than half; oak, hickory, and pine region, 680 square miles; southern prairie, 520 square miles.
Tilled lands : 14,744 acres.—Area planted in cotton, 1,422 acres; in corn, 4,475 acres; in oats, 93 acres.
Cotton production : 469 bales; average cotton product per acre, 0.33 bale, 495 pounds seed-cotton, or 165 pounds cotton lint.

Atascosa is an undulating or somewhat rolling county, watered by a number of creeks tributary to the Nueces river. It is about equally divided between prairie and timbered lands, the latter, known as the black-jack country, being covered with a growth of post and black-jack oaks, hickory, and mesquite, with cottonwood, pecan, willow, etc., along the streams. The soils vary from the sandy loam of the prairies to the deep sands of the timbers, and are underlaid by clays.

The county is sparsely settled, and the chief industry is raising stock, especially sheep, for which the mesquite grasses of the prairies seem to be admirably suited. The amount of tilled lands is small in comparison with the area of the county. They are found principally near the streams, and average about 12 acres per square mile. The long droughts are the chief hinderance to successful farming operations. The cotton acreage is small, that crop as yet receiving but little attention.

San Antonio is the nearest railroad market, to which shipments are made by wagon.

ABSTRACTS FROM THE REPORTS OF F. W. KLEMCKE AND GEORGE W. MUDD, OF SOMERSET.

The uplands are rolling and level. The lands of the county are the fine or coarse sandy and the black shelly prairie. The *fine sandy lands* cover about two-thirds of the county area, and have a timbered growth of post, live and black-jack oaks, mesquite, hickory, cat-claw, and hackberry. The soil is a sandy loam, from 8 inches to 1 foot in depth, with a subsoil of red clay impervious to water, underlaid by sandstone at from 6 to 10 feet. It is easily cultivated, is early, warm, and well drained, and produces cotton, corn, and all varieties of vegetables. Cotton, constituting from two-fifths to two-thirds of the entire crops, grows to a height of from 3 to 4½ feet, the latter being the most productive. There is very little difference, either in the yield or in the rating of the staple, between cotton grown on fresh and that raised from long cultivated land, the product per acre being from 800 to 1,800 pounds of seed-cotton, from 1,425 to 1,665 pounds being required for 475 pounds of lint rating as strict middling. The rainfall has a great influence on the size and quality of the crop, and the plant runs to weed in wet seasons and when too closely planted. Deep plowing and topping has the effect of favoring bolling and restraining the tendency to run to weed. Crab-grass, lamb's-quarter, careless, nettle, and wild millet form the most troublesome weeds on all lands of the county.

Additional from the report of F. W. Klemcke.

Premature frosts do not kill the cotton crops either on the uplands or on the lowlands. Sometimes, though very seldom, when the cotton is planted before the 20th of April, the cool, damp weather causes "sore-shin". If properly cultivated the crop is always certain.

The belt of *coarse sandy* land is 8 miles wide and 30 miles long. The soil is about 4 feet in depth, gray in color, underlaid by clay, and has a natural growth of hickory and black-jack oak. It is easily cultivated in all seasons, and is early, warm, and well drained. It is best adapted to cotton, from which is obtained a very fine lint, rating as middling. The height usually attained by the plant is about 2 or 3 feet; the yield of seed-cotton per acre is from 600 to 1,000 pounds, and from 1,425 to 1,780 pounds are necessary for a 475-pound bale. There appears to be no difference in the above yield after the land has been cultivated many years. No land lies "turned out" in this county. Crab-grass is the only troublesome weed.

The *black prairie shelly* land has a natural growth of mesquite. The soil is a light gravelly loam, about 2 feet in depth; the subsoil is heavier, contains flinty pebbles and white gravel, and is underlaid with gravel and rock at from 7 to 10 feet. The land is early, warm, and in wet seasons ill-drained; also in such times it is difficult to till. It is best adapted to corn, cotton, and small grain. Up to this time (1880) only one-tenth of the cultivated area has been devoted to cotton, but the prospect is good for one-half. The plant usually attains a height of from 4 to 5 feet; but there is a tendency to run to weed in wet weather, for which deep plowing and topping are the remedies applied. In good seasons from 1,200 to 1,800 pounds is the product of seed-cotton per acre from fresh lands, and 1,600 pounds are requisite for 475 pounds of good middling lint. Long cultivation of the land does not seem to affect the above yield. Morning-glory vine, wild millet, and crab-grass are the most troublesome weeds. The soil does not wash or gully on slopes.

Shipments are made by wagon to San Antonio at 75 cents per bale, and thence to New York at $7 50 per bale; also to Mexico.

FRIO.

Population: 2,130.—White, 2,065; colored, 65.
Area: 1,000 square miles.—Woodland, small part; oak, hickory, and pine region, 140 square miles; southern prairie, 860 square miles.
Tilled lands: 5,622 acres.—Area planted in cotton, 543 acres; in corn, 1,574 acres; in wheat, 8 acres.
Cotton production: 156 bales; average cotton product per acre, 0.29 bale, 435 pounds seed-cotton, or 145 pounds cotton lint.

Frio is one of the extreme western cotton counties of the state. Its surface is undulating or rolling, with some prominent points, and consists mostly of sandy prairies of the southwestern region, with a scattering growth of live and post oaks, pecan, and mesquite. The country is very sparsely populated, the ratio being only about two persons per square mile, and its prairies are chiefly devoted to stock-raising. The lands are not much under cultivation, because of the necessity for irrigation, caused by the extreme droughts. The county is watered by the Frio and Leona rivers, from which a supply can be obtained for irrigating purposes. These streams are timbered with elm, ash, willow, etc. San Antonio is the nearest railroad depot to which shipments of cotton are made. The lands under cultivation comprise less than 1 per cent. of the county area, and average 5.6 acres per square mile. This is one of the largest sheep-raising counties in the state, the number reaching 140,222 head.

ABSTRACT FROM THE REPORT OF LEWIS OWINGS, OF IRELAND.

This county has been only recently settled. The uplands are rolling and level table-lands.

The red sandy lands, covering about three-quarters of the county, with its growth of mesquite, live oak, ash, elm, willow, and hackberry, and the black sandy lands along the rivers and creek bottoms, comprise the lands devoted to the cultivation of cotton. The soil of the *red sandy lands*, which is the more important, is easily tilled, and has a depth of from 20 to 25 inches. It is early, warm, and well drained, and produces corn, cotton, and potatoes. Fruit also does well, but it is best adapted to cotton, which grows to a height of from 3 to 5 feet, yielding 1,000 pounds of seed-cotton per acre, from 1,425 to 1,780 pounds of which are required for a 475-pound bale, the rating being good. The plant never runs to weed unless too thick in the drill, the remedy being thinning to a proper stand. Purslane and careless-weed are the most troublesome weeds. No land lies "turned out".

Shipments of cotton are made to San Antonio, as soon as ginned, by wagons, the rate being from $2 50 to $3 per bale.

MEDINA.

(See " Central black prairie region ".)

UVALDE.

(See " Central black prairie region ".)

GOLIAD.

Population: 5,832.—White, 4,166 ; colored, 1,666.

Area: 820 square miles.—Woodland, small part; oak, hickory, and pine region, 180 square miles; southern prairie, 640 square miles.

Tilled lands: 30,547 acres.—Area planted in cotton, 1,779 acres ; in corn, 9,059 acres ; in oats, 273 acres ; in wheat, 372 acres.

Cotton production: 728 bales ; average cotton product per acre, 0.41 bale, 615 pounds seed-cotton, or 205 pounds cotton lint.

Goliad is an undulating prairie county, watered by the Guadalupe river and Blanco creek, which form respectively the eastern and western boundaries, and by the San Antonio river, which flows in a southeast course through its center. These streams and their tributaries are timbered with pecan, oaks, cottonwood, and willow. Mesquite and chaparral bushes, with clumps or motts of live oak, are found abundantly on the prairies. The banks of the San Antonio river are high, and in them, as well as in those of the other smaller streams, there outcrops a whitish clay or adobe (Port Hudson), which was used as the building material in the old Mexican houses and missions. The walls of these buildings were made very thick, to withstand the washing effects of rains, which gives to them the appearance of simple mud houses. The soils of the county vary from dark sandy loam to black waxy calcareous clay on the prairies and gray sandy lands in the timbered uplands along the streams. Goliad is chiefly a stock-raising county. The cotton acreage is small, other crops being more productive and more profitable.

ABSTRACT FROM THE REPORT OF REV. J. E. VERNOR, OF WESATCHE.

The uplands consist of rolling prairie and timbered lands, mostly the former, with black waxy and white sandy soils.

The *black waxy lands* cover about one-fourth of the county, and the soil varies very much. On river bottoms, and also on the prairies, the waxy land is found, though the sandy lands are more plentiful, sometimes extending 25 miles. Scrubby post oak and mesquite, with pecan on the rivers, form the natural timber growth. The soil is a black, sticky, clay loam, very deep, very difficult to till in wet, but much easier in dry seasons, and is early, warm, and well drained. The subsoil is usually a kind of joint clay, which holds water well, but occasionally there is an adobe subsoil strongly impregnated with lime, containing sand or gravel, sometimes rock at from 3 to 30 feet, which produces cotton, corn, and oats. Cotton comprises about one-third of the crops, and grows to a height of from 3 to 5 feet, being most productive at 3 feet. It yields about 950 pounds of seed-cotton per acre, from 1,425 to 1,665 pounds being necessary for 475 pounds of lint. The above figures are not changed after the land has been in cultivation for twenty years. Cocklebur gives trouble to some extent, but crab-grass gives the greatest trouble to the planters on all lands of the county. Very little, if any, land lies "turned out".

The *black sandy land* comprises about five-eighths of the tillable area, and has a growth of post oak in places. The soil is fine sandy or gravelly, from brown to black in color, and from 8 to 30 inches in depth ; it has a hard-jointed, impervious clay subsoil, underlaid by sand or gravel, and sometimes by rock. The land is easily cultivated, is early, warm, and well drained, and best adapted to cotton, to which about one-third of the land under cultivation is devoted, the height usually attained being from 3 to 5 feet, the former being the height at which it is the most productive. The yield is from 800 to 900 pounds of seed-cotton per acre, of which from 1,425 to 1,665 pounds are required for a 475-pound bale. Twenty years' cultivation has no effect either as regards the yield or rating of the staple.

The *white sandy lands,* comprising about one-eighth of the county, extend from 1 to 2 miles, and have a timber growth of post and black-jack oaks. The soil is white and coarse sandy, and has a depth of from 10 to 24 inches, with a subsoil of clay of good quality, such as is used for making brick and earthenware. It is early, warm, well drained, and apparently best adapted to cotton and sweet potatoes, the former, constituting about one-half of the entire crops, growing to a height of from 1 to 4 feet, being the most productive at 2 feet. The yield per acre in seed-cotton, both from fresh land and from land cultivated twenty years, is from 400 to 600 pounds, from 1,425 to 1,665 pounds being necessary for 475 pounds of lint. Drought and occasional wet seasons have a bad effect on the crops; drought prevents the appearance of the caterpillar, and wet seasons produce them.

Shipments are made from August to January, by the Morgan line of steamships, to New York at $4 75, to New Orleans at $3 53, and to Galveston at $2 73 per bale.

OTHER COUNTIES PRODUCING LITTLE OR NO COTTON.

The counties comprising the rest of the southern prairie region to the Rio Grande river are extremely sparsely settled, and are chiefly devoted to stock-raising, very little cotton being grown. For character of land and general features the reader is referred to the regional description on page 32, and for statistical information to Tables I and II at the beginning of the report.

Calhoun and Aransas counties, immediately on the coast, report no cotton ; Refugio, 15 bales ; San Patricio, 2 bales, and also a little sea-island cotton ; Nueces and Duval, none ; Bee, 9 bales ; Live Oak, 4 bales ; Hidalgo, 9 bales ; and Cameron, at the mouth of the Rio Grande, 23 bales.

CALHOUN.—This county is included between Matagorda and Lavaca bays on the east, and San Antonio bay and Guadalupe river on the west. The surface of the country is almost a perfectly level and open prairie, with here and there motts or clumps of live-oak trees. The lands are largely stiff black hog-wallow clays, with areas or belts of sandy prairie soils, underlaid by concretionary and gypseous clays and sandstones, as observed in the bluffs of Lavaca bay and Green lake.

ARANSAS.—One-third of the area is composed of bays, lagoons, and bayous. The surface is level, and is divided between open prairies and lands covered with live-oak and scrubby timber. The lands comprise the black waxy clays and sandy loams common to the southern prairie region, and are but slightly under cultivation. The crops are corn, potatoes, and vegetables. No cotton has been reported from this county, though the sea-island variety would no doubt do well.

Although no cotton has ever been planted in this county, because our greatest interest has always been that of stock, yet I am satisfied that the very best staple of sea-island cotton can be raised here, both on the main coast-line and on the adjacent islands that run parallel with the coast. Up to the past year no cotton had ever been tried within our extreme southwestern counties, with the exception of some in the Rio Grande valley. Last year experiments were made in some of our western counties, and with so much success that this year considerable quantities have been planted in Live Oak, Bee, Goliad, and San Patricio counties, and the prospect is at present so good that two cotton-gins are being built in these counties in the neighborhood of the planted cotton.—*E. A. Perrenot, of Corpus Christi.*

REFUGIO.—This county is very similar to Calhoun in its surface features, being mostly a level and open prairie, intersected by skirts of timbered lands along the streams. The timber growth of the bottoms is white oak, pecan, elm, ash, hackberry, etc.; that of some of the uplands post, live, and black-jack oaks and mesquite. It is watered by many streams flowing into the numerous bays that border it on the south.

The lands of the prairies comprise the black waxy clays, dark and brown sandy loams peculiar to this southern region, with light sandy lands in the timbered sections. All are underlaid by heavy concretionary clays.

SAN PATRICIO.—This is a Gulf county lying between the Aransas and Nueces rivers, and its surface is mostly a prairie, with black calcareous and sandy-loam soils. Mesquite is the chief upland growth of the county, with clumps of live oak, while on the bottom lands there is found elm, ash, cottonwood, and hackberry.

There is a peculiar feature in this county called the "brasada", being an area of upland about 31 square miles, covered with a thick growth of mesquite, interspersed with chaparral and the prickly pear. The land is a rich, dark loam, and would undoubtedly produce well; but scarcely any of it is cultivated, owing to the labor of clearing and preparing the ground.—*Thrall, History of Texas.*

The uplands are level table-lands. The various lands of the county are sandy, occurring in patches on the slopes of hills, in Nueces valley, and on the Aransas river, black hog-wallow uplands comprising about five-eighths of the tillable area out from Nueces valley, along Nueces river, Corpus Christi bay, and Chiltipin creek, and black alluvial bottom on the Nueces river. Of the above the sandy land is the most important as regards the cultivation of cotton, which covers about one-fourth of the county. The timbered growth in the Nueces valley is wesatche and mesquite; on the Aransas river, live, post, and black-jack oaks; and live oak, cottonwood, ash, elm, hackberry, and willow along the Nueces river. The soil of the sandy lands, black in color, is very easily tilled in wet or dry seasons, producing cotton, corn, potatoes (Irish and sweet), sorghum, and all kinds of vegetables. The first forms about 20 per cent. of the crops, corn being the chief product. Wild mint, sunflower, and cocklebur are the troublesome weeds. Very little land lies "turned out". Shipments are made from Corpus Christi to Galveston.—*James O. Gaffney, of San Patricio.*

NUECES.—This county has a level or undulating surface, and consists mostly of prairies, either open or with a low growth of mesquite bushes and trees. Nueces river forms the northeast boundary, and a number of other streams flow through the county to the Laguna Madre. Corpus Christi, the county-seat, is located partly upon a bluff about 50 feet above the water-level, which is thought to be the highest along the entire Texas coast. The lands of the county are said to be a rich sandy loam, very productive in fair seasons. A small proportion of this land is under cultivation, the chief industry of the county being stock-raising. In the southern part of the county, and about 20 miles from Corpus Christi, are the sand hills of the desert, which extend thence to the valley of the Rio Grande.

DUVAL.—The following description is by W. H. Caldwell, of Borjas:

The country around Borjas, both east and west, is a hilly or rolling prairie. The hills are composed of white soft limestone, but underneath this, deeper in the earth, there is a formation of rock-like concrete, which is white and soft, but on exposure to the weather becomes quite hard. Only in rare cases do rocks outcrop in the creeks. The soil is sandy; the hills of red and the valleys or cañons of dark sand, underlaid by clay. The country is a broad prairie, the hills being covered with a black chaparral growth. The valleys are mostly open, and when not so mesquite brush and trees are found. There is no large timber on the prairies. The creeks are marked by motts of elm and hackberry trees of medium size.

BEE.—The surface of the county is rolling, with mostly open prairies, interspersed with areas of timbered lands and watered by numerous streams flowing southward. The timbered lands, it is estimated, cover about one-third of the county, with a scattering growth of post and live oaks, mesquite, etc., and lie mostly on the west of Beeville, the county-seat.

On the east and north there are broad and rolling prairies, well covered with grass, and devoted to grazing purposes. Their soils vary from sandy to black and waxy, and are underlaid by the heavy clays characteristic of this coast prairie region. The best lands are said to lie along the rivers.

LIVE OAK.—The surface of the county is partly undulating and partly level, and is divided by the Nueces river, which flows in an east and southeast course, with numerous tributaries on either side. Open prairies occupy about two-fifths of the county, the rest being covered by a growth of live-oak trees and mesquite on the uplands and elm, cottonwood, pecan, hackberry, etc., on the lowlands of the streams.

The soils vary from a light to a dark sandy loam, and are very productive in good seasons. Limestone occurs near Oakville, and sandstone in other parts of the county.

The uplands of this county are mostly rolling prairies. The soils of the county are dark sandy timbered lands, dark prairies, and light sandy soils, the most important one being the sandy loam, with its timbered growth of mesquite, live oak, hackberry, and mulberry. It is early, warm, and well drained, producing corn, oats, cotton, and sugar-cane. Until 1879 no cotton was raised in the county, but now in 1880 it is estimated that one-third of the crops is of cotton, experiment having proved that its cultivation would be attended with success.—*G. W. Jones, of Oakville.*

HIDALGO.—The lands of the river are very narrow, and approach near the stream at Hidalgo, the county-seat. Here, too, the first hills occur, in which sandstone is said to be the prevailing rock. The lands of this southern part of the county are the only ones under cultivation, and comprise soils varying from sandy to black and clayey. The timber growth is chiefly mesquite, ebony, wesatche, live oak, and Brazil wood on the upland or prairie valleys, and ash, elm, and hackberry on the bottoms. The chief crops are corn, potatoes, and vegetables; but very little cotton is planted. The rest of the county, especially on the north, is mostly sandy, with a scattering growth of moss-covered and scrubby live oak, and forms a part of the desert, which has here a width of about 25 miles. There are many salt lakes in this county, among which *Sal del Rey* is, perhaps, the most noted, being "a mile in diameter, in a flat, surrounded by higher land".

CAMERON.—The following description is from Rev. J. G. Hall, of Brownsville:

The country around Brownsville, and for 100 miles northward, is generally level, and the prevailing growth is mesquite and ebony, though there are many other scrubby varieties. The undergrowth in many places is very heavy. The soil is in belts of from 3 to 8 miles in width, and comprise black waxy and sandy varieties, the latter rather dark in color; but neither has a clay subsoil. The black waxy is the richest, though both are very productive in fair seasons.

For the first 60 or 70 miles above Brownsville the river valley loses itself in the plain, but farther up it becomes narrow, until at a little more than 100 miles it becomes almost nothing. The timber growth is heaviest along the river, though not very dense anywhere. Up to this time there has been very little cotton planted here, but the people are beginning to turn their attention more toward its culture. When there is rain it produces well.

Cotton in this locality often continues to grow for several years in succession unless killed by frosts. This method of culture is not only very uncertain of success, but the staple becomes very inferior. (a)

Mr. L. J. Hynes, living about 30 miles north of Brownsville, owns a large farm and has given much attention to the subject, and he thinks the want of proper labor is the only drawback to the successful culture of cotton. From his own crop, and what he bought from his neighbors, he shipped in one year about 300 bales, which rated as good middling in New York.

BRAZOS ALLUVIAL REGION.

(Comprises all or parts of the counties of Fort Bend, Wharton, Brazoria, and Matagorda.*)

FORT BEND.

Population: 9,380.—White, 1,871; colored, 7,509.

Area: 880 square miles.—Woodland, some; southern prairies, 760 square miles; Brazos alluvial, 120 square miles.

Tilled lands: 38,379 acres.—Area planted in cotton, 10,873 acres; in corn, 16,710 acres; in oats, 284 acres; in sugar-cane, 1,738 acres.

Cotton production: 6,431 bales; average cotton product per acre, 0.59 bale, 885 pounds seed-cotton, or 295 pounds cotton lint.

Fort Bend county is divided into two parts by the Brazos river, which has a very irregular southeasterly course through the county. San Bernard river and Oyster creek are independent streams on the west and east, though small in size until they approach nearly to the coast. The surface of the country is quite level, and the most important feature is the broad alluvial region or delta of the Brazos, which reaches from this county to the coast, and has been called "the sugar-bowl of Texas". It has a width of from 6 to 12 miles in this county, and includes the lands of Oyster creek on the east. Its timber growth is elm, ash, cottonwood, oaks, pecan, and hackberry, with areas of canebrakes, and wild peach undergrowth. The lands near the river are mostly reddish sandy loams, highly prized for their productiveness, and are largely under cultivation.

On the San Bernard river there is much cedar and cypress. The rest of the lands are black and clayey in character, have a prominent growth of elm, and are poorly drained and difficult to till. Sugar-cane is the chief crop on this bottom land, the production of sugar and molasses being very great, viz, 1,827 hogsheads of sugar and 119,079 gallons of molasses. The uplands of the county are level and open prairies, covering three-fourths of the area, with the exception of a narrow strip of post-oak lands on the northeast. The soils vary from stiff and black waxy clays to brown sandy loams, and are very generally devoted to grazing purposes. The heavy concretionary clays peculiar to the southern prairie region underlie them.

The lands under cultivation comprise but 6.8 per cent. of the county area, with an average of 43.6 acres per square mile. Of the latter but 12.4 acres are devoted to the culture of cotton, though the yield per acre is surpassed by only six counties in the state.

ABSTRACT FROM THE REPORTS OF THOMAS B. HOWARD AND W. E. KENDALL, OF HOUSTON.

The lands of the county comprise the first and second bottoms of Oyster creek, alluvial plain on or near the Brazos river, and level black and gray prairie uplands, partly hog-wallow in character.

The *bottom lands* of the Brazos river and immediate tributaries occupy about one-fifth of the county area, and embrace about four-fifths of the cultivated land of the county. The soil is a rich alluvium; chocolate color prevails, but varies to brown and black; depth to change of color, 3 feet. Down to 30 or 40 feet the material consists of strata of sandy and stiff brown loam from 3 to 5 feet thick, all being good

---

a Samples of cotton from stalks of four, three, and one year's growth, respectively, have been submitted for microscopical and expert examination, and the results show that the lint from the three-year-old stalk is much the shortest and weakest, though the widest of the three.

soil. Such is the bottom from within 8 miles of the Gulf of Mexico to 500 miles up on either side of the river. The natural growth is ash, elm, hackberry, pecan, cottonwood, sycamore, linden, yaupon, wild peach, cane, and a great variety of oaks. The Brazos bottoms comprise four classes, viz: (1) Canebrakes; (2) wild peach brakes; (3) pecan, oak, and ash growth; (4) elm flats. The canebrake variety is sandiest, chocolate-colored; the richest has produced two 500-pound bales per acre. When the soil is neither too wet nor dry it is easily tilled, and is early and warm, but ill drained. The soil is well adapted to cotton, corn, sugar-cane, sweet potatoes, red (anti-rust) oats, and millet, and these are the chief crops; but corn and cotton are chief among these. About one-half the cultivated area is planted in cotton. The plant grows to the height of 4 feet in dry seasons, 8 feet in wet, and 6 feet in good seasons. It inclines to run to weed when heavy showers are frequent late in June, July, and August, for which shallow cultivation with the sweep is the best remedy. Topping is frequently resorted to.

The seed-cotton product per acre of fresh land varies from 1,500 to 2,000 pounds, 1,545 pounds making a 475-pound bale of good lint. After thirty years' successive cotton production (without manure) the yield is the same; after forty years it is, in a favorable season, 1,700 pounds, ratio of seed to lint and quality as on fresh land. Corn yields have fallen off one-fourth in forty years. The troublesome weeds are cocklebur, careless-weed, morning-glory, and crab-grass. For several years after the war much of this land lay "turned out"; that amount is now one-twelfth, and is due to the scarcity of laborers, many of the negroes having gone to the towns.

Additional abstract by T. B. Howard.

The brown, blackish and black, stiff prairie, partly hog-wallow in character, comprises three-fifths of the county area. It extends from the Sabine river to the Rio Grande, and from 50 to 80 miles from the Gulf inland, and supports vast herds of cattle and horses. The soil is from 2 to 5 feet deep, the underlying material consisting of strata of clay, black and mulatto-colored, to a depth of 40 feet. Tillage is difficult when the soil is too wet or too dry; it must be broken early in spring. The soil is late, cold, ill-drained, and best adapted to cotton and grasses; but a small amount of it is planted in cotton. The plant grows from 3 to 5 feet high. The seed-cotton product per acre of the best is from 800 to 1,200 pounds in good seasons, 1,560 pounds making a 475-pound bale of lint, shorter than that of the bottom soil. The quantity and quality do not decline by cultivation (unmanured). The cocklebur and careless-weed are the most troublesome.

The condition of things relative to cotton production is gradually improving in Texas.

Cotton is shipped as soon as baled by wagon or rail to Houston, Galveston, or to any convenient town where there is a compress; rate per bale, $1 50 per 100 miles.

WHARTON.

Population: 4,549.—White, 917; colored, 3,632.
Area: 1,170 square miles.—Woodland, one-fifth; one-fifth alluvial; four-fifths southern prairie region.
Tilled lands: 22,735 acres.—Area planted in cotton, 5,563 acres; in corn, 9,477 acres; in oats, 5 acres; in wheat, 5 acres; in sugar-cane, 92 acres.
Cotton production: 3,182 bales; average cotton product per acre, 0.57 bale, 855 pounds seed-cotton, or 285 pounds cotton lint.

The surface of Wharton county is quite level, with a gradual fall to the south, and is watered by many streams that find their way independently to the coast. The Colorado river divides it into two parts, its wide alluvial bottoms furnishing the best and richest lands of the county. These bottoms, as well as those of the San Bernard, are heavily timbered with cottonwood, ash, elm, cypress pecan, etc., and their soils are principally dark alluvial loams, that in fair seasons are capable of producing from 1,500 to 2,000 pounds of seed-cotton per acre. The other streams are bordered by skirts of timber, but otherwise the surface of the county consists of open prairies, well covered with grasses and devoted to grazing purposes. The soils of these prairies comprise the usual sandy and black waxy varieties, and are underlaid by calcareous concretionary clays. But 3.3 per cent. of the entire area of Wharton county is under cultivation, with an average of 21.2 acres per square mile. The crops comprise corn, cotton, sugar-cane, and vegetables, the former having the largest acreage. The average cotton product per acre of the county, including both bottoms and uplands, was in 1879 surpassed by only eight counties in the state. The acreage of that crop was, however, not quite one-fourth of the lands in cultivation.

Shipments are made by railroad to Galveston or Houston.

BRAZORIA.

Population: 9,774.—White, 2,250; colored, 7,524.
Area: 1,400 square miles.—Woodland, more than half; southern prairies, 640 square miles; Brazos alluvial, 760 square miles.
Tilled lands: 28,415 acres.—Area planted in cotton, 5,402 acres; in corn, 13,044 acres; in oats, 348 acres; in sugar cane, 3,359 acres.
Cotton production: 3,484 bales; average cotton product per acre, 0.64 bale, 960 pounds seed-cotton, or 320 pounds cotton lint.

Brazoria, one of the counties that border the Gulf, has a very level surface, and is about equally divided between prairie and timbered lands. Its most important feature is the Brazos river delta, a large body of land covering the western half of the county, and including the bottom lands also of Oyster creek and San Bernard river. In the immediate vicinity of the Brazos river and Oyster creek there are belts of red clayey alluvial lands, half a mile or more in width, which are above overflow, and comprise the best farming lands of the county. They have a timber growth of oaks, among which live oak is most prominent, elm, pecan, ash, etc., and an undergrowth of cane, and are very generally under cultivation, yielding in fair seasons, and in the absence of caterpillars, a bale or more of cotton per acre. Between these belts the country is swampy and poorly drained, and the lands consist of heavy, black clayey soils, with a predominant growth of ash and elm, interspersed with areas of black sandy or "wild peach land", so called because of the prominence of that growth. (See analyses of soils, page 45.)

On the east of Oyster creek there are broad and open prairies, covered with little else than grass, and devoted exclusively to grazing purposes. The lands that border the bottom region in a narrow belt are black, waxy clays, somewhat hog-wallow in character, but the greater part of the prairies are brown sandy loams, and all are underlaid by the heavy concretionary clays peculiar to the southern prairie region. The lands under cultivation in Brazoria county are confined almost entirely to the better class that border the streams, and comprise about 3 per cent. of the county area, averaging but about 20 acres per square mile. Sugar-cane is the principal crop, and the county is foremost in the state in the amount of sugar and molasses produced, viz, 2,440 hogsheads of sugar and 175,530 gallons of molasses. For this reason the Brazos alluvial region has been aptly termed "the sugar-bowl of Texas". Cotton is the third crop in acreage in the county (3.9 acres per square mile), and its average yield is surpassed but by three counties in the state.

There is in this county quite a natural curiosity, known as Damon's mound, which is worthy of note. It is a round conical elevation about 200 feet above the surrounding level prairie. This mound covers an area of about half a mile in diameter, with a gradual and nearly uniform ascent on every side. It is some 20 miles from the nearest part of the Gulf, and is situated between the Brazos and Bernard rivers, 10 miles from the former and 4 from the latter, the whole country being nearly a level with this single exception. It is contiguous to the largest and finest body of timber in the country, consisting chiefly of cedar of superior quality. The mound is composed extensively of the finest limestone covered with earth. There is no other limestone or stone of any kind known to exist within 50 miles of the coast.—(*M. S. Munson in the Texas Almanac.*)

ABSTRACT FROM THE REPORT OF DAVID NATION, OF COLUMBIA.

The uplands of this county are devoted principally to grazing purposes. The varieties of soil may be classed as follows: The black and red sandy alluvial of the larger streams, covering about one-fifth of the surface of the county; the black waxy lands; and the black sandy.

The most important with reference to cotton is the *alluvial soil*, which has a natural timber growth of live, pin, and overcup oaks, elm, ash, hackberry, peach, and pecan. The depth of the soil before it changes color is 18 inches, but in reality it is between 30 and 40 feet deep. It is early, warm, well drained, easily cultivated, and produces cane, cotton, corn, and potatoes, being best adapted to the cane. About one-half the crops consists of cotton, which grows to a height of 5 feet in dry and from 5 to 10 feet in wet seasons, and there is a tendency of the plant to run to weed in wet seasons and when deprived of its fruit by the boll-worm. The yield per acre of seed-cotton is 2,000 pounds, and 1,900 pounds are required for 475 pounds of lint. Fifty years of cultivation does not seem to affect the above product. The troublesome weeds are hog and cocklebur, the former growing to a height of 25 feet. About one-half the land now lies "turned out", which, when again taken into cultivation, produces as well as new land.

The *black waxy lands* form a small proportion of the lands of the county, the natural timber growth being generally elm. The soil has a depth of 18 inches, with a subsoil similar to it, but not quite so stiff. It is very difficult of cultivation in wet seasons, is late, cold, and ill-drained, and seems best adapted to cotton, which constitutes 75 per cent. of the entire crops. The height usually attained by the plant is from 3 to 5 feet, being most productive at 4 feet. It yields 1,800 pounds of seed-cotton per acre, and 1,900 pounds are requisite for a 475-pound bale. No decrease is observed after fifty years' cultivation. Topping is employed to prevent running to weed. Coffee-weed and cocklebur are the most troublesome weeds on this land. About one-half the land lies "turned out", which produces as well as new land when again taken in.

The *black sandy peach soil*, covering about one-quarter of the county, with its natural growth of peach, pecan, hackberry, live oak, and mulberry, and interspersed with prairies, is a fine and black sandy loam about 18 inches deep. It is early, warm, well drained, and easily tilled, and is best adapted to cane. Cotton, forming one-half the entire crops, grows to a height of from 5 to 11 feet, and yields 3,000 pounds of seed-cotton per acre, 1,900 pounds being necessary for 475 pounds of lint. The above product is not changed after fifty years' cultivation. But very little land lies "turned out". Hog, Jerusalem oak, and cocklebur constitute the most troublesome weeds.

Shipments are made in October and November, by boat and rail, to Houston and Galveston at the rate of $1 25 per bale.

MATAGORDA.
(See "Southern prairie region".)

CENTRAL BLACK PRAIRIE REGION.

(It comprises all or parts of the counties of Red River,* Lamar,* Fannin,* Grayson,* Cooke, Montague, Wise, Denton, Collin, Hunt, Delta, Hopkins,* Rains,* Van Zandt,* Kaufman, Rockwall, Dallas, Tarrant, Parker, Hood, Erath, Somervell, Johnson, Ellis, Navarro,* Hill, Bosque, Comanche,* Hamilton, Lampasas, Coryell, McLennan, Limestone,* Falls, Bell, Milam,* Williamson, Burnet,* Travis, Caldwell, Hayes, Blanco, Gillespie, Kerr, Kendall, Comal, Guadalupe, Bexar, Medina, Bandera, and Uvalde.)

RED RIVER.
(See "Red river alluvial region".)

LAMAR.
(See "Red river alluvial region".)

FANNIN.
(See "Red river alluvial region".)

GRAYSON.
(See "Red river alluvial region".)

COOKE.

Population : 20,391.—White, 19,560; colored, 831.

Area : 900 square miles.—Woodland, about one-third; central black prairie region, 650 square miles; lower cross timbers, 250 square miles.

Tilled lands : 98,160 acres.—Area planted in cotton, 27,795 acres; in corn, 32,353 acres; in oats, 4,388 acres; in wheat, 7,960 acres.

Cotton production : 11,547 bales; average cotton product per acre, 0.42 bale, 630 pounds seed-cotton, or 210 pounds cotton lint.

Cooke is one of the northern counties of the state, and, although bounded on the north by the Red river, has not been included in the group of Red river counties, because the bottom lands of that river have comparatively a small representation within its borders. These lands have a timber growth of walnut, pecan, ash, hackberry, elm, and cottonwood.

The surface of the country is for the most part a high and rolling prairie, with the usual black waxy or black sandy soils and rotten limestone (Cretaceous) of the central region. The eastern part of the county is occupied by the belt of lower cross timbers, which, with a width of about 10 miles, passes through it from north to south. Its growth is principally post and black-jack oaks and hickory; its soil is gray and very sandy, with a yellowish subsoil, and its surface rolling and somewhat broken, with much ferruginous sandstone and gravel. Deep beds of white sand are often found on the edges and within the limits of this belt. The upland prairies extend north from Gainesville to the banks of the river, where the limestone forms abrupt bluffs 250 feet in height. The soil of this prairie is mostly a dark sandy loam. The lands under cultivation average 109 acres per square mile.

Corn is the chief crop of the county, cotton being next with its average of 30.9 acres per square mile. Stock-raising is a prominent industry of the county.

ABSTRACT FROM THE REPORT OF W. W. HOWETH, OF GAINESVILLE.

The bottom lands of the county are the richest, comprising the red sandy loams of Red river and the black sandy or waxy soils of Trinity river. The uplands are partly prairie and partly timbered, the latter being all sandy, and the prairies vary from sandy to black waxy in character. These lands are all more or less cultivated in cotton.

The *black and red sandy soils* cover about one-half of the county, embracing chiefly its eastern and northern portions. Its timber growth is post and black-jack oaks and hickory. The soils are mahogany and black coarse sandy loams 18 inches thick. The subsoils are a light grayish yellow, impervious clay, which, when exposed to the atmosphere, falls to pieces as lime does; it contains fossil shells, and is underlaid by white limestone at from 8 to 10 feet. The soil is early, warm, well drained, easily cultivated, and apparently best adapted to cotton, to which one-third of its area is devoted. Cotton and corn are the chief crops of this region. The cotton-plant on this soil grows from 4 to 6 feet high, but is most productive at 4 feet. It inclines to run to weed in wet seasons, or when the boll-worm destroys its fruit. The seed-cotton product per acre, either from fresh land or from land fifteen years under cultivation, is 1,200 pounds, 1,665 pounds making a 475-pound bale of lint, which rates in the market as middling. The ratio of seed to lint and the quality of the staple are about the same, whether the land be fresh or old. The most troublesome weeds are cocklebur, sunflower, careless-weed, and crab-grass. None of this land lies "turned out".

The *black waxy prairie soil* covers about two-fifths of this region, and occurs in large bodies, extending from 5 to 10 miles in each direction. Its only natural growth is grass. The soil is a black loose loam from 12 to 18 inches and sometimes 4 and 5 feet deep to a change of color. The heavier subsoil is leachy, and one-half of its cultivated area being occupied by cotton. The soil is easy to cultivate in dry weather; if wet, it is adhesive and difficult to till, but it soon dries, and is not sticky. It is early, warm, well drained, and about equally well adapted to corn and cotton, one-half of its cultivated area being occupied by cotton. The usual height attained by the plant is 3½ feet, but it is most productive at 3 feet; it inclines to run to weed in very wet weather, or when the boll-worm destroys its fruit. The seed-cotton product per acre is 1,000 pounds, 1,665 pounds making a 475-pound bale of lint, which rates as good middling. After fifteen years' cultivation the product ratio of seed to lint and quality of staple are the same as in the case of fresh land. The cocklebur, rag-weed, and Spanish nettle are the most troublesome weeds on this soil. None of this land lies "turned out".

Early cotton is sometimes injured by late frosts in the spring; late cotton is injured sometimes by early frosts in autumn. Cotton on the lowlands is generally the best; therefore the bottom or valley lands are preferred to uplands.

Cotton is shipped by rail in November and December from Gainesville to Saint Louis at $4 50, or to Galveston at $4 per bale.

MONTAGUE.

Population : 11,257.—White, 11,210; colored, 47.

Area : 900 square miles.—Woodland, greater part; central black prairie, 140 square miles; northwestern red loam, 40 square miles; upper cross timbers, 710 square miles.

Tilled lands : 48,834 acres.—Area planted in cotton, 10,947 acres; in corn, 15,571 acres; in oats, 1,018 acres; in wheat, 2,101 acres.

Cotton production : 4,172 bales; average cotton product per acre, 0.38 bale, 570 pounds seed-cotton, or 190 pounds cotton lint.

Montague is the extreme northwestern county of the central prairie region, and has an average population of 12.6 persons per square mile. Its surface is hilly, with broad and open prairies on the east, diversified with narrow skirts of timber along the streams. The timbered area is very large, and comprises the belt of upper cross timbers which passes south from Red river into the counties on the south. The belt here is quite wide, and has the usual growth of post and black jack oaks and a deep sandy soil.

The extreme western part of the county is included in the northwestern prairie region, and is hilly, with some high peaks; among them the Victoria peak is a prominent feature. The county is watered by the Red river and its small tributaries on the north and the headwaters of some of the tributaries of the Trinity on the south. Montague, the county-seat, is situated on the "divide" between these two rivers, which reaches from the southwest corner to the river on the northeast.

The lands of the eastern prairies are of the black waxy character of the central region, and where tillable are as productive as in other counties of the region. The land of the "timbers" is sandy, and in the lowlands very productive. Its upland growth is mostly scrubby post and black-jack oaks; in the bottoms cottonwood, pecan, ash, hackberry, etc. The lands under cultivation average 54.9 acres per square mile, and the crops comprise corn, cotton, oats, and potatoes. Corn has a larger acreage in this county than any other crop. The average of cotton is 12.3 acres per square mile. The open prairies are generally devoted to stock grazing.

WISE.

Population: 16,601.—White, 16,436; colored, 165.
Area: 900 square miles.—Woodland, about one-half; central black prairie, 500 square miles; upper cross timbers, 400 square miles.
Tilled lands: 84,081 acres.—Area planted in cotton, 21,352 acres; in corn, 27,400 acres; in oats, 2,267 acres; in wheat, 4,121 acres.
Cotton production: 7,231 bales; average cotton product per acre, 0.34 bale, 510 pounds seed-cotton, or 170 pounds cotton lint.
The surface of Wise county is high and rolling, and the eastern portion is a broad prairie, known as the "grand prairie", having a black waxy soil, and interspersed with narrow skirts of timber along the streams, while the western portion is covered with the post-oak and black-jack growth of the "upper cross timbers". The county is watered by the west fork of the Trinity river and its numerous tributaries. These streams are said to have an immense fall, and their banks are high, rendering the bottom lands free from overflow. Their timber growth is walnut, pecan, ash, elm, etc. The upland timbered lands, comprising one-half of the area of the county, have a gray sandy soil, interspersed with small areas of a reddish sandy loam, and have a growth of post, Spanish, burr, and black-jack oaks. Lands under cultivation average 93.4 acres per square mile. In this county the acreage in corn is much greater than that of any other crop. The average in cotton is 23.7 acres per square mile.

ABSTRACT FROM THE REPORT OF J. M. HOLMES, OF DECATUR.

The county is about equally divided between prairie and timber. The eastern part is almost an entirely black waxy prairie. On the west are timbers, with small interspersed prairies. The bottom lands are subject to overflows, but if reclaimed are very rich. The various lands devoted to cotton culture are the gray and black sandy, the black waxy prairie, in some places hog-wallow, and the red or chocolate sandy.

The *dark gray sandy land*, comprising the timbered part, is the most important in reference to cotton. It covers about one-half of the county, and has a natural growth of post and black-jack oaks on the uplands, and post and Spanish oaks, elm, ash, pecan, hackberry, and walnut on the creeks and rivers. The soil is 2 feet in depth, with a red-clay subsoil, underlaid by rock at from 10 to 12 feet. It is easily tilled in wet seasons, and is early, warm, and well drained. The timbered portions are best adapted to corn and cotton, the latter forming one-third of the entire crops, while the prairie lands are most favorable to the production of wheat, oats, and barley. The height usually attained by cotton is about 4 feet, at which it is the most productive; but too much rain causes the plant to run to weed. From 1,200 to 1,500 pounds is the product per acre of seed-cotton. Sunflower, lamb's-quarter, bur, and careless are the most troublesome weeds in this and in the red lands. Considerable damage is done by the washing of the soil on slopes, the valleys being to some extent injured. Horizontalizing and hillside ditching, when well performed, check the damage.

The *black waxy prairie land* comprises about four-tenths of the tillable area. The soil is 2 feet deep; lower down it is of a lighter color, but grows darker by being exposed to the sun. Rock is found at from 2 to 10 feet. The soil is late, cold, and well drained, producing cotton and small grain, the former comprising one-third of the entire crop, and growing to a height of 3 feet. As in the last soil, too much rain inclines the plant to run to weed, which is obviated to some extent by topping. The yield of seed-cotton from land which has been under cultivation 15 years is, as on fresh land, from 800 to 1,000 pounds, 1,720 pounds being necessary for 475 pounds of lint, which rates as good middling. Sunflower and cocklebur are the troublesome weeds. No land lies "turned out". There is not so much washing of the soil in this case as in the last, no damage being done to the valleys. Good results have been attained by ditching.

The *red or chocolate land* constitutes about one-tenth of the agricultural district of the county, occurring in spots all over the timbered or sandy portion. Post, Spanish, burr, and black-jack oaks, and occasionally elm, form the natural timber growth. The soil is from 2 to 4 feet thick, the subsoil being similar but heavier, and is underlaid by sand at from 5 to 10 feet. It is early, warm, and well drained, and produces corn, wheat, oats, and cotton. The last comprises one-tenth of the entire crops, grows to a height of from 3 to 4 feet, and tends to run to weed in continued wet weather, topping being the remedy applied. From 1,000 to 1,500 pounds for fresh, and from 1,000 to 1,200 pounds for land cultivated for five years are the products per acre of seed-cotton, 1,720 pounds being in each case necessary for 475 pounds of lint, rating as good middling. The hilly land is considerably damaged by the soil washing, but the valleys do not suffer to any great extent. Efforts have been made to check the washing by means of horizontalizing and hillside ditching, with good results.

Shipments are made from 1st of November to the 25th of December by wagon to Fort Worth, thence to Galveston or New York by railroad, from $4 50 to $5 being the rate per bale.

DENTON.

Population: 18,143.—White, 17,071; colored, 1,072.
Area: 900 square miles.—Woodland, a little more than one-third; central black prairie region, 580 square miles; lower cross timbers, 320 square miles.
Tilled lands: 110,220 acres.—Area planted in cotton, 29,785 acres; in corn, 35,326 acres; in oats, 6,233 acres; in wheat, 12,103 acres.
Cotton production: 11,568 bales; average cotton product per acre, 0.39 bale, 585 pounds seed-cotton, or 195 pounds cotton lint.
Denton is mostly a rolling prairie county, and is well watered by Clear creek and its tributaries, which flow into the Trinity river. The lower cross timbers pass through it from north to south. This belt has a width of about 10 miles, and is covered by a growth of post and black-jack oaks, some underbrush, and has a deep sandy

and gravelly soil. Its surface is broken, and a considerable quantity of red and yellow ferruginous sandstone is found on the hills. The soil is said to be from 12 to 24 inches deep, with a somewhat clayey subsoil. On either side of this belt are prairie belts of black sandy soils, mixtures, as it were, of the sands of the timbers and the black waxy clays that form the lands of the rest of the prairies.

Rotten limestone (Cretaceous) is the prevailing rock of these prairies, and is found outcropping on the hills and sometimes in the banks of the creeks.

The county is sparsely settled, the average being about 20 persons per square mile. The prairies are mostly given up to stock grazing, for which the great abundance of grass is admirably suited. Corn, cotton, and wheat are the chief crops in the order in which they are named. The lands under cultivation comprise 19.1 per cent. of the county area, averaging 122.5 acres per square mile. The cotton acreage is about 33.1 acres per square mile.

ABSTRACT FROM THE REPORT OF J. W. EVANS, OF PILOT POINT.

The lands of this county are black waxy prairie and light and black sandy timbered lands. Only the sandy lands will be described. These sandy timbered lands extend 8 miles west, 20 miles north, and 10 miles south. The soil varies from a fine sandy to a coarse sandy and gravelly loam, is 18 inches deep, and bears a natural timber growth of post and black-jack oaks. The subsoil is heavier, and is hard-pan in some small spots and leachy in others. It contains soft "black gravel" and dark-brown pebbles, and is underlaid by gravel and sand-rock from 10 to 30 feet. The soil is early, warm, and well drained, and tillage is easy under all circumstances. It is apparently best adapted to cotton, the chief export crop; corn and potatoes are also raised, but chiefly for local consumption.

Cotton comprises about three-fifths of all crops on this land. The plant attains heights varying from 5 to 10 feet, but is most productive at 5 feet. It runs to weed in wet seasons or on manured land, and topping and throwing dirt from the row are practiced as remedies to restrain it and favor bolling. The seed-cotton product per acre varies on fresh land from 800 to 1,200 pounds, and from 1,600 to 1,665 pounds make a 475-pound bale, the lint rating in the market as middling. Two years' cultivation increases the seed-cotton product from 1,500 to 1,800 pounds; the seed is then heavier (it does not mature on fresh land), but the staple is better. The most troublesome weeds are crab-grass, horse, smart, careless, sunflower, and cocklebur. No cultivated land has yet been "turned out", but large bodies of land are yet lying out which have never been cultivated.

Shipments are made by wagon to Sherman at $1 per bale.

COLLIN.

Population: 25,983.—White, 24,003; colored, 1,980.

Area: 880 square miles.—Woodland, very little; all central black prairie region.

Tilled lands: 170,577 acres.—Area planted in cotton, 48,236 acres; in corn, 52,255 acres; in oats, 10,834 acres; in wheat, 24,242 acres.

Cotton production: 22,145 bales; average cotton product per acre, 0.46 bale, 690 pounds seed-cotton, or 230 pounds cotton lint.

Collin is chiefly a high and rolling prairie county, with belts of timbered lands along the streams and on some of the uplands, and is watered by the east fork of the Trinity river and its tributaries, flowing southward. The bottom lands of these streams have a dark, silty alluvial soil, and a timber growth of black walnut, pecan, oak, elm, honey-locust, bois d'arc, and hackberry. The river lands are wide in places, but are not much under cultivation. The prairies have a black waxy and often a hog-wallow soil, and a stiffer yellowish clay subsoil. On some of the hills the soils are thin, and the rotten limestone (Cretaceous) that underlies the entire county comes frequently to the surface, but in the valleys and on the broad table-lands the soils are deep and present excellent agricultural features. (See analysis of soil, page 36.)

Collin is chiefly an agricultural county, 30.3 per cent. of its area being under tillage, with an average of 193.8 acres per square mile. It is the chief corn and oats county of the state, the former being its chief crop, while in the production of wheat it ranks as third.

As a cotton county it stands fourth in the state in total production. Its acreage per square mile is 54.8, the highest but five in the list of counties.

ABSTRACTS FROM THE REPORTS OF W. G. MATTHEWS, OF PLANO, AND A. G. GRAVES, JR., AND GILES G. HOUSTON, OF M'KINNEY.

The relative amount of river and creek bottom land is small in this county, and of this only a small part is in cultivation. Seven-eighths of the soil of the county is what is commonly designated the "black waxy soil" of northern Texas. It extends (from Plano) 15 miles west, 40 northwest and north, 40 northeast and east, and 60 miles southeast, south, and southwest. This land is nearly all prairie, timber occurring chiefly along the water-courses. Where occurring on the highlands the growth is scrubby, and consists of oaks, elms, bois d'arc, ash, pecan, hackberry, honey-locust, and black walnut. The soil has a depth varying from 1 to 6 feet; its color is black, except that on points where the surface has been washed off it is reddish brown. When dry, it is light and mellow; when wet, it is heavy and putty-like, or waxy. It is calcareous, and the greater part is underlaid by a stratum of soft, white limestone or marl. Tillage is easy in dry, but difficult in wet seasons, and is easier on high than on low, hog-wallow places. The soil is early, warm, naturally well drained, and is best adapted to corn, wheat, cotton, oats, and sorghum. Millet, barley, sweet potatoes, the earlier Irish potatoes, and other root crops are raised, but the yields are smaller than they are on sandier lands.

About one-half of the cultivated land is planted in cotton. The plant usually attains a height of from 2 to 3½ feet on higher and from 3 to 5 feet on lower lands, 4 feet being considered the most productive height. It is inclined to run to weed only in very wet seasons, and topping the plant is the most successful remedy. The average seed-cotton product per acre of land, fresh or old, is about 1,000 pounds, from 1,425 to 1,545 pounds making a 475-pound bale of lint, which rates high in the market. In the amount or quality of cotton produced old land does not appreciably differ from fresh land. The chiefly troublesome weeds are Spanish nettles, buffalo-burs, cocklebur, crab-grass, smart-weed, purslane, sunflower, careless-weed, and morning-glory.

The soil of the county is very uniform in character, consisting of rolling and black waxy prairies. There are many spots of hog-wallow, which disappear and cultivate kindly on slopes, but remain tough when the general surface is flat. The climate is very favorable to cotton growing, the only hindering circumstances being late and early frosts, heavy rains in connection with cold north winds, and droughts. The low "hog-wallow" land is most liable to frosts, and it often happens in the same field, the parts of which vary not more than 12 feet in elevation, that the cotton only in the lower parts will be injured by frost. The heavy rains injure the crop in its early stages; and the drought occurs when the bolls are forming, and the shedding of bolls is a consequence. But these things do not generally result in serious damage to the cotton crop. This region has, so far, been comparatively free from insect pests.

Shipments are made as soon as cotton is ginned, by railroad, to Galveston, New Orleans, or Saint Louis, prices ranging from $4 50 to $5 per bale.

HUNT.

Population: 17,230.—White, 16,015; colored, 1,215.
Area: 870 square miles.—Woodland, very little; all central black prairie region.
Tilled lands: 111,797 acres.—Area planted in cotton, 25,906 acres; in corn, 29,157 acres; in oats, 6,314 acres; in wheat, 7,385 acres.
Cotton production: 10,805 bales; average cotton product per acre, 0.42 bale, 630 pounds seed-cotton, or 210 pounds cotton lint.

Hunt is one of the border counties of the central prairie region, and its surface is undulating and diversified with prairies and belts of timbered lands, the former occurring mostly on the northwest. The county is well watered by numerous small streams. Those on the northwest are tributaries of the Trinity river; those on the northeast and south flow into the Sulphur fork and Sabine, respectively.

The prairies have the black clayey lands and underlying rotten limestone peculiar to the central prairie region. They are not as rolling and broken as those in the counties farther west, and all of the lands may be considered as tillable. Some of the prairies on the east have sandy soils. The sandy timbered lands, comprising one-third of the county, extend sometimes 10 miles in each direction, and have a growth of post oak, black-jack, and black oak. Cultivated lands comprise 20.1 per cent. of the county area, with an average of 128.5 acres per square mile.

Corn is the chief crop of the county, its acreage being larger than that of any other. Cotton ranks next, with an average of 29.8 acres per square mile.

ABSTRACT FROM THE REPORT OF WILLIAM R. HOWARD, M. D., OF WHITE ROCK.

The uplands of the county are rolling, and comprise partly black sandy prairies, partly black hog-wallow, waxy prairies, and partly timbered lands.

Of the three kinds of soils cultivated in cotton, that of the *black waxy, hog-wallow prairies* is the chief, occurring in bodies of 300 acres each, some of it having a natural timber growth of elm, bois d'arc, honey-locust, hackberry, swamp dogwood, red-bud, rattan vines, and briers. The soil has an average depth of 3 feet, and covers one-third of this region. The subsoil is heavier, grayish in color, sometimes bluish, and is impervious to water when undisturbed. It contains in many places an abundance of fossil marine univalve shells from 3 to 6 inches in diameter, underlaid at from 5 to 10 feet by soft, white limestone, and in places by a so-called "black slate", which emits the odor of petroleum. Tillage of this soil is rather difficult in wet, but easy in dry seasons; and no matter how hard and cloddy the soil is when broken up, the clods are disintegrated or rather soaked by the first rain. The soil is early and warm, has generally good natural drainage, and is apparently best adapted to cotton, one-half the cultivated land being devoted to its production. The other chief crops of this region in the order of their acreage are corn, oats, and wheat. The cotton-plant attains a height of from 2 to 4 feet on this soil, but is most productive at 2½ or 3 feet. It is inclined to run to weed when it follows corn on fresh land, or when such land is deeply plowed. Among several methods to prevent this and favor bolling shallow plowing or bedding on the hard ground has been tried with favorable results. The seed-cotton product per acre of fresh land is from 1,000 to 1,600 pounds, 1,425 pounds (including toll for ginning) being the minimum amount required to make a 475-pound bale of lint. The product of old land is about the same in amount as that of fresh. The plant grows less to weed, but yields more bolls. A little less seed-cotton is needed to make a bale of lint, and the staple is nearly equal to that from fresh land. The staple is especially fine when the crop has been preceded by a crop of small grain. None of this land has yet been impoverished by successive cultivation. Cocklebur, crab-grass, pig- (*C. album*), rag-, and careless-weeds are the most troublesome on this soil.

The *sandy land* comprises one-third of the county. It is a fine sandy and gravelly loam, its color gray blackish, but chiefly black, and its depth varies from 3 to 30 inches. The prairie portion of it bears a natural growth of grass. This soil varies in fertility through nearly all degrees. The heavier and leachy subsoil contains hard "black gravel" and rounded pebbles generally, but in places it is wholly free from them, and is underlaid by sand, gravel, and white and soft limestone at from 20 to 30 feet. Tillage is always easy, and the soil is early, warm, and well drained, and apparently best adapted to cotton. Of the cereals oats mature best, and corn does well on parts of it in wet seasons. Cotton occupies one-half its cultivated part of this soil, the usual and most productive height attained by the plant being 3 feet. Deep plowing and fresh land incline the plant to run to weed, shallow cultivation and topping obviating the tendency. The seed-cotton product per acre of fresh land is from 1,000 to 1,300 pounds, from 1,425 to 1,545 pounds making a 475-pound bale of lint, which rates as middling. After ten years' cultivation the product per acre varies from 700 to 1,300 pounds (the soil itself in different places being variable to this extent), and 1,425 pounds are then needed for a 475-pound bale of lint, which compares favorably with that from fresh land. Crab-grass and pig- and careless-weeds are the most troublesome. About 3 per cent. of this land originally cultivated now lies "turned out"; it improves by rest. Slopes are seriously damaged by washing and gullying of the soil, but the washings do not injure the valleys.

A *mixed land,* or *sumac and collard land*, covers one-third of the region, and is formed by the mixture of the soils just described. The soil has a blackish color, which extends 24 or 30 inches below the surface, and is composed of coarse sand and clay. A part is prairie, and bears sumac and collard, and the rest is timbered with post oak, water oak, cottonwood, and wild plum, and has also thickets of thorny underbrush. The subsoil is lighter than the surface soil, but is impervious; it is underlaid by sand, gravel, and white rock at from 3 to 30 feet. Tillage is easy at any season, and the soil is early, warm, well drained, and apparently best adapted to cereals and cotton. Cotton occupies one-half its cultivated area, the usual and most productive height attained by the plant being 3 feet. The seed-cotton product per acre of fresh land is from 1,000 to 1,800 pounds, and 1,545 pounds are needed for a 475-pound bale of lint, which rates in the market as good middling. Where rotation of crops is reasonably practiced there is little or no diminution in the product of seed-cotton per acre, even after twenty years' cultivation. From 1,425 to 1,545 pounds of seed-cotton from old land are required to make a 475-pound bale of lint, which compares favorably with that from fresh land. The most troublesome weeds are crab-grass, cockleburs, pig-weed, and three

776

varieties of careless-weeds, the thorny variety being the most formidable. None of this land has yet been "turned out", on account of decline in productiveness. The soil on the slopes is liable to wash or gully, and if not prevented serious damage to the slopes results in this way; but the washings do not injure the lower lands.

On the lowlands cotton starts later, grows more to weed, and is liable to be frost-killed in the fall. Nearly all the uplands produce cotton well. Wind-storms sometimes damage the crop on the higher prairies, often blowing out the staple as fast as the bolls are opened.

Cotton is shipped as soon as baled, by railroad, to Sherman or Terrell at the rate of $3 50 per bale.

DELTA.

Population: 5,597.—White, 4,999; colored, 598.

Area: 260 square miles.—Woodland, small part; oak, hickory, and pine region, 20 square miles; central black prairie region, 240 square miles.

Tilled lands: 29,389 acres.—Area planted in cotton, 8,940 acres; in corn, 9,199 acres; in oats, 1,902 acres; in wheat, 1,409 acres.

Cotton production: 4,911 bales; average cotton product per acre, 0.55 bale, 825 pounds seed-cotton, or 275 pounds cotton lint.

Delta is a small triangular-shaped county on the eastern edge of the central prairie region, and is partly included in the oak and hickory uplands. It lies between the forks of the Sulphur river. The prairies of the western part of the county are quite level or undulating, with black waxy or black sandy lands, and are diversified with timbered areas along the streams. It is underlaid by the white rotten limestone of the Cretaceous. The prairie lands are very productive, yielding in ordinary seasons from 800 to 1,000 pounds of seed-cotton per acre. The eastern part of the county has a timber growth of post oak, hickory, etc., and a sandy soil with a subsoil of yellowish clay, more or less sandy. These lands also produce well, and seem to be preferred to the black prairies, as being more easily tilled and as productive.

Corn, cotton, oats, and wheat are the chief crops, and are named in the order of their predominance. Lands under cultivation average 113 acres per square mile. The acreage devoted to cotton is an average of 34.4 acres per square mile. The average yield per acre for 1879 was about 825 pounds of seed-cotton, the county ranking as eleventh in the state in this regard.

HOPKINS.

(See "Oak, hickory, and pine region".)

RAINS.

(See "Oak, hickory, and pine region".)

VAN ZANDT.

(See "Oak, hickory, and pine region".)

KAUFMAN.

Population: 15,448.—White, 13,471; colored, 1,977.

Area: 830 square miles.—Woodland, small part; oak, hickory, and pine region, 90 square miles; central black prairie region, 720 square miles; brown-loam prairie region, 20 square miles.

Tilled lands: 84,317 acres.—Area planted in cotton, 26,659 acres; in corn, 24,386 acres; in oats, 4,522 acres; in wheat, 8,921 acres.

Cotton production: 10,668 bales; average cotton product per acre, 0.40 bale, 600 pounds seed-cotton, or 200 pounds cotton lint.

The surface of Kaufman county is rolling, and is watered by the tributaries of Trinity river, flowing in a southerly course. The southeastern part of the county is covered with the gray sandy soil of the post-oak uplands region of eastern Texas, and has its characteristic timber growth. The rest of the county is an open prairie, except along the water-courses, where there is a growth of elm, bois d'arc, etc. The soil of the prairies is usually black and waxy, except near the timbers, where it becomes more sandy. It is several feet in depth, and is underlaid by the limestone of the Cretaceous. On the west this rock is soft, or of the "rotten" variety, but at Terrell it is overlaid by the hard fossilliferous variety that forms the uppermost stratum in this part of the state.

This county does not form an exception to others of the state in being sparsely settled, the proportion of population being about 18.6 per square mile. Lands under cultivation average 101.6 acres per square mile. Cotton is the chief crop, its acreage being an average of 32.1 per square mile.

The average yield of seed-cotton for 1879 was not large, probably because of the drought of that year, which was felt all over the state.

ABSTRACT FROM THE REPORT OF H. B. M'CORKLE, OF ELMO.

The surface of the county is equally divided between timber and prairie lands. The bottom lands, having a black alluvial, shelly soil, are well timbered, and are better adapted to cotton, corn, sweet potatoes, and vegetables than to small grain, being preferred on account of drought. The uplands comprise black sandy and black waxy land and gray sandy land. That best adapted to cotton is the *black sandy and black waxy upland,* which abounds on all the creeks, and covers nine-tenths of the county. In some localities there is a growth of post, black, black-jack, and red oaks, hickory, elm, and an undergrowth of dogwood, sassafras, grape-vine, and mulberry. The soil is 2 feet deep, is early, warm, and well drained, and easily tillable. The subsoil is a yellow or reddish clay, containing, sometimes, large pebbles, and is underlaid by soft limestone at from 4 to 20 feet. All kinds of grain grow well, although the soil is best adapted to cotton and corn.

777

Two-thirds of the acreage is devoted to cotton, which usually reaches on black sandy lands a height of 4 feet, and on black waxy soil 3½ feet. If the season is such that moisture is kept within 4 inches of the surface, the cotton has a tendency to run to weed, which is remedied by the use of the scooter-plow close to the plant and by topping. Fourteen hundred pounds is the yield per acre of seed-cotton for fresh lands. For lands which have been in cultivation 4 years, 1,000 pounds for upland and 1,500 pounds for bottom land is the product per acre of seed-cotton; 1,685 pounds is, in both cases, the amount necessary to pay toll (one-twelfth) and make 475 pounds of lint. Cotton produced from the fresh land commands a higher price than that from land which has been under cultivation. The most troublesome weeds in this region are careless, hog, Jamestown, and cocklebur. On the gray sandy lands the trouble arises from crab-grass. No land lies turned out.

As soon as the cotton is baled it is shipped by railroad to Saint Louis, Galveston, and New Orleans, the rate being $4 25 per bale.

ROCKWALL.

Population: 2,984.—White, 2,898; colored, 86.
Area: 150 square miles.—Woodland, very little; all central black prairie region.
Tilled lands: 26,443 acres.—Area planted in cotton, 5,786 acres; in corn, 6,715 acres; in oats, 961 acres; in wheat, 2,515 acres.
Cotton production: 2,630 bales; average cotton product per acre, 0.45 bale, 675 pounds seed-cotton, or 225 pounds cotton lint.

Rockwall is the smallest county in the state. Its surface is principally a gently undulating prairie, whose soil is of the black waxy nature common to the central prairie region, and produces from 800 to 1,000 pounds of seed-cotton per acre. The streams of the county are very small, and are usually timbered with a growth of elm, pecan, etc., but the lands are not much under cultivation. More than one-fourth of the county area is under tillage, averaging 176.3 acres per square mile. Corn has a larger acreage than any other crop of the county, cotton ranking next, with its average of 38.6 acres per square mile. The yield per acre is high in comparison with the general average of the state.

ABSTRACT FROM THE REPORT OF WILLIAM H. PRICE, OF ROCKWALL.

Only a very small portion of the land of this county is lowland; such, though exceedingly rich, is mostly in timber, but may in time be brought into cultivation. Drought is the greatest difficulty to be encountered in the cultivation of cotton. The lands devoted to cotton comprise the black waxy prairie, known as hog-wallow and smooth land, there being but little difference in quality, and the sandy (both light sandy and rawhide, or tough) land. *Black waxy prairie land* is the most important, covering about nine-tenths of the county, and has a growth of bois d'arc, live oak in spots, elm, ash, and pecan in bottoms. The soil is from 3 to 8 feet in depth, early, warm, and well drained, and produces wheat, oats, corn, and cotton. It is best adapted to wheat and cotton, the latter, constituting about one-third of the crops, growing to a height of 4 feet, and tending to run to weed in seasons which are warm and moderately moist, and when well tilled. Land fifteen years under cultivation produces more than fresh lands, the yield from the former being about 1,000 pounds of seed-cotton per acre, 1,545 pounds for 475 pounds of lint. Buffalo-bur (this is a monster), sunflower, and a variety of the careless form the most troublesome weeds. No land lies "turned out". Cotton needs much less rain than any other crop; wheat is matured before the drought sets in.

Shipments are made, in September, October, and November, by railroad, to Terrell and to Galveston at the rate of $4 50 per bale.

DALLAS.

Population: 33,488.—White, 28,530; colored, 4,958.
Area: 900 square miles.—Woodland, small part; central black prairie region, 770 square miles; lower cross timber, 130 square miles.
Tilled lands: 190,542 acres.—Area planted in cotton, 44,377 acres; in corn, 44,004 acres; in oats, 8,306 acres; in wheat, 26,854 acres.
Cotton production: 21,469 bales; average cotton product per acre, 0.52 bale, 780 pounds seed-cotton, or 260 pounds cotton lint.

Dallas is a high and rolling prairie county, with skirts of timbered lands lying along the streams, and it is well watered by the Trinity river (flowing in a rather diagonal course through its center southeastwardly) and its many tributaries. The bottom lands of the streams, and especially of the river, have a dark and deep silty alluvial soil, underlaid by a stiff clay, and are capable of producing in ordinary seasons as much as 1,000 pounds of seed-cotton per acre.

The timber growth consists of cottonwood, pecan, ash, elm, etc. Between the river bottom and the prairie uplands there is a broad open prairie valley several miles in width, bounded by high bluffs or ridges of the white Cretaceous limestones. The soil at the foot of the ridges is usually black and waxy, but becomes more and more sandy toward the river, and finally, in the edge of the timbered bottoms, there are sometimes found deep beds of white sand. This Trinity valley "lies beautifully", has a very gentle undulating surface, and is apparently easily tilled. From Dallas it extends westward into Tarrant county, following the course of the river. A mesquite growth occurs in localities. (See analysis of soil, page 44.)

The prairie uplands are high and rolling, interspersed with strips of timbered lands, and have a black waxy, or, in places, a black sandy soil, the rotten limestone is often found outcropping.

The city of Dallas has an elevation of 468 feet above the sea. There are two cotton compresses and a cottonseed-oil mill located here.

Dallas is an agricultural county, 33.1 per cent. of its area being under tillage, or an average of 211.7 acres per square mile. It is also the principal wheat county in the state, the acreage of that crop being greater than in any other county. Cotton and corn are, however, the chief crops, their acreages being very nearly the same. In total production the county ranks fifth, and in product per acre fourteenth in the state. Its acreage per square mile is 49.3 acres.

The lands upon which cotton is cultivated are the black prairie, commonly known as the black waxy or hog-wallow, the black sandy prairie, and the light or white sandy. The black waxy constitutes the chief soil, covering about eight-tenths of the county, and extending north to Red river 80 miles, south 75 miles, east from 40 to 60 miles, and west from 70 to 100 miles.

The *black prairie land* has no timber. The soil is a black clay loam from 1 to 8 feet in depth, very difficult to till in wet weather, but quite the reverse in dry seasons. It is an early, warm, well-drained soil, and seems to be best adapted to corn. The subsoil is similar to the soil, but is a little heavier, and is underlaid by soft limestone, which is impervious to water, causing in very wet seasons what we call "poison earth", the result of which is that vegetation, especially that having tap-roots, dies. The cause of this has never been understood.

The crops of the county, with their average yield per acre, are: corn, from 40 to 60 bushels; wheat, from 15 to 20 bushels; cotton, 1,200 pounds of seed-cotton; oats, from 40 to 70 bushels; rye, from 20 to 30 bushels; Irish potatoes, from 60 to 80 bushels; and sweet potatoes, from 100 to 150 bushels. Cotton forms three-tenths of the total crops planted, attaining a height of from 3½ to 6 feet; at the former height it is most productive. It runs to weed in very wet seasons, and also when the boll-worm causes shedding, but otherwise it fruits very heavily. Topping is the method used by some planters to restrain the running to weed and to favor bolling, and the result is beneficial where the cotton-plants are not too thick. The staple rates the same on old and new land. The older the land the better it is, none being "turned out". Horse-weed, nettle, cocklebur, hog-, and careless-weed are apparently the weeds which are the greatest source of trouble to planters. Crab-grass troubles them but little.

About one-tenth of the tillable lands of the county consist of *black sandy prairie*, having in places a brushy growth of swamp dog-wood, haw, wild china, and hackberry. The soil resembles fine rifle powder, being a fine sandy loam from 1 foot to 2 feet in depth; it has a subsoil composed of a very compact red, or in some cases blue clay, containing black, ferruginous pebbles, and is underlaid by gravel and white limestone at from 2 to 3 feet. The land can be easily tilled in either wet or dry seasons, as it never becomes hard, is early, warm, and usually well drained, and is best adapted to cotton and corn. One-third of the land is devoted to cotton, which grows to the height of from 4 to 5 feet, the former being the most productive. Excessive rains are the cause of the plant's running to weed, which is in some degree restrained, when the plant is not too thick, by topping. The yield of cotton is the same as on the last soil. The careless-weed is the most troublesome on this soil.

The *light or white sandy bottom lands* constitute one-tenth of the tillable lands, and have a natural growth of post, black-jack, and red oaks, hickory, red elm, and grape-vines. The soil is from 1 to 2 feet deep, and is underlaid by a red clay hard-pan, mixed with sand to a certain extent, and containing ferruginous pebbles. The soil, which is best adapted to cotton and corn, is early, warm, and well drained, and very easily tillable in either wet or dry seasons. Cotton comprises about one-third of the crops, and the growth is from 5 to 6 feet, 5 feet being the most productive. On fresh land from 1,200 to 1,500 pounds of seed-cotton are raised per acre; from 800 to 1,000 pounds is the yield on land which has been under cultivation for ten years, in which case 1,545 pounds are needed for a 475-pound bale, whereas on fresh land 1,425 pounds is the necessary amount. There is no difference in the rating of the staple from the two soils. The boll-worm and too much rain, in this case as in the others, cause the plant to run to weed, the same remedy being applied. About one-twentieth of the land is "turned out", and, after resting for five or six years produces, when again cultivated, about one-third less than it did originally. Careless- and hog-weeds are troublesome, but crab-grass is extremely so.

Black waxy bottom land is not much planted in cotton, being cold and late and subject to frost in spring. A large proportion of our land lies high and dry and in large bodies, and our planters much prefer it for cotton. Frost affects the plants 8 or 10 days later than on the bottom land.

Shipments are made, when the prices are good, usually to Saint Louis by railroad; to eastern mills at $7 50 or to Liverpool at $9 75 per bale, or to Galveston.

TARRANT.

Population: 24,671.—White, 22,488; colored, 2,183.
Area: 900 square miles.—Woodland, about one-third; central black prairie region, 610 square miles; lower cross timbers, 290 square miles.
Tilled lands: 143,440 acres.—Area planted in cotton, 27,821 acres; in corn, 38,496 acres; in oats, 7,055 acres; in wheat, 26,481 acres.
Cotton production: 10,950 bales; average cotton product per acre, 0.39 bale, 585 pounds seed-cotton, or 195 pounds cotton lint.

The surface of Tarrant county is high and rolling, and is well watered by the Trinity river and its tributaries. The belt of lower cross timbers passes through it from north to south east of Fort Worth, the county-seat. This belt is about 10 miles wide, and has a deep sandy soil over a clayey subsoil, associated with beds of brownish ferruginous gravel. (See analysis, page 29.) In the central part of the belt there are low hills of sandstone and conglomerate. Near Handley, a station near the western edge, these timbers are seen to be underlaid by the limestone of the prairies, and quantities of the Cretaceous fossil *gryphæa* are found in the beds of the small streams. The lowlands of these streams have a rich brown loam soil, very productive, and in places rather extensive; the uplands, on the contrary, are not very fertile, except where the subsoil comes near to the surface. The river bottom lands are rich and productive and well timbered, but seem to be but little under cultivation. The prairie valleys lying between them and the high uplands are broad, and have a black clayey soil, with some mesquite growth.

The rest of the county is a high and rolling prairie, with black waxy lands, deep in the valleys but thin on the hills, the underlying rotten limestone coming very generally to the surface and outcropping on the sides in ledges. Near the timbers the usual black sandy soils occur.

About one-fourth of the county area is under cultivation. Tarrant ranks next to Dallas, or second in the state, in the acreage given to wheat, and first in the state in the number of bushels produced. Corn is, however, its chief crop. Cotton has an acreage but little larger than that of wheat, or an average of 30.9 acres per square mile.

ABSTRACT FROM THE REPORT OF MR. BENJAMIN STUART, OF HANDLEY.

The kinds of land cultivated in cotton in this county are black waxy or hog-wallow prairie land, red sandy timbered land, and black sandy land.

The *black waxy prairie land* is of uniform character to depths varying from 1 foot to 6 feet to the underlying limestone, and it is very black, without sand or grit, and very adhesive when wet. It is all prairie, and embraces three-fourths of this county, extending 125 miles north, 200 or more miles south, 150 miles east, and 175 miles west. The underlying limestone is generally white, inclined to be soft, pulverizes under a wagon wheel, and occurs in small lumps. The soil is well drained, but is later than the sandy soils. Tillage is usually easy, but is difficult when the soil is too wet. This land is well adapted to wheat and cotton, but is often too dry for corn. One-third of its cultivated area is planted in cotton. The plant usually attains the height of 4 feet, and is most productive at that or 6 inches less. It inclines to run to weed in very wet seasons; but topping will restrain its growth, and cause it to spread and to boll better. The seed-cotton product per acre of fresh land is from 1,500 to 2,000 pounds. Ten years' cultivation causes no diminution of production, and there is but little difference in the quality of the staple. Very little of this land lies "turned out", and the best quality is almost inexhaustible. None of it is yet "worn out", but it is believed that deeper tillage and rest would improve some of it. The most troublesome weed is cocklebur. The valley lands are improved by the washings from the uplands.

The *red sandy timbered land*, covering about one-fifth of the county, extends the entire length of the cross timbers, and is from 10 to 20 miles wide. Post oak is its characteristic growth. The soil is fine, red, sandy, and from 1 foot to 2 feet deep; the subsoil is generally a red clay. The soil is early, warm, and well drained, always easily cultivated, and is apparently best adapted to cotton and corn. Of wheat it produces a good quality, but the yield is insufficient. Fully one-half the cultivated soil is planted in cotton. The plant attains a height of from 4 to 6 feet usually, and is more productive at the medium; it inclines to run to weed only in wet seasons. The product per acre of fresh land in good seasons is 2,000 pounds. This soil produces very well for a few years and then declines. The staple from old land is a little inferior in quality to that from new land. A very small amount of this land lies "turned out", and it does not improve so much by rest and deep plowing as the black waxy soil does. Crab-grass is the chief of weeds on this soil, and is very troublesome in wet seasons. The extent of the damage done to slopes by washing and gullying of the soil is rather serious; the washing, however, improves the lower lands. No special efforts have been made to check the damage to slopes.

The *black sandy land* is chiefly prairie, and occurs in small bodies. It is a black, fine sandy loam from 1 foot to 4 feet deep, and rests on limestone. This soil is early, warm, well drained, and easily tilled, and is apparently best adapted to corn and cotton. One-third of its area is planted in cotton. In fair seasons the plant attains a height of 5 feet, and it is most productive at from 4 to 5 feet. It is inclined to run to weed only in wet seasons. The seed-cotton product per acre of fresh land is from 1,500 to 2,000 pounds, of a quality already noted for the other soils, and is no less after ten years' cultivation. Very little of this land lies "turned out", and has not again been cultivated; but it is supposed that rest and deep plowing would restore its fertility. The damage done to slopes by washing and gullying is very slight, and no efforts have been made to check it. The washings improve the quality of the lower lands. Sunflower and careless-weed are the most troublesome. With good seasons the lands of this county always produce a bale of cotton per acre; but they often fail to produce so much, owing to drought, which causes it to shed its forms. This is the greatest difficulty with which we have to contend in raising cotton.

Shipments are made from October to January either to Saint Louis, New York, New Orleans, or Galveston.

PARKER.

Population: 15,870.—White, 15,250; colored, 620.

Area: 900 square miles.—Woodland, greater part; central black prairie region, 310 square miles; upper cross timbers, 590 square miles.

Tilled lands: 78,707 acres.—Area planted in cotton, 15,036 acres; in corn, 24,987 acres; in oats, 2,253 acres; in wheat, 12,306 acres.

Cotton production: 4,454 bales.—Average cotton product per acre, 0.30 bale, 450 pounds seed-cotton, or 150 pounds cotton lint.

Parker county is hilly and broken, and is about equally divided between prairie and timbered lands. It is watered by the Brazos river and its tributaries on the west and southwest, and by the small tributaries of the Trinity on the east. The wide belt of upper cross timbers passes through it from the north to the Brazos river. Its eastern limit is 3 miles to the east of Weatherford, the county-seat; its western, at or near the county-line. Its continuity is, however, broken by a range of high and bald prairie hills a few miles west of the town, which present bold and abrupt sides to the west, and overlook the broad timbered region still westward. Cretaceous limestones outcrop in ledges on the sides of these hills, and contain an abundance of the fossils of the formation.

The lands of the timbers are sandy, with also a yellowish sandy subsoil, underlaid by sandstone at a depth of several feet. This rock is being quarried for grindstones. The timber growth of the belt is mostly post and black-jack oaks. The valley lands have a dark-loam soil, and are said to produce 800 pounds of seed-cotton per acre. The sandy uplands are not much under cultivation. The open prairies have the usual black waxy soil, which are tillable only in the valleys between the hills, whose sides and summits are mostly covered with the Cretaceous limestones, and a thin soil often filled with gryphæas. These prairies are mostly devoted to the grazing of stock, and are but little under cultivation.

The tilled lands average 87.4 acres per square mile, and the crops comprise corn, cotton, small grain, and potatoes. Parker is one of the chief wheat-producing counties of the state, and ranks as ninth. The acreage devoted to corn is greatest, that of cotton being but little more than that of wheat, and averaging 16.7 acres per square mile. The county stands low in the list of counties with regard to product per acre.

Shipments of cotton are made by railroad eastward.

HOOD.

Population: 6,125.—White, 5,927; colored, 198.

Area: 490 square miles.—Woodland, greater part; central black prairie region, 80 square miles; upper cross timbers, 410 square miles.

Tilled lands: 34,819 acres.—Area planted in cotton, 7,139 acres; in corn, 10,427 acres; in oats, 605 acres; in wheat, 4,355 acres.

Cotton production: 1,966 bales; average cotton product per acre, 0.28 bale, 420 pounds seed-cotton, or 140 pounds cotton lint.

The surface of Hood county is rolling and somewhat hilly, with a few high and prominent peaks. Through its center, from northwest to southeast, flows the Brazos river, its bottoms and adjoining uplands forming a belt of timbered lands from 5 to 10 miles wide. The rest of the county is chiefly an open prairie, interspersed with narrow belts of timbered lands lying along the small streams. Comanche peak is the most prominent point in these prairies, and can be seen from a great distance. It has an elevation of 600 feet above the Brazos river. Its sides are abrupt, exposing the different beds of Cretaceous limestones and fossils, the lowest of which is very similar in character to the hard and partly siliceous rock occurring in the western part of Erath county. The soil of the prairie valley lands is black and waxy in character, more or less sandy in localities, and very productive. The timbered uplands of the river have a sandy soil, varying in depth from 10 to 18 inches, and a reddish clay subsoil, and are known as "post-oak lands", from the predominance of that growth. The river bottoms comprise both the first, or those liable to overflow, and the second bottoms, which are not thus liable, and are largely in cultivation. The latter have a deep red sandy loam soil and a growth of live and post oaks, pecan, sumac, etc. (See analysis, page 45). These river lands (upland and bottom) comprise the greater part of the cultivated lands of the county, which average 71 acres per square mile. Corn has the largest acreage, that of cotton being next, with an average of 14.6 acres per square mile.

ABSTRACT FROM THE REPORT OF G. E. WALLS, OF GRANBERRY.

The *post oak lands* of the river are considered the best of the county. They yield more per acre, the soil is warmer than any other, and cotton starts off better and is two weeks earlier; the land also stands severe droughts better. The soil is sandy, and has a depth of 18 inches, with a red-clay subsoil from 10 to 40 feet deep. The *black prairie lands* cover the largest part of the county. They are easily tilled, and are best adapted to wheat. Cotton comprises one-third of the crops, grows 5 feet high, and is most productive at 4 feet, yielding 1,250 pounds of seed-cotton per acre. Topping the plant is practiced to prevent its running to weed. Crab-grass is most troublesome on these prairie lands.

Shipments of cotton are made to Cleburne or to Fort Worth.

ERATH.

Population: 11,796.—White, 11,539; colored, 257.

Area: 1,000 square miles.—Woodland, nearly all; central black prairie region, 40 square miles; northwestern red-loam region, 250 square miles; upper cross timbers, 710 square miles.

Tilled lands: 61,647 acres.—Area planted in cotton, 14,220 acres; in corn, 19,702 acres; in oats, 1,822 acres; in wheat, 5,832 acres.

Cotton production: 2,857 bales; average cotton product per acre, 0.20 bale, 300 pounds seed-cotton, or 100 pounds cotton lint.

Erath is a rolling and somewhat hilly county, situated on the west side of the central prairie region and partly included in the northwestern red-loam region. The belt of upper cross timbers passes through the county, but is interrupted by high and bald prairie ridges of the central prairie region, whose sandstone and limestone rocks, with characteristic fossils, are found outcropping on their sides and summits. The timbers occupy the low valley lands between these ridges. Its soil is in many places but little else than a deep white sand, especially on the west of Stephenville, the county-seat. On the prairies there are occasional clumps of live oaks, the soil being a dark sandy loam or stiff clay. The population of the county is very sparse, being only an average of about 12 persons per square mile. Lands under cultivation average 61.6 acres per square mile. Corn is the chief crop, its acreage being a third greater than that of cotton, which averages 14.2 acres per square mile. The yield in seed-cotton for 1879 was only 300 pounds.

ABSTRACT FROM THE REPORT OF J. G. O'BRIEN, OF DUBLIN.

The uplands of the county are mostly rolling, two-thirds being timbered with post oak, the rest being open and rocky prairies, with black waxy soils. The bottom lands of Leon river and tributary creeks have a fine black sandy soil, and are tillable. The lands devoted to cotton comprise deep black fine sandy, a lighter grade of the black sandy, and a mixture of black waxy and sandy.

The *black sandy timbered land* is best adapted to the cultivation of cotton, and extends 25 miles to the southeast, about the same distance to the north and east, with some alternations, and about 10 miles southwest, changing to a lighter grade in the west. Post oak principally, with some live oak, cottonwood, hackberry, sumac, and pecan, is the natural timber growth. The soil is a black fine sandy loam 3 feet in depth, having a subsoil of impervious red or pipe-clay, the pipe-clay being generally on creek bottoms and prairies. It contains gravel, and is underlaid by sand and gravel. The soil is early, warm, tolerably well drained, and remarkably easily tilled in dry seasons. The chief crops of the county are: for the market, cotton, corn, wheat, and oats; for home use, potatoes, fruits, millet, and hay. The lowlands are best adapted to wheat; but at least one-half the crops planted is in cotton. The uncertainty of rain is the greatest drawback, and good acreage of cotton could be made if there was plenty of rain and an early spring. The late frosts occasionally kill the cotton, but as planting is usually done about the middle of April the effect of the frost is not great. Cotton usually attains a height or from 2 to 6 feet, the height at which production is the best being 3 or 4 feet. Cotton runs to weed during very wet seasons, which is prevented and bolling facilitated by topping. From fresh land the product per acre in seed-cotton is from 300 to 800 pounds, rating as low middling, from 1,475 to 1,660 pounds, according to the variety of cotton, being required to make a 475-pound bale. After the land has been in cultivation for three years the yield per acre of seed-cotton is from 750 to 2,500 pounds, according to the season, 1,900 pounds being necessary to make 475 pounds of lint of better staple. Sunflower, cocklebur, and occasionally crab-grass and purslane, are the most troublesome weeds, although in many localities the careless-weed, nettle, and lamb's-quarter are the greatest source of annoyance. None of this land lies "turned out".

The lighter grade black sandy land is commonly known as the *second-rate black sandy*. It comprises about one-sixth of the tillable land, occurring only in spots, the natural timber being squatty post oak. The soil is a light, blackish, fine sandy loam, from 9 to 36 inches in depth, and easily tillable in either wet or dry seasons; and is early, warm, well drained, and best adapted to cotton and corn. The subsoil is generally a clay, containing white angular gravelly pebbles. Two-thirds of the crop planted is cotton, which reaches a height of from 18 to 30 inches, the latter being most productive; it runs to weed in very wet seasons, though not generally so dispose. On fresh land the product per acre of seed-cotton is from 300 to 500 pounds, 1,660 pounds being required for a 475-pound bale. The rate is low middling for fresh land. For land three years under cultivation it is better, the yield per acre for such land being from 1,000 to 1,400 pounds of seed-cotton, 2,000 pounds of which are needed for a 475-pound bale.

The mixture of black sandy and black waxy is commonly designated as *black waxy prairie land*, and, like the previously-described land, it occurs only in spots, and forms about one-sixth of the surface of the county. The soil is a fine silty, shelly, slightly putty-like prairie soil, 2 inches deep, not easily tillable in wet seasons, but more so in dry ones; it is late, cold, and well drained, and is best adapted to corn and wheat. The subsoil is mostly pipe-clay, sometimes rock, containing hard black gravel, underlaid by rock at from 2 to 4 feet. Very little cotton is grown on this land, the height attained being about 1 or 2 feet. The fresh lands yield from 200 to 400 pounds of seed-cotton per acre; on the land after three years' cultivation the yield is from 700 to 800 pounds, the lint rating as good ordinary.

Shipments are made during the fall by means of wagon to Fort Worth and Waco, the rate being $2 or $2 50 per bale.

SOMERVELL.

Population: 2,649.—White, 2,621; colored, 28.

Area: 200 square miles.—Woodland, small part; central black prairie region, 160 square miles; upper cross timbers, 40 square miles

Tilled lands: 15,609 acres.—Area planted in cotton, 4,030 acres; in corn, 5,629 acres; in oats, 238 acres; in wheat, 1,603 acres.

Cotton production: 1,066 bales; average cotton product per acre, 0.26 bale, 390 pounds seed-cotton, or 130 pounds cotton lint.

Somervell is one of the smallest counties in the state, and is divided by the Brazos river, which flows through it in a zigzag course from north to south. The surface of the country is rolling, with a few prominent bald hills and peaks, and, with the exception of the river bottoms and their adjoining uplands, is an open prairie. Rotten limestone, is the prevailing rock. The soil of the prairies is a black waxy clay or adobe, and is not much under cultivation, being chiefly devoted to grazing purposes. On the edge of these prairies this soil becomes commingled with the sands of the timbered lands, but retains its black color, and is known as black sandy soil. The uplands near the river have chiefly a timber growth of post oak and a gray sandy soil, very productive, and are to some extent under cultivation. The red alluvial loam of the river bottoms is preferred for the crops of the county, and is the one chiefly under cultivation. Tilled lands average 78 acres per square mile, the average of cotton being 20.2 acres.

ABSTRACT FROM THE REPORT OF SCOTT MILAM, OF GLENROSE.

The lands of the county are the alluvial loam of the Brazos river, black waxy, mulatto, black sandy, and sandy post oak.

The chief soil is the *alluvial loam* of the river bottom, which comprises one-fortieth of the whole county. The timber growth of these bottoms is cottonwood, poplar, black walnut, pecan, ash, elm, and cedar. The soil is a black sandy loam, sometimes mulatto in color, from 1 foot to 3 feet deep, with a yellowish clay subsoil, which occasionally contains pebbles. The soil is early, well drained, and easily tilled, yielding about 40 bushels of wheat, 60 bushels of corn, or about 1,080 pounds of seed-cotton per acre, making 500 pounds of lint. Cotton comprises one-fourth of the crops, the chief of which are wheat, corn, cotton, oats, barley, rye, millet, and Hungarian grass; also peaches, cherries, and grapes. Cotton grows to a height of from 4 to 5 feet, being most productive at the latter, and seldom inclines to run to weed, except in the wet, warm weather in June; topping is the remedy applied. The yield per acre of seed-cotton on old land is, as on fresh land, 1,000 pounds, 1,600 pounds on fresh and from 1,545 to 1,720 pounds on old land being necessary for a 475-pound bale of middling and low middling lint. Careless, crab-grass, purslane, and cocklebur are the most troublesome weeds. None of this land lies "turned out"; it does not wash on slopes.

River bottom lands are generally preferred for cotton, although the post-oak lands average quite as much, and stand the drought much better. Cold nights on the last of April and first of May generally give cotton what is known by farmers and planters as "sore-shin". In the fall the Rocky mountain locust or grasshopper sometimes injures the crop.

As soon as ginned, cotton is hauled at the rate of $1 50 per bale to Fort Worth by wagon, and thence shipped to Galveston by railroad at 1½ cents per pound.

JOHNSON.

Population: 17,911.—White, 17,337; colored, 574.

Area: 690 square miles.—Woodland, small part; central black prairie region, 520 square miles; lower cross timbers, 170 square miles.

Tilled lands: 134,842 acres.—Area planted in cotton, 40,446 acres; in corn, 38,151 acres; in oats, 5,528 acres; in wheat, 14,339 acres.

Cotton production: 13,778 bales; average cotton product per acre, 0.34 bale, 510 pounds seed-cotton, or 170 pounds cotton lint.

The surface of Johnson county is high and rolling, but the greater part is an open prairie, with a few prominent hills. The belt of lower cross timbers passes through from north to south immediately east of Cleburne, the county-seat. This belt has a width of 10 or 15 miles, and retains the characteristic features of deep sandy lands, ferruginous sandstone, brown and reddish gravel, and a growth of post and black-jack oaks that are seen in other counties. At Cleburne it occupies a valley, being much lower than the general level of the prairies. Its own surface is, however, somewhat hilly in places.

The prairie lands are of the black waxy character peculiar to the central region, free from timber, and devoted principally to stock-grazing. (See analysis, page 36.) Rotten limestone outcrops on the hills, but is deeply covered by the soil in the valleys. The country is watered by the headwaters of Chambers and Noland's creeks, the Brazos river touching the southwestern corner.

Johnson is an agricultural county, 30.5 per cent. of its area being under cultivation, averaging 195.4 acres per square mile. Corn has the largest acreage, that of cotton averaging 58.6 acres per square mile.

ABSTRACTS FROM THE REPORTS OF J. B. ALLARD, E. E. SKIPPER, AND W. A. MENAFEE, OF CLEBURNE.

The uplands of the county are mostly rolling prairies, and the lands under cotton cultivation comprise the black waxy of the prairies and of the valleys of Noland's river, the sandy lands of the cross timbers, and the sandy and mahogany of the prairies.

The most important soil is the *black waxy*, of which one-third of this county is composed. The natural timber is post oak in the cross timbers, with some black-jack, hickory, and elm, pecan, walnut, ash, hackberry, cottonwood, and various other kinds on the water-courses. The soil is a black prairie clay from 2 to 5 feet in depth, underlaid in the black lands sometimes by a yellowish clay, but mostly by gravel and limestone, and in the timbers mostly by red clay, gravel and sand-rock occasionally; the subsoil itself is underlaid by sand, gravel, and rock at from 2 to 10 feet. The soil is early, warm, and well drained, and is easily tillable in dry seasons.

The chief crops are corn, wheat, oats, and cotton, each of which does equally well in favorable seasons. Early frosts prevent early planting. Planting is generally done from the 1st to the 20th of April. The June and July drought frequently damages the cotton crop, causing it to shed its bolls, and also producing "motes" in the lint, which pass through the gin. Cotton comprises one-third of the crops, growing from 2 to 4 feet high on the black, and from 2½ to 5 feet on the sandy lands. It is most productive at 3 feet on the former, and 4 on the latter, but runs to weed in warm and wet springs and summers, and yields from 1,000 to 2,000 pounds of seed-cotton per acre, the staple rating from middling to middling fair. After twenty years' cultivation the yield is about the same as on fresh land, except on the sandy lands, where there is a slight falling off. Rag-weed on the black lands, and rag-weed and crab-grass on the sandy lands, are most troublesome. No lands have been turned out to rest. Only the sandy lands are liable to wash and gully on slopes.

As fast as cotton is ginned it is hauled by wagon to Cleburne, Fort Worth, Dallas, or Waco, the freight being $1 per bale to Fort Worth.

ELLIS.

Population: 21,294.—White, 18,755; colored, 2,539.

Area: 950 square miles.—Woodland, very little; all central black prairie region.

Tilled lands: 172,084 acres.—Area planted in cotton, 52,172 acres; in corn, 42,899 acres; in oats, 5,533 acres; in wheat, 18,500 acres.

Cotton production: 18,956 bales; average cotton product per acre, 0.36 bale, 540 pounds seed-cotton, or 180 pounds cotton lint.

Ellis is an open prairie county, with a surface partly rolling and partly level, and watered by the Trinity river and its tributaries, which flow eastward, the river forming its eastern boundary. These streams usually have narrow skirts of sandy lands along their borders, timbered mostly with post oak. The river lands have a deep and dark alluvial soil and a timber growth of walnut, ash, elm, pecan, bois d'arc, and cottonwood, and are generally subject to overflow, and therefore not under cultivation.

The prairie lands near the timbers are black sandy in character and very productive, but over the greater part of the county they are black and waxy, with a stiff yellowish subsoil, underlaid by the white rotten limestone that is characteristic of the central prairie region. (See analysis, page 36.) The yield per acre is about 750 pounds of seed-cotton in fair seasons.

Ellis is chiefly an agricultural county, the lands under cultivation comprising 28.3 per cent. of its area, and averaging 181 acres per square mile.

Cotton is the chief crop, its acreage being greater than that of any other crop, and is surpassed by but three counties in the state, viz, McLennan, Washington, and Fayette. Its cotton average per square mile is 54.9 per cent., that of the counties of Johnson, Washington, Fayette, Camp, and Robertson being greater. The average product per acre for 1879 was low in comparison with very many other counties. In the production of wheat Ellis county ranks as fifth.

ABSTRACTS FROM THE REPORTS OF S. C. TALLEY, OF CHAMBERS CREEK; G. W. COOPER, OF BRISTOL; W. HAMLETT, OF MILFORD, AND JAMES E. SMITH, OF WAXAHACHIE.

On the lowlands the cotton is liable to injury from heavy spring rains, which cause it to have the sore-shin, and in killed by frosts from two to four weeks earlier than on the uplands; still the bottom land, where it can be cultivated fourth to one-third more cotton per acre, because it endures the summer droughts better. The cultivated land c different varieties: The black upland prairie, which embraces at least 90 per cent. of all the cultivated lands of loam all above overflow, being deposits from the uplands; and the black sandy soil along the Trinity river.

The *black waxy prairie* soil, which is the most important, is from 3 to 15 feet in depth, with a subsoil of seldom reached except when digging wells, and does not lose its identity after being mixed with the surface s when undisturbed, and contains pebbles and shells. Limestone is found at from 10 to 35 feet. Mesquite is th not too wet, the soil is early; it is rather difficult to till in wet but easy in dry seasons, producing cotton, corn, w potatoes, though best adapted to cotton, corn, and oats, from one-third to one-half of all the crops planted bein to a height of from 2 to 5 feet, producing most at 3 feet, and tending to run to weed in wet seasons in July an rapid cultivation are the remedies applied. The yield per acre from fresh land is from 500 to 1,000 pounds; fr after one year's cultivation; from 800 to 1,200 pounds after two years' cultivation, and from 1,000 to 1,500 pou cultivation. In each of the above cases the amount necessary for 475 pounds of lint is from 1,425 to 1,900 pound staple in all cases is middling. Numerous varieties of careless, rag, sunflower, cocklebur, sand briers, and nett weeds.

The *gray sandy lands* cover about 2 per cent. of the tillable area, and occur along or near the streams. Post oa locust, with some pecan, comprise the natural growth. The soil, 2 feet in depth, has a subsoil of bluish yellow c underlaid by limestone and joint clay at 12 feet. It is easily tilled in wet and moderately so in dry seasons, and is e well drained. In warm, wet weather the cotton runs to weed. The usual height to which it grows is 2 feet, yie cotton per acre, which yield is not altered by cultivation, the lint rating as second class. Spanish nettl constitute the troublesome weeds. No land lies "turned out". The same may be said of all lands of the count

Shipments are usually made as soon as ginned, by wagon, to the nearest depot, and thence by rail to Gal Louis, the rate being $4 50 per bale.

e weeds.

en made to

by wagon being

are miles; upper cross

s; in oats, 723 acres;

d-cotton, or 85 pounds

Lampasas creeks, and

They have a timber nd abrupt, with ledges black waxy soils and along the streams, with their rocky character, tion, and are devoted to tton acreage is small as e, while the product per

785

acre for 1879 (0.17 of a bale) was about equal in all of them, varying from 195 to 330 pounds of seed-cotton. This extremely small average for 1879 is due entirely to the unusual drought that prevailed in that year over western Texas. The lands are naturally as productive as lands of the same character in other counties of the region, whose yield in this same year was several times greater, and in good seasons is about 750 pounds of seed-cotton. The tilled lands of the county are chiefly devoted to corn, its acreage being nearly double that of cotton, which averages 7 acres per square mile.

LAMPASAS.

Population: 5,421.—White, 5,248; colored, 173.
Area: 850 square miles.—Woodland, nearly one-fourth; central black prairie region, 700 square miles; northwestern red loam, 150 square miles.
Tilled lands: 28,435 acres.—Area planted in cotton, 4,611 acres; in corn, 9,153 acres; in oats, 760 acres; in wheat, 3,633 acres.
Cotton production: 628 bales; average cotton product per acre, 0.14 bale, 210 pounds seed-cotton, or 70 pounds cotton lint.

Lampasas is a high and rolling prairie county, with high and abrupt ridges standing out so prominently over the surface that they have received the name of "mountains". These hills are largely destitute of timber, with the exception of many cedar brakes on their sides. Rotten limestone is the prevailing rock of these hills, outcropping in ledges and bluffs, but underneath this there is found in localities a sandstone, the lowest of the Cretaceous series of rocks. It is estimated that two-thirds of the surface of the county is an open prairie, having mostly the black waxy lands peculiar to the central prairie region. (See analysis, page 36.) The western part of the county has more timber, and the lands are sandy and belong to the red-loam region. The county is watered by the Colorado river and its tributaries on the west and Lampasas creek and its small tributaries on the east. A number of fine sulphur springs occur near the town of Lampasas, and are a great place of resort for people of central Texas. The prairies are mostly used for grazing purposes, as the population is sparse. The farms lie along the streams, the soil being of a black waxy or black sandy character and highly productive. The lands under cultivation average 33.4 acres per square mile. The average yield per acre of both corn and cotton for 1879 was very small, due evidently to the extreme drought of that year.

ABSTRACT FROM THE REPORT OF THOMAS J. DURRETT, OF LAMPASAS.

Three kinds of lands are found in this county, viz: Black waxy, in what is called the open valleys; cove and table-lands, some of the latter having a red clay subsoil; and grayish sandy next to the creek banks.

The chief soil is the *black waxy prairie*, which forms two-thirds of the tillable land of the county, extending 15 or 20 miles in a northwesterly direction, and about the same to the southeast. There is on this land no natural timber. On the creeks grow mesquite, elm, cottonwood, and burr, post, live and black-jack oaks, sycamore, sumac, some walnut, wild china, and chittim wood.

The *black soil* is a heavy prairie clay loam, from 18 to 20 inches in depth, with a dark reddish and dove-colored clayey, leachy subsoil, containing hard gravel, rounded pebbles on all streams, and is underlaid by gravel and concrete at from 5 to 15 feet. The soil is easily tillable in either wet or dry seasons, and is late (depending on the "northers" more than anything else), warm, and well drained. The chief crops are corn, wheat, oats, cotton, millet or Hungarian grass, and sweet potatoes. Cotton forms about one-third of the crops, growing to a height of about 3½ feet. Very wet seasons, and also deep cultivation when young, are favorable conditions for causing the plant to run to weed, the remedy for which, besides increasing the bolling, is surface culture. The yield per acre of seed-cotton is for fresh lands from 1,200 to 1,800 pounds; on lands under cultivation for thirteen years the yield is the same; from 1,426 pounds to 1,665 pounds are necessary in both cases to make a 475-pound bale of lint. The rating of the staple from fresh land is not so good as that from lands which have been under cultivation. Careless-weeds, cocklebur, and Spanish bur are the most troublesome weeds. Crab-grass is not troublesome. No land lies "turned out", and there is very little washing of the soil.

Shipments are made from October to Christmas, by means of wagons, to Round Rock, in Williamson county, the rate being from $1 50 to $2 per bale.

CORYELL.

Population: 10,924.—White, 10,539; colored, 385.
Area: 950 square miles.—Woodland, very little; all central black prairie.
Tilled lands: 78,763 acres.—Area planted in cotton, 19,688 acres; in corn, 22,993 acres; in oats, 2,733 acres; in wheat, 8,506 acres.
Cotton production: 3,331 bales; average cotton product per acre, 0.17 bale, 255 pounds seed-cotton, or 85 pounds cotton lint.

The surface of Coryell county is rolling or hilly, and is watered by Leon river and Cowhouse creek, which flow in a southerly course, and are separated by a line of hills partly timbered with live and post oaks. The greater part, probably two-thirds of the county, is an open prairie of black waxy land, tillable only in the valleys because of the rocky nature of the hills, rotten limestone outcropping everywhere. Timber is quite scarce, comprising post oak and mountain cedar. These prairies are almost entirely given up to grazing purposes, the county being very sparsely settled. The lands under cultivation average 82.9 acres per square mile, 20.7 of which are devoted to the culture of cotton.

ABSTRACT FROM THE REPORT OF THOMAS WILLIAMSON, OF PIDCOCK RANCH.

The lands of the county comprise the black prairie uplands and dark soils of the Cowhouse valley above overflow. The soils of the uplands do not vary in quality, and are black and rich, in tracts variously estimated from 10 to 200 acres. Cotton on the lowlands is from two to four weeks later than on the uplands, but usually matures well.

The *Cowhouse valley* is the chief cotton region of the county, but is not extensive, comprising but a small proportion of the county area. Its timber growth is pecan and elm. The hills have usually a growth of live and post oaks. These prairie soils have a depth of about 2 feet, and are underlaid at 10 or 20 feet by soft limestone. The soil is difficult to cultivate in wet weather, but easy in dry. It is late and ill drained, the chief crops being cotton, corn, wheat, oats, millet, sorghum, sweet and Irish potatoes. About one-third of the crops is in cotton, but the soil is best adapted to corn, wheat, and oats. Cotton grows to a height of 4 or 5 feet, runs to weed in wet weather, and produces 1,000 pounds of seed-cotton per acre, the lint rating as middling. After ten years' cultivation its yield decreases to 700 pounds, and rates as low middling, 1,680 pounds being then required for a 475-pound bale of lint. The careless-weed is the most troublesome. The soil does not wash readily, and scarcely any of it is "turned out".

In November, December, and January cotton shipments are made by wagon to Waco, and thence by railroad to Galveston, the rate being $4 50 per bale.

McLENNAN.

Population: 26,934.—White, 19,276; colored, 7,658.
Area: 1,080 square miles.—Woodland, nearly one-fifth; central black prairie, 980 square miles; lower cross timbers, 100 square miles.
Tilled lands: 203,882 acres.—Area planted in cotton, 53,394 acres; in corn, 48,357 acres; in oats, 9,091 acres; in wheat, 18,682 acres.
Cotton production: 12,777 bales; average cotton product per acre, 9.24 bale, 360 pounds seed-cotton, or 120 pounds cotton lint.

McLennan, one of the central counties of the state, is divided by the Brazos river, which crosses it from northwest to southeast. The surface of the county consists of high and rolling prairies, and, along the river and its tributaries, belts of timbered lands. The timbered river uplands are broad and sandy, and have a growth of post oak and other timber. The subsoil is clayey in character, and the lands are said to produce as much as 700 pounds of seed-cotton per acre. The bottom lands have a red-loam soil, and are by many considered the best lands in the county. The timber growth is cottonwood, pecan, elm, etc. Rotten limestone (Cretaceous) underlies these bottom lands, outcropping in the banks of the river at Waco and elsewhere. On the prairies this rock is again found on the hills, where it approaches very near the surface; but in the valleys it is deeply covered by the soil which has accumulated from the hillsides. These prairie lands are of the black waxy nature peculiar to the central region, but near the sandy timbered lands the soil becomes more or less mixed with sand, forming what is termed black sandy soil, or terminus of the lower cross timbers. (See analysis, page 36.)

Lands under cultivation in this county comprise 29.5 per cent. of the area, and average 188.8 acres per square mile. There are but five counties having a greater proportion of tilled lands, viz, Washington, Dallas, Johnson, Collin, and Grayson.

McLennan ranks as first in the state in quantity of wheat product, though the acreage of that crop is less than in three other counties. Cotton is, however, the chief crop, but while in acreage it ranks as third, it is only nineteenth in the state in the number of bales for 1879. Its average acreage per square mile is 49.4.

ABSTRACTS FROM THE REPORTS OF J. H. EARLE AND D. R. GURLEY, OF WACO, AND C. A. WESTBROOK, OF MASTERSVILLE.

The bottoms of the Brazos river comprise a large body of rich lands, having a red or chocolate clay and sandy soil, covered with a growth of cottonwood, pecan, hackberry, elm, and boxwood. Beds of sand and gravel underlie this soil at a depth of 15 feet. The other lands of this section devoted to the cultivation of cotton are the black rolling prairie and the hog-wallow prairies.

The most important of the above is the *Brazos bottom land*, the soil of which, under proper management, is easily tilled in dry seasons or in wet ones. It is early, warm, and well drained, and produces cotton, corn, wheat, and oats, though it is apparently best adapted to cotton and corn, the former constituting two-thirds of the crops. The height usually attained by the plant is 5 feet, at which it is most productive, although in wet seasons it sometimes reaches as high as 6 or even 8 feet, when it runs to weed. Land after being cultivated for 15 years shows no difference as far as the yield and the rating of the cotton are concerned. From fresh land the product per acre in seed-cotton is 1,600 pounds, 1,545 pounds being required for a 475-pound bale, the rating being strict good middling. Sunflower and cocklebur are the most troublesome weeds. No land lies "turned out".

The *black rolling or upland prairie lands* cover about nine-tenths of this region, and extend beyond the limits of the county. The soil of these lands is from 2 to 20 feet thick, and is underlaid by soft white limestone at different depths. It is easily cultivated in dry seasons, and is late, warm, well drained, and best adapted to wheat and oats, cotton forming one-twentieth of the crops and growing to a height of 3 feet, at which it is most productive. The yield of this soil per acre in seed-cotton is from 800 to 1,000 pounds, the rating being middling; 1,555 pounds are necessary for a 475 pound bale of lint. There is no change in the above after many years cultivation.

Cotton forms about 50 per cent. of the crops grown on the *hog-wallow lands*, which cover about 6 per cent. of this section, and have a growth of mesquite. The soil is a black adobe, 1 foot in depth, with a clay subsoil. It is very difficult to cultivate, and is late, cold, and badly drained. Cotton and corn seem best adapted to it, the former growing to a height of 3 feet, and running to weed in wet seasons. The soil produces 500 pounds of seed-cotton per acre, 1,565 pounds being required for a 475-pound bale of lint. Cultivated lands, even after 10 years, show no appreciable difference either in the yield or in the rating, which is middling. Sunflower and cocklebur are the most troublesome weeds.

The effect of frost on the uplands or on the lowlands is just about the same. The bottom lands are the best for cotton, notwithstanding that the cotton-worm generally attacks the lowlands about two weeks before it does the prairie lands.

Shipments are made all through the season, by wagon, to Waco at 50 cents, and thence to Galveston at $4 per bale.

LIMESTONE.
(See "Oak, hickory, and pine region".)

FALLS.

Population : 16,240.—White, 9,565 ; colored, 6,675.
Area : 780 square miles.—Woodland, a large part; oak, hickory, and pine region, 60 square miles; central black prairie region, 460 square miles; brown loam prairie, 260 square miles.
Tilled lands : 114,867 acres.—Area planted in cotton, 39,669 acres ; in corn, 29,943 acres ; in oats, 1,200 acres ; in wheat, 953 acres.
Cotton production : 12,495 bales; average cotton product per acre, 0.32 bale, 480 pounds seed-cotton, or 160 pounds cotton lint.

Falls county is divided into two parts by the Brazos river, which flows through it from northwest to southeast. The western division, locally known as "West Falls", is mostly a rolling prairie country with black waxy soils, except on the southwest corner, where the lands are sandy and have a growth of mesquite and a few scattering post-oak trees. Immediately adjoining the bottom lands of the Brazos there is a strip of timbered uplands, 3 or 4 miles wide, having a somewhat sandy soil and a heavy growth of post and Spanish oaks, elm, ash, pecan, and cedar. Some of the best cedar brakes in the county are on this side of the river.

The Brazos bottom lands are of the reddish clayey loam character peculiar to those rivers whose sources are in the extreme northwest. They are wide, very heavily timbered with cottonwood, walnut, pecan, elm, etc., and are highly prized for their great productiveness.

That part of the county east of the river is known as the Blue Ridge, from a low ridge of that name 10 miles east of Marlin, the county-seat. The upper portion of this section is mostly a rolling and open prairie, with black waxy soils and outcropping rotten limestone (Cretaceous), the rest being generally sandy and timbered with mesquite and post oak. (See analysis, page 36.) Eastward from the river lands to Marlin there is but little timber, the country with its red clayey soils being known as "weed prairies". From Marlin eastward to Big Sandy creek, 3 miles distant, the soil is sandy and the soil is of the black clayey character, with a growth of mesquite and some post oak and an occasional prairie. Big creek, 7 miles east of Marlin, has a rich black bottom land about 2 miles in width, part of which is a mesquite prairie. The Blue Ridge lies between this creek and the Little Brazos, and is not more than 50 feet high, but is a prominent object in these almost level lands. The west side is very abrupt in places, but in others is a gradual slope. The eastern side has a very gradual slope to the Little Brazos. This stream has very little bottom lands until near the southern boundary-line of the county, but is usually well timbered with elm, ash, post, and burr oaks, and some cedar.

Falls is principally an agricultural county, its cultivated lands averaging 147.3 acres per square mile. It is also one of the chief cotton counties of the state, there being but fourteen counties having each a greater cotton acreage, and but nine whose average acreage per square mile is greater (50.9). Its rank is 20 as regards the number of bales produced. Its yield per acre is small in comparison with other counties, there being 89 having a higher product.

ABSTRACTS FROM THE REPORTS OF P. LEA, OF WEST FALLS; A. E. WATSON, OF MARLIN; AND E. C. M'CULLOUGH
OF MORESVILLE.

The lands of the county under cultivation in cotton are the alluvial of the Brazos river, the black waxy prairies, sandy prairies, and post-oak uplands.

Of the various qualities of land in the county, the *red clay soils* of the Brazos bottom are the most productive, but comprise only about one-twentieth of the tillable area. Its growth is hackberry, pecan, hickory, elm, and cottonwood. The soil has a depth of many feet, and is easily tilled in all seasons. The chief products are corn and cotton, but it seems to be best adapted to the latter, yielding from 1,500 to 2,000 pounds of seed-cotton per acre. From one-half to two-thirds of the cultivated lands is planted in cotton. The stalk grows to a height of from 5 to 10 feet, and is most productive at 6 feet ; from 1,425 to 1,660 pounds of seed-cotton make 475 pounds of lint, which rates very high in the market. The cocklebur and careless weed are most troublesome.

The *black waxy prairie lands*, which comprise about two-thirds of the lands of the county, are well drained, and are almost equal to the Brazos bottoms, producing an average of 1,200 pounds of seed-cotton per acre. The rotten limestone underlies it at 20 feet, though often coming nearer the surface. The soil is a black tenacious clay from 2 to 6 feet deep. The yellow subsoil is often mixed with lumps of the decomposed rock, and is underlaid by joint clay. Corn, cotton, wheat, and oats all do well on these prairies. Cotton comprises one-fourth of the crops, grows to a height of 3½ feet, producing a grade of lint rating as low middling, 475 pounds being obtained from 1,660 pounds of seed-cotton. Long cultivation affects the productiveness very little, if at all.

The *post-oak and black-jack upland* along the river bottom has a gray sandy soil 18 inches deep and a clay subsoil containing water-worn pebbles. The soil is easily cultivated, early, warm, and well drained, and best adapted to cotton and corn. The former grows to a height of 2 feet, and produces, when the land is fresh, about 1,000 pounds of seed-cotton per acre, 1,660 pounds making 475 pounds of lint, which rates as "good ordinary". After eight years' cultivation the yield decreases to 600 pounds of seed-cotton per acre, and 1,780 pounds are required to make 475 pounds of lint. Crab-grass is most troublesome. These uplands wash readily, doing serious damage, but do not injure the black land of the valleys.

The *sandy prairies* of the eastern part of the county have a fine sandy soil 18 inches in depth, and are underlaid by a red clay. They have a scattering growth of elm, oak, and mesquite, are early, warm, and well drained, and are best adapted to cotton, which grows to a height of 2 feet and produces 1,000 pounds of seed-cotton, which rates as good ordinary. After ten years' cultivation the yield is only 800 pounds. Crab-grass is the most troublesome.

Shipments are made by railroad, from October to February, to Marlin and Galveston, the rates being from $4 to $5 per bale.

BELL.

Population : 20,518.—White, 18,783 ; colored, 1,735.
Area : 1,000 square miles.—Woodland, very little ; all central black prairie.
Tilled lands : 129,039 acres.—Area planted in cotton, 37,826 acres ; in corn, 40,475 acres ; in oats, 5,169 acres ; in wheat, 47,000 acres.
Cotton production : 9,217 bales ; average cotton product per acre, 0.25 bale, 360 pounds seed-cotton, or 120 pounds cotton lint.

788

Bell, one of the central counties of the state, is high and rolling, and mostly an open prairie, with timbered lands along its water-courses. It is well watered by Leon river and Lampasas creek and their tributaries, which unite to form Little river, a tributary of the Brazos. These streams have some large bodies of rich alluvial lands from one-half to one mile in width, and they are mostly in cultivation where above overflow. They have a large growth of cottonwood, oaks, walnut, mulberry, ash, elm, etc. On the low uplands, near the bottoms, are cedar brakes and live oaks. The prairies are rolling, with outcropping rotten limestone on the hills and deep, black, calcareous soils in the valleys. They yield about 800 pounds of seed-cotton per acre. The cultivated lands average 129 acres per square mile. Corn is the chief crop of the county, though there is not a very great difference between its acreage and that of cotton, whose average is 37.8 acres per square mile. The population is very sparse, being about 20 persons per square mile.

ABSTRACT FROM THE REPORTS OF A. J. HARRIS, OF BELTON, AND MORITZ MAEDGEN, OF TROY.

The western part of the county is hilly, with some table-lands and valleys of black prairie. The eastern, southern, and northern portion is a solid body of rich land, one-fourth of it creek and river valleys of alluvial and sandy loam, the rest of rolling black prairie. On the hills the limestone outcrops in abundance, but the lowlands have a deep soil. The latter are properly the first and second bottoms of the creeks, although mostly open prairie, and are high and dry and never overflow.

Cotton is cultivated on all of these lands, the chief soil being the *black prairie*. The rainfall in the summer season, from July to September, is generally insufficient, but there is no other obstacle to the production of cotton in this county. The prairies are bare of timber, with occasional spots of hackberry, elm, and pecan. The soil has a depth of about 3 feet, and is underlaid by a joint clay, nearly white, and slightly yellowish. Occasionally a small area, having the disintegrated rotten limestone for its subsoil, forms a gray soil by cultivation. The soil is easily cultivated in dry weather, but in wet weather is so sticky as to be almost unmanageable. It remains cold longer in the spring than sandy lands, retarding the growth of cotton, and making it more liable to injury from the summer's drought. The soil is well drained by its natural slopes. The chief crops are cotton, corn, wheat, and oats, and the soil is equally well adapted to all. The proportion of cotton planted is from one-fourth to one-fifth; it grows to a height of from 3 to 5 feet, and the higher the stalk the more productive it is, yielding from 800 to 1,000 pounds of seed-cotton per acre, which, after twenty years' cultivation, is not diminished. About 1,495 pounds of seed-cotton make 475 pounds of lint, the quality being the same from old and from fresh lands, and rating as middling. The most troublesome weeds are the careless, bull-nettle, and bur, and dewberry vines. The soil does not wash, nor is any "turned out". Along the streams the growth consists of cottonwood, burr oak, elm, walnut, hickory, white oak, mulberry, bois d'arc, ash, post oak, black-jack, and sycamore. Near the streams are live and Spanish oaks and cedars. These lands are from one-half to a mile wide, and are very productive.

ABSTRACT FROM THE REPORT OF JOHN T. DULANY, OF BELTON.

The chief cotton land has a *black prairie soil* from 1 inch to 10 inches in depth, with an occasional growth of pecan, hackberry, and live oak. Elm and pecan grow on the creek and river bottoms. The soil is underlaid by soft rock and joint clay, and can be easily cultivated in all seasons. The soil is early, warm, and well drained, and produces cotton, corn, oats, and barley; wheat does not make a profitable crop. About one-third of the crops is cotton, which, when seasonable, reaches a height of from 3 to 5 feet, and inclines to run to weed in continued wet weather; no remedy has been applied. The yield is from 1,000 to 1,500 pounds of seed-cotton per acre, from 1,545 to 1,780 pounds being necessary for 475 pounds of lint. There is no perceptible difference between the yield nor the rating of the staple from fresh land or from cultivated land, it being classed as middling. The careless, bull-nettle, and the cocklebur are the troublesome weeds.

Shipments are made in October and November, by mule wagons, to Taylor station, on the International and Great Northern railroad, and thence to Galveston, the rates being $1 to Taylor and from $4 25 to $4 50 to Galveston per bale.

MILAM.

"See (Oak, hickory, and pine region)."

WILLIAMSON.

Population: 15,155.—White, 13,520; colored, 1,635.

Area: 1,100 square miles.—Woodland, a large part; part central prairie region; rest northwestern red-loam region.

Tilled lands: 141,862 acres.—Area planted in cotton, 18,528 acres; in corn, 26,995 acres; in oats, 8,834 acres; in wheat, 7,901 acres.

Cotton production: 4,017 bales; average cotton product per acre, 0.23 bale, 345 pounds seed-cotton, or 115 pounds cotton lint.

Williamson is largely a prairie county, especially that part lying east of Georgetown, the county-seat. On the west of this town, and extending to Liberty Hill, not far from the county-line, there is a high and hilly belt of country, very broken, and covered with a growth of post and black-jack oaks and a reddish sandy soil. Its surface is covered with a limestone, inclosing nodules and masses of variegated and flinty material; on weathering, this rock presents a rough and jagged surface. At the foot of these hills, on the east, is found the white and soft rotten limestone of the Cretaceous, having an easterly dip and containing the fossils of the formation. This latter limestone underlies the country eastward to the county-line, where the Tertiary sands and clays are found. The prairies on the west of the hills are much more broken, and occur in smaller bodies than those of the east, but the lands are nearly the same. Near the timbers the usual change takes place from the black waxy to the black sandy. The cultivated lands of the county comprise 20.2 per cent. of its area, averaging 129 acres per square mile. Of these, 16.8 acres are in cotton.

ABSTRACT FROM THE REPORTS OF ANDREW J. NELSON, OF ROUND ROCK, AND R. E. TALBOT, OF GEORGETOWN.

The chief agricultural lands are the black waxy prairies, covering about one-half of the county. The bottom lands have a growth of Spanish, burr, post, and white oaks, elm, walnut, pecan, hackberry, willow, sycamore, mulberry, cedar, and cottonwood.

The *prairie soil* is a black stiff clay, from 2 to 5 feet in depth, with a subsoil of yellow clay, containing some "black gravel" and white gravel pebbles, and is underlaid by limestone at 15 feet. It is easy to till in dry seasons, but difficult in wet, and is early, warm, and well drained. The productions, with their average yields per acre, are: Cotton, 800 pounds of seed-cotton; corn, 40 bushels; wheat, 12 bushels; oats, 60 bushels; also, barley and rye. Cotton and corn seem best adapted to the soil, the former constituting one-third of the crops, the height usually attained by it being from 3 to 4 feet; the latter is the most productive. In wet weather there seems to be an inclination to run to weed, which can be restrained by topping. From 1,435 to 1,545 pounds of seed-cotton are required for 475 pounds of lint, the rating being good middling. After twenty years' cultivation there is no appreciable difference in the yield of the land.

Cocklebur, rag-weed, careless, nettle, and sunflower are the most troublesome weeds on this land. The soil of the uplands washes readily on slopes.

Additional abstract of R. E. Talbot.

The *black hog-wallow prairies* comprise one-fourth of the area of the county, and having less surface soil than the black prairies, is more subject to drought. It is underlaid by decomposed limestone at 2 feet, and is best adapted to corn and wheat, though one-sixth of the cultivated lands are devoted to cotton. The soil is late, cold, ill-drained, and difficult to till in wet seasons, but better in moderately dry seasons. Cotton grows to a height of 3 feet, yielding 600 pounds of seed-cotton per acre when fresh and after forty years' cultivation. The lint rates as good middling. This soil has the same troublesome weeds as the black waxy.

The *sandy loam soils* of the *post oak* and *cedar lands* comprise one-fourth of the lands of the county. The former lie in the eastern part of the county, and have an area of 25 by 10 miles; the latter cover the hills on the west with an area of 5 by 30 miles. The soil has a depth of 1 foot. The yellow subsoil is underlaid and mixed with pebbles, gravel, and sand. The soil is best adapted to cotton, corn, and small grain. Cotton grows to a height of 2 or 3 feet, and runs to weed in wet seasons. Deep plowing is the remedy applied to prevent running to weed, and also to favor bolling. The yield per acre in cotton-seed is for fresh lands 500 pounds, which is reduced to 475 pounds after the land has been in cultivation ten years, the lint rating as good middling. The soil washes readily, doing serious damage to the uplands, but not to the valleys. The troublesome weeds are cocklebur, rag- and careless- weeds. In this as in other counties drought seems to be the principal drawback to the successful raising of cotton.

Shipments are made in November and December, by rail, to Houston at $3 65, and to Galveston at $4 40 per bale.

BURNET.

(See "Northwestern red-loam region".)

TRAVIS.

Population: 27,028.—White, 18,410; colored, 8,618.
Area: 1,000 square miles.—Woodland, one-eighth; all central black prairie region.
Tilled lands: 86,724 acres.—Area planted in cotton, 29,500 acres; in corn, 30,882 acres; in oats, 4,779 acres; in wheat, 4,048 acres.
Cotton production: 9,271 bales; average cotton product per acre, 0.31 bale, 465 pounds seed-cotton, or 155 pounds cotton lint.

Travis is a rolling prairie county, and is divided by the Colorado river, flowing through it in a southeasterly course. The bottom lands of this stream, as well as of others that water the county, are well timbered with pecan, elm, cottonwood, and hackberry. (See analyses, page 47.) The country west and northwest from Austin is hilly and broken, the summits having a growth of cedar and Spanish oaks; the rest of the county is largely prairie, the monotony being broken only by the timber of the streams or a few scattering oaks and clumps of mesquite. It is estimated that the prairies, with their black clayey lands, cover about five-eighths of the surface of the county. Cretaceous rotten limestone is the prevailing rock, and is found underlying the lands and forming ledges in the hills. The lands of the river bottom are wide, and have a reddish clay loam soil, which, near the uplands, changes to a black clayey character, somewhat similar to that of the prairie. Immediately adjoining the river there are commonly low and narrow flats of a deep sandy soil, subject to overflow, and of little or no value. The rest of the bottom lands are very generally under cultivation.

Tilled lands embrace 13.6 per cent. of the county area, averaging 86.7 acres per square mile. Of these 29.5 acres are in cotton.

ABSTRACT FROM THE REPORTS OF E. H. ROGERS AND SON AND J. J. WHELESS, OF AUSTIN.

Although the early-planted cotton in the lowlands is likely to be killed by the late frosts, still, because of their much greater yield, they are preferred to the uplands. This county seldom fails to return a fair crop. The dry weather of this part of the state is preferable to wet, because the latter is favorable to the coming of the grasshopper, a more deadly enemy than the drought. The lands devoted to cotton cultivation comprise the rich black prairie, both along the creek bottoms and also on the uplands, the black sandy lands of the Colorado river, and a light sandy low bottom land.

The *black prairie lands* cover about three-fourths of the tillable area of the county, mesquite, with a few patches of live oak and clumps of chaparral, forming the natural timber growth. The soil is from 2 to 3 feet in depth, is black waxy, and on the very high prairies there are outcroppings of white rotten limestone. Near the foot of the hills, where the deposit is deep, the subsoil is a heavy yellow clay; generally, though, it is limestone. The soil is easy to till in dry seasons, as it is then not tenacious, but in wet weather it is especially difficult. It is early, well drained, and warm, producing cotton, corn, wheat, and oats, but apparently it is best adapted to cotton and corn, the former comprising from one-half to two-thirds the crops planted. Cotton grows to a height of from 2 to 4, or even 5 feet, at which it seems to be the most productive. In wet seasons, and when too thick, it runs to weed, which can be prevented by topping. It yields from 1,200 to 1,500 pounds of seed-cotton per acre, and 1,485 pounds make a 475-pound bale of lint. Thirty years' cultivation makes no appreciable difference either in the productiveness of the soil or in the character of the staple, unless it be that the fiber is a little shorter. Cocklebur, tie-vines, Spanish bur, and morning-glory are the most troublesome weeds. These seem to be on all lands of the county.

The *Colorado river bottom lands* have a soil of reddish clay loam, with a great deal of sand next to the river. They comprise about one-sixth of the lands of this region, the natural timber growth being pecan, elm, hackberry, box-elder, cedar, cottonwood, and in some places mesquite. The depth of the soil is from 3 to 6 feet, with a subsoil of rocky, gravelly clay, containing drift pebbles, etc., underlaid by fine sand and gravel, the former being found at 12 feet. It is best adapted to cotton and corn, is easily cultivated in all seasons, and is warm, early, and well drained, two-thirds of the tillable lands being devoted to cotton. This grows to a height of from 6 to 8 feet, and yields from 1,600 to 2,000 pounds of seed-cotton per acre, 1,665 pounds of which are necessary for a 475-pound bale. The staple rates from middling to fine from fresh lands, and about the same from lands after ten years' cultivation, except that the staple is not quite so long. Very little land lies "turned out".

The soil of the *light-brown sandy bottom lands* is covered by a timber growth of elm, willow, and cottonwood, and occurs only in places along the water-courses. The soil is 2 feet in depth, with a red-clay subsoil, impervious when undisturbed; contains white pebbles, and is underlaid by sand and gravel at 10 feet. The land is early, warm, well drained, and best adapted to corn and hay. One-fourth of the crops is in cotton, which grows to a height of from 5 to 6 feet; 1,800 pounds is the product per acre of seed-cotton, and from 1,485 to 1,665 pounds make 475 pounds of lint, which rates from middling to fair. In wet weather the plant inclines to run to weed, which may be restrained by topping. After thirty years' cultivation there is no apparent change in the yield. Cocklebur is the most troublesome weed. No land lies "turned out".

The *black bottom sandy land* comprises about one-sixth of the tillable area, and extends the whole length of the river from east to west. Its natural timber growth is elm and hackberry. The soil is a fine black or brown sandy, from 3 to 4 feet deep; the subsoil is heavier, consists of a dark red clay, which bakes hard where exposed to the sun and wind, is very impervious when undisturbed, and contains flinty pebbles, "black gravel," and white gravel. It is underlaid by fine sand and gravel, sand being found at 12 feet. The soil is easily tillable in all seasons, as there is enough sand to prevent sticking; it is early when well drained, and is best adapted to cotton and corn. About one-half the crops planted is in cotton, which usually attains a height of about 4 feet, producing well at that height. The plant inclines to run to weed in wet weather; and topping is the remedy applied. The product per acre of seed-cotton from fresh or from lands that have been under cultivation thirty years is 2,000 pounds, 1,485 pounds being necessary for 475 pounds of lint. Very little land lies "turned out", and this, when again cultivated, produces well. Cocklebur, tie-vine, and sunflower are the most troublesome weeds.

The *light ashy land*, comprising about one-third of the cultivated lands, is in some places sandy and in others quite rocky, and extends in all directions, but less toward the northeast, black soils being there found. The natural timber growth is post and black-jack oaks and mesquite. The soil is fine, sandy, and gravelly, whitish gray in color, and from 6 inches to 1 foot in depth. The subsoil is a red clay, containing small rocks, in some places white gravel, and is underlaid by sand and gravel. The soil is early, warm, and well drained, and easily tilled in all seasons, and is apparently best adapted to cotton and potatoes. About two-thirds of the tillable area is devoted to cotton, which usually grows to a height of 6 feet, in wet seasons higher; 5 feet is the most productive height. On newly cleared land, in wet seasons, there is a tendency to run to weed, which is restrained by topping the plant at 5 feet in July or August. On fresh land the product per acre of seed-cotton is from 1,000 to 1,400 pounds, 1,665 pounds being requisite for 475 pounds of lint, rating from middling to fair. After the land has been under cultivation for ten years the yield is reduced to 600 or 800 pounds of seed-cotton per acre, 1,720 pounds being necessary for 475 pounds of lint, the staple being a little shorter than that from fresh land. Some land lies "turned out", not producing well when again cultivated. The soil washes readily on slopes, doing serious damage, and to some extent injuring the valleys. No efforts have been made to check the damage. Cocklebur and crab-grass are the troublesome weeds, the latter being a great pest on this third-rate land.

Cotton is hauled to Austin, as soon as baled, at the rate of 50 cents per bale, and thence by railroad to Galveston or to New Orleans, freight being about $6 per bale.

CALDWELL.

Population : 11,757.—White, 7,723; colored, 4,034.

Area : 540 square miles.—Woodland, greater part; oak, hickory, and pine region, 400 square miles; central black prairie region, 140 square miles.

Tilled lands : 54,914 acres.—Area planted in cotton, 18,906 acres ; in corn, 18,393 acres ; in oats, 1,364 acres ; in wheat, 2,566 acres.

Cotton production : 7,609 bales ; average cotton product per acre, 0.40 bale, 600 pounds seed-cotton, or 200 pounds cotton lint.

Caldwell, one of the southeastern border counties of the central region, though having a large proportion of open prairie, is well timbered with post oak, hickory, etc. Its surface is undulating and well watered by numerous creeks. The northern and western part of the county is of the black waxy prairie character of the central region, while the rest is partly dark sandy prairie and partly oak and hickory sandy uplands. The rocks of the county are limestones of the Cretaceous on the west, and red ferruginous sandstone of the Tertiary hills near Luling and northward. In Williamson's prairie, south of Lockhart, the county-seat, there have been found an abundance of well-preserved Tertiary Eocene fossils.

The prairies vary in breadth from 6 to 30 miles, and are interspersed with streams having a timber growth of live oak, elm, ash, hickory, and cottonwood. Lockhart is situated in a grove of live oaks, which are festooned with long moss (*Tillandsia usneoides*), and an open prairie stretches away immediately on the west and south. The town is supplied with water from the Lockhart springs, 20 in number.

Caldwell is an agricultural county, the lands under cultivation comprising 15.9 per cent. of its area, an average of 101.7 acres per square mile. Cotton is a prominent crop, with an average of 35 acres per square mile and a yield per acre greater than that for the state. The prairies are largely devoted to stock grazing.

The uplands of the county are rolling and level, comprising hog-wallow prairies and timbered sandy loams, and some of the prairies, though black, are rocky and covered with a growth of mesquite.

The lands devoted to the cultivation of cotton comprise black sandy loam, light post-oak sandy, and black waxy prairie. The soil best adapted to cotton is the *black sandy loam*, although the black prairie stands the drought well and a good yield is obtained from it, but it is hard to get a stand on it. The black sandy loam comprises one-quarter, the light post-oak sandy one-quarter, and the black waxy one-half of the county. The first two occur only in spots.

The natural timber of the light post-oak sandy lands is pecan, elm, hickory, and post, and black-jack oaks; it is underlaid by a subsoil of red clay. The black waxy is from 2 to 6 feet in depth; the subsoil is mainly concrete, though in some cases it is joint clay, and is underlaid by rock at from 4 to 90 feet. The soil is not easily tillable in dry seasons, and is early and well drained.

The chief crops of the county are cotton, corn, and some wheat. Cotton forms one-half of the total crops, the height usually obtained being from 4 to 5 feet; in wet weather there is an inclination to run to weed, but this is restrained to some extent by topping, which also favors bolling. The product per acre of seed-cotton, when the land is fresh, is 1,000 pounds, 1,780 pounds being necessary for a 475-pound bale; when clean the staple rates as good, ordinary and middling. After four years' cultivation the product per acre is from 1,200 pounds to 1,500 pounds. The most troublesome weeds are tie-vines, cockleburs, and sunflowers. The black waxy soil does not wash readily; the sandy does, and sometimes the damage by such washings is quite serious.

The shipments are made chiefly from September to January by means of wagons and railroads to Galveston, Houston, and New York, the rates ranging from $3 75 to $5 per bale.

HAYES.

Population : 7,555.—White, 6,076; colored, 1,479.
Area : 680 square miles.—Woodland, very little; all central black prairie.
Tilled lands : 32,711 acres.—Area planted in cotton, 9,868 acres; in corn, 10,749 acres; in oats, 2,223 acres; in wheat, 2,789 acres.
Cotton production : 3,441 bales; average cotton product per acre, 0.35 bale, 525 pounds seed-cotton, or 175 pounds cotton lint.

Hayes is a prairie county, but its surface is undulating and somewhat rolling on the east, and hilly and mountainous on the west, where there is an abundant growth of Spanish and live oaks, cedar, elm, mesquite, etc. It is watered by the San Marcos river and numerous small tributary streams, all flowing southeastward. There are a number of excellent springs in various localities. The lands of the county are the black, waxy soil of the prairies and the sandy soils of the narrow skirts of timbers, underlaid by Cretaceous rotten limestones. Lands under cultivation average 48.1 acres per square mile, and the crops of the county are corn, cotton, small grain, and fruits. The soils are very productive, yielding from 500 to 1,000 pounds of seed-cotton per acre. The prairies are largely devoted to stock grazing. Corn is, however, the chief crop, its acreage being much greater than that of cotton. The latter has an average of 14.5 acres per square mile, which is 30.2 per cent. of the lands under cultivation. The county is sparsely settled, with an average of about eleven persons per square mile.

Shipments of cotton are made either to Austin on the north, or to the railroad stations on the south, the county lying about midway between the two points.

BLANCO.

Population : 3,583.—White, 3,415; colored, 168.
Area : 710 square miles.—Woodland, some; central black prairie region, 580 square miles; northwestern red loam, 130 square miles.
Tilled lands : 16,090 acres.—Area planted in cotton, 3,039 acres; in corn, 5,382 acres; in oats, 597 acres; in wheat, 2,106 acres.
Cotton production : 690 bales; average cotton product per acre, 0.23 bale, 345 pounds seed-cotton, or 115 pounds cotton lint.

Blanco is a hilly and broken prairie county, and is chiefly devoted to stock raising. It is watered by the Perdernales river and tributaries. The lands of the county are almost entirely of the black, waxy character common to the central prairie region.

The timber growth of the county is post and live oaks, pecan, some hickory, etc. The county is sparsely settled, with an average of five persons per square mile. The lands under cultivation embrace but 3.5 per cent. of the county area, an average of 22.7 acres per square mile. Of the latter, 4.3 acres are devoted to the culture of cotton.

There are two classes of lands employed in the cultivation of cotton, namely, the black stiff prairie and the sandy creek lands, with a sandy or gravelly subsoil. The chief soil is the *black waxy prairie*, which forms nine-tenths of the county, and extends 20 miles northward, 50 miles in a southerly direction, and about 150 miles to the west. The natural growth of the timbered portion is post, Spanish, black-jack, and shin oaks, cedar, pecan, elm, and cottonwood. The soil is a black, heavy clay loam 2 feet in depth, the subsoil being mostly red clay, underlaid by rock at from 4 to 6 feet. It is a warm, early, well drained, and in dry seasons easily tillable soil.

The chief crops of the county are corn, wheat, oats, cotton, sorghum, and grasses. Summer droughts do more harm to the crops than anything else. Cotton and wheat are best adapted to the soil, the former amounting to one-third of the crops. The height usually attained by cotton is from 2 to 8 feet, the most productive height being about 3½ feet. When the season is wet and the cotton late there is a tendency to run to weed. There is but little, if any, difference between the yield of fresh land and that which has been under cultivation twenty years, the product per acre in seed-cotton being from 1,500 to 1,800 pounds, 1,780 pounds of which are necessary to make a 475-pound bale of lint. The rating is middling to good middling, either for fresh land or for that from land which has been under cultivation for twenty years. The most troublesome weeds are sunflowers and cockleburs. None of the land lies "turned out", nor does it wash.

November and December are the months in which shipments are usually made, being hauled by wagons to Austin and San Antonio at $2 per bale.

GILLESPIE.

Population : 5,228.—White, 5,096; colored, 132.

Area : 980 square miles.—Woodland, a little; central black prairie region, 620 square miles; northwestern red loam, 160 square miles; table-lands, 200 square miles.

Tilled lands : 10,127 acres.—Area planted in cotton, 4,082 acres; in corn, 5,297 acres; in oats, 527 acres; in wheat, 3,533 acres.

Cotton production : 767 bales; average cotton product per acre, 0.19 bale, 285 pounds seed-cotton, or 95 pounds cotton lint.

Gillespie is one of the most western of the cotton counties of the state, and lies west from Austin. The surface of the country is hilly or mountainous, with timbered areas and broad valley lands of open mesquite prairies. The Perdernales river, with its tributaries, flows in an easterly course through the lower part of the county, while on the north a few small tributaries of the Colorado river flow northeast. Most of the county is included in the dark or black prairie region of the Cretaceous, its limestones forming the hills of the south. On the north are the red sandy soils, sandstones, granites, and other rocks of the western region. The east and west divide between the tributaries of the two rivers mentioned probably marks the line between the two regions. Fredericksburg, the county-seat, is said to be 1,500 feet above the sea.

The population of Gillespie county is almost exclusively German, and averages 5.3 persons per square mile. The lands under cultivation comprise about 1.6 per cent. of the county area, averaging 10.3 acres per square mile, of which 4.2 is devoted to cotton culture. Corn is the chief crop, cotton and wheat ranking next. Their respective yields were very small for the year 1879, the average of seed-cotton being but 285 pounds.

ABSTRACTS FROM THE REPORTS OF THOMAS B. SPLITTGERBER AND ADOLPH WEISS, OF FREDERICKSBURG, AND B. F. WHITE, OF MARTINSBURG.

The soils devoted to cotton are the black and yellow lowlands, lying on slopes in patches; the dark sandy mesquite prairies; the black sandy loam of Perdernales river; and the post-oak soils of the southeast.

The *black waxy prairies* are the chief lands of the county, covering two-thirds of its area, and have a scattering growth of post and live oaks and mesquite. They occur along the limestone hills and mountains, and in the valleys between them. The soil is a black waxy clay from 1 foot to 4 feet deep, and is underlaid by heavy red clay, which is very difficult to till in wet weather, but very easy in dry. The chief crops are cotton, corn, wheat, rye, oats, sweet and Irish potatoes. Cotton comprises one-third of the crops, and grows to a height of from 3 to 4 feet, yielding from 800 to 1,000 pounds of seed-cotton, 1,485 pounds being required for a 475-pound bale of lint. After five years' cultivation the soil improves, and yields from 1,000 to 1,500 pounds of seed-cotton, with no change in other respects. Careless and purslane weeds are the most troublesome.

The *post-oak uplands* extend from west to east about 20 miles and from north to south about 25 miles, and have a growth of post and black-jack oaks and hickory. The soil is a black or yellowish fine sandy loam 18 inches in depth, with a subsoil of orange-red loam, which becomes like the soil by cultivation. It is underlaid by sand-rock at a depth of from 12 to 15 feet. The soil is easily tilled in wet as well as in dry seasons, is early, warm, and well drained, and produces wheat, cotton, potatoes, and sorghum. About one-third of the crops is of cotton, which grows to a height of about 3½ feet, producing 800 pounds of seed-cotton when fresh. A few years' cultivation improves the land, the yield increasing to 1,000 pounds. From fresh land 1,545 pounds of seed-cotton are required for a 475-pound bale of lint, but otherwise only 1,495 pounds. Crab-grass and worm-weed are the most troublesome weeds.

The *dark mesquite prairies* comprise about one-third of the lands of the county, and extend from west to east about 20 miles and from north to south about 18 miles. They have a natural timber growth of live and Spanish oaks and mesquite. The soil is a light, fine, sandy loam, black in color, and 3 feet in depth. The subsoil is a tough yellow clay, which bakes very hard where exposed, but becomes like the soil by cultivation. It is quite impervious when undisturbed, and contains hard-rounded pebbles, and is underlaid by lime-rock at from 5 to 10 feet. The soil is rather difficult to till in wet seasons, but usually not troublesome. It is early when well drained, and apparently is best adapted to cotton, corn, potatoes, and sorghum. Cotton forms about one-third of the crops here, and usually is most productive at a height of 3 feet. The cotton-plant has never been known to run to weed here. The seed-cotton product per acre is about 700 pounds on fresh land, 1,545 pounds being necessary to make a 475-pound bale of lint. The seed-cotton product per acre, after three years' cultivation, is 900 pounds, and 1,495 pounds then make a 475-pound bale of lint, which rates about the same as that from fresh land. The most troublesome weeds are sunflower, cocklebur, and crab-grass. None of these lands lie "turned out".

The *black loam soils* of Perdernales river and small patches on the mountains cover about one-third of the county, and are scattered about in areas varying from 50 to 5,000 acres. The natural growth is pecan, elm, and hackberry. The soil is a black heavy clay loam, from 8 to 10 feet deep, with a tough yellowish black clay subsoil, which bakes very hard where exposed, but gradually becomes like the surface soil. It is quite impervious when undisturbed, and contains hard white gravel, and sometimes large pebbles inclosing sea shells; it is underlaid by rather hard sandy rock at from 5 to 15 feet. The soil is very difficult to till in wet seasons, is late and well drained, and is best adapted to corn and sorghum. About one-fifth of these lands is devoted to cotton, which usually grows to a height of about 2½ feet, and is most productive at that height. Cotton has never been known to run to weed on these lands. The seed-cotton product per acre of fresh land is 600 pounds, and 1,545 pounds are required for a 475-pound bale of lint. After three years' cultivation the yield is increased to 800 pounds, then 1,495 pounds are necessary for a 475-pound bale of lint, which rates the same as that from fresh land. The most troublesome weeds are sunflower and cocklebur. No land lies "turned out".

The *post-oak lands* in the southeast have a fine sandy soil from 6 to 8 inches in depth of a brown to red color; its subsoil is a red loam, containing flint pebbles. It produces cotton, corn, wheat, and oats, is early, warm, and well drained, and readily tillable in either wet or dry seasons.

The lowlands are preferred, because the cotton grows faster, although it is later, and is liable to be killed by early frosts. It is said to grow well, and with ordinary care a full crop is assured. The fiber is of a superior quality, and commands the highest price in the market. Drought is the only hinderance to cotton growing, and that is becoming less frequent than formerly.

Shipments are made from September to January, by wagon, to Austin or San Antonio, the rate being $2 50 per bale.

KERR.

Population : 2,168.—White, 2,075; colored, 93.
Area : 1,100 square miles.—Woodland, a little; all central black prairie.
Tilled lands : 9,481 acres.—Area planted in cotton, 469 acres; in corn, 1,348 acres; in oats, 185 acres; in wheat, 1,134 acres.
Cotton production : 72 bales; average cotton product per acre, 0.15 bale, 225 pounds seed-cotton, or 75 pounds cotton lint.

Kerr is one of the extreme western organized counties in the central region. It has a very small population, averaging about two persons per square mile. The surface of the country is hilly and broken, and watered by the headwaters of the Guadalupe river. The valley of this river is said to be from 1 to 3 miles wide, and is covered in places with timber, while in others the prairie extends for miles. Like the adjoining counties, Kerr is largely devoted to stock raising, and but 1.3 per cent. of the area is under cultivation, averaging 8.6 acres per square mile. The people give but little attention to the culture of cotton. The proportion of tilled lands given to this crop was, in 1879, only about 4.9 per cent., or four-tenths of an acre per square mile. The first crop was planted in 1870.

ABSTRACT FROM THE REPORT OF W. P. COLEMAN, OF KERRVILLE.

The surface of the county is hilly, but the valley lands are level between the hills and the river. Some of the lands are timbered, and some are not. The lands devoted to cotton culture lie in patches along the river and creeks, the same kind never extending to any great distance. There are three kinds, namely, the black valley, the clay loam, and the gray valley soil.

The chief soil is the *black valley land*, which covers about two-thirds of the county, the natural growth being live, Spanish, and post oaks. The soil is a heavy black clay loam, 18 inches deep, with a subsoil of red or yellowish clay, underlaid by gravel at 4 or 5 feet. It is an early, warm, and well-drained soil, in wet seasons difficult and in dry seasons easily cultivated. The chief crops of the county are cotton, wheat, oats, and rye. Cotton and corn do very well, but oats are best adapted to the soil. Between one-third and one-fourth of the crops planted consist of cotton, which usually attains a height of from 3 to 4 feet, at which it is most productive, running to weed only in very wet seasons. Topping is the remedy applied. The yield per acre of seed-cotton is altogether dependent on the season, varying all the way from 400 to 1,500 pounds, 1,545 pounds being the necessary amount for a 475-pound bale of lint. The rating is from middling to good middling. After the land has been in cultivation ten years the yield is from 600 to 1,500 pounds of seed-cotton per acre, being, as in case of fresh land, dependent on the season, 1,485 pounds being necessary for a 475-pound bale. The rating is generally improved the longer the land is cultivated. The most troublesome weeds in this, as well as in the other two soils, are the sunflower and careless-weed. No land lies "turned out"; this also applies to the other two soils. There is very little washing of the soil.

The *post-oak land* comprises but a small part of the county, occurring generally in small patches. When it extends for any distance, it is only up and down the river and creeks. There is very little natural timber on these lands—some live-oak trees and bushes. The soil is a light gray silt from 15 to 16 inches deep, early, warm, well drained, and easy to till in either wet or dry seasons. The subsoil is yellowish clay, underlaid by gravel, which sometimes is found near the surface. Cotton comprises about one-third of the crops. The height attained is from 3 to 4 feet, either of which is equally good for production. The soil yields 1,300 pounds of seed-cotton per acre both when fresh and after seven years' cultivation, 1,485 pounds being necessary for a 475-pound bale of middling lint. Careless-weed is the most troublesome.

Shipments are made by wagon to San Antonio, and thence by rail to Galveston.

KENDALL.

Population : 2,763.—White, 2,588; colored, 175.
Area : 670 square miles.—Woodland, very little; all central black prairie.
Tilled lands : 9,410 acres.—Area planted in cotton, 1,808 acres; in corn, 3,657 acres; in oats, 655 acres; in wheat, 1,167 acres.
Cotton production : 286 bales; average cotton product per acre, 0.16 bale, 240 pounds seed-cotton, or 80 pounds cotton lint.

Kendall is a hilly and broken county, well watered by the Guadalupe river and tributaries and Cibolo creek. It is largely a prairie country, with a black-loam soil, but the tillable lands are in small bodies. There is an abundant supply of timber, consisting of live, post, white, and black-jack oaks; cedar, elm, walnut, and a variety of wild apple, plum, cherry, etc. The timbered lands are said to cover two-thirds of the county. While this is an excellent stock country, it is also largely devoted to agriculture, the crops being cotton, corn, wheat, oats, and potatoes. Corn is the chief crop. The low average yield per acre of seed-cotton, as shown by the census returns for 1879, is perhaps due to the extreme drought of that season. Other crops of that year were almost failures. Lands under cultivation comprise 2.2 per cent. of the county area, an average of 14 acres per square mile. Of the latter 2.7 acres are devoted to the culture of cotton.

ABSTRACT FROM THE REPORT OF C. H. CLAUSS, OF BOERNE.

Kendall county is situated in the mountainous part of western Texas. The area of tillable lands is smaller than that of the pasture lands of the mountains, and therefore the farms are small, containing not more than 40 or 50 acres.

The lands devoted to the cultivation of cotton are the strong black post oak, mixed sometimes with flinty pebbles and reddish clay, the black prairie, and a light sandy river bottom soil.

The *strong black post oak soil*, the one best adapted to cotton, has been under cultivation for fifteen years, and still yields as good a crop as ever. The cotton stalk reaches a height of 4 feet, and yields 1,900 pounds of seed-cotton per acre, making one-third of its weight of clean lint.

The *black prairie soil* is well adapted to cotton, which grows 3 feet high and yields 1,500 pounds of seed-cotton per acre. Manuring is necessary after a cultivation of seven or eight years.

The *light sandy river bottoms* produce a low stalk, not more than 12 or 18 inches high, but when manured it will yield as much as the black prairie lands.

Cotton culture is in this county being constantly increased, the crop withstanding the dry seasons being better than other crops. The planters cultivate only what they are able to attend to themselves without hired help, and therefore the staple and quality are much better.

Cotton is shipped to Mexico and Galveston, and some to San Antonio.

COMAL.

Population: 5,546.—White, 5,276; colored, 270.

Area: 670 square miles.—Woodland, very little; all central black prairie.

Tilled lands: 33,414 acres.—Area planted in cotton, 5,860 acres; in corn, 8,990 acres; in oats, 861 acres; in wheat, 2,898 acres.

Cotton production: 2,102 bales; average cotton product per acre, 0.36 bale, 540 pounds seed-cotton, or 180 pounds cotton lint.

The county of Comal, situated in the southern part of the central prairie region, is rolling and hilly in character, the largest part of its surface being an open mesquite prairie, with black waxy and black sandy soils. The hills, or mountains, as they are called, because of their prominence, with their elevations of 300 feet, are too rough and rocky for tillage.

The streams are timbered with black and post oaks, walnut, hickory, pecan, elm, etc. The Comal river is said to have a fall of 40 feet in a distance of 3 miles, furnishing good water-power, which is partially utilized. The Guadalupe river is the principal stream of the county, flowing through it in a southeast course.

Among the crops of the county fruits of many kinds are said to be largely and successfully cultivated. The population is largely German, especially in and near the town of New Braunfels, the county-seat. The county is not thickly settled, the average per square mile being but 8.3 persons. Nearly 8 per cent. of the county area is under cultivation, averaging 40.9 acres per square mile. Corn is the chief crop, though cotton, with its average of 8.7 acres per square mile, is a prominent product. Much attention is given to stock raising.

ABSTRACT FROM THE REPORT OF R. WIPPRECHT, OF NEW BRAUNFELS.

About two-thirds of this county is a rolling, black waxy prairie, and the remainder mountainous and hilly, rising at once 300 feet above the prairie. The growth on the prairies is mesquite, and along the streams live and post oaks, elm, hackberry, and pecan.

The *prairies* are the chief cotton lands, with a black clay soil from 5 to 25 feet in depth, having a subsoil which in some places is a yellow clay with strata of gravel, and in others a yellow-grayish loam, impervious (and hence used for cisterns), and underlaid by a kind of blue impervious clay of unknown thickness. The land is very difficult to till in wet seasons, and in dry seasons good teams are required. It is early and ill drained, and produces crops of corn, cotton, wheat, oats, sweet potatoes, and sorghum. Cotton comprises one-third of the crops, and grows to a height of 5 feet, producing 1,300 pounds of seed-cotton per acre, 2,090 pounds being required for a 475-pound bale of lint, which rates as good middling. Ten years' cultivation reduces the yield to one-fourth less than that on fresh land, and requires 1,185 pounds for a 475-pound bale of middling lint. The morning-glory (*Convolvulus*) vine is most troublesome on these prairie lands. The soil washes readily on slopes, but the damage is not serious.

The *hilly uplands* are covered with a growth of cedar, live and post oaks, black-jack, pecan, elm, walnut, cypress, and mesquite. The soil is a gravelly loam, brown to black in color, and in places has an abundance of fossil shells. It is about 3 feet deep, and is underlaid by a subsoil of gravel and clay, or by rotten limestone. Cotton grows to a height of 4 feet, yielding about 1,000 pounds of seed-cotton per acre, the lint rating as good middling. After ten years' cultivation the yield is 800 pounds. The soil washes readily, doing serious damage in places, but not to the valleys below.

Shipments are made to Marion station, and thence to Galveston by railroad at $4 50 per bale.

GUADALUPE.

Population: 12,202.—White, 8,747; colored, 3,455.

Area: 710 square miles.—Woodland, about one half, oak, hickory, and pine region, 380 square miles; central black prairie region, 330 square miles.

Tilled lands: 69,680 acres.—Area planted in cotton, 16,469 acres; in corn, 23,501 acres; in oats, 2,260 acres; in wheat, 4,483 acres.

Cotton production: 6,531 bales; average cotton product per acre, 0.40 bale, 600 pounds seed-cotton, or 200 pounds cotton lint.

Guadalupe, lying in the southern part of the central prairie region, is largely a prairie county, rather rolling, and watered by the Guadalupe river, which flows through it, and by San Marcos river and Cibolo creek, which form its northeast and southwest boundaries.

The northwestern half of the county is covered by the black waxy prairie lands of the central region, on which a mesquite growth is abundant, with occasional motts or clumps of oak. Rotten limestone is the prevailing rock, but its outcrops are not as frequent as in the more hilly counties of the region. The soil is deep and very productive.

Adjoining these prairies on the southeast are others having a black sandy soil, but the belt is narrow and irregular. The extreme southeast part of the county is covered with a growth of mesquite and post oak, and properly belongs to the oak and hickory uplands that extend from the northeast into this section of the state.

Guadalupe is largely an agricultural county, 15.3 per cent. of its area being under cultivation, an average of 98.1 acres per square mile. Cotton is a prominent crop, though not the chief one, its average being 23.2 acres per square mile. The prairies are generally devoted to stock grazing.

The cotton lands of the county are the black waxy, the sandy, and the bottom soils.

The *black waxy prairies* are considered the chief cotton soils in the county, and extend about 50 miles east of Marion and north and west beyond the county-line. The growth on the prairies is mesquite and scattering post oak, with excellent grasses for grazing purposes. The soil is several feet deep, with beds of gravel and a clay understratum below it. As is usual with these black prairies, the soil is very difficult to cultivate in wet seasons. It is early, warm, and well drained, producing good crops of cotton, corn, wheat, oats, rye, barley, sorghum, and sweet potatoes. One-half of the land under cultivation is in cotton, which grows to a height of 5 feet, yielding about 1,700 pounds of seed-cotton per acre, 1,545 pounds making 475 pounds of lint, which rates as middling fair in market. There seems to be no change in the yield or the quality of the staple after twenty-five years' cultivation. Morning-glory vines and crab-grass are most troublesome.

The *sandy lands*, lying in the southeastern part of the county, have a growth of post oak and mesquite and a fine sandy soil varying in color from gray to brown and red. The soil is easily cultivated both in dry and wet seasons, producing good crops of cotton and all kinds of grain. Cotton grows to a height of 6 feet, producing 1,700 pounds of seed-cotton per acre. Grass burs are the most troublesome weeds. Bottom lands cover a very small area in the county.

Shipments of cotton are made by railroad from Marion station to Galveston at $4 50 per bale.

BEXAR.

Population: 30,470.—White, 26,603; colored, 3,867.

Area: 1,180 square miles.—Woodland, small part; oak, hickory, and pine region, 140 square miles; central black prairie, 1,040 square miles.

Tilled lands: 54,200 acres.—Area planted in cotton, 4,273 acres; in corn, 14,601 acres; in oats, 2,159 acres; in wheat, 1,597 acres.

Cotton production: 1,543 bales; average cotton product per acre, 0.36 bales, 540 pounds seed-cotton, or 180 pounds cotton lint.

Bexar county, of which San Antonio is the county-seat, is mostly a high and rolling prairie county, and is well watered by the San Antonio river and its tributaries. The prairie lands have a few scattering live-oak trees, and in places a thick growth of mesquite. The bottoms are rich and well timbered with mesquite, elm, hackberry, cottonwood, and pecan.

In the southern part of the county there is a strip of oak uplands with a gray sandy soil and yellow clay subsoil, the chief cotton land of that section. The prairies have usually a black waxy or bog-wallow soil, sandy in some localities, and in the eastern part of the county are underlaid by occasional beds of gravel and pebbles. The prairies cover the largest part of the county, and are almost exclusively devoted to the grazing of herds of cattle. Corn is the chief crop, its acreage being more than three times that of any other.

Previous to the late war there was little or no cotton produced in this county, and even now its acreage is small, averaging only 3.6 acres per square mile. The population is almost entirely concentrated in and around the city of San Antonio.

The uplands consist of black bog-wallow prairies. Those of the Cibolo and Saledo creeks vary, being in patches of from 10 to 1,000 acres, and on the Medina river from 100 to 1,000 acres.

The lands along the creeks are a dark loam soil, timbered with mesquite, elm, hackberry, and pecan; the adjoining prairie valleys are covered with mesquite and a few scattering oaks.

The chief land of this portion of the county is the *upland prairie*, with thin black bog-wallow clayey soils, interspersed with patches of a sandy nature. Live oak occurs in motts on this prairie, and mesquite is abundant. The depth of the soil is 2 feet, which is underlaid by a heavier clay subsoil, which, when exposed, bakes hard, but gradually becomes pulverized, and contains pebbles. The land is difficult to cultivate in wet weather, the chief crops being corn, wheat, oats, cotton, and potatoes. It seems best adapted to oats, as in some instances the yield has amounted to 110 bushels per acre. Cotton forms one-third of the crops, and grows to the height of 4 or 5 feet. The average yield is about 800 pounds of seed-cotton per acre, 1,665 pounds being required for a 475-pound bale. It rates as good ordinary. Sunflower, cocklebur, hog-weed, and crab-grass are the weeds giving the most amount of trouble.

The *sandy uplands* consist of post oak and hickory timbered lands, interspersed with some prairies. They extend about 10 miles east and west, and about 15 miles north and south. The soil is a fine sandy loam, 2 feet in depth, over a heavier subsoil. It is early, warm, well drained, and best adapted to corn, cotton, and sweet potatoes. About one-third of the crops is in cotton. The height usually attained by the plant is between 4 and 5 feet; but when the season is very wet there is a tendency to run to weed, and no remedy is applied to restrain it. The product in seed-cotton per acre from fresh land is from 800 to 1,500 pounds; after four years the yield is diminished to from 500 to 1,200 pounds, depending upon seasons and cultivation. In both cases the amount requisite for 475 pounds of lint is 1,785 pounds. Burs, crab-grass, and careless-weed are the most troublesome weeds. No land lies "turned out". The soil washes on slopes, but the damage is not of a serious nature. The late frosts often kill early planted cotton on the bottom lands, while that of the adjoining uplands would not be at all injured. Previous to the war this was a stock-raising county.

ABSTRACT FROM THE REPORT OF THEO. E. S. TRIP, OF SAN ANTONIO.

(Lands of the southern part of the county.)

The lowlands are more apt to damage the young cotton than the uplands. The soils used consist of three varieties, viz: (1) Gray loamy valley land, lying mostly on the west side of the Medina river. (2) Black loamy valley land, principally on the east side of the Medina river. (3) Gray sandy land on Elm creek and Atascosa river.

The natural growth of the *gray loam*, which is the chief soil devoted to cotton cultivation and comprises one-half of the region, is mesquite and live oak. The depth is 18 inches, and it has a subsoil resembling hard-pan, except in its not being able to hold water, and is underlaid by yellow clay at about 3 feet. The soil, which produces cotton, corn, oats, and wheat, is early, well drained, and easily

700

tilled in either wet or dry seasons. Very little cotton is raised; the height of the plant is usually 4 feet, yielding about 1,200 pounds of seed-cotton per acre, and requiring 1,600 pounds for a 475-pound bale, and there seems to be no decrease in the yield of the land or in the rating of the staple even after twenty-five years' cultivation. Cocklebur and sunflower form the most troublesome weeds, although all weeds can be kept down by proper cultivation. No land lies "turned out". There have not been any efforts made to check the damage arising from the washings of the soil.

The *black loamy or waxy land* forms about one-fourth of the region, and lies in spots all over the county. It has a natural growth of mesquite and a little live oak. The soil is a black loam, with a subsoil similar to that of the last soil, which is very difficult to cultivate in wet seasons, but is best adapted apparently to corn, cotton, and oats, and is early, warm, and well drained. About one-fifth of the land is devoted to cotton, which attains a height of from 4 to 5 feet, the latter the most desirable. It never runs to weed. The land seems to be inexhaustible, as there appears to be no difference in the yield from fresh or from cultivated land, in both cases it being from 1,200 to 1,400 pounds of seed-cotton per acre, 1,600 pounds being necessary for a 475-pound bale, rating as middling. The remarks made above concerning weeds, etc., apply also to this soil and to the following one.

The *gray sandy lands*, which constitute the larger portion of the tillable lands of this section, have a gray sandy soil, with a natural growth of post oak principally, with some live oak and mesquite brush. The subsoil is yellow clay, with gravel in spots. The soil seems best adapted to cotton (which constitutes about one-half the crop), corn, and sweet potatoes. It is early, warm, and well drained, and tolerably easy to till in wet, but not so easy in dry seasons. Cotton usually attains a height of from 4½ to 5 feet, never runs to weed, and yields from 900 to 1,000 pounds of seed-cotton per acre on fresh and old land, 1,660 pounds being necessary for a 475-pound bale. Rating is good or ordinary.

Cotton is usually sold to merchants or cotton agents at the gin, and then shipped by rail from San Antonio to Houston and Galveston, freight being from $4 10 to $5 per bale.

MEDINA.

Population: 4,492.—White, 4,209; colored, 283.
Area: 1,300 square miles.—Woodland, a little; mostly central black prairie region.
Tilled lands: 16,987 acres.—Area planted in cotton, 685 acres; in corn, 11,600 acres; in oats, 1,069 acres; in wheat, 1,008 acres.
Cotton production: 289 bales; average cotton product per acre, 0.42 bale, 630 pounds seed-cotton, or 210 pounds cotton lint.

Medina, one of the western counties of the state, is principally a stock-raising section. The surface of the country is hilly and broken, and is largely timbered, with a belt of post-oak lands beginning west of Castroville and extending southeastward into the adjoining counties. Black waxy and hog-wallow prairie lands are found in localities.

The county is sparsely settled, with an average of more than three persons and 13.1 acres of tilled land per square mile. Corn is the chief crop of the county, cotton having an acreage of only 4 per cent. of the lands under cultivation, though its average yield is more than that for the state at large.

ABSTRACT FROM THE REPORT OF DR. A. WADGYMAR, OF SAN ANTONIO.

The uplands of the county are hilly, partly black prairie and partly hog-wallow, varying greatly from one ridge to another, being in patches of from 3 to 8 acres each. Sandy, loamy (so-called post oak) black hog-wallow and alluvial river bottom are the kinds of lands employed in cotton cultivation.

The chief soil is the *sandy, loamy post oak*, which averages from 1½ to 2 feet in depth; its subsoil is a tough bluish clay This soil predominates in the eastern and northern parts of the county, and produces one-third of all the cotton grown. The natural timber growth is post oak and mesquite. The subsoil is underlaid by soft rock at from 4 to 50 feet. The chief crops of the county are corn, tobacco, and cotton. The soil is early when well drained, and is best adapted to corn and cotton. Cotton usually attains a height of from 4 to 5 feet, but is most productive when at 4 feet. The tendency to run to weed is great in rainy seasons, and also is owing to neglect in cultivation. The free use of the plow and the hoe will tend to increase the production of bolls. The product per acre of seed-cotton is from 1,800 to 2,300 pounds on fresh land, or on land after 20 years' cultivation. The soil washes readily on slopes. Sometimes the damage so arising is quite serious, and in some years the valleys suffer considerable injury from the washings of the uplands, but no efforts have been made to check this evil. The most troublesome weeds are the burdock and stickle grass. None of the land now lies "turned out".

The *black prairie hog-wallow*, commonly designated as upland soil, and forming one-sixth of all the farming land, is from 9 to 30 inches in depth, and has a subsoil of tough bluish clay, intermixed with flint pebbles, the underlying rock being limestone. The natural growth is live and black-jack oaks and mesquite. The soil is best adapted to cotton, which forms nearly all the upland crops, and the height at which it is most productive is about 3 feet. The running to weed, owing to neglect in cultivation, may be restrained and bolling favored by plowing and hoeing. The lands yield, even after ten years' cultivation, 700 pounds of seed-cotton per acre. The most troublesome weed is the stickle grass. Very little land now lies "turned out", and when again taken into cultivation it produces well.

The *alluvial river bottom lands*, comprising one-half the lands of the county, extend along the Medina, Hondo, and Francisco Perez rivers for a distance of 26 miles. The natural growth is cypress, pecan, live oak, hackberry, and willow. Cotton in the lowlands is liable to be damaged by overflow in rainy seasons, growing profusely in leaves, and yields less than the uplands; but the lowlands are preferred to the uplands, because, owing to the late, dry seasons and long droughts, the cotton in the latter is most likely to dry out and die. The soil has a thick layer of humus and a depth of 3 feet, and is best adapted to corn; the subsoil is gravel, containing large flinty pebbles, underlaid by sandstone at 8 feet. Cotton forms one-half of the crops planted, and grows to a height of 5 or 6 feet. Overflow and neglect in cultivation cause the plant to run to weed, and remedy is the same as in the case of soil previously described. Fresh land produces 1,800 pounds of seed-cotton per acre, and the yield is the same after the land has been in cultivation for ten years. The most troublesome weeds are burdock and Spanish needles. None of the land lies "turned out".

Shipments are usually made after the picking, by wagon, to San Antonio, and thence by rail to Saint Louis, at $5 per bale.

BANDERA.

Population: 2,158.—White, 2,127; colored, 31.
Area: 1,000 square miles.—Woodland, very little; all central black prairie.
Tilled lands: 11,628 acres.—Area planted in cotton, 223 acres; in corn, 3,641 acres; in oats, 259 acres; in wheat, 1,200 acres.
Cotton production: 52 bales; average cotton product per acre, 0.23 bale, 345 pounds seed-cotton, or 115 pounds cotton lint.

Bandera is a high, hilly, and broken prairie county, very sparsely settled, and principally devoted to stock-raising. The streams of the eastern and southern part of the county are tributaries of the San Antonio and the Nueces rivers. But little attention is given to the culture of cotton, there being only about 2 per cent. of the tilled lands in that crop.

The soil is mostly the stiff black prairie land of the central black prairie region, underlaid by soft white limestone (Cretaceous). The county is very sparsely populated, the average being about 2.2 persons per square mile; that of lands under cultivation is 11.6 acres per square mile, or 1.8 per cent. of the county area.

John Christall, of Bandera, writes:

There is not enough cotton grown in this county to form data upon which any calculations could be made. The chief cotton soil is that of the valleys, which is black, from vegetable mold. The natural timber is live, post, and Spanish oaks, pecan, and cedar. The soil is 3 feet deep, having a subsoil varying from gravelly to clay. The land is early, warm, well drained, and easily tillable in either wet or dry seasons. The chief crops are corn and wheat, corn being the one best adapted to the soil.

UVALDE.

Population: 2,541.—White, 2,478; colored, 63.
Area: 1,550 square miles.—Woodland, a little; central black prairie, 610 square miles; southern prairies, 270 square miles; table-lands, 670 square miles.
Tilled lands: 3,466 acres.—Area planted in cotton, 141 acres; in corn, 1,345 acres; in oats, 91 acres; in wheat, 407 acres.
Cotton production: 53 bales; average cotton product per acre, 0.38 bale, 570 pounds seed-cotton, or 190 pounds cotton lint.

The surface of Uvalde county is rolling and broken, especially on the north, and is watered by a number of streams flowing southward. The southern part of the county is mostly a prairie, interspersed with timbered lands along the various streams, and included in the southwestern prairie region; the northern portion is hilly, with outcropping Cretaceous limestones, and embraces the black prairie lands of the central region, which are too broken for cultivation except in small areas. The crops of the county are corn, wheat, oats, etc., but a system of irrigation is necessary, because of the dryness of the seasons. The population does not average two persons per square mile, and stock raising is the chief occupation. Very little cotton is cultivated, owing in part to the great distance from market and the difficulty of transportation, as well as to the local causes mentioned. The lands under cultivation average 2.2 acres per square mile.

T. W. Redman, of Uvalde, writes:

About two-thirds of the county on the south is a rolling prairie, with heavy timber on the streams, consisting of mesquite, live oak, elm, and pecan, with some cypress, hackberry, and sycamore. On the north it is hilly, and is known as a part of the Anakacha range. Solid white limestone is abundant, with an occasional stratum of flint bowlders.

NORTHWESTERN RED-LOAM PRAIRIE REGION.

Comprises all or parts of the cotton counties of Clay, Baylor, Archer, Jack, Young, Throckmorton, Jones, Shackelford, Stephens, Palo Pinto, Erath,* Eastland, Callahan, Taylor, Coleman, Brown, Comanche, San Saba, McCulloch, Mason, Llano, Burnet, Williamson,* Travis,* Blanco,* and Gillespie.*

BORDER COUNTIES OF THE COTTON REGION (with brief descriptions): Wichita, Baylor, Archer, Throckmorton, Jones, Shackelford, Callahan, Taylor, McCulloch, and Mason.

OTHER COUNTIES (not described): Hardeman, Wilbarger, Knox, Haskell, Runnels, Concho, Menard, and Kimble.

CLAY.

Population: 5,045.—White, 5,019; colored, 26.
Area: 1,100 square miles.—Woodland, very little; all northwestern red-loam prairies.
Tilled lands: 24,538 acres.—Area planted in cotton, 3,289 acres; in corn, 8,778 acres; in oats, 1,343 acres; in wheat, 2,282 acres.
Cotton production: 1,155 bales; average cotton product per acre, 0.35 bale, 525 pounds seed-cotton, or 175 pounds cotton lint.

Clay is one of the Red river counties of the northwestern prairie region. Its surface is high and rolling, with prominent hills and ridges. The country is mostly an open prairie, with skirts of timbered lands along the streams, and a growth of oaks, walnut, ash, elm, pecan, cottonwood, hackberry, mesquite, and bois d'arc. The county is well watered by the Little and Big Wichita rivers and their tributaries, all flowing into Red river.

Clay is chiefly a stock-raising county, for which its broad prairies are admirably suited. The lands have a red loam soil, very productive in fair seasons, yielding 800 pounds of seed-cotton per acre. The lands under cultivation comprise 3.5 per cent. of the area, an average of 22.3 acres per square mile. Corn is the chief crop, its acreage being more than twice that of cotton, which has an average of 3 acres per square mile. Gainesville is the nearest railroad point, to which cotton is hauled by wagon for shipment.

ABSTRACT FROM THE REPORT OF WILLIAM M. POPE, OF BUFFALO SPRINGS.

The upland soil consists chiefly of red prairie in bodies of from 160 to 500 acres, and a less amount of black prairies. These bodies are interspersed with groves of post-oak timber. The soil is chiefly a red loam, 18 inches deep, which contains soft, limy pebbles, and is underlaid by soft sandstone at from 10 to 90 feet. The soil is easily tilled, early, well drained (for the most part), and best adapted to corn, cotton, and sweet potatoes. Cotton is the second crop of the county. The plant grows from 2½ to 3 feet high, and inclines to run to weed in wet weather, the remedy for which is to plow close to the roots. The seed-cotton product per acre is 800 pounds, 1,665 pounds making a 475-pound bale of second grade lint. The second year the staple is better and the proportion of seed is less. The rag-weed is most troublesome. On the uplands cotton can be planted ten days earlier, and fall frosts are three weeks later; therefore uplands are preferred. Cotton is shipped during the winter to Galveston and to Saint Louis.

JACK.

Population: 6,626.—White, 6,508; colored, 118.
Area: 870 square miles.—Woodland, some; all northwestern red-loam prairie.
Tilled lands: 29,338 acres.—Area planted in cotton, 4,751 acres; in corn, 10,990 acres; in oats, 230 acres; in wheat, 1,866 acres.
Cotton production: 1,444 bales; average cotton product per acre, 0.30 bale, 450 pounds seed-cotton, or 150 pounds cotton lint.

Jack is a rolling and somewhat hilly county, with open prairies and timbered lands, and is watered by some of the headwaters of the Trinity river, which flow in an easterly direction. The prairies cover the largest portion of the county, and have reddish sandy loam soils, mesquite grasses, and an occasional low growth of mesquite trees. (See analysis, page 37.) In the valley lands of these prairies the outcropping limestones (Carboniferous) frequently give to the soils a stiff black, calcareous nature, and this is the character of the lands along some of the streams, where there is a growth of burr and spotted oaks, elm, and hackberry. Post oak is perhaps the most prominent timber growth of the county, covering large bodies of the uplands, and is associated with black-jack oak on the ridges and hills. The ridges and chains of hills have usually a trend northeast and southwest, with abrupt sides to the southeast, narrow summits, capped with heavy beds of red sandstones, and gradual descents on the west into the broad open valleys, which, after a width of a few miles, are again terminated by another and similar chain.

The valley of Keechi creek, about 6 miles wide, is well timbered, and has a dark sandy loam soil, which is said to produce 1,000 pounds of seed-cotton per acre. In the southern part of the county are the post, red, and black-jack oak lands of the upper cross timbers, with deep sandy soils and associated red sandstones.

Jack is largely a stock-raising county, and its grassy prairies are well adapted to that purpose. The population is rather sparse, the average being not quite eight persons per square mile. Cultivated lands average 33.7 acres per square mile. Cotton is not a very prominent crop, its acreage comprising in the census year only about 16.2 per cent. of the lands under cultivation. Its average yield per acre was small.

ABSTRACT FROM THE REPORT OF C. M. SNODGRASS, OF JACKSBORO'.

This county consists mostly of uplands, which embrace both prairie and timber lands. Three kinds of soils may be distinguished: the gray sandy, varying in color from gray to red, the black sandy, and the black waxy lands. The chief soil is the *grey sandy*, constituting about two-thirds of the tillable area. Mesquite and post oak on the uplands and burr and spotted oaks, elm, and hackberry on creeks and rivers form the timber growth. The soil is a fine sandy loam, 18 inches in depth, and overlies a subsoil which is a mixture of red and yellow clay, very deep, and which acts as a fertilizer when mixed with the soil. Rock is found at 90 feet. The land is easily cultivated, is early and well drained, and produces cotton, corn, and small grain. One-third of the crops is in cotton, which grows to a height of from 3 to 6 feet, running to weed in very wet seasons. Eight hundred pounds of seed-cotton are obtained per acre from fresh land or from land after thirty years' cultivation, 1,495 pounds being necessary for 475 pounds of lint, which rates as good, the staple from lands long cultivated rating better. Cocklebur and sunflower are the most troublesome weeds. No land lies turned out. There is considerable washing of the soil, but no serious damage arises therefrom.

Cotton is hauled by wagon to Fort Worth in November and December at $2 50 per bale.

YOUNG.

Population: 4,726.—White, 4,709; colored, 17.
Area: 900 square miles.—Woodland, a large part; all northwestern red-loam region.
Tilled lands: 23,122 acres.—Area planted in cotton, 2,049 acres; in corn, 9,181 acres; in oats, 114 acres; in wheat, 1,947 acres.
Cotton production: 554 bales; average cotton product per acre, 0.27 bale, 405 pounds seed-cotton, or 135 pounds cotton lint.

The surface of Young county is rolling and broken, with high and prominent ridges that usually trend southwestward. These hills are formed largely of sandstone and conglomerate, frequently capped with red sandstone, and are timbered with a growth of post and black-jack oaks. Fossils of the Carboniferous period are found in some of the hills near Graham, the county-seat, and the sandstones that underlie them in the bed of the streams are saline in character. The valley lands lying between the ridges are sometimes open prairies, with some mesquite and scattering oak growth, and have a sandy soil.

The Brazos river pursues its tortuous course through the southern part of this county, with open valleys of reddish loam soils on either side, bounded by bold and rocky bluffs. These lands are said to produce from one-half to a bale of cotton per acre, and are the chief cotton lands of the county. The rest of the county is watered by streams that flow southward and are tributary to the Brazos. From Belknap mountain on the west there is said to be a rolling or undulating prairie that extends 100 miles north to Red river.

The lands under cultivation comprise 4 per cent. of the county area, with an average of 25.7 acres per square mile. Of the latter only 2.3 acres are devoted to the culture of cotton. The crops comprise corn, wheat, oats, rye, barley, and cotton, the acreage of the two former being the largest. Stock-raising also receives much attention in Young county.

STEPHENS.

Population : 4,725.—White, 4,700; colored, 25.

Area : 900 square miles.—Woodland, much; all northwestern red-loam prairie.

Tilled lands : 18,042 acres.—Area planted in cotton, 686 acres; in corn, 3,824 acres; in oats, 254 acres; in wheat, 2,187 acres.

Cotton production : 137 bales; average cotton product per acre, 0.20 bale, 300 pounds seed-cotton, or 100 pounds cotton lint.

Stephens county has a surface very similar to those counties already described, viz, rolling and broken, with prominent timbered ridges, and watered by streams flowing northward into the Brazos river. These ridges are largely formed of fossiliferous (*Productus, spirifer,* etc.) strata, overlaid by conglomerates and sandstones, and underlaid by crinoidal limestones, as seen in the valleys. The upper stratum of sandstone on the hills near Breckenridge, the county-seat, is solid, and has a thickness of about 4 feet. On its surface are commonly found fragments of sandstone, accompanied by rounded masses of red hematite, having frequently bright or specular surfaces; silicified wood also occurs.

The lands of the valleys are mostly open prairies, with mesquite and a scattering oak growth, and have soils varying from black clayey to a reddish, sandy loam. They are said to yield finely, even in very dry seasons, producing as much as 600 pounds of seed-cotton per acre. In good seasons the yield is said to be 1,200 pounds.

The valleys on Hubbard's creek are never forgotten by one who sees them. Level almost as a billiard-table, and covered with the finest of mesquite grass, which remains green nearly all winter, it would be difficult to find anything more beautiful and picturesque.—*Thrall.*

Stephens is chiefly a stock-raising county, and but a small proportion of its area (3.1 per cent.) is under cultivation, the average being 20 acres per square mile. The crops of the county are corn, wheat, cotton, oats, etc., the first two having the largest acreage. The average acreage of cotton is eight-tenths of an acre per square mile.

PALO PINTO.

Population : 5,885.—White, 5,797; colored, 88.

Area : 900 square miles.—Woodland, much; all northwestern red-loam prairie.

Tilled lands : 24,468 acres.—Area planted in cotton, 4,292 acres; in corn, 9,301 acres; in oats, 305 acres; in wheat, 2,425 acres.

Cotton production : 885 bales; average cotton product per acre, 0.21 bale, 315 pounds seed-cotton, or 105 pounds cotton lint.

The surface of Palo Pinto county is rolling and broken, and is divided by the Brazos river, which flows through it from northwest to southeast in a very irregular course. On the west and north are many high hills and ridges, with broad valleys of open mesquite prairie and timbered lands, and while often precipitous on the east, they have a gradual slope to the west, and are usually capped with crinoidal limestones and cherty rocks, or by their overlying red sandstone. In the eastern part of the county (east of the county-seat) the hills seem to terminate at the river (where heavy beds of pebble conglomerate occur), and from thence to the Parker county-line the country is rather level, and is timbered with a post and black-jack oak growth. The soil is sandy, with fragments of sandstone, has a tall growth of sedge-grass, and abounds in gopher holes. Underlying it, as seen in the east bank of the river, are strata of whitish sandstone with an exposed thickness of 50 feet.

The valley lands between the hills are the chief farming lands of the county. Their soils are red sandy loams, interspersed with areas of black waxy clay lands, and timbered with a growth of live and post oaks, mesquite, pecan, etc.

The lands under cultivation average 25.5 acres per square mile, or 34 per cent. of the county area. The corn crop has the largest acreage, that of cotton comprising 17.5 per cent. of the tilled lands, or an average of 4.5 acres per square mile.

ABSTRACT FROM THE REPORT OF J. A. M'LAREN, OF COKELAN.

The uplands of this county consist of rolling table-lands and prairies, and the soils are black waxy, gray mesquite, and sandy loams. The *sandy loam lands* comprise one-half of the tillable lands of the county. The growth is live, post, and burr oaks, elm, pecan, and mesquite. The soil is about 18 inches in depth. The subsoil is a tenacious clay; and sand, gravel, and rock are found at 10 feet. The land is early, warm, and well drained, and easily tilled under all circumstances. Corn and wheat form the chief crops, wheat being best adapted to the soil. Cotton, forming about one-fifth of the entire crops, grows to a height of from 3½ to 5 feet, and runs to weed only during very wet seasons. Topping is the remedy applied to restrain it. The yield per acre of seed-cotton is from 800 to 1,000 pounds, of which 1,425 pounds are requisite for a 475-pound bale of lint, rating as good middling. The effect of cultivation cannot as yet be estimated, as this (1879) is only the third season in which cotton has been grown. The most troublesome weeds are careless, lamb's-quarter, sunflower, cocklebur, horse-nettles, and many others.

Cotton is hauled as soon as ginned to Fort Worth, the rate of freight being 30 cents per 100 pounds.

ERATH.

(See "Central black prairie region".)

EASTLAND.

Population: 4,855.—White, 4,837; colored, 18.
Area: 900 square miles.—Woodland, some; all northwestern red-loam prairie.
Tilled lands: 19,752 acres.—Area planted in cotton, 3,264 acres; in corn, 5,867 acres; in oats, 89 acres; in wheat, 1,941 acres.
Cotton production: 742 bales; average cotton product per acre, 0.23 bale, 345 pounds seed-cotton, or 115 pounds cotton lint.

The surface of Eastland county is rolling, with high ridges on the north and south, and is watered by the Leon river and tributaries. It is largely covered with a growth of post and black-jack oaks, with large mesquite prairies, on which there is a scattering growth of live oak.

The dividing ridge between the waters of Leon river and Hubbard's creek consists of a succession of bold, rocky hills, east of which the county is covered with a dense growth of post, black-jack, and other oaks, and is a fine country for hogs. On the west there are some fertile valleys, covered with mesquite grass, with good post oak timber convenient.—*Thrall.*

The county is sparsely populated, and a comparatively large proportion (3.4 per cent.) of its area is under cultivation, with an average of 21.9 acres per square mile. It is chiefly a stock-raising county, far from railroad facilities. The lands are well described in the following abstract:

ABSTRACT FROM THE REPORT OF A. J. STUART, OF EASTLAND.

The soil of the uplands is generally sandy, with occasional small prairies of black, sticky land. There are some large prairies of black waxy land on which live oak and mesquite once grew. The lands devoted to the cultivation of cotton comprise the dark sandy and black waxy of the first and second bottoms and valleys, sandy post oak land, and the black prairie and mesquite lands of the uplands.

The *dark or black valley land* is the most important, and constitutes about one-eighth of the county and one-half of the cultivated lands. Its growth is pecan, spotted oak, walnut, cottonwood, elm, and hackberry. The depth of the soil, which is a dark and waxy loam, is 3½ feet, its subsoil being a light yellowish clay, and in places gravelly. It is underlaid by rock at 20 feet. The soil is easily cultivated in wet seasons; but in dry seasons, when not well broken up, it is cultivated with difficulty. It is early, warm, well drained, and produces corn, wheat, barley, and cotton, cotton and wheat being best adapted to it. About one-third of the tillable area is devoted to cotton, which attains a height of from 4 to 5 feet, being most productive at the latter. The yield per acre of seed-cotton is 800 pounds, but were it not for the droughts 1,600 pounds would be the product; 1,545 pounds of seed-cotton make 475 pounds of lint, rating as middling. Twelve years' cultivation of the land does not decrease the above yield or lower the rating of the staple. Only a small portion of the land has been under cultivation ten years. The troublesome weeds are horse-nettle, broom-weed, sunflower, and cocklebur. The valleys are very level, and do not wash to any appreciable extent.

The *post-oak uplands* comprise about one-half of the county and one-fourth of the cultivated land, and have a growth of post and black-jack oaks. The soil is a dark, grayish, fine sandy loam 12 inches deep. The subsoil is usually a clay, red and hard when dry, and sticky when wet. It overlies sand, gravel, and rock at 25 feet. The soil is easily cultivated at all times, is early, warm, and well drained, and is best adapted to corn, cotton, potatoes, and wheat. About one-third of the crop is in cotton, whose growth is 3½ feet, 4 feet being the most productive height; it produces from 500 to 1,000 pounds of seed-cotton per acre, 1,545 pounds of which are required for a 475-pound bale, which rates as middling. The yield is not diminished in any way after the land has been under cultivation for five years.

The *black prairie and mesquite lands* have a growth of mesquite and a few scattering live and post oaks. This land comprises about one-quarter of the lands under cultivation, and about the same proportion of the county. The soil is a black prairie loam 1 foot in depth, having a lighter subsoil of yellowish clay, in some places a red clay, and in others gravelly; it contains white gravel and flinty pebbles. Sand, gravel, and rock are found at 15 feet. The land is easily cultivated in wet seasons, but not so in dry ones. It is early, warm, and well drained. The soil is best adapted to wheat and cotton, the latter, forming five-fifths of the entire crops, growing to a height of 3½ feet, 5 feet being the most productive. It yields from 500 to 1,000 pounds of seed-cotton per acre, which after four years is increased from 800 to 1,400 pounds, 1,545 pounds being necessary for 475 pounds of lint, which rates as middling. There are no very troublesome weeds on this land, but hog-weed and cocklebur cause some slight trouble. No land lies turned out; neither is there any running to weed of the cotton-plant on any of the lands of the county.

In this county dry weather has damaged cotton more than any other evil. The land generally being fresh and never properly brought into cultivation, has suffered more from drought than it would have done otherwise.

Shipments are made in November and December, by wagon, to Fort Worth at $3 per bale.

COLEMAN.

Population: 3,603.—White, 3,568; colored, 33.
Area: 1,040 square miles.—Woodland, some; all northwestern red-loam prairie.
Tilled lands: 17,017 acres.—Area planted in cotton, 796 acres; in corn, 4,333 acres; in oats, 90 acres; in wheat, 1,568 acres.
Cotton production: 243 bales; average cotton product per acre, 0.31 bale, 465 pounds seed-cotton, or 155 pounds cotton lint.

Coleman, one of the western border counties of the cotton region, lies on the north side of the Colorado river, into which flow the many streams that water the country. The surface is undulating, with several high and prominent peaks in the central and northern portions; the southern portion is mostly open prairies.

The soils are black and sandy loams, and very productive, the crops being corn, wheat, rye, oats, cotton, and all of the vegetables. There is plenty of timber for fencing and building purposes. The grasses are excellent, and the county is finely adapted to stock raising.—*Thrall.*

The country is sparsely populated, and but a small proportion (2.1 per cent.) of the area is under cultivation, with an average of 13.7 acres per square mile. Of the latter but six-tenths of an acre is devoted to cotton.

The live-stock comprises 60,334 head of cattle, 28,419 sheep, and 4,336 hogs.

51 C P

BROWN.

Population: 8,414.—White, 8,291; colored, 123.
Area: 1,200 square miles.—Woodland, much; central black prairie, 60 square miles; northwestern red loam, 1,140 square miles.
Tilled lands: 45,655 acres.—Area planted in cotton, 4,254 acres; in corn, 12,408 acres; in oats, 516 acres; in wheat, 7,814 acres.
Cotton production: 998 bales; average cotton product per acre, 0.23 bale, 345 pounds seed-cotton, or 115 pounds cotton lint.

The surface of Brown county is rolling and broken, with high and prominent ridges and hills; on the south and west there are said to be broad prairies. It is watered by numerous creeks flowing southward into the Colorado river, which forms a part of the southern boundary. The hills or mountains, some of which have broad summits, are usually timbered with post oak, or sometimes with only a low scrub or brush growth, as on the south. The soils are sandy, often red in color, and in places are filled with masses of white and pinkish quartz fragments. The hilly portion of the county is but little inhabited. The valleys between the hills and along Pecan creek are usually rather open or covered mostly with a mesquite growth, interspersed with sandy post-oak lands. The soil is a stiff red loam, more or less clayey, and very productive, and similar to the lands of San Saba county. Limestones outcrop in many of these valleys, while the hills are often capped with sandstones and quartzites.

The lands under cultivation comprise 5.9 per cent. of the county area, with an average of 38 acres per square mile. The chief crops are corn, wheat, cotton, oats, potatoes, etc., the acreage of cotton being 3.5 acres per square mile.

Brown is an excellent stock-raising county. White labor is almost exclusively used, the wages being from $10 to $15 per month.
Shipments are made to Fort Worth by wagon.

COMANCHE.

Population: 8,608.—White, 8,529; colored, 79.
Area: 930 square miles.—Woodland, greater part; central black prairie, 170 square miles; northwestern red loam, 180 square miles; upper cross timbers, 580 square miles.
Tilled lands: 44,191 acres.—Area planted in cotton, 9,301 acres; in corn, 14,267 acres; in oats, 460 acres; in wheat, 5,074 acres.
Cotton production: 2,098 bales; average cotton product per acre, 0.23 bale, 345 pounds seed-cotton, or 115 pounds cotton lint.

The surface of Comanche county is rolling, but in places it is hilly. The eastern part is mostly an open prairie; the western and middle is generally covered with a timber growth of post and black-jack oaks, and belongs to the upper cross timbers belt, but is interspersed with prairies. The county is watered by the Leon river and its tributaries, flowing southeastward. The lands of the prairies are of the black waxy and calcareous character common to the central prairie region, of which they are a part, and are underlaid by stiff clays and the limestones of the Cretaceous formation. They are covered with grasses, and are generally used for stock grazing. The timbered uplands are sandy to a depth of from 12 to 18 inches, and are somewhat pebbly and underlaid by reddish clay subsoils. That portion of the region between the Comanche and Leon rivers on the east is very level. The soils are easily tilled, and produce an average of about 500 pounds of seed-cotton per acre. The valley lands of the streams are narrow, and have a dark loam soil, with a timber growth of pecan, walnut, elm, post oak, etc. Mustang grape-vines are abundant. It is largely a stock-raising county. The lands under cultivation comprise 7.4 per cent. of its area, with an average of 47.5 acres per square mile. Of these about 10 acres for each mile is devoted to the culture of cotton, corn being the chief crop.

ABSTRACT FROM THE REPORT OF W. L. SARTWELL, OF COMANCHE.

The uplands are rolling, with some high hills or table-lands, interspersed with prairies of black and sandy soils and sandy post-oak lands.

The most important soil for cotton cultivation is the *black upland prairie*. Its growth is mesquite and scattering post oaks. About one-sixth of the lands of the county belong to this variety. The soil, which varies in character and color, is 2 feet deep. The subsoil is a tough yellow clay, baking hard when exposed, impervious when undisturbed, but is much improved by cultivation; it is underlaid by limestone at from 5 to 10 feet. The soil is easily cultivated in wet seasons, but quite difficult in dry ones. It is early and well drained, and produces wheat, corn, and other grains, being best adapted to cotton as a sure crop. There is an occasional trouble from droughts, which dwarf the plant. Cotton grows to a height of from 3 to 4 feet, yielding 1,000 pounds of seed-cotton per acre, the amount necessary for a 475-pound bale being 1,545 pounds. The staple rates as fair. The effect of cultivation of the land cannot, as yet, be estimated, as this (1879) is only the third or fourth year in which cotton has been planted in the county. Careless, cocklebur, and sunflower are the most troublesome weeds on all the soils.

The *sandy post-oak land* covers about two-thirds of the surface of the county, and has a natural timber growth of post and black-jack oak. The soil is a grayish sandy loam, about 2 feet deep, overlying a yellow clay subsoil, which is underlaid by sand-rock at 20 feet. It is easily cultivated, and is early, warm, and well drained. The chief productions are cotton and corn, both of which do well, the former constituting about one-fourth of the whole crops. The plant grows to a height of from 3 to 5 feet, and yields 1,000 pounds of seed-cotton per acre, 1,485 pounds of which are necessary for 475 pounds of lint, rating as fair.

The *dark loam alluvial lands*, with a natural timber growth of mesquite and oak, comprise one-sixth of the lands of the county. The soil is 10 feet deep, is cultivated with difficulty in wet seasons, and is early, warm, and well drained, and best adapted to grains. The subsoil is clay, overlying rock at 20 feet. Cotton, forming about one-tenth of the entire crops, grows to a height of from 5 to 6 feet, and yields 1,000 pounds of seed-cotton per acre, 1,665 pounds being requisite for a 475-pound bale, rating as ordinary.

Shipments are made from Comanche .... inclusive by wagon, to Fort Worth and Waco, and thence to Galveston, the rate of freight being $2 50 to Fort Worth and $7 to Galveston.

SAN SABA.

Population: 5,324.—White, 5,183; colored, 141.
Area: 1,130 square miles.—Woodland, much; all northwestern red-loam region.
Tilled lands: 21,075 acres.—Area planted in cotton, 2,819 acres; in corn, 8,281 acres; in oats, 675 acres; in wheat, 3,148 acres.
Cotton production: 400 bales; average cotton product per acre, 0.14 bale, 210 pounds seed-cotton, or 70 pounds cotton lint.

San Saba county is bounded on the north and east by the Colorado river, into which all of the streams flow. The surface of the county is hilly and broken, the valley lands along the streams and between the hills comprising almost the only tillable lands. The rocks vary from the cherts, conglomerates, and sandstones of the mountains usually to the underlying limestones of the valleys, all belonging, so far as known, to the Palæozoic series. The lands of the county vary from the sandy soils of the post-oak uplands to the brown and red loams and black waxy prairies and timbered lands of the valleys and bottoms of the San Saba river. (See analysis, page 47.) The prairies have usually a growth of mesquite and scattering live and post oaks, while that of the bottoms comprises pecan, elm, sycamore, cottonwood, etc. Cedar, black-jack, and other oaks, etc., are found on the hills. The lands under cultivation comprise 2.9 per cent. of the county area, an average of 18.7 acres per square mile. They are better adapted to grain than to any other crop, and but a comparatively small acreage is given to cotton. The seasons are so droughty that irrigation is often resorted to.

The average yield per acre of the crops is said to be: corn, 5 bushels; wheat, 0.4 bushels; oats, 13 bushels.

ABSTRACT FROM THE REPORT OF J. FRAZER BROWN, OF SAN SABA.

The timbered lands along the creeks (tributary to the Colorado river) have an alluvial soil, and black prairie lands extend from this to the rocky hills on the north and gray to the orange red sandy land on the south. The timber consists of elm, pecan, hackberry, willow, and live oak. The creek bottoms are from 100 yards to 1 mile wide.

The *black mesquite prairies* have a black sandy loam soil about 2 feet thick. A whitish, calcareous loam and a yellow clay constitute the subsoil of most of the black lands, while the gray and red lands have a red-clay subsoil. The clays are impervious, and contain flinty, rounded pebbles. The subsoils are underlaid by rock at 10 feet. The soil is easily tilled when dry, but with difficulty when too wet; it is cold but well drained, and is best adapted to small grains. The chief crops of this region are wheat and corn. One-fifth of the cultivated area of these lands is planted in cotton. The plant grows from 4 to 7 feet high, and is most productive at about 5 feet. It inclines to run to weed in wet weather, and as a remedy some have tried topping about July 1, also in the dark of the moon of August, with good results. The seed-cotton product per acre of fresh land is 1,700 pounds in good seasons, 1,615 pounds then making a 475-pound bale of low middling to good ordinary lint; but in dry seasons it takes 1,900 pounds to make such a bale. This land is still fresh, and has been cultivated only a few years. The cocklebur, careless-weed, and another that has lately appeared, are the most troublesome weeds. The drainage from higher lands is conducted upon cultivated fields, fertilizing and irrigating the same, and almost insuring a crop. The only hinderance to the cotton crop is a deficiency of rain about every fourth year. The gray and red sandy soils of this section produce on the average as much as the black loams, because it withstands the droughts the best. This is the case where there is a red-clay subsoil.

Cotton is shipped in November and December, by wagon, to Round Rock and to Austin at 50 cents per 100 pounds, and thence by rail to Galveston.

LLANO.

Population: 4,962.—White, 4,896; colored, 66.
Area: 900 square miles.—Woodland, much; all northwestern red-loam prairie.
Tilled lands: 17,553 acres.—Area planted in cotton, 2,247 acres; in corn, 7,700 acres; in oats, 209 acres; in wheat, 1,145 acres.
Cotton production: 469 bales; average cotton product per acre, 0.21 bale, 315 pounds seed-cotton, or 105 pounds cotton lint.

The surface of Llano county is broken and somewhat mountainous. It is generally timbered with mesquite, post and live oaks, pecan, and mountain cedar, and is watered by the Llano river, which flows east through the middle of the county and unites with the Colorado at the boundary. A number of the mountains are composed of granites and other metamorphic rocks, and copper, gold, and other minerals are reported by the state geologist as accompanying them. The Enchanted Rock and Packsaddle mountains are two of the most prominent. Between the hills and mountains there are broad valleys with rich clayey lands, very deep, which comprise the chief agricultural lands of the county, and are described in the abstract below.

Llano is chiefly a stock-raising county, there being but 3 per cent. of its area under cultivation, or an average of 19.5 acres per square mile. A fair percentage (12.8) of cotton is planted, although the county is so far from railroad facilities and markets.

ABSTRACT FROM THE REPORT OF C. M. COGGIN, M. D., OF BLUFFTON.

The surface of the county is rolling and broken, having mostly a red-clay and sandy soil in the valleys and black lands in the bottoms on the rivers. There is some black hog-wallow soil on the mountains.

The chief soil is the *red clay on the uplands*, covering about one-fourth of the surface of the county, and running with each ledge of the mountains with a width of from one-fourth to one-half mile, the natural timber growth of which is mesquite, pecan, and post and live oaks. The soil is several feet deep, and is underlaid by sand and gravel at from 8 to 10 feet. It is easily tilled, and is early, warm, and well drained. Corn, cotton, wheat, oats, barley, and Hungarian grass form the chief crops. About one-fourth of the cultivated land is in cotton, but the soil seems best adapted to cotton, wheat, and barley. The height usually attained by the plant is 4 feet, yielding 850 pounds of seed-cotton per acre, 2,020 pounds being necessary for a 475-pound bale of lint, rating very good. Cultivation of the land for ten years does not affect the above product or the rating of the staple. There is a tendency of the plant to run to weed in July or August if there is too much rain, but no remedy has as yet been tried. The uplands are preferred, because on them the plant runs less to weed than on the river bottoms. No land lies "turned out". On our soils there are no troublesome weeds, this being a frontier county.

Cotton is hauled by wagon to Austin, Red Rock, and Galveston at 50 cents per bale, the time being from October to March.

BURNET.

Population: 6,855.—White, 6,607; colored, 248.

Area : 1,000 square miles.—Woodland, much; central black prairie, 350 square miles; northwestern red loam, 650 square miles.

Tilled lands : 37,168 acres.—Area planted in cotton, 7,024 acres; in corn, 14,187 acres; in oats, 1,997 acres; in wheat, 5,173 acres.

Cotton production : 1,399 bales; average cotton product per acre, 0.20 bale, 300 pounds seed-cotton, or 100 pounds cotton lint.

Burnet county is bounded on the west partly by the Colorado river, which flows southward until near the lower part of the county, when it turns almost at right angles to the east. The surface of the country is rough and broken, with high timbered hills and rather narrow valleys of mesquite prairies. A large part of the county is said to be covered with dense cedar brakes, and it is generally rocky. There is also much post and live oak.

The lands of the Colorado river and tributaries have a red or chocolate-colored loam, timbered with a growth of cottonwood, elm, hackberry, pecan, etc. The lands of San Gabriel and its tributaries are black alluvial loams. The southern and western part of the county is included in the northwestern red-loam region, and its rocks are reported to be principally sandstones, with large granite outcrops. On the northeast and other parts of the county the Cretaceous limestones are found, giving to the low prairie valleys a black calcareous soil.

Burnet county is sparsely settled, and the lands under cultivation comprise 5.8 per cent. of its area, averaging 37.2 acres per square mile, and are chiefly confined to the valley and bottom lands of the streams. Corn is the chief crop, the average of cotton being but 7 acres per square mile.

ABSTRACT FROM THE REPORT OF A. SCHROETER, OF DOUBLE HORN.

The lowlands are the first bottoms of the Colorado river and numerous small flats along different creeks; then the elm flats, or second bottoms, lie just above these, with their growth of elm and mesquite.

The uplands are mostly prairies, with a variety of soils. The cotton lands are river valley lands, comprising about 30 per cent. of those under cultivation. The black mesquite lands (about 20 per cent.), and the elm flats, lands sheltered from the dry, bleaching west winds, are generally preferred for cotton, as these winds prevail during the spring, when the plants are young and tender.

The *river lands* extend along the Colorado river for 25 or 30 miles through the county, and have usually a red sandy loam soil 2 feet or more in depth, underlaid by a heavier red-clay loam, sometimes containing rounded pebbles, and is itself underlaid by a limestone at from 30 to 40 feet. The growth on this land is post oak, hackberry, black-jack, and pecan. The soil is easily cultivated, and produces corn, cotton, oats, and wheat. It is best adapted to corn, though about 40 per cent. of cotton is planted. The height of cotton on this soil is 3½ feet; it yields 1,500 pounds of seed-cotton per acre, 1,485 pounds being required for 475 pounds of lint. It rates as good middling in the market. After ten years' cultivation no change is observed in either the productiveness of the soil or the quality of the staple. Grass is most troublesome. The soil washes or gullies very slightly.

Black mesquite flats are found in almost every part of the county, and have a scattering growth of mesquite and post oak. The soil is a black prairie clay, 18 inches in depth, underlaid by lighter subsoil, which contains soft, white fragments of gravel. Limestone underlies this at from 6 to 8 feet. It is an early and warm soil if well drained, and is best adapted to wheat. Cotton reaches a height of 3 feet on this soil, is not troubled with weeds to any extent, and produces as well as on the river lands.

The *elm flats* are scattered over the county, and have a heavy clay soil, mixed with sand at a depth of 18 inches, underlaid by limestone at 6 feet. Their growth is elm and mesquite. The soil is well drained, not difficult to till in wet seasons, and is best adapted to corn and oats. Cotton grows to a height of 3 feet, seldom runs to weed, and produces 1,500 pounds of seed-cotton per acre, the lint rating as middling. Purslane is the most troublesome weed.

Shipments of cotton are made before Christmas, by wagon, to Austin, freight per bale being $2 50.

WILLIAMSON.
(See " Central black prairie region".)

TRAVIS.
(See " Central black prairie region".)

BLANCO.
(See " Central black prairie region".)

GILLESPIE.
(See " Central black prairie region".)

BORDER COUNTIES OF THE COTTON REGION.

Wichita county, producing 43 bales of cotton; Baylor, 83; Archer, 43; Throckmorton, 10; Jones, 19; Shackelford, 5; Callahan, 86; McCulloch, 54; Mason, 64; with Gillespie, Kerr, Bandera, and Uvalde, of the central prairie region, form a western border for the Texas cotton region of 1879, reaching from the Red river to the Nueces, or, in other words, to a tier of counties on the Rio Grande which do not produce cotton. Wilbarger, Hardeman, Knox, Haskell, Taylor, Runnels, Concho, and Kimble form a nearly unbroken north and south line still west of the border cotton counties, with lands adapted to cotton but reporting none for market. These counties are not even all organized.

Cotton is planted as farming begins. Stock raising is the predominant interest in all this sparsely settled region. There is some mesquite growth in part of the region, and a little other timber; cedars on the most broken parts, and some live, post, and black-jack oaks, pecan, cottonwood, elm, and walnut, especially near streams.

The following brief descriptions are given of the counties in which any cotton is produced; but for statistical information the reader is referred to Tables I and II, at the beginning of the report:

WICHITA.—The surface is mostly a rolling and hilly prairie, with tillable lands along the streams, timbered with cottonwood and mesquite trees. The amount of tilled lands is very small (4.2 acres per square mile), and they are chiefly devoted to corn. Cotton is little else than an experiment at present, though a successful one, with a product per acre larger than in very many counties whose production is very great. The soil of the prairie is the red sandy loam common to this region.

BAYLOR.—The surface is generally an open rolling and broken prairie, with a brushy mesquite growth along the streams. The Brazos and Big Wichita rivers and their tributaries flow through the county, but their waters are mostly unfit for use because of their salty and brackish character. The soil of the prairies is a red sandy loam, associated with veins of gypsum, and as yet but little under cultivation.

ARCHER.—The surface is an open and rolling prairie, very rough in places, and having but little growth even on the streams. There is some post oak in places. The county is watered by numerous small streams, all flowing northeastward into the Red river. The lands of the county have a reddish sandy loam soil, and there are said to be some fine valley lands on several of the creeks.

THROCKMORTON.—The surface is broken and hilly, and is well timbered with live and post oaks and mesquite on the uplands, and pecan, cottonwood, and hackberry on the creek bottoms. The soil is generally a red loam, with areas of black clayey lands on the south. The tillable lands lie along the streams. The acreage of tilled lands is small, and is nearly entirely devoted to corn and wheat crops. The county is one of the extreme western of those producing any cotton at all, and would have been left out of the list entirely had not an enterprising farmer determined in 1879 to plant it as an experiment. The following description is given by Charles McCormick, of Throckmorton:

The face of the country is rolling, sometimes broken into hilly ranges. The soil is on the whole above the average of the region, and a good portion of it is very choice land, finely adapted to the growth of cotton, corn, wheat, rye, oats, millet, etc. Much of the soil is of a reddish or mulatto nature, similar to the Brazos river lands; a portion of it is of a black sandy character, some sticky. Gypsum beds occur in Haskell, the adjoining county on the west. The first cotton ever raised in this county was planted in 1879 by J. T. Reff, and notwithstanding the fact that it was an unprecedentedly dry year he produced three-fourths of a bale per acre.

JONES.—The surface is broken, with high ranges of hills and abrupt bluffs of sandstone and limestone (Cretaceous). "A range of sand hills several miles wide runs north of and parallel with the Elm fork." The growth of the uplands is mostly mesquite—on the hills some live oak and cedar, and on the streams elm, pecan, and hackberry, with some post oak, cottonwood, etc. "The soil is a red loam, more or less sandy, becoming darker in the southeastern corner of the county."

SHACKELFORD.—The surface is broken, with a high range of hills forming the "divide" between the waters of the Clear fork of the Brazos river and Hubbard's creek. These hills are formed of sandstone and limestone, and are densely timbered, while the valleys have generally a growth of mesquite trees. The lands are of the red sandy loam peculiar to the region, but are not much under cultivation.

CALLAHAN.—This county has a rolling and broken surface, with high ridges and prominent hills, two of the most prominent being East and West Caddo peaks, on the southeast. The northern part of the county is drained by tributaries of the Brazos, the southern by those of the Colorado river. The county is about equally divided between prairie and timber. It is a fine grazing county, with a fair proportion of good arable land. There is an abundance of good timber and pure water, and the soil is rich, particularly in the valleys. The lands comprise the red and dark sandy soils already described in the adjoining counties.

William H. Parvin, of Belle Plain, reports that cotton was first raised in this county in 1877.

TAYLOR.—No cotton was reported by the census enumerators as having been produced in this county in 1879. The following abstract, however, from the reports of Messrs. N. N. Browne and J. S. Porter, of Buffalo Gap, affirms that cotton has been successfully raised in small quantities:

One-fifth of the county is mountainous; the rest is level or rolling prairie and mesquite, elm, and pecan valleys. There are, strictly speaking, no lowlands. The soils comprise many varieties: dark, light, and red loams; dark, or a red and stiff hog-wallow; and some heavy beds of sand. These are the timbered lands of the county, covered with post-oak; live oak is abundant in places. The mountains have considerable cedar, and frequently along streams there is a growth of elm, pecan, hackberry, plum, cherry, walnut, and willow.

The chief soil is the dark loam, comprising about one-third of the county, which occurs in areas of from 4 to 5 miles in width, and has a natural growth of mesquite trees and mesquite grass. The soil is a heavy loam, frequently putty-like in texture, varying in color from dun and brown to black, and its depth is about 2 feet. The subsoil is generally a reddish clay; sometimes it is of a light color and intermixed with pebbles, and is underlaid by sand and gravel, and then by red clay at about 20 feet. The soil is nearly always easily tilled, is changeable in regard to warmth and cold, is well drained, and best adapted to wheat, oats, millet, corn, potatoes, sorghum, and squashes, and probably not quite a fiftieth of its area is devoted to cotton culture. The average height of the cotton-plant is 4 feet, which is probably the most desirable height, as the plant is not inclined to run to weed too much. The seed-cotton product per acre of fresh land is about 1,200 pounds, 1,545 pounds of which make a 475-pound bale of lint. In counties east of here there is but little difference in yield, etc., after the first thirty or forty years' cultivation. The troublesome weeds are sunflower, horse-nettle, milkweed, and cocklebur. None of this land lies "turned out". The soil washes some in places, but is generally too level to be injured or to damage the valleys by the washings.

The red-loam soil comprises probably about one-fourth of the county, and is chiefly confined to the numerous creeks running north to the Brazos river. The natural growth is mesquite trees and mesquite grass. The soil is a heavy clay loam, often stiff, mahogany to orange-red in color, and from 5 to 6 feet deep. The subsoil varies; sometimes it is red clay, and sometimes sand and gravel, is leachy, contains some pebbles, and is underlaid by sand and gravel, and in places by rock at from 15 to 20 feet. The soil is easily tilled, rarely too wet, is early, warm (changeable), well drained, and but very little of it is devoted to cotton. The plant varies from 2½ to 5 feet in height, 3½ to 4 feet being the most desirable. With too much rain and cultivation the plant inclines to run to weed; this rarely occurs, and is remedied by topping when in bloom. The seed-cotton product, etc., is the same as on the dark loam soil.

The *red stiff "hog-wallow" land* occurs in bodies, the largest being about 2 miles across; it bears (naturally) mesquite trees and mesquite grass. The soil is from 2 to 6 feet deep. The subsoil is generally pure clay, but has gravel in some places, and is underlaid by sandstone at various depths. This is probably our richest soil, but the heaviest to cultivate; it is late, cold, and well drained. A very small part of it is planted in cotton. The height of the plant has not been well noted; it would probably grow quite tall. In favorable seasons the seed-cotton product per acre of fresh land is from 1,200 to 1,500 pounds, 1,545 pounds making a 475-pound bale of lint. It is not likely that forty years' cultivation (unmanured) would make any difference in the quantity or quality of the cotton product of this land. The troublesome weeds are the sunflower and cocklebur. Few slopes are in cultivation; at any rate, the country is too level to admit of serious damage to slopes by washing and gullying.

The county being only recently settled, not much cotton has yet been planted, but, so far, results are satisfactory. The greatest success in cotton production, judging from three years' trial, cannot here be expected, on account of the springs being usually too dry to insure a good stand every year, and because a portion of the crop is liable to destruction by the high winds that usually prevail during the fall; and during the spring, and until the middle of June, comes the occasional "norther", reducing the temperature in an hour's time to the freezing point of water. This norther season is generally succeeded by long hot droughts.

Cotton is sent as soon as baled, by wagons, to Fort Worth and Waco at from $2 to $3 per bale, and then shipped by rail to Galveston at $4 per bale.

McCULLOCH.—This county lies on the south side of the Colorado river, into which the northern part is drained by small streams. Through the central part flows Brady's creek in an easterly course into the San Saba river, which comes from the southwest. The surface of the county is hilly and broken with prairie valley lands having brown and red loam and black waxy soils covered with a growth of mesquite, and very similar in character to the lands of San Saba county.

MASON.—The surface of Mason county is rolling and broken, and is largely timbered with post and black-jack oaks on the northwest. It is watered chiefly by the Llano river and tributaries, the San Saba river crossing the northwest corner of the county. It is said to be the best timbered county in western Texas. Pecans grow in great quantities on the rivers. The central and southwest portions are said to abound in mesquite flats, with much outcropping granite rock. The lands embrace the red sandy and black loam soils common to this western prairie region.

The following description is given by H. M. Holmes, of Mason:

The surface of the county is very uneven. The rivers have but little bottom land; the uplands have red sandy loam and black loam soils and a growth of post, live, and black-jack oaks. The most important with reference to cotton culture is the *red sandy*, which covers about one-half the county. Its depth is from 4 to 10 feet, overlying decomposed granite. Limestone and shales underlie the black loam. The chief crops are corn, oats, rye, cotton, and wheat. About one-tenth of the cultivated lands is devoted to cotton, which yields from 750 to 1,000 pounds of seed-cotton per acre, 1,425 pounds being required for a 475-pound bale. The year 1879 was the first year in which cotton was planted in the county, and, unfortunately for the experiment, the season was one of long drought. The soil washes readily on slopes, and no efforts have been made to check the damage, which is sometimes of a serious nature. Creek beds have sometimes been filled up by these washings. Jamestown and bur weed are most troublesome weeds on this soil.

Cotton is shipped in November, by wagon, to Austin, the rate of freight being three-fourths of a cent per pound.

PART III.

CULTURAL AND ECONOMIC DETAILS

OF

COTTON PRODUCTION.

REFERENCE LIST

OF

NAMES AND ADDRESSES OF CORRESPONDENTS.

[The numbers preceding the names of counties are used in Part III to designate the person giving any special answer.]

RED RIVER ALLUVIAL COUNTIES.

Bowie.—H. J. H. BREUSING, Texarkana, Ark., August 5, 1880.
Red River.—T. H. YOUNG, Clarksville, March 6, 1880.
Grayson.—(1) M. T. BRACKETT, Sherman, March 4, 1880; (2) J. P. HOPSON, Sherman, December 26, 1879.
Fannin.—(1) THOMAS LIGHTFOOT, Bonham, April 20, 1880; (2) GIDEON SMITH, Bonham, April 25, 1880; (3) JOHN L. BLAIR, Honey Grove, January 29, 1880.

OAK, HICKORY, AND PINE REGION.

Hopkins.—B. M. CAMP, Sulphur Springs, January 30, 1880.
Titus.—J. W. JACKSON, Mount Pleasant, January 31, 1880.
Morris.—JAMES M. BAKER, Wheatville, July 26, 1880.
Cass.—J. J. FOWLER, Linden, August 16, 1880.
Harrison.—(1) W. T. WARE, Jefferson, February 2, 1880; (2) H. V. SENTELL, Jefferson, April 10, 1880; (3) W. J. CAVEN, Marshall, March 28, 1880; (4) THOMAS STEELE, Elysian Fields, December 27, 1880.
Upshur.—J. M. GLASCO, Gilmer, March 22, 1880.
Wood.—J. H. NEWSOM, Mineola, January 31, 1880.
Van Zandt.—G. J. CLOUGH, Ben Wheeler, January 5, 1880.
Navarro.—(1) W. INGRAM, Rural Shade, March 8, 1880; (2) M. DRANE, Corsicana, April 16, 1880; (3) JAMES N. BRACEWELL, Corsicana, June 1, 1880.
Henderson.—N. P. COLEMAN, Athens, January 31, 1880.
Rusk.—(1) C. B. RICHARDSON, Henderson, January 5, 1880; (2) J. D. WOODWARD, M. D., Overton, January 26, 1880.
Panola.—H. FYKE, Carthage, February 8, 1880.
Shelby.—JOHN HOLT, Center Post-Office, January 3, 1881.
Nacogdoches.—R. P. WHITE, Nacogdoches, March 6, 1880.
Cherokee.—(1) J. T. WALKER, Etna (Smith county), September 15, 1880; (2) W. F. THOMPSON, Jacksonville, October 18, 1880.
Anderson.—(1) WILLIAM HAMLETT, sr., M. D., Beaver, January 1, 1880; (2) W. H. TUCKER, Palestine, February 2, 1880.
Freestone.—H. MANNING, Butler, February 13, 1880.
Limestone.—C. M. BELL, M. D., Tehuacana, January 16, 1880; J. Z. ADAMS, Kosse, 1880.
Houston.—C. E. DOUGLASS, Crockett, December 30, 1879.
Trinity.—(1) J. W. HAMILTON, Centralia, December 23, 1879; (2) SAMUEL T. ROBB, Trinity, December 24, 1879; (3) W. E. SHEFFIELD, Trinity, January 5, 1880.
Angelina.—E. L. ROBB, Homer, January 10, 1880.
Sabine.—C. W. HAMMOCK, Milam, 1880.
Jasper.—L. C. WHITE, Jasper, August 31, 1880.
Orange.—JOSEPH BUNN, Bunn's Bluff, 1880.
Hardin.—P. S. WATTS, Hardin, March 1, 1880.
Polk.—JOHN P. KALE, Livingston, January 1, 1880.
Madison.—P. K. GORE, Midway, January 5, 1880.
Grimes.—(1) P. D. SAUNDERS, Gibbon's Creek, February 20, 1880; (2) A. R. KILPATRICK, M. D., Navasota, May 15, 1880; (3) C. H. EHINGER, Navasota, February 18, 1880; (4) ROBERT D. BLACKSHEAR, Navasota, February 10, 1880.
Robertson.—H. D. PENDERGAST, Calvert, February 1, 1880.
Milam.—WILLIAM V. HEFLEY, Cameron, February 14, 1880.
Brazos.—J. W. BICKHAM, Bryan, March 16, 1880.
Burleson.—HILLARY RYAN, Caldwell, July 1, 1880.
Lee.—(1) Rev. A. J. LOUGHRIDGE, Tanglewood, May 18, 1880; (2) ROBERT H. FLANNIKEN, Tanglewood, February 4, 1880; (3) C. B. LONGLEY, Giddings, January 28, 1880.
Bastrop.—(1) JOHN FAWCETT, Smithville, January, 1880; (2) W. A. HIGHSMITH, Snake Prairie, December 25, 1880.
Gonzales.—B. W. BROTHERS, Harwood Station, February 8, 1880.
Wilson.—J. W. ANDERSON, Sutherland Springs, January 24, 1880.

150
808

COAST AND SOUTHERN PRAIRIE REGION.

Jefferson.—W. M. CAMPBELL, Beaumont, October 26, 1880.
Chambers.—M. BYERLY, Wallisville, February 4, 1881.
Galveston.—WILLIAM J. JONES and SIDNEY.SCUDDER, Galveston, January 8, 1880.
Harris.—(1) S. P CHRISTIAN, Lynchburg, 1881; (2) ROBERT BLALOCK, Lynchburg, September 7, 1880.
San Jacinto.—GREENE B. BYRD, Cold Springs, December 24, 1879.
Waller.—P. S. CLARKE, Hempstead, February 10, 1880.
Washington.—O. H. P. GARRETT, Brenham, February 14, 1880.
Fayette.—HENRY B. RICHARDS, La Grange, January 1, 1880.
Colorado.—(1) JOHN KNIPSCHEER and F. BOETTCHER, January 30, 1880; (2) W. T. McLEARY, M. D., Weimar, January 31, 1880; (3) W. H. CARLTON, Columbus, January 19, 1880.
Austin.—(1) MARTIN M. KENNY, Belleville, October 14, 1880; (2) J. H. KRAUCHER, Millheim, February 25, 1880.
Fort Bend.—(1) THOMAS B. HOWARD, Houston, June 24, 1880; (2) W. E. KENDALL, Houston, June 1, 1880.
Brazoria.—DAVID NATION, Columbia, February 24, 1880.
Lavaca.—(1) HENRY K. JUDD, Halletteville, January 10, 1880; (2) JOHN WILLIAMS, Williamsburg, January 15, 1880.
De Witt.—A. G. STEVENS, Concreto, April 10, 1880.
Karnes.—THOMAS BUCKMAN, Helena, April 3, 1880.
Atascosa.—(1) F. W. KLEMCKE, Somerset, January 22, 1880; (2) GEORGE. W. MUDD, Somerset, March 8, 1880.
Frio.—LEWIS OWINGS, Ireland Post-Office, September 23, 1880.
Aransas.—E. A. PERRENOT, Corpus Christi, 1880.
Live Oak.—G. W. JONES, Oakville, February 10, 1880.
Goliad.—Rev. J. E. VERNOR, Weeatche, January 30, 1880.
Victoria.—THOMAS R. COCKE, M. D., Victoria, January 5, 1880.
Jackson.—GEORGE F. HORTON, Texana, 1880.
San Patricio.—JAMES O. GAFFNEY, San Patricio, May 26, 1880.

CENTRAL PRAIRIE REGION.

Cooke.—W. W. HOWETH, Gainesville, December 10, 1880.
Hunt.—WILLIAM R. HOWARD, White Rock, March 18, 1880.
Collin.—(1) A. G. GRAVES, jr., McKinney, February 15, 1880; (2) GILES G. HOUSTON, McKinney, January 21, 1880; (3) W. G. MATHEWS, Plano, February 8, 1880.
Denton.—J. W. EVANS, Pilot Point, December 30, 1879.
Wise.—J. M. HOLMES, Decatur, August 16, 1880.
Tarrant.—BENJAMIN STUART, Handley, June 1, 1880.
Hood.—G. E. WALLS, Granbury, 1880.
Dallas.—(1) W. W. ROSS, Dallas, August 13, 1880; (2) JOHN H. COLE, Dallas, 1880.
Rockwall.—WILLIAM H. PRICE, Rockwall, December 27, 1879.
Kaufman.—H. B. McCORKLE, Elmo, October 19, 1880.
Ellis.—(1) G. W. COOPER, Bristol, March 12, 1880; (2) JAMES E. SMITH, Waxahatchie, June 19, 1880; (3) GEORGE W. HAMLETT, Milford, January 28, 1880; (4) S. C. TALLEY, Chambers' Creek, 1880.
Johnson.—W. A. MENAFEE, Cleburne, January 20, 1880; J. B. ALLARD and E. E. SKIPPER, Cleburne.
Erath.—J. G. O'BRIEN, Dublin, April 20, 1880.
Somervell.—SCOTT MILAM, Glenrose, May 25, 1880.
Bosque.—T. W. ARCHIBALD, Clifton, January 28, 1880.
Hill.—(1) JOHN P. COX, Hillsboro', February 17, 1880; (2) D. D. SANDERSON, Whitney, April 30, 1880; (3) W. S. THOMAS, Irene, 1880.
Coryell.—THOMAS WILLIAMSON, Pidcock Ranch, December 24, 1879.
McLennan.—(1) J. H. EARLE and D. R. GURLEY, Waco, February 5, 1880; (2) C. A. WESTBROOK, Mastersville, January 20, 1880.
Falls.—(1) A. E. WATSON, Marlin, January 15, 1880; (2) ED. C. McCULLOUGH, Mooresville, January 15, 1880; (3) P. LEA, West Falls, February 26, 1880.
Bell.—(1) MORITZ MAEDGEN, Troy, January 29, 1880; (2) A. J. HARRIS, Belton, January 22, 1880; (3) JOHN T. DULANY, Belton, December 29, 1879.
Lampasas.—THOMAS J. DURRETT, Lampasas, April 6, 1880.
Williamson.—(1) R. E. TALBOT, Georgetown, February 10, 1880; (2) ANDREW J. NELSON, Round Rock, April 3, 1880.
Travis.—(1) J. J. WHELESS, P. O. box 285, Austin, February 4, 1880; (2) ED. H. ROGERS & SON, Austin, March 30, 1880.
Blanco.—JOHN W. SPEER, Blanco, January 29, 1880.
Bexar.—(1) R. B. EVANS, Selma, February 17, 1880; (2) THEO. E. S. TRIP, San Antonio, February 10, 1880.
Medina.—Dr. A. WADGYMAR, San Antonio, April 29, 1880.
Guadalupe.—AUGUST EBERT, Marion, January 7, 1880.
Caldwell.—JOHN B. HOLT, Lockhart, August 12, 1880.
Kendall.—C. H. CLAUSS, Boerne, August 25, 1880.
Gillespie.—(1) THEO. B. SPLITTGERBER, Fredericksburg, February 8, 1880; (2) ADOLPH WEISS, Fredericksburg, January 31, 1880; (3) B. F. WHITE, Martinsburg, March 17, 1880.
Kerr.—W. P. COLEMAN, Kerrville, October 27, 1880.
Bandera.—JOHN CHRISTALL, Bandera City, March 1, 1880.
Uvalde.—T. W. REDMAN, Uvalde.

NORTHWESTERN RED-LOAM REGION.

Clay.—WILLIAM M. POPE, Buffalo Springs, October 27, 1880.
Jack.—C. M. SNODGRASS, Jacksboro', February 25, 1880.
Palo Pinto.—J. A. McLAREN, Cokelan, March 25, 1880.
Eastland.—A. J. STUART, Eastland, February 16, 1880.
Taylor.—(1) N. N. BROWNE, Buffalo Gap, May 7, 1880; (2) J. S. PORTER, Buffalo Gap, 1880.
Comanche.—W. L. BARTWELL, Comanche, March 6, 1880.
San Saba.—J. FRAZER BROWN, San Saba, January 1, 1880.
Mason.—HENRY M. HOLMES, Mason, March 25, 1880.
Llano.—C. M. COGGIN, M. D., Bluffton, March 23, 1880.
Burnet.—A. SCHROETER, Double Horn, January 20, 1880.
Throckmorton.—CHARLES McCORMICK, Throckmorton.

ADDITIONAL CORRESPONDENTS FROM WHOM INFORMATION HAS BEEN RECEIVED.—Christ. Dietert, Kerrville; W. A. Proctor, Paint Rock; J. F. Gordon, Coleman; James W. Ward, Corpus Christi; James T. Otey, Clarendon; D. L. Switzer and W. W. Blake, Jasper; E. K. Smith, McDade; C. A. Ricks, Homer; W. D. Willis, Livingston; Victor Bracht, Rockport; William H. Caldwell, Borjas; William H. Parvin, Belle Plain; R. A. Hutchison, Archer; F. W. Voight, Nacogdoches; T. J. Chambers, Liberty; T. W. Laney, Lockhart; H. F. Best, Texarkana; G. Salmon, Decatur; J. Brockman, Fredericksburg; J. W. Hackworth, Brenham; E. D. Sim, Victoria; Rev. R. M. Loughridge and J. T. Somervell, Marlin; J. R. Self, Corsicana; F. M. Graves, Hamilton; B. F. Duren, Crockett, and others.

SUMMARY OF ANSWERS TO SCHEDULE QUESTIONS.

The following pages embrace the answers to the question schedules that were sent to each cotton county of the state. They are presented in a condensed form, to enable the reader to obtain at a glance that information which would require much time and trouble if the answers were given in detail from each county in the state. Extracts from the schedule answers are given under most of the questions in addition to the general summary, and the writer can be identified either by the given county name or by a number prefixed to that name in the list of correspondents.

TILLAGE, IMPROVEMENT, ETC.

1. Usual depth of tillage (measured on land-side of furrow)? What draft is employed in breaking up?

The usual depth is from 2 to 4 inches, sometimes less, on the sandy uplands of the oak and hickory region and in the southern and northwestern prairie regions; 5 to 8 inches on the bottom lands of the state and in the central prairie region. The usual draft is one horse or mule on the sandy lands and two animals on the heavier lands of the state.

2. Is subsoiling practiced? If so, with what implements, and with what results?

OAK, HICKORY, AND PINE REGION: It is not practiced in twenty counties; in twelve counties it is practiced, but only "a very little" or "exceptionally", with a subsoil plow, scooter, or with diamond pointed bull-tongue plows; results are always good, and in several cases yields are reported to have increased from 30 to 50 per cent. *Brazos:* Results are good on heavy prairie soil; it is rarely practiced on sandy or timbered soil. Does no good on sandy soils. *Titus:* Very little, only on bottom lands; chiefly for corn, rarely for cotton. It is done by a scooter following a turn-plow; results are very fine for corn. 2 *Anderson:* Very little, only on old and worn lands, with subsoil plows of from 16 to 20 inch standards; results are good. *Harrison, Limestone,* and *Lee:* Very little; yields are greater, and crops endure extremes of wet and dry weather better.

CENTRAL BLACK PRAIRIE REGION: In twenty-four counties it is not practiced; in eight it is practiced a little; by following in the furrow of a turn-plow with a subsoil plow, bull-tongue, or another turn-plow, yields are increased from 20 to 30 per cent. 2 *Fannin:* Results are good where the soil is deep enough, or where the subsoil is impervious. 1 *Collin:* Very deep plowing has been practiced on a small scale with oxen without any decided results; heavy rains pack the soil together again. 2 *Navarro:* Subsoiling increases yields and enables crops to endure longer droughts. 1 *Dallas:* To a small extent; land has been plowed a second time with the same plow crossways at the same or 4 inches greater depth; land so treated in the fall will produce corn the following season in spite of the severest droughts.

SOUTHERN AND NORTHWESTERN PRAIRIE REGIONS: Only in eight counties. *Galveston:* Highly beneficial, except on sandy land. 2 *Colorado:* With fine results on all lands. *Llano* and *Taylor:* Yields are increased one-third, and crops endure droughts better.

3. Is fall-plowing practiced? With what results?

In twenty-two counties it is practiced, though very little, because of cotton picking, but with good results. Its objects are in three counties to turn the stubble under; in four counties to improve the soil and increase the yields; in one county to prepare the ground for sowing small grain. 1 *Anderson:* If it were practiced, it would facilitate the washing and gullying of the soil by the heavy rains. *Limestone:* Results are very satisfactory; the soil becomes more friable, vegetation is decomposed, and insects are destroyed. *Houston:* Results are good on stiff lands. *Wilson:* The soil endures drought better in the summer following; good results. *Colorado:* It is a good way to rid the soil of weeds and trash, and should be done before vegetation dies. *Atascosa:* Results are good if the rainfall is not too great, so that the soil washes and gullies. *Live Oak:* All the farming land is broken in the fall or early winter. *Leeson:* Results are good when it is again plowed in spring, but it can rarely be done before January; the latter is also true in *Galveston, Washington,* and *Fort Bend.*

4. Is fallowing practiced? Is the land tilled while lying fallow or only "turned out"? With what result in either case?

It is practiced very little throughout the state. The lands are in some of the counties, especially in the oak and hickory sandy region, only turned out. Such land is sometimes cultivated while thus resting. *Harrison:* After a year's rest an ordinary cereal crop may be obtained if the land is tilled while resting; otherwise the crop would consist of crab-grass and other weeds. One or two years of rest increases yields from 10 to 15 per cent. *Jasper:* Land is "turned out" or pastured, and improves if not severely tramped and eaten off by stock or rooted by hogs, either of which is ruinous.

5. Is rotation of crops practiced? If so, of how many years' course, and in what order of crops? With what result?

Rotation is practiced to some extent in many of the counties, but there is no regular system or order of crops, each farmer suiting his own convenience. Cotton and corn most generally alternate on the sandy timbered lands and southern prairies for a series of years, sometimes with other crops, while in the black prairie region wheat and oats are also sometimes planted after corn or cotton. *Harrison :* On fresh land corn and cotton alternate for nine or ten years ; then cotton alone is raised until the yield falls below 600 or 700 pounds of seed-cotton per acre, when the land is "turned out" or rested ; sometimes oats follow cotton. *Anderson :* The usual practice consists in raising cotton from three to six years on the same soil, then corn from one to three years ; pease, oats, and small patches of sweet potatoes are also raised. *Bell :* Not regularly. The best farmers follow cotton with corn or wheat, and corn with wheat, oats, or cotton, and never raise the same kind from the same land more than two consecutive years. *Fayette :* By some in three years' courses. Oats are sown just after removing corn from the land in the fall ; in the following May the oats are harvested and sweet potatoes are planted ; cotton is planted on the same land in the third year. *Fort Bend :* Stiff lands are best suited to cotton, and are exclusively devoted to that crop.

RESULTS.—*Jasper :* The soil endures longer. *Titus* and *Wise :* Fertility is maintained without manuring. *Burleson* and *Grimes :* Corn yields nearly 100 per cent. and cotton 20 per cent. more. *Anderson* and *Hopkins :* Discourages insect pests. *Hill :* (Black prairies) cotton bolls better, and corn is more certain. *Jack :* (Northwest) cotton is our fertilizer ; anything grows well after it.

6. What fertilizers or other direct means of improving the soil, are used by you, or in your region? With what results? Is green-manuring practiced? With what results?

In the timbered and sandy lands of the state fertilizers are used to a slight extent ; forty-seven of the counties report the application of cotton-seed or composts to the land by a few of the farmers. The yields are variously estimated to be increased from 15 to 300 per cent. In the black prairies of the central region, and the still comparatively fresh lands of the coast and northwestern regions, fertilizers are not thought necessary, there being as yet no apparently diminished yield. Green-manuring is practiced but little. *Nacogdoches* and *Sabine :* The prevailing practice in this eastern region is to shift the fencing so as to include fresh land, rather than to manure the old. *Harrison :* Very little effort is made to improve the soil by any means or material, in spite of the very profitable returns that might be realized. The practice (and a bad one it is) in this region is to use the soil for corn and cotton until it ceases to produce profitably, when it is abandoned in favor of fresh soil, which in turn is put through the same course. The land "turned out" soon becomes thickly studded with pine, persimmon, sedge-grass, and briers. After lying out seven or eight years, if not too rolling, it produces fairly well when again cultivated. Of late there is an apparent inclination to improve the old lands by pasturing stock. This must in a few years become a necessity, as there will soon be little available virgin soil left. *Limestone :* Little other than barn-yard manure is used, and 99 per cent. of that is allowed to waste. *Grimes :* Cotton-seed and barn-yard manure are used a little, chiefly in gardens and orchards or on sandy lands ; they double the yields, and are profitable even on the richest soils. Cow-pease are raised only on small patches ; they always improve the soil. 2 *Fannin :* None of consequence, though manuring would pay well on our best Red river lands, and better on the lighter soils. When cotton-seed is applied directly to corn in the hill, at the rate of 10 bushels to an acre, the yield of corn is increased 10 bushels per acre. Green-manuring was formerly practiced, but is not now, owing to the system of labor now prevailing. Cow-pease are most satisfactory as a feed crop and fertilizer. I have cultivated a piece of river bottom land twelve years successively in cotton without any diminution in quantity or perceptible deterioration in the quality of the product. The stalks are never allowed to be burned, but by dragging a heavy bush over the field they are ground to small fragments, which are easily plowed under. The average yield of lint-cotton on this land has been 500 pounds or more per acre ; in 1879 it was 625 pounds per acre. There are other lands adjacent of the same quality, which by a system of raking and burning of the corn and cotton stalks, etc., have been so impoverished that they do not produce a third or half as much as when fresh ; and the soil has lost its mellowness, and is tilled with more difficulty. There is hardly any doubt that our deepest and best soils would last forever if stock were not allowed to tramp the ground, wet or dry, and eat what is left of the crop, and cotton-seed were all returned to the soil. Under such circumstances the soil and the yields would even improve to an astonishing degree. So far as cotton-growing is concerned, our best soils would be inexhaustible if all except the lint be returned to them. A most pernicious practice is that of turning stock into the field as soon as the cotton is picked to feed on what is left of the bolls, foliage, and even smaller branches, and then burning the remainder ; in addition to which the soil is tramped and packed in all kinds of weather.

7. How is cotton-seed disposed of? If sold, on what terms, or at what price?

There are oil-mills at Dallas, Hempstead, Bryan, Galveston, Navasota, and Calvert (also at Shreveport, Louisiana), and in the neighboring counties to these places much seed is sold to the mills at from 5 to 10 cents per bushel. Along the railroads, and at the chief stations, seed is also sold to buyers, who ship to these mills. In counties at a distance some seed is sold at much lower prices. Throughout the state the seed is otherwise either fed to cattle or allowed to rot and go to waste, except in the eastern counties, where much is returned to the soil. The seed is in some counties used as fuel for steam-engines.

8. Is cottonseed-cake used with you for feed or manure?

In the vicinity of the cotton-seed oil mills, and at points on some of the railroads, the cake is used to some extent as feed for stock, especially milch cows ; as a manure it is seldom used. In other portions of the state the cake has not been introduced, and is scarcely known. *Grimes :* Sheep, cattle, horses, and mules eat it greedily when mixed with equal parts of corn-meal or bran. It is also used as manure alone for growing fruits and vegetables, for which purposes it is equal, if not superior, to guano. Cottonseed-oil mills were at first considered a great curse in this community, for they consumed the seed which should have been fed to stock and returned to the soil. The negroes especially would sell the last seed in the fall, and then depend upon owners for *seed* to plant in spring. 812

Farmers have, however, during this winter (1879–'80) arrived at a different conclusion. Trial uses of the products that remain after removing the oil from the seed have determined that for feeding stock of all kinds they are far superior to the seed itself, superior to corn and fodder ; they produce more milk when fed to dairy cows than any other feed yet tried. The cotton-seed cake, meal, and hulls are also cheaper than other kinds of feed. What has heretofore been wasted will hereafter be utilized. Those who first opposed the factory are now its strongest supporters, and agree that it is *very* profitable to the planter to sell the seed to the oil factory and buy the resulting hulls and cake for feeding and fertilizing purposes.

PLANTING AND CULTIVATION OF COTTON.

9. What preparation is usually given to cotton land before bedding up?

Fall plowing is sometimes done on old stubble land, but the almost universal practice is simply spring plowing and bedding after the stalks have been knocked down and sometimes burned.

10. Do you plant in ridges? How far apart?

Cotton is planted in ridges throughout the state, except in some of the western counties of the prairie regions, where the land is not thrown up in ridges. *Hood:* "On account of dry seasons the practice of ridging is being abandoned, thus diminishing the liability of the soil to become dry about the roots of the plants." The usual distances given between cotton rows are from 3 to 4 feet on uplands and from 4 to 5 feet on bottom or rich lands, where the plant has a vigorous growth.

11. What is your usual planting time?

The earliest dates are from March 1 to 15, reported from *Bastrop, Angelina, Wilson, Caldwell, San Patricio,* and *De Witt:* From March 15 to April 1 by twenty-four counties of the southern portion of the state; from April 1 to 15 by a large majority of counties, and from April 15 to May 15 by seventeen counties of the central prairie region. *Kaufman:* June planting will mature in favorable seasons. *Sabine:* Cotton planted in the first week of May succeeded best in five of seven years' experience.

12. What variety of cotton do you prefer?

There are twenty-seven different names given as representing different varieties, though it is more than probable that the most of them are but supposed improvements on some of those well known in other states. Those most commonly mentioned are the Schuback or storm-proof variety, said to retain its cotton in the boll during high winds, and preferred in the open black prairie country of the central region, and mentioned by forty counties; the Dixon variety, preferred in the timbered and sandy lands, and mentioned by twenty-four counties; the Petit Gulf variety, by fifteen counties; the Cheatham and Hurlong varieties, each mentioned ten times; Meyers, four times; the Sugar-loaf, Hefley, and South American, three times each; Bagley, Peeler, Moon, and Armstrong, two times each; Matagorda Silk, Poor-man's Relief, Bohemian, and others, once each. The sea-island long staple and Kemp's long staple are also mentioned once each. ? *Harrison:* The best plan is to select the best seed from common varieties and cultivate thoroughly and judiciously. *McLennan:* The best seed, without regard to name, is obtained from the best farmers, who make selections annually from the best part of their crops. *Fort Bend:* Varieties from Tennessee and northern Georgia produce the largest yields in this (coast) region, especially the Dixon, from northern Georgia. *Brazoria:* The seed brought yearly from the extreme northern part of the state or from the Indian territory afford the largest yields and by early maturity escape the ravages of the caterpillar.

WORM-PROOF COTTON.—Mr. L. C. White, of Jasper, writes that after a number of years' trial he has succeeded in producing a hybrid variety of cotton that is entirely worm-proof. It also grows and yields well, and is an early variety, as was shown in the fact that his crop, planted on the 4th of April, had matured and been gathered by the last of August. The following experiments made to test the immunity of such cotton against the attacks of the caterpillar may be of interest: ? *Trinity:* In September the worms destroyed a field of cotton not more than 200 yards from the garden in which a worm-proof variety from Arkansas was growing. I pulled up a stalk covered with worms and set it down in the midst of the worm-proof cotton and they refused to eat it. I then put on some of the most voracious looking worms I could find in the field, but even they refused to dine upon it. The worm-proof cotton continued to fruit till frost. My opinion is that it will remain worm-proof as long as the leaves continue as bitter as they have for the past two years. What effect the climate may have on this bitter quality remains to be seen. This cotton yields finely, is easy to pick, and the lint is long and fine, and is classed as good middling. *Angelina:* The worms attacked the crops of a worm-proof variety from Arkansas, but not until other varieties had been entirely eaten up by them. The opinion among the farmers is that young worms can do nothing with it, as its leaves are very thick and rough; it has large and heavy branches from the ground up, and they bear full and large bolls.

13. How much seed is usually used per acre?

Two bushels in twelve counties, 1 or 1½ bushels in thirteen counties, and one-half bushel in *Limestone* and *Milam*, of the timbered and sandy region of eastern Texas. One bushel in twenty-two counties, one-half bushel in *Hood, Bosque,* and *Lampasas,* of the central black prairie region, and two bushels in six counties of the western red-loam region. In the coast counties and in a few of those of regions mentioned the number of bushels is greater. *De Witt* and *San Patricio,* of the coast, each report one-half bushel.

14. What implements do you use in planting?

Throughout the state any plow that is convenient for making a furrow is used for planting, the bull-tongue plow most generally, the scooter next, and the shovel and turn-plow often. In some instances the seed is covered with a sweep or cultivator; very often with a board attached to a plow-stock; more frequently with the harrow, and sometimes with brush, block, or log. The "cotton-seed planters" vary from the rudest to the most improved; they are designated "home-made" in several reports, and as "keg planters" in several others. In most cases the kind of "planter" is not specified.

15. Are "cotton-seed planters" used in your region? What opinion is held of their efficacy or convenience?

They are used more or less throughout the state, in the eastern timbered region, the central prairie region, and a few of those of the western red-loam and southern prairie regions. They seem to be home-made implements, and opinions regarding them are various, a large number (twenty-six) of the central prairie counties regarding them as time-, seed-, and labor-saving machines, planting regularly and uniformly, and making after-cultivation easy. Opinions concerning them are not expressed in the majority of reports from the rest of the state. *Wood:* The land here is too stumpy and rooty for their use. *Nacogdoches:* They have been laid aside for the next generation. *Titus:* The few in use are not a success. *Burnet:* They do not plant thick enough. *Somervell:* They are more convenient, but less efficient than hands. *Falls:* Successful only on light soils. *Cooke:* Almost universally adopted.

16. How long usually before the seed comes up?

The time varies from three to ten days, with an average of about seven days, and is dependent upon depth of seed below the surface and the temperature and moisture of the soil. Early planting requires a longer time for the plant to appear than if planted late.

17. At what stage of growth do you thin out your stand, and how far apart?

Usually throughout the state when the third or fourth leaf appears, or as soon as a stand is assured. The crop is first chopped out with hoes, leaving a number of plants in a bunch, which are afterward thinned to one or two plants for each hill. The distance apart depends on the character of the soil and consequent growth of the plant. Fourteen counties of the oak and hickory region report from 10 to 18 inches; fifteen counties from 18 to 24 inches, and a few counties as much as 36 inches. In the black prairie region twenty-two counties report from 12 to 20 inches, others a greater distance. In other regions the usual distance is from 18 to 24 inches, except in the Brazos alluvial lands and Frio county, where as much as 36 or 48 inches is given. In *San Patricio* sea-island cotton is thinned when about 18 inches high to single plants 36 inches apart.

18. Is your cotton liable to suffer from "sore-shin"?

OAK, HICKORY, AND PINE REGION: In three counties it rarely occurs; in twenty-four counties it occurs more or less, but only when the weather in the spring is wet, cool, and backward, or the nights are cold and windy, or when cotton has been planted too early. *Madison:* It appears early in the season if the crop is allowed to become weedy. In ten counties it does not occur, and is not known in some of them.

CENTRAL BLACK PRAIRIE REGION: It is rare and exceptional in eleven counties; it occurs in other eleven counties only in wet, cold, backward springs, or when cotton is planted too early. *Tarrant:* Cold weather causes "sore-shin". In fourteen counties it does not appear, and in some of them is not known.

NORTHWESTERN REGION: In *Palo Pinto* slightly; in *Taylor* slightly, owing to cold winds; and in *San Saba*, but not in the other counties.

SOUTHERN PRAIRIE REGION: Very little or rarely in six counties; in five counties only in cold, wet, late springs, or if cotton is planted too early. It does not appear in four counties. *Austin* and *Fayette:* Yes; if hoed carelessly or if too young. *Colorado* and *Lavaca:* In cold, late springs, or when damaged by careless and early hoeing.

19. What after-cultivation do you give, and with what implements?

The usual method is first to "bar off" or run a plow close to the plant, throwing the dirt from it. Then the crop is thinned out with hoes, and the dirt is thrown back to the plant. The method after this differs greatly; the majority of farmers give a surface cultivation with sweeps or shovel-plows to keep down the grass, while others plow out the middles with a turning-plow first, and then simply use sweeps. A number of hoeings are given to the plants through the season till "laid by". The following extracts from reports are given: *Harrison:* A plowing every ten to twelve days until about July 15, when the crop is laid by; first stir the soil and throw a little to the row with the scooter or small shovel-plow, then clean out the row with hoes; plow again with sweep or shovel, or, if the weather be wet or the field grassy, the turn-plow is used; two or three hoeings are given. *Titus:* Three days after thinning side up with a small sweep, next plow out with a long shovel, after which the solid sweep, or (what is better) a short scooter, with heel-sweep attached, is used. *Cherokee:* First throw soil immediately about the plants, then keep down the grass and weeds until the crop shades the ground; sweeps are used, and quite successfully, where the ground was broken before planting. *Trinity:* Dirt is thrown to the row with a solid sweep or bull-tongue plow, and the ground is then kept free from weeds the best way possible. The turn-plow and scraper are also used. *Upshur* and *Freestone:* Bar off or throw the dirt from the row, thin to a stand, sweep near the rows, break out the middles, and sweep again. *Grimes:* Bar off, thin to a stand, throw dirt to the row with plows and hoes until the crop is laid by; sweeps and double-shovel cultivators are used; plowing is shallow. *Burleson:* Some bar off with the turning-plow and then use sweeps; others use sweeps altogether. *Milam:* Usually plow first with the cultivator, then deep in the middles with shovel or bull-tongue plows; repeat until the bolls open. The practice varies with seasons. *Collin:* Bulky cultivators, double shovels, sweeps, and hoes are used; the turn-plow is used on flat lands, where the ridges should be kept higher. The chief thing is to keep the grass down. *Bell:* Double shovels, sweeps, and sulky cultivators are used; in ordinary seasons the crop is plowed once in two weeks to keep weeds down; oftener in wet, and less frequently in dry seasons; the less cultivated the better. *Gillespie:* When rows are not ridged the soil is thrown from them toward the middles with a scraper or double shovel; the stand is then thinned, weeds are then kept down with double shovel, sweep, or cultivator, and hoe until the bolls appear. *Erath:* Bar off, thin to a stand, hoe once, and plow about twice, using turn-plows, sweeps, bull-tongues, or scooters. *Travis:* Three plowings and two hoeings after thinning to a stand, using sweeps, double shovels; progressive farmers use cultivators with four shovels, which run astride the row. *Harris:* Bar off with bull-tongue plow, hoe out, and return the soil to the row with sweeps; the shovel-plow is sometimes used. *Fort Bend:* Four to six workings are given; first with the hoe and turn-plow, afterward with the sweep (and hoe if necessary); cultivators are used to a limited extent, but they cause the plants to run too much to weed. *Colorado:* The bull-tongue, shovel, harrow, sweep, cultivator, and (if weeds become large) the turn-plow are used, but chiefly the sweep; sometimes a final hoeing is given.

20. What is the height usually attained by your cotton before blooming? When do you usually see the first blooms?

The usual height on the timbered uplands and prairies is from 10 to 18 inches, and on the bottom lands from 18 to 24 or 30 inches. The earliest dates in which the first blooms are seen are about the last of April, in *Bastrop* and *Victoria;* early in May in nine counties of the coast region; about the middle of May in two counties of the coast, and in *Brazos, Lee,* and *Robertson,* and other extreme southern counties of the timbered region; the last of May or early in June in the central counties of the state, and about the last of June or early in July in the northern counties. 2 *Trinity:* About one month from the time of planting.

21. When do the bolls first open?

The earliest date is from May 15 to June 1, in *Victoria* county; June 15 in *Lee* and *Bastrop,* of the oak and hickory region; late in June in *Grimes,* of the same region, and in four counties of the coast region; early in July in other southern counties of the state; usually the last of July in the central, east, and west counties, and from August 1 to 15 in the northern counties. In the northwestern red-loam region the dates are July in *Clay* and *San Saba,* September in *Llano* and *Taylor,* and August in the other counties. 1 *Bexar:* Bolls open about forty days after blooming.

814

22. When do you begin your first picking? How many pickings do you usually make?

About July 10 in *De Witt*, July 15 in *Lavaca* and *Brazoria*, and later in July in a large number of the southern counties. From August 1 to 10 in *Bell* and *Gillespie* of the central prairie region, *Clay* and *Jack* of the northwestern region, and the other southern counties of the coast and timbered regions. The middle of August in the central or interior counties of the state, and about September 1 in the northern counties of the eastern timbered region, and in the greater number of those of the central black prairie region, and also in the northwestern region. The latest dates are October 1 in *Llano* and *Taylor*. Three pickings are usually given in most of the counties, the work continuing until the crop is gathered.

23. Do you ordinarily pick all your cotton?

The crop is usually all gathered, excepting such as is lost by storms or by falling to the ground, or that which, opening late, is too much scattered to justify picking. *Polk:* About one-fourth is left in the field. *Wilson:* 100 pounds of seed-cotton per acre are usually left. *Grayson* and *Fort Bend:* One-tenth is wasted or left in the field.

24. At what date does picking usually close?

In the greater number of counties from December 1 to 30. In November in *Navarro, Anderson, Wilson, Lee, Brazos, Gillespie, Medina, Palo Pinto, San Saba, Jack,* and seven counties of the coast region. In October in *Chambers* and *Austin*. In *Bowie*, February 1.

25. At what time do you expect the first "black frost"?

OAK, HICKORY, AND PINE REGION: Throughout the region usually from the 1st to the 15th of November. The following counties report frosts in October, from the 15th to the 30th: *Bowie, Titus, Harrison, Wood, Henderson, Rusk, Nacogdoches, Cherokee, Anderson, Madison, Burleson,* and 3 *Lee*. (1 and 2 *Lee* report that black frost is not known in that county.)

CENTRAL BLACK PRAIRIE REGION: From November 15 to 30 in all of the counties of the region except the following, which report its appearance during the last of October: *Cooke, Fannin, Tarrant, Dallas,* 2 *Navarro,* 2 *Falls,* and 3 *Gillespie*.

NORTHWESTERN REGION: In November in *Clay, Comanche,* and *San Saba,* December in *Llano* and *Mason,* and October in *Jack* and *Palo Pinto* counties.

SOUTHERN PRAIRIE REGION: November in fifteen counties; December in *Chambers, Live Oak, Colorado,* and *Jefferson*. In *Fort Bend* "the average time for the appearance of 'black frost' for the past forty years has been November 15".

26. Do you pen your seed-cotton in the field or gin as picking progresses?

The majority of farmers throughout the state either pen their cotton in the fields (some piling it on the ground) or place it securely under shelter until the picking season is nearly over, or until good prices induce them to gin it for market. Others gin as picking progresses (or when enough for a bale), especially in the central prairie region, where in the counties of *Hunt, Collin, Dallas, Erath, Falls, Williamson,* and *Bell* the practice is very general; also in *Colorado, Austin,* and *Karnes*, of the coast region, and *Hopkins* and *Sabine*, of the eastern counties. *Harrison* and *Titus:* Some pile it on the ground; a bad practice, as it gets moist, heats, and turns yellow. *Waller:* Penned in the field and hauled to gin at the end of each week. *Victoria:* Field pens are a thing of the past.

GINNING AND BALING.

27. What gin do you use? How many saws? What motive power—steam, horses, or mules?

Pratt's gins, with from 40 to 100 saws, is reported in forty-four counties; Gullett's, with from 45 to 180 saws, in thirty-one; Brown's, with from 40 to 80 saws, in nineteen; Winship's, with from 45 to 80 saws, in seven; the Chatham, with from 50 to 60 saws, in five; the Eagle, with from 40 to 60; the Carver, with from 45 to 60, and the Etna, with from 50 to 60 saws, each in three; the Hulsey and Hall gins, with from 45 to 80 saws, each in two; the Billup, Massey, Excelsior, Kingsland, Fergerson, Schadwick, Phœnix, Tarver, Centennial, Rose, and Logan gins, with from 50 to 80 saws, in one county each. The use of steam-power is reported in 81 counties; horse or mule in 58; water-power in 10. More lint separated in a given time by steam, but a better quality of the staple is produced where horse-power is used. *Jack, Colorado, Jasper, Lavaca, Lee,* and *Gillespie:* On account of safety and cheaper insurance horse- or mule-power is preferable. 2 *Anderson:* One-fourth of the gins are run by steam-power, the balance by mules, horses, or oxen. *Kaufman:* Previous to May, 1880, there had not been a gin in *Frio* county; likewise in *San Saba,* previous to September of the same year.

28. How much clean lint do you make in a day's run of 10 hours?

Pratt's gin of 80 saws, with steam-power, will make from 5,000 to 7,500 pounds (*Colorado*); 5,000 pounds (*Falls*); 4,000 pounds (*Red River, Hill,* and *Falls*). With mule-power, from 960 to 1,300 pounds (*Taylor*); 75 saws, with steam-power, 3,500 pounds (*Atascosa*); 70 saws, with steam-power, 4,000 pounds (*Henderson*); 65 saws, with steam-power, 2,000 pounds (*Karnes*); 60 saws, with steam-power, 5,000 pounds (*Grimes*); 4,500 pounds (*Harrison*); 3,750 pounds (*Jefferson*); 3,000 pounds (*Bexar*); 2,500 pounds (*Fayette*); 2,000 pounds (*Williamson*); 50 saws, with steam- or mule-power, 1,500 pounds (*Harrison, Panola, Shelby, Harris,* and *Nacogdoches*); 40 saws, with horse-power, 800 pounds (*Hardin*).

Gullett's gin of three stands, of 60 saws each, or 180 saws, with steam-power, will make 8,500 pounds (*Falls*); 80 saws, with steam, 5,000 pounds (*Navarro*); 4,000 pounds (*Lampasas*); 3,500 pounds (*Collin*); 70 saws, with steam, 4,500 pounds (*Travis*); 4,000 pounds (*Navarro*); 60 saws, with steam, from 6,000 to 7,000 pounds (*Hunt*); 4,500 pounds (*Comanche*); 2,500 pounds (*Chambers* and *Grayson*); 60 saws, with horse-power, from 2,000 to 2,500 pounds (*Hunt*); 60 saws, steam, 2,000 pounds (*McLennan*); with mule-power, 2,500 pounds (*San Saba*); 40 saws, with horse-power, 1,000 pounds (*Jasper*).

Carver gin of 90 saws, with steam-power, will produce 500 pounds every half hour, or 10,000 pounds in a day's run (*Grimes*).

The Brown gin, 80 saws, with steam, 5,000 pounds (*San Jacinto*); 2,500 pounds (*Eastland*); 60 saws, with steam, 2,500 pounds (*Angelina*); with mule-power, 2,000 pounds (*Clay*); 50 saws, with mule-power, 2,000 pounds (*Fannis*).

The Winship gin, 80 saws, with steam, 2,500 pounds (*Eastland*); 60 saws, with steam, 3,500 pounds (*Hamilton*); 3,000 pounds (*Fannin*); 50 saws, with mule-power, 2,500 pounds (*Cherokee*).

The Chatham gin, 80 saws, with steam, 4,000 pounds (*Hill*); 50 saws, with steam, 5,000 pounds (*Trinity*).

The Hulsey and Logan gin, 50 saws, with mule-power, 1,200 pounds (*Morris*). The Tarver gin, 60 saws, with steam, 3,500 pounds (*Harris*). The Etna gin, 50 saws, with mule-power, 1,775 pounds (*Cherokee*). The Centennial gin, 50 saws, with mule-power, 1,500 pounds (*Harrison*). The Rose gin, 60 saws, with steam, 4,500 pounds (*Harrison*). The Eagle gin, 60 saws, with steam, 3,000 pounds (*Fannin*); with mule-power, 2,000 pounds (*Anderson*). The Billup gin, 50 saws, with horse-power, 1,500

pounds (*Anderson*). Hulse gin, 60 saws, with mule-power, 2,500 pounds (*Fannin*). Schadwick's gin, 60 saws, with mule-power, 3,600 pounds (*Llano*); 85 pounds lint for 10 saws for 10 hours is good work (*Grimes*).

29. How much seed-cotton on an average is required for a 475-pound bale of lint?

In sixteen counties, 1,425 pounds; in three counties, 1,495 pounds; in twenty-three counties, as much as 1,545 pounds; in twenty-five counties, 1,665 pounds; in five counties, 1,725 pounds; in six counties, 1,780 pounds; in five counties, 1,900

pounds; in *Llano, Lavaca*, and *Fayette*, 2,000 pounds, and in *Trinity*, 2,130 pounds. The greatest number of high estimates are from counties outside of the sandy timbered region of the eastern part of the state.

30. What press do you use for baling? What press is generally used in your region? What is its capacity per day?

Brooks' press is reported in thirty-one counties; Reynolds' in fourteen; old-fashioned wooden and compass presses each in six; iron screw press, Williams' and Farmers and Planters', each in four; the Southern Standard and Gray's, each in two; Winship's and the Grasshopper presses, each in three; the Colburn, Wilson, Smith, McGowan, Eclipse, Schadwick's, Self-return screw, Albertson segment screw, Simmond's, and Caruthers' and Crenshaw's, each in one. Brooks' press, with 6 men and 2 mules, will pack 30 bales in 10 hours (*Wood*); with 3 men and 1 horse, 15 bales (*San Saba*); with steam-power, 12 bales (*De Witt*); with 3 men and 2 horses, from 9 to 15 bales (*Madison*); with 2 men and 2 horses, from 10 to 12 bales (*Bell*); with 2 men and 1 horse, 10 bales (*Somervell, Grimes,*

Johnson, and others). Reynolds' press, with steam-power, will pack 20 bales (*Ellis*); from 10 to 12 bales (*Titus*); from 8 to 10 bales (*Atascosa*); with from 4 to 5 men and 1 mule, from 15 to 20 bales (*Harrison*); with horse-power, 10 bales (*Ellis*). The wooden press, with 4 men and 1 horse, will pack 16 bales (*Collin*); from 10 to 12 bales (*Robertson*); with 8 men and 2 horses, 12 bales (*Brazoria*); with 2 men and 1 horse, 10 bales (*Somervell and Victoria*). The iron-screw press with steam-power will pack from 15 to 20 bales (*Upshur*); with 4 men and 1 horse, 16 bales (*Collin*); with 3 men and 1 mule, from 8 to 10 bales (*Fayette*). The "Self-return screw press" will pack 20 bales while others pack 10 bales (*Navarro*). The capacity of other presses run by horse-power is given at 10 or 12 bales.

31. Do you use rope or iron ties for baling? If the latter, what fastening do you prefer? What kind of bagging is used?

The use of iron ties is universal throughout the state. The preference for the arrow or buckle fastening is reported in forty-five counties; no preference from eight counties. The Beard hook is preferred in *Navarro, Brazoria,* and *Williamson*; both arrow and Beard in *Falls*; Davis hook in *Coryell*; alligator fastening in *Sabine*; either the buckle or Beard hook in *Brazos*; Schadwick's fastening in *Llano*. The use of double

anchor bagging is reported by forty-two counties; jute, 2 pounds per yard, by twenty-two; "India", by nineteen; Texas mills, 1½ pounds per yard, by six; Kentucky, by eight; manila, by four; hemp, by three; greenleaf, gunny, and bark each, by two; and Saint Louis, Indiana, Dundee, grass, Eureka, and elephant bagging are reported each by one county.

32. What weight do you aim to give your bales? Have transportation companies imposed any conditions in this respect?

All the counties excepting twelve report 500 pounds. Railroad freight charges are almost universally by the bale, regardless of weight. Forty counties report that merchants deduct $1 per bale for all bales weighing less than 400 pounds. In *Tarrant* the deduction is $2; in *Rusk*, from $1 50 to $2 50; in *Brazos* and *Robertson*, one-half cent per pound. Bales are discounted if less than 450 pounds in *Titus* and *Sabine*; in *Johnson*, $2 50 per bale. In *Lavaca*, if less than 300 pounds; in *Van Zandt*, if less than 350 pounds; in *Colorado* and *Grayson*, $1 per bale if less than 300 pounds. *Bell:* If a bale weighs between 400

and 450 pounds it is discounted by merchants one-quarter per cent. of market value, and if between 350 and 400 pounds one-half per cent. *Houston* and *Karnes:* When cotton is lost carriers pay for actual weight. *Jasper:* Bales are required to be entirely covered. *Collin:* Freight charges are extra on bales exceeding 500 pounds in weight, but no deduction is made on bales weighing less. *Navarro:* For short distances the charges are per bale; for long distances, per 100 pounds. *San Saba* and *Eastland:* Farmers have no intercourse with transportation companies.

DISEASES, INSECT ENEMIES, ETC.

33. By what accidents of weather, diseases, or insect pests is your cotton crop most liable to be injured (caterpillar, boll-worm, shedding, rot of boll, rust, blight)? At what dates do these several pests or diseases usually make their appearance, and to what cause is the trouble attributed by your farmers?

OAK, HICKORY, AND PINE REGION: The caterpillar and boll-worm are of common occurrence in the following counties: *Bowie, Hopkins, Henderson, Harrison, Rusk, Panola, Nacogdoches, Cass, Cherokee, Anderson, Houston, Trinity, Hardin, Madison, Grimes, Brazos, Lee,* and *Gonzales,* occasionally in *Red River* and *Navarro,* and rarely in *Milam*. The time of appearance varies from June to October. The caterpillar is common in *Titus,* but comes too late to do much damage; is more dreaded than anything else in *Angelina* and *Sabine.* Hot days and cold nights about May 15 favor the growth of mildew to feed the caterpillar in *Jasper.* Does little harm in *San Jacinto* and *Robertson.* It occurs to some extent in *Morris, Wood,* and *Wilson.* The boll-worm appears generally in *Titus,* and is the worst enemy of all; it often destroys one-third of the crop,

being present from the dropping of cotton-blooms to maturity of the crop. Also, in *Morris, Van Zandt, Wood,* and *Freestone;* occasionally in *Angelina* and *Sabine.* Aphides are of common occurrence in *Morris, Upshur, Henderson, Nacogdoches,* and *Brazos;* "attributable to cold wet springs." Shedding is common in all of the counties of this region except *Wood, Van Zandt, Rusk, Shelby, Houston, Jasper, Hardin, Madison, San Jacinto,* and *Milam,* and is generally caused by extreme conditions of the weather, wet or dry. Rust and rot of bolls occur commonly in *Bowie, Titus, Cass, Harrison, Upshur, Panola, Angelina, Anderson, Trinity, Polk, Madison* (when too much shaded by foliage), *Grimes, Brazos, Lee, Nacogdoches, Sabine, Robertson;* generally attributable to wet autumns. Rust is found in *Hopkins, Freestone, Bastrop,* and *Red River.* Blight is of

816

general occurrence in *Red River, Hopkins, Titus, Cass, Brazos, Lee, Trinity*, and *Bastrop;* occasionally in *Cherokee* and *Anderson* in July, and is confined to special spots, where the plants invariably die; the cause must lie in the soil. Drought causes trouble in *Hopkins, Wood, Rusk, Freestone, Limestone, Grimes, Robertson*, and *Wilson;* "undoubtedly attributable to uniform south or southeast winds without changes of temperature either way." Excessive rains damage the cotton crop more than anything else (*Red River*).

CENTRAL BLACK PRAIRIE REGION: The caterpillar appears extensively in *Grayson, Burnet, Hunt, Tarrant, Dallas, Rockwall, Bosque, Navarro, Coryell, Travis, Medina, Guadalupe, Caldwell, Gillespie*, and *Kerr;* to some extent in *Collin, Somervell*, and *Lampasas;* rarely in *Falls, Blanco*, and *Denton*. In *Fannin* and *Wise* it is always too late to do any damage. Time of appearance varies from early in the summer to late in the fall. The boll-worm occurs generally in 28 counties of the region. The worms are, in most cases, attributed to too much rain and cool nights. Aphides are common in *Tarrant* and *Dallas*, and occasional in *Fannin*. The army-worm is found in *Bexar* county, being attributed to a moth called the candle-fly; and in *Kendall*, where it is considered as a ore destructive to cotton crops than anything else. Shedding is of common occurrence in all of the counties of this region, excepting *Hamilton, Burnet, Comal*, and *Guadalupe;* it is owing to extreme states of the weather, wet or dry. Rot of bolls and rust are of general occurrence in *Fannin, Denton, Dallas*, and *Kaufman;* occur to some extent in *Hunt* and *Collin*, and are never heard of in *Bexar*. Rot of bolls occurs in *Tarrant, Coryell*, and *Blanco;* rarely in *Travis*. Rust appears quite commonly in *Wise*. Blight is a source of injury to the cotton crops in *Fannin, Wise, Hamilton, Bell*, and *Bosque;* to some extent in *Hunt, Collin, Hill*, and *Williamson;* rarely in *Travis*, and never heard of in *Bexar*. Drought occur in *Bosque, Navarro, Falls, Bell, Williamson*, and *Bexar*. All these troubles are attributed entirely to the weather in most of the counties.

"On the high and extensive prairies, where cotton grows and matures to perfection, it is blown out by the constant south winds almost as fast as it opens. To save it by immediate picking is impracticable where there is much to pick" (*Fannin*).

"Shedding is attributed to a partial arrest of the supply of plant-food, and the consequent insufficiency to maintain the large number of bolls; hence their death" (*Erath*).

"When the young plants are about five or six days old they are often destroyed, when the nights are warm and damp, by night-ants, beetles, and cut-worms. The only way to compensate for this trouble is to plant an abundance of seed, and thus make liberal allowance for these pests. Sometimes on

the finest looking plants, loaded with foliage, blooms and bolls are observed to die on spots of ground scattered over as much as 10 varas, apparently not from any fault of the soil, for the trouble occurs in spots. The root seems first to be affected; it is found covered with mold" (*Kendall*).

NORTHWESTERN REGION: The caterpillar never causes any serious trouble in *Comanche;* they are rarely found in *Eastland*. The boll-worm is of common occurrence in *Jack, Palo Pinto*, and *Llano;* occasionally in *Taylor*. The grasshopper is troublesome in *San Saba* and *Palo Pinto*. Shedding damages the crop in *Jack, Eastland, Taylor, Comanche*, and *Llano*. Rust is a source of trouble in *Llano*, due to a lack of sunshine, and appears soon after heavy rains. Excessive rains also do damage. Blight appears to some extent, in spots, in *Taylor*. Drought occurs in *Jack, Eastland*, and *Taylor*. The web-worm is sometimes injurious on black bottom lands in *Comanche* when cotton is coming up, and is attributable to cool nights.

SOUTHERN PRAIRIE REGION: The caterpillar and boll-worm are of common occurrence in *Chambers, Galveston, Fayette, Colorado, Austin, Washington, Jefferson, Harris, Waller, Fort Bend* ("if not checked, destroys the crop from August 15 to 25"), in *Brazoria, Lavaca, De Witt, Karnes, Atascosa, San Patricio, Frio, Live Oak;* is the chief pest in *Goliad* county, appearing any time in June to late in August. If it comes early a half crop or more will mature after it disappears. In *Victoria* "the later it comes the less the damage it does; if in August an average crop will still mature; it is the chief pest". The time of its appearance, and also that of the boll-worm, varies from about June to October, attributable to wet weather in the majority of cases. The boll-worm is common in *Chambers, Galveston, Fayette, Colorado, Austin,* and *Washington;* does not do much damage in *Fort Bend;* is occasionally found in *Goliad*, but rarely in *Lavaca*. The web-worm is found in *Galveston* and *De Witt*. The army-worm is a source of injury to the cotton crop in *Lavaca* and *De Witt*. Aphides are found in *Colorado* and *Washington*, owing to cold, wet springs. Shedding is of common occurrence in *Galveston, Harris, Waller, Fayette, Colorado, Austin, Fort Bend, Brazoria, Lavaca* (after drought), *De Witt, Atascosa, Goliad* (after drought), *Victoria*, and *Washington;* to some extent in *Karnes*. Rot of bolls occurs quite commonly in *Chambers, Galveston, Fayette, Colorado, Fort Bend, Lavaca, Goliad, Victoria*, and *Washington*. The cause is generally attributed to wet weather. Rust damages the cotton crops in *Jefferson* (due to plowing when wet), *Chambers, Galveston* (on some soils), and *Colorado* (in wet weather of April and May). Blight is found in spots in *Austin;* it does very little damage in *Fort Bend*. Frosts occasion trouble in *Colorado, Austin*, and *Goliad*.

34. What efforts have been made to obviate it, and with what success?

The majority of counties report no efforts to obviate the diseases and pests. The moths of the caterpillar and boll-worm are in *Titus, Trinity, Fayette*, and *McLennan* sometimes decoyed at night by lights placed in basins of water and oil, and thus caught. Shedding and boll rot are obviated in *Titus, Grimes, Lee, Angelina*, and *Jack*, and a few other counties by deep plowing. *Titus:* To avoid rust, underdraining; and to avoid blight, harrowing is done soon after the rains, in order to break the crust and allow air to reach the roots. *Grimes:* If corn and peas are planted a year or two, the diseases are less damaging to the succeeding cotton crop. *Ellis:* Early planting and deep plowing are practiced to obviate the effects of drought; the other pests so rarely appear that the farmer is wholly unprepared for them. *Bell:* Nothing is done, for the reason that the cause of the blight is not known here. On the blighted or "dead spots" potatoes rot, and the Osage orange (bois d'arc) dies before the third year, but cereals remain unaffected. *Kendall:* The caterpillar is sought after by a gray linnet and several other small birds; insectivorous birds, however, are scarce in this region. I believe that the common European sparrow would do good service against pestiferous insects, and would also recommend that flocks of tur-

keys, especially hens with their broods, be kept in the cotton fields when pests are liable to appear. There are also many varieties of wasps, ants, and lizards, that prey eagerly upon the cotton-worms in this region. *Comanche:* Plowing immediately after the plants come up successfully prevents damage by cut worms. *San Saba:* Generally nothing is done. Winter plowing would turn up, expose to frost, and thus favor the destruction of insect eggs. *Austin:* The "dying out in spots" is to some extent remedied by green manuring. *Brazoria:* Early planting, with seed from northern counties, and early and rapid cultivation have been successfully practiced. *Fannin:* Some or most of these pests and hinderances may be obviated by planting corn and cotton together on the same land; for example, let every third row be corn; then of every three acres planted one produces corn and two produce cotton. The yield of the acre of corn under such circumstances is much greater than in the case of corn planted exclusively. The yield of cotton is also improved in quantity and quality. The corn should be planted as early as possible; then by the time the cotton is up it is protected by the corn against the cool, spring winds. The rows should be made east and west, because the damaging winds are north and

52 C P

817

south. Such protection is considerable through May. and even in June, up to which time cotton, so planted, has a more vigorous appearance than that planted the usual way. From about June 15 until the foliage is stripped from the cornstalks (which should be done by July 15) there is a perceptible hesitation in the growth of the cotton foliage. The plants are then observed to be leaning away from the corn, and to be crowding toward the center of the cotton strip. This ceases, and the cotton again spreads when the cornstalks are stripped. While the growth of the foliage is retarded the bearing is not affected, and the quality of the lint is probably improved. Cotton so planted is not injured by aphides, even if they do appear, nor by the caterpillar, boll-worm, etc. It is well known that the boll-worm never commences near corn, or near any shade, but that these summer and fall pests always begin in the interior of a cotton field, and will exhaust this part before going to the exterior, to which, even then, only the grown worms will venture. For this reason many plant corn and cotton in alternate parallel strips, always with good results. On the prairies already mentioned is to be observed the great advantage of the standing rows of cornstalks, which here prevent the constant south winds from tangling and blowing out the cotton as fast as the bolls open.

35. Is rust or blight prevalent chiefly on heavy or ill-drained soils? Do they prevail chiefly in wet or dry, cool or hot seasons?

They prevail chiefly on ill-drained soils, both sandy and heavy; on nearly all flat and bottom lands and the uplands black waxy and hog-wallow prairies of the central region, and on the flat prairies of the coast region; on some of the red and black lands of the eastern part of the state, and sometimes on sandy uplands, and apparently without regard to seasons, though the majority of counties report cool and wet seasons, and others dry and hot, wet and hot, and cool and dry seasons. On this point, however, the answers vary greatly even in the same agricultural region and as regards the same character of land. The following replies are given. *Colorado:* It occurs chiefly in wet springs when days are warm and nights are cool, and is most common on poor, cold, wet, sandy soil, especially that which has produced cotton successfully. Where corn has grown one season it is not so bad. 1 *Cherokee:* They are perhaps a little more common on the heavy red and the light mahogany soils; seasons, tenacity of soil, or drainage seem to make no difference. *Henderson, Hill, Fayette,* and 1 *Travis:* Rust and blight cause no trouble; but there are spots of from 1 to 100 plants where cotton dies; peach-trees also die, and potatoes rot. These spots are on any kind of soil, but more commonly on the dark colored kind. 2 *Travis:* Rust and blight do no serious damage here; they appear in dry, hot seasons, and are most common on black land which is underlaid by chalk rock. *Fannin:* They are not peculiar to any kind of soil. Rust prevails in either extreme of wet or dry seasons, is most common on heavy soils, and is always stopped by change of season. Blight is caused by an alkali or brackish ingredient in the soil. It occurs in spots, which will not produce any root crops, but will produce any cereal or other crop the essential part of which is above ground, except cotton. Cotton suddenly wilts down at any stage of growth; on examination the roots appear as if they had been limed. *Dallas, Bexar,* and *other counties:* They occur in spots of a few square yards to an acre on the flat and stiff hog-wallow and all low valley lands. *Bell:* In spots alike on all lands and in all seasons. *Jasper:* In low wet places at bases of hills. *Wise:* Where the sandy and waxy soils join. *Titus:* On bottoms and moist depressions of the uplands. *Houston:* On stiff post oak and prairie soils. *Victoria:* On low flats of black land. *Austin:* On sandy uplands and ill-drained bottoms, especially when drought is followed by heavy rains. *Fort Bend:* On stiff brown soils. *Navarro:* On sandy mesquite lands (low and flat) when too wet in spring and suddenly dries out. *Madison, Panola, Red River,* and *Trinity:* On light gray sandy soils. *Bowie:* On hickory land.

36. Is Paris green used as a remedy against the caterpillar? If so, how, and with what effect?

It is not used in a majority of counties, the caterpillar usually appearing too late to do much damage. Laborers are very much afraid of the effects of the poison, both on themselves and on the work-stock; the plants also are often killed or injured by it. It is applied either in solution, by means of water-pots, or in the dry state, mixed with flour or resin. A fresh application is necessary after rains and to any new leaves that may appear, and its use in a great majority of cases has not proved successful. *Harrison:* Where 15 acres per hand are cultivated in cotton its use is considered impracticable. Even if applied in any form to the extent of one-fourth pound per acre, it will cause the leaves to shrivel. *San Jacinto:* "Three-fourths" of a pound to 40 gallons of water, applied with a fountain pump or other improved sprinkler, a sure exterminator, if the weather is dry. *Grimes:* Yes; it is sprinkled on in solution or sifted on the plants in the form of powder, mixed with flour; it is generally, but not always, effectual, and often checks the growth of the plant. Arsenic is also used in the same way. *Wilson:* The aqueous solution is sprinkled on the plant; it kills the worm, but checks the plant's growth, though the latter will soon grow off rapidly again if not too badly poisoned. Arsenic and other poisons are also used. *Travis:* Paris green and arsenic in solution are sprinkled upon the plants; they effectually destroy the worm. Negroes are afraid of the poison, and will not pick cotton where it has been used. 1 *Colorado:* Yes; by sprinkling its solution, or sifting the powder and powdered resin on the plants while wet with dew. The effect is good, but the material is too costly, and the application too troublesome. Arsenic is better; it is applied while the worms are young at the rate of 1 pound in 200 gallons of solution to 6 acres. *Lavaca:* Yes; by sprinkling it upon the plants at the worm's first appearance and repeating if necessary; in wet weather it is very difficult to kill it. Arsenic is also used, but Paris green alone is preferred; both are certain death to the worm.

LABOR, AND SYSTEM OF FARMING.

37. What is the average size of farms or plantations in your region? Is the prevalent practice "mixed farming" or "planting"?

Farms vary greatly in size in every county, and each answer gives usually a minimum and maximum. The largest farms are 3,000 acres in *Harrison;* 1,500 acres in *Falls* and *Hill;* 1,000 in *Waller, Robertson, Bastrop, Grimes, Fort Bend, San Jacinto,* and *Travis;* 500 in *Cass, Henderson, Clay, Jack, Lampasas, Collins, De Witt, Red River, Fannin, Brazos, Bosque, Austin,* and *Colorado;* 300 to 400 in twelve counties; 100 to 250 in other counties. Averages are from 25 to 30 acres in *Frio, Live Oak,* and *Wilson;* 40 acres in *Shelby, Angelina, Hood, Gillespie, Kerr,* etc. *Harris,* and *San Patricio;* 50 acres in *Wood, Jasper, Gonzales, Somervell, Comanche, Chambers,* and *Victoria;* 75 acres in *Houston, Morris, Upshur, Van Zandt,* and *Limestone;* 100 acres in ten counties; 150 acres in *Fayette, Rockwall, Burleson, Dallas,* and *Caldwell,* and 200 acres in *Titus* and *Rusk;* 250 in *Brazoria,* and 300 in *Cherokee.* "Mixed farming" is the prevalent practice throughout the state, with the exception of a few counties, in which "planting" is also done.

38. Are supplies raised at home or imported, and if the latter, where from? Is the tendency toward the raising of home supplies increasing or decreasing?

Corn is usually produced in sufficient quantities for home consumption, as is also wheat in many of the central prairie counties. Other supplies are in part imported from Saint Louis, Kansas City, and other western cities, and in part from New Orleans.

The tendency toward the raising of home supplies is decreasing in *Denton*, *Jackson*, and *Harris*; unvarying in *Panola*, *Freestone*, *Jefferson*, *Waller*, and *Nacogdoches*; and is increasing in the other counties.

39. Who are your laborers chiefly?

OAK, HICKORY, AND PINE REGION: Whites chiefly in nine counties, viz: *Van Zandt*, *Wood*, *Sabine*, *Limestone*, *Henderson*, *Angelina*, *Navarro*, *Wilson*, and *Lee*. Negroes chiefly in *Red River*, *Harrison*, *Rusk*, *Freestone*, *Houston*, *Bastrop*, *Grimes*, *Madison*, *Burleson*, and *Jasper*. In all other counties of the region the proportion is about equal. In *Polk* "the negroes occupy different parts of the county from the whites". Germans are reported in *Wilson* and *Lee*, Mexicans in *Wilson*.

CENTRAL BLACK PRAIRIE REGION: White laborers predominate in all of the counties of this region except in *McLennan*, *Fannin*, *Collin*, *Falls*, *Rockwall*, *Dallas*, *Travis*, *Williamson*, and *Caldwell*,

where the proportion of whites and negroes is about equal. Germans are reported in *Medina*, *Bell*, *Lee*, *Bexar*, *Gillespie*, *Blanco*, *Comal*, *Washington*, *Dallas*, *Travis*, *Victoria*, Mexicans in *Bexar* and *Caldwell*.

SOUTHERN PRAIRIE REGION: Whites predominate only in *Kerr*, *Live Oak*, and *Goliad*. In five other counties whites and negroes are in about equal proportions, while in all others the negroes predominate. Polish laborers are reported in *Karnes* and *Gonzales*. Germans in *Harris*, *Colorado*, *Fayette*, and *Washington*.

NORTHWESTERN REGION: Whites predominate in all of the counties.

40. How are wages paid; by the year, month, or day, and at what rates? When payable?

Daily wages are payable weekly or at the close of each day's service. In other cases wages are payable monthly in thirty counties; monthly or yearly, according to terms, in eight counties; on demand at any time after being earned in twenty-five counties; at end of time of service, or when the work is done, in twelve counties; and in twenty counties a part is paid during the year (in cash or supplies), and full payment is made at the close of the season or when crops are sold. Wages are from $8 to $12 per month in twenty-eight counties; from $8 to $15 in nineteen counties; from $10 to $16 in *Henderson*, *Burnet*, and

Waller; from $12 50 to $15 in eight counties; from $12 50 to $20 in *Erath*; from $10 to $20 and board in *Wood*; $15 with or $20 without board in *Hopkins*; $15 in *Live Oak*, *Denton*, *Comanche*, *Jefferson*, *Hunt*, and *San Saba*; from $15 to $16 in *Dallas*; from $15 to $20 in *McLennan* and *Goliad*; $16 in *Limestone*; $18 in *Gonzales*, and $20 in *Bandera*. Daily rates are usually from 50 to 75 cents throughout the state; from 50 cents to $1 per day in *Lee*, *Rusk*, *Comal*, *Gillespie*, and *Collin*; and $1 in *San Jacinto*, *Jefferson*, and *Bandera*.

41. Are cotton farms worked on shares? Are any supplies furnished by owners?

The share system prevails very generally throughout the state, except in *Jasper* and *Karnes*, where but few farms are thus worked. Supplies, consisting of implements, teams, and their feed, are often furnished by the owners, who receive in return one-half of all the crops. When the renter furnishes his own supplies, the owner of the land receives one-fourth of the

cotton and one-third of the grain and other products. Buildings and improvements are included with the farm; gins and presses only when they belong to the farm. Should the laborer receive his board in addition to farm and implements, he receives one-third of the crop.

42. Does your system give satisfaction? How does it affect the quality of the staple? Does the soil deteriorate or improve under it?

The share system gives very general satisfaction in 67 counties of the 80 reporting, and in the others not so great, because of the unreliability of the laborer. In 32 counties the share systems are reported as not affecting the quality of the staple. In 10 counties the quality is improved. In 4 counties it deteriorates. In 3 counties it deteriorates under the one-half share system. In 6 counties the staple suffers from bad and careless handling. The staple is better handled when the laborer owns one-half. In 39 counties the soil is reported as

deteriorating under the share system if restorative means are not resorted to. In *Red River* the soil deteriorates very little. In *Robertson* the soil is affected alike by all systems. In 18 counties the soil maintains its fertility. In 24 counties it improves if well managed. *Colorado*: The share systems are satisfactory to married tenants, but not entirely to owners nor to unmarried tenants. Picking is badly done by negroes; Germans and Bohemians gather their cotton with care and thus produce a staple of superior quality.

43. Which system (wage or share) is the better for the laborer? Why?

The following is a summary of answers in favor of each system:

SHARE SYSTEM.—It pays the laborer more fully for all labor bestowed; he makes more, is apt to stay with the crop and save it all, and habits of industry are encouraged; he can raise most of his provisions; in good seasons he can double what wages he would have received; he enjoys greater liberty, has a home, occupation, and support for himself and family; he has money in the bank and live-stock about his farm; he would spend his wages as fast as received; he risks nothing but his labor, and his share is net gain; he can employ additional help, and increase his income proportionally; he can

make use of his family in cotton-picking time, and in keeping cows, poultry, and a garden.

WAGE SYSTEM. Because the laborer is better satisfied, and makes more in the end; because he consumes his share in supplies; shares with cotton at so low a price do not pay him; he cannot go in debt; he mortgages his prospective share of the crop, and he takes no risk in a poor crop, because the negro is usually negligent, improvident, and has a lack of judgment which disqualifies him for success under the share system. He is not easily defrauded out of his share; he lives extravagantly under the share system; wages are certain; crops sometimes fail.

44. What is the condition of the laborer?

Generally good throughout the state, except in *Angelina*, *Hardin*, *Milam*, *Grimes*, *Denton*, *Lampasas*, *Llano*, *Chambers*, *Goliad*, *Atascosa*, *Brazoria*, *Frio*, *San Patricio*, and *De Witt*. In *Robertson* and *Upshur* they are jolly and happy, and in some instances in better condition than their employers. *Grimes*:

The negro as a rule is shabby, lazy, careless, indolent, and therefore thriftless and poor. *Fannin*: Well provided, healthy, and vigorous, and are improving. *Dallas*: Thrifty and of average intelligence. *Travis*: Good, but immediately dependent on their daily earnings. *Bexar*: Whites do well, and soon acquire homes; Mexicans provide nothing for the immediate future; negroes sometimes do a little better. *Lavaca:* The thrifty have acquired homes of their own. *Fort Bend:* Laborers have horses, mules, wagons, cattle, hogs, etc. They are now better satisfied, and more cheerful and industrious than formerly. Many of the negroes are buying small tracts of land (in some cases from their former masters, whom they have never left), and are making comfortable homes. *Harrison:* Their condition (negroes) is good, bad, and indifferent. The good class are in a thriving condition. They own live-stock of all kinds, and many have small farms; they are also disposed to make use of opportunities for intellectual and moral im-

provement. The second and third classes are composed chiefly of those just arriving at maturity. Their aspirations go little beyond a sufficiency of tobacco, rum, and (costly) brass jewelry. Some of them will labor all the year and spend their shares before they are entirely gathered. Some strive to appear genteel, but care not for to-morrow. There is prevalent among them a rather exaggerated idea of freedom. *Collin:* The whites are generally content and prosperous; the negroes are improvident, not caring for the future if they have two weeks' rations on hand. Their condition is poor, but that is their own fault.

45. What proportion of negro laborers own land, or the houses in which they live?

One-half in *Victoria* and *San Saba;* one-fourth in *Madison* and *Lavaca;* one-fifth in *Van Zandt;* one-sixth in *Sabine* and *Fort Bend;* one-tenth in fourteen counties; one-twentieth in fourteen counties, and a very small proportion in all other counties.

46. What is the market value per acre of the land in your region? What rent is paid?

OAK, HICKORY, AND PINE UPLANDS: Prices, from $1 to $5 for unimproved land, and from $10 to $20 for improved. Rents, from $3 to $5 per acre.

CENTRAL PRAIRIE REGION: Prices average about $5 for unimproved (less than that in a few counties), and from $10 to $25 for improved land, and even higher near railroads and towns. Rents are from $3 to $5, and seldom higher.

NORTHWESTERN REGION: Prices are from 50 cents to $3 for unimproved, and from $8 to $10 for improved; sometimes higher. Rents are from $1 to $3; for grazing purposes in *Mason,* 2½ cents.

SOUTHERN PRAIRIE REGION: From $1 to $3 for unimproved ($5 for some land in *Colorado*), and from $5 to $25 for improved lands. Rents, from $2 to $5 per acre; in *Victoria,* $8 for well-fenced land.

47. How many acres or bales per hand is your customary estimate?

OAK, HICKORY, AND PINE REGION: On the sandy pine lands of the southeast, about 3 bales or 10 acres; on the better class of uplands in the rest of the region, from 4 to 6 bales, or from 10 to 15 acres in cotton alone, or 8 acres in cotton and 15 in corn. On bottom lands, from 8 to 10 bales. *Grimes:* The white laborer cultivates from 15 to 20 acres—two-thirds of it in cotton; the negro cultivates 12 acres, one-half of which is in cotton. *Harrison:* One man and a mule can cultivate 30 acres.

CENTRAL PRAIRIE REGION: Usually from 6 to 10 acres or from 4 to 6 bales, or from 15 to 20 acres in cotton and other crops, or 5 bales of cotton and 150 bushels of corn. *Grayson* and *Comal:* One

hand can cultivate 10 acres of cotton, but can pick only 5 or 6 acres or bales.

NORTHWESTERN REGION: From 4 to 5 bales or 12 acres of cotton. *Taylor:* With help to thin out, a good hand can easily cultivate 20 acres. *Jack:* Ten acres of cotton, 10 of corn, and 5 of wheat.

SOUTHERN PRAIRIE REGION: Usually from 3 to 5 bales. *Fort Bend:* The negro can cultivate about 4 acres and gather 2½ bales of cotton. *Fayette* and *Lavaca:* Five or 6 bales, or 10 acres of cotton and 10 of corn.

48. To what extent does the system of credits or advances upon the growing cotton crop prevail in your region?

It is not prevalent in *Burnet, Gillespie, Clay, Palo Pinto, Eastland, Frio,* and *Live Oak* counties; to a very small extent in *Hopkins, Van Zandt, Cooke, Dallas, Grayson, Denton, Johnson, Tarrant, Hill, Lavaca, Karnes, Goliad, Blanco, Victoria, Rockwall, Titus, Wilson, Comal, Harris, De Witt, Hardin, Chambers, Jefferson, Guadalupe, Blanco, Bexar,* and *Atascosa.* In other cotton counties of the state it prevails very largely, usually to one-half or three-fourths, and sometimes to the full value of a crop. In a few of the counties it is declining. As a rule, the land-owner is made responsible for any supplies that merchants may advance to tenants or share-laborers. *Robertson:* Local or Galveston merchants advance supplies to about $30 per bale at 8 per cent. interest. *Grimes:* About four-fifths of the farmers ob-

tain advances of goods; planter pledges to merchant, the merchant makes advances as far as he feels safe, and at the close of the season generally takes all the crop. Mortgages are sometimes given before the crop is planted, and *very few* can raise a crop without assistance. Merchants sell goods at cash rates, but charge 1 per cent. per month on all credits. *Colorado:* Besides obtaining supplies from merchants, the tenant also obtains on credit milch cows, corn, meat, etc., from the farm-owner. The merchant always makes money, while the land-owner suffers loss when, from fault of season or tenant, the crop partially or entirely fails. It sometimes takes three years to pay for what was spent in eight months.

49. At what stage of its production is the cotton crop usually covered by insurance?

Not at all in fifty-five counties; only when baled or stored preparatory to shipment in the majority of other counties. About planting time in *Shelby;* when the bolls have begun to open in *Morris, Jack, Hunt,* and *Kaufman.* When in the gin-house

in *Rusk, Robertson, Grimes, Limestone, Navarro, McLennan, Galveston, Titus, Collin, Ellis, Taylor, Harris, Waller, Colorado, Brazoria,* and some other counties.

50. What are the merchants' commissions and charges for storing, handling, shipping, insurance, etc., to which your crop is subject? What is the total amount of these charges against the farmer per pound or bale?

Commissions are almost universally 2½ per cent. on gross sales. Storage, from 25 to 50 cents per bale for the first month, and 25 cents per month after that. Handling, 25 cents; shipping, 25 cents; insurance, one-fourth per cent. of its market value, or from 6 to 25 cents per bale per month. Weighing, from 7 to 15 cents per bale; inspection, from 10 to 15 cents and drayage from 5 to 25 cents per bale. The total amount of these charges, including freight, vary from 50 to $6 in eighteen counties, and as high as $7 50 in *Falls, Collin,*

Gonzales, Polk, Jasper, and *Hopkins,* and from $8 to $8 75 in *Tarrant* and *Blanco.* Without freight the charges per bale vary from 12 cents in *Brazoria* to 50 cents in *Washington* and *Travis,* $1 25 in *Bosque,* $1 50 in *Bell* and *Upshur,* $1 75 in *Navarro* and *Harris,* $2 50 in *Hill,* and $3 50 in *Angelina.* Cotton is usually sold to local buyers at railroad stations at from 1 to 2 cents below Galveston and New York quotations, and the farmers avoid the above charges, except that for weighing.

51. What is your estimate per pound of the cost of production in your region, exclusive of such charges, and with fair soil and management?

The lowest estimates are 3½ cents per pound in *Madison, Coryell, Brazoria;* from 4 to 5 cents in *Wilson, Wood, Red River, Trinity, Burnet, Erath, Dallas, Gillespie, Fannin, Hill, Travis, Jack, Eastland, Live Oak,* and *Jefferson;* 6 cents in *Milam, Robertson, Morris, Gonzales, Anderson, Harrison, Lee, Somervell, Bexar, Ellis, Denton, Cooke, Grayson, Galveston, Harris, Fort Bend,* and *Austin.* From 7 to 8 cents in all other counties except *Houston, Cherokee, Grimes, Williamson, Blanco, McLennan, Lavaca, Fort Bend,* and 2 *Austin,* where the estimate is from 9 to 10 cents per pound.

Sabine: After cotton is ready to pick it costs $18 50 per 500-pound bale to deliver it at the shipping point ready for sale. For example:

To picking 15½ cwt. of seed-cotton at 50 cents per cwt.	$7 75
To nine days' board of hand while picking	2 25
To hauling to gin	1 50
To ginning	3 00
To baling and ties	2 00
To hauling to the river	2 00
	18 50

The cost of delivering is of course greater where the production is more remote from shipping points.

Cost of each item of labor and material expended in the cultivation of an acre of cotton.

Items.	COUNTY.			
	Navarro.	Bell.	Gillespie.	Brazoria.
Rent	$2 00	$4 50	$3 00	$5 00
Fencing, repairs, and interest on ...	1 00		7 00	50
Knocking stalks		50	1 00	30
Pulling and burning stalks			1 00	10
Listing			1 50	40
Bedding with hoes			1 75	
Breaking up	1 00	1 50	6 00	
Harrowing		15	1 25	
Splitting middles			35	40
Laying off		25	75	10
Bedding up		1 50	1 50	
Splitting middles			35	30
Knocking off beds	15		1 00	
Planting, opening	15	25	40	
dropping	05	15	25	12
covering	15	25	40	10
Replanting	05		25	05
Seed	05	05	25	50
Thinning	1 00	75	50	30
Number of plowings	1 50	3 00	1 00	60
Number of hoeings	25	1 00	2 00	50
Wear and tear of implements	50			
Total	8 85	13 85	31 50	9 77
Other expenses.				
Picking. per hundred-weight	75	50 to 75	75	60
Hauling to gin	3 50	1 25	1 00	
Ginning, per hundred-weight	25	25	1 30	30

NOTES ON THE ABOVE TABLE.

Bell county: The original cost of fencing, repairs, etc., depends on number of acres in inclosure. Knocking down stalks is not usually done. Harrowing is not general. Hauling to gin costs about 12½ cents per 100 pounds. The usual toll for ginning is one-twelfth of the cotton. It is impossible to indicate with certainty the cost of raising and gathering an acre of cotton. It is much more some years than others. It depends greatly on the seasons; the better the seasons the greater the cost and the greater the profit.

COST OF PICKING 100 POUNDS OF SEED-COTTON.—*Bowie:* 75 cents early in the fall, and from $1 to $1 25 later in the season. *Fannin:* From 75 to $1. *Wise:* 75 cents and board and $1 without board. *Washington:* 80 cents. *Gillespie* and *Victoria:* 75 cents. *Caldwell:* 70 cents. *Liberty:* From 50 cents to $1. *Nacogdoches:* From 50 to 75 cents.

INDEX TO COTTON PRODUCTION IN TEXAS.

REPORT

ON

COTTON PRODUCTION IN THE INDIAN TERRITORY,

WITH A BRIEF DESCRIPTION OF

THE AGRICULTURAL FEATURES OF A PORTION OF THE COUNTRY.

BY

R. H. LOUGHRIDGE, Ph. D.,

SPECIAL AGENT.

TABLE OF CONTENTS.

LETTER OF TRANSMITTAL.

BERKELEY, CALIFORNIA, *June* 1, 1882.

To the SUPERINTENDENT OF CENSUS.

DEAR SIR: I transmit herewith a report on the cotton production of the Indian territory, with a general description of its agricultural features, by Dr. R. H. Loughridge, special agent.

The omission of the census enumeration in the territory has necessitated the substitution of an estimate derived from personal inquiry and from correspondence and other sources for a detailed table of production. In the absence of any connected description of the surface features of this interesting region, Dr. Loughridge undertook a personal exploration under the auspices of the Census Office during months of 1880. From the notes of this exploration, from the data contained in the several reports of United States expeditions, and finally from correspondence and inquiry by word of mouth, the description hereinafter given has been compiled. It will be found to present a picture differing in several respects from the popular conception, especially of the more remote portions of the territory, and will, it is hoped, lead to a more just estimate of its capabilities than has heretofore been largely prevalent even among those who considered themselves well informed.

Very respectfully,

E. W. HILGARD,
Special Agent in charge of Cotton Production.

Professor E. W. HILGARD,
Special Agent in charge of Cotton Production.

DEAR SIR: I have the honor to transmit herewith my report on the cotton production of the Indian territory, with also a very brief description of the agricultural features of the country. The material from which the report is compiled was mostly obtained by me in a hasty trip through the territory during the month of May, 1880. Dependent largely on stages or private conveyances for transportation, I was able during this short period to visit but few points distant from the line of railway, viz, Tahlequah, Ockmulgee, Wewoka (Seminole nation), Webber's Falls, Boggy depot, Tishomingo (opposite Gainesville, Texas), and on the east the Kiamitia Creek country. The report can therefore be only a general one for the territory at large, with details concerning the country visited. Assistance was also kindly given me by the Presbyterian missions at Tallahassee, in the Creek nation, and at Wewoka, in the Seminole country, as well as by persons whose names are given in the list of correspondents. The tables of population and leading productions were obtained from the report of the commissioner of Indian affairs for 1880.

Very respectfully,

R. H. LOUGHRIDGE,
Special Agent.

TABULAR STATEMENT

OF

POPULATION, TILLED LAND, AND LEADING PRODUCTIONS

OF THE

FIVE COTTON-PRODUCING NATIONS.

POPULATION, TILLED LAND, AND LEADING PRODUCTIONS OF THE COTTON-PRODUCING NATIONS OF THE INDIAN TERRITORY. (a)

Nation.	POPULATION.		TILLED LAND.	PRODUCTIONS.			
	Total.	Number who can read.	Acres.	Corn.	Wheat.	Oats and barley.	Vegetables.
				Bushels.	Bushels.	Bushels.	Bushels.
Cherokee	19, 720	16, 000	92, 398	726, 042	58, 424	52, 568	190, 000
Creek	15, 000	3, 500	65, 000	200, 000	75, 000	20, 000	150, 000
Seminole	2, 667	450	17, 000	220, 000		2, 000	25, 000
Choctaw	15, 900	11, 000	100, 000	1, 200, 000	200, 800	80, 000	150, 000
Chickasaw	6, 000	3, 000	40, 000				50, 000

a From the report of the Commissioner of Indian Affairs, 1880.

841

PART I.

PHYSICO-GEOGRAPHICAL AND AGRICULTURAL DESCRIPTION

OF THE

INDIAN TERRITORY.

PHYSICAL AND AGRICULTURAL FEATURES

OF THE

INDIAN TERRITORY.

The Indian territory, lying north of Texas and west of Arkansas, covers an area of about 69,000 square miles, and is divided up among a large number of Indian tribes. Five of these tribes, the Cherokees, Creeks, Seminoles, Choctaws, and Chickasaws, are half civilized, and well supplied with schools, churches, and books printed in their own native languages (though English is now largely spoken among the people), and are largely engaged in farming. A system of public schools, with a seminary for each sex, was established among the Cherokees nearly forty years ago, and is wholly supported by the nation. In each of the other nations large manual-labor mission schools have been supported largely from the annuities. Each nation holds its land in common, an individual being deemed owner only of his improvements; and when abandoned, the land may be occupied by others. Their form of government is similar in many respects to that of the states, nearly all of their chief men having received a common-school and some of them a collegiate education. Numerous whites have been adopted into the tribes, and there are also many negroes, formerly slaves of the Indians. These tribes occupy the eastern part of the territory. The Pottawatomie nation should also perhaps be added to this list. The other tribes are not so far advanced in civilization, and some of them are still mainly dependent upon hunting and fishing for subsistence. The territory of the six tribes first mentioned will alone be described in detail in this report, as it is only among these tribes that cotton is planted. The surface of the country embraced in the territory is varied in its topographical characters, but is mostly an open prairie, generally rolling, and in places hilly and mountainous, drained by three large rivers, the Arkansas, Canadian, and Red, and their many tributaries. These rivers flow eastward, and their beds are broad and mostly filled with quicksand and sand-bars, though in time of low water the streams themselves are quite narrow.

Going westward from the line of the state of Arkansas we enter a region broken, hilly, and mountainous, and mostly timbered, interspersed with small prairies, and presenting but a small proportion of tillable lands. This region, beginning on the northeast of the territory, embraces the eastern and southeastern parts of the Cherokee nation and the greater part of the Choctaw nation southward nearly to the Red river and westward to within a few miles of the Missouri, Kansas, and Texas railroad. In addition to this, the Shawnee mountains extend along the southern side of the territory, beginning nearly from the line of the Chickasaw nation. Still westward we enter the great rolling and treeless prairies of the Cherokee and Creek and the western part of the Choctaw nations, a country interspersed on the south by prominent sandstone ridges, and interrupted throughout only by the narrow timbered belts of the streams, almost the only signs of life being the herds of cattle upon these plains.

These prairies extend westward a short distance into the Seminole and Chickasaw nations to a broken and timbered region of hills in the former and to the cross timbers in the latter nation. Still westward from these narrow belts lie the red-loam and clay prairie lands, and then the arid gypsum plains, interspersed with sandstone hills this entire country being generally destitute of water and almost of trees, even along the large water-courses, (a) On the southwest the Wichita mountains, with their high and sharp peaks of granite, stand out prominently on the plain, and among them are seen occasional groves of post oaks.

On the southeast, in the southern part of the Chickasaw and Choctaw nations, there is a belt of black prairies, extending from the "cross timbers" eastward, at first very broad, but narrowing eastward, and terminating before the line of the state of Arkansas is reached.

a The descriptions by Captain Marcy and others differ from the indications of the land-office map as regards the abundance of the streams laid down on the latter.

7

CLIMATE.—The *temperature* of the territory from Fort Gibson, in the Cherokee nation, south and west to Fort Sill, varies comparatively little, except in the extreme portions of the country, and then but a few degrees. The following is taken from the tables compiled by Mr. Schott, of the Smithsonian Institution, and represents averages or means of the observations of many years:

.	Spring.	Summer.	Autumn.	Winter.	Year.
	Degrees.	*Degrees.*	*Degrees.*	*Degrees.*	*Degrees.*
Fort Gibson	61.08	79.13	61.44	40.35	60.48
Fort Towson	62.23	78.92	61.09	43.74	61.50
Fort Washita	62.56	79.63	63.02	43.53	62.18
Fort Sill (southwest)		79.34	58.38		

The highest temperature recorded was 116° at Fort Gibson in the year 1834, and the lowest, 20°, at the same place in 1857, and also at Fort Sill (on the southwest), in 1873.

Rainfall.—The rainfall of the eastern part of the territory is naturally greater than upon the table-lands of the west, and also greater in the timbered region of the southeast than in the prairie region of Fort Gibson and the west. The following table will show the precipitation in inches for each season of the year at points on the east, southeast, and west:

	Spring.	Summer.	Autumn.	Winter.	Year.
Fort Gibson	11.44	9.65	9.30	6.57	36.96
Fort Towson	15.65	14.36	12.23	8.94	51.08
Fort Washita	11.24	10.43	10.01	6.35	38.03
Fort Sill	8.44	8.20	7.49	4.39	28.52

Snow falls quite frequently to the depth of a few inches, but seldom remains on the ground for more than a day or two. Occasionally a depth of a foot or more is reached.

During the spring and summer months the prevailing winds are from the southeast and south, but during the autumn and winter months they are mostly from the northeast and north; in the northern part of the territory the wind frequently blows from the northwest. Thunder-storms are frequent during the warm and hot months, and are sometimes accompanied by hail; but tornadoes or very destructive winds seldom occur.

The following is from Rev. R. M. Loughridge, of the Presbyterian mission in the Creek nation:

During the winter season there is in this country much snow and ice, the snow sometimes, though rarely, reaching a depth of 15 to 18 inches. The temperature has been known to fall from 9 to 15 degrees below zero, and at such times the Arkansas river freezes over, the ice being so thick and firm that loaded wagons are driven over on it. In the winter of 1849 the cold was very severe, and the whole country was covered with snow several inches deep; then rain and sleet fell on that, forming a compact sheet of ice over the whole prairie and woodland, which remained for seven weeks. In the summer months north winds or "northers" occasionally blow, but they are not so frequent as in winter, and are also rather oppressively close and warm.

GEOLOGY.—The eastern part of the territory, embracing a region extending southward nearly to Red river and westward beyond the Creek nation, is made up almost entirely of the representative sandstones, limestones, etc., of the Coal Measures, the former rock capping the mountains of the east, and becoming the prevailing feature in the lower hills and country westward, while the limestone, which appears prominently in the mountain sides and valleys of the east, disappears almost entirely on the west, or is exposed only in the beds of the largest streams. Coal mines are extensively worked on the south of the Canadian river by companies who have leased them from the nation. The Permian is said to cover an area south of the Wichita mountains on the southwest, while the remainder of the western part of the territory is thought to belong to the Triassic and Jurassic, excepting the region of the mountains, which are of granitic structure, their granites flesh-colored, and associated with greenstone, quartz, porphyry, etc. Another granitic area, as observed in my recent trip, occurs in the eastern part of the Chickasaw nation, Tishomingo being situated in the belt. This outcrop is in a region having a width of about 3 miles and a length northeast and southwest of about 15 or 20 miles. Biotite mica and flesh-colored crystals of feldspar enter into the composition of the rock, which also is traversed by much dark-blue trap. On the south, along Red river, and extending eastward from the Chickasaw nation, is a belt of the Cretaceous, represented by the rotten limestone, covered in places, especially along the immediate upland river front and on the southeast, by the sands and clays of later age. East of Tishomingo the rock breaks off suddenly, facing the west in high cliffs. The peculiar belt of timbered country on the west, known as the *cross timbers*, is of undetermined age; but whatever may underlie the top material at 20 to 30 feet, or perhaps less, it can hardly be questioned that the ferruginous sandstones, pebble conglomerates, sands, and clays that form this surface material are Quaternary. Their origin will be a matter of doubt until their extent northward is fully ascertained. (a)

a Their outlines, as given on the general agricultural map that accompanies the general report, were taken from the charts of the Pacific railroad reports. Captain Marcy states that they extend from Texas as far north as the Arkansas river.

AGRICULTURAL SUBDIVISIONS OR REGIONS.—The topographical divisions outlined above differ from each other also in the character of their lands, and the following agricultural regions are easily recognized, and for convenience placed in three general divisions—*timbered uplands, river alluvial or bottom lands,* and *prairies.*

Timbered uplands:
    Red loam and mountainous region of the east.
    Pine hills of the southeast.
    Cross timbers of the west.
    Wichita mountain and granitic regions.
    River uplands.
Alluvial or river bottom lands (timbered).
Prairies:
    Light sandy central prairies.
    Black and stiff prairies (Cretaceous) of the south.
    Western regions of red loam and gypsum prairies.

TIMBERED UPLANDS.

The following portions of the territory are embraced in this division: chiefly the eastern portion of the Cherokee and Choctaw nations, designated as the *red loam and mountainous region;* the southeastern part of the Choctaw nation, designated as the *sandy pine lands;* two belts of timbered lands entering the Chickasaw nation from Texas, known as the "*cross timbers*"; and narrow belts along the large streams, and broad areas lying within the angles formed by the junction of the streams, designated as *river uplands.* These subdivisions are best considered separately, as they differ from each other in their more prominent features.

THE MOUNTAINOUS AND RED-LOAM REGION.

The region thus designated covers a very large area in the eastern part of the territory, and is bounded on the west by a line extending southwest from Tahlequah, in the Cherokee nation, to the Arkansas river, a few miles above the mouth of the Canadian river; still southward, with its western limit within a few miles of the Missouri, Kansas, and Texas railroad, it extends to Atoka, in the Choctaw nation. Here the country becomes more level and sandy, forming a belt extending westward to Tishomingo, in the Chickasaw nation, and eastward to the Arkansas state line, while on the south it is limited by the open and black prairie region.

The greater part of this region is too rocky, broken, and mountainous for cultivation, and, though many of the mountains have broad summits, their soils are too sandy and thin for fertility. The Sans Bois mountains are said to be 2,000 feet above the valleys. The valley lands are mostly narrow, and present but few desirable agricultural features. The bottom lands of the Illinois river average one-fourth of a mile in width; but on the immediate south of the Arkansas river the valleys between the hills seem to be broader than on the north, and are interspersed with small undulating and fertile prairies. One of these narrow prairies reaches from the Poteau river westward not far from and parallel with the Arkansas river to Sans Bois creek. These uplands on each side of the latter river, and extending back several miles, are said to be comparatively well settled and under cultivation, the crops being corn and cotton. In the extreme southern part of the region the lands are more level and very sandy, gradually merging into the *pine and sand hills* of the southeast.

The most thickly settled portion of the region is that in the Cherokee nation immediately south and east of Tahlequah, where the country is comparatively level, and the lands, comprising sandy and cherty soils and clay subsoils, are largely under cultivation.

The following analyses are given to show the composition of the soils of the timbered uplands that are under tillage. The first borders the mountainous country of the Cherokee nation; the other is a sample of the more level lands of the southern part of the Choctaw nation:

No. 15. *Sandy upland soil,* with cherty gravel, from near Park Hill, 5 miles south of Tahlequah, Cherokee nation. Depth taken, 12 inches; depth to yellow clay subsoil, 18 inches; timber growth, oaks and hickory.

No. 18. *Gray sandy soil,* from Boggy Depot, Choctaw nation. Depth taken, 12 inches; timber growth, blackjack and post oaks, and some hickory.

Timbered sandy uplands.

	CHEROKEE NATION.	CHOCTAW NATION.
	PARK HILL.	BOGGY DEPOT.
	Cherty soil.	Soil.
	No. 15.	No. 16.
Insoluble matter	85.920 } 92.650	88.796 } 92.896
Soluble silica	6.730	4.100
Potash	0.179	0.161
Soda	0.059	0.085
Lime	0.072	0.170
Magnesia	0.187	0.136
Brown oxide of manganese	0.166	0.061
Peroxide of iron	3.431	1.582
Alumina	0.881	2.434
Phosphoric acid	0.126	0.117
Sulphuric acid	0.144	0.073
Water and organic matter	2.113	2.507
Total	99.929	100.181
Hygroscopic moisture	3.283	3.090
absorbed at	26.5 C.°	29.0 C.°

In both of these soils there is a fair percentage of potash for such sandy lands. There is also a fair amount of phosphoric acid, but a deficiency of lime in the first soil, and the application of the latter element would be of very great benefit. The percentages of sulphuric acid seem excessive, and are doubtless errors.

THE SANDY SHORT-LEAF PINE LANDS.

This region embraces a section of the timbered region lying in the southeastern part of the Choctaw nation. Its area is comparatively small, and its surface is rolling and somewhat hilly, timbered with short-leaf pine, oaks, and some hickory. The soil is sandy, often contains red gravel, and is underlaid by clay beds, resting upon Cretaceous rotten limestone, which is usually exposed along the streams, and frequently gives rise to black prairie lands. The lands will produce an average of 800 pounds of seed-cotton per acre. This is said to be the chief cotton-growing section of the territory, the crop being chiefly produced by whites and sold at the nearest railroad town in Texas.

THE CROSS TIMBERS.

This region enters the territory from Texas in two belts, known respectively as the upper and the lower cross timbers, each having a width of from 15 to 20 miles, and separated from each other by a prairie region of about 15 miles. Southward the two belts extend into Texas to and beyond the Brazos river, preserving the same characters throughout. The lower timbers in Texas form a trough-like depression in the prairie region (in some places its hills rising, however, above them), being bordered on each side by the black and stiff prairies, the soils of the two regions presenting a very strong and interesting contrast, and this feature continues in the territory until the two belts of timber unite. The lands of the lower belt are sandy for a depth of 10 or 15 inches, but are generally underlaid by a yellowish loam or clay, and support a growth of post, Spanish, and black-jack oaks, and some hickory. The lands of the upper belt are mostly a deep sand of little fertility, and bear a stunted growth of oaks. Both belts, with their rolling and timbered surfaces, stand out prominently on these broad and generally level and treeless prairies.

GRANITIC LANDS.

These are embraced mostly in two regions, the one lying in the southeastern part of the Chickasaw nation around Tishomingo, the other on the southwest, in the Comanche country, and forming the Wichita mountains. In the first of these the granite belt proper is about 3 miles wide and 15 or 20 miles long, extending in a southwestern and northeastern course near Boggy Depot. Its surface is hilly, and it is well timbered with oaks and some other growth, the timbered lands also reaching eastward many miles further to the black prairies, and along their northern border to the Arkansas line. Granite outcrops in large masses at Tishomingo, its materials, on disintegration, producing a sandy and often gravelly soil, with clay subsoils, which are highly productive. In many localities the soil is mostly a heavy sand. In some of the deep gullies east of Tishomingo beds of white clay from 30 to 50 feet in thickness are exposed.

THE WICHITA MOUNTAIN COUNTRY.—In the southwestern part of the territory is a region described by Captain Marcy as comprising "groups or clusters of detached peaks of conical form (indicating a volcanic origin), with smooth level glades intervening; and rising as they do perfectly isolated from all surrounding eminences upon the plateau of the great prairies, their rugged and precipitous granite sides almost denuded of vegetation, they present a very peculiar and imposing feature in the topographical aspect of the country". The rock is a flesh-colored granite, with hornblende, greenstone, etc., producing excellent soils. Good water and some post-oak woodland is found in the valleys, while on the mountains are raspberries, gooseberries, and currants. Grapes and plums are also abundant, the latter (the Chickasaw plum) growing on bushes from 2 to 6 feet high. Pecan, walnut, ash, elm, cottonwood, wild china, willow, and mesquite occur to some extent on the banks of Otter creek south of the mountains, but otherwise the country is a level plain, destitute of water or timber. Between the northern extremity of the mountains and Red river there are, in places, continuous chains of sand-hills from 25 to 50 feet high, "destitute of all herbage except a few plum bushes and grape-vines." The country is generally barren and sandy.

TIMBERED RIVER UPLANDS.

Along the larger streams within the agricultural region of the territory the bottom lands are very generally bordered by a belt of timbered uplands, abruptly rising sometimes 100 feet above them; it often happens, however, that the prairies approach to the very edges of the bluffs. These belts are narrow and well timbered with red, post, black-jack, and other oaks, hickory, and sassafras, with sumac and other undergrowth. The soils are always deep sands, more or less gravelly, underlaid by red and yellow clays at a depth of from 12 to 24 inches. These lands are not very extensive, the largest bodies occurring chiefly along the north side of the Arkansas river to Grand river, including heavy beds of white sand along the Canadian to its mouth and along Red river. They are said to be good cotton lands, and capable of yielding from 800 to 900 pounds of seed-cotton per acre for a few years, but are durable.

In the southern part of the Chickasaw nation the Red river uplands embrace some lower and narrow tracts of sandy lands, called "black-jack flats", because of the predominance of that timber, though post oak is also largely intermingled with it, forming an open region a mile or more in width, with little or no undergrowth. They are said to yield about 1,200 pounds of seed-cotton per acre.

The following analyses show the chemical composition of some of these lands:

No. 1. *Gray sandy soil* from the country between the Verdigris and the Arkansas rivers, and not far from their junction in the Creek nation; taken 18 inches deep. Timber growth, post and red oaks, hickory, and sassafras.

No. 2. *Red clay subsoil* of the above, taken from 18 to 24 inches.

No. 8. *Sandy soil* of Canadian uplands near Eufaula, Creek nation. Depth taken, 12 inches; red-clay subsoil reached at about 24 inches; timber growth, oaks and hickory.

No. 24. *Black-jack flats* of Red river, from the southern part of the Chickasaw nation, and opposite Gainesville, Texas. Depth taken, 12 inches; subsoil not reached; timber growth, black-jack and post oaks, and some hickory.

Timbered uplands bordering river bottoms.

	CREEK NATION.			CHICKASAW NATION.
	FOUR MILES WEST OF VERDIGRIS RIVER.		NEAR EUFAULA.	"BLACK-JACK FLATS" OF RED RIVER.
	Sandy soil.	Red-clay subsoil.	Sandy soil.	Dark soil.
	No. 1.	No. 2.	No. 8.	No. 24.
Insoluble matter	88.870 } 97.042	78.258 } 85.865	90.202 } 95.341	90.170 } 95.880
Soluble silica	1.872	7.615	4.085	5.710
Potash	0.084	0.250	0.138	0.251
Soda	0.010	0.080	0.028	0.088
Lime	0.082	0.110	0.132	0.207
Magnesia	0.079	0.380	0.151	0.618
Brown oxide of manganese	0.082	0.180	0.149	0.205
Peroxide of iron	0.947	3.521	1.678	1.658
Alumina	0.779	8.486	2.453	1.218
Phosphoric acid	0.095	0.130	0.104	0.061
Sulphuric acid	0.108	0.143	0.043	0.097
Water and organic matter	0.798	3.825	1.873	2.119
Total	100.059	100.810	100.088	100.877
Hygroscopic moisture	1.040	3.070	3.852	3.015
absorbed at	24.8 C.°	24.4 C.°	26.8 C.°	27.9 C.°

The sample of soil No. 1 is little else than sand, and is perhaps not a fair representative of the uplands of that region, though these deep sands are very prevalent. The subsoil, with its large amount of alumina, is deficient in phosphoric acid, and has but a fair percentage of potash and lime. The sandy lands of Eufaula are much better than the above, though still low in potash, and contain fair amounts of potash, lime, and phosphoric acid. Durability, however, cannot be expected of them.

The *black-jack flats* of Red river are very deficient in phosphoric acid, but have fair amounts of potash and lime, which would render them thrifty for a short time.

Altogether, these river uplands cannot be considered as very desirable for farming purposes, except for deep-rooted crops, such as cotton, which could reach the more fertile underclays. Comparatively little of the lands are under cultivation, and much of that originally tilled now lies turned out because of its impoverished condition.

PRAIRIE LANDS.

The prairies comprise the greater part of the territory, and, as already stated, may be divided into four distinct classes, viz, *Sandy prairies* (Palæozoic) of the central part of the territory, *black sandy and clayey* prairies (Cretaceous) of the south, *red-loam* prairies (Palæozoic) of the west, and the *gypsum plains* (Triassic) of the extreme west. The latter two will be included in one group for convenience of description. Besides these there are small red-loam prairies in the eastern and northeastern parts of the country, of which a special description has not been thought necessary.

SANDY AND OPEN PRAIRIES.

The region thus designated covers the northern and western part of the Cherokee nation, nearly all of the Creek, and the western part of the Choctaw nation, and extends still westward into the adjoining nations. The central and northern portion of the region is mostly an open prairie but little diversified with timbered belts, and reaches northward from the north fork of the Canadian river through the Cherokee nation, Ockmulgee being on its western edge and Tahlequah on the eastern, excepting that corner lying south of the latter place and included between the Illinois and the Arkansas rivers, which is largely timbered, broken, and mountainous. The prairies in the Creek country are interspersed with high and prominent bald or treeless ridges, from the sides of which ledges of sandstone are seen to outcrop. This rock is also often exposed on the lower hills and in some of the valleys, making the soil thin and worthless for farming purposes. Good grass covers all of the prairies and hills, and furnishes fine grazing facilities. The amount of hay cut in 1880 from the prairies aggregated 125,500 tons.

The country west of Ockmulgee and south of the Arkansas river to the timbered belt on Boggy creek is quite hilly, and the high ridges are often colored with conglomerates and a timbered growth of oaks. Large open and rolling sandy loam prairies occur everywhere as far west as Wewoka, in the Seminole country, and sandstone is the prevailing rock, as in the region just described. Limestone often outcrops at the foot of the hills on the south, in the Choctaw nation, and on the extreme east in the region of Tahlequah, Cherokee nation, producing spots of stiff calcareous soils along the margins of the creeks, but otherwise the lands of this and of the entire prairie region are of a light sandy loam character, in many places covered with a small brownish ferruginous gravel. But little, if any, of these lands are under cultivation, not only because they are thin and best adapted to grazing purposes, but because the people prefer living in the timbered regions along the streams, where wood and water are plentiful.

The timbered uplands that occur in the prairie region are mostly covered with a deep sandy soil resting on heavy clays. They have a post and black-jack oak growth, and are mostly too poor for continued cultivation. Much gravelly and cherty ridge, as well as rocky land, is found between Fort Gibson and Tahlequah, in the Cherokee nation.

The following analyses have been made to show the chemical composition of the prairie lands of the region:

No. 14. *Sandy prairie loam*, with chert, from near Park Hill, 5 miles south of Tahlequah, Cherokee nation; taken 12 inches deep.

No. 3. *Sandy prairie loam* from near Muscogee, Creek nation; taken 15 inches deep.

No. 10. *Sandy prairie loam* from the Seminole mission, near Wewoka, Seminole nation. Depth taken, 18 inches.

Sandy prairie lands.

	CHEROKEE NATION. PARK HILL. No. 14.	CREEK NATION. MUSCOGEE. No. 8.	SEMINOLE NATION. WEWOKA. No. 10.
Insoluble matter	84.500 } 89.207	86.410 } 91.610	84.176 } 88.966
Soluble silica	4.707	5.200	4.790
Potash	0.225	0.364	0.261
Soda	0.041	0.069	0.087
Lime	0.063	0.112	0.148
Magnesia	0.233	0.136	0.249
Brown oxide of manganese	0.126	0.201	0.100
Peroxide of iron	2.024	1.781	2.587
Alumina	2.056	2.461	4.418
Phosphoric acid	0.194	0.136	0.117
Sulphuric acid	0.073	0.075	0.097
Water and organic matter	3.296	3.185	3.165
Total	99.552	100.140	100.485
Hygroscopic moisture	4.428	3.551	4.054
absorbed at	29.4 C.°	24.0 C.°	27.0 C.°

The above soils differ from each other comparatively little in their most important constituents, with the exception of the alumina. Nos. 10 and 14 were taken from places 70 miles apart, and yet bear a very close resemblance, showing that these prairie lands are quite uniform in composition, except in lower localities, where the underlying limestone, shale, or other material can affect them. The analyses show that the lands have fair percentages of all the elements necessary to thriftiness, and were depth and the physical conditions also favorable they would make good farming lands. As it is, they are generally too thin (the underlying sandstone approaching too near the surface), and it is only in the lowlands, where the soil has accumulated to great depth, that farms might be successfully kept up.

BLACK PRAIRIE REGION (CRETACEOUS).

In the southern part of the Choctaw and in the southeastern part of the Chickasaw nation there is an open prairie region, treeless and more or less rolling, that is characterized by heavy and stiff clay lands of usually a black color and many feet in depth, underlaid by the whitish rotten limestone of the Cretaceous formation. This is the northern limit of the great central belt of Texas, and is similar to that region in all of its features. Its most westerly occurrence is between the upper and lower cross timbers, and its greatest width is in the southeastern part of the Choctaw nation, where it reaches from 2 miles north of Caddo south to the timbered uplands of Red river. Eastward it becomes more and more narrow, until near the Arkansas state line the prairies disappear almost altogether, and its black calcareous lands are found only in places along the streams among the pine uplands, and with a characteristic growth of bois d'arc (known also as Osage orange). Much of the prairie land is sandy in character, and is easily tilled; but very little is under cultivation, the more sandy soils of the timbers being preferred.

OTHER PRAIRIE REGIONS.

Passing westward from the sandy loam prairies of the central part of the territory, we reach a region of red loam prairie lands in the Pottawatomie and Chickasaw nations, which extend northward into Kansas. The exact limits of this region are not known, but near the eastern border of the Comanche and Wichita countries the great gypsum prairies begin, and extend westward through the territory and northward into Kansas. These two regions are continuations of the same in Texas, and are probably similar to them in their chief features. The red-loam lands are not as prominent as in Texas, and appear chiefly in the valleys along the streams.

Paul's valley, on the Washita river, 60 miles above Tishomingo, in the Chickasaw nation, is a noted locality. Lying in a bend of the river, it has a width of about a mile and a length of five miles. Its soil is a very fertile red loam, and all of the valley is said to be under-cultivation, chiefly in corn. Its relation to the river is that of a prairie bottom. Kickapoo and Jourdan's flats are other prairie valleys lying still northwest of Paul's valley, and similar to it in character.

The character of this entire western region is said to be that of a broad and arid plain, mostly high and level, but broken and hilly in places, interspersed with sand-hills, and having sandy lands but little suited to cultivation. Gypsum occurs in the greatest abundance on the surface of the prairies and in thick beds in the hills, making the waters of the streams mostly unfit for use.

ALLUVIAL LANDS.

The four or five large rivers, the Arkansas, its Red Fork, Canadian and its North Fork, and Red river, all have their sources in the great plains of the west, and are often bordered on both sides by high prairie plateaus. They have little valley lands and little or no timber growth, except some scattering cottonwood and willow, until far within the territory. The timber then increases in quantity and variety, and when the better class of uplands is reached on the western border of the country, belonging to the more civilized tribes, we find these bottom lands quite heavily timbered with black walnut, pecan, ash, elm, oaks, hickory, etc., with cottonwood and its associates only in the first or lowest bottoms. The beds of the streams, especially of the Arkansas and Canadian rivers, are covered with deep white sand, which forms ever-changing sand-bars, and "quicksand beds" where covered with water.

In the eastern half of the territory the river beds of the Arkansas and Canadian are very wide from bank to bank, though in low-water seasons the streams themselves are quite narrow, and in places are easily forded.

The bottom lands of the rivers are usually very wide either on one side or the other of the stream, and embrace two bottoms or terraces, known as the *first* and *second bottoms*.

The *first bottom*, or the lowest, and immediately along the stream, mostly narrow and more or less subject to overflow at high-water seasons, is usually composed of a red sandy soil, very deep, supporting a timber growth of large cottonwood, etc., as above. The soils of the first bottoms of Red river are mostly heavy red clays, which are derived from the red clay beds of the gypsum region of the West.

In the following analyses the composition of some of the first bottom soils of the rivers is shown:

No. 16. *Red sandy loam* of Arkansas river, Webber's falls, Cherokee nation. Depth taken, 12 inches; timber growth, cottonwood, walnut, pecan, etc., with cane undergrowth.

No. 6. *Red sandy soil* of Canadian river, near Eufaula, Creek nation. Depth taken, 18 inches; timber growth, chiefly cottonwood.

No. 21. *Red sandy loam* of Washita river, near Tishomingo, Chickasaw nation. Depth taken, 12 inches; heavy timber growth.

No. 23. *Red clay soil* of Red river, in Chickasaw nation, opposite Gainesville, Texas. Depth taken, 10 inches; timber growth, walnut, pecan, ash, elm, etc.

No. 26. *Red clay soil* of Red river, near the mouth of Kiamitia creek, Cherokee nation. Depth 10 inches; timber growth, ash and elm mostly.

River first bottom lands.

	ARKANSAS RIVER.	CANADIAN RIVER.	WASHITA RIVER.	RED RIVER.	
	CHEROKEE NATION.	CREEK NATION.	CHICKASAW NATION.	CHICKASAW NATION.	CHOCTAW NATION.
	Red sandy loam.	Red sandy soil.	Red sandy loam.	Red clay soil.	Red clay soil.
	No. 16.	No. 6.	No. 21.	No. 23.	No. 26.
Insoluble matter	87.590 } 92.210	89.770 } 94.801	90.190 } 93.640	65.765 } 72.383	68.050 } 77.913
Soluble silica	4.660	5.031	8.450	6.618	9.863
Potash	0.286	0.117	0.141	0.405	0.345
Soda	0.070	0.044	0.077	0.090	0.065
Lime	0.285	1.084	1.258	2.933	1.116
Magnesia	0.412	0.021	0.134	2.623	1.217
Brown oxide of manganese	0.132	0.075	0.096	0.065	0.196
Peroxide of iron	1.971	0.925	1.290	4.661	5.374
Alumina	1.353	0.628	1.205	8.347	8.345
Phosphoric acid	0.135	0.117	0.068	0.170	0.238
Sulphuric acid	0.061	0.068	0.114	0.090	0.080
Carbonic acid		0.800	0.749	1.707	0.952
Water and organic matter	2.589	1.408	1.849	6.908	4.906
Total	99.750	100.061	100.113	100.362	100.331
Humus	0.806			1.069	0.862
Available inorganic	0.480			0.723	1.488
Available phosphoric acid	0.014			0.068	0.061
Available silica	0.308			0.308	0.682
Hygroscopic moisture	3.542	3.165	3.153	9.962	9.568
absorbed at	26.5 C.°	25.5 C.°	27.0 C.°	27.7 C.°	27.7 C.°

In the red sandy loams of the Arkansas, Canadian, and Washita rivers there is a fair amount of potash, and, in the first two, of phosphoric acid. The latter element is deficient in the Washita soil. A matter of special note is the large percentage of lime in all of these soils, and especially in that of the Canadian river, which has so little clay in its composition. The Red river clay lands are very stiff, and their analyses show large amounts of potash, lime, and magnesia, as well as of iron and alumina. The percentages of phosphoric acid are only fair for such soils, though sufficient to insure great fertility for a number of years. The humus is high, and the analysis shows it to hold, in an available condition, about one-third of the phosphoric acid of the soil. In the red sandy loam of Arkansas river the humus percentage is greater than in one of the red clay soils of Red river; but there is a less amount of available phosphoric acid, which is due probably to the smaller amount of lime and to the comparative absence of clay, a retentive element.

The *second bottom*, occupying a terrace about 10 or 15 feet above the first, is very heavily timbered with walnut, pecan, ash, elm, etc., and has usually a dense undergrowth of cane, briers, etc., which affords cattle both shelter and sustenance in the winter months. This terrace is broad, sometimes extending nearly half a mile from the river, and has a dark loam soil, deep and very highly productive, capable of yielding a bale or more of cotton per acre if the plants were properly restrained from running to weed and the seasons were long enough to enable the bolls to mature. These may be considered as the chief cotton lands of the territory, those of the Red river and the eastern portion of the Arkansas river in the Cherokee nation being more generally under tillage.

The following analyses show the composition of these soils from the several rivers:

No. 5. *Dark clay loam second-bottom soil*, Arkansas river, north of Muscogee, Creek nation; taken 12 inches deep. Timber growth large, with dense undergrowth.

No. 7. *Dark red loam* of Canadian river, near Eufaula, Creek nation; taken 12 inches deep; bottom narrow and timbered.

No. 9. *Dark clayey loam* of North Fork river, near Eufaula, Creek nation. Depth taken, 12 inches; entire depth of soil, 24 inches. This land is said to have yielded 1,700 pounds of seed-cotton per acre.

No. 22. *Dark sandy loam*, second bottom of Washita river, near Tishomingo, Chickasaw nation. Depth taken, 12 inches to deep red subsoil.

No. 25. *Dark clayey loam* of second bottom of Red river, near mouth of Kiamitia creek, Choctaw nation. Depth taken, 12 inches; well timbered, and having a cane undergrowth.

Second bottom river lands.

	CREEK NATION.			CHICKASAW NATION.	CHOCTAW NATION.
	ARKANSAS RIVER.	CANADIAN RIVER.	NORTH FORK RIVER.	WASHITA RIVER.	RED RIVER.
	Dark clay loam.	Dark red loam.	Dark clayey loam.	Dark sandy loam.	Dark loam.
	No. 5.	No. 7.	No. 9.	No. 22.	No. 25.
Insoluble matter	67.280 } 80.820	80.310 } 82.230	74.070 } 84.760	80.365 } 83.666	76.660 } 85.060
Soluble silica	13.540	1.920	10.690	4.301	9.100
Potash	0.144	0.201	0.447	0.304	0.404
Soda	0.089	0.074	0.082	0.084	0.089
Lime	0.756	0.177	0.575	0.028	0.465
Magnesia	0.944	0.157	0.624	0.169	0.619
Brown oxide of manganese	0.229	0.080	0.078	0.081	0.169
Peroxide of iron	4.186	1.820	3.311	1.895	3.286
Alumina	7.741	1.568	5.984	1.614	3.944
Phosphoric acid	0.394	0.199	0.186	0.065	0.163
Sulphuric acid	0.167	0.080	0.105	0.019	0.073
Water and organic matter	4.696	1.902	4.743	2.597	5.750
Total	100.106	100.480	99.784	100.152	99.947
Hygroscopic moisture	0.882	1.704	7.966	2.283	6.772
absorbed at	34.5 C.°	26.0 C.°	25.5 C.°	26.0 C.°	27.0 C.°

The percentage of potash is large in the samples of soil from the Red, Washita, and North Fork rivers, and is rather small in the clayey soil of the Arkansas river. There are fair amounts of phosphoric acid in all, except that of Washita river, and this is also very deficient in lime. In the averages of lime they all fall below the first-bottom soils. Taken altogether, the soils of the second bottoms of the rivers do not show anything remarkable in their composition. With the exception of the Washita soil, they are good soils chemically and physically, with sufficient amounts of each important element to make them thrifty and durable under cultivation.

Cotton as a crop, except along the immediate borders of Texas and Arkansas, has been comparatively unknown among the Indians until within the last few years. A few attempts had been made to raise small patches of cotton in the interior of the territory, but these mostly failed because of ignorance as to the proper methods of culture. The freeing of the negro slaves of the Indians, the building of the Missouri, Kansas, and Texas railroad from Saint Louis through the heart of the agricultural region of the territory, the greater influx of whites among the several tribes, and a greater tendency toward speaking the English language on the part of the Indians, resulting in more general relations with the whites, have brought about an improved and greatly enlarged system of agriculture, and with this the introduction of cotton as a general crop in a great part of the territory. It is true that comparatively little cotton is produced by the real or "full-blood" Indians, who are still chiefly dependent upon their small farms of corn and potatoes and upon the raising of stock, but the more wealthy and intelligent, especially on the south and east, do have their fields of cotton.

The culture of cotton is said to have been introduced among the Indians of the southern part of the Choctaw nation in 1850, and it has been kept up since that time with a gradually increasing acreage. It finds a ready market at the railroad towns in Texas immediately south of Red river. In the Chickasaw nation its culture on any notable scale was begun about 1873, and is now carried on chiefly by white settlers. One farm of corn and cotton on Red river is said to contain 1,600 acres. In the Seminole and the Pottawatomie nations cotton was first planted in 1879, and its culture is almost altogether confined to the river and creek bottoms.

In the Creek nation the lands along the Canadian river are the chief cotton lands. Some cotton is planted along the Verdigris river, and a very little along the Arkansas as far north as the thirty-sixth parallel, or within 10 miles of the northern boundary-line of- the nation. Its culture was begun only within the past few years, and is now carried on chiefly by negroes and whites.

The Cherokees began to plant cotton in 1874 or 1875 from seed that was distributed among them. The limit of its culture is on Little river, about 10 miles northeast of Tahlequah. It has been grown at a distance of 40 miles from that town, but the planters became discouraged because of its running to weed and failure to mature.

The amount of cotton raised in the territory in 1879 has been estimated at 17,000 bales, from 25,000 acres. This is simply an estimate, as no census was taken among the Indians in 1880. As already stated, the greater part of this was produced in the southern part of the territory, comparatively little having come from the interior. The following statement of cotton shipments between July, 1879, and July, 1880, has been furnished by the railroad agents at the several stations named, and will give an idea of the distribution of cotton acreage over the territory, except in the eastern part of the Cherokee nation and the southern parts of the Choctaw and Chickasaw nations: Muscogee, on the Arkansas river, 562 bales; Eufaula, on the Canadian river, 1,100 bales; Stringtown, south of the Canadian river, none; Atoka, 900 bales; Caddo, 554 bales. These two latter places are in the southern part of the territory.

The planters of the Red river section haul their cotton to the nearest railroad stations in Texas, Caddo only receiving only that produced in more contiguous localities. Eufaula receives nearly all of that produced among the Seminoles. Gins have been erected in Muscogee and the chief towns southward, and one is in operation in the Seminole nation.

Analyses of soils of the Indian territory, made for the Tenth Census.

Number.	Name.	Locality.	Nation.	Depth in inches.	Vegetation.	Analyst.
	THICKNED SANDY UPLANDS.					
15	Sandy upland soil	Five miles south of Tahlequah.	Cherokee.	12	Oaks and hickory.	C. Cory.
16	Gray upland soil	Boggy depot.	Choctaw.	12	Black-jack and post oaks; some hickory.	J. R. Durrett.
1	...do...	Fork of Verdigris and Arkansas rivers.	Creek.	18	Post and red oaks, hickory, and sassafras.	Do.
2	Red-clay subsoil			18 to 24		Do.
3	Sandy upland soil	Near Eufaula.		12	Oaks and hickory.	H. McCalley.
24	Black-jack flat of Red river.	Opposite Gainesville, Texas.	Chickasaw.	12	Black-jack and post oaks; some hickory.	C. Cory.
	RIVER BOTTOM LANDS. *First bottoms.*					
18	Arkansas river, red sandy loam.	Webber's Falls.	Cherokee.	12	Cottonwood, walnut, pecan, etc.	C. Cory.
6	Canadian, red sandy soil.	Near Eufaula.	Creek.	18	Chiefly cottonwood.	J. R. Durrett.
21	Washita, red sandy loam.	Near Tishomingo.	Chickasaw.	12	Cottonwood, etc.	C. Cory.
22	Red river, red-clay soil.	Opposite Gainesville, Texas.	...do...	10	Walnut, ash, pecan, elm, etc.	J. R. Durrett.
26		Near mouth of Kiamitia creek.	Cherokee.	16	Ash and elm.	Do.
	Second bottoms.					
5	Arkansas river, dark clay loam.	North of Muscogee.	Creek.	12	As in first bottom, with cane undergrowth.	C. Cory.
7	Canadian, dark-red loam.	...do...	...do...	12	...do...	Do.
23	North fork, dark clayey loam.	Near Tishomingo.	Chickasaw.	12	...do...	Do.
25	Washita, dark sandy loam.		Chickasaw.	10	...do...	H. McCalley.
24	Red river, dark clayey loam.	Near mouth of Kiamitia creek.	Choctaw.	12	...do...	C. Cory.
	SANDY PRAIRIE LANDS.					
16	Sandy and clayey prairie loam.	Five miles south of Tahlequah.	Cherokee.	12	Open prairie.	J. R. Durrett.
19	Sandy prairie loam.	Near Muscogee.	Creek.	15	...do...	C. Cory.
19	...do...	Wewoka.	Seminole.	18	...do...	H. McCalley.

* See Humus table.

Humus percentages.

	No. 16.	No. 22.	No. 26.
Humus	0.808	1.069	0.962
Available inorganic	0.490	0.722	1.450
Available phosphoric acid	0.094	0.605	0.651

PART II.

DESCRIPTION OF COTTON-PRODUCING NATIONS.

DESCRIPTION OF COTTON-PRODUCING NATIONS.

CHEROKEE NATION.

The Cherokee Indians number (in 1880) 19,720 persons, and the territory occupied by them covers about 7,860 square miles in the northeastern corner of the territory. The surface of the country north of Tahlequah, the capital town, is mostly a rolling grassy prairie, with light sandy soils, timbered only along the streams, and devoted generally to stock grazing. On the east of Tahlequah, along the Arkansas line, the country becomes hilly, broken, and rocky. It is largely timbered, and its soils are similar in character to those of the red-loam region of the adjoining portions of Arkansas.

The country lying southeast and east of the Illinois river embraces the roughest and most mountainous of the entire nation, and is well timbered throughout, being the western spur of the Boston mountains of Arkansas. A few small open prairies occasionally occur. The mountains rise several hundred feet above the valleys, their sides being rocky and precipitous, and their summits usually present broad table-lands of sandy and gravelly soils, which are not under cultivation. Smaller hills, covered with deep masses of chert fragments, appear often, while sandstone outcrops abundantly in the mountains.

The valleys between the mountains are narrow, and have red-loam soils, well timbered with oak, hickory, and other growth. Each valley is usually watered by a small stream, along which are located the few farms of this region. The country becomes less mountainous toward the Arkansas line, and large areas of good and tillable lands appear. The soil is often sandy, but is underlaid by red and yellow clay subsoils. Westward of the Illinois river to the Grand river the country is hilly and broken, interspersed with cherty ridges and a few mountain chains toward the Arkansas river on the south. Many small open prairies occur, their soils enriched and made stiff and waxy by outcropping limestones. The timbered portions of the region have cherty and gravelly lands, with clay subsoils, and are considered quite productive. (See analysis, page 10.) A number of bald or treeless hills also occur, but the mountains are well timbered.

Within 12 miles of Fort Gibson, on the Grand river, the limestone disappears, and is overlaid by the sandstones, which are prominent in the prairies to the south and westward, and which produce a rather dark sandy soil. (See analysis, page 13.) On the west of Grand river the country is rolling and well timbered.

South of the Arkansas river, in the angle formed by it and the Canadian, the country is mostly an open and rolling prairie—a part of the large prairie region that extends westward through the Creek country. In this section there are a few hills and ridges timbered with oaks and having deep sandy soils. Rocky fragments, sometimes of trunks covered with impressions of coal plants, are also very abundant. The two rivers are bordered by timbered bottoms, and these by belts of high timbered and sandy uplands. The open prairies are here interspersed with a few bald sandstone ridges, and are entirely devoted to stock grazing.

From the above it will appear that a large proportion of the lands of the Cherokee country are comparatively unfit for cultivation, being either too mountainous and rocky, as in the east, or too thin and light, as is the case with a large part of the prairie region.

The bottom lands of the rivers are often broad, and afford excellent farming lands. Those of the Arkansas embrace two bottoms or terraces; the first or lowest is narrow, more or less subject to overflow, and is heavily timbered, cottonwood being most prominent. The soil is a dark red sand or loam, very deep, said to be capable of yielding from 2,000 to 2,500 pounds of seed-cotton per acre. The second bottom varies in width from 1 to 1½ miles, and has a great variety of timber growth, prominent among which is walnut, pecan, oak, and hickory. There is also usually a dense cane undergrowth. The soil is a dark sandy loam, highly productive under cultivation. (See analysis, page 14.) Cotton is planted on these lands, but is said to open first on the first bottoms, the rich lands of the second causing the plant to run to weed.

In 1879 the lands under cultivation, according to the report of the Indian bureau, embraced 92,306 acres. The farms lie chiefly along the streams and in the latter class of timbered lands, and are mostly distant from the main thoroughfares. Cotton is a new crop among the people, its culture having been introduced in 1876. At present it is confined mostly to the southern part of the nation, along the Arkansas and Canadian rivers, whose sandy and timbered border uplands are said to yield the best staple, as well as a crop two weeks earlier than on the bottom lands. There are comparatively few negroes among the Cherokees, and the laborers are therefore native full-blood and half-breed Indians and the few whites who have become citizens.

The tribe is said to be rapidly improving in agricultural pursuits, and now produces nearly all of its own necessary supplies. The productions in 1880 were 726,042 bushels of corn, 58,424 bushels of wheat, and 52,568 bushels of oats and barley.

The kinds of soils devoted to the cultivation of cotton are the loamy and sandy bottoms and the level or undulating sandy uplands. The chief soil is the *river bottom* land of the Arkansas river, including also the bottoms of Saltsaw, Illinois, Canadian, and Grand rivers, and Lee's creek, with a timber growth of cottonwood, oak, walnut, ash, hickory, pecan, mulberry, etc. The soil is a sandy loam, mahogany or black colored, and 4 feet deep. The chief crops of the region are cotton, corn, wheat, oats, and potatoes, and the soil is best adapted to cotton and tobacco. The usual and most productive height is from 4 to 5 feet. The plant inclines to run to weed on rich land or during wet seasons, which topping and close planting restrains. One thousand pounds of seed-cotton per acre is the yield on fresh land, and 1,425 pounds from upland or 1,660 pounds from bottom make a 475-pound bale of good lint. After two years' cultivation the product is 1,750 pounds, and the same amount from upland or bottom makes a 475-pound bale of lint, which rates about the same as that from fresh land. Crab-grass and cockleburs are the most troublesome weeds. None of this land lies "turned out".

Shipments are made during the fall and spring months, by railroad and river, to Saint Louis, Memphis, or New Orleans at from $3 to $5 per bale.

CREEK NATION.

The territory occupied by the Creek or Muscogee tribe is bounded on the south by the Canadian river, and on the north in part by the Arkansas river, and covers an area of about 5,025 square miles. It is very sparsely settled away from the railroad towns, the village of Ockmulgee being the largest inland place. The population is 15,000.

The surface of the country presents somewhat varying features, but is mostly a rolling and open prairie, with occasional mountainous ridges, and is watered by a number of large streams and their small tributaries, along whose immediate banks lie timbered bottom lands. Along the larger streams the banks are bordered by belts of high and sandy uplands, timbered with post, red, and black-jack oaks, hickory, sumac, and dogwood. Near the junction of the Verdigris and the Arkansas these respective belts unite and form quite a large timbered region, which is covered with deep white sands over beds of red and yellow loams, the whole underlaid (as shown in the beds of the rivers) by slates, shales, and crinoidal limestones.

The Verdigris river is bordered 5 miles north of the old site of Tallahassee mission by large lakes of clear water, lined with marsh flags or rushes and large areas of pond lilies. Forests of pecan trees and an abundant growth of cottonwood, walnut, elm, ash, etc., cover the rather wide bottoms of both this and the Arkansas river. The bed of the Verdigris river is very rocky, and the stream is fordable in but few places, whereas the bed of the Arkansas is very wide, and is covered with deep quicksands, the fording places being constantly changed by the current.

The large open prairies on the south of the Arkansas river are more rolling and hilly than those on the north, and are almost entirely treeless (except along the streams) as far west as Ockmulgee, where the mountains are mostly timbered. Sandstone is the prevailing rock everywhere, often coming to the surface, and producing thin sandy soils little suited to cultivation; luxuriant grasses, however, cover the prairies. On the west of Ockmulgee, after crossing the timbered uplands of the Deep Fork river, we find the country broken and interspersed with partly timbered and partly treeless ridges, the valleys being for the most part open and undulating. This character of country prevails between the North Fork and the Canadian rivers, but as these streams approach each other it becomes more and more densely timbered, and in the region of the railroad we find an almost exclusive timber growth and deep sandy soils very similar to those along the Arkansas river.

The lands of the nation embrace three chief varieties: the sandy prairies, the deep sands of the timbered regions, and the river bottoms. The first of these covers the greater part of the country, and has been described; the timbered lands, while having a deeper soil, are too sandy to be either durable or very productive after a few years' cultivation, except where the red subsoil comes near the surface. They are excellent fruit lands, and are to a large extent under cultivation with other crops. (See analyses of soils, page 13.)

The *bottom lands* are the chief farming lands of the nation, and yield fine crops of corn and cotton. They comprise a first bottom of sand, subject to overflow, and a *second bottom* of usually greater width, heavily timbered with a great variety of growth. The soil is a dark loam, often very sandy, but at other times passing into a stiff clay, and capable of yielding a bale of cotton per acre. (See analysis, page 14.)

There are some broad and level loam lands along Caney creek (west of Muscogee) that are largely under cultivation by negroes, the former slaves of the Indians, who have formed a settlement there.

Cotton is not a prominent crop in this nation, though planted to some extent as far up the Arkansas river as Wealaka, near the thirty-sixth parallel of latitude. It is raised chiefly along the Canadian and North Fork rivers in isolated patches of a few acres each, and mostly by negroes. The number of acres under cultivation in 1880 was 65,000, and from this was produced 200,000 bushels of corn, 78,000 bushels of wheat, and 20,000 bushels of oats and barley, besides a very large amount of vegetables.

The lowlands comprise the sandy alluvial land of the Arkansas and Canadian rivers and their tributaries. The uplands are hilly and rolling, and mostly prairie.

The cotton soil is the *fine sandy loam* of the uplands with a red-clay subsoil. The chief crops are corn, beans, wheat, oats, sorghum, sweet potatoes, and cotton. The soil is best adapted to cotton and corn, but one-third of its tilled area is devoted to the latter crop. The usual height of the plant on the uplands is from 3 to 4 feet; on the bottoms, from 5 to 7 feet, but is most productive at 4 feet.

On new ground, or when the plant is not well cultivated on old ground, it inclines to run to weed, and good cultivation or topping in the dark of the moon in the months of July or August restrains the plant. The average yield of seed-cotton per acre from fresh land is 1,800 pounds, and 1,900 pounds of first picking, or from 2,020 to 2,160 pounds of late picking, make a 475-pound bale of lint, rating as good as any. The uplands are good for thirty years' cultivation in cotton; the bottoms are inexhaustible. The staple from old land is better than that from fresh land. Cocklebur is the most troublesome weed. None of this land lies "turned out".

The slopes wash readily, and the damage is serious to them, but the valleys are not much injured. A few efforts, by horizontalizing, have been made to check the damage, with partial success.

Cotton is shipped as soon as possible by railroad to Saint Louis at $3 per bale.

SEMINOLE NATION.

This tribe is but a branch or offshoot of the Creeks, and has the same language and customs. The territory occupied by it is comparatively small, and embraces about 312 square miles, presenting a narrow strip of country north and south, bordered on the north by the North Fork and on the south by the Canadian river. Wewoka and Little rivers flow through it respectively eastward and southeastward. All of these streams have good clay and loam bottom lands, bordered by sandy post-oak uplands, and are almost the only lands under cultivation. The surface of the country presents three prominent features or divisions: (1) An open and rolling prairie country on the east, almost treeless, and having a light sandy soil resting upon shales and sandstone, covered with grass, and devoted exclusively to stock grazing. (See analysis, page 13.) Its hills are sometimes capped with pebble conglomerates. (2) A hilly, timbered, and very broken country in the central part, extending 9 miles west of the village of Wewoka. Its lands are poor and sandy, and have a yellow sandy subsoil and a growth chiefly of black-jack oaks, but they are said to be too broken and rough for cultivation. (3) A red loam and clay country on the west, partly open prairies and partly timbered, and but little settled.

It is estimated that one half of the territory of the Seminoles is unsuited for agricultural purposes, and one-half of the remainder comprises the open prairies of the east.

This tribe in 1880, according to the reports of the Indian bureau, numbered about 2,667 persons; and the lands under cultivation embraced about 17,000 acres, yielding 220,000 bushels of corn, 2,000 bushels of oats and barley, and a large amount of vegetables.

The crops of the nation are corn, some small grain, and potatoes. Cotton was first introduced in 1879, and results show that the bottom lands alone are suited to it. It there grows to a height of about 4 feet, while on the uplands it seldom reaches 2 feet. Indians are the chief laborers. There are many negroes in the nation, but they usually have their own farms of about 4 acres each. The usual wages are 50 cents per day. Sufficient supplies are raised in the nation for their own use. The methods of cotton culture are the same as among the Creeks.

CHOCTAW NATION.

The tribe of Choctaw Indians occupies a large territory on the southeast embraced between the Canadian and Arkansas rivers on the north and the Red river on the south, with the state of Arkansas on the east. This area of about 10,450 square miles is mostly drained by tributaries of the Red river flowing southeastwardly.

The surface of the country is varied in character, and presents the following prominent features:

First.—A region of open and rolling sandy prairies extends from McAllister southward, the line of railroad to Atoka nearly marking their eastern limit, and westward from a few miles east of the railroad into the Chickasaw nation. These prairies are interrupted by timbered lands along the streams and elsewhere; the soils are sandy, and rest mostly on sandstone, and on the south are filled with a small ferruginous gravel. These prairies are not under cultivation, their grasses affording an excellent range for cattle.

Second.—The larger portion is a mountainous, hilly, and very broken region, and includes the line of the Shawnee hills on the northwest, and nearly all of the country on the north and east lying between the Missouri, Kansas, and Texas railroad and Arkansas state line, and from the northern boundary southward to within 30 or 40 miles of Red river. The Sans Bois mountains form a high divide between the waters of the Canadian and Red rivers; but the rest of the region is too rocky and broken for cultivation, and the arable lands lie only in narrow tracts along the streams. The country is well timbered throughout, and is interspersed on the north with a few small open prairies. Sandstones and conglomerates are the prevailing rocks, with shales in the valleys and some granite on the north, the region being a part of the red-loam division of Arkansas. Southward for a few miles, and forming a border belt extending westward south of Atoka into the Chickasaw nation, the country is not so hilly or broken, and the soil is deep and sandy, with a yellowish underclay and a timber growth of oak and hickory. (See analysis, page 10.) This belt is found along the railroad to within 3 miles of Caddo (where the country opens up into a region of black calcareous prairies), and extends eastward to Arkansas, merging on the southeast into the pine and sand hills or yellow-loam region.

Third.—An open and rolling black prairie country (that forms the northern part of the great central prairie region of Texas) lies in the southern part of the nation, and an extreme width from 3 miles north of Caddo to Red river gradually become more and more narrow to the east, and near the Arkansas line finally disappears, except along the borders of the streams, where small areas of black lands appear, the uplands themselves here belong to the region of sand and pine hills or yellow loam region of Arkansas and Texas. These prairies are underlaid by Cretaceous rotten limestone, with beds of fossils. The soil is a stiff waxy clay, very deep, partly hog-wallow, in dry weather shrinking with innumerable cracks, and in wet seasons is very tenacious and difficult to till. Portions of these lands are sandy in character, though still black, and are more under cultivation than the stiffer varieties.

Fourth.—This group embraces the bottom lands of the large streams, which are sometimes very extensive, and afford excellent farming lands. They are heavily timbered with cottonwood, walnut, pecan, ash, elm, etc., and embrace red sandy soil and dark loams, and sometimes heavy clays. The bordering uplands are usually sandy, with an oak growth. (See analysis, page 14.)

The nation has a population of about 15,800, according to the report of the Indian agent for 1880. The lands under cultivation embrace about 100,000 acres, and lie chiefly in the western and southern parts of the country. The crops are corn, small grain, and cotton. The latter crop is planted chiefly on the south and southeast, much of it being hauled to Paris and to Clarksville, in Texas, and there sold.

The crop has, however, been looked upon with favor only within the past eight years, and its acreage is now thought to comprise about one-fourth of the tilled lands of the southern parts of the nation. Its yield is said to be from 600 to 900 pounds of seed-cotton per acre. The crop is produced chiefly by negroes and whites, the Indians as a class not caring to work much. From Atoka, on the border of the upper prairie region, 900 bales of the crop of 1869 were shipped, but a large part of this probably came from the Chickasaw nation, on the west. The production of other crops was 1,200,000 bushels of corn, 200,000 bushels of wheat, 50,000 bushels of oats and barley, and a large amount of vegetables.

ABSTRACT FROM THE REPORT OF G. B. HESTER, OF BOGGY DEPOT.

The lowlands comprise the first and second bottoms of Red river and Clear Boggy creek, occurring in small bodies of from 2 to 20 acres in area. The uplands are level table-land and prairie. The chief crops of the region are corn and cotton. Cotton is usually grown on the uplands or level table-land, and has not been raised here until within the last six years. The chief soil cultivated in cotton is the *sandy loam*, extending east 15 or 20 miles, south 9 miles, west and north 50 or more miles, with a timber growth of black-jack and post oaks and dogwood. On the bottoms the timber growth is red and water oaks and bois d'arc.

The soil is a sandy loam, some prairie, black colored, and from 8 inches to 2 feet deep. The subsoil is usually a red, clammy and sticky clay, and contains soft sticky pebbles. The soil is easy to till in all seasons, and is early, warm, and well drained. Both corn and cotton do well on this land, and about one-fourth of the tilled land is planted in cotton, which usually grows from 2¼ to 6 feet high, but is most productive at a medium of these heights. The plant never runs to weed on prairie or uplands, but on bottom lands it does, and topping restrains it, although but little practiced. From 600 to 900 pounds is the seed-cotton product from fresh land, 1,680 pounds making a 475-pound bale of middling to low middling lint. After three years' cultivation it takes from 1,545 to 1,600 pounds to make a bale of lint, which rates about the same as that from new land. Lamb's-quarter, hog-weed, purslane, rag-weed, crab-grass, and a tough thorny weed are the most troublesome. After long cultivation the land always produces best after resting one, two, or three years. It washes badly on slopes, and very seriously where the farms lie idle. The valleys are greatly benefited by the washings. Nothing has been done to check the damage to the slopes.

There is not much cotton planted on the low or bottom lands, as it usually runs to weed too much, and does not mature as early as that on the uplands.

Cotton is shipped as soon as possible, by the Missouri, Kansas, and Texas railroad, to Saint Louis, at $3 50 per bale.

CHICKASAW NATION.

The country occupied by the Chickasaw Indians, lying in the central and southern parts of the territory, covers an area of 7,267 square miles. The surface of the country is somewhat varied in its features, though the greater part is an open prairie, interspersed on the east with timbered belts along the stream, and also by two large timbered regions. One of the latter embraces a large rolling and broken region of deep sandy lands. Tishomingo, the capital of the nation, is situated in this region, which is part of the timbered belt of the Choctaw nation of the east. It differs, however, from the latter in embracing a large region of granite outcrops. The land of this region has a deep sandy and gravelly soil, underlaid in places by heavy beds of white clay (probably from granite decomposition), and timbered with oaks, hickory, etc. This granite outcrop is about 3 miles wide and 18 miles in length northeast and southwest. Three miles west of Tishomingo the prairies again appear.

Another timbered region is that of the cross timbers, which enter the nation from Texas in two belts, the upper and lower, separated from each other by an open black prairie, but soon uniting to form one region (according to the reports of government surveys), and extending far northward. The two belts, before uniting, are each about 15 miles broad, and their surfaces rolling and somewhat broken, and covered with a deep sandy soil. The growth of the lower belt is post, Spanish, and black-jack oaks, with some hickory; that of the upper belt a scrubby post oak on poorer soils.

The prairies which cover mostly the rest of the nation are of three chief kinds :

First.—The *black sandy*, sometimes hog-wallow, prairies of the southeast, underlaid by Cretaceous rotten limestone, and being a continuation of the great central black region of Texas. The lands are rolling and mostly treeless, covered with grass, and devoted to grazing purposes.

Second.—The *sandy prairies* of the northeast, with timbered belts along the streams, the soil light sandy in character.

Third.—The *red-loam* prairies of the western part of the nation, also given up entirely to stock grazing.

The bottom lands of the streams are the chief agricultural lands of the nation. Those of Red river embrace the usual narrow *first bottom* of the red sandy lands, partly timbered with cottonwood and subject to overflow, and the *second bottom* of red and dark loams and clays, timbered with walnut, pecan, ash, and elm. In the bends of the river these lands are very extensive, while on the opposite side the bluffs rise almost directly from the water's edge. There are also *post-oak* and *black-jack flats* on the borders of these bottoms that are said to yield well, though having a sandy soil and subsoil. (See analysis, page 11.) These, with the bottom lands, are the chief cotton lands of the nation, and yield from 700 to 1,000 pounds of seed-cotton per acre.

The bottom lands of the Washita river also embrace a narrow red sandy first bottom and a red and dark loam and clayey second bottom, the latter often quite wide and well timbered. (See analysis, page 14.)

To the northwest, however, the timber becomes less and the prairies often approach near the river, producing prairie valleys or flats. Of these the most noted is Paul's valley, situated 60 miles above Tishomingo. Its width is said to be about a mile and its length five miles. Its soil is a red loam, and is almost entirely under cultivation in grain. Kickapoo and Jourdan's flats, lying 25 and 30 miles still above Paul's valley, are also noted for their high fertility.

The Chickasaws in 1880 numbered 6,000 persons, and the lands in cultivation were estimated at 40,000 acres. The crops embrace corn, small grain, tobacco, and cotton. The latter is produced chiefly on the Red river lands, though some is raised along the Canadian river in the north. In 1879 a little was said to be planted in Kickapoo flat, on the Washita river, and this may be considered the extreme northwest limit of production, though in reality but an experimental crop. Cotton culture is carried on almost entirely by whites who have settled among the Indians, and was first begun about 10 years ago. The methods of culture are the same as practiced in the adjoining portions of Texas. Other productions are not given.

THE POTTAWATOMIE NATION.

The country occupied by the Pottawatomies covers an area of about 900 square miles, and is bordered on the south by the Canadian river, and on the north by the North Fork. Little river flows eastward through the central part.

The surface of the country is high and partly rolling, one-half of it comprising sandy uplands, timbered with black and post oaks and hickory, and the remainder is mostly an open and treeless prairie of red-loam and sandy lands.

The bottom lands of the rivers are chiefly cultivated in crops of corn and a little cotton, the latter having been but recently introduced in the nation. These lands have dark sandy soils, well timbered with walnut, pecan, cottonwood, ash, and elm, and said to yield over 1,000 pounds of seed-cotton per acre.

ABSTRACT FROM THE REPORT OF ELIJAH CAMBRON, OF OBERLIN.

The lowlands of the region are the alluvial lands of the South Canadian river. The uplands are rolling and level table-lands and prairie, one-half prairie and the remainder timbered. The chief crops are corn, Irish and sweet potatoes, and cotton.

The cotton soil is the *black and yellow sandy lands,* comprising the greater portion of this region, and having a natural timber growth of black and post oaks and hickory on part of the uplands, and elm, walnut, pecan, cottonwood, and ash on the bottoms.

The soil is sandy loam, black or yellow colored, with a depth of 1 foot. The soil is easy to till, and is best adapted to corn and cotton. A very limited amount of the tilled land is devoted to cotton; the plant grows usually 4 feet high, and is most productive at that height, inclining to run to weed if there is too much rain. The seed-cotton product per acre from fresh or from old land is from 1,200 to 1,300 pounds. The yield increases every year, and 1,425 pounds make a 475-pound bale of lint, which rates better from old than from new land. Sunflower and careless weeds are the most troublesome weeds. None of this land lies turned out. It washes on the slopes, but no damage is done to them or to the valleys. Dry and warm weather favors cotton culture in this region.

Cotton is hauled in wagons to nearest railroad station and shipped to Saint Louis.

863

PART III.

CULTURAL AND ECONOMIC DETAILS

OF

COTTON PRODUCTION.

REPORTS RECEIVED FROM CORRESPONDENTS.

Cherokee nation.—Rev. STEPHEN FORMAN, Tahlequah, March 30, 1880.
Choctaw nation.—G. B. HESTER, Boggy Depot, 1880.
Creek nation.—JOHN A. FORMAN, Muscogee, February 25, 1880.
Pottawatomie nation.—ELIJAH CAMBRON, Oberlin, August 16, 1880.

28

866

ANSWERS TO SCHEDULE QUESTIONS.

TILLAGE, IMPROVEMENT, ETC.

1. What is the usual depth of tillage, and what draft is employed in breaking up? Is subsoiling, fall plowing, or fallowing practiced?

Usual depth of tillage is from 3 to 4 inches; with 1 horse in the Cherokee and Choctaw nations, and with 2 horses, mules, or a yoke of oxen in the Creek and Pottawatomie nations. Neither subsoiling nor fallowing are practiced in any nation, and fall plowing only to some extent in the Creek and Choctaw nations.

2. Is rotation of crops practiced? If so, how many years' course, and in what order of crops? With what results?

Cherokee: Rotation of crops is practiced with cotton, corn, sweet potatoes, oats, and wheat in no regular order, but with good results. *Choctaw:* Wheat and oats do not do well; corn and cotton are the only crops planted, except sweet potatoes, for home use. There are some farmers in this nation who have planted corn for 15 years without change. *Creek* and *Pottawatomie:* Rotation of crops is not practiced.

3. What fertilizers, or other direct means of improving the soil, are used by you or in your region? Is green manuring practiced?

Creek: Cotton-seed, barn-yard manure, prairie grass, leaves, bones, etc.; the results are good. *Choctaw:* Notwithstanding the great benefit which would be derived from the use of fertilizers, none are used. *Cherokee* and *Pottawatomie:* No fertilizers are used.

Green manuring is not practiced in any of the nations.

4. How is cotton-seed disposed of? If sold, on what terms, or at what price? Is cotton-seed cake used with you for feed or manure?

Creek: Cotton-seed is partly shipped to Saint Louis at 10 cents per bushel; partly fed to cattle, partly used as manure, and partly wasted. *Cherokee:* Shipped to Little Rock and Saint Louis oil-mills at $8 per ton. *Pottawatomie:* Mostly used as feed for cattle; when sold, the price is 8 cents per bushel. *Choctaw:* Usually fed to cattle. Cotton-seed cake is used as a manure, mixed with barn-yard manure, for cotton and vegetables in the Creek and Choctaw nations, as feed for cattle in the Pottawatomie nation, and not at all in the Cherokee nation.

PLANTING AND CULTIVATION OF COTTON.

5. What preparation is usually given to cotton land before bedding up? Do you plant in ridges, and how far apart? What is the usual planting time?

Choctaw and *Pottawatomie:* Spring plowing. *Creek* and *Cherokee:* No preparation is given. Planting in ridges is the general practice. *Choctaw:* From 3 to 3½ feet apart. *Cherokee* and *Pottawatomie:* Four feet. *Creek:* Four feet on uplands; from 5 to 6 feet on bottoms. The usual planting time is the middle of May in the Choctaw, and the middle of April in the other nations.

6. What variety of cotton do you prefer, and how much seed is used per acre? What implements do you use in planting?

The variety preferred in the Creek nation is the Cheatham and the Texas long staple; in the other nations no preference is expressed. One bushel of seed is usually used per acre. The implements are the common bull-tongue plows to open the land with, and the seed is then mostly planted by hand. In the Cherokee nation cotton-seed planters are in use to some extent, and are well thought of.

7. How long usually before your seed comes up? At what stage of growth do you thin out your stand, and how far apart?

Cherokee: The plant appears in three weeks, and the stand is thinned out at the formation of the fourth leaf, and at about 18 inches apart. *Creek:* Comes up in from 6 to 10 days (depending on the weather), and is thinned out when the fourth or sixth leaf appears, and at 10 inches apart. *Choctaw:* Comes up in from 4 to 7 days, and is thinned out to from 12 to 18 inches apart as soon as large enough. *Pottawatomie:* Comes up in a week; is thinned out to 18 inches when the plant is a month old.

8. What after-cultivation do you give, and with what implements? Is your cotton liable to suffer from "sore-shin"?

Cherokee: A scraper is first used, and then the plants are chopped out to a stand; a sweep follows this, then the harrow, and again the sweep, the hoe being used near the plants. The dirt is after this thrown to the plant with a turning plow, and cultivation finished with the hoe if necessary. *Creek:* Bar off with small turning plows, and afterward throw the dirt back with small shovels. *Choctaw:* After-cultivation is usually given with cast and bull-tongue plows and sweeps. *Pottawatomie:* With common implements and double shovels. Cotton does not suffer with "sore-shin" in the Cherokee and Pottawatomie nations, but does to a small extent in the Choctaw and Creek nations "if planted too thick and too early".

9. What is the height usually attained by your cotton before blooming? When do you usually see the first blooms? When do the bolls first open?

Choctaw: The height usually attained is from 12 to 20 inches. *Cherokee:* About 18 inches. *Creek:* From 18 to 24 inches. *Pottawatomie:* Two feet and upward. *Choctaw:* First blooms are seen from the 5th to the 8th of June. *Cherokee:* July 1, and sometimes sooner. *Pottawatomie:* About July 1. *Creek:* About July 4. The bolls usually open from August 1st to the 4th.

10. When do you begin your first picking? How many pickings do you usually make, and when?

Cherokee: The first picking begins August 25, between which date and Christmas three pickings are made. *Choctaw:* The first picking commences September 1; from two to three pickings are made from September to December. *Pottawatomie:* First picking begins about the 1st of September; two pickings are made from September to November. *Creek:* Picking is continuous, commencing September 10; from two to three pickings are usually made, cotton being picked as fast as needed and able to be gathered.

11. When do you begin your first picking? How many pickings do you usually make, and when?

Cherokee: The first picking begins August 25. *Choctaw* and *Pottawatomie:* About the 1st of September. *Creek:* September 10. *Cherokee:* Three pickings are made between August 25 and Christmas. *Choctaw:* Two to three from September to December. *Pottawatomie:* Two in September, October, and November. *Creek:* Cotton is picked as fast as it is needed and able to be gathered, from two to three pickings being made.

12. Do you ordinarily pick all your cotton? At what date does picking usually close? At what time do you expect the first black frost?

Cotton is reported as being all picked in each of the nations. *Pottawatomie:* Picking usually closes in November. *Choctaw:* From the 1st to the 10th of December. *Cherokee:* December 25. *Creek:* From the 1st of January to the 1st of February. Black frost appears the last of September in the Choctaw nation, the 15th of October in the Creek and Cherokee nations, and in November in the Pottawatomie nation.

13. Do you pen your seed-cotton in the field, or gin as the picking progresses?

Creek and *Pottawatomie:* Seed-cotton is penned in the field. *Choctaw:* Usually haul to gin as fast as possible. *Cherokee:* In some cases it is penned in the field; in others ginned as picking progresses.

GINNING AND BALING.

14. What gin do you use? How many saws? What motive power, steam or horse? How much clean lint do you make in a day's run of ten hours? How much seed-cotton is required for a 475-pound bale of lint?

Pottawatomie: The Eagle gin of 60 saws, with steam-power, makes 3,000 pounds of clean lint per day. The Remington needle gin of 60 saws, with steam-power, 2,800 pounds of lint per day. *Choctaw:* The Phœnix gin of 60 saws, with steam-power, 2,200 to 2,500 pounds of lint per day. *Cherokee:* Pratt's, Emery's, and Carver's, of from 50 to 70 saws each; some prefer steam, others mule power; they make about 500 pounds of lint per day for every ten saws. In the Choctaw nation 1,700 pounds are required for a bale of lint, while in the other nations about 1,425 are necessary.

15. What press do you use for baling? What press is generally used in your region? What is its capacity per day?

Cherokee: The press generally used is the Wilson, with a capacity, when run by four men and one horse, of from 16 to 18 bales. The old-fashioned Georgia wooden screw press is also in use. *Choctaw:* The Farmers' press, with a capacity of five bales. *Creek:* Tapy's' power-press; its capacity, when run by four men and horses, is 4 bales.

16. Do you use rope or iron ties for baling? If the latter, what fastening do you prefer? What kind of bagging is used? What weight do you aim to give your bales?

The use of iron ties is reported in all the nations. *Choctaw:* The arrow fastening is preferred. *Creek:* The button. *Cherokee:* The square buckle. "Hemp or jute" bagging is used generally, and 500 pounds is the usual weight of bales of cotton.

DISEASES, INSECT ENEMIES, ETC.

17. By what accidents of weather, diseases, or insect pests is your cotton crop most liable to be injured? To what cause is the trouble attributed by your farmers, and is rust or blight prevalent chiefly on heavy or ill-drained soils? Do they prevail chiefly in wet or dry, cool or hot seasons?

Pottawatomie: The caterpillar, boll-worm, shedding, and rot of bolls, all of which make their appearance late in August. *Cherokee:* The cotton crop is injured chiefly by wet weather; also by early frost in the fall. *Creek:* Hail-storms are the only trouble; there are no insects. *Choctaw:* Shedding to some extent, a little rust, storms and droughts, injure the cotton crop. Rust and blight are most common on low, ill-drained soils and in wet seasons in the Creek nation, and do not occur at all in other nations.

LABOR AND SYSTEM OF FARMING.

18. What is the average size of farms?　Is the prevalent practice mixed farming or planting?　Are supplies raised at home or imported?

Farms contain from 3 to 100 acres in the Choctaw nation, 20 acres in the Creek, 75 in the Cherokee, and 160 in the Pottawatomie. The prevalent practice is mixed farming, and the tendency to raising home supplies is increasing, though this is already very generally done in the Cherokee and Pottawatomie nations. In the Creek nation flour is imported, and in the Choctaw nation "all of the flour and the greater part of the bacon and corn are brought from Kansas".

19. Who are your laborers chiefly?　How are wages paid?　At what rates, and when payable?

Cherokee and *Pottawatomie:* Laborers are white, no negroes; wages are $12 per month, payable when the work is done. *Creek:* Laborers are of all classes except Chinese, and usually share the crop; otherwise they are paid $15 per month, one-half being paid at the end of the month and the remainder at the close of the season. *Choctaw:* Laborers are usually whites and negroes; Indians work very little; laborers usually receive a share of the crop.

20. Are cotton farms worked on shares?　Are any supplies furnished by the owners?

Creek: Cotton farms are worked on shares; and when the owner furnishes supplies, teams, and implements, except gin and press, he receives one-half of the crop. *Pottawatomie:* The owner furnishes supplies, but no implements, and receives one-half the crop. *Choctaw:* Neither supplies nor implements are furnished by the owner, whose share of crops is one-fourth of the cotton and one-third of the corn. *Cherokee:* The share system is not practiced.

21. Does your system give satisfaction?　How does it affect the soil or the quality of staple?　Which system (share or wage) is best for the laborer?

Each system gives satisfaction in all of the nations, and the staple improves. The soil also improves under cultivation under either system, except in the Choctaw nation. The share system is preferred in the Creek nation because the laborer is more interested in the crop, and in the Choctaw nation because farmers cannot pay cash. Prompt cash payments are considered best in the Cherokee nation.

22. What is the condition of laborers?　What proportion of negro laborers own land or the houses in which they live?　How many acres or bales per hand is your customary estimate?

Cherokee and *Pottawatomie:* Good. *Creek:* Improving; nearly all negroes own land and houses. *Choctaw:* Generally poor; all the negroes could own land if they choose. Estimate: From 1 to 5 bales in the Choctaw and Pottawatomie, 7 acres in the Creek, and 10 acres or 10 bales in the Cherokee nation.

23. To what extent does the system of credits or advances upon the growing cotton crop prevail in your region?　At what stage is the growing crop insured?

Choctaw: The system of credits and advances prevails almost universally, and without advances from the merchant no cotton would be raised. *Creek:* It prevails to a great extent. *Cherokee:* No advances are made by merchants. The growing crop is not insured in any of the tribes.

24. What are the merchants' commissions and charges for storing, handling, shipping, insurance, etc., to which your crop is subject?　What is the total amount of these charges against the farmer per pound, or 500-pound bale?

Choctaw: Merchants generally buy the seed-cotton and ship it direct to Saint Louis. *Creek:* Merchants buy seed-cotton and gin it. In 1879 the price paid was 2.5 cents per pound. *Cherokee:* The total amount of the merchants' charges is $5 per bale.

25. What is your estimate of the cost of production in your region, exclusive of such charges, and with fair soil and management?

Choctaw: About $2 per one hundred pounds of seed-cotton, including rent. *Cherokee:* $30 per bale, for tillage and gathering. *Creek:* About 8 cents per pound.

INDEX TO COTTON PRODUCTION IN INDIAN TERRITORY.

GENERAL INDEX TO COTTON PRODUCTION.

NOTE.—In the following index the information regarding counties and the names of persons who have furnished information for the reports are omitted. For such references and for details of minor importance see the index of each state.

	Part	Page of special report	General folio (at bottom of page)
Bolling not favored in Georgia by deep culture	II	149	406
Bolling of cotton-plants favored and running to weed prevented—			
In Alabama by:			
Application of fertilisers	II	81–148	91–158
Breaking the land very shallow	II	129	139
Deep preparation of the land	II	143	153
Deep tillage	II	96	96
Early planting...............	II	110, 143, 148	130, 133, 158
Giving more space between the plants	II	129, 139	139, 149
Not plowing too near the plant	II	106	116
Planting every second or third row with corn.	II	129	139
Plowing close to the plant	II	131–139	131–149
Rapid and light cultivation.............	II	143, 148	153, 158
Shallow culture............	II	81–147	91–152
Thinning out to proper distance.........	II	108	118
Topping the plant.........................	II	78–145	88–155
Underdrainage	II	112, 126	122, 138
In Arkansas by:			
Bedding the land high	I	77	613
Close plowing and cutting lateral roots ...	I	50–83	586–629
Drainage and cultivation	I	84, 82	600, 618
Early planting............	I	77	613
Late culture..........	I	56	592
Planting smaller varieties	I	55	591
Shallow cultivation	I	50–91	586–627
Topping (in a majority of counties)	I	50–94	586–630
In Florida by:			
Application of fertilisers	II	39, 43, 48, 54	219, 223, 228, 234
Early planting............	II	40, 54	220, 234
Flat weeding	II	56	236
Importation of new seed from Georgia and South Carolina.	II	40, 50	220, 230
Late plowing	II	48	228
Light cultivation	II	41	221
Proper distance between plants...........	II	40, 41, 53, 54	220, 221, 233, 234
Shallow culture	II	50, 53	230, 233
Thorough cultivation	II	59	239
Topping the plant.............	II	40, 41, 48, 49, 50, 60	220, 221, 228, 229, 230, 240
In Georgia by:			
Application of fertilisers	II	71–156	397–422
Deep preparation of the land...........	II	103, 111, 141, 142	369, 377, 407, 408
Drainage	II	148, 156	414, 434
Early planting..........	II	110, 137	376, 403
Planting closer in the drill............	II	72, 73, 77	337, 338, 343
Plowing near the plant and breaking lateral roots.	II	100, 114	366, 380
Proper distance between plants	II	121	387
Shallow cultivation	II	73–137	383–403
Thick planting	II	97	363
Topping the plant	II	70–156	396–434
Use of an early variety of seed...........	II	97	363
Use of marl.............	II	131	397
Use of prolific seed...	II	143	409
"Working neglect of the crop"...........	II	197	422
In Indian territory by:			
Close planting...	I	22	800
Good cultivation ...	I	23	800
Topping the plant	I	22, 24	800, 802
In Louisiana by:			
Deep plowing..........	I	72	174
Drainage	I	82	184
Fertilisers	I	64	166
Plowing close to the plant	I	45, 66	147, 168
Shallow cultivation	I	44, 48, 50	146, 150, 152
Thinning the plants	I	48	150
Topping the plant	I	44–73	168–175

	Part	Page of special report	General folio (at bottom of page)
Bolling of cotton-plants favored and running to weed prevented—continued.			
In Mississippi by:			
Application of fertilisers or lime...........	I	88, 90, 91, 134, 137, 139	290, 292, 293, 336, 338, 341
Deep plowing, throwing soil from the plant, and cutting lateral roots.	I	113, 115, 130, 725, 125, 130	315, 317, 322, 327, 329, 332
Drainage	I	88, 130	290, 332
Early planting...........	I	95, 111, 112, 126, 131, 137	297, 313, 314, 328, 333, 339 e
Judicious culture	I	101, 104, 107, 115, 121	303, 306, 309, 317, 233
Making rows farther apart	I	89, 111	290, 313
Shallow culture...........	I	90–135	292–337
Topping the plant	I	92, 96, 104, 110, 111, 136	294, 298, 306, 313, 313, 340
In Missouri by:			
Shallow tillage.................	I	16	514
Topping the plant	I	16, 18	514, 516
In North Carolina by:			
Application of fertilisers or lime...........	II	31–59	563–591
Closer planting	II	59	591
Deep cultivation	II	56	588
Deep plowing..........	II	43, 56	577, 588
Early cultivation	II	31, 34, 39, 42	563, 566, 571, 574
Marling	II	35, 42	567, 574
Thinning out	II	53	585
Thorough draining............	II	35, 36, 39, 42, 45, 56	567, 568, 571, 574, 577, 588
Thorough subsoiling............	II	56	588
Topping the plant............	II	30–54	562–586
In South Carolina by:			
Application of fertilisers............	II	58, 60	515, 516
Planting short-limbed varieties of cotton ...	II	59	515
Plowing close to the plant	II	59	515
Topping	II	59	515
Underdrainage.........	II	59	515
In Tennessee by:			
Application of manure	I	52, 58, 61, 71, 76, 92	424, 430, 433, 443, 448, 464
Close plowing to cut lateral roots	I	50–54, 58, 59	429–433, 430, 431
Deep plowing in preparation of the land ...	I	81	453
Early planting........	I	52, 56, 57, 66, 81, 90	424, 428, 429, 438, 453, 462
Planting the seed thick in the drill	I	81	453
Rapid culture and early laying-by	I	52	424
Reducing the height of the ridge..........	I	88	460
Rolling the seed in plaster and planting early.	I	87	459
Running no center furrow when bedding ..	I	52	424
Shallow cultivation	I	48–91	420–463
Thinning the stalks	I	73	445
Topping the plant	I	50–90	422–462
Turning out the middles............	I	54	466
In Texas by:			
Bedding on bad ground	I	116	776
Close planting	I	102	760
Deep plowing..........	I	109, 132	767, 790
Early planting............	I	72, 84	730, 742
Plowing close to the plant and breaking lateral roots.	I	66–141	724–799
Rapid cultivation	I	75, 125	733, 783
Shallow culture...................	I	65, 85, 90, 113, 116, 128	723, 743, 748, 771, 776, 786
Thinning out the plants	I	72, 90, 98	726, 748, 756
Thorough drainage.................	I	62, 70, 79	720, 728, 737
Thorough tillage.................	I	62, 66, 70, 84, 88, 126	720, 724, 728, 742, 746, 797
Throwing soil from the plant..............	I	61, 72, 87, 90, 117	730, 730, 745, 751, 773
Topping the plant (in a majority of counties).	I	60–142	718–806

	Part	Page of special report.	General folio (at bottom of page).
Condition and nationality of, and wages paid to, laborers in:			
Alabama	II	155, 156	165, 166
Arkansas	I	104, 105	540, 541
California	I	190, 131	788, 789
Florida	II	70, 71	250, 251
Georgia	II	173, 178	436, 450
Indian territory	I	21	369
Louisiana	I	88, 84	195, 196
Mississippi	I	154	656
Missouri	I	27, 38	525, 526
North Carolina	II	77	509
South Carolina	II	60–68	516–523
Tennessee	I	43, 104	415, 476
Texas	I	161, 162	819, 820
Virginia	II	21	643
Conditions imposed by transportation companies as to weight of bales in:			
Alabama	II	155	165
Arkansas	I	102	688
Florida	II	69	249
Georgia	II	170	446
Louisiana	I	81	193
Mississippi	I	152	354
Missouri	I	27	525
North Carolina	II	75	507
South Carolina	II	56	514
Tennessee	I	102	474
Texas	I	158	816
Virginia	II	20	642
Conecuh river, Alabama, drainage system of	II	19	29
Contents of volume on cotton culture. (See back of title page.)			
Contra Costa Mountain range, California, elevation and description of.	II	46	704
Cooper River marls, occurrence of, in South Carolina.	II	11	467
Coosa coal-field of Alabama, area and description of..	II	36, 37–39	36, 47–39
Coosa river, Alabama, drainage system of	II	9, 10	19, 20
Coosa Valley region, Alabama:			
Area, geological features, and subdivisions of the region and its outlines.	II	17–25	27–35
Cotton product per acre in, and its relation to population.	II	61–68	71–72
Extent and structure of, and section showing topographical features.	II	18	28
Coquina, character and extent of, in Florida	II	27	207
Coral formation, extent of, in Florida	II	26	206
Corn, acreage and production of, in:			
Alabama	II	5, 6	15, 16
Arkansas	I	5, 6	541, 542
California	I	3, 4	661, 662
Florida	II	4	184
Georgia	II	6–8	272–274
Indian territory	I	3	341
Kentucky (in Report on Tennessee)	I	110	482
Louisiana	I	5, 6	197, 198
Mississippi	I	5, 6	367, 368
Missouri	I	4	502
North Carolina	II	5, 6	527, 528
South Carolina	II	4	460
Tennessee	I	6–8	378–380
Texas	I	7–10	563–566
Virginia	II	3	625
Corn, acreage greater than that of cotton in Arkansas.	I	20	575
Corn, soil ingredients withdrawn by (General Discussion).	I	50	62
Correspondents, abstracts of reports of, in monograph on:			
Alabama	II		99–113
Arkansas	I	38–60	506–522
California	I		
Georgia	II	70–158	386–424
Indian territory	I	22–25	360–363
Louisiana	I	44–73	156–175
Mississippi	I	88–142	300–345
Missouri	I	15–15	513–516
North Carolina	II	30–34	502–506
South Carolina	II	54–56	510–514
Tennessee	I	48–95	420–464
Texas	I	80–148	718–806
Virginia	II	12–14	634–636
Correspondents, names and addresses of, in:			
Alabama	II	150–152	160–162
Arkansas	I	96	532
California	I	125	783
Florida	II	96	246
Georgia	II	160–163	436–426
Indian territory	I	32	360
Louisiana	I	76	178
Mississippi	I	146	348
Missouri	I	24	522
North Carolina	II	72	504
South Carolina	II	50	506

	Part	Page of special report.	General folio (at bottom of page).
Correspondents, names and addresses of, in—cont'd.			
Tennessee	I	94–96	466–468
Texas	I	150–152	808–810
Virginia	II	18	640
Corundum, occurrence of, in South Carolina	II	10	466
Cost of cotton picking in:			
Arkansas	I	101	537
Florida	II	68	248
Georgia	II	176	442
Mississippi	I	155	357
North Carolina	II	78	511
South Carolina	II	55	511
Texas	I	183	821
Virginia	II	20	642
Cost of cotton picking in Mexico (in Report on California).	II	131	789
Cost of cotton production, estimated, in:			
Alabama	II	156	166
Arkansas	I	107	543
California	I	76	734
Florida	II	71	251
Georgia	II	175	441
Indian territory	I	31	369
Louisiana	I	85	187
Mississippi	I	155	357
Missouri	I	28	526
North Carolina	II	78	510
South Carolina	II	66	522
Tennessee	I	105	477
Texas	I	153	821
Virginia	II	21	643
Cost of cotton production, itemized, in:			
Alabama	II	156	166
Arkansas	I	107	543
California	I	76	734
Georgia	II	175, 176	441, 442
Louisiana	I	85	187
Missouri	I	28	526
North Carolina	II	78	510
Tennessee	I	105	477
Texas	I	153	821
Cost of drayage in:			
Arkansas	I	107	543
Louisiana	I	85	187
Mississippi	I	155	357
North Carolina	II	78	510
Tennessee	I	105	477
Texas	I	152	820
Cost of sale, charges, and insurance on cotton crop in:			
Alabama	II	156	166
Arkansas	II	106, 107	542, 543
Florida	II	71	251
Georgia	II	174	440
Indian territory	I	31	369
Louisiana	I	85	187
Mississippi	I	155	357
Missouri	I	28	526
North Carolina	II	78	510
Tennessee	I	104, 105	476, 477
Texas	I	152	820
Virginia	II	21	643
Côte Blanche island, Louisiana, location of	I	23	125
Côte Gelée, Louisiana, description of	I	24, 50	126, 161
Cotton, acreage and production of, in:			
Alabama	II	3–6, 60	13–16, 70
Arkansas	I	3–6, 39, 40	519–542, 575, 576
Florida	II	3, 4, 29	183, 184, 209
Georgia	II	3–8, 54, 55	269–274, 320, 321
Kentucky (in Report on Tennessee)	I	109	481
Louisiana	I	3, 4, 83, 86	193, 196, 198
Mississippi	I	3, 4	351, 502
North Carolina	II	3–6	525–528
South Carolina	II	3	459
Tennessee	I	3–8	375–380
Texas	I	3–6, 49, 51	707, 709
Virginia	II	3, 10	625, 632
Cotton acreage and tilled land in Louisiana, greatest disproportion between.	I	39	141
Cotton, after-cultivation of, in:			
Alabama	II	154	164
Arkansas	I	100	536
California	I	125	733
Florida	II	68	248
Georgia	II	167	433
Indian territory	I	30	368
Louisiana	I	80	182
Mississippi	I	150	352
Missouri	I	26	524
North Carolina	II	74	506
South Carolina	II	55–56	511–514
Tennessee	I	99, 100	471, 472
Texas	I	156	814
Virginia	II	20	642

58 C P

Lightning Source UK Ltd.
Milton Keynes UK
UKHW020048231118
332756UK00005B/129/P